BRITISH MUSEUM

GENERAL CATALOGUE OF PRINTED BOOKS

Photolithographic edition to 1955

Volume 31

BUTT—CALD

PUBLISHED BY
THE TRUSTEES OF THE BRITISH MUSEUM

LONDON 1965

Printed in England by
Balding + Mansell, London and Wisbech

BUTT (Andor)

—— Crisis in Christendom. A symposium of great ghosts. pp. 89. *Watts & Co.: London*, 1942. 8°. **8011.** aa. **19.**

BUTT (Archibald Willingham) The Letters of Archie Butt. Edited by Lawrence F. Abbott. [With illustrations, including a portrait.] pp. xxviii. 395. *William Heinemann: London; printed in U.S.A.*, 1924. 8°. **10906.** c. **10.**

—— Taft and Roosevelt. The intimate letters of Archie Butt, military aide. [With a portrait.] 2 vol. pp. xxiv. vii. 862. *Doubleday, Doran & Co.: Garden City, N.Y.*, 1930. 8°. **010920.** d. **9.**

BUTT (Arthur N.) William Caxton, mercer & courtier, author & printer . . . Illustrated by numerous fac-similes of types and wood-cuts. Reprinted from "Things in General," *etc.* pp. 31. *The Author: London*, 1878. 8°. **11899.** f. **12.** (**8.**)

BUTT (Audrey)

—— *See* Baxter (Paul T. W.) and Butt (A.) The Azande, and related peoples of the Anglo-Egyptian Sudan and Belgian Congo. 1953. 8°. [*Ethnographic Survey of Africa.* East Central Africa. pt. 9.] Ac. **2272.** c/**31.** (**1.**)

—— The Nilotes of the Anglo-Egyptian Sudan and Uganda. [With a bibliography and a map.] pp. 198. *International African Institute: London*, 1952. 8°. [*Ethnographic Survey of Africa.* East Central Africa. pt. 4.] Ac. **2272.** c/**31.** (**1.**)

BUTT (Beatrice May) Alison. By the author of 'Miss Molly' [i.e. B. M. Butt], *etc.* 3 vol. 1883. 8°. *See* Alison. **12635.** u. **10.**

—— Ann: a brief tragedy, and A Free Pass. By the author of "Miss Molly" [i.e. B. M. Butt]. pp. 139. [1907.] 8°. *See* Ann. **012629.** h. **45.**

—— Dan Riach, Socialist. By the author of 'Miss Molly' [i.e. B. M. Butt], *etc.* pp. 369. 1908. 8°. *See* Riach (Dan) **012625.** dd. **30.**

—— Delicia. By the author of 'Miss Molly,' 'Eugenie,' etc. [i.e. B. M. Butt.] Second edition. pp. vi. 342. 1879. 8°. *See* Delicia. **12618.** i. **3.**

—— Eugénie. By the author of "Miss Molly" (B. M. Butt). pp. 245. *W. Blackwood & Sons: Edinburgh & London*, 1877. 8°. **12638.** n. **6.**

—— A Friend. [A tale.] By the author of "Miss Molly" [i.e. B. M. Butt]. pp. 24. 1891. 12°. *See* Friend. **4412.** dd. **30.** (**3.**)

—— Geraldine Hawthorne. A sketch. By the author of 'Miss Molly,' 'Delicia,' etc. [i.e. B. M. Butt.] pp. viii. 311. 1882. 8°. *See* Hawthorne (Geraldine) **12643.** bbb. **4.**

—— The Great Reconciler. By the author of "Miss Molly" [i.e. B. M. Butt]. pp. 463. 1903. 8°. *See* Reconciler. **012628.** bb. **17.**

—— Ingelheim. By the author of "Miss Molly" [i.e. B. M. Butt]. 3 vol. 1892. 8°. *See* Ingelheim. **012637.** f. **2.**

—— Keith Deramore. By the author of "Miss Molly" [i.e. B. M. Butt]. pp. 379. 1893. 8°. *See* Deramore (Keith) **012630.** e. **33.**

—— Miss Molly. pp. vi. 292. *W. Blackwood & Sons: Edinburgh & London*, 1876. 8°. **12638.** d. **2.**

—— Pearls—Tears. *See* Eros. Eros. Four tales. vol. 2. 1880. 8°. **12636.** e. **13.**

BUTT (Beatrice May) and **BUTT** (Geraldine)

—— Lads and Lasses . . . [Tales.] With a frontispiece by W. G. Wills. pp. 132. *R. Grant & Son: Edinburgh; Simpkin, Marshall & Co.: London*, [1876.] 16°. **4417.** de. **2.**

BUTT (Boswell) *Esq., pseud.* [i.e. Charles Henry Ross.] *See* also Ross (C. H.)

—— The Great Gun, an eccentric biography . . . Edited [or rather, written] and illustrated by C. H. Ross. pp. 96. *Ward, Lock & Tyler: London*, [1865.] 8°. **12350.** d. **7.**

BUTT (Brian Alford)

—— The Beauty of Land's End. [A photographic guide.] *Jarrold & Sons: Norwich*, [1953.] 8°. [*Magna-Crome Books.*] W.P. **3517/26.**

BUTT (Brian Alford) and **BUTT** (Jane)

—— Falmouth Panorama. A pictorial souvenir, *etc.* *Jarrold & Sons: Norwich*, [1955.] 16°. **010368.** a. **50.**

BUTT, afterwards **RUMFORD** (*Dame* Clara Ellen) *D.B.E.* *See* Ponder (Winifred) Clara Butt: her life-story, *etc.* [With portraits.] 1928. 8°. **010855.** f. **17.**

—— How to become a Successful Singer. *See* Singer. How to Become a Successful Singer, *etc.* [1912.] 8°. **7896.** pp. **38.**

BUTT (Drinkwater) Practical Retouching, including directions for the after treatment of the negative generally. pp. 78. *Iliffe & Sons: London*, 1901. 8°. **08909.** e. **15.**

—— Second edition. pp. 78. *Iliffe & Sons: London*, 1904. 8°. **08909.** e. **42.**

BUTT (Ferdinand H.)

—— *See* Johannsen (Oskar A.) and Butt (F. H.) Embryology of Insects and Myriapods, *etc.* 1941. 8°. W.P. **3430/55.**

BUTT (George) *D.D.* *See* Bible.—*Isaiah.* [*English.*] Isaiah Versified. By G. Butt. 1785. 8°. **219.** h. **2.**

—— *See* Valpy (Richard) Poems . . . spoken at Reading School. To which is added some account of the lives of the Rev. Mr. Benwell and the Rev. Dr. Butt, *etc.* 1804. 8°. **992.** k. **22.**

—— Poems. [With a portrait.] 2 vol. *Printed for the Author: Kidderminster*, 1793. 8°. **79.** e. **11, 12.**

—— The Religious Importance of Sunday Schools. A discourse, preached in the Church of Tenbury . . . the 3d of June, 1787, *etc.* pp. 27. *N. Rollason: Kidderminster*, [1787.] 8°. **4474.** bb. **10.**

—— A Sermon, occasioned by the death of the Hon. Lady Winnington, preached . . . December 21, 1794. pp. 19. *G. Gower: Kidderminster*, [1794.] 8°. **1026.** f. **3.** (**15.**)

—— A Sermon preached at the Octagon Chapel, in . . . Bath, on the day the late Bishop of Worcester [i.e. James Johnson] was buried. pp. 22. *J. & J. Fletcher: Oxford*, 1775. 4°. **682.** e. **24.** (**6.**)

—— [Another copy.] **1417.** k. **24**

—— A Sermon preached in Bewdley Chapel before . . . Lord Westcote . . . and . . . the Bailiff and Corporation of Bewdley, on the 27th of September, 1792. pp. 22. *George Gower: Kidderminster*, [1792.] 8°. **114.** b. **64.** (**2.**)

BUTT (George) *D.D*

—— A Sermon preached in the Cathedral of Worcester, on the 7th of March 1795, at the Assizes, *etc.* pp. 29. *Holl & Brandish: Worcester,* [1795.] 8°. **1026**. f. 3. (**16**.)

—— A Sermon upon His Majesty's Proclamation, preached in the Parish Church of Kidderminster . . . the 3rd of June, 1792. pp. 22. *G. Gower: Kidderminster; T. Cadell: London,* [1792.] 8°. **114**. b. **64**. (**1**.)

—— A Sermon upon the General Fast, preached in . . . Kidderminster, on . . . the 19th of April, 1793. pp. 21. *G. Gower: Kidderminster,* [1793.] 8°. **1026**. f. 3. (**14**.)

—— Sermons. [Mostly preached in the Chapel Royal.] 2 vol. *George Gower: Kidderminster,* 1791. 8°. **4460**. gg. 3.

—— The Spanish Daughter. By the Rev. G. Butt . . . Revised and corrected by his daughter, Mrs. Sherwood. [A novel. With a memoir of the author.] 2 vol. *Knight & Lacey; M. A. Nattali: London,* 1824. 8°. N. **249**.

BUTT (George) *Solicitor.*

—— *See* Wiltshire. The Poll of the Freeholders of . . . Wilts . . . Transcribed . . . by G. Butt. [1819.] 4°. **10361**. c. **31**.

—— A Peep at the Wiltshire Assizes. A serio-ludicrous poem. By one who is but an attorney [i.e. G. Butt]. pp. xiv. 92. [1819.] 8°. *See* Wiltshire Assizes. **11642**. aa. **12**.

—— Suggestions as to the Conduct and Management of a County Contested Election . . . With an appendix of the statutes on county election, *etc.* pp. xvi. 151. lxxxiii. *James Duncan: London,* 1826. 8°. **514**. b. **21**.

BUTT (George) *Vicar of Chesterfield.* Sermon preached in the Parish Church of Chesterfield, on the day of the funeral of the Duke of Wellington. pp. 24. *T. Hatchard: London,* 1852. 12°. **10815**. a. **55**.

BUTT (George Baseden) Invitation to Poetry. A book for the young. pp. 132. *Gerald Howe: London,* [1932.] 8°. **20016**. e. 4.

—— Madame Blavatsky. [With a portrait.] pp. xi. 269. *Rider & Co.: London,* [1926.] 8°. **10790**. h. 6.

—— Modern Psychism. [On spiritualism and theosophy.] pp. viii. 318. *Cecil Palmer: London,* 1925. 8°. **08632**. e. **24**.

BUTT (George Edward) The Class Meeting: how its usefulness may be promoted. An address, *etc.* pp. 12. *Alden's Printing & Publishing Offices: Oxford,* 1874. 8°. **4139**. b. **1**. (**23**.)

—— My Travels in North West Rhodesia or a missionary journey of sixteen thousand miles. [With plates, including a portrait.] pp. xiii. 283. *E. Dalton: London,* [1910?] 8°. **10098**. a. **12**.

BUTT (George Medd) *See* Shower (*Sir* Bartholomew) Reports of Cases adjudged in the Court of King's Bench . . . The third edition: forming part of the complete series of law reports . . . from mss. of Sir B. Shower and others . . . by G. Butt, *etc.* 1836. 8°. **1243**. g. **19**.

BUTT (Geraldine) *See* Butt (Beatrice M.) and Butt (G.) Lads and Lasses, *etc.* [1876.] 16°. **4417**. de. 2.

—— Black and White. An Anglo-Indian story for young readers, *etc.* pp. 127. *J. Hogg: London,* [1893.] 8°. **4412**. l. 8.

BUTT (Geraldine)

—— Christmas Roses. Tales for young persons. pp. 256. *W. Blackwood & Sons: Edinburgh & London,* 1877. 8°. **12638**. aaa. **20**.

—— Esther, a story for children . . . Woodcut and chromograph illustrations. pp. 271. *M. Ward & Co.: London & Belfast,* 1878. 8°. **12809**. cc. **31**

—— How Molly Made Peace [and other tales]. *See* Girl. Every Girl's Stories. 1895. 8°. **012808**. eee. 5.

—— Martin Craghan. [A tale.] pp. 16. *S.P.C.K.: London,* [1875.] 16°. **4416**. aa. **89**. (**10**.)

—— My Picture, and other poems. pp. 48. *Houlston & Sons: London; R. Hobson: Wellington, Salop,* 1874. 8°. **11650**. f. **28**.

—— Sapphire—Truth. *See* Eros. Eros. Four tales. vol. 1. 1880. 8°. **12636**. e. **13**.

—— A Sprig of Heather. [A novel.] Illustrated, *etc.* pp. 234. *M. Ward & Co.: London & Belfast,* 1878. 8°. [" *Blue-Bell " Series.*] **12601**. bbb. 5.

BUTT (Geraldine) and BUTT (J. G.)

—— John Smith, and other stories. pp. 96. *W. Oliphant & Co.: Edinburgh,* 1880 [1879]. 8°. **12809**. g. **47**.

BUTT (Harold Thomas Hayward) First Aid Illustrated . . . New edition revised by Dr. A. Frew . . . assisted by Harold Jowitt . . . Standard edition, *etc.* *Eng.* pp. 96. *Longmans & Co.: London,* [1937.] 8°. **07481**. ff. **71**.

—— Ikusiza Aba Limele . . . (First Aid Illustrated.) [Illustrations, with titles in English, Zulu, Xosa and Sesuto.] Revised, 1934. (2nd edition.) pp. 72. *Prevention of Accidents Committee of the Rand Mutual Assurance Co.: Johannesburg,* 1934. 8°. **07481**. ff. **46**.

—— First Aid Illustrated. Msaidizi wa watu waliojeruhiwa. Omujanjabi w'abalwade . . . New edition revised by Dr. A. Frew . . . assisted by Harold Jowitt . . . East African edition, English, Swahili, Luganda. pp. 95. *Longmans & Co.: London,* 1938. 8°. **07481**. ff. **77**.

—— Kubalilo Kwafwa Bachenwa. Kutandisa wo Lasiwa . . . First Aid Illustrated. (Revised by Dr. A. Frew . . . assisted by Harold Jowitt. Northern Rhodesian edition.) *Eng., Bemba & Nyanja.* pp. xvi. 96. *Longmans & Co.: London,* 1938. 8°. **07481**. bb. **14**.

—— First Aid Illustrated. Usizo Iokuqala. Ukusiza aɓalimele. Thuso ea pele kotsing . . . New edition revised by Dr. A. Frew . . . assisted by Harold Jowitt . . . South African edition with text in English, Zulu, Xhosa, Sesotho, *etc.* pp. 95. *Longmans & Co.: London,* 1938. 8°. **07481**. ff. **74**.

—— Kubalilo kwafwa bachenwa. Kutandisa wo lasiwa . . . First Aid Illustrated. (New edition, revised by A. Frew.) pp. xvi. 96. *Longmans, Green & Co.: London,* 1947. 8°. **7382**. r. **40**.

—— First Aid Illustrated . . . Revised by Dr. A. Frew . . . Assisted by Harold Jowitt, *etc.* (Southern Rhodesian edition.) *Eng., Shona, Sindebele & Cinyanja.* pp. xxiii. 96. *Longmans, Green & Co.: London,* 1950. 8°. **7483**. aaa. **8**.

BUTT (Hugh R.) and **SNELL** (Albert Markley)

—— Vitamin K . . . Illustrated. [With a bibliography.] pp. x. 172. *W. B. Saunders Co.: Philadelphia & London,* 1941. 8°. **7384**. b. **9**.

BUTT (Isaac) *See* Martin (Bon L. H.) Daniel Manin, and Venice in 1848-49 . . . With an introduction by I. Butt. 1862. 8°. **10633**. a. **5**.

—— *See* Ovidius Naso (P.) [*Fasti.—English.*] Ovid's Fasti translated into English prose by I. Butt. 1833. 12°. **11355**. bb. **27**.

—— *See* Virgilius Maro (P.) [*Georgica.—English.*] The Georgics of Virgil. Translated into English prose, with an appendix of critical and explanatory notes, by I. Butt. 1834. 12°. T. **1995**. (**1**.)

—— *See* White (Terence de V.) The Road of Excess. [A biography of I. Butt. With portraits and plates.] [1946.] 8°. **10825**. eee. **53**.

—— Berkeley. [A discourse upon his character and writings.] 1866. *See* English Literature. The Afternoon Lectures on English Literature, *etc.* ser. 3. 1863, *etc.* 8°. **11826**. aa. **19**. (**6**.)

—— Chapters of College Romance. First series. pp. 344. *C. J. Skeet: London*, 1863. 8°. **12631**. bb. **6**.

—— The Gap of Barnesmore: a tale of the Irish highlands, and the Revolution of 1688. [By I. Butt.] 3 vol. 1848. 8°. *See* Barnesmore. N. **2707**

—— The History of Italy, from the abdication of Napoleon I., with introductory references to that of earlier times. 2 vol. *Chapman & Hall: London*, 1860. 8°. **9165**. f. **12**.

—— Home Government for Ireland. Irish federalism! Its meaning, its objects, and its hopes . . . Fourth edition. pp. 68. *Irish Home Rule League: Dublin*, 1874. 8°. **8145**. df. **10**.

The running title reads: "Irish Federalism."

—— An Introductory Lecture, delivered before the University of Dublin in Hilary Term 1837. [On political economy.] pp. 71. *W. Curry, Jun. & Co.: Dublin*, 1837. 8°. T. **2090**. (**6**.)

—— Irish Corporation Bill. A speech delivered at the Bar of the House of Lords . . . in defence of the City of Dublin, *etc.* pp. 95. *James Fraser: London*, 1840. 8°. **1390**. h. **20**.

—— The Irish Deep Sea Fisheries. A speech delivered at a meeting of the Home Government Association of Ireland . . . the 17th of October, 1871. pp. 25. *Irish Home Rule League: Dublin*, 1874. 8°. **8145**. ee. **3**. (**6**.)

—— Irish Life in the Castle, the Courts and the Country. [By I. Butt.] 3 vol. 1840. 12°. *See* Irish Life. N. **2118**.

—— The Irish People and the Irish Land: a letter to Lord Lifford; with comments on the publications of Lord Dufferin and Lord Rosse. pp. 298. *John Falconer: Dublin; W. Ridgway: London*, 1867. 8°. **8145**. dd. **7**.

—— The Irish Querist: a series of questions proposed for the consideration of all who desire to solve the problem of Ireland's social condition. pp. 40. *John Falconer: Dublin*, 1867. 8°. **8146**. c. **10**. (**1**.)

—— Irish University Education. A speech, *etc.* pp. 52. *M. H. Gill & Son: Dublin*, 1877. 8°. **8146**. cc. **14**. (**6**.)

—— Land Tenure in Ireland; a plea for the Celtic race . . . Second edition. pp. 104. *John Falconer: Dublin*, 1866. 8°. **8146**. cc. **18**.

—— *See* Hewitt (James) *Viscount Lifford.* A Plea for Irish Landlords. A letter to Isaac Butt, Esq., Q.C. [On his "Land Tenure in Ireland."] 1867. 8°. **8146**. cc. **15**. (**1**.)

BUTT (Isaac)

—— The Liberty of Teaching Vindicated. Reflections and proposals on the subject of Irish national education. With an introductory letter to the Right Honourable W. E. Gladstone, *etc.* pp. xxxi. 173. *W. B. Kelly: Dublin; Simpkin, Marshall & Co.: London*, 1865. 8°. **8308**. bb. **18**.

—— National Education in Ireland. A speech, *etc.* pp. 24. *J. McGlashan: Dublin*, 1854. 8°. **8364**. d. **52**.

—— The Poor-Law Bill for Ireland Examined, its provisions, and the report of Mr. Nicholls contrasted with the facts proved by the Poor Inquiry Commission, in a letter to Lord Viscount Morpeth. pp. 47. *B. Fellowes: London*, 1837. 8°. T. **2162**. (**2**.)

—— A Practical Treatise on the new Law of Compensation to Tenants in Ireland, and the other provisions of the Landlord and Tenant Act, 1870; with an appendix of statutes and rules. pp. lvi 647. *John Falconer: Dublin; Butterworths: London*, 1871. 8°. **6503**. c. **3**.

—— The Problem of Irish Education: an attempt at its solution. pp. ix. 117. *Longmans & Co.: London*, 1875. 8°. **8306**. ee. **33**.

—— *See* Bagwell (Richard) A Plea for National Education, in answer to Mr. Butt's proposal for its destruction. [An answer to "The Problem of Irish Education."] 1875. 8°. **8306**. d. **7**. (**14**.)

—— "The Rate in Aid." A Letter to the Right Hon. the Earl of Roden. pp. 75. *James McGlashan: Dublin*, 1849. 8°. **8275**. e. **9**.

—— Speech of I. Butt, Esq. delivered at the great Protestant meeting in Dublin . . . February 13, 1840. From the Dublin Statesman and Record. pp. 16. *F. Baisler: London*, [1840 ?] 8°. **8145**. c. **7**.

—— The Transfer of Land, by means of a judicial assurance; its practicability and advantages considered, in a letter to Sir Richard Bethell, M.P. pp. 129. *Hodges, Smith & Co.: Dublin*, 1857. 8°. **6325**. c. **5**.

—— A Voice for Ireland. The famine in the land. What has been done, and what is to be done. Reprinted from "The Dublin University Magazine." pp. viii. 59. *James McGlashan: Dublin*, 1847. 8°. **8275**. d. **6**. (**6**.)

The running title reads: "The Famine in the Land."

—— Zoology and Civilization. A lecture, delivered before the Royal Zoological Society of Ireland. pp. 32. *James McGlashan: Dublin*, 1847. 16°. **1251**. b. **17**.

BUTT (J. G.) *See* Butt (Geraldine) and Butt (J. G.) John Smith, and other stories. 1880. 8°. **12809**. g. **47**.

BUTT (Jane)

—— *See* Butt (Brian A.) and Butt (J.) Falmouth Panorama, *etc.* [1955.] 16°. **010368**. a. **50**.

BUTT (Jeremiah) *See* Veal (Edward) Good Deeds Done for God's House. Or, a Sermon preached on the occasion of the death of Dr Jeremiah Butt. 1694. 4°. **1416**. d. **61**.

BUTT (Joannes Marten) Tentamen medicum inaugurale, de spontanea sanguinis separatione, *etc.* pp. 62. *Apud G. Gordon & Socios: Edinburgi*, 1760. 8°. T. **76**. (**7**.)

—— [Another edition.] 1769. *See* Sandifort (E.) Thesaurus dissertationum, *etc.* vol. 2. 1768, *etc.* 4°. **41**. g. **9**.

BUTT (John) Memoirs of the late Anthony Metcalfe-Gibson. pp. 118. *T. Wilson: Kendal*, 1903. 8°. **10827**. ff. **8**.

BUTT (*Sir* JOHN) Sir John Butt: a farce. In two acts. [By Eaglefield J. Smith.] pp. 56. *Edinburgh*, 1798. 8°. **11777**. b. **23**.

BUTT (JOHN EVERETT)

— *See* DYSON (Henry V. D.) and BUTT (J. E.) Augustans and Romantics, 1689–1830, *etc.* 1940. 8°. **11872.g.21/3.**

— *See* DYSON (Henry V. D.) and BUTT (J. E.) Augustans and Romantics, 1689–1830, *etc.* 1950. 8°. **11872.g.22/3.**

— *See* POPE (Alexander) [*Works.—English.*] The Twickenham Edition of the Poems of A. Pope. General editor: J. Butt. 1939, *etc.* 8°. W.P. **9589**.

— *See* POPE (Alexander) [*Works.—English.*] The Twickenham Edition of the Poems of Alexander Pope, *etc.* (vol. IV. Imitations of Horace with An Epistle to Dr. Arbuthnot and the Epilogue to the Satires. Edited by J. Butt.) 1939, *etc.* 8°. W.P. **9589/4**.

— *See* POPE (Alexander) *the Poet.* [*Works.—English.*] The Twickenham Edition of the Poems of Alexander Pope. General editor: J. Butt. 1953, *etc.* 8°. W.P. B. **455**.

— *See* POPE (Alexander) *the Poet.* [*Works.—English.*] The Twickenham Edition of the Poems of Alexander Pope, *etc.* (vol. 4. Imitations of Horace, with An Epistle to Dr. Arbuthnot and The Epilogue to the Satires. Edited by J. Butt.) 1953, *etc.* 8°. W.P. B. **455**.

— *See* POPE (Alexander) *the Poet.* [*Epistle to Dr. Arbuthnot.*] An Epistle to Dr. Arbuthnot . . . Edited by J. Butt. 1954. 8°. W.P. **6815/34**.

— *See* VOLTAIRE (F. M. A. de) [*Candide.*] Candide; or, Optimism. Translated by J. Butt. 1947. 8°. W.P. **513/4**.

— The Augustan Age [of English literature]. pp. 152. *Hutchinson's University Library: London,* 1950. 8°. [*Hutchinson's University Library.* no. 43.] W.P. **1413/43**.

— A Bibliography of Izaak Walton's "Lives." *Oxford,* 1930. 4°. [*Oxford Bibliographical Society. Proceedings & Papers.* vol. 2. pt. 4.] **N.L.25.a.**

— Editorial Problems in Eighteenth-Century Poetry. [On editing the poetry of Pope.] *In:* POTTER (George R.) Editing Donne and Pope, *etc.* pp. 11–22. [1953?] 8°. **11923**. c. **23**.

— Fielding. pp. 35. *Longmans, Green & Co.: London,* 1954. 8°. [*Bibliographical Series of Supplements to "British Book News."* no. 57.] W.P. **9502/57**.

— Pope's Taste in Shakespeare . . . A paper, *etc.* pp. 21. 1936. 8°. *See* LONDON.—III. *Shakespeare Association.* Ac. **9489**. b/**10**.

BUTT (JOHN MARTEN) A Commentary on the Prophecy of Daniel, relating to the Seventy Weeks. pp. 40. *J. Hatchard: London,* 1807. 12°. **3185**. aa. **50**.

— A Commentary upon the Last Vision of the Prophet Daniel, contained in the 10th, 11th, and 12th chapters: being a sequel to the Commentary on the Seventy Weeks, *etc.* pp. 74. *J. Hatchard: London,* 1808. 12°. **3125**. de. **2**. (**1**.)

— The Divinity of the Apocalypse demonstrated by its fulfilment: in answer to Professor Michaelis [i.e. to his "Einleitung in die . . . Schriften des Neuen Bundes"] pp. 313. *T. Holl: Worcester; J. Hatchard: London* 1809. 12°. **3187**. a. **68**

BUTT (JOHN MARTEN)

— The Genuineness of the Book of Enoch investigated. pp. 92. *L. B. Seeley & Son: London,* 1837. 8°. **3166**. df. **28**.

— A Key to the Prophet Isaiah, *etc.* [By J. M. Butt.] pp. vii. 40. 1823. 12°. *See* BIBLE.—*Appendix.—Isaiah.* [*Miscellaneous.*] **3166**. b. **7**.

— The Pilgrimage of Theophilus to the City of God. [By J. M. Butt.] pp. 257. 1812. 8°. *See* THEOPHILUS. **1119**. d. **28**.

— Queries on the Doctrine of the Church of England respecting Baptism, *etc.* [By J. M. Butt.] pp. 72. 1824. 12°. *See* ENGLAND.—*Church of England.* [*Appendix.*] **4325**. aa. **30**.

— The Revelation of St. John, compared with itself and the rest of Scripture . . . The second edition, revised and corrected. (An Appendix, *etc.*—Notes, *etc.*—A Second Part of Notes, *etc.*—A Third Part of Notes, *etc.*) 5 pt. *G. Gower: Kidderminster,* 1804, 02–06. 8°. **3187**. b. **19**.

BUTT (JOHN WILLIAM) *See* MUSGRAVE (*Sir* Richard) *Bart.* The Origin of Orangemen . . . With other extracts from Sir R. Musgrave's Memoirs of the Rebellions in Ireland . . . By . . . J. W. Butt. 1813. 8°. **8145**. bbb. **1**. (**1**.)

— A Short and Plain Address to Christians, on the necessity of uniting faith with practice. pp. 24. *R. Thorogood: Downham,* 1818. 12°. **4402**. b. **15**.

BUTT (JOSEPH) successively *Bishop of Cambysopolis* and *Archbishop of Nicopsi.* *See* LITURGIES.—*Latin Rite.—Rituals.*—I. *Abridgments and Extracts.* The Rite of Marriage. The Nuptial Mass and the Form of Blessing without the Mass; with an instruction by the Rt. Rev. Bishop Butt. 1915. 8°. **3366**. de. **36**

BUTT (JOSEPH V.)

— *See* UNITED STATES OF AMERICA.—*Congress.—Library.—Hispanic Foundation.* Latin American Periodicals current in the Library of Congress. Prepared by M. M. Wise, with the aid of . . . J. V. Butt. 1941. 4°. **11924**. d. **40**.

BUTT (K.) The Reverse of the Picture. An art reverie. [With a frontispiece by E. Œ. Somerville.] pp. 47. *R. Grant & Son: Edinburgh,* 1888. 8°. **12806**. r. **14**.

BUTT (KATHLEEN M.) Ptahlīth. Some Indian and other stories. pp. 191. *W. Newman & Co.: Calcutta,* 1897. 12°. **012627**. e. **71**.

BUTT (MARTHA HAINES) Antifanaticism: a tale of the South. pp. xii. 268. *Lippincott, Grambo & Co.: Philadelphia,* 1853. 12°. **12706**. d. **8**.

BUTT, afterwards **SHERWOOD** (MARY MARTHA)

WORKS.

— The Works of Mrs. Sherwood, *etc.* [With plates, including a portrait.] 16 vol. *Harper & Bros.: New York,* 1855. 12°. **12272**. dd. **1**.
Each volume has an additional titlepage, engraved.

TWO OR MORE WORKS.

— My Three Uncles; and The Swiss Cottage. pp. 64. *Darton & Clark: London,* [1825?] 16°. **4411**. a. **17**.

— The Hedge of Thorns . . . Third edition. (On the Formation of Sin in the Heart, or, the Story of the apples. [From "The History of the Fairchild Family."]—The Denials of him who would not deny himself. [A tale by Jane Taylor.]) pp. 79. *American Sunday School Union: Philadelphia,* 1827. 12°. **864**. h. **4**.

BUTT, afterwards **SHERWOOD** (MARY MARTHA) [TWO OR MORE WORKS.]

—— Mary Grant; or, the Secret fault . . . Revised by the Committee of Publication. (Obedience to Parents.) pp. 72. *American Sunday School Union: Philadelphia*, 1827. 12°. **864**. h. **5**.

—— The Mail Coach; and The Old Lady's Complaint. pp. 64. *Darton & Clark: London*, [1830 ?] 16°. **4416**. a. **15**.

—— The Little Woodman and his Dog Cæsar, and The Orphan Boy . . . New edition, illustrated. pp. 138. *Houlston & Wright: London*, 1860. 12°. **12807**. a. **41**.

—— The Little Woodman, and his Dog Cæsar. (Stolen Sweets.—Little Things.) pp. 64. *A. Hislop & Co.: Edinburgh*, [1869.] 16°. **12808**. ee. **30**.

—— The Lily Series. 6 vol.

1. Flowers of the Forest. pp. 108.
2. The Young Forester. pp. 108.
3. The Little Woodman and his Dog. pp. 108.
4. The Little Beggars. pp. 108.
5. The Two Orphans; or the Roman baths. pp. 108.
6. Joan the Trustworthy. pp. 108.

R. Carter & Bros.: New York, 1871. 12°. **4413**. b. **9**.

—— The Little Woodman, and his Dog Caesar. (Ambrose the Blacksmith.) pp. 72. *W. P. Nimmo: Edinburgh*, 1871. 16°. **12808**. e. **17**.

—— The Little Woodman, and The May-Bee. pp. iv. 92. *F. Warne & Co.: London*, [1875.] 32°. **4418**. aa. **54**.

—— The Lost Trunk. (The Good Nurse.) pp. 62. *Book Society: London*, [1877.] 16°. **12809**. b. **22**.

—— Martin Crook, and the Rose and Nightingale. pp. 62. *Book Society: London*, [1877.] 16°. **12809**. aaa. **7**.
The author's name is given only on the cover.

—— Mrs. Sherwood's Juvenile Library . . . New edition. 3 vol.

1. The Fall of Pride. 2. Grandmamma Parker. 3. The Rose and the Nightingale. 4. Frank Beachamp. pp. 218.
1. The Heron's Plume. 2. Duty is Safety. 3. Martin Crook. 4. Jack the Sailor Boy. pp. 230.
1. The White Pigeon. 2. The Lost Trunk. 3. Think before you Act. 4. The Traveller. pp. 254.

W. Swan Sonnenschein & Allen: London, 1880. 8°. **12808**. de. **6**.

—— The History of Little Henry and his Bearer, and other stories (The Orphan Boy—Soffrona and her cat Muff). pp. 91. *Ward, Lock & Co.: London & New York*, [1883.] 8°. **12810**. aaa. **57**.

—— Charles Lorraine: or, the Young Soldier . . . Copyright edition, illustrated. (Reflections on the Hours of the Night. [In verse.]) pp. 128. *Houlston & Sons: London*, [1887.] 8°. **4417**. k. **10**.

—— The Juvenile Library. By Mrs. Sherwood. Containing a selection from her popular stories for young people. With . . . illustrations by Mary Sibree. pp. 377. *Swan Sonnenschein & Co.: London*, 1891. 8°. **012803**. ee. **25**.
Previous edition 1880.

—— Margot and the Golden Fish. (The Story of Little Martin.—Edwy and The Echo.—The Old Story of Mrs. Howard.) Re-told by Amy Steedman. Pictures by M. D. Spooner. pp. 96. *T. C. & E. C. Jack: London & Edinburgh*, [1908.] 8°. [*Grandmother's Favourites*.] **012804**. dd.

SINGLE WORKS.

—— Arzoomund . . . Second edition. pp. 101. *Houlston & Son: Wellington, Salop*, 1829. 12°. N. **1800**. (**1**.)

BUTT, afterwards **SHERWOOD** (MARY MARTHA) [SINGLE WORKS.]

—— The Ayah and Lady. *See* infra: The Lady and her Ayah.

—— Bible History, or, Scripture its own interpreter, illustrated, from the birth, to the death of Moses . . . Revised and enlarged. pp. xi. 204. *Knight & Lacy: London*, 1823. 12°. **3127**. b. **20**.

—— Biography Illustrated. pp. 163. *Darton & Clark: London*, [1836.] 16°. **10601**. a. **36**.

—— The Bitter Sweet. 2 pt. *Wellington, Salop*, [1830 ?] 8°. [*Houlston's Series of Tracts*. no. 19, 20.] **4410**. l. **1**.

—— The Blessed Family. (4th edit.) pp. 16. *W. Whittemore: London*, 1824. 8°. **4411**. de. **11**. (**5**.)

—— [Another edition.] pp. 16. *Houlston & Co.: London*, [1830 ?] 12°. **4422**. ee. **43**. (**3**.)

—— The Blind Man and Little George. pp. 15. *W. Whittemore: London*, [1824 ?] 12°. **4411**. de. **11**. (**6**.)

—— [Another edition.] pp. 15. *Houlston & Co.: London*, [1830 ?] 12°. **4422**. ee. **43**. (**10**.)

—— The Broken Hyacinth, or, Ellen and Sophia . . . Revised by the Committee of Publication. pp. 106. *American Sunday School Union: Philadelphia*, 1832. 12°. **864**. k. **18**.

—— The Busy Bee . . . Sixth edition. pp. 30. *F. Houlston & Son: Wellington, Salop*, 1822. 24°. **012806**. de. **27**. (**10**.)

—— Caroline Mordaunt; or, the Governess. pp. 214. *Darton & Clark: London*, [1853.] 12°. **1362**. e. **20**.

—— Charles Lorraine; or, the Young soldier, *etc*. 5 pt. *Houlston & Son: London*, [1830 ?] 12°. **4422**. ee. **43**. (**6**.)

—— Copyright edition, illustrated. pp. 109. *Houlston & Wright: London*, [1866.] 8°. **4414**. ff. **9**.

—— The Children of the Hartz Mountains. *See* infra: The Little Beggars.

—— The Christmas Carol. pp. 70. *Darton & Clark: London*, [1839.] 12°. **4413**. aa. **73**. (**1**.)

—— A Chronology of Ancient History, illustrated by parallel streams of time . . . With illustrative extracts from the ancient poets. 2 vol. *Longman & Co.: London*, 1826, 27. 8°. **799**. b. **2**.

—— Clara Stephens; or, the White rose . . . Revised by the Committee of Publication. pp. 144. *American Sunday School Union: Philadelphia*, 1827. 8°. **864**. i. **31**.

—— The Convent of St. Clair. pp. 74. *Thomas Melrose: Berwick*, 1833. 12°. **12804**. eee. **19**.

—— Conversations on the Bible, *etc*. *See* infra: Scripture Prints, *etc*.

—— The Cottage in the Wood. (No. 41, 42 of Houlston's Series of Tracts.) [With titlepages bearing the imprint: Houlston & Co.: London.] 2 pt. *In*: Narrative Tracts, moral and religious . . . Second series. [c. 1860.] 12°. **4431**. b. **64**.

—— The De Cliffords: an historical tale. By Mrs. Sherwood [or rather, by Sophia Streeten, afterwards Kelly, assisted by Mrs. Sherwood]. pp. 314. *Darton & Co.: London*, 1847. 12°. **12621**. b. **18**.

—— [Another issue.] *London*, [1847.] 8°. [*Parlour Library*. vol. 193.] **12600**. bbb.

BUTT, afterwards **SHERWOOD** (MARY MARTHA) [SINGLE WORKS.]

—— Do what you can. pp. 12. *London*, [1830 ?] 8°. [*Houlston's Series of Tracts.* no. 71.] **4410**. l. **1**.

—— Do your own Work. pp. 12. *London*, [1830 ?] 8°. [*Houlston's Series of Tracts.* no. 67.] **4410**. l. **1**.

—— The Druids of Britain. pp. 16. *Darton & Co.: London*, [1840 ?] 12°. **12804**. ff. **34**.

—— The Dry Ground. pp. 14. *Houlston & Son: Wellington, Salop*, 1827. 16°. T. **963***. **(10.)**

—— Second edition. pp. 15. *Houlston & Son: Wellington, Salop*, 1828. 24°. **012806**. de. **28**. **(4.)**

—— Dudley Castle. [A tale.] pp. 108. *W. Darton & Son: London*, [1834.] 12°. **12614**. ccc. **12**.

—— Duty is Safety; or, Troublesome Tom. *See* infra: The Holiday Keepsake.

—— Easy Questions for a Little Child . . . Tenth edition. pp. 47. *F. Houlston & Son: Wellington, Salop*, 1829. 24°. **012806**. de. **27**. **(3.)**

—— A Sequel to Mrs. Sherwood's Easy Questions for a Little Child. By E. O. B. [i.e. E. O. Bull.] 1848. 32°. *See* B., E. O. **4406**. a. **22**.

—— Emancipation. pp. 150. *Houlston & Son: Wellington, Salop*, 1829. 12°. N. **1800**. (**2**.)

—— Ermina; or, the second part of Juliana Oakley. pp. 108. *American Sunday School Union: Philadelphia*, 1827. 12°. **864**. h. **3**.

—— [Another edition.] pp. viii. 170. *Houlston & Son: London*, 1831. 12°. **012803**. de. **31**.

—— [Another copy.] **12804**. eee. **18**.

—— The Errand-Boy. pp. 35. *F. Houlston & Son: Wellington, Salop*, 1819. 12°. **12804**. de. **56**. **(3.)**

—— [Another edition.] Revised by the Committee of Publication. pp. 34. *American Sunday School Union: Philadelphia*, 1830. 12°. **864**. g. **55**.

—— The Fairchild Family. *See* infra: The History of the Fairchild Family.

—— The Fairy Knoll. pp. 153. *H. K. Lewis: London*, 1848. 18°. **4415**. c. **13**.

—— The Fall of Pride. pp. 62. *Book Society: London*, [1877.] 16°. **12809**. aaa. **5**.

—— The Father's Eye . . . Stereotype edition. pp. 38. *Thomas Melrose: Berwick*, 1833. 12°. **12314**. df. **6**. **(2.)**

—— The Fawns. pp. 15. *Houlston & Son: Wellington, Salop*, 1828. 24°. **1210**. b. **52**. **(3.)**

—— [Another copy.] **012806**. de. **28**. **(2.)**

—— The Flowers of the Forest. By the author of "Little Henry and his Bearer" [i.e. M. M. Butt, afterwards Sherwood]. pp. 108. 1830. 12°. *See* FLOWERS. **12836**. a. **3**.

—— The Flowers of the Forest. By the author of "Little Henry and his Bearer" [i.e. M. M. Butt, afterwards Sherwood]. Third edition. pp. 108. 1834. 12°. *See* FLOWERS. **12822**. a. **36**.

—— The Flowers of the Forest. By the author of "Little Henry and his Bearer" [i.e. M. M. Butt, afterwards Sherwood]. pp. 108. 1839. 12°. *See* FLOWERS. **012803**. de. **29**.

BUTT, afterwards **SHERWOOD** (MARY MARTHA) [SINGLE WORKS.]

—— As Flores do Bosque. Pelo redactor de Minino Henry e seo servo [i.e. M. M. Butt, afterwards Sherwood]. pp. 97. 1835. 12°. *See* FLORES. **4399**. i. **28**.

—— The Fountain of Living Waters . . . By the author of "Little Henry and his Bearer" [i.e. M. M. Butt, afterwards Sherwood]. pp. 30. [1825 ?] 12°. *See* FOUNTAIN. **863**. f. **30**. **(2.)**

—— [Another copy.] T. **980***. **(7.)**

—— Frank Beauchamp, or, the Sailor's Family. *See* infra: The Juvenile Forget-me-not.

—— A General Outline of Profane History . . . Second edition. pp. xi. 297. *Houlston & Son: Wellington, Salop*, 1823. 12°. **9009**. a. **3**.

—— The Gipsy Babes. A tale of the last century. pp. 64. *F. Houlston & Son: Wellington, Salop*, 1826. 12°. **4413**. e. **62**.

—— The Gipsy Babes. A tale of the last century . . . Second edition. pp. 64. *Houlston & Son: Wellington, Salop*, 1827. 12°. **12804**. df. **29**. **(6.)**

—— The Golden Chain . . . Embellished with cuts by Bewick [i.e. R. E. Bewick]. pp. 85. *Thomas Melrose: Berwick*, 1830. 8°. **4416**. cc. **16**.

—— The Governess; or, the Little female academy. By Mrs. Sherwood. [Recast by Mrs. Sherwood from the work of the same name by Sarah Fielding.] pp. iv. 250. *F. Houlston & Son: Wellington, Salop*, 1820. 12°. **4415**. f. **2**.

—— Fifth edition. pp. iv. 252. *Houlston & Son: London*, 1832. 8°. **4415**. f. **13**.

—— The History of Emily and her Mother. [An extract from "The Governess."] pp. 66. *F. Houlston & Son: Wellington, Salop*, 1826. 12°. **012806**. i. **33**. *With an engraved frontispiece dated* 1825.

—— Fourth edition. pp. 66. *Houlston & Son: London*, 1831. 12°. **4399**. de. **33**.

—— Histoire d'Émilie Nugent . . . Traduite de l'anglais de Mrs. Sherwood [i.e. from "The History of Emily and her Mother"]. pp. 48. *Houlston, Mère & Fils: Wellington, Salop*, 1825. 8°. **4414**. cc. **22**.

—— Grandmamma Parker, or, the Father's return. *See* infra: The Juvenile Forget-me-not.

—— The Happy Choice; or, the Potters' common. *See* infra: The Potters' Common.

—— The Hedge of Thorns. pp. 98. *J. Hatchard: London*, 1819. 12°. N. **1802**.

—— The Heron's Plume. pp. 62. *Book Society: London*, [1877.] 16°. **12809**. aaa. **2**.

—— The Hills. pp. 15. *Houlston & Son: Wellington, Salop*, 1828. 24°. **1210**. b. **52**. **(5.)**

—— [Another copy.] **012806**. de. **27**. **(6.)**

—— The History of Emily and her Brothers . . . Twelfth edition. pp. 30. *F. Houlston & Son: Wellington, Salop*, 1824. 24°. **012806**. de. **27**. **(5.)**

—— The History of Emily and her Mother. *See* supra: The Governess.

—— The History of George Desmond; founded on facts which occurred in the East Indies, and now published as a useful caution to young men going out to that country. [By M. M. Butt.] pp. 290. 1821. 8°. *See* DESMOND (George) **12614**. bb. **9**.

BUTT, afterwards **SHERWOOD** (Mary Martha) [Single Works.]

—— The History of Henry Milner, a little boy, who was not brought up according to the fashions of this world . . . The second edition. pt. 1, 3, 4. *J. Hatchard & Son: London*, 1823–37. 12°. N. **1007**. (**1**.), **1008***, **1008****.
Pt. 1 *only is of the second edition. Imperfect; wanting pt.* 2.

—— Fifth edition [of pt. 1, 2.] pp. viii. 466. *J. Hatchard & Son: London*, 1835. 12°. **4415**. bbb. **13**.

—— The History of John Marten, a sequel to the Life of Henry Milner. pp. 517. *J. Hatchard & Son: London*, 1844. 12°. **1362**. i. **7**.

—— The History of Little George and his Penny . . . Fourteenth edition. pp. 29. *F. Houlston & Son: Wellington, Salop*, 1828. 24°. **012806**. de. **28**. (**10**.)

—— The History of Little Henry and his Bearer . . . Thirteenth edition. pp. 139. *F. Houlston & Son: Wellington, Salop*, 1819. 12°. **4413**. e. **63**.
With an additional titlepage, engraved.

—— The History of Little Henry and his Bearer, *etc.* [By M. M. Butt, afterwards Sherwood.] pp. 69. 1832. 12°. *See* Henry. **864**. i. **20**.

—— New edition. pp. 103. *T. J. Allman: London*, 1859. 18°. **4414**. b. **26**.

—— [Another edition.] Little Henry and his Bearer. pp. 62. *T. Nelson & Sons: London*, 1859. 16°. **4414**. a. **17**.

—— A new edition, *etc.* pp. 96. *Routledge, Warne, & Routledge: London*, 1864. 16°. **4415**. a. **22**.

—— Copyright edition . . . illustrated. pp. iv. 107. *Houlston & Wright: London*, 1866. 8°. **4415**. ccc. **13**.

—— [Another edition.] pp. 50. [1870.] 16°. *See* Henry. **12808**. ee. **17**. (**1**.)

—— [Another edition.] pp. 64. *A. Hislop & Co.: Edinburgh*, [1870.] 16°. **4413**. a. **13**.

—— [Another edition.] pp. 72. *W. P. Nimmo: Edinburgh*, 1871. 16°. **4412**. a. **69**. (5.)

—— [Another edition.] pp. 96. *W. Swan Sonnenschein & Co.: London*, [1884.] 16°. **12810**. a. **13**.

—— Histoire du petit Henri; traduite de l'anglois . . . par L. Sémonin. pp. 146. *Houlston, Mère & Fils: Wellington, Salop*, 1820. 12°. **1210**. f. **45**.
With an additional titlepage, engraved.

—— [Another copy.] Histoire du petit Henri, *etc.* *Wellington*, 1820. 12°. **600**. i. **23/83**.

—— Der kleine Heinrich und sein Träger . . . Aus dem Englischen übersetzt. pp. 72. *Neu-York*, [1850 ?] 8°. **4416**. bb. **18**.

—— The History of Little Lucy and her Dhaye . . . Second edition. pp. 151. *F. Houlston & Son: Wellington, Salop*, 1825. 12°. **4415**. aaa. **20**.
With an additional titlepage, engraved.

—— The History of Lucy Clare. By the author of "Susan Gray" [i.e. M. M. Butt, afterwards Sherwood], *etc.* pp. 147. *See* Clare (Lucy) 1815. 12°. T. **980***. (**1**.)

—— Fourteenth edition. pp. 137. *F. Houlston & Sons: Wellington, Salop*, 1824. 12°. **12809**. df. **47**.

—— The History of Lucy Clare . . . New edition. pp. 137. *Houlston & Stoneman: London*, 1853. 12°. **04422**. aa. **50**.

BUTT, afterwards **SHERWOOD** (Mary Martha) [Single Works.]

—— [Another edition.] 1882. 8°. *See* Clare (Lucy) **12600**. g. **26**.

—— [Another edition.] pp. 111. *J. Gemmell: Edinburgh*, 1883. 8°. **4419**. i. **41**.

—— [Another edition.] pp. 111. *Hodder & Stoughton: London*, [1887.] 8°. **4413**. n. **19**.

—— The History of Mary Saunders. pp. 16. *Houlston & Co.: London*, [1830 ?] 12°. **4431.a.111.(7.)**

—— The History of Mrs. Catharine Crawley. pp. 101. *F. Houlston & Son: Wellington, Salop*, 1824. 12°. **4415**. aaa. **19**

—— The History of Susan Gray; as related by a Clergyman: designed for the benefit of young women when going into service, &c. [By M. M. Butt, afterwards Sherwood.] A new edition. pp. 164. 1815. 12°. *See* Clergyman. **4907**. aa. **8**.

—— A new edition. pp. 143. *F. Houlston & Sons: Wellington, Salop*, 1825. 12°. **12809**. df. **45**.

—— [Another edition.] pp. 96. [1830 ?] 24°. *See* Clergyman. **4906**. a. **76**.

—— Parlour edition. pp. iv. 134. *Houlston & Wright; S. W. Partridge & Co.: London*, [1869.] 8°. **4416**. ccc. **13**.

—— [Another edition.] pp. 178. *J. Blackwood & Co.: London*, [1869.] 12°. **4413**. aaa. **12**.

—— [Another edition.] pp. 142. *Gall & Inglis: Edinburgh*, [1870.] 16°. **12808**. ee. **21**.

—— [Another edition.] pp. 192. *G. Routledge & Sons: London*, 1880. 8°. **4422**. k. **26**.

—— [Another copy.] **4420**. b. **8**.

—— [Another edition.] pp. 176. *J. Gemmell: Edinburgh*, 1883. 8°. **4419**. i. **40**.

—— [Another issue.] *Edinburgh*, 1883. 8°. **12600**. g. **21**. (2.)

—— [Another edition.] pp. 176. *Hodder & Stoughton: London*, [1887.] 8°. **4413**. n. **15**.

—— The History of the Fairchild Family; or, the Child's manual: being a collection of stories calculated to shew the importance and effects of a religious education. (Pt. 3 by Mrs. Sherwood, and her daughter, Mrs. Streeten.) 3 pt. *J. Hatchard: London*, 1818–47. 12°. **1362**. f. **1**.

—— The History of the Fairchild Family . . . Second edition [of pt. 1]. pp. 302. *J. Hatchard: London*, 1818. 12°. **04422**. aaa. **11**.

—— Fourth edition, corrected [of pt. 1]. pp. 302. *J. Hatchard & Son: London*, 1819. 12°. **4406**. i. **10**.

—— Fifth edition [of pt. 1]. pp. 300. *J. Hatchard & Son: London*, 1822. 8°. **1078**. h. **38**.

—— [Another edition of pt. 1.] [With "Some account of the authoress," signed: J. M.] pp. vi. 213. *Ward, Lock & Tyler: London*, [1875.] 8°. [*Rose Library.*] **12209**. cc. **14**. (**1**.)

—— [Another edition of pt. 1–3.] 3 pt. pp. 572. *Hatchards; G. Routledge & Son: London*, 1876. 8°. **12803**. d. **1**.

—— [Another edition of pt. 1.] pp. viii. 300. *Ward, Lock & Tyler: London*, [1876.] 8°. **12804**. dd. **10**.

—— [Another edition of pt. 1.] pp. vi. 213. *Ward, Lock & Co.: London,* [1879.] 8°. [*Lily Series.*] **12704**. h. 4.

—— [Another edition of pt. 1–3.] 3 pt. pp. 542. *J. Nisbet & Co.: London,* [1889.] 8°. **4410**. o. **31**.

—— [Another edition of pt. 1, 2.] Edited with introduction by Mary E. Palgrave. With illustrations by Florence M. Rudland. pp. xxxiii. 470. *Wells Gardner & Co.: London,* 1902. 8°. **12809**. o. **35**.

—— Die Familie Fairschild . . . nach der französischen Uebersetzung deutsch bearbeitet [by Adalbert von der Recke-Volmerstein]. [Pt. 1.] pp. viii. 425. *Düsselthal,* 1839. 8°. **012803**. df. **19**.

—— The Fairchild Family . . . Re-told by Jeanie Lang [from pt. 1, 2]. Pictures by Evelyn Beale. pp. 111. *T. C. & E. C. Jack: London & Edinburgh,* [1908.] 8°. [*Grandmother's Favourites.*] **012804**. dd.

—— [Another edition, abridged, of pt. 1, 2.] Edited by Lady Strachey. Containing eight full page illustrations in colour by Miss Sybil Tawse. pp. vii. 354. *A. & C. Black: London,* 1913. 8°. **012803**. h. **81**.

—— The History of Theophilus and Sophia. pp. 127. *Houlston & Son: Wellington, Salop,* 1818. 12°. **012807**. de. **13**.

—— Sixth edition. pp. 127. *F. Houlston & Son: Wellington, Salop,* 1822. 12°. **4416**. aa. **20**.

—— [Another edition.] The Shepherd of the Pyrenees . . . Revised by the Committee of Publication. pp. 54. *American Sunday School Union: Philadelphia,* [1830 ?] 12°. **864**. g. **57**.

—— [Another edition.] The History of Theophilus and Sophia . . . Eleventh edition. pp. 127. *Houlston & Son: London,* 1836. 12°. **012803**. de. **32**.

—— The Holiday Keepsake. [Consisting of: "Sisterly Love," "The Traveller," "Duty is Safety," "Jack the Sailor Boy."] pp. 256. *Darton & Clark: London,* [1841.] 16°. **1210**. e. **10**.

—— Duty is Safety: or, Troublesome Tom . . . Fifth edition. [Extracted from the "Holiday Keepsake."] *Darton & Hodge: London,* 1864. 16°. **12835**. aa. **43**.

—— Duty is Safety; or, Troublesome Tom. [Extracted from "The Holiday Keepsake."] *Book Society: London,* [1877.] 16°. **12809**. aaa. **6**.

—— Jack, the Sailor Boy. [Extracted from "The Holiday Keepsake."] *Book Society: London,* [1877.] 16°. **12809**. aaa. **1**.

—— The Traveller. [Extracted from "The Holiday Keepsake."] *Book Society: London,* [1877.] 16°. **12809**. aaa. **4**.

—— Home. pp. 15. *Houlston & Son: Wellington, Salop,* 1828. 24°. **1210**. b. **52**. (**1**.)

—— [Another copy.] **012806**. de. **27**. (**9**.)

—— The Hop-picking. 2 pt. *London,* [1830 ?] 8°. [*Houlston's Series of Tracts.* no. 61, 62.] **4410**. l. **1**.

—— The Idiot Boy. pp. 15. *Houlston & Son: Wellington, Salop,* 1828. 24°. **1210**. b. **52**. (**4**.)

—— [Another copy.] **012806**. de. **28**. (**6**.)

—— The Indian Pilgrim; or, the Progress of the pilgrim Nazareenee . . . from the city of the Wrath of God to the city of Mount Zion. Delivered under the similitude of a dream, *etc.* pp. viii. 214. *F. Houlston & Son: Wellington, Salop,* 1818. 8°. **4413**. cc. **13**.

—— Second edition. pp. viii. 214. *F. Houlston & Son: Wellington, Salop,* 1818. 8°. **4414**. g. **20**.

—— Third edition. pp. viii. 214. *F. Houlston & Son: Wellington,* 1820. 12°. **4409**. gg. **3**.

—— Sixth edition. pp. viii. 214. *F. Houlston & Son: Wellington, Salop,* 1826. 12°. **4413**. k. **11**.

—— Seventh edition. pp. viii. 214. *Houlston & Son: London, Wellington, Salop,* 1832. 12°. **4416**. h. **11**.

—— The Indian Pilgrim . . . New edition. pp. viii. 214. *Houlston & Stoneman: London,* 1846. 12°. **4408**. k. **42**.

—— New edition, illustrated. pp. vi. 324. *Houlston & Wright: London,* 1858. 8°. **4417**. h. **22**.

—— The Infant's Grave . . . Second edition. pp. 75. *F. Houlston & Son: Wellington, Salop,* 1825. 12°. **4414**. aa. **14**.

—— The Infant's Progress from the Valley of Destruction to Everlasting Glory. pp. 237. *F. Houlston: Wellington, Salop,* 1821. 8°. **4410**. k. **2**.

—— The Infant's Progress . . . Third edition. pp. iv. 238. *F. Houlston & Son: Wellington, Salop.,* 1823. 12°. **4408**. k. **40**.

—— The Infant's Progress . . . Fourth edition. pp. iv. 238. *F. Houlston & Son: Wellington, Salop,* 1825. 12°. **12835.b.47.**

—— [Another edition.] Revised by the Committee of Publication. pp. vi. 197. *American Sunday School Union: Philadelphia,* 1829. 12°. **864**. k. **17**.

—— The Infant's Progress . . . Fifth edition. pp. iv. 238. *Houlston & Son: London,* 1830. 12°. **12835.b.48.**

—— Sixth edition. pp. iv. 238. *Houlston: London,* 1835. 12°. **4399**. ee. **33**.

—— Eleventh edition. pp. iv. 238. *Houlston & Stoneman: London,* 1847. 12°. **4410**. o. **36**.

—— The Infant Pilgrim's Progress from the Valley of Destruction to Everlasting Glory . . . New edition. [With plates.] pp. viii. 366. *Houlston & Stoneman: London,* 1856. 8°. **04422**. b. **31**.

With an additional titlepage, engraved.

—— The Infirmary . . . Nineteenth edition. pp. 35. *Houlston & Co.: London,* [1846.] 16°. **4422**. aa. **6**. (**1**.)

—— Intimate Friends . . . Second edition. pp. 70. *Houlston & Son: London,* 1834. 12°. **4413**. e. **64**.

—— An Introduction to Astronomy. Intended for little children. pp. vii. 56. *F. Houlston & Son: Wellington Salop,* 1817. 12°. T. **971***. (**5**.)

—— Second edition. pp. vii. 54. *F. Houlston & Son: Wellington, Salop,* 1818. 12°. **9504**. aaa. **8**. (**3**.)

—— An Introduction to Astronomy . . . Third edition. pp. 54. *F. Houlston & Son: Wellington, Salop,* 1819. 12°. **8561**. a. **54**.

—— Eighth edition. pp. vii. 54. *Houlston & Son: London & Wellington, Salop,* 1831. 12°. **8560**. aa. **6**.

BUTT, afterwards **SHERWOOD** (Mary Martha) [Single Works.]

—— An Introduction to Geography. Intended for little children. pp. vii. 136. *F. Houlston & Son: Wellington, Salop*, 1818. 12°. **10004**. aa. **34**.

—— Fourth edition. pp. vii. 136. *F. Houlston & Son: Wellington, Salop*, 1828. 12°. **10004**. aa. **35**.

—— It is not my Business. pp. 12. *Houlston & Son: London*, [c. 1835.] 8°. [*Houlston's Series of Tracts.* no. 81.] **4410**. l. **1/81**.

—— Jack the Sailor Boy. *See* supra: The Holiday Keepsake.

—— Joan; or, Trustworthy. (No. 31, 32 of Houlston's Series of Tracts.) [With titlepages bearing the imprint: Houlston & Co.: London.] 2 pt. *In:* Narrative Tracts, moral and religious . . . Second series. [c. 1860.] 12°. **4431**. b. **64**.

—— Joys and Sorrows of Childhood. (The Loss of the Rhone.) pp. 171. *Darton & Clark; London*, [1844.] 18°. **1362**. d. **14**.

With an additional titlepage, engraved.

—— Juliana Oakley . . . Illustrated . . . Fourth edition. pp. 119. *Knight & Lacey: London*, 1825. 12°. N. **358**. (**2**.)

—— [Another edition.] Revised by the Committee of Publication. Second edition. pp. 88. *American Sunday School Union: Philadelphia*, 1827. 12°. **864**. h. **2**.

—— Seventh edition. pp. 164. *Houlston & Son: London*, 1837. 12°. **012803**. de. **55**.

—— Julietta di Lavenza. *Eng.* pp. 208. *J. Hatchard & Son: London*, 1841. 8°. **1362**. a. **35**.

—— The Juvenile Forget-me-not. [Consisting of: "Think before you Act," "Frank Beauchamp," "Grandmama Parker" and "Uncle Manners."] pp. 254. *Darton & Clark: London*, [1841.] 16°. **1210**. e. **9**.

—— Frank Beauchamp; or, the Sailor's family. [Extracted from "The Juvenile Forget-me-not."] *Book Society: London*, [1877.] 16°. **12809**. aaa. **3**.

—— Grandmamma Parker; or, the Father's return. [Extracted from "The Juvenile Forget-me-not."] *Book Society: London*, [1877.] 16°. **12809**. b. **24**.

—— Think before you Act. [Extracted from "The Juvenile Forget-me-not."] pp. 64. *Book Society: London*, [1877.] 16°. **12809**. b. **19**.

—— The Lady and her Ayah, an Indian story. By the author of Little Henry and his Bearer [i.e. M. M. Butt, afterwards Sherwood], *etc.* pp. 108. 1816. 12°. *See* Lady. **4414**. aa. **41**.

—— [Another edition.] The Ayah and Lady . . . Fourth edition. pp. 56. *Christian Literature Society for India: London & Madras; Madras* printed, 1902. 8°. **012199**. ee. **4/12**.

—— The Lady in the Arbour. pp. 15. *Houlston & Son: Wellington, Salop*, 1827. 16°. T. **963***. (**9**.)

—— Second edition. pp. 15. *Houlston & Son: Wellington, Salop*, 1828. 24°. **012806**. de. **28**. (**8**.)

—— The Lady of the Manor. Being a series of conversations on the subject of Confirmation. Intended for the use of the middle and higher ranks of young females. [With plates.] 7 vol. *F. Houlston & Son: Wellington, Salop*, 1825–29. 12°. N. **308–310**.
Vol. 1, 2 are of the second edition.

—— New edition. 5 vol. *Houlston & Wright: London*, 1860. 8°. **04412**. ee. **8**.

—— The Lambourne Bell. pp. 20. *W. Whittemore: London*, [1824 ?] 12°. **4411**. de. **11**. (**7**.)

—— The Latter Days. pp. vii. 273. *R. B. Seeley & W. Burnside: London*, 1833. 8°. **693**. c. **16**.

—— The Life of Mrs. Sherwood, chiefly autobiographical; with extracts from Mr. Sherwood's journal during his imprisonment in France and residence in India. Edited by her daughter, Sophia Kelly. [With a portrait.] pp. xii. 600. *Darton & Co.: London*, 1854. 8°. **1373**. h. **7**.

With an additional titlepage, engraved.

—— [Another edition, enlarged.] The Life and Times of Mrs. Sherwood, 1775–1851, from the diaries of Captain and Mrs. Sherwood. Edited by F. J. Harvey Darton. [With illustrations, including portraits.] pp. xiv. 519. *Wells Gardner & Co.: London*, 1910. 8°. **010827**. h. **9**.

—— The Life of Mrs. Sherwood, edited and abridged by Isabella Gilchrist. [With a portrait.] pp. 220. *Robert Sutton: London*, 1907. 8°. **10855**. b. **34**.

—— Little Arthur . . . Sixth edition. pp. 15. *F. Houlston & Son: Wellington, Salop*, 1826. 24°. **012806**. de. **28**. (**3**.)

—— The Little Beggars. pp. 36. *W. Whittemore: London*, 1824. 12°. **4411**. de. **11**. (**8**.)

—— The Little Beggars. 2 pt. *Houlston & Son: London*, [c. 1830.] 12°. **4431**. a. **111**. (**1**.)

—— [Another edition.] The Children of the Hartz Mountains; or, the Little beggars . . . Revised by the Committee of Publication. pp. 36. *American Sunday School Union: Philadelphia*, [1830 ?] 12°. **864**. g. **54**.

—— Little Henry and his Bearer. *See* supra: The History of Little Henry, *etc.*

—— The Little Momiere. pp. 226. *J. Hatchard & Son: London*, 1833. 12°. **12804**. gg. **5**.

—— [Another copy.] N. **929**. (**1**.)

—— Little Robert and the Owl . . . Eighth edition. pp. 31. *F. Houlston & Son: Wellington, Salop*, 1828. 24°. **012806**. de. **27**. (**2**.)

—— The Little Sunday-School Child's Reward . . . Fifteenth edition. pp. 15. *F. Houlston & Son: Wellington, Salop*, 1828. 24°. **012806**. de. **28**. (**12**.)

—— The Little Woodman, and his Dog Cæsar . . . Twenty-first edition. [With illustrations.] pp. 106. *Houlston & Co.: London*, [1850 ?] 12°. **12835**. aa. **1**.

—— The Little Woodman and his Dog Cæsar, and other stories. pp. 128. *Milner & Sowerby: Halifax*, 1865. 32°. **12842.1.29.**

—— The Little Woodman and his Dog Cæsar. [With illustrations.] pp. 62. *Seeley, Jackson & Halliday; S. W. Partridge & Co.: London*, [1869.] 4°. **12807**. f. **7**.

—— [Another edition.] pp. 32. *William Macintosh: London*, 1870. 32°. **4413**. a. **71**. (**1**.)

—— [Another edition.] pp. 32. *Haughton & Co.: London*, [1873.] 32°. **4409**. a. **66**. (**8**.)

—— [Another edition.] With illustrations. pp. 122. *G. Routledge & Sons: London,* [1878.] 8°. **12808**. d. **10**.

—— [Another edition.] pp. 64. *Partridge & Co.: London,* [1894.] 8°. **4399**. de. **22**.

—— [Another edition.] pp. 61. *Jarrold & Sons: London,* 1901 [1900]. 8°. **04410**. g. **26**.

—— The Loss of the Rhone. *See* supra: Joys and Sorrows of Childhood.

—— Lucy Clare . . . A new edition. pp. 123. *Milner & Co.: London,* [1885 ?] 8°. **04422**. a. **44**.

—— Maria and the Ladies, and other tales. By Mrs. Sherwood [or rather, by her daughter Sophia Kelly]. 6 pt. *Darton & Co.: London,* [1855 ?] 16°. **012803**. de. **103**.

—— Mary Anne. By the author of "Little Henry and his Bearer" [i.e. M. M. Butt, afterwards Sherwood], *etc.* pp. 36. [1820 ?] 12°. *See* MARY ANNE. T. **983***. (**7**.)

—— Mary Anne. By the author of "Little Henry and his Bearer" [i.e. M. M. Butt, afterwards Sherwood] . . . Second edition. pp. 36. [1823 ?] 12°. *See* MARY ANNE. **012803**. de. **44**.

—— Third edition. pp. 36. [1825 ?] 12°. *See* MARY ANNE. **863**. f. **28**. (**2**.)

—— The May-Bee. [A religious tract.] pp. 16. *American Tract Society: New York,* [1820 ?] 32°. **4422**. aa. **49**. (**8**.)

—— The May-Bee . . . Sixth edition. [With illustrations.] pp. 29. *F. Houlston & Son: Wellington, Salop,* 1825. 12°. **12835**. a. **51**.

—— Memoirs of Sergeant Dale, his daughter, and the orphan Mary. [By M. M. Butt, afterwards Sherwood.] pp. 98. 1816. 12°. *See* DALE (Thomas) *Sergeant*. **12803**. a. **61**.

—— Memoirs of Sergeant Dale . . . [By M. M. Butt, afterwards Sherwood.] Revised by the Committee of Publication. pp. 86. 1830. 12°. *See* DALE (Thomas) *Sergeant*. **864**. i. **11**.

—— Nineteenth edition. pp. 99. *Houlston & Son: London,* 1831. 12°. **12809**. df. **46**.

—— New edition. pp. 99. *Houlston & Stoneman: London,* [1845 ?] 12°. **012803**. e. **19**.

—— The Monk of Cimiés. pp. 428. *W. Darton & Son: London,* [1837 ?] 8°. N. **1488**.

—— [Another edition.] The Monk . . . New and improved edition. pp. 360. *Simpkin, Marshall & Co.: London; J. M. Burton & Co.: Ipswich,* [1855.] 12°. **4417**. c. **10**.

—— My Aunt Kate. pp. 72. *Houlston & Son: Wellington, Salop,* 1828. 12°. T. **983***. (**8**.)

—— My Uncle Timothy: an interesting tale for young persons. pp. 94. *Knight & Lacey; Harrison & Stephens: London,* 1825. 12°. N. **358**. (**1**.)

—— The Nun. [By M. M. Butt, afterwards Sherwood.] pp. 326. 1833. 8°. *See* NUN. **693**. c. **17**.

—— [Another edition.] pp. 326. 1836. 8°. *See* NUN. **12621**. c. **25**.

—— [Another edition.] pp. iv. 202 [282]. 1856. 12°. *See* NUN. **4417**. c. **31**

BUTT, afterwards **SHERWOOD** (MARY MARTHA) [SINGLE WORKS.]

—— New edition. pp. vi. 279. *Sampson Low & Co.: London,* [1857.] 8°. **4417**. h. **21**.

—— [A reissue.] *Simpkin, Marshall & Co.: London,* [1860.] 8°. **12618**. b. **9**.

—— [Another edition.] pp. 278. *Ward, Lock & Tyler: London,* [1876.] 8°. [*Rose Library.*] **12209**. cc. **14**. (**2**.)

—— The Nursery Maid's Diary. pp. 20. *W. Whittemore; Wightman & Cramp: London,* [1820 ?] 12°. **4418**. ccc. **39**.

—— Obedience. pp. 87. *T. Melrose: Berwick,* 1830. 12°. **012807**. de. **41**.

—— Obedience . . . Second edition. pp. 86. *Thomas Melrose: Berwick,* 1831. 12°. **12830**. e. **21**.

—— The Oddingley Murders. [An account of two murders in Oddingley, Worcs., 24 and 25 June 1806.] pp. 18. *Houlston & Son: London,* 1830. 12°. T. **1434**. (**5**.)

—— Sequel to the Oddingley Murders. pp. 18. *Houlston & Son: London,* 1830. 16°. **4415**. a. **66**. (**1**.)

—— Old Times. 2 pt. *Houlston & Son: London,* [c. 1830.] 8°. [*Houlston's Series of Tracts.* no. 23, 24.] **4410**. l. **1/23**, **24**.

—— The Orange Grove. pp. 29. *Houlston & Son: Wellington, Salop,* 1829. 8°. T. **1433**. (**4**.)

—— The Orange Grove . . . New edition. pp. 29. *Houlston & Wright: London,* [1860 ?] 12°. **12835**. a. **3**.

—— The Orphans of Normandy, or, Florentin and Lucie . . . Second edition. pp. 145. *J. Hatchard & Son: London,* 1822. 12°. **12811**. a. **15**.

—— Fourth edition. pp. 159. *J. Hatchard & Son: London,* 1825. 12°. **12804**. gg. **6**.

—— The Parson's Case of Jewels. pp. ix. 247. *Thomas Melrose: Berwick,* 1837. 12°. **942**. a. **13**.

—— The Penny Tract. pp. 20. *Houlston & Co.: London,* [1830 ?] 12°. **4431.a.111.(3.)**

—— Père la Chaise. [A tale.] pp. 100. *F. Houlston & Son: Wellington, Salop,* 1823. 24°. **4416**. c. **20**.

—— Second edition. pp. 100. *F. Houlston & Son: Wellington, Salop,* 1827. 12°. **12804**. ff. **8**.

—— [A reissue.] Père la Chaise . . . Second edition. *Houlston & Son: London,* 1834. 12°. **04422**. a. **72**.

—— Poor Burruff . . . Second edition. pp. 15. *F. Houlston & Son: Wellington, Salop,* 1828. 24°. **012806**. de. **27**. (**7**.)

—— The Poor Man of Colour: or, the Sufferings, privations, and death of Thomas Wilson, in the suburbs of the British metropolis. pp. 23. *W. Whittemore, etc.: London,* [1830 ?] 12°. **4416**. h. **10**.

—— The Potters' Common. 4 pt. *W. Whittemore: London; Houlston & Son: Wellington,* 1822–23. 12°. **4416**. aa. **21**.

—— [Another edition.] 4 pt. *Houlston & Son: London,* [1830 ?] 12°. **4422**. ee. **43**. (**12**.)

—— [Another edition.] The Happy Choice; or, the Potters' common . . . Revised by the Committee of Publication. pp. 69. *American Sunday School Union: Philadelphia,* 1830. 12°. **864**. i. **29**.

BUTT, afterwards SHERWOOD (MARY MARTHA) [SINGLE WORKS.]

—— The Pulpit and the Desk. pp. 57. *Houlston & Son: Wellington, Salop*, 1827. 12°. T. **969***. **(9.)**

—— The Rainbow. pp. 15. *F. Houlston & Son: Wellington, Salop*, 1828. 24°. **1210**. b. **52**. **(8.)**

—— [Another copy.] **012806**. de. **27**. **(8.)**

—— The Re-captured Negro . . . Second edition. pp. 72. *F. Houlston & Son: Wellington, Salop*, 1821. 12°. **4415**. aaa. **18**.

—— [Another edition.] Dazee, or the Re-captured Negro. pp. 47. *W. & J. Gilman: Newburyport* [*Mass.*], 1822. 12°. **4986**. a. **60**.

—— The Red Book. By the author of "Little Henry and his Bearer" [i.e. M. M. Butt, afterwards Sherwood]. Fourth edition. pp. 56. 1836. 12°. *See* BOOK. **12809**. df. **48**.

—— [Another edition.] pp. 36. [1845 ?] 12°. *See* BOOK. **4422**. ee. **1**.

—— Religious Fashion; or, the History of Anna . . . Revised by the Committee of Publication. pp. 138. *American Sunday School Union: Philadelphia*, 1827. 12°. **864**. g. **56**.

—— The Rose. A fairy tale . . . Eighth edition. pp. 27. *F. Houlston & Son: Wellington, Salop*, 1827. 24°. **012806**. de. **28**. **(9.)**

—— The Rosebuds. pp. 15. *Houlston & Son: Wellington, Salop*, 1828. 24°. **1210**. b. **52**. **(2.)**

—— [Another copy.] **012806**. de. **28**. **(5.)**

—— Roxabel. 3 vol. *Houlston & Son: London*, 1830, 31. 8°. N. **802**, **803**.

—— [A reissue of vol. 1.] Roxabel. *London*, 1831. 12°. **12650**. a. **104**.

—— Sabbaths on the Continent. pp. 136. *T. Ward & Co.: London*, 1835. 12°. **1123**. a. **38**.

—— Scripture Prints [illustrating Genesis], with explanations in the form of familiar dialogues. pp. viii. 254. *R. B. Seeley & W. Burnside: London*, 1831. 8°. **3128**. bb. **21**.
The titlepage is slightly mutilated.

—— [Another edition.] Conversations on the Bible [i.e. on Genesis] . . . Illustrated, *etc.* pp. vii. 254. *R. B. Seeley & W. Burnside: London*, 1841. 8°. **3128**. bbb. **24**.

—— Sea-side stories. [With plates.] pp. 144. *Darton & Clark: London*, [1838.] 16°. **1210**. b. **41**.

—— A Series of Questions and Answers, illustrative of the Church Catechism. pp. 39. *Houlston & Son: Wellington, Salop*, 1827. 16°. T. **963***. **(16.)**

—— [Another copy.] **012806**. de. **28**. **(11.)**

—— Shanty the Blacksmith. A tale of other times. pp. 169. *Darton & Clark: London*, [1844.] 12°. **012638**. p. **5**.
With an additional titlepage, engraved.

—— The Shepherd of the Pyrenees. *See* supra: The History of Theophilus and Sophia.

—— Sisterly Love. *See* supra: The Holiday Keepsake.

—— Social Tales for the Young. pp. 230. *William Darton & Son: London*, [1835 ?] 12°. **12830**. e. **29**.

—— Social Tales for the Young . . . New edition, with additions. pp. 247. *W. Darton & Son: London*, [1841.] 12°. **012807**. e. **14**.

—— Soffrona and her Cat Muff. pp. 31. *Houlston & Son: Wellington, Salop*, 1828. 24°. **1210**. b. **52**. **(11.)**

—— [Another copy.] **012806**. de. **27**. **(1.)**

—— Third edition. pp. 31. *Houlston & Son: London & Wellington, Salop*, 1832. 16°. **012808**. e. **22**.

—— Southstone's Rock. pp. 91. *Houlston & Son: Wellington, Salop*, 1828. 12°. N. **358**. **(3.)**

—— [Another copy.] **12806**. aaa. **8**.

—— Stories Explanatory of the Church Catechism . . . Ninth edition. pp. iv. 308. *F. Houlston & Son: Wellington, Salop*, 1822. 12°. **4416**. h. **9**.

—— Eighteenth edition. pp. iv. 308. *Houlston & Son: London*, 1835. 12°. **4399**. l. **34**.

—— New edition, with an introduction by the Rev. W. Meynell Whittemore. pp. viii. 424. *Houlston & Stoneman: London*, 1855. 8°. **4417**. c. **9**.
With an additional titlepage, engraved.

—— Stories on the Lord's Prayer. By Mrs. Sherwood. [With the text.] pp. 110. 1860. 16°. *See* LORD'S PRAYER. [*English.*] **4414**. a. **45**.

—— The Story Book of Wonders. By Mrs. Sherwood. [Descriptions by Mrs. Sherwood, with poems by various authors.] pp. 136. *Thomas Nelson: London & Edinburgh*, 1849. 16°. **12805**. d. **30**.

—— Susannah; or, the Three guardians . . . Revised by the Committee of Publication, *etc.* pp. 90. *American Sunday School Union: Philadelphia*, 1829. 12°. **864**. g. **58**.

—— Think before you Act. *See* supra: The Juvenile Forget-me-not.

—— The Thunder-Storm. pp. 15. *Houlston & Son: Wellington & Salop*, 1828. 24°. **1210**. b. **52**. **(6.)**

—— [Another copy.] **012806**. de. **28**. **(7.)**

—— The Traveller. *See* supra: The Holiday Keepsake.

—— The Turnpike-House. (No. 51, 52 of Houlston's Series of Tracts.) [With titlepages bearing the imprint: Houlston & Co.: London.] 2 pt. *In:* Narrative Tracts, moral and religious . . . Second series. [c. 1860.] 12°. **4431**. b. **64**.

—— Two Dolls. pp. 31. *F. Houlston & Son: Wellington, Salop*, 1826. 24°. **012806**. de. **28**. **(1.)**

—— The Two Knights, or, Delancey Castle. A tale of the Civil Wars. [With plates.] pp. vi. 302. *Darton & Co.: London*, [1851.] 12°. **12622**. a. **39**.

—— The Two Sisters; or, Ellen and Sophia. By the author of "Little Henry and his Bearer" [i.e. M. M. Butt, afterwards Sherwood], *etc.* pp. 108. 1827. 12°. *See* ELLEN. **863**. f. **10**.

—— Uncle Manners, or, Self-Will cured. *See* supra: The Juvenile Forget-me-not.

—— Victoria. pp. 231. *J. Hatchard & Son: London*, 1833. 12°. N. **973**. **(2.)**

BUTT, afterwards **SHERWOOD** (MARY MARTHA) [SINGLE WORKS.]

—— Waste not, Want not. 4 pt. *W. Whittemore: London; Houlston & Son: Wellington,* 1824. 12°. **4411**. de. **11**. (**9**.)

—— [Another edition.] 4 pt. pp. 72. [1825 ?] 12°. *See* WASTE. **863**. f. **29**.

—— [Another edition.] 4 pt. pp. 95. *R.T.S.: London,* [1879.] 8°. **4420**. k. **9**.

—— The White Pigeon. pp. 62. *Book Society: London,* [1877.] 16°. **12809**. aaa. **8**.

—— The Wish; or, Little Charles . . . Revised by the Committee of Publication. pp. 15. *American Sunday School Union: Philadelphia,* 1827. 24°. **864**. a. **44**. (**4**.)

—— The Wishing-Cap, *etc.* pp. 16. *American Tract Society: New York,* [1820 ?] 32°. **4422**. aa. **49**. (**9**.)

—— Fifth edition. pp. 29. *Houlston & Son: Wellington, Salop,* 1822. 32°. **12804**. de. **55**. (**8**.)

—— Eighth edition. pp. 29. *F. Houlston & Son: Wellington, Salop,* 1827. 24°. **012806**. de. **27**. (**4**.)

—— The Wishing Cap . . . New edition. [With cuts.] pp. 29. *Houlston & Sons: London,* [1871 ?] 32°. **12823**. a. **76**.

—— The Young Forester. 4 pt. *London,* [1830 ?] 8°. [*Houlston's Series of Tracts.* no. 1–4.] **4410**. l. **1**.

WORKS EDITED BY M. M. BUTT, afterwards SHERWOOD.

—— *See* BUTT (George) *D.D.* The Spanish Daughter. By the Rev. G. Butt. Revised and corrected by his daughter, Mrs. Sherwood. [With a memoir of the author.] 1824. 8°. N. **249**.

APPENDIX.

—— *See* SMITH (Naomi G. R.) The State of Mind of Mrs. Sherwood. A study. 1946. 8°. **11864**. aa. **44**.

—— *See* TABOR (Margaret E.) Pioneer Women, *etc.* (ser. 3. Mrs. Sherwood, Isabella Bird, *etc.* [With a portrait.]) 1925, *etc.* 8°. **10804.1.31.**

BUTT, afterwards **SHERWOOD** (MARY MARTHA) and **STREETEN**, afterwards **KELLY** (SOPHIA)

—— Boys will be Boys: or, the Difficulties of a schoolboy' life. A schoolboy's mission. pp. viii. 315. *Darton & Co.: London,* 1854. 12°. **4417**. d. **5**.

—— The Golden Garland of Inestimable Delights. pp. 383. *J. Hatchard & Son: London,* 1849. 12°. **12805**. h. **17**.

—— The Mirror of Maidens in the days of Queen Bess. pp. 348. *Thomas Hatchard: London,* 1851. 12°. **12622**. b. **11**.

—— Victorine Durocher, or the Blessings of peace. 1850. *See* TOULMIN, afterwards CROSLAND (Camilla) The Young Lord, *etc.* 1849, *etc.* 12°. **012803**. de. **96**.

BUTT (NEWBERN ISAAC) *See* HARRIS (Franklin S.) and BUTT (N. I.) The Fruits of Mormonism. 1925. 8°. **4744**. bbb. **38**.

—— *See* HARRIS (Franklin S.) and BUTT (N. I.) Scientific Research and Human Welfare. 1924. 8°. **08709**. b. **45**.

BUTT (PERCY LOVEL) *See* KEIGWIN (Richard P.) Lanyard Lyrics . . . Illustrated by P. L. Butt. [1914.] 8°. **11649**. h. **49**.

BUTT (RICHARD GATHORNE) *See* LONDON.—III. *Stock Exchange.* The Calumnious Aspersions contained in the Report of the Sub-Committee of the Stock-Exchange . . . refuted in so far as regards . . . R. G. Butt, *etc.* [1814.] 8°. **1414**. h. **22**. (**4**.)

—— *See* RANDOM DE BÉRENGER (Charles) *Baron de Beaufain.* The Trial of C. Random de Berenger . . . R. G. Butt . . . and H. Lyte, for a Conspiracy, *etc.* 1814. 8°. **518**. l. **17**.

BUTT (THOMAS) *See* LITURGIES.—*Church of England.* [*Common Prayer.—Catechism.—English.*] The Church Catechism, as taught . . . by . . . the Rev. T. Butt. 1846. 24°. **1353**. a. **49**.

—— A Sermon preached . . . at the primary visitation of the Lord Bishop of Lichfield and Coventry, September 11, MDCCCXXXVI. pp. 39. *J. G. & F. Rivington: London,* 1836. 8°. T. **2053**. (**15**.)

—— Sermons preached in the Parish Church of Trentham. pp. xvi. 415. *J. G. & F. Rivington: London,* 1838. 8°. **696**. d. **20**.

BUTT (WILLIAM) *Secretary of the Royal Toxophilite Society.* *See* FORD (Horace A.) The Theory and Practice of Archery . . . Revised . . . by W. Butt. 1887. 8°. **7907**. e. **41**.

BUTT (*Sir* WILLIAM) *See* BUTTS.

BUTT (YURY MIKHAILOVICH)

—— *See* YUNG (V. N.) Технология вяжущих веществ. [By A. N. Bokov, Yu. M. Butt, and others.] Под общей редакцией . . . В. Н. Юнг. 1947. 8°. **8764**. f. **15**.

BUTTA (GIOVANNI)

—— Collezione Butta. Monete pontificie e di zecche italiane. La vendita all'asta pubblica avrà luogo il 28 giugno 1939, *etc.* pp. 119. pl. xxv. *Roma,* 1939. 4°. **07757**. d. **4**.

BUTTACALICE ( ) *Arciprete.* Alcuni cenni caratteristici sul progetto dell'erezione del gran ponte sulla Veneta Laguna. pp. 68. *Venezia,* 1831. 8°. T. **2261**. (**7**.)

BUTTAFOCO (ANTOINE SEMIDEO LOUIS FRANÇOIS DE) *Count.* *See* BUTTAFUOCO.

BUTTAFOCO (ANTONIO)

—— Journal. (1744–1756.) pp. 72. 1913. *See* BASTIA.—*Société des Sciences Historiques et Naturelles de la Corse.* Bulletin, *etc.* fasc. 355–357. 1882, *etc.* 8°. Ac. **2861**.

BUTTAFOCO (MATHIEU DE) *Count.* *See* BUTTAFUOCO (Matteo)

BUTTAFUOCO (ANTOINE SEMIDEO LOUIS FRANÇOIS DE) *Count.* Fragments pour servir à l'histoire de Corse de 1764 à 1769, *etc.* (Abrégé et considérations d'histoire, de politique et d'économie publique sur l'île de Corse, par le comte Mathieu de Buttafoco.—Corrrespondance de Mathieu Buttafoco avec J. J. Rousseau, *etc.*) pp. 187. *Bastia,* 1859. 8°. **9150**. e. **11**.

BUTTAFUOCO (GAETANO)

—— Dizionario corografico dei ducati di Parma, Piacenza e Guastalla. Compilato per cura del professore G. Buttafuoco. pp. xxxvii. 118. *Milano,* 1845–47. 8°. [*Dizionario corografico-universale dell'Italia.* vol. 2. pt. 2.] **10129**. f. **5**.

Published in three parts.

BUTTAFUOCO (MATTEO) *Count.* Correspondance . . . avec J. J. Rousseau. *See* BUTTAFUOCO (A. S. L. F. de) *Count.* Fragments pour servir à l'histoire de Corse, *etc.* 1859. 8°. **9150**. e. **11**.

BUTTAFUOCO (MATTEO) *Count.*

—— Original Letters . . . to J. J. Rousseau. *See* ROUSSEAU (J. J.) [*Correspondence.*] Original Letters, *etc.* 1799. 8°. **1455.** c. **20.**

—— [Another edition.] *See* ROUSSEAU (J. J.) [*Correspondence.*] Original Letters, *etc.* 1820. 8°. **10910.** aaa. **5.**

—— Abrégé et considérations d'histoire, de politique et d'économie publique sur l'île de Corse. [Extracts from chap. 3–6 of the complete work.] *See* BUTTAFUOCO (A. S. L. F. de) *Count.* Fragments pour servir à l'histoire de Corse, *etc.* 1859. 8°. **9150.** e. **11.**

—— Observations . . . sur la réponse de M. Saliceti. pp. 16. [*Paris*, 1791.] 8°. F. **994.** (**5.**)

BUTTALL (ELIZABETH) *See* HARRIS (Rice) A Sermon occasioned by the Death of Mrs. Elizabeth Buttall, *etc.* [1767.] 4°. **1416.** d. **63.**

BUTTAONI (ALEXANDER) Alexandri Buttaoni . . . Dissertatio in titulum codicis de vendendis rebus civitatis. pp. 38. *Romæ*, 1815. 4°. **899.** f. **4.** (**11.**)

BUTTAONI (DOMINICUS) *Bishop of Fabriano and Matelica.* Dominici Buttaoni . . . Episcopi Fabrianensis, et Mathilicensis epistola pastoralis ad clerum, et populum utriusque diœcesis. pp. xv. *Romae*, 1806. 4°. T. **85*.** (**2.**)

—— [Another copy.] **1356.** k. **5.** (**29.**)

BUTTAR (CHARLES) The Anatomy of the Brain and Nervous System.—The Physiology of the Brain and Nervous System. *See* RHODES (Geoffrey) The Mind at Work, *etc.* 1914. 8°. **8469.** ee. **13.**

BUTTARI (ALESSANDRO) *See* JANNICOLI (F.) Ragguaglio della vita, e morte del sacerdote A. Buttari, *etc.* 1742. 4°. **4865.** dd. **26.**

BUTTARI (FILIPPO) *See* BALIRIO (E.) *pseud.* [i.e. F. Buttari.]

BUTTARI (GIOVANNI BATTISTA) Devasagayam Pillai's Conversion and Martyrdom, from contemporary accounts. Translated from the Italian of Fr. J. B. Buttari, S.J. By the Rev. P. Dahmen, S.J. pp. 32. *St. Joseph's College Press: Trichinopoly*, 1908. 8°. **4888.** c. **24.** (**6.**)

BUTTATS (FRANTS) De abscessuum curatione dissertatio inauguralis, *etc.* pp. 37. *Gottingae*, [1796.] 4°. T. **604.** (**10.**)

—— Observations pratiques sur différentes maladies. pp. viii. 41. pl. III. *William Thorne: Londres*, 1801. 4°. T. **16.** (**9.**)

BUTTBERG (JESSIE M. B.) Higher French Sentences. (Key to Higher French Sentences.) 2 vol. *Blackie & Son: London & Glasgow*, 1937. 8°. **12952.** pp. **40.**

BUTTE-DES-MOULINS, *Section de la.* *See* PARIS.—*Section du Palais-Royal.*

BUTTE (GEORGE CHARLES) Amerikanische Prisengerichtsbarkeit mit besonderer Berücksichtigung der verfassungsrechtlichen Schwierigkeiten, die für die Vereinigten Staaten von Amerika der Ratifikation des internationalen Prisengerichtsabkommens entgegenstehen. [With a bibliography.] pp. vii. 172. *Heidelberg*, 1913. 8°. **06616.** e. **16.**

—— [Die Frage der Panamakanalabgaben.] Great Britain and the Panama Canal: a study of the tolls question. [Translated from an article in the "Jahrbuch des Völkerrechts."] pp. 77. 1913. 8°. **6955.** de. **11.**

BUTTE (GEORGE CHARLES)

—— Rechtsverhältnisse der Indianer in den Vereinigten Staaten mit besonderer Berücksichtigung des Eigentums an Grund und Boden. Vortrag . . . Separatabdruck aus den Blättern für vergleichende Rechtswissenschaft und Volkswirtschaftslehre, *etc.* pp. 48. *Berlin*, 1913. 8°. **08175.** aa. **47.** (**5.**)

—— The Legal Status of the American Indians; with special reference to the tenure of Indian lands . . . A translation of an address, *etc.* pp. 39. [1913 ?] 8°. **6616.** de. **17.** (**4.**)

BUTTE (HEINRICH) Stift und Stadt Hersfeld im 14. Jahrhundert. Mit einem Anhang: Die Stadt Hersfeld bis zum Beginn des 15. Jahrhunderts, und 14 Urkundenbeilagen. pp. 167. *Marburg*, 1911. 8°. **10256.** ff. **43.**

BUTTE (WILHELM) Die Biotomie des Menschen; oder die Wissenschaft der Natur-Eintheilungen des Lebens als Mensch, als Mann und als Weib . . . Hierzu ein lithographirtes Blatt. pp. xxxiv. 592. *Bonn*, 1829. 8°. **541.** b. **27.**

—— Die polnisch-russische Angelegenheit, unter den Gesichts-Punkten rascher, definitiver . . . Erledigung . . . Ein Nachtrag zu seiner Kriegs-Frage, von W. Butte. pp. xiv. 82. *Leipzig*, 1831. 8°. **8093.** aaa. **11.**

—— Statistisch-politisch- und kosmopolitische Blikke in die Hessen-Darmstädtischen Lande. (Beilagen, *etc.*) 2 pt. *Giesen & Darmstadt*, 1804. 8°. **10250.** aa. **12.**

BUTTEAUD (ÉDOUARD) *See* DORMOY (   ) and DORMOY (   ) *Madame.* Vocabulaire tahitien-français, *etc.* (Révisé par MM. Cadousteau et Butteaud.) 1890. 8°. **12910.** a. **65.**

—— —— 1894. 8°. **12910.** a. **59.**

BÜTTEL (   ) [For the German surname of this form:] *See* BUETTEL.

BUTTEL (C. D. VON) Ueber die Geltung des römischen Rechts und das Verlangen nach freierer Gerichtsverfassung. Eine Vorlesung gehalten im literarisch-geselligen Verein zu Oldenburg am 5. Sept. 1845. pp. 67. *Oldenburg*, 1846. 8°. **5207.** c. **21.** (**1.**)

BUTTEL (FR.) Practische Erfahrungen über Dornsche Dächer nebst . . . einem Anhange: über die Anwendung der flachen Dächer bei ökonomischen Gebäuden. [With plans.] 2 Hft. pp. 50. *Neubrandenburg & Friedland*, 1841, 42. 8°. **7814.** bbb. **41.** (**1.**)

BUTTELL (MARIE PIERRE)

—— Religious Ideology and Christian Humanism in German Cluniac Verse. A dissertation, *etc.* pp. ix. 289. *Catholic University of America Press: Washington*, 1948. 8°. [*Catholic University of America. Studies in German.* vol. 21.] Ac. **2692.** y/**10.**

BUTTELL (MARY FRANCES)

—— The Rhetoric of St. Hilary of Poitiers. A dissertation, *etc.* pp. xiv. 175. *Catholic University of America Press: Washington*, 1933. 8°. [*Catholic University of America. Patristic Studies.* vol. 38.] Ac. **2692.** y/**16.**

BUTTEL-REEPEN (HUGO VON) Apistica: Beiträge zur Systematik, Biologie, sowie zur geschichtlichen und geographischen Verbreitung der Honigbiene, Apis mellifica, L., ihrer Varietäten und der übrigen Apis-Arten . . . Mit 8 Textfiguren. 1906. *See* BERLIN.—*Museum für Naturkunde.* Mitteilungen, *etc.* Bd. 3. Hft. 2. 1898, *etc.* 8°. Ac. **2926.**

BUTTEL-REEPEN (HUGO VON)

—— [Aus dem Werdegang der Menschheit.] Man and his Forerunners . . . Incorporating accounts of recent discoveries in Suffolk and Sussex. Authorized translation by A. G. Thacker. With a frontispiece, 70 figures in the text and 3 tables. pp. x. 96. *Longmans & Co.: London*, 1913. 8°. **10007**. f. **36**.

—— Sind die Bienen Reflexmaschinen? Experimentelle Beiträge zur Biologie der Honigbiene. pp. vi. 82. *Leipzig*, 1900. 8°. **7299**. h. **19**.

—— Über Fensterurnen. Mit 58 Abbildungen. 1925. *See* OLDENBURG.—*Oldenburger Verein für Altertumskunde und Landesgeschichte*. Oldenburger Jahrbuch, *etc*. vol. 29. 1918, *etc*. 4°. Ac. **5392/2**.

BUTTENSHAW (DIANA MARGUERITE)

—— Dominic. Days in the life of a boy who lived in a forest. pp. 207. *Frederick Muller: London*, 1943. 8°. **12827**. eee. **14**.

—— Incident in Ismalia. pp. 188. *Hodder & Stoughton: London*, 1953. 8°. NNN. **3969**.

—— Journey to Venice. pp. 287. *Hodder & Stoughton: London*, 1949. 8°. NN. **39433**.

—— An Oak for Posterity. pp. 190. *Hodder & Stoughton: London*, 1952. 8°. NN. **9718**.

—— The One Black Swan. pp. 191. *Hodder & Stoughton: London*, 1955. 8°. NNN. **6067**.

—— Patrick . . . Illustrated by Raymond Sheppard. pp. 278. *Macmillan & Co.: London*, 1939. 8°. **12817**. aa. **19**.

—— Pepito of Guadiaro . . . Illustrated by Margaret Horder. pp. 186. *Frederick Muller: London*, 1948. 8°. **12832**. bb. **41**.

—— Say not Good-Night. pp. 316. *Hodder & Stoughton: London*, 1943. 8°. NN. **33916**.

—— The Sleeping Princess. pp. 333. *Hodder & Stoughton: London*, 1941. 8°. NN. **32996**.

—— The Villach Road. pp. 256. *Hodder & Stoughton: London*, 1947. 8°. NN. **37401**.

BUTTENWIESER (MOSES) *See* BIBLE.—*Job*. [*Polyglott*.] The Book of Job. By M. Buttenwieser. 1922. 8°. **01902**. a. **17**.

—— —— 1925. 8°. **01903**. a. **12**.

—— *See* BIBLE.—*Psalms*. [*English*.—*Prose Versions*.] The Psalms. Chronologically treated, with a new translation, by M. Buttenwieser. 1938. 8°. **03089**. ee. **12**.

—— *See* ELIJAH, *the Prophet*. Die hebräische Elias-Apokalypse . . . Mit Erläuterungen . . . und einer Einleitung, nebst . . . Übersetzung . . . von M. Buttenwieser. 1897. 8°. **04034**. g. **8**.

—— The Prophets of Israel from the eighth to the fifth century. Their faith and their message. pp. xxii. 350. *Macmillan Co.: New York*, 1914. 8°. **03187**. df. **62**.

BUTTER.

—— Butter and Cheese, and Adieu to Cold Winter. [Songs.] *Leonard Deming: Boston & Middlebury*, [1840?] *s. sh*. 4°. **11630**. f. **7**. (**124**.)

BUTTER, *Brueder, Schriftgiesserei*. *See* SCHRIFTGIESSEREI BRUEDER BUTTER.

BUTTER (ALFRED) Midsummer Eve: a tale. [By A. Butter.] 3 vol. 1842. 12°. *See* MIDSUMMER EVE. N. **2243**.

BUTTER (DONALD) Outline of the Topography and Statistics of the Southern Districts of Oud'h, and of the cantonment of Sultanpur-Oud'h. [With maps.] pp. 183. *G. H. Huttmann: Calcutta*, 1839. 8°. **1298**. l. **2**.

—— Snake-bite Curable, and Hydrophobia Preventible. pp. 27. *Smith, Elder & Co.: London*, 1873. 8°. **7442**. aaa. **25**.

BUTTER (FRANCIS J.) Locks and Lockmaking, *etc*. pp. xi. 135. *London*, [1926.] 8°. [*Pitman's Common Commodities and Industries*.] **07077**. f. **1/101**.

—— Second edition. pp. xi. 132. *London*, [1931.] 8°. [*Pitman's Common Commodities and Industries*.] **07077**. f. **1/128**.

BUTTER (GULIELMUS) *See* BUTTER (William)

BUTTER (HENRY) A Correct Abstract of the new Act for ascertaining and establishing Uniformity of Weights & Measures . . . Second edition. pp. 36. *H. C. Hodson: London*, 1825. 12°. T. **1079**. (**10**.)

—— The Etymological Spelling Book; being an introduction to the spelling, pronunciation, and derivation, of the English language, *etc*. pp. 137. *Simpkin & Marshall: London*, 1830. 12°. **829**. b. **49**.

—— Ninth edition . . . revised, *etc*. pp. vii. 136. *W. Simpkin & R. Marshall: London*, 1833. 12°. **12982**. aaa. **7**.

—— Forty-third edition. pp. vii. 144. *Simpkin, Marshall & Co.: London*, 1840. 8°. **1212**. k. **45**.

—— The hundred and eleventh edition, revised, *etc*. pp. 158. *Simpkin, Marshall & Co.: London*, 1848. 16°. **1212**. k. **59**.

—— Two hundred and thirty-eighth edition, revised. pp. 158. *Simpkin & Co.: London*, 1860. 8°. **12983**. b. **29**.

—— New and revised edition, *etc*. pp. 158. *Simpkin Marshall & Co.: London*, [1897.] 8°. **12981**. df. **1**.

—— The Etymological Spelling-Book . . . New and revised edition, *etc*. pp. 158. *Simpkin, Marshall & Co.: London*, 1941. 8°. **12987**. a. **21**.

—— Gradations in Reading and Spelling. 3 pt. pp. 108. *W. Simpkin & R. Marshall: London*, [1829.] 8°. T. **1433**. (**8**.)

—— Twenty-first edition. pp. 180. *Whittaker & Co., etc.: London*, 1839. 12°. **1212**. k. **44**.

—— Thirty-fifth edition. pp. vi. 178. *Whittaker & Co.: London*, 1848. 16°. **1211**. a. **26**.

—— The Gradual Primer, upon an entirely new and original plan. Tenth edition. pp. 71. *Simpkin, Marshall & Co.: London*, 1839. 12°. **1212**. l. **18**.

—— Forty-fifth edition, revised and enlarged. pp. 78. *Simpkin & Co.: London*, 1858. 16°. **12985**. a. **73**

—— Maiden, Prepare to Become a Happy Wife and Mother. An address to young women on marriage. pp. 32. *S. W. Partridge & Co.; W. Macintosh: London*, 1868. 8°. **8415**. aa. **49**. (**4**.)

—— [Another edition.] Happy Home: a simple address to an English maiden. . . . Formerly called 'Maiden, prepare.' pp. 32. *W. H. Guest: London*, [1873.] 8°. **8416**. i. **4**. (**1**.)

BUTTER (Henry)

—— Marriage for the Million: for the lads and lasses of the working classes. pp. 15. *G. J. Stevenson; S. Palmer: London*, 1872. 8°. **8435**. aaa. **1**. **(7.)**

—— Second thousand. pp. 15. *W. H. Guest: London*, 1875. 8°. **8416**. d. **9**. **(1.)**

—— Tangible Arithmetic and Geometry . . . illustrated by figures and . . . cubes, *etc.* pp. 35. *Simpkin, Marshall & Co.: London*, 1840. 12°. **1394**. c. **36**.

—— What's the Harm of Fornication? The question answered. By Paterfamilias [i.e. H. Butter]. pp. 16. 1864. 8°. *See* Paterfamilias. **8415**. bbb. **30**.

—— [Another edition.] Is the Pleasure worth the Penalty? A common-sense view of the leading vice of the age. pp. 16. *Job Caudwell: London*, 1865. 8°. **8415**. bbb. **22**.

—— [Another edition.] What's the Harm? A young man's question, answered. By the author of 'Butter's Spelling.' Formerly called 'Is the Pleasure?' etc. pp. 16. *W. H. Guest: London*, [1880.] 8°. **8416**. d. **9**. **(2.)**

BUTTER (Hermann) Die Kunst zu inseriren. Eine Sammlung von originellen Muster-Annoncen, *etc.* pp. 40. *Saaz*, 1880. 8°. **7943**. g. **15**.

BUTTER (Jacob) A Review of Dr. Hawker's Letter to an Undergraduate, in defence of the Church Articles, &c. against the questions proposed by the Bishop of Peterborough, to candidates for Holy Orders . . . Connected with some remarks on Dr. Hawker's Poor Man's Prayer Book. Comprising also an answer to the pamphlet entitled "The Retrospective Summary of Dr. Hawker's Ministerial Life, &c." Preceded by an epitome of the Reformation. pp. 100. *L. J. Higham: London; E. Nettleton: Plymouth*, 1825. 8°. **4107**. e. **14**.

BUTTER (John) Remarks on Irritative Fever, commonly called the Plymouth Dock-Yard Disease; with Mr. Dryden's detailed account of the fatal cases including that of the lamented surgeon, Dr. Bell, *etc.* pp. xviii. 302. *Congdon & Hearle: Devonport*, 1825. 8°. **1168**. h. **26**.

BUTTER (Nathaniel)

—— *See* Day (Martin) Doomes-Day: or, A Treatise of the resurrection of the body. Delivered in 22. sermons, *etc.* [Edited by N. Butter.] 1636. 8°. **4452**. bb. **6**.

BUTTER (Oskar)

—— *See* Beneš (E.) *President of Czechoslovakia.* Locarno a Svaz Národů. Ministr Beneš o konferenci locarnské, *etc.* (Řídí . . . O. Butter.) 1925. 8°. **08028**. a. **73**.

BUTTER (Oskar) and **DORAZIL** (V.) Чехословацкая Республика. Обзор духовной, политической, экономической и общественной жизни. Составлен под редакцией О. Буттера и В. Доразила. [With illustrations and maps.] pp. 177. *в Праге*, 1924. 8°. **10215**. dd. **2**.

BUTTER (Oskar) and **RUML** (Bohuslav)

—— Encyclopédie tchécoslovaque. Collection publiée sous la direction de O. Butter et B. Ruml. [With illustrations and maps.] 3 vol.

1. Industrie et commerce. Rédigé par Jaroslav Veselý. pp. xxi. 594. 1923.
2. Communications. Rédigé par Jan Smetana. pp. xli. 365. 1927.
3. Agriculture. Rédigé par Vladislav Brdlík. pp. xlvii. 882. 1928.

Paris, Prague, 1923–28. 8°. **12208**. p. **2**.
No more published.

BUTTER (Peter Herbert)

—— Shelley's Idols of the Cave. [A study of the imagery in Shelley's poetry.] pp. vii. 228. *University Press: Edinburgh*, 1954. 8°. [*Edinburgh University Publications. Language & Literature.* no. 7.] W.P. **5688**. c/**7**.

BUTTER (William) An Account of Puerperal Fevers, as they appear in Derbyshire, and some of the counties adjacent. pp. viii. 124. *T. Payne: London*, 1775. 8°. **1177**. d. **12**. **(1.)**

—— [Another edition, without the cases.] *See* London.—iii. *Sydenham Society.* Essays on the Puerperal Fever, *etc.* 1849. 8°. Ac. **3837/19**.

—— Dissertatio medica et chirurgica de arteriotomia. pp. 40. *Hamilton, Balfour & Neill: Edinburgi*, 1761. 8°. T. **73**. (4.)

—— An Improved Method of opening the Temporal Artery, also a new proposal for extracting the cataract . . . To which are now added, a miscellaneous introduction, and cases, and observations . . . tending to illustrate the good effects of arteriotomy, in various diseases of the head. pp. viii. 213. *J. Robson, etc.: London*, 1783. 8°. **1186**. i. **3**.

—— A Method of Cure for the Stone chiefly by Injections, *etc.* [With a plate.] pp. iv. 84. *Hamilton, Balfour & Neill: Edinburgh*, 1754. 12°. T. **431**. **(2.)**

—— A Treatise on the Disease commonly called Angina pectoris. pp. 62. *J. Johnson: London*, 1791. 8°. T. **991**. **(12.)**

—— A Treatise on the Infantile Remittent Fever. pp. 50. *J. Robson: London*, 1782. 8°. **1177**. d. **12**. **(2.)**

—— A Treatise on the Kinkcough. With an appendix, containing an account of hemlock and its preparations. pp. ix. 206. *T. Cadell: London*, 1773. 8°. T. **104**. **(2.)**

—— [Another copy.] **1172**. g. **10**. **(1.)**

—— *See* Treatise. Animadversions on a late Treatise on the Kink-Cough [by W. Butter], *etc.* 1774. 8°. **1172**. g. **10**. **(8.)**

BUTTERBAUGH (Grant Illion)

—— A Bibliography of Statistical Quality Control. pp. viii. 114. 1946. 8°. *See* Seattle.—*University of Washington.—College of Economics and Business.—Bureau of Business Research.* **11926**. aaa. **23**.

—— A Bibliography of Statistical Quality Control. Supplement. pp. 141. *University of Washington Press: Seattle*, 1951. 8°. **11927**. pp. **2**.

BUTTERBAUGH (Wayne Edgar) Industrial Traffic Management. A survey of its relation to business. pp. viii. 172. *Washington*, 1930. 8°. [*U.S. Bureau of Foreign and Domestic Commerce. Domestic Commerce Series.* no. 39.] A.S. **130/2**.

—— Principles of Importing. [With plates.] pp. xxi. 473. *D. Appleton & Co.: New York & London*, 1924. 8°. **08245**. ee. **29**.

—— Transportation. pp. xxiv. 342. *Alexander Hamilton Institute: New York*, [1931.] 8°. [*Modern Business.*] W.P. **8864/30**.

BUTTERCUP. Little Buttercup and Jenny Wren. A book for the young. By the author of "How to Enter into Rest" [i.e. Harriet Hamilton], *etc.* pp. viii. 127. *Morgan & Scott: London*, [1873.] 8°. **12803**. bbb. **13**.

BUTTERCUP.

—— Little Buttercup's Picture Book. With ninety-six pages of illustrations [and explanations in prose and verse]. pp. 96. *G. Routledge & Sons: London,* 1881 [1880]. 4°. **12807**. i. **29**.

—— [Another copy.] **12807**. i. **23**.

BUTTERCUP FARM. Buttercup Farm. [A coloured picture-book with explanatory verses.] *E. Nister: London; E. P. Dutton & Co.: New York; Nuremberg* [printed], [1892.] *obl.* fol. **1876**. b. **18**.

—— Buttercup Farm. [Short stories, with illustrations.] *Ernest Nister: London; E. P. Dutton & Co.: New York; printed in Bavaria,* [1901.] 4°. **12812**. c. **26**.
A different publication from the preceding.

BUTTERCUPS. Buttercups and Daisies. [In verse. With coloured illustrations.] *R.T.S.: London,* [1872.] 8°. **12807**. cc. **10**.

—— Buttercups and Daisies. A picture story-book for little people . . . By J. D., author of "Smiles & Dimples," *etc.* [1900.] 8°. *See* D., J. **012803**. h. **56**.

—— Buttercups and Daisies; or, Short stories for little folk. pp. 61. *Darton & Co.: London,* 1855. 12°. **12806**. d. **10**.

—— Buttercups and Daisies and other pretty flowers. [In verse, with coloured illustrations.] *S.P.C.K.: London,* [1866.] 4°. **12806**. h. **58**.

—— Buttercups and Daisies for Little Children. [In verse.] With illustrations by Oscar Pletsch. Printed in colours, *etc.* pp. 94. *G. Routledge & Sons: London & New York,* [1876.] 8°. **12807**. ccc. **16**.

BUTTERFIELD NEWS.

—— Butterfield News. *See* BUTTERFIELD (W. P.) LTD. News and Views.

BUTTERFIELD (AVICE LOUIS) Lyrics. *A. L. Butterfield: [London,]* 1933. 8°. **011641**. ee. **52**.
Typewritten.

—— The Witch and the Friar. First story. *A. L. Butterfield: [London,]* 1934. 4°. **12604**. i. **27**.
Typewritten. No more published.

BUTTERFIELD (CONSUL WILLSHIRE) *See* WASHINGTON (George) *President of the United States of America.* [*Letters.*] The Washington-Crawford Letters. Being the correspondence between G. Washington and W. Crawford, from 1767 to 1781, concerning Western Lands . . . Chronologically arranged and carefully annotated. By C. W. Butterfield. 1877. 8°. **10921**. i. **2**.

—— *See* WASHINGTON (George) *President of the United States of America.* [*Letters.*] Washington-Irvine Correspondence. The official letters which passed between Washington and Brig.-Gen. William Irvine, and between Irvine and others, concerning military affairs in the West from 1781 to 1783. Arranged and annotated with an introduction . . . By C. W. Butterfield. 1882. 8°. **9615**. ee. **17**.

—— History of Brulé's Discoveries and Explorations, 1610–1626 . . . With a biographical notice of the discoverer, *etc.* pp. xii. 184. *Helman-Taylor Co.: Cleveland,* 1898. 8°. **9551**. d. **6**.

—— History of George Rogers Clark's Conquest of the Illinois and the Wabash Towns 1778 and 1779, *etc.* [With a biography of the author by W. H. Hunter.] pp. xix. 815. *F. J. Heer: Columbus,* 1904. 8°. **09605**. b. **6**.

BUTTERFIELD (CONSUL WILLSHIRE)

—— History of the Discovery of the Northwest by John Nicolet in 1634, with a sketch of his life. pp. ix. 113. *R. Clarke & Co.: Cincinnati,* 1881. 8°. **10460**. b. **11**.

—— History of the Girtys: being a concise account of the Girty Brothers—Thomas, Simon, James and George, and of their half-brother, John Turner—also of the part taken by them in Lord Dunmore's war, in the Western border war of the Revolution, *etc.* pp. xiii. 425. *R. Clarke & Co.: Cincinnati,* 1890. 8°. **9916**. c. **7**.

—— History of the University of Wisconsin . . . With biographical sketches of its chancellors, presidents, and professors. [With portraits.] pp. viii. 233. *University Press Co.: Madison,* 1879. 8°. **8366**. dd. **10**.

—— History of Wisconsin. *See* JEFFERSON, *County of, Wisconsin.* The History of Jefferson County, *etc.* 1879. 8°. **10409**. h. **5**.

—— [Another issue.] *See* ROCK, *County of, Wisconsin.* The History of Rock County, *etc.* 1879. 8°. **10409**. h. **4**.

—— [A reissue.] *See* COLUMBIA, *County of, Wisconsin.* The History of Columbia County, *etc.* 1880. 4°. **10409**. h. **21**.

—— [A reissue.] *See* IOWA, *County of, Wisconsin.* History of Iowa County, *etc.* 1881. 4°. **10408**. h. **9**.

—— [Another issue.] *See* LA FAYETTE, *County of, Wisconsin.* History of La Fayette County, *etc.* 1881. 4°. **10408**. h. **8**.

BUTTERFIELD (DANIEL) Camp and Outpost Duty for Infantry, *etc.* pp. 124. *Harper & Bros.: New York,* 1863. 12°. **8826**. aaa. **14**.

BUTTERFIELD (EDWARD) Report dated the 3rd January 1913 on the Cocos Island Group. *See* COCOS ISLANDS. Reports on the Cocos Islands, *etc.* 1913. fol. I.S. BU. **100/35**.

BUTTERFIELD (F.) [A collection of remedies.] *F. Butterfield: Bingley,* [1914.] 32°. **945**. d. **7**.

BUTTERFIELD (*Sir* FREDERICK WILLIAM LOUIS) The Battle of Maldon, and other renderings from the Anglo-Saxon; together with original verse. By F. W. L. B. [i.e. Sir F. W. L. Butterfield.] pp. xi. 59. [1900.] 8°. *See* B., F. W. L. **011651**. i. **42**.

—— The Crevasse. A dramatic study. pp. 39. *Parker & Son: Oxford,* 1903. 8°. **11779**. ddd. **26**.

—— My West Riding Experiences. [With portraits.] pp. 207. *Ernest Benn: London,* [1928.] 8°. **010855**. e. **40**.

—— Passing Notes of a Visit to the Cape, 1930. pp. 21. *Alexander Moring: London,* 1930. 8°. **10094**. aa. **4**.

BUTTERFIELD (HARRY MORTON)

—— Bush Berry Culture in California. pp. 56. *Berkeley,* 1947. 8°. [*California Agricultural Extension Service.* Circular. no. 80.] Ac. **2689**. gdb/**2**.

—— Production of Easter Lily Bulbs. pp. 34. *Berkeley,* 1947. 8°. [*California Agricultural Extension Service.* Circular. no. 132.] Ac. **2689**. gdb/**2**.

BUTTERFIELD (HARRY ROBERT FREDERICK)

—— Index to the Laws of the Tanganyika Territory in force on the 31st day of December, 1933, *etc.* pp. xii. 94. 1935. 8°. *See* TANGANYIKA TERRITORY. [*Miscellaneous Official Publications.*] C.S. c. **209/3**. (**1**.)

BUTTERFIELD (HENRY) Homilies for Earnest Enquirers. The spiritual doctrines contained in the first four Homilies of the Church of England . . . plainly set forth. pp. 115. *L. & G. Seeley: London*, 1839. 12°. **4461**. c. **7**.

—— What Should the Church Do ? or, Self-denial instead of mendicant appeals to the government and the people, *etc.* pp. 28. *J. B. Brown: Windsor*, 1839. 8°. T. **2437**. (**3**.)

BUTTERFIELD (HENRY S.) *See* DUPANLOUP (F. A. P.) *Bishop of Orleans.* The Future Œcumenical Council. A letter . . . Translated by H. S. Butterfield . . . and E. Robillard. 1869. 8°. **5016**. bb. **16**.

—— *See* WOLTER (M.) The Roman Catacombs . . . Translated . . . by H. S. Butterfield. 1867. 8°. **7707**. a. **25**.

BUTTERFIELD (HERBERT) *See* LAFFAN (Robert G. D.) Select Documents of European History, *etc.* (vol. 3. 1715–1920. Edited by H. Butterfield.) 1930, *etc.* 8°. **9071**. bb. **7**.

—— Christianity and History. pp. vi. 146. *G. Bell & Sons: London*, 1949. 8°. **9010**. c. **2**.

—— Christianity, Diplomacy and War. (The Beckley Social Service Lecture.) pp. 125. *Epworth Press: London*, 1953. 8°. **8012**. a. **65**.

—— Christianity in European History. pp. 63. *Oxford University Press: London*, 1951. 8°. [*Riddell Memorial Lectures.* ser. 23.] Ac. **1342**. b/2. (**23**.)

—— [A reissue.] Christianity in European History, *etc.* *Collins: London*, 1952. 8°. **4889**. bb. **24**.

—— The Englishman and his History. pp. x. 139. *University Press: Cambridge*, 1944. 8°. [*Current Problems.* no. 19.] W.P. **147/19**.

—— George III, Lord North and the People, 1779-80. pp. xi. 407. *G. Bell & Sons: London*, 1949. 8°. **9505**. c. **17**.

—— The Historical Novel. An essay. pp. 113. *University Press: Cambridge*, 1924. 8°. **011850**. c. **27**.

—— History and Human Relations. pp. 254. *Collins: London*, 1951. 8°. **9012**. aa. **15**.

—— Lord Acton. pp. 24. *G. Philip & Son: London*, 1948. 8°. [*Historical Association. General Series.* no. G.9.] W.P. **3175/9**.

—— Man on his Past. The study of the history of historical scholarship. pp. xvi. 237. *University Press: Cambridge*, 1955. 8°. [*Wiles Lectures given at the Queen's University, Belfast.* 1954.] Ac. **1522**. b. (**1**.)

—— Napoleon. pp. 143. *Duckworth: London*, 1939. 8°. [*Great Lives.*] W.P. **6397/83**.

—— The Origins of Modern Science, 1300–1800. pp. x. 217. *G. Bell & Sons: London*, 1949. 8°. **8713**. de. **17**.

—— The Peace Tactics of Napoleon, 1806–1808. pp. viii. 395. *University Press: Cambridge*, 1929. 8°. **09076**. b. **22**.

—— The Reconstruction of an Historical Episode. The history of the enquiry into the origins of the Seven Years' War. Being the eighteenth lecture on the David Murray Foundation in the University of Glasgow, delivered on 20th April, 1951. pp. 43. *Jackson, Son & Co.: Glasgow*, 1951. 8°. [*Glasgow University Publications.* no. 91.] Ac. **1487**.

BUTTERFIELD (HERBERT)

—— The Statecraft of Machiavelli. [With a portrait.] pp. 167. *G. Bell & Sons: London*, 1940. 8°. **08008**. d. **68**.

—— The Statecraft of Machiavelli. pp. 167. *G. Bell & Sons: London*, 1955. 8°. **8012**. de. **29**.

—— The Study of Modern History. An inaugural lecture, *etc.* pp. 34. *G. Bell & Sons: London*, 1944. 8°. **9010**. de. **8**.

—— The Whig Interpretation of History. pp. vi. 132. *G. Bell & Sons: London*, 1931. 8°. **09007**. bb. **41**.

BUTTERFIELD (HERBERT E.) The Scientific Manufacture of Jams & Allied Products. pp. 36. *Richardsons: St. Albans*, [1926.] 8°. **07942**. ccc. **51**.

BUTTERFIELD (JANE) *See* N., H. Observations on the Case of Miss Butterfield, *etc.* 1776. 8°. **112**. b. 49.

—— *See* SANXAY (Edmund) A Letter to Mr Sanxay . . . occasioned by his . . . conduct, in the prosecution of Miss Butterfield, *etc.* 1775. 8°. **518**. g. **15**. (**5**.)

—— *See* SCAWEN (William) Circumstances of the Death of Mr. Scawen, with . . . particulars relative to Miss J. Butterfield, *etc.* 1775. 8°. **1131**. e. **16**.

—— The Trial of Jane Butterfield for the wilful murder of William Scawen, Esq; . . . Taken in short-hand by Joseph Gurney and William Blanchard. pp. 53. *W. Owen; G. Kearsly: London*, 1775. fol. **516**. m. **12**. (**3**.)

—— [Another copy.] **115**. k. **22**.

—— [Another copy.] C. **71**. g. **2**. (**6**.)

BUTTERFIELD (JOHN WARREN) *See* UNITED STATES OF AMERICA.—*Treasury.*—*Office of Comptroller.* A Digest of the Decisions in the Office of the Second Comptroller of the Treasury, *etc.* [vol. 1 compiled by J. W. Butterfield.] 1869, *etc.* 8°. A.S. **461**.

BUTTERFIELD (JOSEPH) *See* BIBLE.—*Psalms.* [*English.*—*Prose Versions.*] The Psalter . . . arranged and pointed for chanting, by J. Butterfield. 1842. 12°. **3406**. aa. **13**.

BUTTERFIELD (JOSEPH) *of Melbourne.* *See* DIRECTORIES.—*Melbourne.* The Melbourne Commercial Directory . . . Compiled by J. Butterfield. [1854, *etc.*] 8°. P.P. **2642**. d.

BUTTERFIELD (KENYON LEECH) Chapters in Rural Progress. (Second impression.) pp. ix. 251. *University of Chicago Press: Chicago*, 1909. 8°. **08276**. b. **31**.

—— Christianity and Rural Civilization. *See* CHRISTIAN WORK. Principles and Methods of Christian Work, *etc.* [1928.] 8°. W.P. **8731/6**.

—— The Country Church and the Rural Problem. The Carew Lectures at Hartford Theological Seminary, 1909. pp. viii. 153. *University of Chicago Press: Chicago*, 1911. 8°. **4499**. i. **14**.

—— The Farmer and the New Day. pp. 311. *Macmillan Co.: New York*, 1919. 8°. **08282**. aa. **13**.

BUTTERFIELD (LINDSAY P.) Floral Forms in Historic Design, mainly from objects in the Victoria & Albert Museum . . . Selected and drawn by L. P. Butterfield. With preface and descriptive notes by W. G. Paulson Townsend. pl. XVIII. *B. T. Batsford: London*, [1922.] fol. Tab. **710**. c. 2.

BUTTERFIELD (LOUIS HENRY) Charles Churchill and "A Fragment of an Epic Poem." [Attributing to Churchill the poem included in "The Works of John Hall-Stevenson." Reprinted from "Harvard Studies and Notes in Philology and Literature."] *Harvard University Press: Cambridge, Mass.*, 1933. 8°. **11857. b. 44.**

BUTTERFIELD (LYMAN HENRY)

—— *See* JEFFERSON (Thomas) *President of the United States of America.* The Papers of Thomas Jefferson . . . L. H. Butterfield and M. R. Bryan, associate editors. 1950, *etc.* 8°. **10893.a.1.**

—— *See* RUSH (Benjamin) *the Elder.* Letters of Benjamin Rush. Edited by L. H. Butterfield. 1951. 8°. [*Memoirs of the American Philosophical Society.* vol. 30.] Ac. **1830/8.**

—— The American Interests of the Firm of E. and C. Dilly, with their letters to Benjamin Rush, 1770–1795. *In:* The Papers of the Bibliographical Society of America. vol. 45. pp. 283–332. 1951. 8° **N.L.27.d.**

—— John Witherspoon comes to America. A documentary account, *etc.* [With plates, including a portrait.] pp. xiv. 99. 1953. 8°. *See* PRINCETON, *New Jersey.—Princeton University.—Library.* **10891. bb. 34.**

BUTTERFIELD (MARGUERITE) *See* BROWN (Dorothy L.) and BUTTERFIELD (M.) Bozo the Woodchuck, *etc.* [1933.] 8°. **12837.aa.1.**

—— *See* TIDYMAN (Willard F.) and BUTTERFIELD (M.) Teaching the Language Arts. 1951. 8°. W.P. **12179/85.**

BUTTERFIELD (OLIVER MACKINLEY)

—— Love Problems of Adolescence, *etc.* [A thesis.] pp. viii. 212. *Teachers College, Columbia University: New York*, 1939. 8°. **8417. d. 13.**

BUTTERFIELD (PAUL KENYON) The Diplomacy of the Bagdad Railway, 1890–1914. Inaugural-Dissertation, *etc.* pp. 82. *Göttingen*, 1932. 8°. **8236. f. 20.**

BUTTERFIELD (PHILIP DOUGLAS)

—— How to make your Confession. A primer for members of the Church of England, *etc.* pp. 54. *S.P.C.K.: London*, 1952. 8°. **3479. a. 44.**

BUTTERFIELD (ROBERT) Maschil. Or, a Treatise to give instruction, touching the state of the Church of Rome since the Councell of Trent, whether shee be yet a true Christian Church. And if she have denied the foundation of our faith. For the vindication of . . . the L. Bishop of Exeter, from the cavills of H. B. [i.e. Henry Burton] in his book intituled The seven Vialls. pp. 134. *H. L.* [*H. Lownes*] *& R. Y.* [*R. Young*] *for N. Butter:* [*London,*] 1629. 8°. **857. b. 7.**

—— *See* BURTON (Henry) *Rector of St. Matthews, Friday Street.* Babel no Bethel. That is, the Church of Rome no true visible Church of Christ. In answer to Hugh Cholmley's Challenge, and Rob: Butterfields Maschil, *etc.* 1629. 4°. **108. d. 30.**

—— *See* SPENCER (Thomas) Maschil Unmasked. In a treatise defending this sentence of our Church: vidz. The present Romish Church hath not the nature of the true Church. Against the publick opposition of Mr. Cholmley, and Mr. Butterfield, *etc.* [1629.] 4°. **108. a. 43.**

BUTTERFIELD (ROLAND POTTER)

—— Monastery and Manor. The history of Crondall. [With plates.] pp. xi. 138. *E. W. Langham: Farnham*, 1948. 8°. **010368. b. 42.**

BUTTERFIELD (ROLAND POTTER)

—— Padre Rowlands of Ceylon. [With portraits.] pp. viii. 182. *Marshall, Morgan & Scott: London & Edinburgh*, [1930.] 8°. **4907. dd. 27.**

BUTTERFIELD (THOMAS EDWARD) Steam and Gas Engineering. A text covering power generating apparatus utilizing energy released by the combustion of fuels. pp. xv. 481. *Macmillan & Co.: London; Brooklyn* printed, [1929.] 8°. **8769. d. 16.**

BUTTERFIELD (W. P.) **LTD.**

—— News and Views. The W. P. Butterfield house magazine. no. 8–21. Autumn 1951—Winter 1955. *Shipley*, 1951–55. 4°.

[Continued as:]

Butterfield News. Jan. 1956, *etc.* *Shipley*, 1956– . 8°. **P.P. 5793. eaa.**

Wanting no. 10, 15.

BUTTERFIELD (W. RUSKIN)

—— History of St. Clement's Caves, Hastings. pp. 7. [c. 1935.] 8°. **010368. a. 58.**

BUTTERFIELD (WALTER H.) *See* ALLEN (Richard D.) Providence Inventory Test in Music. By R. D. Allen . . . W. H. Butterfield, *etc.* [1932, *etc.*] 4°. **7894. h. 12.**

BUTTERFIELD (WILLIAM) *D.D., Ph.D.*

—— Be Ye Perfect. pp. 80. *Burns, Oates & Co.: London*, 1944. 8°. **4398. aaa. 115.**

BUTTERFIELD (WILLIAM) *of Adam Street, Adelphi.*

—— *See* BARBER (Mary) *M.B.* Some Drawings of ancient Embroidery, *etc.* [Edited by W. Butterfield.] 1880. fol. **1809. a. 14.**

—— Church Seats and Kneeling Boards . . . With an appendix by Richard Foster . . . Second edition. pp. 11. *Rivingtons: London*, 1886. 8°. **7807. f. 17. (11.)**

—— Third edition. pp. 12. *Rivingtons: London*, 1880. 8°. **08230.b.50.(7.)**

—— Elevations, Sections, and Details, of Saint John Baptist Church, at Shottesbroke, Berkshire. pp. 7. pl. x. 1844. fol. *See* OXFORD.—*Oxford Society for Promoting the Study of Gothic Architecture, etc.* **1263. g. 17. (4.)**

BUTTERFIELD (WILLIAM A.) How to tune your own Piano. The vibratory lock-system and divided temperament, *etc.* pp. 24. *W. A. Butterfield: Boston*, [1910.] 8°. **7898. pp. 21. (3.)**

BUTTERFIELD (WILLIAM HENRY)

—— Effective Personal Letters . . . Second edition, revised and enlarged. pp. xvii. 389. *Prentice-Hall: New York*, 1951. 8°. **012987. ee. 16.**

—— Successful Collection Letters. pp. xvii. 250. *McGraw-Hill Book Co.: New York & London*, 1941. 8°. **08228. bb. 63.**

BUTTERFIELD (WILLIAM JOHN ATKINSON) *See* LEEDS (Frank H.) and BUTTERFIELD (W. H. A.) Acetylene, *etc.* 1903. 8°. **08715. aaa. 2.**

—— —— 1910. 8°. **2244. d. 13.**

—— *See* ROSS (Hugh C.) and CROPPER (J. W.) The Problem of the Gasworks Pitch Industries & Cancer, *etc.* (With some observations by W. J. A. Butterfield.) 1912. 8°. **07306. g. 32. (5.)**

—— Gas Manufacture: the chemistry of. A practical handbook, *etc.* pp. xiv. 375. *C. Griffin & Co.: London*, 1896. 8°. **8716. bbb. 51.**

BUTTERFIELD (WILLIAM JOHN ATKINSON)

—— Second edition, revised, with a new chapter on acetylene, *etc.* pp. xv. 448. *C. Griffin & Co.: London*, 1898. 8°. **8716.** c. **24.**

—— The Chemistry of Gas Manufacture . . . Third edition, with illustrations. vol. 1. pp. ix. 259. *C. Griffin & Co.: London*, 1904. 8°. **8716.** bb. **56.**
No more of this edition published.

—— Fourth edition, *etc.* vol. 1. pp. ix. 267. *C. Griffin & Co.: London*, 1907. 8°. **8716.** bb. **12.**
No more of this edition published.

—— Lectures on Chemistry in Gas-Works. pp. 71. 1913. 8°. *See* LONDON.—III. Royal *Institute of Chemistry.* **08909.** a. **20.** (**5.**)

BUTTERFIELD (WILLIAM THOMAS) Notes on the Worsted Industry. A paper read at the autumnal meeting of the Institute of Chartered Accountants . . . 1913. pp. 74. *Gee & Co.: London*, 1913. 8°. **07942.** i. **42.** (**5.**)

BUTTERFILL (HENRY HOLT) First Principles of Mechanical and Engineering Drawing, *etc.* pp. xii. 211. *Chapman & Hall: London*, 1897. 8°. **8768.** ccc. **14.**

BUTTERFLIES. Butterflies in their Floral Homes, with Butterfly Fables indited by a Dreamer in the Woods. [Coloured plates, with descriptions in verse.] ff. 9. *Paul Gerrard: London*, [1858.] fol. **1347.** l. **16.**

BUTTERFLY. The Butterfly. A humorous and artistic monthly. *See* PERIODICAL PUBLICATIONS.—*London.*

—— The Butterfly. A series of literary papers. *See* PERIODICAL PUBLICATIONS.—*Warrington.*

—— The Butterfly's Ball, and the Grasshopper's feast. [A poem. By William Roscoe. With engravings from drawings by William Mulready.] *J. Harris: London*, 1807. 16°. C. **40.** a. **57.** (**1.**)
Printed on one side of the leaf only.

—— [Another edition.] With neat engravings on wood. ff. 31. *Dean & Munday: London*, [1830?] 12°. **012806.** de. **23.** (**15.**)
Printed on one side of the leaf only. The illustrations are different from those in the edition of 1807.

—— [Another edition.] The Butterfly's Ball. *T. Goode: London*, [1854.] 32°. **11622.** a. **33.** (**13.**)

—— Butterfly's Ball. [Adapted from William Roscoe's "The Butterfly's Ball and the Grasshopper's Feast."] pp. 8. *W. Walker & Son: Otley*, [1850?] 12°. **12805.** aa. **49.** (**1.**)

—— The Butterfly's Birth-day. By the author of the Butterfly's Ball [i.e. William Roscoe]. [With plates.] pp. 15. *Longman & Co.; J. Harris: London*, [1809.] 16°. **012806.** de. **8.** (**5.**)

—— Day-dreams. By a Butterfly. [A poem.] pp. 156. *J. M. Creighton: Kingston, C.W.*, 1854. 12°. **11644.** c. **69.**

—— The Golden Butterfly. A novel. By the authors of 'Ready-money Mortiboy' [i.e. Sir Walter Besant and James Rice], *etc.* 3 vol. *Tinsley Bros.: London*, 1876. 8°. **12636.** m. **11.**

—— I'd be a Butterfly. [A song. By Nathaniel Thomas Haynes Bayly.] *In*: The Crying Family, and I'd be a Butterfly. [1835?] *s. sh.* 4°. **11630.** f. **7.** (**132.**)

—— I'd be a Butterfly. [By T. H. Bayly.] (The Mountain Maid.—The Irish Recruit.) [Songs.] *Ryle & Co.: London*, [1840?] *s. sh.* 4°. **11621.** b. **18.** (**25.**)

—— [Another copy.] **11621.** b. **18.** (**29.**)

—— [Another copy.] C. **116.** h. **2.** (**11.**)

BUTTERFLY ANNUAL. *See* PERIODICAL PUBLICATIONS.—London.—*Butterfly.*

BUTTERFLY BIRTHDAY BOOK. The Butterfly Birthday Book. *M. Ward & Co.: London*, [1888.] 16°. **11601.** aa. **41.**

BUTTERFLY COLLECTING. Butterfly and Moth Collecting . . . With brief descriptions of many species, fully illustrated. Second edition, revised, rearranged and enlarged. pp. 112. *L. U. Gill: London*, 1901. 8°. **7296.** b. **10.**

BUTTERFLY SERIES. The Butterfly Series of Complete Stories from "The Young Ladies' Journal." *See* PERIODICAL PUBLICATIONS.—London.—*Young Ladies' Journal.*

BUTTERFLY (BACHELOR) The Veritable History of Mr. Bachelor Butterfly, *etc.* [A series of plates, taken from the "Histoire de M. Cryptogame" in the French newspaper "L'Illustration."] *D. Bogue: London*, 1845. *obl.* 8°. **1322.m.81.**

BUTTERICK PUBLISHING COMPANY. [Miscellaneous booklets and patterns.] [*New York*, 1931– .] 12° & 4°. **7742.** p. **17.**

—— The Butterick Cook Book. *See* JUDSON (Helena)

—— Butterick Dressmaking Book. pp. 95. *Butterick Co.: New York*, [1940.] 4°. **07743.** dd. **4.**

—— Butterick Dressmaking Book. pp. 80. *Butterick Co.: New York*, [1946.] 4°. **7744.** d. **14.**

—— Butterick Dressmaking Book. pp. 80. *New York*, [1949.] 4°. **7744.** gg. **10.**

—— Butterick New Sewing Book. (Editor: Eileen Heagney.) pp. 80. [*New York*, 1952.] 4°. **7744.d.35.**

—— [A reissue.] Butterick New Sewing Book. *New York*, [1953.] 4°. **7744.** gg. **45.**

—— Butterick Sewing and Dressmaking Book. pp. 63. *New York*, [1944.] 4°. **7744.** d. **10.**

—— The New Butterick Cook-Book. *See* ROSE (Flora)

BUTTERIS (VALENTINE) Butteris's Guide to the Dart, Dartmouth and the neighbourhood, *etc.* pp. 62. *V. Butteris: Dartmouth*, 1852. 8°. **10351.** f. **22.**

—— [Another edition.] pp. 62. *V. Butteris: Dartmouth*, [1855?] 12°. **10351.** cc. **25.**

BUTTERLEY COMPANY.

—— Ad rem . . . The house magazine of the Butterley Company, *etc.* no. 5, *etc. Derby*, 1953– . 4°. P.P. **5793.** bty.
Wanting no. 7.

BUTTERLEY, afterwards **SMITHERS** (CECILIA) When the Light is softly gleaming. [A hymn.] [1903.] *s. sh.* fol. **1897.** b. **33** (**51.**)

BUTTERS (A. FRIEDRICH) Emanuel Tremellius, erster Rector des Zweibrücker Gymnasiums. Eine Lebensskizze, *etc.* pp. 38. *Zweibrücken*, 1859. 8°. **4886.** e. **41.** (**6.**)

BUTTERS (FREDERIC CHARLES)

—— Branscombe. The parish and the church. [With illustrations.] pp. 29. *Sydney Lee: Exeter*, [1949.] 8°. **07822.** df. **60.**

BUTTERS (FREDERIC KING) *See* ROSENDAHL (C. O.) A Monograph on the Genus Heuchera. By C. O. Rosendahl . . . F. K. Butters, *etc.* 1936. 8°. [*Minnesota Studies in Plant Science.* vol. 2.] Ac. **2692.** k/10.

BUTTERS (Friedrich) *See* Butters (A. F.)

BUTTERS (Fritz) Sinngemässe gynäkologische Therapie im alten Griechenland. pp. 68. *Würzburg*, 1937. 8°. **07680.** aaa. **40.**

BUTTERS (Henry Augustus) Harry Butters, R.F.A. "An American Citizen." Life and war letters. Edited by Mrs. Denis O'Sullivan. With twelve photographs, *etc.* pp. 297. *J. Lane Co.: New York*, 1918. 8°. **010880.** e. **19.**

BUTTERS (J. Friedrich) Führer durch Bad Dürkheim in der Rheinpfalz und seine Umgebungen. [With a map.] pp. viii. 113. *Dürkheim*, 1868. 12°. **7470.** aaa. **12.**

BUTTERS (John Keith)

—— Corporate Mergers. [By] J. K. Butters, John Lintner, William L. Cary. Assisted by Powell Niland. pp. xviii. 364. *Division of Research, Graduate School of Business Administration, Harvard University: Boston*, 1951. 8°. [*Effects of Taxation.*] **8204.a.83/4.**

—— Inventory Accounting and Policies. [By] J. K. Butters . . . Assisted by Powell Niland. pp. xvii. 330. *Division of Research, Graduate School of Business Administration, Harvard University: Boston*, 1949. 8°. [*Effects of Taxation.*] **8204.a.83/1.**

—— Investments by Individuals. [By] J. K. Butters . . . Lawrence E. Thompson . . . Lynn L. Bollinger. pp. xxxiv. 533. *Division of Research, Graduate School of Business Administration, Harvard University: Boston*, 1953. 8°. [*Effects of Taxation.*] **8204.** a. **83/6.**

BUTTERS (John Keith) and **LINTNER** (John Virgil)

—— Effect of Federal Taxes on Growing Enterprises. pp. ix. 226. *Division of Research, Graduate School of Business Administration, Harvard University: Boston*, 1945. 8°. **08226.** eee. **13.**

BUTTERS (Laurence) *See* Fairbairn (James) *Engraver.* Fairbairn's Crests of the Families of Great Britain and Ireland . . . Revised by L. Butters, *etc.* [1860.] 8°. **9904.** pp. **6.**

—— *See* Knight (F.) *Engraver*, and Butters (L.) Knight & Butters' Crests of Great Britain & Ireland, *etc.* [1885.] 8°. **2400.** g. **4.**

BUTTERS (M.) *See* London.—iii. *Queenswood Literary Union.* The Net. [Edited by M. Butters and Miss McMillan.] 1885, *etc.* 8°. P.P. **5870.** d. (**2.**)

BUTTERSACK (Felix Eberhard)

—— *See* Villaret (A. H. A.) and Paalzow (F. F. O.) Sanitätsdienst und Gesundheitspflege im Deutschen Heere . . . Unter Mitwirkung von Oberstabsarzt Dr. Buttersack [and others] . . . herausgegeben, *etc.* 1909. 8°. M.L. d. **19.**

BUTTERSWORTH (Jane) *See* Branch (Elizabeth) *the Elder.* The Cruel Mistress. Being the genuine trial of E. Branch and her daughter for the murder of J. Buttersworth, *etc.* 1740. 8°. **518.** f. **69.**

—— *See* Branch (Elizabeth) *the Elder.* The Trial of Mrs. Branch, and her Daughter for the murder of J. Buttersworth, *etc.* [1740.] 8°. **1416.** d. **13.**

BUTTERTON (George Ash) Parochial Sermons, on various subjects. pp. ix. 268. *J. Hathard & Son: London*, 1845. 8°. **1357.** e. **11.**

—— A Sermon delivered at St. John's Church, Wakefield . . . on the occasion of the death of W. Thistlethwaite, *etc.* pp. 16. *Longman & Co.: London*, 1836. 4°. **10347.** g. **2.** (**2.**)

BUTTERWECK (Joseph Seibert) The Problem of teaching High School Pupils how to study, *etc.* [A thesis.] pp. vi. 116. *Teachers College, Columbia University: New York*, 1926. 8°. **20017.** l. **37.**

BUTTERWORTH, *Penang.—Town Council.*

—— Statement of Revenue and Expenditure for the year ended 31st December 1954 [*etc.*]. *Kuala Lumpur*, 1955- . fol. C.S. b. **406/4.**
Issued as supplements to the Federation of Malaya Government Gazette.

BUTTERWORTH, *South Africa.—Public Library.* Catalogue of Books and List of Rules, *etc.* pp. 48. *Cape Town*, 1893. 8°. **011902.** e. **22.** (**9.**)

BUTTERWORTH AND CO.

—— Butterworth's Annotated Legislation Service. *See* England. [*Laws and Statutes.*—iv. *Emergency Legislation.*] Butterworth's Emergency Legislation Service, *etc.*

—— Butterworths Commercial Controls. *See* England. [*Laws and Statutes.*—iv. *Commercial Controls.*]

—— Butterworths' Commercial French Handbook. *See* Blouet (H.)

—— Butterworths' Company Precedents. *See* Sutton (Ralph) and Williams (W. J.)

—— Butterworths' Digest of Leading Cases on Workmen's Compensation. *See* Knocker (Douglas) Workmen's Compensation Digest.

—— Butterworths' Digest of Workmen's Compensation Cases. *See* Periodical Publications.—*London.*

—— Butterworth's Emergency Legislation Service. *See* England. [*Laws and Statutes.*—iv. *Emergency Legislation.*]

—— Butterworths' Empire Law List and Directory. *See* Directories.—*Law.*

—— Butterworths' Five Years' Digest. *See* Stone (Gilbert)

—— Butterworths Index and Noter-up to S.A.L.R. *See* Africa, *South.* [Union of South Africa.]—*Supreme Court.* The South African Law Reports.

—— Butterworths' Loose Leaf Collection of Forms and Notes. *See* Underhill (Arthur)

—— Butterworth's Modern Text Books. *London*, 1950- . 8°. W.P. **14721.**

—— Butterworths Modern Trends Series. *See* Horder (Thomas J.) *Baron Horder.* Modern Trends Series, *etc.*

—— Butterworths' Rating Appeals. 1913–1925 [*etc.*]. *London*, 1925- . 8°. W.P. **12970.**

—— Butterworths' Standard Law Book Series. *London*, 1909- . 8°. **6144.** s. **1**, *etc.*

—— Butterworths Taxation Statutes Service. *See* Blann (Basil E. J.)

—— Butterworths' Ten Years' Digest of Reported Cases, 1898–1907. *See* Clarke (Sidney W.)

—— Butterworths' Twentieth Century Statutes, Annotated. *See* England. [*Laws and Statutes.*—iii. 1900 *to date.*]

—— Butterworths' Workmen's Compensation Cases. *See* Periodical Publications.—*London.* Workmen's Compensation Cases.

—— Butterworths' Yearly Digest of Reported Cases. *See* England.—*Supreme Court of Judicature.*

BUTTERWORTH COURIER.

—— The Butterworth Courier. *See* ENGLAND.—*Royal Air Force.—Butterworth Station, Malaya.*

BUTTERWORTH (A. E.) The Commission of H.M.S. Glory, Flag Ship of Commander-in-Chief, China Station, 1900–1904 . . . With an introduction by Lionel Yexley. [With plates.] pp. ix. 153. 6. *Westminster Press: London*, 1904. 8°. [" *Log* " *Series.*] **08806**. bb. **11**.

—— The Log of H.M.S. " Bedford," China Station, 1907–09. [With plates.] pp. 131. *Westminster Press: London*, 1909. 8°. [" *Log* " *Series.*] **08806**. bb. **25**.

BUTTERWORTH (ADELINE M.) William Blake, mystic. A study . . . Together with Young's Night Thoughts: nights I & II. With illustrations by William Blake and frontispiece Death's Door, from Blair's 'The Grave.' ff. 14. pp. 42. *Liverpool Booksellers Co.: Liverpool; Simpkin, Marshall & Co.: London*, 1911. 4°. **7856**. ff. **15**.

BUTTERWORTH (ALAN) District Administration in Madras, 1818–1857.—District Administration in Madras, 1858–1918. *See* DODWELL (Henry H.) The Indian Empire, 1858–1918, *etc.* 1932. 8°. [*Cambridge History of the British Empire.* vol. 5.] **2090.a.**

—— The Formation of Madras. pt. 1. pp. 83. *Hickmott & Co.: Camberley*, 1932. 8°. **9056**. bb. **34**. *No more published.*

—— Some Madras Trees. pp. xi. 228. *Methodist Publishing House: Madras*, 1911. 8°. **07073**. ee. **6**.

—— The Southlands of Siva: some reminiscences of life in Southern India. pp. x. 258. *John Lane: London*, 1923. 8°. **010056**. f. **42**.

—— The Substance of Indian Faith. [Selected passages from Indian religious writings.] pp. ix. 151. *A. Butterworth: Camberley*, 1926. 8°. **04503**. e. **35**.

BUTTERWORTH (ALAN) and **VENUGOPĀLA CHEṬṬI**, *V.*

—— A Collection of the Inscriptions on Copper-Plate and Stones in the Nellore district. Made by Alan Butterworth . . . and V. Venugopaul Chetty. [With translations and plates.] 3 vol. pp. xi. 1520. 1905. 8°. *See* MADRAS, *Presidency of.* **14058**. c. **11**.

BUTTERWORTH (ALEXANDER)

—— Flow of Harmonics in a Metropolitan-Type Supply System feeding a Large Rectifier Load. pp. 20. pl. 6. *Leatherhead*, 1950. 4°. [*British Electrical and Allied Industries Research Association. Technical Report.* no. M/T 110.] W.P. **9138/515**. *Reproduced from typewriting.*

—— The Impedance of Steel Conduit used as an Earth-Continuity Conductor. By A. Butterworth [and others], *etc. Leatherhead*, 1951. 4°. [*British Electrical and Allied Industries Research Association. Technical Report.* no. V/T 111.] W.P. **9138/708**.

—— Reduction of Sheath Losses by Auxiliary Conductors. ff. 8. pl. 5. *London*, 1940. 4°. [*British Electrical and Allied Industries Research Association. Technical Report.* Reference F/T 144.] W.P. **9138/348**.

BUTTERWORTH (ALEXANDER) and **KLEWE** (HANS ROBERT JULIUS)

—— Interference from Zero-Phase Sequence Currents in a System with Insulated Neutral—Delabole Tests. pp. 24. pl. 6. *Leatherhead*, 1949. 4°. [*British Electrical and Allied Industries Research Association. Technical Report.* no. M/T 101.] W.P. **9138/551**. *Reproduced from typewriting.*

BUTTERWORTH (ALEXANDER) and **KLEWE** (HANS ROBERT JULIUS)

—— The Study of Balanced Harmonics in an Overhead Ring Main System. East Cornwall tests. pp. 25. pl. 4. *Leatherhead*, 1950. 4°. [*British Electrical and Allied Industries Research Association. Technical Report.* no. M/T 105.] W.P. **9138/541**.

BUTTERWORTH (*Sir* ALEXANDER KAYE) *See* BUTTERWORTH (George S. K.) George Butterworth, 1885–1916. [The editorial notes signed: A. K. B., i.e. Sir A. K. Butterworth.] 1918. 4°. **10823**. k. **28**.

—— The Law relating to Maximum Rates and Charges on Railways . . . By A. K. Butterworth . . . assisted by Arthur Reginald Butterworth . . . and F. H. Cripps-Day. (Analysis of the Railway Rates and Charges Confirmation Acts, 1891 and 1892, as issued by the Board of Trade.) 2 pt. *Butterworth & Co.: London*, 1897. 8°. **08235**. h. **52**.

—— The Practice of the Railway & Canal Commission, being the Railway & Canal Commission Rules, 1889, and the Railway and Canal Traffic Acts, 1854, 1873 and 1888. With notes and index, and a compendium of the practice. pp. 79. 1889. 8°. *See* ENGLAND. [*Laws and Statutes.*—IV. *Railways and Canals.*] **6376**. f. **15**.

—— Road Accidents. A pedestrian's grievance, or, the law as it is and as it should be, *etc.* pp. 15. *Pedestrians' Association: London*, [1932.] 8°. **6426**. b. **59**.

—— A Treatise on the Law relating to Rates and Traffic on Railways and Canals, with special reference to the Railway and Canal Traffic Act, 1888, and an appendix of statutes, rules, etc. By A. K. Butterworth . . . assisted by Charles Edward Ellis. pp. xxxii. 234. 108. *Butterworths: London*, 1889. 8°. **08235**. h. **7**.

—— Second edition. pp. xxxii. 264. 165. *Butterworths: London*, 1889. 8°. **6376**. f. **16**.

BUTTERWORTH (ANNIE) Manual of Household Work and Management. pp. xv. 195. *Hutchinson & Co: London*, [1903.] 8°. **07943**. l. **6**.

—— Second edition, revised and enlarged. pp. xv. 200. *Longmans & Co.: London*, 1906. 8°. **07943**. m. **46**.

—— Third edition, revised and enlarged. pp. xvi. 235. *Longmans & Co.: London*, 1913. 8°. **07942**. ee. **41**.

—— Manual of Household Work and Management . . . (Third edition.) New impression. pp. xvi. 235. *Longmans, Green & Co.: London*, 1922. 8°. **7950**. aa. **34**.

—— Fourth edition, revised and enlarged. pp. xvi. 248. *Longmans & Co.: London*, 1926. 8°. **07943**. cc. **2**.

—— Seventh edition. pp. xvi. 250. *Longmans & Co.: London*, 1940. 8°. **7943**. v. **47**.

BUTTERWORTH (ARTHUR REGINALD) *See* BENJAMIN (Judah P.) A Treatise on the Law of Sale of Personal Property . . . Fifth edition by W. C. A. Ker . . . and A. R. Butterworth. 1906. 8°. **6306**. p. **8**.

—— *See* BUTTERWORTH (*Sir* Alexander K.) The Law relating to Maximum Rates and Charges on Railways . . . By A. K. Butterworth . . . assisted by A. R. Butterworth, *etc.* 1897. 8°. **08235**. h. **52**.

—— Australian Federation and the Privy Council. pp. 52. *Sweet & Maxwell: London*, 1900. 8°. **8156**. df. **27**. **(6.)**

—— Bankers' Advances on Mercantile Securities other than bills of exchange and promissory notes. pp. xv. 208. *Sweet & Maxwell: London*, 1902. 8°. **6375**. de. **25**.

—— The Criminal Evidence Act, 1898, with introductory chapter and practical notes. pp. xv. 107. 10. *Sweet & Maxwell: London*, 1898. 8°. **6485**. ee. **4**.

BUTTERWORTH (BASIL)

—— *See* BONNELL (David G. R.) and BUTTERWORTH (B.) Brick Clays of North-East Scotland . . . Part II. Report on analyses and physical tests. By D. G. R. Bonnell . . . and B. Butterworth, *etc.* 1946. fol. [*Geological Survey of Great Britain. Wartime Pamphlets.* no. 47.] B.S. **38.** g/**8.**

—— *See* BONNELL (David G. R.) and BUTTERWORTH (B.) Clay Building Bricks of the United Kingdom, *etc.* 1950. 8°. B.S. **46/38.**

—— Bricks and Modern Research. [With plates.] pp. xiii. 160. *Crosby Lockwood & Son: London,* 1948. 8°. **7948.** aa. **20.**

—— Clay Building Bricks. Their manufacture, properties and testing with notes on the efficiency of brickwork. [With plates.] pp. iv. 24. *London,* 1948. 8°. [*National Building Studies.* Bulletin. no. 1.] B.S. **38A/12.**

BUTTERWORTH (BENJAMIN) Commercial Union between Canada and the United States. [With a portrait.] *See* NEW YORK.—*Canadian Club.* Canadian Leaves, *etc.* 1887. 4°. **12356.** l. **16.**

BUTTERWORTH (CHARLES COLLIER)

—— The English Primers, 1529–1545: their publication and connection with the English Bible and the Reformation in England. [With plates and a bibliography.] pp. xiii. 340. *University of Pennsylvania Press: Philadelphia,* 1953. 8°. **2008.e.**

—— [Another copy.] The English Primers, 1529–1545. pp. xiii. 340. *Philadelphia,* 1953. 8°. **3458.** ee. **1.**

—— The Literary Lineage of the King James Bible, 1340–1611. pp. xi. 394. *University of Pennsylvania Press: Philadelphia,* 1941. 8°. **3130.** bb. **3.**

BUTTERWORTH (E.) **AND SON.** Durable Copy Book. pp. 22. *J. Whittle & R. H. Laurie: London,* 1819. 4°. **1267.** d. **7.**

—— Elegant Extracts for Butterworth & Son's new Universal Penman, *etc.* [Engraved by J. Menzies.] *Edinburgh,* 1809. *obl.* 4°. **1810.** a. **3.** (**3.**)

—— New Copies written by Butterworth and Son. Engraved by W. Salomon. *W. Salomon: Paris,* [1825?] *obl.* 8°. **871.h.52.(3.)**

BUTTERWORTH (E.) *Calligrapher.* Butterworth's Young Arithmetician's Instructor; containing specimens of writing, with directions, *etc.* pp. 51. *Oliver & Boyd: Edinburgh,* [1815.] 4°. **1268.** f. **19.**
Printed on one side of the leaf only.

BUTTERWORTH (EDWIN) A Concise History of Lancashire. pt. 1. pp. 126. *James Gilbert: London,* [1847?] 8°. **10349.** c. **8.** (**2.**)
No more published?

—— An Historical Account of the Towns of Ashton-under-Lyne, Stalybridge, and Dukinfield. pp. 177. v. *T. A. Phillips: Ashton,* 1842. 12°. **10351.** bbb. **39.**

—— Historical Sketches of Oldham . . . With an appendix containing the history of the town to the present time. pp. 255. *John Hirst: Oldham,* 1856. 8°. **10358.** aa. **11.**

—— A Statistical Sketch of the County Palatine of Lancaster. pp. xl. 168. *Longman & Co.: London,* 1841. 12°. **797.** f. **7.**

—— [Another copy.] **10349.** c. **8.** (**1.**)

BUTTERWORTH (EDWIN)

—— Views on the Manchester & Leeds Railway, drawn from nature, and on stone, by A. F. Tait; with a descriptive history, by E. Butterworth. pp. 34. *Bradshaw & Blacklock: London,* 1845. fol. Maps **17.** e. **19.**

BUTTERWORTH (ELSIE MARY) *See* LYDE (Lionel W.) and BUTTERWORTH (E. M.) The Where and Why Geographies. 1925, *etc.* 8°. **10003.r.13.**

—— The Teaching of Geography in France. A comparative study, *etc.* pp. v. 137. *London,* 1922. 8°. [*Blackie's Library of Pedagogics.*] **08310.** de. **26/2.**

BUTTERWORTH (ELSIE P.) *See* AMAR (J.) The Human Motor, *etc.* (Translated by E. P. Butterworth and G. E. Wright.) 1920. 8°. **08282.** b. **17.**

BUTTERWORTH (ETHEL)

—— Jimmy Jumbo's Exciting Day. Story and pictures by E. Butterworth. *Lutterworth Press:* [*Redhill,* 1945.] 8°. **12830.** b. **41.**

BUTTERWORTH (FRANK NESTLE) *See* also BLUNDELL (Peter) *pseud.* [i.e. F. N. Butterworth.]

—— The Engineer Afloat, his training, work, and pay. With full particulars of the Board of Trade Examinations. pp. 84. *Technical Publishing Co.: London,* 1914. 8°. **08806.** aaa. **25.**

BUTTERWORTH (GEORGE) Deerhurst. A parish of the Vale of Gloucester. [With plates.] pp. vii. 184. *William North: Tewkesbury; Simpkin, Marshall & Co.: London,* [1888?] 8°. **10352.** bbb. **46.**

—— Second and revised edition. pp. ix. 252. *William North: Tewkesbury; Simpkin, Marshall & Co.: London,* [1890.] 8°. **10352.** g. **8.**

—— A Few more Words about Extinction; addressed especially to thoughtful working men. [A reply to H. S. Warleigh's pamphlet "A Demonstration of the extinction of evil persons and evil things." pp. 64. *C. A. Bartlett: London; T. Kerslake & Co.: Bristol,* 1873. 8°. **4380.** b. **49.** (**13.**)

—— Notes on the Priory and Church of Deerhurst, Gloucestershire. pp. 28. *W. North: Tewkesbury,* 1878. 12°. **10347.** aa. **1.** (**10.**)

—— [Another edition.] A Short Account of the Ecclesiastical Buildings of Deerhurst, Gloucestershire. [With plates.] pp. 22. *William North: Tewkesbury,* [1900?] 8°. **07815.** a. **22.**

—— Remarks on a Pamphlet written by Rev. H. S. Warleigh, and entitled "A Demonstration of the extinction of evil persons and of evil things." pp. 52. *C. A. Bartlett: London; T. Kerslake & Co.: Bristol,* 1872. 8°. **4380.** b. **49.** (**12.**)

BUTTERWORTH (GEORGE SAINTON KAYE) *See* SHARP (Cecil J.) The Country Dance Book. (pt. 3, 4 described by C. J. Sharp and G. Butterworth.) 1909, *etc.* 8°. **07911.** de. **89.**

—— *See* SHARP (Cecil J.) The Country Dance Book, Part III (IV) . . . Described by C. J. Sharp and G. Butterworth. 1927, *etc.* 8°. **7917.** de. **96.**

—— *See* SHARP (Cecil J.) The Morris Book, *etc.* (pt. 5 by C. J. Sharp and G. Butterworth.) 1907, *etc.* 8°. **7912.** ee. **32.**

—— George Butterworth, 1885–1916. [A diary and letters, with a memoir signed: R. O. M., i.e. Reginald O. Morris, and other additional matter. The editorial notes signed: A. K. B., i.e. Sir Alexander Kaye Butterworth.] pp. 127. *Printed for private circulation: York & London,* 1918. 4°. **10823.** k. **28.**

BUTTERWORTH (George Sainton Kaye)

—— George Sainton Kaye Butterworth, born July 12th, 1885, killed in action August 5th, 1916. Extract from The Times, August 12th, 1916. [With letters reproduced from typewriting.] [1916.] 8°. **010826**. f. **19**.

BUTTERWORTH (George William) *See* Clemens (T. F.) *Alexandrinus*. Clement of Alexandria, with an English translation by G. W. Butterworth, *etc.* 1919. 8°. **2282**. d. **52**.

—— *See* Origen. Origen on First Principles . . . Translated . . . together with an introduction and notes, by G. W. Butterworth. 1936. 8°. **3805**. ee. **16**.

—— British-Israelism, *etc.* pp. 7. *Press & Publications Board of the National Assembly: London,* [1937.] 8°. **04034**. l. **1**.

—— The Church and Spiritualism. pp. 10. *Press & Publications Board of the Church Assembly: London,* [1937.] 8°. **8634**. cc. **29**.

—— Churches, Sects and Religious Parties. pp. 155. *S.P.C.K.: London,* 1936. 8°. **20010**. e. **10**.

—— Various Sects and Doctrines . . . Reprinted from " Churches, Sects and Religious Parties." pp. 47. *S.P.C.K.: London,* 1938. 8°. **4135**. df. **56**.

—— The Devotional Use of the Bible. pp. 23. *S.P.C.K.: London,* 1948. 16°. [*Inner Life Series.* no. 2.] **4110**. aaa. **8/2**.

—— Jesus, Leader of Man. A study on the claims of Jesus on man and society. pp. 177. *Religious Education Press: Wallington,* 1952 [1953]. 8°. **4227**. l. **10**.

—— Our Christian Heritage: six simple lectures on English Church history; for use with lantern slides. pp. 104. *Press & Publications Board of the Church Assembly: London,* 1937. 8°. **20031**. d. **17**.

—— Short Notes on Bible Study, *etc.* 3 pt. *S.P.C.K.: London,* 1924. 8°. **03127**. g. **52**.

—— Spiritualism and Religion. pp. ix. 196. *S.P.C.K.: London,* 1944. 8°. **8634**. ff. **42**.

—— The Story of the Church. 3 pt.

1. How God's Message came to Britain.
2. The Building of the English Church.
3. The Expansion of the English Church.

Press & Publications Board of the Church Assembly: London, 1939. 8°. **20032**. f. **50**.

—— A Study of Church History to the end of the thirteenth century. pp. 168. *Student Christian Movement: London,* 1927. 8°. **4532**. aa. **22**.

BUTTERWORTH (H. H.) Robin Hood's Miracle; and other stories. By H. H. Butterworth, Blanche Willis Howard, and other noted authors. [With plates.] *D. Lothrop & Co.: Boston,* [1878.] 8°. **12809**. i. **5**.

BUTTERWORTH (Harold H.) Poems. pp. 46. *A. H. Stockwell: London,* [1907.] 8°. **11650**. cc. **40**.

BUTTERWORTH (Henry) A Catalogue of Law Books, in general use, of the best editions . . . Second edition, corrected and enlarged. pp. 129. *Henry Butterworth: London,* 1820. 8°. **11902**. aaa. **3**.

—— A Catalogue of the Books in the Library of the College of Advocates in Doctors' Commons. [Compiled by H. Butterworth.] pp. 236. 1818. 8°. *See* London.—iii. *College of Advocates in Doctor's Commons.* **620**. g. **22**.

BUTTERWORTH (Henry)

—— Memoir of the late Henry Butterworth, F.S.A. Reprinted, with additions, from the " Gentleman's Magazine," *etc.* pp. 8. [1861.] 8°. **10816**. de. **18**. (3.)

BUTTERWORTH (Hezekiah) *See* Rice (Adams T.) Pinocchio . . . Dramatized from the translation of the Italian fairy tale of H. Butterworth. [1931.] 8°. **11791**. r. **21**.

—— Brother Jonathan. [A novel.] pp. xi. 246. *D. Appleton & Co.: New York,* 1903. 8°. **012707**. aa. **48**.

—— In the Boyhood of Lincoln. A tale of the Tunker schoolmaster and the times of Black Hawk. pp. vii. 266. *D. Appleton & Co.: London,* 1892. 8°. **10883**. c. **14**.

—— [Another copy, with a different titlepage.] *D. Appleton & Co.: New York,* 1892. 8°. **012807**. f. **5**.

—— In the Land of the Condor. A story of Tarapaca. [With plates.] pp. 192. *Baptist Tract & Book Society: London; Philadelphia* printed, 1898. 8°. **04410**. k. **44**.

—— The Pilot of the Mayflower. A tale of the children of the pilgrim republic . . . Illustrated. pp. viii. 248. *D. Appleton & Co.: New York,* 1898. 8°. **012703**. ee. **6**.

—— Songs of History. Poems and ballads upon important episodes in American history. pp. 183. *New England Publishing Co.: Boston,* 1887. 8°. **11686**. ee. **27**.

—— South America. A popular illustrated history of the struggle for liberty in the Andean Republics and Cuba. [With plates.] pp. xxi. 266. *Doubleday & McClure Co.: New York,* 1898. 8°. **9770**. b. **9**.

—— The Story of Magellan and the Discovery of the Philippines . . . Illustrated, *etc.* pp. x. 235. *D. Appleton & Co.: New York,* 1899. 8°. **10633**. f. **40**.

—— The Story of the Hymns; or, Hymns that have made a history, *etc.* [With portraits.] pp. 256. *American Tract Society: New York,* [1875.] 12°. **4999**. bb. **5**.

—— The Treasure Ship. A tale of Sir William Phipps, the regicides, and the inter-charter period in Massachusetts . . . Illustrated, *etc.* pp. x. 251. *D. Appleton & Co.: New York,* 1899. 8°. **012707**. m. **6**.

—— Zigzag Journeys in Acadia and New France . . . Fully illustrated. pp. 320. *Estes & Lauriat: Boston,* 1885. 4°. **10470**. bbb. **4**.

—— Zigzag Journeys in Australia; or, a Visit to the Ocean World . . . Fully illustrated. pp. 319. *Estes & Lauriat: Boston,* [1891.] 4°. **10492**. ee. **20**.

—— Zigzag Journeys in Northern Lands. The Rhine to the Arctic . . . Fully illustrated. pp. 320. *Estes & Lauriat: Boston,* 1884. 4°. **10108**. e. **11**.

—— Zigzag Journeys in the Antipodes . . . Fully illustrated. pp. 320. *Estes & Lauriat: Boston,* [1889.] 4°. **10055**. df. **19**.

—— Zig-zag Journeys in the British Isles . . . Fully illustrated. pp. 320. *Estes & Lauriat: Boston,* [1890.] 4°. **010358**. f. **5**.

—— Zigzag journeys in the Levant, with a Talmudist story-teller . . . Fully illustrated. pp. 304. *Estes & Lauriat: Boston,* 1886. 4°. **10077**. bbb. **15**.

—— Zigzag Journeys in the Occident. The Atlantic to the Pacific . . . Fully illustrated. pp. 320. *Estes & Lauriat: Boston,* 1883. 4°. **10413**. h. **13**.

BUTTERWORTH (Hezekiah)

—— [A reissue.] Zigzag Journeys in the Western States of America, *etc.* *Dean & Son: London,* [1884.] 8°. **10413.** h. **19.**

—— A Zigzag Journey in the Sunny South; or, Wonder tales of early American history . . . Fully illustrated. pp. 320. *Estes & Lauriat: Boston,* 1887. 4°. **9605.** ee. **16.**

BUTTERWORTH (Horace)

—— How To. A book of tumbling, tricks, pyramids and games. pp. 155. *The Author: Chicago,* 1899. 8°. **7919.** aa. **66.**

BUTTERWORTH (James) *Baptist Minister.*

—— [Circular letter, 1783.] An Exhorta-tion to the Religious Education of Children: being a circular letter from the Elders and Messengers of the several Baptist Churches meeting at Aulcester [and elsewhere, i.e. the Midland Association] . . . met in association at Bromsgrove . . . June 11 and 12, 1783. Prepared by J. Butterworth. pp. 36. 1795. 8°. *See* England. — *Churches, etc.* — *Baptists.* — *Midland Association.* **4183.** aaa. **48.**

BUTTERWORTH (James) *of Oldham.* The Antiquities of the Town, and a complete history of the trade of Manchester: with a description of Manchester and Salford, *etc.* pp. v. 302. xii. *Printed for the Author: Manchester,* 1822. 12°. **10368.** e. **29.**

—— [Another copy.] **10349.** e. **14.** (**2.**) *Imperfect; wanting the engraved frontispiece, the first of the preliminary leaves, pp.* 45–177, *and all after p.* 298.

—— [A reissue.] A Complete History of the Cotton Trade . . . To which is added an account of . . . the town of Manchester. By a person concerned in the trade [i.e. J. Butterworth]. 1823. 12°. *See* History. **10360.** cc. **43.**

—— An Historical and Descriptive Account of the Town and Parochial Chapelry of Oldham . . . including some biographical sketches of remarkable persons, natives or residents thereof: together with a directory. [With maps.] pp. xii. 211. *J. Clarke: Oldham,* 1817. 12°. **10358.** d. **37.**

—— [Another copy.] **10349.** e. **14.** (**3.**) *Imperfect; wanting the maps and all after p.* 175.

—— [Another edition.] History and Description of the Parochial Chapelry of Oldham . . . Second edition, *etc.* [With plates.] pp. x. 194. *J. Dodge: Oldham,* 1826. 12°. **577.** c. **15.**

—— An Historical and Topographical Description of the Town and Parish of Bury . . . 1829. With memorial introduction and bibliography. pp. xiii. 23. *Albert Sutton: Manchester,* 1902. 8°. **010360.** ee. **38.**

—— History and Description of the Town and Parish of Ashton-under-Lyne . . . and the village of Dukinfield, *etc.* pp. 188. *Thomas Cunningham: Ashton,* 1823. 8°. **578.** c. **23.**

—— A History and Description of the Towns and Parishes of Stockport, Ashton-under-Lyne, Mottram-long-den-dale, and Glossop, with some Memoirs of the late F. D. Astley, Esq. . . . and extracts from his poems, *etc.* 2 pt. *W. D. Varey: Manchester,* 1827, 28. 8°. **10360.** c. **25.** *Privately printed. Imperfect; wanting the woodcuts of Stockport and Mottram churches. Interleaved.*

BUTTERWORTH (James) *Phonographer. See* Bible.—*New Testament.* [*English.*] The New Testament lithographed in the reporting style . . . of phonography by J. Butterworth. [1864, *etc.*] 8°. **12991.** c. **4.**

—— *See* Bible.—*Matthew.—Selections.* [*English.*] The Sermon on the Mount. Lithographed in the corresponding style of phonography, by J. Butterworth. [1866.] 8°. **12991.** bb. **10.**

—— *See* Bible.—*Matthew.—Selections.* [*English.*] The Sermon on the Mount. Lithographed in the reporting style of phonography, by J. Butterworth. [1866.] 12°. **12991.** bb. **16.**

—— *See* Franklin (Benjamin) *LL.D.* The Autobiography of Benjamin Franklin. [Transcribed into phonographic script by J. Butterworth.] [1889.] 8°. **12991.** bb. **63.**

—— *See* Grindon (Leopold H.) Extracts from Life . . . Lithographed in the corresponding style of phonography. By J. Butterworth. 1866. 18°. **12991.** bb. **15.**

—— *See* Periodical Publications.—*London.* The Cabinet . . . containing readings in phonography . . . Conducted by J. Butterworth. [1863, *etc.*] 8°. P.P. **1893.** b.

—— *See* Periodical Publications.—*London.* The Weekly Phonographer . . . Edited . . . by J. Butterworth. [1868, *etc.*] 8°. P.P. **1893.** ba.

BUTTERWORTH (James) *Wesleyan Methodist Minister.* Adventures in Boyland. Pages from a boys' club scrap-book. pp. 192. *Epworth Press: London,* 1926. 8°. **04192.** aaa. **26.**

—— Bees' Wings and Ruby Queens, or, a Private's digressions. pp. 59. *C. H. Kelly: London,* [1918.] 8°. **4017.** dg. **20.**

—— Byways in Boyland, *etc.* p. 158. *Epworth Press: London,* 1925. 8°. **4193.** i. **30.**

—— Clubland. pp. 238. *Epworth Press: London,* 1932. 8°. **20016.** aa. **42.**

BUTTERWORTH (James E.) Practical Painting & Decorating, *etc.* pp. 189. *English Universities Press: London,* 1936. 8°. **7941.** p. **13.**

BUTTERWORTH (John) *Baptist Minister. See also* Christophilus, *pseud.* [i.e. J. Butterworth.]

—— *See* Bible.—*Appendix.—Concordances.* [*English.*] A New Concordance . . . by J. Butterworth, *etc.* 1785. 8°. **220.** e. **2.**

—— —— 1812. 8°. **3104.** aaa. **7.**

—— —— [1838.] 8°. **3109.** g. **6.**

—— —— 1851. 8°. **3050.** d. **13.**

BUTTERWORTH (John) *of Oldham.* Cotton, and its Treatment in the various processes of opening, carding, and spinning . . . To which is added directions for the examination of cotton fibre, yarns, &c., under the microscope. pp. 71. *Hirst & Rennie: Oldham,* [1881.] 8°. **7945.** bbb. **10.**

BUTTERWORTH (John Blackstock)

—— *See* Cheshire (Geoffrey C.) The Modern Law of Real Property . . . With an appendix on the Rent Acts by J. B. Butterworth. 1954. 8°. **6307.** d. **8.**

BUTTERWORTH (Joseph) **AND SON.** A Catalogue of Modern Law Books, also of Old Reports. pp. viii. 96. *London,* 1826. 12°. **1128.** b. **15.**

BUTTERWORTH (Joseph) **AND SON.**

—— A General Catalogue of Law Books . . . The sixth edition, corrected and enlarged. pp. xix. 252. *London*, 1819. 12°. **1128. b. 14.**
Earlier editions are entered under BUTTERWORTH *(Joseph) Bookseller.*

BUTTERWORTH (Joseph) *Assistant Registrar of the Rochdale County Court.* *See* England.—*County Courts.* Rules and Orders . . . Edited by J. Butterworth. 1857. 12°. **6405. a. 15.**

—— Pearse's County Court Guide. Edited by J. Butterworth, *etc.* pp. 24. *Whittaker & Co.: London*, 1872. 12°. **6405. a. 42. (9.)**

—— A Practical Hand-Book for the use of Suitors in the County Courts; with a table of fees. pp. 23. *Whittaker & Co.: London; Aldis & Pearson: Rochdale*, [1856.] 12°. **6375. a. 43. (1.)**

BUTTERWORTH (Joseph) *Bookseller.* A General Catalogue of Law-Books. pp. 4. 102. *Printed for the Compiler: London*, 1801. 12°. **883. i. 26.**

—— The third edition corrected. pp. xv. 203. *J. Butterworth: London*, 1812. 12°. **11903. bb. 22.**

—— [Another copy.] **270. c. 17.**
The sixth edition is entered under BUTTERWORTH *(Joseph)* AND SON.

BUTTERWORTH (Joseph) *M.P.* *See* Evans (John) *LL.D., of Islington.* Complete Religious Liberty vindicated . . . With remarks on the . . . correspondence between . . . J. Ivimey and J. Butterworth, *etc.* 1813. 8°. **4135. d. 13.**

—— *See* Sibthorp (Richard W.) The Substance of a Sermon preached . . . on the Sunday following the interment of J. Butterworth. [1826.] 4°. **4906. h. 6. (2.)**

—— *See* Watson (Richard) *Wesleyan Minister.* A Sermon on the death of J. Butterworth. 1826. 4°. **4906. h. 6. (1.)**

BUTTERWORTH (Joseph Henry) "Not yours, but you." A sermon, *etc.* pp. 16. *Joseph Masters: London*, 1850. 8°. **4475. e. 19.**

BUTTERWORTH (Julian Edward)

—— *See* Morrison (John C.) The Intermediate District in New York State. Special studies prepared under the direction of J. C. Morrison . . . and J. E. Butterworth, *etc.* 1948. 8°. A.S. n. **192/8.**

—— The County Superintendent in the United States. pp. v. 50. *Washington*, 1932. 8°. [*U.S. Office of Education. Bulletin.* 1932. no. 6.] A.S. **202.**

—— The Parent-Teacher Association and its Work. pp. ix. 149. *Macmillan Co.: New York*, 1928. 8°. **08311. bb. 47.**

—— Principles of Rural School Administration. pp. xvi. 379. *Macmillan Co.: New York*, 1926. 8°. [*Rural Education Series.*] **08311.h.99/3.**

BUTTERWORTH (Julian Edward) and **DAWSON** (Howard Athalone)

—— The Modern Rural School . . . With chapters by Stanley Warren [and others], *etc.* pp. xii. 494. *McGraw-Hill Book Co.: New York*, 1952. 8°. [*McGraw-Hill Series in Education.*] W.P. **12179/84.**

BUTTERWORTH (Lawrence)

—— Circular Letter. The Elders and Messengers of the several Baptist Churches, meeting at Aulcester [and elsewhere] . . . being met in association at Evesham . . . on the 2d and 3d days of June, 1789, *etc.* pp. 8. [1789.] 8°. *See* England.—*Churches and Religious Bodies.—Baptists.—Midland Association.* **4135. aa. 100. (25.)**

—— The Super-excellency of the Christian Religion displayed: or, a Treatise on natural and revealed religion . . . To which is added, an answer to the Rev. Mr. Lindsey's popular argument against the Divinity of the Lord Jesus Christ. pp. xii. 150. *Printed for the Author: London*, 1781. 12°. **4014. cc. 9.**

—— Thoughts on Moral Government and Agency, and the origin of moral evil; in opposition to the doctrine of absolute, moral, Christian, and philosophical necessity. Also, strictures on Dr. Priestley's correspondence with Dr. Price, on the same subject. pp. viii. 357. *Printed for the Author: Evesham*, 1792. 8°. **4256. e. 19.**

—— [Another edition.] pp. viii. 357. *Printed for the Author: Evesham*, 1792. 8°. **4256. cc. 4.**

BUTTERWORTH (Lionel Milner Angus) *See* Marson (Percival) Glass and Glass Manufacture . . . Revised and enlarged by L. M. Angus-Butterworth. 1932. 8°. **07077. f. 1/133.**

—— —— 1936. 8°. **07077.f.1/149.**

—— *See* Marson (Percival) Glass and Glass Manufacture . . . Revised and enlarged by L. M. Angus-Butterworth, *etc.* 1949. 8°. **07077. f. 1/153.**

—— The Manufacture of Glass. pp. xii. 274. *Sir Isaac Pitman & Sons: London*, 1948. 8°. **7940. f. 28.**

—— Old Cheshire Families & their Seats. [With plates.] pp. 218. xviii. *Sherratt & Hughes: Manchester*, 1932. 8°. **09917. de. 11.**

BUTTERWORTH (M. A.) Tales and Poems of a Grandmother. pp. 137. *J. M. Dent & Co.: London*, 1900. 8°. **012806. ee. 17.**

—— Now cook me the Fish. 146 fresh-water fish recipes collected by Margaret Butterworth. pp. 102. *Country Life: London*, 1950. 8°. **7949. e. 34.**

BUTTERWORTH (Marianne) Portraiture of a Father, *etc.* [Letters of Thomas Stock and others, edited, with a memoir, by M. Butterworth.] pp. 289. *C. Whittingham: London*, [1859.] 8°. **4907. bb. 25.**
Printed for private circulation.

BUTTERWORTH (S.)

—— Structural Analysis by Moment Distribution, *etc.* pp. vii. 119. *Longmans, Green & Co.: London*, 1949. 8°. **08535. g. 22.**

BUTTERWORTH (Stephen)

—— Electrical Characteristics of Overhead Lines. [With charts.] pp. 238. *Leatherhead*, 1954. 8°. [*British Electrical and Allied Industries Research Association. Technical Report.* no. O/T 4.] W.P. **9138/758.**

BUTTERWORTH (Theodore) The Combined Geography, Grammar and Arithmetic. Standard 2, 3. *J. B. Ledsham: Manchester; Simpkin, Marshall & Co.: London*, [1879, 80.] 8°. [*World School Series.*] **12200. aa. 36/14.**

BUTTERWORTH (Theron H.) Mr. Samuel Whiskers. A play in three scenes and an epilogue from the story of "The Roly-Poly Pudding" by Beatrix Potter. Adapted by T. H. Butterworth. pp. 19. *F. Warne & Co.: London & New York*, [1933.] 8°. **11781. b. 71.**

BUTTERWORTH (Thornton) Thornton Butterworth's Thrillers. 4 vol. *Thornton Butterworth: London,* 1929. 8°. **012614**. b. **1**.

BUTTERWORTH (William) *Drum-Major in the 12th Regiment of Foot.* The Conversion, Experience and Labours of Willm Butterworth . . . written by himself . . . Revised and corrected by A. Scott. pp. 26. *J. Nicholson: Lees,* 1807. 12°. **4906**. de. **25**. (**2**.)

BUTTERWORTH (William) *pseud.* [i.e. Henry Schroeder.] Three Years Adventures of a Miner, in England, Africa, the West Indies, South-Carolina, and Georgia. pp. x. 492. *Edwd Baines: Leeds,* [1822.] 12°. **615**. g. **23**.

BUTTERWORTH (William John) The Madras Road Book, *etc.* (Edition 1839.) pp. 164. 72. *George Calder: Madras,* 1839. 8°. **10055**. bb. **14**.

BUTTERY (Eliza) Advice to Boys. [With a poem, entitled: "Come to God."] pp. 3. *Printed by the Author: London,* [1887.] 8°. **1879**. cc. **8**. (**7**.)

—— Britannia. Song. *Printed by the Composer: London,* 1887. 8°. **11602**. dd. **13**. (**1**.)

—— The Doomed Bridal. pp. 2. *Printed by the Composer: London,* [1887.] 8°. **1871**. e. **1**. (**204**.)

—— The Mysteries of Hampton Court Palace. pp. 11. *Printed by the Author: London,* 1890. 8°. **8632**. g. **24**. (**8**.)

—— The Spectre Knight. Song. pp. 2. *Printed by the Composer: London,* [1887.] 8°. **1875**. d. **9**. (**126**.)

BUTTERY (John A.) Why Kruger made War, or Behind the Boer scenes . . . With two chapters on the past and future of the Rand and the mining industry by A. Cooper Key. pp. vii. 298. *William Heinemann: London,* 1900. 8°. **8155**. de. **31**.

BUTTES (Henry) Dyets Dry Dinner: Consisting of eight seuerall Courses: 1. Fruites. 2. Hearbes. 3. Flesh. 4. Fish. 5. Whitmeats. 6. Spice. 7. Sauce. 8. Tabacco. All serued in after the order of Time vniuersall. *Tho. Creede for William Wood: London,* 1599. 8°. **C. 31**. b. **8**.

The recto of each leaf of the text is printed in Roman type, the verso in black letter.

BUTTES (*Sir* William) *See* Butts (*Sir* W.) *the Younger.*

BUTTET (Charles de) Aperçu de la vie de Xavier de Maistre, d'après sa correspondance, des notes et des souvenirs de famille. [With plates, including portraits.] pp. 219. *Grenoble,* 1919. 8°. **10657**. h. **5**.

BUTTET (Marc de) Les Alpins. Étude militaire sur les troupes cantonnées dans les Alpes et chargées de les défendre. pp. 224. *Thonon-les-Bains,* 1894. 8°. **10196**. f. **18**.

BUTTET (Marc Antoine de) Le Caualier de Sauoye, ou Response au Soldat françois [by P. de l'Hostal]. [By M. A. de Buttet.] Plus, vn discours . . . seruant d'apologie contre les faussetez, impertinences, & calomnies du Caualier de Sauoye. pp. 216. 1607. 12°. *See* French Soldier. **1193**. c. **6**. (**4**.)

—— *See* French Soldier. Le Citadin de Genéue, ou Response au "Caualier de Sauoye." 1606. 8°. **9200**. aa. **1**.

BUTTET (Marc Claude de) *See* Burdin (C.) Notice sur la vie & les œuvres du poète M.-C. de Buttet. [1873.] 4°. **10659**. h. **1**.

BUTTET (Marc Claude de)

—— *See* Mugnier (F.) Marc-Claude de Buttet . . . Notice sur sa vie, ses œuvres . . . et sur ses amis. L'Apologie pour la Savoie [by M. C. de Buttet]. Le Testament de M. C. de Buttet. 1896. 8°. [*Mémoires et documents publiés par la Société savoisienne d'histoire et d'archéologie.* sér. 2. tom. 10.] **Ac. 5240**.

—— *See* Ritter (E.) Recherches sur le poète Claude de Buttet et son Amalthée. 1887. 8°. **011840**. f. **17**. (**8**.)

—— Œuvres poétiques . . . précédées d'une notice sur l'auteur et accompagnées de notes par le Bibliophile Jacob. 2 tom. *Paris,* 1880. 8°. **011483**. ee. **6**.

—— [Selected poems.] *See* French Poets. Les Poètes françois depuis le xii. siècle jusqu'à Malherbe. tom. 5. 1824. 8°. **2285**. e. **5**.

—— Le Caualier de Sauoye, ou response au Soldat françois. [By M. A. de Buttet; sometimes attributed to M. C. de Buttet.] 1607. 12°. *See* French Soldier. **1193**. c. **6**. (**4**.)

BUTTETOURT (John) *Baron de Buttetourt.* *See* Botetourt (J. de)

BUTTEVILLE (Ludovic Guignard de) *See* Guignard de Butteville.

BUTTFIELD (James) The Threefold Cord; or, Musings on faith, hope, and love. [Poems.] pp. 144. *J. Heaton & Son: Leeds; Houlston & Stoneman: London,* 1854. 8°. **11648**. b. **47**.

BUTTFIELD (James Walter) The Allotment Observatory, Piccadilly Downs. pp. 30. *London,* 1926. 4°. **12352**. h. **39**.

—— The Hut Dwellers' Legacy, or, the Treasures of a prehistoric island. In which the secrets of a Surrey hill are revealed by its own chronology and literature, *etc.* [With a portrait.] pt. 1. pp. 36. *The Author: London,* 1913. 8°. **07709**. bb. **1**.
No more published.

—— Lay-Figure Frivolity. The dance of the 20th century. [*London,* 1925.] *s. sh.* fol. **1879**. cc. **6**. (**48**.)

—— The Next Peace. Being a sequel to the recent publication entitled "The Next War." pp. 8. [*The Author:*] *London,* 1915. 8°. **8610**. d. **11**.

—— The Picture-Stones of Prehistoric Man, *etc.* pp. 7. pl. iv. [*The Author:*] *London,* 1920. 4°. **7708**. ee. **62**.

—— The "Pit Circle," otherwise ancient "nest-earth" cypher of prehistoric astronomy. [*London,* 1924.] *s. sh.* fol. **1887**. a. **9**. (**24**.)

BUTTFIELD (William) Free Communion an Innovation: or, an Answer to Mr. John Brown's pamphlet, entitled, The House of God opened and His table free, &c. pp. vi. 46. *G. Keith; J. Johnson: London,* 1778. 8°. **4139**. c. **23**.

BÜTTGENBACH ( ) [For the German surname of this form:] *See* Buettgenbach.

BUTTGENBACH (André) Le Mouvement rexiste et la situation politique de la Belgique. Extrait de la Revue des sciences politiques, *etc.* pp. 68. *Bruxelles,* 1937. 8°. **8079**. eee. **13**.

BUTTGENBACH (H.) *See* Katanga. Carte géologique du Katanga, et notes descriptives par . . . H. Buttgenbach. 1908. fol. [*Annales du Musée du Congo Belge.* Minéralogie, géologie et paléontologie. sér. 2. tom. 1. fasc. 1.] **Ac. 2959**. c. (**1**.)

BUTTGENBACH (H.)

—— Description des minéraux du Congo belge. pp. 31. *Bruxelles*, 1910. fol. [*Annales du Musée du Congo Belge.* Minéralogie, géologie et paléontologie. sér. 1. tom. 1. fasc. 1.] Ac. **2959.** c. (**1.**)

—— Introduction à l'étude des roches ignées. pp. 136. pl. IV. *Paris, Liége; Liége* [printed], 1939. 8°. **07107.** k. **61.**

—— Minéralogie du Congo belge. [With a map.] pp. 183. 1926. *See* LIÈGE, *City of.—Société Royale des Sciences de Liège.* Mémoires, *etc.* sér. 3. tom. 13. 1843, *etc.* 8°. Ac. **2961.**

—— Quelques Notes sur l'Afrique du Sud. pp. 15. *Bruxelles*, 1904. 8°. [*Publications de la Société d'Études coloniales de Belgique.*] Ac. **2348/3.**

BUTTGERALD (CHARLES) Von Herz zu Herz. Gedichte. pp. vi. 216. *Leipzig*, 1892. 8°. **11528.** aaa. **68.**

BUTTI (ADELE)

—— Byron in Grecia. Carme. pp. 19. *Venezia*, 1875. 8°. **11431.** ff. **12.**

BUTTI (ANGELO)

—— *See* CORIO (B.) Storia di Milano, *etc.* (vol. 2. 3. Riveduta e annotata dal prof^e A. Butti e da L. Ferrario.) 1855, *etc.* 8°. **1318.** g. **13**

BUTTI (ATTILIO) *See* CELLINI (Benvenuto) *Artist.* La Vita di Benvenuto Cellini. Illustrata da note di A. Butti, *etc.* 1910. 8°. **10632.** p. **1.**

—— *See* DECEMBRIO (P. C.) Petri Candidi Decembrii Opuscula historica. A cura di A. Butti, F. Fossati, *etc.* 1925, *etc.* 8°. [*MURATORI* (*L. A.*) *Rerum Italicarum scriptores.* tom. 20. pt. 1.] **9168.** l.

—— Studi Pariniani. pp. 172. *Torino*, 1895. 8°. **011824.** de. **63.**

BUTTI (ENRICO ANNIBALE) L'Anima. Memorie di Alberto Sàrcori. [A novel.] pp. 274. *Milano*, 1894. 8°. **12471.** k. **18.**

—— L'Automa. Romanzo. Quarta edizione riveduta. pp. viii. 344. *Milano*, 1897. 8°. **12471.** k. **19.**

—— La Corsa al piacere. Dramma in cinque atti. pp. 317. *Milano*, 1900. 8°. **11714.** bb. **3.**

—— Fiamme nell'ombra, dramma in tre atti. Il Cuculo, commedia giocosa in tre atti. 2 pt. *Milano*, 1907. 8°. **11714.** bb. **11.**

—— Il Gigante e i Pigmei. Commedia in quattro atti. Con prefazione e polemica. pp. xxviii. 146. *Milano*, [1904.] 8°. **11714.** bb. **7.**

—— L'Incantesimo. Romanzo. pp. 380. *Milano*, 1897. 8°. **12471.** k. **20.**

—— Intermezzo poetico, dramma burlesco in quattro atti. Il frutto amaro, commedia in tre atti. Vortice, dramma in quattro atti. Edizione postuma con prefazione biografica di Luciano Zùccoli. pp. xvi. 242. *Milano*, 1912. 8°. **11714.** bb. **26.**

BUTTIG (ANDREAS) *See* BIBLE.—*New Testament.* [*Greek.*] *Ἡ Καινη Διαθηκη.* Novum Testamentum, ad probatissimos codices studiose revisum . . . industria J. G. Pritii: editio tertia . . . aucta et emendata, *etc.* [Edited by A. Buttig.] 1724. 12°. **219.** a. **3, 4.**

—— De emphasi verbi σπλαγχνιζομαι, ad Marc. VIII. 3. *See* HASE (T.) and IKEN (C.) Thesaurus novus theologico-philologicus, *etc.* tom. 2. 1732. fol. **L.16.f.2.**

BUTTIGEIG (GUISEPPE) *See* BUTTIGIEG.

BUTTIGELLA (BONIFACIO) *Bishop of Lodi.* Tractatus de regulanda vita illustris et excelse domine domine Blanche, etc. [By B. Buttigella?] 1909. 4°. [*Vita di Bonacosa da Beccalòe, etc.*] *See* BLANCHE [of Savoy], *Consort of Galeazzo II., Duke of Milan.* **4829.** dg. **10.**

BUTTIGIEG (GIUSEPPE) *See* CASTRIQUE (L. J. A.) In the Privy Council. On appeal from the Royal Court of the island of Malta . . . L. J. A. Castrique, Appellant; versus Giuseppe Buttigieg, Respondent. Appellant's case. [1855.] fol. **1487.z.12.(2.)**

—— *See* CASTRIQUE (L. J. A.) In the Privy Council. On appeal from the Royal Court of the island of Malta. Between Louis J. A. Castrique, Appellant; and Giuseppe Buttigieg, Respondent. Appendix. [1855.] fol. **1487.z.12.(3.)**

—— *See* CASTRIQUE (L. J. A.) In the Privy Council. On appeal from the Royal Court of Appeal of the island of Malta. Between Louis J. A. Castrique, Appellant, and G. Buttigeig, Respondent. Case for Respondent. [1855.] fol. **1487.z.12.(1.)**

BUTTIGNONI (GIUSTO) La Messa "Iste confessor" di Palestrina a S. Giusto. Critica e polemica. pp. 38. *Trieste*, 1894. 8°. **7899.** ee. **6.** (**4.**)

BÜTTIKOFER.

—— [For the German surname of this form:] *See* BUETTIKOFER.

BÜTTIKOFER (J.) Mededeelingen over Liberia. Resultaten van eene onderzoekingsreis, door J. Büttikofer en C. F. Sala in de jaren 1879–1882, samengesteld door J. Büttikofer. Met een kaart. pp. xvi. 147. *Amsterdam; Utrecht*, 1883. 4°. [*Tijdschrift van het Aardrijkskundig Genootschap gevestigd te Amsterdam.* Bijbladen. dl. 3. no. 7.] Ac. **6094.**

—— Reisebilder aus Liberia. Resultate geographischer, naturwissenschaftlicher und ethnographischer Untersuchungen während der Jahre 1879–1882 und 1886–1887 . . . Mit Karten . . . Tafeln, *etc.* 2 Bd. *Leiden*, 1890. 8°. **10096.** gg. **7.**

BUTTILIERIUS RANCAEUS (ARMANDUS JOANNES) *See* LE BOUTHILLIER DE RANCÉ (Armand J.)

BUTTIN (CHARLES) Catalogue de la collection d'armes anciennes européennes et orientales de Charles Buttin. [Begun by C. Buttin and completed by François Buttin. With a portrait.] pp. 284. pl. XXXII. *Rumilly*, 1933. 8°. **07805.** d. **42.**

—— Le Guet de Genève au XVme siècle et l'armement de ses gardes. (Extrait de la Revue Savoisienne.) pp. 127. *Genève, Annecy*, 1910. 8°. **08821.** f. **8.**

—— Une Prétendue armure de Jeanne d'Arc. 1913. *See* PARIS.—*Société Nationale des Antiquaires de France.* Mémoires, *etc.* sér. 8. tom. 2. 1817, *etc.* 8°. Ac. **5331.**

BUTTIN (FRANÇOIS) *See* BUTTIN (C.) Catalogue de la collection d'armes anciennes européennes et orientales de Charles Buttin. [Completed by F. Buttin.] 1933. 8°. **07805.** d. **42.**

BUTTIN (LOUIS) Essai comparatif des pharmacopées Helvetica, Germanica, Gallica, Belgica & Austriaca d'après les dernières éditions de ces ouvrages. pp. 58. *Schaffhouse*, 1873. 4°. **7509.** i. **2.**

BUTTIN (PAUL)

—— Le Drame du Maroc. [With plates and a map.] pp. 240. *Paris*, 1955. 8°. **09062. aa. 48.**

BUTTINGER (E.) Practische beschrijving van de wijze van reiniging, vuilnisverzameling en mestbereiding te Groningen, met eene plaat, *etc.* pp. 29. *Groningen*, 1870. 8°. **8775.** dd. **33.** (**10.**)

BUTTINGER (JOSEPH)

—— Am Beispiel Österreichs. Ein geschichtlicher Beitrag zur Krise der sozialistischen Bewegung. pp. 668. *Köln*, [1953.] 8°. **9316.** aa. **8.**

—— In the Twilight of Socialism. A history of the revolutionary socialists of Austria. (Translated from the German by E. B. Ashton.) pp. x. 577. *Weidenfeld & Nicolson: London; printed in U.S.A.*, 1954. 8°. **08074.e.19.**

BUTTINGHA WICHERS (JOHAN VAN) *See* WICHERS.

BUTTINGHA WICHERS (PETRUS ADRIANUS VAN) *See* WICHERS.

BÜTTINGHAUSEN ( ) [For the German surname of this form:] *See* BUETTINGHAUSEN.

BUTTINONI (FRANCESCO) Petizione dei 32 ufficiali rimossi della Brigata Piemonte. [Signed by F. Buttinoni and others.] pp. 14. *Torino*, 1862. 8°. **8827.** aaa. **47.**

BUTTISHOLZ. Jahrzeitbücher des Mittelalters . . . 18. Der Kirche in Buttisholz, Ct. Lucern. Mitgetheilt vom Vereinsvorstande J. Schneller. 1870. *See* EINSIEDELN.—*Historischer Verein der fünf Orte Lucern, Uri, Schwyz, Unterwalden und Zug.* Der Geschichtsfreund, *etc.* Bd. 25. 1843, *etc.* 8°. Ac. **6940.**

BUTTIVANT (SAMUEL) A Brief Discovery of a threefold estate of Anti-Christ now extant in the world: viz. A description of 1. The true and false Temple, 2. The false Ministery, and 3. The false Churches. Whereunto is added the Trial of one George Fox in Lancashire, with his Answer to eight articles exhibited against him . . . also certain queries upon a petition lately presented to the Parliament from divers Gentlemen and others in Worcester-shire, *etc.* [Edited by Samuel Buttivant.] pp. 19. *For Giles Calvert: London*, 1653. 4°. **1415.** b. **10.**

—— *See* ENGLAND.—*Parliament.—Petitions and Addresses to Parliament.*—1653. The Worcester-shire Petition . . . defended . . . in answer to XVI. queries, printed in a book called: A Brief Discovery of the threefold estate of Antichrist, *etc.* 1653. 4°. E. **693.** (**18.**)

BUTTJER (B.) Geschichte der Verfassungen und Rechtsamen Ostfrieslands und Harrlingerlands, sowie Entwickelungen über die Natur der sog. suspendirten Gefälle u.s.w. mit anderen Eigenthümlichkeiten und Besonderheiten der Provinz, &c. pp. 63. 104. *Leer*, 1867. 8°. **5606.** ccc. **18.**

BUTTKE (ERIKA) Balzac als Dichter des modernen Kapitalismus. pp. 104. *Berlin*, 1932. 8°. [*Romanische Studien.* Hft. 26.] **12952.** ppp. **1/26.**

BUTTLAR (CURT TREUSCH VON) *See* TREUSCH VON BUTTLAR.

BUTTLAR (FRIEDRICH OTTO VON) *See* CONSTANTINE, *Abbot of Fulda* [F. O. von Buttlar].

BUTTLAR (J. L. VON) Das Wesentliche der Sternkunde nach den neuesten Entdeckungen in leicht fasslicher Aufstellung zum Selbstunterricht . . . Mit 2. grossen Sternkarten. pp. vi. 194. *Königsberg*, 1854. 8°. **8562.** c. **5.**

BUTTLAR (RUDOLPH VON) *Baron.* Forstkultur-Verfahren in seiner Anwendung und seinen Folgen zu der Forstwirthschaft für Waldbesitzer und Forstmänner mitgetheilt . . . Mit einer Tafel Abbildungen. pp. viii. 165. *Cassel*, 1853. 8°. **7077.** c. **10.**

BUTTLAR-BRANDENFELS (HORST JULIUS LUDWIG OTTO TREUSCH VON) *Baron.* *See* TREUSCH VON BUTTLAR-BRANDENFELS.

BUTTLE (IDA M.)

—— Hymns for Anniversary Services. Editors: I. M. Buttle, H. Vincent Capsey, H. J. Staples (T. W. Cowap, W. J. Doidge, F. B. Westbrook). New series. no. 27–29. *London*, [1947.] 8°. **3438.** k. **21.**

—— Musical Moments in the Sunday School. [With musical notes.] pp. 88. *H. V. Capsey: London*, [1939.] 8°. **7893.** pp. **21.**

BUTTLE (N.) *See* BULL (William J.) Life after Death. A sermon preached . . . on the death of Mr. N. Buttle, *etc.* [1867.] 8°. **4479.** aaa. **46.** (**3.**)

BUTTLER (EVA VON) *See* CHRISTIANY (L.) Eva von Buttler, die Messaline und Muckerin, als Prototyp der "Seelenbräute," *etc.* 1870. 8°. **4886.** aaa. **33.**

BUTTLER (SAMUEL) *See* BUTLER.

BUTTLER (*Sir* TOBY) An Elegy on the very much lamented death of Sir Toby Buttler, *etc.* [*Dublin*, 1721.] *s. sh.* fol. **11602.** i. **1.** (**2.**)

BUTTLER (WERNER)

—— Die Bandkeramik in ihrem nordwestlichsten Verbreitungsgebiet. 1930. *See* BERLIN.—*Archaeologisches Institut des Deutschen Reiches.—Römisch-Germanische Kommission.* Bericht über die Fortschritte der römisch-germanischen Forschung, *etc.* (Bericht der Römisch-Germanischen Kommission. no. 19.) 1905, *etc.* 8°. Ac. 5388/4.

—— Der donauländische und der westische Kulturkreis der jüngeren Steinzeit. Mit . . . 5 Karten. pp. 108. pl. 24. *Berlin & Leipzig*, 1938. 4°. [*Handbuch der Urgeschichte Deutschlands.* Bd. 2.] W.P. **12415/2.**

—— Ein Hinkelsteingefäss aus Köln-Lindenthal und seine Bedeutung für die Chronologie der rheinischen Bandkeramik. (Germania: Sonderabdruck.) [With plates.] *Berlin*, [1935.] 8°. **7706.** s. **4.**

BUTTLES (BRUCE)

—— America's New Army. pp. 48. *Pilot Press: London*, [1942.] 8°. [" *March of Time* " *Series.* no. 6.] **11794.m.1.(c.)/6.**

BUTTLES (JANET R.) The Queens of Egypt, *etc.* pp. xi. 250. pl. xx. *A. Constable & Co.: London*, 1908. 8°. **09061.** eee. **25.**

BUTTLEWSI (RUDOLFUS) *See* BUTTLEWSKI (C. F. R.)

BUTTLEWSKI (CAROLUS FRIDERICUS RUDOLFUS) De embolia adiposa. Dissertatio inauguralis, *etc.* pp. 32. *Regimonti*, [1864.] 8°. **7386.***e. (**32.**)

BUTTLEWSKI (RUDOLFUS) *See* BUTTLEWSKI (C. F. R.)

BUTTMANN (ALEXANDER) *See* APOLLONIUS, *Alexandrinus, Dyscolus.* Des Apollonius Dyskolos vier Bücher über die Syntax. Übersetzt und erläutert von A. Buttmann. 1877. 8°. **12923.** dd. **18.**

—— *See* BUTTMANN (P. C.) Philipp Buttmann's Griechische Grammatik. Herausgegeben und bearbeitet von A. Buttmann, *etc.* 1869. 8°. **12924.** c. **4.**

BUTTMANN (ALEXANDER)

—— *See* BUTTMANN (P. C.) Dr. P. Buttmann's Intermediate or Larger Greek Grammar, *etc.* [Revised by A. Buttmann.] 1840. 8°. **624.** e. **6.**

—— —— 1841. 8°. **12924.** c. **35.**

—— —— 1851. 8°. **12923.** d. **22.**

—— Die deutschen Ortsnamen, mit besonderer Berücksichtigung der ursprünglich wendischen in der Mittelmark und Niederlausitz. pp. iv. 183. *Berlin,* 1856. 8°. **12963.** d. **6.**

—— Einige nachträgliche Bemerkungen zu den Vertheidigungsschriften gegen die Angriffe namentlich von Striez, Stahl, Kunze und Schede auf die Erklärung vom 15 August. pp. 31. *Potsdam,* 1845. 8°. **3910.** c. **21.**

—— Grammatik des neutestamentlichen Sprachgebrauchs. Im Anschlusse an Ph. Buttmann's Griechische Grammatik bearbeitet von A. Buttmann. pp. xvi. 374. *Berlin,* 1859. 8°. **3226.** e. **19.**

—— A Grammar of the New Testament Greek . . . Authorized translation [by J. H. Thayer], with numerous additions and corrections by the author. pp. xx. 474. *W. F. Draper: Andover* [*Mass.*], 1873. 8°. **12924.** p. **3.**

—— [A reissue.] A Grammar of the New Testament Greek, *etc. Andover, Mass.,* 1876. 8°. **12924.** g. **27.**

—— Die griechischen anomalen Verba in systematischer Folge. Als Anhang zur Buttmannschen griech. Grammatik ausgearbeitet von A. Buttmann. pp. viii. 35. *Potsdam,* 1859. 8°. **12924.** c. **13.**

—— [Another edition.] pp. 24. *Berlin,* 1875. 8°. **12902.** d. **1.** (**22.**)

BUTTMANN (AUGUST)

—— *See* DEMOSTHENES. [*In Midiam.—Greek.*] Demosthenis Oratio in Midiam cum annotatione critica et exegetica. Curavit Philippus Buttmannus . . . Editio altera, aucta atque iterum recognita [by the original editor's son, A. Buttmann]. 1833. 8°. **834.** h. **25.**

—— Agesilaus, Sohn des Archidamus. Lebensbild eines spartanischen Königs und Patrioten. Nach den Quellen mit besonderer Berücksichtigung des Xenophon dargestellt. pp. xii. 294. *Halle,* 1872. 8°. **10605.** df. **8.**

—— De Dicaearcho, ejusque operibus, quae inscribuntur Βιος Ἑλλαδος et Ἀναγραφη Ἑλλαδος. pp. 60. *Nurnburgi,* [1833?] 4°. T. **6*.** (**2.**)

—— Friedrich Wilhelm IV. der Deutsche, oder die weltgeschichtliche Aufgabe Preussens. Festrede zur Feier des Geburtstages Sr. Majestät des Königs Friedrich Wilhelm IV., *etc.* pp. 26. *Prenzlau,* 1848. 8°. **10703.** bb. **25.**

—— Die Schicksals-Idee in Schillers Braut von Messina und ihr innerer Zusammenhang mit der Geschichte der Menschheit. pp. xii. 128. *Berlin,* 1882. 8°. **11840.** f. **22.** (**9.**)

BUTTMANN (HUGO) De musculis crocodili. Dissertatio, *etc.* pp. 32. *Halae,* [1826.] 8°. **7386.c.8.(12.)**

BÜTTMANN (PAUL) Carl Winter's Dream. A fairy romance. pp. 240. *Elliot Stock: London,* 1895. 8°. **012808.** m. **7.**

BUTTMANN (PHILIPP CARL) *See* ARATUS, *of Soli.* Arati Phaenomena et Diosemea . . . Edidit P. Buttmannus. *Gr.* 1826. 8°. **995.** a. **20.** (**3.**)

BUTTMANN (PHILIPP CARL)

—— *See* DEMOSTHENES. [*In Midiam.—Greek.*] Demosthenis oratio in Midiam, cum annotatione critica et exegetica curavit P. Buttmannus, *etc.* 1833. 8°. **834.** h. **25.**

—— *See* DEMOSTHENES. [*In Midiam.—Greek.*] Demosthenis Midias . . . reprinted from Buttmann's text, and comprising extracts from his commentaries, *etc.* 1862. 8°. **11391.** b. **23.**

—— *See* FRONTO (M. C.) M. Cornelii Frontonis Reliquiæ . . . P. Buttmanni . . . animadversionibus instructas . . . edidit B. G. Niebuhrius, *etc.* 1816. 8°. **68.** b. **9.**

—— *See* HOMER. [*Odyssey.—Greek.*] Homeri Odyssea cum scholiis veteribus, *etc.* [With the notes and preface from Buttmann's edition of the Scholia.] 1827. 8°. **995.** k. **6, 7.**

—— *See* HOMER. [*Scholia.*] Scholia antiqua in Homeri Odysseam . . . edita a P. Buttmanno, *etc.* 1821. 8°. **832.** f. **22.**

—— *See* KLENZE (C. A. C.) P. Buttmann und die Gesetzlosen, *etc.* [With the "Pragmatische Statuten der gesetzlosen Gesellschaft" drawn up by him.] 1834. 8°. **5511.** bbb. **9.**

—— *See* LOWE (M. S.) Bildnisse jetztlebender Berliner Gelehrten mit ihren Selbstbiographieen. (Sammlung 3. Philipp Buttmann.) 1806. 8°. **10708.** dd. **50.**

—— *See* MEIEROTTO (J. H. L.) Ueber die Sitten und Lebensart der Römer in verschiedenen Zeiten der Republik. Dritte, verbesserte, mit Zusätzen vermehrte, Ausgabe. [Edited by P. C. Buttmann.] 1814. 8°. **1307.** d. **4.**

—— *See* PERIODICAL PUBLICATIONS.—*Berlin.* Museum der Alterthumswissenschaft. Herausgegeben von F. A. Wolf und P. Buttmann. 1807, *etc.* 8°. P.P. **4957.**

—— *See* QUINTILIANUS (M. F.) M. Fabii Quintiliani De institutione oratoria libri duodecim, *etc.* [Vol. 4 edited by P. Buttmann.] 1798, *etc.* 8°. **166.** h. **10–15.**

—— *See* SOPHOCLES. [*Philoctetes.—Greek.*] Sophoclis Philoctetes græce. Cum suis selectisque aliorum notis edidit P. Buttmann. 1822. 8°. **1348.** c. **33.** (**1.**)

—— *See* WOLF (Christian W. F. A.) and BUTTMANN (P. C.) Museum antiquitatis studiorum, *etc.* 1808. 8°. **11312.** d. **35.**

—— Aelteste Erdkunde des Morgenländers. Ein biblisch-philologischer Versuch. pp. x. 68. *Berlin,* 1803. 8°. **1122.** g. **5.**

—— Philippi Buttmanni Auctarium animadversionum in Platonis Gorgiam et Theaetetum. 1805. *See* PLATO. [*Two or more Works.—Greek.*] Platonis dialogi selecti, *etc.* vol. 2. 1802, *etc.* 8°. **525.** h. **16.**

—— Ausführliche griechische Sprachlehre . . . Zweite, verbesserte und vermehrte Ausgabe. (Mit Zusätzen von C. A. Lobeck.) 2 Bd. *Berlin,* 1830, 39. 8°. **12924.** bb. **31.**

—— A Catalogue of Irregular Greek Verbs, with all the tenses extant . . . [Extracted from P. C. Buttmann's "Ausführliche griechische Sprachlehre."] Translated and edited with explanatory notes and a very copious index by the Rev. J. R. Fishlake. pp. xi. 288. *John Murray: London,* 1837. 8°. **827.** f. **20.**

—— Third edition. pp. x. 362. *John Murray: London; Jena printed,* 1866. 8°. **12924.** aaa. **44.**

—— Buttmann und Schleiermacher über Heindorf und Wolf. pp. 16. *Berlin,* 1816. 8°. **11312.** bb. **18.**

BUTTMANN (Philipp Carl)

—— Epimetron de rarioribus quibusdam verborum formis. *See* Bos (L.) Lamberti Bos Ellipses græcæ, *etc.* 1825. 8°. **12923**. e. 6.

—— Griechische Grammatik . . . Elfte, durchaus vermehrte und verbesserte Ausgabe. pp. xii. 476. *Berlin,* 1824. 8°. **624**. d. 25.

—— Vierzehnte, vermehrte und verbesserte Ausgabe. pp. vi. 490. *Berlin,* 1833. 8°. **826**. e. 1.

—— Zwei und zwanzigste Auflage. (Herausgegeben und bearbeitet von Alex. Buttmann.) pp. viii. 591. *Berlin,* 1869. 8°. **12924**. c. 4.

—— Dr. Philip Buttmann's Intermediate or Larger Greek Grammar, translated . . . by D. Boileau, Esq. With a biographical notice of the author. Edited, with a few notes, by E. H. Barker. pp. xxvii. 457. *Printed for the Editor; Black, Young & Young: London,* 1833. 8°. **624**. d. 27. (1.)

—— [Another edition.] Buttmann's Larger Greek Grammar . . . Translated . . . with additions, by Edward Robinson. pp. 494. *Flagg, Gould & Newman: Andover [Mass.],* 1833. 8°. **624**. h. 12.

—— [Another edition.] Dr. P. Buttmann's Intermediate or Larger Greek Grammar [revised by A. Buttmann], translated . . . with a biographical notice of the author [by D. Boileau]. Edited by Dr. Charles Supf. pp. xviii. 485. *Black & Armstrong: London,* 1840. 8°. **624**. e. 6.

—— Second edition. pp. xviii. 485. *Whittaker & Co.: London,* 1841. 8°. **12924**. c. 35.

—— [Another edition.] A Greek Grammar for the use of High Schools and Universities . . . Revised and enlarged by . . . Alexander Buttmann. Translated from the eighteenth German edition by Edward Robinson. pp. xi. 517. *Harper & Bros.: New York,* 1851. 8°. **12923**. d. 22.

—— *Γραμματικη της ἑλληνικης γλωσσης ἐκ της Γερμανιστι γεγραμμενης Φ. Βουτμαννου μεταφρασθεισα και μεταρρυθμισθεισα ὑπο Στεφανου Οἰκονομου, etc.* pp. ιη'. 510. *'Εν Βιεννῃ,* 1812. 8°. **869**. c. 18.

—— Table of the Personal endings of a Greek Verb. From Buttmann [i.e. from his "Griechische Grammatik"]. (Tense formation table. By Ph. Skene.—On the use of the tables. [Signed: P. S.]) *Boosey & Sons: [London,]* 1827. *s. sh.* 8°. **1881**. a. 1. (44.)

—— Practical Rules for Greek Accents and Quantity. From the German of P. Buttmann and F. Passow by Moses Stuart. [Extracts from Buttmann's "Griechische Grammatik," with a translation of Passow's "Die Lehre vom Zeitmaasse der griechischen Sprache."] pp. 107. *Flagg & Gould: Andover [Mass.],* 1829. 12°. **826**. c. 31.

—— *See* Buttmann (A.) Grammatik des neutestamentlichen Sprachgebrauchs. Im Anschlusse an Ph. Buttmann's Griechische Grammatik bearbeitet von A. Buttmann. 1859. 8°. **3226**. e. 19.

—— *See* Buttmann (A.) Die griechischen anomalen Verba in systematischer Folge. Als Anhang zur Buttmannschen griech. Grammatik ausgearbeitet, *etc.* 1859. 8°. **12924**. c. 13.

—— —— 1875. 8°. **12902**. d. 1. (22.)

—— *See* Krueger (C. W.) Kritische Briefe über Buttmann's Griechische Grammatik, *etc.* 1846. 8°. **826**. a. 31.

—— *See* Trollope (William) *M.A., of Pembroke College, Cambridge.* A Greek Grammar to the New Testament . . . Arranged as a supplement to Dr. P. Buttmann's "Intermediate or Larger Greek Grammar." 1842. 8°. **624**. d. 36.

—— Griechische Schul-Grammatik . . . Neunte, verbesserte Auflage. pp. iv. 388. *Berlin,* 1831. 8°. **12923**. aaa. 15.

—— Greek Grammar, translated from the German [by E. Everett]. pp. xi. 292. *Richard Priestley: London,* 1824. 8°. **624**. d. 26.

—— Third edition, *etc.* pp. vii. 336. *Hilliard & Co.: Boston,* 1831. 8°. **826**. e. 17.

—— *Φιλιππου Βουττμαννου Ἑλληνικη γραμματικη, δις μεν προεκδοθεισα, νυν δε πρωτον εἰς τρια μερη προς εὐχερειαν διαιρεθεισα, και μετρικῃ θεωριᾳ ἀπαρτισθεισα, εἰς χρησιν των σχολειων του Ἰονιου Κρατους, ἐπιταγῃ των της δημοσιας παιδειας ἐπιμελητων.* [Translated by S. Oikonomos.] 4 pt. *Κερκυρᾳ,* [1843.] 8°. **12924**. c. 15.

—— Greek Grammar, principally abridged [by G. Bancroft] from that of Buttmann, for the use of Schools. pp. iv. 112. *Cummings, Hilliard & Co.: Boston,* 1824. 12°. **12923**. aaa. 9.

—— *See* Kreuser (J.) Griechische Accentlehre nach der Buttmann'schen Schul-Grammatik für Schulen geordnet, *etc.* 1827. 8°. **12924**. bbb. 46.

—— Lexilogus, oder Beiträge zur griechischen Wort-Erklärung, hauptsächlich für Homer und Hesiod . . . Dritte Auflage. 2 Bd. *Berlin,* 1837, 60. 8°. **12924**. aaa. 43.

Bd. 2 is of the second edition.

—— Lexilogus; or, a Critical Examination of the meaning and etymology of numerous Greek words and passages, intended principally for Homer and Hesiod . . . Translated and edited, with explanatory notes . . . by the Rev. J. R. Fishlake. pp. xv. 597. *John Murray: London,* 1836. 8°. **624**. f. 18.

—— Third edition, revised. pp. xv. 586. *John Murray: London,* 1846. 8°. **12923**. de. 20.

—— Fifth edition. pp. xv. 586. *John Murray: London,* 1861. 8°. **12924**. p. 2.

—— Synopsis of Buttmann's Lexilogus. *See* Homer. [*Iliad.—Greek.*] Homer's Iliad: Books i., ii., iii., *etc.* 1856. 8°. **11315**. b. 22.

—— Mythologus, oder gesammelte Abhandlungen über die Sagen des Alterthums. 2 Bd. *Berlin,* 1828, 29. 8°. **696**. h. 10.

—— Über das Leben des Geschichtschreibers Q. Curtius Rufus. In Beziehung auf A. Hirts Abhandlung über den selben Gegenstand. pp. 32. *Berlin,* 1820. 8°. **10605**. bb. 22.

—— Über den Mythos der Sündflut . . . Zweite verbesserte Ausgabe. pp. 64. *Berlin,* 1819. 8°. **1107**. b. 19. (1.)

BUTTMANN (Philipp Carl Johann Ludwig) *See* Bible.—*New Testament.* [*Greek.*] Novum Testamentum graece . . . recensuit . . . P. Buttmann. 1856. 8°. **3020**. b. 30.

—— —— 1860. 8°. **3020**. b. 31.

—— —— 1862. 8°. **3015**. bb. 3.

—— —— 1886. 8°. **2047**. f. 5.

BUTTMANN (PHILIPP CARL JOHANN LUDWIG)

—— See BIBLE.—*New Testament.* [*Polyglott.*] Novum Testamentum graece et latine . . . P. Buttmannus . . . graecae lectionis auctoritates apposuit. 1842, *etc.* 8°. **1214.** e. **6, 7.**

—— Recensus omnium lectionum quibus Codex Sinaiticus discrepat a textu editionis Novi Testamenti cui est titulus: N. T. graece ad fidem potissimum codicis Vaticani B recensuit . . . Philippus Buttmann Lipsiae Ed. II. 1860. Ed. III. 1865. pp. viii. 123. *Lipsiae*, 1865. 8°. **3020.** aaa. **4.**

—— Was gehört dazu, ein Mitglied der evangelischen Kirche zu sein? Geschrieben in Bezug auf seine Unterzeichnung der Berliner Erklärung vom 15.—26.—August c. pp. 16. *Berlin*, 1845. 8°. **3910.** cc. **22.**

BUTTMANN (RUDOLF) See KOENIG (D.) David Königs Beschreibung der Konstitution des Herzogtums Zweibrücken . . . Herausgegeben von R. Buttmann, *etc.* 1900. 8°. **9340.** g. **13.**

BUTTMANN (WALTHER) Die niedere Geodäsie, ein Stiefkind im preussischen Staats-Organismus, *etc.* pp. 24. *Berlin*, 1875. 8°. **7078.** de. **1.** (**5.**)

BUTTMANNUS (PHILIPPUS CAROLUS) See BUTTMANN (Philipp C.)

BÜTTNER ( ) [For the German surname of this form:] See BUETTNER.

BUTTNER (CHRISTOPHORUS ANDREAS) De origine mali, *etc.* See FEUERLEIN (J. W.) Iacobi W. Feuerlini . . . Observationes eclecticæ ex controversiis de metaphysica Leibnitio-Wolfiana, *etc.* pt. 7. [1725.] 4°. **525.** e. **15.** (**8.**)

—— Lemmata quaedam antiquitatum Norimbergensium, *etc.* *Praes.* C. G. Schwarz. pp. 16. *Altorfii*, [1726.] 4°. **1054.** h. **23.** (**14.**)

BUTTNER (CHRISTOPHORUS GOTTLIEB) Dissertatio anatomica de peritonaeo, *etc.* *Resp.* M. Scheiba. See HALLER (A. von) *Baron.* Disputationum anatomicarum . . . volumen I, *etc.* 1746, *etc.* 4°. **45.** e. **14.**

BUTTNER (DAVID) Dissertatio inauguralis medica de morbis recte distinguendis, *etc.* *Praes.* Friedrich Hoffmann. *Halæ Magdeburgicæ*, [1718.] 4°. **1185.** f. **12.** (**8.**)

—— [Another copy.] **T. 528.** (**14.**)

BUTTNER (FRANCISCUS) Dissertatio inauguralis medica de probabilitatibus medicis, *etc.* pp. 32. [*Altorf*, 1722.] 4°. **T. 511.** (**31.**)

BUTTNER (JACQUES LOUIS) A Fleshless Diet. Vegetarianism as a rational dietary. pp. v. 287. *F. A. Stokes Co.: New York*, 1910. 8°. **7405.** dd. **25.**

BÜTTNER (LINA) See SACHER-MASOCH (L. von) [Gute Menschen, *etc.*] Hitelezők mint házasságszerzők . . . Fordította B. Büttner L. [1884.] 8°. [*Magyar könyvesház.* foly. 12.] **739.** bb. **26.**

—— See SACHER-MASOCH (L. von) [Gute Menschen, *etc.*] A szerelmes szerkesztőség . . . Fordította B. Büttner L. [1884.] 8°. [*Magyar könyvesház.* foly. 13.] **739.** bb. **27.**

—— Egy rút kis leány története. Elbeszélés fiatal leányok számára. Az én édesem. Rajz. B. Büttner Linától. pp. 126. *Budapest*, 1879. 8°. **12809.** m. **25.**

BUTTNERUS (ANDREAS) De sudore Christi sanguineo; utrum naturalis fuerit? Disquisitio physica . . . iterum emendatius edita. *Praes.* C. Posnerus. *Sumtibus J. J. Bauhoferi: Jenæ*, 1665. 4°. **480.** a. **7.** (**17.**)

BUTTNERUS (CHRISTOPHORUS ANDREAS) See BUTTNER.

BÜTTNERUS (DANIEL) See BUETTNER.

BUTTNERUS (THEOPHILUS) Dissertatio inauguralis medica de medicamentorum apparatu compendiario diffusiori anteponendo, *etc.* *Praes.* J. H. Schulze. pp. 26. *Halae Magdeburgicae*, [1739.] 4°. **7306.** f. **10.** (**17.**)

BUTTOLPH'S ALDGATE, *Parish of.* See SAINT BOTOLPH, *Aldgate, Parish of.*

BUTTOLPH (FRANK E.) [A collection of menu cards of dinners and reports of celebrations in the United States of America, 1890–1904; formed by Miss F. E. Buttolph.] 3 vol. [1890–1904.] 8°, *etc.* See COLLECTION. C. **120.** f. **2.**

BUTTON. Button, and Button-Hole: with a character of the Drabs, and the change of Old-hat. In three familiar epistles in verse. pp. 8. *A. Moore: London*, 1723. fol. **11630.** h. **10.**

BUTTON BULLETIN. See UNITED STATES OF AMERICA.—*National Button Society.*

BUTTON HOLE GARLAND. The Button Hole Garlang [*sic*]. Compos'd of four excellent new songs, *etc.* pp. 8. [*Newcastle?* 1750?] 8°. **C.110.bb.11.(21.)**

BUTTON'S BAY. A Description of the Coast, Tides, and Currents, in Button's Bay, and in the Welcome; being the North-West Coast of Hudson's Bay . . . taken from Scrog's, Crow's, Napier's, and Smith's Journals . . . Also from the discoveries made in 1742 . . . shewing . . . a probability, that there is a passage from thence to the Western Ocean of America. pp. 24. *J. Robinson: London*, [1750?] 8°. **10460.** d. **26.**

BUTTON, *Family of.* See LE GRAND, alias BUTTON, *Family of.*

BUTTON (ARTHUR MICHAEL) A Popular and Practical Treatise upon the origin, nature, symptoms, and treatment of Spermatorrhœa, *etc.* pp. xii. 267. *Tallant & Co.: London*, 1861. 8°. **7640.** a. **16.**

BUTTON (BENJAMIN) Raphael and his Works, *etc.* pp. 24. *Printed for private circulation*, 1890. 4°. **7808.** bbb. **31.** (**1.**)

BUTTON (BERYL W.)

—— Intimate Talking. A selection of essays. pp. 20. *Arthur H. Stockwell: Ilfracombe*, 1954. 8°. **8474.** aa. **42.**

BUTTON (BILLY) Billy Button's Disastrous Journey to Brentford and back. Embellished with neat engravings. pp. 29. *Dean & Munday: London*, [1830?] 12°. **012806.** de. **23.** (**13.**)

BUTTON (CHARLES) A Descriptive Catalogue of Chemical Apparatus . . . manufactured and sold by C. Button, *etc.* pp. 95. pl. 5. *Vizetelly Bros. & Co.: [London,]* 1846. 12°. **1143.** f. **14.**

BUTTON (CHARLES) and **DE LA RUE** (WARREN)

—— A Series of Tables of the elementary and compound bodies systematically arranged, *etc.* pt. 1. ff. 20. *De la Rue & Co.: London*, 1843. fol. **718.** k. **21.**
Printed on one side of the leaf only.

BUTTON (CLIFFORD NORMAN) Out of Focus. Short talks to boys and girls. pp. 92. *Epworth Press: London*, [1928.] 8°. **8403.** ee. **24.**

BUTTON (DICK) *See* BUTTON (Richard T.)

BUTTON (EDWARD) Rudiments of Ancient History, sacred and prophane . . . from the Creation . . . to the Birth of Christ. By way of question and answer, *etc.* pp. xxiv. 374. *C. Ward & R. Chandler: London,* 1739. 12°. **9009**. aa. **4**.

—— The second edition. pp. xxiv. 374. *S. Birt: London,* 1745. 12°. **1311**. a. **13**.

—— The third edition. pp. xxiv. 374. *W. Johnston: London,* 1757. 12°. **9005**. cc. **7**.

BUTTON (EUSTACE HARRY) *See* HAKE (Guy D. G.) and BUTTON (E. H.) Architectural Drawing, *etc.* 1929. 8°. **07815**. eee. **26**.

—— *See* HAKE (Guy D. G.) and BUTTON (E. H.) Architectural Drawing, *etc.* 1948. 8°. **07822**. e. **27**.

BUTTON (FRED SMITH) A Historical and Detailed Description of the Sewage Disposal Works [of Burnley]. pp. 38. 1893. 4°. *See* BURNLEY. **8777**. cc. **32**.

BUTTON (HENRY) Flotsam and Jetsam. Floating fragments of life in England and Tasmania. An autobiographical sketch, with an outline of the introduction of responsible government. [With illustrations, including portraits.] pp. xx. 479. *A. W. Birchall & Sons: Launceston, Tasmania,* [1910.] 8°. **010854**. e. **18**.

BUTTON (HENRY ELLIOT) System in Musical Notation . . . With preface by Sir Edward Elgar. pp. xv. 76. *London,* [1920.] 8°. [*Novello's Music Primers.* no. 91.] **W.P.A.900/91.**

BUTTON (HOWARD) Notes on Principles of Profit-Sharing and Labour Co-Partnership. pp. 18. *Boyle, Son & Watchurst: London,* [1918.] 8°. **08285**. b. **42**.

BUTTON (J.) *Captain.* Algiers Voyage in a iournall or briefe reportary of all occurrents hapning in the fleet of ships sent out by the King his most excellent Maiestie, as well against the pirates of Algiers, as others . . . The accidents of euery particular moneth . . . being in this discouery, expressed by one that went along in the voyage. [The verse preface to the reader signed: I. B., i.e. J. Button.] 1621. 4°. *See* B., I. **1093**. b. **82**.

—— [Another copy.] G. **7096**.

BUTTON (JOHN)

—— The Lewes Library Society; a poem. pp. x. 28. *Printed by C. Whittingham; sold by W. Button & Son; J. Johnson: London,* 1804. 4°. **11657**. m. **5**.

BUTTON (JOHN V.) The Brighton and Lewes Guide . . . With four engravings and a map. pp. iv. 79. *J. Baxter: Lewes,* 1805. 12°. **10351**. c. **47**. (**1**.)

—— *Begin.* An English Grammar School will be opened on the 11th of July, 1791, at Lewes, by John Button, *etc.* (An address to the public on the advantages of an English Grammar School.) [A reprint.] pp. 4. [1888.] 4°. **8364**. f. **16**. (**4**.)

—— Exercises on Elocution; or, Poems, select and original, principally intended for public recitation: compiled and written by J. V. Button. pp. viii. 231. *J. Baxter: Lewes,* 1805. 12°. **1347**. c. **10**.

BUTTON (M. M. KESSLER) *See* KESSLER-BUTTON.

BUTTON (PEARL) *pseud.* Brummagem Love, pure, false, unrequited & fatal. A good, bad, and indifferent story. pp. 37. *W. R. Oliver: London,* [1932.] 8°. **12625**. ppp. **3**.

BUTTON (RALPH) Catalogus librorum [e] bibliothecis selectissimis doctissimorum virorum, viz. D. Radulphi Button . . . D. Thankfull Owen . . . Accessit in fine bibliotheca Reverendi Viri D. Gulielmi Hoeli Sussexiæ. Quorum auctio habebitur Londini . . . septimo die Novembris 1681, *etc.* 3 pt. MS. NOTES [of prices and names of buyers]. [*London,*] 1681. 4°. **11906**. e. **25**.

BUTTON (RICHARD TOTTEN)

—— Dick Button on Skates. [With illustrations, including portraits.] pp. 217. *Prentice-Hall: Englewood Cliffs,* 1955. 8°. **7919**. ff. **53**.

BUTTON (T. C.) *See* also ALTON, *pseud.* [i.e. T. C. Button.]

—— The Equipment of Volunteer Infantry. pp. 25. *Chiswick Press: London,* 1874. 8°. **8831**. bb. **42**. *Printed for private circulation.*

—— [Genealogical notes on the Betthone or Bitton Family.] pp. 14. [*Printed for private circulation: London,* 1890.] 8°. **9916**. a. **20**.

—— Something about Works of Art, more particularly engravings: being paragraphs selected from a lecture thereon. pp. 15. *Chiswick Press: London,* 1885. 8°. C. **41**. b. **24**.

Printed for private circulation. One of three copies printed on vellum.

BUTTON (*Sir* THOMAS) *See* CLARK (George T.) *Archaeologist.* Some Account of Sir R. Mansel . . . and of Admiral Sir T. Button, *etc.* 1883. 8°. **10817**. i. **25**.

—— The Voyage of Sir Thomas Button. 1612. *See* FOX (Luke) The Voyages of Captain Luke Foxe of Hull, and Captain Thomas James of Bristol, in search of a North-West passage, *etc.* vol. 1. 1894. 8°. Ac. **6172/70**.

BUTTON (THOMAS DE) *Bishop of Exeter.* *See* BITTON.

BUTTON (WILFRED ALAN) Principles of the Law of Libel and Slander. pp. xxiii. 255. *Sweet & Maxwell: London,* 1935. 8°. **6145**. t. **23**.

—— Principles of the Law of Libel and Slander . . . Second edition. pp. xxiii. 255. *Sweet & Maxwell: London,* 1946. 8°. **6147**. bb. **11**.

BUTTON (WILLIAM) *Baptist Minister.* National Calamities Tokens of the Divine Displeasure: a sermon preached . . . on February 28, being the day appointed for a General Fast. pp. 33. *Printed for the Author: London,* 1794. 8°. **4478**. h. **7**. (**3**.)

—— Remarks on a Treatise, entitled, The Gospel of Christ worthy of all acceptation . . . by Andrew Fuller . . . In a series of letters to a friend. pp. viii. 105. *J. Buckland:* [*London,*] 1785. 12°. **1355**. a. **37**.

—— *See* FULLER (Andrew) A Defence of a Treatise, entitled, the Gospel of Christ worthy of all acceptation; containing a reply to Mr Button's remarks, *etc.* 1787. 12°. **4255**. aaa. **1**. (**2**.)

BUTTON (*Sir* WILLIAM) *Bart.* *See* BAYLY (Francis) An Antidote against Immoderate Sorrow for the Death of our Friends . . . In a sermon preached . . . at the funeral of Sr William Button. 1660. 4°. E. **1026**. (**5**.)

BUTTON (WILLIAM H.) The Margery Mediumship. Comments upon Mr. Thorogood's report on the fingerprint phenomena of the Margery mediumship . . . Reprinted from the Journal of the American S.P.R. pp. 8. [*New York*, 1934.] 8°. **8633**. h. **32**.

BUTTONERUS (GULIELMUS) *See* WORCESTER (William)

BUTTONS. The Three Buttons. A faery tale. pp. 18. *Bosworth & Harrison: London*, 1864. 4°. **12807**. cc. **18**.

BUTTONS, *a Dog*. Buttons' Bit. The story of a patriotic dog. *Hudson Printing Co.: Boston*, [1918.] 16°. **012331**. de. **32**.

BUTTONSHAW (THOMAS) A Defence of a late Book, intituled, A Plain Account of the nature and end of the Sacrament of the Lord's-Supper, [by Benjamin Hoadly,] in reply to the several answers to it, as Dr. Brett, Dr. Warren, Mr. Bowyer, *etc.* pp. iv. 439. *Stephen Austen: London*, 1747. 8°. **4326**. e. **16**.

BUTTREE (JULIA M.) The Rhythm of the Redman in song, dance and decoration . . . Introduction, art section, and illustrations by Ernest Thompson Seton. pp. xv. 280. *A. S. Barnes & Co.: New York*, 1930. 8°. **07896**. i. **38**.

BUTTRESS (FREDERICK ARTHUR)

—— Agricultural Periodicals of the British Isles, 1681–1900, and their Location. Compiled by F. A. Buttress. 1950. 8°. *See* CAMBRIDGE.—*University of Cambridge.—Department of Agriculture.—School of Agriculture.* **11926**. ff. **42**.

—— World List of Abbreviations of Scientific, Technological and Commercial Organizations. pp. ix. 261. *Leonard Hill: London*, 1954. 8°. **12945.b.26.**

—— [Another copy.] **12224**. dd. **1**.

BUTTREY (DOUGLAS NORTON)

—— Cellulose Plastics. pp. 127. pl. IV. *London*, 1947. 8°. [*Cleaver-Hume Monographs on Plastics.*] W.P. **5699/1**.

—— Plasticizers. With . . . tables, *etc.* pp. viii. 175. *Cleaver-Hume Press: London*, 1950. 8°. **8896**. e. **15**.

BUTTRICK (GEORGE ARTHUR)

—— *See* BIBLE. [*English.*] The Interpreter's Bible, *etc.* [Edited by G. A. Buttrick and others.] [1952, *etc.*] 8°. **3091.ff.1.**

—— The Christian Fact and Modern Doubt. A preface to a restatement of Christian faith. pp. xv. 311. *C. Scribner's Sons: New York, London*, 1934. 8°. **04018**. h. **30**.

—— Jesus Came Preaching. Christian preaching in the new age, *etc.* pp. xii. 239. *C. Scribner's Sons: New York, London*, 1932. 8°. [*Lyman Beecher Lectures on Preaching.* 1931.] **Ac.2692.mfg.(6.)**

—— The Parables of Jesus. pp. xxx. 274. *Hodder & Stoughton: London; printed in U.S.A.*, [1928.] 8°. **03226**. eee. **41**.

—— The Parables of Jesus. pp. xxx. 274. *Harper & Bros.: New York & London*, [1928.] 8°. **3228**. b. **51**.

BUTTRICK (HELEN GOODRICH) Principles of Clothing Selection, *etc.* pp. xii. 185. *Macmillan Co.: New York*, 1923. 8°. **07742**. aa. **18**.

BUTTRICK (JOHN ARTHUR)

—— *See* WILLIAMSON (Harold F.) and BUTTRICK (J. A.) Economic Development, *etc.* 1954. 8°. **8208**. bb. **40**.

BUTTRICK (PHILIP LAURANCE)

—— Forest Economics and Finance. pp. xviii. 484. *J. Wiley & Sons: New York; Chapman & Hall: London*, [1943.] 8°. **8231**. h. **60**.

—— The Mountain Laurel, *etc.* (Kalmia latifolia. Connecticut's State flower.) pp. 28. *New Haven*, 1924. 8°. **7054**. cc. **7**. *Marsh Botanical Garden Publication.* no. 1.

—— Politics and Perpetual Rights—some aspects of grazing on the National Forests . . . Reprinted from Journal of Forestry, *etc.* *Society of American Foresters: [Washington*, 1928.] 8°. **07076**. l. **53**.

—— Public and Semi-Public Lands of Connecticut. [With maps.] pp. 151. *Hartford*, 1930. 8°. [*State Geological and Natural History Survey of Connecticut. Bulletin.* no. 49.] A.S. c. **94**.

BUTTRICK (TILLY) Voyages, Travels and Discoveries of Tilly Buttrick, Jr. pp. 58. *Printed for the Author: Boston*, 1831. 12°. **10026**. b. **12**.

—— [Another copy.] **10003**. bb. **28**.

—— Buttrick's Voyages, Travels, and Discoveries, 1812–1819. Reprint of the original edition: Boston, 1831. 1904. *See* THWAITES (Reuben G.) Early Western Travels, 1748–1846, *etc.* vol. 8. 1904, *etc.* 8°. **9551.dd.25.**

BUTTRINI (FRANCESCO) *See* DANTE ALIGHIERI. [*Divina Commedia.—Italian.*] "Lectura Dantis" genovese, *etc.* [Inferno, Canto 11, interpreted by F. Buttrini.] 1904, *etc.* 8°. **11421**. bbb. **33**.

BUTTRIS SHINGHASHUN. *See* BATRIS-SIMHĀSANA.

BUTTS (ALFRED BENJAMIN) Public Administration in Mississippi, *etc.* [A thesis.] pp. 278. *Jackson*, 1919. 8°. [*Publications of the Mississippi Historical Society. Centenary Series.* vol. 3.] Ac. **8407**.

BUTTS (ALLISON) *See* KEFFER (R.) Methods in Non-Ferrous Metallurgical Analysis . . . Prepared for publication by A. Butts. 1928. 8°. **8901**. d. **1**.

—— *See* STOUGHTON (Bradley) and BUTTS (A.) Engineering Metallurgy, *etc.* 1926. 8°. **7112.ee.21/1.**

—— —— 1930. 8°. **7112.ee.21/3.**

—— —— 1938. 8°. **7112.ee.21/7.**

—— *See* STOUGHTON (Bradley) Engineering Metallurgy . . . [By] B. Stoughton . . . A. Butts, *etc.* 1953. 8°. **8774**. bb. **31**.

—— Copper. The science and technology of the metal, its alloys and compounds. Prepared under the editorial supervision of Allison Butts, *etc.* [By various authors. With illustrations.] pp. xii. 936. *Reinhold Publishing Corporation: New York*, 1954. 8°. [*American Chemical Society Monograph Series.* no. 122.] Ac. **3934/5**.

—— A Textbook of Metallurgical Problems, *etc.* pp. xiv. 425. *McGraw-Hill Book Co.: New York & London*, 1932. 8°. [*Metallurgical Texts.*] **7112.ee.21/4.**

—— Metallurgical Problems . . . Second edition [of "Textbook of Metallurgical Problems"]. pp. xii. 446. *McGraw-Hill Book Co.: New York & London*, 1943. 8°. [*Metallurgy and Metallurgical Engineering Series.*] W.P. **13077/2**.

BUTTS (Amy) *See* Edgar (John G.) Cavaliers and Roundheads . . . With illustrations by A. Butts. 1862. 8°. **9525**. a. **14**.

—— Sixteen Illustrations to the Idylls of the King. Drawn and etched on copper by A. Butts. pl. xvi. *Day & Son: London*, [1863.] fol. **1751**. a. **10**.

BUTTS (Asa K.) *See* Besant (Annie) [*Single Works.*] Marriage . . . With a sketch of the life of Mrs. Besant. Edited by A. K. Butts. [1879.] 16°. **8416**. bbb. **32**.

BUTTS (B. S.) A Romance of the Daisy, and other poems. [With a portrait.] pp. 79. *A. H. Stockwell: London*, [1910.] 8°. **011650**. f. **27**.

BUTTS (Barbara)

—— *See* Scharlieb (*Dame* Mary D.) *D.B.E.*, and Butts (B.) England's Girls and England's Future. 1917. 16°. [*National Council for Combating Venereal Diseases.* N.C.26.] **7642.de.1/26.**

BUTTS (Charles) *See* Weller (Stuart) The Geology of Hardin County . . . By S. Weller, with the collaboration of C. Butts, *etc.* 1920. 8°. [*Illinois State Geological Survey. Bulletin.* no. 41.] A.S. i. **26**.

—— The Appalachian Plateau and Mississippi Valley. *See* Ruedemann (R.) and Balk (R.) Geology of North America, *etc.* vol. 1. 1939, *etc.* 8°. W.P. **13433/1**.

—— Economic Geology of the Kittanning and Rural Valley Quadrangles, Pennsylvania. pp. 198. pl. x. *Washington*, 1906. 8°. [*U.S. Geological Survey. Bulletin.* no. 279.] A.S. **212/2**.

—— Southern Appalachian Region. By C. Butts, G. W. Stose and Anna I. Jonas. pp. iv. 94. pl. 27. *Washington*, 1932. 8°. [*International Geological Congress. xvi session. United States*, 1933. *Guidebook.* no. 3.] **7110.b.1/3.**

BUTTS (Charles) and **MOORE** (Elwood S.)

—— Geology and Mineral Resources of the Bellefonte Quadrangle, Pennsylvania. [With maps.] pp. vi. 111. pl. 12. *Washington*, 1936. 8°. [*U.S. Geological Survey. Bulletin.* no. 855.] A.S. **212/2**.

BUTTS (E. L.) *of Montreux.* This is not your Rest, and other poems. By E. L. B. Montreux [i.e. E. L. Butts ?]. pp. 95. [1879 ?] 8°. *See* B., E. L., *Montreux.* **11653**. bbb. **14**.

BUTTS (Edmund Luther) Manual of Physical Drill, United States Army. pp. vi. 175. *D. Appleton & Co.: New York*, 1897. 8°. **8832**. bb. **33**.

BUTTS (Edward) Statement No. 1. The Swastika. [With illustrations.] pp. 42. *Franklin Hudson Publishing Co.: Kansas City*, 1908. 4°. **7702**. h. **44**.

—— The Triskelion. [On the Aztec calendar. With illustrations.] pp. 63. *Burton Publishing Co.: Kansas City*, [1925.] 4°. **7708**. ee. **42**.

BUTTS (George Manning) *See* Frazier (Rowland W.) and Butts (G. M.) The Factories Act, 1937. 1937. 8°. **20031**. h. **31**.

—— The Law of Food and Drugs. pp. lxxii. 603. 1940. 8°. *See* England.—*Laws and Statutes.*—iv. *Sale of Food and Drugs.* **6428**. t. **7**.

—— The New County Court Procedure. pp. xvi. 151. *Solicitors' Law Stationery Society: London*, 1936. 8°. **6191**. ff. **7**.

—— The New County Court Procedure . . . Second edition. pp. xi. 179. *Solicitors' Law Stationery Society: London*, 1942. 8°. **6192**. b. **1**.

BUTTS (George Manning)

—— Modern County Court Procedure . . . Third edition [of "The New County Court Procedure"]. pp. xviii. 159. *Solicitors' Law Stationery Society: London*, 1952. 8°. **6193**. b. **7**.

BUTTS (Halleck A.)

—— Trends in Japan's Trade and Industries. pp. ii. 26. *Washington*, 1929. 8°. [*U.S. Bureau of Foreign and Domestic Commerce. Trade Information Bulletin.* no. 642.] A.S. **128/3**.

BUTTS (Henry) *Master of Corpus Christi College, Cambridge.* *See* C., B. Puritanisme the Mother, Sinne the Daughter . . . Heerunto is added, as an appendix, A Funerall Discourse touching the . . . deathes of . . . Doctour Price Deane of Hereford, and Doctour Butts Vice-Chancellour of Cambridge. 1633. 8°. **3936**. b. **29**. **(4.)**

BUTTS (Henry) *of Nickerson, Kansas.* The Oliver Typewriter Instructor. Latest work on typewriters with double shift. pp. 25. *Nickerson*, 1904. 4°. **07942**. f. **2**.

BUTTS (Isaac) Protection and Free Trade: an inquiry whether protective duties can benefit the interests of a country in the aggregate, *etc.* [The editor's preface signed: W. W. E. With a portrait.] pp. 190. *G. P. Putnam's Sons: New York*, 1875. 12°. **8206**. b. **25**.

BUTTS (Isaac R.) Book-Keeping; and method of keeping ship's accounts. *See* Branson (Ware) The Art of Sail-making, *etc.* 1860. 12°. **8806**. c. **20**.

—— The Business Man's Assistant. Part i. Containing useful forms of legal instruments . . . adapted to the wants of business men . . . By I. R. Butts, assisted by an attorney . . . Thirty fourth thousand. pp. 96. *I. R. Butts: Boston*, 1847. 12°. **6615**. aaa. **13**.

—— The Creditor's & Debtor's Assistant, or the Mode of collecting debts, *etc.* (Trader's & mechanic's laws of trade.) pp. 108. *I. R. Butts: Boston*, 1849. 12°. **6615**. aaa. **14**.

—— Manual of Admeasurement. The United States Tonnage Law of 1864, with an analysis of the mode of measuring ships and vessels, *etc.* pp. 68. *I. R. Butts & Co.: Boston*, 1865. 12°. **6835**. aa. **31**.

—— The Merchant's and Mechanic's Assistant, being a collection of rules and practical tables for the use of commercial houses & those interested in ships . . . Second edition. pp. 252. *I. R. Butts: Boston*, 1857. 12°. **1393**. d. **12**.

—— The Tinman's Manual and Builder's and Mechanic's Handbook . . . Fourth edition. pp. 204. 2. *I. R. Butts & Co.: Boston*, 1867. 12°. **7814**. b. **9**.

BUTTS (Marie) *See* Le Braz (A.) The Lightkeeper. Translated by M. Butts. 1916. 8°. **12548**. s. **22**.

—— *See* Rabelais (F.) Rabelais pour la jeunesse . . . Texte adapté par M. Butts, *etc.* [1910.] 8°. **012548**. b. **30**.

—— *See* Rossello (P.) [Les Précurseurs du Bureau International d'Éducation.] Forerunners of the International Bureau of Education . . . Abridged and translated by M. Butts, *etc.* [1944.] 8°. **08310**. ee. **104**.

—— Education for Peace. pp. 9. *Friends Peace Committee: London; Northern Friends Peace Board: York*, [1943.] 8°. **08425**. f. **92**.

BUTTS (Marie)

—— Héros ! Épisodes de la Grande Guerre. Avec 47 illustrations de F. Bovard et 8 portraits hors texte. pp. 394. *Paris; Lausanne* [printed], [1915.] 8°. **9082.** e. **21.**

BUTTS (Mary Francis) *See* Hope (David) Sennen Pamphlet Series. (no. 1. Mary Butts, Fire bearer.) [1937, *etc.*] 8°. W.P. **6778/1.**

—— Armed with Madness. pp. 224. *Wishart & Co.: London*, 1928. 8°. NN. **14238.**

—— Ashe of Rings. pp. 304. *Three Mountains Press: Paris*, 1925. 8°. **012614.** d. **3.**

—— (First English edition, revised.) pp. 313. *Wishart & Co.: London*, 1933. 8°. NN. **20887.**

—— The Crystal Cabinet. My childhood at Salterns. [With a portrait.] pp. viii. 279. *Methuen & Co.: London*, 1937. 8°. **010821.** g. **6.**

—— Death of Felicity Taverner. pp. 267. *Wishart & Co.: London*, 1932. 8°. NN. **22612.**

—— Last Stories. pp. 265. *Brendin Publishing Co.: London*, 1938. 8°. NN. **29314.**

—— The Macedonian. pp. xi. 211. *William Heinemann: London*, 1933. 8°. **12646.** e. **14.**

—— Scenes from the Life of Cleopatra. [A novel.] pp. x. 286. *William Heinemann: London, Toronto*, 1935. 8°. NN. **23987.**

—— Several Occasions. (Stories.) pp. 231. *Wishart: [London,]* 1932. 8°. **012601.** i. **21.**

—— Speed the Plough, and other stories. pp. 222. *Chapman & Hall: London*, 1923. 8°. NN. **8662.**

—— Traps for Unbelievers. pp. 51. *Desmond Harmsworth: London*, 1932. 8°. **4370.** ee. **21.**

—— Warning to Hikers. pp. 36. *Wishart & Co.: [London,]* 1932. 8°. [*Here & Now Pamphlets.* no. 6.] W.P. **9881/6.**

BUTTS (Richard Vladimirovich) Изъ Берлина. (Изъ Эдинбурга.—Изъ Лондона.—Изъ Парижа.—Изъ Вѣны.—Заграничныя письма.—Изъ "Хирургическаго Вѣстника," *etc.*) 7 pt. [*Saint Petersburg*, 1886, 87.] 8°. **7305.** ee. **14.**

BUTTS (Robert) successively *Bishop of Norwich* and *of Ely*. The Charge of . . . Robert, Lord Bishop of Ely, deliver'd to the Reverend the Clergy of his diocese . . . at his Primary Visitation, *etc.* pp. 26. *Fletcher Gyles: London*, 1740. 4°. **4445.** cc. **10.**

—— The Charge of . . . Robert, Lord Bishop of Norwich, to the Reverend the Clergy of his diocese, in the Primary Visitation of the same in the year MDCCXXXV. pp. 22. *Fletcher Gyles: London*, 1736. 4°. **694.** k. **18.** (**6.**)

—— [Another copy.] **4445.** e. **15.**

—— A Sermon preach'd before the . . . House of Lords in the Abbey Church at Westminster . . . June 11, 1737, being the anniversary of his Majesty's happy accession to the throne. pp. 23. *Fletcher Gyles: London*, 1737. 4°. **693.** f. **5.** (**13.**)

—— [Another copy.] **226.** f. **4.** (**6.**)

BUTTS (Robert) *of Lewisham.* Butts' Historical Guide to Lewisham, Ladywell, Lee, Blackheath and Eltham. pp. vi. 121. *Robert Butts: Lewisham*, 1878. 8°. **010368.** de. **45.**

BUTTS (Robert Freeman)

—— The American Tradition in Religion and Education. pp. xiv. 230. *Beacon Press: Boston*, 1950. 8°. **4745.** l. **5.**

One of the " Beacon Press Studies in Freedom and Power."

—— The College Charts its Course. Historical conceptions and current proposals. pp. xvi. 464. *New York & London*, 1939. 8°. [*McGraw-Hill Series in Education.*] W.P. **12179/14.**

—— A Cultural History of Education, *etc.* pp. ix. 726. *McGraw-Hill Book Co.: New York & London*, 1947. 8°. [*McGraw-Hill Series in Education.*] W.P. **12179/44.**

—— [A Cultural History of Education.] A Cultural History of Western Education . . . Second edition. pp. xii. 645. *McGraw-Hill Book Co.: New York*, 1955. 8°. [*McGraw-Hill Series in Education.*] W.P. **12179/112.**

BUTTS (Sophie Michell) *See* Turgenev (I. S.) [*Вешнія Воды.*] Ivan Turgénieff's Spring Floods. Translated . . . by Mrs. S. M. Butts, *etc.* 1874. 8°. **12209.** ccc. **6.**

BUTTS (Thomas) *American Trade Commissioner.*

—— Exports of Electrical Equipment from Germany 1913–1927. pp. ii. 27. [*Washington*, 1928.] 8°. [*U.S. Bureau of Foreign and Domestic Commerce. Trade Information Bulletin.* no. 548.] A.S. **128/3.**

BUTTS (Thomas) *Muster Master General.*

—— *See* Blake (William) *Artist.* [*Letters.*] Letters from William Blake to Thomas Butts, 1800–1803, *etc.* [With a letter from T. Butts to W. Blake.] 1926. 4°. **10906.** h. **18.**

BUTTS (William) *See* Arensberg (Walter C.) Francis Bacon, William Butts and the Pagets of Beaudesert. [Maintaining that Francis Bacon and William Shakespeare were the pseudonyms of William Butts, son of Sir William Butts and Lady Anne Cooke Bacon.] 1929. 8°. **011761.** f. **20.**

BUTTS (*Sir* William) *the Elder.* *See* Clippingdale (Samuel D.) Sir William Butt, M.D.: a local link with Shakespeare. [1916.] 8°. **010856.** e. **4.**

BUTTS (*Sir* William) *the Younger.* *See* Dallington (*Sir* Robert) A Booke of Epitaphes made upon the death of Sir W. Buttes. [1583 ?] 8°. **11623.** a. **12.**

BUTTSTÄDT (   ) [For the German surname of this form:] *See* Buttstaedt.

BUTTSTAEDT (Johann Heinrich) *See* Ziller (E. R. T.) Johann Heinrich Buttstädt, *etc.* 1934. 8° & *obl.* 4°. **07899.** ee. **23.**

—— Ut, mi, sol, re, fa, la, tota musica et harmonia æterna, oder Neu-eröffnetes, altes, wahres, eintziges und ewiges fundamentum musices, entgegen gesetzt dem neu-eröffneten Orchestre [of Johann Mattheson], *etc.* pp. 176. *Erffurt; Leipzig*, [1715.] 4°. Hirsch I. **97.**

—— [Another copy.] Ut, mi, sol, re, fa, la, tota musica et harmonia æterna, *etc.* *Erffurt: Leiptzig*, [1715.] 4°. **785.** e. **39.**

Imperfect: wanting pl. II. D. *With two copies of pl.* I. D.

—— *See* Mattheson (Johann) Das beschützte Orchestre . . . worinn . . . des lange verbannet gewesenen Ut, mi, sol, re, fa, la todte—nicht tota—Musica [of J. H. Buttstaedt] . . . zu Grabe gebracht . . . wird. 1717. 12°. **785.** b. **37.**

BUTTSTETT (Franz Vollrath)

—— *See* Kern (H.) Franz Vollrath Buttstett, 1735–1814, *etc.* [With a portrait.] 1939. 8°. W.P. **13605/4.**

BUTTSTETT (Johann Heinrich) *See* Buttstaedt.

BUTT-THOMPSON (Frederick William) *See* Thompson.

BUTTURA (Antonin) *See* Buttura (Charles A.)

BUTTURA (Antonio) *See* Alamanni (L.) *the Elder.* La Coltivazione . . . Publicata da A. Buttura. 1821. 16°. **11426. a. 9.**

—— *See* Ariosto (L.) [*Orlando Furioso.*] L'Orlando Furioso . . . Publicato da A. Buttura. 1840. 16°. **11426. bbb. 1.**

—— *See* Boileau-Despréaux (N.) L'Art poétique . . . Traduit en vers italiens par A. Buttura. 1806. 8°. **1065. h. 28.**

—— *See* Dante Alighieri [Smaller Collections.—*Italian.*] Opere poetiche . . . Per diligenza e studio di A. Buttura. 1823. 8°. **11421. f. 19.**

—— *See* Dante Alighieri. [*Smaller Collections.*] Opere poetiche di Dante Alighieri. [Edited by A. Buttura.] 1836. 8°. **11420. d. 10.**

—— *See* **Dante Alighieri.** [*Single Works.—Divina Commedia.—Complete Texts.—Italian.*] **La Divina Commedia . . . Publicata da A. Buttura.** 1820. **16°. 11421. aa. 3.**

—— *See* Dante Alighieri. [*Divina Commedia.*—Complete Texts:—*Italian.*] La Divina Commedia . . . Publicata da A. Buttura. 1829. 32°. **11421. a. 28.**

—— *See* Gray (Thomas) *the Poet.* [*Elegy written in a Country Churchyard.*] L'Elegia di Gray. [Translated by A. Buttura.] 1806. 8°. [*Boileau-Despréaux* (*N.*) *L'Art poétique . . . traduit en vers italiens, etc.*] **1065. h. 28.**

—— *See* Gray (Thomas) *the Poet.* [*Elegy written in a Country Churchyard.*] L'Elegia . . . sopra un cimitero di campagna tradotta . . . in più lingue, *etc.* [Including an Italian translation in terza rima by A. Buttura.] 1817. 8°. **11632. cc. 4.**

—— —— 1843. 8°. **1465. k. 23.**

—— *See* Macchiavelli (N.) [*Il Principe.*] Il Principe . . . Publicato da A. Buttura. 1825. 16°. **524. a. 18. (1.)**

—— *See* Metastasio (P. A. D. B.) Opere scelte . . . Publicate da A. Buttura. 1823. 16°. **1088. b. 27.**

—— —— 1840. 16°. **1088. b. 25.**

—— *See* Petrarca (F.) [*Canzoniere.—Italian.*] Le Rime . . . Publicate da A. Buttura. 1820. 16°. **11421. de. 3.**

—— *See* Racine (J.) [*Iphigénie.*] L'Ifigenia . . . Recata in versi italiani da A. Buttura. 1815. 12°. **636. b. 24.**

—— *See* Tasso (T.) [*Aminta.—Italian.*] Aminta . . . Publicata da A. Buttura. 1828. 16°. **524. a. 18. (2.)**

—— *See* Tasso (T.) [*La Gerusalemme Liberata.—Italian.*] La Gerusalemme liberata . . . Publicata da A. Buttura. 1820. 16°. **11421. de. 5.**

—— Poesie. pp. 216. *Parigi,* 1811. 12°. **1062. d. 22.**

—— A Napoleone il Grande, ricorrendo il compleanno della sua incoronazione a Rè d'Italia. Ode. [With a French prose translation.] pp. 19. *Parigi,* 1807. 12°. **11429. b. 6.**

With the imperial arms of France stamped on the binding.

BUTTURA (Antonio)

—— Discorso pronunciato . . . nella Sala d'Istruzion pubblica, *etc.* [On the education of children.] pp. viii. *Verona,* 1797. 8°. **8306. ee. 32.**

—— Il Genio, canto lirico, nel compleanno dell'incoronazione a Rè d'Italia di Napoleone il Grande, *etc.* pp. 15. [*Paris,*] 1808. 8°. **1063. i. 3. (4.)**

—— **Hommage à la gloire de Desaix. Ode au peuple français. Traduction [in prose] de l'italien précédée du texte.** ***Ital. & Fr.*** **pp. 14.** ***Paris,*** **an VIII [1799/1800]. 8°. 1065. l. 43. (7.)**

—— La Nascita di Giove. [*Paris,*] 1808. 8°. **T. 950. (6.)**

—— Ode à la France, à l'occasion de la paix continentale. Texte italien, suivi de la traduction [in prose]. pp. 14. [*Paris,* 1801.] 8°. **1062. k. 3.**

—— I Quattro poeti italiani, con una scelta di poesie italiane dal 1200 sino a' nostri tempi. Publicati da A. Buttura. pp. x. 751. *Parigi,* 1833. 8°. **11436. i. 44.**

—— Scelta di poesie italiane d'autori antichi, publicate da A. Buttura. pp. 270. *Parigi,* 1820. 32°. **11436. a. 75.**

Tom. 7 of the "Biblioteca poetica italiana scelta e publicata da A. Buttura."

—— Scelta di poesie italiane d'autori dell'età media, dal 1500 al 1700. Publicate da A. Buttura. pp. 316. *Parigi,* 1821. 16°. **11436. aa. 25.**

—— Scelta di poesie italiane d'autori moderni, publicate da A. Buttura. pp. 310. *Parigi,* 1822. 32°. **11436. a. 74.**

Tom. 30 of the "Biblioteca poetica italiana scelta e publicata da A. Buttura."

BUTTURA (Antonio) and **RENZI** (Angelo)

—— Dictionnaire général italien-français . . . entièrement refait par Renzi . . . et augmenté . . . Deuxième édition. pp. xvi. 1279. *Paris,* 1861. 8°. **12944.cc.18.**

BUTTURA (Charles Antonin) Des fièvres éruptives sans éruption, et particulièrement de la scarlatine sans exanthème. pp. 44. *Paris,* 1857. 8°. **7561. e. 63. (7.)**

—— L'Hiver à Cannes. Les bains de mer de la Méditerranée, les bains de sable. pp. 92. *Paris,* 1867. 8°. **7687. aaa. 11.**

—— L'Hygiène publique à Cannes. pp. 16. *Cannes,* 1871. 8°. **7687. aa. 60. (7.)**

—— Thèse pour le doctorat en médecine. (Questions sur diverses branches des sciences médicales.) pp. 31. *Paris,* 1839. 4°. [*Collection des thèses soutenues à la Faculté de Médecine de Paris.* An 1839. tom. 3.] **7371. a. 3.**

BUTTURINI (Annibale) *pseud.* [i.e. *Cardinal* Enrico Noris? or Franciscus Sparaverius?] *See* also Noris (E.) *Cardinal.*

—— *See* also Sparaverius (F.)

—— Thraso Macedonicus Plautino sale perfrictus. [A satire on works written by F. Macedo using the pseudonym Henricus Hausen.] pp. 14. *Lovanii* [*Padua?*], 1707. fol. **1229. i. 5. (2.)**

Other editions are entered under Corradini (Annibale) pseud.

BUTTURINI (MATTIA) *of Salò*. *See* FIORINI (V.) Chi inventò la bandiera tricolore. [Followed by "Osservazioni" by M. Butturini.] 1897. 8°. **9903**. f. **40**. (4.)

—— Gasparo da Salò, inventore del violino moderno. Studio critico. pp. 95. *Salò*, 1901. 8°. **7899**. d. **38**.

BUTTURINI (MATTIA) *Professor of Greek in the University of Pavia*. Omero pittore delle passioni umane, discorso. *See* C., G. Scelte orazioni italiane, *etc.* 1833. 12°. **12301**. c. **19**.

—— I Veneziani, e le nozze. Inno greco . . . volgarizzato da Giuseppe Compagnoni. pp. xxiii. **L.P.** *Venezia*, 1792. 12°. T. **2278**. (**12**.)

—— Zaira. Dramma nuovo per musica, *etc.* [By M. Butturini. In verse. Based on Voltaire's "Zaïre."] pp. 64. 1797. 8°. *See* ZAÏRE. **905**. c. **5**. (4.)

BUTTY (BENOÎTE) *See* SAINTE-JUSTINE, *Mère* [B. Butty].

BUTTY (ENRIQUE)

—— **Introducción a la física matemática. vol. 2. pp. 444.** ***Buenos Aires***, **1934. 8°. 08535. l. 28.**
Imperfect; wanting vol. 1.

BUTTZ (HENRY ANSON)

—— *See* BIBLE.—*Romans*. [*Greek*.] The Epistle to the Romans in Greek, in which the text of Robert Stephens . . . is compared with the texts of the Elzevirs, Lachmann, Alford . . . By H. A. Buttz. 1895. 8°. **3266**. ff. **11**.

BUTURAS (ATHANAS) *See* BOUTOURAS (Athanasios Ch.)

BUTURLIN (ALEKSYEI PETROVICH) *See* N. (Th.) Путеводитель по Ярославской губерніи, составленный, подъ руководствомъ . . . А. П. Бутурлина . . . Ѳ. Н-мъ [i.e. by Th. Ya. Nikol'sky] и изданный . . . Н. М. Журавлевымъ. 1859. 8°. **10292**. i. **4**.

BUTURLIN (AUGUST) *See* GIGLIOLI (E. H.) Note intorno agli animali vertebrati raccolti dal conte A. Boutourline e dal dʳ L. Traversi ad Assab e nello Scioa negli anni 1884–87. 1888. 8°. [*Annali del Museo Civico di Storia Naturale di Genova*. ser. 2. vol. 6.] Ac. **2809**.

BUTURLIN (DMITRY PETROVICH) Исторія смутнаго времени въ Россіи въ началѣ XVII вѣка. (Приложенія.) 3 част. *Санктпетербургъ*, 1839–46. 8°. **9455**. ee. **1**.

—— Военная исторія походовъ россіянъ въ XVIII столѣтіи . . . переведена . . . А. Хатовымъ. [том. 4 translated by A. Kornilovich.] (Планы и карты, *etc.*) 3 част. 4 том. 1819–23. 8° & *obl.* 8°. *See* RUSSIA.—*Army*.—*Главный Штабъ*. **9079**. d. **1**.

—— Histoire militaire de la campagne de Russie en 1812. [Translated, by the author? from the Russian.] 2 tom. *Paris*, 1824. 8°. **1055**. d. **24**.

—— Atlas. [*Paris*, 1824.] fol. Maps **12**. e. **23**.

—— *See* DAVUIDOV (D. V.) Замѣчанія на некрологію Н. Н. Раевскаго, *etc.* [Containing extracts from the Russian translation of D. P. Buturlin's "Histoire militaire de la campagne de Russie en 1812."] 1832. 8°. **8820**. a. **23**. (**1**.)

—— Précis des événemens militaires de la dernière guerre des Espagnols contre les Français. pp. 88. *St. Pétersbourg*, 1818. 8°. **1323**. f. **13**.

—— Tableau de la campagne d'automne de 1813, en Allemagne depuis la rupture de l'armistice jusqu'au passage du Rhin par l'armée française; avec une carte topographique des environs de Leipzig. Par un officier russe [i.e. D. P. Buturlin]. pp. xi. 200. 1817. 8°. *See* GERMANY. [*Appendix.—History and Politics.*—II.] **1055**. e. **10**.

BUTURLIN (DMITRY PETROVICH)

—— Darstellung des Feldzugs im Spätjahr 1813 in Deutschland . . . von einem russischen Offizier. [A translation of "Tableau de la campagne d'automne de 1813 en Allemagne" by D. P. Buturlin.] Deutsch bearbeitet von F. v. Kausler. [With tables and a map.] pp. xvi. 167. 1819. 8°. *See* GERMANY. [*Appendix.—History and Politics.*—II.] M.L. aa. **84**.

BUTURLIN (DMITRY PETROVICH) *Count*. Catalogue des livres de la bibliothèque de S. E. M. le comte de Boutourlin; revu par MM. Ant.-Alex. Barbier . . . et Charles Pougens, *etc.* pp. 758. *Paris*, 1805. 8°. **270**. k. **8**.

—— Catalogue de la bibliothèque de . . . M. le comte D. Boutourlin. [The compiler's preface signed: G. L. I. G. A ****, i.e. E. Audin de Rians.] 9 pt. *Florence*, 1831. 8°. **821**. k. **17**.

BUTURLIN (P.) *See* RUSSIA.—*Greek Church*.—*Synod*. Mémoire . . . par . . . Comte D. Tolstoy sur l'activité de l'Administration Ecclésiastique Orthodoxe depuis juin 1865 jusqu'à janvier 1866. Traduit par P. Boutourlin. 1867. 8°. **3926**. f. **19**. (**6**.)

—— *See* SAMARIN (Yu. Th.) [Іезуиты и ихъ отношеніе къ Россіи.] Les Jésuites et leurs rapports avec la Russie . . . Traduit . . . par P. Boutourlin. 1867. 8°. **4092**. h. **11**.

—— [О календаряхъ юліанскихъ и григоріанскихъ.] Des calendriers julien et grégorien . . . Traduit du russe par l'auteur. pp. 91. *Paris*, 1865. 12°. **8560**. aaa. **6**.

BUTURLIN (PETR DMITRIEVICH) *Count*. Стихотворенія Графа П. Д. Бутурлина, собранныя и изданныя послѣ его смерти Графинею Я. А. Бутурлиной. [With a portrait.] 2 част. pp. xxv. 252. *Кіевъ*, 1897. 8°. **011586**. l. **18**.
The date on the wrapper is 1898.

BUTURLIN (SERGYEI ALEKSANDROVICH) *See* RUSSIA.—*Центральный Исполнительный Комитетъ Совѣтовъ*.—*Комитетъ Содѣйствія Народностямъ Сѣверныхъ Окраинъ*. Советский Север . . . Под редакцией П. Г. Смидовича, С. А. Бутурлина, *etc.* 1929, *etc.* 8°. **10292.h.39.**

—— *See* ZHITKOV (B. M.) and BUTURLIN (S. A.) Матеріалы для орнитофауны Симбирской губерніи, *etc.* 1906. 8°. [*Записки Императорскаго Русскаго Географическаго Общества по Общей Географіи*. том. 41. no. 2.] Ac. **6130/2**.

BUTURLIN (THEDOR MIKHAILOVICH) *Count*. Необычайные, но истинные приключения графа Федора Михайловича Бутурлина, описанные по семейным преданиям московским ботаником Х. и иллюстрированные фитопатологом У. 1924. 8°. *See* KH. **12591**. ppp. **36**.

BUTURLINA (T. T.) and **KUPRINA-VUISOTSKAYA** (V. B.)

—— Советская избирательная система. Методическое пособие. pp. 37. *Москва*, 1951. 8°. **8095**. l. **58**.
The titlepage headed: Академия Педагогических Наук РСФСР, Институт Методов Обучения. Part of a series entitled "Заочная методическая консультация."

BUTURLINA (YA. A.) *Countess*. *See* BUTURLIN (P. D.) *Count*. Стихотворенія . . . изданныя . . . Графинею Я. А. Бутурлиной. 1897. 8°. **011586**. l. **18**.

BUTUSOV (VIKTOR PAVLOVICH)

—— *See* DUBOSHIN (V. N.) and KOTOV (V. S.) Англо-русский авиационный словарь . . . Под редакцией инж. В. П. Бутусова и инж. М. Н. Чаусского. 1950. 8°. **12975**. o. **24**.

BUTUTUS (GERARDUS) *See* GERARDUS, *Bituricensis.*

BUTUZOV (V. V.) Словарь особенныхъ словъ, фразъ и оборотовъ англійскаго народнаго языка и употребительнѣйшихъ американизмовъ, не введенныхъ въ обыкновенные словари. Настольная книга, *etc.* pp. viii. 373. *Санктпетербургъ*, 1867. 16°. **12984**. aaa. 2.

BUTY (PIERRE LÉON) Remarques sur les appareils employés dans le traitement des fractures compliquées. Des atelles plâtrées combinées avec la suspension élastique. pp. 40. *Paris*, 1872. 4°. [*Collection des thèses soutenues à la Faculté de Médecine de Paris.* An 1872. tom. 3.] **7373**. n. 9.

BUTYAGINA (VARVARA) Лютики. [Poems. With a preface by A. V. Lunacharsky.] pp. 44. *Петербург*, 1921. 8°. **011586**. cc. 14.

BUTYROLAMBIUS (NECTARIUS) *pseud.* [i.e. JOHANN MUELLER, *Pastor of St. Peter's, Hamburg*, or JOHANN MOLLER, *of Hamburg.*] *See* ANTENOR, *pseud.* [i.e. J. B. Schupp.] Etwas Neues von Lobe und Redligheit Antenors und seinen drey Palm Eseln Butyrolambio, Bernd Fabro, und Justo Soporino. 1659. 12°. **8410**. de. **18**. (**8**.)

—— Der Bücher-Dieb Antenors, empfangen und wider abgefertiget durch Nectarium Butyrolambium, *etc.* [A criticism of "Der Bücher-Dieb," by J. B. Schupp.] pp. 58. *Pieter Jansoon: Amsterdamm* [*Hamburg*], [1658.] 12°. **8410**. de. **18**. (**5**.)

BUTYROLAMBIUS (NECTARIUS) *pseud.* [i.e. JOHANN MUELLER, *Pastor of St. Peter's, Hamburg*, or JOHANN MOLLER, *of Hamburg.*]

—— *See* ANTENOR, *pseud.* [i.e. J. B. Schupp.] Unschuld des Antenors, gewiesen von einem Bekanten doch Unpartheischen. [An answer to "Der Bücher-Dieb Antenors, empfangen und wieder abgefertiget durch Nectarium Butyrolambium."] 1659. 12°. **8410**. de. **18**. (**7**.)

—— *See* SCHUPP (J. B.) Abgenöthigte Ehren-Rettung Joh. Balth. Schuppii. [An answer to "Der Bücher-Dieb Antenors, empfangen und wieder abgefertiget durch Nectarium Butyrolambium."] 1660. 12°. **8410**. de. **18**. (**2**.)

BUTZ (CASPAR) *See* PERIODICAL PUBLICATIONS.—*Chicago.* Deutsch-amerikanische Monatshefte . . . Herausgegeben von C. Butz. 1864, *etc.* 8°. P.P. **3639**. d.

BUTZ (ERHARD) Trauerrede auf den . . . Herrn Gallus, aus der adelichen Familie von Leith in Schottland, des . . . Stiftes der Schotten bey St. Jakob in Regensburg, und des Klosters zu Erfurt . . . würdigsten Abten . . . gehalten bey seinem Grabe den 20 Novemb. 1775. pp. 27. [*Ratisbon?* 1775.] fol. **4885**. f. **11**.

BUTZ (FRIEDRICH CARL) Der englische Januskopf. [Impressions of travel.] pp. 148. *Mainz*, [1928.] 8°. **010360**. b. **14**.

BUTZ (GUSTAV) *See* MUELLER (Adolf) *Poet.* Plattdeutsche Gedichte, *etc.* [Edited by G. Butz.] 1876. 16°. **11526**. cc. **13**.

BUTZ (HANS) *Oberstleutnant.*

—— Die K. B. Gebirgs-Artillerie-Abteilung Nr. 2. Nach den amtlichen Kriegstagebüchern bearbeitet von H. Butz . . . Mit 9 Skizzen. pp. 99. *München*, 1921. 8°. [*Erinnerungsblätter deutscher Regimenter.* Bayerische Armee. Hft. 5.] **8836**. e. 2/5.

BUTZ (HANS) *Professor Dr.*, and **BOETTGER** (THEODOR)

—— Das Zahnalter des Pferdes . . . Mit 28 Abbildungen. pp. vi. 80. *Hannover* [1946.] *obl.* 8°. **07295**. k. **52**.

BUTZ (JOHANNES) Disputatio medica inauguralis de hydrocephalo, *etc.* *Praes.* J. C. Brotbequius. pp. 16. *Typis J. A. Cellii: Tubingæ*, 1661. 4°. T. **557**. (**20**.)

BUTZ (RICHARD) Untersuchungen über die physiologischen Functionen der Peripherie der Netzhaut. Inaugural-Dissertation, *etc.* pp. 142. *Dorpat*, 1883. 8°. **7407**. aa. **6**.

BUTZ (WILHELM) Wir Schweizer und der Deutschen-Hass! pp. 46. *Zürich*, 1918. 8°. **08072**. cc. **32**.

BUTZBACH. Butzbachische reformierte Gerichts Ordnung, *etc.* [Issued by Louis IV., Landgrave of Hesse, 9 May 1578.] *See* SAUR (A.) Fasciculus Iudiciarii ordinis singularis, *etc.* Tl. 2. 1589. fol. **705**. l. **18**.

BUTZBACH (JOHANNES) *See* KNOD (G. C.) Zur Kritik des Johannes Butzbach. [With reference to the "Auctarium de scriptoribus ecclesiasticis."] 1891. 8°. [*Annalen des Historischen Verein für den Niederrhein.* Hft. 52.] Ac. **7335**.

—— *See* LETTS (Malcolm H.) Johannes Butzbach, a wandering scholar of the fifteenth century. [1917.] 8°. **010705**. i. **7**.

—— *See* RUEHL (Carl) *Dr.* Das Auctarium de scriptoribus ecclesiasticis des Johannes Butzbach. 1937. 8°. **20013**. i. **10**.

—— Chronica eines fahrenden Schülers oder Wanderbüchlein des Johannes Butzbach. Aus der lateinischen Handschrift übersetzt und mit Beilagen vermehrt von D. J. Becker. pp. xvi. 299. *Regensburg*, 1869. 8°. **010705**. e. **39**.

—— Wanderbüchlein. Chronika eines fahrenden Schülers . . . Übersetzt von Dr. D. J. Becker. pp. 127. *Leipzig*, [1912.] 8°. [*Insel-Bücherei.* no. 26.] **012213**. de. **1/26**.

—— The Autobiography of Johannes Butzbach, a wandering scholar of the fifteenth century. Translated from the German by Robert Francis Seybolt and Paul Monroe. pp. vii. 159. *Edwards Bros.: Ann Arbor*, [1933.] 8°. **010709**. df. **42**.

Reproduced from typewriting.

—— Mittheilungen über Alexander Hegius und seine Schüler sowie andere gleichzeitige Gelehrte, aus den Werken des Johannes Butzbach . . . Von Pastor Karl Krafft und Dr. W. Crecelius. 1871. *See* ELBERFELD.—*Bergischer Geschichtsverein.* Zeitschrift des Bergischen Geschichtsvereins, *etc.* Bd. 7. 1863, *etc.* 8°. Ac. **7340**.

BUTZE (E.) *See* DURAMA DE OCHOA (D.) Die Emancipation der Sklaven auf Cuba . . . Übersetzt von E. Butze. 1864. 8°. **8156**. aa. **55**. (**9**.)

BUTZE (GEORG) Der selbständige Teil der Magdeburgischen Chronik von Georg Butze, 1467–1551. 1899. *See* MUNICH.—*Königliche Akademie der Wissenschaften.* Die Chroniken der deutschen Städte vom 14. bis in's 16. Jahrhundert. Bd. 27. 1862, *etc.* 8°. Ac. **714/3**.

BUTZER (ALBERT GEORGE) You and Yourself, *etc.* [Sermons.] pp. viii. 117. *Harper & Bros.: New York & London*, 1933. 8°. **4486**. de. 38.

BUTZER (MARTIN) *See* BUCER.

BUTZER (MARTINUS ARNOLDUS) *Resp.* *See* HEISTER (L.) Dissertatio medico-chirurgica de hydrocele. 1755. 4°. [*HALLER* (*A. von*) *Baron. Disputationes chirurgicæ selectæ, etc.* tom. 3.] **7481**. ff. 20.

BUTZIGER (GUSTAV) *See* JAHRHUNDERT. Das neunzehnte Jahrhundert des Thierreichs . . . Mit poetischen Einleitungen von G. Butziger, *etc.* [1843, *etc.*] 8°. **12550.** cc. **7.**

—— D und T——Durst und Tod . . . [Satirical poems.] Zweite Auflage. pp. 161. *Leipzig,* 1847. 8°. **11527.** dd. **26.**

BUTZKE (E. L.) Denkschrift über den Weichselzopf. Ein Beitrag zur Begründung einer rationellen Pathologie und Therapie desselben . . . Neuer Abdruck. pp. 242. *Berlin,* 1859. 8°. **7610.** bb. **9.**

BUTZKE (HERMANN) Die Gefahr des neuen Zolltarifs. pp. 21. *Berlin,* [1926.] 8°. [*Flugschriften der Deutschen Liga für Menschenrechte.* no. 32.] **08072.** dd. **66/32.**

BUTZKE (LUDOLPHUS ERNESTUS) De efficacia bromi interna experimentis illustrata. Dissertatio inauguralis medica, *etc.* pp. 35. *Berolini,* [1829.] 8°. **7460.** aa. **54.** (2.)

BÜTZLER ( )

—— [For the German surname of this form :] *See* BUETZLER.

BUTZMANN (KURT)

—— Aktualgenese im indirekten Sehen, *etc.* 1940. *See* PERIODICAL PUBLICATIONS.—*Leipsic.* Archiv für die gesamte Psychologie, *etc.* Bd. 106. 1903, *etc.* 8°. P.P. **1253.** bd.

BUTZNER (JANE)

—— *See* UNITED STATES OF AMERICA.—*Convention for framing the Constitution.* Constitutional Chaff. Rejected suggestions of the Constitutional Convention of 1787, with explanatory argument. Compiled by J. Butzner, *etc.* 1941. 8°. **8175.dd.16.**

BÜTZOVIUS (NICOLAUS JOACHIMUS OLAUS) *Resp. See* HANSEN (Hans) *Provst of Skjelby and Gunderslev.* Disputatio physica prior de sonorum quorundam in chordis conspiratione, *etc.* [1707.] 4°. **1185.** c. **19.** (9.)

BÜTZOW. *See* BUETZOW.

BUTZOW (CAROLUS FRIDERICUS) Dissertatio medica inauguralis, de iis quae homines contagio pestilentiali magis obnoxios faciunt, *etc.* pp. 53. *Lugduni Batavorum,* 1777. 4°. T. **597.** (15.)

BUTZOW (HENRICUS) *Resp.* Theses de magis, *etc. Praes.* N. J. Lunde. pp. 8. *Havniæ,* [1709.] 4°. **8630.** e. **24.**

BUUCK (CHRISTIAN HEINRICH) Die Meuterei auf der preussischen Bark "Adolph Werner." Verklarung abgelegt vor dem Amte zu Bremerhaven . . . von Capitain C. H. Buuck, und seiner Mannschaft. pp. 22. *Bremen & Bremerhaven,* 1853. 8°. **1295.** b. **30.** (2.)

BUUL (HENRICUS JOANNES VAN) *Jansenist Bishop of Haarlem. See* SANTEN (J. van) *Jansenist Archbishop of Utrecht,* and BUUL (H. J. van) Illustrissimorum et reverendissimorum DD. J. van Santen . . . et H. J. van Buul . . . Epistola ad Summum Pontificem Pium IX, de literis apostolicis, *etc.* 1853. 8°. **3925.** cc. **28.**

BUULTJENS (ALFRED ERNEST) *See* PERIODICAL PUBLICATIONS.—*Colombo.* The Buddhist, *etc.* (vol. 2 edited by A. E. Buultjens.) 1888, *etc.* 8°. P.P. **636.** cn.

BUUREN (ADRIAAN DIEDERIK VAN) Gedichten. Tweede druk. pp. 141. vii. *Helder,* [1870.] 16°. **11557.** de. **18.**

—— Solide menschen. Blijspel in één bedrijf. pp. 23. *Purmerende,* [1868 ?] 8°. **11754.** aa. **65.** (2.)

BUUREN (ANNA MARIA ADRIANA JOHANNA VAN) Clara. [A novel.] 2 dl. *Arnhem,* 1883. 8°. **12580.** o. **2.**

BUUREN (HANS VAN)

—— De Consolidatie van de onafhankelijkheid der Verenigde Staten van Amerika, 1763–1795. Proefschrift, *etc.* [With sketch-maps.] pp. 266. [*Utrecht,* 1949.] 8°. **9617.** d. **4.**

BUUREN (MARIE VAN) *See* BUUREN (Anna Maria A. J. van)

BUURMAN (PETRUS) *See* BURMANNUS.

BUURMAN (ULRICH) Erläuterungen und Aufsätze zur Einführung in Goethes Faust, *etc.* pp. xi. 115. *Leipzig,* 1901. 8°. **11852.** de. **12.**

—— Kurzer Wegweiser durch Goethes Faust . . . Zweite Auflage. pp. 81. *Bremen,* 1934. 8°. **11856.** b. **6.**

BUURT (HADRIANUS) Hadriani Buurt Dissertatio philosophica, qua existentia Dei contra atheos probatur. *See* BUDDEUS (J. F.) Ioan. F. Buddei . . . Theses theologicae de atheismo et superstitione, *etc.* 1737. 8°. **4016.** bb. **8.**

BUUS (ERIK)

—— *See* MIKKELSEN (K.) *Bishop of Viborg.* Knud Mikkelsens Glosser, dansk tekst, og Thords artikler. Udgivet af E. Buus. 1951, *etc.* 8°. [*Danmarks gamle landskabslove.* Bd. 4. Tillæg.] Ac. **9879/8.**

BUVALELLI (RAMBERTINO) Rambertino Buvalelli, trovatore bolognese, e le sue rime provenzali. Per Giulio Bertoni. pp. 76. *Dresden,* 1908. 8°. [*Gesellschaft für romanische Literatur.* Bd. 17.] Ac. **8955.**

BUVARSTVO.

—— Буварство с черничарство и пашкулопреработване, *etc.* [By Iv. Kozhukharov, Dim. Khristov and Iord. Irinchev.] pp. 224. *София,* 1951. 8°. **7081.** g. **1.**

BUVAT (JEAN) Gazette de la Régence, janvier 1715—juin 1719. Publiée d'après le manuscrit inédit . . . par le comte E. de Barthélemy. pp. 352. *Paris,* 1887. 12°. **9220.** c. **4.**

—— Journal de la Régence—1715–1723 . . . Publié pour la première fois . . . précédé d'une introduction et accompagné de notes . . . par Émile Campardon. 2 tom. *Paris,* 1865. 8°. **9220.** ee. **11.**

—— Mémoire-journal de Jean Buvat, écrivain de la Bibliothèque du Roi, 1697–1729. Publié par Henri Omont. (Extrait de la Revue des Bibliothèques.) pp. 123. *Paris,* 1900. 8°. **010661.** d. **3.**

BUVÉE (BARBE) *See* GARNIER (S.) Barbe Buvée, en religion, sœur Sainte-Colombe, et la prétendue possession des Ursulines d'Auxonne, *etc.* 1895. 8°. **8632.** f. **34.**

BUVERT (V. V.)

—— *See* TRANSPORT. Сухопутный транспорт леса, *etc.* [By V. V. Buvert and others.] 1951. 8°. **7081.** bb. **14.**

BUVEURS. Les Buveurs de sang. [A socialist pamphlet occasioned by the Congrès des étudiants de Liége, 1865. By Odilon Delimal.] pp. 32. *Bruxelles,* 1865. 12°. **8275.** aaa. **13.** (4.)

BUVIGNIER (AMAND) Statistique géologique, minéralogique, minérallurgique et paléontologique du departement de la Meuse, *etc.* pp. li. 694. *Paris,* 1852. 8°. **7107.** aaa. **12.**

—— Atlas. pp. 52. pl. XXXII. *Paris,* 1852. fol. **1824.** d. **32.**

BUVIGNIER (Charles Jean Victor) Note sur les archives de l'Hôtel-de-Ville de Verdun, Meuse. pp. 120. *Metz*, 1855. 8°. 10170. dd. 29.

BUVIGNIER (Firmin) Le Retour des aigles. Au Prince Louis-Napoléon, Président de la République. [A poem.] pp. 12. *Paris*, 1852. 8°. 11481. g. 14.

BUVIGNIER (Marie) *See* Paris.—*Bibliothèque Nationale.* [*Manuscrits.*] Collections Emmery et Cloüet-Buvignier sur l'histoire de Metz et de la Lorraine . . . Inventaire, *etc.* 1919. 8°. [*Mettensia.* vol. 7.] Ac. 5331/4.

BUVIGNIER-CLOÜET (Madeleine) Chevert, lieutenant général des armées du roi 1695–1769. Son origine, sa naissance, sa vie, *etc.* [With plates, including portraits.] pp. iv. 300. *Verdun*, 1888. 8°. 010661. m. 33.

—— Observations sur la manière dont M. Labande juge l'abbé Cloüet . . . Réponse à quelques notes de l'Étude sur l'organisation municipale de la ville de Verdun [by L. H. Labande], et à une lettre adressée à M. le rédacteur du Courrier de Verdun, 11 septembre 1891. pp. 71. *Verdun*, 1891. 8°. 11826. i. 42. (2.)

BUVINGTON (G. F. J.) Chanticleer's Wireless Talks on Poultry, *etc.* pp. 113. *Sir I. Pitman & Sons: London*, [1926.] 8°. 07295. eee. 30.

BUVRY (Jacob du) *See* Du Buvry.

BUVRY (L.) *See* Berlin.—*Acclimatisations-Verein.* Zeitschrift für Acclimatisation, *etc.* (Neue Folge. Herausgegeben von Dr. L. Buvry.) 1858, *etc.* 8°. Ac. 3568.

—— Algerien und seine Zukunft unter französischer Herrschaft, *etc.* pp. xx. 266. *Berlin*, 1855. 8°. 10096. d. 10.

—— Anbauversuche mit ausländischen Nutzpflanzen in Deutschland angestellt auf Veranlassung des Akklimatisations-Vereins in Berlin. Herausgegeben von . . . Dr. L. Buvry. pp. viii. 131. 1868. 8°. *See* Berlin.—*Acclimatisations-Verein.* 1145. h. 18.

BUWALDA (H. S.)

—— *See* Sipma (P.) Lyts Frysk wirdboek, *etc.* (dl. 2. Nederlânsk-Frysk. Gearstallers: H. S. Buwalda, *etc.*) 1944, *etc.* 8°. 12974. h. 2.

BUWINKHAUSEN DE WALMEROD (Nicolaus) Oratio . . . pro Germania. *See* Frederick Achilles, *Prince of Wurtemberg.* F. A. D. W. Consultationis de principatu inter provincias Europæ, editio secunda, *etc.* 1620. 4°. C. 79. b. 16.

—— [Another edition.] *See* Frederick Achilles, *Prince of Wurtemberg.* F. A. D. W. Consultatio de principatu inter provincias Europæ, *etc.* 1626. 8°. 712. e. 1.

—— [Another edition.] *See* Frederick Achilles, *Prince of Wurtemberg.* F. A. D. W. Consultatio de principatu inter provincias Europæ, *etc.* 1635. 8°. 712. e. 2.

BUX (Alla) *See* Allāh-Bakhsh.

BUX (Kuda) *See* Khudā Bakhsh, calling himself K. B. Duke.

BUXADÉ (José) España en Crisis. La bullanga misteriosa de 1917. Historial crítico de ella, *etc.* pp. 338. *Barcelona*, [1918.] 8°. 8042. cc. 35.

BUXADERAS (E.) *See* Oller (N.) Cuentos y Novelas. Traducción castellana de E. B. (E. Buxaderas), *etc.* 1896. 8°. 12489. aa. 25.

BUXALANCE. Por la villa de Buxalance. Con la ciudad de Cordoua, en respuesta á su informacion. [A pleading. By — Marquez de Cisneros.] ff. 10. [1620?] fol. 1322. l. 6. (23.)

BUXAREO ORIBE (Félix) *See* Buenos Ayres, *City of.* —*Biblioteca Nacional.* Catálogo de la Donación Félix Buxareo Oribe. [With a portrait.] 1935. 8°. 11911. a. 75.

BUXBAUM (Alexander Julius) Quibus rebus catarrhı et rheumatismus inter se conveniant, quibus differan Dissertatio inauguralis pathologica, *etc.* pp. 32. *Berolini*, [1835.] 8°. 7385.*a. (6

BUXBAUM (Andreas) Catechesis medica per modu dialogi proposita, *etc.* *Impensis C. Forberger. Martisburgi*, 1695. 12°. 544. d. 1

—— Disputatio inauguralis medica de ventriculi inflation *etc.* *Praes.* J. Vesti. *J. G. Hertzl: Erfurt* [1686.] 4°. T. 594. (10

—— [Another copy.] 1185. b. 17. (28
The titlepage is mutilated.

—— Dissertationem de variolis, hactenus in patria grassati quam . . . publicæ Philiatrorum censuræ subjicit Buxbaum. *Praes.* Johannes Bohn. pp. 28. *Typ E. Fiebig: Lipsiæ*, [1679.] 4°. 1179. g. 12. (

—— [Another copy.] T. 596. (1

BUXBAUM (Anselmus Guthmann) Theses medicæ febre miliari puerperarum, *etc.* pp. 24. *Giess* 1729. 4°. T. 533. (45

BUXBAUM (Béni) *See* Winternitz (W.) Fortschrit der Hydrotherapie. Festschrift zum vierzigjährig Doctorjubiläum des Prof. Dr. W. Winternitz . . . herau gegeben von Dr. A. Strasser und Dr. B. Buxbaum. 1897. 8°. 7462. ee. 4

—— Lehrbuch der Hydrotherapie, *etc.* pp. xi. 381. *Leipzig*, 1900. 8°. 7461. i. 2

—— Special Hydrotherapy. *See* Winternitz (W.) Hydro therapy, Thermotherapy, Heliotherapy, and Phototherapy *etc.* 1902. 8°. [Cohen (*S. S.*) *A System of Physiolog Therapeutics, etc.* vol. 9.] 7462. i. 1

BUXBAUM (Edith)

—— Your Child makes Sense. A guidebook for parents . . With a contribution by Florence L. Swanson, *etc.* pp. xv. 204. *George Allen & Unwin: London*, 1951. 8 07581. ee. 5

BUXBAUM (Eduard) and **LEHR** (Hans)

—— 250 Rechenaufgaben zum Vierjahresplan. pp. 40. *Wien*, 1939. 8°. 8218. g. 2

BUXBAUM (Emil) Carl Philipp Freiherr v. Diez, K bayr. charakt. General der Kavallerie, 1769–1850. [Wi a portrait.] pp. viii. 80. *Berlin*, 1893. 8°. 10707. dd. 4

—— "Die Chevaulegers." Zeichnung von H. Goetze. Te von E. Buxbaum. *Berlin*, [1887.] fol. [*Das deutsc Heer in Einzeldarstellungen.* Lfg. 4.] 1857. b. 2

—— Friedrich Wilhelm Freiherr von Seydlitz, Königlic Preussischer General der Kavallerie. 1721–1773 . . Neue Auflage. [With a portrait and maps.] pp. 155. xxvi. *Rathenow*, 1890. 8°. 010707. h. 2

—— [Friedrich Wilhelm Freiherr von Seydlitz.] Seydl von . . . 4. Auflage, *etc.* (Vermehrt durch Beiträge d Freiherrn Rudolph von Seydlitz-Kurzbach.) [With plate including portraits.] pp. xi. 216. *Leipzig*, 1907. 4°. M.L. bb. 4

—— Thatenbuch der deutschen Reiterei, *etc.* pp. viii. 25 *Berlin & Leipzig*, 1900. 8°. M.L. m. 3

BUXBAUM (Franz)

—— Die Phylogenie der nordamerikanischen Echinocactee Trib. Euechinocactineae F. Buxb, *etc.* *In:* Österreichisc Botanische Zeitschrift. Bd. 98. pp. 44–104. 1951. 8 P.P. 213

BUXBAUM (GUTMANNUS) Disputatio medica inauguralis de peste, *etc.* *A. Elzevier: Lugduni Batavorum,* 1697. 4°. **1185. h. 3. (6.)**

BUXBAUM (JOANNES CHRISTIANUS) Jo. Christiani Buxbaums Enumeratio plantarum accuratior in agro Hallensi locisque vicinis crescentium una cum earum characteribus et viribus qua variæ nunquam antea descriptæ exhibentur. Cum præfatione Friderici Hoffmanni . . . de methodo compendiosa plantarum vires et virtutes in medendo indagandi. [With plates.] pp. 342. *Halæ Magdeb.,* 1721. 8°. **988. c. 15.**

—— [Another copy.] **968. d. 8.**

—— [Another copy.] **968. d. 7.**
Imperfect; wanting the frontispiece.

—— Plantarum minus cognitarum centuria I.(–V.) complectens plantas circa Byzantium & in Oriente observatas. 5 pt. MS. NOTES. *Petropoli,* 1728–40. 4°. **448. g. 5, 6.**

—— [Another copy.] **35. e. 11.**

—— [Another copy of centuria IV.] **788. i. 37.**

—— *See* GRISEBACH (A. H. R.) Spicilegium florae rumelicae et bithynicae . . . Accedunt species quas . . . plene descriptas reliquerunt Buxbaum [in his "Plantarum minus cognitarum centuria I.(–V.)"], Forskål, *etc.* 1843, *etc.* 8°. **1253. d. 24.**

BUXBAUM (LIBMANNUS) Disputatio medica inauguralis de hydrope. *A. Elzevier: Lugduni Batavorum,* 1697. 4°. **1185. h. 3. (5.)**

BUXBAUM (PHILIPP) In Feldgrau. Heldentaten hessischer Krieger aus Deutschlands grösster Zeit, *etc.* pp. 183. *Giessen,* [1917.] 8°. **9083. aa. 40.**

—— Der Kleegrasbau, nach den im östlichen Odenwalde gemachten Erfahrungen für den praktischen Landwirth bearbeitet, *etc.* pp. 89. *Darmstadt,* 1875. 8°. **7077. b. 11.**

—— Der Moosbauer. Roman aus dem Odenwälder Volksleben. pp. 178. *Giessen,* [1906.] 8°. **012554. a. 20.**

—— Von Jägern und Wildschützen. Erzählungen aus dem Odenwälder Volksleben.
Bd. 1. Die Heckenrose. pp. 128.
Giessen, [1907.] 8°. **012554. a. 21.**
Imperfect; wanting Bd. 2.

BUXBAUM (RICHARD)

—— Die Anlagewerte in der Bilanz bei schwankender Währung. pp. 141. *Frankfurt am Main,* 1922. 8°. **8207. t. 30.**

BUXBAUMERL (JODOCUS) *See* TRAUGOTT (Johann) *pseud.* Nach belieben Kraut und Rüben! Dichtungen für Kinder . . . Mit Bildern von J. Buxbaumerl, *etc.* [1851.] 12°. **11527. b. 22.**

BUXDORF (DIETRICH VON) *Bishop of Naumburg. See* BOCKSDORF (Theodericus von)

BUXDORFIUS (JOANNES) *See* BUXTORFIUS.

BUXEDA DE LEYVA ( ) Historia del reyno de Iapon y descripcion de aquella tierra, y de algunas costumbres, cerimonias, y regimiento de aquel reyno: con la relacion de la venida de los embaxadores del Iapon a Roma, para dar la obediencia al Summo Pontifice . . . [Re]copilada por el Doctor Buxeda de Leyua. ff. 179 [176]. *Impressa en casa de P. Puig, acosta de A. Hernandez: Çaragoça,* 1591. 8°. **1434. a. 17.**
The titlepage is mutilated.

—— [Another copy.] **G. 6689.**

BUXERIUS (CLAUDIUS) *See* BOISSIÈRE (Claude de)

BUXERIUS (PETRUS) *See* BOISSERIUS.

BUXHALL.

—— The Parish Registers (from 1558 to 1700). *See* COPINGER (Walter A.) History of the Parish of Buxhall, *etc.* 1902. 4°. **10358. h. 20.**

BUXHOEVEDEN (SOPHIE) *Baroness.* Before the Storm, *etc.* [Reminiscences.] pp. xiv. 331. *Macmillan & Co.: London,* 1938. 8°. **10858. b. 16.**

—— A Cavalier in Muscovy. [A biography of General Patrick Gordon. With plates, including portraits.] pp. xiv. 325. *Macmillan & Co.: London,* 1932. 8°. **010815. i. 35.**

—— Left Behind. Fourteen months in Siberia during the Revolution, December 1917—February 1919 . . . With illustrations. pp. xii. 182. *Longmans & Co.: London,* 1929. 8°. **010290. f. 13.**

—— The Life & Tragedy of Alexandra Feodorovna, Empress of Russia. A biography, *etc.* [With plates, including portraits.] pp. xxii. 360. *Longmans & Co.: London,* 1928. 8°. **010795. dd. 44.**

BUXHOEWDEN (ALBERT VON) *Bishop of Livonia. See* ALBERTUS, *Bishop of Livonia.*

BUXHOEWDEN (PETER WILHELM VON) *Baron.* Beiträge zur Geschichte der Provinz Oesell . . . Mit einem illuminirten Wappen von Oesell. pp. xii. 293. *Riga & Leipzig,* 1838. 8°. **10260. cc. 24.**

BUXHÖWDEN ( ) [For the German surname of this form:] *See* BUXHOEWDEN.

BUXIIS (JOANNES ANTONIUS DE) successively *Bishop of Accia* and *of Aleria. See* ANDREAS (Joannes)

BUXON (HARVEY) Our Remarkable Fledger. [A novel.] pp. viii. 418. *Digby, Long & Co.: London,* 1900. 8°. **012641. aaa. 6.**

BUXTEHUDE (DIETRICH) *See* FERNSTRÖM (J.) Dietrich orgemester. En bok om Buxtehude. 1937. 8°. **07899. df. 63.**

—— *See* GRUSNICK (B.) Dietrich Buxtehude. Leben und Werke. [1937.] 8°. **7899.1.41.**

—— *See* HEDAR (J.) Dietrich Buxtehudes Orgelwerke. Zur Geschichte des norddeutschen Orgelstils. [With musical quotations and facsimiles.] 1951. 8°. **7901. c. 12.**

—— *See* PIRRO (A.) Dietrich Buxtehude. 1913. 8°. **7899. t. 16.**

—— *See* STAHL (Wilhelm) *Domorganist in Lübeck.* Dietrich Buxtehude, *etc.* [1937.] 8°. Hirsch **2836.**

—— *See* STAHL (W.) *Domorganist in Lübeck.* Franz Tunder und Dietrich Buxtehude. 1920. 8°. [*Zeitschrift des Vereins für Lübeckische Geschichte und Altertumskunde.* Bd. 20.] Ac. **7078.**

BUXTON. Buxton and Matlock, and other poems. pp. 10. [1877?] 4°. **11650. i. 2.**

—— Buxton Illustrated. A pictorial and descriptive souvenir, *etc.* (Fourth edition.) *Bournemouth,* 1905. *obl.* 8°. [*Mate's Illustrated Guides.*] **10369. p. 9.**

—— The Cabinet Album of Buxton Views. *E. White: Buxton; printed in Germany,* [1896.] 8°. **10352. bbb. 53.**

BUXTON.

—— A Description of Buxton, and the adjacent country; or the new guide, *etc.* pp. 63. *J. Harrop: Manchester,* 1790. 8°. **7462.** aaa. **33.** (**2.**)

—— [Another copy.] **291.** b. **48.**

—— [Another edition.] pp. 84. *J. Harrop: Manchester,* 1792. 8°. **10351.** aaa. **37.**

—— A Month at Buxton; or a Description of the town and neighbourhood . . . To which is added, a concise description of Matlock . . . Fourteenth edition, corrected. pp. 46. *John Goodwin: Bakewell,* [1829?] 12°. **10360.** bb. **22.**

—— Pocket Guide to Buxton. A guide to Buxton and its environs, *etc.* pp. 30. *John Heywood: Manchester,* [1869.] 16°. **10358.** a. **38.** (**2.**)
One of "John Heywood's Pocket Guides."

—— The Residential Attractions of Buxton . . . and District. *Hampson Bros.: Buxton,* [1940.] 8°. **8287.** h. **9.**

—— Souvenir of Buxton. (22 photographic views.) [*Boots: Nottingham,* 1904.] *obl.* 4°. **10352.** f. **46.**

—— The Stranger's Pocket Companion and Guide to Buxton and neighbourhood. pp. 23. *J. C. Bates: Buxton,* [1873?] 8°. **10369.** a. **61.**

—— [Another edition.] pp. 32. *C. F. Wardley: Buxton,* 1886. 16°. **10358.** de. **19.** (**1.**)

—— To Buxton. A poem in four cantos, by J. C. W., *etc.* 1886. 12°. *See* W., J. C. **11602.** e. **29.** (**10.**)

—— *Bureau of Information.* Buxton, "the Mountain Spa" . . . Written and compiled by J. M. Scott. pp. 80. *E. J. Burrow & Co.: Cheltenham,* [1916.] 8°. **10360.** s. **9.**

—— [Another edition.] pp. 36. *Buxton,* [1919.] 8°. **010352.** ff. **15.**

Buxton Advertising Committee.

—— The "Borough" Guide to Buxton, the Mountain Spa. (Issued under the auspices of the Buxton Advertising Committee.) pp. 48. *E. J. Burrow & Co.: Cheltenham,* [1912?] 8°. **10354.** a. **164.**

—— *Buxton Bath Charity.* [For the joint reports of the Devonshire Hospital and Buxton Bath Charity after the foundation of the Devonshire Hospital in 1859:] *See* infra: *Devonshire Hospital.*

—— *Buxton Literary Society.* Buxton Literary Society. (The Buxton Literary Society Magazine.) no. 1–4. [*Buxton,*] 1920–24. 4°. P.P. **6083.** ik.
No. 1 *is lithographed.*

—— *Devonshire Hospital.* Devonshire Hospital and Buxton Bath Charity . . . Annual Report for the year 1867 (1895). 2 pt. *Buxton,* 1868, 96. 8°. **7686.** b. **65.**

Free Public Library and Museum.

—— Third [*etc.*] Annual Report. Buxton, *etc.* *Buxton,* [1892– .] 8° **A.R.233.**
Imperfect; wanting the 4*th to* 20*th,* 29*th and* 31*st Reports.*

—— Museum Guide, *etc.* pp. 19. *Buxton,* [1930?] 8°. **07804.** bbb. **3.**

—— *Redfern's Museum.* Catalogue of the Museum. *See* POOLE'S CAVERN. A Description of Poole's Cavern, Buxton, *etc.* 1875. 8°. **7708.** aa. **44.** (**3.**)

BUXTON BATH CHARITY. *See* BUXTON.

BUXTON DIAMONDS. The Buxton Diamonds; o Grateful Ellen. pp. 107. *W. Darton & Son: Londo* [1820?] 12°. **12803.** aa. **1**

BUXTON GUIDE. The New Buxton Guide, *etc.* (A ne edition, enlarged.) pp. 81. *James Swinnerto Macclesfield,* 1823. 12°. **10347.** aa. **8.** (

—— [Another edition.] pp. 60. *Printed for the Autho Leek,* 1837. 12°. **10352.** f.

BUXTON, *Family of.* *See* BEAUMONT (George F.) Pa cocke's House, Coggeshall. With some notes on th families of Paycocke and Buxton, *etc.* [1905.] 4°. **9915.** de.

—— *See* BUXTON (Charles L.) The Buxtons of Coggeshall. 1910. 4°. **9904.** v. **1**

—— *See* SQUIBB (George D.) Belfield and the Buxtons. 1954. 8°. **9918.** bbb. **3**

BUXTON ( ) *Bookseller.* A Catalogue of the Stoc in trade of Mr. Buxton, Bookseller, of Blackman Stree Southwark, which will be sold by auction . . . Octob the 28th, 1816, and five following days, *etc.* pp. 41. *W. Smith & Co.: London,* 1816. 8°. **130.** k. **9.** (**6**

BUXTON ( ) *of Albany?* A Lecture on Analog Out-Analogized, being the doctrine of ontology extende proving by incontestable analogies, the earth to be e dowed with animality, *etc.* pp. 29. *Printed for the Autho Albany,* 1841. 8°. **8706.** aaa. **1**

BUXTON (ALBERT SORBY) A Short Account of the Brun Family, and Samuel Brunts' Charity. [With illustr tions.] pp. 35. *"Mansfield Reporter" Co.: Mansfiel* 1911. 4°. **9914.** r.

BUXTON (ALFRED BARCLAY) *See* BIBLE.—*Genesis.* [*Kar mojong.*] Genesis, *etc.* [Translated by W. E. Owen an A. B. Buxton.] 1933. 8°. **3068.** aa. **1**

—— *See* BIBLE.—*Matthew.* [*Ngala.—Uele dialect.*] Matay [Translated by A. B. Buxton and J. A. Barney.] 1927. 8°. **03068.** ee. **10**

—— *See* BIBLE.—*Mark.* [*Ngala.—Uele dialect.*] Samb Malamu na Mako. [Translated by A. B. Buxton.] 1916. 8°. **03068.** h. **2**

—— *See* GRUBB (Norman P.) Alfred Buxton of Abyssin and Congo, *etc.* [With portraits.] 1942. 8°. **20047.** aaa.

—— "Evangelise to a Finish to Bring Back the King. pp. 35. *London,* [1935.] 8°. [*Inter-Varsity Missionar Papers.* no. 1.] W.P. **11292/**

—— The First Seven Years of the Heart of Africa Missio (1913–1919.) [With plates and a map.] pp. 86. [1920.] 8°. *See* LONDON.—III. *Worldwide Evangelisatio Crusade.—Heart of Africa Mission.* **4763.** e. **3**

—— [Another edition.] The First Seven Years of the Hea of Africa Mission (1913–1919), and A Triplet of Year 1920–1922 . . . With "Nine Years Ago and Now," b Mrs. C. T. Studd. (3rd edition.) pp. 124. 1923. 8 *See* LONDON.—III. *Worldwide Evangelisation Crusade.— Heart of Africa Mission.* **4763.** aa. **6**

—— [Another edition.] The First Ten Years of the Heart o Africa Mission (1913–1922) . . . With "Nine Year Ago and Now," by Mrs. C. T. Studd. (4th edition. pp. 124. 1924. 8°. *See* LONDON.—III. *Worldwid Evangelisation Crusade.—Heart of Africa Mission.* **4763.** bb. **21**

BUXTON (ALFRED BARCLAY)

—— The Four Winds of Ethiopia, *etc.* [With plates.] pp. 83. *Durham & Sons: Blackburn*, [1935.] 8°. **10094. a. 35.**

—— Nala Missionary Methods. A description and scriptural explanation of them, *etc.* pp. 11. *Heart of Africa Mission: London*, [1920.] 4°. **4764. ff. 34.**

—— A Triplet of Years (1920–1922) . . . Sequel to "The First Seven Years," With "Nine Years Ago and Now," by Mrs. C. T. Studd. (Worldwide Evangelisation Crusade and Heart of Africa Mission.) pp. 37. *Graham & Heslip: Belfast*, [1923.] 8°. **4763. aa. 59.**

BUXTON (ALFRED SAINT CLAIR) Ophthalmic Hints, *etc.* pp. x. 51. *Whiting & Co.: London*, 1890. 8°. **7610. de. 38.**

BUXTON (ANDREW RICHARD) Andrew R. Buxton, the Rifle Brigade. A memoir [consisting chiefly of his letters from the front]. Edited by Edward S. Woods. [With plates, including portraits.] pp. ix. 294. *Robert Scott: London*, 1918. 8°. **010856. e. 27.**

BUXTON (ANTHONY)

—— Fisherman Naturalist. pp. 190. pl. 39. *Collins: London*, 1946. 8°. **7006. e. 35.**

—— Happy Year. The days of a fisherman-naturalist. [With plates.] pp. 191. *Collins: London*, 1950. 8°. **7008. de. 3.**

—— Sport in Peace and War. pp. viii. 119. *A. L. Humphreys: London*, 1920. 8°. **7912. ccc. 16.**

—— Sporting Interludes at Geneva. [With plates.] pp. 115. *Country Life: London*, 1932. 4°. **20016. d. 21.**

—— Travelling Naturalist. [With plates.] pp. 224. *Collins: London*, 1948. 8°. **7006. cc. 46.**

BUXTON (AUBREY)

—— The King in his Country. [An account of the game shooting activities of King George VI. With plates, including portraits.] pp. ix. 139. *Longmans, Green & Co.: London*, 1955. 8°. **010807. h. 37.**

BUXTON (BARCLAY FOWELL)

—— *See* BUXTON (Barclay G.) The Reward of Faith in the Life of Barclay Fowell Buxton, 1860–1946. [With portraits.] 1949. 8°. **4909. b. 14.**

—— The Baptism of the Holy Ghost: the essential preparation for all Christian work. A few words on Acts I & II. pp. 39. *S. W. Partridge & Co.: London*, [1891.] 8°. **4371. a. 3. (7.)**

—— The Book of Jonah. pp. 53. *Japan Evangelistic Band: London*, [1930.] 8°. **3186. de. 55.**

—— The Book of Ruth: its message for Christians to-day. pp. 62. *Japan Evangelistic Band: London*, [1929.] 8°. **03166. de. 48.**

—— Following hard after God. A letter. pp. 9. *Japan Evangelistic Band: London*, 1947. *obl.* 16°. **4398. a. 99.**

—— Heavenly Places. Four Bible readings on holiness. pp. 40. *Japan Evangelistic Band: London*, [1935.] 8°. **04478. e. 61.**

—— Life's Possibilities. Addresses. [Selected from "The Still Small Voice."] pp. 75. *Japan Evangelistic Band: London*, 1949. 8°. **4481. aaa. 11.**

BUXTON (BARCLAY FOWELL)

—— The Royal Anointing. pp. 22. *Japan Evangelistic Band: London*, [1936.] 12°. **03166. de. 57.**

BUXTON (BARCLAY GODFREY)

—— The Reward of Faith in the Life of Barclay Fowell Buxton, 1860–1946. [With portraits.] pp. 274. *Lutterworth Press: London*, 1949. 8°. **4909. b. 14.**

BUXTON (BERTHA H.) *See* also BEE, *Auntie*, *pseud.* [i.e. B. H. Buxton.]

—— *See* also BEE (B. H.) *pseud.* [i.e. B. H. Buxton.]

—— Fetterless, though Bound Together. 3 vol. *Tinsley Bros.: London*, 1879. 8°. **12639. k. 10.**

—— [Another edition.] pp. 381. *G. Routledge & Sons: London, New York*, 1880. 8°. **12619. aaaa. 15.**

—— From the Wings. A novel. 3 vol. *Tinsley Bros.: London*, 1880. 8°. **12640. aaa. 11.**

—— New edition. pp. viii. 341. *Tinsley Bros.: London*, 1885. 8°. **12624. l. 5.**

—— Great Grenfell Gardens. 3 vol. *Tinsley Bros.: London*, 1879. 8°. **12639. n. 5.**

—— [Another edition.] pp. 381. *G. Routledge & Sons: London, New York*, 1880. 8°. **12619. bbb. 28.**

—— Jennie of "The Prince's." A novel. [By B. H. Buxton.] 3 vol. 1876. 8°. *See* JENNIE. **12636. m. 3.**

—— [Another edition.] pp. 448. [1877.] 8°. *See* JENNIE. **12619. bbb. 9.**

—— Little Pops: a nursery romance . . . Second edition. pp. 148. *Newman & Co.: London*, 1881. 8°. **12808. d. 31.**

—— Many Loves. [Tales.] 3 vol. *Tinsley Bros.: London*, [1880.] 8°. **12640. n. 11.**

—— Nell—on and off the Stage. [A novel.] 3 vol. *Tinsley Bros.: London*, [1879.] 8°. **12640. e. 8.**

—— New edition. pp. viii. 341. *Tinsley Bros.: London*, 1884. 8°. **12622. k. 3.**

—— Sceptre and Ring. A novel. 3 vol. *Tinsley Bros.: London*, 1881. 8°. **12642. aaa. 5.**

—— Won! By the author of "Jennie, of 'The Prince's'" [i.e. B. H. Buxton.] 3 vol. 1877. 8°. *See* WON. **12625. k. 9.**

—— [Another edition]. pp. 384. 1878. 8°. *See* WON. **12619. aaaa. 4.**

BUXTON (BERTHA H.) and FENN (WILLIAM WILTHEW)

—— A Noble Name: a novel . . . With other stories by W. W. Fenn. 3 vol. *F. V. White & Co.: London*, 1883. 8°. **12643. k. 4.**

—— New and revised edition. pp. vi. 342. *John Hogg: London*, [1887.] 8°. **012633. g. 41.**

—— Oliver Gay. A rattling story of field, fright, and fight, *etc.* pp. 163. *Newman & Co.: London*, 1880. 8°. **12640. a. 7.**

BUXTON (BERTINE) My First Book of Prayers . . . Illustrated by Horace J. Knowles. *Athenæum Press: London*, 1932. 16°. **03456. de. 121.**

BUXTON (BERTRAM HENRY) *See* BEEBE (Silas P.) and BUXTON (B. H.) Outlines of Physiological Chemistry. 1904. 8°. **08909. ee. 37.**

BUXTON (Bessie Raymond)

—— Begonias and How to Grow Them. [With plates.] pp. x. 163. *Oxford University Press: New York*, 1946. 8º. **7034**. aaa. **10**.

—— History of the South Church, Peabody, *etc. In:* The Essex Institute Historical Collections. vol. 87. 1951. 8º. Ac. **1760/3**.

BUXTON (Charles) How to Stop Drunkenness. [An article reprinted from the North British Review. Edited by T. B. Smithies.] pp. v. 80. *S. W. Partridge: London*, [1864.] 8º. **8435**. aaa. **43**.

—— [Another edition.] pp. v. 80. *S. W. Partridge & Co.: London*, [1868.] 8º. **8435**. aaa. **44**.

—— [Another edition.] pp. 80. *Church of England Temperance Society: London*, [1901.] 8º. **8436**. g. **12**.

—— Opinions of Charles Buxton . . . Brewer, on the Sale and Use of Strong Drink. From an article in the "North British Review," *etc.* [An abridgment of "How to Stop Drunkenness."] (Second edition.) pp. 15. [*Job Caudwell: London*, 1860?] 16º. **8435**. aa. **29**.

—— (Third edition.) pp. 15. [*Job Caudwell: London*, 1860?] 16º. **8435**. aa. **30**.

—— (Fourth edition.) pp. 15. [*Job Caudwell: London*, 1865?] 16º. **8435**. aa. **31**.

—— (Sixth edition.) pp. 15. [*Heywood & Co.: London*, 1870.] 8º. **8435**. aa. **32**.

—— The Ideas of the Day on Policy. pp. vi. 111. *John Murray: London*, 1866. 8º. **8006**. ee. **10**.

—— Third edition. pp. vi. 154. *John Murray: London*, 1868. 8º. **8006**. ee. **11**.

—— Italy, *etc. See* London.—iii. *Young Men's Christian Association.* Lectures delivered before the . . . Association . . . from November 1851, to February 1852. 1852. 8º. **4461**. d. **15**.

—— Limitations to Severity in War. [1855.] *See* Cambridge Essays. Cambridge Essays, *etc.* [1855, *etc.*] 8º. P.P. **6119**. cc.

—— Memoirs of Sir Thomas Fowell Buxton, Baronet. With selections from his correspondence. Edited by his son, C. Buxton. [With a portrait.] pp. xvi. 600. *John Murray: London*, 1848. 8º. **1452**. f. **1**.

—— Second edition. pp. xvi. 614. *John Murray: London*, 1849. 8º. **1452**. f. **2**.

—— Third edition. pp. xi. 508. *John Murray: London*, 1849. 16º. **1155**. b. **18**.

—— [Another edition.] With an inquiry into the results of emancipation. New edition. [With a portrait.] pp. xxvi. 260. *John Murray: London*, 1860. 12º. **1155**. c. **5**.

—— [A reissue.] *London*, 1872. 12º. **10817**. aaa. **40**.

—— [Another edition.] (With an introduction by Earl Buxton.) pp. xlvii. 272. *J. M. Dent & Sons: London & Toronto*, [1925.] 8º. [*Everyman's Library*.] **12206.p.1/576.**

—— Sir Thomas Fowell Buxton, Bart. Ein Bild des englischen Lebens . . . Entworfen nach "Memoirs of Sir Th. Fowell Buxton, Bart." . . . von A. v. Treskow. Volks-Ausgabe. pp. xii. 297. *Berlin*, 1854. 8º. **10825**. b. **41**.

BUXTON (Charles)

—— Das Leben des Sir Thomas Fowell Buxton . . . deutsch bearbeitet von Dr. Bernhard Brandis. pp. viii. 318. *Hamburg*, 1855. 12º. [*Lebensbilder aus der Geschichte der inneren Mission.* no. 8.] **4804**. aaa. **35**.

—— Notes of Thought . . . Preceded by a biographical sketch, by Rev. J. Llewelyn Davies. [With a portrait.] pp. 62. 294. *John Murray: London*, 1873. 8º. **8407**. df. **17**.

—— Second edition. pp. 52. 209. *John Murray: London*, 1883. 8º. **8464**. bb. **3**.

—— Opinions of Charles Buxton . . . Brewer, on the Sale and Use of Strong Drink. *See* supra: How to Stop Drunkenness.

—— The Questions raised by the Mutiny. 1857. *See* Cambridge Essays. Cambridge Essays. [1855, *etc.*] 8º. P.P. **6119**. cc.

—— Self-Government for London. The leading ideas on which a constitution for London should be based. A letter to the Right Hon. H. A. Bruce, *etc.* pp. 24. *Metropolitan Municipal Association: London*, 1869. 8º. **1303**. d. **18**.

—— Sir Thomas More. A lecture. *See* Gurney (John H.) Evening Recreations, *etc.* 1856. 8º. **9005**. b. **19**.

—— Slavery and Freedom in the British West Indies. pp. 92. *Longman & Co.: London*, 1860. 8º. **8156**. a. **17**.

—— Speech . . . on the Treatment of the Rebels in India. pp. 12. *J. E. Taylor: London*, 1858. 8º. **08023**. bb. **4**. (**1**.)

—— A Survey of the System of National Education in Ireland. pp. 33. *John Murray: London*, 1853. 8º. **8307**. g. **5**. (**14**.)

—— A Survey of the System of National Education in Ireland . . . Second edition. pp. 33. *John Murray: London*, 1853. 8º. **8029**. dd. **14**. (**6**.)

—— The Theory of the Construction of Birds, with hints for the management of museums. pp. 72. *A. & G. A. Spottiswoode: London*, 1854. 8º. **7207**. a. **23**. *Not published.*

BUXTON (Charles Louis) *See* Tristram (Henry B.) *the Younger.* The Land of Moab . . . With . . . illustrations by C. L. Buxton and R. C. Johnson. 1873. 8º. **2356**. a. **16**.

—— The Buxtons of Coggeshall. [Edited by E. H. Pelham. With plates, including portraits.] pp. 107. *P. L. Warner: London*, 1910. 4º. **9904**. v. **11**.

BUXTON (Charles Roden) *See* Buxton (Noel E.) afterwards Noel-Buxton (N. E.) *Baron Noel-Buxton*, and Buxton (C. R.) The War and the Balkans. 1915. 8º. **08027**. a. **56**.

—— *See* De Bunsen (Victoria) Charles Roden Buxton. A memoir. [With portraits.] 1948. 8º. **10862**. aa. **5**.

—— *See* Periodical Publications.—*London.* The Independent Review. (The Albany Review. Editor, C. R. Buxton.) 1907, *etc.* 8º. P.P. **5939**. bi.

—— The ABC Home Rule Handbook. Edited by C. R. Buxton. pp. 276. 1912. 8º. *See* London.—iii. *Home Rule Council.* **8146**. f. **3**.

—— The Alternative to War. A programme for statesmen. pp. 176. *G. Allen & Unwin: London*, 1936. 8º. **08008**. a. **32**.

BUXTON (Charles Roden)

—— The Case for an Early Peace. pp. 7. *Friends' Peace Committee: London*, [1940.] 8°. **08028**. c. **80**.

—— Companies and Conscience: Justice and Dividends. pp. 4. *S.P.C.K.: London*, 1908. 8°. [*Pan-Anglican Papers*. S.A. 4a.] **4108**. cc. **35**.

—— Electioneering Up-to-Date. With some suggestions for amending the Corrupt Practices Act . . . With three additional chapters on the case of Thanet, by J. C. Haig. pp. 90. *Francis Griffiths: London*, 1906. 8°. **8139**. de. **41**.

—— In a Russian Village. pp. 96. *Labour Publishing Co.: London*, 1922. 8°. **10290**. aaa. **55**.

—— Inter-Continental Peace. *See* Woolf (Leonard S.) The Intelligent Man's Way to Prevent War, *etc.* 1933. 8°. **08425**. e. **65**.

—— Memorandum on Territorial Claims and Self-Determination. pp. 7. *London*, 1919. 8°. [*Union of Democratic Control. Pamphlet.* no. 29a.] **08008**. bb. **51/29**a.

—— Peace this Winter: a reply to Mr. Lloyd George. *National Labour Press: London, Manchester*, [1916.] 8°. **8138**. h. **1**. (**160**.)

—— A Politician Plays Truant. Essays on English literature. pp. 203. *Christophers: London*, 1929. 8°. **11824**. ppp. **9**.

—— A Practical, Permanent, and Honourable Settlement of the War. Lectures intended to be delivered at Devonshire House . . . on Jan. 3rd, 10th, and 17th, 1916. pp. 21. *National Labour Press: London*, [1916.] 8°. **08027**. aaa. **56**.

—— Prophets of Heaven & Hell. Virgil, Dante, Milton, Goethe. An introductory essay. [On the Aeneid, the Divine Comedy, Paradise Lost and Faust.] pp. xv. 115. *University Press: Cambridge*, 1945. 8°. **11866**. a. **13**.

—— The Race Problem in Africa, *etc.* pp. 59. *L. & V. Woolf: London*, 1931. 8°. [*Merttens Lecture.* 1931.] W.P. **8328/4**.

—— The Secret Agreements (concluded during the war between the Allied Governments). With a preface . . . and nine maps. pp. 19. *National Labour Press: Manchester & London*, [1918.] 8°. **08028**. dd. **20**.

—— Towards a Lasting Settlement . . . Edited by C. R. Buxton. pp. 216. *G. Allen & Unwin: London*, 1915. 8°. **8425**. p. **28**.

—— Turkey in Revolution . . . With 33 illustrations and a map. pp. 285. *T. Fisher Unwin: London, Leipzig*, 1909. 8°. **9136**. ff. **28**.

—— Verbatim Report of a Debate held at Lindsey Hall, Kensington . . . January 24th, 1917 . . . "That a peace is now obtainable which will convince Germany that aggression does not pay." Pro: Mr. C. R. Buxton. Con.: Mr. G. G. Coulton, *etc.* pp. 30. [1917.] 8°. *See* London.—iii. *Union of Democratic Control.—Hammersmith and Chiswick Branch.* **08028**. dd. **31**.

BUXTON (Charles Roden) and **BUXTON** (Dorothy Frances)

—— The World after the War. pp. 155. *G. Allen & Unwin: London*, 1920. 8°. **08028**. e. **33**.

BUXTON (Charles Sydney)

—— *See* Furniss (Henry S.) *Baron Sanderson.* Charles Sydney Buxton. A memoir, *etc.* [With portraits.] 1914. 8°. **10862**. d. **3**.

BUXTON (Clare Emily) *See* Buxton (Edward N.) On Either Side of the Red Sea . . . By H. M. B., C. E. B. [i.e. C. E. Buxton], *etc.* 1895. 8°. **10076**. ee. **11**.

BUXTON (Constance May) Side Lights upon Bible History . . . With illustrations. pp. viii. 299. *Macmillan & Co.: London*, 1892. 8°. **3149**. d. **6**.

BUXTON (Cyril Raymond)

—— *See* Eaton (Richard S.) German Technical Reader . . . By R. S. Eaton . . . H. S. Jackson . . . C. R. Buxton. 1950. 8°. **12965**. i. **1**.

BUXTON (David) The Past and Present Condition of the Education of the Deaf. *See* Praed (Rosa C. M.) For Their Sakes, *etc.* 1884. 8°. **12357**. i. **28**.

—— The Queen's English: a paper read before the Liverpool Philomathic Society during its thirty-third session, *etc.* pp. 45. *Cleaver: London; Adam Holden & C. W. Townshend: Liverpool*, 1858. 8°. **012987**. bb. **14**.

BUXTON (David Roden) Russian Mediaeval Architecture. With an account of the Transcaucasian styles and their influence in the West. pp. xi. 112. pl. 108. *University Press: Cambridge*, 1934. 4°. **7820**. p. **6**.

—— Travels in Ethiopia. [With plates.] pp. 200. *Lindsay Drummond: London*, 1949. 8°. **10095**. ppp. **11**.

BUXTON (Dorothy Frances)

—— *See* Angell (Norman) *pseud.*, and Buxton (D. F.) You and the Refugee, *etc.* 1939. 8°. **12208**. a. **2/29**.

—— *See* Buxton (Charles R.) and Buxton (D. F.) The World after the War. 1920. 8°. **08028**. e. **33**.

—— *See* Jebb (Eglantyne) Save the Child! A posthumous essay . . . Edited by D. F. Buxton, *etc.* 1929. 8°. **08311**. a. **18**.

—— *See* Prison. I was in Prison. Letters from German pastors. Edited [and translated] by D. F. Buxton, *etc.* 1938. 8°. **3913**. de. **18**.

—— The Challenge of Bolshevism. A new social ideal. pp. 95. *G. Allen & Unwin: London*, 1928. 8°. **08286**. d. **15**.

—— The Economics of the Refugee Problem, *etc.* pp. 46. *Focus Publishing Co.: London*, [1939.] 8°. **8287**. df. **38**.

—— The Religious Crisis in Germany. pp. 11. *Kulturkampf Association: London*, [1938.] 16°. **3910**. de. **10**.

BUXTON (Dorothy Frances) and **FULLER** (Edward) *Editor of "The World's Children."*

—— The White Flame. The story of the Save the Children Fund, *etc.* pp. xiii. 91. *Longmans & Co.: London*, 1931. 8°. **8277**. v. **27**.

BUXTON (Dudley Wilmot) *See* Waring (Edward J.) A Manual of Practical Therapeutics . . . Edited by D. W. Buxton, *etc.* 1886. 8°. **7460**. aa. **2**.

—— Anæsthetics, their Uses and Administration. pp. xii. 164. *London*, 1888. 8°. [*Lewis's Practical Series.*] **07481**. a. **6**.

—— Second edition. pp. xiv. 222. *London*, 1892. 8°. [*Lewis's Practical Series.*] **07481**. a. **16**.

—— Third edition. pp. xvi. 320. *London*, 1900. 8°. [*Lewis's Practical Series.*] **07481**. a. **33**.

—— Fourth edition. pp. viii. 415. *London*, 1907. 8°. [*Lewis's Practical Series.*] **07481**. a. **43**.

BUXTON (DUDLEY WILMOT)

—— Fifth edition. pp. xiv. 477. pl. VIII. *London*, 1914. 8°. [*Lewis's Practical Series.*] **07481**. aa. **17**.

—— Sixth edition. pp. xiv. 548. *London*, 1920. 8°. [*Lewis's Practical Series.*] **07481**. aa. **26**.

BUXTON (EDITH) Chocolate & Cream. [Tales of African missions.] pp. 31. *Graham & Heslip: Belfast*, [1926.] 8°. **4763**. bb. **37**.

BUXTON (EDWARD JOHN MAWBY)

—— The Redstart, *etc.* [With plates.] pp. xii. 180. *Collins: London*, 1950. 8°. [*New Naturalist Monograph.*] W.P. **12018/3**.

—— Sir Philip Sidney and the English Renaissance. [With plates, including a portrait.] pp. xi. 283. *Macmillan & Co.: London*, 1954. 8°. **10864**. b. **21**.

BUXTON (EDWARD JOHN MAWBY) and **LOCKLEY** (RONALD MATHIAS)

—— Island of Skomer. A preliminary survey of the natural history of Skomer Island, Pembrokeshire, undertaken for the West Wales Field Society and edited by John Buxton and R. M. Lockley. [With plates.] pp. 164. 1950. 8°. *See* WALES.—*West Wales Field Society.* **7210**. b. **36**.

BUXTON (EDWARD NORTH) The ABC of Free Trade. An address, *etc.* pp. 31. 1882. 8°. *See* LONDON.—III. *Cobden Club.* **8228**. bb. **33**. (3.)

—— Revised edition. pp. 32. [1888.] 8°. *See* LONDON.—III. *Cobden Club.* **8228**. bb. **34**. (4.)

—— Revised edition. pp. 43. *Cassell & Co.: London*, 1903. 8°. **8229**. aaa. **51**. (8.)

—— Epping Forest. [With plates and maps.] pp. xii. 147. *Edward Stanford: London*, 1884. 8°. **10368**. dd. **31**.

—— (Second edition.) pp. xii. 139. *Edward Stanford: London*, 1885. 8°. **10350**. aa. **32**.

—— Third edition. pp. xii. 137. *Edward Stanford: London*, 1890. 8°. **10360**. bb. **60**.

—— Fourth edition revised, with new chapters, *etc.* pp. xii. 175. *Edward Stanford: London*, 1897. 8°. **10349**. d. 29.

—— Fifth edition revised, *etc.* pp. xii. 175. *Edward Stanford: London*, 1898. 12°. **010358**. ee. 2.

—— Sixth edition revised, *etc.* pp. xii. 175. *Edward Stanford: London*, 1901. 12°. **10351**. f. **60**.

—— Seventh edition revised, *etc.* pp. xii. 177. *Edward Stanford: London*, 1905. 12°. **010358**. ee. **19**.

—— Eighth edition revised. pp. xii. 179. *Edward Stanford: London*, 1911. 8°. **010358**. ee. **58**.

—— Ninth edition revised, *etc.* pp. xii. 182. *Edward Stanford: London*, 1923. 8°. **2367**. a. **7**.

—— On Either Side of the Red Sea. With illustrations of the granite ranges of the Eastern Desert of Egypt, and of Sinai. By H. M. B. [i.e. Hannah Maud Buxton], C. E. B. [i.e. Clare Emily Buxton] and T. B. [i.e. Theresa Buxton.] With an introduction and footnotes by E. N. Buxton. [Edited by E. N. Buxton.] pp. viii. 163. *Edward Stanford: London*, 1895. 8°. **10076**. ee. **11**.

—— Short Stalks: or, Hunting camps north, south, east, and west . . . With numerous illustrations [and with maps]. 2 ser. *Edward Stanford: London*, 1892, 98. 8°. **7908**. dd. 24.

BUXTON (EDWARD NORTH)

—— Second edition [of ser. 1]. pp. xiii. 405. *Edward Stanford: London*, 1893. 8°. **7906**. dd. **1**

—— Two African Trips, with notes and suggestions on bi game preservation in Africa . . . With illustrations an map. pp. xiii. 209. *Edward Stanford: London*, 1902. 8 **10094**. e. **2**.

BUXTON (ETHELDREDA MARY WILMOT) *See* BIBLE.—*Old Testament.*—*Selections.* [*English.*] Stories from th Old Testament. By E. M. Wilmot-Buxton. 1909. 8°. **012203**. f. **31/**

—— *See* BIBLE.—*New Testament.*—*Selections.* [*English*] Stories from the New Testament. By E. M. Wilmo Buxton. 1910. 8°. **012203**. f. **31/**

—— *See* FIRDAUSĪ. The Book of Rustem. Retold . . . E. M. Wilmot-Buxton. 1907. 8°. **12411**. p. **1/1**

—— *See* HAWTHORNE (Nathaniel) A Wonder Book . . Edited by E. M. Wilmot-Buxton. [1920.] 8°. **012207.aaa.1/12**

—— *See* KINGSLEY (Charles) [*Miscellaneous Works.*] Th Heroes . . . Edited by E. M. Wilmot-Buxton. [1920.] 8°. **012207.aaa.1/139**

—— *See* MABINOGION. Kilhugh and Olwen, and oth stories from the "Mabinogion." Retold by E. M. Wilmo Buxton. [1913.] 8°. **12451.cc.2/8**

—— Adventures Perilous: being the story of . . . Fath John Gerard, S.J., *etc.* pp. xiii. 230. *Sands & Co London & Edinburgh*, 1919. 8°. **4902**. de. **3**

—— Alcuin. pp. 222. *Harding & More: London*, 1922. 8 [*Catholic Thought & Thinkers Series.*] W.P. **5723/**

—— The Ancient World. Outlines of ancient history for th middle forms of schools . . . With twelve maps an twenty illustrations. pp. xxvii. 244. *Methuen & Co London*, 1904. 8°. **9004**. g. **2**

—— Anselm . . . With nine illustrations by Morris Meredi Williams. pp. 192. *G. G. Harrap & Co.: Londo* 1915. 8°. [*Heroes of All Time.*] **010603**. c. **1/1**

—— A Book of English Martyrs . . . Illustrated by M. Mere dith Williams. pp. xv. 242. *Burns & Oates: Londo* 1915. 8°. **4804**. f. **2**

—— A Book of Noble Women . . . With sixteen illustra tions. pp. viii. 307. *Methuen & Co.: London*, 1907. 8 **10600**. r. **1**

—— Britain Long Ago. Stories from old English and Celt sources. Retold by E. M. Wilmot-Buxton. pp. xv. 24 *G. G. Harrap & Co.: London*, 1906. 8°. [*Told through t Ages.*] **12411**. p. **1/**

—— Old Celtic Tales. (Selected from "Britain Long Ago." pp. 128. *G. G. Harrap & Co.: London*, [1909.] 8°. [*A Time Tales.* no. 1.] **012804**. d. **1/**

—— [A reissue.] pp. 135. *London*, 1927. 8°. **12805**. e. **6** *With the addition of exercises.*

—— Tales of Early England. (Selected from "Britai Long Ago.") pp. 160. *G. G. Harrap & Co.: Londo* [1910.] 8°. [*All Time Tales.* no. 6.] **012804**. d. **1/**

—— [A reissue.] pp. 168. *London*, 1926. 8°. **12805**. e. **5** *With the addition of exercises.*

—— By Road and River: a descriptive geography of th British Isles . . . With twelve illustrations and twelv maps. pp. viii. 154. *Methuen & Co.: London*, 1909. 8° **10351**. ccc. **3**

BUXTON (ETHELDREDA MARY WILMOT)

—— A Catholic History of Great Britain, *etc.* pp. xiii. 336. *Burns, Oates & Co.: London,* 1921. 8°. **09504. de. 57.**

—— Easy Stories from English History. pp. viii. 128. *Methuen & Co.: London,* 1905. 8°. [*The Beginner's Books.*] **012203. f. 31/1.**

—— Sixth edition. pp. viii. 128. *Methuen & Co.: London,* 1911. 8°. [*The Beginner's Books.*] **012203. f. 31/7.**

—— English History Reader. Comprising an account of the leading events of each century from the Roman invasion to the present day. For the upper standards. pp. vii. 190. *Skeffington & Son: London,* 1903. 8°. **9502. c. 6.**

—— Faust and Marguerite. Retold by E. M. Wilmot-Buxton. Illustrated by Norman Little. pp. 95. *T. Nelson & Sons: London,* [1912.] 8°. [*World's Romances.*] **12451.cc.2/3.**

—— Founded upon a Rock. Stories for children from English church history. pp. viii. 134. *Skeffington & Son: London,* 1895. 8°. **4705. aaa. 36.**

—— Gildersleeves. pp. 349. *Sands & Co.: Edinburgh, London,* 1921. 8°. **NN. 7149.**

—— Highroads of Empire History. (Highroads of History. Book VIII.) pp. 256. *T. Nelson & Sons: London,* 1909. 8°. [*Royal School Series.*] **12202. cc. 3/163.**

—— Highroads of General History. (Highroads of History. Book IX.) pp. 334. *T. Nelson & Sons: London,* [1910.] 8°. [*Royal School Series.*] **12202. cc. 3/163.**

—— A History of Great Britain from the coming of the Angles to the year 1870 . . . With twenty maps. pp. xii. 335. *Methuen & Co.: London,* 1908. 8°. **9502. ee. 7.**

—— Second edition. pp. xii. 335. *Methuen & Co.: London,* 1909. 8°. **9502. ee. 19.**

—— Fifth edition. pp. xii. 335. *Methuen & Co.: London,* [1915.] 8°. **9503. c. 20.**

—— Seventh edition, enlarged. pp. xii. 354. *Methuen & Co.: London,* 1921. 8°. **09506. df. 10.**

—— Eighth edition. pp. xii. 354. *Methuen & Co.: London,* 1924. 8°. **09506. g. 12.**

—— A Junior History of Great Britain. [With maps.] pp. xi. 210. *Methuen & Co.: London,* 1910. 8°. **9505. bbb. 31.**

—— Third edition. pp. xi. 210. *Methuen & Co.: London,* 1915. 8°. **9504. e. 30.**

—— Eighth edition, revised. pp. xi. 212. *Methuen & Co.: London,* 1924. 8°. **09506. g. 9.**

—— A Little Book of St. Francis & his Brethren . . . With 5 illustrations, *etc.* pp. 46. *Burns, Oates & Co.: London,* 1920. 8°. **4830. aa. 13.**

—— Makers of Europe. Outlines of European history for the middle forms of schools . . . With twelve maps. pp. xii. 260. *Methuen & Co.: London,* 1902. 8°. **9072. b. 17.**

—— Ninth edition, enlarged. pp. xii. 268. *Methuen & Co.: London,* 1908. 8°. **9073. aaa. 25.**

—— Eighteenth edition, revised. pp. xii. 268. *Methuen & Co.: London,* 1920. 8°. **09073. cc. 21.**

BUXTON (ETHELDREDA MARY WILMOT)

—— Taoısıgh Eorpa .i. "The Makers of Europe" . . . Mícheál Ó Siochfhradha d'aistrigh. pp. x. 272. *Oifig Díolta Foillseacháin Rialtais: Baile Átha Cliath,* 1933. 8°. **09076. a. 58.**

—— Old Celtic Tales. *See* supra: Britain Long Ago.

—— The Pageant of British History . . . With two plates in colour and eight other illustrations. pp. x. 164. *London,* 1913. 8°. [*Methuen's Historical Readers.*] **09505.g.44/3.**

—— The Red Queen. pp. ix. 292. *Burns, Oates & Co.: London,* 1923. 8°. **NN. 8453.**

—— The Roses of Liscawen.—"Doctor" Marjorie. *See* SWAN, afterwards SMITH (Annie S.) The Girl who helped, and other stories. By A. S. Swan, E. M. Wilmot-Buxton, *etc.* [1914.] 8°. BURNETT. **012807. aa. 21.**

—— St. Francis of Assisi . . . With nine illustrations. pp. 190. *G. G. Harrap & Co.: London,* 1925. 8°. [*Heroes of All Time.*] **010603. c. 1/27.**

—— A Short World History. pp. viii. 219. *Methuen & Co.: London,* 1921. 8°. **09009. bb. 43.**

—— A Social History of England from Anglo-Saxon times, for upper and middle forms. pp. xii. 222. *Methuen & Co.: London,* 1920. 8°. **9512. b. 43.**

—— Stories from Modern History. pp. vi. 122. *Methuen & Co.: London,* 1909. 8°. **09009. bb. 53.**

—— Second edition. pp. vi. 122. *Methuen & Co.: London,* 1919. 8°. **09009. bb. 52.**

—— Stories from Old French Romance. pp. 119. *Methuen & Co.: London,* 1910. 8°. **12403. e. 32.**

—— Stories from Roman History. pp. viii. 117. *Methuen & Co.: London,* 1907. 8°. [*The Beginner's Books.*] **012203. f. 31/8.**

—— Stories from Scottish History . . . With a map. pp. vii. 157. *Methuen & Co: London,* 1912. 8°. **09009. bb. 51.**

—— The Story of Hildebrand, St. Gregory VII. pp. ix. 165. *Burns, Oates & Co.: London,* 1920. 8°. [*Heroes of the Church.*] **4856. de. 12/2.**

—— The Story of Jeanne d'Arc . . . With eight illustrations by Chas. A. Buchel, *etc.* pp. 191. *G. G. Harrap & Co.: London,* 1914. 8°. [*Heroes of All Time.*] **010603. c. 1/1.**

—— [Another edition.] pp. 191. *G. G. Harrap & Co.: London,* 1924. 8°. **4823. f. 3.**

—— The Story of the Crusades . . . With sixteen illustrations by M. Meredith Williams. pp. 286. *G. G. Harrap & Co.: London,* 1911. 8°. **9055. bb. 39.**

—— The Struggle with the Crown, 1603–1715 . . . Illustrated by May Gibbs. pp. 224. *G. G. Harrap & Co.: London,* 1912. 8°. **9510. cc. 17.**

—— Tales of Early England. *See* supra: Britain Long Ago.

—— Told by the Northmen. Stories from the Eddas and Sagas. pp. xviii. 246. *G. G. Harrap & Co.: London,* 1908. 8°. [*Told through the Ages.*] **12411. p. 1/4.**

—— Tales from the Eddas. (Taken from "Told by the Northmen.") pp. 160. *G. G. Harrap & Co.: London,* [1909.] 8°. [*All Time Tales.* no. 4.] **012804. d. 1/4.**

BUXTON (Etheldreda Mary Wilmot)

—— Wales . . . Containing twelve full-page illustrations in colour. pp. viii. 87. *A. & C. Black: London,* 1911. 8°. [*Peeps at Many Lands.*] **010026**. g. **1/37**.

—— Wee Folk, Good Folk. A fantasy . . . Illustrated by F. M. Cooper. pp. vii. 88. *Sampson Low & Co.: London,* 1889. 4°. **12807**. p. **12**.

BUXTON (Gene)

—— The Bees Wedding. Illustrated by Kenneth Hunter. pp. 63. *Quality Press: London,* [1947.] 8°. **012826**. h. **69**.

BUXTON (George) *M.A.*

—— *See* Bovey (Wilfrid) The French Canadians Today . . . Adapted and abridged . . . by G. Buxton. 1942. 8°. **12208**. a. **2/94**.

—— L'Influence de la Révolution américaine sur le développement constitutionnel du Canada, 1774–1791. pp. xv. 128. *Paris,* 1929. 8°. **9555**. s. **13**.

BUXTON (George) *Political Writer.* The Political Quixote; or, the Adventures of the renowned Don Blackibo Dwarfino and his trusty squire, Seditiono; a romance . . . founded on one of Wooler's Castles in the Air (which appeared in the Black Dwarf, March 3d, 1819), *etc.* pp. vi. 70. *C. Chapple: London,* 1820. 12°. **8138**. aaa. **1**.

BUXTON (Georgius) Dissertatio medica inauguralis de amaurosi, *etc.* pp. 19. *G. Hamilton & J. Balfour: Edinburgi,* 1756. 8°. **T. 309. (3.)**

—— [Another copy.] **T. 353. (2.)**

—— [Another copy.] **T. 311. (3.)**

BUXTON (German) A Treatise on Algebra, *etc.* pp. 208. *Printed for the Author: London,* 1819. 8°. **530**. g. **16**.

BUXTON (Gurney Harry Lionel)

—— *See* Somerville (T. V.) Tests on a Whirlwind Aircraft in the Royal Aircraft Establishment 24-ft. Wind Tunnel . . . By T. V. Somerville . . . G. H. L. Buxton. 1953. 4°. [*Aeronautical Research Council. Reports and Memoranda.* no. 2603.] **B.S. 2/2.**

—— The Effect of Tab Mass-Balance on Flutter . . . By G. H. L. Buxton [and others], *etc.* pp. 18. *London,* 1951. fol. [*Aeronautical Research Council. Reports and Memoranda.* no. 2418.] **B.S. 2/2.**

BUXTON (Gurney Harry Lionel) and **MINHINNICK** (I. T.)

—— Expressions for the Rates of Change of Critical Flutter Speeds and Frequencies with Inertial, Aerodynamic and Elastic Coefficients. pp. 71. *London,* 1951. 4°. [*Aeronautical Research Council. Reports and Memoranda.* no. 2444.] **B.S. 2/2.**

BUXTON (Hannah) *Lady.* Memorials of Hannah Lady Buxton. From papers collected by her granddaughters. [With plates after designs by Catherine E. Buxton, and with a portrait.] pp. 258. *Bickers & Son: London,* 1883. 4°. **010856**. e. **16**.
Printed for private circulation.

BUXTON (Hannah Maud) *See* Buxton (Edward N.) On Either Side of the Red Sea . . . By H. M. B. [i.e. H. M. Buxton], C. E. B., *etc.* 1895. 8°. **10076**. ee. **11**.

BUXTON (Harold Jocelyn) *Bishop of Gibraltar. See* Buxton (Noel E.) afterwards Noel-Buxton (N. E.) *Baron Noel-Buxton.* Travels and Politics in Armenia. By N. Buxton, M.P., and the Rev. H. Buxton, *etc.* 1914. 8°. **2356**. a. **20**.

BUXTON (Harold Jocelyn) *Bishop of Gibraltar.*

—— Adventures with the Bulgarian Army, 1912–13. pp. 46. *Charles Jenkinson: Thaxted,* [1913.] 8°. **09004**. bb. **20. (10.)**

—— Trans-Caucasia. [With plates.] pp. x. 99. *Faith Press: London,* [1926.] 8°. **9456**. a. **47**.

BUXTON (Harold Jocelyn) *Bishop of Gibraltar,* and **SHARPE** (Frederick)

—— Handbook to the Church of St. Mary the Virgin, Launton, Oxfordshire. Compiled . . . by H. J. Buxton . . . and F. Sharpe. [With illustrations.] pp. 15. *Launton Parochial Church Council: [Launton,]* 1952. 8°. **07822**. c. **14**

BUXTON (Harry John Wilmot) Waiting. Advent.—The Leading of the Child Jesus, Christmas.—Self Blindness. Lent. 1875. *See* Fowle (Edmund) Plain Preaching to Poor People, *etc.* ser. 9. 1875, *etc.* 12°. **4462**. a. **26**

—— i. Short Sermons for Children. Twenty-three sermons. ii. Bought with a Price. Nine sermons from Ash Wednesday to Easter Day. 2 pt. *London,* 1906. 8°. [*Skeffingtons' Sermon Library.* vol. 2.] **4475**. ff. **1/2**
Reissues of the editions of 1876 *and* 1897 *respectively.*

—— Until the Harvest.—The Voices of God. *See* Harvest Festival Sermons. Harvest and Flower Festival Sermons, *etc.* 1897. 8°. **4477**. ee. **24**

—— The Acceptable Year. *See* Victoria, *Queen of Great Britain and Ireland.* [*Biography.*—ii. *Jubilee,* 21 *June* 1887.] Sermons for the Jubilee, *etc.* 1887. 8°. **4466**. ee. **12**

—— The Battle of Life. A series of mission sermons, *etc.* pp. x. 229. *Skeffington & Son: London,* 1889. 8°. **4479**. b. **30**

—— [Another copy.] **4479**. e. **1**.

—— The Best Place for God's People. 1874. *See* Fowle (Edmund) Plain Preaching to Poor People, *etc.* ser. 8. 1875, *etc.* 12°. **4462**. a. **26**

—— Bible By-Ways. Fifteen plain sermons. pp. vii. 147. *Skeffington & Son: London,* 1911. 8°. **4474**. de. **12**

—— Bible Object Lessons. Thirty plain sermons, including many for the principal church seasons. pp. xi. 281. *Skeffington & Son: London,* 1903. 8°. **4479**. eee. **25**

—— New and cheaper edition. pp. xi. 261. *Skeffington & Son: London,* 1916. 8°. **4473**. d. **20**

—— Bought with a Price. Nine sermons from Ash Wednesday to Easter Day. pp. vi. 106. *Skeffington & Son: London,* 1897. 8°. **4479**. ee. **19**.

—— Bread in the Wilderness. Twelve plain addresses to communicants. pp. vii. 93. *Skeffington & Son: London,* 1901. 8°. **4476**. ee. **37**

—— By Word & Deed. Being a complete set of plain sermons for the year on the parables & miracles. pt. 1. *Skeffington & Son: London,* 1892. 8°. **4479**. e. **15**.
Imperfect; pt. 1 *only.*

—— [Another edition.] 2 vol. *Skeffington & Son: London,* 1893. 8°. **4477**. ee. **3**

—— New edition. 2 vol. *Skeffington & Son: London,* [1936.] 8°. **4480**. de. **10**

—— A Changed Earth. A plain sermon, *etc.* pp. 12. *William Skeffington: London,* 1874. 8°. **4479**. cc. **47**. **(9.)**

BUXTON (Harry John Wilmot)

—— The Children's Bread. Short sermons to children. pp. x. 133. *W. Skeffington & Son: London*, 1883. 8°. **4466.** aaa. **24.**

—— Common Life Religion. Thirty plain sermons, including many for the principal church seasons. pp. xii. 266. *Skeffington & Son: London*, 1902. 8°. **4475.** i. **19.**

—— The Crown. *See* George v., *King of Great Britain and Ireland.* [*Biography.*—ii. *Coronation.*] Sermons for the Coronation of King George v, *etc.* 1911. 8°. **4466.** ee. **31.**

—— Day by Day Duty. Thirty plain sermons, including many for the principal church seasons. pp. xi. 258. *Skeffington & Son: London*, 1905. 8°. **4479.** l. **13.**

—— Dreams and Realities. A sermon on the Pan-Anglican Congress. pp. 14. *Skeffington & Son: London*, 1908. 8°. **4473.** h. **28.** **(14.)**

—— England's Watchword. A sermon for the Nelson centenary. pp. 12. *Skeffington & Son: London*, 1905. 8°. **10601.** de. **23.** (**5.**)

—— English Painters . . . With a chapter on American painters by S. R. Koehler. [With illustrations.] pp. xiii. 226. *Sampson Low & Co.: London*, 1883. 8°. [*Illustrated Handbooks of Art History.*] **07808.** de. **13/2.**

—— Full of Days and Honour. A plain sermon on the death of Her Majesty Queen Victoria. pp. 15. *Skeffington & Son: London*, [1901.] 8°. **10806.** dd. **8.** (**1.**)

—— God with Us. *See* Transvaal War. [1899–1902.] Three Plain Sermons for the Day of Intercession . . . in respect of the War in South Africa, *etc.* [1900.] 8°. **4475.** g. **56.** (**5.**)

—— God's Heroes. A series of plain sermons. pp. x. 233. *Skeffington & Son: London*, 1890. 8°. **4462.** dd. **6.**

—— [A reissue.] *London*, 1907. 8°. [*Skeffingtons' Sermon Library.* vol. 7.] **4475.** ff. **1/6.**

—— The Goodness of the Lord. *See* Fruits. The Kindly Fruits of the Earth. A series of . . . sermons, *etc.* 1889. 8°. **4479.** aa. **39.**

—— Holy-Tide Teaching. A complete course of plain sermons for all the saints' days, the chief holy days, etc. pp. viii. 224. *Skeffington & Son: London*, 1893. 8°. **4477.** ee. **5.**

—— In Many Keys. Thirty sermons on thirty psalms, *etc.* pp. x. 270. *Skeffington & Son: London*, 1901. 8°. **4478.** i. **13.**

—— "In Watchings Often." Being twenty-eight short devotional readings, one for each day in Advent. pp. viii. 128. *Skeffington & Son: London*, 1891. 8°. **4399.** aa. **1.**

—— Led by a Little Child. Short addresses or readings for children. pp. x. 142. *Skeffington & Son: London*, 1886. 8°. **4479.** c. **16.**

—— The Life of Duty. A year's plain sermons on the Gospels or Epistles. 2 vol. *Skeffington & Son: London*, 1885. 8°. **4479.** bbb. **9.**

—— The Life of Service. pp. viii. 223. *Skeffington & Son: London*, 1912. 8°. **4465.** ee. **21.**

—— The Life worth Living. Mission sermons. pp. x. 201. *W. Skeffington & Son: London*, 1882. 8°. **4466.** aaa. **14.**

—— The Lighthouse on the Rock. A series of short sermons to children. pp. x. 143. *Skeffington & Son: London*, 1887. 8°. **4479.** b. **14.**

BUXTON (Harry John Wilmot)

—— The Lights of Home. Thirty plain sermons, including many for the principal church seasons. pp. 263. *Skeffington & Son: London*, 1907. 8°. **4475.** ff. **8.**

—— The Lord's Song: plain sermons on hymns. pp. x. 201. *W. Skeffington & Son: London*, 1880. 8°. **4466.** aa. **25.**

—— [A reissue.] pp. xii. 201. *London*, [1912.] 8°. [*Skeffingtons' Sermon Library.* vol. 11.] **4475.** ff. **1/10.**

—— [A reissue.] *London*, [1933.] 8°. **04478.** k. **46.**

—— The Master's Message. A series of plain sermons. pp. x. 244. *Skeffington & Son: London*, 1891. 8°. **4478.** dd. **10.**

—— Mission Sermons for a Year. pp. xxiv. 498. *W. Skeffington & Son: London*, 1878. 8°. **4466.** ff. **2.**

—— New and Contrite Hearts. Forty brief meditations for Lent. pp. viii. 146. *Skeffington & Son: London*, 1888. 8°. **4401.** n. **36.**

—— Notes of Sermons for the Year. A series of 80 short sermons for the Sundays, the chief holy days, and all the saints' days of the Christian year, *etc.* 4 pt. *Skeffington & Son: London*, 1909, 10. 8°. **4466.** ee. **24.**

—— The Old Road. Thirty plain sermons, including many for the principal church seasons. pp. xii. 225. *Skeffington & Co.: London*, 1909. 8°. **4466.** ff. **6.**

—— Parable Sermons for Children. pp. x. 125. *W. Skeffington & Son: London*, 1884. 8°. **4466.** c. **21.**

—— Pictures from the Acts of the Holy Apostles . . . Illustrated by Wyndham Hughes. *Mowbray & Co.: Oxford, London*, [1891.] 4°. **4827.** f. **5.**

—— Pictures from the Gospels . . . Illustrated by Wyndham Hughes. *Mowbray & Co.: Oxford, London*, [1888.] 4°. **4807.** eee. **9.**

—— The Pilgrim Band. A series of sermons. pp. xi. 193. *Skeffington & Son: London*, 1886. 8°. **4479.** b. **10.**

—— Prayer and Practice. Sixty-one plain sermons on the Collects, *etc.* pp. xii. 431. *Skeffington & Son: London*, 1894. 8°. **4466.** cc. **7.**

—— Second impression. pp. xii. 431. *Skeffington & Son: London*, 1908. 8°. **4474.** k. **1.**

—— The Pure Crown. *See* Edward vii., *King of Great Britain and Ireland.* [*Biography.*—ii. *Coronation.*] Sermons for the Coronation of King Edward vii, *etc.* 1902. 8°. **9930.** bbb. **56.**

—— Readings for Mothers' Meetings. pp. 173. *Skeffington & Son: London*, 1907. 8°. **4193.** ff. **8.**

—— Scenes and Stories from the New Testament . . . Engravings by Wyndham Hughes. Letterpress by Rev. H. J. Wilmot Buxton. *Mowbray & Co.: Oxford, London*, [1893.] 4°. **3105.** e. **2.**

—— [Another copy.] **3105.** e. **5.**

—— [Another edition.] *A. R. Mowbray & Co.: Oxford, London*, 1903. 4°. **3225.** ff. **17.**

—— Scenes and Stories from the New Testament, *etc.* [A selection.] 2 ser. *Mowbray & Co.: Oxford, London*, [1894.] 4°. **3105.** e. **4.**

—— [Another copy.] **3105.** e. **7.**

BUXTON (Harry John Wilmot)

— Scenes and Stories from the Old Testament . . . Engravings by Wyndham Hughes. Letterpress by Rev. H. J. Wilmot Buxton. *Mowbray & Co.: Oxford, London,* [1893.] 4°. **3105.** e. **1.**

— [Another copy.] **3105.** e. **3.**

— [Another copy.] **3105.** e. **6.**

— The School of Christ. Plain sermons to children on the Lord's Prayer and the Ten Commandments. pp. viii. 137. *Skeffington & Sons: London,* 1895. 8°. **4478.** de. **12.**

— Seeing Jesus. Advent. 1876. *See* Fowle (Edmund) Plain Preaching to Poor People, *etc.* ser. 10. 1875, *etc.* 12°. **4462.** a. **26.**

— Services for Parochial Missions . . . Second edition. pp. 12. *W. Skeffington & Son: London,* 1883. 12°. **3455.** dd. **18.** (**2.**)

— The Sheathed Sword. *See* Transvaal War. [1899–1902.] Three Plain Sermons for the Day of Thanksgiving in respect of the War in South Africa, *etc.* [1900.] 8°. **4475.** f. **62.** (**3.**)

— [Another edition.] *See* Transvaal War. [1899–1902.] Three Plain Sermons on Thanksgiving in respect of the conclusion of the War in South Africa, *etc.* [1902.] 8°. **4473.** h. **23.** (**1.**)

— Short Sermons for Children. pp. 175. *W. Skeffington & Son: London,* 1876. 8°. **4465.** a. **12.**

— Soldiers of Christ. A series of plain sermons. pp. x [ix]. 212. *Skeffington & Son: London,* 1888. 8°. **4479.** bb. **46.**

— The Straight Furrow. *See* Season. In Due Season. A collection of sermons, *etc.* 1903. 8°. **4476.** aa. **113.**

— Sunday Lessons for Daily Life. Being one hundred and twenty sermons for the Christian year. 2 vol. *Skeffington & Son: London,* 1896. 8°. **4462.** ee. **14.**

— Sunday Sermonettes for a Year. pp. xv. 225. *Skeffington & Son: London,* 1883. 8°. **4466.** bbb. **9.**

— [A reissue.] *London,* [1912.] 8°. [*Skeffingtons' Sermon Library.* vol. 12.] **4475.** ff. **1/11.**

— The Sweet o' the Year. A novel. pp. 214. *Skeffington & Son: London,* 1887. 8°. **12625.** f. **9.**

— Thankfulness. A sermon on thanksgiving for the recovery from illness of His Majesty King Edward vii. pp. 13. *Skeffington & Son: London,* [1902.] 8°. **4475.** f. **64.** (**7.**)

— [Another edition.] pp. 14. *Skeffington & Son: London,* [1902.] 8°. **9930.** ccc. **65.** (**4.**)

— The Things of Cæsar and the Things of God. A plain sermon on Sunday observance. pp. 15. *Skeffington & Son: London,* 1907. 8°. **4473.** h. **28.** (**9.**)

— Towards the Close of a Great Century. (Sermons.) pp. viii. 84. *Skeffington & Son: London,* 1899. 8°. **4478.** f. **86.**

— The Tree of Life. Plain sermons on the fruits of the spirit. pp. x. 270. *Skeffington & Son: London,* 1898. 8°. **4478.** de. **28.**

— Two Sermons for the Celebration of the Eightieth Birthday of Her Majesty Queen Victoria. i. A Glorious Retrospect. By the Rev. H. J. Wilmot Buxton . . . ii. A Royal Bridge-Maker. By the Rev. G. Wingfield Hunt. pp. 31. *Skeffington & Son: London,* 1899. 8°. **4475.** f. **56.** (**1.**)

BUXTON (Harry John Wilmot)

— Waterside Mission Sermons. 2 ser. *W. Skeffington: London,* 1874, 75. 8°. **4464.** a. **7.**

— [A reissue of ser. 2.] Mission Sermons. Second series. pp. 251. *London,* 1907. 8°. [*Skeffingtons' Sermon Library.* vol. 8.] **4475.** ff. **1/7.**

— Words by the Way. 57 short plain village sermons for the Christian year. 4 pt. pp. 443. *Skeffington & Son: London,* 1899, 1900. 8°. **4479.** e. **49.**

— Anecdotes and Illustrations for Pulpit Use. Selected from the works of the Rev. H. J. Wilmot-Buxton. Compiled by the Rev. G. A. C. Smith. pp. 211. *Skeffington & Son: London,* 1913. 8°. **04376.** e. **7.**

BUXTON (Harry John Wilmot) and **POYNTER** (*Sir* Edward John) *Bart.*

— German, Flemish and Dutch Painting. [With illustrations.] pp. xiv. 244. *Sampson Low & Co.: London,* 1881. 8°. [*Illustrated Text-Books of Art.*] **07808.** de. **13/7.**

BUXTON (Harry Wilmot) *See* England. [*Laws and Statutes.—*iv. *Mercantile Marine.*] The Master Mariners' Hand-book, and Shipowner's Vade-mecum of Mercantile Marine Law . . . With a copious introduction & practical notes . . . By W. Buxton. 1852. 8°. **6835.** a. **8.**

BUXTON (Helen A. Wilmot) Little Friends.—On the Mountains.—Gretchen, or the Enchanted palace. *See* Tale. Please Tell Me a Tale. 1885. 8°. **12811.** c. **29.**

BUXTON (Isaac) Dissertatio inauguralis physiologica, enarrans ruminationis humanae casum, *etc.* pp. 16. *Gottingae,* [1802.] 4°. T. **992.** (**22.**)

— An Essay on the use of a Regulated Temperature in Winter-Cough and Consumption: including a comparison of the different methods of producing such a temperature in the chambers of invalids. pp. xii. 176. *Cox: London,* 1810. 8°. **1187.** a. **23.**

BUXTON (James Basil) and **GLOVER** (R. E.)

— Tuberculin Tests in Cattle. Observations on the intradermal tuberculin test in cattle with special reference to the use of synthetic medium tuberculin. pp. v. 94. *London,* 1939. 8°. [*A.R.C. Report Series.* no. 4.] B.S. **32/6.**

BUXTON (James Basil) and **MAC NALTY** (*Sir* Arthur Salusbury) *K.C.B.* The Intradermal Tuberculin Test in Cattle. Collected results of experience. pp. 64. *London,* 1928. 8°. [*Medical Research Council. Special Report Series.* no. 122.] B.S. **25/8.**

BUXTON (James Walton Fowell) The Elements of Military Administration. First part. Permanent system of administration. pp. xiii. 560. *Kegan Paul & Co.: London,* 1883. 8°. [*Military Handbooks for Officers & Non-Commissioned Officers.* vol. 4.] **8837.** de. **1/16.**
No more published.

BUXTON (John) *Dramatist.*

— *See* Drayton (Michael) Poems of Michael Drayton. Edited with an introduction by J. Buxton. 1953. 8°. W.P. **3362/11.**

— Atropos, and other poems. pp. vii. 46. *Macmillan & Co.: London,* 1946. 8°. **11657.** c. **88.**

— Judas. A play in four acts. pp. 67. *Basil Blackwell: Oxford,* 1938. 8°. **11782.** a. **2.**

— A Marriage Song for the Princess Elizabeth, November 20th, 1947. pp. 15. *Macmillan & Co.: London,* 1947. 8°. **11656.** g. **29.**

BUXTON (John) *Dramatist.*

—— "Such Liberty." [Poems.] pp. vii. 40. *Macmillan & Co.: London*, 1944. 8°. **11657. dd. 51.**

—— Westward. [A poem.] pp. 44. *Jonathan Cape: London*, 1942. 8°. **11657. dd. 3**

BUXTON (John) *Naturalist.* *See* Buxton (Edward J. M.)

BUXTON (John) *of Shadwell.* A Letter to John Buxton, of Shadwell, Esq; on the contests relative to the ensuing election for the county of Norfolk. [By Robert Potter?] pp. 24. [*London?*] 1768. 8°. **8135. bb. 85. (1.)**
With a MS. note stating that this was said to be written by Mr. Potter, with some assistance from W. DeGrey, Baron Walsingham, and Leonard Buxton.

—— [Another copy.] **8133. c. 12.**

—— A Letter to the Author of a Letter to John Buxton, Esq., of Shadwell, on the contests relative to the ensuing election for the county of Norfolk. [By Thomas Inyon?] pp. 20. [*London?*] 1768. 8°. **8135. bb. 85. (3.)**

—— A Letter to the Author of a Letter to Mr. Buxton. In which it is proved that the design of that letter has been entirely misunderstood and that the author of it is the real friend of Sir Edward Astley and Mr. Coke. [By Samuel Cooper?] pp. 34. MS. NOTE. [*London?*] 1768. 8°. **8135. bb. 85. (2.)**

—— Remarks on the Letter to John Buxton, Esq. (Appendix consisting of extracts from the celebrated Letter concerning libels, general warrants and the seizure of papers, *etc.*) [By Richard Gardiner?] 2 pt. MS. NOTE. *London*, 1768. 8°. **8135. bb. 85. (4.)**

BUXTON (John Colin Whitfield)

—— Rural Studies . . . Illustrated with photographs and line drawings by Arnold Bond. *J. M. Dent & Sons: London*, 1951– . 8°. W.P. **4181.**

BUXTON (John Harry Wilmot) *See* Buxton (Harry J. W.)

BUXTON (John Leycester Dudley) Dental Pathology. pp. 193. *E. & S. Livingstone: Edinburgh*, 1927. 8°. [*Outlines of Dental Science.* vol. 7.] **07612.e.22/7.**

—— Dental Surgery. pp. 172. *E. & S. Livingstone: Edinburgh*, 1927. 8°. [*Outlines of Dental Science.* vol. 8.] **07612.e.22/8.**

—— Handbook of Mechanical Dentistry, *etc.* pp. vii. 269. *J. & A. Churchill: London*, 1921 [1920]. 8°. **7611. d. 31.**

BUXTON (Leland William Wilberforce) The Black Sheep of the Balkans . . . With an introduction by Aubrey Herbert. [With a map.] pp. 191. *Nisbet & Co.: London*, 1920. 8°. **08026. a. 25.**

—— Count Blitski's Daughter. pp. 271. *Christophers: London*, [1925.] 8°. NN. **11136.**

—— The Devil's River. pp. 283. *G. Allen & Unwin: London*, 1924. 8°. NN. **9907.**

BUXTON (Leonard) *See* Buxton (John) *of Shadwell.* A Letter to John Buxton, Esq; on the contests relative to the ensuing election for the county of Norfolk. [By R. Potter with the assistance of L. Buxton?] 1768. 8°. **8135. bb. 85. (1.)**

BUXTON (Leonard Halford Dudley) *See* Garrod (Dorothy A. E.) Excavation of a Mousterian Rock-Shelter at Devil's Tower, Gibraltar. By D. A. E. Garrod, L. H. D. Buxton, *etc.* 1928. 8°. **07708. l. 62.**

BUXTON (Leonard Halford Dudley)

—— *See* Marett (Robert R.) Custom is King. Essays presented to R. R. Marett . . . Edited by L. H. D. Buxton. 1936. 8°. **010006. g. 37.**

—— China: the land and the people . . . With a chapter on the climate by W. G. Kendrew. [With maps.] pp. xiii. 333. pl. xvi. *Clarendon Press: Oxford*, 1929. 8°. **010055. aaa. 36.**

—— Cross-Cousin Marriages in Ashanti. *See* Rattray (Robert S.) Religion & Art in Ashanti, *etc.* 1927. 8°. **04503. g. 56.**

—— The Eastern Road. [Sketches of travels in China and Japan.] pp. xii. 268. pl. xix. *Kegan Paul & Co.: London; E. P. Dutton & Co.: New York*, 1924. 8°. **010055. e. 45.**

—— From Monkey to Man, *etc.* pp. 76. *London*, 1929. 8°. [*Routledge Introductions to Modern Knowledge.* no. 2.] W.P. **9709/2.**

—— Guide to the Larmer Grounds and the Antiquities of Cranborne Chase. Edited by L. H. D. Buxton. pp. 16. pl. III. 1929. 8°. *See* Farnham, *Dorset.—Pitt-Rivers Museum.* **010360. aa. 61.**

—— The Peoples of Asia. [With a bibliography.] pp. xiii. 271. pl. viii. *Kegan Paul & Co.: London; A. A. Knopf: New York*, 1925. 8°. [*History of Civilization.*] **09009. e. 1/14.**

—— The Pitt-Rivers Museum, Farnham. General Handbook. Edited by L. H. D. Buxton. pp. 63. pl. xxvi. 1929. 8°. *See* Farnham, *Dorset.—Pitt-Rivers Museum.* **07805. ee. 37.**

—— Primitive Labour. pp. viii. 272. *Methuen & Co.: London*, 1924. 8°. **08285. de. 28.**

BUXTON (Leonard Halford Dudley) and **GIBSON** (Strickland)

—— Oxford University Ceremonies. pp. xii. 168. pl. iv. *Clarendon Press: Oxford*, 1935. 8°. **08367. aa. 11.**

BUXTON (Louisa Caroline) *See* Bickersteth (Edward H.) *Bishop of Exeter.* The Master's Will. A sermon . . . upon the death of Mrs. S. Gurney Buxton. 1879. 16°. **4422. aa. 12. (10.)**

BUXTON (Lucy) Hay Harvest, and other poems. pp. 47. *John Lane: London; John Lane Co.: New York*, 1918. 8°. **011648. eee. 45.**

BUXTON (Mary Aline) Kenya Days . . . Illustrated. [With a map.] pp. xi. 242. *E. Arnold & Co.: London*, 1927. 8°. **10094. cc. 11.**

BUXTON (Maud)

—— The Manuscripts of Miss Buxton, at Shadwell Court, Norfolk. [Calendared by Augustus Jessopp.] 1903. *See* England.—*Royal Commission on Historical Manuscripts.* First [*etc.*] Report. (55. Report on Manuscripts in Various Collections. vol. 2.) 1870, *etc.* fol., *etc.* **Bar.T.1.(55.)**

BUXTON (Noel Edward) afterwards **NOEL-BUXTON** (Noel Edward) *Baron Noel-Buxton.*

—— *See* Anderson (Mosa) Noel Buxton. A life, *etc.* [With portraits.] 1952. 8°. **10857. f. 31.**

—— *See* De Bunsen (Victoria) and Buxton (N. E.) afterwards Noel-Buxton (N. E.) *Baron Noel-Buxton.* Macedonian Massacres, *etc.* [1907.] *obl.* 8°. **8027. a. 29.**

BUXTON (NOEL EDWARD) afterwards **NOEL-BUXTON** (NOEL EDWARD) *Baron Noel-Buxton.*

—— *See* EVANS (THOMAS P. C.) Foreign Policy from a Back Bench, 1904–1918. A study based on the papers of Lord Noel-Buxton, *etc.* 1932. 8°. **09077. aa. 30.**

—— *See* PHILLIPSON (Coleman) and BUXTON (N. E.) afterwards NOEL-BUXTON (N. E.) *Baron Noel-Buxton.* The Question of the Bosphorus and Dardanelles. 1917. 8°. **08026. dd. 20.**

—— Europe and the Turks . . . With maps. pp. xi. 143. *John Murray: London,* 1907. 8°. **8027. bb. 43.**

—— (Second edition, revised with new matter.) pp. xi. 118. *Methuen & Co.: London,* 1912. 8°. **8028. aaa. 37.**

—— Poland. Speech by the Right Hon. Lord Noel-Buxton. (House of Lords. Extract from official report.) pp. 7. *London,* [1939.] 8°. **08028. d. 57.**

—— Travels and Politics in Armenia. By N. Buxton, M.P., and the Rev. Harold Buxton. With an introduction by Viscount Bryce, and a contribution on Armenian history and culture by Aram Raffi. With illustrations and a map. pp. xx. 274. *Smith, Elder & Co.: London,* 1914. 8°. **2356. a. 20.**

—— Travels and Reflections. [With plates.] pp. 223. *G. Allen & Unwin: London,* 1929. 8°. **010028. ee. 17.**

—— With the Bulgarian Staff . . . With illustrations. pp. xvi. 164. *Smith, Elder & Co.: London,* 1913. 8°. **9136. de. 27.**

BUXTON (NOEL EDWARD) afterwards **NOEL-BUXTON** (NOEL EDWARD) *Baron Noel-Buxton,* and **BUXTON** (CHARLES RODEN)

—— The War and the Balkans. pp. 112. *G. Allen & Unwin: London,* 1915. 8°. **08027. a. 56.**

BUXTON (NOEL EDWARD) afterwards **NOEL-BUXTON** (NOEL EDWARD) *Baron Noel-Buxton,* and **EVANS** (T. P. CONWIL)

—— Oppressed Peoples and the League of Nations. [With maps.] pp. x. 230. *J. M. Dent & Sons: London & Toronto,* 1922. 8°. **08028. de. 110.**

BUXTON (NOEL EDWARD) afterwards **NOEL-BUXTON** (NOEL EDWARD) *Baron Noel-Buxton,* and **HOARE** (WALTER)

—— Temperance Reform. *See* BRITISH EMPIRE. The Heart of the Empire, *etc.* 1901. 8°. **08277. ff. 64.**

BUXTON (NOEL EDWARD) afterwards **NOEL-BUXTON** (NOEL EDWARD) *Baron Noel-Buxton,* and **LEESE** (CHARLES LEONARD)

—— Balkan Problems and European Peace. pp. 135. *G. Allen & Unwin: London,* 1919. 8°. **08026. aaa. 48.**

BUXTON (NOEL SAINT JOHN GREY DUDLEY) *See* CANTLIE (*Sir* James) *K.B.E.* British Red Cross Society First-Aid Manual . . . By St. J. D. Buxton . . . Sixth edition [of "First-Aid Manual," by Sir J. Cantlie], *etc.* 1932. 16°. **W.P. 1831/1b.**

—— *See* CANTLIE (*Sir* James) *K.B.E.* British Red Cross Society First-Aid Manual . . . By St. J. D. Buxton, *etc.* 1944. 16°. **W.P. 1831/1c.**

BUXTON (NOEL SAINT JOHN GREY DUDLEY)

—— *See* ENGLAND.—*British Red Cross Society.* Note Book with Diagrams for use during attendance at Red Cross courses of First Aid. Edited by St. J. D. Buxton, *etc.* 1940. 8°. **20036.a.1/296.**

—— *See* WAKELEY (*Sir* Cecil P. G.) *K.B.E.,* and BUXTON (N. St. J. G. D.) Surgical Pathology. 1929. 8°. **07482. aa. 5**

—— Arthroplasty. pp. vii. 126. pl. 2. *Pitman Medical Publishing Co.: London,* 1955. 8°. **7484. l. 14**

—— First Aid Catechism. Compiled from First Aid Manual [i.e. British Red Cross Society Manual no. 1.] by St. J. D. Buxton. pp. 64. *Cassell & Co.: London,* [1928.] 16°. **07481. de. 26**

The titlepage headed: British Red Cross Society.

—— British Red Cross Society . . . Manuel de premiers soins . . . Traduction française de la huitième édition . . . par St J. D. Buxton. [A translation by Arthur Rohan of the "First-Aid Manual" originally written by Sir James Cantlie.] pp. xiv. 307. [1942.] 8°. *See* ENGLAND.—*British Red Cross Society.—Mauritius Branch.* **7483. aaa. 4**

—— Orthopædics. 1936. *See* MAINGOT (R. H.) Post-Graduate Surgery, *etc.* vol. 2. 1936, *etc.* 8°. **7324.b.3/2.**

BUXTON (OLIVE VIOLET) and **MAC KAY** (P. M. MACULLOCH)

—— The Nursing of Tuberculosis . . . Illustrated. pp. 124 *John Wright & Sons: Bristol,* 1947. 8°. **7689. e. 6**

BUXTON (PATRICK ALFRED) *See* LONDON.—III. *British Museum.—Department of Zoology.* [*Arthropoda.*] Insects of Samoa and other Samoan Terrestrial Arthropoda. (pt. 9 fasc. 1. Description of the Environment.—fasc. 2. Summary. By P. A. Buxton.) 1927, *etc.* 8°. **7298. w. 1**

—— *See* WATERSTON (James) Fleas as a Menace to Man and Domestic Animals . . . Revised by P. A. Buxton. 1937. 8°. **W.P. 3036/39**

—— —— 1937. 8°. **W.P. 3036/39a**

—— Animal Life in Deserts. A study of the fauna in relation to environment, *etc.* [With plates.] pp. xv. 176. *E. Arnold & Co.: London,* 1923. 8°. **07207. eee. 44**

—— [A reissue.] Animal Life in Deserts, *etc.* *London,* 1955. 8°. **7211. aa. 18**

—— Les Conditions de la vie animale dans les déserts. *See* HACHISUKA (M.) Le Sahara, *etc.* vol. 1. pt. 1. 1932, *etc.* 4°. **Ac. 6035. b/4.**

—— The Louse. An account of the lice which infest man, their medical importance and control. pp. ix. 115. *E. Arnold & Co.: London,* 1939. 8°. **07299. ee. 71.**

—— The Louse, *etc.* (Second edition.) pp. viii. 164. *Edward Arnold & Co.: London,* 1947. 8°. **07299. ee. 85**

—— The Natural History of Tsetse Flies. An account of the biology of the genus Glossina—Diptera, *etc.* [With a bibliography.] pp. xviii. 816. pl. 47. *H. K. Lewis & Co.: London,* 1955. 8°. [*London School of Hygiene and Tropical Medicine. Memoir.* no. 10.] **Ac. 2666. c/4. (10.)**

—— Researches in Polynesia and Melanesia. An account of investigations in Samoa, Tonga, the Ellice Group, and the New Hebrides, in 1924, 1925. (Parts I–IV, relating principally to medical entomology, by P. A. Buxton assisted by G. H. E. Hopkins.—Parts V–VII, relating to human diseases and welfare, by P. A. Buxton.) [With plates.] 2 vol. *London,* 1927, 28. 4°. [*Memoir Series of the London School of Hygiene and Tropical Medicine.* no. 1, 2.] **Ac.2666.c/4.(1,2.)**

BUXTON (PATRICK ALFRED)

—— Trypanosomiasis in Eastern Africa, 1947. pp. 44. *H.M. Stationery Office: London*, 1948. fol. [*Colonial Office. Tsetse Fly and Trypanosomiasis Committee. Reports.*] **B.S. 7/44.**

BUXTON (PATRICK ALFRED) and **UVAROV** (*Sir* BORIS PETROVICH) *K.C.M.G.*

—— A Contribution to our Knowledge of Orthoptera of Palestine. (Extrait du Bulletin de la Société royale entomologique d'Égypte.) *Le Caire*, 1924. 8°. **07299. f. 51.**

BUXTON (RAYMOND)

—— Broken Liebestraum. [A novel.] pp. 208. *G. G. Swan: London*, 1944. 8°. **NN. 34551.**

—— Midsummer Madness. pp. 144. *Modern Fiction: London*, [1950.] 8°. **Cup.367.c.44.**

—— Modern Story no. 6 [*etc.*]. Edited by R. Buxton. *Modern Fiction: London*, 1949- . 8°. **W.P. 3880.**

—— No Gentle Lady. pp. 128. *Modern Fiction: London*, [1949.] 8°. **12651. d. 65.**

—— A Rope for the Gal called Lou. pp. 136. *Modern Fiction: London*, [1950.] 8°. **12650. a. 41.**

BUXTON (RAYMOND) and **BENNISON** (BEN)

—— The Black Wraith; or, See how they run. pp. 93. *Stanley Baker: Richmond*, 1952. 8°. **12646. e. 21.**

BUXTON (RICHARD) *Compiler of "The Sculptured Garland."*

—— *See* LANDOR (Walter S.) The Sculptured Garland, *etc.* (Chosen and arranged by R. Buxton.) 1948. 4°. **11656. g. 35.**

BUXTON (RICHARD) *of Manchester.*

—— A Botanical Guide to the Flowering Plants, Ferns, Mosses and Algæ, found indigenous within sixteen miles of Manchester, with some information as to their agricultural, medicinal and other uses . . . Together with a sketch of the author's life; and remarks on the geology of the district. pp. xxi. 168. *Longman & Co.: London; Abel Heywood: Manchester*, 1849. 12°. **7030. c. 8.**

—— Second edition, with corrections and additions. pp. xxi. 207. *Simpkin, Marshall & Co.: London; Abel Heywood: Manchester*, 1859. 8°. **7032. c. 9.**

BUXTON (RICHENDA) The Servant of the Lord [and other essays], *etc.* pp. xiv. 187. *Masters & Co.: London*, 1906. 8°. **04403. e. 31.**

BUXTON (ROBERT HUGH) *See* BRADLEY (Arthur G.) A Book of the Severn . . . With sixteen illustrations in colour by R. H. Buxton. 1920. 8°. **010352. i. 12.**

BUXTON (RUFUS ALEXANDER NOEL) *Baron Noel-Buxton.*

—— The Ford, *etc.* [A poem.] pp. 32. *Caravel Press: London*, 1955. 8°. **11661. bb. 9.**

—— No Smooth Journey. [A poem.] pp. 22. *Basil Blackwell: Oxford*, 1938. 8°. **11656. a. 46.**

—— Without the Red Flag. pp. 24. *Basil Blackwell: Oxford*, 1936. 8°. **11655. aaa. 63.**

BUXTON (SAINT JOHN DUDLEY) *See* BUXTON (Noel St. J. G. D.)

BUXTON (*Mrs.* SAMUEL GURNEY) *See* BUXTON (Louisa C.)

BUXTON (STANLEY) Stanley Buxton; or, the Schoolfellows . . . By the author of "Annals of the Parish" [i.e. John Galt], *etc.* 3 vol. *H. Colburn & R. Bentley: London*, 1832. 12°. **N. 888.**

BUXTON (SYDNEY CHARLES) *Earl Buxton. See* BUXTON (Charles) Memoirs of Sir Thomas Fowell Buxton, Bart., *etc.* (With an introduction by Earl Buxton.) [1925.] 8°. **12206.p.1/576.**

—— *See* LONDON.—III. *Mr. Tuke's Fund.* Emigration from Ireland . . . With statements by Mr. Tuke, Mr. S. Buxton, *etc.* [1883.] 8°. **08285. g. 16. (2.)**

—— *See* SMITH (*Sir* Hubert L.) *G.C.B.*, and NASH (Vaughan) The Story of the Dockers' Strike . . . With an introduction by S. Buxton. [1889.] 8°. **8276. aa. 41.**

—— The Arguments for and against the Three F's. With a brief exposition of the Land Act of 1870, etc. . . . Enlarged from the "Contemporary Review." pp. 20. *Strahan & Co.: London*, [1881.] 8°. **8145. f. 4. (3.)**

—— Chinese Labour. The Transvaal Ordinance analysed, together with the British Guiana Ordinance. pp. 23. *Liberal Publication Department: London*, 1904. 8°. **08157. ee. 78.**

—— Edward Grey, Bird Lover and Fisherman. pp. 18. *Privately printed*, 1933. 8°. **10856. m. 23.**

—— Electoral Purity and Economy. pp. 23. *London & Counties Liberal Union: London*, 1882. 8°. **8138. cc. 8. (9.)**

—— Proposed Draft Amendments to the Corrupt Practices Bill. Being an appendix to Mr. S. Buxton's "Electoral Purity and Economy," *etc.* [By the same author.] pp. 11. *National Press Agency: London*, [1882.] 8°. **8132. ee. 16. (3.)**

—— Finance and Politics; an historical study. 1783–1885. 2 vol. *John Murray: London*, 1888. 8°. **2240. bb. 5.**

—— Fishing and Shooting . . . With illustrations by Archibald Thorburn and from prints. pp. xiv. 268. *John Murray: London*, 1902. 8°. **07905. i. 49.**

—— General Botha. [With portraits and maps.] pp. xv. 347. *John Murray: London*, 1924. 8°. **010760. f. 4.**

—— A Handbook to Political Questions of the Day. Being the arguments on either side. pp. xi. 134. *John Murray: London*, 1880. 8°. **8139. bb. 13.**

—— Second edition. pp. xv. 140. *John Murray: London*, 1880. 8°. **8139. df. 5.**

—— Third edition. pp. xv. 170. *John Murray: London*, 1881. 8°. **8139. df. 8.**

—— Fifth edition. pp. xvi. 188. *John Murray: London*, 1885. 8°. **8139. bb. 35.**

—— Sixth edition. Revised and enlarged. pp. xvii. 226. *John Murray: London*, 1885. 8°. **8139. e. 6.**

—— Seventh edition. Revised and with new subjects. pp. xxvii. 282. *John Murray: London*, 1888. 8°. **8139. df. 12.**

—— Eighth edition. Revised and with new subjects. pp. xxii. 436. *John Murray: London*, 1892. 8°. **8139. e. 7.**

—— Ninth edition. [With supplement.] 2 pt. *John Murray: London*, 1892, 1900. 8°. **8139. e. 16.**

—— [Another copy.] **08139. aaa. 2.**

—— Eleventh edition. pp. xx. 442. *John Murray: London*, 1903. 8°. **2238. cc. 10.**

BUXTON (SYDNEY CHARLES) *Earl Buxton.*

—— A Manual of Political Questions of the Day, *etc.* [An abridgment of "A Handbook to Political Questions of the Day."] (Fourth edition.) pp. 168. *Cassell & Co.: London,* 1891. 8°. **8176.** dg. **11.**

—— The Arguments on either Side of the Fiscal Question, *etc.* [Extracted from "A Handbook to Political Questions."] pp. 82. *John Murray: London,* [1904.] 8°. **08225.** f. **23.**

—— (Second impression.) pp. 82. *John Murray: London,* 1904. 8°. **08225.** f. **30.**

—— The Imperial Parliament. [A series of handbooks on political questions.] Edited by S. Buxton. 13 vol. *Swan Sonnenschein & Co.: London,* 1885–1909. 8°. **8139.** bbb. **44.**
This set includes two editions of the volume on "Representation" and three of that on "Local Option."

—— The Irish Land Bill of 1870, and the Lords' and Tories' amendments thereon. pp. 23. *National Press Agency: London,* [1881.] 8°. **8146.** c. **2.** (**2.**)

—— Mr. Gladstone as Chancellor of the Exchequer. A study. pp. viii. 197. *John Murray: London,* 1901. 8°. **010817.** e. **26.**

—— Mr. Gladstone's Irish Bills; what they are and the arguments for them. pp. vi. 25. *National Press Agency: London,* 1886. 8°. **8146.** c. **4.** (**1.**)

—— "Over Pressure" and Elementary Education. pp. viii. 124. *Swan Sonnenschein & Co.: London,* 1885. 8°. **8310.** aaa. **34.**

—— Report of a Speech delivered . . . March 12, 1904. *See* LONDON.—III. *Eighty Club.* "The Chinese Question" and "Retaliation," *etc.* [1904.] 8°. **8138.** aaa. **45.** (**7.**)

—— The War. Its cost, finance and legacies . . . Reprinted . . . from the 'National Review.' pp. 24. *Liberal Publication Department: London,* 1903. 8°. **08139.** c. **117.**

BUXTON (SYDNEY CHARLES) *Earl Buxton,* and **BARNES** (*Sir* GEORGE STAPYLTON) *K.C.B.*

—— A Handbook to the Death Duties. pp. viii. 109. *John Murray: London,* 1890. 8°. **8228.** aaa. **17.**

BUXTON (*Mrs.* SYDNEY CHARLES) *See* BUXTON (Constance M.)

BUXTON (THERESA) *See* BUXTON (Edward N.) On Either Side of the Red Sea . . . By H. M. B. . . . T. B. [i.e. T. Buxton], *etc.* 1895. 8°. **10076.** ee. **11.**

BUXTON (*Sir* THOMAS FOWELL) 1*st Bart.* *See* BINNEY (Thomas) Sir Thomas Fowell Buxton, Bart. A study for young men, *etc.* 1849. 16°. [*Lectures to Young Men delivered before the Young Men's Christian Association.* 1849.] **4461.** d. **12.** (**2.**)

—— —— 1864. 8°. [*Lectures delivered before the Young Men's Christian Association.* vol. 4.] **4462.** aaa. **22.**

—— —— 1871. 8°. **10825.** aa. **33.**

—— *See* BUXTON (Charles) Memoirs of Sir Thomas Fowell Buxton, Baronet. With selections from his correspondence, *etc.* [With a portrait.] 1848. 8°. **1452.** f. **1.**

—— —— 1849. 8°. **1452.** f. **2**

—— —— 1849. 8°. **1155.** b. **18.**

BUXTON (*Sir* THOMAS FOWELL) 1*st Bart.*

—— —— 1860. 8°. **1155.** c.

—— —— 1872. 8°. **10817.** aaa. **4**

—— —— [1925.] 8°. **12206.p.1/576**

—— *See* BUXTON (Charles) Sir Thomas Fowell Buxton, Ba[r] Ein Bild des englischen Lebens, *etc.* 1854. 8°. **10825.** b. **4**

—— *See* BUXTON (Charles) Das Leben des Sir Thom[as] Fowell Buxton, *etc.* 1855. 12°. [*Lebensbilder aus d[er] Geschichte der inneren Mission.* no. 8.] **4804.** aaa. **3**

—— *See* GELDART (Hannah R.) The Man in Earnest: S[ir] T. F. Buxton. 1852. 18°. **4903.** c. **8**

—— *See* HOARE (Edward N.) *Dean of Waterford.* A Letter [to] Thomas Fowell Buxton, Esq., M.P., in reply to his spee[ch] on the Irish Tithe Bill. 1836. 8°. **T. 2133.** (**6**

—— *See* IRENAEUS, *pseud.* A Letter to Thomas Fow[ell] Buxton, Esq., M.P., on the subject of his reported speec[h] April 2, 1835, in the debate upon Lord John Russell[']s Resolution. 1835. 8°. **T. 1909.** (**11**

—— *See* MAC DONNELL (Alexander) *Esq.* A Letter to Tho[mas] Fowell Buxton, Esq., M.P., in refutation of his allegation[s] respecting the decrease of the slaves in the British Wes[t] India Colonies. 1833. 8°. **8156.** df. **4**

—— *See* MOTTRAM (Ralph H.) Buxton the Liberato[r.] [With a portrait.] [1946.] 8°. **10861.** b. **3**

—— *See* MUDGE (Zachariah A.) The Christian Statesman[;] a portraiture of Sir T. F. Buxton, *etc.* [1865.] 8°. **10817.** aa. **2**

—— *See* PUGH (S. S.) Sir Thomas Fowell Buxton, Bart[.] *etc.* [1903.] 8°. **10600.** bb. **13.** (**3**

—— —— [1906.] 8°. [*Six Heroic Men, etc.*] **04429.** k. **2**

—— *See* READ (Paul) Lord John Russell, Sir Thoma[s] Fowell Buxton and the Niger Expedition, *etc.* 1840. 8° **1389.** g. **44.** (**1**

—— *See* WESTLAKE (Richard) Sir Thomas Fowell Buxto[n,] Bart., and the Slave Trade, *etc.* 1894. 8°. **8156.** df. **22.** (**13**

—— [Speech in the House of Commons. 23 June 1825. *See* ENGLAND.—*Parliament.*—*House of Commons.* [*Proceedings.*—II.] Substance of the Debate in the House o[f] Commons . . . on Mr. Buxton's Motion, respecting th[e] destruction of the Methodist Chapel in Barbadoes. 1825. 8°. **8155.** de. **2.** (**1**

—— The African Slave Trade. [With a map.] pp. xv. 240. *John Murray: London,* 1839. 8°. **1389.** g. **2**

—— The Remedy; being a sequel to the African Slave Trade[.] [With a map.] pp. xvi. 278. *John Murray: London[,]* 1840. 8°. **1389.** g. **23.** (**2.**

—— [Another edition.] pp. 152. *W. Clowes & Sons[:] London,* [1840?] 8°. **8156.** aaa. **16**
"This edition is not to be published."

—— The African Slave Trade and its Remedy. (Secon[d] edition.) [With a map.] pp. viii. vi. 582. *John Murray: London,* 1840. 8°. **8156.** c. **25**
With this work is bound up a "Prospectus of the Societ[y] for the Extinction of the Slave Trade and for the Civilisatio[n] of Africa."

—— Der afrikanische Sklavenhandel und seine Abhülf[e] . . . Aus dem Englischen übersetzt von G. Julius. Mi[t] einer Vorrede: Die Nigerexpedition und ihre Bestimmung, von Carl Ritter. Mit einer Karte. pp. lxx. 453. *Leipzig,* 1841. 8°. **8156.** bb. **25**

BUXTON (*Sir* THOMAS FOWELL) 1*st Bart.*

—— Abridgment of Sir T. Fowell Buxton's Work on the African Slave Trade and its Remedy. With an explanatory preface and an appendix. pp. 68. *John Murray: London*, 1840. 8°. **8156**. e. **8**. (**7**.)

—— [Another copy.] **8156**. c. **1**. (**6**.)

—— Second edition. pp. 71. *John Murray: London*, 1840. 8°. **1389**. g. **39**.

—— Extracts and Remarks from the Work of Sir Thomas Fowell Buxton, on "The Slave Trade and Remedy" for Central and Western Africa, applied to Madagascar and East Africa [by H. Ibbotson]. pp. 16. *L. Clark: [London*, 1841.] 8°. **8156**. e. **8**. (**9**.)

—— An Inquiry, whether Crime and Misery are produced or prevented, by our present system of prison discipline. Illustrated by descriptions of the Borough Compter, Tothill Fields, *etc.* [With an appendix, "containing an account of the prisons at Ilchester and at Bristol."] 2 pt. *J. & A. Arch: London*, 1818. 8°. **1127**. c. **9**. (**2**, **3**.)

—— [Another copy, without the appendix.] **8285**. bbb. **56**. (**12**.)

—— Second edition. pp. vii. 171. *J. & A. Arch: London*, 1818. 8°. **6059.b.8.**

—— Fifth edition. pp. 179. *A. Constable & Co.: Edinburgh*, 1818. 12°. **6058.pp.18.**

—— [Selections from "An Inquiry," etc., translated into French.] *See* CUNNINGHAM (Francis) *Philanthropist.* Notes recueillies en visitant les prisons de la Suisse, *etc.* 1820. 8°. **8073**. dd. **17**.

—— Ricerca quali delitti e calamità sono prodotte o prevenute dal presente sistema di disciplina delle carceri in Inghilterra . . . Versione dall'inglese. 1821. *See* RACCOLTA. Raccolta di trattati . . . di legislazione e giurisprudenza criminale. tom. 3. 1821, *etc.* 8°. **706**. h. **2**.

—— A Letter to the Right Hon. Lord John Russell . . . on certain allegations recently made in the House of Commons in the debate on Sir George Strickland's motion for the abolition of negro apprenticeship. pp. 15. *J. Hatchard & Son: London*, 1838. 8°. T. **2386**. (**6**.)

—— Observations on the West-India Company Bill [of 21 March 1825] as printed and read a second time on . . . March 29, 1825. [By T. F. Buxton.] pp. 32. 1825. 8°. *See* ENGLAND.—*Parliament.*—*Bills.*—II. T. **1153**. (**7**.)

—— [Another copy.] Observations on the West-India Company Bill [of 21 March 1825], *etc.* [By T. F. Buxton.] 1825. 8°. *See* ENGLAND.—*Parliament.* [*Bills.*—II. [1825. March 21.] [*Appendix.*—*West India Company.* **6837**. d. **14**.

—— Severity of Punishment. Speech . . . in the House of Commons . . . May 23rd, 1821, on the bill "for mitigating the severity of punishment in certain cases of forgery," *etc.* pp. 70. *J. & A. Arch: London*, 1821. 8°. **1127**. c. **9**. (**5**.)

—— [Another copy.] Severity of Punishment. Speech . . . May 23rd, 1821, *etc. London*, 1821. 8°. **8140**. e. **40**. (**5**.)

—— [Another edition.] pp. 49. *J. & A. Arch: London*, 1822. 8°. **8135**. ccc. **6**. (**5**.)

—— [Another copy.] **6056**. b. **22**.

—— The Speech of Thomas Fowell Buxton, Esq., at the Egyptian Hall, on the 26th November, 1816, on the subject of the distress in Spitalfields. To which is added the report of the Spitalfields Association, *etc.* pp. 20. *William Phillips: London*, 1816. 8°. **1103**. h. **32**.

BUXTON (*Sir* THOMAS FOWELL) 1*st Bart.*

—— The Substance of the Speech of Thos. Fowell Buxton, Esq. M.P. in the House of Commons, March 2d, 1819, on the motion of Sir James Mackintosh, Bart., "that, a select committee be appointed, to consider of so much of the criminal laws as relates to capital punishments or felonies," *etc.* pp. 24. *J. & A. Arch: London*, 1819. 8°. **6485**. b. **5**.

—— Enquiry into the Consequences of the present Depreciated Value of Human Labour, &c. &c. In letters to Thos. Fowell Buxton, Esq., M.P. pp. 116. *Longman & Co.: London*, 1819. 4°. **8207**. g. **7**. (**1**.)

BUXTON (*Sir* THOMAS FOWELL) 3*rd Bart. See* RUSSELL (*Right Hon.* George W. E.) Lady Victoria Buxton . . . With some account of her husband (Sir T. F. Buxton), *etc.* [With a portrait.] 1919. 8°. **010856**. ee. **24**.

—— England and Africa. A lecture, *etc.* [With a map.] pp. 24. *Edward Stanford: London*, 1878. 8°. **8154**. ee. **4**.

BUXTON (TRAVERS) William Wilberforce. The story of a great crusade. [With plates, including portraits.] pp. 187. *R.T.S.: London*, [1903.] 8°. **04429**. l. **19**.

—— [A reissue.] *London*, [1933.] 8°. **4909**. aaa. **12**.
Without two of the plates, and with the addition of a foreword.

BUXTON (*Lady* VICTORIA) *See* NOEL (*Hon.* Roden B. W.) The Collected Poems of Roden Noel, *etc.* [With an introductory note by Lady Victoria Buxton.] 1902. 8°. **11609**. dd. **11**.

—— *See* RUSSELL (*Right Hon.* George W. E.) Lady Victoria Buxton . . . With portraits. 1919. 8°. **010856**. ee. **24**.

BUXTON (WILLIAM LEONARD) Mearham. pp. vii. 310. *Longmans & Co.: London*, 1927. 8°. NN. **12723**.

BUXTON (WILLIAM ORRELL) *See* PITMAN (*Sir* Isaac) AND SONS. Pitman's Advanced Book-keeping . . . Revised edition by W. O. Buxton. [1918, *etc.*] 8°. **08532**. df. **21**.

—— *See* PITMAN (*Sir* Isaac) AND SONS. Pitman's Book-keeping Simplified . . . Chapters on reserves, and the formation of joint stock companies, by W. O. Buxton, *etc.* [1912.] 8°. **8503**. ccc. **33**.

—— *See* PITMAN (*Sir* Isaac) AND SONS. Pitman's Book-keeping Simplified . . . Thoroughly revised edition, by W. O. Buxton. [1916.] 8°. **8503**. ee. **42**.

—— Book-keeping. pp. vii. 150. *London*, [1915.] 8°. [*Pitman's Practical Primers of Business.*] **08226**. aaa. **1/11**.

—— Book-keeping Simplified . . . Revised and enlarged edition [of "Pitman's Book-keeping Simplified"]. [With answers to exercises.] 2 pt. *Sir I. Pitman & Sons: London*, 1933. 8°. **08206**. eee. **6**.

BUXTON (WILLIAM PITT WILBERFORCE) The Lodge opened. Arranged and adapted by W. P. W. Buxton. [With songs and musical notes.] *See* TEMPLAR ENTERTAINER. The Templar Entertainer, *etc.* [1877.] 8°. **12331**. aaaa. **2**.

BUXTON (WILMOT) *See* BUXTON (Harry W.)

BUXTORF (ANDREAS)

—— *See* GEIGY (J. R.) *S.A.* 15 Years of Geigy Pest Control. (Editors: A. Buxtorf and M. Spindler.) 1954. fol. L.R. **400**. a. **15**.

BUXTORF (AUGUST) *Capitaine au 34e régiment d'artillerie de Campagne.* En Italie avec la 24e division d'infanterie française, septembre–décembre 1918. Dessins de Bernard Naudin. pp. 146. *Nancy,* [1920.] 8°. **09084**. aa. **34**.

BUXTORF (AUGUST) *of Basle.*

—— Die Anfänge der geologischen Erforschung des nordschweizerischen Juragebirges. Rektoratsrede, *etc.* pp. 23. *Basel,* 1940. 8°. [*Basler Universitätsreden.* Hft. 11.] Ac. **604**. f.

—— Geologie der Umgebung von Gelterkinden im Basler Tafeljura. Mit . . . einer geolog. Karte, *etc.* pp. ix. 106. *Bern,* 1901. 4°. [*Beiträge zur geologischen Karte der Schweiz.* Lfg. 41.] Ac. **2866**/**5**.

BUXTORF (AUGUST JOHAN) Die Reise nach der Birs-Quelle samt einer kurzen Beleuchtung der ohnferne . . . befindlichen römischen Steinschrift auf Pierre-Pertuis, *etc.* [With plates.] 1756. *See* BRUECKNER (D.) Versuch einer Beschreibung . . . der Landschaft Basel, *etc.* Stück 14. 1764, *etc.* 8°. **956**. d. **27**.

BUXTORF (CARL) *See* CARPENTARII (G.) Die Reformationschronik des Karthäusers Georg, übersetzt . . . durch K. Buxtorf. 1849. 8°. **4535**. c. **9**. (4.)

BUXTORF (JOHANN) *See* BUXTORFIUS (Johannes)

BUXTORF (JOHANN JACOB) *See* BUXTORFIUS (Johannes J.)

BUXTORF (K.) *Pfarrer in Stettfurt.* Die dringendsten Aufgaben der protestantischen Apologetik in der Gegenwart. Referat, *etc.* pp. 29. *Basel,* 1875. 8°. **3913**. e. **2**. (**15**.)

BUXTORF (KARL) *See* BUXTORF (Carl)

BUXTORF (PETER)

—— Die lateinischen Grabinschriften in der Stadt Basel. pp. 224. *Basel,* 1940. 8°. [*Basler Beiträge zur Geschichtswissenschaft.* Bd. 6.] W.P. **9213**/**6**.

BUXTORF-FALKEISEN (CARL) *See* KNEBEL (Johannes) *Capellanus in Basilea.* Chronik des Kaplans J. Knebel, *etc.* [Edited by C. Buxtorf-Falkeisen.] 1851, *etc.* 8°. **09327**. aaa. **29**.

—— Baslerische Stadt- und Landgeschichten aus dem sechszehnten Jahrhundert. 3 Abt. *Basel,* 1868 [1863–68]. 8°. **9304**. ee. **26**.
Published in parts.

—— Baslerische Stadt- und Landgeschichten aus dem siebzehnten Jahrhundert. 3 Hft. *Basel,* 1872–77. 8°. **9304**. ee. **30**.

—— Johannes Buxtorf Vater, Prof. ling. hebr. 1564–1629, erkannt aus seinem Briefwechsel. pp. 46. *Basel,* 1860. 8°. **4886**. c. **71**. (**5**.)

BUXTORFFIUS (GERHARDUS) *See* BUXTORFFIUS (Gerlacus)

BUXTORFFIUS (GERLACUS) Consilium II. G. Buxtorfj . . . Articulus I. agit de jure lustrationis . . . II. De jure sequelæ . . . III. De jure statuendi . . . IV. De jure collectandi, *etc.* *See* KLOCKIUS (C.) C. Klockii . . . tractatus . . . de contributionibus, *etc.* (Fasciculus . . . consultationum, *etc.*) 1656. fol. **5505**. i. **3**.

—— [Another edition.] *See* KLOCKIUS (C.) C. Klockii . . . tractatus . . . de contributionibus, *etc.* (Fasciculus . . . consultationum, *etc.*) 1676. fol. **1234**. k. **18**.

—— Gerlaci Buxtorffii Dissertatio ad XVII. priora capita Aureae Bullae Caroli IV. *See* GERMANY. [*Appendix.—History and Politics.*—II.] Repræsentatio Reipubl. Germanicæ, *etc.* 1657. 4°. **169**. e. **19**.

BUXTORFIUS (GERHARDUS) *See* BUXTORFFIUS (Gerlacus

BUXTORFIUS (JOHANNES) *the Elder.* *See* ANSGARIU (M.) לקט קציר רבותינו sive Spicilegium defectus lex corum Rabbinicorum variorum potissimum Buxtorf utriusque, in brevi dissertatione coacervatum, *etc.* [1704.] 4°. **619**. e. **8**. (4

—— *See* BIBLE.—*Old Testament.* [*Polyglott.*] תשועתך ' באמרתך . . . הכ״ד החדשים וכו׳ [The Old Testament, wit Aramaic versions, and the commentaries of Rash Abraham Ibn Ezra, David Ḳimḥī and others. Revise and edited by J. Buxtorfius the Elder.] [1618, *etc.*] fc **8**. g. **1**–

—— *See* BIBLE.—*Appendix.—Old Testament.—Concordance* [*Hebrew.*] The Hebrew Concordance, adapted to th English Bible, disposed after the manner of Buxtorf . . by J. Taylor, *etc.* 1754, *etc.* fol. **685**. l.

—— *See* BIBLE.—*Lamentations.* [*Latin.*] איכה sive Jeremi vatis Lamentationes . . . cum . . . commentariis . . è Buxtorfiis Bibliis magnis excerptis, *etc.* 1651. 4°. **3166**. bb.

—— *See* BUXTORF-FALKEISEN (C.) Johannes Buxto Vater . . . erkannt aus seinem Briefwechsel. 1860. 8°. **4886**. c. **71**. (5

—— *See* KAUTZSCH (E. F.) Johannes Buxtorf der Älter Rectorats-Rede, *etc.* 1879. 8°. **010705**. h. 4

—— *See* MARTINIUS (P.) Grammatica ebræa Martini Buxtorfiana. Seu, Grammatica P. Martinii . . . quam e . . . aliorum grammaticis, prȩcipue verò cl. Buxtor . . . S. Amana . . . correxit, *etc.* 1634. 8°. **12903**. aaa. **12**. (1

—— *See* SELIG (G.) Compendia vocum hebraico-rabbin carum, quæ partim ex Buxtorfio . . . collegit G. Seli *etc.* 1780. 8°. **12904**. aa. 1

—— *See* SENNERTUS (A.) Compendium lexici ebræi pleniori . . . concinnatum e concordantiarum opere . . . Jo Buxtorfii autore A. Sennerto. 1663. 4°. [TROSTIUS (M *Cl. V. M. Trosti Grammatica ebraea.*] **63**. l.

—— Iohan. Buxtorfii De abbreviaturis hebraicis liber novu & copiosus: cui accesserunt operis Talmudici brev recensio . . . Item Bibliotheca rabbinica nova, ordin alphabethico disposita. pp. 335. *Typi C. Waldkirchii: Basileæ,* 1613. 8°. **826**. a. **1**. (1.

—— Editione hac secunda omnia castigatiora, *etc.* pp. 472. *Impensis L. Regis: Basileæ,* 1640. 8°. **621**. d.

—— [Another edition.] Editione hac novissima omni castigatiora, luculentis adnotationibus illustrata, & nov abbreviaturis librorumque titulis aucta. 2 pt. *Herbornæ Nassauiæ,* 1708. 8°. **58**. a.

—— Joann. Buxtorfii Epitome grammaticæ Hebrææ . . . a publicum scholarum usum proposita. Adjecta succinct de mutatione punctorum vocalium instructio, & textuu Psalmorumque aliquot Hebraicorum Latina interpretati *etc.* pp. 119. *Ex officina Rogeri Daniel: Londin* 1653. 8°. **621**. d.

—— [Another edition.] Aucta & emendata per I. Buxtorfiu filium. Cui tandem accessit Christiani Schotani appendi ad pleniorem etymologiæ κατασκευην. Editio non pp. 147. *Ex officina Johannis Redmayne: Londin* 1666. 8°. **12932**. aaa. 4

—— [Another edition.] Hanc editionem secundam, su ductu patris, procuravit [R]odolphus Leusdenus. pp. 172 *J. Luchtmans: Lugduni Batavorum,* 1691. 8°. **12903**. a. **2**. (1.
The titlepage is slightly mutilated.

BUXTORFIUS (JOHANNES) *the Elder.*

— Editio nona, *etc.* (Recensita a J. Buxtorfio fil.) pp. 176. *Basileæ*, 1710. 8°. **12904.** a. **25.**

— Editio quarta. (Emendata, illustrata et aucta a J. Leusden.) pp. 176. *Lugduni Batavorum*, 1716. 8°. **12906.** a. **27.**

— Editio quinta. pp. 176. *Lugduni Batavorum*, 1761. 8°. **12903.** a. **46.**

— A Short Introduction to the Hebrew Tongue, being a translation of . . . J. Buxtorfius' Epitome . . . By John Davis . . . Whereunto is annexed an English interlineall interpretation of some Hebrew texts of the Psalmes, for . . . beginners, *etc.* pp. 114. *Roger Daniel, for Humphrey Moseley: London*, 1656. 8°. E. **1639.** (2.)
The imprint has been corrected in a contemporary hand to " 13 *Novemb.* 1655."

— Johannis Buxtorfii Epitome radicum hebraicarum et chaldaicarum complectens omnes voces, tam primas quàm derivatas, quæ in Sacris Bibliis . . . extant: interpretationis fide, exemplorum Biblicorum copia . . . locupletata, *etc.* pp. 983. *C. Waldkirch: Basileæ*, 1607. 8°. **621.** d. **2.**

— [Another edition.] Johannis Buxtorfii Lexicon hebraicum et chaldaicum . . . Accessit lexicon breve rabbinico-philosophicum, *etc.* pp. 954. *Typis C. Waldkirchii: Basileæ*, 1615. 8°. **1476.** a. **16.**

— Editio tertia . . . recognita. pp. 960. *L. König: Basileæ*, 1621. 8°. **12904.** aa. **17.**

— Editio quarta, *etc.* pp. 974. *L. König: Basileæ*, 1631. 8°. **621.** d. **4.**

— Editio quinta, de novo recognita, *etc.* pp. 976. *Sumptibus hæredum L. König: Basileæ*, 1645. 8°. **12903.** aaa. **10.**

— Editio sexta . . . recognita . . . & emendata. Huic sextæ editioni accessit abbreviaturarum συλλογη, ex optimis authoribus concinnata. pp. 999. *Typis J. Junii, & M. Bell; sumptibus R. Whitakeri & S. Cartwright: Londini*, 1646. 8°. **12903.** aa. **31.**

— [Another edition.] Accessere huic editioni radices ebraicæ, cum versione germanica & belgica [or rather, Dutch only]. pp. 976. *sumptibus J. Jansonii Junioris: Amstelodami*, 1654. 8°. **12903.** aaa. **11.**
With an additional titlepage, engraved, and dated 1655.

— [Another edition.] pp. 976. *J. König: Basileæ*, 1655. 8°. **621.** d. **5.**

— Editio septima, *etc.* pp. 976. *J. König: Basileæ*, 1663. 8°. **12904.** aaa. **20.**

— Editio octava, *etc.* pp. 976. *J. König & Fil.: Basileæ*, 1676. 8°. **621.** d. **6.**

— Editio nona, *etc.* pp. 976. *Typis & sumptibus J. L. König & J. Brandmylleri: Basileæ*, 1689. 8°. **12904.** aaa. **35.**

— Editio decima, *etc.* pp. 976. COPIOUS MS. NOTES. *Sumptibus F. Plateri & J. P. Richteri: Basileæ*, 1698. 8°. **825.** c. **22, 23.**
Interleaved.

— Editio undecima, *etc.* (Subsidium memoriae primum, onomasticum, *etc.*—Subsidium memoriae secundum, analogicum, *etc.*) [With a portrait.] 2 pt. *Basileæ*, 1710. 8°. **12903.** aaa. **9.**

BUXTORFIUS (JOHANNES) *the Elder.*

— Editio novissima, *etc.* 2 pt. pp. 976. *Basileæ*, 1735. 8°. **12904.** a. **36.**

— [Another edition.] Digessit . . . auxit, atque illustravit Fr. Josephus Montaldi, *etc.* 4 tom. *Romæ*, 1789. 8°. **12903.** cc. **29.**

— Editio nova, sedulo recensita. pp. 616. *A. & J. M. Duncan: Glasguæ*, 1824. 8°. **621.** i. **32.**

— A Transcript of Buxtorf's Primitives [from the " Lexicon hebraicum "]; with the leading signification to every word in English. pp. 103. *J. Evans: Carmarthen*, 1812. 12°. **12904.** aaa. **28.**

— Explicatio carminis Saadiae quod . . . exhibet numerum quoties quaelibet alphabeti litera in tota Scriptura contineatur. *See* ELIJAH, *Ben Asher, the Levite.* Uebersetzung des Buchs Massoreth Hammassoreth, *etc.* 1772. 8°. **4034.** ccc. **24.**

— Ioh. Buxtorfii Grammaticae Chaldaicae et Syriacae libri III . . . Cum facili vocabulorum difficilium explicatione grammatica, & pravorum ad veram linguae analogiam collatione. Inserta quoque passim est Dialectus talmudica & rabbinica. pp. 416. *L. König: Basileæ*, 1615. 8°. **825.** a. **35.**

— Editio emendatissima. pp. 450. *L. & E. König: Basileæ*, 1685. 8°. **58.** a. **21.**

— Johann. Buxtorfii Institutio epistolaris hebraica, cum epistolarum hebraicarum familiarium centuria, ex quibus . . . quinquaginta punctis vocalibus animatæ, versione latina & notis illustratæ sunt. Adjectus est . . . index: item abbreviaturarum epistolicarum succincta explicatio. pp. 279. *Typis C. Waldkirchii: Basileæ*, 1610. 8°. **826.** a. **1.** (2.)

— [Another copy.] **1085.** k. **12.**
With the autograph of Isaac Casaubon on the titlepage.

— [Another edition.] Accessit appendix variarum epistolarum R. Majemonis & aliorum . . . Rabbinorum, quas recensuit J. Buxtorfius fil. pp. 462. *Sumptibus L. Regis: Basileæ*, 1629. 8°. **1085.** k. **13.**

— [Another copy.] **3128.** b. **21.** (2.)

— Johannis Buxtorfii P. Lexicon chaldaicum talmudicum et rabbinicum . . . Nunc demum, post patris obitum . . . in lucem editum a Johanne Buxtorfio filio, *etc.* [With a portrait.] coll. 2680. *L. König: Basileæ*, 1639. fol. **629.n.20.**
With an additional titlepage, engraved.

— [Another issue.] *Basileæ*, 1640. fol. **66.** h. **4.**

— [Another edition.] Denuo edidit et annotatis auxit . . . Bernardus Fischerus. 2 vol. pp. xxvii. 1322. *Lipsiae*, 1869, 75 [1866–75]. 4°. **012904.d.2.**
Published in parts. The wrapper of fasc. 1 *reads:* " *Denuo editum . . . a Dr. Ph. B. Fischer . . . et Dr. Ph. Hermanno Gelbe.*"

— [Another issue.] *Asher & Co.: Londini; [Leipsic printed,]* 1874, [75.] 4°. **12904.** f. **14.**
Without the titlepage of vol. 2.

— Lexicon hebraicum et chaldaicum. *See* supra: Epitome radicum hebraicarum.

— Johannis Buxtorfii Manuale hebraicum et chaldaicum . . . Editio quarta, castigatior. pp. 383. *L. Köning: Basileæ*, 1619. 12°. **12901.** aaa. **10.**

BUXTORFIUS (JOHANNES) *the Elder.*

—— Editio quinta, *etc.* [With a preface by J. Buxtorfius the Younger.] pp. 383. *L. Köning: Basileæ,* 1631. 12°. **12904.** a. **12.**

—— [Another edition.] pp. xii. 386. *E Typographeo Clarendoniano: Oxonii,* 1807. 12°. **63.** l. **8.**

—— Joh. Buxtorfii . . . Specimen phraseologiæ V. T. hebraicæ, exhibens . . . phrases aliquam multas, adjecta passim difficiliorum succincta explicatione. pp. 96. *Francofurti,* 1717. 8°. **12904.** aa. **6.**

—— Synagoga judaica: Das ist, Jüden Schul: Darinnen der gantz Jüdische Glaub und Glaubensubung, mit allen Ceremonien, Satzungen, Sitten und Gebräuchen, wie sie bey ihnen . . . im Brauche: auss ihren eigenen Bücheren und Schrifften . . . grundlich erkläret . . . Jetzt erstmals . . . an Tag gegeben. pp. 730. *S. Henricpetri: Basel,* 1603. 8°. **4033.** de. **7.** (**1.**)

—— Schoole der Jooden, begrypende het geheele Joodsche geloof . . . Af nieuws overzien, en met nieuwe kopere platen door J. Luyken verçierd. Hier agter is bygevoegt een Reden-strydt tusschen een Jood en een Christen, waar in het Christen geloof werd verdedigt. Derde druk. 2 pt. *Rotterdam,* 1731. 8°. **4034.** bb. **27.**
With an additional titlepage, engraved.

—— Synagoga iudaica; hoc est, Schola Iudæorum, in quâ natiuitas, institutio, religio, vita, mors, sepulturaq; ipsorum . . . a M. I. Buxdorfio . . . graphice descripta est. Addita est mox per eundem Iudæi cum Christiano disputatio de Messia nostro. Quæ vtraque germanica nunc latinè reddita sunt operâ & studio M. Hermanni Germbergii . . . Accessit Ludouici Carreti epistola, de conuersione eius ad Christum, *etc.* pp. 644. MS. NOTES [by I. Casaubon]. *Apud G. [Antonium]: Hanou[iæ],* 16[04]. 12°. **848.** b. **19.**
The titlepage is mutilated.

—— Johannis Buxtorfii Synagoga judaica, auspiciis authoris jam olim Latinitate donata [by David Le Clerc], nunc primum in vulgus emissa. [Edited by Johannes Buxtorfius the Younger.] pp. 498. *L. König: Basileæ,* 1641. 8°. **4034.** bb. **28.**

—— Tertia hac editione, de novo restaurata, & . . . in . . . augustiorem formam redacta, a J. Buxtorfio, filio, *etc.* pp. 779. *Sumptibus Authoris, apud J. J. Deckerum: Basileæ,* 1661. 8°. **4034.** b. **43.**
With an additional titlepage, engraved.

—— Quarta hac editione revisa . . . a Joh. Jacobo Buxtorfio. pp. 779. *Impensis E. König & Filiorum: Basileæ,* 1680. 8°. **482.** a. **18.**

—— [Another edition.] 1745. *See* UGOLINUS (B.) Thesaurus antiquitatum sacrarum, *etc.* tom. 4. 1744, *etc.* fol. **686.** k. **4.**

—— Translation, by way of abridgment, of Buxtorf's Latin Account of the Religious Customs and Ceremonies of the Jews. *See* STEHELIN (John P.) Rabbinical Literature . . . Appendix, *etc.* 1748. 8°. **219.** g. **1.**

—— Excerptum e libro cui titulus est Synagoga iudaica . . . Hanouiæ edito anno 1614, *etc.* [From Chap. 20 of H. Germbergius's version.] [*Paris?* 1617?] 12°. **8050.** aaa. **23.** (**22.**)

—— Johannis Buxtorfii Thesaurus grammaticus linguæ sanctæ hebrææ . . . Adjecta Poeseos hebraicæ accurata tractatio; lectionis rabbinicæ solida instructio, lectionis hebræo-germanicæ usus & exercitatio. pp. 671. *Typis C. Waldkirchii: Basilea,* 1609. 8°. **12903.** aa. **28.**

BUXTORFIUS (JOHANNES) *the Elder.*

—— Editio tertia, cum . . . indice. pp. 690. *Impens[...] L. Regis: Basilea,* 1620. 8°. **621.** d. [...]

—— Editio quinta, *etc.* pp. 690. *Impensis hære[...] L. Regis: Basilea,* 1651. 8°. **12903.** aaa. [...]

—— Editio sexta, recognita à Johanne Buxtorfio, fili[...] pp. 669. *Impensis J. Buxtorfi, Junioris: Basile[...]* 1663. 8°. **63.** l. [...]

—— Tiberias; sive Commentarius masorethicus; q[...] primum explicatur quid Masora sit; tum histo[...] Masoretharum ex Hebræorum annalibus excutitur . Secundò clavis Masoræ traditur . . . denique . . analytica Masoræ explicatio in primum caput Genes[...] proponitur, *etc.* pp. 324. *L. König: Basileæ Rauracoru[...]* 1620. 4°. **3129.** e. [...]

—— [Another edition.] Recognitus & additamentis n[...] paucis hinc inde locupletatus a Johanne Buxtorfio [...] Editionem hancce novam accurante Johan. Jaco[...] Buxtorfio. pp. 108. *Impensis J. Buxtorfii: Basile[...]* 1665. fol. **8.** g. **4.** ([...]

—— [Another edition.] pp. 430. *Sumptibus J. Buxtorf[...] Basileæ,* 1665. 4°. **220.** i. [...]

—— J. Buxtorfii Tractatus brevis de prosodia metr[...] Hebræorum. 1766. *See* UGOLINUS (B.) Thesau[...] antiquitatum sacrarum, *etc.* vol. 31. 1744, *etc.* fol. **686.** l. [...]

BUXTORFIUS (JOHANNES) *M.D.* Dissertatio inaugur[...] medica de visu, *etc.* [With a diagram.] pp. 23. *Basileæ,* [1728.] 4°. **1179.** h. **9.** [...]

BUXTORFIUS (JOHANNES) *Nephew of Johannes Jaco[...] Buxtorfius.* Johannis Buxtorfii . . . ספר לבוצים s[...] Catalecta philologico-theologica. Accedunt manti[...] loco virorum celeberrimorum Casauboni, Heinsii, Uss[...] Waltoni, Schickardi, aliorumque epistolæ ad J. Buxtorfi[...] patrem & filium nunc primum in lucem editæ. pp. 49[...] *Basileæ,* 1707. 8°. **4373.** a. [...]

—— Johannis Buxtorfii Dissertationes varii argume[...] Accedit G. S. Doctoris angli, Diatriba de judicio pa[...] culari. pp. 186. *Basileæ,* 1725. 8°. **245.** h. [...]

—— Specimen prælectionum aliquot, *etc.* *Basi[...]* 1712. 8°. **731.** b. **3.** [...]

BUXTORFIUS (JOHANNES) *the Younger. See* ANSGAR[...] (M.) לקט קציר רבותינו sive Spicilegium defectus l[...] corum rabbinicorum variorum potissimum Buxtorf[...] utriusque, *etc.* [1704.] 4°. **619.** e. **8.** [...]

—— *See* BUXTORFIUS (Johannes) *the Elder.* Joann. Buxt[...] Epitome grammaticæ hebrææ . . . Aucta & emendata[...] I. Buxtorfium filium, *etc.* 1666. 8°. **12932.** aaa. [...]

—— —— 1710. 8°. **12904.** a. [...]

—— *See* BUXTORFIUS (Johannes) *the Elder.* Joha[...] Buxtorfii Institutio epistolaris hebraica . . . Acc[...] appendix variorum epistolarum R. Majemonis & ali[...] . . . Rabbinorum, quas recensuit J. Buxtorfius fil. 1629. 8°. **1085.** k[...]

—— *See* BUXTORFIUS (Johannes) *the Elder.* J. Buxt[...] P. Lexicon chaldaicum . . . Nunc demum . . . in lu[...] editum a J. Buxtorfio filio, *etc.* 1639. fol. **629.n.**[...]

— —— 1640. fol. **66. h. 4.**

— —— 1869, *etc.* 4°. **012904.d.2.**

— —— 1874. 4°. **12904. f. 14.**

— *See* BUXTORFIUS (Johannes) *the Elder.* Johannis Buxtorfii Manuale hebraicum et chaldaicum, *etc.* [Edited by J. Buxtorfius the Younger.] 1631. 12°. **12904. a. 12.**

— *See* BUXTORFIUS (Johannes) *the Elder.* Johannis Buxtorfii Synagoga judaica, *etc.* [Edited by J. Buxtorfius the Younger.] 1641. 8°. **4034. bb. 28.**

— —— 1661. 8°. **4034. b. 43.**

— —— 1680. 8°. **482. a. 18.**

— *See* BUXTORFIUS (Johannes) *the Elder.* Johannis Buxtorfii Thesaurus grammaticus linguæ sanctæ hebrææ . . . Editio sexta, recognita a J. Buxtorfio, filio. 1663. 8°. **63. l. 9.**

— *See* BUXTORFIUS (Johannes) *the Elder.* J. Buxtorfii P. Tiberias, sive Commentarius masorethicus . . . Recognitus & additamentis non paucis hinc inde locupletatus a J. Buxtorfio fil., *etc.* 1665. fol. **8. g. 4. (3.)**

— —— 1665. 4°. **220. i. 9.**

— *See* GERNLER (L.) Oratio parentalis . . . J. Buxtorfii beatis manibus dicata, *etc.* [1665.] 4°. **489. a. 9. (2.)**

— *See* LAURENTIUS (G.) Corpus et syntagma confessionum fidei, *etc.* (Articuli confessionis Basileensis. De quorum *ὀρθοδοξίᾳ* . . . præsidibus . . . T. Zvingero . . . J. Buxtorfio . . . conferetur.) 1654. 4°. **849. l. 10.**

— *See* MOSES, *ben Maimon.* [*Guide of the Perplexed.*] Rabbi Mosis Majemonidis liber מורה נבוכים Doctor perplexorum . . . in linguam latinam . . . conversus, a J. Buxtorfio. 1629. 4°. **01937. f. 12.**

— *See* SCHNEDERMANN (G.) Die Controverse des L. Cappellus mit den Buxtorfen über das Alter der hebräischen Punctation, *etc.* 1879. 8°. **12901. e. 27. (18.)**

— Johannis Buxtorfii, filii . . . Dissertationes philologico-theologicæ, *etc.* 7 pt. *Sumptibus hæred. L. König: Basileæ,* 1645 [1642–45]. 4°. **12904. df. 30.**

— [Another edition.] Accesserunt R. Isaaci Abarbenelis . . . aliquot elegantes & eruditæ dissertationes . . . Ab eodem ex hebræa in latinam linguam versæ: cum indice locorum Scripturæ explicatorum & illustratorum. pp. 499. *Impensis J. Buxtorfii: Basileæ,* 1662. 4°. **482. a. 17.**

— Johannis Buxtorfii fil. . . . Anticritica: seu Vindiciæ veritatis hebraicæ: adversus Ludovici Cappelli Criticam quam vocat sacram, ejusq; defensionem: quibus sacrosanctæ editionis Bibliorum hebraicæ authoritas . . . à variis ejus . . . sophismatis; quamplurima loca a temerariis censuris, & variarum lectionum commentis, vindicantur, *etc.* pp. 1026. *Sumptibus hæredum L. Regis: Basileæ,* 1653. 4°. **217. g. 7.**

— J. Buxtorfii Dissertatio de conviviis veterum Hebræorum. 1765. *See* UGOLINUS (B.) Thesaurus antiquitatum sacrarum, *etc.* vol. 30. 1744, *etc.* fol. **686. l. 10.**

— J. Buxtorfii Dissertatio de literarum hebraicarum genuina antiquitate. 1765. *See* UGOLINUS (B.) Thesaurus antiquitatum sacrarum, *etc.* vol. 28. 1744, *etc.* fol. **686. l. 8.**

— *See* CAPPEL (L.) *the Younger.* Ludovici Cappelli diatriba de veris et antiquis Ebræorum literis. Opposita D. J. Buxtorfii de eodem argumento dissertationi, *etc.* 1645. 12°. **621. a. 14.**

—— J. Buxtorfii dissertatio de nomine יהוה. *See* RELAND (A.) Decas exercitationum philologicarum de vera pronuntiatione nominis Jehova, *etc.* 1707. 8°. **12904. aa. 21.**

—— Johannis Buxtorfii fil. . . . Dissertatio, de sponsalibus et divortiis. Cui accessit Isaaci Abarbanelis Diatriba de excidii pœna, cujus frequens in lege, & in hac ipsa materia fit mentio. pp. 195. *Sumptibus hæred. L. Regis: Basileæ,* 1652. 4°. **859. g. 8. (2.)**

—— [Another copy.] **220. f. 15. (2.)**

—— [Another edition.] 1765. *See* UGOLINUS (B.) Thesaurus antiquitatum sacrarum, *etc.* vol. 30. 1744, *etc.* fol. **686. l. 10.**

—— J. Buxtorfii Epistola de recte instituendo studio rabbinico. 1748. *See* PERIODICAL PUBLICATIONS.—*Zurich.* Museum helveticum, *etc.* pt. 9. 1746, *etc.* 8°. **248. c. 28.**

—— Johannis Buxtorfii, fil. . . . Exercitationes ad historiam, 1. Arcæ fœderis. 2. Ignis sacri et cœlestis. 3. Urim et Thummim. 4. Mannæ. 5. Petræ in deserto. 6. Serpentis ænei. Quibus sacra hæc Vet. Testamenti mysteria . . . enucleantur, *etc.* pp. 492. *Typis G. Deckeri: Basileæ,* 1659. 4°. **220. f. 15. (1.)**

—— J. Buxtorfii Dissertatio de manna. [From the "Exercitationes."] 1747. *See* UGOLINUS (B.) Thesaurus antiquitatum sacrarum, *etc.* vol. 8. 1744, *etc.* fol. **686. k. 8.**

—— J. Buxtorfii fil. Historia arcæ fœderis. [From the "Exercitationes."] 1747. *See* UGOLINUS (B.) Thesaurus antiquitatum sacrarum, *etc.* vol. 8. 1744, *etc.* fol. **686. k. 8.**

—— J. Buxtorfii Historia ignis sacri et coelestis, sacrificia consumentis. [From the "Exercitationes."] 1749. *See* UGOLINUS (B.) Thesaurus antiquitatum sacrarum, *etc.* vol. 10. 1744, *etc.* fol. **686. k. 10.**

—— J. Buxtorfii Historia Urim et Thummim. [From the "Exercitationes."] 1751. *See* UGOLINUS (B.) Thesaurus antiquitatum sacrarum, *etc.* vol. 12. 1744, *etc.* fol. **686. k. 12.**

—— Johannis Buxtorfii, fil. . . . Florilegium hebraicum: continens elegantes sententias, proverbia, apophthegmata, similitudines: ex optimis quibusque, maximè vero priscis Hebræorum scriptoribus, collectum, *etc.* pp. 390. *Impensis hæred. L. König: Basileæ,* 1648. 8°. **12903. a. 44.**

—— Ioh. Buxtorfius Spenero, S.D. *See* GEDIKE (F.) Epistolarum selectissimarum . . . decas, *etc.* 1745. 4°. **117. n. 55.**

—— Lexicon chaldaicum et syriacum, quo voces omnes . . . quotquot in sacrorum Vet. Testamenti librorum Targumim, seu paraphrasibus chaldaicis, Onkeli in Mosen, Jonathanis in Prophetas, & aliorum authorum in Hagiographa: item in Targum Hierosolymitano . . . denique in Novi Testamenti translatione syriaca reperiuntur . . . copiose . . . describuntur, *etc.* pp. 640. *Ex officina L. Regis: Basileæ,* 1622. 4°. **12903. bb. 11.**

—— Maimonidis vita descripta a J. Buxtorfio fil. in præfatione ad More Nevochim. 1747. *See* UGOLINUS (B.) Thesaurus antiquitatum sacrarum, *etc.* vol. 8. 1744, *etc.* fol. **686. k. 8.**

—— Iohannis Buxtorfii filii . . . Tractatus de punctorum vocalium et accentuum in libris Veteris Testamenti hebraicis, origine, antiquitate & authoritate; oppositus Arcano punctationis revelato Ludovici Cappelli. pp. 437. *Sumptibus hæredum L. König: Basileæ,* 1648. 4°. **859. g. 8. (1.)**

—— [Another copy.] **218. h. 22.**

BUXTORFIUS (Johannes Jacobus) *See* Buxtorfius (Johannes) *the Elder*. Johannis Buxtorfii patris Synagoga judaica . . . Quarta hac editione . . . revisa . . . à J. J. Buxtorfio. 1680. 8°. **482. a. 18.**

—— *See* Buxtorfius (Johannes) *the Elder*. J. Buxtorfii P. Tiberias . . . Editionem hancce novam accurante J. J. Buxtorfio. 1665. fol. **8. g. 4. (3.)**

—— —— 1665. 4°. **220. i. 9.**

BUXTORFIUS (Johannes Ludovicus) Observationes medicæ, *etc. Praes.* J. R. Hess. pp. 8. *Basileæ*, [1753.] 4°. **B. 141. (9.)**

—— Specimen observationum medicarum, *etc. Praes.* J. R. Stehelin. pp. 8. *Basileæ*, [1753.] 4°. **B. 141. (10.)**

BUXY (B. de) Le Secret de Lusabran. pp. 317. *Paris*, [1888.] 12°. **012547. g. 22.**

BUY.

—— Buy, sell & exchange. *See* Periodical Publications.—*Thornton Heath.*

BUY ME. Buy Me! Leach's Summer Annual. *See* Periodical Publications.—*Middlesbrough.*

BUY ( ) *See* Halévy (Léon) and Buy ( ) La Madone. Drame, *etc.* 1840. 8°. [*Magasin théâtral.* tom. 27.] **11735. i. 27. (11.)**

—— *See* Halévy (Léon) and Buy ( ) [La Madone.] Um Quadro. Drama, *etc.* 1846. 8°. [*Archivo theatral.* tom. 8. no. 93.] **11726. c. 18.**

BUY (Abel) Essai sur l'ulcère simple de l'estomac, *etc.* pp. 34. *Paris*, 1862. 4°. [*Collection des thèses soutenues à la Faculté de Médecine de Paris.* An 1862. tom. 2.] **7373. d. 13.**

BUY (Paul) Histoire naturelle et médicale des Ixodes. 1907. *See* Lyons.—*Société Linnéenne de Lyon.* Annales. Nouvelle série. tom. 53. 1847, *etc.* 8°. **Ac. 2847/2.**

BUYAKEVICH (Melety) *Archimandrite of the Monastery of the Caves at Kiev. See* Melety.

BUYALSKY (Iliya Vasil'evich) Eliae Buialsky . . . Tabulae anatomico-chirurgicae, operationes ligandarum arteriarum maiorum exponentes . . . Анатомико-хирургическія таблицы, *etc. Lat. & Russ.* pp. iv. 32. pl. xiv. *Санктпетербургъ*, 1828. fol. **1899.f.35.**
With an additional titlepage in Russian only, engraved.

BUYANOV (A. F.)

—— Новые волокна. Под редакцией проф. Н. В. Михайлова. Издание второе. pp. 46. *Москва*, 1953. 8°. **7744. df. 7.**
Научно-популярная библиотека. вып. 55.

BUYANOV (V. I.)

—— *See* Lesik (B. V.) Первичная обработка конопли. [By B. V. Lesik and V. I. Buyanov.] 1954. 8°. **7081. a. 23.**

BUYAT (Jean Claude) La Vérité à la France ou Cause et remède de nos malheurs . . . Deuxième édition. pp. 240. *Lyon*, 1871. 8°. **8051. d. 12.**

BUYAT (Jean Marie Anthelme) Notice sur la vie et la mort de Jean-Marie-Anthelme Buyat . . . Par un prêtre du diocèse de Belley. pp. xii. 211. *Lyon*, 1852. 12°. **4865. aaa. 11.**

BUYAT (L. A. Fouilloud) *See* Fouilloud-Buyat.

BUYCK (Jacob) Aanteekeningen van Pastoor J Buyck, over de stemming der katholieke gemeente er Regeering van Amsterdam tijdens het "Geus Word der Stad. Medegedeeld door Dr. R. Fruin. 1895. Utrecht.—*Historisch Gezelschap, etc.* Bijdragen mededeelingen, *etc.* dl. 16. 1877, *etc.* 8°. **Ac. 75**

BUYCKX (Etienne J. E.)

—— Recherches sur un dryinide Aphelopus indivisus, par de cicadines. *In:* Carnoy (J. B.) La Cellule, *etc.* ton fasc. 1. pp. 61–155. 1948. fol. **742**

BUYDECKI (Floryan) *See* Bujdecki.

BUYENS (Frans) *pseud.* [i.e. **Ferdinand Borges.**]

—— Andreas Latzko. Rebel tegen het onrecht, strijder de vrede . . . Illustraties Marcel Payot. pp. 59. *Antwerpen*, 1954. 8°. **11853.** w

—— Beschouwingen rondom het werk van Achilles Mus [With a portrait.] pp. 44. *Gent*, 1952. 8°. **11870.** bb

BUYER. *See* Periodical Publications.—*Capetown.*

—— The Buyer's Companion: containing—p calculator; discounts, *etc.* pp. 14. [1883.] 16°. **8548.** a

—— The Buyer's Guide to Print. [With plates.] pp. 88. *County Associations: London*, [1955.] 4°. **7947.** dd.

—— The Buyer's Guide to the Dairy & Ice Cream Indust *See* Directories.—*Dairies.*

BUYER (Jacques) *See* Buerius (Jacobus)

BUYERS. Buyers' Guide to Branded Goods. *See* Pe dical Publications.—London.—*Shoe and Leather Re*

—— Buyers' Guide to Hull's Industries. *See* Directorie *Hull.*

—— Buyers' Guide to Scottish Industries. *See* Directo —*Scotland.*

—— The Buyers' Guide to the Manufacturing Towns Manufacturers of Great Britain. *See* Periodi Publications.—*London.*

—— Buyers' Guide to the Motor Trade of Great Bri and the Empire. *See* London.—iii. *Society of M Manufacturers and Traders.*

BUYERS (William) Christianity in the East. pp. iv. *John Snow: London*, 1842. 12°. **4766.** b

—— Letters on India: with special reference to the sp of Christianity. pp. xii. 295. *John Snow: Lon* 1840. 12°. **1126.** e.

—— Recollections of Northern India; with observation the origin, customs and moral sentiments of the Hind and remarks on the country, and principal places on Ganges, &c. pp. 548. *John Snow: London*, 1848. 8 **4765.** d.

BUYES (Joannes) Disputatio medica inauguralis atrophia, *etc. A. Elzevier: Lugduni Batavor* 1685. 4°. **1185. g. 17.**

BUYESIUS (Jean) Mond-sluyting, over de saken Amelandt. [Signed: "Post nubila Phoebus," i.e. J. Bu sius ?] Mitsgaders den brieff van mijn Heer Foppius Aitsema, gesonden aen de Hog. Mog. Heeren Sta Generael deser Vereenigde Provincien, streckende verantwoordinge van sijn persoon ende handel. [1637 ?] 4°. *See* Amelandt. **11755. e. 12.** (

BUYKEN (THEA)

—— See PLANITZ (H.) and BUYKEN (T.) Bibliographie zur deutschen Rechtsgeschichte. 1952. 8°. **2727.g.2.**

—— See PLANITZ (H.) and BUYKEN (T.) Die Kölner Schreinsbücher des 13. und 14. Jahrhunderts, *etc.* 1937. 8°. Ac. **7028.** b/35.

—— Enea Silvio Piccolomini. Sein Leben und Werden bis zum Episkopat. pp. xii. 78. 50*. *Bonn & Köln,* 1931. 8°. **4856.** dd. **14.**

BUYKEN (THEA) and **CONRAD** (HERMANN) *Gerichtsassessor.*

—— Die Amtleutebücher der kölnischen Sondergemeinden. Herausgegeben von T. Buyken und H. Conrad. pp. xi. 285. *Weimar,* 1936. 8°. [*Publikationen der Gesellschaft für rheinische Geschichtskunde.* no. 45.] Ac. **7028.** b/33.

BUYL (ADOLPHE) *See* WAUTERS (A. J.) Bibliographie du Congo . . . Avec la collaboration de M. A. Buyl. 1895. 8°. **011899.** i. **8.**

BUYLLA (ADOLFO) *See* ARBOLEYA MARTÍNEZ (M.) En las Garras de Cuatro Sabios, Buylla, Posada, *etc.* 1904. 8°. **1414.** i. **32.**

—— El Instituto del Trabajo. Datas para la historia de la reforma social en España. Por A. Buylla . . . Adolfo Posada . . . Luis Morote . . . Con un discurso preliminar de José Canalejas y Méndez . . . y una memoria acerca de los Institutos del Trabajo en el extranjero, por J. Uña y Sarthou. pp. A–I. clxvii. 342. *Madrid,* 1902. 8°. **08275.** bb. **4.**

BUYLLA Y ALEGRE (A.) See CASAL JULIAN (G.) Memorias de historia natural y médica de Asturias . . . Reimpresas y anotadas por A. Buylla y Alegre, *etc.* 1900. 8°. **7680.** e. **31.**

BUYN (LOUIS ANTOINE PIERRE FRANÇOIS) Grondeigendom op Java. pp. 30. *Breda,* 1865. 8°. **8022.** dd. **34.** (**3.**)

—— Het Ontwerp van wet tot vaststelling der gronden, waarop ondernemingen van landbouw en nijverheid in Nederlandsch-Indië kunnen worden gevestigd . . . beoordeeld door . . . L. A. P. F. Buijn. pp. 24. *Breda,* 1865. 8°. **5686.** b. **34.** (**6.**)

—— Het Regt tot eene volkomen onbelemmerde gedachteuiting. Eene strafregtelijke proeve. pp. xi. 107. *Amsterdam,* 1867. 8°. **5686.** b. **14.**

—— La Liberté de la parole. Étude de droit criminel. pp. xv. 111. *Amsterdam,* 1867. 8°. **6056.** e. **34.**

—— De Roeping van het Nederlandsche volk. Een woord tot de kiezers bij de stembus van 30 October 1866. pp. 14. *Delft,* 1866. 8°. **8079.** e. **1.**

BUYNAND (JEAN FRANÇOIS ANNE) *See* TRIOMPHE. Triomphe de l'Évangile . . . Traduit de l'espagnol . . . par J. F. A. B. . . . des E. . . . [i.e. J. F. A. Buynand des Échelles.] 1805. 8°. **C.108.bbb.15.**

—— —— 1841. 8°. **4015.** e. **17.**

BUYNO-ARCTOWA (MARYA) Słoneczko. Powieść. Wydanie trzecie. Z rysunkami Wandy Romeykówny. pp. 157. *w Warszawie,* 1930. 8°. **012591.** aaa. **78.**

BUYS-MAN. *See* BUISMAN.

BUYS (A.) *of Utrecht.* *See* FORTINI (P.) Moet de priester niet trouwen? . . . Vertaald en met aanteekeningen voorzien door A. Buys. 1864. 12°. **5061.** aa. **18.**

BUYS (A.) *of Utrecht.*

—— Antiek of modern? Twee brieven aan Ds. Blaauw en Dr. Meijboom . . . Naar aanleiding van de door hen inde Remonstrantsche Kerk, te Utrecht uitgesproken leerredenen. pp. 35. *Utrecht,* 1865. 8°. **3925.** i. **39.** (**3.**)

—— Er op of er onder! De twee levenskwestiën van ons land: de koloniale- en de onderwijs-kwestie. pp. 16. *Utrecht,* [1868.] 8°. **8081.** aaa. **23.** (**9.**)

—— Maria en de Mariadienst. Eene Mariologische studie . . . Met een brief aan den heer J. A. Alberdingk Thijm. pp. iv. 96. *Amsterdam,* 1868. 8°. **4784.** aaa. **20.**

—— Mr. Groen van Prinsterer en zijne Javaantjes. Vier vragen van Mr. Groen van Prinsterer aan de konservatieve partij over het koloniale vraagstuk. Beantwoord door A. Buys. pp. 60. *Amsterdam,* 1869. 8°. **8022.** dd. **35.** (**10.**)

—— Een Nebukadnézars lot, of Wat zal er van Dr. Zaalberg nog worden? Eene physiologische studie. pp. 40. *Kampen,* 1868. 8°. **3925.** i. **37.** (**3.**)

—— Neërlands toekomst. Een kort maar bondig woord aan de kiezers . . . Tweede druk. pp. 8. *Utrecht,* 1868. 8°. **8081.** b. **3.**

—— Het Regeeringsbeleid van Graaf van Zuylen, in de Limburg-Luxemburgsche aangelegenheden, voor 't volk verduidelykt. pp. 23. *Utrecht,* 1868. 8°. **5686.** a. **31.**

BUYS (ABRAHAMUS) Disputatio juridica inauguralis de transactionibus, *etc.* pp. 29. *Lugduni Batavorum,* [1719.] 4°. **501.** f. **23.** (**19.**)

BUYS (ALFRED) Observations pratiques sur la prononciation, notamment sur celle de la langue française, *etc.* pp. 32. *Amsterdam,* 1863. 8°. **12952.** ee. **18.** (**7.**)

BUYS (B. G. F.)

—— *See* STRIDIRON (J. G.) Handboek der bedrijfseconomische statistiek. Door Dr. J. G. Stridiron . . . met medewerking van B. G. F. Buys [and others], *etc.* 1943. 8°. **08535.** k. **8.**

BUYS (COENRAAD DE) *See* SCHOEMAN (Agatha E.) Coenraad de Buys, the first Transvaler, *etc.* 1938. 8°. **10761.** eee. **49.**

BUYS (D. W.) *See* DUTCH EAST INDIES.—*Indisch Comité voor Wetenschappelijke Onderzoekingen.* Midden-Oost-Borneo Expeditie 1925. Uitgave van het Indisch Comité voor Wetenschappelijke Onderzoekingen. Met medewerking van . . . D. W. Buijs, *etc.* 1927. 8°. **10058.** s. **8.**

BUYS (EGBERT) *See* SEWEL (W.) A Compleat Dictionary, English and Dutch . . . Reviewed and augmented . . . by E. Buys, *etc.* 1766. 4°. **12972.** g. **18.**

—— A New and Complete Dictionary of Terms of Art. Containing a sufficient explication of all words . . . made use of to expres any art, science, custom . . . machine, &c. . . . Dat is, Nieuw en volkomen konstwoordenboek, *etc.* 2 vol. *Amsterdam,* 1768, 69. 4°. **1332.** i. **3.**

—— Nieuw en volkomen woordenboek van konsten en weetenschappen, *etc.* 10 dl. *Amsteldam,* 1769–78. 8°. **734.** c. **1–10.**

BUYS (ELLA) *See* MITCHELL (Edith) *of Cape Town.* [Table Mountain Fairy Tales.] Ou Vader Tafelberg. Sprokies vir kinders . . . Vertaal deur Ella Buys, *etc.* [1937.] 8°. **12450.** p. **22.**

BUYS (H.)

—— De Practische bruikbaarheid van de plasmajodium-bepaling en van de meting van radioactief jodium in de urine voor de beoordeling der schildklierfunctie . . . With a summary. Proefschrift, *etc.* pp. 58. *Utrecht,* [1951.] 8°. **7643. b. 42.**

BUYS (HANS BRANDTS)

—— De Passies van Johann Sebastian Bach. [With musical examples and with facsimiles.] pp. 379. pl. 11. xx. *Leiden,* 1950. 8°. **7900. f. 26.**

—— Het Wohltemperirte clavier van Johann Sebastian Bach . . . Ontstaan, geschiedenis en bouw van het werk . . . Voorzien van tabellen en verlucht met vele notenvoor-beelden. Overdacht en op schrift gesteld door H. Brandts Buys. Tweede druk. pp. x. 322. *Arnhem,* 1944. 8°. **7900. f. 9.**

BUYS (J. M.)

—— Voortrekker-plegtighede. pp. 64. *Bloemfontein,* 1936. 8°. [*Union of South Africa. Voortrekkers. Amp-telike uitgawe.* no. 6.] **W.P. 5824/6.**

BUYS (J. M.) and **DALEBOUT** (J. A.) Kom ons speel—. (Spele vir groot en klein.) pp. 63. *Bloemfontein,* 1932. 8°. **12973. aa. 32.**

BUYS (JAN) *See* BUSAEUS (Joannes)

BUYS (JOANNES THEODORUS) *See* BUYS (Johannes T.)

BUYS (JOHANNES THEODOOR) *See* HOETINK (G. C. R.) De Noodzakelijkheid en mogelijkheid der grondwetsherziening tegenover Prof. Buys verdedigd. [A criticism of "Beden-kelijke leuzen," an article contributed by J. T. Buys to "De Gids."] 1881. 8°. **8081. h. 4. (1.)**

—— *See* HOOGENDIJK (A.) Eenige beschouwingen over "Een Nieuw leven," geschetst door . . . J. T. Buys, *etc.* [On an article contributed by J. T. Buys to "De Gids."] 1867. 8°. **8246. dd. 24. (5.)**

—— *See* NABER (S. A.) Vier tijdgenooten [i.e. J. T. Buys and others], *etc.* 1894. 8°. **10759. f. 30.**

—— *See* PERIODICAL PUBLICATIONS.—*Amsterdam.* De Gids, *etc.* [1863–93 edited by J. T. Buys and others.] 1837, *etc.* 8°. **P.P. 4595.**

—— De Grondwet. Toelichting en kritiek. 3 dl. *Arnhem,* 1883–88. 8°. **8081. g. 29.**

—— De Hypotheekbank, haar wezen en hare waarde. pp. ii. 95. *Haarlem,* 1861. 8°. **8227. g. 44. (9.)**

—— Het Moderne staatsbegrip. Inwijdingsrede, *etc.* 1869. *See* LEYDEN.—*Academia Lugduno-Batava.* Annales academici. 1864/65. 1840, *etc.* 4°. **Ac. 940.**

—— Mr. S. Vissering. (23. Juni 1818—22. Augustus 1888.) *See* NABER (S. A.) Karakterschetsen van vermaarde Nederlanders, *etc.* 1906. 8°. **10760. cc. 10.**

—— De Nederlandsche staatsschuld sedert 1814 . . . Vier voorlezingen, *etc.* pp. 176. *Haarlem,* 1857. 8°. **8227. e. 22.**

—— Het Regt van de Tweede Kamer. Een woord aan de kiezers. pp. 58. *Haarlem,* 1866. 8°. **8081. e. 2. (1.)**

—— *See* KEMPER (J. de B.) Vooruitgang. Getrouwe handhaving der grondwet . . . Met bedenkingen tegen . . . de brochure van Prof. Buijs [i.e. "Het Regt van de Tweede Kamer"]. 1866. 8°. **8079. cc. 18.**

—— *See* LION (I. J.) Dertien professoren en Prof. G. J. Buijs' "Regt van de Tweede Kamer" wederlegd, *etc.* 1866. 8°. **8081. k. 1.**

BUYS (JOHANNES THEODOOR)

—— Specimen juridicum inaugurale de jure cogitata com-municandi ex juris communis principiis regendo, *etc.* pp. viii. 116. [*Utrecht,*] 1850. 8°. **6025. c. 11**

—— Studiën over staatkunde en staatsrecht . . . [A collec-tion of articles contributed to "De Gids."] Uitgegeven onder toezicht van Mr. W. H. de Beaufort . . . en Mr A. R. Arntzenius. 2 dl. *Arnhem,* 1894, 95. 8°. **8010. g. 10**

Imperfect ; wanting all after p. 480 *of dl.* 2.

—— Voorlezingen over de circulatie-banken meer bijzonde in Frankrijk, Groot-Britannië en de Vereenigde Staten van Noord-Amerika, *etc.* pp. 180. *Haarlem,* 1856. 8°. **8227. e. 21**

—— Het Wezen van den constitutionelen regeringsvorm Inwijdingsrede, *etc.* pp. 46. *Haarlem,* 1862. 8°. **8008. dd. 1**

—— [Another edition.] 1866. *See* LEYDEN.—*Academia Lugduno-Batava.* Annales academici. 1862/63. 1840, *etc.* 4°. **Ac. 940**

BUYS (LUCIEN) La Science de la quantité, précédée d'un étude analytique sur les objets fondamentaux de l science. pp. 563. *Bruxelles,* 1880. 8°. **8507. f. 21**

BUYS (M. M.)

—— Juta se Spellys. 6 pt. *Kaapstad & Johannesbur* [1939, 32.] 12°. **12972. aa. 3**

BUYS (MARIUS) Batavia, Buitenzorg en de Preange Gids voor bezoekers en toeristen. pp. x. 158. *Batavia* 1891. 8°. **10055. aaa.**

—— Duinenburg. Schetsen en herinneringen. pp. 236. *Leiden,* 1901. 8°. **012331. k. 1.**

—— In het hart der Preanger. pp. 214. *Leiden,* 1900. 8° **10055. df. 4**

—— Mr. Jan Rudolf Thorbecke herdacht . . . Met portre Tweede druk. pp. 16. *Tiel,* 1872. 8°. **10759. i.**

—— Twee jaren op Sumatra's Westkust. pp. vii. 440. *Amsterdam,* [1886.] 8°. **10055. b.**

—— Twee maanden op Borneo's Westkust. Herinneringe pp. xi. 230. *Leiden,* 1892. 8°. **010057. e.**

BUYS (MARIUS ADRIANUS BRANDTS) *See* VLOTEN (J. va Nederlandsche baker- en kinderrijmen . . . Met melodi bijeengebracht door M. A. Brandts-Buys. [1894.] 8°. **011556. f.**

BUYS (MATTHAEUS) Disputatio juridica inauguralis evictionibus, *etc.* pp. 25. *Lugduni Batavoru* [1716.] 4°. **501. f. 21. (2**

BUYS (P.) *Priest, of St. Walburga's Church, Antwerp.* Noot (H. K. N. van der) *Begin.* Alle waere vaderland worden verzogt, *etc.* [An invitation to attend a M to be celebrated by P. Buys in the church of Walburga's at Antwerp on the saint's day of H. K. van der Noot.] [1790.] *s. sh.* 4°. **107. g. 23. (1**

BUYS (P. H. A. MARTINI) and **KOCK** (ANNE WILL THEODOOR) [Korte beschrijving der groote vaste spo wegbruggen in Nederland.] Notice sur les grands po fixes pour chemins de fer dans les Pays-Bas . . . Ava propos de M. N. Th. Michaëlis, *etc.* pp. viii. 131. pl. *Rotterdam,* 1885. 8°. **8768. l.**

—— Atlas. pl. 18. *Rotterdam,* 1885. *obl.* fol. **1801. b.**

BUYS (PAULUS) *See* EVERDINGEN (W. van) Het Lev van Mr. Paulus Buys, *etc.* 1895. 8°. **10759. f.**

BUYS (PAULUS)

—— See ROGIER (L. J.) Paulus Buys en Leicester, *etc.* 1948. 8°. **10862. cc. 12.**

BUYS (PETRUS) *See* BIBLE.—*New Testament.* [*Dutch.*] Het Nieuwe Testament . . . Op nieuw herzien en zorgvuldig naar den Griekschen en Latijnschen text verbeterd door P. Buys. 1846. 12°. **3035. aa. 22.**

—— Rome en Utrecht, of Korte schets van den oorsprong, voortgang en tegenwoordigen staat hunner drie hoofdgeschillen . . . Tweede herziene druk. pp. xv. 192. *Amsterdam,* 1864. 8°. **04685. d. 2.**

BUYS (R. VAN BRAKELL)

—— Drie dichteressen uit het Victoriaanse tijdperk. Christina Rossetti, Emily Brontë, Elizabeth Barrett Browning. [With plates, including portraits.] pp. 352. *Amsterdam,* [1947.] 8°. **011840. m. 67.**
Hoogtepunten der Engelse cultuur. no. 3.

—— Gestalten uit de Persische mystiek. pp. 142. *Deventer,* [1938.] 8°. **04503. i. 42.**

—— Poëzie en leven. pp. 39. *Deventer,* [1946.] 8°. **11868. aaa. 11.**

BUYS (W. R. VAN BRAKELL) Het Godsbegrip bij Spinoza. Een inleiding tot het monisme. pp. 147. *Utrecht,* 1934. 8°. **08459. i. 52.**

—— Het Ideën-drama van Friedrich Hebbel. pp. 133. *Utrecht,* 1937. 8°. **11860. bb. 10.**

—— John Keats. Een strijd om het dichterschap . . . Met vier afbeeldingen [including portraits]. pp. 156. *Naarden,* [1946.] 8°. **11866. cc. 15.**

BUYS (WILHELMUS) *the Elder.* Oratio de conscientia. *Apud viduam Petri Boeteman: Amstelædami,* 1677. 4°. **8409. d. 47. (6.)**

BUYS (WILHELMUS) *the Younger.* Disputatio juridica inauguralis de jure dotium, *etc.* pp. 23. *Lugduni Batavorum,* [1719.] 4°. **501. f. 23. (18.)**

BUYS (WILLEM) De Windmolens aan de Zaanstreek, 1439–1918. Met vele aanteekeningen en vertrouwbare gegevens op de windmolens betrekking hebbend. pp. viii. 143. *Koog-Zaandijk,* 1919. 8°. **010271. f. 36.**

BUYSAERT (GILBERTE GEPTS) *See* GEPTS-BUYSAERT (G.)

BUYS BALLOT (CHRISTOFFEL HENDRIK DIRK) *See* BALLOT.

BUYSCH ( ) *See* MUENCHEN-GLADBACH. Der Kreis Gladbach . . . Schriftleitung: Kreissyndikus Dr. Buysch. 1929. 4°. **10250. i. 17.**

BUYSCHER (LAMBERTUS) Disputatio medica inauguralis de hæmorrhagia, *etc.* *A. Sas: Hardervici,* 1676. 4°. **1185. i. 17. (11.)**

BUYS DE GRAAF (A.) *See* GRAAF.

BUYSE (FERDINAND) The Curiosities of France; being a hand book for the use of English visitors to France . . . Collection de curiosités en France, *etc.* *Eng. & Fr.* pp. 155. *Paris,* 1854. 16°. **10172. a. 24.**

BUYSE (L. J.) *See* BIBLE.—*Luke.* [*Lendu.*] Luka dza buku. [Translated by Mrs. L. J. Buyse and Mrs. C. R. Webber.] 1933. 8°. **03068. k. 35.**

—— *See* BIBLE.—*John, Gospel of.* [*Lendu.*] Yohana dza buku. [Translated by Mrs. L. J. Buyse and B. L. Litchman.] 1933. 8°. **03068. k. 34.**

BUYSE (OMER) Les Écoles professionnelles et les écoles d'art industriel en Allemagne et en Autriche, *etc.* pp. 320. *Bruxelles,* 1896. 8°. **8311. b. 39.**

—— Une Expérience d'éducation professionnelle et sociale des masses. Les Écoles du Travail pour soldats belges internés en Hollande, 1914–1918, *etc.* pp. 63. pl. XIX. *Bruxelles,* [1926.] 8°. **08286. c. 7.**

BUYSE (TH. C.) *See* MARNE, *River.* Les Batailles de la Marne . . . Traduit . . . par T. C. Buyse, *etc.* 1917. 8°. **09082. bbb. 44.**

BUYSEN (A. VAN) *See* BRANDENBURG, *House of.* [Twenty-seven engraved medallions of various members of the House of Brandenburg, for the most part by A. van Buysen.] [1720?] 4°. **1486.gg.25.**

BUYSEN (JOANNES) Dissertatio inauguralis juridica de imperio viri in mulierem, secundum jus naturale et civile hodiernum, *etc.* pp. 23. *Leodii,* [1821.] 4°. **498. f. 5. (11.)**

BUYSEN (PAUL) *See* BUSIUS (Paulus)

BUYSERO (CORNELIS) Cornelis Buijsero te Bantam, 1616–1618. Zijn brieven en journaal, met inleiding en bijlagen uitgegeven door Dr. J. W. IJzerman. pp. xxiv. 272. *'s-Gravenhage,* 1923. 8°. **10759. cc. 5.**

BUYSERO (DIDERIK) *See* BUYSERO (Dirk)

BUYSERO (DIRK) *See* ASTARTO. Astrate, koning van Tyrus; treurspel. [A translation by D. Buysero of P. Quinault's "Astrate, roi de Tyr."] 1670. 4°. **11755. f. 39. (2.)**

—— —— 1697. 8°. **11755. aa. 40. (1.)**

—— —— 1720. 8°. **11735. a. 4.**

—— *See* TERENTIUS (P.) *Afer.* [*Heautontimorumenos.—Dutch.*] Pub. Terentii Heautontimorumenos ofte Selfsqeller [*sic*], in Nederduydtsche rijmen naar ghevolgt door D. Buysero. 1662. 4°. **11755. f. 39. (1.)**

—— Tooneelpoëzy. [With plates.] 2 dl. [1747.] 8°. **11755. aaa. 7.**
With an additional titlepage, engraved. A collection of 12 *separate pieces published at different dates between* 1680 *and* 1733, *issued with a collective titlepage.*

—— Arete, of Stryd tusschen de plicht en min. Treurspel. [In verse.] pp. 48. *J. Lescailje: [Amsterdam,]* 1992 [1692]. 8°. **11755. a. 12.**

—— Blyde inhalinge van den onverwinnelijksten helt Willem de Derde, Koning van Engeland, Vrankrijk, Schotland en Yerland, *etc.* [In verse.] *Dordregt,* 1691. 4°. **11755. f. 39. (4.)**

—— Dirck Buysero's " Korte beschrijvinge van Parys " 1667. Opnieuw uitgegeven met inleiding, bronnenstudie en aanteekeningen door Dr. R. J. Willemyns. [With plates.] pp. xv. 153. *Antwerpen,* 1942. 8°. [*Uitgave van de Vereeniging der Antwerpsche Bibliophielen.* Nieuwe reeks. no. 1.] **Ac.9629/2.(2.)**

—— Op het beklaaglijk en ontydig afsterven van de doorlugtigste en grootmagtigste Vorstin Maria Stuart, Koninginne van Engeland, Schotland, Vrankryk, en Ierland. Overleden den 7 January 1695. [In verse.] *J. Dale: Amsterdam,* 1695. 4°. **11755. f. 39. (5.)**

—— De Schoonste, of het Ontzet van Schevening; blyspel. [In verse.] pp. 45. *'s Gravenhage,* 1717. 8°. **11754. b. 69. (1.)**

BUYSERO (Dirk)

—— De Triomfeerende min, vredespel. Gemengt met zang en snaarenspel, vliegwerken en balletten. Door D. B. (D. Buysero.) [In verse. With musical notes.] pp. 23. 66. *Voor d'erfgenaamen van J. Lescailje: Amsterdam*, 1680. 4º. **11755. f. 39. (3.)**

—— Vredezang over den gemaakten peis de Rijswijk, door D. B. [i.e. D. Buysero.] pp. 13. 1697. 4º. *See* B., D. **11755. f. 39. (6.)**

BUYSERS (Immetjen Heertjes) *See* Pronck (A.) Liefdens-vastigheydt: vertoond, op 't gewenschte Bruylofs-Feest, van . . . A. P. Pronck . . . met . . . I. H. Buysers, *etc.* [1663.] *obl.* 8º. **11556. aa. 1. (11.)**

BUYSING (Duco Johannes Storm) Bouwkundige leercursus ten gebruike der Koninklijke Akademie voor de Zee- en Landmagt. Handleiding tot de kennis der waterbouwkunde voor de kadetten der Genie . . . Tweede druk. 2 dl. *Breda*, 1854, 57. 8º. **8775. b. 42.**

—— Atlas. pp. 7. 7. pl. xliv. lii. 1858. fol. **1801. f. 9.**

—— De Kust van Noord- en Zuid-Holland. pp. 8. *Amsterdam*, 1860. 8º. **8776. b. 56. (7.)**

BUYSMAN. *See* Buisman.

BUYSMAN (J.) Amsterdam en de spoorwegen, *etc.* pp. 8. *Amsterdam*, 1860. 8º. **8235. c. 91. (11.)**

BUYSSCHAERT (Joris) *See* Musseley (J.) and Buysschaert (J.) Geschiedenis van Ledeghem. 1912. 8º. **10271. bbb. 28.**

BUYSSE (Arthur) De Anarchisten en de strafwet . . . Voordracht, *etc.* pp. 31. *Gent*, 1897. 8º. **08282. g. 34. (11.)**

BUYSSE (Cyriel) *See* Mussche (A.J.) Cyriel Buysse. Een studie, *etc.* [With a portrait.] 1929. 4º. **11823. w. 9.**

—— *See* Puymbrouck (H. van) Cyriel Busse en zijn land. [With portraits.] 1929. 8º. **11822. v. 17.**

—— *See* Steyns (D. B.) De Vlaamsche schrijver Cyriel Buysse. Zijne wereld en zijne kunst. 1911. 4º. **011852. dd. 20.**

—— 't Bolleken, *etc.* pp. 235. *Bussum*, 1906. 8º. **012581. bb. 41.**

—— Daarna. pp. 288. *Amsterdam*, [1904.] 8º. **012581. b. 48.**

—— Emile Claus, mijn broeder in Vlaanderen. [With plates, including portraits.] pp. 69. *Gent, Bussum*, [1926.] 4º. **7859. pp. 1.**

—— Émile Zola. [With a portrait.] 1904. *See* Mannen. Mannen van beteekenis in onze dagen, *etc.* dl. 35. afl. 8. 1870, *etc.* 8º. **10602. de. 18. (7.)**

—— Het "Ezelken." Wat niet vergeten was. pp. 245. *Bussum*, 1910. 8º. **12581. r. 14.**

—— Le Bourriquet. Traduit . . . par Pierre Maes. Avant propos de Maurice Maeterlinck. 2e édition. pp. 251. *Paris*, 1920. 8º. **012582. b 16.**

—— Het Gezin van Paemel. Drama in vier bedrijven. pp. 53. *Gent*, [1903.] 8º. **11755. e. 20.**

—— Guustje en Zieneken. Schetsen uit het boerenleven. pp. 56. *Gent*, 1887. 8º. **12316. d. 48. (2.)**

—— In de natuur. pp. 245. *Bussum*, 1905. 8º. **012581. bb. 34.**

—— 'k Herinner mij . . . Tweede druk. pp. 170. *Bussum*, 1928. 8º. **010760. df. 13.**

—— Kerels. pp. 196. *Gent*, 1927. 8º. **012582. d. 58.**

—— 'n Leeuw van Vlaanderen. pp. 257. *Amsterdam*, [1901.] 8º. **012581. aaa. 56.**

—— Lente. pp. 215. *Bussum*, 1907. 8º. **012581. bb. 54.**

—— Het Leven van Rozeke van Dalen. Roman, *etc.* 2 dl. *Bussum*, 1905. 8º. **012581. bb. 37.**

—— De Nachtelijke aanranding. pp. 183. *Bussum*, 1912. 8º. **012581. g. 62.**

—— L'Agression nocturne. Roman flamand inédit, *etc.* (Traduit par Pierre Maes.) 1931. *See* Periodical Publications.—*Paris.* Les Œuvres libres, *etc.* no. 126. 1921, *etc.* 8º. **12208. ee. 126.**

—— Oorlogsvisioenen. pp. 249. *Bussum*, 1914. 8º. **12581. t. 10.**

—— Het Recht van den sterkste. pp. 237. *Amsterdam*, 1893. 8º. **012581. k. 17.**

—— De Schandpaal. pp. 227. *Gent*, 1928. 8º. **12581. t. 15.**

—— Schoppenboer. pp. 304. *Amsterdam*, 1898. 8º. **012581. aaa. 12.**

—— Stemmingen. pp. 172. *Bussum*, 1911. 8º. **012354. f. 5.**

—— Sursum Corda. 2 dl. *Amsterdam*, [1895.] 8º. **12591. ee. 27.**

—— Tantes. pp. 170. *Gent*, [1925.] 8º. **012582. d. 38.**

—— Te lande. pp. 255. *Amsterdam*, 1900. 8º. **012581. f. 76.**

—— Twee werelden, *etc.* [With a portrait.] pp. 301. *Gent*, 1931. 8º. **12583. w. 9.**

—— Typen. pp. 253. *Gent*, [1926.] 8º. **012582. c. 70.**

—— Uit het leven. pp. 237. *Gent*, 1930. 8º. **012582. dd. 47**

—— Uit Vlaanderen. pp. 234. *Amsterdam*, 1899. 8º. **012331. i. 9**

—— Uleken. Van oud en jong. [With a portrait.] pp. 204 *Gent & Bussum*, 1926. 8º. **012582. d. 48**

—— Van arme menschen. pp. 248. *Amsterdam* [1902.] 8º. **012581. dd. 33**

—— Van hoog en laag. Het eerste levensboek. pp. 156. *Bussum*, 1913. 8º. **12580. q. 19**

—— Het Volle leven, *etc.* pp. 233. *Bussum*, 1908. 8º. **12581. pp. 2**

—— Een Vroolijk drietal. pp. 118. *L. B. Hill: London* 1916. 8º. **12582. a. 4**

—— De Vroolijke tocht. pp. 135. *Bussum*, 1911. 8º. **12355. s. 31**

—— Wroeging. pp. 220. *'s-Gravenhage*, [1896.] 8º. **12580. k. 40**

—— Zomerleven, *etc.* pp. vii. 312. *Bussum*, 1915. 8º. **12354. ppp. 12**

BUYSSENS (E.) Calvinism in the "Faerie Queene" o Spenser. Extrait de la Revue belge de philologie e d'histoire, *etc.* [*Brussels*, 1926.] 8º. **011824. bb. 27**

UYSSENS (ERIC)

— Speaking and Thinking from the Linguistic Standpoint. (Reprinted from: Thinking and Speaking.) *North-Holland Publishing Co.: Amsterdam*, 1954. 8°. **012902. t. 27.**

UYSSENS (PAUL)

— Le Pithécanthrope était-il un pygmée? Considérations sur la généalogie humaine, inspirées par les recherches récentes sur l'ancienneté et les caractères de certains hommes fossiles. pp. 48. *Bruxelles*, 1937. 8°. **10009. ppp. 2.**

— Les Trois races de l'Europe et du monde. Leur génie et leur histoire, *etc.* pp. 269. *Bruxelles*, 1936. 8°. **10009.y.6.**

UYSSON (LOUIS) *See* LA GUESLE (J. de) Rémonstrances faictes . . . par Monsieur de la Guesle . . . & feu Monsieur maistre Loys Buysson . . . pour avoir justice du parricide de deffunct Henry III, *etc.* 1610. 4°. **1195. c. 4. (1.)**

UYSSONIUS (CLAUDIUS) Claudii Buyssonii . . . Partitiones; quibus iuris ciuilis brevis idea exprimitur. Tertia editio denuo recognita ab auctore & aucta. ff. 40. *Apud P. Candelarium: Cadomi*, 1586. 8°. **5254. a. 17. (1.)**

UYSSONIUS (PETRUS) Definitiones iuris vtriusque, *etc.* ff. 68. *Apud P. Candelarium: Cadomi*, 1586. 8°. **5254. a. 17. (2.)**

UYST (LEONARD) Nieuwe gedichten. pp. 95. *Brussel*, 1899. 8°. **011556. eee. 15.**

— Verhalen en verzen. pp. 94. *Brussel*, 1897. 8°. **011556. eee. 7.**

— Willem Sanger. Tafereelen uit het leven eens dichters. [In verse.] pp. 136. *Brussel*, 1882. 16°. **11565. df. 32.**

UYTAERS (EVARISTUS) Brockley in Pre-Reformation Times. [With plates.] pp. 74. *Augustinian Library: London*, 1920. 8°. **010368. e. 36.**

UYTAERT (ÉLIO MARIE)

— *See* EUSEBIUS, *Bishop of Emesa.* Eusèbe d'Émèse. Discours conservés en Latin, *etc.* [Edited by E. M. Buytaert.] 1953, *etc.* 8°. **W.P. 7396/26.**

— *See* EUSEBIUS, *Bishop of Emesa.* L'Héritage littéraire d'Eusèbe d'Émèse. Étude critique et historique. Textes. Par É. M. Buytaert. 1949. 8°. [*Bibliothèque du Muséon.* vol. 24.] **P.P. 1927. d.**

— L'Authenticité des dix-sept opuscules contenus dans le MS. T. 523 sous le nom d'Eusèbe d'Emèse. *In:* Revue d'histoire ecclésiastique. vol. 43. no. 1/2. pp. 5–89. 1948. 8°. **Ac. 2646/3.**

UYTEN (MARTINUS VAN)

— *See* CURIONE (L.) La Notomia delle cancellaresche corsiue, & altre maniere di lettere . . . Libro secondo. (Martin[s] van buyten sculpsit hoc opus.) 1588. *obl.* 4°. **1322.m.47.(1.)**

— *See* CURIONE (L.) Il Teatro Delle Cancellaresche corsiue per Secretari et altre maniere di Lettere. Libro terzo. (Martin. uan Buyten Hollandus sculpsit.) 1593. *obl.* 4°. **1322.m.47.(2.)**

UYTENDIJK (FREDERIK JACOBUS JOHANNES)

— Die Abstufung der willkürlichen Musckelspannung. *In Civitate Vaticana*, 1940. 8°. [*Pontificia Academia Scientiarum. Commentationes.* vol. 4. no. 13.] **Ac. 101. b/5.**

BUYTENDIJK (FREDERIK JACOBUS JOHANNES)

— Algemene theorie der menselijke houding en beweging. Als verbinding en tegenstelling van de physiologische en de psychologische beschouwing. pp. 570. *Utrecht; Antwerpen*, 1948. 8°. **8473. ee. 40.**
Part of the "Universitaire bibliotheek voor psychologie."

— Le Football. Une étude psychologique. pp. 52. *Paris, Bruges* [printed], 1952. 8°. **8475. aa. 45.**
Part of "Textes et études philosophiques."

— Grondproblemen van het dierlijk leven. pp. 231. *Antwerpen*, 1938. 8°. **7206. ppp. 13.**

— Psychologie der dieren. pp. 6. 254. *Haarlem*, 1920. 8°. [*Volksuniversiteits bibliotheek.*] **12211. s. 1/3.**

— De Psychologie van de roman. Studies over Dostojevskij. pp. 111. *Utrecht, Brussel*, 1950. 8°. **11861. e. 57.**

— [De Psychologie van den hond.] The Mind of the Dog. Authorized translation by Lilian A. Clare. Illustrated. pp. 215. *G. Allen & Unwin: London*, 1935. 8°. **07295. aa. 17.**

— [Het Spel van mensch en dier als openbaring van levensdriften.] Wesen und Sinn des Spiels. Das Spielen des Menschen und der Tiere als Erscheinungsform der Lebenstriebe. pp. 164. pl. 15. *Berlin*, [1933.] 8°. **7206. pp. 3.**

— Traité de psychologie animale . . . Traduit par A. Frank-Duquesne. pp. xv. 362. *Paris*, 1952. 8°. [*Logos. Introduction aux études philosophiques.*] **W.P. 2490/8.**

— De Vrouw. Haar natuur, verschijning en bestaan. Een existentieel-psychologische studie. (Derde herziene druk.) pp. 358. *Utrecht, Antwerpen*, 1952. 8°. **8417. f. 33.**

— Wege zum Verständnis der Tiere. [With plates.] pp. 264. *Zürich, Leipzig*, [1938.] 8°. **07206. h. 14.**

BUYTENDIJK (FREDERIK JACOBUS JOHANNES) and **MEESTERS** (A.)

— Duration and Course of the Auditory Sensation. *In Civitate Vaticana*, 1942. 8°. [*Pontificia Academia Scientiarum. Commentationes.* vol. 6. no. 11.] **Ac. 101. b/5.**

BUYTENDIK (WILLEM VAN) Essay philosophique sur la vérité et la raison. pp. 74. *Amsterdam*, 1739. 4°. **702. d. 4. (5.)**

BUYTENDORP (JOHANNES BAPTIST AUGUSTINUS) Philippe Quinault, sa vie, ses tragédies et ses tragi-comédies. [With a portrait.] pp. 196. *Amsterdam*, 1928. 8°. **10657. ff. 15.**

BUYTENDORP (K. B. A.)

— *See* TEIXEIRA DE MATTOS (L. F.) De Waterkeeringen, waterschappen en polders van Zuid-Holland, *etc.* (dl. 7. Door K. B. A. Buijtendorp.) 1906, *etc.* 8°. **08777. dd. 1.**

BUYTENDYCK (ALBERTUS) *Resp. See* VRIES (Gerard de) *Professor of Philosophy at Utrecht.* Disputationum selectarum prima, *etc.* disp. 27. 1674, *etc.* 4°. **525. d. 3. (21.)**

— Disputatio philosophica; qua disquiritur, Num admittenda sint spatia imaginaria? *etc. Praes.* G. de Vries. *M. à Dreunen: Ultrajecti*, 1678. 4°. **536. g. 2. (18.)**

BUYTENDYK (GOSUINUS VAN) Disputatio medica inauguralis de epilepsia. *Praes.* M. Leydekker. pp. 28. *Trajecti ad Rhenum*, 1715. 4°. **1185. k. 17. (28.)**
Cropped.

BUYTENDYK (SIMON HENRICUS) *See* HARDERWIJK.—*Hervormde Gemeente.* Adres van den Kerkeraad . . . aan de Synode, met een toelichtend woord van S. H. Buijtendijk. 1864. 8°. **3925. i. 38. (1.)**

—— De Zaligsprekingen des Heeren. Achttal leerredenen. pp. iv. 191. *Doesborgh*, [1866.] 8°. **4423. aaa. 8.**

BUYTENHEM (ISAAK DAVID VAN) Dissertatio juridica inauguralis de gabella emigrationis, quæ jure patrio vocatur Exu-Geld, *etc.* *Praes.* C. H. Trotz. pp. 37. *Trajecti ad Rhenum*, 1757. 4°. **T. 50*. (11.)**

BUYTENWECH (WILLEM) *See* COSTUMES. [A collection of engravings, etchings and woodcuts of various sizes, mainly representing the costumes of different nations, by or after W. Buytenwech and other artists from the fifteenth to the seventeenth centuries.] **146. i. 10.**

BUYTENWEG (WILLEM) *See* BUYTENWECH.

BUYTEVEST (REINERUS) Disputatio medica inauguralis de angina, *etc.* pp. 12. *T. Hoorn: Lugduni Batavorum*, 1663. 4°. **1185. g. 5. (55.)**

BUYTRAGO (JUAN DE) *See* CAXA DE LERUELA (M.) Restauración de la Abundancia de España, *etc.* [Edited by J. de Buytrago.] 1732. 4°. **08227. de. 24.**

BÜYTWECH (WILLEM) *See* BUYTENWECH.

BUYUJU OYUNU. Orta-Oyounou. Théâtre populaire turc. Texte turc, avec transcription et traduction hongroise par Ignace Kúnos [of the popular play, "Büjüdžü," "a Varázsló"] . . . Extrait du journal "Nyelvtudományi Közlemények" de l'Académie d. Sc. hongroise. [By I. Kúnos in collaboration with Mazhar Efendi.] pp. 63. 32. *Budapest*, 1888. 8°. **14479. b. 5.**
The Turkish text was printed at Constantinople.

—— [Another issue.] Orta-Ojunu. (Türkisches Volksschauspiel.) Török népszinjáték. Följegyezte, fordítással és jegyzetekkel ellátta Dr. Kúnos Ignácz [in collaboration with Mazhar Efendi]. Különnyomat a Magyar Tudományos Akadémia kiadásában megjelenő "Nyelvtudományi Közlemények" XXI. kötetéből. *Budapest*, 1888. 8°. **14479. b. 2.**
The date on the wrapper is 1889.

BUYZE (HENRIK GIJSBERT)

—— Over de omzettingen van foliumzuurconjugaat door enzymen van het maag-darmkanaal—van normale personen en lijders aan pernicieuse anaemie. Proefschrift, *etc.* [With a summary in English.] pp. 76. *'s-Gravenhage*, [1949.] 8°. **08909. t. 13.**

BUZ, *pseud.* Comic Illustrated Multiplication. By Buz and Fuz. *Dean & Son: London*, [1867.] 8°. **8505. bbb. 11.**

—— Current American Notes By "Buz!" [A parody on the American Sketches of Charles Dickens.] pp. 80. [*London*, 1842 ?] 8°. **12316. k. 45.**

—— A Dish of Gossip off the Willow Pattern, by Buz, and plates to match by Fuz. pp. 32. *Alex. Laidlaw: London*, [1867.] 8°. **11648. bbb. 46.**

—— Dolby and Father. By "Buz." [A satire on Charles Dickens.] pp. 53. *P. S. Wynkoop & Son: New York*, 1868. 12°. **12621. aa. 13.**

BUZ (NICOLAS) *See* LE BORGNE (N.)

BUZA (JÁNOS) Növénytan. A középtanodák V-ik osztálya részére keszítette Buza J., *etc.* pp. iv. 194. 1882. 8°. *See* SÁROSPATAK.—*Sárospataki Irodalmi Kör.* **07028. f. 13.**

BUZA (LÁSZLÓ) Diktatura és kisebbségvédelem. *Szeged*, 1936. 8°. [*Acta litterarum ac scientiarum Reg. Universitatis Hung. Francisco-Iosephinae.* Sectio juridico-politica. tom. 10. fasc. 2.] **Ac. 833.**

—— Az Europai válság a nemzetközi jog tükrében, *etc.* pp. *Szeged*, 1939. 8°. [*A M. Kir. Ferencz József-Tudományegyetem barátai egyesületének jog- és államtudományi szakosztályában tartott előadások.* no. 32.] **Ac. 833**

—— A kisebbségek jogi helyzete a békeszerződések és nemzetközi egyezmények értelmében, *etc.* [With bibliography.] pp. xx. 432. 1930. 8°. *See* PEST.—*Magyar Tudományos Akadémia.* **6916. dd.**

—— Magyarország katonai ellenőrzése a nemzetközi jog szempontjából. pp. 19. *Budapesten*, 1925. 8°. **06916. f.**

—— A Nemzetek Szövetségének szerepe az alkalmazhatatlanná vált nemzetközi jogszabályok reviziójánál s a rebus sic stantibus klauzula, *etc.* pp. 112. *Szeged*, 1931. [*Acta litterarum ac scientiarum Reg. Universitatis Hung. Francisco-Iosephinae.* Sectio juridico-politica. tom. 5.] **Ac. 833.**

BUZACARINUS (FRANCISCUS) *See* ISOCRATES. [*Nicoclem.—Latin.*] *Begin.* [fol. 2, *recto*:] Franciscus Buzacarinus Magnifico Federico Cornelio Patauii praetori integerrimo salutem. p. d., *etc.* [fol. 3, *recto*:] Isocratis oratio ad Nicoclem . . . per Franciscum Buzacharinum e Graeco in Latinum traducta, *etc.* [1480 ?] 4°. **IA. 208**

BUZACOTT (AARON) *the Elder.* *See* BIBLE. [*Rarotongan.*] Te Bibilia Tapu ra, *etc.* [Translated by J. Williams, C. Pitman and A. Buzacott; the whole revised by Buzacott.] 1851. 8°. **3070. d.**

—— —— 1872. 8°. **3070. g.**

—— —— 1888. 8°. **3070. g.**

—— —— 1895. 8°. **3068. df.**

—— *See* BIBLE.—*Hagiographa.* [*Rarotonga.*] Te Salomo te maata i tataia e Davida ra, *etc.* (Te Maseli Solomona.—Koheleta.—Te Sire a Solomona. [Translated by A. Buzacott.]) 1841. 12°. **1106. b.**

—— *See* BIBLE.—*Leviticus.* [*Rarotonga.*] E aite anga no Levitiku. I kiritiia e te Rev. A. Buzacott ; no roto i tuatua a te Rev. A. A. Bonar. [A commentary Leviticus. With the text.] 1856. 12°. **3068. aa.**

—— *See* BUNYAN (John) [*Pilgrim's Progress, Pt.* 1 *Rarotonga.*] Te Tere no te Tuitarere mei teianei ao ki ao a muri atu, *etc.* [Translated by A. Buzacott.] [1846.] 12°. **C. 58. b.**

—— *See* SUNDERLAND (James P.) and BUZACOTT (A.) *Younger.* Mission Life in the Islands of the Pacific. Being a narrative of the life and labours of the Rev. Buzacott, *etc.* [With a portrait.] 1866. 8°. **4745. aaa.**

—— Te Akataka Reo Rarotonga. Or, Rarotongan and English grammar. pp. 78. *Mission Press*: *Rarotonga*, 1854. 12°. **12907. aa.**
Interleaved.

—— Te au tuatua i akarukeia'i. Te ekalesia i Roma. E aronga tei akono i te tuatua mou e orai. [A catechism on the errors of the Church of Rome, in the Rarotongan language, by A. Buzacott.] pp. 20. 1844. 16°. ROME.—*Church of.* [*Appendix.*] **3940. a.**

BUZACOTT (AARON) *the Younger.* *See* SUNDERLAND (James P.) and BUZACOTT (A.) Mission Life in the Islands of the Pacific, *etc.* 1866. 8°. **4745. aaa.**

BUZÁGH (Aladár) [Kolloidik.] Colloid Systems. A survey of the phenomena of modern colloid physics and chemistry . . . Translated by Otto B. Darbishire . . . Edited by William Clayton, *etc.* pp. xix. 311. *Technical Press: London*, 1937. 8°. **8903.** dd. **66.**

BUZAGLO (Abraham) A Treatise on the Gout; wherein . . . the facility of a . . . cure . . . by . . . muscular exercise is established . . . The third edition, corrected and enlarged. pp. 70. *H. Sharp: London*, 1778. 8°. **7305.** de. **12.** (2.)

BUZAGLO (Shalom) *See* Duschinsky (C.) Jacob Kimchi and Shalom Buzaglo. 1914. 8°. **4516.** ee. **33.**

BUZAIRIES (Louis Alban) Biographies limouxines. pp. 228. *Limoux*, 1865. 8°. **10658.** aaa. **4.**

—— De l'influence des ovaires sur l'organisme de la femme. Tribut académique, *etc.* pp. 35. *Montpellier*, 1830. 4°. **1181.** f. **1.** (5.)

BUZANÇAIS, Charles Paul François de Beauvilliers, *Count de.* *See* Beauvilliers (C. P. F. de) *Duke de Saint Aignan.*

BUZANDO, *le Nain.* Buzando le nain. pp. 48. *Paris*, 1859. 8°. [*Bibliothèque bleue.* no. 19.] **12430.** m. **2.**

BUZANO (Pietro)

—— La Geometria differenziale in Italia dal 1939 al 1945, *etc.* [With a bibliography.] pp. 27. *In Civitate Vaticana*, 1946. 8°. [*Relationes de auctis scientiis tempore belli.* no. 12.] Ac. **101.** b/**6.** (**12.**)

BUZANSKY (Mark) Человеческий документ. Мой побег из ангарской ссылки. pp. 139. 1931. 8°. *See* Russia.—*Общество Бывшихъ Политическихъ Каторжанъ и Ссыльно-Поселенцевъ, etc.* **010790.** h. **61.**

BUZANTINA CHRONIKA. *Βυζαντινα χρονικα.* *See* Russia.—*Академия Наук СССР.*

—— *Βυζαντινα χρονικα.* [New series.] *See* Russia.—*Академия Наук СССР Истории.*

BUZANTINON HEMEROLOGION. *Βυζαντινον ἡμερολογιον.* *See* Ephemerides.

BUZANTINON MOUSEION. *Βυζαντινον Μουσειον.* *See* Athens.

BUZANTIOLOGIKE HETAIREIA. *Βυζαντιολογικη Ἑταιρεια.* *See* Athens.

BUZANTION. *Βυζαντιον.* Revue internationale des études byzantines. *See* Periodical Publications.—*Brussels.*

BUZANTIOS (Alexandros Kalphoglou) *Ἠθικη στιχουργια του περιωνυμου στιχουργου Ἀλεξανδρου Καλφογλου Βυζαντιου προς τον ἐν Βουκουρεστιῳ ἀνεψιον αὐτου, εὑρεθεισα . . . ἐπι ἐτους* 1797, *etc.* *See* Kremos (G. P.) *Ἐπιστολαι Γ. Π. Κρεμου, etc.* 1870. 8°. **10905.** ccc. **3.**

BUZANTIOS (Alexandros S.) *Ἐργα Α. Σ. Βυζαντιου. (Τα κυριωτερα πνευματικα δημουργηματα.) Ἐκδιδονται ὑπο Γρηγοριου Σ. Βυζαντιου.* [With a portrait.] pp. ιϛ'. 401. *Ἐν Ἀθηναις*, 1902. 8°. **12265. f. 11.**

—— *Ποιηματα.* [With a note signed: *Ἀλεξανδρος Ρ. Ραγκαβης.*] pp. 40. *See* Kalligas (P.) *Θανος Βλεκας, etc.* τομ. 3. [1890.] 8°. **012589.** e. **50.**

—— L'Insurrection de Candie et le gouvernement français. pp. 24. *Leipzig*, 1867. 8°. **8028.** bb. **68.** (**8.**)

—— *Σωκρατης και Ἀριστοφανης. Ποιημα, etc.* (*Λυρικα ποιηματια.*) pp. 48. *Ἀθηνησι*, 1862. 8°. **11586.** aa. **73.** (4.)

BUZANTIOS (Antonios) *Χρηστοηθεια, προς διακοσμησιν ἠθων των Νεων πανυ λυσιτελης. Ἐκ της Λατινιδος μεν ποτε εἰς ἁπλην μετενεχθεισα φρασιν, κοσμηθεισα δε τῳ καλλει του ἑλληνικου χαρακτηρος και ἐν τινι προσαυξυνθεισα χαριν των σπουδαιων ὑπο του . . . Ἀντωνιου του Βυζαντιου ἠδη δευτερον ἀκριβως διορθωθεισα τυποις ἐξεδοθη.* pp. 46. *Ἐνετιησιν*, 1803. 12°. **637.** f. **11.** (2.)

BUZANTIOS (Chrestos S.) *See* Thiers (L. A.) *President of the French Republic.* *Ἱστορια του Ναπολεοντος, ἐπιμελως ἐρανισθεισα ἐκ των του Α. Θιερσου γαλλικων ἱστορικων συγγραμματων*—Histoire de la Révolution française et Histoire du Consulat et de l'Empire—*ὑπο Χ. Σ. Βυζαντιου, etc.* 1860, *etc.* 8°. **9220.** d. **18.**

—— *Ἐγχειριδιον Ἐθνοφυλακος. Συλλογη νομων και διαταξεων, κανονισμων και διδασκαλιων στρατιωτικων ἀσκησεων και ὑπηρεσιων . . . ἐκδοθεν ὑπο Χ. Σ. Βυζαντιου . . . παρα τῳ Ὑπουργειῳ των Στρατιωτικων.* pp. κδ'. 799. β'. pl. 69. 7. 1863. 8°. *See* Greece.—*Army.* **8826.** aa. **17.**

—— *Ἱστορια του τακτικου στρατου της Ἑλλαδος, ἀπο της πρωτης συστασεως του κατα το* 1821 *μεχρι των* 1832. pp. ϛ'. 186. *Ἐν Ἀθηναις*, 1837. 8°. **1312.** d. **2.**

—— *Ἱστορια των κατα την Ἑλλην. Ἐπαναστασιν ἐκστρατειων και μαχων . . . ὡν συμμετεσχεν ὁ τακτικος στρατος, ἀπο του* 1821 *μεχρι του* 1833, *etc.* pp. η'. 431. *Ἐν Ἀθηναις*, 1874. 8°. **9136.** d. **6.**

BUZANTIOS (Demetrios K. Chatze Aslane) *Ἡ Βαβυλωνια ἠ ἡ κατα τοπους διαφθορα της ἑλληνικης γλωσσης. Κωμῳδια εἰς πραξεις πεντε . . . Ἐκδοσις δευτερα, etc.* pp. 113. *Ἐν Ἀθηναις*, 1840. 8°. **1343.** i. **21.**

—— *Ἐκδοσις τεταρτη. Ἀπαραλλακτως τυπωθεισα ὑπο Ἐμμ. Γεωργιου Σαμιου.* pp. 100. *Ἐν Ἀθηναις*, 1861. 8°. **11758.** e. **8.**

—— [Another edition.] pp. 99. *Ἐν Ἀθηναις*, [1890.] 16°. **11758.** aa. **25.** (3.)

—— *Ἡ Γυναικοκρατια. Κωμῳδια εἰς πεντε πραξεις, etc.* pp. ϛ'. 90. *Ἐν Ἀθηναις*, 1841. 8°. **1343.** i. **20.** *Imperfect; wanting pp.* 3, 4.

—— *Μυθοι, μυθιστοριαι και διηγηματα ἠθικα και ἀστεια . . . Ἐκδιδεται το δευτερον ὑπο Ἐμμ. Γεωργιου Σαμιου.* pp. 120. *Ἀθηνησι*, 1861. 8°. **12430.** aa. **19.**

BUZANTIOS (Gregorios S.) *See* Buzantios (A. S.) *Ἐργα . . . Ἐκδιδονται ὑπο Γ. Σ. Βυζαντιου.* 1902. 8°. **12265.** f. **11.**

BUZANTIOS (Hierotheos) *See* Hierotheos, *Buzantios.*

BUZANTIOS (Konstantios) *Archbishop of Mount Sinai, Patriarch of Constantinople.* *See* Konstantios.

BUZANTIOS (Michael Chourmouzes) *See* Chourmouzes (M.)

BUZANTIOS (Serapheim) *Metropolitan of Arta.* *See* Serapheim.

BUZANTIOS (Skarlatos D.) *Ἡ Κωνσταντινουπολις ἠ περιγραφη τοπογραφικη, ἀρχαιολογικη καὶ ἱστορικη της περιωνυμου ταυτης μεγαλοπολεως . . . Μετα . . . εἰκονων και . . . πινακων, etc.* 3 tom. *Ἀθηνησιν*, 1851–69. 8°. **10125.** e. **20.**

—— *Λεξικον ἑλληνικον και γαλλικον . . . ἐκδοθεν . . . ὑπο Ἀ. Κορομηλα, etc.* 2 pt. *Ἀθηνησιν*, 1846. 8°. **12924.** m. **3.**

—— Édition seconde stéréotype. 2 pt. *Athènes*, 1856. 8°. **12994.f.3.**

—— [Another copy.] **12923.** f. **14.**

BUZANTIOS (Skarlatos D.)

—— *Λεξικον ἐπιτομον της ἑλληνικης γλωσσης, etc.* pp. δ'. 1463. *Ἀθηνησιν*, 1839. 4°. **2053.b.**

—— [Another copy.] **826. i. 4.**

—— *Λεξικον της ἑλληνικης γλωσσης. Συντεθεν μεν . . . ἐπι τη βασει παντων των ἀχρι τουδε ἐκδεδομενων ἑλληνικων λεξικων, ἰδιως δε του ἐν Παρισιοις ἐκδιδομενου θησαυρου του Ἑρρικου Στεφανου . . . Οἷς προσετεθη ἐπι τελους και Λεξικον ἐπιτομον των . . . κυριων ὀνοματων, ἐκδοθεν δε στερεοτυπως ὑπο Ἀνδρεου Κορομηλα, etc.* 3 τομ. *Ἐν Ἀθηναις*, 1852. 4°. **12923. f. 2.**

—— *Λεξικον της καθ' ἡμας ἑλληνικης διαλεκτου, μεθηρμηνευμενης εἰς το ἀρχαιον ἑλληνικον και το γαλλικον μετα προσθηκης γεωγραφικου πινακος των νεωτερων και παλαιων ὀνοματων ὑπο Σ. Δ. του Βυζαντιου.* pp. λθ'. 394. *Ἐν Ἀθηναις*, 1835. 8°. **826. e. 8.**

—— *Ἐκδοσις δευτερα, etc.* pp. ζ'. 505. *Ἀθηνησι*, 1857. 8°. **12924. c. 25.**

—— *Ἐκδοσις τριτη, ἐπηυξημενη, etc.* pp. να'. 676. *Ἐν Ἀθηναις*, 1874. 8°. **12924. cc. 6.**

BUZANTIOS (Skarlatos D.) and **RIZOS RANKABES** (Alexandros)

—— *Ἑλληνικη χρηστομαθεια (ἡ συλλογη τεμαχιων) ἐκ των δοκιμωτερων ἑλληνων πεζογραφων και ποιητων, μετα σχολιων γραμματικων, ἱστορικων και γεωγραφικων, και μετ' ἐπιτομων φιλολογικων και κριτικων ἐκθεσεων . . . Ἐκδοσις πεμπτη στερεοτυπος, etc.* 5 τομ. *Ἐν Ἀθηναις*, 1853, 51, 52. 8°. **12265. dd. 12.**

Tom. 2 is of the fourth edition.

BUZANTIS. *Βυζαντις. Ἐπιθεωρησις των βυζαντιακων σπουδων.* See Athens.—*Βυζαντιολογικη Ἑταιρεια.*

BUZAREINGUES (Charles Girou de) *See* Girou de Buzareingues.

BUZAREINGUES (Louis Girou de) *See* Girou de Buzareingues.

BÚZÁS (Győző) A németes összetételek története . . . Különnyomat a Magyar Nyelvőrből. pp. 48. *Budapest*, 1907. 8°. [*Nyelvészeti füzetek.* no. 41.] **012901. d. 1/41.**

BUZATO (Lodovico) Vn Stupendissimo caso il quale e interuenuto in Alemagna, ad vna terra chiamata Sleborg, *etc. Appresso L. Zannetti: Roma*, 1593. 8°. **4662. aaa. 7.**

Cropped.

BUZĂU, Dionisie Romano, *Bishop of.* [1865-73.] *See* Dionisie Romano.

BUZBY (George) *See* Busby.

BUZECCHI-TASSIS (Costanza) *See* Paola Elisabetta, *Founder of the Istituto delle Suore d. S. Famiglia* [Costanza Cerioli].

BUZEK (Józef) Historya polityki narodowościowej rządu Pruskiego wobec Polaków od traktatów Wiedeńskich [of 1815] do ustaw wyjątkowych z r. 1908. pp. xxiii. 569. 1909. 8°. *See* Leopol.—*Związek Naukowo-Literacki.* **Ac. 8975/4.**

—— Studya z zakresu administracyi wychowania publicznego. I. Szkolnictwo ludowe. pp. 479. *we Lwowie*, 1904. 8°. [*Archiwum Naukowe.* dział 1. tom 1. zesz. 2.] **Ac. 764.**

BUZEK (Kamil) *See* Tůma (J.) Josef Tůma. (Sborník vzpomínek.) K šedesátým jeho narozeninám napsali: K. Buzek, E. Havelka, *etc.* 1925. 8°. **08311. f. 63.**

BUZELINUS (Gabriel) *See* Bucelinus.

BUZELINUS (Joannes) Annales Gallo-Flandriæ: in quibus . . . ea omnia enarrantur, quæ per Gallo-Flandriam euenere, aut intra fines suos extraue Gallo-Flandri gesserunt: ac denique Regum Franciæ . . . Comitum Flandriæ . . . Tornacensium atque Atrebatensium Episcoporum . . . series ac successio contexitur, *etc.* pp. 629. *M. Wyon: Duaci*, 1624. fol. **156. g. 3.**

—— Gallo-Flandria, sacra et profana, in qua vrbes, oppida . . . et pagi præcipui Gallo-Flandrici tractus describuntur; horumque omnium locorum antiquitates, religio, mores . . . proponuntur. Dein Annales Gallo-Flandriæ. 2 vol. *M. Wyon: Duaci*, 1625, 24. fol. **C. 73. g. 11.**

Vol. 2 is another copy of the "Annales Gallo-Flandriæ."

BUZELLO (Arthur) Der Wundstarrkrampf beim Menschen, *etc.* pp. xiv. 260. *Stuttgart*, 1929. 8°. [*Neue deutsche Chirurgie.* Bd. 45.] **07482. dd. 1/45.**

BUZELLO (Herbert) Kritische Untersuchung von Ernst Mach's Erkenntnistheorie. pp. 94. *Berlin*, 1911. 8°. [*Kantstudien.* Ergänzungshft. 23.] **P.P. 1253. bba.**

BUZELLO (Siegfried) Der ausländische und der deutsche Buchhandel. Ein Vergleich der organisatorischen Entwicklungstendenzen. pp. 127. *Berlin*, 1930. 8°. [*Volkswirtschaftliche Studien.* Hft. 32.] **W.P.14651/32.**

BUZENAC (Ernest) Étude sur les charbons. pp. 156. *Paris*, 1906. 8°. **07107. l. 47.**

BUZENET (Jean Jules Alfred) Du chancre de la bouche, son diagnostic différentiel, *etc.* pp. 78. *Paris*, 1858. 4°. [*Collection des thèses soutenues à la Faculté de Médecine de Paris.* An 1858. tom. 3.] **7373. b. 1.**

BUZENET (Prosper) Thèse pour le doctorat en médecine, *etc.* (Questions sur diverses branches des sciences médicales.) pp. 23. *Paris*, 1844. 4°. [*Collection des thèses soutenues à la Faculté de Médecine de Paris.* An 1844. tom. 3.] **7371. e. 8.**

BUZENGEIGER (Carl Heribert Ignatius) *See* Feuerbach (C. W.) Eigenschaften einiger merkwürdigen Punkte des geradlinigen Dreiecks . . . Mit einer Vorrede von K. Buzengeiger. 1822. 4°. **8529. dd. 4.**

BUZENGEIGER (Karl Heribert Ignatius) *See* Buzengeiger (Carl H. I.)

BUZENIN (Hieronymus a) *See* Bużeński (Hieronim)

BUZENIN (Matthias de) successively *Bishop of Przemysl* and *of Kujawy.* *See* Pstroconius.

BUŻEŃSKI (Hieronim) Regestrum perceptorum pecuniarum privatorum proventuum S. Mtis. R. a die prima mensis Januarii ad diem ultimam Decembris anni 1576 sub administratione officii regni thesaurariatus . . . H. a Buzenin, *etc.* pp. 51. [1881.] *See* Źródła. Źródła dziejowe. (tom 9. Księgi podskarbińskie.) 1876, *etc.* 8°. **9456. aa. 19.**

BUŻEŃSKI (Stanisław) *Dean of Vermland.* Vita . . . B. Raphaelis Proszoviani Ordinis Minorum S. Francisci . . . Varthæ quiescentis, *etc.* [The dedication signed: S. B. D. V. C. G., i.e. Stanislaus Bużeński Decanus Varmiensis Canonicus Gnesnensis.] pp. 143. 1686. 4°. *See* G., S. B. D. V. C. **1232. a. 15.**

UŻEŃSKI (Stanisław) *Dean of Vermland.*

— Żywoty Arcybiskupów Gnieźnieńskich, Prymasów Korony Polskiéj i Wielkiego Księstwa Litewskiego, od Wilibalda do Andrzeja Olszowskiego włącznie . . . Z niewydanego dotąd rękopismu łacińskiego na język polski przełożył Michał Bohusz Szyszko. Wstęp i wiadomość o założeniu Arcybiskupstwa, tudzież o jedénastu Późniejszych Prymasach, do zgonu Księżęcia Michała Poniatowskiego, dodał Mikołaj Malinowski. 5 tom. *Wilno*, 1852–60. 8°. **4886**. g. **5**.

UZENVAL (Nicolas Choart de) *Bishop of Beauvais. See* Choart de Buzenval.

UZER (Anton) Handbuch der Zahnheilkunde, *etc.* pp. xii. 340. *Berlin*, 1867. 8°. **7611**. df. **30**.

— Das Medizinal- und Sanitätswesen im Herzogtum Sachsen-Meiningen mit Rücksicht auf die Reichsgesetzgebung . . . Bearbeitet von . . . A. Buzer und mitgeteilt von . . . Carl Buzer, *etc.* 7 pt. 1896–1900. *See* Meiningen.—*Verein für Meiningische Geschichte und Landeskunde.* Schriften, *etc.* Hft. 23–25, 27–29, 35. 1888, *etc.* 8°. Ac. **7114**.

UZER (Carl) *See* Buzer (A.) Das Medizinal- und Sanitätswesen im Herzogtum Sachsen-Meiningen . . . Bearbeitet von . . . A. Buzer und mitgeteilt von . . . C. Buzer. 1896, *etc.* 8°. [*Schriften des Vereins für Sachsen Meiningische Geschichte und Landeskunde.* Hft. 23–25, 27–29, 35.] Ac. **7114**.

UZÉSCA (Sima) *See* Ionnescu-Gion (G. I.) Din istoria Bassarabilor. I. Sima stolnicésa Buzésca. (Cu douĕ portrete.) 1903, *etc.* 8°. **9136**. bbb. **56**.

UZESKUL (Vladislav Petrovich)

— Античность и современность. Современныя темы въ античной Греціи. Изданіе 2-е, дополненное. pp. iv. 210. *С.-Петербургъ*, 1914. 8°. **07704**. eee. **51**.

— Введеніе въ исторію Греціи. Лекціи. pp. v. 535. *Харьковъ*, 1903. 8°. **9026**. dd. **8**.

— Всеобщая история и ее представители в России в XIX и начале XX века. *Ленинград*, 1929– . 8°. [*Труды Комиссии по Истории Знаний.* no. 7, *etc.*] Ac. **1125**. sa.

— Историческіе Этюды, *etc.* pp. vi. 406. *С.-Петербургъ*, 1911. 8°. **09008**. g. **19**.

— Наукові записки. Праці Науково-дослідчої катедри історії европейської культури. Присвячується почесному голові Катедри академіку В. П. Бузескулу з нагоди 70-річчя його народження. Випуск III. (Ученые записки . . . Scientific Magazine, *etc.*) [With a portrait.] *Russ.* pp. 454. pl. VII. 1929. 8°. *See* Kharkov.—*Науково-Дослідча Катедра Історії Европейської Культури.* **12352**. y. **30**.

— Открытия XIX и начала XX века в области истории древнего мира . . . Восток. (Древне-греческий мир.) 2 част. *Петербург*, 1923, 24. 8°. **7705**. pp. **1**.

UZETA (Manuel) and **BRAVO** (Felipe) Diccionario geográfico, estadístico, histórico, de las Islas Filipinas, *etc.* 2 tom. *Madrid*, 1850, 51. 8°. **10056**. f. **22**.

UZEŬ. *See* Buzău.

UZEWINCKEL (Georgius) *See* Feuerlein (J. W.) Medicinam intellectus sive logicam exponent . . . respondentes V. H. Regenfus . . . G. Buzewinckel, *etc.* [1716 ?] 4°. **525**. e. **15**. (**10**.)

UZHANSKY (Osip Evsevievich) *See* Menger (A.) Право на полный продуктъ труда. Переводъ . . . О. Е. Бужанскаго. 1906. 8°. **08282**. cc. **49**.

— Die gewerblichen Genossenschaften Belgiens. pp. viii. 93. *Leipzig*, 1900. 8°. [*Staats- und socialwissenschaftliche Forschungen.* Bd. 18. Hft. 3.] **8205**. pp. **1**. (**3**.)

BUZHINSKY (Gavriil) *Bishop of Ryazan and Murom. See* Gavriil.

BUZICIUS (Theodericus) *See* Muehlpforth (J. F.) De Theoderico Buzicio ejusque genere et patria, *etc.* [1731.] 4°. **1197**. c. **11**. (**20**.)

—— *See* Thilo (J. C.) De Theoderico Buzicio ejusque genere et patria, *etc.* [1730.] 4°. **1197**. c. **11**. (**19**.)

BUZIN (J.) La Bourse et ses opérations. Explications pratiques, *etc.* pp. 96. *Paris*, 1887. 12°. **8228**. bb. **18**.

BUZINOV (Aleksyei) В.Ф.Г. За Невской заставой. Записки рабочего Алексея Бузинова. С предисловием Б. Горева. pp. 176. *Москва, Ленинград*, 1930. 8°. **10795**. p. **13**.

BUZIO (Vincenzo) *See* Butio.

BUZIUS (Hieronymus Maria) *See* Berti (G. L.) Jo. Laurentii Berti . . . librorum XXXVII. de theologicis disciplinis accurata synopsis quam . . . in lucem . . . edit F. H. M. Buzius, *etc.* 1789. 8°. **3558**. bb. **7**.

—— De locis theologicis. *See* Berti (G. L.) Jo. Laurentii Berti . . . De theologicis disciplinis, *etc.* tom. 10. 1792. 8°. **1350**. k. **2**.

BUZJĀNĪ. *See* Muḥammad ibn Muḥammad (Abū al-Wafā) *al-Buzjānī.*

BUZ'KO (D.) Смерть Івана Матвієвича. Хроника на 4 розділи. pp. 69. *Харків*, 1926. 8°. **20002**. e. **31**.

BUZNA (Alajos) *See* Domaniczky (I.) Katonai szótár. Német-magyar rész . . . Szerkesztették Domaniczky I. . . . Buzna A., *etc.* 1892. 8°. **12975**. b. **3**.

BUZNIKOV (Vladimir Ionovich) Лесотехнические продукты. pp. 16. *Петроград*, 1922. 8°. [*Богатства России.*] Ac. **1125**. i/6.

BUZÓ GOMES (Sinforiano)

—— Indice de la poesía paraguaya. Presentado y anotado por S. Buzó Gomes. pp. 384. *Asunción, Buenos Aires*, 1943. 8°. **11453**. bb. **8**.

BUZONNIÈRE (Léon de) Histoire architecturale de la ville d'Orléans. 2 tom. *Paris*, 1849. 8°. **10171**. g. **27**.

—— Voyage en Écosse, ou Itinéraire général de l'Écosse . . . Orné de quatre gravures. pp. viii. 479. *Paris*, 1832. 8°. **10370**. cc. **23**.

BUZORINI (Ludwig) Grundzüge einer Pathologie und Therapie der psychischen Krankheiten, mit kritischem Rückblicke auf die bisher bestandenen Lehren. pp. viii. 178. *Stuttgart & Tübingen*, 1832. 8°. **7660**. cc. **10**.

—— Luftelectricität, Erdmagnetismus und Krankheitsconstitution . . . Mit einer Charte. pp. xii. 227. *Belle-Vue bei Constanz*, 1841. 8°. **7687**. bb. **2**.

—— Untersuchungen über die körperlichen Bedingungen der verschiedenen Formen von Geisteskrankheiten, *etc.* pp. 150. *Ulm*, 1824. 8°. **1191**. h. **33**.

BUZOT, *Family of. See* Tyssandier (L.) Un Gouverneur de Paris. Le général Lecointe. Les Buzot et les Caffieri. 1897. 8°. **010664**. f. **11**.

BUZOT (Charlemagne Adrien) and **CAFFIERI** (Joseph Corentin) Au Conseil des Cinq-Cents, les héritiers Buzot. [A protest against the claims of M. A. V. Buzot to the property of her late husband, F. N. L. Buzot.] [*Paris*, 1797 ?] *s. sh.* 8°. **F. 949**. (**12**.)

BUZOT (François Nicolas Léonard) *See* Davy (J. N.) Études sur la Révolution française. Les Conventionnels de l'Eure, Buzot, Duroy, *etc.* 1876. 8°. **9226**. h. **1**.

BUZOT (François Nicolas Léonard)

—— *See* Hérissay (J.) Un Girondin. François Buzot, député de l'Eure à l'Assemblée constituante et à la Convention, 1760–1794. 1907. 8°. **010663**. h. 5.

—— Convention nationale. Discours . . . sur la famille des Bourbons, *etc.* pp. 6. [*Paris*, 1792.] 8°. F. **926**. (10.)

—— Opinion d'un patriote germain, sur la motion du citoyen Buzot [to banish the members of the Orleans family]. pp. 4. [*Paris*, 1792?] 8°. F.R. **126**. (27.)

—— Convention nationale. Opinion . . . sur le jugement de Louis XVI. pp. 12. [*Paris*, 1793?] 8°. F. **914**. (28.)

—— Convention nationale. Rapport et projet de décret sur la garde des 83 départemens, *etc.* pp. 11. [*Paris*, 1792?] 8°. F. **1255**. (10.)

—— [Another copy.] F. **250**. (3.)

—— Convention nationale. Rapport fait au nom de la Commission des Neuf . . . sur une loi contre les provocateurs au meurtre & à l'assassinat. pp. 7. [*Paris*, 1793?] 8°. F. **1255**. (9.)

—— [Another copy.] Rapport fait au nom de la Commission des Neuf . . . sur une loi contre les provocateurs au meurtre & à l'assassinat. [*Paris*, 1793?] 8°. R. **97**. (15.)

—— [Another issue.] Rapport fait au nom de la Commission des Neuf, *etc.* [*Paris*, 1793?] 8°. F.R. **217**. (26.)

—— Lettres de F. N. L. Buzot . . . à ses commettans. pp. 28. *Paris*, 1793. 8°. F. **1033**. (10.)

—— Mémoires sur la Revolution française, par Buzot . . . précédés d'un précis de sa vie et de recherches historiques sur les Girondins; par M. Guadet. [With an appendix containing speeches by Buzot.] pp. 112. 364. *Paris*, 1828. 8°. **1195**. g. **17**.

—— Mémoires de François-Nicolas-Louis Buzot. *See* Petion de Villeneuve (J.) Mémoires inédits de Pétion, *etc.* 1866. 8°. **10661**. g. **11**.

—— Projet de décret proposé par M. Buzot . . . dans la séance du [21 May 1791]. Division du Corps législatif en deux sections de discussion. pp. 3. [*Paris*, 1791?] 8°. F.R. **75**. (15.)

—— [Another copy.] Projet de décret . . . dans la séance du [21 May 1791], *etc.* [*Paris*, 1791.] 8°. R. **73**. (10.)

BUZOT (François Nicolas Louis) *See* Buzot (F. N. Léonard)

BUZOT (Marie Anne Victoire) *See* Buzot (C. A.) and Caffieri (J. C.) Au Conseil des Cinq-Cents, les héritiers Buzot. [A protest against the claims of M. A. V. Buzot to the property of her late husband, F. N. L. Buzot.] [1797?] *s. sh.* 8°. F. **949**. (12.)

BUZUKU (Gjon)

—— *See* Bible.—*New Testament.—Liturgical Epistles and Gospels.* [*Albanian.*] Monumenti mâ i vjetri i giûhës shqype. D. Gjon Buzuku—1555., *etc.* 1930. 8°. **03025**. i. **25**.

BUZURG IBN SHAHRIYĀR, *al-Rām-Hurmuzī.* ['Ajā'ib al-Hind.] Livre des merveilles de l'Inde . . . Texte arabe publié d'après le manuscrit de M. Schefer, collationné sur le manuscrit de Constantinople, par P. A. van der Lith. Traduction française par L. Marcel Devic. Avec quatre planches coloriées, *etc.* *Arab. & Fr.* pp. 310. *Leide*, 1883–1886. 4°. **14565**. d. 3.

BUZURG IBN SHAHRIYĀR, *al-Rām-Hurmuzī.*

—— The Book of the Marvels of India. From the Ara by L. Marcel Devic. (Translated into English by Pe Quennell.) pp. vi. 163. *G. Routledge & Sons: Lond* 1928. 8°. [*Golden Dragon Library.*] **14005**. d.

—— Les Merveilles de l'Inde, ouvrage arabe inédit du siècle. [By Buzurg ibn Shahriyār.] Traduit pour première fois d'après un manuscrit de la . . . mosquée Sainte-Sophie, à Constantinople; avec introducti notes, index . . . par L. Marcel Devic. pp. xxx. 220. 1878. 16°. *See* India. **14565**. b.

BUZŪRGMIHR. Ganjeshâyigân. *Pehlevi, Gujarati & E* *See* Peshotan Behrāmjī Saṃjaṇa. Ganjesháyagán, 1885. 8°. **14990**. f

BUZWELL (James) *pseud.* Buzwell's Gludstone. Ta at Hawhawden: being a record of the opinions convictions of W. E. Gludstone, LL.D., M.P. by Ja Buzwell. [A satire upon W. E. Gladstone, by the aut of "Letters to my son Herbert."] pp. 91. *Tinsley Br* *London*, 1884. 16°. **8139**. a

BUZY (Antonie Carrère de) *See* Carrère de Buzy.

BUZY (Denys) Introduction aux paraboles évangéliq pp. xxiii. 476. *Paris*, 1912. 8°. **03226**. de

—— Saint Jean-Baptiste. Études historiques et critiq pp. xii. 411. *Paris*, 1922. 8°. **4807**. aaa.

—— The Life of S. John the Baptist . . . Freely adapted w much additional matter by John M. T. Barton. pp. xx. *Burns, Oates & Co.: London*, 1933. 8°. **2216**. a.

—— Les Symboles de l'Ancien Testament. pp. vi. 421. *Paris*, 1923. 8°. **03149**. de.

—— [Vie de Sœur Marie de Jésus crucifié.] Life of Servant of God Sister Mary of Jesus Crucified . Translated by the Rev. A. M. O'Sullivan. [With pla including a portrait.] pp. 311. *Sands & Co.: Lon* [1926.] 8°. **4863**. a.

BUZY (J. B.) Dom Maugérard. Histoire d'un bib graphe lorrain de l'ordre de Saint-Benoît au XV siècle. [Followed by "La Chapelle Sainte-Anne d'Argor Meuse."] pp. 303. *Châlons-sur-Marne*, 1882. 8°. **4865**. dd

BUZZ.

—— Buzz. The magazine of H.M.S. Royal Harold. Royal Harold, *H.M.S.*

BUZZ ( ) *See* J *** (Niklas) *Pastor an Pfarrkirche zu **.* Des Niklas J *** Pastor an Pfarrkirche zu ** Abbitte an das baiersche I diger-Institut, *etc.* [A rejoinder to Heinrich Bra defence of Direktor Buzz against a charge of plagiari By J. M. Sailer.] [1780.] 8°. **3908**. bbb. **10**.

BUZZA (Gertrude Kessen) and **ACOCK** (Mur Marion) Ear-training in French Dictation. pp. 77. *London*, 1936. 8°. [*Harrap's Modern Language Series*] **12213**. a. 1/3

—— Pupil's edition. pp. 54. *London*, 1938 [1937]. 8°. [*Harrap's Modern Language Series.*] **12213**. a. 1/4

—— Répétition. Modern French exercises for middle for 3 bk. *London & Toronto*, 1928. 8°. [*Dent's Mod Language Series.*] **12215.e.1/11**

BUZZA (Gertrude Kessen) and **HURT** (Evelyn Els

—— La Langue franç Grammaire à l'usage des classes moyennes et supérieu pp. 246. *John Murray: London*, 1920. 8°. **12951**. aaa.

BUZZACCARINI (Francesco) *Marquis.* Nell'occasione delle faustissime nozze del nobile marchese F. Buzzaccarini e della nobile contessa Angiola da-Rio, *etc.* [Signed: A. D. C.] 1824. 8°. *See* C., A. D. **11431.** cc. **39.**

BUZZAGLIA (Filippo Ruggieri) *See* Ruggieri Buzzaglia.

BUZZANI (Guiseppe Saverio) Strano avvenimento di una chicchera a caffé. Lettera, *etc.* pp. 19. *Torino,* 1778. 8°. **7482.** h. **4.** (**3.**)

BUZZANO, *near Turin.—Monastery of St. Thomas. See* Thomas, *Saint and Apostle, Monastery of, at Buzzano.*

BUZZARD (Charles Norman)

—— The Bumble Bee. Special visual aid book for schools. (Enlarged reproductions of J. Yunge-Bateman's illustrations to " Bomba, the Bumble Bee.") pl. 8. [" *Daily Mail " School-Aid Department: London,* 1946.] *obl.* fol. Cup. **1247.** c. **41.**

—— Shining Hours . . . [Autobiographical reminiscences, mainly of bee-keeping.] Illustrated by J. Yunge-Bateman. pp. 192. *Collins: London,* 1946. 8°. **7296.** b. **49.**

BUZZARD (*Sir* Edward Farquhar) *K.C.V.O. See* Athanassio-Benisty (M.) Clinical Forms of Nerve-Lesions . . . Edited with a preface by E. Farquhar Buzzard, *etc.* 1918. 8°. **07305.** ccc. **13.**

—— *See* Athanassio-Benisty (M.) Treatment & Repair of Nerve Lesions . . . Edited with a preface by E. Farquhar Buzzard. 1918. 8°. **07305.** ccc. **12.**

—— *See* Babinski (J.) and Froment (J.) Hysteria or Pithiatism . . . Edited, with a preface, by E. Farquhar Buzzard, *etc.* 1918. 8°. **07305.** ccc. **4.**

—— *See* Yeo (Isaac B.) A Manual of Medical Treatment or Clinical Therapeutics. New edition by I. B. Yeo . . . R. Crawfurd . . . and E. F. Buzzard, *etc.* 1909. 8°. **7439.** aa. **6.**

—— —— 1913. 8°. **7439.** aa. **11.**

—— An Outline of Neurology and its Outlook, *etc.* pp. 24. *London,* 1929. 8°. [*Earl Grey Memorial Lecture.* no. 11.] Ac. **2671.** g.

BUZZARD (*Sir* Edward Farquhar) *K.C.V.O.,* and **GREENFIELD** (Joseph Godwin)

—— Pathology of the Nervous System. pp. xv. 334. *Constable & Co.: London,* 1921. 8°. **07660.** i. **45.**

BUZZARD (Frank Anstie) *See* Fortresses. Fortresses and Military Engineering in Recent Literature . . . Translated by Capt. F. A. Buzzard. 1907. 8°. [*Professional Papers of the Corps of Royal Engineers.* ser. 4. vol. 1. no. 7.] Ac. **4354.**

BUZZARD (Thomas) *See* Brinton (William) Intestinal Obstruction . . . Edited by T. Buzzard, *etc.* 1867. 8°. **7620.** aa. **18.**

—— Clinical Aspects of Syphilitic Nervous Affections. pp. xi. 148. *J. & A. Churchill: London,* 1874. 8°. **7641.** b. **36.**

—— Clinical Lectures on Diseases of the Nervous System. pp. xvi. 466. *J. & A. Churchill: London,* 1882. 8°. **7630.** dd. **30.**

—— On Some Forms of Paralysis from Peripheral Neuritis . . . The Harveian lectures for 1885. pp. viii. 147. *J. & A. Churchill: London,* 1886. 8°. **7641.** aaa. **15.**

BUZZARD (Thomas)

—— On the Simulation of Hysteria by organic disease of the nervous system. pp. vii. 113. *J. & A. Churchill: London,* 1891. 8°. **7630.** de. **15.**

—— Scorbutus. *See* Reynolds (*Sir* John R.) *Bart.* A System of Medicine. vol. 1. 1866, *etc.* 8°. **07305.** h. **29.**

—— With the Turkish Army in the Crimea and Asia Minor [1855, 56]. A personal narrative . . . With eight illustrations by the author, and two maps. pp. viii. 310. *John Murray: London,* 1915. 8°. **9078.** ee. **13.**

BUZZARDS. Doorga; or, the Indian coolie's Eldorado in the West Indies. By the Buzzards. pp. 46. *Calcutta Central Press Co.: Calcutta,* [1884.] 8°. **12330.** h. **27.** (**3.**)

BUZZATI (Dino)

—— Un Caso clinico. Commedia, *etc.* pp. 183. [*Milan,*] 1953. 8°. **11716.** aa. **35.** *La Medusa degli italiani.* vol. 85.

—— [Il Deserto dei Tartari.] The Tartar Steppe. Translated by Stuart C. Hood. pp. 214. *Secker & Warburg: London,* 1952. 8°. **12472.** b. **12.**

BUZZATI (Giulio Cesare) *See* Bar (C. L. von) [Das internationale Privat- und Strafrecht.] Teoria e pratica del diritto internazionale privato. Traduzione . . . a cura del prof. G. C. Buzzati. 1915. 8°. [*Biblioteca di scienze politiche ed amministrative.* ser. 3. vol. 11. pt. 1.] **8005.** l.

—— *See* Brunialti (A.) Biblioteca di scienze politiche, *etc.* (ser. 3. Diretta dai professori A. Brunialti, O. Ranelletti, G. C. Buzzati.) 1883, *etc.* 8°. **8005.** i–l.

—— *See* Triepel (H.) [Völkerrecht und Landesrecht.] Diritto internazionale e diritto interno. Traduzione italiana con note a cura del prof. G. C. Buzzati. 1913. 8°. [*Biblioteca di scienze politiche ed amministrative.* ser. 3. vol. 9. pt. 1.] **8005.** k.

—— *See* Ullmann (E. von) [Völkerrecht.] Trattato di diritto internazionale pubblico. Traduzione italiana . . . a cura del prof. G. C. Buzzati. 1914. 8°. [*Biblioteca di scienze politiche ed amministrative.* ser. 3. vol. 9. pt. 2.] **8005.** k.

—— L'Offesa e la difesa nella guerra secondo i moderni ritrovati. Studio di diritto internazionale. pp. 388. *Roma,* 1888. 8°. **6955.** f. **5.**

—— [Trattato di diritto internazionale privato secondo le convenzioni dell'Aja.] Le Droit international privé d'après les conventions de La Haye. 1. Le Mariage, d'après la Convention du 12 juin 1902. Traduction française . . . par Francis Rey. pp. xvi. 507. *Paris,* 1911. 8°. **06916.** g. **16.** *No more published.*

—— L'Urto di navi in mare. Studio di diritto internazionale privato. pp. 122. *Padova; Verona,* 1889. 8°. **6955.** f. **6.**

BUZZEGOLI (Alberto Giuseppe) Dell'acqua marziale di Rio nell'isola dell'Elba e dell'uso di essa in medicina e chirurgia, *etc.* pp. xx. 259. *Firenze,* 1762. 8°. **665.** e. **21.**

BUZZELL (Francis) The Great Lakes Naval Training Station. A history . . . Illustrated from photographs. pp. 212. *Small, Maynard & Co.: Boston,* [1919.] 8°. **08806.** cc. **11.**

BUZZELL (JOHN)

—— A Religious Magazine. (A Religious Magazine, containing a short history of the Church of Christ gathered at Durham, N.H., in the year 1780. Also a particular account of late reformations and revivals of religion. By J. Buzzell.—A Religious Magazine, containing an account of the United Churches of Christ commonly called Free-Will Baptist.) vol. 1. no. 1—vol. 2. no. 8. Jan. 1811—Sept. 1822. 1811–22. 8°. *See* PERIODICAL PUBLICATIONS.—*Portland, Maine.* Mic. A. **364**. (2.)

BUZZELL (JONATHAN JOHN) *See* POOLE (George W.) and BUZZELL (J. J.) Letters that Make Good . . . Edited by G. W. Poole, J. J. Buzzell, *etc.* 1914. 4°. **10902**. g. **33**.

BUZZER. The Buzzer. *See* ENGLAND.—*Army.* [*Magazines, etc. of Unspecified Units.*]

—— The Buzzer. *See* also ENGLAND.—*National Union of Disabled Ex-Service Men.*—*Leeds Branch.*

BUZZETTI (ANTONIUS) De utilitate seminum colchici autumnalis in rheumatismo chronico, aliisque affectionibus, dissertatio inauguralis, *etc.* pp. 27. *Ticini Regii,* 1822. 8°. **7383***. c. **7**. (**18**.)

BUZZETTI (CURZIO) Sul clima di Ferrara e della sua provincia. pp. 36. *Pavia,* 1868. 8°. **7687**. bb. **29**. (**2**.)

—— I Venti . . . Lettura, *etc.* pp. 67. *Milano,* 1872. 16°. **8755**. a. **48**. (**5**.)

BUZZETTI (JOSÉ L.)

—— Planificación y desarrollo de las obras públicas. El plan de obras públicas 1944–1949. pp. 221. *Montevideo,* 1945. 8°. **8288**. d. **65**.

BUZZETTI (PIETRO) Documenti della Rezia Chiavennasca anteriori al XIV° secolo, pubblicati per cura di P. Buzzetti. pp. vii. 78. *Como,* 1903. 8°. **10136**. i. **7**.

—— Regesto per documenti di Carate-Lario. pp. vii. 110. *Como,* 1914. 8°. **10132**. h. **26**.

BUZZETTI (ULPIANO) Teoria del commercio internazionale, con una nota sui salari e sul commercio internazionale. Studi. pp. 164. *Milano,* 1877. 8°. **8247**. bbb. **3**.

BUZZETTI (VINCENZO) Teologali di Vincenzo Buzzetti . . . con discorso proemiale dell'abate Carlo Gazola. pp. xii. 159. *Piacenza,* 1826. 8°. T. **2482**. (**2**.)

BUZZI (ANDREAS VON) Dramatischer Nachlass. [The editor's preface signed: R. v. B., i.e. R. von Buzzi.] pp. v. 373. *Wien,* 1866. 16°. **11745**. bbb. **14**.

BUZZI (FAUSTO) Beitrag zur Würdigung der medikamentösen Seifen unter Zugrundelegung von Seifen in flüssiger und weicher Form. pp. 76. *Hamburg & Leipzig,* 1891. 8°. [*Dermatologische Studien.* Reihe 2. Hft. 6.] P.P. **3015**. e. (**2**.)

BUZZI (FRANCESCO) Nuove sperienze fatte sull'occhio umano.—Correzioni degli stromenti del sig. Mejan per curare la fistola lacrimale. 1782. *See* AMORETTI (C.) and SOAVE (F.) Opuscoli scelti sulle scienze, *etc.* tom. 5. 1778, *etc.* 4°. **981**. h. **5**.

BUZZI (GIANCARLO)

—— Grazia Deledda. pp. 170. *Milano,* 1952. 8°. *Pubblicazioni della Facoltà di Lettere e Filosofia della Università di Pavia.* no. 3. **11865**. i. **31**.

BUZZI (GIROLAMO) Storia di Gamondio antico or Castellazzo di Alessandria, *etc.* 4 vol. *Alessandria,* 1863–65. 8°. **10129**. g. **26**.

—— Le Tombe de' padri greci e latini, *etc.* pp. 480. *Torino,* 1848. 8°. **4828**. d. **8**.

BUZZI (GIULIO) *See* BOBBIO.—*Benedictine Monastery.* Codice diplomatico del Monastero di S. Colombano di Bobbio, *etc.* (vol. 2. A cura di C. Cipolla e G. Buzzi.—vol. 3. A cura di G. Buzzi.) 1918. 8°. [*Fonti per la storia d'Italia.* no. 53, 54.] **Ac. 6543. (32.)**

—— *See* RAVENNA, *Archbishopric of.* Regesto della chiesa di Ravenna . . . A cura di V. Federici e G. Buzzi. 1911, *etc.* 8°. [*Regesta chartarum Italiae.* no. 7, 15.] **9150**. p. **1/6**.

BUZZI (MASSIMILIANO) *See* OVIDIUS NASO (P.) [*Works.—Latin and Italian.*] [The Works of Ovid.] (Delle epistole di P. Ovidio Nasone da Ponto libri quattro. [Translated by M. Buzzi.]) 1745, *etc.* 4°. [*MALATESTA* (*G. R.*) *Corpus omnium veterum poetarum Latinorum, etc.* tom. 29.] **77**. d. **5**.

BUZZI (OMOBONO) La Divisione incominciata dalla destra, e da un ordine qualunque. Dialogo tra Didascolo, Sefisto e Loghisto. pp. 42. *Chiavenna,* 1877. 8°. **8506**. cc. **10**. (**4**.)

BUZZI (PAOLO) Il Carme di Napoleone Bonaparte. pp. 28. *Milano,* 1901. 4°. **11422**. k. **21**.
One of an edition of 100 copies.

—— Rapsodie Leopardiane. [Poems.] pp. 328. *Milano,* 1898. 8°. **11429**. ccc. **10**.

BUZZI (PIETRO) *See* MANCINI (G. B.) Practical Reflections on the Figurative Art of Singing . . . Translated by P. Buzzi. [1912.] 8°. **7897**. p. **3**.

BUZZI (R. VON) *See* BUZZI (A. von) Dramatischer Nachlass. [The editor's preface signed: R. v. B., i.e. R. von Buzzi.] 1866. 16°. **11745**. bbb. **14**.

BUZZI BONFICHI (FRANCESCA) Vantaggi della donna istruita, *etc.* pp. 165. *Torino,* 1841. 8°. **1387**. c. **24**.

BUZZICONI (GIUSEPPE) La Bibliografia di Cavour. pp. 46. *Torino,* 1898. 8°. **11905**. aa. **46**.

BUZZONI (EMILIO) Dio, Chiesa e Stato. Ragione, verità e giustizia. pp. 93. *Milano,* 1885. 8°. **8032**. c. **1**. (**6**.)

B — VA (EK.)

—— *See* RISTORI (A.) afterwards CAPRANICA DEL GRILLO (A. *Marchioness.* Этюды и воспоминанія. Переводъ Ек Б — вой. 1904. 8°. **11796**. aa. **18**

B—VIĆ (B.) *See* POPOVIĆ (T. Lj.)

B . . . . VICH (D. N.) Сказки и преданія народовъ Кавказа. Обработаны по различнымъ источникамъ Д. Н. Б . . . . вичемъ. pp. 52. *Москва,* [1895.] 8°. **12431**. df. **3**

B . . . . . VO (D. D.) Дворцовое Село Островъ. Истори ческое описаніе Д. Д. Б . . . . . во [i.e. D. D. Blagovo Archimandrite Pimen], *etc.* [An offprint.] pp. 29. *Москва,* 1875. 8°. **10291**. f. **22**

BW. En Samtale mellem Hans Nielsen og Jens Olsen om Barnedaaben, til Bestyrkelse for dem, som ville blive Kirkens Samfund. Af Bw. pp. 16. *Ringsted* 1859. 8°. **4419**. bb. **34**

B——W. Wene-Saksa-Eesti keeli kõneajud, nende keelt rutuseks kättesaamiseks. Russisch-deutsch-estnisch Gespräche. Разговоры русско-нѣмецко-эстскіе. [Th preface signed: B——w.] pp. vi. 130. *Dorpa* 1877. 8°. **12976**. d. **3**

B——W, *Mr.* An Answer to Mr. B——w's [i.e. Richar Blacow's] Apology, as it respects his King, his country, hi conscience, and his God. By a Student of Oxford. pp. 3(*W. Bizett: London,* 1755. 8°. **1414**. b. **2**(

. . . . W (IL.) Ueber die historische Bedeutung der Verhandlungen der Moskauer Synode im Jahre 1551. [Signed: Il. B . . . . w.] *See* BODENSTEDT (F. M. von) Russische Fragmente, *etc.* Bd. 1. 1862. 8°. **9455. bb. 21.**

VANIKWA. *See* CAMPBELL (Dugald) *Missionary.* Ten Times a Slave, but freed at last. (The thrilling story of Bwanikwa.) [1916.] 8°. **4763. de. 33.**

VCLE (THOMAS) *See* BULKELEY.

VLCHYR-ESKIR-HYR. An Abstract of the Present State of the Mines of Bwlchyr-Eskir-Hyr and of the material proceedings of the Committee appointed for the management thereof. pp. 4. [*London*, 1700.] fol. **522. m. 12. (50.)**

— [Another edition.] (The Second Abstract of the State of the Mines of Bwlchyr-Eskir-Hyr, *etc.*) 2 pt. *London*, 1700. 8°. **444. a. 4.**

— The Third Abstract of the State of the Mines of Bwlchyr Eskir-Hir . . . From the thirtieth day of April last, inclusive, to this present nineteenth day of December, 1700. pp. 4. *F. Collins: London*, 1700. fol. **1487.1.10.(4.)**

— [Another copy.] **522. m. 12. (47.)**

— The Fourth Abstract of the State of the Mines of Bwlchyr Eskir-hir . . . from the 10th day of December last, inclusive, to this present 5th day of May, 1701. pp. 4. *Freeman Collins: London*, 1701. fol. **1487.1.10.(6.)**

— [Another copy.] **522. m. 12. (48.)**

— A List of the Names of all the Partners in the Lead Mines of Bwlchyr Eskir Hir . . . the tenth day of December, 1694, *etc.* [1695.] *s. sh.* fol. L.R. **305. a. 7. (5.)**

VLETIN CYMRY'R GROES. *See* WALES.—*Church in Wales.—Provincial Youth Council.*

W-R (A - - CH - B - LD) A Faithful Account of Mr. A - - ch - b - ld B - w - r's [i.e. Archibald Bower's] Motives for leaving his office of Secretary to the Court of Inquisition, *etc.* [Edited by Richard Barron.] pp. 8. [1750.] 8°. **T. 1613. (7.)**

— [Another edition.] *See* LISBON. A Letter from a Clergyman at London to the remaining disconsolate inhabitants of Lisbon, *etc.* 1756. 8°. **T. 1620. (8.)**

VRDD. Bwrdd Addysg. *See* ENGLAND.—*Board of Education.*

— Bwrdd yr Athrofa Unedig. *See* WALES.—*Calvinistic Methodist Church.—Bwrdd yr Athrofa Unedig.*

VRDD NWY CYMRU. *See* ENGLAND.—*Gas Council.—Wales Gas Board.*

VTHYN. Bwthyn bach y bryn. [A child's reading book.] rhan 1, 2. *Educational Publishing Co.: Cardiff*, [1910.] 4°. **12978. cc. 18.**

— [Another edition.] 3 rhan. *Educational Publishing Co.: Cardiff*, [1920.] 8°. **12978. bb. 46.**
Rhan 1 *is a reissue of the preceding.*

.

— By og bygd. *See* OSLO.—*Norsk Folkemuseum.*

. **Y,** *Docteur.* Promenades historiques dans le pays de Liége, par le docteur B . . y [i.e. J. P. P. Bovy]. [With maps.] tom 1, 2. *Liége*, 1838, 39. 8°. **1300. e. 5.**
Imperfect; wanting tom. 3.

- - - - Y, *Dr.* *See* PAUL (George) An Account of a Discourse . . . occasion'd by Dr. B - - - - - y's [i.e. R. Bentley's] Answer to the Discourse of Free-thinking [by A. Collins], *etc.* 1713. 8°. **4136. b. 60.**

B - - - - - Y, *Dr.*

— Five Extraordinary Letters suppos'd to be writ to Dr. B - - - - y [i.e. R. Bentley], upon his edition of Horace, and some other matters of great importance. pp. 22. *John Morphew: London*, 1712. 8°. **T. 723. (7.)**

— [Another copy.] **T. 2074. (1.)**

— [Another copy.] **237. e. 33. (3.)**

B - - - Y, *General.* General B - - - y's [i.e. Lord Blakeney's] Account to His Majesty concerning the loss of Minorca. [A political satire.] [*London*, 1756?] *s. sh.* fol. C. 113. hh. 3 (11.)

B - - - - Y, *Lord.* A Letter to the Right Honourable Lord B - - - - y [i.e. Lord Blakeney]. Being an inquiry into the merit of his defence of Minorca. [By Israel Mauduit.] pp. 47. *R. May: London*, 1757. 8°. **518. g. 16. (10.)**

— [Another copy, with a different titlepage.] *R. Baldwin: London*, 1757. 8°. **E. 2048. (8.)**

— Second edition. pp. 47. *R. May: London*, 1757. 8°. **T. 1053. (10.)**

— A Full Answer to an Infamous Libel, intituled, a Letter to Lord B — y, being, an enquiry into his defence of Minorca. To which is prefixed an exact plan of Fort St. Philip's, *etc.* pp. 47. *W. Reeve: London*, 1757. 8°. **1045. f. 6. (4.)**

— [Another copy.] **E. 2049. (3.)**

B——Y, *Mr.* *See* J., T. A Letter of Compliment, to the ingenious author of a Treatise on the Passions . . . with a critical enquiry into the theatrical merit of Mr. G——k, Mr. Q——n and Mr. B——y [i.e. S. Barry], *etc.* [1747.] 8°. **641. f. 8. (2.)**

— *See* TREATISE. A Treatise on the Passions, so far as they regard the stage; with a critical enquiry into the theatrical merit of Mr. G——k, Mr. Q——n, and Mr. B——y [i.e. S. Barry], *etc.* [1747?] 8°. **641. f. 8. (1.)**

B - - Y, *Reverend D - -.* A Vindication of the Reverend D - - B - - y [i.e. Dr. Berkeley], from the scandalous imputation of being author of a late book, intitled Alciphron, or the Minute Philosopher. To which is subjoined, the predictions of the late Earl of Shaftsbury concerning that book. Together with an appendix and an advertisement. pp. 104. *A. Millar: London*, 1734. 8°. **702. g. 4. (7.)**

BY-AND-BY. By-and-By, and other stories, *etc.* pp. 216. *Presbyterian Board of Publication: Philadelphia*, [1869.] 12°. **4413. b. 10.**

— By-and-Bye may never come. [A religious tract.] pp. 16. *Wertheim, Macintosh & Hunt: London*, [1860.] 8°. **4418. e. 23.**

BY COACH MAGAZINE. *See* PERIODICAL PUBLICATIONS.—*Birmingham.*

BY KENT AND SKERNE. By Kent and Skerne. [A magazine.] *See* DARLINGTON.—*Polam Hall.*

BY SEA AND SHORE. *See* PERIODICAL PUBLICATIONS. —*Birmingham.*

BY-STANDER. *See* BYSTANDER.

BY STAR AND CANDLELIGHT SERIES. By Star and Candlelight Series. *Frank Juckes: Birmingham*, 1937– . 8°. **W.P. 12195.**

BY YOURSELF LANGUAGE SERIES.

— The 'By Yourself' Language Series. 6 pt. *G. Bell & Sons: London*, 1940–51. 8°. **012902. r. 15.**
Containing two editions of "German by yourself."

B . . . . . . Y (B . . . . DE) [Projet d'éducation militaire nationale.] [With a dedicatory epistle to the Marquis de la Fayette, signed: B . . . . de B . . . . . . y, i.e. François Babié de Bercenay.] pp. 60. [*Paris ?* 1790.] 8°. **F. 11. (6.)**
Imperfect; wanting the titlepage, and all before p. 3.

B . . . Y (C. DE) Olivier. [A tale. The introduction signed: C. de B . . . y, i.e. H. de Thabaud de Latouche ?] pp. 144. *Bruxelles,* 1826. 12°. **12518.** ccc. **16.**

B——Y (THERESE VON) *See* Sz . . . . Y (F. von) *Count.* Ein Wort über animalischen Magnetismus . . . nebst Beschreibung des ideo-somnambülen Zustandes des Fräuleins T. von B——y zu Vasárhely im Jahre 1838, *etc.* 1840. 8°. **7410.** cc. **2.**

BYA (MAUNG MAUNG) *See* MAUNG BYA, *Maung.*

BYADULYA (ZMITROK) *pseud.* [i.e. S. E. PLAVNIK.]

—— Збор твораў у чатырох тамах, *etc.* [With a portrait.]
том 1. Апавяданні, 1912–1939. pp. 451. 1951.
том 2. Вершы і паэмы. pp. 442. 1952.
том 3. Салавей. Язэп Крушынскі. pp. 524. 1953.
том 4. Язэп Крушынскі. У дрымучых лясах. pp. 572. 1953.
Мінск, 1951–53. 8°. **012266.** a. **2.**

—— Избранное. Перевод с белорусского. (Составители М. Климкович и М. Бядуля. Перевод Б. Яковлева.) pp. 639. *Москва,* 1953. 8°. **12266.** i. **7.**

BYAKONT (SIMEON ELEVTHERY THEDOROVICH) *See* ALEXIS, *Saint, Metropolitan of Russia.*

BYALEVICH (ANTON PETROVICH)

—— Жывая рака. pp. 165. *Мінск,* 1955. 8°. **11588.** p. **32.**

BYALIK (BORIS A.)

—— *See* RUSSIA.—*Союз Советских Писателей СССР.* Проблемы социалистического реализма. Сборник, *etc.* [Edited by B. A. Byalik and others.] 1948. 8°. **11868.** c. **10.**

—— А. М. Горький и принцип партийности литературы. *In:* Советская литература. Сборник. pp. 60–111. 1948. 8°. **11868.** e. **1.**

—— Горький в борьбе с театральной реакцией. [With a portrait.] pp. 189. 1938. 8°. *See* RUSSIA.– Всероссийское *Театральное Общество,*
11795.aa.46.

—— Горький и театр. *In:* GRIFOR'EV (M. S.) Советский театр. pp. 131–188. 1947. 8°. **11798.** b. **21.**

—— Драматургия М. Горького советской эпохи. [With plates, including a portrait.] pp. 317. *Москва,* 1952. 8°. **11870.** aa. **4.**
The titlepage headed: Академия Наук СССР. Институт Мировой Литературы имени А. М. Горького.

—— Эстетические взгляды Горького. [With a portrait.] pp. 228. *Ленинград,* 1939. 8°. **11863.** b. **23.**

BYALIK (GAVRIIL LOSIFOVICH)

—— Широкополосные усилители. pp. 102. *Москва, Ленинград,* 1951. 8°. **08757.** bb. **41.**
Массовая радио-библиотека. вып. 104.

BYALIK (KH. N.)

—— Разсказы . . . Переводъ съ еврейскаго. Третье изданіе. pp. 220. *Берлинъ,* 1922. 8°. **12519.** d. **9.**

BYALL (S.)

—— *See* WALTON (Charles F.) Farm Production of Sc Sirup. By C. F. Walton . . . S. Byall. 1938. 8°. [*l Department of Agriculture. Farmers' Bulletin.* no. 17 A.S.

BYALOBZHESKY (G. V.)

—— *See* IVANOV (F. M.) and BYALOBZHESKY (G. V.) Иск ственные камни. 1954. 8°. **07822.** p.

—— Снег и лёд. pp. 64. *Москва, Ленинград,* 1951. 8 **08756.** aaa
Научно-популярная библиотека. вып. 36.

BYALUINITSKY-BIRULYA (ALEKSYEI ANDREEV Очерки изъ жизни птицъ полярнаго побере Сибири . . . Съ 8 таблицами, *etc.* (Научные резу таты Русской Полярной Экспедиціи, *etc.*) pp. xxxvi. *С.-Петербургъ,* 1907. 4°. [*Mémoires de l'Acadé Impériale des Sciences de St.-Pétersbourg.* sér. 8. Cl physico-mathématique. vol. 18. no. 2.] Ac. **112**

—— Скорпіоны, *etc.* вып. 1. pp. 224. *Петрогр* 1917. 8°. [*Фауна Россіи. Паукобразныя.* том вып. 1.] Ac. **1125.** n.
Imperfect; wanting вып. 2.

—— Фаланги-solifuga. (Ordo solifuga.) [With a summ in German.] pp. vii. 175. pl. I. *Москва, Ленинг* 1938. 8°. [*Фауна СССР.* / Нов. сер. no. 17. *Паукообразные.* том вып. 3.]
Ac.1125.n/3.(9

BYALUINITSKY-BIRULYA (VITOL'D KAETANOVIC

—— *See* MOSCOW.—*Третьяковская,* afterwards *Госуда венная Третьяковская, Галлерея.* В. Н. Бакш В. К. Бялыницкий-Бируля, *etc.* [A catalogue o exhibition. With autobiographical notes and plates cluding portraits.] 1944. 8°. **7960.** a

BYALUY (GRIGORY ABRAMOVICH)

—— *See* GARSHIN (V. M.) Сочинения. Ре ция, вступительная статья и примечания Г. А. Бял 1938. 8°. **12266.**

—— *See* GARSHIN (V. M.) Сочинения. (Подготовка тек вступительная статья и примечания Г. А. Бялого.) 1951. 8°. **12266.**

—— В. Г. Короленко. [With portraits.] pp. 370. *Мо Ленинград,* 1949. 8°. **10794.** b

—— В. М. Гаршин. Критико-биографический оч [With a portrait.] pp. 107. *Москва,* 1955. 8°. **10798.** e.

BYAM (EDWARD) *See* BYAM (Edward S.) Chronolog Memoir . . . of Henry, John and Edward Byam, [1854.] 12°. **4906.** e.

—— —— 1862. 4°. **4906.** f. **25.**

BYAM (EDWARD SAMUEL) *See* SHADRACH (A.) The B slider's Mirror . . . Translated . . . by E. S. Byam. 1845. 16°. **1361.** h.

—— Chronological Memoir of the three Clerical Bret Pastors of the Reformed Church of England and Ire . . . Henry, John and Edward Byam, *etc.* pp. 132. *James Briddon: Ryde,* [1854.] 12°. **4906.** e.

—— [Another edition.] pp. 82. *R. Mason: Tenby,* 1862 **4906.** f. **25.**

—— Genealogical Table of the Sovereigns of England, the Norman Conquest to the present time, shewing descents, births, accessions, marriages, deaths, and a *etc.* [A roll.] *Printed for the Proprietor: Lon* 1812. *s. sh.* fol. **11.**

BYAM (Edward Samuel)

—— Retrospect of the Literary Avocations and Performances of E. S. Byam . . . By himself. pp. 20. *Binns & Goodwin: Bath*, [1851.] 8°. **10855. c. 20. (4.)**
One of an edition of fifty copies, printed for private circulation.

BYAM (Edwin Colby) Théodore Barrière, Dramatist of the Second Empire. [With a portrait and a bibliography.] pp. 338. *Baltimore*, 1938. 8°. [*Johns Hopkins Studies in Romance Literatures and Languages.* Extra volume. no. 13.] **Ac. 2689/6.**

BYAM (George) Wanderings in some of the Western Republics of America, with remarks upon the cutting of the great ship canal through Central America. [With plates.] pp. xii. 264. *J. W. Parker: London*, 1850. 12°. **10480. b. 3.**

—— Wild Life in the interior of Central America. pp. viii. 253. *J. W. Parker: London*, 1849. 16°. **10480. b. 2.**

—— Wildes Leben im Innern von Central-Amerika . . . Aus dem Englischen von M. B. Lindau. pp. 208. *Dresden*, 1850. 8°. **010481. d. 12.**

BYAM (Henry) *See* Byam (Edward S.) Chronological Memoir . . . of Henry, John and Edward Byam, *etc.* [1854.] 12°. **4906. e. 35.**

—— —— 1862. 4°. **4906. f. 25. (18.)**

—— A Returne from Argier. A sermon preached at Minhead . . . the 16. of March, 1627. at the re-admission of a relapsed Christian into our Church. *See* Kellet (Edward) A Returne from Argier, *etc.* 1628. 4°. **693. f. 20. (6.)**

BYAM (John) *See* Byam (Edward S.) Chronological Memoir . . . of Henry, John and Edward Byam, *etc.* [1854.] 12°. **4906. e. 35.**

—— —— 1862. 4°. **4906. f. 25. (18.)**

BYAM (Ricardus Scott) Tentamen medicum de administratione antiphlogistica, *etc.* pp. 29. *Balfour & Smellie: Edinburgi*, 1775. 8°. **T. 334. (11.)**

—— [Another copy.] **T. 160. (3.)**

—— [Another copy.] **T. 285. (8.)**

BYAM (William) *Lieut.-Colonel, R.A.M.C.* Trench Fever. *See* Lloyd (Ll.) *Lieut., R.A.M.C.* Lice and their Menace to Man, *etc.* 1919. 8°. **20036.a.1/110.**

—— Trench Fever, a louse-borne disease. By Major W. Byam [and others] . . . With . . . a summary of the report of the American Trench Fever Commission by Lieut. R. H. Vercoe. pp. xvi. 196. *Henry Frowde; Hodder & Stoughton: London*, 1919. 8°. [*Oxford Medical Publications.*] **20036.a.1/120.**

BYAM (William) *Lieut.-Colonel, R.A.M.C.*, and **ARCHIBALD** (*Sir* Robert George)

—— The Practice of Medicine in the Tropics. By many authorities. Edited by W. Byam . . . and R. G. Archibald. 3 vol. pp. xxii. xx. xx. 2550. pl. xcvi. *Henry Frowde; Hodder & Stoughton: London*, 1921–23. 8°. [*Oxford Medical Publications.*] **20036.a.1/445.**

BYAM (William) *Lieut.-General, Governor of Guiana.* *See* Crijnssen (Abraham) Een der artikelen van het verdrag tusschen A. Crijnsen en W. Byam, *etc.* 1917. 8°. **9406. ee. 13.**

—— An Exact Relation of the most execrable attempts of John Allin committed on the person of his Excellency Francis Lord Willoughby of Parham, Captain General of the Continent of Guiana. pp. 12. *For Richard Lowndes: London*, 1665. 4°. **1132. b. 49.**

BYAM (William) *Lieut.-General, Governor of Guiana.*

—— [Lieut[t]-Gen[ll] Byam's Journall of Guiana 1665–1667.] Verhaal van de inneming van Paramaribo, 1665, door Generaal William Byam, medegedeeld door George Edmundson. *Eng.* 1898. *See* Utrecht.—*Historisch Gezelschap, etc.* Bijdragen, *etc.* dl. 19. 1877, *etc.* 8°. **Ac. 7510/8.**

—— Surinam Justice. In the case of several persons proscribed by certain usurpers of power in that colony. Being a publication of that perfect relation of the beginning, continuance, and end of the late disturbances in the Colony of Surinam, set forth under that title, by W. Byam . . . And the vindication of those gentlemen, sufferers by his injustice, from the calumnies wherewith he asperseth them in that relation. Couched in the answer thereunto by Robert Sanford. pp. 50. *Printed for the Author: London*, 1662. 4°. **1061. g. 81.**

BYAM (William) *Phrenologist.* Explanation of the new Physiognomical System of the Brain, according to D[rs] Gall and Spurzheim, *etc.* *W. Byam: London*, 1818. *s. sh.* fol. **L.R.110.d.6.(76.)**

BYAM SHAW (Eveline) *See* Shaw (Eveline B.) afterwards Winkworth (E.)

BYANGWA (Yusufu) Enyimba ze gwanga enkulu. [Luganda songs.] pp. 33. [*Lukiko*, 1931.] *obl.* 8°. **12911. de. 40.**

BYANS (Charles Joseph Vernier de) *See* Vernier de Byans.

BYARD (Betty Adelaide Mary) Through a Glass darkly. [A novel.] pp. 218. *George Roberts: London*, 1929. 8°. **012602. i. 22.**

BYARD (Dorothy R.) Not Creatures but Creations. [Poems.] pp. 58. *Fowler Wright: London*, [1930.] 8°. **011644. h. 127.**

BYARD (John) and **WRIGHT** (Richard) *Surgeon.* A True State of the Case of Sir John Curzon . . . by John Byard and Richard Wright, Surgeons, in vindication of themselves from a false and malicious report spread abroad, that the said Sir J. Curzon died of a mortification of his leg, occasioned by their ill management, *etc.* pp. 18. *S. Hodgkinson: Derby*, 1727. 8°. **7680. a. 27.**

BYARNE, Lyonnet Laborey, *Sieur de.* *See* Laborey.

BYARS (Louis T.)

—— *See* Blair (Vilray P.) Cancer of the Face and Mouth . . . By V. P. Blair . . . L. T. Byars, *etc.* 1941. 8°. **7612. d. 2.**

BYARS (William Vincent) The Glory of the Garden, and other odes, sonnets and ballads in sequence. With a note on the relations of the Horatian ode to the Tuscan sonnet. pp. 102. *Gazlay Bros.: New York*, [1896.] 8°. **011652. f. 88.**

—— Homeric Memory Rhymes, and the principles of melody in poetry. pp. 18. *W. V. Byars: South Orange, N.Y.*, [1895.] 8°. **011824. e. 63. (11.)**

BYAS (Hugh)

—— Government by Assassination. [On the recent history of Japan.] pp. ix. 369. viii. *G. Allen & Unwin: [London,]* 1943. 8°. **09059. aa. 30.**

—— The Japanese Enemy. His power and his vulnerability. pp. 88. *Hodder & Stoughton: London*, 1942. 8°. **8024. aaa. 4.**

BYAS (Hugh)

—— The Japanese Enemy, *etc.* pp. ix. 107. *A. A. Knopf: New York,* 1942. 8°. **8024. aa. 36.**

—— Why Britain is Fighting. pp. 18. *British Embassy: Tokyo,* 1940. 8°. [*British Information Series.* no. 8.] **B.S.14/158.(8.)**

BYASS (Bob) Bo-Peep, a dialogue between Bob Byass, late Quæstor of the Fiscus, and Simon George, a country gentleman: together with two merry songs . . . Dedicated to the Freeholders and Freemen of Corporations in Ireland. pp. 12. *Dublin,* 1714, 15. 4°. **8145. dd. 8.**

BYASS (Owen) Gentle Dew. pp. 284. *Eldon Press: London,* 1933. 8°. **NN. 20056.**

—— Service from Ladies. A romantic satire. pp. 288. *John Long: London,* 1939. 8°. **NN. 29850.**

—— The Strangers. pp. 287. *John Long: London,* [1940.] 8°. **NN. 31462.**

BYASS (William) Christ's Instructions to his Followers concerning the suffering Galileans; a sermon, *etc.* pp. 26. *S. Hooper: London,* 1756. 8°. **T. 1659. (14.)**

—— [Another copy.] **225. g. 1. (4.)**

BYASSON (Henri) Essai sur la relation qui existe à l'état physiologique entre l'activité cérébrale et la composition des urines. pp. 68. *Paris,* 1868. 4°. [*Collection des thèses soutenues à la Faculté de Médecine de Paris.* An 1868. tom. 2.] **7373. i. 6.**

—— [Another issue.] pp. 66. *Paris,* 1868. 8°. **7407. f. 43.**

BYASSON (Henri) and **FOLLET** (Antonin)

—— Étude sur l'hydrate de chloral et le trichloracétate de soude. pp. 64. *Paris,* 1871. 8°. **7460. e. 7.**

BYASSON (Jean) Aperçu sur la péripneumonie inflammatoire. Tribut académique, *etc.* pp. 20. *Montpellier,* [1804.] 4°. **1180. e. 10. (13.)**

BYASSON (Louis) Essai sur les causes des dyspepsies et sur leur traitement par l'eau minérale de Mauhourat, *etc.* pp. 68. *Paris,* 1874. 4°. [*Collection des thèses soutenues à la Faculté de Médecine de Paris.* An 1874. tom. 3.] **7374. a. 8.**

BYATT (Henry) Before the Dawn. One act play. pp. 19. *Joseph Williams: London,* [1902.] 8°. **11779. aa. 77. (8.)**

—— The Brothers. Original drama, in one act. pp. 12. *London, New York,* [1888.] 12°. [*French's Acting Edition.* vol. 130.] **2304. h. 21. (14.)**

—— The Flight of Icarus. pp. 247. *Sisley's: London,* 1907. 8°. **012634. aaa. 23.**

—— The Golden Age; or, Pierrot's sacrifice. An original idyllic musical play, *etc.* pp. 16. *Joseph Williams: London,* [1898.] 8°. **11781. dd. 44. (2.)**

—— [A reissue.] *London,* [1911.] 8°. **11779. a. 66. (2.)**

—— Das goldene Zeitalter oder Pierrot's Entsagung. Musikalisches Idyll in einem Akt . . . Deutsche Übertragung von Willy Alexander Kastner. pp. 16. *Joseph Williams: London,* [1907.] 8°. **11779. ff. 56. (6.)**

—— Land o' Gold. A novel. pp. viii. 277. *Sisley's: London,* [1907.] 8°. **012626. aaa. 3.**

BYATT (Henry)

—— Third edition. pp. viii. 277. *Bohemian Publishing Co.: London,* [1913.] 8°. **12624. ee. 16.**

—— Purple and White. A romance. pp. 316. *R. A. Everett & Co.: London,* 1905. 8°. **012632. a. 12.**

—— The Real Man. pp. 319. *John Long: London,* 1909. 8°. **012623. b. 17.**

—— The Testament of Judas. [A novel.] pp. 318. *John Long: London,* 1908. 8°. **012625. aaa. 11.**

BYBEL- EN BIDVERENIGING. *See* Capetown.

BYBILAKIS (E.) Neugriechisches Leben, verglichen mit dem Altgriechischen; zur Erläuterung beider. pp. xiv. 74. *Berlin,* 1840. 8°. **802. b. 29.**

BYBLIS. *See* Periodical Publications.—*Paris.*

BYBLIUS (Philo) *See* Philo, *Byblius.*

BYBLUS, François Marie Henri Agathon, *Bishop of.* [1846–1862.] *See* Pellerin.

BYCHELBERG (Udo Horst)

—— *See* Danielcik (H. P.) and Bychelberg (U. H.) Deutsche Rechtskunde. 1939. 8°. **05656. g. 14.**

BYCHELBERG (Werner von)

—— Technisches Taschenwörterbuch in französischer und deutscher Sprache . . . 1. Teil: Deutsch-Französisch. pp. 246. *Berlin,* 1943. 16°. **012902. l. 23.** *Siemens' Technische Taschenwörterbücher.* Bd. 3. Tl. 1.

BYCHER-NOJES. *See* Periodical Publications.—*Warsaw.*

BYCHOWIEC (Józef) *See* Brose (C. G.) [Ansichten über unsern gesellschaftlichen Zustand in seinem ganzen Umfange.] Obraz niniejszego społecznego Europy stanu . . . Przekładał z języka niemieckiego J. Bychowiec. 1816. 8°. **8026. b. 36.**

BYCHOWSKI (Gustaw)

—— Dictators and Disciples from Caesar to Stalin. A psychoanalytic interpretation of history, *etc.* pp. 264. *International Universities Press: New York,* [1948.] 8°. **010604. bb. 39**

—— Słowacki i jego dusza. Studjum psychoanalityczne. pp. 485. *Warszawa, Kraków,* 1930. 8°. **11858. aa. 13**

BYCK (J.) *See* Negruzzi (C.) Opere alese. [Edited by J. Byck and others.] 1935. 8°. **12591. ppp. 46.**

—— *See* Rosetti (A.) and Byck (J.) Gramatica limbii române, *etc.* 1945. 8°. **12944. e. 2**

BYCONILL (*Sir* John) *See* Biconyll.

BYCONYLLE (William) *See* Bicknell (Algernon S.) Excerpta Biconyllea. A forgotten Chancellor (William Byconylle), *etc.* 1900. 8°. **09915. dd. 13**

BYCRAFT (E. S.) Labour, Capital, and Consumption. A paper, *etc.* pp. 12. *Co-operative Union: Manchester,* [1890.] 8°. **8276. aa. 59. (3.**

BYCROFT LTD. Bread Baking in New Zealand. A treatise on practical bread making compiled by Bycroft Limited, flourmillers, Auckland, N.Z. pp. 252. *Whitcombe & Tombs: Auckland,* [1934.] 8°. **7943. v. 4**

BYCULLA SCHOOLS. Byculla Schools. Rules for Girls' School. [*Bombay,* 1865?] 8°. **4765. df. 2. (7.**

DAND I.O.G.T. GOOD TEMPLAR.

GOOD TEMPLARS, *Independent Order of.—Gordon Ark of Safety Lodge.*

Y DE B N, *M. l'Abbé.* La Folle soirée, parodie du Mariage de Figaro, en un acte, prose et vaudevilles . . . Par M. l'abbé B y de B n [i.e. F. L. Bonnefoy de Bonyon, or rather, by Louis Laus de Boissy]. pp. 75. *Gattières*, 1784. 8°. **11738. a. 15. (4.)**

DERHAND.

— Byderhand. U dagboekie. *See* EPHEMERIDES.

DESKÚTY̆ (SÁNDOR) Az Osztrák-Magyar Monarchia véderejének szervezete. pp. 415. *Budapest*, 1891. 8°. **8823. n. 9.**

DGOSZCZ. *See* BROMBERG.

— *Bernardinerkloster. See* infra: *Klasztor Księdzy Franciszkanów (Bernardynów).*

Biblioteka Miejska w Bydgoszczy.

— Dziesięciolecie Bibljoteki Miejskiej w Bydgoszczy. (Stronę redakcyjną i graficzną opracowali... Witold Belza i... Teodor Brandowski.) pp. 285. pl. xv. *Bydgoszcz*, 1931. 4°. **11902. v. 28.**

— *Christ-katholische Gemeinde.* Die Spaltung in der christ.-kathol. Gemeinde zu Bromberg, dargelegt von dem Vorstande derselben. pp. 30. *Bromberg*, 1845. 8°. **3910. c. 17.**

— *Klasztor Księdzy Franciszkanów (Bernardynów).* Die Chronik des Bernardinerklosters zu Bromberg. Übersetzung im Auszuge nebst Anmerkungen und verbindendem Texte . . . Vom Oberlehrer Dr. Erich Schmidt. *Ger.* 2 pt. *Bromberg*, 1900, 01. 8°. **4662. ee. 9.**

DGOSZCZ, *Regierungsbezirk of.*

— Uebersicht der Bestandtheile und Verzeichniss aller Ortschaften des Bromberger Regierungsbezirks. pp. 118. *Bromberg*, 1818. 4°. **10255. bbb. 7.**

DGOSZCZY (BARTŁOMIEJ z) *See* BARTHOLOMAEUS, *of Bromberg.*

DLOWSKI (JAN) Exposé succinct des principaux moyens employés pour maintenir les fractures réduites. Thèse, *etc.* pp. 28. *Montpellier*, 1841. 4°. **1182. c. 8. (14.)**

DRAES.

— Bydraes tot opvoedkunde. *See* COETZEE (J. C.)

DŽOVSKÝ (ALOIS) *See* VERCONSIN (E.) and LESBAZEILLES (E.) Dluh z mladosti. Činohra . . . Z frančiny přeložil A. Bydžovský. 1874. 8°. [*Divadelní ochotník. Nové sbírky sv.* 62.] **11758. p. 9. (2.)**

DŽOVSKÝ (BOHUMIL)

— Bedřich Procházka. [With a portrait and a bibliography.] pp. 18. *v Praze*, 1934. 8°. [*Česká Akademie Věd a Umění. Separately published obituaries.*] **Ac. 799/20. (20.)**

— Jan Sobotka. [With a portrait and a bibliography.] pp. 45. *v Praze*, 1932. 8°. [*Česká Akademie Věd a Umění. Separately published obituaries.*] **Ac. 799/20. (27.)**

E-COER. *See* BYEKOER.

E-GONES. *See* BYGONES.

BYE (ADRIAEN DE) Disputatio juridica inauguralis de divortiis et repudiis, *etc. Praes.* T. H. van den Honert. pp. 19. *Lugduni Batavorum*, [1720.] 4°. **501. f. 23. (36.)**

The titlepage is engraved.

BYE (ARTHUR EDWIN) Pots and Pans, or, Studies in still-life painting. [With plates.] pp. xiii. 236. *Princeton University Press: Princeton; Oxford University Press: London*, 1921. 8°. **7860. f. 28.**

BYE (CARL ROLLINSON)

—— Developments and Issues in the Theory of Rent. pp. vi. 133. *Columbia University Press: New York*, 1940. 8°. **8204. cc. 22.**

BYE (CORNELIUS) *See* DEMETRIUS, *Saint and Martyr.* S. Demetrii martyris acta ex editione C. Byei. 1864. 8°. [*MIGNE (J. P.) Patrologiæ cursus completus, etc.* Series græca. tom. 116.] **2002. a.**

—— [For editions of the " Acta Sanctorum " continued by C. Bye and others:] *See* BOLLANDUS (J.) and HENSCHENIUS (G.)

—— Réponse de l'ancien des Bollandistes, Corneille de Bye, au Mémoire de M. Des Roches touchant le Testament de S. Remi, inséré au deuxième tome des Nouveaux mémoires de l'Académie impériale & royale des Sciences & Belles-Lettres, établie à Bruxelles, donnés au jour cette année 1780. pp. 50. *Bruxelles*, 1780. 8°. **4372. g. 10. (5.)**

BYE (JACOBUS DE) Disputatio medica inauguralis de hydrope in genere, *etc. A. Elzevier: Lugduni Batavorum*, 1688. 4°. **1185. g. 18. (34.)**

BYE (JACQUES DE) *See* BIE.

BYE (JANUS GISBERTUS THIERRY DE) Disputatio juridica inauguralis de peculiari navium maritimarum dominio, *etc.* pp. 74. *Trajecti ad Rhenum*, 1837. 8°. **6825. aaa. 14.**

BYÉ (JEAN)

—— Contribution à l'étude des molybdates. 1945. *See* PERIODICAL PUBLICATIONS.—*Paris.* Annales de chimie. (Annales de physique.) Onzième ser. tom. 20. 1789, *etc.* 8°. P.P. **1495. aa.**

BYE (JOHAN DE) *See* V., H. V. Ernstigen brief van een borger van Leiden over de vreemde proceduuren gehouden bij . . . Mr. G. van Hoogeveen tegen twee . . . borgers der zelver stad . . . Met de Remonstrancie van J. de Bije, en de sententie daar op gevolgt. 1664. 4°. T. **2258. (24.)**

—— Remonstrantie ofte ootmoedig vertoog aen de E.E. A.A. Heeren, Burge-Meesteren, en Regeerderen . . . der stadt Leyden. pp. 27. *Gedruckt voor den Autheur: [Leyden,]* 1666. 4°. T. **2258. (26.)**

—— De Vredes, en liefdes bazuyne. Behelsende, een apologia. Ofte nootzakelijke, christelijke verdediging van, ende door Johan de Bye. Tot behoud, zijner goede naam, en faam, tegens alle on-christelijke lasteringen, *etc.* pp. 72. *Gedrukt voor den Autheur: [Leyden,]* 1664. 4°. T. **2258. (21.)**

—— Kort vervolch, van de Vredes, en liefdes bazuyne van Johan de Bye: helder uyt-galmende, den tegenwoordigen toestant, vanden Remonstrantschen byenkorf binnen Leyden, *etc.* pp. 8. *J. Hermanus: [Leyden,]* 1665. 4°. T. **2258. (22.)**

BYE (LILIAN)

—— Finner i Finnmark. [With plates and a map.] pp. 179. *Oslo*, 1939. 8°. **010281. l. 18.**

BYÉ (MAURICE)

—— *See* JULLIOT DE LA MORANDIÈRE (L.) and BYÉ (M.) Les Nationalisations en France et à l'étranger . . . Publié sous la direction de L. Julliot de la Morandière, M. Byé, *etc.* 1948, ~~etc.~~ 8°. **8208.q.16.**

—— *See* TRUCHY (H.) and BYÉ (M.) Les Relations économiques internationales. 1948. 8°. **8207. k. 20.**

—— Le Port de Gênes. Son activité, son organisation, sa fonction économique. pp. xvi. 269. *Lyon; Paris,* 1927. 8°. [*Annales de l'Université de Lyon.* Nouvelle série. II. Droit, lettres. fasc. 40.] **Ac.365.(b.)**

BYE (NICOLAUS DE) Disputatio juridica inauguralis de injuriis, *etc.* pp. 16. *Lugduni Batavorum,* [1716.] 4°. **501. f. 21. (33.)**
The titlepage is engraved.

BYE (RAYMOND TAYLOR)

—— Principles of Economics . . . Third edition. pp. vii. 508. *F. S. Crofts & Co.: New York,* 1936. 8°. **08206. i. 70.**

—— Social Economy and the Price System. An essay in welfare economics. pp. viii. 356. *Macmillan Co.: New York,* [1950.] 8°. **8204. e. 39.**

BYE (RAYMOND TAYLOR) and **BLODGETT** (RALPH HAMILTON) Getting and Earning. A study of inequality. pp. vii. 274. *F. S. Crofts & Co.: New York,* 1937. 8°. **8287.de.34.**

BYE (RAYMOND TAYLOR) and **HEWETT** (WILLIAM WALLACE)

—— Applied Economics, *etc.* pp. vi. 655. *A. A. Knopf: New York,* 1928. 8°. **8207. v. 11.**

—— Applied Economics . . . Fourth edition, completely revised. pp. viii. 718. *Appleton-Century-Crofts: New York & London,* [1947.] 8°. **8204. f. 22.**

BYEFIELD (I.) *pseud.* [i.e. JOHN FREIND.] *See* BYFIELDE.

BYEKOER. De Bye-Coer. Friesc almanak. *See* EPHEMERIDES.

BYEL (GABRIEL) *See* BIEL.

BYEL'CHIKOV.

—— [For the Russian surname in this form:] *See* BEL'CHIKOV.

BYELETSKY.

—— [For the Russian surname in this form:] *See* BELETSKY.

BYELEV. *See* BIELEV.

BYELKE (STEN) *See* JACOBSEN (J. P.) Niels Lyhne. Roman danois en français par S. Byelke & S. Voirol. 1898. 18°. **012590. ee. 51.**

BYEN. *See* BIJEN.

BYER (HERBERT) To the Victor. A novel. pp. 277. *Doubleday, Doran & Co.: Garden City, N.Y.,* 1936. 8°. **A.N. 3289.**

BYER (HERMAN B.) Prison Labor in the United States, 1932. Prepared under the direction of H. B. Byer, *etc.* pp. v. 216. *Washington,* 1933. 8°. [*U.S. Bureau of Labor Statistics. Bulletin.* no. 595.] **A.S. 111.**

BYER (JAN DE) *See* BEYER.

BYERLEY (FRANCES)

—— *See* HICKS (Phyllis D.) A Quest of Ladies, *etc.* history of the school conducted by M. and F. Byerl [1949.] 8°. **08368. b.**

BYERLEY (FREDERICK JOHN) *See* JARDINE (Frank) a (A.) Narrative of the overland expedition of the Mess Jardine from Rockhampton to Cape York, Queensla Compiled from the Journals of the brothers . . . F. J. Byerley. 1867. 8°. **10492. f.**

BYERLEY (HUBERT FRANK) Songs of the War and Fa and Hope. pp. 29. *W. H. Barrell: Portsmouth,* [1918.] **011648. f.**

BYERLEY (ISAAC) The Fauna of Liverpool. pp. 124. *A. Hall, Virtue & Co.: London; A. Holden: Liverp* 1856. 8°. **7207. dd.**

BYERLEY (J.) *See* BYERLEY (Lucy)

BYERLEY (*Sir* JOHN) *See* MACKEY (Sampson A.) marks on the Cabinet Cyclopædia [of D. Lardner] and geological globe [of Sir J. Byerley] relative to the pc motion. 1824. 12°. **8562. a. 3.**

BYERLEY (JOHN SCOTT) *See* also RIPON (John Sc *pseud.* [i.e. J. S. Byerley.]

—— *See* MACCHIAVELLI (N.) [*Il Principe.*] The Pr . . . Translated from the original Italian . . . To w is prefixed an introduction, shewing the close anal between the principles of Machiavelli and the action Buonaparte. By J. S. Byerley. 1810. 8°. **8005. f. 42.**

—— *See* SAINT-VENANT (de) *Madame.* Leopold Circe . . . Translated by J. S. Byerley. 1807. 12°. **12510. b.**

—— The Conscript, a serio-comic romance. [Based on Lemaire's "Le Conscrit."] 2 vol. *C. Chapple: Lon* 1807. 12°. **12611. aaa**

—— Love's Lyrics, or, Cupid's carnival. Original and tr lated. pp. 174. *C. Chapple: London,* 1807. 8°. **11687. a.**

BYERLEY (L. W.) "In Merry Portsmouth Town." story of the days of Lord Anson. pp. 200. *A. H. Stockwell: London,* [1905.] 8°. **04412. k.**

BYERLEY (LUCY) Amy's Secret; or, the Blue silk d [By L. Byerley.] pp. 64. [1883.] 8°. *See* AMY. **4420. bb.**

—— [Another edition.] pp. 64. [1911.] 8°. *See* AMY. **04429. i.**

—— [Another edition.] pp. 64. [1919.] 8°. *See* AMY. **12810. de. 1.**

—— The Queen's Oak. pp. 64. *R.T.S.: London,* [1886.] [*Little Dot Series.*] **4420. a. 4**

—— Ruth Arnold, or, the Country cousin. pp. 128. *R.T.S.: London,* [1884.] 16°. **4422. ddd**

—— Ruth Arnold. [An abridgment.] pp. 32. [*R.T London,* 1913.] 8°. [*Bouverie Series of Penny Sto* no. 71.] **4430. ee.**

BYERLEY (MARIA)

—— *See* HICKS (Phyllis D.) A Quest of Ladies, *etc.* history of the school conducted by M. and F. Bye [1949.] 8°. **08368. b**

YERLEY (Thomas) *See* also Collet (Stephen) *pseud.* [i.e. T. Byerley.]

— *See* also Percy (Reuben) *pseud.* [i.e. T. Byerley.]

— *See* Periodical Publications.—*London.* The Mirror of Literature, Amusement and Instruction, *etc.* [1823–26. Edited by T. Byerley.] 1823, *etc.* 8°. P.P. **5681**.

— On Characteristic Signatures, *etc.* *See* Lumley (Edward) The Art of Judging the Character of Individuals from their Handwriting and Style, *etc.* 1875. 16°. **12991**. b. **29**.

ERLY (Alpheus Edward) The Beginning of Things in Wellington and Waterloo Counties. With particular reference to Guelph, Galt and Kitchener . . . Illustrated by Leslie Marsh. pp. 106. *Guelph Publishing Co.: Guelph,* 1935. 8°. **010470**. bb. **30**.

— Fergus, or the Fergusson-Webster settlement, with an extensive history of North-East Nichol . . . Indexed and illustrated with many rare photographs. pp. x. 372. *Elora Express: Elora,* 1934. 8°. **010470**. bb. **20**.

ERLY (Perry)

— Pacific Coast Earthquakes. [With illustrations.] pp. vii. 38. *Eugene,* 1952. 8°. [*Oregon State System of Higher Education. Condon Lectures.*] W.P. **2733/6**. *With an errata slip.*

— The Registration of Earthquakes at the Berkeley Station and at the Lick Observatory Station (Earthquakes in Northern California and the Registration of Earthquakes at Berkeley, Mount Hamilton, Palo Alto, San Francisco, Ferndale, Fresno, Mineral) from April 1, 1930, to Sept. 30, 1930 [*etc.*]. By P. Byerly [and others]. Bulletin of the Seismographic Stations. vol. 2. no. 20, *etc.* 1931– . 8°. & 4°. *See* Berkeley, *California.—University of California.* Ac. **2689**. ge.

ERLY (William Elwood) An Elementary Treatise on Fourier's Series and spherical, cylindrical, and ellipsoidal harmonics, with applications to problems in mathematical physics. pp. ix. 287. *Ginn & Co.: Boston,* 1895. 8°. **08533**. i. **3**.

— Elements of the Differential Calculus, with examples and applications, *etc.* pp. xv. 258. *Ginn & Co.: Boston,* 1888. 8°. **8535**. d. **14**.

— Elements of the Integral Calculus, with a key to the solution of differential equations . . . (With a short table of integrals. Compiled by B. O. Peirce.) Second edition, revised, *etc.* 2 pt. *Ginn & Co.: Boston,* 1889. 8°. **8531**. df. **3**.

— Harmonic Functions . . . Fourth edition, enlarged. pp. 66. *J. Wiley & Sons: New York,* 1906. 8°. [*Mathematical Monographs.* no. 5.] **8507**. g. **16/5**.

— An Introduction to the use of Generalized Coördinates in Mechanics and Physics. pp. vii. 118. *Ginn & Co.: Boston,* [1916.] 8°. **08709**. b. **19**.

ERN (E. von) Bilder aus Griechenland und der Levante, *etc.* pp. viii. 344. *Berlin,* 1833. 8°. **10250**. aaa. **16**.

ERN (Georg von) Deutsch-Ostafrika und seine weissen und schwarzen Bewohner. pp. 42. *Berlin,* 1913. 8°. [*Koloniale Abhandlungen.* Hft. 68, 69.] **10024**. g. **1/40**.

ERS (Amy Irene) *See* Byers (Irene)

ERS (Charles Francis)

— *See* Rogers (James S.) Man and the Biological World. By J. S. Rogers . . . C. F. Byers. 1942. 8°. **7008**. c. **1**.

BYERS (Charles Francis)

—— *See* Rogers (James S.) Man and the Biological World. [By] J. S. Rogers . . . C. F. Byers, *etc.* 1952. 8°. **7008**. c. **30**.

BYERS (Chester) Roping. Trick and fancy rope spinning . . . Illustrated. pp. xix. 105. *G. P. Putnam's Sons: New York, London,* 1928. 8°. **07912**. ff. **44**.

BYERS (D. B.) The Christian Sabbath, viewed briefly in the light of Scripture, chronology and history, and the claims of Sabbatarians shown to be untenable, *etc.* pp. 195. *W. F. Schneider: Cleveland, O.,* [1879.] 16°. **4355**. de. **3**.

BYERS (Douglas S.)

—— *See* United States of America.—*Society for American Archaeology.* Memoirs of the Society for American Archaeology . . . D. S. Byers, editor. 1941, *etc.* 8°. Ac. **5797**. (**2**.)

BYERS (Edward) The British Empire, its origin and destiny. [An exposition of the "Anglo-Israelite" theory.] pp. 175. *J. T. Pattison: Ottawa,* 1921. 8°. **04033**. f. **30**.

BYERS (Edward Elmer)

—— *See* Berger (Kathleen Lutz) afterwards Root (K. B.) and Byers (E. E.) Dictation for the Medical Secretary, *etc.* [1952.] 8°. **012991**. df. **37**.

BYERS (Horace Greeley)

—— *See* Brown (Irvin C.) and Byers (H. G.) The Chemical and Physical Properties of Dry-Land Soils and of their Colloids. 1935. 8°. [*U.S. Department of Agriculture. Technical Bulletin.* no. 502.] A.S. **800/2**.

—— *See* Holmes (Robert S.) *Chemist.* The Chemical Composition of Soils and Colloids of the Norfolk and related Soil Series. By R. S. Holmes . . . H. G. Byers. 1938. 8°. [*U.S. Department of Agriculture. Technical Bulletin.* no. 594.] A.S. **800/2**.

—— *See* Hough (George J.) and Byers (H. G.) Chemical and Physical Studies of certain Hawaiian Soil Profiles. 1937. 8°. [*U.S. Department of Agriculture. Technical Bulletin.* no. 584.] A.S. **800/2**.

—— *See* Lakin (Hubert W.) and Byers (H. G.) Selenium Occurrence in Certain Soils in the United States, *etc.* 1948. 8°. [*U.S. Department of Agriculture. Technical Bulletin.* no. 950.] A.S. **800/2**.

—— *See* Middleton (Howard E.) Physical and Chemical Characteristics of the Soils from the Erosion Experiment Stations. By H. E. Middleton . . . H. G. Byers. 1932, *etc.* 8°. [*U.S. Department of Agriculture. Technical Bulletin.* no. 316, 430.] A.S. **800/2**.

—— *See* Slater (C. S.) Trace Elements in the Soils from the Erosion Experiment Stations . . . By C. S. Slater . . . and H. G. Byers. 1937. 8°. [*U.S. Department of Agriculture. Technical Bulletin.* no. 552.] A.S. **800/2**.

—— *See* Whetstone (Richard R.) Boron Distribution in Soils and Related Data. By R. R. Whetstone . . . H. G. Byers. 1942. 8°. [*U.S. Department of Agriculture. Technical Bulletin.* no. 797.] A.S. **800/2**.

—— Selenium Occurrence in certain Soils in the United States, with a discussion of related topics. ~~pp. 48.~~ *Washington,* 1935–. 8°. [*U.S. Department of Agriculture. Technical Bulletin.* no. 482, 530, 601, etc.] A.S. **800/2**.

—— A Study of the Reduction of Permanganic Acid by Manganese Dioxide. Dissertation, *etc.* pp. 53. *Chemical Publishing Co.: Easton, Pa.,* 1899. 8°. **8909**. dd. **22**. (**3**.)

BYERS (HORACE ROBERT)

—— General Meteorology. Published formerly under the title Synoptic and Aeronautical Meteorology. pp. x. 645. *McGraw-Hill Book Co.: New York & London*, 1944. 8°. **8753**. e. **11**.

—— Summer Sea Fogs of the Central California Coast. *Berkeley, Cal.*, 1930. 8°. [*University of California Publications in Geography*. vol. 3. no. 5.] Ac. **2689**. g/**38**.

—— Synoptic and Aeronautical Meteorology. [With maps.] pp. ix. 279. pl. 6. *McGraw-Hill Book Co.: New York & London*, 1937. 8°. **8753**. aaa. **37**.

—— Thunderstorm Electricity, *etc.* (Edited by H. R. Byers.) pp. viii. 344. *University of Chicago Press: Chicago*, 1953. 8°. [*University of Chicago Committee on Publications in the Physical Sciences. Monographs.*] Ac. **2691**. dt. (4.)

BYERS (HORACE ROBERT) and **STARR** (VICTOR P.)

—— The Circulation of the Atmosphere in High Latitudes during Winter, *etc.* pp. ii. 34. *Washington*, 1941. 4°. [*U.S. Weather Bureau. Monthly Weather Review.* suppl. no. 47.] **A.S.875/8.**

BYERS (IRENE)

Full name: AMY IRENE BYERS.

—— Adventure at Fairborough's Farm. pp. 151. *Epworth Press: London*, 1955. 8°. NNN. **6848**.

—— The Adventure of the Floating Flat . . . Illustrated by Robert Johnston. pp. vii. 232. *Thomas Nelson & Sons: London*, 1952. 8°. **12819**. h. **40**.

—— [A reissue.] The Adventures of the Floating Flat, *etc.* *London*, 1955. 8°. **12830**. bb. **54**.

—— Catherine of Corners. pp. 192. *Max Parrish: London*, 1955. 8°. NNN. **7162**.

—— The Circus, and other verses for children . . . Illustrated by Donald Craig. pp. 64. *Frederick Muller: London*, 1946. 8°. **11657**. ff. **6**.

—— Mystery at Barber's Reach . . . Illustrated by A. E. Batchelor. pp. 192. *Frederick Muller: London*, 1950. 8°. **12833**. aa. **34**

—— The Mystery of Midway Mill. pp. 200. *Hutchinson & Co.: London*, [1955.] 8°. NNN. **6932**.

—— Our Outdoor Friends . . . With illustrations by Constance Marshall. First (—fourth) set, *etc.* *Meiklejohn & Son: London*, [1949–52.] 8°. 12830. h. 29.

—— The First [*etc.*] Book of Our Outdoor Friends . . . Illustrated by Constance Marshall. *Meiklejohn & Son: London*, 1952– . 8°. W.P. A. **568**.

—— Out and about Tales . . . Illustrated by Paxton Chadwick. 12 pt. *House of Grant: London, Glasgow*, 1954. 16°. **12842.1.28.**

—— Tim of Tamberly Forest. pp. 184. *Max Parrish: London*, 1954. 8°. **12838**. aa. **8**.

—— The Young Brevingtons. pp. 192. *Max Parrish: London*, 1953. 8°. **12834**. i. **7**.

BYERS (JAMES BROOFF) *See* PHILIPPS (Charles) Sermons preached in the Parish Churches of Pembroke . . . To which is appended the funeral discourse preached . . . by the Rev. J. B. Byers. [1854.] 12°. **4462**. e. **27**.

BYERS (JOHN) *Bard of Liddesdale.* Hamely Border Musings. [With a portrait.] pp. 248. *Alexander Gardner: Paisley*, 1913. 8°. **011649**. eee. **20**.

BYERS (JOHN) *of Haslingden.* Theonomia; or Di Laws. By one whom the Lord hath visited. Addr to the Evangelical Churches of the Christian World [Signed: J. B., i.e. John Byers.] pp. 24. 1883. *See* B., J. **04375**. df. **38**.

BYERS (JOHN) *Surveyor.* *See* BYRES.

BYERS (JOHN WILLIAM) Sayings, Proverbs, and Hu of Ulster. pp. 66. *W. Strain & Sons: Belfast*, 1904. **12316**. i

BYERS (M. E. SELINA) Agnes Hope; or, the You example. A tale of the times, etc. pp. iv. 215. *B & Goodwin: London*, [1855.] 8°. **4417**. f

BYERS (MARGARETTA)

—— Designing Women. The art, technique, and co being beautiful. By M. Byers. With Consuelo Kam Illustrated by Jane Miller, *etc.* pp. 285. *John M London*, 1939. 8°. **8417**.

BYERS (MORTON LEWIS) Economics of Railway Opera pp. ix. 673. *Engineering News Publishing Co.: New* 1908. 8°. **08235**. c

BYERS (NORMAN R.) A Doubtful Loss. [A no pp. 223. *Digby, Long & Co.: London*, 1896. 8°. **012626**. g

—— World Commerce in its relation to the British E . . . With an introduction by W. R. Lawson. pp. *P. S. King & Son: London*, 1916. 8°. **08228**. f

BYERS (PETER SMITH) *See* FULLER (Samuel) *D.D. Andover, Mass.* Memorial to P. S. Byers . . . at funeral, *etc.* 1856. 8°. **4986**. dd. **21**.

BYERS (RALPH)

—— The Armour of Light, and fifty-one other tales children. pp. 127. *Independent Press: Lon* 1951 [1952]. 8°. **12830**. f.

BYERS (ROBERT PATERSON) Blessedness Explained. pp. 95. *H. R. Allenson: London*, [1927.] 8°. **04375**. df.

—— The Chemical Elements Interpreted. pp. 26. *Superuniversity Publications: Boston*, [1938.] 8°. **8899**.

—— The Invisible Library. pp. 20. *D. Gestetner: Lon* [1935.] 8°. **08466**. e. *Reproduced from typewriting.*

—— Our Thirty Capacities. pp. 24. *Meador Press: Bo* [1936.] 8°. **08466**. e.

—— The Reference Library and its Patrons. [A lectur psychology.] pp. 20. *R. P. Byers: London*, 1935. **11911**. a. *Reproduced from typewriting.*

—— The Six Physical Elements. pp. 25. *Superunive Publications: Boston*, [1938.] 8°. **8710**. de.

—— The Thousand Forms of Disease. pp. 29. *Superuniversity Publications: Boston*, [1938.] 8°. **7440**. df.

BYERS (SAMUEL HAWKINS MARSHALL) Florence, pp. 32. *Zurich*, [1881.] 8°. [*Illustrated Europe.* no. **10108**. de.

—— Twenty Years in Europe. A Consul-General's mem of noted people, with letters from General W. T. She . . . Profusely illustrated. pp. 320. *R McNally & Co.: Chicago & New York*, [1900.] 8°. **010881**. de.

BYERS (SELINA) *See* BYERS (M. E. S.)

BYERS (SPARKS) The Lamb of God. A sermon, *etc.* pp. 30. *A. E. Binns: Bath,* 1834. 8°. **4476. f. 18.**

BYERS (THOMAS)

—— Addresses on Ireland. By . . . T. Byers . . . and . . . Fred. C. Gibson. *Irish Mission Office: Belfast,* [1948–] 16°. **W.P.13978.**

—— Ireland's Need and how to meet it . . . Address, *etc.* [With a portrait.] pp. 16. *Irish Mission Office: Belfast,* [1946.] 8°. **4480. ee. 32.**

—— "Making St. Patrick's Vision Come True." Darkness and Light in Ireland. By the Right Rev. T. Byers . . . and The Ireland of To-morrow. By Rev. Fred C. Gibson. *Irish Mission Office: Belfast,* [1946.] 8°. **4175. a. 114.**

BYERS (TIMOTHY) The Objective Character of Christian Faith. A sermon preached before the University of Cambridge, *etc.* pp. 23. *Deighton, Bell & Co.: Cambridge,* 1860. 8°. **4478. d. 8.**

BYERS (WILFRED)

—— Carnival Time, and other poems. pp. 16. *Arthur H. Stockwell: Ilfracombe,* 1952. 8°. **11657. l. 23.**

BYERS (WILLIAM GORDON MATTHEW) A Study of the Ocular Manifestations of Systemic Gonorrhœa, with reports of cases of this nature. pp. 131. [*Montreal,*] 1908. 8°. [*Studies from the Royal Victoria Hospital, Montreal.* vol. 2. no. 2.] **07306. k.**

BYERS (WINIFRED) *See* BOTREL (T.) Songs of Botrel . . . Translated by W. Byers. [1916.] 8°. **011483. aa. 18.**

BYERS-BARR (R. A.) *See* BARR.

BYESS (WILLIAM F.)

—— *See* PÉREZ GALDÓS (B.) Doña Perfecta. Adapted for early reading with notes, exercises, and vocabulary by W. F. Byess and W. E. Stiefel, *etc.* [1940.] 8°. **12944. c. 7.**

BYETT (H.) Alfred Williams, Ploughboy, Hammerman, Poet & Author . . . Reprinted from "The Swindon Advertiser," with additional matter. [With portraits.] pp. 95. *Swindon Press: Swindon,* 1933. 8°. **10823. b. 27.**

BYETT (JESSIE DOROTHEA)

—— *See* HENNEY (Ethel) and BYETT (J. D.) Laundrywork in School. 1936. 8°. **7943. v. 46.**

—— *See* HENNEY (Ethel) and BYETT (J. D.) Laundrywork in School, *etc.* 1951. 8°. **7949. de. 29.**

—— *See* HENNEY (Ethel) and BYETT (J. D.) Modern Home Laundrywork. 1934. 8°. **7943. p. 47.**

—— *See* HENNEY (Ethel) and BYETT (J. D.) Modern Home Laundrywork. 1940. 8°. **07943. i. 112.**

—— *See* HENNEY (Ethel) and BYETT (J. D.) Modern Home Laundrywork. 1953. 8°. **7950. aa. 29.**

BYEUS (CORNELIUS) *See* BYE.

BYEWAYS. Byeways of Two Cities. By the author of "The Romance of the Streets" [i.e. Godfrey Holden Pine], *etc.* pp. 308. *Hodder & Stoughton: London,* 1873. 8°. **4192. aaa. 38.**

BYFEILD (ADONIRAM) *See* BYFIELD.

BYFEILD (NICHOLAS) *See* BYFIELD.

BYFIELD, *Massachusetts.—Dummer Academy.* Catalogue of the Officers and Students of Dummer Academy, *etc.* [The preface signed: W. D. N., i.e. William Dummer Northend.] [With a plate.] pp. 53. *Salem,* 1844. 8°. **8366. e. 30.**

BYFIELD (ADONIRAM) *See* BYFIELD (Nicholas) The Rule of Faith . . . Published . . . by . . . A. Bifield. 1626. 4°. **3505. cc. 52.**

—— *See* CHAMBERS (Humphrey) *D.D.* An Apology for the Ministers . . . of . . . Wilts in their actings at the election of Members for the approaching Parliament, *etc.* [By H. Chambers, A. Byfield and others.] 1654. 4°. **E. 187. (4.)**

—— *See* S., H. Adoniram Byfeild of the last Edition. Or, an Expostulation with him concerning the book . . . entituled The Reasons presented by the Dissenting brethren, *etc.* 1648. 4°. **E. 443. (32.)**

—— A Brief View of Mr. Coleman his New-Modell of Church Government, delivered by him in a late sermon, upon Job 11. 20 [entitled "Hopes deferred and dashed"]. [By A. Byfield?] 1644. 4°. *See* COLEMAN (Thomas) *Preacher at St. Peter's, Cornhill.* **E. 307. (8.)**

—— A Letter sent from a Worthy Divine [i.e. A. Byfield?], to the Right Honourable the Lord Maior of the City of London [Sir R. Gurney]. Being a true relation of the battaile fought betweene his Majesties forces, and his Excellency the Earle of Essex, *etc.* 1642. *s. sh.* fol. *See* GURNEY (*Sir* Richard) **105. f. 17. (18.)**

—— [Another edition.] 1642. 4°. *See* GURNEY (*Sir* Richard) **E. 124. (21.)**

—— The Summe of the Principles. Or, a Collection of those Principles of Religion, which are set down in a little treatise, called, The Principles, or Patterne of wholesome words, *etc.* *See* BYFIELD (Nicholas) The Principles, *etc.* 1630. 12°. **3557. a. 1.**

—— [Another edition.] *See* BYFIELD (Nicholas) The Principles, *etc.* 1634. 12°. **3559. a. 8**

—— [Another edition.] 1637. *See* BYFIELD (Nicholas) The Marrow of the Oracles of God, *etc.* 1636. 12°. **4400. m. 42.**

—— [Another edition.] 1662. *See* BYFIELD (Nicholas) The Principles, *etc.* 1665, *etc.* 12°. **4408. c. 20.**

BYFIELD (NATHANAEL) *See* CHAUNCY (Charles) *Pastor of the First Church in Boston.* Nathanael's Character display'd. A sermon, preach'd the Lord's Day after the funeral of the Honourable N. Byfield, *etc.* 1733. 8°. **4985. bb. 1.**

—— An Account of the late Revolution in New-England. Together with the declaration of the gentlemen, merchants, and inhabitants of Boston and the country adjacent. April 18. 1689, *etc.* pp. 20. *For Ric. Chiswell: London,* 1689. 4°. **1061. g. 76.**

—— [Another edition.] pp. 26. *New York,* 1865. 4°. [*Sabin's Reprints.* Quarto series. no. 1.] **9603. g. 2. (1.)**

—— [Another edition.] pp. 20. 1868. *See* BOSTON, *Massachusetts—Prince Society.* The Publications of the Prince Society. The Andros Tracts. vol. 1. 1865, *etc.* 4°. **Ac. 9503/4.**

BYFIELD (NICHOLAS) *See* BREREWOOD (Edward) A Learned Treatise of the Sabaoth, written . . . to Mr N. Byfield . . . With Mr Byfields answere and Mr Brerewoods Reply. 1630. 4°. **700. d. 54.**

—— —— 1631. 4°. **700. b. 9. (1.)**

BYFIELD (NICHOLAS)

—— *See* BYFIELD (Richard) The Doctrine of the Sabbath Vindicated, in a confutation of a treatise of the Sabbath written by M. Edward Breerwood against M. Nic. Byfield, *etc.* 1631. 4°. **700**. b. **9**. (2.)

—— A Commentary vpon the three first chapters of the first Epistle Generall of S[t] Peter, *etc.* [Edited by William Gouge. With the text.] 3 pt. 1637. fol. *See* BIBLE.—*Peter.—Selections.* [*English.*] **3266**. g. **16**.

—— A Commentary; or, Sermons vpon the second chapter of the first epistle of Saint Peter, *etc.* [Edited by William Gouge. With the text.] pp. 922. 1623. 4°. *See* BIBLE.—*Peter.—Selections.* [*English.*] **3266**. cc. **21**.

—— Directions for the priuate reading of the Scriptures . . . The third edition. pp. 95. *W. Stansby for N. Butter: London*, 1626. 12°. **3125**. a. **12**.

—— The fourth edition. Wherein the analyticall tables are much and profitably inlarged, and helps prescribed to those that cannot write or read: By Jo: Geree . . . Whereunto is annexed a pithy Direction to reconcile places of scripture which seem repugnant. 2 pt. *M. F.* [*Miles Fletcher*] *for P. Stephens: London*, 1648. 12°. **3107**. a. **49**.

—— An Exposition upon the Epistle to the Colossians . . . Being the substance of neare seauen yeeres weeke-dayes sermons, *etc.* [With the text.] 3 pt. 1615. fol. *See* BIBLE.—*Colossians.* [*English.*] **3266**. g. **15**.

—— [Another edition.] Corrected and amended. 3 pt. 1617. fol. *See* BIBLE.—*Colossians.* [*English.*]
C.123.g.16.

—— The fourth edition, corrected and amended. 1649. fol. *See* BIBLE.—*Colossians.* [*English.*] **3265**. dd. **11**.

—— The Marrow of the Oracles of God. Or diuers treatises, containing directions about six of the waightiest things can concerne a Christian in this life . . . The sixth edition. pp. 767. *T. C.* [*T. Cotes*] *for R. R.* [*R. Rounthwaite*]*: London*, 1628. 12°. **4401**. b. **29**.

—— The seuenth edition. 6 pt. pp. 767. *Printed by Iohn Legatt; sold by P. Stephens and C. Meredith: London*, 1630. 12°. **4403**. bb. **41**.

—— The tenth edition. (The Summe of the Principles. Or, a collection of those principles of religion, which are set down in the little treatise, called, The Principles or Patterne of wholesome words, *etc.* [The dedicatory epistle signed: Adoniram Byfield.]) 6 pt. pp. 767. *Printed by Ioh*[*n Legatt: London*], 16[36]. 12°. **4400**. m. **42**.
"The Summe of the Principles" bears the imprint "Io. Dawson for Philemon Stephens & Christopher Meredith, 1637." *The general titlepage is mutilated.*

—— The eleventh edition. (The Principles, or the Paterne of wholesome words . . . The eleaventh edition, corrected and amended.) 2 pt. *Printed by Iohn Legatt: London*, 1640. 12°. **851**. g. **9**.
"The Principles" has an additional titlepage, stating it to be of the sixth edition and bearing the imprint "Jo. Dawson for Philemon Stephens & Christopher Meredith, 1637."

—— Thirteenth edition. pp. 528. *Printed by John Field; sold by Peter Dring: London*, 1660. 12°. **4410**. b. **10**.
The titlepage of the twelfth edition of "The Principles, or the Pattern of Wholesome Words" follows p. 440, *but the tract itself is wanting.*

—— The Paterne of Wholsome Words. Or a collection of such Truths as are of necessity to be believed vnto saluation . . . And withall the seuerall vses such Principles should be put to, are abundantly shewed, *etc.* pp. 525. *F. K.* [*Felix Kingston*] *for Samuel Man: London*, 1618. 8°. **3560**. a. **14**.

BYFIELD (NICHOLAS)

—— [Another edition.] The Principles, or, the Patterne of Wholesome Words . . . The third edition, corrected and amended. pp. 479. *W. Stansby for Phile. Stephens and Christ. Meredith: London*, 1627. 12°. **3557**. a. **11**.

—— The fourth edition, *etc.* (The Summe of the Principles, *etc.* [The dedicatory epistle signed: Adoniram Byfield.]) 2 pt. *Io. Beale for Philemon Stephens and Christopher Meredith: London*, 1630. 12°. **3557**. a. **1**.

—— The fifth edition, *etc.* (The Summe of the Principles, *etc.*) 2 pt. *G. Miller for Philemon Stephens and Christopher Meredith: London*, 1634. 12°. **3559**. a. **8**.

—— The sixth edition, *etc.* pp. 479. *Jo. Dawson for Philemon Stephens and Christopher Meredith: London*, 1637. 12°. **1016**. c. **26**.

—— The Principles, or, The Pattern of wholsome words . . . The sixth Edition, *etc.* *London*, 1637. 12°. Mic. A. **587**. (**10**.)

MICROFILM *of a copy of the preceding in Cambridge University Library. Made by University Microfilms*, 1954.

—— The seventh edition, *etc.* (The Sum of the Principles, *etc.*) 2 pt. pp. 407. *E. T. for Peter Dring: London*, 1665. 12°. **4408**. c. **20**.
The titlepage of "The Sum of the Principles" bears the imprint "E. T. for Philemon Stephens, 1662."

—— The Rule of Faith: or, an Exposition of the Apostles Creed . . . Published . . . by . . . Adoniram Bifield. pp. 563. *G. M.* [*G. Miller*] *for Philemon Stephens & Christopher Meredith: London*, 1626. 4°. **3505**. cc. **52**.

—— Sermons vpon the first chapter of the first Epistle generall of Peter, *etc.* [With the text.] pp. 512. 1617. 8°. *See* BIBLE.—*Peter.—Selections.* [*English.*] **3266**. ccc. **7**

—— Sermons upon the ten first verses of the third chapter of the first Epistle of S. Peter . . . Being the last that were preached by . . . N. Byfield . . . Published since the Authors death by William Gouge. [With the text.] pp. 235. 1626. 4°. *See* BIBLE.—*Peter.—Selections* [*English.*] **4452**. bb. **4**

—— [Another copy, imperfect.] C. **71**. d. **26**. (**3**.)

—— The Signes, or, an Essay concerning the assurance o Gods love and mans salvation; gathered out of the holy Scriptures . . . Newly corrected and amended. pp. 78. *A. M. for Henry Overton: London*, 1637. 12°. **1019**. e. **43**

BYFIELD (RICHARD) The Doctrine of the Sabbath Vindicated, in a confutation of a treatise of the Sabbath, writte by M. Edward Breerwood against M. Nic. Byfield, *et* pp. 227. *Felix Kyngston, for Philemon Stephens & Christopher Meredith: London*, 1631. 4°. **700**. b. **9**. (2.)

—— [Another copy.] **484**. a. **31**. (**1**.)

—— The Gospels Glory, without prejudice to the Law shining forth in the Glory of God, the Father, the Sonne the Holy Ghost, for the Salvation of Sinners, *etc.* pp. 37 *E. M. for Adoniram Byfield: London*, 1659. 8°. E. **1864**. (**1**

—— The Light of Faith: and, Way of holinesse. Shewin what to belieue, and for what to striue together, *et* pp. 444. *T. H.* [*T. Harper*] *for Ph. Stephens an Ch. Meredith: London*, 1630. 12°. **4410**. a.

—— The Lord's Day, the Sabbath day. Or, a briefe Answ to some materiall passages, in a late Treatise of th Sabbath-day [by Francis White, Bishop of Ely]. Digeste dialogue-wise between two Divines A & B . . . The 2. ed tion much enlarged, with a second part and postscrip [By R. Byfield?] pp. 62. 1636. 4°. *See* LORD'S DAY. **4355**. b.

BYFIELD (Richard)

—— *See* White (Francis) successively *Bishop of Carlisle, of Norwich,* and *of Ely.* An Examination and Confutation of a Lawlesse Pamphlet [by Richard Byfield?], intituled, A briefe Answer to a late Treatise of the Sabbath-Day, *etc.* 1637. 4°. **4355.** e. **5.**

—— The Power of the Christ of God, or a Treatise of Power, as it is originally in God the Father, and by him given to Christ his Sonne, *etc.* pp. 46. *R. Cotes for Jo. Bellamie & Ralph Smith: London,* 1641. 4°. **4105.** a. **9.**

—— [Another copy.] E. **170.** (**10.**)

—— Temple-defilers defiled, wherein a true Visible Church of Christ is described. The evils and pernicious errours, especially appertaining to schisme, anabaptisme and libertinisme, that infest our Church, are discovered . . . Delivered in two sermons preached at the lecture in Kingston upon Thames, Feb. 20. & 27. 1644, *etc.* pp. 40. *John Field for Ralph Smith: London,* 1645. 4°. **4455.** b. **5.**

—— [Another copy.] E. **278.** (**20.**)

—— [A reissue, without the epistle dedicatory.] . A Short Treatise describing the true Church of Christ, *etc. For Ralph Smith: London,* 1653. 4°. T. **1562.** (**1.**)

—— Zions Answer to the Nations Ambassadors, according to instructions given by Isaiah from Gods mouth: In part unfolded in a sermon preached before the Honourable House of Commons at their solemne fast, Junii 25. 1645. *Printed by John Field for Ralph Smith: London,* 1645. 4°. E. **289.** (**12.**)

BYFIELD (Robert) Sectum: being the universal directory in the art of cutting; containing unerring principles upon which every garment may be made to fit the human shape, with ease and elegance, *etc.* pp. vii. 131. pl. 25. *H. S. Mason: London,* 1825. 8°. **1044.** k. **3.**

BYFIELD (Timothy) The Artificial Spaw, or Mineral-waters to drink: imitating the German spaw-water, *etc.* pp. 70. *James Rawlins for the Author: London,* 1684. 12°. **1171.** e. **20.** (**2.**)

—— A Closet Piece. The experimental knowledge of the ever-blessed God, the Father, the Son, the Holy Ghost, according to revelation in the Holy Scriptures; and to be experienc'd in the hearts of all true believers. pp. 100. *J. Roberts: London,* 1721. 8°. **479.** b. **50.**

—— Directions tending to Health and Long Life, &c. pp. 32. *Printed for the Author: London,* 1717. 8°. **1162.** f. **18.** (**3.**)

—— A Short and Plain Account of the late-found Balsamick Wells at Hoxdon, *etc.* pp. 55. *Sold by Christopher Wilkinson: London,* 1687. 8°. **1171.** e. **20.** (**4.**)

—— A Short but full Account of the Rise, Nature, and Management of the Smal-Pox, and other putrid fevers, with their proper remedy. pp. 20. *J. Morphew: London,* 1711. 8°. **1174.** d. **46.** (**2.**)

—— Some Long-vacation Hours Redeem'd. The Christian Examiner, *etc.* 2 pt. *John Penn: London,* 1720, 21. 8°. **702.** b. **7.** (**3.**)

—— Two Discourses: one of consumptions, with their cure . . . The other contains some rules of health. pp. 31. *For Dorman Newman: London,* 1685. 4°. **1187.** e. **3.** (**1.**)

—— The Devil and the Doctor; or, the Tragi-Comic consultation: an anthypochondriac satyr, for suppressing the turgent bile of the quacks. By Doctor Byfielde. [A reissue of "Mandragora; or, the Quacks: a poem," here purporting to be by T. Byfield.] pp. 111. *J. Bettenham: London,* 1719. 8°. **1077.** k. **16.**

—— [Another copy.] **161.** l. **19.**

BYFIELD (Timothy)

—— A Letter to the Learned Dr. Woodward. By Dr. Byfielde. [A satire on J. Woodward's "State of Physic and Diseases." Signed: J. Byfielde. By John Freind? intending to suggest the authorship of T. Byfield.] pp. 51. *James Bettenham: London,* 1719. 8°. **1172.** g. **7.** (**3.**)

—— The third edition. pp. 51. *Thomas Bickerton: London,* 1719. 8°. **117.** k. **8.**

—— A Letter to the Fatal Triumvirate [i.e. J. Freind, R. Mead and Salusbury Cade]: in answer to that pretended to be written by Dr. Byfield: and shewing reasons why Dr. Woodward should take no notice of it. [By John Harris.] pp. 23. *J. Bettenham: London,* 1719. 8°. **1172.** g. **8.** (**2.**)

—— The Two Sosias: or the true Dr. Byfield at the Rainbow Coffee-House, to the pretender in Jermyn-Street. In answer to a letter wrote by him, assisted by his two associates, with a preface relating to the late famous exploits of the facetious Dr. A. Tripe [i.e. to William Wagstaffe's satires on the controversy], *etc.* [A satire on J. Friend and R. Mead, defending Woodward's "State of Physic and Diseases," and objecting to the use of Byfield's name.] [By John Woodward?] pp. 58. *J. Bettenham: London,* 1719. 8°. **551.** a. **10.** (**4.**)

BYFIELDE (J.) *See* Byfield (Timothy)

BYFLEET.—*Brooklands Aerodrome.* B.A.M. Brooklands Aerodrome Magazine. vol. 1. no. 1.—vol. 4. no. 2. Oct. 1932—Feb.–Mar. 1935. *Byfleet,* 1932–35. 4°. P.P. **1563.** ads.
Subsequently incorporated in "The Sports Car."

BYFORD (Charles Thomas)

—— *See* Hemmens (Harry L.) A Very Gallant Gentleman. Charles Thomas Byford, 1872–1948. [With a portrait.] [1948.] 8°. **4910.** a. **36.**

—— Peasants and Prophets. Baptist pioneers in Russia and South Eastern Europe . . . Second edition. pp. xi. 152. *J. Clarke & Co.: London,* [1913.] 8°. **4715.** aa. **43.**

—— The Soul of Russia. pp. 396. *Kingsgate Press: London,* [1914.] 8°. **3926.** e. **22.**

BYFORD (Gertrude) Examination Scales. For the use of candidates preparing for the Local Centre Examinations of the Associated Board of the R.A.M. & R.C.M. Intermediate & Advanced Grades. Grouped with hints as to method of practice. pp. 12. *Augener: London,* [1907.] 8°. **7898.** t. **9.** (**4.**)

BYFORD (Henry Turman) *See* Byford (William H.) The Practice of Medicine and Surgery applied to the Diseases and Accidents incident to Women . . . Fourth edition (by W. H. Byford and H. T. Byford), *etc.* 1888. 8°. **7580.dd.1.**

—— To Panama and back. The record of an experience. [With plates.] pp. 384. *W. B. Conkey Co.: Chicago,* [1908.] 8°. **010480.** de. **50.**

BYFORD (Samuel) Reminiscences of Chipping Barnet and Monken Hadley from A.D. 1816 to 1891. pp. 44. *Stephen Baldock: Barnet,* 1891. 8°. **10348.** ccc. **57.** (**4.**)

BYFORD (William Heath) The Philosophy of Domestic Life. pp. 174. *Lee & Shepard: Boston,* 1869. 8°. **8404.** b. **28.**

—— The Practice of Medicine and Surgery applied to the Diseases and Accidents incident to Women. pp. 566. *Lindsay & Blakiston: Philadelphia,* 1865. 8°. **7580.** e. **14.**

BYFORD (WILLIAM HEATH)

—— Third edition. Thoroughly revised and rewritten, *etc.* pp. 682. *Lindsay & Blakiston: Philadelphia*, 1881. 8°. **7580**. cc. **7**.

—— Fourth edition (by W. H. Byford and H. T. Byford). Revised rewritten and very much enlarged, *etc.* pp. 820. *J. & A. Churchill: London*, 1888. 8°. **7580**. dd. **1**.

BYFORD-JONES (W.) *See* JONES.

BYGARRURES. *See* BIGARRURES.

BYGATE (J. E.) The Cathedral Church of Durham . . . With forty-four illustrations. pp. 117. *London*, 1899. 8°. [*Bell's Cathedral Series.*] **04705**. c. **17**.

—— (New edition.) pp. 120. *London*, 1922. 8°. [*Bell's Cathedral Series.*] **04705**. c. **51**.

BYGD. *See* PERIODICAL PUBLICATIONS.—*Copenhagen.*

BYGDÉN (ANDERS LEONARD) *See* BENZELSTIERNA (G.) G. Benzelstjernas censorsjournal, 1737–1746. Utgifven af L. Bygdén, *etc.* [1884, *etc.*] 8°. Ac. **9072/3**.

—— Svenskt anonym- och pseudonym-lexikon. Bibliografisk förteckning öfver uppdagade anonymer och pseudonymer i den svenska litteraturen. 2 bd. pp. 1051. ii. 1898–1915. 8°. *See* UPSALA.—*Svenska Literatursällskapet.* **2038.c.**

—— [Another copy.] Ac. **9072/13**.

BYGDÉN (ARTUR)

—— Heliga Birgittas reliker. Av Artur Bygdén . . . Nils Gustaf Gejvall . . . Carl Herman Hjortsjö. pp. 111. pl. xx. *Lund*, 1954. 8°. **7801**. c. **52**.

—— Sankt Eriks skrin genom tiderna. *In:* THORDEMAN (B. J. N.) Erik den helige, *etc.* pp. 321–396. 1954. 8°. **7801**. c. **58**.

—— Silicium als Vertreter des Kohlenstoffs organischer Verbindungen. Inaugural-Dissertation, *etc.* pp. viii. 189. *Uppsala*, 1916. 8°. **8904**. b. **25**.

BYGDÉN (LEONARD) *See* BYGDÉN (Anders L.)

BYGELIUS (JOANNES RODOLPHUS) Series atque ordo consulum reipub. Tigurinæ a Rodolpho Brunone vsque ad tempora nostra. [*Zurich*, 1577.] 8°. **11409**. ccc. **13**. (**1**.)

BYGGINGAR-BREF. Byggingar-Bref. [Blank form of agreement between landlord and tenant as used in Iceland.] [*Reykjavik?* 1780?] 4°. **867**. l. 8. (8.)

BYGGMÄSTEREN.

—— Byggmästeren . . . Organ för Stockholms Byggnadsföreningen og Svenska Arkitektföreningen. *See* STOCKHOLM.—*Stockholms Byggnadsförening.*

BYGGNADSMATERIALUTREDNING. *See* SWEDEN.—*Socialdepartementet.*

BYGNING.

—— En Bygning vi rejser. Den politiske arbejderbevægelses historie i Danmark. [By Oluf Bertolt, Ernst Christiansen and Poul Hansen.] 3 pt. *København*, 1954, 55. 8°. **9424**. gg. **10**.

BYGOD (*Sir* FRANCIS) A treatise cōcernynge impropriations of benefices. **B.L.** *Printed by Tho. Godfray: Lōdon*, [1535?] 8°. **696**. a. **34**.

—— [Another copy.] C. **37**. a. **28**. (**1**.) *Imperfect; wanting the first 4 leaves, including the titlepage.*

BYGONES. Bye-Gones, relating to Wales, and the Border Countries. *See* PERIODICAL PUBLICATIONS.—*Oswestry.*

BYGOTT (JOHN) Eastern England. Some aspects of its geography with special reference to economic significance . . . Illustrated by specially compiled maps and diagrams. pp. xv. 358. *G. Routledge & Sons: London*, 1923. 8°. **010368**. e. **101**.

—— Hale's Diagram Geographies. General editor: John Bygott. *Robert Hale: London*, 1939– . 4°. W.P. **12344**.

—— An Introduction to Mapwork and Practical Geography. pp. viii. 246. *University Tutorial Press: London*, 1934. 8°. **010005**. ee. **22**.

—— (Second edition.) pp. viii. 246. *University Tutorial Press: London*, 1938. 8°. **10004**. pp. **21**.

—— An Introduction to Mapwork and Practical Geography. (Third edition.) pp. viii. 251. *University Tutorial Press: London*, 1947. 8°. **10001**. ee. **36**.

—— An Introduction to Mapwork and Practical Geography. (Fourth edition.) pp. viii. 251. *University Tutorial Press: London*, 1952. 8°. **010004**. eee. **5[illegible]**

—— An Introduction to Mapwork and Practical Geography. (Fifth edition.) pp. viii. 251. *University Tutorial Press: London*, 1955. 8°. **010005**. c. **[illegible]**

—— Lincolnshire, *etc.* [With plates and a map.] pp. xii. 28[illegible] *Robert Hale: London*, 1952. 8°. [*County Books Series.*] W.P. **1690/5[illegible]**

—— A Regional Geography of the World for School. pp. x. 362. *University Tutorial Press: London*, 1932. 8°. [*School Examinations Series.*] **12207.aaa.1/6**

—— Two Soldier Brothers. "Bert"—Lieutenant Walter Bertram Wood . . . "Ted"—Second Lieutenant Edwi[illegible] Leonard Wood, *etc.* [With plates, including portraits.] pp. ix. 176. *Jarrolds: London*, [1919.] 8°. **010855**. cc. **1**

BYGOTT (JOHN) and **JONES** (A. J. LAWFORD)

—— The King's English and how to write it, *etc.* pp. 242. *Jarrold & Sons: London*, [1903.] 8°. **12981**. dd. **1**

—— Fourteenth edition. pp. 297. *Jarrolds: London*, [1918.] 8°. **12980**. e.

—— New and revised edition. pp. 270. *Jarrolds: London*, 1923. 8°. **12980**. e. **1**

—— Points in Punctuation, *etc.* pp. 105. *Jarrold & Sons: London*, [1905.] 8°. **12984**. ee. **3**

—— Fourth edition. pp. 105. *Jarrold & Sons: London*, [1908.] 8°. **12985**. e. **5**

BYGRAVE (BULSTRODE) *See* LONGITUDE (The.) *pseu[illegible]* [i.e. B. Bygrave?]

BYGRAVE (CH.) Quelques considérations sur l'extracti[on] des dents, les inconvénients de la clef de Garengeot, et supériorité des nouveaux daviers anglais. (Extrait de Gazette des hôpitaux.) pp. 18. *Paris*, 1859. 8°. **7610**. b. **49**. (

BYGRAVE (ROBERT) The Case of Mr. Bygrave, late Cl[erk] of the Papers of the Fleet. [A petition to recover mon[ey] of which Bygrave alleged he had been defrauded [by] T. Bambridge.] pp. 3. [*London*, 1729.] fol. C. **116**. i. 4. (**8**

BYHAN (ARTHUR) *See* PUŞCARIU (S.) Studii istroromâne de S. Puşcariu . . . în colaborare cu D—nii M. Bartoli . . . A. Byhan. I. Texte 1906. 8°. [*Annalele Academii Române.* ser. 2. tom. 28. Memoriile secţiunii literare.] Ac. **743.**

—— *See* PUŞCARIU (S.) Studii istroromâne în colaborare cu M. Bartoli . . . A. Byhan. II [*etc.*]. 1926, *etc.* 8°. [*Academia Română. Studii şi cercetări.* vol. 11, 16, *etc.*] Ac. **743/43.**

—— Die alten Nasalvokale in den slavischen Elementen des Rumänischen. 1898. *See* LEIPZIG.—*Institut für Rumänische Sprache.* Erster [*etc.*] Jahresbericht, *etc.* no. 5. 1894, *etc.* 8°. Ac. **9831.**

—— La Civilisation caucasienne. Préface et traduction du Dr George Montandon, *etc.* pp. 259. pl. XXIV. *Paris,* 1936. 8°. **10008.** p. **23.**

—— Die Entwicklung von e vor nasalen in den lateinischen Elementen des Rumänischen. 1896. *See* LEIPZIG.—*Institut für Rumänische Sprache.* Erster [*etc.*] Jahresbericht, *etc.* no. 3. 1894, *etc.* 8°. Ac. **9831.**

—— Istrorumänisches Glossar. 1899. *See* LEIPZIG.—*Institut für Rumänische Sprache.* Erster [*etc.*] Jahresbericht, *etc.* no. 6. 1894, *etc.* 8°. Ac. **9831.**

BYINGTON (CYRUS) *See* BIBLE.—*New Testament.* [*Choctaw.*] The New Testament, *etc.* [Translated by A. Wright and C. Byington.] 1848. 8°. **3070.** b. **58.**

—— —— 1857. 8°. **3070.** b. **50.**

—— —— 1881. 8°. **3068.** de. **34.**

—— Holisso anumpa tosholi. An English and Choctaw Definer; for the Choctaw academies and schools, *etc.* pp. 252. *S. W. Benedict: New York,* 1852. 8°. **12907.** a. **42.**

BYINGTON (EDWIN HALLOCK) The Quest for Experience in Worship. pp. xii. 211. *Doubleday, Doran & Co.: Garden City, New York,* 1929. 8°. **3474.** a. **4.**

BYINGTON (EZRA HOYT) The Puritan as a Colonist and Reformer. [With plates.] pp. xxvi. 375. *Gay & Bird: London; Cambridge, U.S.A.* [printed], 1899. 8°. **4744.** dd. **16.**

—— The Puritan in England and New England . . . With an introduction by Alexander McKenzie. [With plates.] pp. xl. 406. *Roberts Bros.: Boston,* 1896. 8°. **4744.** ee. **32.**

—— [Another copy with a different titlepage.] *Sampson Low & Co.: London; Cambridge, U.S.A.* [printed], 1896. 8°. **4744.** ee. **33.**

—— Fourth edition. With a chapter on witchcraft in New England. [With plates.] pp. xlii. 457. *Little, Brown & Co.: Boston,* 1900. 8°. **4745.** de. **12.**

BYINGTON (MARGARET F.)

—— Organizing a Public Welfare Committee in Spring County. Edited by M. F. Byington. pp. x. 82. *Columbia University Press: New York,* 1941. 8°. [*New York School of Social Work Publications.*] **8286.** bb. **67/10.**

BYINGTON (STEVEN TRACY) *See* ELTZBACHER (P.) Anarchism . . . Translated by S. T. Byington. 1908. 8°. **08277.** ee. **47.**

—— *See* MUNCHAUSEN, *Baron,* Baron Munchausen's Narrative . . . With . . . notes by S. T. Byington, *etc.* [1928.] 8°. **012403.** de. **79.**

BYINGTON (STEVEN TRACY)

—— *See* SCHILLER (J. C. F. von) [*Die Jungfrau von Orleans.*] Schillers Jungfrau von Orleans. Edited with introduction, notes, and vocabulary by P. S. Allen . . . and S. T. Byington. [1909.] 8°. **012203.** e. **10/32.**

—— *See* STIRNER (Max) *pseud.* The Ego and His Own . . . Translated . . . by S. T. Byington, *etc.* 1912. 8°. **012552.** ee. **49.**

BYK (ALFRED) Die Zustandsgleichungen in ihren Beziehungen zur Thermodynamik. 1906. *See* PERIODICAL PUBLICATIONS.—*Halle.* Annalen der Physik. Vierte Folge. Bd. 19. Hft. 3. 1877, *etc.* 8°. P.P. **1487.**

BYK (S. A.) Der Hellenismus und der Platonismus. pp. 45. *Leipzig,* 1870. 8°. **8464.** eee. **30.** (3.)

—— Die vorsokratische Philosophie der Griechen in ihrer organischen Gliederung dargestellt. 2 Tl. *Leipzig,* 1876, 77. 8°. **8460.** h. **10.**

—— Die Physiologie des Schönen. pp. vi. 286. *Leipzig,* 1878. 8°. **7808.** bb. **7.**

—— Rechtsphilosophie. Der letzte Grund des Rechts und seine practischen Consequenzen, *etc.* pp. ix. 244. *Leipzig; Utrecht* [printed], 1882. 8°. **6006.** g. 8.

BYKER AND HEATON YOUTH CENTRE. *See* NEWCASTLE-UPON-TYNE.

BYKER HILL FRIENDLY SOCIETY. Rules, Articles, & Regulations, of the Byker Hill Friendly Society . . . Instituted February IV, M.DCCC.XXV. pp. 12. *John Marshall: Newcastle upon Tyne,* 1826. 12°. **8275.** bb. **4.** (**10.**)

BYKOV ( ) [For the Russian surname in this form:] *See* BUIKOV.

BYKOWSKA (MAURYCJA) *See* BIKOVS'KA (M.)

BYKOWSKI (LEON) *See* BIKOVS'KY (Lev)

BYKOWSKI (LUDWIK JAXA) Badania eksperymentalne nad znaczeniem współzawodnictwa. Ze studjów nad młodzieżą szkolną. (Recherches expérimentales sur le rôle de l'émulation.) pp. 79. *Warszawa,* 1923. 8°. [*Wydawnictwa komisji pedagogicznej Ministerstwa W. R. i O. P.* no. 4.] **S.K.11.**

BYKOWSKI (PIOTR JAXA) Pamiętniki Włóczęgi. Z csasow przejścia XVIII do XIX wieku. [The preface signed: Ludwik***.] Ogłosił P. J. Bykowski [or rather written by him]. 4 tom. 1872. 8°. *See* LUDWIK * * *. **12589.** g. **38.**

—— Urodzenie. Dramat w trzech aktach z prologiem, *etc.* [By P. J. Bykowski.] pp. 104. 1860. 8°. *See* URODZENIE. **11758.** aaa. **92.**

BYL (ARMAND) *See* PERIODICAL PUBLICATIONS.—*Antwerp.* Jurisprudence du Port d'Anvers . . . Par J. Conard, *etc.* (Continuée par F. de Kinder . . . A. Byl.) 1856, *etc.* 8°. P.P. **1376.** c.

BYL (ARTHUR)

—— *See* TOULOUSE-LAUTREC-MONFA (H. M. R. de) Yvette Guilbert. Drawn by H. de Toulouse Lautrec. Described by A. Byl, *etc.* 1898. fol. **1899.** r. **15.**

BYL (FLEMING VOLTELIN VAN DER) *See* VAN DER BYL.

BYL (ISAAC) *See* BIJL.

BYL (JOOST) *See* BIJL.

BYL (PAUL ANDRIES VAN DER) Plantsiektes: hul oorsaak en bestryding. pp. vii. 404. *Kaapstad*, 1928. 8°. **07028**. b. **47**.

BYLAERT (JOANNES JACOBUS) Nieuwe manier om plaet-tekeningen in 't koper te brengen, van een, twee of meer couleuren . . . Aengetoond en uitgevoerd door J. J. Bylaert. (Nouvelle manière de graver en cuivre . . . Traduit du Hollandais par L. G. F. Kerroux.) [With plates.] *Dutch & Fr.* pp. 77. *Leiden*, 1772. 8°. **565**. c. **11**.

BYLAND ( ) *See* also BYLANDT.

BYLAND (HANS) Der Wortschatz des Zürcher Alten Testaments von 1525 und 1531 verglichen mit dem Wortschatz Luthers. Eine sprachliche Untersuchung. pp. vi. 84. *Berlin*, 1903. 8°. **3186**. h. **40**.

BYLAND (JOHN) Catalogue of Patriotic Literature. To be obtained at the office of "England," *etc.* [By J. Byland.] pp. 16. [1884.] 8°. *See* PERIODICAL PUBLICATIONS.—London.—*England*. **11904**. d. **20**. **(8.)**

—— [Another edition.] The Politician's Guide: containing a . . . catalogue of political literature, *etc.* (Second edition.) pp. 32. *"England" Office: London*, [1884.] 8°. **8139**. bb. **24**. **(2.)**

BYLANDT (CARL JOAN EMILIUS VAN) *Count*. Le Rôle des églises wallonnes à notre époque. *See* ROCHEDIEU (P.) L'Origine des églises wallonnes, *etc.* 1889. 8°. **4533**. ff. **18**. **(7.)**

BYLANDT (CHARLES MALCOLM ERNEST GEORGE VAN) *Count*. Order of Service at the Dutch Church, Austin Friars . . . in commemoration of his late Excellency Charles Malcolm Ernest George, Count de Bylandt, *etc.* [Chiefly consisting of the translation of an address by S. de Waard.] pp. 10. [*London*, 1893.] 8°. **10601**. d. **33**. **(10.)**

BYLANDT (DMITRY LOUIS VAN) *Count*. Het Blokkade-Recht. Academisch proefschrift, *etc.* pp. 158. *'s Gravenhage*, 1880. 8°. **8009**. k. **7**.

BYLANDT (FREDERIK SIGISMUND VAN) *Count*. *See* GEELVINCK (J.) Missive aan den . . . Heere F. S. Grave van Byland . . . over de gehoudene conversatie . . . den 16 November 1783. [1784.] 8°. **934**. f. **9**. **(2.)**

—— *See* VRIES (H. de) *of Amsterdam*. De Gehoudene conversatie tusschen den . . . Heere F. S. Grave van Byland . . . en Mr. Joan Geelvinck . . . den 16 November 1783. In een waar daglicht gesteld. 1784. 8°. **934**. f. **9**. **(1.)**

—— Antwoord . . . aan . . . Mr. Johan Geelvinck op zyn . . . Missive aan zyn Hoog Welgeboren gezonden, *etc.* [On their conversation of 16 Nov. 1783.] pp. 8. [*Amsterdam*, 1784.] 8°. **934**. f. **9**. (**4**.)

—— De Brief van den . . . Heere Mr. Joan Geelvink . . . aan F. S. Grave van Byland . . . over de gehoudene conversatie in 't Heeren logement, te Amsterdam, den 16 November 1783, door den laastgenoemde beantwoord, *etc.* pp. 27. *Amsterdam*, 1784. 8°. **934**. f. **9**. **(3.)**

—— Eenige bedenkingen over de zeemagt van de Republiek. [By Count F. S. van Bylandt.] pp. 35. 1783. 8°. *See* NETHERLANDS.—*United Provinces.—Navy*. [*Appendix*.] **934**. f. **9**. **(15.)**

BYLANDT (FREDERIK WILLEM CAREL PIETER VAN) *Count*.

—— Het Diplomatisch beleid van Hieronymus van Beverningk, gedurende de jaren 1672–1678. Academisch proefschrift, *etc.* pp. x. 136. 12. *'s-Gravenhage*, 1863. 8°. **9405**. ee. **37**.

BYLANDT (HENRI DE) *Count*. Les Races de chiens, leurs origines, points, descriptions, *etc.* pp. 1160. *Bruxelles*, 1897. 4°. **7294**. h. 9.

—— Dogs of all Nations: their varieties, characteristics, points, *etc.* [With illustrations.] *Eng., Fr., Ger. & Dutch.* 2 vol. *Kegan Paul & Co.: London; printed in Holland*, 1905. fol. **7294**. h. 22.

BYLANDT (LODEWYK VAN) *Count*. *See* BERNARD (François) *of Leyden*. De Memorie van Lodewyk, Graave van Byland . . . getoetst aan den toetssteen van het gezond verstand en van de waarheid, *etc.* 1783. 8°. **934**. f. **9**. **(5.)**

—— *See* CATO-BATAVUS, *pseud.* Brief van Cato-Batavus . . . over de onlangs voorgevallene rencontre, tusschen het Esquader van den Schout by Nagt Grave van Byland, en dat van den Commodore Fielding. [1780.] 8°. **934**. f. **9**. **(6.)**

—— *See* RUYTER (M. A. de) De Schimmen van Michiel de Ruiter . . . de Engelsche Admiraalen Blaake, Georg Askue, Prins Robbert, Sprag, de Fransche Admiral de Graaf van Estrée en een Voornaam Neerlandsch Koopman . . . Met elkander spreekende: over het voorgevallene tusschen het Esquador der Hollandische Schout-by-Nagt Byland en de Engelsche Commandore Fielding, *etc.* [1780.] 8°. **934**. e. **16**. **(10.)**

BYLANDT-HALT (J. G. VON) *Count*. *See* MASCAMP (H.) Henrici Mascampii Disquisitio de patria Justiniani quam . . . defendendam suscipiet J. G. Comes de Byland-Halt. 1708. 4°. **589**. d. **23**. **(3.)**

BYLANDT PALSTERCAMP (A. DE) *Count*. Théorie des volcans. 3 tom. *Paris*, 1835. 8°. **551**. d. 1.

—— Atlas. pl. 16. *Paris*, 1836. fol. **650**. a. **10**.

BYLANDT-RHEIDT (ARTHUR) *Count*, and **MARESCH** (OTTO) Wirkung und Gebrauch der k.k. österr. Feld- und Gebirgs-Geschütze . . . Mit 2 Tafeln, *etc.* pp. viii. 149. *Wien*, 1872. 8°. **8823**. i. 4.

BY-LAWS. By-Laws for —— Co-operative Society with unlimited liability. [For adoption by societies applying for registration in India.] pp. 7. *Alipore*, 1913. fol. **5319**. h. **21**.

BYLDENSNYDER (HINRIK) *See* BELDENSNYDER (Henrik)

BYLER (HENRICUS CAROLINUS VAN) Henrici Carolini van Byler Libellorum rariorum, partim editorum, partim ineditorum, fasciculus primus. pp. 299. *Groningae*, 1733. 8°. **123**. b. **17**.

BYLER (LUCAS) Has de ictero flavo theses . . . publicè examinandas proponit L. Byler. [1618.] *See* GENATHIUS (J. J.) Decas I. [*etc.*] disputationum medicarum select. *etc.* decas 2. 1618, *etc.* 4°. **1179**. g. 3. (16.)

BYLERTIUS (ANTONIUS) Antonii Bylertii Carmen de Lingæ scholarumque ejus initiis processibus & incrementis 1734. *See* HOVEN (J. D. van) and MOLFENGER (A. S.) Verosimilia sacra et profana, *etc.* fasc. 3. 1732, *etc.* 8°. **12258**. bbb. 7

BYLES (ALFRED THOMAS PLESTED) *See* LULL (Ramón) The Book of the Ordre of Chiualry . . . Edited by A. T. P. Byles. 1926. 8°. Ac. **9925/124**

—— *See* PISAN (Christine de) The Book of Fayttes of Armes and of Chyualrye. Translated . . . by W. Caxton . . Edited by A. T. P. Byles. 1932. 8°. Ac. **9925/144**

—— *See* PISAN (Christine de) The Book of Fayttes of Armes and of Chyvalrye . . . Edited by A. T. P. Byles . . . Reissued with corrections. 1937. 8°. Ac. **9925/157**

BYLES (ARTHUR HOLDEN) The P.S.A. What it is, and how to start it. pp. 42. *J. Clarke & Co.: London* 1891. 8°. **08276**. f. **21**. **(11.**

BYLES (BRIDGET) *See* HEWLETT, afterwards COPLE (Esther) Memorials of Practical Piety, as exemplified in the lives of Miss M. Beuzeville . . . and Mrs. B. Byles, *etc.* 1830. 12°. **4920**. bbb. **11**

BYLES (C. B.) The First Principles of Railway Signalling, including an account of the legislation in the United Kingdom affecting the working of railways and the provision of signalling and safety appliances. pp. viii. 146. *Railway Gazette: London*, 1910 [1909]. 8°. **08767**. a. **25**.

BYLES (CHARLES EDWARD) *See* HAWKER (Robert S.) Cornish Ballads, and other poems. Edited, with an introduction, by C. E. Byles, *etc.* 1904. 8°. **11607**. bbb. **30**.

—— *See* HAWKER (Robert S.) Footprints of Former Men in Far Cornwall . . . Edited, with introduction, by C. E. Byles, *etc.* [1903.] 8°. **012331**. i. **32**.

—— *See* HAWKER (Robert S.) Stones Broken from the Rocks . . . Edited by C. E. Byles. 1922. 8°. **4371**. aa. **43**.

—— *See* PLUTARCH. [*Vitae Parallelae.—Abridgments and Selections.—English.*] Greek Lives from Plutarch. Newly translated by C. E. Byles, *etc.* [1907.] 8°. **10606**. k. **8**.

—— *See* TARN (Arthur W.) and BYLES (C. E.) A Record of the Guardian Assurance Company, *etc.* 1921. 8°. **08245**. i. **4**.

—— Cornish Breakers, and other poems. pp. 48. *Printed for the Author: London*, 1909. 16°. **011651**. h. **75**.

—— The Life and Letters of R. S. Hawker, *etc.* [With portraits.] pp. xxviii. 689. *John Lane: London & New York*, 1905. 8°. **2216**. b. **11**.

—— Rambles in Bookland: an English reading-book for junior forms. Edited by C. E. Byles. pp. 224. *London*, [1908.] 8°. [*Arnold's Literary Reading-Books.*] **012203**. f. **3/5**.

—— Rupert Brooke's Grave, and other poems. pp. 57. *Erskine Macdonald: London*, 1919. 8°. **011648**. ff. **39**.

BYLES (FREDERICK GLYDE) William Byles. By his youngest son. [With plates, including portraits, and a genealogical table.] pp. 150. *Printed for private circulation: Weymouth*, 1932. 8°. **010822**. e. **37**.

BYLES (FREDERICK GLYDE) and **LEAF** (E. MATTHEW)

—— "Old Times at t'Bay." A play in four scenes. ff. 20. [*Robin Hood's Bay*, 1941.] 4°. **11780**. dd. **55**. *Reproduced from typewriting.*

BYLES (GEORGE) Reveries in Confinement: a poem, *etc.* pp. iii. 25. *T. Skelton: Southampton*, [1804.] 4°. **11642**. f. **46**.

—— Reveries in Confinement . . . Second edition, *etc.* pp. iii. 21. *T. Skelton: Southampton*, [1804.] 4°. **11661**. dd. **17**.

—— The Vicissitudes of Human Life, and other poems. Illustrated with notes. pp. xxiii. 104. *Printed for the Author: Norwich*, 1809. 12°. **11632**. aaa. **7**.

BYLES (HARRIET) *See* PRICE (Ernest J.) and BYLES (H.) Scenes from the Life of John Milton. A play. [1925.] 8°. **011779**. h. **59**.

BYLES (JOHN) The Boy and the Angel, being Sunday morning talks to the children. pp. 214. *T. Fisher Unwin: London*, 1893. 8°. **012330**. g. **41**.

—— Dick Whittington; or, the Young traveller. A New Year's address to Sunday School boys & girls. pp. 16. *Sunday School Union: London*, [1880.] 16°. **4422**. h. **14**. (**6**.)

BYLES (JOHN)

—— The Legend of St. Mark. Being Sunday morning talks to the children. pp. viii. 188. *T. Fisher Unwin: London*, 1899. 8°. **4371**. de. **35**.

—— [Another edition.] pp. 141. *Alston Rivers: London*, 1906. 8°. **4377**. de. **27**.

—— Spring Blossoms and Summer Fruit; or, Sunday morning talks to the children. pp. 142. *T. Fisher Unwin: London*, 1888. 8°. **4400**. p. **28**.

—— (New edition.) pp. 144. *Alston Rivers: London*, 1905. 8°. **04403**. ee. **12**.

—— What Jesus said on six great subjects; or, Six Sermons on the testimony of Jesus. To which is added a sermon "Robert Elsmere; or, the lost faith." pp. 96. *S. B. Spaull: London*, [1889.] 8°. **4479**. bb. **49**.

BYLES (*Right Hon. Sir* JOHN BARNARD) *One of the Justices of the Court of Common Pleas.*

—— Byles on Bills of Exchange. *See* infra: A Treatise on the Law of Bills of Exchange.

—— A Discourse on the Present State of the Law of England, the proposed schemes of reform, and the proper method of study, *etc.* pp. 42. *S. Sweet: London*, 1829. 8°. T. **1240**. (**12**.)

—— Foundations of Religion in the Mind and Heart of Man. pp. x. 157. *John Murray: London*, 1875. 8°. **4380**. bb. **34**.

—— Observations on the Usury Laws, and the effect of the recent alterations; with suggestions for the permanent amendment of the law, and the draft of an act for that purpose. pp. 167. *S. Sweet: London*, 1845. 12°. **1380**. c. **7**.

—— A Practical Treatise of the Law of Bills of Exchange, Promissory Notes, Bank-Notes, Bankers' Cash Notes, & Checks; with an appendix of statutes, and the new forms of pleading . . . Second edition, greatly enlarged. pp. l. 368. *S. Sweet: London*, 1834. 12°. **515**. a. **16**.

—— Third edition, enlarged. pp. lv. 436. *S. Sweet: London*, 1839. 12°. **1129**. a. **26**.

—— Fourth edition, enlarged. pp. lxvii. 536. *S. Sweet: London*, 1843. 8°. **1380**. f. **11**.

—— A Treatise of the Law of Bills of Exchange. The fifth edition. pp. lxiv. 494. *S. Sweet: London*, 1847. 8°. **1380**. g. **3**.

—— The sixth edition. pp. lxvi. 517. *S. Sweet: London*, 1851. 8°. **6405**. d. **1**.

—— Fourth American, from the sixth London edition. With additional notes, illustrating the law and practice in this country, by Hon. George Sharswood. pp. 670. *T. & J. W. Johnson & Co.: Philadelphia*, 1856. 8°. **6405**. d. **2**.

—— The seventh edition, with notes from the third American edition. pp. lxxi. 556. *H. Sweet: London*, 1857. 8°. **6375**. c. **5**.

—— The eighth edition, with notes from the fourth American edition. pp. lxx. 550. *H. Sweet: London*, 1862. 8°. **6405**. d. **3**.

—— The ninth edition, with notes from the fourth American edition. pp. lxx. 569. *H. Sweet: London*, 1866. 8°. **6375**. bb. **6**.

—— The eleventh edition, with notes from the fifth American edition, by Maurice Barnard Byles, *etc.* pp. lxviii. 571. *H. Sweet: London*, 1874. 8°. **6375**. aaa. **1**.

BYLES (*Right Hon. Sir* John Barnard) *One of the Justices of the Court of Common Pleas.*

—— Sixth American, from the eleventh London edition, with notes . . . by Maurice Barnard Byles . . . With additional notes . . . by Hon. George Sharswood. pp. lxiii. 783. *T. & J. W. Johnson & Co.: Philadelphia*, 1874. 8º. **6375**. f. **1**.

—— The twelfth edition, with notes from the sixth American edition, 1874, by Maurice Barnard Byles. pp. lxx. 580. *H. Sweet: London*, 1876. 8º. **6375**. c. **36**.

—— The thirteenth edition, with notes from the sixth American edition, 1874, by Maurice Barnard Byles. pp. lxxi. 575. *H. Sweet: London*, 1879. 8º. **6375**. cc. **14**.

—— The fourteenth edition, with notes from the sixth American edition, 1874, by Maurice Barnard Byles . . . and Archie Kirkman Loyd. pp. lxviii. 592. *Sweet & Sons: London*, 1885. 8º. **6375**. c. **39**.

—— The fifteenth edition. By Maurice Barnard Byles . . . and Archie Kirkman Loyd. pp. lxx. 584. *Sweet & Maxwell: London*, 1891. 8º. **6376**. h. **15**.

—— The sixteenth edition by Maurice Barnard Byles . . . . . and Walter John Barnard Byles. pp. lxx. 582. *Sweet & Maxwell: London*, 1899. 8º. **6376**. pp. **21**.

—— The seventeenth edition by Walter J. Barnard Byles and Eric R. Watson. pp. cvi. 464. 5–52. *Sweet & Maxwell: London*, 1911. 8º. **6405**. v. **8**.

—— The eighteenth edition . . . By Walter J. Barnard Byles . . . and A. W. Baker Welford. pp. lxxx. 442. *Sweet & Maxwell: London*, 1923. 8º. **6374**. t. **13**.

—— The nineteenth edition . . . By A. W. Baker Welford. pp. lxxvi. 447. *Sweet & Maxwell: London*, 1931. 8º. **6378.bbb.2.**

—— A Treatise on the Law of Bills of Exchange . . . The twentieth edition. With colonial notes. By A. W. Baker Welford. pp. lxxix. 656. *Sweet & Maxwell: Stevens & Sons: London*, 1939. 8º. **6405.1.2.**

—— [A Treatise on the Law of Bills of Exchange.] Byles on Bills of Exchange . . . Twenty-first edition. By Maurice Megrah. pp. lxxvii. 439. *Sweet & Maxwell: London*, 1955. 8º. **2016**. g.

—— [Another copy.] 6307.bb.10.

—— Sophisms of Free-Trade and Popular Political Economy Examined. By a Barrister [i.e. Sir J. B. Byles]. Second edition. pp. xvi. 226. 1850. 8º. *See* Barrister. **8205**. a. **18**.

—— Ninth edition, *etc.* pp. xii. 343. 1870. 8º. *See* Barrister. **8246**. aaa. **30**.

—— A new edition with an introduction and notes by William Samuel Lilly . . . and Charles Stanton Devas. pp. lxi. 424. *John Lane: London & New York*, 1904. 8º. **08207**. ee. **40**.

—— *See* Barrister. Free Trade and its so-called Sophisms: a reply to "Sophisms of Free Trade, etc. examined by a Barrister" [i.e. Sir J. B. Byles], *etc.* 1850. 12º. **8245**. a. **54**.

—— *See* Pearson (Robert) *Wharfinger*. Free Trade. A reply to "Sophisms of Free Trade . . . by a Barrister" [i.e. Sir J. B. Byles.] 1850. 8º. **8245**. b. **56**.

BYLES (John Beuzeville) *See* Ricketts (Thomas F.) The Diagnosis of Smallpox . . . Illustrated from photographs by J. B. Byles, *etc.* 1908. 8º. **07561**. k. **35**.

BYLES (Lilian S.) A Flower Alphabet for Children. [I verse.] pp. 31. *A. H. Stockwell: London*, [1925.] 8º. **011645**. f. **9**

BYLES (Marie Beuzeville) By Cargo Boat & Mountai The unconventional experiences of a woman on tran round the world, *etc.* [With plates, including portraits pp. 315. *Seeley, Service & Co.: London*, 1931. 8º. **010028**. ee. **2**

BYLES (Mather) *the Elder.* *See* Eaton (Arthur W. H The Famous Mather Byles, *etc.* [With portraits 1914. 8º. **4987**. bb.

—— Affection on Things Above. A discourse delivered the Thursday lecture in Boston, *etc.* pp. 20. iii. *J. Edwards & H. Foster: Boston*, 1740. 8º. **4486**. aa. **66**. (

—— The Character of the Perfect and Upright Man . . Boston . . . mdccxxix. [A reprint.] *See* New En land Sermons. Early New England Sermons, 172 1794, *etc.* [1939.] 4º. W.P. **1879**

—— A Discourse on the Present Vileness of the Body, and future glorious change by Christ . . . The second editi pp. 23. *T. & J. Fleet: Boston*, 1771. 8º. **4486**. bb.

—— An Elegy . . . on the Death of . . . the Honoura Daniel Oliver. pp. 4. *See* Prince (Thomas) *of Bost N.E.* The Faithful Servant Approv'd at Death, *etc.* 1732. 8º. **4985**. bb. **47**. (

—— A Poem on the Death of his late Majesty King Geo . . . and the accession of our present Sovereign K George ii. pp. v. [*Boston*, 1727.] 8º. **11686**. c.

—— Poems on Several Occasions . . . Reproduced from t edition of 1744. With an introduction by C. Lenn Carlson. pp. xxxvii. 104. *Columbia University Pres New York*, 1940. 8º. [*Facsimile Text Society. Publi tion.* no. 49.] Ac. **97**

—— The Prayer and Plea of David, to be delivered fr Blood-Guiltiness, improved in a sermon . . . before execution of a young negro servant, for poisoning infant. pp. 20. *Samuel Kneeland: Boston*, 1751. 8º **4487**. dd. **6**.

—— A Sermon on the Nature and Necessity of Convers . . . The third edition. pp. 15. *T. & J. Fl Boston*, 1771. 8º. **4486**. b.

—— The Vanity of Every Man at his Best Estate. funeral sermon on the Honorable William Dummer, pp. 24. 3. *Green & Russell: Boston*, 1761. 8º. **4486**. bb. **59**.

BYLES (Mather) *the Younger.* Divine Power and An displayed in Earthquakes. A sermon, *etc.* pp. 31. *S. Kneeland: Boston*, 1755. 8º. **4486**. b.

—— A Sermon, delivered March 6th 1760. Being a appointed . . . as a Public Thanksgiving, for the signal successes, granted to the British arms. pp. 22. *Timothy Green: New-London*, 1760. 8º. **4486**. a.

—— A Debate between the Rev. Mr. Byles, late Pastor of first Church in New-London, and the Brethren of t Church . . . By A. Z. Esq. [i.e. Benjamin Gal 1768. 8º. *See* Z., A., *Esq.* **4183**. aa.

BYLES (Maurice Barnard) *See* Byles (*Right Hon.* John B.) *One of the Justices of the Court of Common Pl* A Treatise on the Law of Bills of Exchange . . . eleventh edition . . . with notes from the fifth Ameri edition, by M. B. Byles, *etc.* 1874. 8º. **6375**. aaa

BYLES (MAURICE BARNARD)

—— 1874. 8º. **6375**. f. **1**.

—— 1876. 8º. **6375**. c. **36**.

—— 1879. 8º. **6375**. cc. **14**.

—— 1885. 8º. **6375**. c. **39**.

—— 1891. 8º. **6376**. h. **15**.

—— 1899. 8º. **6376**. pp. **21**.

BYLES (NATHANIEL) *See* CURTIS (William) *of Lynn Regis.* A Sketch for the Pillory, recommended to the perusal of . . . Squire Byles and Collier Matland his tool, *etc.* [With a letter addressed to him.] [1790 ?] 8º. **1414**. d. **76**. (**1**.)

—— *See* CURTIS (William) *of Lynn Regis.* Two Letters, addressed to Nathaniel Byles, and Collier Matland, Esqs; containing a complete refutation of a certain lying, and libellous production, lately obtruded upon the public, under the signature of the last of these respectable gentlemen. [1790.] 8º. **1414**. d. **76**. (**3**.)

BYLES (PHOEBE G.) *See* ASHBY (Arthur W.) and BYLES (P. G.) Rural Education, *etc.* 1923. 8º. **08311**. de. **77**.

BYLES (R. B.) The Card Index System: its principles, uses, operation, and component parts. pp. x. 99. *London,* [1911.] 8º. [*Pitman's Practical Primers of Business.*] **08226**. aaa. **1/8**.

BYLES (ROUSSEL DAVIDS) *See* BIBLE. [*English.*] St. Edmund's College Series of Scripture Handbooks. (The Second Epistle of Saint Paul to the Corinthians. With introduction and notes by R. D. Byles.) 1897, *etc.* 8º. **03127**. ee. **5/3**.

BYLES (W. DUNCAN) Blackheath, and the story of a sea ball, or sink hole. pp. 7. *W. A. Feurtado: Jamaica,* 1890. 8º. **12620**. dd. **21**. (**3**.)

—— The Ghost at John Crow House. A tale of Spanish Town, 60 years ago. pp. 12. *W. A. Feurtado: Kingston, Jamaica,* 1889. 8º. **12315.h.61.(5.)**

BYLES (WALTER JOHN BARNARD) *See* BYLES (*Right Hon. Sir* John B.) *One of the Justices of the Court of Common Pleas.* A Treatise on the Law of Bills of Exchange . . . The sixteenth edition by M. B. Byles . . . and W. J. B. Byles. 1899. 8º. **6376**. pp. **21**.

—— 1911. 8º. **6405**. v. **8**.

—— 1923. 8º. **6374**. t. **13**.

BYLES (WILLIAM) *See* BYLES (Frederick G.) William Byles. [With portraits and a genealogical table.] 1932. 8º. **010822**. e. **37**.

—— William Byles. [Appreciations, reprinted from the "Bradford Observer." With a portrait.] pp. 47. *For private circulation:* [*Bradford,* 1891.] 8º. **10803**. e. **17**. (**3**.)

BYLEVELD (FRANCISCUS PETRUS) Dissertatio historico-juridica, de Comite Leycestrio quondam Confoederatis Belgii Regionibus praefecto, *etc.* pp. 127. *Lugduni Batavorum,* 1819. 4º. **10816**. f. **18**.
One of an edition of twelve copies printed on large paper.

BYLEVELD (H. VAN)

—— Nederland in Frankrijk. De zuidergrens der Nederlanden. pp. 166. *Antwerpen,* 1941. 8º. **10169**. aaa. **31**.

BYLICA (MARCIN) *See* BIRKENMAJER (L. A.) Marcin Bylica z Olkusza oraz narzędzia astronomiczne, które zapisał Uniwersytetowi Jagiellońskiemu w roku 1493 . . . Rzecz, *etc.* 1893. 8º. [*Rozprawy Akademii Umiejętnosci. Wydział matematyczno-przyrodniczy.* ser. 2. tom 5. no. 1.] Ac. **750/14**.

—— Martini Biem de Ilkusz Poloni Nova calendarii romani reformatio. Opusculum ad requisitionem v-ti Concilii Lateranensis A.D. 1516 compositum . . . Nunc primum edidit Ludovicus Birkenmajer. pp. xv. 114. *Cracoviae,* 1918. 8º. [*Editionum Collegii ad historiam scientiarum mathem.-naturalium perscrutandam vol.* 1.] Ac. **750/111**.

BYLINA (MICHAŁ) List X. Michała Byliny . . . do X. Antoniego Kuryłowicza . . . pisany a . . . do druku podany. Roku panskiego 1787. (Odpis X. Antoniego Kuryłowicza . . . na list . . . M. Byliny . . . dany w . . . roku 1788.) [On the right of the Clergy of the Church of Rome in Poland to the tithes from land held by persons belonging to the Eastern Church.] 2 pt. *w Lublinie,* [1788.] 4º. **3926**. b. **3**.

BYLIN-ALTHIN (MARGIT)

—— The Sites of Ch'i Chia P'ing and Lo Han T'ang in Kansu. 1946. *See* STOCKHOLM.—*Östasiatiska Samlingarna.* Bulletin no. 18. 1929, *etc.* 8º. Ac. **5566**.

BYLL (KLAAS JANSE) Waaragtig verhaal van het voorgevallene binne Enkhuizen . . . in een briev van een scheepstimmerman in Enkhuizen aan zijn vriend in Amsterdam. pp. 7. [*Enkhuizen,* 1782.] 8º. **934**. e. **15**. (**1**.)

BYLL (THOMAS) A Godly Song, entituled, A farewell to the World, made by a Godly Christian, named Thomas Byll, being the Parish Clerke of West-Felton, as he lay upon his Death-bed, shewing the vanitie of the World, and his desire to be dissolved. (The Soules Petition at Heaven Gate.) 𝕭.𝕷. 2 pt. *For Henry Gossen: London,* [1630 ?] fol. **Rox.I.136,137.**

BYLLAARDT (LEONARDUS VAN DEN) Aan de leden van het Toneel-öeffenend Gezelschap, onder de zinspreuk: Tot Onderling Vermaak . . . by de intrede van 't jaar 1800. pp. 4. [*The Hague ?* 1800.] 8º. **11556**. g. **38**. (**3**.)

—— Aan de leden van het Tooneel-öeffenend Gezelschap, onder de spreuk: Tot Onderling Vermaak . . . by de intrede van 't jaar 1801, *etc.* pp. 2. [*The Hague,* 1801 ?] 8º. **11556**. g. **38**. (**4**.)

—— Aan de leden van het Tooneel-öeffenend Gezelschap, onder de spreuk: Tot Onderling Vermaak . . . by de intrede van 't jaar 1802, *etc.* pp. 3. [*The Hague ?* 1802.] 8º. **11556**. g. **38**. (**5**.)

BYLLYNGE (EDWARD) *See* BILLING.

BYLOFF (FRITZ) Hexenglaube und Hexenverfolgung in den österreichischen Alpenländern. pp. xi. 194. *Berlin & Leipzig,* 1934. 8º. **8633**. h. **22**.

—— Die Land- und peinliche Gerichtsordnung Erzherzog Karls II. für Steiermark vom 24. Dezember 1574; ihre Geschichte und ihre Quellen. pp. 111. *Graz,* 1907. 8º. [*Forschungen zur Verfassungs- und Verwaltungsgeschichte der Steiermark.* Bd. 6. Hft. 3.] Ac. **7197/2**.

—— Das Verbrechen der Zauberei—Crimen magiae. Ein Beitrag zur Geschichte der Strafspflege in Steiermark. pp. viii. 440. *Graz,* 1902. 8º. **6056**. f. **28**.

BYLOU (ANNA) Chronicum Genealogicum, eller: underwisning på någon gammal slächt, med åthskilliga tidahändelser; fordom sammanskrefne af Anna Fickes dotter Bylou . . . och widare af Herr Lars Siggesson . . . samt af . . . Erik Sparre . . . upptecknade. [Edited by Johan Peringskiöld.] pp. 20. 60. *Stockholm,* 1718. 4º. **137**. a. **26**. (**6**.)

BYLSKI (Leopold) Rzut oka na kwestyę polską w dobie obecnej. pp. 132. *Kraków*, 1910 [1909]. 8°. **8094**. i. **29**.

BYLUND (Erik)

—— Glommersträsk by i Arvidsjaurs socken. En näringsgeografisk studie. [With an English summary.] pp. xi. 118. *Uppsala*, 1947. 8°. [*Geographica*. no. 19.] Ac. **1077**. k.

BYLWERF (Gulielmus) Disputatio medica inauguralis de cancro, *etc*. pp. 14. *Lugduni Batavorum*, 1706. 4°. **1185**. h. **6**. (**27**.)

BYMAALSLAG. *See* Oslo.—*Norsk Samlag*.

BYMAN (Johannes) Råd och anvisningar beträffande hönsens skötsel . . . Med 9 figurer i texten. pp. 26. *Stockholm*, 1903. 8°. [*Studentföreningen Verdandis småskrifter*. 117.] **08282**. c. **1/117**.

BYMHOLT (B.) Geschiedenis der Arbeidersbeweging in Nederland. pp. 22. li. 736. *Amsterdam*, 1894 [1893, 94]. 8°. **08275**. m. **45**.

Published in parts.

BYNAEUS (Antonius) Antonii Bynæi De calceis Hebræorum libri duo. Cum tabulis æneis elegantissimis, & indicibus uberrimis. Accedit Somnium de laudibus critices. pp. 412. 38. *Ex officina viduæ Caspari, & T. Goris: Dordraci*, 1682. 12°. **848**. b. **1**.

—— [Another edition.] pp. 267. 24. *Ex officina T. Goris: Dordraci*, 1695. 4°. **222**. g. **18**.

—— De calceis Hebræorum libri ii. 1765. *See* Ugolinus (Blusius) Thesaurus antiquitatum sacrarum, *etc*. vol. 29. 1744, *etc*. fol. **686**. l. **9**.

—— Antonii Bynæi De morte Jesu Christi liber primus (—tertius). Commentarius amplissimus. 3 vol. *G. Borstius: Amstelædami*, 1691–98. 4°. **222**. h. **22–24**.

—— Antonii Bynæi De natali Jesu Christi libri duo. Accedit dissertatio de Jesu Christi circumcisione. pp. 582. 34. *G. Borstius: Amstelædami*, 1689. 4°. **221**. g. **5**.

—— Antonii Bynæi Somnium, *etc* .pp. 21. *G. à Poolsum: Trajecti ad Rhenum*, 1675. 4°. **536**. f. **7**. (**11**.)

BYNE, *Family of*.

—— *See* Renshaw (Walter C.) Searches into the History of the Family of Byne or Bine of Sussex. 1913. fol. **9906**. w. **31**.

BYNE (Arthur) *See* Stapley, afterwards Byne (M.) and Byne (A.) Spanish Gardens and Patios, *etc*. 1924. 4°. **7030**. s. **17**.

BYNE (Arthur) and **STAPLEY**, afterwards **BYNE** (Mildred)

—— Decorated Wooden Ceilings in Spain. A collection of photographs and measured drawings, with descriptive text. pp. x. 222. [1920.] fol. *See* New York.—*Hispanic Society of America*. L.R. **262**. d. **12**.

—— Decorated Wooden Ceilings in Spain. [With plates.] pp. xii. 112. *New York & London*, 1920. 8°. [*Hispanic Notes & Monographs*.] Ac. **9729/9**. (**6**.)

—— Provincial Houses in Spain. pp. x. pl. 190. *William Helburn: New York*, 1925. fol. Cup. **1247**. f. **7**.

—— Rejería of the Spanish Renaissance. A collection of photographs and measured drawings, with descriptive text. pp. vii. 101. pl. xxvi. 1914. fol. *See* New York. —*Hispanic Society of America*. **1757**. c. **1**.

BYNE (Arthur) and **STAPLEY**, afterwards **BYI** (Mildred)

—— Spanish Architecture of the Sixteenth Century, pp. xxii. 436. pl. lxxx. 1917. 4°. *See* New York *Hispanic Society of America*. **07815**. i.

—— Spanish Interiors and Furniture, *etc*. (Second printi 2 vol. pp. ix. pl. 300. *William Helburn: New Y* 1928. fol. L.R. **294**. b.

—— Spanish Ironwork . . . With one hundred and fi eight illustrations. pp. xxiii. 143. 1915. 8°. New York.—*Hispanic Society of America*. **07808**. g.

BYNE (Magnus) The Scornfull Quakers answered, their Railing Reply refuted. pp. 123. *Willi Bentley for Andrew Crook: London*, 1656. 4°. **105**. c.

—— *See* Lawson (Thomas) *Quaker, of Lancashire*. Lip of Truth Opened . . . A few words agains book, written by M. Bine . . . which he calls, Scornful Quakers answered, *etc*. 1656. 4°. E. **889**.

BYNE (Mildred Stapley) *See* Stapley, afterwa Byne (M.)

BYNG (Alice Harriet Frederica) *Countess of Straff See* Bible.—*New Testament*.—*Selections*. [*Engl* Selection of Texts from the Tauchnitz Edition of New Testament . . . Compiled and arranged by Countess of Strafford, *etc*. 1912. 4°. **03127**. h.

—— *See* Gower (*Lord* Francis Leveson) afterwards Eger (F.) *Earl of Ellesmere*. Personal Reminiscences of the D of Wellington . . . Edited, with a memoir of Lord Ellesm by his daughter Alice, Countess of Strafford, *etc*. 1903. 8°. **010817**. ee.

—— *See* Greville (Henry W.) Leaves from the Diar Henry Greville. Edited by the Viscountess Enfield. 1883, *etc*. 8°. **2406**. c

—— Blameless Knights; or, Lutzen and La Vendée. pp. *Hatchards: London*, 1876. 8°. **9073**. de

—— The Dayrells. A domestic story. pp. 286. *F. Warne & Co.: London*, 1866. 8°. **12806**. ee.

—— Evening Thoughts on Holy Writ. A series of sl lay sermons for use in private households, *etc*. pp. xii. *Skeffington & Son: London*, 1897. 8°. **4477**. eee

BYNG (Andrew) For editions of the Authorised Ver of the Bible, of which A. Byng was one of the translato *See* Bible. [*English*. 1611, *etc*.]

BYNG (Arthur H.) *See* Wilkins (John) *of Stanst Essex*. The Autobiography of an English Gameke . . . Edited by A. H. Byng and S. M. Stephens, 1892. 8°. **07905**. h.

BYNG (Douglas) Byng Ballads . . . Decorated in co and line by Clarke Hutton. *John Lane: Lon* [1932.] 8°. **11644**. l.

—— More Byng Ballads . . . Decorated by Clarke Hutt *John Lane: London*, 1935. 8°. **11654**. c.

BYNG (Edward Stanley) Communications and Manufacturer . . . A lecture, *etc*. [With plates.] pp. *Eyre & Spottiswoode: London*, 1934. 4°. [*Post O Green Papers*. no. 4.] B.S. **31**

BYNG (Edward Stanley) and **ROBINSON** (Geo Allen)

—— Education in Industrial Management. pp. 28. *Loughborough*, [1937.] 8°. [*Association of Techn Institutions. Miscellaneous pamphlets*.]

W.P.4362/11.(

BYNG (Eleanor) *Viscountess Torrington.* "Over the Garden Wall." A story of racing and romance. pp. 288. *Hutchinson & Co.: London,* [1924.] 8°. **NN. 9565.**

BYNG (Emily Georgina) *Countess of Strafford.* Friends and Foes at the Cross of Jesus. A service of song . . . for use on Good Friday, *etc.* pp. xviii. 96. *Skeffington & Son: London,* 1893. 8°. **3406.** cc. **49.**

BYNG (Florence) '93, or, the Revolution amongst the flowers, *etc.* pp. 59. *T. Fisher Unwin: London,* 1892. 4°. **12803.** g. **39.**

BYNG (*Hon. Mrs.* Francis) *See* Byng (Emily Georgina) *Countess of Strafford.*

BYNG (Francis Edmund Cecil) *Earl of Strafford.* Friends and Foes of Jesus Christ, and other sermons. pp. viii. 271. *Skeffington & Son: London,* 1881. 8°. **4466.** ee. **2.**

—— A Funeral Sermon. Sermon preached in Little Casterton Church . . . on the death of a parishioner. pp. 13. *Langley: Stamford,* 1860. 8°. **900.** g. **28.** (**8.**)

—— "Multis ille bonis flebilis occidit." A sermon preached . . . on the occasion of the funeral of his late R.H. the Prince Consort, *etc.* pp. 13. *Langley: Stamford,* 1862. 8°. **900.** g. **28.** (**9.**)

—— The Seasons of the Year, and of our Lives, considered in four sermons, *etc.* pp. 53. *W. Skeffington: London,* 1873. 16°. **4402.** bb. **32.**

—— The Sorrow of Sin. Ten sermons, *etc.* pp. 159. *William Skeffington: London,* 1870. 8°. **4462.** cc. **7.**

—— Waiting. [A sermon.] *See* Message. The Fourfold Message of Advent. 1870. 8°. **4463.** aa. **29.**

BYNG (*Hon.* Frederick) On Improving the Dwellings of the Poor. *See* Talbot (Charles J. C.) *19th Earl of Shrewsbury.* Meliora: or, Better times to come, *etc.* 1852. 8°. **8275.** a. **55.**

—— Smithfield and Newgate Markets. pp. 26. *James Ridgway: London,* 1851. 8°. **8425.** e. **3.**

—— *See* Challis (Thomas M.) Smithfield and Newgate Markets, as they should and might be. An answer to the Hon. F. Byng. 1851. 8°. **8776.** b. **26.**

BYNG (G.) *Manufacturer.*

—— Protection. The views of a manufacturer. pp. xi. 255. *Eyre & Spottiswoode: London,* 1901. 8°. **08226.** h. **53.**

BYNG (George) *M.P. for Middlesex.* *See* Middlesex.—*Freeholders.* The Whole Proceedings, and Resolutions of the Freeholders of the County of Middlesex. Also a . . . debate on the parliamentary conduct of Mr. Byng and Mr. Mainwaring, the present representatives of the county, *etc.* 1800. 8°. **1102.** i. **75.**

BYNG (George) *1st Viscount Torrington.* *See* Eelbeck (H.) Epinicion Anglicanum ad illum magnanimum ac equitem illustrissimum D. Georgium Bingium, arrogantium de clade Hispanorum, cui munus classis præfecti . . . delatum erat. [1719 ?] 8°. **1213.** m. **16.** (**2.**)

—— The Byng Papers. Selected from the letters and papers of Admiral Sir George Byng, First Viscount Torrington and of his son Admiral the Hon. John Byng, and edited by Brian Tunstall. [*London,*] 1930– . 8°. [*Publications of the Navy Records Society.* vol. 67, 68, 70, *etc.*] Ac. **8109.**

—— An Account of the Expedition of the British Fleet to Sicily, in the years 1718, 1719 and 1720, under the command of Sir G. Byng . . . Collected from the Admiral's manuscripts, *etc.* [The dedication signed: T.C., i.e. Thomas Corbett.] 1739. 8°. *See* C., T. **593.** c. **20.**

BYNG (George) *1st Viscount Torrington.*

—— [Another edition.] A True Account, *etc.* pp. 118. *Printed and sold by the Booksellers: London,* 1739. 8°. **806.** a. **9.**

—— Memoirs relating to the Lord Torrington. Edited by John Knox Laughton. pp. xii. 203. *London,* 1889. 4°. [*Publications of the Camden Society.* N.S. no. 46.] Ac. **8113/132.**

—— Sir George Byng's Garland, containing I. Sir George Byng's Fight with the Spaniards. II. An Alarm for War. pp. 8. *W. W.* [*William Wood*]: *Lincoln,* [1750 ?] 12°. **11621.** b. **5.** (**17.**)

BYNG (George) *7th Viscount Torrington.* *See* Henderson (John M.) The History of the Rebellion in Ceylon, during Lord Torrington's government, *etc.* 1868. 16°. **9056.** bb. **20.**

—— On Farm Buildings; with a few observations on the state of agriculture in the County of Kent. (Appendix. Specification for building a farmstead, *etc.*) pp. 111. pl. 3. *Ridgway: London,* 1845. 8°. **1252.** c. **53.**

—— Speech . . . on the affairs of Ceylon, in the House of Lords, April 1, 1851. With an appendix, *etc.* pp. 42. *G. Woodfall & Son: London,* 1851. 8°. **8022.** e. **1.** (**2.**)

BYNG (Hugh Edward Cranmer) *See* Yang (Chu) Yang Chu's Garden of Pleasure . . . With an introduction by H. Cranmer-Byng. 1912. 8°. **14003.** a. **41.**

—— Dialect & Songs of Essex. pp. 34. *Denham & Co.: Colchester,* 1934. 8°. **010360.** a. **104.**

—— The Diddycoy. An Essex comedy in three acts, *etc.* *See* Essex.—*Essex Play Society.* Essex Plays. vol. 1. [1933, *etc.*] 8°. W.P. **10388/1.**

—— The Magic Mawkin, and other Essex tales. pp. 66. *Benham & Co.: Colchester,* [1935.] 8°. **12626.** r. **16.**

—— Old Cottage Tales, *etc.* [1933.] *See* Essex.—*Essex Play Society.* Essex Plays. vol. 2. [1933, *etc.*] 8°. W.P. **10388/2.**

—— The Old-Time Essex Speech and Humour. Two papers on Essex dialect, its ancestry and interest . . . Reprinted from the Herts and Essex Observer and the Essex County Standard. pp. 23. *Benham & Co.: Colchester,* [1933.] 8°. **12984.** aa. **77.**

—— The Queen's Ring, and Annie the Come b' Chance. pp. 69. *Benham & Co.: Colchester,* [1937.] 8°. [*Essex Plays.* vol. 3.] W.P. **10388/3.**

BYNG (**Hugh Edward Cranmer**) **and BYNG** (**Lancelot Alfred Cranmer**)

—— A Romance of the Fair, and other stories. pp. 114. *Roxburghe Press: London,* [1897.] 8°. **012625.** ee. **22.**

BYNG (John) *Viscount Torrington.* The Torrington Diaries, containing the tours through England and Wales of the Hon. John Byng, later fifth Viscount Torrington, between the years 1781 and 1794. Edited, with an introduction, by C. Bruyn Andrews, *etc.* [With plates, including a portrait.] 4 vol. *Eyre & Spottiswoode: London,* 1934–38. 8°. **10353.** b. **19.**

—— The Torrington Diaries . . . Edited, with an introduction, by C. Bruyn Andrews and abridged into one volume by Fanny Andrews, *etc.* pp. vii. 528. *Eyre & Spottiswoode: London,* 1954. 8°. **10892.** c. **16.**

BYNG (JOHN) *Viscount Torrington.*

—— Clouds & Sunshine by an English Tourist of the Eighteenth Century. Part I of the tour of 1789 from the Torrington diaries by the Hon. John Byng, 1743–1813. Edited by Cyril Bruyn Andrews. [With plates.] pp. 53. *R. P. Smith: Marlow,* [1934.] 8°. **010352. bbb. 24.**

BYNG (*Hon.* JOHN) *See* ACCOUNT. A Full and Particular Account of a . . . Dreadful . . . Apparition [i.e. Admiral Byng's ghost] which appeared to a certain Great Man, *etc.* [1757 ?] *s. sh.* fol. **C.113.hh.3.(25.)**

—— *See* A - - - - - - Y, *L - - - ds of the.* A Letter to the Right Honourable the L - - - ds of the A - - - - - - y [i.e. the Lords of the Admiralty, by the Hon. Sarah Osborn, on behalf of Admiral Byng]. [1757.] *s. sh.* fol. **C.113.hh.3.(14.)**

—— *See* B - - - -, *A - - - - - l.* A Dialogue between the Ghost of A - - - - - l B - - - - [Admiral Byng], and the substance of a G - - - - l [Lord George Sackville], *etc.* [1759 ?] 8°. **905. d. 8. (1.)**

—— *See* B——, *A——l.* A Real Defence of A——l B——'s [Admiral Byng's] conduct. By a Lover of Truth and a Friend to Society. [A satire.] 1756. 8°. **1414.d.83.(5.)**

—— *See* BARCLAY (Isaac) Some Friendly and Seasonable Advice to Mr. Admiral Byng [upon his approaching trial by court martial]. [1756.] *s. sh.* fol. **515. l. 6. (31.)**

—— *See* BERTIE (*Lord* Robert) *General.* A Letter to Lord Robert Bertie, relating to his conduct in the Mediterranean, and his defence of Admiral Byng. 1757. 8°. **518. g. 19. (7.)**

—— *See* B — G. A Late Epistle to Mr C - - - - - - - - - d [i.e. John Cleveland]. [A lampoon in verse on Admiral Byng.] [1756.] *s. sh.* fol. **1865. c. 4. (153.)**

—— *See* B——G, *Admiral.* Admiral B - - g's Answer to the Friendly Advice, or the Fox out of the pit and the geese in. [1756.] *s. sh.* fol. **1881. c. 3. (91.)**

—— *See* B——G, *Admiral.* Admiral B - - - - g in Horrors at the Appearance of the Unhappy Souls, who was killed in the engagement crying for revenge. [In verse. With a woodcut.] [1756.] *s. sh.* fol. **T. 1070. (1.)**

—— *See* B——G, *Admiral.* A Narrative of the Proceedings of Admiral B - - - g and of his conduct off Mahon the 20th of May. By an Officer of the Squadron. [1756.] 8°. **T. 1054. (8.)**

—— *See* B——G, *Admiral.* A Rueful Story, or Britain in tears, being the conduct of Admiral B——g in the late engagement off Mahone with a French fleet the 20. of May 1756. [1756.] 8°. **T. 1070. (1*.)**

—— *See* B——G, *A——l.* The State of Minorca, and its Lost Condition when A - - - - - l B - - g appeared off that island. [1757.] 8°. **8132. a. 7.**

—— *See* BUNG (   ) *Admiral.* The New Art of War at Sea, *etc.* [A satire on Admiral Byng.] [1756.] *s. sh.* 4°. **1852. d. 1. (9.)**

—— *See* CHARLES I., *King of Great Britain and Ireland.* [*Appendix.*] Charles premier, roi d'Angleterre, condamné à mort par la nation angloise. Et Bing, amiral anglois, fusillé par ordre de la même nation. Entretiens de leurs ombres aux Champs Élisées. 1757. 12°. **8133. a. 20.**

—— *See* C——LL, *Captain.* Queries addressed to Captain C——ll [i.e. F. Cornwall, with reference to his evidence before the court martial for the trial of Admiral Byng]. [1757.] *s. sh.* fol. **228. e. 35. (12.)**

BYNG (*Hon.* JOHN)

—— *See* ENGLAND.—*Parliament.—House of Lords.* [*Pr ceedings.*—II.] The Proceedings [1 and 2 Mar. 1757] of t . . . Lords . . . upon the Bill, intituled, An Act to relea from the obligation of the oath of secrecy, the members the court-martial appointed for the tryal of Admir J. Byng, *etc.* 1757. fol. **C.113.hh.3.(18.**

—— *See* ENGLAND.—*Admiralty.* [*Appendix.*] Letter to t Lords of the Admiralty [from the Hon. Sarah Osborn on behalf of her brother, Admiral Byng]. 1757. *s. sh.* f **228. e. 35. (1**

—— *See* FORBES (*Hon.* John) Admiral Forbes's Reaso for not signing Admiral Byng's Dead Warrant. 1757. *s. sh.* fol. **228. e. 35. (1**

—— *See* GIBRALTAR. Some Queries on the Minutes of t Council of War held at Gibraltar the fourth of May las from which good reasons may be drawn, for a nob colonel's [Lord Robert Bertie's] having taken so large part in the defence of Admiral B——g. 1757. 8°. **518. g. 19. (**

—— —— 1757. 8°. **228. e. 35. (**

—— *See* LONDON.—III. *Tower of London.* More Birds for t Tower, *etc.* [A ballad on the conduct of the Duke Newcastle in relation to Admiral Byng.] [1756 ?] *s. sh.* fol. **C.113.hh.3.(6.**

—— *See* M——D——N. The Sham Fight . . . as it w acted . . . in the M——d——n, *etc.* [A satire Admiral Byng.] 1756. 8°. **1346. f. 4**

—— *See* MEDITERRANEAN SEA. A Serious Apology a Modest Remarks on the Conduct of a certain Admi [i.e. Admiral Byng] in the Mediterranean, *etc.* 1756. 4°. **G. 14482. (**

—— *See* MEDITERRANEAN SEA. A Modest Apology for t Conduct of a certain Admiral [i.e. Admiral Byng] in t Mediterranean, *etc.* [Based on the "Serious Apology." 1756. 8°. **1202. g.**

—— *See* MINORCA. The Block and Yard Arm. A ne ballad, *etc.* [Against Admiral Byng.] [1756.] *s. sh.* fo **1876. f. 1. (15**

—— *See* OSBORN (*Hon.* Sarah) The Honourable M Osborne's Letter to the Lords of the Admiralty. [C behalf of Admiral Byng.] [1757.] *s. sh.* fol. **C.113.hh.3.(27.**

—— *See* PITT (William) *Earl of Chatham.* A Letter to t Right Hon. William Pitt, Esq; being an impart vindication of the conduct of the Ministry . . . in answ to the aspersions cast upon them by Admiral Byng a his advocates. 1756. 8°. **228. e. 34. (**

—— *See* RAY. A Ray of Truth darting thro' the thick clou of falshood, *etc.* [A pamphlet in favour of Admi J. Byng.] [1756.] fol. **1884.b.25.(44**

—— *See* RESIGNATION. The Resignation: or, the Fox o of the pit and the geese in, with B - - - - g [i.e. Admi Byng] at the bottom. 1756. 8°. **1103. g.**

—— *See* SMITH (Thomas) *Admiral.* A Letter to Admi Smith, president of the court martial, for the tryal of t hon. J. Byng, *etc.* 1757. 8°. **228. e. 35. (1**

—— *See* TEMPORA. Oh! Tempora. Oh! Mores, *etc.* lampoon in verse on Admiral Byng.] 1756. *s. sh.* fol. **1865. c. 4. (15**

BYNG (*Hon.* JOHN)

—— *See* TRITON. To the People of England. [An address on behalf of Admiral Byng.] [1757.] *s. sh.* fol. **C.113.hh.3.(13.)**

—— *See* TUNSTALL (William C. B.) Admiral Byng and the Loss of Minorca. [With portraits.] 1928. 8°. **010815. g. 22.**

—— *See* W——E, C——. Some Reasons for believing sundry Letters and Papers ascribed in three late publications to Admiral Byng [i.e. " An Appeal to the People," " A Letter to a Member of Parliament," and " Some Further Particulars in relation to Admiral Byng "], not only spurious, but also an insidious attempt to prejudice the Admiral's character, *etc.* [1756.] 8°. **228. e. 34. (6.)**

—— The Byng Papers. Selected from the letters and papers of Admiral Sir George Byng . . . and of his son Admiral the Hon. John Byng and edited by Brian Tunstall. [With portraits and maps.] 1930– . 8°. [*Publications of the Navy Records Society.* vol. 67, 68, 70, *etc.*] *See* BYNG (George) 1*st Viscount Torrington.* **Ac. 8109.**

—— Admiral Byng's Defence, as presented by him, and read in the Court January 18, 1757 . . . containing a very particular account of the action on the 20th of May, 1756, off Cape Mola, *etc.* [With an appendix of letters.] 2 pt. *J. Lacy: London,* 1757. 8°. **1132. c. 47. (1.)**

—— [Another copy of pt. 1.] **518. g. 19. (3*.)**

—— [Another copy of pt. 1.] **E. 2214. (6.)**

—— An Appeal to the People: containing, the genuine and entire letter of Admiral Byng to the Secr. of the Ad——y . . . Part the first. (Part the second. On the different deserts and fate of Admiral Byng and his enemies, *etc.*) 2 pt. *J. Morgan: London,* 1756, 57. 8°. **228. e. 34. (2, 3.)**

—— [Another copy of pt. 1.] **518. g. 19. (2.)**

—— [Another copy of pt. 1.] **T. 1053. (9.)**

—— [Another copy of pt. 1.] **E. 2213. (5.)**

—— [Another copy of pt. 1.] **E. 2215. (4.)**

—— An Exact Copy of a Remarkable Letter from Admiral Byng to the Right Hon. W—— P——, Esq; dated March 12, 1757, two days before his execution. pp. 22. *J. Reason: London,* 1757. 8°. **T. 1688. (5.)**

—— [Another copy.] **518. g. 19. (8.)**

—— [Another copy.] **228. e. 35. (14.)**

—— A Further Address to the Publick. Containing genuine copies of all the letters which passed between A——l B——g and the S——ry of the A——ty [i.e. the Secretary of the Admiralty, John Cleveland]; from the time of his suspension, to the twenty-fifth of October last. With proper remarks and reflections on the unprecedented treatment he has met with since his confinement. 2 pt. 1757. 8°. *See* B——G, *A——l.* **518. g. 19. (10.)**

—— [Another copy.] **E. 2048. (7.)**

—— [Another copy.] **228. e. 35. (3.)**

—— [Another copy.] **G. 14828. (3.)**

—— The Original Paper delivered by Admiral Byng to the Marshal just before his execution, *etc.* [*London?* 1757.] *s. sh.* fol. **C.113.hh.3.(22.)**

—— Admiral Byng's Complaint. [A ballad, beginning: " Come all you true Britons and listen to me."] [*London,* 1756?] *s. sh.* fol. **C.113.hh.3.(8.)**

BYNG (*Hon.* JOHN)

—— [Another edition.] All is out - - - or, Admiral Byng. [*London,* 1756?] *s. sh.* fol. **C.113.hh.3.(9.)**

—— Boh Peep-Peep Boh, or A——l Bing's apology to the Fribbles. A new ballad. [*London,* 1756?] *s. sh.* fol. **C.113.hh.3.(7.)**

—— Bungiana, or an Assemblage of What-d'ye-call-em's, in prose and verse, that have . . . appeared relative to the conduct of a certain naval commander [i.e. Admiral Byng], now first collected in order to perpetuate the memory of his wonderful atchievements. pp. 44. *J. Doughty: London,* 1756. 8°. **6875. aa. 38.**

—— Byng return'd; or, the Council of expedients. [A satirical print, with verses.] [1756?] *s. sh. obl.* fol. **C.121.g.9.(213.)**

—— A Candid Examination of the Resolutions and Sentence of the Court-Martial on the Trial of Admiral Byng . . . In a letter to the gentlemen of the Navy. By an Old Sea Officer. pp. 38. *J. Cooke: London,* 1757. 8°. **518. g. 19. (4.)**

—— [Another copy.] **E. 2214. (1.)**

—— [Another copy.] **E. 2215. (3.)**

—— [Another copy.] **228. e. 35. (9.)**

—— The Case of the Hon. Admiral Byng, ingenuously represented . . . Likewise his letter to the Secretary of the Admiralty . . . also two letters from M. Voltaire & the Marshal Duke de Richlieu to Mr. Byng. With an account of his execution . . . Also an elegy on his death, *etc.* pp. 63. *H. Owen: London,* 1757. 8°. **228. e. 35. (1.)** *Imperfect; wanting the portrait.*

—— A Collection of several Pamphlets, very little known, some suppressed letters, and sundry detached pieces . . . relative to the case of Admiral Byng. pp. 125. *T. Lacy: London,* 1756. 8°. **T. 1053. (8.)**

—— [Another copy.] **228. e. 34. (4.)**

—— Essential Queries relating to the Condemnation and Execution of Admiral Byng. [*London?* 1757.] *s. sh.* fol. **C.113.hh.3.(19.)**

—— Impartial Reflections on the Case of Mr. Byng, as stated in an Appeal to the People, etc. and a Letter to a Member of Parliament, etc. pp. 47. *S. Hooper: London,* 1756. 8°. **228. e. 34. (7.)**

—— A Key to the Trial of Admiral Byng: or, a Brief state of facts relating to the action in the Mediterranean on the 20th of May, 1756, *etc.* *London,* [1756.] fol. **C.113.hh.3.(17.)**

—— A Letter to a Gentleman in the Country, from his friend in London: giving an authentick and circumstantial account of the confinement, behaviour, and death of Admiral Byng, as attested by the gentlemen who were present. pp. 48. *J. Lacy: London,* 1757. 8°. **518. g. 19. (11.)**

—— [Another copy.] **E. 2048. (9.)**

—— [Another copy.] **E. 2213. (7.)**

—— [Another copy.] **228. e. 35. (16.)**

—— A Letter to a Member of Parliament in the Country, from his friend in London, relative to the case of Admiral Byng: with some original papers and letters which passed during the expedition. pp. 31. *J. Cooke: London,* 1756. 8°. **518. g. 19. (6.)**

BYNG (*Hon.* JOHN)

—— [Another copy.] E. 2213. (6.)

—— [Another copy.] E. 2215. (2*.)

—— [Another copy.] 228. e. 34. (1.)

—— Observations on the Twelfth Article of War: wherein the nature of negligence, cowardice, and disaffection, is discussed . . . and the difference between error of judgment and negligence clearly stated . . . and exemplified in the case of the late Admiral Byng . . . In a letter to the President of the late Court Martial. By a Plain Man [i.e. David Mallet]. pp. 83. *W. Owen: London*, 1757. 8°. 228. e. 35. (6.)

—— Past Twelve o'Clock, or Byng's ghost. [In verse. A satire on the Duke of Newcastle.] [*London*, 1757.] *s. sh.* fol. 1876. f. 1. (165.)

—— [Another copy.] C.113.hh.3.(23.)

—— The Portsmouth Grand Humbug: or, a Merry dialogue between a Boatswain and his mate on board the Monarch, relating to Admiral Byng, *etc.* [*London?* 1757.] *s. sh.* fol. C.113.hh.3.(30.)

—— The Shooting of Admiral Byng, on board the Monarque, March 14, 1757. [An engraved plate, with descriptive letterpress and "a copy of a paper delivered by the Hon. Admiral Byng, to W. Brough, Esq., Marshal . . . before his death,"] [*London?* 1757.] *obl.* fol. C.113.hh.3.(21.)

—— Some Further Particulars in relation to the Case of Admiral Byng. From original papers, &c. . . . By a Gentleman of Oxford. pp. 70. *J. Lacy: London*, 1756. 8°. 518. g. 19. (5.)

—— [Another copy.] E. 2215. (5.)

—— [Another copy.] 228. e. 34. (5.)

—— The Sorrowful Lamentation and Last Farewell to the World of Admiral Byng. [A ballad.] [*London*, 1757.] *s. sh.* fol. 1876. f. 1. (164.)

—— The Speech of the Hon[ble] Admiral Byng, intended to have been spoken on board the Monarque at the time of his execution, *etc.* pp. 6. *T. Lindsey: London*, [1757.] fol. C.113.hh.3.(20.)

—— Testament politique de l'amiral Byng, traduit de l'anglois. pp. 259. *Portsmouth* [*Paris?*], 1759. 12°. 8133. a. 13.

—— Testament politique de l'amiral Byng, traduit de l'anglois. pp. 259. *Portsmouth* [*Paris?*], 1759. 12°. M.L. n. 1/32. (26.)

—— Testamento político del Almirante Bing: en el que se manifiestan las maxîmas del partido Realista para sojuzgar al Pueblo Inglés . . . Traducido del francés por Don Antonio Rato. pp. 272. *Valencia*, 1780. 8°. 8133. b. 24.

—— To the worthy Merchants and Citizens of London. [Urging the execution of sentence on Admiral Byng.] [*London*, 1757.] *s. sh.* fol. 515. l. 6. (32.)

—— The Trial of the Honble Admiral Byng, at a Court-Martial held . . . for an enquiry into his conduct, while he commanded in the Mediterranean. Together with his defence; likewise an appendix containing all the papers read in court, and several others, *etc.* [Reported by Thomas Cook.] [With a portrait.] pp. v. 479. 45. 71. *J. Lacy: London*, 1757. 8°. 228. e. 36.

—— [Another copy.] 518. g. 18.
Imperfect; wanting the portrait.

—— [Another copy of pp. v. 1–320.] 518. e. 21. (8.)

BYNG (*Hon.* JOHN)

—— [Five charts illustrating the engagement on the 20 May, 1756.] Publish'd . . . 1757, for Adm[l] Byng Trial in two vol[s] octavo. [*London*, 1757.] fol. C.113.hh.3.(3.

—— The Trial of the Honourable John Byng, at a Cou Martial, as taken by Mr. Charles Fearne . . . To whi are added, a copy of their Lordships memorial to t King, in relation to the sentence passed upon Admi Byng [and other documents], *etc.* pp. 130. 19. *R. Manb London*, 1757. fol. 515. l. 6. (3

—— [Another copy.] C.113.hh.3.(2
In this copy are inserted two engraved portraits of Admi Byng, and a plate representing his execution; a portrait Admiral Lord Torrington; a MS. note by General Sir Byng and an engraving of Womersley Hall. P. 3 of t copy differs slightly from that of the preceding.

—— [Another edition.] pp. 308. 84. *J. Hoey, et Dublin*, 1757. 8°. 6875. c.

—— The Trial of Vice-Admiral Byng . . . Together with Admirals defence, taken down in short-hand. [abridgment.] pp. 48. *J. Reason: London*, 1757. 8°. 518. g. 19. (

—— Zuverlässige Lebens-Geschichte des grosbritannisch Admirals . . . Johan Byng, *etc.* pp. 156. *Frankf & Leipzig*, 1757. 8°. 10816. aa.

BYNG (JOHN LAUNCELOT CRANMER)

—— *See* BYNG (Pattee) *Viscount Torrington.* Pattee Byn Journal, 1718–1720. Edited by J. L. Cranmer-Byng. 1950. 8°. [*Publications of the Navy Records Soci* no. 88.] Ac. 81

—— *See* EAST. The Wisdom of the East. (The Wisdom the East Series.—Edited by L. Cranmer-Byng, S. Kapodia; Alan W. Watts; J. L. Cranmer-Byng.) 1904, *etc.* 8°. 14003. a. 1,

BYNG (JULIAN HEDWORTH GEORGE) *Viscount Byng of Vi* *See* VINCENT (*Sir* Charles E. H.) *K.C.M.G.* Vincen Police Code . . . Revised by the Commissioner of Pol of the Metropolis [i.e. Viscount Byng of Vimy]. 1931. 06055. de.

BYNG (*Hon. Mrs.* JULIAN HEDWORTH GEORGE) *See* BY (Marie E.) *Viscountess Byng of Vimy.*

BYNG (LANCELOT ALFRED CRANMER) *See* BYNG (Hugh E. and BYNG (L. A. C.) A Romance of the Fair, *etc.* [1897.] 8°. 012625. ee.

—— *See* EAST. The Wisdom of the East. (Edited by Cranmer-Byng, S. A. Kapadia.) 1904, *etc.* 8°. 14003. a. 1,

—— *See* ḤĀFIẒ, *Shīrāzī.* The Rubáiyát of Háfiz. Transla with introduction by Syed Abdul Majid . . . Rende into English verse by L. Cranmer-Byng. 1910. 8°. 14003. a.

—— *See* ḤAMMO, *Sidi.* The Songs of Sidi Hammo . . . verse renderings by L. Cranmer Byng. 1907. 8°. 14599. h.

—— *See* HUI LI The Life of Hiuen-Tsiang . . . With preface by L. Cranmer-Byng. 1911. 8°. 2318. f.

—— *See* MERLIN. Selections from the Prose Merlin. Edi by L. Cranmer-Byng. 1930. 8°. W.P. 933

—— *See* NIẒĀMĪ, *Ganjavī.* Lailí and Majnún. From Persian of Nizami, by James Atkinson. Re-edited, w an introduction, by L. Cranmer Byng. 1905. 8°. 757. bb.

BYNG (LANCELOT ALFRED CRANMER)

—— *See* SA'DĪ. [*Gulistān.—English.*] The Rose-Garden of Sa'di. Selected and rendered, with introduction, by L. Cranmer-Byng. 1905. 8°. **14003**. a. **9**.

—— *See* SHIH CHING. The Odes of Confucius. Rendered by L. Cranmer-Byng. 1904. 8°. **14003**. a. **1**.

—— [Poems.] *See* SEXTET. A Sextet of Singers, *etc.* [1896.] *obl.* 8°. **11652**. de. **80**.

—— Daisies of the Dawn. [Poems.] pp. 108. *Roxburghe Press: London; T. B. Banks & Co.: Guernsey,* [1896.] 8°. **011652**. l. **58**.

—— An English Rose. [Poems.] pp. 48. *Elkin Matthews: London,* 1906. 8°. **011651**. g. **75**.

—— A Feast of Lanterns. [An anthology of Chinese poems.] Rendered with an introduction by L. Cranmer-Byng. pp. 95. *John Murray: London,* 1916. 8°. [*Wisdom of the East Series.*] **14003**. a. **54**.

—— A Lute of Jade; being selections from the classical poets of China, rendered with an introduction by L. Cranmer-Byng. pp. 116. *John Murray: London,* 1909. 8°. [*Wisdom of the East Series.*] **14003**. a. **29**.

—— The Never-Ending Wrong, and other renderings of the Chinese from the prose translations of Professor Herbert A. Giles, *etc.* (English Poems.) pp. 131. *Grant Richards: London,* 1902. 8°. **011651**. eee. **101**.

—— Poems of Paganism; or, Songs of life and love. By "Paganus"—L. Cranmer-Byng. pp. 112. *Roxburghe Press: London,* 1895. 8°. **011652**. f. **66**.

—— [Another copy.] **011652**. f. **89**.

—— Romance of the East Series. Edited by L. Cranmer-Byng. 3 vol. *John Murray: London,* 1909. 8°. **14005**. d. **1–3**.

—— Salma. A play in three acts. pp. xiii. 110. *John Murray: London,* 1923. 8°. **011779**. h. **8**.

—— Tomorrow's Star. An essay on the shattering and remoulding of a world. pp. 179. *Golden Cockerel Press:* [*London,*] 1938. 8°. **Cup.510.af.12.**

—— The Vision of Asia. An interpretation of Chinese art and culture. pp. xi. 306. *John Murray: London,* 1932. 8°. **07805**. bb. **26**.

—— The Vision of Asia, *etc.* pp. xvi. 306. *John Murray: London,* 1939. 8°. **07804**. c. **15**.

—— The Vision of Asia, *etc.* pp. ix. 306. *John Murray: London,* 1947. 8°. **7802**. aa. **32**.

—— Voices in the Twilight. [Poems.] pp. 88. *Watts & Co.: London,* 1897. 8°. **011651**. l. **2**.

BYNG (LUCY MARGARET SCHOMBERG) *See* BEZA (M.) Doda . . . Translated . . . by L. Byng. [1925.] 8°. **012591**. cc. **55**.

—— *See* BEZA (M.) Rays of Memory . . . Translated . . . by Mrs. L. Byng. 1929. 8°. **012352**. cc. **74**.

—— *See* CREANGĂ (I.) Recollections, *etc.* [Four stories selected from the works of I. Creangă.] (Translated . . . by L. Byng.) 1930. 8°. **012591**. ee. **6**.

—— *See* ZAMFIRESCU (D.) Sasha . . . Translated . . . by L. Byng, *etc.* [1927.] 8°. **012591**. cc. **59**.

—— Roumanian Stories. [By various authors.] Translated . . . by L. Byng. pp. xv. 287. *John Lane: London, New York,* 1921. 8°. **012590**. aaa. **70**.

BYNG (MARIE EVELYN) *Viscountess Byng of Vimy.* Anne of the Marshland. pp. 319. *Holden & Hardingham: London,* [1914.] 8°. **NN. 2314**.

—— [Another edition.] pp. 20. *McClelland & Stewart: Toronto,* [1921.] 8°. **12602**. v. **14**.
A registration copy, containing the first chapter only.

—— [Another edition.] pp. 309. *McClelland & Stewart: Toronto,* [1921.] 8°. **NN. 10987**.

—— Barriers. pp. 380. *Holden & Hardingham: London,* [1912.] 8°. **NN. 417**.

—— [Another edition.] pp. 28. *McClelland & Stewart: Toronto,* [1921.] 8°. **012603**. **cc**. **26**.
A registration copy, containing the first chapter only.

—— [Another edition.] pp. 371. *McClelland & Stewart: Toronto,* [1921.] 8°. **12710**. a. **5**.

—— Up the Stream of Time. [Memoirs. With plates, including portraits.] pp. 274. *Macmillan Co. of Canada: Toronto,* 1945. 8°. **10861.aa.31.**

BYNG (MAX) and **BELL** (F. G.) A Popular Guide to Commercial and Domestic Telephony. pp. xii. 152. *General Electric Co.: London,* 1898. 8°. **8756**. cc. **9**.

BYNG (N. W.) In a Street—In a Lane. [Poems.] pp. 64. *Elkin Matthews: London,* 1908. 8°. **11647**. ff. **54**.

—— The Lawless Lover. A tale of the road. pp. 247. *Methuen & Co.: London,* 1926. 8°. **NN. 12187**.

—— She of the Green Hair; and, The Poet's House. (The Poet's Garden.) [Poems.] pp. vii. 51. *Madgwick, Houlston & Co.: London,* [1911.] 8°. **011650**. de. **61**.

BYNG (PATTEE) *Viscount Torrington.*

—— Pattee Byng's Journal, 1718–1720. Edited by J. L. Cranmer-Byng. [With plates, including a portrait.] pp. xxxii. 311. *London,* 1950. 8°. [*Publications of the Navy Records Society.* no. 88.] **Ac. 8109**.

BYNG (*Lady* RACHEL THEODORA) Angora Wool Farming. *Watmoughs: Idle,* [1924.] 8°. **7076**. aa. **58**.

—— How to Make Money by Angora Rabbit Breeding and Wool Farming. 2 pt. *Watmough's: Idle,* [1925, 26.] 8°. **7296**. c. **49**.

—— Mr. Jim & the Brownies . . . With photographic illustrations. pp. ix. 237. *Andrew Melrose: London & New York,* 1922. 8°. **7001**. cc. **7**.

—— Pamela's Dream History of England, *etc.* [A tale.] pp. 211. *Mills & Boon: London,* 1923. 8°. **012807**. bb. **46**.

—— Pamela's Dream History of England. A play. [Based on the author's tale of that name.] pp. 89. *Mills & Boon: London,* 1923. 8°. **011779**. gg. **69**.

—— Six Plays for Girl Guides, especially introducing first aid, nature study, *etc.* pp. 92. *C. A. Pearson: London,* 1920. 8°. **011779**. g. **79**.

BYNG (*Hon.* ROBERT) *See* BAXTER (Thomas) *Attorney General of Barbados.* A Letter from a Gentleman at Barbados . . . concerning the administration of the Governor B - - - - - g [i.e. the Hon. R. Byng]. 1740. 8°. **1416**. c. **44**.

BYNG (WILLIAM BATEMAN) Thoughts on the first Rainbow, in connection with certain geological facts. [By W. B. Byng.] pp. 16. 1852. 8°. *See* THOUGHTS. **1254**. g. **34**.

BYNG-HALL (C.) *See* HALL.

BYNG-HALL (FREDERICK FELIX WEICHS) *See* HALL.

BYNGHAM (DION) Creative Simplicity. pp. 31. *Bureau of Cosmotherapy: Leatherhead; C. W. Daniel Co.: London,* 1937. 8°. [*Pan Pamphlets.* no. 3.] W.P. **7223/3.**

BYNKERSHOEK (CORNELIUS VAN) *See* DELPECH (J.) *Professeur de droit administratif.* Bynkershoek, *etc.* 1904. 8°. [*Les Fondateurs du droit international, etc.*] **06955.** h. **18.**

—— *See* NUMAN (O. W. S.) Cornelis van Bynkershoek, zijn leven en zijne geschriften, *etc.* 1869. 8°. **6006.** i. **4.** (**3.**)

—— *See* PHILIPSE (J. H.) Iacobi Hermanni Philipse Oratio de Cornelio Bynkershoekio, *etc.* 1823. 4°. **10604.** h. **23.** (**1.**)

—— —— 1824. 4°. [*Annales Academiae Groninganae.* 1821–22.] Ac. **939.**

—— *See* PHILLIPSON (C.) Cornelius van Bynkershoek. [1908.] 8°. **06955.** h. **23.**

—— Cornelii van Binkershoek . . . opera omnia . . . Edidit et praefatus est B. Philippus Vicat. (Jo. Gottl. Heineccii Praefatio quam iuris Romani observationum libris IV prioribus . . . praemiserat.—Francisci Caroli Conradi . . . Praefatio quam Bynkershoekii varii argumenti opusculis . . . praemiserat.) 2 tom. *Coloniae Allobrogum,* 1761. fol. **500.** h. **11, 12.**

—— Editio quinta a quamplurimis mendis perpolita. 4 tom. *Neapoli,* 1766. 4°. **5255.** e. **18.**

—— [Another edition.] [With a portrait.] 2 tom. *Lugduni Batavorum,* 1767. fol. **14.** c. **9.**

—— Cornelii van Bynkershoek . . . Ad L. Ἀξιωσις IX. de lege Rhodia de jactu liber singularis. Et de dominio maris dissertatio. 2 pt. *Hagæ Batavorum,* 1703. 8°. **877.** c. **19.** (**2.**)

—— [Another copy.] **877.** e. **14.**

—— Cornelii van Bynkershoek . . . Ad L. Lecta XL. Dig. de Reb. cred. si cert. pet. [of Julius Paulus], liber singularis & Dissertatio de pactis juris stricti contractibus incontinenti adjectis. Editio secunda. Accedit de auctore auctoribusve authenticarum, quas vocant, diatriba. 3 pt. *F. Haaringh: Lugduni-Batavorum,* 1699. 8°. **877.** c. **19.** (**1.**)

—— De dominio maris dissertatio . . . A photographic reproduction of the second edition [or rather of pp. 352–424 of the second edition of the author's "Opera minora"], 1744. With an English translation by Ralph Van Deman Magoffin, and an introduction by James Brown Scott. pp. 107. 352–429. *Oxford University Press: New York,* 1923. 4°. [*Classics of International Law.*] Ac. **1866/3.** (**12.**)

—— De foro legatorum liber singularis. A monograph on the jurisdiction over ambassadors in both civil and criminal cases . . . A photographic reproduction of the text of 1744 with an English translation by Gordon J. Laing . . . and an introduction by . . . Jan de Louter. pp. xxx. 135. 427/571. 24a. *Clarendon Press: Oxford; Geoffrey Cumberlege: London,* 1946. 4°. [*Classics of International Law.* no. 21.] Ac. **1866/3.** (**22.**)

—— [Another copy.] De Foro legatorum liber singularis, *etc. Oxford, London,* 1946. 8°. [*Classics of International Law.* vol. 21.] Ac. **1866/3.** (**23.**)
With an errata slip inserted.

BYNKERSHOEK (CORNELIUS VAN)

—— [Liber singularis de foro legatorum.] Traité du juge compétent des ambassadeurs, tant pour le civil, que pour le criminel. Traduit du latin . . . par Jean Barbeyrac. pp. xxxvi. 304. *La Haye,* 1723. 8°. **228.** b. **15.**

—— Traité du juge competent des ambassadeurs . . . Traduit . . . par Jean Barbeyrac . . . Seconde edition, revue & augmentée dans les notes du traducteur. *See* WICQUEFORT (A. van) L'Ambassadeur et ses fonctions, *etc.* 1730. 4°. **1474.** c. **25.**

—— Seconde édition, revuë & augmentée dans les notes du traducteur. pp. xvi. 200. *See* WICQUEFORT (A. van) L'Ambassadeur et ses fonctions, *etc.* tom. 2. 1746. 4°. **6955.** f. **33.**

—— Cornelii van Bijnkershoek . . . Observationes tumultuariae. Ediderunt E. M. Meijers, A. S. de Blécourt, H. D. J. Bodenstein [and others]. 4 tom. *Harlemi,* 1926–62. 4°. **5321.** f. **12.**

—— Systematisch compendium der Observationes tumultuariae . . . Samengesteld door Mr. M. S. van Oosten. pp. xxi. 277. *Haarlem,* 1962. 8°. **5321.** f. **12.** a.

—— Cornelii van Bynkershoek . . . Observationum iuris Romani libri quatuor. In quibus plurima juris civilis aliorumque auctorum loca explicantur & emendantur. pp. 446. *Lugduni Batavorum,* 1710. 4°. **497.** b. **16.**

—— Editio secunda. pp. 446. *Lugduni Batavorum,* 1735. 4°. **5207.** aaa. **7.**

—— De usu artis criticæ in jurisprudentia. [Extracted from the preface to the "Observationum juris Romani libri quatuor."] 1769. *See* OPUSCULA. Variorum opuscula ad cultiorem jurisprudentiam adsequendam pertinentia. tom. 2. 1769, *etc.* 8°. **1375.** c. **1.**

—— Cornelii van Bynkershoek . . . Observationum juris Romani libri quatuor, quatuor prioribus additi, nempe V VI. VII. & VIII, *etc.* pp. 570. *Lugduni Batavorum,* 1733. 4°. **5207.** aaa. **7***

—— Cornelii van Bynkershoek . . . Opuscula varii argumenti, nunc primum collecta . . . cum præfatione D. Francisci Caroli Conradi. 2 tom. *Halæ,* 1729. 4°. **5684.** b. **9.**

—— Cornelii van Bynkershoek . . . Quaestionum juris privati libri quatuor: quarum plerisque insertae sunt utriusque in Hollandia curiae res de his ipsis quaestionibus judicatæ. [With a portrait.] pp. 744. *Lugduni Batavorum,* 1744. 4°. **5686.** aa. **5.**

—— Cornelii van Bynkershoek Quæstionum juris publici libri duo, quorum primus est de rebus bellicis, secundus de rebus varii argumenti. pp. 384. *Lugduni Batavorum,* 1737. 4°. **498.** d. **19.**

—— Quaestionum juris publici libri duo. (Vol. I. A photographic reproduction of the edition of 1737, with a list of errata and a portrait of Bynkershoek. Vol. II. A translation . . . by Tenney Frank, with an introduction by J. de Louter.) 2 vol. *Clarendon Press: Oxford, London* 1930. 8°. [*Classics of International Law.*] Ac. **1866/3.** (**15.**)

—— Treatise of Captures in War. By Richard Lee. [An enlarged translation of "De rebus bellicis," lib. 1 of the "Quæstiones iuris publici" of C. van Bynkershoek. pp. 264. 1759. 8°. *See* LEE (Richard) *Barrister-at-law.* **517.** c. **15.**

—— Second edition, corrected. With additional notes [by the editor, Thomas Hartwell Horne]. pp. viii. 240. *W. Clarke & Sons: London,* 1803. 8°. **18.** a. **5.**

BYNKERSHOEK (CORNELIUS VAN)

—— A Treatise on the Law of War. Translated from the . . . Latin . . . Being the first book of . . . Quæstiones juris publici. With notes, by Peter Stephen Du Ponceau. pp. xxxiv. 216. *Philadelphia*, 1810. 8°. [*American Law Journal.* vol. 3.] **P.P. 1352.**

—— A Treatise on the Law of War, *etc.* *Philadelphia*, 1810. 8°. [*American Law Journal.* vol. 3.] Mic. A. **215.** (2.)
MICROFILM *of a copy of the preceding in the Law Library of the University of Michigan. Issued by University Microfilms, Ann Arbor,* 1948. *American Periodical Series,* 1800–25, *no.* 113.

BYNNE (OWEN HENRY) Short Studies in Modern Oxford. pp. 67. *A. T. Shrimpton & Son: Oxford,* 1886. 8°. **8364. aaa. 31.** (5.)

BYNNER (EDWIN LASSETTER) *See* HALE (Lucretia P.) and BYNNER (E. L.) An Uncloseted Skeleton. [1888.] 16°. **12704. aa. 7.**

—— Agnes Surriage. pp. 418. *Trübner & Co.: London,* [1886.] 8°. **12707. k. 6.**

—— [A reissue.] *Ticknor & Co.: Boston,* 1887. 8°. **12704. m. 22.**

—— [A reissue.] *Sampson Low & Co.: London,* 1890. 8°. **012705. g. 48.**

—— The Begum's Daughter, *etc.* pp. vi. 473. *Little, Brown & Co.: Boston,* 1890. 8°. **012705. ee. 48.**

—— [Another issue.] *Sampson Low & Co.: London,* 1890. 8°. **012705. f. 23.**

—— Damen's Ghost. [By E. L. Bynner.] pp. iv. 313. 1881. 8°. *See* DAMEN (   ) **12207. ee. 9.**

—— Penelope's Suitors. pp. 68. *Ticknor & Co.: Boston,* 1887. 8°. **12705. a. 31.**

—— Tritons. A novel. pp. 406. *Lockwood, Brooks & Co.: Boston,* 1878. 8°. **12706. ee. 19.**

BYNNER (WITTER)

—— *See* CHIANG (Shao-ch'üan) The Jade Mountain. A Chinese anthology . . . Translated by W. Bynner from the texts of Kiang Kang-hu. 1929. 8°. **11093. d. 14.**

—— *See* EURIPIDES. [*Iphigenia in Tauris.—English.*] Iphigenia in Tauris. An English version by W. Bynner. 1915. 8°. **11707. df. 12.**

—— *See* LAO TZŬ. The Way of Life, according to Laotzu. Translated by W. Bynner. 1946. 8°. **15235. bb. 19.**

—— *See* TUCKERMAN (Frederick G.) The Sonnets of Frederick Goddard Tuckerman. Edited, with an introduction, by W. Bynner. 1931. 8°. **011686. aaa. 23.**

—— *See* WALTON (Eda L.) Dawn Boy . . . With an introduction by W. Bynner. [1925.] 8°. **011686. f. 75.**

—— Selected Poems . . . Edited by Robert Hunt. With a critical preface by Paul Horgan. pp. lxxvi. 258. vii. *A. A. Knopf: New York, London,* 1936. 8°. **11688. l. 52.**

—— Cake. An indulgence. [A play, in verse.] pp. 169. *A. A. Knopf: New York, London,* 1926. 8°. **11791. aa. 1.**

—— Eden Tree. [Poems.] pp. 111. *A. A. Knopf: New York,* 1931. 8°. **011686. c. 32.**

—— Indian Earth. [Poems.] pp. xvi. 77. *A. A. Knopf: New York,* 1929. 8°. **011686. c. 20.**

BYNNER (WITTER)

—— Journey with Genius. Recollections and reflections concerning the D. H. Lawrences, *etc.* [With plates, including portraits.] pp. xvii. 361. *Peter Nevill: London, New York,* 1953. 8°. **10884. l. 5.**

—— The Persistence of Poetry. pp. 29. *Book Club of California: San Francisco,* 1929. 8°. **Cup.510.pt.4.**

—— Take away the Darkness. [Poems.] pp. xv. 176. *Alfred A. Knopf: New York,* 1947. 8°. **11688. p. 28.**

—— Tiger. [A play.] pp. 48. *Mitchell Kennerley: New York,* 1913. 8°. **11791. cc. 37.**

—— W. B. in California. A tribute. [In verse.] (Presented to Mr. Witter Bynner by his students, friends and colleagues at a dinner, May 1919.) pp. viii. 63. *Privately printed: Berkeley,* 1919. 8°. **011686. h. 12.**

BYNNS (RICHARD) Conscience void of Offence. A sermon preach'd at the Assizes held at Stafford, August the 9th 1710, *etc.* pp. 19. *John Morphew: London,* 1710. 8°. **225. h. 11.** (8.)

—— Evil Communications. A sermon preach'd at the Assizes held at Stafford, August the 7th. 1712, *etc.* pp. 20. *London; for Michael Johnson: Litchfield; Henry Norman: Stafford,* 1712. 8°. **695. f. 2.** (7.)

—— [Another copy.] **225. h. 11.** (9.)

—— The Office of the Ministry accounted for, in a sermon preach'd before the . . . Bishop of Coventry & Lichfield, at his primary visitation, *etc.* pp. 24. *R. Clavell: London,* 1701. 4°. **226. g. 17.** (6.)

—— A Sermon preached before the Honourable House of Commons, January 30. 1692. pp. 31. *Edw. Jones, for William Crooke: in the Savoy,* 1693. 4°. **694. e. 13.** (2.)

—— [Another copy.] **226. h. 4.** (4.)

—— [Another copy.] A Sermon preached . . . January 30. 1692. *In the Savoy,* 1693. 4°. **1482. c. 30.** (8.)
Imperfect; wanting the half-title.

—— [Another issue.] A Sermon preached before the Honourable House of Commons, January 30. 1692. pp. 31. *Printed by Edw. Jones, for William Crooke: In the Savoy,* 1693. 4°. **4481. aaa. 37.** (4.)
With a different publisher's advertisement.

BYNOE (CHARLES AUGUSTUS) *See* STEAD (William T.) Wanted: a Sherlock Holmes! . . . A strange true story of to-day. [On the case of Dr. C. A. Bynoe.] 1895. 8°. **6495. aa. 54.**

BYNTZE (VICENTZ) *See* YAÑEZ PINZON (V.)

BYNUM (ERNEST T.) Das Leben des M. Junius Brutus bis auf Caesars Ermordung. pp. 49. *Halle,* 1898. 8°. **10600. g. 3.** (5.)

BYNUM (JESSE ATHERTON) Speech . . . on the Motion of Mr. Wagener to be excused from serving on the investigating committee to examine into the defalcation of Samuel Swartwout. In the House of Representatives, January, 1839. pp. 13. *Blair & Rivers: Washington,* 1839. 8°. **8226. e. 19**

BYNUM (JOSEPHINE M.)

—— *See* ORMSBY (Waterman L.) The Butterfield Overland Mail . . . Edited by L. H. Wright and J. M. Bynum 1942. 8°. W.P. **9803/32**

BYNUM (LINDLEY) *See* SHALER (William) Journal of a Voyage between China and the North-Western Coast of America made in 1804 . . . Introduction by L. Bynum, *etc.* 1935. 8°. **10497. e. 2.**

BYNUM (Lindley) and **JONES** (Idwal)

—— Biscailuz, Sheriff of the New West, *etc.* [With plates, including portraits.] pp. 208. *William Morrow & Co.: New York*, 1950. 8º. **10892**. b. **7**.

BYNUM (Mary L.) *See* MacCreery (Walter G.) and Bynum (M. L.) The Coffee Industry in Brazil. 1930. 8º. [*U.S. Bureau of Foreign and Domestic Commerce. Trade Promotion Series.* no. 92.] A.S. **126/2**.

—— International Trade in Coffee. [With a map.] pp. viii. 103. *Washington*, 1926. 8º. [*U.S. Bureau of Foreign and Domestic Commerce. Trade Promotion Series.* no. 37.] A.S. **126/2**.

BYNWALTH (Matthias) Das Vaterunser, ausgelegt durch Matthiam Bynwalth, Prediger zu Gdantzk, 1525. Herausgegeben von Hermann Freytag. Haushaltungsbüchlein. Herausgegeben von Otto Clemen. pp. 41. *Leipzig*, 1910. 8º. [*Flugschriften aus den ersten Jahren der Reformation.* Bd. 4. Hft. 2.] **3907**. bbb. **4**. (**2**.)

BYPRODUCT.

—— Byproduct. The journal of the Sheffield University Chemical Society. *See* Sheffield.—*University of Sheffield.—Sheffield University Chemical Society.*

BYR (Bob) *pseud.* [i.e. Carl Robert Emmerich von Bayer.] *See* Byr (Robert) *pseud.*

BYR (C.) *pseud.* [i.e. Conrad Beyer.] Erzherzog Karls Liebe und der Kampf um den Niederwald. Roman. 2 Bd. *Stuttgart*, 1888. 8º. **012553**. f. **42**.

—— Dritte Auflage. 2 Bd. *Stuttgart*, 1890. 8º. **012553**. k. **24**.

BYR (Robert) *pseud.* [i.e. Carl Robert Emmerich von Bayer.] *See* also Bayer (C. R. E. von)

—— *See* Handbuch. Handbuch für die Kavallerie—Mannschafts-Schulen . . . II. Auflage. Durchgesehen und nach den neuesten Vorschriften umgearbeitet von Robert Byr. 1862. 16º. M.L. aa. **90**.

—— *See* Meissner (A.) Mosaik, *etc.* [The preface signed: Robert Byr.] 1886. 8º. **12249**. ee. **4**.

—— Alpröslein. [Poems.] pp. 122. *Prag*, 1860. 16º. **11527**. aa. **8**.

—— Andor. Roman. 3 Bd. *Jena*, 1883. 8º. **12555**. aaaa. **24**.

—— Andor. Romans . . . Przekład Filipa Sulimierskiego. 3 tom. pp. 372. *Warszawa*, 1884. 8º. **012553**. aa. **72**.

—— Anno Neun und Dreizehn. Biografisches Gedenkblatt aus den deutschen Freiheitskämpfen. 2 Bd. *Innsbruck*, 1865. 8º. **10705**. aaa. **38**.

—— Aquarelle. [Tales.] 2 Bd. *Jena*, 1892. 8º. **012554**. g. **36**.

—— Auf der Station. Skizzen und Novellen aus dem Soldaten-Leben . . . Erstes Bändchen. pp. 181. *Berlin*, 1865. 16º. **12550**. aa. **39**.
No more published.

—— Cantonirungs-Bilder. 2 Bd. *Prag*, 1860. 8º. **12553**. dd. **12**.

—— Castell Ursani. Roman. 3 Bd. *Jena*, 1885. 8º. **12554**. cc. **36**.

—— Ein deutsches Grafenhaus. Roman. 1865. *See* Periodical Publications.—*Berlin.* Deutsche Roman-Zeitung. Jahrg. 2. Bd. 3. 1864, *etc.* 8º. P.P. **4736**. ie.

BYR (Robert) *pseud.* [i.e. Carl Robert Emmerich von Bayer.]

—— [Another edition.] 3 Bd. *Berlin*, 1866. 8º. **12551**. dd. **17**.

—— Dora. Roman. 2 Bd. *Jena*, 1886. 8º. **12555**. e. **16**.

—— Edwiesen. Roman. 2 Bd. *Jena*, 1888. 8º. **012553**. e. **33**.

—— Einige Ansichten über leichte Reiterei. pp. 37. *Prag*, 1861. 8º. **7906**. g. **28**. (**3**.)

—— Die Einnahme der Stadt, des Passes und Schlosses Bregenz durch die Schweden im Jahre 1647 . . . Nebst einem Plane . . . und einem Anhange bisher unveröffentlicht gebliebener Documente. pp. 16. *Lindau*, 1873. 8º. **9315**. g. **22**. (**4**.)

—— Der Eisenwarm. Roman. 2 Bd. *Stuttgart*, 1894. 8º. **012554**. g. **66**.

—— Gita. Roman. 4 Bd. *Leipzig*, 1877. 8º. **12554**. h. **11**.

—— Der Kampf um's Dasein. Roman. 5 Bd. *Jena*, 1869. 8º. **12552**. ee. **10**.

—— Larven. Roman. 4 Bd. *Leipzig*, 1876. 8º. **12554**. c. **19**.

—— Lydia. Roman. pp. 308. *Stuttgart & Leipzig*, 1883. 8º. **12555**. c. **34**.

—— Mit eherner Stirn. Roman. 1867. *See* Periodical Publications.—*Berlin.* Deutsche Roman-Zeitung. Jahrg. 4. Bd. 3, 4. 1864, *etc.* 4º. P.P. **4736**. ie.

—— [Another edition.] 4 Bd. *Berlin*, 1868. 8º. **12550**. de. **12**.

—— Oestreichische Garnisonen. Roman aus dem Militairleben. 4 Bd. *Hamburg*, 1863. 8º. **12548**. ccc. **14**.

—— Parodien. Maupassant, "Der Maler." Prévost, "Die Vase." Zola, "Sein Modell," etc. *München*, [1902.] 8º. **12315**. k. **36**.

—— Quatuor. Novellen. 4 Bd. *Leipzig*, 1875. 8º. **12552**. i. **8**.

—— Rutschepeter. Roman. 2 Bd. *Stuttgart*, 1892. 8º. **012554**. g. **32**.

—— Sesam. Roman. 3 Bd. *Stuttgart & Leipzig*, 1881 [1880]. 8º. **12554**. g. **39**.

—— Sphinx. Roman. 3 Bd. *Berlin*, 1870. 8º. **12553**. e. **11**.

—— Sternschnuppen. Roman. 2 Bd. *Jena*, 1897. 8º. **012552**. b. **18**.

—— Ein stolzes Herz. Roman. pp. 346. *Jena*, 1891. 8º. **012553**. h. **56**.

—— Vierundzwanzig Stunden Hausarrest. Eine Soldatengeschichte aus der guten alten Zeit. pp. 116. *Berlin*, [1890.] 8º. **012553**. g. **38**.

—— Waisenmädchenhaar. Roman. 2 Bd. *Berlin & Leipzig*, [1891.] 8º. **012553**. l. **36**.

—— Waldidyll. Roman. pp. 232. *Stuttgart*, 1889. 8º. **012553**. i. **6**.

—— Der Weg zum Glück. Roman. 3 Bd. *Stuttgart*, 1890. 8º. **012553**. k. **41**.

—— Der Weg zum Herzen. Erzählung . . . Zweite Auflage. pp. 223. *Leipzig*, 1881 [1880]. 8º. **12554**. f. **33**.

BYR (ROBERT) *pseud.* [i.e. CARL ROBERT EMMERICH VON BAYER.]

—— Droga do serca. Powieść . . . Przekład z niemieckiego. pp. 136. [*Warsaw*, 1882.] 8°. **12590**. bbb. **33**.

—— Am Wendepunkt des Lebens. Roman. 3 Bd. *Jena*, 1881. 8°. **12553**. f. **2**.

—— Wie es weiter noch kam. Roman. pp. 311. *Jena*, 1888. 8°. **012553**. f. **39**.

—— Wozu? Roman. 2 Bd. *Stuttgart*, 1891. 8°. **012553**. l. **18**.

—— Wrak. Zwei Erzählungen. (Bd. 1, 2. Trümmer. Bd. 3, 4. Der Tuwan von Panawang.) 4 Bd. *Leipzig*, 1873. 8°. **12547**. eee. **9**.

BYRAM (GEORGE M.) and **JEMISON** (GEORGE MEREDITH)

—— Some Principles of Visibility and their Application to Forest Fire Detection. pp. 61. *Washington*, 1948. 8°. [*U.S. Department of Agriculture. Technical Bulletin.* no. 954.] A.S. **800/2**.

BYRAM (HAROLD MOORE) Some Problems in the Provision of Professional Education for College Teachers, *etc.* [A thesis.] pp. vi. 210. *Teachers College, Columbia University: New York*, 1933. 8°. **08385**. f. **46**.

BYRAM (JOHN Q.) Principles and Practice of Filling Teeth with Porcelain. With 132 illustrations. pp. 120. *Consolidated Dental Manufacturing Co.: New York; C. Ath & Sons: London*, [1908.] 8°. **07610**. i. **19**.

BYRAM (LÉO) *pseud.* [i.e. LOUIS DREVET.] Mon ami Fou-Than'. Roman de mœurs chinoises. pp. 288. *Paris*, [1912.] 8°. **12550**. t. **21**.

BYRAM (WILLIAM JAMES) *See* AESCHYLUS. [*Prometheus Vinctus.—English.*] Prometheus Bound . . . Translated . . . by W. J. Byram. 1922. 12°. **11707**. df. **33**.

BYRCA. *See* BIRKA.

BYRCH (HENRICUS) Disputatio medica inauguralis, de dolore colico, *etc. T. ab Ackersdyck: Trajecti ad Rhenum*, 1669. 4°. **1185**. k. **11**. (**29**.)

BYRCHE (WILLIAM) A Sermon preach'd at the Consecration of Edward Lord Bishop of Lichfield and Coventry, at Lambeth Chappel, November 17, 1717. pp. 16. *James Holland: London*, 1717. 4°. **225**. g. **20**. (**7**.)

—— [Another copy.] **L.P.** **694**. k. **10**. (**4**.)

BYRCHENSHA (RALPH) *See* BIRCHENSHA.

BYRD, *Family of. See* BYRD (William) The Younger. The Writings of Colonel William Byrd, *etc.* [With an introduction, "The Byrd Family in Virginia."] 1901. 8°. **12296**. h. **6**.

BYRD (BOB) Ka-Zar, King of Fang and Claw. pp. 252. *Wright & Brown: London*, [1937.] 8°. NN. **27223**.

BYRD (COLIN B.) Discovering Charles. A comedy in one act. pp. 24. *H. F. W. Deane & Sons: London*, [1937.] 8°. [*Year Book Press Series of Plays.*] W.P. **2236/126**.

BYRD (HIRAM) Forty Notifiable Diseases, *etc.* pp. iv. 74. *World Book Co.: Yonkers-on-Hudson*, 1922. 8°. **07561**. ee. **22**.

BYRD (JOHN DYMOND)

—— Naming the Twins and other poems (for children), *etc.* pp. 44. *Celtic Book Co.: Cardiff*, 1945. 8°. **11658**. aaa. **48**.

BYRD (JOHN WALTER) The Born Fool. [A novel.] pp. 316 *Chatto & Windus: London*, 1917. 8°. NN. **4538**

BYRD (JOSIAS) Loues Peereles Paragon, or, the Attributes, and progresse of the Church. A sermon preached in St Maries in Oxford, *etc.* pp. 27. *Printed by Ioseph Barnes: Oxford*, 1613. 4°. **4474**. c. **100**.

BYRD (KENNETH FREDERIC)

—— The Preparation of Consolidated Balance Sheets of Holding and Subsidiary Companies. (Reprinted from "The Accountant.") pp. 35. *Gee & Co.: London*, 1946. 8°. **8218**. a. **14**.

BYRD (MARY E.) A Laboratory Manual in Astronomy. pp. ix. 272. *Ginn & Co.: Boston*, 1899. 8°. **8562**. b. **54**.

BYRD (OLIVER ERASMUS)

—— Health Instruction Yearbook, 1943(–1952). [1943–52.] 8°.
[Continued as:]
Health Yearbook, 1953 [*etc.*]. [1953– .] 8°. *See* PERIODICAL PUBLICATIONS.—*Stanford.* P.P. **2487**. fcp.

—— School Health Sourcebook. Compiled by O. E. Byrd. [With a bibliography.] pp. vii. 373. *Stanford University Press: Stanford*, [1955.] 8°. **7583**. cc. **19**.

—— Textbook of College Hygiene. pp. xv. 443. *W. B. Saunders Co. Philadelphia & London*, 1953. 8°. **7393**. ee. **8**.

BYRD (PAUL FRANCIS) and **FRIEDMAN** (MORRIS DAVID)

—— Handbook of Elliptic Integrals for Engineers and Physicists, *etc.* pp. xii. 355. *Springer-Verlag: Berlin; Lange, Maxwell & Springer: London, New York*, 1954. 8°. **8536**. bb. **26**.
Grundlehren der Mathematischen Wissenschaften in Einzeldarstellungen. Bd. 67.

BYRD (REBECCA) A Testimony concerning R. Byrd. Printed by direction of the Yearly Meeting of Friends, held in London, 1835. pp. 15. 1835. 8°. *See* FRIENDS, *Society of.* **4920**. d. **21**.

BYRD (RICHARD EVELYN) *See* ADAMS (Harry) Beyond the Barrier with Byrd. An authentic story of the Byrd Antarctic Exploring Expedition, *etc.* [1932.] 8°. **010460**. ee. **44**.

—— *See* FOSTER (Coram) Rear Admiral Byrd and the Polar Expeditions, *etc.* [With portraits.] 1930. 8°. **010460**. de. **20**.

—— *See* GREEN (Fitzhugh) Dick Byrd, Air Explorer, *etc.* [With portraits.] 1928. 8°. **010884**. de. **63**.

—— *See* HILL (Joe) and HILL (O. D.) In Little America with Byrd, *etc.* [1937.] 8°. **010460**. l. **3**.

—— *See* MILLER (Francis T.) Byrd's Great Adventure, *etc.* [1930.] 8°. **010460**. g. **19**.

—— *See* MURPHY (Charles J. V.) Struggle. The life and exploits of Commander R. E. Byrd, *etc.* [With portraits.] 1928. 8°. **10885**. aaa. **13**.

—— *See* O'BRIEN (John S.) By Dog Sled for Byrd, *etc.* [With portraits.] 1931. 8°. **010460**. eee. **21**.

—— *See* RIOTOR (L. E. E.) Byrd au Pôle sud, *etc.* [With portraits.] 1932. 8°. **010460**. ff. **4**.

—— *See* SIPLE (Paul) A Boy Scout with Byrd, *etc.* 1931. 8°. **010460**. f. **20**.

BYRD (Richard Evelyn)

—— *See* Siple (Paul) Scout to Explorer. Back with Byrd in the Antarctic, *etc.* [With a portrait.] 1936. 8°. **010460. f. 29.**

—— *See* United States of America.—*Department of the Interior.—Division of Territories and Island Possessions.—Antarctic Service.* Reports on Scientific Results of the United States Antarctic Service Expedition 1939–1941 [under the leadership of Rear-Admiral R. E. Byrd. With a portrait]. 1945. 4°. [*Proceedings of the American Philosophical Society.* vol. 89. no. 1.] Ac. **1830.**

—— Alone. [An account of the author's experiences at the Advance Base during the American Antarctic Expedition of 1933–34.] pp. xi. 302. *Putnam: London,* 1938. 8°. **010460. g. 58.**

—— Antarctic Discovery. The story of the second Byrd Antarctic Expedition, *etc.* [First published under the title "Discovery." With plates, including a portrait, and maps.] pp. xxi. 421. *Putnam: London,* 1936. 8°. **010460. h. 25.**

—— Exploring with Byrd. Episodes from an adventurous life, compiled and revised by Rear Admiral R. E. Byrd . . . Illustrated with photographs [including a portrait]. pp. vii. 241. *G. P. Putnam's Sons: New York,* 1937. 8°. **010460. g. 49.**

—— Little America: aerial exploration in the Antarctic & the flight to the South Pole, *etc.* [With plates, including a portrait, and maps.] pp. xvi. 422. *G. P. Putnam's Sons: London,* 1931. 8°. **010460. h. 14.**

—— Skyward. Man's mastery of the air as shown by the brilliant flights of America's leading air explorer [the author] . . . 48 illustrations [including portraits]. pp. xv. 359. *G. P. Putnam's Sons: New York, London,* 1928. 8°. **010884. h. 14.**

BYRD (Russell A.)

—— Driving to Live. pp. 249. *Pacific-Western Publishing Co.: Los Angeles,* [1948.] 8°. **08245. k. 102.**

BYRD (Sam)

—— Small Town South. [Autobiographical reminiscences of Carolina.] pp. 237. *Houghton Mifflin Co.: Boston,* 1942. 8°. **10889. b. 10.**

BYRD (Samuel) *See* Bird.

BYRD (Sigman) Tall Grew the Pines. pp. 273. *D. Appleton-Century Co.: New York, London,* 1936. 8°. A.N. **3124.**

BYRD (William) *the Elder.*

—— [For the "Essay upon the Government of the English Plantations on the Continent of America," sometimes attributed to W. Byrd:] *See* American.

BYRD (William) *Musician.*

—— *See* Becker (Oscar) *of Cologne.* Die englischen Madrigalisten. W. Byrd, *etc.* 1901. 8°. Hirsch **2840.**

—— *See* Fellowes (Edmund H.) William Byrd, *etc.* 1923. 8°. **07896.** de. 3.

—— —— 1928. 8°. **07896.** h. 56.

—— —— 1936. 8°. **07896.** e. 23.

—— *See* Fellowes (Edmund H.) William Byrd, *etc.* 1948. 8°. **7900.** c. 24.

BYRD (William) *Musician.*

—— *See* Hadow (*Sir* William H.) William Byrd, 1623–1923, *etc.* [1923.] 8°. Ac. **1186/8**

—— *See* Howes (Frank S.) William Byrd. [With a portrait. 1928. 8°. **10602.** p. 4/

—— Psalms, Sonnets and Songs of Sadness and Piety [Without the Psalms. The words only.] 1879. *See* Arber (Edward) An English Garner, *etc.* vol. 2. 1877, *etc.* 8°. **12269.** cc. 12

—— [Another edition.] 1903. *See* Arber (Edward) An English Garner. (Shorter Elizabethan Poems.) 1903, *etc.* 8°. **2324.** e. **9/10**

—— The Second Book of Songs and Sonnets. [The words only.] 1903. *See* Arber (Edward) An English Garner, *etc.* 1903, *etc.* 8°. **2324.** e. **9/1**

—— Songs of Sundrie Natures, *etc.* [The words only.] 1879. *See* Arber (Edward) An English Garner, *etc.* vol. 2. 1877, *etc.* 8°. **12269.** cc. 12

—— [Another edition.] 1903. *See* Arber (Edward) An English Garner, *etc.* 1903, *etc.* 8°. **2324.** e. **9/1**

BYRD (William) *of Marnhull.*

—— *See* Friends, *Society of.* A Testimony concerning William Byrd, *etc.* 1836. 8°. **4716.** b. **24.** (4

BYRD (William) *the Younger.*

—— *See* Beatty (Richmond C.) William Byrd of Westover, *etc.* [With portraits.] 1932. 8°. **010885.** df.

—— The Westover Manuscripts: containing the History of the Dividing Line betwixt Virginia and North Carolina; a Journey to the Land of Eden, A.D. 1733; and a Progress to the Mines. Written from 1728 to 1736, and now first published. pp. iv. 143. *E. & J. C. Ruffin: Petersburg* [*Va.*], 1841. 8°. **1431.** k.

—— History of the Dividing Line and other tracts [viz. "A Journey to the Land of Eden," "A Progress to the Mines," "The Proceedings of the Commissioners appointed to lay out the Bounds of the Northern Neck," "An Essay on Bulk Tobacco," "Miscellaneous Papers"]. From the papers of W. Byrd. [The editor's introduction signed: T. H. W., i.e. Thomas H. Wynne.] 2 vol. *Richmond, Va.,* 1866. 4°. **10410.** bbb.
Printed for private circulation. No. 2, 3 of "Historical Documents from the Old Dominion."

—— [Another copy.] **10410.** f. 3
One of ten copies printed on large paper.

—— The Writings of Colonel William Byrd . . . Edited by John Spencer Bassett. Illustrated. [With an introduction by the editor, "The Byrd Family in Virginia."] pp. lxxxviii. 461. *Doubleday, Page & Co.: New York,* 1901. 8°. **12296.** h.

—— Another Secret Diary of William Byrd of Westover 1739–1741. With letters & literary exercises, 1696–1726. Edited by Maude H. Woodfin. Translated and collated by Marion Tinling. [With plates.] pp. xlv. 490. *Dietz Press: Richmond, Va.,* 1942. 8°. **10888.** g. 2

—— Description of the Dismal Swamp and a Proposal to drain the Swamp . . . Edited by Earl Gregg Swem. pp. 32. *Metuchen,* 1922. 8°. [*Heartman's Historical Series.* no. 38.] **9617.k.1/38**

—— Representation of Mr. Byrd concerning Proprietary Governments, *etc.*—Proposalls humbly submitted to the Lords of the Councill of Trade and Plantations for sending the French Protestants to Virginia. [From a MS. note book.] *See* American. An Essay upon the Government of the English Plantations on the Continent of America, *etc.* 1945. 8°. **08157.** g. 7

BYRD (WILLIAM) *the Younger.*

—— The Secret Diary of William Byrd of Westover, 1709–1712. Edited by Louis B. Wright and Marion Tinling. [With plates.] pp. xxviii. 622. *Dietz Press: Richmond, Va.*, 1941. 8°. **10887. h. 24.**

BYRDAL (HENRI CHRISTIAN VALDEMAR) De udnævnte Landsthingsmænd. pp. 112. *København*, 1906. 8°. **8092. ee. 42.**

BYRDAL (VALDEMAR) *See* BYRDAL (Henri C. V.)

BYRDE ( ) *Mrs.*, and **PEARSON** (ADA T.) Bread, Butter, Pastries and Cakes in India and the Colonies. A concise manual for the use of housewives . . . Second edition. pp. viii. 115. *Thacker, Spink & Co.: Calcutta*, 1916. 8°. **07942. aa. 23.**

BYRDE (CHARLOTTE ELEANOR)

—— Poems. Original and translated. pp. 59. *Athenæum Press: London*, [1928.] 8°. **11657. ff. 41.**

BYRDE (ELSIE) The Polish Fairy Book. Translated and adapted . . . by E. Byrde. With illustrations . . . by Livia Kádár. pp. 231. *T. Fisher Unwin: London*, 1925. 8°. **012403. df. 18.**

BYRDE (HENRY CHARLES WALLER) A System for learning quickly the English Morse Alphabet. *Gale & Polden: Aldershot*, [1914.] 8°. **1879. c. 11. (12.)**

BYRDE (KATHERINE CONSTANCE) *Begin.* God's great love for us. [A religious tract.] *Bristol*, [1916.] 32°. **4420. a. 21. (1.)**

—— The Great Spiritual Warfare: its promise & reward. pp. 14. *Bristol*, [1917.] 32°. **4420. a. 21. (3.)**

—— Our Flags and their Significance. pp. 24. 1920. *obl.* 8°. *See* BRISTOL.—*Bristol British-Israel Association.* **4033. de. 44.**

—— The Trumpet shall Sound. [A religious tract. By] K. C. B. [i.e. K. C. Byrde.] pp. 12. [1917.] 32°. *See* B., K. C. **4420. a. 21. (2.)**

BYRDE (LOUIS)

—— The Evangelistic Method, China. pp. 4. *Society for Promoting Christian Knowledge: London*, 1908. 8°. [*Pan-Anglican Papers.* S.D. 2g.] **4108. cc. 35.**

BYRDE (MARGARETTA) The Interpreters. A story of cross-purposes. pp. 336. *T. Fisher Unwin: London*, 1905. 8°. **012631. dd. 30.**

—— The Searchers, *etc.* (Second impression.) pp. 452. *T. Fisher Unwin: London*, 1902. 8°. [*First Novel Library.*] **12622. p. 1/2.**

BYRDE (OWEN RICHARD AUGUSTUS) *See* EURIPIDES. [*Hercules Furens.—Greek.*] Heracles. With introduction and notes by O. R. A. Byrde. 1914. 8°. **11707. de. 43.**

BYRDE (RICHARD AUGUSTUS) High Aims at School. School sermons . . . With a preface by the Rev. H. A. James. pp. vii. 134. *Elliot Stock: London*, 1899. 8°. **4473. e. 35.**

—— Cheap edition. pp. vii. 134. *Elliot Stock: London*, 1900. 8°. **4479. f. 29.**

BYRDE (*Sir* WILLIAM) *See* PRICE (Sampson) The Two Twins of Birth and Death. A sermon . . . upon the occasion of the funeralls of Sir W. Byrde. 1624. 4°. **1415. b. 63.**

BYRDSALL (F.) The History of the Loco-Foco, or Equal Rights Party, its movements, conventions and proceedings. With short characteristic sketches of its prominent men. pp. 192. *Clement & Packard: New-York*, 1842. 12°. **1447. d. 19.**

BYRES, *Family of.* *See* GILL (Andrew J. M.) The Families of Moir and Byres. 1885. 4°. **9905. g. 2.**

BYRES (JAMES) Hypogæi, or, Sepulchral Caverns of Tarquinia, the capital of antient Etruria . . . Edited by Frank Howard. [Plates, with introductory letterpress.] *F. Howard: London*, [1842.] fol. **559*. h. 7.**

BYRES (JOHN) References to the Plan of the Island of Dominica, as surveyed from the year 1765 to 1773. pp. 30. *S. Hooper: London*, 1777. 8°. **10470. c. 21.**

—— References to the Plan of the Island of St Vincent, as surveyed from the year 1765 to 1773. pp. 8. *S. Hooper: London*, 1777. 8°. **10470. c. 22.**

BYRG (JUSTUS) *See* BUERGI (Jost)

BYRHTFERTH. *See* CLASSEN (Carl M.) Über das Leben und die Schriften Byrhtferds, eines . . . Gelehrten . . . um das Jahr 1000, *etc.* 1896. 4°. **11850. i. 39.**

—— *See* SINGER (Charles) and SINGER (D. W.) Byrhtferd's Diagram, *etc.* (A restoration: Byrhtferd of Ramsey's Diagram of the Physical and Physiological Fours.) [1917.] 4°. **8561. k. 27.**

—— **Byrhtferth's Manual, A.D. 1011. Now edited for the first time from MS. Ashmole 328 in the Bodleian Library . . . with an introduction, translation . . . by S. J. Crawford. *London*, 1929– . 8°. [*Early English Text Society. Original series.* 177, *etc.*] Ac. 9925/133.**

—— [Another copy.] **Ac. 9927/131.**

—— *See* HENEL (H.) Studien zum altenglischen Computus. [With special reference to Byrhtferth's Manual.] 1934. 8°. **W.P. 7720/26.**

—— Bridferti Ramesiensis Monachi Vita Sancti Dunstani. 1853. *See* MIGNE (J. P.) Patrologiæ cursus completus, *etc.* tom. 139. 1844, *etc.* 4°. **2000. e.**

BYRHTNOTH. *See* LABORDE (Edward D.) Byrhtnoth and Maldon. [1936.] 8°. **20029. g. 1.**

—— [For editions of "The Battle of Maldon," sometimes called "The Death of Byrhtnoth":] *See* MALDON, *Battle of.*

BYRIEL (CAI)

—— *See* BRÜEL (E.) International Straits, *etc.* (pt. 1. Translated by C. Byriel.) 1947. 8°. **6956. dd. 1.**

BYRKA. *See* BIRKA.

BYRKLINUS (JACOBUS) *See* ZIMMERMANN (J. J.) *Professor of Theology, etc.* Meditatio sacra complectens salutaria quædam monita ad verum . . . usum sacræ cœnæ, *etc.* (Pars posterior . . . assumente J. Byrklino.) 1746, *etc.* 4°. **474. b. 13. (16.)**

BYRN ( ) *Solicitor.* *See* HUDLESTON ( ) *Inn-Keeper in Ballogh.* An Account of a Barbarous and Bloody Murder committed on the body of Mr Hudleston . . . by one Byrn a sollicitor. 1725. fol. **C.133.g.7.(27.)**

BYRN (EDWARD W.) The Progress of Invention in the Nineteenth Century. pp. viii. 476. *Munn & Co.: New York*, 1900. 8°. **08766. bb. 14.**

BYRN (G.) An Epistle from G. Byrn to Miss Kennedy, the night before his execution at Kilkenny. pp. 22. *Pat. Byrne: Dublin,* 1781. 8°. **1478**. d. **20**. (**3**.)

BYRN (Marcus Lafayette) The Artist and Tradesman's Companion; embracing the manufacture and the application of varnishes . . . instructions for working enamel . . . the art of glazing . . . of staining wood and metal; imitation of fancy woods . . . etc., entirely simplified. With illustrations. pp. xi. 214. *Stearns & Co.: New York,* 1853. 12°. **7954**. c. **11**.

—— The Complete Practical Distiller . . . With . . . engravings. pp. 198. *H. C. Baird: Philadelphia,* 1868. 12°. **7954**. b. **15**.

—— The Mystery of Medicine Explained; a family physician, and household companion, *etc.* (Fortieth edition. Revised and improved.) pp. 474. *M. L. Byrn: New York,* 1872. 8°. **7390**. ee. **22**.

—— The Repository of Wit and Humor; comprising more than one thousand anecdotes, &c. . . . Selected and arranged by M. L. Byrn. pp. 392. *J. P. Jewett & Co.: Boston,* 1853. 8°. **12315**. f. **22**.

BYRN (R. G.) The Commission of H.M.S. Archer, Australian Station. 1900–1904. pp. 88. *Westminster Press: London,* 1904. 8°. [*"Log" Series.*] **08806**. bb. **10**. (**1**.)

BYRNE (Alexander S.) Observations on the Best Means of Propelling Ships . . . Second edition. pp. 47. *C. S. Francis: New-York; J. H. Francis: Boston,* 1841. 8°. **1397**. e. **35**. (**1**.)

BYRNE (Alfred T.)

—— Medical Services for the Future. By Alfred T. Byrne . . . Public Utilities. By F. P. Russell pp. 10. 5. *J. Duffy & Co.: Dublin,* [1944.] 8°. [*Reconstruction Pamphlets.* no. 2 & 5.] **08218.a.13/2 & 5.**

BYRNE (Anna Dorothea) *Lady.* Dame Anna Dorothea Birne . . . and Sir John Birne Bart. an infant . . . Appellants. George Hartpole . . . and others, Respondents. The appellants case. pp. 3. [*London,*] 171$\frac{7}{8}$. fol. **19**. h. **1**. (**56**.)

—— Dame Anna Dorothea Byrne . . . and Sir J. Byrne, an infant . . . Appellants . . . George Hartpole [and others] . . . Respondents . . . Respondents case. pp. 4. [*London,* 1718.] fol. **19**. h. **1**. (**57**.)

BYRNE (Austin Thomas) A Treatise on Highway Construction . . . Fifth revised and enlarged edition, *etc.* pp. xliii. 1040. *J. Wiley & Sons: New York,* 1908. 8°. **08766**. d. **42**.

—— Modern Road Construction. A practical treatise on the engineering problems of road building, *etc.* pp. 187. 6. *American Technical Society: Chicago,* 1919. 8°. **08767**. eee. **54**.

BYRNE (Austin Thomas) and **PHILLIPS** (Alfred Edward)

—— Masonry Construction. pp. 91. *See* Encyclopaedias. Cyclopedia of Carpentry and Contracting, *etc.* vol. 2. 1910. 8°. **07942**. g. **5**.

BYRNE (Brendan)

—— Three Weeks to a Better Memory . . . Cartoons by Richard Decker. pp. xiv. 233. *John C. Winston Co.: Philadelphia, Toronto,* [1951.] 8°. **08460**. k. **4**.

BYRNE (Brian Oswald Donn) *See* Macauley (Thurston) Donn Byrne, Bard of Armagh. [With a portrait.] [1929.] 8°. **10824**. df. **15**.

—— —— [1930.] 8°. **10824**. df. **23**.

BYRNE (Brian Oswald Donn)

—— *See* Wetherbee (Winthrop) Donn Byrne. A bibli graphy. 1949. 8°. **11927**. b.

—— An Alley of Flashing Spears, and other stories. pp. v. 250. *Sampson Low & Co.: London,* [1933.] 8°. NN. **1987**

—— Blind Raftery and his Wife, Hilaria. pp. 124. *Sampson Low & Co.: London,* [1925.] 8°. **012638**. dd. **5**

—— Brother Saul. pp. 475. *Sampson Low & Co.: Londo* [1927.] 8°. NN. **1276**

—— Changeling, and other stories. pp. vii. 407. *Sampson Low & Co.: London,* [1924.] 8°. NN. **1011**

—— Crusade. pp. 240. *Sampson Low & Co.: Londo* 1928. 8°. NN. **1372**

—— A Daughter of the Medici, and other stories. pp. v. 28 *Sampson Low & Co.: London,* [1933.] 8°. NN. **2095**

—— Destiny Bay. pp. vii. 432. *Sampson Low & Co. London,* 1928. 8°. NN. **1462**

—— The Foolish Matrons. pp. 383. *Harper & Bros. New York & London,* 1920. 8°. NN. **650**

—— [Another edition.] pp. 313. *Sampson Low & Co. London,* [1923.] 8°. NN. **903**

—— The Golden Goat. pp. 156. *Sampson Low & Co. London,* [1930.] 8°. NN. **1616**

—— Hangman's House. pp. x. 406. *Sampson Low & Co. London,* [1926.] 8°. NN. **1154**

—— [Another edition.] pp. 288. *John Lane: London* [1936.] 8°. [*Penguin Books.* no. 24.] **12208.a.1/24**

—— Teaċ an Ċroċadóra .i. Hangman's House . . . Seosa Mac Grianna do ċuir Gaeḋilg air. pp. 564. Oifig Díolta Foillseaċáin Rialtais: Bail Áta Cliat, 1935. 8°. **875**. i. **79**

—— The Hound of Ireland, and other stories. pp. v. 250. *Sampson Low & Co.: London,* [1934.] 8°. NN. **21595**

—— Ireland, the rock whence I was hewn . . . Foreword b the Right Hon. T. P. O'Connor. [With plates.] pp. xxi. 104. *Sampson Low & Co.: London,* [1929.] 8°. **10390**. de. **38**

—— The Island of Youth, and other stories. pp. v. 282. *Sampson Low & Co.: London,* [1932.] 8°. NN. **22608**

—— Messer Marco Polo, *etc.* [A novel.] pp. 147. *Century Co.: New York,* 1921. 12°. **012603**. ff. **43**

—— [Another edition.] pp. 151. *Sampson Low & Co. London,* [1921.] 8°. **12601**. ff. **43**

—— [Another edition.] pp. v. 122. *Sampson Low & Co. London,* [1930.] 8°. **012600**. l. **5**

—— Marco Polo. Seán Mac Maoláin a rinne an leagan Gaeḋilge. pp. 187. Oifig Díolta Foillseaċáin Rialtais: Baile Áta Cliat, 1938. 8°. **012643**. n. **110**.

—— Poems, *etc.* pp. viii. 44. *Sampson Low & Co.: London,* 1934. 8°. **11654**. b. **19**.

—— The Power of the Dog. [With a portrait.] pp. 473. **F.P.** *Sampson Low & Co.: London,* 1929. 8°. **012604**. bb. **46**.

BYRNE (Brian Oswald Donn)

—— The Power of the Dog. pp. 331. *Penguin Books: Harmondsworth, New York,* 1947. 8°. [*Penguin Books.* no. 552.] **12208**. a. **1/552.**

—— Neart na Cú-niṁe. Séan Mac Maoláin a rinne an leagan Gaeḋilge. pp. 761. Baile Áta Cliat, 1940. 8°. **12643**. ppp. **23**.

—— Rivers of Damascus, and other stories. pp. 312. *Sampson Low & Co.: London,* 1931. 8°. NN. **18129**.

—— Sargasso Sea, and other stories. pp. vii. 344. *Sampson Low & Co.: London,* 1932. 8°. NN. **21593**.

—— Stories without Women, *etc.* pp. 330. *Hearst's International Library Co.: New York,* 1915. 8°. NN. **3152**.

—— [Another edition.] pp. v. 282. *Sampson Low & Co.: London,* [1931.] 8°. NN. **17529**.

—— The Strangers' Banquet. pp. 351. *Harper & Bros.: New York & London,* 1919. 8°. NN. **5938**.

—— An Untitled Story. pp. 156. *Sampson Low & Co.: London,* [1925.] 8°. NN. **11072**.

—— The Wind Bloweth. pp. 310. *Sampson Low & Co.: London,* [1922.] 8°. NN. **8338**.

—— [Another edition.] Illustrated by George Bellows. pp. 393. *Century Co.: New York,* 1922. 8°. NN. **21594**.

BYRNE (Charles Alfred) and **FULGONIO** (Fulvio) Gabriella. A lyric drama in one act . . . The English version by M. Marras, *etc. Eng. & Ital.* pp. 27. *R. Cocks & Co.: London,* 1893. 8°. **11725**. b. **24**. (4.)

BYRNE (Charlotte) *See* Dacre, afterwards Byrne.

BYRNE (D. P.) An Exposition of the Medical Treatment of S. M. Watson. pp. 36. *Boston,* 1841. 12°. **7680**. a. **71**. (1.)

BYRNE (Dawson) The Story of Ireland's National Theatre: the Abbey Theatre, Dublin. [With plates, including portraits.] pp. xi. 196. *Talbot Press: Dublin & Cork,* 1929. 8°. **011795**. i. **42**.

BYRNE (Desmond) *See* Byrne (John F. D.)

BYRNE (Dolly) *See* Varesi (Gilda) and Byrne (D.) Enter Madame, *etc.* 1921. 8°. **11791**. de. **11**.

BYRNE (Donn) *See* Byrne (Brian O. D.)

BYRNE (E.) *B.Sc.*

—— *See* Leach (John A.) Australian Nature Studies . . . Revised by E. Byrne. 1952. 8°. **7008**. df. **15**.

BYRNE (E.) *Examining Officer, Customs, Liverpool.* Gauging. pp. 83. *Sheppard & Co.: London,* [1906.] 8°. **8229**. a. **40**.

BYRNE (Elizabeth) *See* Westminster Abbey. The History and Antiquities of Westminster Abbey . . . Illustrated with . . . engravings by Woolnoth, Byrne, *etc.* 1856. 4°. **1782**. c. **9**.

BYRNE (Ethna) Bourdaloue moraliste. pp. 504. *Paris,* 1929. 8°. **4863**. g. **16**.

BYRNE (Eugene Hugh) Genoese Shipping in the Twelfth and Thirteenth Centuries. pp. ix. 159. *Cambridge, Mass.,* 1930. 8°. [*Mediaeval Academy of America. Publication.* no. 5.] **Ac.2684/2.(5.)**

BYRNE (Fanny) *See* Byrne (Miles) Memoirs of M. Byrne . . . Edited by his widow (F. Burne). 1863. 8°. **10826**. f. **4**.

—— —— 1907. 8°. **010827**. f. **12**.

—— *See* Byrne (Miles) M. Byrne. Mémoires d'un exilé irlandais de 1798, édités par sa veuve (F. Byrne), *etc.* 1864. 8°. **10826**. f. **5**.

BYRNE (Francis David) *B.A.* (*Lond.*) *See* Apuleius (L.) *Madaurensis.* [*Asinus Aureus.—English.*] The Golden Ass . . . Newly translated, with introduction and notes, by F. D. Byrne. [1905.] 8°. **12403**. aaa. **40**.

BYRNE (Francis David) *Rev.* Prayers for the People. pp. x. 153. *Burns & Oates: London,* 1896. 8°. **3456**. df. **69**.

BYRNE (Francis X. A.) Commencement Address . . . Ateneo de Manila. pp. vi. [*Manila,* 1925.] 8°. **8385**. dd. **27**.

BYRNE (Frank) An Irish Stew, *etc.* [Tales.] pp. 63. *St. Catherine Press: London,* [1916.] 8°. **012331**. g. **90**.

BYRNE (Frederick) *See* Haemmerlein (Thomas) *a Kempis.* Vera Sapientia . . . Translated . . . by the Right Rev. Mgr. Byrne. 1904. 8°. **04403**. ee. **9**.

BYRNE (G. M.)

—— The Lower Fourth at Rimington. pp. 208. *Gerald G. Swan: London,* [1948.] 8°. **12832**. b. **33**

BYRNE (George)

—— Love tested: Love triumphant. pp. 74. *M. H. Gill & Son: Dublin,* 1951. 8°. **4397**. e. **2**.

—— The Veil upon the Heart. [On the approach to God through prayer.] pp. viii. 103. *M. H. Gill & Son: Dublin,* 1947. 8°. **3458**. aaa. **68**.

BYRNE (Gerald)

—— Borstal Boy. The uncensored story of Neville Heath. pp. 144. *John Hill Productions:* [*London,* 1954.] 8°. **10863.aa.51.**

—— John George Haigh: acid bath killer, *etc.* [With a portrait.] pp. 143. *Headline Publications: London,* [1950.] 8°. **6058**. aa. **8**.

BYRNE (Harriet Anne) *See* Manning (Caroline) The Effects on Women of Changing Conditions in the Cigar and Cigarette Industries. By C. Manning and H. A. Byrne. 1932. 8°. [*U.S. Department of Labor. Women's Bureau. Bulletin.* no. 100.] A.S. **166**.

—— *See* Manning (Caroline) and Byrne (H. A.) The Employment of Women in the Sewing Trades of Connecticut, *etc.* 1935. 8°. [*U.S. Department of Labor. Women's Bureau. Bulletin.* no. 109.] A.S. **166**.

—— *See* Peterson (Agnes L.) and Byrne (H. A.) A Survey of the Shoe Industry in New Hampshire. 1935. 8°. [*U.S. Department of Labor. Women's Bureau. Bulletin.* no. 121.] A.S. **166**.

—— The Age Factor as it relates to Women in Business and the Professions. pp. v. 66. *Washington,* 1934. 8°. [*U.S. Department of Labor. Women's Bureau. Bulletin.* no. 117.] A.S. **166**.

—— The Effects of the Depression on Wage Earners' Families. A second survey of South Bend. pp. v. 31. *Washington,* 1936. 8°. [*U.S. Department of Labor. Women's Bureau. Bulletin.* no. 108.] A.S. **166**.

BYRNE (HARRIET ANNE)

—— Employment in Hotels and Restaurants. pp. vii. 105. *Washington*, 1936. 8°. [*U.S. Department of Labor. Women's Bureau. Bulletin.* no. 123.] A.S. **166**.

—— The Health and Safety of Women in Industry. pp. v. 23. *Washington*, 1935. 8°. [*U.S. Department of Labor. Women's Bureau. Bulletin.* no. 136.] A.S. **166**.

—— Unattached Women on Relief in Chicago, 1937. By H. A. Byrne and Cecile Hillyer. pp. v. 84. *Washington*, 1938. 8°. [*U.S. Women's Bureau. Bulletin.* no. 158.] A.S. 166.

—— Women Office Workers in Philadelphia. pp. v. 17. *Washington*, 1932. 8°. [*U.S. Department of Labor. Women's Bureau. Bulletin.* no. 96.] A.S. **166**.

—— Women Unemployed Seeking Relief in 1933. pp. v. 19. *Washington*, 1936. 8°. [*U.S. Department of Labor. Women's Bureau. Bulletin.* no. 139.] A.S. **166**.

—— Women who Work in Offices. I. Study of employed women. II. Study of women seeking employment. pp. v. 27. *Washington*, 1935. 8°. [*U.S. Department of Labor. Women's Bureau. Bulletin.* no. 132.] A.S. **166**.

—— Women's Employment in West Virginia. pp. v. 27. *Washington*, 1937. 8°. [*U.S. Department of Labor. Women's Bureau. Bulletin.* no. 150.] A.S. **166**.

BYRNE (HARRIET ANNE) and **BLAIR** (BERTHA)

—— Industrial Home Work in Rhode Island, with special reference to the lace industry. pp. v. 27. *Washington*, 1935. 8°. [*U.S. Department of Labor. Women's Bureau. Bulletin.* no. 131.] A.S. **166**.

BYRNE (HARRY J.)

—— Investment of Church Funds. A study in administrative law . . . A dissertation, *etc.* pp. xi. 206. *Catholic University of America Press: Washington*, 1951. 8°. [*Catholic University of America. Canon Law Studies.* no. 309.] Ac. **2692**. y/**21**.

BYRNE (HENRY EDWARD) Byrne Simplified Shorthand . . . Sixth edition. pp. 27. *Byrne Publishing Co.: Tyler, Texas*, [1908.] 8°. **12991**. cc. **40**.

BYRNE (HOWARD)

—— Without Assignment. A personal guide to free lance photo journalism, its business technique & practice. [With illustrations.] pp. 199. *Focal Press: London, New York*, 1951. 8°. **11868**. dd. **44**.

BYRNE (HUBERT J.)

—— The Teacher and his Pupils. (Illustrated by C. W. Bruce.) pp. 185. *Oxford University Press: London*, 1953. 8°. [*Teachers' Library.*] W.P. **12070/4**.

BYRNE (J. C.) Emigrant's Guide to New South Wales Proper, Australia Felix, and South Australia . . . Eighth edition. [With a map.] pp. iv. 128. *Effingham Wilson: London*, 1848. 24°. **10491**. a. **54**.

—— Emigrant's Guide to Port Natal . . . With a map of the Colony. pp. iv. 99. *Effingham Wilson: London*, 1848. 24°. **1304**. a. **18**.

—— Sixth edition, revised. pp. 140. *Effingham Wilson: London*, 1850. 8°. **10097**. a. **39**.

—— Emigrant's Guide to the Cape of Good Hope . . . With a map of the Colony. pp. 91. *Effingham Wilson: London*, 1848. 12°. **1304**. a. **19**.

BYRNE (J. C.)

—— Second edition. pp. 91. *Effingham Wilson: Lond* 1848. 24°. **1304**. a.

—— Twelve Years' Wanderings in the British Colonies, fr 1835 to 1847. 2 vol. *Richard Bentley: London*, 1848. **1430**. k.

BYRNE (J. PATRICK) *Writer of Verse.*

—— A Poem: The Green Tree. *Gayfield: Dublin*, 1941. **11656**. f.

BYRNE (J. R.) *Lieutenant, N.Z.F.A.* New Zealand Artill in the Field, 1914–18. [With plates, including portra and maps.] pp. xii. 314. 1922. 8°. *See* NEW ZEALA Military Forces.—*New Zealand Contingent, British Expe tionary Force.—New Zealand Field Artillery.* **09084**. bb.

BYRNE (JACK)

—— Gunswift. pp. viii. 238. *G. G. Swan: London*, 1943. **12727**. c.

BYRNE (JACQUES) The Legend. A lyric tragedy in act, *etc.* pp. 17. *Chappell & Co.: New York*, [1919.] **11791**. e.

BYRNE (JAMES) *See* O'GALLAGHER (James) successiv *R.C. Bishop of Raphoe* and *of Kildare*. The Sermons the Right Rev. Dr. Gallagher, translated from the origi Irish by J. Byrne, *etc.* 1835. 12°. **4461**. aaa.

BYRNE (JAMES) *Coachman.* The Irishman in Lond Byrne versus Parkins: the celebrated speech of Phillips, Esq. The whole of the trials at the Court King's Bench, in the case of Byrne v. Parkins . February 16th, 1824, *etc.* pp. 16. *G. Hebert: Lon* 1824. 8°. **6495**. bb. **2**. (

—— Sketch of the Life, and Unparalleled Sufferings of Ja Byrne, late coachman to the Honourable John Jocel brother to . . . the Lord Bishop of Clogher. Toget with some observations on the conduct of the Joce family, *etc.* pp. iv. 36. *T. Dolby: London*, [1822.] 8 **6495**. bb. **2**. (

—— Subscription for James Byrne. [An appeal, with a of subscribers.] *T. Dolby: [London*, 1822.] *s. sh.* 8°. **6495**. bb. **2**. (

BYRNE (JAMES) *Dean of Clonfert.* General Principles of Structure of Language. 2 vol. *Trübner & Co.: Lon* 1885. 8°. **12901**. g.

—— Second edition. 2 vol. *Kegan Paul & Co.: Lon* 1892. 8°. **12901**. f.

—— *See* SCHULENBURG (A. C. von der) *Count.* Über Verschiedenheiten des menschlichen Sprachba Eine Studie über das Werk des James Byr Principles of the Structure of Language. 1895. 8 **12902.g.16.(6**

—— The Influence of Foreign Literature on English Lite ture. 1866. *See* ENGLISH LITERATURE. The Aftern Lectures on English Literature, *etc.* ser. 3. 1863, *etc.* 8°. **11826**. aa. **19**.

—— The Influence of National Character on English Lite ture. *See* ENGLISH LITERATURE. The Afternoon L tures on English Literature, *etc.* ser. 1. 1863, *etc.* 8° **11826**. aa. **17**.

—— A Letter on the Irish Church Question, addressed to Right Hon. W. E. Gladstone, M.P. pp. 46. *Hod Smith & Co.: Dublin*, 1867. 8°. **4165**. aaa.

BYRNE (James) *Dean of Clonfert.*

—— Naturalism and Spiritualism: six discourses on those forms of theistical infidelity; preached before the University of Dublin, at the Donnellan Lecture. pp. iv. 184. *Hodges, Smith & Co.: Dublin,* 1856. 8°. **4015.** d. 5.

—— On the General Principles of the Establishment and Endowment of Religious Bodies by the State, with special reference to Ireland.—The Influences exerted on Ireland by the Irish Church Establishment. *See* Ireland.—*Church of Ireland.* Essays on the Irish Church. 1866. 8°. **4165.** f. 4.

—— Origin of the Greek, Latin, and Gothic Roots. pp. vi. 359. *Trübner & Co.: London,* 1888 [1887]. 8°. **12902.** e. **35.**

—— Second edition. pp. viii. 359. *Kegan Paul & Co.: London,* 1893. 8°. **12902.** dd. **38.**

BYRNE (James) *Lawyer, of New York. See* Burlingham (Charles C.) Heidelberg and the Universities of America. [Edited by C. C. Burlingham, J. Byrne and others.] 1936. 8°. **8358.** ccc. **34.**

—— Foreclosure of Railroad Mortgages. *See* Phases. Some Legal Phases of Corporate Financing, *etc.* 1917. 8°. **06616.** df. **25.**

BYRNE (James) *of Byrne & Co., Ltd.* Byrne's Guide to Company Formation, *etc.* pp. 103. *Byrne & Co.: London,* [1901.] 8°. **08227.** g. **67.**

BYRNE (James) *pseud.* [i.e. Edward William Garnett.]

—— *See* also Garnett (E. W.)

—— Lords and Masters. A play in three acts. pp. 62. *Sidgwick & Jackson: London,* 1911. 8°. **11775.** ff. **50.** (**2.**)

BYRNE (James) *Weaver.* The Advantage of Reading the Scriptures, exemplified in the history of James Burne, of Kilberry, in Ireland; with observations thereon by an Irish clergyman, to whom he was well known. pp. 12. *R.T.S.: London,* [1823?] 12°. **4422.** k. **48.** (**11.**)
No. 126 *of a numbered series.*

—— [Another edition.] pp. 12. *London,* [1830?] 12°. [*First Series Tracts of the Religious Tract Society.* no. 126.] **863.** k. **9.**

BYRNE (James J.) Handbook of the Catholic Evidence Guild. pp. 119. 1922. 8°. *See* London.—iii. *Catholic Evidence Guild.* **3940.** aa. **63.**

BYRNE (James Patrick) A Handy Book on the Law and Practice of Patents for Inventions . . . Second edition. pp. 158. *Davis & Son: London,* 1860. 8°. **6375.** a. 4.

—— The New Law of Divorce and Matrimonial Causes applicable to Ireland; with the Acts 21 & 22 Vic., c. 85 and 21 & 22 Vic., c. 108, popularly explained. pp. xi. 117. *E. J. Milliken: Dublin,* 1859. 12°. **5176.** aa. **30.**

—— A Treatise on the Law and Practice of Parliamentary Elections in Ireland, from the creation of the vacancies to the final decision of the Election Committees. With an appendix of forms and statutes, *etc.* pp. viii. 244. *Hodges, Smith & Co.: Dublin,* 1865. 12°. **6325.** a. **12.**

BYRNE (Janet) *pseud.* [i.e. Jane Besemeres.] *See* also Besemeres (J.)

—— Patsy's First Glimpse of Heaven. pp. 103. *Cassell, Petter & Galpin: London,* [1873.] 16°. **4413.** ccc. **10.**

—— [A reissue.] *Tubbs & Brook: Manchester,* [1878.] 16°. **4420.** aa. 4.

BYRNE (Janet) *pseud.* [i.e. Jane Besemeres.]

—— Picture Teaching for Young and Old. pp. 184. *Cassell Petter & Galpin: London & New York,* [1869.] 8°. **12807.** f. **72**

—— Picture Teaching Series of Books for the Young. 3 pt.

1. Picture Reading.
2. Picture Geography.
3. Picture Lessons on the Life of Christ.

Cassell, Petter & Galpin: London, [1873.] 8°. **12810.** de. **34.**
A reissue in separate parts of pt. 1, 4 *and* 5 *of "Picture Teaching for Young and Old."*

—— Scraps of Knowledge . . . With . . . illustrations. Second edition. pp. 192. *Cassell, Petter & Galpin: London & New York,* [1872.] 4°. **12806.** f. **32.**

BYRNE (John) *Chairman to Sir Richard Cox.* The Humble Petition of John Byrne, a poor old man, formerly chairman to Sir Richard Cox, Bart. [On the subject of wages due to the petitioner by his former employer. A petition for relief addressed to Parliament and to the citizens of Dublin.] [*Dublin,* 1750?] *s. sh.* fol. **1890.** e. **5.** (**240.**)

BYRNE (John) *Civil Engineer. See* Byrne (Oliver) The Miscellaneous Mathematical Papers of Oliver Byrne . . . Collected and edited by J. Byrne. 1848. 8°. **8530.** c. **17.** (**1.**)

—— *See* Byrne (Oliver) and Byrne (J.) The Fallacies of Our Own Time. 1844. 8°. **1386.** h. **15.**

—— Anti-Phrenology, or, a Chapter on humbug. pp. 36. *The Author: Washington,* 1843. 8°. **8530.** c. **17.** (**3.**)
An enlarged edition of this work, entitled "Fallacy of Phrenology" and forming pt. 1 *of "The Fallacies of Our Own Time," is entered under* Byrne *(Oliver) and* Byrne *(John).*

BYRNE (John) *M.D.* Clinical Notes on the Electric Cautery in Uterine Surgery. pp. 68. *W. Wood & Co.: New York,* 1873. 8°. **7641.** g. **20.**

—— Researches and Observations on Pelvic Hæmatocele. pp. 44. *William Wood: New York,* 1862. 8°. **7620.** aaa. **57.** (**1.**)

BYRNE (John) *Writer of Verse.* Poems on Moral and Religious Subjects. pp. 207. *W. Curry & Co.: Dublin,* [1846.] 12°. **11643.** i. **18.**

BYRNE (John Francis) ***Assistant Professor of Electrical Engineering, Ohio State University.***

—— **Radio Transmission Characteristics of Ohio at Broadcast Frequencies. pp. iii. 18.** ***Columbus, O.,*** **1932. 8°. [*Ohio State University.* Engineering. *Experiment Station Bulletin.* no. 71.]** Ac. **2685.** gb/4. (**71.**)

BYRNE (John Francis) *of Dublin.*

—— Silent Years. An autobiography with memoirs of James Joyce and our Ireland. pp. xi. 307. *Farrar, Straus & Young: New York,* 1953. 8°. **10864.** f. **5.**

BYRNE (John Francis) *of Ringwood. See* Aesop. [*English.—Collections.*] The Fables of Æsop, and other fabulists. In verse. By J. F. Byrne. 1835. 8°. **12304.** ccc. **35.**

—— *See* Ovidius Naso (P.) [*Epistolae Heroidum.—English.*] Ovid's Epistles, translated into verse, by J. F. Byrne. 1858. 8°. **11388.** aaa. **30.**

—— Four Letters on the Corn Laws, addressed to the Right Hon. Sir Robert Peel, Bart. pp. 19. *E. Palmer & Son: London,* 1841. 8°. **8244.** c. **71.** (**3.**)

BYRNE (JOHN FRANCIS DESMOND)

—— Australian Writers. pp. 288. *R. Bentley & Son: London*, 1896. 8°. **011851**. e. 4.

BYRNE (JOHN J.) *Writer on Tailoring.*

—— Perfection. An illustrated manual for artist tailors, exhibiting a . . . method of laying patterns on goods, *etc.* pp. 129. *Trübner & Co.: London; N.Y.* printed, [1889.] *obl.* fol. **1807**. a. 16.

—— Practical Tailoring . . . Revised by Z. W. Shaw. Part three.—Vests. pp. 39. *J. Williamson Co.: London*, [1895.] 8°. **7743**. cc. 36.

BYRNE (JOHN RICE) Diocesan School-Inspection. pp. 31. *Macmillan & Co.: London*, 1870. 8°. **8305**. aaa. 17.

—— Lives of Light & Leading. Biographical sketch of some eminent divines of the last three centuries . . . Reprinted from "Church Bells." pp. iv. 99. "*Church Bells*": *London*, 1904. 8°. **4903**. f. 65.

—— Sermons in Different Styles. Preached at St. James's Church, Piccadilly. pp. vi. 84. *William Skeffington: London*, 1860. 8°. **4464**. a. 15.

BYRNE (JOSEPH)

—— *See* NEW ZEALAND. [*Laws.*—III.] [1922. no. 39.] **Macdonald's Law relating to Workers' Compensation in New Zealand . . . By J. W. Macdonald . . . assisted by . . . J. Byrne. (Supplement no. 9, 1945. Edited by J. Byrne.)** 1934. 8°. **6608**. dd. 4a.

—— Bhagalpur. [With a map and supplementary statistical tables.] pp. xiv. 181. *Calcutta*, 1911. 8°. [*Bengal District Gazetteers.*] I.S. BE. **226**.

BYRNE (JOSEPH GRANDSON) Clinical Studies on the Physiology of the Eye, *etc.* pp. x. 144. *H. K. Lewis & Co.: London*, 1934. 8°. **07611**. ee. 29.

—— On the Physiology of the Semicircular Canals and their relation to Seasickness. pp. ix. 569. *J. T. Dougherty: New York; H. K. Lewis: London*, 1912. 8°. **7406**. ee. 20.

—— Seasickness and Health. A manual for travellers. pp. 128. *H. K. Lewis: London; New York* printed, 1912. 8°. **07620**. de. 8.

—— Studies on the Physiology of the Eye, *etc.* pp. xii. 428. *H. K. Lewis & Co.: London*, 1933. 8°. **2256**. g. 20.

—— Reissue with supplement and new index, *etc.* pp. xii. 440. *H. K. Lewis & Co.: London*, 1938. 8°. **7406**. s. 27.

—— Studies on the Physiology of the Eye . . . Second reissue with supplements, *etc.* pp. xii. 469. *H. K. Lewis & Co.: London*, 1942. 8°. **7406**. s. 37.

—— Studies on the Physiology of the Middle Ear, *etc.* pp. xi. 298. *H. K. Lewis & Co.: London*, 1938. 8°. **7407**. pp. 3.

BYRNE (JULIA CLARA) The "Beggynhof;" or the City of the Single. By the author of "Gheel; or, the City of the Simple" [i.e. J. C. Byrne]. pp. xv. 176. 1869. 8°. *See* BEGGYNHOF. **4071**. bb. 10.

—— Cosas de España. Illustrative of Spain and the Spaniards as they are. vol. 1, 2. *Alexander Strahan: London & New York*, 1866. 8°. **10162**. d. 7.
No more published.

—— Curiosities of the Search-Room. A collection of serious, and whimsical wills. By the author of "Flemish Interiors" [i.e. J. C. Byrne], *etc.* pp. ix. 407. 1880. 8°. *See* CURIOSITIES. **6355**. bb. 20.

BYRNE (JULIA CLARA)

—— De Omnibus Rebus. An old man's discursive rambl on the road of everyday life. By the author of "Flem Interiors" [i.e. J. C. Byrne]. With . . . illustrations R. Caulfield Orpen. pp. xxiii. 343. 1888 [1887]. 8°. RES. **12357**. m.

—— Feudal Castles of France. Western provinces. By author of "Flemish Interiors" [i.e. J. C. Byrne] . Illustrated from the author's sketches. pp. xviii. 360. 1869. 8°. *See* FRANCE. [*Appendix.—Descriptions,* **010171**.

—— Flemish Interiors. By the writer of "A Glance beh the Grilles" [i.e. J. C. Byrne]. pp. xv. 359. [1856.] *See* FLEMISH INTERIORS. **4784**. a.

—— Gheel, the City of the Simple. By the author "Flemish Interiors" [i.e. J. C. Byrne]. pp. xvi. 195. 1869. 8°. *See* GHEEL. **7660**. aa.

—— A Glance behind the Grilles of Religious Houses France, *etc.* [By J. C. Byrne.] pp. xvi. 316. 1855. *See* FRANCE. [*Appendix.—Miscellaneous.*] **4632**. a.

—— Gossip of the Century. Personal and traditi memories social, literary, artistic, &c. By the autho "Flemish Interiors" [i.e. J. C. Byrne], *etc.* (Social Hc with Celebrities; being the third and fourth volume "Gossip of the Century." by the late Mrs. W. Pitt By . . . Edited by her sister, Miss R. H. Busk, *etc.*) [W plates, including a portrait of the author.] 4 vol. *W & Downey: London*, 1892, 98. 8°. **012330**.

—— Pictures of Hungarian Life. By the author of "Flem Interiors" [i.e. J. C. Byrne] . . . Illustrated by author. pp. x. 401. 1869. 8°. *See* HUNGARIAN LIF **10210**. bb.

—— Realities of Paris Life. By the author of "Flem Interiors" [i.e. J. C. Byrne], *etc.* 3 vol. 1859. 8°. PARIS. [*Appendix.—Miscellaneous.*] **10173**. c.

—— Red, White, and Blue: sketches of military life. By author of "Flemish Interiors" [i.e. J. C. Byrne]. 3 1862. 8°. *See* RED. **8834**. f

—— Social Hours with Celebrities. *See* supra: Gossip the Century.

—— Undercurrents Overlooked. By the author of "Flem Interiors" [i.e. J. C. Byrne], *etc.* 2 vol. 1860. *See* UNDERCURRENTS. **8276**. c.

BYRNE (KEVIN)

—— Family Prayers and Mixed Marriages. pp. 16. *Cath Truth Society: London*, 1950. 8°. **3943**. aaa.

BYRNE (*Sir* LAURENCE AUSTIN)

—— *See* ENGLAND.—*Home Office.—Departmental Comm on Depositions.* Report of the Departmental Commi on Depositions, *etc.* [Chairman, Mr. Justice Byrne.] 1949. 8°. B.S. **18/40**. (1

BYRNE (LEE) Check List Materials for Public Sc Building Specifications, *etc.* [A thesis.] pp. vii. 195. *Teachers College, Columbia University: New Y* 1931. 8°. **07815**. aa.

BYRNE (LETITIA) *See* AMSINCK (P.) Tunbridge W . . . The etchings executed by L. Byrne. 1810. 4°. **190**. e.

BYRNE (LIONEL STANLEY RICE) *See* FUGGER, *Famil Barons of Kirchberg and Weissenhorn.* The Fugger N Letters. Second series . . . Translated by L. S. Byrne, *etc.* 1926. 8°. **10906**. b.

BYRNE (LIONEL STANLEY RICE)

—— *See* SOMERVILLE (Annesley A.) and BYRNE (L. S. R.) A First German Writer. 1900. 8°. **12963. e. 37.**

—— —— 1901. 8°. **12963. e. 45.**

—— *See* SOMERVILLE (Annesley A.) and BYRNE (L. S. R.) Primary German Exercises. 1894. 8°. **12962. c. 35.**

—— —— 1894. 8°. **12962. c. 34.**

—— —— 1897. 8°. **12963. bbb. 49.**

—— —— 1901. 8°. **12963. e. 46.**

—— *See* SOMERVILLE (Annesley A.) and BYRNE (L. S. R.) A Primer of German Grammar. 1894. 8°. **12962. c. 32.**

—— —— 1894. 8°. **12962. c. 33.**

—— —— 1896. 8°. **12962. c. 38.**

—— —— 1899. 8°. **12962. cc. 20.**

—— —— 1903. 8°. **12963. e. 54.**

BYRNE (LIONEL STANLEY RICE) and **CHURCHILL** (ERNEST LEE)

—— Changing Eton. A survey of conditions based on the history of Eton since the Royal Commission of 1862–64. [With plates.] pp. ix. 278. *Jonathan Cape: London,* 1937. 8°. **08364. g. 54.**

—— A Comprehensive French Grammar, with classified vocabularies. pp. xxi. 515. *Basil Blackwell: Oxford,* 1950. 8°. **012955. b. 1.**

—— Exercises and Vocabularies for A Comprehensive French Grammar. pp. v. 320. *Basil Blackwell: Oxford,* 1951. 8°. **012955. b. 6.**

—— The Eton Book of the River. With some account of the Thames and the evolution of boat-racing. pp. xvii. 262. pl. LXIII. *Spottiswoode, Ballantyne & Co.: Eton,* 1935. 4°. **2270. bb. 26.**

—— The Eton Book of the River, *etc.* (Second edition.) pp. xvi. 228. pl. LXIII. *Alden & Blackwell: Eton,* 1952. 4°. **7921. cc. 29.**

BYRNE (LUCIUS WIDDRINGTON) *See* ELLIS (Arthur L.) The Trustee Acts . . . Sixth edition by L. W. Byrne. 1903. 8°. **6355. aaa. 47.**

—— *See* HOLT (Ernest W. L.) and BYRNE (L. W.) Third (—Sixth) Report on the Fishes of the Irish Atlantic Slope. 1910, *etc.* 8°. [*Department of Agriculture and Technical Instruction for Ireland. Fisheries Branch. Scientific Investigations.* 1908. no. 4, 5. 1910. no. 6. 1912. no. 1.] **C.S.A.22/19.**

BYRNE (MARIE JOSÉ) Prolegomena to an Edition of the Works of Decimus Magnus Ausonius. [A thesis. With a bibliography.] pp. 101. *New York,* 1916. 8°. [*Columbia University Studies in Classical Philology.*] **Ac. 2688/15. (5.)**

BYRNE (MARJORIE)

—— Mr. & Mrs. Mouse, and other poems. pp. 16. *Arthur H. Stockwell: Ilfracombe,* 1946. 8°. **11655. ee. 95.**

BYRNE (MARY) Murder at the "Signal." pp. 256. *John Long: London,* [1936.] 8°. **NN. 26312.**

BYRNE (MARY E.) *See* DUBLIN.—*Royal Irish Academy.* Catalogue of Irish Manuscripts . . . By T. F. O'Rahilly (M. E. Byrne). 1926, *etc.* 8°. **W.P.4196.**

—— *See* FRÁECH. Táin Bó Fraích. Edited by M. E. Byrne and M. Dillon. 1933. 8°. [*Mediaeval and Modern Irish Series.* vol. 5.] **Ac. 9955. b.**

BYRNE (MATTHEW J.) *See* LOMBARDUS (Petrus) *R.C. Archbishop of Armagh.* The Irish War of Defence, 1598–1600. Extracts from the De Hibernia Insula Commentarius . . . Edited, with introduction and translation, by M. J. Byrne. 1930. 8°. **W.P. 9829/1.**

—— *See* O'SULLEVAN (Philippus) Ireland under Elizabeth . . . Being a portion of the history of Catholic Ireland . . . Translated . . . by M. J. Byrne. 1903. 8°. **9508. c. 3.**

—— Library Musings. pp. 67. *The Kerryman: Tralee,* 1927. 8°. **11908. a. 59.**

BYRNE (MAY) Ingram Place. A novel. By a Cape Colonist [i.e. M. Byrne]. 2 vol. 1874. 8°. *See* INGRAM PLACE. **12638. e. 11.**

—— Power's Partner. 3 vol. *Hurst & Blackett: London,* 1876. 8°. **12621. i. 8.**

BYRNE (MILES) Memoirs of Miles Byrne, chef de bataillon in the service of France . . . Edited by his widow (Fanny Byrne). [With a portrait.] 3 vol. *G. Bossange & Cie: Paris,* 1863. 8°. **10826. f. 4.**

—— A new edition with an introduction by Stephen Gwynn. 2 vol. *Maunsel & Co.: Dublin,* 1907. 8°. **010827. f. 12.**

—— Mémoires d'un exilé irlandais de 1798, édités par sa veuve (Fanny Byrne). Traduction . . . par A. Hédouin. [With a portrait.] 2 tom. *Paris,* 1864. 8°. **10826. f. 5.**

—— Some Notes of an Irish Exile of 1798: being the chapters from the Memoirs of Miles Byrne relating to Ireland. pp. 301. *Maunsel & Co.: Dublin,* [1910.] 8°. **010827. f. 37.**

—— Deoraiḋe Gaeḋil ag eaċtraḋ ar Ḃliain a 1798. Nioclás Tóibín d'aistriġ, *etc.* pp. 346. Oifig Díolta Foillseaċáin Rialtais: Baile Áṫa Cliaṫ, 1937. 8°. **10856. l. 15.**

BYRNE (MURIEL SAINT CLARE)

—— *See* HENRY VIII., *King of England.* The Letters of King Henry VIII . . . Edited by M. St. C. Byrne. 1936. 8°. **010920. f. 55.**

—— *See* MUNDAY (Anthony) John a Kent & John a Cumber. [Edited by M. St. Clare Byrne.] 1923. 4°. **Ac. 9923. (48.)**

—— *See* RUSSELL (Francis) *2nd Earl of Bedford.* "My Lord's Books." The library of Francis, second Earl of Bedford. [Edited with an introduction by M. St. C. Byrne and G. S. Thomson.] [1931.] 8°. **11912. aa. 67.**

—— *See* SAINLIENS (C. DE) The Elizabethan Home, *etc.* (Edited by M. St. C. Byrne.) [1925.] 8°. **C. 102. i. 1/4.**

—— —— 1930. 8°. **010360. bbb. 15.**

—— *See* SAINLIENS (C. DE) The Elizabethan Home . . . Edited by M. St. Clare Byrne. 1949. 8°. **010368. k. 85.**

—— *See* SAINLIENS (C. DE) The French Littelton . . . With an introduction by M. St Clare Byrne. 1953. 8°. **012955. b. 16.**

BYRNE (MURIEL SAINT CLARE)

—— *See* SAYERS (Dorothy L.) and BYRNE (M. S. C.) Bridgeheads. Edited by D. L. Sayers and M. S. C. Byrne. 1941, *etc.* 8°. **012213**. bb. **7**.

—— *See* SAYERS (Dorothy L.) and BYRNE (M. St. C.) Busman's Honeymoon, *etc.* 1937. 8°. [*Famous Plays of* 1937.] **11778**. ppp. **33**.

—— *See* SHAKESPEARE (W.) [*Smaller Collections of Plays.*] The New Eversley Shakespeare, *etc.* (King Henry VIII. Edited by M. St. C. Byrne.) 1935, *etc.* 8°. **011768.ff.8/23.**

—— *See* SHAKESPEARE (W.) [*King Henry VIII.*] King Henry VIII . . . Edited by M. St. C. Byrne, *etc.* 1937. 8°. **012209.d.1/53.**

—— *See* TOPSELL (Edward) The Elizabethan Zoo, *etc.* [Extracts from E. Topsell's "Historie of Foure-footed Beastes" and "Historie of Serpents," with additional matter taken from Philemon Holland's translation of Pliny's "Natural History." Edited by M. St. C. Byrne.] 1926. 4°. C. **102**. i. **1/9**.

—— Aldebaran. [Poems.] pp. 63. *B. H. Blackwell: Oxford,* 1917. 8°. ["*Adventurers All*" *Series.* no. 14.] **011604**. g. **31/14**.

—— Bibliographical Clues in Collaborate Plays. [With special reference to "The Downfall of Robert Earl of Huntington" and "The Death of Robert Earle of Huntington."] (Reprinted from the Transactions of the Bibliographical Society.) *London,* 1932. 8°. **11912**. b. **69**.

—— Common or Garden Child. A not-unfaithful record. pp. 187. *Faber & Faber: London,* 1942. 8°. **10859**. r. **16**.

—— Elizabethan Handwriting for Beginners . . . Reprinted from The Review of English Studies, *etc.* pp. 12. *Sidgwick & Jackson: London,* [1925.] 8°. **07943**. bb. **26**.

—— Elizabethan Life in Town and Country . . . With eleven illustrations. pp. x. 294. *Methuen & Co.: London,* 1925. 8°. **10368**. ccc. **53**.

—— Second edition, revised, with an introduction. pp. xxii. 295. *Methuen & Co.: London,* 1934. 8°. **010352**. bb. **52**.

—— Elizabethan Life in Town and Country . . . Fourth edition, revised and enlarged. pp. xxiv. 302. *Methuen & Co.: London,* 1946. 8°. **09506**. h. **41**.

—— Elizabethan Life in Town and Country, *etc.* (Sixth edition, revised.) pp. xxiv. 302. *Methuen & Co.: London,* 1950. 8°. **9501**. a. **10**.

—— Elizabethan Life in Town and Country, *etc.* (Seventh edition, revised.) pp. xxiv. 802. *Methuen & Co.: London,* 1954. 8°. **9525**. de. **22**.

—— Havelok the Dane, Childe Horn, William and the Werwolf, told from the originals by M. St. C. Byrne. Illustrated by E. M. Ball. pp. 175. *Jonathan Cape: London,* 1929. 8°. [*Children's Library.* ser. 3. no. 5.] **12827.b.1/5.**

—— A History of Shakespearean Production. [The catalogue of an exhibition prepared by M. S. C. Byrne.] pp. 35. *Arts Council of Great Britain: London,* 1947. 8°. W.P. **12368/71**.

BYRNE (MURIEL SAINT CLARE) and **MANSFIELD** (CATHERINE HOPE)

—— Somerville College, 1879–1921 . . . With an introductory chapter by Mrs. T. H. Green . . . and seven illustrations by Edmund H. New. pp. vi. 99. *University Press: Oxford,* [1922.] 8°. **08364**. de. **14**.

BYRNE (OLIVER) *See* EUCLID. [*Elementa.*] The Doctrine of Proportion clearly developed . . . or, the Fifth book of Euclid simplified. By O. Byrne. 1841. 8°. **1140**. d. **27**.

—— *See* EUCLID. [*Elementa.*] The First Six Books of the Elements of Euclid, in which coloured diagrams and symbols are used instead of letters . . . By O. Byrne. 1847. 4°. **C.117.e.2.**

—— *See* SCOTT (Robert) *Cotton Manufacturers.* The Practical Cotton Spinner . . . Corrected and enlarged . . . by O. Byrne. 1851. 8°. **7954**. d. **24**. (**1**.)

—— The Miscellaneous Mathematical Papers of Oliver Byrne . . . Collected and edited by John Byrne. pt. 1. pp. 81. *Maynard: London,* 1848. 8°. **8530**. c. **17**. (**1**.)
No more published.

—— The American Engineer, Draftsman, and Machinist's Assistant, *etc.* pp. 128. pl. XIV. *C. A. Brown & Co.: Philadelphia,* 1853. 4°. **1262**. h. **14**.

—— Appleton's Dictionary of Machines, Mechanics, Enginework, and Engineering, *etc.* [Edited by O. Byrne.] 2 vol. 1852. 4°. *See* APPLETON (Daniel) AND Co. **08767**. k. **18**.

—— The Calculator's Constant Companion, for practical men, machinists, mechanics and engineers. pp. 288. *J. W. Moore: Philadelphia,* 1854. 12°. **1393**. a. **8**.

—— The Calculus of Form. [By O. Byrne.] [1870?] 4°. *See* CALCULUS. C. **40**. i. **5**.

—— The Creed of Saint Athanasius proved by a Mathematical Parallel. [A satire. By O. Byrne.] pp. viii. 6. 1839. 8°. *See* ATHANASIAN CREED. [*Appendix.*] **1119**. i. **16**.

—— [Another copy.] **3504**. f. **10**. (**3**.)

—— Description and Use of the Byrnegraph: an instrument for multiplying, dividing and comparing lines, angles, surfaces, and solids. pp. 38. **L.P.** *C. & J. Adlard: London,* 1846. 8°. **1394**. k. **13**.

—— [Another copy.] **8530**. c. **17**. (**2**.)
Imperfect; wanting the last leaf containing a list of the author's works.

—— Dual Arithmetic. A new art. 2 pt. *Bell & Daldy: London,* 1863, 67. 8°. **8504**. cc. **18**.

—— New issue. With a complete analysis. pp. vi. 85. *Bell & Daldy: London,* 1864. 8°. **8504**. cc. **19**.
Containing "An Analysis of Dual Arithmetic" only.

—— The Essential Elements of Practical Mechanics, based on the principle of work; designed for engineering students. pp. xi. 360. *E. & F. N. Spon: London,* 1867. 8°. **08768**. aa. **30**.

—— General Method of Solving Equations of all degrees; applied particularly to equations of the second, third, fourth, and fifth degrees. pp. 31. *E. & F. N. Spon: London,* 1868. 8°. **8529**. bbb. **32**. (**9**.)

[BY]RNE (OLIVER)

—— The Geometry of Compasses; or, Problems resolved by the mere description of circles, and the use of coloured diagrams and symbols. *C. Lockwood & Co.: London,* 1877. 8°. **8534**. b. **1**.

—— The Handbook for the Artisan, Mechanic, and Engineer, *etc.* pp. 483. pl. XI. *T. K. Collins, Jr.: Philadelphia,* 1853. 8°. **8765**. d. **18**.

—— How to Measure the Earth with the assistance of Railroads. pp. 12. *Currie & Bowman: Newcastle,* 1838. 8°. **716**. f. **21**.

—— Lectures on the Art and Science of War: addressed to Irish-American citizen soldiers. [With diagrams.] pp. 42. *Patrick Donahoe: Boston,* 1853. 8°. **8824**. f. **27**. (**2**.)

—— Mechanics: their principles and practical applications. pp. 182. *De Witt & Davenport: New York,* [1853.] 12°. **8765**. b. **32**.

—— The Mechanics' Manual: a pocket companion for working carpenters, joiners, *etc.* pp. 128. *J. M. Fairchild & Co.: New York,* 1856. 16°. **1392**. a. **40**.

—— New and Improved System of Logarithms . . . Also, an appendix, containing tables of trigonometrical formulæ, *etc.* pp. xii. 106. *William Day: London,* 1838. fol. **715**. l. **14**.

—— Pocket-Book for Railroad and Civil Engineers. Containing new, exact, and concise methods for laying out railroad curves, switches, *etc.* pp. 163. *C. Shepard & Co.: New York,* 1856. 12°. **1392**. b. **54**.

—— The Pocket Companion for Machinists, Mechanics and Engineers, *etc.* pp. 144. pl. III. *Dewitt & Davenport: New York,* 1851. 12°. **8765**. a. **9**.

—— The Practical, Complete and Correct Gager, containing a description of Parker and Byrne's patent calculating instruments; with their use and applications. pp. xvii. 328. *A. H. Bailey & Co.: London,* 1840. 8°. **1394**. g. **5**.

—— The Practical Metal-Worker's Assistant: containing the arts of working all metals and alloys . . . with the application of . . . electro-metallurgy to manufacturing processes, *etc.* pp. 577. *H. C. Baird: Philadelphia,* 1851. 8°. **7955**. d. **24**.

—— A new, revised, and improved edition, with additions by John Scoffern . . . William Clay, William Fairbairn . . . and James Napier, *etc.* pp. 652. *H. C. Baird: Philadelphia,* 1864. 8°. **7943**. cc. **45**.

—— The Practical Model Calculator, for the engineer, mechanic, machinist, *etc.* pp. 591. *H. C. Baird: Philadelphia,* 1852. 8°. **8765**. e. **15**.

—— Index to the Practical Model Calculator. *H. C. Baird: Philadelphia,* 1851. 8°. **7954**. d. **24**. (**2**.)

—— A Short Practical Treatise on Spherical Trigonometry, *etc.* pp. xi. 37. *A. J. Valpy: London,* 1835. 8°. **716**. f. **20**.

—— Spons' Dictionary of Engineering, Civil, Mechanical, Military and Naval; with technical terms in French, German, Italian and Spanish. Edited by O. Byrne (by Byrne and Spon). pp. vii. viii. 3131. *E. & F. N. Spon: London,* 1869–74. 8°.

BYRNE (OLIVER)

—— Supplement . . . Edited by Ernest Spon. pp. 1168. *E. & F. N. Spon: London,* 1879–81. 8°. *Imperfect; wanting pp.* 737–740. **8769.h.14.**

—— Tables of Dual Logarithms, Dual Numbers, and corresponding Natural Numbers, *etc.* pp. 40. 74. 38. 90. *Bell & Daldy: London,* 1867. 4°. **8504**. e. **26**.

—— Byrne's Treatise on Navigation and Nautical Astronomy, *etc.* pp. xvi. 5–218. 462. *The Author: Jersey City & Maidstone; Edinburgh & London* printed, 1875. 4°. **8805**. ff. **4**.

—— [A reissue.] *R. Bentley & Son: London,* 1877. 4°. **8806**. h. **1**.

—— The Young Dual Arithmetician; or, Dual arithmetic . . . Designed for elementary instruction, *etc.* pp. xii. 144. 58. *Bell & Daldy: London,* 1866. 12°. **8505**. bb. **22**.

—— Second edition, revised and amended. pp. xii. 206. *E. & F. N. Spon: London,* 1871. 12°. **8506**. bbb. **23**.

—— The Young Geometrician; or, Practical geometry without compasses. pp. vii. 62. *Chapman & Hall: London,* 1865. 8°. **8530**. h. **28**.

BYRNE (OLIVER) and **BYRNE** (JOHN)

—— The Fallacies of Our Own Time . . . Fallacy of Phrenology. [An enlarged edition of "Anti-Phrenology," by J. Byrne.] pp. 79. *Sherwood, Gilbert & Piper: London,* 1844. 8°. **1386**. h. **15**. *No more published.*

BYRNE (OLIVER) and **HULL** (HENRY WILLIAM)

—— Exemplary Institute for Mathematics, Engineering, Classics and General Literature, Surrey Villa, near Lambeth Palace. Principals: Oliver Byrne . . . and Henry William Hull. (Prospectus.) pp. 8. *W. Barnes: London,* [1845?] 8°. **8365**. b. **48**. (**1**.)

BYRNE (PADDY) Paddy Byrne's Connaught College. [In verse and prose.] To which is added, Big Black Turf. [A song.] pp. 8. *Wholesale & Retail Book Warehouse: Dublin,* [1825?] 16°. **1078**. k. **12**. (**43**.)

—— [Another copy.] **1078**. e. **15**. (**1**.)

BYRNE (PATRICK) *Biographer.*

—— Lord Edward Fitzgerald. [With a portrait.] pp. 252. *Talbot Press: Dublin,* 1955. 8°. **10864**. i. **8**.

—— The Wildes of Merrion Square: the family of Oscar Wilde. pp. 224. *Staples Press: London, New York,* 1953. 8°. **10861**. ee. **47**.

BYRNE (PATRICK) *of Inchicore.*

—— An Evening in the Green Hills; or, the Complaint of the dogs on taxation. [In verse.] pp. vi. 58. *J. F. Fowler: Dublin,* 1869. 16°. **11649**. cc. **17**. (**7**.)

BYRNE (PATRICK JOHN) *See* NORTHAMPTON, *County of.* County of Northampton. [Certificates of the surgeon, of the under-sheriff and others, and of the coroner's court to the execution and death of P. J. Byrne.] [1878.] *s. sh.* fol. **1881**. c. **16**. (**67**.)

—— Execution of Sergeant Patrick John Byrne, for the murder of Quarter-master Sergt. Brooks and Paymaster Sergeant Griffiths, *etc.* [*Arlidge: Northampton,* 1878.] *s. sh.* fol. **1881**. c. **16**. (**73**.)

BYRNE (PATRICK ROBERT) *See* GAYER (Charles) Persecution of Protestants in the year 1845, as detailed in a full and correct report of the trial (Gayer versus Byrne) at Tralee, *etc.* 1845. 8°. **3942. d. 13.**

BYRNE (*Sir* PETER) *Bart.* The Case of Sir Peter Byrne, Baronet. [On a bill brought into Parliament to meet the difficulties caused by the will of Sir Francis Leicester.] pp. 3. [*London*, 1744?] fol. (S.P.R.) **358. b. 4. (22.)**

BYRNE (REGINALD) Examination Questions in Banking and Finance, together with answers thereto. pp. 129. *Coaching Association: London*, [1931.] 8°. **08225. a. 27.**

—— Examination Questions on Banking, Financial Knowledge and Foreign Exchange . . . Second edition. pp. 235. *Coaching Association: London*, [1933.] 8°. **08228. de. 37.**

—— Examination Questions in Company Law, together with answers thereto. pp. 108. *Coaching Association: London*, [1931.] 8°. **6405. bbb. 19.**

—— Second edition. pp. 330. *Coaching Association: London*, [1933.] 8°. **6405. bbb. 24.**

—— Examination Questions in General Commercial Knowledge, together with answers thereto. pp. 210. *Coaching Association: London*, [1931.] 8°. **08225. a. 25.**

—— Examination Questions in Mercantile Law, together with answers thereto. pp. 157. *Coaching Association: London*, [1931.] 8°. **6836. df. 22.**

—— Examination Questions in Partnership Law, together with answers thereto. pp. 65. *Coaching Association: London*, [1931.] 8°. **6405. bbb. 18.**

—— (Second edition.) pp. 153. *Coaching Association: London*, [1933.] 8°. **6405. bbb. 25.**

—— Examination Questions on Bankruptcy and Deeds of Arrangement, together with answers thereto. pp. 123. *Coaching Association: London*, [1931.] 8°. **6405. bbb. 20.**

—— Second edition. pp. 183. *Coaching Association: London*, [1932.] 8°. **6405. p. 23.**

—— Examination Questions on Economics, together with answers thereto. pp. 239. *Coaching Association: London*, [1932.] 8°. **8207. a. 36.**

—— Examination Questions on Executorship, together with answers thereto. Also a summary of the law relating to estate duty on companies. pp. 189. *Coaching Association: London*, [1931.] 8°. **6405. p. 21.**

—— Second edition. pp. 212. *Coaching Association: London*, [1934.] 8°. **6405. bbb. 26.**

—— Examination Questions on Liquidations and Receivers, together with answers thereto. pp. 129. *Coaching Association: London*, [1932.] 8°. **6405. bbb. 22.**

—— Examination Questions on Statistics, together with answers thereto. [By R. Byrne.] pp. 86. [1931.] 8°. *See* EXAMINATION QUESTIONS. **08534. de. 56.**

—— 109 Examination Questions on General Financial Knowledge, together with answers thereto. pp. 187. *Coaching Association: London*, [1934.] 8°. **08235. l. 27.**

BYRNE (SIMON) A New Song called Byrne's Victory. Together with Mary's Dream. The Banks of Invarary. The Boarding School Lasses. pp. 8. *Wholesale & Retail Book Warehouse: Dublin*, [1830?] 16°. **1078. k. 12. (10.)**

—— [Another copy.] **1078. k. 25. (12.)**

BYRNE (STAFFORD) The Laughing Cavalier. A romanti[c] comedy, *etc.* ff. 80. [*The Author: London*, 1934.] 4°. **011779. l. 7**

Typewritten.

BYRNE (THEODORE EDGAR DICKSON) Lunacy and Law together with hints on the treatment of idiots. pp. 41. *H. K. Lewis: London*, 1864. 8°. **6095. b. 26. (7**

BYRNE (THOMAS S.) *See* ALZOG (J. B.) [Universa[l]geschichte der christlichen Kirche.] Manual of Univers[al] Church History . . . Translated . . . by F. J. Pabisc[h] . . . and Rev. T. S. Byrne. 1874, *etc.* 8°. **4531. g.**

—— —— 1879, *etc.* 8°. **2010.d**

BYRNE (VINCENT) Occasional Sermons. [With a por[trait.] pp. vii. 309. *Browne & Nolan: Dublin*, [1937.] 8° **4480. de.**

BYRNE (WALTER) *See* STONE (Richard) Richard Ston[e] Esq; and others, Apellants [*sic*]. W. Byrne, Responden[t]. The apellant's [*sic*] case, *etc.* [1722.] fol. **19. h. 2. (17**

—— *See* STONE (Richard) Richard Stone, Esq; [and other[s] . . . Appellants. W. Byrne Esquire, Respondent. Th[e] respondent's case. [1722.] fol. **19. h. 2. (18**

—— Walter Byrne, Esq; and John Byrne, Gent. Appellant[s]. Thomas Acton, Esq; Respondent. The appellants cas[e]. pp. 3. [*London*, 1721.] fol. **19. h. 1. (218**

—— Walter Byrne, Esquire; and John Byrne, Gent. Appe[l]lants. Thomas Acton, Esquire, Respondent. Th[e] respondent's case. pp. 3. [*London*, 1721.] fol. **19. h. 1. (219**

BYRNE (WILLIAM) *Barrister-at-Law.* *See* O'CONNOR (*Righ[t] Hon. Sir* James) The Irish Justice of the Peace . . . B[y] J. O'Connor . . . assisted, as to vol. II. by W. Byrn[e]. 1915. 8°. **6503. d. 2**

BYRNE (WILLIAM) *Distiller, of Comber.* The Northe[rn] Banking Company against William Byrne . . . Extrac[t] of the proceedings in this matter, in the Insolvent Cour[t] Queen's Bench; Bankrupt Court; Chancery, *etc.* [B[y] W. Byrne.] pp. 188. *W. & G. Agnew: Belfast*, 1853. 8 **8223. b. 4**

BYRNE (WILLIAM) *Engraver.* *See* CRIRIE (James) Scottis[h] Scenery . . . with engravings by W. Byrne . . . fro[m] views painted by G. Walker, *etc.* 1803. 4°. **11642. h. 3**

—— *See* HEARNE (Thomas) *Artist.* Antiquities of Gre[at] Britain, illustrated in views of monasteries . . . E[n]graved by W. Byrne . . . from drawings made by [T.] Hearne, *etc.* 1807. *obl.* fol. **2061.c**

—— Britannia Depicta; a series of views, with brief descri[p]tions, of the most interesting and picturesque objects [in] Great Britain engraved from drawings by Messrs. Hearn[e], Farington, Smith, Turner, Alexander, &c. By W. Byr[ne] [and others], *etc.* 6 pt. *T. Cadell & W. Davies: Londo[n]*, 1806–18. *obl.* fol. **1899.cc.12**

—— Scottish Scenery. Twenty views engraved by W. Byr[ne] . . . from pictures by G. Walker . . . With brief descri[p]tions. pl. xx. 1807. *obl.* 4°. See WALKER (George) F.S.A.E. **187. c.**

BYRNE (WILLIAM) *of Cheltenham.* Poems. pp. 109. *Groombridge & Sons: London; James Hogg: Edinburg[h]*, 1855. 8°. **11648. b.**

BYRNE (WILLIAM A.) A Light on the Broom . . . [Poems] Second thousand. pp. viii. 98. *M. H. Gill & So[n]: Dublin*, 1904. 8°. **011651. e. 7**

RNE (WILLIAM JAMES) *See* BEVEN (Thomas) Negligence in Law . . . Fourth edition by W. J. Byrne . . . and A. D. Gibb. 1928. 8°. **6327.c.12.**

— *See* BROOM (Herbert) A Selection of Legal Maxims . . . The ninth edition. By W. J. Byrne. 1924. 8°. **2016.f.**

— *See* GALE (Charles J.) A Treatise on the Law of Easements . . . The tenth edition by W. J. Byrne. 1925. 8°. **6305. t. 10.**

— *See* WILLIAMS (Joshua) Principles of the Law of Personal Property . . . The eighteenth edition by . . . T. C. Williams . . . assisted by W. J. Byrne. 1926. 8°. **2017. c.**

— A Dictionary of English Law. pp. xliv. 942. *Sweet & Maxwell: London,* 1923. 8°. **6145. r. 2.**

RNE (*Mrs.* WILLIAM PITT) *See* BYRNE (Julia C.)

RNELL (GEORGE J.) A Bible Course, simply arranged, *etc.* 2 pt. *Soldiers' Christian Association; Pickering & Inglis: London, Glasgow,* [1929.] 8°. **03127. g. 53.**

RNES (DANIEL) A Short Address to the English Colonies in North-America. [On negro slavery.] [*Wilmington?* 1775.] *s. sh.* fol. **L.7.a.3.(73.)**

— [Another edition.] pp. 2. [*Wilmington?* 1775.] *s. sh.* fol. **1850. c. 6. (5.)**

RNES (GARRETT DAVIS)

— *See* HART (James S.) and BYRNES (G. D.) Scoop. 1930. 8°. **A.N. 430.**

— Fashion in Newspapers. pp. 74. *Columbia University Press: New York,* 1951. 4°. [*Handbook for Editors.* no. 2.] **Ac. 2688. pb.**

— Food in Newspapers. pp. 20. [*New York,* 1951.] 4°. [*Handbook for Editors.* no. 1.] **Ac. 2688. pb.**

RNES (JAMES FRANCIS)

— Address . . . at the Overseas Press Club, New York City. February 28, 1946. pp. 14. *Washington,* 1946. 8°. [*U.S. Department of State, United States—United Nations Information Series.* no. 4.] **A.S. 420/93.**

— Report on First Session of the Council of Foreign Ministers . . . October 5, 1945. pp. 10. 1945. 8°. *See* UNITED STATES OF AMERICA.—*Department of State.* **A.S. 419/77.**

— Speaking Frankly. [An account of the conferences on a peace settlement held in 1945 and 1946, with observations on foreign policy. With portraits.] pp. xii. 324. *William Heinemann: London, Toronto; U.S.A.* printed, [1947.] 8°. **09101. aa. 13.**

— U.S. Aims and Policies in Europe. By the Secretary of State [i.e. J. F. Byrnes]. pp. 12. *Washington,* 1946. 8°. [*U.S. Department of State. European Series.* no. 18.] **A.S. 420/90.**

YRNES (JOHN PATRICK KING)

— Your Money and your Life. pp. 20. *Epworth Press: London,* 1950. 8°. [*Beckly Occasional Papers.* no. 5.] **W.P. 3395/5.**

YRNES (LAWRENCE HENRY) Church Membership: its duties and privileges . . . Second edition. pp. 45. *W. Mack: Bristol; Book Society: London,* 1874. 16°. **4412. a. 71. (3.)**

— The Pastor's Glory and Joy: a sermon, *etc.* pp. 24. *John Snow: London,* 1851. 8°. **4475. c. 15.**

BYRNES (MICHAEL) The Boat Race: a reminiscence. [In verse.] pp. 30. *Henry Vickers: London,* [1877.] 8°. **11602. e. 5. (6.)**

BYRNES (ROBERT FRANCIS)

—— Antisemitism in Modern France. *Rutgers University Press: New Brunswick,* [1950– .] 8°. **W.P. 4146.**

BYRNES (ROBERT STEEL)

—— Endeavour, and other poems. pp. 105. *Queensland Authors & Artists' Association: Brisbane,* 1954. 8°. **11685. f. 7.**

BYRNES (THOMAS E.) The Inevitable Hour. A play in one act. pp. 28. *Samuel French: New York, Los Angeles,* [1939.] 8°. **11792. aa. 55.**

BYRNES (THOMAS F.)

—— Darkness and Daylight in New York. Criminal life and detective experiences in the great metropolis, *etc.* *See* CAMPBELL (Helen S.) Darkness and Daylight, *etc.* 1892. 8°. **10413. t. 3.**

—— Professional Criminals of America. [With portraits.] pp. 433. *Cassell & Co.: New York,* [1886.] 8°. **6057. f. 1.**

BYRNS (J. M.) *See* HERTY (Charles H.) *the Younger.* The Physical Chemistry of Steel-making: deoxidation of steel with aluminium. By C. H. Herty . . . J. M. Byrns. 1930. 8°. [*Mining and Metallurgical Investigations. Cooperative Bulletin.* no. 46.] **Ac. 3190.**

BYROM (BEPPY) *See* BYROM (Elizabeth)

BYROM (BLANCHE) Calvary. pp. 15. *Diprose, Bateman & Co.: London,* 1924. 8°. **11643. dd. 21.**

—— [Another edition.] pp. 15. *E. Mathews & Marrot: London,* 1928. 16°. **011644. de. 122.**

—— Hyacinthus. pp. 8. *Diprose, Bateman & Co.: London,* 1924. 8°. **11643. dd. 22.**

—— Ode to a Butterfly. pp. 8. *Diprose, Bateman & Co.: London,* 1924. 8°. **11643. dd. 20.**

—— Quand même. [Poems.] *Eng.* pp. xxii. 152. *Privately published: London,* 1914. 8°. **011652. m. 71.**

—— Twisted Scarlet. Poems in prose and verse. pp. 39. *Diprose, Bateman & Co.: London,* 1922. 8°. **11651. d. 52.**

—— The Water Bearer. *Diprose, Bateman & Co.: London,* 1924. 8°. **011648. h. 71.**

BYROM (ELIZABETH)

—— Beppy Byrom's Diary. An eye-witness account of Bonnie Prince Charlie in Manchester. With illustrations, many previously unpublished, and notes by W. H. Thomson. [With portraits.] pp. 96. *W. H. Thomson: Manchester,* [1954.] 8°. **010807.i.32.**

—— The Journal of Elizabeth Byrom in 1745. Edited by Richard Parkinson . . . Reprinted from vol. II. part II. of the remains of John Byrom. pp. 32. 1857. 4°. *See* MANCHESTER.—*Chetham Society.* **10855. f. 1.**

BYROM (JAMES) The Iron Gates. [A novel.] pp. 283. *R. Hale & Co.: London,* 1936. 8°. **NN. 26621.**

BYROM (JOHN) *Fellow of Trinity College, Cambridge.* *See* ALEXIS. Alexis; or, the Distrest shepherd . . . In imitation of that celebrated poem [by J. Byrom] in the six-hundred and third Spectator. [1740?] fol. **1870. d. 1. (25.)**

BYROM (JOHN) *Fellow of Trinity College, Cambridge.*

—— *See* BAILEY (John E.) John Byrom's Journal, Letters, &c., 1730–31. [On a notebook containing MS. entries by Byrom and his daughter.] 1882. 8°. **10854**. g. **13**.

—— *See* GAWTRESS (William) A Practical Introduction to the Science of Short Hand, upon the general principles of . . . Dr. Byrom. 1819. 8°. **1043**. g. **45**.

—— *See* HOBHOUSE (Stephen H.) William Law and Eighteenth Century Quakerism. Including some unpublished letters and fragments of William Law and John Byrom. [With a portrait.] 1927. 8°. **4908**. eee. **6**.

—— *See* HOOLE (Elijah) Byrom and the Wesleys . . . With a portrait of Dr. Byrom. 1864. 8°. **4906**. dd. **39**. (**4**.)

—— *See* IMMORTALITY. The Immortality of the Soul. A poem. Book the first. Translated from the Latin [of Isaac Hawkins Browne, by J. Byrom]. 1754. 4°. **11630**. e. **13**. (**10**.)

—— *See* JONES (G. W.) *Stenographer.* Byrom Improved. Method against memory; or a royal road to short hand, *etc.* [1832?] 8°. **T. 1421**. (**5**.)

—— *See* NIGHTINGALE (Joseph) A Letter to a Friend; containing a comparative view of the two systems of short-hand, respectively invented by Mr. Byrom and Dr. Mavor. 1811. 8°. **T. 183**. (**5**.)

—— —— 1814. 8°. **787**. h. **46**. (**4**.)

—— *See* NIGHTINGALE (Joseph) Rational Stenography . . . founded on the principles of the late John Byrom, *etc.* 1823. 12°. **7942**. b. **35**. (**4**.)

—— *See* ROFFE (Robert C.) A Catechism of Short-Hand, upon the system of Dr. John Byrom . . . For the use of schools, *etc.* 1834. 12°. **1268**. a. **18**. (**2**.)

—— *See* ROFFE (Robert C.) The Grand Master [i.e. J. Byrom]. Being some extracts from the . . . correspondence of R. C. Roffe . . . with . . . Thomas Molineux, *etc.* 1860. 4°. **10920**. f. **25**.

—— *See* ROFFE (Robert C.) Stenographical Accidence, or Byrom's system of short hand, made easy, *etc.* 1833. 12°. **T. 1534**. (**9**.)

—— *See* THOMSON (Wilfred H.) "Christians Awake." Written by John Byrom, *etc.* [With a portrait and a facsimile.] [1948.] *obl.* 8°. **3438**. g. **31**.

—— *See* THOMSON (Wilfred H.) "Christians Awake." Written by J. Byrom, *etc.* [With a portrait.] [1949.] *obl.* 8°. **3438**. g. **37**.

—— *See* THOMSON (Wilfrid H.) John Byrom's Birthplace. Manchester. [1955.] 8°. **010368**. v. **36**.

—— *See* THOMSON (Wilfrid H.) Previously Unpublished Byromiana relating to J. Byrom, *etc.* 1954. 8°. **10863**. f. **72**.

—— *See* THOMSON (Wilfrid H.) The Story of Christians Awake, written by J. Byrom, *etc.* [With a portrait.] [1948.] *obl.* 8°. **3438**. g. **25**.

—— *See* WALKER (C.) *Stenographer.* Stenography . . . Comprising an abridgment of the . . . system by Byrom, *etc.* 1823. 12°. **7942**. aaa. **37**.

—— The Beggar and the Divine.—Armelle Nicholas's Account of Herself. *See* PIECES. Pious Pieces in verse, *etc.* 1821. 12°. **11641**. aaa. **42**.

BYROM (JOHN) *Fellow of Trinity College, Cambridge.*

—— The Poems of John Byrom. Edited by Adolphus William Ward. 3 vol. *Manchester,* 1894–1912. 4°. [*Chetham Society. Remains, etc.* New ser. vol. 29, 30, 34, 35, 70.] **Ac. 8120**.

—— The Private Journal and Literary Remains of John Byrom. Edited by Richard Parkinson. [With a portrait and genealogical tables.] 2 vol. *Manchester,* 1854–57. 4°. [*Chetham Society. Remains, etc.* vol. 32, 34, 40, 44.] **Ac. 8120**.

—— Armelle Nicolas's Account of Herself. *See* infra: The Experience of Armelle Nicolas.

—— Christians, Awake, Salute the Happy Morn. [A hymn.] *Castell Bros.: London; printed in Bavaria,* [1890.] 16°. **3433**. de. **29**.

—— Egumberriko Canticobat. (Traduit [by Edward Spencer Dodgson], en imitation du basque du 16ᵉ siècle, de l'hymne célèbre "Christians awake!" composé . . . par J. Byrom.) [*Oxford,* 1907.] *s. sh.* fol. **1879**. c. **12**. (**124**.)

—— *See* HILTON (Robert) Christmas and Manchester; or, the Story of "Christians Awake" [the hymn by J. Byrom]. [1931.] 16°. **4906**. a. **81**.

—— The Experience of Armelle Nicolas. [In verse.] Second edition, 1859. [By J. Byrom. Edited by C. P. Brown.] pp. 4. 1859. 8°. *See* NICOLAS (A.) **11647**. e. **1**. (**40**.)

—— Armelle Nicolas's Account of Herself. Third edition, 1859. From the Arminian Magazine . . . for 1795; where Dr. Byrom is named as the writer, *etc.* pp. 4. 1859. 8°. *See* NICOLAS (A.) **11621**. h. **1**. (**46**.)

—— Doctor Byrom's Letter to Mr. Comberbach (in defence of rhyme), *etc.* [In verse.] *See* COMBERBACH (Roger) *the Younger.* A Dispute, *etc.* [1755?] 8°. **11824**. cc. **6**

—— Miscellaneous Poems. 2 vol. *J. Harrop: Manchester* 1773. 8°. **239**. k. **16, 17**

—— [Another copy.] **L.P.** **992**. k. **2, 3**

—— [Another edition.] The Poems of John Byrom. (The Life of John Byrom. By Mr. Chalmers.) *See* CHALMERS (Alexander) The Works of the English Poets, *etc.* vol. 15. 1810. 8°. **11613.c.1.**

—— [Another edition.] Miscellaneous Poems, by J. Byrom . . . To which are added his life and notes by the editor. [With a portrait.] 2 vol. *James Nichols: Leeds,* 1814. 8°. **993**. l. **7**.

—— Careless Content. (Reprinted from "Miscellaneous Poems," 1814.) pp. iv. 7. *Cock Robin Press: Chichester,* 1932. 8°. [*Cock Robin Series.* no. 1.] **11602.f.36/1.**

—— A Slang Pastoral: being a parody on a celebrated poem of Dr. Byron's [*sic*]. Written by Ralph Tomlinson. [A parody of the poem beginning "My Time, O ye Muses was happily spent," first printed in vol. 8 of "The Spectator." With the original text.] pp. 11. *Printed for the Editor: London,* 1780. 4°. **11633**. g. **9**

—— A Review of the Proceedings against Dr. Bentley, in the University of Cambridge: in answer to a late pretended Full and Impartial Account, &c. With some remarks upon Sergeant Miller's Account of that University . . . By N. O., M.A. of the same University [i.e. J. Byrom; sometimes attributed to R. Bentley himself]. pp. 82. 1719. 8°. *See* O., N., *M.A.* **699**. h. **4**. (**6**.)

—— Tunbridgiale, a poem: being a description of Tunbridge . . . By the author of My Time, O ye Muses, &c. [i.e. J. Byrom.] pp. 11. 1726. 4°. *See* TUNBRIDGE WELLS. **840**. h. **4**. (**11**.)

BYROM (JOHN) *Fellow of Trinity College, Cambridge.*

—— The Universal English Short-Hand; or, the Way of writing English, in the most easy, concise . . . manner Invented by J. Byrom . . . Now published from his manuscripts. pp. ix. 92. *Joseph Harrop: Manchester,* 1767. 8°. **787**. h. **46**. (2.)

—— [Another copy.] **58**. g. **36**.

—— *See* MOLINEUX (Thomas) *of Macclesfield.* An Introduction to Mr. Byrom's Universal English Short Hand, *etc.* 1804. 8°. **12991**. g. **36**.

—— —— 1813. 8°. **12991**. g. **71**.

—— —— 1823. 8°. **12991**. g. **74**.

—— *See* PALMER (John) *Stenographer.* A New Scheme of Short-Hand; being an improvement upon Mr. Byrom's Universal English Short-Hand. 1774. 8°. **1043**. g. **3**.

—— An Abridgement of Mr. Byrom's Universal English Short-Hand . . . The second edition. [The editor's advertisement signed: T. M., i.e. Thomas Molineux.] 1796. 8°. *See* M., T. **12991**. d. **35**.

—— An Easy Introduction to Byrom's Universal English Short Hand, being an abridgment of that celebrated system . . . by an eminent professor [i.e. C. Walker]. A new and improved edition. pp. 30. pl. 3. *B. Blake: London,* 1825. 12°. **7942**. aaa. **28**.

—— Selections from the Journals & Papers of John Byrom, poet-diarist-shorthand writer, 1691–1763. Edited with notes and biographical sketches of some of his notable contemporaries by Henri Talon, *etc.* [With plates, including a portrait.] pp. xvi. 336. *Rockliff: London,* [1950.] 8°. **012274**. g. **4**.

—— A Catalogue of the Library of the late John Byrom, *etc.* pp. 249. *Printed for private circulation: London,* 1848. 4°. **11899**. ee. **34**.

—— [Another copy.] **822**. b. **31**.

BYROM (JOHN) *Rector of Stanton-Quintin, Wilts.* The Necessity of Subjection, asserted in an assise-sermon, *etc.* pp. 26. *For Benj. Took: London,* 1681. 4°. **226**. i. **3**. (**7**.)

BYROM (MOLLY)

—— Jockey Silks . . . With illustrations by Richard Kennedy. [A tale.] pp. 214. *H. F. & G. Witherby: London,* 1950. 8°. **12833**. ff. **10**.

BYROM (ROBERT MICHAEL)

—— Thus spake Zumperhinck. A comic satire . . . With drawings by the author. pp. 115. *Andrew Moore: London,* 1953. 8°. **012332**. aa. **53**.

BYROM (SAMUEL) An Irrefragable Argument fully proving, that to discharge great debts is less injury, and more reasonable, than to discharge small debts, *etc.* pp. 28. *London,* 1729. 8°. **517**. f. **11**. (**9**.)

BYROM (THOMAS HENRY)

—— *See* CHRISTOPHER (John E.) and BYROM (T. H.) Modern Coking Practice, *etc.* 1952. 8°. **7947**. b. **68**.

—— The Physics and Chemistry of Mining. An elementary class-book, *etc.* pp. xii. 160. *C. Lockwood & Son: London,* 1905. 8°. **07109**. i. 8.

—— Second edition, revised. pp. xii. 196. *C. Lockwood & Son: London,* 1912. 8°. **07109**. i. **25**.

BYROM (THOMAS HENRY)

—— Fifth edition, enlarged, *etc.* pp. xvi. 232. *London,* 1924. 8°. [*Lockwood's Technical Manuals.*] W.P. **7056/10**.

BYROM (THOMAS HENRY) and **CHRISTOPHER** (J. E.)

—— Modern Coking Practice, including the analysis of materials and products. A handbook for those engaged in coke manufacture and the recovery of bye-products, *etc.* pp. xi. 156. *C. Lockwood & Son: London,* 1910. 8°. **07945**. g. **36**.

—— Modern Coking Practice. By J. E. Christopher . . . Including the analysis of materials and products by T. H. Byrom . . . Second edition. 2 vol. 1917. 8°. *See* CHRISTOPHER (J. E.) and BYROM (Thomas H.) **07942**. cc. **6**.

—— Third edition, enlarged. 2 vol. 1921. 8°. *See* CHRISTOPHER (J. E.) and BYROM (Thomas H.) **07942**. c. **6**.

BYROM (WILLIAM) Sketches from Life. I. Alice Jevons. II. The Heiress of Hallstead. pp. 156. *A. Hall, Virtue & Co.: London,* 1852. 12°. **12625**. c. **1**.

BYRON FOUNDATION LECTURE. *See* NOTTINGHAM.—*University of Nottingham.*

BYRON MONOGRAPHS. *See* AUSTIN, *Texas.—University of Texas.*

BYRON SOCIETY. *See* LONDON.—III.

BYRON, *Lord.* The Self-Deceived: or, the History of Lord Byron. [A novel.] (An Appeal to the Public, by F. and J. Noble, booksellers, from the aspersions cast on them by the anonymous editor of the London Magazine. With a few words to Mr. Baldwin, *etc.*) 2 vol. *F. & J. Noble: London,* 1773. 12°. **12613**. g. **4**.
The " Appeal " has separate pagination and is imperfect, wanting pp. 30, 31.

BYRON, *Mr.* The History of Mr. Byron and Miss Greville. [A novel.] 2 vol. *F. Noble & J. Noble: London,* 1767. 12°. **12612**. ee. **4**.

—— [Another edition.] 2 vol. pp. 261. *W. Colles: Dublin,* 1768. **12612**. cc. **8**.

BYRON (   ) *Miss.* The Bachelor's Journal, inscribed, without permission, to the girls of England . . . Edited by Miss Byron. 2 vol. *A. K. Newman & Co.: London,* 1815. 12°. N. **2035**.

—— Celia in search of a Husband. By a Modern Antique [i.e. Miss Byron ?]. 2 vol. 1809. 8°. *See* CELIA. **12612**. ff. **7**.

—— The English Exposé; or, Men and women " abroad " and " at home " . . . By a Modern Antique [i.e. Miss Byron ?]. 4 vol. 1814. 12°. *See* ENGLISH EXPOSÉ. **12612**. bbb. **8**.

—— The Englishman. A novel. 6 vol. *A. K. Newman & Co.: London,* 1812. 12°. **012611**. e. **47**.

—— The English-woman. A novel. 5 vol. *Lane, Newman & Co.: London,* 1808. 12°. **1478**. dd. **2**.

—— Hours of Affluence, and Days of Indigence. A novel, *etc.* 4 vol. *Lane, Newman & Co.: London,* 1809. 12°. N. **2507**.

—— The Spinster's Journal . . . By a Modern Antique [i.e. Miss Byron ?]. 3 vol. 1816. 12°. *See* SPINSTER. N. **2190**.

BYRON (   ) *Mrs., Author of "Anti-Delphine."* *See* STRUTT (Elizabeth)

BYRON (*Hon.* ADA AUGUSTA) *See* LEIGH (*Hon.* A. A.)

BYRON (ANNE ISABELLA NOEL) *Baroness Byron.* *See* BYRON (A. I. N.) *Baroness Wentworth.*

BYRON (ANNE ISABELLA NOEL) *Baroness Wentworth.* *See* BYRON (George G. N.) *Baron Byron.* [*Hebrew Melodies.*] Hebrew Melodies. [With a MS. note by Lady Byron.] 1815. 8°. Ashley **5454*.**

—— *See* BYRON (George G. N.) *Baron Byron.* [*Appendix.—Biography and Criticism.*] A Narrative of the Circumstances which attended the Separation of Lord and Lady Byron, *etc.* 1816. 8°. **1164.** g. **38.**

—— *See* HOBHOUSE (John C.) *Boron Broughton.* Contemporary Account of the Separation of Lord and Lady Byron, *etc.* 1870. 8°. Ashley **2742.**

—— *See* MACKAY (William) *Publisher.* The True Story of Lady Byron's Life . . . Christmas comic version. 1869. 8°. **11649.** cc. **23.** **(13.)**

—— *See* MAYNE (Ethel C.) The Life and Letters of Anne Isabella, Lady Noel Byron, *etc.* [With portraits.] 1929. 8°. **10824.** h. **9.**

—— *See* MILBANKE (Mary C.) *Countess of Lovelace.* A Portrait [by James Ramsay] mis-named Lady Byron, *etc.* 1918. 8°. **7860.** ff. **7.**

—— *See* MILBANKE (Ralph G. N.) *Earl of Lovelace.* Lady Noel Byron and the Leighs: some authentic records of certain circumstances in the lives of Augusta Leigh, and others of her family, that concerned Anne Isabella, Lady Byron, *etc.* 1887. 8°. Ashley **2747.**

—— *See* STOWE (Harriet E. B.) Lady Byron Vindicated, *etc.* 1870. 8°. **10855.** aaa. **18.**

—— —— 1870. 8°. **10855.** aaa. **19.**

—— To Ada.—To a Friend—Miss * * *. [Poems.] *See* BYRON (George G. N.) *Baron Byron.* [*Appendix.—Biography and Criticism.*] Byron painted by his Compeers, *etc.* 1869. 8°. **10856.** aaa. **26.** (4.)

—— Remarks occasioned by Mr. Moore's Notices of Lord Byron's Life. pp. 15. *Richard Taylor: [London,* 1830.] 8°. **10855.** c. **20.** (2.)

—— [Another edition.] A Letter to Thomas Moore, Esq. occasioned by his Notices of the Life of the late . . . Lord Byron. pp. 19. *Marsh & Miller: London,* [1830.] 8°. **10803.** b. **7.** (7.)

—— [Another edition.] Remarks occasioned by Mr. Moore's Notices of Lord Byron's Life. *See* M., J. The True Story of Lord & Lady Byron as told by Lord Macaulay, Thomas Moore, *etc.* [With a portrait of Lady Byron.] [1869.] 8°. **10856.** a. **6.**

—— What De Fellenberg has done for Education. [By A. I. N. Byron, Baroness Wentworth?] pp. xlix. 105. 1839. 8°. *See* FELLENBERG (P. E. von) **722.** b. **41.**

—— Lady Byron's Responsive "Fare thee well!" . . . Third edition. (Conciliator to Lady Byron.) [Two poems. With a portrait of Lord Byron.] pp. 16. *Richard Edwards: London,* 1816. 8°. **11642.** bbb. **58.**

—— Lady Byron's Reply to her Lord's Farewell. With referential notes to the lines in Lord Byron's poem, particularly alluded to, by her Ladyship. pp. 16. *J. Pearse: London,* 1825. 8°. Ashley **334.**

BYRON (ANNE ISABELLA NOEL) *Baroness Wentworth.*

—— Life of Lady Byron, compiled from the best authorities, together with a summary of the "True Story" told by Mrs. H. B. Stowe. With descriptive matter, private letters, and . . . particulars of the great scandal. To which is appended a vindication of Lord Byron with . . . portraits, *etc.* (Police News edition.) pp. 16. [*London,* 1870?] 8°. **10803.** g. **18.** **(4.)**

—— Lines addressed to Lady Byron. [By Mrs. E. Cockle.] pp. 6. *S. Hodgson: Newcastle,* 1817. 8°. **11632.** g. **60.** **(11.)**

—— Vindication of Lady Byron. pp. xv. 352. *R. Bentley & Son: London,* 1871. 8°. **10855.** df. **10.**

BYRON (BENJAMIN) Report of a Sermon, preached at the Independent Chapel, Lincoln, by the Rev. B. Byron. As taken in short-hand, by Robinson Taylor. pp. iv. 33. *E. B. Drury: Lincoln,* 1829. 8°. T. **1280.** **(6.)**

BYRON (CHRISTOPHER)

—— The Christian Ascent. Instructions on the life of Christian devotion. pp. 31. *Church Union; Church Literature Association: London,* 1950. 8°. **4397.** bb. **45.**

—— The Glorious Liberty. An elementary introduction to Christian prayer. pp. viii. 103. *Church Union Church Literature Association: London,* 1952. 8°. [*Beacon Books.* no. 4.] W.P. **4244/4.**

BYRON (EDWARD) Fallacies in the Art of Singing. *H. J. Pickard: Leicester,* [1908.] 8°. **7899.** ee. **18.** **(3.)**

BYRON (ELIZA) The Art of Dressmaking. pp. 15. *Wood Printing Works: Dublin,* [1897.] 8°. **7742.** bb. **46.**

BYRON, afterwards STRUTT (ELIZABETH) *See* STRUTT.

BYRON (F. NOËL) Athenian Days. [Poems.] pp. 31. *Elkin Mathews: London,* 1919. 8°. **011648.** de. **50.**

BYRON (FRANCIS ERIC) *See* BLAIR (Robert W.) and BYRON (F. E.) Notes on Damar Penak. 1927. 8°. **C.S.B.437/4.(4.)**

BYRON (FREDERICK ERNEST CHARLES) *Baron Byron.* The Gorge. [A fantasy.] pp. 112. *John Murray: London,* 1934. 8°. **12602.** tt. **16.**

BYRON (*Mrs.* G. F.) *See* GILLINGTON, afterwards BYRON (May C.)

BYRON (GEORGE ANSON) *Baron Byron.* *See* MACRAE (James) *Botanist.* With Lord Byron at the Sandwich Islands in 1825, *etc.* 1922. 8°. **10493.** f. **14.**

—— Voyage of H.M.S. Blonde to the Sandwich Islands, in the years 1824–1825. Captain the Right Hon. Lord Byron Commander. [By Maria Graham. With plates, including a map.] pp. x. 260. *John Murray: London,* 1826. 4°. **792.** k. **19.**

—— An Examination of Charges against the American Missionaries at the Sandwich Islands, as alleged in the Voyage of the ship Blonde (Captain the Right Hon. Lord Byron, commander), and in the London Quarterly Review. [Reprinted from the "North American Review."] pp. 67. *Hilliard, Metcalf & Co.: Cambridge* [*Mass.*], 1827. 8°. **4765.df.10.(2.)**

BYRON (GEORGE GORDON DE LUNA) *See* DE GIBLER (   ) alias GEORGE GORDON DE LUNA BYRON.

BYRON (George Gordon Noel) *Baron Byron.*

Arrangement.

WORKS.

—— The Poetical Works of Lord Byron. From the last London edition. 2 vol. *Cummings & Hilliard: Boston,* 1814. 12°. **11612**. de. **1**, **2**.

—— The Works of the Right Hon. Lord Byron. 2 vol. *John Murray: London,* 1815. 8°. **11604**. f. **25**.
This collection consists of works previously published separately between 1812 *and* 1818, *with collective titlepages bearing the date* 1815 *prefixed to each of the volumes.*

—— The Works of the Right Honourable Lord Byron. 8 vol. *John Murray: London,* 1815–20. 8°. **11604**. bbb. **24**.
Vol. 1–4, *dated* 1815, *bear the words* " *In four volumes* " ; *vol.* 5, *dated* 1817, " *In five volumes* "; *vol.* 6, 7 *and* 8, *dated respectively* 1818, 1819 *and* 1820, *do not state the number of volumes.*

—— [Another issue.] *London,* 1815–20. 8°. **11611**. aa. **9–16**.
Without the half-titles.

—— [Another edition of vol. 1–5.] 5 vol. *John Murray: London,* 1817. 8°. **1466**. a. **1**.

—— The Works of the Right Honourable Lord Byron. [With plates.] 8 vol. *John Murray: London,* 1818–20. 8°. **239**. f. **39–46**.
Previous edition 1815–20.

—— The Works of the Right Honourable Lord Byron. 13 vol. *Gerard Fleischer: Leipsick,* 1818–22. 12°. **012273**. df. **3**.

—— The Works of Lord Byron. 3 vol. *John Murray: London,* 1819. 8°. **11611**. g. **2**.

—— The Works of the Right Honourable Lord Byron. Comprehending all his suppressed poems. Embellished with a portrait and a sketch of his Lordship's life . . . Second edition. 6 vol. *Galignani: Paris,* 1819. 12°. **11609**. de. **28**.

—— The Works of Lord Byron. 7 vol. *John Murray: London,* 1819–25. 8°. **11612**. l. **1**.
A made-up set. Vol. 1–3 *are of the edition of* 1819. *Vol.* 4–7 *bear the imprint of J. & H. L. Hunt. Vol.* 4, 1825, *contains* " *Sardanapalus,* " " *The Two Foscari* " *and* " *Cain.* " *Its titlepage originally read:* " *The Works of Lord Byron. In eight volumes. Vol.* viii," *but a slip bearing the no.* iv *has been pasted over the original numeration. Vol.* 5, 1824, *contains* " *Marino Faliero* " *and* " *Prophecy of Dante.* " *Its titlepage originally read:* " *The Works of Lord Byron. In eight volumes. Vol.* vii," *but a blank slip has been pasted over the last two figures of the numeral. The titlepage of vol.* 6, 1824, *reads:* " *The Works of Lord Byron. In seven volumes. Vol.* vi." *The text of this volume is a duplicate of that contained in vol.* 7 *of the edition of* 1824, 25 *entered below. The titlepage of vol.* 7 *reads:* " *The Works of Lord Byron. In seven volumes. Vol.* vii." *The text of this volume is a duplicate of that of vol.* 6 *of the edition of* 1824, 25.

—— The Works of Lord Byron. 5 vol. *John Murray: London,* 1821. 8°. **11604**. bbb. **25**.

—— The Works of Lord Byron, comprehending the suppressed poems. Embellished with a portrait, and a sketch of his life. 16 vol. *A. & W. Galignani: Paris,* 1822–24. 12°. **11612**. ee. **9**.
In this copy the biographical " *Sketch* " *mentioned on the titlepage of vol.* 1 *has been replaced by an anonymous* " *Life* " *written after* 1824.

—— The Works of Lord Byron. vol. 5–7.

Vol 5. Hours of Idleness.—Translations and Imitations.—Fugitive Pieces.—English Bards and Scotch Reviewers.—Miscellaneous Poems. 1824.
Vol. 6. Werner.—Heaven and Earth.—Translation. Morgante Maggiore. 1824.
Vol. 7. The Age of Bronze.—The Island.—The Vision of Judgment.—The Deformed Transformed. 1825.

Knight & Lacey: London, 1824, 25. 8°. **1164**. g. **13–15**.
Vol. 1–4 *were not published in this edition. The titlepages to vol.* 6 *and* 7 *read:* " *The Works of Lord Byron. In seven volumes. J. & H. L. Hunt: London.* " *These volumes have each an additional half-title and titlepage bound in at the end. The additional titlepage in vol.* 6 *reads:* " *The Works of Lord Byron. In eight volumes. Vol.* vii. 1824 "; *that in vol.* 7 *reads:* " *In eight volumes. Vol.* viii. 1825." *A* " *Notice to the binder* " *inserted in vol.* 6 *and* 7 *reads:* " *In order that each purchaser of the two concluding volumes of Lord Byron's Works may be enabled with them to complete his particular set, whatever edition he possesses, an extra titlepage is given with each—there being several editions in print, comprising the same works in different numbers of volumes.* " *The text of vol.* 7 *is a duplicate of that of vol.* 6 *of the made-up set of* 1819–25.

—— [Another issue of vol. 6, 7.] The Works of Lord Byron, *etc.* 1824 [1824, 25]. 8°. *See* infra: [*Smaller Collections.*] **11613**. c. **10**.

—— The Complete Works of Lord Byron. With a biographical and critical notice by J. W. Lake. [With a portrait.] 7 vol. *Baudry: Paris,* 1825. 8°. **11611**. ee. **2–8**.

—— The Works of Lord Byron, including the suppressed poems. [With " The Life of Lord Byron " by J. W. Lake, a facsimile of a letter from Lord Byron to the editor of " Galignani's Messenger," and a portrait.] pp. xliii. 716. *A. & W. Galignani: Paris,* 1826. 8°. **11642**. g. **35**.

—— The Works of Lord Byron, *etc. Paris,* 1827. 8°. G. **18677**.
A reissue on fine paper of the preceding. The portrait is printed on India paper. An earlier state of the portrait is also included.

—— [Another edition.] pp. xl. 718. *A. & W. Galignani: Paris,* 1828. 8°. **11611**. ee. **9**.

—— The Works of Lord Byron, including his suppressed poems, *etc.* [With a portrait and a facsimile letter.] pp. xliii. 716. *A. & W. Galignani: Paris,* 1827. 8°. **11613**. c. **3**.
A different edition from the preceding.

—— The Works of Lord Byron. [With a portrait.] 4 vol. *John Murray: London,* 1828. 12°. **11611**. a. **5–8**.

—— The Works of Lord Byron. 6 vol. *John Murray: London,* 1829. 8°. **11604**. bbb. **26**.

—— The Works of Lord Byron. 4 vol. *John Murray: London,* 1829. 12°. **11611**. a. **11**, **12**.

—— The Works of Lord Byron. [With a portrait.] 4 vol. *John Murray: London,* 1830. 16°. **11604**. ccc. 4.

—— The Works of Lord Byron. 6 vol. *John Murray: London,* 1831. 16°. **11612**. a. **14–19**.
Vol. 1–4 *are reissues of the four volumes of the edition of* 1830.

—— [Another edition.] The Works of Lord Byron. *John Murray: London,* 1831. 12°. G. **18565–70**.
Vol. 1–4 *are reissues of the four volumes of the duodecimo edition of* 1829; *vol.* 5 *and* 6 *are duplicates of vol.* 5 *and* 6 *of the sextodecimo edition of* 1830.

—— [Another copy of vol. 5, 6.] **1164**. a. **1**, **2**.

—— The Complete Works of Lord Byron, including his Lordship's suppressed poems, with others never before published. [With "The Life of Lord Byron abridged from the life by J. W. Lake, a facsimile of a letter from Lord Byron to the editor of "Galignani's Messenger," and a portrait.] pp. xxiv. 730. *A. & W. Galignani: Paris,* 1831. 8°. **11611**. b. **1**.
Previous edition 1828.

—— The Works of Lord Byron: with his letters and journals, and his life, by Thomas Moore. [Edited by John Wright.] 17 vol. *John Murray: London,* 1832, 33. 8°. **12271**. p. **1**.
Each volume has an additional titlepage, engraved. The printed titlepages of vol. 1–12 *bear the words "In fourteen volumes"; that of vol.* 17 *bears the words "In seventeen volumes."*

—— [A reissue.] *London,* 1835, 32, 33. 8°. **991**. f. **4–20**.
The printed titlepages of vol. 1 *and* 12 *bear the words "In seventeen volumes." Vol.* 2–11 *and* 13–17 *are duplicates of the corresponding volumes of the preceding.*

—— The Complete Works of Lord Byron, reprinted from the last London edition, with considerable additions, now first published; containing notes and illustrations by Moore, Walter Scott, Campbell [and others] . . . and a complete index; to which is prefixed a life, by Henry Lytton Bulwer. [With a facsimile of a letter from Lord Byron to the editor of "Galignani's Messenger," and a portrait.] pp. xxxiii. 935. *A. & W. Galignani & Co.: Paris,* 1835. 8°. **11611**. g. 3.
Previous edition 1831.

—— The Complete Works of Lord Byron from the last London edition . . . To which is prefixed the life of the author by John Galt. pp. 11. cxxii. 954. *Baudry's European Library; A. & W. Galignani & Co.: Paris,* 1837. 8°. **11611**. h. 4.
A different edition from the preceding.

—— The Works of Lord Byron. Complete in one volume. With notes by Thomas Moore, Esq., Lord Jeffrey, Sir Walter Scott . . . &c. &c. [With a portrait.] pp. viii. 827. *John Murray: London,* 1837. 8°. **1466**. i. **25**.
With an additional titlepage, engraved.

—— The Poetical Works of Lord Byron. In eight volumes. (Letters and Journals of Lord Byron: with notices of his life, by Thomas Moore.) 44 vol. *John Murray: London,* 1839, 30. 4°. C. **44**. e–g.
*These copies of these two works, originally published in eight and two volumes respectively, have been expanded by the addition of Byron's "Letter to **** ******, on the Rev. W. L. Bowles' strictures on the life and writings of Pope . . . Second edition" and other printed matter, views, portraits, autograph letters and signatures, the whole collected by William Watts. Each volume has a special titlepage reading "The Poetical Works, Letters and Journals of Lord Byron: with notices of his life. By Thomas Moore" and dated* 1844. *With a* MS. *index in folio.*

BYRON (George Gordon Noel) *Baron Byron.* [Works.]

—— The Complete Works of Lord Byron, reprinted from the last London edition, containing besides the notes and illustrations by Moore, Walter Scott [and others] . . . considerable additions and original notes, with a most complete index; to which is prefixed a life, by Henry Lytton Bulwer. [With a portrait and facsimiles.] pp. xxxiii. 935. *A. & W. Galignani & Co.: Paris,* 1842. 8°. **11611**. h. **22**.
Pp. 887–908 *are slightly mutilated.*

—— The Poetical Works of Lord Byron. Complete in one volume. Collected and arranged, with illustrative notes by Thomas Moore, Lord Jeffrey, Sir Walter Scott . . . &c. &c. With a portrait, *etc.* pp. viii. 827. *John Murray: London,* 1845. 8°. **11611**. g. **6**.
A reissue of the edition of 1837. *With an additional titlepage, engraved.*

—— The Poetical Works of Lord Byron . . . Collected and arranged, with illustrative notes by Thomas Moore [and others] . . . With a portrait, *etc.* pp. viii. 827. *John Murray: London,* 1847. 8°. **11658**. h. **14**.
With an additional titlepage, engraved. A reissue of the edition of 1845.

—— The Works of Lord Byron; in verse and prose. Including his letters, journals, etc. With a sketch of his life. [Edited by FitzGreene Halleck. With plates.] pp. xxviii. 319. 627. *S. Andrus & Son: Hartford,* 1847. 8°. **1340**. n. **13**.

—— The Poetical Works of Lord Byron . . . Collected and arranged, with the notes and illustrations of Thomas Moore, Lord Jeffrey, Sir Walter Scott [and others] . . . With portrait, *etc.* pp. viii. 827. *John Murray: London,* 1850. 8°. **11609**. h. **21**.
A reissue of the edition of 1845. *With an additional titlepage, engraved.*

—— The Works of Lord Byron: with a life and illustrative notes, by William Anderson. [With plates, including a portrait.] 2 vol. *A. Fullarton & Co.: Edinburgh,* [1850.] 8°. **11611**. k. **1**, **2**.
Each volume has an additional titlepage, engraved.

—— The Poetical Works of Lord Byron. Containing the Giaour, Bride of Abydos . . . Also several attributed and suppressed poems not included in other editions. With a memoir, by Henry Lytton Bulwer. pp. xlviii. 641. *H. G. Bohn: London,* 1851. 12°. **11611**. a. **13**.
With an additional titlepage, engraved, reading "Lord Byron's Poetical Works."

—— The Complete Works of Lord Byron, reprinted from the last London edition . . . To which is prefixed a life by Thomas Moore [abridged] . . . With a portrait. Second edition. pp. xlviii. 1004. *Joseph Baer: Frankfort,* 1852. 8°. **11611**. h. **15**.

—— The Illustrated Byron. With upwards of two hundred engravings from original drawings by Kenny Meadows, Birket Foster, Hablot K. Browne, Gustave Janet, and Edward Morin. pp. viii. 632. *Henry Vizetelly: London,* [1854, 55.] 8°. **11611**. k. **3**.
Published in parts.

—— The Poetical Works of Lord Byron. A new edition. [With a portrait.] 6 vol. *John Murray: London,* 1855, 56. 8°. **11611**. g. **8–10**.

—— The Poetical Works of Lord Byron, complete. New edition, the text carefully revised. [With portrait.] pp. viii. 685. *John Murray: London,* 1857. 8°. **11611**. d. **5**.

— The Poetical Works of Lord Byron. Collected and arranged with notes by Sir Walter Scott, Lord Jeffrey [and others] . . . New and complete edition. With portrait and illustrative engravings. pp. x. 827. *John Murray: London*, 1859. 8°. **11601**. k. 9.
A reissue of the edition of 1850. *Published in parts. With two additional titlepages, one printed, one engraved.*

— The Poetical Works of Lord Byron. With life. (In this edition objectionable pieces have been excluded.) pp. xix. 514. *Gall & Inglis: Edinburgh*, [1859.] 8°. **11611**. bb. 2.
With an additional titlepage, engraved.

— The Poetical Works of Lord Byron. With illustrations by Keeley Halswelle. [With "The Life of Lord Byron" by Alexander Leighton, and a portrait.] pp. xxii. 673. *W. P. Nimmo: Edinburgh*, 1861. 8°. **11611**. aaa. 2.
With an additional titlepage reading: "Poems by Lord Byron."

— The Poetical Works of Lord Byron. [With a portrait.] 10 vol. *Little, Brown & Co.: Boston*, 1861. 8°. **11611**. aa. 18–27.

— The Poetical Works of Lord Byron. Collected and arranged with notes by Sir Walter Scott, Lord Jeffrey [and others] . . . New and complete edition. With portrait and illustrative engravings. pp. x. 827. *John Murray: London*, 1863. 8°. Ashley **2711**.
A reissue of the edition of 1859, *without the engraved titlepage and frontispiece. Imperfect; wanting the additional printed titlepage?*

— The Poetical Works of Lord Byron: with life of the author, and copious notes . . . Illustrated. Family edition. pp. xv. 702. *Milner & Sowerby: London*, 1865. 8°. **11661.ee.10.**
With an additional titlepage, engraved.

— The Works of Lord Byron . . . Second edition. With the portrait of the author. 5 vol. *Leipzig*, 1866. 8°. *Bernhard Tauchnitz: Leipzig*, 1866. 8°. [*Collection of British Authors.* vol. 8–12.] **12267.a.1/34.**

— The Poetical Works of Lord Byron complete. New edition, the text carefully revised. pp. viii. 685. *John Murray: London*, 1867. 8°. **11611**. bbb. 8.
A reissue of the edition of 1857.

— The Poetical Works of Lord Byron, with life of the author, and copious notes . . . Illustrated. pp. xv. 702. *Milner & Sowerby: London & Halifax*, 1867. 8°. **11612**. i. 13.
With an additional titlepage, engraved. A reissue of the edition of 1865.

— The Poetical Works of Lord Byron. With illustrations [by Keeley Halswelle]. New edition, carefully revised. [With "The Life of Lord Byron" by Alexander Leighton.] pp. 437. *W. P. Nimmo: Edinburgh*, [1868.] 8°. **11611**. g. 11.
Previous edition 1861. *With an additional titlepage, engraved.*

— The Poetical Works of Lord Byron. Reprinted from the original editions, with explanatory notes, etc. pp. vii. 638. *F. Warne & Co.: London*, [1869.] 8°. [*Chandos Classics.*] **12204.ff.1/4.**

— The Poetical Works of Lord Byron: with life and portrait, and sixteen illustrations, by F. Gilbert. pp. xv. 457. *John Dicks: London*, [1869.] 8°. **11609**. bbb. 4.

— [Another copy.] **11611**. c. 11.

— The Poetical Works of Lord Byron. Complete in one volume. Collected and arranged, with illustrative notes by Thomas Moore, Lord Jeffrey [and others] . . . With a portrait, *etc.* pp. 829. *D. Appleton & Co.: New York*, 1869. 8°. **11611**. h. 7.
With an additional titlepage, engraved.

— The Poetical Works of Lord Byron. Edited, with a critical memoir, by William Michael Rossetti. Illustrated by Ford Madox Brown. pp. xx. 604. *E. Moxon, Son & Co.: London*, 1870. 8°. **11611**. d. 6.
With an additional titlepage, engraved.

— [Another copy.] **11611**. cc. 5.

— [A reissue.] *London*, [1872.] 8°. **11611**. d. 7.

— The Complete Poetical Works of Lord Byron. With an introductory memoir by William B. Scott. With illustrations [including a portrait]. pp. 750. *G. Routledge & Son: London*, [1874.] 8°. **11611**. d. 22.

— The Poetical Works of Lord Byron. Illustrated edition. [With a portrait.] pp. vi. cliv. 614. *Virtue & Co.: London*, [1874.] 8°. **11611**. g. 12.
With an additional titlepage, engraved.

— The Poetical Works of Lord Byron. pp. vii. 604. *Ward, Lock & Co.: London*, [1878.] 8°. **11611**. ccc. 13.
A reissue of the edition published by E. Moxon, Son & Co. in 1870, *without the memoir and the illustrations.*

— The Poetical Works of Lord Byron, *etc.* pp. vi. cliv. 614. *Virtue & Co.: London*, [1878, 79.] 8°. **11611**. h. 6.
A reissue of the edition of 1874. *Published in parts. The wrappers bear the words "Pictorial edition."*

— Poems. pp. xxxii. 719. *G. Routledge & Sons: London*, [1880.] 8°. **11609**. e. 25.

— The Poetical Works of Lord Byron, *etc.* 10 vol. *Houghton, Mifflin & Co.: Boston*, [1880?] 8°. [*British Poets.*] **11613**. e. 1/31.
A reissue of the edition of 1861.

— The Poetical Works of Lord Byron. Edited, with a critical memoir, by W. M. Rossetti. Illustrated by Thomas Seccombe [or rather, by Ford Madox Brown]. pp. xx. 604. *Ward, Lock & Co.: London*, [1880.] 8°. [*Moxon's Popular Poets.*] **11604.ee.29/1.**
With an an additional titlepage, engraved, bearing the imprint "E. Moxon, Son & Co.: London." A reissue of the edition of 1870; *previously issued in* 1878 *without the memoir and the illustrations by Ford Madox Brown.*

— [A reissue.] *London*, [1881.] 8°. **11609**. h. 18.
Without the additional titlepage and the frontispiece, the latter being replaced by a portrait. With different illustrations from the preceding, that facing p. 410 *signed: "M. W. Ridley."*

— The Poetical Works of Lord Byron. With life. Engravings on steel. pp. xviii. 576. *Gall & Inglis: Edinburgh*, [1881.] 8°. **11604**. df. 2.

— The Poetical Works of Lord Byron. Reprinted from the original editions, with life, explanatory notes, etc. (The "Albion" edition.) pp. xvi. 720. *F. Warne & Co.: London*, [1881.] 8°. **11609**. g. 22.

— The Complete Poetical Works of Lord Byron, with an introductory memoir by William B. Scott. [With plates, including a portrait.] pp. 750. *G. Routledge & Sons: London*, 1883. 8°. **11607**. f. 9.
A reissue of the edition of 1874, *with additional plates.*

—— The Poetical Works of Lord Byron. With original and additional notes. 12 vol. *Suttaby & Co.: London; Scribner & Welford: New York,* 1885 [1884]. 4°. **11609.** ee. 6.

—— The Complete Poetical Works of Lord Byron, with an introductory memoir by William B. Scott. 3 vol. *G. Routledge & Sons: London,* 1886 [1885]. 8°. **11609.** bbb. 35.

Previous edition 1883.

—— The Poetical Works of Lord Byron. Edited by Mathilde Blind. 2 vol.

Miscellaneous Poems.
Childe Harold. Don Juan. [Abridged.]

Walter Scott: London, 1886. 8°. [*Canterbury Poets.*] **11604.** aa. **16.**

No more published.

—— The Complete Poetical Works of Lord Byron. With an introductory memoir by William B. Scott. pp. 750. *G. Routledge & Sons: London,* 1887. 8°. **11611.** e. **27.**
A reissue of the edition of 1883, *without the plates.*

—— [A reissue.] *London,* 1890. 8°. **012207.** e. **24.**
With some of the plates of the edition of 1883.

—— The Poetical Works of Lord Byron. With original and additional notes. 12 vol. *Griffith Farran, Okeden & Welsh: London,* [1891, 92.] 8°. **11612.** de. **30.**
A reissue of the edition published by Suttaby & Co. in 1885. *The wrappers bear the words " The Bijou Byron."*

—— The Poetical Works of Lord Byron. Reprinted from the original editions, with explanatory notes, &c. pp. x. 668. *E. H. Wells: London,* [1895?] 8°. **11658.** a. **81.**

—— Lord Byrons Werke, in kritischen Texten mit Einleitungen und Anmerkungen herausgegeben von Eugen Kölbing. 2 Bd.

Bd. 1. The Siege of Corinth.
Bd. 2. The Prisoner of Chillon, and other poems.

Weimar, 1896. 8°. **11611.** dd. **8.**
No more published.

—— The Poetical Works of Lord Byron. (Oxford Miniature Byron.) 4 vol. *Henry Frowde: London,* 1896. 16°. **11612.** dg. 3.
Printed on Oxford India paper.

—— The Works of Lord Byron. Edited by William Ernest Henley. (vol. 1. Letters, 1804–1813.) [With a portrait.] pp. xix. 469. *William Heinemann: London,* 1897 [1896]. 8°. **12272.** dd. 2.
No more published.

—— [Another copy.] Ashley **5294.**

—— The Poetical Works of Lord Byron. [With a portrait.] pp. xvi. 727. *Bliss, Sands & Co.: London,* [1897.] 8°. [*Apollo Poets.*] **11607.** g. **23.**

—— The Works of Lord Byron. A new, revised and enlarged edition, with illustrations [including portraits]. 13 vol.

Poetry . . . Edited by Ernest Hartley Coleridge. 7 vol. 1898–1904.
Letters and Journals . . . Edited by Rowland E. Prothero. 6 vol. 1898–1901. **2040.c.& 12276.aa.6.**

John Murray: London, 1898–1904. 8°.
A " Bibliography of Lord Byron's Poetical Works " forms part of vol. 7 *of the " Poetry."*

—— [Another issue.] *London,* 1898–1904. 4°. **12270.** i. 4.
Some of the plates differ from those of the preceding issue.

—— [Another copy.] Ashley **2712.**

—— The Poetical Works of Lord Byron. (Oxford edition.) [With a portrait.] pp. x. 924. *Henry Frowde: London,* 1904. 8°. **11609.** d. **28.**

—— The Complete Poetical Works of Lord Byron. [Edited, with a biographical sketch, by P. E. More. With a portrait.] pp. xxi. 1055. *Houghton Mifflin Co.: Boston & New York,* [1905.] 8°. [*Cambridge Edition of the Poets.*] **011604.** ff. **13/11.**

—— The Poetical Works of Lord Byron. The only complete and copyright text in one volume. Edited, with a memoir, by Ernest Hartley Coleridge. [With a portrait.] pp. lxxii. 1048. *John Murray: London,* 1905. 8°. **11604.** dd. **1.**

—— The Shorter Poems of Byron. (The Longer Poems.—The Dramas & Satires.) [With portraits.] 3 vol. *George Newnes: London; Charles Scribner's Sons: New York,* [1906.] 8°. **11611.** df. **15.**
With an additional titlepage to each volume.

—— The Poems and Plays of Lord Byron. (With an introduction by Professor W. P. Trent.) 3 vol. *J. M. Dent & Sons: London; E. P. Dutton & Co.: New York,* [1910.] 8°. [*Everyman's Library.*] **12206.p.1/483.**

—— The Poetical Works of Lord Byron. With introduction by W. M. Rossetti. [With a portrait.] pp. xxiv. 836. *Ward, Lock & Co.: London,* [1911.] 8°. **11643.** i. **34.**

—— Poems. (New revised edition.) 3 vol. *J. M. Dent & Sons: London; E. P. Dutton & Co.: New York,* 1948. 8°. [*Everyman Library.* no. 486–488.] **12206.** p. **1/775.**

French.

—— Œuvres complètes de Lord Byron, traduites de l'anglais par MM. A.-P. et E.-D. S. [i.e. Amédée Pichot and Eusèbe de Salle]; troisième édition, entièrement revue et corrigée. (Essai sur le génie et le caractère de Lord Byron, par A. P . . . . t [i.e. A. Pichot]; précédé d'une notice préliminaire, par M. Charles Nodier. Extraits de la quatrième édition des Œuvres complètes de Lord Byron—six volumes in-8°, ornés de vignettes. [With an essay " Sur la mort de Lord Byron," and a translation of his " Heaven and Earth."]) [With a portrait.] 15 tom. *Paris,* 1821–24. 12°. **11612.** a. **5–12.**
Tom. 1–10 *only are of the third edition. The half-titles of tom.* 11–13, 15 *read: " Œuvres de Lord Byron. Inédites.* I(–III, V)." *The volume entitled " Essai sur le génie et le caractère de Lord Byron, etc." bears no series title, but was probably published as tom.* 14.

—— Quatrième édition, entièrement revue et corrigée par A. P . . . . t (A. Pichot); précédée d'une notice sur Lord Byron par M. Charles Nodier; ornée de vignettes. [With a portrait.] 8 tom. *Paris,* 1823, 22–25. 8°. **12271.** k. **11.**
Each volume has an additional titlepage, engraved.

—— Œuvres complètes de Lord Byron, avec notes et commentaires, comprenant ses mémoires publiés par Thomas Moore, et ornées d'un beau portrait de l'auteur. Traduction nouvelle par M. Paulin Paris. 13 tom. *Paris,* 1830, 31. 8°. **11609.** g. **6–12.**

—— Œuvres complètes de Lord Byron, traduction nouvelle d'après la dernière édition de Londres, par Benjamin Laroche . . . Avec les notes et commentaires de Sir Walter Scott, Thomas Moore, Francis Jeffrey . . . etc. les variantes du texte; précédées de l'histoire de la vie et des ouvrages de Lord Byron, par John Galt. [With a portrait.] 4 tom. *Paris,* 1836, 37. 8°. **1466.** k. **1–4.**

—— Œuvres complètes de Lord Byron. Traduction de M. Amédée Pichot. Onzième édition, accompagnée de notes historiques et littéraires. [With plates, including a portrait.] pp. 820. *Paris*, 1842. 8°. **12269**. h. 4.
Previous edition 1823–25.

—— Œuvres de Lord Byron, traduites en vers français par Orby Hunter & Pascal Ramé. tom. 1–3. *Paris*, 1845. 8°. **11611**. g. 7.
No more published.

—— Œuvres complètes . . . Traduites par Benjamin Laroche. Septième édition revue et corrigée avec soin par le traducteur. 4 sér. *Paris*, 1851. 8°. **12273**. aaa. 7.

—— Œuvres de Lord Byron. Traduction nouvelle précédée d'un essai sur Lord Byron par Daniel Lesueur [pseudonym of Jeanne Loiseau]. [With a portrait.] 2 vol.
Heures d'oisivité—Childe Harold. pp. xxviii. 397. 1891.
Le Giaour—La Fiancée d'Abydos—Le Corsair—Lara, etc. pp. 451. 1892.
Paris, 1891, 92. 12°. **11612**. bbb. 21.
No more published.

German.

—— Lord Byron's sämmtliche Werke. Herausgegeben von Dr. Adrian. [The translation by G. N. Bärmann, O. L. B. Wolff, K. L. Kannegiesser, A. Hungari, P. von Haugwitz, Ph. A. G. von Meyer and the editor. With " Byron's Leben," by Ph. A. G. v. Meyer, and a portrait.] 12 Tl. *Frankfurt*, 1830, 31. 12°. **11611**. c. 8–10.

—— Lord Byron's sämmtliche Werke. Nach den Anforderungen unserer Zeit neu übersetzt von Mehreren. Zweite unveränderte Ausgabe. [The translation by Ernst Ortlepp, Franz Kottenkamp, Hermann Kurz and others.] 10 Bd. *Pforzheim*, 1842. 16°. **1466**. a. 2.

—— Lord Byrons sämmtliche Werke . . . Frei übersetzt von Adolf Seubert. 3 Bd. *Leipzig*, [1874.] 8°. **11612**. aaa. 1.

—— Lord Byron's Werke. Uebersetzt von Otto Gildemeister. . . . Vierte Auflage. 6 Bd. *Berlin*, 1888. 8°. **11607**. de. 8.

—— Byron's sämmtliche Werke. Von Adolf Böttger. Achte Auflage. 8 Bd. *Leipzig*, 1901. 8°. **11609**. dd. 10.

—— Byrons Werke. Übersetzt von A. Böttger, W. Grüzmacher, R. Imelmann, A. H. Janert, W. Schäffer, H. Stadelmann, A. Strodtmann. Herausgegeben von Friedrich Brie. Kritisch durchgesehene und erläuterte Ausgabe. [With portraits.] 4 Bd. *Leipzig*, [1912.] 8°. **12275**. a. 12.

Greek.—Modern Greek.

—— *Τα άπαντα του Βυρωνος.* 3 tom. *'Εν 'Αθηναις*, 1895. 8°. **11611**. g. 19.

Italian.

—— Opere complete di Lord Byron, voltate dall'originale inglese in prosa italiana da Carlo Rusconi, con note ed illustrazioni del volgarizzatore nonchè dei signori Moore, Walter Scott, Campbell . . . ec. ec. a cui si aggiungono i dialoghi di Lord Byron compilati da M. Medwin, un saggio sul di lui genio [translated from Amédée Pichot's " Essai sur le génie et le caractère de Lord Byron"], una prefazione, e un'appendice, parte desunti da altri scritti, parte tradotti, parte originali. 2 vol. pp. xxxix. 1561. *Padova*, 1842. 8°. **11611**. g. 4, 5.

—— Opere di Lord Giorgio Byron, precedute da un saggio intorno al genio e al carattere del medesimo [translated from Amédée Pichot's " Essai sur le génie et le caractère de Lord Byron "]. pp. 711. *Napoli*, 1886. 8°. **12271**. h. 6.
A different translation from the preceding.

—— [A reissue of pp. 1–668.] *Napoli*, 1891. 8°. **11612**. h. 3.

Polish.

—— Poezye Lorda Byrona w tłumaczeniu polskiém. Wydane staraniem B. M. Wolffa. Tom 1. Wędrówki Czajld-Harolda. (Z angielskiego przełożył M. Budzyński.) pp. 256. *Petersburg*, 1857. 12°. **11611**. aa. 17.
No more published.

Russian.

—— Сочиненія Лорда Байрона въ переводахъ русскихъ поэтовъ, изданныхъ подъ редакціею Н. В. Гербеля. 5 том. *С.-Петербургъ*, 1864–66. 16°. **11611**. dd. 1, 2.

—— Байронъ. (Библіотека великихъ писателей. Подъ редакціей С. А. Венгерова.) [With illustrations.] 3. том. *С.-Петербургъ*, 1904, 05. 8°. **11641**. h. 17.

Spanish.

—— Obras Completas. (Edición preparada y dirigida por D. Francisco Gallach Palés.) *Madrid*, 1930– . 8°. W.P. **6835**.

SMALLER COLLECTIONS.

—— [Nine poems, not previously published.] *See* HOBHOUSE (John C.) *Baron Broughton.* Imitations and Translations, *etc.* 1809. 8°. **1164**. k. 8.

—— Fare Thee Well, a poem. A Sketch from Private Life, a poem. pp. 12. *Barry & Son: Bristol*, 1816. 8°. **11647**. e. 50. (2.)

—— Fare Thee Well! and other poems. pp. 32. *John Robertson: Edinburgh*, 1816. 8°. **11649**. cc. 22. (2.)

—— An Ode [" We do not curse thee, Waterloo! "]. On the Star of the Legion of Honour. Napoleon's Farewell. Fare Thee Well. And a sketch, &c. pp. 24. *Van Winkle & Wiley: New York*, 1816. 8°. **11642**. bbb. 6.

—— Poems on his Domestic Circumstances. I. Fare Thee Well! II. A Sketch from Private Life. By Lord Byron. With the Star of the Legion of Honour, and other poems. [Seven poems, including two spurious.] pp. 31. *W. Hone: London*, 1816. 8°. **11642**. d. 31.
Imperfect ; wanting the half-title.

—— Second edition. pp. 31. *W. Hone: London*, 1816. 8°. **11641**. d. 15.

—— Sixth edition. Containing eight poems. [With a portrait.] pp. 31. *W. Hone: London*, 1816. 8°. **11643**. bb. 23.

—— [Another copy.] **11645**. cc. 10
Imperfect ; wanting the portrait and pp. 31, 32.

—— Eighth edition. Containing nine poems, *etc.* pp. 32. *W. Hone: London*, 1816. 8°. **11645**. cc. 16.

—— Poems on his Domestic Circumstances. By Lord Byron . . . To which is prefixed the life of the noble author Eleventh edition. [Seven poems, including two spurious With a portrait.] pp. 32. *R. Edwards: London*, 1816. 8° **11659**. h. 89

BYRON (George Gordon Noel) *Baron Byron.* [Smaller Collections.]

—— Fifteenth edition. Containing nine poems. pp. 40. *W. Hone: London,* 1816. 8°. **11642.** c. 46

—— Poems on his Domestic Circumstances . . . By Lord Byron . . . Seventeenth edition, containing nine poems. [With a portrait.] pp. 32. *W. Hone: London,* 1816. 8°. **11606.** bb. **22.** (**1.**)

—— Poems on Domestic Circumstances. Fare Thee Well! A Sketch from Private Life . . . With the Star of the Legion of Honour, and other poems. [Seven poems, including two spurious.] pp. 24. *J. Bumpus: London,* 1816. 8°. **11626.** g. **12.**
The half-title reads: " New Poems."

—— Poems on his Domestic Circumstances, etc. etc. By Lord Byron. Second edition. [Twenty poems, including six spurious.] pp. vi. iv. 50. *W. Sheppard: Bristol,* 1816. 12°. G. **18564.**

—— Lord Byron's Poems, on his own Domestic Circumstances. Fare Thee Well. [Containing " Fare Thee Well " and " A Sketch from Private Life."] pp. 15. *W. Espy: Dublin,* 1816. 8°. **11641.** c. 7.

—— Poems on his Domestic Circumstances . . . By Lord Byron . . . Twenty-third edition. Containing nine poems, *etc.* pp. 32. MS. NOTES. *W. Hone: London,* 1817. 8°. **992.** l. **18.**

—— [Another copy.] **11645.** bb. **61.** (**3.**)

—— Three Poems, not included in the Works of Lord Byron. Lines to Lady J——. The Ænigma [by Catherine Maria Fanshawe]. The Curse of Minerva. pp. 18. *Effingham Wilson: London,* 1818. 8°. **11641.** bbb. **20.**

—— Beppo: Mazeppa: Ode to Venice: a Fragment: a Spanish Romance: and Sonnet translated from Vittorelli. pp. 165. *John Murray: London,* 1820. 12°. **11641.** aaa. **17.**

A separate issue of vol. 8 *of the Works of Byron, published in the same year.*

—— The Works of the Right Honourable Lord Byron; containing English Bards, and Scotch Reviewers; the Curse of Minerva, and the Waltz, an apostrophic hymn. [Including " The Enigma " by Catherine Maria Fanshawe. With a portrait.] pp. viii. 151. *M. Thomas: Philadelphia,* 1820. 8°. **11642.** c. **20.**

—— [Another copy.] **11643.** bb. **2.**
Without the portrait.

—— The Beauties of Lord Byron: with a sketch of his life, and a dissertation on his genius and writings, by Thomas Parry. pp. xi. 312. *J. Sudbury: London,* 1823. 12°. **20098.** a. 3.

—— Poems, on his Domestic Circumstances, by the Right Honourable Lord Byron: to which are added, several choice pieces from his Lordship's works. [Twenty-four poems, including four spurious.] pp. 47. *J. Limbird: London,* 1823. 12°. **11643.** a. **48.** (**3.**)
Imperfect; wanting pp. 29, 30.

—— Miscellaneous Poems, on his Domestic and other Circumstances. By Lord Byron. [Twenty-five poems, including six spurious and " Enigma " by Catherine Maria Fanshawe.] pp. 48. *Hodgson & Co.: London,* 1823. 16°. **1075.** d. **10.** (**2.**)

—— Miscellaneous Poems, including those on his Domestic Circumstances. By Lord Byron. To which are prefixed memoirs of the author, and a tribute to his memory by Sir Walter Scott. [Twenty-five poems, including six spurious and " Enigma " by Catherine Maria Fanshawe.] pp. 72. *John Bumpus: London,* 1824. 12°. **11643.** a. **48.** (**5.**)

BYRON (George Gordon Noel) *Baron Byron.* [Smaller Collections.]

—— The Works of Lord Byron . . . Containing Werner, a tragedy; Heaven and Earth, Morgante Maggiore, Age of Bronze, Island, Vision of Judgment, and Deformed Transformed. 2 vol. *John & Henry L. Hunt: London,* 1824 [1824, 25]. 8°. **11613.** c. **10.**
Four additional titlepages reading: " The Works of Lord Byron. In seven volumes. vol. VI. 1824 "; " *vol.* VII. 1825 " *; and " The Works of Lord Byron. In eight volumes. vol.* VII. 1824 " *and " vol.* VIII. 1825 " *are bound in at the end.*

—— The Age of Bronze. (The Island.) [1825 ?] 12°. **11642.** b. **57.** (**4.**)

Pp. 169–244 *of a larger collection.*

—— Lara. A tale. (Manfred. A dramatic poem.) *W. Dugdale: London,* [1825 ?] 12°. C. **58.** bb. **4.**
Pp. 137–216 *of a larger collection.*

—— The Miscellaneous Poems of Lord Byron, consisting of Hours of Idleness, English Bards, Curse of Minerva, &c. &c. With portrait and vignette. pp. xi. 204. *T. & J. Allman: London; John Aderson Jun.: Edinburgh,* 1825. 24°. **011652.** h. **185.**

With an additional titlepage engraved.

—— Miscellaneous Poems on his Domestic and other Circumstances. By Lord Byron. [Twenty-nine poems, including six spurious and " Enigma," by Catherine Maria Fanshawe.] pp. 54. *William Cole: London,* 1825. 12°. **11645.** aa. **64.**

—— The Miscellaneous Poems of Lord Byron. pp. 94. *Benbow: London,* 1825. 12°. **11642.** a. **8.**

—— Poems. By the Right Honourable Lord Byron; with his memoirs. *Jones & Co.: London,* 1825. 8°. Ashley **5457.**

Imperfect; wanting all after p. 74.

—— Poems by the Right Honourable Lord Byron; with his memoirs. [With a portrait.] pp. xiv. 174. *Jones & Co.: London,* 1825. 32°. **011652.** de. **35.**
With an additional titlepage, engraved, reading: " Select Poetical Works, of Lord Byron."

—— Don Juan Complete; English Bards and Scotch Reviewers; Hours of Idleness; The Waltz; and all the other minor poems. pp. 574. *J. F. Dove: London,* 1827. 12°. **11643.** a. **31.**
With an additional titlepage, engraved.

—— Don Juan; Hours of Idleness; English Bards and Scotch Reviewers; The Waltz; and other poems. 2 vol. *J. F. Dove: London,* 1828. 12°. **11611.** a. **9, 10.**
These volumes are numbered 5 *and* 6 *respectively on the binding, thus continuing the numeration of the four volume edition of Byron's Works published by John Murray in the same year.*

—— Life and Select Poems of Lord Byron arranged &c. by C. Hulbert. pp. 84. *Sold by all the Booksellers: London,* [1828.] 12°. **11642.** a. **10.**

—— The Beauties of Byron, consisting of selections from his works. By J. W. Lake. pp. viii. 230. *Baudry; Bobée & Hingray: Paris,* 1829. 16°. **11612.** aa. **28.**

—— Fugitive Pieces and Reminiscences of Lord Byron: containing an entire new edition of the Hebrew Melodies, with the addition of several never before published . . . Also some original poetry, letters and recollections of Lady Caroline Lamb. By I. Nathan. pp. xxxvi. 196. *Whittaker, Treacher & Co.: London,* 1829. 8°. **1164.** f. **7.**

—— [Another copy.] Ashley **336.**

RON (GEORGE GORDON NOEL) *Baron Byron.* [SMALLER COLLECTIONS.]

— The Miscellaneous Works of Lord Byron. Containing Werner, a tragedy; Heaven and Earth; Morgante Maggiore; Age of Bronze; The Island; Vision of Judgment; and The Deformed Transformed. 2 pt. *Hunt & Clarke: London,* 1830. 8°. **1465. h. 4.**

— The Select Works of Lord Byron. Containing: Hours of Idleness; English Bards and Scotch Reviewers; Cain, a mystery; and Miscellaneous Poems. [With a portrait.] pp. 63. *Printed for the booksellers: London,* 1833. 16°. **11659. a. 4.**

— The Beauties of Byron, consisting of selections from his works. By Alfred Howard, Esq. pp. 212. *Thomas Tegg: London,* [1835?] 12°. **11643. a. 33.**
Previous edition 1829.

— A new edition. pp. 192. *T. Tegg & Son: London,* 1837. 12°. **11642. bbb. 70.**

— The Beauties of Byron & Burns, being a collection of poems by the above authors. pp. 128. *W. Howe: Hull,* 1837. 32°. **11647. a. 84. (1.)**

— Dramas. 2 vol. *John Murray: London,* 1837. 12°. **11609. ee. 3.**
Each volume has an additional titlepage, engraved.

— Miscellanies. 3 vol. *John Murray: London,* 1837. 12°. **11609. ee. 4.**
Each volume has an additional titlepage, engraved.

— Tales. 2 vol. *John Murray: London,* 1837. 8°. **11609. ee. 5.**
Each volume has an additional titlepage, engraved.

— The Siege of Corinth, Beppo, Mazeppa, The Island, Parisina, Prisoner of Chillon. 6 pt. *John Murray: London,* 1842. 12°. **11652. a. 98. (5.)**
With an additional titlepage, engraved. "The Prisoner of Chillon" is imperfect, wanting all after p. 22.

— Lord Byron's Tales: consisting of the Giaour, the Bride of Abydos, the Corsair, Lara; with all the notes. Hebrew Melodies, and other poems. pp. 256. *William Milner: Halifax,* 1845. 16°. **11646. a. 3.**

— The Giaour, and the Bride of Abydos. pp. 154. *H. G. Clarke & Co.: London,* 1848. 16°. **1155. a. 17. (1.)**

— The Select Works of Lord Byron . . . With . . . life of the author. pp. xii. 372. *William Milner: Halifax,* 1848. 32°. **11607. eee. 10.**

— Tales and Poems . . . With forty-six illustrative engravings on steel by Edward Finden, from designs by Henry Warren. pp. 290. *Wm. S. Orr & Co.: London,* 1848. 8°. **11656. f. 67.**
With an additional titlepage, engraved.

— Lord Byron's Poetical Works: with life and notes by Allan Cunningham [or rather, by A. Cunningham, author of "The Revolutions of Europe"] . . . Illustrated. Family edition. [With a portrait.] pp. xxii. 544. *Charles Daly: London,* [1850?] 12°. 11612. i. 14.
With an additional titlepage, engraved.

— Poems. [Containing "Hours of Idleness," "English Bards and Scotch Reviewers" and "Poems on Domestic Circumstances."] pp. vi. 46. *See* BRITISH POETS. Cabinet Edition of the British Poets. vol. 2. 1851. 8°. **2504. o. 1.**

— Beppo and Don Juan. 2 vol. *John Murray: London,* 1853. 8°. **1466. a. 4.**

BYRON (GEORGE GORDON NOEL) *Baron Byron.* [SMALLER COLLECTIONS.]

—— Dramas. 2 vol. *John Murray: London,* 1853. 8°. **1466. a. 3.**
Previous edition 1837.

—— Miscellanies. 2 vol. *John Murray: London,* 1853. 8°. **1466. a. 5.**
Previous edition 1837.

—— Tales and Poems. pp. 358. *John Murray: London,* 1853. 8°. **1466. a. 7.**
Previous edition, entitled "Tales," 1837.

—— Selections from the Writings of Lord Byron . . . By a Clergyman [i.e. Whitwell Elwin]. 2 vol. *John Murray: London,* 1854. 8°. **1155. c. 6.**

—— Poems by the Right Honourable Lord Byron; with his Memoirs. pp. xvi. 174. *T. Nelson & Sons: London,* 1855. 32°. **11601. a. 6.**

—— Poems. By Lord Byron. With eight illustrations, by Birket Foster, John Gilbert, etc. [With a "Life of Lord Byron," signed: W. R.] pp. xxxii. 539. *Routledge, Warne & Routledge: London,* 1859. 8°. **11603. ee. 4.**

—— Eastern Tales . . . comprising the Corsair, Lara, the Gaiour, the Bride of Abydos, and the Siege of Corinth. With the author's original introductions and notes. Illustrated. pp. 265. *David Bogue: London,* [1859.] 8°. **11611. bb. 3.**

—— A Selection from the Works of Lord Byron. Edited and prefaced by Algernon Chas. Swinburne. pp. xxxii. 244. *London,* 1866. 8°. [*Moxon's Miniature Poets.*] **11602. bbb. 32.**

—— The Hebrew Melodies and Childe Harold. pp. 166. *Perkins Institution for the Blind: Boston,* 1871. 4°. **13008. a. 33.**
Printed in embossed Roman type.

—— Songs by Lord Byron. pp. 278. *Virtue & Co.: London,* 1872. 8°. **11622. aaa. 12.**

—— [Another copy.] **11622. aaa. 2.**

—— Byron's Siege of Corinth and Ode to Napoleon Buonaparte. With notes for students for the first examination in arts, University of Madras, 1877. pp. 56. *Addison & Co.: Madras,* 1876. 12°. **11643. bbb. 15. (18.)**

—— Favorite Poems. By Lord Byron. Illustrated. pp. 127. *J. R. Osgood & Co.: Boston,* 1877. 16°. **11644. e. 11.**

—— Poetry of Byron, chosen and arranged by Matthew Arnold. pp. xxxvi. 276. **L.P.** *Macmillan & Co.: London,* 1881. 8°. **2308. d. 6.**

—— A Selection from the Works of Lord Byron. Edited and prefaced by Algernon Chas. Swinburne. pp. xxxii. 244. *Ward, Lock & Co.: London,* [1885.] 16°. [*Moxon's Miniature Poets.*] **11602. bbb. 44.**
Previous edition 1866.

—— Byron's Prisoner of Chillon und Siege of Corinth. Mit bibliographischem Material, litterarischer Einleitung und sachlichen Anmerkungen . . . herausgegeben von J. G. C. Schuler. pp. vi. 94. *Halle,* 1886. 8°. **11646. g. 54.**

—— Gems from Byron. With an introduction by the Rev. Hugh Reginald Haweis. pp. 158. *London,* 1886. 8°. [*Routledge's World Library.* no. 33.] **12207. ee. 24.**

BYRON (George Gordon Noel) *Baron Byron*. [Smaller Collections.]

—— Poems of Lord Byron. Carefully selected. 2 vol. *Cassell & Co.: London*, [1886.] 32°. **11607**. cc. **2**.

—— Lord Byron. 1788–1824. [Selections, edited by the Hon. Roden Noel.] [1891.] *See* Miles (Alfred H.) The Poets and the Poetry of the Century, *etc.* vol. 2. [1891, *etc.*] 8°. **11603**. cc. **20/2**.

—— Adieu, Adieu! my Native Shore.—The Destruction of Sennacherib.—Sonnet on Chillon.—The Isles of Greece.—On this day I complete my thirty-sixth-year. *See* Murison (William) Shorter Poems by Burns, Byron and Campbell. With introduction and notes by W. Murison. 1893. 8°. **12201**. df. **1/4**.

—— [Another edition.] *See* Murison (William) Shorter Poems by Burns, Byron, *etc.* 1895. 8°. **12201**. df. **1/5**.

—— Selections from Byron. *See* English Poetry. The Revival of English Poetry, *etc.* 1898. 8°. **11602**. ccc. **32**.

—— Selections from the Poetry of Lord Byron. Edited with an introduction and notes by Frederic Ives Carpenter. pp. lviii. 412. *H. Holt & Co.: New York*, 1900. 8°. **11611**. df. **5**.

—— Poems of Lord Byron. Selected and arranged for use in schools by C. Linklater Thomson. pp. ix. 67. *A. & C. Black: London*, 1901. 8°. **11609**. bb. **34**.

—— Byron. Selected Poetry. By J. Wight Duff. pp. lxv. 388. *Edinburgh & London*, 1904. 8°. [*Blackwood's English Classics.*] **12270**. de. **16/1**.

—— Byron's Songs, *etc.* pp. 270. *J. J. Keliher & Co.: London*, 1904. 8°. [*Kelkel Series.*] **7898**. ee. **79/4**.

—— Poems by Lord Byron. With an introduction by Arthur Symons. pp. ix. 281. *Blackie & Son: London*, [1904.] 8°. [*Red Letter Library.*] **012209**. fff.**1/19**.

—— Love Poems of Byron. pp. xi. 136. *John Lane: London & New York*, 1905. 12°. [*Lover's Library.*] **11607**. aaaa. **1/13**.

—— Ode to Napoleon, &c. (Selections from Byron.) pp. 24. *London*, [1905.] 8°. [*Blackie's English Classics.*] **012200**. e. **3/63**.

—— Byron's Love Songs. pp. 18. *T. N. Foulis: Edinburgh & London*, [1906.] 12°. [*Roses of Parnassus.* no. 18.] **11604**. dg. **17/18**.

—— With Byron in Italy. A selection of the poems and letters of Lord Byron, relating to his life in Italy. Edited by Anna Benneson McMahan. With sixty illustrations from photographs. pp. xxi. 327. *T. Fisher Unwin: London*, 1907 [1906]. 8°. **10854**. de. **15**.

—— Byron's Shorter Poems. Selected and edited, with notes and an introduction, by Ralph Hartt Bowles. pp. xxxviii. 229. *New York*, 1907. 8°. [*Macmillan's Pocket English and American Classics.*] **12199**. a.**1/16**.

—— Poems of Lord Byron. Selected & with an introduction by Charles Whibley. pp. lii. 262. *T. C. & E. C. Jack: Edinburgh*, [1907.] 8°. [*Golden Poets.*] **011604**. e. **1/9**.

—— Selections from Byron. The Prisoner of Chillon, Mazeppa, and other poems. Edited with introduction and notes by Samuel Marion Tucker. pp. xliii. 101. *Ginn & Co.: Boston*, [1907.] 8°. [*Standard English Classics.*] **012203**. f. **39/7**.

BYRON (George Gordon Noel) *Baron Byron*. [Smalle[r] Collections.]

—— Selections from the Poetry of Lord Byron. Edited wit[h] an introduction and notes by Frederic Ives Carpente[r]. pp. lviii. 412. *G. Bell & Sons: London*, 1908. 8[°]. [*English Readings.*] **12271**. w. **7/**
A reissue of the edition of 1900.

—— Prisoner of Chillon. Mazeppa. Lament of Tass[o]. pp. 48. *Clarendon Press: Oxford*, [1909.] 8°. [*Oxfo[rd] Plain Texts.*] **12271**. w. **8/**

—— Love Poems of Byron. pp. viii. 63. *A. L. Humphrey[s]: London*, 1911. 16°. **11612**. dg. **1**

—— Selected Poems of Lord Byron. pp. x. 436. *Oxford University Press: London*, 1913. 8°. [*Worl[d's] Classics.*] **012209**. df. **9**

—— Selected Poems of Byron. [Edited by] William Robe[rt]son. pp. 191. *G. G. Harrap & Co.: London*, [1913.] 1[6°]. [*King's Treasury of Literary Masterpieces.*] **012208**. de. **6/1**

—— Selections from the Poetry of Lord Byron. Chil[de] Harold, cantos iii., iv., etc. pp. viii. 120. *Lond[on]*, 1913. 8°. [*Bell's English Texts.*] **12199**. ccc. **4**

—— Song of the Greek Poet. A Moorish Ballad. *Johnso[n], Hickborn & Co.: London*, [1913.] 8°. **11641**. b. **6**
Printed for private circulation.

—— Selections from the Poems of Lord Byron. Edited [by] A. Hamilton Thompson. pp. xliv. 178. *University Pres[s]: Cambridge*, 1920. 8°. [*English Romantic Poets.*] **11611.bbb.48/5**

—— Poems of Lord Byron. Selected and arranged [in] chronological order, with a preface, by H. J. C. Grierso[n]. pp. xxx. 397. **F.P.** *Chatto & Windus: London*, 1923. [8°.] **11642**. g. **4**
Printed at the Florence Press.

—— Selections from Byron. Compiled by M. F. D[...]. pp. 158. *John Hamilton: London*, [1926.] 8°. [*Wedgwo[od] Series.*] **11607**. aaaa. **18**

—— With Byron in Love. Compiled by Walter Littlefie[ld] with introduction and notes. [Selected poems a[nd] letters.] pp. 319. *J. H. Sears & Co.: New Yo[rk]*, [1926.] 8°. [*Royal Collection.*] **012209.bb.2/8**

—— An Introduction to Byron. Edited by Guy N. Poco[ck]. pp. 191. *J. M. Dent & Sons: London & Toron[to]*, [1927.] 8°. [*King's Treasuries of Literature.* no. 154.] **012207**. aaa. **1/**

—— Poems. Introduction by Arthur Symons. pp. ix. 281. *London & Glasgow*, [1927.] 12°. **11632**. de.
Previous edition 1904.

—— Selections from Byron . . . Edited by W. Roy Mack[...]. pp. iv. 92. *A. & C. Black: London*, 1927. 8°. [*Socra[tic] Booklets.* no. 15.] **012213.p.3/15**

—— Selections from Byron's Poems. pp. 32. *Lond[on]*, [1927.] 8°. [*Brodie Books.* no. 28.] W.P. **8579/**

—— The Shorter Byron . . . Chosen and edited by Ern[est] Rhys. pp. xxi. 215. *R. Holden & Co.: Lond[on]*, 1927. 8°. **11602**. ff.

—— Byron. [Selected poems.] pp. 31. *Ernest Ben[n]: London*, [1928.] 8°. [*Augustan Books of Engl[ish] Poetry.* ser. 2. no. 26.] **11605.cc.12/8**

—— Selections from Byron. A selection in the light of his l[ife] and times by Hamish Miles. pp. 286. *Jonathan Ca[pe]: London*, 1930. 8°. [*Travellers' Library.*] **012208.m.1/5**

—— Selections from Byron. Poetry and prose. Edited w[ith] an introduction by D. M. Walmsley. pp. vii. 216. *Lond[on]*, 1931. 8°. [*Methuen's English Classics.*] W.P. **6815/**

RON (George Gordon Noel) *Baron Byron.* [Smaller Collections.]

— Selections from the Poetry of Byron. Edited by John Bullocke. pp. xxvii. 196. *Ginn & Co.: London,* [1931.] 8°. [*Selected English Classics.*] 012213.h.4/8.

— Lyrical Poems. Selected and arranged in chronological order (by E. du Perron). Wood engraving by J. Buckland Wright. pp. 67. *Halcyon Press: [London;] Maastricht* printed, 1933. 8°. Cup.510.g.13.

— Byron. Satirical and critical poems. Edited by Joan Bennett. pp. xiv. 214. *University Press: Cambridge,* 1937. 8°. 11655. f. 8.

— Byron, Poetry & Prose. With essays by Scott, Hazlitt, Macaulay, etc. With an introduction by Sir Arthur Quiller-Couch and notes by D. Nichol Smith. [With a portrait.] pp. xi. 207. *Clarendon Press: Oxford,* 1940. 8°. 12274. h. 28.

— [Selections from Byron's poems and letters.] *See* Bull (Charles R.) Regency Poets, *etc.* 1941. 8° 12299.b.60/1.

— Byron for To-day. Selected and with an introduction by Roy Fuller. pp. 143. *Porcupine Press: London,* 1948. 12°. 11658. e. 41.

— Byron. Poems, selected and introduced by Patric Dickinson. pp. 62. *Grey Walls Press: London,* 1949. 8°. [*Crown Classics.*] W.P. 2809/31.

— Byron. Selections from Poetry, Letters & Journals . . . Edited by Peter Quennell. pp. ix. 879. *Nonesuch Press: London,* 1949. 8°. 12275. ee. 4.

— George Gordon, Lord Byron. A selection from his poems. By A. S. B. Glover. pp. 365. *Penguin Books: Harmondsworth,* 1954. 8°. [*Penguin Poets.* no. D 26.] 12208. a. 6/26.

English and Armenian.

— [Select poems by Byron with Armenian translations; together with pieces of Armenian prose translated into English by Lord Byron.] *See* English Poets. Beauties of English Poets. 1852. 12°. 17046. a. 12.

— [Another edition.] Lord Byron's Armenian Exercises and Poetry. pp. 167. *Venice, in the Island of S. Lazzaro,* 1886. 12°. 17046. a. 16.
The date on the wrapper is 1870.

English and French.

— Rough Hewing of Lord Byron in French, with the English text. By Francis D'Autrey. pp. 233. *J. W. Kolckmann: London,* 1869. 8°. 11612. bbb. 13.

English and German.

— Drei Lieder.—Finsterniss.—Hebräische Lieder. (In deutscher Uebersetzung mit gegenübergedrucktem Original.) *See* Moore (Thomas) *the Poet.* Dichtungen von Moore und Byron, *etc.* 1852. 16°. 11643. bb. 33. (3.)

English and Italian.

— Parisina. Il Prigioniero di Chillon. Versione col testo a fronte, introduzione e commento a cura di Aldo Ricci, *etc.* pp. viii. 185. *Firenze,* [1924.] 8°. 011644. de. 18.

Czech.

— Korsár. Lara. Básnické povídky . . . Přeložil Čeněk Ibl. pp. 128. *v Praze,* 1885. 8°. [*Poesie světová.* pt. 23.] 011586. df. 51.

Danish.

— Udvalgte dramatiske Digte og Fortællinger af Byron. Oversatte af Edv. Lembcke. [With a portrait.] 2 Bd. *Kjøbenhavn,* 1873, 76. 8°. 11609. ccc. 2.

BYRON (George Gordon Noel) *Baron Byron.* [Smaller Collections.]

—— Manfred, Fangen paa Chillon og Mazeppa. Oversat af Alfred Ipsen. pp 36. *København,* [1888.] 16°. 11781. a. 13. (3.)

—— Beppo. Domm iagssynet . . . Oversatte af Alfred Ipsen. pp. 88. *København,* 1891. 8°. 11601. dd. 9. (8.)

Dutch.

—— Navolgingen van Lord Byron. Door Nicolaas Beets. De gevangene van Chillon. Mazeppa. Parisina. Fragmenten. Joodsche zangen. Verscheiden gedichten. Nieuwe, herziene uitgave. Vermeerderd met een woord over Byrons poëzy. pp. xi. 170. *See* Beets (N.) Gedichten, *etc.* 1848. 8°. Hoogleraar te Utrecht. 11555. c. 7.

—— Gedichten van Lord Byron. Door J. J. L. ten Kate. Eerste volledige uitgave. [Parisina, The Giaour, Manfred, Cain.] pp. 242. *Leiden,* [1870.] 8°. 11643. e. 8.

French.

—— [Select poems, translated into French verse by D. Bonnefin.] *See* Bonnefin (D.) Écrin poétique de la littérature anglaise. 1841. 8°. 11604. ff. 3.

—— Le Prisonnier de Chillon, Lara, Parisina. Poëmes de Lord Byron, traduits en vers, et poésies diverses par H. Gomont. pp. viii. 228. *Paris; Nancy,* 1862. 12°. 11642. bb. 4.

—— Chefs-d'œuvre de Lord Byron, traduits en vers français par A. Regnault. 2 tom. *Paris,* 1874. 8°. 11612. g. 1.

—— [Another copy.] 11609. i. 9.

—— Les Deux Foscari, tragédie historique. Beppo, poème humoristique. Traduction en vers, ornée de 15 vignettes, par Achille Morisseau. pp. xiii. 258. *Paris,* 1881. 8°. 11777. g. 1.

German.

—— Kain. Ein Mysterium. Mazeppa . . . Aus dem Englishen übersetzt von Friederike Friedmann. pp. 154. *Leipzig,* 1855. 16°. 11611. a. 14.

—— Lord Byron's Mazeppa, Korsar und Beppo. In das Deutsche übertragen von Wilhelm Schäffer. pp. 138. *Leipzig,* 1864. 8°. 11642. aa. 17.

—— Dichtungen von Lord Byron. Deutsch von Wilhelm Schäffer (Bdchn. 3 von Adolf Strodtmann). 3 Bdchn. *Hildburghausen,* 1865–72. 8°. [*Bibliothek ausländischer Klassiker.* Bd. 11, 122, 142.] 12209.e.1/13–15.

—— Byron-Anthologie. Auserwähltes aus Lord Byron's Dichtungen, übertragen von Eduard Hobein. pp. 187. *Schwerin,* 1866. 8°. 11611. bbb. 7.

—— Lord Byrons dramatische Werke. Deutsch von W. Grüzmacher. Manfred. Kain. Himmel und Erde. Sardanapal. 2 pt. pp. 323. *Hildburghausen,* 1870. 8°. [*Bibliothek ausländischer Klassiker.* Bd. 112, 113.] 12209.e.1/20.

—— Die Braut von Abydos. Der Traum. Zwei Gedichte . . . Im Versmass des Originals übertragen von Dr. Otto Riedel. pp. 80. *Hamburg,* 1872. 16°. 11643. a. 25.

—— Lord Byrons lyrische Gedichte. Ausgewählt und übersetzt von Heinrich Stadelmann. pp. 132. *Hildburghausen,* 1872. 8°. [*Bibliothek ausländischer Klassiker.* Bd. 145.] 12209.e.1/17.

—— Poetische Erzählungen von Lord Byron . . . [The Giaour, The Bride of Abydos, The Corsair, Lara, The Siege of Corinth, Beppo, Mazeppa, The Island.] Übersetzt und mit einem Vorwort versehen von Alexander Neidhardt. 4 pt. *Halle,* [1903.] 8°. 11611. i. 5.

Hungarian.

—— Manfred.—Mazeppa. [With other poems. Translated by L. Horváth.] 2 pt. *See* Horváth (L.) Byron lord' élete 's munkái. rész. 2, 3. 1842. 8°. **1466**. b. **19**.

Italian.

—— Poemi di Lord G. Byron tradotti dall'originale inglese da Pietro Isola. [The Prisoner of Chillon, Parisina, The Siege of Corinth, Lara.] pp. 204. *Torino,* 1827. 8°. **11643**. g. **29**.

—— Poemi di Lord G. Byron, tradotti dall'originale inglese da Pietro Isola. [The Prisoner of Chillon, Parisina, The Siege of Corinth, Lara, The Bride of Abydos, The Island, and other poems.] 2 vol. *Lugano,* 1832. 8°. **11607**. bb. 3.

—— Poemi di Giorgio Lord Byron, recati in italiano da Giuseppe Nicolini. [The Bride of Abydos, Parisina, The Corsair, Lara.] Con alcuni componimenti originali del traduttore. pp. 433. *Milano,* 1834. 8°. **1465**. h. **6**.

—— Poemi di Giorgio Lord Byron, recati in italiano da Marcello Mazzoni. pp. 239. *Milano,* 1838. 8°. **993**. f. **55**.

—— Poemi di Giorgio Lord Byron, recati in italiano da Giuseppe Nicolini. Nuova edizione eseguita su quella del 1837 riveduta ed aumentata dal traduttore. 2 vol. *Milano,* 1842. 12°. **1466**. b. **7**.

—— Marino Faliero, e I Due Foscari, tragedie . . . Versione dall'originale inglese del P. G. B. Cereseto. pp. 304. *Savona,* 1845. 8°. **1344**. h. **10**.

—— Opere di Giorgio Lord Byron. [Childe Harold, The Bride of Abydos, Parisina, The Corsair, Lara, The Prisoner of Chillon, The Siege of Corinth, The Giaour, The Lament of Tasso, Cain, Manfred, Marino Faliero, The Two Foscari. Translated by G. Gazzino, G. Nicolini and others.] Precedute da alcune avvertenze critiche sulle stesse [by Bernardino Marotta] e da un discorso di Cesare Cantù. Prima edizione napolitana adorna di figure incise. [With a portrait.] pp. xvi. 504. *Napoli,* 1853. 8°. **11611**. f. 5.

—— Tragedie di Giorgio Lord Byron. Traduzione del cav. Andrea Maffei. Sardanapalo. Marino Faliero. I Due Foscari. pp. 493. *Firenze,* 1862. 8°. **11779**. aaa. **46**.

—— Caino, Cielo e terra, Un Sogno, La Sposa promessa d'Abido, Parisina, Il Prigioniero di Chillon, Le Tenebre, L'Addio, Ricordi giovanili. *See* Maffei (A.) Poeti inglesi e francesi . . . Traduzioni di A. Maffei. 1870. 8°. **11420**. bb. **7**.

—— Il Pellegrinaggio d'Aroldo.—La Parisina, il Beppo e La Sposa d'Abido. [Translated by Giacinto Casella.] *See* Casella (G.) Opere edite e postume, *etc.* vol. 1. 1884. 8°. **12225**. b. **1**.

Polish.

—— Poezye Lorda Byrona tłumaczone, Giaur przez Adama Mickiewicza, Korsarz przez Edwarda Odyńca. Wydanie Alexandra Jelowickiego. pp. xiv. 202. *w Paryżu,* 1835. 12°. **11612**. aaa. **19**. **(1.)**

—— Pięć poematów Lorda Birona przełożył Franciszek Dzierżykraj Morawski. [Manfred, Mazeppa, The Siege of Corinth, Parisina, The Prisoner of Chillon.] pp. 272. *Leszno,* 1853. 8°. **11611**. d. 4.

Portuguese.

—— A Peregrinação de Childe Harold.—Sardanapalo. Tr gedia . . . adaptada á scena. *See* Pinheiro Guimarõe (F. J.) Traducçoes Poeticas. 1863. 8°. **11452**. g. **2**

Roumanian.

—— Din ckpiepiлe л8i Lord Byron партѣ ııı tpaд8ce де Eлiad. (Prisonierul de Chillon.—Lamantatiile lui Tassu.— Beppo n8otate Italianъ.) pp. 74. *Б8к8peщi,* 1834. 8 **11633**. e.

Russian.

—— Драмы. Переводы И. А. Бунина, Н. А. Брянског Вступит. статьи В. М. Жирмунского и А. А. Смирнов pp. 347. *Петербург, Москва,* 1922. 8°. **011779**. m. **1**

—— Избранные произведения, *etc.* (Составление и реда ция переводов Р. М. Самарина. Вступительная стат А. Елистратовой.) [With a portrait.] pp. 501. *Моск* 1953. 4°. **12643**. t. **1**

—— Каинъ. Манфредъ. Небо и земля. Переводъ И. Бунина. pp. 187. *Берлинъ,* 1921. 8°. **11658**. e. **3**
The wrapper bears the title " *Мистерiи.*"

Spanish.

—— Odas a Napoleon . . . Traduccion castellana. pp. 60. *Paris,* 1830. 12°. **11646**. cc. **9**. **(1**

—— Poemas de Lord Byron, con notas, comentarios aclaraciones. [Lara, The Siege of Corinth, Parisin Mazeppa, Childe Harold, Lament of Tasso, Beppo Primera version española, en vista de la última edicio Por Ricardo Canales. [In prose.] pp. 352. *Barcelon* [1876.] 8°. **11611**. dd.

—— Cuatro poemas de Lord Byron. Traducidos en vers castellano por Antonio Sellen. Parisina. El Prisionero d Chillon. Los Lamentos del Tasso. La Novia de Abydos [With an introduction by A. Lopez Prieto.] pp. 111. *New York,* 1877. 12°. **11646**. b. **59**

—— Lord Byron. (Poemas.) [The Corsair, Lara, Darkness six Hebrew Melodies, The Lament of Tasso. Translate into Spanish prose; with an introduction by R. Ginard d la Rosa.] pp. 191. *Madrid,* 1880. 16°. [*Bibliotec Universal. Coleccion de los mejores autores antiguos modernos.* tom. 63.] **739**. a. **63**

—— D. Juan . . . seguido de las Lamentaciones del Tass . . . Version [in prose] de J. A. R. Ilustrado con dibujo á la pluma por R. Escaler. pp. 414. *Barcelona* 1883. 8°. **11633**. bbb. **4**

—— Poemas dramaticos de Lord Byron. Caín. Sardaná palo. Manfredo. Traducidos en verso castellano po D. José Alcalá Galiano, con una carta prólogo de D Marcellino Menéndez y Pelayo. pp. xxxvi. 382. *Madri* 1886. 8°. **12231**. d. **1**

—— Poemas líricos. Selección, versión y prólogo de Marí Alfaro. pp. 72. *Madrid,* 1945. 8°. **11659**. de. **15**
Colección Adonais. no. 18.

—— Lord Byron. [Selected poems translated by various writers.] pp. 81. *Barcelona,* [1922.] 8°. **11647**. aa. **82**.

Swedish.

—— Byrons poetiska berättelser. (Öfversättning af Tali Qualis [pseudonym of C. V. A. Strandberg].) hft. 1–8.

1. Mazeppa. 1853.
2. Belägringen af Korinth. 1854
3. Fången på Chillon. 1854.
4. Parisina. 1854.
5. Beppo. 1854.
6. Giaurn. 1855.
7. Bruden från Abydos. 1855.
8. Ön. 1856.

Stockholm, 1853–56. 8°. **11644**. g. **19**
Imperfect; wanting hft. 9 *and* 10, *containing respectivel* " *Korsaren* " *and* " *Lara.*"

LETTERS AND JOURNALS.

— [Private correspondence of Lord Byron, including his letters to his mother written from Portugal, Spain, Greece, and other parts of the Mediterranean in the years 1809, 1810 and 1811. Connected by memorandums and observations forming a memoir of his life from the year 1808 to 1814. By R. C. Dallas, Esq.] pp. 19–168. [1824.] 4°. C. **59**. i. 4.
The titlepage, which is in MS., *bears the note:* "*The following sheets are the whole that were printed when an injunction was obtained from the Court of Chancery . . . to restrain the publication of the work on the 7th July* 1824."

— [Another copy.] Ashley **4755**.

— Correspondence of Lord Byron, with a friend, (R. C. Dallas.) including his letters to his mother, written from Portugal, Spain, Greece, and the shores of the Mediterranean, in 1809, 1810 and 1811. Also recollections of the poet, by the late R. C. Dallas . . . and a continuation and preliminary statement of the proceedings by which the letters were suppressed in England, at the suit of Lord Byron's executors. By the Rev. A. R. C. Dallas. 3 vol. *A. & W. Galignani: Paris,* 1825. 12°. **10920**. d. 3.

— [Another copy.] Ashley **324**.

— Letters and Journals of Lord Byron: with notices of his life, by Thomas Moore. 2 vol. *John Murray: London,* 1830. 4°. **841**. m. **16, 17**.

— [Another copy, with plates, autograph letters, etc., inserted.] 14 vol. *See* supra: Works. The Poetical Works of Lord Byron, *etc.* vol. 31–44. 1839, *etc.* 4°. C. **44**. f, g.

— Letters and Journals of Lord Byron, with notices of his life, by Thomas Moore. 4 vol. *A. & W. Galignani: Paris,* 1830, 31. 12°. **10923**. df. 3.

— [Another edition.] [With a portrait.] pp. 512. *A. & W. Galignani: Paris,* 1831. 8°. **10855**. ee. **7**.

— Third edition, with forty-four engravings [including a portrait], *etc.* 3 vol. *John Murray: London,* 1833. 8°. **841**. g. **40**.

— [Another copy.] **1203**. e. **2**.

— Life, Letters, and Journals of Lord Byron. [Edited by Thomas Moore.] Complete in one volume. With notes. pp. xix. 735. *John Murray: London,* 1838. 8°. **10860**. c. **10**.
With an additional titlepage, engraved.

— The Life of Lord Byron, with his Letters and Journals. By Thomas Moore. A new edition, complete in one volume. With portraits, *etc.* pp. xix. 735. *John Murray: London,* 1847. 8°. **10827.h.33.**
With an additional titlepage, engraved, bearing the date 1846. *A reissue of the edition of* 1838.

— Life of Lord Byron: with his Letters and Journals. By Thomas Moore. [With a portrait.] 6 vol. *John Murray: London,* 1851. 8°. **10923**. a. 1.
With additional titlepages, engraved.

— [A reissue.] The Life, Letters and Journals of Lord Byron, *etc. London,* 1860 [1859, 60]. 8°. **10855**. f. 12.
Published in parts.

— The Life, Letters and Journals of Lord Byron. By Thomas Moore . . . New and complete edition, *etc.* pp. xix. 735. *John Murray: London,* 1866. 8°. **010881**. k. **54**.
A reissue of the edition of 1838. *With an additional titlepage, engraved, dated* 1860.

— The Unpublished Letters of Lord Byron. Edited, with a critical essay of the poet's philosophy and character, by H. S. Schultess-Young. pp. viii. 251. *R. Bentley & Son: London,* 1872. 8°. Ashley **2709**.

— The Letters and Journals of Lord Byron; with notices of his life. By Thomas Moore. New and revised edition, with twelve illustrations. pp. 1080. *Chatto & Windus: London,* 1875 [1874]. 8°. **10856**. bbb. **7**.

— [Letters from Byron to the Rev. Francis Hodgson.] *See* Hodgson (James T.) Memoir of the Rev. Francis Hodgson, *etc.* 1878. 8°. **4903**. ee. **18**.

— The Works of Lord Byron. Edited by William Ernest Henley. (vol. 1. Letters, 1804–1813.) [With a portrait.] pp. xix. 469. 1897 [1896]. 8°. *See* supra: Works. **12272**. dd. **2**.

— The Letters and Journals of Lord Byron. Selected. With introduction by Mathilde Blind. pp. xvi. 346. *Walter Scott: London,* 1886. 8°. [*Camelot Classics.*] **12205**. ff. **9**.

— Letters and Journals . . . Edited by Rowland E. Prothero. 6 vol. 1898–1901. *See* supra: Works. The Works of Lord Byron, *etc.* 1898, *etc.* 8° **12276.aa.6.**

— [Another issue.] *See* supra: Works. The Works of Lord Byron, *etc.* 1898, *etc.* 4°. **12270**. i. 4.

— The Confessions of Lord Byron. A collection of his private opinions of men and matters, taken from the new and enlarged edition of his Letters and Journals. Arranged by W. A. Lewis Bettany. [With a portrait.] pp. xxviii. 402. *John Murray: London,* 1905. 8°. **10856**. cc. 8.

— Lord Byron's Correspondence, chiefly with Lady Melbourne, Mr. Hobhouse, the Hon. Douglas Kinnaird, and P. B. Shelley. With portraits. Edited by John Murray. [With a portrait.] 2 vol. *John Murray: London,* 1922. 8°. **2410**. b. **19**.

— [Another copy.] Ashley **2713**.

— Lord Byron in his Letters. Selections from his letters and journals. Edited by V. H. Collins. With a portrait. pp. xvi. 301. *John Murray: London,* 1927. 8°. **10905**. f. **6**.

— [Another copy.] MS. NOTES [by the editor]. **10906**. g. **8**.

— The Ravenna Journal . . . Mainly compiled at Ravenna in 1821, and now for the first time issued in book form. With an introduction by the Right Honourable Lord Ernle. pp. 100. 1928. 8°. *See* London.—III. *First Edition Club.* Ac. **9670**. c/**10**.

— [Another copy.] Ashley **2714**.

— Selected Letters of Byron. Edited by V. H. Collins. pp. vii. 166. *Clarendon Press: Oxford,* 1928. 8°. **010905**. e. **65**.

— Seventeen Letters of George Noel Gordon, Lord Byron, to an unknown lady, 1811–1817. (The text derived from the suppressed Unpublished Letters of Lord Byron, edited by H. S. Schultess-Young, London, 1872.) Edited, with introduction and notes, by Walter Edwin Peck. pp. 50. *Covici-Friede: New York,* 1930. fol. Ashley **4756**.

— [Another copy.] Ashley **4765**.

BYRON (George Gordon Noel) *Baron Byron.* [Letters and Journals.]

—— The Letters of George Gordon, 6th Lord Byron. Selected by R. G. Howarth . . . Illustrated . . . by . . . portraits. pp. xxii. 471. *J. M. Dent & Sons: London; E. P. Dutton & Co.: New York,* 1933. 8°. **2410. b. 21.**

—— [Another edition, abridged.] pp. xxi. 393. *J. M. Dent & Sons: London; E. P. Dutton & Co.: New York,* 1936. 8°. [*Everyman's Library.*] **12206.p.1/721.**

—— Byron. A self-portrait. Letters and diaries, 1798 to 1824. With hitherto unpublished letters in two volumes edited by Peter Quennell. [With portraits.] 2 vol. *John Murray: London,* 1950. 8°. **10862. e. 29.**

—— Mémoires de Lord Byron, publiés par Thomas Moore; traduits de l'anglais par Mme Louise Sw.-Belloc. 5 tom. *Paris,* 1830. 8°. **1452. g. 2.**

—— Correspondance de Lord Byron avec P. B. Shelley, Lady Melbourne, Mr. Hobhouse, l'Hon. Douglas Kinnaird. Publiée par John Murray. Traduit de l'anglais par F. Laroche. Avec un portrait. 2 tom. *Paris,* [1924.] 8°. **010905. e. 55.**

—— Lord Byron's Briefwechsel mit einem Freunde und seiner Mutter in den Jahren 1809–1811; nebst Erinnerungen und Beobachtungen von R. C. Dallas. Mit Lord Byrons Bildniss . . . Aus dem Französischen ins Teutsche übertragen durch Marum Samuel Mayer. pp. 403. *Stuttgart,* 1825. 8°. **010921. e. 12.**

—— Lord Byron. Eine Autobiographie nach Tagebüchern und Briefen. Mit Einleitung und Erläuterungen. Von Eduard Engel. Ergänzungsband zu Byrons Werken. Zweite Auflage. pp. xx. 231. *Berlin,* 1876. 8°. **10854. e. 1.**

—— Viaggi (in Italia e nella Grecia) di Lord Byron, descritti da lui medesimo. [Letters.] *See* Cantù (C.) Lord Byron. Discorso, *etc.* 1833. 12°. **10854. a. 22.**

—— Byron's Letters in Italian. *In:* Origo (Iris) *Marchioness.* The Last Attachment. The story of Byron and Teresa Guiccioli as told in their unpublished letters, *etc.* pp. 425–477. 1949. 8°. **10862. c. 5.**

—— *See* Borgese Freschi (M.) L'Appassionata di Byron. Con le lettere inedite fra Lord Byron e la contessa Guiccioli, *etc.* [With facsimiles.] [1949.] 8°. **10923. aaa. 51.**

—— [For editions of the "Letter to **** ******, on the Rev. W. L. Bowles' Strictures on the life and writings of Pope," first published in 1821:] *See* infra: Single Works.

—— Lord Byron. A fac-simile of an interesting letter written by Lord Byron, dated 15th January 1809 . . . An essay affording a curious insight into his character and early views of leading men, *etc.* *Joseph Thomas: London,* 1876. 4°. **10921. g. 1.**

PARLIAMENTARY SPEECHES.

—— The Parliamentary Speeches of Lord Byron. Printed from the copies prepared by his Lordship for publication. pp. 44. *Rodwell & Martin: London,* 1824. 8°. **T. 1130. (3.)**

—— [Another copy.] **Ashley 2708.**

SINGLE WORKS.

Address for the Opening of Drury Lane Theatre.

—— Address, written by Lord Byron [for the opening of Drury Lane Theatre]. *See* London.—iii. *Drury Lane Theatre.* The Genuine Rejected Addresses, *etc.* 1812. 8°. **993. a. 27.**

Appendix.

—— A Critique, on the Address written by Lord Byron which was spoken at the opening of the New Theatre Royal, Drury Lane, October 10, 1812. By Lord —— pp. 18. *T. Bayley: London,* [1812 ?] 8°. **11805. dd. 25. (1.**

The Age of Bronze.

—— The Age of Bronze; or, Carmen seculare et annus haud mirabilis. [By Lord Byron.] pp. 36. 1823. 8°. *See* Age. **11643. bbb. 17. (6.**

—— [Another copy.] **Ashley 2704**

—— [Another copy.] **Ashley 5456***

—— Second edition. pp. 36. 1823. 8°. *See* Age. **11646. ff. 2**

—— Third edition. pp. 36. 1823. 8°. *See* Age. **11643. bbb. 18. (1.**

Beppo.

—— Beppo, a Venetian Story. [By Lord Byron.] pp. 49. 1818. 8°. *See* Beppo. **C. 71. c. 2**

—— [Another copy.] **Ashley 268**

—— Second edition. pp. 49. 1818. 8°. *See* Beppo. **11641. bbb. 1**

—— Third edition. pp. 49. 1818. 8°. *See* Beppo. **11645. cc. 2**

—— Beppo . . . Fourth edition. [By Lord Byron.] pp. 5 1818. 8°. *See* Beppo. **11658. g. 163. (**

—— Fifth edition. pp. 51. *John Murray: Londo* 1818. 8°. **992. l. 4. (7**

—— Sixth edition. pp. 51. *John Murray: Londo* 1818. 8°. **1344. l. 21. (1**

—— Seventh edition. pp. 51. *John Murray: Londo* 1818. 8°. **11645. g. 1**

English and French.

—— Beppo . . . Traduit en vers français [by S. Clogenson avec texte anglais en regard. pp. 159. *Pari* 1865. 12°. **11642. aaa.**

Dutch.

—— Beppo, eene Venetiaansche vertelling. Naar he Engelsch van Lord Byron. *See* Lennep (J. van) Vert lingen en navolgingen in poezy. 1834. 8°. **11641. g. 2**

—— Additional Stanzas to the First, Second, and Thi editions of Beppo. pp. 2. [*John Murray: Londo* 1818.] *s. sh.* 8°. **Ashley 268**
Printed for private circulation.

Appendix.

—— A Poetical Epistle from Alma Mater to Lord Byro occasioned by the following lines in a tale called "Beppo But for those children of the "mighty mother's," T would-be wits, and can't-be gentlemen. pp. 18. *Deighton & Sons; Goode: Cambridge,* 1819. 8°. **992. i. 24. (**

The Bride of Abydos.

—— The Bride of Abydos. A Turkish tale. pp. 72. *John Murray: London,* 1813. 8°. **C. 71. e. 1**
With errata slip and ms. *corrections.*

BYRON (George Gordon Noel) *Baron Byron*. [Single Works.—The Bride of Abydos.]

— [Another copy.] The Bride of Abydos . . . Second edition. *London*, 1813. 8°. **11659**. d. **8**.

— [Another copy.] Ashley **2621**.

— [Another issue.] *London*, 1813. 8°. **11642**. cc. **28**. (**2**.)
With the errata corrected.

— [Another copy.] Ashley **2622**.

— Second edition. pp. 72. *John Murray: London*, 1813. 8°. **11641**. f. **10**.

— Third edition. pp. 72. *John Murray: London*, 1813. 8°. **11643**. bbb. **17**. (**1**.)

— [Another copy.] Ashley **5454**.

— Fourth edition. pp. 72. *John Murray: London*, 1813. 8°. **11643**. c. **7**.

— Fifth edition. pp. 72. *John Murray: London*, 1813. 8°. **11643**. c. **6**.

— Sixth edition. pp. 72. *John Murray: London*, 1814. 8°. **11646**. ff. **16**.

— [Another copy.] **11643**. l. **14**. (**3**.)

— Seventh edition. pp. 72. *John Murray: London*, 1814. 8°. **11641**. cc. **10**.

— Eighth edition. pp. 72. *John Murray: London*, 1814. 8°. **11643**. c. **5**.

— [Another copy.] The Bride of Abydos . . . Eighth edition. *London*, 1814. 8°. **11661**. c. **7**. (**2**.)

— Ninth edition. pp. 72. *John Murray: London*, 1814. 8°. **11643**. k. **31**. (**2**.)

— Tenth edition. pp. 71. *John Murray: London*, 1814. 8°. **11645**. cc. **27**.

— [Another issue.] The Bride of Abydos . . . Tenth edition. [With plates.] *London*, 1814. 8°. **11659**. b. **33**. (**2**.)

— Eleventh edition. pp. 71. *John Murray: London*, 1815. 8°. **11643**. bbb. **17**. (**4**.)

— [Another edition.] pp. 48. *Thomas Wilson: London*, 1825. 12°. C. **58**. bb. **4**. (**1**.)

— The Bride of Abydos, *etc*. pp. 48. *John Murray: London*, 1842. 12°. **11652**. a. **98**. (**2**.)

— [Another edition.] pp. 39. [*Clarke: London*, 1844.] 8°. **1155**. c. **1**. (**3**.)

Czech.

— Lorda Byrona Nevěsta z Abydu. Pověst turecká . . . Přeložil Josef V. Frič. pp. 66. *v Praze*, 1854. 16°. **11643**. bb. **33**. (**4**.)

Dutch.

— De Abydeensche verloofde. Uit het Engelsch . . . door Mr. J. van Lennep. pp. 67. *Amsterdam*, 1826. 8°. **11641**. g. **8**.

Polish.

— Narzeczona z Abydos. Powieść turecka. 1838. *See* Odyniec (A. E.) Tłómaczenia. tom 2. 1838, *etc*. 8°. **11585**. c. **39**.

Appendix.

— *See* Dimond (William) The Bride of Abydos: a romantic drama . . . From Lord Byron's celebrated poem, *etc*. [1866.] 12°. **2304**. f. **15**. (**7**.)

1–9

BYRON (George Gordon Noel) *Baron Byron*. [Single Works.—The Bride of Abydos.]

—— *See* Harfenton (E. R.) Zuleika, ein Seelengemälde in vier Schilderungen, frei nach Byron's "Braut von Abydos" dargestellt. 1845. 8°. **1464**. f. **8**.

British Bards.

—— *See* infra: English Bards, and Scotch Reviewers.

Cain.

—— Cain; a mystery. *See* infra: Sardanapalus. Sardanapalus . . . The Two Foscari . . . Cain, *etc*. 1821. 8°. **642**. i. **33**.

—— Cain; a mystery. By the author of Don Juan. pp. 93. 1822. 12°. *See* Cain. **11779**. a. **22**.

—— Cain; a mystery . . . To which is added a letter from the author to Mr. Murray, the original publisher. pp. 24. *R. Carlile: London*, 1822. 8°. **09525**. k. **35**. (**3**.)

—— Cain; a mystery . . . To which is added a letter from the author to Mr. Murray . . . Second edition. pp. 23. *R. Carlile: London*, 1822. 8°. **11779**. cc. **7**.

—— [Another copy.] **11779**. cc. **15**.

—— [Another edition.] pp. 72. *H. Gray: London*, 1822. 12°. **11779**. b. **25**.
With an additional titlepage, engraved.

—— [Another edition.] pp. 85. *W. Benbow: London*, 1824. 12°. **11642**. a. **61**. (**4**.)

—— [Another edition.] pp. 63. *W. Dugdale: London*, 1826. 12°. **011781**. l. **5**. (**2**.)

—— [Another edition.] With notes; wherein the religion of the Bible is considered in reference to acknowledged philosophy and reason. By Harding Grant. pp. xvi. 432. *William Crofts: London*, 1830. 8°. **641**. d. **21**.

—— [Another copy.] Ashley **5295**.

—— [Another edition.] pp. 47. *J. Watson: London*, 1832. 8°. **1344**. c. **46**.

—— [Another copy.] Ashley **325**.

—— [Another edition.] [1879?] 8°. [*Dicks' Standard Plays*. no. 203.] **11770**. bbb. **4**.
A reissue of part of "The Poetical Works of Lord Byron" published by John Dicks in 1866.

—— [Another edition.] With introduction, notes and appendix by B. Uhlemayr. *C. Kock's Verlagsbuchhandlung: Nürnberg*, 1907. 8°. **11779**. i. **22**.

—— [Another edition.] Translated into French verse and refuted . . . Preceded by a letter addressed to Lord Byron . . . by Fabre d'Olivet, mdcccxxiii. Done into English by Nayán Louise Redfield. [Byron's original text, with a translation of Fabre d'Olivet's Refutation.] pp. xi. 265. *G. P. Putnam's Sons: New York & London*, 1923. 8°. **11643**. k. **35**.

—— [Another edition.] pp. 88. *London; Vienna printed*, [1924.] 16°. [*Holerth Library*. no. 6.] **012207**. g. **2/6**.

Czech.

—— Kain. Dramatická báseň . . . Přeložil J. Durdík. pp. 117. *v Praze*, 1871. 8°. [*Poesie světová*. pt. 1.] **011586**. df. **51**.

Dutch.

—— Cain. Misterie-spel . . . Metrische vertaling met inleiding en aanteekeningen door Dr. S. A. Kok. pp. 160. *'s-Gravenhage*, 1906. 8°. **11775**. g. **28**.

Esperanto.

—— Kain . . . Tradukis A. Kofman. pp. ix. 102. *Nurnbergo,* 1896. 8°. **11778.** a. **1.**

French.

—— Caïn, mystère dramatique en trois actes . . . traduit en vers français, et réfuté dans une suite de remarques philosophiques et critiques, précédé d'une lettre adressée à Lord Byron, sur les motifs et le but de cet ouvrage, par Fabre d'Olivet. pp. 248. *Paris,* 1823. 8°. **11779.** bb. **46.**

—— [Another copy.] **11738.** e. **30.** (**5.**)

German.—Judaeo-German.

—— *See* infra : *Yiddish.*

Greek.

—— Gaisford Greek Verse, 1925 . . . Cain, Act III, from 'Where is thy brother Abel ?' Translated into iambics by Henri Nicolas De Villiers. pp. 7. *Basil Blackwell: Oxford,* 1925. 8°. **11641.** df. **57.**

Polish.

—— Kain. Poemat dramatyczny . . . przełożył A. Pajgert. pp. 125. *Lwów,* 1868. 8°. **11779.** c. **30.**
Published as a supplement to the "Dziennik literacki."

Yiddish.

—— [Lord Byron's Cain. Yiddish translation by Nathan Horowitz.] [*London,* 1925.] 8°. **11633.** de. **61.**
Cuttings from a newspaper. With a MS. *title.*

Appendix.

—— *See* ADAMS (Thomas) *Author of "A Scourge for Lord Byron."* A Scourge for Lord Byron; or, "Cain, a mystery" unmasked. 1823. 8°. **11601.** dd. **10.** (**6.**)

—— *See* BATTINE (William) Another Cain, a mystery. [A reply to Byron's "Cain."] 1822. 12°. **11643.** bb. **32.** (**7.**)

—— *See* BRITANNICUS, *pseud.* Revolutionary Causes: with . . . a postscript containing strictures on Cain, *etc.* 1822. 8°. **8138.** b. **12.**

—— *See* CAIN. Another Cain. A poem. [A reply to Byron's "Cain."] 1822. 8°. T. **1063.** (**6.**)

—— *See* HARNESS (William) The Wrath of Cain: a Boyle Lecture, *etc.* [A reply to Byron's "Cain."] 1822. 8°. **4473.** c. **13.** (**5.**)

—— *See* HARROVIENSIS, *pseud.* A Letter to Sir Walter Scott, Bart., in answer to the remonstrance of Oxoniensis on the publication of Cain, a Mystery, by Lord Byron. 1822. 8°. **11840.** ccc. **10.** (**3.**)

—— *See* HOWELL (Owen) Abel: written . . . in reply to Lord Byron's Cain. 1843. 12°. **11650.** cc. **13.** (**4.**)

—— *See* LAYMAN. A Layman's Epistle to a certain Nobleman. [Addressed to Lord Byron, with special reference to his "Cain."] 1824. 8°. **11643.** bbb. **18.** (**3.**)

—— *See* OXONIENSIS, *pseud.* A Remonstrance addressed to Mr. John Murray, respecting a recent publication [i.e. Byron's "Cain"]. 1822. 8°. T. **1166.** (**10.**)

—— *See* PHILO MILTON, *pseud.* A Vindication of the Paradise Lost, from the Charge of exculpating "Cain," a mystery. 1822. 8°. T. **1166.** (**11.**)

—— *See* SCHAFFNER (A.) Lord Byron's Cain und sein Quellen. 1880. 8°. **11840.** f. **15.** (**11.**

—— *See* WILKINSON (Henry) *of York.* Cain, a poem . . containing an antidote to the impiety and blasphemy o Lord Byron's Cain, *etc.* 1824. 8°. **11645.** cc. **8**

CHILDE HAROLD'S PILGRIMAGE.

Cantos I, II.

—— Childe Harold's Pilgrimage. A romaunt. [Cantos and II. With fourteen other poems.] pp. vi. 226. *John Murray: London,* 1812. 4°. C. **57.** f. **16**

—— [Another copy.] C. **28.** m. **14**
With part of an autograph letter from Byron to the Re Robert Walpole inserted.

—— [Another copy.] Ashley **4723**

—— The second edition. [With twenty other poems. pp. xii. 300. *John Murray: London,* 1812. 8°. **992.** l. **2**

—— [Another copy.] Childe Harold's Pilgrimage . . . Th second edition. *London,* 1812. 8°. **11659.** d.

—— [Another copy.] **989.** b. **2**

—— Third edition. pp. xii. 300. *John Murray: Londo* 1812. 8°. **11643.** l.

—— Fourth edition. pp. xii. 300. *John Murray: Londo* 1812. 8°. **11642.** e. **34.** (**1**

—— Fifth edition. pp. xvi. 300. *John Murray: Londo* 1812. 8°. **11643.** l.

—— The sixth edition. pp. xvi. 300. *John Murray London,* 1813. 8°. **11645.** ff. **4**

—— Seventh edition. [With twenty-nine other poems pp. xvi. 296. *John Murray: London,* 1814. 8°. **11642.** g.

—— Eighth edition. pp. xii. 296. *John Murray: Londo* 1814. 8°. **11643.** k. **2**

—— [Another copy.] **11643.** l. **14.** (**1**

—— Tenth edition. pp. xii. 302. *John Murray: Londo* 1815. 8°. **11643.** l.

—— Eleventh edition. pp. xii. 274. *John Murray: Londo* 1819. 8°. **11645.** ff. **1**

—— [Another edition.] Edited with introduction and note by H. F. Tozer . . . Third edition. *Clarendon Press Oxford,* 1907 [1910]. 8°. **2292.a.19.**
A reissue of parts of the complete edition, published i 1907, with the titlepage and table of contents of that editio

—— [Another edition.] Edited with introduction and note by the Rev. J. C. Scrimgeour. pp. xliii. 182. *Macmillan & Co.: London; Calcutta* [printed], 1914. 8° **11644.** dd. **8**

—— Childe Harold's Pilgrimage. Canto II. Edited by Joh Downie. pp. 47. *London,* 1901. 8°. [*Blackie's Englis Classics.*] **012200.** e. **3/3**

English and Italian.

—— To Thyrza.—A Thyrsa. [Stanzas beginning "An thou art dead, as young and fair," appended to th second edition of Childe Harold's Pilgrimage, Cantos and II.] *See* WIEL (T.) Versioni da Thomas Gray, *et* 1906. 8°. **11602.** h. **2**

BYRON (George Gordon Noel) *Baron Byron.* [Single Works.—Childe Harold's Pilgrimage.—*Cantos I, II.*]

Italian.

—— Pellegrinaggio d'Aroldo. Traduzione di Giovanni Giovio. [Cantos I, II.] pp. xxxiii. 122. *Milano,* 1866. 8°. **11643.** aaa. **57.**

Canto III.

—— Childe Harold's Pilgrimage. Canto the third. pp. 79. *John Murray: London,* 1816. 8°. Ashley **2619. (1.)**

—— [Another copy, with a different titlepage.] **992.** l. **3. (1.)**

—— [Another copy.] **B. 690. (4.)**

—— [Another copy.] Ashley **2619. (2.)**

—— [Another copy, with minor variations.] pp. 76 [79]. Ashley **2619. (3.)**

—— [Another copy.] Ashley **2620.**

—— [Another edition.] Edited by John Downie. pp. 47. *London,* 1901. 8°. [*Blackie's English Classics.*] **012200.** e. **3/36**a.

—— [Another edition.] Edited with introduction and notes by H. F. Tozer . . . Third edition. *Clarendon Press: Oxford,* 1907 [1912]. 8°. **11653.** ccc. **59.**
A reissue of parts of the complete edition published in 1907, *with the titlepage and table of contents of that edition, and an additional titlepage dated* 1912 *for Canto III.*

—— Childe Harold's Pilgrimage. Canto III. (Goldsmith's Traveller and Deserted Village. With an introduction by A. T. Quiller-Couch.) 2 pt. *Clarendon Press: Oxford,* [1912.] 8°. **11604.** de. **36.**
"*Goldsmith's Traveller and Deserted Village*" *is a reissue of the edition first published in* "*Select English Classics*" *edited by A. T. Quiller-Couch.*

—— Childe Harold . . . Canto III. Stanzas I.–LX. With biographical sketch and explanatory notes. pp. 40. *London & Glasgow,* [1882.] 8°. [*Collin's English Classics.*] **12204.** b. **23/1.**

Canto IV.

—— Childe Harold's Pilgrimage. Canto the fourth. pp. xiv. 257. *John Murray: London,* 1818. 8°. Ashley **2690. (1.)**

—— [Another copy.] pp. xiii. 257. Ashley **2690. (6.)**
In this copy a new paragraph of seven lines has been inserted on p. 160 *and pp.* 155–160 *have been re-set. Sig.* A, *containing the titlepage, dedicatory preface and list of contents, is probably a proof-sheet.*

—— [Another copy, with a preface re-set.] pp. xiv. 257. Ashley **2690. (2.)**

—— [Another copy.] Ashley **2690. (3.)**
In this copy alterations have been made to footnotes, and pp. 217–219 *and* 226–233 *have been re-set.*

—— [Another copy, with minor variations.] **992.** l. **3. (2.)**

—— [Another copy.] Ashley **2690. (4.)**

—— [Another copy, without the Errata list.] Ashley **2690. (5.)**

—— [Another edition.] Edited with introduction and notes by H. F. Tozer . . . Third edition. *Clarendon Press: Oxford,* 1907 [1913]. 8°. **11644.** dd. **3.**
A reissue of parts of the complete edition published in 1907, *with the titlepage and table of contents of that edition.*

BYRON (George Gordon Noel) *Baron Byron.* [Single Works.—Childe Harold's Pilgrimage.—*Canto IV.*]

—— Venice. From Lord Byron's Childe Harold. [Canto IV. Stanzas 1–29.] With thirty original drawings made in Venice by Linley Sambourne. *Bradbury, Agnew & Co.: London,* 1878. fol. **1872.** c. **5.**

—— Childe Harold . . . Canto IV. Stanzas 1–48, and 140–186. With biographical sketch and explanatory notes. pp. 48. *London & Glasgow,* [1882.] 8°. [*Collins' English Classics.*] **12204.** b. **23/1**a.

—— Byron's Childe Harold. Canto IV. Stanzas I.–XLVIII.; CXL.–CLXXXVI. With illustrative notes. Edited by Thomas Morrison. pp. 64. *Gall & Inglis: London & Edinburgh,* [1882.] 8°. [*British School Series.*] **12201.** cc. **35/1.**

English and Armenian.

—— Childe Harold's Pilgrimage. Italy. [The text of Canto IV with an Armenian verse translation by L. M. Alishan.] pp. 147. *Venice,* 1872. 16°. **17046.** a. **15.**

Italian.

—— L'Italia, Canto IV. del Pellegrinaggio di Childe Harold . . . tradotto da Michele Leoni. pp. 77. MS. NOTES. *Italia,* 1819. 8°. **1164.** g. **16.**

—— L'Italia. Canto di Lord Byron accomodato all'indole del verso italiano da M. Missirini. Pubblicato per cura del Prof. F. Longhena. pp. 95. *Milano,* 1848. 8°. **11647.** f. **27.**

—— Italia. Canto . . . tradotto da A. Maffei. pp. 190. *Firenze,* 1872. 8°. **11643.** e. **1.**

—— Roma descritta da Giorgio Lord Byron nel Pellegrinaggio del Giovine Aroldo. [Extracted from Canto IV.] Versione dall'Inglese di P. Isola. pp. 22. *Novi-Ligure,* 1870. 8°. **11436.** f. **61.**

Cantos III, IV.

—— Childe Harold's Pilgrimage . . . Cantos III. and IV. Edited with notes and an introduction by J. H. Fowler. pp. xiv. 136. *Macmillan & Co.: London,* 1906. 8°. [*English Literature for Secondary Schools.*] **012273.** de. **2.**

—— [Another edition.] Edited with introduction and notes by H. F. Tozer . . . Third edition. *Clarendon Press: Oxford,* 1907 [1910]. 8°. **2292.a.19.**
A reissue of parts of the complete edition published in 1907, *with the titlepage and table of contents of that edition, and an additional titlepage without imprint for Cantos III, IV.*

—— Byron. Childe Harold's Pilgrimage. Cantos III., IV. Edited by B. J. Hayes. [With an introduction and notes.] pp. xxxii. 140. *W. B. Clive: London,* [1932.] 8°. **11640.** df. **26.**

—— Selection from Byron's Childe Harold's Pilgrimage Cantos III and IV. With introduction and notes by E. D. A. Morshead. pp. xvi. 79. *Percival & Co.: London,* 1893. 8°. [*English Classics for Schools.*] **12201.** df. **1/6**

—— [A reissue.] Byron's Childe Harold's Pilgrimage Cantos III. and IV. The text reduced, *etc.* *Rivington Percival & Co.: London,* 1894. 8°. [*English Classics for Schools.*] **12201.** df. **1/7**

—— Childe Harold. Canto III . . . XXI–XXVIII (Canto IV. CXXVIII–CXLV, CLXXVIII–CLXXXIV.) *See* Ellis (Adele) Chosen English . . . With short biographies and notes *etc.* 1896. 8°. **12270.** de. **1**

—— Byron's Childe Harold's Pilgrimage. Cantos III and IV, *etc. Rivingtons: London,* [1900.] 8°. [*English Classics for Schools.*] **12201. df. 1/50.**
A reissue of the edition of 1894.

Cantos I–IV.

—— Childe Harold's Pilgrimage. A romaunt, in four cantos. 2 vol. *John Murray: London,* 1819. 8°. **11645. aaa. 31.**

—— [Another edition.] pp. 182. *W. Dugdale: London,* 1825. 12°. **11642. a. 61. (1.)**

—— [Another edition.] pp. 162. *W. Dugdale: London,* 1826. 12°. **11645. df. 10.**

—— Childe Harold's Pilgrimage. [With a portrait.] 2 vol. *A. & W. Galignani: Paris,* 1827. 16°. **11659. a. 50.**

—— [Another edition.] MS. NOTES. pp. vi. 161. *Thomas Colmer: London,* 1827. 16°. **11642. a. 51.**

—— Childe Harold's Pilgrimage. 2 vol. *Du Jardin-Sailly Bros.: Brussels,* 1829. 32°. **11659. de. 22.**

—— [Another edition.] pp. 333. *F. Campe & Co.: Nuremberg & New York,* [1831.] 12°. **11643. a. 37.**

—— [Another edition.] pp. 270. *John Duncombe: London,* [1831?] 12°. **11646. bbb. 68.**

—— [Another edition.] pp. 329. *John Murray: London,* 1837. 8°. **11609. ee. 1.**

—— [Another edition.] pp. vi. 171. *C. Daly: London,* 1839. 16°. **11630. a. 42.**

—— Childe Harold's Pilgrimage. A romaunt. [With illustrations, including a portrait.] pp. xvi. 227. *John Murray: London,* 1841. 8°. **11656. f. 57.**

—— [Another edition.] [With illustrations.] pp. xvi. 320. *John Murray: London,* 1841. 8°. **840. i. 11.**
With an additional titlepage, engraved and mounted.

—— [A reissue.] Childe Harold's Pilgrimage, *etc. London,* 1845. 8°. **11658. ff. 29.**

—— Childe Harold's Pilgrimage. A romaunt. [With a portrait.] pp. 331. *John Murray: London,* 1851. 12°. **11661. a. 5.**
With an additional titlepage, engraved, bearing the date 1842.

—— [Another edition.] pp. xii. 311. *John Murray: London,* 1853. 16°. **1466. a. 6.**

—— [Another edition.] Erklärt von Ferd. Brockerhoff. 2 Bdchn. *Berlin,* 1854, 55. 8°. [*Sammlung englischer Schriftsteller.* Bdchn. 7, 9.] **11603.d.21.**

—— [Another edition.] Illustrated from original sketches. pp. 329. *John Murray: London,* 1859. 8°. **C. 109. b. 2.**

—— A new edition. pp. 60. *John Murray: London,* 1860. 8°. **11641. a. 12.**

—— New edition. pp. 192. *John Murray: London,* 1860. 8°. **11641. a. 13.**

—— [Another edition.] With a memoir by William Spalding . . . Illustrated. pp. 180. *C. Griffin & Co.: London,* [1866.] 8°. **11641. aaa. 18.**

—— Illustrated edition. pp. 329. *John Murray: London,* 1869 [1868]. 4°. **11642. e. 26.**
A reissue of the edition of 1859.

—— Childe Harolde's Pilgrimage . . . New edition. pp. xii. 311. *John Murray: London,* 1870. 8°. **11657. e. 11.**

—— [Another edition.] With notes. pp. 180. *W. & R. Chambers: London & Edinburgh,* 1877. 12°. **11645. de. 12**

—— [Another edition.] With explanatory notes. Edited by W. Hiley. pp. xxii. 168. *Longmans & Co.: London* 1877. 8°. **11646. aaa. 3**

—— Édition classique par J. Darmesteter. pp. xxxv. 342. *Paris,* 1882. 18°. **11644. ccc. 40**

—— [Another edition.] Edited, with introduction and notes, by H. F. Tozer. pp. 336. *Oxford,* 1885. 8°. [*Clarendon Press Series.*] **12205. t. 19**

—— [Another edition.] Erklärt von August Mommsen. pp. xxxvi. 367. *Berlin,* 1885. 8°. **11653. f. 47**

—— [Another edition.] Illustrated. pp. 236. *Ticknor & Co.: Boston,* 1886. 8°. **11645. ff. 41**

—— [Another edition.] pp. 192. *London,* 1886. 8°. [*Cassell's National Library.* vol. 6.] **12208.bb.15/6**

—— [Another edition.] pp. 320. *G. Routledge & Sons: London,* 1888. 16°. **12208. aaaa.**

—— [Another edition.] pp. 249. *G. Routledge & Sons: London,* 1892. 8°. [*Sir John Lubbock's Hundred Books.* no. 29.] **012207.1.1/29**

—— [Another edition.] With introduction and notes by H. G. Keene. pp. xx. 255. *London,* 1893. 8°. [*Bell's English Classics.*] **012272. aaaa. 1/34**

—— [Another edition.] Avec une notice, des arguments et des notes en français par E. Chasles. pp. xxvi. 264. *Paris,* 1893. 8°. **11646. de. 21**

—— [A reissue.] *Paris,* 1894. 12°. **11647. a. 86**

—— [Another edition.] Edited by the Rev. E. C. Everard Owen. pp. lxii. 236. *London, New York,* [1897.] 8°. [*Arnold's British Classics for Schools.*] **012200. gg. 2/1**

—— [Another edition.] [Edited by Israel Gollancz.] pp. xii. 310. *J. M. Dent & Co.: London,* 1898. 8°. [*Temple Classics.*] **012200.de.8/13.**

—— [Another edition.] Edited with notes and an introduction by E. E. Morris. 2 vol. *Macmillan & Co.: London,* 1899. 8°. **11646. eee. 38**

—— [Another edition.] pp. 192. *London,* 1904. 8°. [*Cassell's National Library.* New series. no. 40.] **012209.ff.1/40.**

—— [Another edition.] With biographical introduction by Hannaford Bennett. pp. 159. *London,* 1905. 8°. [*John Long's Carlton Classics.*] **12204. p. 11/1**

—— [Another edition.] Edited with introduction and notes by Andrew J. George. pp. xxxiv. 282. *New York,* 1907. 8°. [*Macmillan's Pocket American and English Classics.*] **12199.a.1/9.**

—— [Another edition.] 4 pt. *Clarendon Press: Oxford,* [1909.] 8°. [*Oxford Plain Texts.*] **12271. w. 8/**

—— Childe Harold's Pilgrimage. pp. 192. *London,* 1909. 8°. [*Cassell's Little Classics.* no. 4.] **012202. eeee. 2/**
A reissue of the edition of 1904.

—— [Another edition.] Edited by A. Hamilton Thompson. pp. xxii. 286. *University Press: Cambridge,* 1913. 8°. [*Pitt Press Series.*] **2322. bb. 1**

BYRON (George Gordon Noel) *Baron Byron.* (Single Works.—Childe Harold's Pilgrimage.—*Cantos I–IV.*]

—— [Another edition.] Edited with introduction and notes by David Frew. pp. xii. 216. *Blackie & Son: London,* 1918. 8°. **11643**. aa. **62**.

—— [Another edition.] With illustrations by Sir Francis Cyril Rose. pp. 236. *Harrison: Paris,* 1931. 4°. **11641**. h. **18**.

—— Childe Harold. Edited with introduction and notes by H. F. Tozer . . . Third edition. pp. 336. *Clarendon Press: Oxford,* 1937. 8°. **11657**. aa. **51**.
A reissue of the edition published by the Clarendon Press in 1907.

—— Childe Harold's Pilgrimage. Edited by A. Hamilton Thompson. pp. xxii. 286. *University Press: Cambridge,* 1937. 8°. [*Pitt Press Series.*] **2322**. de. **184**.
A reissue of the edition of 1913.

English and Italian.

—— Aroldo—Childe Harold. Versione col testo a fronte, introduzione e note a cura di Aldo Ricci. 3 vol. *Firenze,* [1924–28.] 8°. **11630**. aa. **21**.

English and Japanese.

—— Lord Byron's Childe Harold's Pilgrimage. Canto the First. Stanzas 15–22. [1905?]. 4°. Crach. Tab. **3**. e. (**6**.)
An extract from a periodical, pp. 110–112.

Bulgarian.

—— Чайлдъ Харолдъ. Отъ английски: Н. Вранчевъ. Второ издание. pp. 205. *София,* 1925. 12°. **11630**. aa. **25**.

Czech.

—— Childe-Haroldova Pout. Přeložila Eliška Krásnohorská. pp. 245. *v Praze,* 1890. 8°. **11646**. df. **12**.

Danish.

—— Junker Harolds Pilgrimsfart . . . Oversat af Adolf Hansen. pp. 237. *Kjøbenhavn,* 1880. 8°. **11609**. ccc. **5**.

French.

—— Le Pélerinage de Childe Harold. Traduction en vers français par E. Quiertant. pp. viii. 266. *Paris,* 1861. 8°. **11642**. e. **3**.

—— Childe Harold . . . Traduit en vers français par L. Davésiès de Pontès. 2 tom. *Paris,* 1862. 12°. **11649**. aaa. **1**.

—— Le Pèlerinage de Childe Harold. Version en vers avec notes explicatives par Gabriel Leprévost. pp. vi. 275. *Paris,* 1910. 8°. **11645**. cc. **59**.

German.

—— Ritter Harold's Pilgerfahrt . . . Im Versmass des Originals übersetzt von Zedlitz. pp. xvi. 381. *Stuttgart & Tübingen,* 1836. 8°. **11646**. ff. **23**.

—— Byron's Ritter Harold. Von A. Böttger. Diamant-ausgabe. pp. 194. *Leipzig,* 1846. 16°. **11646**. aaa. **62**.

—— Childe Harold's Pilgerfahrt . . . Aus dem Englischen im Versmass des Originals übersetzt von A. Büchner. pp. xxiii. 342. *Frankfurt,* [1853.] 16°. **11642**. a. **11**.

—— Harold's Pilgerfahrt . . . Uebersetzt von E. von Monbart. pp. 143. *Köln,* 1865. 8°. **11642**. f. **29**.

—— Childe Harolds Pilgerfahrt . . . Deutsch von A. H. Janert. pp. 191. *Hildburghausen,* 1868. 8°. [*Bibliothek ausländischer Klassiker.* Bd. 87.] **12209.e.1/16.**

—— Jung Harold's Pilgerfahrt . . . Metrisch übersetzt von Ferdinand Schmidt. pp. 132. *Berlin,* 1869. 16°. **11645**. aa. **61**.

Hungarian.

—— Childe Harold. Byron után anya nyelvéből magyarra forditotta Bickersteth Johanka. pp. 211. *Genfben,* 1857. 8°. **11642**. d. **30**.

—— [Another copy.] **11642**. dd. **6**.

Italian.

—— Il Pellegrinaggio d'Aroldo. Poema . . . tradotto da C. Faccioli. pp. xii. 249. *Firenze,* 1873. 8°. **11643**. b. **1**.

Polish.

—— Pielgrzymka Czajlda Harolda. Poema . . . zpolszczone przez W. z Baworowa, wydane przez J. D. cz. 1. Pieśń I.–II. pp. viii. 79. x. MS. CORRECTIONS. *we Lwowie,* 1857. 12°. **11643**. bbb. **15**. (**14**.)
No more published.

—— Poezye Lorda Byrona w tłumaczeniu polskiém. Wydane staraniem B. M. Wolffa. tom I. Wędrówki Czajld-Harolda. 1857. 12°. *See* supra: Works.—*Polish.* **11611**. aa. **17**.

Russian.

—— Чайльдъ-Гарольдъ. Переводъ В. Фишера. Под редакцией А. Е. Грузинскаго. Съ иллюстраціями [including a portrait]. pp. 79. *Москва,* 1912. 8°. **11656**. c. **51**.

Swedish.

—— Childe Harolds pilgrimsfärd . . . öfversatt af A. F. Skjöldebrand. pp. 192. *Stockholm,* 1832. 8°. **1464**. f. **9**.

Selections.

—— Byron's Childe Harold's Pilgrimage—slightly abridged. With introduction, notes and questions by G. A. Sheldon. pp. xii. 138. *London,* 1933. 8°. [*Rivington's English Classics for Schools.*] **012208.a.7/6.**

—— Thirty Illustrations of Childe Harold. [With selections from the text.] The original drawings produced expressly for the Art-Union of London. ff. 1–12, 14–29, 29*, 30. pl. I–XII, XIV–XXVII, XXIX, XXIX*, XXX. 1855. 4°. *See* London.—III. *Art Union.* **7868.d.15.**

Appendix.

—— *See* Gordon (Rosa) Childe Archie's Pilgrimage. [A parody.] 1873. 8°. **11648**. e. **56**.

—— *See* Dalgado (D. G.) Lord Byron's Childe Harold's Pilgrimage to Portugal critically examined. 1919. 8°. Ac. **190**/**21**.

—— *See* Harold. Lines to Harold [i.e. to Lord Byron, author of "Childe Harold's Pilgrimage"]. 1841. 12°. **11602**. e. **4**. (**6**.)

—— *See* Harold, *Childe.* Childe Harold's monitor, or, Lines occasioned by the last canto of Childe Harold, *etc.* 1818. 8°. **992**. i. **22**. (**2**.)

—— *See* Harold, *Childe.* Childe Harold's Pilgrimage to the Dead Sea, *etc.* [An imitation.] 1818. 8°. **992**. i. **21**. (**4**.)

—— *See* Hobhouse (John C.) *Baron Broughton.* Historical Illustrations of the Fourth Canto of Childe Harold, *etc.* 1818. 8°. **1164**. g. **17**.

—— *See* HOBHOUSE (John C.) *Baron Broughton.* Historical Illustrations of the Fourth Canto of Childe Harold, *etc.* 1818. 8°. Ashley **2717.**

—— *See* KOELBING (E.) Zur Textüberlieferung von Byron's Childe Harold. Cantos I, II, *etc.* 1896. 8°. **011851.** h. **14.** (**7.**)

—— *See* LAMARTINE DE PRAT (M. L. A. de) Nouvelles Meditations poétiques . . . Le Dernier chant du Pélerinage d'Harold, *etc.* 1871. 8°. **11482.** cc. **26.**

—— *See* LAMARTINE DE PRAT (M. L. A. de) [Le Dernier chant du Pèlerinage d'Harold.] The Last Canto of Childe Harold's Pilgrimage. [Translated from the French.] 1827. 8°. **1161.** g. **18.**

—— *See* LAMARTINE DE PRAT (M. L. A. de) The Last Canto of Harold's Pilgrimage . . . Rendered into English verse by the author of " The Poetry of Earth," *etc.* 1848. 12°. **1161.** f. **36.**

—— *See* LEWIS (Robert T.) A Commentary & Questionnaire on Childe Harold, Canto III (Canto IV), *etc.* 1927. 8°. **11859.** a. **1/42, 43.**

—— *See* MAIER (H.) *Dr. Phil.* Entstehungsgeschichte von Byrons " Childe Harold's Pilgrimage," Gesang I. und II. 1911. 8°. **11851.** s. **25.**

—— *See* MOLL (O. E. E.) Der Stil von Byron's Child Harold's Pilgrimage. 1911. 8°. **11860.e.22/10.**

—— *See* PAKOWSKA (R.) Polskie przekłady poematów Byrona " Childe Harold " i " Manfred." [With a portrait.] 1938. 8°. **11862.** d. **8.**

—— *See* SARBOT, *Old, pseud.* Brum: a Parody. [A satire on local celebrities at Birmingham, in the form of a parody of Byron's " Childe Harold's Pilgrimage."] [1866.] 8°. **11602.** ee. **9.** (**1.**)

—— The Childe Harold and the Excursion, *etc.* [Signed: J. B.] [1842.] 8°. *See* B., J. **11826.** d. **38.** (**4.**)

—— Thirty Illustrations of Childe Harold, *etc.* 1855. 4°. *See* supra: *Selections.* **7868.d.15.**

THE CORSAIR.

—— The Corsair, a tale. pp. xi. 100. *John Murray: London,* 1814. 8°. **11642.** cc. **28.** (**3.**)
Without sig. I, *containing six additional poems, which formed part of the original issue of this work.*

—— [Another copy.] C. **57.** l. **11.**

—— [Another copy.] Ashley **2628.**

—— [Another copy, with six additional poems.] pp. xi. 108. Ashley **2629.**
A made-up copy, the additional poems having been inserted later.

—— [Another copy.] pp. xi. 100. Ashley **2627.**
Without the additional poems. In this copy the words " The End " and the printer's imprint have been added on p. 100.

—— [Another issue.] The Corsair, *etc.* [With plates.] *London,* 1814. 8°. **11659.** b. **33.** (**3.**)

—— Second edition. pp. xi. 108. *John Murray: London,* 1814. 8°. **11646.** ff. **22.**
With the additional poems. A made-up copy, sig. I *containing the additional poems having been inserted from a later edition.*

—— Third edition. pp. xi. 100. *John Murray: London,* 1814. 8°. **11643.** h. **13.**
Without the additional poems.

—— Fourth edition. pp. xi. 108. *John Murray: Londo* 1814. 8°. **11645.** g. **3**
With the additional poems.

—— Fifth edition. pp. xi. 108. *John Murray: Londo* 1814. 8°. **11646.** dd.

—— [Another edition.] From the fifth London editio pp. 108. *Eastburn, Kirk & Co.: New York,* 1814. 12° **1465.** a. **3**

—— Sixth edition. pp. xi. 108. *John Murray: Londo* 1814. 8°. **11642.** e. **34.** (

—— [Another copy.] The Corsair . . . Sixth edition. *London,* 1814. 8°. **11661.** c. **7.** (

—— [Another copy.] **11643.** l. **14.** (

—— Seventh edition. pp. xi. 108. *John Murray: Londo* 1814. 8°. **1466.** g. **5**

—— [Another copy.] **11643.** k. **31.** (

—— Ninth edition. pp. xi. 112. *John Murray: Londo* 1815. 8°. **11649.** f. **18.** (

—— Tenth edition. pp. 114. *John Murray: Londo* 1818. 8°. **11646.** dd.

—— [Another edition.] pp. 72. *W. Dugdale: Londo* 1825. 12°. C. **58.** bb. **4.** (

—— The Corsair, *etc.* pp. 55. *B. Cormon & Blanc: Pa & Lyons,* 1835. 24°. **012987.** a. **2.** (
Part of " The Select Poetical Works of Lord Byron."

—— The Corsair: a tale. pp. 80. *John Murray: Londo* 1842. 12°. **11652.** a. **98.** (

—— [Another edition.] [*Clarke: London,* 1844.] 8°. **1155.** c. **1.** (

—— [Another edition.] pp. 122. *A. K. Murray & C London,* 1867. 16°. **11642.** a. **5**

Hungarian.

—— A Kalóz . . . Angolból forditotta Kacziány Gé pp. 74. *Budapest,* 1892. 16°. [*Olcsó könyvtár.* sz. 311 **12215.a.1/311**

Italian.

—— Il Corsaro, novella di Lord Byron; versione in pro di L. C. pp. v. 131. *Torino,* 1819. 8°. **1465.** h. **2.** (
The titlepage is engraved.

—— Seconda edizione riveduta dall'autore. pp. 123. *Milano,* 1820. 8°. **11431.** ccc. **27.** (

—— Il Corsaro . . . Versione del cavaliere L. Seren Honorati. pp. 95. *Bologna,* 1870. 12°. **11643.** bbb. **10.** (1

—— Il Corsaro . . . Versione di C. Rosnati. pp. 96. *Pav* 1879. 8°. **11645.** ff. **2**

Polish.

—— Korsarz. Powieść. 1841. *See* ODYNIEC (A. Tłomaczenia. tom 3. 1838, *etc.* 8°. **11585.** c. **3**

—— Korsarz. Powieść. pp. 66. *Warszawa,* [1918?] 8°. **11660.** aa. **1**
Bibljoteczka uniwers. ludowych i młodzieży szkoln no. 203.

BYRON (GEORGE GORDON NOEL) *Baron Byron.* [SINGLE WORKS.—THE CORSAIR.]

Spanish.

—— El Corsario. pp. 272. *Valencia,* 1832. 32°. **11647. a. 85.**

Swedish.

—— Corsaren. (Öfversättning af Talis Qualis [pseudonym of C. W. A. Strandberg].) pp. 96. *Stockholm,* 1868. 8°. **011557. h. 15.**

Appendix.

—— *See* BOULAY-PATY (E. F. C.) and LUCAS (H. J. J.) Le Corsaire. Poème dramatique . . . d'après Byron, *etc.* 1901. 8°. **11740. h. 25.**

—— *See* GALZERANI (G.) Il Corsaro, azione mimica, *etc.* [Founded on Byron's poem.] 1826. 8°. [*MERELLI (B.) Il Precipizio, etc.*] **906. f. 15. (3.)**

—— *See* ROSSETTI (G. P. G.) Il Corsaro, scene melodrammatiche, con cori, tratte dal Corsaro di Lord Byron, *etc.* [1830.] 12°. **11725. bb. 10. (2.)**

—— *See* ROSSETTI (G. P. G.) Medora e Corrado, cantata melodrammatica . . . tratta dal Corsaro di Lord Byron. [1832.] 8°. **T. 1317. (1.)**

—— *See* VERNOY DE SAINT-GEORGES (J. H.) and MAZILIER (N.) Le Corsaire, ballet-pantomime, *etc.* [Founded on Byron's poem.] 1856. 8°. **11740. e. 11. (5.)**

—— *See* WOCQUIER (C.) Le Corsaire, poême en quatre chants, d'après Byron, *etc.* 1861. 8°. **11643. bbb. 15. (15.)**

—— Hone's Lord Byron's Corsair. Conrad, the Corsair: or, the Pirates' Isle. A tale. By Lord Byron. Adapted as a romance. pp. 16. *W. Hone: London,* 1817. 8°. **G. 18981. (7.)**

THE CURSE OF MINERVA.

—— The Curse of Minerva. [By Lord Byron.] [With the autograph of Samuel Rogers and two amendments in his hand.] pp. 25. 1812. 4°. *See* MINERVA. Ashley **4725.**

—— [Another edition.] pp. 24. *De-Silver & Co.: Philadelphia,* 1815. 8°. **11647. f. 31.**

—— Third edition. pp. 21. *Galignani: Paris,* 1818. 12°. **8050. d. 60. (2.)**

—— [Another copy.] **11609. de. 29. (2.)**

—— Fourth edition. pp. 21. *Galignani: Paris,* 1820. 12°. **11642. aa. 61. (2.)**

—— [Another copy.] Ashley **5295***

—— Sunset from the Parthenon . . . Fac-simile of the first page [of the MS. of "The Curse of Minerva"], *etc.* [Edited by Earl Stanhope. *Window & Grove:* [*London,*] 1875. 4°. **11661. c. 17.**

THE DEFORMED TRANSFORMED.

—— The Deformed Transformed; a drama. pp. 88. *J. & H. L. Hunt: London,* 1824. 8°. **11658.g.163.(3.)**
In this copy sig. F *is misprinted* G.

—— [Another copy.] **T.1065.(7.)**

—— [Another copy.] Ashley **2707.**
In this copy sig. F *is similarly misprinted.*

—— Second edition. pp. 88. *J. & H. L. Hunt: London,* 1824. 8°. **11643. bbb. 17. (7.)**

—— [Another edition.] pp. 52. [1825?] 12°. **11642. b. 57. (3.)**
Part of a larger collection?

—— [Another edition.] *London,* [1875?] 8°. [*Dicks' Standard Plays.* no. 113.] **11770. bbb. 4.**

BYRON (GEORGE GORDON NOEL) *Baron Byron.* [SINGLE WORKS.—THE DEFORMED TRANSFORMED.]

Hungarian.

—— Lord Byron' Elváltoztatott idomtalanjából töredék. Lukács Móricztól. [Act 1 only. In verse.] [1840.] *See* EÖTVÖS (J.) *Baron.* Budapesti Árvizkönyv, *etc.* köt 4. 1839, *etc.* 8°. **1206. i. 3.**

Appendix.

—— *See* VARNHAGEN (H.) Über Byron's dramatisches Bruchstück "Der umgestaltete Missgestaltete," *etc.* 1905. 4°. **11850. v. 4.**

DON JUAN.

Cantos I, II.

—— Don Juan. [Cantos I and II. By Lord Byron.] pp. 227. 1819. 4°. *See* JUAN, *Don.* **C. 57. g. 32.**

—— [Another copy.] Ashley **4732.**

—— A new edition. pp. 227. 1819. 8°. *See* JUAN, *Don.* **11642. d. 3.**

—— [Another copy.] Don Juan . . . A new edition, 1819. 8°. *See* JUAN, *Don.* **Cup.401.g.13.**

—— [Another edition.] An exact copy from the quarto edition. pp. 117. 1819. 8°. *See* JUAN, *Don.* **11645. ff. 6.**

—— [Another edition.] pp. 192. 1819. 8°. *See* JUAN, *Don.* **11633. b. 61.**

—— A new edition. pp. 227. 1820. 8°. *See* JUAN, *Don.* **11641. bbb. 25.**

—— [Another edition.] pp. 227. 1820. 8°. *See* JUAN, *Don.* **11645. bb. 48.**

—— [Another copy.] **11648. dd. 14.**

—— [Another copy.] **C. 58. bb. 6. (1.)**

—— [Another edition.] An exact copy from the quarto edition. pp. 117. 1820. 4°. *See* JUAN, *Don.* **11643. k. 22. (1.)**

—— Don Juan . . . Second edition. pp. 192. 1820. 12°. *See* JUAN, *Don.* **11659. df. 48.**

—— A new edition. pp. 227. 1822. 8°. *See* JUAN, *Don.* **11643. k. 6.**

Roumanian.

—— Don Juan . . . Poema epica. Tradusâ de I. Eliade. [Cantos I, II. In prose.] pp. 183. *Bucuresci,* 1847. 4°. **11644. g. 35.**

Russian.

—— Донъ Жуанъ, поэма Лорда Байрона. Переводъ Н. Жандра. (Я перевелъ одну Первую Пѣснь Донъ Жуана.) pp. 89. *Санктпетербургъ,* 1846. 8°. **11641. c. 9.**

—— Донъ-Жуанъ . . . Глава первая. Переводъ Н. А. Маркевича. pp. 164. *Лейпцигъ,* 1862. 16°. **11643. a. 58.**

Cantos III, IV, V.

—— Don Juan, Cantos III, IV and V. [By Lord Byron.] pp. 218. **L.P.** 1821. 8°. *See* JUAN, *Don.* **C. 57. l. 10.**

—— [Another copy.] *L.P.* Ashley **4733.**

—— [Another edition.] pp. 218. 1821. 8°. *See* JUAN, *Don.* **C.58.bb.6.(2.)**

—— [Another edition.] pp. 218. 1821. 8°. *See* Juan, *Don.* **11645.** bb. **49.**

—— [Another edition.] pp. 14. 1821. 8°. *See* Juan, *Don.* **11643.** k. 22. (2.)

—— Don Juan. Cantos iii. iv and v. pp. 215. 1822. 12°. *See* Juan, *Don.* **11659.** df. **47.**

—— Fifth edition, revised and corrected. pp. 222. 1822. 8°. *See* Juan, *Don.* **11643.** k. 27.

Cantos I–V.

—— Don Juan. [Cantos i–v.] With a preface by a Clergyman. pp. x. 226. *Hodgson & Co.: London,* 1822. 12°. **11642.** a. **7.**

—— A new edition, with notes. And three engravings after Corbould. pp. 180. [1823.] 12°. **11642.** aa. **21.** *See Juan, Don.*

—— [Another edition.] A correct copy from the original edition. [With coloured illustrations by I. R. Cruikshank.] pp. 215. [1826?] 8°. *See* Juan, *Don.* **11643.** g. **17.**

Italian.

—— Aidea. Episodio del Don Giovanni. Saggio d'una traduzione completa di V. Betteloni. [Extracted from Cantos ii–iv.] pp. x. 149. *Verona,* 1875. 8°. **11645.** f. **1.**

Cantos VI, VII, VIII.

—— Don Juan, Cantos vi, vii, viii. pp. 186. 1823. 12°. *See* Juan, *Don.* **11659.** df. **46.**

—— Don Juan. Cantos vi.—vii.—and viii. [By Lord Byron.] pp. vii. 184. **L.P.** 1823. 8°. *See* Juan, *Don.* Ashley **4734.**

—— [Another edition.] pp. vii. 184. 1823. 12°. *See* Juan, *Don.* C. **58.** bb. **7.** (1.)

—— [Another edition.] pp. vii. 184. 1825. 8°. *See* Juan, *Don.* **11645.** g. **13.**

—— [Another edition.] [1825?] 8°. **11643.** k. **22.** *Pp.* 165–291 *of a collection of Byron's poems.*

—— Eulogy on Colonel Boon. [From "Don Juan," Canto viii, stanzas 61–67.] *See* Boone (Daniel) Life and Adventures, *etc.* 1916. 4°. [*Heartman's Historical Series.* no. 17.] **9617.k.1/17.**

Spanish.

—— El Sitio de Ismaïl, novela heróica. [Don Juan. Cantos vii, viii.] pp. 184. *Paris,* 1830. 12°. **1465.** a. **31.**

Cantos IX, X, XI.

—— Don Juan, Cantos ix, x, xi. pp. 145. 1823. 12°. *See* Juan, *Don.* **11659.** df. **45.**

—— Don Juan. Cantos ix.—x.— and xi. [By Lord Byron.] pp. 151. **L.P.** 1823. 8°. *See* Juan, *Don.* Ashley **4735.**

—— [Another copy.] Don Juan. Cantos ix.—x.—and xi. 1823. 12°. *See* Juan, *Don.* C. **58.** bb. **7.** (2.)

—— [Another edition.] pp. 151. 1823. 12°. *See* Juan, *Don.* **11658.e.49.**

Cantos VI–XI.

—— Don Juan. Cantos vi.—vii.—viii. (ix.—xi.) [By Lord Byron.] pp. 221. 1823. 12°. *See* Juan, *Don.* **11647.** aa. **80.** (1.)

Cantos XII, XIII, XIV.

—— Don Juan. Cantos xii.—xiii.—and xiv. [By Lo Byron.] pp. 168. **L.P.** 1823. 8°. *See* Juan, *Don.* Ashley 47

—— [Another edition.] pp. 170. 1823. 12°. *See* Jua *Don.* **992.** b. **3.** (

—— [Another copy.] Don Juan. Cantos xii.—xiii.—a xiv. pp. 170. 1823. 12°. *See* Juan, *Don.* **11654.** a.

—— [Another copy.] C. **58.** bb. **8.** (

—— [Another edition.] pp. 83. 1823. 18°. *See* Juan, *D* **11643.** a. **48.** (

—— [Another edition.] pp. 83. 1823. 12°. *See* Jua *Don.* **11647.** aa. **80.** (

—— [Another edition.] pp. 164. 1824. 12°. *See* Jua *Don.* **11643.** b.

—— [Another copy.] Don Juan, Cantos xii, xiii, xiv. 1824. 12°. *See* Juan, *Don.* **011652.** g. **1**

Cantos XV, XVI.

—— [Another copy.] Don Juan, Cantos xv, xvi. 1824. 12°. *See* Juan, *Don.* **11659.** df.

—— Don Juan. Cantos xv. and xvi. [By Lord Byro pp. 129. **L.P.** 1824. 8°. *See* Juan, *Don.* Ashley 47

—— [Another edition.] pp. 130. 1824. 12°. **992.** b. **3.** (

—— [Another copy.] C. **58.** bb. **8.** (

—— [Another edition.] pp. 62. 1824. 12°. *See* Juan, *D* **11647.** aa. **80.** (

—— [Another edition.] pp. 125. 1824. 8°. *See* Juan, *D* **11643.** b.

Cantos I–XVI.

—— Don Juan. A poem. [Cantos i—xvi.] 5 pt. *W. Benbow: London,* 1822 [1824]. 12°. **11646.** aaa.

A made-up edition of the complete poem. Cantos i– xii–xiv, xv, xvi, and probably Cantos vi–xiii, w printed by Sudbury. Cantos ix–xi were printed by Benb and form part of a larger collection.

—— [Another edition.] With a preface by a Clergyma 5 pt. *Hodgson & Co.: London,* 1823 [1824]. 12°. **11646.** cc.

This edition of the complete poem is made up of edition of Cantos i–v published by Hodgson & Co. 1822, *the editions of Cantos vi–viii, ix–xi and xii–x published by John Hunt in* 1823, *and that of Cantos xv, x published by John Hunt in* 1824.

—— Don Juan. A poem. 2 vol. *James Kay: Edinburg* 1825. 12°. **11659.** de.

—— [Another edition.] 2 vol. *Printed for the Bookselle London,* 1826. 8°. **11642.** c.

—— [Another edition.] pp. xii. 432. *William Clar London,* 1826. 16°. **11642.** a.

—— [Another edition.] pp. 430. *Printed for the Propriet London,* 1826. 32°. **11647.** dg.

—— [Another edition.] With a short biographical memoir of the author [signed: Z.]. pp. ix. 537. *T. & J. Allman: London*, 1827. 12°. **1467. a. 29.**

—— [Another edition.] 2 vol. *Printed for the Booksellers: London*, 1828. 8°. **11645. aa. 3.**

—— [Another edition.] 2 vol. 1828. 12°. *See* Juan, *Don*. G. **18571, 72.**

—— Don Juan, in sixteen cantos, with notes. pp. 359. *Printed for the booksellers: London*, 1831. 12°. **11659. a. 1.**

—— [Another edition.] pp. xvi. 432. *J. Thompson: London*, 1832. 32°. **991. b. 36.**

—— [Another edition.] pp. 359. *Scott & Webster: London*, 1833. 12°. **11644. bbb. 46.**

—— [Another edition.] pp. 359. MS. NOTES. *Printed for the Booksellers: London*, 1835. 12°. **11642. aa. 14.**

—— [Another edition.] 2 vol. *John Murray: London*, 1837. 8°. **11609. ee. 2.**

—— [Another edition.] pp. 438. *H. G. Bohn: London*, 1849. 12°. **11641. a. 10.**

—— [Another edition.] With illustrations. pp. xvi. 431. *Charles Daly: London*, [1850?] 16°. **11647. dg. 96.**

—— Lord Byron's Don Juan. With life and original notes, by A. Cunningham . . . and many illustrations on steel. pp. xii. 456. *C. Daly: London*, 1852. 12°. **11656. h. 38.**
With an additional titlepage, engraved.

—— [Another edition.] pp. 431. *Milner & Sowerby: Halifax*, 1857. 8°. **11644. e. 86.**

—— [Another edition.] pp. 431. *G. Routledge & Sons: London*, [1874.] 12°. **11643. a. 41.**

—— [Another edition.] pp. 359. *Chatto & Windus: London*, 1875. 16°. **12209. bbb. 6.**

—— [Another edition.] pp. 476. *G. Routledge & Sons: London*, 1886. 8°. **11647. ee. 19.**

—— [Another edition.] pp. 476. *G. Routledge & Sons: London*, 1886. 8°. **11646. ff. 29.**

—— A new, revised and enlarged edition with illustrations. Edited by Ernest Hartley Coleridge. pp. xvi. 612. *John Murray: London*, 1906. 8°. **11647. eee. 6.**

—— (The Campion edition.) pp. 426. *A. M. Philpot: London*, 1924. 8°. **C. 98. g. 9.**
One of twenty-five copies in Niger leather.

—— [Another edition.] With 93 illustrations & decorations by John Austen. pp. xi. 408. *John Lane: London; Dodd, Mead & Co.: New York*, 1926. 8°. **11632. dd. 3.**

—— [Another edition.] Edited with an introduction by Frank H. Ristine. pp. xvii. 493. *Macmillan Co.: New York*, 1927. 8°. [*Modern Readers' Series.*] **012201. bb. 1/11.**

—— Don Juan. With an introduction by Peter Quennell. pp. 526. *John Lehmann: London*, 1949. 8°. [*Chiltern Library.*] **W.P. 1548/22.**

Danish.

—— Don Juan . . . Metrisk bearbeidet efter den engelske Original af H. Schou. Hft. 1. pp. 16. *Fredericia*, 1854. 4°. **11642. e. 39.**
No more published.

—— Don Juan. Oversat paa Dansk af Holger Drachmann. Med Indlednings- og Slutningsdigte af Oversætteren. 2 Bd. *Kjøbenhavn*, 1880–1902. 8°. **11647. dd. 5.**
Published in parts.

French.

—— Don Juan de Lord Byron. Traduction nouvelle [by Paul Lehodey], précédée d'une préface de M. Legouvé, *etc.* pp. xi. 450. *Paris*, [1869.] 12°. **11646. bbb. 54.**

German.

—— Byron's Don Juan übersetzt von O. Gildemeister. 2 vol. *Bremen*, 1845. 8°. **1464. g. 3.**

—— Byron's Don Juan von A. Böttger. Diamantausgabe. pp. 413. *Leipzig*, 1849. 8°. **11646. aa. 36.**

—— Byron's Don Juan. Deutsch von W. Schäffer. 2 Tl. *Hildburghausen*, 1867. 8°. [*Bibliothek ausländischer Klassiker.* Bd. 47, 48.] **12209.e.1/18,19.**

Italian.

—— Il Don Juan . . . Recato in altrettante stanze italiane dal cavaliere E. Casali. pp. xx. 548. *Milano*, 1876. 8°. **11647. ee. 2.**

Polish.

—— Don Żuan Lorda Bajrona. Pieśń pierwsza, przełożona przez Wiktora z Baworowa. pp. 60. v. *Tarnopol*, 1863. 8°. **11643. bbb. 18. (4.)**
The first volume only of this translation, containing Canto I.

—— Don Juan. Przekład Edwarda Porębowicza. Wydanie nowe przerobione. pp. 631. **L.P.** *Warszawa*, 1922. 8°. **011604. f. 60.**

—— [Another edition.] 2 tom. *Warszawa*, 1922. 8°. [*Wielka Bibljoteka.* no. 14, 15.] **012208.d.2/14.15.**

Spanish.

—— Don Juan . . . Traduccion de F. Villalva. 2 tom. *Madrid*, 1876. 8°. **11645. bbb. 56.**

—— [Another edition.] 2 tom. *Madrid*, [1916.] 8°. **11644. i. 25.**

Swedish.

—— Don Juan . . . Första sången. Med upplysande och utwalde noter. Öfversatt ifrån engelska originalet. pp. 80. *Stockholm*, 1838. 8°. **1465. c. 31. (6.)**
No more published.

—— Don Juan. (Öfversättning af Carl Wilh. Aug. Strandberg.) 2 dl. *Stockholm*, 1857–65. 8°. **11641. f. 13.**
Published in parts.

Selections.

—— The Beauties of Don Juan: containing those passages only which are calculated to extend the real fame of Lord Byron. 2 vol. *James Cawthorn: London*, 1828. 8°. **11656. h. 36.**

Spurious Cantos and Imitations.

—— *See* Baxter (George R. W.) Don Juan Junior: a poem, by Byron's Ghost. Edited [or rather, written] by G. K. W. Baxter. 1839. 8°. **1164. g. 30.**

—— *See* Buckstone (John B.) Don Juan, *etc.* (A romantic drama founded on Lord Byron's poem.) [1887.] 8°. [*Dicks' Standard Plays.* no. 828.] **11770. bbb. 4.**

—— *See* Thomas (John Wesley) An Apology for "Don Juan," *etc.* [A satire on Byron's poem.] 1850. 8°. **11643.** aa. **29.**

—— *See* Thomas (John Wesley) Byron and the Times; or, an Apology for "Don Juan," *etc.* 1855. 8°. **11649.** cc. **46.**

—— *See* Wetton (Harry W.) The Termination of the Sixteenth Canto of Lord Byron's Don Juan. By H. W. Wetton. 1864. 8°. **11651.** bb. **32.**

—— An Apology for "Don Juan." Cantos i., ii. [A satire on Byron's poem. By John Wesley Thomas.] pp. 98. 1824. 8°. *See* Juan, *Don.* **992.** b. **4.**

—— Don Juan, canto the third. [By William Hone?] pp. 58. 1819. 8°. *See* Juan, *Don.* **1164.** f. **12.**

—— Don Juan. Canto the third. pp. 103. 1821. 8°. *See* Juan, *Don.* **1164.** h. **14.**

—— Don Juan. Canto the seventeenth. pp. 56. 1870. 8°. *See* Juan, *Don.* [*Anonymous editions of Byron's Don Juan.—Spurious Cantos and Imitations.*] **011650.** f. **87.** (**1.**)

—— [Another copy.] Ashley **5301.**

—— Don Juan. Cantos xvii and xviii. pp. 60. [1825.] 12°. *See* Juan, *Don.* **11643.** aa. **58.** (**3.**)

—— Don Juan: with a biographical account of Lord Byron and his family; anecdotes of his Lordship's travels and residence in Greece, at Geneva, &c. . . . With a portrait . . . Canto iii. pp. viii. 156. *William Wright: London,* 1819. 8°. **11657.** g. **59.**

—— Don Juan Reclaimed; or, his Peregrination continued, from Lord Byron. By W. C. [i.e. William Cowley.] 1840. 8°. *See* C., W. **1164.** f. **25.**

—— Juan Secundus. Canto the first. pp. 46. 1825. 8°. *See* Juan Secundus. T. **1061.** (**2.**)

—— The New Don Juan. The introduction. By Gerald Noel Byron. And the last canto of the original Don Juan, from the papers of the Countess Guiccioli. By George Lord Byron [or rather, by G. N. Byron]. pp. 61. *G. Head: London,* [1880.] 8°. **11643.** i. **17.**

—— A Sequel to Don Juan. [By G. W. M. Reynolds.] pp. 239. *Paget & Co.: London,* [1843.] 8°. **11643.** d. **1.**

—— Second edition. pp. 239. *Paget & Co.: London,* [1845?] 8°. **11649.** h. **51.**

—— The Seventeenth Canto of Don Juan, in continuation of the unfinish'd poem by Lord Byron. Intended as the first canto of the remaining eight which are wanting to complete that author's original design of extending the work to twenty-four. pp. iv. 144. *W. Wilson: London,* 1829. 8°. **992.** b. **3.** (**3.**)

—— Some Rejected Stanzas of "Don Juan," with Byron's own curious notes . . . The whole written in double rhymes, after Casti's manner . . . From an unpublished manuscript in the possession of Captain Medwin. A very limited number printed. pp. 5. *Printed at Charles Clark's Private Press: Great Totham, Essex,* 1845. 4°. **1466.** h. **2.**
Printed on one side of the leaf only.

—— Twenty Suppressed Stanzas of Don Juan in refere to Ireland, with Byron's own curious historical notes, *See* Pindar (Peter) *Esq., the Younger, pseud.* Geor Revel-ations, *etc.* 1838. 8°. **11643.** bbb. **14.**

Appendix.

—— *See* Alonzo (S.) Giorgio Byron. Attraverso " Giovanni." 1931. 8°. **11429.** g.

—— *See* Boyd (Elizabeth F.) Byron's Juan. A critical study. 1945. 8°. **11865.** d.

—— *See* Trueblood (Paul G.) The Flowering of Byr Genius. Studies in Byron's Don Juan. [1945.] 8°. **11864.** d.

—— The Centenary of Don Juan. (Reprinted from American Journal of Philology.) [Signed: S. C. C., Samuel C. Chew.] [1919.] 8°. *See* C., S. C. Ashley 5

—— 'Don John,' or Don Juan unmasked; being a key to mystery, attending that remarkable publication (by I Byron); with a descriptive review of the poem, extracts. Third edition enlarged, with a plate. pp *William Hone: London,* 1819. 8°. **8135.** ccc. **5.**

—— Gordon, a tale. A poetical review of Don Juan. pp. *T. & J. Allman: London,* 1821. 8°. **11642.** e.

—— Remarks, Critical and Moral, on the Talents of Byron, and the Tendencies of Don Juan. By the au of Hypocrisy, a satire, *etc.* [The dedication sig C. C. C., i.e. Charles Caleb Colton.] 1819. 8°. *Se* C. C. **1087.** c. **31.**

—— [Another edition.] Remarks on the Talents of Byron, and the tendencies of Don Juan. 1819. 8°. C., C. C. **527.** k. **12.**

Don Juan.—*Dedication to Don Juan.*

—— Dedication to Don Juan. pp. 16. *Effingham Wi London,* 1833. 8°. Ashley

The Dream.

—— *See* infra: The Prisoner of Chillon.

English Bards, and Scotch Reviewers.

First Version.

—— The British Bards, a satire. [By Lord Byron.] pp ms. additions and corrections. [1808.] 4°. British Bards. MS. Eg.

Enlarged Version.

First Edition and Reprints of the First Edition.

—— [Another edition, enlarged.] English Bards, and Sc Reviewers. A satire. [By Lord Byron.] pp. 54. [1809.] 12°. *See* English Bards. Ashley

—— [Another issue, with the addition of a preface.] pp. vi. 54. Ashley

—— [Another copy.] **11645.** bb
Interleaved with the variations of other editions, in ms

—— [Another edition, probably spurious.] pp. vi. 54. [1809?] 12°. *See* English Bards. C. **59.**

—— [Another copy.] C. **59.**
Imperfect; wanting the half-title.

BYRON (George Gordon Noel) *Baron Byron.* [Single Works.—English Bards, and Scotch Reviewers.]

—— [Another edition.] pp. vi. 54. [1812.] 12°. *See* English Bards. Ashley **319.**

—— [Another copy.] **11642.** bbb. **69.**
Imperfect; wanting the half-title.

Second Edition.

—— Second edition, with considerable additions and alterations. pp. vii. 85. *James Cawthorn: London,* 1809. 8°. **992.** g. **21.** (**2.**)

—— [Another copy.] Ashley **309.**

—— [Another copy.] Ashley **317.**
With a ms. *note purporting to be in Byron's handwriting, but in fact by the forger De Gibler, calling himself George Gordon Byron.*

Third Edition and Reprints of the Third Edition.

—— Third edition. pp. vii. 85. *James Cawthorn: London,* 1810. 8°. **11630.** bbb. **39.**
The watermarks are dated 1804, 1805 *and* 1807.

—— [Another copy.] G. **18974.**

—— [Another copy.] Ashley **310.**

—— Third edition. pp. vii. 85. *James Cawthorn: London,* 1810 [1812?]. 8°. **11643.** i. **26.**
The watermark is dated 1812.

—— [Another copy.] Ashley **312.**

—— Third edition. pp. vii. 73 [85]. *James Cawthorn: London,* 1810 [1817?]. 8°. **1465.** h. **17.**
The watermarks are dated 1815 *and* 1817.

—— [Another copy, with a different titlepage and heading to the preface.] **11645.** bbb. **36.**

—— [Another issue.] English Bards, and Scotch Reviewers; a satire . . . Third edition. *London,* 1810 [1817?]. 8°. **1481.** aaa. **54.**
The watermarks are dated 1815 *and* 1817.

—— [Another copy.] Ashley **2612.**
In this copy the watermarks are dated, 1815, 1816 *and* 1817.

—— Third edition. pp. vii. 73 [85]. *James Cawthorn: London,* 1810 [1817?]. 8°. Ashley **313.**
The watermark is dated 1817.

—— Third edition. pp. vii. 85. *James Cawthorn: London,* 1810 [1817?]. 8°. Ashley **2613.**
The watermark is dated 1817.

—— Third edition. pp. vii. 85. *James Cawthorn: London,* 1810 [1817?]. 8°. Ashley **2614.**
The watermark is dated 1817.

—— Third edition. pp. vii. 85. *James Cawthorn: London,* 1810 [1818?]. 8°. Ashley **314.**
The watermark is dated 1817.

—— Third edition. pp. vii. 85. *James Cawthorn: London,* 1810 [1818?]. 8°. Ashley **2615.**
The watermark is dated 1818.

—— Third edition. pp. vii. 81. *James Cawthorn: London,* 1810 [1818?]. 8°. **11645.** bbb. **35.**
The watermark is dated 1818.

—— [Another copy.] **11643.** c. **53.** (**2.**)

—— [Another copy.] Ashley **2616.**

BYRON (George Gordon Noel) *Baron Byron.* [Single Works.—English Bards, and Scotch Reviewers.]

—— English Bards and Scotch Reviewers . . . First American from the third London edition. pp. viii. 86. *E. Morford, Willington, & Co.: Charleston, S.C.,* 1811. 8°. **11613.** e. **15.**

Fourth Edition and Reprints of the Fourth Edition.

—— Fourth edition. pp. vii. 85. *James Cawthorn: London,* 1810. 12°. Ashley **2610.**
The watermark is "G & RT" and is undated.

—— [Another copy.] English Bards, and Scotch Reviewers, etc. *London,* 1810. 12°. **11656.** p. **57.**

—— Fourth edition. pp. vii. 85. *James Cawthorn; Sharpe & Hailes: London,* 1811. 8°. **11645.** bbb. **33.**
The watermark is "J Whatman 1805."

—— [Another copy.] Ashley **311.**

—— Fourth edition. pp. vii. 85. *James Cawthorn: London,* 1810 [1812?]. 8°. **11641.** f. **11.**

—— [Another copy.] English Bards, and Scotch Reviewers, etc. *London,* 1810 [1812?]. 8°. **11659.** bb. **3.**

—— [Another copy.] **11643.** k. **30.**

—— [Another copy.] Ashley **2617.**

—— Fourth edition. pp. vii. 85. *James Cawthorn; Sharpe & Hailes: London,* 1811 [1812?]. 8°. **1164.** f. **36.**
The watermark is dated 1812.

—— [Another copy.] **11645.** bbb. **34.**

—— [Another copy.] Ashley **315.**

—— Fourth edition. pp. vii. 85. *James Cawthorn; Sharpe & Hailes: London,* 1811 [1814?]. 8°. **1465.** h. **1.**
The watermark is dated 1814.

—— [Another copy.] **11643.** c. **52.**

—— English Bards, and Scotch Reviewers . . . Fourth edition. pp. 85. *James Cawthorn; Sharpe & Hailes: London,* 1811 [1815?]. 8°. **11658.** g. **44.**
Without a watermark.

—— Fourth edition. pp. vii. 85. L.P. *James Cawthorn; Sharp & Hailes: London,* 1811 [1815?]. 8°. **11645.** h. **15.**
Without a watermark.

—— [Another copy.] Ashley **2618.**

—— Fourth edition. pp. vii. 85. *James Cawthorn; Sharpe & Hailes: London,* 1811 [1816?]. 8°. Ashley **316.**
The watermark is dated 1816.

—— [Another copy.] Ashley **5453**

—— Fourth edition. [With a portrait.] pp. vii. 85. *James Cawthorn; Sharp & Hailes: London,* 1811 [1817?]. 8°. **11645.** bb. **61.** (**1.**)
Interleaved with revisions of the text from various editions. Containing also pp. 1–6, 29–32, 49–52, 59, 60, 79–82 *of the text of the first edition similarly interleaved, and an additional preface and postscript.*

—— Fourth edition. pp. 71. *James Cawthorn: London,* [1819?] 8°. Ashley **318.**
The watermark is dated 1819.

— [A facsimile of a copy of the octavo fourth edition of 1811, containing MS. notes by Byron. Edited by Sir John Murray.] pp. xix. vii. 85. 1936. 4°. *See* London.—III. *Roxburghe Club.* C. **101**. d. **27**.

Fifth and Subsequent Editions.

— Fourth [or rather, fifth] edition. pp. 83. MS. NOTE [by R. C. Dallas]. *James Cawthorn; Sharpe & Hailes: London,* 1811 [1812]. 8°. C. **59**. g. **19**.
The suppressed fifth edition, for which no titlepage was printed. A titlepage from the fourth edition has been supplied in this copy, which is without the preface and postscripts.

— Fifth edition, with additions. pp. v. 87. *J. Cawthorn: London,* 1816. 8°. Ashley **2611**.
A reissue of the suppressed fifth edition.

— [Another edition.] pp. 54. *A. T. Goodrich & Co.: New York,* 1817. 12°. **11646**. de. **19**.

— English Bards and Scotch Reviewers . . . Ode to the land of the Gaul. Sketch from Private Life. Windsor Poetics, &c. . . . Second edition. pp. 84. *Galignani: Paris,* 1818. 12°. **11650**. cc. **20**. (4.)
The half-title reads: "Suppressed Poems."

— [Another copy.] **1346**. a. **36**. (2.)

— Third edition. pp. 84. *Galignani: Paris,* 1819. 12°. **11642**. b. **49**.

— [Another copy.] **11642**. aa. **61**. (1.)

— English Bards and Scotch Reviewers, *etc.* pp. 64. *English Repository of Arts: Brussells,* 1819. 8°. **11641**. d. 14.

— [Another edition.] pp. 5. 68. *P. G. Ledouble: Geneva,* 1820. 12°. **11641**. a. 9.

— English Bards and Scotch Reviewers. A satire. Ode to the Land of the Gaul. Sketch from Private Life. Windsor Poetics, etc. . . . Fourth edition. pp. 82. *Galignani: Paris,* 1821. 12°. **11658**. ee. **97**.

— [Another edition.] pp. 53. *Hodgson & Co.: London,* 1823. 16°. **1075**. d. **10**. (1.)

— [Another edition.] pp. 61. *Benbow: London,* 1823. 12°. **11646**. aa. **71**. (2.)

— A new edition, with a life of the author. To which is added, Fare Thee Well, a poem. pp. 54. *James Starke: Glasgow,* 1824. 12°. **11643**. a. **48**. (4.)

— English Bards and Scotch Reviewers, *etc.* pp. 50. *W. Dugdale: London,* 1825. 12°. **11649**. cc. **21**. (5.)

— A new edition, with a life of the author. To which is added, Fare Thee Well: a poem. pp. xiv. 34 [40]. *M'Intosh & Co.: Glasgow,* 1825. 12°. **11646**. aa. **13**.

— English Bards and Scotch Reviewers. *See* British Satirist. The British Satirist, *etc.* 1826. 12°. **11601**. b. 3.

— A new edition. pp. vii. 80. *T. Kay: London,* 1827. 8°. **11643**. h. **12**.

— [Another edition.] *See* Gifford (William) *Editor of "The Quarterly Review."* Gifford's Baviad and Mæviad, *etc.* 1827. 12°. **11644**. bb. **56**.

— A new edition, with a life of the author: to which is added 'Fare Thee Well' and other poems. pp. 128. *W. Milner: Halifax,* 1834. 8°. **944**. c. **10**.

Appendix.

— *See* Koenig (Carl) *Dr. phil.* Byrons English Bards Scotch Reviewers. Entstehung und Beziehungen zur genössischen Satire und Kritik. [1914.] 8°. **11825**. d.

— *See* Mongrelites. The Mongrelites . . . A satiric po *etc.* (An imitation of Byron's "English Bards and Sc Reviewers.") 1866. 8°. **11687**. ccc. **37**.

— Critique, from the Edinburgh Review, on Lord Byr Poems [i.e. "Hours of Idleness"]. Which occasic "English Bards and Scotch Reviewers." 1820. 8°. infra: Hours of Idleness. [*Appendix.*] **11824**. ee. 3.

— Deutsche Dramatiker und Hamburger Kritiker. Satyre, Byron's English Bards and Scotch Revie frei und zeitgemäss nachgebildet vom Verfasser "Mohammed" [i.e. G. F. Daumer?]. pp. 15. *Be* 1857. 8°. **11526**.

Fare Thee Well.

— Fare Thee Well! [A poem. By Lord Byron.] pp [1816.] 4°. *See* Fare. C. **59**.

— [Another copy.] Ashley 2

Appendix.

— A Reply to Fare Thee Well!!! Lines addresse Lord Byron . . . Second edition. pp. 12. *Plumm Brewis: London,* 1816. 8°. **992**. i. **21**.

Fugitive Pieces.

— Fugitive Pieces. [By Lord Byron.] pp. 66. FEW CORRECTIONS [by the author?]. [1806.] 4°. *See* Pie Ashley

— A fac-simile reprint of the suppressed edition of [Edited by H. Buxton Forman.] pp. x. 66. *Pr for private circulation: London,* 1886. 4°. **11647**. g

— [Another copy.] Ashley 4

— [Another edition.] Reproduced from the first edi With a bibliographical note by Marcel Kessel. pp. 66 *New York,* 1933. 8°. [*Facsimile Text Society.* s vol. 8.] Ac. **9730**.

— [Another copy.] Ashley

— *See* Roe (Herbert C.) The Rare Quarto Editio Lord Byron's "Fugitive Pieces" described, 1919. 8°. Ashley 5

The Giaour.

— The Giaour, a fragment of a Turkish tale. [By Byron.] pp. 41. 1813. 4°. *See* Giaour. Ashley

— [Another copy.] The Giaour . . . Fifth edition, *etc.* *London,* 1813. 8°. **11643**.
Wanting the dedication to Samuel Rogers.

— [Another copy.] Ashley **2626**

— [Another copy, with a different titlepage.] ***F.P.*** *John Murray: London,* 1813. 8°. **11643**. bbb. **17**

— [Another copy.] Ashley
— [Another copy.] Ashley **2626**
— [Another copy.] **F.P.** Ashley

— A new edition, with some additions. pp. 47. *John Murray: London,* 1813. 8°. **11641**.

— [Another copy.] Ashley **2626**

RON (GEORGE GORDON NOEL) *Baron Byron.* [SINGLE WORKS.—THE GIAOUR.]

— Third edition, with considerable additions. pp. 53. *John Murray: London,* 1813. 8°. Ashley **2626**. (3.)

— [Another copy, with the addition of an advertisement on the verso of the half-title.] **1466**. g. **58**.

— [Another copy.] Ashley **2626**. (4.)

— Fourth edition, with additions. pp. 58. *John Murray: London,* 1813. 8°. Ashley **2626**. (5.)

— Fifth edition, with considerable additions. pp. 66. *John Murray: London,* 1813. 8°. **11659.c.35.(1.)**

— Sixth edition. pp. 66. *John Murray: London,* 1813. 8°. **11642**. cc. **28**. (1.)

— [Another copy.] Ashley **2626**. (7.)

— Seventh edition, with some additions. pp. 75. *John Murray: London,* 1813. 8°. **1466**. g. **55**.

— [Another copy.] Ashley **2626**. (8.)

— The Giaour . . . Eighth edition, with some additions. pp. 75. *John Murray: London,* 1813. 8°. Ashley **2626**. (9.)

— The ninth edition. pp. 75. *John Murray: London,* 1814. 8°. **11643**. c. **4**.
Imperfect; wanting the half-title.

— [Another copy.] The Giaour . . . The ninth edition. *London,* 1814. 8°. Ashley **2626**. (**10**.)

— The tenth edition. pp. 75. *John Murray: London,* 1814. 8°. **11641**. cc. **11**.

— [Another copy.] The Giaour . . . The tenth edition. *London,* 1814. 8°. Ashley **2626**. (**11**.)
Without the publisher's advertisements at the end.

— [Another copy.] **11643**. l. **14**. (2.)

— The eleventh edition. pp. 75. *John Murray: London,* 1814. 8°. **11645**. cc. **14**.

— [Another copy.] The Giaour . . . The eleventh edition. *London,* 1814. 8°. **11661**. c. **7**. (1.)

— The twelfth edition. pp. 75. *John Murray: London,* 1814. 8°. **11646**. ff. **18**.

— The Giaour . . . Thirteenth edition. pp. 75. *John Murray: London,* 1815. 8°. **11658**. c. **93**.

— The fourteenth edition. pp. 75. *John Murray: London,* 1815. 8°. **11643**. h. **7**.

— [Another copy.] **11659**. b. **33**. (1.)

— [Another edition.] pp. 51. *W. Dugdale: London,* 1825. 12°. **11642**. a. **61**. (6.)

— [Another edition.] pp. 67. *John Murray: London,* 1842. 12°. **11649**. cc. **16**. (2.)

— [Another copy.] The Giaour, *etc.* *London,* 1842. 12°. **11652**. a. **98**. (1.)

— [Another edition.] pp. 40. [*Clarke: London,* 1844.] 8°. **1155**. c. **1**. (5.)

German.

— Der Gauer. Bruchstück einer türkischen Erzählung . . . Nach der siebenten englischen Ausgabe im Deutschen metrisch bearbeitet. pp. 70. *Berlin,* 1819. 12°. **11603**. de. **22**. (1.)

BYRON (GEORGE GORDON NOEL) *Baron Byron.* [SINGLE WORKS.—THE GIAOUR.]

Greek.—Modern Greek.

—— *Ποιηματα Βυρωνος. Ὁ Γκιαουρ. Τεμαχιον τουρκικου διηγηματος. Μεταφρασις Αἰκατερινης Κ. Δοσιου.* [With introduction by K. N. Dosios.] *Ἐκδιδεται το δευτερον ὑπο Ἀρ. Κ. Δοσιου.* pp. ι. 69. *Ἀθηνησι,* 1873. 4°. **11642**. h. **26**.

—— [Another edition.] pp. 91. *ἐν Ἀθηναις,* [1890?] 8°. **11647**. de. **37**.

Russian.

—— Гяуръ Байрона. Перевелъ Е. Мишель. pp. 49. *Санктпетербургъ,* 1862. 8°. **11642**. g. **29**.

—— *See* ONORATO (R.) "Il Giaurro" di Lord Byron. 1905. 8°. **11870**. f. **21**.

HEAVEN AND EARTH.

—— Heaven and Earth, a mystery. [By Lord Byron.] pp. 35. 1823. 16°. *See* HEAVEN. **1075**. d. **10**. (3.)

—— [Another edition.] pp. 35. 1824. 12°. *See* HEAVEN. **11642**. b. **57**. (6.)

—— [Another edition.] pp. 36. [1825?] 12°. *See* HEAVEN. C. **58**. bb. **4**. (5.)

French.

—— Le Ciel et la terre. Mystère, *etc.* *See* P . . . T (A.) Essai sur le génie et le caractère de Lord Byron par A. P . . . t [i.e. Amédée Pichot], *etc.* 1824. 12°. **11612**. a. **12**. (1.)

Polish.

—— Niebo i ziemia. Dramma liryczne. [1841.] *See* ODYNIEC (A. E.) Tłómaczenia. tom 3. 1838, *etc.* 8°. **11585**. c. **39**.

Russian.

—— Небо и Земля. Мистерія. *See* BUNIN (I. A.) Разсказы и стихотворенія, *etc.* 1912. 8°. **012264**. c. **6**.

HEBREW MELODIES.

—— Hebrew Melodies. pp. 53. *John Murray: London,* 1815. 8°. **1478**. b. **14**.

—— [Another copy.] Hebrew Melodies. *London,* 1815. 8°. **Cup.400.b.38.**
With half titles and titlepages for Byron's Works, 1815, *and John Murray's catalogue for June* 1815 *bound in after the text.*

—— [Another copy.] Ashley **2672**.

—— [Another copy.] Ashley **2673**.
Without the advertisement of Rogers's "Jacqueline" on the verso of sig. E 4.

—— [Another copy.] MS. NOTE [by Lady Byron]. Ashley **5454***.

—— [Another copy.] **992**. l. **4**. (1.)
Imperfect; wanting sig. E 4.

—— [Another edition.] pp. 36. *W. Dugdale: London,* 1823. 12°. **11643**. a. **48**. (2.)

—— [Another edition.] pp. 22. *W. Dugdale: London,* 1825. 12°. **11642**. b. **57**. (2.)

—— [Another copy.] **11643**. a. **48**. (6.)

—— Hebrew Melodies. pp. 35. *De La More Press: London,* 1902. 8°. [*De La More Booklets.*] **012208**. de. **9/1**.

English and German.

—— Hebräische Gesänge aus dem Englischen des Lord Byron von F. Theremin. Mit beigedrucktem englischen Text. pp. viii. 87. *Berlin,* 1820. 12°. **11602.** e. **18.** (**1.**)

English and Hebrew.

—— שירי ישרון . . . Hebrew Melodies . . . translated by Dr. S. Mandelkern. pp. 45. *Leipzig,* 1890. 8°. **01980.** a. **31.**

Danish.

—— Jødiske Sange. Oversatte af J. Andresen-Halmrast. pp. 41. *Christiania,* 1889. 16°. **011586.** f. **27.** (**1.**)

German.

—— Lord Byron's Hebräische Gesänge. Aus dem Englischen übertragen und mit sachlichen Einleitungen und Bemerkungen versehen von E. Nickles. pp. 112. *Karlsruhe,* 1863. 8°. **11643.** bbb. **15.** (**16.**)

German.—Judaeo-German.

—— *See* infra: *Yiddish.*

Italian.

—— Melodie ebraiche . . . Versione di P. P. Parzanese. pp. xii. 47. *Napoli,* 1837. 16°. **11602.** e. **25.** (**1.**)

Swedish.

—— Hebreiska melodier . . . Öfversatta af T. Lind. pp. 41. *Helsingfors,* 1862. 8°. **11601.** d. **14.** (**7.**)

Yiddish.

—— [Lord Byron's "Hebrew Melodies." Translated by Nathan Horowitz.] [*London,* 1920.] 8°. **11641.** de. **69.**
Cuttings from a newspaper.

—— Byron's Hebrew Melodies. Yiddish translation by Nathan Horowitz. pp. 16. "*Express*" *Printers: London,* 1925. 8°. **11633.** bb. **60.**

—— [Another copy.] MS. CORRECTIONS. **11633.** bb. **61.**

—— [Another copy.] MS. CORRECTIONS. **11654.** bbb. **17.**

Appendix.

—— *See* BEUTLER (C. A.) Über Lord Byron's "Hebrew Melodies," *etc.* 1912. 8°. **011853.** d. **10.**

—— *See* OELBERMANN (H.) Germanische Melodien. Theilweise frei nach Lord Byron's hebräischen Melodien. 1862. 8°. **11526.** aaa. **66.** (**5.**)

HOURS OF IDLENESS.

—— Hours of Idleness, a series of poems, original and translated. [Forty poems, of which twenty-eight are reprinted from "Poems on Various Occasions," and twelve are new.] pp. xiii. 187. *S. & J. Ridge: Newark,* 1807. 8°. **11641.** c. **6.**
In this copy sig. D 3 *is a cancel.*

—— [Another copy.] **992.** b. **2.**

—— [Another copy.] Ashley **303.**

—— [Another copy.] Ashley **304.**
In this copy the original sig. D 3 *is included in addition to the cancel.*

—— [Another edition.] pp. xiii. 187. *S. & J. Ridge: Newark,* 1807. 8°. **11642.** d. **37.**
A portrait of Byron dated 1819 *is inserted.*

—— [Another copy.] Ashley **2606.**

—— [Another edition.] Poems Original and Translated . . Second edition. pp. viii [vii]. 174. *S. & J. Ridg Newark,* 1808. 8°. Ashley **30**
Sig. U 4 *containing the first thirty-two lines of* "*Childi Recollections,*" *which it was intended to cancel, has be retained in error.*

—— [Another edition.] Poems Original and Translat . . . Second edition. pp. viii [vii]. 174. *S. J. Ridge: Newark,* 1808 [1811?]. 8°. **11646.** ccc.
The watermark is dated 1811.

—— [Another copy.] Ashley **30**

—— [Another edition.] Hours of Idleness . . . Second e tion. [With "Critique extracted from the Edinbur Review, no. 22, for January 1808."] pp. 158. *Galignani: Paris,* 1819. 8°. **11609.** de. **29.** (

—— [Another edition.] pp. 158. *Galignani: Paris,* 1819. 8 **1346.** a. **36.** (

—— [Another edition.] pp. viii. 160. *W. T. Sherwi London,* 1820. 8°. **11642.** c. **4**

—— [Another copy.] Ashley **269**

—— [Another copy.] Ashley **5294**

—— [Another edition.] pp. viii. 160. *Sherwin & C London,* 1820. 8°. **11645.** g.

—— [Another copy.] Ashley **26**

—— Third edition. pp. 158. *Galignani: Paris,* 1820. 1 **11645.** bb.

—— [Another edition.] pp. 159. *A. & W. Galignar Paris,* 1822. 12°. **11643.** c. **53.** (

—— Hours of Idleness, a series of poems, original and tra lated. By a noble author [i.e. Byron]. pp. 183. 1822. 12°. *See* HOURS. **C. 117.** a.

—— [Another copy.] **11643.** aa.

—— Hours of Idleness . . . A new edition. pp. iii. 184. *J. Starke: Glasgow,* 1825. 12°. **11643.** a. **48.** (

Appendix.

—— Critique, from the Edinburgh Review, on Lord Byro Poems [i.e. "Hours of Idleness"]. Which occasion "English Bards and Scotch Reviewers." pp. 8. *W. T. Sherwin: London,* 1820. 8°. **11824.** ee. **3.** (

—— [Another copy.] Ashley **271**

—— Extract of the Review of Lord Byron's Hours of Id ness, from the Edinburgh Review, *etc.* pp. 8. *Wilt & Son: London,* 1820. 8°. Ashley **529**

THE IRISH AVATAR.

—— The Irish Avatar. [By Lord Byron.] pp. 8. [1821.] *See* IRISH AVATAR. Ashley **26**

THE ISLAND.

—— The Island, or Christian and his comrades. pp. 94. *John Hunt: London,* 1823. 8°. **11649.** f. **15.** (

—— [Another copy.] Ashley **270**

—— Second edition. pp. 94. *John Hunt: London,* 1823. 8 **11643.** bbb. **18.** (

—— Third edition. pp. 94. *John Hunt: London,* 1823. 8 **11645.** g. **1**

[BY]RON (GEORGE GORDON NOEL) *Baron Byron.* [SINGLE WORKS.]

— [Another edition.] pp. 95. *A. & W. Galignani: Paris,* 1823. 8º. **11650.** cc. **21.** (4.)

THE LAMENT OF TASSO.

— The Lament of Tasso. pp. 19. *John Murray: London,* 1817. 8º. Ashley **2684.**

— [Another copy.] **11646.** f. **69.**
Imperfect; wanting the half-title.

— Second edition. pp. 18. *John Murray: London,* 1817. 8º. **11645.** cc. **20.**

— Third edition. pp. 18. *John Murray: London,* 1817. 8º. **11643.** f. **12.**

— Fourth edition. pp. 18. *John Murray: London,* 1817. 8º. **11645.** cc. **19.**

— Fifth edition. pp. 18. *John Murray: London,* 1817. 8º. **992.** l. **4.** (6.)

— Sixth edition. pp. 18. *John Murray: London,* 1818. 8º. **11645.** cc. **21.**

English and Italian.

— Lamento del Tasso . . . Recato in italiano da M. Leoni. pp. ix. 27. *Pisa,* 1818. 4º. **11642.** f. **42.**

Italian.

— Traduzione del Lamento del Tasso. [By Gaetano Polidori.] *See* POLIDORI (G.) La Magion del Terrore, *etc.* 1843. 16º. **1463.** b. **26.**

— Il Lamento di Tasso . . . portato in versi italiani. *See* GODIO (G.) Il Lamento di Tasso, *etc.* 1873. 8º. **11427.** f. **27.** (4.)

LARA.

— Lara, a tale. Jacqueline, a tale [by Samuel Rogers]. pp. 128. 1814. 8º. *See* LARA. C. **58.** b. **30.**

— [Another copy.] Lara, a tale. Jacqueline, a tale. 1814. 8º. *See* LARA. C. **59.** g. **33.**

— [Another copy.] Ashley **322.**

— Lara, a tale . . . Fourth edition. pp. 70. *John Murray: London,* 1814. 8º. **11643.** bbb. **17.** (3.)
Without "Jacqueline."

— [Another issue, with additions.] pp. 74. *John Murray: London,* 1814. 8º. **11642.** cc. **28.** (4.)
Imperfect; wanting the half-title.

— Lara. A tale . . . Fifth edition. pp. 74. *John Murray: London,* 1815. 8º. **11659.** b. **33.** (4.)

— Fifth edition. pp. 74. *John Murray: London,* 1817. 8º. **11645.** g. **31.**

— Lara. A tale. pp. 52. *W. Dugdale: London,* 1824. 12º. **11659.** df. **65.**

— Lara: a tale. pp. 53. *John Murray: London,* 1842. 12º. **11652.** a. **98.** (4.)

— [Another edition.] Illustrated by C. B. Birch. pp. 11. *Art Union of London: London,* 1879. *obl.* fol. **1875.** a. **20.**

Italian.

— Il Lara de Lord Byron. Tradotto dal Signor G. Ce Bazoldo . . . con giunta di tre altre traduzioni dall'inglese, una dal tedesco, e tre canzoni dell'autore. pp. xi. 138. *Parigi,* 1828. 24º. **11641.** a. **11.**

BYRON (GEORGE GORDON NOEL) *Baron Byron.* [SINGLE WORKS.—LARA.]

Serbocroatian.

—— Лара . . . Србски од А. Поповића. pp. 72. *у Новом Саду,* 1860. 16º. **11586.** df. **31.** (2.)

Spanish.

—— Lara . . . Traducción directa del inglés por Natalio Plaza. pp. 127. *Madrid,* [1922.] 16º. **11645.** de. **76.**

Swedish.

—— Lara. (Öfversättning af Talis Qualis [pseudonym of Carl Wilhelm August Strandberg].) pp. 64. *Stockholm,* 1869. 8º. **11557.** aaa. **32.**

LETTER ON BOWLES'S STRICTURES ON POPE.

—— Letter to **** ****** [i.e. John Murray], on the Rev. W. L. Bowles' Strictures on the life and writings of Pope. pp. 55. *John Murray: London,* 1821. 8º. Ashley **2701.**

—— [Another issue, with six pages of "Addenda to be inserted in page 31, line 15."] pp. 55. 6. *London,* 1821. 8º. Ashley **2702.**

—— Second edition. pp. 61. *John Murray: London,* 1821. 8º. **11643.** h. **6.**

—— Letter to **** ****** [i.e. John Murray], on the Rev. W. L. Bowles' Strictures on the life and writings of Pope . . . Third edition. pp. 61. 2. *John Murray: London,* 1821. 8º. **11873.** f. **8.**

—— [Another edition.] pp. 81. *A. & W. Galignani: Paris,* 1821. 12º. **11805.** b. **46.** (1.)

Appendix.

—— *See* BOWLES (William L.) A Final Appeal to the Literary Public, relative to Pope . . . To which are added, some remarks on Lord Byron's conversations, as far as they relate to the same subject and the author, *etc.* 1825. 8º. **1162.** h. **14.** (1.)

—— *See* BOWLES (William L.) Two Letters to the Right Honourable Lord Byron, in answer to his lordship's Letter to **********, on the Rev. W. L. Bowles's Strictures on the life and writings of Pope, *etc.* 1821. 8º. **11805.** d. **17.**

—— —— 1821. 8º. [*The Pamphleteer.* vol. 18.] P.P. **3557.** w.

—— —— 1822. 8º. **11805.** h. **9.**

—— *See* MACDERMOT (Martin) A Letter to the Rev. W. L. Bowles, in reply to his letter to Thomas Campbell, Esq. and to his two letters to the Right Hon. Lord Byron; containing a vindication of their defence of the poetical character of Pope, *etc.* 1822. 8º. [*The Pamphleteer.* vol. 20.] P.P. **3557.** w.

MANFRED.

—— Manfred, a dramatic poem. pp. 80. *John Murray: London,* 1817. 8º. Ashley **2685.**
With the printer's imprint on the verso of the titlepage.

—— [Another copy.] **643.** f. **21.** (6.)
With the printer's imprint on the verso of the half-title.

—— [Another copy.] Ashley **2686.**

—— [Another copy, with a different titlepage.] Ashley **2687.**

—— [Another copy.] C. **57.** l. **9.** (2.)
Imperfect; wanting the half-title.

—— Second edition. pp. 80. *John Murray: London,* 1817. 8°. **11779**. f. **20**.
Without the half-title to the Notes.

—— [Another edition.] pp. 81. *British Press: Brussels,* [1817?] 8°. **11779**. aaa. **45**.

—— [Another edition.] pp. 35. *W. Dugdale: London,* 1824. 12°. **11642**. a. **61**. (**3**.)

—— [Another edition.] pp. 41. *W. Dugdale: London,* 1826. 12°. **011781**. l. **5**. (**1**.)

—— [Another edition.] Manfred. A choral tragedy, in three acts. pp. 41. *London,* 1864. 12°. [*Lacy's Acting Edition of Plays.* vol. 60. no. 1.] **2304**. f. **5**. (**1**.)

—— [Another edition.] *London,* [1875?] 8°. [*Dicks' Standard Plays.* no. 59.] **11770**. bbb. **4**.

—— [Another edition.] Decorated by Frederick Carter. With an introduction by the artist. *Fanfrolico Press: London,* 1929. fol. C. **100**. k. **17**.
One of an edition of thirty copies.

English and German.

—— Manfred. A tragedy. (Manfred . . . Teutsch von Adolf Wagner.) pp. 239. *Leipzig,* 1819. 8°. **1346**. c. **27**.

—— Manfred. Ein dramatisches Gedicht. [Translated by Woldemar Starke. With the English text.] pp. 140. *München,* 1912. 4°. **11642**. h. **34**.

English and Greek.

—— Greek Tragic Verse. Byron, 'Manfred,' Act II. Scene II. 'It may be that I can aid thee' to Scene III. 'Wreak further havoc for me.' By Kenneth Robert Brooks, *etc.* (Gaisford Prize for Greek Verse, 1936.) pp. 11. *Basil Blackwell: Oxford,* 1936. 8°. **20029**. d. **20**.

Bohemian.

—— Manfred. Báseň dramatická. Přeložil Jaroslav Vrchlický. (Rediguje Jaroslav Kvapil.) pp. 81. *v Praze,* 1901. 8°. **11646**. df. **13**.

Bulgarian.

—— Манфредъ. Отъ английски Н. Вранчевъ. Второ издание. pp. 75. *София,* 1926. 12°. **11630**. aa. **24**.

Catalan.

—— Manfret. Poema dramatic en 3 actes. Traducció de Michêl Ventura Balaña. pp. 72. *Reus,* 1905. 12°. **11655**. a. **79**.

Danish.

—— Manfred . . . Oversat af P. F. Wulff. pp. 107. *Kjøbenhavn,* 1820. 12°. **1344**. b. **11**.

—— Manfred . . . Oversat af E. Lembcke. pp. 109. *Kjøbenhavn,* 1843. 8°. **1344**. c. **32**.

Dutch.

—— Manfred. Een dramatisch gedicht naar Lord Byron, door J. R. Steinmetz. pp. xv. 59. *Amsterdam,* 1857. 8°. **11779**. a. **19**.

—— Byron's Manfred . . . Metrische vertaling . . . van W. Gosler. pp. vii. 78. *Heusden,* 1882. 8°. **11774**. e. **2**. (**8**.)

French.

—— Manfred, poëme dramatique . . . Traduit par Madame la comtesse de Lalaing . . . Seconde édition. pp. 61. *Bruxelles,* 1852. 8°. **11781**. f. **6**.

—— Manfred . . . Adaptation nouvelle, en vers, de Moreau. pp. vii. 28. *Paris,* 1887. 8°. **11779**. aaa. **11**. (1

—— Manfred . . . Traduction en vers par C. Trébla. pp. *Toulouse,* 1888. 8°. **11740**. bbb.

German.

—— Byron's Manfred. Einleitung, Uebersetzung und merkungen. Ein Beitrag zur Kritik der gegenwärti deutschen dramatischen Kunst und Poesie, von Posg [i.e. G. F. W. Suckow]. pp. 212. *Breslau,* 1839. 8°. **11771**. e.

—— Lord Byron's Manfred. Deutsch von H. von Kös pp. 86. *Leipzig,* 1858. 16°. **11779**. a.

—— Byron's Manfred. Erklärt und übersetzt von L. Fr tag. pp. 158. *Berlin,* 1872. 16°. **11779**. a.

—— Manfred. Dramatische Dichtung in drei Abtheilun von Lord Byron. Musik von Robert Schumann. pp. *Leipzig,* [1879.] 8°. [*Breitkopf & Härtel's Textbiblioth* no. 66.] **11747**. ccc. **1**/

—— Text der Gesänge zu: Manfred, dramatisches Gedi von Byron. Musik von Robert Schumann. pp. 7. *Leipz* [1879.] 8°. [*Breitkopf & Härtel's Textbibliothek.* no. 6 **11747**. ccc. **1**/

—— Manfred. Dramatisches Gedicht von Byron. Musik v Robert Schumann. Verbindende Dichtung für Konze aufführungen von R. Pohl. pp. 48. *Leipzig,* 1907. [*Breitkopf & Härtel's Textbibliothek.* no. 382.] **11747**. ccc. **1/3**

German.—Judaeo-German.

—— **See infra: *Yiddish.***

Greek.—Modern Greek.

—— *'Ο Μαμφρεδ. Δραματικον ποιημα . . . Μεταφρα 'Ε. Γκρην.* pp. 79. *ἐν Πατραις,* 1864. 8°. **11643**. bbb. **19**. (

Hungarian.

—— Manfred . . . Angolból forditotta: Dr. Kludik Im Byron és a világfájdalom. Irta: Dr. Kludik Im Második kiadás. pp. 112. *Szolnok,* 1884. 8°. **11779**. aa.

—— Manfred . . . **Forditotta Ábrányi Emil.** pp. 98. *Budapest,* 1891 [1890]. 8°. **11778**. aaa.

Italian.

—— Manfredo, poema drammatico . . . versione in pr [By Silvio Pellico.] *See* Pellico (S.) Tragedie, 1859. 8°. **2298**. f.

Polish.

—— Manfred . . . Przekład wolny na wiersz polski p M. Chodźkę, wydanie ozdobione z rysunkami. pp. 89 *Paryż,* [1859.] 8°. **11647**. f.

Roumanian.

—— Manfred. Poemă dramatică în treĭ acte, dupe L Byron. *See* Stoenescŭ (T. M.) Teatru, *etc.* 1896. **11758**. e.

Russian.

—— Манфредъ. Драматическая поэма. *See* Bunin (I. Стихотворенія 1903–06 г., *etc.* [1912.] 8°. **011586**. g.

Serbocroatian.

— Manfred. Dramska pjesan u tri razdjela . . . U mjerilu izvornika preveo Stjepan Miletić. pp. 76. *Zagreb,* 1894. 8°. **11646.** e. **48.**

Spanish.

— Manfredo, poema dramatico . . . Traducido en verso directamente del Inglés al Castellano por D. J. Alcalá Galiano y Fernandez de las Peñas. pp. xiii. 85. *Madrid,* 1861. 8°. **11779.** b. **26.**

— Manfredo y Oscar de Alva, version castellana de A. R. Chaves. pp. xix. 78. *Madrid,* 1876. 8°. **11645.** ee. **22.**

Yiddish.

— [Lord Byron's Manfred. Yiddish translation by Nathan Horowitz.] [1925?] 8°. **11644.** d. **65.**
Cuttings from a newspaper. With a MS. *title.*

Appendix.

— *See* ANTON (H. S.) Byron's Manfred, *etc.* 1875. 8°. **11840.** f. **3.** (**5.**)

— *See* DUENTZER (H.) Göthe's Faust . . . Nebst . . . zwei Anhängen: über Byron's Manfred und Lessing's Doktor Faust. 1836. 12°. **11824.** c. **39.** (**2.**)

— *See* PAKOWSKA (R.) Polskie przekłady poematów Byrona "Childe Harold" i "Manfred." [With a portrait.] 1938. 8°. **11862.** d. **8.**

— *See* ROETSCHER (H. T.) Manfred . . . in ihrem inneren Zusammenhange entwickelt, *etc.* 1844. 4°. **11649.** f. **8.**

— *See* THEOLOG. Manfred, dramatische Dichtung von Lord Byron, aus ihrem Grundgedanken erklärt, *etc.* [1898.] 8°. **011850.** f. **85.**

— *See* VARNHAGEN (H.) De rebus quibusdam compositionem Byronis dramatis quod Manfred inscribitur praecedentibus, *etc.* 1909. 8°. **11853.** k. **17.**

MARINO FALIERO.

— Marino Faliero, Doge of Venice. An historical tragedy, in five acts. With notes. The Prophecy of Dante, a poem. pp. xxi. 261. *John Murray: London,* 1821. 8°. **11643.** k. **28.**

— [Another copy.] Ashley **2697.**

— [Another issue, with additions.] *London,* 1821. 8°. **992.** l. **5.**
In this issue p. 101 *is misnumbered* 110.

— [Another copy.] Ashley **2698.**

— Second edition. pp. xxi. 261. *John Murray: London,* 1821. 8°. **11779.** h. **21.**

— [Another edition.] pp. xxi. 261. *John Murray: London,* 1823. 8°. **11626.** bbb. **21.**

— [Another edition.] pp. 162. *John Murray: London,* 1842. 12°. **11649.** cc. **16.** (**3.**)
Without "The Prophecy of Dante."

— [Another edition.] Erklärt von Fr. Brockerhoff. pp. 196. *Berlin,* 1853. 8°. [*Sammlung englischer Schriftsteller.* Bdchn. 2.] **11603.** d. **20.**

— [Another edition.] *London,* [1877?] 8°. [*Dicks' Standard Plays.* no. 153.] **11770.** bbb. **4.**

German.

— Marino Faliero. Doge von Venedig . . . Freie Übersetzung von T. Preyer. pp. 147. *Frankfurt,* 1883. 4°. **11779.** h. **6.**

—— Lord Byron's Marino Faliero. Für das Herzoglich Sachsen-Meiningen'sche Hoftheater übersetzt und bearbeitet von A. Fitger. pp. 84. *Oldenburg,* [1886.] 8°. **11781.** g. **29.**

MAZEPPA.

—— Mazeppa, a poem. pp. 71. *John Murray: London,* 1819. 8°. **11641.** c. **8.**
In this copy p. 70 *bears the printer's imprint.*

—— [Another copy.] Ashley **2691.**

—— [Another copy.] Ashley **2692.**
In this copy p. 70 *is blank.*

—— [Another copy.] **992.** l. **4.** (**8.**)
Imperfect; wanting the last leaf.

—— Second edition. pp. 69. *Galignani: Paris,* 1819. 8°. **11609.** de. **28.** (**1.**)

—— [Another edition.] pp. 35. *W. Dugdale: London,* 1824. 12°. **11642.** b. **57.** (**1.**)

—— [Another edition.] Mazeppa, or the Wild horse of the Ukraine: a poem. pp. 48. *T. Goode: London,* [1854?] 32°. **528.** m. **23/66.**

—— The Knight's Tour in a continuous and uninterrupted ride over 48 boards or 3072 squares. Adapted from Byron's "Mazeppa" by H. Eschwege. *Silsbury Bros.: Shanklin,* 1896. 8°. **11647.** ee. **37.**

Czech.

—— Mazeppa. Přeložil Antonin Klášterský. pp. 41. *v Praze,* [1895?] 8°. **11603.** aa. **27.** (**3.**)

—— Druhé opravené vydání. pp. 43. *v Praze,* 1922. 8°. **11632.** c. **67.**

German.

—— Mazeppa, nach Lord Byron. *See* FREILIGRATH (F.) Nachgelassenes von F. Freiligrath. 1883. 8°. **11641.** de. **8.**

Italian.

—— Mazeppa. Traduzione . . . di T. Virzì. pp. 63. *Palermo,* 1876. 8°. **11643.** d. **2.**

Polish.

—— Mazeppa. Powieść. [1843.] *See* ODYNIEC (A. E.) Tłómaczenia. tom 5. 1838, *etc.* 8°. **11585.** c. **39.**

Ruthenian.

—— *See* infra: *Ukrainian.*

Ukrainian.

—— "Мазепа"—поема. [Translated by D. Zahul.] *See* BORSHCHAK (I.) and MARTEL (R.) Іван Мазепа, *etc.* 1933. 8°. **20002.** f. **8.**

Appendix.

—— *See* CORTESI (A.) Mazeppa. Ballo storico, *etc.* [Based on Lord Byron's poem.] 1841. 8°. **906.** g. **12.** (**11.**)

—— *See* ENGLAENDER (D.) Lord Byrons Mazeppa, *etc.* 1897. 8°. **011851.** ee. **20.**

—— *See* MAZEPA (Ivan) *Hetman of the Cossacks.* Mazeppa Travestied: a poem, *etc.* [A parody of Lord Byron's poem.] 1820. 8°. **1466.** g. **38.**

BYRON (George Gordon Noel) *Baron Byron.* [Single Works.—Mazeppa.]

—— *See* Milner (Henry M.) Mazeppa, a romantic drama in three acts, dramatised from Lord Byron's poem, *etc.* [1830?] 12°. [*Cumberland's Minor Theatre.* vol. 5.] **643.** a. **3.**

—— —— 1874. 12°. **2304.** g. **14.** **(9.)**

—— —— [1885.] 8°. [*Dicks' Standard Plays.* no. 620.] **11770.** bbb. **4.**

Monody on the Death of R. B. Sheridan.

—— Monody on the Death of the Right Honourable R. B. Sheridan, written at the request of a friend, to be spoken at Drury Lane Theatre. [By Lord Byron.] pp. 12. 1816. 8°. *See* Sheridan (*Right Hon.* Richard B. B.) [*Appendix.*] **Ashley 2678.**

—— [Another copy.] **992.** i. **18.** **(5.)**
In this copy the word "mourn" has been substituted for "weep" in the first line on p. 11.

—— [Another issue.] C. **57.** l. **8.**
In this issue p. 11 *has been re-set.*

—— [Another copy.] **Ashley.2677**

—— New edition. pp. 11. *John Murray: London,* 1817. 8°. **11641.** bbb. **19.**

—— New edition. pp. 11. *John Murray: London,* 1818. 8°. **11645.** cc. **9.**

Observations upon "Observations."

—— Observations upon "Observations." A second letter to John Murray, Esq. on the Rev. W. L. Bowles's Strictures on the life and writings of Pope. Now first published. [1872.] 8°. T. **1166.** **(8*.)**
An extract, consisting of pp. 381–416, *from vol.* 6 *of the seventeen volume edition of the "Works of Lord Byron" published by John Murray in* 1832, 33.

Ode to Napoleon Buonaparte.

—— Ode to Napoleon Buonaparte. [By Lord Byron.] pp. 14. 1814. 8°. *See* Napoleon i., *Emperor of the French.* [*Appendix.*] **11644.** h. **27.**

—— [Another copy.] Ashley **2671.**

—— The second edition. pp. 14. 1814. 8°. *See* Napoleon i., *Emperor of the French.* [*Appendix.*] **11645.** cc. **13.**

—— The third edition. pp. 15. 1814. 8°. *See* Napoleon i., *Emperor of the French.* [*Appendix.*] **11643.** bbb. **15.** **(4.)**

—— Ode to Napoleon Buonaparte . . . [By Lord Byron.] The fourth edition. pp. 15. 1814. 8°. *See* Napoleon i., *Emperor of the French.* [*Appendix.*] **11661.** c. **7.** (4.)

—— The seventh edition. pp. 17. 1814. 8°. *See* Napoleon i., *Emperor of the French.* [*Appendix.*] **11643.** bbb. **8.**

—— [Another copy.] **11643.** l. **14.** **(5.)**

—— The ninth edition. pp. 17. 1814. 8°. *See* Napoleon i., *Emperor of the French.* [*Appendix.*] **11646.** ff. **19.**

—— Ode to Napoleon Buonaparte . . . [By Lord Byron.] Tenth edition. pp. 17. 1814. 8°. *See* Napoleon i., *Emperor of the French.* [*Appendix.*] **11659.** c. **54.**

—— Twelfth edition. pp. 17. *John Murray: London,* 1816. 8°. **11645.** cc. **12.**

—— Thirteenth edition. pp. 17. *John Murray: London,* 1818. 8°. **11633.** cc. **3.** **(6.)**

BYRON (George Gordon Noel) *Baron Byron.* [Single Works.]

Ode to the Framers of the Frame Bill.

—— A Political Ode by Lord Byron [entitled "Ode to the Framers of the Frame Bill"], hitherto unknown as his production. [Edited by John Pearson.] pp. 11. *John Pearson: London,* 1880. 8°. C. **71.** e. 1
Privately printed. One of an edition of 100 *copies. Printed on one side of the leaf only.*

—— [Another copy.] Ashley **271**

On John William Rizzo Hoppner.

—— On John William Rizzo Hoppner, born at Venice on the eighteenth of January 1818. [A poem, with translation in eleven languages. By Lord Byron.] pp. 14. [1818.] 8°. *See* Hoppner (John W. R.) Ashley **32**

Parisina.

—— Parisina. A poem. [By Lord Byron.] *See* Corinth. The Siege of Corinth, *etc.* 1816. 8°. **11642.** g. **2**

—— Second edition. *See* Corinth. The Siege of Corinth, *etc.* 1816. 8°. **992.** l. **4.** (2

—— Third edition. *See* Corinth. The Siege of Corinth, *etc.* 1816. 8°. **11643.** bbb. **19.** (4

French.

—— Parisina, poème de Lord Byron [translated by A. Krafft] et fragment de Nicolas de Ferrare, drame [by A. Krafft] . . . Avec commentaires, *etc.* pp. xiv. 55. *Paris* 1900. 8°. **11646.** f. **7**

—— Parisina, et poésies diverses. Traduction de Benjamin Laroche, *etc.* pp. xii. 136. *L. B. Hill: Londres* [1920.] 32°. **945.** dd.

German.

—— Parisina. [Translated into German verse by J. V. Cirkel.] *See* Cirkel (J. V.) Gedichte, *etc.* 1825. 8°. **11526.** ee. **3**

Italian.

—— Parisina. Poema . . . Traduzione italiana in versi. pp. 27. *Milano,* 1821. 8°. **11601.** aa. **48.** (2

Appendix.

—— *See* Brown (W. S.) *Dramatist.* Parisina: an opera from the poem of Lord Byron. [1896.] 8°. **11781.** gg. **21.** (12

—— *See* Romani (F.) Parisina. Dramma serio, *etc.* (Tratt da un poemetto di Lord Byron.) 1836. 12°. **906.** c. **9.** (4

—— —— 1838. 8°. **905.** a. **2.** (2

—— —— [1840?] 8°. **906.** d. **5.** (3.

—— —— 1841. 8°. **906.** g. **12.** (3.

—— —— 1858. 12°. **905.** i. **9.** (5

—— *See* Romani (F.) Parisina; a serious opera, *etc.* [By F. Romani, based on the "Parisina" of Lord Byron 1838. 12°. **11725.** bb. **11.** (2

—— —— 1838. 12°. **1342.** c. **2**

Poems, 1816.

—— Poems. pp. 38. *John Murray: London,* 1816. 8°. Ashley **2675**

—— [A reissue.] pp. 39. *London,* 1816. 8°. Ashley **5455**
With the addition of a poem to Samuel Rogers.

—— Second edition. pp. 39. *John Murray: London* 1816. 8°. **992.** l. **4.** (4.

—— [Another copy.] Ashley **2676**

—— Traduction de l'ode de Lord Byron, sur la bataille de Waterloo. [" We do not curse thee, Waterloo ! " Extracted from " Poems," 1816.] Par Aristide Guilbert. pp. 28. *Hunt & Clark: Londres,* 1826. 8°.
T. 960. (23.)

Poems on Various Occasions.

—— Poems on Various Occasions. [By Lord Byron. Fifty-one poems, of which thirty-nine are reprinted from " Fugitive Pieces," and twelve are new.] pp. 11. 144. 1807. 8°. *See* Poems. C. 28. b. 9.

—— [Another copy.] Ashley **2605**.

Poems Original and Translated.

—— *See* supra : Hours of Idleness.

The Prisoner of Chillon.

—— The Prisoner of Chillon, and other poems. pp. 60. *John Murray: London,* 1816. 8°. Ashley **2681**.

—— [Another copy.] 992. l. 4. (3.)
Imperfect; wanting the last leaf.

—— [Another copy.] **11642**. cc. 28. (6.)
Imperfect; wanting the last leaf.

—— [Another edition.] pp. 29. *Hignou & Co.: Lausanne,* 1818. 8°. **11643**. bbb. **17**. (5.)

—— [Another edition.] pp. 35. *W. Chubb: London,* 1824. 12°. **11642**. a. **61**. (2.)

—— [Another edition.] pp. 18. [*London,* 1825 ?] 12°.
C. **58**. bb. 4. (4.)

—— [Another edition.] pp. 32. *Barbezat & Delarue: Geneva,* 1830. 16°. **11649**. cc. **16**. (**1**.)

—— [Another edition.] The Prisoner of Chillon . . . Le Prisonnier de Chillon . . . précédé d'une notice historique sur le château de Chillon par D. Martignier. pp. 46. *Martignier & Chavannes: Lausanne,* 1857. 8°.
11643. bbb. 14. (7.)

—— [Another edition.] (Illuminated by W. & G. Audsley. Chromolithographed by W. R. Tymms.) *Day & Son: London,* [1865.] 4°. **11651**. m. **8**.

—— [Another edition.] With notes, *etc.* pp. 32. *London,* [1875.] 16°. [*Allman's English Classics for Elementary Schools.*] **12205**. cc. 8/4.

—— [Another edition.] With life, notes, grammatical & miscellaneous questions, &c. &c. by R. S. Davies. pp. 24. *A. Brown: Hull,* [1877.] 12°. [*Brown's Series of English Classics.*] **12202**. dg. **13**/**1**.

—— [Another edition.] With life and notes, *etc.* pp. 35. *J. B. Ledsham: Manchester; Simpkin, Marshall & Co.: London,* [1879.] 8°. [*World School Series.*]
12200. aa. **36**/**15**.

—— [Another edition.] With prefatory and explanatory notes. pp. 32. *London, Glasgow,* 1879. 16°. [*Blackie's School Classics.*] **12200**. c. **15**/**3**.

—— [Another edition.] The Prisoner of Chillon . . . and part of the 3rd Canto of Child Harold. With a short description of the castle and a notice of the chief historical events and legends connected with its history. Selected from authentic sources by an English resident . . . Fourth edition. pp. 59. *Loertscher & Son: Vevey,* 1880. 8°.
11601. dd. 9. (**1**.)

—— [Another edition.] The Prisoner of Chillon . . . With life, introduction, notes, etc. pp. 36. *Fallon & Co: Dublin,* [1896.] 8°. [*School and College Series.*]
012202. h. **3**/**9**.

—— [Another edition.] With notes . . . by the Rev. H. Evans. pp. 36. *Blackie & Son: Dublin,* 1896. 8°. [*English Classics for Intermediate Schools and Colleges.*]
12274.df.8/2.

—— [Another edition.] Kritischer Text mit Einleitung und Anmerkungen herausgegeben von E. Kölbing. pp. xxiv. 97. *Weimar,* 1898. 8°. [*Englische Textbibliothek.* no. 1.] **12273**. c. **21**/**1**.

—— The Prisoner of Chillon. Prose version. *See* Carleton (A. E. M.) Outlines of English Literature 1789–1815, *etc.* 1901. 8°. **11852**. b. **40**.

—— The Prisoner of Chillon, by Lord Byron. A Christmas Carol, by Charles Dickens. Edited by James H. Cousins, with introductory essays . . . notes, *etc.* 2 pt. *Dublin,* [1910.] 8°. [*Maunsel's Intermediate Text-Books.*]
12199. b. **2**/**1**.

—— [Another edition.] The Prisoner of Chillon, and other poems. pp. 96. *Siegle, Hill & Co.: London,* [1911.] 32°. [*Langham Booklets.*] **944**. b. **106**.

—— Byron's Dream, illustrated by Mrs. Lees. [Originally published in " The Prisoner of Chillon, and other poems."] *Dickinson & Co.: [London,]* 1849. fol. **1268**. i. 24.
Printed in gold on one side of the leaf only.

Czech.

—— Vězeň Chillonský. Přeložil Antonín Klášterský. pp. 28. *v Praze,* [1895 ?] 8°. **11603**. aa. **27**. (2.)

—— Druhé, opravené vydání. pp. 31. *v Praze,* 1922. 8°.
11632. c. **68**.

French.

—— Le Prisonnier de Chillon. *See* Huguenot. Bonivard à Chillon, *etc.* 1892. 8°. **11740**. d. **16**. (**1**.)

German.

—— Der Gefangene von Chillon. Dichtung . . . In deutscher Uebersetzung mit historischer Einleitung von M. von der Marwitz. pp. xi. 16. *Vevey & Lausanne,* [1865.] 16°. **11645**. cc. 34. (3.)

—— Der Gefangene von Chillon . . . Uebersetzt von J. G. Hagmann. pp. 29. *St. Gallen & Leipzig,* [1892.] 16°.
11601. cc. **21**. (3.)

Greek.—Modern Greek.

—— *Το 'Ενυπνιον.* [Translated by Ch. A. Parmenides. Originally published in " The Prisoner of Chillon, and other poems."] *See* infra: Sardanapalus. [*Greek.—Modern Greek.*] *Σαρδαναπαλος, etc.* 1865. 8°. **11779**. c. **29**.

Icelandic.

—— Bandinginn í Chillon og Draumurinn . . . Steingrimur Thorsteinson íslenzkaði. (Ágrip af æfi Byrons og athugasemdir.) pp. 70. *Kaupmannahöfn,* 1866. 12°.
11754. a. **8**.

The Prophecy of Dante.

—— The Prophecy of Dante, a poem. *See* supra : Marino Faliero. Marino Faliero, *etc.* 1821. 8°.
11643. k. **28**.

—— [Another issue, with additions.] *See* supra: Marino Faliero. Marino Faliero, *etc.* 1821. 8°. **992**. l. 5.

—— Second edition. *See* supra: Marino Faliero. Marino Faliero, *etc.* 1821. 8°. **11779**. h. **21**.

—— [Another edition.] *See* supra: Marino Faliero. Marino Faliero, *etc.* 1823. 8°. **11626**. bbb. **21**.

—— [Another edition.] pp. 32. *W. Dugdale: London,* 1825. 12°. **11642**. a. **61**. (**5**.)

—— [Another edition.] With critical and explanatory notes by L. W. Potts. (Cantos I. II.) pp. 32. *London, Glasgow,* 1879. 16°. [*Blackie's School Manuals.*] **12200**. c. **14/1**.

English and Italian.

—— La Profezia di Dante . . . Tradotta in terza rima da L. da Ponte. (The Apostrophe to the Ocean, in the fourth canto of Child Harold, translated in ottava rina [*sic*]. By L. da Ponte.) pp. 72. *R. E. W. A. Bartow: Nuova-Jorca,* 1821. 12°. **11644**. ee. **3**.

—— La Profezia di Dante . . . Tradotta in terza rima da L. da Ponte. Seconda edizione, con note ed aggiunte di varie poesie originali. [With a portrait.] pp. 100. *R. & W. A. Bartow: Nuova-Jorca,* 1822. 12°. **11661**. a. **3**.

French.

—— La Prophétie du Dante. [A prose translation by B. Laroche.] *See* Dante Alighieri. [*Smaller Collections.—French.*] Œuvres de Dante Alighieri, *etc.* 1842. 12°. **11421**. c. **9**.

—— La Prophétie du Dante . . . Traduction libre [by Sébastian Rhéal]. 1846. *See* Dante Alighieri. [*Smaller Collections.*] Dante Alighieri. La Divine Comédie, *etc.* (Le Paradis. Troisième cantique, *etc.*) 1843, *etc.* 8°. **011420**. dd. **52**.

Italian.

—— La Profezia di Dante . . . Tradotto in terzine italiane da Edoardo Roncaldier. pp. 62. *Roma, Milano,* [1904.] 8°. **11644**. eeee. **54**.

Spanish.

—— La Profecía del Dante . . . Traducido del Frances por A. M. Vizcayno, *etc.* pp. 28. *México,* 1850. 8°. **11824**. dd. **36**. (**7**.)

Ravenna Journal.

—— *See* supra: Letters and Journals.

Sardanapalus.

—— Sardanapalus, a tragedy. The Two Foscari, a tragedy. Cain, a mystery. pp. viii. 439. *John Murray: London,* 1821. 8°. **642**. i. **33**.

—— [Another copy.] Ashley **2699**.

—— Sardanapalus . . . The Two Foscari . . . Cain, *etc.* pp. viii. 329. *John Murray: London,* 1821. 8°. **11614**. bb. **2**.

Consisting of "Sardanapalus" and "The Two Foscari" without "Cain."

—— [Another edition.] pp. 179. *John Murray: London,* 1823. 8°. **1347**. c. **24**.

—— [Another edition.] pp. 134. *John Murray: London,* 1829. 8°. **11779**. aaa. **1**.

—— Sardanapalus, King of Assyria. A tragedy. In fiv acts . . . Adapted for representation by C. Kear pp. 56. *London,* [1853.] 12°. [*Lacy's Acting Edition* *Plays.* vol. 11. no. 5.] **2304**. d. **15**. (**5**

—— Lord Byron's Historical Tragedy of Sardanapalu Arranged for representation by Charles Calvert, *et* pp. vii. 51. *John Heywood: Manchester,* [1875?] 8°. **011781**. e. **11**

—— Lord Byron's Historical Tragedy of Sardanapalu Arranged for representation, in four acts, by Charl Calvert. pp. vii. 56. *John Heywood: Mancheste* [1877?] 8°. **11777**. b. **17**. (**2**

—— Sardanapalus, *etc.* *London,* [1877?] 8°. [*Dick Standard Plays.* no. 50.] **11770**. bbb.

French.

—— Sardanapale, tragédie imitée de Lord Byron par L. Alvi pp. xviii. 122. *Bruxelles,* 1834. 8°. **11779**. aa. **5**

German.

—— Sardanapal . . . Bühnenbearbeitung nach der Uebe setzung von Adolf Böttger, mit einem "Vorspiel" vo Max Zerbst. pp. 117. *Jena,* 1888. 8°. **11779**. bb. **1**

—— Lord Byron's Sardanapal . . . Frei übertragen und fi die Bühne bearbeitet von Josef Kainz. pp. 214. *Berli* 1897. 8°. **11781**. d. **3**

Greek.—Modern Greek.

—— *Σαρδαναπαλος, τραγῳδια του Λορδου Βυρωνος Μεταφρασθεισα ἐκ του ἀγγλικου. Ὁ Υἱος της Δουλης κα Εὐγενια, ὑπο Χρηστου Α. Παρμενιδου.* (*Ὁ Πατροκτονος κατα τον* Victor Hugo.—*Το Ἐνυπνιον ἐκ των του Βυρωνο —Το Ὁραμα του Βασιλοπαιδος Ἀλφρεδου.*) [The pros story *Εὐγενια,* the verses *Υἱος της Δουλης* and *Ὁραμα* b Parmenides, the translator of the other works. Wit notes.] pp. η′. 400. *ἐν Ἀθηναις,* 1865. 8°. **11779**. h. **5**

Italian.

—— Sardanapalo. Tragedia in 5 atti. pp. 91. *Milan* 1884. 8°. **11644**. ccc. **4**

Polish.

—— Sardanapal . . . Przekład Fryderyka Krauze'g Wydanie redakcyi Biblioteki Warszawskiéj. pp. 13 *Warszawa,* 1872 [1871]. 8°. **11781**. g. **3**

Russian.

—— Сарданапалъ . . . Переводъ Е. Зарина. (Из Библіотеки для чтенія №12–го 1860 года.) pp. 12 *Санктпетербургъ,* 1860. 8°. **11771**. g.

Swedish.

—— Sardanapalus: sorgespel i fem akter . . . Försvenska och för scenen behandladt af N. Arfvidsson. pp. 154. *Stockholm,* 1864. 8°. **11779**. aa. **5**

Appendix.

—— *See* Becque (H.) Sardanapale, opéra en trois act imité de Lord Byron, *etc.* 1867. 12°. **11739**. bbb. **3**. (**14**

—— *See* Berton (P.) Sardanapale. Opéra en trois acte d'après Byron, *etc.* 1882. 18°. **11740**. e. **15**. (**2**

—— *See* Tennyson (Alfred) *Baron Tennyson.* [*Appendix* Description of an important Collection of Holograp Manuscript Poems by Lord Tennyson; also the holograp manuscript of "Sardanapalus" by Lord Byron. [1914.] 8°. **011903**. d. 1. (**4**

The Siege of Corinth.

—— The Siege of Corinth. A poem. Parisina. A poem. [By Lord Byron.] pp. 89. 1816. 8°. *See* Corinth. **11642**. g. **25**.

—— [Another copy.] The Siege of Corinth, *etc.* 1816. 8°. *See* Corinth. **11659**. b. **33**. (**5**.)

—— [Another copy.] C. **57**. l. **9**.

—— [Another copy.] Ashley **2679**.

—— Second edition. pp. 89. 1816. 8°. *See* Corinth. **992**. l. **4**. (**2**.)

—— [Another copy.] **11642**. cc. **28**. (**5**.)

—— [Another copy.] Ashley **2680**.

—— Third edition. pp. 89. 1816. 8°. *See* Corinth. **11643**. bbb. **19**. (**4**.)

—— The Siege of Corinth. A poem. pp. 44. *W. Dugdale: London*, 1824. 12°. **11649**. cc. **21**. (**4**.)

—— [Another edition.] [With notes.] pp. 62. *National Society's Depository: London*, 1879. 16°. [*Lines from the Poets.* no. 4.] **11603**. cc. **19**.

—— [Another edition.] Mit Einleitung und Anmerkungen herausgegeben von E. Kölbing. pp. lx. 155. *Berlin*, 1893. 8°. **11644**. cc. **63**.

—— [Another edition.] With introduction and notes by P. Hordern. pp. xii. 64. *London*, 1914. 8°. [*Bell's English Classics.*] **012272**. aaaa. **1/40**.

Dutch.

—— Het Beleg van Corinthe, uit het Engelsch van Lord Byron. Door Mr. J. van Lennep. pp. 59. *Amsterdam*, 1831. 8°. **11641**. g. **9**.

Spanish.

—— El Sitio de Corinto. Traducido del Francés al Castellano. pp. 85. *Paris*, 1828. 16°. **11642**. a. **19**.

A Sketch from Private Life.

—— A Sketch from Private Life. [A satire on Mrs. Clermont. In verse. By Lord Byron.] pp. 4. [1816.] 4°. *See* Sketch. C. **57**. i. **29**.

—— [Another copy.] **Ashley 2674.**

—— [Another copy.] ms. notes [by Lord Byron]. Ashley **2670**.

A proof copy.

Appendix.

—— *See* Sketch. A Sketch from Public Life: a poem founded upon recent domestic circumstances, *etc.* [A reply to Byron's "A Sketch from Private Life."] 1816. 8°. **11642**. bbb. **32**.

—— *See* Tyro, *pseud.* A Sketch from Public Life, and a Farewell: a poem. By Tyro. [A reply to Byron's "A Sketch from Private Life."] 1816. 8°. Ashley **2716**.

The Two Foscari.

—— The Two Foscari, a tragedy. *See* supra: Sardanapalus. Sardanapalus . . . The Two Foscari . . . Cain, *etc.* 1821. 8°. **642**. i. **33**.

—— [Another edition.] [*London*, 1825?] 12°. **11642**. b. **57**. (**5**.)

Pp. 227–297 *of a larger work.*

—— [Another edition.] *London*, [1874?] 8°. [*Dicks' Standard Plays.* no. 73.] **11770**. bbb. **4**.

Spanish.

—— Los Dos Foscaris. Drama histórico en cinco actos y en verso, por D. Manuel Cañete. [Adapted from the "Two Foscari" of Lord Byron.] pp. 24. *Madrid*, 1846. 4°. **1343**. n. **11**. (**10**.)

Appendix.

—— *See* Escudier (M.) and (L.) Les Deux Foscari, tragédie lyrique en quatre actes, imitée de Lord Byron. 1849. 8°. **2296**. b. **7**.

The Vision of Judgment.

—— The Two Visions; or, Byron v. Southey. Containing The Vision of Judgment by Dr. Southey . . . also another Vision of Judgment, by Lord Byron. pp. 72. *W. Dugdale: London*, 1822. 12°. **11642**. a. **63**. (**2**.)

—— The Vision of Judgment. By Quevedo Redivivus [i.e. Lord Byron]. Suggested by the composition so entitled by the author of "Wat Tyler" [i.e. Robert Southey]. pp. 14. 1824. 8°. *See* Quevedo, *Redivivus, pseud.* **11645**. cc. **5**.

—— [Another edition.] The Vision of Judgment. By Quevedo Redivivus (Lord Byron). *See* Southey (Robert) [*A Vision of Judgment.*] A Vision of Judgment, *etc.* 1824. 16°. **1075**. d. **10**. (**4**.)

—— [Another edition.] *See* Southey (Robert) [*A Vision of Judgment.*] Visions of Judgment. [1824?] 12°. Ashley **332**.

—— [Another edition.] pp. x. 48. *University Press: Cambridge*, 1926. 8°. [*Cambridge Plain Texts.*] W.P. **6501/44**.

—— [Another edition.] Edited by E. M. Earl. With Southey's Vision of Judgment as an appendix. pp. 78. *Oxford University Press: London*, 1929. 8°. **11632**. de. **55**.

—— [Another edition.] *See* Southey (Robert) [*A Vision of Judgment.*] A Vision of Judgement, *etc.* 1932. 8°. C. **98**. f. **24**.

Waltz.

—— Waltz: an apostrophic hymn. By Horace Hornem, Esq. [i.e. Lord Byron.] pp. 27. 1813. 4°. *See* Hornem (Horace) *pseud.* Ashley **4726**.

—— [Another edition.] pp. 30. 1821. 12°. *See* Hornem (Horace) *pseud.* **11644**. g. **57**.

—— [Another edition.] pp. 30. [1821?] 8°. *See* Hornem (Horace) *pseud.* **11645**. bb. **61**. (**2**.)

—— [Another edition.] [With four "Fugitive Pieces" by Lord Byron, and "Enigma" by C. M. Fanshawe.] pp. 39. 1821. 8°. *See* Hornem (Horace) *pseud.* **1164**. g. **36** (**1**.)

—— [Another copy.] Ashley **5456**.

—— [Another edition, with an additional poem by Lord Byron, and without "Enigma."] pp. 36. 1821. 12°. *See* Hornem (Horace) *pseud.* C. **58**. c. **11**.

Werner.

—— Werner, a tragedy. pp. viii. 188. *John Murray: London*, 1823. 8°. **11659.c.35.(3.)**

—— [Another copy.] **Ashley 2705.**

BYRON (GEORGE GORDON NOEL) *Baron Byron.* [SINGLE WORKS.]

—— [Another copy.] **T. 1065. (6.)**
In this copy the words "The End" and the printer's imprint have been added on p. 188.

—— [Another copy.] **Ashley 2706.**

—— [Another edition.] With the stage business, *etc.* pp. 75. *M. Douglas: New York,* 1848. 8°. **11781.** gg. **19.** (1.)

—— Werner . . . Printed from the acting copy, *etc.* pp. 77. *G. H. Davidson: London,* [1850?] 12°. [*Cumberland's British Theatre.* vol. 46. no. 380.] **642.** a. **25.**

—— [Another edition.] 1865. *See* BRITISH DRAMA. The British Drama. Illustrated. vol. 3. 1864, *etc.* 8°. **11770.** bbb. **11.** (9.)

—— [Another edition.] pp. 77. *London,* [1866.] 12°. [*Lacy's Acting Edition of Plays.* vol. 70. no. 8.] **2304.** f. **15.** (8.)

—— [Another edition.] *London,* [1874?] 8°. [*Dicks' Standard Plays.* no. 3.] **11770.** bbb. **4.**
A reissue of the edition of 1865.

—— [Another issue.] Werner, *etc.* [*London,* 1874?] 8°. **11784.** aa. **48.** (13.)
Part of "Dicks' British Drama."

—— [Another edition.] pp. 256. *G. Routledge & Sons: London,* 1887. 16°. **12208.** aaaa. **5.**

Appendix.

—— *See* STOEHSEL (C.) Lord Byron's Trauerspiel "Werner" und seine Quelle, *etc.* 1891. 8°. [*Erlanger Beiträge zur englischen Philologie.* Hft. 11.] **12984.** g. **16.**

EXTRACTS.

—— Byron. With four . . . plates & twenty . . . illustrations [including portraits]. pp. 79. *William Collins: London,* 1941. 8°. [*The English Poets in Pictures.*] **W.P.10933/3.(2.)**

—— The Byron Birthday Book. Compiled and edited by James Burrows. *S. Tinsley & Co.: London,* 1879 [1878]. 16°. **11601.** bb. **26.**

—— Second thousand. *David Bogue: London,* [1880.] 16°. **11601.** bb. **37.**

—— Byroniana. The opinions of Lord Byron on men, manners and things: with the parish clerk's album kept at his burial place, Hucknall Torkard. [The editor's preface signed: J. M. L.] pp. xv. 148. *Hamilton, Adams & Co.: London,* 1834. 16°. **1164.** a. **35.**

Italian.

—— A' miei amici. [Extracts from Childe Harold and The Corsair, and The Tear, translated into Italian verse by P. Isola.] pp. 27. *Novi,* [1870?] 8°. **11646.** ff. **24.** (13.)

WORKS EDITED, TRANSLATED, OR WITH CONTRIBUTIONS BY BYRON.

—— *See* AUGEREAN (Y.) A Grammar, Armenian and English. (Exercises in the Armenian language [comprising an apocryphal Epistle of the Corinthians to St. Paul and his Epistle in reply, both translated by Lord Byron].) 1819. 8°. **2056.** a.

—— —— 1832. 8°. **12903.** aa. **26.**

—— *See* PERIODICAL PUBLICATIONS.—*London.* The Liberal, *etc.* [With contributions by Lord Byron.] 1822, *etc.* 8°. P.P. 5825.

BYRON (GEORGE GORDON NOEL) *Baron Byron.* [WORKS EDITED, TRANSLATED, OR WITH CONTRIBUTIONS BY BYRON.]

—— *See* PERIODICAL PUBLICATIONS.—London.—*The Liberal.* Lord Byron, Leigh Hunt and the "Liberal," *etc.* [Extracts from "The Liberal," including contributions by Byron.] [1925.] 8°. **010856.** g. **3**

WORKS WITH MS. NOTES BY BYRON.

—— *See* CRISSO (A.) *pseud.* Versi. [With the autograph of and a MS. note by Lord Byron.] 1816. 12°. C. **28.** f. **1**

—— *See* VAUCLUSE. Retour de la fontaine de Vaucluse &c. [With an autograph of and a MS. note by Lord Byron.] 1805. 8°. C. **28.** f.

DOUBTFUL OR SUPPOSITITIOUS WORKS.

—— Arnaldo; Gaddo; and other unacknowledged poems by Lord Byron, and some of his contemporaries; collected [or rather, written] by Odoardo Volpi [pseudonym of Edward N. Shannon]. (The Comedy of Dante Alighieri translated by Odoardo Volpi. [Containing only the first 10 Cantos of the "Inferno."]) 2 pt. *W. F. Wakeman: Dublin,* 1836. 8°. **993.** h. **11.** (1, 2
A later edition entitled "Tales, Old and New, with other lesser poems, etc.," is entered under SHANNON (Edward P.)

—— [Another copy.] **993.** h. **12.** (1–2

—— A Farrago Libelli. A poem, chiefly imitated from the first satire of Juvenal. [By Lord Byron?] pp. 24. 1806. 8°. *See* FARRAGO. Ashley **30**

—— In the Matter of the Stowe Scandal. Lord Byron's Defence. [In verse. Signed: Byron. By Henry Savile Clarke.] pp. 14. *London,* 1869. 4°. **11650.** cc. **18.** (5.

—— Lord Byron's Farewell to England; with three other poems, viz. Ode to St. Helena, To my Daughter, on the morning of her birth, and To the Lily of France. [By John Agg.] pp. 31. *J. Johnston: London,* 1816. 8°. **11641.** bbb. **17**

—— [Another copy.] Ashley **2682**

—— Second edition. pp. 31. *J. Johnston: London,* 1816. 8°. **11641.** bbb. **18**

—— Lord Byron's Pilgrimage to the Holy Land. A poem . . . To which is added, The Tempest, a fragment. [By John Agg.] pp. 72. *J. Johnston: London,* 1817. 8°. **11602.** ff. **13.** (2.
The second edition, entitled "A Pilgrimage to the Holy Land," is entered under PALESTINE.

—— Reflections on Shipboard, by Lord Byron. pp. 16. *Printed for the Author: London,* 1816. 8°. **992.** l. 4. (5.

—— The Vampyre; a tale, by the Right Honourable Lord Byron [or rather by J. W. Polidori]. (Extract of a letter from Geneva [by J. Mitford], containing an account of Lord Byron's residence in the island of Mitylene). pp. 84 *Sherwood, Neeley & Jones: London,* 1819. 8°. C. **133.** d. **4**

—— [Another copy, with a different titlepage.] **C.133.d.3.**

—— [Another copy.] **12604.** g. **3**
Imperfect; wanting the half-title.

—— El Vampiro. Novela. Por Lord Byron [or rather by J.W.Polidori]. pp. 112. *Paris,* 1829. 8°. **11646.** cc. 9. (2.

APPENDIX.

BIOGRAPHY AND CRITICISM.

—— *See* ACKERMANN (R.) Lord Byron. Sein Leben, seine Werke, sein Einfluss auf die deutsche Litteratur. 1901. 8°. **10856.** g. **17.**

BYRON (George Gordon Noel) *Baron Byron.* [Appendix.—Biography and Criticism.]

—— *See* Åman-Nilsson (G.) Byron-dramat. Randanteckningar till André Maurois' och Ethel C. Maynes Byronbiografier. 1930. 8°. **10824**. aaa. **26**.

—— *See* Åman-Nilsson (G.) Lord Byron och det sekelgamla förtalet, *etc.* [With reference to Lord Byron's relations with Mrs. Ada Augusta Leigh.] 1915. 8°. **010826**. f. **23**.

—— *See* Åman-Nilsson (G.) Medora Leigh. Ett apokryfiskt blad i lord Byrons historia. 1927. 8°. **010855**. de. **36**.

—— *See* Aston (James) *Poetical Writer*, and Aston (Edward) Pompeii, and other poems. To which is added, a dissertation on Lord Byron. 1828. 16°. **993**. g. **2**.

—— *See* Austin (Alfred) *Poet Laureate.* A Vindication of Lord Byron. 1869. 8°. **C.134.b.7.(4.)**

—— *See* Bagnall (Edward) Lord Byron [a poem], with remarks on his genius and character. 1831. 8°. **T. 1398**. **(10.)**

—— *See* Balslev (C. F.) *Writer on Literature.* Lord Byron. Mennesket og Digteren. 1930. 8°. **10823**. aa. **14**.

—— *See* Barabás (Á.) Goethes Wirkung in der Weltlitteratur. Goethe, Byron und Madách. 1903. 8°. **011840**. k. **78**.

—— *See* Bellamy (Robert L.) Byron the Man. 1924. 8°. **010855**. aaa. **63**.

—— *See* Belloc (Louise S.) Lord Byron. 1824. 8°. **1164**. g. **20**.

—— *See* Benbow (William) A Scourge for the Laureate, in reply to his infamous letter of the 13th of December, 1824, meanly abusive of the deceased Lord Byron, *etc.* [1825?] 12°. **11840**. b. **27**. **(1.)**

—— *See* Beppo. Beppo in London, *etc.* [A satire on Lord Byron.] 1819. 8°. **11601**. g. **27**. **(5.)**

—— *See* Beppo, *a Noble Venetian, pseud.* More News from Venice, *etc.* [A satire on Lord Byron.] 1818. 8°. **1465**. g. **6**. **(1.)**

—— *See* Bernardi (J.) Lord Byron e il generale Angelo Mengaldo. [1866?] 16°. **10631**. a. **25**.

—— *See* Best (John R.) afterwards Beste (J. R. D.) Satires, *etc.* (Infidelity and Catholicism of Lord Byron.) 1831. 12°. **993**. a. **2**.

—— *See* Birkedal (U.) Lord Byrons Liv og Digtning. [With a portrait.] [1917.] 8°. **10855**. f. **32**.

—— *See* Björkman (E.) Lord Byron. 1916. 8°. **10855**. aa. **51**.

—— *See* Blaquiere (Edward) Narrative of a Second Visit to Greece, including facts connected with the last days of Lord Byron, *etc.* 1825. 8°. **790**. h. **17**.

—— *See* Bleibtreu (C.) Byron der Uebermensch, sein Leben und sein Dichten. [1897.] 8°. **10856**. ee. **15**.

—— *See* Bleibtreu (C.) Das Byron-Geheimnis. 1912. 8°. **010826**. ee. **2**.

—— *See* Bluemel (H. M.) Die Unterhaltungen Lord Byron's mit der Gräfin Blessington als ein Beitrag zur Byronbiographie kritisch untersucht, *etc.* 1900. 8°. **10856**. ee. **20**.

BYRON (George Gordon Noel) *Baron Byron.* [Appendix.—Biography and Criticism.]

—— *See* Bolonakes (M. D.) *Λογος ἐπι τῃ ἑκατονταετηριδι του θανατου του Λορδου Βυρωνος, etc.* 1925. 8°. **12301**. r. **16**.

—— *See* Borgese Freschi (M.) L'Appassionata di Byron. Con le lettere inedite fra Lord Byron e la contessa Guiccioli, *etc.* [With portraits.] [1949.] 8°. **10923**. aaa. **51**.

—— *See* Born (S.) Lord Byron. Vortrag, *etc.* 1883. 8°. [*Oeffentliche Vorträge gehalten in der Schweiz.* Bd. 7. Hft. 4.] **12201**. e. **1**.

—— *See* Borst (William A.) Lord Byron's First Pilgrimage. 1948. 8°. Ac. **2692**. ma/3.

—— *See* Boutet de Monvel (R.) La Vie de Lord Byron, *etc.* 1924. 8°. **010855**. aaa. **56**.

—— *See* Brandes (G. M. C.) [*Works.*] Shelley und Lord Byron. Zwei litterarische Charakterbilder. Mit besonderer Berücksichtigung der Frauengestalten in ihrem Leben. 1894. 8°. **011850**. h. **36**.

—— *See* Brandl (Alois) Byron im Kampf mit der englischen Politik, *etc.* 1915. 8°. **012301**. ee. **28/20**.

—— *See* Brecknock (Albert) Byron. A study of the poet in the light of new discoveries. [With portraits.] 1926. 8°. **010855**. cc. **44**.

—— *See* Brecknock (Albert) The Pilgrim Poet, Lord Byron of Newstead, *etc.* 1911. 8°. **010854**. h. **14**.

—— *See* Briscoe (Walter A.) Byron, the Poet . . . Illustrated by portraits, *etc.* 1924. 8°. **011850**. bb. **73**.

—— *See* Brouzas (Christopher G.) Byron's Maid of Athens, *etc.* 1949. 8°. [*West Virginia University. Philological Papers.* vol. 7.] Ac. **2691**. tf.

—— *See* Brouzas (Christopher G.) Teresa Macri, the "Maid of Athens," 1797–1875. [1947.] 8°. **10796**. dd. **13**.

—— *See* Brydges (*Sir* Samuel E.) *Bart.* An Impartial Portrait of Lord Byron as a Poet and a Man, *etc.* 1825. 12°. **1088**. h. **20**. **(1.)**

—— *See* Brydges (*Sir* Samuel E.) *Bart.* Letters on the Character and Poetical Genius of Lord Byron. 1824. 8°. **1087**. g. **20**.

—— *See* Bull (John) *pseud.* [i.e. John Gibson Lockhart.] John Bull's Letter to Lord Byron, *etc.* [With a portrait.] 1947. 8°. **11868**. c. **15**.

—— *See* Bull (John) *pseud.* [i.e. John Gibson Lockhart.] Letter to the Right Hon. Lord Byron. By John Bull. 1821. 8°. C. **58**. e. **2**.

—— *See* Butler (Eliza M.) Goethe and Byron. [1950.] 8°. **Ac.2673.b/3.**

—— *See* Byron (Anne I. N.) *Baroness Wentworth.* Life of Lady Byron . . . To which is appended a vindication of Lord Byron, *etc.* [1870?] 8°. **10803**. g. **18**. **(4.)**

—— *See* Byron (Anne I. N.) *Baroness Wentworth.* Remarks occasioned by Mr. Moore's Notices of Lord Byron's Life. 1830. 8°. **10855**. c. **20**. **(2.)**

—— *See* Calcaño (J.) Tres Poetas pesimistas del siglo xix. (Lord Byron. Shelley. Leopardi.) Estudio crítico. 1907. 8°. **11840**. t. **21**.

—— *See* Calvert (William J.) Byron, Romantic Paradox. 1935. 8°. **010821**. f. **21**.

BYRON (George Gordon Noel) *Baron Byron.* [Appendix. —Biography and Criticism.]

—— *See* Cantoni (F.) Byron e la Guiccioli a Bologna. 1927. fol. **10855**. h. **33**.

—— *See* Cantoni (F.) La Prima dimora di Lord Byron a Bologna. 1926. fol. **10855**. h. **34**.

—— *See* Cantù (C.) Lord Byron and his Works: a biography and essay, *etc.* [1883.] 8°. **10854**. aaa. **11**.

—— *See* Castelain (M.) Byron. [With a portrait.] 1931. 8°. **010855**. de. **57**.

—— *See* Castelar y Ripoll (E.) *President of the First Spanish Republic.* Vida de Lord Byron. 1873. 8°. **10855**. b. **22**.

—— *See* Castelar y Ripoll (E.) *President of the First Spanish Republic.* Life of Lord Byron and other sketches, *etc.* 1875. 8°. **10856**. cc. **1**.

—— *See* Castelar y Ripoll (E.) *President of the First Spanish Republic.* Lord Byron élete, *etc.* [1876.] 8°. [*Magyar Könyvesház.* foly. 2.] **739**. bb. **16**.

—— *See* Cato, *pseud.* Cato to Lord Byron on the Immorality of his Writings, *etc.* 1824. 8°. **11861**. b. **50**.

—— *See* Cato, *pseud.* [i.e. George Burges.] Cato to Lord Byron on the Immorality of his Writings. 1824. 8°. **11826**. dd. **33**. (**1**.)

—— *See* Chambers (Raymond W.) Ruskin—and others—on Byron. 1925. 8°. [*English Association. Pamphlet.* no. 62.] Ac. **2664**.

—— *See* Chew (Samuel C.) Byron in England: his fame, *etc.* [With a bibliography.] 1924. 8°. **011850**. bb. **72**.

—— *See* Chew (Samuel C.) The Dramas of Lord Byron. A critical study. 1915. 8°. W.P. **1449/8**.

—— *See* Chew (Samuel C.) The Relation of Lord Byron to the Drama of the Romantic Period, *etc.* 1914. 8°. **11826**. f. **45**.

—— *See* Chiarini (G.) Studi e ritratti letterari . . . Byron, *etc.* 1900. 8°. **11853**. aaa. **21**.

—— *See* Churchman (Philip H.) Byron and Espronceda, *etc.* 1909. 8°. **11840**. tt. **14**.

—— *See* Churchman (Philip H.) Lord Byron's Experiences in the Spanish Peninsula in 1809, *etc.* [1909.] 8°. **10803**. f. **10**. (**3**.)

—— *See* Clark (Cumberland) Dickens & Democracy, and other studies. (Byron's Life and Works.) 1930. 8°. **010855**. de. **30**.

—— *See* Clarke (Isabel C.) Shelley and Byron, *etc.* [With portraits.] 1934. 8°. **010825**. h. **13**.

—— *See* Claus (W.) Byron und die Frauen, *etc.* 1862. 8°. **10854**. d. **9**. (**1**.)

—— *See* Clinton (George) Memoirs of the Life and Writings of Lord Byron. [With copious extracts from his works.] 1825. 8°. **1164**. g. **26**.

—— *See* Cobos (F. J.) La Muerte de Lord Byron. 1899. 8°. **10600**. g. **1**. (**2**.)

—— *See* Cogniard (H.) and Burat de Gurgy (E.) Byron à l'école d'Harrow, *etc.* 1834. 24°. G. **19521**.

—— *See* Collas (A.) The Authors of England. A series of medallion portraits . . . With illustrative notices, *etc.* (Lord Byron.) 1838. 4°. **821**. eee. **20**.

—— *See* Collas (A.) The Authors of England. A series medallion portraits, *etc.* (Lord Byron.) 1861. 4°. **10855**. h.

—— *See* Crawshay (Rose M.) Byron—Shelley—Keats Memoriam Endowed Yearly Prizes, *etc.* (Essay on Byro "Fare Thee Well," "A Sketch" and "Lines on hear Lady Byron was Ill.") [1893.] 8°. **011824**. e. **63**.

—— *See* Dallas (Robert C.) Recollections of the Life of Lo Byron, from the year 1808 to the end of 1814 . . . which is prefixed an account of the circumstances leadi to the suppression of Lord Byron's correspondence wi the author, and his letters to his mother, lately announc for publication. 1824. 8°. **1164**. g.

—— *See* Dallois (Joseph) Études morales et littéraires propos de Lord Byron, *etc.* 1890. 12°. **011824**. de.

—— *See* Danube. Die Donau-Reise . . . Nebst . . . einig Nachrichten über den Aufenthalt des Lord Byron Griechenland. (Lord Byron und das Mädchen v Athen.) 1839. 12°. **10106**. bb.

—— *See* De Beer (Esmond S.) and Seton (W.) Byronia The archives of the London Greek Committee, *etc.* [1926.] 8°. **010855**. i.

—— *See* Dick (William) *M.A. Lond.* Byron & his Poet 1913. 8°. **11863.a.11/1**

—— *See* Doerken (H.) Lord Byron's Subjektivismus seinem Verhalten zur Geschichte, untersucht an sein Verserzählungen. 1929. 8°. W.P. **7720/**

—— *See* Donner (J. O. E.) Lord Byrons Weltanschauu 1897. 4°. [*Acta Societatis Scientiarum Fennicae.* tom. no. 4.] Ac. **1094**,

—— *See* Draper (Frederick W. M.) The Rise and Fall of t French Romantic Drama, with special reference to t influence of Shakespeare, Scott, and Byron. 1923. 8°. **011795**. c. **4**

—— *See* Drinkwater (John) *Poet.* The Pilgrim of Eternit Byron—a conflict. 1925. 8°. **010856**. b.

—— *See* Du Bos (C.) Byron, et le besoin de la fatalité. 1929. 8°. **10824**. df.

—— *See* Du Bos (C.) Byron and the Need of Fatality, e [With a portrait.] 1932. 8°. **10823**. e.

—— *See* Duff (John W.) Byron and Aberdeen. 1902. 4°. **10604**. f. **18**. (

—— *See* Dyboski (R.) Byron. Studium. 1927. 8°. **11878.f.2**

—— *See* Eberty (F.) Lord Byron. Eine Biographie. 1862. 8°. **10854**. b. **2**

—— *See* Edgcumbe (Richard J. F.) Byron: the last phas 1909. 8°. **010854**. ee. **1**

—— *See* Eggert (G.) Lord Byron und Napoleon. 1933. 8 **12203**. ff. **1/18**

—— *See* Eichler (A.) John Hookham Frere . . . Se Einfluss auf Lord Byron. 1905. 8°. **12984**. h. **1/2**

—— *See* Eimer (M.) Byron und der Kosmos. Ein Beitr zur Weltanschauung des Dichters, *etc.* 1912. 8°. **12981**. p. **1/3**

BYRON (George Gordon Noel) *Baron Byron.* [Appendix. —Biography and Criticism.]

—— *See* Eimer (M.) Die persönlichen Beziehungen zwischen Byron und den Shelleys, *etc.* 1910. 8°. **12981**. p. **1/32**.

—— *See* Eisser (M.) Lord Byron als Kritiker, *etc.* 1932. 8°. **11878.k.19.**

—— *See* Eliades (P. D.) *'Ο Βυρων και ἡ 'Ελλας.* 1949. 8°. **10862**. d. **30**.

—— *See* Elliott (Ebenezer) Love, a poem . . . To which is added, The Giaour, a satirical poem. (Addressed to Lord Byron.) 1823. 8°. **11644**. h. **20**.

—— *See* Elton (Oliver) The Present Value of Byron, *etc.* [1925.] 8°. Ashley **5470**.

—— *See* Elze (C. F.) Lord Byron. 1870. 8°. **10855**. ee. 9.

—— —— 1881. 8°. **10854**. ee. 8.

—— —— 1886. 8°. **10854**. f. 17.

—— *See* Elze (C. F.) Lord Byron: a biography, *etc.* 1872. 8°. **2408**. e. 5.

—— *See* Engel (C. E.) Byron et Shelley en Suisse et en Savoie, mai–octobre 1816, *etc.* 1930. 8°. **10823**. k. **1**.

—— *See* Erlangen.—*Academia Fridericiana.—Englisches Seminar.* Byroniana und anderes aus dem Englischen Seminar in Erlangen, *etc.* [Including a "Katalog der Byron-Abteilung des Englischen Seminars."] 1912. 8°. **011852**. dd. **40**. (4.)

—— *See* Estève (E.) Byron et le romantisme français. Essai sur la fortune et l'influence de l'œuvre de Byron en France de 1812 à 1850. 1907. 8°. **11851**. tt. **10**.

—— *See* Farinelli (A.) Byron e il byronismo, *etc.* 1924. 8°. **011840**. a. **28**.

—— *See* Ferriman (Z. D.) Some English Philhellenes. (8. Lord Byron.) 1917, *etc.* 8°. **10804.bbb.20/8.**

—— *See* Fletcher (William) *Valet to Lord Byron.* Lord Byron's Illness and Death, *etc.* 1920. 4°. **10854**. cc. 25.

—— *See* Flower (Robin E. W.) Byron and Ossian, *etc.* 1928. 8°. **Ac.2673.b/3.**

—— *See* Foà (G.) Lord Byron . . . Studio critico-storico. 1935. 8°. **010822**. de. 38.

—— *See* Fox (*Sir* John C.) The Byron Mystery. 1924. 8°. **010856**. f. 24.

—— *See* Fuess (Claude M.) Lord Byron as a Satirist in Verse. 1912. 8°. Ac. **2688/16**. (**1**.)

—— *See* Fuhrmann (L.) Die Belesenheit des jungen Byron, *etc.* 1903. 8°. **10827**. bb. 35.

—— *See* Gabrielson (A.) Rime as a Criterion of the Pronunciation of Spenser . . . Byron, *etc.* 1909. 8°. **11840**. t. 16.

—— *See* Galt (John) *Novelist.* The Life of Lord Byron. 1830. 8°. **1157**. b. 24.

—— —— 1830. 8°. **10855**. aaa. **11**.

—— —— 1845. 12°. **12205**. b. 90.

—— —— [1908.] 8°. **12203**. r. 8/20.

BYRON (George Gordon Noel) *Baron Byron.* [Appendix. —Biography and Criticism.]

—— *See* Gamba (P.) *Count.* A Narrative of Lord Byron's Last Journey to Greece, *etc.* 1825. 8°. **280**. h. **24**.

—— —— 1825. 8°. **10854**. aaa. **22**.

—— *See* Gardiner (Marguerite) *Countess of Blessington.* Conversations of Lord Byron with the Countess of Blessington. 1834. 8°. **1164**. g. **29**.

—— *See* Gardiner (Marguerite) *Countess of Blessington.* Conversations of Lord Byron with the Countess of Blessington, *etc.* [With a portrait.] 1850. 8°. **10859**. pp. **3**.

—— *See* Gardiner (Marguerite) *Countess of Blessington.* [A Journal of the Conversations of Lord Byron with the Countess of Blessington.] Conversations de Lord Byron avec la comtesse de Blessington, *etc.* 1833. 8°. **10863**. ff. **46**.

—— *See* Gardiner (Marguerite) *Countess of Blessington.* A Journal of the Conversations of Lord Byron with the Countess of Blessington, *etc.* 1893. 8°. **10854**. d. **11**.

—— *See* Garrod (Heathcote W.) Byron . . . A lecture, *etc.* 1924. 8°. **011852**. h. **87**.

—— *See* Gerard (William) Byron re-studied in his Dramas, *etc.* 1886. 8°. **11850**. aaa. **12**.

—— *See* Giardini (G.) Il Pessimismo di Giorgio Byron. 1914. 8°. **11825**. c. 49.

—— *See* Gillardon (H.) Shelley's Einwirkung auf Byron. 1898. 8°. **011852**. c. 7. (1.)

—— *See* Gillington, afterwards Byron (May C.) A Day with Lord Byron. [1910.] 8°. **10600**. bbb. 2/2.

—— *See* Goode (Clement T.) Byron as Critic. 1923. 8°. **011850**. d. **31**.

—— *See* Gordon (Armistead C.) Allegra. The story of Byron and Miss Clairmont, *etc.* 1927. 8°. **010855**. e. **11**.

—— *See* Gordon (*Sir* Cosmo) Life and Genius of Lord Byron. 1824. 8°. T. **1091**. (**11**.)

—— —— 1824. 8°. [*The Pamphleteer.* vol. 24.] P.P. **3557**. w.

—— *See* Graham (William) *Editor of "The Twentieth Century."* Last Links with Byron, *etc.* 1898. 8°. **10856**. bbb. **16**.

—— *See* Gray (Austin K.) Teresa. The story of Byron's last mistress [i.e. Teresa, Countess Guiccioli], *etc.* [With portraits.] 1948. 8°. **010632**. bb. **29**.

—— *See* Gray (Duncan), The Life and Work of Lord Byron. [With a portrait.] 1945. 8°. *F. L. A.* W.P. **1035**/4.

—— *See* Green (Andrew J.) Did Byron write the poem To Lady Caroline Lamb? [1928.] 8°. Ashley **2771***.

—— *See* Gribble (Francis H.) The Love Affairs of Lord Byron. 1910. 8°. **010827**. ee. 31.

—— *See* Grieg (J. N. B.) De Unge døde . . . Keats . . . Byron, *etc.* [With a portrait.] 1932. 8°. **11855**. d. **12**.

—— *See* Grierson (*Sir* Herbert J. C.) Lord Byron: Arnold and Swinburne, *etc.* [1921.] 8°. [*Warton Lecture on English Poetry.* no. 11.] Ac. **1186/7**.

—— *See* Guiccioli (T.) *Countess,* afterwards Rouillé de Boissy (T. de) *Marchioness.* Lord Byron jugé par les témoins de sa vie. My Recollections of Lord Byron, *etc.* 1869. 8°. **10855**. ee. **10**.

—— —— 1869. 8°. **2408**. c. 5.

—— *See* Hamann (A.) Sketches of English Literature. (Hft. 5. A Short Sketch of the Life and Works of Byron.) 1910. 8°. **011824. cc. 71.**

—— *See* Hamann (A.) A Short Sketch of the Life and Works of Byron, *etc.* 1895. 4°. **11825. r. 7. (6.)**

—— *See* Hartmann (Heinrich) *Dr., of Tangerhütte.* Lord Byrons Stellung zu den Klassizisten seiner Zeit: Rogers, Campbell, Gifford, Crabbe und Moore, *etc.* 1932. 8°. **11855. aaa. 15.**

—— *See* Hawkes (Charles P.) Authors-at-Arms. The soldiering of six great writers (Lord Byron [and others]), *etc.* 1934. 8°. **010825. h. 19.**

—— *See* Henson (Herbert H.) successively *Bishop of Hereford* and *of Durham.* Byron. The Rede lecture for 1924. 1924. 8°. **010855. aaa. 59.**

—— *See* Hobhouse (John C.) *Baron Broughton.* Contemporary Account of the Separation of Lord and Lady Byron; also of the destruction of Lord Byron's memoirs. 1870. 8°. Ashley **2742.**

—— *See* Hohenhausen (E. von) Rousseau, Göthe, Byron, ein kritisch-literarischer Umriss, *etc.* 1847. 8°. **11824. bb. 49. (1.)**

—— *See* Holzhausen (P.) Bonaparte, Byron und die Briten, *etc.* 1904. 8°. **10600. ff. 22.**

—— *See* Hunt (James H. L.) Lord Byron and Some of His Contemporaries, *etc.* 1828. 8°. **841. m. 15.**

—— —— 1828. 8°. **10854. ee. 16.**

—— —— 1828. 8°. **2408. a. 4.**

—— *See* Irving (Washington) An Unwritten Drama of Lord Byron, *etc.* 1925. 8°. **011852. dd. 24.**

—— *See* James (David G.) Byron and Shelley. [1951.] 8°. **Ac.2673.b/3.**

—— *See* Jeaffreson (John C.) The Real Lord Byron. New views of the poet's life. 1883. 8°. **10856. d. 17.**

—— *See* Jónsson (S.) Byron, 1788–1824–1924, *etc.* [A review of "Byron in England: his fame and after-fame," by S. C. Chew.] 1924. 12°. **10824. a. 28.**

—— *See* Jowett (Henry) Byron. [1884.] 8°. **10803. de. 7. (4.)**

—— *See* Kaklamanos (D.) The Centenary of Byron's Death in England: two addresses, *etc.* 1924. 16°. **11825. de. 40.**

—— *See* Kennedy (James) *M.D., of H.M. Medical Staff.* Conversations on Religion with Lord Byron and others, *etc.* 1830. 8°. **1164. g. 28.**

—— *See* Kennedy (James) *M.D., of H.M. Medical Staff.* Conversations on Religion with Lord Byron and Others, *etc.* 1830. 12°. **4381. ee. 38.**

—— *See* Knight (George W.) Byron's Dramatic Prose. [1953.] 8°. [*Byron Foundation Lecture.* 1953.] Ac. **2673.** b/**3.**

—— *See* Knight (George W.) Lord Byron, *etc.* [A study. With a portrait.] 1952. 8°. **10863. bb. 47.**

—— *See* Knott (John) *A.M., M.D.* (*Univ. Dub.*) The Last Illness of Lord Byron, *etc.* 1912. 8°. Ashley **5464.**

—— *See* Koeppel (E.) Byron . . . Fordította Esty Jánosné, *etc.* 1913. 8°. Ac. **825/197.**

—— *See* Kraeger (H.) Der Byronsche Heldentypus. 1898. 8°. **11854. r. 1**

—— *See* Krug (W. G.) Lord Byron als dichterische Gest in England, Frankreich, Deutschland und Amerika, *etc.* 1932. 8°. **11878.c.3**

—— *See* La Hire (Jean de) *pseud.* Les Voyages passion A Venise, dans l'ombre de Byron. [1915.] 8°. **10130. df.**

—— *See* Lake (J. W.) *Author of the Life of Byron.* The I of Lord Byron. 1826. 16°. **1164. a.**

—— —— 1827. 16°. **1164. a.**

—— *See* Lange (H.) Der dämonische Byron, *etc.* 1935. **11859. b.**

—— *See* Layman. A Layman's Epistle to a certain No man. [Addressed to Lord Byron, with special referenc his "Cain."] 1824. 8°. **11643. bbb. 18.**

—— *See* Le Bourdellès (R.) Giacomo Leopardi. L Byron en Suisse, en Italie et en Grèce, *etc.* 1901. 12° **011853. g.**

—— *See* Leigh (Elizabeth M.) Medora Leigh, a history an autobiography . . . With . . . a commentary on charges brought by Mrs. Beecher Stowe. 1869. 8°. **10855. bb.**

—— *See* Leonard (William E.) Byron and Byronism America. 1905. 8°. **11853. t**

—— *See* Lewes (Louis) Lord Byron. 1897. 8°. **12249. m.**

—— *See* Light. Light or Darkness? A poem. With marks on Lord Byron's detractors. 1870. 8°. **11650. e.**

—— *See* Lines. Lines addressed to a Noble Lord [i.e. I Byron], *etc.* 1815. 8°. **11645. bbb.**

—— *See* Loforte-Randi (A.) Nelle letterature strani (ser. 5. W. Shakespeare—Lord Byron, *etc.*) 1899, *etc.* **11840.**

—— *See* Lorenzo y D'Ayot (M.) Shakespeare, Lord By y Chateaubriand, como Modelos de la Juventud Liter *etc.* 1886. 8°. **11826. h. 42.**

—— *See* Lovell (Ernest J.) His Very Self and V Collected conversations of Lord Byron, *etc.* 1954. 8 **12275.**

—— *See* Lueder (A.) Lord Byron's Urteile über It und seine Bewohner, ihre Sprache, Litteratur und Ku 1893. 4°. [*Jahresbericht der Drei-König-Schule* . . *Wiener-Neustadt* . . . 1893.] **11840. tt.**

—— *See* Lumbroso (A. E.) *Baron.* Il Generale Menga Lord Byron e l'ode On the Star of the Legion of Ho Con un saggio di bibliografia byroniana. 1903. fol. **1870. b.**

—— *See* Luther (A.) Byron. Heine. Leopardi. Drei träge. 1904. 8°. **11826. o.**

—— [For editions of Macaulay's essay on "Moore's Li Lord Byron":] *See* Macaulay (Thomas B.) *B Macaulay.* [*Essays.*]

—— *See* Mackay (George E.) Lord Byron at the Arme Convent. 1876. 8°. **10855. aa**

BYRON (George Gordon Noel) *Baron Byron*. [Appendix. —Biography and Criticism.]

—— *See* Maramotti (G.) Giorgio Byron e il poeta reggiano Enrico Casali. 1931. 8°. **10634**. a. **38**.

—— *See* Marjarum (Edward W.) Byron as Skeptic and Believer. 1938. 8°. [*Princeton Studies in English*. no. 16.] Ac. **1833/5**.

—— *See* Martin (Leonard C.) Byron's Lyrics. [1948.] 8°. **11867**. h. **6**.

—— *See* Mason (Edward T.) Personal Traits of British Authors. (vol. 1. Byron, Shelley, *etc.*) 1885. 8°. **10854**. bbb. **22**.

—— *See* Maurois (A.) *K.B.E.* Byron. 1930. 8°. **12237**. ppp. **5/7, 8**.

—— *See* Maurois (A.) *K.B.E.* Byron . . . Translated, *etc.* [With portraits.] 1930. 8°. **10824**. b. **15**.

—— *See* Maychrzak (F.) Lord Byron als Uebersetzer, *etc.* 1895. 8°. **011850**. k. **17**. (**6**.)

—— —— 1896. 8°. **11852**. e. **33**.

—— *See* Mayne (Ethel C.) Byron, *etc.* [With portraits.] 1912. 8°. **010827**. k. **19**.

—— —— 1924. 8°. **010856**. h. **37**.

—— *See* Medwin (T.) Conversations of Lord Byron, *etc.* 1824. 8°. **10859**. pp. **2**.

—— *See* Medwin (Thomas) Journal of the Conversations of Lord Byron: noted during a residence with his Lordship at Pisa, in the years 1821 and 1822. 1824. 4°. **841**. m. **14**.

—— —— 1824. 8°. **10856**. ee. **11**.

—— —— 1824. 12°. **10856**. de. **2**.

—— —— 1824. 8°. **10856**. de. **7**.

—— —— 1832. 8°. **1157**. b. **23**.

—— *See* Medwin (Thomas) Les Conversations de Lord Byron, *etc.* 1824. 12°. **11612**. a. **13**.

—— *See* Medwin (Thomas) Gespräche mit Lord Byron, *etc.* 1824. 8°. **10855**. bb. **20**.

—— *See* Medwin (Thomas) Exposure of the Mis-Statements contained in Captain Medwin's pretended "Conversations of Lord Byron." 1824. 8°. Ashley **2730**.

—— *See* Megyery (I.) Lord Byron. Életrajz-tanulmány. 1889. 8°. **10854**. bbb. **31**.

—— *See* Melchior (F.) Heinrich Heines Verhältnis zu Lord Byron. 1903. 8°. **11852**. a. **27**.

—— *See* Meneghetti (N.) Lord Byron a Venezia. [1910.] 8°. **10827**. ee. **27**.

—— *See* Milbanke (Ralph G. N.) *Earl of Lovelace*. Astarte. A fragment of truth concerning George Gordon Byron, sixth Lord Byron, *etc.* 1905. 4°. **10855**. f. **22**.

—— —— 1921. 8°. **010855**. bb. **16**.

—— *See* Miller (Barnette) Leigh Hunt's Relations with Byron, *etc.* 1910. 8°. Ac. **2688/13**. (**16**.)

—— *See* Miller (Joaquin) Trelawny with Shelley and Byron. 1922. 8°. **010856**. dd. **24**.

—— *See* Millingen (Julius) Memoirs of the Affairs of Greece . . . With various anecdotes relating to Lord Byron, and an account of his last illness and death. 1831. 8°. **1053**. g. **12**.

BYRON (George Gordon Noel) *Baron Byron*. [Appendix. —Biography and Criticism.]

—— *See* Mitford (John) *Journalist*. The Private Life of Lord Byron, *etc.* [1836?] 8°. **1452**. c. **28**.

—— *See* Mondot (A.) Histoire de la vie et des écrits de Lord Byron, *etc.* 1860. 12°. **10826**. bb. **15**.

—— *See* Moore (Joseph S.) Byron: his biographers and critics, *etc.* 1869. 8°. **10601**. cc. **30**. (**1**.)

—— *See* Moorman (Frederic W.) Byron. 1915. 8°. [*Cambridge History of English Literature*. vol. 12.] **11870.g.1.**

—— *See* Morvay (G.) Byron Magyarországon, *etc.* [With a bibliography.] 1913. 8°. [*Koeppel* (*E.*) *Byron*.] Ac. **825/197**.

—— *See* Muoni (G.) La Fama del Byron e il Byronismo in Italia. 1903. 8°. **011853**. g. **59**. (**4**.)

—— *See* Muoni (G.) La Leggenda del Byron in Italia. 1907. 8°. **10856**. df. **26**.

—— *See* Muoni (G.) Poesia notturna preromantica, *etc.* (La leggenda del Byron in Francia. [A review of Edmond Estève's "Byron et le romantisme français."]) 1908. 8°. **11850**. bb. **29**. (**2**.)

—— *See* Murray (John) *Publisher, Albemarle Street, the Elder*. Notes on Captain Medwin's Conversations of Lord Byron. [1824.] 8°. **841**. g. **27**.

—— *See* Murray (*Sir* John) *K.C.V.O., the Elder*. Lord Byron and his Detractors. (Astarte. Lord Byron and Lord Lovelace. By John Murray.—Lord Lovelace on the separation of Lord and Lady Byron. By R. E. Prothero.) 1906. 4°. C. **101**. e. **20**.

—— *See* Newstead, *Notts.*—*Newstead Abbey*. Newstead Abbey: its present owner, with reminiscences of Lord Byron. [1857.] 8°. **10351**. dd. **9/5**.

—— *See* Nichol (John) *Professor of English Literature in the University of Glasgow*. Byron. 1880. 8°. **2326**. b. **8**.

—— *See* Nicolini (G.) Vita di Giorgio Lord Byron. 1835. 16°. **1164**. f. **8**.

—— *See* Nicolson (*Hon.* Harold G.) Byron. The last journey, *etc.* 1924. 8°. **010856**. dd. **22**.

—— *See* Nicolson (*Hon. Sir* Harold G.) *K.C.V.O.* Byron. The last journey, *etc.* 1940. 8°. **2407**. bb. **17**.

—— *See* Nicolson (*Hon. Sir* Harold G.) *K.C.V.O.* Byron. The last journey, *etc.* 1948. 8°. **10862**. b. **11**.

—— *See* Nicolson (*Hon. Sir* Harold G.) *K.C.V.O.* The Poetry of Byron. 1943. 8°. [*English Association. Presidential Address*, 1943.] Ac. **2664/13**.

—— *See* Noel (*Hon.* Roden B. W.) Life of Lord Byron. [With a bibliography by J. P. Anderson.] 1890. 8°. **10601**. dd. **8**.

—— *See* Olguin (F. J. de) El Libro de Andres Maurois sobre Lord "Byron." Rectificación a sus conceptos sobre John Edward Trelawny. 1930. 8°. **10823**. d. **2**.

—— *See* Oxonian. The Radical Triumvirate; or Infidel Paine, Lord Byron, and Surgeon Lawrence, colleaguing with the patriotic Radicals to emancipate mankind from all laws human and divine, *etc.* 1820. 8°. **8135**. ccc. **30**. (**5**.)

—— *See* Parry (William) *Major of Lord Byron's Brigade*. The Last Days of Lord Byron; with his Lordship's opinions on various subjects, *etc.* 1825. 8°. **1164**. g. **25**.

—— *See* PASTON (George) *pseud.*, and QUENNELL (P. C.) "To Lord Byron." Feminine profiles, based upon unpublished letters, *etc.* [With portraits.] 1939. 8°. **10922.** c. 9.

—— *See* PICHOT (A.) Essai sur la vie, le caractère, et le génie de Lord Byron. 1830. 12°. **10855.** a. **28.**

—— *See* POLIDORI (John W.) The Diary of Dr. John William Polidori, 1816, relating to Byron, *etc.* 1911. 8°. **010854.** df. **47.**

—— *See* POPMA (T.) *Dr.* Byron en het byronisme in de Nederlandsche letterkunde. 1928. 8°. **11824.** t. **26.**

—— *See* PORTA (A.) Byronismo italiano. 1923. 8°. **11824.** tt. **4.**

—— *See* PRATT (Willis W.) Byron at Southwell. The making of a poet. With new poems and letters from the rare books collections of the University of Texas. [With a portrait.] 1948. 8°. W.P. **11315/1.**

—— *See* PRATT (Willis W.) Lord Byron and his Circle. A calendar of manuscripts in the University of Texas Library, *etc.* 1947. 8°. **11869.** i. **16.**

—— *See* PRAZ (M.) La Fortuna di Byron in Inghilterra. [With portraits.] 1925. 8°. **010856.** aa. **18.**

—— *See* PRENTIS (Stephen) An Apology for Lord Byron, *etc.* [In verse.] 1836. 8°. **993.** l. **33.**

—— *See* P . . . . T (A.) Essai sur le génie et le caractère de Lord Byron, *etc.* 1824. 12°. **11612.** a. **12.** (**1.**)

—— *See* PUGHE (F. H.) Studien über Byron, *etc.* 1902. 8°. **12981.** p. **1/8.**

—— *See* PUJALS (E.) Espronceda y Lord Byron. [With portraits.] 1951. 8°. [*Anejos de Cuadernos de literatura.* no. 7.] Ac. **132/16.** (**3.**)

—— *See* QUENNELL (Peter C.) Byron. 1934. 8°. W.P. **6397/28.**

—— *See* QUENNELL (Peter C.) Byron. The years of fame. [With portraits.] 1935. 8°. **010822.** e. **16.**

—— *See* QUENNELL (Peter C.) Byron. The years of fame. 1950. 8°. W.P. **14536/4.**

—— *See* QUENNELL (Peter C.) Byron: the years of fame. 1954. 8°. **12208.** a. **1/982.**

—— *See* QUENNELL (Peter C.) Byron in Italy. [With portraits.] 1941. 8°. **10859.** s. **17.**

—— *See* QUENNELL (Peter C.) Byron in Italy. 1951. 8°. W.P. **14536/8.**

—— *See* QUENNELL (Peter C.) Byron in Italy. 1955. 8°. **12208.** a. **1/1057.**

—— *See* RABBE (F.) Les Maîtresses authentiques de Lord Byron. 1890. 18°. **10854.** aaa. **36.**

—— *See* RAINERI (L.) Le Vite di Dante Alighieri . . . di Giorgio Lord Byron, *etc.* 1860. 8°. **10630.** cc. **11.**

—— *See* RAVA (L.) Lord Byron e P. B. Shelley a Ravenna, e Teresa Guiccioli Gamba, *etc.* 1929. 8°. **10824.** aaa. **19.**

—— *See* RAYMOND (Dora N.) The Political Career of Lord Byron. [1925.] 8°. **010856.** b. **15.**

—— *See* READ (Sir Herbert E.) Byron. [With a portrait.] 1951. 8°. W.P. **9502/8.**

—— *See* REINSBERG DUERINGSFELD (I. von) *Baro* Byron's Frauen. 1845. 8°. **1460.**

—— *See* RENNES (J. J. van) Bowles, Byron and the P Controversy. 1927. 8°. **11824.**

—— *See* RENZULLI (M.) Il Peccatore: Byron, *etc.* [1935.] 8°. **010822.** de

—— *See* REUL (P. de) La Poésie anglaise de Wordswo Keats. (Byron.) 1933. 8°. **11854.** v

—— *See* RICE (Richard A.) Lord Byron's British Re tion, *etc.* 1924. 8°. [*Smith College Studies in M Languages.* vol. 5. no. 2.] Ac. 18

—— *See* RICHTER (H.) Lord Byron, *etc.* 1929. 8°. **10824.** k

—— *See* ROBERTSON (John G.) Goethe and Byron, [With portraits.] 1925. 8°. [*Publications of the En Goethe Society.* New ser. vol. 2.] Ac.

—— *See* RODOCANACHI (E.) Byron, 1788–1824. [Wi portrait.] [1924.] 8°. **010856.**

—— *See* ROTH (G.) La Couronne poétique de Byron. T choisis et publiés par G. Roth. 1924. 8°. **011850.** c

—— *See* SALVO (C. de) *Marquis.* Lord Byron en Italie Grèce; ou aperçu de sa vie et de ses ouvrages, *etc.* 1825. 8°. **1164.** g

—— *See* SCHEIDACKER (Frances) Lord Byron and Chaworth. 1935. 8°. **010822.** de

—— *See* SCHMIDT (Immanuel) Byron im Lichte ur Zeit, *etc.* 1888. 8°. [*Sammlung gemeinverständ wissenschaftlicher Vorträge.* Neue Folge. Hft. 51.] **12249.**

—— *See* SCHMIDT (Otto) *Lehrer an der städt. höh. Mäd schule zu Greifswald.* Rousseau und Byron. Ein Be zur vergleichenden Litteraturgeschichte des Revolut zeitalters. 1890. 8°. **011840.**

—— *See* SCHMIDT (Theodor F. K.) Das Verhalter Romantiker zur Public School—Cowper, Shelley, B *etc.* 1935. 8°. **11857.** aa

—— *See* SCHREMPF (C.) Lord Byron stirbt für Griechen *etc.* [With a portrait.] [1938.] 8°. **2404.**

—— *See* SCHULTS (U.) Het Byronianisme in Nederland [1929.] 8°. **11822.**

—— *See* SCOTT (*Sir* Walter) *Bart.* [*Character of Lord B* Character of Lord Byron. 1824. 8°. [*The Pamph* vol. 24.] P.P. 355

—— *See* SCOTT (*Sir* Walter) *Bart.* [*Appendix.*] A Disc on the Comparative Merits of Scott and Byron, as W of Poetry, *etc.* 1824. 8°. **011840.**

—— *See* SÉCHÉ (A.) and BERTAUT (J.) Lord Byron, *et* [1909.] 8°. **10602.** p

—— *See* SIMHART (M.) Lord Byrons Einfluss au italienische Literatur. 1909. 8°. **11822.** r.

—— *See* SIMMONS (J. W.) *of Philadelphia.* An Inquir the Moral Character of Lord Byron. 1826. 8°. **1164.**

—— *See* SPASOWICZ (W.) Байронизмъ у Пушки Лермонтова. Съ приложеніемъ краткой біо Лорда Байрона составленной Б. Степанцемъ. 191 **011852.** dd.

— *See* SPENDER (Edward H.) Byron and Greece. [With portraits.] 1924. 8°. **010854. i. 37.**

— *See* STEFANOV (K.) Байронъ, поетътъ на свободата и на мировата скърбь, *etc.* 1930. 8°. [*Годишникъ на Софийския Университетъ. Историко-филологически факултетъ.* кн. 26. но. 2.] **Ac. 1137. (1.)**

— *See* STOKOE (Frank W.) German Influence in the English Romantic Period . . . With special reference to Scott . . . and Byron. 1926. 8°. **011853. w. 64.**

— *See* STOWE (Harriet E. B.) Lady Byron vindicated. A history of the Byron controversy, *etc.* 1870. 8°. **10855. aaa. 18.**

— *See* STOWE (Harriet E. B.) The Stowe-Byron Controversy: a complete résumé of all that has been written and said upon the subject . . . Together with an impartial review of the merits of the case, *etc.* [1869.] 8°. **010854. de. 22.**

— *See* STRAUMANN (H.) Byron and Switzerland. [1948.] 8°. **Ac.2673.b/3.**

— *See* STYLES (John) *D.D.* Lord Byron's Works viewed in connexion with Christianity . . . a sermon, *etc.* 1824. 8°. **T. 1040. (1.)**

— *See* SWINBURNE (Algernon C.) Wordsworth and Byron. [1884.] 8°. **Ashley 5142.**

— *See* SYMON (James D.) Byron in Perspective. 1924. 8°. **010856. b. 7.**

— *See* THOMPSON (L. C.) More Magic dethroned. [On the influence of Shelley on Byron and Keats.] [1935.] 8°. **Ashley 4560.**

— *See* THOMSEN (G.) Om Lord Byron, *etc.* 1845. 8°. **10855. c. 17.**

— *See* THOUGHTS. Thoughts on what has been called Sensibility of the Imagination; with practical illustrations from the lives of Petrarch, Sterne and Byron, *etc.* 1839. 12°. **1087. c. 23.**

— *See* TRELAWNY (Edward J.) The Last Days of Shelley and Byron, *etc.* [With a portrait.] 1952. 8°. **10863. bb. 18.**

— *See* TRELAWNY (Edward J.) Recollections of the Last Days of Shelley and Byron. 1858. 8°. **10855. b. 1.**

— —— 1858. 8°. **10856. aa. 15.**

— —— 1878. 8°. **2408. c. 9.**

— —— 1887. 8°. **10855. b. 20.**

— —— [1905.] 8°. **12204. p. 2/23.**

— —— 1906. 8°. **10855. aa. 42.**

— —— 1933. 8°. [*SHELLEY (P. B.) The Life of Percy Bysshe Shelley, etc.*] **20016. f. 26.**

— *See* TRELAWNY (Edward J.) The Relations of Lord Byron and Augusta Leigh. With a comparison of the characters of Byron and Shelley, *etc.* [Letters.] 1920. 4°. **C. 57. i. 19. (4.)**

— *See* TRIKOUPES (S.) Funeral Oration . . . delivered at Mesolongi . . . April 18, 1824, on the death of Lord Byron. 1856. 8°. [*FELTON (Cornelius C.) Selections from Modern Greek Writers, etc.*] **12226. b. 17.**

—— *See* TRIKOUPES (S.) Translation of the Funeral Oration delivered . . . 10th/22nd April, 1824, in honour of . . . Lord Byron. 1836. 8°. **10855. bbb. 23. (2.)**

—— *See* 'UMAR KHAIYĀM. [*English.—Other versions.*] Life's Echoes. By " 'Tis True ! " A possible elucidation of the mysteriously cryptic " tesselations " made mostly by Byron, Fitzgerald, and others from Omar Qayyam's " Ruba'iyat." [1923.] 4°. **C. 43. g. 17.**

—— *See* VESELOVSKY (A. N.) Байронъ, біографическій очеркъ. Съ двумя фототипіями *etc.* 1902. 8°. **10854. h. 19.**

—— —— 1914. 8°. **10854. h. 22.**

—— *See* VINCENT (Eric R. P.) Byron, Hobhouse and Foscolo, *etc.* [With a portrait.] 1949. 8°. **11856. ff. 73.**

—— *See* VULLIAMY (Colwyn E.) Byron. With a view of the kingdom of cant and a dissection of the Byronic ego. [With a portrait.] 1948. 8°. **10861. ee. 18.**

—— *See* WARD (James) *of Nottingham.* Lord Byron's Lameness, *etc.* 1915. 8°. **010826. de. 18.**

—— *See* WEDDIGEN (F. H. O.) Lord Byron's Einfluss auf die europäischen Litteraturen der Neuzeit, *etc.* 1884. 8°. **11825. o. 16. (5.)**

—— *See* WESTENHOLZ (F. von) Ueber Byrons historische Dramen, *etc.* 1890. 8°. **011824. h. 31. (7.)**

—— *See* WHITE (William) *Bookseller.* The Calumnies of the " Athenæum " Journal exposed. Mr. White's letter . . on the subject of the Byron, Shelley, and Keats MSS. 1852. 8°. **011840. h. 56. (1.)**

—— *See* WIESCHKE (E.) Lord Byron. Versuch einer Strukturanalyse, *etc.* 1932. 8°. **11878.e.22.**

—— *See* WILLIAMS (Edward E.) Journal of Edward Ellerker Williams, companion of Shelley and Byron in 1821 and 1822, *etc.* 1902. 8°. **10827. f. 13.**

—— *See* WINDAKIEWICZ (S.) Walter Scott i Lord Byron w odniesieniu do polskiej poezyi romantycznej. 1914. 8°. **011851. aa. 11.**

—— *See* ZACCHETTI (C.) Lord Byron e l'Italia. [1920.] 8°. **011853. a. 76.**

—— *See* ZDZIECHOWSKI (M.) Byron i jego wiek, *etc.* 1894, *etc.* 8°. **011850. k. 28.**

—— *See* ZHIRMUNSKY (V. M.) Байрон и Пушкин, *etc.* 1924. 8°. **011840. dd. 71.**

—— An Address to the Right Hon. Lord Byron, with an opinion on some of his writings. By F. H. B. 1817. 8°. *See* B., F. H. **992. i. 15. (7.)**

—— An Address to the Right Hon. Lord Byron with an opinion on some of his writings. By F. H. B., *etc.* 1819. 8°. *See* B., F. H. **11658. aaa. 178.**

—— Anecdotes of Lord Byron, from authentic sources; with remarks illustrative of his connection with the principal literary characters of the present day. [By Alexander Kilgour. With a portrait.] pp. xvi. 207. *Knight & Lacey: London,* 1825. 12°. **1164. f. 5.**

—— Byron painted by his Compeers; or, All about Lord Byron, from his marriage to his death, as given in the various newspapers of his day, shewing wherein the American novelist [Harriet Beecher Stowe] gives a truthful account, and wherein she draws on her own morbid imagination. [With two original poems by Lady Byron.] pp. 112. *Samuel Palmer: London,* 1869. 8°. **10856. aaa. 26. (4.)**

BYRON (George Gordon Noel) *Baron Byron.* [Appendix.—Biography and Criticism.]

—— [Another copy.] Byron painted by his Compeers, *etc.* *London,* 1869. 8°. Ashley **343**.

—— Byroniana. Bozzies and Piozzies. pp. vii. 104. *Sherwood, Jones & Co.: London,* 1825. 8°. T. **1167**. (**9**.)

—— Les Dernières années de Lord Byron. [L]es Rives du lac de Genève—L'Italie—La Grèce. Par l'auteur de Robert Emmet [i.e. Louise de Cléron, Countess d'Haussonville]. pp. 269. *Paris,* 1874. 12°. **10855**. aaa. **8**.

—— Despair; a vision. Derry Down and John Bull; a simile. Being two political parodies on "Darkness," and a scene from "The Giaour," by Lord Byron. Together with A Love Letter from John Bull to Liberty, and a Farewell Address, *etc.* [In verse.] pp. 19. *Printed for the Author: London,* 1820. 8°. G. **18982**. (**21**.)

—— Second edition, *etc.* ms. notes in pencil. pp. 19. *Printed for the Author: London,* 1820. 8°. **C.131.d.11.(9.)**

—— La Jeunesse de Lord Byron. Par l'auteur de Robert Emmet [i.e. Louise de Cléron, Countess d'Haussonville]. pp. 281. *Paris,* 1872. 12°. **10855**. aaa. **9**.

—— The Late Lord Byron. (Copied from the Irish Times.) [An obituary notice.] [1824.] *s. sh.* 4°. **10825**. bbb. **19**. (**5**.)
Pp. 397, 98 *of an unidentified periodical.*

—— A Letter of Expostulation to Lord Byron, on his present pursuits; with animadversions on his writings and absence from his country in the hour of danger. 1822. *See* Periodical Publications.—*London.* The Pamphleteer, *etc.* vol. 19. 1813, *etc.* 8°. P.P. **3557**. w.

—— The Life, Writings, Opinions, and Times of the Right Hon. George Gordon Noel Byron, Lord Byron . . . By an English gentleman, in the Greek military service, and comrade of his Lordship. Compiled from authentic documents and from long personal acquaintance. [With a portrait.] 3 vol. *Matthew Iley: London,* 1825. 8°. **1164**. g. **21**.

—— [Another copy.] **10855**. ee. **6**.

—— Lord Byron jugé par les témoins de sa vie. [By the Countess Teresa Guiccioli.] 2 tom. *Paris,* 1868. 8°. **10855**. ee. **8**.

—— Lord Byron's Liebes-Abenteuer. Aus dem Englischen übersetzt von F. Reiter. 2 Bd. *Sondershausen,* [1862.] 8°. **10855**. a. **32**.

—— Memoirs of the Life and Writings of the Right Honourable Lord Byron, with anecdotes of some of his contemporaries. [By John Watkins.] pp. xvi. 428. *H. Colburn & Co.: London,* 1822. 8°. **1164**. g. **18**.

—— Des Lords Byron Lebensbeschreibung nebst Analyse und Beurtheilung seiner Schriften. Aus dem Englischen. Mit dem Bildnisse des Lords Byron. [Extracted and translated by A. G. Gebhardt from "Memoirs of the Life and Writings of the Right Hon. Lord Byron," by John Watkins.] pp. x. 246. *Leipzig,* 1825. 8°. **10855**. a. **4**.

—— Narrative of Lord Byron's Voyage to Corsica and Sardinia, during the summer and autumn of the year 1821. Compiled from minutes made during the voyage by the passengers; and extracts from the journal of his Lordship's yacht, the Mazeppa, kept by Captain Benson. [A fabrication.] pp. viii. 79. *J. Limbird: London,* 1824. 8°. **10151**. aaa. **14**.

BYRON (George Gordon Noel) *Baron Byron.* [Appendi —Biography and Criticism.]

—— [Another copy.] Narrative of Lord Byron's Voyage Corsica and Sardinia, *etc.* *London,* 1824. 8°. Ashley **33**

—— [Another edition.] pp. xii. 94. *A. & W. Galegnan* *Paris,* 1825. 12°. **10854**. aaa.

—— A Narrative of the Circumstances which attended t Separation of Lord and Lady Byron; remarks on h domestic conduct, and a complete refutation of t calumnies circulated by public writers. pp. 22. *R. Edwards: London,* 1816. 8°. **1164**. g. **3**

—— A Review of the Character and Writings of Lord Byro [By Willard Phillips.] (Reprinted from "The Nor American Review.") pp. xvi. 158. *Sherwood, Gilbert Piper: London,* 1826. 8°. **10856**. aa.

—— Review of the Life and Character of Lord Byron. [C. W. Le Bas.] Extracted from the British Critic April, 1831. pp. viii. 95. *J. G. & F. Rivington: Lond* 1833. 8°. T. **1473**. (

—— [Another copy.] Review of the Life and Character Lord Byron, *etc.* *London,* 1833. 8°. **4431**. a. **41**. (**1**

—— The Shade of Byron: a mock heroic poem, containi strange revelations not hitherto disclosed, with copio notes and references . . . A preface, with the autho comments on the so-called true "Story," by Mrs. Stow And a repudiation of the charges hurled against t memory of Lord Byron and his beloved sister, A Augusta. (Second edition.) vol. 1. pp. xxiii. 401. *James Burns: London,* [1871.] 8°. **11650**. f.
No more published.

—— The True Story of Lord & Lady Byron . . . in answ to Mrs. Beecher Stowe. [The introduction signed: J. M i.e. John Mitford.] [1869.] 8°. *See* M., J. **10856**. a.

—— Uriel: a poetical address to . . . Lord Byron, writt on the continent: with notes, containing strictures on t spirit of infidelity maintained in his works . . . A several other poems. pp. x. 127. *Hatchard & So* *London,* 1822. 8°. **11645**. dd.

—— [Another copy.] Uriel; a poetical address to . . Lord Byron, *etc.* *London,* 1822. 8°. **11657**. ff. **1**

—— Vie privée et amours secrètes de Lord Byron . . . Tr duit de l'anglais . . . par M. F. [A translation of "T Private Life of Lord Byron," by John Mitford.] 2 tom *Paris,* 1837. 12°. **1452**. a. **1**

Miscellaneous.

—— *See* Aberdeen, *City of.—Grammar School.* Proceedin at the Presentation to Aberdeen Grammar School Statue of Lord Byron, *etc.* 1923. 8°. **010856**. c.

—— *See* Athens.—*Ἱστορικη και Ἐθνολογικη Ἑταιρ της Ἑλλαδος.—Μουσειον.* Souvenirs de Lord Byro Exposition organisée . . . à l'occasion du centenaire de mort du poête. [A catalogue.] 1924. 8°. **10857**. a.

—— *See* Bagnall (Edward) Lord Byron. [A poem.] Wi remarks on his genius and character. 1831. 8°. T. **1398**. (**1**

—— *See* Barber (Thomas G.) Byron—and where he is buri [With portraits.] 1939. 8°. **10858**. g.

—— *See* Barber (Thomas G.) Hucknall Torkard Churc its history and Byron associations, *etc.* [1925.] 8°. **04705**. bb.

—— *See* Bedford (John H.) Wanderings of Childe Harol A romance of real life, *etc.* [A satire on Lord Byro 1825. 12°. N. **2**

BYRON (George Gordon Noel) *Baron Byron.* [Appendix. —Miscellaneous.]

—— *See* Bernard (Edward) *Genealogist.* Pedigree of George Gordon Sixth Lord Byron, *etc.* 1870. *s. sh.* fol. **9905**. aa. **1**.

—— *See* Cassidy (Appolonia H.) George Gordon, 6th Baron, Lord Byron of England, *etc.* [A film scenario.] [1946.] fol. **11780**. dd. **61**.

—— *See* Cline (Clarence L.) Byron, Shelley and their Pisan Circle. 1952. 8°. **10863**. b. **7**.

—— *See* Cruikshank (George) Forty Illustrations of Lord Byron. [1825.] 8°. Ashley **2732**.

—— *See* Diem (C.) Lord Byron als Sportsmann. [With a portrait.] [1950.] 8°. **10863**. aa. **30**.

—— *See* Drinkwater (John) *Poet.* 'Ωδη προς τον Βυρωνα . . . Missolonghi. April 19th. 1824–1924. *Eng. & Gr.* [1924.] *s. sh.* 4°. Ashley **3105**.

—— *See* Driver (Henry A.) Byron and "The Abbey." A few remarks upon the poet, elicited by the rejection of his statue by the Dean of Westminster, *etc.* 1838. 8°. **1164**. f. **38**.

—— *See* Edgcumbe (Richard J. F.) History of the Byron Memorial. 1883. 8°. **10803**. g. **5**. (8.)

—— *See* Finden (Edward F.) Finden's Illustrations of the Life and Writings of Lord Byron, *etc.* 1833, *etc.* 4°. **841**. m. **18–20**.

—— *See* Finden (Edward F.) and Finden (W.) [Finden's Byron Beauties.] Lord Byron's Frauen-Kranz. 1845. 8°. **11660**. ee. **26**.

—— *See* Finden (William) and Finden (E. F.) Finden's Byron Beauties, *etc.* 1836. 4°. **1754**. b. **14**.

—— *See* Foa (E.) *pseud.* Le Chien de Lord Byron, *etc.* [1890.] 32°. **12809**. aa. **48**.

—— *See* Hobhouse (John C.) *Baron Broughton.* [Recollections of a Long Life.] Napoléon, Byron et leurs contemporains, *etc.* [1910.] 8°. **10862**. ee. **36**.

—— *See* Howitt (William) A Poets' Thoughts at the Interment of Lord Byron. 1824. 8°. T. **1060**. (9.)

—— *See* Illiberal. The Illiberal! Verse and prose from the North!! . . . Dedicated to My Lord Byron in the South!!, *etc.* [1822.] 8°. Ashley **2722**.

—— *See* Intze (O.) Byroniana, *etc.* [1914.] 12°. **011904**. aaa. **10**.

—— *See* Korninger (S.) Lord Byron und Nikolaus Lenau. Eine vergleichende Studie. 1952. 8°. [*English Miscellany.* no. 3.] P.P. **5939**. cbc.

—— *See* London.—iii. *First Edition Club.* Bibliographical Catalogue of First Editions, proof copies & manuscripts of books by Lord Byron exhibited . . . January 1925. 1925. 4°. Ac. **9670**. ca.

—— *See* London.—iii. *British Museum.—Department of Printed Books.* Byron. An excerpt from the General Catalogue of Printed Books in the British Museum. 1939. fol. Cup. **1247**. i. **52**.

—— *See* Lorimer (Laurie) To Byron. [Verses.] [c. 1870.] *s. sh.* 4°. **11658**. h. **33**.

—— *See* Mayfield (John S.) Notes on Lord Byron's Infirmity. 1927. 8°. Ashley **5303**.

BYRON (George Gordon Noel) *Baron Byron.* [Appendix. —Miscellaneous.]

—— *See* Meadows (Lindon) *pseud.* The Byron Oak. Written after a recent visit to Newstead Abbey. [1860?] *s. sh.* 4°. Ashley **2740**.

—— *See* New York.—*Keats-Shelley Association of America.* Keats-Shelley Journal. A periodical devoted to Keats . . . Byron . . . and their circles. 1952, *etc.* 8°. P.P. **3437**. bkd.

—— *See* Newstead Abbey. The Roe-Byron Collection, Newstead Abbey. [With a portrait.] 1937. 8°. **011899**. m. **34**.

—— *See* Nottingham.—*Nottingham Mechanics' Institution.* Catalogue of the Byron Exhibition, held in the Minor Hall of the Institution . . . 1915. [1915.] 8°. Ashley **5465**.

—— *See* Origo (Iris M.) *Marchioness.* The Last Attachment. The story of Byron and Teresa Guiccioli, *etc.* [With portraits.] 1949. 8°. **10862**. c. **5**.

—— *See* Quevedo, *Redivivus, pseud.* A Spiritual Interview with Lord Byron, in which his lordship gave his opinion and feelings about his new monument, *etc.* [1880?] 8°. **08631**. f. **11**. (1.)

—— *See* Reid (Whitelaw) Byron. Address, *etc.* 1910. 4°. **11871**. d. **11**.

—— *See* Sinker (Robert) The Statue of Byron in the Library of Trinity College, Cambridge, *etc.* [1881?] 8°. **07807**. i. **6**. (4.)

—— *See* Sydney, *pseud.* "Sydney's" Letter to the King; and other reported correspondence connected with the exclusion of Lord Byron's monument from Westminster Abbey. 1828. 12°. T. **1221**. (12.)

—— *See* Wise (Thomas J.) A Bibliography of the Writings in Verse and Prose of George Gordon Noel, Baron Byron. With letters illustrating his life and work and particularly his attitude towards Keats. [With a portrait.] 1932, *etc.* 4°. C. **57**. f. **25**.

—— *See* Wise (Thomas J.) A Byron Library. A catalogue of printed books, manuscripts and autograph letters by George Gordon Noel, Baron Byron, *etc.* [With a portrait and facsimiles.] 1928. 4°. C. **57**. f. **21**.

—— [A collection of cuttings from newspapers and periodicals relating to Lord Byron.] 2 vol. 1812–80. fol., *etc.* **1764**. a. **11**.

—— Byron and Byroniana. A catalogue of books. pp. ix. 126. *Elkin Mathews: London,* [1930.] 8°. **S.C.Elkin Mathews.**

—— [Another copy.] Ashley **2774**.

—— The Byron Gallery. A series of historical embellishments to illustrate the poetical works of Lord Byron. *Smith, Elder & Co.: London,* 1833. 8°. **7868**. f. **26**.

—— The Byron Gallery: a series of historical embellishments, illustrating the poetical works of Lord Byron. A new and enlarged edition, with descriptive letter-press. *Smith, Elder & Co.: London,* 1838. 8°. **7865.pp.26.**

—— The Byron-Shelley-Keats In Memoriam Yearly Prizes for the best Essay in English written by a woman . . . Jubilee edition. (Prize Essays no. 2.) 2 vol. *R. M. Crawshay: Cathedine,* [1887, 88.] 8°. Ashley **1645**, **46**.

—— A Catalogue of a Collection of Books, late the property of a Nobleman [Lord Byron] about to leave England on a tour . . . which will be sold by auction by Mr. Evans . . . on Friday, April 5, and following day. pp. 13. ms. notes of prices. [1816.] 8°. *See* Evans (Robert H.) **S.C.Evans.5.(6.)**

BYRON (GEORGE GORDON NOEL) *Baron Byron.* [APPENDIX. —MISCELLANEOUS.]

—— Catalogue of the Library of the late Lord Byron, to which is added the library of a gentleman, deceased. Which will be sold by auction, by Mr. Evans, at his house, no. 93, Pall Mall, on Friday, July 6, and two following days, *etc.* pp. 27. MS. NOTES OF PRICES. *London,* 1827. 8°. **S.C.Evans.30.**
Interleaved.

—— [Another edition.] Reprinted with an introductory essay by Gilbert H. Doane. pp. 7. *Privately printed,* 1929. 8°. Ashley **2773. (1.)**
One of an edition of 100 *copies.*

—— [Another copy.] Ashley **2773. (2.)**

—— Historical Illustrations of Lord Byron's Works, in a series of etchings, by Reveil, from original paintings, by A. Colin. [With accompanying text.] *Charles Tilt: London; Paris* [printed], 1833. 8°. **11641. cc. 12.**

—— The Home and Grave of Byron; an historical and descriptive account of Newstead Abbey, Annesley Hall, and Hucknall-Torkard, *etc.* pp. 78. *Longman & Co.: London,* [1852.] 8°. **10350. a. 47.**

—— [Another edition.] The Home and Grave of Byron . . . Also Remarks on the architecture of Newstead Abbey . . . by Arthur Ashpitel . . . New edition, enlarged and revised. pp. 80. *Longman & Co.: London,* [1855?] 8°. **10351. b. 64.**

—— Illustrations to the Works of Lord Byron. The drawings by Chalon, Leslie, Harding . . . Engraved under the superintendence of Mr. Charles Heath. [With illustrative extracts from Byron's works.] *A. Fullarton & Co.: London,* [1846?] 4°. **789. f. 30.**
With an additional titlepage, engraved, reading "Heath's Illustrations," etc.

—— Lord Byron in the Other World.—Lord Byron's Immortality, *etc.* [By W. Davenport.]—Death of Lord Byron. [By Mrs. Henry Rolls.] *See* BOOK. [The Book of Spirits and Tales of the Dead.] [1825?] 8°. **11642. bbb. 58. (2.)**

—— Lord Byron International Memorial Fund, *etc.* [An appeal by A. Lynch and J. C. Squire.] [1925.] 4°. **10825. k. 39.**
Not published.

—— Lord Byron vindicated, and Mr. Campbell answered. [In answer to Thomas Campbell's defence of Lady Byron.] pp. 48. *Marsh & Miller: London,* 1830. 8°. Ashley **338.**

—— Remarks on the Exclusion of Lord Byron's Monument from Westminster Abbey. [By J. C. Hobhouse, Baron Broughton.] pp. 48. [*Privately printed: London,*] 1844. 8°. **C. 58. e. 33.**

—— [Another copy.] Remarks on the Exclusion of Lord Byron's Monument from Westminster Abbey. [By J. C. Hobhouse.] [*London,*] 1844. 8°. Ashley **340.**

—— Thoughts on Byron. [Signed: G. B., i.e. George Bealby?] [1919?] 8°. *See* B., G. **11869. df. 34.**

—— To the Departed. Stanzas to the memory of Lord Byron. pp. 16. *J. Hatchard & Son: London,* 1825. 8°. **T. 1061. (13.)**

BYRON (GERALD NOEL) The New Don Juan. The introduction. By G. N. Byron. And the last canto of the original Don Juan, from the papers of the Countess Guiccioli. By George Lord Byron [or rather, by G. N. Byron]. pp. 61. [1880.] 8°. *See* BYRON (George G. N.) *Baron Byron.* [*Don Juan.—Spurious Cantos and Imitations.*] **11643. i. 17.**

BYRON (GERTRUDE) "Poor Angela." pp. 316. *Andrew Melrose: London,* [1920.] 8°. NN. **649**

BYRON (GORDON)

—— Give Yourself a Chance. The seven steps to succes pp. x. 266. *World's Work: Kingswood, Surrey,* 1946. 8 **8412. a. 7**

BYRON (H. T.) *See* BYRON (Henry James)

BYRON (HENRY JAMES) *See* H., J. C. [*Vocabulari etc.—English Slang.*] The Slang Dictionary, *etc.* COPIO MS. NOTES [by H. J. Byron and W. C. Hazlitt]. 1864. **C. 45. c. 2**

—— *See* PERIODICAL PUBLICATIONS.—*London.* Mirth . Edited by H. J. Byron. 1877, *etc.* 8°. **P.P. 5441.**

—— *See* TALFOURD (Francis) and BYRON (H. J.) The Mil and his Men. A burlesque mealy-drama, *etc.* [1860.] 1 **2304. e. 19. (1**

—— Aladdin; or, the Wonderful scamp! An origi burlesque extravaganza, in one act. [In verse.] pp. 4 *London,* [1861.] 12°. [*Lacy's Acting Edition of Pla* vol. 50.] **2304. e. 24. (1**

—— [Another edition.] With slight alterations, and entire new songs and music, selected, and adapted to circun stances by J. H. Leslie R.A. and E. A. P. Hobday, *e* pp. 45. *Civil & Military Gazette Press: Lahor* 1882. 8°. **011779. f. 19. (1**

—— [Another edition.] pp. 47. *Bombay,* 1885. 8°. **011779. f. 2**

—— Ali Baba; or, the Thirty-nine thieves . . . A burlesq extravaganza in one act. [In verse.] pp. 38. *Londo* [1864.] 12°. [*Lacy's Acting Edition of Plays.* vol. 5 **2304. f. 4. (1**

—— The Babes in the Wood! And the good little fai birds! A burlesque drama, in one act. [In vers pp. 30. *London,* [1859.] 12°. [*Lacy's Acting Edition Plays.* vol. 41.] **2304. e. 15. (1**

—— Beautiful Haidée; or, the Sea nymph and the Sall rovers. A new and original whimsical extravaganz Founded on the poem of Don Juan, the Ballad of Lo Bateman, and the Legend of Lurline. pp. 31. *Londo* [1863.] 12°. [*Lacy's Acting Edition of Plays.* vol. 58.] **2304. f. 3. (**

—— Beauty and the Beast: a grand comic Christmas pant mime . . . as first performed at the Royal English Ope Covent Garden, *etc.* [In verse.] pp. 16. *Published sold in the Theatre: London,* [1862.] 8°. **11781. b. 43. (1**

—— Blow for Blow. An original drama, in a prologue a three acts. pp. 54. *London; New York,* [1875.] 12 [*French's Acting Edition of Plays.* vol. 101.] **2304. g. 19. (**

—— [A reissue.] Blow for Blow, *etc.* *London; New Yo* [1875.] 12°. [*French's Acting Edition.* no. 1501.] **11791. t. 1/12**

—— Blue Beard! From a new point of hue. A burlesq extravaganza. [In verse.] pp. 38. *London,* [1861.] 1 [*Lacy's Acting Edition of Plays.* vol. 49.] **2304. e. 23. (**

—— Bow Bells. An original comic drama, in three ac pp. 48. *London; New York,* [1881.] 12°. [*Frenc Acting Edition of Plays.* vol. 117.] **2304. h. 8. (1**

—— The Bride of Abydos; or, the Prince, the pirate, and t pearl. An original oriental burlesque extravaganza. [verse.] pp. 24. *London,* [1858.] 12°. [*Lacy's Acti Edition of Plays.* vol. 36.] **2304. e. 10. (**

[B]YRON (HENRY JAMES)

— Camaralzaman and the Fair Badoura; or, the Bad Djinn and the good spirit. An extravaganza. [In verse.] pp. 42. *London*, [1872.] 12°. [*Lacy's Acting Edition of Plays*. vol. 94.] **2304**. g. **12**. **(9.)**

— Cinderella; or, the Lover, the lackey, and the little glass slipper. A fairy burlesque extravaganza. [In verse.] pp. 45. *London*, [1861.] 12°. [*Lacy's Acting Edition of Plays*. vol. 49.] **2304**. e. **23**. **(8.)**

— [A reissue.] Cinderella, *etc.* *Samuel French: London; Samuel French & Son: New York*, [1875.] 12°. [*Lacy's Acting Edition*. no. 728.] **11791**. t. **1/1210**.

— The Corsican "Bothers"; or, the Troublesome twins. An original burlesque extravaganza. Founded on a famous romantic drama [i.e. "The Corsican Brothers" by E. P. Basté and Count X. A. de Montépin]. pp. 44. *London*, [1871.] 12°. [*Lacy's Acting Edition of Plays*. vol. 88.] **2304**. g. **6**. **(10.)**

— "Courtship"; or, the Three caskets. A comedy, in three acts. pp. 48. *London; New York*, [1884.] 12°. [*French's Acting Edition of Plays*. vol. 120.] **2304**. h. **11**. **(8.)**

— Cyril's Success. A comedy in five acts, *etc.* pp. 46. *R. M. De Witt: New York*, [1870?] 12°. **11783**. a. **15**. (**3**.)

— Cyril's Success. An original comedy, in five acts. pp. 78. *London*, [1871.] 12°. [*Lacy's Acting Edition of Plays*. vol. 89.] **2304**. g. **7**. **(1.)**

— Daisy Farm; an original drama, in four acts. pp. 50. *London; New York*, [1879.] 12°. [*French's Acting Edition of Plays*. vol. 115.] **2304**. h. **6**. **(9.)**

— 1863; or, the Sensations of the past season. With a shameful revelation of Lady Somebody's secret. A comical conglomerative absurdity, in one act. [In verse.] pp. 30. *London*, [1864.] 12°. [*Lacy's Acting Edition of Plays*. vol. 61.] **2304**. f. **6**. **(11.)**

— The Enchanted Wood, or, the Three transformed princes. A fairy extravaganza. [In verse.] pp. 28. *Samuel French: London; New York*, [1874.] 12°. [*Lacy's Acting Edition of Plays*. vol. 99.] **2304**. g. **17**. **(15.)**

— An English Gentleman: or, the Squire's last shilling. An original drama . . . in four acts. pp. 52. *London; New York*, [1887.]. 12°. [*French's Acting Edition of Plays*. vol. 126.] **2304**. h. **17**. **(5.)**

— Esmeralda; or, the "Sensation" goat! A new and original burlesque extravaganza, in one act. [In verse.] pp. 42. *London*, [1862.] 12°. [*Lacy's Acting Edition of Plays*. vol. 52.] **2304**. e. **26**. **(14.)**

— Fine Feathers, an original modern drama, in three acts and a prologue. *London; New York*, [1884.] 12°. [*French's Acting Edition of Plays*. vol. 120.] **2304**. h. **11**. **(7.)**

— Fra Diavolo! Or, the Beauty and the brigands. A new and original burlesque burletta. [In verse. Founded on A. E. Scribe's play.] pp. 34. *London*, [1858.] 12°. [*Lacy's Acting Edition of Plays*. vol. 35.] **2304**. e. **9**. **(12.)**

— Der Freischutz; or, the Bill! the Belle!! and the Bullet!!! An original burlesque [of J. F. Kind's "Der Freischütz"]. [In verse.] pp. 35. *London*, [1869.] 12°. [*Lacy's Acting Edition of Plays*. vol. 81.] **2304**. f. **26**. **(15.)**

— The Gaiety Gulliver. [A farce.] pp. 41. *Aubert's Steam Printing Works: [London*, 1880?] 8°. **11779**. g. **6**. **(4.)**

BYRON (HENRY JAMES)

—— The Garibaldi "Excursionists." An apropos sketch, in one act. pp. 18. *London*, [1861.] 12°. [*Lacy's Acting Edition of Plays*. vol. 48.] **2304**. e. **22**. **(14.)**

—— George de Barnwell. A burlesque pantomime opening. [In verse.] pp. 34. *London*, [1863.] 12°. [*Lacy's Acting Edition of Plays*. vol. 57.] **2304**. f. **2**. **(2.)**

—— The Girls. An original modern comedy in three acts. pp. 52. *London; New York*, [1887.] 12°. [*French's Acting Edition of Plays*. vol. 126.] **2304**. h. **17**. **(14.)**

—— Giselle; or, the Sirens of the Lotus Lake. A fanciful, comical, musical legend. pp. 26. *London*, [1872.] 12°. [*Lacy's Acting Edition of Plays*. vol. 93. **2304**. g. **11**. **(2.)**

—— The "Grin" Bushes! or, the "Mrs." Brown of the "Missis"-sippi. A burlesque extravaganza, in one act. Founded on the famous Adelphi drama of "The Green Bushes" [by J. B. Buckstone]. pp. 36. *London*, [1865.] 12°. [*Lacy's Acting Edition of Plays*. vol. 64.] **2304**. f. **9**. **(10.)**

—— A Hundred Thousand Pounds. An original comedy, in three acts. pp. 48. *London*, [1868.] 12°. [*Lacy's Acting Edition of Plays*. vol. 77.] **2304**. f. **22**. **(14.)**

—— [A reissue.] A Hundred Thousand Pounds, *etc.* *London*, [1871.] 12°. [*Lacy's Acting Edition*. no. 1154.] **11791**. t. **1/1219**.

—— Ill-Treated Il Trovatore; or, the Mother, the maiden, & the musicianer. A new burlesque extravaganza. [Based on S. Cammarano's "Il Trovatore."] pp. 38. *Thomas Hailes Lacy: London*, [1863?] 12°. **11785**. aa. **15**.

—— [A reissue.] Ill-treated Il Trovatore, *etc.* *London*, [1871.] 12°. [*Lacy's Acting Edition.*] **2304**. f. **3**. **(12.)**

—— Ivanhoe. In accordance with the spirit of the times. An extravaganza. [In verse.] pp. 48. *London*, [1864.] 12°. [*Lacy's Acting Edition of Plays*. vol. 59.] **2304**. f. **4**. **(8.)**

—— Songs, duetts, trios, &c. in the new extravaganza of Ivanhoe. pp. 16. *London*, [1863.] 12°. [*Lacy's Acting Edition of Plays*. suppl. vol. 2.] **2304**. i. **2**. **(7.)**

—— Jack the Giant Killer; or, Harlequin King Arthur, and yᵉ Knights of yᵉ Round Table. A burlesque extravaganza, preceding a mirthful, magical, comical, Christmas pantomime. [In verse.] pp. 31. *London*, [1859.] 12°. [*Lacy's Acting Edition of Plays*. vol. 43.] **2304**. e. **17**. **(15.)**

—— La! Sonnambula! Or, the Supper, the sleeper, and the merry Swiss boy. An original operatic burlesque extravaganza. [In verse.] pp. 36. *London*, [1866.] 12°. [*Lacy's Acting Edition of Plays*. vol. 66.] **2304**. f. **11**. **(6.)**

—— Lady Belle Belle; or, Fortunio and his seven magic men. A Christmas fairy tale, in one act. [In verse.] pp. 44. *London*, [1864.] 12°. [*Lacy's Acting Edition of Plays*. vol. 61.] **2304**. f. **6**. **(10.)**

—— The latest edition of the Lady of Lyons; or, Two-penny pride and penny-tence. A burlesque extravaganza. [In verse. A burlesque founded on the drama by E. G. E. L. Bulwer-Lytton.] pp. 27. *London*, [1858.] 12°. [*Lacy's Acting Edition.*] **2304**. e. **8**. **(15.)**

—— [A reissue.] The Very Latest Edition of the Lady of Lyons, *etc.* *Samuel French: London; Samuel French & Son: New York*, [1874.] 12°. [*Lacy's Acting Edition*. no. 510.] **11791**. t. **1/1226**.

—— [Another edition.] pp. 30. *London*, [1859.] 12°. [*Lacy's Acting Edition of Plays*. suppl. vol. 1.] **2304**. i. **1**. **(21.)**

—— The Lancashire Lass; or, Tempted, tried, and true. A domestic melodrama, in a prologue and four acts. pp. 60. *London; New York*, [1879.] 12°. [*French's Acting Edition of Plays*. vol. 115.] **2304**. h. **6**. (**11**.)

—— The Lion and the Unicorn: a grand, nursery, versery, comical Christmas pantomime, *etc.* [In verse.] pp. 16. *Published & sold in the Theatre: London*, [1864.] 8°. **11781**. b. **43**. (**15**.)

—— Little Don Giovanni. A burlesque. [In verse.] pp. 38. *London*, [1867.] 12°. [*Lacy's Acting Edition of Plays*. vol. 72.] **2304**. f. **17**. (**11**.)

—— Lord Bateman; or, the Proud young porter and the fair Sophia. A burlesque. Founded on the loving ballad of "Lord Bateman." pp. 36. *London*, [1871.] 12°. [*Lacy's Acting Edition of Plays*. vol. 87.] **2304**. g. **5**. (**5**.)

—— Lucia di Lammermoor; or, the Laird, the lady, and the lover. A new and original operatic burlesque extravaganza. [In verse. Founded on the opera by S. Cammarano.] pp. 35. *London*, [1867.] 12°. [*Lacy's Acting Edition of Plays*. vol. 72.] **2304**. f. **17**. (**12**.)

—— Lucretia Borgia, M.D.; or, la Grande doctresse. An original burlesque extravaganza. [Founded on a famous opera [i.e. "Lucrezia Borgia" by F. Romani]. pp. 32. *London*, [1871.] 12°. [*Lacy's Acting Edition of Plays*. vol. 87.] **2304**. g. **5**. (**2**.)

—— The Maid and the Magpie; or, the Fatal spoon! A burlesque burletta [in verse], founded on the opera of "La Gazza ladra" [by G. M. S. C. Gherardini]. pp. 36. *London*, [1859.] 12°. [*Lacy's Acting Edition of Plays*. vol. 37.] **2304**. e. **11**. (**12**.)

—— Married in Haste; an original comedy in four acts. pp. 52. *London; New York*, [1879.] 12°. [*French's Acting Edition of Plays*. vol. 115.] **2304**. h. **6**. (**13**.)

—— Mazeppa! A burlesque extravaganza, in one act. [In verse.] pp. 39. *London*, [1865.] 12°. [*Lacy's Acting Edition of Plays*. vol. 46.] **2304**. e. **20**. (**15**.)

—— Mazourka; or, the Stick, the Pole, and the Tartar. A burlesque extravaganza, in one act, founded on a famous French ballet, entitled "Le Diable à quatre" [by Adolphe de Leuven and N. Mazillier]. [In verse.] pp. 36. *London*, [1865.] 12°. [*Lacy's Acting Edition of Plays*. vol. 63.] **2304**. f. **8**. (**10**.)

—— [A reissue.] Mazourka, *etc. London*, [1867.] 12°. [*Lacy's Acting Edition*. no. 940.] **11791**. t. **1/1215**.

—— Miss Eily O'Connor. A new and original burlesque [in verse] founded on the great sensation drama of the Colleen Bawn [by D. L. Bourcicault]. pp. 35. *London*, [1862.] 12°. [*Lacy's Acting Edition of Plays*. vol. 53.] **2304**. e. **27**. (**1**.)

—— The Motto: I am "all there." A new and original burlesque, founded on the Lyceum drama of the "Duke's Motto." pp. 43. *London*, [1864.] 12°. [*Lacy's Acting Edition of Plays*. vol. 59.] **2304**. f. **4**. (**5**.)

—— Not such a Fool as he looks. An original eccentric comedy, in three acts. pp. 54. *London; New York*, [1884.] 12°. [*French's Acting Edition of Plays*. vol. 120.] **2304**. h. **11**. (**10**.)

—— [Another issue.] Not such a Fool as he looks, *etc. London; New York*, [1884?] 12°. **11785**. aa. **14**. *French's Standard Drama*. no. 392.

—— The Nymph of the Lurleyburg; or, the Knight and the Naiads. A spectacular extravaganza. [In verse.] pp. 36. *London*, [1859.] 12°. [*Lacy's Acting Edition of Plays*. vol. 43.] **2304**. e. **17**. (**13**.)

—— Old Sailors; original comedy, in three acts. pp. 42. *London; New York*, [1880.] 12°. [*French's Acting Edition of Plays*. vol. 116.] **2304**. h. **7**. (**2**.)

—— Old Soldiers; an original comedy, in three acts. pp. 40. *London; New York*, [1879.] 12°. [*French's Acting Edition of Plays*. vol. 113.] **2304**. h. **4**. (**11**.)

—— The Old Story! An original comedy, in two acts. pp. 32. *London*, [1861.] 12°. [*Lacy's Acting Edition of Plays*. vol. 51.] **2304**. e. **25**. (**8**.)

—— The Orange Tree and the Humble Bee; or, the Little princess who was lost at sea. A new extravaganza. pp. 34. *London*, [1872.] 12°. [*Lacy's Acting Edition of Plays*. vol. 93.] **2304**. g. **11**. (**7**.)

—— Orpheus and Eurydice; or, the Young gentleman who charmed the rocks. A comical classical love tale, in one act. [In verse.] pp. 44. *London*, [1864.] 12°. [*Lacy's Acting Edition of Plays*. vol. 61.] **2304**. f. **6**. (**7**.)

—— Eurydice; or, Little Orpheus and his lute. A grand burlesque extravaganza, being a second edition of "Orpheus and Eurydice," *etc.* pp. 39. *London*, [1872.] 12°. [*Lacy's Acting Edition of Plays*. vol. 92.] **2304**. g. **10**. (**2**.)

—— "Our Boys": an original modern comedy. pp. 48. *London; New York*, [1880.] 12°. [*French's Acting Edition of Plays*. vol. 116.] **2304**. h. **7**. (**3**.)

—— [A reissue.] "Our Boys," *etc. London; New York*, [1880.] 12°. [*French's Acting Edition*. no. 1728.] **11791**. t. **1/1206**.

—— [Another edition.] pp. iv. 58. *Gouda*, [1885.] 8°. [*Library of English Literature*. no. 2.] **12268**. b. **7**. (**2**.)

—— [A reissue.] "Our Boys," *etc. London; New York*, [1901.] 12°. [*French's Acting Edition*. no. 1728.] **11791**. t. **1/1205**.

—— Our Boys. A comedy in three acts. pp. 57. *London; New York*, [1923?] 8°. [*French's Acting Edition*.] **11791**. t. **1/699**.

—— [Our Boys.] Staří-Mladí, aneb: Naši hoši. Obraz ze života ve třech jednáních . . . Přeložil A. Pulda. Radostné shledání. Činohra . . . Dle A: z Kotzebue vzdělal A. Reinwart. pp. 90. *v Praze*, [1880.] 8°. [*Divadelni ochotník*. Nové sbírky sv. 182.] **11758**. p. **21**. (**2**.)

—— Paid in Full. A novel. 3 vol. *J. Maxwell & Co.: London*, 1865. 8°. **12634**. m. **3**.

—— [Another edition.] pp. iv. 460. *J. Maxwell & Co.: London*, 1865. 8°. **12618**. g. **21**.

—— [A reissue.] *Ward, Lock & Co.: London*, [1881.] 8°. **12619**. bbb. **33**.

—— Pan. An original classical pastoral. [In verse.] pp. 36. *London*, [1866.] 12°. [*Lacy's Acting Edition of Plays*. vol. 66.] **2304**. f. **11**. (**8**.)

—— Pandora's Box. A mythological extravaganza, in one act. [In verse.] pp. 42. *London*, [1875.] 12°. [*Lacy's Acting Edition of Plays*. vol. 76.] **2304**. f. **21**. (**13**.)

—— Partners for Life. An original comedy in three acts. pp. 48. *London; New York*, [1878.] 12°. [*Lacy's Acting Edition of Plays*. vol. 108.] **2304**. g. **26**. (**15**.)

—— The Pilgrim of Love! A fairy romance, in one act. pp. 39. *London*, [1860.] 12°. [*Lacy's Acting Edition of Plays*. vol. 45.] **2304**. e. **19**. (**11**.)

— Princess Spring-Time; or, the Envoy who stole the king's daughter. An original fairy extravaganza. Founded on a story by the Countess d'Anois. pp. 30. *London*, [1866.] 12°. [*Lacy's Acting Edition of Plays.* vol. 64.] **2304.** f. **9.** (**14.**)

— The Prompter's Box . . . An original domestic drama, in four acts. pp. 48. *London; New York*, [1884.] 12°. [*French's Acting Edition of Plays.* vol. 120.] **2304.** h. **11.** (**9.**)

— Punch. A comedy in three acts. pp. 48. *London; New York*, [1887.] 12°. [*French's Acting Edition of Plays.* vol. 126.] **2304.** h. **17.** (**10.**)

— Puss in a new Pair of Boots; a new & original burlesque extravaganza. [In verse.] pp. 36. *W. H. Swanborough:* [*London*,] 1862. 12°. **11781.** b. **42.** (**11.**)

— Robert Macaire; or, the Roadside inn turned inside out. An original burlesque extravaganza. pp. 40. *London*, [1872.] 12°. [*Lacy's Acting Edition of Plays.* vol. 93.] **2304.** g. **11.** (**3.**)

— Robinson Crusoe; or, Harlequin Friday and the king of the Caribee Islands! A grotesque pantomime opening. [In verse.] pp. 30. *London*, [1861.] 12°. [*Lacy's Acting Edition of Plays.* vol. 49.] **2304.** e. **23.** (**7.**)

— Robinson Crusoe. Burlesque. By H. T. [or rather, H. J.] Byron, W. S. Gilbert, T. Hood, H. S. Leigh, Arthur Sketchley and "Nicholas." Haymarket Theatre, July 5th, 1867. [1930?] 8°. **C.132.g.6.(3.)**
Typewritten.

— The Rosebud of Stingingnettle Farm; or, the Villanous squire and the virtuous villager, *etc.* [A play.] pp. 12. *London*, [1867.] 82°. [*Lacy's Sensation Series.*] **11781.** df. **30.** (**6.**)

— [Another edition.] pp. 12. *London; New York*, [1903.] 8°. [*French's Acting Edition of Plays.* Sensation ser. no. 8.] **2304.** i. 4. (**8.**)

— [Another edition.] With . . . new songs, dances and dialogue, specially arranged & adapted . . . by John H. Leslie. pp. 12. *"Albion" Press: Mooltan*, 1884. 8°. **011779.** f. **19.** (**5.**)
Inserted is a copy of "'I'm not quite so sure about that!' Topical song, etc."

— Sensation Dramas for the Back Drawing Room. pp. 101. *T. H. Lacy: London*, [1864.] 8°. **11781.** d. **29.** (**4.**)

— Sour Grapes. Original comedy in four acts. pp. 62. *London; New York*, [1887.] 12°. [*French's Acting Edition of Plays.* vol. 126.] **2304.** h. **17.** (**15.**)

— Timothy to the Rescue. An original farce, in one act. pp. 19. *London*, [1865.] 12°. [*Lacy's Acting Edition of Plays.* vol. 63.] **2304.** f. **8.** (**9.**)

— £20 a year—all found; or, Out of a situation refusing twenty. Being an apropos sketch, *etc.* pp. 18. *London; New York*, [1880.] 12°. [*French's Acting Edition of Plays.* vol. 116.] **2304.** h. **7.** (**5.**)

— "Uncle." A new and original farcical piece, in three acts. pp. 42. *London; New York*, [1884.] 12°. [*French's Acting Edition of Plays.* vol. 120.] **2304.** h. **11.** (**6.**)

— Uncle Dick's Darling. An original drama, in three acts. pp. 42. *London; New York*, [1907.] 12°. [*French's Acting Edition of Plays.* vol. 154.] **2304.** h. **45.** (**15.**)

— War to the Knife. An original comedy, in three acts. pp. 31. *London*, [1866.] 12°. [*Lacy's Acting Edition of Plays.* vol. 67.] **2304.** f. **12.** (**3.**)

— [Another edition.] pp. 24. *New York*, [1869.] 8°. [*De Witt's Acting Plays.* no. 44.] **11791.** ccc. **4/44.**

— Weak Woman: a new and original comedy, in three acts. pp. 43. *London; New York*, [1878.] 12°. [*French's Acting Editions of Plays.* vol. 112.] **2304.** h. 3. (**4.**)

— A Grand Comic Christmas Pantomime, entitled Whittington and his Cat! or, Harlequin King Kollywobbob, and the Genius of Good Humour, *etc.* [In verse.] pp. 27. *A. Harris: London*, 1862. 8°. **11781.** b. **43.** (**12.**)

— William Tell, with a vengeance! Or, the Pet, the patriot, and the pippin. A grand new and original burlesque. [In verse.] pp. 39. *London*, [1868.] 12°. [*Lacy's Acting Edition of Plays.* vol. 78.] **2304.** f. **23.** (**2.**)

— Wrinkles; a tale of time. An original comedy. pp. 53. *London; New York*, [1879.] 12°. [*French's Acting Edition of Plays.* vol. 115.] **2304.** h. **6.** (**10.**)

— Bits of Burlesques, being extracts from the extravaganzas of H. J. Byron. pp. 46. *Samuel French: London; New York*, 1877. 8°. **11779.** b. **3.** (**6.**)

BYRON (JAMES M.) *See* REES (John) *Minister of Crown Street Chapel, Soho.* The Restoration of the Joy of God's Salvation and the Upholding of His free Spirit earnestly implored. A sermon . . . with notes, containing an appeal to . . . the Rev. J. Byron . . . respecting his attack upon the author . . . in the Cheltenham Chronicle, under the signature of Amor Veritatis, *etc.* 1817. 8°. **4473.** bb. **1.** (**7.**)

— Antinomianism unmasked; Error detected; and Falsehood confuted: including observations on election, reprobation, imputed righteousness, and finished salvation; in a series of letters, addressed to the editor of the Cheltenham Chronicle, and the Reverend John Rees . . . Containing a reply to certain remarks in his pamphlet, entitled, "A Sermon, preached at Portland Chapel, Cheltenham." pp. 105. *Printed for the Author: Cheltenham*, [1817.] 8°. **4256.** c. **13.**

— *See* REES (John) *Minister of Crown Street Chapel, Soho.* A Defence of Truth; being an answer to a pamphlet, entitled "Antinomianism unmasked," *etc.* [1818.] 8°. **4257.** i. **4.** (**4.**)

— Thoughts on the Evil of Persecution, occasioned by the rioting at Newent. Including a friendly address to the inhabitants. pp. 60. *D. Walker: Glocester*, 1806. 8°. **4135.** e. **9.** (**1.**)

BYRON (JAN)

— It Will Happen Again, unless the world shapes a new way of political leadership. [Revised edition.] pp. 64. *A. H. Stockwell: Ilfracombe*, [1941.] 8°. **8011.** a. **4.**

BYRON (JOHN) *Baron Byron.* *See* BRERETON (*Sir* William) *Bart.* Sir William Brereton's Letter concerning the Surrender of the City of Chester . . . together with the articles agreed on betwixt both parties [i.e. Sir W. Brereton and John Byron, Baron Byron], *etc.* 1645. 4°. **E. 320.** (**20.**)

— *See* BRERETON (*Sir* William) *Bart.* Letters from Sir William Brereton, Sir Thomas Middleton, Sir John Meldrum, of the great Victory . . . given them . . . And, how they routed, and totally dispersed His Majesties Forces, under the command of the Lord Byron, *etc.* 1644. 4°. **E. 10.** (**4.**)

BYRON (JOHN) *Baron Byron.*

—— *See* DEVEREUX (Robert) *3d Earl of Essex.* A True Relation of a great battle fought betwixt the Earle of Essex and Prince Robert their forces: also the manner of the death of Sir John Byron, *etc.* 1642. 4°. **E. 118. (17.)**

—— *See* ENGLAND. [*Miscellaneous Public Documents, etc.*—III. Charles I.] A Message from His Majesty to the House of Peeres, the 11 of Feb. 1641 [O.S.]. Concerning his acceptance of Sir John Coniers, in the place of Sir John Byron to be Lieutenant of the Tower. 1642. *s. sh.* fol. **C.122.h.4.(52.)**

—— *See* ENGLAND.—*Parliament.* [*Parliamentary Proceedings.*—II.] A Declaration of the Lords and Commons [13 Sept. 1642] . . . Concerning an insolent letter sent to Mr. Clarke . . . from Sir J. Biron . . . whereunto is annexed a coppy of the said letter. 1642. 4°. **E. 116. (46.)**

—— *See* ISACK (I.) A Famous Victory obtained by Sir W. Brewerton, Sir T. Fairfax, [and] Sir W. Fairfax in a pitcht Battle against the Lord Byron . . . at the raising of the Siedge of Namptwich, *etc.* 1644. 4°. **E. 31. (6.)**

—— *See* WALES. Bloudy Newes from Wales declaring the proceedings of the Lord Byron for the King, *etc.* 1648. 4°. **E. 462. (9.)**

—— *See* WILKINSON (Thomas) *of Carnarvon.* Bloudy Newes from the Lord Byron, in Wales, declaring the proceedings of the Royall Party, *etc.* 1648. 4°. **E. 463. (15.)**

—— Two Letters from the Lord Byron to . . . the Marques of Newcastle, the one dated the 2. of January, and the other the 5. of January, 1643, *etc.* pp. 7. *Stephen Bulkley: York,* 1643 [1644]. 4°. **601. aa. 12.**

—— Letters from the Lord Byron to the King. *See* CHARLES I., *King of Great Britain and Ireland.* [*Letters and Speeches.*—II.] The King's packet of Letters, *etc.* 1645. 4°. **E. 304. (22.)**

—— A Letter written by the Lieutenant of the Tower [i.e. Lord Byron] to the Parliament, in defence of himselfe, *etc.* *See* NEWS. A Little True Forraine Newes, *etc.* 1641. 4°. **E. 131. (36.)**

—— The True Coppy of a Letter sent from Sir J. Byron, Lieutenant of the Tower, to the House of Commons, *etc.* *See* DIGBY (George) *2nd Earl of Bristol.* A Letter sent to the Hon. George Lord Digby, in Flushing, *etc.* 1641. 4°. **E. 134. (6.)**

—— The True Coppy of a Letter from Sir John Byron, *etc.* *See* CAVALIERS. A True and Perfect Relation of the . . . Taking of 46 rebellious Cavalliers at Brackly . . . under the command of Sir J. Byron, *etc.* 1642. 4°. **E. 117. (11.)**

—— Declaration to the Kingdom . . . with his lordships speech in the head of his army at Brees-heath. *See* JONES (Robert) *of Shrewsbury?* A Great and Bloody Fight in Shropshire, *etc.* 1648. 4°. **E. 457. (18.)**

—— Februar 1. 1645. Articles for the surrender of the city of Chester with the castle and fort: agreed on between the commissioners appointed on the behalf of John Lord Byron . . . on the one part, and the commissioners on the behalf of Sir William Brereton . . . on the other part. pp. 6. *For Rich. Cotes: London,* 1645 [1646]. 4°. **E. 320. (1.)**

—— The Lord Byrons First Articles presented to Sir William Brereton before the surrender of the city of Chester: wherein the great ambition of that party doth appear, *etc.* pp. 8. *For John Field: London,* 1645 [1646]. 4°. **E. 322. (10.)**

BYRON (JOHN) *Baron Byron.*

—— Sir John Byrons Relation to the Secretary of the la Westerne Action [at Devizes]. Between the Lord Wi mott and Sir William Waller. On Thursday, July 1 1643. With a list of both their Forces, and of their Losse pp. 7. *Stephen Bulkley: York,* 1643. 4°. **1103. d. 77. (**

BYRON (JOHN) *M.A., Fellow of Trinity College, Cambrid* *See* BYROM.

BYRON (JOHN) *of Mablethorpe St. Mary, Lincolnshire.*

—— *See* BETHELL (Richard) *Baron Westbury.* In the Ho of Lords. Between John Byron, John Blades [and othe . . . Appellants, and the Rev. Thomas Lovick Coop Respondent . . . The case of the appellants. [1841.] **1487.z.3.(1**

—— *See* SIMPKINSON (John A. F.) and ANDERDON (O.) the House of Lords. Between John Byron, John Bla [and others] . . . Appellants. And the Rev. T. Cooper, Respondent . . . Case of the respondent. [1841.] fol. **1487.z.3.(2.**

BYRON (*Hon.* JOHN) *See* CAMPBELL (Alexander) *M shipman of H.M.S.* "*Wager.*" The Sequel to Bulke and Cummins's Voyage to the South Seas, or the A ventures of Capt. Cheap, the Hon. Mr. Byron . . . a others, late of His Majesty's Ship the Wager, *etc.* 1747. **978. l.**

—— *See* DISCOVERIES. New Discoveries concerning t World, and its Inhabitants . . . Comprehending all t discoveries made in the several voyages of Commodo now Admiral, Byron, Captains Wallis, Carteret, *etc.* 1778. 8°. **978. h.**

—— *See* HAWKESWORTH (John) *LL.D., Essayist.* Relati des voyages entrepris par ordre de Sa Majesté Britanniq . . . par . . . Byron . . . Carteret . . . Wallis . . . Coc *etc.* 1774. 8°. **010498. a.**

—— *See* HAWKESWORTH (John) *LL.D., Essayist.* Geschic der See-Reisen nach dem Südmeere, welche von . Byron . . . Wallis . . . Carteret und . . . Cook . . . ausgefü worden sind, *etc.* 1775. 8°. **010498. a.**

—— *See* WHITE (Thomas) *Captain, R.N.* Naval Research or, a Candid inquiry into the conduct of Admirals Byr Graves . . . in the actions off Grenada, Chesapeak, *etc.* 1830. 8°. **806. b.**

—— An Account of a Voyage round the World, in the Ye MDCCLXIV, MDCCLXV, and MDCCLXVI. By the Honoura Commodore Byron, in His Majesty's Ship the Dolph *See* HAWKESWORTH (John) *LL.D., Essayist.* An Accou of the Voyages undertaken . . . for making discover in the Southern Hemisphere, *etc.* vol. 1. 1773. 4°. **455. a.**

—— An Account of a Voyage round the World, in the ye MDCCLXIV, MDCCLXV, and MDCCLXVI. *In:* HAWK WORTH (John) *LL.D., Essayist.* An Account of t Voyages undertaken . . . for making discoveries in t Southern Hemisphere, *etc.* vol. 1. pp. 1–165. 1773. 8°. **010028. p.**

—— An Account of a Voyage round the World, in the ye MDCCLXIV, MDCCLXV, and MDCCLXVI. *In:* HAWK WORTH (*John*) *LL.D., Essayist.* An Account of t Voyages undertaken . . . for making Discoveries in t Southern Hemisphere, *etc.* (Second edition.) vol. pp. 1–139. 1773. 4°. **G. 74**

—— [Another edition.] *See* HAWKESWORTH (John) *LL. Essayist.* An Account of the Voyages undertaken . for making discoveries in the Southern Hemisphere, vol. 1. 1775. 8°. **10026. d.**

—— [Another edition.] *See* HAWKESWORTH (John) *LL.D., Essayist.* An Account of the Voyages undertaken . . . for making discoveries in the Southern Hemisphere, *etc.* 1789. 12°. **10025.** aaa. **1.**

—— [Another edition.] *See* MAVOR (William F.) General Collection of Voyages, *etc.* vol. 3–5. 1810. 12°. **10027.** a.

—— Voyage autour du monde en 1764, 1765 et 1766, par le commodore Byron, sur le vaisseau le Dauphin. *See* DUPONCHEL (A.) Nouvelle bibliothèque des voyages, *etc.* tom. 1. [1841, *etc.*] 8°. **1424.** e. **1.**

—— John Byrons . . . Reise um die Welt, in den Jahren 1764 und 1765 . . . Mit einem Anhange, worinnen eine vollständige Beschreibung der Patagonischen Küsten . . . enthalten ist. [The translator's preface signed: C. H. K.] pp. xxx. 286. *Frankfurt & Leipzig,* 1769. 8°. **10028.** df. **6.**

—— Viage del Comandante Byron al rededor del mundo . . . traducido del Ingles, é ilustrado con notas . . . por el Dr Dn Casimiro de Ortega. [With a plate and a map.] pp. 245. *Madrid,* 1769. 4°. **10026.** d. **6.**

—— Segunda edicion, en que se añade el Resumen historico del viage emprendido por Magallanes, y concluído por . . . Juan Sebastian del Cano (su autor C. de Ortega). 2 pt. *Madrid,* 1769. 4°. **978.** i. **28.**

—— [Another copy.] **304.** f. **1.**

—— The Voyage of Commodore Byron round the World. [An abridgment.] *See* MOORE (John H.) A New and Complete . . . Collection of Voyages and Travels, *etc.* vol. 1. [1780?] fol. **10003.** f. **2.**

—— Voyage round the World performed by the Hon. Commodore Byron, *etc.* [Slightly abridged and rewritten.] *See* WILSON (Robert) *Editor of Voyages.* Voyages of Discoveries round the World, *etc.* 1806. 12°. **10026.** cc. **24.**

—— Tocht van den Kommandeur Byron. [Extracts from Admiral Byron's account of his voyage round the World.] *See* HAWKESWORTH (John) *LL.D., Essayist.* Reizen rondom de wereld, *etc.* (Verkort verhaal.) 1774. 4°. **10002.** c. **23.** (**2.**)

—— Voyages de Byron. 1764. [Extracts from Admiral Byron's account of his voyage round the World.] 1848. *See* ROUSIER (   ) *Abbé.* Bibliothèque religieuse, morale, littéraire de l'enfance et de la jeunesse, *etc.* 1843, *etc.* 12°. **12203.** cc. **14.**

—— Beschreibung einer Reise um die Erdkugel, angestellt . . . im Jahre 1764, *etc.* [Abridged.] 1831. *See* CAMPE (J. H.) Sämmtliche Kinder- und Jugendschriften, *etc.* Bdchn. 19. 1831, *etc.* 8°. **12807.** bbb.

—— The Narrative of . . . the Honourable John Byron . . . containing an account of the great distresses suffered by himself and his companions on the coast of Patagonia from the year 1740, till their arrival in England, 1746. With a description of St. Jago de Chili . . . Also a relation of the loss of the Wager man of war, *etc.* pp. viii. 257. *S. Baker & G. Leigh; T. Davies: London,* 1768. 8°. **978.** h. **30.**

—— [Another copy.] **671.** f. **11.**

—— [Another copy.] **1045.** g. **9.** (**1.**)

—— [Another copy.] **304.** d. **6.**

—— The Narrative of the Honourable John Byron . . . containing an account of the great distresses suffered by himself and his companions on the coast of Patagonia, from the year 1740, till their arrival in England, 1746 . . . The second edition. pp. viii. 257. *S. Baker & G. Leigh; T. Davies: London,* 1768. 8°. **010481.** c. **34.**

—— The Narrative of the Honourable John Byron . . . containing an account of the great distresses suffered by himself and his companions on the coasts of Patagonia, *etc.* pp. xii. 268. *S. Baker & G. Leich; T. Davies: London,* 1778. 12°. **1472.** aa. **5.**

—— [Another edition.] pp. xii. 264. *S. Baker & G. Leich* [*Leigh*]: *London,* 1780. 12°. **10481.** a. **12.**

—— [Another edition.] pp. xii. 268. *W. Bancks: Wigan,* 1784. 12°. **10480.** a. **2.**

—— The Narrative of the Honourable John Byron . . . containing an account of the great distresses suffered by himself and his companions on the coasts of Patagonia, *etc.* pp. x. 193. *S. Baker & G. Leigh; T. Davies: London,* 1785. 12°. **10482.** aa. **43.**

—— [Another edition.] pp. 185. *S. Wilkinson: Morpeth,* 1812. 12°. **10481.** aa. **7.**

—— [Another edition.] pp. 115. *Oliver & Boyd: Edinburgh,* 1814. 12°. **10481.** a. **10.**

—— [Another edition.] The Narrative of the Honourable John Byron . . . To which is prefixed, a biographical sketch of . . . the author. pp. xv. 158. *James Johnston: Aberdeen,* 1822. 12°. **10480.** a. **1.**

—— [Another edition.] Byron's Narrative of the Loss of the Wager Man of War, *etc.* pp. 180. *W. Folds & Son: Dublin,* 1822. 12°. **863.** f. **46.**

—— [Another edition.] pp. 171. *Society for promoting the United and Scriptural Education of the Poor of Ireland: Dublin,* [1825?] 12°. **4422.** d. **39.**

—— [Another edition.] The Narrative of the Hon. John Byron, *etc.* pp. 155. *S.P.C.K.: London,* 1842. 12°. **10026.** a. **19.**

—— Foul Weather Jack: being the Narrative of the Hon. John Byron, *etc.* pp. 64. *John Neale: London,* 1844. 12°. **10497.** aaa. **19.** (**3.**)

—— [Another edition.] The Wreck of the "Wager" and subsequent adventures of her crew. Narratives of the Hon. J. Byron and of his fellow-midshipman, Isaac Morris. pp. 192. *London,* [1896.] 8°. [*Blackie's School and Home Library.*] **012200.g.4/5.**

—— [A reissue.] *London,* [1925.] 8°. **012604.** aa. **5.**

—— Relato del honorable John Byron . . . que contiene una esposicion de las grandes penurias sufridas por él i sus compañeros en la costa de la Patagonia . . . Traducido al castellano de la primera edicion inglesa publicada en 1768, por José Valenzuela D. pp. xiii. 155. *Santiago de Chile,* 1901. 8°. **10480.** aa. **31.**

—— A Voyage round the World, in . . . the Dolphin, commanded by the Honourable Commodore Byron . . . By an Officer on board the said ship. [With plates.] pp. 186. *J. Newbery; F. Newbery: London,* 1767. 8°. **10026.** d. **12.**

—— [Another edition.] pp. 222. *J. Hoey: Dublin,* 1767. 12°. **10026.** bb. **24.**

—— Commodore Byron, to Magellanica. [An extract from "A Voyage round the World in . . . the Dolphin."] 1768. *See* CALLANDER (John) Terra Australis cognita, *etc.* vol. 3. 1766, *etc.* 8°. **566.** c. **3.**

BYRON (LESLEY) Opportunist Sinn Feiners. [A novel.] pp. 134. *Heath Cranton: London,* [1921.] 8°. **NN. 6949.**

BYRON (Lionel Dawson) Israel, or the Simultaneousness of the " Fulness " of the Gentiles, the " Fulness " of the Jews, the Coming of the Lord and the end of time. pp. 22. *Simpkin, Marshall & Co.: London*, 1877. 8°. **4033**. f. 6. (16.)

—— The Origin and Nature of Baptism, *etc.* pp. 46. *Simpkin, Marshall & Co.: London*, 1875. 8°. **4325**. aaa. 19.

—— Water Baptism; or, did Christ ever command anyone either to baptize or to be baptized with water? With an appendix, containing an adjustment of certain . . . remarks upon " The Origin and nature of baptism," which have recently appeared in the " Gospel Standard." pp. 36. *Simpkin, Marshall & Co.: London*, 1875. 8°. **4325**. aaa. 1. (8.)

—— " What saith the Scripture ? " Or, a plea for the name and person of the " One Mediator between God and men, the man Christ Jesus." pp. 19. *Simpkin, Marshall & Co.: London*, 1876. 8°. **4372**. f. 1. (6.)

BYRON (Marguerite)

—— Cloth of Gold. A collection of poems. pp. 31. *Arthur H. Stockwell: Ilfracombe*, [1955.] 8°. **11658**. aa. 140.

BYRON (Mary) Dawn and Dusk in the High Veld, *etc.* [Tales.] pp. x. 276. *Longmans & Co.: London*, 1931. 8°. **012601**. i. 18.

—— The Owls: a book of verses. pp. 48. *T. M. Miller: Cape Town*, [1920.] 8°. **011648**. df. 138.

—— A Voice from the Veld . . . [Poems.] With a foreword by Sir J. Percy Fitzpatrick. pp. x. 77. *J. M. Dent & Sons: London*, 1913. 8°. **011651**. h. 97.

BYRON (May Clarissa) *See* Gillington, afterwards Byron.

BYRON (Medora Gordon) *pseud.* Zameo; or, the White warrior! An operatic romance . . . By Medora Gordon Byron, a Minor . . . To which is prefixed a memoir of Miss Byron . . . [a jeu d'esprit, representing the author as a natural daughter of Lord Byron] written by Mrs. Jane Briancourt, *etc.* pp. 40. *London*, [1834.] 12°. [*Duncombe's Edition of the British Theatre.* vol. 15.] **2304.a.8.**

—— [A reissue, with a different titlepage, and without the memoir.] Zameo: a melodrama . . The only edition correctly marked, by permission, from the prompter's book, *etc.* *J. Duncombe & Co.: London*, [1840 ?] 12°. **11779**. a. 41. (4.)

BYRON (Robert) *See* also Waughburton (Richard) *pseud.* [i.e. R. Byron and C. Sykes.]

—— *See* Sykes (Christopher) Four Studies in Loyalty. [Including an essay on Robert Byron. With a portrait.] 1946. 8°. **012359**. cc. 22.

—— The Appreciation of Architecture. pp. 63. pl. xvi. *Wishart & Co.: London*, 1932. 4°. [*Adelphi Quartos.* vol. 1.] **012208.1.7/1.**

—— The Byzantine Achievement. An historical perspective, A.D. 330–1453. pp. xiii. 345. pl. xvi. *G. Routledge & Sons: London*, 1929. 8°. **9042**. c. 4.

—— An Essay on India. pp. viii. 175. *G. Routledge & Sons: London*, 1931. 8°. **8022**. a. 65.

—— Europe in the Looking-glass. Reflections of a motor drive from Grimsby to Athens. pp. 229. *G. Routledge & Sons: London*, 1926. 8°. **010106**. g. 15.

—— First Russia Then Tibet. [With plates.] pp. xvi. 328. *Macmillan & Co.: [London,]* 1933. 8°. **2352**. g. 4.

—— How we Celebrate the Coronation. [On the demolition of historic buildings in London.] (Reprinted from the Architectural Review.) pp. 31. *Architectural Press: London*, 1937. 8°. **010349**. bb. 22.

BYRON (Robert)

—— Imperial Pilgrimage. [With plates.] pp. 72. *London Transport: London*, 1937. 8°. [*London-in-your-Pocket Series.*] **W.P. 12092/2.**

—— The Road to Oxiana. [With plates.] pp. ix. 341. *Macmillan & Co.: London*, 1937. 8°. **010075**. ff. 26.

—— The Road to Oxiana, *etc.* pp. 292. *John Lehmann: London*, 1950. 8°. [*Library of Art and Travel.*] **W.P. 13755/5.**

—— Shell Guide to Wiltshire. A series of views . . . Edited by R. Byron. [With maps.] pp. 62. *Architectural Press: London*, 1935. 4°. [*Shell Guides.*] **W.P. 10927/3.**

—— [A reissue.] Shell Guide to Wiltshire, *etc.* *Faber & Faber: London*, [1939.] 4°. [*Shell Guides.*] **W.P.10927/22.**

—— The Station. Athos: treasures and men. [With plates.] pp. 292. *Duckworth: London*, 1928. 8°. **10127**. e. 14.

—— The Station. Athos: treasures and men, *etc.* [With plates.] pp. 263. *John Lehmann: London*, 1949. 8°. [*Library of Art and Travel.*] **W.P. 13755/2.**

BYRON (Robert) and **RICE** (David Talbot)

—— The Birth of Western Painting . . . Illustrated from the paintings of Mistra and Mount Athos, of Giotto and Duccio, and of El Greco, *etc.* pp. xviii. 236. pl. 94. *G. Routledge & Sons: London*, 1930. 4°. **7860**. r. 36.

BYRON (W. H. Smith) Why I Killed Him . . . With illustrations by Matthew Stretch. [A novel.] pp. 98. *Digby, Long & Co.: London*, [1893.] 8°. **012634**. g. 58

BYRON (William) *Baron Byron.*

—— *See* London.—iii. *Star and Garter Tavern, Pall Mall.* A circumstantial and Authentic Account of a late unhappy affair which happened at the Star and Garter Tavern, *etc.* [An account of a duel fought between William Chaworth and Lord Byron.] 1765. 4°. **8425**. i. 17.

—— Representation of the Court at the trial of Lord Byron. [A plan.] [*London*, 1765.] *s. sh.* 4°. **1879**. c. 1. (124.)

—— The Trial of William Lord Byron . . . for the Murder of William Chaworth, Esq; before . . . the House of Peers, *etc.* pp. 47. *Samuel Billingsley: London*, 1765. fol. **6485**. h. 2.

BYRON-BRADLEY (J.) *See* Bradley.

BYRON-WEBBER (Ronald) *See* Webber.

BYRRNE (E. Fairfax) Entangled. 3 vol. *Hurst & Blackett: London*, 1885. 8°. **12620**. p. 5

—— A Fair Country Maid. [A novel.] 3 vol. *R. Bentley & Son: London*, 1883. 8°. **12643**. d. 12

—— The Heir without a Heritage. A novel. 3 vol. *R. Bentley & Son: London*, 1887. 8°. **012639**. i. 14

—— Milicent. A poem. pp. 262. *C. Kegan Paul & Co. London*, 1881. 8°. **11653**. c. 31

BYRT (George William)

—— John Clifford. A fighting Free Churchman. [A biography. With plates, including portraits.] pp. 192. *Kingsgate Press: London*, 1947. 8°. **4910**. aa. 30

BYRT (George William)

—— Stream of the River. An attempt to tell the story of a Free Church—West End Baptist Church, Hammersmith, on the background of its place and period 1793–1943. [With plates.] pp. 150. *Kingsgate Press: London,* 1944. 8°.* **4716**. aa. **2**.

BYRT (Mabel Evelyn)

—— Call of the River. [A tale. With plates.] pp. 127. *Country Life: London,* 1955. 8°. **7211**. a. **30**.

BYRT (Richard) The Great Trap of George Booth, Henry Newman . . . with a true relation of their intrapping of Richard Byrt of London. Likewise False Swearers discover'd, *etc.* pp. 109. *For the Author: London,* 1659. 8°. **6495**. aaa. **6**.

BYRTH (Henry Stewart) None like unto Ahab: a sermon, *etc.* pp. 16. *J. Parker & Co.: London & Oxford,* [1877.] 8°. **4478**. cc. **3**. (**16**.)

—— Paul before Agrippa: a sermon, *etc.* pp. 15. *T. Roworth: Manchester; J. Parker & Co.: London & Oxford,* [1877.] 8°. **4479**. bb. **4**.

BYRTH (Thomas) *See* Moncreiff (George R.) The Soldier's Rest. A sermon . . . on the death of the Rev. T. Byrth, *etc.* [1849.] 8°. **4905**. c. **48**

—— *See* Tobin (John) *Incumbent of St. John's, Liscard.* A Sermon on the death of the Rev. T. Byrth. 1849. 8°. **4905**. c. **56**.

—— A Curate's Farewell Address to his Parishioners. pp. 29. *Talboys & Wheeler: Oxford,* 1826. 8°. **4407**. g. **11**.

—— God Justifieth the Ungodly. A sermon, *etc.* pp. 32. *J. H. Parker: Oxford,* 1840. 8°. T. **2449**. (**12**.)

—— A Letter to the Rev. John Hamilton Thorn, containing strictures on some remarks in his sermon, entitled, "Christianity not the property of critics and scholars, but the gift of God to all men" . . . Second edition. pp. 46. *Henry Perris: Liverpool,* 1839. 8°. **4225**. bb. **8**.

—— Memoir [of Thomas Tattershall]. *See* Tattershall (Thomas) Sermons, *etc.* 1848. 8°. **4460**. e. **21**.

—— Observations on the Neglect of the Hebrew Language, and on the best mode of promoting its cultivation among the clergy. pp. 41. *Hatchards: London,* 1832. 8°. **4109**. b. **23**. (**1**.)

—— Remains of Thomas Byrth . . . with a memoir of his life, by the Rev. G. A. Moncreiff. pp. v. 444. *T. Hatchard: London; Webb & Hunt: Liverpool,* 1851. 8°. **3755**. c. **3**.

—— A Selection of Hymns for the use of Wallasey Church. Second edition. [The editor's preface signed: T. B., i.e. T. Byrth.] pp. 104. 1844. 12°. *See* B., T. **3433**. de. **62**. (**5**.)

—— Transubstantiation contradicted by Scripture, Reason, and Experiment. [A sermon.] *See* Rome, *Church of.* [*Appendix.*] A Course of Sermons on the Principal Errors of the Church of Rome, *etc.* 1838. 12°. **1119**. f. **28**.

—— The Unitarian Interpretation of the New Testament based upon defective scholarship, or dishonest and uncandid criticism. *See* Unitarianism. Unitarianism Confuted, *etc.* 1839. 8°. **1120**. k. **20**.

—— *See* Thom (John H.) A Letter to the Rev. Thomas Byrth, *etc.* [In criticism of a lecture by him, entitled "The Unitarian Interpretation of the New Testament based upon defective scholarship."] 1839. 8°. **4225**. bb. **62**.

BYRUM (Enoch Edwin) The Secret of Prayer. How and why we pray. pp. 209. *F. H. Revell Co.: New York,* [1912.] 8°. **3457**. k. **32**.

BYRUTE. Byrutės Dainos, *etc.* Laida 1. pp. 32. *Vilniuje,* 18861 [1861?]. 16°. **11586**. a. **10**. (**3**.)
The wrapper bears the imprint: Tilžėje, 1891.

BYSACK (Govinda Chandra) *See* Govindachandra Vaiśākha.

BYSACK (Nemy Churn) *See* Nimāicharaṇa Vaiśākha.

BYSCHER (Joannes Godofredus) Dissertatio philosophico medica inauguralis de perturbatione animi atque corporis, *etc.* *Praes.* L. Heisterus, *etc.* pp. 32. *Helmstadii,* 1738. 4°. **7306**. e. **15**. (**15**.)

BYSCHOFF. *See* Bischof.

BYSDRAGUS (Gerardus) *Bishop of Thessalonica.* *See* Busdragus.

BYSE (Charles)

—— *See* Bible.—*Revelation.* [*French.*] Apocalypse, sens interne, *etc.* [Swedenborg's "Apocalypsis revelata" abridged, translated and edited by C. Byse.] [c. 1920.] 8°. **3716**. n. **7**.

—— Au Bengale. Babou Keshoub Chander Sen. Un réformateur religieux et social . . . Avec portrait. pp. vi. 320. *Lausanne,* 1892. 8°. **10606**. bb. **39**.

—— De l'autorité en matière de foi. Conférence. pp. 36. *Paris,* 1870. 8°. **3902**. g. **42**. (**7**.)

—— Ère nouvelle. Refonte du crédo protestant, *etc.* pp. 103. *Lausanne,* [1916.] 8°. **3716**. n. **6**.

—— L'Homme-dieu, *etc.* pp. 240. *Lausanne,* [1920.] 8°. **3716**. n. **2**.

—— Lettre ou symbole? Étude historique sur le double sens de l'Écriture, *etc.* pp. 258. *Lausanne,* [1914.] 8°. **3716**. n. **4**.

—— Le Mariage idéal et ses contrefaçons. Étude morale, *etc.* [On Swedenborg's "Delitiæ sapientiæ de amore conjugali."] pp. 144. *Lausanne,* [c. 1915.] 8°. **3716**. n. **1**.

—— La Providence d'après Swédenborg, *etc.* [On "Sapientia angelica de divina providentia."] pp. 151. *Lausanne,* [1917.] 8°. **3716**. n. **5**.

—— Le Scientisme et Swédenborg. Étude critique. [With special reference to Mary Baker Eddy.] pp. 257. *Lausanne,* [1915.] 8°. **3716**. n. **3**.

—— Swédenborg. [Lectures. With plates, including portraits.] 5 tom. *Lausanne,* 1911–13. 8°. **3716**. b. **7**.

BYSE (Fanny) Milton on the Continent. pp. 6. [*Printed for private circulation: Lausanne?* 1890?] 8°. **10803**. e. **23**. (**6**.)

—— Milton on the Continent. A key to L'Allegro and Il Penseroso, *etc.* [With the text.] pp. 77. 1903. 8°. *See* Milton (J.) [*L'Allegro and Il Penseroso.*] **11630**. bbb. **31**.

—— [A reissue, with the addition of an appendix.] pp. 95. 1903 [1909]. 8°. *See* Milton (John) [*L'Allegro and Il Penseroso.*] **11856**. aaa. **18**.

BYSE (*Mrs.* L. J.) *See* Bible.—*New Testament.* [*Lendu, Batha.*] Kothi pi ma gothaba Yesu Kristu ma na di thi dingana tso gbani na o ku na lo. [Translated by Mrs. L. J. Byse.] 1936. 8°. **03068**. k. **84**.

BYSELEY, *Family of.* See BEAZLEY (Frank C.) Pedigree of Byseley, Bisley or Beazley of Newington and Warborough, Co. Oxon; Ryde and Alverstoke, Co. Southampton; and Oxton, Co. Chester, *etc.* 1928. 8°. **9907.e.38.**

BYSET (JOHN) *See* BATTEN (Edmund C.) The Charters of the Priory of Beauly, with notices . . . of the family of the founder John Byset. 1877. 8°. Ac. **8241/6.**

BYSH (JOHN) Bysh's British Spelling Book, *etc.* *J. Bysh: London,* [1861.] 16°. **12983.** a. **6.**

—— Bysh's New Progressive Series. No. 1.—The alphabets, Roman and Italic. [A folding card.] *J. Bysh: London,* [1861.] 8°. **12983.** e. **5.**

—— Bysh's Pictorial A B C, or Alphabet of all nations. *J. Bysh: London,* [1861.] 12°. **12985.** bbb. **26.** (3.)

BYSHBURY. Byshbury. [An extract from vol. 2 of Stebbing Shaw's "History and Antiquities of Staffordshire."] *Nichols & Son: London,* [1801.] fol. **134.** f. **10.** (2.)

BYSHOP (HENRY) *Postmaster General.* An Advertisement from Henry Byshop Esquire, his Majesties Post-Master General. [*London,* 1660?] *s. sh.* fol. **C.112.h.4.(19.)**

BYSHOP (JOHN) *See* BISHOP (John) *Recusant Papist.*

BYSINIA. *See* BISIGNANO.

BYSKOV (JENS)

—— Christian den x.s Danmark. Udvikling og Fremdrift i Tiden 1912–1947. Under Redaktion af . . . J. Byskov, *etc.* [With illustrations.] 2 vol. [*Copenhagen,* 1948.] 4°. **010281.** s. **1.**

BYSSANDER (ADAM) Oratio . . . de scholarum dignitate, *etc.* *See* SELNECCER (N.) Pædagogii illustris Gandershemij inauguratio, *etc.* 1571. 8°. **8309.** aa. **32.**

BYSSE (HENRI DE THIARD DE) *Cardinal.* *See* THIARD DE BISSY.

BYSSHE (EDWARD) *Author of "The Art of English Poetry."* *See* BULSTRODE (*Sir* Richard) Original Letters written to the Earl of Arlington by Sir Richard Bulstrode, *etc.* [Edited by E. Bysshe.] 1712. 8°. E. **1997.** (2.)

—— *See* XENOPHON, *the Historian.* [*Memorabilia.—English.*] The Memorable Things of Socrates . . . Translated into English [by E. Bysshe], *etc.* 1712. 8°. **523.** i. **8.**

—— *See* XENOPHON, *the Historian.* [*Memorabilia.—English.*] The Memorable Things of Socrates . . . By E. Bysshe. 1722. 8°. **8463.** cc. **39.**

—— —— 1758. 12°. **8460.** aaa. **29.**

—— —— 1889. 8°. **12208.bb.15/158.**

—— —— 1904. 8°. [*Cassell's National Library.* New series. vol. 49.] **012209.ff.1/49.**

—— The Art of English Poetry: containing, I. Rules for making verses. II. A dictionary of rhymes. III. A collection of the most natural, agreeable, and noble thoughts . . . that are to be found in the best English poets. 3 pt. *R. Knaplock: London,* 1702. 8°. **11633.** bb. **8.**

—— The second edition, corrected and improved. 3 pt. *Sam. Buckley: London,* 1705. 8°. **1480.** aaa. **7.**

—— The fifth edition. 3 pt. *J. Churchill: London,* 1714. 12°. **238.** g. **1, 2.**

BYSSHE (EDWARD) *Author of "The Art of English Poetry."*

—— The Art of English Poetry . . . The sixth edition corrected and enlarged. (First volume.) 2 pt. *O. Loyd, etc.: London,* 1718. 12°. **11603.** i. **46.**
Imperfect; wanting vol. 2.

—— The seventh edition, corrected and enlarged. 2 vol. *R. Wilkin: London,* 1724. 12°. **11824.** b. **33.**

—— The seventh edition, corrected and enlarged. 2 vol. *A. Bettesworth: London,* 1725. 12°. **992.** d. **3.**

—— The eighth edition, corrected and enlarged. 2 vol. *F. Clay: London,* 1737. 12°. **11602.** bbb. **9, 10.**

—— The ninth edition, corrected and enlarged. 2 vol. *Hitch & Hawes: London,* 1762. 12°. **11603.** cc. **18.**

—— [Another copy of sig. N5–O12 of vol. 2.] **1162.** c. **38.** (1.)

—— Rules for making English Verse. [Extracted from "The Art of English Poetry."] *See* HOOD (Thomas) *the Younger.* Practical Guide to English Versification, *etc.* 1877. 8°. **2308.** a. **12.**

—— The British Parnassus: or, a Compleat common-place-book of English poetry . . . alphabetically digested . . . To which is prefix'd, a Dictionary of rhymes. 2 vol. *J. Pemberton; J. Morphew: London,* 1714. 12°. **992.** d. **1, 2.**

—— [Another copy.] **238.** g. **3.**

—— [A reissue.] The Art of English Poetry, vol. the III^{d}. and IVth. Which, with the two former volumes, make a compleat common-place-book of English poetry, *etc.* *W. Taylor: London,* 1718. 12°. **1346.** c. **32.**
Imperfect; wanting vol. 4.

—— The Art of English Poetry, 1708. With an introduction by A. Dwight Culler. pp. vi. 36. *Los Angeles,* 1953. 8°. [*Augustan Reprint Society. Publication.* no. 40.] W.P. **2367.** a/**40.**

BYSSHE (*Sir* EDWARD) [For Heraldic Visitations made by Sir E. Bysshe and by his deputies:] *See* ENGLAND.—*College of Arms.* [*Visitations.*]

—— *See* PALLADIUS, successively *Bishop of Helenopolis* and *of Aspona.* Παλλαδιου περι των της 'Ινδιας ἐθνων . . . nunc primum in lucem protulit . . . E. Bissæus, *etc.* *Gr. & Lat.* 1665. 4°. **149.** b. **4.**

—— *See* UPTON (NICLAUS) Nicolai Uptoni De studio militari, libri quatuor . . . E. Bissæus e codicibus MSS. primus publici juris fecit, notisque illustravit. 1654. fol. **M.L.f.17.**

—— Bibliotheca Bissæana: sive Catalogus librorum in omni arte & linguâ præstantissimorum, quos . . . undecunque conquisitos, eleganter etiam compingi, et dorsis deauratis ornari curavit . . . Edoardus Bissæus . . . Horum auctio habebitur Londini 15 die Novembris in ædibus Joannis Dunmore, *etc.* (A Catalogue of Sir Edward Bish's books of heraldry.) pp. 70. 4. MS. NOTES OF PRICES [*London,* 1679.] 4°. **C.120.c.2.(11.**

—— [Another copy.] MS. NOTES OF PRICES. **11906.** e. **11**
Without the catalogue of Books of heraldry.

BYSSHE (PERCY SHELLEY) The Charlatans. [A novel. pp. 320. *Everett & Co.: London,* 1909. 8°. **012626.** aaa. **11**

BYSTANDER. *See* CITIZEN. A Reply to a Most Parti[al] Pamphlet entitled, a Letter from a By-Stander to th[e] commissioners for rebuilding the bridge at Bristol. 1762. 8°. **101.** k. **2**

BYSTANDER.

—— *See* STRATFORD (Ferdinando) Observations on the Letter by a By-Stander, Bristol printed in the year 1760. 1762. 8°. **101. k. 10.**

—— Animadversions on the Rev. Mr. E. Harwood's . . . letter to the Rev. Mr. Caleb Evans [upon the confession of faith made by him at his ordination]. By a By-Stander. pp. 39. *S. Farley: Bristol,* 1767. 8°. **4136. f. 2. (1.)**

—— The Bystander. [A satire.] pp. vii. 50. *M. Hingeston: London,* 1772. 8°. **8132. de. 1. (6.)**

—— The Bystander. A monthly review, *etc. See* PERIODICAL PUBLICATIONS.—*Toronto.*

—— The Bystander, a monthly supplement. *See* PERIODICAL PUBLICATIONS.—*London.* The Saturday Journal, *etc.*

—— The By-Stander, or, Universal Weekly Expository. *See* PERIODICAL PUBLICATIONS.—*London.*

—— The Catholick Gamesters, or a Dubble Match of Bowleing . . . To the tune of, The Plot in the Meal-Tub . . . Published by a By-stander, *etc.* [With an engraving representing incidents in the Popish Plot.] [*London?* 1680?] *s. sh.* fol. **1865. c. 19. (50.)**

—— Common Sense: in some free remarks on the efficiency of the moral change . . . By a By-stander. pp. 52. *S. Inslee & A. Car: New-York,* 1772. 4°. **4402. dd. 14.**

—— Confession and Absolution. A letter to the Right Reverend the Lord Bishop of Exeter on his late correspondence with the very Rev. the Dean of Exeter, from a Bystander. pp. 28. *Longman & Co.: London,* 1852. 8°. **4107. d. 16.**

—— The Consequences of Laying an Additional Duty on Spirituous Liquors, candidly considered. By a Bystander. pp. 24. *H. Whitridge: London,* 1751. 8°. **8225. b. 25.**

—— Domestic Economy, Gymnastics, and Music: an omitted clause in the Education Bill. By a Bystander [i.e. Patrick Fraser]. pp. 24. *W. P. Kennedy: Edinburgh,* 1855. 8°. **8308. e. 15.**

—— Fair Play is a Jewel: or, the Language and conduct of the discussers' discussed; in which the case is fairly stated respecting the Bishop of Salisbury's late Charge, and Mr. Wansey's Letter . . . Occasioned by a pamphlet, entitled "Rights of Discussion." By a By-Stander. pp. 63. *J. Easton: Salisbury,* 1799. 8°. **4105. bb. 15.**

—— A Letter from a By-stander [signing himself J. H.] containing . . . objections to the Bill . . . for the better prevention of clandestine marriages, *etc.* 1753. 8°. *See* H., J. **T. 1705. (1.)**

—— A Letter from a By-stander to a Member of Parliament: wherein is examined What necessity there is for the maintenance of a large regular land-force in this island; what proportions the revenues of the Crown have born to those of the people, at different periods . . . and whether the weight of power in the regal or popular scale now preponderates. [By Corbyn Morris.] pp. 114. *J. Roberts: London,* 1741. 8°. **1103. f. 15. (1.)**

—— The second edition. pp. 112. *J. Roberts: London,* 1742. 8°. **1398.d.49.**

—— [Another copy.] A Letter from a By-stander to a Member of Parliament . . . The second edition. [By Corbyn Morris.] *London,* 1742. 8°. **8833. a. 50. (1.)**

BYSTANDER.

—— [Another copy.] **293.k.30.(2.)**

—— [Another copy.] *J. Roberts: London,* 1742. 8°. **T. 1813. (10.)**
Imperfect; wanting the half-title.

—— [Another copy.] **T. 1111. (3*.)**
Imperfect; wanting the half-title.

—— The third edition. pp. 112. *J. Robinson: London,* 1743. 8°. **T. 1111. (5.)**

—— *See* CARTE (Thomas) A Full and Clear Vindication of the Full Answer to a Letter from a Bystander, *etc.* 1743. 8°. **9510. c. 8.**

—— *See* CARTE (Thomas) A Letter to the Reverend Mr. Thomas Carte, author of the Full Answer to the Letter from a Bystander, *etc.* 1743. 8°. **1093. d. 97.**

—— *See* H——, R——, *Esq.* A Full Answer to the Letter from a By-Stander, wherein his false calculations and misrepresentations of facts in the time of King Charles II. are refuted, *etc.* 1742. 8°. **1103. f. 15. (3.)**

—— A Proper Answer to the By-stander [i.e. to "A Letter from a By-stander" by C. Morris]. Wherein is shewn I. That there is no necessity for . . . the maintenance of a large regular . . . land force in this island. II. That by keeping up a standing army for preventing an invasion, we shall at last render it certain and successful, *etc.* [By William Pulteney, Earl of Bath?] pp. 78. *T. Cooper: London,* 1742. 8°. **1103. f. 15. (2.)**

—— [Another copy.] **8833.a.50.(2.)**

—— [Another copy.] **T. 1813. (5.)**

—— Observations and Illustrations, on a pamphlet . . . entitled, Minutes of the case of Waithman & Co. v. Birch, determined in the Insolvent Debtors' Court, November 9, 1816 . . . By a Bystander. pp. 29. *J. Ross: London,* [1818.] 8°. **518. e. 23. (13.)**

—— Public Competitions. Public Works. A letter to the Right Honourable the First Commissioner of Her Majesty's Works and Public Buildings. By a Bystander. pp. 12. *J. E. Taylor: London,* 1858. 8°. **07807. i. 24. (3.)**

—— Remarks on the Answer of the Reverend Mr. M——n [i.e. M. Madan], to the Faithful Narrative of Facts [by J. Kimpton], relating to the late presentation of Mr. H——s [i.e. T. Haweis] to the Rectory of Al—w—le [i.e. Aldwinkle] in Northamptonshire . . . By a By-Stander. pp. 27. *J. Lee: London,* 1767. 8°. **4103. aaa. 16.**

—— [Another copy.] **1482. c. 5. (3.)**

—— A Review of the Recent Proceedings connected with the proposal for the erection of a Chapel attached to Cheltenham College . . . By a By-stander. pp. 30. *H. Davies: Cheltenham; Hall, Virtue & Co.: London,* [1856.] 8°. **4108. d. 12.**

—— A True State of the Case concerning the Good and Evil which the Bill for the Naturalization of the Jews [26 George II. c. 26] may bring upon Great Britain. With some remarks on the speeches of Sir J—— B——d [i.e. Sir John Barnard.] and H——s Fra——y, Esq. [i.e. Nicholas Fazakerley] upon the said bill. By a Bystander. pp. 32. *J. Noon; R. Baldwin: London,* 1753. 8°. **1093. e. 40.**

—— [Another copy.] **T. 2231. (8.)**

—— [Another copy.] **111. e. 13.**

BYSTERUS (Jacobus) Dissertatio medica inauguralis de nephritide, *etc.* pp. 31. *Lugduni Batavorum*, 1734. 4°. **1185. i. 10. (6.)**

BYSTERUS (Symon Lucas) *See* Claessen (D.) Rotterdamsche Moort, begaen door den Dijckgraef Duyn Claessen, op de ghevanckenisse des eerw: ende godtsalighen S. L. Bysterus, *etc.* 1621. 4°. **T. 2251. (9.)**

BYSTERVELDT (Hadrianus a) *See* Damman (H.)

BYSTERVELT (Hermannus van) Disputatio theologica de generatione ex sanguinibus, ex voluntate carnis, & ex voluntate viri, ad Johan. I. vers. 13, *etc.* *Praes.* J. à Marck. *A. Elzevier: Lugduni Batavorum*, 1693. 4°. **T. 2172. (10.)**

BYSTRICKÝ (Rudolf)

—— Mírová smlouva s Německem s hlediska mezinárodního práva. Referát z diskuse fakulty mezinárodních vztahů Karlovy university k německé otázce. pp. 102. *Praha*, 1954. 8°. **8029. d. 79.**

BYSTŘINA (Otakar) Hanácká Legenda. Kresby Adolfa Kašpara. [With glossary.] pp. 158. *v Novém Jičíně*, 1904. 8°. **12450. ccc. 16.**

BYSTRÖM (H.) Handbok för befälhafvare inom handelsflottan. pp. 308. *Stockholm*, 1891. 8°. **8806. dd. 16.**

—— [Sveriges lastageplatser.] The Loading Ports of Sweden. Translated and improved by Kurt Asker. pp. 106. *C. Wilson: London*, [1880.] 8°. **10496. cc. 7.**

BYSTRÖM (Jakob Jacobsson) En frikyrklig banbrytare, eller F. O. Nilssons lif och verksamhet. [With illustrations, including a portrait.] pp. 293. *Stockholm*, 1910. 8°. **4888. e. 49.**

BYSTRÖM (Johan Niklas)

—— *See* Nyman (T.) Johan Niklas Byström. Ett konstnärsöde, *etc.* [With illustrations, including portraits.] 1939. 4°. **7876. t. 8.**

—— Byström's skulptur-galleri, innefattande en cykel af konstnärens förnämsta arbeten efter i Rom gjorde afteckningar, *etc.* [With verses by various authors.] (Minnesteckning öfver Johan Nicl. Byström . . . Föredrag af Wilhelm Wohlfahrt.) 3 hft. *Stockholm*, 1849. fol. **1753. c. 1.**

BYSTRÖM (Johan Thomas) Utlåtande, efter hållen syn å Lunds Domkyrka, till Domkyrko-Rådet i Lund, afgivet den 27. Mars 1860. pp. 16. *Lund*, [1860.] 4°. **7814. bbb. 12.**

BYSTRÖM (Olof)

—— *See* Bellman (Carl M.) Dikter av Carl Michael Bellman. (dl. 2. Fredmans epistlar. Kommentar. Utgiven av O. Byström.) 1916, *etc.* 8°. [*Svenska författare.* 5.] **Ac. 9070.**

BYSTRÖM (Tryggve)

—— *See* Berglund (L.) Strömbergs synonymordbok. (Huvudmedarbetarna: L. Berglund, T. Byström [and others].) 1953. 8°. **12973. d. 40.**

BYSTRÖM-LINDHAGEN (Agnes)

—— *See* Galsworthy (John) [*Smaller Collections.*] En Fejd. Noveller. Till svenska av A. Byström-Lindhagen. 1926. 8°. **12651. g. 34.**

BYSTROŃ (Andrzej) Polityczny program oświatowy. pp. 51. *Kraków*, 1914. 8°. **8095. ff. 11.**

BYSTROŃ (Jan)

—— *See* Alexis, *Saint, of Rome.* [*Other Versions.*] Żywot świętego Alexego wyznawcy i żywot świętego Eustachiusza męczennika. Druk Krakowski z roku 1529. Wydał i objaśnił J. Bystroń. [1894.] 8°. [*Akademya Umiejętności. Sprawozdania Komisyi Językowej.* tom 5. no. 9.] **Ac. 750/29.**

—— *See* Romans. Historye Rzymskie. Gesta Romanorum. Wydał Dr. J. Bystroń. 1894. 8°. [*Akademya Umiejętności. Biblioteka pisarzow polskich.* no. 29.] **Ac. 750/45.**

—— Lessings Epigramme und seine Arbeiten zur Theorie des Epigramms. pp. 56. *Krakau*, 1889. 8°. **011840. h. 56. (3.)**

—— O użyciu genetivu w języku polskim. Przyczynek dó historycznej składni polskiej. [1895.] *See* Cracow.—*Akademya Umiejętności, etc.* Rozprawy . . . Wydział Filologiczny. ser. 2. tom 7. no. 2. 1874, *etc.* 8°. **Ac. 750/13.**

—— Przyczynek do historyi języka polskiego z początku XV. wieku, na podstawie zapisków sądowych w Księdze Ziemi Czerskiej. [1891.] *See* Cracow.—*Akademya Umiejętności, etc.* Sprawozdania Komisyi Językowej, *etc.* tom 4. no. 6. 1880, *etc.* 8°. **Ac. 750/29.**

BYSTROŃ (Jan Stanisław)

—— *See* Polish Silesia. Pieśni ludowe z polskiego Śląska, *etc.* (tom 1. Wydał i komentarzem zaopatrzył J. St. Bystroń.) 1927, *etc.* 8°. **Ac. 750/129.**

—— Człowiek i książka, *etc.* [With plates.] pp. 200. *Warszawa*, 1935. 8°. **11912. a. 63.**

—— Dzieje obyczajów w dawniej Polsce, wiek XVI–XVIII, *etc.* [With plates.] 2 tom. *Warszawa*, [1934.] 4°. **2364. h. 12.**

—— Etnografia Polski. pp. 232. *w Poznaniu*, 1947. 8°. **10008. n. 2.**

—— Komizm. [With illustrations, including portraits.] pp. 540. *Lwów, Warszawa*, [1939.] fol. **L.R. 280. b. 9.**

—— Księga imion w Polsce używanych. pp. 376. *Warszawa*, 1938. 8°. **012902. n. 1.**

—— Kultura ludowa. pp. 462. *Warszawa*, 1936. 8°. **8358. c. 147.**

—— Łańcuch szczęścia i inne ciekawostki. [Essays.] pp. 230. *Warszawa*, 1938. 8°. **12359. b. 19.**

—— Literaci i grafomani z czasów Królestwa Kongresowego 1815–1831. Dwanaście portretów, *etc.* [With portraits.] pp. 272. *Lwów, Warszawa*, [1938.] 8°. **11862. b. 29.**

—— Megalomanja narodowa. Źródła—teorje—skutki. pp. 28. *Warszawa*, 1924. 8°. **08008. aa. 1.**

—— Megalomanja narodowa [and other essays]. pp. 268. *Warszawa*, 1935. 8°. **012403. k. 25.**

—— Nazwiska polskie. pp. viii. 243. *Lwów*, 1927. 8°. [*Lwowska bibljoteka slawistyczna.* tom 4.] **011903.dd.48/4.**

—— Polska pieśń ludowa. Wybór. Opracował Jan St. Bystroń. pp. 170. *Kraków*, [1921.] 8°. [*Bibljoteka narodowa.* ser. 1. no. 26.] **W.P. c. 656. a/26.**

—— Przysłowia polskie. pp. 260. 1933. 8°. *See* Cracow.—*Akademya Umiejętności, etc.* **Ac. 750/139.**

—— Publiczność literacka. pp. 411. *Lwów, Warszawa*, 1938. 8°. **11861. c. 12.**

BYSTROŃ (JAN STANISŁAW)

—— Socjologja. Wstęp informacyjny i bibljograficzny. pp. 154. *Warszawa,* 1931. 8°. **8288**. cc. **6**.

—— Tło ogólne kultury polskiej XVII i XVIII wieku. *See* LAM (S.) Polska, jej dzieje i kultura, *etc.* tom 2. [1937.] fol. L.R. **276**. b. **9**.

—— Typy ludowe J. P. Norblina. 27 tablic, *etc.* (Résumé. Les types populaires de J. P. Norblin.) pp. 66. *Kraków,* 1934. 4°. [*Wydawnictwa Muzeum Etnograficznego w Krakowie.* no. 6.] Ac. **6231**. d.

—— Wstęp do ludoznawstwa polskiego. pp. viii. 176. *we Lwowie,* 1926. 8°. [*Lwowska bibljoteka slawistyczna.* tom 2.] **011903.dd.48/2.**

BYSTROW (A.) *See* BUISTROV (A. E.)

BYSTROW (PETER) Über die angeborene Trichterbrust. Inauguraldissertation, *etc.* (Separatabdruck aus dem "Archiv für Orthopädie, Mechanotherapie und Unfallchirurgie.") pp. 21. *Wiesbaden,* 1907. 8°. **7307**. ee. **13**. (**2**.)

BYSTRYANSKY (V. A.) *See* BUISTRYANSKY.

BYSTRZONOWSKI (LUDWIK) *Count.* *See* PERIODICAL PUBLICATIONS.—*Paris.* Kraj i emigracya, *etc.* [Edited by L. Bystrzonowski.] [1835, *etc.*] 8°. P.P. **4864**. d.

—— Notice sur le réseau stratégique de la Pologne pour servir à une guerre de partisans . . . Extrait du Spectateur militaire, *etc.* pp. 45. *Paris,* 1842. 8°. **10290**. bbb. **16**.

—— O Algieryi, a głównie o wypadkach zaszłych w tym kraju od zajęcia onego przez Francuzów. Przez L. hr. B. . . . Wydanie J. N. Bobrowicza. [By Count L. Bystrzonowski.] 2 tom. 1846. 8°. *See* B . . ., L., *Hr.* **9061**. a. **17**.

—— Sur la Serbie dans ses rapports européens avec la question d'Orient. pp. vii. 180. *Paris,* 1845. 8°. **1250**. e. **25**.

BYSTRZONOWSKI (WOJCIECH) Polak sensat w liscie, w komplemenćie polityk, humanistá w dyskurśie, w mowách státystá, náprzykład dány szkolney młodzi od X. W. Bystrzonowskiego. *w Wilnie,* 1733. 8°. **8403**. bbb. **9**.

BYSTRZYCKI (JAN) Krasiński a Kajsiewicz. [On their personal relations. With portraits.] 2 cz. pp. 136. *Kraków,* 1912. 8°. **010790**. e. **41**.

BYSTRZYCKI (MARCIN) *See* HAUR (J. K.) Oekonomika Ziemianska Generalna . . . z nowym przydatkiem geometryi gospodarskiey, napisaney od . . . M. Bystrzyckiego, *etc.* 1757. fol. **5758**. g. **2**.

BYTAL PUCHEESEE. *See* BAITĀL-PACHĪSĪ.

BYTAL-PUCHISI. *See* BAITĀL-PACHĪSĪ.

BYTEMEISTER (HEINRICH JOHANN) Henrici Johannis Bytemeister Bibliothecæ appendix sive Catalogus apparatus curiosorum artificialium et naturalium, subjunctis experimentis a possessore editus . . . Editio altera auctior, *etc.* [With plates, including a portrait.] pp. 58. pl. XXVIII. [*Helmstadt,* 1735.] 4°. **458**. b. **25**.

—— Catalogus Bibliothecæ Lautensackianæ . . . a. MDCCXXXVII. Cellis Lyneburgicis die 1. Aug. et seqq. auctione publica distrahendæ . . . secundum materiarum ordinem dispositus atque editus ab H. J. Bytemeister. 3 pt. MS. NOTES OF PRICES. *Helmstadii,* [1737.] 8°. **271**. b. **21**.

BYTEMEISTER (HEINRICH JOHANN)

—— Commentarius historicus de augustæ domûs Brunsvigio-Luneburgensis meritis in rem literariam, *etc.* pp. 168. *Helmstadii,* 1730. 4°. **819**. g. **11**.

—— Henrici Johannis Bytemeisteri Delineatio rei numismaticæ . . . Editio III. correctior. pp. 109. *Argentorati,* 1744. 8°. **790**. b. **3**. (**3**.)

—— M. Henr. Joh. Bytmeisteri Dissertatio de sela contra Gottlieb [i.e. Henr. Gottlieb Reine]. 1767. *See* UGOLINUS (Blasius) Thesaurus antiquitatum sacrarum, *etc.* vol. 32. 1744, *etc.* fol. **686**. l. **12**.

BYTHELL (JOHN WILLIAM) Salopia, The News-room, and other poems. pp. xii. 252. *Houlston & Stoneman: London,* 1841. 8°. **1164**. c. **29**.

BYTHELL (WILLIAM) The Trials of William Bythell, William Hartley, William Ladds, and Thomas Tothill, at the Sessions House in the Old Bayly, for misdemeanors. pp. 2. *Richard Baldwin: London,* 1695. fol. **515**. l. **6**. (**23**.)

BYTHELL (WILLIAM JAMES STOREY) and **BARCLAY** (ALFRED ERNEST) X-Ray Diagnosis and Treatment. A text-book for general practitioners and students. [With plates.] pp. xii. 147. *Oxford University Press; Hodder & Stoughton: London,* 1912. 8°. [*Oxford Medical Publications.*] **20036.a.1/87.**

BYTHESEA (GEORGE) A Sermon preached at Igtham, in Kent before the New Amicable Society, established in that parish, on Monday, the 8th of June, 1795, *etc.* [By G. Bythesea.] pp. 14. 1802. 8°. *See* IGHTHAM.—*New Amicable Society.* **4473**. e. **4**. (**7**.)

BYTHEWOOD (WILLIAM MEECHAM) *See* ENGLAND.—*Laws and Statutes.*—IV.—*Savings Banks.* A Collection of all the Acts of Parliament relating to Banks for Savings in England. With explanatory notes . . . By W. M. Bythewood. 1824. 12°. C.T. **125**. (**1**.)

—— A Course of Reading for Students in the several branches of the profession of Law. *See* WYNNE (Edward) *Barrister-at-Law.* Eunomus . . . The fifth edition; with numerous additional notes . . . by W. M. Bythewood. 1822. 12°. **6145**. a. **34**, **35**.

—— A Selection of Precedents, from the best modern manuscript collections, and drafts of actual practice . . . forming a system of conveyancing; with dissertations and practical notes. By W. M. Bythewood . . . continued by Thomas Jarman. (Index in two parts by George Sweet.) vol. 4–10. *S. Sweet; R. Pheney: London,* 1827– . 8°. **511**. b. **13–20**.

Imperfect; wanting vol. 1–3. vol. 5 is of the second edition.

—— The second edition, corrected, with additions, by James Stewart. (vol. 4–9. By William Palmer Parken and James Stewart.—An Appendix shewing the alterations effected by the recent acts with the precedents rendered necessary by them. By J. Stewart.) 9 vol. *S. Sweet; R. Pheney; Saunders & Benning: London,* 1828–34. 8°. **511**. b.**4–12**.

—— A Selection of Precedents . . . by . . . W. M. Bythewood . . . and Thomas Jarman . . . The third edition, by George Sweet. [vol. 8. pt. 1 by W. Stokes. vol. 11 by G. Sweet and A. Bisset.] vol. 1–7, vol. 8. pt. 1, vol. 9, 11. *S. Sweet; H. Sweet: London,* 1841, 39–61. 8°. **6305**. h. **7**.

No more published.

—— New edition, by Cayley Shadwell. vol. 1. *Shaw & Sons: London,* 1850. 8°. **6305**. e. **3**.

No more published.

BYTHEWOOD (WILLIAM MEECHAM)

—— [Another edition.] Bythewood & Jarman's System of Conveyancing . . . Fourth edition by Leopold George Gordon Robbins. (Supplement. By the editor and Arthur Turnour Murray.) 8 vol. *Henry Sweet: London*, 1884–93. 8º. **6306**. cc. **1**.

—— *See* SWEET (George) Recent Statutes relating to the Practice of Conveyancing, *etc.* (Supplement to the title "Purchase Deeds" in Jarman & Bythewood's Conveyancing.) 1850. 8º. **6306**. r. **21**.

—— *See* SWEET (George) The Statute, 7 & 8 Vict. Cap. 76, intituled An Act to Simplify the Transfer of Property, *etc.* (Published as a supplement to the ninth volume of Bythewood and Jarman's Conveyancing.) 1844. 8º. **1380**. k. **5**.

—— Bythewood & Jarman. A compendium by Charles Edward Cree, assisted by Donald C. L. Cree . . . of the Precedents in Conveyancing by the late W. M. Bythewood, Thomas Jarman & George Sweet. 2 vol. *Sweet & Maxwell: London*, 1915. 8º. **6306**. r. **1**.

—— Second edition. By Stuart L. Bathurst . . . and Donald C. L. Cree . . . assisted by Albert S. Oppé . . . A. R. Taylour . . . and K. Richard A. Hart (and Norman H. Oldham). 2 vol. *Sweet & Maxwell: London*, 1926. 8º. **6305**. s. **1**.

—— Bythewood & Jarman's Law of Leases. Fifth edition revised, with additions, by Norman H. Oldham . . . (Founded on the preliminary dissertation in the fourth edition of Bythewood & Jarman's Conveyancing Precedents.) Reprinted from . . . "The Conveyancer." pp. xii. 285. *Sweet & Maxwell: London*, 1923. fol. **6325**. y. **16**.

BYTHNER (BARTHOLOMAEUS) Fraterna & modesta ad omnes per vniuersam Europam Reformatas Ecclesias, earumque . . . moderatores ac defensores, pro vnanimi, in toto religionis Euangelicæ negotio consensu inter se constituendo exhortatio. A pio & erudito theologo [i.e. B. Bythner] nomine fratrum Euangelicæ professionis in regno Poloniæ existentium, ante aliquot annos scripta, *etc.* pp. 258. 1618. 8º. *See* EUROPE.—*Reformed Churches*. **1011**. d. **12**.

—— *See* STARKE (Arnold) "Fraterna Exhortatio," 1607/1618 . . . Mit einem Anhang über den Verfasser der Schrift, B. Bythner, *etc.* 1937. 8º. [BERGER (*Carl*) *Gottes Wille und die geschichtliche Wirklichkeit, etc.*] **04374**. gg. **41**.

BYTHNER (VICTORINUS) Clavis linguæ sanctæ universas voces Pentateuchi sententiis biblicis comprehendens, earumq; analysin critice exhibens, *etc.* pp. 135. MS. NOTES. *Ex officina R. Daniel: Cantabrigiæ*, 1648. 8º. **12903**. aa. **17**.

—— לשון לםודים. Lingua eruditorum. Hoc est, nova et methodica institutio linguæ sanctæ, usui eorum quibus fontes Israëlis plene intelligere, & ex illis limpidissimas aquas haurire, curæ cordique est, accommodata. pp. 224. *Typis Guil. Turner; impensis Authoris: Oxoniæ*, 1638. **622**. d. **38**.

—— לשון למודים Lingua eruditorum: sive Methodica institutio linguæ sanctæ . . . Cui addita est introductio ad linguam Chaldæam Veteris Testamenti . . . Editio novissima, *etc.* pp. 134. *Ex officina Jacobi Flesher: Londini*, 1650. 12º. **1473**. b. **40**.

—— [Another edition.] Cui addita est introductio ad linguam chaldæam Veteris Testamenti. . . . Editio novissima ultimam manum authoris iam passa. pp. 132. *Typis J. Flesher; apud J. Hart: Londini*, 1664. 12º. **12904**. a. **11**.

BYTHNER (VICTORINUS)

—— [Another edition.] pp. 135. *Typis T. Roycroft; Apud J. Hart: Londini*, 1675. 12º. **12903**. aa. **9**.

—— [Another edition.] Victorini Bythneri Institutio linguæ sanctæ, cui addita est Introductio ad linguam chaldæam Veteris Testamenti, auctore eodem. Editio nova, accurante Rev. J. A. Hessey. 2 pt. *Impensis S. Bagster & Fill.: Londini*, 1853. 8º. **12903**. d. **10**.

—— Sceleton Institutionis hebrææ Victorini Bythneri, una cum schemate conjugationum hebraicarum *etc.* *See* BIBLE.—*Song of Solomon.* [*Hebrew.*] Epithalamium mysticum Salomonis, *etc.* 1677. 8º. **01902**. a. **19**.

—— Lyra prophetica Davidis regis sive Analysis critico-practica Psalmorum . . . Insuper Harmonia hebræi textus cum paraphrasi chaldæa & versione græca LXXII interpretum . . . Cui ad calcem addita est Brevis institutio linguæ hebrææ & chaldææ, *etc.* pp. 342 [352]. 69. 46. *Typis J. Flesher: Londini*, 1650. 4º. **3089**. gg. **5**.

—— [A reissue.] *Typis J. Flesher; Apud C. Bee: Londini*, 1653. 4º. **672**. d. **1**.

—— [Another copy.] **E. 478**.

—— [Another edition.] pp. 352. 69. 46. *Typis J. Flesher: Londini; Apud G. Morden: Cantabrigiæ*, 1664. 4º. **3089**. gg. **6**.

—— [Another edition.] pp. 352. 69. 46. *Typis E. Flesher: Londini; Apud G. Morden: Cantabrigiæ*, 1679. 4º. **3089**. dd. **13**.

—— The Lyre of David; or, an Analysis of the Psalms . . . To which is added a Hebrew and Chaldee Grammar . . . Translated by the Rev. Thomas Dee . . . To which are added, by the translator, a Praxis of the first eight psalms and tables of the imperfect verbs. pp. vii. 375. *John Cumming: Dublin*, 1836. 8º. **690**. d. **29**.

—— New edition, most carefully revised . . . with numerous . . . additions . . . by N. L. Benmohel. pp. xxx. 365. ii. *Cumming & Ferguson: Dublin*, 1847. 8º. **1215**. d. **4**.

—— עמיר קציר רב Manipulus messis magnæ. Sive Grammatica exemplaris XXXII sententiis, CCLXVII vocibus, omn[illegible] vocibus, omne id quod ad tò technikòn Linguæ Sanct[illegible] pertinet, complectens, *etc.* *Typis Thomæ Paine: Londin*[illegible] 1639. 8º. **622**. d. [illegible]
Interleaved.

BYTHNERUS (CAROLUS HENRICUS) Hypopiasm[illegible] Paulinus. Ex 1. Cor. ix. vers. xxvii, *etc.* *Praes.* J. [illegible] Dannhauer. *J. Pickel: Argentorati*, 1650. 4º. **1014**. e. **5**[illegible]

BYTHNERUS (VICTORINUS) *See* BYTHNER.

BYTHWAY (EDWARD MELVILLE)

—— The Old Swansea Potteries and Swansea-Nantga[illegible] China Works. A souvenir. [With photographs.] *Ern*[illegible] *Davies & Co.: Swansea*, 1926. 8º. **07813**. ee.

BYTHWAY (JOHN EDWARD) Facts on the Sunday Questio[illegible] showing how far the Lord's-Day differs from the Sabbat[illegible] *etc.* pp. vi. 49. *Elliot Stock: London*, 1882. 8º. **4372**. df. **12**. [illegible]

—— On Mr. F. R. Statham's Articles on the Transv[illegible] Question, contributed to the "Manchester Guardian," 1896. pp. 78. *Printed for private circulation*, [1903.] **8157**. de.

YTKOWSKI (ZYGMUNT) Gerhart Hauptmanns Naturalismus und das Drama. pp. 208. *Hamburg & Leipzig*, 1908. 8°. [*Beiträge zur Ästhetik*. Bd. 11.] **011824**. k. **50/11**.

— Stanisław Przybyszewski. *See* LEOPOL.—*Związek Naukowo-Literacki*. Charakterystyki literackie, *etc.* 1902. 8°. Ac. **8975**.

YTOVETZSKI (PAVEL L.)

— *See* CORMACK (Maribelle) A Recruit for Abe Lincoln, *etc.* [Written in collaboration with P. L. Bytovetzski.] 1942. 8°. **12726**. bb. **4**.

— *See* CORMACK (Maribelle) Road to Down Under, *etc.* (Written in collaboration with P. L. Bytovetzski.) [1944.] 8°. **12727**. aaa. **3**.

— How to master the Violin. A practical guide for students and teachers. pp. 108. *Oliver Ditson Co.: Boston*, [1917.] 8°. **7894**. bb. **24**.

YTTNER (ANDERS)

— *See* RUSSELL (Bertrand A.) *Earl Russell*. [Sceptical Essays.] Skeptiska essäer. (Till svenska av A. Byttner.) 1950. 8°. **08460**. k. **17**.

— *See* RUSSELL (Bertrand A. W.) *Earl Russell*. [Human Society in Ethics and Politics.] Moral och politik. (Till svenska av A. Byttner.) 1955. 8°. **8413**. b. **17**.

— *See* RUSSELL (Bertrand A. W.) *Earl Russell*. [The Impact of Science on Society.] Vetenskap och samhälle. (Till svenska av A. Byttner.) 1952. 8°. **8474**. aa. **49**.

— *See* RUSSELL (Bertrand A. W.) *Earl Russell*. [Philosophical Essays.] Mystik och logik, och andra essäer. (Till svenska av A. Byttner.) 1954. 8°. **8473**. p. **48**.

— *See* SCHUMPETER (J. A.) [Ten Great Economists.] Stora nationalekonomer, *etc.* (Översatt och redigerad av A. Byttner.) 1953. 8°. **8208**. ccc. **8**.

— *See* UTLEY (Freda) Desillusionen Sovjet, *etc.* (Översättningen är utförd av Anders Byttner.) [1949.] 8°. **10292**. pp. **35**.

BYTTON (THOMAS DE) *Bishop of Exeter*. *See* BITTON.

BYTZOWIUS (HENRICUS CHRISTOPHORUS) Observationes circa Jovem Elicium, *etc.* *Def.* M. Hassing. pp. 19–32. *Hafniæ*, [1717.] 4°. **704**. e. **24**. (**23**.)

B'YUIK (TOMAS) *See* BEWICK (Thomas)

BYUISSON (ET'EN) *See* BUISSON (Étienne) *of Leysin*.

BYULER (THEDOR ANDREEVICH) *Baron*. *See* BANTUISH-KAMENSKY (N. N.) Обзоръ внѣшнихъ сношеній Россіи по 1800 годъ, *etc.* [Edited by Baron Th. A. Byuler.] 1894, *etc.* 8°. **8027**. i. **40**.

— *See* CATHARINE II., *Empress of Russia*. [*Letters.—Original Languages*.] Политическая переписка Императрицы Екатерины II. (Изданъ барономъ Ф. А. Бюллеромъ, при содѣйствіи магистра Ульяницкаго.) 1885, *etc.* 8°. [*Сборникъ Императорскаго Русскаго Историческаго Общества*. том. 48, 51, 57, 67, 87, 97, 118, 135, 145.] Ac. **7886**.

BYULLETEN'. Бюллетень. *See* PERIODICAL PUBLICATIONS.—*London*.

— Бюллетень астрономических институтов Чехословакии. *See* PRAGUE.—*Československá Akademie Věd*.

BYULLETEN'.

— Бюлетень Богословсько-педагогічної Академії. *See* MUNICH.—*Богословсько-педагогічна Академія*.

— Бюллетень Главного ботанического сада. *See* RUSSIA.—*Академия Наук СССР*. —*Главный Ботанический Сад*.

— Бюллетень Государственного Издательства. *See* RUSSIA.—*Государственное Издательство*, afterwards *Объединение Государственных Издательств*.

— Бюллетень Института по изучению истории и культуры СССР. *See* MUNICH.—*Институт по Изучению СССР*. Ac. **7357/4**.

— Бюллетень культурной информации. *See* BULGARIA.—*Министерство на Информацията и на Изкуствата.—Отдел на Културни Връзки с Чужбина*.

— **Бюллетень Извѣстій Государственнаго Контроля.** *See* RUSSIA.—***Государственный Контроль.***

— **Бюллетень Оппозиции—Большевиков-Ленинцев.** *See* PERIODICAL PUBLICATIONS.—*Paris*.

— Бюллетень Польской Академии Наук. *See* WARSAW.—*Polska Akademia Nauk*.

— Бюллетень посевной кампании. *See* RUSSIA.—*Народный Комиссаріатъ Земледѣлія*.

— Бюллетень Русского Общества Помощи Беженцам в Великобритании. *See* LONDON.—III. *Русское Общество Помощи Беженцам в Великобритании*.

— Бюллетень Союзнической Комиссии по Австрии. *See* AUSTRIA.—*Allied Commission for Austria*.

— Бюлетень Союзу Українських Національних Демократів у Злучених Державах. *See* UNITED STATES OF AMERICA.—*Союз Українських Національних Демократів у Злучених Державах*.

— Бюллетень строительной техники. *See* RUSSIA.—*Центральный Институт Информации по Строительству*.

— Бюллетень финансового и хозяйственного законодательства. *See* RUSSIA. [*Laws, etc.*—C. *Finance*.]

BYULLETENI.

— Бюллетени Ликвидаціоннаго Отдѣла Народнаго Комиссаріата Торговли и Промышленности. *See* RUSSIA.—*Народный Комиссариат Торговли и Промышленности.—Ликвидационный Отдел*.

— **Бюллетени Рукописного отдела.** *See* RUSSIA.—***Академия Наук.—Институт Русской Литературы (Пушкинский Дом).***

BYUNIAN (IOANN) *See* BUNYAN (John)

BYURO. **Бюро Научной Организаціи Труда.** *See* TARTAR SOCIALIST SOVIET REPUBLIC.—***Татарскій Совѣтъ Профессіональныхъ Союзовъ.***

— **Бюро по Евгенике. (Бюро но Генетике и Евгенике.—Бюро по Генетике.)** *See* RUSSIA.—*Академия Наук СССР*. —***Комиссія по изученію Естественныхъ Производительныхъ Силъ Россіи.***

— **Бюро Уполномоченныхъ Русскихъ Почвовѣдовъ.** *See* MOSCOW.

BYVANCK (ALEXANDER WILLEM)

— Het Brevier van Beatrix van Assendelft . . . door Dr. A. W. Byvanck en Mgr. Lagerwey. Achtten lichtdruckplaten med inleidning. pp. 27. pl. XVIII. *Leiden*, 1943. fol. L.R. **294**. b. **35**.

BYVANCK (Alexander Willem)

—— Excerpta Romana. De bronnen der Romeinsche geschiedenis van Nederland, *etc.* 3 dl. *'s-Gravenhage*, 1931–47. 8°. [*Rijks Geschiedkundige Publicatiën.* no. 73, 81, 89.] **9405**. p.

—— Gids voor de bezoekers van het Museum Meermanno-Westreenianum. I. Bewerkt door A. W. Byvanck. pp. xv. 279. pl. XXXII. 1912. 8°. *See* Hague.—*Museum Meermanno-Westreenianum.* Ac. **956**/2.

—— Het Hellenisme en zijn strijd in de antieke wereld. Rede, *etc.* pp. 35. *'s-Gravenhage*, 1922. 8°. **9041**. c. 3.

—— De Kunst der oudheid. *Leiden*, 1946– . 8°. W.P. **1379**.

—— De Middeleeuwsche boekillustratie in de Noordelijke Nederlanden. [With illustrations.] pp. 83. *Antwerpen*, 1943. 8°. **7866**. ppp. **57**. *Maerlantbibliotheek.* no. 10.

—— La Miniature dans les Pays-Bas septentrionaux. Traduit . . . par Mlle Adrienne Haye. pp. 185. pl. c. *Paris ; Bruges* [printed], 1937. 4°. Cup. **1247**. c. 14.

—— De Platen in de Aratea van Hugo de Groot [i.e. the edition of the "Syntagma Arateorum" edited by H. de Groot in 1600] . . . With a summary: The illustrations in the Aratea of Hugo Grotius, and a list of illustrated astronomical manuscripts. pp. 67. *Amsterdam*, 1949. 8°. [*Mededelingen der Koninklijke Nederlandsche Akademie van Wetenschappen.* Afd. Letterkunde. Nieuwe reeks. dl. 12. no. 2.] Ac. **944**. (2.)

—— Les Principaux manuscrits à peintures de la Bibliothèque Royale des Pays-Bas et du Musée Meermanno-Westreenianum à la Haye. pp. 155. lxvii. 1924. fol. *See* Paris.—*Société Française de Reproductions de Manuscrits à Peintures.* Ac. **9811**. c/6.

—— Le Strade romane nei Paesi Bassi, *etc.* pp. 18. pl. IV. *Roma*, 1938. 8°. [*Quaderni dell' Impero.* Le grandi strade del mondo romano. no. 7.] Ac. **103**. b/5. (3.)

—— De Tabula Peuteringiana [*sic*] en de Romeinsche wegen in Nederland. [1930.] *See* Blok (P. J.) De Romeinsche tijd en de Frankische tijd. 1929, *etc.* 8°. [*Geschiedkundige Atlas van Nederland.*] **Maps.144.a.2.**

—— Varia historica, aangeboden aan Professor Doctor A. W. Byvanck ter gelegenheid van zijn zeventigste verjaardag door de Historische Kring te Leiden. [With plates, including a portrait.] pp. 285. 1954. 8°. *See* Leyden.—*Historische Kring te Leiden.* **09009**. g. 17.

—— De Voorgeschiedenis van Nederland . . . Vierde, opnieuw verbeterde en aangevulde druk. pp. xii. 251. pl. XXXVI. *Leiden*, 1946. 8°. **7711**. b. **28**.

BYVANCK (Alexander Willem) and **HOOGEWERFF** (Godefridus Joannes)

—— Noord-Nederlandsche miniaturen in handschriften der 14^e^, 15^e^ en 16^e^ eeuwen. Verzameld en beschreven door Dr. A. W. Byvanck . . . en Dr. G. J. Hoogewerff. 4 pt. *'s-Gravenhage*, 1921–25. fol. MS. Facs. **238**.

BYVANCK (Willem Gertrud Cornelis) *See* Bijvanck.

BYVORTIUS (Matthias) *See* Baudius (D.) Dominici Baudii Orationes . . . Edente M. Byvortio. 1619. 8°. **1090**. h. 4. (2.)

BYWAART (Gerardus) Disputatio medica inauguralis de asthmate, *etc.* *Apud A. Elzevier: Lugduni Batavorum*, 1683. 4°. **1185**. g. **16**. (21.)

BYWATER (Abel) *See* Bible.—*Song of Solomon.* [*English.—Sheffield Dialect.*] The Song of Solomon, in the Sheffield Dialect . . . By A. Bywater. 1859. 16°. **3050**. a. **42**. (6.)

—— Popery Unveiled: containing 1st, some observations upon the subject of Catholic emancipation. 2d, A refutation of the principal doctrines laid down in the Catholic Bishops' declaration; and 3d, A chronology of the Popes, *etc.* pp. 32. *J. Blackwell: Sheffield*, 1826. 8°. **3938**. cc. **21**.

—— The Sheffield Dialect. [A series of papers in that dialect, with a glossary.] pp. xii. 283. *G. Chaloner: Sheffield*, 1839. 16°. **1077**. c. **23**.

—— Second edition. pp. 295. *W. Evans & Co.: London*, 1854. 12°. **1077**. c. **77**.

—— Third edition. pp. 311. *W. Nicholson & Sons: Wakefield ; T. Rodgers: Sheffield*, 1877. 8°. **12330**. d. **40**.

BYWATER (Hector Charles) *See* Baumeister (A.) [Spione durchbrechen die Front.] Spies Break Through . . . Translated and introduced by H. C. Bywater, *etc.* 1934. 8°. **09080**. aaa. **40**.

—— *See* Ellsberg (Edward) "On the Bottom" . . . Edited . . . by H. C. Bywater. 1929. 8°. **8804**. bbb. **1**.

—— *See* Hurd (*Sir* Archibald S.) and Bywater (H. C.) From Heligoland to Keeling Island, *etc.* 1914. 8°. **9085**. de. **1/19**.

—— Cruisers in Battle. Naval 'Light Cavalry' under fire 1914–1918. [With plates.] pp. xvi. 276. *Constable & Co.: London*, 1939. 8°. **08805**. b. 12.

—— The Great Pacific War. A history of the American-Japanese campaign of 1931–33. pp. ix. 317. *Constable & Co.: London*, [1925.] 8°. **12707**. h. **27**.

—— Navies and Nations. A review of naval developments since the Great War. pp. vii. 285. *Constable & Co.: London*, 1927. 8°. **08806**. d. **36**.

—— Sea-Power in the Pacific. A study of the American-Japanese naval problem . . . With 4 maps and a chart. pp. ix. 334. *Constable & Co.: London*, 1921. 8°. **08806**. c. **50**.

—— [New edition.] With a new preface and appendices recast and brought up to date. pp. xxv. 327. pl. IV. *Constable & Co.: London*, 1934. 8°. **08806**. cc. **36**.

—— A Searchlight on the Navy. pp. vii. 308. *Constable & Co.: London*, 1934. 8°. **8804**. e. **17**.

—— New edition, *etc.* pp. x. 308. *Constable & Co.: London*, 1935. 8°. **8805**. df. **20**.

—— Their Secret Purposes. Dramas and mysteries of the naval war . . . With a chart of the post-Jutland battle fleets. pp. x. 311. *Constable & Co.: London*, 1932. 8°. **09080**. aa. **50**.

BYWATER (Hector Charles) and **FERRABY** (Herbert Cecil)

—— Strange Intelligence. Memoirs of Naval Secret Service. [With a map.] pp. ix. 299. *Constable & Co.: London*, 1931. 8°. **09080**. aaa. **15**.

—— [A reissue, with the addition of a Foreword by Sir Reginald Hall.] *London*, 1934. 8°. **09080**. aaa. **45**.

— See ARISTOTLE. [*Poetica.—English.*] Aristotle's Art of Poetry . . . [Translated by I. Bywater.] With an introduction and explanations by W. H. Fyfe. 1940. 8°. **011313. a. 4.**

— See ARISTOTLE. [*Works.—English.*] The Works of Aristotle translated into English, *etc.* vol. 11. De poetica. Translated by I. Bywater.) 1908, *etc.* 8°. **08461. f. 51.**

— See ARISTOTLE. [*Ethica Nicomachea.—Greek.*] Aristotelis Ethica Nicomachea recognovit breviqe adnotatione critica instruxit I. Bywater. 1890. 8°. **8408. g. 27.**

—— [1912.] 8°. [*Scriptorum Classicorum Bibliotheca Oxoniensis.*] **11305.dd.**

— See ARISTOTLE. [*Poetica.—Greek.*] Aristotelis De arte poetica liber. Recognovit brevique adnotatione critica instruxit I. Bywater. 1898. 8°. **11312. q. 21.**

—— 1911. 8°. **11305.dd.**

— See ARISTOTLE. [*Poetica.—Greek and English.*] *Ἀριστοτελους περι ποιητικης.* Aristotle on the Art of Poetry. A revised text, with critical introduction, translation and commentary by I. Bywater. 1909. 8°. **011313.b.19.**

— See ARISTOTLE. [*Poetica.—English.*] Aristotle on the Art of Poetry. Translated by I. Bywater, *etc.* 1920. 8°. **11313. f. 14.**

— See HERACLITUS, *of Ephesus.* Heracliti Ephesii reliquiae. Recensuit I. Bywater, *etc.* 1877. 8°. **8460. ee. 18.**

— See HERACLITUS, *of Ephesus.* The Fragments of the Work of Heraclitus of Ephesus on Nature. Translated from the Greek text of Bywater, *etc.* 1889. 8°. **8460. ee. 39.**

— See JACKSON (William W.) *Rector of Exeter College, Oxford.* Ingram Bywater. The memoir of an Oxford scholar, 1840–1914. 1917, *etc.* 8°. **010856. ff. 21.**

— See PERIODICAL PUBLICATIONS.—*London.* The Journal of Philology, *etc.* [vol. 8–33 edited by I. Bywater and others.] 1868, *etc.* 8°. **P.P. 4970. c.**

— Contributions to the Textual Criticism of Aristotle's Nicomachean Ethics. pp. vii. 70. *Clarendon Press: Oxford,* 1892. 8°. **11312. f. 50.**

— Elenchus librorum vetustiorum apud * * [i.e. I. Bywater] hospitantium. pp. 142. [1911.] 8°. See CATALOGUES. **011904. aaa. 18.**

— The Erasmian Pronunciation of Greek, and its Precursors: Jerome Aleander, Aldus Manutius, Antonio of Lebrixa. A lecture. pp. 27. *Henry Frowde: London, Oxford,* 1908. 8°. **012901. i. 23. (2.)**

— Four Centuries of Greek Learning in England. Inaugural lecture . . . 1894. pp. 20. *Clarendon Press: Oxford,* 1919. 8°. **11313. c. 32.**

— A Letter to the Rev. John Wordsworth . . . on . . . a statement in his recent letter to Mr. C. S. Roundell, M.P. pp. 8. *E. Baxter: Oxford,* 1880. 8°. **8367. b. 19. (8.)**

[BY]WATER (JOHN) An Essay on the History, Practice and Theory of Electricity. [With two plates.] pp. iii. 127. *Printed for the Author: London,* 1810. 8°. **956. b. 10.**

— New Theory of the Leyden Phial. Founded on experiments, *etc.* pp. 60. *E. B. Robinson: Nottingham,* 1803. 12°. **8757. aa. 43.**

—— Observations on the Deviation of the Compass, with illustrative remarks on its magnetic principles. To which is added the description of a plan to remedy the above defect in navigation. pp. 46. *Longman & Co.: London,* 1820. 8°. **533. e. 42.**

—— Physiological Fragments; or, Sketches of various subjects intimately connected with the study of Physiology. pp. 119. *Baldwin, Cradock & Joy: London,* 1819. 8°. **784. i. 3. (1.)**

—— [Another edition.] To which are added, Supplementary observations, to shew that vital and chemical energies are of the same nature and both derived from solar light. pp. 158. *R. Hunter: London,* 1824. 8°. **728. d. 2.**
Sig. A–G 2 *are a reissue of the sheets of the edition of* 1819.

—— Remarks on the Principles and Use of the Barometer. pp. 14. *Melling & Co.: Liverpool,* 1831. 8°. **8704. de. 11. (5.)**

BYWATER (JOHN C.) The Mystery Solved; or, a Bible expose of the spirit rappings. Showing that they are not caused by spirits of the dead, but by evil demons, or devils. pp. 119. *Advent Harbinger Office: Rochester [N.Y.],* 1852. 12°. **8631. bbb. 34. (1.)**

BYWATER (T.) A New and Improved Liverpool Tide Table and Almanac for the year 1836. pp. 48. [1835.] 16°. See EPHEMERIDES. **T. 1989. (15.)**

BYWATER (WILLIAM EDWIN) Fishers of Men. pp. 135. *Independent Press: London,* 1938. 8°. **20032. ee. 15.**

—— The Power of Thought. pp. 140. *Thorsons: London,* 1943. 8°. [*"Life My Teacher" Books.* no. 3.] **W.P. 6892/3.**

BYWATER (WITHAM MATTHEW) A Brief Sketch of the History of the Royal Athelstan Lodge of Antient Free and Accepted Masons constituted no. 159, February 27, 1769, subsequently no. 10, and now no. 19. pp. 19. 1869. 8°. See FREEMASONS.—*Royal Athelstan Lodge, no.* 19. **4784. bb. 26.**

—— Notes on Lau: Dermott . . . and his work. pp. vi. 57. *Privately printed: London,* 1884. 8°. **10827. b. 37.**

BYWATERS (FREDERICK EDWARD FRANCIS)

—— See DUDLEY (Ernest) *Novelist.* Bywaters and Mrs. Thompson. [With portraits.] 1953. 8°. **W.P. B. 246/3.**

—— See PARMITER (Geoffrey V. de C.) Reasonable Doubt. [Accounts of the trials of F. E. F. Bywaters and Edith J. Thompson, and others.] 1938. 8°. **6496. bbb. 18.**

—— See THOMPSON (Edith J.) The Case of Thompson and Bywaters. [1932.] 8°. **6057. p. 18/2.**

—— Trial of Frederick Bywaters and Edith Thompson. Edited by Filson Young. [With portraits.] pp. xxxii. 261. *W. Hodge & Co.: Edinburgh & London,* 1923. 8°. [*Notable British Trials Series.*] **6496. d. 1/9.**

BYWATERS (FREDERICK JAMES) The Clergy of Sawston, 1197–1937. pp. 16. [*Sawston,* 1937.] 8°. **20031. bbb. 22.**

—— Willingham Parish Church. pp. 16. *Crampton & Sons: Sawston,* [1939.] 8°. **07816. cc. 88.**

BYWATERS (Hubert William) An Inquiry into the Chemical Mechanism concerned in the Absorption of Protein and Carbohydrate Foods . . . Thesis, *etc.* pp. 69. *R. F. Hunger: London*, 1908. 8°. **07305. h. 45. (9.)**

—— Modern Methods of Cocoa and Chocolate Manufacture. pp. xii. 316. *J. & A. Churchill: London*, 1930 [1929]. 8°. **08244. i. 68.**

BYWAYMAN, *pseud.*

—— Call of the Road. Trails in Wanderland. By 'Bywayman.' Illustrated by Patterson. pp. 135. *R.T.S.—Lutterworth Press: London*, 1939. 8°. **010358. n. 16.**

BYZANTINE ART. Histoire de l'art byzantin. *See* Diehl (Charles) *Archaeologist.*

—— Monuments de l'art byzantin. *See* France.—*Ministère de l'Instruction Publique, etc.* **7806. w.**

BYZANTINE CAPITALS. Byzantinische Capitaeler aus verschiedenen Kirchen Deutschlands, Frankreichs, und Englands . . . Herausgegeben von v. R. [1844, 45.] fol. *See* R., v., *Königlicher Lehrer der Architectur, etc.* **1734. c. 6.**

BYZANTINE COLLECTION. Collection byzantine. *See* Paris.—*Association Guillaume Budé.*

BYZANTINE EMPIRE.

—— Forma imperii byzantini. *Bruxelles*, 1939– . fol. [*Corpus bruxellense historiae byzantinae.*] L.R. **283. d. 4.**

BYZANTINE HISTORY. Corpus byzantinæ historiæ. *Gr. & Lat.* 26 vol.

'Ιωαννου του Καντακουζηνου ἀποβασιλεως 'Ιστοριων βιβλια δ'., *etc.* 3 pt. pp. 1058. 1645 [1646]. **196. h. 2–4.**

Γεωργιου του Κεδρηνου Συνοψις ἱστοριων . . . Item Ioannes Scylitzes Curopalates, excipiens ubi Cedrenus desinit. 2 pt. 1647. **196. h. 5, 6.**

Νικητου 'Ακωμινατου Χωνιατου 'Ιστορια, *etc.* pp. 464. 1647. **196. h. 7.**

Georgius Codinus Curopalata, De officiis Magnæ Ecclesiæ et Aulæ Constantinopolitanæ, *etc.* pp. 422. 1648. **196. h. 8.**

De byzantinæ historiæ scriptoribus . . . publicam in lucem e Luparæa Typographia emittendis . . . Προτρεπτικον. Proponente P. Labbe. ('Εκλογαι περι πρεσβεων.—Eclogæ historicorum de rebus byzantinis. 3 pt. 1648. **196. h. 9. (1.)**

Θεοφυλακτου Σιμοκαττου . . . 'Ιστοριας βιβλια η'., *etc.* pp. 256. 1647 [1648]. **196. h. 9. (2.)**

Του ἐν ἁγιοις πατρος ἡμων Νικηφορου Πατριαρχου Κωνσταντινουπολεως 'Ιστορια συντομος, *etc.* pp. 88. 1648. **196. h 9. (3.)**

Anastasii bibliothecarii Historia ecclesiastica, *etc.* (Anastasii Historia de vitis romanorum pontificum.) 2 pt. 1649. **196 h. 10.**

Λαονικου Χαλκοκονδυλου 'Αποδειξις ἱστοριων δεκα . . . Cum Annalibus Sultanorum, ex interpretatione I. Leunclauii, *etc.* pp. 506. 1650. **196. h. 11.**

Γεωργιου του 'Ακροπολιτου . . . Χρονικη συγγραφη . . . Ioelis Chronographia compendiaria & Ioannis Canani Narratio de bello CP., *etc.* (Ducæ Michaelis Ducæ nepotis Historia byzantina. Accessit chronicon breve.) 2 pt. 1651. **196. h. 12.**

'Αννης της Κομνηνης . . . 'Αλεξιας, *etc.* pp. 507. 1651. **197. h. 1.**

Γεωργιου Μοναχου και Συγκελλου γεγονοτος . . . Ταρασιου πατριαρχου Κωνσταντινουπολεως Χρονογραφια ἀπο 'Αδαμ μεχρι Διοκλητιανου . . . Et Nicephori Patriarchæ CP. Breuiarium chronographicum, *etc.* 2 pt. 1652. **197. h. 2.**

Του ἐν ἁγιοις πατρος ἡμων Θεοφανους Χρονογραφια . . . Leonis Grammatici Vitæ recentiorum impp., *etc.* pp. 676. 1655. **197. h. 3.**

Κωνσταντινου του Μανασση Συνοψις ἱστορικη, *etc.* (Georgii Codini et alterius cuiusdam anonymi excerpta de antiquitatibus Constantinopolitanis . . . Accedunt Manuelis Chrysolaræ epistolæ tres de comparatione veteris et nouæ Romæ. Et Imp. Leonis cognominis Sapientis oracula . . . Addita est etiam Explicatio officiorum sanctæ et magnæ Ecclesiæ, *etc.*) 2 pt. 1655. **197. h. 4.**

Histoire de l'Empire de Constantinople sous les empereu[rs] françois, diuisée en deux parties, dont la premi[ère] contient l'Histoire de la conquéte de la Ville de Co[n]stantinople . . . écrite par Geoffroy de Ville-Hardou[in] . . . La seconde contient vne Histoire générale de [ce] que les François & les Latins ont fait . . . da[ns] l'Empire de Constantinople, *etc.* (Recueil de plusieu[rs] chartes, et autres pièces, pour seruir à l'Histoire [des] François.) 3 pt. 1657. **197. h.**

'Αγαθιου Σχολαστικου Περι της 'Ιουστινιανου βασιλειας βιβ[λια] πεντε, *etc.* ('Αγαθιου Σχολαστικου 'Επιγραμματα.) pp. 1[…] 1660. **197. h.**

Του κυρου Μιχαηλ Γλυκα Σικελιωτου Βιβλος χρονικη, [*etc.*] pp. 387. 1660. **197. h.**

Operum Procopii Cæsariensis tomi duo. Accesseru[nt] Nicephori Bryennii Commentarii. 2 tom. 1662, 63. **197. h. 8,**

'Ιωαννου Κιννα μου . . . 'Ιστοριων λογοι ἑξ . . . Accedu[nt] Caroli du Fresne . . in Nicephori Bryennii . . . An[næ] Comnenæ . . . et ejusdem Ioannis Cinnami Histori[am] Comnenicam notæ . . . His adiungitur Pauli Silentia[rii] Descriptio Sanctæ Sophiæ, *etc.* pp. 602. 1670. **197. h.**

Historiæ byzantinæ scriptores post Theophanem, [*etc.*] pp. 494. 1685. **197. h.**

Chronicon orientale. Latinitate donatum ab Abraha[mo] Ecchellensi, *etc.* pp. 264. 1685. **197. h.**

'Ιωαννου του ἀσκητου του Ζωναρα . . . Χρονικον. 2 to[m.] 1686, 87. **197. h. 13,**

Πασχαλιον, seu Chronicum Paschale a mundo condito, [*etc.*] pp. lii. 614. 1688. **198. h.**

Νικηφορου του Γρηγορα 'Ρωμαϊκη ἱστορια, *etc.* pp. 8[…] 1702. **198. h.**

E typographia regia: Parisiis, 1645–1702. fol. **196. h. 2–12, 197. h. 1–14, 198. h. 1,**

—— Corpus byzantinæ historiæ. [A reprint of the Pa[ris] Corpus, and of sundry other volumes printed at Paris a[nd] elsewhere, but not included in the Paris Corpus.] 36 v[ol.]

De byzantinæ historiæ scriptoribus. Editio secunda [ad] Luparæam fideliter expressa. ('Εκλογαι περι πρεσβειω[ν] —Eclogæ historicorum de rebus byzantinis.—Προκοπ[ιου] Καισαρεως των κατ' αὐτον ἱστοριων τετρας πρώτη. 3 [pt.] 1729. **804. i. 2./**

Προκοπιου Καισαρεως των κατ' αὐτον ἱστοριων τετρας δευτε[ρα,] *etc.* (Προκοπιου Καισαρεως 'Ανεκδοτα.—Προκοπιου K[αι]σαρεως Περι των του δεσποτου 'Ιουστινιανου κτισματ[ων] λογοι ἑξ.) 3 pt. pp. 480. 1729. **804. i. 2./**

'Αγαθιου Σχολαστικου Περι της 'Ιουστινιανου βασιλειας βιβ[λια] πεντε, *etc.* ('Αγαθιου Σχολαστικου 'Επιγραμματα.—Θ[εο]φυλακτου Σιμοκαττου 'Ιστοριων βιβλια η'.) 2 pt. pp. 3[…] 1729. 804. i. 2/.

Πασχαλιον, *etc.* pp. xlvii. 390. coll. 395–560. 1729. 804. i. 2/

Γεωργιου Μοναχου . . . Χρονογράφια . . . Et Niceph[ori] Patriarchæ CP. Breviarium chronographicum, *etc.* 2 [pt.] 1729. 804. i. 2/.

Του ἐν ἁγιοις πατρος ἡμων Θεοφάνους Χρονογραφια . [. .] Leonis Grammatici Vitæ recentiorum impp., *etc.* 2 [pt.] 1729. 804. i. 2/

Νικηφορου Καισαρος του Βρυεννιου 'Υλη ἱστοριας, *etc.* pp. […] 1729. 804. i. 2,

Του ἐν ἁγιοις πατρος ἡμων Νικηφορου Πατριαρχου Κωνστ[αν]τινουπολεως 'Ιστορια συντομος, *etc.* pp. 59. 1729. 804. i. 2,

Γεωργιου του Κεδρηνου Συνοψις ἱστοριων, *etc.* (Excerpta [ex] Breviario historico Joannis Scylitzæ Curopalatæ.) 2 [pt.] 1729. 804. i. 2/4

Του κυρου Μιχαηλ Γλυκα . . . Βιβλος χρονικη, *etc.* pp. 2[…] 1729. 804. i. 2/4

'Ιωαννου του ἀσκητου του Ζωναρα . . . Χρονικον, *etc.* 2 v[ol.] 1729. **804.** i. 2

'Αννης της Κομνηνης . . . 'Αλεξιας, *etc.* (Caroli du Fres[ne] in Annæ Comnenæ Alexiadem notæ.) 2 pt. 1729. **804.** i. 2/

'Ιωαννου Κιννα μου . . . 'Ιστοριων λογοι ἑξ . . . Accedu[nt] Caroli du Fresne . . . notæ . . . His adjungitur Pa[uli] Silentiarii Descriptio Sanctæ Sophiæ, *etc.* pp. 2[…] 1729. **804.** i. 2/

Κωνσταντινου του Μανασση Συνοψις ἱστορικη, *etc.* pp. 1[…] 1729. **804.** i. 2/

Νικητου 'Ακωμινατου Χωνιατου 'Ιστορια, *etc.* pp. 373. 1729. **804.** i. 2/

Γεωργιου του 'Ακροπολιτου . . . Χρονικη συγγραφη . [. .] Joelis Chronographia compendiaria, & Joannis Can[ani] Narratio de bello CP., *etc.* 2 pt. 1729. **804.** i. 2/

Γεωργιου του Παχυμερη Μιχαηλ Παλαιολογος, *etc.* Specim[en] sapientiæ Indorum veterum.) 2 pt. 1729. **804.** i. 2/

Γεωργιου του Παχυμερη 'Ανδρονικος Παλαιολογος, *etc.* 2 pt. 1729. 804. i. 2/8.
'Ιωαννου του Καντακουζηνου ἀποβασιλεως 'Ιστοριων βιβλια δ'., *etc.* 3 pt. pp. 724. 76. 1729. 804. i 2/9.
Λαονικου Χαλκοκονδυλου . . . 'Αποδειξις ἱστοριων δεκα . . . Cum Annalibus Sultanorum, *etc.* pp. 380. 804. i. 2/10.
Historiæ byzantinæ scriptores post Theophanem, *etc.* pp. 443. 1729. 804. i. 2/10.
Chronicon orientale, latinitate donatum ab Abrahamo Ecchellensi, *etc.* pp. 216. 1729. 804. i. 2/11.
Chronicon orientale Petri Rahebi Ægyptii, primum ex arabico latine redditum ab A. Ecchellensi . . . nunc nova interpretatione donatum a Josepho Simonio Assemano . . . Accessere . . . dissertationes IV. pp. 270. 1729. 804. i 2/11.

Georgii Codini et alterius cujusdam anonymi excerpta de antiquitatibus Constantinopolitanis . . . Accedunt Manuelis Chrysolaræ epistolæ tres . . . Et Imp. Leonis . . . oracula . . . Addita est etiam Explicatio officiorum sanctæ ac magnæ Ecclesiæ, *etc.* pp. 211. 1729. 804. i. 2/11
Georgius Codinus Curopalata, De officiis Magnæ Ecclesiæ et Aulæ Constantinopolitanæ, *etc.* pp. 262. 1729. 804. i. 2/11.
Notitia dignitatum, *etc.* pp. 52. 1729 804. i. 2/11.
Anastasii Bibliothecarii Historia ecclesiastica, *etc.* (Anastasii Historia de vitis romanorum pontificum.) 2 pt. 1729. 804. i. 2/12.
Ducæ . . . Historia byzantina . . . Accessit Chronicon breve, *etc.* pp. 203. 1729. 804. i. 2/12.
Του ἐν ἁγιοις πατρος ἡμων Θεοφυλακτου 'Αρχιεπισκοπου Βουλγαριας Παιδεια βασιλικη, *etc.* pp. 20. 1729. 804. i. 2/12.
Νικηφορου του Γρηγορα 'Ρωμαϊκη ἱστορια, *etc.* 2 pt. 1729. 804. i. 2/13.

Histoire de l'Empire de Constantinople . . . Divisée en deux parties, dont la première contient l'Histoire . . . écrite par Geoffry de Ville-harduin . . . La seconde contient une Histoire générale, *etc.* (Recueil de plusieurs chartes.) 3 pt. 1729. 804. i. 2/13.
Historia byzantina duplici commentario illustrata. Prior familias ac stemmata imperatorum . . . complectitur: alter descriptionem urbis Constantinopolitanæ, *etc.* 4 pt. 1729. 804. i. 2/14.
Imperium orientale . . . Opera & studio Domni Anselmi Banduri. 2 tom. 1729. 804. i. 2/15.
Josephi Genesii De rebus Constantinopolitanis a Leone Armenio ad Basilium Macedonum libri quatuor, nunc primum editi. (Georgii Phranzæ Chronicon.—Joannis Malalæ Historia chronica.—Leonis Allatii Συμμικτα.) 4 pt. 1733. **804.i.2/16.**

Venetiis, 1729, 33. fol. **804.i.2.**

— Corpus scriptorum historiae byzantinae. Editio emendatior et copiosior, consilio B. G. Niebuhrii . . . instituta, opera ejusdem Niebuhrii, I. Bekkeri, L. Schopeni, G. Dindorfii aliorumque philologorum parata (auctoritate Academiae Litterarum Regiae Borussicae continuata). 50 vol. *Gr. & Lat. Bonnae*, 1828–97. 8°. **2071.f–h.**
The volumes are not numbered. Some are printed at Leipzig. The words "Auctoritate Academiae," etc. appear on those published in and after the year 1832.

— Historiæ byzantinæ scriptores tres græco-latini, uno tomo simul nunc editi. I. Nicephori Gregoræ . . . Byzantinæ historiæ libri XI . . . [The Latin version by H. Wolfius.] II. Laonici Chalcocondylæ . . . Historia de origine ac rebus gestis imperatorum turcicorum, ab Ogusiorum primordio usque ad Mechemetis primi annum XIII . . . nunc primum græcè edita & emendata. (C. Clausero interprete). III. Georgii . . . Acropolitæ Chronicon constantinopolitanum. [Edited and translated by T. Dousa.] Accesserunt indices necessarij. *Gr. & Lat.* 3 pt. *Apud P. de la Rouiere: Coloniæ Allobrogum*, 1615. fol. **589. i. 23**

— Плачевно паденiе Константинопола, 1453 Цариграда несрећне године. Изъ Бизантински Iсторiя с' грчкогъ [of M. Ducas] на србски езикъ преведено и iсторичкимъ примѣтбама умножено. Георгiемъ Хаџићъ [*sic*], *etc.* pp. 84. *у Новомъ Саду*, 1853. 8°. **9135. bb. 8.**

BYZANTINE INSTITUTE. *See* PARIS.

BYZANTINE MUSIC. Monumenta musicae byzantinae. *See* HØEG (C.)

BYZANTINE PATRIARCHATE. Le Patriarcat byzantin. Recherches de diplomatique, d'histoire et de géographie ecclésiastiques. *See* BUCHAREST.—*Institut Français d'Études Byzantines.*

BYZANTINE RESEARCH FUND. The Church of Our Lady of the Hundred Gates—Panagia Hekatontapyliani—in Paris. By H. H. Jewell and F. W. Hasluck. pp. xii. 78. pl. 14. *Macmillan & Co.: London*, 1920. fol. **7815. r. 11.**

—— The Church of Saint Eirene at Constantinople. By Walter S. George . . . With an historical notice by Alexander Van Millingen . . . and an appendix on the Monument of Porphyrios by A. M. Woodward . . . and A. J. B. Wace. pp. xiv. 87. pl. 29. *Oxford University Press: London*, [1913.] fol. **1736. e. 4.**

—— The Church of the Nativity at Bethlehem. By W. Harvey, W. R. Lethaby, O. M. Dalton, H. A. A. Cruso, and A. C. Headlam. Illustrated from drawings & photographs by W. Harvey & others. Edited by R. Weir Schultz. pp. xi. 76. pl. 12. *B. T. Batsford: London*, 1910. fol. **7815. r. 6**

BYZANTINISCH-NEUGRIECHISCHE JAHRBÜCHER. *See* PERIODICAL PUBLICATIONS.—*Berlin.*

BYZANTINISCHE CAPITAELER. *See* BYZANTINE CAPITALS.

BYZANTINISCHE ZEITSCHRIFT. *See* PERIODICAL PUBLICATIONS.—*Leipzig.*

BYZANTINISCHES ARCHIV. *See* KRUMBACHER (C.)

BYZANTINOSLAVICA. *See* PRAGUE.—*Slovanský Ústav.*—*Byzantologická Komise.*

BYZANTINUS (ELUTHERIUS) *pseud.* An Historical Enquiry after the Author of the Creed commonly called Athanasian. pp. 36. *J. Roberts: London*, 1720. 8°. **701. f. 9. (12.)**

BYZANTINUS (STEPHANUS) *See* STEPHEN, *of Byzantium.*

BYZANTION. *See* PERIODICAL PUBLICATIONS.—*Brussels.* *Βυζαντιον.*

BYZANTIOS (ALEXANDRE S.) *See* BUZANTIOS.

BYZANTIUM. *See* also CONSTANTINOPLE.

—— Byzantium. [A prize poem. By G. S. Venables.] pp. 8. *Talbot & Ladds: Cambridge*, [1830.] 8°. **C. 59. e. 9. (12.)**

BYZANTIUS, PHILO. *See* PHILO, *Byzantius.*

BYZANTIUS (CHARLES D.) *See* BUZANTIOS (Skarlatos D.)

BYZANTIUS (STEPHANUS) *See* STEPHEN, *of Byzantium.*

BYZYNIUS (LAURENTIUS) Laurentii Byzynii . . . Origo et diarium belli Hussitici ab. an. CIↃCCCCXIV ad CIↃCCCCXXIII. 1724. *See* LUDEWIG (J. P. von) Reliquiæ manuscriptorum omnis ævi diplomatum, *etc.* tom 6. 1720, *etc.* 8°. **122. a. 9.**

B. . Z. . D, *M. l'Abbé.*

—— Projet de cahier des trois ordres réunis de Paris. Par M. l'abbé B . . Z . . D. [i.e. Gabriel Brizard.] [With "Suite, *etc.*" also by G. Brizard.] 1789. 8°. *See* D., B . . Z . ., *M. l'Abbé.* **910. c. 11. (14.)**

BZOVIUS (ABRAHAMUS) La Vita di Paolo Quinto . . . tradotta dal R.P.F. Luigi Bartolommei.—Aggiunta del R.P.F. A. Bzovio . . . alla Cronologia ecclesiastica del Reuer. P.F. O. Panuinio . . . Tradotta dal Reuer. D. Domenico Belli. *See* SACCHI (B.) *de Platina.* Historia delle vite de' Sommi Pontefici, *etc.* 1622. 4°. **4856.** g. **21.**

—— Annalium ecclesiasticorum post illustriss. et reuerendiss. D.D. Cæsarem Baronium . . . tomus XIII.(–XVIII.), *etc.* 6 tom. *Apud A. Boetzerum: Coloniæ Agrippinæ,* 1616–27. fol. **481.** i. **7–9.**
The titlepages are engraved. The volumes are numbered consecutively with those of Baronius's "Annales ecclesiastici."

—— *See* DUNS (J.) *Scotus.* F. Ioannis Duns Scoti . . . in primum et secundum Sententiarum quæstiones subtilissimæ . . . Accesserunt . . . Apologia pro ipso contra P. A. Bzouium, *etc.* [A reply by H. MacCaghwell, Archbishop of Armagh, to a passage in the "Annales Ecclesiastici." 1620. fol. **3835.** f. **4.**

—— *See* GEWOLD (C.) Defensio Ludouici IV. Imp. . . . contra A. Bzouium. [A reply to passages in the "Annales Ecclesiastici."] 1618. 4°. **167.** b. **20.**

—— *See* HERWART AB HOHENBURG (J. G.) Ludouicus quartus Imperator defensus. Bzouius iniuriarum postulatus, *etc.* [A reply to passages in the "Annales Ecclesiastici."] 1618, *etc.* 4°. **1200.** cc. **4.**

—— *See* JANSSENIUS (N.) *a Dominican Friar.* R.P. F. Nicolai Ianssenii . . . Animaduersiones & scholia, in Apologiam . . . de vita et morte, Ioannis Duns Scoti, aduersus R.P. F. A. Bzouium [in the "Annales Ecclesiastici"], *etc.* 1622. 8°. **847.** e. **13.**

—— *See* THADÆI (D.) Nitela Franciscanæ religionis, et abstersio sordium quibus eam conspurcare frustra tentauit A. Bzouius [in the "Annales Ecclesiastici"], *etc.* 1627. fol. C. **65.** gg. **14.**

—— Historiæ Ecclesiasticæ ex . . . Cæsaris Baronii . . . Annalibus aliorumq; viror. illust. ecclesiasticis historicisq; monumentis, tomus I.(II.) Auctore A. Bzouio. (Historiæ ecclesiasticæ ex . . . A. Bzouii . . . Annal. . . . liber decimus tertius: Auctore J. F. Matenesio.) 3 tom. *Sumptibus A. Boetzeri: Coloniæ Agrippinæ,* 1617. fol. **1232.** k. **1.**

—— Nomenclator sanctorum professione medicorum, anniuersariam quorum festiuitatem vniuersalis celebrat Ecclesia. pp. 39. *Sumptibus A. Boetzeri hæredum: Coloniæ Agrippinæ,* 1623. 12°. **1181.** a. **7.**

—— Paulus Quintus Burghesius. P. O. M. pp. 88. *Ex typographia S. Paulini: Romæ,* 1626. 4°. C. **80.** a. **9.** (**1.**

—— La Vita di Paolo Quinto . . . Tradotta dal R.P.F. Luigi Bartolammei. *See* SACCHI (B.) *de Platina.* Le Vite de' Pontefici, *etc.* 1715. 4°. **484.** b. **6.**

—— [Another edition.] 1730. *See* SACCHI (B.) *de Platina.* Le Vite de' Pontefici, *etc.* pt. 2. 1730, *etc.* 8°. **4855.** dd. **15.**

—— [Another edition.] 1763. *See* SACCHI (B.) *de Platina.* Storia delle Vite de' Pontefici, *etc.* tom. 4. 1760, *etc.* 4°. **4856.** g. **22.**

—— Pontifex Romanus, seu, de pręstantia officio, auctoritate virtutib⁹ felicitate, rebusq; præclare gestis Summorum Pontificum, a D. Petro usque ad Paulum Quintum, commentarius. pp. 660. *Apud A. Boetzerum: Coloniæ Agrippinæ,* 1619. fol. **484.** f. **7.**

BZOVIUS (ABRAHAMUS)

—— [Another edition.] *See* ROCABERTI (J. T. de) *Arc[h]bishop of Valencia.* Bibliotheca maxima pontificia, *et[c.]* tom. 1. 1698, *etc.* fol. **484.** e.

—— Retractatio . . . de electione Ludouici IV. *See* NIGG[…] (E.) Bona opera Ludouici IV., *etc.* 1628. 12°. **1193.** a.

—— Siluester II. Caesius Aquitanus Pont. Max. . . . A[d]iuncta est Vita S. Adalberti. m. ab eodem Siluestro edit[a] studio . . . Bzouij . . . vindicata, et notis illustrata. 2 p[t.] *Typis Vaticanis: Romæ,* 1629. 4°. C. **83.** d. **2**

—— Sacrum pancarpium quadragesimale. Ex floribus sacr[æ] scripturæ, et SS. patrum, super Euangelia quæ in profest[is] & Dominicis diebus totius Quadragesimæ leguntur, *et[c.]* pp. 309. *Apud Societatem Minimam: Venetiis,* 1611. 4° **848.** h. **7.** (**1**

—— [Sert]um gloriae S. Hyacinthi Poloni vitam et laud[e] ipsius octo concionibus & septem orationibus complecten[s] Studio . . . A. Bzouii . . . confectum, atq; collectum [The sermons written and the orations collected b[y] A. Bzovius.] pp. 228. *Apud M. A. Zalterium: Veneti[is,]* 1598. 4°. **4828.** aa. **2**
Several leaves are slightly mutilated.

—— Tutelaris Silesiæ, seu De vita rebusq; preclarè gest[is] B. Ceslai Odrouansii . . . commentarius, *etc.* pp. 36. *In officina A. Petricouij: Cravouiæ,* 1608. 4°. **1124.** h. **16.** (**5**

BZOWSKI (ABRAHAMUS) *See* BZOVIUS.

BZOWSKI (KONSTANTY)

—— Geografia. Podręcznik na III klasę gimnazjalną. pp. 229. *Zrzeszenie Profesorów i Docentów w Wielki[ej] Brytanii: Londyn,* 1946. 8°. **10004.** bb. **5**

—— Geografja Polski. Podręczni[k] szkolny dla młodzieży . . . Z licznemi rysunkami i ma[p]kami. Wydanie IV. pp. 209. *Kalisz,* 1921. 8°. **010290.** eee.

C.

Where **initials** *apparently denoting an author's name are adopted as headings, the* **last letter** *is taken as representing a surname unless the typography or evidence from the book itself shows that the surname is represented by one of the preceding letters.*

—— *See* A. Essai historique . . . sur les lanternes . . . P[ar] une société de gens de lettres. [The dedicatory epist[le] signed: A. B. C. D. By J. F. Dreux du Radier, A. I[.] Camus, J. Lebeuf and F. L. Jamet.] 1755. 12°. **811.** b.

C.

—— *See* A. A Religious Demurrer, concerning Submissi[on] to the Present Power: contained in a letter . . . fro[m] some peaceable and truth-seeking gentlemen in t[he] countrey, *etc.* [Signed: A.B.C.D.–.] [1649.] 4°. E. **530.** (**1**

—— —— [1649.] 4°. **100.** e. (**1**

C. *See* AFRICAN. Annexation of the Transvaal, *etc.* [Wi[th] a preface signed: C.] [1878.] *obl.* fol. **1890.** a.

C. *See* AGAMYA GURU PARAMAHAMSA. Śri Brahma Dhàr[a,] *etc.* [With a preface signed: C.] 1905. 8°. **4505.** eee. **2**

C. *See* ALFIERI (V.) *Count.* [*Letters.*] Notizie e lette[re] inedite di V. Alfieri, *etc.* [Signed: C., i.e. Giusep[pe] Campori, the editor.] [1851?] 8°. **10631.** c. **48.** (

C. *See* Alfieri (V.) *Count.* [*Single Works.*] Felipe Segundo . . . Tragedia . . . Traducida por C., en 1820. 1924. 8°. [*Instituto de Literatura Argentina. Sección de documentos.* tom. 1. no. 4.] **Ac. 2694**. bc.

C * * *. *See* Alissan de Chazet (A. R. P. d') and C * * *. Champagnac et Suzette. Comdie[*sic*]-vaudeville . . . par Chazet et C * * * [i.e. Nicolas Fontaines de Cramayel], *etc.* [1800.] 8°. **11738**. c. **1**. (**1**.)

C. *See* Campbell (Thomas) *the Poet.* The Poetical Works of Thomas Campbell. [The preface signed: C.] 1856. 8°. **11611**. aaa. **3**.

C. *See* Carey (Mathew) Female Wages and Female Oppression. [No. 1 and 2 signed: C.] [1835.] 8°. **8415**. h. **14**.

C. *See* Carpenteius (J.) Sanctissimi patris Benedicti vita. [With an English verse translation. The preface signed: C.] 1881. 8°. **11403**. bbb. **12**.

C. *See* Chamillart (G.) Généralité de Caen. Recherche de la noblesse faite en 1666 et années suivantes par Messire G. Chamillart . . . Publiée . . . par un membre de la Société des Antiquaires de Normandie. [The preface signed: C.] 1887. 8°. **9904** i. **35**.

C. *See* Frederick Charles Nicholas, *Prince of Prussia.* A Military Memorial . . . Edited from the German, with an introduction [signed: C., i.e. Charles H. Chambers]. 1866. 8°. **8826**. ccc. **15**.

C.

—— *See* Gallison (John) Christian Biography. A memoir of John Gallison, *etc.* [Here attributed to W. E. Channing, in a preface, signed: C.] 1828. 12°. **4986**. de. **22**. (**3**.)

C. *See* Goethe (J. W. von) [*Tasso.—English.*] Goethe's Torquato Tasso. Translated into English verse. [The translator's preface signed: C., i.e. J. Cartwright.] 1861. 8°. **11748**. d. **18**.

C . . . . *See* Heliodorus, *Bishop of Tricca.* Histoire éthiopique . . . Avec des notes de M. Coray, C . . . ., etc. 1822. 8°. **12410**. f. **22**.

C. *See* How (Samuel) How's Sermon . . . on the Sufficiency of the Spirit's Teaching . . . To which is added a brief sketch of his life, and the life of the Rev. Thomas Goodwin, *etc.* [The introduction signed: C.] 1835. 12°. **4479**. aaa. **3**. (**2**.)

C. *See* Jouanneau (   ) Discussions du Code civil dans le Conseil d'État . . . Par MM. Jouanneau, L., C., et Solon. 1805, *etc.* 4°. **707**. e. **13**.

C * * *. *See* Lemaitre (Frédérick) *the Elder*, and C * * *. Le Vieil artiste, ou la Séduction, mélodrame . . . Par MM. F. Lemaître et C * * * [i.e. Baron Alphonse de Chavanges]. 1826. 8°. **11738**. cc. **15**. (**5**.)

C. *See* Milton (J.) [*Selections.*] The Poetry of Milton's Prose; selected from his various writings; with notes, and an introductory essay. [The advertisement signed: C., i.e. Robert Carruthers.] 1827. 12°. **716**. b. **24**.

C.

—— *See* Netherlands.—*Nederlandsce Vereeniging tot Afschaffing van Alcoholhoudenen Dranken.* De Grondslag en het beginsel der Ned. Vereeniging tot Afschaffing van Sterken Drank . . . Met een naschrift, ten antwoord aan den schrijver C. in den Tijdspiegel van Junij 1859. 1859. 8°. **8435**. d. **66**. (**8**.)

C * * *. *See* P., D., *Député de* * * *. Consultation épistolaire touchant l'opinion par ordre ou par tête. [A letter seeking advice on the manner of voting in the States-General; with the reply, signed: C * * *, i.e. J. A. J. Cérutti.] [1789.] 8°. **F. 30**. (**7**.)

C. *See* Philadelphus (Eutropius) *pseud.* Eutropii Philadelphi Oeconomische Balance . . . Aus dem Dänischen übersetzt durch C. 1760. 8°. **228**. c. **40**. (**2**.)

C. *See* Planché (James R.) Charles the xii, *etc.* [With German notes and a preface signed: C., i.e. Hermann Croll.] 1855. 16°. **11771**. a. **1**.

C * * *. *See* Romagnesi (J. A.) and C * * *. Les Fées, comedie . . . Par Messieurs Romagnesi & C * * * [i.e. Michel Cotelli, called Procope Couteaux]. 1753. 12°. [*Nouveau théatre italien.* tom. 9.] **241**. i. **12**.

C. *See* Shakespeare (W.) [*Collected Poems.*] The Poems of Shakespeare, *etc.* [The editor's advertisement signed: C.] 1856. 8°. **11607**. bb. **18**.

C. *See* Weaver (Richard) *Collier.* A Voice from the Coal-Pit. Seven addresses . . . With a brief biographical notice [signed: C.]. [1861.] 8°. **4406**. cc. **11**.

C. An Address on the Corn Laws. By a Protectionist. [Signed: C.] pp. 42. *J. Hatchard & Son: London,* 1846. 8°. **8245**. d. **19**.

—— [Another copy.] **8245**. d. **18**.

C. The American Firemen. Essays, lurid leaves, sketches, sparks. A standard work on fire matters. [The preface signed: C., i.e. Henry L. Champlin.] pp. 256. *H. L. Champlin: Boston,* 1875. 12°. **8715**. aa. **39**.

C. Antonio Scarpa in Modena. Estratto dall'Indicatore modenese, *etc.* [Signed: C., i.e. Giuseppe Campori.] pp. 15. [*Modena,* 1851?] 8°. **10631**. c. **48**. (**4**.)

—— Appunti intorno Lodovico Antonio Muratori. (Estratto dall'Indicatore modenese.) [Signed: C., i.e. Giuseppe Campori.] pp. 16. [*Modena,* 1851?] 8°. **10631**. c. **48**. (**3**.)

C. The Army in its Medico-Sanitary Relations. (Three papers, reprinted from the Edinburgh Medical Journal.) [The preface signed: C.] pp. 84. *Sutherland & Knox: Edinburgh,* 1859. 8°. **7686**. d. **40**. (**3**.)

C. The Assailant Assailed. Being a vindication of Mr. Kean, by C. author of Letters on the Portland Vase, *etc.* pp. 34. *Fearman's Public Library: London,* 1819. 8°. **011795**. f. **14**. (**1**.)

—— Second edition. pp. 39. *Fearman's Public Library: London,* 1819. 8°. **11777**. bb. **3**. (**3**.)

C. Athanasion. Second edition, with notes and corrections. Also, Miscellaneous Poems. By the author of "Christian Ballads," &c. [The dedication signed: C., i.e. Arthur C. Coxe.] pp. 187. *Wiley & Putnam: New-York,* 1842. 12°. **1466**. d. **5**.

C . . . . Bilder ur fantasien och verkligheten. Af C . . . . [i.e. Clara Sandströmer]. 2 ser. *Stockholm,* 1872, 73. 8°. **12581**. dd. **12**.

C * * *. Le Blason de France, ou Notes curieuses sur l'édit concernant la police des armoiries. [The dedication signed: C * * *, i.e. Thibaut Cadot. With plates.] pp. 174. *C. de Sercy: Paris,* 1697. 8°. **137**. a. **32**.

C. Bremen und der Zollverein. Eine Denkschrift. Der Bremischen Handelskammer überreicht von C. pp. 80. *Bremen,* 1868. 8°. **8245**. bbb. **62**. (**8**.)

C. Catalogue of Books selected from the Library of an English Amateur. [The preface signed: C., i.e. G. E. S. M. Herbert, Earl of Carnarvon. With plates.] 2 pt. *Printed for private circulation: London*, 1893, 97. fol. **667.k.3.**

C. Cenni biografici intorno al g. c. ed avvocato nobile Giuseppe Robolini, Pavese. Estratti dal n. 25 della Gazzetta provinciale di Pavia, *etc.* [Signed: C.] pp. 16. *Pavia*, 1840. 8°. **10602. h. 14.** (4.)

C. Le Cercle des femmes. Comédie. [In verse. The dedication signed: C., i.e. Samuel Chappuzeau.] pp. 60. *J. Girin & B. Rivière: Lion*, [1662?] 12°. **11736. aa. 20.**

C. Choice Consolation for the Suffering Children of God. Compiled from the writings of Leighton, Romaine, Cecil, Newton, Winslow, *etc.* [The preface signed: C.] pp. 155. *E. P. Dutton & Co.: Boston*, 1864. 8°. **4410. c. 16.**

C. Christian Ballads. [The dedication signed: C., i.e. Arthur C. Coxe.] pp. 138. *Wiley & Putnam: New York*, 1840. 12°. **1466. c. 21.**

C. Christian Socialism. Two papers contributed to the "Weekly Churchman" by C. pp. 24. *W. H. Burnett: Middlesbrough; Hamilton, Adams & Co.: London*, [1885.] 8°. **8275. aa. 31.** (2.)

C. Christmas Holidays; or, a Visit at home, *etc.* [Signed: C.] pp. 34. *American Sunday School Union: Philadelphia*, [1830.] 12°. **864. g. 13.**

—— [Another issue.] 1830. *See* CABINET. The Juvenile Cabinet, *etc.* 1830, *etc.* 12°. **864. h. 44.**

C * *. Collection choisie de plantes et arbustes. Avec un abrégé de leur culture, *etc.* (Auswahl von Pflanzen und Gesträuchen, *etc.*) [The preface signed: C * *, i.e. J. P. de Clairville. With plates.] *Fr. & Ger.* vol. 1. pp. 125. *Zuric*, 1796. 4°. **442. g. 14.**

C. Conte Gaetano Tonani. (Estratto dall'Indicatore modenese.) [Signed: C., i.e. Giuseppe Campori.] [*Modena*, 1851?] 8°. **10631. c. 48.** (5.)

C. A Correspondence between a Roman Catholic Priest, and a Protestant Layman . . . To which is subjoined, an Address to Roman Catholic readers; also a Challenge to the Roman Catholic Clergy of Ireland . . . and an Appeal to the King, his ministers, and Protestants of every denomination, on the subject of the idolatry of the Church of Rome. [The priest's contributions signed: C., / Those of the Protestant layman signed: L. Edited by the latter.] pp. 111. *Anne Watson; Martin Keene: Dublin*, 1821. 8°. / i.e. David Clark. **3942. c. 8.**

—— *See* CORRESPONDENCE. A Refutation of an Insidious Pamphlet, entitled "A Correspondence between a Roman Catholic Priest and a Protestant Layman." 1822. 8°. **3940. cc. 1.** (9.)

C * *. Critique de la charlatanerie, divisée en plusieurs discours, en forme de panégyriques, faits & prononcés par elle-même. [The dedication signed: C * *.] Premier discours. *Paris*, 1726. 12°. **74. a. 6.**

Imperfect; wanting the second Discourse.

C . . . . .

—— De par le comte d'Artois, Roi de Botani-Bay, aux terres australes et peuplades de malfaiteurs échappés de l'échauffaud et des galères anglaises. [Signed: C . . . . ., or G . . . . .] pp. 20. *Londre*, 1799. 8°. **F. 421.** (8.)

A previous edition, without the author's initial, entitled "Le Comte d'Artois, roi de Botani-Bay, à tous les fuyards, etc." is entered under Charles x., *King of France.*

C. Della istituzione delle Guardie Svizzere in Italia e particolamente in Modena. (Estratto dall'Indicatore modenese.) [Signed: C., i.e. Giuseppe Campori.] pp. 8. [*Modena*, 1852?] 8°. **8827. bbb. 50.** (4.)

C. La Dernière bordée du fort de la Double-Couronne. Souvenirs et anecdotes du siége de Paris. [The dedication signed: C.] pp. xi. 183. *Paris*, 1872. 12°. **9080. b. 17.**

C. The Disobedient Mouse: a fable. [Signed: C.] *See* S., C. M. The Bundle of Sticks, *etc.* 1848. 32°. **1163. a. 33.**

C . . . . . Du but et de l'importance des Humanités. (Par H. D. Nouvelle édition.) [The author's preface signed: C . . . . .] [1888.] 8°. *See* D., H. **8311. aa. 3.**

C. The Earth Measured . . . With comprehensive table. By a member of the Chicago Astronomical Society. [Signed: C., i.e. Elias Colbert.] pp. 40. *For private circulation: Chicago*, 1898–99. 8°. **8563. bb. 33.**

—— Second edition. pp. 40. *For private circulation: Chicago*, 1899. 8°. **8563. bb. 34.** (7.)

C. Edward E. Powers. (Obituary notice.) [Signed: C., i.e. Henry W. Cushman.] *See* POWERS (Edward E.) Last Will and Testament . . . of E. E. Powers. 1856. 8°. **4986. f. 45.** (14.)

C. The Eltham Tragedy Reviewed. By C. [i.e. Newton Crosland.] pp. 16. *F. Farrah: London*, 1871. 8°. **6496. aaa. 2.**

Later editions are entered under the author's name.

—— *See* POOK (Edmund W.) A Full Report of the Speeches delivered at the Blackheath Meeting on the Pook v. Farrah Libel Case, for the publication of a pamphlet [by C., i.e. Newton Crosland] entitled the Eltham Tragedy Reviewed. [1871.] 8°. **6496. bb. 20.**

C. An Essay on the Antiquities of Great Britain and Ireland . . . Designed as an introduction to a larger work . . . In answer to an objection against revealed religion. [Five letters, signed: C., i.e. David Malcolm.] pp. 48. *T. & W. Ruddiman: Edinburgh*, 1738. 8°. **812. d. 12.**

—— [Another copy.] *See* COLLECTION. A Collection of Letters, in which the imperfection of learning . . . and a remedy for it, are hinted, *etc.* 1739. 8°. **577. e. 24.**

C. Essays on Providence, as connected with the political systems of these "last days" in the United Kingdom and United States. [Signed: C.] pp. 185. *Thomas Drysdale: Portobello*, 1844. 8°. **4379. a. 29.**

C. Le Fabbricerie. Un delitto di leso buon senso. [Signed: C., i.e. Antonio Caucino?] pp. 12. *Torino*, 1868. 8°. **8246. cc. 41.** (7.)

C. Francesco Mirandola. (Estratto dall'Indicatore modenese.) [Signed: C., i.e. Giuseppe Campori.] pp. 12. [*Modena*, 1851?] 8°. **10631. c. 48.** (7.)

—— Galeazzo Marescotti. (Estratto dall'Indicatore modenese.) [Signed: C., i.e. Giuseppe Campori.] pp. 8. [*Modena*, 1851?] 8°. **10631. c. 48.** (6.)

C.

—— Gedanken über die taktischen Bewegungen der gegenwärtigen Zeit. *See* infra: Tankar om nutidens taktisk rörelser.

—— Idées et réflexions sur les mouvements de la tactique moderne. *See* infra: Tankar om nutidens taktisk rörelser.

C. Gedichte von C. (Carl xv.) Aus dem Schwedischen. pp. 48. 1866. 8°. *See* CHARLES XV., *King of Sweden and Norway.* **11565. a. 58. (6.)**

C. Geology and Genesis; or, the Two teachings contrasted. By "C." To which is appended, the Controversy between Dr. Baylee and "C.," on the harmony between Genesis and geology. pp. x. 158. *Whittaker & Co.: London,* 1857. 8°. **4375. d. 11.**

C. Il Giardino pubblico in Modena. (Estratto dall'Indicatore modenese.) [Signed: C., i.e. Giuseppe Campori.] pp. 4. [*Modena,* 1852?] 8°. **1298. m. 11. (50.)**

C. Guide to American Income Tax, Super Tax, and Excess Profits Tax, with examples. Foreign liability. Compiled . . . by "C." [i.e. E. R. Cason.] pp. 56. *C.: London,* 1917. 8°. **6617. a. 18.**

—— A Guide to the existing American Income Tax as it affects British Investors and Companies . . . Compiled . . . by "C." [i.e. E. R. Cason.] pp. 23. *"C.": London,* [1917.] 8°. **06617. de. 17.**

C.** Die gute und zufriedene Wahl. Ein Lustspiel in vier Aufzügen. Von C**. pp. 126. 1791. *See* GERMAN STAGE. Deutsche Schaubühne. Jahrg. 3. Bd. 6. 1788, *etc.* 8°. **752. a. 1/30.**

C. Histoire des ioyaux, et des principales richesses de l'Orient & de l'Occident. Tirée des diuerses relations des plus fameux voyageurs de nôtre siecle. Piece curieuse . . . Suiuie d'vne description exacte des regions & des lieux, dont il est parlé dans cette histoire. [The dedication signed: C.] pp. 180 [182]. *I. H. Widerhold: Geneue,* 1667. 12°. **954. b. 38.**
With an additional titlepage, engraved.

—— [Another copy.] **446. a. 40.**

—— The History of Jewels, and of the Principal Riches of the East and West. Taken from the relation of divers of the most famous travellers of our age, *etc.* [Translated from the French of C.] pp. 128. 1671. 8°. *See* HISTORY. **954. b. 39.**

—— [Another copy.] **446. a. 25. (2.)**

—— [Another copy.] **7107. aa. 46.**

C. L'Histoire du Royaume de Nauarre, contenant de roy en roy, tout ce qui y est aduenu de remarquable des son origine . . . Tiree des meilleurs historiens . . . par l'vn des Secretaires Interprettes de sa Maiesté. [The dedication signed: C., i.e. Gabriel Chapuis.] pp. 876. *Chez Nicolas Gilles: Paris,* 1596. 8°. **1058. a. 16.**

—— [Another copy.] **9220. ccc. 11.**
Imperfect; wanting the genealogical table.

C. Home Thoughts. By C. [i.e. Maria McIntosh Cox.] pp. 311. *Gay & Bird: London; Cambridge, U.S.A.* printed, 1901. 8°. **8411. ee. 27.**

C.

—— I.M.H. By C. [i.e. Maurice Baring.] pp. 7. *Printed for Maurice Baring by Stanley Morison: London,* 1924. 4°. Ashley **4687. (2.)**
No. 17 *of twenty-five privately printed copies.*

C. A Letter to a Member of a Christian Church. [Signed: C.] pp. 8. *T. Phillips: Northampton,* [1840?] 8°. **4422. h. 19. (1.)**

C——. Letters from the Cape of Good Hope, in reply to Mr. Warden [i.e. "Letters written on board . . . the Northumberland and at St. Helena"]; with extracts from the great work now compiling for publication under the inspection of Napoleon. The third edition. [The preface signed: C——, i.e. B. E. O'Meara.] pp. vii. 206. *James Ridgway: London,* 1817. 8°. **285. i. 5.**

C. Lettre au citoyen Méhée de la Touche. [On his pamphlet entitled "Denonciation au Roi, *etc.*" Signed: C.] pp. 18. *Paris,* 1814. 8°. **T. 2169. (1.)**

C . . . . . Lettre d'un Constituant de l'an VIII, au citoyen R . . . M . . ., sur l'exécution d'un article de l'acte constitutionnel. [Signed: C . . . . .] pp. 10. [*Paris,* 1801.] 8°. **F.R. 93. (26.)**

C. Lexiade, oder drei Bücher von dem Leben und den Thaten des . . . Bürgermeisters Liberius Servilius Lex. In vierzehn Gesängen, *etc.* [Signed: C.] pp. 207. *Berlin,* 1878. 8°. **11527. df. 15.**

C. Life. [An introduction to sex knowledge.] By C. pp. 13. *J. M. Dent & Sons: London,* [1926.] 8°. **08407. ee. 34.**

C.****.** Mémoires et négociations secrètes de la cour de France, touchant la paix de Munster. Contenant les lettres, réponses, mémoires & avis secrets envoiez de la part du Roi, de S. E. le Cardinal Mazarin, & de Mr. le Comte de Brienne . . . aux plénipotentiaires de France à Munster, afin de leur servir d'instruction pour la paix générale. Avec les dépêches & les réponses desdits plénipotentiaires. [The compiler's dedication signed: C.******., i.e. Nicolas Clément. Edited by Jean Aymon.] 4 tom. *Amsterdam,* 1710. 8°. **122. a. 16–19.**

C. Memoirs of Mirabeau. Mémoires biographiques, littéraries, et politiques, de Mirabeau, *etc.* [Signed: C. A review, extracted from a periodical.] [1836.] 8°. **R. 85. (32.)**

C——. Memoirs of the C—— & L—— Families; with an account of their misfortunes, afflictions, and disappointments. Written by one of its suffering members, for the benefit of the others. [The dedication and address to the reader signed: C.] pp. xi. 107. *Printed for the Author: London,* 1829. 12°. **1414. a. 63.**

—— [Another copy.] **1414. a. 3.**

C. Neues Maler-Lexicon zum Handgebrauch für Kunstfreunde. Nebst Monogrammen. [The editor's preface signed: C., i.e. Friedrich Campe.] pp. xxxii. 362. *Nürnberg,* 1833. 8°. **1422. b. 19.**

—— [Another copy.] **1043. e. 23.**

C. The New Biblical Atlas, and Scripture Gazetteer; with descriptive notices of the Tabernacle and the Temple. [The editor's introduction signed: C.] pp. 96. pl. XII. *R.T.S.: London,* [1851.] 8°. **3104. c. 13.**

C. Nieuwjaarswensch van Thomasvaêr, op de bruiloft van Kloris en Roosje, uitgesproken door den heer J. Tjasink in den Amsterdamschen Schouwburg. Januarij 1860. [A dialogue in verse. Signed: C.] pp. 16. *Amsterdam,* 1860. 8°. **11556. d. 47. (8.)**

C. Notice sur le lieutenant-colonel du génie Audé. [Signed: C.] *See* AUDÉ (P. A.) Nouvelles expériences sur la poussée des terres, *etc.* 1849. 8°. **8765. d. 4.**

C. Observations on the Question between the Church and the Committee of Privy Council, which appeared in the form of letters to the editor of the 'Guardian' newspaper with the signature 'C.' Collected and revised by the author [i.e. John A. Frere]. pp. 36. *J. Deighton: Cambridge,* 1848. 8°. **8305. e. 9.**

—— [Another copy.] **4109. bb. 1.**

C*.** Osservazioni sull'Olimpiade [of Metastasio]. Del C***. *See* METASTASIO (P. A. D. B.) Osservazioni di varj letterati, *etc.* tom. 2. 1785. 12°. **639. a. 16.**

C. Oudvlaemsche liederen en andere gedichten der XIVe en XVe eeuwen. [The editor's preface signed: C., i.e. C. L. Carton. With musical notes.] pp. viii. 540. 31. *Gent,* [1849.] 8°. [*Maetschappy der Vlaemsche Bibliophilen.* ser. 2. no. 9.] Ac. **9035/2.**

C * * * *. Patronage of Irish Genius. Two letters, shewing the utter unfitness . . . of erecting a bridge over the Liffey . . . as the National testimonial of His Majesty's . . . visit to Ireland . . . Also, proving the wisdom . . . of erecting a National Gallery . . . [By] C * * * * . . . Second edition. pp. 34. *Dublin,* 1823. 8°. **7805.** b. **33.** **(2.)**

C. Petit traité de l'amour des femmes pour les sots. [The dedication signed: C., i.e. Louis de Champcenetz.] pp. 57. *Petersbourg* [*Paris ?*], 1788. 12°. **8416.** aaa. **45.**

C. The Pope and the Quarterly Review; a letter to the Lord Chancellor. [Signed: C.] pp. 8. *Thomas Hatchard: London,* 1851. 8°. **3938.** e. **22.**

C. The Presence of God. [Signed: C.] pp. 14. *James Burns: London,* 1841. 12°. [*Tracts on Christian Doctrine.* vol. 1. no. 6.] **1353.** a. **10.**

C . . . . . Procès de la Reine d'Angleterre [i.e. Caroline of Brunswick]. Par C . . . . . [With a portrait.] 2 tom. *Paris,* [1820.] 12°. **6055.** a. 3.

C. The Providence of God. [Signed: C.] pp. 12. *James Burns: London,* 1841. 12°. [*Tracts on Christian Doctrine.* vol. 2. no. 24.] **1353.** a. **10.**

C. Reply to Lord Byron's "Fare thee well." [A poem. Signed: C., i.e. Mrs. E. Cockle.] *S. Hodgson: Newcastle,* 1817. 8°. **11632.** g. **60.** **(10.)**

C. Rough Pencillings of a Rough Trip to Rangoon in 1846. [Signed: C., i.e. Colesworthey Grant.] pp. x. 49. *Thacker, Spink & Co.: Calcutta,* 1853. 8°. **10056.** f. **16.**

—— [Another copy.] **10058.** s. **17.**

—— Rural Life in Bengal; illustrative of Anglo-Indian suburban life; more particularly in connection with the planter and peasantry . . . Letters from an artist in India to his sisters in England . . . By the author of "Anglo-Indian Domestic Life" . . . Illustrated with one hundred and sixty six engravings. [Signed: C., i.e. Colesworthey Grant.] pp. xli. 203. *W. Thacker & Co.: London,* 1860. 8°. **10057.** e. **38.**

C. En Samling dikter af C. [i.e. Charles XV, King of Sweden and Norway]. pp. 242. *Stockholm,* [1863.] 8°. **11565.** dd. 3.

C. A Serious Address to the Electors of Great-Britain, on the subject of short parliaments, and an equal representation. [Signed: C.] pp. 31. *J. Debrett: London,* 1782. 8°. **8138.** bb. **29.**

C. The Silent Teacher; or, Words for the weary, the lonely, and the afflicted. [The preface signed: C.] pp. 190. *R.T.S.: London,* [1874.] 8°. **4412.** h. **14.**

C . . . . Små-plancher till ledning vid fisk-odling. Af G . . . . [i.e. G. C. U. Cederström]: m. fl. pp. 19. pl. XIV. *Stockholm,* 1859. 8°. **7290.** a. **42.**

C. Le Soldat poltron. Comedie. [In verse. The preface signed: C., i.e. J. Chevalier.] pp. 48. *G. Quinet: Paris,* 1668. 12°. **163.** c. **19.**

C. Suite de l'Europe viuante, contenant la relation d'vn voyage fait en Allemagne aux mois d'Auril, May, Iuin, Iuillet & Aoust de l'année M.DC.LXIX. Où l'on void quelle est la face presente de plusieurs Estats d'Électeurs et de Princes de l'Empire, l'origine de leurs maisons, leur accroissement & leurs alliances, auec les portraits des Princes & des Princesses, suiuis des eloges des personnes les plus illustres de ce temps, *etc.* [The dedication signed: C., i.e. Samuel Chappuzeau.] pp. 556. *I. H. Widerhold: Genève,* 1671. 4°. **800.** g. 7.

C. [La Suitte et le mariage du Cid. Tragi-comedie. [verse. The dedication signed: C., i.e. Urbain Chevrea pp. 83. [*T. Quinet: Paris,* 1638.] 12°. **163.** b.
Imperfect; wanting the titlepage.

C.

—— [Tankar om nutidens taktiska rörelser.] Gedanken üb die taktischen Bewegungen der gegenwärtigen Zeit. V C. [i.e. Charles XV., King of Sweden and Norway] a dem Schwedischen von Hilder, *etc.* pp. 32. *Königsbe* [1868.] 8°. **8829.** bbb. **43.** (

—— [Tankar om nutidens taktiska rörelser.] Idées réflexions sur les mouvements de la tactique moderr par C. [i.e. Charles XV., King of Sweden and Norway], e pp. 55. *Stockholm,* 1868. 8°. **8828.** h.

C. Le Theâtre françois, diuisé en trois livres, où il e traité, I. De l'vsage de la comedie. II. Des autheurs q soûtiennent le theâtre. III. De la conduite des comedie [The dedication signed: C., i.e. Samuel Chappuzeau.] *Lion; R. Guignard: Paris,* 1674. 12°. **11735.** aaa.

C. Thought Not a Function of the Brain: a reply to t arguments for materialism advanced by Mr. W. Lawren in his Lectures on Physiology. [The preface signed: pp. 80. *C. & J. Rivington: London,* 1827. 8°. **7410.** bb.

C. Thoughts Versified. By C. [i.e. Anna Caroline Steel pp. 86. *E. & C. Joscelyne: Braintree,* 1860. 8°. **11645.** df.

C. Three Political Sketches. By C. [In verse.] pp. 8. *Steel & Jones: London,* 1881. 8°. **11645.** ee. **46.** **(1.**

C. Tiptree Races. [A song. Signed: C., i.e. Charl Clark.] 1844. *s. sh.* 8°. *See* CLARK (Charles) *Esq., Great Totham, Essex.* [A Collection of broadsides, *etc.*] 1833, *etc.* 8° & fol. **1890.** d.

C . . . . To Maaneder i Slutteriet. Af C . . . . [i.e. Ass D. Cohen.] Andet Oplag. pp. 48. *Kjøbenha* 1858. 8°. **10761.** aaa. **48.** (

C. Two Letters upon the Application of the Nitric Acid Medicine. From the Bombay Courier, *etc.* [Signe C.] pp. 24. *Courier Press: [Bombay,* 1796.] 12°. **B. 655.** **(1**

—— [Another edition.] Some Letters upon the Application the Nitric Acid to Medicine, *etc.* [Containing a thi letter. Signed: C.] pp. 33. *Courier Press: [Bomba* 1797. 8°. **B. 558.** (

C.

—— The Two Supremacies. A letter to the Lord Lyndhur [Signed: C.] pp. 16. *Thomas Hatchard: Lond* 1851. 8°. **3938.** b.

—— [Another copy.] **3940.** dd. **7.** (

C. Village Rhymes. [The dedication signed: C.] *R. Seeley & W. Burnside: London,* 1831. 12°. **994.** a.

C. A Vindication of the Earl of Carnarvon's Asserti respecting the Expences of the War: in answer to t reporter of the substance of the speech of Lord Auckla in the House of Lords on Friday, 20th March, 1801. which is added, a copy of Lord Auckland's speech, therein reported. [Signed: C., i.e. H. Herbert, Earl Carnarvon?] pp. 27. *J. Debrett: London,* 1801. 8°. **8135.** c.

C * * *. Virginie. Tragedie. [The dedication signe C * * *, i.e. J. G. de Campistron.] pp. 67. *E. Luca Paris,* 1683. 12°. **636.** c. **27.** (

—— [Another copy.] Virginie, *etc.* *Paris,* 1683. 12°. **86.** i. **10.** (

C. The Work and Profits of an Insurance Agency. [The preface signed: C.] pp. 146. *Thomas Murby: London,* 1877. 8°. **8226.** aaa. 3.

C. The Yeomanry Cavalry of Worcestershire, 1914–1922. By C. [With plates and maps.] pp. viii. 251. 1926. 4°. *See* ENGLAND.—*Army.—Cavalry.—Queen's Own Worcestershire Hussars.* **9083.** c. 6.

C.

— xx. Umrisse zur Undine von Friedrich Baron de la Motte Fouqué. (C. inv. L. Schnorr v. K.sc.) [Engravings from designs by Karl Joseph Prince von Clary und Aldringen.] pl. 20. [*Leipsic,* 1816.] *obl.* 8°. **1322.m.79.**

C. and **L.** El Clown y el Cocinero. Disparate en un acto, tomado del Francés . . . por los Señores C. y L., *etc.* pp. 5. [*Madrid,* 1865.] 4°. **11725.** h. 20.

C..* and **O..*.** Dresdener Kunstzustände. No. 1. Malerei . . . Allen Künstlern gewidmet von C..* und O..*. pp. 29. *Dresden & Leipzig,* 1843. 12°. **786.** d. 35.

C. . . . and **SÉDAINE** (MICHEL JEAN) Les Sabots, opéra-comique en un acte, mêlé d'ariettes; par Mrs. C. . . . [i.e. Jacques Cazotte] & Sédaine, *etc.* pp. 24. *Paris,* 1777. 8°. [*Recueil général des opéra bouffons, etc.* tom. 1.] **11735.** b. 2.

C . . ., *Ab . . . .* Novelle galanti, in ottava rima, dell'Ab . . . C . . . [i.e. G. B. Casti.] Nuova edizione corretta, e ricorretta. pp. 306. *Londra,* 1793. 8°. **80.** k. 29.

C., *l'Abbé.* *See* B * * *, *le R.P.* L'Esprit du Pape Clément XIV . . . Traduit de l'italien par l'Abbé C. [Or rather, written by Joseph Lanjuinais.] 1775. 12°. **3677.** a. 4.

C * * *, *l'Abbé.* Les Amours de Napoléon III. Par l'abbé C * * *. [With illustrations.] pp. 165. *Paris,* [1880.] 8°. **10659.** f. 20.

—— [Another copy.] **10661.** s. 14.

C * *, *l'Abbé.* Louis XVI et Madame Élisabeth sa sœur. Par l'Abbé C * *. pp. 203. *Paris,* [1853?] 12°. **10659.** b. 5.

C * * * * *, *Ainé, de Marseille.* Jean dé Cassis oou Martégué, imitation burlesque de Jean de Paris, mêlée de contes, saillies et bons mots, attribués aux anciens habitans du Martigues, en un acte et en vers Provençaux . . . Par C * * * * * Ainé, de Marseille [i.e. — Carvin, the elder.] pp. 45. *Marseille,* 1816. 8°. **11739.** d. 13. (1.)

—— Seconde édition. pp. 28. *Marseille,* 1829. 12°. **1343.** a. 12.

C . . . . ., *Ami de la Loi.* A mes concitoyens. [Concerning the irruption of the mob into the Tuileries on 20 June 1792. Signed: C . . . . . Ami de la Loi.] pp. 6. [*Paris,* 1792.] 8°. **F. 890.** (11.)

C * * *, *Ancien Administrateur.* Discussion de l'article 17 du projet de loi sur l'organisation des colléges électoraux. [Signed: C * * *, ancien Administrateur.] pp. 8. [*Paris,* 1816.] 8°. **1141.** h. 14. (19.)

C * * *, *Avocat.* Le Secret révélé, ou Lettre à un magistrat de province sur les Protestans. [Signed: C * * *, Avocat.] pp. 81. [*Paris?* 1787.] 8°. **F.R. 169.** (1.)

C . . ., *il B . . . C . . . G . . . .* Consiglio tra Medici, e de Tommaso. [In verse. Signed: Il B . . . C . . . G . . . C . . . .] [*Naples,* 1820.] *s. sh.* fol. **8032.** m. 10. (2.)

C., *B^on de.* *See* LA COUR DE LA GARDIOLLE (L. M. de) Quatre lettres sur l'expédition d'Égypte . . . 1798. [With a prefatory note signed: Bon de C., i.e. Baron de Cabiron.] 1880. 4°. **9078.** i. 3.

—— *See* LA COUR DE LA GARDIOLLE (P. de) Guerre de Sept Ans. Rosback. [With a prefatory note signed: Bon de C., i.e. Baron de Cabiron.] 1883. 4°. **9078.** i. 4.

—— Quelques documents. [Relating to the history of the Régiment de Dauphiné in 1789–1791–1792, to the history of the French Protestants, etc. The editor's preface signed: Bon de C., i.e. Baron de Cabiron.] pp. 66. *Nîmes,* 1884. 4°. **4630.** f. 2.
No. 15 *of an edition of sixty copies.*

C * *, *le C.* Ode à la calomnie, en réponse à la Queue de Robespierre [by J. C. H. Méhée de la Touche, published under the pseudonym "Felhemési"]. (Par le C. C * * [i.e. M. J. B. de Chénier].) pp. 8. [*Paris,* 1794.] 8°. **935.** b. 17. (10.)

—— [Another copy.] **F. 358.** (4.)

—— [Another copy.] **F. 357.** (4.)

C., *il Cavaliere.* Risposta del Cavaliere C. al discorso sul debito pubblico del Senat. G., *etc.* pp. 46. *Italia,* 1801. 8°. **8207.** e. 2. (5.)

C * *, *le C^en.* Une Étincelle de raison, ou Opinion du C^en C * *, sur le gouvernement révolutionnaire, *etc.* pp. 79. *Paris,* an III [1795]. 8°. **F. 1104.** (9.)

C * * *, *le Chev. de, Lieut. Colonel au Service de S.M.C.* Le Véritable esprit militaire, ou l'Art de rendre les guerres moins funestes. [The dedication signed: Le Chev. de C * * *, Lieut. Colonel au Service de S.M.C.] 2 tom. *Liége,* 1774. 8°. **8827.** f. 43.

C., *le Chevalier de.*

—— Lettres d'amour d'une religieuse, escrites au Chevalier de C., officier françois en Portugal. [Five letters, first published in Paris in 1669 under the title "Lettres portugaises, traduites en françois." Commonly attributed to Marianna Alcoforado. Translated, or perhaps originally composed in French, by Gabriel Joseph de Lavergne, Count de Guilleragues. The preface to this edition contains the statement: "Le nom de celuy auquel on les a écrites est Monsieur le Chevalier de Chamilly, & le nom de celuy qui en a fait la traduction est Cuilleraque." The Chevalier is usually identified as Noël Bouton, Marquis de Chamilly, and Cuilleraque as the Count de Guilleragues.] pp. 50. *Chez Pierre du Marteau: Cologne,* 1669. 12°. **1085.** b. 5.

—— Lettres d'amour d'une religieuse portugaise. Escrites au Chevalier de C., officier françois en Portugal. [The five letters commonly attributed to Marianna Alcoforado, preceded by seven others, also first published in Paris in 1669 under the title "Lettres portugaises," and then stated to be the work of "une femme du monde," the whole numbered consecutively]. (Réponces du Chevalier de C.) Enrichies & augmentées de plusieurs nouvelles lettres, fort tendres & passionnées de la Presidente F. [i.e. Anne Ferrand] à Mr. le Baron de B. Dernière édition. pp. 310. *J. van Ellinckhuysen: La Haye,* 1696. 12°. **10909.** aa. 26.
In the preface to this edition the name of the "translator" is given as "Guilleraque."

—— [Another edition.] pp. 310. *J. van Ellinckhuysen: La Haie,* 1701. 12°. **10909.** a. 20.

—— [Another edition.] pp. 310. *A. de Hondt: La Haye,* 1701. 12°. **1094.** cc. 19.

—— [Another edition.] pp. 373. *La Haye,* 1716. 12°. **1094.** g. 15

C., *le Chevalier de.*

—— Lettres d'amour d'une religieuse portugaise, écrites au Chevalier de C. . . . Augmentées de plusieurs nouvelles lettres, & de différentes pièces de poésie. Nouvelle édition. tom. 2. *La Haye*, 1742. 12°. **1094**. g. **17**.
Imperfect; wanting vol. 1, *containing the* " *Lettres portugaises,*" *parts* I *and* II, *their* " *Réponses,*" *and the* " *Lettres . . . de la Présidente F. à Mr. le Baron de B.*"

—— [Another edition.] Lettres d'amour d'une religieuse portugaise, écrites au Chevalier de C. . . . [The twelve letters, alternating with those of the two sets of replies first published by Loyson and by Philippes respectively.] Augmentées de plusieurs nouvelles lettres, & de différentes piéces de poésie. Nouvelle édition. 2 tom. *C. G. Seyffert: Londres*, 1760. 12°. **1094**. g. **16**.

—— [Another edition.] 2 tom. *C. G. Seyffert: Londres*, 1777. 12°. **10905.cc.5.**

—— Five Love-Letters from a Nun to a Cavalier. Done out of French into English, by Sir Roger L'Estrange. The second edition. (Cinque lettres d'amour d'une religieuse portugaise. Escrites au Chevalier de C., *etc.*) pp. 168. 1702. 12°. *See* NUN. **1081**. b. **4**. (**2**.)

—— Réponces du Chevalier de C. aux Lettres d'amour d'une religieuse en Portugal. Edition nouvelle. [Eleven letters, consisting of the five replies to the " Lettres portugaises," Part I, first published by Loyson, Paris, 1669, followed by the six replies to the same letters first published by Philippes, Grenoble, 1669.] *See* supra: Lettres d'amour d'une religieuse portugaise, *etc.* 1696. 12°. **10909**. aa. **26**.

—— [Another edition.] *See* supra: Lettres d'amour d'une religieuse portugaise, *etc.* 1701. 12°. **10909**. a. **20**.

—— [Another edition.] *See* supra: Lettres d'amour d'une religieuse portugaise, *etc.* 1701. 12°. **1094**. cc. **19**.

—— [Another edition.] *See* supra: Lettres d'amour d'une religieuse portugaise, *etc.* 1716. 12°. **1094**. g. **15**.

C * * *., *le Citoyen.* Exposition de quelques principes politiques, et de quelques opinions religieuses (que le Citoyen C * * * [i.e. Jean Chas] se propose d'établir et de publier dans son Tableau historique . . . de la monarchie anglaise, depuis la descente de Jules-César jusqu'à la paix de 1783, *etc.*) pp. 130. [*Paris*, 1795?] 8°. R. **668**. (**2**.)

C., *Citoyen français, Membre du Point-central des Arts et Métiers céans au Louvre.* Les Élémens du contrat social, ou le Développement du droit naturel de l'homme sur la propriété. Par C., Citoyen français, Membre du Point-central des Arts et Métiers céans au Louvre [i.e. Claude Romieux]. pp. 15. *Paris*, 1792. 8°. F.R. **86**. (**10**.)

C . . . ., *le Comte de.* Cris de guerre et devises des états de l'Europe, des provinces et villes de France et des familles nobles de France, d'Angleterre, des Pays-Bas . . . Par le comte de C. . . . [i.e. Albert Cohen de Vinkenhoef]. pp. 168. *Paris*, 1852. 12°. **9930**. b. **13**.
The date on the wrapper is 1853.

C * * *, *le Comte de.* Séjour de dix mois en France, par un émigré, qui n'avoit pu sortir de Toulon en Décembre 1793, et ne s'est sauvé de France que par l'élargissement des prisonniers de Paris, en Août 1794 . . . On y trouve la relation complette du siége de Lyon, l'histoire de La Vendée, et celle des Chouans. Par le Comte de C * * *. pp. 198. *Hambourg*, 1795. 8°. **1322**. c. **14**.

—— Séjour de dix mois en France . . . Seconde partie. Par le Comte de C * * *. pp. 124. *De Boffe, etc.: Londres*, 1795. 8°. **10658**. bb. **11**. (**2**.)

C——, *Countess.* Beauty's Aids, or, How to be beautiful. [By] the Countess C—. pp. vii. 240. *Sands & Co.: London*, 1901. 8°. **07943**. g. [illegible]

C * * * *, *le Cte de.* L'Armee française, sa mission et s[a] histoire, 496–1852. Par le Cte de C * * * * [i.e. Cou[nt] Eugène de Civry]. pp. viii. 246. *Paris*, 1852. 8°. **1319**. f.

C . . . ., *Curé de* * * *. De la conduite des curés dans [les] circonstances présentes, ou bien Lettre d'un curé [de] campagne à son confrère, député à l'Assemblée nationa[le] sur la conduite à tenir par les pasteurs des âmes, dans [les] affaires du jour. [Signed: C. . . ., Curé de * * *, i[.e.] Augustin Barruel.] pp. 16. *Paris*, 1790. 8°. F.R. **138**. (

—— [Another copy.] F. **114**. (**1**

C., *D. of. See* R., *Lord.* A Dialogue between Lord R[ussell's] [i.e. Lord William Russell's] Ghost and the D. of [C.] [Dean of Canterbury, i.e. John Tillotson.] [1683.] *s. sh.* f[ol.] [TILLOTSON (*John*) *Archbishop of Canterbury. A Let[ter] written to my Lord Russel, etc.*] **1852**. d. **1**. (**1**

C., *il Dottore. See* MATTEI (C.) *Count.* La Scienza nuova [del] conte Cesare Mattei e la scienza vecchia del dottore C. 1880. 8°. **14537**. b. **9**. (

C——., *Dr. See* TURNER (John) *Vicar of Greenwich.* [A] Farther Vindication of the Soul's . . . Immortality, [in] answer to Dr. C——'s [i.e. W. Coward's] Farther though[ts] upon his second thoughts concerning human Soul, *etc.* 1703. 4°. **698**. f. **3**. (**1**

C., *Dr.* The Present State of Russia, in a letter to a frie[nd] at London; written by an eminent person (Dr. C. [i.e.] Samuel Collins]) residing at the great Tzars Court [at] Mosco for the space of nine years. Illustrated with ma[ny] copper plates. [The editor's preface signed: N. [B.]] pp. 141. *J. Winter for D. Newman: London*, 1671. [8°.] **1056**. b.
The author is referred to as " *Dr. C.*" *in* " *The Statio[ner] to the Reader.*" *At the end is a list of books sold by Dorm[an] Newman in which the book is advertised under the autho[r's] name.*

—— [Another copy.] **150**. a. [illegible]

—— [Another copy.] G. **151**[illegible]

C . . . . . ., *Dr.* Unmusikalische Noten zu Richard Wagne[r's] " Judenthum in der Musik " Von Dr. C . . . . . . pp. [illegible] *München*, 1869. 8°. **7895**. c. **48**. (**1**

—— [Another copy.] Unmusikalische Noten zu Richa[rd] Wagner's " Judenthum in der Musik." Von Dr. C . . . . *München*, 1869. 8°. Hirsch **4914**. (

C . . . . ., *Dr.*, and **O . . . . . .**, G. Der Cheiroelectrom[ag]netismus oder die Selbstbewegung und das Tanzen [der] Tische—Tischrücken. Eine Anweisung in Gesellschaf[t] das merkwürdige Phänomen einer neu entdeckt[en] menschlichen Urkraft hervorzubringen . . . mitgetheilt v[on] Dr. C . . . . . und G. O . . . . . . pp. 16. *Berl[in]*, 1853. 16°. **8631**. aa. **38**. (

C., *Dr., a Person of Great Skill in Chymistry. See* SUCHT[EN] (A. von) Alex. Van Suchten Of the Secrets of Antimo[ny] . . . Translated . . . by Dr. C., a person of great s[kill] in chymistry [i.e. Daniel Cable], *etc.* 1670. 12°. **1033**. f.

C * *, *Duchess of.* The Affecting History of the Duchess [of] C * *, who was confined nine years in a horrid dunge[on,] *etc.* [Translated by Maria Josepha, Lady Stanley [of] Alderley, from " Histoire de la Duchesse de C * *" contained in tom. 2 of the " Adèle et Théodore " [of] Madame de Genlis.] pp. 36. *Dean & Munday: Lond[on]*, [1820?] 12°. **10630**. a. [illegible]

C * *, *Duchess of.*

—— [Another edition.] pp. 24. *Thomas Richardson: Derby,* [1830?] 12°. **12316. ee. 15. (4.)**

—— [Another edition.] The Inhuman Husband, or the Sad narrative of the Dutchess of C——, who was excluded for nine years from the sight of the sun, *etc.* pp. 24. *Orlando & Hodgson: London,* [1830?] 12°. **12315. d. 27. (6.)**

C——, *Duchess of.* The Dutchess of C——s Memorial. (General Fielding's answer to the Dutchess of C——'s Memorial.) [Being two satirical ballads on Barbara Palmer, Duchess of Cleveland, and Robert Fielding.] [*London,* 1707?] *s. sh.* fol. **1872. a. 1. (158.)**

C., *E. of.* A Modest Apology for the Ancient and Honourable Family of the Wrongheads. In a letter to the Right Honourable the E. of C - - - -. 1744. 8°. *See* WRONGHEADS. **8132. b. 90.**

C——., *Family of.* Memoirs of the C—— & L—— Families; with an account of their misfortunes, afflictions, and disappointments. Written by one of its suffering members, for the benefit of the others. [The dedication and address to the reader signed: C.] 1829. 12°. *See* C. **1414. a. 63.**

C., *Feldwebel.* Souvenirs de guerre d'un sous-officier allemand (le Feldwebel C.), 1914–1915–1916. Publiés avec une préface par Louis-Paul Alaux. pp. 256. *Paris,* 1918. 8°. **09082. d. 11.**

C * * *, *Frau von.* Schweizersinn. Lustspiel in drei Aufzügen. Nach dem französischen Manuskript: L'Émigré von der Frau von C * * * [i.e. Isabelle Agnès Élizabeth de Charrière], übersetzt von dem Herausgeber der Friedens-Präliminarien [i.e. Ludwig Ferdinand Huber.] pp. 56. *Berlin,* 1794. 8°. **11748. e. 30.**

C * * *, *General.*

—— Kleines Kriegshandbuch für Offiziere. Abriss der angewandten Taktik aller Waffen, der Generalstab und der Parteigängerkrieg. Vom General C*** [i.e. Wojciech Chrzanowski]. Mit . . . Tafeln . . Ins Deutsche übertragen. pp. viii. 180. *Halle,* 1852. 8°. **M.L. i. 31.**

C—, *Graduate of Trinity College, Cambridge.* The Useful Arts of the Greeks and Romans.—Illustrations of the State of the Useful Arts in Other Nations and Times. *See* MARTIN (Samuel) *Minister of Westminster Chapel.* The Useful Arts, *etc.* 1851. 8°. **7955. a. 44.**

C * * *, *Gräfin.* Briefe und Tagebuch-Blätter von Gräfin C * * *. pp. 213. *Wien,* 1865. 8°. **8406. f. 2.**

C——, *His Ex——y Lord.* A Vindication of His Ex——y the Lord C—— [i.e. John Carteret, Earl of Granville] from the charge of favouring none but Toryes, High-Churchmen, and Jacobites. [By Jonathan Swift, Dean of St. Patrick's.] pp. 37. *Dublin,* 1730. 8°. **8145. a. 7.**

C., *His R.H. the D. of.* The Trial of His R.H. the D. of C. [Duke of Cumberland] July 5th, 1770 for criminal conversation with Lady Harriet G - - - - - - - - - - r [Grosvenor] [or rather Henrietta, Lady Grosvenor]. To which is prefixed, an introductory discourse upon the ancient and modern punishments of adultery . . . Including all the letters which have passed between His R.H. and her Ladyship, *etc.* pp. 60. *John Walker: London,* 1770. 8°. **1132. d. 6.**

Imperfect; wanting the frontispiece.

—— [Another edition.] pp. 66. *John Walker: London,* 1770. 8°. **1132. c. 62.**

C - - - - -, *Lady.*

—— The Whim!!! or, the Maid-stone bath. A Kentish poetic. Dedicated to Lady Worsley. (Said to be written by Lady C - - - - -.) pp. vi. 14. *J. Williams: London,* 1782. 4°. **11631. g. 31. (5.)**

C——, *Lord.* *See* B——s, *Monsieur.* An Historical View of the Principles, Characters, Persons, &c. of the Political Writers in Great Britain. Viz. Mr P——y [i.e. W. Pulteney, Earl of Bath], Lord C—— [i.e. John Carteret, Earl Granville], *etc.* 1740. 8°. **1418. f. 23.**

C., *Lord.* *See* CONSIDERATIONS. Serious Considerations on the Present State of Affairs . . . In a letter to the Lords B. and C. [i.e. William Pulteney, Earl of Bath, and John Carteret, Earl of Granville.] 1744. 8°. **8132. b. 3.**

C., *Lord.* Life of Lord C. [i.e. Lord Cardigan]. [A song.] *Birt: London,* [1841.] *s. sh.* fol. **1876. e. 1. (45.)**

C * * *, *M.* Histoire critique des journaux. Par M. C * * * (Camusat). [The editor's preface signed: B. D. M. E. A., i.e. Jean Frédéric Bernard.] 1734. 12°. *See* CAMUSAT (D. F.) **274. a. 24.**

C * * *, *M.* Lettres critiques, sur divers écrits de nos jours, contraires à la religion et aux mœurs. Par M. C * * *. 2 pt. *Londres,* 1751. 8°. **722. c. 65.**

C * * *, *M.* Tableau de toutes especes de successions, régies par la Coutume de Paris; et computation des dégrés de parenté, suivant le Droit Civil et le Droit Canon. Par M. C * * * (Castel). Suivi du texte de la Coutume de Paris. 1785–88. 32°. *See* CASTEL ( ) **705. a. 1, 3–8, 10–16.**

C., *M. de.*

—— Lettre de M. de C. à M. de L. (Quelques éclaircissements sur ce qui s'est passé à la Chambre des Comptes de cette province, dans la séance du 8 de ce mois.) pp. 13. [*Rennes?* 1788.] 8°. **911. c. 1. (5.)**

C . . . ., *le M . . . . . de.* Mémoire sur l'esclavage et sur la traite des nègres. Par le M . . . . . . de C . . . . pp. 52. *A. Dulau & Co.: Londres,* 1798. 8°. **B. 491. (14.)**

C . . ., *le M . . . . de.*

—— Nouvelle lettre à M. Rousseau de Genève, sur celle qui parut de lui, il y a quelques mois, contre la musique françoise. Par le M . . . . de C . . . [Sometimes attributed to the Marquis de Chastellux.] pp. 10. [*Paris,*] 1754. 8°. **Hirsch I. 117.**

C . . . . ., *M. de, Membre de l'Académie d'Amiens.*

—— Dissertation sur l'emplacement du champ de bataille ou César défit l'armée des Nervii et de leurs alliés, par M. de C . . . . ., Membre de l'Académie d'Amiens [i.e. L. N. J. J. de Cayrol]. pp. 62. *Amiens,* 1832. 8°. **803. f. 14.**

C * * *, *M., des Arcades de Rome.* *See* V., P., *Docteur.* De l'énormité du duel, traité traduit de l'italien . . . Par M. C * * * des Arcades de Rome [i.e. — Cousin], *etc.* 1783. 12°. **501. a. 25.**

C * * *, *M. l'Abbé.* Lettre de M. l'Abbé C * * * à un ecclésiastique du diocèse de F * *. pp. 11. [*Paris?* 1791?] 12°. **F.R. 161. (18.)**

C * *, *M. l'Abbé, Chanoine à la Métropole d'Albi.* *See* JEANNE MARGUERITE, *de Miséricorde, Carmelite.* Le Banquet sacré . . . Retraite annuelle . . . Revue et corrigée par M. l'Abbé C * *, chanoine à la Métropole d'Albi [i.e. Jean Augustin Émile Caraguel]. [1844.] 12°. **4401. p. 4.**

C., *M. le C.*

—— L'Emprisonnement D. C. D., présenté au roy. [The drop-head title reads: "L'Emprisonnement de M. le C. C., envoyé au roy." In verse.] *In:* FOURNIER (E.) Variétés historiques et littéraires, *etc.* tom. 8. pp. 211–216. 1857. 12°. **12234**. aa. **8**.

C., *M. le C. de.* *See* VINCI (L. da) Recueil de testes de caractere & de charges dessinées par Leonard de Vinci . . . & gravées par M. le C. de C. [i.e. A. C. P. de Tubières de Grimoard de Pestels de Levis, Count de Caylus.] 1730. 8°. **562***. b. **18**. (**1**.)

C . . . . ., *M. le Chevalier de, des Académies de Lyon, Dijon, Rouen, Marseille, Hesse, Cassel, etc.*

—— Les États-généraux de Cythère, imitation très libre de l'italien du comte Algarotti . . . par M. le Chevalier de C . . . . . [i.e. Michel de Cubières-Palmézeaux]. pp. 32. 1789. 8°. **F**. **511**. (**2**.)

—— L'Homme-d'état imaginaire, comédie . . . par M. le Chevalier de C * * *, des Académies de Lyon, Dijon, Rouen, Marseille, Hesse-Cassel, &c. [i.e. Michel de Cubières de Palmézeaux.] [Based on "Den politiske Kandestøber" by Baron Ludvig af Holberg.] pp. xix. 136. *Paris*, 1789. 8°. **911**. c. **18**. (**1**.)

—— [Another copy.] **164**. c. **50**.

—— L'Homme-d'état imaginaire, comédie . . . par M. le chevalier de C * * * [i.e. Michel de Cubières de Palmézeaux]. [With a Norwegian translation of the preface.] *See* FOSS (Kåre) Konge for en dag, *etc.* 1946. 8°. **11868**. c. **12**.

C * * *., *M. le Comte de.* *See* CASSINI (G. D.) Fragment d'un poème sur l'astronomie. [Signed by the translator: M. le Comte de C * * *, i.e. Jean Dominique, Count de Cassini?] [1780?] 4°. **B**. **728**. (**18**.)

C * * *, *M. le Comte de.* Les Dangers d'un amour illicite, ou le Mariage mal assorti. Histoire véritable: par M. le Comte de C * * *. 2 pt. *Gattey: Londres*, 1789. 12°. **12518**. aa. **30**.

C . . ., *M. le Cte de.* Les Contes rémois par M. le Cte de C . . . [i.e. Count L. M. J. de Riche de Chevigné]. Dessins de E. Meissonier. Troisième édition. [In verse.] pp. 239. *Paris*, 1858. 8°. **11482**. f. **13**.

C * * *, *M. le Duc de.*

—— Catalogue de tableaux anciens, choisis dans les diverses écoles, et formant le riche cabinet de M. le duc de C*** [identified in a MS. note as the Duke de Caraman], *etc.* [Catalogue of a sale due to take place on 10–12 May, 1830.] pp. 58. MS. PRICES. *Paris*, 1830. 8°. **562**. e. **74**. (**17**.)

C . . . ., *M. le Vte de.*

—— Notice de tableaux, gravures, porcelaines et objets de curiosité, dont la vente aura lieu après le décès de M. le Vte de C . . . . le lundi 3 juillet 1826, *etc.* pp. 8. MS. PRICES. [*Paris*,] 1826. 8°. **562**. e. **63**. (**1**.)

C . . . . ., *Mad. la D^sse de.*

—— Opuscules de Mad. la D^sse de C . . . . . [i.e. Louise Honorine, Duchess de Choiseul]. *See* CHOISEUL (E. F. de) *Duke de Choiseul and d'Amboise.* Mémoires, *etc.* tom. 2. 1790. 8°. **285**. k. **15**.

C * * *, *Madame.* Amelia Mansfield. Translated from the French of Madame C * * *, author of Malvina & Claire d'Albe [i.e. Sophie Cottin]. 4 vol. *Gameau & Co.: London*, 1803. 12°. **12611**. a. **21**.
Imperfect; wanting the titlepage to vol. 2.

C * * * *, *Madame.* Malvina. By Madame C * * * *, autl ress of Clare d'Albe and Amelia Mansfield [i.e. Sop Cottin]. Translated from the French, by Miss Gunni 4 vol. *T. Hurst: London*, 1804. 12°. **N**. **27**
Imperfect; wanting pp. 197, 198 *of vol.* 4.

—— The second edition. 4 vol. *C. Chapple: Lond* 1810. 12°. **12510**. bb.

C * * *, *Madame de.*

—— Amélie de Saint-Far, ou la Fatale erreur; par Mad de C***, auteur de Julie, ou J'ai sauvé ma rose. [Vario attributed to Félicité de Choiseul-Meuse and to Mad Guyot. With engraved frontispieces.] 2 tom. *Hambourg & Paris*, 1816. 12°. **12520**. aa

C * * *, *Madame de.* Lettres historiques et galantes, Madame de C * * * [i.e. Anne Marguerite Petit du Noy Ouvrage curieux. 7 tom. *Cologne* [*The Hag* 1707–18. 12°. **12510**. aaaa.
Tom. 2 *is of the fourth edition, and bears the date* 1 *Tom.* 1 *and* 6 *are imperfect; wanting the plates.*

—— Quatrième edition, revûë & corrigée. tom. 1–6. *Col* [*The Hague*], 1714, 11–13. 12°. **1085**. a.
A made-up copy; tom. 1, 2 *are of the fourth edit tom.* 3 *of the second, tom.* 4–6 *of the first. Imperf wanting tom.* 7.

—— Cinquième edition, revuë & corrigée. tom. 1–3. *Cologne* [*The Hague*], 1733, 12. 12°. **1085**. a.
Tom. 3 *is of the second edition. Imperfect; wan tom.* 4–7.

C * * * *, *Madame de.* A Winter in Paris; or, Memoir Madame de C * * * *: written by herself. [A nov 3 vol. *Henry Colburn: London*, 1811. 12°. **12623**. e

C—, *Major.*

—— Indian Horse Notes. An epitome of useful informa . . . Seventh edition, completely revised. pp. 119. *Thacker, Spink & Co.: Calcutta*, 1912. 8°. **7295**. p.

—— Indian Notes about Dogs, their diseases treatment. Compiled by Major C——, author of "H Notes." Second edition, revised and enlarged. pp. viii. 115. *Thacker, Spink & Co.: Calcutta*, 1881. **7295**. aaa.

—— Fourth edition. pp. viii. 118. *Tha Spink & Co.: Calcutta*, 1889. 8°. **7293**. aa

—— Sixth edition. pp. viii. 118. *Thacker, Spink & Calcutta*, 1896. 8°. **7293**. aaa

C * * * *, *Marquis de.* Lettre du marquis de C * * * * comte de F * * * contre le divorce. pp. 19. *P* [1790.] 8°. **F**. **536**.

C . . . . ., *Me. de.* *See* BROWN (Thomas) Thomas B . . . Traduit de l'anglais, par M^e de C . . . . . 1806. **12808**. r

C . . . ., *Membre de la Chambre des Députés.* *See* LET Lettre à un membre de la Chambre des Députés, [The editor's preface signed: C . . . ., Membre chambre des députés.] 1816. 8°. **1141**. h. **8**.

C * * *, *Monsieur, avocat au Parlement.*

—— Lettre de Monsieur D***, à Monsieur C***, avoca Parlement. [1790.] 8°. *See* D***, *Monsieur.* **F**. **586**

C * * *, *Monsieur de.* L'Honneur considéré en lui-mêm relativement au duel . . . Par Monsieur de C * * * — de Champdevaux?]. pp. xv. 391. *Paris*, 1752. **721**. c

C * * *, *Monsieur de.* Pharamond, tragédie. Par Monsieur de C * * * [i.e. L. de Cahusac]. [In verse.] pp. 76. *Paris,* 1736. 8°. **164.** c. **52.**

C . . ., *Monsieur de.* Poesies nouuelles, et autres oeuures galantes. De Monsieur de C . . . [i.e. Bénech de Canterac]. (Poesies morales et chrestiennes de Monsieur de C.— Lettres choisies et galantes de Monsieur de C . . .. Reueuës & augmentées en cette seconde edition.) 2 pt. *J. Girard: Paris,* 1665, 64. 12°. **11483.** aa. **5.**
With an additional titlepage, engraved.

C. * *, *Monsieur de.* Recueil de letres tant en prose qu'en vers. Sur le livre (de Monsieur de C. * * [i.e. F. de Salignac de la Mothe Fénelon, Archbishop of Cambray]) intitulé, Explication des maximes des Saints. [Edited by J. B. Bossuet, successively Bishop of Condom and of Meaux.] pp. 96. 1699. 8°. **3902.** bb. **8.** (**2.**)

C., *Mr. See* KING (Thomas) *Controversial Writer.* A Check to Uncharitableness . . . To which is added, A Farther Check to Uncharitableness: in answer to a sermon preached in Grub-Street, by Mr. C., *etc.* 1791. 12°. **4378.** c. **29.**

C., *Mr. See* NETHERLANDS.—*United Provinces.* [*Appendix.*] Extracts from a work called Breeden Raedt aen de Vereenighde Nederlandsche Provintien . . . Translated . . . by Mr. C. 1850. 12°. **8079.** bb. **6.**

C * * *, *Mr.* Atlas historique, ou Nouvelle introduction à l'histoire, à la chronologie & à la géographie ancienne & moderne; réprésentée dans de nouvelles cartes . . . Par Mr C * * * [i.e. H. A. Chatelain] avec des dissertations sur l'histoire de chaque état, par Mr. Gueudeville [and — Garillon]. tom. 2. pt. 2, 3, 4, 6. *Amsterdam,* 1708–19. fol. Maps **49.** f. **6.**
Imperfect; wanting tom. 1, *and pt.* 1, 5, 7 *of tom.* 2.

—— Troisiesme édition, révuë corrigée & augmentée. (Supplément . . . avec des dissertations . . . par Mr H. P. de Limiers.) 7 tom. *Amsterdam,* 1721, 14–20. fol. **209.** i. **4–7.**
Tom. 4–7 *are of the first edition.*

—— Carte du gouvernement ecclésiastique d'Angleterre, *etc.* [A facsimile of pl. 50 of the "Atlas Historique."] *Paris,* 1939. *s. sh.* fol. **1856.** g. 3. (**38.**)

C., *Mr.* Bristol Drollery. Poems and songs. By Mr. C. [Signed: N. C.] 1674. 8°. *See* C., N. C. **39.** b. **52.**

C . . . ., *Mr.* Kantteekeningen op het Handboek der geschiedenis van het Vaderland, van Mr. G. Groen van Prinsterer. Door Mr. C . . . . [With a note by the author, J. J. de Rovere van Breugel, signed in MS.: Cuchlinus.] dl. 1, 2. *Nijmegen,* 1857. 8°. **9415.** h. **26.**
No more published.

C——, *Mr.* A Short Account of the Last Hours of Mr. C——. pp. 16. *J. K. Campbell: London,* [1854 ?] 16°. **4409.** a. **65.** (**1.**)

C., *Mr.* An Union to be Subjection, proved from Mr. C.'s own words in his Arguments for and against. In two parts. Part I. . . . By an Irish Logician. [With reference to "Arguments for and against an Union between Great Britain and Ireland, considered" by Edward Cooke.] pp. 40. *J. Rice: Dublin,* 1799. 8°. **8145.** de. **9.** (**7.**)

C - - - - - - - -, *Mr.* Upon the Death of that Incomparable Princess, Q. Mary: with an address to His Majesty. By Mr. C - - - - - - - -. [In verse.] *Heirs & Successors of Andrew Anderson: Edinburgh,* 1695. *s. sh.* fol. **1875.** d. **6.** (**56.**)

C * * *, *Mr.*

—— Vente d'une collection de tableaux, des trois écoles, composant le cabinet de Mr. C * * * [identified in a MS. note as — Chartier], dont la vente se fera . . . 10 et . . . 11 septembre 1817, *etc.* pp. 8. MS. NOTES AND PRICES. [*Paris,*] 1817. 8°. **562.** e. **37.** (**19.**)
The dates of sale are altered in MS. *to* 12 *and* 13 *September.*

C., *Mr., Curé de Bury près de Condé.* Emigration de Dumourier, ou Extrait d'une lettre de Mr. C. curé de Bury pres de Condé à son neveu philosophe à Louvain. pp. 3. [1793.] 8°. **8050.** d. **63.** (**26.**)

—— [Another copy.] Émigration de Dumourier, *etc.* [1793.] 8°. **9415.** c. **18.** (**35.**)

C * * * * *, *Mr., de Marseille.* Mesté Barna, marchand de vin ei grands carmés . . . Comédie en un acte et en vers provençaux, par Mr. C * * * * *, de Marseille [i.e. — Carvin]. pp. 36. *Marseille,* 1809. 8°. **1343.** g. **16.** (**1.**)

C * * *, *Mr. le M** de.*

—— Lettres d'un citoyen des États-unis à un Français, sur les affaires présentes. Par Mr le M** de C*** [i.e. M. J. A. N. Caritat, Marquis de Condorcet]. 2 pt. *Philadelphie,* 1788. 8°. R. **186.** (**14.**)
The imprint is fictitious.

C., *Mr. le Syndic.* Copie de la lettre écrite par Mr. le Syndic C. [i.e. Jean Louis Chouet], à Mr. * * *, en datte du 7me octobre 1735. [With reference to "Mémoire justificatif pour Jean Trembley."] pp. 8. [*Geneva,* 1735.] 4°. **8074.** i. **19.** (**3.**)

—— [Another copy.] **8074.** i. **12.** (**15.**)

C., *Mr., M. de la R. de G. See* F. DE LA C., *Madame de.* Mémoire de Madame de F. de la C. [de Falques de la Cépèdes] contre Mr. C. M. de la R. de G. [i.e. Mr. Celesia, Ministre de la République de Gènes.] 1758. 8°. **1080.** k. **17.**

C——, *Mrs.* Belinda, or, the Fair Fugitive. A novel. By Mrs. C—— . . . A new edition. 2 vol. *G. Allen: London,* 1789. 12°. **12611.** bb. **7.**

C . . . ., *Officier de la Marine.* Observations, sur le rapport fait à l'Assemblée nationale, et le projet de décret proposé par M. Cavalier, au nom du Comité de Marine, dans la séance du soir, du 8 décembre 1791. [Signed: C . . . ., Officier de la Marine.] pp. 15. [*Paris,* 1791.] 4°. **936.** f. **14.** (**42.**)

C., *Philopatris.* The True Lawe of Free Monarchies. Or the reciprock and mutuall dutie betwixt a free King, and his naturall Subiects. [The advertisement to the reader signed: C. Φιλοπατρις, i.e. James I., King of Great Britain and Ireland.] *Printed by T. C.: London,* 1603. 8°. **720.** a. **32.** (**4.**)

—— [Another edition.] *Printed by T. C.: London,* 1603. 8°. **1196.** c. **32.** (**2.**)

—— [Another edition.] pp. 16. *Printed & sold by T. P.: London,* 1642. 4°. E. **238.** (**23.**)

—— Assertio Juris Monarchici in Regno Scotorum: seu de mutuis Regis Scotiæ, & Subditorum ejus officiis, dissertatio politica. [The preface signed: C. Philopatris, i.e. James I., King of Great Britain and Ireland. A translation of "The True Lawe of Free Monarchies."] pp. 26. 1653. 4°. **601.** aa. **6.** (**1.**)

—— [Another copy.] G. **3803.** (**14.**)

C . . . . ., *Prêtre.* Lettre intéressante d'un prêtre réfractaire de Lyon, à un de ses amis de Mâcon, en date du 19 octobre 1791, *etc.* [Signed: C . . . . . prêtre.] pp. 4. [1791.] 8°. F.R. **139.** (**31.**)

C . . . . ., *le Prince de.* Memento politique par le Prince de C . . . . . pp. 95. *Paris*, 1844. 8°. **8051**. df. **19**.

C., *the R - - - H - - - - - -, Lord.* The Heroic Epistle answered: by the R - - - H - - - - - - Lord C—— [i.e. William Craven, 1st Earl Craven]. [A satire. With reference to "An Heroic Epistle to Lord Craven" by William Combe.] pp. 11. *J. Wilkie: London*, 1776. 4°. T. **667**. (5.)

—— [Another copy.] **162**. l. **73**.

C * * * *, *Sieur.* See PERIODICAL PUBLICATIONS.—*Rotterdam.* Nouveau journal des sçavans, dressé par le Sieur C * * * * [i.e. E. Chauvin]. 1694, *etc.* 12°. **942**. n. **8, 9**.

C., *le Sieur.* L'Escole des Muses, dans laquelle sont enseignées toutes les reigles qui concernent la poësie françoise. Recueillies par le Sieur C. [i.e. F. Colletet]. pp. 95. *L. Chamhoudry: Paris*, 1656. 12°. **11824**. aa. **6**.

C * * *, *Le sieur de.*

—— Dictionarium latino-gallicum. [By "Le sieur de C***."] pp. 350. *In:* Dictionnaire universel françois & latin, *etc.* tom. 3. 1704. fol. **12955**. f. **2**.

—— Dictionarium universale latino-gallicum. [Another edition of "Dictionarium latino-gallicum."] pp. 330. 236. *In:* Dictionnaire universel françois et latin, *etc.* tom 5. 1721. fol. **1487.a.1.**

—— Dictionarium universale latino-gallicum. pp. 530. *In:* Dictionnaire universel françois et latin, *etc.* tom. 7. 1752. fol. **68**. h. **4**.

—— Dictionarium latino-gallicum. pp. 364. 92. *In:* Dictionnaire universel françois et latin, *etc.* tom 8. 1771. fol. **1332**. l. **1-8**.

C . . ., *le Sieur de.* Poesies nouuelles, et autres oeuures galantes. Du Sieur de C . . . [i.e. Bénech de Cantenac]. (Poesies morales, et chrestiennes du Sieur de C.—Lettres choisies et galantes du Sieur de C . . . . .) pp. 253. *T. Girard: Paris*, 1662. 12°. **11483**. aa. **7**.
With an additional titlepage, engraved.

C., *S^r^.* Les Bagolins, comedie. Par le Sr C. [The dedication signed: C. D. L. B.] pp. 27. *F. Lammiga: Amsterdam*, 1682. 12°. **163**. b. **5**.

C., *el T. de.* Diálogo casero. El Aquador, la Cocinera, y el Insurgente. [Signed: El T. de C.] [*Mexico*,] 1810. 4°. **9770**. aaa. **12**. (**15**.)

C * * *, DE. Les Petits avis d'un républicain monarchiste. Par De C * * *. pp. 29. *Lyon*, 1871. 8°. **8051**. de. **1**. (**7**.)

C . . ., DE, *Citoyen Actif.* See LAMETH (C. M. F. de) *Count, pseud.* Lettre de M. le Cte C. de Lameth, à M. le Chr. de B. adressée à l'Assemblée nationale; par un Citoyen de l'Anjou, *etc.* [The dedication signed: C . . . Citoyen actif.] [1789.] 8°. F. **585**. (**9**.)

C * * * (DE) *M.*

—— See LALANDE ( ) *Ancien Secrétaire de la Présidence de la Chambre des Pairs.* Catalogue de lettres autographes provenant des cabinets de feu M. Lalande . . . et de M. de C***, *etc.* 1850. 8°. **11900**. bbb. **1**. (**10**.)

C., V. See HAUPT (Carl) *Pastor von Lerchenborn.* Vom deutschen Volksthum, *etc.* [With a "Nachwort," signed: v. C.] 1871. 16°. **8074**. aa. **59**.

C., V. Abhandlung vom Torfe, dessen Ursprung, Nachwuchs, Aufbereitung, Gebrauch und Rechten. Zweite Auflage. [The preface signed: v. C.] pp. 96. *Giessen*, 1801. 8°. **967**. i. **13**.

C * * *, VON. See LA B * * *, *Marquis de.* La Corresponde[nce] amusante sur les evenemens de nos jours. Oder gewechselten Briefe . . . des Marqu. de la B * * * [und] eines deutschen Edelmanns von C * * *, *etc.* 1743. 8° **8050**. bb. **5**.

C., A. See ANDREIS (A. J. F. B. de) Leben und Wir[ken] des hochwürdigen Herrn Felix von Andreis . . . üb[er]setzt von A. B. und A. C. 1866. 8°. **4886**. bb.

C., A. See APHORISMES. Aphoris[mes] d'astrologie tirée de Ptolemée, Hermes . . . Traduit[s en] françois par A. C., *etc.* 1657. 12°. **8610**. a.

C., A. See B., B. de, and C., A. Histoire d'un atome [de] carbone, depuis l'origine des temps jusqu'à ce jour, 1864. 12°. **8704**. aaa. **33**.

C., A. See BOURDALOUE (L.) [*Sermons.—Two or m[ore] Sermons.*] Practical Divinity . . . Translated from French of Bourdaloue . . . by A. C. [i.e. Anth[ony] Carroll.] 1776. 12°. **4423**. f

C., A. See BURNS (Robert) *the Poet.* [*Smaller Collecti[ons]*] The Poetical Works of Robert Burns . . . To whic[h is] prefixed, a sketch of his life [signed: A. C., i.e. Alexa[nder] Chalmers]. 1804. 8°. **11609**. aa.

—— —— 1813. 24°. **11630**. aa.

—— —— 1817. 12°. **11612**. aa.

—— —— 1823. 8°. **1346**. c. **17**

C., A. See C., J., *Jun.*, and C., A. The United States [and] Canada, as seen by two Brothers [J. C., Jun. and A. [C.]] *etc.* 1862. 8°. **10408**.

C., A. See C., T. Prince Perindo's Wish . . . Illustr[ated] by A. C. 1874. 8°. **12804**. i.

C., A. See CAVEDONE (G.) Due novelle aggiunte i[n] codice del MCCCCXXXVII, *etc.* [The editor's preface sig[ned] A. C., i.e. Antonio Cappelli.] 1866. 8°. **12226**. bbb. **12**.

C., A.

—— See CHEYNE (John) Essays on Partial Derangeme[nt of] the Mind, *etc.* [The editor's preface signed: A. C. A. Cheyne.] 1843. 8°. **1191.1.**

C., A. See COOPER (Mary) *Mrs., of London.* Memoirs o[f the] late Mrs. Mary Cooper, *etc.* [Extracts from her [diary] and correspondence. The editor's advertisement sig[ned] A. C., i.e. Dr. Adam Clarke.] 1814. 12°. **4903**. ccc

C., A. See EDMOND, *pseud.* [i.e. E. Crosnier], and C., A. Pièce en perce, comédie . . . par Mm. Edmont et A. [i.e. Armand Croizette], *etc.* 1819. 8°. **11738**. c. **29**.

C., A.

—— See GIRARD DES BERGERIES (Jacob) Moïse sans [voile] ou Explication des types et des figures de l'Ancien T[esta]ment, *etc.* [The editor's advertisement signed: A. C.] 1828. 8°. **3156**. aa

C., A. See GLASS (Thomas) *Puritan.* A Mite from T[hree] Mourners (J. V., W. A., A. C.): in memorial of T. C *etc.* [1666.] *s. sh.* fol. Lutt.

C., A. See ITALY.—*Ministero dell' Interno.* Raccolta [di] circolari di massima emanate dal Ministero dell'Int[erno] *etc.* [The compilers' preface signed: T. G., A. C.] 1867. 8°. **8032**.

C., A. See LAMARTINE DE PRAT (M. L. A. de) The S[tone]cutter of St.-Point: being a translation from the F[rench] . . . by A. C. 1886. 8°. **12200**. aa. 2

C., A. *See* Ochino (B.) Fouretene Sermons . . . concernyng the predestinacion and eleccion of god . . . Translated out of Italian . . . by A. C. [i.e. Anne Cooke.] [1550?] 8º. **C. 12. c. 22.**

—— *See* Ochino (B.) Sermons . . . Translated . . . by A. C. [i.e. Anne Cooke.] [1570?] 8º. **C. 53. gg. 12.**

C., A. *See* Periodical Publications.—*Milan.* Non ti scordar di me . . . Compilata per cura di A. C. [i.e. Antonio Corbellini.] [1832, *etc.*] 12º. **P.P. 6980.**

C., A. *See* Possevino (G. B.) *the Younger.* Discours de la vie de Sainct Charles Borromée . . . Traduict . . . par A. C., *etc.* 1611. 8º. **862. g. 3.**

C., A. *See* Robertson (William) *D.D., the Historian.* Storia del regno dell'imperatore Carlo Quinto . . . Traduzione . . . di A. C. con note e confutazioni del traduttore. 1835. 4º. **10708. f. 38.**

C., A. *See* Roergas de Serviez (J.) Le Mogli dei dodici Cesari . . . Traduzione . . . di A. C. 1820, *etc.* 12º. **1198. c. 1.**

C., A. *See* Rome, *Church of.—Congregatio Rituum.* Urbis et orbis. Repositionis nominis S. Joseph in litaniis majoribus discursus, *etc.* [The editor's preface signed: A. C., i.e. A. E. A. Carion?] 1862. 12º. **4826. aa. 5.**

C., A. *See* Thomas, *Aquinas, Saint.* [*Lauda Sion.—Italian.*] Parafrasi della sequenza Lauda Sion Salvatorem, *etc.* [The dedication signed: A. C., i.e. Agostino Coltellini.] 1659. 12º. **11427. df. 23. (2.)**

C., A. *See* Vernon (John) *Nonconformist Minister.* Bochim. Sighs poured out by some troubled hearts (J. T., J. M., A. C., W. A.), and tendred towards continuing the precious savour of the good name of . . . J. Vernon, *etc.* [1667.] *s. sh.* fol. **Lutt. I. 153.**

C., A. *See* W., R. The Christian Priest. A poem sacred to the memory of . . . Dr. Samuel Clarke . . . with his Character [signed: A. C.]. 1729. 8º. **11631. e. 67.**

C., A. Almanach de la Principauté de Monaco . . . Par A. C. [i.e. Antoine Cauvin.] [1833.] 8º. *See* Ephemerides. **P.P. 2386. e.**

C., A. An Answer [signed: A. C.] to a late Treasonable Pamphlet, entituled, Treason in Grain, &c. for which pamphlet Edward Fitz-Harris lies condemned. pp. 2. *By N. T.: London,* 1681. *s. sh.* fol. **816. m. 2. (19.)**

C., A. An Answere to a Letter of a Iesuited Gentleman, by his Cosin, Maister A. C. [i.e. Anthony Copley] concerning the {Appeale; State, Iesuits.} pp. 122. [*F. Kingston: London,*] 1601. 4º. **860. k. 28.**

C., A. An Answer to a Pamphlet [by Daniel Featley] intituled, The Fisher catched in his owne net . . . By A. C. [a Catholic, i.e. John Floyd.] (An Appendix containing an answere to some untruthes.) pp. 86. [*St. Omer?*] 1623. 4º. **C. 26. h. 18. (3.)**

C., A. The Art of Writing Short-Hand Made Easy, *etc.* [The preface signed: A. C., i.e. Alexander Crome.] pp. 15. pl. 3. *J. Crome: Sheffield,* [1798.] 12º. **7942. aaa. 33. (2.)**

C., A. Beawtie dishonoured, written under the title of Shores Wife. [In verse. The epistle dedicatory signed: A. C., i.e. Anthony Chute.] pp. 54. *By John Wolfe: London,* 1593. 4º. **C. 39. c. 12.**

C., A. The Bibliographical Miscellany; or, Supplement to the Bibliographical Dictionary. [The preface signed: A. C., i.e. Adam Clarke.] 2 vol. 1806. *See* Dictionary. A Bibliographical Dictionary, *etc.* 1802, *etc.* 12º. **619. b. 30, 31.**

C., A. The Book of Prophecy Opened: or, a Plain discovery of the hidden treasure of wisdom and knowledge, contained in the book with seven seals, *etc.* [The preface signed: A. C., i.e. Alexander Clark.] pp. xii. 257. *Printed for the Author: London,* 1779. 8º. **3165. aa. 52.**

C., A. The Case Restated; or an Account of a conversation with a Papist, concerning a book intitled, the Case stated between the Church of Rome, and the Church of England, &c. [by Charles Leslie?]. In a letter from a gentleman in the country to his friend in London. [Signed: A. C., i.e. Archibald Campbell?] pp. 100. [*London,*] 1713. 8º. **3936. c. 9.**

C., A.

—— Catalogue of the Engraved Portraits in the Royal College of Physicians. [The compiler's preface signed: A. C., i.e. Arnold Chaplin.] 2 vol. [1925.] fol. *See* London.—iii. *Royal College of Physicians.* Dept. of Prints & Drawings.

C., A.

—— Cenni biografici di Carlo Fea. [The introduction signed: A. C., i.e. Antonio Coppi. With a bibliography.] pp. 7. *Roma,* 1836. 4º. **10634. i. 49.**

C., A. Christian Liberty described in a sermon preached in the Collegiate Church at Westminster, by a Minister of Suffolke . . . A. C. [i.e. Alexander Chapman.] *I. W.* [*John Windet*], *for Matthew Lawe: London,* 1606. 4º. **4473. aaa. 14.**

C., A. Le Comte de Rémusat—François-Marie-Charles—Ministre des Affaires Étrangères de la République Française. Sa vie politique et littéraire. [Signed: A. C.] Nouvelle édition. pp. 29. *Montauban,* 1873. 16º. **10661. a. 3.**

C., A. Crítica sobre el dictamen de la Comision especial del Consejo [or rather, Congreso] de Veracruz acerca de la resistencia del Sr. Obispo de Puebla [F. P. Vazquez] á obedecer el decreto núm. 54 de aquella Legislatura, que trata de estincion de Conventos, *etc.* [Signed: A. C.] pp. 35. *Puebla,* 1834. 4º. **9770. bb. 23. (7.)**

C., A.

—— De danske Kongeborges Mysterier eller hemmelige Hofhistorier ved A. C. [i.e. L. J. Flamand]. pp. 318. *Kjøbenhavn,* 1857. 8º. **9425. a. 4.**

C., A. A Day in Dublin: a poem. [The prefatory epistle signed: A. C.] pp. iv. 19. *John Whitworth: Dublin,* 1807. 12º. **11643. aa. C.**

C., A. Della impudenza letteraria. Sermone parenetico di A. C. [i.e. Agatopisto Cromaziano, pseudonym of Appiano Buonafede] contro un libro intitolato Memorie anedote spettanti alla vita ed agli studj di F. Paolo Servita raccolte e ordinate da Francesco Griselini. pp. 84. [*Lucca,* 1760?] 8º. **1371. h. 10.**

C., A. The English Oracle: or, A Late prophecy of the miseries that will happen this next year, 1679. [A satire upon almanac-makers.] By A. C. pp. 8. *Printed for W. M.: London,* 1679. 4º. **12316. dd. 35.**

C., A. Examen critique du projet de loi relatif à l'Armée et à la Garde nationale mobile amendé par la Commission du Corps législatif. Exposé d'un nouveau plan d'organisation militaire. [The preface signed: A. C.] pp. 176. *Paris,* 1867. 8º. **8828. ee. 21.**

C., A. The Footstep to Mrs. Trimmer's Sacred History For the instruction and amusement of little children. [The preface signed: A. C.] pp. 117. *J. Marshall & Co.: London*, 1785. 12°. **843.** g. **32.** (**1.**)

C., A. The Garden. [Signed: A. C., i.e. Abraham Cowley.] *See* Poems. Poems upon Divers Occasions, *etc.* 1667. 8°. **1076.** h. **28.**

C., A. Giornale dell'incendio dell'Vessuuio dell'anno M.DC.LX. con le osseruationi matematiche. [The dedication signed: A. C., i.e. Accademico Cosentino. By G. B. Zupi.] pp. 15. *I. de'Lazari: Roma*, 1660. 4°. **444.** b. **49.**

—— [Another copy.] **664.** b. **23.** (**2.**)

C., A. Hymns on the Litany. By A. C. [i.e. Ada Cambridge, afterwards Cross.] pp. 73. *J. H. & J. Parker: Oxford & London*, 1865. 8°. **11647.** aaa. **39.**

C., A. "If." Dohnavur Fellowship. [The preface signed: A. C., i.e. Amy Carmichael.] pp. vii. 82. *S.P.C.K.: London*, 1938. 12°. **04402.** f. **71.**

C., A. In Memoriam A. C. [i.e. Annie Chapman. Verses, signed: I. M. C., i.e. John Mitchel Chapman.] 1871. 8°. *See* C., I. M. **11648.** a. **4.** (**2.**)

C., A. Inventario de una Colección de Libros de Arte que reune A. C. pp. 641. *Madrid*, 1911. 12°. **011899.** e. **12.**

C., A.

—— Juvenilia . . . Unpublished. [The foreword signed: A. C., i.e. Arthur Crichton.] pp. 48. *The Author: London*, 1812. 8°. **11658.** ee. **4.**

C., A. Il Latino nel concetto di Dante e dell'età sua. Nota filologica. [Signed: A. C.] pp. 31. *Monza*, 1903. 8°. **11422.** e. **18.** (**1.**)

C., A. A Letter [signed: A. C.] to a Friend. Shewing the illegall proceedings of the two Houses of Parliament: and observing God's aversenesse to their actions,. Which caused the authours returne to the King and his alleagiance. pp. 17. *Oxford* [*London*], 1645. 4°. **1093.** c. **1.**

C——, A——. Letters addressed to the Right Honorable the Earl of Liverpool and the Right Honorable Nicholas Vansittart. [Signed: A. C.] 1820. *See* Periodical Publications.—*London*. The Pamphleteer, *etc.* vol. 16. 1813, *etc.* 8°. **P.P. 3557.** w.

C., A. The London-Citizen Exceedingly Injured: or, a British Inquisition display'd, *etc.* [The dedication signed: A. C.] 1739. 8°. *See* Cruden (Alexander) **1415.** f. **39.**

C., A. Les Lyonnaises, ou Lettres à un ami au sujet d'un procès. Par A. C. [i.e. A. Chataing] . . . Première lettre, suivie de quelques réflexions sur la république actuelle. Octobre 1890. pp. 24. *Lyon*, 1890. 8°. **8051.** e. **42.**

C., A. La Maintenue des Roys, contre les assassins endiablez. Le prix d'outrecuidance, & Los de l'Vnion. [An allegorical engraving in honour of Henry IV. of France, with a dedication to him, signed: A. C.] [*Paris?* 1590.] *s. sh.* fol. **1853.** e. **5.** (**40.**)
The engraving is a much altered copy of one published under the title of "Eigentliche Beschreibung dess verstorbenen Königs Henrici 3., etc."

C., A. Maximilien et la monarchie au Mexique. Par A. C. pp. 87. *Paris*, 1867. 8°. **8179.** bb. **15.**

C., A. Memoria storico-giuridica sulla istituzione del fidecommesso Falconieri con documento allegato, di A. C. (Albero genealogico della casa Falconieri.) pp. 40. *Roma*, 1901. 4°. **9905.** c. **48.**

C., A. Les Normands au combat naval de l'Écluse 24 juin 1340. [Signed: A. C.] pp. 11. *Rouen*, 1872. 8°. **8806.** de. **38.** (**7.**)

C., A.

—— Obrona Warszawy. Wrzesień 1939 roku. Wydanie drugie. [The preface signed: A. C.] pp. 30. *M. I. Kolin: London*, [1941.] 8°. **09101.** a. **49.**

C., A. Ode sur le retablissement de la santé de Monseigneur [i.e. Louis, the Dauphin]. [In Latin and French. The Latin signed: A. C., the French signed: A. M.] pp. 7. *Paris*, 1701. 4°. **11474.** h. **27.** (**15.**)

C., A. Our Courts of Law [i.e. those of India], and how to improve them. By A. C. . . . Revised edition. pp. iii. 27. v. *K. R. Press: Madras*, 1882. 8°. **6146.** bbb. **24.** (**3.**)

C., A. Oxford v. Cambridge at Lords June 30th, 1892. M. R. Jardine, b. Streatfeild, 140. V. T. Hill, b. Hill, c. Wells, 114. "Never say die." [In verse. Signed: A. C., i.e. Albert Craig.] [*London*, 1892.] *s. sh.* 8°. **11647.** e. **1.** (**177.**)

C., A. Pensieri e voti pel coordinamento idraulico degli scoli col nuovo sistema dei fiumi del Padovano e proposta generale di un nuovo piano direttivo dei consorzi. Discorsi due di A. C. pp. 56. *Padova*, 1858. 8°. **8775.** cc. **29.** (**2.**)

C., A. Pools and the Valley of Vision. [Poems. The preface signed: A. C., i.e. Amy Carmichael.] pp. 61. *S.P.C.K.: London*, [1938.] 8°. **11654.** bb. **72.**

C., A. The Quinquennial Proceedings of two Administrations. 1881 to 1891 . . . By A. C. pp. 62. *W. Barton: London*, 1892. 8°. **8138.** de. **11.**

C., A. Ragguagli di Roma nel secolo XV, estratti da un articolo del Sig. G. Voigt pubblicato nel Taschenbuch, anno IV, Lipsia 1833, tradotti da A. C. *See* Italian Historical Archives. Archivio storico italiano, *etc.* Appendice. tom. 3. 1842, *etc.* 8°. **P.P. 3557.** a.

C., A. Rime di poeti italiani del secolo XVI. [The editor's preface signed: A. C., i.e. Antonio Cappelli.] pp. vii. 158. *Bologna*, 1873. 8°. **12226.** c. **11.** (**1.**)
Disp. 133 *of "Scelta di curiosità letterarie, etc."*

C., A. La Rivoluzione de' pazzi contro Mastro Giorgio, cercando la libertà. [In verse. Signed: A. C.] [*Naples*, 1820.] *s. sh.* fol. **8032.** m. **8.** (**12.**)

—— [Another copy.] **8032.** m. **8.** (**14.**)

C., A.

—— A Satyre. The Puritan and the Papist. By a scholler in Oxford. [A poem. Signed: A. C., i.e. Abraham Cowley.] pp. 9. [*H. Hall: Oxford*,] 1643. 4°. **1478.** dd. **4**[illegible]

C., A. A Sermon preach'd at Edinburgh, on Thursday the thirtieth of January M.DCC.VII. being the anniversary of the martyrdom of K. Charles I. By A. C., one of the suffering Clergy there [i.e. Andrew Cant]. pp. 30. [*Edinburgh*,] 1707. 4°. **4475.** b. **3**[illegible]
Slightly cropped.

—— A Sermon preach'd at Edinburgh on Tuesday the xxx. of January M.DCC.XI. being the anniversary of the martyrdom of K. Charles I. By one of the suffering clergy there. [The dedication signed: A. C., i.e. Andrew Cant.] pp. 20. [*Edinburgh*,] 1711. 4°. **4475.** bb. **2**[illegible]

—— A Sermon preach'd in one of the Meeting-Houses in Edinburgh, on Monday, January 31, 1715. Being the anniversary of the martyrdom of King Charles the First. By A. C. [i.e. Andrew Cant.] pp. 24. *George Stewart: Edinburgh*, 1715. 4°. **92.** i. **6**[illegible]

, A.

— A Sermon preached on the xxx day of January 170$\frac{2}{3}$ at Edinburgh, by one of the suffering clergy of the Kingdom of Scotland. [The preface signed: A. C., i.e. Andrew Cant.] pp. 29. *Printed for the Author: Edinburgh,* 1703. 4°. **4475**. bb. **28**.

, A. Some Remarks upon a book [by George Whitehead], entitled, Christ's Lambs defended against Satan's rage, &c. Being the Quaker's answer to The Quakers' unmask'd, &c. In a letter to E. S. Esq; [signed: A. C.]. *See* PENNYMAN (John) The Quakers Unmask'd, *etc.* 1691. 4°. **4106**. h. **4**. (**1**.)

, A. Souvenirs du siège de Paris. Une page d'histoire de la défense nationale, 1870–1871. [The dedication signed: A. C., i.e. A. Chaix.] pp. 118. *Paris,* 1890. 4°. **9079**. d. **15**.

, A. A Synopsis or Abridgement of the Holy Scriptures. [Signed: A. C.] *See* LOWTH (William) *Prebendary of Winchester.* Directions for the Profitable Reading of the Holy Scriptures, *etc.* 1769. 12°. **217**. d. **15**.

, A. True Relations of Sundry Conferences had betweene certaine Protestant Doctours (Francis White, Daniel Featly) and a Iesuite called M. Fisher . . . with defences of the same . . . By A. C. [a Catholic, i.e. John Sweet?] (An Appendix containing An Answere to some Untruthes, obiected by D. White, and D. Featly, against M. Fisher's Relations, or Writings.) pp. 74. 73–86. [*St. Omer,*] 1626. 4°. **3939**. b. **4**.
Cropped. Imperfect; wanting "An Answer to a Pamphlet, intituled The Fisher catched in his own net," and "A Reply to D. Whyte and D. Featly."

— *See* LAUD (WILLIAM) *Archbishop of Canterbury.*

— A Relation of the Conference betweene William Lawd . . . and Mr Fisher the Jesuite . . . With an answer to such exceptions as A. C. [i.e. John Sweet?] takes against it [in "True Relations of sundry Conferences betweene certaine Protestant Doctours and a Iesuite called M. Fisher"]. 1639. fol. **480**. d. **8**. (**1**.)

— —— 1673. fol. **480**. d. **9**.

— —— 1686. 4°. **3936**. i. **29**.

— —— 1901. 8°. **2206**. c. **4**.

, A. Le Vicomte de Taunay. Esquisse biographique. [Signed: A. C.] *See* ESCRAGNOLLE-TAUNAY (A. de) *Viscount.* La Retraite de Laguna, *etc.* 1913. 8°. **9771**. df. **22**.

, A. A View of the Posture of Affairs in Europe, both in Church and State . . . Written by a gentleman, by way of a letter. [The dedication signed: A. C.] pp. 84. *James Knapton: London,* 1701. 8°. E. **1977**. (**4**.)

, A. A Vindication of Lieut. Gen. Cromwell and Com. Gen. Ireton against the scandalous Aspersions cast upon them in a posted Libell signed by one Tompson. And likewise a true state of the case concerning the said Tompson. By A. C. pp. 6. *For L. Chapman: London,* 1647 [1648]. 4°. E. **431**. (**7**.)

, A. "The Way into the Holiest"; or, Talks on the Tabernacle. By A. C. pp. 90. *C. J. Thynne & Jarvis: London,* [1928.] 8°. **04478**. e. **13**.

, A. What is the Church? By A. C. pp. 310. *London Literary Society:* [*London,*] 1884. 8°. **4376**. b. **2**.

, A., and **C.**, P. The Tyrannical Usurpation of the Independent Cloak over the Episcopal Gown. By A. C. & P. C. [A ballad.] *Gideon Andrews: London,* 1663. *s. sh.* fol. **C.121.g.9.(8.)**

C., A., and **D.**, B. Whist Studies: being hands of w played through, according to the system of Cavendish, and in illustration of the principles laid down in that work. By A. C. [i.e. James Innes Minchin] and B. D. [i.e. F. Arbuthnot.] pp. 78. *Smith, Elder & Co.: London,* 1863. 8°. **7913**. b. **30**.

C., A., and **M.**, F. The Newcastle upon Tyne Church High School, 1885–1935. [The editors' preface signed: A. C., F. M. With plates.] pp. 103. 1935. 8°. *See* NEWCASTLE-UPON-TYNE.—*Newcastle-upon-Tyne Church High School.* **08364**. ff. **60**.

C., A., and **V.**, T. Jesus, Maria, Joseph, or, the Devout Pilgrim, of the Ever Blessed Virgin Mary, in his holy exercises, affections, and elevations. Upon the sacred mysteries of Jesus, Maria, Joseph. Published for the benefit of the pious Rosarists by A. C. and T. V. [i.e. A. A. Crowther and T. V. F. Sadler], religious monks of the Holy Order of S. Bennet. pp. 648. *Amsterdam,* 1657. 12°. **699**. a. **44**.

—— [Another edition.] pp. 301. *Amsterdam,* 1663. 8°. C. **53**. i. **22**.
With an additional titlepage, engraved. With the arms of Catharine of Braganza, Queen Consort of Charles II, stamped on the binding.

—— [Another copy.] **699**. a. **10**.
Imperfect; wanting the engraved titlepage.

C . . . ., A., *Ancien Avoué.* *See* VIGNERTE (B.) and C . . . ., A. Manuel juridique et pratique de l'irrigateur, *etc.* 1846. 12°. **1253**. a. **23**.

C., A., *Capitaine de Chasseurs.* Étude sur la cavalerie, sa tactique, son rôle, et sa réorganisation. Par A. C., Capitaine de Chasseurs. Suite de l'Étude sur les causes de nos désastres, *etc.* pp. 35. *Auch, Paris,* 1871. 8°. **8829**. e. **38**. (**8**.)

—— Étude sur les causes de nos désastres et la réorganisation de l'Armée. Par A. C., Capitaine de Chasseurs. pp. 24. *Toulouse,* 1871. 8°. **8829**. e. **38**. (**7**.)

C., A., *Carb.* Medici in Turchia, del Carb. A. C. [A political satire in verse.] [*Naples,* 1820.] *s. sh.* fol. **8032**. m. **10**. (**6**.)

C., A., *Cittadino.* Giampietro-eremita, del Cittadino A. C. [A political satire in verse.] [*Naples,* 1820.] *s. sh.* fol. **8032**. m. **10**. (**8**.)

C., A., *il Dottore.* *See* TABE. Della tabe dorsale . . . Tradotto dall'Inglese dal dottor A. C., *etc.* 1785. 8°. **7383***. b. **2**. (**14**.)

C., A., *Dr.* *See* BRONZINO (A.) Dello starsi. Capitoli tre burleschi, *etc.* [The dedication signed: A. Dr C., i.e. Angelo Cornello.] 1821. 8°. T. **68***. (**18**.)

C., A., *Esq.* *See* GRETTON (Phillips) Remarks upon Two Pamphlets [entitled "A Dissertation on Liberty and Necessity," and "A Philosophical Enquiry concerning Human Liberty"] written by the late A. C. Esq; [i.e. Anthony Collins] concerning human liberty and necessity, *etc.* 1730. 8°. **1020**. m. **2**. (**2**.)

—— A Dissertation on Liberty and Necessity: wherein the process of ideas, from their first entrance into the soul, until their production of action, is delineated. With some remarks upon the late Reverend Dr. Clarke's reasoning on this point. And an epistle dedicatory to Truth . . . By A. C. Esq; [i.e. Anthony Collins.] pp. vii. 23. *J. Shuckburgh: London,* 1729. 8°. **113**. g. **35**.

C., A., *Esq.*

—— *See* JACKSON (John) *Rector of Rossington.* A Defense of Human Liberty . . . To which is added, a Vindication of Human Liberty: in answer to a Dissertation on liberty and necessity. Written by A. C., Esq. [i.e. Anthony Collins.] 1730. 8°. **T. 1960. (8.)**

C * *, A * *, *Esq.* A Letter from the late A * * C * * Esq. [i.e. Anthony Collins] to the Rev[d] Dr. C * * M * * * * [i.e. Conyers Middleton] on his examination of the Lord Bishop of London's Discourses concerning the use and intent of prophecy. With some occasional references to the Free Enquiry, *etc.* [A satire.] pp. iv. 74. *S. Austen: London,* 1750. 8°. **3224. b. 16.**

C., A., *Fr., Augustinianus.* Arnolphus, malè Malus cognominatus, seu justa defensio, qua Arnolphi, Bavariæ ducis . . . facta, fata, fama a veterum æquè ac recentiorum scriptorum obtrectationibus, fabulis & convitiis vindicantur . . . per Fr. C. Augustinianum [i.e. Agnellus Caendler]. pp. 162. *Monachii,* 1735. 4°. **1199. h. 5.**

C., A., *il G . . . M . . . C . . . .* Confessione di Giampietro. [A political satire, in verse. Signed: Il G . . . M . . . C . . . A. C.] [*Naples,* 1820.] *s. sh.* fol. **8032. m. 10. (9.)**

—— *See* P., T. Risposta all'autore della Confessione di Giampietro [Il G . . . M . . . C . . . A. C.]. 1820. *s. sh.* fol. **8032. m. 10. (10.)**

—— Il Gigante di Palazzo, e la capo di Napoli. [In verse. Signed: Il G . . . M . . . C . . . A. C.] [*Naples,* 1820.] *s. sh.* fol. **8032. m. 10. (11.)**

C., A., *Generosus.*

—— Ad Populum: or, a Lecture to the people. Held forth long since, but never understood nor believed till now: notwithstanding, this is the sixth repitition. With a Satyre against Separatists. [By] A. C. Generosus. [Two works, of which the first is certainly, and the second probably, by Peter Hausted.] 2 pt. 1660. 8°. **E. 1822. (2.)**

—— A Satyre against Seperatists, or, the Conviction of chamber-preachers, and other chismatickes contrary to the discipline of this our Protestant profession. By A. C. Generosus. [Sometimes attributed to Abraham Cowley; more probably by Peter Hausted. In verse.] pp. 8. *Printed for A. C.: London,* 1642. 4°. **164. k. 4.**

—— [Another copy.] **E. 126. (28.)**

—— [Another edition.] A Satyre against Separatists, or, the Conviction of chamber-preachers, *etc.* [Sometimes attributed to Abraham Cowley; more probably by P. Hausted.] pp. 8. *Printed for A. C.: London,* 1642. 4°. Ashley **516.**

—— *See* SATIRE. A Satyre against the Cavaliers: penned in opposition to the Satyre against Separatists [by "A. C. Generosus"]. 1643. *s. sh.* fol. **1870. d. 1. (9*.)**

C., A., *Gent.* *See* GEIER (John) Thespis on Tryal . . . Translated . . . by A. C. Gent. 1887. 8°. **012202. de. 46.**

C., A., *Liverpool.* Imaginary Stories of the Isle of Man [in verse], by A. C., Liverpool. pp. 16. [*Liverpool?* 1894.] *obl.* 8°. **11686. a. 59.**

C., A., *M.* *See* BONALD (L. G. A. de) *Viscount.* Esprit de M. de Bonald . . . avec une notice sur l'auteur de ce recueil par M. A. C. 1870. 12°. **12236. aa. 7.**

C * * *, A * * *, *M.* M. Dupinceau, ou le Peintre d'enseigne, facétie en un acte, mêlée de couplets, par M. A * * *. C * * * [i.e. Armand Croizette]. pp. 38. *Paris,* 1808. 8°. **11738. c. 28. (1.)**

C., A., *M.A.* An Essay concerning Church Governme out of the excellent writings of Calvin and Beza. By C., M.A. [i.e. Alexander Cunningham.] 1689. 4°. **3900. bb.**

—— [Another edition.] 1692. 4°. **108. c.**

C., A., *M.A., of Trinity College, Cambridge.* The Telegra and Telegrapheme Controversy, as carried on in a friend correspondence between A. C. and H., both M.A.s Trinity College, Cambridge. pp. 48. *Rivingtons: Londo* 1858. 8°. **12923. d.**

C., A., *Missionaire.* Dictionnaire annamite-latin. Par professeur de séminaire. [The preface signed: A. Missionaire.] pp. ii. 361. *Hongkong,* 1928. 8°. **12906. p.**

C., A., *Mr.* Another Letter of Mr. A. C. [i.e. Anthony Cople to his Dis-Iesuited kinseman, concerning the Appea State, Iesuites. Also a third letter of his, Apologeticall himselfe against the calumnies contained against him in certaine Iesuiticall libell, intituled, A manifestation folly and bad spirit, &c. [by R. Parsons]. pp. 83. [*London,*] 1602. 4°. **853. f.**

C——, A——, *of H——.* An Elegy Sacred to the Memo of A—— C—— of H——. pp. iv. [*Edinburg* 1780?] 4°. **11633. bbb. 42.**

C., A., *Officier d'Infanterie.* Notice militaire et historique s l'ancienne ville de Lambœse, province de Constanti Par A. C. Officier d'Infanterie [i.e. Xavier Amé Charpentier], *etc.* pp. 100. pl. 11. *Paris,* 1860. 8°. **10095. d.**

C., A., *le P., Prêtre Mariste.* *See* DICTIONARIES. [*Vocab laries, etc.—Latin-Iaian.*] Dictionnaire latin-uvea à l'usa des élèves du Collège de Lano. Par les missionnai Maristes. Revu par le P. A. C., Prêtre mariste [i.e. Colomb]. 1886. 8°. **12902. cc. 53**

—— *See* P., F., *le P., Missionnaire Mariste.* Notes gramm ticales sur la langue de Lifu . . . d'après les manuscr du P. F. P. . . . par le P. A. C., Prêtre mariste [A. Colomb]. 1882. 8°. **12907. e.**

C., A., *le P., S.M.*

—— *See* FRENCH-WAGAP-ENGLISH DICTIONARY. Dictionnaire français-wagap-anglais wagap-français . . . Revu et mis en ordre par le P. A. C s.m. [i.e. A. Colomb.] 1891. 8°. **12910. d. 2**

—— *See* NAKETI. Vocabulaire des mots les p usuels de la langue de Nékété et de Thyo . . . Mis en or par le P. A. C., s.m. [i.e. A. Colomb.] [1889.] 8°. **012901. h. 8.**

—— *See* TOGA-FRENCH DICTIONARY. Dictionnaire toga-français et français-to anglais . . . précédé d'une grammaire et de quelq notes sur l'archipel. Par les missionnaires Mari [Joseph Chevron and Pierre Bataillon]. Revu et mis ordre par le P. A. C., s.m. [i.e. A. Colomb.] 1890. **12902. cc. 5**

—— *See* WAGAP. La Tribu de Wagap, Nouvelle-Calédo ses mœurs et sa langue. D'après les notes d'un missi naire mariste, coordonnées par le P. A. C., s.m. A. Colomb.] 1890. 8°. **12910. g.**

—— Essai de grammaire de la langue de Viti, d'après manuscrits des missionnaires Maristes coordonnés, pa P. A. C., s.m. [i.e. A. Colomb.]. pp. 148–288. 1884. *See* FRANCE.—*Œuvre de Saint-Jérôme pour la publicat des travaux philologiques des missionnaires.* **12902. cc. 5**

, A., *Philomath*. A New Almanack for the Year of our Lord, 1708. Containing astrological judgments for the weather, and monthly observations . . . By A. C. Philomath [i.e. Andrew Cumpsty]. 1708. 12°. *See* EPHEMERIDES. **P.P. 2477.** c.

, A., *Professeur de philosophie.* *See* SANSEVERINO (G.) Éléments de la philosophie chrétienne . . . Traduit . . . par A. C. Professeur de philosophie [i.e. the Abbé Corriol], *etc.* 1876. 8°. **8467.** gg. **2.**

, A., *S.* A Manual of Controuersies. Wherin the Catholique Romane faith in all the cheefe pointes of controuersies of these daies is proued by holy Scripture. By A. C., S. [i.e. Anthony Champney.] pp. 166. *Printed by Peter Buray: Paris,* 1614. 12°. **3932.** aa. **4.**

, *Lady* A., and *Lady* H. Recollections of Rome in 1843. [Coloured lithographs, from designs] by the Ladies A. and H. C. [i.e. the Ladies Augusta Sarah and Honoria Louisa Cadogan.] *Dickinson & Son: London,* [1845?] fol. Dept. of Prints & Drawings.

, A. DE. *See* LANGE (Joachim) Court exposé des maximes de philosophie de Mr. Wolf . . . Traduit . . . par A. de C. 1737. 8°. [*Recueil de nouvelles pièces philosophiques, etc.*] **717.** d. **21.**

, A. A. DE, *Conseiller privé du Roi.* *See* PRUSSIA.—[*Laws, etc.*—II.]—Frederick II. called *the Great, King.* Code Frédéric; ou Corps de droit pour les États de sa Majesté le Roi de Prusse . . . Traduit . . . par A. A. de C. Conseiller privé du Roi [i.e. A. A. de Campagne], *etc.* 1751, *etc.* 8°. **230.** g. **25.**

, A. B. *See* CHÂTEILLON (S.) Opera, *etc.* (Calumnia of Valsch-wroegen. In Nederlantsch vertaelt, *etc.* [The translator's preface signed: A. B. C., i.e. Cornelis Adriaenz Boomgaert.] 1613. 4°. **T. 2243.** (**4–8.**)

, A. B. *See* EHRENFRIED (J. F. C. S.) Das andere Wort des Laien J. F. C. S. Ehrenfried in Sachen der sogenannten protestantischen Freunde . . . nebst einem Vorworte an den Verfasser der vier ersten Gegenkönige, Herrn A.B.C. 1845. 8°. **3910.** cc. **26.**

, A. B. *See* GONIN, *Maître.* Der frantzösische Eulenspiegel, mit Kupffern und kurtzen Anmerckungen versehen von A. B. C. [i.e. Johann F. Bachstrom.] 1738. 8°. **12316.** ccc. **29.**

, A. B. *See* LACOMME (J.) Nouveau système d'arithmétique, *etc.* [The editor's introduction signed: A. B. C.] 1862. 8°. **8505.** cc. **42.** (**4.**)

, A. B. *See* MUELLER (Theodor) *Evang. luth. Pastor zu Embden.* Beleuchtung des A. B. C. Büchleins: Die vier ersten Gegenkönige, *etc.* 1845. 8°. **3910.** b. **94.**

, A. B. *See* PISTORIUS (H. A.) Die Herren J. Steinbrecher . . . und A. B. C., *etc.* [Containing a reply to " Die vier ersten Gegenkönige " of A. B. C.] 1845. 8°. **3910.** cc. **61.**

, A. B. [Religious tracts, and cuttings from " The Family Churchman," for the most part entitled " Devotional Paper." Signed: A. B. C., i.e. A. B. Cobb.] 7 pt. *G. J. W. Pitman: London,* [1894, 95.] 8°. **764.** i. **19.** (**15.**)

, A. B. Anciennes familles de Normandie. Le Forestier du Buisson-Sainte-Marguerite. Croquis généalogiques depuis le xve siècle. Par un Membre de la Société des Antiquaires de Normandie et du Conseil héraldique de France. [The preface signed: A. B. C., i.e. A. C. Du Buisson de Courson.] pp. 78. *Versailles,* 1888. 8°. **9916.** bb. **12.**

C., A. B. The Bank of England and the Discount Houses. By A. B. C. pp. 8. *Richardson Bros.: London,* 1860. 8°. **8226.** b. **79.** (**17.**)

—— *See* X. The Grievance of the Discount Houses. [In reply to " The Bank of England and the Discount Houses " by A. B. C.] 1860. 8°. **8227.** b. **70.** (**6.**)

C., A. B. Britons, Awake!!! By A. B. C. pp. 15. *Kegan Paul & Co.: London,* 1885. 8°. **8139.** b. **18.** (**9.**)

C., A. B. Contestacion á " El Universal " de Méjico [in its comments on a pamphlet by J. M. Barrundia. Signed: A. B. C.]. pp. 20. *Guatemala,* 1890. 8°. **8180.** e. **20.** (**4.**)

C., A. (B.) The Controversy concerning Free-Will, and Predestination, set in a true light and brought to a short issue. In a letter to a friend. [Signed: A. (B.) C.] pp. 26. *J. Roberts: London,* 1728. 8°. **1019.** l. **6.** (**4.**)

C., A. B. The Countrey-Mans Rudiments: or, an Advice to the farmers in East-Lothian how to labour and improve their ground. [The preface signed: A, B, C. By John Hamilton, 2nd Baron Belhaven.] pp. 48. *Heirs of A. Anderson: Edinburgh,* 1699. 8°. **7077.** aaa. **13.**

C., A. B. Francis and Day's " Music made Easy." Designed for school and private use by A. B. C., *etc.* pp. 33. *Francis, Day & Hunter: London,* [1904.] 8°. **7895.** b. **53.** (**3.**)

C., A. B. The Hardship and Danger of Subscriptions, represented, in a letter to the Reverend Dr. Powell, with remarks upon his sermon [entitled " A Defence of the Subscriptions required in the Church of England "], preached before the University of Cambridge, on the Commencement Sunday, 1757. [Signed: A. B. C.] pp. 31. *J. Waugh; W. Fenner: London,* 1758. 8°. **698.** i. **12.** (**10.**)

C., A. B. Indian Finance and Government. By A. B. C. pp. 44. *Hatchards: London,* 1884. 8°. **8023.** e. **11.** (**9.**)

C., A. B. Inverse Elementary Tactics of Cavalry; comprising simple, compound, and partial inversions, with the application of them to regimental, extensive, and auxiliary lines, also, the conversion of the squadron. By A. B. C. pp. 56. *Thomas Bosworth: London,* 1855. 8°. **8828.** b. **21.**

C., A. B. Joseph " the Dreamer." His mission to the world, via Egypt. [Signed: A. B. C.] pp. 7. *Bales & Wilde: Chesterfield & Clay Cross,* [1899.] 8°. **4371.** eee. **31.** (**8.**)

C., A. B. Lausus & Lydia, with Madam Bonso's Three Strings to her Bow; or, Three Bows to her String!!! [The dedication signed: A. B. C., i.e. Sarah Lawrence.] pp. vii. 78. *W. Earle: London,* 1806. 8°. **11779.** c. **31.**

C., A. B. A Letter from a Country Justice of the Peace to an Alderman of the City of London, &c. concerning the Bishop of Salisbury's [i.e. Gilbert Burnet's] Speech in the House of Lords, upon the Bill against Occasional Conformity. [Signed: A. B. C.] pp. 24. *London,* 1704. 4°. **4136.** b. **13.**

C., A. B. A Letter to the Right Honourabel the Earl of Chesterfield [signed: A. B. C.] upon the present posture of affairs in Ireland; with some remarks on a late anonimous Paper, without a title, but in the manner of a Letter, to some Right Honourable. pp. 24. [*Dublin?*] 1755. 8°. **8145.** bb. **12.**

C., A. B. Light at Evening Time; or, Narratives of missionary labour amongst the sick. [The preface signed: A. B. C.] pp. 237. *T. Nelson & Sons: London,* 1868. 8°. **4193.** aaa. **63.**

C., A. B. Lines, on Dick Wharton's Promise to the Freemen not to Enterfere [*sic*] in the Present Contest. [A verse lampoon on Richard Wharton, apparently referring to his attitude in the Durham County Parliamentary election, 1807. Signed: A. B. C.] *Brockett: Durham*, [1807.] *s. sh.* 8°. **1850**. d. **26**. (**50**.)

C., A. B. Mémoire des coupe-jarrets à leurs représentans. [Signed: A. B. C. q.q. D. E. F. q.q. G. H. I. q.q.] pp. 8. [*Brussels ?*] 1791. 8°. **107**. f. **45**.

C., A. B. Observations on the Improvement Controversy; containing a reply to the "Remarks" [by X. Y. Z.] on a statement by the Commissioners who support the west line of the southern approach, *etc.* [Signed: A. B. C.] pp. 15. *T. Ireland: Edinburgh*, 1834. 8°. **6573**. bb. **9**. (**16**.)

C., A. B. A Plain Account of Vaccination; designed for the heads of families . . . by A. B. C. pp. 58. *Renshaw & Rush: London*, 1833. 12°. **T. 1585**. (**2**.)

C., A. B. Die politische Colica, oder das Reissen in Leibe der Schulkrancken Menschen welche in mancherley zustanden ohne Leibs Schmertzen zu Bette liegen, Niemanden sonst als hohen und gelehrten Leuten zur belustigung vorgestellet durch A. B. C. [i.e. Johann Riemer.] pp. 352. *J. Fritzsche: Leipzig*, 1680. 12°. **12314**. aa. **49**.

C., A. B. Recherches nobiliaires en Normandie. Par un Gentilhomme normand sous-préfet et antiquaire 1866–1876. [The preface signed: A. B. C., i.e. A. C. Du Buisson de Courson.] pp. 570. *Caen*, 1876. 8°. **9916**. aa. **3**.

C., A. B.

—— La Réunion de la Belgique à la Hollande, serait-elle avantageuse ou désavantageuse à la Belgique? Par A. B. C. [i.e. Jean Joseph van Bouchout.] pp. 83. *Bruxelles*, [1814.] 8°. **8081**. de. **48**.

C., A. B. Roma e il prossimo cholera!!! Osservazioni. [By A. B. C.] pp. 30. *Roma*, 1885. 8°. **7306**. cc. **20**. (**7**.)

C., A. B. A Short History of the Revolution in Scotland. In a letter from a Scotch gentleman in Amsterdam to his friend in London. [Signed: A. B. C.] pp. 16. *London*, 1712. 8°. **601.e.37.**

—— [Another copy.] **114**. g. **37**.

—— [Another edition.] pp. 20. *London*, 1717. 8°. G. **15508**. (**2**.)

—— [Another edition.] *See* Lindsay (Colin) *Earl of Balcarras.* An Account of the Affairs of Scotland, *etc.* 1754. 8°. **1325**. c. **20**.

C., A. B. Short Readings for Advent. By the compiler of "Short Readings for Lent" (A. B. C.). pp. 47. *S.P.C.K.: London*, 1886. 8°. **4419**. bb. **9**.

—— Short Readings for Lent. [The preface signed: A. B. C.] pp. 72. *S.P.C.K.: London*, 1881. 8°. **4421**. f. **16**.

—— Short Readings from Easter to Trinity. By the compiler of "Short Readings for Lent." [The preface signed: A. B. C.] pp. 79. *S.P.C.K.: London*, 1908. 8°. **04429**. c. **130**.

C., A. B. Theatralische Belustigungen nach französischen Mustern. Erste Sammlung. [Signed: A. B. C., i.e. G. C. Pfeffel.] pp. 176. *Frankfurt & Leipzig*, 1765. 8°. **11747**. aa. **53**.

Imperfect; wanting Samml. 2–5.

C., A. B. Theology of Linguistics. [Signed: A. B. C., i. Alonzo B. Chapin.] pp. 30. *P. A. Rice: Mercersbur* 1852. 8°. **12901**. i.

C., A. B. A True Account of Land Forces in England; ar provisions for them, from before the reputed Conque downwards: and of the regard had to foreiners. In letter to A. B. C. T. T. T. &c. [i.e. John Trenchard ar W. Moyle.] With animadversions upon their Argume and History of standing armies, *etc.* pp. 72. *J. Nut London*, 1699. 4°. **8826**. c.

The caption-title reads "A Second Letter to A B C D E &c."

C., A. B.

—— "True and Firm." Biography of Ezra Cornell, found of the Cornell University. A filial tribute. [The prefa signed: A. B. C., i.e. Alonzo B. Cornell. With a portrait pp. 322. *A. S. Barnes & Co.: New York*, 1884. 8°. **10882**. dd.

C., A. B. The Unbishoping of Timothy and Titus. Or, briefe elaborate Discourse, prooving Timothy to be n Bishop . . . of Ephesus, nor Titus of Crete; and that th power of ordination, or imposition of hands, belong iure divino to Presbyters, as well as to Bishops, and not t Bishops onely . . . (A briefe Exhortation to the Arch bishops and Bishops of England in respect of the presen Pestilence.) By a Wellwisher to Gods truth and people [The dedication signed: A. B. C., i.e. William Prynne. pp. 165 [173]. [*J. F. Stam: Amsterdam*,] 1636. 4°. **700**. g. **6**. (**6**.

—— [Another copy.] The Vnbishoping of Timothy an Titus, *etc.* [*Amsterdam*,] 1636. 4°. C. **132**. h. **34**. (**4**

C., A. B. What Every Fresher Should Know. Some sug gestions for those starting university life. By A. B. C pp. 16. *W. Hodge & Co.: Glasgow & Edinburgh* [1930.] 8°. **08364**. de. **55**

—— The University Code . . . By A. B. C. [A revise and enlarged edition of "What Every Fresher Shoul Know."] pp. 19. *W. Hodge & Co.: Edinburgh* [1932.] 8°. **08364**. de. **56**

C., A. B. The Word Book; or, Twenty-four stories, wit twenty-four woodcuts, chiefly in three letters . . . B A. B. C. assisted by the other letters of the alphabet Fourth edition. pp. 48. *J. Harris: London*, [1820?] 12° **012806**. f. **2**

At the end are inserted slips bearing nineteen addition woodcuts.

C., A. B., *Ciudadano ecuatoriano.* La Revolucion del 8 d Setiembre de 1876 en el Ecuador. Por A. B. C., Ciuda dano ecuatoriano. pp. 82. *Lima*, 1877. 8°. **900**. g. **31**. (**8**.

C., A. B., *Esq., Second Professor of the Otaheite.* *See* Bank (*Right Hon. Sir* Joseph) *Bart.* An Epistle from Mr. Bank . . . to Oberea, Queen of Otaheite. Transfused by A. B. C Esq. Second Professor of the Otaheite, *etc.* [1773.] 4° **1346**. k. **45**

C., A. B., *In Coll. SS. Trin. apud Cant. olim discipulus* *See* Priapic Poem. Auctoris ignoti carmen priapeiun . . . denuo perpetua annotatione illustravit, atque i lucem edidit A.B.C. in Coll. SS. Trin. apud Cant. olin discipulus. [The text of an unpublished ballad attribute to W. M. Thackeray, with a Latin translation by W. C. A Ker.] 1896. 8°. C. **57**. e. **67**

C., A. B., *Jesuite.* *See* Dering (*Sir* Edward) 1*st Bart.* A Discourse of Proper Sacrifice in way of answer to A. B. C. Jesuite, another Anonymus of Rome, *etc.* 1644. 4°. E. **51**. (**13**.

C., A. B., *Quaker*. *See* PHILOGAMUS, *pseud.* Marriage Defended, *etc.* (A Reply to the Late Whimsical Letter, originally wrote by A. B. C. Quaker.) 1741. 8°. **8415**. f. **1**.

C., *Sir* A. B. The Famous Daily Courant of Thursday Nov. 28. 1734. Written by Sir A. B. C. upon the subject of the pill-plot, *etc.* *See* D'ANVERS (Caleb) *pseud.* The Famous Dedication to the Pamphlet, entitled, A Dissertation upon Parties, *etc.* [1735?] 8°. T. **1109**. (**7**.)

C., A. C. The Ladye Chace: a ballad. By the author of "Christian Ballads" (A. C. C. [i.e. Arthur C. Coxe]). Edited by Francis Phillip Nash . . . Cabinet edition. pp. 150. *Lippincott & Co.: Philadelphia*, 1877. 16°. **11687**. bbb. **5**.

—— Saul, a Mystery . . . By the author of "Christian Ballads," *etc.* [The dedication signed: A. C. C., i.e. Arthur C. Coxe.] pp. 297. *D. Appleton & Co.: New York; H. S. Parsons: Hartford*, 1845. 8°. **1344**. i. **50**.

C., A. C. The Stray Notes of a Wayfarer. By A. C. C. pp. 176. *Roxburghe Press: London*, [1898.] 8°. **012356**. h. **31**.

C., A. C., and **G.**, C. W. The Langshan Fowls: their history and their merits. By A. C. C. [i.e. A. C. Croad] and C. W. G. [i.e. C. W. Gedney.] Illustrated, *etc.* pp. 47. *"Live Stock Journal": London*, 1877. 8°. **7204**. aaa. **8**. (**10**.)

—— Second edition. pp. 48. *"Live Stock Journal": London*, 1880. 8°. **7204**. b. **11**. (**5**.)

C., A. C. L. S., and **T.**, T. E. H. The Making of the Military Shot. Instruction in rifle shooting. [The preface signed: A. C. L. S.-C., i.e. Arthur Christopher Lancelot Stanley Clarke, and T. E. H. T., i.e. Thomas Edgar Hugh Taylor.] pp. 32. *W. S. Paine & Co.: Hythe*, [1930.] 8°. **8822**. bb. **36**.

C., A. C. P. "The Love of God has conquered." By A. C. P. C. pp. 8. *J. E. Hawkins: London*, [1882.] 16°. **4422**. aa. **35**. (**2**.)

C., A. C. T. Some Scriptural and Theoretical Difficulties considered. By a Bible Student. [The preface signed: A. C. T. C.] pp. 40. *George Herbert: Dublin*, 1874. 8°. **3149**. b. **18**.

C., A. D.

—— *See* CHIFFLET (Jean J.) Le Faux Childebrand relegué aux fables, *etc.* [A reply to "Le Vray Childebrand" by A. D. C., i.e. C. de Combault, Count d'Auteuil.] 1688. 4°. [*Miscellania Chifletiana*. vol. 3.] **604**. e. **5**.

C., A. D. *See* OLDKNOW (J.) and C., A. D. The Priest's Book of Private Devotion, compiled and arranged by two priests [i.e. J. Oldknow and A. D. Crake]. [The preface signed: A. D. C., i.e. A. D. Crake.] 1877. 16°. **3435**. ccc. **12**.

—— Æmilius: a tale of the Decian & Valerian persecutions. [The preface signed: A. D. C., i.e. Augustine D. Crake.] pp. ii. 302. *A. R. Mowbray & Co.: Oxford; Simpkin, Marshall & Co.: London*, 1871. 8°. **12707**. b. **5**.

—— The Bread of Life: a manual of instruction and devotion for the Blessed Sacrament. [The preface signed: A. D. C., i.e. Augustine D. Crake.] pp. 141. *A. R. Mowbray: Oxford; Simpkin, Marshall & Co.: London*, 1869. 16°. **4327**. aa. **23**.

—— Second edition. pp. ii. 141. *A. R. Mowbray & Co.: Oxford; Simpkin, Marshall & Co.: London*, 1870. 16°. **4327**. aa. **24**.

C., A. D.

—— Fourth edition. pp. ii. 197. *A. R. Mowbray & Co.: Oxford; Simpkin, Marshall & Co.: London*, 1872. 16°. **3457**. aa. **48**.

—— The Garden of Life. A manual of devotion . . . By the author of "The Bread of Life," &c. &c. [The preface signed: A. D. C., i.e. Augustine D. Crake.] pp. ii. 212. *A. R. Mowbray & Co.: London, Oxford*, 1873. 12°. **4405**. ee. **24**.

C., A. D.

—— Hillhead High School Club, 1902–1952. [The preface signed: A. D. C., i.e. Alastair Douglas Campbell. With plates.] pp. 63. 1952. 8°. *See* GLASGOW.—*Hillhead High School.—Hillhead High School Club.* **8369**. de. **30**.

C., A. D. Nell'occasione delle faustissime nozze del nobile marchese Francesco Buzzaccarini e della nobile contessa Angiola da-Rio. Anacreontica. [Signed: A. D. C.] *Padova*, 1824. 8°. **11431**. cc. **39**.

C., A. D. Offices for the Hours of Prime, Sext, and Compline, with special antiphons & chapters for the Seasons of the Church, *etc.* [The prefatory note signed: A. D. C., i.e. Augustine D. Crake.] pp. 36. *A. R. Mowbray & Co.: Oxford; Simpkin, Marshall & Co.: London*, 1871. 16°. **3456**. aaa. **68**. (**5**.)

C., A. D. Reglas gramaticales para aprender la lengua Española y Francesa, confiriendo la vna con la otra, segun el orden de las partes de la oration Latinas. [The dedication signed: A. D. C., i.e. A. de Corro.] (Dialogo en que particularmente se tratan las cosas acaecidas en Roma el año de M.D.XXVII, *etc.* [By A. de Valdés.]) 2 pt. *Por Ioseph Barnes: Oxford*, 1586. 8°. C. **63**. f. **33**.

The titlepage of the second tract bears the fictitious imprint: Impresso en Paris. Imperfect; wanting sig. E 1 *of the first tract.*

C., A. D. Simple Prayers for School-Boys. [The prefatory note signed: A. D. C., i.e. Augustine D. Crake.] pp. 54. *A. R. Mowbray: Oxford; J. Masters: London*, 1867. 12°. **3455**. aa. **26**.

—— Simple Prayers: a manual of instruction and devotion for schoolboys . . . Second edition, enlarged. [The preface signed: A. D. C., i.e. Augustine D. Crake.] pp. v. 117. *A. R. Mowbray & Co.: Oxford; Simpkin, Marshall & Co.: London*, 1870. 16°. **876**. a. **29**.

—— Simple Prayers: a manual of instruction and devotion for school girls . . . Second edition, enlarged. [Adapted from the second edition of "Simple Prayers for School-Boys." The preface signed: A. D. C., i.e. Augustine D. Crake.] pp. 117. *A. R. Mowbray & Co.: Oxford; Simpkin, Marshall & Co.: London*, 1870. 16°. **876**. a. **15**.

C., A. D. Le Vray Childebrand, ou Response au traitté iniurieux de M. Chifflet . . . contre le Duc Childebrand, frere du Prince Charles Martel . . . Par vn bon François. (Discours, ou remarques, en forme de critique, sur les differentes opinions de l'origine plus apparente de l'auguste maison d'Austriche.—Apologie pour la tres-auguste . . . maison de France, dite la troisiesme race.) [The prefatory letter signed: A. D. C., i.e. C. de Combault, Baron d'Auteuil.] 3 pt. *P. Lamy: Paris*, 1659. 4°.

9903.d.14.

C., A. D., *Citoyen du département de la Seine Inférieure.* Réflexions sur les communaux, & la necessité de les livrer à l'agriculture. Par A. D. C. citoyen du département de la Seine inférieure. A Rouen, 25 mars 1792, *etc.* pp. 20. *Rouen*, 1792. 8°. F.R. **247**. (**4**.)

C., A. D. B. A. D. D. L. N. D. Qu'est-ce qu'une révolution? Par l'auteur du Réveil aux Parisiens. [Signed: A. D. B. A. D. D. L. N. D. C.] pp. 8. [1792.] 8°. F. **979**. (4.)

C., A. D. L. *See* Cocher. Le Parfait Cocher, ou l'Art d'entretenir, & de conduire un équipage, *etc.* [By P. J. Mancini Mazarini, Duke de Nevers. The dedicatory epistle signed: A. D. L. C., i.e. F. A. Aubert de la Chenaye des Bois.] 1744. 12°. **7905**. bbb. **2**.

C., A. D. L. *See* Ditton (Humphry) La Religion Chrétienne démontrée par la résurrection de Notre Seigneur Jesus-Christ . . . Traduit . . . par A. D. L. C. [i.e. A. Boisbeleau de la Chapelle.] 1728. 8°. **4015**. cc. **12**.

—— *See* Periodical Publications.—London.—*The Tatler.* Le Philosophe nouvelliste, traduit de l'anglois . . . par A. D. L. C. [i.e. A. Boisbeleau de La Chapelle], *etc.* 1735. 8°. **012612**. e. **6**.

C., A. D. L. Dictionnaire militaire, *etc.* [The dedicatory epistle signed: A. D. L. C., i.e. F. A. Aubert de la Chenaye des Bois.] pp. 583. *Lausanne & Geneve,* 1743. 12°. **1140**. b. **10**.

C., A. D. V. Adolphe de Waldheim, ou le Parricide innocent. Nouvelle allemande. Extraite du Journal d'un jeune militaire, recueillie et publiée par A. D. V. C. [i.e. A. du Voisin-Calas.] pp. 218. *Paris,* 1802. 12°. **12510**. cc. **6**.

C., A. E.

—— *See* Bunyan (John) [*Pilgrim's Progress, Pt. 2.—Dutch.*] Eens Christens reyse naa de euwigheid: tweede diel . . . in 't Neederduidsch vertaalt . . . Door A. E. C. 1723. 12°. **04411**. b. 15.

C., A. E. *See* Drummond (Henry) *F.R.S.E.* [The Greatest Thing in the World.] Die Grootste gawe . . . Afrikaanse vertaling deur A. E. C. 1932. 32°. **4372**. eee. **8**.

C., A. E. *See* Ellis (John) *M.D.* Scetticismo e divina revelazione, *etc.* [The translator's preface signed: A. E. C.] 1886. 8°. **4105**. de. **13**.

C., A. E.

—— The Family of Corbet. Its life and times. (By A. E. C. [i.e. Augusta Elizabeth Corbet.]) [With plates and genealogical tables.] 2 vol. *St. Catherine's Press: London,* [1915, 18.] 4°. **9904**. w. **7**.

C., A. E. Hymns and their Stories. By A. E. C. With a preface by Edgar C. S. Gibson, *etc.* pp. 201. *S.P.C.K.: London,* 1894. 8°. **4430**. aaa. 4.

C., A. E. Kinderfreunden. Von A. E. C. . . . A simple German reading-book. pp. 80. *Clarendon Press: Oxford,* 1903. 8°. **12963**. f. 22.

—— Ma première visite à Paris. Par A. E. C. pp. 106. *Imprimerie de l'Université: Oxford,* 1905. 8°. **010169**. ff. **11**.

—— [A reissue, with the addition of exercises by E. R. Wyatt.] pp. 128. *Oxford,* 1905 [1915]. 8°. **12952**. r. 19.

C., A. E.

—— The Yale Excavation at Dura-Europos. [Signed: A. E. C. i.e. Alice Elizabeth Chase.] [1944.] 4°. *See* New Haven, *Connecticut.—Yale University.—Gallery of Fine Arts.* Ac. **2692**. moa/**7**.

C., A. F. Boyhood, and other poems. By A. F. C. pp. viii. 64. *W. Blackwood & Sons: Edinburgh & London,* 1868. 8°. **11647**. bb. 35.

C., A. F. Good out of Evil; or the History of Adjai, the African slave-boy; an authentic biography of the Rev S. Crowther, native Church missionary in Abbeokuta West Africa. By A. F. C. [i.e. A. F. Childe.] Second edition. Edited by the Rev. C. F. Childe. pp. viii. 112. *Wertheim & Macintosh: London,* 1852. 16°. **4903**. c. **71**
An earlier edition is entered under Lady.

C., A. F. The Show Australian Terrier. [The preface signed: A. F. C. With plates.] pp. 21. [*Hazell Watson & Viney: London & Aylesbury,* 1934.] 8°. **07295**. a. **51**

C., A. F. D. D., *Mr.* *See* Gazola (G.) [Il Mondo ingannato da falsi medici.] Préservatif contre la charlatanerie des faux medecins . . . Traduit . . . par Mr A. F. D. D. C [i.e. A. F. D. de Coulange.] 1735. 8°. **1172**. c. **8**. (2.

C., A. F. T.

—— Première lettre à M. le comte Decazes, en réponse à so discours sur la liberté individuelle. Par A. F. T. C. [i.e Adolphe Fr. T. Chevalier.] pp. 76. *Paris,* 1817. 8°. R. **134**. (4.

C., A. H. S. *See* L., W. H. Winchester College Notions By three Beetleites. [The preface signed: W. H. L J. F. R. H., and A. H. S. C., i.e. William H. Lawson John F. R. Hope and Alfred H. S. Cripps.] 1901. 8°. **8365**. de. 39

C., A. J. *See* Lake (Edward) *D.D.* Officium eucharisticum *etc.* [The editor's preface signed: A. J. C., i.e. Alban James Christie.] 1843. 16°. **1219**. a. **17**

C., A. J. The Little Captain. A tale of the sea. By A. J. C pp. 96. *Johnstone, Hunter & Co.: Edinburgh,* [1865.] 16° **4415**. aa. **18**

C., A. J. Notes on the Influence of Sir Walter Scott on George Eliot. By A. J. C. pp. 15. *A. Baxendine & Sons Edinburgh,* 1923. 8°. **011851**. c. **41**

C., A. J., *Ouvrier voironnais.* Lois de Kepler. Simplicit des mouvements des corps célestes . . . Corrections faire subir à la 2e et à la 3e lois. Par A.-J. C., Ouvrie voironnais. pp. 108. *Voiron,* 1892. 8°. **8561**. aaaa. **46**

C., A. J. de. Presupuestos de 1881–82. La unificacion de l deuda: su necesidad y sus consecuencias para la desa hog^a^da gestion de la hacienda, mediante la consolidacio de la deuda flotante por ejercicios cerrados, y la reduccio considerable de los actuales déficits. Por A. J. de C pp. 68. *Madrid,* 1880. 8°. **8229**. de. **30**. (1

C., A. J. D. De Vereenigde weduwen. Huisselyk tafere in twee bedryven, door A. J. D. C. [i.e. A. J. de Craene. pp. 50. *Gent,* 1851. 12°. **11755**. b. **91**. (3.

C., A. K. Litany for use at Children's Services . . . B A. K. C. *H. D. Kermode: Macclesfield,* [1923.] 16°. **3405**. aa. **61**

C., A. L. *See* Bath.—*Bath "Mutual Aid" Photographic Club.* Camera Notes . . . Edited by H. Roland Batema and A. L. C. (vol. 1. no. 9—vol. 2. no. 18. Edited b H. R. Bateman and A. L. Curtis.) 1903, *etc.* 4°. P.P. **1912**. e

C., A. L. *See* Taylor (Frederick W.) Études sur l'organisa tion du travail dans les usines, *etc.* [The editor's intro duction signed: A. L. C.] 1907. 4°. **7105**. h. **1**

C., A. L. A.B.C. to the Girl Guide Handbook. Six specime evenings for officers. [The preface signed: A. L. C., i.e A. L. Cruikshank.] pp. 12. [1914.] 8°. *See* England *—Girl Guides Association.* **8827**. aaa. **58**

—— Second edition. pp. 10. [1916.] 8°. *See* England.—*Girl Guides Association.* **8822**. aa. **17**

C., A. L. A Memorial of the Titanic Disaster portrayed in rhyme. [Signed: A. L. C., i.e. Annie L. Clements.] [1912.] 8°. **011686. dg. 12.**

C., A. L. The Sjögren Automatic System of Fire Arms. [Signed: A. L. C., i.e. Arnold L. Chevallier.] pp. 14. *Normal Powder & Ammunition Co.: London,* [1910.] 16°. **8824. aaa. 29.**

C., A. L. C.

—— The Spiritual Teaching of the East. By A. L. C. C. pp. 20. *Buddhist Society: London* [1944.] 8°. [*Foundations of Peace Series.* no. 5.] **W.P. 548/5.**

C., A. L. D. L. P. D. Réponse à Monseigneur le commandant du château, ou au geolier des cachots des Isles de Sainte-Marguerite; sur M. d'Eprémesnil et sur les États-Généraux. [Signed: A. L. D. L. P. D. C. A reply to A. J. M. Servan's anonymous pamphlet "Avis au public et principalement au tiers-état."] pp. 27. [1789.] 8°. **935. b. 1. (11.)**

—— [Another copy.] **F. 416. (3.)**

C., A. L. L. Tichborne or Orton? The "crucial test" tested. By A. L. L. C. Being a review of the photographic test suggested in a recent pamphlet "for use in cases of disputed identity," *etc.* pp. 15. pl. IV. *Chiswick Press: London,* 1874. 8°. **6495. b. 55. (12.)**

C., A. L. M. Rome. [The dedication signed: A. L. M. C., i.e. A. L. de Coulibeuf, Marchioness de Blocqueville.] pp. 418. *Paris,* 1865. 8°. **10130. dd. 23.**

C., A. L. O. The Story of a Dark Plot; or, Tyranny on the frontier. By A. L. O. C. [On the dismissal of William W. Smith, a temperance agitator, from the service of the Canadian Pacific Railway. With plates, including a portrait.] pp. 197. *J. Lovell & Son: Montreal,* 1898. 8°. **8436. c. 26.**

C., A. L. T. M. Les Promenades printanieres de A. L. T. M. C. [i.e. A. Le Tartier, médicin champenois.] ff. 198. *Chez G. Chaudiere: Paris,* 1586. 16°. **012356. de. 11.**

C., A. M. *See* PRAYERS. Prayers when the Door is Shut . . . By a Lady deceased. With additions by A. M. C. 1870. 8°. **876. b. 3.**

C., A. M. "Afterward," and other stories. By A. M. C. [With plates.] pp. 149. *Drummond's Tract Depot: Stirling,* [1910.] 8°. **04413. ee. 55.**

C., A. M. Guide de l'étranger aux jeux de Monaco. Extrait de l'ouvrage complet, en préparation, sur les moyens employés . . . pour attaquer les chances de jeu, par A. M. C. *See* TIFFEN (Charles H.) The Stranger's Practical Guide to Nice, *etc.* [1860?] 8°. **10174. a. 12.**

C., A. M. A Guide to Nature-printing. Butterflies and Moths. [By A. M. C.] pp. 31. *Harrison: London,* 1879. 8°. **7942. f. 5.**

C., A. M. The Hampstead Garner. [An anthology of poetry written at Hampstead.] Compiled by A. M. C. With a preface by Clement Shorter. pp. viii. 200. *Elliot Stock: London,* 1906. 8°. **11604. e. 32.**

C., A. M. How the Plot Answered, and other stories. By A. M. C. [With plates.] pp. 176. *Drummond's Tract Depot: Stirling,* [1905.] 8°. **04412. i. 57.**

—— The Midnight Message, and other stories. By A. M. C. [With plates.] pp. 162. *Drummond's Tract Depot: Stirling,* [1910.] 8°. **04413. de. 56.**

C., A. M. "On the March"; being the recollections and experiences of an officer's wife, descriptive of a regiment on the march in India in the early seventies. By A. M. C. [i.e. A. M. Clifford.] pp. 45. *Higginbotham & Co.: Madras & Bangalore,* 1904. 8°. **010058. e. 32.**

C., A. M. Stirring Stories. By A. M. C. 12 pt. *Drummond's Tract Depot: Stirling,* [1906.] 16°. **04412. g. 8.**

—— Stories of a Men's Class. Told by themselves. By A. M. C. pp. 155. *Drummond's Tract Depot: Stirling,* [1903.] 8°. **04412. e. 35.**

—— Tom Tester's Mistake, and other narratives. By A. M. C. [With plates.] pp. 149. *Drummond's Tract Depot: Stirling,* [1908.] 8°. **04413. ee. 15.**

—— "Trying to Forget," and other narratives. By A. M. C. [With plates.] pp. 156. *Drummond's Tract Depot: Stirling,* [1905.] 8°. **04412. k. 65.**

—— "Two Words did it," and other narratives. By A. M. C. pp. 159. *Drummond's Tract Depot: Stirling,* [1903.] 8°. **04412. f. 65.**

—— Walking Backwards, and other narratives. By A. M. C. [With plates.] pp. 160. *Drummond's Tract Depot: Stirling,* [1909.] 8°. **04413. f. 22.**

C., A. M.

—— Westhorpe Manor: a tale of the days of persecution. [Signed: A. M. C.] (The Snow Maiden. By Augusta Marryat.—The Story of a Coin. By Theo. Gift.) pp. 32. *Catholic Truth Society: London,* [1890.] 8°. **3943.aa.94.**

C., A. M., *Signor, Accademico di Montecchio e di Corneto.* Istruzione per coltivare il lino, e la canapa d'Olanda, nei terreni dello Stato Pontificio, pubblicata dal Signor A. M. C. Accademico di Montecchio e di Corneto, *etc.* pp. viii. *Roma,* 1785. 4°. **7074. k. 2. (2.)**

C., A. N., *le P., Reg. de l'Ordre de S. Aug.* Le Tableu de la bido del parfet crestia . . . Fait per le P. A. N. C. Reg. de l'Ordre de S. Aug. (Père Amilha.) 1673. 8°. *See* AMILIA (B.) **11498. b. 16.**

C., A. N. C. L., *Panthemus, P.P.P.* *See* STAHL (G. E.) Herrn George Ernst Stahls . . . Gründliche Abhandlung von Abschaffung des Missbrauchs . . . Aus dem Lateinischen ins Teutsche übersetzt. [The translator's preface signed: A. N. C. L. C. Panthemus. P.P.P.] 1739. 8°. **07306. df. 4. (2.)**

C., A. N. D. M. *See* ANDRÉS (Juan) *Jesuit.* Storia d'ogni litteratura . . . breviata ed annotata per A. N. D. M. C. [i.e. A. Narbone?], *etc.* 1836. 12°. **616. f. 28.**

C., A. N. E. *See* LORGION (E. J. D.) The Pastor of Vliethuizen . . . Translated from the Dutch. [The translator's preface signed: A. N. E. C.] 1861. 4°. **3925. k. 13.**

C., A. P. *See* PERIODICAL PUBLICATIONS.—*Oporto.* O Bardo, jornal de poesias ineditas. Redactores A. P. [i.e. A. Pinheiro Caldas]—F. X. de Novaes. 1857. 8°. **P.P. 4111.**

C., A. P. The Church of God. Can a Christian leave it? A dialogue. By A. P. C. Revised. pp. 12. *Bible Truth Depot: Hull,* [1898.] 24°. **04420. de. 3. (5.)**

C., A. P.

—— Eternal Life and the Holy Ghost. By A. P. C. (Lord Adelbert P. Cecil.) [1890?] 32°. *See* CECIL (*Lord* A. P.) [MISSING.]

C., A. P. Gulde Compas, waer in kort eñ levendich afghepeylt wort het groot verschil der Remonstranten ter eener, ende de Ware Ghereformeerde ter ander zijden . . . Door A. P. C. (Ioabs Kus, *etc.*) [An attack on the Arminians.]) 1618. 4°. **700**. h. **25**. (**13**.)

C., A. P. The King's Son. A dream. [Signed: A. P. C.] pp. 25. *Campbell: London,* 1854. 12°. **4412**. ee. **14**. (**1**.)

C., A. P.

—— A Short summary of the Epistle to the Ephesians. By A. P. C. [i.e. Lord Adalbert P. Cecil.] pp. 62. *George Cooper: London,* [1882?] 8°. **3266**. a. **38**.

C., A. P. Songs in the Wilderness. By A. P. C. [i.e. Agnes P. Carter.] pp. 105. *D. Walther; W. G. Bartlett: London,* [1845.] 12°. **11644**. aaa. **40**.

C., A. P. K. 'Comfort ye My People.' A record of severe suffering and of great consolation. [The preface signed: A. P. K. C.] pp. 176. *T. Woolmer: London,* 1881. 16°. **4920**. a. **39**.

C., A. P. P. *See* Bossuet (J. B.) successively *Bishop of Condom* and *of Meaux.* [*Two or more Works.*] De la connaissance de Dieu et de soi même . . . Avec . . . une notice bibliographique [signed: A. P. P. C., i.e. A. P. P. Caron]. 1846. 12°. **4405**. g. **23**.

C., A. R. *See* Emerson (R. W.) Emerson Year Book. Selections from the essays of R. W. Emerson. By A. R. C. 1893. 8°. **012356**. e. **11**.

C., A. R. *See* Goethe (J. W. von) [*Selections.—English.*] Goethe Year Book. Selections . . . by A. R. C. 1894. 12°. **12251**. e. **7**.

C., A. R. Immanuel's Land, and other pieces. [Poems.] By A. R. C. [i.e. Annie R. Cousin.] pp. 267. *J. Nisbet & Co.: London,* 1876. 8°. **11650**. df. **23**.

C., A. R. El Regimiento de Infanteria de Ordenes militares expedicionario, se justifica de la supuesta satisfacción dada á este ilustre pueblo á nombre de su oficialidad por algun intruso [i.e. F. Barrera? signing himself: J. A. A.]. [Signed: A. R. C.] *México,* [1821.] 4°. **9770**. bb. **9**. (**4**.)

—— Ataque á los Serviles, *etc.* [Signed: J. R. A reply to "El Regimiento de Infanteria de Ordenes militares expedicionario, se justifica, *etc.*"] [1821.] 4°. *See* R., J. **9770**. bb. **9**. (**8**.)

—— El Honor marcial sostenido, *etc.* [Signed: J. R., F. J. C., J. F.] [A reply to "El Regimiento de Infanteria de Ordenes militares expedicionario, se justifica, *etc.*"] 1821. 4°. *See* R., J. **9770**. bb. **7**. (**39**.)

C., A. R. I.

—— *See* Gattefossé (R. M.) [Formulaire de parfumerie et de cosmetologie.] Formulary of Perfumery and of Cosmetology. A translation by A. R. I. C., *etc.* 1952. 8°. **7946**. e. **85**.

—— *See* Gattefossé (René M.) and Jonquières (H.) [Technique des produits de beauté.] Technique of Beauty Products. A translation by A. R. I. C., *etc.* 1949. 8°. **7384**. b. **32**.

C., A. S. Novella disparatoria do Gigante sonhado, obra jocoseria . . . escrita por A. S. C. *etc.* pp. 8. *Lisboa,* 1745. 8°. **12314**. ccc. **15**.

C., A. S. The Two Ways of Christian Life. Reprinted, with additions, from "Church Work." [Signed: A. S. C.] pp. 24. *Joseph Masters: London,* 1862. 8°. **4193**. cc. **12**.

C., A. S. A Renascence of the Irish Art of Lace-makin Illustrated by photographic reproductions of Irish lac . . . Introductory notes and descriptions by A. S. C. [i Alan S. Cole.] pp. 40. *Chapman & Hall: Lond* 1888. 8°. **7743**. c.

C., A. S. A. L. O. "My Lady's Garden." [A tale. T dedication signed: A. S. A. L. O. C.] pp. 15. *Thompson: Saffron Walden,* [1908.] 8°. **12629**. i. **1**

C., A. S. I.

—— *See* Valerius Flaccus (C.) Argonauticon . . . li viii. Post L. Canionem . . . ab A. S. I. C. emenda *etc.* 1604. 8°. **1483**. b. 1

C., A. S. M. Short Doggerel Tales. By A. S. M. [Limericks, illustrated.] ff. 21. *Bickers & So London,* [1891.] 4°. **12331**. h. **3**

C., A. S. O. Harold; or, Following the footprints. A. S. O. C. pp. 139. *J. F. Shaw & Co.: Lond* [1877.] 12°. **12809**. b. **1**

C., A. T. *See* Bible.—*Selections.* [*English.*] Day after Da A. T. C. [Scripture texts, illustrated by poetical extract 1874. 16°. **4410**. g. **1**

—— —— [1883.] 16°. **4418**. bb. **2**

C., A. T. M. Entier discours de la vertu et proprieté d bains de Plumbieres . . . Par A. T. M. C. [i.e. A. Toignar ff. 46. *Chez I. Hulpean: Paris,* 1581. 16°. **1171**. a. **33**. (

Sig. A2 *recto, intended to contain part of the publishe address to the reader, is blank.*

C., A. V. Nieuwe-jaars Zegenwensch van den volder en zes aanstekers der lantarenen, van het vierde-deel geteke met de letter D. aan de . . . inwoonders van 's Gravenha op het ingaen van het jaer 1696. [In verse. Signe A. V. C.] *'s Gravenhage,* [1696.] *s. sh.* fol. **1870**. d. **1**. (**19**

C., A. V. "Then shall be Great Tribulation"; or, Solemn warning. By A. V. C. pp. 64. *Pickeri & Inglis: Glasgow,* [1934.] 8°. **03187**. g. **1**

C., A. W. *See* Graham (Maria) afterwards Callcott (M *Lady.* Description of the Annunziata dell'arena, [The illustrator's postscript signed: A. W. C., i.e. Augustus W. Callcott.] 1835. fol. **7816**. i.

C., A. W. H. The Charitable Administration of an East E Mission District. By A. W. H. C. [i.e. Anson W. Cartwright.] Second edition. pp. 8. *Char Organisation Society: London,* 1872. 8°. **8285**. aaa. **37**. (**1**

—— *See* Langhorne (William H.) Mission Life East London. Being a sequel to "The Charita Administration of an East End Mission District," A. W. H. C. 1876. 8°. **4193**. b.

C * * * * (Ab *) *Signore.*

—— Raccolta di poesie, o siano Novelle galanti del signo Ab * C * * * * [i.e. G. B. Casti]. 2 tom. 1790. 12°. **11431**. bbb.

C. (Ad.) Album. Le Pélerinage d'Ars, illustré de 14 gravu et 8 culs-de-lampe d'après Fonville et Dubief. Avec texte . . . Par Ad. C. [With plates.] pp. 84. *Ly* 1852. 8°. **10171**. g.

C * * * * * (Al.) *See* Secrets. Ce sont les Secres des dam . . . Avec . . . une introduction, des notes et un appendi par les drs. Al. C * * * * * [i.e. Alexandre Colson] & Ch.-E C * * * * 1880. 8°. **7581**. df. **2**

C * * (Ant.) *See* Crevier (J. B. L.) Abrégé de l'Histoi des empereurs, de Crévier, suivant le plan de cet auteu par Ant. C * *. 1819. 12°. **9040**. bbb. [i.e. Antoine Caillot]

C * * (Ant.)

—— Plus de printemps, plus de violettes: vivent les lis et les œillets blancs. [Signed: Ant. C**, i.e. Antoine Caillot.] pp. 4. [*Paris*, 1815. 8°.] R. **130**. (**16**.)

C., B. *See* Bassano. Nozze Pasolini-Zanelli Baroni-Semitecolo. [Laws of the commune of Bassano concerning the care of vineyards. The dedication signed: B. C., B. Z.] 1874. 8°. **5357**. c. 3.

—— *See* Bassano. In occasione delle nozze dell'egregio avvocato Dr. Giambattista Talin colla nob. donzella Caterina Maello. [A sumptuary ordinance of the commune of Bassano. The dedication signed: B. C.] 1874. 8°. **9006**. f. **1**. (**7**.)

C., B. *See* Bell (Thomas) *Protestant Controversial Writer* The Catholique Triumph: conteyning, a Reply to the pretensed Answere of B. C., a masked Iesuite, lately published against the Tryall of the New Religion, *etc.* [In answer to "Bels Trial examined . . . By B. C., student in diuinitie," i.e. Philip Woodward.] 1610. 4°. **874**. k. 3.

C., B. *See* F., C. and C., B. The Book of Speed. [The editors' note signed: C. F., B. C.] 1934. 4°. **08770**. dd. **2**.

C., B. *See* Fox (George) *Founder of the Society of Friends.* The Foxonian Quakers, dunces, lyars and slanderers, proved out of George Fox's Journal, and other scriblers; particularly B. C. [i.e. Benjamin Coole] his Quakers no Apostates, *etc.* 1697. 12°. **4152**. a. **8**.

C., B. *See* H., C. The Perfect Husbandman . . . By C. H., B. C. [i.e. Barnaby Googe] and C. M., *etc.* [Another edition of Googe's translation of "Foure Bookes of Husbandry" by Conrad Heresbach, with Gervase Markham's additions.] 1658. 4°. E. **928**. (**1**).

C., B. *See* Martin (Josiah) *of the Society of Friends.* A Vindication of Women's Preaching, as well from Holy Scripture . . . as from the paraphrase and notes of . . . John Locke, on 1 Cor. xi, wherein the Brief Observations of B. C. [i.e. Benjamin Coole] on the said paraphrase and notes . . . are fully consider'd. 1717. 8°. **4152**. ee. **4**.

C., B. *See* Periodical Publications.—*London.* The Holiday Annual . . . Edited by a B. C. [1878, *etc.*] 8°. P.P. **6700**. k.

C., B. Adiós á Cuba. Recuerdos de un Cubano. Por B. C. [i.e. Bernardo Coya.] pp. 270. *Burgos*, 1900. 8°. **9772**. c. **33**.

C., B. The Apostles Creed better than the Assembly's Catechism: or, the Doctrine of Christ and his Apostles concerning the Unity and Trinity, defended against the Sabellian and Tritheistick errors of the times. In a letter to the Reverend Mr. Cumming. [Signed: B. C., i.e. Benjamin Chandler.] pp. 91. *John Noon: London*, 1720. 8°. **698**. i. **8**. (**8**.)

C., B. Autentiche prove contro i Gesuiti moderni, loro affigliati, ed il celebre dialettico M°. R°. Frassinetto. Appendice all'opuscolo di C. B. Per B. C. In risposta a P. G. Seconda edizione. pp. 75. *Italia*, 1847. 8°. **4092**. e. **10**.

C., B. The Church and the Meeting-House. A dialogue. [Signed: B. C.] pp. 23. *Groombridge: London; Hearn & Whitmarsh: Salisbury*, 1838. 12°. **908**. c. **5**. (**1**.)

C., B. Clésinger, 1814–1883. Notice biographique [signed: B. C.]. Catalogue des œuvres. Préface de Remy de Gourmont. 2e édition. pp. 27. *Paris*, 1903. 8°. **10601**. cc. **28**. (**4**.)

C., B. Croquemitaine. Par B. C. [A tale for children.] pp. 64. *Rouen*, [1860?] 16°. **12804**. a. **13**.

C., B. Cupid in Quest of Beauty: or, Venus at Stratford. A lampoon. By the author of The British Apollo. [The preface signed: B. C.] pp. 8. *London*, 1709. 8°. **1481**. aaa. **3**.

C., B. Discours veritable des affaires presentes, enuoyé au Roy de la Grand' Bretagne par vn certain quidan de la Cour du très-chrestien Roy de France & de Nauarre. [The "Discours" signed: B. C. The dedicatory epistle signed: D. S. L.] pp. 23. 1616. 8°. **1192**. h. **27**. (**5**.)

C., B. Earth's Thousand Voices. A daily text book of nature with quotations from Scripture and the poets. Compiled by B. C. *H. R. Allenson: London*, [1927.] 32°. **11603**. de. **37**.

C., B. Kunst und Leben. u.B.C. *Leipzig*, 1869. 8°. **7806**. cc. 5.

C., B. The Ladies' Monitor, being a series of letters, first published in Bengal, on the subject of female apparel, tending to favour a regulated adoption of Indian costume . . . By the author of A Vindication of the Hindoos. [The author's introduction signed: B. C., i.e. John Scott-Waring. The preface to the reader signed: M——.] pp. 226. *Printed for the Author: London*, 1809. 8°. **1043**. g. **49**.

C., B.

—— La Marche de la révolution. [Signed: B. C., i.e. Benjamin Henri Constant de Rebecque.] *In:* Napoleon i., *Emperor of the French.* [*Appendix.*] Napoléon, la révolution, famille des Bourbons, *etc.* 1815. 8°. R. **130**. (**14**.)

C., B. Marie von Kollenau, oder: die deutsche Hausmutter. Ein Original-Trauerspiel in fünf Aufzügen von B. C. 1794. *See* German Stage. Deutsche Schaubühne. Bd. 66. 1788, *etc.* 8°. **752**. a. **1/66**.

C., B. A New Exposition of the Horse's Hoof. [Signed: B. C., i.e. Bracy Clark.] [*London*, 1820.] *s. sh.* 4°. **779**. i. **22**. (**8**.)

C., B. Obituary.—Sept. 20. At Greenwich Hospital, Vice-Adm. Sir Thomas M. Hardy, Bart., *etc.* [Signed: B. C., i.e. Bolton Corney.] (Extracted from the Gentleman's Magazine.) *H. S. Richardson: Greenwich*, 1839. *s. sh.* 8°. **10803**. d. **2**. (**3**.)

C., B. On the Vices of Horses. By B. C. [i.e. Bracy Clark.] pp. 8. *London*, 1839. 4°. **779**. i. **23**. (**14**.)

—— [Another copy.] **779**. i. **23**. (**20**.)

—— Original Remarks on the General Framing of the Horse. Illustrated by plates . . . By B. C. [i.e. Bracy Clark.] Second edition. pp. 20. *Richards: London*, 1842. 4°. **779**. i. **23**. (**1**.)

C., B. Parish of St. Mark's, Collingwood [in the diocese of Melbourne]. [Signed: B. C.] pp. 12. *Heath & Cordell: Geelong*, 1859. 12°. **4183**. a. **68**. (**3**.)

C., B. Puritanisme the Mother, Sinne the Daughter. Or a Treatise, wherein is demonstrated . . . that the fayth and religion of the Puritans, doth forcibly induce its professours to the perpetrating of sinne . . . Written by a Catholike Priest . . . Heerunto is added, as an appendix, a Funerall Discourse touching the . . . deathes of . . . Doctour Price, Deane of Hereford, and Doctour Butts, Vice-Chancellour of Cambridge. By the same authour. [The dedicatory epistle signed: B. C.] pp. 184. [*St. Omer*,] 1633. 8°. **3936**. b. 29. (4.) *Cropped.*

C., B. The Quakers cleared from being Apostates: or the Hammerer defeated, and proved an impostor. Being an answer to a scurrilous pamphlet, falsly intituled, William Penn and the Quakers either Apostates or Impostors; subscribed Trepidantium Malleus [i.e. Samuel Young]. With a postscript, containing some reflections on a pamphlet, intituled, The Spirit of Quakerism, and the danger of their divine revelation, laid open. By B. C. [i.e. Benjamin Coole.] pp. 95. *Printed & sold by T. Sowle: London*, 1696. 8°. **4152**. ff. **1**. (**3**.)

C., B. Rascunhos sobre a grammatica da lingua portugueza por B. C. pp. 108. *Rio de Janeiro*, 1881. 8°. **12901**. i. **31**. (**1**.)

C., B.

—— Religion at Home; being a series of conversations, between a mother and her daughter, on important Scripture subjects. By the author of "Meditation with self-examination for every day in the year." [The preface signed: B. C., i.e. Benjamin Clark.] pp. xii. 180. *W. S. Orr & Co.: London*, 1844. 16°. **1362**. a. **21**.

C., B. Sacred Emblems; with miscellaneous pieces, moral, religious, and devotional: in verse. [The preface signed: B. C.] pp. 132. *W. Birchall: London*, 1828. 12°. T. **1219**. (**17**.)

C., B. Some Account of the Circulation of the Blood in the Foot of the Horse. By B. C. [i.e. Bracy Clark.] pp. 8. *Richards: London*, [1842.] 4°. **779**. i. **23**. (**2**.)

C., B. Thy Wonderful Works. A daily text book of nature with quotations from Scripture and the poets. [The compiler's foreword signed: B. C.] *G. J. Galloway: London*, [1938.] 16°. **4400**. n. **41**.

C., B.

—— Two Conversions and the reasons for them. (Why I Gave Up Protestantism. [Signed: B. C.]—Where Does Christ Rule and Teach? [By Charles F. Trusted.]) pp. 16. *Catholic Truth Society: London*, 1922. 8°. **3943**. aa. **279**.

C., B., *Fr.*

—— *See* FRANCISCANS. *Third Order of.* Riaghuil Threas Uirḋ S. Froinsias . . . ar na cur a nosa a nGáoiḋilg le bráthair áiriḋe dord an náoṁathar ċéudna Fr. B. C. [i.e. Bernard Conny.] 1641. 12°. C. **53**. a. **41**.

C., B., *in D.* Die Landtagswahl in München und die Abstinenz-Politik. Ein Mene-Tekel an alle ehrlichen Patrioten . . . von B. C. in D. pp. 19. *Augsburg*, 1875. 8°. **8074**. e. **3**. (**5**.)

C., **B.** ***Mrs. Oswald Chambers.***

—— Oswald Chambers. His life and work, *etc.* [Appreciations and extracts from letters. Edited by B. Chambers. With plates, including portraits.] pp. 411. *Simpkin, Marshall: London*, 1933. 8°. **2216**. aa. **7**.

—— (Second edition.) pp. 445. *Simpkin, Marshall: London*, 1938. 8°. **20032**. ee. **32**.

C., B., *Student in Divinitye.*

—— The Dolefull Knell, of Thomas Bell. That is, a full and sounde answer, to his pamphlet, intituled, The Popes Funeral. Which he published, against a treatise of myne, called, The Fore-runner of Bels Downefal . . . By B. C. Student in Diuinitye [i.e. Philip Woodward], *etc.* pp. 414. *Printed at Roane* [*Laurence Kellan: Douai*,] 1607. 8°. **3936**. bb. **42**.

The preliminaries are the work of a different printer, probably Pierre Auroi of Douai.

C., B., *Student in Divinitye.*

—— *See* BELL (Thomas) *Protestant Controversial Writer.* [The Tryall of the New Religion. Wherein it is proued that the] late Faith and Doctrine of the Church of Rome, is indeede the New Religion. [In answer to "The Dolefull Knell, of Thomas Bell . . . By B. C. Student in Diuinitye," i.e. Philip Woodward.] 1608. 4°. **3932**. dd. **22**.

—— *See* BELL (Thomas) *Protestant Controversial Writer.* The Catholique Triumph: conteyning, a Reply to the pretensed Answere of B. C., a masked Iesuite, lately published against the Tryall of the New Religion, *etc.* [In answer to "Bels Trial examined . . . By B. C., student in diuinitie," i.e. Robert Parsons.] 1610. 4°. **874**. k. **3**.

C., B., *Vestryman of Mary-le-Bone.* An Exposure of the Corruption of the Saxon Name Arm's Housen into Alms Houses; and of some other Norman corruptions. By B. C., Vestryman of Mary-le-Bone [i.e. Bracy Clark] pp. 8. *R. & J. E. Taylor: London*, [1844.] 4°. **779**. i. **23**. (**22**.

C * * *, B. DE. Lettre à Monsieur le duc de * * * * en répons aux Questions d'un bon patriote. [Signed: B. de C * * *. pp. 22. [1788.] 8°. F. **28**. (**5**.

—— [Another copy.] R. **20**. (**6**.

—— [Another edition.] *See* FRANCE. [*Appendix.—Histor and Politics.—Miscellaneous.*] Questions sur les affaire présentes de l'État, 1788, *etc.* 1788. 8°. F. **24**. (**12**.

C * * *, B. DE, *Mr.* Entendons-nous! Dissertation sur Mémoire des Princes présenté au Roi. Par Mr B. d C * * *. pp. 14. *Londres; se trouve à Paris* [*Par* printed], 1789. 8°. R. **16***. (**5**.

C——, B—— DI. Letter of an Italian Refugee on his Exil addressed to the Countess Dowager of Belmore. [Signed B—— di C——, i.e. Baron Gaetano Borso di Carminati pp. 134. *Sherwood, Gilbert & Piper: London*, 1827. 8°. **9165**. dd. **1**

C . . . . ., B . . . . . DI, *Conte.* Saggio sopra la politica e legislazione romana, del Conte B . . . . . de C . . . . . [i. Count G. U. Bottone di Castellamonte.] pp. 286. 1772. 8°. C.T. **105**. (**3**

—— [Another copy.] **521**. b. **3**

C., B. A.

—— Letters from B. A. C. [i.e. Boyce Albert Combe.] Afghanistan, 1878–80, *etc.* pp. 212. *J. Davy & Son London*, 1880. 8°. **9059**. df.

Printed for private circulation.

C., B. B., *Vicaire de la Cathédrale* (*de Dijon*). Noti historique et liturgique sur les cloches de St.-Bénign cathédrale de Dijon. Bénédiction solennelle de tr nouvelles cloches, le dimanche 15 mars, 1863 par Mo seigneur Rivet, évêque de Dijon. (2e édition.) [Signe B.-B. C., Vicaire de la Cathédrale.] pp. 34. *Dij* 1863. 8°. **7707**. aaa.

C . . ., B . . . C . . . Francisco Borbone regni utriusq Siciliæ principi hæredi, vicarium ius, potestatemque regnum universum obtinenti, epigramma. (Hende syllabi.) [Signed: B . . . C . . . C . . . .] [*Napl* 1820.] *s. sh.* fol. **8032**. m. **10**. (**2**

C., B. C. D., *M. le C. d.* Lythographie sicilienne, ou Catalog raisonné de toutes les pierres de la Sicile . . . Par M. C. d. B. C. d. C. [i.e. Michał Jan Borch.] pp. x. 50. *Naples*, 1777. 4°. **457**. d. **9**. (

—— [Another copy.] **443**. f.

C., B. D. S. Brief van B. D. S. C. aen M. D. Burgermeester tot Solathurn, aengaende de belangen van de Switserse Cantons, *etc.* pp. 20. [1689.] 4°. **8074. c. 20. (7.)**

C., B. D. S.

—— Continuacion de los Verdaderos Intereses de los Principes Christianos, en carta escrita a vn Regidor de la Ciudad de Soloturno, Cabeza de vno de los Cantones Catolicos de la Republica de los Esguizaros, traducida del Francès. [A translation of " Lettre de B. D. S. C. à M. D. Bourguemestre de Soleurre, sur les interêts des cantons suisses," a sequel to " Les veritables interêts des princes de l'Europe, dans les affaires presentes, ou Reflexions sur un escrit venu de France, sous le titre de Lettre de Monsieur .... à Monsieur . . . sur les affaires du temps."] pp. 23. [1689 ?] 4°. *See* CHRISTIAN PRINCES. **1445 f. 17. (76.).**

C., B. E. J. A Fool's " Passion ", and other poems. By B. E. J. C. pp. 76. *Eglington & Co.: London,* 1892. 8°. **011653. n. 94.**

C., B. F. C. Ethics or Anarchy: an essay concerning the relation of modern philosophy to morals and religion. [The preface signed: B. F. C. C., i.e. B. F. C. Costelloe.] pp. vii. 100. *Catholic Truth Society: London,* 1895. 8°. **3939. ccc. 17.**

C., B. G. and A., M. C. Ai Vakavuvuli sa bale ki na vei ka me caka e na Vakasucu Gone e Viti. [Instructions relative to the management of childbirth, native midwives and mothers. Signed: B. G. C., M. C. A., i.e. Bolton Glanvill Corney and May Christina Anderson.] pp. 8. [1902.] 8°. *See* FIJI. **07580. f. 20.**

C., B. H. A Letter to Jeremiah Harman, Esq. . . . on the circulating medium of the Kingdom and the means of diminishing the practice of forgery. [Signed: B. H. C.] pp. 40. *R. Hunter: London,* 1818. 8°. **B. 497. (5.)**

C., B. H. Précis des lois devant donner aux mariages célébrés par les ministres des églises chrétiennes les mêmes effets légaux que ceux obtenus par les mariages célébrés par un officier de l'état civil, *etc.* [The preface signed: B. H. C.] pp. 20. *Maurice,* 1916. 8°. **06605. b. 10.**

C., B. I. D. P. E., *Mr.* Recherches sur l'origine du despotisme oriental. Ouvrage posthume de Mr. B. I. D. P. E. C. [i.e. N. A. Boulanger, ingénieur des ponts et chaussées.] [Edited by Baron P. H. D. von Holbach.] pp. xxxii. 435. [*Geneva,*] 1761. 12°. **8005. aaa. 9.**

—— [Another edition.] pp. xvi. 255. [*Geneva,*] 1762. 8°. **8005. de. 17.**

C., B. J., *Dr.* Indice alphabetico e remissivo dos decretos e ordens das Cortes geraes, extraordinarias e constituintes da Nação portugueza . . . com designação das suas datas, pagina e numero. Pelo Dr. B. J. C. [i.e. Bernardo José de Carvalho.] pp. 39. *Coimbra,* 1823. 4°. **9180. ccc. 6. (12.)**

C., B. J. S. P. Douri-Vinhaida: poema epico-burlesco, offerecido aos lavradores do vinho do Alto Douro. Por B. J. S. P. C. [i.e. Bernardino Joaquim da Silva Carneiro.] pp. 40. *Porto,* 1822. 8°. **11452. aa. 8.**

C., B. L. Warhafftige Abbildung aller itzo im Krieg begriffenen hohen Potentaten und dero Generals, durch Beibringung verschiedener aus Betrachtung dero Actionen gezogenen Remarques erläutert, nahmentlich Ihr. Kays. Maj. Josephi, König Carls in Spanien, Königin Annæ von Engeland . . . Mit einem Entwurff von der sehr curieusen Kunst, die Gemüther der Menschen zu erkennen, *etc.* [The " Entwurff " signed: B. L. C.] 2 pt. *Cöln,* 1707. 4°. **580. d. 27. (14.)**

C., B. M. Traicté du delict commun, et cas privilegié: ou de la puissance legitime des iuges seculiers sur les personnes ecclesiastiques. Par B. M. C. [i.e. Bénigne Milletot.] pp. 132. *N. Roysset: Paris,* 1611. 4°. **878. f. 3. (6.)**

—— [Another edition.] Reueu, corrigé, & augmenté. pp. 132. *F. du Carroy: Paris,* 1612. 12°. **697. d. 41.**

C., B. M. S. *See* CLOUGH (A. H.) Selections from the Poems of Arthur Hugh Clough. [The preface signed: B. M. S. C.] 1894. 8°. **11612. bb. 26.**

C., B. P. Senatus deorum de præsentibus afflictissimæ et periclitantis Germaniæ miseriis, & reducendâ pace. [Signed: B. P. C., i.e. Bogislav Philipp von Chemnitz.] pp. 51. 1627. 4°. **1054. h. 9. (18.)**

—— [Another edition.] *Apud J. Janssonium: Holmiæ,* [1645 ?] 12°. **1193. a. 4. (1.)**

C., B. R. Lines occasioned by the much lamented Death of Her Royal Highness Princess Charlotte. [Signed: B. R. C.] *D. Cox: Southwark,* 1817. *s. sh.* 8°. **1879. c. 12. (146.)**

C., B. S. Ode to the New River. [Signed: B. S. C., i.e. B. S. Coupe.] [*London ?* 1890.] *s. sh.* fol. **1870. d. 1. (140.)**

C., B. T. C. A. Observações sobre o voto, que Domingos Alves Branco Moniz Barreto, como eleitor da parochia do Sacramento da Corte do Rio de Janeiro apresentou no dia 25 de Dezembro de 1821 na Junta Eleitoral para a installação do governo desta provincia. Nas quaes se mostra, que semelhante voto he contrario ao pacto Social da Nação Portugueza, e aos direitos . . . das provincias do Brasil, escriptas ror [*sic*] hum Amigo da união, e da justiça. [The dedicatory epistle signed: B. T. C. A. C.] pp. 65. *Lisboa,* 1822. 4°. **9180. ccc. 7. (9.)**

C. (BEATRIX S.) ' Benediction.' A meditation in verse. [Signed: Beatrix S. C.] pp. 16. *Elliot Stock: London,* 1892. 16°. **11601. aa. 47. (3.)**

C., C. *See* BOLTON (Robert) *Puritan Divine.* A Threefold Treatise: containing the Saints sure and perpetuall Guide, *etc.* [The editor's dedicatory epistle signed: C. C.] 1634. 4°. **1360. l. 7.**

C., C. *See* BRUGES. [*Appendix.*] Het Boek van al't gene datter gheschiedt is binnen Brugghe, sichtent jaer 1477, 14 Februarii, tot 1491. Uitgegeven door CC. [i.e. Charles Louis Carton.] 1859. 8°. [*Maetschappy der Vlaemsche Bibliophilen.* ser. 3. no. 2.] **Ac. 9035/2.**

C., C.

—— *See* CASSANDER (Georgius) Oratio in laudem urbis Brugensis. [The editor's preface signed: C. C., i.e. C. L. Carton.] 1847. 4°. **Ac. 5517/4. (26.)**

C., C.

—— *See* CROMWELL (Oliver) *Lord Protector of the Commonwealth of England, etc.* [*Appendix.—Biography.—*II. 1657. *April, May.*] Treason's Master-piece: or, a Conference held at Whitehall between Oliver the late Usurper, and a Committee of the then pretended Parliament, *etc.* [The preface signed: C. C.] 1680. 8°. **1104. b. 28.**

C., C. *See* DEVEREUX (Robert) *2nd Earl of Essex.* Apologie . . . vanden Grave van Essex, teghen de ghene die hem . . . schelden als beletter des vredes ende ruste zijnes vaderlandts . . . Ouergheset door C. C. [i.e. Kaspar Koolhaas.] 1603. 4°. **E. 1940. (4.)**

C * * *., C * * *. *See* EDGEWORTH (Maria) Léonora . . . Traduit . . . par C * * *. C * * *. [i.e. C. Chenel.] 1807. 12°. **12808. t. 13.**

C., C. *See* ERASMUS (D.) [*Moriae Encomium.*] Elogio della pazzia . . . recato in italiano . . . ed arricchito delle annotazioni . . . del volgarizzatore, C. C. 1819. 12°. **1079. g. 24.**

C., C. *See* HEMELSDAELE, *Abbey of.* Chronique et cartulaire de l'abbaye de Hemelsdaele, publiés par C. C. et F. V. [i.e. C. L. Carton and F. van de Putte.] 1858. 4°. [*Recueil de chroniques, chartes, et autres documents concernant l'histoire et les antiquités de la Flandre-Occidentale.* sér. 1.] Ac. **5517/4. (6.)**

C., C. *See* HOMER. [*Iliad.—English.*] The Episode of Hector and Andromache . . . Attempted in English hexameters: by C. C. [i.e. Charles Chorley.] [1867.] 8°. **11655. e. 10. (5.)**

—— *See* HORATIUS FLACCUS (Q.) [*Carmina and Epodi.—Selections.—English.*] Horatian Metres, attempted in English. By C. C. [i.e. Charles Chorley.] [1867.] 8°. **11655. e. 10. (4.)**

C., C. *See* LONDON.—III. *Hospital for Poor French Protestants.* The Charter and By-laws . . . of the Hospital for Poor French Protestants, *etc.* [The introduction signed: C. C.] 1876. 8°. **6345. b. 11.**

—— *See* LONDON.—III. *Hospital for Poor French Protestants.* The Charter and By-Laws . . . of the Hospital for Poor French Protestants, *etc.* [With an introduction signed: C. C.] 1892. 8°. **7681. b. 53.**

C., C. *See* LUCANUS (M. A.) [*Pharsalia.—Latin.*] Marci Annæi Lucani . . . Pharsalia, *etc.* [The "præfatiuncula" signed: C. C.] 1815. 12°. **11355. a. 4.**

C., C. *See* M., J., and C., C. Jack Frost and Betty Snow, *etc.* [The dedication signed: J. M. and C. C., i.e. J. M. Chanter and Charlotte Chanter.] 1858. 16°. **12807. b. 53.**

C., C. *See* MANNING (Henry E.) *Cardinal, Archbishop of Westminster.* The Teaching of Christ. A selection of sermons from the Anglican writings of the late Henry Edward Manning. [The editor's preface signed: C. C.] 1899. 8°. **4476. df. 13.**

C., C. *See* NICHOLAS, *Saint, Abbey of, at Furnes, Flanders.* Chronicon et cartularium abbatiæ Sancti Nicolai Furnensis . . . et Chronicon Bethaniæ seu Domus S. Josephi Furnensis; ediderunt F. V. N. C. C. [i.e. F. van de Putte and C. L. Carton.] 1849. 4°. [*Recueil de chroniques, chartes, et autres documents concernant l'histoire et les antiquités de la Flandre-Occidentale.* sér. 1.] Ac. **5517/4. (4.)**

C., C. *See* PARIS.—*Bibliothèque Nationale.* [*Manuscrits.*] Heures dites de Henri IV. Reproduction réduite des 60 peintures du manuscrit latin 1171 de la Bibliothèque nationale. [The preface signed: C. C., i.e. Camille Couderc.] [1908.] 8°. MS. Facs. **119.**

C., C. *See* PERIODICAL PUBLICATIONS.—*Paris.* Revue protestante, *etc.* [The editor's introduction to the first number signed: C. C., i.e. Charles Augustin Coquerel.] 1825, *etc.* 8°. P.P. **56. b.**

C., C. *See* TASSO (T.) [*Rime.—English.*] From the Italian of Tasso's Sonnets; by C. C. [i.e. C. Chorley. Verse translations.] [1867.] 8°. **11655. e. 10. (3.)**

C., C. *See* TER DOEST, *Abbey of.* Chronique de l'abbaye de Ter Doest, par F. V. et C. C. [i.e. F. van de Putte and C. L. Carton.] 1845. 4°. [*Recueil de chroniques, chartes, et autres documents concernant l'histoire et les antiquités de la Flandre-Occidentale.* sér. 1.] Ac. **5517/4. (4.)**

C., C. *See* TERENTIUS (P.) *Afer.* [*Works.—Latin.*] Terentii, Afri, comœdiæ sex, *etc.* [The "præfatiuncula" signed: C. C.] 1815. 12°. **11707. a.**

C., C. *See* VORMEZEELE, *Abbey of.* Chronicon Vormeselen per F. V. et C. C. [i.e. F. van de Putte and C. L. Carto 1847. 4°. [*Recueil de chroniques, chartes, et autres do ments concernant l'histoire et les antiquités de la Fland Occidentale.* sér. 1.] Ac. **5517/4.** (

C., C. *See* WILLIAMS (Helen M.) Souvenirs de la Révolut française, *etc.* [The translator's advertisement signe C. C., i.e. Charles Augustin Coquerel.] 1827. 8°. **1442. g.**

C., C. [**A collection of broadsides,** chiefly satirical son parodies, etc., printed at the private press of Charles Cla from 1833 to 1862, the majority signed: C. C., i.e. Clark.] 1833–62. 8° & fol. *See* CLARK (Charles) *Esq., Great Totham, Essex.* **1890. d.**

C., C. Al campo di Don Carlos. Memorie di un Carli italiano. Gennaio 1874. [By C. C.] pp. 95. *Bolog* [1874.] 8°. **9180. aa.**
The author's initials are disclosed in the introductory n

C., C. Anecdotes of Alamayu, the late King Theodore's s By C. C. [With a portrait.] pp. 72. *W. Hunt & C London,* [1870.] 16°. **10605. a.**

C., C. An Answer to the Marquesse of Worcester his Re to the Kings Paper. [The address to the reader, by author of the "Answer," signed: C. C., i.e. Christop Cartwright.] *See* CHARLES I., *King of Great Britain Ireland.* [*Letters and Speeches.*—II.] Certamen relig sum: or, a Conference between the late King of Engla and the late Lord Marquesse of Worcester, *etc.* 1651. **858. g.**

—— [A reissue.] *See* CHARLES I., *King of Great Britain Ireland.* [*Letters and Speeches.*—II.] Certamen relig sum, *etc.* 1652. 4°. **858. g**

C., C. Ane Brief Explanation of the Life, or a Prophecie of Death, of the Marquis of Argyle, with diverse verses th upon . . . Composed in Scottish rhyme by C. C. Lordship's old Servitor, *etc.* [Reprinted from the edit of Inverlochie, 1656.] pp. 12. [1820?] 4°. **11601. ddd. 6.**

C., C. Converssationi famigliari frà due forestieri sul pu della uera ed unica relligione christiana . . . Dedicato al Sig^r: Gulielmo Burnetti da C. C. pp. 131. *Francof* 1711. 12°. **4017. de.**

C., C. Di alcune opere biografiche. Annotazione. Estra dall'Effemeridi letterarie di Roma, *etc.* [Signed: C. i.e. Clemente Cardinali.] pp. 25. *Roma,* 1822. 8°. **7702. cc. 10.** (

—— Explicatio literarum et notarum frequentius in anti Romanorum monimentis occurrentium . . . Annotazi [A critical article on the above work. Signed: C. C., Clemente Cardinali.] Estratta dall'Effemeridi letter di Roma, *etc.* pp. 12. *Roma,* 1822. 8°. **7702. cc. 10.**

C., C. The Father of the City of Eutopia, or the Su road to riches. Being a narrative of the remarkable and adventures of an elevated bear, *etc.* [A satire. dedication signed: C. C.] pp. iv. 22 [20]. *J. Co London,* 1757. 8°. **906. k. 7.**

C., C. Fictions et réalités polonaises. [Signed: C. pp. 121. *Saint-Pétersbourg,* 1864. 8°. **10292. h.**

C., C. The First Gift; or, Ruth Noble's friends. By C. C. pp. 217. *R.T.S.: London*, [1882.] 8°. **4420.** m. **33.**

C., C. Giftie the Changeling. By C. C. With illustration. pp. 96. *F. Warne & Co.: London*, [1869.] 16°. **12807.** aa. **28.**

C., C. "If." [A religious tract. Signed: C. C.] pp. 10. *Marshall Bros.: London*, [1895.] 32°. **4420.** aa. **62.** (**2.**)

C., C.

—— The Invitation of God. [Signed: C. C.] pp. 8. *Gospel Proclamation Society: [London*, 1950.] 8°. **4397.** aa. **70.**

C., C. Iscrizioni antiche collocate ne' muri della Scala Farnese, e spiegate da D. Pietro de Lama . . . Lettera del Dottore Giovanni Labus a D. Pietro de Lama intorno a due iscrizioni Vellejati . . . Tavola alimentaria Vellejate detta Trajana, restituita alla sua vera lezione da D. Pietro de Lama. Annotazione. (Estratto dall'Effemeridi Letterarie di Roma.) [A critical article on the above books. Signed: C. C., i.e. Clemente Cardinali.] pp. 21. *Roma*, 1821. 8°. **7702.** cc. **10.** (**15.**)

C., C. Jesus Hostia; or, the Real Presence of Our Lord in the Holy Eucharist. [The preface signed: C. C. With plates.] pp. xi. 136. *Anthonian Press: Dublin*, [1931.] 8°. **4323.** df. **38.**

C., C. Memoria istorico-fisica del terremoto accaduto in Lombardia li 12 maggio 1802. Di C. C. (Ciro Caparrotti.) 1802. 8°. *See* CAPARROTTI (C.) **7109.** e. **28.**

C., C. The Narrow Way. [Verses. Signed: C. C.] pp. 8. *J. Masters & Co.: London*, [1877.] 8°. **11643.** bb. **35.** (**12.**)

C., C. Het Nieuwe Hoornse speel-werck, bestaende uyt verscheyden ernstige en vroolijcke gezangen en gedichten van C. G. v. d. H. en C. G. K. [i.e. C. Groenvelt, P. Y. van der Hof and C. G. Kleyn] &c. Versamelt door C. C. [i.e. C. Croock.] Tweede druk, vermeerdert, en in nette ordre gebragt. pp. 437. *Hoorn*, 1732. 8°. **11556.** bb. **10.**
With an additional titlepage, engraved.

C., C. Notes on the Doctrines of the Sacraments, according to the Church of England . . . By a Lay Member. [The preface signed: C. C. With an appendix, signed: A Constant Reader.] pp. 15. xii. *D. Batten: Clapham*, 1844. 12°. **908.** c. **5.** (**2.**)

C., C. Ode sacra tricolos tetrastrophos ad psalmun [*sic*] .45. iuxta Hebr. Verit. expensum in tranquillum ex turbulentiss. rerum statum diuinis. C. M. victorijs partum et stabilitum Anno Dñi. 1544. Aemsterodami natalitijs Dñi ferijs cantanda ex more scripta per C. C. [i.e. Cornelius Crocus] pueritię in antiqua schola formatorem. (Idem Psal. . . . pene ad verbum ex Hebreo conuersus per eundem C. C.) **G.L.** [1544.] 8°. *See* BIBLE.—*Psalms.*—*Selections.* [*Latin.*—*Single Psalms.*—XLVI. (45.)] **11408.** aa. **39.** (**2.**)

C., C. The Old Bachelor. [A satirical poem. Signed: C. C., i.e. Charles Clark.] *Great Totham*, [1855 ?] *s. sh.* fol. **1890.** d. **19.**

C., C. A Prologue spoken by Mr. Elrington, on the 22d of April, being the birth-day of his Excellency Lord Carteret. Written by C. C. [i.e. Charles Carthy.] (Epilogue, spoken by Mr. Griffith . . . By the same.) *Pressick Rider & Thomas Harbin: Dublin*, 1725. *s. sh.* fol. **C.121.g.8.(74.)**

—— [Another copy.] **1890.** e. **5.** (**98.**)

C., C. Prose varie del cavaliere A. Mustoxidi Corcirese con aggiunta di alcuni versi, *etc.* (Estratto dall'Effemeridi letterarie di Roma.) [A critique of the above work. Signed: C. C., i.e. Clemente Cardinali.] pp. 19. [*Rome*, 1821.] 8°. **7702.** cc. **10.** (**22.**)

C., C. Riviera Nature Notes, a popular account of the more conspicuous plants and animals of the Riviera and the Maritime Alps. [The preface signed: C. C., i.e. George Edward Comerford Casey.] Second edition, with . . . plates, *etc.* pp. xv. 402. *Bernard Quaritch: London*, 1903. 8°. **7002.** f. **40.**

C., C. Sad and Serious Thoughts; or, the Sense and meaning of the late Act concerning marriages: explained in a letter, *etc.* [Signed: C. C.] [*London*, 1653.] 4°. **E. 713.** (**8.**)

C., C. Several Queries, relating to an Act of Parliament . . . entituled An Act for the discharge out of prison such insolvent debtors as shall serve . . . in Her Majesty's Fleet or Army. Sent in a letter, by a Gentleman in the Country, to his Friend, a Counsellor at Law in London. With his answer thereto, *etc.* [The letter signed: C. C.; the answer signed: E. G.] pp. 12. *London*, 1704. 4°. **8122.** bb. **35.** (**14*.**)

C., C. The Song of the Brat; or, a Mother's manifold miseries, *etc.* [Signed: C. C., i.e. Charles Clark.] *Great Totham*, 1855. *s. sh.* fol. **1890.** d. **19.**

C., C. Sulla Divina Commedia di Dante di mano del Boccacci, cantica I. Inferno. Roveta negli occhi santi di Bice: annotazione. Estratto dall'Effemeridi letterarie di Roma, *etc.* [Signed: C. C., i.e. Clemente Cardinali.] pp. 21. *Roma*, 1822. 8°. **011421.bbb.8.**

C., C. Sunday Alphabet. By C. C. [In verse.] (Illuminated by Owen Jones.) *Day & Son: London*, [1861.] *obl.* 8°. **1264.** a. **6.**

C., C. Sylla's Ghost: a satyr against ambition, and the last horrid plot. [In verse. The dedication signed: C. C.] pp. 12. *Printed by John Harefinch: London*, 1683. fol. **11602.** i. **27.** (**3.**)

C., C. Tactical Talks and Tramps. By Sextus. 4th edition, revised, with diagrams. [The introduction signed: C. C., i.e. William Charles Christie.] pp. 114. *Baily & Woods: Cirencester*, 1914. 16°. **8823.** a. **35.**

C., C. Translations. By C. C. [i.e. Charles Chorley.] [In verse.] pp. 29. *J. R. Netherton: Truro*, 1866. 8°. **11655.** e. **10.** (**1.**)

—— Translations. By C. C. [i.e. Charles Chorley.] [In verse.] pp. 31. *J. R. Netherton: Truro*, 1866. 8°. **11655.** e. **10.** (**2.**)
A different work from the preceding.

C., C. Triumph, and other poems. By C. C. pp. 23. *Chapman & Hall: London*, 1916. 16°. **011649.** de. **79.**

C., C. Gli Ultimi giorni del carnevale di Milano nel 1848. [In verse. Signed: C. C.] [*Genoa*, 1848.] *s. sh.* fol. **804.** k. **13.** (**204.**)

C., C. Ventidue anni di sventure di un Garibaldino raccontate da un uffiziale dei volontari, *etc.* [The dedication signed: C. C.] pp. 64. *Firenze*, [1870 ?] 16°. **10631.** aa. **36.** (**2.**)

C., C. Verse. By C. C. [i.e. Charles Chorley.] [With a portrait.] pp. 30. *J. R. Netherton: Truro*, [1867.] 8°. **11655.** e. **10.** (**6.**)

—— Verse. By C. C. [i.e. Charles Chorley.] pp. 24. *J. R. Netherton: Truro*, [1867.] 8°. **11655.** e. **10.** (**7.**)
A different work from the preceding.

C., C. La Vie de tres-haute . . . Henriette-Marie de France, reyne de la Grand' Bretagne. [The dedication signed: C. C., i.e. Charles Cotolendi.] pp. 326. *M. Gueroult: Paris*, 1690. 8°. **G. 1880.**

C., C. A Voice to the Young, from a Death-Bed. [A religious tract. Signed: C. C.] pp. 24. *Seeley, Jackson & Halliday: London; Dixon: Cambridge,* [1860.] 32°. **4986. a. 61. (7.)**

—— A Voice to the Young, from a Death-Bed. [Signed: C. C., i.e. Charles Clayton.] pp. 8. *Seeley, Jackson & Halliday: London; Dixon: Cambridge,* 1859. 8°. **4480. b. 17. (2.)**

C., C., and **B.**, A. Brevi cenni biografici sulla vita dell'illustre statista italiano Conte Camillo Benso di Cavour. Editi per cura di due operai. [The introduction signed: C. C. ed A. B.] pp. 16. *Torino,* 1873. 8°. **10630. ee. 1. (6.)**

C., C., and **C.**, E. The Sphynx: a new and original collection of double acrostics. By C. C. and E. C. pp. ii. 87. *Harrison & Sons: London,* 1867. 8°. **12304. bb. 39.**

—— A Key to the Sphynx: a new and original collection of double acrostics. By C. C. and E. C. pp. 23. *Harrison & Sons: London,* 1867. 16°. **12316. aaa. 46.**

C., C. and **G.**, D.

—— The English in Love. A museum of illustrative verse and prose pieces from the 14th cent. to the 20th. Assembled by C. C. and D. G. [i.e. Catherine R. Carswell and Daniel George.] pp. 559. *Martin Secker: London,* 1934. 8°. **12298. dd. 7.**

—— A National Gallery. Being a collection of English characters. Compiled by C. C. & D. G. [i.e. Catherine R. Carswell and Daniel George.] pp. viii. 535. *Martin Secker: London,* 1933. 8°. **12298. df. 18.**

C., C., and **V.**, E. V. Las Campanetas. Joguina en un acte y en vers, arreglada á la escena catalana per C. C.—E. V. V. [i.e. Eduardo Vidal Valenciano], *etc.* pp. 24. *Barcelona,* 1873. 8°. **11725. ee. 6. (11.)**

C . . . . ., C., *Abbé.* Album descriptif des fêtes et cérémonies religieuses à l'occasion du jubilé de 700 ans du Saint-Sang, à Bruges, précédé de l'abrégé d'un essai sur l'histoire du Saint-Sang . . . Par l'Abbé C. C . . . . . [i.e. C. L. Carton]. Contenant 30 planches, *etc.* pp. 78. *Bruges,* 1850. 8°. **4685. h. 9.**

C., C., *Abbé, Prêtre du diocèse de Lyon.* La Tante: notice historique sur Antoinette Montet, fondatrice du Séminaire de Verrières, Loire. Par l'abbé C. C. Prêtre du diocèse de Lyon. pp. 36. *Lyon,* 1868. 12°. **4867. a. 13.**

C., C., *Dott.* I Capi d'arte di Bramante da Urbino nel Milanese. Memorie storico-artistiche raccolte per cura del Dott. C. C. [i.e. C. Casati.] [With plates.] pp. 115. *Milano,* 1870. 8°. **07822.e.39.**

C., C., *Great Totham, Essex.* Tiptree Races: a comic punning poem. By "C. C." [i.e. Charles Clark] Great Totham, Essex. pp. 32. *P. H. Youngman: Maldon,* 1833. 8°. **T. 1529. (2.)**

C., C., *Mr, Propriétaire.*

—— Lettres socialistes. Première lettre. Pourquoi le socialisme? Mai 1850. Par Mr C. C., propriétaire [i.e. Charles Victor Charpillet]. pp. iv. 134. *Paris,* 1850. 8°. **R. 142. (11.)**

C., C., *of Gray's Inn, Esquire.* Another Word to Purpose against The Long Parliament Revived [by Thomas Philips, pseud.]. By C. C. of Grays-Inne, Esq; pp. 20. *For Thomas Dring: London,* 1660. 4°. **518. k. 1. (12.)**

—— [Another copy.] **E. 1053. (5.)**

C., C., *of Gray's Inn, Esquire.*

—— A Word to Purpose: or, a Parthian Dart, shot ba to 1642, and from thence . . . to 1659 . . . and n sticks fast in two substantial queries, I. concerning Legality of the Second Meeting of some of the Lo Parliament-Members. Also, a Fools Bolt shot i Wallingford House . . . concerning a free state. [C. C.] pp. 15. 1659. 4°. *See* WORD. **E. 985.**

—— The second impression, with addition. pp. 15. 1659. 4°. *See* WORD. **T. 1933.**

C., C., *le Sieur.* La Stimmimachie, ou le grand com des medecins modernes touchant l'usage de l'antimo Poëme historicomique . . . par le Sieur C. C. [i.e. Carneau.] pp. 112. *I. Paslé: Paris,* 1656. 8°. **1143. a.**

—— [Another copy.] **1161.**

C., C. A. Brief Gleanings from the Ministry of C. A Twelve cards, *etc.* [*G. Morrish:*] *London,* [1932.] *obl.* **04420. f.**

—— "The High Priest of Our Confession." Four addre at Newton Abbot, by C. A. C. pp. 48. *G. Morr London,* [1902.] 8°. **4422. cc.**

C., C. A.

—— Laetitia et gratulatio publica occasione recens co tuti regni Hungariae Palatini [i.e. of Archduke Jo Antony John]. Vulgata per C. A. C. [i.e. Count A Cziráky.] pp. 10. *Posonii,* 1796. 4°. **10797. f**

C., C. A.

—— An Outline of the Revelation. By C. A. C. pp. *Stow Hill Bible Depôt & Publishing Office: Newport, London,* [1923.] 8°. **3268. aa**

C., C. A. C. *See* GRANIER (M.) Conferences upon Hom pathy . . . Translated . . . by H. E. W. [i.e. H Wilkinson] & C. A. C. C. [i.e. C. A. C. Clark.] 1859. **7391. c**

C., C. B. Hints of a Plan to remedy the evils of the Laws . . . in answer to the suggestions on refor parochial government of Thomas Walker, M.A. C. B. C. pp. 12. *Effingham Wilson: London,* 1834. **C.T.208.(1**

C., C. C. Remarks, Critical and Moral, on the Talen Lord Byron, and the tendencies of Don Juan. B author of Hypocrisy, a satire, with notes and anec political and historical. [The dedication signed: C. i.e. Charles C. Colton.] pp. 52. *Printed for the A London,* 1819. 8°. **1087. c. 3**

—— [Another copy.] Remarks on the Talents of Lord I and the Tendencies of Don Juan. [The dedication si C. C. C., i.e. C. C. Colton.] [1819.] 8°. **526. l.**

—— [Another copy.] **8407. dd. 3**

—— [Another edition.] pp. 56. [1819.] 8°. **527. k. 1**

—— [Another copy.] **1387. h.**

C., C. C. DE

—— *See* DARINEL, *Pasteur des Amadis, pseud.* [i.e. Boileau de Buillon.] La Sphere des deux mondes posée en François par Darinel pasteur des Amadis. vn Epithalame . . . Commenté, glosé, & enrich plusieurs fables Poeticques, par G. B. D. B. C. C N. L. Oubli. 1555. 4°. **532.**

C., C. D. Copie d'vne lettre escrite à vne âme d touchant les dispositions qu'il faut auoir en la pra des vertus, *etc.* [Signed: C. D. C.] pp. 44. *G. Schoeuarts: Bruxelles,* 1642. 12°. **4409. a. 5**

C., C. D., *Sr. de Welles*. *See* Bosco (Antonio) *Antiquarian.* La Chasteté victorieuse en l'admisable conuersion de S. Valerian espoux de Saincte Cecile . . . De la traduction de C. D. C. Sr de Welles. 1617. 8°. **860**. h. **8**. (**2**.)

C., C. D. S. La Doctrine de Iesus-Christ, nostre Seigneur: et celle, de Robert, Cardinal Bellarmin, Iesuiste [in his "Tractatus de potestate Summi Pontificis in rebus temporalibus"], touchant les roys et princes, rapportée l'une à l'autre, *etc.* [The dedication signed: C. D. S. C.] pp. 27. 1611. 8°. **860**. c. **25**. (**3**.)

—— [Another edition.] 1611. *See* Millétot (B.) Traicté du delict commun, *etc.* pt. 2. 1611. 8°. **857**. g. **11**. (**7**.)

C., C. E.

—— Questions on the First Series of Chepmell's Short Course of History. [The "advertisement" signed: G. E. C.] pp. 64. *Whittaker & Co.: London*, 1851. 12°. **1308**. b. **18**.

C., C. E. Useful Hints on how to take care of and keep in order the Pianoforte. By C. E. C. [i.e. C. E. Cope.] pp. 13. *A. E. Jympson: St. Leonard's-on-Sea*, [1891.] 16°. **7899**. a. **17**. (**2**.)

C., C. F. Advertising for Retailers. A handy guide. [The introduction signed: C. F. C.] pp. 72. *Home Trade Publishing Co.: London*, [1905.] fol. **8228**. k. **48**.

C., C. F. Bencoolen to Capricorno. A record of wrecks at Bude, 1862 to 1900. [The preface signed: C. F. C.] pp. 121. *J. E. Cornish: Manchester*, 1902. 8°. **08805**. ee. **47**.

C., C. F. The Land-Assessment and the Landed Tenures of Canara. [The preface signed: C. F. C., i.e. Frederick Chamier.] pp. 88. *German Mission Press: Mangalore*, 1853. 8°. **8023**. cc. **6**.

C., C. F. Sacred Poetry. Selected by C. F. C. [i.e. Caledon F. Cocks ?] *Tydenhangre Press*, [1842 ?] 16°. **11602**. aa. **8**.

—— [Another copy.] **1075**. c. **10**.

C., C. F. P.

—— The Theocracy and the Law of National Caducity: a reply to recent dissertations on the "temporal power," in the New Review, Spectator, Contemporary Review, etc., by the author of "Civil Principality," etc. [The introduction signed: C. F. P. C., i.e. C. F. P. Collingridge.] pp. 103–173. *Burns & Oates: London; Benziger Bros.: New York*, [1893.] 8°. **3940**. cc. **17**. (**3**.)
The pagination continues that of the same author's pamphlet "The Temporal Power of the Pope."

C., C. G. *See* Bergmueller (J. B.) Der Maassstab Gottes, oder die Berechnung göttlicher Zahlen in der heiligen Schrift, *etc.* [With a preface signed: C. G. C.] 1778. fol. **L.16.h.4.**

C., C. G. *See* Bible.—*Selections.* Christ and His People, *etc.* [The compilers' preface signed: C. G. C. and L. B.] [1896.] 12°. **3128**. eee. **57**.

C., C. G. *See* Vaughan (Henry) *Vicar of Crickhowel.* Memoir and Remains of the Rev. H. Vaughan. [The advertisement signed: C. G. C.] 1842. 12°. **1372**. d. **13**.

C., C. G. Entdeckung der gantzen Jüdischen Synagog, oder immerwährender Ceremoniel-Calender . . . aus dem Hebräischen ins Teutsche übersetzt, und zusammen getragen durch einen Proselyten, C. G. C. pp. 60. [*Nuremberg ?* 1740 ?] 8°. **12903**. bbb. **15**. (**3**.)
Cropped.

C., C. G., *L.L.O.* Jüdischer Dolmetscher, oder Hebräisch- und Teutsche Vocabula . . . heraus gegeben von . . . C. G. C., L.L.O. pp. 83. *Nürnberg*, 1735. 8°. **12903**. bbb. **15**. (**1**.)

C., C. G. C. D. G., *Il G.* La Coltivazione de' gelsi, e propagazione de' filugelli in Sardegna. (Moriografia sarda.—Seriografia sarda. Dal G. C. G. C. D. G. C. [i.e. Giuseppe Cossu.]) 1788, *etc.* 8°. *See* Cossu (G.) **1254**. e. **7**.

C., C. H.

—— Innsbruck and its Environs. By C. H. C., *etc.* [The preface signed: Charlotte H. Coursen.] 1899. 8°. *See* Coursen (Charlotte H.) **10201**. bbb. **2**.

C., C. H. Ornamental Lathework for Amateurs . . . By C. H. C. [i.e. C. H. Caunter.] pp. 121. pl. xxii. *P. Marshall & Co.: London*, [1914.] 8°. **07816**. a. **2**.

C., C. H. P. Mr. Balfour and Conceivable Cures for Imagined Ills. By C. H. P. C. [i.e. Charles H. P. Christie.] pp. 48. *Effingham Wilson: London*, 1903. 8°. **08226**. h. **71**.

C., C. H. T. Notes on the North-Western Provinces of India. By a District Officer. Second edition. [The preface signed: C. H. T. C., i.e. Sir Charles H. T. Crosthwaite.] *W. H. Allen & Co.: London*, 1870. 8°. **10058**. bb. **7**.

C., C. I. C. A. L. Der nützliche und curiöse Künstler, oder neu- und wohl-approbirtes Hauss- und Kunst-Buch . . . mitgetheilet und zum Druck befördert von C. I. C. A. L. C. pp. 800. *Nürnberg*, 1728. 8°. **7807**. aa. **15**.

C., C. J. Margaret, and other poems. By C. J. C. pp. 120. *William Skeffington: London*, 1871. 8°. **11647**. ccc. **23**.

C., C. J. Sonnets: by C. J. C. [i.e. Charles J. Cruttwell.] *Private Press of H. & E. Daniel: Frome*, 1856. 16°. **C**. **99**. a. **13**.

C., C. K. Die neue Reformation. [A poem. Signed: C. K. C.] *See* K., C. W. Die katholische Kirche ist die allein wahre, *etc.* 1845. 16°. **3911**. a. **35**.

C., C. L. *See* H., A. I., and C., C. L. Poetical Gems. A birthday book . . . Compiled by A. I. H. and C. L. C. [1896.] 32°. **11601**. a. **58**.

C., C. L. The Bazaar. [A tract against bazaars.] [Signed: C. L. C.] pp. 24. *Love & Barton: Manchester; Simpkin, Marshall & Co.: London*, [1850.] 24°. **4415**. b. **14**.

C., C. L. Devotions for Daily Use. [The preface signed: C. L. C., i.e. Hon. Charles L. Courtenay.] pp. vii. 72. *J. Masters & Co.: London*, 1875. 32°. **3457**. a. **34**.

—— How to come to Christ. By the author of "Our New Life in Christ." Edited by a Parish Priest. [The preface signed: C. L. C., i.e. Hon. Charles L. Courtenay.] pp. 45. *Joseph Masters: London*, 1873. 8°. **4402**. b. **8**.

—— Our New Life in Christ. Edited by a Parish Priest. [The preface signed: C. L. C., i.e. Hon. Charles L. Courtenay.] pp. viii. 91. *Joseph Masters: London*, 1863. 8°. **4406**. aa. **65**.

C., C. L. Mrs. Poynter's Missionary Box. A tale. By C. L. C., *etc.* pp. 47. *S.P.C.K.: London*, [1879.] 16°. **4422**. b. **12**. (**6**.)

C., C. L. A Sequel to "Our New Life in Christ"; or the Presence of Jesus on the Altar, *etc.* [The preface signed: C. L. C., i.e. Hon. Charles L. Courtenay.] pp. vi. 95. *Joseph Masters: London*, 1872. 8°. **4324**. aaa. **30**.

C., C. L. W. A Guide to Battle Abbey, by C. L. W. C. [i.e. Catherine Lucy Wilhelmina, Duchess of Cleveland.] pp. 75. vi. *Ticehurst Bros.: Battle & Hastings*, [1879.] 16°. **10347**. b. **7**. (8.)

C., C. M. Etthundradesjutton Bref, 1859–1862. Framställande gudaktighetens hemlighet. Utgifne af C. M. C. [i.e. C. M. Carlander.] pp. 340. *Stockholm*, 1864. 8°. **4410**. d. **16**.

—— Hans Majestät Konung Oscar II.s bibliografi, 1849–1887. Utgifven af C. M. C. [i.e. C. M. Carlander], *etc.* pp. 19. *Stockholm*, 1888. 4°. **11901**. d. **26**. (1.)

C., C. M. How She came into her Kingdom; a romance. [The dedication signed: C. M. C., i.e. Charlotte M. Clark.] pp. 337. *Jansen, McClurg & Co.: Chicago*, 1878. 8°. **12703**. ff. **11**.

C., C. M.

—— John Vassall and his Descendants. By one of them. [The foreword signed: C. M. C., i.e. Charles M. Calder.] pp. 40. *S. Austin & Sons: Hertford*, [1920.] 8°. **9906**. e. **33**.

C., C. M. The Legislation of 1889; or, One year of Conservative & Unionist government. [Signed: C. M. C.] pp. 19. *Conservative Central Office: London*, 1890. 8°. **8138**. e. 5. (**11**.)

C., C. M. Was God the Dominant Factor in securing Victory in the Great War? By a Layman. [The preface signed: C. M. C.] pp. 23. *C. J. Thynne: London*, 1921. 8°. **04375**. de. **34**.

C., C. P. The Case of Arnold v. Arnold, on the construction of Order 16, Article 33, and of Order 66, of the General Orders of May, 1845: decided by the Lord Chancellor, 8th May, 1847. [The preface signed: C. P. C., i.e. Charles P. Cooper.] pp. 19. *V. & R. Stevens & G. S. Norton: London*, 1847. 8°. **6190**. e. **7**.

C., C. P.

—— Record Commission. Remarks upon the "Reply of Francis Palgrave, Esq. to those portions of the statements drawn up by Mr. C. P. Cooper, which relate to the editor of the new edition of the Rolls of Parliament," &c. [The preface signed: C. P. C., i.e. Charles Purton Cooper. The text in fact written by Sir Nicholas H. Nicolas.] pp. 31. *London*, 1832. 8°. **619**. i. **19**. (3.)

—— [Another copy.] **619**. i. **25**. (4.)

—— **A Refutation of so much of the Calumnies against the Lord Chancellor contained in the last number of the Quarterly Review in an article upon the pamphlet [edited by Sir Denis le Marchant] entitled "The Reform Ministry and the Reformed Parliament," as relates to the appointment of Mr. James Brougham to the offices of Clerk of Patents and Registrar of Affidavits. [The preface signed: C. P. C., i.e. Charles P. Cooper.] pp. 22.** *London*, 1833. 8°. T. **2014**. (5.)

C., C. R.

—— Non Nobis, Domine. A sermon preached at Itchen Stoke on the day of thanksgiving for the victory at Tel-el-Kebir. [The dedication signed: C. R. C., i.e. C. R. Conybeare.] pp. 12. *Jacob & Johnson: Winchester*, [1882.] 8°. **4477**. dd. **28**. (5.)

C., C. R. Nuovo canto dei Subalpini e Liguri. [Signed: C. R. C.] pp. 4. [1848?] 8°. **804**. k. **13**. (83.)

C., C. R. Those Things which God prepared for them that love Him. A sermon preached at St. Mary's, Itchen-Stoke, *etc.* [The dedication signed: C. R. C., i.e. Charles R. Conybeare.] pp. 11. *Parker & Co.: Oxford, London*, 1881. 8°. **4478**. e. **92**. (2.)

C., C. S. *See* Liturgies.—*Church of England.—Occasion Offices.—Consecration of Churches.—Lancing.* The For and Order for the Consecration of the Chapel of S. Ma and S. Nicolas, Lancing, *etc.* [With an explanatory no signed: C. S. C., i.e. Cyril S. Cobb.] 1911. 8°. **3408**. f. **16**. (2

C., C. S. The Church in the World, and the Church of t First-born: or, an Affectionate address to Christi ministers upholding Oxford Tract doctrines. [Signe C. S. C.] pp. 84. *R. B. Seeley & W. Burnside: Londo* 1840. 8°. **1114**. b. **3**

C., C. S. Fly Leaves. By C. S. C., author of "Verses a Translations" [i.e. Charles S. Calverley]. pp. iv. 120. *Deighton, Bell & Co.: Cambridge*, 1872. 8°. **11652**. aa. **1**

—— Verses and Translations. By C. S. C. [i.e. Charles Calverley.] pp. vi. 203. *Deighton, Bell & Co Cambridge*, 1862. 8°. **11650**. aaa. **2**

—— Third edition, revised. pp. vi. 201. *Deighton, Bell & Co Cambridge*, 1865. 8°. **11650**. aaa. **2**

—— Fourth edition, revised. pp. viii. 214. *Deighto Bell & Co.: Cambridge*, 1871. 8°. **11652**. aa. **1**

—— Sixth edition. pp. viii. 214. *Deighton, Bell & Co Cambridge*, 1877. 8°. **11646**. eee. **5**

C., (C. Saint C.) Scraps on the Great Scrap of 14–15. chronicle of facts, falsehoods and fantasies inspired the world's gigantic Hun hunt . . . [Collected b C. St. C. C. [i.e. C. St. C. Cameron.] pp. 61. *Calcutt* [1915.] 8°. **011604**. ff.

C. (Cælius S.)

—— *See* Dion Cassius. Agrippae ad Octauium Caes. Aug tum oratio, contra Monarchiam, ex Dione Lib. lii Cæ S. C. [i.e. C. S. Curio] interprete. (Mecoenatis Oratio Monarchia, Ad Cæs. Augustum, ex Dionis Lib. lii. Cæ S. C. interprete.) 1589. 8°. [*Nicolai Machiavelli Pr ceps Ex Sylvestri Telii . . . traductione diligenter em data, etc.*] **521**. c.

C. (Ch.) A Sad Memoriall of Henry Curwen Esquire, t most worthy and onely child of Sr Patricius Curwen . who . . . departed this life August: 21. being Sunda 1636. in the fourteenth yeare of his age, *etc.* [T dedication signed: Ch. C., i.e. Charles Croke.] pp. 32. *Printed by W. Turner: Oxford*, 1638. 4°. **113**. f.

C. * * * * (Ch. Ed.) *See* Sachy (E. de) Essais sur l'histo de Péronne. [The editor's preface signed: Ch. E C****.] 1866. 8°. **10171**. g. **2**

C * * * * (Ch. Ed.)

—— *See* Secrets. Ce sont les secres des dames . . . A . . . une introduction, des notes et un appendice par D^rs Al. C***** [i.e. A. Colson] & Ch.-Ed. C** [i.e. E. Chojecki]. 1880. 8°. **7581**. df.

C. (Ch. O.) *See* Laudynowa (S.) A World Problem, (pt. 2. Translated by C. Sypniewski and Ch. O. C.) 1920. 8°. **4515**. df.

C. (Ch. P. D. D.) Corinne ressuscitée. Continuation roman de Madame la baronne de Staël Holstein intit Corinne, ou l'Italie. [Edited by E. Veroni; the edito preface containing part of a letter from the author, signe Ch. P. D. D. C.] pp. xv. 279. *Chez l'Éditeur: Londr* 1815. 12°. **837**. b.

The half-title reads: "M. Anastase, ou Corir ressuscitée."

(Charles) *See* Baudelaire (C. P.) [*Two or more Works.*] Charles Baudelaire. Souvenirs, *etc.* (Biographie. [Signed: Ch. C., i.e. C. Cousin.]) 1872. 8°. **10663.** bbb. **4.**

. . . . . (Charles) *de la Société des Amis des Livres.* Voyage dans un grenier. Par Charles C . . . . . [i.e. C. Cousin]. (Bouquins, faïences, autographes & bibelots.) [With plates.] pp. 270. *Paris,* 1878. 8°. **12350.** l. **6.**
With an additional titlepage.

, D. *See* Boive (A.) La Saincte chronologie, *etc.* (Seconde partie. Dans laquelle sont contenuës diuerses matieres curieuses concernantes le Christ manifesté en chair. Auec la vie de ses euangelistes & apostres. Par D. C.) 1661. 8°. **4807.** aaaa. **1.**

, D. *See* C., P. and C., D. A Proposal for Regulating Cars and Carts, &c. [Signed: P. C. and D. C.] [1694 ?] fol. **816.** m. **7.** **(130.)**

— —— [1694 ?] fol. **816.** m. **7.** **(131.)**

, D. *See* Charles I., *King of Great Britain and Ireland,* [*Eikon Basilike.*] *Εἰκων βασιλικη.* Ou portrait roial, *etc.* [The translator's dedicatory letter prefixed to the second part signed: D. C., i.e. D. Cailloué.] 1649. 12°. **E. 1255.**

, D. *See* Dass (Vikmali) Songs of a Sudra: being translations . . . By D. C. 1920. 8°. **11648.** df. **67.**

* * *, D. *See* Fouquet (C. L. A.) *Count de Belle-Isle.* Le Codicille, et l'esprit, ou Commentaire des maximes politiques de M. le maréchal duc de Bell' Isle . . . le tout publié par [or rather, written by] Monsieur D. C * * * [i.e. F. A. de Chevrier], *etc.* 1762. 8°. **8006.** aa. **44.** **(1.)**

, D. *See* Grebner (P.) Prédiction, où se voit comme le Roy Charles II . . . doit estre remis aux royaumes d'Angleterre, Escosse & Irlande, *etc.* [The editor's dedication signed: D. C., i.e. D. Cailloué.] 1650. 16°. **600.** a. **25.**

, D. *See* Mackey (Albert G.) A Lexicon of Freemasonry, *etc.* [The editor's preface signed: D. C.] [1884.] 8°. **4782.** c. **4.**

* * *, D *. *See* Periodical Publications.—London.—*The Freeholder.* Le Freeholder, *etc.* [The translator's dedication signed: D * C * * *.] 1727. 12°. **1389.** c. **6.**

, D. *See* Playfere (Thomas) Ten Sermons, *etc.* [The dedication signed: D. C.] 1610. 8°. **4452.** aa. **8.**

, D. *See* Pray (G.) George Pray, Steph. Katona, et Danielis Cornides, epistolae exegeticae in dispunctionem A. Ganoczy, cum appendicula ad L. K. [Signed: D. C., i.e. D. Cornides.] 1784. 8°. **9315.** bbb. **29.**

, D. *See* Tassoni (A.) *Count.* [*La Secchia rapita.*] Le Seau enlevé, *etc.* [The translator's dedication signed: D. C., i.e. —— de Cedors.] 1759, *etc.* 12°. **1063.** b. **30.**

, D. *See* Wordsworth (W.) *Poet Laureate.* The Wanderer, *etc.* [The introduction signed: D. C., i.e. Derwent Coleridge.] 1863. 8°. **11642.** aa. **13.**

, D. The Account Audited and Discounted; or, a Vindication of the Diatribe against Doctor Hammonds Paradiatribees. By D. C. [i.e. Daniel Cawdry.] pp. 438. *Ralph Wood for M. Wright: London,* 1658. 8°. **E. 1850.**

, D. Auuertimento importantissimo d'vn gentil'huomo Francese in forma di risposta alle dimande d'vn Caualier Curioso, sopra il giusto soggetto della guerra d'Italia. Con la giustificazione di Monseigneur il Contestabile [*sic*]. Tradotto dal Francese in Italiano. [Signed: D. C.] pp. 20. 1626. 4°. **9166.** cc. **15.**

C. D. A Dictionary of Music Terms, *etc.* [The preface signed: D. C., i.e. Douglas Clayton.] pp. 50. *Douglas Clayton: Croydon,* [1932.] 16°. **7898.** e. **60.**

C., D. An Essay towards the Deciding of the so much, and so long controverted case of Usury . . . As also, some animaduersions upon the resolution of the case of usury, by a Reverend, and very learned doctor (D. H.). By D. C. pp. 18. *For John Rothwell: London,* 1661. 4°. **8226.** a. **5.**

C., D. Fencing. [On dissimulation.] By D. C. pp. 45. *W. & H. S. Warr:* [*London,*] 1862. 16°. **8407.** aa. **45.**

C., D. La Honte de Babilon, comprise en deux parties. Par D. C. ff. 103. *Seden,* 1612. 8°. **3900.** b. **38.**
The imprint is probably fictitious.

C., D. Injunctions illustrated by Scripture and enforced by the Writings of Eminent Divines: compiled by a Governor of the Foundling Hospital, for the benefit . . . of young persons who have been brought up there, *etc.* pp. iv. 126. *H. S. Warr: London,* 1877 [1876]. 8°. **8410.** bbb. **22.**

C., D. Leading Articles on the Licensing Question and the sale of liquors on Sunday, contributed to the Licensed Victuallers' Guardian 1867–1868. By "D. C." pp. 76. *James Wyld:* [*London,* 1868.] 8°. **8435.** cc. **13.**

—— Leaves on Licensing. [By] "D. C." pp. 88. *James Wyld:* [*London,* 1869.] 8°. **8435.** cc. **14.**

C., D. A Letter from a Citizen to J - - - B - - -, Esq; Member of Parliament, relating to the York Buildings Company's affairs. [Signed: D. C.] pp. 4. [1725 ?] fol. (S.P.R.) **357.** b. **7.** **(48.)**

C., D. The Matter of Manner. By D C. pp. 110. *H. S. Pratt: Sudbury,* 1863. 8°. **8408.** bb. **20.**

C., D. Melo-drama en un acto, que en celebridad de la victoria conseguida por las armas españolas en la Andalucía se representó en el teatro de esta M. N. Y. L. ciudad de Cadiz, *etc.* [The dedication signed: D. C.] pp. 19. *Málaga,* [1808 ?] 4°. **8042.** bb. **6.** **(27.)**

C., D. Métamorphose des Isles Fortunées. A la reyne douairière de la Grande Bretagne. Ode. [With other poems. The dedicatory letter signed: D. C., i.e. D. Cailloué.] pp. 56. *See* Charles I., *King of Great Britain and Ireland.* [*Eikon Basilike.*] *Εἰκων βασιλικη.* Ou portrait roial, *etc.* 1649. 12°. **E. 1255.**

C., D. Notizie e osservazioni su di un antica epigrafe greca trovata in Selinunte di Sicilia e sulle illustrazioni fattene sinora. [Signed: D. C.] pp. 29. *Livorno,* 1872. 8°. **7709.** bb. **21.**

C., D. Poems: by D. C. pp. 96. *Printed for private circulation:* [*London,*] 1854. 8°. **11646.** eee. **11.**

—— [Another issue.] *Printed for private circulation:* [*London,*] 1855. 8°. **11646.** ee. **35.**

C., D. Politike discoursen handelende in ses onderscheide boeken van steeden, landen, oorlogen, kerken, regeeringen en zeeden. Beschreven door D. C. [i.e. J. de la Court.] 2 vol. *I. Ciprianus: Amsterdam,* 1662. 8°. **231.** b. **36.**
The titlepage is engraved.

C., D. The Reign of Fancy, a poem. With notes. Lyric tales, *etc.* [The author's preface signed: D. C., i.e. David Carey.] pp. 179. *Vernor & Hood: London,* 1804. 8°. **11641.** bbb. **5.**

C., D. Relation de ce qui s'est passé en Catalogne. (Suite de la relation, *etc.*) [The dedicatory letter signed: D. C., i.e. — de Caissel.] 2 pt. *G. Quinet: Paris*, 1678, 79. 12°. **9078. aaa. 15.**

—— [A reissue of pt. 1.] *Paris*, 1679. 12°. **1196. a. 20.**

C., D. Simo, comœdia. [In verse. The dedication signed: D. C.] pp. 55. *Londini*, 1702. 4°. **78. d. 4.**

C., D. Superstitio superstes: or, the Reliques of Superstition newly revived. Manifested in a discourse concerning the holinesse of Churches, and bowing towards the Altar. Whereunto is added a censure of two letters, touching the same subject, by D. C. pp. 60. *A. N. for I. M.: London*, 1641. 4°. **117. f. 11.**

—— [Another issue.] pp. 60. *Printed for P. W.: London*, 1641. 4°. **E. 178. (5.)**
With an additional titlepage, bearing the imprint "Printed by A. N. for I. M."

C., D.

—— Воззваніе къ миру. Примиреніе враждующихъ и соединеніе противоположностей и раздвоеній. Сочиненіе D. C. [i.e. of D. Chernushenko]. pp. 22. [1889.] 8°. *See* CHERNUSHENKO (D. N.) **8425. c. 70. (7.)**

C., D., *Dottore.* *See* MATTEI (C.) *Count.* La Scienza nuova del conte Cesare Mattei e la scienza vecchia del dottore C. (del dottore D. C. Medico.) [A reply by Count C. Mattei to Dr. D. C.'s criticism of his "Elettromiopatia."] 1880. 12°. **14537. b. 9. (1.)**

C * * *, D., *M.* Mémoires sur l'agriculture du Boulonnois et des cantons maritimes voisins. Par M. D. C * * * [i.e. Baron G. L. M. Dumont de Courset]. pp. iii. 260. *Boulogne*, 1784. 8°. **452. d. 13.**

C . . . ., D . . . ., *M.* Révolutions de Paris, ou Récit exact de ce qui s'est passé dans la capitale, & particulièrement de la prise de la Bastille, depuis le 11 juillet 1789 jusqu'au 23 du même mois. Par M. D. . . . C . . . . [i.e. — de Courtive], *etc.* [*Paris*,] 1789. 8°. **F. 56**. (10.)**

—— [Another copy.] Révolutions de Paris, *etc.* [*Paris*,] 1789. 8°. **R. 62. (2.)**

C * * *, D., *Monsieur.* Histoire de Stanislas I. Roi de Pologne . . . Par Monsieur D. C * * * [i.e. J. G. de Chevrières or P. de Cantillon ?]. 2 tom. *Francfort*, 1740. 8°. **10795. a. 25.**

—— The History of Stanislaus I . . . To which is added, A Relation of his Retreat from Dantzick . . . written by himself. Translated from the French ["Histoire de Stanislas I . . . Par Monsieur D. C * * *," i.e. J. G. de Chevrières or P. de Cantillon ?]. pp. 248. 1741. 12°. *See* STANISLAUS I. [Lezczyński], *King of Poland.* **1436. b. 44.**

—— *See* CZARNOWSKI (J. N.) Stanisław Leszczyński i Polska w pierwszej połowie XVIII wieku, *etc.* [A plagiarism of the work entitled "Histoire de Stanislas I., roi de Pologne . . . Par Monsieur C.*** D."] 1858. 8°. **9455. c. 21.**

C., D., *le S.* *See* SAVARY DE BRÈVES (F.) Relation des voyages de Monsieur de Breues . . . Ensemble un traicté faict l'an 1604. entre le Roy Henri le Grand, & l'Empereur des Turcs. Et trois discours dudit Sieur. Le tout recueilly par le S. D. C. [i.e. le Sieur du Castel.] 1628. 4°. **567. f. 22.**

C., D., *le S.* Voiage de Levant fait par le commandement du Roy en l'année 1621. Par le Sr. D. C. [i.e. L. Deshayes, Baron de Courmenin.] [With maps.] pp. 404. *A. Taupinart: Paris*, 1624. 4°. **790. i. 22. (2.)**
The titlepage is engraved.

—— Seconde édition. pp. 495. *A. Taupinart: Paris*, 1629. 4°. **981. d. 9.**

C., D. A. Spirit, Fire & Dew. Poems written in South Afric By D. A. C. pp. 48. *Basil Blackwell: Oxford*, 1938. 8° **11655. ff. 7**

C., D. A. DE. Diccionario del Dialecto Gitano. Orígen costumbres de los Gitanos . . . Por D. A. de C. pp. 239. *Barcelona*, 1851. 16°. **12907. a. 3**

C., D. A. Y. *See* A. y C., D.

C., D. A. H. Y. *See* H. y C.

C., D. A. P. C., *Insulana.* *See* JACOB (P. L.) *Bibliophi pseud.* Serões de Walter Scott . . . (A Barba.) Traduzi por D. A. P. C. C., Insulana. 1851. 8°. **012330. e. 66. (**

C., D. A. V. *See* ACOSTA (J. de) *Jesuit.* Historia Natural Moral de las Indias . . . Dala á luz . . . D. A. V. C. 1792. 4°. **9551. f.**

C., D. A. V. *See* PÉREZ DE OLIVA (F.) Las Obras d Maestro F. Perez de Oliva . . . Dalas á luz . . . D. A. V. [i.e. Don A. Valero Chicarro ?] 1787. 8°. **12230. a. 2**

C., D. A. V. *See* THOMAS [More] *Saint, Lord High Chancell of England.* La Utopia de Tomás Moro . . . Dala à l . . . D. A. V. C. 1790. 8°. **8005. c. 2**

C., D. C., *le Sieur.* *See* BOCCACCIO (G.) [*Teseide.—Frenc* La Theseyde . . . Traduicte . . . en François, par le sie D. C. C. 1597. 12°. **245. c. 3**

C., D. D. J. D. S. Na simultanea publicacam, e acto d felicissimos desposorios da . . . Dona Maria, Princeza d Brazis . . . com . . . Dom Pedro, Infante de Portug *etc.* [A sonnet, signed: D. D. J. d. S. C.] [*Lisb* 1760.] *s. sh.* fol. **9181. e. 4. (4**

C., D. F. A. R. DE, *el D.* Al Señor General Don F. M. Call y á los valientes vencedores de Quautla. Cancion P. D. D. F. A. R. de C. [*Mexico*,] 1812. 4°. **11451. bbb. 45. (1**

—— [Another copy.] **11451. bbb. 45. (1**

C., D. F. C. P. *See* BIBLE. [*Latin.*] Sacra Biblia, vulg editionis . . . Ope & opera D. F. C. P. C. [i.e. F. Chemina 1664. 12°. **1408. d. 12,**

C., D. F. E. *See* AYOS. Los Dos Ayos. Comedia . Traducida P. D. F. E. C. [i.e. Don F. E. Castrillón], 1808. 4°. **1342. e. 6.**

—— *See* SORDO. El Sordo en la Posada. Drama en actos en verso. Traducido del Frances . . . Por D. F C. [i.e. D. F. E. Castrillon.] 1808. 4°. **1342. e. 6.**

C., D. F. M. E. Y. *See* E. Y C., D. F .M.

C., D. F. M. S. C. A. F. I. R. Elogio istorico dell'insi letterato Girolamo Gigli. [Signed: D. F. M. S. C. A. F R. C.] pp. xliv. *See* GIGLI (G.) Collezione comp delle opere . . . di Girolamo Gigli, *etc.* vol. 1. 1797. **630. d**

C., D. F. P. P. Francilia, pastora do Tejo. Poezias D. F. P. P. C. [i.e. Dona F. de P. Possollo da Cos pp. 248. *Lisboa*, 1816. 8°. **11452. bb.**

—— Henriqueta de Orleans, ou o Heroismo. Nouella . por D. S. [or rather F.] P. P. C. [i.e. Dona F. de P. Poss da Costa.] Segunda ediçao. 2 tom. *Lisboa*, 1829. 8 **12491. aaa**

C., D. F. P. Y. *See* P. Y C., D. F.

C., D. G. Observations on the Readjustment of Taxati and the substitution of a more simple mode of collect a revenue than at present pursued, *etc.* [Signed: D. G. pp. 12. *James Ridgway: London*, 1845. 8°. **1391. e. 38.**

D. H. B. Premier Volume du Recueil, contenant les choses mémorables aduenues soubs la Ligue, qui s'est faicte & esleuée contre la Religion Reformée, pour l'abolir. (Le Second Recueil, *etc.*) [The preface to the "Second recueil" signed: D. H. B. C., i.e. S. Goulart.] 2 pt. [*La Rochelle ?*] 1587,89. 8°. **1193.** c. **30, 31.**
The "Premier volume du recueil" includes "Lettre d'un Gentilhomme Catholique François, contenant breue Responce aux calomnies d'vn certain pretendu Anglois" and "Fidelle Exposition sur la Declaration du Duc de Mayenne, contenant les Exploicts de guerre qu'il a fait en Guyenne," dated 1586 *and* 1587 *respectively.*

— [Another edition of the "Second Recueil."] pp. 869. [*La Rochelle ?*] 1590. 8°. **1059.** b. **10.**

D. I. A., *Abogado*, and **H. Y M.,** D. M., *Abogado.* Ley para el Gobierno de las Provincias, comentada, concordada y anotada . . . por D. I. A. C. y D. M. H. y M. Abogados, *etc.* pp. 250. *Madrid*, 1864. 16°. **5383.** a. **8.**

, D. J.

— *See* JULIETA. Julieta y Romeo . . . Traducido por D. J. C. 1828. 8°. **11729.** a. **10.**

, D. J. *See* TANCRED, *the Crusader.* El Tancredo . . . Traducido por D. J. C. 1837. 8°. **11728.** de. **3.** (**1.**)

, D. J. Catecismo Político arreglado á la Constitucion de la Monarquía Española; para ilustracion del pueblo . . . y uso de las escuelas de primeras letras. Por D. J. C. pp. 103. *Palma*, 1812. 8°. **8042.** a. **4.** (**2.**)
With an additional titlepage, engraved.

— [Another edition.] pp. 94. *Méjico*, 1820. 16°. **8009.** a. **41.**

, D. J. Historical Sketch of St. Mary's, Holly Place, Hampstead, London, N.W. [The preface signed: D. J. C.] pp. 53. *J. Hewetson & Son: London*, 1916. 8°. **20020.** e. **44.**

, D. J. A., *Cura de Montuenga.* Censura Crítica de la pretendida Excelencia y Antigüedad del Vascuence, por D. J. A. C., Cura de Montuenga [i.e. J. A. Conde. An attack on P. P. de Astarloa y Aguirre's "Apología de la Lengua bascongada"]. pp. 85. *Madrid*, 1804. 12°. **12907.** aaa. **16.**

— Reflexiones Filosóficas en defensa de la Apología de la Lengua Bascongada [by P. P. de Astarloa y Aguirre]: ó respuesta á la Censura Crítica del Cura de Montuenga (D. J. A. C. [i.e. J. A. Conde]). pp. 119. *Madrid*, 1804. 8°. **12906.** a. **28.**

— Censura Crítica del Alfabeto Primitivo de España, y pretendidos monumentos literarios del Vascuence. Por D. J. A. C., Cura de Montuenga [i.e. J. A. Conde. An attack on a work by J. B. de Erro y Azpiroz, entitled "Alfabeto de la lengua primitiva de España"]. pp. 70. *Madrid*, 1806. 8°. **829.** c. **20.**

— Critique de l'Alphabet primitif de l'Espagne et des prétendus monumens de la langue basque; par D. J. A. C., curé de Montuenga [i.e. J. A. Conde]. Traduite par extrait . . . par M. Eloi Johanneau. *See* ERRO Y AZPIROZ (J. B. de) Alphabet de la langue primitive de l'Espagne, *etc.* [1808.] 8°. **1331.** g. **25.**

— *See* ERRO Y AZPIROZ (J. B. de) Observaciones Filosóficas en favor del Alfabeto primitivo, ó respuesta . . . á la Censura critica del Cura de Montuenga (D. J. A. C. [i.e. J. A. Conde]). 1807. 4°. **628.** i. **28.**

, D. J. A., *el Lic.* El Tirano de la Europa Napoleon I°. Manifiesto que a todos los pueblos del mundo, y principalmente a los Españoles presenta el Lic. D. J. A. C. pp. 47. *Madrid*, 1808. 16°. **1389.** a. **24.**

— [Another edition.] pp. 24. *Valencia*, 1808. 4°. **9180.** c. **10.** (**53.**)

C., D. J. D. Crisol de Fidelidad. Manifestation, que haze el Principado de Cathaluña de las Causas de alta congruencia, que le han obligado à tomar las armas para defender su libertad . . . Escriviolo D. J. D. C. pp. 64. *Barcelona*, 1713. 4°. **1197.** g. **7.**

C., D. J. DE S. Convite cortesano de la fama a los fieles y nobles Españoles, para ver coronar a los que aclama la España antigua y nueva sus dos soles . . . que traslada . . . D. J. de S. C. [On the coronation of Charles IV.] pp. 47. [*Madrid*,] 1789. 8°. **830.** a. **35.** (**6.**)

— Gracias pedidas y negadas con gracia à unos forasteros que solicitaban posada en Madrid para ver los reales festejos. Recocidas por D. J. de S. C. pp. 16. [*Madrid*, 1789 ?] 8°. **830.** a. **35.** (**5.**)

C., D. J. F. P. Carta crítica al autor de las notas de Don Quixote [J. A. Pellicer], en la que se descubre el verdadero autor de su famosa historia, á quien Cervántes da el nombre de Cide Hamete Ben-engeli. Por D. J. F. P. C. pp. 12. *Madrid*, [1800.] 8°. Cerv. **507.** (**2.**)

— *See* PELLICER (J. A.) Carta en castellano con posdata poliglota: en la qual Don J. A. Pellicer y Don J. A. Conde . . . responden á la carta critica que un anonimo [D. J. F. P. C.] dirigió al autor de las Notas del Don Quixote, desaprobando algunas de ellas. 1800. 8°. Cerv. **507.** (**3.**)

C., D. J. H. Y. *See* H. Y C., D. J.

C., D. J. J. R. Escena unipersonal. Don Liquido, ó el Currataco vistiendose. Por D. J. J. R. C. [In verse.] pp. 7. *Valencia*, 1813. 4°. **1342.** e. **6.** (**4.**)

C., D. J. M. R. DEL, *Capitan.* Manifiesto político que á todos los verdaderos Españoles, fieles . . . vasallos de . . . Fernando Séptimo presenta el Capitan D. J. M. R. del C., natural y vecino de la villa de Marchena. pp. 16. *Sevilla*, 1808. 4°. **8042.** bb. **6.** (**1.**)

C., D. J. M. V. Jubilo de Xalapa y su Exército acantonado en los dias 27 y 28 de Junio de 1808. Poema de D. J. M. V. C. pp. 16. *México*, [1808 ?] 4°. **11451.** bbb. **6.** (**32.**)

C., D. L. Historia Cientifica, Politica, y Ministerial del Excmo. Señor D. Lorenzo Arrazola. Escrita por D. L. C. [With a portrait.] 2 pt. *Madrid*, 1850. 8°. **10632.** d. **15.**

C., D. L., *le Citoyen.* Idée sommaire d'un grand travail. 1° Sur la nécessité . . . de l'instruction; 2° Sur tous les genres de difficultés qui s'opposent à ses progrès; 3° Sur l'applanissement de ces mêmes difficultés; au moyen d'une collection complète . . . de toutes les connoissances humaines . . . Par le Citoyen D. L. C. pp. 40. *Paris*, an VIII [1799/1800]. 8°. **F. 497.** (**14.**)

C., D. L., *le Sieur.* Le Language müet, ou l'Art de faire l'amour sans parler, sans écrire & sans se voir. Par le Sieur D. L. C. [Based on "Histoire de Youssuf-Bey et de Gul-Beyaz" in Du Vignau's "Le Secrétaire turc."] pp. 44. *G. Horthemels: Middelbourg*, 1688. 12°. **1043.** b. **13.** (**1.**)

— [A reissue.] pp. 44. *P. Mortier: Amsterdam*, [1690 ?] 8°. **012356.** de. **32.**

C., D. L. B. D. Les Francs fripons dans le Libraire banqueroutier et le Mercure au gibet. [A satire. Signed: D. L. B. D. C.] pp. 33. *L. le Sincère: Cologne*, 1684. 12°. **1081.** g. **20.** (**2.**)

C., D. L. F. Opera seria en un acto. El Tirano de Ormuz, por D. L. F. C. [i.e. L. F. Comella ?], *etc.* [In verse.] pp. 12. *Valencia*, 1813. 4°. **1342.** e. **6.** (**5.**)

C., D. L. G., le S.

—— Histoire ionique des vertueuses et fidèles amours de Poliphile Pyrenoise & de Damis Clazomenien. De l'inuention du S. D. L. G. C. ff. 398. *A. L'Angelier: Paris*, 1602. 12°. **12511. aaaa. 36.**

C., D. L. G. D., *le Sieur, Avocat en Parlement.* La Conduite des François justifiée, ou Observations sur un écrit anglois intitulé: Conduite des François à l'égard de la Nouvelle-Écosse . . . Par le Sieur D. L. G. D. C. Avocat en Parlement [i.e. G. A. F. S. de La Grange de Chessieux. A reply to "The Conduct of the French in regard to Nova Scotia" by Thomas Jeffereys]. pp. viii. 256. *Utrecht*, 1756. 12°. **8154. a. 4.**

C., D. M. *See* CHILI. Revolución del reino del Chile . . . Traducida . . . por D. M. C. 1822. 4°. **9770. bb. 13. (30.)**

—— *See* MEXICO. [*Appendix.*] Resumen Histórico de la Insurreccion de Nueva España . . . Traducido . . . por D. M. C. 1821. 4°. **9770. bb. 9. (18.)**

—— *See* NAPOLEON I., *Emperor of the French.* [*Notes, Extracts, etc.*] Máximas y pensamientos del prisionero de Santa Elena . . . Traduccion . . . al Castellano por D. M. C. 1821. 8°. **8406. a. 30.**

C., D. M. De la liberté et de la restriction dans les échanges entre les peuples, et des traités de commerce; par D. M. C. pp. 54. *Paris*, 1845. 8°. **935. i. 39. (1.)**

C., D. M.

—— Dorothy's Poems. By her Mama. [The introduction signed: D. M. C.] pp. vii. 56. *R. Clay, Sons, & Taylor: London*, 1870. 16°. **11659. df. 23.**
Privately printed.

C., D. M. Tonadilla, la Huérfana . . . por D. M. C., *etc.* pp. 8. *Barcelona*, 1858. 4°. **11726. g. 5. (37.)**
Printed on yellow paper.

C., D. M. A. DE. *See* DORAT (C. J.) [Lettre du Comte de Comminges.] Carta del Conde de Cominges á su Madre . . . traducida . . . por D. M. A. de C. 1803. 8°. **11450. a. 10. (1.)**

C., D. M. I. Breues reflexiones, acerca de los decretos de nombramiento de una Comision Regia, para informar sobre el estado de la administracion de las Islas de Cuba y Puerto-Rico, por D. M. I. C. pp. 16. *Madrid*, 1839. 8°. **8155. bb. 36. (7.)**

C., D. N. F. *See* HYPATIA. Hipatia . . . Novela historica . . . Traducida . . . por D. N. F. C. 1857. 8°. **12622. a. 1.**

C., D. N. N., *la Marquise. See* EPHEMERIDES. Almanach nocturne à l'usage du Grand Monde . . . Par Madame la Marquise D. N. N. C. 1740. 12°. **12315. aa. 32.**

C., D. N. Q. S. *See* TAMBURINI (P.) Verdadera Idea de la Santa Sede . . . Traducida por D. N. Q. S. C., *etc.* 1826. 8°. **4051. cc. 36.**

C., D. P. *See* ALADDIN. Historia de Aladin . . . traducida del francés por D. P. C., *etc.* 1847. 4°. **12330. h. 23. (10.)**

C., D. P. Crinoliniad, an epic poem, published in cantos; by D. P. C. [i.e. Daniel P. Carter.] pp. 24. *E. Tipper: West Maitland*, 1867. 8°. **11688. d. 32. (8.)**
Containing Canto II. only.

C., D. P. L. Le Tombeau de Monsieur Servin. [A panegyric. Signed: D. P. L. C.] pp. 15. *I. Bessin: Paris*, 1626. 8°. **10661. aaa. 5. (6.)**

—— [Another copy.] **1193. h. 15. (1.)**

C., D. R. *See* KINNIBURGH (R.) Eachdraidh na ainmidhean ainmicht' anns na Sgriobtuiribh, *etc.* [The preface signed: D. R. C., i.e. D. R. Collie.] 1838. 24°. **3127. aa. 2**

C., D. R.

—— Chums, or an Experiment in Economics. By D. R. C. Edited and published by Gertrude Ogden Tubby. pp. 31 *New York*, [1908.] 8°. **04422. bb. 3**

C., D. R. Essai de pensées morales sur les qualités d'une femme mariée. [The dedication signed: D. R. C.] pp. 32. *Helmstedt*, 1751. 8°. **T. 910. (3**

C., D. R. Tesoro de la Cria de Gallinas, Palomas y Pavos. De su alimento y propagacion, modo de formar y poblar los gallineros y palomares . . . Por D. R. C. pp. 144. *Madrid*, 1858. 8°. **7294. c. 1**

C., D. S. P. El Libro de las Carreras. Guia del estudiante de los padres de familia para 1868. Reseña de todas las carreras que hay en España . . . Recopilada y arreglada por D. S. P. C. pp. 208. *Barcelona*, 1868. 8°. **8409. aaa.**

C., D. S. P. P. Henriqueta de Orleans . . . Novella . . . por D. S. [or rather F.] P. P. C., *etc.* 1829. 8°. *See* C., D. F. P. P. **12491. aaa.**

C., D. Y. Howetoon.—Records of a Scottish village. By a Residenter. [The preface signed: D. Y. C., i.e. Ala Reid.] pp. 193. *J. & R. Parlane: Paisley*, [1892.] 8°. **012330. f.**

C., E. *See* ALVAREZ GATO (J.) Cancionero inédito de Juan Alvarez Gato, *etc.* [The editor's introduction signed: E. C., i.e. E. Cotarelo y Mori.] 1901. 8°. **11451. b.**

C., E. *See* AUBERT DE VERTOT D'AUBEUF (R.) The History of the Revolution of Portugal . . . Translated into English, *etc.* [The dedication signed: E. C.] 1758. 8°. **1445. b. 1**

C., E. *See* BÉDÉ DE LA GORMANDIÈRE (J.) The Mass displayed, *etc.* [The preface signed: E. C., i.e. Edward Chaloner ?] 1619. 4°. **3932. dd. 2**

C., E. *See* BIBLE.—*Psalms.* [*English.—Miscellaneous Metrical Versions.*] A New Metrical Version of the Psalms . . By C. F. and E. C. [i.e. C. Foster and Elizabeth Colling] 1838. 12°. **692. d.**

C., E. *See* BIBLE.—*Psalms.—Selections.* [*English.—Sing Psalms.*] The Bridegroom-King. A meditation on Psalm XLV., *etc.* [The editor's preface signed: E. C.] [1875.] 12°. **3090. aa. 4**

C., E. *See* BIBLE.—*Gospels.* [*Suto.*] Livangeli tsa Yesu Kereste . . . Traduits par E. C. et S. R. [i.e. Eugene Casalis and Samuel Rolland.] 1839. 8°. **1110. g. 2**

C., E. *See* C., C. and C., E. The Sphynx . . . By C. C. and E. C. 1867. 8°. **12304. bb. 3**

C., E. *See* C., C. and C., E. A Key to the Sphynx . . By C. C. and E. C. 1867. 16°. **12316. aaa. 4**

C., E. *See* C., R. H. Selections in Prose and Verse from the papers of R. H. C. [The editor's preface signed: E. C. i.e. Edward Cheney.] 1871. 4°. **12352. dd.**
[i.e. R. H. Cheney.]

C., E. *See* CAVALCANTI (G.) Rime. Con introduzione e appendice bibliografica di E. C. [i.e. E. Cecchi.] 1910. 8 **11436. h. 2**

C., E. *See* CERVANTES SAAVEDRA (M. de) [*Poems.—Spanish.*] Epístola á Mateo Vázquez dirigida en 157 desde Argel . . . Con introducción y algunas notas [by E. C., i.e. E. Cotarelo y Mori]. 1905. 8°. **011451. f. 4**

E. *See* CHEVALIER (M.) L'Industrie et l'octroi de Paris, *etc.* [With an introduction signed: E. C.] 1867. 8°. **8246.** ff. **28.**

E. *See* COLERIDGE (Sara) *the Younger.* Memoir and Letters of Sara Coleridge. Edited by her daughter. [The editor's preface signed: E. C., i.e. Edith Coleridge.] 1873. 8°. **10921.** e. **12.**

—— —— 1873. 8°. **10856.** bbb. **8.**

—— —— 1873. 8°. **10856.** bbb. **9.**

—— —— 1874. 8°. **10856.** bb. **6.**

E. *See* CROOKE (Samuel) *Divine.* The Guide vnto True Blessednesse, *etc.* [With "an admonitorie preface" signed: E. C.] 1614. 8°. **699.** b. **37.** (**1.**)

—— *See* CROOKE (Samuel) *Divine.* The Guide vnto True Blessednesse, *etc.* [With an "Admonitory Preface" signed: E. C.] 1632. 8°. **1481.** bb. **11.** (**1.**)

—— —— 1640. 8°. **4406.** aaa. **16.** (**1.**)

E. *See* EURE-ET-LOIR. *Department of.* Eure et Loir. Invasion prussienne 1870-71. Rapports des Maires, *etc.* [The introduction signed: E. C.] 1872. 8°. **9078.** ccc. **4.**

E. *See* FELLENS (J. B.) Vita privata e politica di Luigi Napoleone . . . Compendiata sull'originale francese da E. C., *etc.* 1853. 8°. **10658.** g. **14.**

E. *See* FULLER (Francis) *M.A., the Younger.* Medicina Gymnastica, *etc.* [The dedication signed: E. C.] 1777. 8°. **41.** d. **24.**

E. *See* JACKSON (Henry K.) Experiments in making Ensilage during the wet season of 1888. [The editor's preface signed: E. C., i.e. Ernest Clarke.] 1889. 8°. **7073.** de. **13.** (**7.**)

E. *See* JULYOT (F.) Les Elegies de la belle fille lamentant sa virginité perdue. Réimpression complète, publiée d'après l'édition originale de 1557, *etc.* [The editor's preface signed: E. C.] 1873. 8°. **11474.** bbb. **2.**

E.

—— *See* LA FONTAINE (J. de) [*Doubtful or Supposititious Works.*] **Fable inédite de La Fontaine, découverte, annotée et publiée par un bibliophile de province. [The editor's preface signed: E. C., i.e. E. J. Castaigne.]** 1862. 8°. **12304.** h. **12.** (**6.**)

E. *See* LEDRU-ROLLIN (A. A.) The Decline of England. [The preface signed: E. C.] 1850. 8°. **8007.** c. **21.**

E. *See* LONGUS. Les Amours pastorales de Daphnis et de Chloé, *etc.* [The "Discours préliminaire" signed: E. C.] 1803. 12°. C. **41.** d. **16.**

. . . ., E. *See* LUC ( ) *le Sieur, pseud.* Une Commission de censure . . . Seconde édition, publiée, revue et augmentée, par E. C. . . . [i.e. E. Cavé] et G. F. D. 1827. 8°. **11738.** bbb. **34.** (**7.**)

E.

—— *See* NIGHTINGALE (Florence) Note sull'assistenza ai malati . . . Tradotte e abbreviate da E. C. [i.e. E. Comparetti.] 1887. 8°. **7689.** a. **8.**

E. *See* PAPISTS. A Dialogue agaynst the Tyrannye of the Papistes. Translated . . . by E. C. 1562. 8°. **3932.** aa. **11.**

E. *See* PERIODICAL PUBLICATIONS.—*London.* The Downside Review. (An Index to the Writers & Principal Contents of the Downside Review. Volumes I–XXV. 1880–1906. Compiled by E. C.) 1880, *etc.* 8°. P.P. **6123.**

C., E. *See* PETRARCA (F.) [*Selections.*] Sentenze, massime e proverbj estratti dalle rime di Messer F. Petrarca, con annotazioni da E. C. [i.e. E. Cestari.] 1838. 8°. **11422.** aaa. **25.**

C., E.

—— *See* ŠINKO (E.) Četrnaest dana. (Preveo E. C.) 1947. 8°. **12594.** c. **4.**

C., E. *See* WELLS (Christopher) Discourses, &c. on Several Subjects. [The dedication signed: E. C.] 1800. 8°. **4454.** i. **6.**

C., E. *See* WILTSHIRE. The Wiltshire Petition for tythes, explained . . . By E. C. and R. E. 1653. 4°. E. **690.** (**12.**)

C., E. An A. B. C. or Holy Alphabet, conteyning some plaine Lessons gathered out of the Word, to the number of the Letters in the English Alphabet, to enter young beginners in the Schoole of Christ. [The advertisement to the reader signed: E. C.] pp. 125. *I. N.* [*John Norton*] *for William Shefford: London,* 1626. 8°. **03504.** ee. **11.**

C., E. An Abstract of what was spoke in Parliament, by E. C. [i.e. George Mackenzie, Earl of Cromarty, on the proposed Union of England and Scotland.] 1705. 4°. **8142.** a. **5.**

Imperfect; wanting all after p. 4.

C., E. "Among the Brambles," and other lessons from life . . . By E. C., author of "Lord, I hear of Showers of Blessings" [i.e. Elizabeth Codner], *etc.* pp. viii. 248. *J. Nisbet & Co.: London,* 1880. 8°. **12809.** h. **10.**

C., E. Baily's Interpreter, in six languages. English, French, German, Italian, Spanish, Portuguese. By E. C. pp. 111. *A. H. Baily & Co.: London,* 1862. *obl.* 16°. **12901.** aa. **2.**

—— Baily's London: in six rambles. To which are added excursions to the interesting localities ten miles round. [The author's preface signed: E. C. With a map.] pp. 159. *Baily Bros.: London,* 1862. 8°. **10349.** aaa. **2.**

—— Londres et ses environs; ce qu'il faut y voir, et comment le voir. [The author's preface signed: E. C. Translated from "Baily's London." With a map.] pp. 159. *Baily Frères: Londres,* 1862. 8°. **10349.** aaa. **3.**

C., E. Baptismal Regeneration. Baptism by faith: being a letter, in reply to the Rev. C. H. Spurgeon's one question "Do you believe that Baptism regenerates?" [Signed: E. C.] pp. 3. *John Wallis: London,* [1864.] 12°. **4325.** aaa. **20.**

C., E. "Behind the Cloud," and other lessons from life . . . By E. C., author of "Lord, I hear of Showers of Blessings" [i.e. Elizabeth Codner], *etc.* pp. xii. 288. *J. Nisbet & Co.: London,* 1885. 8°. **4401.** n. **10.**

C., E. Broadlands as it was. [The dedication signed: E. C., i.e. Edward Clifford. Reminiscences. With plates.] pp. 191. *Printed for private circulation: London,* 1890. 8°. **010825.** ee. **50.**

C., E. Christians Worshipping in the Last and Perilous Times. [Signed: E. C.] pp. 32. *Kaines: Southampton,* [1867.] 16°. **3185.** a. **29.**

C., E.

—— The Daniells in India. Reprinted from Vol. XLII, Part II, of Bengal: Past & Present. [Signed: E. C., i.e. Sir H. E. A. Cotton. With reproductions of two aquatints by T. and W. Daniell.] pp. 4. *Calcutta,* [1934.] 4°. **9057.** i. **13.** (**2.**)

C., E. Death and Life—Union and Glory; or, Truths connected with the Lord's Supper. [Signed: E. C.] pp. 46. *Shrubshall: Brighton,* 1864. 8°.
4372. df. **34.** (3.)

C., E.

—— The Dying Soldier's Victory. [Signed: E. C.] pp. 8. *J. F. Shaw: London; W. Innes: Edinburgh,* [c. 1855.] 8°.
4431. a. **90.**

Pp. 1, 2 *are slightly cropped.*

C., E. An Enquiry into the Causes of Robbery, by Assistant Linen Drapers, etc., with a plan for its prevention. Suggested by the late confessions of a delinquent. By one of the Trade. [Signed: E. C.] pp. 15. *G. Parsonage: London,* 1828. 8°. T. **1242.** (8.)

C., E. The Eucharistic Hymns of the Church, *etc.* [The editor's prefatory notice signed: E. C.] pp. 32. *Joseph Masters: London,* 1871. 32°. **3435.** aaa. **53.** (7.)

C., E. An Exhibition Ode and City Poem, by E. C. pp. 67. *J. Menzies & Co.: Edinburgh & Glasgow,* 1888. 16°.
11651. c. **50.**

C., E. A Faithful Account, of the Present State of affairs, in England, Scotland, and Ireland: or, the Remarkable transactions and proceedings . . . in these kingdoms, since the discovery of the horrid Popish Plot, anno . . . 1678 to this present year, 16$\frac{89}{90}$ . . . By E. C. pp. 184. *For Tho. Beaver: London,* 1690. 12°. **599.** a. **35.**

C., E.

—— A forme of Prayer to be vsed in all Christian families. [The Prefatory epistle signed: E. C., i.e. E. Chapman.] B.L. *Christopher Barker: London,* 1583. 8°.
3406. a. **12.**

Sig. C[8] D[4]. *Also issued as part of "A Catechisme with a Prayer annexed, meete for all Christian families."*

C., E. Here is something of Concernment in Ireland . . . a warning and a charge to you is, that you stand clear . . . Never to be uphoulders of those priests, *etc.* [Signed: E. C., i.e. Edward Cooke]. pp. 4. [1660 ?] 4°.
4152. f. **21.** (18.)

C., E. Histoire de la persécution révolutionnaire dans le département du Jura, 1789–1800. [The epilogue signed: E. C.] pp. 357. *Lons-le-Saunier,* 1893. 8°. **4630.** df. 3.
The date on the wrapper is 1894.

C., E. Histoire des trois glorieuses journées 22, 23, 24 février, 1848. [Signed: E. C.] pp. 40. [*Paris,* 1848.] 12°.
1321. a. **34.**

C******, E****.

—— Instructive Hints, in easy lessons for children. By E**** C****** [i.e. Elizabeth Coltman, afterwards Heyrick]. pp. 106. *Darton, Harvey & Darton: London,* 1816. 12°. **8306.** a. **30.**

C., E. Die Katzenmusik und die Vorkämpfer studentischer Ehre. Ein offenes Wort an die Berliner Studentenschaft. Von E. C. pp. 12. *Berlin,* [1874.] 12°. **8357.** bb. 5.

C., E. A Letter from E. C. [i.e. George Mackenzie, Earl of Cromarty] to E. W. [i.e. the Earl of Wemyss] concerning the Union [of Scotland with England]. pp. 16. [*Edinburgh,* 1706.] 4°. **8142.** bb. **10.**

C., E. The Life of John Gay, author of the Beggar's Opera, &c. [The author's dedication signed: E. C., i.e. Edmund Curll.] pp. 72. *E. Curll: London,* 1733. 8°.
1416. g. 61.

C., E.

—— The Life of the Late Honourable Robert Price, Esq one of the Justices of His Majesty's Court of Common Pleas. [With "A True Copy of the Last Will and Testament of Mr. Justice Price" and an appendix. The author's dedication signed: E. C., i.e. Edmund Curll. 3 pt. *Printed by the Appointment of the Family: London* 1734. 8°. **613.** k. **17.** (2

—— [Another copy.] **1418.** f. **1**

—— [Another copy.] **613.** k. **17.** (2

—— [Another copy.] G. **14862.** (1

C., E. Lines on the Lamented Death of Sir John Moore . . By E. C. [i.e. E. Cockle.] pp. 11. *D. N. Shury London,* 1810. 4°. **11632.** g. **60.** (13

C., E. Little Lilla; or, the Way to be happy. By E. C., *etc.* pp. vi. 246. *Seeley & Co.: London,* 1865. 8°.
12804. cc. 2

C., E. Memoirs of the Life and Writings of Matthew Tindal LL.D. with a history of the controversies wherein he was engaged. [The author's dedication signed: E. C., i.e. Edmund Curll.] pp. 64. *E. Curll: London,* 1733. 8°.
1418. h. 4

C., E. La Monarchie sans révolution. [Signed: E. C.] pp. 12. *Paris,* [1888.] 12°. **8052.** bbb. **10.** (5

C., E. Morals from the Churchyard; in a series of cheerful fables. With illustrations, by H. K. Browne. [The author's preface signed: E. C., i.e. Edward Caswall pp. viii. 120. *Chapman & Hall: London,* 1838 16°.
1210. g. **2**

C., E. Mornings at Mildmay. Notes of lessons from the Beatitudes. By E. C., author of "Behind the Cloud [i.e. Elizabeth Codner], *etc.* pp. 123. *S. W. Partridge & Co. London,* 1887. 8°. **3225.** bb.

C., E. Notes and Various Readings to Shakespeare, part the first containing, All's Well that ends Well, Anthony and Cleopatra . . . With a general glossary. [The "Advertisement to the reader" signed: E. C., i.e. Edward Capell 2 pt. *E. & C. Dilly: London,* [1775.] 4°. **644.** k. **1**

—— Notitia Dramatica; or, Tables of ancient plays, from their beginning to the Restoration of Charles the second so many as have been printed, with their several editions faithfully compiled . . . by E. C. [i.e. Edward Capell], *etc.* [1774.] 4°. **11902.** h.

C., E. Osservazioni sui consigli di prefettura nella prossima riforma della legge comunale provinciale. [Signed E. C.] pp. 12. *Chieti,* 1864. 8°. **8033.** aa. 52. (1

C., E. Our Children, how to rear and train them. A manual for parents, *etc.* [The preface signed: E. C.] pp. 280. *Cassell & Co.: London,* [1874.] 8°. **8306.** bb. 3

C., E. Poems, by E. C. pp. 48. *John Hernaman Newcastle-upon-Tyne,* 1853. 8°. **11646.** eee. 1

C., E. The Poor Doubting Christian drawn to Christ . . By E. C. The 4th impression. B.L. *For John Wright London,* 1669. 16°. **4412.** a. 1

C., E. A Practical Discourse of God's Sovereignty: with other material points deriving thence . . . The third impression. [The author's "Accompt of this Treatise and Publication" signed: E. C., i.e. Elisha Coles the Elder pp. 415. *Ben. Griffin for E. C.: London,* 1678. 8°.
4257. bb. 4

An earlier edition, in which the author's initials do not appear, is entered under DISCOURSE.

C., E. The Precious Stones of the Bible: descriptive and symbolical . . . With two maps. By a Physician. [The preface signed: E. C., i.e. Edward Clapton.] *J. Nisbet & Co.: London*, 1878. 8°. **3127. k. 32.**

C-----, E-----.

—— A Proposal for the better Supplying the City of Dublin, with Corn and Flour; being heads of a bill intended to be laid before the Parliament, at their next meeting. [The introduction signed: E----- C-----, identified in a MS. note as Edmond Costello.] pp. 16. *Richard Watts: Dublin*, 1757. 8°. **8145. aaa. 24.**

C., E. The Rarities of Richmond: being exact descriptions of the Royal Hermitage and Merlin's Cave. With his life and prophecies. [The author's dedication signed: E. C., i.e. Edmund Curll.] [With plates.] ~~5 pt.~~ pp. 211. *E. Curll: London*, 1736. 8°. **8630. f. 31. (1.)**

—— The second edition, *etc.* pp. 211. *E. Curll; J. Read: London*, 1736. 8°. **G. 3404.**

C., E. La Routine militaire. [The dedication signed: É. C.] pp. ix. 207. *Paris*, 1880. 12°. **8823. bb. 17.**

C., E. The Scots Remonstrance or Declaration; concerning the restoring their declared King to his just rights and priviledges; with their raising an army of 25000 men. [Signed: E. C.] Also a more exact relation of the resolute deportment of the late Marquess of Montross . . . at the time of his execution. Together, with the Lord Hoptons letter to divers of the gentry in Cornwall, and Devonshire, *etc.* pp. 6. *For G. H.: [London,]* 1650. 4°. **E. 602. (17.)**

C., E. Sir Richard Bulkeley's Remarks on the Caveat against New Prophets [by Edmund Calamy] consider'd, in a letter to a friend. [Signed: E. C., i.e. Edmund Calamy. In reply to "An Answer to several Treatises lately published on the subject of the Prophets," by Sir R. Bulkeley.] pp. 16. *Thomas Parkhurst: London*, 1708. 8°. **4105. bb. 32.**

C., E. A Sketch of the Character of the late Lord Erskine, extracted from the Morning Chronicle, with some slight alterations and additions. [Signed: E. C., i.e. Emily Calcraft.] ~~pp. 8.~~ 1824. *See* PERIODICAL PUBLICATIONS.—*London.* The Pamphleteer, *etc.* vol. 23. 1813, *etc.* 8°. **P.P. 3557. w.**

C., E. The Society of Operative Stonemasons. The London Lockout. [Signed: E. C.] [*London?* 1914.] *s. sh.* 8°. **1879. c. 2. (136.)**

C., E. Some Part of the Life and Death of Mrs. Elizabeth Egleton, *etc.* [The epistle dedicatory signed: E. C., i.e. E. Clayton?] pp. 24. *London*, 1705. 12°. **857. h. 28.**

C., E. Statute Mongery. The results, the remedy. By E. C. pp. 29. *P. S. King & Son: London*, 1901. 8°. **08275. b. 8. (3.)**

C., E. The Sunday Excursion and the Week-Day Excursion. [Signed: E. C., i.e. E. Clare.] pp. 16. *William Macintosh: London*, [1870.] 16°. **4418. d. 20.**

—— [Another edition.] pp. 30. *W. Hunt & Co.: London*, [1872.] 16°. **4402. e. 55.**

C., E. Tables of the Geography of Great Britain and Ireland . . . Prepared at the request of the Committee of the Home and Colonial School Society. Second edition, enlarged. [The preface signed: E. C.] pp. viii. 37. *R. Groombridge & Sons: London*, 1857. 8°. **10350. a. 15.**

C., E.

—— The Taunton-Dean Letter, from E. C. to J. F. at the Grecian Coffee-house. *London*, 1701. *s. sh.* fol. **1856. g. 14. (83.)**

C., E. Thomas Rolph, D.C.M. A tribute by a few friends, E. C., W. D., B. E., W. H. S., E. W. With a foreword by W. G. Turner. pp. 35. *C. A. Hammond: London*, 1937. 8°. **10856. b. 31.**

C., E. The Tragedie of Mariam, the Faire Queene of Iewry. Written by that learned, vertuous, and truly noble Ladie, E. C. [i.e. Elizabeth Cary, Viscountess Falkland. Formerly attributed to Lady Elizabeth Carew.] *Thomas Creede for Richard Hawkins: London*, 1613. 4°. **162. c. 28.**

—— [Another copy.] **C. 34. c. 9.**
Imperfect; wanting the last two leaves which have been supplied in MS.

—— [Another copy.] **G. 11221.**
The titlepage is mutilated.

C., E.

—— Triduum to St. Joseph, and short prayers for obtaining his assistance. Translated and compiled by E. C. pp. 16. *Catholic Truth Society: London*, [1890?] 16°. **3943. a. 53.**

C., E. A True and Perfect Narrative of the Inhumane Practices, occasioned by the damnable positions of Jesuites and Papists, towards Protestants at home and abroad; being a relation of several horrid and barbarous murthers and treasons committed by them. Which may serve as a supplement to the narrative made by Mr. John Smith, *etc.* [The epistle dedicatory signed: E. C.] pp. 31. *For Samuel Day: London*, 1680. fol. **193. d. 11. (9.)**

—— [Another issue.] *For Samuel Tidmarsh: London*, 1680. fol. **G. 19902. (2.)**

—— A Defence of the Innocency of the Lives, Practice, and Doctrine of the English Preists, Jesuits, and Papists. relating to the crimes of murther and treason, vnjustly charged on them by E. C. in his narrative [i.e. "A True and Perfect Narrative of the Inhumane Practices of Jesuites and Papists"], wherein are discouered his gross mistakes . . . of the English Papists, *etc.* [By John Warner.] pp. 32. 1680. 4°. **860. i. 12. (6.)**

C., E. Two Letters concerning the Present Union [of Scotland and England], from a Peer in Scotland to a Peer in England. (From E. C. [i.e. George Mackenzie, Earl of Cromarty] to E. W. [the Earl of Wemyss.]) pp. 28. 1706. 4°. **8142. b. 11.**

C., E. The Unveiling of the Everlasting Gospel: with the Scripture philosophy of happiness, holiness and spiritual power, *etc.* [The preface signed: E. C., i.e. Ebenezer Cornwall.] pp. 270. *Hamilton, Adams & Co.: London*, 1848. 12°. **1361. b. 15.**

C., E. Versuche in westphälischen Gedichten von E. C. [i.e. F. A. Consbruch.] [With a preface signed: C. J. R.] pp. 136. *Frankfurt*, 1751. 8°. **11526. dd. 2.**

C., E. A Visit to my Discontented Cousin. Reprinted, with additions, from "Fraser's Magazine." [The dedication signed: E. C., i.e. Baron James Moncreiff.] pp. 311. *Longmans & Co.: London*, 1871. 8°. **12331. f. 18.**

C., E. War Scenes: and other verses. By "E. C." pp. 104. *Hamilton, Adams & Co.: London*, 1862. 8°. **11649. bb. 22.**

C., E. We Must Discover . . . E. C., the compiler. pp. viii. 176. *Simpkin, Marshall & Co.: London*, 1919. 8°. **08311. ff. 21.**

C., E. Welmeenende en openhartige vaderlands-gezinde zang in beantwoordinge van die, van den door een Schoot op't Scheeveninge Strand ontwaakten, en uit den dood verreezenen . . . Ridder Jacob Cats. [In verse. Signed: E. C.] pp. 4. [1782 ?] 8°. **934. g. 12. (13*.)**

C., E. While they are with us. [Tales. The preface signed: E. C.] pp. 176. *R.T.S.: London*, [1865.] 12°. **4414. bbb. 18.**

C., E.

—— Why, Sir, it's better and better. With a word to the striving one, the doubting one, the happy one. [Signed: E. C., i.e. Edward Crowley.] pp. 16. *Kaines: Southampton; C. Morrish; W. H. Broom: London*, [1865.] 8°. **4410. b. 52. (7.)**

C., E. Zur Eisenbahn-Frage. Von E. C. pp. 29. *Prag*, 1866. 8°. **8235. bb. 73. (8.)**

C., E., *Ancien négociant*, and **V.**, E. Mars 1877.—Notes sur la marine marchande à l'occasion de la révision des traités de commerce et de navigation. (Septembre 1877.—Nouvelles notes sur la marine marchande, *etc.*) [Signed by E. C., Ancien négociant, and E. V.] 2 pt. *Paris*, 1877. 8°. **8807. ee. 10. (5.)**

C., E., *Britannicus*. A Letter from E. C. to E. N., concerning the Advantages of a Fishery. [Signed: E. C. Britannicus.] pp. 4. *James Watson: Edinburgh*, 1709. fol. **12350. m. 18. (25.)**

C., E., *Doctor of the Civil Law*. A Full and Final Proof of the Plot from the Revelations: whereby the testimony of Dr. Titus Oates, and Mr. Will. Bedloe is demonstrated to be jure divino, and all colours and pretences taken away that might hinder the obstinate from assenting to the truth and sincerity of their evidence . . . By E. C. Doctor of the Civil Law. pp. 12. *For Thomas Simmons, and Jacob Sampson: London*, 1680. fol. **T. 1*. (62.)**

—— [Another copy.] **193. d. 11. (18.)**

C., E., *Esq.* Descriptive Catalogue of Articles exhibited by the Royal Society of Arts, Jamaica . . . at the International Exhibition, 1862. By E. C., Esq. [i.e. Edward Chitty.] pp. 18. 1862. 8°. *See* LONDON.—III. *International Exhibition of* 1862. [*Jamaica.*] **7957. d. 11.**

C., E., *Esquier*. Emaricdulfe. Sonnets written by E. C. Esquier. [A facsimile, with an introduction, of the edition printed in 1595 at London, by Matthew Law.] *See* LONDON.—III. *Roxburghe Club*. A Lamport Garland, *etc.* 1881. 4°. **C. 101. d. 14.**

C., E., *Journaliste*, and **M.**, DE, *Journaliste*. Biographie des 750 représentants à l'Assemblée législative élus le 13 mai 1849. Par deux journalistes. [The preface signed: E. C.—De M., journalistes.] pp. 256. *Paris*, 1849. 12°. **10662. c. 18.**

C., E., *Knight*. A Little Treatise of Baile and Mainprize. Written by E. C., Knight [i.e. Sir Edward Coke], *etc.* B.L. pp. 32. *For William Cooke: London*, 1635. 4°. **6191. a. 7.**

—— The second edition, corected and enlarged. B.L. pp. 33. *For William Cooke: London*, 1637. 4°. **6281. aa. 5.**

C., E., *Nephew of Lady Rebecca Romney.*

—— *See* BAYNES (Paul) A Helpe to true Happinesse, *etc.* [The epistle dedicatory signed: E. C.] 1622. 12°. **1481. bb. 3.**

—— *See* BAYNES (Paul) A Helpe to true Happinesse, *etc.* [The dedication signed: E. C.] 1635. 12°. Mic. A. **587. (1.)**

C., E., *Nephew of Lady Rebecca Romney.*

—— *See* BAYNES (Paul) Two Godly and Fruitfull Treatises, *etc.* [The editor's preface signed: E. C.] 1619. 12°. **873. b. 14.**

C., E., *Professeur*, and **L.** (GL.) *Maître de conférence à l'Institut catholique de Paris.* Textes de droit coutumier classés et mis en ordre par MM. E. C., professeur, et Gl. L., maître de conférence à l'Institut catholique de Paris. Coutume de Paris. pp. 26. *Paris*, 1884. 8°. **5423. bb. 15.**

C., E. DE.

—— *See* FREEMAN (Edward A.) Gl'Imperatori illirici e la loro patria. (Versione di E. de C. dall'inglese.) [A translation of "The Illyrian Emperors and their Land" from "Historical Essays . . . Third series."] 1878. 8°. [*Bullettino di archeologia e storia dalmata.* anno 1. pp. 65–69, 81–85, 97–103, 116–120, 132–138, 148–152, 162–172.] P.P. **1897. h.**

C., E. DE, *Ancien rédacteur en chef de la Revue européenne.* *See* OZANAM (A. F.) Deux chanceliers d'Angleterre, *etc.* [The preface signed: E. de C., ancien rédacteur en chef de la Revue européenne.] 1836. 8°. **1130. e. 13.**

C., E. DE, *Mr.* Du droit de tester, par Mr E. de C. [i.e. Count E. de Cornulier-Lucinière.] pp. 94. *Orléans*, 1872. 8°. **5424. dd. 3. (4.)**

C., E. DEL. Camila, ó la Virtud triunfante. Novela original de E. del C. [i.e. Estanislao del Campo.] pp. 119. *Buenos Aires*, 1856. 8°. **12491. g. 33. (2.)**

C., E. A.

—— *See* GIANNI. Gli Sponsali di Gianni e di Bianchetta. Poema. [The preface signed: E. A. C., i.e. E. A. Cigogna, who purports to be the editor but is in fact the author of the whole.] 1819. 8°. **T. 2290. (6.**

—— *See* PETRARCA (F.) [*Canzoniere.*— Cantos.] Centone tratto dal canzoniere di Messer Francesco Petrarca, *etc.* [The editor's dedication signed: E. A. C., i.e. E. A. Cigogna .] 1857. 8°. **11422. d. 27. (4.)**

C., E. A. Catechism of Outpost Duty. [The introduction signed: E. A. C.] pp. 31. *W. Clowes & Sons: London*, 1881. 16°. **8831. a. 47.**

C., E. A. Cenni storici intorno Paolo de Campo de Catania già corsaro indi eremita del secolo XV, e conghietture che le ossa scoperte . . . sotto la mensa dell'altar maggiore di Santo Stefano protomartire di Venezia sieno del B. Bonsembiante Badoardo. [The dedication signed: E. A. C., i.e. E. A. Cigogna.] pp. 32. *Venezia*, 1836. 8°. **10631. d. 31. (5.)**
With an engraved frontispiece, and two proofs of the same.

C., E. A. Esai de sinplificacion du français en vue de le fair accepter come langue internacionale. Par E. A. C. [i.e. E. A. Clerc.] pp. 151. *Lyon*, 1863. 8°. **12953. h. 5.**

C., E. A. Le Fatum. Par E. A. C. [i.e. E. A. Carrière.] pp. 155. *Paris*, 1864. 8°. **8007. cc. 7.**

C., E. A. Lettere di uomini illustri scritte a M. Antonio Bonciario. [The editor's preface headed: E. A. C., i.e. E. A. Cigogna, a chi legge.] pp. 41. *Venezia*, 1839. 8°. **10905. i. 8.**

C., E. A. Memento, si in luce ambulamus societatem habemus ad invicem. By E. A. C. pp. 16. *S.P.C.K.: London*, 1905. 16°. **4499. a. 41.**
The title on the cover reads: "Ad clerum: A solemn reminder."

—— [Another edition.] pp. 19. *S.P.C.K.: London*, 1914. 16°. **4499. a. 63.**
The title on the cover reads: "Ad clerum. A solemn reminder."

E. A.

— [Another edition.] *Warren & Son: Winchester*, [1925.] 16°. **4498. a. 87.**
The title on the cover reads: "Ad clerum. A solemn reminder."

E. A. F. Sammlung derer vornehmsten Landes-Verträge des Fürstenthums Minden . . . verfertiget von E. A. F. C. [i.e. E. A. F. Culemann.] pp. 290. 1748. 8°. *See* MINDEN. **1193. g. 24.**

E. A. R. Personal Adventures of "Prince Ananda"—E. A. R. C.—for the first time presented to the British public. pp. 40. *John Heywood: Manchester*, [1904.] 8°. **10600. de. 32. (2.)**

E. B. *See* CHRISTY (George) George Christy's Ethiopian Joke Book . . . Compiled and arranged by . . . E. C. B. [*sic.*] [The preface signed: E. B. C., i.e. E. B. Christy.] [1858.] 12°. **12352. aa. 45. (4.)**

E. B. The Gown in the Pulpit: is it legal? and, is it worth while? By E. B. C. Second thousand. pp. 14. *William Poole: London*, [1878.] 16°. **4108. de. 14. (3.)**

— Fifth edition, with preface, *etc.* pp. 10. *Elliot Stock: London*, 1883. 8°. **4109. i. 1. (7.)**

— Will the Foundation Bear? An examination of the opening pages of "The One Offering . . . by the Rev. M. F. Sadler" . . . By E. B. C., author of "The Gown in the Pulpit," *etc.* pp. 16. *William Poole: London*, 1880. 16°. **4422. b. 2. (8.)**

E. C. Golden Days of Childhood, by E. C. C.. *etc.* pp. 16. *Dean & Son: London*, [1879.] fol. [*Royal Series of Picture Books.*] **12823. e. 56/4.**

— The Travels and Adventures of Funny Dog Tray. By E. C. C. Illustrations in chromo colours. pp. 16. *Dean & Son: London*, [1879.] fol. **12823.e.56/2.**
With an additional titlepage, reading: "Dog Tray's Travels." [Royal Series of Picture Books.]

E. D. *See* WASSON (David A.) Poems. [The editor's preface signed: E. D. C.] 1888. 4°. **11688. df. 6.**

E. D. L. I. Apologie catholique contre les libelles, declarations, aduis, et consultations faictes, escrites, & publiees par les Liguez perturbateurs du repos du Royaume . . . Par E. D. L. I. C. [i.e. E. de L'Allouette, Iurisconsulte, possibly a pseudonym of P. de Belloy.] ff. 124. 1585. 8°. **1058. b. 22. (2.)**

— [Another copy.] **284. a. 24.**

— [Another edition.] pp. 328. 1585. 8°. **8052. bb. 19.**

— [Another edition.] pp. 248. 1586. 12°. **1193. c. 4. (8.)**
Slightly cropped.

— A Catholicke Apologie against the Libels, Declarations, Aduices, and Consultations made, written, and published by those of the League, perturbers of the quiet estate of the Realme of France. Who are risen since the decease of the late Monsier, the Kings onely brother. By E. D. L. I. C. [i.e. E. de L'Allouette, Iurisconsulte, possibly a pseudonym of P. de Belloy.] B.L. ff. 139. FEW MS. NOTES. *For Edward Aggas: London*, [1590?] 8°. **3901. b. 5.**

— *See* ROBERT [Bellarmino], *Saint, Cardinal, Archbishop of Capua.* [Responsio ad praecipua capita apologiae, quae falso catholica inscribitur, pro successione Henrici Navarreni, *etc.*] Reply to the Principal Points of the Argument, which is falsely entitled Catholic, for the Succession of Henry of Navarre to the Kingdom of France [i.e. to the "Apologie catholique," signed: E. D. L. I. C.], *etc.* [1950.] 4°. **3902. i. 15.**

C., E. E. Jessie M'Kinnon. [A tale.] By E. E. C. pp. 64. *Johnstone, Hunter & Co.: Edinburgh*, 1881. 16°. **12638. a. 16.**

C., E. E. Little Nellie's Days in India. By E. E. C. pp. 80. *R.T.S.: London*, [1883.] 8°. **4420. bb. 54.**

C., E. E. Piers de Gaveston. By E. E. C. 2 vol. *Whittaker & Co.: London*, 1838. 12°. **N. 1634.**

C., E. E. Short Khaskura Phrases. [The preface signed: E. E. C.] pp. 66. *Pioneer Press: Allahabad*, [1880?] 8°. **12903. aaa. 29. (2.)**

C., E. E. Stray Leaves, by E. E. C. [i.e. E. E. Chapman.] [Poems.] pp. xii. 75. *H. Berrill: Potton*, 1874. 8°. **11645. df. 27.**
The author's name occurs on the cover.

C., E. H. Christ for Me. By E. H. C. pp. 12. *J. S. Robertson: Edinburgh*, [1885.] 8°. **4422. bbb. 37. (6.)**

C., E. H. Practical Potato Cultivation. By E. H. C. pp. 12. *Drane's: London*, [1918.] 8°. **07078. de. 18.**

C., E. J.

—— Guide to Darell Aisle in Little Chart Church. [Signed: E. I. C., i.e. E. I. Cheesman.] (Reprinted 1920 and 1927.) pp. 4. *W. N. Clark: Charing*, 1913 [1927]. 8°. **9907. a. 21.**

C., E. J. The Gathered Lilies. By E. J. C. pp. 23. *Morgan & Scott: London*, [1876.] 16°. **4422. aa. 8. (6.)**

C., E. J. Mathematics and Reality. [Signed: E. J. C., i.e. Edward J. Clifford.] pp. 7. *G. B. Flower & Sons: London*, [1936.] 8°. **08534. e. 59.**

—— The Mechanism of the Wave Vortex Atom. [Signed: E. J. C., i.e. Edward J. Clifford.] [*London*, 1932.] 8°. **08710. aaa. 21.**

C * * *, E. J., *l'Abbé.* Souvenirs de voyage, ou les Vacances en Auvergne. Itinéraire du Puy-de-Dome . . . Par l'Abbé E. J. C * * *. [Variously attributed to J. Chaumette and E. J. Cosse.] pp. 375. *Clermont-Ferrand*, 1857. 12°. **10173. bb. 5.**

C . . ., E . . . J . . ., *M*ⁿ *∴ Rég*ʳ *∴* Nécessaire maçonnique, par E . . . J . . . C . . . Mⁿ ∴ Régʳ ∴ [i.e. E. J. Chappron.] pp. 114. *Paris; Amsterdam* [printed], 5812 [1812]. 12°. **4783. aaa. 1.**

C., E. L. *See* MILDMAY (Carew A. St. J.) Sermons, *etc.* [With a memorial notice signed: E. L. C.] [1879.] 8°. **4465. f. 13.**

C., E. L.

—— Sister Nannie [i.e. Anna Tempo]. A sketch of her life and work. [The foreword signed: E. L. C.] pp. 25. *Woman's Christian Temperance Union: [Cape Town*, 1939?] 8°. **4910. a. 55.**

C., E. L. B., and **B.**, M. Daily Footsteps in the Church's Path. Compiled by E. L. B. C. and M. B. With a preface by the Rev. T. B. Dover. pp. ix. 409. *Rivington, Percival & Co.: London*, 1895. 8°. **3457. dd. 45.**

C., E. M.

—— *See* CATECHISM. Catechism of Confirmation. Translated and adapted from the French. By a Priest of the diocese of Oxford. [The introduction signed: E. M. C.] [1879.] 16°. **3456. c. 55. (6.)**

—— *See* KNITTING TEACHER. The Knitting Teacher's Assistant . . . New edition, edited by E. M. C., author of "Ladies' Knitting" [i.e. Elvina M. Corbould], *etc.* 1877. 16°. **7742**. aaa. **3**.

—— *See* TEACHER. The Teacher's Assistant in Needle-Work . . . Edited by E. M. C., author of "Knitting" [i.e. Elvina M. Corbould], *etc.* 1877. 16°. **7742**. aaa. **2**.

C., E. M. Ad Te Domine, *etc.* [A devotional anthology. The editor's introduction signed: E. M. C.] pp. 40. *Guild of Health: London*, [1928.] 16°. **04402**. ff. **62**.

C., E. M. Embroidery and Art Needlework Designs. By E. M. C. [i.e. Elvina M. Corbould.] pp. 12. pl. 10. *Hatchards: London*, [1879.] 8°. **1751**. c. **6**.

—— The Knitter's Note Book. By the author of "The Lady's Knitting Book" (E. M. C. [i.e. Elvina M. Corbould]), *etc.* pp. 62. [1890.] 16°. *See* KNITTER. **7743**. aa. **17**.

—— The Lady's Crewel Embroidery Book. With one dozen designs in outline for tracing, and a book of directions for wools and working. By E. M. C., author of Ladies Knittings [i.e. E. M. Corbould], *etc.* *Hatchards: London*,[1878.] 8°. **7743**. bbb. **15**.

—— The Lady's Crewel Embroidery Book. Second series . . . By E. M. C., author of Lady's Crewel Embroidery Book, first series [i.e. Elvina M. Corbould], *etc.* *Hatchards: London*, [1879.] 8°. **7743**. bbb. **20**.

—— The Lady's Crochet-Book . . . By the author of "The Lady's Knitting Book" (E. M. C. [i.e. Elvina M. Corbould]), *etc.* 1874. 16°. *See* LADY. **7742**. aa. **13**.

—— The Lady's Crochet-Book. First series . . . By E. M. C. [i.e. Elvina M. Corbould.] pp. 64. *Hatchards: London*, 1885. 16°. **7743**. aa. **37**.

—— The Lady's Crochet-Book. Second series . . . By E. M. C., author of 'The Lady's Knitting-Books' [i.e. Elvina M. Corbould], *etc.* pp. 62. *Hatchards: London*, 1876. 16°. **7742**. aa. **41**.

—— The Lady's Crochet-Book. Third series. By E. M. C., author of 'The Lady's Knitting-Books' [i.e. Elvina M. Corbould], *etc.* pp. 63. *Hatchards: London*, 1877. 16°. **7742**. aa. **42**.

—— The Lady's Crochet Book . . . By E. M. C. [i.e. Elvina M. Corbould], *etc.* 4 ser. *Hatchards: London*, 1878. 16°. **7743**. aaa. **14**.

—— The Lady's Knitting-Book. By E. M. C. [i.e. Elvina M. Corbould], *etc.* pp. 63. *Hatchards: London*, 1874. 16°. **7743**. aa. **24**.

—— The Lady's Knitting-Book. Third series. By E. M. C., author of 'The Lady's Crochet-Book' [i.e. Elvina M. Corbould], *etc.* pp. 60. *Hatchards: London*, 1875. 16°. **7743**. aa. **38**.

—— The Lady's Knitting-Book. Third series. . . . By E. M. C., author of 'The Lady's Crochet-Book' [i.e. Elvina M. Corbould] . . . Sixth thousand, *etc.* pp. 63. *Hatchards: London*, 1876. 16°. **7743**. aaa. **13**.

—— The Lady's Knitting-Book. Fourth series. By E. M. C., author of 'The Lady's Crochet-Book' [i.e. Elvina M. Corbould], *etc.* pp. 62. *Hatchards: London*, 1875. 16°. **7743**. aa. **40**.

—— The Lady's Knitting-Book. First(—third) series. By E. M. C., author of 'The Lady's Crochet-Book' [i.e. Elvina M. Corbould] . . . Fourth edition, revised and enlarged. *Hatchard: London*, 1875. 16°. **7743**. aa. **1**.
Ser. 2 *and* 3 *are of the first edition.*

—— The Lady's Knitting-Book . . . By E. M. C., author of 'The Lady's Crochet-Book' [i.e. Elvina M. Corbould], *etc.* 4 ser. *Hatchards: London*, 1876. 16°. **7743**. aa.

—— The Lady's Netting-Book. By E. M. C., author of the "Lady's Knitting and Crochet Books" [i.e. Elvina M. Corbould]. pp. 63. *Hatchards: London*, 1876. 16°. **7743**. aa.

—— The Lady's Work-Book. First series . . . By the author of The Lady's Knitting Books, *etc.* [The preface signed: E. M. C., i.e. Elvina M. Corbould.] pp. 64. *Hatchards: London*, 1876. 16°. **7743**. aa.

—— The Lady's Work-Book. Second series . . . By E. M. C., author of 'The Lady's Knitting-Books' [i.e. Elvina M. Corbould], *etc.* pp. 63. *Hatchards: London*, 1876. 16°. **7743**. aa. **3**

C., E. M. El Moledor Constitucional al Pensador Megicano. [On the author's dealings with printers. Signed: E. M. C.] pp. 5. *Puebla*, 1820. 4°. **9770**. bb. **27**. (55

C., E. M. Mother's Knitter. By E. M. C. [i.e. Elvina M. Corbould.] Containing some patterns of things for little children. pp. 38. *Hatchards: London*, 1882. 16°. **7743**. aa. **1**

C., E. M. On Tears. [Signed: E. M. C., i.e. Ethel Mary Callard.] *C. M. R. Brooke: Chipperfield*, [1934.] 8°. **7383**. pp. **4**

C., E. M. Popular Geography of Plants; or, a Botanical excursion round the world: by E. M. C. [i.e. Maria E. Catlow.] Edited by Charles Daubeny. pp. xl. 370. pl. 2 *Lovell Reeve: London*, 1855. 8°. **7030**. b. **1**

—— [A reissue.] Plants of the World and where they grow. *Routledge & Co.: London*, 1865. 8°. **7030**. bb. **1**

C., E. M. Through Faith to Sacraments. A simple course of Sunday school lessons. By E. M. C. pp. 64. *Talbot & Co.: London*, [1924.] 8°. **4323**. aaaa. **3**

C., E. M. The Useful Knitter . . . By E. M. C. [i.e. Elvina M. Corbould], *etc.* 2 pt. *Hatchards: London*, 1887. 16°. **7742**. aa.

C., E. M. A. D. O. *See* E., A. B. C. D. Novembris monstrum . . . Made publique . . . by E. M. A. D. O. C. 1641. 12°. **11623**. a. **1**

C., E. M. P. *See* TOLFREE (Arthur P.) Speaking is Fun, *etc.* (Rhymes by E. M. P. C. [and others.]) 1938. 8°. **11806**. a.

C., E. N. *See* LITURGIES.—*Church of England.*—*Common Prayer.*—*Catechism.* [*English.*] The Catechism. With additional questions and answers for school and home. Compiled by E. N. C. [1896.] 16°. **03504**. e. **3**. (

C., E. N. *See* TURMEDA (A.) Disputa de l'Ase. Versió p E. N. C., *etc.* 1928. 8°. W.P. **4906/**

C., E. P. *See* CAMPBELL (Duncan H.) Sermons by the Venerable Duncan Houston Campbell. [The editor's dedication signed: E. P. C., i.e. E. P. Campbell.] 1882. 8°. **4477**. h.

C., E. R. *See* CONDER (Josiah) *Editor of "The Patriot."* Hymns of Prayer, Praise, and Devout Meditation, *etc.* [The editor's preface signed: E. R. C., i.e. Eustace Conder.] 1856. 12°. **3437**. e. **2**

C., E. R. *See* WILLIAMS (John) *Missionary to the South Seas.* Farewell to Viriamu [i.e. the Rev. John Williams.] [Three poems, signed respectively: J. C., J. E. C., E. R. C.] 1838. 12°. **11633**. b. **5**

C., E. R. An Order for the Solemnization of Matrimony: together with an Order for the Burial of the Dead. [The preface signed: E. R. C., i.e. Eustace R. Conder.] pp. 23. *John Snow: London*, 1854. 8°. **3407**. c. **1**.

—— (New edition.) To which are added Scripture passages suitable to baptismal services. [The preface signed: E. R. C., i.e. Eustace R. Conder.] pp. 30. *John Snow: London*, [1859.] 8°. **3407**. c. **2**.

C., E. S. Home Reminiscences. [Poems. The dedication signed: E. S. C., i.e. Elizabeth S. Abbot, Lady Colchester.] pp. 84. [1861.] 8°. **11646**. cc. **12**.
Unpublished. Imperfect; wanting the titlepage. The description is taken from the running title.

C., E. S. Schediasma de vitiis Paparum adversus eorundem infallibilitatem. [The preface headed: " Lectori benevolo E. S. C. salutem."] pp. 68. *Coloniæ*, 1699. 4°. **4856**. aaa. **8**.

C., E. S. Ward and Lock's Pictorial and Historical Handbook to Scotland . . . With . . . maps and town plans. [The preface signed: E. S. C.] 3 pt. [1890.] 8°. *See* WARD, LOCK AND Co. [*Guide Books.*] [Scotland.] **10369**. aaa. **38**.

—— Ward & Lock's Pictorial Guide to Windsor and its Castle; with excursions in the neighbourhood. Maps, plans, *etc.* [The preface signed: E. S. C. Based on Bernard B. Woodward's " Windsor Castle, picturesque and descriptive."] pp. vi. 196. [1887.] 8°. *See* WARD, LOCK AND Co. [*Guide Books.*] [Windsor.] **010347.de.180.**

C., E. T. *See* LITURGIES.—*Church of England.—Common Prayer.—Baptismal Offices.* [*English.*] An Order of Service to be used on the Ministration of Public Baptism of Infants. [The preface signed: E. T. C., i.e. Edward T. Cardale.] 1866. 8°. **3406**. cc. **43**.

C., E. T. Friends in Need. [In verse. Signed: E. T. C., i.e. Edward T. Craig.] [1893.] *s. sh.* fol. **1865**. c. **8**. (**26**.)

C., E. T. Is a Religious Use of Images and Pictures as much opposed to the Gospel as to the Law. By the author of " Petras," " Petra-Kleis," *etc.* [Signed: E. T. C.] pp. 11. *Hamilton, Adams & Co.: London; Noyes & Friend: Brighton*, [1869.] 8°. **4379**. bbb. **51**. (**3**.)

C., E. T. Notes of a Sermon on Sudden Death, by E. T. C. *W. Simpson: Folkestone*, [1847 ?] 8°. **4477**. aa. **133**. (**1**.)
Imperfect; wanting all after p. 8.

C., E. T.

—— The Story of the Gainsborough Parish Church of All Saints. By E. T. C. Illustrated. pp. 16. *British Publishing Co.: Gloucester*, [1948.] 8°. **07822**. aaa. **88**.

C., E. V. The Promised Land; or, Nine years—gold mining, hunting, and volunteering—in the Transvaal. By E. V. C. pp. 226. *Blades, East & Blades: London*, 1884. 8°. **10095**. bb. **4**.

C., E. W. *See* COLLIER (Joseph A.) The Dawn of Heaven . . . With a brief biographical sketch of the author [signed: E. W. C., i.e. E. W. Collier]. 1865. 12°. **4410**. ccc. **13**.

C., E. W. A Consolidated Index to Paver's Marriage Licences, 1567–1630, printed in the " Yorkshire Archæological Journal." [The introduction signed: E. W. C., i.e. Ely W. Crossley.] pp. 152. *Wakefield*, 1912. 8°. [*Yorkshire Archæological Society.* Extra series. vol. 2.] Ac. **5652/11**.

C., E. W. L. Jeanne de Rentaille. Ketchen. [Two tales.] By E. W. L. C. [i.e. E. W. L. Cawston.] pp. 122. *Printed for private circulation: London*, 1896. 8°. **012807**. e. **68**.

C. (EDM.) *See* FENNER (William) *B.D.* The Soul's Looking-glasse, *etc.* [The " epistle to the reader " signed: Edm. C., i.e. Edmund Calamy.] 1640. 8°. **4408**. c. **23**.

—— —— 1643. 8°. **4410**. k. **18**.

C . . . . . (EDUARD VON) *Baron.*

—— Italien und die Karte von Europa. Deutsche Antwort auf La Gueronnière's Napoleon III. und Italien, und E. de Girardin's Europa im Jahre 1860. Zweite Auflage. [Signed: Eduard Freiherr von C . . . . ., i.e. Eduard Ferdinand Baron von Callot.] pp. 56. *Leipzig*, 1859. 8°. **8010.a.20.**

—— Napoleon der Dritte und Europa. [Signed: Eduard Freiherr von C * * * * *, i.e. Eduard Ferdinand Baron von Callot.] pp. 21. *Leipzig*, 1860. 12°. **8010.a.36.**

—— Napoleon III. der Mann der grössten Attentate des neunzehnten Jahrhunderts. Von einem Conservativen. [Signed: Eduard Freiherr von C . . . . ., i.e. Eduard Ferdinand Baron von Callot.] pp. 75. *Cöln*, 1859. 8°. **8052**. dd. **12**.

C . . . (ELISA) *Mlle.* *See* PARIS. [*Appendix.—Miscellaneous.*] Aux Ministres!!! Nouvelle pétition des filles publiques de Paris . . . rédigée par Mlle Elisa C . . ., *etc.* 1830. 8°. **12316**. i. **14**. (**4**.)

C. (ÉLISABETH)

—— L'Amour et la peur. Lettres et pages de journal. pp. 336. [*Paris*,] 1950. 8°. **10666**. a. **27**.

—— [L'Amour et la peur.] Love and Fear. Letters and some pages from a diary. By Elizabeth C. Translated by Gerard Hopkins. pp. 316. *Jonathan Cape: London*, 1952. 8°. **010921**. pp. **67**.

C—— (ELIZABETH) *See* TIMPSON (Thomas) Elizabeth C——; or, Early piety. 1824. 12°. T. **982***. (**2**.)

C * * * * * (ELIZABETH) *See* C * * * * * (Henry) Memoirs of Henry and Elizabeth C * * * * *, *etc.* 1840. 12°. **4986**. a. **57**. (**3**.)

C—— (ELLEN) Poems. By Ellen C—— [i.e. Ellen Culley]. pp. 70. *Charles Westerton: London*, 1855. 12°. **11646**. ccc. **13**.

C . . . . (EMMA KEYSERLING) *Countess.* *See* KEYSERLING-C . . . . (E.) *Countess.*

C * * * (ERNEST) Appel suprême adressé au souverain pontife, aux évêques, et au clergé du monde catholique. Par Ernest C * * *, 1871, 1872. pp. xi. 187. *Paris*, 1872. 12°. **3902**. bb. **5**.
The title on the cover reads: " Appel suprême au clergé catholique."

C., F. *See* ANFOSSI (F.) La Ragione e la fede in collera con F. C. [i.e. F. Carrega] per la sua dissertazione sulla legge del divorzio. 1814. 8°. **5175**. de. **5**. (**1**.)

C., F. *See* BIBLE.—*Song of Solomon.* [*English.*] The Unlettered Believer's Interpretation of the Song of Songs, *etc.* [The preface signed: F. C.] [1881.] 8°. **3166**. de. **15**.

C., F. *See* BONAVENTURA, *Saint, Cardinal, etc.* [*Legenda Sancti Francisci.*] The Life of the most Holy Father S. Francis, *etc.* [With a dedicatory epistle signed: F. C.] 1635. 16°. **C.122.b.37.**

C., F. *See* C., F. P. and C., F. Mudge and her Chicks, *etc.* [The dedication signed: F. P. C. and F. C., i.e. F. P. Cotton and Frances Collins.] 1880. 8°. **12809**. k. **30**.

C., F.

—— *See* COMALADA (M.) [*Spill de la Vida Religiosa.—Irish.*] Emanuel . . . Ar na cur anosa a ngaoidilg lé bratair airide dórd S. Fronsias [i.e. Florence Conroy, Archbishop of Tuam], *etc.* 1616. 8°. C. **69**. d. **8**.

C., F. *See* DYKSTRA (W.) De Gierigheid bedriegt de wijsheid. Blijspel. Overgebracht . . . door F. C. 1866. 8°. **11754**. e. **62**. (**2**.)

C., F. *See* ENGLAND.—*Parliament.* [*Petitions, etc.*] An Address to the Legislature, including the substance of a letter to the Honorable George Rose, M.P. [signed: F. C.] on subjects connected with the vital interests of the Empire. 1817. 8°. **1102**. f. **12**. (**6**.)

C., F. *See* JOHNSON (Samuel) *LL.D.* Lives of the most eminent English Poets, *etc.* [The introductory notice signed: F. C.] 1868. 8°. **10854**. aaa. **24**.

C., F.

—— *See* LA FONTAINE (A. H. J.) La Fedeltà a prova . . . Tradotta da F. C. 1826. 12°. **11716**. a. **6/19**.

C., F. *See* MACAULAY (Thomas B.) *Baron Macaulay.* [*Essays.—Milton.*] An Essay on the Life and Works of John Milton. [The introductory notice signed: F. C.] 1868. 8°. **11824**. aaa. **29**. (**2**.)

C., F. *See* MAGGI (C. M.) Commedie e rime . . . corredate di note da F. C. [i. e. F. Cherubini.] 1816. 12°. **11714**. aa. **14**.

C., F. *See* MAGUIRE (Robert) *Rector of St. Olave's Southwark.* A Chapter for the Living in Memory of the Dead, *etc.* [With an introduction signed: F. C.] 1856. 8°. **4906**. f. **8**.

C., F. *See* MATTHIEU (P.) *Historian.* The Historie of S. Elizabeth, *etc.* [With "A Commonitory to the reader" signed: F. C.] 1633. 8°. C.122.c.39.

C., F. *See* MUḤAMMAD RAFĪ', called SAUDĀ. Free-Trade a Bunya's Owl (a satire of Hindoostan adapted to the times), *etc.* [The adapter's preface signed: F. C.] 1849. 8°. **8138**. bb. **112**. (**3**.)

C., F. *See* NASH (Caroline) The Sacred Bee, *etc.* [The editor's preface signed: F. C., i.e. F. Clemence.] 1850. 12°. **11648**. aa. **68**.

C., F. *See* RICHSTAETTER (C.) [Eine moderne deutsche Mystikerin.] A Daughter of the Cross . . . Translated by F. C. 1928. 8°. **4888**. cc. **50**.

C., F. *See* SOUBEN (J.) [L'Esthétique du dogme chrétien.] The Beauty of Christian Dogma, *etc.* [The translator's preface signed: F. C.] 1900. 8°. **3558**. c. **16**.

C., F. Les Agraviados d'Espagne. Suivi de notices sur les hommes qui ont joué un rôle dans les affaires d'Espagne depuis l'abolition de la Constitution des Cortès en 1823. Par F. C. [i.e. J. F. Caze.] pp. 92. *Paris*, 1827. 8°. **8042**. cc. **25**. (**3**.)

C., F. Anonymous Poems. [The preface signed: F. C.] pp. iv. 60. *Richard Bentley: London*, 1850. 8°. **11646**. c. **52**.

C., F. Aquileja's Patriarchengräber. Monographische Skizzen von F. C. [i.e. F. C. A. Coronini, Count von Cronberg.] pp. ix. 287. *Wien*, 1867. 8°. **10130**. aaa. **24**.

C., F. L'Arbre du Bon Dieu, à Cortessem, par F. C. [i.e. F. Capitaine.] pp. 9. *Tongres*, 1862. 8°. **7032**. bb. **37**. (**2**.)

C., F. The Beginning, Progresse and Conclusion of the late Troubles in France &c. Faithfully observed, and written from a gentleman now in Paris, to a person of honour in this kingdome. Dated at Paris March 23. 1649. [Signed: F. C.] pp. 5. *London*, 1649. 4°. E. **548**. (**15**.)

C., F. Carta en que se describe lo mas notable de las funciones de la proclamacion del Rey Nuestro Señor Fernando VII°. en la Villa y Corte de Madrid. [Signed: F. C.] pp. 12. *Madrid*, [1808.] 4°. **9180**. c. **10**. (**27**.) *Cropped.*

C., F. Common Needs, Common Methods. A uniform system of registration of the literature of the British Empire. [Signed: F. C., i.e. F. B. F. Campbell.] [*London*, 1897.] *obl.* fol. **11900**. k. **10**. (**2**.)

C., F. Conversion de Pierre Marcha en l'église de Saint-Ouen à Rouen, précédée d'une notice par P. Le Verdier. (Ample et fidelle narré de l'heureuse conversion de Pierre Marcha, Sieur de Pras, *etc.* [The dedication signed: F. C.]) pp. vi. 23. *Rouen*, 1905. 8°. [*Société des Bibliophiles Normands. Miscellanées.* sér. 4. no. 7.] Ac. **8938/30**.

C., F. I Delitti della famiglia Bourbone dacchè regna nelle Due Sicilie 1734–1848; e la veridica storia dello scoprimento del cholera morbus avvenuto in Sicilia (scritto da un Siracusano). Compilazione di F. C. pp. 24. *Genoa*, 1848. 8°. **8032**. d. **68**. (**2**.)

C., F. Les Diuertissemens de Forges. Où les auantures de plusieurs personnes de qualité sont fidellement d'écrites [*sic*]. Nouuelle. [The dedication signed: F. C. With a plate.] pp. 404. *C. Barbin: Paris*, 1663. 12°. **12517**. a. **15**.

C., F. The Elements of the Currency plainly stated and practically discussed. By F. C. pp. 33. *Robert Hardwicke: London*, 1856. 8°. **8227**. d. **6**.

C., F. L'Estat nouueau de la France, dans sa perfection . . . Enrichy de nouuelles figures & de tous les blazons des officiers de la couronne. [The dedication signed: F. C.] 2 pt. pp. 682. *E. Loyson: Paris*, 1661. 12°. **608**. b. **2**.

C., F. Free Trade: its moral, social, commercial, agricultural, and political results. An essay for the prize offered by the Anti-Corn-Law-League. By F. C. pp. 43. *W. E. Painter: London*, 1852. 8°. **8246**. c. **47**. (**9**.)

C., F. The Great Holiday. A tale. By F. C. pp. 174. *E. Longhurst: London*, [1874.] 8°. **12803**. ccc. **17**.

C., F. La Guerre civile en Amérique et l'esclavage. Par F. C. pp. 31. *Paris*, 1861. 8°. **8177**. d. **84**. (**3**.)

C., F. An Inquiry into the National Debt and Sinking Fund. By F. C. pp. 32. *Robert Hardwicke: London*, 1856. 8°. **8227**. c. **10**.

—— The Politics and the Political Economy of Weak Governments. By F. C. pp. 47. *Robert Hardwicke: London*, 1858. 8°. **8138**. d. **14**.

—— Preliminaries of Peace between Protection & Free-Trade: or, Cheap bread compatible with both. By F. C. pp. 36. *W. E. Painter: London*, 1852. 8°. **8246**. d. **11**.

—— Present Condition and Future Prospects of the Country in reference to Free Trade and its recent application. By F. C., author of "Remarks on the cost of producing wheat in foreign countries," &c. pp. 48. *W. E. Painter: London*, 1846. 8°. **8245**. d. **20**.

C., F. Royal Military Exhibition, 1890. Official Catalogue and Guide. [The preface signed: F. C.] pp. xxii. 196. [1890.] 8°. *See* London.—iii. *Royal Military Exhibition, 1890.* **7959. aaa. 47.**

—— Third edition. pp. xxii. 226. 1890. 8°. *See* London.—iii. *Royal Military Exhibition,* 1890. **7959. aaa. 51.**

C., F. Signs and Temper of the Times. An anonymous pamphlet. [Signed: F. C.] pp. 39. *Robert Hardwicke: London,* 1859. 8°. **8138. c. 21.**

C., F. Two Letters: the one from a Dutchman to his correspondent in England [signed: F. C.] the other an answer from the said correspondent [signed: J. G.]. In which most things of note, that relate to or have been transacted in this Hostility, are very fully handled, *etc.* pp. 21. 1673. 4°. **8132. bb. 17.**

—— [Another copy.] **8079. bbb. 3.**

C......., F........ The Mélange, containing the Lunarian, a tale, in five cantos. Wonders, in two parts. The Picture Gallery, in nine cantos. And various other pieces, in verse. By F........ C....... [i.e. Frederick Corfield]. pp. vi. 334. *J. Poole: Taunton,* 1819. 8°. **991. l. 12.**

C., F. On Safari. Experiences of a gunner in the East African Campaign. By F. C. pp. 90. *J. C. Juta & Co.: Cape Town,* 1917. 8°. **9081. eee. 17.**

C., F. The Pyramid Platform of Gizeh. [The preface signed: F. C.] pp. 38. *Edward Stanford: London,* 1898. 8°. **7701. b. 5. (11.)**

C., F. Remerciement de Messieurs les Prouinciaux à Messieurs les Préuost des Marchands et Escheuins de la ville de Paris sur la glorieuse & triomphante entrée de leurs Majestez en leur bonne ville de Paris, en vers burlesque. [Signed: F. C.] pp. 8. *J. B. Loyson: Paris,* 1660. 4°. **11482. h. 6.**

C., F. Sixteen Humorous Songs, by F. C. [i.e. Frank Collin.] pp. 16. *W. H. Eves: London,* [1881.] 8°. **11645. ee. 46. (12.)**

C., F. Sobre la Contratacion de Efectos Publicos. Del monopolio de los agentes de Bolsa. [Signed: F. C.] pp. 22. *Madrid,* 1857. 16°. **8226. aa. 27. (2.)**

C * * *., F. Soirées bermudiennes, ou Entretiens sur les évènemens qui ont opéré la ruine de la partie française de l'isle Saint-Domingue . . . Par F. C * * *. un de ses précédens colons [i.e. F. Carteau]. pp. xlii. 306. *Bordeaux,* 1802. 8°. **F. 715. (1.)**

C., F. A Talk about District Visiting. By F. C., *etc.* pp. 15. *Marshall Bros.: London,* [1895.] 16°. **4420. aa. 62. (3.)**

C., F. Wild Mike and his Victim. By the author of "Misunderstood." [Signed: F. C., i.e. Florence Montgomery.] pp. 146. *R. Bentley & Son: London,* 1875. 8°. **12638. ccc. 6.**

The author's name appears on the binding.

C., F., *Captain, "The King's" (Liverpool) Regt.* Maxims and Notes on the Art of Command for junior officers. Collected by a Territorial Officer. [The preface signed: F. C., Captain, "The King's" (Liverpool) Regt., i.e. F. Campbell.] pp. 61. *Hugh Rees: London,* 1917. 16°. **8826. aa. 68.**

C., F., *Gent.* A Poem on the Death of the Countess of Sunderland. By F. C. Gent. pp. 8. *J. Roberts: London,* 1716. fol. **11602. i. 26. (5.)**

C., F., *a Lover of his Countrey.*

—— Wealth discovered: or, an Essay upon a late expedient for taking away all impositions, and raising a revenue without taxes . . . By F. C., a lover of his countrey (Francis Cradocke), *etc.* 1661. 4°. *See* Cradocke (Francis) **1471.df.12.**

C.·., F.·., *Professeur de langue française, etc.* Le Petit répertoire maçonnique, contenant ce qu'il est indispensable de savoir sur les trois grades symboliques, tant au rite français qu'au rite écossais; par F.·. C.·., Professeur de langue française [i.e. Frère Colin], *etc.* pp. 113. *Paris,* 1829. 12°. **4783. b. 16.**

C., F. A. *See* Canonico. Lettera di un Canonico ad uno de' suoi amici su la vicinanza della fine del mondo. Tradotta dal francese da F. A. C. 1790. 8°. **4380. bbb. 46. (9.)**

C., F. A. *See* Cervantes Saavedra (M. de) [*Don Quixote.—Finnish.—Abridgments.*] Michaël Cervanteen Don Quixote de la Mancha . . . nuorisoa varten vapaasti toimitti A. Th. Paban. Vanhemman, jo loppuun myydyn suomennoksen toinen painos, jonka korjaili F. A. C. [i.e. F. A. Castrén.] 1876. 8°. **12489. aaa. 44.**

C., F. A. Egypt; its highways and byways. With some peeps into nooks and corners of Cairo and Alexandria. By F. A. C. pp. iv. 84. *William Clowes: London,* 1882. 8°. **010096. e. 26.**

C., F. A. Eminentissimo ac R^mo D^no Domino Savo Mellini, S. Romanæ Ecclesiæ Cardinali dignissimo, *etc.* [A congratulatory ode. Signed: F. A. C.] [1679.] *s. sh.* fol. **T.101.(2.)**

The date is given in the form of a chronogram.

C., F. A. Life's Medley. [Verses.] By F. A. C. pp. 79. *C. W. Daniel Co.: London,* 1931. 8°. **11640. de. 16.**

—— Llandovery, and other poems. With a play, The Battle of Souls. By F. A. C., author of "Shadows, and other poems." pp. 48. *C. W. Daniel Co.: London,* 1930. 8°. **011644. g. 151.**

—— Shadows, and other poems. By F. A. C. pp. 31. *C. W. Daniel Co.: London,* 1930. 8°. **011644. h. 43.**

C., F. A., *Lieut., R.N.*

—— The Duty of Humanity, and the Sin of Cruelty to Animals, proved and illustrated. (Reprinted, with additions, from a tract by Lieut. F. A. C—, R.N.) pp. 16. *Scottish Society for the Prevention of Cruelty to Animals: Edinburgh,* 1840. 8°. **4431. ee. 3. (14.)**

C., F. A. d. La Provincia de la Mancha contra el Diccionario Burlesco. [Signed: F. A. d. C.] pp. 8. *México,* 1812. 4°. **9180. ccc. 2. (52.)**

C., F. A. de S. Memoria historica ácerca da perfida e traiçoeira amizade ingleza . . . por F. A. de S. C. [i.e. F. de Assis Castro e Mendonça.] pp. 261. *Porto,* 1840. 8°. **8042. a. 44.**

C., F. A. di. Teatro fisicosmografico: ovvero Trattato di cosmografia . . . Da F. A. di C. pp. 154. *J. Bettenham: Londra,* 1724. 8°. **1135. b. 17.**

C., F. A. B. *See* Ryckel (J. G. à) La Vie de S. Gertrude . . . Traduicte en françois par F. A. B. C. 1639. 12°. **4824. aa. 4.**

C., F. B. Myosotis. Bilder, intryck och minnen ur naturen, lifvet och dikten, af F. B. C. [i.e. F. B. Cöster.] pp. vi. 328. *Stockholm,* 1853. 8°. **12350. bb. 10.**

C., F. B. The Quadrupeds' Pic-Nic. [In verse. The preface signed: F. B. C.] pp. 32. *William Pickering: London*, 1840. 16°. **11641**. de. **57**.

C., F. B. F. Summer Thoughts for a Winter's Eve, *etc.* [Signed: F. B. F. C., i.e. F. B. F. Campbell.] [1896.] 8°. **011651**. g. **8**.

C., F. B. L. M. *See* DANTE ALIGHIERI. [*Divina Commedia.—Italian.*] La Divina Commedia . . . corretta, spiegata e difesa da F. B. L. M. C. [i.e. Fra Baldassare Lombardi, Minor Conventuale.] 1791. 4°. **11422.b.28.**

C., F. C. *See* CANTALAMESSA CARBONI (G.) Ricerche sulla vita del commendatore A. Caro, *etc.* (Cenni biografici di G. Cantalamessa Carboni. [Signed: F. C. C., i.e. F. Cantalamessa Carboni.]) 1858. 8°. **12225**. ee. **3**.

C., F. C. Autre plus briefve response au sermon du cordelier, contenant la conference ou plutost la difference de Iesus-Christ de Sainct François. [Signed: F. C. C.] *See* CORDELIER. Sermon du cordelier, *etc.* 1833. 8°. **11475**. a. **53**. (**4**.)

C., F. C. La Missione di Nuova Norcia nell'Australia. Per F. C. C. Varietà. [Extracted from "Letture cattoliche di Napoli."] pp. 64. *Napoli*, 1868. 16°. **4744**. a. **15**.

C., F. C. Musings of an Exile. [In verse.] By F. C. C. [i.e. Francis C. Carter.] pp. 28. *Thacker, Spink & Co.: Calcutta & Simla*, 1927. 8°. **11654**. b. **40**.

—— A Romance of Thakote, and other tales. By F. C. C. [i.e. Francis C. Carter.] pp. 100. *Thacker Spink & Co.: Calcutta*, 1889. 8°. **012634**. f. **27**.

C., F. C. DE. *See* BENTHAM (Jeremy) [*Single Works.*] Táctica de las Asambleas Lejislativas . . . Traducida . . . por F. C. de C. 1835. 8°. **8009**. a. **30**.

C., F. C. DE.

—— Comedie op den reghel
Bedwonghen liefde baert veel onrust', leet en' pijn:
Maer vry verkoren trouw is heyl en' medecijn.
Verthoont den 18. October vanden Jare 1635. op de Camer der Violieren. Door F. C. de C. [i.e. Frans de Coninck.] *Jan Huyssens: Antwerpen*, [1635.] 4°. **11754**. g. **81**. (**2**.)

—— Tragycomedie op den reghel.
De Liefde en 'tgeual speelt somwijl met den mensch:
Maer waere trouw en deucht brenght hem noch tot sijn wensch.
Vertoont op de Camer der Violieren, den eersten September deur F. C. de C. [i.e. Frans de Coninck.] *Ian Huyssens: Antwerpen*, 1636. 4°. **11754**. g. **81**. (**1**.)
Bound up with three other plays of the Camer der Violieren and preceded by an engraving bearing the MS. *title "Tonneel spele van F. C. de Conde."*

C., F. C. D.

—— Herdersche ongestadicheyt op den sin Gheen liefde sonder strijdt: speelwys verthoont op de Camer vande Gulde van Sint Lucas diemen noempt de Violiere . . . Den 18. October. 1638. [The author's postscript signed: F. C. D. C., i.e. Frans de Coninck.] *Jan Huyssens: Antwerpen*, 1638. 4°. **11754**. g. **81**. (**4**.)

C., F. C. H. DE. Comedia original en tres actos. El Mayordomo Felíz. Por F. C. H. de C. [In verse.] pp. 27. *Madrid*, 1798. 4°. **1342**. e. **6**. (**3**.)

C., F D. Philipiques, contre les Bulles, et autres pratiques de la faction d'Espagne. Pour . . . Henry le Grand . . . Roy de France & de Nauarre. [The dedication signed: F. D. C., i.e. F. de Clary.] 2 pt. *Tours*, 1611. 8°. **3900**. aaa. **2**.

C., F. D. Poems, chiefly devotional. [The dedication signed: F. D. C., i.e. Frances D. Cartwright.] pp. 55. *G. Woodfall: London*, 1835. 8°. **1164**. e. **28**.

C., F. D., *Lyonnois*. Histoire generale des Larrons, diuisee en trois livres . . . Par F. D. C. Lyonnois [i.e. F. de Calvi]. (Inuentaire general de l'histoire des Larrons.—Suitte de l'Inuentaire, *etc.*) 3 pt. *R. Baragnes: Paris*, 1631. 8°. **1073**. c. **17**.
An earlier edition of pt. 1 *attributed to "le sieur d'Aubrincourt" is entered under* AUBRINCOURT (de) *Sieur*.

—— [Another edition.] 3 pt. *A. Coulon: Paris*, 1639. 8°. **012330**. e. **46**.

—— [Another edition.] 3 pt. *J. Berthelin: Rouen*, 1645. 8°. **1414**. a. **16**.

—— [Another edition.] 3 pt. *P. Borde: Lyon*, 1652. 8°. **12330**. bbb. **25**.

—— [Another edition.] 3 pt. *C. Malassis: Rouen*, 1657. 8°. **12330**. bbb. **32**.

—— Histoire generale des larrons, *etc.* 3 pt. *Antoine Ferrand: Rouen*, 1666. 8°. **012332**. a. **12**.

C., F. D., *Miss*.

—— *See* RIEGO NUÑEZ (E. A. del) Egloga que con la gloriosa ocasion de celebrar . . . el ascenso del . . . Conde de Campomanes, al gobierno del . . . Consejo de Castilla: escribia Don. E. del Riego Nuñez, *etc.* (Otras varias composiciones suyas poeticas, traducidas al ingles por Miss F. D. C. [F. D. Cartwright] por . . . Dr. J. Bowring, *etc.*) 1846. 12°. [RIEGO Y NUÑEZ (*R. del*) *The Principal Part of the Romancero de Riego, etc.*] **1464**. c. **18**

C * * *, F * * * D * * *, *Mr.* Les Vertus du beau-sexe par Mr. F * * * D * * * C * * * [i.e. F. Bruys ?]. Ouvrage posthume. pp. viii. 327. *La Haye*, 1733. 12°. **1081**. f. **7**.

C., F. D. C. G. D. Jubilos de Portugal . . . expressados na grandiosa festividade de Touros com que . . . applaudi o Senado a elevaçaõ ao trono do augustissimo senhor D Jozé I. Escrevia F. D. C. G. D. C. [In verse.] *Madrid* 1752. 4°. T. **1542**. (**22**.

C., F. D. G. Diálogo entre un Frances y un Español. [O religion. Signed: F. D. G. C.] pp. 8. *México* 1820. 4°. **9770**. bb. **3**. (**13**.

C., F. E. A.

—— Response d'vn ecclésiastique à vn de ses amis de prouince de Languedoc. Sur vne censure publiée . . contre la probabilité des opinions dans la morale, *et* [Signed: F. E. A. C. On the "Censure d'un livre anon me, intitulé Apologie pour les Casuistes . . . Faite p Messeigneurs les Evesques d'Alet, Pamiés, *etc.*"] pp. 1 [1658.] 4°. **860**. l. **18**. (**11**

C., F. E. D. M. S. M., *P.* Dissertazione (sopra la venu del vero Messia) scritta in forma di lettera diretta all'ebr Tranquillo Corcos dal P. F. E. D. M. S. M. C. pp. 130. *Viterbo*, 1772. 8°. **4034**. i. **1**

C., F. F. A. C. M. *See* CERTANI (G.) Vita del prodigioso Patrizio, *etc.* [The editor's preface signed: F. F. A. M. C.] 1757. 8°. G. **57**

C., F. F. M. V. Notizie della vita di Pietro Andrea Vallot *etc.* [The dedication signed: F. F. M. V. C., i.e. F F. M. Vallotti, Carmelitano.] pp. xxxii. *Bolog* 1786. 12°. **10630**. a.

C., F. G. *See* Webb (Maria) The Penns and Peningtons of the Seventeenth Century, *etc.* [The editor's introduction, signed: F. G. C.] 1891. 8°. **4903.** df. **45.**

C., F. G. Betrachtungen über das heilige Bündniss besonders in Vergleich mit ähnlichen Ereignissen des sechszehnten Jahrhunderts. [The preface signed: F. G. C.] pp. xxiii. 120. *Hamburg,* 1817. 8°. **1439.** g. **13.** (**2.**)

C., F.-G. Observations sur l'ouvrage de M. T. Colani: Jésus-Christ et les croyances messianiques de son temps, par un pasteur de l'Église Réformée. [The preface signed: F.-G. C.] pp. 84. *Paris; Strasbourg,* 1864. 8°. **4378.** cc. **12.**

C., F. G. El Señor F. G. C. y el contrato Grace. pp. 30. *Lima,* 1887. 4°. **8180.** k. **9.** (**2.**)

C., F. G., *Bachelier en théologie.* *See* Affinati d'Acuto (J.) Le Monde renversé san-dessus dessous . . . Mis en françois par F. G. C., Bachelier en théologie [i.e. F. G. Cornuère], *etc.* 1610. 8°. **4372.** b. **8.**

C., F. H. A Few Words of Counsel to the Parents of a New-born Child. [Signed: F. H. C.] pp. 12. *H. & C. Best: Hobart Town,* [1849?] 12°. **4407.** cc. **3.**

—— [Another edition.] pp. 12. *Oxford; Rivington: London,* 1850. 12°. **4326.** d. **16.**

C., F. H. af. Afhandling om rätta sättet at finna segelarean til linie-skepp och dåraf rundhultens längder. [The dedication signed: F. H. af C., i.e. F. H. af Chapman.] pp. 48. *Carlskrona,* 1793. 4°. **8805.** e. **34.** (**2.**)
Interleaved.

—— Plates. pl. xxvi. [1793.] *obl.* fol. **1899.c.13.**

—— Dimensioner på wirke och järn til fem sorter linie-skepp, samt längd och tjocklek på master och rundhult, salningar och eselhufvun, til samma skepp. Af F. H. af C. [i.e. F. H. af Chapman.] ff. 29. *Carlscrona,* 1796. 8°. **8805.** d. **11.**
Imperfect; wanting the volume of plates, issued separately.

—— Dimensioner på wirke och järn til nio sorter fregatter och trenne mindre bevärade fartyg, samt längd och tjocklek på master och rundhult salningar och eselhufvun til samma fartyg, af F. H. af C. [i.e. F. H. af Chapman.] ff. 27. *Carlskrona,* 1798. *obl.* 4°. **8531.** a. **1.**
Imperfect; wanting the volume of plates, issued separately.

C., F. I. F. C. R. S. T. P. A. P. Antithesis Augustini et Calvini. Authore F. I. F. C. R. S. T. P. A. P. C. [i.e. J. Fronteau.] pp. 257. *Parisiis,* 1651. 12°. **4255.** a. **10.**

C., F. J. *See* R., J. El Honor Marcial sostenido por las Leyes, *etc.* [Signed: J. R., F. J. C., J. F.] 1821. 4°. **9770.** bb. **7.** (**39.**)

C., F. J. Four Old Plays. Three interludes: Thersytes, Jack Jugler, and Heywood's Pardoner and Frere: and Jocasta, a tragedy by Gascoigne and Kinwelmarsh. With an introduction and notes. [The introduction signed: F. J. C., i.e. Francis J. Child.] pp. xxxiv. 288. *George Nichols: Cambridge [Mass.],* 1848. 8°. **11771.** ddd. **2.**

—— Notice of William Thaddeus Harris, Esq. prepared for and published in the January number of the New England Historical and Genealogical Register, for 1855. [Signed: F. J. C., i.e. Francis J. Child, with a preface signed: S. G. D., i.e. Samuel G. Drake.] pp. 14. *S. G. Drake: Boston,* 1855. 8°. **10880.** b. **36.** (**4.**)
One of an edition of six copies; with an autograph letter by the author inserted.

C., F. Le G. Cécile Booysen . . . A brief memoir. [Signed: F. Le G. C., i.e. Frederick Le Gros Clark. With a portrait.] pp. 11. [*Printed for private circulation: London,* 1937.] 8°. **10826.** i. **45.**

C., F. M. Lily's Garden, and other tales. By F. M. C. With six illustrations, *etc.* pp. 32. *Dean & Son: London,* 1875. 16°. **12804.** de. **16.**

C., F. M. Love—the Singer. By F. M. C. [Poems.] pp. 165. *Madgwick, Houlston & Co.: London,* [1911.] 8°. **011650.** de. **59.**

C., F. M. Which shall we have? Mrs. G. O. M.—The Grand Old Madam [i.e. W. E. Gladstone]—or The Hertfordshire Man [i.e. the Marquis of Salisbury]! Period 1886. [A play.] Written for the Annual Meeting of the Hoddesdon Conservative Association . . . By F. M. C. (2nd edition.) pp. 11. *W. Clark: Hoddesdon,* [1887.] 8°. **11778.** c. **1.** (**4.**)

C., F. M. del. Reflexiones en Contestacion al Artículo comunicado inserto en el Universal numero 169, ó sea á la que se dice resolucion de las cuestiones sobre America, propuestas por . . . Valentin Ortigosa en 1813, reimpresas en el propio periodico num. 157. [Signed: F. M. del C.] pp. 192. *Madrid,* 1821. 8°. **8180.** a. **4.**

C., F. M. A. H. A. O. S. O. Luna sub pedibus . . . Leopoldo . . . Imperatori Romanorum . . . pro pace Turca supplex . . . F. M. A. H. A. O. S. O. C. [i.e. A. Hacki.] [In verse.] *Typis Abbatialibus: Olivæ,* [1693.] fol. **1871.** d. **2.** (**8.**)

C., F. M. A. H. A. O. S. T. D. P. A. O. G. & P. G. S. R. M. S. P. P. Arbos una, nemus — — . . . Heroum procerum Godziemba illustrissimo . . . Domino D. Stanislao in Lubraniec Dąmbski senatorum, antistitum, phœnici immortalis gloriæ nidô composita â F. M. A. H. A. O. S. T. D. P. A. O. G. & P. G. S. R. M. S. P. P. C. [i.e. M. A. Hacki.] [In verse.] [*Oliva,* 1692?] fol. **1871.** d. **2.** (**2.**)

C., F. M. A. H. D. V. A. O. S. O. C. S. T. D. P. A. O. G. & P. G. S. R. M. P. I. C. S. P. P. S. Io Triumphe! Majestatibus Regni Poloniarum serenissimis Joanni iii. Regi . . . Mariæ Casimiræ Reginæ . . . Teresiæ Cunegundi . . . Ducissæ Bavariæ Alexandro & Constantino Principibus . . . Io! Triumphe! [Signed: F. M. A. H. D. V. A. O. S. O. C. S. T D. P. A. O. G. & P. G. S. R. M. P. I. C. S. P. P. S. C., i.e. M. A. Hacki. In verse.] [*Oliva,* 1694.] fol. **1871.** d. **2.** (**5.**)

C., F. M. I. Em Applauso do M. R. P. M. doutor Fr. Joaquim de S. Joseph . . . Soneto. [Signed: F. M. I. C.] [*Lisbon,* 1760?] *s. sh.* fol. **9181.** e. **4.** (**41.**)

C., F. M. M. M. Los Famosos Traidores refugiados en Francia convencidos de sus crímenes . . . Por F. M. M. M. C. [i.e. M. Martínez, Mercenario Calzado.] pp. 20. *Madrid,* 1814. 4°. **9180.** ccc. **10.** (**8.**)

C., F. P. The Manchester Clerical Book Society, 1831–1931. [Signed: F. P. C., i.e. F. P. Cheetham.] pp. 15. 1931. 8°. *See* Manchester.—*Manchester Clerical Book Society.* **011904.** ee. **53.**

C., F. P., and **C.**, F. Mudge and her Chicks. [A tale.] By a brother and sister. [The dedication signed: F. P. C. and F. C., i.e. F. Percy Cotton and Frances Collins.] pp. 288. *Griffith & Farran: London,* 1880. 8°. **12809.** k. **30.**

C., F. P. D. B. P. Le Tableau parfait de la vie spirituelle et religieuse es vies de Sainte Boue et Sainte Dode, fondatrices de l'Abbaie roiale de S. Pierre de Reims. [The dedication signed: F. P. D. B. P. C., i.e. P. de Beauvais.] pp. 233. *A. Pottier: Reims,* 1655. 8°. C. **47.** c. **11.**

C., F. P. da M. R. Saggio della vita de' Cappuccini liguri illustri in virtù, dottrina e santità, tratto fedelmente dalle cronache dell'ordine . . . da un religioso dello stess'ordine, *etc.* [The preface signed: F. P. da M. R. C.] pp. 384. *Genova*, 1822. 4°. **4867**. df. **32**.

C., F. P. F. A Recepção de hum Maçon: farça. Dada á luz por F. P. F. C. [i.e. F. de P. Ferreira da Costa.] pp. 28. *Lisboa*, 1827. 4°. **11726**. c. **32**. (**5**.)

C., F. S. D. I. Lettre à Monseigneur le Marquis de Fontenay-Marveil, ambassadeur de sa Maiesté à Rome. Sur le trespas de Monseigneur l'Éminentissime Cardinal Duc de Richelieu. [Signed: F. S. D. I. C., i.e. Frère Séraphim de Jesus Christ, pseudonym of Léon de Saint Jean.] 1838. *See* Cimber (M. L.) *pseud.* Archives curieuses de l'histoire de France. sér. 2. tom. 5. 1834, *etc.* 8°. **805**. b. **7**.

C., F. T. Cutchacutchoo; or, the Jostling of the innocents. (Second edition.) [In verse. The dedication signed: F. T. C.] pp. xii. 29. *C. Lewis: Dublin*, [1805.] 8°. **1346**. g. **37**.

—— [Another edition.] Cutchacutchoo, *etc.* (Second edition.) pp. 43. *C. Lewis: Dublin*, [1805.] 12°. **11641**. b. **61**. (**2**.)

—— [Another copy.] **1465**. d. **23**.
The titlepage is mutilated.

—— *See* Dublin. Dublin Run Mad!!! or, Remarks on Cutchacutchoo, *etc.* 1805. 12°. **11641**. b. **61**. (**4**.)

—— *See* Epistle. Poetical Epistle from the Right Hon. Lady —— . . . Addressed to the delinquent author of a poem entitled Cutchacutchoo, *etc.* 1805. 12°. **11641**. aaa. **19**.

—— *See* History. The History of Cutchacutchoo. [By John W. Croker. A reply to "Cutchacutchoo, or the Jostling of the Innocents," by F. T. C.] 1805. 12°. **11641**. b. **61**. (**3**.)

—— *See* Quizz, *pseud.* The Croaker . . . Addressed to the author of Cutchacutchoo, *etc.* 1805. 12°. **11641**. b. **61**. (**5**.)

C., F. V. *See* Curio (C. S.) Een seer schoone Dialogus . . . van den Roomschen Pasquillo ende Marforio . . . Nu eerst uiten Latiinsche in de Nederduytsche tale ouerghesett. [The heading of the translator's dedication signed: F. V. C.] 1567. 8°. **3925**. a. **18**.

C., F. W. *See* Fletcher (William) *One of the Justices of the Court of Common Pleas in Ireland.* The Charge of Judge Fletcher to the Grand Jury of the County of Wexford, *etc.* [The editor's preface signed: F. W. C.] 1814. 8°. **6503**. b. **17**.

C., F. W. Sherryana. By F. W. C. [i.e. F. W. Cosens.] Illustrated by Linley Sambourne. pp. 54. *London*, [1886.] *obl.* 8°. **7077**. aa. **19**.

C., F. X. Relaçam de alguns Combates, e de todas as Prezas que tem havide este prezente anno entre os Inglezes e Francezes . . . Por F. X. C. pp. 7. *Lisboa*, 1757. 4°. **1196**. c. **33**. (**11**.)

C., F. Z. *See* Charlin, afterwards Perrin (L.) called Labé. Œuvres, *etc.* [The preface signed: F.-Z. C.] 1845. 12°. C. **29**. e. **16**.

C. (Félix D.) Charles Stuart, ou le Château de Woodstock, mélodrame en trois actes . . . Tiré du roman de Sir Walter-Scott. Paroles de M. Félix D. C. [i.e. F. de Croisy; assisted by J. B. E. Cantiran de Boirie, and A. N. Béraud], *etc.* pp. 48. *Paris*, 1826. 8°. **11738**. bb. **20**. (**2**.)

C. (Fidelio F. A.) *pseud.* [i.e. Joseph Brodie.] *See* Fidelio, *F. A. C.*

C. (Francesco) *See* Foresti (J. P.) *Bergomensis.* Supplementum Supplementi de le chroniche uulgare . . . p Francesco .C. Fiorentino uulgarizato : ⁊ historiato. 1520. fol. **9006**. i. **10**.

C * * (Franz Anton Wenzel von) Schlesischer Robinson, oder Frantz A. Wentzels v. C * * eines schlesischen Edelmanns denckwürdiges Leben, seltsame Unglücks-Fälle und ausgestandene Abentheuer, *etc.* 2 Tl. *Breslau & Leipzig*, 1723, 24. 8°. **12555**. aa. **24**.

C. (Fréd.) La Crise ecclésiastique dans le canton de Vaud. Par Fréd. C. [i.e. F. Chavannes.] Extrait de la Revue suisse, *etc.* pp. 64. *Neuchâtel*, 1846. 8°. **3900**. ccc. **4**. (**1**.)

C., G. *See* Bacon (Francis) *Viscount St. Albans.* [*Confession of Faith.*] Confessio fidei Francisci Baconi . . . Nunc denuo typis excusa, cura . . . G. C. [i.e. G. Cantor.] 1896. 8°. **4371**. d. **34**.

C., G. *See* Bullinger (H.) [*Sermonum Decades.*] Sermons on the Sacraments. [The editor's preface signed: G. C.] 1840. 8°. **1122**. g. **1**.

C., G.

—— *See* C., M. L. Biographical Notes on Sir Ernest Barker and Thomas Greenwood, *etc.* [The notes on Sir E. Barker signed: M. L. C.; those on T. Greenwood signed: G. C.] [1950.] 8°. **10863**. de. **5**.

C., G. *See* Du Moulin (Pierre) *the Elder.* The Anatomy of the Mass . . . Together, with a learned Treatise of Traditions, translated by G. C. 1750. 12°. **3902**. aa. **17**.

—— *See* Du Moulin (Pierre) *the Elder.* A learned Treatise of Traditions . . . Faithfully done into English by G. C. 1631. 8°. **3900**. b. **33**.

C., G. *See* Estella (D. de) The Contempte of the World, and the vanitie thereof . . . Translated out of Italian into Englishe, *etc.* [The epistle signed: G. C.] 1584. 12°. **8406**. aa. **31**.

—— —— 1622. 8°. **4404**. e. **31**.

C., G. *See* Euistor (F.) *the Palaeopolite, pseud.* Divine Dialogues, *etc.* [The address of the publisher to the reader signed: G. C.] 1713. 8°. **4380**. bb. **21**.

C., G. *See* Franco (N.) Dix plaisans dialogues . . . Traduits d'Italien en François. [The dedicatory epistle signed: G. C., i.e. G. Chappuys.] 1579. 16°. **1094**. a. **6**.

C., G. *See* French Gentleman. Dialogue facetieux d'un Gentil-homme françois, se complaignant de l'amour, *etc.* [The editor's note signed: G. C., i.e. G. Chartener.] 1847. *obl.* 16°. **11498**. a. **19**.

C., G. *See* Hipolito. The True History of the tragicke Loves of Hipolito and Isabella, *etc.* [Preceded by verses addressed "To the volume," signed: G. C.] 1628. 8°. **12613**. a. **17**.

—— —— 1633. 8°. **12613**. a. **18**.

C., G. *See* Jonson (Ben) The Masque of Queenes, *etc.* [The editor's introduction signed: G. C.] 1930. fol. C. **100**. l. **12**.

C., G. *See* Lazarillo, *de Tormes.* [*English.*] The Adventures of Lazarillo de Tormes, *etc.* [The preface signed: G. C.] 1821. 12°. **12490**. aaa. **28**. (**1**.)

C., G. *See* Letters. Letters from a Sister. [The editor's preface signed: G. C., i.e. George Cooke.] [1841.] 12°. **4422**. h. **16**. (**9**.)

C., G. *See* LONDON.—III. *London Missionary Society.* Centenary of the London Missionary Society, 1895. Scheme of monthly addresses, *etc.* [The preface signed: G. C.] [1894.] 8°. **4767.** a. **14.** (7.)

C., G.

—— *See* LOUVET DE COUVRAY (J. B.) [Les Amours du chevalier de Faublas.] The Amours of the Chevalier de Faublas ... translated [by G. C.], *etc.* 1822. 16°. C. **133.** b. **4.**

C., G. *See* LUCRETIUS CARUS (T.) [*Italian.*] Di Tito Lucrezio Caro della natura delle cose, libri VI. Tradotti da Alessandro Marchetti. [The editor's dedication signed: G. C., i.e. G. Conti.] 1761. 12°. **238.** k. **37.**

C., G.

—— *See* M., P. The Christians Combat . . . Englished by G. C. [i.e. George Chapelin.] 1591. 12°. **1473.** aa. **3**

C., G. *See* MARTIGIANI (G. B.) Divozioni alla santissima Vergine Maria . . . raccolte dalla buona memoria del Reverendo D. G. B. Martigiani, *etc.* [The editor's preface signed: G. C.] 1784. 8°. **4380.** e. **8.** (4.)

C., G. *See* MILAN.—*Pinacoteca di Brera, etc.* Catalogo della R. Pinacoteca di Milano, *etc.* [With an introduction signed: G. C.] 1896. 8°. **7858.** m. **19.**

C., G. *See* MILI (C.) *pseud.* Operette di Callimaco Mili indirizzate al molto reverendo Padre Vincenzo Domenico Fassini . . . da G. C. 1767. 12°. [CALOGIERA (*A.*) *Nuova raccolta d'opuscoli scientifici, etc.* tom. 15.] **247.** a. **15.**

C., G. *See* MONTANUS (A.) Het Leven, bedryf, en oorlogsdaaden van Wilhelm den Derden . . . En 't eerste deel vervolgt door G. C. 1703. 8°. **1448.** a. **14.**

C., G. *See* SANCASSANI (D. A.) Tre lettere inedite, *etc.* [The editor's preface signed: G. C., i.e. G. Campori.] 1856. 8°. **10909.** h. **19.** (3.)

C., G. *See* WEIDENFELD (J. S.) Four Books . . . concerning the Secrets of the Adepts, *etc.* [The translator's preface signed: G. C.] 1685. 4°. **1033.** i. **18.** (1.)

C——, G. The Almanack for the Year 1797, according to the true time, *etc.* [The introduction signed: G. C——.] pp. xx. 1797. 12°. *See* EPHEMERIDES. P.P. **2513.** ga. (1.)

C., G.

—— The Art of G. C. [i.e. Gopeṣa-chandra Chakravartī], *etc.* [1950.] 8°. *See* GOPEṢA-CHANDRA CHAKRAVARTĪ. **7871.** d. **21.**

C., G. Il Balilla. Inno da cantarsi il giorno 10 gennaio dalle donne portoriane. [Signed: G. C.] [*Genoa,* 1848.] *s. sh.* 4°. **804.** k. **13.** (179.)

C., G. Breaking the Line. Statement of facts, in the nature of memoir, leading to and connected with the great battle of the 12th of April, 1782, between the fleet of Great Britain, commanded by Lord Rodney, and that of France, under the Compte de Grasse. By an Old Naval Officer, *etc.* [The author's letters in the appendix signed: G. C.] pp. xv. 52. xxxv. *J. J. Hadley: Cheltenham,* 1830. 8°. **806.** b. **19.**

C., G. Bref Instruction pour tous estats . . . Par G. C. [i.e. F. de Corlieu.] Nouvellement corrigé & augmenté. *M. Bernard: Pont-a-Mousson,* 1609. 8°. C. **48.** a. **12.** *Printed in "caractères de civilité." The editions of* 1558 *and* 1559 *are entered under* VEILROC (*F.*) *pseud.*

C., G. Breviuscula introductio ad logicam . . . Editio secunda, ab auctore recognita & emendata. [The preface signed: G. C.] pp. vi. 70. *Typis J. Mosman & Sociorum, impensis Joannis Paton: Edinburgi,* 1722. 12°. **1211.** e. **32.** (2.)

C., G. Carl Fichtner. Eine Skizze seines Lebens, und künstlerischen Wirkens. Von G. C. [i.e. Prince Konstantin Czartoryski.] Mit dem photographischen Portrait des Künstlers. pp. 56. *Wien,* 1865. 8°. **10707.** g. **19.** (6.)

C., G. Cwyn Dafydd Evans, Caerynarfon, yr hwn a gollodd ei olwg yn Nghloddfa Matilda, ger Lanberis, drwy daniad ergyd, Medi 25, 1848. [A poem. Signed: G. C.] pp. 4. *J. Jones: Llanrwst,* [1848 ?] 8°. C.**116.b.25.(87.)**

C., G. The Excellency and Equity of God's Law, and the unreasonableness of sin . . . By G. C. pp. 103. *J. Bagnall: Ipswich,* 1729. 8°. **874.** d. **8.**

C., G. La Festa facta per li Ciptadini Romani allo Magnifico Juliano in Capitolio: con la dechiaratione delle historie: ⁊ de tutte le altre cose. [Signed: G. C.] [1513.] 4°. C. **32.** g. **11.** (11.)

C., G. From Portsmouth to Peking via Ladysmith with a Naval Brigade. [The preface signed: G. C.] pp. 151. *Hong Kong Daily Press: Hong-Kong; London,* 1901. 8°. **9061.** ccc. **36.**

C., G.

—— La Giovinezza di Giorgio IV d'Inghilterra. [A novel. The Preface signed: G. C., i.e. Guido Campi.] pp. x. 645. *Mantova,* 1888. 8°. **12471.** d. **34.**

C., G. Li Gran triumphi facti a Maximilian maria Sforza, Duca de Milano nela sua iocundissima intrata. [Signed: G. C.] [1512.] 4°. C. **32.** g. **11.** (15.)

C., G. Hanes bachgen a frathwyd gan gi cynddeiriog. [Translated from "John Boltwood."] [Signed: G. C.] pp. 8. *I. Davies: Trefriw,* [1807.] 8°. **875.** a. **40.** (4.)

C——, G——. Humanity: a poem: inscribed to George Boden Esq. By G—— C——. pp. 23. *Charles Marsh: London,* 1766. 4°. **11633.** g. **10.**

C., G. A pleasant comedy entituled: An humerous dayes myrth . . . By G. C. [i.e. George Chapman.] *Printed by Valentine Syms: London,* 1599. 4°. C. **34.** c. **14.**

—— [Another issue.] *London,* 1599. 4°. C. **12.** g. **4.** (2.)

C., G. I want to see the Queen. [Verses. Signed: G. C.] pp. 7. *Gospel Tract Depot: London,* [1901.] 16°. **04420.** de. **8.** (16.)

C., G. Liberty of Conscience asserted and vindicated. By a learned country-gentleman, *etc.* [The preface signed: G. C., i.e. George Care ?] pp. 27. *For Jonathan Robinson: London,* 1689. 4°. **698.** g. **19.** (1.)

—— [Another copy.] T. **1675.** (3.)

C., G. A Little Looking-Glass for the Times, or, a brief remembrancer for Pennsylvania . . . By G. C. . . . 1764. [A poem.] 1913. *See* PERIODICAL PUBLICATIONS. —*New York.* The Magazine of History, *etc.* Extra number 22. 1905, *etc.* 4°. P.P. **3437.** bab.

C., G. The Marriage Laws considered, with the view of diminishing prostitution and infanticide. [Signed: G. C.] pp. 29. *William Downing: Birmingham,* [1883.] 8°. **5176.** bbb. **23.** (5.)

C., G. La Metà di Quaresima. [Signed: G. C. L'Autore delle Reminiscenze.] [1850 ?] *s. sh.* fol. **1879.cc.15.(111.)**

C., G. Miscelánea instructiva y amena.—Coleccion escogida de escritos sobre todas materias, en prosa y en verso, *etc.* [The preface signed: G. C.] 2 tom. *Merida de Yucatán,* 1849. 8°. **12230.** aa. **11.**

C., G. The Nation and the Sabbath. [The advertisement signed: G. C.] pp. 31. *Seeley & Co.: London; Ward: Canterbury*, [1851.] 8°. **4355. b. 17.**

—— (Second edition, enlarged.) pp. 82. *Seeley & Co.: London; Ward: Canterbury*, [1851.] 8°. **4355. b. 18.**

C., G. The New Commandment. By G. C. [A religious tract.] pp. 16. *J. F. Shaw & Co.: London*, [1874.] 16°. **4422. aa. 2. (1.)**

C., G. Notizie istoriche relative a Francesco Sforza, che fu il primo fondatore del Grande Ospitale di Milano, con altre notizie particolari intorno le vicende di si interessante luogo pio. [The dedication signed: G. C., i.e. G. Cavallotti.] pp. 73. *Milano*, 1829. 8°. **10630. dd. 2. (3.)**

C., G. Observations on the Amalgamation of the Regiments of Royal and Indian Artillery and Engineers: with proposals for an improved organization and system of promotion for the British Artillery Service. By an Officer. [The preface signed: G. C., i.e. Francis R. Chesney.] pp. 78. *Smith, Elder & Co.: London*, 1861. 8°. **8838.bb.9.**

C., G. The Poetical Museum. Containing songs and poems on almost every subject. Mostly from periodical publications. [The preface signed: G. C., i.e. George Caw.] pp. viii. 392. *G. Caw: Hawick*, 1784. 8°. **11621. b. 34.**

C., G. Rambles by the Rivers, in the Woods, and by the Streams. True stories in verse. By G. C. pp. 141. *G. Cooper: London*, [1877.] 16°. **11652. df. 34.**

C., G. La Révolution politique et la révolution sociale. Par G.-C. pp. 11. *Paris*, 1848. 8°. **935. i. 37. (3.)**

C., G. Rhymes. By G. C. [i.e. G. Cross.] pp. 64. *W. A. Scripps: London*, 1819. 12°. **11601. aaa. 30. (2.)**
Printed for private circulation.

C., G. Ricordi per le truppe di fanteria in campagna. [The preface signed: G. C.] pp. 148. [1848.] 16°. **8033. a. 38. (7.)**

C., G. Saggio di callologia ed estetica, di G. C. pp. xiv. 464. *Milano*, 1889. 8°. **11824. df. 42.**

C., G. The Sampler Series. [Signed: G. C., i.e. Grace Christie.] 6 no. *J. Pearsall & Co.: London*, [1911–13.] 4°. **7743. d. 33.**

C., G. Scelte orazioni italiane attinenti alle arti, alle lettere, ed alle scienze, recitate nelle più celebri università ed accademie d'Italia raccolte . . . per cura del professore G. C. pp. 316. *Londra*, 1833. 12°. **12301. c. 19.**

C., G. Serie cronologica della rappresentazioni drammatico-pantomimiche poste sulle scene dei principali teatri di Milano dall'autunno 1776 sino all'intero autunno 1818. Compilazione di G. C. [i.e. G. Chiappari.] [With three continuations bringing the lists up to 30 June 1824.] 4 vol. *Milano*, 1818–25. 8°. **11795. bb. 26.**
and with plates.

—— [Another copy.] Serie cronologica delle rappresentazioni drammatico-pantomimiche poste sulle scene dei principali teatri di Milano . . . Compilazione di G. C. [i.e. Giuseppe Chiappari.] *Milano*, 1818–25. 8°. Hirsch **1319.**

C., G. Severall Grounds, Reasons, Arguments, and Propositions, offered to the Kings Most Excellent Majesty, for the improvement of his revenue in the First-Fruits, and Tenths: Annexed to the petition of James, Earl of Northhampton, Viscount Hereford, Sir William Farmer, Baronet, George Carew, Esq; *etc.* [Signed: G. C., i.e. George Carew?] B.L. [1660.] *s. sh.* fol. **1851. c. 10. (83*.)**

C., G. Sulla conservazione di S.S. R.M. il re Carlo Alberto . . . Inno popolare. [Signed: G. C.] [*Genoa*, 1848.] *s. sh.* fol. **804. k. 13. (340.)**

C., G. Sventura d'amore. Novella del secolo XVIII di G. C. pp. 22. *Firenze*, 1876. 8°. **12315. ccc. 24. (8.)**

C., G. Tarifsagen og Arbeiderklassens Interesser i Frihandelen, nærmest med Hensyn til Rigsraadets foregaaende og eventuelle Behandling af Tarif-Udkastet. Af G. C. pp. 66. *Kjøbenhavn*, 1863. 8°. **8247. aaa. 32. (2.)**

C., G.

—— A Treatise of Mathematicall Physick. Or a briefe Introduction to Physick, by judiciall astrologie . . . Written by G. C. [A new edition of the work written originally by G. C., Gent. Practicioner in Phisicke.] *See* DARIOT (C.) Dariotus Redivivus, *etc.* 1653. 4°. **8610. c. 56.**

C., G. A Tribute to the Principles, Virtues, Habits and Public Usefulness of the Irish and Scotch early settlers of Pennsylvania. By a Descendant. [The preface signed: G. C., i.e. George Chambers.] pp. 171. *M. Kieffer & Co.: Chambersburg, Pa.*, 1856. 8°. **10411. g. 30.**

C., G. Las Víctimas del Japón. [A political skit. Signed: G. C.] pp. 12. *Puebla*, 1820. 4°. **9770. bb. 28. (9.)**

C., G. Zurded Gwirionez ha Plijadur. Dre G. C. pp. 30. *Bible Truth Depot: Hull*, [1900.] 16°. **887. a. 11.**

C., G., and **R.**, H. C.

—— Nasik and the Gospel. The story of a hundred years of Christian witness, 1832–1932. Compiled by two Nasik Missionaries, *etc.* [The authors' note signed: G. C., H. C. R., i.e. Grace Helen Cookson and Henry Cecil Read. With plates.] pp. xiii. 81. *H. C. Read: Nasik*, 1932. 8°. **20019. h. 19.**

C., G., *A.M.* Justice done to the Sacred Text, and the Nature of the Kingdom, or Church of Christ asserted. A sermon . . . By G. C., A.M. [A rejoinder to Benjamin Hoadly's sermon "The Nature of the Kingdom or Church of Christ."] pp. 24. *Printed for the Author: London* 1717. 8°. **111. g. 26**

C., G., *an Affectionate Friend, and true Servant of his Grac the Duke of Buckingham's.* A Reply to the Answer of th Man of No Name [i.e. "A Short Answer to His Grace th D. of Buckingham's Paper"], to His Grace the Duke o Buckingham's Paper of Religion, and Liberty of Conscienc [i.e. "A Short Discourse upon the Reasonableness o men's having a Religion, or Worship of God"]. By G. C an Affectionate Friend, and true Servant of his Grac the Duke of Buckingham's [i.e. George Care]. pp. 36. *John Leake for Luke Meredith: London*, 1685. 4°. **700. f. 13. (3**

—— [Another copy.] **G. 5083. (4**

C., G., *Bardd Clwyd.* Cerdd Molawd Dyffryn Clwy [Signed: G. C.] pp. 4. *J. Jones: Llanrws* [1830?] 8°. **C.116.b.25.(53**

C., G., *Il C.* *See* JULIA, *Daughter of Augustus.* Corri pondenza tra Giulia ed Ovidio, *etc.* [The editor's prefa signed: Il C. G. C.] 1872. 8°. **12471. b. 3**

C., G., *il C.* Il Cicisbeo per giustizia consulto del C. G. pp. 47. [*Venice*, 1741.] 4°. **721. f. 3**

C., G., *Coll. Med. Lond. M.D.* Generale Materiæ Medic Compendium in tabulam accuratam redactum . . . Auto G. C., Coll. Med. Lond. M.D. [i.e. William Carter.] *Ap Gul. Carter: [London*, 1707.] 8°. **777. f.**
Printed on one side of the leaf only.

C., G., *Gent.* On the Crowing-Cock, and Lyon Couchant: or, a Poem to express the Gallantry of our Royal Chanticlere . . . Writ on the news of the surrender of Namur to our English Arms, anno 1696 . . . to congratulate His Majesties happy return to London, *etc.* [Signed: G. C. Gent. With an emblematical engraving.] [*London?* 1696.] *s. sh.* fol. C. **20.** f. **2.** (**206.**)

C., G., *Gent., Practicioner in Phisicke.* A Treatise of Mathematicall Phisicke, or briefe Introduction to Phisicke, by Iudiciall Astronomy . . . Written by G. C. gent. Practicioner in Phisicke, *etc.* *See* DARIOT (C.) A Briefe and most easie Introduction to the Astrologicall Judgement of the Starres . . . Augmented and amended by G. C., *etc.* 1598. 4°. **1141.** a. **42.**

C., G., *Italiano residente a Londra.* La Conciliazione del governo italiano col Vaticano. Per G. C. Italiano residente a Londra [i.e. Giuseppe Clemente]. pp. 24. *Napoli*, 1887. 8°. **8033.** f. **47.**

C., G., *a Lover of his Country.* Severall Considerations, offered to the Parliament concerning the improvement of Trade, Navigation, and Comerce, more especially the old draperies and other woolen manufactures of England: by G. C. a Louer, of his country [i.e. George Carew]. pp. 8. [1675.] 4°. **712.** g. **52.** (**7.**)

—— [Another copy.] **104.** m. **51.**

C., G., *a Lover of Peace and Truth.* Scotland's Present Circumstances, and the Present Duty of Private Christians, with reference thereunto . . . By a Lover of Peace and Truth, G. C. pp. 116. [*Samuel Arnot*:] *Edinburgh*, 1718. 4°. **1354.** f. **3.**

The author's initials on the titlepage have been partially defaced.

C., G. D. Illustrazione di un gran quadro a olio di Paolo Barbotti. [Signed: G. d. C.] pp. 20. *Pavia*, 1858. 8°. **7856.** aaa. **28.** (**6.**)

C., G. v. Der Bischof Dräseke und sein achtjähriges Wirken im Preussischen Staate, von G. v. C. pp. 70. *Bergen*, 1840. 8°. **4887.** a. **21.**

C., G. A. *See* ARMSTRONG (Edmund J.) Poems by the late E. J. Armstrong. [With a preface signed: G. A. C.] 1865. 8°. **11648.** bb. **4.**

C., G. A. *See* C., J. M. and C., G. A. A Small Dictionary of Colloquial Bengali Words. By J. M. C. [i.e. Joseph M. Culshaw] & G. A. C. [i.e. G. A. Cowley.] 1901. 8°. **12906.** de. **24.**

C., G. A.

—— Guide to St George's Chapel, Windsor. Compiled by G. A. C. Second edition. pp. 22. *T. Ingalton*: *Eton*, 1855. 12°. **10362.** de. **1.**

C., G. A. Ordine del Conclaue per la creatione del nuouo Papa. Con le prouisioni . . . per la sedia vacante di Gregorio XV. . . . Con la lista di tutti gl'Illustriss. e Reuerendiss. Cardinali, quali hoggi viuono, e da chi furono creati. Dato in luce da G. A. C. *N. Tebaldini*: *Bologna*, 1623. 4°. **4855.** bb. **22.**

C., G. B. *See* BRUNTON (Richard L.) A Brief Memoir of Ellen Hamer B. [i.e. E. H. Brunton], *etc.* [With an obituary notice of R. L. Brunton, signed: G. B. C.] [1869.] 16°. **4906.** aa. **67.** (**16.**)

C., G. B. Capricio di G. B. C. pubblicato nell'occasione che la nobile signora contessa Orsola Mocenigo si fa sposa col nobile signor Giovanni-Venezze. *Padova*, 1819. 12°. **11436.** aa. **35.**

C., G. B. It is for Man to Choose. [By] G. B. C. [i.e. Georgina de B. Bowen-Colthurst. In verse.] pp. 16. *Elkin Mathews*: *London*, 1921. 8°. **011648.** df. **163.**

C., G. B. Plots, Conspiracies and Attempts of domestick and forraigne enemies, of the Romish Religion, against the Princes, and Kingdomes of England, Scotland, and Ireland. Beginning with the Reformation of Religion under Queene Elizabeth, unto this present yeare, 1642. Briefly collected by G. B. C. pp. 28. *For Ralph Rounthwait*: *London*, 1642. 4°. **E. 121.** (**29.**)

—— The second edition. Whereunto is added, The present rebellion in Ireland, the cruell practises in France against the Protestants, the murther of Henry the 3d and Henry the 4th by the Popish French faction. pp. 46. *G. M. for Ralph Rounthwait*: *London*, 1642. 4°. **701.** e. **5.** (**1.**)

C., G. B. Sul Monte dei Paschi de Siena. Lasciate il Monte com' è. Osservazioni di G. B. C. pp. 34. *Firenze*, 1862. 8°. **8225.** ee. **39.** (**4.**)

C., G. B. Sul progetto ministeriale di un istituto di credito fondiario ed agricolo. Osservazioni di G. B. C. pp. 40. *Firenze*, 1862. 8°. **8225.** dd. **41.** (**6.**)

C., G. C. L'Alboino in Italia. Drama per musica, *etc.* [The dedication signed: G. C. C., i.e. G. C. Corradi.] pp. 57. *Il Nicolini*: *Venezia*, 1691. 12°. **906.** l. **4.** (**2.**)

C., G. C. Bulògna travajâ dal guêrr zivil di Lambertazz e di Geremi. Poemètt scherzèvol fatt da G. C. C. (Conte Gregorio Casali), *etc.* 1827. 12°. *See* CASALI BENTIVOGLIO PALEOTTI (G. F. M.) *Count.* **11431.** aaa. **35.**

C., G. C. Canzone della pulice ridicolosa, e bella, sopra vna vechia, & vna giouane che si spulicauano vna sera . . . Di G. C. C. [i.e. G. C. Croce.] *Gli eredi del Cochi*: *Bologna*, 1635. 8°. **1071.** g. **10.** (**14.**)

—— Lamento della pouertà per l'estremo freddo del presente anno M.D.LXXXVII. di G. C. C. [i.e. G. C. Croce.] *Per lo Cochi*: *Bologna*, 1620. 8°. 1071.h.43.(10.)

—— Lamento di tutte le arti del mondo e di tutte le città, e terre d'Italia, per le poche facende che si fanno alla giornata. Di G. C. C. [i.e. G. C. Croce.] *Modona*, 1588. 8°. **1071.** c. **63.** (**8.**)

—— Lamento, et esclamatione fatta dal Duca di Birone avanti la sua morte. Di G. C. C. [i.e. G. C. Croce.] pp. 13. *Gli heredi di Gio. Rossi*: *Bologna*, 1603. 8°. **10604.** aa. **12.** (**3.**)

C., G. C. L., *Docteur en médecine de la Faculté de Montpellier.* L'École du chirurgien, ou les Principes de la chirurgie françoise . . . Par G. C. L. C. docteur en médecine de la Faculté de Montpelier [i.e. G. C. Le Clerc]. pp. 138. *E. Michallet*: *Paris*, 1684. 12°. **782.** b. **11.**

C., G. D. Disamina degli scrittori, e dei monumenti risguardanti S. Rufino, vescovo, e martire di Asisi . . . Seguono tre appendici. I. Serie dei vescovi di Asisi . . . II. Dei documenti. III. Iscrizioni romane della città e vicinanze di Asisi, *etc.* [The dedication signed: G. D. C., i.e. G. di Costanzo.] pp. xxiii. 542. pl. x. *Asisi*, 1797. 4°. **4828.** g. **20.**

C., G. D., *M.* Histoire de l'isle de Corse contenant en abrégé les principaux événemens de ce pays, *etc.* (Par M. G. D. C. [i.e. J. F. Goury de Champgrand.] pp. xvi. 296. *Nancy*, 1749. 8°. **596.** a. **37.**

C., G. D., *Mr.* Journal d'un voyage de Genève à Londres, en passant par la Suisse, entremelé d'avantures tragiques. Par Mr. G. D. C. pp. 184. 1783. 12°. **10196.** bb. **39.** (**1.**)

C., G. D., *le P.* Relations nouvelles du Levant; ou Traités de la religion, du gouvernement, et des coûtumes des Perses, des Armeniens, et des Gaures . . . Composés par le P. G. D. C. [i.e. G. de Chinon] & donnés au public par le sieur L. M. P. D. E. T. (L. Moréri.) pp. 481. *I. Thioly*: *Lyon*, 1671. 12°. **1053.** b. **31.**

—— [Another copy.] **280.** f. **29.**

C., G. D., *le Sieur.*

—— Histoire tragicomique de nostre temps, sous le nom de Splendor & de Lucinde . . . par le sieur G. D. C. (Guil. de Coste.) 1624. 8°. *See* COSTE (G. de) **1072.** b. **5.**

C., G. D. B. Il Libro delle meraviglie, o Spiegazione dei fenomeni della natura fatta a' fanciulli da G. D. B. C. pp. 237. *Firenze,* 1869. 8°. **8705.** b. 2.

C., G. E. Complete Baronetage. Edited by G. E. C. [i.e. George E. Cokayne.] 5 vol. *W. Pollard & Co.: Exeter,* 1900–06. 8°.

—— [Another copy.] Complete Baronetage. Edited by G. E. C. [i.e. George E. Cokayne.] *Exeter,* 1900–09. 8°. **9918.** f. 2.

—— Index . . . together with an appendix, *etc.* pp. 91. *W. Pollard & Co.: Exeter,* 1909. 8°. **2101.b.**

—— Complete Peerage of England, Scotland, Ireland, Great Britain and the United Kingdom, extant, extinct or dormant; alphabetically arranged and edited by G. E. C. [i.e. George E. Cokayne.] 8 vol. *G. Bell & Sons: London,* 1887–98. 8°. **9914.t.**
From vol. 2 *onwards W. Pollard & Co.: Exeter share the publication with G. Bell & Sons.*

—— The Complete Peerage of England, Scotland, Ireland . . . By G. E. C. [i.e. George Edward Cokayne.] New edition, revised and much enlarged. Edited by the Hon. Vicary Gibbs. (vol. 4. Edited by the Hon. V. Gibbs with the assistance of H. A. Doubleday; vol. 5. Edited by the Hon. V. Gibbs and H. A. Doubleday; vol. 6. Edited by H. A. Doubleday, Duncan Warrand and Lord Howard de Walden; vol. 7–9, 13. Edited by H. A. Doubleday and Lord Howard de Walden; vol. 10. Edited by H. A. Doubleday, Geoffrey H. White and Lord Howard de Walden; vol. 11 [*etc.*] Edited by Geoffrey H. White.) *St. Catherine Press: London,* 1910– . 4°. **2101.a.**

—— [Another copy.] **9915.r.1.**

—— [Another copy.] **9918.d.**

—— Some Notice of Various Families of the Name of Marsh. Compiled by G. E. C. [i.e. George E. Cokayne.] pp. 56. *W. Pollard & Co.: Exeter,* 1900. 8°. [*The Genealogist.* New series. vol. 16. suppl.] **2100.** a.

—— State of the Peerage of Ireland, at and since the time of the Union, 1801 to 1888. Also list of the Knights of St. Patrick . . . 1783 to 1888. Edited by G. E. C. [i.e. George E. Cokayne.] From The Genealogist, *etc.* pp. 58. *G. Bell & Sons: London,* 1889. 8°. **09915.** l. 5.

C., G. E. L. *See* LUCAS (Carl W.) Forms of the Ionic Dialect in Homer, *etc.* [The translator's preface signed: G. E. L. C., i.e. George E. L. Cotton.] 1846. 12°. **832.** c. **47.**

—— The Antiquities of Marlborough College. A lecture, *etc.* [The preface signed: G. E. L. C., i.e. George E. L. Cotton.] pp. 25. *W. W. Lucy: Marlborough,* 1855. 8°. **10347.** d. **10.** (**4.**)

—— Third edition. pp. 28. *William Gale: Marlborough,* 1887. 8°. **010358.** f. **8.** (**8.**)

C., G. F. *See* BIBLE.—*Selections.* [*English.*] Sunday: Quotations from the Bible . . . to which are appended a few remarks, *etc.* [Signed: G. F. C., i.e. George F. Chambers.] 1861. 8°. **4355.** aa. 4.

—— Where are you Going on Sunday? [Signed: G. F. C., i.e. George F. Chambers.] pp. 4. *W. Macintosh: London,* [1864.] 8°. **4406.** g. 2. (49.)

C., G. F. R. History & Genealogy of the Colts of that Ilk and Gartsherrie and of the English & American branches of that family. [The preface signed: G. F. R. C., i.e. George F. R. Colt.] pp. vi. 276. *Printed for private circulation: Edinburgh,* 1887. 8°. **9902.** f. **18.**

C., G. G.

—— Doggerel Verses. By G. G. C. pp. 15. *Privately printed,* [1925?] 8°. **11656.** e. **81.**

C., G. G. Fasciculus carminum stylo Lucretiano scriptorum auctoribus doctis quibusdam viris in sinu Regiæ Scholæ Etonensis Musarum disciplina olim institutis. [The editor's preface signed: G. G. C., i.e. William G. Cookesley.] pp. viii. 52. *Impensis E. P. Williams: Etonæ,* 1839. 8°. **1213.** m. **37.**

C., G. G. What is the Good of Life Assurance? A discussion, with remarks on tontine schemes. By G. G. C. pp. 31. *Imperial Life Office: London,* 1884. 8°. **8229.** bb. **46.** (**3.**)

C., G. H. *See* DUMONT (P. E. L.) Recollections of Mirabeau *etc.* [The translator's preface signed: G. H. C.] 1832. 8°. **2390.** d. **6.**

C., G. K. *See* B., H. The Great Inquiry . . . Ornamented with sharp cuts drawn on the spot by G. K. C. [i.e. G. K. Chesterton.] [1903.] 8°. **012314.** h. **49.**

C., G. L. *See* CHAMBERLIN (Wilbur J.) Ordered to China, *etc.* [The editor's note signed: G. L. C., i.e. G. L. Chamberlin?] 1903. 8°. **09055.** aa. **11.**

C., G. L. Pater Noster; or, Brief meditations on the Lord's Prayer. By G. L. C. pp. 98. *T. Bosworth & Co.: London,* 1886. 8°. **764.** m. **5.** (**12.**)

C., G. L. B. O. Siris: a Chain of Philosophical Reflexions and Inquiries concerning the Virtues of Tar Water . . . By G. L. B. O. C. [i.e. George Berkeley, Bishop of Cloyne.] pp. 261. *R. Gunne: Dublin,* 1744. 8°. **8705.** bb. **6.**

C., G. M. Manual de la Elocuencia Española, arreglado al espiritu del nuevo plan de estudios, por G. M. C. pp. iv. 188. *Madrid,* 1846. 8°. **11805.** b. **33.**

C., G. M. Shadows of Truth; or, Thoughts and allegories in prose and verse. A Sunday-book for young persons. By G. M. C. [With illustrations.] pp. 217. *John Morgan: London,* [1862.] 8°. **4409.** bb. **9.**

C., G. M. The Strike; or, Do you want a new master? [A religious tract.] By G. M. C., author of "Christmas; or, the Shepherds of Bethlehem." pp. 12. *S.P.C.K.: London,* [1862.] 12°. **4417.** aaa. **15.**

C., G. M. D. Éloge historique de Suger, abbé de Saint-Denis, régent du royaume sous le règne de Louis VII . . . Par G. M. D. C. [i.e. Marquis F. G. J. Du Chasteler.] pp. 83. *Amsterdam,* 1779. 8°. **4864.** d. **13.** (**1.**)

C., G. M. F. D. Apologia per la scrittura pubblicata in Milano l'anno MDCCVII. [i.e. "De juribus Rom. Imperii et Mediolani ducatus in civitatibus Parmae et Placentiae" by Luigi Caroelli] ed osservazioni critiche sopra l'Istoria del dominio temporale della Sede Apostolica nel ducato di Parma e Piacenza [by Giusto Fontanini], pubblicata in Roma l'anno MDCCXX. e sopra la Dissertazione istorico-politica, e legale della natura, e qualità delle città di Piacenza e Parma [by Francesco Nicoli]. [The preface signed: G. M. F. D. C., i.e. G. M. F. de Colla.] 2 pt. *Milano,* 1727. fol. **592.** i. **15**

C., G. N. The Crusader: a romaunt; and other poems. By G. N. C. pp. 111. *Newman & Co.: London,* 1879. 8°. **11652.** c. **30**

C., G. N. Il Popolo di Giuda liberato dalla morte per intercessione della regina Ester. Componimento sacro per musica, *etc.* (Poesia di G. N. C.) pp. 16. *Roma*, 1768. 8º. **11715**. ee. **1**. (**2**.)

C., G. P.

—— Dittionario italiano e francese . . . Per M. Filippo Venuti. Corretto e accresciuto di nouo di molte voci e sententie cauate tutti da migliori autori. [Stated in the printers' preface to the reader to be a revised edition of the work of G. P. C., i.e. Jean Pierre Canal.] 1626. 8º. *See* VENUTI (Filippo) *of Cortona*. **627**. c. **5**. (**2**.)

C., G. S. *See* CLEPHANE (Anna J. D. M.) Plays and Poems. [With " Elegies in memory of D.M.C." signed: G. S. C.] 1864. 8º. **11781**. bb. **43**.

C., G. S. Examen critique des anciens historiens d'Alexandre-le-Grand. Seconde édition, considérablement augmentée. [The preface signed: G. S. C., i.e. G. E. J. G. de Clermont-Lodève, Baron de Sainte-Croix. With plates.] pp. xxxii. 924. *Paris*, 1804. 4º. **584**. h. **11**.

C., G. S. Gardens of Light and Shade. By G. S. C. [With plates.] pp. viii. 70. *Elliot Stock: London*, 1886. 8º. **7055**. h. **4**.

C., G. S. A. Cenni su Fra Dolcino. Ricordi e raffronti storici e religiosi, compilati e svolti con note da G. S. A. C. pp. vi. 40. *Torino*, 1887. 8º. **4804**. c. **17**. (**4**.)

—— Nuova edizione, emendata accresciuta e rifatta dall'autore. pp. iv. 89. *Milano*, 1889. 8º. **4866**. g. **10**.

C., G. T. *See* CLARKE (Samuel) *Minister of St. Bennet Fink.* The Duty of Every One that intends to be Saved, *etc.* [The editor's preface signed: G. T. C., i.e. George T. Clark.] 1882. 12º. **4400**. h. **30**.

—— *See* CLARKE (Samuel) *Minister of St. Bennet Fink.* The Saint's Nosegay . . . Reprinted, with a memoir of the author, by his descendant, G. T. C. [i.e. George T. Clark.] 1881. 12º. **4400**. a. **41**.

C., G. U. P. Il Terremoto di Messina. Pensieri di un amico dell'umanità, G. U. P. C. [i.e. G. U. Pagani-Cesa. In verse.] pp. xvii. *Venezia, Padova*, 1783. 8º. B. **746**. (**7**.)

—— [Another copy.] **11431**. e. **17**.

C., G. W. *See* MELYN (C.) Broad-Advice to the United Netherland Provinces . . . Made and arranged from divers true and trusty memories. By J. A. G. W. C. [Here ascribed to C. Melyn.] 1854. 4º. [*Vertoogh van Nieu Nederland, etc.*] **9604**. f. **3**.

C., G. W. *See* WINTHROP (Theodore) Life in the Open Air, *etc.* [The editor's note signed: G. W. C., i.e. George W. Curtis.] 1876. 8º. **12209**. ccc. **8**.

C., G. W. A Book of Family Prayer, compiled chiefly from the devotions of Jeremy Taylor and other divines of the seventeenth century. [The preface signed: G. W. C.] pp. 48. *Longmans & Co.: London*, 1862. 12º. **3456**. b. **49**.

C. (GEO.) *See* PERIODICAL PUBLICATIONS.—*London.* Tidings of Life and Peace. Edited by Geo. C. [i.e. George Cutting.] 1890, *etc.* 8º. P.P. **353**. cmb.

—— Saved or Deceived, Which? By Geo. C. [i.e. George Cutting.] pp. 16. *W. H. Broom & Rouse: London*, [1890.] 32º. **4422**. c. **30**. (**2**.)

—— " Seed Time " Series (of Gospel Books) . . . By Geo. C. (Geo. Cutting.) [1922.] 16º. *See* CUTTING (George) **04420**. f. **42**.

C. (GERHARD R. v.) Ruinen, oder Taschenbuch zur Geschichte verfallener Ritterburgen und Schlösser, *etc.* [The preface to Bd. 1. signed: Gerhard R. v. C.] 5 Bd. *Wien*, 1834, 27, 28. 12º. **10230**. a. **25**.

The title is taken from the titlepages of Bd. 2, 3. *Bd.* 1, 4, 5 *have special titlepages and the general title " Ruinen " occurs on the half titles.*

C. (GF. J.) Attila und rother Frack. Gedanken über das Verhältniss Ungarn's zu Oesterreich und die Neugestaltung des Kaiserstaates. Von Gf. J. C. pp. 39. *Klausenburg*, 1861. 8º. **8074**. ff. **31**. (**1**.)

C. (GYÖRGY) *See* BIBLE. [*Hungarian.*] Magyar Biblia . . . Mellyet . . . Magyar nyelvre forditott . . . Comáromi C. György [i.e. Gy. Csipkes], *etc.* [1718.] 8º. **1410**. c. **12**.

C., H. *See* APPERLEY (Charles J.) The Life of John Mytton . . . With a memoir of Nimrod [signed: H. C.]. [1871.] 8º. **10826**. aaa. **18**.

—— —— [1892.] 8º. **10827**. aaa. **42**.

C., H. *See* ARISTOTLE. [*Rhetorica.—English.*] Aristotle's Rhetoric, *etc.* [The epistle dedicatory signed: H. C.] 1686. 8º. **11805**. bb. **25**.

C., H. *See* BAUDELAIRE (C. P.) [*Selections.*] Some Translations from Charles Baudelaire, Poet and Symbolist. [By] H. C. [1894.] 8º. **11483**. b. **56**.

C., H. *See* BAXTER (Richard) [A Call to the Unconverted.] La Vusch da Deus, caclomma ils Pucconts tiers la Penitentia . . . Mess giu en Rumonsch. [The translator's dedicatory letter signed: H. C., i.e. Hans Caflisch.] 1669. 12º. **4411**. aa. **2**.

C., H. *See* BIBLE.—*Thessalonians.* [*English.*] Lectures vpon the First and Second Epistles of Paul to the Thessalonians; preached by . . . M. Robert Rollock. [The editors' epistle dedicatory signed: H. C., W. A., i.e. Henry Charteris, William Arthur.] 1606. 8º. **3266**. ee. **14**.

C., H. *See* BONATTI (G.) Anima Astrologiæ, *etc.* [The translator's preface signed: H. C., i.e. Henry Coley.] 1676. 8º. **718**. d. **12**.

C., H. *See* BURROWS (John N.) and PLIMPTON (W.) Ritual Notes . . . By the editors of " The Order of Divine Service " (H. C., E. C. R. L. [i.e. H. Cairncross, E. C. R. Lamburn]), *etc.* 1926. 8º. **3474**. aa. **2**.

C., H. *See* CORRIE (Daniel) *Bishop of Madras.* Sermons, with a charge . . . and addresses, *etc.* [The editor's preface signed: H. C., i.e. Henry Corrie.] 1837. 8º. **4461**. i. **6**.

C., H. *See* CULVERWELL (Thomas W.) Meditative Hours . . . With a memoir of the author [signed: H. C., i.e. H. Culverwell]. 1867. 8º. **11646**. cc. **32**.

C., H.

—— *See* GREGORY XIII., *Pope* [Ugo Buoncompagni]. The Popes pittiful Lamentation for the death of his deere darling Don Ioan of Austria . . . Translated . . . by H. C. [1578.] 8º. Mic. A. **696**. (**1**.)

C., H. *See* JOHNSON (Samuel) *LL.D.* Prayers and Meditations, *etc.* [With an introduction signed: H. C.] 1906. 8º. **3455**. h. **36**.

C., H. *See* LAURENT, *de la Résurrection, etc.* The Practice of the Presence of God, *etc.* [The translator's preface signed: H. C.] [1906.] 8º. **04402**. fff. **1/11**.

—— —— [1907.] 8º. **3939**. ee. **10**.

—— —— 1908. 32º. **3940**. a. **53**.

C., H.

—— *See* LAURENT, *de la Résurrection, etc.* The Spiritual Maxims of Brother Lawrence. [The translator's preface signed: H. C.] [1907.] 8°. **3939. ee. 9.**

—— —— [1907.] 8°. **04402. fff. 1/12.**

C., H. *See* NORTHAMPTON, *County of. Begin.* The Addresse of the County of Northampton, to his Excellency the Lord Generall Monck. [Preceded by "An Extract out of a Letter from a Gentleman of Quality, wherein this Addresse was sent up to be printed," signed: H. C.] [1660.] *s. sh.* fol. **1851.c.11.(3.)**

C., H.

—— *See* PARÉ (A.) An Explanation of the Fashion and Use of three and fifty Instruments of Chirurgery. Gathered out of Ambrosius Pareus . . . and done into English . . . by H. C. [i.e. Helkiah Crooke.] 1634. 8°. [*READ (Alexander) M.D., F.R.C.P.* Σωματογραφια ἀνθρωπινη, *etc.*] **782. l. 2.**

C., H. *See* PROTESTANTS. A Seasonable Discourse shewing the Necessity of Union amongst Protestants . . . Also, the charge of persecution, lately maintained against the established religion, by W. P. [i.e. William Penn], H. C. [i.e. Henry Care], and other insignificant scribblers, detected, *etc.* 1688. 4°. **T. 1030. (13.)**

C., H. *See* ROLLOCK (Robert) Certaine Sermons, upon Severall Texts of Scripture, *etc.* [The editors' epistle dedicatory signed: H. C., W. A., i.e. Henry Charteris, William Arthur.] 1634. 8°. **4453. de. 1.**

C., H. *See* SCAPULA (J.) Joannis Scapulæ Lexicon Græco-Latinum, *etc.* [The editor's address signed: H. C., i.e. Henry Cotton.] 1820. fol. **12924. k. 1.**

C., H. *See* TALES. Moral and Instructive Tales, *etc.* [The editor's preface signed: H. C.] [1786.] 8°. **1210. l. 1. (3.)**

—— —— [1790?] 12°. **12804. aaa. 11.**

C., H. Abbregé de l'Histoire Françoyse, auec les Effigies des Roys, tirées des plus rares & excellentz Cabinetz de la France. Par H. C. *Par I. le Clerc: Paris,* 1585. fol. **L.R.404.f.12.**

—— Abbrege de l'Histoire Frãçoise, auec les effigies des Roys, depuis Pharamond iusques au Roy Henry iiij. à present regnant, tirees des plus rares & excellents cabinets de la France. Par H. C. Reueuë & augmentée de nouveau. *Iean le Clerc: Paris,* 1599. fol. **9200. i. 21.**

—— [Another edition.] Reueu, corrigé & augmenté de nouueau, de ce qui s'est passé, iusques à la presente annee 1610. *I. Petit: Rouen,* 1610. fol. **1319. m. 1.**

—— [Another edition.] Reueu, corrigé & augmenté de nouueau, de ce qui s'est passé iusques au mois d'Auril, 1613. pp. 187. *D. Geuffroy: Rouen,* 1613. 8°. **1058. c. 15.**

—— [Another edition.] Reueu, corrigé & augmenté de nouueau, de ce qui s'est passé, iusques au mois de Feburier 1620. *D. Geuffroy: Rouen,* 1620. fol. **595. k. 16. (2.)**

C., H. Animadversions on a Late Paper, entituled, A Letter to a Dissenter upon occasion of his Majesties late Gracious Declaration of Indulgence [signed: T. W., i.e. George Savile, Marquis of Halifax]. By H. C. [i.e. Henry Care.] pp. 40. *For John Harris: London,* 1687. 4°. **T. 2230. (12.)**

—— [Another copy.] **T. 763. (10.)**

—— [Another copy.] **110. f. 14.**

—— [Another edition.] pp. 40. *For J. Harris: London,* 1687. 4°. **116. c. 38.**

C., H.

—— *See* F., S. A Letter to a Friend, concerning the late Answers to a Letter to the Dissenter. [A criticism of "Animadversions . . . By H. C." and "An Answer to a Letter to a Dissenter" by Sir Roger L'Estrange.] [1687.[fol. **T. 2230. (13.)**

C., H. Animadversions upon the Responses of the Athenian Mercury, to the Questions about Infant-Baptism. [Signed: H. C., i.e. Hercules Collins.] pp. 4. [*London,* 1692.] fol. **L.R.404.n.5.(78.)**

C., H. An Answer to the Letter from Edmund Burke, Esq., one of the Representatives of the City of Bristol, to the Sheriffs of that City . . . The second edition. [The advertisement signed: H. C.] pp. 60. *T. Cadell: London,* 1777. 8°. **8177. aa. 13.**
The first edition, issued anonymously the same year, is entered under BURKE *(Right Hon. Edmund) [Letter to the Sheriffs of Bristol.—Appendix.]*

C., H. L'Avenir de Paris, par un ancien élève de l'École normale. [Signed: H. C.] pp. 14. *Paris,* 1871. 8°. **8051. f. 1. (4.)**

C., H. Brief Directions for our more Devout Behaviour in Time of Divine Service. With a short rationale on the Common-Prayer. By H. C. [i.e. Henry Cornwallis.] The second edition. pp. 47. *T. W. for J. Robinson: London,* 1693. 8°. **4402. c. 1. (4.)**

C., H. The Catholike Moderator: or a Moderate Examination of the Doctrine of the Protestants. Prouing against the too rigid Catholikes of these times, and against the arguments especially, of that booke called, The Answer to the Catholike Apologie, that we, who are members of the Catholike, Apostolike, & Roman Church, ought not to condeme the Protestants for heretikes, vntill further proofe be made. First written in French by a Catholike Gentleman (H. C. [i.e. Cardinal Jacques Davy Du Perron]), and now faithfully translated, *etc.* [A translation of "Examen pacifique de la doctrine des Huguenots."] pp. 68. *For Nathaniel Butter: London,* 1623. 4°. **3939. aaa. 38. (1.)**

—— The third impression. [The translator's preface signed: W. W.] pp. 68. *For Nathaniel Butter: London,* 1623. 4°. **C. 46. d. 24.**
The arms of Sir Edward Dering, Bart., are stamped on the binding.

—— The fourth impression. pp. 68. *For Nathaniel Butter: London,* 1624. 4°. **1018. l. 29. (4.)**

—— [Another copy.] **G. 19571. (7.)**

C., H. A College Hall-Book of 1401–2. (Reprinted, with some additions, from Notes and Queries.) [Signed: H. C., i.e. Herbert Chitty.] pp. 15. *Privately printed: London,* [1916.] 8°. **08365. e. 29. (1.)**

C., H. The Country-Curates Advice to his Parishioners . . . By H. C. [i.e. Henry Cornwallis.] pp. 76. *T. W. for J. Robinson: London,* 1693. 8°. **T. 1832. (7.)**

C., H. Diana. Or, The excellent conceitful Sonnets of H. C. [i.e. Henry Constable.] Augmented with diuers quatorzains of honorable and lerned personages. Deuided into viij. decads. *Iames Roberts for Richard Smith: London,* [1584.] 16°. **C. 39. a. 60.**
The date supplied is that found in perfect copies; this copy is cropped. The work was published in 1594. *Imperfect; wanting sig.* F, *which is supplied from the reprint published in* 1818.

—— [Another edition.] [Edited by Samuel W. Singer.] [*London,* 1818.] 8°. **1078. g. 12**
One of an edition of fifty copies.

C., H. A Discourse concerning the Drayning of Fennes and Surrounded Grounds in the sixe Counteys of Norfolke, Suffolke, Cambridge with the Isle of Ely, Huntington, Northampton, and Lincolne. [Signed: H. C.] *London*, 1629. 4°. **725.** c. **35.**

—— [Another copy.] **290.** b. **43.** (**1.**)

C., H. Draconica: or, an Abstract of all the penal-laws touching matters of religion; and the several oaths and tests thereby enjoyned . . . With brief observations thereupon. Published . . . by H. C. [i.e. Henry Care.] pp. 19. *Printed by George Larkin: London*, 1687. fol. **514.** l. **1.** (**16.**)

—— [Another copy.] **515.** k. **22.** (**2.**)

—— [Another copy.] **694.** m. **4.** (**2.**)

—— [Another copy.] **599.** i. **24.** (**25.**)

C., H. Eighteen Sixty-One rhymed to death. [Signed: H. C., i.e. Henry Campkin.] pp. 8. *S. Prentice: [London*, 1862.] 8°. **012314.** i. **2.** (**1.**)

C., H. Elegy on the Death of the Princess Charlotte, *etc.* [Signed: H. C.] *W. Mantz: [London*, 1817.] *s. sh.* 4°. **1879.** c. **12.** (**144.**)

C., H. An Elegie Sacred to the Memory of Sir Edmund-bury Godfrey, Knight; whose body was lately found barbarously murthered, and since honourably interr'd, *etc.* [Signed: H. C., i.e. Henry Case?] *For L. C.* [*Langley Curtis*]: *London*, 1678. *s. sh.* fol. C. **20.** f. **2.** (**112.**)

—— [Another edition.] *For Langley Curtis: London*, 1678. *s. sh.* fol. Lutt. I. 53.

C., H. England's Jests Refin'd and Improv'd. Being a choice collection of the merriest jests . . . yet extant . . . To which are added, XIII. ingenious characters, drawn to the life . . . The third edition with the addition of several jests, not permitted to be printed in the former impressions . . . By H. C. [i.e. Humfrey Crouch.] pp. 185. *For John Harris: London*, 1693. 12°. **12316.** a. **20.**

C., H. The Forrest of Fancy. Wherein is conteined very prety apothegmes, and pleasaunt histories, both in meeter and prose, songes, sonets, epigrams and epistles, of diuerse matter and in diuerse manner. With sundry other deuises, no less pithye then pleasaunt and profytable. [Signed: H. C.] B.L. *Imprinted by Thomas Purfoote: London*, 1579. 4°. C. **39.** c. **36.**

C., H. Fromond's Chantry at Winchester. (Reprinted from Notes and Queries.) [Signed: H. C., i.e. Herbert Chitty.] pp. 14. *Privately printed: London*, [1916.] 8°. **08365.** e. **29.** (**4.**)

C., H.

—— The Greeks and Trojans Warres.
Caus'd by that wanton Trojan Knight Sir Paris
Who ravishes Hellen and her to Troy carries.
The Greeks in revenge, and to fetch her again,
A mighty great Army do quickly ordain.
Imagine you see them besiedging old Troy,
Which after ten years they at th'last destroy,
With a fit allusion, before the conclusion.
Tune is, A Conscionable Caveat. [Signed: H. C., i.e. Humfrey Crouch.] B.L. *F. Grove: London*, [1640?] fol. Rox. III. **158.**

C., H. Her Dignity and Grace. A tale. By H. C. 3 vol. *Chapman & Hall: London*, 1880. 8°. **12640.** g. **9.**

C., H. Hortus Madraspatensis. Catalogue of plants, indigenous and naturalized, in the Agri-Horticultural Society's Gardens, Madras. [The preface signed: H. C., i.e. Hugh F. C. Cleghorn.] pp. v. 26. 1853. 8°. *See* MADRAS.—*Agri-Horticultural Society of Madras.* **7055.** h. **9.**

C., H. The Householders. Another story of the Orkneys. By H. C., author of "Island Notes in Wartime" [i.e. H. Campbell], *etc.* pp. 72. "*Scottish Chronicle*" *Press: Edinburgh*, 1921. 8°. **012603.** ff. **57.**

C., H. "I Won't Go to the Ball." [A religious tract. Signed: H. C.] pp. 14. *Yapp & Hawkins: London*, [1873.] 32°. **4402.** aa. **21.**

C., H. Island Folk Songs. By H. C., author of Island Notes in War Time [i.e. H. Campbell]. pp. 28. *W. R. Mackintosh: Kirkwall*, 1920. 8°. **11607.** c. **31.**

—— Island Notes in War Time. [Concerning the Orkneys.] By H. C. [i.e. H. Campbell], *etc.* pp. 69. "*Scottish Chronicle*" *Press: Edinburgh*, 1918. 8°. **012350.** de. **21.**

—— Jean's Garden and how it grew. By H. C., author of "Island Notes in Wartime," &c. [i.e. H. Campbell.] pp. 52. *W. R. Mackintosh: Kirkwall*, 1927. 12°. **012611.** f. **17.**

C., H. Kin kou ki kouan. [A bibliography. Signed: H. C., i.e. Henri Cordier. Reprinted from "T'oung pao."] pp. 8. *Leide*, 1890. 8°. **11098.** b. **2.**

C., H. Londons Lord have Mercy upon us. A true Relation of five modern Plagues or Visitations in London, with the number of all the diseased that were buried: viz.: the first . . . Anno 1592 . . . the second in the yeare 1603, the third in . . . 1625. The fourth in anno 1630. The fift this now present visitation 1636 . . . Written by H. C. [Sometimes attributed to Humfrey Crouch.] *For Richard Harper: London*, [1637.] *s. sh.* fol. **1870.** d. **1.** (**13.**)

—— Londons Vacation, and the Countries Tearme. Or, A lamentable relation of severall remarkable passages which it hath pleased the Lord to shew on severall persons, both in London, and the country in this present visitation, 1636 . . . With new additions. By H. C. [Sometimes attributed to Humfrey Crouch. In verse.] *For Richard Harper: London*, 1637. 8°. C. **39.** a. **29.** *Slightly cropped.*

C., H. Maudie and the White Cat. By H. C., author of "Island Notes in Wartime" [i.e. H. Campbell]. pp. 42. "*Scottish Chronicle*" *Press: Edinburgh*, 1919. 8°. **12802.** cc. **11.**

C., H.

—— Miscellanea nova et curiosa: the new and curious miscellany: being a series of remarkable incidents . . . extracted from the best English and French authors. To which is added, a collection of poems: several of which were never before published. [Signed: H. C., i.e. Hill Chetwood?] pp. xii. 400. *S. Powell: Dublin*, 1749. 8°. **12298.** ff. **23.**

C., H. The Mystery of Gold and Currency. By H. C. pp. 14. *Effingham Wilson: London*, 1861. 8°. **8227.** b. **6.**

C., H. News from Dublin in Ireland. Relating how Colonell Jones, Governour of the said city, with his forces fell upon the rebells, beat the whole army . . . and forc'd them to a flight. In a letter to a Member of the Honourable House of Commons. [Signed: H. C.] *For John Wright: London*, 1647. 4°. E. **416.** (**22.**)

—— [Another edition.] pp. 9. *Privately printed: Edinburgh*, 1884. 8°. [*Historical Reprints.* no. 7.] **9525.** e. **10.**

C., H. Notices biographiques sur M. l'archiprêtre Coll. [Signed: H. C., i.e. Baron E. F. d'Hénin de Cuvillers. Reprinted from the "Bibliothèque du magnétisme animal."] pp. 12. *Paris*, 1817. 8°. **7410.** b. **1.** (**9.**)

C., H. The Office of the Clerk of the Peace. Shewing the true manner and form of the proceedings at the Court of General Quarter-Sessions of the Peace, *etc.* [The preface signed: H. C.] *See* OFFICE. The Office of the Clerk of Assize, *etc.* 1682. 8°. **883.** e. **11.**

C., H. The Payment of Interest during Construction out of Capital. Is it for the benefit of the public? [Signed: H. C.] pp. 10. [1886.] 8°. **08227.** ee. **66.** (**10.**)

C., H. Peter Little and the Lucky Sixpence; The Frog's Lecture; and other stories. A verse book for my children and their playmates. [The dedicatory poem signed: H. C., i.e. Henry Campkin.] pp. 35. *James Ridgway: London,* 1851. 8°. **11646. f. 60.**

—— Fourth edition. With several new stories added. pp. 69. *Robert Hardwicke: London,* 1861. 8°. **11651.** bb. **39.**

C., H. Phil and the Farm. A story of the Orkneys. By H. C. author of "Island Notes in War-Time" [i.e. H. Campbell], *etc.* pp. 77. *"Scottish Chronicle" Press: Edinburgh,* 1920. 8°. **012602. f. 25.**

C., H. Editio fabulae romanensis exeunte saeculo decimo sexto sermone anglico compositae quae inscripta est: Piers Plainnes Seaven Yeres Prentiship. (By H. C. [i.e. Henry Chettle.]) Curavit Hermannus Varnhagen. pp. iv. 37. *Typis F. Junge: Erlangae,* 1900. 4°. **12403.** g. **24.**

—— Piers Plainnes seauen yeres Prentiship. By H. C. [i.e. Henry Chettle.] [A photographic facsimile.] **B.L.** *I. Danter for Thomas Gosson: London,* 1595 [1910?] 16°. L.R. **263.** a. **8.**

C., H. Sakuntala. [The preface signed: H. C.] pp. x. 91. *Longmans & Co.: London; Calcutta* printed, 1925. 8°. **012403.** de. **46.**

C., H. The School Government Handbooks. [The editor's prefaces: signed: H. C., i.e. Herbert Cornish.]

no. 1. The Education Act, 1902. (Third edition.) pp. 32. 1902.
no. 2. The Education Acts, 1870–1901, as remaining after the total and partial repeals, enacted by the Education Act, 1902 . . . Second edition. pp. 96. 1903.
no. 3. Schemes for the Local Education Committees under section 17 of the Education Act, 1902, etc. pp. 17. 57. 1903.
no. 4. The Education Authorities Directory . . . December, 1903(—1928-29). 1903–[28].
no. 6. The "School Government" Edition and Manual of the Code for Public Elementary Schools, 1904–1905 (—1907-1908). [1904–07.]

Office of the "School Board Chronicle" & "School Government Chronicle": London, 1902–[28]. 8°.
8311.cc.46.& P.P.2506.ama.

The "Education Authorities Directory" is placed at P.P. 2506.ama. It is imperfect; wanting the issues between 1907 *&* 1919. *After the* 1928–29 *issue the Directory was published independently of the series.*

C., H. Sentences, selected and translated from commentaries by the Greek Fathers on the New Testament. [The compiler's preface signed: H. C.] pp. xxvii. 132. xx. *P. Davis & Sons: Pietermaritzburg,* 1879. 8°. **3224.** k. **7.**

C., H. Set on the Great Pot. A sermon upon hospitality, preach'd at a late visitation at Tunbridg in Kent, on 2 Kings IV. 38. [The epistle dedicatory signed: H. C., i.e. Henry Cornwallis.] pp. 31. *Printed for the Sons of the Prophets: London,* 1694. 8°. **111.** a. **31.**

C., H.

—— The Story of Kelvedon. [The foreword signed: H. C., i.e. Helen Corke.] pp. 25. [*Kelvedon,* 1954.] 4°. **10368.** v. **20.**

Reproduced from typewriting.

C., H. Tabulæ Linguarum. Being a set of tables, exhibit at sight the declensions of nouns and conjugations of ve . . . In eight parts. Part I. Containing the Lat Spanish, Portuguese, Italian, French, and Norm [The dedication signed: H. C., i.e. Henry Clark pp. xxiv. 252. *Printed for the Author: London,* 1793. 1 **12901.** bb.

No more published.

C., H. Winchester College Chapel. The headmasters' shiel [The preface signed: H. C., i.e. Herbert Chitty.] pp. 1913. 8°. **9904.** b. **37.**

—— Winchester College Documents. [A selection. Signe H. C., i.e. Herbert Chitty.] pp. 8. [*Winches* 1913.] 8°. **08366.** g.

—— The Winchester Hall-Book of 1406–7. (Reprint with variations and additions, from Notes and Querie [Signed: H. C., i.e. Herbert Chitty.] pp. 17. *Privately printed: London,* [1916.] 8°. **08365.** e. **29.**

—— The Winchester Hall-Book of 1414–5. (Reprint from Notes and Queries.) [Signed: H. C., i.e. Herb Chitty.] pp. 15. *Privately printed: London,* [1916.] **08365.** e. 29. (

C., H., and **G.**, R.

—— Winchester College Hall Windows. note by H. C. [i.e. Herbert Chitty] & R. G. [i.e. Regin M. Y. Gleadowe.] pp. 6. pl. 4. *P. & G. We Winchester,* 1931. 8°. **7807.** i.

C., H., and **T.**, E. The Mysterious Travellers, emblematica represented, through the diverse mazes of this mor scene, *etc.* [Signed: H. C. and E. T., animatus ant patus.] pp. 52. *Printed for the Author: Lond* 1831. 12°. T. **1367.**

—— Fifth edition. pp. 72. *Printed for the Author: Lond* 1853. 12°. **4416.** c.

C., H., *Berlin.* Houston Stewart Chamberlain, Die Gru lagen des neunzehnten Jahrhunderts, besprochen v H. C., Berlin. pp. 44. *Dresden & Leipzig,* 1901. 8°. **8006.** dd.

C., H., *Capitaine de Cavalerie.* Considérations sur la organisation de la cavalerie. Par H. C., capitaine cavalerie. pp. 48. *Paris,* 1871. 8°. **8830.** g.

C., H., *le Comte, Docteur en droit.* Mémoire à l'adresse membres du Congrès antimaçonnique de Trente, par comte H. C., docteur en droit [i.e. Count H. J. Coudenhove-Kalergi]. [A criticism of "Le Diable XIXe siècle" published by G. Jogand-Pagès and C. Ha under the pseudonym "Docteur Bataille."] pp. 40. *Wien; Paris,* 1897 [1896]. 8°. **04785.** l. **4.** (

C., H., *Dr.* A Bank Dialogue between Dr. H. C. [i.e. Hu Chamberle n] and a Country Gentleman. [A satir pp. 4. [*London,* 1696.] fol. **8223.** e. **7.** (

—— An Answer to a Libel entituled, a Dialogue betwe Dr. H. C. [i.e. Hugh Chamberle n] and a Countr Gentleman. pp. 24. *Printed & sold by T. Sow London,* 1696. 4°. T. **1788.** (

C., H. *Dr.*

—— Some Remarks upon a late Nameless and Scurrilo Libel, entituled, a Bank-Dialogue between Dr. H. [i.e. Hugh Chamberle n] and a Country-Gentlema In a letter to a person of quality. *Printed & sold T. Sowle: London,* 1696. fol. **8223.** e. **7.** (**13**

C., H., *Esq.* The Fisher Boy. A poem, comprising his several avocations, during the four seasons of the year . . . By H. E. Esq. [i.e. Samuel W. H. Ireland.] pp. viii. 116. *Vernor, Hood & Sharpe: [London,* 1808.] 8°. **1164**. d. **54**.
The titlepage is engraved.

— [Another copy.] The Fisher Boy, *etc.* [*London,* 1808.] 8°. **11659**. df. **28**.

— The Sailor-Boy. A poem. In four cantos. Illustrative of the navy of Great Britain. By H. C. Esq., author of "The Fisher-Boy" [i.e. Samuel W. H. Ireland]. pp. 208. *Vernor, Hood & Sharpe: London,* 1809. 12°. **1164**. d. **24**.
A presentation copy from the author.

C., H., *Gent.* *See* Agrippa (H. C.) The Glory of Women . . . Translated into . . . heroicall verse, by H. C., Gent. [i.e. Hugh Crompton.] 1652. 12°. E. **1289**. (3.)

C., H., *Gent.* The English Dictionary: or, an Interpreter of hard English words . . . The eleventh edition revised and enlarged. By H. C. Gent. (Henry Cockeram.) 1658. 8°. *See* Cockeram (Henry) **12984**. de. **24**.

— The twelfth edition, revised and enlarged by S. C. [i.e. Samuel Clarke.] *W. Miller: London,* 1670. 12°. **12984**. de. **25**.

C., H., *Gent.* The Plain Englishman's Historian: or, a Compendious chronicle of England . . . By H. C. Gent. pp. 141. *For Langley Curtis: London,* 1679. 12°. G. **5903**.

C., H., *in der Kunst-Rechnungs Lieb- und übenden Societät Der Continuirender.* Historisch-algebraischer sehr nützlicher Zeit-Vertreib, bestehend in 100. sehr raren und seltsamen Geschichts-Erzehlungen, welche . . . colligiret und in die edle Algebram . . . verfasset worden . . . von H. C., in der Kunst-Rechnungs Lieb- und übenden Societät Dem Continuirenden. pp. 462. *Lübeck,* 1714. 8°. **1393**. c. **33**.

C., H., *a Lover of true Protestants.* A Word in Season; being a Parallel between the intended bloody massacre of the people of the Jews, in the reign of King Ahasuerus; and the hellish powder-plot against the Protestants, in the reign of King James. Together with an account of the wicked principles and practices of the Church of Rome . . . By H. C. a lover of true Protestants [i.e. Henry Care]. pp. 47. *For Francis Smith: London,* 1679. 4°. **698**. h. **7**. (2.)

— [Another copy.] **3936**. d. **15**.

C., H., *Madame.* *See* Ampère (A. M.) Journal et correspondance . . . Recueillis par Mme H. C. [i.e. Henriette Cheuvreux.] 1872. 12°. **10662**. df. **23**.

— — [1877.] 12°. **10910**. bb. **7**.

— *See* Ampère (A. M.) The Story of His Love: being the journal and early correspondence of A. M. Ampère . . . Edited by Madame H. C. [i.e. Henriette Cheuvreux], *etc.* 1873. 8°. **10661**. ee. **22**.

— *See* Ampère (A. M.) André-Marie Ampère et Jean-Jacques Ampère. Correspondance et souvenirs . . . Recueillis par Madame H. C. [i.e. Henriette Cheuvreux], *etc.* 1875. 12°. **10909**. cc. **1**.

— — 1875. 12°. **10909**. cc. **4**.

C., H., *Mr.* An Epithalamium. Being stanzas on the most auspicious nuptials of the Right Honourable the Marquess of Carmarthen, and the Lady Elizabeth Harley . . . By Mr. H. C. [i.e. Henry Castleton.] pp. 6. *John Morphew: London,* 1712. fol. **11632**. i. 3.

C., H., *Mr.* More Cheap Riches: or, Heavenly Aphorismes; viz. a third, or rather true first part of the Pocket Companion compleated. Being 300 golden sayings more: faithfully copied out of the manuscripts of Mr. H. C. [i.e. Henry Church] . . . By N. C. Master of Arts of Emanuel Colledg in Cambridg (Nat. Church). pp. 68. *D. M. for J. Rothwell: London,* 1660. 12°. **12305**. a. **12**. (2.)

C., H., *Mr., Minister of the Gospel at K.* Inquisitio Nova, et inter Evangelicos hactenus inaudita; or, a Just and true narrative, of the unjust and illegal process raised and pursued against Mr. H. C. [i.e. Hugh Clanny] Minister of the Gospel at K. [i.e. Kirkbean] by the Presbytery and Synod of D. [i.e. Dumfries] . . . Published by the said Mr. C., *etc.* pp. 79. *London,* 1698. 4°. **4175**. aaa. **16**.

C., H., *of the Church of England.* A True Account of the Doctrine of Christ, and of the Primitive Church, with respect to the Eucharist. Occasion'd by a conference with the author, attack'd by a Romish priest, and continued by letters. Wherein transubstantiation is proved a novel doctrine . . . Also occasionally shewing, the inconsistency of a late sacramentarian piece [by Benjamin Hoadly], call'd, A plain Account of the Nature and End of the Sacrament of the Lord's Supper, with the doctrine of the primitive ages, the Reformes, the Church of England, and our greatest divines. Between H. C. of the Church of England, and A. B. of the Church of Rome. pp. xvi. 144. xi. *F. Gyles: London,* 1736. 8°. **4324**. g. **35**.

C., H., *Officier de Cavalerie.* Le Général, sa mission, son rôle, ses qualités. Extrait des meilleurs auteurs anciens et modernes, par H. C., officier de cavalerie. pp. 75. *Paris,* 1875. 8°. [*Mélanges militaires.* sér. 3. no. 81–85.] **8832**. h. **40**. (2.)

C., H., *Φιλονομιον.* The Character of an Honest Lawyer. By H. C. *Φιλονομιον.* *For Jonathan Edwin: London,* 1676. fol. **12330**. k. **6**.

— [Another edition.] *See* Somers (John) *Baron Somers.* A Collection of Scarce and Valuable Tracts, *etc.* vol. 4. 1748. 4°. **184**. a. **4**.

— [Another edition.] By H. G. *Χιλονομιον* [or rather, by H. C. *Φιλονομιον*]. 1790. 8°. [*Strictures on the Lives and Characters of the most Eminent Lawyers, etc.*] *See* G., H., *Χιλονομιον.* **1419**. g. **52**.

C., *Lady* H. *See* C., *Lady* A., and C., *Lady* H. Recollections of Rome in 1843. By the Ladies A. and H. C. [i.e. Augusta Sarah and Honoria Louisa Cadogan.] [1845?] fol. Dept. of Prints & Drawings.

C., *Lady* H. Something about Bells, told to little folks. By Lady H. C. pp. 16. *Hatchards: London,* 1878. 8°. **7897**. aa. **28**.

C., H. d. Wahrhaffter und in der Natur gegründeter Bericht von der Generation und Regeneration der Metallen . . . auf Danielis Georgii Morhofii Epistel an Joelem Langelottum, durch H. d. C. MDCCXVI., *etc.* *See* Roth-Scholtz (F.) Deutsches Theatrum Chemicum, *etc.* Tl. 1. 1728, *etc.* 8°. **46**. l. **3**.

C***, H. de. *See* Bourdaloue (L.) [*Miscellaneous Writings.*] Instruction générale donnée . . . à Madame de Maintenon. [The editor's note signed: H. de C***, i.e. Marquis R. C. H. de Chateaugiron.] 1819. 12°. **4405**. aaa. **5**.

C***, H. de. *See* Businger (J.) Itinéraire du Mont-Righi . . . Traduit de l'allemand . . . par H. de C*** [i.e. Henri de Crousaz]. 1815. 8°. **794**. f. **29**.

C., H. DE. See PICHLER (C.) Zuléima . . . imité de l'allemand par H. de C. [i.e. Marquis R. C. H. de Chateaugiron.] 1825. 12°. C. **101.** f. **24.**

C., H. DE. See WYSS (J. R.) Voyage dans l'Oberland bernois . . . traduit . . . par H. de C. 1817, *etc.* 8°. **157.** d. **2–4.**

C., H. DE. Caricatures. By H de C. pp. x. 43. *Architectural Press: London,* 1926. 8°. **7855.** e. **67.**

C., H. DE, Vte. Quatre prophéties sur l'avenir de l'Italie. Par le Vte H. de C. pp. 31. *Paris,* 1861. 8°. **8033.** c. **38.** (**6.**)

C., H. A. See W., J. W., and C., H. A. Father Jones of Cardiff . . . By . . . J. W. W. and H. A. C. [i.e. J. W. Ward and Hector A. Coe], *etc.* [1908.] 8°. **4907.** bbb. **35.**

C., H. B. See ARABIN (William S. J.) Arabiniana. [The compiler's preface signed: H. B. C., i.e. Henry B. Churchill.] 1843. 8°. C. **71.** e. **6.**

C., H. B. The Insurrection of the twenty-third July, 1803. [An account of the trials of Robert Emmet and others. The preface signed: H. B. C., i.e. Henry B. Code.] pp. xiii. 110. *Graisberry & Campbell: Dublin,* [1803.] 8°. **6495.** b. **8.**

C., H. B. The Tree of Life, bearing twelve manner of fruits, *etc.* [Religious tracts. The preface signed: H. B. C.] no. 1–3. pp. 5–192. *Blackader & Co.: London,* 1853, [54.] 16°. **4406.** a. **18.**
No more published?

—— [Another copy of no. 1.] **3127.** aa. **7.**

C., H. C.

—— See CARUANA DINGLI (E.) Malta, *etc.* [With a foreword signed: H. C. C.] [1925?] 4°. **7867.** d. **7.**

C., H. C. See EVERYMAN. Everyman. Cantata, *etc.* [With analytical notes by H. C. C., i.e. Henry C. Colles.] [1904.] 4°. **7896.** ee. **42.**

C., H. C. Intercession. [By] H. C. C. pp. 48. *Warren & Son: Winchester; Simpkin & Co.: London,* 1890. 8°. **3457.** h. **30.**

C***, H*** D*. La Mort de tous les criminels. [By] H*** D* C***. pp. 43. *Paris,* 1790. 8°. **F. 517.** (**6.**)

—— La Vie de tous les criminels. [By] H*** D* C***. pp. ii. 8–24. *Paris,* 1790. 8°. **F. 517.** (**6*.**)

C. (H. D'A.) The Gospel of the Glory. By H. d'A. C. [i.e. H. d'A. Champney.] pp. 63. *Stow Hill Bible & Tract Depot: Newport, Mon., London,* [1918.] 16°. **4380.** de. **14.**

C., H. E.

—— Édouard et Suzanne; ou, Le vieux chêne. pp. v. 218. *R. Juigné: Londres,* 1813. 12°. **12520.tt.23.**

C., H. E. The Pot-Luck Cookery Book . . . Compiled by H. E. C. pp. 160. *W. P. Nimmo & Co.: Edinburgh,* [1921.] 8°. **07942.** aa. **94.**

C., H. E. Who Took Shem's Common? A historical sketch. [On the Afghan war.] By H. E. C. pp. 48. *Civil Service Printing & Publishing Co.: London,* 1880. 8°. **8028.** aa. **8.** (**6.**)

C., H. E. A. A Noite, ou o Enterro de Carlota [i.e. Carlota Nogueira], poema de H. E. A. C. [i.e. H. E. d'Almeida Coutinho.] Segunda edição. (Em seguimento acrescem . . . algumas outras poesias do mesmo auctor.) pp. 28. *Porto,* 1841. 8°. **11452.** c. **11.**

C., H. E. A.

—— A Saudade, canto elegiaco; na morte do . . . jo João Alvares d'Almeida Guimaraens. Por H. E. A [i.e. H. E. d'Almeida Coutinho.] pp. 12. *Porto,* 1847. **11452.** cc.

C., H. E. M. M. S., *zu Mayntz.* Kurtzverfasstes Mü Manual, worinn deren silbern und guldenen Münt Aigenschafft, Gewicht . . . Analogi und Proporti Tabellenweiss vor Augen gestellet wird . . . Auth H. E. M. M. S. C. zu Mayntz. pp. 118. *May* 1701. 12°. **8548.** aaa

C., H. E. S. M. A Page in my Life-Story. [Signed: H. S. M. C.] pp. 8. *Drummond's Tract Depot: Stirl* [1901.] 32°. **04420.** de. **9.** (

C., H. F. Duchess Eleanour. A tragedy . . . [In ver By the author of "Old Love and New Fortune," [The prefatory note signed: H. F. C., i.e. Henry Chorley.] pp. 74. *T. H. Lacy: London,* [1854.] 12°. **11781.** c

C., H. F. Illustrated Catalogue of Pictures by Masters of Milanese and allied Schools of Lombardy exhibited . 1898. [Signed: H. F. C., i.e. Sir Herbert F. Coo pp. lxxx. 41. pl. XXVII. 1899. fol. See LONDON III. *Burlington Fine Arts Club.* L.R. **21.** c

C., H. F. Old Love and New Fortune. A play . . . verse.] By the author of "Conti," *etc.* [The pref signed: H. F. C., i.e. Henry F. Chorley.] pp. 92. *Chapman & Hall: London,* 1850. 8°. **1344.** l

C., H. F. Reprint of the Book of Remembrance [i.e. of MS. history of the activities of the Jewish Board Guardians], 1859–1929. [The compiler's postscript sign H. F. C., i.e. Hannah F. Cohen.] pp. 66. [1931.] See LONDON.—III. *Board of Guardians for the Relief of Jewish Poor.* **04033.** g.

C., H. F. Sir John Toughbo, M.P.; or, the Registered l pass. By H. F. C. pp. 63. *Thomas Burleigh: Lond* 1903. 8°. **08275.** b.

C., H. F., *Ancien sous-secrétaire de l'abbé Kneipp.* Gu du Kneippiste. Par H. F. C. ancien sous-secrétaire l'abbé Kneipp. pp. 17. *Bruxelles,* 1893. 12°. **07305.** f. **20.** (

C., H. F. S. D. Le Labyrinthe d'amour, ou Suite des Mu françoises. Recherchee des plus beaux esprits de temps par H. F. S. D. C. pp. 305 [306]. *B. Ancel Lyon,* [1611.] 12°. **1102.** b.
The titlepage is engraved.

—— [Another edition.] Le Premier(—Troisiesme) liure Labyrinthe d'amour, où [*sic*] Suite des Muses folast *etc.* 3 pt. *C. le Villain: Rouen,* 1615. 24°. **11475.** a.

—— [A reprint of the Rouen edition of 1615.] *Bruxell* 1863. 12°. **12234.** dd. **1.** (

—— [Another copy.] **11474.** df.

C., H. G.

—— See ANTWERP.—*Museum Plantin-Moretus.* Specim Types from Matrices at the Plantin-Moretus Museu Cast by H. G. C. [i.e. H. G. Carter], *etc.* 1955. 8°. **11918.** m.

C., H. G. B. L. Englands Present Distractions . . . H. G. B. L. C. 1642. 4°. See G., H., *B.L.C.* **E. 126.** (1

C., H. G. D., *Francopolita.* H. G. D. C. [i.e. Hippoph Galeacii de Corneliis] Francopolitæ Wahrer Bericht v dem alten Königreich Austrasien, und klarer Bewe dass die von Frankreich ersonnene Ober-Rheinisc Dependentien, sich . . . über das ganze Hoch- u Nieder-Teutschland . . . wie auch über einig benac barte Königreich und Länder erstrecken, *etc.* [By P. von Hornick.] pp. 52. 1682. 4°. **596.** f. **23.** (1

C., H. G. D., *Francopolita.*

—— H. G. D. C. [i.e. Hippophili Galeacii de Corneliis] Francopolitæ Wahrer Bericht von dem alten Königreich Lothringen, und klarer Beweis, dass die Französische, von denen Carolinischen Fränkischen Königen, anmasslich hergeführte Sprüche, auf die Über-Rheinische Reichs-Länder allerdings nichtig und untüchtig seyen, *etc.* [By P. W. von Hornick.] pp. 65. 1682. 4°. **9327. c. 40.**

C., H. H. Carey Franklin Coombs. A memoir. [Signed: H. H. C., i.e. Hugh H. Carleton? With a portrait.] (Reprinted from the "Bristol Medico-Chirurgical Journal," together with a contribution from Dr. Coombs himself on "Prognosis in Coronary Thrombosis.") pp. 12. [*Bristol*, 1932.] 8°. **010885. eee. 49.**

C., H. H. The Facts about the Unemployed. An appeal and a warning. By One of the Middle Class. [Signed: H. H. C., i.e. Henry H. Champion.] pp. 16. *Modern Press: London*, 1886. 8°. **08248. i. 30. (4.)**

C., H. H. von. M. Avenarius. Vertheidigung der Bahrdtischen Dogmatik, geprüft und widerlegt von H. H. von C. pp. 56. *Erfurth & Tyrol*, 1777. 8°. **3908. f. 40. (6.)**

C., H. J. *See* Arias (F.) The Charity of Jesus Christ. [With a preface signed: H. J. C., i.e. Henry J. Coleridge.] 1880. 8°. **4227. g. 9.**

—— *See* Avancinus (N.) The Life and Teaching of Jesus Christ, *etc.* [The editor's preface signed: H. J. C., i.e. Henry J. Coleridge.] 1883. 8°. **3605. dd. 41, 42.**

—— *See* Bedingfield (Edmund) The Life of Margaret Mostyn, *etc.* [The editor's preface signed: H. J. C., i.e. Henry J. Coleridge.] 1878. 8°. **3605. dd. 25.**

—— *See* Boero (G.) [Vita del B. Pietro Fabio.] The Life of the Blessed Peter Favre, *etc.* [The translator's preface signed: H. J. C., i.e. Henry J. Coleridge.] 1873. 8°. **3605. dd. 8.**

C., H. J. *See* Claudius (M.) Claudius; or, the Messenger of Wandsbeck, and his message. [Extracts, with a sketch of the author's life. The editor's preface signed: H. J. C.] 1859. 8°. **10707. e. 7.**

C., H. J.

—— *See* Colles (Henry C.) Essays and Lectures. With a memoir of the author by H. J. C. [i.e. Hester Janet Colles.] 1945. 8°. **12355. cc. 41.**

C., H. J. *See* Drużbicki (K.) The Tribunal of Conscience. [With a preface signed: H. J. C., i.e. Henry J. Coleridge.] 1884. 8°. **3605. dd. 48.**

—— *See* Hunter (Thomas) *of the Society of Jesus.* An English Carmelite. The Life of Catharine Burton, *etc.* [The editor's preface signed: H. J. C., i.e. Henry J. Coleridge.] 1876. 8°. **3605. dd. 18.**

—— *See* Ludolphus, *de Saxonia.* The Hours of the Passion, *etc.* [With a preface signed: H. J. C., i.e. Henry J. Coleridge.] 1887. 8°. **3605. dd. 59.**

—— *See* Schmoeger (C. E.) The Life of Anne Catherine Emmerich, *etc.* [The editor's preface signed: H. J. C., i.e. Henry J. Coleridge.] 1874. 8°. **3605. dd. 10.**

—— *See* Séguin (E.) The Life of the Venerable Father Claude de la Colombière, *etc.* [The editor's preface signed: H. J. C., i.e. Henry J. Coleridge.] 1883. 8°. **3605. dd. 40.**

C., H. J. The Art of Furnishing on Rational and Æsthetic Principles. By H. J. C. [i.e. H. J. Cooper.] pp. viii. 116. *H. S. King & Co.: London*, 1876. 8°. **7943. aaa. 16.**

C., H. J.

—— The Story of St. Michael's Church, Pirbright, Surrey. Illustrated. [The dedication signed: H. J. C., i.e. Henry Jones Curtis.] pp. 36. *British Publishing Co.: Gloucester, & London*, [1933.] 8°. **7822. a. 32.**

C., H. J. V. SS. T. Na-treuringe over het vertreck van den . . . Heer D. Lambertus Groen wanneer syn Ee. van Maestricht na Harlem beroepen wierde, November 1667. [In verse. Signed: H. J. V. SS. T. C.] *P. Boucher: Maestricht*, 1667. *s. sh.* fol. **1855.g.8.(9.)**

C., H. K. Sonnets and Verses from Home and Parochial Life. [The prefatory notice signed: H. K. C., i.e. Hubert K. Cornish.] pp. vii. 154. *Joseph Masters: London*, 1856. 12°. **11649. b. 40.**

C., H. K. S. *See* Walton (Izaak) *the Angler.* The Complete Angler . . . With a new introduction and notes, *etc.* [The introduction signed: H. K. S. C., i.e. Henry K. S. Causton.] 1851. 8°. **7905. a. 6.**

C., H. L. *See* Day (Martha) The Literary Remains of Martha Day, *etc.* [The editor's preface signed: H. L. C.] 1834. 8°. **11644. f. 56.**

C., H. L. *See* Kotzebue (A. F. F. von) [*Miscellaneous Writings.*] [Leontine.] Léontine de Blondheim . . . Traduit de l'allemand, avec notes par H. L. C. [i.e. Baron H. L. Coiffier de Verseux.] 1808. 12°. **12614. f. 10.**

C., H . . . L . . . L . . . v. Des Isländers Franz Severin van Ditthefts merkwürdige . . . Reisen zur See, und desselbene vierzigjähriger Aufenthalt auf der schwimmenden Davids-Insel. Aus . . . vielen in englischer und andern Sprachen enthaltenen Nachrichten übersetzt und in Ordnung gebracht von H . . . L . . . L . . . v. C. Zweyte Auflage. pp. 143. *Leipzig & Frankfurt*, 1758. 8°. **10026. b. 7.**

C., H. L. W. Brünhilde. A psychological study. By H. L. W. C. pp. 22. *Theosophical Publishing Society: London*, 1909. 8°. **12450. g. 15. (4.)**

C., H. M.

—— *See* Murray (John) *Publishing Firm.* [*Handbooks for Travellers.—Derbyshire.*] Handbook for Travellers in Derbyshire, Nottinghamshire, Leicestershire, and Staffordshire, *etc.* [The editor's preface signed: H. M. C., i.e. Herbert M. Cundall.] 1892. 8°. **2364. a. 8.**

—— *See* Murray (John) *Publishing Firm.* [*Handbooks for Travellers.—England and Wales.*] Handbook for England and Wales, *etc.* [The editor's preface signed: H. M. C., i.e. Herbert M. Cundall.] 1890. 8°. **2364. a. 12.**

—— *See* Murray (John) *Publishing Firm.* [*Handbooks for Travellers.—Northamptonshire.*] Handbook for Northamptonshire and Rutland, *etc.* [The editor's preface signed: H. M. C., i.e. Herbert M. Cundall.] 1901. 8°. **2364. b. 4.**

—— *See* Periodical Publications.—*London.* The Etcher, *etc.* [The editor's introduction signed: H. M. C., i.e. Herbert M. Cundall.] 1879, *etc.* fol. **P.P. 1931. pck.**

—— English Painters of the Georgian Era. Hogarth to Turner. Biographical notices of the artists, illustrated with . . . photographs after their most celebrated pictures. [The preface signed: H. M. C., i.e. Herbert M. Cundall.] pp. viii. 96. *Sampson Low & Co.: London*, 1876. 4°. **1754. b. 8.**

—— Handbook for Hertfordshire, Bedfordshire, and Huntingdonshire. With maps and plans. [The editor's preface signed: H. M. C., i.e. Herbert M. Cundall.] pp. viii. 19. 260. 1895. 8°. *See* Murray (John) *Publishing Firm.* [*Handbooks for Travellers.—Hertfordshire.*] **2364. b. 31.**

—— A Handbook of Warwickshire. [The editor's preface signed: H. M. C., i.e. Herbert M. Cundall. With maps.] pp. vi. 14. 140. 1899. 8°. *See* Murray (John) *Publishing Firm.* [*Handbooks for Travellers.—Warwickshire.*] **2364. a. 29.**

C., H. M. Historical Retrospect of the Wiltshire Regt., *etc.* [Signed: H. M. C., i.e. Harry M. Carter.] pp. 12. *Gale & Polden: Aldershot*, [1899.] 8°. **8832.bb. 50. (3.)**

C., H. M. The Land of Prince Charlie. By the author of "The Summer Tenant" . . . With . . . illustrations, *etc.* [In prose and verse. The verses signed: H. M. C., i.e. Hugh M. Campbell.] pp. 34. *John Hay: Edinburgh*, 1904. 8º. **10369**. f. **20**.

C., H. N. *See* Coleridge (Samuel T.) [*Prose Works.—Miscellaneous.*] Specimens of the Table Talk of the late Samuel Taylor Coleridge. [The editor's preface signed: H. N. C., i.e. Henry N. Coleridge.] 1835. 8º. **1164**. f. **17, 18**.

—— —— 1836. 8º. **12355**. ppp. **31**.

—— —— 1851. 8º. **1164**. f. **52**.

—— —— [1874.] 8º. **12314**. f. **6**.

—— —— 1884. 8º. **12204**. gg.1/**14**.

C., H. O. *See* Bible.—*Appendix.—Revelation.* [*Pictorial Illustrations.*] The Apocalypse of S. John . . . represented by figures reproduced in facsimile from a ms., *etc.* [The editor's preface signed: H. O. C., i.e. Henry O. Coxe.] 1876. 4º. **C. 101**. d. **9**.

—— Forms of Bidding Prayer, with introduction and notes. [The editor's preface signed: H. O. C., i.e. Henry O. Coxe.] pp. xliv. 203. *J. H. Parker: London*, 1840. 8º. **1113**. b. **35**.

C., H. R. One Trial. A novel . . . By H. R. C. 2 vol. *T. C. Newby: London*, 1860. 12º. **12630**. b. **4**.

C., H. R. Our New Ministers; their position towards the country. By H. R. C. pp. 20. *Joseph Masters: London*, 1858. 8º. **8138**. c. **22**.

C., H. S. *See* Armida. Eine newe, sehr anmüthige und liebreiche History, von der edlen Armida . . . in Hochteutsch vbersetzet. [The translator's dedication signed: H. S. C.] 1633. 8º. **11521**. de. **2**. (**2**.)

C., H. S. Cookery and Domestic Economy for Young Housewives. A new and improved edition. [The preface signed: H. S. C.] pp. 34. *W. & R. Chambers: London & Edinburgh*, 1862. 8º. **7954**. aa. **28**.

C., H. T. Notes on the War. By a Barrister. [Signed: H. T. C., i.e. H. T. Cameron.] pp. 7. *Army Reform Association: London*, 1855. 8º. **8821**. c. **16**. (**1**.)

C—— (Henriette de) Valoé, conte; suivi du Récit de Mr, B**, ou la poule blanche. Par Henriette de C——, auteur des "Premières leçons d'une aimable petite fille," *etc.* pp. viii. 226. *J. Compton: Londres*, 1817. 12º. **12808**. i. **11**.

C. (Henry) *See* Sybarites. Les Sybarites. Roman historique . . . Traduit de l'allemand par Henry C. [i.e. Baron H. L. Coiffier de Verseux.] 1801. 8º. **1102**. cc. **2**.

C***** (Henry) *late of Chatham, Kent.* Memoirs of Henry & Elizabeth C*****, late of Chatham, Kent. pp. iv. 60. *J. S. Clarke: Peterborough*, 1840. 12º. **4986**. a. **57**. (**3**.)

C* (Hippolite) *See* C* (Théodore) Les Enfans du soldat, vaudeville . . . par MM. T. C* [i.e. T. Cogniard], Henri [i.e. P. H. Martin] et Hippolite C* [i.e. H. Cogniard], *etc.* 1832. 8º. **11738**. c. **13**. (**3**.)

C*** (Hippolite) *See* C*** (Théodore) and C*** (H.) La Cocarde tricolore . . . vaudeville . . . par MM. T. C*** [i.e. T. Cogniard] et Hippolite C*** [i.e. H. Cogniard], *etc.* 1831. 8º. **11738**. c. **13**. (**6**.)

C******* (Hugh) *Esq.* The Life of Richard Carew . . . by Hugh C*******, Esq. [i.e. / *See* Carew (Richard) The Survey of Cornwall, *etc.* 1769. 4º. [Pierre Des Maizeaux.] **10353.1.24.**

—— [Another edition.] *See* Carew (Richard) Carew's Survey of Cornwall, *etc.* 1811. 4º. **191**. c. **7**.

C. (Hyppolite) *See* C. (Théodore) and C. (H.) Le Mo . . . folie-vaudeville . . . de MM. T. C. [i.e. T. Cognia et Hyppolite C. [i.e. H. Cogniard], *etc.* 1831. 8º. **11738**. c. **11**.

C., I. *See* also C., J.

C., I. *See* Bedford (Thomas) *B.D., of Queen's Coll Cambridge.* The Sinne vnto Death, *etc.* [With an add to the reader signed: I. C.] 1621. 4º. **4473**. aaa.

C., I. *See* Bible.—*Psalms.—Selections.* [*Dutch.—Si Psalms.*] viii. Uytbreydinge over den achtsten Ps Davids. Door I. C. [i.e. Jacob Cats.] 1642. 4º. **1473.bb**

C., I. *See* Cornwall. [*Appendix.*] New News from C wall . . . Fully related in two letters [the second sign I. C.], *etc.* 1642. 4º. **E. 124**. (

C . . . . . ., I. *See* F., *Dr.* So sprach ein Fürst. [editors' preface signed: I. C . . . . . . und H. B . . . . . 1860. 8º. **12551**. dd.

C., I. *See* Hildersam (Arthur) Lectures vpon the Fourt Iohn, *etc.* [With an address to the reader signed: I i.e. John Cotton.] 1629. fol. **1485.ff.12.(**

—— —— 1632. fol. **3227**.

—— —— 1647. fol. **3090**. e. **38**.

C., I. *See* Letters. Three Severall Letters of Great portance . . . the third [signed: I. C.], concerning late losse of Monmouth, and the possibility of regai it. 1644. 4º. **E. 21**.

C., I. *See* Maritain (J.A.H.) [Éléments de philoso V. ii. La petite logique.] An Introduction to L [The translator's preface signed: I. C.] 1937. 8º. **8471**.

C., I. *See* Melanchthon (P.) [*Letters.*] The epistle of Philip Melancton made vnto . . . Kynge Henry eight . . . newly trāslated out of laten . . . by I. C. 1547. 8º. **227**. a

C., I. *See* Molière (J.B.P. de) [*Le Mé malgré lui.—Spanish.*] El Médicó á Palos. Comedia imitada por I. C. [i.e. I. Celenio, pseudonym of Lea Fernández de Moratín], *etc.* 1815. 4º. **T. 1736**.

—— —— 1817. 4º. **1342**. e. **12**.

C., I. *See* Mommsen (T.) Theodore Mommsen to the Pe of Italy. (Translated from the Italian by I. C.) 1871. 8º. [*Letters on the War between Germany France.*] **8026**. bb.

C., I. *See* Peacock (Thomas) *B.D.* A Narration of Grievous Visitation and Dreadfull Desertion of Peacock, in his last sicknesse, *etc.* [The editor's e to the reader signed: I. C.] 1641. 12º. **4906**. a

C., I. *See* Penn (William) *Founder of Pennsylvania.* Skirmisher defeated and Truth defended; bein answer to a pamphlet, entituled, A Skirmish made Quakerism [here said to be by I. C., i.e. John Cheney 1676. 4º. **T. 407**

C., I. *See* Rodriguez (A.) *Jesuit, of Valladolid.* A and Sure Way to Heauen . . . Translated out of Spa [The dedication signed: I. C.] 1630. 8º. **698**.

C., I. *See* Schurzfleisch (C. S.) Conradi Samuelis Sc fleischii . . . Introductio in notitiam scriptorum ex variis acroasibus et mss. . . . huius uiri collec eruta opera et studio I. C. [i.e. G. Wagner.] 1736. 8º **270**.

—— *See* Schurzfleisch (C. S.) C. S. Schurzfleischii Notitia scriptorum librorumque uarii argumenti, ex uariis ipsius prælectionibus . . . collegit et I. C. [i.e. G. Wagner.] 1735, *etc.* 8º. **818**.

C., I. *See* THEODORET, *Bishop of Cyrus.* The Mirror of Diuine Prouidence, *etc.* [The editor's address to the reader signed: I. C.] 1602. 8°. **4402.** aaa. **33.**

C., I. Alcilia. Philoparthens louing Folly. [Signed: I. C.] Wherevnto is added Pigmalions Image. [By John Marston.] With the Loue of Amos and Laura. [By Samuel Page.] And also Epigrammes by Sir I. H. [i.e. Sir John Harington] and others, *etc.* *For Richard Hawkins: London,* 1613. 4°. C. **39.** c. **62.**
Imperfect; wanting sig. M 2, 3.

— Alcilia. Philoparthens louing Folly. [Signed: I. C.] Wherevnto is added Pigmalions Image. [By W. K., i.e. John Marston.] With the Loue of Amos and Laura. (Written by S. P. [i.e. Samuel Page.]) *For Richard Hawkins: London,* 1619. 8°. C. **39.** a. **37.** (4.)

— Alcilia. Philoparthens louing Folly. [Signed: I. C.] Wherevnto is added, Pigmalions Image [with a dedication signed: W. K., i.e. John Marston]: with the Loue of Amos and Laura. (Written by S. P. [i.e. Samuel Page.]) And also, Epigrammes, by Sir I. H. [i.e. Sir John Harington] and others. The second impression. *For Richard Hawkins: London,* 1628. 4°. C. **39.** c. **13.**

— Alcilia, Philoparthens Louing Follie . . . 1595. Nach dem einzigen Exemplar der ältesten Ausgabe in der Hamburger Stadtbibliothek herausgegeben und eingeleitet von Wilhelm Wagner. Separat-Abdruck aus dem Shakespeare-Jahrbuch, *etc.* pp. 46. *Köthen,* 1875. 8°. **11602.** g. **33.** (**1.**)

— [Another edition.] From the unique exemplar in the Town Library, Hamburg. Edited, with introduction, and notes and illustrations, by the Rev. Alexander B. Grosart. pp. xxxi. 66. *Printed for the subscribers: Manchester,* 1879. 4°. [*Occasional Issues of Unique or Very Rare Books.* vol. 8.] **2326.** g. **8.** (**2.**)
No. 5 of an edition of fifty-one copies.

— [Another edition.] 1882. *See* ARBER (Edward) An English Garner, *etc.* vol. 4. 1877, *etc.* 8°. **12269.** cc. **12.**

— [Another edition.] 1903. *See* ARBER (Edward) An English Garner. (Some Longer Elizabethan Poems.) 1903, *etc.* 8°. **2324.** e. **9/9.**

C., I. Les Amours de Philocaste. Où, par mille beaux & rares accidents, il se void que les variables hazards de la Fortune ne peuuent rien sur la constance de l'Amour. [The dedicatory epistle signed: I. C., i.e. Jacques Corbin.] ff. 144. *I. Gesselin: Paris,* 1601. 12°. **12510.** de. **18.**

C., I. The Character of a Country Committee-man, with the Eare-marke of a Sequestrator. [The dedication signed: I. C., i.e. John Cleveland.] pp. 5. *London,* 1649. 4°. **1093.** c. **5.**

— [Another copy.] E. **571.** (**5.**)

— [Another copy.] The Character of a Country Committee-man, *etc.* *London,* 1649. 4°. Ashley **397.**

C., I. I. C. G. De libertate ecclesiastica . . . Ad viros politicos, qui de controuersia inter Paulum v . . . & Rempublicam Venetam edoceri cupiunt . . . MDVII. [The running title reads, "I. C. De libertate ecclesiastica."] 1611. fol. *See* G., I. C. **495.** k. **6.**

C., I. Do we meet only in the Name of the Lord Jesus? Observations addressed to the Brethren. [Signed: I. C.] pp. 15. *Elliot Stock: London,* 1877. 8°. **4135.** e. **3.** (**18.**)

C., I. An Elegie offered up to the Memory of that late faithfull Servant of God, Mr. Jeremiah Burroughs, *etc.* [Signed: I. C.] *Printed by B. A.: London,* 1646. *s. sh.* fol. **669.** f. **10.** (**100.**)

C., I. Epigrammata, ofte Winter-avondts tyt-korting. Door I. C. *A. Bon: Delf,* 1655. 4°. **11555.** e. **42.** (**4.**)

C., I. An Essay upon the Inscription of Macduff's Crosse in Fyfe. By I. C. [i.e. James Cunningham], *etc.* pp. 20. *Printed by the Heir of Andrew Anderson: Edinburgh,* 1678. 4°. **101.** i. **66.**

C., I. The Gyant Whipt by his Godmother; or, a Loving epistle wrote to the most notorious Observator, Monsieur L'Estrange. By the Anti-Papistical I. C. [*London,* 1682?] *s. sh.* fol. **1850.** c. **5.** (**69.**)

C., I. Handelinge van de prædestinatie, perseverantie, ende vrye wille des menschen . . . Tegens de calumnien M. P. Bertij [with reference to his "Aenspraecke aen D. F. Gomarum"], Cupij, ende haren ghevolge. Tot dienste van die van Alckmaer . . . Door een liefhebber der waerheyt, genoemt I. C., *etc.* pp. 23. *J. Andriess: Delft,* 1610. 4°. T. **2240.** (**21.**)

C., I. A Handkercher for Parents Wet Eyes, vpon the Death of Children. A consolatory letter to a friend. [The preface signed: I. C.] pp. 67. *E. A. for Michael Sparkes: London,* 1630. 12°. C. **53.** aa. **19.**

— [Another edition.] Reprinted at the request of divers friends. *See* SPARK (Michael) The Second Part of Crums of Comfort, *etc.* 1652. 24°. C. **53.** gg. **23.**

C., I. Hints upon the Question of Jury Trial, as applicable to the proceedings in the Court of Session. [Signed: I. C., i.e. the Right Hon. Sir Ilay Campbell.] pp. 40. *Mundell, Doig, & Stevenson: Edinburgh,* 1809. 8°. **6573.** b. **34.**

C., I. Iona; or, the Sin of Columcille. By I. C., *etc.* [In verse.] *Dundalgan Press: Dundalk,* [1932.] *obl.* 8°. **11647.** dg. **91.**

C., I. Lettre à la reyne Christine de Suède, sur son abdication et sur sa conuersion. [Signed: I. C.] pp. [11.] *Paris,* 1656. 4°. **8092.** ee. **22.** (**1.**)
Cropped.

C., I.

— Militarie Instructions for the Cavallrie . . . collected out of divers forreigne authors ancient and modern, and rectified and supplied, according to the present practise of the Low-Countrey Warres. [The dedication signed: I. C., i.e. John Cruso.] pp. 108. pl. 16. *Printed by the printers to the Universitie of Cambridge,* 1632. fol. **717.** m. **18.**
With an additional titlepage, engraved. Imperfect; wanting the additional titlepage and pl. 3–5, 8–16.

C., I. Myśli różne o sposobie zakładania ogrodów przez I. C. [i.e. Princess Izabela Fortunata Czartoryska.] (Katalog drzew, krzewów, roślin i kwiatów.) [With plates.] pp. xii. 66. 56. *w Wrocławiu,* 1805. 4°. **7054.** i. **4.**

— Wydanie drugie. pp. vi. 70. 56. *w Wrocławiu,* 1808. 4°. **7005.** g. **9.**
The titlepage is engraved.

C., I. *Begin.* The Newes from Monmouth is this. [A letter. Signed: I. C.] *See* C., P. Three Severall Letters, *etc.* 1644. 4°. E. **21.** (**6.**)

C., I. Peter's Patern: or, the Perfect Path to Worldly Happiness. As it was delivered in a funeral sermon preached at the interrment of Mr. Hugh Peters . . . By I. C. Translator of Pineda upon Job, and one of the Triers [i.e. Joseph Caryl]. [A satire.] pp. 13. *London,* 1659. 4°. E. **995.** (**11.**)

— [Another copy.] **292.** f. **39.** (**5.**)

— [Another edition.] 1745. *See* HARLEIAN MISCELLANY. The Harleian Miscellany, *etc.* vol. 6. 1744, *etc.* 4°. **185.** a. **10.**

— [Another edition.] 1810. *See* HARLEIAN MISCELLANY. The Harleian Miscellany, *etc.* vol. 6. 1808, *etc.* 4°. **2072.g.**

C., I. Plain Reasons why the people called Quakers may in conscience, and ought in duty, to pay Tithes. Published in 1786, and said to be written by a Prelate of this Kingdom. [Signed: I. C.] *See* TRACTS. Tracts on Tithes, *etc.* 1786. 8°. **4152**. a. **56**. (4.)

C., I. Saint Marie Magdalens Conuersion. [A poem. The address to the reader signed: I. C.] [*Douai?*] 1603. 4° C. **39**. e. **51**.

C., I.

—— Thoughts in Verse. By I. C. [i.e. Itys Christie.] pp. 32 *Welbecson Press: London*, [1944.] 8°. **11656**. d. **86**.

C., I. A Pleasant Comedie, called The Two Merry Milke-Maids. Or, the Best words weare the garland. By I. C. *Bernard Alsop, for Lawrence Chapman: London*, [1620.] 4°. **644**. a. **14**.

The date in the imprint has been cut off.

—— [Another copy.] **162**. c. **29**. *Cropped.*

—— [Another edition.] *Printed by Tho. Johnson: London*, 1661. 4°. **643**. d. **43**.

—— [Another edition.] [*Privately printed: London*,] 1914. 8°. [*Tudor Facsimile Texts.*] Tab. **579**. a. **9**. *Interleaved.*

C., I. Wits Interpreter, the English Parnassus. Or, a sure guide to those admirable accomplishments that compleat our English gentry, in the . . . qualifications of discourse, or writing . . . By I. C. [i.e. John Cotgrave.] 3 pt. *For N. Brooke: London*, 1655. 8°. E. **1448**.
The third edition, in which the author is given as J. C., is entered under C., J.

C., I. Ya son Tales los Ladrones que se han hecho Rogaciones. Dialogo entre D. Eleuterio y D. Plutarco. [Signed: I. C.] pp. 8. [*Mexico*,] 1822. 4°. **9770**. bb. **13**. (**55**.)

C., I., and **W.**, I. A Brief Relation of a Wonderful Accident, a dissolution of the earth, in the Forest of Charnwood, about two miles from Loughborough in Leicestershire . . . Published by two lovers of art, I. C. and I. W. pp. 6. *Sold by Nath. Ponder: [London,]* 1679. 4°. **7107**. b. **12**.

—— [Another copy.] G. **16643**. (4.)

C., I., *Doctor in Physicke.*

—— A True Discouery of the Empericke, with the Fugitiue, Physition and Quacksaluer, who display their banners vpon posts: whereby his Maiesties subiects are not onely deceiued, but greatly endangered in the health of their bodies: being very profitable as well for the ignorant, as for the learned: by I. C. Doctor in Physicke (Iohn Cotta). 1617. 4°. *See* COTTA (John) **551**. a. **2**. (**2**.)

C., I., *Gent.* *See* KNIGHT. A poore Knight his Pallace of priuate pleasures . . . Written by a student in Cābridge. And published by I. C. Gent. [A reprint of the edition of 1579.] 1844. 4°. [*Three Collections of English Poetry, etc.*] C. **101**. b. **14**.

C., I., *Mathematician.* A New Prognostication for the Year . . . 1675 . . . wherein is contained the exact day, hour and minut of the new moon . . . the daily disposition of the weather . . . Exactly calculated according to art, for the meridian of the . . . city of Edinburgh . . . By I. C. Mathematician [i.e. James Corss ?]. 1675. 8°. *See* EPHEMERIDES. **8610.aa.64.(4.)**

C., I., *the Meanest Labourer in Christ's Vineyard.* The Mystery of Godlines, or godlinesse in a mystery. Or, the character of a saint, in seeming contradictions. By I. C. the meanest Labourer in Christs Vineyard [i.e. Joseph Caryl ?]. pp. 52. *For Philemon Stephens: London*, 1654. 8°. **4401**. g. **18**.

C., I., *Mr.* Vindiciæ Clavium: or, a Vindication of keyes of the Kingdome of Heaven, into the hands the right owners. Being some animadversions upon tract of Mr. I. C. (Mr. Cotton) called, The Keyes of Kingdome of Heaven, *etc.* 1645. 4°. *See* COTTON (Jo *of Boston, U.S.* **4103**. bbb.

C., I., *Student in Divinity.* The Theatre of Catholique Protestant Religion . . . wherein the zealous Catho may plainelie see the . . . truth . . . of the Catholi Religion . . . Written by I. C. Student in Diuin [i.e. John Colleton]. pp. 32. 632. [*St. Om* 1620. 8°. **3936**. aa.

C., I. A. Harangue sur la reception de Monseigneur Du à la charge de Garde des Sceaux de France. Par J. D [The dedication, in Latin, signed: I. A. C.] 1616. *See* C., J. D. **8050**. bb. **50**.

C . . . . . ., I. B. Les Périgordinismes corrigés. Par I. C . . . . . . [i.e. J. B. Caville]. pp. iv. 68. *Périgu* 1818. 8°. **12950**. f.

C., I. B., *Irish Priest.* A Looking Glasse for New Reform Answering Paul Rainalds, Scotishmans letter perswad his brother to forsake the true ancient Catholike Roman Religion. Made by I. B. C. Irish Priest. pp. *Printed by Thomas Stone: Lion*, [1630 ?] 12°. **3939**. aa.

C., I. C. U. Murmurs from the Slough of Misrule. In se chapters. By I. C. U. C. pp. 92. *London Lite Society: London*, 1887. 8°. **12621**. g

C., I. C. W. President Kruger's Oversight, and its Res [In the form of a parody on Amos, chapter 5.] I. C. W. C. [i.e. J. C. Wyndham Childs ?] *Netherto Worth: Truro* [1902.] 8°. **8155**. df. **71**.

C., I. D. La Cabale des Reformez, tiree nouuellemen puits de Democrite. Par I. D. C. [i.e. Guillaum Reboul ?] pp. 224. *Chez le Libertin: Mompe* 1597. 8°. **702**. a. **22**.

—— [Another edition.] Auec l'Apologie de Reboul icelle. Le tout reueu & corrigé, *etc.* ff. 94. 57. *Ch Libertin: Mompellier*, 1601. 8°. **3900**. a.

C., I. D. Den lydenden ende stervenden Christus. I. D. C. [i.e. Jean de Condé.] [A drama. In verse.] *G. Scheybels: Brussel*, 1652. 8°. **11754**. aaa

—— Den tweeden druck, by den autheur verbetert. pp *G. Scheybels: Brussel*, [1660 ?] 8°. **11754**. a. **71**.

—— [Another edition.] pp. 56. *Weduwe Thieulli A. Colpyn: Antwerpen*, [1660 ?] 8°. **11754**. a

C., I. D. F. C. D. L'Origine des Eglises de France, pro par la succession de ses evêques. Avec la vie de Austremoine, premier Apôtre & Primat des Aquita [The dedication signed: I. D. F. C. D. C., i.e. Dufraisse, chanoine de Clermont.] pp. 521. *E. Michallet: Paris*, 1688. 8°. **4629**. de

C., I. E. B. *See* PERIODICAL PUBLICATIONS.—*London.* Anglers' Diary . . . By I. E. B. C. [i.e. Irwin E. B. 1866, *etc.* 4° & 8°. P.P. **250**

—— *See* PERIODICAL PUBLICATIONS.—*London.* The Sho Diary . . . By I. E. B. C. [i.e. Irwin E. B. Cox.] 1866, *etc.* 4°. P.P. **248**

—— The Country House: a collection of useful inform and recipes . . . Edited by I. E. B. C. [i.e. Irwin Cox.] pp. 143. *Horace Cox: London*, 1866. 8°. **7908**.

C., I. E. B.

—— Third edition, *etc.* pp. 228. *Horace Cox: London,* 1883. 8°. **7908.** c. 5.

—— Facts and Useful Hints relating to Fishing and Shooting . . . to which is added a list of recipes for the management and cure of dogs in disease. Profusely illustrated. Edited by I. E. B. C. [i.e. Irwin E. B. Cox.] pp. 115. *Horace Cox: London,* 1866. 8°. **7908.** c. 3.

—— Third edition. Edited by I. E. B. C. [i.e. Irwin E. B. Cox], *etc.* pp. vi. 293. *Horace Cox: London,* 1874. 8°. **7908.** c. 8.

—— The Farm, Garden, Stable, and Aviary: to which is added some useful information relating to the poultry-yard, bee-keeping, and natural history . . . Edited by I. E. B. C. [i.e. Irwin E. B. Cox.] pp. 171. *Horace Cox: London,* 1866. 8°. **7908.** c. 6.

—— Second edition. 3 pt. *Horace Cox: London,* 1869–71. 8°. **7908.** c. 7.

—— The Gamekeeper's and Game-Preserver's Account Book and Diary. By I. E. B. C. [i.e. Irwin E. B. Cox.] pp. 134. *Horace Cox: London,* 1881. 4°. **7906.** g. 26.

—— The Gamekeeper's Shooting Memorandum Book for 1891. By I. E. B. D. [i.e. Irwin E. B. Cox.] [Blank forms.] *Horace Cox: London,* 1881. *obl.* 16°. **7908.** a. 32.

C., I. F. *See* Poitou. Coustumes . . . de Poictou . . . Ensemble, la conference desdites Coustumes à celle de Paris, & des pays & prouinces plus proches dudit pays de Poictou (par I. F. C. [i.e. Jean François Coutineau?]), *etc.* 1625. 4°. C. **69.** ee. 4.

C., I. F. The Funeral Elogy and Character, of her Royal Highness, the late Princess Sophia: with the explication of her consecration-medal . . . (Elogium et simulacrum principis incomparabilis Divae Sophiae utcunque adumbratum a I. F. C. [i.e. J. F. Cramer].) Translated into English [with the text], and further illustrated, by Mr. Toland. Who has added the character of the King, the Prince, and the Princess. pp. 34. *Bernard Lintott: London,* 1714. 8°. **1418.** g. 58.

—— [Another copy.] T. **1780.** (1.)

—— [Another copy.] **113.** d. 41.

—— [Another copy.] G. **13695.** (1.)

C., I. G. Der Gott und Menschen gefällige Glasskünstler. Abgebildet von I. G. C. pp. 24. *Hildburghausen,* 1770. 4°. T. **940.** (2.)

C., I. L. My Dream; or, the Audience chamber of the Great King. By I. L. C., author of "White Raiment," etc. pp. 18. *J. Masters: London,* 1857. 12°. **4407.** b. 13.

—— "White Raiment"; a lesson for Sunday school teachers and Sunday school girls. By I. L. C. pp. 18. *J. Masters: London,* 1856. 12°. **4417.** a. **99.** (5.)

C., I. M. In Memoriam A. C. [i.e. Annie Chapman.] [Verses, signed: I. M. C., i.e. John M. Chapman.] pp. 16. *J. Parker: Oxford,* 1871. 8°. **11648.** a. 4. (2.)

C., I. M. S. D. Le Limosin. [A political tract, signed: I. M. S. D. C.] pp. 15. [1619.] 8°. **1192.** h. 2. (5.)

C., I. P. Hymns Selected and Original, principally intended to aid the devotional exercises of children and teachers in the Leeds Sunday School Union. Compiled by direction of the Committee. Third edition. [The editor's advertisement signed: I. P. C., i.e. John P. Clapham.] pp. 298. *John Heaton: London,* 1833. 16°. **3435.** bbb. 32.

C., I. P.

—— The Sunday School Hymn Book . . . Eleventh thousand. pp. 310. *Hamilton, Adams & Co.: London,* 1860. 16°. **3437.** b. 24.

C., I. P. D. Mémoires touchant l'établissement d'vne mission chrêtienne dans . . . la Terre Australe, meridionale, antartique, & inconnuë . . . Par vn ecclésiastique originaire de cette mesme terre. [The dedication signed: I. P. D. C., i.e. J. Paulmier de Courtonne.] pp. 215. *C. Cramoisy: Paris,* 1663 [1664]. 8°. **493.** g. 6.

Imperfect; wanting a map, which has been supplied in facsimile. An earlier issue, with a different titlepage, and without the "Aduertissement touchant la publication de cet ouvrage" and the list of errata, is entered under the author's name.

C., I. R. El que se Quemare que Sople. [On matters connected with Guanajuato. Signed: I. R. C.] *Guanajuato,* 1825. *s. sh.* 4°. **9770.** bb. **16.** (7.)

C., I. R. A Rosary from the Rhine. [Poems. The dedication signed: I. R. C.] 1844. 8°. **11644.** eeee. 25.

C., I. R. Transformation. [By] I. R. C. [A religious tract.] pp. 31. *Marshall Bros.: London,* [1900.] 16°. **04420.** f. 1. (1.)

C., I. R. S. M. *See* Philalethes (Eugenius) *pseud.* Lumen de Lumine . . . Übersetzet von I. R. S. M. C. 1750. 8°. **8630.** bbb. 7.

C., I. S. E. St. Leonard; or, the Missionary. A vision. [In verse. The dedication signed: I. S. E. C.] pp. 142. *W. Kent & Co.: London,* 1857. 8°. **11650.** b. 28.

C., I. S. N. P. P. Discursus politicus, oder rathliches Bedencken, von der nothwendigen vnd wichtigen Frag, vnd Bescheidt: ob es heylsam vnd nützlich sey, im heiligen Römischen Reich teutscher Nation, Uniones vnd Bündnussen, auffzurichten . . . Gestelt durch einen erfahrnen Jureconsultum & Historicum. I. S. N. P. P. C. pp. 20. 1618. 4°. **8073.** cc. 17.

C., I. T. A. *See* Sanders (Nicholas) Les Trois liures de Nicolas Sander, touchant l'origine et progres du schisme d'Angleterre . . . Traduits . . . par I. T. A. C. 1587. 8°. **1478.** d. 12.

C., I. V. Τῳ Καθολικῳ Stillingfleeton. Or, an account given to a Catholick Friend, of Dr. Stillingfleets late book against the Roman Church. Together with a short postil upon his text, in three letters, by I. V. C. [i.e. John V. Cane.] [With a preface signed: J. C.] 4 pt. *Printed by Luke Kerchove: Bruges,* 1672. 8°. **699.** c. 47.

With an additional titlepage, bound at the end of pt. 4, reading: "An Account of Dr. Still.'s late Book against The Church of Rome. Together with a short postil upon his text of Fanaticism and Divisions. 1672."

—— *See* Stillingfleet (Edward) *Bishop of Worcester.* An Answer to several late Treatises, *etc.* [Including a reply to "Τῳ Καθολικῳ Stillingfleeton."] 1673. 8°. **1019.** e. 20.

C. (Ida) Heavenly Bridegrooms. An unintentional contribution to the erotogenetic interpretation of religion. By Ida C. . . . With an introduction by Theodore Schroeder . . . Reprint from Alienist and Neurologist, *etc.* pp. 121. iii. *New York,* 1918. 8°. **04504.** g. 2.
[i.e. Ida Craddock.]

C. (Is.) The London New Method and Art of Teaching Children to Spell and Read, *etc.* [The address to the reader signed: Is. C.] pp. 85. *Edmund Parker: London,* 1723. 8°. **12984.** a. 37.

—— [Another issue.] *London,* [1725?] 8°. **12984.** de. 23.

C. (Ismenia S.) Teresa, pagine contemporanee di Ismenia S. C. autrice del Profugo. pp. 301. *Milano*, 1874. 8°. **12471. bb. 7.**

C., J. *See* Aengelen (P. van) De Verstandige hovenier . . . Deesen laetsten druck is merckelijck verbetert, door J. C., *etc.* [1668 ?] 4°. **441. b. 24. (3.)**

C., J. *See* Alice Georgina. Wild Spring Flowers. [The preface signed: J. C.] 1852. 8°. **11647. b. 31.**

—— —— 1852. 8°. **11649. e. 48.**

C., J. *See* Arabia. A Critical Essay on various Manuscript Works, Arabic and Persian, illustrating the history of Arabia . . . Translated by J. C. from a Persian manuscript, *etc.* 1832. 8°. **14003. d. 12.**

C., J. *See* B., E. To all dear Friends & Brethren, *etc.* [Signed: E. B., J. C., J. P., i.e. E. Burrough, John Crook and Isaac Penington.] 1662. 4°. **4151. b. 8.**

—— —— 1662. 4°. **4152. c. 2.**

C., J. *See* B., E., *D.D.* The Rosary's of the B. Virgin Mary and of the most H. Name of Jesus re-printed . . . Answers to three curious letters [the second signed: J. C.], *etc.* 1725. 8°. **C. 53. aa. 33.**

C., J. *See* Bible. [*English.*] The Holy Bible . . . with . . . annotations . . . now placed in due order (by J. C. [i.e. John Canne]), *etc.* 1642, *etc.* fol. **1216. l. 2.**

—— —— 1672. fol. **L.15.d.9.**

—— —— 1679. fol. **695. l. 5, 6. (1.)**

—— —— 1683. fol. **L.18.d.5.(2.)**

—— —— 1715. fol. **L.9.d.3.(2.)**

C., J. *See* Brierley (Roger) A Bundle of Soul-Convincing Truths, *etc.* [With an epistle to the reader signed: J. C., i.e. John Cheney ?] 1670. 8°. **4452. a. 13.**

—— —— 1677. 12°. **874. c. 23.**

C., J. *See* Bunyan (John) [*Pilgrim's Progress.—Abridgments, etc.*] The Story of the Pilgrims' Progress told for Young People. [The preface signed: J. C.] 1858. 8°. **4414. d. 10.**

C., J. *See* C., I. V. *Τω Καθολικω* Stillingfleeton, *etc.* [With a preface signed: J. C.] 1672. 8°. **699. c. 47.**

C., J. *See* C., W. L. Buds of Poesy, *etc.* [The editor's preface signed: J. C.] 1839. 16°. **11646. a. 63.**

C., J. *See* Cassé de Saint-Prosper (A. J.) Historia de Francia . . . Traducida por M. O. y J. C. [i.e. Juan Cortada.] 1840, *etc.* 8°. **1323. i. 8–10.**

C., J. *See* Charles i., *King of Great Britain and Ireland.* [*Trial and Execution.*] The Full Proceedings of the High Court of Justice against King Charles . . . on Saturday the 20. of January, 1648 . . . Translated out of the Latine by J. C., *etc.* 1655. 8°. **E. 1506. (2.)**

C., J. *See* Deacon (George E.) The Lord's Prayer: a course of sermons, *etc.* [The editor's preface signed: J. C.] 1887. 8°. **4478. d. 82. (13.)**

C., J. *See* Doll. The Well-Bred Doll, *etc.* [The translator's preface signed: J. C.] 1853. 8°. **12806. b. 25.**

C., J. *See* Durham (James) *Covenanting Divine.* The Blessednesse of the Death of these that die in the Lord, *etc.* [The editor's dedicatory epistle and address to the reader signed: J. C., i.e. John Carstairs ?] 1682. 8°. **1417. b. 31.**

—— —— 1756. 12°. **4461. aa. 9.**

C., J.

—— *See* Durham (James) *Covenanting Divine.* Christ Crucified, *etc.* [The editor's dedicatory epistle and address to the reader signed: J. C., i.e. John Carstairs ?] 1726. 4°. **3165. df. 20.**

—— —— 1769. 8°. **3165. b. 40.**

—— *See* Durham (James) *Covenanting Divine.* The Unsearchable Riches of Christ, *etc.* [The editor's dedicatory epistle signed: J. C., i.e. John Carstairs ?] 1745. 8°. **1115. a. 39.**

—— —— 1764. 8°. **1476. b. 20.**

—— —— 1786. 12°. **4454. b. 8.**

—— —— 1794. 12°. **4454. aaa. 27.**

C., J. *See* Elliott (William) *Ex-Inspector of Police.* Tracking Glasgow Criminals. [With a preface signed: J. C.] [1904.] 8°. **6057. ee. 17.**

C., J. *See* England. [*Appendix.—History and Politics.—* ii. 1653.] A Relation of the Engagement of the Fleet of the Common-wealth of England . . . With the copy of a letter from the Commissioners of Prize Goods from Dover [signed: J. C., N. F.] touching the said fight, *etc.* 1653. 4°. **E. 688. (8.)**

C., J. *See* F., J., *Minister of the Gospel.* The Dead Saint Speaking, *etc.* [With an address to the reader signed: J. C., i.e. John Collinges.] 1679. 4°. **4903. f. 40.**

C., J. *See* Fox (George) *Founder of the Society of Friends.* Der Heydenen Godts-geleertheyt, gebracht over de hoofden van alle . . . Christenen . . . Uyt het Engelse in't Nederduyts overgeset, door J. C. 1674. 4°. **855. i. 1. (67.)**

C., J.

—— *See* Guadagnoli (A.) [Sulla luna.] Sixains sur la lune . . . traduits . . . par J. C., *etc.* 1836. 8°. **1875. d. 6. (179.)**

C., J. *See* Hamburg.—*Portugiesisch-jüdische Gemeinde.* Aus dem ältesten Protokollbuch der portugiesisch-jüdischen Gemeinde in Hamburg. Uebersetzung und Anmerkungen von J. C. 1909, *etc.* 8°. [*Jahrbuch der Jüdisch-Literarischen Gesellschaft.* vol. 6–11, 13.] **Ac. 8956. d**

C., J. *See* Homer. [*Odyssey.—Greek and English.*] Homeric Ballads, with translations . . . by . . . William Maginn [The editor's preface signed: J. C.] 1850. 8°. **11315. df. 28**

C., J. *See* Ireland.—*Parliament.*—iii. *House of Commons* [*Debates.*] Debates relative to Ireland in . . . 176 and 1764. Taken by a military officer. To which ar added, his remarks on the trade of Ireland, *etc.* [Th dedication signed: J. C., i.e. Sir James Caldwell, Bart.] 1766. 8°. **G. 4805**

C., J. *See* Ireland. [*Appendix.—*ii. *Miscellaneous.*] Th State of the Papist and Protestant Proprieties in th Kingdom of Ireland, *etc.* [The editor's dedicatio signed: J. C.] 1689. 4°. **601. f. 4**

—— —— 1751. 4°. [*Somers* (*John*) *Baron Somers.* *Third Collection of Scarce and Valuable Tract* vol. 3.] **184. a. 1**

—— —— 1814. 4°. [*Somers* (*John*) *Baron Somers.* *Collection of Scarce and Valuable Tracts, etc.* vol. 11] **750. g. 1**

C., J. *See* J., N. Melk voor kinderkens . . . door . . . N. J. Als mede iets van de waerheyt geopenbaert . . . [by] W. S. (Willem Smith.) Voormaels in't Engels gedruckt, ende nu in't Nederduyts overgeset, door J. C. 1673. 4º. **855**. i. **1**. (**64**.)

C., J. *See* Jurieu (P.) A Critical History of the Doctrines and Worships . . . of the Church . . . Done into English. [The dedicatory epistle signed: J. C.] 1705. 8º. **4515**. b. **25**.

C., J. *See* Kingsbridge. A Narrative of the Persecutions against Dissenters in Kingsbridge, *etc.* [The editor's preface signed: J. C.] 1821. 12º. **4371**. aa. **29**. (**12**.)

C***, J. *See* Krick (N. M.) Relation d'un voyage au Thibet, *etc.* [The editor's preface signed: J. C***.] 1854. 12º. **10057**. a. **20**.

C., J. *See* La Mothe (M. C.) *Countess d'Aulnoy.* Memoirs of the Court of England . . . Now made English, *etc.* [The translator's dedicatory epistle signed: J. C.] 1707. 8º. **598**. d. **34**.

—— —— 1708. 8º. **808**. c. **8**.

C., J. *See* MacCheyne (Robert M.) Memoir and Remains of the Rev. R. M. M'Cheyne . . . Abridged from the larger work [of A. A. Bonar]. [The preface signed: J. C.] 1865. 8º. **4955**. aa. **11**.

C., J. *See* Margaret, *Saint, Virgin and Martyr.* La Vie et légende de sainte Marguerite, *etc.* (Corrigée & revue selon la vérité de l'histoire des auteurs orthodoxes . . . Par J. C.) [1740?] 16º. **11474**. a. **44**.

—— —— [1770?] 16º. **11474**. a. **12**.

—— —— [1840?] 12º. **12331**. aa. **50**. (**13**.)

C., J. *See* Martin (Guillaume) *Abbé.* Historia de la Tierra Santa . . . Traducida por M. O. y J. C. [i.e. Juan Cortada.] 1840. 8º. **1323**. i. **11**.

C., J. *See* Milton (John) [*Paradise Lost.—Latin.*] Paradisus Amissa . . . Quod . . . nunc . . . in linguam Romanam transfertur, *etc.* [The translator's dedication signed: J. C.] 1686. 4º. **992**. h. **2**. (**1**.)

C., J. *See* Morales (B.) La Víctima del Despotismo . . . Redactada . . . por J. C. 1836. 8º. **11450**. aa. **12**.

C., J. *See* Muhammad Ṣadik, *Iṣfahānī.* The Geographical Works of Sádik Isfaháni. Translated by J. C., *etc.* 1832. 8º. **14003**. d. **11**.

C., J. *See* Otway (Thomas) Heroick Friendship . . . By the late Mr. Otway. [A spurious work. With a preface signed: J. C.] 1719. 4º. **644**. h. **83**.

C., J. *See* Owen (John) *D.D.* A Treatise of the Dominion of Sin, *etc.* [With an address "To the Serious Reader" signed: J. C., i.e. Isaac Chauncy?] 1739. 8º. **4373**. a. **40**.

—— *See* Owen (John) *D.D.* The True Nature of a Gospel Church, *etc.* [With a preface signed: J. C., i.e. Isaac Chauncy?] 1689. 4º. **4135**. e. **28**.

C., J. *See* Paltock (Robert) The Life and Adventures of Peter Wilkins . . . A new edition . . . revised. [The editor's preface signed: J. C.] 1844. 8º. **1158**. c. **27**.

C., J. *See* Pope (Alexander) *the Poet.* [*Essay on Criticism.—Latin.*] Tentamen de re critica . . . Latine nunc emittente Ushero Gahagan. Illustravit amicus quidam notis aliquot anglicanis, *etc.* [The notes signed: J. C.] 1747. 8º. **11633**. df. **2**.

C., J. *See* Rohan (H. de) *Duke de Rohan.* The Complete Captain . . . Englished by J. C. (Captain Cruso.) 1640. 8º. **9039**. b. **17**.

C., J. *See* Saint-Aubin (C.) Réponse . . . à plusieurs questions proposées par le citoyen J. C sur la hausse des rentes, *etc.* [With the text of the questions.] [1797.] 8º. F. **217**. (**9**.)

C., J. *See* Schiller (J. C. F. von) [*Selections.*] Schiller's politisches Vermächtniss, *etc.* [The editor's preface signed: J. C., i.e. Julius Campe?] 1832. 12º. **1389**. b. **53**. (**1**.)

C., J. *See* Scudéry (G. de) [Discours politique des rois.] Entdeckte Grufft politischer Geheimnüssen, *etc.* [The translator's dedication signed: J. C.] [1662.] 8º. **8010**. a. **10**. (**1**.)

C., J. *See* Shakespeare (William) [*As You Like It.*] The Modern Receipt: or, a Cure for Love. A comedy altered from Shakespeare [i.e. from "As You Like It"]. With original poems, letters, &c. [The dedication signed: J. C. By James Carrington, with the assistance of Daniel Bellamy the younger.] 1739. 12º. **238**. c. **23**.

C., J. *See* Sirr (Joseph d'A.) Westport Darbyism exposed. [Being a reply to the criticisms of J. C. on a tract by P. Pounden, entitled "The Church of Ephesus."] 1843. 12º. **4139**. aaa. **53**.

C., J. *See* Slater (Eliza) Slater's Sententiæ Chronologicæ . . . A new edition with additions . . . by J. C. 1848. 12º. **800**. d. **26**.

C., J. *See* Spring (Gardiner) and Beecher (E.) Religious Revivals, *etc.* [The editor's introduction signed: J. C.] [1859.] 18º. **4417**. a. **85**.

C., J. *See* Stafford.—*Benevolent Society.* An Abstract of the Deed of Settlement of the Benevolent Society at Stafford . . . With a prefaratory [*sic*] discourse . . . by a member [signed: J. C., i.e. John Cheadle?] [1770.] 4º. **8277**. bbb. **40**.

C., J. *See* Townshend (Lee P.) Some Account of General Robert Venables, *etc.* [The editor's introduction signed: J. C., i.e. James Crossley.] 1872. 4º. [*Chetham Society. Remains, etc.* vol. 83.] Ac. **8120**.

C., J. *See* Valentinois. Émile Augier . . . Avec une bibliographie par J. C., *etc.* 1896. 8º. **010664**. ee. **7**.

C., J. *See* Viardot (L.) A Brief History of the Painters of All Schools, *etc.* [The editor's preface signed: J. C.] 1877. 8º. **7855**. p. **18**.

C., J. *See* W. S. Truth Vindicated; or Mr. Keach's sober appeal answered . . . By S.W. J.C. J.L. Lovers of Truth and Peace. 1691. 8º. **3477**. b. **73**. (**2**.)

C., J. *See* Williams (John) *Missionary to the South Seas.* Farewell to Viriamu [i.e. the Rev. John Williams]. [Three poems, signed respectively: J. C., J. E. C., E. R. C.] 1838. 12º. **11633**. b. **57**.

C., J. Ad Augustissimam . . . Annam, primam Mag. Brit. Reginam, de rebus . . . felicissime gestis. Inprimis de optatissima nostra cum Scotis conjunctione . . . oratio. [The dedication signed: J. C.] pp. 19. *H. Clements & J. Morphew: Londini,* 1707. 4º. **012301**. e. **15**. (**5**.)

—— Ad Augustissimam . . . Annam Reginam de felicissimis regni sui initiis, et rebus . . . bene gestis, inprimis de insigni apud Vigum reportata victoria oratio. [The dedication signed: J. C.] pp. 28. *Impensis Johannis Chauntry: Londini,* 1703. 4º. **835**. g. **33**.

C., J. Advice to the Afflicted, admonitory and consolatory; including a " century of inventions " . . . being chapter 32 of a work on suicide, by J. C. pp. 36. *Office of Aris's " Birmingham Gazette " Co.: Birmingham*, 1887. 8°. **8425. b. 57. (6.)**

C., J. Alcilia. Philoparthens louing Folly. *See* C., I.

C., J.

—— The Antiquities of St Peter's, or the Abbey-Church of Westminster . . . Adorn'd with draughts of the tombs, *etc.* (A supplement.) [The preface signed: J. C., i.e. Jodocus Crull.] 2 pt. *J. Nutt, etc.: London*, 1713. 8°. **010349. tt. 45.**

Wanting certain plates?

C., J. Ny amy ny fitandremana ny andro fadina atao hoe, Sabata. [A tract on the observance of the Sabbath, in Malagasy. Signed: J. C., i.e. James Cameron.] pp. 12. [*Antananarivo*, 1832.] 12°. **4355. de. 21. (1.)**

C., J. Annals of the Life and Work of William Shakespeare, collected from the most recent authorities. [The preface signed: J. C., i.e. Joseph Cundall.] pp. 146. *Sampson Low & Co.: London*, 1886. 8°. **11765. bbb. 27.**

C., J. The Annual Gathering of the L & B. Club, January 15th, 1892. [Verses. Signed: J. C.] *J. Dowling & Son: Newcastle*, [1892.] 12°. **1865. c. 8. (12.)**

C., J. The Antiquities of St. Peter's, or the Abbey-Church of Westminster . . . [The preface signed: J. C., i.e. Jodocus Crull.] The second edition. pp. 351. *J. Nutt: London*, 1715. 8°. **10349. bbb. 5. (1.)**

The first edition is entered under C., J., M.D.

C., J. Apologie voor den . . . pensionaris der stad Amsterdam . . . Mr. Engelbert François van Berckel. Vervat in een missive van een heer uit Delft, aan zyn vriend te Amsterdam. Benevens een gelyke missive, *etc.* [Both letters signed: J. C.] pp. 32. *Rotterdam*, [1782.] 8°. **934. e. 14. (2.)**

C., J. The Araignment of Hypocrisie: or, a Looking-glasse for murderers and adulterers . . . Being a fearfull example of Gods judgments on Mr. Barker, Minister of Gods Word at Pytchley . . . who for living in adultery with his neer kinswoman, and concealing the murder of her infant, was with his kinswoman and maid-servant executed at Northampton. With . . . their severall speeches immediately before their deaths. [The epistle to the reader signed: J. C., i.e. John Crowch?] *Printed by John Crowch & T. W.: London*, 1652. 8°. **E. 1290. (3.)**

C., J. La Artilleria Decidida en defensa del Congreso. [Signed: J. C.] pp. 8. *México*, 1822. 4°. **9770. bb. 10. (14.)**

C., J. The Avalonian Guide to the town of Glastonbury, and its Environs. [Signed: J. C., i.e. John Clark.] Second edition. pp. 57. *J. Wakefield: Glastonbury*, 1814. 8°. **10368. bb. 51. (1.)**

—— Eighth edition. pp. 52. FEW MS. NOTES. *J. Clark: Bridgwater*, 1839. 12°. **10360. bb. 49. (5.)**

—— [Another copy.] **10368. bb. 52. (1.)**

C., J. Babies, and how to take care of them, *etc.* [The preface signed: J. C.] pp. 114. *Ward, Lock & Co.: London*, [1879.] 8°. **7581. de. 12.**

C., J. [The Beauty of Devotion: set forth in the humble and devout behaviour of the sincere conformist to the publick worship of the Church of England. By the author of Schism Try'd and Condemned.] [The preface signed: J. C.] pp. 47. [*A. Bettesworth? London*, 1715?] 8°. **4372. f. 35. (1.)**

Imperfect; wanting all before p. 9.

C., J. Ett Besök i Björkheda prestgård. Af J. C., förf. till " Familjen Stark " [i.e. J. C. A. von Hofsten]. pp. 238. *Stockholm*, 1869. 12°. **10281. aa. 23.**

—— Birkheda Vicarage; the story of a woman's influence. From the Swedish of J. A., author of " The Stark Family " [i.e. J. C. A. von Hofsten], *etc.* pp. viii. 237. *S. W. Partridge & Co.: London*, 1874. 8°. **12638. dd. 21.**

—— Et Besøg i Bjørkheda Præstegaard af J. C., Forf. til " Familien Stark " [i.e. J. C. A. von Hofsten]. pp. 210. *Christiania*, 1870. 8°. **12580. df. 10.**

C., J. Betsey Harold's Story. By J. C. pp. 152. *R. A. Elliott: Liverpool*, 1876. 8°. **12638. l. 12.**

C., J. Bibleland: a Scripture epitome. In twenty-two books, *etc.* [In verse. Signed: J. C.] 2 vol. pp. 626. *Printed for private circulation: Edinburgh*, 1876. 8°. **11643. bbb. 37.**

C., J. Birkheda Vicarage . . . From the Swedish of J. C. *See* supra: Ett Besök i Björkheda prestgård, *etc.*

C., J. A Book of Favourite Modern Ballads. Illustrated with fifty engravings, from drawings by the first artists. [The editor's preface signed: J. C.] pp. xiii. 167. *W. Kent & Co.: London*, 1860 [1859]. 4°. **1347. i. 13.**

—— [Another edition.] pp. xiii. 167. *Ward, Lock & Co.: London*, [1865.] 4°. **1347. g. 25**

C., J. Brief Observations concerning Trade, and Interest of Money. By J. C. [i.e. Sir Josiah Child.] (A Tract against Usurie, *etc.* [By Sir Thomas Culpeper.]) pp. 38 *For E. Calvert & H. Mortlock: London*, 1668. 4°. **1029. b. 1. (2, 3.**

—— *See* MANLEY (Thomas) *the Younger.* [U]sury a Six per Cent. examined, and found unjustly charge by Sir Tho. Culpepper, and J. C. [i.e. Sir Josiah Child, in " Brief Observations concerning Trade, and Interest of Money "] with many crimes, *etc.* 1669. 4°. **1029. b. 1. (8**

—— The Brief Observations of J. C. [i.e. Sir Josiah Child concerning Trade and Interest of Money, briefl examined. By H. R. 1668. 8°. *See* R., H. **104. k. 2**

C.*, J.**

—— Brief van den deken van Brussel in antwoord van de vorenstaenden Brief van den deken van Antwerpe [Signed: J. C.***] *In:* D., W. Brief van eenen dek van Antwerpen aen eenen deken van Brussel. pp. 6–1 [1793.] 8°. **8079. c. 22. (2**

C., J. Calendar for Two Hundred Years. By J. C. [circular card.] 1865. **1881. a. 4. (5****

C., J. A Call to Prayer, in two sermons on that subject . . With an account of the principles and practice of th Quakers in the matter of prayer, subjoined: wherein shewed, that the Quakers religion is much wanting prayer . . . By the author of The Skirmish up Quakerism. [The preface signed: J. C., i.e. Jo Cheney.] pp. 152. *London*, 1677. 8°. **4151. aa.**

C., J. Carta al Conciso. [Defending the liberty of the pr against a writer signing himself El Imparcial. Signe J. C.] pp. 11. [*Cadiz*, 1811?] 4°. **1480. dd. 8. (2**

C., J. Catalogue d'une belle collection de lettres autograp de personnages illustres depuis le xve siècle jusqu'à jours composant le cabinet de M. . . . Fr. Égide Su *etc.* [A sale catalogue. The preface signed: J. C., Jacques Charavay.] pp. 138. 1863. 8°. *See* Su (E. F.) **S.C.676.(8**

, J. A Catalogue of the Subscription Library at Kingston upon Hull, *etc.* [The compiler's " advertisement " signed: J. C., i.e. Joseph Clarke.] pp. xxix. 672. 1822. 8°. *See* Hull.—*Subscription Library.* **11900.** h. **9.**

— [Another copy.] **824.** g. **19, 20.**

— [Another copy.] **619.** i. **41.** (**1.**)

, J. A Character of a Diurnal-Maker. By J. C. [i.e. John Cleveland.] pp. 6. *London,* 1654 [1653]. 4°. **E. 720.** (**6.**)

— [Another edition.] pp. 12. *London,* 1654. 8°. **12314.** e. **48.**

— [Another issue.] *See* infra: Poems. By J. C., *etc.* 1654. 8°. **1076.** k. **21.**

— The Character of a Moderate Intelligencer. With some select poems written by the same author. J. C. [i.e. John Cleveland.] pp. 12. [*London,* 1647.] 4°. **E. 385.** (**9.**)

— [Another copy.] The Character of a Moderate Intelligencer . . . Written by the same author, J. C. [i.e. John Cleveland.] [*London,* 1647.] 4°. Ashley **398.**

, J.

— The Charlie's Holiday; or, the Tears of London at the funeral of Tom and Jerry: also, the Death and Last Will of Poor " Black Billy Waters." [Signed: J. C., i.e. James Catnach. Founded on Pierce Egan's " Life in London."] (Second edition.) *Jas. Catnach:* [*London,* 1823 ?] *s. sh.* fol. **1875.** d. **8.** (**99.**)

, J. Clouds in the East, and a Voice out of the cloud. A call to consider the signs of the times and a saying of the Saviour. By an old student of prophecy. [The preface signed: J. C.] pp. 20. *Houlston & Sons: London,* 1876. 8°. **3166.** de. **11.** (**4.**)

, J.

— The Coin-Act. By way of dialogue. Designed for the use of every one that has any thing at all to do with money . . . [An allegory.] By J. C. [With a preface by Rowland Hill.] pp. 24. *Printed for the Author: London,* 1775. 8°. **4410.** d. **17.**

— [Another copy.] **4410.** bbb. **39.** (**5.**)
Slightly cropped.

— [The Coin-Act.] Yr Act am bwyso aur, a osodwyd allan mewn trefn ysprydol, mewn dull o ymddiddan . . . Gan T. C. [A translation of " The Coin-Act . . . By J. C." With a preface by Rowland Hill.] pp. 35. 1775. 12°. *See* C., T. **04411.** de. **14.** (**3.**)

, J. The Compleat Collier: or, the Whole art of working coalmines in the northern parts: M.DCC.VIII. (By J. C.) pp. vi. 55. *M. A. Richardson: Newcastle,* 1845. 8°. [*Reprints of Rare Tracts & Imprints, etc.* Miscellaneous.] **1077.** f. **90.**

One of an edition of 100 *copies.*

J.

— The Conforming Non-Conformist and the Non-Conforming Conformist, pleading the cause of either side against violent opposers, and modestly answering to the many exceptions made by Mr. Baxter against conformity, in his late book, intituled, The Non-Conformists Plea for Peace. By J. C. [i.e. John Cheyney.] pp. 144. *J. M. for J. Robinson: London,* 1680. 8°. **1471.** aa. **27.**

J. A Cure for Jealousie. A comedy, *etc.* [The dedication signed: J. C., i.e. John Cory.] pp. 56. *Richard Harrison: London,* 1701. 4°. **81.** c. **19.** (**1.**)

C., J. Curious Notions, etc. chiefly concerning alcoholic liquors, tobacco, and those who consume them . . . Compiled, edited, and illustrated by J. C. [i.e. John Coulter.] vol. 1. pp. viii. 320. *C. Eason & Son: Belfast,* [1888–90.] 4°. **8435.** e. **18.**
Published in parts.

C., J. De pace ab optima . . . nostra Regina felicissime constituta, carmen gratulatorium. [Signed: J. C.] pp. 8. MS. NOTE [by J. C.]. *Apud Johannem Morphew: Londini,* 1713. 4°. **837.** h. **34.** (**16.**)

C., J.

— The Death, Last Will, and Funeral of " Black Billy " (Billy Waters): also, the Tears of London for the Death of Tom and Jerry. [Signed: J. C., i.e. James Catnach. Founded on Pierce Egan's " Life in London."] (Tenth edition.) *Jas. Catnach:* [*London,* 1823 ?] *s. sh.* fol. **1875.** d. **7.** (**15.**)

— [Another copy.] **1875.** d. **8.** (**100.**)

C., J. A Defence of the True Church called Quakers . . . against the . . . Independants, Separatists or Brownists, Baptists, Fift Monarchy-men, Seekers, and High Notionists of all sorts . . . Written by J. C. [i.e. John Crook ? or John Collens ?], *etc.* pp. 56. *For Thomas Simmons: London,* 1659. 4°. **4152.** f. **21.** (**17.**)

C., J.

— Denmark Vindicated: being an answer to a late treatise called, An Account of Denmark, as it was in . . . 1692 [by Robert Viscount Molesworth]. Sent from a gentleman in the country, to his friend in London. [The dedication signed: J. C., i.e. Jodocus Crull.] pp. 216. *Tho. Newborough & Ed. Mory: London,* 1694. 8°. **1056.** a. **24.**
Another issue in which the dedication is signed: J. C, D., is entered under C., J., D.

C., J. Earl Beaconsfield: a political sketch. [Signed: J. C., i.e. John Cuckson.] pp. 20. *All Saints' Ward Liberal Association: Birmingham,* 1878. 8°. **10825.** b. **9.**

C., J. Earthwork. Practical methods of setting out slopes for excavations and embankments, *etc.* [The preface signed: J. C., i.e. John Carpendale ?] pp. 41. pl. v. *Madras,* 1861. 8°. [*Madras Civil Engineering College Papers.* no. 3.] **14170.** i. **7.**

C——, J——. Election Squibs, Ballads & Broadsides, with other impromptu verses, by J—— C—— [i.e. John Cotton.] pp. 22. *Privately printed: Birmingham,* [1887 ?] 8°. **11601.** f. **36.** (**2.**)

C., J. An Elegie, upon the Death of the most incomparable, Mrs. Katharine Philips, the glory of her sex . . . By J. C. [*London,* 1664.] *s. sh.* fol. Lutt. I. **117.**

C., J.

— An Elegy on the Queen . . . A Lament for Caroline, the Rose of England. [Signed: J. C., i.e. James Catnach ?] *Catnach:* [*London,* 1821.] *s. sh.* fol. **1852.** c. **9.** (**81.**)

C., J. An Encouragement for all true Britains. [A song. Signed: J. C.] *See* Williams (Andrew) *Merchant of Dublin.* Victorious Newes from Waterford, *etc.* 1642. 4°. **E. 144.** (**1.**)

C., J. Englands Troubles Anatomized. Wherein is related the rise, cause, beginning, unhappy progresse, of this uncivill War . . . Written by a Captaine, servant to His Majesty, who fights his battels with the Parliament. [The dedication signed: J. C., i.e. J. Cockayne.] pp. 55. *For Richard Tomlins: London,* 1644. 4°. **E. 12.** (**15.**)

C., J. The English, or, Viva-voce Ballot. A new method of secret voting, affording protection to the voter . . . With a plan. Addressed to John Bright, Esq., M.P. [The prefatory letter signed: J. C.] pp. 17. *Judd & Glass: London*, 1859. 8º. **8138.** e. **24.**

C., J. The Foundling; or, the Child of Providence. Written by himself. [Letters signed: J. C., i.e. John Church. With a portrait.] pp. 297 [270]. *Printed for the Author: London*, 1823. 8º. **4903.** ccc. **43.** (**1.**)

C., J. A General Index to the Monthly Review from the commencement of the new series in January 1790, to . . . December, 1816. [The preface signed: J. C.] 2 vol. 1818. 8º. *See* PERIODICAL PUBLICATIONS.—London.—*Monthly Review.* P.P. **5434.**

—— [Another copy.] **268.** f. **10, 11.**

C., J. The Golden Guide to London. Illustrated with map, plans, and . . . engravings, *etc.* [The preface signed: J. C.] pp. viii. 256. *Sampson Low & Co.: London*, 1875. 8º. **10350.** bb. **1.**

C., J. The Great Honour and Advantage of the East-India Trade to the Kingdom, Asserted. [The dedication signed: J. C., i.e. Sir Josiah Child.] pp. 39. *For Thomas Speed: London*, 1697. 8º. **1141.** i. **7.** (**1.**)

—— [Another copy.] **8245.** a. **8.**

C., J. Histoire financière de l'Égypte depuis Saïd Pacha, 1854–1876. [The preface signed: J. C.] pp. viii. 264. *Paris*, 1878. 8º. **8229.** d. **8.**

C., J. Hollands op-komst, oft Bedenkingen op de schaadelijke schriften, genaamt Graafelyke regeeringe, en Interest van Holland, uit-gegeven door V. D. H. [van den Hoven, i.e. P. de la Court] . . . vergadert door J. C. [i.e. Jasper Cattenbaert.] Dezen tweeden druk by den autheur . . . vermeerdert. 2 pt. *J. Princen: Leyden*, 1662. 8º. **157.** b. **6.** (**1.**)

C., J. Hydraulics . . . with notes on the supply of water to, and the drainage of, towns, *etc.* [The preface signed: J. C., i.e. John Carpendale?] pp. 99. 72. *Madras*, 1862. 8º. [*Madras Civil Engineering College Papers.* no. 5.] **14170.** i. **7.**

C., J. Il faut avoir du chic. [In verse. Signed: J. C.] pp. 27. *Bordeaux*, [1890.] 8º. **11483.** ee. **39.** (**6.**)

C., J. The Interest of England in the Matter of Religion, unfolded in the solution of these three questions. I. Q. Whether the Presbyterian party should . . . be rejected and depressed, or protected and encouraged. II. Q. Whether the Presbyterian party may be protected . . . and the Episcopal not deserted . . . III. Q. Whether the upholding of both parties by a just and equal accommodation, be not in itself more desireable . . . Written by J. C. [i.e. John Corbet.] pp. 130. *J. M. for G. T.: London*, 1660. 8º. E. **2121.** (**3.**)

—— The Second Part of the Interest of England in the Matter of Religion, unfolded in a deliberative discourse . . . Written by J. C. [i.e. John Corbet.] pp. 132. *For G. T.: London*, 1660 [1661]. 8º. E. **1857.** (**2.**)

C., J. A Just Reprimand to Daniel de Foe. In a letter [signed: J. C., i.e. James Clark] to a gentleman in South Britain. [A reply to certain statements made by Defoe in his "History of the Union," respecting a sermon preached by J. Clark.] pp. 8. *Alexander Henderson: Edinburgh*, [1709.] 4º. **1103.** f. **60.**

C., J. Leaves for the Pocket-Book. An alphabetical l of French words and phrases of frequent occurrence English literature & conversation; with their pr nunciation and meaning. [The preface signed: J. C.] *W. Kent & Co.: London*, [1861.] 16º. **12954.** a. **44.** (

C., J. A Lesson for all True Christians . . . By J. C. ballad.] B.L. *Printed by and for A. M.: Lond* [1670?] *s. sh.* fol. Rox. II. 2

C., J. A Letter of a Clergyman to his Parishioners; bei an expostulatory address on their breach of the Sabba and neglect of all religion. [Signed: J. C., i.e. Jo Courtney.] pp. 3. [1810?] fol. **1203.** k. **12.** (

C., J. Lettre à un gentilhomme allemand, touchant genie & la force de la langue angloise, par rapport au s & à la prononciation . . . Some Thoughts of the Geni and Potestas of the English Language . . . In a letter t High-Dutch gentleman. [Signed: J. C.] *Fr. & E* pp. 20. *Joseph Downing: London*, 1708. 4º. **628.** i. **3.** (

C., J. The Literature relating to New Zealand. A bibl graphy. [The prefatory note signed: J. C., i.e. Jam Collier.] pp. 235. *G. Didsbury: Wellington*, 1889. 8º. **2771.lp.1**

C., J. Little Mary and her Doll, *etc.* [The introductory n signed: J. C.] pp. 30. *David Bogue: London*, [1852.] **12806.** b.

—— Little Mary's Primer, *etc.* ["A Few Words to t Teacher" signed: J. C.] *David Bogue: Lond* 1847. 8º. **12982.** a.

—— [A reissue.] *London*, [1852.] 8º. **12806.** b.

—— Little Mary's Reading Book, *etc.* ["A Few Wo to the Teacher" signed: J. C.] pp. 32. *David Bog London*, [1848.] 8º. **12985.** b.

—— [A reissue.] *London*, [1852.] 8º. **12806.** b.

—— Little Mary's Scripture Lessons, illustrated, *etc.* [Signe J. C.] *David Bogue: London*, [1847.] 8º. **3126.** a.

—— [A reissue.] *London*, [1852.] 8º. **12806.** b.

—— Little Mary's Spelling-Book, *etc.* [The preface signe J. C.] pp. 32. *David Bogue: London*, 1849. 8º. **12982.** a.

—— [A reissue.] *London*, [1852.] 8º. **12806.** b.

C., J. Love in the East; or, Adventures of twelve hou A comic opera in three acts. Written by the author the Strangers at Home, *etc.* [The dedication sign J. C., i.e. James Cobb.] pp. 81. *W. Lowndes: Lond* 1788. 8º. **643.** h. **11.** (

C., J. Magic Squares: new methods, embracing a gene method. [The preface signed: J. C., i.e. James Cra pp. 64. *R. S. Barrie: Dundee*, 1885. 16º. **8503.** aa. **39.**

—— [Another copy.] **8534.** aa.

C., J. Magna Charta: containing that which is very m the sence and agreement of the good people of th nations, nothwithstanding their differences relating worship. Humbly tendered to those that are in emin place . . . as some further essay in order to a w grounded unity, peace and settlement, *etc.* [Signe J. C.] *For Francis Smith: London*, 1659. *s. sh.* fol. **669.** f. **22.** (**1**

., J. The Melancholy Cavalier. Or, Fancy's master-piece. A poëm, by J. C. pp. 28. *Printed for C. R.: [London,]* 1654. 8°. **E. 1493. (3.)**

., J. Miscellaneous Poems. By J. C. pp. xxxv. 103. *W. J. Bradley: London,* [1856.] 8°. **11649. c. 38.**

., J. My Jewels. By the author of "Little Ships on the Sea of Life." (New Year's Address, 1889.) [Signed: J. C.] pp. 24. *Morison Bros.: Glasgow,* [1889.] 8°. **4372. f. 36. (14.)**

., J. My Lady's Cabinet, decorated with drawings and miniatures. [Reproductions. The editor's preface signed: J. C.] *Sampson Low & Co.: London,* 1873. fol. **7855. i. 11.**

., J. Naturales de Galicia. [A patriotic call to arms. Signed: J. C.] [1808.] *s. sh.* fol. **9770. k. 5. (26.)**

., J. The Neglected Wealth of Ireland Explored. Or, a plain view of the great national advantages which may be obtained by compleating the navigation of the River Shannon . . . By J. C. pp. 46. *M. Mills: Dublin,* 1778. 8°. **8246. bb. 8.**

., J. A New Charge against J. C. [i.e. Sir John Clotworthy.] Or, A Bone to pick for such poore English-Irish as walk at Westminster without their dinners. pp. 7. *[London,]* 1647. 4°. **E. 442. (7.)**

., J. A New Fiction, As Wee Were: A. I. M. E. 1. M. 1. D. 2. F. 4. The Scene White-Hall, *etc.* [A satire, mostly in verse. An epigram headed "Par l'Autheur" is signed: J. C.] pp. 6. *J. C. for the Author: London,* 1661. 4°. **E. 1088. (3.)**

., J.

—— The Nonconformists Plea for the Conformists: or, The Church of England and the Dissenters reconciled . . . Wherein is endeavoured to be proved, that it is not unlawful for those commonly called Nonconformists to hear ministers of the Church of England, *etc.* [A prefatory letter by the author signed: J. C., i.e. James Cheak?] pp. 36. *Printed for James Cheak & sold by Benj. Harris: London,* 1683. 4°. **1477. b. 58.**

., J. Observations on the Life and Writings of Edmund Spenser. [Signed: J. C.] *See* Spenser (E.) *the Poet.* [*Works.*] The Works of Edmund Spenser, *etc.* 1840. 8°. **840. i. 7.**

., J. Olde ffrendes wyth newe Faces. Adorn'd with sutable sculptures. [Old ballads and tales. The editor's note to the reader signed: J. C., i.e. Joseph Crawhall.] *Field & Tuer: London,* 1883. 4°. **1876. c. 26.**

., J. One Sheet against the Quakers, detecting their errour and mis-practice in refusing to reverence men outwardly . . . By J. C. [i.e. John Cheyney *etc.*] pp. 8. *For Richard Butler: London,* 1677. 4°. **700. e. 28. (2.)**

., J. Paisley School Board of 1873 & 1876. Illustrated by the election cartoons of Mr. J. E. Christie, etc. Founded on reports in the Paisley and Renfrewshire Gazette. [The editor's introduction signed: J. C.] pp. 160. *J. & J. Cook: Paisley,* 1879. 8°. **8365. f. 2.**

., J. The Picture Gallery, or, Sketches from the life of the Spirit King. [A temperance tract.] By J. C. pp. 108. *W. Tweedie: London,* 1863. 12°. **8435. aa. 10.**

* * *, J. Pisciceptologie, ou l'Art de la pêche à la ligne; discours sur les poissons . . . la pêche aux filets et autres instruments; suivi d'un traité des étangs, viviers, fossés, réservoirs, et les moyens d'en tirer avantage . . . Par J. C * * * [i.e. J. Cussac]. pp. xxiv. 388. pl. xxviii. *Paris,* 1816. 12°. **236. g. 13.**

C * * *, J.

—— Pisciceptologie . . . Terminé par un précis des lois et réglemens sur la pêche. Deuxième édition. pp. xxiv. 388. 326–336. pl. xxviii. *Paris,* 1820. 12°. **7908. aaaa. 1.**

—— Troisième édition. pp. xvi. 416. pl. xxviii. *Paris,* 1823. 12°. **785. c. 22.**

C., J. Poems. By J. C. pp. 63. *A. H. Stockwell: London,* 1923. 8°. **011645. eee. 42.**

C., J. Poems. By J. C. [i.e. John Cleveland.] With additions. (Letters.—The Character of a London-Diurnall.—The Character of a Country-Committee-Man, *etc.*) 2 pt. *[London,]* 1651. 8°. **11626. a. 11.**

—— [Another edition.] 2 pt. *[London,]* 1651. 8°. **1465. a. 36.**

—— [Another edition.] pp. 77. *[London,]* 1651. 8°. **1465. a. 37.**

—— [Another edition.] [With a portrait.] pp. 107. *[London,]* 1653. 8°. **G. 18851.**

—— [Another edition.] Poems. By J. C. [i.e. John Cleveland], *etc.* (A Character of a Diurnal-Maker.) 2 pt. *W. S. [William Sheares]: London,* 1654. 8°. **1076. k. 21.**

C., J. A Poetry Book for Children, *etc.* [The editor's prefatory verses signed: J. C.] pp. 144. *George Bell: London,* 1854. 8°. **11647. d. 3.**

C., J. The Point of Church-Unity and Schism Discuss'd, by a Nonconformist with respect to the church-divisions in England. [Signed: J. C., i.e. John Corbet.] pp. 67. *For Thomas Parkhurst: London,* 1679. 8°. **697. a. 54.**

C., J. The Precious Name of Jesus. [Signed: J. C.] pp. 8. *R. Weston: London,* [1820?] 8°. **4411. i. 42. (2.)**

C., J. Quakerism Proved to be Gross Blasphemy and Antichristian Heresie. By J. C. [i.e. John Cheney.] pp. 31. *For Richard Butler: London,* 1677. 4°. **702. d. 11. (4.)**

—— [Another copy, with a different titlepage.] **4151. b. 27.**

—— Quakerism Subverted: being a further discovery and confutation of the gross errours of the Quakers; published and maintained by William Penn and others of that sect . . . By J. C. [i.e. John Cheyney.] pp. 37. *London,* 1677. 4°. **700. e. 28. (1.)**

C., J. Quercus Regia in Agro Staffordiensi, non, ut olim, Jovi, sed jam Jehovæ . . . Deo Caroli, totiúsqu; Britanniæ Servatori, sacra. [Signed: J. C., i.e. John Cole.] *[London,* 1660?] *s. sh.* fol. **Lutt. i. 186.**

C., J. The Rational Dissenter, soberly professing his Stedfast Belief in the Thirty-Nine Articles. By J. C. pp. 36. *Eman. Matthews: London,* 1716. 8°. **4136. c. 1. (4.)**

C., J. Reasons for Passing the Bill for Relieving and Employing the Poor of this Kingdom humbly offered. [Signed: J. C.] *[London,* 1699?] *s. sh.* fol. **816. m. 15. (51.)**

C., J. Regalías de los Excmos. Gobernadores de los Estados Libres Americanos [i.e. those of Mexico]. [Signed: J. C.] pp. 12. *[Mexico,* 1825.] 4°. **9770. bb. 16. (15.)**

C., J. A Remonstrance of Piety and Innocence; containing the last devotions and protestations of several Roman-Catholicks, condemned and executed on account of the plot . . . To which are annexed certain lessons, psalms and prayers . . . proper for the present exigence of the times. Hereunto is also added a summary of Roman Catholick principles, in reference to God and the King, *etc.* [Signed: J. C., i.e. James Corker.] pp. 190. *London,* 1683. 12°. **1372. a. 33.**

C., J. A Reply to the Absolution of a Penitent, according to the directions of the Church of England, &c. [Signed: J. C., i.e. Jeremy Collier.] pp. 11. [1696.] 4°. **4107. aa. 69.**

C., J. Rules and Maxims for a Holy Life and Happy Death. By J. C. The second edition. pp. 24. *J. Buckland: London*, 1772. 8°. **4422. d. 15. (1.)**

C., J. The Rustick Rampant, or Rurall Anarchy affronting monarchy: in the insurrection of Wat Tiler. By J. C. [i.e. John Cleveland.] [With a portrait.] pp. 154. *For F. C.: London*, 1658. 8°. **E. 2133. (1.)**
Previous editions, entitled "The Idol of the Clownes," are entered under WAT, *Tyler.*

—— [Another copy.] **292. a. 37.**

—— [Another copy.] MS. NOTES. **G. 3523.**

C., J. Sacred Hymns for the Children of God, in the Days of their Pilgrimage. By J. C. [i.e. John Cennick.] pp. xxxii. 220. *B. Milles: London*, 1741. 12°.
Imperfect; wanting pp. 5–8. **3436. e. 24.**

—— The second edition. pp. xxii. 343. *B. Milles: London*, 1741. 12°. **3436. e. 1. (1.)**

—— Sacred Hymns for the Children of God, in the Days of their Pilgrimage. By J. C. [i.e. John Cennick.] 2 pt. *The Author: London*, 1742. 12°. **3436. e. 1. (2.)**
A different collection from the preceding.

C., J. Schism Try'd and Condemn'd by the sentiments of the most eminent writers among the Dissenters . . . By a Lay-Hand. [The preface signed: J. C.] pp. 52. *J. Woodward: London*, [1715?] 8°. **698. h. 15. (2.)**

—— [Another copy.] **T. 1781. (3.)**

—— The second edition. pp. 49. *J. Woodward: London*, [1715?] 8°. **110. f. 3. (1.)**
"Schism Try'd and Condemn'd: containing the sentiments of the foreign Reformed Churches . . . Part II," which does not contain the author's initials, is entered under REFORMED CHURCHES.

C., J. Schleswig-Holstein: an historical survey. By a Manchester Merchant. [Signed: J. C.] pp. 28. *Franz Thimm: Manchester*, 1864. 8°. **8092. aa. 6.**

C., I. A Scripture Catechism for the Instruction of Youth, *etc.* [The preface signed: J. C., i.e. John Campbell.] pp. 36. *M. Ogle: Glasgow*, 1801. 12°. **1018. h. 8. (2.)**

C., J. The Seasons Moralised: a poem . . . By J. C. pp. 48. *W. E. Painter: London*, 1847. 12°. **1467. a. 4.**

C., J. The Secret of Life: a drama. In three acts. By J. C. [i.e. J. Coatsworth.] pp. 62. *Samuel Tinsley: London*, [1876.] 16°. **11781. a. 3.**

C., J.

—— [Selsam trougeval tusschen een Spaens edelman en een heydinne.] Tim. Ritzschens verteutschte Spanische Ziegeunerin. Aus dem Holländischen J. C. [i.e. Jacob Cats.] [*Leipsic*, 1656.] 4°. Hirsch III. **874.**
The titlepage is mutilated.

C., J. The Seventy-Fourth Anniversary of the Birth-day of Daniel Webster, celebrated at . . . Boston, January 18, 1856. [The editor's preface signed: J. C., i.e. John Clark?] pp. 95. *Daily Courier: Boston*, 1856. 8°. **10882. ff. 1. (4.)**

C., J. The Sham Beggar. A comedy in two acts. As it is now acting at the Theatre in Dublin, *etc.* [The dedication signed: J. C.] pp. vi. 34. *C. Henderson: London*, 1756. 8°. **161. g. 67.**

C., J. A Short Treatise of the Epidemical Diseases of these times. Communicated by a loyal pen, in a letter to . . Sir G. B., *etc.* [A satire on political and religious events. Signed: J. C.] pp. 30. *Sold by R. Vaughan: London*, [1662?] 8°. **1093. b. 9**

C., J. Slavery in the South; or, What is our present duty to the slaves? By J. C. pp. 15. *Prentiss & Deland: Boston*, 1862. 8°. **8156. bb. 78. (11.**

C., J. Solitude, and other poems, with translations from the "Méditations poétiques" of Lamartine, and from Metastasio [i.e. from his canzonetta "La Libertà"]. By J. C. [i.e. J. Churchill?] [With the text of the translated poems.] pp. 141. *Hookham: London*, [1830?] 8°. **11643. f. 4**

C., J. Some Arguments to prove, I. The certain salvation of the Christened infants of ungodly as well as of godly Christian parents, dying before actual sin . . . V. With an enquiry into Mr. Baxter's doctrine of particular churches, and terms of church-unity, and detection thereof as faulty. By J. C. [i.e. John Cheyney.] pp. 62. *For J. Robinson: London*, 1680. 8°. **4324. g. 1**

C., J. Some Reasons why the People called Quakers do absent from the Publique way of Worship . . . And also why they cannot swear at all . . . Presented . . . by J. C. [i.e. John Crook.] pp. 8. [1665.] 4°. **224. a. 42. (47**

C., J. Songs, Madrigals and Sonnets. A gathering of some of the most pleasant flowers of old English poetry. Set in borders, *etc.* [The preface signed: J. C., i.e. Joseph Cundall.] *Longman & Co.: London*, 1849. 16°. C. **30. a.**

C., J. Spiritual Life. Poems on several divine subjects relating both to the inward experience and outward practice of Christianity. [The dedication signed: J. C., i.e. James Craig.] pp. xxv. 214. *J. Davidson & Co.: Edinburgh*, 1727. 12°. **11631. a. 1**

C., J. The Stark Family; a sketch from real life. From the Swedish of J. C., author of "Birkheda Vicarage" [i.e. J. C. A. von Hofsten], *etc.* pp. viii. 247. *S. W. Partridge & Co.: London*, 1874. 8°. **12638. dd. 2**

C*********, J. The Stranger; or, the New Man of Feeling. [The dedication signed: J. C********] pp. 138. *James Cundee & M. Jones: [London,]* 1806. 8°. **12614. ee.**

C., J. Strength in Weakness. A sermon preached at the funeral of Mrs. Martha Brooks . . . To which are added some experiences of the grace and dealings of God observed and gathered by a near relation of the said Mrs. Brooks [i.e. by her husband, Thomas Brookes]. By J. C. [i.e. John Collins.] pp. 39. *For John Hancock: London*, 1676. 4°. **1415. b. 5**

C., J. Strictures on Military Discipline, in a series of letters . . . in which is interspersed some account of the Scotch Brigade in the Dutch service. By an Officer. [Signed: J. C., i.e. James Cuninghame.] pp. viii. 212. *John Donaldson: London*, 1774. 8°. **58. c. 1**

C., J. The System of Short-hand, practised by Mr. Thomas Lloyd, in taking down the debates of Congress; and now . . . published for general use, by J. C. [i.e. John Carey.] pp. 16. *H. & P. Rice: Philadelphia*, 1793. 12°. **1042. b. 7**

C., J. Tekel, Dan. v. 27: a modern claim to the gifts of the Holy Spirit examined. [A review of an address by George McClelland, entitled: "The End of this Dispensation, *etc.*" Signed: J. C., i.e. John Craig.] (Reprinted from the "Messenger of the Churches.") pp. 8. *A. & W. R. Wilson: Edinburgh*, [1867.] 8°. **764. f.**

C., J. Thesaurus Brevium, or a Collection of approved forms of writs, and pleadings . . . Collected and published . . . by J. C. The second edition corrected and enlarged. **B.L.** pp. 310. *W. Rawlins for T. Basset: London,* 1687. fol. **5805**. f. **18**.

C., J. Thomas Carlyle: a study. By J. C. [With a portrait.] pp. 138. *John Heywood: Manchester,* 1881. 8°. **10856**. de. **3**.

C., J. The Three Saint Stephen's Days. [A tale.] By J. C. pp. 24. *C. Le Feuvre: Jersey,* 1857. 12°. **4414**. b. **73**. (**1**.)

C., J. Topicks in the Laws of England. Containing media, apt for argument, and resolution of law cases: also an exposition of severall words, not touched by former glossaries. [The dedication signed: J. C., i.e. John Clayton.] pp. 138. *R. L. for William Leake: London,* 1646. 8°. **510**. a. **3**.

Another copy, in which the dedication is signed with the author's name, is entered under CLAYTON *(John) of the Inner Temple.*

C., J. A Touch-Stone: whereby the Protestant religion, as it stands at this day in England may be tryed . . . Also it may appear hereby that the people called Quakers are the true Protestants in practice, and principle . . . By a friend to all that love pure religion . . . J. C. [i.e. John Collens.] [With "an epistle, or preface, to the reader," by Tho. Salthouse.] pp. 18. *For Robert Wilson: London,* 1660. 4°. **4375**. b. **10**.

C., J. A Treatise on Short Whist. By J. C. [i.e. James Clay.] *See* BALDWIN (John L.) The Laws of Short Whist, *etc.* 1864. 16°. **7913**. b. **26**.

—— [Another edition.] *See* BALDWIN (John L.) The Laws of Short Whist, *etc.* 1866. 16°. **7913**. aaa. **11**.

C., J. A True Discovery of the Ignorance, Blindness, and Darkness of those who are called Magistrates about Carlile in Cumberland . . . [By] J. C. [i.e. John Camm?] (The Examination and accusation of Geo. Fox. [By G. Fox?]) pp. 19. *For G. Calvert: London,* 1654. 4°. E. **740**. (**8**.)

C., J. A True Information to the Nation, from the People called Quakers. Being a brief account of the proceedings of some of the magistrates in and about . . . London, against the aforesaid people . . . By J. C. [i.e. John Crook?] pp. 14. [*London,*] 1664. 4°. **4152**. f. **20**. (**2**.)

—— Twenty Cases of Conscience Propounded to the Bishops, or others who are called Fathers in God . . . As also some of the reasons why many godly people refuse to worship with the multitude. By J. C. [i.e. John Crook.] pp. 8. *For Robert Wilson: London,* [1667?] 4°. **4151**. b. **26**.

C., J. The Two Merry Milke-Maids. By J. C. *See* C., I. A Pleasant Comedie, called The Two Merry Milke-Maids.

C., J. A Vindication of Oaths and Swearing in Weighty Cases, as lawful and useful under the Gospel. By J. C. [i.e. John Cheney] . . . The second edition. pp. 38. *For R. Butler: London,* 1680. 4°. **4105**. de. **3**. (**5**.)

C., J. Waiting for an Answer. A truthful record of God's goodness towards a living witness. By J. C. pp. 48. *S. W. Partridge & Co.: London,* 1869. 16°. **4906**. b. **71**. (**11**.)

C., J. A Warning for Swearers, by the example of God's judgments shewed upon a man [i.e. John Duncalf] born near . . . Wolverhampton . . . who had stolen a Bible . . . and falsly forswore it, wishing he might rot, if he were guilty . . . which . . . immediately fell upon him . . . Also, a relation of God's judgments shewed upon a woman . . . who falsly forswore herself, and dyed in a short time after, *etc.* [A ballad. Signed: J. C.] **B.L.** *W. Thackeray, T. Passenger & W. Whitwood: London,* 1677. *s. sh.* fol. Rox. III. **38, 39**.

C., J. Wits Interpreter: the English Parnassus. Or, a sure guide to those admirable accomplishments that compleat our English gentry, in the . . . qualifications of discourse or writing . . . The 3d edition with many new additions, by J. C. [i.e. John Cotgrave.] pp. 520. *For N. Brook: London,* 1671. 8°. **243**. k. **32**.

The 1655 *edition* "*By I. C.*" *is entered under C., I.*

—— [Another copy.] G. **10378**.

Imperfect; wanting the publisher's address to the reader.

C., J.

—— The Woes of Caroline. [Signed: J. C., i.e. James Catnach?] (Bow thy Head thou Lily Pale.—The Poor Royal Stranger without any Home.) [Verses on Queen Caroline.] *Catnach:* [*London,* 1820.] *s. sh.* 4°. **1852**. b. **9**. (**6**.)

C., J. A Word in Season to all in Authority. With weighty considerations what persons, practices and things, doth chiefly cause division and contention . . . Published by a lover of truth and the Kingdoms peace, J. C. [i.e. John Collens.] (The Conclusion. [Signed: J. A., i.e. John Anderdon.]) pp. 26. *For Robert Wilson: London,* 1660. 4°. **4152**. b. **9**.

C., J. De Wyse jaer-beschryver, vertoonende den hemelsloop, een onfeylbaren almanack, oorsprong en vastetijt der heylige dagen. Item, Ontdeckingh van wonderlijcke wercking der natuur . . . Nu . . . vermeerdert en verbetert. Door J. C. [i.e. J. Coler.] [An abridgment of Coler's "Calendarium perpetuum."] coll. 256. *C. J. Zwol: Amsterdam,* 1658. 4°. **7953**. bb. **21**.

C., J., and **MAC C.** (J.) A Net for the Fishers of Men; and the same which Christ gave to his Apostles. Wherein the points controverted betwixt Catholicks and Sectaries are . . . vindicated . . . By two gentlemen, late converts. [The dedication signed: J. C., J. M'C.] pp. 48. *London,* 1723. 12°. **3935**. aa. **1**.

—— New edition. pp. 80. *Keating & Brown: London,* 1827. 32°. **908**. b. **14**. (**2**.)

C., J., *Abbé.*

—— *See* ANSELM, *Saint, Archbishop of Canterbury.* [*Single Works.*] Méditations de Saint Anselme . . . Traduction nouvelle. Par M. l'abbé J. C. 1859. 8°. **3805**. df. **44**.

C., J., *A.M.* The Desertion [i.e. the desertion of the Throne by James II.] Discuss'd. In a letter to a country gentleman. By J. C. A.M. [i.e. Jeremy Collier.] pp. 16. [*London,* 1689.] 8°. T. **1710**. (**1**.)

C., J., *B.A.* Suggestions for Thought on the Permanence of Individuality. By J. C., B.A. pp. 20. *A. Roberts, Woodall & Venables: Oswestry; Hamilton, Adams & Co.: London,* 1870. 8°. **8467**. c. **28**. (**8**.)

C., J., *Capitaine d'Artillerie.* Études sur la campagne de 1796–97 en Italie. Par J. C. capitaine d'artillerie. pp. 306. *Paris,* 1898. 8°. **09078**. cc. **4**.

C * * *, J., *Curé Constitutionnel.* Instruction en forme de lettre d'un curé constitutionnel du département de Mayenne et Loire, à ses paroissiens. [Signed: **J. C * * ***, curé constitutionnel et membre de la Société des amis de la constitution d'Angers.] pp. 46. L'an trois de la Liberté [1791]. 8°. F.R. **151**. (**20**.)

C., J., *D.*

—— Denmark Vindicated: being an answer to a late treatise called, An Account of Denmark, as it was in the year 1692 [by Robert, Viscount Molesworth]. Sent from a gentleman in the country, to his friend in London. [The dedication signed: J. C, D., i.e. Jodocus Crull.] pp. 216. *Tho. Newborough; Ed. Mory: London,* 1694. 8°. **152**. b. **19**.

Another issue, in which the dedication is signed: J. C., is entered under C., J.

C., J., *D.D.* See BIBLE.—*Song of Solomon.—Selections.* [*English.*] The Intercourses of Divine Love betwixt Christ and the Church . . . as metaphorically expressed . . . in the second chapter of the Canticles: opened . . . in several lecture-sermons . . . By J. C. D.D. [i.e. John Collinges.] 1676. 4°. **3165. b. 36.**

C., J., *D.D.* Contemplations on the Life & Glory of Holy Mary the Mother of Jesus. With a daily office agreeing to each mystery thereof . . . By J. C. D.D. [i.e. John Cross.] pp. 103. *Paris*, 1685. 8°. **T. 1851. (1.)**

—— [Another copy.] **222. e. 13. (1.)**

—— See MARY, *the Blessed Virgin.* An Account of the Life and Death of the Blessed Virgin . . . And a Preface in answer to the Apology [by J. C. D.D., i.e. John Cross] for the Contemplations, *etc.* 1687. 4°. **485. b. 31.**

C., J., *D.D.* Defensative Armour, against four of Sathan's most fiery darts: viz. temptations to atheistical and blasphemous impressions and thoughts, self-murther, despair, and presumption . . . By J. C. D.D. [i.e. John Collinges.] pp. 336. *For Benjamin Alsop: London*, 1680. 8°. **4409. d. 19.**

C., J., *D.D.* An Enquiry into the Nature, Necessity, and Evidence of Christian Faith, in several essays. Part I. Of faith in general, and of the belief of a Deity. By J. C. D.D. [i.e. John Cockburn.] pp. 68. *For William Keblewhite: London*, 1696. 8°. **480. a. 36.**
Pt. 2 was published under the author's name.

C., J., *D.D.* The Weavers Pocket-Book: or, Weaving spiritualized. In a discourse . . . To which also are added . . . moral and spiritual observations, relating to that and other trades. By J. C. D.D. [i.e. John Collinges.] pp. 156. *A. Maxwell for T. Parkhurst: London*, 1675. 8°. **873. d. 9.**

—— [Another copy.] **4403. e. 15. (1.)**
The titlepage is mutilated. Imperfect; wanting sig. I 8, K 1, L 7, 8.

C., J., *de "Lo Rat Penat."* Los Malteses en Valencia. Notas heráldico-genealógicas de los apellidos de familias Valencianas procedentes de Malta. Por J. C. de "Lo Rat Penat" [i.e. J. Caruana y Reig, Baron de San Petrillo]. pp. x. 167. pl. 7. *Valencia*, 1911. 8°. **9904. d. 12.**

C * * *, J., *du faubourg Saint-Antoine.* Journal d'un insurgé malgré lui. Par J. C * * * du faubourg Saint-Antoine. pp. xi. 490. *Paris*, 1849. 12°. **1321. a. 32.**

C——, J——, *Esq.* A Letter addressed to J—— C——, Esq. [i.e. John Cobbold] containing some observations on his late conduct and proceedings as Lord of the Manor. [By Robert Small?] pp. 87. *T. Dolby: London*, 1816. 8°. **10358. d. 1. (5.)**

C., J., *Esq.* Thirty-Six Views in Scotland, chiefly from drawings by J. C. Esq. With descriptions. *J. & J. Boydell: London*, 1791. *obl.* 4°. **195. c. 28. (1.)**
"Thirty-six Views in Scotland, with descriptions. A second set" is entered under SCOTLAND. [*Appendix.—Topography and Travels.*]

C., J., *Gent.* The Candidates Guide: or, the Electors rights decided. Shewing the determination of the rights of elections, by the Hon[ble] the Commons of Great Britain . . . in all controverted elections for the counties and boroughs in South Britain, from . . . 1624 to 1730. The second edition, corrected and improved. To which is added the like determinations . . . for North Britain since the Union . . . By J. C. Gent. [i.e. J. Cowley.] pp. 64. *J. Brindley: London*, 1735. 16°. **809. c. 19.**

—— [Another copy.] **8133. aa. 2. (3.)**

C., J., *Gent.* An English-Greek Grammar . . . By J. C. Gent. pp. 62. *London*, 1658. 8°. **E. 1720. (2.)**

C., J., *Gentleman.* See INDEPENDANT CATECHISM. The Independents Catechism. The second edition. Corrected and amended, by J. C. Gentleman. 1654. 4°. **E. 731. (9.)**

C., J., *J. C[tus].* Naufragia publicanorum esse, nec jus permittit, nec ratio. Thesis nupèr in Academia Cantabrigiensi, ad æquitatem juris civilis Romanorum adstructa, adversùs raptores hodiernos. Aucta denuo, & asserta ad aures licentiatorum, in jure Angliæ communi . . . Accessit brevissimà exegesis juris repræsaliarum. Auctore J. C. J. C[to]. pp. 48. *Typis Gulielmi Godbid, impensis Edovardi Dod: Londini*, 1657. 4°. **517. c. 10. (4.)**

C., J., *Jun.*, and **C.**, A. The United States and Canada, as seen by two brothers [J. C., Jun. and A. C.] in 1858 and 1861. pp. 137. *Edward Stanford: London*, 1862 [1861]. 8°. **10408. c. 6.**

C., J., *Junior.* Letters, occasioned by a recent controversy, between R. R. Esq. [i.e. Richard Ryland] and the Rev. J. C. [i.e. John Clayton senior]. Second edition enlarged. [Signed: J. C. junior.] 1805. 8°. *See* CLAYTON (John) *Minister of the Poultry Chapel.* **4405. h. 10.**

C., J., *late Vice-President of the Birmingham Microscopists' and Naturalists' Union.* Collecting & Preserving Freshwater Algæ, by J. C., late Vice-President of the Birmingham Microscopists' and Naturalists' Union, *etc.* pp. 8. *Naturalists' Publishing Co.: Birmingham*, [1891.] 8°. **7074. e. 9. (4.)**

—— Third edition, *etc.* pp. 8. *Naturalists' Publishing Co.: Birmingham*, [1893.] 8°. **07031. de. 3. (4.)**

C., J., *M.* See MANGIN (E.) Nouveau traité complet du jeu de billard . . . Préface par M. J. C. [i.e. J. Caillet.] 1876. 12°. **7915. bbb. 4. (1.)**

C., J., *M.A.* A New-Years Gift: being an help to heart-converse . . . Alphabetically digested . . . By J. C., M.A. *Tho. Parkhurst: London*, 1690. *s. sh.* fol. **C.121.g.9.(8.)**
Cropped.

C., J., *M.D.* The Antiquities of St. Peters, or the Abbey Church of Westminster . . . by J. C. M.D. [i.e. Jodocus Crull] . . . With draughts of the tombs, *etc.* pp. 351. *John Morphew: London*, 1711. 8°. **577. c. 16**

—— [Another copy.] **1123. k. 18**

—— [Another copy.] **1481. b. 18**

C., J., *M.D.* Charity commended . . . By J. C. M.D. *Se*[*e*] infra: Medici Catholicon.

C., J., *M.D.* A Dissertation on the Method of Inoculating the Small-Pox; with critical remarks on the several authors who have treated of this disease. By J. C M.D. [i.e. Jacobo de Castro.] pp. 48. *T. Bickerton London*, 1721. 8°. **1174. h. 21. (5.**

—— [Another copy.] **T. 374. (1.**

—— [Another copy.] **T. 433. (4.**
Cropped.

C., J., *M.D.* An Historical and Critical Review of the Civi[l] Wars in Ireland, from the reign of Queen Elizabeth, t[o] the Settlement under King William. Extracted fro[m] Parliamentary records . . . and other authentic material[s] By J. C. M.D. [i.e. John Curry.] pp. xxi. 447. *J. Hoe[y] & T. T. Faulkner: Dublin*, 1775. 4°. **9509. dd. 9**

C., J., *M.D.* Medici Catholicon, or a Catholick Medicine for the Diseases of Charitie. By J. C., M.D. [i.e. John Collop.] pp. 134. *For Humphrey Moseley: London,* 1656. 12°. **E. 1637. (2.)**

—— [A reissue.] Charity commended, or, a Catholick Christian soberly instructed. pp. 134. *London,* 1667. 8°. **3936. aaa. 1.**

C., J., *M.D.* The Practice of Salivating Vindicated: in answer to Dr. Willoughby's translation of Mons. Chicoyneau's pamphlet against mercurial salivations, in which the anti-venereal vertue of Mercury is prov'd to depend on salival evacuations, &c. . . . By J. C. M.D. [i.e. Joseph Cam.] pp. 56. *J. Peele: London,* 1724. 8°. **1175. k. 7. (5.)**

—— [Another copy.] **117. m. 7.**

C., J., *M.D.R.* A Compleat History of the Affairs of Spain, from the first Treaty of Partition, to this present time . . . The second edition . . . By J. C. M.D.R. [i.e. Jodocus Crull.] pp. 532. *Jos. Barns: London,* 1708. 8°. **9073. df. 11.**

C., J., *Med. D.* See DELLON (C.) A Voyage to the East-Indies, *etc.* [The translator's dedicatory epistle signed: J. C. Med. D., i.e. Jodocus Crull.] 1698. 8°. **1470.b.29.**

—— Memoirs of Denmark, containing the life and reign of the late K. of Denmark Norway &c. Christian v. together with an exact account of the rise and progress of those differences now on foot betwixt the two Houses of Denmark and Holstein Gottorp . . . By J. C. Med. D. [i.e. Jodocus Crull], *etc.* pp. 157. *John Nutt: London,* 1700. 8°. **1056. c. 24.**

C., J., *Medicinæ Professor.* See PRINCIPLES. The Principles of the most Ancient and Modern Philosophy . . . Translated out of the English into Latin . . . and now again made English. By J. C. Medicinæ Professor. 1692. 8°. **702. c. 15.**

C., J., *a Member of the Philadelphia Bar.* See SMITH (Richard) *Lieutenant in the United States Infantry.* The Trials of Richard Smith . . . and Ann Carson . . . Taken in short hand by J. C., a member of the Philadelphia Bar [i.e. James Carson]. [1816.] 8°. **6615. aaa. 4. (2.)**

C., J., *Membre effectif de la Société internationale d'études sociales et politiques.* La Question sociale résolue, précédée du testament philosophique d'un penseur. [The preface signed: J. C. membre effectif de la Société internationale d'études sociales et politiques.] pp. 250. *Bruxelles,* 1893. 8°. **08277. g. 6.**

C., J., *Merchant.* Proposals for Regulating the Silver Coyne, bearing the charge of it, producing a circulation, and securing it to the kingdom. By J. C. Merchant. [1696?] *s. sh.* fol. **8223. d. 38. (12.)**

C., J., *Merchant in Dublin.* A National Credit; for a National Use. Written by J. C. Merchant in Dublin (John Collis). [1705.] 8°. *See* COLLIS (John) **8225. aa. 6.**

C——, J--, *Mr., a Mercer at Aldgate.* See E--, J., *Mr.* Tryal before the Lord Cheif Justice R-y---d [i.e. Raymond] at at [*sic*] Guild Hall between Mr J-- C—— a mercer at Aldgate . . . and Mr J. E-- for criminal conversation with his wife, *etc.* [1730?] *s. sh.* fol. **515. l. 15. (58.)**

C., J., *of Lincoln's-Inn, Esq.* By J. C. of Lincoln's-Inn, Esq. [i.e. Jamineau Chevely.] Appendix to his pamphlet, containing thoughts on the easy reduction of the National Debt. With a proposal—if all other projects fail—for the National Debt paying itself off in a few years; and comments on some late publications on this subject, *etc.* [1780?] 8°. **E. 2162. (1.)**
Imperfect; wanting all after p. 10.

C., J., *of M.H. Oxon.* See HELMONT (J. B. van) Van Helmont's Workes . . . done into English by J. C. sometime of M.H. Oxon. [i.e. John Chandler, of Magdalen Hall.] 1664. fol. **549. l. 27.**

C., J., *of the Inner Temple, Gent.* Stage-Coaches Vindicated: or, Certain animadversions and reflections upon several papers writ by J. C. of the Inner Temple, Gent. [i.e. John Cressett] against stage-coaches, *etc.* pp. 6. [*London,* 1672?] fol. **816. m. 12. (162.)**

C., J., *Philologo.-Polit.* See PERIODICAL PUBLICATIONS.—*Amsterdam.* Europische Mercurius, *etc.* [1707–1718 edited by J. C. Philologo-Polit.] 1690, *etc.* 4°. **P.P. 3444. d.**

C., J., *Prof. Reg.* See OXFORD.—*University of Oxford.—Convocation.* Oratiuncula habita in domo Convocationis, Oxon. die Oct. 27. 1756 [by William King]. Publicavit, et illustravit notis criticis, politicis, et satiricis J. C. Prof. Reg. [i.e. Robert Jenner, Juris Civilis Professor Regius.] [A mock criticism by W. King of his own speech, parodying Jenner's Latin style.] pp. xvi. 24. *Apud Bibliopolas Oxonienses: Oxonii; W. Owen: Londini,* 1757. 4°. **732. g. 17.**

C., J., *R. dé S.-P.* Nouès dé J. C., R. dé S.-P. [i.e. Jean Cazaintre, Ritou dé Sant-Papoul] diouçéso dé Carcassouno. pp. 32. *Carcassouno,* 1810. 12°. **11498. b. 8.**

C., J., *Rector of W. N.* Obedience to Magistrates Recommended, in a discourse . . . preached September the ninth, 1683 . . . by J. C. Rector of W. N. [i.e. Jonathan Clapham, Rector of Wramplingham, Norfolk.] pp. 35. *T. S. for E. Giles: London,* 1683. 4°. **226. g. 10. (8.)**

C., J., *Rev.* See CLAYTON (John) *Minister of the Poultry Chapel.* Letters, occasioned by a recent controversy, between R. R. Esq. [i.e. Richard Ryland] and the Rev. J. C. [i.e. John Clayton, Independent Minister, Weigh House], *etc.* 1805. 8°. **4405. h. 10.**

—— *See* PINDAR (P.) *Esq., pseud.* The Golden Calf . . . A poem . . . dedicated to the Rev. J. C. [i.e. John Clayton, Independent Minister, Weigh House] and his three sons, *etc.* [A satire.] [1815?] 8°. **11633. cc. 1. (2.)**

C., J., *Rev.* Millennial Liberty, or a Prophetic view of the Messiah's kingdom, a poem . . . By the Rev. J. C. [i.e. James Creighton?] pp. 17. *London,* 1788. 8°. **11641. bb. 15.**

—— Poetic Miscellanies. Written occasionally, and addressed to the author's relatives, and particular friends. By the Rev. J. C. [i.e. James Creighton.] pp. 83. *London,* 1791. 8°. **11641. bb. 16.**

C., J., *Rev., a Brother.* A Sermon preached at Bury St. Edmunds . . . 31st of August, 1772, before a . . . body of Free and Accepted Masons, there assembled to constitute the Royal Edmund Lodge. By the Rev. J. C. a Brother. pp. viii. 15. *W. Green: Bury,* 1773. 4°. **4476. cc. 19.**

C., J., *a Sincere Desirer of the Peace and Purity of all Christ's People.* A Branch of Quakerism cut off: or a Vindication of our common custom of naming the dayes and months after their usual names . . . By J. C., a sincere desirer of the peace and purity of all Christ's people, *etc.* pp. 6. *For Richard Butler: London,* 1676. 4°. **4151. c. 146.**

C., J., *Teacher and Translator of English and Portuguese.* O Livro Novo de Soletrear Inglez e Portuguez, *etc.* (A New English and Portuguese Spelling-Book . . . By J. C. teacher and translator of both languages.) pp. 143. *William Reeve: London,* 1747. 12°. **12941. aa. 37.**

C., J. A. *See* CONGREVE (William) Nova Tragedia intitulada A Noiva de Luto . . . traduzida . . . por J. A. C. [i.e. J. A. Cardoso de Castro.] 1788. 4°. **11725. b. 32. (1.)**

—— —— 1817. 8°. **1346. b. 24.**

C., J. A. En Felíz Anuncio de los Dias de Nuestro Catolico, Amado Monarca el Señor Don Fernando VII. dixo J. A. C. [In verse.] pp. 4. [*Mexico*, 1808?] 4°. **11451. bbb. 43. (13.)**

C., J. A. An English Churchman's Answer, from Scripture, reason, and antiquity, to the question: Why do you take your children to be baptized? Original edition by J. A. C. [i.e. James A. Colbeck.] A revised edition by G. H. Colbeck. pp. 16. *Mowbray & Co.: Oxford*, [1896.] 16°. **4371. de. 24. (7.)**

C., J. A. Historia revelationum Christophori Kotteri, Christinæ Poniatoviæ, Nicolai Drabicij, et qvæ circa illas variè acciderunt, usqve ad earundem anno 1657 publicationem & post publicationem. [The dedication signed: J. A. C., i.e. J. A. Komenský.] pp. 272. 1659. 4°. **1368. h. 17. (3.)**

First published in 1657 *under the title* "*Lux in tenebris.*"

C., J. A. The Lord's Prayer. [no. 1, 3–5, 7, signed: J. A. C.] 7 pt. 1848–50. *See* SERMONS. Plain Sermons for the Poor. vol. 1. no. 6, 11, 16, 20, 27, 34, 37. 1848, *etc.* 24°. **4461. a. 48.**

C., J. A. Remarques sur le voyage de M. J. Acerby, en Suède, Finlande et Laponie, par J. A. C. [i.e. J. A. Correa.] pp. 39. *Brunswick*, 1804. 4°. **10105. f. 5. (2.)**

C., J. A.

—— The Truth respecting Italy and Piedmont. Diplomatic revelations by a secret agent of Count Cavour. [Signed: J. A. C., i.e. J. A. Curletti. A translation of " La Vérité sur les hommes et les choses du royaume d'Italie ", by J. A. Curletti, edited by J. F. Griscelli, Baron da Rimini.] pp. 33. *W. Jeffs: London*, 1862. 8°. **8033. b. 63. (5.)**

C., J. A. DA. Novo Combate que tiveram os Napolitanos com os Mouros, *etc.* [Signed: J. A. da C.] pp. 8. *Lisboa*, 1758. 4°. **9004. gg. 33. (24.)**

C., J. A. S. K. D. *See* HOLBERG (L. af) *Baron*. Moralische Fabeln . . . Übersetzt durch J. A. S. K. D. C. [i.e. J. A. Scheibe, Königlichen Dänischen Capellmeister.] 1751. 8°. **012305. f. 1.**

—— *See* HOLBERG (L. af) *Baron*. Peter Paars . . . übersetzt von J. A. S. K. D. C. [i.e. J. A. Scheibe, Königlichen Dänischen Capellmeister.] 1750. 8°. **1160. b. 1.**

C., J. A. Y. *See* A. Y C., J.

C., J. B. A Discourse delivered in the Catholic Apostolic Church, Gordon Square, on the occasion of . . . opening the Church for public worship, Christmas Eve, 1853. (By J. B. C. [i.e. J. B. Cardale.]) Reprinted. pp. 15. *G. J. W. Pitman: London*, 1905. 8°. **764. f. 4. (11.)**

C., J. B. Ireland in the Magic Lantern. Reading. The Lakes of Killarney and Glengariff, viâ Cork and Bantry. [Signed: J. B. C.] pp. 47. *W. Lawrence: Dublin*, [1894.] 8°. **10348. d. 20. (10.)**

C., J. B. Man. [A tract. Signed: J. B. C., i.e. J. B. Cardale.] pp. 5. *H. Teape & Son: London*, 1850. 12°. **764. g. 14. (3.)**

Printed for private circulation.

C**, J. B. Lou Novy para. Coumediou prouvençalou, en tres acte. [In the dialect of Arles.] Per J. B. C** [i.e. J. B. Coye]. pp. 62. *Cracouviou*, 1743. 8°. **11498. c. 23.**

C., J. B. A Venice Looking-Glasse: or, a Letter [signed: J. B. C.] . . . written . . . from London to Rome by a Venetian clarissimo to Cardinal Barberino, Protector of the English nation, touching these present distempers . . . Faithfully rendred out of the Italian into English. pp. 22. [*London*,] 1648. 4°. **E. 525. (19.)**

C., J. B. Veritas et æquitas constitutionis Unigenitus theologicè demonstrata seu 101. Quenelli propositiones confutatæ ex locis theologicis, Scripturis, Conciliis, Definitionibus Pontificum, SS. Patribus, ratione. Editio altera. [The dedication signed: J. B. C., i.e. J. B. Caers.] pp. 134. *Gandavi*, 1724. 12°. **5015. a. 13.**

C., J. B., *ein Liebhaber Ober-Lausitzischer Antiquitäten.* Memoria Heidenreichiana, oder Historischer Bericht von dem Leben, Lehre . . . Reformation und Aembtern M. Laurentii Heidenreichs . . . so wohl auch dessen Kinder, insonderheit Esaias Heidenreichs . . . ingleichen Johannis Heidenreichs . . . Der Nachwelt mitgetheilet . . . von einem Liebhaber Ober-Lausitzischer Antiquitäten J. B. C. [i.e. J. B. Carpzov.] pp. 138. *Leipzig*, 1717. 8°. **10703. aaa. 3. (3.)**

The titlepage is cropped.

C., J. B., *Prêtre de la Congrégation des Missions Étrangères.* Les Lieux saints, ou Notes d'un missionnaire pélerin en Palestine . . . Par J. B. C. Prêtre de la Congregation des Missions-Étrangères. pp. xii. 304. *Roanne*, 1869. 12°. **10076. aaa. 18.**

C., J. B. DE, *Padre, Beneficiado na Santa Basilica Patriarcal de Lisboa.* Roteiro terrestre de Portugal . . . pelo Padre J. B. de C. Beneficiado na Santa Basilica Patriarcal de Lisboa [i.e. J. B. de Castro] . . . Quinta ediçaõ. pp. xv. 190. *Lisboa*, 1814. 8°. **10162. aa. 3**

C., J. B. V. F. The Reclaimed Papist. Or the Process of a Papist Knight reformd by a Protestant Lady with the assistance of a Presbyterian minister and his wife an Independent. And the whole conference, wherby that notable reformation was effected. [The dedication signed: J. B. V. F. C., i.e. John B. V. Canes.] pp. 221 [*London*,] 1655. 8°. **699. a. 40**

—— [Another copy.] **E. 1650. (1.**

C., J. C. *See* H., J. R., and C., J. C. Athletica . . . By J. R. H. [i.e. James R. Hakewill] & J. C. C. 1871. 8°. **7905. aaa. 16**

C., J. C. The Law of Man at variance with the Law of God A speech on the marriage question delivered in the Synod of the Diocese of Sydney. [The preface signed: J. C. C. i.e. James C. Corlette.] pp. 45. *J. Cook & Co. Sydney; T. Bosworth: London*, 1876. 8°. **8416. cc. 1. (20.**

—— [Another copy.] **764. k. 2. (15.**

C., J. C. Neue holländische Grammatica, oder Hinlänglich Anleitung vor die Hochteutsche . . . die holländisch Sprache . . . zu schreiben und zu sprechen. Nieuw Hollandsche Grammatica, *etc.* [The preface signed J. C. C.] pp. 328. *Amsterdam*, 1741. 8°. **829. a.**

C., J. C. Le Péril social dévoilé. Par l'auteur de Grandeu ou décadence future de la nation française. [The prefac signed: J. C. C.] pp. 488. *Bruxelles*, 1877. 8°. **8051. aa. 4**

C., J. C. Pro Patria et pro Petri Sede. L'Action catholiqu en France. [The preface signed: J. C. C.] pp. 80. *Paris*, 1891. 8°. **3900. h. 49. (9**

C., J. D. *See* COWPER (W.) *the Poet.* [*Poetical Works.— Miscellaneous Collections.*] An Original and Singula Poem, and a Fragment . . . To which are appended, humble counterpart and attempt to finish such exquisit stanzas [by J. D. C.], *etc.* [1816?] *s. sh.* fol. **1865. c. 8. (8**

C., J. D. *See* Liturgies.—*Church of England.* [*Adaptations of Latin Liturgical Books.*] A Companion to Confession and Holy Communion. Translated and arranged from the ancient English Offices of Sarum use. By a Layman. [The editor's note signed: J. D. C., i.e. John D. Chambers.] 1853. 12°. **3395. a. 6.**

—— *See* Liturgies.—*Church of England.* [*Adaptations of Latin Liturgical Books.*] The Encheiridion, or Daily Hours of private devotion, according to Sarum use. Translated and arranged by a Layman of the English Church, *etc.* [The advertisement signed: J. D. C., John D. Chambers.] 1860. 16°. **3395. a. 29.**

C., J. D. A Catalogue of the Pictures, Prints, Drawings, etc. in possession of the Worshipful Company of Painter-Stainers at Painters' Hall. [The preface signed: J. D. C.] ff. 21. 1908. 8°. *See* London.—II. *Livery Companies.—Painter-Stainers.* **7854. p. 1.**

C., J. D.

—— Egyptian Art in the Brooklyn Museum Collection. [Photographs, with explanatory text signed: J. D. C., i.e. John D. Cooney.] 1952. 4°. *See* New York.—*Brooklyn Institute of Arts and Sciences.—Museums.* **07705. bb. 56.**

C., J. D. Harangue sur la reception de Monseigneur Du Vair à la charge de Garde des Sceaux de France. Par J. D. C. [The dedication, in Latin, signed: I. A. C.] pp. 19. *D. Langlois: Paris,* 1616. 8°. **8050. bb. 50. (1.)**

C., J. D. Yeddie: an incident and a poem. By W. P. Balfern. [The narrative of the incident signed: J. D. C.] pp. 7. *J. Clarke & Co.: London,* 1870. 8°. **4413. bbb. 12.**

C., J. D. D. Les Agréemens et les chagrins du mariage. Nouvelle galante, *etc.* [The dedication signed: J. D. D. C.] pp. 148. *J. van Ellinkhuysen: La Haye,* 1692. 12°. **12315. aa. 12.**

C., J. D. D., *Monsieur.* L'Honneste homme et le scelerat . . . par Monsieur J. D. D. C. pp. 272. *M. Brunet: Paris,* 1699. 12°. **837. a. 9.**

C., J. E. *See* Williams (John) *Missionary to the South Seas.* Farewell to Viriamu [i.e. the Rev. John Williams]. [Three poems, signed respectively: J. C., J. E. C., E. R. C.] 1838. 12°. **11633. b. 57.**

C., J. E.

—— Hymns for use in Manchester College, Oxford. [The editor's preface signed: J. E. C., i.e. Joseph E. Carpenter.] *Privately printed: Oxford,* 1894. 8°. **03440. i. 22.**

C., J. E. The New Comic Almanack for 1835 (1836). [The preface to the 1836 edition signed: J. E. C., i.e. J. E. Carpenter.] 2 pt. 1835, [36.] 8°. *See* Ephemerides. **P.P. 2465. b.**

C., J. E., *ein des Berg- und Hütten-Wercks erfahrner Liebhaber.* *See* Ercker (L.) Aula Subterranea . . . vermehrt und verbessert durch J. E. C., einem des Berg- und Hütten-Wercks . . . erfahrnen Liebhaber, *etc.* 1736. fol. **443. h. 13. (1.)**

C., J. E. M., *Rakotonirainy.* Origine et valeur des cérébrales dans la langue malgache. Par Rakotonirainy J. E. M. C. pp. 16. *Tananarive,* 1935. 8°. **12911. f. 47.**

C., J. F. *See* Bungener (L. L. F.) What the Christmas Tree teaches us . . . From the French of F. Bungener. [Signed: J. F. C.] [1863.] 16°. **4409. aa. 12.**

C., J. F.

—— *See* Czechowski (M. B.) Thrilling and Instructive Developments: an experience of fifteen years as Roman Catholic clergyman, *etc.* [The editor's preface signed: J. F. C.] 1862. 12°. **4885. aa. 12.**

C., J. F. *See* Eagar (John H.) The Doctrine of the Trinity defended against the attacks of J. F. C. [i.e. James F. Clarke], *etc.* 1864. 8°. **4225. aa. 20.**

C., J. F. *See* Hanet-Cléry (J. B. C.) A Faithful Servant, *etc.* [The translator's preface signed: J. F. C., i.e. James F. Cobb.] [1874.] 16°. **10661. b. 20.**

C., J. F. The Christmas Tree. A parable—from the German. [Signed: J. F. C.] pp. 32. *Wertheim, Macintosh & Hunt: London,* [1863.] 16°. **4414. a. 18.**

C., J. F. A Letter on Baptism, *etc.* [Signed: J. F. C.] pp. 47. *G. Morrish: London,* [1877.] 32°. **4324. a. 3.**

C., J. F. Poems and Essays: inspirational. By J. F. C. pp. 75. *Masters & Lee: Syracuse, N.Y.,* 1867. 8°. **8631. bb. 46. (6.)**

C., J. F. Vindiciæ nominis Germanici contra quosdam obtrectatores Gallos. (J. F. C. [i.e. Joannis Frederici Crameri] Epistola ad F. B. Carpzovium. [In answer to "Les Entretiens d'Ariste et d'Eugène" by D. Bouhours.]) pp. 64. *Apud H. Wetstenium: Amstelodami,* 1694. 8°. **1088. c. 13. (3.)**

C., J. F., and C., L. Exotics; attempts to domesticate them. [Translations in verse from various authors.] By J. F. C. and L. C. [i.e. James F. and Lilian R. Clarke.] pp. 141. *J. R. Osgood & Co.: Boston,* 1875. 12°. **11688. aa. 3.**

C., J. G. *See* Atkins (Henry M.) Ascent to the Summit of Mont Blanc. [The introduction signed: J. G. C., i.e. John G. Children.] 1838. 8°. **1413. g. 7.**

C., J. G. Christoffer Polhem och hans werk. En teckning för folket af J. G. C. [i.e. J. G. Carlén.] pp. 27. *Stockholm,* 1861. 8°. [*Öreskrifter för folkläsning.* no. 7.] **12206. cc. 1.**

C., J. G. The Decayed but Reviving Churchyard Yew, Offwell, Devon. [A poem. The preface signed: J. G. C., i.e. John G. Copleston.] pp. 19. 1832. 8°. **11645. g. 53. (2.)**

C., J. G. Maxims for Children. [Signed: J. G. C.] *J. Groom: London & Birmingham,* [1855 ?] *s. sh.* 4°. **1879.cc.15.(11.)**

—— Maxims for Mothers. [Signed: J. G. C.] *J. Groom: London & Birmingham,* [1855 ?] *s. sh.* 4°. **1879.cc.15.(12.)**

C., J. G. Mémoires pour servir à la connoissance des affaires politiques et économiques du royaume de Suède jusqu'à la fin de la 1775me année . . . Avec figures & XLIII. tables. [The dedication signed: J. G. C., i.e. J. G. Canzler.] 2 tom. pp. x. 431. *Londres* [*Berlin*], 1776. 4°. **1197. d. 1.**

—— [Another copy.] **150. d. 22.**
Imperfect ; wanting tables XVIII–XLIIB.

C., J. G. A Prayer for this Time of War. [Signed: J. G. C., i.e. James G. Cowan.] *W. Skeffington: London,* [1854.] *s. sh.* 12°. **4406. g. 1. (7.)**

C., J. G. La Question portugaise. [Articles on the right of Don Pedro to the throne of Portugal and on his administration, three signed: J. G. C.] pp. 26. [1852.] 8°. **8042. cc. 4.**

C., J. G. El Verdadero Amante de la Constitucion. [Signed: J. G. C. Strictures on the pamphlet signed: A. R., entitled: "El Amante de la Constitucion."] pp. 12. *Puebla*, 1820. 4°. **9770**. bb. **28**. (**7**.)

C., J. G., and **P.**, J. S. Prayers for Sunday Schools. [The preface signed: J. G. C., i.e. James G. Cowan, J. S. P.] pp. 12. *William Skeffington: London*, 1863. 12°. **3456**. aaa. **53**.

C., J. G. DE LA. Cartilla Social, ó Breve instruccion sobre los derechos y obligaciones de la sociedad civil. Publícala para el uso de la Juventud Mejicana J. G. de la C. pp. 60. *Méjico*, 1833. 12°. **8403**. a. **41**. (**1**.)

C., J. G. DE LA. La Lotería. [Signed: J. G. de la C.] pp. 16. *México*, 1844. 12°. **8226**. aa. **26**. (**3**.)

C., J. G. H. *See* MATTHIAS, *Emperor of Germany*. Acta coronationis Mathiæ II. in regem Hungariæ ... e synchrono ... manuscripto in lucem edita. [The editor's preface signed: J. G. H. C., i.e. Joseph Grossinger.] 1784. 4°. **9325**. dd. **11**.

C., J. G. ST. C. The Rubber Restriction Ready Reckoner & Note Book. By "Tapper." [Signed: J. G. St. C. C.] pp. i. 20. *Commercial Press: Kuala Lumpur*, [1925.] 4°. **08548**. dd. **47**.

C., J. H. Benhanan: and other allegories. By J. H. C. pp. 38. *J. Nisbet & Co.: London*, 1851. 16°. **4415**. d. **70**. (**3**.)

C*****, J. H. Les Dicts de Poissy. Par J.-H. C*****. Avec une préface de M. Octave Noël. pp. xi. 259. *Poissy*, 1874. 12°. **11483**. bb. **22**.

C., J. H. Historical Tales for Young Protestants. [The preface signed: J. H. C., i.e. J. H. Crosse.] pp. viii. 180. *R.T.S.: London*, [1857.] 12°. **4416**. e. **12**.

—— [Another edition.] pp. viii. 188. *R.T.S.: London*, [1878.] 8°. **4420**. ccc. **1**.

—— [Another edition.] pp. 192. *R.T.S.: London*, [1883.] 8°. **4420**. c. **9**.

C., J. H.

—— A Puritan Editor (Henry Wilkinson). [Signed: J. H. C., i.e. James H. Colligan. Reprinted from the "Journal of the Presbyterian Historical Society of England."] [1939.] 8°. **20048**. bb. **3**.

C., J. H., *Esq., Barrister-at-Law*. Some Observations on the Projected Union between Great Britain and Ireland, and the inexpediency of agitating the measure at this time. By J. H. C. Esq., Barrister at Law. pp. 35. *Wm. McKenzie: Dublin*, 1798. 8°. **8145**. de. **11**. (**4**.)

C., J. H. D. Parkstone Phantasies; or, Whispers of the pinewoods ... By J. H. D. C. [i.e. J. H. D. Cochrane.] [In verse.] *Ralph & Brown: Parkstone*, [1901.] 8°. **11650**. ff. **16**.

C., J. H. L. Who is this Spurgeon? (Fourth edition.) [Signed: J. H. L. C.] pp. 8. *William Freeman: London*, [1863.] 8°. **4135**. bb. **13**.

—— Who is this Spurgeon? (Tenth edition.) [Signed: J. H. L. C.] pp. 8. *William Freeman: London; James Seaward: Greenwich*, [1863.] 8°. **4431**. bb. **24**.

C., J. I. Noticias Biographicas do Desembargador José Accursio das Neves por J. I. C. [i.e. J. I. Cardoso.] pp. 12. *Lisboa*, 1849. 8°. **10632**. bb. **32**.

C., J. J. *See* TOPLADY (Augustus M.) Family Prayers, *etc.* [The editor's preface signed: J. J. C.] 1831. 12°. **3456**. df. **16**.

C., J. J.

—— —— 1834. 12°. **3455**. ccc.

—— —— 1845. 8°. **3456**. dd.

—— —— 1852. 8°. **3455**. b.

C., J. J. La Docilidad y Gratitud de los Mexicanos, ¿ Co ha sido correspondida por Iturbide? [Signed: J. J. pp. 19. *Puebla*, 1823. 4°. **9770**. bb. **28**. (

C., J. J. D. Ramounet, ou lou Paysan agenez, tournat d guerro. Pastouralo en lengatge d'Agen. Aumentado quantitat de bers qu'eron estats oublidats à la prum impression, & courrijado, *etc.* [The dedication sign J. J. D. C., i.e. J. J. de Courtete. In verse.] pp. 90. *Bourdeu*, 1740. 12°. **11498**. aa.

C., J. K. The Education Riddle Answered. How to so the problem by means of a policy, non-party and sectarian, which would be just to, and would satisfy, parents, sects, and parties, and be the most helpful to children. By J. K. C. [With a portrait.] pp. 15. *Modern Private University: Westcliff on Sea*, [1908.] **8304**. ff. **10**.

—— [Another copy, with a different titlepage.] **8306**. de. **29**.

C., J. K. Intemperance. An ethical poem ... By J. K [i.e. James Casey.] pp. 56. *J. Duffy & Sons: Dub* 1876. 8°. **11652**. b

—— Our Thirst for Drink: its cause and cure. A poem . By J. K. C. author of ethical poem on Intempera [i.e. James Casey]. pp. 115. *J. Duffy & So Dublin*, 1879. 8°. **11653**. aa.

—— Tyndall and Materialism. Gladstone and the Vati Decrees. Two epistles in verse. By J. K. C. [i.e. Ja Casey.] pp. 23. *J. Duffy & Sons: Dublin*, 1875. 8° **011644**. e.

C., J. L. Ad Justitiam. Ode. [Signed: J. L. C.] pp. 4. [1701?] 4°. **837**. k. **11**.

C., J. L. La Dama con Treinta Mil Novios. Extracto d curioso capricho. [Signed: J. L. C.] pp. 7. *Ca* [1810?] 4°. **9180**. c. **10**.

—— [Another copy.] **1323**. k. **18**. (

C., J. L. B. Nueva coleccion de piezas en prosa y en ve sacadas de varios autores españoles, tales son S Cervantes, Quevedo, etc. Por J. L. B. C. [i.e. J. L Cormon.] Tercera edicion. (Nouvelle collection morceaux en prose et en vers, *etc.*) 2 tom. *L* 1823. 12°. **1162**. a.

C., J. L. D. De Kapel van den Heyligen Naem, in de Pr heeren-Kerk, te Gend. Geschiedkundig verhael, J. L. D. C. [i.e. J. L. de Clercq.] Tweeden druk. pp. *Gend*, 1840. 12°. **12580**.

C., J. L. M. *See* BARBA (A. A.) [Arte de los Meta Berg-Büchlein ... übersetzet von J. L. M. C. Johann Lange, medicinae candidato.] 1676. 8°. **446**. a

—— —— 1739. 8°. **954**. a

—— *See* BESCHREIBUNG. Naturgemässe Beschreibung Coffee, Thee, Chocolate, Tabacks ... übersetzet d J. L. M. C. [i.e. Johann Lange, medicinae candidat 1684. 12°. **B. 227**.

—— *See* BOYLE (*Hon.* Robert) [The Aerial Noctil Die lufftige Noctiluca ... übersetzet durch J. L. M [i.e. Johann Lange, medicinae canditatum.] 1682. **1035**. b.

C., J. L. M.

— See Bunyan (J.) [*Holy War.*] Der Helige Krieg . . . Übersetzet von J. L. M. C. [i.e. Johann Lange, medicinae candidato.] 1751. 8°. **4415. ee. 39. (1.)**

— See Cyrenaeus, *pseud.* Cyrenæi Philalethæ Erklärung über die sechs chymischen Pforten des . . . Philosophi G. Riplæi . . . übersetzet durch J. L. M. C. [i.e. Johann Lange, medicinae candidatum.] 1689. 8°. **1143. a. 39.**

— See Flamel (N.) Des berühmten philosophi Nicolai Flamelli chymische Wercke . . . über gesetzt von J. L. M. C. [i.e. Johann Lange, medicinae candidato.] 1681, *etc.* 8°. **1034. g. 18. (1.)**

— See Kelley, otherwise Talbot (E.) Edouardi Kellæi . . . tractatus duo . . . De lapide philosophorum, una cum Theatro astronomiæ terrestri . . . nunc primum in lucem editi curante J. L. M. C. [i.e. Johann Lange, medicinae candidato.] 1676. 8°. **1033. e. 16. (5.)**

— See Lancillotti (C.) [Guida alla chimica.] Der brennende Salamander . . . Übersetzet durch J. L. M. C. [i.e. Johann Lange, medicinae candidatum.] 1681. 8°. **1033. a. 18.**

— See Micigno (P.) Michael Sendivogii Leben . . . übersetzet . . . durch J. L. M. C. [i.e. Johann Lange, medicinae candidatum.] 1683. 12°. **1400. a. 36.**

— See N., S. Aula lucis . . . übersetzt durch J. L. M. C. [i.e. Johann Lange, medicinae candidatum.] 1690. 8°. [*Wunderliche Begebenheiten unbekandten Philosophi, etc.*] **1035. f. 34. (2.)**

— See Nodus. Nodus sophicus enodatus, *etc.* (Kinder-Bett des Steins der Weisen . . . übersetzet durch J. L. M. C. [i.e. Johann Lange, medicinae candidatum.]) 1692. 8°. **1033. e. 57.**

C., J. M. *See* Alphonso Maria [de' Liguori], *Saint, etc.* [*Collections.*] Reflections on Spiritual Subjects, *etc.* [The preface signed: J. M. C.] 1849. 16°. **4415. d. 9.**

C., J. M. *See* C., M. D. The Tripled Crown. A book of English, Scotch and Irish verse for the age of six to sixteen. Chosen and arranged by three of that age. [The preface signed: M. D. C., M. W. C., J. M. C., i.e. M. D., M. W., and Joanna M. Cannan.] 1908. 8°. **11603. i. 17.**

C., J. M. *See* Ornsby (Robert) The Life of St. Francis de Sales, *etc.* [The preface signed: J. M. C., i.e. John M. Capes.] 1856. 8°. **4865. a. 30.**

C., J. M. *See* Squier (E. G.) Honduras . . . Edicion corregida y ampotada por J. M. C. 1908. 8°. **010480. de. 51.**

C., J. M. *See* Wilson (John) *D.D., President of Trinity College, Oxford.* Recollections of Past Years; or, Family notices of the late Rev. John Miller. [With memorial verses signed: J. M. C., i.e. J. M. Chapman.] [1858.] 8°. **11648. aa. 1. (1.)**

C., J. M. Á la Nacion Mexicana. [A political pamphlet. Signed: J. M. C.] pp. 8. *México,* 1822. 4°. **8180. bb. 9.**

C., J. M. An Address to British Christians, on the importance and necessity of a revival of religion . . . By a Minister of the Gospel. [The advertisement signed: J. M. C., i.e. John M. Cramp.] pp. 24. *Holdsworth & Ball: London,* 1832. 12°. **4371. aaaa. 21. (9.)**

C., J. M. The "Christian Casket" containing . . . interesting and improving material, selected from the writings of many of the most gifted men . . . By J. M. C. pp. 224. *P. M. Cranenburgh: Calcutta,* 1860. 8°. **3752. b. 3.**

C., J. M. Con la razon y sin armas se desmoronó un imperio. [Signed: J. M. C.] [*Mexico,* 1823.] *s. sh.* fol. **9770. k. 8. (1.)**

C., J. M. Exhortacion á los Españoles. [On colonial independence. Signed: J. M. C.] pp. 7. *México,* 1822. 4°. **9770. bb. 11. (24.)**

C., J. M. Imputed Righteousness, "The Righteousness of God." A dialogue. By J. M. C. pp. 42. *J. B. Bateman: London,* 1860. 12°. **4226. b. 20.**

C., J. M. Meekness. [Signed: J. M. C.] 1849. *See* Sermons. Plain Sermons for the Poor. no. 23. 1848, *etc.* 24°. **4461. a. 48.**

C., J. M. Monetary System. The injury, insufficiency, and inconvenience of a gold standard and circulating medium, stated, with a proposed substitute. By J. M. C. pp. 31. *R. Groombridge: London,* 1837. 8°. **1139. i. 8. (2.)**

C., J. M. Noticia extraordinaria de Durango. [Signed: J. M. C.] [*Mexico,* 1823.] *s. sh.* fol. **9770. k. 7. (127.)**

C., J. M. Nuevo Calendario Religioso, *etc.* [The preface signed: J. M. C.] 1876. 8°. *See* Ephemerides. **P.P. 2595. f.**

C., J. M. Palabrita á los Serviles. [Signed: J. M. C.] pp. 8. *México,* 1822. 4°. **9770. bb. 12. (42.)**

C., J. M. Proyecto de Ley. [On freedom of testamentary disposition. Signed: J. M. C.] pp. 7. *México,* 1822. 4°. **9770. bb. 13. (13.)**

C., J. M. Restoration: a parochial tract. [Signed: J. M. C.] pp. 16. *William Skeffington: London,* 1867. 16°. **4411. aaa. 57. (1.)**

C., J. M. Saint Sophia in Ramazán. Second edition. [Signed: J. M. C., i.e. James M. Campbell.] pp. 9. *Bombay Gazette Steam Press: Bombay,* 1897. 8°. **4506. df. 11. (2.)**

C., J. M. Satisfaccion que se da al señor coronel don Angel Perez Palacios. [An account of the retraction by H. La Garza of the charges made by him in the anonymous pamphlet entitled: "Diario del Ahorcado y Descuartizado." Signed: J. M. C., i.e. J. M. Campos.] *México,* 1834. *s. sh.* fol. **9770. k. 12. (100.)**

C., J. M. Wreck of the North-German Emigrant Ship "Deutschland," off the Kentish Knock, on December 7th, 1875. [Signed: J. M. C., i.e. John M. Chapman.] [1876 ?] 8°. **11648. a. 4. (3.)**

C., J. M., and C., C. Jack Frost and Betty Snow, *etc.* [The dedication signed: J. M. and C. C., i.e. J. M. Chanter and C. Chanter.] 1858. 16°. *See* M., J., and C. C. **12807. b. 53.**

C., J. M., and C., G. A. A Small Dictionary of Colloquial Bengali Words. By J. M. C. & G. A. C. [i.e. Joseph M. Culshaw and G. A. Cowley.] pp. 125. *Methodist Publishing House: Calcutta,* 1901. 8°. **12906. de. 24.**

C., J. M., *de l'Académie des Sciences, Arts, et Belles Lettres de Dijon.* Encyclopédie élémentaire, ou Rudiment des sciences et des arts . . . Par J. M. C. de l'Academie des Sciences, Arts, et Belles Lettres de Dijon [i.e. J. M. Crommelin]. 3 tom. *Autun,* 1775. 12°. **827. b. 47.**

C., J. M., *Lic.*

— Apuntamientos para contestar á las observaciones que acaba de publicar el sr. D. M. Atristain en contra de las que se hicieron acerca de la sentencia pronunciada . . . en el negocio . . . sobre pesos que seguian las señoras doña M. de los Angeles y doña L. Lardizábal, contra la testamentaría de la señora doña A. Obregon. [Signed, Lic. J. M. C., i.e. J. M. Cuevas.] *México,* 1859. 8°. **6784. e. 1. (6.)**

C., J. M. DE LA, *el P., Escolapio.* Elementos de Geografía de la Isla de Cuba, con un mapa . . . por el P. J. M. de la C., escolapio [i.e. Juan Miracle de la Concepción] . . . Segunda edición corregida y aumentada. pp. 69. *Habana,* 1875. 8°. **10470.** aa. **6.**

C., J. M. F. El Militar Imparcial. [Signed: J. M. F. C.] pp. 4. *Puebla,* 1820. 4°. **9770.** bb. **27.** **(54.)**

C., J. M. F. A. L. D. *See* ART. L'Art de désopiler la rate . . . Nouvelle édition, revue & augmentée par J. M. F. A. L. D. C. [i.e. J. Manoury, F.A., Libraire de Caen.] 178873 [1773]. 12°. **12316.** ee. **25.**

C., J. M. R. Calendario Manual . . . que arregla al meridiano de México J. M. R. C. [1833.] 16°. *See* EPHEMERIDES. P.P. **2589.** ah.

C., J. M. T. DE. *See* GUSMÃO (A. de) *Cavalheiro professo na Ordem de Christo.* Collecção de varios escritos ineditos politicos e litterarios . . . que dá á luz publica J. M. T. de C. 1841. 8°. **12230.** a. **13.**

C., J. M. V. Poesías Varias en Loor de la Independencia. Su autor J. M. V. C. pp. 36. *México,* 1821. 4°. **11451.** bbb. **44.** **(26.)**

C., J. N. *See* LITURGIES.—*Latin Rite.—Combined Offices.*—I. *Holy Week Offices.* L'Office de la Semaine Sainte, selon le Messel et Breuiaire Romain . . . Traduit en françois, *etc.* [The translator's dedication signed: J. N. C.] 1662. 8°. C. **46.** e. **23.**

C., J. N. Memorabilia seculorum XV, XVI, XVII & XVIII, versibus numerabilibus & mnemonicis, tempus rerum, quibusvis proprium, exhibentibus . . . inclusa; opera J. N. C. pp. 32. 1706. 4°. **1479.** aaa. **4.**

C., J. N. Observaciones á los Europeos. Por un Americano. [Signed: J. N. C.] 2 pt. *México,* 1821. fol. **9770.** k. **5.** **(149.)**

C., J. N. A. J. R. L. P. D. Queja ó Reclamacion de España a todos los Franceses de Honor y Rectitud, con una breve refutacion de los once diarios recibidos de Madrid. Por J. N. A. J. R. L. P. D. C. pp. 34. *México,* 1808. 4°. **9180.** e. **6.** **(39.)**

—— [Another copy.] **9180.** ccc. **2.** **(15.)**

C., J. O. Remarks on the Annuity-Tax and Seat-Rents. Written for the Committee of inhabitants, by J. O. C. pp. 31. *Printed for the Committee: Edinburgh,* 1828. 8°. **4175.** c. **11.**

C., J. P. *See* BARLOW (William R.) Notes on Ammunition, *etc.* [The editor's preface signed: J. P. C., i.e. John P. Cundill.] 1877. 8°. **8831.** i. **2.**

C., J. P. *See* BASSE (William) The Pastorals and other works of William Basse. [With an introduction signed: J. P. C., i.e. John P. Collier.] [1870.] 4°. **2326.** c. **10.** **(5.)**

—— *See* CHETTLE (Henry) Patient Grissil . . . With an introduction [signed: J. P. C., i.e. John P. Collier] and notes. 1841. 8°. Ac. **9485/5.**

—— *See* CHURCHYARD (Thomas) The firste (second) Parte of Churchyardes Chippes, *etc.* [With an introduction signed: J. P. C., i.e. J. P. Collier.] [1870 ?] 4°. **2326.** c. **1.** **(1.)**

—— *See* CHURCHYARD (Thomas) A light Bondell of livly discourses called Churchyardes Charge, *etc.* [With an introduction signed: J. P. C., i.e. J. P. Collier.] [1870 ?] 4°. **2326.** c. **1.** **(2.)**

—— *See* D., N. An Antidote against Melancholy: made up in pills, *etc.* [With an introduction signed: J. P. C., i.e. John P. Collier.] [1870.] 4°. **11621.** f. **1.**

C., J. P.

—— *See* DIALOGUE. A dialogue bytwene the comm secretary and Jalowsye, touchynge the vnstableness Harlottes. [With an introduction signed: J. P. C., John P. Collier.] [1842 ?] 4°. **11623.**

—— *See* DRAYTON (Michael) Endimion and Phœbe, [With an introduction signed: J. P. C., i.e. Joh Collier.] [1870 ?] 4°. **11623.** d.

—— *See* DRAYTON (Michael) The Shepheards Garland, [With an introduction signed: J. P. C., i.e. Joh Collier.] [1870 ?] 4°. **11623.** d.

—— *See* GREENE (Robert) *the Poet.* A Quip for an Up Courtier, *etc.* [With an introduction signed: J. P i.e. John P. Collier.] [1870.] 4°. **2326.** c. **8.**

—— *See* GUILPIN (Edward) Skialetheia, *etc.* [With introduction signed: J. P. C., i.e. John P. Collier.] [1870.] 4°. **2326.** c. **8.**

—— *See* HARVEY (Gabriel) Foure Letters, and cer Sonnets, *etc.* [With an introduction signed: J. P i.e. John P. Collier.] [1870.] 4°. **2326.** c. **8.**

—— *See* HARVEY (Gabriel) A New Letter of No Contents, *etc.* [With an introduction signed: J. P i.e. John P. Collier.] [1870.] 4°. **2326.** c. **9**

—— *See* HARVEY (Gabriel) Pierces Supererogation, [With an introduction signed: J. P. C., i.e. Joh Collier.] [1870.] 4°. **2326.** c. **9**

—— *See* LICHFIELD (Richard) *pseud.* The Trimmin Thomas Nashe, *etc.* [With an introduction sig J. P. C., i.e. John P. Collier.] [1870.] 4°. **2326.** c. **10**

—— *See* NASH (Thomas) *Satirist.* Have with you to Sa Walden, *etc.* [With an introduction signed: J. P. C John P. Collier.] [1870.] 4°. **2326.** c. **10**

—— *See* NASH (Thomas) *Satirist.* Pierce Penilesse Supplication to the Diuell. [With an introduction si J. P. C., i.e. John P. Collier.] [1870.] 4°. **2326.** c. **9**

—— *See* ROWLANDS (Samuel) Humors Looking G [With an introduction signed: J. P. C., i.e. Jo Collier.] [1870.] 4°. **2326.** c. **1**

—— *See* SPAIN. [*Appendix.—History and Politics.*] Coppie of a Discourse written by a Gentleman, em in the late Voyage to Spaine and Portingale, *etc.* [W introduction signed: J. P. C., i.e. John P. Collier.] [1870.] 4°. **2326.** c. **10.**

—— *See* STUBBES (Phillip) The Anatomie of Abuse [With an introduction signed: J. P. C., i.e. Jo Collier.] [1870.] 4°. **2326.** c. **1**

—— A Few Odds and Ends, for cheerful friends. A C mas gift. [Verses. The "notice" signed: J. P. C John P. Collier.] pp. ii. 51. *Printed for private circu only,* 1870. 4°. **11650.**

C., J. P.

—— Law without Gravity. By J. P. C. Illustrated by Starke. [Verses.] pp. x. 53. *Justice of the Chichester,* 1953. 8°. **11659.**

C., J. P. Letters on Christian Missions. By a Layn the Church of England. [The preface signed: J. i.e. Julius P. Caesar.] pp. iv. 83. *G. C. Hay Calcutta,* 1858. 8°. **4193.**

C., J. P. Mein Zeitvertreib im Dichten. [Signed: J. pp. 84. *Coburg,* 1761. 8°. **11526.** df. **2**

C., J. P. Moustiques, littéraires et politiques de l'an passé. [Verses. The titlepage headed: J. P. C.] pp. 82. *Paris*, 1895. 12°. **11483**. eee. **41**.

C., J. P. Nine Historical Letters of the Reign of Henry VIII: written by Reginald Pole, Thomas Cromwell, Michael Throckmorton and Thomas Starkey. Copied from the originals. [The editor's introduction signed: J. P. C., i.e. John P. Collier.] pp. ii. 48. *For private circulation only: London*, 1871. 4°. **2326**. c. **5**.

C., J. P. Lou Pâté dé moussu lou cura, ou lou songi dé Janet. Par J.-P. C. pp. 8. *Marseille*, [1857.] 8°. **11498**. f. **59**. (**10**.)

C., J. P.

—— Poetic Justice. By J. P. C. Illustrated by Leslie Starke. [Verses.] pp. xii. 84. *Stevens & Sons: London*, 1947. 8°. **11659**. e. **36**.

C., J. P. Skjæbnens Luner. Original Novelle af J. P. C. [Extracted from the "Nordiske Uge-Journal."] [*Copenhagen*, 1870?] 8°. **12581**. df. **30**.
Imperfect; wanting all after p. 16.

C., J. P. Ved Øresund. Sangspil i 1 Akt, a J. P. C. pp. 16. [*Copenhagen*, 1870?] 8°. **11754**. f. **11**.

C., J. P.

—— The Way of Prayer. A manual of daily prayers and readings. [The prefatory note signed: J. P. C., D. T., W. W.] pp. 48. [1940.] 16°. *See* ENGLAND.—*Unitarian and Free Christian Churches.—General Assembly.* **03456**. de. **170**.

C., J. P. J. DA S., *Bacharel.* Apanhamento de Decisões sobre Questões de Liberdade, publicadas en diversos periodicos forenses da Corte, feito pelo Bacharel J. P. J. da S. C. [i.e. J. P. J. da Silva Caroatá.] pp. 137. *Bahia*, 1867. 8°. **6785**. aa. **10**.

C., J. P. L. Un Enfant de Marie, ou le Vénérable Jean Berchmans de la Compagnie de Jésus. Par un père de la même compagnie. [The dedication signed: J. P. L. C., i.e. L. J. M. Cros.] pp. 324. *Paris*, 1863. 18°. **4885**. aa. **9**.

C., J. P. L., *el Ciudadano.* Cantares Políticos por el ciudadano J. P. L. C. pp. 60. *Madrid*, 1873. 8°. **11450**. b. **10**. (**2**.)

C., J. R. Historia Veteris Testamenti antediluviana ex recentioribus Gallorum, Anglorum, Italorum, Germanorum, Belgarum &c. scriptis collecta . . . atque selectis observationibus illustrata a J. R. C. pp. 82. *Lipsiæ*, 1722. 4°. **3149**. d. **23**.

C., J. R. Lest We Forget. By J. R. C. [i.e. John R. Crawford.] pp. 126. *Simpkin, Marshall & Co.: London*, 1897. 8°. **8139**. de. 4.

—— [Another copy.] **8139**. de. **8**.

C., J. R. Prayers. J. R. C. pp. 51. *Gowans & Gray: London & Glasgow*, 1917. 16°. **03456**. de. **12**.

C., J. R. Voces de un Misionero para despertar á las almas que estan abismadas en las ilusiones de este mundo . . . Segunda edicion. [Signed: J. R. C.] pp. 21. *Lima*, 1889. 8°. **011451**. f. **14**. (**2**.)

C., J. R. DE. Más vale Tarde que Nunca. Sobre la Independencia que emprendieron los Americanos el año de 1821, y primero de ella. [Signed: J. R. de C.] [*Mexico*, 1821.] 4°. **11451**. bbb. **44**. (**19**.)

C., J. S. *See* A., E. A Month in the Coasting Trade . . . By E. A., J. S. C., and J. A. R. 1877. 8°. **8807**. aaa. **9**.

C., J. S. *See* AELFRIC, *Grammaticus, Abbot of Eynsham.* An Anglo-Saxon Homily on St. Gregory's Day. With an English translation by E. Elstob, *etc.* [With a preface signed: J. S. C.] 1839. 8°. **4452**. f. **2**.

C., J. S. *See* COLLIER (Jane) An Essay on the Art of Ingeniously Tormenting, *etc.* [The editor's advertisement signed: J. S. C.] 1805. 8°. **245**. f. **14**.

—— —— 1806. 12°. **12352**. bbb. **26**.

C., J. S.

—— *See* CURWEN (John) How to observe Harmony, *etc.* [The editor's preface signed: J. S. C., i.e. John S. Curwen.] [1890?] 4°. **7891**. a. **59**.

C., J. S.

—— *See* STAHL (G. E.) Georg. Ernest. Stahlii . . . Fundamenta chymiae, *etc.* [The editor's preface signed: J. S. C., i.e. J. S. Carl.] 1723, *etc.* 4°. **44**. f. **12**.

—— —— 1746, *etc.* 4°. **1033**. i. **25**.

C., J. S. Lays of the Heart, being an ode to the memory of a father and other poems. By J. S. C. [i.e. John S. Clark.] pp. 97. *Smith, Elder & Co.: London*, 1836. 8°. **993**. i. **11**.

C., J. S. Seven New Short Stories. By J. S. C. pp. 120. *Mather & Archer: Lower Mitcham*, [1915.] 8°. **012621**. e. **6**.

C . . . . , J. S., *Senex.* Témoinage spiritualiste d'outre-tombe sur le magnétisme humain, fruit d'un long pélérinage par J. S. C . . . . . . Senex. Publié et annoté par l'abbé J.-B. Loubert. pp. lvi. 134. *Paris*, 1860. 8°. **8631**. dd. **11**.

C., J. S. F. On the Revealed Course of Events from the Rapture of the Heavenly Saints to the Restitution of All Things. By J. S. F. C. pp. 12. *T. Weston: London*, 1903. 8°. **04420**. i. **44**. (**4**.)

C., J. T. *See* BUCHMAN (Frank N. D.) Live Wires, *etc.* [The editors' preface signed: J. T. C., B. R. E., H. V.] 1938. 8°. **20092**. a. 4.

C., J. T. Some few Personal Recollections of Sir Thomas Dyke Acland. [Signed: J. T. C., i.e. Sir John T. Coleridge.] pp. 31. [*Printed for private circulation:*] *Exeter*, [1872.] 12°. **10855**. dh. **28**.

C., J. T. DE. El Comerciante de Perlas. Novela americana, escrita por J. T. de C. pp. 360. *Paris*, 1869. 12°. **12490**. bbb. **21**.

C., J. T. L. *See* TURRETINUS. [De iis, qui ultimis seculis divinas revelationes iactant.] Preservatif contre le fanatisme, *etc.* [The translator's preface signed: J. T. L. C., i.e. J. T. le Clerc.] 1723. 8°. **850**. f. **13**.

C. (J. TH.) *P.P.P.T.* Philosophiæ Wolffianæ, ex græcis et latinis auctoribus illustratæ, maxime secundum animæ facultatem cognoscendi consensus cum theologia, per præcipua fidei capita. Auctore J. Th. C. P.P.P.T. [i.e. Israel Gottlieb Canz.] pp. 951. *Francofurti & Lipsiæ*, 1737. 8°. **526**. e. **30**.

C., J. V. Diaphanta: or, Three Attendants on Fiat Lux. Wherin Catholik religion is further excused against the opposition of severall adversaries. 1 Epistola ad Odoenum, against Dr. Owen. 2 Epistola ad Croesum, against Mr. Whitby. 3 Epistola ad Ampibolum [*siç*], against Dr. Taylor. And by the way an answer is given to Mr. Moulin, Denton and Stillingfleet. [Signed: J. V. C., i.e. John B. V. Canes.] pp. 411. 1665. 8°. **3935**. a. **36**.

C., J. V.

—— [A reissue.] Three Letters declaring the strange odd Proceedings of Protestant Divines, when they write against Catholicks: by the example of Dr. Taylor's Dissuasive against Popery; Mr. Whitbies Reply in behalf of Dr. Pierce against Cressy; and Dr. Owens Animadversions on Fiat Lux. Written by J. V. C. [i.e. John B. V. Canes], *etc.* 1671. 12°. **3935.** aaa. **6.**

—— An Epistle to the Authour of the Animadversions, upon Fiat Lux [i.e. John Owen] in excuse and justification of Fiat Lux against the said Animadversions. [Signed: J. V. C., i.e. John B. V. Canes.] pp. 111. 1663. 8°. **874.** f. **6.**

C., J. V. Montserrat. Glosas a la carta collectiva de los obispos españoles. [By J. V. C., i.e. Joan Vilar Costa. With the text of the letter.] pp. xv. 389. 1938. 4°. *See* Spain.—*Bishops.* Ac. **2006.** c.

C., J. V., *Mr., a Friend to men of all Religions.* Fiat Lux: Or, A general Conduct to a right understanding in the great Combustions and Broils about Religion here in England. Betwixt Papist and Protestant, Presbyterian & Independent . . . By Mr. J. V. C. a Friend to Men of all Religions [i.e. John B. V. Canes]. pp. 368. 1661. 8°. E. **2266.**

—— The second edition reviewed and enlarged by the authour, *etc.* pp. 396. 1662. 8°. **4139.** a. **30.**

—— The third edition, reviewed and enlarged by the authour, *etc.* pp. 344. 1665. 8°. **4139.** aaa. **10.**

—— *See* Protestant. Animadversions on a Treatise intituled Fiat Lux, *etc.* 1662. 8°. **1019.** c. **16.**

—— *See* Whitby (Daniel) *D.D.* *Δος που στω.* Or, an Answer to sure footing . . . wherein the rule and guide of faith . . . are . . . vindicated; from the . . . petty flirts of Fiat Lux, *etc.* 1666. 8°. **1019.** e. **17.**

C., J. W. *See* Aristophanes, *the Poet.* [*Aves.—English.*] The Birds of Aristophanes. Translated by J. H. Frere. [The editor's preface signed: J. W. C., i.e. John W. Clark.] 1883. 8°. **11705.** de. **5.**

C., J. W. Elements of Geography; for the use of young children. By the author of "Stories from the History of England." [The introduction signed: J. W. C., i.e. Right Hon. John W. Croker.] pp. 94. *John Murray: London,* 1829. 12°. **570.** c. **44.**

—— Third edition. pp. 96. *John Murray: London* 1835. 12°. **793.** c. **34.**
The fourth edition, entitled "Progressive Geography for Children" is entered below.

C., J. W. The German Reformation of the Nineteenth Century; or, a Sketch of the rise, progress and present position of those who have recently separated themselves from the Church of Rome; with a short notice of the state of Protestantism in Prussia, Austria, Bavaria and the Prussian Baltic Provinces. By the German correspondent of "The Continental Echo." [The preface signed: J. W. C.] pp. xx. 469. *John Snow: London,* 1846. 8°. **1368.** f. **16.**

C., J. W. Mary M'Neill; or, the Word remembered. A story of humble life. By J. W. C., author of 'Alice Lowther,' *etc.* pp. 145. *Johnstone, Hunter & Co.: Edinburgh,* 1863. 16°. **4414.** aa. **15.**

—— [Another edition.] pp. 144. *Johnstone, Hunter & Co.: Edinburgh,* [1875.] 16°. **4418.** bbb. **7.**
With an additional titlepage.

C., J. W. The Militia as an Army of Reserve. By J. W. C. pp. 16. *Thomas Hatchard: London,* 1856. 8°. **8828.** a. **20.**

C., J. W. The One Baptism: a tract for the times. By J. W. C. *J. Paul: London,* 1864. 8°. **4325.** cc. **22.**

C., J. W. Our Dwellings warmed. As they are and as they might be; with a chapter on ventilation. By J. W. C. pp. 48. *Lockwood & Co.: London,* 1875. 8°. **7814.** aa. **6.**

C., J. W. Phases of Thought. By J. W. C. 2 no.
no. 1. Materialism. A sketch of the life and writings of John Stewart, *etc.* pp. 16.
no. 2. Unitarianism. A sketch of the life and writings of Joseph Priestley. pp. 16.
Farrah & Dunbar: London, 1861. 8°. **4014.** c. **79.** **(5.)**

C., J. W. Progressive Geography for Children. By the author of "Stories for Children." Fourth edition, revised. [The introduction signed: J. W. C., i.e. Right Hon. John W. Croker.] pp. 72. *John Murray: London,* 1847. 12°. **793.** a. **48.**
Previous editions, entitled "Elements of Geography," are entered above.

C., J. W. Quakerism and the Church: being my reasons for leaving the Society of Friends and joining the Church. By J. W. C. [i.e. John W. Cudworth.] pp. 93. *F. B. Kitto: London,* 1870. 8°. **4152.** cc. **13.**

—— "Ritualism" or "Quakerism?" Being remarks on a pamphlet by J. W. C. [i.e. J. W. Cudworth], entitled "Quakerism and the Church." [By] J. B. [i.e. John Bellows], *etc.* 1870. 8°. *See* B., J. **4151.** e. **16.** **(9.)**

C., J. W.

—— Stories selected from the History of England, from the Conquest to the Revolution. For children. Third edition. [The preface signed: J. W. C., i.e. Rt. Hon. John Wilson Croker.] pp. [180.] *John Murray: London,* 1817. 12°. **12835.aa.64.**
The last leaf is mutilated.

—— Stories selected from the History of England, from the Conquest to the Revolution. For children. Fourth edition. [The preface signed: J. W. C., i.e. Right Hon. John Wilson Croker.] pp. vi. 180. *John Murray: London,* 1818. 18°. **12835.aa.65.**

—— Stories selected from the History of England . . . Fourteenth edition, *etc.* [The preface signed: J. W. C., i.e. Right Hon. John W. Croker.] pp. xii. 205. *John Murray: London,* 1847. 16°. **1210.** f. **37.**

C., J. W. d. Brieven uit Engeland aan mijn' vriend Z. Door J. W. d. C. (J. W. del Campo.) 1862. 8°. *See* Campo (J. W. del) **10349.** g. **1.**

C., J. W. B. The Royal Marriage, canzonet. Prepared for the Prince of Wales, and the Princess Alexandra of Denmark. By the loyal poet, J. W. B. C. [*London,* 1863.] *s. sh.* 8°. **11621.** h. **1.** **(64.)**

C. (J. Wilson)

—— Tales of a Grandfather on English History; being a collection of stories taken from the History of England, by J. Wilson C. [i.e. J. W. Croker.] Continued to Queen Victoria by Pearson. pp. xvi. 264. *J. H. Truchy: Paris,* 1840. 12°. **9505.** aa. **34.**

C—— (John Newton) *See* Newton (John) *Rector of St Mary Woolnoth.* Sixty-eight Letters . . . to a Clergyman *etc.* [The preface signed: John Newton C——.] 1845. 12°. **4410.** c. **33**

. (JUNIEN) *See* G. (Auguste) Les Petits maraudeurs . . . tableau . . . par Auguste G., Junien C. [i.e. J. Champeaux], *etc.* 1823. 8°. **11738.** cc. **18.** (**10.**)

., K. *See* DEMOSTHENES. [*Two or more Works.—English.*] Several Orations of Demosthenes . . . English'd . . . by several hands, *etc.* (The Second Philippick, by K. C. [i.e. Knightley Chetwood.]) 1702. 12°. **236.** e. **39.**

., K. *See* LITURGIES.—*Church of England.—Common Prayer.—Collects.* [*English.*] Daily Helps from the Collects. Compiled and arranged by K. C. [1886.] 8°. **3477.** aa. **8.**

., K.

— *See* MASARYK (T. G.) *President of Czechoslovakia.* Hovory s T. G. Masarykem. [Recounted by K. Č., i.e. K. Čapek.] 1936. 8°. **2402.** d. **21.**

., K. *See* STEIN (C. H. von) Aus dem Nachlass von H. von Stein. Dramatische Bilder, *etc.* [With a preface signed: K. C.] 1888. 8°. **12252.** f. **1.**

., K. Cambria. [Poems, entitled "The Ancient Harper," "An Address to the Dee," "On a Stream in Carmarthenshire," "A Welsh Dingle." Each signed: K. C.] 4 pt. [1865 ?] 8°. **11651.** bbb. **42.**

., K. Dew Drops. [Poems, each signed: K. C.] 1874. 8°. **011653.** f. **16.**

Printed on one side of the leaf only.

., K. Good Counsell, to the Petitioners for Presbyterian Government, that they may declare their faith before they build their church. [Signed: K. C., i.e. Katherine Chidley.] [*London*, 1645.] *s. sh.* fol. **669.** f. **10.** (**39.**)

., K.

— Mlčení s T. G. Masarykem. [By K. Č., i.e. Karel Čapek. With a bibliography.] pp. 30. *Praha*, 1936. 8°. **11858.** c. **81.**

., K. An Ode in imitation of Pindar on the Death of the Right Honourable Thomas Earl of Ossory. By K. C. pp. 6. *For Samuel Carr: London*, 1681. fol. **163.** n. **46.**

., K. Pilgrims of Fashion. A novel. By K. C. pp. xvi. 337. *Trübner & Co.: London*, 1862. 12°. **12632.** k. **3.**

., K. Songs of Many Days. By K. C. pp. 99. *M. Ward & Co.: London*, 1882. 8°. **11653.** g. **25.**

., K. Thumbnail Essays. By K. C. [i.e. K. Collins.] pp. viii. 253. *S. C. Brown, Langham & Co.: London*, 1905. 8°. **12355.** dd. **16.**

., K., *Pastor.* Die Stöckersche Bewegung und der evangelische Geistliche. Ein Beitrag zur Erörterung über das Verhältniss des Christenthums zur Politik, von Pastor K. C. pp. 31. *Berlin*, 1884. 8°. **3911.** aa. **60.** (**5.**)

., K. v. Einige Worte über den Alpenstreit von K. v. C. Zweite Auflage. pp. 14. *Wasserburg*, 1869. 8°. **1145.** i. **5.** (**6.**)

., K. A. *See* JANVIER (P. D.) [Sœur Saint-Pierre.] Sister Saint Peter . . . Translated by K. A. C. 1886. 12°. **4867.** aa. **33.**

., K. H. Brief van een Heer te Rotterdam aan zijn vriend te Utrecht, over het eclatante geval . . . Petrus Hofstede . . . bejeegend, en de gevolgen, *etc.* [Signed: K. H. C.] pp. 8. [1783.] 8°. **934.** e. **10.** (**10.**)

., K. I. Mairi of Callaird. A West Highland tale, translated from the Gælic as orally collected. Versified: and dedicated to Mac Cailein Mòr, Duke of Argyll, by a kinswoman. K. I. C. [i.e. Katherine I. Campbell], *etc.* [With a preface by J. F. Campbell.] pp. vi. 99. [*Privately printed*, 1878 ?] 4°. **11595.** cc. **3.**

C., K. L. *See* TEELINCK (W.) Het Nieuwe Jeruzalem . . . Naar de oorspronkelijke uitgave van 1652, in de hedendaagsche spelling overgebracht. [The editor's preface signed: K. L. C.] 1884, *etc.* 8°. **4372.** e. **31.**

C., L. *See* A., A., and C., L. First Course of Exercises, *etc.* 1884. 8°. **12953.** bb. **51.**

—— *See* A., A., and C., L. A Synopsis of the Rules of the French Grammar, *etc.* 1884. 8°. **12950.** cc. **3.**

C., L. *See* APPEAL. An Earnest Appeal for Medical Freedom. [With an introduction, signed: L. C.] 1877. 8°. **7306.** de. **6.** (**4.**)

C., L. *See* BYRON (G. G. N.) *Baron Byron.* [*The Corsair.—Italian.*] Il Corsaro . . . versione in prosa di L. C. 1819. 8°. **1465.** h. **2.** (**1.**)

—— —— 1820. 8°. **11431.** ccc. **27.** (**3.**)

C., L. *See* C., J. F., and C., L. Exotics; attempts to domesticate them. By J. F. C. and L. C. [i.e. J. F. and Lilian R. F. Clarke.] 1875. 12°. **11688.** aa. **3.**

C . . . ., L . . . . *See* CONSTANTIA. Constantia in de Balcon, of the Vrye Entrée, zynde het zeldzaam leeven van eene welbekende, genaamd L . . . . C . . . . alias Klein Tapster. 1804. 16°. **12580.** a. **4.**

C., L. *See* CORROZET (G.) Le Tresor de l'histoire de France . . . Diuisé en deux parties. La premiere . . . enrichie de plusieurs curieuses recherches & pieces autentiques . . . par L. C. [i.e. L. Coulon], *etc.* 1645, *etc.* 8°. **9220.** ccc. **13.**

C., L. *See* COURTAUX (T.) Notice historique sur les seigneurs de la baronnie de la Bôve, *etc.* [With an introduction signed: L. C.] 1901. 8°. **9903.** dd. **16.**

C - - - - - - -, L - - - . *See* MOORE (John) *Apothecary.* An Epistle . . . to L - - - C - - - - - - - [i.e. John Carteret, Earl Granville] upon his Treatise of Worms [i.e. the Treaty of Worms]. [1743.] fol. **C. 57.** g. **7.** (**13.**)

C., L. *See* ROTHSCHILD (C. de) Letters to a Christian Friend on the Fundamental Truths of Judaism . . . Translated from the German. [With a dedication signed: L. C.] 1869. 8°. **4034.** cc. **24.**

C., L. *See* ROULLET DE LA BOUILLERIE (F. A. M.) successively *Bishop of Carcassonne* and *Archbishop of Perga.* The Eucharist and the Christian life. Translated . . . by L. C. 1875. 8°. **4257.** aaa. **1.**

C., L. *See* T., *le R. D.* Discours contre la transubstantiation . . . Traduit par L. C., *etc.* 1685. 12°. **4327.** aa. **9.**

C., L. L'Aigle républicaine. 17ᵉ édition. Élection de Louis-Napoléon. L'Ombre de l'Empereur à son neveu Louis-Napoléon. [Signed: L. C., i.e. L. de Chaumont, pseudonym of L. Guillemin.] *Paris*, [1848.] *s. sh.* fol. **1880.** c. **1.** (**169.**)

C., L. Amoret, or, Policy defeated; in a satyrical dialogue between Mopsus and Damon. [The dedication signed: L. C.] pp. 11. *For Daniel Brown: London*, 1682. 4°. **1346.** f. **57.**

C., L. Bibliographie. Le Mystère des Trois Doms [by S. Pra] joué à Romans en MDIX publié d'après le manuscrit original . . . par feu Paul-Émile Giraud . . . et Ulysse Chevalier. [A critique, signed L. C.] pp. 16. *Romans*, [1887 ?] 8°. **011902.** m. **20.** (**6.**)

C., L. Biografia del Libertador Simon Bolívar, o la Independencia de la América del Sud. Reseña histórico-biográfica por L. C. [i.e. Lorenzo Campano.] pp. 180. *Paris*, 1868. 12°. **10882.** aa. **39.**

C., L. "Children busy, children glad, Children naughty, children sad." Pictures by T. Pym. Stories by L. C. [i.e. Lucy Clifford.] pp. 40. *Wells Gardner & Co.: London*, [1881.] 4°. **12808**. dd. **60**.

C., L. Chwila teraźniéjsza i posłannictwo Polski, przez L. C. [i.e. by L. Chrzanowski.] pp. 18. *Paryż*, 1846. 8°. **8093**. aaa. **44**. (**3**.)

C., L. Les Dires d'un vieux maître d'école, médaillé de Sainte-Hélène, sur le concours ouvert en 1860-61 entre les instituteurs publics par S. Exc. le Ministre de l'Instruction publique. [Signed: L. C.] pp. 48. *Paris*, 1862. 12°. **8309**. aaa. **44**. (**3**.)

C., L. Giuoco degli scacchi. Del finale di torre e cavallo contro torre. Esempi diversi con note ed aggiunte. [The postscript signed: L. C., i.e. Luigi Centurini.] pp. 30. *Genova*, 1853. 8°. **7906.aaa.19.**

C., L. Het groote Liedeboek van L. C. [i.e. L. Clock.] Inhoudende veelderhande schriftuerlijcke liedekens, vermaningen, leeringen, ghebeden, *etc.* *G. Rooman: Haerlem*, 1604. 16°. **3437**. aaa. **1**.

C., L. John Elliott the Reformed, *etc.* [The preface signed: L. C.] pp. 216. *Usher & Strickland: Boston*, 1841. 18°. **10880**. aa. **19**.

C., L. Mártos y la Izquiérda. Por C. L. [Signed: L. C.] 1883. 12°. *See* L., C. **8042**. a. **39**. (**1**.)

C., L. Le Musée de Douai depuis son origine jusqu'à ses derniers accroissements. [The preface signed: L. C., i.e. L. Crépin.] pp. 128. *Douai*, 1867. 8°. **7807**. a. **49**. (**2**.)

C., L. L'Ordre du jour, chanson nouvelle. Extrait du journal le Pacificateur, *etc.* [Signed: L. C.] pp. 4. *Paris*, [1792.] 8°. **F**. **545**. (**15**.)

C., L. Parere su i principj artistici che hanno servito di guida al Sig. Cavaliere Niccola Matas per il suo disegno della facciata di S. Maria del Fiore di Firenze. [Signed: L. C.] pp. 16. [*Florence*, 1845.] 8°. **7807**. c. **41**. (**17**.)

C., L. Paris républicain. Recueil chantant. Par L. C., auteur du Bon pasteur [i.e. L. de Chaumont, pseudonym of L. Guillemin]. 2e édition. *Paris*, [1848.] fol. **1871**. e. **1**. (**29**.)

—— 15e édition. [*Paris*, 1848.] fol. **1850**. a. **1**. (**9**.)

C., L. Poor Daddy Long-Legs, and other stories. By L. C. With illustrations. pp. 69. *Hodges, Figgis & Co.: Dublin*, 1885. 4°. **12810**. cc. **55**.
The author's initials appear on the cover as: L. E. C.

C., L. Prayers for Individuals. Consisting of the Daily Devotions . . . by the late Rev. Samuel Merivale: together with prayers for a second week from various sources, and occasional prayers and collect, *etc.* [The editor's preface signed: L. C., i.e. Lant Carpenter.] pp. 186. *William Browne: Bristol*, 1829. 12°. **3457**. ddd. **11**.

C * * *, L. Prière pour la France. Dernier vœu de l'Archevêque de Paris [i.e. D. A. Affre], *etc.* (Par L. C * * *, auteur de: A genoux devant le Christ [i.e. L. de Chaumont, pseudonym of L. Guillemin].) [*Paris*, 1848.] *s. sh.* fol. **1852**. d. **1**. (**23**.)

C., L. La Promenade de Livry. [The dedication signed: L. C.] 2 vol. *C. Barbin: Paris*, 1678. 12°. **12512**. cc **31**.

C., L. Recueil de poësies de diuers autheurs, *etc.* [The dedication signed: L. C. The compiler's name given in the privilege as L. Chamhoudry.] 1661. 12°. *See* Chamhoudry (L.) **11481**. aa. **53**.

C . . . . , L. Regrets et repentir de Buonaparte dit Napolé[on] et sa réponse aux critiques. [Signed: L. C . . . . .] pp. [*Paris*, 1814.] 8°. **8052.k.11.(15**

—— [Another copy.] **8052**. k. **16**. (

C., L. Séminaire de la Garlière et Maison-École de Bonn[es] Sœurs, à Sondée dans la paroisse de Saint-Laurent-[de-] Cuves. [Signed: L. C.] 1893. *See* Avranches.—*Soci[été] Archéologique d'Avranches.* Mémoires, *etc.* tom. 11. 1842, *etc.* 8°. Ac. **52**

C., L. Serie di biografie contemporanee, per L. C. [W[ith] portraits.] vol. 1, 2. *Torino*, 1853. 16°. **10603**. a.
Imperfect; wanting vol. 3.

C., L. The Story of Little Louise, and her brother Euge[ne]. By L. C. pp. 63. *G. Morrish: London*, 1884. 12°. **12810**. aa.

C., L. Tractatus aliquot chemici singulares summ[um] philosophorum arcanum continentes. 1. Liber de princi[piis] naturæ, & artis chemicæ, incerti authoris. 2. J. Be[...] Angli tractatulus novus, & alius Bernhardi Comitis Tre[vi]rensis, ex gallico versus. Cum fragmentis Edua[rdi] Kellæi H. Aquilæ Thuringi & Joh. Isaaci Hollan[di.] 3. Fratris Ferrarii tractatus integer, hactenus fere s[up]pressus, & in principio & fine plus quam dimidia pa[rte] mutilatus. 4. Johannis Daustenii Angli Rosarium, [The editor's preface signed: L. C., i.e. L. Co[m]bachius.] 4 pt. *Sumptibus S. Köhlers: Geismar* 1647. 8°. **1033**. e.

C., L. Under Mother's Wing. By L. C. author of stories "Children busy, children glad, children naughty, child[ren] sad" [i.e. Lucy Clifford]. Illustrated by J. K. pp. 3[...] *Wells Gardner & Co.: London*, [1885.] 4°. **12805**. w.

C., L., and **B.**, F. P. Nouveau traité d'arithméti[que] décimale . . . Par L. C. [i.e. L. Constantin] et F. P. B. [i.e.] M. Bransiet, called in religion Frère Philippe] . Trente-neuvième édition, revue et corrigée, *etc.* pp. 3[...] pl. iv. *Liége*, 1847. 8°. **8506**. bbb.

—— [Another edition.] Par F. P. B. [i.e. M. Bransiet], pp. iv. 376. 1869. 8°. *See* B., F. P. **8506**. bbb.

—— *See* B., F. P. Solutions des problèmes du Nouv[eau] traité d'arithmétique décimale . . . Par F. P. B., 1847. 8°. **8506**. bbb.

C., L., and **H.**, A. E. Simple Instructions for the Lay[ing] Out of the Dead. By two Queen's Nurses—L. C. [and] A. E. H. [i.e. Amelia E. Hastings.] With preface by Rev. E. F. Russell. pp. 8. *Queen's Nurses: Richm[ond]* [1912.] 16°. **07306**. de. **15**.

C * * *, L., *Amateur*. Académie universelle des jeux . Précédé d'un coup d'œil général sur le jeu . . . Par L. C * Amateur [i.e. C. Y. Cousin d'Avallon]. pp. xvi. 460. *Paris*, 1825. 12°. **7913**. b.

C., L., *Citoyen du district de S. Nicolas du Chardon[net].* Réflexions offertes à l'attention de MM. des soix[ante] districts de la ville de Paris. [Signed: L. C. Citoyen [du] district de S. Nicolas du Chardonnet.] pp. 8. *P[aris]*, 1789. 8°. **F**. **624**. (

C., L., *Colonel réformé des Grenadiers royaux en* 1791. Le[ttre] d'un Colonel de Grenadiers royaux réformés à un off[icier] supérieur de la Garde Nationale de Paris, ou extrai[t de] quelques idées militaires. [Signed: L. C. Colonel réfo[rmé] des Grenadiers royaux en 1791.] pp. 26. *P[aris]*, 1791. 8°. **F**. **252**.

C., L., *a Friend of the inslaved Communality.* A Generall Charge, or, Impeachment of High-Treason, in the name of Justice Equity, against the Communality of England; as was presented by Experienced Reason. Anno 1647. With the speech of Experienced Reason to the Communality of England . . . Likewise the Communalities objections to the said articles. With the answer of Experienced Reason . . . This penned by L. C., a friend of the inslaved Communality [i.e. Laurence Clarkson]. pp. 28. *London*, 1647. 4°. **103**. a. **27**.

—— [Another copy.] E. **410**. **(9.)**

C . . ., L . . ., *M.* Le Philosophe, ami de tout le monde, ou Conseils désintéressés aux litterateurs. Par M. L . . . C . . . [i.e. L. Coste] qui n'est point litterateur. pp. 36. *Sophopolis* [*Paris*], 1760. 12°. **11826**. aaa. **6**.

C., L., *One of the Universality.* A Single Eye All Light, no Darkness; or Light and Darkness One . . . This revealed in L. C. one of the universality [i.e. Laurence Clarkson]. *Imprinted* [*by Gilles Calvert*] *at London, in the yeer that the powers of heaven and earth was, is, and shall be shaken, yea damned, till they be no more for ever* [1650]. 4°. E. **614**. **(1.)**

C., L., *Philalethes.* Some Animadversions upon a case [viz. an action of escape against Stephen Mosdel] inserted in a book lately printed, entituled Modern Reports. Or Select cases adjudged in the Courts of King's Bench Chancery Common Pleas and Exchequer since the restoration of His Majesty King Charles the Second. [By Anthony Colquitt. Signed: L. C. Philalethis [*sic*].] pp. 12. *Printed for the Author: London*, 1682. fol. T. **925**. **(3.)**

C . . . ., L . . . ., *le R. Père.* See Le Plat (J.) Confession publique de Monsieur Le Plat . . . Premiere édition, ornée des notes &c. par le R. Père L . . . . C . . . . 1787. 8°. **107**. c. **60**.

C., L., *Sig.* Notizie di Odessa (scritte dal Sig. L. C.). [With a map.] pp. 35. *Firenze*, 1817. 8°. **10291**. e. **32**.

C., L. A. D.

—— Réponse aux Questions du Citoyen Dard. [Signed: L. A. D. C., i.e. Léonard André Du Cloux. A reply to "Genève de 1793, et Genève de 1796. Questions patriotiques adressées à tous les Genevois qui veulent garder leur serment civique" by H. B. Dard.] [1794.] 8°. **8073**. dd. **6**.

—— See Dard (H. B.) Réplique aux réponses normandes qui ont été faites aux Questions patriotiques du citoyen Dard, par l'anonime L. A. D. C. 1796. 8°. **8074**. i. **14**. **(22.)**

C., L. B. D. R. S. Christine, reine de Suède, tragédie en trois actes; par L. B. D. R. S. C. [i.e. Baron J. A. de Réveroni Saint-Cyr.] pp. 46. *Paris*, 1816. 8°. **11738**. m. **37**. **(9.)**

—— Mademoiselle de Lespinasse, ou l'Esprit et le cœur, comédie en un acte et en vers, par L. B. D. R. S. C. [i.e. Baron J. A. de Réveroni Saint-Cyr.] pp. 36. *Paris*, 1817. 8°. **11738**. m. **37**. **(6.)**

—— Les Partis, ou le Commérage universel, comédie en trois actes et en vers, par L. B. D. R. S. C. [i.e. Baron J. A. de Réveroni Saint-Cyr.] pp. 55. *Paris*, 1817. 8°. **11738**. m. **37**. **(11.)**

—— Le Sybarite, ou le Voluptueux, comédie en trois actes et en vers, par L. B. D. R. S. C. [i.e. Baron J. A. de Réveroni Saint-Cyr.] pp. 47. *Paris*, 1817. 8°. **11738**. m. **37**. **(8.)**

C., L. B. S. Gramophone Adjustments and Repairs . . . By "L. B. S. C." pp. 77. *P. Marshall & Co.: London*, [1929.] 8°. **08769**. aaa. **10**.

C., L. B. S.

—— How to build "Princess Marina," an L.M.S. Mogul Class in 3½-ins. gauge. By L. B. S. C. pp. 52. *Mechanics: London*, 1949. 8°. **8769**. g. **41**.

C., L. B. S.

—— The Live Steam Book. By "L.B.S.C." (Revised.) pp. xiv. 209. *Percival Marshall & Co.: London*, 1954 [1955]. 8°. **8236**. m. **8**.

C., L. B. S.

—— "Maisie:" words and music. By "L. B. S. C." [A model locomotive construction manual.] pp. viii. 131. *Percival Marshall & Co.: London*, [1952.] 8°. **8774**. b. **9**.

C., L. B. S. Shops, Shed, & Road. A handbook on the construction and fitting of details and accessories for small power steam locomotives. By "L. B. S. C." . . . Illustrated. pp. 176. *P. Marshall & Co.: London*, [1930.] 8°. **8769**. bb. **32**.

C., L. B. S.

—— [Shops, Shed and Road.] The Live Steam Book. By "L. B. S. C." pp. xiv. 199. *Percival Marshall & Co.: London*, [1950.] 8°. **08773**. cc. **10**.

C., L. C. See Bible.—*Selections.* [*English.*] The Stations of the Cross in the Words of Holy Writ. By L. C. C. 1900. 32°. **3939**. a. **15**. **(1.)**

C., L. C. See Freytag (G.) [Soll und Haben.] Debit and Credit. Translated . . . by L. C. C. [i.e. Lucy C. Cumming, afterwards Smith.] 1857. 8°. **12552**. d. **13**.

—— See Grillparzer (F.) Sappho, a tragedy . . . Translated by L. C. C. [i.e. Lucy C. Cumming, afterwards Smith.] 1855. 8°. **11746**. c. **17**.

C., L. C., *Cen, Sén.* Le Cen L. C. C., Sén. [i.e. Count J. B. Le Couteulx de Canteleu], à un de ses collègues, sur une lettre d'un Anglais (M. H.) qu'il lui a communiquée. pp. 23. [1802.] 8°. **523**. e. **10**. **(4.)**

C. (L. Ch.) Déisme. [Signed: L. Ch. C.] pp. 54. *Nice*, 1864. 8°. **4378**. cc. **53**. **(3.)**

C., L. D. See Goldsmith (Oliver) *the Poet.* [*The Vicar of Wakefield.*] La Familia de Primrose. Novela moral . . . Traducida . . . por D. A. B. y L. D. C. 1833. 16°. **12604**. aa. **4**.

C., L. D., *Mr.* Journal, ou Suite du voyage de Siam. En forme des lettres familieres fait en m.dc.lxxxv et m.dc.lxxxvi. par Mr. L. D. C. [i.e. F. T. de Choisy.] pp. 377. *P. Mortier: Amsterdam*, 1688. 12°. **979**. b. **26**.

—— [Another copy.] **1048**. a. **28**.

The first Paris edition of 1687 *entitled* "*Journal du voyage de Siam*" *is entered under C., M. L. D. Other editions are entered under the author's name.*

C., L. D. D. D. L. C. C. R. A. L. E. E. L. F. D. L. N. L. P. L. Étrennes pour l'année 1789, ou Almanach historique à l'usage du Tiers-État. Par L. D. D. D. L. C. C. R. A. L. E. E. L. F. D. L. N. L. P. L. C. 1788. (Catéchisme historique.) pp. 155. [1788.] 8°. R. **48**. **(20.)**

C., L. D. R. P. I. See Horatius Flaccus (Q.) [*Ars Poetica.—Latin.*] Q. Horatii Flacci ad Pisones epistola, *etc.* [The dedicatory epistle signed: L. D. R. P. I. C., i.e. L. Desprez, Rhetoricae Professor in Cardinalitio.] 1674. 12°. **1002**. a. **20**.

C., L. E. *See* LITURGIES.—*Church of England.—Common Prayer.—Collects.* [*English.—Metrical Versions.*] The Collects in Verse. By L. E. C. [1888.] 16°. **3406**. de. **7**.

C., L. E. Pantheism, and other essays. By L. E. C. [i.e. Louisa Emily, Lady Cohen.] pp. 103. *Kegan Paul & Co.: London,* 1926. 8°. **012352**. cc. **3**.

C., L. E. Poor Daddy Long-Legs and other stories. By L. C. [The author's initials given on the cover as: L. E. C.] 1885. 4°. *See* C., L. **12810**. cc. **55**.

C., L. F.

—— *See* CLARKE (James F.) Messages of Faith, Hope, and Love, *etc.* [The editor's preface signed: L. F. C., i.e. Lilian R. F. Clarke.] 1895. 8°. **4399**. cc. **1**.

C., L. F.

—— Extracts from the Diary of a Living Physician. Edited [or rather written] by L. F. C. [A collection of anecdotes.] pp. vi. 195. 1851. 8°. *See* EXTRACTS. 12622. c. 5.

C., L. G. Étude archéologique sur le manuscrit bilingue de Montpellier désigné sous le nom d'Antiphonaire de Saint Grégoire. Par un Supérieur de Séminaire. [Signed: L. G. C.] pp. 48. *Paris, Lyon,* 1875. 8°. **7704**. b. **6**. **(19.)**

—— [Another copy.] **7706**. g. **5**. **(4.)**

C., L. I. Camp Equipment. By L. I. C. [With plans.] pp. 37. *Pioneer Press: Allahabad,* 1907. 8°. **07943**. k. **60**. **(1.)**

C., L. J. A Few More Notes on Southam. Its church and some old customs of by-gone days. [The preface signed: L. J. C.] pp. 34. *A. J. Chambers & Son: Southam,* 1913. 8°. **010352**. aaa. **25**.

C., L. J. Rev. Mother Agatha Verhelle, Foundress of the Society of the Religious of Christian Instruction, 1786–1838. [Signed: L. J. C.] pp. 46. *Burleigh Press: Bristol,* [1934.] 8°. **20019**. bb. **45**.

C . . ., L. J. DE. Extract uyt eenen brief uyt Namen van den 22 September 1790. [Signed: L. J. de C.] [*Brussels,* 1790.] *s. sh.* 8°. **8079**. c. **21**. **(32.)**

C., L. J. C. D., *M.* Analyse de plusieurs Polychrestes ultra-marins, leurs usages, et proprietés . . . Par M. L. J. C. D. C. [i.e. L. Joly.] pp. x. 105. *Paris,* 1736. 12°. **778**. e. **58**.

C., L. L. The Country Parson's Wife. Being intended as a continuation of and companion for Herbert's Country Parson. By the author of "Recollections of Sark," *etc.* [The preface signed: L. L. C., i.e. Louisa L. Clarke.] pp. v. 93. *J. Hatchard & Son: London,* 1842. 8°. **1361**. f. **6**.

C., L. L. M. Le Manuel du chirurgien d'armée. Ou l'Art de guerir methodiquement les playes des arquebuzades . . . Par L. L. M. C. pp. 344. *M. Villery: Paris,* 1686. 12°. **783**. c. **21**.

—— Seconde édition, revû & corrigé: par L. L. M. C. pp. 348. *L. d'Houry: Paris,* 1693. 12°. **783**. c. **24**.
The titlepage is mutilated.

C., L. M. Alcune memorie sulla vita del sacerdote Fran.co Fed.co Castagneri, *etc.* [The dedication signed: L. M. C.] pp. 111. *Torino,* 1868. 16°. **4864**. aa. **46**.

C., L. M. The Science of Food. A text-book . . . By L. M. C. [i.e. L. M. Cole.] pp. viii. 126. *G. Bell & Sons: London,* 1883. 8°. **7945**. aaa. **33**.

C., L. M. DE LA C. Gone Home: or Loving memories of L. M. de la C. C. by her friend C. S. 1881. 16°. *See* S., C. **4956**. a. **12**.

C., L. N. H. Considérations sur le décret de l'Assemblée Nationale [of 19 June 1790] relatif à la noblesse héréditaire, aux noms, aux titres, & aux armoiries. [Signed: L. N. H. C.] pp. 24. [1790.] 8°. **F.R. 128**. **(16.)**

C., L. O. S. *See* ZAGATA (P.) Cronica della città di Verona, *etc.* [The editor's preface signed: L. O. S. C., i.e. G. A. Cavazzani.] 1745, *etc.* 4°. **661**. e. **14**.

C., L. S. *See* also COLCHESTER (Linzee S.)

C., L. S. Lettre à M. Joly de St. Vallier (sur son Histoire raisonnée des opérations militaires de la derniere guerre). [Signed: L. S. C.] pp. 39. [*Amsterdam?* 1783.] 8°. **F. 589**. **(20.)**

C., L. S. Talks with my Lads on religious principle and practice in daily life. By L. S. C. Preface by Canon Seymour Coxe. pp. xi. 160. *Elliot Stock: London; MacNiven & Wallace: Edinburgh,* 1900. 8°. **4400**. p. **33**.

C., L. S.

—— A Short History of the Organs of Wells Cathedral. [By L. S. C., i.e. Linzee Sparrow Colchester . . . With plates.] 1951. 8°. *See* WELLS.—*Cathedral Church.—Friends of Wells Cathedral.* 7900. e. 24.

—— A Short History of the Organs of Wells Cathedral. 2nd edition. pp. 23. 1953. 8°. *See* WELLS.—*Cathedral Church.—Friends of Wells Cathedral.* **7889**. a. **57**.

—— Stained Glass in Wells Cathedral. [The preliminary note signed: L. S. C. Various editions.] 1952– . 8°. *See* WELLS.—*Cathedral Church.—Friends of Wells Cathedral.* 7812. df. 18.

C., L. S. D. *See* JESUITS. [*Letters from Missions.*] Les Miracles merueilleux aduenus aux Indes Orientales, *etc.* [A translation of Nicolas Pimenta's Annual Letter, dated 1 Dec. 1600. The translator's preface signed: L. S. D. C.] 1603. 8°. **860**. h. **23**.

C., L. T. A Few Indian Stories. By L. T. C., author of "Through the Eye of a Needle" [i.e. Lionel James]. pp. 117. *Pioneer Press: Allahabad,* 1895. 8°. **012627**. m. **22**.

C., L. T., *Mrs.* Songs under His Shadow. Original, and translated from the German. By Mrs. L. T. C. pp. 111. *S. W. Partridge & Co.: London,* [1880.] 8°. **11653**. de. **43**.

C., L. T. D., *Mr.* Nouvelles recherches sur la langue, l'origine & les antiquités des Bretons . . . par Mr L. T. D. C. [i.e. T. M. de La Tour d'Auvergne Corret.] pp. 196. *Bayonne,* 1792. 8°. **1322**. a. **6**.

C., L. V. Las Abanturos d'un campagnard à Toulouso, per L. V. C. [i.e. L. C. Vestrepain.] [In verse.] 2me édition. pp. 16. *Toulouse,* 1837. 8°. **11498**. h. **18**.

C., L. V., *gewesener Keyserlicher Maiestat Stallmeister.* Ritterliche Reutter-Kunst, dariñen ordentlich begriffen wie mã . . . die ritterliche, vnd adeliche Vbung der Reutterey, bevorab in Teutschland . . . gebrauchen vnd vnderscheiden möge . . . Dessgleichen ein . . . Vnderricht der Marstallerey, vnd Rossartzeney . . . Durch . . . L. V. C. gewesener Keyserlicher Maiestat Stallmeister, *etc.* ff. ccliiii. *Getruckt durch M. Lechler, in Verlegung M. Feyrabends: Franckfurt,* 1584. fol. **7905**. k. **15**. **(1.)**

L. W. A Verie Perfect Discourse, and order how to know the age of a horse, and the diseases that breede in him, with the remedies to cure the same: as also, The description of euery vayne, and how and when to let him blood, according to the diuersitie of the disease: as hath been proued by the Author. L. W. C. [With a woodcut.] B.L. pp. 37. *W. W. [W. White] for Thomas Pauier: London,* 1601. 4°. **C. 27. c. 36.**

— [Another edition.] B.L. MS. NOTES. *W. W. [W. White] for Thomas Pauier: London,* 1610. 4°. **C.31.f.16.(2.)**

The last five leaves are mutilated.

— [Another edition.] *Iohn Norton, for Robert Bird: London,* 1630. 4°. **B. 426. (1.)**

(Louis) Fictions guerrières anglaises. [By Louis C. With maps.] pp. 256. *Paris,* [1910.] 8°. **11851. w. 25.**

M. *See* Bell (Thomas) *Professor of Philology in the College of Edinburgh.* Nehemiah the Tirshatha, *etc.* [With an address to the reader, signed: M. C.] 1692. 8°. **4454. aaa. 18.**

* *, M. *See* Boethius (A. M. T. S.) [*De Consolatione Philosophiae.—French.*] La Consolation de la philosophie . . . Traduction nouvelle par M. C.* * * [i.e. L. Colesse]. 1772. 12°. **8407. ccc. 2.**

M. *See* Cervantes Saavedra (M. de) [*Novelas.—Spanish.*] Novelas, *etc.* [Edited by M. C., i.e. M. Catalina.] 1883. 16°. **12231. aa. 4.**

M. *See* Christian Man. How and whither a Chrysten man ought to flye the horryble Plague of the Pestilence. A sermon, *etc.* (Translated by M. C. [i.e. Miles Coverdale] out of hye Almayne.) [1564.] 8°. **4428. a. 5.**

M. *See* England.—*Church of England.* [*Appendix.*] An Apologie or answere in defence of the Churche of Englande, *etc.* [Edited by M. C., i.e. Matthew Parker, Archbishop of Canterbury.] 1564. 8°. **C. 12. c. 12.**

, M. *See* Guillaume (L.) and C., M. Dieu et diable, *etc.* 1903. 8°. **4015. i. 18. (4.)**

, M. *See* Hamilton (Alexander) *General in the service of the United States.* Alexander Hamilton's Report on the subject of Manufactures . . . To which are prefixed, two prefaces by the editor [signed: M. C., i.e. Mathew Carey]. 1827. 8°. **8246. e. 31.**

M. *See* Hirsch (M.) Die Weintraubenkur or Grape-Cure . . . Translated by M. C. 1846. 8°. **1172. l. 1. (4.)**

M. *See* Horatius Flaccus (Q.) [*Carmina.—English.*] The Odes of Horace. Book first. Translated into English verse by M. C. 1871. 8°. **11375. aaa. 19.**

, M. *See* Longfellow (Henry W.) Miles Standish. El Halcón de Ser Federigo. Los Pájaros de Killingworth. [With a " Noticia biográfica y literaria " signed: M. C.] 1893. 8°. **11687. aa. 45.**

* * * * *, M. *See* Poerner (C. W.) Instruction sur l'art de la teinture . . . Ouvrage traduit de l'allemand, par M. C * * * * *, *etc.* 1791. 8°. **959. e. 22.**

, M. *See* Rio de Janeiro.—*Bibliotheca Nacional.* Catalogo da Collecção Salvador de Mendonça. [The preface signed: M. C.] 1906. 8°. **11908. s. 10.**

, M. *See* Romancero. Romancero Selecto, *etc.* [Edited by M. C., i.e. M. Catalina.] 1883. 16°. **12231. aa. 5.**

, M. *See* Schurzfleisch (C. S.) Orthographia romana ex acroasibus v.c. Conradi Samuelis Schurzfleischii, collecta a M. C., *etc.* 1707. 8°. **827. d. 15.**

C., M. *See* Socinus (F. P.) De baptismo aquæ disputatio . . . Cui accesserunt . . . I. Responsiones ad . . . notas A.D. in disputat. de baptismo. II. Responsio ad M. C. (Mart. Czechovitzii) notas in appendice libri ipsius de pædobaptismo, *etc.* 1613. 8°. **4226. c. 12. (2.)**

C., M. *See* Vega Carpio (L. F. de) [*Miscellaneous Works.*] La Dorotea, *etc.* [Edited by M. C., i.e. M. Catalina.] 1886. 16°. **12231. aa. 6.**

C., M. *See* Wiclif (John) [*Works.*] Wicklieffes Wicket, *etc.* (Ouerseene by M. C. [i.e. Miles Coverdale.]) [1548.] 8°. **1360. a. 3.**

—— —— [1548 ?] 8°. **G. 11996.**

C., M. An Account of the Fair Intellectual-Club in Edinburgh: in a letter to a honourable member of an Athenian Society there. By a young Lady, the Secretary of the Club. [Signed: M. C.] pp. 32. *J. McEuen & Co.: Edinburgh,* 1720. 4°. **741. b. 1.**

C * *, M. Abdolonime, ou le Roi berger, comédie-héroïque en trois actes et en vers, imitée de l'italien [i.e. from Metastasio's " Il Re Pastore "]; par M. C * * [i.e. J. B. Collet de Messine]. pp. 52. *Paris,* 1780. 8°. **11738. c. 15. (1.)**

C * *, M. Almanach des Grâces, étrennes chantantes; dédié au beau sexe, par M. C * * [i.e. A. C. Cailleau], *etc.* pp. 276. *Paphos, Paris,* 1784. 12°. **011483. de. 48.**

C., M. Alte und neue Wehrverfassung, Bürgerbewaffnung, und Volkswehr. Von M. C. pp. 16. *Breslau,* 1848. 8°. **8825. bbb. 37. (1.)**

C., M. Aventures singulières de M. C. (Ciangulo) contenant le recit abbregé des desordres qui se commettent dans les convents [*sic*], et de ce qu'il a éprouvé de la cruauté de l'Inquisition, *etc.* 1724. 8°. *See* Ciangulo (M.) **1124. a. 52.**

C * * *, M. Batailles, combats et victoires des armées françaises en Russie et en France, jusqu'à la bataille de Waterloo. Par M. C * * *. [With a plate.] pp. 108. *Paris,* [1825 ?] 12°. **9078. aaa. 14.**

C . . . . ., M. Cahier de la déclaration des droits du peuple; et contrat de constitution de l'État. Pour les députés aux États-Généraux. Par M. C . . . . . [i.e. J. L. Carra]. pp. 19. 1789. 8°. **R. 41. (6.)**

C * *, M.

—— Catalogue d'une belle collection d'estampes, anciennes et modernes . . . quelques dessins et tableaux, provenant du cabinet de M. C**; par Pieri Bénard. Cette vente se fera les . . . 27 . . . 28 et . . . 29 décembre 1824, *etc.* pp. 40. MS. PRICES. *Paris,* [1824.] 8°. **562. e. 57. (15.)**

C. * * *, M.

—— Catalogue d'une collection de tableaux des trois écoles, provenant du cabinet de M. C. * * * [identified in a MS. note as — Constantin]. Par A. Pérignon . . . Dont la vente aura lieu les . . . 18 et 19 mars 1816, *etc.* pp. ii. 31. MS. PRICES. [*Paris,*] 1816. 8°. **562. e. 33. (15.)**

C * *, M. Le Club de la Raison, par M. C * *. [A political satire.] pp. 16. *Paris,* 1790. 8°. **F. 377. (6.)**

C., M. Comments on " Light on the Path." [A commentary, expanding the text of the original.] (By M. C. [i.e. Mabel Collins.]) *See* B., H. P. First Steps in Occultism, *etc.* 1895. 16°. **8632. aa. 38.**

C * * *., M. Correspondance entre M. C * * *. [i.e. J. A. J. Cérutti] et le comte de Mirabeau, sur le Rapport de M. Necker, et sur l'Arrêt du Conseil du 29 décembre, qui continue pour six mois, force de monnoie au papier de la caisse-d'escompte. pp. 60. 1789. 8°. **523. d. 4. (2.)**

—— [Another copy.] **R. 84. (6.)**

C * * *., M.

—— See Riquetti (H. G.) Count de Mirabeau. [*Letters.*] Observations sur la correspondance de M. le comte de Mirabeau avec M. C * * * [i.e. J. A. J. Cérutti], *etc.* 1789. 8°. **910. c. 16. (6.)**

—— See Riquetti (H. G.) *Count de Mirabeau.* [*Appendix.*] Correspondance entre le diable et M. le comte de Mirabeau, sur celle de M. C. [i.e. J. A. J. Cérutti] & l'Histoire secrete . . . &c. [i.e. L'Histoire secrète de la cour de Berlin.] 1789. 8°. **F.R. 54. (19.)**

—— Réponse à la Correspondance de M. C * * * [i.e. J. A. J. Cérutti] et le comte de Mirabeau. [By C. A. de Calonne.] pp. 48. *Londres*, 1789. 8°. **910. c. 16. (4.)**

—— [Another copy.] **F. 284. (2.)**

C., M. A Daughter to be proud of. [A tale.] By M. C. pp. 80. *R.T.S.: London*, [1891.] 8°. **4429. de. 14.**

C., M. Della libertà ed eguaglianza civile. Istruzione al popolo di M. C. pp. 15. [*Genoa*, 1848.] 8°. **8007. b. 4.**

C., M. A Discourse of the Terrestrial Paradise, aiming at a more probable discovery of the true situation of that happy place of our first parents habitation. [The dedicatory epistle signed: M. C., i.e. Marmaduke Carver. With a map.] pp. 167. *Printed by James Flesher: London*, 1666. 8°. **4375. aa. 12.**
Another copy with a different titlepage is entered under the author's name.

—— [Another copy.] **G. 19519.**

C., M. Each Sex in their Humour: or, the Histories of the families of Brightley, Finch, Fortescue, Shelburne, and Stevens. Written by a Lady of Quality, *etc.* [A novel. With a prefatory note headed "The Editor to the Reader," but in fact written by the author, signed: M. C.] 2 vol. *Printed for the Editor: London*, 1764. 12°. **12612. e. 10.**

C., M. An Elegy on the . . . Death of Mr. W. Bentley, *etc.* (Printed for the author, M. C.) [1751 ?] *s. sh.* fol. **C. 20. f. 2. (251.)**

C * * * * * *, M. Essai sur l'histoire de Longwy, par M. C * * * * * * [i.e. — Clauteaux, notaire de Longwy], suivi de considérations relatives à l'industrie et au commerce de cette ville, et de notices biographiques sur les hommes illustres qui y ont prit naissance. [The latter part by E. A. Bégin.] pp. 207. *Metz*, 1829. 8°. **576. f. 15.**

C., M. Estratto dalla Gazzetta Piemontese. 22 settembre 1832. [An appreciation of articles on the calculus by Baron A. L. Cauchy. Signed: M. C.] [*Turin*, 1832.] *s. sh.* 4°. **T. 27*. (6.)**

C., M. The Explorers, and other poems. By M. C. [i.e. Catherine E. M. Mackay, afterwards Martin.] pp. vii. 270. *George Robertson: Melbourne*, 1874. 8°. **11652. a. 3.**

C., M. Gardening Don'ts. By M. C. [i.e. Marion Chappell.] Coloured frontispiece . . . and seventeen photographs, *etc.* ff. 56. *Bickers & Son: London*, 1912. 16°. **07029. ff. 10.**

C . . . . ., M. Gasconiana, ou Recueil des hauts faits et jeux d'esprit des enfans de la Garonne. Par M. C . . . . . [i.e. C. Y. Cousin]. pp. vi. 178. *Paris*, 1801. 12°. **12316. b. 8.**

C., M. Indicacion contra los Enemigos de la Independencia. [Signed: M. C.] [*Mexico*, 1823 ?] *s. sh.* fol. **9770. k. 9. (112.)**

C., M. L'Isle déserte, comédie en un acte et en vers, p M. C. [i.e. J. B. Collet de Messine.] pp. 45. *Par* 1758. 8°. **11738. a. 29. (**

C * * * * *., M.

—— Les Jésuites condamnés par leurs maximes et par le actions . . . Par M. C * * * * * [i.e. P. N. Collin d'Ambl pp. 61. *Paris*, 1825. 8°. **4092. e.**

C. * * *, M.

—— Lettre de M. C.*** à M. D.***, membre du Club d Jacobins. [A plea in favour of moderation.] pp. 8. [1791.] 8°. **R. 157. (3**

C., M. A Letter from a Merchant in London, to his cor spondent abroad. In which the present state of affairs impartially consider'd. [Signed: M. C.] pp. 20. *C. Corbett: London*, 1739. 8°. **T. 1110. (**

C., M. A Letter written by a Jesuite to the Queens Majes March, xxii wherein he useth divers subtle insinuations her Majesty for the Kings Majesties repealing and recalli of the lawes and proclamations against the Jesuits, prie and recusants. With a brief consideration of the reaso intimated in the letter, and a just confutation of the [The letter signed: M. C.] *For John Watkins: Lond* [1642.] 4°. **E. 141. (**

C * * *, M. Lettre à M. * * *, suivie d'un discours prono en 1781 dans une assemblée particulière, sur l'administ tion de M. Necker; et du plan d'une loterie projettée faveur du commerce, produisant cent millions en circu tion. Par M. C * * * [i.e. A. Carrière-Doisin]. pp. 45. *Lausanne*, 1788. 8°. **F. 19. (**

C * * *, M. Lettre de M. C * * * [i.e. J. A. J. Cérutti] à M de * * * *, au sujet de deux billets ridicules que M. L * * * [i.e. L. L. F. Duke de Brancas] a fait courir imprimer. pp. 18. 1789. 8°. **F.R. 46. (**

—— [Another copy.] **F. 61. (**

—— See Brancas (L. L. F. de) *Duke.* Lettre de Mada la marquise de . . . au comte de Lauraguais sur Cérutti, *etc.* [On the "Lettre de M. C * * * à Mad. * * * * au sujet de deux billets ridicules."] 1789. **F. 578. (**

C * * *, M.

—— Lettres sur l'opéra. Par M. C*** [i.e. C. N. Coch pp. 24. 5–86. *Paris*, 1781. 12°. **7891. a.**

C., M.

—— Light on the Path . . . Written down by M. C. Mabel Collins] with notes by the author. [With Comments published in "Lucifer," together w "Through the Gates of Gold" by the same auth pp. 92. 114. *Theosophical University Press: Cov* 1949. 8°. **8634. ccc.**

C., M. Little Arthur's History of England. [The pref signed: M. C., i.e. Maria Graham, afterwards L Callcott.] 2 vol. *Murray: London*, 1835. 12°. **598. a. 16,**
The editions of 1856, 1866 *and* 1872 *are entered under author's name.*

—— A new edition, with continuation to the year 18 pp. viii. 272. *T. J. Allman: London*, 1874. 8°. **9504. bbb.**

—— [A reissue.] *G. Routledge & Sons: London*, [1875.] **9503. bb.**

* * * *, M. M. de Calonne tout entier, tel qu'il s'est comporté dans l'administration des finances, dans son commissariat en Bretagne, &c. &c. Avec une analyse de sa Requête au Roi, & de sa Réponse à l'écrit de M. Necker . . . Par M. C * * * * [i.e. J. L. Carra]. 2 pt. *Bruxelles*, 1788. 8°. **R. 32. (8.)**

., M. Metrica Descripcion de las solemnes Fiestas, que en este Hispalico Theatro se han hecho a . . . Maria Santissima, con el título de La Antigua . . . Describela la devocion de M. C. *Sevilla*, [1738.] 4°. **11451. e. 38. (3.)**

* * *, M. La Monarchie vengée des attentats des républicains modernes, ou Réfutation de l'ouvrage de M. de la Vicomterie, intitulé les Crimes des rois de France. Par M. C * * *. pp. lxiv. 134. *Paris*, 1791. 8°. **F.R. 118. (1.)**

., M. A Most true and exact Relation of that as honourable as unfortunate Expedition of Kent, Essex, and Colchester. By M. C. [i.e. Matthew Carter], a loyall actor in that engagement, anno dom. 1648. pp. 214. [*London*,] 1650. 8°. **600. b. 8.**

—— [Another copy.] **292. a. 50.**
Imperfect; wanting the titlepage.

., M.

—— The Mysterious Protector: a novel. Dedicated to Lady Crespigny. [The author's dedication signed: M. C.] 2 vol. *George Robinson: London*, 1805. 12°. **012643. tt. 49.**

., M. National Lyrics for the Army and Navy. By a British Soldier. Second edition. [The dedication signed: M. C., i.e. Michael Constable.] pp. 72. *James M'Glashan: Dublin*, 1848. 12°. **11645. a. 73. (3.)**

., M. A New Arrangement of the entered Apprentice's Song. To be sung,—as a duet,—by Bros. Pio Nono and Lord Ripon, on the occasion of the contemplated visit of the Ex-Grand Master to the Pope. [Signed: M. C., i.e. Matthew Cooke.] [1874.] *s. sh.* 8°. **11621. h. 1. (92.)**

* * * * *, M. Observations sur l'ouvrage publié par M. Patte . . . sous le titre d'Essai sur l'architecture théatrale. Par M. C * * * * *. [With a folding plate.] pp. 24. [*Paris*, 1783 ?] 12°. **1103. b. 15. (3.)**

., M. Odds and Ends, done up in parcels to suit all readers, *etc.* Extracts from "The People's Magazine." [The editor's preface signed: M. C.] pp. viii. 184. *S.P.C.K.: London*, [1872.] 8°. **12331. aaaa. 25.**

., M. Le Onoranze funebri e religiose a Niccolò Tommaseo il 2 e 7 maggio in Firenze. Relazione. (Estratto delle Letture di Famiglia.) [The compiler's introductory remarks signed: M. C.] pp. 16. [*Florence*, 1874.] 8°. **10630. dd. 2. (16.)**

. . . . ., M . . . . . Per le faustissime nozze della Signora Luigia Ascari col Signor Carlo Rusconi. (Anacreontica.) [Signed: M . . . . . C . . . . .] pp. 8. *Vicenza*, 1818. 16°. **11436. aa. 12. (2.)**

., M. Una Poesia tangente. El Canto biblico. Compuesto por M. C. (Ierusalen Destruida. [Signed: C. P. G.]) pp. 16. *Caracas*, 1850. 16°. **11451. aaa. 12.**

C., M. Polémique impérialiste. [By] M. C. pp. 165. *Paris*, [1878.] 12°. **8051. bb. 11.**

., M. Reglas da moralitat a prudienscha cun proverbis, las amprimas en prosa, ils auters en riema . . . Mess en Ramonsch suenter ilg urden da Sigr. Dr. Georg Friedr. Seiler en sieu cudisch, titulau: Allgemeines Lesebuch für Stadt- und Landschulen . . . tras M. C. [i.e. M. Conradi ?] pp. 64. *Coira*, 1812. 8°. **885. d. 3. (1.)**

C * * *, M. La Ressource des théâtres, pièce en un acte. Par M. C * * * [i.e. F. A. de Chevrier], *etc.* pp. 42. *Paris*, 1760. 8°. **11738. c. 6. (1.)**

C * * *, M. Satires. Par M. C * * * [i.e. J. M. B. Clément]. pp. xxxvi. 175. *Amsterdam, Paris*, 1786. 8°. **1161. g. 10.**

—— [Another copy.] **86. c. 3**

C., M. The Secret of the Dawn. By M. C. pp. 27. *A. L. Humphreys: London*, 1915. 4°. **4418. h. 45.**

C., M. The Story of our British Ancestors. By M. C. [i.e. Mrs. M. Cooke], *etc.* pp. 85. *Covenant Publishing Co.: London*, 1927. 12°. **04033. de. 55.**

C * * *, M. Tableau de toutes especes de successions, régies par la Coutume de Paris . . . Par M. C * * * (Castel), *etc.* 1785, *etc.* 32°. *See* CASTEL ( ) **705. a. 1–16.**

C., M. The Torn Cloak. By M. C. [i.e. Mrs. M. Cooke.] Brief sketches of the history of our race, from King Solomon to the present day, *etc.* pp. 39. *Covenant Publishing Co.: London*, 1926. 8°. **04033. de. 52.**

—— Second edition. pp. 39. *Covenant Publishing Co.: London*, 1928. 8°. **04034. e. 64.**

C., M. The True Christian's Deligh[t] that fears God and honours his King. [A collection of prayers. The introductory epistle signed: M. C.] pp. 67. *Printed for J. D.*, 1684. 12°. **3455. a. 56.**
The titlepage is mutilated.

C., M. The Two Portions: which is yours ? By M. C. pp. 16. *James Carter: London*, [1894.] 16°. **4422. aaa. 73. (9.)**

C * * *, M. Les Vendeurs d'argent ou les Deux porte-feuilles, comédie en deux actes, et en prose . . . Par M. C * * * [i.e. J. M. Collot d'Herbois]. pp. 24. *Nyons*, [1791.] 8°. **11738. c. 17. (5.)**

C., M. Vies des saints de l'atelier. [The editor's preface signed: M. C., i.e. M. Cornudet.] 7 pt. *Paris*, [1862–65.] 12°. **4827. aa. 10.**
Imperfect; wanting the life of St. Aquilas.

C., M. Wild Flowers from Many Fields, or, Thoughts in verse, on various subjects, by M. C. pp. 71. *W. D. Jenkins: Wallingford*, 1867. 8°. **11649. e. 61.**

C., M. The Words and Deeds of Joshua Davidson. Two letters from a lady in London to her friend in Paris. [Signed: M. C.] pp. 15. *James Burns: London*, 1880. 8°. **12352. b. 44. (10.)**

C., M., and W., G. DE S. Confidences: being six months in the lives of Melisande and Geraldine. By M. C. and G. de S. W. pp. 296. *Limpus, Baker & Co.: London*, 1903. 8°. **012638. aaa. 36.**

C., M., *il A. See* GRAY (Thomas) *the Poet.* [*Elegy, etc.—Translations.*] Elegia inglese del signor Tomasso Gray sopra un cimitero de campagna trasportata in verso italiano dall'A. M. C. [i.e. M. Cesarotti.] 1772. 8°. **79. c. 13.**

C., M., *Amateur, de Lyon.*

—— Catalogue d'une riche et belle collection de tableaux . . . provenant du cabinet de M. C., amateur, de Lyon [i.e. — Coulet], dont la vente aura lieu . . . les . . . 15 . . . 16 et . . . 17 novembre 1831, *etc.* pp. iv. iv. 52. *Paris*, 1831. 8°. **562. e. 75. (7.)**

C * * *, M., *Ancien Avocat au Parlement de Paris.* Cours gastronomique, ou les Dîners de Manant-ville, ouvrage anecdotique, philosophique et littéraire; seconde édition . . . par feu M. C * * *, ancien avocat au Parlement de Paris [i.e. Charles Louis Cadet de Gassicourt]. pp. xx. 18–364. *Paris*, 1809. 8°. **1037. h. 17.**

C . . . , M., *Ancien Curé.* La Fille du mandarin. Par M. C . . ., ancien curé [i.e. — Corrier]. pp. xii. 258. *Paris,* 1861. 12°. **4417. aaa. 16.**

C . . . , M., *Av. au Parl. et C. R.* *See* FRANCE. [*Laws, etc.*—II.] Réglemens sur les matieres ecclésiastiques. (Avec des notes . . . Par M. C . . . Av. au Parl. et C. R. [i.e. A. G. Camus, avocat au Parlement et censeur royal.]) 1788. 32°. **705. a. 15, 16.**

C . . . . , M., *Avocat.* De la nécessité de montrer à la nation, avant la prochaine législature, le bon et le mauvais des travaux de ses députés. Par M. C . . . . . Avocat. [1791.] 8°. **F.R. 51. (16.)**

—— [Another copy.]

De la nécessité de montrer à la nation, avant la prochaine législature, le bon et le mauvais des travaux de ses députés. Par M. C . . . . avocat. [1791.] 8°. **R. 70. (17.)**

C * * *, M., *Avocat à la Cour Royale de Paris.* Buonaparte peint par lui-même dans sa carrière militaire et politique, par M. C * * *, avocat à la Cour royale de Paris [i.e. A. S. G. Coffinières]. pp. viii. 534. *Paris,* 1814. 8°. **8050. g. 2.**

C * * *, M., *Chanoine du Diocèse.* Instructions et prières chrétiennes, à l'usage des religieuses Ursulines et des personnes du sexe. Le tout recueilli et mis en ordre par M. C * * *, chanoine du diocèse [i.e. G. Chardon]. Cinquième édition, corrigée et considérablement augmentée. pp. 668. *Riom & Clermont,* [1790 ?] 12°. **3457. dd. 36.**

C. * * *, M., *ci-devant Membre de plusieurs Académies.* L'Espion de la Révolution française. Par M. C.* * *, ci-devant membre de plusieurs académies [i.e. I. M. Crommelin]. 2 tom. *Paris,* 1797. 8°. **907. g. 11.**

A later edition published at Frankfort in 1799, *with the title* "*Histoire secrète de l'espionnage pendant la Révolution*" *is entered under* FRANCE. [*Appendix.—History and Politics.—Revolution of* 1789.]

—— [Another copy.] **F. 1323. (1.)**

C., M., *Confessor to the English Nuns at Paris.* *See* DU PLESSIS (A. J.) *Cardinal, Duke de Richelieu.* The Principall Points of the Faith of the Catholike Church . . . Englished by M. C. Confessor to the English Nuns at Paris [i.e. Thomas Carre, pseudonym of Miles Pinkney]. 1635. 8°. **3901. aaa. 8.**

—— *See* JESUS CHRIST. [*De Imitatione Christi.—English.*] Of the Following of Christ . . . Reviewed and in diuers things corrected by M. C. Confessor to the English Nuns at Paris [i.e. Thomas Carre, pseudonym of Miles Pinkney]. Who also added the authours life in this last edition. [The translation by Anthony Hoskins.] 1636. 16°. **IX. Eng. 55.**

C . . . . . , M., *D.M.P.* *See* L * * * *, *M.* Nouveaux élémens de botanique . . . Troisième édition, revue . . . par M. C . . . . ., D.M.P. 1815. 12°. **7029. aaa. 29.**

C . . . . , M., *de L . . . . .* *See* L . . . ., M. C . . . . de.

C * *, M., *de l'Académie Royale des Sciences, Inscriptions et Belles-Lettres de Châlons-sur-Marne.* Encyclopédie littéraire, ou Nouveau dictionnaire raisonné et universel d'éloquence et de poësie . . . Par M. C * *, de l'Académie royale des Sciences, Inscriptions & Belles-Lettres de Châlons-sur-Marne [i.e. Étienne Calvel]. 3 tom. *Paris,* 1772. 8°. **71. b. 23–25.**

C * * * *, M., *Député du Département de l'Arriége.* Opinion de M. C * * * *, député du département de l'Arriége [i.e. M. J. J. L. Calvet ?] sur cette question : établira-t-on, ou non, un Comité diplomatique ? pp. 3. *Paris,* [1791 ?] 8°. **F.R. 56. (5.)**

C., M., *Fellow of the Theosophical Society.* The Idyll of the White Lotus. By M. C., Fellow of the Theosophical Society [i.e. Mabel Collins.] pp. 141. *Reeves & Turner: London,* 1884. 8°. **12619. c. 6.**

—— Light on the Path. A treatise written for the personal use of those who are ignorant of the Eastern wisdom, and who desire to enter within its influence. Written down by M. C., Fellow of the Theosophical Society [i.e. Mabel Collins.] pp. 31. *Reeves & Turner: London,* 1885. 16°. **8410. aa. 36.**

—— [Another edition.] pp. 30. *Scottish Press: Madras,* 1885. 16°. **8410. aa. 40.**

—— [Another edition.] pp. 31. *Cupples, Upham & Co.: Boston,* 1886. 8°. **8410. bbb. 39.**

—— [Another edition.] pp. 36. *Aryan Theosophical Society: New York,* [1886 ?] 12°. **8410. bb. 39.**

—— New edition, with notes by the author. pp. 40. *George Redway: London,* 1888. 8°. **8410. aa. 39.**

C * * *, M., *Homme de lettres et membre de plusieurs sociétés savantes.* Notice des livres de la bibliothèque de M. C * * *, homme de lettres et membre de plusieurs sociétés savantes, etc. Dont la vente se fera . . . les 2 janvier 1813 et jours suivans, *etc.* pp. 23. *Paris,* 1814. 8°. **S.C. 533.**

C., M., *Leodiensis, SS. Theologiae Doctor.* *See* FRANCE.—*Church of France.—Assemblée Générale du Clergé.* Œcumenica cathedræ apostolicæ authoritas . . . asserta et vindicata . . . In quo tractatu vindicantur . . . tum ea, quæ Emanuël à Schelestrale adversùs Maymbourgum reposuit . . . tum quæ author Regalis sacerdotij, ac Leodiensis SS. Theologiæ Doctor M. C. in lucem ediderunt circa cleri gallicani præinsinuatas propositiones [with reference to "Tractatus de libertatibus Ecclesiæ gallicanæ" by A. Charlas, published under the initials M. C., S. Theol. Doctor], *etc.* 1689. fol. **3851. b. 7.**

C., M., *Membre de la Société Théosophique.* Lumière sur le sentier. Traité pour l'usage . . . de ceux qui, ne connaissant pas la sagesse orientale, désirent en recevoir l'influence. Transcrit par M. C. membre de la Société théosophique [i.e. Mabel Collins, afterwards Cook]. [A translation of "Light on the Path." The translator's preface signed: F. K. G.] pp. 45. *Paris,* 1887. 8°. **8410. aa. 42.**

C., M., *P.* A Briefe Admonition to all English Catholikes, concerning a late Proclamation set forth against them . . . Togeather with the confutation of a pamphlet, newly published, cõcerning a decree of the Sorbon at Paris &c. and an Epistle to Doctor King, in the behalfe of the Iesuites. By M. C. P. [i.e. Michael Christopherson, Priest, pseudonym of Michael Walpole.] pp. 135. [*St. Omer,*] 1610. 4°. **3936. d. 16.**

C * * * *, M., *Professeur d'histoire naturelle à l'Université de S * * * * * * *.* Réflexions sur les observations de M. de Beauvois . . . touchant le traité sur l'origine des champignons de M. de Necker . . . par M. C * * * * professeur d'histoire naturelle à l'université de S * * * * * * *. pp. 70. *Nuremberg,* 1788. 8°. **7032. d. 11.**

C., M., *S. Theol. Doctor.* Tractatus de libertatibus Ecclesiæ gallicanæ, continens amplam discussionem declarationis factæ ab illustrissimis archiepiscopis, & episcopis, Parisiis mandato Regio congregatis, anno M.DC.LXXXII . . . Auctore M. C. S. Theol. Doctore [i.e. A. Charlas]. pp. 820. *Apud M. Hovium: Leodii,* 1684. 4°. **3901. ff. 6.**

—— [Another edition.] pp. 818. *Apud M. Hovium: Leodii,* 1689. 4°. **700. d. 48.**

M., *S. Theol. Doctor.*

— *See* FRANCE.—*Church of France.—Assemblée Générale du Clergé.* Œcumenica cathedræ apostolicæ authoritas. Ex occasione quatuor cleri Gallicani propositionum anno M.DC.XXCII. in Parisiensi ecclesiastico conventu editarum, asserta et vindicata . . . In quo tractatu vindicantur insuper tum ea, quæ Emanuël à Schelestrale adversùs Maymbourgum reposuit . . . tum quæ author Regalis sacerdotij, ac Leodiensis SS. Theologiæ Doctor M. C. in lucem ediderunt circa cleri gallicani præinsinuatas propositiones [with reference to "Tractatus de libertatibus Ecclesiæ gallicanæ" by A. Charlas, publisher under the initials M. C., S. Theol. Doctor], *etc.* 1689. fol. **3851.** b. **7.**

M., *S. Theologiae Doctor.* Causa regaliæ penitus explicata, seu responsio ad dissertationem R. P. F. Natalis Alexandri de jure regaliæ, quæ habetur inter ejus selecta Historiæ ecclesiasticæ capita . . . Autore M. C. S. Theologiæ Doctore [i.e. A. Charlas]. pp. 728. *H. Foppin: Leodii,* 1685. 4°. **5125.** cc. **1.**

M., *Sig.* Lettera del sig. M. C. al cel. sig. M. G. [A review of A. Comparetti's "Observationes anatomicæ de aure interna comparata."] pp. lvi. [*Padua,* 1790.] 8°. **7420.** aa. **22.**

M.-D.-L., *Sr., Religieuse de Saint-Thomas.* Vie de Mère Marie-Ephrem, Religieuse de Saint-Thomas-de-Villeneuve, Aix, Provence . . . Par Sr M.-d.-l.-C., Religieuse de Saint-Thomas. 1871. 8°. *See* M.-D.-L.-C., *Sr., Religieuse de Saint-Thomas.* **4867.** de. **49.**

. . ., M. DE. *See* CARVER (Jonathan) Voyage dans les parties intérieures de l'Amérique septentrionale . . . Ouvrage traduit . . . par M. de C . . . . [i.e. J. E. Montucla], *etc.* 1784. 8°. **1431.** f. **18.**

. ., M. DE. *See* P . . . ., *Curé du Bailliage de Provins.* Réponse au Cincinnatus moderne, ou au militaire laboureur. [A reply to a letter written to J. Necker by M. de C . . ..] [1789 ?] 8°. F.R. **136.** **(9.)**

M. DE. *See* ROME, *Church of.*—Pius VI., *Pope.* [1775–1799.] Sur les brefs du Pape . . . Discussion . . . Suivie d'un supplément relatif à l'Instruction pastorale & à l'Ordonnance de M. de C. [i.e. C. C. C. d'Agault de Bonneval, Bishop of Pamiers] de juin 1791, *etc.* [1791.] 8°. F.R. **156.** **(21.)**

M. DE. *See* ROUSSEAU (J. J.) [*Botanique.*] Le Botaniste sans maître, ou Manière d'apprendre seul la botanique . . . Continuée et complettée . . . par M. de C. [i.e. J. P. de Clairville.] 1805. 12°. B. **216.** **(5.)**

* *, M. DE. *See* SEDLEY (Cornelia) Cornelia Sedley . . . Traduit de l'anglois par M. de la Montagne, *etc.* [tom. 2, 3 translated by M. de C * * *.] 1789. 8°. **12808.** s. **23.**

M. DE.

— Catalogue d'une collection du meilleur choix de tableaux . . . provenant du cabinet de M. de C. Dont la vente aura lieu, le 1er. mars [1819], *etc.* pp. 18. MS. NOTES AND PRICES. [*Paris,*] 1819. 8°. **562.** e. **42.** **(23.)**

* *, M. DE. Catalogue de lettres autographes et de manuscrits provenant du cabinet de M. de C * * * [i.e. Pierre Capelle]. Supplément, *etc.* [A sale catalogue.] pp. 98. *Paris,* 1851. 8°. S.C. **673.** **(4.)**

M. DE.

— Catalogue de tableaux et autres objets de curiosité, formant le cabinet de M. de C. [identified in a MS. note as M. de Franqueville Colcaute.] Dont la vente . . . se fera le . . . 3 mars [1817], *etc.* pp. 15. MS. NOTES AND PRICES. *Paris,* [1817.] 8°. **562.** e. **36.** **(12.)**

C * * *, M. DE. Lettre curieuse d'un aristocrate converti, aux quatre-vingt-trois départemens du royaume. (Sur la solemnité du Pacte fédératif, et sur la réception qu'on a faite aux députés.) [Signed: M. de C * * *.] pp. 24. *Paris,* 1790. 8°. F. **379.** **(6.)**

—— [Another copy.] Lettre curieuse d'un aristocrate converti, *etc.* *Paris,* 1790. 8°. R. **181.** **(28.)**

C., M. DE. Récit d'un de MM. au sujet de M. de C. [i.e. C. A. de Calonne.] Du 10 août 1787. pp. 22. [1787.] 8°. **911.** b. **9.** **(3.)**

—— [Another copy.] R. **32.** **(5.)**

C * * *, M. DE, *Académicien-Associé.* Observations sur la musique, et principalement sur la métaphysique de l'art. (Par M. de C * * *, Académicien-Associé [i.e. M. P. G. de Chabanon].) pt. 1. pp. xx. 215. *Paris,* 1779. 8°. **7807.** e. **14.** **(1.)**
No more of this edition published. Subsequently incorporated in "De la musique considérée en elle-même," published in 1785 *under the author's name.*

C * * *, M. DE, *Bibliophile anglais.* Bibliographie anecdotique et raisonnée de tous les ouvrages d'Andréa de Nerciat. Par M. de C * * *, bibliophile anglais. Édition ornée du portrait inédit de Nerciat, *etc.* pp. 63. *J. A. Hooygs: Londres;* [*printed in Belgium ?*] 1876. 8°. Tab. **603.** a. **26.**

C., M. A. *See* A., E. O., and C., M. A. Dottie's Pets, *etc.* [1883.] 4°. **12805.** s. **14.**

C., M. A. *See* FALLON (D.) Poesías. [The editor's preface, signed: M. A. C., i.e. M. A. Caro.] [1875 ?] 8°. **11451.** de. **31.**

C., M. A. *See* FERNÁNDEZ DE PIEDRAHITA (L.) successively *Bishop of Santa Marta* and *of Panama.* Historia General de las Conquistas del Nuevo Reino de Granada, *etc.* [The editor's preface signed: M. A. C.] 1881. 8°. **9772.** eee. **2.**

C., M. A. *See* HUGELMANN (Gabriel) *Journalist.* Españolas . . . Traducidas . . . por M. A. C. y G. A. L. [i.e. M. A. Comes and G. A. Larrosa.] 1852. 8°. **11474.** f. **24.**

C., M. A. *See* NITSCHE (G.) Golden Thoughts on a Holy Life, translated . . . by M. A. C. [1883.] 32°. **4400.** e. **33.**

C., M. A. *See* STOLZ (A.) "Give us this Day our Daily Bread," *etc.* [The translator's biographical note signed: M. A. C.] [1886.] 8°. **4407.** f. **7.**

C., M. A. *See* TAULER (J.) Golden Thoughts on the Higher Life . . . [Selections from "Medulla Animae" and "Nachfolgung des armen Lebens Christi."] Translated by M. A. C., *etc.* [1897.] 8°. **4399.** aaa. **49.**

—— *See* TAULER (J.) Golden Thoughts from the Book of Spiritual Poverty [i.e. "Nachfolgung des armen Lebens Christi"] . . . Translated by M. A. C., *etc.* [1897.] 8°. **4399.** aaa. **50.**

C., M. A.

—— **Amy's Dream. A Christmas story. By M. A. C., author of "Better than Fairies" [i.e. M. A. Cooke] . . . Second thousand. pp. 11.** ***Provost & Co.: London,*** **[1870.] 8°. 11652. a. 12.**
***The first edition is entered under* UNKNOWN.**

—— Fourth thousand. pp. 15. *W. H. Beer & Co.: London,* [1886.] 8°. **11602.** c. **27.** **(2.)**

—— **The Bailiff's Cross: a Guernsey legend. By M. A. C., author of "La Haye du Puits," "The Hole in the Roof," &c. [i.e. M. A. Cooke], *etc.* pp. 48.** ***Provost & Co.: London,*** **[1875.] 8°. 12638. aa. 54.**

C., M. A.

—— Beauty: a Christmas story, founded on the "Ugly Duck" [of Hans Andersen]. By the author of "Amy's Dream," *etc.* [Signed: M. A. C., i.e. M. A. Cooke.] pp. 26. *W. Maillard: Guernsey,* [1860?] 16°. **11647. a. 66. (3.)**

—— **Better than Fairies. A Christmas story, suggested by a real incident. By M. A. C., author of "Santa Claus" [i.e. M. A. Cooke], *etc.* pp. 23. *Simpkin, Marshall & Co.: London,* 1864. 24°. 11649. a. 76. (5.)**

—— Fourth thousand. pp. 15. *Provost & Co.: London,* [1870.] 8°. **11650. e. 44.**

—— Fifth thousand. pp. 15. *Provost & Co.: London,* [1879.] 8°. **11649. cc. 22. (8.)**

C., M. A. The Call. Verses by M. A. C. [With a preface by Dugald Macfadyen. The whole written by D. Macfadyen?] pp. 33. *Marshall Bros.: London,* [1916.] 8°. **011649. de. 109.**

C., M. A. Cameron Hall: a story of the Civil War. By M. A. C. [i.e. Mary A. Cruse.] pp. 543. *J. B. Lippincott & Co.: Philadelphia,* 1867. 8°. **12705. dd. 19.**

C., M. A. Catalogue d'une petite collection de livres rares et précieux . . . provenant du cabinet de M. A. C. dont la vente se fera le mercredi 4 mai 1853, *etc.* pp. iii. 48. MS. NOTES OF PRICES. *Paris,* 1853. 8°. **11902. f. 27.**

C., M. A. The Children's Kettledrum. [A picture-book, with verses.] By M. A. C. pp. 60. *Dean & Son: London,* [1881.] 4°. **12805. l. 30.**

—— A new edition, *etc.* pp. 40. *Dean & Son: London,* [1883.] 4°. **12810. d. 44.**

—— [Another issue of pp. 1–22.] *Dean & Son: London,* [1883.] 4°. **12805. u. 3.**

C., M. A. The Christmas Tree. [A poem, founded on Hans Andersen's "Grantræet." Signed: M. A. C., i.e. M. A. Cooke] pp. 24. [*Guernsey,* 1859.] 16°. **11647. a. 66. (2.)**

—— Second edition. pp. 15. *Provost & Co.: London,* [1877.] 16°. **12314. a. 44. (10.)**

—— Third edition. pp. 15. *W. H. Beer & Co.: London,* 1886. 8°. **11602. e. 27. (3.)**

C., M. A. Enthusiasm not Religion. A tale. By the late M. A. C. pp. xvi. 192. *J. Masters: London,* 1848. 16°. **1362. b. 16.**

C., M. A. The Exhibition Bible Stall. By the author of "Amy's Dream," *etc.* [A poem, signed: M. A. C., i.e. M. A. Cooke] pp. 15. *William Maillard: Guernsey,* 1862. 16°. **11647. a. 60.**

C., M. A. Fresh-Gathered Pictures and Lays. By M. A. C. pp. 7, 8. 17–30. *Dean & Son: London,* [1883.] 4°. **12807. k. 38.**

C., M. A.

—— A Legend of La Haye du Puits. A Guernsey home. By M. A. C., author of "Better than Fairies," "Santa Claus," &c. [i.e. M. A. Cooke.] Third edition. (Amy's Dream. A Christmas story. By M. A. C., author of "The Bailiff's Cross" . . . Third thousand.—Better than Fairies. A Christmas story . . . By M. A. C., author of "Santa Claus" . . . Fifth thousand.—Santa Claus. A Christmas story. By M. A. C., author of "Amy's Dream" . . . Second edition.—Marion; or, the Two crowns, by M. A. C., author of "The Bailiff's Cross" . . . Second edition.—Marie de Saint Roman: an incident of the sixteenth century. By M. A. C., author of "Better than Fairies," "Santa Claus," &c. Second edition.) 6 pt. *Provost & Co.: London,* [1882.] 8°. **11653. ee. 32.**
The title on the cover is: "The Legend of Haye du Puits & Other Stories."

C., M. A.

—— Marie de Saint Roman: suggested by an incident [of] the sixteenth century. By M. A. C. author of "Bett[er] than Fairies" ["Santa Claus," etc.] [i.e. M. A. Cooke], *etc.* pp. 22. *Frederick Le Lievre: Guernsey,* 1865. 16°. **11649. cc. 20. (**

—— **Marion; or the Two crowns. By the author of "Amy['s] Dream," "Charlie, the shipwrecked boy," *etc.* [Signed M. A. C., i.e. M. A. Cooke.] pp. 15. *William Maillard: Guernsey,* 1859. 16°. 11647. a. 66. (1**

—— [Another copy.] **11602. e. 18. (1**

C., M. A. The Mignonette; a gift for all seasons. [A[n] anthology of verse and prose. The editor's preface signe[d] M. A. C.] [With plates.] pp. 288. *D. Appleton & Co[.]: New York,* [1856.] 8°. **12706. f. 1**

C., M. A. The Recruiting Cantata of His Majesty's Hon[ourable] and Honour Guards. By M. A. C. pp. iii. 90. iv. *London Headquarters of "The Art and Practick" H.M.H.H.G.: London,* [1909.] 8°. **011650. de. 2**

C., M. A. Ten Types of Commercial Travellers. By M. A. [C.] pp. 86. *John Heywood: Manchester,* [1893.] 8°. **012330. g. 3**

C., M. A., *Vicar.* "Essays for the Times." Addressed to th[e] Church of England Working Men's Society, by M. A. C[.] Vicar [i.e. Michael A. Camilleri]. (First essay. Whenc[e] arose the Reformation of the Church of England[.]) pp. iv. 24. *C. A. Bartlett & Co.: London[;] H. N. Nichols: Wantage,* 1877. 8°. **4109. aaa.**
No more published.

C., M. A. DI. Dantes Alighierius ad Italos. (Elegia[.]) [Signed: M. A. di C.] pp. 8. FEW MS. NOTES. *Florenti[ae],* 1867. 8°. **11422. f. 16. (6**

C., M. A. C. DE, *Député du Bailliage de C. aux États-Générau[x].* Symbole des états, ou Profession de foi nationale. P[ar] M. A. C. de C. député du bailliage de C. aux État[s-]Généraux [i.e. Edme Aubert.] [The text of the Athanasia[n] Creed in Latin, with a parody in French.] pp. 13. [1789.] 8°. *See* ATHANASIAN CREED. [*Latin.*] **F. 381. (12**

C., M. A. E. A Beginning without an End. An allegor[y.] By M. A. E. C. pp. iv. 144. *Robt. Hardwicke: Londo[n,]* 1855. 8°. **4417. d.**

—— Jews and Gentiles; or, the Mystery of redemption [in] the two covenants, and the two witnesses in Revelatio[n] xi. explained by Scripture evidence alone. Being [a] reply to a pamphlet and its supplement entitled "T[he] Coming Struggle among the Nations" . . . By M. A. E. C[.] author of "A Beginning without an End," *etc.* pp. vi. 240. *Wertheim & Macintosh: London,* 1857. 8[°.] **3186. a. 3**

C., M. B. *See* GESSNER (S.) The Death of Abel, done in[to] blank verse from the translation, by Mrs. Mary Collyer 1761 . . . By M. B. C. 1840. 8°. **1064. e. 2**

C., M. B. Events of England in Rhyme; or, a List of t[he] chief occurrences of English history from 55 B.C. [to] A.D. 1866. By M. B. C. pp. 46. *Longmans & Co[.]: London,* 1867. 16°. **11648. aa. 2**

C., M. B.

—— **Scenes and Stories little known. Chiefly in Nort[h] Wales. [In verse.] By M. B. C. [i.e. M. B. Clough] pp. 92. *Pring & Price: Mold., Whittaker & Co.: Londo[n,]* 1861. 16°. 11650. a. 2**

C., M. B. Y. *See* B. Y C., M.

C., M. C. Cricket on the Brain. By M. C. C. pp. 80. *T. Fisher Unwin: London*, 1905. 4°. **12316**. dd. **40**.

C., M. C. Motherhood: its duties and comforts. By M. C. C. pp. 32. *S.P.C.K.: London*, [1879.] 16°. **4422**. e. **8**. **(11.)**

C., M. C. Photo-Chromography: an easy method of colouring photographs . . . By M. C. C. pp. 10. *William Barnard: London*, [1871.] 8°. **787**. c. **68**.

C., M. C. Short Notes of a last Sickness. [Signed: M. C. C.] pp. 12. *Wertheim, Macintosh & Hunt: London*, [1860.] 12°. **4920**. a. **35**. **(12.)**

C., M. C. Thoughts on Marriage, for the unmarried. By M. C. C., pp. 32. *S.P.C.K.: London*, [1878.] 16°. [i.e. M. C. Carr.] **4422**. aa. **5**. **(12.)**

C., M. C. What are you going to do with the Reform Bill? A letter to the conservatives of England. [Signed: M. C. C.] pp. 20. *James Ridgway: London*, 1860. 8°. **8138**. c. **23**.

C***, M. C*** DE.

—— Sujets importans de délibérations pour les États Généraux de 1789; ouvrage auquel on a joint l'article Loterie, tel qu'il a été composé pour l'Encyclopédie méthodique . . . Par M. C*** de C*** [i.e. M. A. Caminade de Castres]. pp. 92. *Londres*, 1789. 8°. R. **54**. (3.)

C., M. C. I. H. D. L'Ambition de l'Espagnol en son artifice par luy faict, en la solemnité de la vueille de la S. Iean Baptiste . . . Par M. C. I. H. D. C. pp. 13. *I. Brunet: Paris*, 1614. 8°. **1193**. h. **10**. (4.)

C., M. C. P. S. M. D. *See* N., N. Réflexions d'un Portugais sur le Mémoire du R.P. Général des Jésuites [L. Ricci] présenté au Pape Clément XIII . . . Traduites en françois, avec une préface . . . par M. C. P. S. M. D. C. [i.e. P. O. Pinault.] 1760. 12°. **4091**. e. **48**.

C., M. D. *See* LICQUET (F. I.) Rouen . . . Translated by M. D. C., *etc.* 1846. 12°. **10171**. aa. **32**.

—— *See* LICQUET (F. I.) Rouen . . . Translated . . . by M. D. C. and M. H. Barguet. 1857. 12°. **10172**. a. **20**.

C., M. D. *See* MEXIA (P.) Trois dialogues de M. P. Messie, *etc.* [The translator's dedicatory epistle signed: M. D. C., i.e. M. de Coste-Blanche.] 1593. 8°. **535**. b. **37**.

C., M. D. *See* MORLENT (J.) Historical and Picturesque Voyage from Havre to Rouen . . . Translated . . . by M. D. C. 1843. 12°. **10174**. aa. **5**.

—— *See* MORLENT (J.) Voyage from Havre to Paris . . . Translated by M. D. C. 1841. 12°. **10171**. a. **32**.

C., M. D. *See* SOTO (F. de) Histoire de la conqueste de la Floride, par les Espagnols, sous Ferdinand de Soto. Écrite en portugais par un Gentil-homme de la ville d'Elvas. Par M. D. C. [i.e. S. de Broé, Seigneur de Citri de la Guette.] 1685. 12°. **9555**. aaa. **8**.

C., M. D. *See* VIDA (M. H.) *Bishop of Alba.* Le Ieu des Eschets. Traduction en vers français du poëme latin de Vida De ludo scacchorum par M. D. C., *etc.* 1862. 12°. **11481**. b. **34**.

C., M. D. Chronicles of Christopher Columbus. A poem in three cantos. By M. D. C. [i.e. Moncure D. Conway.] pp. x. 315. *Kegan Paul & Co.: London*, 1882. 8°. **11653**. cc. 34.

C., M. D. Des mots à la mode, et des nouvelles façons de parler. Avec des observations sur diverses maniéres d'agir & de s'exprimer. Et un discours en vers sur les mêmes matiéres. (By M. D. C., i.e. François de Callières.] pp. 175. *C. Barbin: Paris; J. Leonard: Bruxelles*, 1692. 12°. **236**. e. **42**.
The initials occur in the privilege. A later edition, without the author's initials, is entered under MOTS.

—— Du bon et du mauvais usage dans les manières de s'exprimer. Des façons de parler bourgeoises. Et en quoy elles sont différentes de celles de la cour. Suitte des Mots à la mode. [By M. D. C., i.e. F. de Callières.] pp. 241. *Claude Barbin: Paris*, 1693. 12°. **11805**. aaa. **1**.
The initials occur in the privilege. A later edition without the author's initials is entered under USAGE.

C., M. D. Essais sur les mœurs, ou point de constitution durable sans mœurs; ouvrage adressé à l'Assemblée nationale . . . Par M. D. C. [i.e. L. C. de Cressy.] pp. 160. *Paris*, 1790. 8°. **112**. d. **28**.

C***, M. D. Les Orphelins; conte moral, mis en action en forme de pièce dramatique, en cinq actes et en prose. Par M. D. C*** [i.e. J. P. Costard]. pp. 119. *Paris*, 1767. 8°. **11738**. aa. **19**. **(2.)**

C., M. D. Passages from some Journals, and other poems. By M. D. C. [i.e. Moncure D. Conway], *etc.* pp. ix. 184. *Kegan Paul & Co.: London*, 1886. 8°. **11653**. dd. **26**.

—— Three Lyrical Dramas. Sintram, the Friends of Syracuse, the Lady of Kynast. By M. D. C. [i.e. Moncure D. Conway.] pp. 161. *Kegan Paul & Co.: London*, 1886. 8°. **11781**. g. **28**.

C., M. D. The Tripled Crown. A book of English, Scotch and Irish verse for the age of six to sixteen. Chosen and arranged by three of that age. [The preface signed: M. D. C., M. W. C., J. M. C., i.e. M. D., May W. and Joanna M. Cannan.] pp. 304. *Henry Frowde: London*, 1908. 8°. **11603**. i. **17**.

C., M. D., *de l'Académie Française.* Le Dictionnaire des arts et des sciences. Par M. D. C. de l'Académie françaíse [i.e. T. Corneille]. 2 tom. *See* PARIS.—*Académie Française.* Le Dictionnaire de l'Académie française, *etc.* tom. 3, 4. 1694. fol. **12953**. k. **3**.

—— Nouvelle édition, revûe, corrigée & augmentée par M. **** de l'Académie royale des Sciences [i.e. B. Le Bovier de Fontenelle]. 2 tom. *Paris*, 1731. fol. **12953**. k. **6**.

C., M. D. D. L. P. D. Fables nouvelles, et autres pièces en vers. Par M. D. D. L. P. D. C. [i.e. J. F. Dreux du Radier.] Avec un examen critique des principaux fabulistes anciens & modernes. pp. xxvi. 101. *Paris*, 1744. 12°. **637**. c. **23**.

C., M. D. F. R., and **F.**, A. Difesa del Regio Fisco contra l'arrendamento del ducato à botte, da esaminarsi nel Regio Collateral Consiglio, *etc.* [Signed: M. D. F. R. C., & A. F.] [1729.] 4°. *See* NAPLES, *Kingdom of.*—*Regio Fisco.* **5357**. b. **1**.

C., M. D. L. Mémoire sur la prochaine tenue des États-généraux, et sur les objets qui doivent y être mis en délibération. Par M. D. L. C. pp. 15. *Villefranche*, 1788. 8°. F. **34**. **(11.)**

C., M. D. L. Nouvelles toutes nouvelles. Par M. D. L. C. [i.e. —— Le Chevalier de Mailly.] [With a plate.] pp. 287. *Amsterdam*, 1710. 12°. **1094**. aa. **24**.

C., M. D. L. Projet de cahier pour le tiers-état du bailliage et de la vicomté de Paris. Par M. D. L. C. pp. 29. 1789. 8°. F.R. **35.** (4.)

C., M. D. L. Le Toledan. [A novel. By M. D. L. C., i.e. J. Regnauld de Segrais.] 5 tom. *A. de Sommaville: Paris*, 1647–55. 8°. **243.** i. **16–20.**
The initials occur in the privilege at the end of tom. 1.

—— Seconde édition. 5 pt. *G. de Luyne: Paris*, 1654, 49–55. 8°. G. **17658–62.**
Tom. 1 *only is of the second edition.*

C., M. D. L., *Mr.* L'Hommage du sentiment, suivi d'une fable, sur le rétablissement de la santé du Roi. Par Mr. M. D. L. C. [i.e. M. de La Chesnaye.] pp. 13. *W. Gillman: Rochester*, 1789. 12°. **12305.** bbb. **40.** (**1.**)

—— Quelques fables, suivies de quelques vers. Par Mr. M. D. L. C. [i.e. M. de La Chesnaye.] pp. 35. *W. Gillman: Rochester*, 1789. 12°. **12305.** bbb. **40.** (**2.**)

C., M. D. L. M. Réponse aux différens écrits publiés contre la comédie des Philosophes [of C. Palissot de Montenoy], ou Parallèle des Nuées d'Aristophane, des Femmes sçavantes [of Molière], du Méchant [of J. B. L. Gresset], et des Philosophes. Par M. D. L. M. C. [i.e. H. I. de La Marche Courmont.] pp. 76. [*Paris*,] 1760. 8°. **241.** i. **26.** (**11.**)

C., M. D. M. C. D. M. A. E. Malicia dos homens contra a bondade das mulheres . . . Escrita por M. D. M. C. D. M. A. E. C. pp. 8. *Lisboa*, 1759. 4°. [*Bondade das mulheres contra a malicia dos homens, etc.* pt. 2.] **12314.** d. **34.** (**6.**)

C., M. E. The Legend of St. Christopher. [In verse. Signed: M. E. C.] pp. 20. *Catholic Truth Society: London*, [1896.] 32°. **11603.** aaa. **3.** (**5.**)

C., M. E. A Short Account of Holy Cross Abbey. By M. E. C. pp. 30. *Edward Ponsonby: Dublin*, 1868. *obl.* fol. **7814.** ppp. **11.**

C., M. E., *Docteur en théologie. See* CHAPELON (J.) Œuvres complettes . . . Recueillies par M. E. C., docteur en théologie, *etc.* 1820. 8°. **11498.** h. **52.**

C., M. E. B. The Prayers of Scripture, and their answers. By M. E. B. C. pp. iv. 80. *William Macintosh: London*, 1866. 8°. **4410.** b. **11.**

C., M. F. *See* APULEIUS (L.) *Madaurensis.* [*Asinus Aureus.—Spanish.*] Las Metamorfósis de Apuléo . . . Traduccion libre al castellano, por un aficionado. [The translator's preface signed: M. F. C.] 1844. 8°. **12403.** aaaa. **1.**

C., M. F. An Illustrated History of Ireland: from the earliest period. By M. F. C. [i.e. Mary F. Cusack.] With historical illustrations by Henry Doyle. pp. xxiv. 581. *Longmans & Co.: London*, 1868. 8°. **9509.** bb. **21.**

C., M. F. DE.

—— *See* CHATEAUBRIAND (F. R. de) *Viscount.* Petit manuel à l'usage des hommes monarchiques et immobiles . . . Par M. F. de C. [Extracts from the controversial works of Chateaubriand, with a commentary.] 1819. 8°. R. **139.** (**4.**)

C., M. G. Geroglíficos para el Arco que se Puso en la Hacienda de Rancho-Grande para el Recibimiento del Sr. Brigadier D. Pedro Celestino de Negrete. Dispuesto por M. G. C. *Guadalajara*, 1821. 4°. **11451.** bbb. **44.** (**13.**)

—— [Another copy.] **11451.** bbb. **44.** (**14.**)

C., M. G. A Manual of Prayers for the use of Servants. By M. G. C. pp. 60. *William Macintosh: London*, [1867.] 16°. **3455.** aa. **7**

C., M. G. Riflessioni sul trattato d'alleanza tra le Repubbliche Cisalpina e Francese, di M. G. C. [i.e. M. Gioja.] pp. 24. *Italia* [*Lecco*], 1798. 8°. T. **862.** (**9.**)

C., M. G. C. D. Nouveautés du Palais Royal, ou Livres nouveaux des charlatans, des roués, &c. de la France, accompagnés de notes impartiales. Par M. G. C. D. C. pp. 27. [*Paris*,] 1789. 8°. F. **386.** (**14.**)

C., M. G. D. Mémoires de Monsieur de Bordeaux, intendant des finances. Par M. G. D. C. [i.e. G. de Courtilz de Sandras.] 4 tom. *Amsterdam*, 1758. 12°. **12510.** aaa. **15.**

C., M. G. F. D. A. * * C. D. Ce que c'est que constitution, et suite des élections et de la répartition des pouvoirs, décrites aux réflexions constitutionnelles, qui, avec l'établissement des codes sur les troupes, finances, affaires étrangères, marine, etc., feront une constitution réelle, pour établir la liberté et la souveraineté des peuples et le bonheur des monarques . . . Par M. G. F. D. A. * * C. D. C. pp. 62. *Paris*, 1791. 8°. F.R. **82.** (**9.**)

—— Réflexions constitutionelles et remède conciliatoire aux trois maux politiques qui nous affligent. Par M. G. F. D. A. * * C. D. C. pp. 59. *Paris*, 1790. 8°. F.R. **79.** (**5.**)

C., M. G. M. A. V. DI C. DI. Memorie ecclesiastiche e civili di Città di Castello. Raccolte da M. G. M. A. V. di C. di C. [i.e. G. Muzi, Bishop of Città di Castello.] Con dissertazione preliminare sull'antichità ed antiche denominazion di detta città. 7 vol. *Citta di Castello*, 1842–44. 8°. **10136.** i. **1.**

C., M. G. T. Desengaño de Falsas Imposturas. [The first part signed: M. G. T. C., i.e. M. G. Toral Cabañas.] 1811. 8°. *See* TORAL CABAÑAS (M. G.) **9770.** aaa. **15.** (**3.**)

C., M. H. Fifty per Cent. Dividend. Showing how certain good dividend-paying stocks may be made to yield a return equivalent to a dividend of 50 per cent. per annum . . . By M. H. C. [i.e. Montague H. Cockle.] pt. 1. pp. 14. *Sold only by subscription: London*, 1898. 8°. **08228.** h. **28.**

C., M. H. Mysterium: Mysteriorum Mundanorum. Das ist: Ein Welt- vnd Geldgeheimnuss, oder kurtze Satyra vnd freyer Discurs. Darinnen offentlich recht vnd respectivè theologico-poltice [*sic*] von dem grossen Mangel, so bey Reichen vnd Armen mit grossem klagen vnd seufftzen in der gantzen Christenheit im schwang gehet, tractirt . . . wird . . . Auffs kürtzte . . . proponirt von M. H. C. pp. 32. 1620. 4°. **8225.** d. **64.**

C., M. H. The Old Art of Tatting. By an Englishwoman, *etc.* [Signed: M. H. C.] pp. 36. *Hollway & Son: Bath*, [1870?] *obl.* 16°. **7742.** a. **90.**

C., M. H. F. G. F. M. H. F. G.F.C. [i.e. M. H. Fuhrmann.] Musicalische Strigel, *etc.* [1715?] 8°. *See* F., M. H., *G.F.C.* **7898.** aaaa. **37.**

C., M. I. P., *Evesque de Belley.* Les Relations morales. De M. I. P. C. Evesque de Belley. 1638. 8°. *See* CAMUS (J. P.) successively *Bishop of Belley* and *of Arras.* **1073.** c. **14.**

C., M. J. Ab-sa-ra-ka, Home of the Crows: being the experience of an officer's wife on the Plains, and marking the vicissitudes of peril and pleasure during the occupation of the new route to Virginia City, Montana, 1866–7, and the Indian hostility thereto, *etc.* [The dedication signed: M. J. C., i.e. Margaret Irvin Carrington.] pp. 284. *J. B. Lippincott & Co.: Philadelphia*, 1868. 8°. **10410.** aaa. **19.**

M. J. Catalogue of the Chief Portion of the Library of the late James C. Culwick. [The prefatory note signed: M. J. C., i.e. M. J. Culwick.] 4 pt.
See CULWICK (James C.) 1908. 8°. 011901. e. 35.

M. J. The Mother's Sabbath Assistant. Three hundred questions and answers. By M. J. C. pp. 52. S. B. Oldham: Dublin, 1854. 12°. 3128. a. 70. (2.)

M. J. M. DE C. E V. Festejando o Regimento da cavallaria do Caes. Com hum Te Deum em acçaõ de graças o beneficio, com que milagrosamente livrou Deos a vida do nosso Soberano . . . (Soneto. De M. J. M. de C. e V. C., soldado do mesmo regimento.—Illuminando-se toda a praça na noite antecedente á festa . . . Soneto.) 2 pt. [*Lisbon*, 1758.] fol. 4783. e. 5. (13.)

M. L.

Biographical Notes on Sir Ernest Barker and Thomas Greenwood. Issued in connection with the unveiling of plaques in their honour at the Bredbury and Romiley Branch of the Cheshire County Library . . . 12th October 1950. [The notes on Sir E. Barker signed: M. L. C., i.e. M. L. Cousins; those on T. Greenwood signed: G. C. With portraits.] [1950.] 8°. 10863. de. 5.

M. L. Catalogue des tableaux, livres, dessins, aquarelles gouaches, sépias, gravures, lithographies, photographies miniatures, bronzes et objets divers composant le cabinet de M. L. C. [i.e. L. Constantin.] [With MS. correspondence concerning the collection.] pp. 70. [*Paris*,] 1876. 8°. 11899. cc. 24.

M. L. Clarie's Little Charge. By M. L. C., author of 'Lonely Lily." pp. 136. *J. F. Shaw & Co.: London*, 1871.] 8°. 12808. eee. 5.

., M. L. Essai sur les erreurs et les superstitions. Par M. L. C . . . [i.e. J. L. Castilhon]. pp. 411. *Amsterdam*, 1765. 12°. 8631. aaa. 14.

M. L. Left at Home; or, the Heart's resting place. By M. L. C. pp. 144. *J. F. Shaw & Co.: London*, [1875.] 12°. 12808. l. 33.

M. L. Lonely Lily. By M. L. C. Second edition. pp. 94. *J. F. Shaw & Co.: London*, [1870.] 16°. 4413. aaa. 13.

M. L. The New-Zealander on London Bridge; or, Moral ruins of the modern Babylon. By M. L. C. pp. 67. S. *Tinsley & Co.: London*, 1878. 8°. 8139. b. 1. (1.)

M. L. Our Great Consoler in Life & Death. Short devotional readings by M. L. C. pp. viii. 109. S.P.C.K.: *London*, 1915. 8°. 3455. ddd. 39.

M. L. Some Time in Ireland. A recollection. [The preface signed: M. L. C.] pp. vii. 317. *London*, 1874. 8°. 10390. bbb. 3.

M. L. Things concerning Jesus, out of "The Law of Moses," "The Prophets," and "The Psalms." St. Luke XXIV. 27, 44. Short readings for Lent. [The preface signed: M. L. C.] pp. 105. *Skeffington & Son: London*, 1901. 8°. 3456. ee. 53.

M. L., *Esq.* See SÉGUR (L. P. de) *Count.* Le Tems. New song of old time, by M. de Segur; with the English translation, by M. L. C. Esq.) 1799. 8°. [POPE *Alexander*) *the Poet. Windsor Forest, etc.*] 992. h. 24. (5.)

M. L. A. D., *Docteur de Sorbonne.* Lettre à M. L. A. D. C. docteur de Sorbonne. Où il est prouvé par plusieurs raisons tirées de la philosophie, & de la theologie, que les cometes ne sont point le presage d'aucun malheur, *etc.* By Pierre Bayle.] pp. 574. *P. Marteau: Cologne*, 1682. 12°. 531. e. 19.

C., M. L. C. D. La Mort de Louis XVI, poème épico-élégiaque. Par M. L. C. D. C. pp. 43. *Paris*, 1815. 8°. R. 12. (21.)

C., M. L. D. Journal du voyage de Siam fait en M.DC.LXXXV. et M.DC.LXXXVI. Par M. L. D. C. [i.e. F. T. de Choisy.] pp. 416. *S. Mabre-Cramoisy: Paris*, 1687. 4°. G. 7193.

C., M. L. D. S. M. C. A. Réfutation de l'ouvrage de M. l'évêque-duc de Langres, ayant pour titre: Sur la forme d'opiner aux États-Généraux. Par M. L. D. S. M. C. A. C. [i.e. L. P. de Saint-Martin.] pp. 54. [*Paris*, 1789.] 8°. F. 28. (6.)

C., M. L. M. D.

—— Lettre d'un hermite de la forêt de Sénart, M. L. M. D. C. [i.e. M. le marquis de Condorcet], aux auteurs du Journal de Paris. *See* GLUCK (C. W. von) Mémoires pour servir à l'histoire de la révolution opérée dans la musique par M. le chevalier Gluck. 1781. 8°. Hirsch.I.310.

C., M. L. P. D. Histoire des amours du grand Alcandre. (Par M. L. P. D. C. [i.e. Marguérite Louise Princesse de Conti.]) *See* HENRY III., *King of France.* [*Biography.* —I.] Recueil de diverses pièces, *etc.* 1662. 12°. 611. a. 13.

—— Histoire des amours du grand Alcandre [i.e. Henry IV., King of France]. (Par M. L. P. D. C.) [Attributed to Louisa Margaret de Bourbon, Princess de Conti.] *In:* Recueil de diverses pièces servant à l'histoire de Henry III., *etc.* pp. 223–310. 1666. 12°. 1471. e. 40.

C., M. M. *See* BREWSTER (*Sir* David) A Short Life of Sir Isaac Newton. [The editor's introduction signed: M. M. C.] 1864. 12°. 10825. aa. 36. (4.)

C., M. M.

—— *See* CLARKE (Blackburn) Occasional Hymns. [The editor's preface signed: M. M. C., i.e. M. M. Clarke.] [1907.] 8°. 3433. f. 19.

C., M. M. Five Years of Theosophy . . . Essays, selected from "The Theosophist" [by M. M. C.]. Second and revised edition. pp. vi. 385. 1894. 8°. *See* PERIODICAL PUBLICATIONS.—Bombay.—*The Theosophist.* 8632. m. 15.

C., M. M. Home Education. An address to mothers. [Signed: M. M. C.] pp. 14. *S.P.C.K.: London*, 1894. 8°. 4429. c. 21. (15.)

C., M. M. Jacobæidcs metricæ portio v. Salutare Jacobæum . . . explicans . . . Das ist: Jacobs, des Patriarchen Heils-Begierde, im I. Buch Mos. am 49/18. zubefinden: gesang-weise verfasset von M. M. C., *etc. Lat. & Ger. Altenburg*, 1649. 8°. 897. aa. 2. (8.)

C., M. M. Manifestacion de la Provincia de Galicia, sobre las altercaciones acerca de la Inquisicion, publicada en el periódico titulado el Sensato, quarto trimestre del jueves 14 de mayo de 1812, *etc.* [Signed: M. M. C.] pp. 4. *México*, 1812. 4°. 9180. ccc. 2. (46.)

C., M. M. Representaciones de Varios Ilustrísimos Señores, Arzobispos y Obispos de España, dirigidas al soberano congreso de las Cortes generales y extraordinarias del regno pidiendo el restablecimiento del santo tribunal de la Inquisicion, al exercicio de sus funciones . . . Dalas á luz M. M. C. pp. 19. *Cadiz*, 1812. 4°. 9180. dd. 2. (9.)

C., M. N. The Pilgrim with the Ancient Book. And other sacred poems. By M. N. C. pp. xii. 180. *W. Hunt & Co.: London*, 1868. 8°. 11648. cc. 19.

C., M. N. Readings and Prayers for Every Day in Lent. [The preface signed: M. N. C.] pp. 135. *Skeffington & Son: London*, 1907. 8°. **3457**. bbb. **77**.

C., M. N. Sacred Poems: "Come and See," "De profundis," etc., etc. By M. N. C. pp. 22. *W. Hunt & Co.: London; G. Short: Bath*, 1867. 16°. **11648**. aa. **76**. **(10.)**

—— Sacred Poems: Paraphrases, etc. By M. N. C. pp. 54. *W. Hunt & Co.: London; G. Short: Bath*, 1868. 16°. **11648**. a. **86**. **(11.)**

—— Sacred Poems: Sabbath, Sacramental, and Holy Days, etc. By M. N. C. pp. 48. *W. Hunt & Co.: London; G. Short: Bath*, 1867. 16°. **11648**. a. **86**. **(10.)**

C., M. M.

—— The Tallyman's Vocabulary. [The preface signed: M. M. C., i.e. Mo Jo-lien.] pp. 11. [*Hong Kong*, 1913.] 8°. **11095**. a. **44**.
Later editions were included in "English Made Easy," by the same author.

C., M. O. A Memorial History of the Campbells of Melfort, Argyllshire . . . By M. O. C. (M. O. Campbell.) 1882. 4°. *See* CAMPBELL (Margaret O.) **9915**. f. **3**.

C., M. P., *Docteur de Sorbonne.*

—— *See* CAMUS (J. P.) *Bishop of Belley.* L'Esprit de Saint François de Sales . . . recueilli de divers écrits de M. J.-P. Camus . . . Par M. P. C., docteur de Sorbonne [i.e. Pierre Collot], *etc.* 1816. 8°. **3706**. p. **6**.

—— Explication des premières vérités de la religion . . . Par M. P. C., Docteur de Sorbonne [i.e. Pierre Collot]. Nouvelle édition. pp. 510. *Paris*, 1763. 8°. **3558**. ee. **7**.

C . . . , M. P . . . . . . C . . . D. Dissertations physico-théologiques, touchant la conception de Jésus Christ dans le sein de la Vièrge Marie sa mère. Et sur un tableau de Jésus-Christ qu'on appelle la Sainte Face, & qu'on a voulu faire passer pour une image constellée. Par M. P . . . . . . C . . . D. C . . . . [i.e. J. Pierquin, curé de Chatel]. pp. 261. *Amsterdam*, 1742. 8°. **850**. d. **23**.

C., M. P. J. M. P. A., *Citoyen actif.* Bilan de la nation, ou Situation des finances de la France avec des observations importantes, servant de réfutation de l'extrait raisonné des rapports du Comité des finances. Par M. P. J. M. P. A. C., citoyen actif [i.e. P. J. Messange, procureur au Châtelet]. pp. 38. *Paris*, 1790. 4°. **936**. e. **18**. **(6.)**

C . . . . . . (M. Ph. L.) Le Préjugé excusable, ou Il voulait et ne voulait pas. Comédie en cinq actes et en vers, par M. Ph. L. C . . . . . . [i.e. P. L. Candon]. pp. 99. *Marseille*, 1811. 8°. **11738**. a. **41**. **(7.)**

—— Les Supercheries, ou Elle voulait et ne voulait pas, comédie en cinq actes et en vers. Par M. Ph. L. C . . . . . . [i.e. P. L. Candon]. pp. 136. *Marseille*, 1809. 8°. **11738**. a. **41**. **(6.)**

C., M. R. S. Le Vaisseau Amiral, ou Forbin et Delville, opéra en un acte; paroles de M. R. S. C. [i.e. R. Saint Cyr], *etc.* pp. 41. *Paris*, 1805. 8°. **11738**. m. **37**. **(10.)**

C., M. S. Blades and Flowers: poems for children. By M. S. C., author of "Twilight Thoughts" [i.e. Mary S. Claude], *etc.* pp. ix. 85. *Grant & Griffith: London*, 1856 [1855]. 8°. **11648**. b. **18**.

C., M. S. Consideration; or, Modern Christianity compared with the Bible. By M. S. C. pp. iii. 169. *Simpkin, Marshall & Co.: London*, 1847. 16°. **1360**. g. **17**.

C., M. S. The Life of Moses. By M. S. C. pp. iv. 88. *Hatchards: London*, 1888. 8°. **4805**. e.

C., M. S. Little Poems for Little People. By M. S. [i.e. Mary S. Claude], *etc.* pp. 80. *Chapman & Hal London*, [1847.] 12°. **11645**. a. 2

—— [Another edition.] pp. 89. *Hamilton, Adams & Co London*, [1866.] 8°. **11648**. bb. 3

—— Natural History in Stories for Little Children. B M. S. C., author of "Twilight Thoughts" [i.e. Ma S. Claude] . . . With illustrations by Harrison Weir. pp. 104. *Addey & Co.: London*, 1854. 12°. **12806**. b. 5

—— Enlarged edition, *etc.* pp. 208. *Hamilton, Adams & Co Simpkin, Marshall & Co.: London*, [1863.] 8°. **7205**. aa. 1

C., M. S. Plain Thoughts on Holy Communion. [Signe M. S. C.] pp. 11. *Rivingtons: London*, 1878. 16°. **4422**. e. **7**. (4

—— Second edition, revised. pp. 12. *Rivingtons: Londo* 1879. 16°. **4422**. e. **7**. (

—— Third edition, revised. pp. 12. *Rivingtons: Londo* 1880. 16°. **4422**. e. **21**. (4

—— Fourth edition, revised. pp. 12. *Rivingtons: Londo* 1882 [1881]. 16°. **4422**. aa. **29**. (

—— Fifth edition, revised. pp. 12. *Rivingtons: Londo* 1883. 16°. **4422**. aa. **44**. (

C., M. S. Thoughts about Familiar Things. Poems, f school and leisure hours. By M. S. C., author of "Tw light Thoughts," etc. [i.e. Mary S. Claude.] pp. 23. *G. H. & J. Smyth & Co.: Liverpool*, 1852. 8°. **11646**. dd. **13**. (1

—— Twilight Thoughts. By M. S. C., author of "Lit Poems for Little People" [i.e. Mary S. Claude]. pp. 1 *Chapman & Hall: London*, 1848. 12°. **1362**. g.

C., M. S., *Don.* El Hombre Convencido á la Razon, ó Muger prudente. Comedia nueva en tres actos . . . P Don M. S. C. pp. 33. [*Madrid*, 1790.] 4°. **1342**. e. **6**. (

C., M. T. Flowers from the Battle-Field, and other poe By M. T. C. pp. 36. *H. B. Ashmead: Philadelph* 1864. 12°. **11687**. aa.

C * * * * * * *. (M. Th. A. B. D.) *Conseiller au Parlement Paris.* Parallèle entre la constitution faite par l'Assembl nationale, et la constitution démandée par les cahi du peuple . . . Par M. Th. A. B. D. C * * * * * * Conseiller au Parlement de Paris [i.e. Th. A. Bourrée Corberon ?]. pp. vi. 74. *En Brabant*, 1791. 8°. **F.R. 81**. (

C., M. V. *See* ENGLISH POST. Engelsche post, tot Rott dam gekomen, *etc.* [Two letters, the second signe M. V. C.] 1653. 4°. **1889**. d. **2**. (

—— *See* LONDON.—IV. [*Appendix.—Miscellaneous.*] Tw brieven uyt Londen geschreven, *etc.* [The second lett signed: M. V. C.] 1653. 4°. **8122**. c. 6

C., M. W. *See* C., M. D. The Tripled Crown. A book English, Scotch and Irish verse for the age of six to si teen. Chosen and arranged by three of that age. [T preface signed: M. D. C., M. W. C., J. M. C., i.e. M. I M. W., and J. M. Cannan.] 1908. 8°. **11603**. i.

C., M. W. Infant Baptism: is it from Heaven, or of me . . . By the author of "The Bible and Slavery," [The introduction signed: M. W. C.] pp. 16. *Willi Macintosh: London*, [1876.] 16°. **4372**. d. **7**. (

C., M. W. Reply to an Enquiry concerning a Proposal to Amend the Bank Act of 1844, contained in a letter, from Mr. Samuel Smith to the Liverpool Chamber of Commerce, dated 13th Nov., 1873. [Signed: M. W. C., i.e. M. W. Collet?] pp. 13. [*London*, 1874.] 8°. **08226**. h. **14**. (**6**.)

C., M. W. Songs of the Free, and Hymns of Christian Freedom. [By various authors. The dedication signed: M. W. C.] pp. 227. *Isaac Knapp: Boston*, 1836. 8°. **11687**. b. **20**.

C., M. Y. Poesias Dedicadas al Señor de la Salud de Puruándiro, por . . . M. Y. C. Por la singular merced de haber libertado á la población de la asoladora epidemia del cólera morbo de 1850. pp. 20. *México*, 1850. 8°. **11450**. bb. **38**.

C*** (Mario) *See* Orcel Dumolard (H. F. E. E.) and C*** (M.) Callot à Nancy, comédie anecdotique . . . Par MM. Dumolard et Mario C*** [i.e. A. M. Coster], *etc.* 1813. 8°. **11738**. dd. **38**. (**1**.)

—— *See* Orcel Dumolard (H. F. E. E.) and C*** (M.) Les Expédients, comédie . . . par MM. Dumolard et Mario C*** [i.e. A. M. Coster], *etc.* 1811. 8°. **11738**. dd. **38**. (**2**.)

—— *See* Orcel Dumolard (H. F. E. E.) and C*** (M.) Le Roman d'un jour, comédie . . . par MM. Dumolard et Mario C*** [i.e. A. M. Coster], *etc.* 1812. 8°. **11738**. dd. **38**. (**5**.)

C—— (Mary) *See* Teacher. The Warning Voice; or Reflections on the death of Mary C——, *etc.* [1852.] 16°. **4903**. b. **30**.

C—— (Mary Ann) A Letter to a Bible Class; or, a Voice from the grave, of an humble lacemaker (Mary Ann C——); with a short memoir. pp. 30. *Partridge & Oakey: London*, 1849. 16°. **4905**. a. **2**.

C. (Mary Elizabeth) "Leaning on her Beloved." A memorial of M. E. C. (Mary Elizabeth C.) [With a portrait.] pp. 120. *J. Nisbet & Co.: London*, 1857. 8°. **4906**. d. **40**.

C. (Michael) An Irishman's Dying Testimony. [On the death of Michael C——.] 1848. 32°. *See* Irishman. **4415**. b. **15**.

C------- (M---y) The Ladies Defence: or, the Bride-woman's counsellor answer'd: a poem . . . Written by a Lady. [The epistle dedicatory signed: M---y C-------, i.e. Mary Lady Chudleigh. A reply to "The Bride Womans Counsellor," by John Sprint.] pp. 23. *John Deeve: London*, 1701. fol. ✗ **11630**. g. **6**.
✗ A later edition is entered under LADIES.

C. (Myles) *See* Austria.—*Landtag.* The Supplicacion: that the nobles and comons of Osteryke made lately, *etc.* [With a preface by Miles Coverdale, headed "Myles. C. to the Reader."] [1543?] 8°. **4661**. a. **4**.

C., N. *See* Clagett (William) *D.D.* Seventeen Sermons preach'd upon several occasions, *etc.* [The editor's preface to vol. 2 signed: N. C., i.e. Nicholas Clagett.] 1699. 8°. **227**. b. **25, 26**.

C., N. *See* Fabricius (W.) *von Hilden.* Lithotomia Vesicæ . . . done into English by N. C., *etc.* 1640. 8°. **1189**. d. **7**.

C., N. *See* Wesley (John) John Wesley's Journal. Abridged edition. [The editor's preface signed: N. C., i.e. Nehemiah Curnock.] 1903. 8°. **4905**. aa. **65**.

—— —— [1906.] 8°. **4902**. de. **16**.

—— —— [1914.] 8°. **12207**. r. **3**.

C., N. Achitophel, or, the Picture of a wicked politician, *etc.* [The epistle dedicatory signed: N. C., i.e. Nathanael Carpenter.] pp. 64. [*H. Lownes & R. Young*] *for M. S.* [*M. Sparke: London*], 1629. 4°. **4375**. b. **11**.

C., N. Bristol Drollery. Poems and songs. By Mr C. [The dedicatory poem signed: N. C.] pp. 102. *For Charles Allen: London*, 1674. 8°. C. **39**. b. **52**.

C., N. Carmen Elegiacum, England's Elegie, or Lamentation . . . By N. C. Whereunto is added a reasonable motion, and lamentation, in the behalfe of such of the Clergie, as are questioned in the parliament, for their places, &c. pp. 6. [*London*, 1643.] 4°. E. **99**. (**31**.)

C., N. Copie d'une lettre du camp d'Arville, du 9 octobre 1790. [Signed: N. C.] [*Brussels?* 1790.] *s. sh.* 8°. **8079**. c. **21**. (**35**.)

C., N. The German History Continued. The seventh part. Wherein is conteyned the principall passages of the last summer, *etc.* [The epistle to the reader signed: N. C.]. 1634. *See* Sweden. [*Appendix.—History and Politics.*—ii.] The Swedish Intelligencer, *etc.* pt. 7. 1632, *etc.* **C.133.c.1.**

C., N. A Modest and True Account of the Chief Points in Controversie between the Roman Catholics, and the Protestants: together with some considerations upon the sermons of a divine of the Church of England [i.e. John Tillotson, Archbishop of Canterbury]. By N. C. [Probably by Cornelius Nary, but also attributed to Nicholas Colson.] pp. 301. *Antwerp*, 1696. 8°. **3936**. aa. **32**.

—— [Another edition.] pp. 292. *Antwerp*, 1705. 8°. **3936**. aa. **21**.

—— An Answer to a Popish Book, intituled, a True and Modest Account of the Chief Points in Controversie, between the Roman Catholicks and the Protestants. Together with some considerations upon the sermons of a divine of the Church of England. By N. C. [i.e. Cornelius Nary? or Nicholas Colson?], *etc.* [By Lewis Atterbury the younger.] pp. 224. *W. Hawes: London*, 1706. 8°. **3936**. bb. **33**.

C., N. Opera profitteuole, e necessaria, cauata dall'auttore, dall'esperienza d'vna larga pratica per migliorar & conseruar la Laguna di Venetia, *etc.* [The dedication signed: N. C.] pp. 76. *A. Ramellati: Milano*, 1675. 4°. **173**. c. **2**.

C., N. The Principall Passages of Germany, Italy, France, and other places for these last sixe moneths past, historically reduced to time, place, and action, till the end of the yeare 1636 . . . All faithfully taken out of good originals by an English Mercury. [The address "To the Readers" signed: N. C.] (The Continuation of the Actions, Passages, and Occurences . . . in the upper Germanie, *etc.*—Diatelesma. The Moderne History of the World, *etc.*—Diatelesma. The second part of the Modern History of the World, *etc.*—Diatelesma: The fifth part or number. Comprehending the principall actions of Germany, France, Spaine, and the Neatherlands, *etc.*) 5 pt. *For Nath. Butter, & Nicholas Bourne: London*, 1636. 4°. **9073**. bbb. **2, 2***.
Pt. 2 bears the imprint "printed by E. P. [E. Purslow] for N. Butter, etc."; pt. 3–5 bear the imprint "Printed by T. Harper for N. Butter, etc."

C., N. Psychometry and Thought-Transference, with practical hints for beginners. By N. C. And an introduction. By Henry S. Olcott . . . Second edition. pp. v. 38. *Proprietors of the "Theosophist": Madras*, 1901. 8°. **7410**. f. **18**.
The first edition "by N. C. F. T. S.," is entered under C., N., F.T.S.

C., N. A Saxon Historie, of the Admirable Adventures of Clodoaldus and his Three Children. Translated out of French, by Sr T. H. [i.e. Sir Thomas Hawkins.] [The epistle dedicatory signed: N. C.] pp. 104. *E. P. [E. Purslow] for H. Seile: London,* 1634. 4°. G. **10461.**

—— [Another copy.] 95. b. **21.**
The titlepage is slightly mutilated.

C., N. A Sermon preached at the Ordination of an Elder and Deacons in a Baptized Congregation in London. By N. C. [i.e. Nehemiah Coxe.] pp. 46. *For Tho. Fabian: London,* 1681. 4°. **226.** g. **1.** (**7.**)

—— [Another copy.] **873.** e. **78.**
Imperfect; wanting the last leaf containing the bookseller's advertisement.

C., N.

—— **Vrymoedige aanmerkingen op het berucht werkje [by Baron J. D. van der Capellen, Heer tot den Poll], betyteld: Aan het volk van Nederland. In eenen brief van een' heer te Utrecht aan zynen vriend in s' Gravenhage. [Signed: N. C.] pp. 14. [1781.] 8°. 934. h. 4. (8.)**

C., N., *Citoyen actif.* Départ des filous et des brigands de Paris, controlés sur le visage de la lettre F. Prononcé . . . par N. C. citoyen actif. pp. 8. [*Paris,* 1791.] 8°. F. **369.** (**14.**)

C., N., *Cosmopolitanus.* Philosophia libera, duplici exercitationum decade proposita . . . Authore N. C. Cosmopolitano [i.e. Nathanael Carpenter]. Cui præit paradoxon, ignorantem docto præferendum esse. pp. 220. *Sumptibus Hulsianis: Francofurti,* 1621. 8°. **527.** g. **5.**

C., N., *F.T.S.* Psychometry and Thought-Transference, with practical hints for experiments. By N. C., F.T.S. And an introduction by H. S. Olcott. pp. v. 35. *Proprietors of the "Theosophist": Madras,* 1886. 8°. **8470.** dd. **33.** (**4.**)

C., N., *M.A.* Hell, with the Everlasting Torments thereof asserted . . . By N. C. M.A. pp. vii. 58. *E. Smith: London,* [1750?] 8°. T. **1825.** (**4.**)

C., N., *Monsieur.* Les Femmes sçavantes, ou Bibliothèque des dames, qui traite des sciences qui conviennent aux dames, de la conduite de leurs études, des livres qu'elles peuvent lire, et l'histoire de celles qui ont excellé dans les sciences. Par Monsieur N. C. pp. 348. *Amsterdam,* 1718. 12°. **1031.** e. **7.**

C., N., *Papist.* See GRETTON (Phillips) A Vindication of the Doctrines of the Church of England, in opposition to those of Rome . . . In which the objections of N. C. Papist, against Archbishop Tillotson . . . are particularly considered. [A reply to "A Modest and True Account of the Chief Points in Controversie between the Roman Catholics, and the Protestants," published under the initials N. C. and attributed to Cornelius Nary.] 1725. 8°. **226.** a. **12.**

C . . ., N., *Prêtre de la Congrégation de la Mission.* Dernières paroles et adieux qu'adresse à ses paroissiens N. C . . ., prêtre de la Congrégation de la mission, *etc.* pp. 30. [*Paris,* 1791.] 8°. F. **139.** (**2.**)

C., N., *a Servant of Christ, and of his Church assembled at Orpington in Kent.* A Rule for Ministers and People, whereby they may see how they are engaged one towards another, by Gods word . . . By N. C., a servant of Christ, and of his Church assembled at Orpington in Kent. pp. 12. *For Giles Calvert: London,* 1654. 4°. E. **806.** (**5.**)

C . . . . ., N., *Vrywilliger der Stad Loven.* Categoriek antwoord van N. C . . . . . vrywilliger der stad Loven, aen den Kyzer en Koning Leopold over zyn manifest van den 14 October 1790. pp. 7. [1790.] 8°. **8079.** c. **17.** (**31.**)

C., N., *a Weaver, of London.* The Great Necessity and Advantage of preserving our own Manufacturies; being an answer to a pamphlet [by Sir Josiah Child], intitul'd, The Honour and Advantage of the East-India Trade, &c. By N. C., a Weaver of London. pp. 30. *For T. Newborough: London,* 1697. 8°. **1029.** a. **29.**

C., N. A. The Prince in Calcutta; or Memorials of His Royal Highness the Duke of Edinburgh's visit in December, 1869. Being a collection of descriptive accounts, *etc.* [The editor's preface signed: N. A. C.] pp. 144. *Barham, Hill & Co.: Calcutta,* [1870.] 8°. **9930.** bb. **12.**

C., N. B. *See* STOBO (R.) Memoirs of Major Robert Stobo, *etc.* [The editor's introduction signed: N. B. C., i.e. Neville B. Craig.] 1854. 12°. **10825.** a. **16.**

C., N. D. Le Cabinet du Roy de France, dans lequel il y a trois perles precieuses d'inestimable valeur: par le moyen desquelles Sa Majesté s'en va le premier monarque du monde, & ses suiets du tout soulagez. [The dedicatory epistle headed: "Au Roy de France . . . N. D. C."—i.e. N. Barnaud du Crest—"paix & salut."] pp. 647. 1581. 8°. **C.125.aa.1.**

—— [Another copy.] **284.** a. **7.**

—— [A reissue.] 1582. 8°. **1059.** b. **20.** (**1.**)

C., N. D. Les Causes principales du surhaussement des monnoyes de France, & la maniere d'y remedier, à la conseruation des finances du Roy & du royaume. Presenté à la royne par N. D. C. [i.e. N. de Coquerel.] pp. 59. *Veufue N. Roffet: Paris,* 1612. 8°. **1103.** a. **7.** (**4.**)

C., N. J. Vozes Metricas, e sentidas a' morte do augusto, e senhor rei D. Pedro III . . . Por N. J. C. [i.e. N. J. Columbina.] pp. 8. *Lisboa,* 1786. 4°. **11452.** c. **49.** (**36.**)

C., N. L. *See* HIPPOLYTUS, *Saint, Bishop of the Port of Rome.* Vray discours du regne de l'Antechrist . . . Traduict . . . par N. L. C. [i.e. N. Le Clerc de Juigné.] 1579. 8°. **701.** c. **1.** (**2.**)

C., N. L. *See* SAUVAGE (T. M. F.) and C., N. L. Une Aventure de Faublas, ou le Lendemain d'un bal masqué, comédie-vaudeville . . . par T. Sauvage et N. L. C. [i.e. N. Lecouturier.] 1818. 8°. **11738.** n. **4.** (**2.**)

C., N. L., *Ancien directeur auxiliaire des subsistances militaires.* Pétition au Sénat sur l'administration militaire principalement au point de vue de la justification des dépenses et des finances. [Signed: N. L. C.] pp. iv. 66. *Nantes,* 1867. 8°. **8824.** dd. **41.** (**2.**)

C., N. L., *Ferrarese.* Indice manuale delle cose più rimarcabili in pittura, scultura, architettura, della città e borghi di Ferrara, compilato da N. L. C. Ferrarese [i.e. L. N. Cittadella]. pp. 175. *Ferrara,* 1844. 16°. **795.** a. **43.**

C. (NN. S.) *See* NN., *S.C.*

C., O. The Conduct and Character of Count Nicholas Serini, Protestant Generalissimo of the Auxiliaries in Hungary . . . With his parallels Scanderbeg & Tamberlain, *etc* [The preface signed: O. C. With engraved plates, including portraits.] pp. 168. *For Sam. Speed: London* 1664. 12°. G. **1328**

C., O.

—— An Elegy on the Usurper O. C. [i.e. Oliver Cromwell] by the author of Absalom and Achitophel, published to shew the loyalty and integrity of the poet. [With a postscript signed: J. D., purporting to be by John Dryden, but in fact consisting of satirical verses against him.] *See* D., J C. **20.** f. **6.** (**12.**

O. Everybody his own Private Secretary. By O. C. pp. 29. *Richard Bentley: London*, 1870. 8°. **7945**. e. **10**.

O. Reminiscences of Cambridge Life. By O. C. [i.e. Alfred H. Lawrence.] pp. viii. 176. *Printed for private circulation: London*, 1889. 8°. **8364**. aa. **57**.

O. Runæ Medelpadicæ ab importuna crisi breviter vindicatæ, auctore O. C. [i.e. Olof Celsius, the Elder.] pp. 36. *Upsaliæ*, 1726. 4°. **T.2218.(8.)**

O. The Unrepealed Sentence. [A religious tract. Signed: O. C.] pp. 8. *W. Hunt & Co.: London*, 1875.] 8°. **4422**. f. **1**. **(15.)**

O. A. En Blick i universum. Skapelse-etyder af O. A. C. [i.e. O. A. Carlstén.] pp. 110. *Stockholm*, 1864. 8°. **8705**. cc. **27**. **(4.)**

O. B. The Legend of Naworth. By O. B. C. [i.e. Owen B. Cole.] [In verse.] pp. 20. *James M'Glashan: Dublin*, 1846. 8°. **11645**. f. **46**. **(5.)**

O. B. The Raid of St. Armand, a Canadian eclogue. [Signed: O. B. C.] pp. 8. [*Portishead*, 1870?] 8°. **011650**. k. **90**. **(4.)**

O. D. Nella fausta circostanza del maritaggio di Alessandro Maria Frattini di Roma e Giuseppa Catrani di Tiferno a dimostrazione di vero gradimento ai novelli sposi uno de' più prossimi agnati O. D. C. [i.e. O. D. Catrani.] [Verses by various authors.] pp. 27. *Roma*, 1827. 8°. **899**. d. **12**. **(10.)**

O. H. Family Prayers for Four Weeks. By O. H. C. pp. viii. 172. *J. Nisbet & Co.: London*, 1901. 8°. **3457**. ddd. **23**.

O. K. When All was Young. A series of childhood pictures. By O. K. C. pp. 116. *A. H. Stockwell: London*, 1919. 8°. **010855**. cc. **16**.

O. M. *See* Madison, *Wisconsin.—State Library of Wisconsin.* Catalogue of the State Library of Wisconsin, 1872. [The preface signed: O. M. C., i.e. Obadiah M. Conover.] 1872. 8°. **11904**. f. **29**.

O. P. Einige Worte über die nützlichsten und dringendsten Land- und Wasser-Strassen in Ungarn, zur Erleichterung der Ausfuhr. Von O. P. C. [i.e. Baron C. Pidoll von Quintenbach.] Zweite verbesserte und vermehrte Auflage, nebst einer Uebersichts-Charte. pp. 46. *Wien*, 1844. 8°. **1391**. f. **28**. **(3.)**

O. R. B. A Few Remarks on Spiritualism. By O. R. B. C. pp. 9. *Waterlow & Sons: London*, [1920.] 8°. **8633**. bb. **10**.

O. S. Chimes of Song. (Random rhymes.) By O. S. C. pp. 93. *Charles Hallett: Bath*, 1889. 12°. **11648**. aaa. **57**.

O. T. Team-Training and Teamcraft. With a chapter on Ashburton Shield teams. By O. T. C. pp. v. 102. *W. W. Greener: London*, [1914.] 8°. **07906**. de. **64**.

P. *See* C., A., and C., P. The Tyrannical Usurpation of the Independent Cloak over the Episcopal Gown. 1663. *s. sh.* fol. **C.121.g.9.(8.)**

P. *See* Canzun. La Canzun davart il senn [by J. C. F. von Schiller], vertida en Romonsch de la surselva tras P. C. [i.e. P. Corai.] [1850?] 8°. **885**. d. **28**.

P. *See* Dinika. Dinika ndRatiahavana mianakavy. [The editor's preface signed: P. C.] 1875. 8°. **4371**. aa. **22**.

C., P. *See* Drummond (William) *of Hawthornden.* Poems, *etc.* [The editor's preface signed: P. C., i.e. Peter Cunningham.] 1852. 8°. **11607**. c. **10**.

C., P. *See* Letters. Three Severall Letters of Great Importance. The first [signed: P. C.], containing the brave exploits of the Lyme Men at Axmister, *etc.* 1644. 4°. **E. 21**. **(6.)**

C * * * *, **P** * *. *See* Locke (John) *the Philosopher.* [*Thoughts concerning Education.*] De l'éducation des enfans. Traduit . . . Par P * * C * * * * [i.e. P. Coste]. 1695. 8°. **722**. b. **32**.

C., P. *See* Malsburg (E. F. G. O. von der) *Baron.* Ernst Friedrich Georg Otto's von der Malsburg poetischer Nachlass und Umrisse aus seinem innern Leben. Von P. C. [i.e. P. von Callenberg.] 1825. 8°. **11521**. d. **17**.

C., P. *See* Modernist. Letters to His Holiness Pope Pius x. By a Modernist. [With an introduction signed: P. C.] 1910. 8°. **3942**. df. **15**.

C., P. *See* Riquetti (H. G.) *Count de Mirabeau.* Esprit de Mirabeau, *etc.* [The editor's preface signed: P. C., i.e. P. J. B. P. Chaussard.] 1797. 8°. **1141**. c. **19**.

C., P. *See* Tentzel (A.) Andreæ Tenzelii . . . medicinisch-philosophisch- und sympathetische Schrifften . . . Zusammen heraus gegeben von P. C. 1725. 8°. **1474**. aaa. **9**. **(2.)**

C., P. *See* Villiers (P. de) *Abbé.* [Pensées et réflexions sur les égaremens des hommes.] Reflections on Men's Prejudices against Religion . . . Translated from the French. [The dedication signed: P. C.] 1709. 8°. **4376**. ee. **3**.

C., P. *See* Waller (John T.) *Rector of Kilcoman.* The Mass. [Letters to the "Limerick Chronicle," in answer to letters signed: P. C.] 1882. 8°. **3939**. de. **14**.

C., P. Un Ancien de la Cambre. A travers l'Afrique équatoriale. [The dedication signed: P. C., i.e. Puck Chaudoir.] pp. 364. *Liége*, [1905.] 8°. **010097**. g. **45**.

—— Un Ancien de la Cambre. Au pays des pagodes. [The dedication signed: P. C., i.e. Puck Chaudoir.] pp. 352. *Liége*, [1905.] 8°. **010058**. e. **39**.

C., P. Brief van een heer uit Utrecht aan zyn vrind te Amsterdam. Behelzende verscheide byzonderheeden betreklyk tot een vast Corps-de-Marine: waarin beweezen wordt, dat 't zelve onontbeerlyk is ter dekkinge van de Republicq, *etc.* [Signed: P. C.] pp. 20. 1784. 8°. **934**. h. **15**. **(9.)**

C., P. Celebration of Burns's Birthday at Mr. Hastie's. [An account of "Burns's punch-bowl." Signed: P. C.] [*London?* 1865.] 8°. **10856**. c. **18**.

C., P. Complainte au sujet de Georges Cadoudal, *etc.* *See* Cadoudal (G.) Vie privée de Georges Cadoudal, *etc.* [1804.] 12°. **F. 1302**. **(1.)**

C., P. Description de la façade et de l'intérieur de la cathédrale de Milan. [The preface signed: P. C. With folding plates.] pp. 61. *Milan*, 1844. 8°. **7814.a.28.**

C . . . ., **P** . . . . . Entretien politique sur le meilleur des gouvernemens. [The dedication signed: P . . . . . C . . . .] pp. 162. *Paris*, an XI [1803]. 8°. **F. 1107**. **(4.)**

C., P. O Futuro das Ordens Religiosas em Portugal. Offerecido ao clero portuguez por um presbytero vimaranense. [The introduction signed: P. C., i.e. C. J. de Mello.] pp. 63. *Braga*, 1858. 8°. **4071**. aa. **13**.

C., P. Guerra Eterna á los Serviles. [Signed: P. C.] no. 4, 7, 8. *México*, 1823. fol. **9770**. k. **7**. (**87**.)

—— *See* Fernández Aguado (M.) Guerra contra la Guerra Eterna á los Serviles en su num. 4. 1823. *s. sh.* fol. **9770**. k. **7**. (**88**.)

C., P. Hvorledes er det fat med det juridiske Studium, og hvad kan der gjøres derved? Nogle Bemærkninger af P. C. pp. 32. *Kjøbenhavn*, 1861. 8º. **5705**. aaa. **9**.

C., P. Las Ilustres Americanas. De la influencia de las mujeres en la sociedad; y acciones ilustres de varias americanas. [Signed: P. C.] pp. 59. *Caracas*, 1826. 8º. **10882**. aa. **34**.

C., P. A Letter to the Author of the Defence of the Bishop of Chichester's Sermon upon King Charles's Martyrdom. [Signed: P. C.] pp. 32. *T. Payne: London*, 1732. 8º. E. **2024**. (**4**.)

—— The second edition. pp. 32. *T. Payne: London*, 1732. 8º. **4106**. c. **58**. (**6**.)

—— A Letter to the Author of the Vindication of Mr. Nation's Sermon: in which the importance of faith, in matters of religion, and particularly as to the doctrine of the Deity of our Saviour, is consider'd: and the Assembly of the United Ministers of Devon and Cornwall is farther defended. To which is added, a second letter to Mr. Nation, in answer to his vindication of himself. By P. C. pp. 70. *London; Aaron Tozer: Exon*, 1732. 8º. **4225**. bb. **9**.

—— The second edition. In which is added a postscript, being a 3d letter to Mr. Nation, *etc.* *Aaron Tozer: Exon*, 1732. 8º. **4225**. aaa. **12**.
Imperfect; containing the postscript only.

—— Charity and Sincerity Defended; in a reply to Mr. P. C.'s Letter to the Author of the Vindication of Mr. Nation's Sermon, *etc.* [Signed: M. T.] 1732. 8º. *See* T., M. **4474**. f. **90**.

—— A Letter to the Right Reverend the Lord Bishop of Chichester. Occasion'd by his Lordship's sermon on January 30. 1732. The second edition. [Signed: P. C.] pp. 30. *T. Payne: London*, 1732. 8º. **4106**. c. **58**. (**5**.)

—— The third edition. pp. 30. *T. Payne: London*, 1732. 8º. **1104**. b. **33**.

—— *See* P., C. A Defence of the Bishop of Chichester's Sermon upon K. Charles's Martyrdom. In answer to Mr. P. C.'s letter. 1732. 8º. **4474**. e. **86**.

C., P. Mutatus Polemo [by A. B., Novice]. Revised, by some epistolary observations of a Country Minister, a friend to the Presbyterian Government [signed: P. C.] . . . Whereunto is annexed a large Tractate, discussing the causes betwixt Presbyter, Scotland and Independent, England. As it was sent to the Reviser, and penned by C. H. Esquire. pp. 56. *For Robert White: London*, 1650. 4º. E. **616**. (**3**.)

C., P. Notizie della vita e degli studj di Pietro Verri che precedono le di lui opere economiche nella raccolta degli economisti italiani di P. C. [i.e. P. Custodi.] pp. 62. *Milano*, 1804. 8º. **10631**. d. **31**. (**2**.)

C., P. Nouveau conducteur de l'étranger à Bordeaux, contenant la description des monuments et curiosités du département de la Gironde, l'itinéraire de Bordeaux à Royan et à Arcachon. Par P. C. [i.e. P. Chaumas.] Quatre gravures et plan de Bordeaux, *etc.* pp. ii. 78. *Bordeaux*, 1861. 12º. **10173**. aaa. **45**.

—— Nouvelle édition. pp. ii. 80. *Bordeaux*, 1866. 12º. **10169**. a. **10**.

C., P. P. C. Check-Figure System. [Signed: P. C.] pp. [*G. W. Choppin: London*, 1934.] 8º. **8533**. aa.

C., P. Parole del Balilla ai Soffioni. [A satire, in ve Signed: P. C.] [*Genoa*, 1847?] *s. sh.* fol. **804**. k. **13**. (**1**

C., P. Pyrologia curiosa & experimentalis, i.e. Ignis scr nium exactum . . . Auctore P. C. [i.e. P. Casa pp. 293 [393]. *Sumptibus J. H. Laurer: Hano* 1689. 4º. **538**. c.

C., P. Rhapsodies mirifiques. [Verses.] pp. 139. *Pa* 1875. 12º. **11482**. e.

C., P. A Short and Impartial View of the Manner Occasion of the Scots Colony's Coming away from Dar In a letter to a person of quality. [Signed: P. C., Philo-Caledon, pseudonym of Andrew Fletcher of Saltou pp. 40. [*Sold by J. Vallange & J. Wardlaw: Edinbur* 1699. 4º. **8245**. bb.

C., P.

—— Simples remarques sur la première édition des Cha et chansons populaires de la France. (Extrait du Bull du bibliophile.) [Signed: P. C.] pp. 61. *Pa* 1909. 8º. Hirsch **19**
One of an edition of 100 *copies.*

C., P. The Three Establishments concerning the Pay of Sea-Officers, *etc.* [The preface signed: P. C. Wit folding table.] pp. xxviii. 50. *London*, 1705. 8º. **534**. b. **23**.

—— [Another copy.] E. **2188**.

C., P. A Visitation of Love unto All People. [Sign P. C., i.e. Priscilla Cotton.] pp. 4. *For Thomas Simmo London*, 1661. 4º. **4152**. f. **4**. (

C., P. Vite dei romani pontefici da S. Pietro fino all' regnante, tratte dai migliori autori con annotazi [The dedication signed: P. C.] 2 tom. *Vene* 1827, 29. 8º. **4855**. c.

C., P., and **C.,** D. A Proposal Humbly offer'd to the C sideration of the Commons of England . . . for raisin farther Supply towards the erecting and maintenance the intended College or Hospital at Greenwich, (A Proposal for regulating cars and carts, &c.—By P. and D. C.) [*London*, 1694?] *s. sh.* fol. **816**. m. **7**. (**1**
The signature D. C. has been altered in MS. *to G. D.*

—— [Another edition.] [*London*, 1694?] *s. sh.* fol. **816**. m. **7**. (**1**

C., P., and **GUYOT DE MERVILLE** (Michel) Roman, comédie en trois actes en vers. Par Mrs P. [i.e. Procope Couteaux] et G. de Merville. pp. 124. *Paris*, 1746. 8º. **164**. e.

C., P., and **K.,** S. An Address, &c. (To the Society Baptized Believers, meeting in the Black Friars, Can bury.) [Signed: P. C., S. K.] pp. 15. *Thomas Sm Canterbury*, 1784. 8º. **4139**. c.

C., P., *Canonico.* Analisi del contratto di denaro dat frutto, e conciliazione delle opinioni sulla giustizia medesimo, del canonico P. C. Pubblicata da al difensori del dogma cattolico intorno al mutuo. pp. 2 *Venezia*, 1841. 8º. **1391**. d.

C . . . . . ., P . . . ., *Citoyen de Millau.* Ode aux Fran sur leur projet de descente en Angleterre; par P . C . . . . . ., citoyen de Millau, *etc.* pp. 14. *Mil* an 12 [1804]. 8º. F. **551**.

., P., *Dr. of Divinity and Midwifery.* The Exaltation of Christmas Pye. As it was delivered in a preachment at Ely House. By P. C. Dr. of Divinity and Midwifery. pp. 11. 1659. 4°. **12316.** c. **52.**

— [Another copy.] **698.** g. **14.** **(10.)**
Imperfect; wanting all after p. 8.

., P., *I.* *See* SAVONAROLA (G.) [*Two or more Works.*] La Simplicité de la vie chrétienne, et quelques autres œuvres spiritüelles . . . traduites en françois par un pere de la Compagnie de Jesus. [The translator's dedication signed: P. C., I., i.e. P. Chahu.] 1672. 12°. **220.** a. **6.**

., P., *M.D., a Lover of Religion and his Country.* An Exact Collection of Many Wonderful Prophesies relating to the Government of England, &c. since the first year of the reign of King James I. to this present time. All of which have been truly fulfilled and accomplished . . . By P. C. M.D. a lover of religion and his country. [In verse.] pp. 16. *J. Baker: London,* 1714. 4°. **164.** n. **1.**

, P., *Merc. Lond.* Tunbrigialia. P. C. Merc. Lond. [i.e. Peter Causton] ad G. F. [A Latin poem. The author's name is formed by the initial letters of the first twelve verses.] 1686. 8°. *See* CAUSTON (Peter) **1213.** f. **42.**

., P., *Mr.* *See* CHOMEL (P. J. B.) Réponse de M. Chomel . . . à deux lettres écrites par Mr P. C. [i.e. P. Collet] sur la botanique. [1697.] 8°. **B. 95. (2.)**

., P., *Mr.* *See* NATION (William) A Vindication of Mr. Nation's Sermon, in a letter to Mr. P. C. 1732. 8°. **4474.** dd. **42.**

— *See* P., C. A Defence of the Bishop of Chichester's Sermon upon K. Charles's Martyrdom. In answer to Mr. P. C.'s letter. 1732. 8°. **4474.** e. **86.**

, P., *Mr.* Entretiens sur la clôture religieuse. Par Mr P. C. (Collet.) pp. 148. 1697. 12°. *See* COLLET (Pierre), *Prieur de St. Edmé.* **1351.** a. **27.**

, P., *Officier de l'Armée française.* La Puissance maritime de l'Angleterre. Par P. C. officier de l'Armée française. Avec 18 cartes. pp. vii. 158. *Paris,* 1887. 8°. **8807.** ee. **31.**

., P., *Procureur général des Missions de la Chine, de la Compagnie de Jésus.* Histoire d'une Dame chrétienne de la Chine (Madame Candide Hiu petitte fille du Grand Chancellier de la Chine). Où par occasion les usages de ces peuples, l'établissement de la religion, les manieres des missionnaires, & les exercices de pieté des nouveaux chrétiens sont expliquez. [Signed: P. C. Procureur general des Missions de la Chine, de la Compagnie de Jesus, i.e. P. Couplet. Translated from the Latin by P. J. d'Orléans.] pp. 152. *E. Michallet: Paris,* 1688. 12°. **862.** h. **26.**

— [Another copy.] **4985.** a. **30.**

, P., *Prof. Dr.* Symbola Renati. Eine Lebens-Erinnerung. 2. Auflage. [The preface signed: Prof. Dr. P. C., i.e. S., afterwards P. S. Cassel.] pp. xvi. 72. *Berlin,* 1870. 16°. **11528.** a. **11.**

, P. DE. *See* KALBOS (A.) *Καλβου και Χρηστοπουλου λυρικα, etc.* (Odes nouvelles de Kalvos . . . traduites par l'auteur des Helléniennes, P. de C. [i.e. J. P. G. Pauthier.]) 1826. 12°. **1160.** d. **12.**

C., P. A.

—— *See* BAUDERON DE SÉNECÉ (A.) Lettre de Clément Marot à Monsieur de ***, touchant ce qui s'est passé, à l'arrivée de Jean-Baptiste de' Lulli, aux Champs-Élysées. [The editor's preface signed: P. A. C., i.e. Paul Antoine Cap.] 1825. 8°. Hirsch **3586.**

C., P. A. Antwort auff Luthers Sendtbrieff, geschribenn gen Augspurg an den Cardinal, Ertzbischoffen zu Mentz Churfürsten *7c.* P. A. C. [i.e. Paulus Bachmann.] M.D.XXX. [With a preface by J. Dobneck.] [*A. Weissenhorn? Augsburg?*] 1530. 4°. **3905.** ee. **103.**

—— Ein Maulstreich dem Lutherischen lügenhafftigen weyt auffgespertem Rachẽ, das Closterlebẽ zulestern vñ schendẽ. Itzlichem Christlicher warheit liebhaber, nütz-lich zu lesen. P. A. C. [i.e. Paulus Bachmann.] *Gedruckt durch W. Stöckel: Dressden,* 1534. 4°. **3906.** e. **112.**

C., P. A.

—— Fifty Years with the Cambridge University Press, 1882–1932. By P. A. C. pp. 34. *University Press: Cambridge,* 1932. 8°. **011908.** de. **42.**
Printed for private circulation.

C., P. A. Operetta d'ordinanze quadre di terreno, & di gente, & altre, con alcuni quesiti intorno all'ordinanze diuerse. Di P. A. C. [i.e. P. A. Cataldi.] pp. 16. *S. Bonomi: Bologna,* 1618. 4°. **8534.** bb. **25.** **(5.)**

C., P. A. Gli Ostrogoti in San Vito al Tagliamento. Frammento primo di cronaca contemporanea per P. A. C. [i.e. A. Cicuto.] pp. 44. *Padova,* 1869. 8°. **7708.** d. **26.** **(13.)**

C., P. A. Principios de Derecho de Jentes Real i Positivo. (Reimpresión del largo artículo de la "Gaceta mercantil" de Buenosaires . . . i de la "Carta particular" que le sirve de comentario.) [By various authors. The editor's address signed: P. A. C.] pp. 24. *Bogoga* [sic], 1847. 8°. **8179.** b. **67.** **(2.)**

C., P. A. Tauola del leuar del sole et del mezo di per ciascun giorno dell'anno. Calculata l'Anno 1587. alla latitudine della Città di Bologna da P. A. C. [i.e. P. A. Cataldi.] 1587. *s. sh.* fol. *See* EPHEMERIDES. **1882.** c. **1.** **(166.)**

C, P. A.,** *Theat. Ord.* Betrachtungen über die Nachtmalsbulle. Aus dem Italiänischen des P. A. C**. Theat. Ord. [i.e. C. A. Pilati di Tassulo] übersetzt. pp. viii. 346. *Freyberg* [*Zürich*], 1770. 8°. **5017.** aa. **19.**

C., P. C. *See* CONSOLAZIUN. Consolatiun della olma devotiusa, *etc.* [The editor's preface signed: P. C. C.] 1731. 12°. **885.** i. **1.**

—— —— 1731. 12°. **885.** h. **16.**

—— —— 1749. 12°. **885.** g. **18.**

C., P. C.

—— Carroll Atwood Wilson, 1886–1947. [Signed: P. C. C.] pp. 17. *Bibliographical Society of America: New York,* 1948. 8°. **10891.** b. **38.**

C., P. D. Anticoton, ou Refutation de la lettre declaratoire du pere Cotton. Liure ou est prouué que les Jesuites sont coulpables & autheurs du parricide execrable commis en la personne du roy . . . Henry IIII, *etc.* [The dedication signed: P. D. C. Generally attributed to C. de Plaix, but also to Jean Du Bois, P. Du Coignet, and P. Du Moulin.] pp. 56. [*Lyons?*] 1610. 8°. **1192.** g. **9.** **(1.)**

—— [Another edition.] pp. 74. 1610. 8°. **860.** d. **9.** **(1.)**

C., P. D.

—— [Another copy.] **1192**. g. **9**. **(13.)**
Imperfect; wanting the last leaf containing the errata.

—— [A reissue.] [1611.] *See* Jesuits. Recueil de plusieurs escrits, *etc.* 1611, *etc.* 8°. **860**. d. **10**. **(3.)**

—— Nouvelle édition, augmentée de quelques remarques, et précédée d'une dissertation historique et critique sur ce fameux ouvrage. pp. 148. *La Haye*, 1738. 8°. **860**. d. **20**. **(1.)**

—— [Another issue.] Anticoton . . . Nouvelle edition, *etc.* pp. 148. *In:* Rasiel de Selva (H.) *pseud.* Histoire de l'admirable Dom Inigo de Guipuscoa. tom. 2. 1738. 8°. **1371**. c. **3**.

—— [A reissue.] Anti-Cotton: nouvelle edition . . . précédée d'une dissertation historique et critique, *etc.* pp. 169. *In:* Rasiel de Selva (H.) Histoire de l'admirable Dom Inigo de Guipuscoa, *etc.* tom. 2. 1758. 8°. **686**. d. **32**.

—— Anti-Coton, or a Refutation of Cottons Letter Declaratorie: lately directed to the Queene Regent, for the Apologizing of the Iesuites Doctrine, touching the killing of Kings. A Booke, in which it is proued that the Iesuites are guiltie, and were the Authors of the late execrable Parricide, committed vpon the Person of the French King, Henry the fourth, of happy memorie. [The dedication signed: P. D. C.] To which is added a Supplication of the Vniuersitie of Paris, for the preuenting of the Iesuites opening their schooles among them . . . Both translated . . . by G. H. [i.e. George Hakewill?] Together with the Translators animaduersions vpon Cottons Letter. pp. 82. *T. S. [T. Snodham] for Richard Boyle: London,* 1611. 4°. **4091**. f. **9**.

—— Anti-Coton, or a Refutation of Cottons Letter Declaratorie, *etc.* pp. 76. *T. S. [T. Snodham] for Richard Boyle: London,* 1611. 4°. **108**. d. **22**.

—— Anti-Cotton: or, a Refutation of Cotton's Letter Declaratory . . . To which is added a Large New Preface and Postscript, fully proving the Doctrine of Murdering Kings to be the Jesuits Doctrine, and vindicating Anti-Cotton from all Objections. pp. xvi. 69. 62. *Randall Taylor: London,* 1689. 4°. **860**. k. **22**. **(3.)**

—— [Another copy.] Anti-Cotton: or, a Refutation of Cotton's Letter Declaratory, *etc.* 1689. 4°. **108**. d. **23**.
Imperfect; wanting the "Vindication."

—— Anti-Coton . . . oft wederlegginghe vanden verclaringbrief van Pater Cotton, *etc.* *See* Cotton (Pierre) Brief dienende tot verclaringe van de leere der Vaderen Jesuijten, *etc.* 1610. 4°. T. **2421**. **(23, 24.)**

—— *See* Montgommery (L. de) *Seigneur de Courbouzon.* Le Fleau d'Aristogiton. Ou Contre le calomniateur des Peres Iesuistes, sous le tiltre d'Anticoton. 1610. 8°. **860**. d. **9**. **(2.)**

—— —— 1610. 8°. **1192**. g. **11**. **(6.)**

—— *See* Montgommery (L. de) *Seigneur de Courbouzon.* Den Aristogitonschen dorsch-vlegel, oft Teghen den lasteraer der vaderen Jesuyten, onder den titel van Anti-Coton, *etc.* 1610. 4°. T. **2421**. **(25.)**

—— Response apologetique à l'Anticoton et à ceux de sa suite . . . Par vn père de la Compagnie de Iesus [i.e. F. Bonald? or P. Cotton?] pp. 320. *M. Gaillard: Paris,* 1610. 8°. **1192**. g. **11**. **(13.)**

C., P. D.

—— Seconde edition, reueuë & augmentée par l'authe[ur]. pp. 283. *I. Cottereau: Paris,* 1611. 8°. **860**. b. **16**. (

—— *See* H., D. Le Contr'assassin, ou Response [à] l'apologie des Iesuites [i.e. to the "Response apo[lo]getique à l'Anticoton"], faite par un pere de la co[m]pagnie de Iesus, *etc.* 1612. 8°. **860**. b.

C., P. D., *Gent.* Complementum Fortunatarum Insularu[m] P. ii. sive Galathea vaticinans. Being part of an Epith[a]lamium upon the auspicious match of the Most Puissa[nt] . . . Charles ii. and the Most Illustrious Catharin[e] Infanta of Portugal. With a description of the Fortuna[te] Islands. Written originally in French, by P. D. C. Gen[t.] [i.e. P. D. Cardonnel] and since translated by him in Lat[in] and English. With the translations also of the Descri[p]tion of S. James's Park, and the late Fight at S. Luca[r] by Mr. Ed. Waller. The Panegyrick of Charles ii. [b]y Mr. Dreyden. And other peeces, *etc.* [With engrav[ed] portraits.] 4 pt. *Printed by W. G.: London,* 1662. 8°. G. **1150**

—— [Another copy.] **11474**. b.
Imperfect; wanting the two additional leaves at the e[nd] and the portraits, which are replaced by a portrait of Phi[li]bert, Count Grammont. With a cutting from the Europe[an] Magazine, by Francis Allison, describing the book.

—— [Another copy.] G. **1150**
Imperfect; wanting the two additional leaves at the en[d]. Wanting also the two original portraits, for which two othe[rs] are substituted.

C., P. D., *M.* Coup d'œil utile, s'il fixe l'attention de m[es] concitoyens, par M. P. D. C. pp. 18. [*Paris,*] 1788. 8° **934**. c. **6**. (

—— [Another copy.] Coup-d'œil utile s'il fixe l'attention [de] mes concitoyens. 1788. 8°. R. **187**. (

C., P. D., *one of the Gentlemen of His Majesty's Privy Chamb[er].* *See* Le Fèvre (N.) *Chemist.* A Compendious Body [of] Chymistry . . . Rendred into English by P. D. C., [etc.] 1664. 4°. **43**. d.

—— —— 1670. 4°. **1142**. h.

C., P. E. Du rôle des femmes dans l'agricultu[re]. Esquisse d'un institut rural féminin par P. E. C. [i.e. P. E. Cazeaux.] pp. 196. *Paris,* 1869. 12°. **1145**. b.

C., P. E. Gespräch in dem Reiche der Todten über die Bi[bel] und Talmud . . . zusammen getragen von . . . P. E. (Christfels), *etc.* 1737. 4°. *See* Christfelss (P. E.) **4033**. b.

C., P. E. P. F. V. D. G. Consejo de Guerra Celebrado en Día 27. de Septiembre de 1808, *etc.* [Satirical vers[es] against the French, signed: P. E. P. F. V. D. G. C.] [1808.] *s. sh.* fol. **L.R.21.a.17.(38.**

C., P. F. Amici della repubblica nemigi [*sic*] d'Ital[ia]. [Signed: P. F. C. With an address to the citizens [of] Milan by Filippo Villani.] *Genova,* [1848.] *s. sh.* fol. **804**. k. **13**. **(25**

C., P. F. Eine militairische Denkschrift von P. F. C. [i.e. Frederick Charles Nicholas, Prince of Prussia] v[on] französischer Seite kritisch beleuchtet—im Spectate[ur] militaire—[by F. de La Fruston]; für die Kamerad[en] aller deutschen Armeen verdeutscht und mit Anmerkung[en] versehen von dem Verfasser der Schrift: "Die französisc[he] Armee auf dem Exercirplatze und im Felde." pp. vii. 6 *Berlin,* 1862. 8°. **8828**. f. **17**. (

C., P. F. Visita del Re di Danimarca a Firenze nel 1708. [Signed: P. F. C.] pp. 88. *Firenze*, 1886. 8°. **10761**. h. **7**.

C., P. G. S. D. L. Les Efforts et assauts eaictz [*sic*] et donnez à Lusignē la vigile de Noel, par Monsieur le duc de Mōpensier, *etc.* [In verse. Signed: P. G. S. D. L. C., i.e. the Sieur de la Coste?] 1575. 8°. **285**. a. **37**. (**2**.)

C., P. H. B. SS. Patrum, et Ecclesiae Doctorum de Passione D. N. I. C. sententiae selectissimae . . . collectae a P. H. B. C., *etc.* pp. 864. *Styrae*, 1769. 8°. **4227**. b. **16**.

C., P. I. L. B. *See* LIEFDE-VLAMMEN. Goddelyke liefde-vlammen . . . Af-gebeeld door . . . Koopere figuuren. Neffens haar verzen, aanmerkingen, gezangen, en ziel-zuchtingen. Ten meerendeel door P. I. L. B. C. [i.e. J. Luyken?] 1711. 8°. **12305**. aaa. **18**.

C., P. J. Philopatriana, den Zeeuwschen burgervaderen toegewyd, gedurende de onlusten onder eenige landlieden in Walcheren ontstaan. Tweede druk. [Signed: P. J. C.] pp. 11. *Amsterdam*, [1778.] 8°. **934**. g. **17**. (**31**.)

C., P. L. *See* BACON (Francis) *Viscount St. Albans*. [*Selections*.] Verulamiana . . . To which is prefixed a life of the author. By the editor. [The editor's preface signed: P. L. C., i.e. P. L. Courtier.] 1803. 12°. **8407**. d. **21**.

C., P. L. *See* LANGLE DE CARY (F. L. A. M. de) Souvenirs de commandement, *etc.* [The editor's preface signed: P. L. C., i.e. P. L. J. C. M. de Langle de Cary?] 1935. 8°. **09079**. bb. **13**.

C., P. L. C. L. D. Lettres sur la Suisse . . . P. L. C. L. D. C. [i.e. par le comte Léopold de Curti.] pt. 1, 2. *Altona*, 1797. 8°. **1428**. i. **7**.
No more published.

C., P. M. *See* GERTRUDE, *Saint*, called *the Great, of the Convent of Helffede*. Preces Gertrudianæ . . . Libellus . . . a quodam B. Gertrudi addictissimo sacerdote compilatus. [The dedication signed: P. M. C.] 1706. 12°. **4400**. ff. **40**.

C., P. M. Notes on Mess Management. By P. M. C. pp. 28. *Simpkin, Marshall & Co.: London*, 1899. 8°. **8831**. ee. **39**.
The title on the cover reads: "Hints on Mess Management."

C., P. M. L., *au R.D.* *See* L., P. M., *au R.D.C.*

C., P. M. L. M. D. Jeux d'esprit et de memoire, ou Conversations plaisantes avec des personnes les plus distinguées de l'état . . . Avec quelques particularitez qui se sont passées sous le règne de Loüis le Grand. P. M. L. M. D. C. [i.e. par Monsieur le marquis de Châtres, P. J. Brodeau.] pp. 196. *Frédéric le Jeune: Cologne*, 1694. 8°. **012314**. e. **25**.

C . . . . . ., P . . P . . . . ., c.-d . . . . . I . . . . -K . . . ., *à K* . . . .

—— Observations grammaticales et morales sur Figaro . . . précédées d'un Discours à MM. les comédiens ordinaires du Roi, et suivies de quelques Réflexions sur les trente volumes des Œuvres de Voltaire, livrés au public par M. de Beaumarchais. (Parodie du vaudeville de Figaro.) [Signed: P . . P . . . . . C . . . . . ., c.-d . . . . . I . . . .-K . . . ., à K . . . .] pp. xvi. 48. 32. *Du séjour de la Vérité, chez l'Ingénu* [*Paris*], 1785. 8°. F. **564**. (**4**.)

C., P. S., *delle S.P.* Annotazioni sincere dell' autore dell' Elogio premiato di Amerigo Vespucci, per una seconda edizione. [Signed: P. S. C. delle S. P., i.e. Padre S. Canovai delle Scuole Pie.] pp. xvi. [*Florence*, 1790?] 4°. **10630**. aaa. **19**.

C., P. U. D. *See* P., M. J. M. C. E. Primeiros Ensaios para o Exame Imparcial da Questão . . . Se a Companhia geral da agricultura das vinhas do Alto Douro he ou não util que exista? . . . por M. J. M. C. E. P., P. U. D. C., *etc.* [1850?] 8°. **7074**. dd. **22**.

C., P. V. B. Le Karesme et mœurs du politique, où il est amplement discouru de sa maniere de viure, de son Estat & Religion. Par P. V. B. C. pp. 20. *Par Pierre-des-Hayes: Paris*, 1589. 8°. **3900**. aa. **47**. (**9**.)

C., P. V. D. P. Narratio in qua tractatur de apparitione, abjuratione, cōversione, & synaxi Illustrissimæ Principis Carlottæ Catharinæ Trimolliæ Principissæ Condęi . . . P. V. D. P. C. [i.e. J. Teixeira?] (Narratio quarta.) pp. 62. *See* TEIXEIRA (José) Rerum ab Henrici . . . majoribus gestarum, epitome, *etc.* 1598. 8°. **521**. a. **36**. (**2**.)

—— [Another edition.] pp. 53. *See* GARRETA (R.) La Conversion de la princesse de Condé à Rouen, *etc.* 1901. 8°. Ac. **8939/43**.

C., P. V. DE M. E. *See* M. E C., P. V. de.

C., P. V. P. *See* TORRES BOLLO (D. de) La Nouuelle histoire du Perou, *etc.* [The translator's preface signed: P. V. P. C., i.e. P. V. Palma Cayet.] 1604. 8°. **10480**. a. **19**.

C., P. W. Review of the d'Hauteville Case: recently argued and determined in the Court of General Sessions, for the City and County of Philadelphia. By a member of the Boston Bar. Reprinted from . . . the Law Reporter. [The advertisement signed: P. W. C., i.e. Peleg W. Chandler.] pp. 44. *Weeks, Jordan & Co.: Boston*, 1841. 8°. **6616**. de. **2**. (**8**.)

C. (PE.) Vues utiles à l'économie publique, à l'établissement de diverses manufactures, & à l'augmentation du commerce de la Provence & de Marseille. [The dedication signed: Pe. C., i.e. Pierre Conte.] pp. 47. [*Marseilles*, 1780.] 8°. **8207**. e. **2**. (**1**.)

C. * * * (PETRUS) Institutiones theologiæ, scholasticæ, quas ad usum seminariorum è propriis suis prælectionibus contraxit Petrus, C. * * * [i.e. Pierre Collet] . . . Editio septima. 2 tom. *Parisiis*, 1771. 12°. **1350**. c. **15**, **16**.

—— Institutiones theologicæ, quas e fusioribus suis, editis et ineditis, ad usum seminariorum, contraxit Petrus, C. * * * [i.e. Pierre Collet] . . . Editio septima. 5 tom. *Parisiis*, 1771. 12°. **1350**. c. **10**.

C., Q. Essai historique sur le Docteur Swift, et sur son influence dans le gouvernement de la Grande Bretagne, depuis 1710, jusqu'à la mort de la reine Anne, en 1714; suivi de notices historiques sur plusieurs personnages d'Angleterre, célèbres dans les affaires et les lettres. [The "discours préliminaire" signed: Q. C., i.e. Quintin Crawfurd.] pp. xxxi. 504. *Paris*, 1808. 4°. **814**. k. **3**.

—— [Another copy.] G. **1707**.

C., Q.

—— Our Trip to Canton. Contributed by "the Boys and Girls." Edited by the old Q. C. pp. 23. *Noronha & Co.: Hongkong*, 1887. 4°. **10055**. p. **12**.
Interleaved with photographs.

C., Q. Over One Thousand Useful and Entertaining Legal Facts for One Shilling. By Q. C. *Richardson & Best: London*, [1879.] 8°. **6145**. aaa. **40**.

—— [Another edition.] *Diprose & Bateman: London*, [1885.] 8°. **6146**. aa. **34**.

C., R. *See* ANSELM, *Saint, Archbishop of Canterbury.* [*Single Works.*] Cur Deus homo, *etc.* [With a life of Saint Anselm, signed: R. C.] [1889.] 8°. **3605**. g. **3/1**.

C., R. *See* ATTERBURY (Francis) *Bishop of Rochester.* [*Letters.*] Letters which passed between Bishop Atterbury and Mr. Dean Stanhope on . . . Baptism in private, *etc.* [The editor's covering letter signed: R. C., i.e. Caleb Parfect, Rector of Cuxton.] 1758. 8°. **4105**. aaa. **1**. (**8**.)

C., R. *See* B., M. The R.F.C. Alphabet . . . Illustrated by R. C. [i.e. R. Cooper.] 1915. *obl.* 8°. **12316**. f. **56**.

C., R. *See* BENNETT (Mary) Don't Tell, *etc.* [The editor's preface signed: R. C.] [1858.] 12°. **12807**. b. **20**.

C., R. *See* BOSWORTH (William) *Gent.* The Chast and Lost Lovers, *etc.* [With a preface and dedication signed: R. C.] 1651. 8°. E. **1236**. (**2**.)

—— —— 1906. 8°. [SAINTSBURY (*J. E. B.*) *Minor Poets of the Caroline Period.* vol. 2.] **11607**. ee. **13**.

C., R. *See* BURNS (Robert) *the Poet.* [*Smaller Collections.*] The Poetical Works of Robert Burns. To which are now added notes, *etc.* [The editor's preface signed: R. C., i.e. Robert Chambers.] 1838. 8°. **1340**. m. **17**. (**3**.)

—— *See* BURNS (Robert) *the Poet.* [*Letters and Journals.*] The Prose Works of Robert Burns, with . . . notes . . . by the present editor. [The editor's preface signed: R. C., i.e. Robert Chambers.] 1839. 8°. **1340**. m. **17**. (**2**.)

C., R. *See* C., W., and C., R. Shipwrecks and Tales of the Sea. [Edited by W. and R. C., i.e. William and Robert Chambers.] 1860. 8°. **12622**. a. **13**.

—— *See* C., W., and C., R. Tales for Home Reading. [Edited by W. and R. C., i.e. William and Robert Chambers.] [1865.] 8°. **12620**. aaa. **24**.

—— *See* C., W., and C., R. Tales for Young and Old. [Edited by W. and R. C., i.e. William and Robert Chambers.] 1865. 8°. **12620**. aaa. **25**.

C., R. *See* COMMANDER. The Accomplished Commander . . . Published . . . by R. C. 1689. 12°. **534**. **a**. **14**.

C., R. *See* CURRIE (James) *M.D., of Liverpool.* The Life of Robert Burns, *etc.* [The preface signed: R. C., i.e. Robert Chambers.] 1838. 8°. **1340**. m. **17**. (**1**.)

C., R. *See* ELSIE, *pseud.* Stories without Names . . . By Elsie. [The preface signed: R. C.] 1900. 8°. **04410**. l. **43**.

C., R. *See* ESTIENNE (Henri) *le Grand.* A World of Wonders . . . Translated out of the . . . French copie. [The translator's preface signed: R. C.] 1607. fol. **585**. i. **21**.

—— —— 1608. fol. **87**. h. **16**.

C., R. *See* FORBES (*Sir* William) *Bart.* Memoirs of a Banking House. [The editor's preface signed: R. C., i.e. Robert Chambers.] 1860. 8°. **8223**. b. **46**.

C., R. *See* FRANCIS [de Sales], *Saint, Bishop of Geneva.* Philothea: or, an Introduction to a devout life . . . Newly translated . . . By R. C. [i.e. R. Challoner?], *etc.* 1770. 12°. **4412**. k. **26**.

C., R. *See* G. Gone Home. A record of the sudden call of R. C. [1885.] 32°. **4422**. aa. **47**. (**6**.)

C., R.

—— *See* HAINAULT. Gouvernement du pays d'Haynna[ut] depuis le trépas de l'archiduc Albert . . . 1621. [Th[e] editors' preface signed: H. D. et R. C., i.e. H. F. Delmott[e] and R. H. G. Chalon.] 1835. 8°. [*Société des Bibliophiles de Mons. Publications.* no. 1.] Ac. **904**[...]

C., R. *See* 'IMĀD AL-DĪN, *Native Minister in Amritsar.* [...] Mahommedan brought to Christ, *etc.* [With a prefac[e] signed: R. C., i.e. Robert Clark.] 1869. 8°. **4986**. bbb. **38**. (**19**[...]

C., R. *See* K., P. Nomenclatura trilinguis Anglo-Latin[o-] Graeca . . . The sixth edition, carefully revised and co[r]rected, by R. C., *etc.* 1704. 8°. **1481**. d. **2**[...]

—— —— [1720?] 8°. **12933**. bb. **4**. (**2**[...]

C., R. *See* K., T. Veritas Evangelica; or, the Gospe[l] Truth . . . Published by R. C. 1687. 4°. **222**. e. **15**. (**3**[...]

C., R. *See* LA MURE (J. M. de) Histoire des ducs d[e] Bourbon et des comtes de Forez, *etc.* [The editor's prefac[e] signed: R. C., i.e. Régis de Chantelauze.] 1860, *etc.* 4°. **9914**. dd. **2**[...]

C., R. *See* LILY (William) *the Grammarian.* The Roy[al] Grammar . . . rendred plain . . . by a supplement [of] things defective . . . By R. C. 1685. 8°. **12934**. a. **4**. (**1**[...]

C., R. *See* MACFARLAN (Patrick) A Vindication of th[e] Church of Scotland, *etc.* [The editor's preface signed[:] R. C.] 1850. 12°. **4735**. c. [...]

C., R. *See* MONGINOT (F. de) A Resolution of Doubts . . faithfully rendred according to the French Copie, *e*[*tc.*] [The translator's dedication signed: R. C.] 1618. 4°. **702**. d. **4**[...]

C., R. *See* P., T. The English and French Cook . . . B[y] T. P., J. P., R. C., *etc.* 1674. 12°. **7953**. a. **5**[...]

C., R. *See* RUGGLE (George) Ignoramus: a comedy . . Translated into English by R. C. [i.e. Robert Codrington.] 1662. 4°. C. **34**. f. **1**[...]

C., R. *See* TRAVERS (Rebecca) A Testimony for God[s] Everlasting Truth . . . testifying against . . . R. C. [i.e. Robert Cobbit] and his work entitled: "God's Trut[h] attested according to Scripture", *etc.* 1669. 4°. C. **32**. c. **22**. (**16**[...]

C., R.

—— *See* VŒU. Le Vœu du héron; poème, *etc.* [Th[e] editors' preface signed: R. C. & Ch. D., i.e. R. H. C[.] Chalon and C. Delecourt.] 1839. 8°. [*Société des Bibliophiles de Mons. Publications.* no. 8.] Ac. **904**[...]

C., R. [Sermon on Lamentations iii.] *See* D., J. Tw[o] Sermons on the Third of the Lamentations of Ieremie . . The one by I. D. [i.e. John Dod] the other by R. C. [i.e. Robert Cleaver.] 1608. 4°. **3109**. c. **9**. (**6**[...]

—— [Another edition.] *See* D., I. Two Sermons on th[e] Third of the Lamentations, *etc.* 1610. 4°. **4476**. g. **12**[...]

—— [Another edition.] *See* D., I. Two Sermons on th[e] Third of the Lamentations, *etc.* 1618. 4°. **1356**. g. **3**[...]

C., R. Arboricultura, ó Manual teórico práctico del arbo[ri]lista. Contiene la propagacion, cultivo y enfermedade[s] de los árboles así frutales como silvestres, por R. C[.] pp. 264. *Madrid*, 1865. 8°. **7077**. cc. **14**

C., R. The Caledonian Heroine; or, the Invasion and fall of Sueno the Dane. In two cantos. [The dedication signed: R. C., i.e. Robert Colvill.] pp. 30. *W. Ruddiman & Co.: Edinburgh*, 1771. 4°. **11632.** e. **11.**

C., R.

—— Carmen Deo Nostro, Te Decet Hymnus. Sacred Poems, collected, Corrected, Augmented, Most humbly Presented to my Lady the Countsse [*sic*] of Denbigh by her most deuoted Seruant R. C. [i.e. Richard Crashaw], *etc.* [With engravings.] pp. 130. *Peter Targa: Paris*, 1652. 8°. E. **1598.** (**1.**)

—— [Another copy.] G. **11497.**

—— [Another copy.] **238.** g. **8.**
In this copy the spaces for the engravings have been left blank.

—— [Another copy.] **238.** f. **36.**
Imperfect; wanting pp. 11, 12, 19, 20, 31, 32, 47, 48, 55, 56, 67, 68, 73, 74, 79, 80, 85, 86, 93, 94.

C......., R...... The Catholick Christian instructed in the Sacraments, Sacrifice, Ceremonies and Observances of the Church. By way of question and answer. By R..... C....... [i.e. Richard Challoner]. pp. xxiv. 261. *London*, 1737. 12°. **3504.** b. **53.**

—— [Another edition.] pp. xxiv. 261. *London*, 1753. 12°. **3506.** a. **26.**

C., R.

—— A Century of Family Shipowning. John Cory and Sons Limited, 1854–1954. [The author's note signed: R. C., i.e. Raymond Cory? With illustrations, including portraits.] pp. 51. [1954.] 8°. *See* Cory (John) and Sons. **8290.** bb. **24.**

C., R. Certaine Tables shewing the interest of any summe of money whatsoeuer vnto 60 yeeres . . . By R. C. *See* Record (Robert) The Ground of Arts, *etc.* 1623. 8°. **8506.** b. **3.**

—— [Another edition.] *See* Record (Robert) The Ground of Arts, *etc.* 1636. 8°. **8505.** aa. **51.**

—— [Another edition.] *See* Record (Robert) Records Arithmetick, *etc.* [1646.] 8°. **8532.** aaa. **22.**

C., R.

A comparison of the life of man,
Concerning how fickle his estate doth stand,
Flourishing like a tree, or vine, or dainty flower,
Or like a ship, or raine, that's turn'd each houre.

[A ballad, signed: R. C., i.e. Richard Climsell?] B.L. *For Francis Coules: London*, [1635?] fol. Rox. I. **44.**

C., R. The Compleat Midwife's Practice enlarged . . . The second edition corrected, by R. C., I. D., M. S., T. B., Practitioners of the said art. With a full supply of those rare secrets which Mr. Culpeper in his brief treatise of midwifry, and other English writers, have . . . omitted. pp. 309. *For Nath. Brook: London*, 1659. 8°. E. **1723.** (**1.**)

The first edition, "by T. C., I. D., M. S., T. B.," is catalogued under C., T.

—— The third edition enlarged, with the addition of Sir Theodore Mayern's rare secrets, *etc.* pp. 321 [322]. *For Nath. Brook: London*, 1663. 8°. **1177.** b. **7.**

—— Fifth edition . . . enlarged, by John Pechey, *etc.* pp. 351. *For H. Rhodes: London*, 1698. 8°. **778.** b. **44.**

C., R. The Conformists Charity to Dissenters, and Concurrence with the Favour granted them in the Act for Toleration: proved from the works of the most eminent divines of the Church of England. [The preface signed: R. C.] pp. 68. *J. R. for John Salusbury: London*, 1689. 4°. T. **750.** (**3.**)

C., R. The Conformists Sayings: or, the Opinion and arguments of Kings, Bishops, and several divines lately assembled in Convocation, in favour of those who dissent from the present ceremonies of publick worship. By a Minister of the Church of England. [The preface signed: R. C.] pp. 68. *Printed for the Author: London*, 1690. 4°. T. **747.** (**5.**)

C., R. Constant, faire, and fine Betty. Being the Youngmans praise, of a curious Creature.

Faire shee was, and faire indeed;
And constant alwayes did proceed.

[A ballad, signed: R. C., i.e. Richard Climsell?] B.L. *For Iohn Wright the younger: London*, [1635?] fol. Rox. I. **66.**

C., R. The Copie of a Letter [signed: R. C., i.e. [Robert Cecil, Earl of Salisbury]] to the Right Honourable the Earle of Leycester, Lieutenant generall of all her Maiesties forces in the vnited Prouinces of the lowe Countreys . . . With a report of certeine petitions and declarations [praying for the execution of the sentence on Mary Queen of Scotland] made to the Queenes Maiestie at two seuerall times, from all the Lordes and Commons lately assembled in Parliament. And her Maiesties answeres thereunto by herselfe deliuered, *etc.* pp. 32. *Imprinted by Christopher Barker: London*, 1586. 4°. C. **33.** b. **3.**

—— [Another copy.] **292.** f. **28.**

—— [Another copy.] G. **6144.**
Imperfect; wanting sig. A 1 *containing a cut of the Royal Arms.*

—— Copye van eenen brief [signed: R. C., i.e. [Robert Cecil, Earl of Salisbury] ~~Richard Crompton?~~] aen den E. den Graue van Leycester . . . Met een verhael, van seker begeerten ende verthooningen aen de Con. Majesteyt . . . Noch is hier bygevoecht, eē warachtige copye vande proclamatie onlancx gepubliceert by de Co. Ma. tot verclaringhe vande sententie onlancx ghegheuen tegen de Coninginne vā Scotlant. Mitsgaders eenighe brieuen gheschreuen by de Schotsche Coninginne, aen den verrader Anthony Babington, *etc.* *Ghedruct by R. Schilders: Middelburgh*, 1587. 4°. C. **33.** b. **24.** (**12.**)

—— [Another copy.] T. **1716.** (**10.**)

—— La Copie d'vne lettre [signed: R. C., i.e. [Robert Cecil, Earl of Salisbury]] inscrite à . . . Monseigneur le Comte de Lecestre . . . Auec vn recit de certaines requestes . . . faictes . . . à la Maiesté de la Royne, de la part de tous les Seigneurs & de la Communauté dernierement assemblez aux Estats. Ensemble, les responces sus cela doneés [*sic*] par sa Maiesté mesme, *etc.* pp. 28. *Imprimé par C. B.: Londres*, 1587. 4°. C. **55.** d. **19.**

C., R. A Copie of a Letter which came from Scotland, the first of September, 1641. to a Gentleman in London. [Signed: R. C.] *See* Scotland. [*Appendix.—History and Politics.*] From Scotland. Two Coppies of letters; the one sent from his Majestie, Aug. 31, *etc.* 1641. 4°. E. **171.** (**9.**)

C., R. Counsel of European Nations. By R. C. pp. 24. *Elliot Stock: London*, 1917. 8°. **8425.** ppp. **24.**

C., R. A cruell murther committed lately upon the body of Abraham Gearsy, who liv'd in the parish of Westmill, in the County of Harford, by one Robert Reeve and Richard Reeve . . . for which fact Robert was prest to death, on Munday the 16. of March, and the Tuesday following Richard was hang'd, *etc.* [A ballad, signed: R. C., i.e. Richard Climsell?] B.L. *For John Wright, Junior: London*, [1635.] fol. Rox. I. **488.**

C., R. The Cry of Newgate, with the other prisons in, and about London: in which dismal holes . . . are imured about three hundred persons . . . of the . . . people . . . called Quakers, for no other cause, but for their unspotted testimonies in God, held in clear consciences. By R. C. [i.e. Richard Crane.] pp. 12. *London*, 1662. 4°. **4151**. a. **134**.

C., R. Death's loud Allarum: or, a perfect description of the frailty of mans life, with some admonitions to warne all men and women to repentance. [A ballad, signed: R. C., i.e. Richard Climsell?] 𝕭.𝕷. *For John Wright the Young[er]: London*, [1635?] fol. Rox. I. **78**.
Cropped.

C., R. A Direct Way, whereby the plainest man may be guided to the waters of Life . . . by R. C. [i.e. Roger Cotton.] 𝕭.𝕷. pp. 247. *Imprinted by George Eld; sold by Iohn Wright: London*, 1610. 8°. **4412**. aa. **14**.

C., R. A Discourse concerning the True Notion of the Lords Supper. By R. C. [i.e. Ralph Cudworth the younger.] pp. 73. *For Richard Cotes: London*, 1642. 4°. **702**. d. **8**. **(11.)**

C., R. Divine Hymns, and other Extempory Poems. By R. C. pp. 23. *Printed for the Author: London*, 1695. 12°. **1163**. b. **12**.

C., R. Dr Ibbotson's Case shewn to be no sufficient precedent for assessing Parsons, Vicars &c. to Poor-Rates for Tithes they don't occupy, commonly called compositions. In a letter . . . To which is annexed, another letter, shewing that a proportion of such compositions may be claimed to the day of the death of the incumbents, *etc.* [Signed: R. C., i.e. Caleb Parfect, Rector of Cuxton.] pp. 24. MS. NOTES [by the author]. *Samuel Baker: London*, 1750. 8°. **4105**. aaa. **1**. **(3.)**

C., R. Eight very Serious and Considerable Queries, humbly tendred to the . . . consideration of the godly and greatly honoured promoters of the Reformation of the Church or Churches of Jesus Christ in England. By a weak and obscure, yet most cordiall, indeavourer to advance that glorious designe. [Signed: R. C.] pp. 8. *London*, 1646. 4°. E. **506**. **(14.)**

C., R. An Elegie Sacred to the Immortal Memory of . . . Margaret Lady Smith . . . Dedicated to . . . Edward Savage Esquire . . . her . . . lamenting Husband. Composed by . . . R. C. [i.e. Robert Codrington.] (Epicedium in obitum . . . Margaretæ Smith, cujus piis Manibus litavit . . . R. C.) [*London*, 1630?] 4°. **11626**. d. **7**.
Imperfect; wanting sig. A 4.

C., R. Epigrammatum sacrorum liber. [The dedication signed: R. C., i.e. Richard Crashaw.] pp. 79. *Ex Academiæ Typographeo: Cantabrigiæ*, 1634. 8°. **11409**. c. **20**.

C., R. An Expedient towards the Establishing of a Worthy Body of Parochial Resident Clergy throughout the whole Kingdom. In a letter to a friend. [Signed: R. C.] (A Solemn and Moving Form made use of by a pious lady in giving in her impropriate tithes to the Church.) pp. 16. *London*, 1769. 8°. **4108**. bb. **5**.

C., R. The Forlorne Traveller:

Whose first beginning was pleasure and joy,
But his riotous spending wrought his decay,
Hee tooke delight to spend and rore,
And at the last dy'd very poore.

[A ballad, signed: R. C., i.e. Richard Climsell.] 𝕭.𝕷. *For F. Coules: London*, [1635?] fol. Rox. I. **524**.

C., R. Gems of Sacred Literature. [The editor's pref signed: R .C., i.e. Richard Cattermole.] 2 vol. *J. W. Parker: London*, 1841. 8°. **1110**. b.
With an engraved half-title reading: "British Sac Prose Writers."

C., R. God's holy Name magnified, and his Truth exalt by the testimony of his Faithful Servants who ha suffered the cruel penalty of Banishment from their Nat Country by the Rulers thereof: as also an Abstract their names . . . [By] R. C. [i.e. Richard Crane] . Unto which is annexed Englands sad estate and co dition lamented. Written by George Fox the young *etc.* pp. 25. [*London*,] 1665. 4°. **4151**. b.

C., R. A Godly Form of Householde Gouernement: the ordering of priuate Families, according to the direct of Gods word. Whereunto is adjoyned . . . The seue duties of the Husband towards his wife: and the wi dutie towards her husband . . . Gathered by R. C. [Roger Carr.] pp. 392. *Thomas Creede Thomas Man: London*, 1598. 8°. **4411**. df.

—— [Another edition.] pp. 384. *Felix Kingston Thomas Man: London*, 1600. 8°. **874**. f.

—— [Another edition.] pp. 384. *Thomas Creede Thomas Man: London*, 1603. 8°. **4402**. g.

—— [Another edition.] Now newly perused, amended, a augmented by Iohn Dod, and Robert Cleuer. pp. 386. *For Thomas Man: London*, 1612. 8°. **4405**. e.

—— [Another edition.] *Printed by the Assignes of Thom Man; sold by Iohn Clarke: London*, 1630. 8°. **8416**. de.

C., R.

—— His Majesty's Propriety, and Dominion on the Britti Seas Asserted: together with a true account of th Neatherlanders insupportable insolences . . . To which added, an exact mapp, containing the isles of Gre Brittain, and Ireland . . . by an experienced han [The epistle dedicatory signed: R. C., i.e. Robert Codrin ton. With a portrait of Charles II.] pp. 176. *T. Ma for Andrew Kembe: London*, 1665. 8°. G. **1616**

—— [Another copy.] **292**. d.
Imperfect; wanting the map.

C., R. Historia de la América del Sur desde su descubrimien hasta nuestros dias . . . Por un Americano. [The pr face signed: R. C.] pp. vii. 427. *Barcelona*, [1878.] **9771**. eee.

—— The History of South America . . . By an America [The preface signed: R. C.] Translated from the Spani by Adnah D. Jones. With maps and index by the tra lator. pp. vi. 345. *Swan Sonnenschein & Co London*, 1899. 8°. **9770**. dd.

C., R. The History of Huntingdon, from the earliest to t present times; with an appendix containing the chart of Charles I. under which the borough is now governe [The preface signed: R. C., i.e. Robert Carruther pp. ix. 338. *A. P. Wood: Huntingdon*, 1824 8°. **10352**. b.

C., R. The Household Birth-Day Book, and marriage an obituary register. With the dates of births, marriag and deaths of over one thousand eminent men an women. Compiled by the editor of "Bible Words f Birth-Days," *etc.* [The preface signed: R. C.] pp. 38 *W. P. Nimmo & Co.: Edinburgh*, 1879. 16°. **10602**. a.

C., R. John Hadlands advice; or, a warning for all young men that have meanes, advising them to forsake lewd company, cards, dice and queanes. [A ballad, signed: R. C., i.e. Richard Climsell.] B.L. *For Francis Coules: London*, [1635?] fol. Rox. I. **522**.

—— The Joviall Broome man: or,
A Kent Street Souldiers exact relation
Of all his Travels in Every Nation, *etc.*
[A ballad, signed: R. C., i.e. Richard Climsell?] B.L. *For Richard Harper: London*, [1640?] fol. Rox. I. **166**.

—— The Kind-hearted Creature: or,
The prettest Jest that er'e you knew,
Yet I'le say nothing but what is true, *etc.*
[A ballad, signed: R. C., i.e. Richard Climsell?] B.L. *For F. Coules: London*, [1640?] fol. Rox. III. **166**.

C., R. A Lamentation over thee O London, with thy rulers and people, who hast slighted the day of thy visitation, *etc.* [Signed: R. C., i.e. Richard Crane.] pp. 5. *London*, 1665. 4°. **4152**. bb. **102**.

C., R. A Letter from an Officer of quality in the Parliament's Army in Munster, to a worthy member of the House of Commons. [Signed: R. C.] *See* O'BRIEN (Murrough) *Earl of Inchiquin*. More Victories lately obtained in Ireland, *etc.* 1647. 4°. E. **409**. **(2.)**

C., R. A Letter to a Friend concerning Usury. Wherein are mentioned all the arguments formerly written for and against the abatement of interest. Collected out of four tracts on that subject: One by Sir Thomas Culpeper Senior, in 1621. Another by Sir Thomas Culpeper Junior, in 1668. The third by Sir Josiah Child, in 1668. And the fourth by Mr. Thomas Manley, in 1669. By R. C. pp. 30. *London*, 1690. 12°. T. **1593**. **(3.)**

C., R. The Long Parliament is not Revived by Tho. Philips. Or, An Answer to Tho. Philips his Long Parliament Revived. By R. C. pp. 6. *For N. W.: London*, 1660. 4°. **518**. k. **1**. **(13.)**

—— [Another copy.] E. **1050**. **(8.)**

—— [Another edition.] 1808. *See* COBBETT (William) *M.P.* Cobbett's Parliamentary History, *etc.* vol. 4. Appendix. 1808, *etc.* 8°. **B.S.Ref.11.**

—— [Another copy.] **287**. h. **4**.

—— [Another edition.] 1812. *See* SOMERS (John) *Baron Somers*. A Collection of Scarce and Valuable Tracts, *etc.* vol. 7. 1809, *etc.* 4°. **750**. g. **7**.

C., R. Memoirs of the Life and Administration of William Cecil Baron Burleigh . . . Including a parallel between the state of government then and now. To which is prefixed a preface to the People of Britain. Together with an appendix of original papers. [Signed: R. C., i.e. Raphael Courteville.] pp. xxxii. 151. *Printed for the Author: London*, 1738. 4°. G. **2149**.

C., R. Minerva, or, the Art of Weaving: containing the antiquity, utility and excellency of weaving. Written in verse . . . by R. C. pp. 47. *For Joseph Moxon: London*, 1677. 4°. **1044**. i. **25**.
Reissued in 1682 *with the title:* "*The Triumphant Weaver.*"

C., R. The Number of Alehouses shewn to be extremely Pernicious to the Publick. In a letter to a Member of Parliament. By the V. of S. in Kent. [Signed: R. C.] pp. 36. *Printed for the Author: London*, 1758. 8°. **103**. l. **30**.

C., R. Ohio Valley Historical Series. Miscellanies. [The editor's preface signed: R. C., i.e. Robert Clarke.] 1. A Tour in Ohio . . . in 1805. By Josiah Espy. 2. Two Western Campaigns in the war of 1812. By Samuel Williams. 3. The Leatherwood God. By R. H. Taneyhill. 3 pt. *R. Clarke & Co.: Cincinnati*, 1871. 8°. [*Ohio Valley Historical Series.* no. 7.] **9602**. g. **13**.

C., R. On the Existence of the Soul after Death: a dissertation opposed to the principles of Priestley, Law, and their respective followers. By R. C. [i.e. Richard Laurence, Archbishop of Cashel.] [With two MS. letters respecting the death of the archbishop.] pp. iv. 114. *J. G. & F. Rivington; London; J. H. Parker: Oxford*, 1834. 8°. **4374**. f. **11**.

—— [Another copy.] T. **1484**. **(6.)**

C., R. Phyladelphian Principles: or, a Discourse proving from the writings of many learned men, that the way to promote unity in the Church, is not by a general uniformity . . . but in the exercise of mutual charity . . . Written by a Peaceable Moderator. [The preface signed: R. C.] pp. 76. *London*, 1689. 4°. **4135**. aaa. **7**.

C., R. A pleasant new Dialogue; or, the discourse between the Serving-man and the Husband-man.
The lofty pride must bated bee,
And praise must goe in right degree.
[A ballad, signed: R. C., i.e. Richard Climsell?] B.L. *For F. Coules: London*, [1635?] fol. Rox. I. **98**.

C., R. Poetica stromata, or, a Collection of sundry peices in poetry: drawne by the known and approved hand of R. C. [i.e. Richard Corbet, Bishop of Norwich.] pp. 121. MS. NOTE. [*London?*] 1648. 8°. **C.117.a.31.**

—— [Another copy.] C. **58**. cc. **24**.

—— [Another copy.] G. **18845**.

C., R. The Politick Maid; or,
A dainty new ditty,
Both pleasant and witty:
Wherein you may see
The maides policie.
[A ballad, signed: R. C., i.e. Richard Climsell?] B.L. *For Thomas Lambert: London*, [1640?] fol. Rox. I. **306**.

C., R. The Present Condition of Dublin in Ireland; with the manner of the siege and how it is straitened, by the Marquesse of Ormond, L. Inchequin, &c. Represented in two letters [signed: R. C.] from a Colonell in Dublin, *etc.* pp. 6. *For Henry Crips, & Lodowick Lloyd: London*, 1649. 4°. E. **562**. **(11.)**

C., R. Pretty Nannie; or,
A dainty, delicate new Ditty,
Fit for the Country, Town or Citty, *etc.*
[A ballad, signed: R. C., i.e. Richard Climsell?] B.L. *For Tho. Lambert: London*, [1640?] fol. Rox. I. **322**.

C., R. The Prodigals Pilgrimage. A poem. Wherein is contained all the remarkable passages occurring from his birth to his return. [The dedication signed: R. C.] pp. 24. *For J. Nutt: London*, 1698. 4°. **164**. l. **12**.

C., R. Reasons and Considerations touching the Lawfulnesse of removing out of England into . . . America. [Signed: R. C., i.e. Robert Cushman.] *See* PLYMOUTH, *Mass.* A Relation . . . of the . . . Proceedings of the English Plantation settled at Plimoth, &c. 1622. 4°. C. **33**. c. **7**.

C., R.

—— Reasons and Considerations touching the Lawfulness of removing out of England into the parts of America. [Signed: R. C., i.e. Robert Cushman.] *In:* Collections of the Massachusetts Historical Society. ser. 2. vol. 9. pp. 64–73. 1832. 8°. Ac. **8400**.

C., R. Reasons for Repose, addressed to a Christian subject to temporary alarms respecting the truth of the Scriptures . . . Second edition. [Signed: R. C., i.e. Richard Cecil.] pp. 36. *T. Williams: London,* [1804.] 12°. **4372**. aa. **30**. **(4.)**

C., R. The Representation of Minorities. By R. C. pp. 32. *William Ridgway: London,* 1868. 8°. **8138**. bbb. **19**.

C., R. A Sailor's Story; or, Where am I going? *etc.* [A religious tract. Signed: R. C.] pp. 12. *Andrews Bros.: London,* 1897. 16°. **4420**. e. **2**. **(5.)**

C., R. Salvation laid on its Right Foundation: or, the Free Grace of God prov'd to be the only ground of, and to have the alone stroke in, the matter of our salvation. Being the sum of two sermons . . . By an admirer of grace, *etc.* [Signed: R. C.] pp. 32. *Printed, & sold by R. Baldwin: London,* 1698. 4°. **4473**. d. 4. (4.)

C., R. A Scholasticall Discourse, demonstrating this conclusion, that, admitting Erastus Senior's reasons for true, neither the Pope, nor those called Bishops in the Church of Rome, are Bishops either in order or jurisdiction. Wherein is answered all which is alledged by Erastus Senior [in the work, "Erastus Senior . . . demonstrating . . . that those called Bishops . . . in England are no Bishops"] against the order and jurisdiction of the Bishops of the Church of England. By R. C. pp. 27. *J. G. for R. Royston: London,* 1663. 4°. **3935**. b. **23**.

C., R. The Shepherd and the Sheep. By R. C. pp. 15. *G. Morrish: London,* [1892.] 32°. **4422**. c. **37**. **(3.)**

C., R. Something spoken in Vindication & Clearing of the People of God called Quakers; that they have not forfeited their liberty in the Declaration . . . by any plots, *etc.* [Signed: R. C., i.e. Richard Crane.] [*For Robert Wilson: London,* 1660.] *s. sh.* fol. **4152**. aaaa. **50**.

—— Jets tot verantwoordinge van het Volk Gods Quakers genaemdt: dat sy hare vryheid in de Declaratie niet verbeurt hebben . . . Getrouwelijk vergeset, uit de Engelsche, in de Nederlandsche Tale. [Signed: R. C., i.e. Richard Crane.] [1660?] *s. sh.* fol. **855**. i. **1**.

C., R. A Table Alphabeticall, contayning and teaching the true writing and vnderstanding of hard vsuall English words, borrowed from the Hebrew, Greeke, Latine, or French, &c. . . . Set forth by R. C. [i.e. Robert Cawdrey] newly corrected and much inlarged . . . The 3. edition. *T. S. for Edmund Weauer: London,* 1613. 8°. **12981**. aa. **32**.

—— The fourth edition. *W. I. for Edmund Weauer: London,* 1617. 12°. **828**. a. **31**.

C., R. A Treatise concerning the Regulation of the Coyn of England, and how the East-India Trade may be preserved and encreased. By R. C. [i.e. Roger Coke.] pp. 44. *For Roger Clavel: London,* 1696. 4°. **8223**. b. 3.

—— [Another copy.] **104**. f. **43**.

—— [Another copy.] A Treatise concerning the Regulation of the Coyn of England . . . By R. C. [i.e. Roger Coke.] *London,* 1696. 4°. **1473**. bb. **35**. **(17.)**

—— [Another copy.] **1473**. bb. **35**. **(18.)**

C., R. The Triumphant Weaver: or, the Art of Wea[ving] discuss'd and handled . . . Written all in verse for divertisement of all . . . who are naturally inclin'd [to] the serious study . . . of the said art, *etc.* [The pre[face] signed: R. C.] pp. 47. *For J. Deacon: [Lond[on],* 1682. 4°. **11626**. bb[.]
A reissue of the edition of 1677 *entitled:* "*Minerva, [or] the Art of Weaving,*" *etc.*

C., R. True Newes from Hull. Being a perfect relation [of a] conspiracy there by divers cavaliers comming in disgu[ise] habits, and entring themselves as souldiers, who inten[ded] to have surprised the towne, and . . . killed Sir J[ohn] Hotham . . . By R. C. pp. 8. *For Fr. Wright: Lon[don],* 1642. 4°. E. **130**. (

C., R. A True Report of the late good successe in Irela[nd] from thence received in London, May 2. 1642. [Sign[ed] R. C.] pp. 6. *Printed by Matthew Simmons: Lon[don],* 1642. 4°. E. **146**. (

C., R. The Union of Christ and the Church; in a shad[ow]. By R. C. [i.e. Ralph Cudworth.] pp. 35. *R. Bishop: London,* 1642. 4°. **8416**. f.

C., R., *Chaplain to an English Regiment.* The History of [the] English College at Doway, from its first foundatio[n in] 1568, to the present time. As also a particular descrip[tion] of the college, gardens, &c. . . . Collected from orig[inal] manuscripts, letters and unquestionable informat[ion] upon the place. By R. C., Chaplain to an English R[egi]ment [i.e. Charles Dodd]. pp. 36. *Bernard Lint[ot]: London,* 1713. 8°. **1367**. c.

—— [Another copy.] G. **19579**.

—— [Another copy.] G. **19580**.

—— A Modest Defence of the Clergy and Religious, [in a] discourse directed to R. C. [i.e. Charles Dodd] ab[out] his History of Doway College. With an accoun[t of] the matters of fact misrepresented in the said hist[ory]. [By Thomas Hunter, S.J.] pp. 143. 1714. 8°. **702**. f. **7**.

—— [Another copy.] G. **19580**.

C . . . ., R . . . ., *D.D.* *See* Jesus Christ. [*De Imitatione Christi.—English.*] The Following of Ch[rist] . . . Newly translated into English by R . . . . C . . . ., D.D. [i.e. Richard Challoner.] 1737. 24°. I.X. Eng.

—— —— 1744. 24°. I.X. Eng. **1**

—— —— 1779. 12°. I.X. Eng. **1**

C., R., *D.D.* *See* Manual. A Manual of Prayers, and ot[her] Christian Devotions. Revised and corrected, with la[rge] additions, by R. C. D.D. [i.e. Richard Challoner.] 1758. 12°. **3455**. cc.

C——, R——, *D.D.*

—— *See* Manual. A Manual of Prayers . . . Revised and [cor]rected, with large additions, by R—— C——, D.D. [i.e. Richard Challoner.] 1800. 12°. **3458**. bb.

C., R., *Doctor of Divinity.* A Brief Survey of the Lord [of] Derry his Treatise of Schism [i.e. Bishop John Bra[m]hall's "Just Vindication of the Church of England"] wherein he intends to cleare the Protestant Church fr[om] schism, and to lay the fault upon the Roman Chur[ch]. By R. C., Doctor of Divinity [i.e. Richard Smith, Bish[op] of Chalcedon]. pp. 144. ms. notes. *Paris,* 1655. 12 **3935**. aa.

C., R., *Esq.* Lithobolia: or, the Stone-Throwing Devil. Being an exact and true account, by way of journal, of the various actions of infernal spirits . . . at a place call'd Great Island in the Province of New-Hantshire in New-England . . . By R. C. Esq; [i.e. Richard Chamberline] *etc.* pp. 16. *Printed & sold by E. Whitlook: London,* 1698. 4°. G. **19148.**
Slightly cropped.

—— [Another copy.] C. **33.** c. **39.**
Slightly cropped.

—— [Another edition.] *William Abbatt: Tarrytown, N.Y.,* 1923. 8°. [*Magazine of History.* Extra no. 90.] P.P. **3437.** bab.

—— *See* DEAN (John W.) Lithobolia, *etc.* [An account of the tract thus entitled.] [1889.] 8°. **8632.** g. **25.** (**6.**)

C., R., *Esquire.* *See* HUARTE (J.) Examen de Ingenios. The Examination of Mens Wits . . . Englished . . . by R. C., Esquire [i.e. Richard Carew]. 1594. 4°. **528.** f. **2.**

—— —— 1596. 4°. **528.** g. **28.**

—— —— 1604. 4°. **1250.** c. **13.**

—— —— 1616. 4°. **528.** e. **30.**

—— *See* TASSO (T.) *the Poet.* [*Gerusalemme Liberata.—Italian and English.*] Godfrey of Bulloigne; or, the Recouerie of Hierusalem . . . translated into English by R. C. Esquire [i.e. Richard Carew], *etc.* 1594. 4°. **1073.** g. **32.**

C., R., *Gent.* *See* CERVANTES SAAVEDRA (M. de) [*Supposititious Works.*] The Troublesome and Hard Adventures in Love . . . Translated into English by R. C. Gent. 1652. 4°. E. **647** (**1.**)

—— *See* IRELAND.—*Roman Catholics.* A Declaration sent to the King of France and Spayne from the catholiques or rebells in Ireland . . . Translated out of French by R. C. Gent. [i.e. Robert Codrington?] 1642. 4°. E. **145.** (**7.**)

C., R., *Gent.* The Happie Mind, or, a Compendious direction to obtaine the same shewing it's sundry passions by an interview of the foure complections . . . By R. C. Gent. pp. 198. [*London,*] 1640. 12°. **8405.** a. **13.**
The titlepage is engraved.

C., R., *Gent.* The Times' Whistle: or, a Newe daunce of seven satires, and other poems: compiled by R. C., Gent. [i.e. Richard Corbet, Bishop of Norwich?] Now first edited . . . by J. M. Cowper. pp. xxxviii. 178. 1871. 8°. *See* LONDON.—III. *Early English Text Society.* Ac. **9925**/**40.**

C., R., *Gentleman.* *See* FUMÉE (M.) *Sieur de Genillé.* The Historie of the Troubles of Hungarie . . . Newly translated out of French into English by R. C., gentleman [i.e. Rooke Churche]. 1600. fol. C. **22.** f. **13.**

C., R., *M.A.* *See* LUTHER (Martin) [*Tischreden.*] The Prophecyes of . . . M. Luther . . . Collected by R. C., M.A. 1664. 4°. G. **19623.**

C., R., *Master of Arts.* *See* LLOYD (Lodowick) The Marrow of History . . . Corrected and revived by R. C., Master of Arts [i.e. Robert Codrington]. 1659. 4°. **10604.** b. **14.**

C., R., *Mover of " the suggested protest against the doctrine of baptismal regeneration."* *See* CLERICUS. A Defence of the Baptismal Service of the Church of England . . . In a letter addressed to " R. C.," mover of " the suggested protest against the doctrine of baptismal regeneration," *etc.* 1839. 12°. **4327.** bbb. **14.**

C——, R——, *Mr.* A Just Character of the Revd. Mr Boyce. [In verse.] Written by M^r R—— C—— [i.e. Richard Choppin]. [*Dublin?* 1728?] *s. sh.* fol. **1890.** c. **5.** (**16.**)

C., R., *Mr., P. and Bachelor of Divinitie.* Palestina. Written by Mr R. C. P. and Bachelor of Diuinitie [i.e. Robert Chambers, Priest.] [A legendary and allegorical romance founded on the Gospels.] pp. 200. *Imprinted by Bartelmew Sermartelli: Florence,* 1600. 4°. C. **25.** e. **18.**

C., R., *of Anthony, Esquire.*

—— The Excellencie of the English Tongue by R. C. of Anthony Esquire [i.e. Richard Carew] to W. C. *See* N., M. Remaines, concerning Britaine, *etc.* 1614. 4°. **980.** f. **3.**

—— [Another edition.] *See* N., M. Remaines, concerning Britaine, *etc.* 1623. 4°. **1303.** c. **1.**

—— [Another edition.] *See* CAMDEN (William) Remains concerning Britain, *etc.* 1674. 8°. **292.** b. **1.**

C., R., *of the Middle Temple, Esq.* Arcana Parliamentaria: or, Precedents concerning elections, proceedings, privileges, and punishments in Parliament. Faithfully collected out of the common and statute law of this realm . . . By R. C. of the Middle Temple, Esq; To which is added, the authority, form, and manner of holding Parliaments, by . . . Sir Tho. Smith. pp. 116. *For M. Gilliflower: London,* 1685. 12°. **516.** a. **26.**

C., R., *of the Middle Temple, Esq.* The Female Apologist. A satire. [In verse.] Occasion'd by the Monthly Memoir of a celebrated British Lady. By R. C., of the Middle Temple, Esq. pp. 15. [*For H. Stibbs:*] *London,* 1748. 4°. **11630.** c. **8.** (**16.**)

C., R., *lu Patriota pe' sentemiento.* Curaggio, e consiglio a li patriote napolitane, *etc.* [In verse. Signed: R. C., lu patriota pe' sentemiento.] *Nnapole,* 1820. *s. sh.* fol. **8032.** m. **10.** (**26.**)

C., R., *Philo-Presbyter.* An Instructive Catechism; being a preservative for young and old to avoid schism. By R. C., Philo-Presbyter. The twelfth eddition [*sic*]. pp. 8. *Newry,* [1785?] 12°. **12331.** b. **34.** (**19.**)

C., *Sir* R. Serious Considerations for repressing of the Increase of Iesuites, Priests and Papists, without shedding of blood. Written by Sir R. C. [i.e. Sir Robert B. Cotton.] pp. 52. [*London,*] 1641. 4°. **702.** d. **8.** (**1.**)

—— [Another copy.] T. **773.** (**8.**)

C., *Sir* R., *Knight and Baronet.* A Short View of the Reign of King Henry III. . . . By Sir R. C. Knight and Baronet [i.e. Sir Robert B. Cotton]. pp. 28. *For Richard Janeway: London,* 1681. 4°. **9510.** aaa. **3.**

C., R. A. *See* ALPHONSO MARIA [de' Liguori], *Saint, Bishop of Sant' Agata dei Goti.* The Month of Mary. [Extracted from " The Glories of Mary." The editor's preface signed: R. A. C., i.e. Robert A. Coffin.] 1872. 16°. **3457.** a. **40.**

C., R. A. March in Scotland, 1929. [Historical notes on the itinerary of a route march of the 14th Bn. London Regiment—The London Scottish. Signed: R. A. C., i.e. Ronald A. Coates.] pp. 15. [*Printed for private circulation:*] *London,* [1929.] 16°. **010369.** df. **2.**
With the autograph of C. W. Train, V.C.

C., R. C. *See* A., J., and C., R. C. Ballads from the Portugueze. Translated & versified by J. A. and R. C. C. [i.e. John Adamson and Richard C. Coxe.] 1846. 8°. **11452.** bbb. **15.**

C., R. C. *See* Bible.—*Selections.* [*English.*] Companion of the Sick, *etc.* [The editor's preface signed: R. C. C.] 1868. 8°. **4412.** c. **10.**

C., R. C.

—— The Mercy at Marsden Rocks: a true tale. [The preface signed: R. C. C., i.e. Richard Charles Coxe.] pp. 15. *M. A. Richardson: Newcastle,* 1844. 8°. **1077.** f. **83.** (**2.**)

—— [Another copy.] **11650. cc. 20. (13.)**

—— The Snow Shroud: or, the lost bairn o' Biddleston Edge. [The preface signed: R. C. C., i.e. Richard Charles Coxe.] pp. 20. *M. A. Richardson: Newcastle,* 1845. 8°. **1077.** f. **83.** (**4.**)

—— [Another copy.] **11650. cc. 20. (14.)**

C., R. D. *See* Cholera. The Cholera. Preservation from its ravages, and its treatment. Extracted from a French publication, by R. D. C. 1866. 8°. **7561.** c. **19.**

C., R. D. Noueaux recits, ou Comptes moralisez . . . Par du Roc sort Manne. [The "Advertisement aux Lecteurs" signed: R. D. C., i.e. —— Romannet du Cros.] 1575. 16°. *See* Du Roc sort Manne, *pseud.* [i.e. —— Romannet du Cros.] C. **4.** a. **14.**

C., R. D. M. A. H. A. O. S. O. C. S. T. D. P. A. O. G. & P. G. S. R. M. I. C. S. P. P. S. Candor Illæsus . . . Christopheri Leopoldi Comitis a Schafgotsche . . . heroicorum operum compendium ab obligatissimo calamo & animo R. D. M. A. H. A. O. S. O. C. S. T. D. P. A. O. G. & P. G. S. R. M. I. C. S. P. P. S. C. [i.e. Reverendi Domini Michaelis Antonii Hacki Abbatis Olivæ Sancti Ordinis Cisterciensis Sanctæ Theologiæ Doctoris Protonotarii Apostolici Officialis Gedanensis et Pomeraniæ Generalis Serenissimæ Regiæ Majestatis Intimi Camerarii Secretarii Portuum Prussiæ Secreti Commissarii.] [In verse.] *Typis Abbatialibus: Olivæ,* [1694.] fol. **1871.** d. **2.** (**11.**)

—— Sapientia cum Principe cuncta componens heroico inpectore . . . Eberhardi de Danckelman Domini in Breskens . . . Vivat! è voto . . . R. D. M. A. H. A. O. S. O. C. S. T. D. P. A. O. G. & P. G. S. R. M. I. C. S. P. P. S. C. [i.e. M. A. Hacki.] [In verse.] *Typis Abbatialibus: Olivæ,* [1694.] fol. **1871.** d. **2.** (**12.**)

C., R. D. M. A. H. A. O. S. O. C. S. T. D. P. A. O. G. & P. G. S. R. M. P. S. P. P. S. Regalis Hymen . . . Maximiliani Emmanuelis . . . Bavariæ . . . Ducis . . . cum serenissima Teresa Cunegunde Regni Poloniarum . . . Principissa Virgine sponsalibus sacris decantatus . . . per R. D. M. A. H. A. O. S. O. C. S. T. D. P. A. O. G. & P. G. S. R. M. P. S. P. P. S. C. [i.e. M. A. Hacki.] [In verse.] *Typis Abbatialibus: Olivæ,* [1694.] fol. **1871.** d. **2.** (**4.**)

C., R. D. M. A. H. A. O. S. O. C. S. T. D. P. A. O. G. & P. G. S. R. M. S. P. P. Spei augustæ solatia Regni Poloniæ Majestatum . . . Joannis III. Regis . . . Mariæ Casimiræ Reginæ publico orbis Christiani voto decantata . . . R. D. M. A. H. A. O. S. O. C. S. T. D. P. A. O. G. & P. G. S. R. M. S. P. P. C. [i.e. M. A. Hacki.] [In verse.] [*Oliva,* 1691.] fol. **1871.** d. **2.** (**3.**)

C., R. E. *See* F., K., and C., R. E. Memoirs of the Life of Elizabeth Fry . . . Edited by two of her daughters. [The preface signed: K. F., R. E. C., i.e. Katherine Fry and Rachel E. Cresswell.] 1847. 8°. **1373.** i. **1.**

—— Memories of her Mother [i.e. Elizabeth Fry], in a letter to her sisters, by R. E. C. [i.e. Rachel E. Cresswell.] pp. 86. *Printed for private circulation: Lynn,* 1845. 4°. **4905.** bbb. **22.**

C., R. E. Moderation versus Total Abstinence, and ot dialogues. By R. E. C. pp. 32. *National Tempera Publication Depôt: London,* [1880.] 8°. **8436. aa. 20.**

—— Something more dangerous than Fire. And ot dialogues. By R. E. C. pp. 30. *National Tempera Publication Depôt: London,* [1880.] 8°. **8436. aa. 20.**

C., R. E. Space for Every Man. Addressed to . . . L Ashley. [The dedication signed: R. E. C., i.e. Rac E. Cresswell.] pp. 43. *Hatchard: London,* [1849.] 8° **8275.** d. **1.**

C., R. F. Deducção filosofica da desegualdade dos sexo de seus direitos politicos por natureza. Auctor R. F. [i.e. R. Ferreira da Costa.] pp. 45. *Lisboa,* 1822. **8415. aa. 48.**

C., R. F. Owen's School Book of Poetry. [The pref signed: R. F. C., i.e. R. F. Cholmeley.] pp. 104. *Educational Supply Association: London,* [1914.] 8°. **11607.** c.

C . . ., R . . . . . F . . . . . , *R.P.* *See* Alithinolo (Eudoxius) *pseud.* Alithinologia sive veridica repo [*sic*] ad Invectiuam Mendaciis . . . fœtam in pluri Antistites . . . Hibernos à R.P. R . . . . . F . . . . . C . [i.e. Richard Ferral, Cappucino] Congregationi de paganda fide . . . exhibitam, *etc.* 1664. 4°. **487.** f.

C., R. H. *See* Burns (R.) *the Poet.* [*Works.*] The Work Robert Burns, *etc.* [The editor's preface signed: R. H i.e. R. H. Cromek.] 1814. 12°. **11611.** aa.

C., R. H. *See* Liturgies.—*Church of England.*—*Com Prayer.* The Book of Common Prayer, &c. [With introduction signed: R. H. C.] 1867. 8°. **3406.** bb.

C., R. H. Documents connected with the History of Lud and the Lords Marchers. [The preface signed: R. H i.e. Robert H. Clive. With plates.] pp. vi. 361. *John Van Voorst: London,* 1841. 4°. **2368.** dd

—— [Another copy.] **L.P.** G. **1**

C., R. H. Race Course Guide. Containing a table of r courses, clubs, &c., also the principal Irish and Contine meetings. By R. H. C. (Racing fixtures for 1901.) *Tindall & Co.: Newmarket,* [1901.] 16°. **7908.** de.

C., R. H. The Scottish National Dances: their origin, nat and history. By R. H. C. [i.e. Robert H. Calder.] pp. *D. Wyllie & Son: Aberdeen,* 1928. 8°. **7908.** g.

C., R. H.

—— Selections in Prose and Verse from the Papers of R. F [i.e. R. H. Cheney.] [The editor's preface signed: E. i.e. Edward Cheney.] pp. viii. 195. *Privately prin London,* 1871. 4°. **12352.** dd

C., R. J. Directions for Plain Knitting . . . By R. J pp. 62. *J. Thompson: Cheadle,* [1846.] 16°. **1042.** a.

C., R. J. A Group of Western Scholars. (D. MacFi John Lynch, Roderick O'Flaherty.) By R. J. C. pp *Catholic Truth Society: Dublin,* 1926. 8°. **010803.** de. *The date on the wrapper is* 1927.

C., R. J. Morning Thoughts; or, Devout meditations every day in the year. By R. J. C. [i.e. R. J. Cr pp. iv. 366. *Thomas Laurie: Edinburgh,* 1868. 8°. **4411.** f.

—— [A reissue.] *London,* 1872. 8°. **764.** d.

C., R. J. La Turquie en 1860. Par R. J. C. pp. 31. *Paris*, 1860. 8°. **8028**. b. **88**. (**7**.)

—— Turkey in 1860. By R. J. C. pp. 34. *H. Baillière: London*, 1860. 8°. **8028**. b. **90**. (**10**.)

C., R. L. The Legend of Mandalay Hill . . . By R. L. C. [i.e. R. L. Calogreedy.] pp. 15. *Upper Burma Advertiser Press: Mandalay*, 1926. 8°. **20018**. f. **13**.

C., R. L.

—— A Picture Book of Welsh Porcelain. [The introduction signed: R. L. C.] pp. 32. 1951. 8°. *See* CARDIFF.—*National Museum of Wales*. **7813**. f. **21**.

C., R. L.

—— Songs of Burma. By R. L. C. author of "The Legend of Mandalay Hill" [i.e. R. L. Calogreedy]. pp. 24. *Upper Burma Advertiser Press: Mandalay*, 1926. 8°. **11654**. a. **61**.

C., R. M. The Late Mr. Sorabjee Shapurjee Bengalee, J.P., C.I.E. [Signed: R. M. C., i.e. Rāmakṛishṇa Mādhavarāva Chonkar.] pp. 4. 172. *Sabodh Prakash Press: Bombay*, [1893.] 8°. **10606**. aaa. **32**.

C., R. N. *See* VAUGHAN (Charles J.) *Dean of Llandaff*. Counsel and Might: prayers and meditations adapted from sermons by . . . C. J. Vaughan . . . Compiled by R. N. C. 1879. 16°. **3457**. bbb. **38**.

C., R. N. Life of Rama, the son of Dasaratha, King of Ajodya . . . Compiled from original sources, and accompanied by maps of ancient and modern India. [The preface signed: R. N. C., i.e. Robert N. Cust. With maps.] pp. 30. *Secundra Orphan Press: Agra*, 1854. 8°. **10602**. h. **1**. (7.)

C., R. N. A Life's Trial. By a Sufferer. [Signed: R. N. C. In verse.] pp. 56. *H. Bickers & Son: London*, 1877. 16°. **11653**. a. **21**.

C., R. N. Some Account of the Church of Cockayne Hatley, Bedfordshire. [Signed: R. N. C., i.e. Robert N. Cust. With illustrations by L. C. Cust and others.] pp.10. *W. Nicol: London*, [1851.] fol. **7816.h.48.**
With insertions.

C., R. O. *See* WOLF (Johann W.) Fairy Ballads from the German, rendered into English Verse by R. O. C. 1856. 16°. **11521**. a. **39**.

C., R. O. Breakfast and Savoury Dishes. By R. O. C. [i.e. Rose O. Cole.] pp. 64. *Chapman & Hall: London*, 1885. 8°. **7945**. c. **8**.

—— The Official Handbook for the National Training School for Cookery: containing the lessons on cookery which constitute the course of instruction in the School . . . Compiled by R. O. C. [i.e. Rose O. Cole], *etc*. pp. 416. 1877. 8°. *See* LONDON.—III. *National Training School for Cookery*. **7944**. c. **7**.

—— New and cheaper edition, twenty-sixth thousand. pp. 476. [1897.] 8°. *See* LONDON.—III. *National Training School for Cookery*. **7953**. bbb. **34**.

C., R. O. Salmon Fishing. "Drawn and lithographed" by R. O. C. *R. & A. Ackermann: London*, [1867.] *obl.* 4°. **1754**. a. **15**.

C., R. P. Sola una ley de un renglon, hará feliz la Nacion. [Signed: R. P. C.] pp. 8. *Guadalajara*, 1834. 4°. **9770**. bb. **23**. (**32**.)

C., R. R. and **J.**, S. H.

—— Exercises for Translation. Greek-English. [The preface signed: R. R. C., i.e. Robert Ronald Cameron, and S. H. J.] pp. 76. "*Muses*" *Press: Nicosia*, [1938.] 8°. **012924**. bb. **20**.

—— Exercises for Translation. English-Greek. [The preface signed: R. R. C., i.e. Robert Ronald Cameron, and S. H. J.] pp. 60. "*Muses*" *Press: Nicosia*, [1938.] 8°. **012924**. bb. **19**.

C., R. S. *See* L., W. H. Winchester College Notions. By three Beetleites. [The "preface to second edition" of vol. 1. signed: W. H. L., J. F. R. H., R. S. C., i.e. W. H. Lawson, J. F. R. Hope and R. S. Cripps.] 1910. 8°. **8367**. e. **8**.

C., R. S. *See* LITURGIES.—*Lesser Reformed Bodies.—Spanish Episcopal Church*. The Revised Prayer-Book . . . Translated by R. S. C. [i.e. R. Stewart Clough], *etc*. 1894. 16°. **3425**. e. **21**.

C., R. S. *See* PERIODICAL PUBLICATIONS.—*Oxford*. The Oxford Spectator. Reprinted. [The preface signed: R. S. C., E. N., T. H. W., i.e. R. S. Copleston, and others.] 1869. 8°. P.P. **6117**. h.

C., R. S.

—— *See* SPAIN.—*Spanish Episcopal Church*. A Communication from the Spanish Episcopal Church (translated by R. S. C.), *etc*. [1880?] 8°. **4626**. d. **11**.

C., R. S. Heads of Objections to the Marriage Affinity Bill. [Signed: R. S. C.] pp. 7. [*Edinburgh*, 1869.] 8°. **5175**. aaa. **43**.

C., R. S., *Citoyen*. Elisa, ou le Voyage au Mont-Bernard, opéra en deux actes. Paroles du Citoyen R. S. C. [i.e. Baron J. A. de Réveroni Saint Cyr], *etc*. pp. 44. *Paris*, [1794?] 8°. **11738**. m. **37**. (3.)

C., R. S., *Mr*. Sophie de Pierrefeu, ou le Désastre de Messine, fait historique, en trois actes, paroles de Mr R. S. C. [i.e. Baron J. A. de Réveroni Saint Cyr], *etc*. pp. 44. *Paris*, 1804. 8°. **11738**. m. **37**. (**7**.)

C. (R. SALVAT) *See* SALVAT C.

C., R. T. D. Conversacion entre Don Quijóte de la Mancha y su escudero Sancho Panza, sobre la constitucion. Su autor R. T. D. C. pp. 4. *Avila*, 1820. 8°. **012314**. h. **55**.

C., R. W. *See* AUSTEN (Jane) Volume the First, *etc*. [The editor's preface signed: R. W. C., i.e. Robert W. Chapman.] 1933. 8°. **012603**. a. **30**.

C., R. Y. No more Tears. By R. Y. C. pp. 78. *Christian Book Society: London*, 1874. 8°. **4416**. eee. **11**.

C. (Ro.) A True Historicall Discourse of Muley Hamets rising to the three Kingdomes of Moruecos, Fes, and Sus. The dis-vnion of the three kingdomes, by ciuill warres kindled amongst his three . . . sonnes, Muley Sheck, Muley Boferes, and Muley Sidan. The religion and policie of the More, or Barbarian. The aduentures of Sir Anthony Sherley, and diuers other English gentlemen, in those countries. With other nouelties. [The dedication signed: Ro. C.] B.L. *Thomas Purfoot, for Clement Knight: London*, 1609. 4°. **1198**. c. **20**

—— [Another copy.] **279**. b. **9**.

—— [Another copy.] G. **6675**
Imperfect; wanting sig. A 2, *containing the dedication.*

C. (Ro.)

—— [Another edition.] Collections of things most remarkable in the History of Barbarie. Written by Ro. C. *Se* PURCHAS (S.) Purchas his Pilgrimes, *etc.* pt. 2. 1625. fol. **679.** h. **12.**

C., S. *See* BARTHÉLEMY (J. J.) Œuvres diverses. (pt. 1. Éloge historique de J. J. Barthélemy. [Signed: S. C., i.e. G. E. J. Guilhem de Clermont Lodève, Baron de Sainte Croix.]) [1798.] 8°. **671.** f. **9.**

C., S. *See* BIBLE.—*Gospels.—Harmonies.* [*English.*] A Gospel Harmony of the Events of Good Friday . . . Arranged . . . By S. C. [i.e. S. Croft.] [1877.] 32°. **3224.** de. **15.**

C., S.

—— *See* C., H., *Gent.* The English Dictionary . . . The twelfth edition revised and enlarged by S. C. [i.e. Samuel Clarke.] 1670. 12°. **12984.** de. **25.**

C., S. *See* ENGLAND.—*Parliament.—House of Commons.* [*Proceedings.*—II.] A Full Report of the Debate . . . on the 25th & 26th of February, and 1st & 2nd of March 1813, on the Catholic Question. [The advertisement signed: S. C.] 1813. 8°. **1119.** e. **6.**

C., S. *See* ENGLAND.—*Catholics.* Declaration and Protestation of the Roman Catholics of England, *etc.* [The advertisement signed: S. C.] 1812. 8°. **3942.** b. **76.** (**7.**)

C., S. *See* FOSCOLO (N. U.) The Sepulchres . . . From the Italian of Ugo Foscolo. [Signed: S. C., i.e. Sinclair Cullen ?] [1820 ?] 8°. **11436.** bbb. **74.** (**5.**)

—— *See* FOSCOLO (N. U.) Sulla fortuna dei "Sepolcri" in Inghilterra, *etc.* [An essay by G. Calabritto on the English translations of the poem, including that signed: S. C., published about 1820 and here ascribed to Sinclair Cullen. With the text of the translations.] 1932. 8°. **11857.** a. **4.**

C., S. *See* GUYOT (Arnold H.) The Earth and Man . . . Slightly abridged . . . With corrections and a few notes. [Signed: S. C.] 1852. 8°. **10002.** a. **22.**

C., S. *See* JENYNS (Soame) *M.P.* De l'évidence de la religion chrétienne . . . Troisième édition augmentée . . . de pensées sur la Providence (par S. C. [i.e. G. E. J. Guilhem de Clermont Lodève, Baron de Sainte Croix]). 1797. 12°. **4017.** aaa. **2.**

C., S. *See* LEIGH (Samuel) *Publisher.* Leigh's New Picture of London, *etc.* [The editor's preface signed: S. C.] 1818. 12°. **578.** a. **14.**

C., S. *See* MIDDLETON (Conyers) A Letter from Rome, shewing an exact conformity between Popery and Paganism, *etc.* [With a preface signed: S. C.] 1813. 8°. **1352.** d. **33.**

C., S. *See* ROBERTSON (William) *D.D., the Historian.* Rise of the Reformation, *etc.* [Selected from the second book of Robertson's "History of the Reign of the Emperor Charles V." The advertisement signed: S. C.] 1812. 8°. **4520.** *d.* **1.** (**1.**)

C., S. *See* STEVENSON (Robert L.) Songs of Travel, *etc.* [The editorial note signed: S. C., i.e. Sidney Colvin.] 1896. 8°. **011652.** f. **60.**

—— *See* STEVENSON (Robert L.) The Strange Case of Dr. Jekyll and Mr. Hyde, with other fables. [The editor's note signed: S. C., i.e. Sidney Colvin.] 1896. 8°. **012627.** i. **21.**

C., S.

—— *See* STEVENSON (Robert L.) Weir of Hermiston, [The editor's note signed: S. C., i.e. Sidney Colvin.] 1896. 8°. **012627.** i

—— *See* STEVENSON (Robert L.) A Stevenson Me [The editor's note signed: S. C., i.e. Sidney Colvin.] 1899. 8°. **C. 59.** e

C., S. *See* V., C., and C., S. A Dynastia e a Revoluçã Setembro, ou Nova exposição da Questão Portugue successão. 1840. 8°. **8042.** bbb

C., S. *See* W., G., and C., S. Innocency against Envy By G. W. [i.e. George Whitehead] and C. S. [i.e. Sa Cater ?] 1691. 4°. **4152.** ee. **46**

C., S. *See* WATTS (Isaac) *D.D.* Watts's First Catec and prayers, versified . . . By a Sunday-School Tea [The prefatory note signed: S. C.] [1826.] 4°. **03504.** de. **3**

C., S. Address to the Inhabitants of the Town and P of Montrose, by a Parishioner. [An appeal for cont tions to the funds of the Kirk Session of Mon Signed S. C., pp. 15. *D. Buchanan: Mon* 1803. 8°. [i.e. Susan Carnegie ?] **8285.** bbb

C., S. Aids to the Mastery of German Declensions Irregular Verbs. Arranged by S. C. [i.e. S. Croft.] p *Relfe Bros.: London,* [1891.] 16°. **12901.** aa. **26**

C., S. An Anniversary upon the xxxth of January. *See* infra: The Loyal Remembrancer.

C., S. The Art of Complaisance, or the Means to obli conversation. [The author's introductory letter si S. C.] pp. 180. *For John Starkey: London,* 1673. **8410.** aaa

—— The second edition. pp. 180. *For John Sta London,* 1677. 12°. **1030.** b. **11**

C., S.

—— Blessed Placide Viel. Second Superior General Sisters of the Christian Schools. By S. C. [With trait.] pp. ix. 134. *Burns Oates & Washbourne: L* 1951. 8°. **4889.** a

C., S. A Book of Family Prayers, Morning Service. Clero-Laicus. [The preface signed: S. C.] pp. *W. Lewis: Cardiff,* 1893. 4°. **3455.**

C., S. A Christian Plea for Christians Baptisme: from the grave of apostasie. Or a short treatise, b reproof of some things written by A. R. [i.e. A Ritor] in his treatise intituled, The vanitie of C baptisme. [By] S. C. [i.e. Samuel Chidley.] p *Printed by T. P. & M. S.; sold by B. Allen: L* 1643. 4°. **E. 10**

—— A Christian Plea for Infants Baptisme, or a futation of some things written by A. R. [i.e. A Ritor] in his Treatise, entituled, The second part vanitie and Childishnesse of Infants Baptisme. answer whereof, the lawfulnesse of Infants Bapti defended . . . [By] S. C. [i.e. Samuel Chidley.] p *Printed by T. P. & M. S.; sold by B. Allen: L* 1643. 4°. **E.**

—— [A reissue.] *Printed by H. Allen: London,* 1647. **432**

Cropped.

C., S. Christmas with the Holy Child. A poem by S. C. [i.e. S. Croft.] pp. 37. *Skeffington & Son: London,* [1891.] 8°. **11601.** dd. **14.** (**3.**)

C., S. El Cometa. Papel liberal. [Signed: S. C.] no. 1. pp. 8. *México,* 1822. 4°. **9770.** bb. **10.** (**30.**)

C., S. De l'état et du sort des colonies des anciens peuples . . . avec des observations sur les colonies des nations modernes, & la conduite des Anglois en Amérique. [The dedication signed: S. C., i.e. G. E. J. Guilhem de Clermont-Lodève, Baron de Sainte Croix.] pp. xiv. 336. *Philadelphie* [*Paris*], 1779. 8°. **232.** h. **21.**

C., S. The Divine Sovereignty in Nature and in the Church and the apparent position and call of the Anglican Communion as typified in the Old Testament . . . By S. C. [i.e. S. Croft.] pp. 90. *Church Printing Co.: London,* [1908.] 8°. **4109.** df. **21.**

— Easter with the Risen Christ . . . By S. C. [i.e. S. Croft.] pt. 1. pp. 79. *Church Printing Co.: London,* [1910.] 8°. **011650.** eee. **120.**

No more published.

C., S. An Epistle Apologetical of S. C. (Mr. Cressy) to a Person of Honour [i.e. E. Hyde, Earl of Clarendon] touching his Vindication of Dr. Stillingfleet [i.e. "Animadversions upon a Book, intituled, Fanaticism fanatically imputed to the Catholick Church by Dr. Stillingfleet"]. 1674. 8°. *See* CRESSY (Hugh P., afterwards S.) **698.** b. **35.**

C., S. Epitaphe d'Alphonse Pollot, cy deuant Premier Gentilhomme de la Chambre de son Altesse . . . d'Orange . . . Votiuum hoc carmen . . . scripsit S. C. [*Geneva,* 1668.] *s. sh.* fol. **11408.** f. **59.** (**35.**)

C., S. The Famous and Delectable History of Cleocreton & Cloryana; wherein is set forth the noble and heroick actions of Cleocreton Prince of Hungary . . . Herein is also declared, his constant love to the most beautiful Princess Cloryana, the onely daughter of the Emperor of Persia. [The epistle dedicatory signed: S. C.] B.L. pp. 155. *J. B.* [*John Beale*] *for C. Tyus: London,* [1630 ?] 4°. **1077.** e. **25.**

C., S.

— Form or Freedom. Five colloquies on liturgies, reported by a Manchester Congregationalist [or rather, written by Samuel Clarkson, who signs the preface S. C.]. pp. 60. *Jackson & Walford: London,* [1856.] 8°. **3477.** b. **44.**

C., S. Gospel Events, chronologically arranged. By S. C. [i.e. S. Croft.] pp. 47. *Hayes & Co.: London,* [1879.] 8°. **4372.** d. **7.** (**12.**)

C., S. Hong Kong, "Isle of Beauty." The new handbook & guide . . . Including: the new territories, Canton, Macao. (1928-1929 edition.) [The preface signed: S. C.] pp. 106. *Hongkong,* [1928.] 8°. **010056.** a. **15.**

C., S. A Horrible and Bloody Plot to murder Sir Thomas Fairfax, Sir William Brereton, Sir Thomas Middleton, Colonell Moore, and above one hundred more of the parliament men . . . With the names of the knights . . . and others that were chief actors therein. The copies of the severall indictments, bills, and other parchments and papers . . . With letters from the Committee of Chester, *etc.* [The letters signed: S. C.] pp. 21. *B. Alsop, for E. Griffin: London,* 1646. 4°. **E. 345.** (**20.**)

C., S. An Impartial Enquiry into the Existence and Nature of God . . . with remarks on several authors both ancient and modern and particularly on some passages in Dr. Clarke's "Demonstration of the being and attributes of God" . . . With an appendix concerning the nature and attributes of space and duration. By S. C. [i.e. Samuel Colliber.] pp. 230. *London,* 1718. 8°. **873.** g. **31.**

C., S. Impugnacion [signed: S.C.] del papel titulado: Consejo prudente sobre una de las Garantías [by F. Lagranda]. pp. 8. *México,* 1821. 4°. **9770.** bb. **7.** (**44.**)

C., S. The Indian Prophet, or a Review of Babu K. C. Sen's lecture "Am I an inspired Prophet?" . . . A lecture delivered . . . at Dacca. [The preface signed: S. C., i.e. Sitalākānta Chaṭṭopādhyāya.] pp. 44. *New Press: Dacca,* 1879. 8°. **4503.** b. **1.** (**2.**)

C., S. Japanese Ideas of London and its wonders, its inhabitants, and their manners and customs; described in a letter to his wife at Yokohama. By a Japanese Scout. [The prefatory note signed: S. C., i.e. S. Cockburn. In verse.] pp. 59. *Printed for private circulation: London,* [1873.] 8°. **11652.** aaa. **41.**

C., S. The Life of the Lady Halket. [The dedication signed: S. C.] pp. 58. *Andrew Symson; Henry Knox: Edinburgh,* 1701. 4°. **4887.** de. **13.** (**1.**)

C., S. The Loyal Remembrancer: or, a Poem dedicated to the Queens . . . Majesty, *etc.* [The dedication signed: S. C., i.e. S. Crown.] pp. 6. *Printed by R. Wood: London,* 1650, *but not permitted to be publick till now,* 1660. 4°. **E. 1048.** (**8.**)

—— [Another edition.] An Anniversary upon the xxx[th] of January. 1648. Being a poem dedicated to the Queen, *etc.* [The dedication signed: S. C., i.e. S. Crown.] pp. 11. *Printed by Nathaniel Butter: London,* 1650, *but not permitted to be publick till now,* 1660. 8°. **C. 58.** bb. **25.**

C., S. Mock Poem or Whiggs supplication. [The author's apology signed: S. C., i.e. Samuel Colvil.] 2 pt. *London,* 1681. 8°. **11626.** a. **12.** (**1.**)

—— [Another edition.] pp. 110. *James Watson: Edinburgh,* 1711. 8°. **11633.** a. **61.**

C., S. Multum in Parvo: or, a Reform catechism in three parts . . . To which is added a Bullion catechism, in two parts . . . By S. C. pp. 40. *J. M. Richardson & J. Hatchard: London,* 1811. 8°. **1028.** e. **2.** (**4.**)

C., S. A New Book for Children to learn in. With many wholsome meditations for them to consider . . . By S. C. [i.e. Stephen Crisp.] (Also a Testimony concerning the Father, Son and Spirit . . . Also, the Devil and his works manifested . . . By G. Fox the younger.—The Lamb and His Day Proclaimed. [Signed: H. S., i.e. Humphry Smith.]) pp. 104. *Printed & sold by A. Sowie: London,* 1681. 16°. **629.** a. **10.**

C., S. New System of Reading. By S. C. 3 pt. [*J. Connell & Co.: Glasgow,* 1896.] 8°. **12984.** ee. **12.**

C., S. "Not a Minute to Spare," a thought for the times. By S. C. pp. 86. *William Roberts: Exeter; Hamilton, Adams & Co.: London,* 1855. 12°. **4407.** b. **58.**

C., S. Personal Appearances in Health and Disease. [Signed: S. C., i.e. Sidney Coupland.] pp. 96. *Hardwicke & Bogue: London,* 1879. 16°. [*Health Primers.*] **7404.** d. **37.**

C., S.

—— Pictures into Verse. By S. C. [With illustrations.] pp. 62. [1945 ?] 4°. **7869.** ppp. **3.**

C., S.

—— Polemica Zamboni-Contri. [Signed: S. C., i.e. Siro Contri. On a philosophical controversy between G. Zamboni and the author.] ff. 9. *Verona*, 1947. fol. **8472**. d. **37**.
Reproduced from typewriting.

C., S. Pour le mariage de Monsieur Gabriel Sarasin, & de Mademoiselle Marie Madeleine Pictet, celebré à Geneve le 26. de février M.DC.LXIX. (Elegie.) [Signed: S. C.] [*Geneva?* 1669.] 4°. **11408**. f. **59**. (**8**.)

C., S. Right and Ritual. A friendly conversation on the order enjoined by law. By S. C. [i.e. S. Croft.] With prefatory note and postscript by . . . J. W. Kempe. pp. 40. *Parker & Co.: London*, 1887. 8°. **4108**. de. **33**. (**3**.)

C., S. Sacred Poems. By S. C. pp. 34. *H. W. Roberts: Ware*, 1866. 12°. **11644**. eee. **13**.

C., S. The Scotch Hudibras: or, a Mock poem . . . Corrected and amended, with additions and alterations. [The author's apology signed: S. C., i.e. Samuel Colvil.] 2 pt. *Printed by T. B. & sold by Randal Taylor: London*, 1692. 8°. **238**. b. **9**.

C., S. Se acabaron los Gendarmas por que marchan al Precidio. [Signed: S. C.] pp. 4. *México*, 1826. 4°. **8180**. bbb. **20**. (**6**.)

C., S. A Select Collection of Novels . . . written by the most celebrated authors in several languages . . . and all new translated from the originals by several eminent hands. [The dedication to each volume signed: S. C., i.e. Samuel Croxall.] 6 vol. *J. Watts: London*, 1722, 20, 21. 12°. **12410**. c. **12–17**.

—— [Another copy of vol. 5, 6.] **635**. c. **1**.

—— The second edition, with additions, *etc.* 6 vol. *John Watts: London*, 1729. 12°. **12602**. aaa. **5**.

C., S. A Short History of a Long Travel from Babylon to Bethel. [Signed: S. C., i.e. Stephen Crisp.] The seventh edition. pp. 28. *London*, 1766. 12°. **4416**. aaa. **12**.

—— The eighth edition. pp. 28. *Mary Hinde: London*, 1771. 12°. **4413**. c. **9**.

—— [Another edition.] pp. 24. *J. Fry & Co.: London*, 1777. 12°. **4378**. aa. **6**. (**4**.)

—— The tenth edition. pp. 36. *James Phillips: London*, 1784. 8°. **4415**. bb. **11**.

—— The twelfth edition. pp. 36. *William Phillips: London*, 1818. 12°. **4152**. a. **19**.

C., S. The Sinfulness and Cure of Thoughts. [A sermon. By S. C., i.e. Stephen Charnock.] *See* ANNESLEY (Samuel) A Supplement to the Morning-Exercise, *etc.* 1676. 4°. **855**. k. **14**.

C., S. "The Three Steps," taken; or, the Happy end of Nurse H—— . . . Second edition. [The preface signed S. C.] pp. 36. *J. Groom: London, Birmingham*, 1855. 12° **4407**. b. **29**

C., S. Translations, found in a commonplace book. [Or rather original pieces. By Maurice Baring. The editor's preface signed: S. C.] pp. xxix. *B. H. Blackwell: Oxford*, 1916. 8°. **012305**. k. **22**.

C., S. A Treatise on the Parallactic Angle, extracted fron letter to the late Earl of Macclesfield on that subje To which is added an appendix: containing a compl set of solar and lunar tables, entitled, Tabulæ Dur menses, for computing the places of those luminaries, [The dedication signed: S. C.] 2 pt. *W. Sandl London*, 1766. 4°. **8532**. dd.

C., S. A Trip to Portugal; or, a View of their strength sea and land . . . with the names of their regimen officers, the situation of their frontier towns, and true prospect of their fortifications. To which is add a catalogue of their kings . . . In a letter from a volont at Lisbon. [Signed: S. C.] pp. 72. *John Nu London*, 1704. 8°. **9195**. c.

C., S. The Truth and Excellence of the Christian Religi with the corruptions and additions of the Romish Chur A discourse . . . With a short vindication of Christ loyalty: and a brief historical account of Romish treas and usurpations, since the Reformation. By a hea Professor of reformed Catholic Christianity. [The dedi tion signed: S. C.] pp. 141. *For John Gellibrar London*, 1685. 8°. **867**. a.

C., S. The Two Widows. [In verse. Signed: S. C.] pp *J. F. Shaw & Co.: London*, [1885.] 8°. **11643**. bbb. **23**.

C., S.

—— Wheat: its history, characteristics, chemical compo tion, and nutritive properties. By the Old Norf Farmer, *etc.* [The preface signed: S.C., i.e. Sam Copland.] pp. xvi. 172. *Houlston & Wright: Lond* 1865. 8°. **7075**. aa.

C., S. The Young Man's Calling: or the Whole duty youth . . . Together with remarks upon the lives several . . . young persons [by the editor, Nathan Crouch] . . . and also, divine poems. [The author's preface signed:] S. C. [i.e. Sam Crossman.] pp. 318. *For Natn. Crouch: Lond* 1685 [1695]. 12°. G. **132**
Another edition of S. Crossman's "Young Man's Mo tor," with the addition of the "Remarks." The "Remark are taken from the edition of 1695.

—— [A reissue.] *For Nath. Crouch: London*, 1695. 12°. **4408**. b.

C., S., *A.M.*

—— A Psalm of Thanksgiving to be sung by the Children Christ's-Hospital . . . The words by S. C. A. M. [i.e. Sam Cobb.] [With musical notes.] 1706. *s. sh.* fol. CHRIST'S HOSPITAL. [*Miscellaneous Publications.*] **10350**. g. **12**. (**1**

C., S., *Barrister at Law.* Lex Custumaria: or, a Treatise copy-hold estates, in respect of the { lord, copy-holder } Together with a collection of many cases . . . presider . . . By S. C. Barrister at Law [i.e. Samuel Carter], e pp. 384. *Assigns of R. & E. Atkins for John Walthc London*, 1696. 8°. **6305**. b.

—— The second edition, with additions. pp. 392. *Dan Brown & John Walthoe: London*, 1701. 8°. **514**. e.

C., S., *a Catholick O.S.B.* Fanaticism fanatically imput to the Catholick Church by Doctour Stillingfleet, a the imputation refuted and retorted by S. C. a Catholi O.S.B. [i.e. Serenus Cressy, name in religion of Hugh Cressy.] pp. 188. FEW MS. NOTES. 1672. 8°. **3936**. b. **2**

., S., *Cavaliere.* Lettera del cavaliere S. C. contenente alcune notizie letterarie della Polonia. *See* BRUNI (G. B.) Nuova collezione d'opuscoli letterarii, *etc.* vol. 1. [1824, *etc.*] 4°. **538. l. 23.**

., S., *Esq.* The Law of Executions . . . By S. C., Esq., author of Lex Custumaria [i.e. Samuel Carter]. pp. 323. *Robert Battersby: London,* 1706. 8°. **884. i. 11.**

., S., *Gent.* *See* PEIRCE (James) The Truth and Importance of the Scripture-Doctrine of the Trinity and Incarnation demonstrated: a defence of . . . Mr. Peirces Thirteen Queries, *etc.* (Postscript, with relation to another Answer to the above Queries, written by S. C. Gent.) 1736. 8°. **699. e. 13. (9.)**

., S., *of the Inner-Temple, Esq.* Legal Provisions for the Poor: or, a Treatise of the common and statute laws concerning the poor . . . By S. C. of the Inner-Temple, Esq; [i.e. Samuel Carter] *etc.* pp. 494. *John Walthoe:* [*London,*] 1710. 8°. **1130. a. 33.**

— The fifth edition, *etc.* pp. 387. *J. Walthoe: London,* 1725. 12°. **518.a.10.**

., S., *of the Inner-Temple, Esquire.* Reports of Several Special Cases . . . in the Court of Common Pleas in the 16, 17, 18 & 19 years of King Charles II. to which are added some cases adjudged in the time of Chief Justice Vaughan. By S. C., of the Inner-Temple, Esquire [i.e. Samuel Carter]. B.L. pp. 243. FEW MS. NOTES [by F. Hargrave]. 1688. fol. *See* ENGLAND.—*Court of Common Pleas.* [*Reports.*] **513. k. 16.**

— [Another copy.] **19. b. 8.**

., S., *of the Society of Jesus.* The Garden of our B. Lady. Or a Deuout manner, how to serue her in her Rosary. Written by S. C. of the Society of Iesus [i.e. Sabin Chambers]. pp. 272. [*St. Omer,*] 1619. 8°. C. **26. gg. 1.**

., S., *Preacher at B. F.* Englands Covenant proved lawfull & necessary, also at this time, both by Scripture and reason. Together with sundry answers to the usuall objections made against it. By S. C. Preacher at B. F. [i.e. Samuel Clarke, Preacher at Bennet Fink.] pp. 16. *For Henry Overton: London,* 1643. 4°. E. **60. (5.)**

., S., *Reverend Father, Monk of the Holy Order of Saint Benedict and of the English Congregation.* I. Question, Why are you a Catholick. The answer follows; II. Question, But why are you a Protestant ?—An answer attempted—in vain. Written by the Reverend Father S. C., Monk of the Holy Order of St. Benedict, and of the English Congregation [i.e. Hugh P., afterwards Serenus Cressy]. pp. 72. *London,* 1686. 4°. T. **1866. (1.)**

— [Another copy.] **222. e. 15. (1.)**

., S., *a Roman Catholick.* Roman-Catholick Doctrines no Novelties; or an Answer to Dr. Pierce's Court-Sermon, miscall'd The Primitive Rule of Reformation. By S. C., a Roman Catholick [i.e. Hugh P., afterwards Serenus Cressy]. pp. 322. 1663. 8°. **694. a. 40.**

., S., *le Sieur.* Oeuvres meslées, ou Nouveau recueïl de diverses pieces galantes en vers. Par le Sieur S. C. [i.e. S. Chapuzeau.] *J. H. Widerholdt: Geneve,* 1671. 12°. **11481. a. 11.**

., S., *V.D.M.*

— Peace the End of the Upright. Opened and applied at the interment of . . . Mr. Samuel Clark . . . who slept in Jesus, Feb. 24. 170$\frac{0}{1}$. aetat. 75. at Wiccomb . . With his true, but too short, character. By S. C., V.D.M. [i.e. Samuel Cox.] [With a preface by M. Sylvester.] pp. 96. *J. Robinson: London,* 1701. 8°. **1416. e. 9.**

C . . . . . ., S . . . . . . DE. L'Ecole des pères et mères, ou les Trois infortunées. [Tales. The dedicatory epistle signed: S . . . . . . de C . . . . . ., i.e. A. Sabatier, de Castres.] 2 pt. *Amsterdam,* 1767. 12°. **12518. aa. 12.**

C., S. v. Auch ein Wort über die Ausbildung der Cavallerie, von S. v. C. pp. 90. *Berlin,* 1862. 8°. **8826. dd. 41. (2.)**

— *See* SEIDLER (E. F.) Einiges über die Ausbildung der Reiter und Pferde . . . mit Bezugnahme auf die Brochüre "Auch ein Wort über die Ausbildung der Kavallerie von S. v. C.," *etc.* 1863. 8°. **7293. g. 41.**

C., S. A. *See* COTTON (George E. L.) *Bishop of Calcutta.* Sermons preached to English Congregations in India. [The editor's preface signed: S. A. C., i.e. Sophia A. Cotton.] 1867. 8°. **4464. bbb. 9.**

C., S. A. *See* JAMES V., *King of Scotland.* The Page of James the Fifth of Scotland. Translated from the French by S. A. C., *etc.* 1900. 8°. **012550. b. 4.**

C., S. A. Ancient Devotions for Holy Communion from Eastern and Western Liturgical Sources. Compiled by S. A. C. With an introduction by Abbot Gasquet. pp. xii. 179. *Kegan Paul & Co.: London,* 1905. 8°. **4324. bb. 31.**

— Second edition, with appendix. pp. xiv. 203. *Kegan Paul & Co.: London,* 1908. 8°. **4324. bb. 36.**

C., S. A. Duytsche Academi, tot Amsterdam ghespeelt, op den eersten dach van Oegstmaant, in't Iaar 1619. [By] S. A. C. [i.e. Samuel A. Coster. In verse.] *C. Lodowiicksz: Amsterdam,* 1619. 4°. **11754. bbb. 14.**

C., S. B. P. L. Teutscher Kriegs Ab- und Friedens Einzug, in etlichen Aufzügen bey . . . Fürstlichen Amalfischen Freudenmahl, schauspielweiss vorgestellt, durch S. B. P. L. C. [i.e. S. von Birken.] [In verse.] pp. 40. *Nürnberg,* 1650. 4°. **11522. e. 31. (3.)**

C., S. C. *See* CHEW (Samuel) *Professor of Medicine in the University of Maryland.* Lectures on Medical Education, *etc.* [With a notice signed: S. C. C., i.e. Samuel C. Chew.] 1864. 12°. **7680. a. 28.**

C., S. C. The Centenary of Don Juan. (Reprinted from the American Journal of Philology.) [Signed: S. C. C., i.e. Samuel C. Chew.] [1919.] 8°. Ashley **5467.**

C., S. C. Emigration realized. A poem by S. C. C. pp. v. 82. *Saunders & Otley: London,* 1855. 8°. **11648. b. 4.**

C * * *, S * * * C * * *, *Miss.* *See* BLISS (George) *Perpetual Curate of Funtington.* A Tribute of Affection to the Memory of a Beloved Niece (Miss S * * * C * * * C * * *), *etc.* 1829. 32°. **012806. de. 20. (3.)**

C., S. D. *See* ZARATE (A. de) Histoire de la découverte et de la conquete du Perou, traduite . . . par S. D. C. [i.e. S. de Broé, Seigneur de Citry et de la Guette.] 1716. 8°. **278. a. 11, 12.**

— — 1742. 8°. **9772. a. 15.**

— — 1830. 8°. **790. e. 16.**

C., S. D. Les Fideles seruiteurs du Roy, de la religion reformee . . . Par S. D. C. pp. 14. *Paris,* 1622. 8°. **1192. f. 10. (3.)**

C., S. D. Mémoires de Henry dernier duc de Mont-morency, *etc.* [The dedication signed: S. D. C., i.e. S. du Cros.] pp. 276. *F. Mauger: Paris,* 1665. 12°. **613. a. 16.**

— [Another edition.] pp. 276. *F. Mauger: Paris,* 1666. 12°. **613. a. 17.**

C., S. D., *Mr.* *See* RISI (P.) Observations sur des matières de jurisprudence criminelle. Traduit . . . par Mr. S. D. C. [i.e. François Seigneux de Correvon.] 1768. 8°. **1127. c. 19.**

C., S. D. DE. Verses. By S. D. de C. [i.e. S. Dobrogosta de Chylińska.] pp. 23. *W. & W. Pike & Son: Derby,* 1869. 12°. **11643. bb. 33. (8.)**

C., S. D. M. *See* TROGUS POMPEIUS. [*Latin.*] Justinus . . . Editio accuratissima. Accurante S. D. M. C. [i.e. Cornelius Schrevelius.] 1659. 8°. **1307. d. 20.**

C., S. I. Der geplünderte Postillon; das ist: allerhand seltzame Begebenheiten der Welt . . . allen galanten und verständigen Gemüthern zu fernerm Nachsinnen vorgestellet von S. I. C. [Translated from " Il Corriero svaligiato " of Ferrante Pallavicino.] pp. 109. *Freystadt* [*Gotha*], 1699. 8°. **11746. de. 9. (1.)**

C., S. J. *See* FRANKLAND (*Sir* Edward) *K.C.B.* Sketches from the Life of Edward Frankland . . . Edited and concluded by his two daughters M. N. W. and S. J. C. 1902. 8°. **010827. g. 22.**

C., S. J. The Company of Heaven. Daily links with the household of God. [The compiler's preface signed: S. J. C., i.e. S. J. Crossley.] pp. xviii. 457. *Longmans & Co.: London,* 1901. 8°. **3456. ddd. 34.**

—— New edition. pp. xx. 457. *Longmans & Co.: London,* 1903. 8°. **3456. ddd. 45.**

—— [A reissue.] *H. J. Glaisher: London,* 1917. 8°. **03456. ff. 6.**

—— The Ministry of Angels. By S. J. C. [i.e. S. J. Crossley.] pp. 46. *A. R. Mowbray & Co.: London, Oxford,* 1910. 16°. **4375. de. 26.**

C., S. J. D. Voyage dans la haute Pensylvanie et dans l'État de New-York, par un membre adoptif de la nation Onéida. Traduit et publié par l'auteur des Lettres d'un cultivateur américain [or rather, written by him]. [The dedication signed: S. J. D. C., i.e. M. G. J. de Crèvecœur, calling himself Saint-Jean de Crèvecœur.] 3 tom. *Paris,* 1801. 8°. **278. f. 1–3.**

—— Planches. pl. XI. fol. **150. k. 1.**

C., S. K. Extempore to Walter Scott, Esq., on the publication of the new edition of the Bridal of Triermain, etc. [Signed: S. K. C., i.e. R. P. Gillies ?] pp. 3. [*Edinburgh,* 1819.] 4°. **11641. g. 10.**

C., S. L. *See* BUCKLIN (Sophronia E.) In Hospital and Camp . . . With an introduction by S. L. C. 1869. 8°. **9602. bbb. 21.**

C., S. L. Figures d'Académie pour aprendre à désiner, gravées par S. L. C. [i.e. Sébastien Le Clerc.] *See* DUFRESNOY (C. A.) L'Art de peinture, *etc.* 1673. 12°. **674. a. 32.**

C., S. M.

—— *See* ANDERSON (Lilian M.) and C., S. M. The Flight and the Song, *etc.* [By L. M. Anderson and " S. M. C.," i.e. Sister Mary Catherine, of the Dominican Convent of Saint Catherine of Siena, Torquay.] 1946. 8°. NN. **36174.**

—— *See* ANDERSON (Lilian M.) and C., S. M. [Another edition.] The Flight and the Song. [By] S. M. C. [i.e. Sister Mary Catherine, of the Dominican Convent of Saint Catherine of Siena, Torquay], & L. M. Anderson. 1946. 8°. NN. **36786.**

C., S. M. *See* BIBLE.—*Selections.* [*English.*] The Fish[...] man's Text-book. By S. M. C. [1884.] 12°. **3129. de. [...]**

—— —— 1900. 32°. **03128. de. [...]**

C., S. M.

—— *See* VINCENT [Ferrer], *Saint.* A Christology from t[...] Sermons of St. Vincent Ferrer . . . Selected and translat[...] by S. M. C. [i.e. Sister Mary Catherine, of the Dominic[...] Convent of Saint Catherine of Siena, Torquay.] 1954. 8°. **04423. bb. [...]**

—— Brother Petroc's Return. A story by S. M. C. [i.e. Sis[...] Mary Catherine, of the Dominican Convent of Sa[...] Catherine of Siena, Torquay.] pp. 200. *Chatto [...] Windus: London,* 1937. 8°. **12626. w. [...]**

—— [A reissue.] Brother Petroc's Return. *Lond[...]* 1954. 8°. [*New Phoenix Library.*] W.P. **11527[...]**

—— *See* LAVERY (Emmet G.) Brother Petroc's Return. [...] play.] An adaptation of the novel . . . by S. M. C. [[...] Sister Mary Catherine, of the Dominican Convent [...] Saint Catherine of Siena, Torquay.] **011791. a. [...]**

—— The Dark Wheel. By S. M. C. [i.e. Sister Mary Catheri[...] of the Dominican Convent of Saint Catherine of Sie[...] Torquay.] pp. 217. *Sands & Co.: London,* 1939. 8° **04426. e. [...]**

—— Henry Suso, Saint and Poet. A study by S. M. C., [...] the English Congregation of Saint Catherine of Siena [i[...] Sister Mary Catherine]. [With a portrait.] pp. viii. 1[...] *Blackfriars: Oxford,* 1947. 8°. **4889. aa. [...]**

C., S. M. Light in Darkness. By S. M. C. [Short religio[...] meditations.] pp. 24. *J. Masters & Co.: Londo[...]* 1889. 12°. **4400. ee. [...]**

C., S. M.

—— Margaret, Princess of Hungary. By S. M. C. [i.e. Sis[...] Mary Catherine], *etc.* (Second edition.) pp. viii. 82. *Blackfriars Publications: London,* 1954. 8°. **4832. a. [...]**

—— Once in Cornwall. Being an account of Friar Pete[...] journey in search of the saint and dragon legends of [...] land. By S. M. C. [i.e. Sister Mary Catherine, of [...] Dominican Convent of Saint Catherine of Siena, Torqua[...] pp. viii. 179. *Longmans & Co.: New York, Toron[...]* 1944. 8°. **04412. l. [...]**

C., S. M. Parables for Grown-up Children. By S. M. [...] *etc.* pp. 124. *Sands & Co.: London & Edinburg[...]* 1925. 8°. **04478. de. 5[...]**

C., S. M. Random Rhymes. By S. M. C. pp. vii. 134. *J. Heywood: Manchester,* [1893.] 8°. **11653. d. 5[...]**

C., S. M. The Seven Words on the Cross; and other hym[...] By S. M. C. pp. viii. 96. *Griffith & Farran: Londo[...]* 1884. 16°. **11652. de. 4[...]**

C., S. M. Sgeaċ-Ġeal, agus Aingeal Dé. Dá ḋráma[...] gcóir páistí. S. M. C. do sgríoḃ. pp. 28. A. Tom ⁊ a Ċ.: Duḃlinn, [1932.] 8°. **875. n. 7[...]**

—— Tomáisín, agus an Plúirín Sneaċta. Drámai[...] gcóir na scol. S. M. C. do sgríoḃ. pp. 24. A. Tom ⁊ a Ċ.: Duḃlinn, [1932.] 8°. **875. n. [...]**

C., S. M.

—— The Spark in the Reeds. By S. M. C. [i.e. Sister Ma[...] Catherine, of the Dominican Convent of Saint Catheri[...] of Siena, Torquay.] pp. 249. *Sands & Co.: Londo[...]* [1941.] 8°. **04426. de. 3[...]**

C., S. M.

—— Steward of Souls. A portrait of Mother Margaret Hallahan. By S. M. C. [i.e. Sister Mary Catherine, of the Dominican Convent of Saint Catherine of Siena, Torquay. With plates, including a portrait.] pp. 181. *Longmans, Green & Co.: London,* 1952. 8°. **4907**. aa. **56**.

C., S. M., *Ursuline, Waterford.* Thoughts on the Sacred Heart. By S. M. C., Ursuline, Waterford. pp. 32. *Irish Messenger: Dublin,* 1937. 16°. **04403**. ff. **122**.

C., S. M., and **ANDERSON** (Lilian M.)

—— The Flight and the Song. [By] S. M. C. [i.e. Sister Mary Catherine, of the Dominican Convent of Saint Catherine of Siena, Torquay] & L. M. Anderson. pp. 155. 1946. 8°. *See* Anderson (Lilian M.) and C., S. M. NN. **36786**.

C., S. M. D. *See* Florus (P. A.) L. A. Florus, cum notis integris C. Salmasii . . . accurante S. M. D. C. [i.e. Cornelius Schrevelius], *etc.* 1660. 8°. **1307**. g. **12**.

C., S. M. D., *l'Abbé.* Les Délassemens d'un galant-homme, ou Fruits agréables de la lecture & de la conversation . . . Par l'abbé S. M. D. C. [i.e. Saint Martin de Chassonville.] pp. 316. *Amsterdam,* 1742. 8°. **12331**. aaaa. **21**.

C., S. M. N. Het Leven van Napoleon III, ex-Keizer der Franschen. Populair geschetst door S. M. N. C. [i.e. S. M. N. Calisch.] pp. 61. *Amsterdam,* 1870. 8°. **10661**. bb. **43**.

C., S. O. *See* Scott (*Sir* Walter) *Bart.* [*Waverley Novels.—Appendix.*] Stories from Waverley [or rather, from the Waverley novels] . . . By S. O. C. [i.e. Harriet Barton.] 1870. 16°. **12603**. aa. **14**.

—— —— 1873. 16°. **12603**. aa. **15**.

—— *See* Scott (*Sir* Walter) *Bart.* [*Old Mortality.*] The Story of Old Mortality for children by S. O. C. [i.e. Harriet Barton.] 1872. 16°. **12604**. bb. **27**.

C., S. O. The Miraculous Increase of Jacob's Flock opened and applied, from Genesis xxx. 25. to the end. By S. O. C. and published by Edmund Jones. pp. iv. 139. *J. Oswald: London,* 1753. 8°. **4473**. bb. **13**. (**1**.)

C., S. S. Corn v. Cotton. An attempt to open the case between the manufacturers and the landlords . . . Inscribed to . . . the Duke of Buckingham by the ——S. S. C. 1843. 8°. *See* Corn. **1391**. g. **33**. (**3**.)

C., S. S. Who discovered Australia? [Signed: S. S. C.] pp. 6. *Stillwell & Knight: Melbourne,* 1868. 16°. **10491**. aa. **3**.

C., S. T. The Court and the Kiln. A story on the Church Catechism. By S. T. C., author of "Waggie and Wattie," *etc.* pp. 297. *J. Nisbet & Co.: London,* 1871. 16°. **12808**. eee. **43**.

—— The Harleys of Chelsea Place; or, in Union is strength. By S. T. C., author of 'Waggie and Wattie,' 'Janet Gray,' etc. pp. viii. 192. *Johnstone, Hunter & Co.: Edinburgh,* [1868.] 8°. **12808**. aa. **26**.

—— [Another edition.] pp. viii. 192. *Hodder & Stoughton: London,* 1885. 8°. **4417**. i. **11**.

—— Janet Gray: or, Life as it meets us. By S. T. C. pp. 385. *Nisbet & Co.: London,* 1860. 8°. **12632**. aa. **18**.

—— The Little Doorkeeper; or, Patience and peace. By S. T. C. . . . With four engravings. pp. 218. *Seeley, Jackson & Halliday: London,* 1865. 8°. **12804**. cc. **30**.

C., S. T.

—— Little Facts for Little People. By S. T. C., author of "Waggie and Wattie," etc. With twelve engravings. pp. 162. *Seeley, Jackson & Halliday: London,* 1864. 8°. **4415**. bb. **12**.

—— The Little Fox: or, the Story of Captain Sir F. L. M'Clintock's Arctic Expedition. Written for the young. By S. T. C., author of "Little Facts for Little People," *etc.* pp. 195. *Seeley, Jackson & Halliday: London,* 1865. 8°. **10460**. aa. **19**.

C., S. T. Seeliger Todes-Schlaf gläubiger Christen, welchen, als . . . Hr. Balthasar Grohlig . . . Bürgermeister zu Pirna . . . beerdiget wurde . . . abbilden sollen S. T. C. [In verse.] *M. Bergens Witwe & Erben: Dresden,* [1679.] fol. **11501**. k. **18**. (**11**.)

C., S. T. Sketches of the Victoria Gold Diggings and Diggers as they are. By S. T. C. pt. 1. *H. H. Collins & Co.: London,* 1853. 4°. **10491**. g. **8**.
No more published.

C., S. T. Waggie and Wattie, or Nothing in vain. By S. T. C., author of "Little Facts for Little People," *etc.* pp. 170. *Seeley, Jackson & Halliday: London,* 1875. 8°. **12806**. cc. **8**.

C., S. T., *Master of Arts and Clerk in Holy Orders.* Jael, and other sermons. By S. T. C., Master of Arts and Clerk in Holy Orders. pp. 50. *Simpkin, Marshall & Co.: London,* 1877. 8°. **4479**. c. **1**.

C., S. T. U. *See* Rabelais (F.) The first Book of the Works of Mr. Francis Rabelais, *etc.* (The Second book . . . translated . . . by S. T. U. C. [i.e. Sir Thomas Urquhart.]) 1653. 8°. C. **57**. k. **14**.

C., S. W. *See* Sharswood (George) Popular Lectures on Commercial Law, *etc.* [The advertisement signed: S. W. C., i.e. S. W. Crittenden.] 1856. 8°. **6615**. cc. **13**.

C., S. W.

—— Diligence and its Reward. Preached . . . 1919 by S. W. C. [i.e. Samuel W. Carruthers.] pp. 8. 1919. 8°. **4480**. e. **72**.
Printed for private circulation.

C., S. Y. *See* S. Y C.

C—— (Samuel) The Young Man's Choice; a brief memorial of S. C——. pp. 51. *Wertheim, Macintosh & Hunt: London,* [1861.] 12°. **4986**. a. **58**. (**13**.)

C—— (Sarah) "Heaven our Home"; or, Memorials of Sarah C—— gathered chiefly from her own letters. pp. iv. 104. *Wertheim, Macintosh & Hunt: London,* [1859.] 12°. **4906**. b. **71**. (**4**.)

C. (Sp. Rt.) Division territorial militar. Sevilla, Coruña, Vitoria, Valladolid y Sta. Cruz de Tenerife. Sueño, aparición y comunicaciones del espíritu de Gonzalo Fernández de Córdova. Por Sp. Rt. C. pp. 30. *Madrid,* 1893. 8°. **8042**. a. **39**. (**4**.)

C. (Sr.) Der geöffnete Fecht-Boden, auf welchen durch kurtz gefaste Regeln gute Anleitung zum rechten Fundament der Fecht-Kunst gegeben und gewiesen wird . . . Verfertiget von Sr. C. pp. 53. *Hamburg,* 1706. 12°. **7912**. a. **23**.

C. (Stella) *See* Price (Harry) Stella C. An account of some original experiments in psychical research, *etc.* 1925. 8°. **08632**. e. **27**.

—— *See* Price (Harry) [Stella C.] Expériences scientifiques avec un nouveau médium, Stella C., *etc.* 1926. 8°. **08632**. h. **22**.

C. (Sy.) Ferns of the British Isles described and photographed. By Sy C. [i.e. Sydney Courtauld.] pp. 65. pl. xx. *John Van Voorst: London,* 1877. 8°. **07075.** e. 3.

C., T. *See* Bennit (William) Selections from the Epistles, &c. of William Bennit . . . To which is prefixed a memoir of his religious experience and character. [The editor's preface signed: T. C., i.e. Thomas Chalk.] 1838. 12°. **4152. a. 18.**

C., T. *See* Bible. [*English.*] The English Version of the Polyglott Bible, *etc.* [The editor's preface signed: T. C., i.e. Thomas Chevalier.] 1816, *etc.* 12°. **1106.** b. **17.**

—— —— 1825. 12°. **1407.** f. **2.** (2.)

—— —— 1828. 12°. **3053.** aaa. **14.**

—— —— 1837. 12°. **03051.** de. 6.

C., T. *See* Browne (*Sir* Thomas) [*Single Works.*] Religio Medici. [The editor's preface signed: T. C., i.e. Thomas Chapman.] 1831. 12°. **8410.** e. 9.

C., T.

—— *See* Chester. [*Appendix.*] Chester's Triumph, *etc.* [The editor's introduction signed: T. C., i.e. Thomas Corser.] 1844. 4°. [*Remains historical and literary connected with the Palatine Counties of Lancaster and Chester.* vol. 3.] Ac. **8120.**

C., T. *See* Cicero (M. T.) [*De Officiis.—English.*] Tully's Three Books of Offices in English, *etc.* [The translator's epistle dedicatory signed: T. C., i.e. Thomas Cockman.] 1699. 12°. **8408.** aa. **14.**

C., T.

—— *See* Dandini (G.) [Missione apostolica al Patriarca e Maroniti del Monte Libano.] A Voyage to Mount Libanus, *etc.* [The editor's dedicatory epistle signed: T. C.] 1698. 8°. **790.** d. **22.**

C., T.

—— *See* Devereux (Robert) 3rd *Earl of Essex.* [*Appendix.*] Another Famous Victorie obtained by his Excellencie the Earle of Essex . . . Also, His Majesties proceedings at Oxford, and the great preparations that are made there to entertain the Queen of Bohemia [signed: T. C.]. [1642.] 4°. E. **129.** (6.)

C., T. *See* Durham.—*Cathedral Church.* Sanctuarium Dunelmense et Sanctuarium Beverlacense. [With a preface signed: T. C., i.e. Temple Chevallier.] 1837. 8°. Ac. **8045/5.**

C., T. *See* Fortunatus. The Right, Pleasant, and Variable Tragical History of Fortunatus . . . First penned in the Dutch tongue: there-hence abstracted . . . by T. C. [i.e. Thomas Churchyard ?] 1676. 8°. C. **38.** a. **21.**

—— —— 1682. 8°. **12450.** b. **13.**

—— —— 1740. 12°. **1077.** e. **35.**

C., T. *See* M., J. Letters to a Sick Friend . . . By J. M. [With a preface signed: T. C.] 1682. 8°. **852.** d. **15.**

C., T. *See* Manilius (M.) The Five Books of M. Manilius . . . Done into English verse. With notes. [The translator's "Account of Manilius" signed: T. C., i.e. Thomas Creech.] 1697. 8°. **11385.** bb. **25.**

C., T. *See* Marten (William) Selections from the Diary . . . of the late William Marten, *etc.* [The editor's preface signed: T. C.] 1828. 8°. **1126.** c. 9.

C., T. *See* Micron (M.) A Short and Faythful Instructi . . . for the edyfeing and comfort of the symple Christian *etc.* (Translated by T. C.) [1560 ?] 8°. **4326.** a. **4**

C., T. *See* Penington (I.) *the Younger.* The Testimony Isaac Pennington concerning Liberty of Conscience . . Needfull to be seriously considered of by you,—call Quakers . . . Teste T. C. 1681. 4°. **855.** f. **7.** (

C., T. *See* Plutarch. [*Moralia.—English.*] Plutarch Morals, *etc.* (vol. 3. Symposiacs. By T. C.) 1870. 8°. **2236.** e.

C., T. *See* Ragon (J. M.) Francomasoneria. Ritual d grado de Compañero . . . Traducido por T. C. 1871. 8° **4785.** bbb. **5**

C., T. *See* Smith (Charlotte) *Mrs.* The Natural History Birds, *etc.* [The editor's preface signed: T. C.] 1807. 16°. **7206.** aa. **1**

C., T. *See* Stillingfleet (Edward) *Bishop of Worcest* A Rational Account of the Grounds of Protestant Religio being a vindication of the Lord Archbishop of Canterbur Relation of a Conference, &c. from the pretended answ by T. C. [i.e. Thomas Carwell, otherwise Thorold], *etc.* 1665. fol. **3936.** i. 3

—— —— 1681. fol. **1492.t.1**

—— —— 1844. 8°. **1353.** h.

C., T. *See* W., G. The Censure of a loyall Subject, e [The editor's preface signed: T. C., i.e. Thomas Chur yard.] [1587.] 4°. **600.** c.

C., T.

—— Abridged Life of Rev. Paul Mary Pakenham, C.P. B T. C. Reprinted from "Westmeath Examiner," 194 [*Westmeath Examiner: Mullingen*], 1948. 8°. **4956.** k. **3**

C., T. An Account of the Expedition of the British Fleet Sicily in . . . 1718, 1719, and 1720, under the comma of Sir George Byng, Bart. . . . Collected from t Admiral's manuscripts and other original papers. [T dedication signed: T. C., i.e. Thomas Corbett.] pp. 21 *J. & R. Tonson: London,* 1739. 8°. **593.** c. **2**

—— [Another copy.] **292.** i. **2**

—— [Another copy.] G. **1593**

—— The second edition. pp. 96. *J. & R. Tonson: Londo* 1739. 8°. **9079.** aa. **17.** (1

—— [Another copy.] T. **1053.** (4 *With a* MS. *insertion, entitled,* "*List of the Spanish M of War at the Carraccas.*"

—— The third edition. pp. 94. *J. & R. Tonson: Lond* 1739. 8°. **518.** g. **19.** (

C., T. An Admonition to the People of England: wher are answered, not onely the slaunderous vntrueth reprochfully vttered by Martin [Mar-prelate] the Libell but also many other crimes . . . obiected genera against all Bishops, and the chiefe of the Cleargie, p posely to deface and discredite the present state of t Church. [The address to the reader signed: T. C., i Thomas Cooper, successively Bishop of Lincoln and Winchester.] pp. 244. *Imprinted by the Deputies Christopher Barker: London,* 1589. 4°. C. **37.** d.

—— [Another edition.] pp. 245. *Imprinted by the Deput of Christopher Barker: London,* 1589. 8°. *Imperfect; wanting sig.* A. **C.118.bb.**

C., T.

—— The Advantages which will manifestly accrue to this kingdom by Abatement of interest from six to four per cent. [Signed: T. C., i.e. Sir Thomas Culpeper.] *T. L. for Christopher Wilkinson: London*, 1668. *s. sh.* fol. **T. 100*. (92.)**

C . . . . . ., T . . . . An Apology for the Life of Mr. T . . . . C . . . . . [i.e. Theophilus Cibber], comedian. Being a proper sequel to the Apology for the life of Mr. Colley Cibber, comedian. With an historical view of the stage to the present year. Supposed to be written by himself, *etc.* [A satire.] pp. viii. 144. *J. Mechell: London*, 1740. 8°. **840.** d. **1.**

—— [Another copy.] **277.** d. **19.**

C., T. An Attempt at Vocal English; that is, English spelled as spoken, *etc.* [The preface signed: T. C., i.e. Thomas Clark.] pp. 39. *Privately printed: Aberdeen*, [1844.] 8°. **12985.** ccc. **11.**

C., T. The Autobiography of a Rejected MS. By T. C. [i.e. Sir Thomas Carmichaell.] pp. 103. *Chapman & Hall: London*, 1870. 8°. **12637.** b. **4.**

C., T. A Brief Discovery of the Corruption of the Ministry of the Church of England: or, Three clear and evident grounds from which it will appear that they are no ministers of Christ . . . Published for the information of all, by T. C. [i.e. Thomas Collier.] pp. 36. *London*, 1647. 8°. **E. 1183. (4.)**

C., T.

—— Yr Act am bwyso aur, a osodwyd allan mewn trefn ysprydol, mewn dull o ymddiddan . . . Gan T. C. [A translation of "The Coin-Act. By way of dialogue . . . By J. C." With a preface by Rowland Hill.] pp. 35. *I. Ross: Caerfyrddin*, 1775. 12°. **04411.** de. **14. (3.)**

C., T.

—— A Collection of Temperance Melodies and Hymns, original and select. Compiled under the direction of the Committee of the Leicester Temperance Society. Third edition. [The preface signed: T. C., i.e. Thomas Cook.] pp. 125. [1863.] 32°. *See* LEICESTER.—*Leicester Temperance Society.* **03440.** de. **37.**

C., T. The Compleat Midwifes Practice . . . With instructions of the midwife to the Queen of France (L. Bourgeois) . . . touching the . . . said art . . . By T. C., I. D., M. S., T. B., Practitioners. [With plates, including a portrait of Louise Bourgeois.] pp. 148. 126. *For Nathaniel Brooke: London*, 1656. 8°. **E. 1588. (3.)**

The second and subsequent editions "by R. C., I. D., M. S., T. B.," are entered under C., R.

C., T. Coppie of a Letter from T. C. at Norwich to a friend of his at London. *See* TURNER (Dawson) Narrative of the Visit of . . . Charles II. to Norwich . . . as related by Blomefield and Echard, *etc.* 1846. 8°. **811.** d. **34.**

C., T. A Discovery of the Accursed Thing found in the Foxonian Quakers camp. [Signed: T. C., i.e. Thomas Crisp.] pp. 8. *For T. C.: London*, 1695. 4°. **4152.** d. **1.**

C., T. Dissertations on the Pecuniary Testimonies of the Quakers relative to their refusing to pay tithes and church rates, *etc.* [Signed: T. C., i.e. Thomas Crowley.] pp. 63. [*London*,] 1773. 8°. **T. 402. (9.)**

C., T. The Duty and Support of Believers in Life and Death. On the death of Mrs. Mary Smith, *etc.* [The epistle dedicatory signed: T. C., i.e. Timothy Cruso.] pp. 27. *For Tho. Cockerill; John Smith: London*, 1688. 4°. **1418.** g. **50.**

C., T.

—— An Epistle of Comfort, from one friend to another. *See* infra: Two very Godly and comfortable Letters, written ouer into England, *etc.*

C., T. Evolution. To correspondents on the subject of the eversion. [Signed: T. C., i.e. Tiberius Cavallo ?] pp. 87. *Gower & Smart: Wolverhampton*, [1803 ?] 8°. **716.** c. **34.**

C., T. Four Original Letters, viz. two from a husband to a gentleman, and two from a husband to a wife. [Signed: T. C.] The second edition. pp. 38. *T. Read: London*, 1739. 8°. **1414.** b. **65. (2.)**

C., T.

—— The Glory of Christ, and the Ruine of Antichrist, unvailed, as they are held forth in Revelation, by the Seales, Trumpets and Vialls . . . By T. C. [i.e. Thomas Collier.] pp. 108. 1647. 8°. **3751.** aa. **16. (1.)**

C., T. Great News from Dublin: in a letter from an Irish gentleman to his friend in London. [Signed: T. C.] [*London*,] 1690. *s. sh.* fol. **816.** m. **23. (69.)**

C., T. An Hospitall for the Diseased. Wherein are to bee founde moste excellent and approued medicines . . . With a newe addition. Gathered by T. C. B.L. pp. 78 [76]. *For Edward White: London*, 1579. 4°. **C. 31.** b. **13.**

—— [Another edition.] Newly augmented and enlarged, *etc.* B.L. *Iames Roberts for Edward White: London*, 1595. 4°. **1038.k.34.(1.)**

—— [Another edition.] B.L. *E. Allde for Edward White: London*, 1598. 4°. **C. 54.** e. **2. (1.)**

—— [Another edition.] B.L. *George Purslowe for Edward White: London*, 1619. 4°. **544.** d. **29.**

C., T. Illustrations of Baptismal Fonts. With an introduction by F. A. Paley. [The advertisement signed: T. C., i.e. Thomas Combe.] *John Van Voorst: London*, 1844. 8°. **1265.** c. **7.**

C., T. An Impartial Examination and Refutation of the erroneous Tenets of Thomas Moor in his dangerous writings, intituled Clavis aurea, *etc.* [The address to the reader signed: T. C.] pp. 24. *For Tho. Parkhurst: London*, 1698. 4°. **478.** a. **30. (1.)**

C., T. The Iust Mans Memoriall . . . To the pretious and immortal memory of . . . William Earle of Pembroke . . . A sermon, *etc.* [The epistle dedicatory signed: T. C., i.e. T. Chaffinge.] pp. 39. *Elizabeth Allde for Nathaniel Butter: London*, 1630. 4°. **1417.** f. **10.**

—— [Another copy.] **1417.** f. **11.**

—— [Another copy.] **113.** f. **14.**

C., T. The Key-stone of Grammar Laid; or, the Governess's assistant in simplifying that science. By T. C. pp. 104. *J. Hatchard & Son: London*, 1843. 12°. **828.** a. **10.**

C., T. Labyrinthus Cantuariensis: or Doctor Lawd's Labyrinth. Beeing an answer to the late Archbishop of Canterburies Relation of a Conference between himselfe and Mr. Fisher, etc. Wherein the true grounds of the Roman Catholique religion are asserted, the principall controuersies betwixt Catholiques and Protestants throughly examined, and the Bishops meandrick windings . . . layd open to publique view. By T. C. [i.e. Thomas Carwell, otherwise Thorold.] pp. 415. *Printed by Iohn Billaine: Paris* [*London ?*], 1658. fol. **480.** d. **8. (2.)**

C., T. Memoir of the Church of S. Thomas the Martyr in Oxford. [Signed: T. C., i.e. Thomas Chamberlain.] pp. 12. *J. Parker & Co.: Oxford & London*, 1871. 8°. **10360**. bbb. **51**.

C., T. A More Full and Exact Relation from Reading, of their proceedings there . . . in a letter [signed: T. C.] sent from a Serjeant Major there, *etc.* pp. 5. *Printed by R. Oulton & G. Dexter: London*, 1643. 4°. G. **3949**. (**3**.)

C., T. The New Atlas; or, Travels and voyages in Europe, Asia, Africa, and America . . . Performed by an English gentleman in nine years travel, *etc.* [The preface signed: T. C.] pp. 236. *For J. Cleave & A. Roper: London*, 1698. 8°. **304**. d. **15**.

C., T. Painting. Its rise and progress from the earliest ages to the present time. With sketches of the lives and works of eminent artists and a brief notice of the principal public galleries of art in Europe. [The introduction signed: T. C.] pp. x. 428. *J. P. Jewett & Co.: Boston*, 1846. 12°. **1402**. g. **17**.

C., T. Patie and Peggy: or, the Fair foundling. A Scotch ballad opera as it is acted at the Theatre Royal in Drury Lane by his Majesty's Servants in one act and in verse. [An adaptation of Allan Ramsay's "Gentle Shepherd." The preface signed: T. C., i.e. Theophilus Cibber.] With the musick prefix'd to each song. pp. 34. *J. Watts: London*, 1730. 8°. **11778**. b. **20**.

—— [Another edition.] pp. 30. *J. Watts: London*, 1731. 8°. **161**. g. **68**.

C., T.

—— The Popes Deadly Wound . . . Written by T. C. (Thomas Clark), *etc.* 1635. 12°. *See* CLARK (Thomas) *of Sutton Coldfield.* **3936**. a. **29**.

C., T. Prince Perindo's Wish. A fairy romance for youths and maidens. By T. C. Illustrated by A. C. pp. iv. 84. *Edmonston & Douglas: Edinburgh*, 1874. 8°. **12804**. i. **28**.

C., T. Reasons against passing into a Law a Bill now depending in Parliament for erecting Public Granaries in Dublin, Corke and Belfast. With a new plan for the improvement of tillage in Ireland, *etc.* [Signed: T. C.] pp. 16. *J. Potts: Dublin*, 1766. 8°. **8145**. aaa. **14**.

C., **T.**

—— The Red-Ribbond. News from the Army. In a discourse between a Minister and a Souldier of the state. Written from thence by a minister of God's holy word in the county of Suffolk, who loveth a souldier as he doth his own life: the characters of his name T. C. pp. 8. *Printed for M. S.: London*, 1647. 4°. E. 390. (2.)

The initials T. C. have been expanded in MS. to "T. Coxcombe" by George Thomason.

C., T. A Replye to an answere made of M. Doctor Whitegifte, againste the Admonition to the Parliament. By T. C. [i.e. Thomas Cartwright.] 𝕭.𝕷. pp. 224. [*London*, 1573?] 4°. T. **2108**. (**1**.)

—— [Another copy.] G. **19840**.

—— [Another edition.] 𝕭.𝕷. [*London*, 1573?] 4°. **108**. b. 4.

The first leaf is mutilated; the missing portions are supplied in MS. *Cropped.*

—— *See* WHITGIFT (John) successively *Bishop of Worcester* and *Archbishop of Canterbury.* The Defense of the Aunswere to the Admonition, against the Replie of T. C. [i.e. Thomas Cartwright.] 1574. fol. **475**. d. **18**.

C., T. A Ride to Niagara in 1809. By T. C. (Reprinted from the Portfolio for July–October 1810.) pp. 49. *G. P. Humphrey: Rochester, N.Y.*, 1915. 8°. **10410**. v. **1**

C., T. The River Fal and Falmouth Harbour illustrated. [The preface signed: T. C., i.e. T. A. Cragoe.] pp. 56. *J. R. Netherton: Truro*, [1876.] 16°. **10358**. a.

C., T. The St. James's Tatler: or, the Court of Reque[sts] miscellany, *etc.* [The dedication signed: T. C.] pp. 55. *John Brooks: London*, 1734. 8°. T. **1618**. (7

C., T. A Scheme to drive the French out of all the Contine[nt] of America. [Signed: T. C.] pp. 23. [*London*] 1754. 12°. **8132**. a. **1**

C., T. A Sermon preach'd in the city of York . . . Janua[ry] XIX, 170¾, being the fast day appointed for the late drea[d]ful storm. By T. C. pp. 27. *J. Nutt: Londo[n]* 1704. 4°. **693**. f. 6. (

C., T. A Short Discourse of the New-found-land: co[n]taynig [*sic*] diverse reasons and inducements, for t[he] planting of that country, *etc.* [The dedication signe[d] T. C.] *Printed by the Societie of Stationers: Dubl[in]* 1623. 4°. C. **32**. h.

C., T. Short Whist Register and Summary, with the laws [of] the game, &c. By T. C. pp. 111. *Griffin & Co.* *Portsmouth*, 1876. 12°. **7915**. aaa.

C., T. Strange Newes from the North. Containing a tr[ue] and exact relation of a great and terrible earth-qua[ke] in Cumberland and Westmerland. With the miraculo[us] apparition of three glorious suns that appeared at on[e] . . . Together with the charge against Charles Howa[rd] esquire high sheriff of . . . Cumberland, *etc.* [T[he] "Strange Newes" signed: T. C.] pp. 6. *Printed by J. Clowes: London*, 1650. 4°. E. **603**. (

C., T. A True Relation of His Majesties Proceedings [at] Oxford. [Signed: T. C.] *See* DEVEREUX (Robert) 3 *Earl of Essex.* Another Famous Victorie, *etc.* [1642.] 4°. E. **129**. (

C., T. Two Treatises. 1. The holy exercise of a true Fa[st] described out of Gods word. Written by T. C. . . . 2. T[he] substance of the Lordes Supper. Written by T. W. 2 p *For I. Harison & T. Man: London*, 1610. 12°. **4324**. e.

C., T.

—— Two very Godly and comfortable Letters, written ou[er] into England. The one to a Godly and zealous Lady wherin the Annabaptists errour is confuted: and t[he] sinne against the Holye Ghoste plainly declared. T[he] other an answer to a Godly Merchants Letter . . . Writte[n] by T. C. *Edward Allde for Edward White: Londo[n]* 1589. 12°. L.R. **263**. aa. 2

Photostats of the copy in the library of the New Yor[k] Theological Seminary.

—— An Epistle of Comfort [signed T. C.], from one friend [to] another, wherein the Anabaptists error of desperation [is] briefly confuted, and the sinne against the Holy Gho[st] plainly declared. Whereunto is added certaine effectua[l] prayers. [The first letter from "Two very Godly an[d] comfortable Letters, written ouer into England."] *S[ee]* JOHN, *Chrysostom, Saint, Patriarch of Constantinople.* [*A[d] Theodorum Lapsum.*] An Excellent Treatise touching t[he] restoring againe of him that is fallen, *etc.* [1609.] 12°. **472**. a.

C., T., *Afgewesen Raet van sijn Majesteyt.* Appendix van Engelands apél en beroep, aan de Communs, zijnde de Edelen en Gemeente, vergadert in beyde Huysen des Parlaments . . . Voorstellende 't contrarie intrest van de Natie, tegens de verwilderde uytvoeringen van de secrete Cabale . . . Mitsgaders verhandelende alle de verliesen des Koninkrijks, anno 1672. en 1673. . . . Door T. C. afgewesen Raet van sijn Majesteyt. [By Pierre Du Moulin the younger ?] Uyt het Engels getranslateert na d'autentijke copye. pp. 56. 1673. 4°. **1103.** f. **21.** (**1.**)

—— [Another copy.] **101.** l. **22.**

C., T., *D.D.* *See* LITURGIES.—*Church of England.*—*Common Prayer.*—*Catechism.* [*English.*] The Church-Catechism, with a brief and easie explanation thereof . . . By T. C., D.D. [i.e. Thomas Comber.] 1686. 8°. **3506.** b. **38.** (**3.**)

—— A Discourse of Duels, shewing the sinful nature and mischievous effects of them, and answering the usual excuses made for them . . . By T. C., D.D. [i.e. Thomas Comber.] pp. 66. *Samuel Roycroft for Robert Clavel: London,* 1687. 4°. **491.** d. **5.** (**4.**)

—— The Examiner Examined: being a vindication of the 'History of Liturgies.' By T. C., D.D. [i.e. Thomas Comber.] [A reply to " An Examination of Dr. Comber's Scholastical History of the primitive and general Use of Liturgies . . . By S. B."] pp. 66. *For Robert Clavel: London,* 1691. 4°. **T. 751.** (**9.**)

—— [Another copy.] **3477.** c. **48.**

C——, T., *Esq., Banker.* *See* M——, H., *the late Miss, of Drury-Lane Theatre.* Fine Acting; or a Sketch of the life of the late Miss H. M——, of Drury-Lane Theatre [i.e. Harriet Mellon], and of T. C——, Esq. banker [i.e. Thomas Coutts]. 1815. 8°. **G. 14282.**

C., T., *Esquire.*

—— *See* METEREN (E. van) A True Discourse Historicall, of the succeeding gouernours in the Netherlands . . . Translated and collected by T. C. Esquire [i.e. Thomas Churchyard], and Ric. Ro., *etc.* 1602. 4°. **154.** l. **17.**

C., T., *Esquire.* Morall Discourses and Essayes upon severall select subjects. Written by T. C. Esquire [i.e. Sir Thomas Culpeper the younger]. pp. 184. *S. G. for Charles Adams: London,* 1655. 12°. **527.** a. **23.**

—— [Another copy.] E. **1703.** (**3.**)

C., T., *Esquire.* Vox & Votum Populi Anglicani. Shewing how deeply the nation resents the thought of capitulating, now, with his Majestie, and holding him, as we say at armes-end, if they could. In a letter to . . . the Earle of Manchester. By T. C. Esquire. pp. 14. *London,* 1660. 4°. E. **1025.** (**2.**)

C., T., *Fr.* *See* BIBLE.—*Ecclesiastes.* [*Polyglott.*] El Libro del Eclesiastés, explicado con notas . . . por el P. Mtro. Fr. J. de Jesús Muñoz. [The editor's preface signed: Fr. T. C., i.e. T. J. Cámara y Castro, successively Bishop of Trajanopolis and of Salamanca.] 1881. 16°. **3165.** df. **5.**

C., T., *a Friend to Truth.* A Glasse for the Times by which according to the Scriptures, you may clearly behold the true ministers of Christ, how farre differing from false teachers. With a briefe collection of the errors of our times, and their authors names . . . Also proofes of Scripture by way of confutation of them, by sundry able ministers. Collected by T. C., a friend to truth. pp. 8. *Printed by Robert Ibbitson: London,* 1648. 4°. E. **455.** (**10.**)

C., T., *late of C.C.C. in Oxford.* A Greek English Lexicon containing the derivations and various significations of all the words in the New Testament, with a complete index . . . Whereunto is added a praxis or an explanation of the second of the Romans, and the Greek dialects contained in the New Testament. By T. C. late of C.C.C. in Oxford [i.e. Thomas Cockaine]. pp. 428. *Printed by Lodowick Lloyd: London,* 1658. 8°. **E.1720.(1.)**

C., T., *M.A.* Isagoge ad Dei Providentiam: or, a Prospect of Divine Providence. By T. C. M.A. [i.e. Thomas Crane.] pp. 544. *A. Maxwell for E. Brewster: London,* 1672. 8°. **4402.** c. **18.**

C., T., *Minister of God's Word.* Huls Pillar of Providence erected: or, The Providentiall Columne, setting out Heavens care for deliverance of that people . . . from the . . . Cavaliers, who had for six weeks closely besieged them. By T. C. Minister of Gods Word. pp. 14. *For Ralph Rounthwait: London,* 1644. 4°. E. **37.** (**30.**)

C., T., *One of the Chaplains in the Army.* A More True and an exacter Relation of the Battaile of Keynton, then any formerly. Written by T. C. one of the Chaplains in the Army, and sent to a friend of his, a learned divine in this city, and by him published, *etc.* pp. 5. *For Edward Blackmore: London,* 1642. 4°. E. **128.** (**20.**)

C., T., *Philo-Pharmacopeiae.* Vindiciæ pharmacapolæ; or, an Answer to the Doctors complaints against apothecaries . . . By T. C., Philo-Pharmacopeiæ. [In verse.] [*London,* 1675 ?] *s. sh.* fol. C. **20.** f. **2.** (**382.**)

—— [Another copy.] **777.** l. **1.** (**56.**)

—— [Another copy.] Lutt. II. **228.**

C., T., *Sidn. Collegii, A.M.* *See* FOX (John) *the Martyrologist.* Christus Triumphans. Comœdia Apocalyptica . . . Editore T. C. Sidn. Collegii, A.M. [i.e. Thomas Comber.] 1672. 8°. **11707.** aa. **11.**

C., T., *Sr. Maj. gewesner Rath.* Appendix an Englands Appellation, eingeliefert an die Comuns . . . Worinnen vorgestellet wird das Contrar-Interesse der Nation wider die verwilderte Ausführungen der geheimden Cabel . . . Samt einer Abhandlung alles Verlusts, den unser Königreich Anno 1672. und 1673. . . . empfangen . . . Eröffnet durch T. C. Sr. Maj. gewesnen Rath. [By Pierre Du Moulin the younger ?] Auss dem Engl. übersetzt. pp. 60. *See* ENGLAND.—*Parliament.* [*Petitions and Addresses to Parliament.*—1673.] Englands Appellation, von der Geheimden Cabel, *etc.* 1674. 4°. **8142.** b. **31.**

C., T., *Surgeon.* The Charitable Surgeon: or, the Best remedies for the worst maladies, reveal'd. Being a new and true way of curing, without mercury, the several degrees of the venereal distemper in both sexes . . . By T. C. Surgeon. The second edition, with additions. pp. 74. *Edmund Curll: London,* 1709. 8°. **1175.** b. **12.** (**1.**)

—— *See* SPINKE (John) Quackery unmask'd: or, Reflections on the . . . pamphlet call'd, the Charitable Surgeon, *etc.* 1709. 8°. **1175.** b. **12.** (**2.**)

—— —— 1711. 8°. **1175.** b. **12.** (**2**.**)

C., T., *Traveller.* An Anatomie of the Metamorphosed Ajax . . . by T. C. Traveller [i.e. Sir John Harington], *etc.* *R. Field: London,* 1596. 8°. G. **10364.** (**3.**)
Eight leaves only, sig. L. *Apparently published as a sequel to one of the editions of Sir J. Harington's " A new discourse . . . called the Metamorphosis of Ajax," which ends with sig.* K.

C., T., *a Well-willer to Truth and Peace.* The Schismaticke Sifted through a Sive of the largest size: but is now more purely drest. Wherein the chaffe, the froth, and the scumme of Mr. John Vicars his siftings and paintings prove him to be a lame draughts-man . . . Collected out of his own words, and under his own hand. By T. C. a Well-willer to Truth and Peace. pp. 11. *R. A. for S. W.: London*, 1646. 4º. **E. 342.** (4.)

C., T. A. The Germans. By themselves. [The preface signed: T. A. C., i.e. Sir Theodore A. Cook.] pp. viii. 42. *The Field & Queen: London*, 1914. 8º. **08027.** d. **18.**

—— The Light Side of Horses. [The editor's preface signed: T. A. C., i.e. Sir Theodore A. Cook. With plates.] pp. 107. *Horace Cox: London*, 1912. 8º. **7904.** d. **18.**

C., T. A. A Story Reader for Standard " O." [The preface signed: T. A. C.] 2 pt. *Blackie & Son: London*, [1898.] 8º. **12984.** aaaa. **36.**

C., T. B. *See* La Primaudaye (P. de) The French Academie, *etc.* [The translator's epistle dedicatory signed: T. B. C., i.e. Thomas Bowes, clerk.] 1618. fol. **8408.** i. **11.**

C., T. B. Bristol Channel Harbour of Refuge. A letter to the . . . Mayor of Bristol. [Signed: T. B. C.] pp. 28. *Stanford: London*, 1859. 8º. **8805.** c. **75.** (5.)

C., T. B. A Memoir of Gen. Sir H. D. Harness K.C.B. . . . Reprinted with some additions, from the Royal Engineer Journal. [Signed: T. B. C., i.e. T. B. Collinson.] pp. 27. *Printed for private circulation: London*, 1883. 8º. **10804.** bbb. **17.** (8.)

C., T. C. Facts and Fallacies in Economics. By T. C. C. Preface by Lord Abinger. pp. 179. *Max Goschen: London*, [1913.] 8º. **8276.** a. **86.**

C., T. C. Lettres diplomatiques. Coup d'œil sur l'Europe au lendemain de la guerre . . . Par l'auteur des Lettres militaires publiées dans le Temps pendant le siége. [The preface signed: T. C. C., i.e. T. Colonna Ceccaldi.] pp. 166. *Paris*, 1872. 12º. **8026.** aa. **2.**

C., T. D. Les Îles Mariannes, considérées comme siège d'une colonie de condamnés, de libérés et de travailleurs libres. Extrait de la Revue britannique. [Signed: T. D. C., i.e. T. Du Colombier.] pp. 68. *Bruxelles*, 1862. 8º. **6055.** a. **18.**

C., T. E. Battle-Fields of the South, from Bull Run to Fredericksburg; with sketches of Confederate commanders . . . By an English combatant (T. E. C.). With two maps. 2 vol. *Smith, Elder & Co.: London*, 1863. 8º. **9602.** b. **16.**

C., T. E. The Child's Guide to Holiness. Edited by a Priest. [The preface signed: T. E. C.] pp. 38. *Joseph Masters: London*, 1873. 16º. **4410.** f. **47.** (3.)

—— Second edition. pp. 54. *Houlston & Son: London*, 1876. 16º. **4409.** aaa. **12.**

C., T. E. War, and other short poems. By T. E. C. pp. 82. *Kegan Paul & Co.: London*, 1909. 8º. **011650.** ee. **12.**

C., T. F. Amors Wege, bey ordentlicher Copulirung des . . . Herrn Christian Ehrenfried Charisii . . . und der . . . Jungfer . . . Juliana Catharina Cochen . . . am Tage der Hochzeit in Lübeck . . . vorgestellet von einem abwesenden Freunde. [Signed: T. F. C.] *M. Schmalhertz: Lubeck*, [1695.] fol. **11522.** k. **9.** (8.)

C., T. G. Clavis Pharmacopœia Collegii Dublinensis; or, a True key to the Pharmacopœia of the King and Queen's College of Physicians in Ireland. By T. G. C. [i.e. T. G. Carroll.] pp. 124. *Printed for the Author: Dublin*, 1825. 8º. **777.** d. **26.**

C., T. G. The Labour Trouble and an International Committee. By T. G. C. pp. 15. *Garthmyl, Mont.*, [1912.] 8º. **08248.** a. **30.**

C., T. G. A., *Accademico Fossanese.* Cantata drammatica per le fortunatissime . . . nozze de' nobilissimi signori, il signor marchese Tommaso Scarampi di Villanova, conte di Camino, e la damigella Vittoria Costa di Carrù. [Signed: T. G. A. C., Accademico fossanese, i.e. Teologo G. A. Cauda.] *Torino*, 1782. 8º. **11715.** cc. **7.** (1.)

C., T. H. A Descriptive Tour in Scotland. By T. H. C. [i.e. Chauncy H. Townshend.] pp. x. 395. *Hauman & Co.: Brussels*, 1840. 8º. **791.** h. **11.**

C., T. H. " Is not this a Brand plucked from the Fire ? " (A brief memoir of . . . Robert Langton.) [Signed: T. H. C.] *Read & Co.: Epworth*, [1852.] 12º. **4902.** aaa. **5.**

C., T. H. Journal of a Tour through part of the Western Highlands of Scotland in the summer of 1839, by T. H. C. pp. 85. *Newcastle*, 1839. 12º. **10370.** aa. **2.**

C., T. K. *See* Cheyne (Elizabeth G.) The Voice of One Crying . . . Arranged in cycles by T. K. C. [i.e. Thomas K. Cheyne.] 1912. 8º. **11646.** dd. **44.**

C., T. L. The Great Social Problem . . . The case and the cure constructively outlined, *etc.* [Signed: T. L. C., i.e. T. L. Clark.] [*The Author: London*, 1906.] 8º. **08275.** aaa. **65.** (3.)

C., T. P. B. Canzone 'nn accaseione de la venuta de li Cravonarl a Nnapole di T. P. B. C. [*Naples*, 1820.] *s. sh.* fol. **8032.** m. **10.** (27.)

C., T. R. del. El Septimo Fernando destronado y Davila sitiado. [Signed: T. R. del C.] *México*, 1822. *s. sh.* fol. **9770.** k. **6.** (184.)

C., T. T. *See* Christian Year. Evening Rest; or, Closing thoughts for every day in the Christian year, *etc.* [With a preface signed: T. T. C., i.e. Thomas T. Carter.] 1868. 16º. **3107.** aa. **18.**

C., T. T. Claim of Rights for Christ and the People. Unto the Presbyteries of the Church of Scotland, the . . . petition of sundry members thereof for the General Congregation of the Christian People to act as a concurrent Court with the Presbytery. [Signed: T. T. C.] pp. 4. *C. Zeigler: Edinburgh*, [1842.] 8º. **4175.** g. **10.** (5.)

C., T. T. Manual of Devotion for Sisters of Mercy. Second edition. [The preface signed: T. T. C., i.e. Thomas T. Carter.] 2 vol. *Joseph Masters: London*, 1868. 32º. **3455.** aa. **55.**

C. (Th.) *See* Grémillon (L.) Lettres. [The editor's preface signed: Th. C.] 1890. 12º. **4379.** ff. **14.**

C. (Th.) Die philosophische Bildung und ihre Förderung durch die deutschen Universitäten. Eine Anregung von Th. C. [i.e. Theodor Curti.] pp. 16. *Würzburg*, 1873. 8º. **8356.** b. **54.**

C. (Th. de.) A Questão do Clero. Cartas de um Aldeão [signed: Th. de C.] ao Sr. padre F. Recreio [commenting upon his strictures upon A. Herculano de Carvalho e Araujo]. Primeira carta. pp. 18. *Lisboa*, 1850. 16º. **3901.** aa. **13.**

C. (Th. A. I.) Tradition Catholiq. ou, Traicté de la croyance des Chrestiens d'Asie, d'Europe, & d'Afrique ez dogmes principalement controuersez en ce tẽps . . . Par Th. A. I. C. [i.e. Morton Eudes.] [The dedication signed: Th. A.] 1609. 8º. **701.** d. **31.**
See A. (Th.)

C. (Th. A. I.)

—— Catholique Traditions. Or a Treatise of the beliefe of the Christians of Asia, Europa, and Africa, in the principall controuersies of our time . . . Written in French by Th. A. I. C. [i.e. Morton Eudes.] And translated into English, by L. O. [i.e. Lewis Owen.] pp. 235. *W. Stansby for Henry Fetherstone: London,* 1609. 4°. **3901.** cc. **8.**

—— [Another copy, with a different titlepage.] Translated into English by L. Owen. *London,* 1610. 4°. **3901.** d. **9.**

C * (Théodore) Les Enfans du soldat, vaudeville en deux actes, par MM. T. C * [i.e. T. Cogniard], Henri [i.e. P. H. Martin] et Hippolite C * [i.e. H. Cogniard], *etc.* pp. 48. *Paris,* 1832. 8°. **11738.** c. **13.** (3.)

C * * * (Théodore) and **C * * *** (Hippolite) La Cocarde tricolore, épisode de la guerre d'Alger; vaudeville en trois actes, par MM. T. C * * * [i.e. T. Cogniard] et H. C * * * [i.e. H. Cogniard], *etc.* pp. 64. *Paris,* 1831. 8°. **11738.** c. **13.** (6.)

C. (Théodore) and **C.** (Hyppolite) Le Modèle, croquis d'atelier, folie-vaudeville en un acte de MM. T. C. [i.e. T. Cogniard] et H. C. [i.e. H. Cogniard], *etc.* pp. 22. *Paris,* 1831. 8°. **11738.** c. **11.** (5.)

C. (Tr. R.) *le R.P.* Véritable relation des iustes procédures obseruées au fait de la possession des Vrsulines de Loudun, & au procés de Grandier. Par le R. P. Tr. R. C. [i.e. le Père Tranquille.] pp. 32. *Jean Martin: Paris,* 1634. 12°. **718.** d. **38.** (2.)

C., U. *See* Bargoin (L. A. J.) Soirs d'hiver, *etc.* [With a biographical notice signed: U. C.] 1880. 12°. **12356.** bbb. **29.**

C., U. *See* Pasquée. Pasquée critique et calotenne sôt les affaires de l'medigenne. [The editor's introduction signed: U. C., i.e. Ulysse Capitaine.] 1858. 8°. **11498.** f. **56.** (9.)

—— *See* Periodical Publications.—*Liége.* Nécrologe liégeois, *etc.* [Signed: U. C., i.e. Ulysse Capitaine.] 1856, *etc.* 12°. **P.P. 3826.**

—— Quelques mots sur le lieu de naissance et l'époque du décès de Renkin Sualem, *etc.* [Signed: U. C., i.e. Ulysse Capitaine.] pp. 10. *Liége,* 1857. 8°. **10663.** ee. **25.** (7.)

C., U. D. The Diplomacy of Mr. Ramsay MacDonald. By "U. D. C." (Reprinted from The Labour Monthly.) pp. 19. *London,* [1925.] 8°. **8138.** i. **23.**

C., V. *See* Giordani (P.) Il Peccato impossibile. Frammento inedito . . . annotato e ristampato per cura di V. C. 1883. 8°. **8632.** e. **14.** (1.)

C., V. *See* Leone (Jacopo) Conjuration des Jésuites, *etc.* [The editor's preface signed: V. C., i.e. V. Considérant.] 1848. 8°. **4092.** g. **35.**

C., V. *See* Paris.—*Council of Paris,* 824. Synodus Parisiensis de imaginibus Anno Christi dcccxxiv. Ex vetustissimo codice descripta, & nunc primum in lucem edita [by V. C.]. 1596. 8°. **C. 54.** b. **16.** (2.)

C., V. Colonie italiane. Appunti saltuari sull'Africa di V. C. pp. 46. *Massa,* 1890. 8°. **8155.** f. 5. (3.)

C., V.

—— Décisions nouvelles sur les difficultez et incidens du jeu de l'hombre et de la manière de marquer quand on jouë à la bavaroise. [The dedication signed: V. C.] *In:* Le Jeu de l'hombre, *etc.* pt. 2. 1718. 12°. **7922.** de. **1.**

C., V. Ricordi di un'escursione in Spagna per V. C. pp. 177. *Firenze,* 1888. 8°. **10160.** ee. **26.**

C., V.

—— Silk, Fur and Feather: the trout-fly dresser's year. By "V. C." Being a reprint . . . of a series of articles published in the "Fishing Gazette." pp. 113. *Fishing Gazette: Beckenham,* 1950. 12°. **7919.** d. **24.**

C * * *, V. Tableau général de la Russie moderne, et situation politique de cet empire au commencement du xixe siècle; par V. C * * *, continuateur de l'Abrégé de l'histoire générale des voyages [i.e. Victor Delpuech de Comeiras]. 2 tom. *Paris,* 1802. 8°. **10290.** e. **7.**

C., V. de.

—— *See* Saluzzo (A.) *Bishop of Mariana and Accia.* Visita della diocesi di Mariana ed Accia fatta nell'anno 1740 per deputazione dell'illustrissimo e reverendissimo monsignor Agostino Saluzzo, vescovo. [The editor's preface signed: V. de C., i.e. V. de Caraffa.] 1890. 8°. [*Bulletin de la Société des sciences historiques & naturelles de la Corse.* fasc. 113, 114.] Ac. **2861.**

C * * * * * * * *, V. de, *Mme.* Les Chevaliers normands, en Italie et en Sicile; et considérations générales sur l'histoire de la chevalerie, et particulièrement sur celle de la chevalerie en France. Par Mme V. de C * * * * * * * * [i.e. Victorine Chastenay de Lenty]. pp. 305. *Paris,* 1816. 8°. **1196.** f. **26.**

C * * *, V * * * * de, *Mme.* De l'Asie, ou Considérations religieuses, philosophiques et littéraires sur l'Asie. Par Mme V * * * * de C * * * [i.e. Victorine Chastenay de Lenty]. 4 tom. *Paris,* 1832. 8°. **583.** f. **2.**

C* * * * * * * *, V. de, *Mme.* Du génie des peuples anciens, ou Tableau historique et littéraire du développement de l'esprit humain chez les peuples anciens, depuis les premiers temps connus jusqu'au commencement de l'ère chrétienne. Par Mme V. de C * * * * * * * * [i.e. Victorine Chastenay de Lenty]. 4 tom. *Paris,* 1808. 8°. **581.** d. **18.**

C., V. A. H. L. Ad virum nobilem de cultu Confucii philosophi et progenitorum apud Sinas. [Signed: V. A. H. L. C.] pp. 47. *H. Thieullier: Antverpiæ,* 1700. 12°. [i.e. Jean Daz.] **4767.** a. **2.**

C. V. A. H. L.

—— Parallèle des propositions du P. le Comte, avec quelques autres propositions, adressé à Monsieur le Syndic de la Faculté de Théologie de Paris. [A comparison of passages from L. D. Le Comte's "Nouveaux mémoires sur l'état présent de la Chine" with passages from a work entitled "Perpétuité de la foy, ou Miroir de la religion chrétienne." Signed: V. A. H. L. C., i.e. Charles Le Gobien.] *See* China.—*Jesuits.* Histoire apologétique de la conduite des Jésuites de la Chine, *etc.* 1700. 12°. **4767.a.3.**

C., V. A. V. L. R. Den—Al—Sieck, ghestorven, en' begraven waer in des weereldts verganckelijcke ijdelheyt, de Vier Wtersten, met d'Eeuwigheydt; wt . . . Iacoponus Tudertinus . . . Carolus Scribanus, Mathæus Raderus, Hieremias Drexelius . . . ende andere schrijveren vertooght wort door V. A. V. L. R. C. pp. 143. *H. Aertssens: Antwerpen,* [1631.] *obl.* 8°. **11556.** a. **5.**
The titlepage is slightly mutilated, the date being cut off.

C., V. D. The Dasharathi. A dramatic translation of the Ramayana by V. D. C. [i.e. V. Deṣikāchāri.] pp. 32. "*N.I. Press*": *Tinnevelly,* 1905. 8°. **11778.** l. 5. (2.)

C., V. J. *See* Fonseca (J. da) Novo Diccionario francez-portuguez . . . corrigido e augmentado por V. J. C., *etc.* 1885. 8°. **12941**. e. **32**.

C., V. M. L'Assartu a la Gancia lu jornu 4 Aprili 1860 . . . 432 ottavi siciliani intruncati e cu la rima obbrigata . . . di V. M. C. pp. 119. *Palermo*, 1885. 8°. **11436**. e. **21**.

C., V. M. A Friendly Letter for You. [Signed: V. M. C.] pp. 8. *Drummond's Tract Depot: Stirling*, [1902.] 16°. **04420**. de. **15**. (3.)

C., V. M. Vita di li gluriusi santi martiri Vitu, Mudestu e Crisenza. 350 ottavi intruncati e a rima furzata divisi in cincu canti cu dui sunetti di dedica. [The dedicatory poem signed: V. M. C.] pp. 34. *Palermo*, 1890. 8°. **4829**. b. **25**. (4.)

C., V. P. *See* Faust (Johann) *Dr.* L'Histoire prodigieuse lamentable du Docteur Fauste, *etc.* [Translated from the German of G. R. Widmann. The translator's dedication signed: V. P. C., i.e. Pierre Victor Palma Cayet.] 1616. 12°. **8630**. a. **25**.

C., V. W. Trou-hertighe onderrichtinge, aen alle hooft Participanten en lief-hebbers van de Ge-octroyeerde West-Indische Compagnie, nopende het open stellen van den handel op de cust van Africa, namentlijck, St. Thomé, Guinea, Angola, St. Paulo de Loando . . . Door een trou Lief-hebber, V. W. C. [*Amsterdam?*] 1643. 4°. C. **32**. i. **19**.

C., V. y. *See* V. y C.

C. (Valentin) *le Docteur.* Hygiène physique et morale. Le médecin consolateur. Par le docteur Valentin C. [i.e. J. B. V. Crimotel.] pp. xvi. 200. *Paris, Lyon*, 1868. 12°. **7383**. aa. **10**.

C * * * (Victor) *See* Michaux (A.) and C * * * (V.) Le Code-formulaire portatif du notariat, *etc.* 1864. 4°. **5424**. e. **32**.

C . . . . (Victor)

—— France et Pologne. (Par M. Victor C . . . . [i.e. V. Ciral].) [A poem.] pp. 6. *Auxonne*, 1863. 8°. **11481**. d. **50**. (**16**.)

C., W. *See* **B., M. D.** The River Mole, or Emlyn Stream. A poem, with notes (by W. C. [i.e. William Cotton?]), *etc.* 1839. 8°. **840**. l. **26**.

C., W. *See* Caracciolo (G.) *Marquis of Vico.* The Italian Convert . . . or the life of Galeacius Caracciolus . . . Put into English . . . by W. C. [i.e. William Crashaw.] 1635. 4°. **4867**. cc. **2**.

—— —— 1639. 12°. **4864**. a. **4**.

—— —— 1655. 8°. **1371**. a. **28**.

—— —— 1662. 8°. **4864**. aa. **47**.

C., W. *See* Chicken (Edward) The Collier's Wedding, a poem, *etc.* [The editor's preface signed: W. C. i.e. William Cail.] 1829. 8°. **1077**. f. **35**.

C., W. *See* Clergyman. A Clergyman's Recreation, *etc.* [By William Sewell; the last four poems signed: W. C.] 1831. 8°. **11642**. bb. **27**.

C., W. *See* Coke (*Sir* Edward) The Compleate Copyholder. [With a prefatory epistle signed: W. C.] 1641. 4°. **883**. k. **2**.

—— *See* Coke (*Sir* Edward) [*The Complete Copyholder.*] The Compleate Copy-Holder, *etc.* [The preface signed: W. C.] 1644. 8°. **1481**. ddd. **44**.

—— —— 1668. 8°. **507**. a. **26**.

—— —— 1673. 8°. **507**. a. **27**.

C., W. *See* **Fell, afterwards Fox (Margaret)** An Evid Demonstration to Gods Elect, *etc.* [With a postscri signed: W. C., i.e. William Caton.] 1660. 4°. **4152**. f. **19**. (1

C., W. *See* Francke (Christianus) *Gardelebiensis.* A C ference or Dialogue discouering the sect of Iesuites . Translated by W. C. [i.e. William Charke], *etc.* [1580.] 8°. C. **53**. a.

C., W. *See* Godolphin (Sidney) *Earl Godolphin.* T Fables, in verse, *etc.* [The editor's preface signed: W. i.e. William Coxe.] [1817.] 4°. **785**. k. **36**. (

—— *See* Godolphin (Sidney) *Earl Godolphin.* A Th Fable, *etc.* [The editor's preface signed: W. C., i William Coxe.] [1818.] 4°. **785**. k. **36**. (

C., W. *See* Hendricks (P.) The Backslider bewailed . Translated . . . by W. C. [i.e. William Caton.] 1665. 4°. **4152**. b.

C., W. *See* Herbal. A Boke of the Propreties of Her called an herball. Wherunto is added the time ẏ her . . . shold be gathered . . . Also a generall rule of maner of Herbes drawen out of an auncyent booke Phisyck by W. C. [i.e. William Copland?] [1552?] 8 **449**. a.

—— —— [1553?] 8°. **546**. b.

—— —— [1560?] 8°. **1405**. a.

C . . . . . ., W . . . . . *See* Jesus Christ. The History the Life of Our Lord Jesus Christ. Newly . . . transla . . . by W . . . . . C . . . . . . [i.e. William Crathorne]. [1763.] 12°. **4823**. b.

C., W. *See* La Mothe (M. C.) *Countess d'Aulnoy.* A Coll tion of Novels and Tales of the Fairies. [The dedicati signed: W. C.] 1728. 12°. **12411**. aa.

—— *See* La Mothe (M. C.) *Countess d'Aulnoy.* A Collect of Novels and Tales of the Fairies, *etc.* [The dedicat signed: W. C.] 1766. 12°. **12240**. de.

C., W. *See* Logan (John) *Poet.* A Dissertation on t Governments, Manners, and Spirit of Asia. [The edito advertisement signed: W. C.] 1787. 4°. **583**. h. **11**. (

C . . . ., W . . . . *See* Marsollier (The Life of St. Francis of Sales . . . Done into Engli . . . By W . . . . C . . . . [i.e. Willia Crathorne]. 1737. 8°. **4823**. b.

C., W. *See* Merks (Anna C.) Jesus Triumphant in t Conversion and Death of A. C. Merks. [The editor preface signed: W. C.] 1847. 12°. **1373**. c. 1

C., W. *See* Mugliano (D.) Extraordinary Newes fro Constantinople . . . sent from thence to the Lo Domenico Mugliano . . . Translated by W. C. 1641. 4 **1103**. e. 4

C., W. *See* Pasquale (Carlo) *Viscount di Quente.* Fal complaints. Or the Censure of an vnthankfull min the labour of Carolus Pascalius translated into Englis by W. C., *etc.* 1605. 4°. **8409**. f. 2

C., W. *See* Watson (Sylvia) Life in the Spheres. A seri of messages received from the spirit world by W. C. 1922. 8°. **8633**. aa. 4

C., W. *See* White, otherwise Blacklow (Thomas) *Roma Catholic Priest.* A Manuall of Divine Consideration Translated [by W. C.] out of the original Latine copi 1655. 12°. E. **1710**. (3

C., W. *See* Zins-Penninck (J.) Some Worthy Proverbs . . . Translated by . . . W. C. [i.e. William Caton.] 1663. 4°. **4152. c. 34.**

C., W. An Alarum to England, to prevent its destruction by the loss of trade and navigation . . . By W. C. [i.e. William Carter.] pp. v. 40. *Mary Fabian: London*, 1700. 8°. **1029. e. 62.**

C., W. The Apostolicall Institution of Episcopacy; deduced out of the Premises, by W. C. [i.e. William Chillingworth.] *See* Protestant Divines. Confessions and Proofes of Protestant Divines, *etc.* 1644. 4°. E. **52. (23.)**

C., W. Aus Goethe's Leben. Wahrheit und keine Dichtung. Von einem Zeitgenossen (W. C. [i.e. W. Ludecus]). pp. 83. *Leipzig*, 1849. 8°. **10706. d. 39. (6.)**

—— [Another copy.] **10707. bb. 4.**
Imperfect; wanting the wrapper, on which the initials appear.

C——, W——. A 'Bleak House' Narrative of Real Life: being a faithful detail of facts connected with a suit in the Irish Court of Chancery . . . [The introduction signed: W—— C——.] To which is added . . . Letters on Chancery reform by P. J. Lock King. pp. 66. *H. Elliot: London*, 1856. 8°. **6503. d. 6.**

C., W. Christian Rules proposed to a vertuous soule aspiring to holy perfection, whereby shee may regulate both her time, and actions for the obtaining of her happy end. By her faithfull frend. W. C. [i.e. William Clifford] . . . Renewed, corrected and augmented by the author. pp. 574. 1659. 12°. **4401. k. 49.**

—— The third edition renewed and augmented by the author W. C. [i.e. William Clifford.] pp. 399. 1665. 8°. **4408. c. 32.**

C., W. Coffo Phillo or the Coffyhouse dialoge between Phillonex Britanicus a Englishman, Monsr. le Docteur a German, Monsr. le Statest a Hollander & Monsr. le Braue a French Captⁿ. [The dedication signed: W. C.] pp. 50. 1672. 8°. **712. e. 3.**

C., W. The Copy of a Letter [signed: W. C.] from Sir Thomas Fairfaxes Quarters. [Dated: 1 April 1646.] *See* England. [*Appendix.—History and Politics.*—II. 1646.] Sir Thomas Fairfaxes Letter or Summons sent to Sir John Berkley, *etc.* 1646. 4°. E. **330. (20.)**

—— The Copie of a Letter [signed: W. C.] from Sir Thomas Fairfax's quarters. [Dated: 16 April 1646.] *See* England. [*Appendix.—History and Politics.*—II. 1646.] Sir Thomas Fairfax's Further Proceedings in the West, *etc.* 1646. 4°. E. **333. (23.)**

C., W. A Declaration of the Kings Most excellent Majesties Proceeding with his Army at Oxford and elsewhere. As it was related by a Student from thence. [Two letters, one signed: W. C., the other: T. H.] *For I. Wright: London*, 1642. 4°. E. **84. (12.)**

C., W. A Dialogue concerning this question, Where was your Church before Luther and Caluin . . . By W. C. [i.e. William Crashaw.] *See* Rogers (Henry) *Prebendary of Hereford.* An Answer to Mr. Fisher . . . his five propositions concerning Luther, *etc.* 1623. 4°. **477. a. 33.**

C., W. A Discourse for a King and Parliament: in four sections. Demonstrating I. The inconsistency of a free-state with the scituation of this countrey, and constitution of the people . . . By a moderate and serious pen. [The epistle dedicatory signed: W. C.] pp. 27. *For G. Bedell & T. Collins: London*, 1660. 4°. E. **1021. (12.)**

—— [Another copy.] **100. g. 25.**

C., W. Don Juan reclaimed: or, his Peregrination continued, from Lord Byron. By W. C. [i.e. William Cowley.] pp. iv. 79. *Printed for the Author: Sheffield*, 1840. 8°. **1164. f. 25.**

C., W. The Dutch Suruay: Wherein are related and truly discoursed, the chiefest losses and acquirements which haue past betweene the Dutch and the Spaniards, in these last four years warres of the Netherlands . . . Whereunto are annext the Mansfeldian motiues, directed vnto all Colonels, Lieutenant Colonels . . . and souldiers, whose seruice is engag'd in this present expedition vnder the commaund of . . . Ernestus Earle of Mansfield. [The epistle dedicatory signed: W. C., i.e. William Crosse.] pp. 36. *Edward All-de, for Nathaniel Butter: London*, 1625. 4°. **1055. a. 29.**

C., W. The Edinburgh Miscellany: consisting of original poems, translations, &c. By various hands. [The preface signed: W. C.] The second edition. vol. 1. pp. iv. 271. *J. M'Euen & Co.: Edinburgh*, 1720. 8°. **1078. f. 26.**

C., W.

—— Elizabethan England in Gentle and Simple Life. *See* infra: Polimanteia.

C., W. The Fatall Vesper, or a true and punctuall relation of that . . . accident, hapning on Sunday . . . the 26. of October last, by the fall of a roome in the Black-Friers . . . with the names . . . of such persons as . . . perished, *etc.* [The epistle dedicatory signed: W. C., i.e. William Crashaw ?] *Iohn Haviland for Richard Whitaker: London*, 1623. 4°. G. **19571. (3.)**

C., W. The First (Second) Part of the Renowned Historie of Fragosa King of Aragon. Together with the strange fortunes, and heroicall deedes, performed by his three sons, and the worthy president of love in his faire daughter Flermia . . . Written by W. C. B.L. 2 pt. *Printed by Bernard Alsop: London*, 1646. 4°. C. **57. b. 26.**
The edition of 1656, "*written by W. C. Gent.*," *is entered under C., W., Gent.*

C., W. *Begin.* The Great Designs of Parliaments have ever been, when duties are granted, that the subjects may have as little trouble and disturbance from the officers and collectors as is possible: and therefore the consideration of what followeth is humbly offered . . . to the Honourable House of Commons, before passing the act for a duty to be laid upon houses & windows. [Signed: W. C.] [*London*, 1695 ?] *s. sh.* fol. **816. m. 6. (89.)**

C., W. Hints and Helps to those who visit the Sick. [Signed: W. C.] pp. 47. *S.P.C.K.: London*, [1873.] 16°. **4402. f. 44.**

C., W. The History of Jack Connor. [The dedication signed: W. C., i.e. William Chaigneau.] The second edition, corrected. (Stultus versus Sapientem. In three letters [signed: T. à Stupidius] to The Fool.) 2 vol. *W. Johnston: London*, 1753. 12°. **12612. de. 14.**

—— The third edition corrected. 2 vol. *Abraham Bradley: Dublin*, 1753. 12°. **12612. df. 32. (1.)**

C., W. The History of the Commons Warre of England throughout these three nations: begun from 1640 and continued till this present year 1662. [The epistle dedicatory signed: W. C.] pp. 140. *For Joshua Conyers: London*, 1662. 8°. **599. b. 13. (1.)**

—— [Another copy.] G. **4136.**

—— [Another copy.] G. **4137.**
Imperfect; wanting the frontispiece.

C., W. The Horrors of a Cattle Boat. By an Eye-Witness. [Signed: W. C.] Echo, Nov. 6th and 8th, 1889. pp. 4. *Harrison & Sons: [London,* 1889.] 8°. **8425. f. 27. (4.)**

C., W. Index of Noteworthy Words and Phrases found in the Clementine Writings, commonly called the Homilies of Clement, *etc.* [The preface signed: W. C.] pp. iv. 105. *Macmillan & Co.: London,* 1893. 8°. **3623. aa. 38.**

C., W. The Intentions of the Army discovered in a letter from a Gentleman residing there, to a friend of his in London . . . Written at the head quarters, Junii. 21. 1647. [Signed: W. C.] pp. 7. *London,* 1647. 4°. **E. 393. (13.)**

C., W.

—— Legiendy polskie przez W. C. [i.e. Władysława Chomętowskiego. In verse.] pp. 67. *w Krakowie,* 1862. 8°. **11586. h. 24. (1.)**

C., W. A Letter from His Excellencies Quarters, of a discovery in Sir Thomas Fairfax his army, the enemies thereof . . . With a conference between His Excellency, and the Marquesse of Worcester. Also, a full relation of all the whole proceedings at Ragland Castle . . . Printed by the originall copies, *etc.* [Signed: W. C.] pp. 6. *Printed by Barnard Alsop: London,* 1646. 4°. **E. 351. (13.)**

C., W. A Letter [signed: W. C.] from the Generalls head Quarters to a Member of the House of Commons. [10 March 1645, o.s.] *See* England. [*Appendix.—History and Politics.*—ii. 1646.] His Majesties whole Army in the West conquered, *etc.* 1645 [1646]. 4°. **E. 328. (7.)**

C., W. A Letter [signed: W. C., i.e. Sir William Coventry] written to Dr Burnet, giving an account of Cardinal Pool's secret powers . . . To which are added, two breves [of Pope Julius iii., in Latin] that Cardinal Pool brought over, and some other of his letters . . . never before printed. pp. 40. *For Richard Baldwin: London,* 1685. 4°. **699. f. 1. (18.)**

—— [Another copy.] **3936. d. 17.**

—— [Another copy.] **108. e. 27.**

C., W. Lilliput. A dramatic entertainment, *etc.* [The prefatory letter signed: W. C., i.e. David Garrick.] pp. v. 39. *Paul Vaillant: London,* 1757. 8°. **643. i. 4. (2.)**

—— [Another copy.] **83. a. 19. (3.)**

C., W. A Little Manuel of the Poore Man's Dayly Devotion. . . . By W. C. (Guillaume Clifford.) 1670. 12°. *See* Clifford (William) *Roman Catholic Priest.* **3456. a. 43.**

C., W. Missa Triumphans, or, the Triumph of the Mass; wherein all the sophistical and wily arguments of Mr. de Rodon . . . in his funestuous tract by him called, The Funeral of the Mass, are fully . . . answered. Together with an appendix by way of answer to the translator's preface. By F. P. M., O. P., Hib. [The epistle dedicatory signed: W. C., i.e. William Collins.] pp. 464. 48. *Louain,* 1675. 8°. **3936. a. 19.**
Another copy, with the epistle dedicatory signed: C. W., is entered under W., C.

—— *See* Dérodon (D.) The Funeral of the Mass . . . With an answer to what Mr. W. C. [i.e. William Collins] has since publish'd . . . in a discourse, entitled, Missa triumphans, *etc.* 1716. 8°. **3901. e. 14.**

C., W. The Moderate Enquirer resolved in a plain descript of several objections . . . concerning the contem people, commonly called Quakers . . . Written . . . W. C. [i.e. William Caton.] pp. 36. 1671. 4°. **4152. ee. 18.**

C., W. A more Full Relation of the Continued Successe . . . Sir Thomas Fairfax, at, and since the routing of enemies forces at Torrington. With a . . . list of names of the cheife Commanders . . . killed, wounc and taken . . . Also intercepted letters from Fra giving intelligence of 8000 Foot, 1000 Horse . . readines to send over to assist the King against Parliament . . . and the surprisall of Cardiffe . Certified by letters to severall members of the . House of Commons, *etc.* [The first letter signed: W. pp. 6. *For Francis Coles: London,* 1645 [1646]. 4°. **E. 325.**

C., W. A most worthy Speech spoken by . . . Lieuten General Lesley, to the Scottish Army, at their march over Tweed into Scotland . . . Together, with the gall answer of the officers and soldiers . . . and their tal of a new oath, *etc.* [Signed: W. C.] (The copy of anot letter from Holmby, concerning the proceedings of Kings Maiesty with the Commissioners [signed: Simpson].) *For James Douglas: London,* 1647. 4°. **E. 378. (**

C., W. Mr. George Keith at Turners-Hall, in Philpot L London, in 1696, contradicting Mr. Geo. Keith, at Tolbooth of Aberdeen, in 1668 in fundamental point the Christian faith. Demonstrated by quotations in a letter to himself. By a Moderate Churchr [Signed: W. C.] pp. 12. *Printed & sold by E. Whitl London,* 1696. 4°. **855. f. 4.**
Cropped.

—— Mr. Keith no Presbyterian nor Quaker; but Ge the Apostate; deduced from proofs . . . in a se letter to himself [signed: W. C.]. By the author of former. pp. 20. *Printed by E. Whitlock: Lon* 1696. 4°. **T. 370.**

—— *See* Keith (George) *Rector of Edburton.* A Reprin for the Author of a Libel entituled, George Keitl Apostate. Written by a Church-man. [A reply to ' Keith no Presbyterian nor Quaker; but George Apostate; deduced from proofs . . . in a second let signed: W. C.] By Trepidantium Malleus [i.e. Sa Young]. 1697. 16°. **856. f. 18.**

C., W. Occasional Attempts in verse. By W. C. William Cockin.] pp. xv. 127. *Privately pri Kendal,* 1776. 8°. **11632.**

C., W. Occasional Sermons. By a Clergyman of the Ch of England. [The dedication signed: W. C.] pp *Bell & Daldy: London,* 1861. 16°. **4463.**

C., W. Omnia ad salutem necessaria perspicuè tradu in Sacra Scriptura. [In verse. Signed: W. C.] Ingelo (N.) The Perfection, Authority and Credil of the Holy Scriptures, *etc.* 1659. 8°. **E. 1792.**

C., W. A Particular Account of this last Siege of Mast . . . together with a list of the officers kill'd and wou in the three English Regiments, and the Scotch Regin Being the substance of a letter written out of Holl by a Friend; to a person of quality in London, Sep 1676, *etc.* [Signed: W. C., i.e. William Carr.] pp *For G. Kunholt & Moses Pitt: London,* 1676. 4°. **1193. i**

—— [Another copy.] **G. 5**

C., W. A Plaine Description of the Barmudas, now called Sommer Ilands. With the manner of their discouerie Anno 1609. by the shipwrack and admirable deliuerance of Sir Thomas Gates, and Sir George Sommers . . . [By Silvester Jourdan. The epistle dedicatory signed: W. C.] With an addition, or more ample relation of diuers other remarkeable matters concerning those ilands since then experienced, *etc.* (A Copie of the Articles which Master R. More, Governour Deputie of the Sommer Islands, propounded, *etc.*) B.L. *W. Stansby, for W. Welby: London,* 1613. 4°. **C. 32. c. 24.**
The first part, to sig. D3, *is a reprint of* "*A Discovery of the Barmudas, etc.*" *by S. Jourdan,* 1610.

—— [Another copy.] **G. 7117.**

—— [Another edition.] pp. 24. 1844. *See* FORCE (Peter) Tracts, *etc.* vol. 3. 1836, *etc.* 8°. **1324. g. 3.**

C., W. Poems for Young People. [The editor's preface signed: W. C., i.e. William Chambers.] pp. vii. 173. *Edinburgh,* 1851. 16°. [*Chambers's Library for Young People.*] **12805. b. 35.**

C., W. Poems on Several Occasions. By W. C. pp. 64. *Printed for the Author, & published by R. Taylor: London,* 1684. 8°. **C. 71. b. 17.**

C., W. The Poetical Commonplace Book, consisting of an original selection of standard and fugitive poetry, *etc.* [The preface signed: W. C.] pp. xvi. 388. *John Anderson, jun.: Edinburgh,* 1822. 12°. **11601. bb. 36. (2.)**
i.e. William Clapperton.

C., W. Polimanteia, or, the Meanes lawfull and vnlawfull, to judge of the fall of a common-wealth, against the friuolous and foolish conjectures of this age. Whereunto is added, A letter from England to her three daughters, Cambridge, Oxford, Innes of Court, and to all the rest of her inhabitants: perswading them to a constant vnitie of what religion soever they are, for the defence of our dread soveraigne, *etc.* [The dedication signed: W. C., i.e. William Covell.] *Printed by Iohn Legate: Cambridge,* 1595. 4°. **G. 537.**

C., W.

—— Elizabethan England in Gentle and Simple Life. Being I. England's Address to her three Daughters, the Universities of Cambridge and Oxford, and Lincoln's Inn: from Polimanteia, 1595. [The dedicatory epistle signed: W. C., i.e. William Covell. A reprint of the 1595 edition, the first essay being abridged.] II. A Quest of Enquirie by Women to know whether the tripe-woman was trimmed, 1595. [A reprint of the 1595 edition of "A Quest of Enquirie . . . gathered by Oliuer Oat-meale."] Edited, with introduction and notes and illustrations, by the Rev. Alexander B. Grosart. pp. xxiv. 177. *Printed for the Subscribers: Manchester,* 1881. 4°. [*Occasional Issues of Unique and Very Rare Books.* vol. 15.] **2326. g. 14. (1.)**
No. 5 *of an edition of sixty-two copies.*

C., W. Prayers directed against the Seven Deadly Sins. [The preface signed: W. C.] *J. & J. Barwick: Lancaster,* [1856.] 12°. **3456. aaa. 67. (4.)**

C., W. The Prince of Wales his Coming to Yarmouth, with 19 saile of shipping, & landing an armie for the relief of Colchester. Also a fight between them and the Parliaments forces . . . Certified in a letter from a gentleman of quality in the army. [Signed: W. C.] pp. 6. *Printed by Robert Austin: London,* 1647 [1648]. 4°. **E. 454. (18.)**

C., W. A Proclamation to All of all Sorts by moving a loving question for triall of all Spirits . . . making six humble requests for truth and peace. By a well-wisher to all mens soules. W. C. pp. 23. [*London,*] 1643. 4°. **E. 84. (21.)**

C., W.

—— Proofs of the Impracticability of the Resumption of Cash Payments in the present state of things: founded on some of the principles of the Bullion Report. [Signed: W. C., i.e. Sir William Congreve.] pp. 29. *J. Whiting: London,* 1819. 8°. **B. 497. (14.)**

C., W. Reflections on a Libel [by I. R.] intituled, A Plea for the Apothecaries. [By W. C.] pp. 10. *For Richard Chiswell: London,* 1671. 4°. **551. a. 7.**

C., W. Remarks upon the Reverend W. Whitefield's Letter to the Vicechancellor of the University of Oxford . . . By a late Member of the University of Oxford. [Signed: W. C.] pp. 62. *The Theatre: Oxford,* 1768. 8°. **105. b. 6.**

C., W. A Replie vnto a certaine Libell, latelie set foorth by Fa: Parsons, in the name of vnited Priests, intituled, A Manifestation of the great folly and bad spirit, of certaine in England, calling themselues seculer Priestes. With an addition of a table of such vncharitable words . . . as by him are vttered in the said treatise as well against our parsons, as our bookes, actions, and proceedings. [The prefaces signed: W. C., i.e. William Clarke.] ff. 106. [*London,*] 1603. 4°. **860. i. 6.**

C., W. A Reprint of four Articles, taken . . . from "The London Record." [A reply, signed: W. C., to Bishop Terrot's remarks upon Bishop Daly's "Letters on the subject of the Scottish Episcopal Church."] With an introduction, by the Rev. D. T. K. Drummond, containing some remarks upon a letter recently addressed by the Rev. Mr. Garden, to the . . . Bishop of Cashel. pp. 40. *W. P. Kennedy: Edinburgh,* 1846. 8°. **4175. bb. 35.**

C., W. The River of Life Pilgrims; or, Homeward bound. Who's for the voyage? A sacred allegory. [The preface signed: W. C.] pp. 724. *W. H. Collingridge: London,* [1866, 67.] 8°. **4417. bbb. 34.**
Published in parts.

C., W. A Short Account of the English Concertina, its uses and capabilities, facility of acquirement, and other advantages. By an Amateur. [The preface signed: W. C., i.e. William Cawdell.] pp. 23. *W. Cawdell: London,* 1866. 8°. **7868. a. 18.**

C., W. The Siege of Vienna, a poem. By W. C. pp. 40. *For H. Hills: London,* 1685. 4°. **164. m. 13.**

C., W. Sir Thomas Fairfax His Victorious proceedings in the taking of Launceston, with the magazine and armes . . . Also how Prince Rupert entred Abbington, and was beaten out againe . . . All of which is confirmed by severall letters. [The first letter signed: W. C., the second: J. R.] pp. 8. *For Matthew Walbanke: London,* 1645 [1646]. 4°. **E. 325. (26.)**

—— [Another copy.] **G. 3581. (6.)**

C., W. Too Much and too Little Money. By the author of "A Change of Luck," *etc.* [The dedication signed: W. C.] 2 vol. *Chapman & Hall: London,* 1870. 8°. **12627. f. 5.**

C., W. The Treatie for the Surrendring of Exeter to Sr. Thomas Fairfax . . . with other news from the Prince . . . and other passages of all the affaires at Barnstable, Pendennis and the Mount. These being true copies of letters [signed: W. C., N. T. respectively] examined, *etc.* pp. 7. *For Matthew Walbancke: London,* 1646. 4°. **E. 332. (2.)**

— The True Reporte of the Skirmish fought betwene the States of Flaunders, and Don Ioan, Duke of Austria, with the number of all them that were slayne on both sides. [Signed: W. C.] *William Bartlet: London,* [1578?] 8°. Mic. A. **605.** (13.)

MICROFILM (*negative*) *of the copy in the Folger Shakespeare Library. Made by the Folger Shakespeare Library,* 1955.

C., W. Truth and Trust. [The dedication signed: W. C., i.e. William Chambers.] pp. 144. *Edinburgh,* 1848. 16°. [*Chambers's Library for Young People.*] **12805.** b. **34.**

C., W. The Usurpations of France upon the Trade of the Woollen Manufacture of England briefly hinted at; being the effects of thirty years observations, by which that king hath been enabled to wage war with so great a part of Europe . . . By W. C. [i.e. William Carter.] pp. 30. *For Richard Baldwin: London,* 1695. 4°. **8245.** b. **13.**

— [Another copy.] **8245.** d. **21.**

C., W. The Widowes Ioy: or, Christ his comfortable salutation to a comfortlesse Widow . . . By W. C. pp. 49. *For Iohn Hogdets: London,* 1622. 4°. [i.e. William Cragge.] **873.** e. **40.**

C., W. The Wine Question; or, the Unity of Scripture and science on the subject. [The preface signed: W. C.] pp. 64. *S. W. Partridge & Co.: London,* 1878. 8°. **8435.** b. **5.**

C., W., and **C.,** R. Shipwrecks and Tales of the Sea. [The editors' preface signed: W. & R. C., i.e. William and Robert Chambers.] pp. 192. *W. & R. Chambers: London & Edinburgh,* 1860. 8°. **12622.** a. **13.**

— Tales for Home Reading. [The editors' preface signed: W. & R. C., i.e. William and Robert Chambers.] pp. 224. *W. & R. Chambers: London & Edinburgh,* [1865.] 8°. **12620.** aaa. **24.**

— Tales for Young and Old. [The editors' preface signed: W. & R. C., i.e. William and Robert Chambers.] pp. 224. *W. & R. Chambers: London & Edinburgh,* 1865. 8°. **12620.** aaa. **25.**

C., W., and **M.,** R. An Impartial Representation of the Case of the Poor Cotton Spinners in Lancashire, &c. [Signed: W. C. & R. M., i.e. Ralph Mather.] With a mode proposed to the legislature for their relief, and an humble petition to Her Majesty in their behalf. pp. 16. *R. Mather: London,* 1780. 8°. **523.** g. **23.** (2.)

C., W., *Bach. of the Civill Law.* Decimarum et Oblationum Tabula. A Tithing Table, or Table of Tithes and Oblations, according to the Kings Ecclesiasticall Lawes and Ordinances established in the Church of England . . . Compiled by W. C. Bach. of the Ciuill Law [*London,* c.1625] fol. **816.** m. **22.** (73.)
Imperfect.

— [Another edition.] B.L. *Printed by Thomas Purfoot: London,* 1633. 4°. **517.** b. **7.** (4.)

— [Another copy.] **517.** h. **27.** (1.)

— [Another edition.] *Printed by Thomas Purfoot: London,* 1635. 4°. T. **800.** (4.)

— [Another edition.] Also a . . . summary declaration of composition . . . priviledge, *etc.* pp. 39. *J. T. for Andrew Crook: London,* 1658. 4°. **5155.** a. **47.**

— [Another edition.] pp. 39. *J. T. for Andrew Crook: London,* 1662. 4°. T. **810.** (5.)

— [Another copy.] **517.** h. **27.** (2.)

— [Another copy.] **1104.** c. **31.** (9.)

— [Another edition.] pp. 39. *For Andrew Cr London,* 1665. 4°. **5125.** b

— [Another edition.] pp. 39. *For Andrew Cr London,* 1673. 4°. **701.** i

— [Another edition.] pp. 39. *For R. Scot: Lo* 1676. 4°. **5155.** aa

— [Another edition.] pp. 39. *For R. Scot: Lo* 1683. 4°. **5155.** c.

— [Another copy.] G. **20177**

C., W., *a Churchman, the Quakers Advocate. See* (George) *Founder of the Society of Friends.* The Fox Quakers, dunces, lyars and slanderers, proved o George Fox's Journal . . . Also a Reply to W. Church-man, the Quakers Advocate—his Trepidar Malleus Intrepidanter Malleatus, *etc.* 1697. 12°. **4152.**

C., W., *Coll. Med. London M.D.* Hydro-sidereon: Treatise of ferruginous-waters, especially the Ips Spaw . . . [The dedication signed: W. C. Coll. Med. L M.D., i.e. William Coward?] With a plain demo tion also of the great vanity and folly in buying cheats in selling German-Spaw-water in England pp. 128. *J. Morphew: London,* 1717. 8°. G. **1907**

— [Another copy.] **1171.** h. **2**
The titlepage is mutilated.

C., W., *Esq.* A Discourse—by way of Essay—h offer'd to the Consideration of the Honourable Ho Commons, towards the raising moneys by an excis By W. C. Esq. pp. 22. *Printed for the Authour: L* 169[5/6]. 4°. **712.**

C., W., *Esq; a True Lover of Art and Nature. See* PHILA (Eyraeneus) *Cosmopolita, pseud.* Secrets Reveal' Published for the benefit of all English-men, by Esq; a true Lover of Art and Nature [i.e. William C 1669. 8°. **8905.** a

C., W., *Gent.* The Renowned History of Fragosa, K Aragon; and his three Sonnes: or, the Mirr magnamity, and Cupid's conquest . . . Written, by Gent. pp. 138. *Printed by E. Alsop: L* 1656. 4°. **12431.**
The edition of 1646, "*written by W. C.,*" *is entered* C., W.

C., W., *a Lover of his Country.* Trades Destruct Englands Ruine: or Excise decryed. Where manifested the irregularity and inequality of raising by way of excise to defray the charge of the r By W. C. a Lover of his Country. pp. 8. *L* 1659. 4°. **518.** h.

— [Another copy.] E. **98**

C., W., *M.A.* Clavis Calendaria: or the Liturgy-Ca of the Church of England explain'd. By W. C. pp. 112. *John Nutt: London,* 1700. 12°. **3478.**

C., W., *M.A., Minister of the Gospel.* The Summ o Sermons on the Witnesses, and the Earthquak accompanies their Resurrection. Occasion'd from earthquake . . . By W. C. M.A. Minister of the [i.e. Walter Cross]. pp. 40. *Printed & sold by Jo Robinson: London,* 1692. 4°. **4462.** cc.

— [Another copy.] **111.**

C., W., *M.D.* The Just Scrutiny: or, a Serious enquiry into the modern notions of the soul . . . By W. C., M.D. [i.e. William Coward.] pp. 221. *John Chantry: London,* [1705 ?] 8°. **1019. k. 9. (3.)**

C., W., *M.D.* A Proposal for Raising a Fund to discharge the Debts of the Nation. Humbly recommended to the Hon. House of Commons, by W. C., M.D. [*London,* 1715 ?] fol. **816. m. 6. (12*.)**

C., W., *M.D., C.M., L.C.* The Grand Essay: or, a Vindication of reason and religion against impostures of philosophy . . . To which is added, a brief answer to Mr. Broughton's Psycholo. &c. By, W. C., M.D., C.M., L.C. [i.e. William Coward.] pp. 248. *P. G.; sold by John Chantry: London,* 1704. 8°. **855. d. 13.**

C., W., *an Officer of Major General How's Regiment.* A Poem humbly inscrib'd to His Grace the Duke of Marlborough, occasion'd upon his repeated victories in Flanders. Wrote in the camp by W. C. an Officer of Major General How's Regiment [i.e. William Churchill]. pp. 12. *Benjamin Bragg: London,* 1709. fol. **11642. i. 9. (1.)**

C*****, W., *Rector of K**** W****.* A Caveat to the Will of a certain Northern Vicar. Addressed to the Reverend W. C*****, Rector of K**** W**** [i.e. William Cooper, Rector of Kirby Wiske]. [In verse.] pp. 39. *W. Flexney: London,* 1766. 4°. **11642. h. 23.**

C——, W., *Rev.* A Key to the Psalms; being an easy, concise, and familiar explanation of words, allusions, and sentences in them, selected from substantial authorities . . . By the Rev. W. C—— [i.e. William Cole]. pp. v. 46. *F. Hodson: Cambridge,* 1788. 8°. **3090. d. 4.**

C., W., *Rev., Chaplain of the New Bayley Prison, Manchester.* The Prisoner's Select Manual of Devout Excercises: including forms of visitation and select psalms. By the Rev. W. C., Chaplain of the New Bayley Prison, Manchester. pp. 82. *G. Swindells: Manchester,* 1791. 12°. **694. c. 34. (2.)**

C., W., *Schoolmaster.* An Epitome of Sacred History, for children. With moral reflections and observations. By W. C. Schoolmaster. [With plates.] vol. 1. *London,* 1794. 12°. **3149. a. 2.**
Imperfect; wanting all after vol. 1.

C., W., *a Servant to his King and Country.* Englands Interest by Trade Asserted, shewing the necessity & excellency thereof. Wherein is discovered, that many hundred thousand pounds might be gained to the King and Kingdom, by the due improvement of the product thereof, more particularly by wool . . . By W. C. a Servant to his King and Country [i.e. William Carter]. The second impression, corrected and enlarged. pp. 44. *Printed for the Author: London,* 1671. 4°. **8245. a. 9.**
An earlier edition, entitled: "England's Interest Asserted," in which the author's initials do not occur, is entered under ENGLAND. [*Appendix.—Trade and Commerce.*]

—— [Another copy.] **712. g. 16. (6.)**

—— [Another copy.] **1102. h. 1. (8.)**

—— [Another copy.] **104. m. 50.**

C., *the Honourable Sir* W. The Character of a Trimmer. His opinion of I. The laws and government. II. Protestant religion. III. The Papists. IV. Foreign affairs. By the Honourable Sir W. C. [i.e. Sir William Coventry, or rather by George Savile, Marquis of Halifax.] pp. 43. *London,* 1688. 4°. **T. 763. (43.)**

—— [Another copy.] **E. 1964. (7.)**

—— [Another copy.] **8132. aaa. 16.**
The titlepage is mutilated.

C., *the Honourable Sir* W.

—— [Another copy.] **T. 682. (8.)**
Mutilated.

C*****, *Sir* W******, *Bart.* The Recantation; a poem; inscribed, without permission, to Sir W****** C*****, Bart. [i.e. Sir William Curtis.] pp. 23. *R. Carlile: London,* 1818. 8°. **1103. e. 40. (18.)**

C., W. DE, *Mme.* Catherine Booth, mère de l'Armée du Salut. Par l'auteur de Serge Batourine. [The author's name given in the publisher's advertisement as: Mme W. de C., i.e. E. Ward de Charrière.] pp. 61. *Lausanne; Paris,* 1891. 8°. **4906. de. 25. (4.)**

C., W. A. *See* FINDEN (William) and (E. F.) Views of Ports and Harbours, Watering Places, Fishing Villages, and other picturesque objects on the English Coast. [With descriptive letter-press. The preface signed: W. A. C., i.e. William A. Chatto.] 1838. 4°. **563. e. 4.**

C., W. A. *See* LAW (William) *Author of the "Serious Call."* Law's Serious Call . . . Adapted to the requirements of the present day, by W. A. C. 1905. 8°. **764. a. 28.**

C., W. A.

—— *See* PERIODICAL PUBLICATIONS.—*Newcastle-upon-Tyne.* The Fisher's Garland for 1821 [*etc.*]. (A Collection of Right Merrie Garlands, *etc.* [The issues for 1835–37 signed: W. A. C., i.e. W. A. Chatto.]) 1821, *etc.* 8°. **1077. f. 41.**

C., W. A. Arndt und Kotzebue als politische Schriftsteller. Von W. A. C. [i.e. C. A. Weinhold.] pp. 14. [*Dresden,*] 1814. 12°. **1390. b. 78.**

C., W. A. Elements of Luganda Grammar, together with exercises and vocabulary. By a Missionary of the Church Missionary Society in Uganda. [Compiled from material collected by G. L. Pilkington. The preface signed: W. A. C., i.e. William A. Crabtree.] pp. 260. *S.P.C.K.: London,* 1902. 8°. **12911. f. 11.**

C., W. A. A Premonitory Cry; or, a Note of warning and testimony of hope. [With a printed slip inserted signed: W. A. C., i.e. W. A. Copinger.] pp. 67. 1876. 8°. *See* CRY. **764. k. 2. (1.)**

C., W. A. Who Killed Cockatoo. [A nursery rhyme.] By W. A. C. [i.e. W. A. Cawthorne.] pp. 19. *J. H. Lewis: Adelaide,* [1860 ?] 8°. **11643. bbb. 14. (8.)**

C., W. A., *of Canada West.* Mick Tracy, the Irish Scripture reader; or the Martyred convert & the priest. A tale of facts. By W. A. C., of Canada West. pp. xii. 355. *Book Society: London,* [1863.] 8°. **3942. b. 67.**

—— [Another edition.] pp. vi. 383. *American Baptist Publication Soc.: Philadelphia,* [1867.] 8°. **12707. b. 6.**

C., W. A. B.

—— *See* MURRAY (John) *Publishing Firm.* [*Handbooks for Travellers.—Switzerland.*] A Handbook for Travellers in Switzerland . . . Eighteenth edition. [The reviser's preface signed: W. A. B. C., i.e. William A. B. Coolidge.] 1891. 8°. **10028. bbb. 14.**

—— —— 1892. 8°. **10028. ccc. 29.**

C., W. A. C. St. Paul at Lystra. [In verse. The "Apology" signed: W. A. C. C., i.e. William A. C. Chevalier.] pp. 56. *Hatchard: London,* 1888. 8°. **11781. g. 36.**

C., W. B. Colonial Policy, with hints upon the formation of military settlements. To which are added observations on the boundary question now pending between this country and the United States. [Signed: W. B. C., i.e. W. B. Cooke.] pp. 49. *J. Cochrane & Co.: London,* 1835. 8°. **8154. e. 1. (8.)**

C., W. B. Cursory Observations, occasioned by a late Address to the People called Quakers. To which the Address is prefixed. [The preface signed: W. B. C., i.e. William B. Crafton.] pp. 40. *J. Gales: Sheffield*, 1789. 8°. **1355**. e. 4.

—— A Short Sketch of the Evidence, for the Abolition of the Slave Trade, delivered before a committee of the House of Commons. To which is added, a recommendation of the subject to the serious attention of people in general. [Signed: W. B. C., i.e. William B. Crafton.] pp. 23. *London*, 1792. 12°. **1102**. g. **13**. **(6.)**

—— [Another copy.] **08415**. e. **20**. **(2.)**

—— The third edition, with additions. pp. 24. *M. Gurney: London*, 1792. 8°. **8156**. b. **18**.

C., W. B.

—— Upton Sinclair. Biographical and critical opinions. [By various authors. With a portrait. Signed: W. B. C.] pp. 32. [1931.] 8°. **10889**. aa. **27**.

C., W. C. *See* Busch (Wilhelm) *Artist.* [Schnurrdiburr.] Buzz a Buzz, or the Bees. Done freely into English, by the author of My Bee Book. [The translator's preface signed: W. C. C., i.e. William C. Cotton.] [1872.] 8°. **11649**. eee. **20**.

C., W. C. *See* Ratramnus, *Monachus Corbeiensis.* Ratramni . . . Liber de Corpore et Sanguine Domini. [The editors' preface signed: H. W., W. C. C.] 1838. 12°. **1114**. a. **22**. **(2.)**

—— *See* Ratramnus, *Monachus Corbeiensis.* The Book of Ratramn . . . on the Body and Blood of the Lord, *etc.* [The translators' preface signed: H. W., W. C. C.] 1838. 12°. **1114**. a. **22**. **(1.)**

C., W. C. Victoriaism; or, a Reorganization of the people: moral, social, economical, and political: suggested as a remedy for the present distress. Respectfully addressed to the Right Hon. Sir Robert Peel, Bart. [Signed: W. C. C., i.e. William C. Coward.] pp. 28. *J. Clements; Charles Westerton: London*, 1843. 8°. **1389**. d. **63**. **(2.)**

C., W. D. L. Le Palais des curieux. Où, l'algebre et le sort donnent la decision des questions les plus douteuses: et où les songes et les visions nocturnes sont expliquez selon la doctrine des anciens. [The dedication signed: W. D. L. C., i.e. M. de Vulson, Sieur de la Colombière.] pp. 110 [210]. *N. Oudat: Troyes*, 1655. 8°. **719**. a. **11**.

—— [Another edition.] pp. 158. *J. Oudat: Troyes*, [1656?] 8°. **719**. a. **12**. **(1.)**

C., W. E. *See* Dickens (C.) [*Edwin Drood.*] The Mystery of Edwin Drood . . . Completed in 1914 by W. E. C.[*etc.* [1914.] 8°. [i.e. Walter E. Crisp.] **012602**. h. 2.

C., W. E. Do Departed Spirits Know their Friends on Earth? Yes! By W. E. C. *See* W., J. Across the River, *etc.* 1864. 24°. **4405**. aaa. **39**.

C., W. E. Elvinor. A poem. By W. E. C. pp. vi. 240. *William Poole: London*, [1880.] 8°. **11653**. b. **43**.

C., W. E. The Indian Story-book for Boys and Girls. [With a preface signed: W. E. C.] pp. 160. *Carey Press: London*, [1921.] 8°. **012802**. c. 2.

C., W. E. Royal Festivities during the Holy Fast of Lent. A story of the Atimian Kingdom. By W. E. C. pp. 19. *G. J. Palmer: London*, 1878. 16°. **4422**. h. **3**. **(2.)**

C., W. E. "Very Few Men!" The lament of a country pastor. [Signed: W. E. C., i.e. William E. Chapman.] pp. 4. *S.P.C.K.: London*, [1870.] 8°. **4420**. i. **1**. **(3.)**

C., W. F. The Doctor's Bill or no Doctor's Bill. A word working men and their families. [On provident disp saries. Signed: W. F. C.] pp. 15. *Jarrold & Son Ladies' Sanitary Association: London*, [1878.] 12°. **7306**. aa. **16**.

C., W. G. *Se* Ruskin (John) Fors Clavigera, *etc.* [T editor's preface signed: W. G. C., i.e. William G. Colli wood.] 1896, *etc.* 8°. **8411**. ee.

—— *See* Ruskin (John) Studies in both Arts, *etc.* [T editor's preface signed: W. G. C., i.e. William G. Colli wood.] 1895. fol. **L.R.404.e.**

C., W. G.

—— *See* Ruskin (J.) Verona; and other lectures, *etc.* [T editor's preface signed: W. G. C., i.e. William G. Collir wood.] 1894. 8°. K.T.C. **27**. b.

—— Coniston Tales. Told by W. G. C. [i.e. William Collingwood.] pp. 72. *Wm. Holmes: Ulverst* 1899. 8°. **012331**. ee.

C., W. G. Remarks on Dr. Buckland's View of the Mos Creation, as the last fitting up of the earth: with a noti of the recorded extent of the Deluge. By Eretzseph [Signed: W. G. C., i.e. W. G. Carter.] pp. 56. *Smallfield & Son: London*, 1837. 8°. T. **2128**. (1

C., W. G. Ruskin Exhibition, Coniston, July 21 to Sept. 1900. [A catalogue. The preface signed: W. G. C., i William G. Collingwood.] pp. 36. 1900. 8°. *S* Coniston.—*Ruskin Exhibition.* **1418**. h. **59**. (

C., W. G. Some Account of the Mount Morgan Gold Mi Rockhampton, Queensland. Compiled by W. G. C. pp. "*Daily Northern Argus*": *Rockhampton*, 1885. 8°. **7106**. f. **18**. (

C., W. H. *See* O'Brien (Henry) *B.A.* The Round Tow of Ireland, *etc.* [The editor's preface signed: W. H. C. 1898. 8°. **07708**. i.

C., W. H. *See* Sicily. Letters from Sicily, *etc.* [T editor's preface signed: W. H. C., i.e. William Henry Charlton.] 1850. 8°. **8033**. b. **71**. (

C., W. H. A Fly-Leaf to Beresford-Webb's Germ Grammar. Arranged by W. H. C. [i.e. William Counsell.] pp. 22. *Jackson & Son: Sedberg* 1918. 8°. **12962**. dd. 4

C., W. H.

—— Memoir of William Ellery Channing, with extracts fro his correspondence and manuscripts. [The preface signe W. H. C., i.e. William Henry Channing. With a portrai 3 vol. *John Chapman: London*, 1848. 12°. **4986**. d. 2

—— Memoir of William Ellery Channing, with extracts fro his correspondence and manuscripts. [The preface signe W. H. C., i.e. William Henry Channing. With a portrai 3 vol. *W. Crosby & H. P. Nichols: Boston*, 1848. 12° **4986**. d. 2

The title on the spine reads "Channing's Memoirs."

—— Memoir of William Ellery Channing, with extracts fro his Correspondence and manuscripts. [The preface signe W. H. C., i.e. William H. Channing. With a portrait 2 vol. *G. Routledge & Sons: London*, [1870.] 8°. 4986. bbb. 3

The title on the spine reads "Channing's Memoirs."

C., W. H. Time, Faith, and Energy. Passages in the life Geoffrey Waller. pp. vii. 422. *C. J. Skeet: London* 1868. 8°. **12621**. bbb.

The author's initials appear in the introduction.

C., W. J. English Poetry . . . To be learned by heart . . . For use in the schools of the Collegiate Institution, Liverpool. [The editor's preface signed: W. J. C., i.e. William J. Conybeare.] 4 bk. *Wareing Webb: Liverpool; Longman & Co.: London*, 1844. 12°. **1162**. c. **26–29**.

C., W. J. The Poor Man's Wisdom. [A religious tract. Signed: W. J. C.] pp. 20. [*J. Carter:*] *London*, [1893.] 8°. **4422**. ddd. **55**. **(8.)**

C., W. J. School Chronology; or the Great dates of history, drawn up for the use of the Collegiate Schools, Liverpool. [The preface signed: W. J. C., i.e. William J. Conybeare.] pp. 23. *Longman & Co.: London*, 1845. *obl.* 12°. Second edition. **807**. a. **12**.

C., W. J. The Syrophenician. [A religious tract. Signed: W. J. C.] pp. 16. *J. Carter: London*, [1901.] 32°. **04420**. de. **8**. **(5.)**

C., W. J., *an Old Rider*. Romances of the Wheel, a collection of romantic cycling tales. By W. J. C., an old rider [i.e. W. J. Coppen]. pp. 100. *Iliffe & Son: Coventry*, 1880. 8°. **12641**. c. **31**.

C., W. K. L.

—— *See* Diognetus. [*Epistle to Diognetus.—Greek.*] The Epistle to Diognetus. Greek text. [The preface signed: W. K. L. C., i.e. William K. L. Clarke.] 1930. 8°. W.P. **4683/45**.

C., W. K. L.

—— The Apocrypha. A brief introduction. [Signed: W. K. L. C., i.e. William K. L. Clarke.] pp. 15. *S.P.C.K.: London*, 1940. 8°. [*Little Books on Religion*. no. 178.] W.P. **1307/178**.

—— "Bring the Books." An account of the missionary literature work of the S.P.C.K. [Signed: W. K. L. C., i.e. William K. L. Clarke.] pp. 8. 1934. 8°. *See* England.—*Church of England.—Society for Promoting Christian Knowledge.* **11855**. aaa. **56**. **(2.)**

—— The Catechism Explained. [The preface signed: W. K. L. C., i.e. William K. L. Clarke.] pp. 63. *S.P.C.K.: London*, 1937. 12°. [*Little Books on Religion*. no. 123.] W.P. **1307/123**.

—— Could God become Flesh? [Signed: W. K. L. C., i.e. William K. L. Clarke.] pp. 22. *S.P.C.K.: London*, 1940. 8°. [*Youth Asks Questions*. no. 5.] W.P. **10088/5**.

—— The Prayer Book Calendar Explained. [Signed: W. K. L. C., i.e. William K. L. Clarke.] pp. 22. *S.P.C.K.: London*, 1941. 8°. [*Little Books on Religion*. no. 182.] W.P. **1307/182**.

—— Spiritualism and Psychical Research. A religion and a science. [Signed: W. K. L. C., i.e. William K. L. Clarke.] pp. 47. *S.P.C.K.: London*, 1941. 12°. [*Little Books on Religion*. no. 187.] W.P. **1307/187**.

C., W. L. Buds of Poesy: being the poetical effusions of a youth, W. L. C. [i.e. W. L. Cole ?] Chiefly written prior to his twelfth year. [The editor's preface signed: J. C.] pp. iii. 45. *Simpkin, Marshall & Co.: London*, 1839. 16°. **11646**. a. **63**.

C., W. L. Etoniana, Ancient and Modern. Being notes of the history and traditions of Eton College. Republished from 'Blackwood's Magazine,' with additions. [The preface signed: W. L. C., i.e. William L. Collins.] pp. viii. 238. *W. Blackwood & Sons: Edinburgh & London*, 1865. 8°. **8364**. aa. **32**.

C., W. L.

—— Jervaulx Abbey. [The foreword signed: W. L. C., i.e. William Lorenzo Christie.] pp. 12. *R. Ackrill: Harrogate*, 1924. 8°. **7822**. a. **53**.

—— The Public Schools. Winchester—Westminster—Shrewsbury—Harrow—Rugby. Notes of their history and traditions. By the author of 'Etoniana.' [The preface signed: W. L. C., i.e. William L. Collins.] pp. viii. 414. *W. Blackwood & Sons: Edinburgh & London*, 1867. 8°. **8364**. aa. **33**.

C., W. M. *See* B., E. V. A Children's Summer. Eleven etchings on steel by E. V. B. Illustrated in prose and rhyme by M. L. B. and W. M. C. 1853. *obl.* fol. **1899.cc.59.**

C., W. M. *See* Fearne (Charles) *the Younger*. An Epitome of Fearne on Contingent Remainders . . . By W. M. C. 1878. 8°. **6306**. a. **8**.

C., W. M. *See* Parer (Raymond J. P.) and MacIntosh (J. C.) The Record Flight from London to Calcutta . . . Edited by W. M. C. 1920. 8°. **010025**. ee. **7**.

C., W. M. Deirdre of the Sorrows: an opera. [The preface signed: W. M. C., i.e. W. M. Crofton.] pp. 35. *R. T. White: Dublin*, 1926. 4°. **11778**. ddd. **26**.

C., W. M. Hymenæus: a drama. In two acts. By W. M. C. [In verse.] pp. 16. *Henry Richards: London*, [1840 ?] 8°. **11779**. c. **8**.

C., W. M. Words and Deeds of Nelson. A brief record compiled by W. M. C. pp. 27. *Henry Frowde: London*, [1905.] 8°. **10815**. aa. **26**.

C., W. M. H. Do you love Christ? [Signed: W. M. H. C., i.e. William M. H. Church.] pp. 8. *William Macintosh: London*, [1867.] 16°. **4418**. d. **21**.

—— Sunday: what is it? [Signed: W. M. H. C., i.e. William M. H. Church.] pp. 11. *William Macintosh: London*, 1869. 12°. **4355**. aa. **66**. **(9.)**

C., W. P. *See* Musset (L. C. A. de) All is Fair in Love and War. A drawing-room comedy, *etc.* (An adaptation of A. de Musset's proverbe L'Ane et le ruisseau.) [The preface signed: W. P. C.] 1868. 8°. **11781**. aaa. **41**. **(5.)**

C., W. P. H.

—— *See* Protestants. A Seasonable Discourse shewing the Necessity of Union amongst Protestants . . . Also, the charge of persecution, lately maintained against the established religion, by W. P. H. C. [i.e. William Penn, Henry Care] and other insignificant scribblers, detected, *etc.* 1688. 4°. T. **1030**. **(13.)**

C., W. R. *See* Lenormant (F.) Chaldean Magic, *etc.* [The translator's preface signed: W. R. C., i.e. William R. Cooper.] [1877.] 8°. **2217**. aa. **3**.

C., W. R. An Extraordinary Saviour for an Extraordinary Sinner. By W. R. C. pp. 8. *J. Carter: London*, [1894.] 16°. **04420**. de. **20**. **(2.)**

—— Honey. [A religious tract. Signed: W. R. C.] pp. 12. *J. Carter: London*, [1895.] 24°. **4418**. de. **3**. **(4.)**

—— How can I? How can I?; or, the Dying railway guard. By W. R. C. pp. 8. *J. Carter: London*, [1893.] 8°. **4422**. aaa. **73**. **(2.)**

C., W. R.

—— Life, Liberty and an Object. [A religious tract.] By W. R. C. pp. 16. *J. Carter: London*, [1893.] 8°. **4422**. aaa. **73**. **(3.)**

C., W. R.

—— Life, Liberty and an Object. [A religious tract.] By W. R. C. pp. 16. *J. Carter: London*, [1893.] 8°. **4422**. aaa. **73**. **(3.)**

—— "Mordecai the Jew"; or, the Mighty Unseen Hand. [On the Book of Esther. Signed: W. R. C.] pp. 16. *J. Carter: London*, [1897.] 32°. **03128**. e. **4**. (2.)

C., W. R. Scripture References on the Gifts and Fruits of the Holy Spirit, *etc.* [Signed: W. R. C., i.e. W. R. Caird.] pp. 12. *G. Norman: London*, 1832. 8°. **764**. i. **17**. **(1.)**

C., W. S. R. *See* Canada, *Lower*. [*Messages, etc., of Governors.*] Proclamation of Government. Lord Gosford's Proclamation against the French Canadian Rebels, *etc.* [With a footnote signed: W. S. R. C., i.e. Sir William S. R. Cockburn.] [1841.] *s. sh.* fol. **695**. l. **14**. **(93.)**

—— Scheme for Voting at Elections for Members of the House of Commons. [Signed: W. S. R. C., i.e. Sir William S. R. Cockburn.] pp. 11. *Longman & Co.: London*, 1854. 12°. **8138**. c. **24**.

C. (William) Saved by Grace, and spoiled for this world. [Signed: Wm C.] pp. 16. *J. Carter: London*, [1901.] 16°. **04420**. de. **8**. (4.)

C . . . . . (*Sir* William) *Commodore, Alderman.*

—— Dispatches from Commodore Alderman C . . . . . commanding a light squadron of coal barges in the rear of the expedition for the Scheld, *etc.* [A satire on Sir William Curtis, Bart.] pp. 16. *Thomas Tegg: London*, 1809. 8°. 12330. dd. 13. (4.)

—— [Another copy.] 12330. h. 27. (1.)

C., X. Everyday Life in Cape Colony in time of Peace. By X. C. [i.e. Richard Cadbury.] With three illustrations. pp. 127. *T. Fisher Unwin: London*, 1902. 8°. **010097**. g. **25**.

C., Z. Marriage-Musick or Nuptial Duties, directed in a fatherly admonition to William Beard and Sarah Whiskard, by Z. C., their fatherly friend. [In verse.] [*London*, 1670 ?] *s. sh.* fol. Lutt. II. **136**.

C., Z. A new ballad, called Simony Fair, *etc.* [The author's initials given in MS. as Z. C.] [1675 ?] *s. sh.* fol. *See* Simony Fair. **1870**. d. **1**. (62.)

C., Z., *Minister of the Word.* Fraterna Correptio: or, the saints zeale against sinful altars: delivered in a sermon preached on a day of humiliation for the errors, heresies, & schisms of our times and nations. By Z. C. Minister of the Word [i.e. Zachary Crofton]. pp. 159. *T. R. & E. M. for Robert Gibbs: London*, 1655. 8°. **4474**. b. **99**.

C.-A., J. P. *See* A., J. P. C.

C. A. A. MAGAZINE. *See* London.—III. *Concert Artists' Benevolent Association, etc.*

C A B M A REGISTER.

—— CABMA Register of British Products and Canadian Distributors (CABMA Register of British Industrial Products for Canada). *See* Canada. —*British Canadian Trade Association.*

C. A. B. PAMPHLET.

—— C.A.B. Pamphlet no. 1 [*etc.*]. *See* England.—*National Council of Social Service.*

C.A.C.A. LIBRARY ABSTRACT. *See* England.—*Cement and Concrete Association.*

C.A.C.A. LIBRARY RECORD. *See* England.—*Cement and Concrete Association.*

C.A.C.A. LIBRARY TRANSLATION. *See* England —*Cement and Concrete Association.*

C. A. DE B., *M. de.* *See* B., M. de C. A. de.

C.A.V. ENGINEERING REVIEW.

—— C.A.V. Engineering Review. *See* C.A.V. Ltd.

C.A.V. LTD.

—— C.A.V. Engineering Review. *London*, 1954– . fol. P.P. **1607**. fgh

C.A.W.G. MAGAZINE.

—— The C.A.W.G. Magazine. *See* England.—*Christian Alliance of Women and Girls.* Our Link.

C. B. C. B.: being the Christmas Bulletin of the 2/6th Cyclist Battalion, the Suffolk Regt. *See* England.—*Army.—Infantry.—Regiments.—Suffolk Regiment, 2/6th Cyclist Battalion.*

C.B.B. GAZETTE. *See* England.—*Catholic Boys Brigade.*

C.-B. BOOK. The C.-B. Book. An A.B.C. book for the use of political schools of all denominations. By the author of "The Irish Green Book," &c. [i.e. G. R. Halkett.] [Political cartoons satirising Sir H. Campbell Bannerman.] pp. 30. *Pall Mall Press: London*, [1906.] *obl.* 8°. **12314**. aaaa. **48**

C. B. C.

—— C.B.C. Society and Clinic for Constructive Birth Control. *See* London.—III. *Society and Clinic for Constructive Birth Control.*

C.B.C. BULLETIN. *See* London.—III. *Society and Clinic for Constructive Birth Control.*

C.B.C.O. BROADSHEET. *See* London.—III. *Central Board for Conscientious Objectors.*

C. B. FRY'S MAGAZINE. *See* Periodical Publications.—*London.*

C. B. M. C. NEWS. *See* Manchester.—*Manchester Christian Business Men's Committee.*

C.B.S. UNITS. C.B.S. Units and Standard Paper Tests. An essay towards establishing a normal system of paper testing. By C. F. Cross, E. J. Bevan, Clayton Beadle, and R. W. Sindall. pp. 25. *Wood Pulp, Limited: London*, 1903. 4°. **7944**. dd. **1[illegible]**

C.C.C. TABLES. The C.C.C. Tables for use in conjunction with the Corrector Check-Code. pp. 15. *A. P. Blundell & Co.: London*, [1911.] 8°. **8504**. f. **38**. (1

C.C.H.E. INFORMATION DIGEST. *See* London —III. *Central Council for Health Education.*

C. D. A. ENGINEERS' NOTE BOOK SERIES. *See* London.—III. *Copper Development Association.* Brasses and other Copper-Zinc Alloys, *etc.*

C.D.A. PUBLICATIONS. *See* London.—III. *Copper Development Association.*

C * * * DE P * * *, J. A. S. Dictionnaire de la folie et de la raison . . . Par J.-A.-S. C * * * de P * * * [i.e. J. A. S. Collin de Plancy], *etc.* 2 tom. *Paris*, 1820. 12°. **1093**. h. **2[illegible]**

C. * * * DE STENAY (VICTOR) *See* STENAY (V. de)

C. E ALMEIDA (L. DE)

—— *See* CAINE (*Sir* Thomas H. H.) *K.B.E.* Cidade Eterna. Tradução de L. de C. e Almeida, *etc.* 1943. 8º. **12650**. de. **36**.

—— *See* CAINE (*Sir* Thomas H. H.) *K.B.E.* [The Christian.] O Apóstolo. Tradução . . . de L. de C. e Almeida, *etc.* 1943. 8º. **12650**. de. **18**.

C.E.M.A. ***See* ENGLAND.—*Arts Council of Great Britain.***

C.E.M.A. BULLETIN. *See* ENGLAND.—*Arts Council of Great Britain.*

C.E.M.S. MAGAZINE.

—— C.E.M.S. Magazine. *See* ENGLAND.—*Church of England.* —*Church of England Men's Society.* Men's Magazine.

C.E.M.S. QUARTERLY MAGAZINE.

—— C.E.M.S. Quarterly Magazine. *See* ENGLAND.—*Church of England.—Church of England Men's Society.* Men's Magazine.

C.E.R.A.M.I.C.A.

—— C.E.R.A.M.I.C.A., *etc.* *Barcelona,* 1952– . 8º. W.P. B. **390.**

C.E.T.S. C.E.T.S. War Issue. *See* ENGLAND.—*Church of England.—Church of England Temperance Society.*

C.E. TOPIC HANDBOOK. *See* ENGLAND.—*Christian Endeavour Union of Great Britain and Ireland.*

C. E VASCONCELLOS (ERNESTO JULIO DE) *See* CARVALHO E VASCONCELLOS.

C. É Y., P. D. R. El Brujo y la Bruja en tertulia. P. D. R. C. é Y. pp. 423. *Tarragona,* 1862. 4º. **8630**. h. **15**.

C. ET U., D. J. S. B. C. Manuale equestre, oder Compendium der Reichs-Ritterschaftlichen alt-hergebrachten Rechten, Kayserlichen-Privilegien und Freyheiten . . . Curante D. J. S. B. C. C. & U. [i.e. J. S. Burgermeister.] 2 vol. *Ulm,* 1720, 21. 4º. **26**. h. **23**.

C.F.T.C. *See* FRANCE.—*Confédération française des Travailleurs Chrétiens.*

C.G.I.L. *See* ITALY.—*Confederazione Generale Italiana del Lavoro.*

CGM.

—— CGM. (Clerical Grades monthly.) *See* ENGLAND.—*Civil Service Clerical Association.—Ministry of Health Branch.*

C. —H., B. *See* H., B. C.

C. H. B. S. C: H: B: S: [i.e. Cheetham Hill Bowling Society.] A Kalendar of members & a letter to the President. 1890. 4º. *See* MANCHESTER.—*Cheetham Hill Bowling Society.* [Missing.]

C.H.E.A.M. *See* PARIS.—*Centre de Hautes Études d'Administration Musulmane.*

C.I.C. BULLETIN. *See* ENGLAND.—*Catholic Industrialists' Conference.*

C I E WEEKLY NEWS.

—— *See* CÓRAS IOMPAIR EIREANN. Cuirle na Cire, *etc.*

C.I.M.O. *See* NETHERLANDS. [Kingdom of the Netherlands.]—*Nederlandse Centrale Organisatie voor Toegepast-Natuurwetenschappelijk Onderzoek.—Centraal Instituut voor Materiaalonderzoek.*

C.I.O. *See* COMITÉ INTERNATIONAL OLYMPIQUE.

C.I.O.S. *See* SUPREME HEADQUARTERS, ALLIED EXPEDITIONARY FORCE.—*Combined Intelligence Objectives Sub-Committee.*

C.I.S.I.M. *See* ITALY.—*Commissione Indagini e Studi sull'Industria Meccanica.*

C.I.T. SERIES. "C.I.T." Series. [Religious tracts. Signed: C. I. T.] *See* T., C. I.

C.I.U. *See* ENGLAND.—*Royal Air Force.—Combined Intelligence Unit.*

C. I. V. *See* ENGLAND.—*Army.—Infantry.—City of London Imperial Volunteers.*

C. L. C. I. *See* FAMAGOSTA.—*Commercial and Language Correspondence Institute.*

C.L.C. TOMBOLA COOK BOOK. C.L.C. Tombola Cook Book. A book of recipes tried and tested by ladies of Cornwall and friends of the Cornwall Lacrosse Club. pp. 98. *Cornwall Standard: Cornwall* [*Ont.*], [1909.] 16º. **07943**. de. **9**.

C.L.S. INDIAN BOOKMAN. *See* LONDON.—III. *Christian Literature Society for India, etc.*

C.L.S. WAR PAMPHLET. *See* LONDON.—III. *Christian Literature Society for India, etc.*

C. L. W. S. PAMPHLETS. *See* ENGLAND.—*Church of England.—Church Societies.—League of the Church Militant.*

C.-M., R. DE, *M., Membre de la Société "Les Cent Bibliophiles."*

—— Catalogue de la bibliothèque de M. R. de C.-M. [i.e. R. de Castro-Maya], *etc.* [With plates.] pp. 42. *Paris,* 1932. fol. **11912**. dd. **63**.

C.M.F. *See* ENGLAND.—*Central Mediterranean Force.*

C.M.S. ALMANACK. *See* EPHEMERIDES. The Church Missionary Almanack.

C.M.S. GAZETTE. *See* ENGLAND.—*Church of England.—Church Missionary Society.*

C.M.S. HOME GAZETTE. *See* ENGLAND.—*Church of England.—Church Missionary Society.* The C.M.S. Gazette.

C.M.S. IN THE WORLD TO-DAY SERIES. *See* ENGLAND.—*Church of England.—Church Missionary Society.*

C M S MISSIONARY NOTES.

—— CMS Missionary Notes. *See* ENGLAND.—*Church of England.—Church Missionary Society.* The Quarterly Papers of the Church Missionary Society, *etc.*

C M S NEWS.

—— CMS News. *See* ENGLAND.—*Church of England.—Church Missionary Society.*

C.M.S. NOTES.

—— C.M.S. Notes. *See* ENGLAND.—*Church of England.—Church Missionary Society.* The Quarterly Papers of the Church Missionary Society, *etc.*

C.M.S. VICTORIA HOME AND ORPHANAGE. *See* Kowloon.

C. MINOR.

—— The C. Minor, and the Vicar of Ristock. Two stories. By E. D. N. 1880. 8°. *See* N., E. D. **12640.** a. **6.**

C.M.U.A. HANDBOOK OF NIGHT SHELTER ACCOMMODATION. *See* London.—iii. *Commercial Motor Users' Association.*

C.M.U.A. JOURNAL. *See* London.—iii. *Commercial Motor Users' Association.*

C.N.D.A. MAGAZINE. *See* Mary, *the Blessed Virgin.—Churches and Institutions.*—Clapham.—*Convent of Notre Dame.—Clapham Notre Dame Association.* Clapham Notre Dame Association Magazine.

C.O.'S HANSARD. The C.O.'s Hansard. *See* London.—iii. *No-Conscription Fellowship.*

—— The C.O.s Hansard. A series of reprints from Parliamentary Reports of matters concerning the C.O. *See also* London.—iii. *Central Board for Conscientious Objectors.*

C.N.T. *See* Spain.—*Confederación Nacional del Trabajo.*

C.O.I. REVIEW. *See* England.—*Central Office of Information.*

C.O.M. The C.O.M. (The C.O.M. Magazine.—C.O.M. Monthly Magazine.) *See* Mary, *the Blessed Virgin.—Orders and Associations.—Association des Enfants de Marie Immaculée.* The Child of Mary and St. Agnes's Magazine.

C.O.N. C.O.N. Conscientious Objectors' News. *See* Periodical Publications.—*Bromborough.*

C.O.P.E.C. *See* England.—*Conference on Christian Politics, Economics and Citizenship.*

C.O. WHITMORE, *Barque.* The " C. O. Whitmore " Case. Report of the consular inquiry and judicial proceedings. (Reprinted from the " China Mail.") pp. 1–64. *China Mail: Hongkong,* 1876. 8°. **6955.** cc. **6.**
Imperfect ; wanting pp. 65, 66.

C . . . P . . ., *M. le Marquis de.* Avis au peuple sur les événemens présens et à venir. [In verse.] Suivi d'une chanson sur les affaires du temps ; par M. le marquis de C . . . P . . .. pp. 13. *Où l'on vent* [*Paris*], 1789. 8°. **F. 24. (6.)**

C.-P., J. B. Carta al editor del Buscapie (A. de Castro y Rossi.) Con notas. [Signed: J. B. C.-P.] pp. 21. [*Cadiz,* 1848.] 12°. **12491.** aa. **15.**

C. P. ASSOCIATION. *See* Bebington.—*Catholic Press Association.*

C. P. C.

—— C. P. C. no. 1 [*etc.*]. *See* England.—*National Union of Conservative and Constitutional Associations.—Conservative Political Centre.*

C.P.C. DISCUSSION SERIES. *See* England.—*National Union of Conservative and Constitutional Associations.—Conservative Political Centre.*

C.P.C. POSTAL STUDY COURSES. *See* England.—*National Union of Conservative and Constitutional Associations.—Conservative Political Centre.*

C.P.C. REFERENCE DIGEST. *See* England.—*National Union of Conservative and Constitutional Associations.—Conservative Political Centre.*

C.P. PIECES.

—— C. P. Pieces [i.e. Central Provinces' Pieces] and other verse by S. 1899. 8°. *See* S. **011651.** k. **51**

C.P.S.A. *See* England.—*Clay Pigeon Shooting Association.*

C. PETO BENNETT MAGAZINE. *See* Periodical Publications.—*London.*

C.Q.M. C.Q.M. [A tale. By Alfred Williams.] pp. 37. [*Alfred Williams: Enfield,* 1924.] 8°. **012637.** g. **26.**

C. R. C. R. Chronicle of the Community of the Resurrection. *See* England.—*Church of England.—Community of the Resurrection.*

C. R. C. *See* London.—iii. *Co-operation for the Renewal of Culture.*

C.R.O. BULLETIN. *See* Canada.—*Militia.—Canadian War Records Office.*

C.R.R. COURIER.

—— The C.R.R. Courier. *See* London.—ii. *Corporation of the City.—Library.—Commercial Reference Room.*

C.-S., A. On the Road from Mons. With an Army Service Corps Train. By its Commander. With map and diagrams. [Signed : A. C.-S.] pp. viii. 163. *Hurst & Blackett: London,* 1916. 8°. **9081.** eee. **5**

C.S.C. REVIEW. *See* Birmingham.—Birmingham *Christian Social Council.*

C.S.G. ANNUAL. *See* England.—*Catholic Social Guild.*

C.S.G. BULLETIN. *See* England.—*Catholic Social Guild.*

C.S.G. FIRST TEXT BOOKS. *See* England.—*Catholic Social Guild.*

C.S.G. LAW OF NATIONS SERIES. *See* England.—*Catholic Social Guild.*

C.S.G. YEAR BOOK. *See* England.—*Catholic Social Guild.* The Catholic Social Year Book, *etc.*

C.S.M.A. BULLETIN. *See* England—*Civil Service Motoring Association.*

C.S.M.A. GAZETTE. *See* England.—*Civil Service Motoring Association.*

C.S.S.M. *See* London.—iii. *Children's Special Service Mission.*

C.S.S.M. MANUALS. *See* London.—iii. *Children's Special Service Mission.*

C.T.C. HANDBOOK.

—— C.T.C. Handbook and Guide. *See* England.—*Cyclists' Touring Club.* Handbook & Guide, *etc.*

C.T.C. MONTHLY GAZETTE. *See* England.—*Cyclists' Touring Club.*

C.T.C. TOURING HANDBOOK. *See* England.—*Cyclists' Touring Club.* Handbook & Guide, *etc.*

T.S.I. *See* DUBLIN.—*Catholic Truth Society of Ireland.*

T.S. LEAFLETS. *See* LONDON.—III. *Catholic Truth Society.*

T.S. LECTURES.

— C.T.S. Lectures on the History of Religions. *See* MARTINDALE (Cyril C.)

THREE THREE.

— The Ballad of Reading Gaol. By C.3.3. [i.e. Oscar F. O'F. W. Wilde.] ff. 31. *Leonard Smithers: London,* 1898. 8°. Cup. **401.** f. **23.**
Printed on one side of the leaf only.

— [Another copy.] The Ballad of Reading Gaol, *etc.* *London,* 1898. 8°. Ashley **4612.**

— [Another copy.] T.C. **4.** a. **13.**
Printed on one side of the leaf only. No. 31 *of thirty-one copies on Japanese vellum.*

— Second edition. ff. 31. **F.P.** *Leonard Smithers: London,* 1898. 4°. 11659. d. 3.
Printed on one side of the leaf only.

— [Another copy.] K.T.C. **33.** a. **10.**

— Third edition. ff. 31. *Leonard Smithers: London,* 1898. 4°. K.T.C. **33.** a. **11.**
Printed on one side of the leaf only. No. 57 *of an edition of ninty-nine copies signed by the author.*

— The Ballad of Reading Gaol. By C. 3. 3. [i.e. Oscar F. O'F. W. Wilde.] ff. 39. *Brentano's: New York,* [1902?] 8°. **11659.** a. **12.**
Printed on one side of the leaf only.

V. MAGAZINE. *See* CLYDE VALLEY ELECTRICAL POWER COMPANY.

V.E. LEAFLET. *See* ENGLAND.—*Council for Visual Education.*

V.L. *See* ITALY.—*Corpo Volontari della Libertà.*

W. BULLETIN. *See* PERIODICAL PUBLICATIONS.—Wigan.—*Catholic Worker.*

W.M. The C.W.M. *See* ROWNTREE AND CO.

V NEWS LETTER. *See* ENGLAND.—*Common Wealth.*

W QUARTERLY. *See* ENGLAND.—*Common Wealth.* Common Wealth Review.

W. S. BANK. *See* CO-OPERATIVE WHOLESALE SOCIETY S BANK.

Y G., D. A., *Don.* *See* ARAUJO (F.) Historia veridica de la Judit Española, Cornelia Bororquia . . . Tercera edición corregida y aumentada por Don D. A. C. y, G. 1825. 12°. **4415.** g. **5.**

Y G., E. DE. Manual del Cocinero Cubano . . . Por E. de C. y G. [i.e. E. de Coloma y Garcés.] Edición ilustrada con láminas. pp. 308. *Habana,* 1856. 8°. **7956.** aa. **8.**

Y M., M. *See* FONSECA (D.) Relacion de la Expulsion de los Moriscos del Reino de Valencia, *etc.* [The editor's preface signed: M. C. y M.] 1878. 4°. **9181.** dd. **11.**

Y.M.S. REVIEW. *See* ENGLAND.—*Catholic Young Men's Society.—Birmingham Branch.*

C. Y N., J. A. *See* EUROPA, *Dame.* Una Riña en la Escuela de Doña Europa . . . Traducido del Ingles por J. A. C. y N. 1871. 8°. **8026.** a. **5.**

C. Y P., M. M. DE. Un Español á todos. Segundo discurso. [On Napoleon's invasion of Spain. Signed: M. M. de C. y P.] pp. 20. [*Madrid,* 1808.] 4°. **8042.** bb. **6.** (**26.**)

C. Y S., M. El Hombre que se necesita (D. Carlos de Borbón). Por M. C. y S. pp. 94. *Madrid,* 1898. 8°. **8042.** h. **2.**

C. Y SOBRÓN (FÉLIX) Los Idiomas de la América latina. Estudios biográfico-bibliográficos. pp. 137. *Madrid,* [1875?] 8°. **12910.** aa. **66.**

CÀ. La Cà dei Cani. Cronaca milanese del secolo XIV. Cavata da un manoscritto di un Canattiere di Barnabò Visconti. [A tale. With plates.] pp. 240. *Milano,* 1840. 8°. **12470.** bbb. **11.**

ÇA. Ça été, v'la qu'et fait. [A song.] [1792?] 8°. **F. 364.** (**14.**)
Lithographed.

—— Ça ira. [A satire, chiefly on the Duke of Orleans.] pp. 4. [1791?] 8°. **F. 255.** (**5.**)

—— "Ça Ira." The journal of the West Yorkshire Regiment, *etc.* *See* ENGLAND.—*Army.—Infantry.—Prince of Wales's Own* (*West Yorkshire Regiment*).

—— Ça va. *See* PERIODICAL PUBLICATIONS.—*London.*

C——A, *Minister.* Tevletta. [A spelling-book in Romansch, dialect of the Lower Engadine.] [Signed: C——a, minister, i.e. J. L. Cloetta.] *Strada,* [1820?] 8°. **12941.** aa. **22.**

CÀ D'ORSOLINO. *See* BENEDELLO.

CA' REZZONICO. *See* VENICE.

CA. (Io.) Apologia musices tam vocalis quam instrumentalis et mixtæ. [The dedication signed: Io. Ca., i.e. John Case, M.D.] pp. 77. *Excudebat Iosephus Barnesius: Oxoniæ,* 1588. 8°. **M.K.1.e.15.**

CÀ (STEFANO DALLA) Una Pagina della mia vita, prosa e versi di un prigioniero nel Castello di Udine, l'anno 1851. pp. 104. *Udine,* 1869. 8°. **4867.** b. **11.**

CA. (W.) *a Member of the Army.* A Sad and serious Discourse, upon a terrible Letter, sent by the Ministers of the Province of London, to the Lord General and his council of war. By W. Ca. a Member of the Army. [A reply to the pamphlet by Thomas Gataker and others, entitled " A Serious and faithfull Representation of the Judgements of Ministers of the Gospell within the Province of London."] *For Giles Calvert: London,* 1648. 4°. **103.** b. **20.**

—— [Another copy.] E. **540.** (**3.**)

ČAADAEV (PETER JAKOVLEVIĆ) *See* CHAADAEV (Petr Ya.)

CAAMAÑO (A. MAURET) *See* MAURET CAAMAÑO.

CAAMAÑO (ALFREDO FLORES Y) *See* FLORES Y CAAMAÑO.

CAAMANO (GIOSEPP) *See* CAAMAÑO (José)

CAAMAÑO (JACINTO JIJÓN Y) *See* JIJÓN Y CAAMAÑO.

CAAMAÑO (JOSÉ) Schreiben des Königl. spanischen Gesandten, Ritter von Caamano an den Freistaat der drei Bünde. [A warning against revolutionary agitation. Dated: 16 Apr. 1794.] (Antwort auf obiges Schreiben.) [*Coire,* 1794.] fol. **9304.** g. 4. (**15.**)

CAAMAÑO (José)

—— Bref digl Ambasciadur de Spagna, Cavalier Caamano, alla Republica dils Grischuns. [16 Apr. 1794.] (Risposta sin la precedenta bref.) [*Coire*, 1794.] fol. **9304**. g. 3. (**1**.)

CAAMAÑO (José Francisco Juan María) *See* Diego José, *de Cadiz*.

CAAMAÑO (José Pardiñas Villalovos Soto y Romero de) *See* Pardiñas Villalovos Soto y Romero de Caamaño.

CAAMAÑO (Juan Ángel) *See* Tasso (T.) [*La Gerusalemme Liberata.—Spanish.*] Jerusalen libertada. Poema . . . traducido por D. J. Caamaño y D. A. Ribot, *etc.* 1841. 8°. **11426**. e. **43**.

CAAMAÑO (María de las Nieves) Mistico poema para el dia de la profesion de la reverenda madre Sor Maria de las Nieves Caamaño de Santa Teresa . . . Dispuesto por un pariente de la dicha [i.e. Diego José de Cadiz], *etc.* pp. lv. [*Seville*,] 1782. 4°. **11451**. e. **39**. (**17**.)

CAAMAÑO BOURNACELL (José) Cambados a la luz de la Historia, *etc.* pp. 80. *Santiago*, 1933. 8°. **010160**. ee. **28**.

CAAN (Hendrik Jan) *See* Dijk (J. van) Itinéraire de la Salle d'Orange . . . Traduit par J[hr] Me Henri Jean Caan, *etc.* 1856. 8°. **7856**. c. **6**.

CAAN (Jacobus Janus de la Bassecour) Handleiding tot de kennis van het administratief regt in Nederland. 3 dl. *'s Gravenhage*, 1856–65. 8°. **5684**. bb. **11**.

—— Schets van den regeringsvorm van Nederland van 1515 tot heden . . . Tweede veel vermeerderde uitgave. pp. ix. 230. *'s Gravenhage*, 1866. 8°. **8081**. g. **22**.

—— Schets van het Nederlandsch staatsbestuur ten gebruike bij de hoogere burgerscholen . . . Bijgewerkt tot 1 Januari 1870. pp. xvi. 396. *'s Hage*, 1870. 8°. **8228**. ccc. **29**.

—— De Wet op het lager onderwijs met een aanteekening van Jhr. Mr. J. J. de la B. Caan. pp. 80. *'s Gravenhage*, 1859. 8°. **8309**. df. **35**. (**3**.)

CAARTEN (D. Bicker) Objections to Socialism . . . A lecture, *etc.* pp. 28. *South of England Printing & Publishing Co.: Southampton*, [1893.] 8°. **08275**. ee. **22**. (**20**.)

—— [Another copy.] **08275**. ee. **22**. (**21**.)

CAARTEN (Herman Adriaan Bicker) Bijdrage tot de kennis der hydrocele. Academisch proefschrift, *etc.* pp. x. 75. *Rotterdam*, 1860. 8°. **7620**. c. **25**. (**5**.)

CAB. The Cab. *See* Periodical Publications.—*London.*

CAB TRADE GAZETTE. *See* Periodical Publications.—*London.*

CAB ( ) *Dr.* Lebensverlängerungsmittel, oder Sammlung aller seit Jahrhunderten von den berühmtesten Aerzten aller Reiche der Welt gemachten Erfahrungen und erprobten Mittel, wodurch die Gesundheit erhalten, Krankheiten verhütet . . . das Leben verlängert und ein hohes Alter erreicht werden kann, *etc.* pp. 16. *Ronneburg*, 1853. 16°. **7391**. a. **58**. (**1**.)

CABA (Pedro)

—— Las Cosas: su metafísica y su poesía. *In:* Revista de la Universidad de Buenos Aires. no. 23, 24. jul./sept., oct./dic. 1952. 1952. 8°. Ac. **2694**. a/**10**.

CABABÉ (Michael)

—— *See* England.—*Supreme Court of Judicature.—H[igh] Court of Justice.—Kings Bench Division.* [*Reports.*] R[e]ports of Actions tried in the Queen's Bench Division [of] the High Court of Justice. From Michaelmas Sittin[gs] 1882, to the end of Trinity Sittings, 1885. By M. Caba[bé] . . . and C. G. Ellis. 1883, *etc.* 8°. **6121**. c.

—— *See* Jevons (William S.) The State in relation [to] Labour . . . Edited . . . by M. Cababé, *etc.* 1894. 8[°]. **08139**. aa. **1**.

—— The Freedom of the Seas. The history of a German tra[...] pp. 159. *John Murray: London*, 1918. 8°. **6836**. de.

—— Interpleader and Attachment of Debts in the Hi[gh] Court of Justice, and in the County Courts; togeth[er] with forms, *etc.* pp. xvi. 220. *Maxwell & Son: Lond[on]*, 1881. 8°. **6405**. de.

—— Interpleader in the High Court of Justice, and in t[he] County Courts . . . Second edition [of the first part [of] "Interpleader and Attachment of Debts"]. pp. xiv. 2[...] *W. Maxwell & Son: London*, 1888. 8°. **6405**. de. [...]

—— Attachment of Debts and Receivers by way of equita[ble] execution, in the High Court of Justice, and in t[he] County Courts . . . Second edition [of the second p[art] of "Interpleader and Attachment of Debts"]. pp. xii. 164. *W. Maxwell & Son: London*, 1888. 8°. **6376**. aaa. [...]

—— Interpleader . . . Third edition. pp. xii. 232. *Sweet & Maxwell: London*, 1900. 8°. **6405**. de. [...]

—— Attachment of Debts . . . Third edition. pp. xiv. 1[...] *Sweet & Maxwell: London*, 1900. 8°. **6376**. de. [...]

—— The Principles of Estoppel. An essay. pp. xi. 152. *W. Maxwell & Son: London*, 1888. 8°. **6146**. bb. [...]

—— Time Limit—Monopoly Value and Compensation. [A] criticism of the Licensing Bill, 1908. pp. 71. *Effingham Wilson: London*, 1908. 8°. **6427**. c.

CABAÇO (Antonio Vaz) *See* Vaz Cabaço.

CABADA DANCOURT (Octavio) Le Inquisición [de] Lima. Síntesis de su historia. pp. 123. *Li[ma]*, [1935.] 8°. **20009**. b.

CABADÉ (Ernest) Essai sur la physiologie des épi[thé]liums. [With a plate.] pp. 90. *Paris*, 1867. [*Collection des thèses soutenues à la Faculté de Médecin[e de] Paris.* An 1867. tom. 3.] **7373**. h[...]

CABADÉS MAGÍ (Augustinus) Sacra doctrina in p[...]tione cathed., quae locorum theologicorum explicati[one] regitur, asserenda a P. F. A. Cabadès Magì in Sch[ola] Valentinis, *etc.* pp. 51. *Valentiae Hedetanorum*, 1774. **475**. b.

CABADIJAR (Leandro de) Novisimo Dicciona[rio] Manual Español-Latino y Latino-Español, *etc.* 2 pt. *Barcelona*, 1857. 8°. **12943**. aa.

CABAL. The Cabal. [A political satire, in verse.] [*London*, 1680.] *s. sh.* fol. Lutt. II.

—— [Another copy.] C. **40**. m. **11**. ([...]

—— [Another copy.] C. **20**. f. **2**. (**3**[...]

—— The Cabal; as acted at the Theatre in George-Str[eet] [A political satire, in verse and prose.] pp. 24. *Pri[nted] for : London*, 1763. 12°. **11777**. bb[...]

The publisher's name has been inked out, and tha[t of] R. Marriner substituted in ms.

—— The Cabal: or, a Voice of the politicks. A most pleasant new play song. See THOMAS, *Lord*. Lord Thomas and Fair Ellinor, *etc*. [1670 ?] *s. sh.* fol. C. **39**. k. **6**. (**68**.)

—— The Moderate Cabal. A satyr. [In verse. By Luke Milbourne.] pp. 64. *Sold by the Booksellers: London*, 1710. 8°. **11631**. c. **8**.

CABAL (CONSTANTINO)

—— La Asturias que venció Roma. pp. 420. *Oviedo*, 1953. 8°. **9042**. h. **16**.

—— Las Costumbres Asturianas, su significación y sus orígenes. 2 vol.

El Individuo. pp. 376. 1925.
La Familia: la vivienda, los oficios primitivos. pp. 414. 1931.

Madrid, 1925, 31. 8°. **010160**. de. **59**.
No more published.

—— Covadonga. pp. 384. *Madrid*, [1918.] 8°. **10162**. cc. **21**.

—— Los Cuentos Tradicionales Asturianos. pp. 254. *Madrid*, [1924.] 8°. **012403**. de. **24**.

—— Del Folk-Lore de Asturias. Cuentos, leyendas y tradiciones. pp. xviii. 243. vi. *Madrid*, [1923.] 8°. **12431**. pp. **28**.

—— El Libro de cómo se hacen todas las cosas, *etc*. pp. 340. *Madrid*, 1919. 8°. **012350**. f. **10**.

—— La Mitología Asturiana.

Los Dioses de la Muerte. pp. 271. 1925.
El Sacerdocio del Diablo. pp. 375. 1928.

Madrid, 1925– . 8°. W.P. **13368**.

—— Nicolás Rivero. (Nombres de España.) [With a portrait.] pp. 286. *Oviedo*, 1950. 8°. **10636**. d. **4**.

CABALA.

The books of the Jewish Cabala are entered under their several authors, or if anonymous under the name by which they are known. Collections are entered under the appropriate headings.

—— La Cabala. Commedia. [In verse. By the Marquis F. degli Obizzi.] (Alcune terze rime dello stesso autore.) 2 pt. *Padova*, 1741. 8°. **11715**. bbb. **21**.

—— [A reissue of pt. 1.] La Cabala, *etc*. [By the Marquis Ferdinando degli Obizzi.] 1767. See TEATRO. Il Teatro di villa. [1766, *etc*.] 8°. **240**. l. **32**.

—— Cabala: or, an Impartial account of the Nonconformists' private designs, actings, and ways, from Aug. 24. 1662, to Dec. 25. in the same year. Printed in the year 1663. 1812. See SOMERS (John) *Baron Somers*. A Collection of Scarce and Valuable Tracts, *etc*. vol. 7. 1809, *etc*. 4°. **750**. g. **7**.

—— Cabala, Mysteries of State, in letters of the great Ministers of K. James and K. Charles. Wherein much of the publique manage of affaires is related. Faithfully collected by a Noble Hand. pp. 347. *For M. M. G. Bedell & T. Collins: London*, 1654 [1653]. 4°. E. **221**. (**3**.)

—— Scrinia Sacra; Secrets of Empire, in letters of illustrious persons. A Supplement of the Cabala. In which business of the same quality and grandeur is contained, *etc*. pp. 355 [255]. *For G. Bedel & T. Collins: London*, 1654. 4°. **595**. f. **6**.

—— [Another copy.] E. **228**. (**2**.)

—— Cabala: sive Scrinia sacra. Mysteries of State & Government: in letters of illustrious persons and great agents; in the reigns of Henry the Eighth, Queen Elizabeth, K: James, and the late King Charls. In two parts. In which the secrets of empire, and publique manage of affairs are contained. With many remarkable passages nowhere else published. [A reissue in one volume of "Cabala, Mysteries of State" and "Scrinia Sacra."] 2 pt. *For G. Bedel & T. Collins: London*, 1654. 4°. **595**. f. **5**.

—— [Another edition.] pp. 416. *For G. Bedell & T. Collins: London*, 1663. fol. C. **75**. e. **5**.

—— Cabala, sive Scrinia sacra . . . To which is added in this third edition, a second part, consisting of a choice collection of original letters and negotiations, never before published. 2 pt. *For Tho. Sawbridge; Mat. Gillyflower: London*, 1691. fol. **594**. f. **17**. (**2**.)
With an additional titlepage, engraved.

—— [Another copy.] G. **5079**.

—— Scrinia Ceciliana: Mysteries of State & Government: In letters of the late famous Lord Burghley, and other . . . Ministers of State: in the reigns of Queen Elizabeth, and King James. Being a further additional supplement of the Cabala. As also many remarkable passages . . . no where else published. pp. 228 [223]. *For G. Bedel & T. Collins: London*, 1663. 4°. **595**. f. **8**.

—— [Another copy.] **194**. e. **2**.
At the end are four pages of MS. *entitled, "The Lord Burleigh his advice to Q. Elizabeth in matters of Religion and State."*

—— Cabala spagnuola. See SPANISH CABAL.

—— Cabalæ verior Descriptio. Das ist, Gründliche Beschreibung und Erweisung aller natürlichen und über natürlichen Dingen, wie durch das Verbum fiat alles erschaffen. pp. 64. *G. Wolff: Hamburg*, 1680. 12°. **1033**. c. **64**.

—— Die Kabbala. Ihre Hauptlehren und ihr Verhältniss zum Christenthum. [By Aron Briman.] pp. 58. *Innsbruck*, 1885. 8°. **4034**. h. **45**. (**3**.)

CABALAO. Quando che Cabalao vendeva menole. Con quell'altro Capitolo in Sdruccioli di Francesco Veronese, che comincia "Quanti che hà scorso tutto il mar Atlantico," &c. [In verse.] *Il Bonfadino: Venetia*, 1608. 8°. **1071**. c. **26**. (**14**.)

CABALE. A bas la cabale. [Reproaching those who denounced Napoleon after his fall. Signed: un Anonyme qui n'a jamais vu Buonaparte, i.e. Mme Sophie de Renneville.] pp. 8. MS. NOTE [in Russian]. [*Paris*, 1814.] 8°. **8052**. k. **11**. (**14**.)

—— [Another copy.] **934**. c. **14**. (**13**.)

—— A bas la cabale, lettre d'un volontaire de la Garde Parisienne, à son ami, capitaine de la troupe du centre. 1790. [In vindication of Lafayette.] pp. 8. [*Paris*, 1790.] 8°. F. **247**. (**3**.)

—— La Cabale chimerique, ou refutation de l'histoire fabuleuse . . . que Mr. J. [i.e. P. Jurieu] vient de publier, *etc*. [By P. Bayle.] 1691. 12°. See J., *Mr*. **882**. a. **22**.

—— La Cabale découverte. [A Philippic directed against H. K. N. van der Noot.] pp. 4. [*Brussels*, 1789 ?] 12°. **8079**. c. **2**. (**24**.)

CABALA.

—— Oh que non, il n'y a pas de cabale! Dialogue entre deux honnêtes gens. [A political pamphlet.] pp. 16. *Paris*, [1790?] 8°. R. **199**. (**9**.)

CABALERI (Miguel) *See* Carrillo de Hermida (J.) Atrocidades que Iturbide y Cabaleri han cometido en Jalapa, *etc.* 1823. fol. **9770**. k. **7**. (**20**.)

CABALES (Claudio) Luisa Kiernan. Historia de un centro agricola. [A tale.] pp. 48. *Buenos Aires*, 1891. 8°. **12330**. e. **40**. (**4**.)

ÇABALETA (Juan de) *See* Zavaleta.

CABALL (John)

—— The Singing Swordsman, *etc.* [A novel.] pp. 232. *Michael F. Moynihan: Dublin*, 1953. 8°. NNN. **5039**.

CABALLERIA (Juan) History of San Bernardino Valley from the Padres to the Pioneers. 1810–1851 . . . Illustrated, *etc.* pp. 17–130. *Times-Index Press: San Bernardino, Cal.*, 1992 [1902]. 8°. **10409**. c. **38**.

CABALLERO. El Caballero de Buen Gusto. Comedia en prosa en tres actos. Traducida del Italiano. Por Don Manuel Bellosartes. [A translation of " Il Cavaliere di buon gusto " by Carlo Goldoni.] pp. 32. *Barcelona*, [1806.] 4°. **1342**. e. **5**. (**50**.)

—— Novela del Caballero Invisibile compuesta en equivocos burlescos. 1847. *See* Spanish Authors. Coleccion de los Mejores Autores Españoles. tom. 38. 1835, *etc.* 8°. **12230**. h. **1/38**.

—— [Another edition.] 1854. *See* Aribau (B. C.) Biblio teca de Autores Españoles, *etc.* tom. 33. 1849, *etc.* 8°. **12232.f.1/31.**

CABALLERO DEL FEBO.

—— [For editions of " The Mirrour of Princely deedes and Knighthood: wherein is shewed the worthinesse of the Knight of the Sunne," translated from the " Espejo de Príncipes " of D. Ortuñez de Calahorra:] *See* Mirror.

—— L'Admirable histoire du Chevalier du Soleil. Ou sont racontees les immortelles proüesses de cet inuincible guerrier, & de son frere Rosiclair . . . Traduite en nostre langue par Fançois [*sic*] de Rosset (& Louys Douet). [Translated from the " Espejo de Principes y Cavalleros " of Diego Ortúñez de Calahorra.] 8 pt. *M. Guillemot: Paris*, 1643, 1620–26. 8°. **244**. k. **4–11**.
Imperfect; wanting ff. 58–63 *of pt.* 2 *and the titlepage, dedication and a portion of the table of contents of pt.* 4. *A made-up set, pt.* 2–8 *bearing the imprint of S. Thiboust.*

—— [Another edition.] 8 pt. *M. Guillemot: Paris*, 1643, 25–33. 8°. G. **10409–16**.
A made-up set, pt. 2–8 *bearing the imprint of S. Thiboust.*

—— Histoire du Chevalier du Soleil, de son frère Rosiclair, et de leurs descendants. Traduction libre & abrégée de l'Espagnol [i.e. of " Espejo de Principes y Cavalleros," by D. Ortúñez de Calahorra, with material from the French books of Amadis, and from Flores de Grèce], avec la conclusion tirée du Roman des Romans, du Sieur Duverdier. [By M. A. R. de Voyer d'Argenson, Marquis de Paulmy, and A. G. Contant d'Orville.] 2 tom. *Amsterdam & Paris*, 1780. 12°. **243**. g. **1, 2**.

—— Geschichte des Sonnenritters, seines Bruders Rosiklair, und ihrer Nachkommenschaft. Aus dem Französischen. [Translated, in part by Wilhelm C. S. Mylius, from " Histoire du Chevalier du Soleil, de son frère Rosiclair et de leurs descendants " by M. A. R. de Voyer d'Argenson, Marquis de Paulmy, and A. G. Contant d'Orville.] 2 Bd. *Leipzig*, 1781, 83. 12°. **1477**. bbb. **10**.

CABALLERO DEL FEBO.

—— Il Cauallier del Sole, chi con l'arte militare dipinge la peregrinatione della vita humana . . . Tradotto nuouamente di Spagnuolo in Italiano, per Messer Pietro Lauro. [A translation of the " Peregrinacion de la Vida del Hombre " by P. Hernandez de Villalumbrales.] ff. 198. *Per G. & M. Sessa: Vinegia*, 1557. 8°. **8409**. ccc. **12**.

—— [Another edition.] ff. 198. *Appresso F. & A. Zoppini: Venetia*, 1584. 8°. G. **10122**.

—— [Another edition.] ff. 218. *D. Maldura: Venetia*, 1607. 8°. **12450**. c. **10**. (**2**.)

CABALLERO DEL SOL. *See* Caballero del Febo.

CABALLERO (Arturo) *See* González Fragoso (R.) Fungi novi vel minus cognitarum Horti Botanici Matritense lecti Arturo Caballero. 1917. 8°. [*Trabajos del Museo Nacional de Ciencias Naturales.* Serie botánica. no. 12.] Ac. **2828/3**.

—— Datos Botánicos del Territorio de Ifni, *etc.* [With plates.] 2 pt. *Madrid*, 1935. 8°. [*Trabajos del Museo Nacional de Ciencias Naturales.* Serie botánica. no. 28, 30.] Ac. **2828/3**.

—— Excursión Botánica a Melilla en 1915, *etc.* pp. 39. pl. II. *Madrid*, 1917. 8°. [*Trabajos del Museo Nacional de Ciencias Naturales.* Serie botánica. no. 11.] Ac. **2828/3**.

CABALLERO (Dario Julio) Gramática del Idioma Mexicano, segun el sistema de Ollendorff. pp. 212. *México*, 1880. 8°. **12941**. bbb. **14**.

CABALLERO (Ernesto Giménez) *See* Giménez Caballero.

CABALLERO (E. Marty) *See* Marty Caballero.

CABALLERO (Eduardo Zamora y) *See* Zamora y Caballero.

CABALLERO (Federico García) *See* García Caballero.

CABALLERO (Félix García) *See* García Caballero.

CABALLERO (Fermin Agosto) *See* Morán Bayó (J.) Hacia la Revolución Agraria Española. Tres agraristas españoles. Jovellanos—F. Caballero—Costa. 1931. 8°. **10633**. pp. **15**.

—— Adiciones de Don Fermín Cabellero al " Diccionario " de Muñoz y Romero, *etc.* [Edited, with an introduction by Ángel González Palencia.] *In*: Revista de archivos bibliotecas y museos. tom. 53. no. 2. pp. 253–343. 1947. 8°. P.P. **4074**. k.

—— Obras Critico-geograficas. 20 pt. *Madrid*, 1827–37. 12°. **574**. e. **23**. (**1–11**.)
Pt. 2, 12 *are of the second edition.*

—— Biografía del doctor Don Vicente Asuero y Cortázar. [With a portrait.] pp. 227. *Madrid*, 1873. 8°. **10632**. cc. **2**.

—— Conquenses Ilustres.
II. Melchior Cano. pp. 640. 1871.
IV. Alonzo y Juan de Valdés. pp. 483. 1875.
Madrid, 1871, 75. 8°. **4867**. h. **10**.
Imperfect; wanting vol. 1 *and* 3.

—— Fomento de la Poblacion Rural . . . Tercera edicion, *etc.* pp. xii. 451. *Madrid*, 1864. 8°. **7076**. ee. **9**.

—— Manual Geográfico-administrativo de la Monarquia Española, *etc.* pp. xi. 626. *Madrid*, 1844. 8°. **10161**. b. **5**.

ABALLERO (FERMIN AGOSTO)

— Pericia geográfica de Miguel de Cervantes, demostrada con la historia de D. Quijote de la Mancha. pp. 117. *Madrid*, 1840. 8°. **635**. d. **12**.

— [Another copy.] Cerv. **453**.

— [Another edition.] [Edited, with an introduction, by Módesto Pérez.] pp. 176. *Madrid*, 1918. 16°. [*Biblioteca Universal*. tom. 173.] **739**. b. **92**.

— Reseña Geográfica-estadística de España . . . Segunda edicion. pp. vi. 126. *Madrid*, 1868. 8°. **10160**. aaa. **35**.

ABALLERO (FERNAN) *pseud*. [i.e. CECILIA FRANCISCA JOSEFA ARROM DE AYALA.]

WORKS.

— Obras completas, *etc*. 14 pt. *Madrid*, 1856–58. 8°. **12491**. c. **42**.

— Obras completas. Fernán Caballero y la novela contemporánea, por D. José María Asensio. 17 tom. *Madrid*, 1893–1913. 8°. **012230**. aaa. **3**.

— Nederlandsche uitgave der Werken van Mevr. C. Bohl de Faber—Fernan Caballero—door eene vereeniging van vaderlandsche letterkundigen. No. 1: Spaansche novellen. pp. 340. *Rotterdam*, 1863. 8°. **12491**. g. **3**.
No more published.

— Fernan Caballero's sämmtliche Werke . . . übersetzt von August Geyder. Tl. 1–6. *Breslau*, 1860. 8°. **12489**. cc. **36**.
No more published.

SMALLER COLLECTIONS.

— Cuadros de Costumbres Populares Andaluces. (La Noche de Navidad.—El Dia de Reyes.—Pobre Dolores!—Lucas Garcia.—El Ex-voto.) pp. 278. *Sevilla*, 1852. 8°. **10160**. a. **11**.

— Cuentos y poesías populares andaluces, coleccionados poi Fernán Caballero. pp. xviii. 435. *Sevilla*, 1859. 8°. **12492**. dd. **23**

— Coleccion de Articulos Religiosos y Morales. pp. 306. *Cadiz*, 1862. 8°. **4378**. bbb. **9**.
The date on the wrapper is 1863.

— Relaciones. pp. 293. *Leipzig*, 1862. 8°. [*Colección de Autores Españoles*. tom. 13.] **12230.bb.6/13.**

— Élia, ó la España treinta años ha . . . El Ultimo Consuelo.—La Noche de Navidad.—Callar en Vida y Perdonar en Muerte. pp. 260. *Leipzig*, 1864. 8°. [*Colección de Autores Españoles*. tom. 16.] **12230.bb.6/1**

— La Familia de Alvareda. Novela original de costumbres populares. Lagrimas. Novela de costumbres contemporaneas. pp. vi. 367. *Leipzig*, 1864. 8°. [*Colección de Autores Españoles*. tom. 5.] **12230.bb.6/5.**

— Cuadros de Costumbres. (Vulgaridad y Nobleza.—Simon Verde.—Mas honor que honores.—Lucas García. Obrar bien . . . que Dios es Dios.—El Dolor es una agonia sin muerte.) pp. 300. *Leipzig*, 1865. 8°. [*Colección de Autores Españoles*. tom. 17.] **12230.bb.6/17**

— La Farisea. Las Dos Gracias. Novelas originales . . . Con un prólogo de D. Pedro de Madrazo . . . 2ª edicion. pp. lvi. 286. *Madrid*, 1865. 8°. **12491**. bbb. **17**.

CABALLERO (FERNAN) *pseud*. [i.e. CECILIA FRANCISCA JOSEFA ARROM DE AYALA.] [SMALLER COLLECTIONS.]

—— Cuatro Novelas. (Una en otra.—Un Servilon y un liberalito.—Con mal ó con bien.—Pobre Dolores!) pp. 335. *Leipzig*, 1866. 8°. [*Colección de Autores Españoles*. tom. 20.] **12230.bb.6/20.**

—— La Farisea. Las Dos Gracias y otras novelas escogidas. pp. 314. *Leipzig*, 1867. 8°. [*Colección de Autores Españoles*. tom. 23.] **12230.bb.6/23.**
Previous edition 1865.

—— Un Verano en Bornos. Cosa cumplida . . . solo en la otra vida. Lady Virginia. Tres novelas originales. pp. viii. 286. *Leipzig*, 1873. 8°. [*Colección de Autores Españoles*. tom. 32.] **12230.bb.6/32.**

—— Ultimas producciones de Fernan Caballero. Estar de Mas, relacion y Magdalena, obra inédita. Precedidas de una noticia biográfica . . . por . . . F. de Gabriel y Ruiz de Apodaca. 3 pt. *Sevilla*, 1878. 16°. **12491**. f. **7**.

—— Cuadros de Costumbres. 2 tom. *Madrid*, 1887. 8°. **12489**. i. **22**.
Containing the tales in previous collections of this title with the addition of "*El Ultimo Consuelo*" *and* "*Dicha y Suerte*."

—— Deudas pagadas [and other tales], *etc*. pp. xxxvii. 198. *Madrid*, 1921. 8°. **12490**. tt. **14**.

—— La Noche de Navidad, and Callar en Vida y Perdonar en Muerte . . . Edited, with notes and vocabulary, by Ronald M. MacAndrew. pp. v. 108. *London*, 1929. 8°. [*Longmans' Spanish Texts*.] W.P. **9367/9**.

—— The Castle and the Cottage in Spain. From the Spanish of F. Caballero. By Lady Wallace. [A translation of "Elia," "La Familia de Alvareda," "Callar en Vida y Perdonar en Muerte" and "Pobre Dolores."] 2 vol. *Saunders, Otley & Co.: London*, 1861. 12°. **12491**. d. **23**.

—— Elia: or, Spain fifty years ago. Translated from the Spanish of F. Caballero. (Consolation in Death: or, a Mother's Prayer to the Virgin.) pp. 324. *D. Appleton & Co.: New York*, 1868. 12°. **12490**. bb. **27**.

—— The Bird of Truth, and other fairy tales. By F. Caballero. (Translated by J. H. Ingram.) pp. xi. 241. *W. Swan Sonnenschein & Allen: London*, [1881.] 8°. [*Illustrated Library of Fairy Tales*.] **12411**. ee. **6**.

—— National Pictures. From the Spanish of F. Caballero [i.e. from the "Cuadros de Costumbres."] By the author of "Tasso's Enchanted Ground." pp. vi. 213. *Burns & Oates: London*, 1882. 8°. **12489**. h. **11**.

—— Air built Castles. Stories from the Spanish of F. Caballero . . . Translated by Mrs. Pauli. pp. 240. *London Literary Society: London*, [1887.] 8°. **12489**. bb. 2.

—— Un Été à Bornos traduit par M. Auguste Dumas, roman par lettres . . . suivi de l'Alcazar de Seville traduit par le même, *etc*. pp. 488. *Paris*, 1865. 8°. **12515**. aaa. 4.

—— Nouvelles andalouses, scènes de mœurs contemporaines . . . Traduites de l'espagnol . . . par A. Germond de Lavigne. pp. xi. 363. *Paris*, 1869. 8°. **12491**. c. **14**.

—— [A reissue.] *Paris*, 1882. 8°. **12491**. cc. 40.

—— Deux nouvelles andalouses posthumes de Fernan Caballero ["Estar de Mas" and "Magdalena"]. Précédées de sa vie et ses œuvres par le Cte. de Bonneau-Avenant. pp. 329. *Paris*, 1882. 8°. **12489**. h. 10.

—— [Another copy.] **12490**. dd. **28**.

—— Elbeszélések. Caballero után Szulik Józseftől, *etc.* pp. 48. *Budapest,* [1876.] 8°. [*Magyar Könyvesház.* foly. 4. no. 36.] **739.** bb. **18.**

—— Glück und Glas—.—Bezahlte Schulden. [" Mas Largo es el Tiempo que la Fortuna " and " Deudas Pagadas," translated by M. Spiro.] *See* SPIRO (M.) Meisternovellen spanischer Autoren, *etc.* [1915.] 8°. **12491.** s. **40.**

—— Łukasz Garcia, powieść andaluzyjska . . . z hiszpańskiego.—Paz i Luz. Pokój i Światło. Wspomnienia starego adwokata. Powieść andaluzyjska . . . Z hiszpańskiego. [1871.] *See* RIOS (J. P. de los) Dygnitarze, *etc.* 1871. 8°. [*Biblioteka najciekawszych powieści i romansów.* tom 19.] **12264.** dd.

LETTERS.

—— Cartas de Fernán Caballero. Coleccionadas y anotadas por . . . Diego de Valencina. pp. xvi. 384. *Madrid,* 1919. 8°. **010905.** df. **26.**

—— Epistolario de Fernán Caballero. Una colección de cartas inéditas . . . publicada por Alberto López Argüello, *etc.* pp. 239. 1922. 8°. *See* SANTANDER.—*Sociedad de Menéndez y Pelayo.* **10906.** e. **14.**

—— Cecilia Böhl de Faber—Fernán Caballero—y Juan Eugenio Hartzenbusch. Una correspondencia inédita, publicada por Theodor Heinermann. pp. 262. 1944. 8°. *See* MADRID.—*Instituto Alemán de Cultura.* **10922.** ee. **9.**

—— Cartas inéditas de Fernán Caballero. [Edited, with an introduction, by S. Montoto.] *In:* Boletín de la Real Academia Española. tom. 35. cuad. 146, *etc.* 1955, *etc.* 8°. Ac. **144/16.**

—— [Letter to D. Leopoldo Augusto de Cueto, on Alphonso XII.] *See* ALPHONSO XII., *King of Spain.* Homenaje poético á . . . Don Alfonso XII. . . . Carta de F. Caballero, *etc.* 1875. 8°. **11451.** g. **1.**

—— [Extracts from letters to Antoine de Latour. *Span.*] *See* MOREL-FATIO (A. P. V.) Fernan Caballero, d'après sa correspondance avec A. de Latour. 1901. 8°. [*Bulletin hispanique.* tom. 3. no. 3.] Ac. **8917.**

SINGLE WORKS.

—— El Alcázar de Sevilla. pp. 28. *Sevilla,* 1862. 12°. **10160.** a. **35.**

—— [Callar en Vida y Perdonar en Muerte.] Silence in Life, and Forgiveness in Death. From the Spanish of F. Caballero . . . by J. J. Kelly, *etc.* pp. 105. *T. Richardson & Son: London,* 1883. 8°. [*Tales for the Young.*] **4413.ee.59/6.**

—— Clemencia. Novela de costumbres. pp. 290. *Leipzig,* 1863. 8°. [*Coleccion de Autores Españoles.* tom. 1.] **12230.bb.6/1**

—— [Another edition.] pp. 290. *Leipzig,* 1869. 8°. [*Coleccion de Autores Españoles.* tom. 1.] **12230.bb.6/1a.**

—— Clemencia, traduit . . . par MM. A. de Zappino et A. Marchais. pp. vii. 254. *Paris,* 1863. 12°. **12491.** bbb. **18.**

—— Klemencya . . . Powieść hiszpańska. Przełożył Ajo. pp. 236. *Lwów,* 1889. 8°. [*Biblioteka najciekawszych powieści i romansów.* tom 3.] **12264.** dd.

—— Cuentos, oraciones, adivinas y refranes populares é infantiles, recogidos por F. Caballero. pp. 504. *Madrid,* 1877. 8°. **12356.** a. **8.**

—— [Another edition.] pp. viii. 268. *Leipzig,* 1878. 8° [*Colección de Autores Españoles.* tom. 40.] **12230.bb.6/4**

—— Cuentos y Poesias Populares Andaluces, coleccionada por F. Caballero. pp. xiv. 296. *Leipzig,* 1866. 8° [*Colección de Autores Españoles.* tom. 8.] **12230.bb.**

—— Deudas pagadas. Cuadro de costumbres populares d actualidad, *etc.* [With a preface by M. Cañete.] pp. xxix. 70. *Madrid,* 1860. 8°. **12491.** c. **41.** (6

—— La Familia de Alvareda . . . Edited, with introductio exercises, notes and vocabulary, by William Samu Hendrix . . . and Ernest Herman Hespelt. pp. xx. 27 *Ginn & Co.: Boston,* [1928.] 8°. **012941.** a. **2**

—— The Alvareda Family. A novelette. Translated . . by Viscount Pollington. pp. 300. *T. C. Newby London,* 1872. 8°. **12637.** f. **3**

—— De Familie Alvareda. Naar het Spaansch van F Caballero. pp. 200. *Rotterdam,* 1868. 8°. **12580.** ee. **2**

—— La Famille Alvareda, roman de mœurs populaires . . Traduit par Auguste Dumas, *etc.* [With a prologue b the Duke de Rivas.] pp. xxvii. 460. *Meaux,* 1862. 12°. **12490.** bb. **1**

—— La Gaviota. Novela de costumbres. pp. 279. *Leipzig* 1863. 8°. [*Colección de Autores Españoles.* tom. 2.] **12230.bb.6/2**

—— [Another edition.] pp. 279. *Leipzig,* 1868. 8°. [*Colección de Autores Españoles.* tom. 2.] **12230.** bb **12230.bb.6/2a**

—— [Another edition.] Introduction, notes, and vocabular by George W. Umphrey . . . and F. Sánchez y Escriban [With a portrait.] pp. xx. 260. *Boston,* [1930.] 8° [*Heath's Modern Language Series.*] **12213.** a. **1/26**

—— The Sea-Gull—La Gaviota. From the Spanish of F Caballero. By the Hon. Augusta Bethell. 2 vol. *Richard Bentley: London,* 1867. 8°. **12490.** cc. **2**

—— Medio-pollito. The half-chicken. (Translated from L Gaviota by H. T. Francis.) [Reprinted from Folk-Lore *Sidgwick & Jackson: London,* 1918. 8°. **12489.** t. **1**

—— Lady Virginia. Novel . . . Traduit da Espaniol i Nuove Roman. *See* PUCHNER (J.) Gramatica di Nuove Roman, *etc.* [1897.] 8°. **012901.** i. **7.** (3

—— Lágrimas. Novela de costumbres contemporánea Segunda edicion corregida. pp. 364. *Cadiz,* 1853. 8°. **12490.** g. **2**

—— [Another edition.] pp. xii. 393. *Madrid,* 1858. 8°. **12489.** aaa. **4**

—— [Mas Honor que Honores.] Lepší čest' než důstojenst . . . Ze španělštiny přeložil František Pohunek. pp. 8 *v Praze,* 1883. 8°. [*Hlasy katolického spolku tiskového* rok 1883. čís. 2.] **3605.** bbb. **25.** (6.

—— [Pobre Dolores!] Arme Dolores! Andalusisch Erzählung . . . Aus dem Spanischen von Wilhelm Lange pp. 79. *Leipzig,* [1883.] 16°. **012207.** f. **16.** (11. *No.* 1709 *of the* " *Universal-Bibliothek.*"

—— Un Servilón y un Liberalito, ó Tres almas de Díos . . Con un prológo de D. A. Aparisi y Aguijarro. pp. xviii. 247 *Madrid,* 1902. 8°. **12489.** d. **35**

CABALLERO (FERNAN) *pseud.* [i.e. CECILIA FRANCISCA JOSEFA ARROM DE AYALA.] [SINGLE WORKS.]

—— Servil und liberal . . . Aus dem Spanischen von Wilhelm Lange. pp. 85. *Leipzig*, [1879.] 16°. **012207**. f. **11**. (**8**.)
No. 1239 *of the " Universal-Bibliothek."*

—— Elöitélet és felvilágasodás . . . Forditotta Lászlófy M. pp. 95. *Budapest*, [1881.] 8°. [*Magyar Könyvesház.* foly. 10. no. 99–100.] **739**. bb. **24**.

—— [Un Verano en Bornos.] Un Été à Bornos . . . Traduit de l'espagnol par Don Téotimo T . . .. pp. 515. *Paris*, 1886. 12°. **12489**. i. **12**.

—— Vulgaridad y Nobleza. Cuadro de costumbres populares. pp. xiii. 97. *Sevilla*, 1860. 4°. **12490**. cc. **31**. (**1**.)

WORKS WITH CONTRIBUTIONS BY FERNAN CABALLERO.

—— *See* CAVANILLES (A.) Dialogos politicos y literarios, *etc.* [With a preface by F. Caballero.] 1859. 8°. **12230**. c. **3**.

—— *See* LOPEZ DE AYALA (A.) La Mejor Corona . . . Precédela un prólogo de F. Caballero, *etc.* 1868. 8°. **11726**. bbb. **30**. (**9**.)

APPENDIX.

—— *See* ASENSIO Y TOLEDO (J. M.) Fernan-Caballero. Estudio biográfico. [1893.] 8°. **10601**. a. **41**. (**5**.)

—— *See* COLOMA (L.) Obras completas. (Tom. 17. Recuerdos de Fernán Caballero.) 1944, *etc.* 8°. **12232**. ff. **3**/**17**.

—— *See* COLOMA (L.) Recuerdos de Fernán Caballero. [1910.] 8°. **10633**. b. **2**.

—— *See* MOREL-FATIO (A. P. V.) Fernan Caballero, d'après sa correspondance avec Antoine de Latour. [With extracts.] 1901. 8°. [*Bulletin hispanique.* tom. 3. no. 3.] Ac. **8917**.

—— *See* PALMA (A.) Fernán Caballero, *etc.* [With a portrait.] 1931. 8°. **10633**. s. **6**.

CABALLERO (FRANCISCO DE ASÍS)

—— *See* SCHMITT (Carl) *Professor an der Universität Berlin.* [Donoso Cortés in gesamteuropäischer Interpretation.] Interpretación europea de Donoso Cortés, *etc.* (Traducción de F. de Asís Caballero.) 1952. 8°. **10636**. aa. **9**.

CABALLERO (FRANCISCO LARGO) *See* LARGO CABALLERO. **10635**. b. **21**.

CABALLERO (GREGORIO CALLEJO Y) *See* CALLEJO Y CABALLERO.

CABALLERO (GIMÉNEZ) *See* GIMÉNEZ CABALLERO ( )

CABALLERO (ISAAC PERAL Y) *See* PERAL Y CABALLERO.

CABALLERO (JOAQUÍN) Renuncia justificada del Gobernador interino del Estado de Michoacan, Señador al Congreso de la Union . . . J. Caballero. pp. 38. *Morelia*, 1833. 4°. **8179**. aa. **7**.

CABALLERO (JOCELYNE)

—— *See* UTLEY (F.) [China Story.] El Relato de la China . . . Traducido por O. Dominici y J. Caballero. 1951. 8°. **8024**. cc. **22**.

CABALLERO (JOSÉ) *Lexicographer.*

—— Diccionario General de la Lengua Castellana . . . Por una sociedad de literatos, bajo la direccion de Don J. Caballero. [With a supplement, containing addenda.] 2 pt. *Madrid*, 1849, [51.] 4°. **1331**. k. **16**.

—— Quinta edicion. (Suplemento. Relacion general alfabética de todos los pueblos de España é islas adyacentes, con las cabezas del partido judicial á que pertenecen.) 2 tom. pp. 1466. 82. *Madrid*, 1856. 4°. **12943.w.6.**

—— Octava edicion. 2 tom. pp. 1466. 82. *Madrid*, 1860. 4°. **12943**. g. **8**.

—— Sexta edicion . . . aumentada. 2 tom. pp. 1466. 82. *Madrid*, 1882. 8°. **12943**. f. **12**.

—— Estado general alfabético de todos los pueblos de España e islas adyacentes, con especificacion de las cabezas de partido judicial á que cada uno pertenece. [By J. Caballero. Another issue of the supplement to the 8th edition of the " Diccionario."] pp. 82. 1860. 4°. *See* SPAIN. [*Appendix.—Topography and Travels.*] **10160**. f. **13**.

CABALLERO (JOSÉ AGUSTÍN)

—— *See* CASTRO Y BACHILLER (R. de) A la Memoria de un Maestro de Maestros en el Centenario de su Muerte. Presbítero J. A. Caballero, *etc.* [1937.] 8°. **012301**. m. **1**.

CABALLERO (JOSÉ ALMOINA Y) *See* ALMOINA Y CABALLERO.

CABALLERO (JOSÉ ANTONIO) Guía de Sanlúcar de Barrameda . . . 1905, *etc.* pp. 232. *Jerez*, 1905. 8°. **10162**. b. **19**.

CABALLERO (JOSÉ BENÍTEZ) *See* BENÍTEZ CABALLERO.

CABALLERO (JOSÉ CIPRIANO DE LA LUZ Y) *See* LUZ Y CABALLERO.

CABALLERO (JOSÉ M.) *of New Orleans. See* EGAÑA (J. J.) Sentencias pronunciadas . . . en autos de testamentaría de Don J. I. de Egaña, precedidas de algunas explicaciones que dá al público el ejecutor testamentario Don J. M. Caballero. 1864. 8°. **6785**. b. **1**. (**3**.)

CABALLERO (JOSÉ MARÍA) En la Independencia. *See* POSADA (E.) and IBAÑEZ (P. M.) La Patria Boba, *etc.* 1902. 8°. [*Biblioteca de Historia Nacional.* vol. 1.] **9773.i.2/1.**

CABALLERO (JUAN BARCIA) *See* BARCIA CABALLERO.

CABALLERO (JUAN IGNACIO VEGA Y) *See* VEGA Y CABALLERO.

CABALLERO (LUCAS) Relación de las Costumbres y Religión de los Indios Manasicas . . . Estudio preliminar y edición del MS. de 1706 por Manuel Serrano y Sanz. pp. 43. *Madrid*, 1933. 8°. **20001**. g. **5**.

CABALLERO (LUIS BELLO) *See* BELLO CABALLERO.

CABALLERO (LUIS E. NIETO) *See* NIETO CABALLERO.

CABALLERO (LUIS MARTY) *See* MARTY CABALLERO.

CABALLERO (MANUEL) *See* STEVENSON (Robert L.) La Isla del Tesoro. Novela . . . traducida . . . por M. Caballero. 1889. 12°. **12807**. n. **37**.

—— Album Queretano de la primera Esposición del Estado, en 1882. pp. 75. *México*, 1882. *obl.* fol. **1789**. a. **32**.

CABALLERO (MANUEL)

—— Independencia. Poema en prosa y verso. pp. 32. *Puebla*, 1910. 8º. 11725.ccc.4.

CABALLERO (MANUEL ANTONIO) Discurso que en la apertura de la Real Audiencia de Galicia . . . 1829, pronunció su Regente . . . M. A. Caballero. pp. 38. *Santiago*, [1829.] 4º. 899. c. 23. (1.)

—— Discurso del Señor D. M. A. Caballero, Regente de la Real Audiencia de Galicia . . . á la apertura del Tribunal . . . 1830. pp. 23. *Santiago*, [1830.] 4º. 899. c. 23. (2.)

—— Discurso que en la apertura de la Real Audiencia de Galicia . . . 1831 pronunció su Regente . . . M. A. Caballero. pp. 25. *Santiago*, 1831. 4º. 899. c. 23. (3.)

CABALLERO (MANUEL GARCÍA) *See* GARCÍA CABALLERO.

CABALLERO (MARCOS GONZÁLEZ) *See* GONZÁLEZ CABALLERO.

CABALLERO (MARÍA DEL CARMEN CALDERON DE) *See* CALDERON DE CABALLERO.

CABALLERO (RAMÓN) Diccionario de modismos—frases y metáforas . . . Con un prólogo de Don Eduardo Benot. pp. 1198. *Madrid*, [1898–1900.] 8º. 12941. dd. 8.
Published in parts.

—— Gorjeos del alma. Cantares populares coleccionados por R. Caballero. pp. 192. *Madrid*, 1884. 18º. [*Biblioteca Universal.* tom. 97.] 739. b. 18.

—— Sueños de Madre. Poema en dos cantos. pp. 32. *Madrid*, 1887. 8º. 11451. bbb. 9. (4.)

CABALLERO (RAMÓN DIOSDADO) Bibliothecae scriptorum Societatis Jesu supplementa. 2 pt. *Romæ*, 1814, 16. 4º. 011900.k.21.

—— De prima typographiae hispanicae aetate specimen. pp. xxxvi. 134. *Romæ*, 1793. 4º. 619. l. 21.

—— [Another copy.] 619. l. 22.

—— [Another copy.] G. 911.

—— L'Eroismo di Ferdinando Cortese confermato contro le censure nemiche. pp. 194. *Roma*, 1806. 8º. 12403. aa. 12.

—— Gloria posthuma Societatis Jesu. pt. 1. pp. 150. *Romæ*, 1814. 8º. 1367. i. 9.
No more published.

—— [Osservazioni sulla patria del pittore G. di Rivera.] Observaciones . . . sobre la patria del pintor Josef de Ribera, llamado el Españoleto. Traducidas de la lengua italiana, é ilustradas con algunas notas. pp. 60. *Valencia*, 1828. 4º. 1402. f. 27.

—— [Another copy.] 8305. dd. 17. (9.)

CABALLERO (RICARDO) *See* PERIODICAL PUBLICATIONS.—*Madrid*. La Marina Española, *etc.* [Edited by R. Caballero and others.] 1867, *etc.* 8º. P.P. 4027. f.

—— Cantos del Pueblo. Parafraseados por D. R. Caballero. . . . Precedidos de una carta-prólogo de M. Ossorio y Bernard. pp. xv. 238. *Madrid*, 1884. 8º. 11450. b. 20.

—— Escenas Populares. Cuadros de costumbres basados en los cantares del pueblo. [In verse.] pp. 350. *Cartagena*, 1880. 8º. 11450. f. 19.

CABALLERO (RICARDO) and **PALACIOS SUAREZ** (M.)

—— Guia ilustrada del viajero en Gijón . . . Con . . . dibujos, *etc.* pp. 144. *Gijón, Oviedo*, [1892.] 8º. 10160. aaa. 19.

CABALLERO (SALVADOR BERMÚDEZ DE CASTRO Y O'LAWLOR DÍEZ Y) *Duke de Ripalda* and *Marquis de Lema*. *See* BERMÚDEZ DE CASTRO Y O'LAWLOR DÍEZ Y CABALLERO.

CABALLERO (VALENTÍN) Orientaciones pedagógicas de San José de Calasanz . . . Prólogo de D. Salvador Minguijón. tom. 1, 2. *Barcelona*, 1921. 8º. 08311. f. 49.
No more published.

—— Orientaciones pedagógicas de San José de Calasanz . . . 2.ª edición. pp. 607. *Madrid*, 1945. 8º. 8356. p. 34.
Ser. A, no. 5, *of the Publications of the Instituto "San José de Calasanz" de Pedagogía.*

CABALLERO CALDERÓN (EDUARDO)

—— Discurso inaugural de la Asamblea Cervantina reunida en Sevilla el diá 14 de abril de 1948. pp. 29. *Madrid*, 1948. 8º. 11868. p. 23.

CABALLERO DE PUGA (EDUARDO) Marruecos. Política é intereses de España en este imperio. [With illustrations.] pp. 32. *Madrid*, 1907. 8º. 010097. l. 2. (1.)

CABALLERO-INFANTE (FRANCISCO) Estudio sobre las monedas árabes de Denia. [Reprinted from "El Archivo."] pp. 17. *Denia*, 1889. 4º. 7757. g. 16. (2.)
One of an edition of 100 *copies.*

CABALLERO-INFANTE Y ZUAZO (FRANCISCO) Discursos leídos ante la Real Academia Sevillana de Buenas Letras el 23 de Abril de 1872, por los Señores D. F. Caballero-Infante y Zuazo [on Aristophanes], y Don J. Fernandez Espino [in reply], en el recepción del primero. pp. 56. 1872. 8º. *See* SEVILLE.—*Real Academia Sevillana de Buenas Letras.* Cerv. 636.

CABALLERO POZO (LUIS)

—— Valera y el embrujo andaluz. *In:* Revista de la Universidad de Buenos Aires. época 4. año 7. no. 25, 26. 1953. 8º. Ac. 2694. a/10.

CABALLEROS. Cavalleros de la limpia Concepcion de la Virgen Santissima Nuestra Señora. *See* MARY, *the Blessed Virgin.—Orders, etc.—Order of the Immaculate Conception of the Virgin.*

CABALLERO Y ESTEVAN (TORIBIO TOMÁS) De Oriente á Occidente. Comercio, industria, administración é impuestos de los pueblos antiguos. pp. ix. 522. *San Sebastian*, 1891. 8º. 9008. bbb. 2.

—— La Protección y el libre cambio ante la producción nacional, *etc.* pp. xi. 287. *Madrid*, 1883. 8º. 8229. aaaa. 16.

CABALLERO Y GÓNGORA (ANTONIO) *Archbishop of Santa Fé.* [For official documents issued by A. Caballero y Gongora as Viceroy of New Granada:] *See* NEW GRANADA, *Colony of.* [1550–1819.]—Caballero y Góngora (A.) *Archbishop of Santa Fé, Viceroy.*

—— Aciertos del Rey nuestro Señor en el tiempo, y lugar, en que coloca a Christo sacramentado y le dedica Templo en las nueva Ciudad de San Fernando. Oracion panegyrica, *etc.* pp. 60. *Madrid*, [1750.] 4º. T. 1547. (9.)

—— Panegyris que en honor . . . de la Bendita Santa María de la Cabeza, muger del Glorioso San Isidro . . . dixo . . . A. Cavallero y Gongora. pp. 52. *Madrid*, 1753. 4º. 478. a. 36.

CABALLERO Y GÓNGORA (Antonio) *Archbishop of Santa Fé.*

—— Relación del estado del Nuevo Reino de Granada . . . Año de 1789. *See* Posada (E.) and Ibáñez (P. M.) Relaciones de mando, *etc.* 1910. 8°. [*Biblioteca de Historia Nacional.* vol. 8.] **9773.i.2/8**

CABALLERO Y RODRÍGUEZ (José Agustín)

—— Homenaje al Ilustre Habanero Pbro. Dr. José Agustín Caballero y Rodríguez en el Centenario de su Muerte, 1835–1935. pp. 75. *La Habana,* 1935. 8°. [*Cuadernos de Historia Habanera.* no. 1.] W.P. **9588/4.**

CABALLERO Y VILLALDEA (Sergio) Geografía médica de Pezuela de las Torres, Madrid. [With plates.] pp. 134. *Madrid,* 1932. 8°. **7680. ff. 31.**

CABALLERUS (Petrus) *Praes. See* Gomero (G.) Pro logices examine instituendo . . . rationes afferent . . . G. Gomero, A. Martel, *etc.* [1832.] 8°. **731. f. 30.**

CABALLETE.

—— El Caballete vivo. (Colección de monografías sobre los principales representantes del arte español.) *Madrid, Barcelona,* 1951– . 8°. W.P. **B. 38.**

CABALLÉ Y CLOS (T.)

—— Barcelona Roja. (Dietario de la Revolución, Julio 1936—Enero 1939.) pp. 269. *Barcelona,* [1939.] 8°. **9181. ee. 25.**

CABALLINI (Antonius Stephanus) Josepho Garampio . . . has ex tractatu de jure et justitia theologico-polemicas theses A. S. . . . Eques Caballini . . . d. d. d. l. m. *Praes.* T. M. Soldatus. pp. 4. [*Rome,* 1782.] 4°. **T. 1985. (12.)**

CABALLINI (Domenico) [For official documents issued by D. Caballini as Camerlengo della Ripa Grande:] *See* States of the Church.—*Tribunale delle Ripe.*

CABALLINUS (Gaspar) *pseud.* [i.e. Charles Du Moulin.] De ædilitiis actionibus libellus. *See* Tractatus. Tractatus vniuersi iuris, *etc.* tom. 6. pt. 1. 1584. fol. **499. f. 7.**

—— D. Gasparis Caballini . . . De eo, quod interest. *See* Tractatus. Tractatus vniuersi iuris, *etc.* tom. 5. 1584. fol. **499. f. 6.**
Another edition of this work, entitled "Extricatio labyrinthi de eo, quod interest," 1555, is entered under Du Moulin (*Charles*).

—— De euictionibus. *See* Tractatus. Tractatus vniuersi iuris, *etc.* tom. 6. pt. 1. 1584. fol. **499. f. 7.**

CABALLIS (Franciscus de) *See* Caballus (F.)

CABALLITO. Se lamenta el Caballito por que lo dejan solito. [In verse.] [*Mexico,* 1852.] *s. sh.* 4°. **11450. e. 5. (52.)**

CABALLIS (Marinus de) *See* Cavalli.

CABALLUS (Franciscus) Franciscus Caballus de numero partium ac librorum Physicæ doctrinae Aristotelis Ioanni Aurelio eius filio. [*Matteo Capcasa: Venice,* 1490?] fol. IB. **22738.**
20 *leaves. Sig.* a⁶ b⁶ c⁴ d⁴. 62 *lines to a page.*

—— Tractatus de theriaca. *See* Montagnana (B.) *the Elder.* Consilia Magistri Bartholomei Montagnane, *etc.* 1499. fol. IB. **24651.**

CABALLUS (Franciscus)

—— [Another edition.] *See* Cermisonus (A.) Consilia Cermisoni, *etc.* [1500?] fol. IB. **22950.**

—— [Another edition.] Tractatus de animali theria. *See* Montagnana (B.) *the Elder.* Cōsilia . . . Bartholomei Montagnane, *etc.* 1514. fol. **545. k. 1.**

—— [Another edition.] *See* Montagnana (B.) *the Elder.* Bartholomæi Montagnanæ . . . opera selectiora, *etc.* 1652. fol. **542. i. 7.**

CABALLUS (Ludovicus) De rebus Italiæ nuperrimis ad Cl. Eq. Victorium Ouidam Cantabrigiensem L. Caballi epistola. pp. 33. *Typis Eleutheriis: Londini; Bologna* [printed], 1899. 8°. **8032. cc. 19. (3.)**

CABALLUS (Petrus) Tractatus de omni genere homicidii . . . cum summariis, *etc.* pp. 295. *Apud B. Sermartellium & fratres: Florentiæ,* 1614. 8°. **501. a. 2. (2.)**

CABALLUS (Seraphinus) De Christo iudice laetis animis expectando, oratio . . . 1562 ad Sacrum Oecumenicum Tridentinum Concilium. [*Apud D. Turlinum ad instantiam J. B. Bozolae: Brixiae,* 1562.] 4°. **5016. c. 5.**
Imperfect; wanting all after sig. B.

—— De Christo iudice lætis animis expectando oratio . . . In Dominica prima Aduentus, 1562. Ad Sacrum Oecumenicum Tridentinum Concilium. *Imprimebatur apud Damianum Turlinum; ad instantiam Ioan. Baptistæ Bozolæ: Brixiæ,* 1563. 4°. **1492. p. 14. (13.)**

CABALZAR (Lucius) *the Elder.* Censura tepidorum, oder Bescheltung der Lauen. Das ist eine christliche . . . Predigt, über die Wort Jesu Christi zu dem Engel und der Gemeinde zu Laodicea, aus der Offenbahrung St. Johannis Cap. 3: 15/16, *etc.* pp. 28. [*Coire?*] 1728. 4°. **9304. dd. 5. (19.)**

CABALZAR (Lucius) *the Younger.* Un Antruvidament davart ilg pli grond kunst, c'ei da morir beadameng, cun anchinnas autras canzuns spiritualas. pp. 32. *Cuera,* 1792. 8°. **885. d. 1. (3.)**

CABAN. *See* Oakeley Slate Quarries Company Limited.

CABAÑA (Agustín Moreto y) *See* Moreto y Cabaña.

CABANAC (Victor de Ségur) *Count. See* Ségur-Cabanac.

CABANACH (Poncio) *See* Cabanoch.

CABANAS (A. Álvarez) *See* Álvarez Cabanas.

CABAÑAS (Agustín Moreto y) *See* Moreto y Cabaña.

CABAÑAS (Amalio Gimeno y) *Count de Gimeno. See* Gimeno y Cabañas.

CABAÑAS (Joaquín Ramírez) *See* Ramírez Cabañas.

CABAÑAS (Manuel German Toral) *See* Toral Cabañas.

CABAÑAS (Narciso Sentenach y) *See* Sentenach y Cabañas.

CABAÑAS (Pablo)

—— *See* Jáuregui y Aguilar (J. de) Orfeo. Edición de P. Cabañas. 1948. 8°. **010632. aa. 48.**

CABAÑAS (Pablo)

—— See **Periodical Publications.—Madrid.—*No me olvides.*** **No me olvides . . . Por P. Cabañas. [Extracts arranged in index form.] 1946. 8°. [*Colección de índices de publicaciones periódicas.* no. 2.]** **Ac. 132. cb/6.**

—— Evocación. Poemas. pp. 14. *Madrid,* 1951. 8°. [*Hojas literarias.* supl. 3.] **Ac. 132/16. (4.)**

—— El Mito de Orfeo en la literatura española, *etc.* [With " El Divino Orfeo " by P. Calderón de la Barca, " Orpheo " by R. P. Gabriel Ruiz and " Orfeo, fénix de Turia." With a bibliography and plates.] pp. 408. *Madrid,* 1948. 8°. **Ac. 132/16. (3.)**

CABAÑAS GUEVARA (Luís)

—— Biografía del Paralelo, 1894–1934. Recuerdos de la vida teatral, mundana y pintoresca del barrio más jaranero y bullicioso de Barcelona. [With illustrations.] pp. 314. *Barcelona,* 1945. 8°. **10163. a. 25.**

—— Cuarenta Años de Barcelona, 1890–1930. Recuerdos de la vida literaria, artística, teatral, mundana y pintoresca de la ciudad. [With plates.] pp. 280. *Barcelona,* 1944. 8°. **10163. a. 13.**

CABAÑAS VENTURA (F.) *See* Scott (*Sir* Walter) *Bart.* [*Woodstock.*] Woodstock . . . Traducción de F. Cabañas Ventura. [1922.] 8°. **012634. n. 41.**

CABANE (G.) and **PETIT** (J.) *Metallurgist.*

—— A Study of the Annealing of Rolled Aluminium . . . Translation by F. Hudswell. [With plates.] pp. 8. *Harwell,* 1955. fol. [*A.E.R.E. Lib./Trans.* no. 516.] **B.S. 62/63.**

CABANE (Henri) Histoire du clergé de France pendant la Révolution de 1848. De la chute de Louis-Philippe à l'élection de Louis Bonaparte. 24 février—20 décembre 1848. pp. 252. *Paris,* 1908. 8°. **4630. de. 16.**

CABANE (Philippe de) *See* Cabani (Filippa de') *Countess di Montorio,* called Filippa Catanese.

CABANEL (Alexandre) *See* Chennevière (H. de) A. Cabanel. [A biography. Translated by C. Bell.] 1884. fol. **L.R.407.h.4.**

—— *See* Lafenestre (G.) La Tradition dans la peinture française . . . La peinture française au xixe siècle . . . A. Cabanel, *etc.* [1898.] 12°. **7858. n. 7.**

CABANEL (Daniel) British Scenery. A poetical sketch. By a quondam Oxonian, and Carthusian [i.e. D. Cabanel]. pp. 40. 1811. 4°. *See* British Scenery. **1466. i. 27. (1.)**

—— The Tocsin. (With several minor poems.) By a Member of the Honourable Society of Lincoln's Inn [i.e. D. Cabanel]. pp. 33. 1811. 4°. *See* Tocsin. **1466. i. 27. (2.)**

—— Poems and Imitations. pp. viii. 192. *R. Bickerstaff: London,* 1814. 8°. **993. l. 8.**

CABANELLAS (J. F. Gustave) Propositions et observations sur quelques points de médecine et de chirurgie; thèse, *etc.* pp. 21. *Paris,* 1826. 4°. **1183. i. 5. (7.)**

CABANELLAS (Jaime) Estudios Teatrales. Apuntes sobre el actor. pp. 32. *Palma,* 1861. 4°. **11795. dg. 1. (2.)**

CABANELLAS (Virgilio) De la Campaña de Yebala e 1924. Asedio y defensa de Xauen, *etc.* pp. 149. *Madrid,* [1926.] 8°. **09061. aaaa. 7**

—— Prontuario de Campaña, *etc.* pp. 98. *Cartagen* 1896. 8°. **8826. aa. 2**

—— La Táctica en Cuba, África y Filipinas . . . Apéndice reglamento táctico de infantería, *etc.* pp. 82. *Madri* 1896. 8°. **8831. ee. 41. (4.**

—— Veladas militares. [Essays.] pp. 71. *Cartagen* 1890. 8°. **8831. l. 8. (5.**

CABANELLAS DE TORRES (Guillermo)

—— El Dictador del Paraguay, Dr. Francia. [With plat including portraits and facsimiles.] pp. 397. *Buenos Aires,* 1946. 4°. **10899. aaa.** *Biblioteca de grandes biografías.* ser. B. vol. 12.

CABAÑERO (José Francisco Esponera y) *See* Esponer y Cabañero.

CABANES, José Garriga Nogués y Roig, *Marquis d* *See* Garriga Nogués y Roig.

CABANES, Jourdaine Magdelène Pelet, *Viscountess d* *See* Pelet.

CABANES ( ) *Mag.* Le Masque de Lyon. pp. 18 *Paris,* 1933. 8°. **010168. f. 6**

CABANES (Adrien) Quelques considérations sur l'étic logie et le traitement du choléra épidémique. Thèse, *et* pp. 51. *Montpellier,* 1855. 4°. **7379. c. 17. (14**

CABANES (André Joseph) Thèse pour le doctorat e médecine, *etc.* (Questions sur diverses branches de sciences médicales.) pp. 23. *Paris,* 1838. 4°. **1184. h. 18. (37.**

CABANES (Antoine Joachim) Dissertation sur les dispos tions et les maladies héréditaires en général; thèse, *et* pp. 28. *Paris,* 1827. 4°. **1183. i. 10. (28.**

CABANÈS (Augustin) *See* Brifaut (C.) Souvenirs d'u académicien . . . Avec introduction et notes du docteu Cabanès, *etc.* 1921. 8°. **09225. g. 3**

—— *See* Régis, afterwards Govaerts (J.) Un médecin a service de l'histoire. Le docteur A. Cabanès, *etc.* 1941. 8°. **010665. ppp. 1**

—— *See* Warden (William) Napoléon jugé par un Anglai Lettres de Sainte-Hélène . . . Réponses de Napoléo Avant-propos, notes, documents justificatifs et appendic Par le docteur Cabanès. 1901. 8°. **010661. bb.**

—— Une Allemande à la cour de France. La Princess Palatine [Charlotte Elizabeth]. Les petits talents d grand Fréderic. Un médecin prussien [David Ferdinan Koreff], espion dans les salons romantiques. (Les dernie moments de Frédéric ii.) . . . 85 gravures, *etc.* pp. 398. *Paris,* 1916. 8°. **10707. c. 1**

—— [A reissue.] La Belle-Sœur du Grand Roi. Une All mande à la cour de France, *etc.* *Paris,* [1925.] 8°. **010704. e. 3**

—— Au chevet de l'Empereur (Napoléon). Ouvrage orné d nombreuses illustrations. pp. 440. *Paris,* [1924.] 8°. **10657. bb. 2**

—— Autour de la vie de Bohème. Ouvrage illustré de 1 gravures. pp. 383. *Paris,* [1938.] 8°. **11862. a. 2**

—— Balzac ignoré. pp. 124. *Paris,* 1899. 8°. **10661. i. 3**

CABANÈS (Augustin)

—— Deuxième édition, revue et augmentée. Ouvrage illustré de 36 gravures. pp. 288. *Paris*, [1911.] 8°. **010664. ee. 29.**

—— Le Cabinet secret de l'histoire, ent'rouvert par un médecin. Précédé d'une lettre de M. Victorien Sardou. [ser. 1.] pp. iii. 209. *Paris*, 1895. 12°. **7679. de. 16.**

—— Troisième édition. 2 sér. *Paris*, 1897. 8°. **7679. ee. 10.**

—— The Secret Cabinet of History peeped into by a Doctor. Translated by W. C. Costello and preceded by a letter of M. V. Sardou . . . First series. pp. x. 239. vii. *Charles Carrington: Paris*, 1897. 8°. **7679. bb. 44.**

—— Curious Bypaths of History. Being medico-historical studies and observations, *etc.* [A translation of "Le Cabinet secret de l'histoire," ser. 2.] pp. xxiv. 367. *Charles Carrington: Paris*, 1898. 8°. **09009. d. 10.**

—— Chirurgiens et blessés à travers l'histoire, des origines à la Croix-rouge. Ouvrage illustré de 275 gravures et 1 planche hors texte. pp. 624. *Paris*, [1912.] 4°. **7680. g. 10.**

—— Chirurgiens et blessés à travers l'histoire. Des origines à la Croix-Rouge. [With illustrations.] pp. 624. *Paris*, [1918.] 4°. **7682. dd. 7.**

—— Les Condé. Grandeur et dégénérescence d'une famille princière. [With illustrations, including portraits.] 2 tom. *Paris*, [1932, 33.] 8°. **9917. bbb. 46.**

—— Dans l'intimité de l'Empereur (Napoléon). Ouvrage orné de nombreuses illustrations. pp. 501. *Paris*, [1924.] 8°. **10657. bb. 30.**

—— Dans les coulisses de l'histoire. 4 tom. *Paris*, [1929,] 37. 8°. **09226. df. 17.**

—— L'Enfer de l'histoire, *etc.* [With illustrations.] 2 ser. *Paris*, 1928. 8°. **010604. cc. 23.**

—— Les Énigmes de l'histoire, *etc.* [With plates.] pp. 344. *Paris*, [1930.] 8°. **10655. a. 21.**

—— Les Évadés de la médecine. Th. Renaudot, *etc.* [With plates including portraits.] pp. 382. *Paris*, 1931. 8°. **10655. bbb. 17.**

—— Folie d'Empereur. Une dynastie de dégénérés. Guillaume II jugé par la science. Ouvrage orné de 63 gravures, *etc.* pp. 461. *Paris*, [1915.] 8°. **010705. de. 33.**

—— Fous couronnés . . . Ouvrage orné de 56 gravures. pp. 438. *Paris*, [1914.] 8°. **10600. aaa. 8.**

—— Grands névropathes. Malades immortels. [With plates.] 3 tom. *Paris*, 1930–35. 8°. **10602. pp. 12.**

—— Les Indiscrétions de l'histoire. 6 sér. *Paris*, 1903–09. 8°. **7679. eee. 12.**

—— Légendes & curiosités de l'histoire. Ouvrage illustré, *etc.* 5 sér. *Paris*, [1912–22.] 8°. **9210. e. 24.**

—— Le Mal héréditaire. 2 sér.

Les Descendants de Charles Quint. Ouvrage orné de 63 illustrations [including portraits]. pp. 379. [1926.]
Les Bourbons d'Espagne. Ouvrage orné de 93 illustrations [including portraits]. pp. 340. [1927.]

Paris, [1926, 27.] 8°. **7679. a. 35.**

—— Marat inconnu. L'homme privé, le médecin, le savant d'après des documents nouveaux et inédits. pp. vi. 328. *Paris*, 1891. 12°. **010661. ee. 43.**

CABANÈS (Augustin)

—— Deuxième édition, refondue et très notablement augmentée. Ouvrage orné de cinq planches et de soixante illustrations, *etc.* pp. xii. 559. *Paris*, [1911.] 8°. **010664. ee. 34.**

—— Médecins amateurs . . . Ouvrage illustré de 60 gravures. pp. 382. *Paris*, [1932.] 8°. **010603. ccc. 4.**

—— Mœurs intimes du passé . . . Ouvrage illustré, *etc.* 12 sér. *Paris*, [1910]–36. 8°. **10175. a. 24.**
The volumes are of various editions.

—— Les Morts mystérieuses de l'histoire. Souverains et princes français de Charlemagne à Louis XVII, *etc.* [ser. 1.] pp. xviii. 540. *Paris*, 1901. 8°. **010661. cc. 7.**

—— Nouvelle édition revue, corrigée et augmentée, *etc.* 2 sér. *Paris*, [1910, 11.] 8°. **010664. ee. 46.**

—— La Princesse de Lamballe intime, d'après les confidences de son médecin [J. G. Saiffert]. Sa liaison avec Marie Antoinette.—Son rôle secret pendant la Révolution, *etc.* [With portraits.] pp. 512. *Paris*, [1922.] 8°. **10657. bb. 23.**

—— Les Secrets de l'histoire. pp. 159. *Paris*, 1938. 8°. **09226. e. 15.**

—— The Erotikon. Being an illustrated treasury of scientific marvels of human sexuality . . . Translated from the French by Robert Meadows. pp. xv. 254. pl. 30. *Falstaff Press: New York*, [1933.] 8°. **Cup. 364. g. 10.**

CABANÈS (Augustin) and NASS (Lucien)

—— La Névrose révolutionnaire . . . Orné de 20 gravures, *etc.* pp. xi. 540. *Paris*, 1906 [1905]. 8°. **9230. b. 36.**

—— Poisons et sortilèges. Les Césars. Envouteurs et sorciers. Les Borgia. Deuxième édition. pp. viii. 308. *Paris*, 1903. 8°. **6055. aa. 20.**

—— Poisons et sortilèges. Les Césars . . . Troisième édition, revue et augmentée. pp. viii. 345. *Paris*, 1903. 8°. **6059. c. 3.**

—— Poisons et sortilèges. Deuxième série. Les Médicis. Les Bourbons. La Science au XXe siècle. Deuxième édition. pp. 388. *Paris*, 1903. 8°. **6059. c. 2.**

CABANES (B. León) Des anémies et particulièrement de la chlorose. pp. 48. *Paris*, 1864. 4°. [*Collection des thèses soutenues à la Faculté de Médecine de Paris.* An 1864. tom. 2.] **7373. e. 13.**

CABANES (Charles) *Biographer.* Denys Papin. Inventeur & philosophe cosmopolite, *etc.* [With a portrait.] pp. 285. *Paris*, 1935. 8°. **010665. de. 25.**

CABANES (Charles) *de Thezan.* Dissertation sur les bains considérés thérapeutiquement, *etc.* pp. 22. *Montpellier*, 1823. 4°. **1181. c. 8. (1.)**

CABANES (Francisco Xavier de) *See* S., C. H., *Oficial de Estado Mayor Moscovita.* Ensayo acerca del Sistema Militar de Bonaparte . . . Traducido por Don F. X. Cabanes. 1811. 8°. **1477. b. 11. (14.)**

—— Guia General de Correos, Portas y Caminos del Reino de España. Con un mapa itinerario de la Peninsula. pp. xvi. 295. *Madrid*, 1830. 8°. **573. h. 30.**

—— Historia de las Operaciones del Exército de Cataluña en la Guerra de la Usurpacion, o sea de la independencia de España. Campaña primera. pp. 49. *México* 1810. 4°. **9180. dd. 1. (10.)**

CABANES (Francisco Xavier de)

—— Memoria acerca del modo de escribir la historia militar de la última guerra entre España y Francia, *etc.* pp. 36. *Barcelona*, 1816. 4°. **8823.** c. **35.** (**1.**)

CABANES (Hippolyte) La Levée des prohibitions et le département du Nord. pp. 71. *Lille*, 1860. 12°. **8244.** a. **38.** (**3.**)

CABANES (J. F. M. Cabiran) *See* Cabiran Cabanes.

CABANÉS (J. P.) Œuvres oratoires . . . Sermons divers. 1856. *See* Migne (J. P.) Collection intégrale et universelle des orateurs sacrés, *etc.* tom. 86. 1844, *etc.* 4°. **3676.** bb. **2.**

CABANES (Jean) Essai sur l'ophthalmie aiguë. Tribut académique, *etc.* pp. 36. *Montpellier*, 1824. 4°. **1181.** c. **16.** (**23.**)

CABANES (Jean de) L'Historien sincere sus la guerro doou duc de Savoyo en Prouvenço, en 1707, poème provençal inédit . . . Précédé d'une notice . . . par A. Pontier. pp. xi. 89. *Aix*, 1830. 8°. **11498.** f. **55.** (**1.**)

—— [Another copy.] **1464.** f. **10.**

CABANES (Jean Baptiste) Essai sur les différences qui existent entre les maladies muqueuses et les maladies catarrales, *etc.* [A thesis.] pp. 27. *Montpellier*, [1804.] 4°. **1180.** e. **11.** (**7.**)

CABANES (José Navarro) *See* Navarro Cabanes.

CABANES (Léon)

—— *See* Lamberton (J.) Lamberton, 1867–1943 . . . " Lamberton vu par lui-même." Notes, propos et extraits de lettres réunis par L. Cabanes. 1946. 8°. **7866.** s. **24.**

CABANES (Louis Guillaume) Dissertation sur l'érysipèle. Tribut académique, *etc.* pp. 36. *Montpellier*, 1823. 4°. **1181.** c. **8.** (**12.**)

CABANES (Maurice) Université de France. Faculté de Théologie protestante de Strasbourg. Étude critique de la méthode suivie par les apologètes du deuxième siècle pour la défense du christianisme, et particulièrement par Méliton de Sardes. Thèse, *etc.* pp. 38. *Strasbourg*, 1857. 8°. **3670.** aa. **14.**

CABANES (P. J. Louis) Considérations sur les fièvres rémittentes. Thèse, *etc.* pp. 59. *Montpellier*, 1846. 4°. **1182.** d. **16.** (**3.**)

CABANET (J. F. Benjamin) Considérations sur l'asphyxie, par les vapeurs qui se dégagent de la houille en combustion. Thèse, *etc.* pp. 35. *Montpellier*, 1827. 4°. **1181.** d. **15.** (**8.**)

CABANI (Filippa de') *Countess di Montorio*, called Filippa Catanese. *See* Matthieu (P.) *Historian.* Unhappy Prosperitie, expressed in the histories of Ælius Seianus and Philippa the Catanian. 1632. 4°. **10605.** cc. **2.**

—— —— 1639. 12°. **610.** a. **7.**

—— *See* Matthieu (P.) *Historian.* Favoriten-Fall, oder unglückliche Glückseligkeit Ælius Seianus, *etc.* (Geschichte in welcher Philippa von Cathana als ein Beyspiel unglücklicher Unglückseligkeit [*sic*] vorgestellt wird, *etc.*) 1664. 12°. **12450.** a. **1.**

—— *See* Matthieu (P.) *Historian.* Historie delle prosperità infelici di Elio Seiano, e d' vna femina da Catanea, *etc.* 1620. 8°. **610.** a. **6.**

CABANI (Filippa de') *Countess di Montorio*, called Filippa Catanese.

—— La Catanoise, ou Histoire secrete des mouvemens arrivez au royaume de Naples, sous la Reine Jeanne I. [By N. Lenglet du Fresnoy?] pp. iv. 324. *Paris*, 1731. 8°. **10631.** aa. **25.**
The running title is " Histoire de la Catanoise."

—— [Another copy.] **12511.** aaaa. **13.**

—— Comedia famosa, El Monstruo de la Fortuna [i.e. F. de' Cabani, called Filippa Catanese]. De tres ingenios. [The first jornada by P. Calderón de la Barca, the second by J. Pérez de Montalbán, and the third by F. de Rojas Zorrilla.] 1666. *See* Spain. [*Appendix.—Miscellaneous.*] Primera [*etc.*] parte de comedias escogidas, *etc.* pt. 24. 1652, *etc.* 4°. **11725.** c. **3.**

—— [Another edition.] pp. 32. [1760?] 4°. **1342.** e. **1.** (**44.**)

—— [Another copy.] T. **1734.** (**7.**)

CABANIÉ (B.) Charpente générale théorique et pratique, *etc.* livr. 1. pp. 2. pl. 2. *Paris*, 1848. fol. **1262.** i. **27.**

—— Deuxième édition. 2 tom. *Paris*, 1864. fol. **1803.** d. **10.**

CABANIÉ (Joseph) Thèse pour le doctorat en médecine, *etc.* (Questions sur diverses branches des sciences médicales.) pp. 31. *Paris*, 1839. 4°. [*Collection des thèses soutenues à la Faculté de Médecine de Paris.* An 1839. tom. 3.] **7371.** a. **3.**

CABANIÉ (Louis Clément) Étude sur le traitement des fractures par action immédiate sur les fragments au moyen des vis métalliques. pp. 80. *Paris*, 1871. 4°. [*Collection des thèses soutenues à la Faculté de Médecine de Paris.* An 1871. tom. 2.] **7373.** m. **13.**

CABANILLAS (Alfredo) La Epopeya del Soldado. Desde el desastre de Annual hasta la reconquista de Monte Arruit. pp. 279. *Madrid*, 1922. 8°. **9060.** bb. **30.**

—— Hacia la España Eterna. Crónica y episodios de la guerra, *etc.* pp. 299. *Buenos Aires*, 1938. 8°. **9180.** v. **35.**

CABANILLAS (Julián Cortés) *See* Cortés Cavanillas.

CABANILLAS (Nicolas de) Recherches pour substituer le papier-monnaie au numéraire. Lettre sur la question financière, *etc.* pp. 14. *Le Mans*, 1848. 4°. **8225.** f. **4.**

CABANILLAS (Ramón) Da Terra Asoballada. (Poesías.) pp. 86. *A Cruña*, 1926. 8°. **011451.** h. **28.**

—— No Desterro. (Poesías.) pp. 87. *A Cruña*, 1926. 8°. **011451.** h. **27.**

CABANILLAS (Ramón) and VILLAR PONTE (Antón)

—— O Mariscal. Lênda tráxica. (Traxédia histórica en verso.) pp. 186. *A Cruña*, 1926. 8°. **11728.** aa. **14.**

CABANILLAS GONZALEZ ALARCÍA Y OROGARAY (Nicolas de) *See* Daumas (M. J. E.) Las Caballos del Sahara . . . Traducido . . . por N. de Cabanillas. 1853. 8°. **07291.** ee. **5**

—— Coleccion de los articulos publicados en el Diario Español desde Setiembre de 1854 hasta 30 de Abril de 1855 3 pt. *Madrid*, 1855–57. 8°. **8042.** c. **17**

CABANILLES (Antonio) *See* Cavanilles (Antonio J.)

CABANIS (F.) Le Murier, ses avantages et son utilité dans l'industrie. pp. vii. 162. *Paris*, 1866. 8°. **7075.** bbb. **10**

CABANIS (George Paul Sylvester) Dietwart. Ein Sang von Nordlands Küste. pp. 222. *Berlin*, 1895. 8°. **11528**. b. **76**.

—— Der Menschheitslehrer. Ein Lebensbild des Weisen von Nazareth. pp. 297. *Berlin*, 1898. 8°. **011528**. g. **75**.

CABANIS (Jean) *See* Periodical Publications.—*Cassel*. Journal für Ornithologie . . . herausgegeben von . . . J. Cabanis. 1853, *etc.* 8°. P.P. **2039**. aa.

—— Museum Heineanum. Verzeichniss der ornithologischen Sammlung des Oberamtmann Ferdinand Heine, auf Gut St. Burchard vor Halberstadt. Mit kritischen Anmerkungen und Beschreibung der neuen Arten, systematisch bearbeitet von Dr. J. Cabanis. [Tl. 2–4 prepared by J. Cabanis and F. Heine the younger.] 4 Tl. 1850–63. 8°. *See* Heine (F.) *the Elder*. **7284**. d. **7**.

—— Ornithologische Notizen. i und ii. Besonders abgedruckt aus dem Archiv für Naturgeschichte, *etc. Berlin*, 1847. 8°. **1257**. e. **27**. (**1**.)

—— Sibirische Vögel. Vortrag, *etc. See* Homeyer (E. F. von) Erinnerungsschrift an die Versammlung der deutschen Ornithologen in Görlitz, *etc.* 1871. 8°. **7284**. bb. **22**.

—— Vögel . . . Mit 18 Tafeln, *etc. See* Decken (C. C. von der) *Baron*. Baron Carl Claus von der Decken's Reisen in Ost-Afrika, *etc.* Bd. 3. Abt. 1. 1869, *etc.* 8°. **10097**. i. **35**.

CABANIS (Paul Sylvester) *See* Cabanis (George P. S.)

CABANIS (Pierre Jean Georges) *See* Bruni (G. B.) Delle dottrine psicologiche e cosmogoniche di P. G. G. Cabanis, *etc.* 1825. 4°. [*Nuova collezione d'opuscoli letterarii*. vol. 2.] **538**. l. **23**. (**3**.)

—— *See* Caritat (M. J. A. N.) *Marquis de Condorcet*. Œuvres complètes. [Edited by the Marchioness de Condorcet, with the assistance of P. J. G. Cabanis and others.] 1804. 8°. **630**. g. **31**.

—— *See* Dubois (E. F.) Philosophie médicale. Examen des doctrines de Cabanis et de Gall. 1845. 8°. **7410**. c. **24**.

—— *See* Goethe (J. W. von) [*Stella.—French.*] Stella, pièce de théâtre. Traduction de Cabanis. 1822. 8°. [*Chefs d'œuvre des théâtres étrangers*. tom. 10.] **1342**. h. **10**.

—— *See* Guillois (A.) Le Salon de Madame Helvétius. Cabanis et les idéologues, *etc.* 1894. 12°. **010663**. f. **7**.

—— *See* Homer. [*Iliad.—French.*] Fragment d'une traduction de l'Iliade en vers français, par M. Cabanis. Priam aux pieds d'Achille, *etc.* 1809. 4°. [*Académie Française. Morceaux de poésie lus* . . . 21 *décembre* 1808, *pour la réception de M. de Tracy, élu à la place de feu M. Cabanis.*] **733**. g. **11**. (**23**.)

—— *See* Riquetti (H. G.) *Count de Mirabeau*. [*Miscellaneous Works.*] Travail sur l'éducation publique . . . Publié par P. J. G. Cabanis. 1791. 8°. **1031**. g. **13**. (**1**.)

—— *See* Saint-Arroman (A.) *Chirurgien*. L'Anthanasie de Cabanis, *etc.* 1857. 12°. **7461**. e. **53**. (**8**.)

—— *See* Tissot (Claude J.) Anthropologie spéculative générale, comprenant . . . l'exposition . . . des doctrines de Bichat, de Cabanis, *etc.* 1843. 8°. **1386**. f. **22**.

—— Œuvres complètes . . . accompagnées d'une notice sur sa vie et ses ouvrages. 5 tom. *Paris*, 1823–25. 8°. **1134**. d. **7–11**.

Without the "Notice," which was not published.

CABANIS (Pierre Jean Georges)

—— Corps législatif. Commission du Conseil des Cinq-Cents. Discours prononcé par Cabanis . . . Séance du 3 nivôse an 8. [On the events of 19 brumaire and the establishment of the Consulate.] pp. 4. *Paris*, an 8 [1799/1800]. 8°. F.R. **93**. (**5**.)

—— Corps législatif. Commission du Conseil des Cinq-Cents. Quelques considérations sur l'organisation sociale en général, et particulièrement sur la nouvelle constitution . . . Séance du 25 frimaire an 8. pp. 48. *Paris*, an 8 [1799]. 8°. F. **799**. (**2**.)

—— Corps législatif. Conseil des Cinq-Cents. Discours prononcé . . . à la suite du rapport de la Commission des sept. [On the proposal of the Commission to remove the Corps législatif to St. Cloud and to invest Buonaparte with the command of the Army.] pp. 10. *Saint-Cloud*, an 8 [1799]. 8°. F. **781**. (**13**.)

—— Corps législatif. Conseil des Cinq-Cents. Discours prononcé . . . sur le message du Conseil des Anciens, relatif aux journaux calomniateurs des premières autorités. pp. 6. *Paris*, an 7 [1799]. 8°. F. **524**. (**15**.)

—— [Another copy.] F. **781**. (**14**.)

—— Coup d'œil sur les révolutions et sur la réforme de la médecine. pp. xii. 438. *Paris*, 1804. 8°. **550**. c. **22**.

—— Sketch of the Revolutions of Medical Science, and views relating to its reform . . . Translated . . . with notes, by A. Henderson. pp. xii. 420. *J. Johnson: London*, 1806. 8°. **775**. h. **25**.

—— Du degré de certitude de la médecine. pp. 144. *Paris*, 1798. 8°. **1172**. i. **10**. (**1**.)

—— Nouvelle édition . . . augmentée de plusieurs autres écrits du même auteur. pp. 537. *Paris*, 1803. 8°. **774**. g. **17**.

—— El Grado de certidumbre de la medicina. Memoria . . . Traducida al castellano de la última edicion publicada en . . . 1803. Por el Doctor Don Luis Guarnerio y Allavenia. [With a dedication by Teresa Gil de Guarnerio]. pp. 184. *Madrid*, 1816. 16°. **7680**. a. **1**.

—— Journal de la maladie et de la mort d'Honoré Gabriel Victor Riquetti Mirabeau. pp. 66. *Paris*, 1791. 8°. F. **281**. (**9**.)

—— [Another copy.] **10660**. c. **17**.

—— [Another copy.] **113**. d. **25**.

—— *See* Duchenne (H.) La Dernière maladie de G. H. Riquetti, Cte de Mirabeau . . . D'après le journal de Cabanis, *etc.* [1890.] 8°. **07305**. e. **23**. (**1**.)

—— Opinion . . . sur les réunions s'occupant d'objets politiques. pp. 16. [*Paris*, 1798.] 8°. T. **358**. (**13**.)

—— Rapports du physique et du moral de l'homme . . . précédés d'une table analytique, par M. le comte Destutt de Tracy, et suivis d'une table alphabétique. Nouvelle édition, augmentée d'une notice sur la vie de l'auteur. 3 tom. *Paris*, 1824. 12°. **8464**. a. **14**.

—— Rapports du physique et du moral de l'homme. 2 tom. *Paris*, 1830. 8°. **8471**. g. **64**.

—— *See* Ladevi-Roche (P. J.) Réponse au livre de Cabanis sur les Rapports du physique et du moral, *etc.* 1863. 8°. **8465**. cc. **40**. (**3**.)

CABANIS (Pierre Jean Georges)

—— Serment d'un médecin, *etc.* [In verse.] *See* Révélations. Les Révélations indiscrètes du XVIIIe siècle; par le cardinal de Bernis . . . Cabanis, *etc.* 1814. 12°. **12352. aa. 38.**

—— Cabanis. Choix de textes et introduction par Georges Poyer . . . 10 gravures et portraits. pp. 222. *Paris*, [1910.] 8°. [*Les Grands philosophes français et étrangers.*] **8459. aa. 14/10.**

CABANIS (Richard Schmidt) *See* Schmidt Cabanis.

CABANISS (Allen)

—— Agobard of Lyons, Churchman and Critic. pp. xii. 137. *Syracuse University Press: [Syracuse, N.Y.,]* [1953.] 8°. **4856. l. 21.**

—— Amalarius of Metz. [With a list of his works.] *North-Holland Publishing Co.: Amsterdam*, 1954. 8°. **4888. m. 13**

CABANNE (Georges) Le Rêve de Ferry. (Les nouvelles némésis. 2me épisode.) [In verse.] pp. 15. *Bordeaux*, 1888. 12°. **1883.c.17.(150.)**

CABANNES (Bernard Augustin de) *Baron de Cauna.* Armorial des Landes, *etc.* 3 tom. *Bordeaux*, 1863–69. 8°. **9904. h. 28.**

—— Clergé et noblesse des Landes. Armorial. Deuxième edition. pp. iv. 118. *Bordeaux*, 1864. 8°. **9904. cc. 45.**

—— Souvenir du Congrès scientifique tenu à Pau le 31 mars 1873. Réponses à diverses questions. pp. xiii. 177. *Bordeaux*, 1874. 8°. **8706. c. 22.**

CABANNES (G.)

—— Le Général Lasserre, 1852–1939. [With a portrait.] pp. 201. *Mont-de-Marsan*, 1939. 8°. **010655. cc. 29.**

CABANNES (Marthe) *See* Alizette (M. d')

CABANOCH (Poncio) Prontuario juridico y elementos prácticos para ejercer el arte de edificar sin agravio del vecino. *See* Barcelona. Constituciones de Sanctacilia, *etc.* 1857. 8°. **5385. a. 7.**

CABANON (Bernard) Examen du projet de loi sur les céréales, présenté à la Chambre des Députés, le 17 octobre 1831. pp. 8. *Paris*, 1831. 8°. **712. g. 31. (6.)**

CABANTOUS (J. Amans) Quelques considérations sur la pleurésie gastro-bilieuse, *etc.* [A thesis.] pp. 18. *Montpellier*, an XII [1803]. 4°. **1180. e. 5. (25.)**

CABANTOUS (Louis Pierre François) De l'influence des institutions administratives sur le caractère et la destinée des peuples. *See* Paris.—*Comité* ~~*Impérial*~~ *des Travaux Historiques et* Scientifiques. Mémoires . . . Histoire, *etc.* 1863. 8°. **Ac. 440.**

—— Discours. *See* Saudbreuil (L.) Discours de réception à l'Académie des Sciences . . . d'Aix . . . Discours de M. Cabantous . . . en réponse au récipiendaire. 1861. 8°. **5405. bb. 44.**

CABANTOUS (Marius) Marguerite d'Angoulême et les débuts de la Réforme. Étude historique, *etc.* pp. 130. *Montauban*, 1898. 8°. **010663. l. 19.**

CABANTOUS (Paulin Léon) Diverses manifestations et étiologie du rhumatisme cérébral. [A thesis.] pp. 64. *Montpellier*, 1866. 4°. **7379. g. 4. (7.)**

CABANY (E. Saint Maurice) *See* Saint Maurice Cabany.

CABANYES (Manuel de)

Full name: Manuel de Cabanyes y Ballester.

—— *See* Oyuela (C.) Estudio sobre la vida y escritos del eminente poeta catalan Manuel de Cabanyes. 1881. 8°. **011850. f. 10. (1**

—— *See* Peers (Edgar A.) Les Poesies de Manuel de Cabanyes, *etc.* [With a portrait.] 1933. 8°. **11857. aa. 4**

—— Poesies completes de Manuel de Cabanyes. Preludis de la meva lira. Càntic nupcial. Poesies pòstumes. Versi pròleg i anotació de Alfons Maseres. pp. 102. *Barcelon* [c. 1935.] 8°. **11453. e. 2** *Col·lecció popular Barcino.* vol. 114.

—— El Poeta Cabanyes. Notas biográficas. "Preludios de mi lira" y otros poesías. Documentos. [Edited by Puig y Puig. With portraits.] pp. 167. *Barcelon* 1927. 8°. **10631. i. 4**

—— Producciones escogidas de D. M. de Cabanyes. pp. 26 *Barcelona*, 1858. 8°. **12231. f.**

—— The Poems of M. de Cabanyes. Edited, with introduc tion, notes and bibliography, by E. Allison Peers. pp. vii. 151. *University Press: Manchester Longmans & Co.: London*, 1923. 8°. [*Spanish Texts an Studies.*] **W.P. 6502/**

CABAR FEIDH. *See* England.—*Army.*—*Infantry.*—*Seaforth Highlanders.*

CABARD (Pierre Victor) Quelques considérations su les maladies du sein, et en particulier du cancer de ce organe. pp. 40. *Paris*, 1859. 4°. [*Collection des thèse soutenues à la Faculté de Médecine de Paris.* An 1859 tom. 3.] **7373. b. 15**

CABARET. Cabaret. A film play. [The foreword signed G. R. F., i.e. Giorgio R. Foa.] 1936. fol. *See* F., G. R. **11795. tt. 5**

CABARET GIRL. A Cabaret Girl tells her Life Story pp. 256. *Macfadden Publications: New York*, 1923. 8° [*True Story Series.* no. 1.] **012619.a.2/1**

CABARET (Jean) *d'Orronville.* Histoire de la vie, faict heroiques, et voyages de . . . Louys, III. Duc de Bourbon, *etc.* [Edited by J. Masson.] pp. 409. *F. Huey: Paris*, 1612. 8°. **G. 1464**

—— [Another edition.] Histoire de la vie de Louis, du troisième de Bourbon. 1838. *See* Panthéon. Panthéon littéraire. (Choix de chroniques et mémoires.) 1835, *etc.* 8°. **12200.p.1/3**

—— [Another edition.] La Chronique du bon duc Loys de Bourbon. Publiée . . . par A.-M. Chazaud. pp. xxix. 374. 1876. 8°. *See* Paris.—*Société de l'Histoire de France.* **Ac. 6884/5**

CABARET (Justine) called *Mademoiselle de Chantilly* [Correspondence with Count Moritz of Saxony.] *See* Meusnier ( ) *Citoyen.* Manuscrit trouvé à la Bastille, concernant deux lettres-de-cachet lâchées contre Mademoiselle de Chantilly et M. Favart, par le maréchal de Saxe. 1789. 8°. **935. h. 2**

—— [Another edition.] *See* Meusnier ( ) *Citoyen.* Manuscrit trouvé à la Bastille concernant les lettres de cachet lancées contre Mademoiselle de Chantilly et M. Favart par le maréchal de Saxe. 1768 [1868]. 8°. **935. e. 2**

CABARET BASSE MAISON (Philibert Julien) Propositions et réflexions sur divers points de médecine et de chirurgie ; thèse, *etc.* pp. 24. *Paris,* 1833. 4°. **1184.** e. **14.** (**31.**)

CABARET D'ORRONVILLE (Jean) *See* Cabaret (J.) *d'Orronville.*

CABARET-DUPATY (J. R. Th.) *See* Jouvency (J.) Appendix de diis et heroibus . . . Recensuit vocabulorumque indicem emendavit ac pæne renovavit J. R. J. Cabaret-Dupaty. 1845. 12°. **4504.** a. **39.**

—— *See* Lhomond (C. F.) Epitome historiæ sacræ . . . Hanc editionem annotationibus gallicis auctam . . . recensuit J. R. T. Cabaret-Dupaty. 1843. 12°. **3128.** aa. **15.**

—— *See* Ovidius Naso (P.) [*Metamorphoses.—Latin and French.*] Ovide. Les Métamorphoses; traduction française de Gros, refondue avec le plus grand soin par M. Cabaret-Dupaty, *etc.* 1862. 12°. **11385.** aa. **27.**

—— *See* Palladius Rutilius Taurus Aemilianus. L'Économie rurale . . . Traduction nouvelle par Cabaret-Dupaty. 1843. 8°. **11306.** k. **29.**

—— *See* Seneca (L. A.) [*Works.—Latin and French.*] Œuvres complètes, *etc.* (tom. 2. Consolation à Helvie. Traduction nouvelle par M. Cabaret-Dupaty.) [1826, *etc.*] 8°. **11306.** i. **2.**

—— *See* Virgilius Maro (P.) [*Works.—French.*] Œuvres complètes . . . Traduites . . . par T. Cabaret-Dupaty. 1872. 8°. **11355.** bb. **11.**

—— —— 1892. 8°. **11375.** ee. **29.**

—— Poetæ minores. Sabinus, Calpurnius, Gratius Faliscus, Nemesianus, Valerius Cato, Vestritius Spurinna, Lupercus Servastus, Arborius, Pentadius, Eucheria, Pervigilium Veneris. Traductions nouvelles par M. Cabaret-Dupaty. [With the Latin text.] pp. 419. *Paris,* 1842. 8°. [*Bibliothèque latine-française.* sér. 2.] **11306.** k. **31.**
Inserted is a leaf bearing part of the translation of Sabinus, possibly in the handwriting of the translator.

CABARET-DUPATY (Th.) *See* Cabaret-Dupaty (J. R. T.)

CABARGA (Guillermo Durante de) *See* Durante de Cabarga.

CABARRUS, Emilio Fernandez de Angulo, *Count de See* Fernandez de Angulo.

CABARRUS (Francisco de) *Count.* Cartas sobre los obstáculos que la naturaleza, la opinión y las leyes oponen á la felicidad pública : escritas . . . al Señor Don Gaspar de Jovellanos, y precedidas de otra al Príncipe de la Paz. (Memoria al Rey . . . Carlos iii. para la extincion de la deuda nacional y arreglo de contribuciones en 1783.) 2 pt. *Vitoria,* 1808. 4°. **1390.** e. **22.**

—— Tercera edicion. pp. 366. *Madrid,* 1820. 8°. **1139.** b. **12.**

—— [Another copy.] **1391.** a. **12.**

—— Nueva edición, corregido el texto, *etc.* [With a biographical sketch by E. Ovejero y Maury.] pp. 248. *Madrid,* 1933. 8°. **8004.** ee. **29.**

—— Copia della carta é instruccion á los Diputados generales de la Provincia de Guipuzcoa, Vitoria 6 Sept. 1808. [*Vittoria ?* 1808.] *s. sh.* fol. **T. 18*.** (**64.**)

CABARRUS (Francisco de) *Count.*

—— Elogio de Carlos iii, Rey de España y de las Indias, leido en la Junta General de la Real Sociedad Económica de Madrid de 25 de julio de 1789, *etc.* pp. xlix. *Madrid,* 1789. 4°. **12301.** e. **2.** (**9.**)

—— Elogio del excelentísimo Señor Conde Gausa, *etc.* [With a portrait after Goya.] pp. 97. *Madrid,* 1786. 4°. **9180.** e. **4.** (**1.**)

CABARRUS (Gaston) La Marquise des Escombes. pp. 275. *Paris,* 1885. 12°. **12511.** s. **8.**

CABARRUS (J. A. E.) Essai sur la pneumonie. Tribut académique, *etc.* pp. 27. *Montpellier,* 1827. 4°. **1181.** d. **11.** (**14.**)

CABARRÚS, afterwards **TALLIEN** (Jeanne Marie Ignace Thérésia) *See* Riquet (J. M. I. T. de) *Princess de Chimay.*

CABART (C. F.) *of Vicel.* Essai sur la paralysie, *etc.* [A thesis.] pp. 35. *Paris,* 1815. 4°. **1183.** c. **9.** (**24.**)

CABART (Charles François) Leçons de physique et de chimie . . . Ouvrage complété d'après le dernier programme officiel d'admission à l'École polytechnique et à l'École de Saint-Cyr. [With plates.] 2 pt. *Paris,* 1853. 8°. **8707.** e. **3.**

CABART-DANNEVILLE (Charles Maurice) La Défense de nos côtes. pp. 402. *Paris,* 1895. 8°. **8824.** bbb. **36.**

—— Les Poudres de la guerre et de la marine en France et à l'étranger. pp. vii. 391. *Paris, Nancy,* 1913. 8°. **08821.** de. **45.**

CABASILAS (Nicolaus) *Archbishop of Thessalonica. See* Nicholas [Cabasilas], *Archbishop of Thessalonica.*

CABASILAS (Nilus) *Archbishop of Thessalonica. See* Nilus [Cabasilas], *Metropolitan of Thessalonica.*

CABASILAS (Simeon) *See* Kabasilas (Sumeon)

CABASSE (Charles Jules) Relation médico-chirurgicale de la captivité des prisonniers français chez les Arabes, 1846. pp. 98. *Paris,* 1848. 4°. [*Collection des thèses soutenues à la Faculté de Médecine de Paris.* An 1848. tom. 2.] **7372.** b. **5.**

CABASSE (Prosper) Essais historiques sur le Parlement de Provence, depuis son origine jusqu'à sa suppression, 1501–1770. 3 tom. *Paris,* 1826. 8°. **1128.** e. **27.**

CABASSI (Eustachio) [Letters to G. Tiraboschi. With a biography of Cabassi.] *Ital.* 1894, 95. *See* Tiraboschi (G.) Carteggio fra l'ab. Girolamo Tiraboschi e l'avv. E. Cabassi, *etc.* 1894, *etc.* 8°. [*Memorie storiche e documenti sulla città e sull'antico principato di Carpi.* vol. 6.] Ac. **6502.**

CABASSIUS (Amandus) *See* Quiqueranus Bellojocanus (P.) *Bishop of Senez.* Petri Quiquerani . . . de laudibus Prouinciæ libri. [The editor's dedication signed: A. Cabassius.] 1551. fol. **181.** d. **2.**

CABASSO (Victor)

—— Sur diverses souches de bacilles acido-résistants paratuberculeux saprophytes . . . Thèse, *etc.* pp. 71. *Tunis,* 1941. 8°. **07561.** k. **73.**

CABASSU (Henri)

—— *See* Cabassu (J.) and (H.) Les Chiens, *etc.* 1939. 8°. **07295.** aa. **54.**

CABASSU (Jean) and **CABASSU** (Henri)

—— Les Chiens, *etc.* pp. 187. *Paris*, 1939. 8°. **07295.** aa. **54.**

CABASSUTIUS (Joannes) P. Joannis Cabassutii . . . De discrimine inter episcopos, & presbyteros jam inde ab ipsis Ecclesiae primordiis. *See* Mainz.—*Sodalitas Academica Major Moguntina.* Antiquitates Christianorum, *etc.* 1769. 8°. **1364.** a. **14.**

—— Juris canonici theoria et praxis . . . Editio postrema ab ipso authore recognita & aucta. pp. 600. *Lugduni*, 1709. 4°. **496.** g. **5.**

—— [Another edition.] Ex editione postrema ab ipso authore recognita et aucta. 2 tom. *Ex typ. Richardi Coyne: Dublinii*, 1824. 8°. **5155.** bb. **22.**

—— Notitia conciliorum Sanctæ Ecclesiæ, in qua elucidantur . . . tùm sacri canones, tùm veteres, nouique Ecclesiæ ritus, tùm præcipuæ partes ecclesiasticæ historiæ, *etc.* pp. 508. *Apud A. Bortolum: Venetiis*, 1692. 8°. **1365.** b. **21.**

—— [Another edition.] Accesserunt dissertationes duæ: una doctissimi P. Joan. Mabillon De critica & regulis in ipsa servandis. (Ex tractatu De studiis monasticis . . . Part. ii. cap. xiii.) Altera auctoris anonymi De canonum collectione Isidori, ac decretalibus primorum sæculorum pontificibus adscriptis. Editio nova . . . recognita & indice chronologico Romanorum Pontificum locupletata. pp. 578. *Lovanii*, 1776. 8°. **5018.** a. **17.**

—— R. P. Joannis Cabassutii . . . Notitia ecclesiastica historiarum, conciliorum, & canonum invicem collatorum veterumque juxta, ac recentiorum Ecclesiæ rituum . . . secundum cujusque sæculi seriem, accurate digesta. Editio secunda, ab ipso authore plurimum aucta, & quinque indicibus locupletata, *etc.* pp. 690. *Ex officina Anissoniana, J. Posuel, & C. Rigaud: Lugduni* 1685. fol. **493.** k. **16.**

—— Editio tertia . . . quinque indicibus locupletata, *etc.* pp. 680. *Lugduni*, 1702. fol. **493.** k. **14.**

—— [Another edition.] Synopsis conciliorum seu notitia ecclesiastica historiarum conciliorum et canonum inter se collatorum . . . Editio nova. [The editor's preface signed: A. D. Z.] 3 tom. *Paris*, 1838. 8°. **1125.** e. **28–30.**

—— *See* Eusebius, *Pamphili, Bishop of Caesarea in Palestine.* [*Historia Ecclesiastica.—English.*] The History of the Church . . . In this second edition are added, i. Two maps . . . iv. A chronological index of the Popes and Emperors, taken from Cabassutius [i.e. from his " Notitia ecclesiastica "]. 1709, *etc.* fol. **4531.** h. **5.**

CABAT (Louis) and **FANNING** (George)

—— A New Approach to Spanish, *etc.* *American Book Co.: New York*, [1942– .] 8°. W.P. **11556.**

CABATON (Antoine) *See* Aymonier (E. F.) and Cabaton (A.) Dictionnaire čam-français. 1906. 8°. [*Publications de l'École Française d'Extrême-Orient.* vol. 7.] Ac. **8814.** e.

CABATON (Antoine)

—— *See* Quiroga de San Antonio (G.) Brève et véridiq[ue] relation des évènements du Cambodge . . . Nouvel[le] édition . . . Avec une traduction et des notes par [A.] Cabaton. 1914. 8°. [*Documents historiques et gé[o]graphiques relatifs à l'Indochine.* tom. 2.] **09055.** d. **5**

—— Catalogue sommaire des manuscrits indiens, indo-chin[ois] & malayo-polynésiens. pp. ii. 319. 1912. 8°. *See* Par[is] —*Bibliothèque Nationale.* [*Manuscrits.*] **11899.** d. **3**

—— Catalogue sommaire des manuscrits sanscrits et pāl[is] 2 fasc. 1907, 08. 8°. *See* Paris.—*Bibliothèque Nationa[le]* [*Manuscrits.*] **11908.** c. **5**

—— Les Indes néerlandaises. [With a map.] pp. viii. 382 *Paris*, 1910. 8°. **010058.** ff. **3**

—— Java, Sumatra, and the other islands of the Dutch Ea[st] Indies . . . Translated and with a preface by Berna[rd] Miall. With a map and 47 illustrations. pp. xvi. 376. *T. Fisher Unwin: London, Leipsic*, 1911. 8°. **010058.** ff. **3**

—— Nouvelles recherches sur les Chams. [With plate[s.]] pp. 215. *Paris*, 1901. 8°. [*Publications de l'Éc[ole] Française d'Extrême-Orient.* vol. 2.] Ac. **8814.**

CABATON (M. A. Roland) *See* Roland-Cabaton.

CABAUD (Pierre Alexandre) Quelques considératio[ns] sur l'hépatite et les abcès du foie. Thèse, *etc.* pp. 30. *Montpellier*, 1851. 4°. **7379.** b. 4. (

CABAZA (Berta)

—— *See* Cerda (G.) Vocabulario español de Texas. P[or] G. Cerda, B. Cabaza, *etc.* 1953. 8°. **12944.** h.

CABBAGE HUSBANDRY. Cabbage and Clover Hu[s]bandry. Description of, and directions for cultivati[ng] several curious plants not generally known in Englan[d]. Particularly Hungarian clover, Swedish cabbage, sever[al] new grasses, *etc.* pp. 23. *To be had at Gregg's Coff[ee] House: York-Street, Covent Garden* [*London*], [1774 ?] 8 **116.** k. **2**

CABBALA. *See* Cabala.

CABBEDO (Jorge de) *See* Cabedo.

CABBELJAU (Jonas) *See* Cabeljau.

CABBY, *pseud.* [i.e. W. B. Dean.] Notorious Bushrange[rs] of Tasmania. By Cabby. pp. 166. " *Daily Telegraph* " *Launceston*, 1891. 8°. **6057.** a. **3**

CABÉ (P. Victor) Historique des courses de chevau[x] pp. 427. *Pau*, 1900. 18°. **07905.** h. **4**

CABEÇA (Juan) *See* Cabezas (J.) *Dramatist.*

CABEÇA (Maria de la) *See* Mary [de la Cabeza], *Sai[nt]* *etc.*

CABEÇA DE VACA (Alvar Nuñez) *See* Nuñez Cabe[ça] de Vaca.

CABEÇA DE VACA (Luis de Paracuellos) *See* Par[a]cuellos Cabeça de Vaca.

CABEÇA DE VACA (Pedro de Escobar) *See* Escob[ar] Cabeça de Vaca.

CABEÇAS (Juan) *See* Cabezas (J.) *Calificador del Sa[nto] Oficio.*

CABEDIUS (Antonius) [Latin poems, with a biographi[cal] notice.] *See* Reys (A. dos) Corpus illustrium poetaru[m] lusitanorum, *etc.* tom. 1. 1745, *etc.* 4°. **78.** h.

CABEDIUS (MICHAEL) *See* ARISTOPHANES, *the Poet.* [*Plutus.—Latin.*] Plutus Aristophanis. Comœdia in Latinum conuersa sermonem, authore M. Cabedio. 1547. 8°. **11705. a. 10.**

—— [Latin poems, with a biographical notice.] *See* REYS (A. dos) Corpus illustrium poetarum lusitanorum, *etc.* tom. 1. 1745, *etc.* 4°. **78. h. 1.**

CABEDO (JORGE DE) *See* PORTUGAL. [*Collections of Laws, etc.*] Errata da noua Recopilaçam das Leis, e Ordenações desto Reyno de Portugal [followed by the text of the laws]: com algũas outras aduertencias necessarias, & substanciaes. Feito pello Doutor I. de Cabedo. 1603. fol. **503. h. 12.**

—— *See* PORTUGAL.—*Casa da Supplicação.* Practicarum observationum sive decisionum Supremi Senatus Regni Lusitanniae pars secunda . . . authore G. de Cabedo. 1620. fol. **5383. gg. 9.**

—— *See* PORTUGAL.—*Casa da Supplicação.* Practicarum observationum sive decisionum Supremi Senatus Regni Lusitaniæ. pars prima (secunda) . . . Auctore G. de Cabedo. 1635. fol. **502. g. 12.**

CABEDO (MANUEL BRESCANÉ Y) *See* BRESCANÉ Y CABEDO.

CABEEN (CHARLES WILLIAM) L'Influence de Giambattista Marino sur la littérature française dans la première moitié du XVIIe siècle. Thèse, *etc.* pp. ix. 163. *Grenoble,* 1904. 8°. **11850. tt. 20.**

CABEEN (DAVID CLARK)

—— *See* SARDOU (V.) and MOREAU (E.) *Dramatist.* Madame Sans-Gêne . . . Edited with introduction, notes, and vocabulary by D. C. Cabeen. 1935. 8°. **20002. e. 44.**

—— A Critical Bibliography of French Literature. D. C. Cabeen general editor, *etc.*

1. The Mediaeval Period. Edited by Urban T. Holmes. pp. xxv. 256. 1947.

2. The Sixteenth Century. Edited by Alexander H. Schutz. pp. xxxii. 365. 1956.

4. The Eighteenth Century. Edited by George R. Havens . . . Donald F. Bond. pp. xxx. 411. 1951.

Syracuse University Press: [*Syracuse,*] 1947– . 8°. BB.G. d. 4.

Vol. 2, 4 were printed in Belgium.

—— Montesquieu. A bibliography. 1947. *See* NEW YORK.—*New York Public Library.* Bulletin, *etc.* vol. 51. no. 6–10. 1897, *etc.* 8°. P.P. **6491.** hm.

—— Montesquieu: a bibliography. (Reprinted with revisions and additions from the Bulletin of the New York Public Library.) pp. 87. 1947. 8°. *See* NEW YORK.—*New York Public Library.* **11926. d. 30.**

CABEI (GIULIO CESARE) Imagine dell'huomo, *etc.* pp. 168. *Appresso D. & G. B. Guerra: Venetia,* 1576. 8°. **8406. c. 23.**

—— Ornamenti della Gentildonna Vedoua. Opera . . . nella quale ordinatamente si tratta di tutte le cose necessarie allo stato vedouile, *etc.* pp. 133. *Appresso C. Zanetti: Venetia,* 1574. 8°. **527. f. 9.**

—— Prima parte delle Rime di M. Giulio Cesare Cabei. Nuouamente da lui reuiste & corrette. Aggiuntaui la seconda parte. pp. 369. *Presso E. Regazzola: Vinegia,* 1573. 12°. **1070. a. 13.**

CABEI (GIULIO CESARE)

—— Quarta et ultima parte delle Rime di M. Giulio Cesare Cabei. ff. 32. *Appresso G. Angelieri: Venetia,* 1575. 8°. **1063. d. 12. (1.)**

CABELIAU (PETRUS) *See* CABELJAUW.

CABELIAUW (PETRUS) *See* CABELJAUW.

CABELIAVIUS (JOHANNES) Iohannis Cabeliavii . . . Epistolarum centuria secunda, ad . . . Danielem Heinsium. Adjectum est insuper Corollarium epistolicum. pp. 231 [227]. *Typis I. Ockersovii: Hagæ Comitum,* 1631. 8°. **1084. g. 19.**

CABELIAVIUS (SAMUEL) Positiones philosophicæ miscellaneæ, *etc.* *Praes.* F. Burgersdijck. *Ex officina I. Elseviri: Lugduni Batavorum,* 1624. 4°. **534. c. 36. (48.)**

CABELJAU (JONAS) *See* OVIDIUS NASO (P.) [*Epistolae Heroïdum.—Dutch.*] Treurbrieven der blakende vorstinnen, *etc.* [Translated by J. Cabeljau.] 1657. 8°. **11385. b. 34.**

CABELJAUW (PETRUS) *See* WYNGAARD (B.) and CABELJAUW (P.) Klare, ende krachtige bewijs-redenen, thoonende dat de houder vande Leenbanck tot Leyden en oock alle andere banck-houders . . . niet en konnen, off behooren van't Heylige Avontmaal . . . gheweert te werden. Gestelt van . . . B. Wyngaarden . . . en P. Cabeliauw, *etc.* 1657. 4°. **T. 2257. (18.)**

—— Catholiick memory-boeck der gereformeerde, gestelt tegen het Roomsch-memory-boeck der Paus-gesinde . . . Zijnde een volkomen wederlegginghe van het Memory-boeck van Turano Vekiti, *etc.* 2 dl. *P. Leffen: Leyden,* 1661. 4°. **3925. k. 39.**
With an additional titlepage, engraved.

CABELL, *Family of.* *See* BROWN (Alexander) *American Historian.* The Cabells and their Kin, *etc.* 1895. 8°. **9914. r. 4.**

CABELL (BRANCH) *See* CABELL (James B.)

CABELL (ISA CARRINGTON) Seen from the Saddle [Sketches.] pp. vi. 161. *Harper & Bros.: New York,* 1893. 8°. **012330. de. 6.**

CABELL (JAMES BRANCH) *See* BRUSSEL (Isidore R.) A Bibliography of the Writings of James Branch Cabell, *etc.* [With a portrait.] 1932. 8°. **11928.aa.13/11.**

—— *See* CLEVELAND, *Ohio.—Colophon Club.* A Round-Table in Poictesme. A symposium, *etc.* [In appreciation of J. B. Cabell.] 1924. 8°. **011851. d. 99.**

—— *See* HOLT (Guy) A Bibliography of the Writings of James Branch Cabell. [With a portrait.] 1924. 8°. **11928.aa.13/3.**

—— *See* VAN DOREN (Carl C.) James Branch Cabell. 1926. 8°. **011840. b. 46.**

—— Beyond Life. Dizain des demiurges. [Essays.] pp. 312. *John Lane: London,* 1925. 8°. **012352. g. 76.**

—— The Certain Hour—Dizain des poëtes. [Tales.] pp. 253. *McBride, Nast & Co.: London,* 1917. 8°. NN. **4638.**

—— [Another edition.] pp. 254. *John Lane: London,* 1931. 8°. A.N. **784.**

—— Chivalry . . . Illustrated. pp. vi. 223. *Harper & Bros.: New York & London,* 1909. 8°. **012703. g. 26.**

CABELL (James Branch)

—— [Another edition.] pp. xv. 281. *John Lane: London*, 1928. 8°. **12714. bbb. 22.**

—— The Cords of Vanity. pp. xx. 341. *Doubleday, Page & Co.: London; New York* printed, 1909. 8°. **012705. aaa. 46.**

—— [Another copy, with a different titlepage.] *Hutchinson & Co.: London; New York* printed, 1909. 8°. **012705. bbb. 11.**

—— [Another edition.] pp. xvi. 332. *John Lane: London*, 1925. 8°. **12709. dd. 13.**

—— The Cream of the Jest. A comedy of evasions, *etc.* pp. xii. 250. *John Lane: London; printed in U.S.A.*, 1923. 8°. **NN. 8675.**

—— [Another edition.] Illustrated by Frank C. Papé. pp. xviii. 243. *John Lane: London; printed in U.S.A.*, 1927. 8°. **012630. m. 45.**

—— The Devil's Own Dear Son. (A comedy of the fatted calf.) pp. 198. *Bodley Head: London*, 1950. 8°. **12730. ee. 22.**

—— Domnei, *etc.* *See* infra: The Soul of Melicent.

—— The Eagle's Shadow, *etc.* pp. xi. 256. *Wm. Heinemann: London; New York* printed, 1904. 8°. **012707. bb. 10.**

—— [Another issue.] *Wm. Heinemann: London; Norwood, Mass.* printed, 1904. 8°. **012707. c. 44.**

—— Figures of Earth. A comedy of appearances. pp. xv. 288. *John Lane: London*, 1921. 8°. **NN. 7579.**

—— [Another edition.] With illustrations by Frank C. Papé. pp. xvii. 257. *John Lane: London*, 1925. 8°. **012643. gg. 8.**

—— The First American Gentleman, *etc.* [A novel.] pp. 196. *John Lane: London*, 1942. 8°. **12725. bb. 8.**

—— Gallantry. Dizain des fêtes galantes, *etc.* pp. xxii. 342. *John Lane: London*, 1928. 8°. **12703. aa. 45.**

—— Hamlet had an Uncle. A comedy of honour. pp. xvi. 269. *John Lane: London*, 1940. 8°. **12722. b. 4.**

—— The High Place. A comedy of disenchantment. pp. 309. *John Lane: London*, 1923. 8°. **012705. aaa. 51.**

—— Jurgen. A comedy of justice . . . With illustrations & decorations by Frank C. Papé, *etc.* pp. xvii. 325. *John Lane: London*, 1921. 8°. **12705. k. 36.**

—— [Another edition.] pp. xv. 325. *John Lane: London*, 1923. 8°. **12702. d. 12.**

—— [Another edition.] pp. xv. 325. *John Lane: London*, 1932. 8°. [*Week-End Library.*] **12211. a. 1/40.**
A reduced facsimile, with a different titlepage, of the 1923 *edition.*

—— [A reissue.] *London*, 1938. 8°. [*Bodley Head Library.*] **012213.t.6/13.**

—— Jurgen. pp. 247. *Harmondsworth*, 1940. 8°. [*Penguin Books.* no. 268.] **12208. a. 1/268.**

—— Jurgen . . . With wood engravings by John Buckland Wright. pp. 349. *Golden Cockerel Press: London*, 1949. 8°. **C. 99. i. 31.**
No. 80 *of an edition of* 100 *specially bound copies.*

CABELL (James Branch)

—— The King was in his Counting House. A comedy of common sense. (Reprinted.) pp. xvi. 304. *John Lane: London*, 1939. 8°. **12720. cc. 13.**

—— Ladies and Gentlemen. A parcel of reconsiderations. pp. x. 304. *R. M. McBride & Co.: New York*, 1934. 8°. **010885. ff. 17.**

—— The Line of Love . . . Illustrated in color by Howard Pyle. pp. xi. 290. *Harper & Bros.: New York & London*, 1905. 8°. **012703. g. 5.**

—— [Another edition.] With an introduction by H. L. Mencken. pp. xv. 261. *John Lane: London*, 1929. 8°. **12715. aaa. 16.**

—— The Rivet in Grandfather's Neck. A comedy of limitations. pp. 368. *McBride, Nast & Co.: London & New York; printed in U.S.A.*, 1916. 8°. **NN. 3584.**

—— [Another edition.] pp. 368. *John Lane: London*, 1924. 8°. **12708. aaa. 16.**

—— The Silver Stallion. pp. xv. 312. *John Lane: London*, 1926. 8°. **12711. aa. 3.**

—— [Another edition.] Illustrated by Frank C. Papé. pp. xxv. 359. *John Lane: London*, 1928. 8°. **012603. bb. 9.**

—— Smire. An acceptance in the third person. [A novel.] pp. xi. 311. *Doubleday, Doran & Co.: Garden City, N.Y.*, 1937. 8°. **A.N. 3566.**

—— Some of Us. An essay in epitaphs. pp. 135. *R. M. McBride & Co.: New York*, 1930. 8°. **20016. d. 2.**

—— Something about Eve . . . A comedy of fig leaves. pp. ix. 364. *R. M. McBride & Co.: New York*, 1927. 8°. **12713. b. 8.**

—— [Another edition.] Illustrated by Frank C. Papé. pp. xxi. 376. *John Lane: London; printed in U.S.A.*, [1929.] 8°. **012603. bb. 16.**

—— The Soul of Melicent . . . [Based on an episode in the Roman de Lusignan.] Illustrated in colour by Howard Pyle. pp. 216. *F. A. Stokes Co.: New York*, 1913. 8°. **012703. f. 17.**

—— Domnei. A comedy of woman-worship, *etc.* [A revised edition of "The Soul of Melicent."] pp. viii. 218. *John Lane: London*, 1927. 8°. **12713. aa. 13.**

—— [Another edition.] Illustrated by Frank C. Papé. pp. xvii. 252. *John Lane: London; Norwood, Mass.* printed, 1930. 8°. **012604. d. 10.**

—— Special Delivery. A packet of replies [to imaginary correspondents]. pp. 272. *P. Allan & Co.: London*, [1934.] 8°. **012352. i. 66.**

—— Straws and Prayer-books. Dizain des diversions. pp. 302. *R. M. McBride & Co.: New York*, 1924. 8°. **012352. c. 32.**

—— [Another edition.] pp. 302. *John Lane: London*, 1926. 8°. **012352. c. 47.**

—— There were Two Pirates, *etc.* (A comedy of division.) pp. 127. *Bodley Head: London*, 1947. 8°. **12830. f. 18.**

—— [There were two Pirates.] Il y avait deux pirates . . . Traduction de Marguerite Yerta Méléra. *In:* Les Œuvres libres. Nouvelle série. no. 63. pp. 41–118. 1951. 8°. **12208.ee.288**

CABELL (JAMES BRANCH)

—— These Restless Heads. A trilogy of romantics, *etc.* pp. xiv. 253. *R. M. McBride & Co.: New York*, 1932. 8°. **12349. s. 29.**

—— The Way of Ecben. A comedietta . . . Decorations by Frank C. Papé. pp. viii. 209. *John Lane: London*, 1929. 8°. **A.N. 234.**

—— The White Robe. A saint's summary . . . With illustrations by Robert E. Locher. *John Lane: London; R. M. McBride & Co.: New York; Norwood, Mass.* printed, [1928.] 8°. **C. 98. h. 23.**

—— Between Dawn and Sunrise. Selections from the writings of J. B. Cabell. Chosen with an introduction & initiatory notes by John Macy. pp. xxvii. 291. *John Lane: London; printed in U.S.A.*, [1931.] 8°. **012295. c. 3.**

—— Preface to the Past. [Prefaces from the collected edition of the author's works.] pp. viii. 309. *R. M. McBride & Co.: New York*, [1936.] 8°. **12298. dd. 19.**

CABELL (JAMES BRANCH) and HANNA (ALFRED JACKSON)

—— The St. Johns. A parade of diversities . . . Illustrated by Doris Lee. pp. x. 324. *Farrar & Rinehart: New York, Toronto*, [1943.] 8°. **10413. ppp. 31.** *Part of the series "The Rivers of America."*

CABELL (JAMES LAWRENCE) The Testimony of Modern Science to the Unity of Mankind . . . With an introductory notice by James W. Alexander, D.D. Second edition revised. pp. 370. *R. Carter & Bros.: New York*, 1860. 8°. **10006. b. 7.**

CABELL (JOSEPH CARRINGTON) *See* JEFFERSON (Thomas) *President of the United States of America.* Early History of the University of Virginia, as contained in the letters of T. Jefferson and J. C. Cabell, *etc.* 1856. 8°. **8365. d. 22.**

CABELL (MICHAEL JOHN)

—— The Complex Ions formed by Thorium and Uranium with Complexones. [With graphs.] pp. 14. 4. *Harwell*, 1951. fol. [*Atomic Energy Research Establishment. Report.* no. C/R 813.] **B.S. 62/40. (1.)**

CABELL (NATHANIEL FRANCIS) A Contribution to the Bibliography of Agriculture in Virginia. Edited by Earl G. Swem . . . from the manuscript of N. F. Cabell. pp. 35. 1918. 8°. *See* RICHMOND, *Virginia.—Virginia State Library.* **11912. b. 5.**

—— The New Jerusalem, or New Christian Church. Freely adapted from the memoir of N. F. Cabell, by Elihu Rich. *See* ENCYCLOPAEDIAS. Cyclopædia of Religious Denominations, *etc.* 1853. 8°. **4503. aa. 19.**

—— Reply to Rev. Dr. Pond's "Swedenborgianism Reviewed" . . . With a preliminary letter, by R. K. Crallé. pp. 195. *John Allen: New York*, 1848. 8°. **3716. ccc. 28.**

—— Scripture Argument for the Trine. (On the order proper to the ministry of the New Church.) pp. 88. [1850 ?] 8°. **4139. g. 1. (21.)**

CABELL (WILLIAM LLOYD) *See* ENGLAND.—*Court of Chancery.* [*Reports of Cases.*] The Law Reports. Chancery Appeal Cases, *etc.* [1872–1875 reported by W. L. Cabell and others.] 1866, *etc.* 8°. **5807.a.7.**

—— *See* ENGLAND.—*Supreme Court of Judicature.—High Court of Justice.—Chancery Division.—[Reports of Cases.]* The Law Reports. Division I.—Chancery, *etc.* [1875–1906. Reported by W. L. Cabell and others.] 1876, *etc.* 8°. **Bar. A. 8.**

CABELL (WILLIAM LLOYD)

—— *See* ENGLAND.—*Court of Chancery.* [*Reports of Cases.*] The Law Reports. Equity Cases, *etc.* [1872–1875 reported by W. L. Cabell and others.] 1866, *etc.* 8°. **5807.a.6.**

—— *See* ENGLAND.—*Supreme Court of Judicature.—High Court of Justice.—King's Bench Division.—[Reports.]* The Law Reports. Queen's (King's) Bench Division, *etc.* [1884–1905. The bankruptcy cases removed to the Court of Appeal reported by W. L. Cabell.] 1876, *etc.* 8°. **Bar. A. 9.**

—— *See* ENGLAND.—*Supreme Court of Judicature.—High Court of Justice.—Probate, Divorce and Admiralty Division.* The Law Reports. Probate Division, *etc.* [1900–1905. The cases removed to the Court of Appeal reported by W. L. Cabell and others.] 1876, *etc.* 8°. **5807. a. 13.**

CABELLA (CESARE)

—— *See* CASANOVA (L.) Del diritto internazionale, lezioni . . . ordinate dall'avvocato C. Cabella, *etc.* 1858. 8°. **5326. c. 14.**

—— *See* RIDELLA (F.) La Vita e i tempi di Cesare Cabella. [With portraits.] 1923. 8°. **Ac. 6510. (2.)**

CABELLA (G. B.) Pagine voltresi. Contributo per la storia medioevale e contemporanea. pp. xxxix. 615. *Genova*, 1908. 8°. **10129. cc. 15.**

CABELLA (GIAN GAETANO)

—— Testamento politico di Mussolini. (Intervista con il Duce, 20 aprile XXIII [1945].) [A newspaper report. With facsimiles and a portrait.] pp. 48. *Roma*, 1948. 8°. **10635. a. 54.**

CABELL'ISM. Cabell'ism . . . Cabell'ism proposes a business settlement on the lines of national co-partnery between capital and labour . . . By a Progressive Labour Unionist T. B. I. (Travelled Business Imperialist), *etc.* pp. ix. 147. *Beds. Times Publishing Co.: Bedford*, [1910.] 8°. **08248. e. 18.**

CABELLO (BARTOLOMÉ) Cartas familiares, que D. B. Cabello . . . ha remitido á un amigo suyo. Carta 3. *Murcia*, 1788. 4°. **9180. dd. 5. (1.)** *Imperfect; wanting cartas* 1 *and* 2.

CABELLO (EMMANUEL) Pro publico totius philosophiæ examine in hac regia Divi Marci Academia subeundo sequentia ex historia philosophiæ, logica, physica . . . exponunt candidati, qui subscribuntur Carolini. D. E. Cabello . . . D. E. Calderon [and others], *etc.* (Clarissimo viro . . . J. A. Areche . . . D. Emmanuel Calderon D. O. C. Q. Elegia.) [*Lima*, 1787 ?] 8°. **731. f. 29. (4.)**

CABELLO (FRANCISCO) *Historian and Politician.* Historia de la Guerra última en Aragon y Valencia. Escrita por D. F. Cabello, D. F. Santa Cruz y D. R. M. Temprado. 2 tom. *Madrid*, 1845, 46. 8°. **1323. i. 2.**

CABELLO (FRANCISCO) *Teniente Coronel.* *See* BARRAQUER (J.) and CABELLO (F.) Memoria sobre la Compensacion general de los Errores en la Red Geodésica de España. 1874. 8°. **10160. ff. 3.**

CABELLO (GERARDO) Política Americana. Introducción de un libro inédito. pp. 193. *Lima*, 1892. 8°. **8179. a. 62.**

CABELLO (JOSÉ MARIA BREMON Y) *See* BREMON Y CABELLO.

CABELLO (JUAN) *See* FRANCISCO [Blanco], *de San Joseph.* Memorial dela Vida Christiana. Que compuso en lengua Tagala . . . Fray Francisco de San Joseph . . . Y lo traduxo en lengua Pampanga un Religioso dela Provincia del santissimo Nombre de Jesus de Philippinas del Orden de los Hermitaños de Nuestro Padre San Augustin (Fr. Francisco Coronel o Fray J. Cabello), *etc.* 1696. 4°. **Or. 72. b. 5.**

CABELLO (Nicolas) *See* Defoe (Daniel) Aventuras de Robinson Crusoé . . . Publicadas por Don N. Cabello. 1849. 8°. **12613.** gg. **7.**

CABELLO (Pedro M.) *See* Periodical Publications.—*Lima.* Guia politica, eclesiastica y militar del Peru . . . Por P. M. Cabello. 1865. 12°. **10480.** a. **16.**

CABELLO DE BALBOA (Miguel) Histoire du Pérou . . . Inédite. [Translated from the Spanish ms. by H. Ternaux-Compans.] pp. viii. 331. *Paris,* 1840. 8°. [*Voyages, relations et mémoires originaux pour servir à l'histoire de la découverte de l'Amérique.* vol. 15.] **1196.** i. **8.**

—— Historia del Perú bajo la dominación de los Incas . . . Anotaciones . . . por Horacio H. Urteaga. Biografía de Cabello Balboa, *etc.* [Translated from the French version of H. Ternaux-Compans, by Delia Rosa Romero.] pp. xv. 191. *Lima,* 1920. 8°. [*Colección de libros y documentos referentes a la historia del Perú.* ser. 2. tom. 2.] **9772.** ppp. **21.**

CABELLO DE CARBONERA (Mercedes) La Religion de la Humanidad. Carta al Señor D. J. Lagarrigue. [In reply to his pamphlet on the same subject.] pp. 62. *Lima,* 1893. 8°. **08464.** f. **9.** (2.)

CABELLOS (Pascual Garcia) *See* Garcia Cabellos.

CABELLO Y ASO (Luis) Ensayo de Estética de las Artes del Dibujo, *etc.* lib. 1. pp. xv. 140. *Madrid,* 1875. 8°. **7807.** k. **20.**

—— Estética de las Artes del Dibujo. La Arquitectura, su teoría estética expuesta . . . constituyendo un ensayo de teoría del arte. pp. xv. 400. *Madrid,* 1876. 8°. **07816.** i. **13.**

CABELLO Y LAPIEDRA (Luis María) La Batalla de San Quintín y su Influencia en las Artes Españolas. [With plates, including portraits.] pp. 192. *Madrid,* 1927. 8°. **9073.** aa. **28.**

—— La Casa Española. Consideraciones acerca de una arquitectura nacional . . . Con un prólogo del Barón de la Vega de Hoz. [With illustrations.] pp. xxiii. 167. 1920. 8°. *See* Madrid.—*Sociedad Española de Amigos del Arte.* **7815.** w. **16.**

—— Ciudad Rodrigo. Cuarenta y ocho ilustraciones con texto, *etc. Span., Fr. & Eng.* pp. 27. *Barcelona,* [1916.] 16°. [*El Arte en España.* no. 13.] **7801.a.11/13.**

—— España Artística y Monumental. La Capilla del Relator ó del Oidor de la parroquia de Santa María la Mayor en la ciudad de Alcalá de Henares . . . Fototipias de Hauser y Menet, *etc.* pp. 36. *Madrid,* 1905. 8°. **7814.** g. **16.**

—— González Brabo, el Político Audaz, *etc.* [With portraits.] pp. 120. *Madrid,* 1934. 8°. **20002.** g. **21.**

CABERA (Pedro Pedraza y) *See* Pedraza y Cabera.

CABERO (Gerónymo Ignacio) Oracion funebre, que en las . . . exequias, que la . . . ciudad de Cadiz, dedicò . . . á la . . . memoria del Sr D. Phelipe v. Rey de las Españas, dixo . . . Don G. I. Cabero. pp. 80. *Cadiz,* [1746.] 4°. **4865.** bbb. **15.** (1.)

CABESTAING (Guillaume de) [Poems.] *See* Mahn (C. A. F.) Die Werke der Troubadours, *etc.* Bd. 1. 1846, *etc.* 8°. **1464.** c. **24.**

—— Der Trobador Guillem de Cabestanh. Sein Leben und seine Werke. Von Franz Hüffer. pp. 68. *Berlin,* 1869. 8°. **10660.** e. **29.** (9.)

CABESTAING (Guillaume de)

—— Les Chansons de Guilhem de Cabestanh. Éditées p[ar] Arthur Långfors. pp. xviii. 96. *Paris,* 1924. 8°. [*L[es] Classiques français du moyen âge.* no. 42.] **012201.** cc. **1/4[2]**

—— Les Poésies de Cabestan (avec le texte ancien de s[es] chansons et leur transposition en langue moderne). *S[ee]* Escallier (E.) Le Destin tragique de Guillaume [de] Cabestan le troubadour. 1934. 8°. **10655.** v. **2[?]**

CABESTAN (Guillaume de) *See* Cabestaing.

CABESTANH (Guillem de) *See* Cabestaing (Guillaum[e] de)

CABET (Étienne)

—— *See* Angrand (Pierre) Étienne Cabet et la Républiqu[e] de 1848. 1948. 8°. **09231.h.35/[?]**

—— *See* Beluze (J. P.) Mort du fondateu[r] d'Icarie (Cabet). 1856. 12°. **8277.** d. **34.** (4.)

—— *See* Ephemerides. 1848. Almanach icarien . . Dirigé par M. Cabet. [1847.] 8°. **P.P. 2397.** c

—— *See* Icaria, *Community of.* Célébration du premi[er] anniversaire de la naissance du fondateur d'Icarie ([É.] Cabet). 1857. 12°. **8277.** d. **34.** (6

—— *See* Job, *pseud.* Socialisme. Voyage d'un Autun[ois] en Icarie à la suite de Cabet. 1898. 8°. **08275.** h. **1**

—— *See* Lefuel (E.) L'Individualisme et le communism[e] par les citoyens Lefuel . . . Cabet, *etc.* 1848. 12°. **8275.** a. **62.** (6

—— *See* Lux (H.) Etienne Cabet und der Ikarische Com[-] munismus, *etc.* 1894. 8°. **08275.** ee. **16**

—— *See* Mirecourt (E. de) *pseud.* Histoire contemporaine *etc.* (no. 82. Garnier-Pagès . . . Cabet. [With a portrait.]) 1867, *etc.* 16°. **10661.** aaa. **3[?]**

—— *See* Piotrowski (Sylvester A.) Étienne Cabet and th[e] Voyage en Icarie, *etc.* 1935. 8°. **11872.** bb. **1[?]**

—— *See* Prudhommeaux (J.) Étienne Cabet et les origine[s] du communisme icarien, *etc.* 1907. 8°. **08276.** c. **57**

—— *See* Prudhommeaux (J.) Icarie et son fondateu[r] Étienne Cabet. Contribution à l'étude du socialism[e] expérimental, *etc.* 1907. 8°. **8247.** dd. **2[?]**

—— Bien et mal, danger et salut, après la révolution d[e] février 1848. pp. 60. *Paris,* 1848. 16°. **8052.** b. **1[?]**

—— Cabet à ceux, qui le menacent d'assassinat. Extra[it] du Populaire du 22 avril 1848. pp. 16. *Pari[s],* 1848. 8°. **8275.** e. **63.** (5.

—— Cabet aux Icariens en France. *See* Icaria, *Communit[y] of.* Prospectus. Émigration icarienne, *etc.* 1852. 16°. **8235.** a. **3[?]**

—— [Ce que je ferais si j'avais $500,000.] Ikarische Güter[-] gemeinschaft. Wenn ich $500,000 haette! pp. 12. *Nauvoo, Ill.,* 1854. 8°. **4182.** bbb. **16.** (2.

—— [Comment je suis communiste.] El Comunismo . . Traducido y aumentado con citas y notas intercaladas en e[l] texto. pp. 157. *Buenos Aires,* 1864. 8°. **8205.** aaa. **8**

CABET (Étienne)

—— Curieuse lettre . . . à Louis Napoléon. [Exhorting him to show himself a good republican.] pp. 15. *Paris*, 1851. 8°. **1850. c. 1. (13.)**

—— Dialogue sur les Bastilles, entre M. Thiers et un courtisan. pp. 16. [*Paris*, 1840.] 8°. **8051. cc. 8. (4.)**

—— Eau sur feu, ou Réponse à Timon [i.e. Louis Marie de La Haye, Viscount de Cormenin]. pp. 79. *Paris*, 1845. 16°. **1389. a. 37. (3.)**

—— État de la question sociale en Angleterre, en Écosse, en Irlande et en France. pp. 95. *Paris*, 1843. 16°. **1389. a. 37. (1.)**

—— Le Fondateur d'Icarie (Cabet) aux Icariens. pp. 11. *Paris*, 1856. 12°. **8277. d. 34. (2.)**

—— Guerre de l'opposition contre le citoyen Cabet, fondateur d'Icarie. pp. 72. *Paris*, 1856. 12°. **8277. d. 34. (3.)**

—— Histoire populaire de la Révolution française de 1789 à 1830, précédée d'une introduction contenant le précis de l'histoire des Français depuis leur origine jusqu'aux États-Généraux. 4 tom. *Paris*, 1839, 40. 8°. **1442. h. 12, 13.**

—— Lettre du citoyen Cabet à l'archevêque de Paris, en réponse à son mandement du 8 juin 1851. pp. 47. *Paris; Troyes*, 1851. 8°. **8206. c. 29. (5.)**

—— Opinions et sentiments publiquement exprimés concernant le fondateur d'Icarie (Cabet). [Edited by E. Cabet.] pp. 36. *Paris*, 1856. 12°. **8277. d. 34. (1.)**

—— Le Populaire. Aux communistes icariens. [*Paris*, 1848.] *s. sh.* fol. **1850. b. 7. (6.)**

—— Prospectus. Grande émigration au Texas en Amérique, pour réaliser la Communauté d'Icarie. pp. 7. [*Paris*, 1848.] 8°. **8177. d. 12.**

—— Révolution de 1830 et situation présente—novembre 1833—expliquées et éclairées par les Révolutions de 1789, 1792, 1799 et 1804, et par la Restauration . . . 3e édition. 2 tom. *Paris*, 1833. 12°. **1389. c. 4.**

—— Société fraternelle centrale. Discours du citoyen Cabet [on elections to the National Assembly, and on the Icarian communistic scheme]. 10 pt. *Paris*, 1848. 8°. **8052. f. 4.**

—— Voyage en Icarie, roman philosophique et social . . . Deuxième edition. pp. vii. 566. *Paris*, 1842. 8°. **12510. dd. 1.**

—— [Voyage et aventures de Lord William Garisdall en Icarie.] Путешествие в Икарию. Философский и социальный роман. Перевод . . . под редакцией Э. Л. Гуревича. Комментарии Э. Л. Гуревича и Ф. Б. Шубаевой. Вступительная статья В. П. Волгина. [With portraits.] 2 vol. *Москва, Ленинград*, 1948. 8°. *Москва, Ленинград*, 1948. 8°. [*Предшественники научного социализма.*] **Ac. 1125/222. (8.)**

—— Le Vrai christianisme suivant Jésus Christ. pp. xii. 636. *Paris*, 1846. 12°. **3900. a. 58.**

—— [Another copy.] **3900. a. 63.**

—— Ueber das wahre Christenthum. *See* Scholl (C.) Freie Stimmen aus dem heutigen Frankreich, *etc.* 1865. 8°. **4378. cc. 43.**

CABET (Étienne)

—— Faits préliminaires au procès devant la Cour d'assises contre M. Cabet . . . IIe partie. Persécution à l'occasion des 5 et 6 juin. pp. 28. *Paris*, 1833. 8°. **R. 163. (7.)**

—— Poursuites du gouvernement contre M. Cabet, député de la Côte-d'Or, directeur du Populaire. 2 pt. *Paris*, 1834. 8°. **1131. f. 21. (2.)**

CABEUS (Nicolaus) *See* Aristotle. [*Meteorologica.—Latin.*] Nicolai Cabei . . . in quatuor libros Meteorologicorum Aristotelis commentaria et quæstiones, *etc.* 1646. fol. **C. 54. f. 9.**

—— *See* Chiaramonti (S.) Scipionis Claramontii Cæsenatis de sede cometarum . . . libri duo. In primo continetur defensio sententiæ suæ ab oppugnationibus P. N. Cabei, *etc.* 1648. 8°. **C.113.a.10.(1.)**

—— Philosophia magnetica, in qua magnetis natura penitus explicatur, et omnium quæ hoc lapide cernuntur, causæ propriæ afferuntur . . . Multa quoque dicuntur de electricis, & aliis attractionibus, & eorum causis. Additis figuris variis, *etc.* pp. 412. *Apud I. Kinckium: Coloniæ*, 1629. fol. **536. m. 10.**
With an additional titlepage, engraved.

CABEZA ( ) *Ex-Diputado.* *See* Leon Huerta (L. de) Impugnacion que hace . . . L. de Leon Huerta á las equivocadas ideas que . . . produjeron en el Congreso los Señores Ex-diputados Echevarria y Cabeza, *etc.* 1822. 8°. **8027. b. 4.**

CABEZA (Bernabe Josef) Memoria interesante para la historia de las persecuciones de la Iglesia Católica y sus ministros en España en los ultimos tiempos de cautividad del Señor Don Fernando VII. el Deseado, consignada en la defensa que hizo . . . B. J. Cabeza . . . por los Comisionados del . . . Cabildo Eclesiástico de Cádiz, D. P. J. Cervera . . . M. de Elejaburu y Urrutia, y . . . M. de Cos . . . en la causa que . . . se formó á éstos . . . por el delito de haber consultado á diferentes RR. Obispos y santas Iglesias sobre lo contenido en los decretos de abolicion del santo tribunal de la Inquisicion, *etc.* (Apéndice de documentos.) 2 pt. *Madrid*, 1814. fol. **4625. f. 17.**

CABEZA (Casto Blanco) *See* Blanco Cabeza.

CABEZA (Jesús Fernández) *See* Fernández Cabeza.

CABEZA (Maria de la) *See* Mary [de la Cabeza], *Saint*, *etc.*

CABEZA (María Alegría Fernández) *See* Fernández Cabeza.

CABEZA DE LEÓN (Salvador)

—— Historia de la Universidad de Santiago de Compostela. Materiales acopiados y transcritos por D. Salvador Cabeza de León. Ordenados, completados y redactados por Enrique Fernández-Villamil. Prólogo de Paulino Pedret Casado. [With plates.] 2 tom. *Santiago de Compostela*, 1945–47. 8°. **8356. n. 38.**
The first volume is divided into two parts.

CABEZA DE LEÓN (Salvador)

—— Primicias. [In prose and verse.] pp. xii. 176. *La Coruña*, 1892. 8°. [*Biblioteca gallega.* no. 31.] **12231. g.**

CABEZA DE VACA (Alvar Nuñez) *See* Nuñez Cabeza de Vaca.

CABEZA DE VACA (Manuel) La Posición del Ecuador en el Conflicto Colombo-Peruano. pp. 227. 1934. 8°. *See* Ecuador.—*Ministerio de Relaciones Exteriores.* **20009.** ff. **85.**

CABEZA DE VACA Y QUIÑONES (Pedro de Castro) successively *Archbishop of Granada* and *of Seville. See* Castro Cabeza de Vaca y Quiñones.

CABEZA PEREIRO (Anacleto) Estudios sobre Carolinas. La isla de Ponapé. Geografia, etnografia, historia . . . Con un prólogo del . . . Teniente General D. Valeriano Weyler. [With maps and plans.] pp. xiii. 241. *Manila,* 1895. 8°. **10492.** ee. **30.**

—— [Another copy.] Estudios sobre Carolinas. La Isla de Ponapé, *etc. Manila,* 1895. 8°. **10493.** ff. **55.**

CABEZAS (Juan) *Calificador del Santo Oficio. See* Juan, *de la Concepcion, Coronista, etc.* Satisfacion à las tachas, defectos, y nulidades, que pone en las bulas pontificias de la Sagrada Religion de la Santissima Trinidad . . . Fr. I de Cabeças, *etc.* [1673 ?] fol. **4783.** e. **3.** (**58.**)

—— Argumento legal, en que por diferentes medios, se muestra es Fiscal la defensa del pleyto, que las Familias Calçada, y Descalça de la Sagrada Religion de la Santa Trinidad, dizen contestado, en este S. S. R. C. de Aragon, contra la . . . Orden de nuestra Señora de la Merced, y Redemptores, *etc.* ff. 13. [*Madrid ?* 1672 ?] fol. **4783.** e. **3.** (**48.**)

—— [Another edition.] ff. 13. [*Madrid ?* 1673 ?] fol. **4783.** e. **3.** (**59.**)

—— Defectos, que padecen las llamadas, carta y bullas, que por parte de las Familias Calçada, y Descalça, de la Sagrada Religion de la Santa Trinidad, se han presentado en el pleyto, con nombre de obtenidas, de la Santidad de Innocencio Tercero, y otros Pontifices. ff. 20. [*Madrid ?* 1673 ?] fol. **4783.** e. **3.** (**57.**)

—— Defensa de el papel, que en forma de peticion presentò la Celeste Real Orden de nuestra Señora de la Merced, y Redemptores, en le pleyto pendiente ante el S. S. R. C. de Aragon, en 16. de Iulio de este año de 1672. representando los defectos, que padecen las llamadas bulas, puestas de contrario, por las Familias Calçada, y Descalça de la Sagrada Religion Trinitaria. ff. 39. [*Madrid,* 1672.] fol. **4783.** e. **3.** (**52.**)

—— Disceptacion de dos excepciones oppuestas por las Familias Trinitarias Calçada, y Descalça, à la Mercenaria, de el Orden de nuestra Señora de la Merced, y Redemptores, en el pleyto que passa en el S. S. R. Consejo de Aragon, y otro, en la Nunciatura, entre los Descalços de ambas Familias, *etc.* ff. 10. [*Madrid ?* 1672 ?] fol. **4783.** e. **3.** (**49.**)

—— [Another copy.] **4783.** e. **3.** (**55.**)

—— Respuesta que dà . . . Fray I. Cabeças . . . a vna carta que recibiò con nombre, y firma de Fr. Luis de la SS. Trinidad. [With the letter of Fr. Luis.] ff. 6. [*Madrid ?* 1673 ?] fol. **4783.** e. **3.** (**60.**)

CABEZAS (Juan) *Dramatist.* Primera parte de Comedias, del Maestro I. Cabeça. pp. 496. *I. de Ybar: Çaragoça,* 1662. 4°. **11726.** d. **11.**

—— Matar por Zelos su Dama. Comedia famosa. [In verse.] pp. 28. *Sevilla,* [1750 ?] 4°. **11728.** i. **7.** (**12.**)

—— No hai Castigo contra Amor. Comedia famosa. [In verse.] pp. 32. *Sevilla,* [1750 ?] 4°. **11728.** i. **7.** (**13.**)

—— Relacion prodigiosa, de la comedia: No ay Castigo contra Amor. *Valencia,* [1758 ?] 4°. T. **1953.** (**34.**)

CABEZAS (Juan Antonio)

—— " Clarín." El provinciano universal. [With a portrai pp. 244. *Madrid,* 1936. 8°. **10633.** ppp. 4

—— Concepión Arenal, o el sentido romántico de la justic [With a portrait.] pp. 228. *Madrid,* 1942. 8°. **10633.** ppp.

—— Rubén Darío. Un poeta y una vida. [With plat including portraits.] pp. 294. *Madrid,* 1944. 8°. **010632.** aa.

CABEZAS (Pedro) Canto. [On the rising in Spain agai Napoleon.] pp. 8. [*Mexico ?* 1810 ?] 4°. **11451.** bbb. **6.** (

CABEZAS (Pedro Alcantara) *See* Alcantara Cabez

CABEZAS DE HERRERA (Juan) Apuntes Históric sobre la Organizacion Politico-Administrativa de Filipin pp. 29. *Manila,* 1883. fol. **8155.** g. **2.** (

—— El Gran Ladron (Alonso de Monroy). Apuntes para historia. pp. 219. *Madrid,* 1895. 8°. **10632.** aaa. 4

CABEZAS DÍAZ (Antonio) *See* Spain. [*Laws, etc.*— *Land.*] El Agro y el Municipio. La Reforma Agrar . . . Ordenada, comentada y con formularios por Cabezas Díaz. 1932. 8°. **5385.** b.

CABEZAS L. (Carlos)

—— Estudio y análisis del periodismo en Panamá. *Méx* 1947. 8°. **11868.** de.

CABEZON (Cárlos) Neógrafos Kontemporáneos. Ten tiba bibliográfika, *etc.* pp. 21. *Santiago de Chi* 1896. 8°. **11906.** e. **74.** (

—— [Another copy.] **11902.** h. **17.** (

—— Notas sobre la Reforma Ortográfiqa. pp. 67. *Santiago de Chile,* 1892. 8°. **12901.** bbb. **45.** (

—— La Ortografía Rrazional. pp. 33. *Paris,* 1902. 4°. **012901.** ff. **14.** (

CABEZON (Francisco Xavier Sanchez de) *See* Sanch de Cabezon.

CABEZÓN (Mariano Gutiérrez y) *See* Gutiérrez Cabezón.

CABEZUDO (Didacus Nugno) *See* Nuño Cabezudo.

CABIANCA (Jacopo) Giovanni Tonesio, racconto. pp. 1 *Parigi, Livorno,* 1846. 8°. **12470.** g.

—— Nozze nobilissime Nievo-Bonin. (Alla sposa. [Verse pp. 10. *Rovigo,* 1854. 8°. **11426.** k. **26.** (

—— Il Torquato Tasso. Canti dodici. pp. 364. *Vene* 1858. 8°. **11436.** g.

—— Poesia e amore. Canto inedito del Torquato Tas Poema. (Per le nobilissime nozze Nievo-Bonin.) pp. *Milano,* 1854. 8°. **11426.** l. **12.** (

—— L'Ultimo dei Koenigsmarck. Gaspara Stam Drammi in versi. pp. 180. *Milano,* 1857. 8°. **11715.** cc. **1.** (

—— *See* Königsmark (F. C.) *Count.* Il Conte di Che march. Melodramma serio, *etc.* [Founded on Cabianca's " L'Ultimo dei Koenigsmarck."] [1867.] 8°. **906.** h. **10.**

CABIAS (Jean Baptiste de) Les Merueilles des ba d'Aix en Sauoye. pp. 208. *I. Roussin: Lyo* 1623. 8°. **1171.** f.

CABIATI (Aldo) La Battaglia dell'ottobre 1917. [With maps.] pp. 445. *Milano*, 1934. 8°. [*Storia della guerra italiana.* no. 5.] **9080.n.1/5.**

—— La Conquista dell'Impero. Cronaca ragionata della guerra italo-abissina, 1935-1936. pp. 303. pl. 16. *Milano*, 1936. 8°. **9062.** bbb. **14.**

—— La Riscossa: Altipiani, Grappa, Piave. [With maps.] pp. 386. *Milano*, 1934. 8°. [*Storia della guerra italiana.* no. 6.] **9080.n.1/6.**

CABIATI (Attilio) *See* Agnelli (Giovanni) and Cabiati (A.) Fédération européenne ou Ligue des Nations? 1919. 8°. **8425.** dd. **16.**

—— *See* Launhardt (W.) [Theorie der Tarifbildung der Eisenbahnen.] Teoria della formazione delle tariffe ferroviarie . . . Traduzione . . . di A. Cabiati. 1902, *etc.* 8°. [*Biblioteca dell'economista.* ser. 4. vol. 3.] **8206.** pp. **1.**

—— *See* Price (Langford L. F. R.) La Moneta e i suoi rapporti coi prezzi . . . Traduzione italiana . . . del dott. A. Cabiati. 1905. 8°. [*Biblioteca dell'economista.* ser. 4. vol. 6–8.] **8206.** pp. **1.**

—— Fisiologia e patologia economica negli scambi della ricchezza fra gli stati. pp. 671. *Torino*, 1937. 8°. **8204.** d. **34.**

CABIATI (Ottavio)

—— Nota al Palladio. Allegato alla riproduzione in fac simile de "I Quattro libri dell'architettura" di Andrea Palladio, *etc.* [With illustrations, including a portrait.] pp. 15. [*Milan*, 1945.] fol. **7822.** d. **38.**

CABIATUS (Joannes Evangelista) Pro D. Comite Josepho Vicecomite Scaramutia, cum D. I. C. C. Papiæ C. F. Pallеario, *etc.* [An argument on a question of the recovery of profits on property which formed part of a dower.] [*Milan*, 1720?] fol. **5322.** ee. **21.** (**2.**)

CABIBBE (Giorgio)

—— Antonio Fogazzaro nel giudizio della critica a cent' anni della nascita. Saggio critico. Con una guida analitica degli scritti apparsi su giornali e riviste nella ricorrenza del centenario. pp. 39. Milano, 1943. 8°. **11925.** g. **8.**

CABIBEL, afterwards **CALAS** (Anne Rose) *See* Calas.

CABIÉ (Edmond) *See* Hébrard, *Family of, Seigneurs de Saint-Sulpice.* Guerres de religion dans le Sud-Ouest de la France . . . D'après les papiers des seigneurs de Saint-Sulpice, de 1561 à 1590. Documents transcrits, classés et annotés par E. Cabié. 1906. 4°. **9225.** m. **14.**

—— *See* Hébrard (Jean) *Seigneur de Saint-Sulpice.* Ambassade en Espagne de Jean Ébrard . . . Documents classés, annotés et publiés par E. Cabié. 1903. 8°. **9225.** c. **8.**

—— *See* Templars, *Knights.* Cartulaire des Templiers de Vaour, Tarn. Publié par C. Portal & E. Cabié. 1894. 8°. [*Archives historiques de l'Albigeois.* fasc. 1.] Ac. **235.**

—— Chartes de coutumes inédites de la Gascogne toulousaine. Documents publiés . . . par E. Cabié. pp. 158. *Paris, Auch*, 1884. 8°. [*Archives historiques de la Gascogne.* fasc. 5.] Ac. **6772/2.**

CABIÉ (Edmond)

—— Droits & possessions du comte de Toulouse dans l'Albigeois au milieu du XIIIe siècle. Documents publiés & annotés par E. Cabié. pp. xvi. 207. *Paris*, 1900. 8°. [*Archives historiques de l'Albigeois.* fasc. 6.] Ac. **235.**

CABIÉ (Edmond) and **MAZENS** (Louis)

—— Un Cartulaire et divers actes des Alaman, des de Lautrec et des de Lévis . . . XIIIe et XIVe siècles, publiés par E. Cabié et L. Mazens, *etc.* pp. lxxviii. 235. *Toulouse*, 1882. 8°. **9905.** bbb. **24.**

CABIEN (Michel) *See* Cussy (G. de) Récit fait à l'Assemblée nationale le 4 sept. 1790 . . . de différentes actions courageuses de M. Cabien, *etc.* [1790.] 8°. F. **22.** (**6.**)

CABIESES-MOLINA (Fernando)

—— **Contribución al estudio del sistema nervioso vegetativo cardiovascular en relación con la vida en las alturas. Tesis, *etc.* pp. 124. *Lima*, 1946. 8°. 7393. d. 18. *Universidad Nacional Mayor de San Marcos. Facultad de Medicina.* tom. 29. no. 1.**

CABILDO.

—— Cabildo Eclesiástico de Buenos Aires. *See* Buenos Ayres.—*Cathedral.*—*Chapter.*

—— Cabildo Metropolitano Cesaraugustano. *See* Saragossa.—*Cathedral Church.*—*Chapter.*

CABILLAVUS (Balduinus) *See* Cabilliavus.

CABILLET (E.) Tour de mille pieds. (Motif et possibilité d'élever une tour de mille pieds au centre de Paris.) [With a plate.] pp. 4. *Paris*, 1845. 4°. **1401.** k. **10.**

CABILLIAVUS (Balduinus) Agar secundò exul. [In verse.] pp. 51. *Typis* / Cornely. *Coenesteny: Louany*, 1642. 8°. **1471.e.45.(2.)**
The titlepage is engraved.

—— [Another copy.] Agar secundò exul. *Louany*, 1642. 8°. **11409.** b. **5.** (**2.**)
Imperfect; wanting sig.)(iii, iv, *containing the letter "Ad lectorem."*

—— Balduini Cabillaui . . . Epigrammata selecta. pp. 78. *Ex officina Plantiniana; Antuerpiæ*, 1620. 12°. **11403.** a. **41.** (**2.**)

—— [Another edition.] *See* Bauhusius (B.) Bernardi Bauhusii et B. Cabillavi epigrammata, *etc.* 1634. 16°. **1070.** b. **17.**

—— R. P. Balduini Cabiliaui . . . Epistolarum Heroum et Heroidum libri quatuor. [In verse.] pp. 384. *H. Aertssens: Antuerpiæ*, 1636. 8°. **11408.** aa. **31.**
The titlepage is engraved.

—— [Another copy.] **11409.** b. **5.** (**3.**)
Imperfect; wanting the engraved titlepage, the five following leaves, and the leaf of errata at the end.

—— Balduini Cabilliaui . . . Magdalena. [In verse.] pp. 229. *Ex officina Plantiniana: Antuerpiæ*, 1625. 12°. **1213.** c. **10.**

—— [Another copy.] **1070.** b. **11.**

—— Phosphorus, siue Ioannes Baptista. (Natiuitas, vita, mors. Lyrica, symbolica, epigrammata, elegiæ.) pp. 295. *Typis C. Coenesteny: Louany*, 1642. 8°. **11409.** e. **52.**
The titlepage is engraved. The preliminary quire of four leaves contains the "Explicatio imaginis," preface, etc.

CABILLIAVUS (BALDUINUS)

—— [Another issue.] *Louany*, 1642. 8°. **11409**. b. **5**. (**1**.)
The preliminary quire of eight leaves contains a dedicatory epistle, and a different preface, etc.

—— [Venatio sacra, siue Puer amissus.] [In verse.] pp. 170. [*Typis* / Cornely / *Coenesteny: Louany*, 1642.] 8°. 1471.e.45.(1.)
Imperfect; wanting the engraved titlepage.

—— [Another copy.] [Venatio sacra, siue Puer amissus.] [*Louany*, 1642.] 8°. **11409**. b. **5**. (**2***.)
Imperfect; wanting the titlepage and the eight preliminary leaves containing the dedication and the preface.

—— [Another copy.] **11409**. b. **5**. (**2****.)
Imperfect; wanting the titlepage and the eight preliminary leaves.

CABILONUM. *See* CHALON-SUR-SAÔNE.

CABIN. The Cabin in the Brush. By the author of "Marion through the Brush," *etc.* pp. 249. *J. P. Skelly & Co.: Philadelphia*, 1869. 12°. **12706**. aa. **4**.

CABIN BOY. Answer to the Cabin Boy. [A song.] *J. Pitts: [London*, 1820 ?] *s. sh.* 8°. C. **116**. i. **1**. (**237**.)

—— The Cabin Boy; or, the First step to fame: a new song book, *etc.* pp. 38. *T. & R. Hughes: London*, 1807. 12°. **11602**. e. **28**. (**1**.)

—— The Cabin Boy's Companion. pp. 64. *R.T.S.: London*, [1830 ?] 16°. **864**. a. **16**. (**1**.)

—— The Cabin Boy's Story; a semi-nautical romance, founded on fact. By the author of the "Pirate Doctor," *etc.* pp. xii. 438. *Garrett & Co.: New York*, [1854.] 8°. **12707**. h. **15**.

—— The Handsome Cabin Boy. (The Royal Black Bird.—Greenmount Smiling Anne.—The Undaunted Female.—Captain Colston.—A Dream of Napoleon.) [Songs.] [*Nugent & Co.? Dublin?* 1860 ?] *s. sh. obl.* 4°. **1872**. c. **1**. (**1**.)

—— The Honest Cabin-Boy. pp. 8. *R.T.S.: London*, [1854.] 32°. [*Little Library*.] **4418**. b. **37**.

—— A New Song called The Poor Cabin Boy. To which are added Come all ye jolly Sailors bold, On board the Charming Molly, and Sheelah and Dermot. pp. 8. *Printed for the Hawkers: Belfast*, [1815 ?] 12°. **11621**. b. **15**. (**21**.)

CABIN CONVERSATIONS. Cabin Conversations and Castle Scenes. An Irish story. By the author of "Early Recollections," "A Visit to my Birthplace," &c. &c. [i.e. Selina Bunbury.] pp. 173. *James Nisbet: London*, 1827. 12°. N. **271**. (**3**.)

—— [Another copy.] **4413**. f. **38**. (**3**.)

CABINET.

—— Antiquarian and Topographical Cabinet, containing a series of elegant views [engraved by J. S. Storer and John Greig] of the most interesting objects of curiosity in Great Britain, *etc.* *See* STORER (James S.)

—— Songs, Duets, Trios, Chorusses, &c. in the new comic opera [by Thomas John Dibdin], called The Cabinet, *etc.* pp. 23. *Barker & Son: London*, 1802. 8°. **11779**. b. **27**.

—— The Cabinet. A magazine of original literature, *etc.* *See* PERIODICAL PUBLICATIONS.—*London.*

CABINET.

—— The Cabinet; a repository of polite literature. PERIODICAL PUBLICATIONS.—*Boston, Massachusetts.*

—— The Cabinet; a series of essays, moral and litera [By Archibald Bell.] 2 vol. *Bell & Bradfu Edinburgh*, 1835. 8°. **838**. e. **8**,

—— The Cabinet. By a Society of Gentlemen. *See* PER DICAL PUBLICATIONS.—*Norwich.*

—— The Cabinet: containing, a collection of curious pap relative to the present political contests in Ireland, pp. vi. 86. *See* PATRIOT MISCELLANY. The Pat Miscellany, *etc.* vol. 2. 1756. 8°. **8145**. e. **83***.

—— The Cabinet: containing entertaining selections, f new books of merit, &c. in prose and verse, *etc.* [W engravings.] pp. iv. 219. *Edinburgh; R. Mor & Sons: Perth; David Ogilvy & Son: London*, 1797. **12360**. de.

—— The Cabinet . . . Containing readings in phonogra *etc.* *See* PERIODICAL PUBLICATIONS.—*London.*

—— The Cabinet; or, Monthly report of polite literat *See* PERIODICAL PUBLICATIONS.—*London.*

—— The Cabinet; or, the Selected beauties of literat [Edited by John Aitken.] Second series. pp. vi. 50 *John Aitken: Edinburgh*, 1825. 8°. **991**. l.

—— Le Cabinet de l'amateur et de l'antiquaire. *See* PE DICAL PUBLICATIONS.—*Paris.*

—— Le Cabinet de l'éloquence; ou, la Manière d'écrire lettres . . . Augmenté d'un petit traité des lettres change, billets à ordre, *etc.* pp. 24. *Montbél* [1826 ?] 24°. **12315**. aa. **1**.

—— [Another edition.] pp. 23. *Charmes*, [1845 ?] 24° **12430**. aa. **14**.

—— Cabinet de vénerie. *See* JULLIEN (E.) and LAC (P.)

—— Cabinet der Weissheit: in welchem befindlich sinnr Betrachtungen, moralische Gedancken, philosophi Sprüche . . . auffs neue zum Druck befordert. pp. *In Verlegung E. T. Kinchii: Cöllen*, 1691. 12°. **12355**. a.

—— Le Cabinet des énigmes, des dieux, déesses, & h [Twenty-four plates.] [1680 ?] 4°. **637**. g.
The titlepage is engraved.

—— Cabinet des Estampes de la Ville d'Anvers. ANTWERP.—*Museum Plantin-Moretus.*

—— Le Cabinet des fées. Contenant tous leurs ouvra en huit volumes. tom. 1–3.

tom. 1. Florine.—Contes des fées . . . par Ma comtesse de M****.
tom. 2. Les Nouveaux contes des fées, par Madan M**.
tom. 3. Les Contes des fées, par Madame D*** M. C. La Mothe, Countess d'Aulnoy].

Amsterdam, 1731–35. 12°. **245**. d. **27**
The remaining volumes of the "Cabinet des fées," w were issued without collective titlepages, are entered u the heading appropriate to each volume.

—— Le Cabinet des fées; ou Collection choisie des conte fées, et autres contes merveilleux. Orné de fig 41 tom. *Amsterdam*, 1785–89. 8°. **89**. c. **15–27**, d.
Tom. 38–41 *were published at Geneva and contai addition to the collective titlepages dated* 1788, 89, *sep titlepages dated* 1793.

—— [Another copy of tom. 7–11, 14, 15.] **681.** a. **21–27.**

—— Le Cabinet des princes. pp. 360. *J. Petit: Bruxelles,* 1672. 12°. **8010.** a. **21.**

—— Le Cabinet du philosophe. *See* PERIODICAL PUBLICATIONS.—Paris.—*Le Spectateur françois.*

—— Cabinet du Spectacle de la Nature et de l'Art. *See* PARIS.

—— Le Cabinet historique. *See* PERIODICAL PUBLICATIONS. —*Paris.*

—— Le Cabinet morale [*sic*] & satyrique des dames, ou Recueil d'epigrames, d'inscriptions et de belles pensées en vers, contenant la connoissance de leurs bonnes & foibles qualitez. Ouverture I. pp. 48. *Berlin & Leipzig,* [1760 ?] 12°. **11474.** df. **24.**

—— A Cabinet of Choice Jewels: or, the Christian's joy and gladness, set forth in sundry pleasant new Christmas carrols. pp. 24. *B. Deacon: London,* [1700 ?] 12°. C. **110.** b. **15.**

—— The Cabinet of Curiosities: or, Mirror of entertainment. Being a selection of extraordinary legends . . . authentic and remarkable anecdotes . . . and a variety of other eccentric matter. pp. 36. *Burkett & Plumpton: London,* [1810 ?] 12°. **12330.** aaa. **44.** (**4.**)

—— The Cabinet of Curiosities; or, Wonders of the world displayed. no. 13, 28, 34. *J. Limbird: [London,* 1830 ?] 8°.

—— New Series. pp. iv. 283. *J. Limbird: London,* 1831. 8°. P.P. **3975.**

—— The Cabinet of Foreign Voyages and Travels. *See* PERIODICAL PUBLICATIONS.—*London.*

—— The Cabinet of Gems: gathered from celebrated authors. With . . . illustrations by eminent artists. pp. 160. *W. P. Nimmo: London & Edinburgh,* 1875. 4°. **11651.** g. **18.**

—— The Cabinet of Genius containing frontispieces and characters adapted to the most popular poems, &c. with the poems &c. at large. 2 vol. *C. Taylor: London,* 1787. 4°. **11631.** f. **50.**
Published in parts. The plates bear the dates 1786–89. *The titlepages are engraved.*

—— [Another copy.] **11601.** g. **20.**
The parts are bound in a different order from that in the preceding. Imperfect; wanting the plates.

—— The Cabinet of Life, Wit, and Humour. *See* PERIODICAL PUBLICATIONS.—*Liverpool.*

—— The Cabinet of Love, or, Cupid's pastime. pp. 12. *J. Kendrew: York,* [1810 ?] 12°. **1870.** c. **2.** (**813.**)

—— The Cabinet of Mirth; or, Comic medley . . . By a Lover of Fun. pp. 36. *Thomas Kaygill: [London,* 1810 ?] 18°. **12314.** a. **45.** (**1.**)

—— The Cabinet of Modern Art, and Literary Souvenir. *See* PERIODICAL PUBLICATIONS.—*London.* The Literary Souvenir, *etc.*

—— The Cabinet of Modern Songs and Recitations. pp. xv. 304. *Music-Publishing Co.: London,* [1863.] 16°. **11622.** a. **10.**

—— The Cabinet of Natural History. *See* LARDNER (Dionysius) The Cabinet Cyclopædia, *etc.*

—— A Cabinet of Portraits, consisting of distinguished characters, British and foreign, accompanied with a brief memoir of each person. 2 vol. *William Darton: London,* [1823, 29.] 8°. **10602.** ppp. **9.**

—— The Cabinet of the Arts. A series of engravings by English artists, from original designs, by Stothard, Burney, Harding, *etc.* [Ninety-four plates.] *London,* 1799. 8°. **1401.** i. **25.**

—— The Cabinet of Useful Arts and Manufactures: designed for the perusal of young persons. pp. 180. *Thomas Courtney: Dublin,* 1821. 12°. **7944.** a. **5.**

—— [Another edition.] pp. 180. *W. Wetton: London,* [1825 ?] 12°. **7942.** a. **26.**

—— [Another edition.] pp. 180. *W. Folds & Son: Dublin,* 1825. 12°. **863.** e. **8.**

—— Cabinet Royal de Dresde touchant l'Histoire Naturelle. *See* DRESDEN.—*Königliche Naturalienkammer.*

—— Cabinet Royal des Médailles à la Haye. *See* HAGUE.—*Koninklijk Kabinet van Munten, Penningen en Gesneden Stenen.*

—— Le Cabinet satyrique; ou, Recueil parfaict, des vers piquants & gaillards de ce temps. Tiré des secrets cabinets des Sieurs de Sigognes, Regnier, Motin, Berthelot, Maynard, & autres des plus signalez poëtes de ce siecle. Nouuelle édition, reueuë, corrigée, & de beaucoup augmentée. pp. 669. *P. Billaine: Paris,* 1613 [1623]. 12°. **011483.** a. **69.**

—— Derniere edition, reueuë, corrigee & de beaucoup augmentee. pp. 732. *Paris,* 1632. 8°. **11474.** bb. **27.**

—— Dernière édition, reveuë, corrigée, & de beaucoup augmentée. 2 tom. [*Leyden,*] 1666. 12°. **11474.** de. **10.**

—— [Another copy.] **241.** c. **39, 40.**

—— [Another edition.] 2 tom. *Au Mont Parnasse* [*Amsterdam ?*], 1697. 12°. **11474.** aaa. **11.**

—— [Another edition.] [Edited by Pierre Nicolas Lenglet-Dufresnoy.] 2 tom. *Au Mont Parnasse; de l'imprimerie de messer Apollon* [*Amsterdam ?*], [1700 ?] 12°. **240.b.16,.17.**

—— Nouvelle édition . . . avec glossaire, variantes, notices biographiques, *etc.* 3 tom. *Gand, Paris,* 1859, 60. 8°. **11475.** bb. **4.**

—— Nouvelle edition complète, revue sur les éditions de 1618 et de 1620 et sur celle dite du Mont-Parnasse, sans date. [Edited by P. E. A. Poulet-Malassis.] 2 tom. [*Brussels,*] 1864. 8°. **11475.** ccc. **43.**

—— Première édition complète et critique d'après l'édition originale de 1618, augmentée des éditions suivantes, avec une notice, une bibliographie, un glossaire, des variantes et des notes par Fernand Fleuret & Louis Perceau . . . Texte orné de plusieurs reproductions. 2 tom. *Paris,* 1924. 8°. **011483.** bb. **34.**

—— [Another copy.] **20010.** h. **17.**

—— *See* LACHÈVRE (F.) Le Cabinet satyrique—édition de 1618—et Charles de Besançon. Réponse à M. Fernand Fleuret. 1924. 8°. **011840.** bb. **31.**

—— Eröffnetes Cabinet grosser Herren, oder gegenwärtiger Zustand aller Reiche und Staaten der Welt, *etc.* *See* PERIODICAL PUBLICATIONS.—*Leipsic.*

—— The Golden Cabinet, or, the Compleat fortune-teller. Wherein the meanest capacities are taught to understand their good or bad fortunes, not only in the wheel of fortune . . . but also by . . . palmestry [*sic*] and physiognomy, *etc.* pp. 24. *Printed & sold in London,* [1790 ?] 12°. **12315. aaa. 6. (11.)**

—— [Another issue.] [*London,* 1795 ?] 12°. **1076. l. 1. (13.)**

—— The Juvenile Cabinet. *See* UNITED STATES OF AMERICA.—*American Sunday School Union.*

—— The New Cabinet of Love. Being a choice collection of songs, *etc.* pp. 8. *J. Evans: London,* [1805 ?] 8°. **1077. g. 47. (3.)**

—— Physiognomisches Cabinet für Freunde und Schüler der Menschenkenntniss. Mit eingedruckten Kupfern. [By Friedrich Christoph Müller ?] 3 pt. *Frankfurt & Leipzig; Münster,* 1777–80. 8°. **7410. de. 30.**
Pt. 3 *was issued at Münster.*

—— [Another copy of pt. 1.] **7406. a. 12.**

—— The Pictorial Cabinet: an entertaining and literary miscellany. pp. 204. *J. Harwood: London,* [1845 ?] 8°. **12331. dd. 9.**
With an additional titlepage, engraved.

—— The Pictorial Cabinet of Marvels . . . Embellished with . . . wood engravings . . . and a series of natural history plates . . . printed in oil colours from paintings . . . by Harrison Weir. pp. vii. 508. *J. Sangster & Co.: London,* [1878.] 8°. **8703. f. 9.**
With an additional titlepage, engraved.

—— The Pictorial Cabinet of Marvels, *etc.* pp. vii. 507. *F. Warne & Co.: London & New York,* [1895 ?] 8°. **08710. dd. 33.**
With an additional titlepage, engraved.

—— Politique du Cabinet Russe, *etc.* 1847. 8°. *See* RUSSIA. [*Appendix.—History and Politics.*] **8092. e. 75.**

—— The Rich Cabinet. Furnished with varietie of excellent discriptions, exquisit charracters, witty discourses, and delightfull histories, deuine and morall. Together with inuectiues against many abuses of the time: digested alphabetically into common places. Whereunto is annexed the Epitome of good manners, exttracted from Mr. Iohn de la Casa, Arch-bishop of Beneuenta. [Attributed to Thomas Gainsford.] ff. 166. *I. B. for Roger Iackson: London,* 1616. 8°. **1388. a. 10.**
The " Epitome " is without foliation.

—— A Rich Cabinet of Notable Inventions, perform'd by the M. of W. [i.e. Edward Somerset, 2nd Marquis of Worcester.] [An abridgment of " A Century of the Names and Scantlings, *etc.*"] [1720 ?] 12°. *See* W., *M. of.* **1480. a. 10. (2.)**

—— The Sacred Cabinet of Literature and Art. vol. 1, 2. *S. Gilbert: London,* 1842. 4°. **P.P. 280.**
Imperfect; wanting pp. 101–104 *and two plates of vol.* 1, *and the titlepage and index of vol.* 2.

—— The Vocal & Musical Cabinet: containing the most approved songs, duets, ballads, &c. &c. English, Scotch & Irish . . . With the music, *etc.* vol. **1.** no. 1. 2 pt. *D. S. Maurice: London,* [1810 ?] 12°. **11621. bb. 12. (4, 5.)**
No more published.

CABINET.

—— The Vocal Cabinet. Being a choice collection of adm songs, *etc.* pp. 8. *Pitts: [London,* 1830 ?] 8°. **1077. k. 15. (**

—— The Zoological Cabinet; or, Menagerie of li characters. [A political satire. In verse. With pla pp. 22. *Thomas McLean: London,* 1832. 8°. **T. 1422.**

CABINET ALBUM. The New Cabinet Album of En tainment and Instruction. Embellished with . . . pl pp. viii. 280. *Edward Lacy: London,* [1840 ?] 8°. **12316.**
With an additional titlepage, engraved. Printed on p of various tints.

CABINET ANNUAL REGISTER. *See* PERIOD PUBLICATIONS.—*London.*

CABINET BIRTHDAY BOOK.

—— Royal Cabinet Birthday Book of Quotations Proverbs, with illustrations of 128 varieties of nat grasses. pp. 255. *D. Bryce & Son: Glasgow,* [1884.] **12357. aa.**

CABINET COLLOQUIES. *See* PERIODICAL PUBI TIONS.—*London.*

CABINET CONSTRUCTION. Cabinet Construc pp. vii. 214. *Evans Bros.: London,* [1928.] 8°. [*W worker Series.*] **W.P. 465**

CABINET CYCLOPAEDIA. *See* LARDNER (Diony

CABINET DICTIONARY.

—— The Cabinet Dictionary of the English Language 1871. 8°. *See* ENGLISH LANGUAGE. **12981.**

CABINET GAZETTEER. The Cabinet Gazetteer By the author of the " Cabinet Lawyer." [The pr signed: J. W., i.e. John Wade.] 1853. 12°. *See* **10003. bbb**

CABINET HISTORIAN. *See* PERIODICAL PUB TIONS.—*London.*

CABINET LAWYER. [For editions of " The Ca Lawyer " edited by J. W., i.e. John Wade:] *See* W.

CABINET LIBRARY. The Cabinet Library of S and Celebrated Tracts. 10 no. *Thomas C Edinburgh,* 1835–41. 8°. **1153. i.**
Imperfect; wanting Tract no. 7.

CABINET MAGAZINE. The Cabinet Magazin Literary Olio. *See* PERIODICAL PUBLICATIONS.—*Lo*

CABINET MAKER. The Cabinet Maker. A jour designs. *See* PERIODICAL PUBLICATIONS.—*London.*

—— The Cabinet Maker. A practical guide to the prin of design, and the economical and sound constructi household furniture . . . By various writers. Edit the editor of " The Industrial Self-Instructor." . . . illustrations, *etc.* pp. xii. 178. *Lock & Co.: London,* 1892. 8°. **7817.**

—— [For editions of " The Cabinet-Maker and Upholst Guide . . . From drawings by A. Hepplewhite and (*See* HEPPLEWHITE (A.) AND CO.

—— The Cabinet-Maker's Assistant; a series of o designs for modern furniture, with descriptions & of construction. pp. lxxx. 63. pl. CI. *Blackie & Glasgow,* 1853 [1850–53]. fol. **1268.**
Published in parts.

CABINET MAKER.

—— The Practical Cabinet-Maker, being a collection of working drawings, with explanatory notes. By a Working Man. pp. iv. 128. *Wyman & Sons: London,* [1878.] 8°. **07943. g. 87.**

CABINET MAKER DIARY.

—— The Cabinet Maker Diary. (Cabinet Maker Diary and Furnishers' Compendium.) *See* EPHEMERIDES.

CABINET MAKER SERIES. *See* PERIODICAL PUBLICATIONS.—London.—*Cabinet Maker.*

CABINET MAKER YEAR BOOK. *See* EPHEMERIDES. Cabinet Maker Diary.

CABINET MAKERS. The Cabinet Makers' Monthly Journal of Design. *See* PERIODICAL PUBLICATIONS.—*London.*

—— The Cabinet Makers' Pattern Book: being examples of modern furniture . . . selected from the portfolios of the leading wholesale makers, *etc.* (Second series.) pl. 56. *London,* 1880. 4°. [*Furniture Gazette.* Supplement.] Hendon.

—— The Cabinet Makers' Pattern Book . . . Fourth series. [Eighty plates.] *London,* 1884. fol. [*Furniture Gazette* Supplement.] Hendon

CABINET MINISTER. The Cabinet Minister. By the authoress of "Mothers and Daughters" [i.e. Catherine Frances Gore], *etc.* 3 vol. *Richard Bentley: London,* 1839. 12°. **N. 1605.**

CABINET MISSION TO INDIA. *See* ENGLAND.

CABINET PORTRAIT GALLERY. The Cabinet Portrait Gallery. Photographs by W. & D. Downey. [With descriptive letterpress.] 5 ser. *Cassell & Co.: London,* 1890–94. 4°. **10803. h. 9.**

CABINET THEATRE. *See* LONDON.—III.

CABINETS. The Cabinets Compared; or, an Enquiry into the late and present administration, *etc.* 1828. 8°. *See* ENGLAND. [*Appendix.—History and Politics.*—II. 1828.] **8135. cc. 12.**

CABINETTE (   ) Swiss Drawing Secret: being a new and easy method discovered by Monsieur Cabinette, *etc.* pp. 57. [*J. Patterson: Belfast,* 1867.] 8°. **7856. a. 43.**

CABIN-SAINT-MARCEL (C. J.) De la progression sur un plan horizontal; de l'exercice chez les anciens. pp. 114. *Paris,* 1853. 4°. [*Collection des thèses soutenues à la Faculté de Médecine de Paris.* An 1853. tom. 3.] **7372. f. 5.**

CABIRAN CABANES (J. F. M.) Aperçu sur quelques affections organiques du cœur, et autres maladies qui peuvent les simuler, *etc.* [A thesis.] pp. 22. *Paris,* 1805. 4°. **1182. g. 3. (5.)**

CABIRO, *pseud.* *See* EUROPA, *Dame.* [The Fight at Dame Europa's School.] Slagsmaalet i Fru Europas Skole . . . Efter den engelske Original ved Cabiro. 1871. 12°. **8026. a. 48.**

—— Udvalgte Feuilletoner af Cabiro. pp. 422. *Kjøbenhavn,* 1870. 8°. **12316. bbb. 24.**

CABIRO (JOSEPHUS) Dissertatio medica de dysenteria speciatim maligna, *etc.* pp. 8. *Monspelii,* 1784. 4°. **T. 19. (40.)**

CABIRON (DE) *Baron.* *See* LA COUR DE LA GARDIOLLE (L. M. de) Quatre lettres sur l'expédition d'Egypte . . . 1798. [With a prefatory note signed: Bon de C., i.e. Baron de Cabiron.] 1880. 4°. **9078. i. 3.**

—— *See* LA COUR DE LA GARDIOLLE (P. de) Guerre de Sept Ans. Rosback. [With a prefatory note signed: Bon de C., i.e. Baron de Cabiron.] 1883. 4°. **9078. i. 4.**

—— Quelques documents. [Relating to the history of the Régiment de Dauphiné in 1789—1791—1792, to the history of the French Protestants, etc. The editor's preface signed: Bon de C., i.e. Baron de Cabiron.] pp. 66. 1884. 4°. *See* C., *B[on] de.* **4630. f. 2.**

CABIRON (G. ARMAND) Essai sur l'emploi thérapeutique du feu. Tribut académique, *etc.* pp. 32. *Montpellier,* 1827. 4°. **1181. d. 14. (21.)**

CABISSOL (LOUIS JEAN DOMINIQUE) Quelques considérations sur l'hygiène navale. Tribut académique, *etc.* pp. 23. *Montpellier,* 1831. 4°. **1181. f. 2. (13.)**

CABLAT (CONSTANT) Des fractures du sternum. Thèse, *etc.* pp. 60. *Montpellier,* 1861. 4°. **7379. e. 12. (1.)**

CABLE AND WIRELESS, LTD.

—— Cable and Wireless Limited. Accounts for the year ended 31st December, 1946 [*etc.*], together with report of the directors, *etc.* 1947– . 8°. *See* ENGLAND.—*Post Office.* **B.S. 31/57.**

—— The Cable and Wireless Communications of the World. Some lectures and papers on the subject, 1924-1939. [By directors and officers of Cable and Wireless, Limited.] pp. viii. 282. *Cambridge,* [1939.] 8°. **8759. g. 15.**

—— Mediterranean Tour. Report of a tour of inspection of Mediterranean telegraphic communications undertaken in November–December, 1944, by Sir Edward Wilshaw, chairman of the company, and five senior officials. pp. 38. *London,* [1945.] 8°. **08755. i. 64.**

—— A Tribute to the Men and Women who serve Cable and Wireless. [An illustrated record of the staff luncheon, 26th January, 1943.] pp. 24. *London,* [1943.] 8°. **8231. bb. 63.**

CABLE CODE. Cable Code . . . 100,000 cable words to be cabled instead of numbers given in private code, *etc.* pp. 11. *Lepard & Smiths: London,* [1906.] 8°. **8757. f. 37.**

CABLE CODE CONDENSER. The Cable Code Condenser for reducing the cost of cablegrams, *etc.* pp. 15. *J. Parry & Co.: London,* [1907.] fol. **8758. h. 17.**

CABLE COMMUNICATIONS.

—— The Cable and Wireless Communications of the World. Some lectures and papers on the subject, 1924–1939. [By directors and officers of Cable and Wireless, Limited.] pp. viii. 282. [1939.] 8°. *See* CABLE AND WIRELESS, LIMITED. **8759. g. 15.**

CABLE CONDENSER. The "2 by 5" Cable Condenser. pp. 31. *Hinchliffe & Co.: Manchester,* [1914.] fol. **1805. a. 35.**

CABLE JOINTING. Practical Cable Jointing, *etc.* pp. 215. *W. T. Henley's Telegraph Works Co.: London,* 1932. 8°. **08755. bb. 46.**

—— Second edition. pp. 301. *W. T. Henley's Telegraph Works Co.: London,* 1936. 8°. **08756. a. 66.**

—— Third edition, *etc.* pp. 341. *W. T. Henley's Telegraph Works Co.: London,* 1938. 8°. **08770. aa. 35.**

CABLE RESEARCH. *See* ENGLAND.

CABLE RESEARCH COMMITTEE. *See* ENGLAND.—*Cable Research,* afterwards *Cable Research Committee.*

CABLE RESEARCH HANDBOOKS. *See* ENGLAND.—*Cable Research,* afterwards *Cable Research Committee.*

CABLE SERIES. The Cable Series of Farm and Household Books. 7 no. *Cable Printing & Publishing Co.: London,* [1898, 99.] 12°. **07944. g. 81.**

CABLE (A.) From Electric Chair Victim to Derby Winner. pp. 96. *Hornsey Journal: London,* 1931. 8°. [*F.P. Racing Novels.* no. 86.] **012614. aaa. 1/86.**

CABLE (ALICE MILDRED) *See* FRENCH (Evangeline) A Desert Journal. Letters . . . by E. French, M. Cable, *etc.* 1934. 8°. **2354. a. 25.**

—— *See* FRENCH (Evangeline) A Desert Journal, *etc.* (By E. French, M. Cable, F. French.) 1939. 8°. **2354. a. 31.**

—— *See* MATTER (Percy C.) The Making of a Pioneer, *etc.* [Edited by A. M. Cable and F. L. French.] 1935. 8°. **010822. de. 43.**

—— The Bible in the World. pp. 7. *Bible Reading Fellowship: London,* [1947.] 8°. **3130. a. 27.**

—— The Challenge of Central Asia. A brief survey of Tibet and its borderlands . . . By M. Cable, F. Houghton [and others.] [On missionary work in Asia. With maps.] pp. 136. *World Dominion Press: London,* 1929. 8°. **010056. i. 32.**

—— "Come, Follow." The call to service. [By various authors.] Edited . . . by M. Cable. pp. 64. [1937.] 8°. *See* ENGLAND.—*Inter-Varsity Fellowship of Evangelical Unions.* **04192. aaa. 91.**

—— Debtor to All These. (Address delivered at the Annual Conference of the Central Asian Mission.) pp. 19. *Central Asian Mission: London,* [1946.] 16°. **4768. a. 9.**

—— The Fulfilment of a Dream of Pastor Hsi's. The story of the work in Hwochow. [With plates.] pp. xx. 268. *Morgan & Scott; China Inland Mission: London,* 1917. 8°. **4763. e. 19.**

—— Important to Motorists. [A series of religious tracts.] 4 no. *R.T.S.: London,* [1935.] 12°. **4418. c. 90.**

—— The Powers of Darkness: being a record of some observations in demonology. pp. vi. 20. *China Inland Mission: London,* 1920. 8°. **04375. de. 17.**

—— Whither Central Asia? [With plates.] pp. 39. *Central Asian Mission: London,* [1941.] 8°. **20041. cc. 12.**

CABLE (ALICE MILDRED) and **FRENCH** (FRANCESCA LAW)

—— The Book which Demands a Verdict. [On the dissemination of the Bible.] pp. 125. *S.C.M. Press: London,* 1946. 8°. **3130. aaa. 40.**

—— Ambassadors for Christ. pp. 158. *Hodder & Stoughton: London,* 1935. 8°. **20019. ee. 22.**

—— China: her Life and her People . . . With maps, diagrams and illustrations. pp. 160. *University of London Press: London,* 1946. 8°. **010055. aa. 103.**

CABLE (ALICE MILDRED) and **FRENCH** (FRANCESCA LAW

—— Dispatches from North-West Kansu . . . With illustra tions. pp. vii. 73. *China Inland Mission: Londo* 1925. 8°. **4763. bb. 1**

—— George Hunter, Apostle of Turkestan. [With plate including portraits.] pp. 107. *China Inland Missio London,* 1948. 8°. **4956. k. 3**

—— The Gobi Desert. [With plates and a map.] pp. 303. *Hodder & Stoughton: London,* 1942. 8°. **10055. t.**

—— The Gobi Desert. (Reprinted.) pp. 302. *Hodder Stoughton: London,* 1946. 8°. **10055. t. 1**

—— Grace, Child of the Gobi. [With plates.] pp. 67. *China Inland Mission: London,* [1933.] 8°. **4765. gg. 12**

—— [Another edition.] pp. 63. *Hodder & Stoughton London,* [1938.] 8°. **20032. ee. 5**

—— Journey with a Purpose. [An account of travels i Australia, New Zealand and India. With plates.] pp. 19 *Hodder & Stoughton: London,* 1950. 8°. **10026. pp. 1**

—— A Parable of Jade. pp. 41. *Hodder & Stoughton* [*London,*] 1940. 8°. **7106. a. 1**

—— The Red Lama. [With plates.] pp. 43. *Chin Inland Mission: London,* 1927. 8°. **4764. h. 36**

—— Something Happened. [An account of a missionar journey in China. With plates and a map.] pp. 320. *Hodder & Stoughton: London,* 1933. 8°. **20030. ff. 3**

—— The Story of Topsy, little lonely of Central Asia pp. viii. 212. *Hodder & Stoughton: London,* 1937. 8°. **20031. ee. 58**

—— Through Jade Gate and Central Asia. An account o journeys in Kansu, Turkestan and the Gobi Deser . . . With illustrations and a map. pp. xvi. 304. *Constable & Co.: London,* 1927. 8°. **010055. aa. 12**

—— New popular edition. pp. xv. 304. *Constable & Co. London,* 1932. 8°. **010055. a. 52**

—— (Sixth edition.) pp. 318. *Hodder & Stoughton London,* 1937. 8°. **010056. a. 71**

—— Towards Spiritual Maturity. A book for those who seek it. [With plates.] pp. 194. *Hodder & Stoughton London,* 1939. 8°. **04400. h. 12**

—— Wall of Spears. The Gobi Desert . . . Illustrated by Joan Kiddell-Monroe. pp. 177. *Lutterworth Press: London,* 1951. 8°. **010076. g. 50.**

—— What it means to be a Christian. pp. 24. *Paternoster Press: London,* [1950.] 8°. **04018. n. 6**

—— Why not for the World? The story of the work of Go through the Bible Society. [With a portrait.] pp. 112 1952. 8°. *See* LONDON.—III. *British and Foreign Bibl Society.* **4768. bbb. 54**

—— A Woman who Laughed. Henrietta Soltau, who laughed at impossibilities and cried: "It shall be done." [With portraits.] pp. 240. *China Inland Mission: London,* 1934. 8°. **20018. a. 34.**

CABLE (BEN) Ben Cable. (Tell me, Mary, how to woo thee!—Why did I love?) [Songs.] *J. Paul & Co.:* [*London,* 1840?] *s. sh.* 4°. **C. 116. i. 1. (216.)**

CABLE (Boyd) *pseud.* [i.e. Ernest Andrew Ewart.] Action Front. pp. viii. 269. *Smith, Elder & Co.: London,* 1916. 8°. **09082. b. 16.**

—— Air Men o' War. pp. x. 246. *John Murray: London,* 1918. 8°. **012603. g. 45.**

—— Between the Lines. pp. ix. 272. *Smith, Elder & Co.: London,* 1915. 8°. **9082. ff. 27.**

—— British Battles of Destiny. pp. 341. *T. Nelson & Sons: London,* 1926. 8°. **08821. e. 56.**

—— By Blow and Kiss. The love story of a man with a bad name . . . Second edition. pp. 319. *Hodder & Stoughton: London,* [1914.] 8°. **NN. 2315.**

—— Doing Their Bit. War work at home, *etc.* pp. 134. *Hodder & Stoughton: London,* 1916. 8°. **9082. de. 7.**

—— [Doing Their Bit.] Dans les ateliers de l'Angleterre . . . Avec préface de M. Albert Thomas. pp. viii. 135. *Hodder & Stoughton: London,* 1917. 8°. **09082. a. 88.**

—— A Double Scoop. pp. 288. *Hutchinson & Co.: London,* [1924.] 8°. **NN. 10111.**

—— The Flying Courier. pp. 254. *Wright & Brown: London,* 1936. 8°. **NN. 26302.**

—— Front Lines. pp. xiv. 306. *John Murray: London,* 1918. 8°. **09083. c. 55.**

—— Grapes of Wrath. pp. viii. 268. *Smith, Elder & Co.: London,* 1917. 8°. **09082. cc. 36.**

—— A Hundred Year History of the P. & O.—Peninsular and Oriental Steam Navigation Company . . . 1837–1937. [With plates.] pp. x. 289. *I. Nicholson & Watson: London,* 1937. 4°. **08806. i. 47.**

—— Labour and Profits. pp. 95. *Jarrolds: London,* [1925.] 8°. [*Library of Capitalism.* no. 3.] **012208.aaa.4/3.**

—— Mates. By Boyd Cable . . . Coppinger's Cave. By Nicholas Palmerston, *etc.* pp. 45. *Basil Blackwell: Oxford,* [1929.] 8°. **012603. b. 48.**

—— The Old Contemptibles. pp. xi. 295. *Hodder & Stoughton: London,* [1919.] 8°. **012603. eee. 16.**

—— The Rolling Road. (Stories.) pp. 304. *Hutchinson & Co.: London,* [1923.] 8°. **012628. k. 53.**

—— Stormalong. pp. 250. *Wright & Brown: London,* 1936. 8°. **NN. 26111.**

—— The Wrist-Watch Castaways. By Boyd Cable . . . Galleons. [A poem.] By Lord Dunsany, *etc.* pp. 36. *Basil Blackwell: Oxford,* [1929.] 8°. **012603. b. 49.**

CABLE (Daniel) *See* Basilius Valentinus. Basilius Valentinus . . . Of Natural & Supernatural Things . . . Translated . . . by D. Cable. 1671. 16°. **8905. a. 9.**

—— *See* Suchten (A. von) Alex. van Suchten Of the Secrets of Antimony . . . Translated . . . by Dr. C., a person of great skill in chymistry [i.e. D. Cable], *etc.* 1670. 12°. **1033. f. 35.**

CABLE (Donald Elmer) *See* MacKee (Ralph H.) and Cable (D. E.) A Liquid Sulphur Dioxide Process for Sulphite Pulp. 1925. 8°. **8899. g. 37.**

CABLE (E. M.)

—— The United States-Korean Relations, 1866–1871. [With plates and maps.] pp. 237. *Seoul,* 1938. 8°. [*Transactions of the Korea Branch of the Royal Asiatic Society.* vol. 28.] **Ac. 8828. c.**

CABLE (Emmett James)

—— Science in a Changing World. [By] Emmett James Cable . . . Robert Ward Getchell . . . William Henry Kadesch. Revised edition. pp. xvii. 622. *Prentice-Hall: New York,* 1946. 8°. **8713. de. 3.**

CABLE (Frank T.) The Birth and Development of the American Submarine. [With plates, including portraits.] pp. xix. 337. *Harper & Bros.: New York & London,* 1924. 8°. **08806. k. 27.**

CABLE (George Washington) *See* Baskervill (William M.) Southern Writers, *etc.* (no. 7. George W. Cable.) 1896, *etc.* 8°. **11825. bb. 34.**

—— *See* Biklé (Lucy L. C.) George W. Cable, *etc.* [With portraits.] 1928. 8°. **010884. h. 18.**

—— *See* Dennis (Mary C.) The Tail of the Comet. [Memoirs of G. W. Cable and A. L. P. Dennis. With a portrait.] 1937. 8°. **010885. ff. 59.**

—— Madame Delphine, Carancro and Grande Pointe . . . [Three tales.] Author's edition. pp. 318. *D. Douglas: Edinburgh,* 1887. 8°. **12705. a. 30.**

—— Bon aventure. A prose pastoral of Acadian Louisiana. pp. v. 314. *Sampson Low & Co.: London,* 1888. 8°. **12707. i. 20.**

—— The Busy Man's Bible and how to study and teach it. pp. 95. *Sunday School Union: London,* [1896.] 8°. **03128. f. 2.**

—— Bylow Hill, *etc.* pp. vii. 215. *Hodder & Stoughton: London; New York* printed, 1902. 8°. **012703. l. 44.**

—— The Cavalier. pp. viii. 371. *John Murray: London,* 1901. 8°. **012703. i. 37.**

—— [Another edition.] pp. vii. 311. *Copp, Clark Co.: Toronto,* 1901. 8°. **012622. k. 12.**

—— The Creoles of Louisiana. [With illustrations.] pp. ix. 320. *J. C. Nimmo: London,* 1885 [1884]. 8°. **10409. s. 11.**

—— Dr. Sevier. pp. 528. *David Douglas: Edinburgh,* 1883, [84.] 8°. **12704. o. 29.**

—— [Another edition.] 2 vol. *David Douglas: Edinburgh,* 1884. 8°. **12707. ee. 9.**

—— [Another edition.] pp. 473. *J. R. Osgood & Co.: Boston,* 1885. 8°. **12707. dd. 8.**

—— The Flower of the Chapdelaines. pp. 262. *W. Collins, Sons & Co.: London,* [1919.] 8°. **NN. 5462.**

—— The Grandissimes. A story of Creole life. pp. ix. 448. *C. Scribner's Sons: New York,* 1880. 8°. **12705. ff. 16.**

—— [Another edition.] With an introductory note by J. M. Barrie. pp. xv. 383. *Hodder & Stoughton: London,* 1898. 8°. **012704. f. 63.**

—— [Another edition.] With illustrations by Albert Herter. pp. xi. 491. *Hodder & Stoughton: London; Cambridge, U.S.A.* printed, 1899. 8°. **12706. m. 2.**

—— *See* Junius (E.) *pseud.* Critical Dialogue between Aboo and Caboo on a new book [i.e. "The Grandissimes" by G. W. Cable], *etc.* 1880. 8°. **11826. n. 39.**

—— John March, Southerner. pp. viii. 513. *Sampson Low & Co.: London,* 1895. 8°. **012705. i. 39.**

—— Kincaid's Battery . . . Illustrated by Alonzo Kimball. pp. x. 396. *Hodder & Stoughton: London; New York* printed, 1909. 8°. **012705. aaa. 47.**

CABLE (George Washington)

—— Madame Delphine, a novelette, and other tales. pp. 176. *F. Warne & Co.: London*, [1881.] 8°. **12600. h. 5.**

—— Old Creole Days. pp. 229. *C. Scribner's Sons: New York*, 1879. 8°. **12704. dd. 4.**

—— Author's edition. pp. 260. *David Douglas: Edinburgh*, 1883. 16°. **12704. l. 23.**

—— [Another edition.] With illustrations by A. Herter. pp. viii. 234. *Lawrence & Bullen: London; Cambridge, Mass.* printed, 1897. 8°. **12703. i. 39.**

—— [Another edition.] pp. 228. *Hodder & Stoughton: London*, 1902. 8°. **012707. i. 18.**

—— Jean Roquelin.—La plantation des belles-demoiselles. [From "Old Creole Days."] *See* Bentzon (T.) *pseud.* Récits américains, *etc.* 1888. 12°. **012706. g. 11.**

—— Old Creole Days, *etc.* pp. xv. 303. *Hodder & Stoughton: London; New York* printed, 1943. 8°. **12727. aa. 18.**

—— The Silent South. Together with The Freedman's Case in Equity and The Convict Lease System. pp. vi. 180. *C. Scribner's Sons: New York*, 1885. 12°. **8176. b. 27.**

—— Strange True Stories of Louisiana, *etc.* pp. xi. 350. *C. Scribner's Sons: New York*, 1889. 8°. **012704. l. 11.**

—— Strong Hearts. pp. 255. *Hodder & Stoughton: London*, 1899. 8°. **012703. e. 54.**

CABLE (J. W.) The Engineers' Guide to the Width of Leather Belt required to transmit any given Horse-Power. [*London*, 1895.] *A card.* **1820.h.8.(66.)**

CABLE (John Ray) The Bank of the State of Missouri. pp. 319. *Columbia University Press: New York*, 1923. 8°. [*Studies in History, Economics and Public Law.* vol. 102. no. 2.] **Ac. 2688/2.**

CABLE (Joseph Wesley)

—— Induction and Dielectric Heating. pp. vii. 576. *Reinhold Publishing Corporation: New York*, 1954. 8°. **8717. bb. 32.**

CABLE (Louella E.) *See* Hildebrand (Samuel F.) and Cable (L. E.) Development and Life History of Fourteen Teleostean Fishes at Beaufort, N.C., *etc.* 1930. 8°. [*Bulletin of the Bureau of Fisheries.* vol. 46.] **A.S. 96.**

—— *See* Hildebrand (Samuel F.) and Cable (L. E.) Further Notes on the Development and Life History of Some Teleosts at Beaufort, N.C., *etc.* 1938. 8°. [*U.S. Bureau of Fisheries. Bulletin.* vol. 48. no. 24.] **A.S. 96.**

CABLE (Lucy Leffingwell) *See* Lowell (James R.) Lowell day by day. Selected by L. L. Cable, *etc.* [1910.] 8°. **11604. eee. 40/10.**

CABLE (Mildred) *See* Cable (Alice M.)

CABLE (Richard) Richard Cable, the Lightshipman. By the author of 'Mehalah' [i.e. Sabine Baring Gould], *etc.* 3 vol. *Smith, Elder & Co.: London*, 1888. 8°. **012638. k. 9.**

CABLES (Henry Albert) Diagnosis and Treatment of Diseases. Aphorisms, observations, and precepts on the method of examination and diagnosis of diseases, with practical rules for proper remedial procedure. pp. 298. *J. Keener & Co.: London*, 1911. 8°. [*Medical Guide and Monograph Series.*] **07306. g. 63.**

CABMAN. The Cabman. A monthly journal. S[ee] London.—III. *London Cabmen's Mission.*

—— The Cabman's Daughter. A tale. pp. 128. *J. & R. Maxwell: London*, [1885.] 8°. **12618. a. 1**

—— A Cabman's Faith. pp. 4. *Seeley, Jackson & Hallida[y]: London*, [1858.] 12°. **4380. ee. 16. (**

—— Cabman's Joint Branch (Rank and File) Committ[ee]. *See* London.—III.

—— The Cabman's Punch. *See* London.—III. *Cabma[n's] Joint Branch (Rank and File) Committee.*

CABO. El Cabo de Guardia vigilante del Centinela d[el] Teatro. *See* Periodical Publications.—*Mexico.*

CABO-BERTON. *See* Cape Breton.

CABO-VERDE. *See* Cape Verde.

CABO (José Serrano) *See* Serrano Cabo.

CABOARA (Lorenzo) *See* Romagnosi (G. D.) Op[ere] scelte. (1. Vedute fondamentali sull'arte logica. Edizio[ne] critica a cura e con note di L. Caboara.) 1936, *etc.* [*Reale Accademia d'Italia. Collezione "Varia."* no. 5.] **Ac. 104. fc**

CABOCHE (Alfred Arthur) Essai sur les scroful[es]. Thèse, *etc.* pp. 31. *Montpellier*, 1843. 4°. **1182. c. 19. (2**

CABOCHE (Charles) Les Mémoires et l'histoire en Fran[ce]. 2 tom. *Paris*, 1863. 8°. **9200. g.**

CABOCHE (H. A.) De l'influence de la lésion de l'inner[va]tion, comme cause de la mort; thèse, *etc.* pp. 41. *Pa[ris]*, 1833. 4°. **1184. f. 1.**

CABOCHE DEMERVILLE (Julien)

—— *See* Periodical Publications.—*Paris.* La Maison [de] campagne. Journal illustré des châteaux, des villas, [des] petites et grandes propriétés rurales . . . Rédacteur [en] chef: J.-C. Demerville. 1860, *etc.* 8°. **P.P. 2224.**

—— Les Anim[aux] célèbres, intelligents et curieux. [With illustratio[ns]] pp. 236. *Paris*, [1845.] 8°. **1256. h.**

—— Les Petits Français. (Illustrations de Gava[rni], Géniole [and others].) [Edited by J. Caboche Demervil[le]] pp. xi. 275. *Paris*, 1842. 8°. **012350. de.**

CABOCHON (Francis) *pseud.* [i.e. Philip Bert[ie] Murray Allan.] *See* also Allan (P. B. M.)

—— The Golden Ladies of Pampel[...] [A novel.] pp. 315. *Philip Allan: London*, 1934. **NN. 23**

CABOGA (Herbert W. M. von) *Count.*

—— Die mittelalterliche Burg im Süden und Westen [des] deutschen Sprachgebietes. Erweiterte Ausgabe mit [Hin]weisen für Konservierungen. pp. 75. *Rapper[swil]*, 1951. 8°. **07822. b.** *Regionale Burgenkunde.* Reihe 2. no. 1.

—— Der Orient und sein Einfluss auf den mittelalterli[chen] Wehrbau des Abendlandes. pp. 36. *Madrid*, 1953. **8838. ee.** *Mitteilungen der Castellologischen Kommission.* no.

—— L'Orient et son influence sur la fortification médié[vale] de l'Occident . . . Conférence au IIIe Congrès internati[onal] pour l'étude des châteaux. pp. 16. *Rapperswil*, 1951. **8838. e** *Castellologie internationale.* ser. 1. no. 1.

CABON (Marcel) Diptyque. [Two sketches.] pp. 12. *Port Louis*, 1935. 8°. **12357. s. 19.**
One of an edition of 100 *copies.*

—— Ébauches. [Poems.] pp. 15. *Port Louis*, 1932. 8°. **20002. e. 82.**
One of an edition of 100 *copies.*

—— Fenêtres sur la vie, *etc.* [Poems.] *Port Louis*, 1933. 8°. **20002. h. 34.**

—— Printemps. pp. 12. *Port-Louis*, 1941. 8°. **12547. h. 27.**

—— Roseaux. [Poems.] Illustrations de Jac. Desmarais. *Port-Louis*, 1932. 8°. **20020. b. 14.**
One of an edition of fifty copies.

—— Villa Fomalhaut. pp. 22. *Standard Printing Establishment:* [*Port-Louis*,] 1940. 8°. **012548. h. 21.**

CABON DE MÉSORMEL (Alexandre) De la pneumonie aiguë. Tribut académique, *etc.* pp. 16. *Montpellier*, 1836. 4°. **1181. g. 16. (14.)**

CABONI (Adriana)

—— Le Poesie di Uc de Mataplana. (Estratto da Cultura neolatina.) pp. 6. *Modena*, [1941.] 4°. **11868. pp. 15.**

CABORN (H. N.)

—— *See* Halliday (Alan S.) The New Whirling Arm at the National Physical Laboratory. By A. S. Halliday . . . and N. H. Caborn. 1949. 4°. [*England. Aeronautical Research Council. Reports and Memoranda.* no. 2286.] **B.S. 2/2.**

CABORNE (Warren Frederick) *See* Dowling (Robert) All about Ships and Shipping . . . With a preface by Commander W. F. Caborne. 1909. 16°. **08806. a. 1.**

—— British Merchant Seamen; their training and treatment, *etc.* pp. 48. *London*, 1898. 8°. [*Shipmasters' Society. Course of Papers.* no. 55.] **08805. bb. 1/55.**

—— The Personnel of the Mercantile Marine. pp. 40. *London*, 1897. 8°. [*Shipmasters' Society. Course of Papers.* no. 52.] **08805. bb. 1/52.**

—— Sons of Our Navy. *R. Tuck & Sons: London*, [1917.] fol. [*Father Tuck's "Patriotic" Series.*] **12812. dd. 26.**

CABOS ( ) A Toulouse, ce 6 ventôse, 5e année . . . Copie d'une lettre écrite par le citoyen Cabos cadet, . . . au citoyen Estadens, membre du Conseil des Anciens. [Concerning the arrest of the author.] [1797.] *s. sh.* 4°. **R. 674. (26.)**

CABOS (Alban) *See* Du Faur (G.) *Seigneur de Pibrac.* L'Apologie de la Saint-Barthélemy. [Edited and translated by A. Cabos.] 1922. 8°. **9200. g. 14.**

—— Guy du Faur de Pibrac. Un magistrat poète au xvie siècle, 1528–1584. [With a bibliography.] pp. 500. *Paris, Auch*, 1922. 8°. **10657. dd. 40.**

CABOS (J. P.) La Réjection du Christ. [A sermon.] 1837. *See* Roussel (N.) Galerie de quelques prédicateurs de l'Église Réformée de France, *etc.* 1835, *etc.* 8°. **4426. cc. 8. (1.)**

CABOT, *pseud.* The Musings of a City Clerk. By "Cabot." pp. 239. *Heath Cranton & Ouseley: London*, [1913.] 8°. **012354. g. 5.**

CABOT, *pseud.* [i.e. William George.] Small Street, Bristol: its ancient state and old inhabitants. From The Bristol Times and Mirror, *etc.* [Signed: Cabot.] pp. 4. *Printed for private circulation*, [1885.] 8°. **10347. c. 27. (4.)**
One of an edition of 100 *copies.*

CABOT CALENDAR. *See* Ephemerides.

CABOT SOCIETY. The Cabot Society. [A prospectus.] [*London?* 1845?] 4°. **741. k. 1. (7.)**

CABOT, *Family of.* *See* Briggs (Lloyd V.) History and Genealogy of the Cabot Family, 1475–1927. [With portraits.] 1927. 8°. **09917. e. 6.**

CABOT (Charles) *See* Jallais (A. de) La Corde du pendu. Vaudeville . . . par MM. A. de Jallais, C. Cabot et E. Cadol. 1854. 8°. **11739. g. 88. (9.)**

—— Les Deux barbes. Vaudeville en un acte, *etc.* pp. 8. *Lagny*, [1865.] 4°. **11737. g. 17.**

—— Les Malheurs d'un homme heureux. Vaudeville en un acte. pp. 39. *Paris*, 1866. 8°. **11737. aaa. 41. (6.)**

—— Sous un bec de gaz. Scènes de la vie nocturne, en une nuit. Par MM. C. Cabot, A. de Jallais et Lelarge. pp. 20. *Paris*, 1854. 8°. [*Bibliothèque dramatique.* tom. 58.] **2296. c. 27.**

—— [Another edition.] pp. 6. 1855. *See* Théâtre. Théâtre contemporain illustré. livr. 168, 169. [1852, *etc.*] fol. **2296. h.**

CABOT (Ella Lyman) Character Training. A suggestive series of lessons in ethics . . . Revised, supplemented, and edited for English teachers by Edward Eyles. pp. 384. *G. G. Harrap & Co.: London*, 1912. 8°. **08407. k. 36.**

—— Everyday Ethics. pp. xiii. 439. *G. Bell & Sons: London*, 1907. 8°. **08407. i. 20.**

—— Seven Ages of Childhood. pp. xxxiv. 321. *Kegan Paul & Co.: London; Cambridge, Mass.* printed, 1921. 8°. **08311. ee. 21.**

—— Temptations to Rightdoing. pp. xvii. 311. *Houghton Mifflin Co.: Boston & New York*, 1929. 8°. **4397. ee. 5.**

CABOT (George) *See* Kirkland (John T.) A Discourse delivered . . . after the interment of the Hon. G. Cabot, *etc.* 1823. 8°. **4985. cc. 45. (14.)**

—— [Letters.] *See* Lodge (Henry C.) Life and Letters of George Cabot. 1877. 8°. **10881. eee. 7.**

CABOT (George D.)

—— Priced Catalogue of the State and City Revenue and Tax Stamps of the United States. pp. iii. 138. [*The Author:*] *Weehawken*, 1940. 8°. **08247. g. 59.**

CABOT (Henry Bromfield) *See* Warner (Sam B.) and Cabot (H. B.) Judges and Law Reform. 1936. 8°. [*Survey of Crime and Criminal Justice in Boston.* vol. 4.] **Ac. 2692. an/3.**

CABOT (Hugh) After-Order by Lieut.-Colonel Hugh Cabot, *etc.* [Containing appreciations of the work of No. 22 General Hospital, B.E.F.] [1919.] 8°. *See* England.—*Army.—Medical Services.—No.* 22 *General Hospital, B.E.F.* **1865. c. 4. (60.)**

—— The Doctor's Bill, *etc.* [On contemporary medical practice in America and Europe.] pp. xvi. 313. *Columbia University Press: New York*, 1935. 8°. **7680. e. 55.**

—— Modern Urology. In original contributions by American authors. Edited by H. Cabot . . . Third edition, thoroughly revised, *etc.* 2 vol. *Henry Kimpton: London; printed in America*, 1936. 8°. **07641.** k. **19.**

CABOT (Hugh) and **GILES** (Mary Dodd)

—— Surgical Nursing, *etc.* [With plates.] pp. 428. *W. B. Saunders Co.: Philadelphia & London*, 1931. 8°. **07688.** df. **9.**

—— Surgical Nursing . . . Fourth edition, revised. (reprinted) pp. xii. 513. *W. B. Saunders Co.: Philadelphia & London*, 1945. 8°. **7687.** c. **27.**

CABOT (Hugh) and **KAHL** (Joseph Alan)

—— Human Relations. Concepts and cases in concrete social science. [With plates.] 2 vol. *Harvard University Press: Cambridge, Mass.*, 1953. 8°. **08285.** i. **65.**

CABOT (James Elliot) *See* Emerson (Ralph W.) Emerson's Complete Works. [Edited by J. E. Cabot.] 1883, *etc.* 8°. **2344.** a. **4.**

—— *See* Emerson (Ralph W.) Poems . . . Household edition. [Edited by J. E. Cabot.] 1884. 8°. **11686.** cc. **11.**

—— *See* Periodical Publications.—*Boston, Massachusetts.* The Massachusetts Quarterly Review. [Edited by R. W. Emerson, T. Parker and J. E. Cabot.] 1847, *etc.* 8°. P.P. **6387.**

—— Lake Superior. Narrative. *See* Agassiz (Louis J. R.) Lake Superior: its physical character, *etc.* 1850. 8°. **10410.** e. **2.**

—— A Memoir of Ralph Waldo Emerson. [With a portrait.] 2 vol. pp. viii. iv. 809. *Houghton Mifflin & Co.: Boston & New York*, 1887. 8°. **10883.** bb. **10.**

—— [Another edition.] 2 vol. *Macmillan & Co.: London*, 1887. 8°. **2408.** c. **13.**

CABOT (John) *See* Avezac-Macaya (M. A. P. d') Les Navigations terre-neuviennes de Jean & Sébastien Cabot. Lettre au révérend Leonard Woods, *etc.* 1869. 8°. **10460.** f. **13.**

—— *See* Avezac-Macaya (M. A. P. d') A Letter on the Voyages of John and Sebastian Cabot. 1869. 8°. [*Collections of the Maine Historical Society.* ser. 2. vol. 1.] Ac. **8390.**

—— *See* Barrera Pezzi (C.) Di Giovanni Cabotto, rivelatore del settentrionale emisfero d'America, *etc.* 1881. 4°. **10629.** f. **16.**

—— *See* Beazley (*Sir* Charles R.) John and Sebastian Cabot, *etc.* 1898. 8°. **10803.** ee. **21/3.**

—— *See* Bellemo (V.) Giovanni Caboto. Note critiche. 1894. fol. [*Raccolta di documenti e studi.* vol. 2.] **1899.m.30.**

—— *See* Biggar (Henry P.) The Voyages of the Cabots, *etc.* 1903. 8°. **10460.** df. **5.**

—— *See* Bourne (Edward G.) Original Narratives of the Voyages of J. Cabot. 1906. 8°. [*Olson (J. E.) The Northmen, Columbus and Cabot, etc.*] **9551.** p. **1.**

—— *See* Brown (Rawdon L.) Notices concerning John Cabot and his son Sebastian; transcribed and translated from original manuscripts in the Marcian Library at Venice, *etc.* 1855–6. 8°. [*Miscellanies of the Philobiblon Society.* vol. 2.] Ac. **9120.**

—— *See* Carreras i Valls (R.) Los Catalanes Juan Cab y Cristóbal Colom, *etc.* 1931. 8°. **9551.** bb. **3**

—— *See* Carreras i Valls (R.) Catalunya descobridor d'Amèrica. La pre-descoberta i els Catalans Joan Cab i Cristòfol Colom, *etc.* 1929. 8°. **9551.** g.

—— *See* Carreras i Valls (R.) La Descoberta d'Amèric —Ferrer, Cabot i Colom . . . Contenint un apèndi amb la prova autèntica d'ésser Cabot fill de Catalunya. [1928.] 8°. **9551.** l. **1**

—— *See* Colombo (C.) The Journal of Christopher Columbu . . . and Documents relating to the voyages of Joh Cabot and Gaspar Corte Real, *etc.* 1893. 8°. Ac. **6172/6**

—— *See* Dawson (Samuel E.) The Voyages of the Cabot John and Sebastian, in 1497 and 1498, *etc.* 1894. 4 [*Proceedings and Transactions of the Royal Society Canada.* vol. 12.] Ac. **188**

—— *See* Dawson (Samuel E.) The Voyages of the Cabot Latest phases of the controversy. 1897. 4°. [*Proceeding of the Royal Society of Canada.* ser. 2. vol. 3.] Ac. **188**

—— *See* Deane (Charles) *of Cambridge, Mass.* John an Sebastian Cabot. A study, *etc.* 1886. 8°. **10026.** l.

—— *See* Desimoni (C.) Intorno a Giovanni Caboto Genoves . . . Documenti, *etc.* 1881. 8°. **10604.** g. **4.** (1

—— *See* Dionne (Narcisse E.) John and Sebastian Cabot 1898. 8°. **9551.** dd.

—— *See* England.—*Commissioners of Customs.* "The Cabo Roll." The Customs Roll of the Port of Bristol, A. 1496 to 1499 . . . With an introduction relating to entrie of the royal pension paid to John Cabot, *etc.* 1897. fol. K.T.C. **21.** b. **1**

—— *See* Hakes (Harry) John and Sebastian Cabot, *etc.* 1897. 8°. **10600.** g. **2.** (6

—— *See* Harrisse (Henry) The Cabots. Notes on certai papers (by S. E. Dawson), *etc.* 1898. 8°. **09004.** d. **4.** (1

—— *See* Harrisse (Henry) Did Cabot return from hi Second Voyage? [1898.] 8°. **9009.** dd. **8.** (3

—— *See* Harrisse (Henry) The Discovery of North Americ by John Cabot. The alleged date, *etc.* 1897. 8°. **9551.** bb. **3**

—— *See* Harrisse (Henry) Jean et Sébastien Cabot, le origine et leurs voyages, étude d'histoire critique, *etc.* 1882. 8°. [*Recueil de voyages . . . pour servir à l'histoi de la géographie, etc.* no. 1.] **10024.i.1/**

—— *See* Harrisse (Henry) John Cabot, the discoverer North America, and Sebastian, his son, *etc.* 1896. 8°. K.T.C. **37.** a.

—— *See* Horsford (Eben N.) John Cabot's Landfall 1497, *etc.* 1886. 4°. **1855.** a.

—— *See* Howley (Michael F.) *R.C. Bishop of St. John' Newfoundland.* Cabot's Voyages, *etc.* [1897.] 8°. **10410.** dd. **34.** (3

—— *See* Howley (Michael F.) *R.C. Bishop of St. John' Newfoundland.* Latest Light on the Cabot Controversy. 1903. 8°. **09004.** d. **5.** (8

CABOT (JOHN)

—— *See* KIDDER (Frederic) The Discovery of North America by John Cabot, *etc.* 1878. 8°. **10408. g. 11. (5.)**

—— *See* PORTER (Edward G.) The Cabot Quadri-Centenary Celebrations at Bristol, Halifax and St. John's in June 1897. [1898.] 8°. **9551. d. 5. (8.)**

—— *See* PORTER (Edward G.) Report of the Cabot Proceedings at the Halifax Meeting of the Royal Society of Canada, *etc.* 1897. 8°. **9551. d. 5. (7.)**

—— *See* PROWSE (George R. F.) Cabot's Bacalhaos, *etc.* [1938.] 8°. **1856. g. 14. (10.)**

—— *See* PROWSE (George R. F.) John Cabot's Baccalaos, *etc.* 1940. fol. Cup. **1247. cc. 19.**

—— *See* PROWSE (George R. F.) Cabot's Bona Vista Landfall. 1946. fol. **9551. m. 19**

—— *See* PROWSE (G. R. F.) Cabot's Surveys. 1931. fol. **1854. g. 19.**

—— *See* PROWSE (G. R. F.) The Voyage of John Cabot in 1497 to North America. The time occupied in coasting, also the Island of St. John. Mr. G. R. F. Prowse's further reply to Mr. Henry Harrisse, *etc.* 1897. 8°. **9004. k. 16. (10.)**

—— *See* SERCIA (G.) Giovanni Caboto e la navigazione italiana del suo tempo, *etc.* 1937. 8°. **9171.c.1/5.**

—— *See* STEVENS (Henry) *F.S.A., of Vermont.* Sebastian Cabot—John Cabot. [A review of "The Remarkable Life, Adventures and Discoveries of Sebastian Cabot," by J. F. Nicholls.] 1870. 8°. **10411. aa. 14.**

—— *See* TARDUCCI (F.) Di Giovanni e Sebastiano Caboto. Memorie, *etc.* 1892. 8°. [*Miscellanea di storia veneta.* ser. 2. no. 1.] **Ac.6580/2.(5.)**

—— *See* TARDUCCI (F.) John and Sebastian Cabot, *etc.* 1893. 8°. **9551. i. 23.**

—— *See* THACHER (John B.) The Cabotian Discovery. 1897. 8°. **9551. dd. 11.**

—— *See* WEARE (George E.) Cabot's Discovery of North America. 1897. 8°. **9551. f. 15.**

—— *See* WEARE (George E.) Cabot's Discovery of North America. The dates connected with the voyage of the Matthew, of Bristol. Mr. G. E. Weare's reply to Mr. Henry Harrisse, *etc.* 1897. 16°. **09004. aa. 1. (6.)**

—— *See* WILLIAMSON (James A.) The Voyages of John and Sebastian Cabot. 1937. 8°. [*Historical Association Pamphlet.* no. 106.] Ac. **8116.** b.

—— *See* WILLIAMSON (James A.) The Voyages of the Cabots, *etc.* 1929. 8°. **9551. l. 20.**

—— *See* WINSHIP (George P.) Cabot Bibliography. 1897. 8°. **011900. aa. 17.**

—— —— 1900. 8°. **011904.** ee. **3.**

—— *See* WINSHIP (George P.) John Cabot and the Study of Sources, *etc.* 1898. 8°. **9004. m. 13. (8.)**

—— *See* WINSOR (Justin) The Cabot Controversies and the Right of England to North America, *etc.* 1896. 8°. **9551. d. 5. (4.)**

—— John Cabot. [A biography.] pp. 32. *Pelley Publishers: Asheville, N.C.,* 1937. 8°. **010655. aa. 13.**
Part of the series "Little Visits with Great Americans."

CABOT (JOHN MOORS)

—— Toward our Common American Destiny . . . Speeches and interviews on Latin American problems. [With a portrait.] pp. xvii. 214. *Fletcher School of Law & Diplomacy: [Medford,* 1955.] 8°.
[*Fletcher School Studies in International Affairs.*] **Ac. 2189. (1)**

CABOT (JOSEFA SASTRE DE) *See* SASTRE DE CABOT (J.)

CABOT (JOSEPH)

—— Golden Gates. pp. 287. *Museum Press: London,* 1950. 8°. NNN. **1573.**

—— An Innocent in the Garden. pp. 204. *Hamish Hamilton: London,* 1934. 8°. **07028. a. 57.**

—— Pebble in the Pond. pp. 335. *Hamish Hamilton: London,* 1933. 8°. NN. **2365.**

—— Transit of a Demigod. pp. 286. *Hamish Hamilton: London,* 1933. 8°. NN. **21363.**

CABOT (JUST)

—— Els Iniciadors de la Renaixença. Volum 1: la poesia . . . Text per Just Cabot, *etc.* [An anthology.] pp. 205. *Barcelona,* 1928. 8°. **11453. ee. 12.**
No more published?

CABOT (LOUIS) The Immature State of the Odonata. pt. 1–3. *Cambridge [Mass.],* 1872–90. 4°. [*Memoirs of the Museum of Comparative Zoölogy at Harvard College.* vol. 2. no. 5; vol. 8. no. 1; vol. 17. no. 1.] **Ac. 1736/4.**

CABOT (OLIVER) The Man without a Shadow . . . Illustrated. pp. vii. 340. *D. Appleton & Co.: New York,* 1909. 8°. **012705. c. 13.**

CABOT (P. P.) De la tarsalgie ou arthralgie tarsienne des adolescents. pp. 94. *Paris,* 1866. 4°. [*Collection des thèses soutenues à la Faculté de Médecine de Paris.* An 1866. tom. 2.] **7373. g. 5.**

CABOT (PHILIP) The Sense of Immortality. (The Ingersoll Lecture, 1924.) pp. 50. *Harvard University Press: Cambridge, Mass.,* 1924. 8°. **4256. df. 51.**

CABOT (PHILIP) and **MALOTT** (DEANE WALDO)

—— Problems in Public Utility Management. pp. xii. 624. *A. W. Shaw Co.: Chicago & New York,* 1927. 8°. **08244. h. 45.**

—— Second revised edition. pp. xiv. 632. *McGraw-Hill Book Co.: New York,* 1930. 8°. **08246. g. 67.**

CABOT (RICHARD CLARKE) *See* DRUCKER (Saul) and HEXTER (M. B.) Children Astray . . . Introduction by R. C. Cabot. 1923. 8°. **08282. dd. 40.**

—— The Achievements, Standards and Prospects of the Massachusetts General Hospital . . . Ether Day address, 1919. pp. 22. [*Boston,* 1919.] 8°. **7688. f. 14.**

—— Adventures on the Borderlands of Ethics. pp. viii. 152. *Harper & Bros.: New York & London,* 1926. 8°. **8403. i. 18.**

—— Case Teaching in Medicine. A series of graduated exercises in the differential diagnosis, prognosis and treatment of actual cases of disease. pp. x. 214. *D. C. Heath & Co.: Boston,* 1907. 8°. **7442. d. 9.**

—— Christianity and Sex. pp. vii. 78. *Macmillan Co.: New York,* 1938. 8°. **08416. l. 17.**

CABOT (RICHARD CLARKE)

—— Differential Diagnosis . . . Presented through an analysis of 385 cases . . . Third edition, revised. Profusely illustrated. 2 vol. *W. B. Saunders Co.: Philadelphia & London*, 1916. 8°. **7441**. d. **7**.

—— Fourth edition, revised, *etc.* vol. 1. pp. 781. *W. B. Saunders Co.: Philadephia & London*, 1919. 8°. **7440**. w. **24**.

No more published.

—— Diseases of Metabolism and of the Blood. Animal Parasites. Toxicology. Edited by R. C. Cabot . . . An authorized translation from "Die deutsche Klinik," *etc.* pp. xiv. 649. *D. Appleton & Co.: New York & London*, 1906. 8°. [*Modern Clinical Medicine.*] **7462**. dd. **14/7**.

—— [A reissue.] *New York & London*, 1910. 8°. [*Modern Clinical Medicine.*] **7462**. dd. **14/8**.

—— A Guide to the Clinical Examination of the Blood for diagnostic purposes . . . With colored plates and engravings. pp. xix. 405. *Longmans & Co.: London; New York* printed, 1897. 8°. **7442**. bb. **25**.

—— Fifth revised edition. pp. xx. 549. *Longmans & Co.: London & Bombay; New York* printed, 1904. 8°. **2256**. h. **16**.

—— Honesty. pp. ix. 326. *Macmillan Co.: New York*, 1938. 8°. **8412**. bb. **4**.

—— The Meaning of Right and Wrong. pp. x. 463. *Macmillan Co.: New York*, 1933. 8°. **08408**. g. **31**.

—— Physical Diagnosis of Diseases of the Chest, *etc.* pp. xv. 310. *Baillière & Co.: London; New York* printed, 1901. 8°. **7616**. f. **32**.

—— Third edition, revised and enlarged, *etc.* pp. xxii. 577. *Baillière & Co.: London*, 1906 [1905]. 8°. **7461**. e. **32**.

—— Fourth edition, revised and enlarged, *etc.* pp. xxii. 579. *Baillière & Co.: London; New York* printed, 1910. 8°. **7462**. d. **16**.

—— Fifth edition, revised and enlarged, *etc.* pp. xxi. 519. *Baillière & Co.: London*, 1913. 8°. **7460**. i. **12**.

—— Sixth edition, revised and enlarged, *etc.* pp. xxi. 521. *Baillière & Co.: London; printed in America*, 1916. 8°. **7460**. i. **16**.

—— Seventh edition, revised and enlarged, *etc.* pp. xxi. 527. *Baillière & Co.: London; printed in America*, 1920. 8°. **7462**. dd. **9**.

—— Eighth edition, revised and enlarged, *etc.* pp. xxi. 536. pl. v. *Baillière & Co.: London; York, Pa.* printed, 1923. 8°. **7460**. h. **17**.

—— Ninth edition, revised and enlarged, *etc.* pp. xxi. 536. pl. v. *Baillière & Co.: London; York, Pa.* printed, 1927. 8°. **7460**. dd. **16**.

—— Tenth edition, revised and enlarged, *etc.* pp. xxi. 529. *Baillière & Co.: London; York, Pa.* printed, 1930. 8°. **7462**. cc. **40**.

—— Eleventh edition. pp. xxiv. 540. *Baillière & Co.: London; printed in America*, 1934. 8°. **7580**. r. **12**.
Later editions are *entered under* CABOT (*R. C.*) *and* ADAMS (*Frank D.*).

—— The Serum Diagnosis of Disease. pp. vii. 154. *Longmans & Co.: London*, 1899. 8°. **7460**. d. **44**.

CABOT (RICHARD CLARKE)

—— Social Work. Essays on the meeting-ground of doctor and social worker. pp. xxvii. 188. *Constable & Co. London; Cambridge, Mass.* printed, [1920.] 8°. **08282**. aaa. **11**.

—— Training and Rewards of the Physician. pp. 153. *Philadelphia & London*, 1918. 8°. [*Lippincott's Training Series.*] **012213.aa.2/4**

—— What Men Live By: work, play, love, worship. pp. xxi. 341. *G. G. Harrap & Co.: London; Cambridge, Mass.* printed, 1915. 8°. **08407**. l. **32**.

CABOT (RICHARD CLARKE) and **ADAMS** (FRANK DENNETTE)

—— Physical Diagnosis . . . Twelfth edition. pp. xxii. 846. *Baillière & Co. London*, 1938. 8°. **7439**. ppp. **12**.
Earlier editions are entered under CABOT (*Richard C.*)

—— Cabot and Adams Physical Diagnosis. Thirteenth edition by F. Dennette Adams. pp. xv. 888. *Baillière & Co.: London; printed in America*, 1942. 8°. **7440**. h. **37**.

CABOT (RICHARD CLARKE) and **DICKS** (RUSSELL LESLIE)

—— The Art of Ministering to the Sick. pp. viii. 384. *Macmillan Co.: New York*, 1936. 8°. **4499.m.17**

CABOT (SEBASTIAN) [For works relating to John and Sebastian Cabot:] *See* CABOT (John)

—— *See* BIDDLE (Richard) A Memoir of Sebastian Cabot, *etc.* [With a portrait.] 1915. 8°. **10408**. o. **23**.

—— *See* DEANE (Charles) *of Cambridge, Massachusetts.* Remarks on Sebastin Cabot's Mappe-Monde, *etc.* 1867. 8°. **10408**. g. **21**. (4.)

—— *See* EDEN (Richard) The History of Trauayle in the West and East Indies, *etc.* (Of the Northeast frostie Seas . . . likewise of the viages of that worthie old man Sebastian Cabote, *etc.*) 1577. 4°. **304**. d. **16**.

—— *See* ERRERA (C.) La Spedizione di Sebastiano Cabot al Rio della Plata. 1895. 8°. [*Archivio storico italiano.* ser. 5. tom. 15.] P.P. **3557**. a.

—— *See* FABYAN (Robert) A Note of Sebastian Gabotes voyage of discouerie, taken out of an old Chronicle, *etc.* 1582. 4°. [*H., R. Diuers voyages touching the discouerie of America, etc.*] C. **21**. b. **35**.

—— *See* GANDÍA (E. de) Antecedentes diplomáticos de las expediciones de Juan Díaz de Solís, Sebastián Caboto y Don Pedro de Mendoza. 1935. 8°. **010028**. f. **21**.

—— *See* HARRISSE (Henry) Sébastien Cabot, pilote-major d'Espagne, considéré comme cartographe, *etc.* 1897. 8°. **10412**. gg. **22**. (5.)

—— *See* HARRISSE (Henry) Sébastien Cabot, pilote-majeur d'Espagne, considéré comme navigateur, *etc.* 1897. 8°. **9551**. dd. **5**.

—— *See* HAYWARD (Charles) *American Writer.* Life of Sebastian Cabot. [With a portrait.] 1838. 12°. [*Library of American Biography.* vol. 9.] **10883**. df. **7**.

—— —— [1850?] 12°. [*Library of American Biography.* vol. 9.] **1452**. b. **9**.

CABOT (SEBASTIAN)

—— *See* HAYWARD (Charles) *American Writer.* Life of Sebastian Cabot. 1838. 8°. [*Library of American Biography.* vol. 9.] **10883. df. 7.**

—— *See* HELLWALD (F. A. H. von) *Baron.* Sebastian Cabot. Vortrag, *etc.* 1871. 8°. [*Sammlung gemeinverständlicher wissenschaftlicher Vorträge.* Ser. 6. Hft. 124.] **12249. l. 6.**

—— *See* HERRERA TORDESILLAS (A. de) De Trotsmoedige scheeps-togt van Sebastiaan Gaboto . . . na de Moluccos *etc.* 1707. 8°. [*AA (P. vander) Naaukeurige versameling der gedenk-waardigste zee en land reysen, etc.* vol. 42.] **979. e. 11.**

—— —— 1727. fol. [*AA (P. vander) De Aanmerkenswaardigste . . . zee- en landreizen der Portugeezen, etc.* dl. 2.] **566. l. 6.**

—— *See* MEDINA (J. T.) El Veneciano Sebastián Caboto al servicio de España, *etc.* 1908. fol. **10027. i. 17.**

—— *See* NICHOLLS (James F.) The Remarkable Life, Adventures and Discoveries of Sebastian Cabot, *etc.* [With a portrait.] 1869. 8°. **10817. bbb. 7.**

—— *See* PROWSE (George R. F.) Sebastian Cabot Lied, *etc.* 1942. fol. **9603. g. 20.**

—— *See* RAMUSIO (G. B.) Primo [*etc.*] volume . . . delle Nauigationi et Viaggi raccolto da M. G. B. Ramusio, *etc.* (vol. 2. La nauigatione di Sebastiano Cabota nelle parte Settentrionali.) 1588, *etc.* fol. **C. 79. e. 4.**

—— *See* TYTLER (Patrick F.) Historical View of the Progress of Discovery on the more Northern Coasts of America . . . To which is added an appendix, containing remarks on a late memoir of Sebastian Cabot [by Richard Biddle], *etc.* 1832. 12°. **12203.t.1/9.**

—— *See* WINSOR (Justin) Cabot and the Transmission of English Power in North America, *etc.* 1896. 8°. **09004. d. 1. (8.)**

—— A Memoir of Sebastian Cabot; with a review of the history of maritime discovery. [By Richard Biddle.] Illustrated by documents from the Rolls, now first published. pp. viii. 333. *Hurst, Chance & Co.: London,* 1831. 8°. **1202. k. 9.**

—— [Another copy.] **G. 1930.**

—— [Another edition.] pp. viii. 327. *Carey & Lea: Philadelphia,* 1831. 8°. **10408. f. 21.**

—— Sébastien Cabot, navigateur vénitien, 1497–1557. Étude d'histoire critique, *etc.* [A criticism of Francesco Tarducci's work "Di Giovanni e Sebastiano Caboto. Memorie." Signed: B. A. V., i.e. H. Harrisse.] 1895. 8°. *See* V., B. A. **10602. i. 22. (9.)**

CABOT (STEPHEN PERKINS) Secondary Education in Germany, France, England and Denmark. pp. xii. 110. *Cambridge, Mass.,* 1930. 8°. [*Harvard Bulletins in Education.* no. 15.] **Ac. 2692. bb.**

CABOT (WILLIAM BROOKS) *See* HUBBARD (Mina B.) A Woman's Way through Unknown Labrador, *etc.* [With an introduction by W. B. Cabot.] 1908. 8°. **10460. dd. 26.**

—— In Northern Labrador . . . With many illustrations from photographs. pp. xii. 292. *R. G. Badger: Boston,* [1912.] 8°. **010470. f. 3.**

CABOT (WILLIAM BROOKS)

—— [Another copy, with a different titlepage.] pp. xii. 292. *John Murray: London,* 1912. 8°. **010470. f. 4.**

—— Labrador . . . With many illustrations, *etc.* pp. xiii. 354. *Small, Maynard & Co.: Boston,* [1920.] 8°. **010470. eee. 23.**

—— [A reissue.] *Heath Cranton: London; printed in U.S.A.,* [1922.] 8°. **010470. eee. 24.**

CABOTA (SEBASTIANO) *See* CABOT (Sebastian)

CABOTINES. Les Cabotines. Scènes épisodiques, historiques et critiques, sur les théâtres de Bordeaux. [By A. L. B. Robineau.] 2 pt. *Bordeaux,* [1803.] 8°. **11738. bb. 14. (4.)**

CABOTIUS (VINCENTIUS) Reuerendi in Christo Patris Michaelis Violæi . . . laudatio funebris. *See* VIOLE (M.) Reuerendi in Christo Patris D.D. Michaelis Violæi . . . tumulus. 1592. 4°. **1230. c. 32.**

—— Vincentii Cabotii . . . variarum iuris publici et privati disputationum liber primus (secundus). 1752. *See* MEERMAN (G.) Novus thesaurus juris civilis et canonici, *etc.* tom. 4. 1751, *etc.* fol. **18. h. 9.**

CABOTO (SEBASTIÁN) *See* CABOT.

CABOUAT (JULES) De l'extension du risque professionnel aux entreprises commerciales, aux employeurs et employés non assujettis et aux délégués à la sécurité des ouvriers mineurs, *etc.* 2 tom. *Paris,* 1914, 16. 8°. **5406. e. 16.**

—— Traité des accidents du travail. Exposé du système de responsabilité et d'indemnisation établi par la loi du 9 avril 1898, *etc.* 2 tom. *Paris,* 1901, 07. 8°. **08285. g. 63.**

CABOUL. *See* KABUL.

—— Traité des accidents du travail. Exposé du système de responsabilité et d'indemnisation établi par la loi du 9 avril 1898, *etc.* 2 tom. *Paris,* 1901, 07. 8°. **08285. g. 63.**

CABOULLET (JEAN JACQUES) Dissertation sur le cancer de l'estomac, *etc.* pp. 27. *Paris,* 1817. 4°. **1183. d. 8. (21.)**

CABOURG.

—— Cabourg. (Guides de poche "Borough.") Texte descriptif français et anglais. 3 plans, *etc.* pp. 40. *E. J. Burrow: Cheltenham,* [1910?] 8°. **10354. a. 165.**

CABOUS ONSOR EL MOALI, *Souverain du Djordjan et du Guilan.* *See* KAI-KĀ'ŪS IBN ISKANDAR, called 'UNṢUR AL-MA'ĀLĪ, *Amir of Dailam.*

CABOY (JEAN FIRMIN) De la fièvre puerpérale? pp. 32. *Paris,* 1853. 4°. [*Collection des thèses soutenues à la Faculté de Médecine de Paris.* An 1853. tom. 3.] **7372. f. 5.**

CABRA, FRANCISCO BELDA Y PÉREZ DE NUEROS, *Marquis de.* *See* BELDA Y PÉREZ DE NUEROS.

CABRA (ALPHONSE FRANÇOIS ÉDOUARD) *See* LIBBRECHT (E. J. J.) and CABRA (A. F. E.) Attaque et défense des places. 1895. 8°. **8831. k. 35.**

CABRA (J. PATA DE) *See* PATA DE CABRA.

CABRA (MARCOS DE) Nueva Relacion, y Jacoso [*sic*] Romance, en que se refiere el tragico casamiento de un desgraciado Mozo, llamado Marcos de Cabra, vecino de la Ciudad de Guadarrama, *etc.* *Madrid,* 1764. 4°. **T. 1954. (5.)**

—— [Another edition.] Marcos de Cabra. Nueva relacion y divertido romance, *etc.* *Madrid,* 1853. 4°. **11450. f. 23. (31.)**

CABRA (MARCOS DE)

—— [Another edition.] *Madrid*, 1858. 4°. **11450**. f. **25**. (**1**.)

CABRA (TEODORO JOSEPH DE) Historia Dolorosa, ó Dolores Historiados . . . en que se ve la acervisima Pasion de nuestro Redentor Jesu-Chisto [*sic*], y la compasion de su dolorosisima Madre, *etc*. pp. 32. *Sevilla*, 1786. 4°. **11451**. e. **38**. (**11**.)

CABRAL (A. DE OLIVEIRA) *See* OLIVEIRA CABRAL.

CABRAL (ALEXANDRE)

—— Terra quente, *etc*. [A novel.] pp. 139. *Lisboa*, 1953. 8°. **12493**. bb. **17**.

CABRAL (ALFREDO DO VALLE) *See* VALLE CABRAL.

CABRAL (ANTONIO) Relazione della vita e martirio del venerabil Padre Ignazio de Azevedo, ucciso dagli eretici con altri trentanove della Compagnia di Gesù. Cavata da' processi autentici, *etc*. pp. 202. *Roma*, 1743. 4°. **1371**. k. **26**.

CABRAL (ANTONIO BERNARDO DA COSTA) *Count de Thomar*. *See* COSTA CABRAL.

CABRAL (ANTÓNIO DO AMARAL) *See* AMARAL CABRAL.

CABRAL (ANTÓNIO JACINTO XAVIER)

—— *See* CAMPOS FERREIRA LIMA (H. de) O Gravador António Jacinto Xavier Cabral. 1949. 8°. [*Revista da Universidade de Coimbra*. vol. 16.] Ac. **2699**. c.

—— Explicaçao analitica do quadro alegorico da Regeneração da Monarquia Portugueza, *etc*. [With a portrait.] pp. 18. *Lisboa*, 1822. 8°. **7854**. c. **49**. (**1**.)

CABRAL (ANTONIO LÓPEZ) *See* LÓPEZ CABRAL.

CABRAL (ANTONIO MOREIRA) *See* MOREIRA CABRAL.

CABRAL (ANTONIO MOREIRA LEITE PEREIRA) *See* MOREIRA LEITE PEREIRA CABRAL.

CABRAL (DOMINGO) *See* HIERRO (A. del) El Doctor Don Agustin del Hierro . . . contra . . . el capitan D. Cabral. Sobre diferentes delitos de lesa Magestad in primo capite. [1640?] fol. **1322**. l. **10**. (**1**.)

CABRAL (ENRICO)

—— O Liceu Nacional Salazar. [With plates.] pp. 104. 1945. 8°. *See* PORTUGAL.—*Ministério das Colónias*.—*Agência Geral das Colónias*. **8356**. p. **25**.

CABRAL (ERNESTO GARCIA) *See* GARCIA CABRAL.

CABRAL (ESTEVÃO) Ricerche istoriche, fisiche ed idrostatiche sopra la caduta del Velino nella Nera. Colla dichiarazione di un nuovo metodo per determinare le velocità e la quantità delle acque correnti, ed altro nuovo metodo di elevare l'acqua ne' sifoni a grande altezza. [With plates.] pp. xii. 82. *Roma*, 1786. 8°. **659**. b. **13**. (**5**.)

—— Tratado de agrimensura, *etc*. [With plates.] pp. 90. 1795. 8°. *See* LISBON.—*Academia das Sciencias de Lisboa*. B. **685**. (**3**.)

CABRAL (ESTEVÃO) and RÈ (FAUSTO DEL)

—— Delle ville e de' più notabili monumenti antichi della città, e del territorio di Tivoli. Nuove ricerche. [With a map.] pp. xx. 220. *Roma*, 1779. 8°. **658**. c. **26**.

CABRAL (ESTEVÃO) and RÈ (FAUSTO DEL)

—— [Another copy.] **171**. n. **6**. *Imperfect; wanting the map*.

—— *See* SANCTIS (D. de) Dissertazioni sopra la villa d'Orazio Flacco, *etc*. (Risposta . . . all'appendice dei signori abb. Cabral e del Rè.) 1784. 4°. **658**. i. **20**.

CABRAL (FAUSTINO JOSÉ) Relatorios sobre a epidemia da fevre amarella em Loanda no anno de 1860. pp. 75. *Lisboa*, 1861. 8°. **7561**. c. **66**. (**4**.)

CABRAL (FERNÃO D'ALVARES) *See* ALVARES CABRAL.

CABRAL (FRANCISCO) Copia d'vna lettera . . . al Reuerendo Padre generale di Cocinocù, il primo di settembre, 1577. *See* JESUITS. [*Letters from Missions*.] Lettere del Giappone dell'anno M.D.LXXVII., *etc*. 1579. 8°. **4767**. b. **25**.

—— Nouueaux aduis de l'amplification, du Christianisme es pays et royaulmes du Iappon, enuoyés au R.P. general de la cōpagnie du nom de Iesus, *etc*. ff. 18. 1579. 8°. *See* JESUITS. [*Letters from Missions*.] **866**. e. 2.

—— [Another copy.] G. **6687**. (**2**.)

CABRAL (FRANCISCO ANTONIO) Analyse a hum escrito intitulado Memoria hydrografica das Ilhas de Cabo Verde . . . e censura á carta das Ilhas de Cabo Verde [both by F. A. Cabral] por hum Socio da Sociedade Real Maritima Militar Geografica. pp. 53. *Lisboa*, 1805. 8°. **10498**. a. **1**.

—— [Another copy.] **10498**. a. **21**.

CABRAL (FREDERICO AUGUSTO DE VASCONCELLOS PEREIRA) *See* VASCONCELLOS PEREIRA CABRAL.

CABRAL (GRAÇA ÁLVARES) *See* ÁLVARES CABRAL.

CABRAL (HÉCTOR INCHÁUSTEGUI) *See* INCHÁUSTEGUI CABRAL (H.)

CABRAL (JOAM RIBEYRO) *See* RIBEYRO CABRAL.

CABRAL (JOSÉ CURRY DA CAMARA) *See* CAMARA CABRAL.

CABRAL (JOSÉ VICTORIANO) Viages á Europa . . . 3ª edicion. pp. 252. *Buenos Aires*, 1895. 8°. **10107**. dd. **1**.

CABRAL (JUDICE)

—— Méningites cérébro-spinales. *See* INTERNATIONAL MEDICAL CONGRESS. [Lisbon, 1906.] XV. Congrès international de médecine, *etc*. (section 5. Médecine.) 1906. 8°. Ac. **3699/14**

CABRAL (LUIS D.) Diccionario Naval Argentino, que contiene cinco mil voces de las mas usadas en la marina española, inglesa y sud-americanas. pp. 242. *Buenos Aires*, 1881. 4°. **8806**. dd. **28**

CABRAL (LUIZ GONZAGA PEREIRA) *See* GONZAGA PEREIRA CABRAL.

CABRAL (MANOEL DE PINA) *See* PINA CABRAL.

CABRAL (MANUEL DEL)

—— Antología tierra, 1930–1949. [Poems.] pp. 199. *Madrid*, 1949. 8°. **011451**. h. **103** *Colección "Poesía de España y America. La encina y el mar."* no. 2.

CABRAL (MÁRIO DA VEIGA) *See* VEIGA CABRAL (M. da)

CABRAL (Miguel Osorio) *See* Osorio Cabral.

CABRAL (Morais) *See* Morais Cabral (   )

CABRAL (P. G. T. Veiga) *See* Veiga Cabral.

CABRAL (Pedro Alvares) *See* Alvares Cabral.

CABRAL (Philomeno da Camara Mello) *See* Camara Mello Cabral.

CABRAL (Stefano) *See* Cabral (Estevão)

CABRAL DA ROCHA WERNECK (Heloisa)

—— A Classificação Decimal Universal. Introdução ao Catálogo Geral da Biblioteca da D.E.P. pp. 35. 1938. 8°. *See* Brazil.—*Ministerio da Agricultura.—Directoria de Estatistica da Produção.* **11900.** cc. **100.**

CABRAL DE MELLO (Evaldo)

—— Recife. Uma introdução ao estudo das suas formas e das suas cores. pp. 38. *Recife,* 1952. 8°. **10481.** pp. **28.**

CABRAL DE MELLO E SILVA (José Augusto) Poesias Lyricas . . . Collecção 1ª. pp. 67. v. *Angra,* 1834. 4°. **11452.** e. **35.**
No more published.

CABRAL DE MONCADA (Luís)

—— Estudos de história do direito. 3 vol. 1948–50. 8°. [*Acta Universitatis Conimbrigensis.*] Ac. **2699/3.** (**4.**)

—— Filosofia do direito e do estado. *Coimbra,* 1947 [1949]– . 8°. W.P. **117.**
Colecção studium. no. 57.

—— Subsídios para uma história da filosofia do direito em Portugal. *In:* Revista da Universidade de Coimbra. vol. 13. pp. 298–442. 1937. 8°. Ac. **2699.** c.

CABRAL DE NOROÑA (   ) Reflexiones imparciales sobre la Franc-Masoneria. [Signed: C. N., i.e. —— Cabral de Noroña?] pp. 30. 1818. 8°. *See* N., C. **4783.** aaa. **40.** (**1.**)

CABRAL DE VASCONCELLOS (Paulino Antonio) Poesias. 2 tom. *Porto,* 1786, 87. 8°. **11452.** aaa. **17.**

CABRAL DO NASCIMENTO (João)

—— *See* Baring (*Hon.* Maurice) C. Traduzido . . . por Cabral do Nascimento. [1945?] 8°. **12649.** dd. **8.**

—— *See* Verde (José J. C.) O Livro de Cesário Verde . . . Edição revista por Cabral do Nascimento. 1952. 8°. **11453.** ee. **27.**

—— Cancioneiro. pp. 132. *Lisboa,* 1943. 8°. **11454.** b. **41.**

—— Confidéncia. [Poems.] pp. 107. *Lisboa,* [1946.] 8°. **11454.** b. **40.**

CABRAL GODINHO (Bento Affonso) Breve Memoria historica de algumas antiguidades, e prelados da Sé Eborense. pp. 8. *Coimbra,* 1836. 8°. **10161.** c. **33.**

CABRALIUS (Emmanuelis Pinius) *See* Pina Cabral (Manoel de)

CABRAL TEXO (Jorge)

—— *See* Alberdi (J. B.) Fragmento Preliminar al Estudio del Derecho . . . Noticia preliminar de J. Cabral Texo. 1942. 8°. Ac. **2694.** ea.

—— *See* Palacios (A. L.) Las Islas Malvinas . . . Prólogo del Profesor J. Cabral Texo. 1934. 8°. **010481.** e. **27.**

CABRANES (Diego de) Abito y armadura spiritual. G.L. ff. cclxxxii. *Impressa por F. Diaz: Gualupe; Merida,* 1544. fol. C. **62.** g. **11.**
The date in the colophon is 1545. *The titlepage is cropped and mounted, and the date is altered by erasure to* 1554.

CABRAS (Angelina)

—— Moto vario dei fluidi nei tubi, *etc.* *In Civitate Vaticana,* 1939. 8°. [*Pontificia Academia Scientiarum. Commentationes.* vol. 3. no. 2.] Ac. **101.** b/**5.**

CABRAS (Descuerna) *pseud.* *See* Descuerna-Cabras, *pseud.*

CABRAS (Tommaso) *Count di San Felice.* Roma contemporanea. Scritti postumi. [With a preface by Biagio Chiara.] pp. vii. 195. *Roma,* [1904.] 8°. **10136.** bb. **22.**

CABRÉ (Antonio) *See* Ignatius [Lopez de Recalde, *de Loyola*], *Saint.* Cartas. [Edited by A. Cabré.] 1874, *etc.* 8°. **3706.** de. **5.**

CABRE (C.) Thèse pour le doctorat en médecine, *etc.* (De quelques cas d'entérite typhoïde ou fièvre typhoïde observés à l'hôpital Necker dans le service de M. Delaroque.) pp. 119. *Paris,* 1838. 4°. **1184.** i. **4.** (**21.**)

CABRE (Honoré Auguste Sabatier de) *See* Sabatier de Cabre.

CABRÉ (Jayme José Ardevol y) *See* Ardevol y Cabré.

CABRÉ (Joseph Watson)

—— Planning and Design. [With plates.] pp. 226. *English Universities Press: London,* 1945. 8°. [*E.U.P. Teach Yourself Building Books.*] W.P. **6100/4.**

CABRÉ AGUILÓ (Juan) *See* Hernández-Pacheco (E.) and Cabré Aguiló (J.) Las Pinturas Prehistóricas de Peña Tú, *etc.* 1914. 4°. [*Comisión de Investigaciones Paleontológicas y Prehistóricas. Memoria.* no. 2.] Ac. **2828.** b.

—— *See* Lantier (Raymond) El Santuario Ibérico de Castellar de Santisteban. Por R. Lantier, con el concurso de J. Cabré Aguiló, *etc.* 1917. 8°. [*Comisión de Investigaciones Paleontológicas y Prehistóricas. Memoria.* no. 15.] Ac. **2828.** b.

—— El Arte Rupestre en España, regiones septentrional y oriental . . . Prólogo del Excmo. Sr. Marqués de Cerralbo. pp. xxxii. 229. pl. xxxi. *Madrid,* 1915. 4°. [*Comisión de Investigaciones Paleontológicas y Prehistóricas. Memoria.* no. 1.] Ac. **2828.** b.

—— Azaila. pp. 30. pl. ii. *Barcelona,* 1929. 8°. **7711.** c. **14/3.**

—— Cerámica de Azaila. Museos Arqueológicos de Madrid, Barcelona y Zaragoza. pp. xi. 101. pl. 63. *Madrid,* 1944. fol. [*Corpus vasorum Hispanorum.* fasc. 1.] Ac. **132.** b/**6.**

—— Excavaciones de Las Cogotas, Cardeñosa, Ávila. (pt. 2. Por J. Cabré Aguiló con la colaboración de María de la Encarnación Cabré Herreros.) 2 pt. *Madrid,* 1930, 32. 8°. [*Junta Superior de Excavaciones y Antigüedades.* no. 110, 120.] Ac. **5247.**

CABRÉ AGUILÓ (JUAN)

—— El Paleolítico Inferior de Puente Mocho. Por J. Cabré y Paul Wernert. pp. 23. *Madrid*, 1916. 4°. [*Comisión de Investigaciones Paleontológicas y Prehistóricas. Memoria.* no. 11.] Ac. **2828**. b

—— Las Pinturas Rupestres de Aldeaquemada. pp. 35. pl. II. *Madrid*, 1917. 8°. [*Comisión de Investigaciones Paleontológicas y Prehistóricas. Memoria.* no. 14.] Ac. **2828**. b.

CABRÉ AGUILÓ (JUAN) and **HERNÁNDEZ-PACHECO** (EDUARDO)

—— Avance al Estudio de las Pinturas Prehistóricas del Extremo Sur de España—Laguna de la Janda, *etc.* pp. 35. pl. XIII. *Madrid*, 1914. 4°. [*Comisión de Investigaciones Paleontológicas y Prehistóricas. Memoria.* no. 3.] Ac. **2828**. b.

CABRÉ HERREROS (MARÍA DE LA ENCARNACIÓN) *See* CABRÉ AGUILÓ (J.) Excavaciones de Las Cogotas, Cardeñosa, Ávila. (pt. 2. Por J. Cabré Aguiló con la colaboración de M. de la E. Cabré Herreros.) 1930, *etc.* 8°. [*Junta Superior de Excavaciones y Antigüedades.* no. 110, 120.] Ac. **5247**.

CABREIRA (ANTONIO) ***Count de Lagos.***

—— Calendrier perpétuel de Antonio Cabreira dans les systèmes julien . . . et grégorien . . . Extrait des Trabalhos da Academia de Sciencias de Portugal, *etc.* pp. 4. *Coimbre*, 1915. 8°. **8505**. f. **32**. (**2**.)

—— Les Mathématiques en Portugal. Deuxième défense des travaux. (Avant-propos de Mr. le prof. Emilio Augusto Vecchi.) pp. xxix. 118. *Lisbonne*, 1910. 8°. **8507**. g. **5**. (**4**.)

—— Quelques mots sur les mathématiques en Portugal . . . Avec biographie de l'auteur par . . . A. Santos Lucas. pp. vii. 64. *Lisbonne*, 1905. 8°. **8533**. i. **25**.

—— Sobre o quadrado e o cubo dos polinómios . . . Separata dos Trabalhos da Academia de Sciencias de Portugal, *etc.* pp. 3. *Coimbra*, 1915. 8°. **8505**. f. **32**. (**1**.)

—— Antonio Cabreira, seus servicios e consagrações. Factos e documentos coligidos e publicados . . . por iniciativa dos seus condiscipulos no Liceu de Lisboa, em 1888–1889. [With plates, including portraits.] pp. xvi. 646. *Lisboa*, 1914. 8°. **10633**. cc. **28**.

CABREIRA (GONÇALO RODRIGUEZ DE) *See* RODRIGUEZ DE CABREIRA.

CABREIRA (SEBASTIÃO DRAGO DE BRITO) *See* DRAGO DE BRITO CABREIRA.

CABRELLY (E. A.)

—— Animals on Parade. Illustrations by Thomas Eckersley, *etc. Conrad Press: London*, [1948.] 4°. **7208**. h. **39**.

CABRER (JOSÉ MARIA) Reconocimiento del rio Pepirí-guazu, por D. J. M. Cabrer . . . Extractado de su diario inédito. pp. iv. 11. 1836. 4°. [*Coleccion de obras y documentos relativas á la historia . . . de las provincias del Rio de la Plata.* tom. 4.] **600**. gg. **8**.

CABRERA. Cinq ans de captivité à Cabrera . . . Par l'abbé C. T., *etc.* 1859. 8°. *See* T., C., *Abbé*. **10662**. bbb. **19**.

CABRERA (PONCE DE MOLINA MALO DE) *See* PONCE DE MOLINA MALO DE CABRERA.

CABRERA (ALONSO) *See* GANDÍA (E. de) Historia de Alonso Cabrera y de la Destrucción de Buenos Aires en 1541. 1936. 8°. **9770.v.8.**

CABRERA (ALONSO DE) *Licenciado*. *See* ORTEGA Y ESPINOSA (M.) Por el L^do D. Gaspar Paez de Barrionuevo . . . En la pleuto con el licenciado A. de Cabrera, *etc.* 1660. fol. **1322**. l. **5**. (**6**.)

CABRERA (ALONSO DE) *Predicador*. Sermones . . . Con un discurso preliminar de Don Miguel Mir. pp. xxxii. 709. *Madrid*, 1906. 8°. [*Nueva Biblioteca de Autores Españoles.* tom. 3.] **012199**. k. **1/9**.

—— Sermon . . . á las honras de nuestro Señor el . . . Rey Filipo segundo, *etc.* ff. 31. [1598?] 4°. **4423**. g. **1**. (**3**.)

CABRERA (ÁNGEL LULIO)

—— *See* FERNÁNDEZ DE CÓRDOVA-FIGUEROA DE LA CERDA Y SALABERT (L. J. M.) *17th Duke de Medinaceli*. Aves de Rapiña y su Caza. Ilustraciones de D. A. Cabrera. [1917.] 8°. **7286**. eee. **19**.

—— *See* HOGBEN (Lancelot T.) [Principles of Animal Biology.] Principios de biología animal. (Traducción de Á. Cabrera.) 1951. 8°. **7008**. f. **3**.

—— Catálogo Metódico de las Colecciones de Mamíferos del Museo de Ciencias, *etc.* pp. 147. pl. IV. *Madrid*, 1912. 8°. [*Trabajos del Museo de Ciencias Naturales de Madrid.* Serie zoológica. no. 7.] Ac. **2828/2**.

—— El Concepto de Tipo en Zoología y los Tipos de Mamíferos del Museo de Ciencias Naturales. pp. 32. *Madrid*, 1912. 8°. [*Trabajos del Museo de Ciencias Naturales de Madrid.* Serie zoológica. no. 1.] Ac. **2828/2**.

—— Dos Mamíferos Nuevos de la Fauna Neotropical . . . Con una lámina. pp. 15. *Madrid*, 1913. 8°. [*Trabajos del Museo de Ciencias Naturales de Madrid.* Serie zoológica. no. 9.] Ac. **2828/2**.

—— Genera Mammalium. *Span.* [With plates.] 2 vol. 1919, 25. 8°. *See* MADRID.—*Instituto Nacional de Ciencias Físico-Naturales.—Museo de Ciencias Naturales.* Ac. **2828**. a.

—— Los Grandes Cetáceos del Estrecho de Gibraltar, su pesca y explotación, *etc.* pp. 51. pl. XII. *Madrid*, 1925. 8°. [*Trabajos del Museo de Ciencias Naturales de Madrid.* Serie zoológica. no. 52.] Ac. **2828/2**.

—— Magreb-el-Aksa. Recuerdos de cuatro viajes por Yebala y por el Rif. [With plates.] pp. 270. *Madrid*, 1924. 8°. **010094**. ff. **14**.

—— Mamíferos. Con veintidós láminas en colores, *etc.* pp. xviii. 441. *Madrid*, 1914. 8°. [*Fauna Ibérica.*] Ac. **2828/4**

—— Los Mamíferos de Marruecos, *etc.* pp. 361. pl. XII. *Madrid*, 1932. 8°. [*Trabajos del Museo de Ciencias Naturales de Madrid.* Serie zoológica. no. 57.] Ac. **2828/2**.

—— Mamíferos del Viaje al Pacífico. Verificado de 1862 a 1865 por una comisión de naturalistas enviada por el Gobierno Español. pp. 62. *Madrid*, 1917. 8°. [*Trabajos del Museo de Ciencias Naturales.* Serie zoológica. no. 31.] Ac. **2828/2**.

—— Vernonieas Argentinas—Compositae. [With plates.] 1944. *See* PERIODICAL PUBLICATIONS.—*Buenos Ayres*. Darwiniana, *etc.* tom. 6. no. 3. 1922, *etc.* 8°. P.P. **3862**. cgb

CABRERA (Ángel Lulio)

—— Zoogeografía. pp. 32. *Buenos Aires*, 1933. 8°. **7209**. bb. **31**.

CABRERA (Antonio) Glorias de el Señor Felipe Quinto, Rey de las Españas, *etc.* pp. 416. *Madrid*, 1708. 4°. **281**. d. **1**.

CABRERA (Antonio J.) La Huasteca Potosina. Ligeros apuntes sobre este país. pp. 180. *San Luis Potosí*, 1876. 8°. **10482**. df. **5**.

CABRERA (Antonio Velazquez y) *See* Velazquez y Cabrera.

CABRERA (Aurelio) *See* Hernández-Pacheco (E.) & Estevan Pinturas prehistóricas y dólmenes de la región de Alburquerque, Extremadura . . . según datos y dibujos de A. Cabrera. 1916. 8°. [*Comisión de Investigaciones Paleontológicas y Prehistóricas. Nota.* no. 8.] Ac. **2828**. b/2.

CABRERA (Bernardo de) Proceso contro Bernardo de Cabrera mandado formar por el Rey Don Pedro iv, *etc.* 2 tom. *Barcelona*, 1867. 8°. [*Coleccion de documentos inéditos del Archivo General de la Corona de Aragon.* tom. 32.] **9181**. d.

CABRERA (Blas) Dia- et paramagnétisme et structure de la matière. pp. 79. *Paris*, 1937. 8°. **8710**. ee. **40**.

—— El Estado Actual de la Teoría del Magnetismo. pp. 160. *Madrid*, 1919. 8°. [*Instituto Nacional de Ciencias Físico-Naturales. Laboratorio de Investigaciones Físicas. Memoria de informacion.* no. 1.] Ac. **2828**. c. (**2**.)

CABRERA (C.) *of Arucas, Canary Islands.*

—— Contribution à l'étude de l'endocardite végétante. Thèse, *etc.* pp. 82. *Montpellier*, 1880. 4°. **7379**. m. **3**. (**8**.)

CABRERA (Christóval Ruiz de) *See* Ruiz de Cabrera.

CABRERA (Cristóbal) Instrumento Espiritual. *See* Macías y García (M.) Poetas religiosos inéditos del siglo xvi, *etc.* 1890. 8°. **11450**. de. **45**.

CABRERA (Francisco) ***Fray.***

—— *See* Ximenez Paton (B.) Discurso de los Tufos, *etc.* [With a dedication by F. Cabrera.] 1639. 4°. **7742**. b. **51**.

CABRERA (Jerónimo Luis de)

—— *See* Arenas Luque (F. V.) El Fundador de Córdoba, Don Jerónimo Luis de Cabrera, *etc.* 1939. 8°. **10635**. a. **15**.

CABRERA (Jorge Alfredo de Castroverde y) *See* Castroverde y Cabrera.

CABRERA (José Álvarez) *See* Álvarez Cabrera.

CABRERA (José Manuel Pérez) *See* Pérez Cabrera.

CABRERA (Joseph de) Por el Obispo de la Puebla de los Angeles, su jurisdicion, y dignidad. En el pleyto . . . sobre que no pudo rotular al Guardian de San Francisco del Pueblo de Topoyango, por incurso en las censuras del Canon si quis suadente diabolo . . . Fundase la jurisdicion, y se responde á todo el informe impresso por parte del Procurador de la Religion Serafica, firmado del Doctor Don Ioseph de Vega y Vique. ff. 11. ms. notes. [1670.] fol. **6784**. k. **2**. (**2**.)

CABRERA (Joseph de)

—— Manifestacion de la indemnidad del informe por el Padre Procurador General de San Francisco, de que el Señor Obispo de la Puebla no pudo rotular al Padre Guardian de Topoyango, por incurso en las censuras del Canon: Si quis suadente diabolo. Satisfatoria à la pretenso respuesta por el dicho Señor Obispo, y licenciado Don Ioseph de Cabrera. [By Joseph de Vega y Vic.] ff. 30. ms. notes. [1670.] fol. **6784**. k. **2**. (**3**.)

CABRERA (Joseph Ignacio de) Gloriosa exaltacion, de la mystica piedra maravilla. Sermon fúnebre que en las honras de la R. M. Soror M. P. Trinidad . . . predicó . . . D. J. I. de Cabrera, *etc.* pp. 35. *México*, 1762. 4°. **4986**. cc. **77**.

CABRERA (Juan) Dolor de estómago de Cabrera y bubatismo del gachupin Aza. [Signed: El Payo del Rosario, i.e. P. de Villavicencio.] *México*, 1826. 4°. **9770**. bb. **17**. (**2**.)

CABRERA (Juan de) Crisis política determina el mas florido imperio, y la mejor institucion de principes y ministros, *etc.* pp. 771. *Madrid*, 1719. fol. **8007**. g. **17**.

CABRERA (Juan Alfonso Enriquez de) *Duke de Medina de Rio-Seco.* *See* Enriquez de Cabrera.

CABRERA (Juan Bautista) *Bishop of the Spanish Reformed Church.* *See* England.—*Church of England.* [*Articles of Religion.*] Exposicion . . . de los Treinta y Nueve Artículos de la Iglesia Anglicana. Por . . . E. H. Browne . . . Traducido . . . por J. B. Cabrera. 1867, *etc.* 8°. **3504**. aaa. **63**.

—— *See* Mayor (John E. B.) Bishop Cabrera. [On his episcopal consecration.] [1894.] 8°. **3900**. dd. **2**. (**4**.)

—— *See* Meyrick (James) La Supremacía Papal, examinada por la Antigüedad . . . Traducido . . . por . . . J. B. Cabrera. 1866. 8°. **3939**. aaa. **86**.

—— Himnario para uso de las Iglesias Evangélicas, coleccionado y en parte compuesto por J. B. Cabrera. pp. xv. 362. *Sevilla*, 1871. 16°. **3436**. aaaa. **81**.

—— Poesías Religiosas y Morales. pp. 511. *Madrid*, 1904. 8°. **011451**. g. **44**.
The date on the wrapper is 1907.

CABRERA (Juan Tomas Enriquez de) *Duke of Medina del Rio-Seco.* *See* Enriquez de Cabrera.

CABRERA (Luis) The Mexican Revolution, its causes, purposes and results. *See* Mexico. [*Appendix.*] The Purposes and Ideals of the Mexican Revolution. Addresses, *etc.*, 1917. 8°. [*Annals of the American Academy of Political and Social Science.* January 1917. Suppl.] Ac. **2383**.

CABRERA (Manuel de) Verdad Aclarada, y Desvanecidas Imposturas, con que lo ardiente de una pluma poderosa (Martin de Solis) en esta Nueva España, en un dictamen malinstruido, quiso persuadir, averse acabado y perficionado el año de 1675 la fabrica del Real Desague de la insigne ciudad de Mexico. pp. 123. [*Mexico*, 1688.] fol. **8776**. g. **23**.

CABRERA (Manuel Estrada) *President of Guatemala.* *See* Estrada Cabrera.

CABRERA (Manuel Fernández) *See* Fernández Cabrera.

CABRERA (Maria Rosa Galvez de) *See* Galvez de Cabrera.

CABRERA (Mariana Gertrudis) *See* María Buenaventura, *of the Convent of San Felipe de Jesus, of Mexico.*

CABRERA (Mariano Cordon de) *See* Cordon de Cabrera.

CABRERA (Mathías de Galvez García Madrid y) *See* Galvez García Madrid y Cabrera.

CABRERA (Miguel) Maravilla Americana y conjunto de raras maravillas, observadas . . . en la prodigiosa imagen de Nuestra Sra de Guadalupe de Mexico. pp. 30. *Mexico*, 1756. 4°. **4625**. bb. **5**.

CABRERA (N.) Entrada Pública en Valladolid de la Señora Doña Ana Huarte de Iturbide, *etc.* [By N. Cabrera ?] pp. 5. 1821. 4°. *See* Iturbide (Ana María de) **9770**. bb. **7**. (**22**.)

CABRERA (Pablo)

—— Ensayos sobre etnología argentina. 2.a serie, onomástica indiana de Tucumán. pp. 306. *Buenos Aires*, 1931. 8°. [*Biblioteca de historia argentina y americana.* vol. 9.] Ac. **8592/11**. (**9**.)

—— La Segunda Imprenta de la Universidad de Córdoba, *etc.* pp. 200. 1930. 8°. *See* Cordova.—*Universidad Nacional de Cordoba.* **11917.gg.5.**

CABRERA (Paulo Félix) Teatro Critico Americano; or, a Critical investigation and research into the history of the Americans, *etc.* *See* Rio (Antonio del) Description of the Ruins of an Ancient City, discovered near Palenque, *etc.* 1822. 4°. **796**. ff. **17**.

CABRERA (Petrus de) Fratris Petri de Cabrera . . . De sacramentis in genere, de auxilio præuio, & de baptismo, in tertiam partem [of the Summa Theologica] sancti Thomæ, à quæstione sexagesima vsque ad septuagesimam primam, commentarii & disputationes. pp. 1174. *L. Sanchez: Matriti*, 1611. fol. **3837**. h. **4**.
Imperfect; half of the second leaf of the preface and the whole of the two following leaves have been cut away.

—— Fratris Petri de Cabrera . . . In tertiam partem [of the Summa Theologica, quaest. 1–26] Sancti Thomæ commentariorum et disputationum tomus primus (ii). 2 tom. *A. Barrera: Cordubæ*, 1602. fol. **4061**. h. **2**.
The titlepage is engraved.

CABRERA (Raimundo) *See* Cabrera y Boch.

CABRERA (Ramiro) ¡A Sitio Herrera! Narración de un viaje a la Sierra de los Organos, intercalada con las aventuras revolucionarias del Coronel Don Nicolás de Cárdenas y Benitez, *etc.* [With a portrait.] pp. 360. *Habana*, 1922. 8°. **9773**. aaa. **4**.

CABRERA (Ramon) *1st Count de Morella.* *See* Arjona (E. de) Páginas de la Historia del Partido Carlista. Cárlos vii y D. Ramon Cabrera. 1875. 12°. **9180**. bb. **2**.

—— *See* Arjona (E. de) Pages d'histoire du parti Carliste. Charles vii et D. Ramon Cabrera, *etc.* 1875. 12°. **9181**. de. **1**.

—— *See* Calbo y Rochina de Castro (D.) Historia de Cabrera y de la Guerra Civil en Aragon, Valencia y Murcia, *etc.* 1846, *etc.* 8°. **9181**. e. **9**.

—— *See* Caso (J. I.) La Cuestion Cabrera. [A criticism of "Páginas de la Historia del Partido Carlista. Cárlos vii y Don Ramon Cabrera," by E. de Arjona.] 1875. 8°. **8042**. i. **2**.

CABRERA (Ramon) *1st Count de Morella.*

—— *See* Gonzalez de la Cruz (R.) El Vengador y Sombra de Cabrera . . . Refutacion del Tigre c Maestrazgo . . . historia novela de W. Ayguals de Yz 1849. 8°. **12490**. b. 3

—— *See* Rahden (W. von) *Baron.* Cabrera. Erinnerung aus dem spanischen Bürgerkriege. 1840. 8°. **9180**. ee.

—— *See* Tomás (M.) Ramón Cabrera, *etc.* 1939. 8°. **10635**. e. 2

—— El Caudillo de Morella, poema en el cual se describ la vida y hechos del célebre Cabrera. 2 tom. *Madr* 1849. 8°. **11451**. d.

—— Historia de Cabrera . . . Tercera edicion. pp. 32. *Madrid*, 1846. 4°. **10631**. ee. **31**. (

—— Historia de la vida, hechos de armas y principales suce del Carlista Ramon Cabrera, *etc.* pp. 32. *Vallado* 1851. 4°. **10631**. ee. **32**.

—— Historia del General Carlista Don Ramon Cabrera, pp. 31. [*Madrid*, 1858 ?] 4°. **10631**. ee. **32**. (1

—— [Another edition.] pp. 38. *Madrid*, 1874. 4°. **12330**. l. **3**.

—— Note to the several Lives of Marshal Cabrera. [Sign T. C. G. H., i.e. T. C. G. Horngold.] [1889.] 8°. H., T. C. G. **10601**. f. **4**.

—— Teatro de la Guerra: Cabrera, los Montemolinista Republicanos en Cataluña. Crónica de nuestros d redactada por un testigo ocular de los acontecimient 2 vol. *Madrid*, 1849. 8°. **1323**. i.

CABRERA (Ramon) *2nd Count de Morella.* *See* Moret Prendergast (S.) The Financial Policy of Willi Pitt . . . Translated by R. Cabrera. 1888. 8°. **08229**. df. **12**. (1

CABRERA (Ramon) *Marquis del Ter.* *See* Cabrera (1 *1st Count de Morella.*

CABRERA (Ramon) *Prior of Arroniz.* Diccionario Etimologías de la Lengua Castellana. Obra póstu . . . publicada por Don Juan Pedro Ayegui. (Noti de la vida de Don Ramon Cabrera. Escrita por Don J de Dios Gil de Lara.) 2 tom. *Madrid*, 1837. 4°. **829**. e.

—— Disertacion histórica, en la qual se expone . . . la v disciplina que ha observado la Iglesia de España sobr lugar de las sepulturas, *etc.* *See* Bails (B.) Prue de ser contrario á la práctica de todas las naciones enterrar los difuntos en las iglesias, *etc.* 1785. 8°. **5125**. a.

CABRERA (Rosa)

—— *See* Dickens (Charles) [*David Copperfield.*] Da Copperfield. Versión española de R. Cabrera. [1929.] **012631**. pp.

CABRERA BUENO (Joseph Gonzalez) *See* Gonza Cabrera Bueno.

CABRERA CANTÓ (Fernando)

—— *See* Pantorba (Bernardino de) *pseud.* El Pintor Cab Cantó, *etc.* [With reproductions.] 1945. 8°. **7868**. b.

—— Fernando Cabrera Cantó. Catálogo completo de obras más destacadas. Recopilación y prólogo de Enri Xaudaró, *etc.* [Reproductions.] *Barcel* [1945.] 8°. **7868**. c.

CABRERA DE CORDOBA (LUIS DE) *See* CABRERA DE CORDOVA.

CABRERA DE CORDOVA (LUIS DE) De historia, para entenderla y escrivirla. ff. 110. *L. Sanchez: Madrid,* 1611. 4°. **9007.** e. **20.**

—— Filipe Segundo, Rey de España. pp. 1176. *L. Sanchez: Madrid,* 1619. fol. C. **79.** c. **7.**
The titlepage is engraved.

—— [Another copy.] **178.** d. **4.**
The titlepage is slightly mutilated.

—— [Another edition.] 3 tom. *Madrid,* 1876, 77. 4°. **9181.** v. **2.**

—— Relaciones de las cosas sucedidas en la Córte de España desde 1599 hasta 1614. pp. x. 655. *Madrid,* 1857. 4°. **9180.** h. **23.**

—— Relatio vitæ mortisque Caroli Infantis Philippi II., Regis Hispaniarum filii. *See* SANDOVAL (P. de) successively *Bishop of Tuy* and *of Pampeluna.* Historia captivitatis Francisci I., *etc.* 1715. 8°. **610.** c. **15.**

CABRERA DE NEVARES (MIGUEL) Memoria sobre el estado actual de las Américas, y medio de pacificarlas. pp. 71. *Madrid,* 1821. 8°. **8179.** a. **50.** (**1.**)

—— *See* LULI ( ) Refutacion contra la Memoria presentada por Don M. Cabrera Nevares sobre las Americas. 1821. 8°. **8179.** a. **50.** (**2.**)

CABRERA DOMÍNGUEZ (ARTURO)

—— *See* BUENOS AYRES.—*Biblioteca Nacional.* Catálogo de manuscritos. Papeles de Gregorio Funes—Simón Bolívar —Antonio José de Sucre . . . Prologado por A. Cabrera Domínguez. 1939. 8°. **11925.** d. **10.**

—— *See* BUENOS AYRES.—*Biblioteca Nacional.* Catálogo de manuscritos. Papeles de Gregorio Funes . . . Prólogo de A. Cabrera Domínguez. 1940. 8°. **11925.** d. **11.**

CABRERA GUERRA (M.) *See* BÓRQUEZ SOLAR (A. N.) Campo lírico. Primera siega. [With an introduction by M. Cabrera Guerra.] 1900. 8°. **11452.** ee. **26.**

CABRERA MORALES (FRANCISCO DE) *See* CHACON (A.) Vitæ et res gestæ Pontificum Romanorum et S. R. E. Cardinalium . . . auctoribus A. Ciaconio, F. Cabrera Morales, *etc.* 1630. fol. **4855.** k. **1.**

—— *See* FRANZINI (G.) Las Iglesias de Roma . . . Corregida y augmentada . . . por F. de Cabrera Morales. 1600. 8°. **574.** e. **5.**

—— *See* MORALES POLO (L. de) Epitome de los Hechos, y Dichos del Emperador Trajano . . . Sacala a luz . . . F. de Morales. 1654. 12°. **610.** b. **8.**

CABRERA NUÑEZ DE GUZMAN (MELCHOR DE) *See* SILVESTRE DE GUZMAN (F. M.) *Marquis de Ayamonte.* Por Don Francisco Manuel Siluestre de Guzman . . . Con el señor don Pedro de Velasco Medinilla, *etc.* [A pleading by J. de Valdes and M. de Cabrera Nuñez de Guzman.] [1656 ?] fol. **1322.** l. **11.** (**24.**)

—— Adicion á la Defensa del Marques de Ayamonte. ff. 8. [*Madrid?* 1650 ?] fol. **1322.** l. **1.** (**31.**)

—— Honra nobleza, y excelencias de los libros, que en apoyo, y defensa de su exempcion, e immunidad, propone al Rey . . . M. de Cabrera y Guzman, *etc.* ff. 14. *D. Diaz de la Carrera: Madrid,* 1639. fol. **1322.** l. **9.** (**1.**)

—— *Begin.* Jesus Maria Joseph. Con ocasion de la alcauala impuesta à los libros, *etc.* [A paper recommending the exemption of books from taxation.] ff. 4. [*Madrid?* 1636 ?] fol. **1322.** l. **9.** (**3.**)

CABRERA NUÑEZ DE GUZMAN (MELCHOR DE)

—— *Begin.* El Marques de Ayamonte està preso en las fortalezas de Santorcaz, y Pinto, *etc.* [A pleading in the case for the Marquis.] ff. 5. [1650 ?] fol. **1322.** l. **11.** (**27.**)

—— Memorial, que pone en las manos de Su Magestad, el Convento Real de Santa Maria de los Angeles de Madrid, suplicando sea servido, como su unico patron, darle protector. ff. 9. [*Madrid?*] 1672. fol. **4745.** f. **11.** (**28.**)

—— Por el Marques de Ayamonte. Con el Señor Fiscal. Sobre poner cobro en los bienes del Marques, y aplicarlos a la Real hazienda, y Fisco. ff. 6. [1650 ?] fol. **1322.** l. **11.** (**26.**)

—— Por la Immunidad de los Libros. Al Rey Nuestro Señor. ff. 6. *M. de Quinones: Madrid,* 1636. fol. **1322.** l. **3.** (**39.**)

—— Respuesta a la Informacion del Señor Fiscal. Por . . . Juan Garceran Valmaseda, y . . . Domingo Fernandez Montesinos, presos en la Carcel Real desta Corte, *etc.* ff. 7. [1650 ?] fol. **1322.** l. **11.** (**28.**)

—— *Begin.* Señor. El Marques de Ayamõte ha mas de cinco años que està preso, la causa es averle imputado fue participe en el lebantamiẽto, *etc.* [A pleading in the case of the Marquis.] ff. 13. [1650 ?] fol. **1322.** l. **11.** (**25.**)

—— *Begin.* Señor. Los Libros yà no proponen exempciones, [An address to the king of Spain recommending the exemption of books from taxation.] ff. 6. [*Madrid,* 1636.] fol. **1322.** l. **9.** (**4.**)

CABRERA PIÑÓN (QUERANDY)

—— *See* BLANCA PARÍS (M.) and CABRERA PIÑÓN (Q.) Las Relaciones entre Montevideo y Buenos Aires en 1811. El Virreinato de Elío. 1947. 8°. [MONTEVIDEO.—*Universidad de la República.—Facultad de Humanidades y Ciencias. Revista.* año. 1. no. 2.] **Ac.2694.b/2.**

CABRERA SAQUI (MARIO)

—— *See* SUÁREZ Y ROMERO (A.) Francisco . . . Edición prologada y anotada por M. Cabrera Saqui. 1947. 8°. W.P. **13556/20.**

CABRERA VALDÉS (M. LADISLAO) *See* AREQUIPA.—*Concejo Provincial.* Colección de Algunos Documentos sobre los Primeros Tiempos de Arequipa, *etc.* (Con una introducción histórica por M. L. Cabrera Valdés.) 1924. 8°. **9773.** a. **20.**

CABRERA Y BOBADILLA (ANA OSORIO DE FERNÁNDEZ DE) *Countess of Chinchon.* *See* OSORIO DE FERNÁNDEZ DE CABRERA Y BOBADILLA.

CABRERA Y BOSCH (RAIMUNDO) *See* ALFONSO (R. M.) *of Cuba.* La Reglamentacion de la Prostitucion, Breves apuntes sobre como debe ser en Cuba. [With a preface by R. Cabrera y Bosch.] 1912. 8°. **8285.** bb. **24.**

—— *See* CHACÓN Y CALVO (J. M.) Don Raimundo Cabrera o la evocación creadora, *etc.* [With a portrait.] 1952. 8°. **10899.** c. **12.**

—— *See* SALAZAR Y ROIG (S.) Elogio del Dr. Raimundo Cabrera y Bosch, *etc.* [With portraits.] 1925. 4°. Ac. **8594/9.**

—— *See* SALAZAR Y ROIG (S.) Lope de Rueda y su Teatro. Prólogo de R. Cabrera. [1912.] 8°. **011852.** h. **47.** (**5.**)

—— La Casa de Beneficia y la Sociedad Economica. Sus relaciones con los gobiernos de Cuba. pp. 258. ii. *Habana,* 1914. 8°. **8282.** bb. **4.**

CABRERA Y BOSCH (RAIMUNDO)

—— Cuba y sus Jueces. Rectificaciones oportunas [to F. Rivas Moreno's "Cuba y su Gente"]. pp. 281. 31. *Habana*, 1887. 8°. **8180.** b. **12.**

—— Octava edición ilustrada y aumentada con notas y un apéndice. pp. 335. *Filadelfia*, 1895. 16°. **8180.** a. **32.**

—— Cuba and the Cubans. Translated from the eighth Spanish edition of "Cuba y sus Jueces" by L. Guiteras. Revised and edited by L. E. Levy, and completed . . . by the editor. Illustrated, *etc.* pp. 442. *Levytype Co.: Philadelphia*, 1896. 8°. **8180.** b. **19.**

—— Los Estados Unidos. Reducción de la obra "Triumphant Democracy" de Mr. Andrew Carnegie, con notas, aplicaciones y comentarios. [With special reference to Cuba.] Tercera edición. pp. 249. *Habana*, [1]922. 8°. **08175.** aaa. **27.**

—— Ideales. [A novel.] pp. 322. *Habana*, 1918. 8°. **12489.** ppp. **7.**

—— Mis Buenos Tiempos. Memorias de estudiante. Cuarta edición. pp. 270. *Habana*, 1922. 8°. **10634.** aaa. **28.**

—— I Miei bei tempi. Memorie di uno studente. Traduzione di Angelina Fantoli. pp. 230. *Parigi*, 1921. 8°. **10634.** aa. **20.**

—— Mis Malos Tiempos. pp. 416. *Habana*, 1920. 8°. **9773.** b. **7.**

—— Sacando Hilas. Obra inédita. [With a notice of the author and his work by R. Suárez Solís.] pp. 228. *Habana*, 1922. 8°. **012352.** g. **21.**

—— Sombras que pasan. pp. 254. *Habana*, 1916. 8°. **12489.** tt. **18.**

—— Homenaje popular a Raimundo Cabrera. 9 marzo, 1923. [With a portrait.] *Habana*, [1923.] 8°. **10884.** d. **8.**

CABRERA Y BOSCH (RAIMUNDO) and **GIBERGA** (ELISEO)

—— La Autonomía Universitaria. Informe presentado a la Junta de Inspectores de la Universidad de la Habana . . . Segunda edición. pp. 80. 1926. 8°. *See* CUBA, *Republic of.—Secretaría de Instrucción Pública.* **8385.** b. **25.**

CABRERA Y DÍAZ (AGUSTÍN) Contribución al estudio de los Eunícidos de las costas Cantábricas. Memoria, *etc.* pp. 43. *Barcelona*, 1909. 8°. **7001.** p. **13. (8.)**

CABRERA Y DÍAZ (ANATAEL) Catálogo de las Aves del Archipiélago Canario. 1893. *See* MADRID.—*Sociedad Española de Historia Natural.* Anales, *etc.* tom. 22. 1872, *etc.* 8°. Ac. **2826.**

CABRERA Y GUZMAN (MELCHOR DE) *See* CABRERA NUÑEZ DE GUZMAN.

CABRERA Y HEREDIA (DOLORES) Las Violetas. Poesias. [Edited by Gregorio Romero Larrañaga.] pp. 246. *Madrid*, 1850. 8°. **11451.** b. **18.**

CABRERA Y MERINO (BARTOLOMÉ) Discurso pronunciado en . . . Mazatlan, el 16 de setiembre de 1854 [the anniversary of the proclamation of independence at Dolores in 1810], *etc.* pp. 6. *Puerto de Mazatlan*, 1854. 8°. **12301.** d. **8. (27.)**

CABRERA Y PEÑARRIETA (JOSEPH DE) Defensa, se haze por los Officiales Brazeageros de la Real Casa la moneda: en el pleyto con el Thesorero de ella, so diferentes pretenciones contenidas en los articulos de divission. ff. 33. [*Mexico*, 1684.] fol. **8223.** de. **1.**

CABRERA Y QUINTERO (CAYETANO DE) Escudo Armas de Mexico: celestial proteccion de esta nobilissi ciudad . . . Maria Santissima, en su portentosa ima del Mexicano Guadalupe, milagrosamente apparec . . . el año de 1531, y jurada su principal Patrona passado de 1737, en la angustia, que ocasionò la pestilen *etc.* pp. 522. *Mexico*, 1746. fol. **1230.** f.

CABRERA Y RODRIGUEZ (JOSE AMALIO) Cor Poetica Imperial, dedicada a . . . Maximiliano I . . . su Augusta Esposa . . . Carlota, *etc.* pp. 12. *Mex* 1864. 4°. **11450.** ccc.

CABRERA Y SAQUI (MARIO) *See* ZENEA Y FORNA (J. C.) Poesías. [Edited by M. Cabrera y Saqui.] 1936. 8°. **W.P.13556/**

CABRERIZO (FRANCISCO) Derecho Matrimonial Espa El matrimonio, los hijos, la separación, y el divorcio, arreglo a las novísimas leyes, *etc.* pp. 351. *Ma* 1933. 4°. **5384.** ee

—— Estudios Penitenciarios. Las prisiones de Londres y nuestras. Comparación, enseñanzas que de ella se ded y conclusiones. pp. 219. *Madrid*, 1911. 8°. **6056.** t.

CABRERIZO (MARIANO DE)

—— *See* ALMELA I VIVES (F.) El Editor don Marian Cabrerizo. [With a portrait.] 1949. 8°. [*Cole bibliográfica.* vol. 9.] Ac. **132.** c

—— Comunicado. [A vindica of the author's conduct in connection with the riot Valencia in September 1835.] (Notas.) pp. 9. *C* 1835. 4°. **1444.** e. **8.**

CABRERIZO SÁNCHEZ (FRANCISCO) Cantares dulces, *etc.* pp. 92. *Madrid*, 1899. 8°. **011451.** eee. **12.**

CABRERO (ARTURO PÉREZ) *See* PÉREZ-CABRERO.

CABRERO (LEONCIO) [La Miseria de las Naciones.] Misère des nations. pp. vii. 354. *Nancy*, [1924.] 8° **08229.** a.

CABRERO MIÑON ( ) Buchivacoa. C dedicado al ciudadano Manuel E. Bruzual. Prima a suscriptores de "El Constitucional." pp. 32. *Car* 1864. 8°. **11450.** ee. **10.**

CABREROS AVENDAÑO (ANTONIO) Bonus Phi Magni secessus delineatus. pp. 64. *P. T* *Madridii*, 1637. 4°. **1445.** f. **120.**

—— Memorial en defensa de la inmunidad de los li ff. 4. MS. NOTES. [*Madrid?* 1636?] fol. **1322.** l. **3.**

CABRES (SABATHIER DE) *See* SABATHIER DE CAB

CABREUIL (BARTHÉLEMY) *See* CABROL.

CABREYRA (JOSEPH DE) Naufragio da Nào Senhora de Belem feyto na terra do Natal no cab Boa Esperança, & varios sucessos que teve o capitaõ Jo de Cabreyra, que nella passou à India no anno de . . . Escritos pelo mesmo J. de Cabreyra. pp. 69. *L. Craesbeeck: Lisboa*, 1636. 4°. T. **2232.**

CABREYRA (Joseph de)

—— [A reissue.] *Lisboa*, [1735.] 4°. [*Gomes de Brito* (*B.*) *Historia tragico-maritima, etc.* tom. 3.] **1424**. g. **3**.

—— Naufragio da Nao N. Senhora de Belem, *etc. Port. & Eng.* 1902. *See* Theal (George M.) Records of South-Eastern Africa, *etc.* vol. 8. 1898, *etc.* 8°. **09061**. aa.

CABRIADA (Juan de) Carta filosofica, medico-chymica. En que se demuestra, que de los tiempos, y experiencias se han aprendido los mejores remedios contra las enfermedades, *etc.* pp. 234. *L. A. de Bedmar y Baldivia: Madrid*, 1687. 4°. **1033**. i. **19**.
With an additional titlepage, engraved.

—— *See* Filiatro, *pseud.* Verdad Triunfante . . . escrita por Filiatro, en defensa de la Carta filosofica . . . del Doctor Don I. de Cabriada. 1687. 4°. **1033**. i. **20**.

ČABRIAN (Miroslav)

—— Željeznička vozila i vozna dinamika. Udžbenik za slušače građevnog inženjerstva. pp. 159. *Zagreb*, 1950. 8°. **8774**. cc. 8.

CABRICES (Fernando)

—— Páginas de emoción y de crítica. pp. 55. *Caracas*, 1944. 16°. **11863**. a. **26**.

CABRIÉ (François) Considérations pratiques sur la cataracte. Thèse, *etc.* pp. 56. *Montpellier*, 1839. 4°. **1181**. i. **14**. (**18**.)

CABRIÉ (Louis) Le Troubadour moderne, ou Poésies populaires de nos provinces méridionales, traduites en français; et précédées d'un discours sur la langue et la littérature provençales, depuis leur origine jusqu'à nos jours. pp. lvi. 320. *Paris*, 1844. 8°. **1464**. f. **16**.

CABRIÉ (Louis Pierre Alexandre) Nice et Hyères comparées comme lieu de séjour pour les tuberculeux. Thèse, *etc.* pp. 20. *Strasbourg*, 1859. 4°. [*Collection générale des dissertations de la Faculté de Médecine de Strasbourg.* Année 1859.] **7381*.e.**

CABRIELE (Jacomo) Dialogo . . . nel quale de la sphera, et de gli orti et occasi de le stelle, minutamente si ragiona. ff. 62. *G. de Farri & fratelli: Vinetia*, 1545. 4°. **49**. a. **6**.

—— Regole grammaticali. ff. 36. *G. Griffio: Vinetia*, 1548. 4°. **12942**. a. **23**.

—— [Another edition.] ff. 36. ms. notes. *G. Griffio: Venetia*, [1550 ?] 8°. **627**. c. **33**.

CABRIELIUS (Tryphon) *See* Gabrielle.

CABRIER (G.) Essai sur les moles. Tribut académique, *etc.* pp. 26. *Montpellier*, 1815. 4°. **1180**. h. **5**. (**33**.)

CABRIER (Guillaume Eugène Roch) Essai sur le quinquina. Tribut académique, *etc.* pp. 24. *Montpellier*, 1825. 4°. **1181**. d. **1**. (**11**.)

CABRIÈRES. La Tragédie du sac de Cabrières. Tragédie inédite en vers français du XVIe siècle. Publiée avec une introduction historique par Fernand Benoit . . . et une étude littéraire de J. Vianey. pp. xviii. 93. *Marseille*, 1927. 8°. [*Bibliothèque de l'Institut Historique de Provence.* vol. 2.] Ac. **6770**.

CABRIÈRES (François Marie Anatole de Rovérié de) *Bishop of Montpellier.* *See* Rovérié de Cabrières.

CABRILLO (Juan Rodríguez) *See* Rodríguez Cabrillo.

CABRIÑANA, Julio Urbina y Cevallos-Escalera, *Marquis de.* *See* Urbina y Cevallos-Escalera.

CABRINI (Angiolo) vi. Congresso nazionale del partito socialista italiano. L'Azioni del partito socialista a favore degli emigranti temporanei. Conclusioni del relatore prof. A. Cabrini. pp. 5. 1900. 8°. *See* Italy.—*Partito Socialista Italiano.* **08275**. ee. **76**. (**3**.)

CABRINI (Emilia Siracusa) Lodovico di Varthema alle isole della Sonda. pp. xiii. 257. *Torino*, 1932. 8°. **10497**. a. **38**.

CABRINI (**Frances Xavier**) *See* **Frances Xavier** [**Cabrini**], ***Saint.***

CABRINI (**Francesca Saverio**) *See* **Frances Xavier** [**Cabrini**], ***Saint.***

CABRINI (Francesco) Il Sabbato dedicato a Maria; ossia, Considerazioni sulle grandezze, virtù e glorie della SS. Vergine per tutti i Sabbati dell'anno . . . Nuova edizione accresciuta di esempi. pp. xv. 468. *Venezia, Milano*, 1869. 8°. **4805**. aaa. **3**.

—— Saturday dedicated to Mary. From the Italian . . . With preface and introduction by Father Clarke. pp. xxiii. 458. *Burns & Oates: London*, 1893. 8°. [*Quarterly Series.* vol. 83.] **3605**. dd. **83**.

CABRINI (Gabrielle)

—— Palais de cendre. Roman. pp. 241. [*Paris*,] 1949. 8°. **012551**. n. **39**.

CABRINI (Gallo) Prontuario di legislazione scolastica. Indice delle leggi e dei decreti riguardanti gli asili d'infanzia, le scuole elementari e le scuole normali pubblicati sulla " Gazzetta Ufficiale " dal 1859 al 1914. pp. iv. 190. *Milano*, 1914. 8°. **5373**. h. **35**.

CABRINI (Maria Francesca Saverio) *See* Frances Xavier [Cabrini], *Saint.*

CABRINI (Modestus) Animadversiones de natura et causa proxima aneurysmatis arteriarum, *etc.* pp. 30. *Ticini Regii*, [1830.] 8°. **7383**. d. **10**. (**4**.)

CABRIOLE (John) Les Trois montures de John Cabriole, *etc.* [A story for children, with coloured illustrations.] *Paris*, 1887. 4°. **12806**. u. **13**.

CABRIOLET. Le Cabriolet. [A novel. By Gabriel Mailhol.] pp. 156. *Amsterdam*, 1755. 12°. **12511**. b. **14**.

—— [Another edition.] Avec le Passetems des mousquetaires, ou le tems perdu. Par M. D. B * * [i.e. L. Des Biefs]. pp. 158. *La Haye*, 1760. 8°. **12511**. aaaa. **37**.

CABRIS, Marie Catherine Louise de Clapiers, *Marchioness de.* *See* Clapiers.

CABRIS (   ) Le Costume de la Parisienne au XIXe siècle. pp. 293. *Paris*, 1901. 8°. **7742**. cc. **17**.

CABRISSEAU (Nicolas) *See* Bible.—*New Testament.—Romans.* [*Polyglott.*] Méditations sur l'Épître de S. Paul aux Romains, *etc.* [By N. Le Gros. Edited by N. Cabrisseau.] *Lat. & Fr.* 1736. 12°. **3267**. aa. 5.

—— Instruction chrétienne sur les huit béatitudes par demandes et responses, *etc.* [By N. Cabrisseau.] pp. 402. 1732. 8°. *See* Christian Instruction. **3627**. aa. **9**.

CABRIT (Jean Pierre Hippolyte) De la fièvre typhoïde chez l'adulte. pp. 52. *Paris*, 1845. 4°. [*Collection des thèses soutenues à la Faculté de Médecine de Paris.* An 1845. tom. 3.] **7371**. f. 4.

CABRIT (Marie Antoine Casimir) Des tumeurs érectiles. pp. 41. *Paris*, 1845. 4°. [*Collection des thèses soutenues à la Faculté de Médecine de Paris.* An 1845. tom. 3.] **7371**. f. 4.

CABRITA (F.) *See* Rio de Janeiro.—*Escola Normal do Districto Federal.* Catalogo da Bibliotheca, *etc.* [With a preface by F. Cabrita.] 1896. 8°. **11904**. g. **2**.

CABROL (Auguste) *See* Gelu (A. J. V.) Œuvres complètes . . . Précédées . . . d'une étude biographique et critique par A. Cabrol. 1886. 8°. **11498**. e. **47**.

—— Marseille sous la défense nationale, la commune, l'état de siège, 1870–1876. pp. 168. *Marseille*, 1879. 8°. **9080**. dd. 9.

CABROL (Barthélemy) Ἀλφαβητον ἀνατομικον, hoc est Anatomes elenchus, *etc.* pp. 114. *I. Chouet: Geneuæ*, 1604. 4°. **548**. f. **27**. (1.)

—— Alphabet anatomic, auquel est contenue l'explication exacte des parties du corps humain, *etc.* pp. 110. *Pour C. Michel & G. Linocier: Tournon*, 1594. 4°. **548**. h. **1**. (2.)

—— Epistre . . . repulsiue des enuieux & venimeux propos tenus contre l'autheur des erreurs populaires. *See* Joubert (Laurent) La premiere et seconde partie des erreurs populaires, touchant la medecine, *etc.* 1601, *etc.* 8°. **1039**. c. **3**.

—— Observationes variæ. [On anatomical subjects.] pp. 28. *See* Jasolino (G.) Collegium anatomicum, *etc.* 1668. 4°. **548**. f. **12**.

CABROL (Élie) A la côte, *etc.* [Plays.] pp. 363. *Paris*, 1899. 12°. **11740**. e. **50**.

—— Comédies. Le coucher de la mariée. Les hasards de l'escarpolette. L'arrivée de l'Infante. [In verse.] Dessins de d'Hurcelles, *etc.* pp. 263. *Paris*, 1873. 12°. **11736**. c. **37**.

—— Étienne Marcel, Prévot des Marchands. Drame en cinq actes et huit tableaux, en vers. Orné de six dessins fac-simile des miniatures des Chroniques de Saint-Denis, ayant appartenu à Charles v, *etc.* pp. 317. *Paris*, 1878. 12°. **11740**. bb. **10**.

—— Hoël. Léa—Edmée—Les enfants. [Poems.] Avec trois héliogravures d'après les dessins de d'Hurcelles. pp. 148. *Paris*, 1900. 8°. **011483**. f. **34**.

—— La Première absence. Lettres en vers . . . Avec douze eaux-fortes d'après d'Hurcelles. pp. 203. *Paris*, 1872. 12°. **11482**. cc. **10**.

—— Voyage en Grèce 1889. Notes et impressions. Vingt et une planches en héliogravure, *etc.* pp. 156. *Paris*, 1890. 4°. **10125**. g. **19**.

CABROL (Étienne) Annales de Villefranche de Rouergue, *etc.* 2 tom. *Villefranche*, 1860. 8°. **10171**. cc. **18**.

CABROL (Fernand) *See* France.—*Benedictines.* Bibliographie des Bénédictins de la Congrégation de France, *etc.* [With an introduction by F. Cabrol.] 1889. 8°. **4999**. cc. **42**.

—— *See* Liturgies.—*Latin Rite.—Breviaries.*—i. *The Tridentine Breviary.* The Roman Breviary . . . With an introduction by the Right Rev. F. Cabrol. 1936, *etc.* 8°. **3396.a.60/4.**

—— *See* Liturgies.—*Latin Rite.—Missals.*—i. *The Tridentine Missal.* The Roman Missal in Latin and English . . . Compiled . . . by Dom F. Cabrol. [1921.] 12°. **03366**. g. **79**.

—— —— [1925.] 12°. **3365**. f. **25**.

CABROL (Fernand)

—— *See* Liturgies.—*Latin Rite.—Missals.*—i. *Abridgmen and Extracts.* [*Latin and English.*] The Order ar Canon of the Mass . . . With . . . an historical intr duction by . . . the Lord Abbot of Farnborough Abb (F. Cabrol). 1918. 8°. **3396.a.60/2**

—— *See* Liturgies.—*Latin Rite.—Missals.*—i. *Abridgmen and Extracts.* [*English.*] My Missal. A new missal f the Sundays and Principal Feasts of the Year . . Compiled under the direction of . . . Dom F. Cabrol. [1927.] 12°. **3366**. c. **4**

—— *See* Liturgies.—*Latin Rite.—Rituals.*—i. *Abridgmen and Extracts.* The Layfolk's Ritual . . . With intr ductions by the . . . Lord Abbot (F. Cabrol), *etc.* 1917. 12°. **3366**. de. **4**

—— *See* O'Mahony (Denis) Great French Sermons . . With an introduction by . . . F. Cabrol. [1918.] 8°. **4427**. df. **3**

—— L'Angleterre chrétienne avant les Normands. pp. xxiii. 341. *Paris*, 1909. 8°. [*Bibliothèque d l'enseignement de l'histoire ecclésiastique.*] **2208**. a. **1/1**

—— Bossuet, ses relations avec l'Angleterre. Extra de la "Revue d'histoire ecclésiastique." *Louvain* 1931. 8°. **20002**. h. **2**

—— Le Culte de la Trinité dans la liturgie et l'institution la fête de la Trinité. Excerptum ex "Ephemerid liturgicae." pp. 11. [*Louvain*,] 1931. 8°. **3475**. ff. **5**

—— Dictionnaire d'archéologie chrétienne et de liturgi Publié par le R.P. dom F. Cabrol (et H. Leclercq) avec concours d'un grand nombre de collaborateurs. 15 tom. *Pari* 1903–53. 8°. **2009.e–f**

—— Étude sur la Peregrinatio Silviæ. Les églises d Jérusalem, la discipline et la liturgie au ivᵉ siècle. pp. viii. 208. *Paris, Poitiers*, 1895. 8°. **4533**. eee. **1**

—— Histoire du cardinal Pitra. pp. xx. 432. *Pari* 1893. 8°. **4863**. de. **1**

—— Introduction aux études liturgiques. pp. 169. *Pari* 1907. 8°. BB.A. b.

—— Le Livre de la prière antique. pp. xvii. 573. *Pari* 1900. 18°. **3478**. bbb. **5**

—— Cinquième édition. pp. xvii. 591. *Tour* 1919. 8°. **2202**. a.

—— Liturgical Prayer, its history & spirit . . . Translate by a Benedictine of Stanbrook. pp. xiv. 382. *Burn Oates & Co.: London*, 1922. 8°. **3477**. eeee. **1**

—— Les Livres de la liturgie latine. pp. 165. [*Pari* 1930.] 8°. **3474**. a. **2**

—— The Books of the Latin Liturgy . . . Translated by th Benedictines of Stanbrook. pp. xii. 165. *Sands & Co. London; B. Herder Book Co.: St. Louis, Mo.*, [1932.] 8 [*Catholic Library of Religious Knowledge.* vol. 22.] **03605.g.4/22**

—— [Another copy.] **3474**. a. **3**

—— La Messe en Occident. pp. 240. [*Paris*,] 1932. 8°. **3474**. c.

—— The Mass of the Western Rites . . . Translated b C. M. Antony. pp. xii. 240. *Sands & Co.: Londo* 1934. 8°. **3474**. a. **4**

CABROL (FERNAND)

—— Mabillon et les études liturgiques. pp. 23. *Ligugé*, 1908. 8°. **3479**. c. **2**.

—— Les Origines liturgiques. Conférences, *etc.* pp. viii. 372. *Paris*, 1906. 8°. **3476**. i. 3.

—— La Prière des premiers chrétiens. pp. 277. *Paris*, 1929. 8°. **03456**. eee. **84**.

—— The Prayer of the Early Christians . . . Translated by Dom Ernest Graf. pp. xxvii. 175. *Burns, Oates & Co.: London*, 1930. 8°. **03456**. f. **22**.

—— Saint Benoît. pp. 188. *Paris*, 1933. 8°. **20003**. cc. **14**.

—— Saint Benedict . . . Translated by C. M. Antony. pp. xi. 155. *Burns, Oates & Co.: London*, 1934. 8°. **20017**. aa. 44.

—— The Year's Liturgy. The Sunday, feriæ and feasts of the liturgical year. *Burns, Oates & Co.: London*, 1938– . 8°. **2202.aa.18.**

—— The Holy Sacrifice. A simple explanation of the Mass . . . (The Ordinary of the Mass.) Translated by C. M. Antony. pp. vii. 88. 1937. 8°. *See* LITURGIES.—*Latin Rite.—Missals.*—I. *Abridgments and Extracts.* [*Latin and English.*] **3474**. c. **23**.

CABROL (FERNAND) **and LECLERCQ** (HENRI M.)

—— Monumenta ecclesiae liturgica. (Reliquiae liturgicae vetustissimae ex sanctorum patrum necnon scriptorum ecclesiasticorum monumentis selectæ.) Ediderunt et curaverunt F. Cabrol, H. Leclercq. *Parisiis*, 1900– . 4°. **L.2.cc.1.**

CABROL (HYACINTHE) *See* CABROL (Jean F. H. B.)

CABROL (J. M. MARCEL) Dans quels cas de lésions de l'urèthre doit-on pratiquer l'uréthroplastie, chez l'homme? Thèse, *etc.* pp. 77. *Montpellier*, 1845. 4°. **1182**. d. **12**. (**15**.)

CABROL (JEAN FRANÇOIS HYACINTHE BERNARD) De l'Algérie sous le rapport de l'hygiène et de la colonisation. pp. 54. *Paris*, 1863. 12°. **8155**. aa. 3.

—— De la saignée en général. Thèse, *etc.* pp. 35. *Montpellier*, 1840. 8°. **1181**. i. **19** (3.)

—— Le Maréchal de Saint Arnaud en Crimée . . . Avant-propos, mise en ordre et notes par P. de Régla. Avec 29 lettres inédites du maréchal à sa fille, *etc.* pp. xxii. 376. *Paris*, 1895. 8°. **9080**. g. **10**.

CABROL (JEAN FRANÇOIS HYACINTHE BERNARD) **and TAMISIER** (PAUL)

—— Eaux thermo-minérales chlorurées sodiques de Bourbonne-les-Bains, *etc.* pp. 108. *Paris*, 1858. 8°. **7470**. e. **14**.

CABROL (LOUIS) Dissertation sur l'hépatite aiguë et chronique; thèse, *etc.* pp. 34. *Paris*, 1832. 4°. **1184**. e. 5. (**12**.)

CABROL (P.) *See* SAINT-CHINIAN. Les Martyrs de Saint-Chinian. Dossier . . . recueilli par . . . P. Cabrol. 1920, *etc.* 8°. **09226**. h. **7**.

CABROL (RAOUL) *See* WELLHOFF (E.) Tribuns et haut-parleurs. Illustrations par Cabrol. 1932. 8°. **10655**. bbb. **34**.

CABROL (URBAIN) Documents sur le soulèvement des paysans du Bas-Rouergue, dits "Croquants," au commencement du règne de Louis XIV. Publiés par U. Cabrol. pp. viii. 201. *Rodez*, [1910.] 8°. **9231**. aa. **17**.

—— Histoire de l'atelier monétaire royal de Villefranche-de-Rouergue. [With illustrations and plans.] pp. xv. 291. *Villefranche-de-Rouergue*, 1913. 8°. **7755**. df. **19**.

CABROLIUS (BARTHOLOMAEUS) *See* CABROL (Barthélemy)

CABROLLUS (BARTHOLOMAEUS) *See* CABROL (Barthélemy)

CABRUNI (ALBERTUS) De dote inspectiones A. Cabruni . . . Nova editio cum adjectis legum numeris, aliisque indicationibus . . . et cum quibusdam annotationibus Ant. Succi. pp. 121. *Bononiæ*, 1838. 8°. **5255**. b. **46**.

CABRYE (ÉMILE D.) De la suppression d'enfant. Dissertation, *etc.* pp. 111. *Paris, Rennes*, 1876. 8°. **5425**. eee. **2**.

—— Du droit de rétention. Droit romain.—Ancien droit français.—Droit actuel, *etc.* pp. 216. *Paris*, 1860. 8°. **5405**. bb. **16**.

CABRYE (PIERRE MICHEL) Dissertation sur la variole, *etc.* pp. 15. *Paris*, 1818. 4°. **1183**. e. **5**. (**6**.)

CABU (FRANCIS)

—— Contribution à l'étude de la répartition des Kwés au Katanga. Par F. Cabu . . . avec la collaboration de M. Vanden Brande. *Tervuren*, 1938. fol. [*Annales du Musée du Congo Belge.* Anthropologie et préhistoire. sér. 1. tom. 1. fasc. 4.] Ac. **2959**. c. (**4**.)

CABUCHET (FRANÇOIS) Essai sur l'expression de la face dans l'état de santé et de maladie, *etc.* pp. 94. *Paris*, 1801. 8°. **1182**. b. **6**. (**8**.)

CABUCHET (TOUSSAINT) Histoire des premiers temps de l'Église et de l'Empire jusqu'au premier concile de Nicée, suivie d'une notice historique sur les premiers pères de l'Église jusqu'au IVe siècle. pp. 414. *Paris*, 1842. 8°. **1365**. i. 5.

CABUEÑAS (JUAN MIGUEL DE CARBALLIDO Y) *See* CARBALLIDO Y CABUEÑAS.

CABUL. *See* KABUL.

CABURACCI (FRANCESCO) Rime. [Edited by Alessandro Vandini.] pp. 146. *Per G. Rossi: Bologna*, 1580. 4°. **83**. c. **14**. (**1**.)

—— Trattato . . . Doue si dimostra il vero, & nouo modo di fare le imprese. Con vn breue discorso in difesa dell'Orlando Furioso di M. Lodouico Ariosto. [Edited by Alessandro Vandini.] pp. 94. *Per G. Rossi: Bologna*, 1580. 4°. **637**. g. **28**. (**2**.)

CABURI (FRANCO) L'Austria e l'Italia. Note e appunti di un giornalista italiano a Vienna. pp. xi. 166. *Milano*, 1915. 8°. **08027**. d. **41**.

—— Francesco Giuseppe. La sua vita e i suoi tempi. 2 vol. *Bologna*, 1920, 25. 8°. **10633**. b. **31**.

—— La Germania alla conquista della Russia. pp. 322. *Bologna*, 1918. 8°. **8095**. e. **58**.

—— Italiani e Jugoslavi nell'Adriatico. pp. 137. *Milano*, 1917. 8°. **08026**. aa. **81**.

CABÚS (José D.)

—— Batista: Pensamiento y Acción. Reportaje histórico . . . 1933–1944. [With illustrations, including portraits.] pp. 536. *La Habana*, 1944. 8°. **10481**. y. **33**.

CABUT (Pierre) Mes doutes sur la mort des Jésuites. [By P. Cabut.] pp. 45. [1762.] 12°. *See* Jesuits. [*Appendix.*] **4091**. e. **33**.

—— [Another edition.] *See* Jesuits. [*Appendix.*] Documents historiques . . . concernant la Compagnie des Jésuites. tom. 1. 1827, *etc.* 8°. **04785**. i. **42**.

—— Meine Zweifel in der gegenwärtigen Angelegenheit der Jesuiten 1762. *See* Jesuits. [*Appendix.*] Dokumente zur Geschichte . . . der Gesellschaft Jesu, *etc.* pt. 1. 1841, *etc.* 8°. **1367**. h. **30**.

CABUY (Arthur) Cause divine de la guerre Anglo-Boer. Poésie, *etc.* pp. 26. *Bruxelles*, 1900. 8°. **11482**. dd. 35. (5.)

CABUZEL (A.) Cours de perspective linéaire, *etc.* pl. xxvii. *Paris*, 1878. *obl.* fol. **1765**. a. **1**.

CABY (Antoine Jean Chrysostome Émile) Nouveau mode de traitement de diverses affections des organes génitaux . . . par l'emploi du sous-nitrate de bismuth. pp. 39. *Paris*, 1858. 4°. [*Collection des thèses soutenues à la Faculté de Médecine de Paris.* An 1858. tom. 3.] **7373**. b. **1**.

CACACE (Tito) *See* Starace (A.) Intelligenza dell'art. 1442 delle leggi civili. Nullità della cessione de' diritti litigiosi fatta dall'attore all'avvocato de' convenuti. [By A. Starace, D. de Curtis and T. Cacace.] 1839. 4°. **5373**. g. 20.

—— Boccapianola contra Boccapianola e Girace. Nella Corte Suprema di Giustizia a rapporto del . . . consigliere La Rosa. [By T. Cacace, M. Moreno and L. Romano.] pp. 65. *Napoli*, 1847. 4°. 5373. i. 10.

—— Discorso. *See* Congresso Internazionale Marittimo. [Naples, 1871.] Discorsi inaugurali dei Congressi riuniti internazionale marittimo e delle Camere di Commercio italiane, *etc.* 1871. 8°. 8805. eee. 26.

CACACIUS (Joannes Baptista) Theatrum omnium scientiarum, siue apparatus, quo exceptus fuit . . . D. Innicus de Gueuara . . . in Neapolitana Academia, *etc.* [Complimentary verses and an oration, with emblematical engravings.] ff. 105. *R. Mollus: Neapoli*, 1650. fol. **637**. k. 23.

CAÇADORI. *See* Cazadori.

CACALACA. *See* Periodical Publications.—*Alais.*

CACAN (Désiré) *See* Heures. Heures perdues, retrouvées par A. Danis, D. Cacan, *etc.* 1852, *etc.* 12°. **11481**. c. **13**.

CACAPISTUS (Gerardus) [For editions of the " Consuetudines feudorum " by Obertus de Horto and G. Cacapistus:] *See* Obertus, *de Horto.*

CACASENNO. [For anonymous editions of " Cacasenno " by Adriano Banchieri, published with anonymous editions of " Bertoldo " by G. B. Croce:] *See* Bertoldo.

CACASENO. *See* Cacasenno.

CACASSUS (Jean Baptiste) Des signes de la grossesse utérine simple. Thèse, *etc.* pp. 47. *Montpellier*, 1860. 4°. **7379**. e. 5. (2.)

CACAULT (Christophe) Essai sur l'hémicranie périodiqu[e] irrégulière, ou migraine des gens du monde, *etc.* pp. 42. *Montpellier*, 1818. 4°. **1180**. h. **14**. (6

CACAULT (François) *See* Richer (Édouard) Voyage [à] Clisson . . . Huitième édition. Suivie de notices s[ur] . . . MM. Cacault et Lemot. 1859. 16°. **10169**. de. **4**

—— Corps législatif. Conseil des Cinq-Cents. Rappo[rt] d'une commission sur le mode d'exécution de l'artic[le] 308 de l'acte constitutionnel. Séance du 11 fructidor an [6.] pp. 10. *Paris*, an 6 [1798]. 8°. F.R. **98**. (4

CACAVELAS (Jeremias) *Monk.* *See* Hieremias [Kak[a]belas], *Monk.*

CACCAVALE (Giovanni) Satira delle satire. [A sati[re] on the publications occasioned by the insurrectiona[ry] movement at Naples in 1820.] [*Naples*, 1820.] *s. sh.* fo[l.] **8032**. m. **10**. (36

—— Raccolta di epigrammi del marchese di Caccavone [an[d] others], *etc.* pp. 179. *Napoli*, 1894. 8°. **11422**. bb. **1**

CACCHIATELLI (Domenico) Nuovo sistema di fortific[a]zione. pp. 12. pl. vi. *Roma*, 1819. 4°. **1812**. b. **2**

—— Progetto per la decorazione della facciata della Chie[sa] di S. Maria in Aracœli. [With a plan.] pp. 11. *Pesar[o]*, 1826. 8°. **7807**. c. **41**. (

CACCHIATELLI (P.) and **CLETER** (G.) Le Scienze [e] le arti sotto il pontificato di Pio ix. Edizione second[a.] [Plates with accompanying letterpress.] 124 fasc. *Roma*, 1863–[67]. *obl.* fol. **1789**. b. **2**

CACCHIONE (Costantino) La Scherma per terreno . . e codice del procedimento da adottarsi per duello. pp. 10 *Sarzana*, 1895. 8°. **8425**. e. **2**

CACCIA. Opera noua doue si contiene vna caccia amoro[sa] tramutata a la Bergamasca & battaglie. Et vn biasm[o] della caccia d'amore, & Capitoli bellissimi. [In verse.] [*M. Pagan: Venice*, 1550 ?] 8°. **11427**. aaa. **3**

—— Opera noua doue si contiene vna Caccia Amor[osa] trasmutata alla Bergamasca, *etc.* [In verse.] [1570 ?] **11426.b.4**

—— Opera nova dove si contiene vna caccia amorosa tra[s]tata a la Bergamasca & battaglie, et vn Biasmo della cac[cia] d'amore & Capitoli bellissimi. [1580 ?] 8°. **11429**. aaa.

—— Caccia d'amore, cauata dal Todesco in Italiano ridut[ta] per far vna mascarata, *etc.* [With other pieces in ver[se.] In the Bergamese dialect.] [*Venice ?* 1550 ?] 8°. **11427**. b.

—— Caccia proibita. Abelardo ed Eloisa. pp. 141. *Mila[no,]* [1887.] 32°. **12470**. aaa.

CACCIA (Alma Maria) Breve compendio della vita del[la] serva del Signore Suor Alma Maria Caccia del SS. Sagr[a]mento. pp. xx. 280. *Bergamo*, 1782. 8°. **4867**. aaaa. **4**

CACCIA (Anthony Mario Felix) A Preliminary Note [on] the Development of the Sal in volume and in money-valu[e.] 1908. *See* India.—*Forest Department.* The Indi[an] Forest Records. vol. 1. pt. 2. 1908, *etc.* 8°. **I.S.252/**

CACCIA (Antonio) *Dottor.* Europa ed America. Sce[ne] della vita dal 1848 al 1850. pp. 500. *Mona[co,]* 1850. 8°. **10630**. a.

CACCIA (ANTONIO) *Dottor.*

—— L'Impero celeste. Lettere di un Cinese ad un Europeo pubblicate [or rather, written] dal dottor A. Caccia. [With a map.] pp. 172. 1858. 8°. *See* CHINESE. **10055**. aa. **8**.

CACCIA (ANTONIO) *of Milan.* *See* SARTORIO (M.) Della vita e degli scritti di Antonio Caccia da Milano, *etc.* 1870. 8°. **10630**. bb. **39**. (**13**.)

CACCIA (CHARLES) When are Boys to be Discharged from Reformatories? A letter to Her Majesty's Inspectors of Reformatories. pp. 11. *Yorkshire Printing & Publishing Co.: Hull,* 1861. 12°. **6055**. a. **19**.

CACCIA (EMILIO) Uruguai e missioni. Stato attuale ed avvenire in rapporto colla emigrazione. (Annessovi la carta geografica dell'Uruguai.) pp. 134. *Milano,* 1885. 8°. **4766**. ccc. **27**.

CACCIA (FEDERICO) *Cardinal.* *See* PARAVICINI (B.) Milano sempre grande nel procurare la promozione de' suoi figli alla dignità di padre, e di pastore . . . Circostanze descritte nell'elezione, e nel solenne ingresso fatto in Milano dall'eminentissimo Signor Cardinale Federico Caccia, *etc.* [1697.] 4°. **9930**. g. **52**.

CACCIA (FILIPPO) La Medicina ai tempi di Augusto, *etc.* pp. 41. pl. IV. *Roma,* 1938. 8°. [*Quaderni Augustei.* Studi italiani. no. 14.] Ac. **103**. b/4. (**1**.)

CACCIA (FRANCESCO) Oratione . . . fatta nella morte della Serenissima Infante Donna Caterina d'Austria, Duchessa di Sauoia. ff. 26. *P. Malatesta, ad instanza di G. Bordone & P. Martire Locarni: Milano,* [1598.] 4°. **835**. f. **16**. (**8**.)

Cropped.

—— Francisci Catii oratio ad . . . Clementem VIII., Pont. Max., pro . . . Carolo Emanuele Sabaudiæ Duce . . . habita VII. Kal. Julij 1593, cum ejusdem Ducis nomine obedientiam præstaret . . . Comes Franciscus Martinengus. (Silvij Antoniani . . . responsio.) *Apud A. Zannettum: Romæ,* 1594. 4°. **805**. d. **43**.

CACCIA (FRANCISCUS) Innocentia Apostolica. Die Apostolische Unschuld. Das ist: Innocentii des Eilfften, tugendsambster Lebens-Wandel, ruhmwürdigste Regierung, und gottseeligste Entzuckung, *etc.* pp. 640. *J. P. Andräe: Franckfurt,* 1697. 4°. **484**. a. **27**.

—— Monumentum gloriæ seraphicæ. Das ist: Gedenck-Zeichen seraphischer Ehr, dess . . . Vatters Francisci, und dero Mindern Ordens-Brüdern . . . so das heilige Grab Jesu Christi . . . in die 431. Jahr . . . verwahret . . . auff 15. Jahr verlohren, anjetzo wiederumb . . . recuperiret . . . zusam̄en getragen, und mit schönen Kupffern geziert. pp. 547. *P. Fievet: Wienn,* 1694. 4°. **10076**. bbb. **20**.

CACCIA (GIOVANNI AGOSTINO) *See* CAZZA.

CACCIA (GIOVANNI FRANCESCO) *Count.* Testamento e codicillo del conte Giovanni Francesco Caccia, giureconsulto novarese. Testo originale con traduzione letterale per cura degli avvocati L. Bazzano, A. Tadini, B. Busser. [With a portrait.] pp. 115. *Novara,* 1902. 4°. **10630**. h. **38**.

CACCIA (GIUSEPPE) *See* CACCIA (Joseph)

CACCIA (GUGLIELMO) called IL MONCALVO. *See* NEGRI (Francesco) *of Casale Monferrato.* Il Moncalvo, *etc.* [With a portrait.] 1895, *etc.* 8°. **10602**. l. **1**. (**4**.)

CACCIA (JOANNES) De scrofula. Tentamen inaugurale, *etc.* pp. 15. *Ticini Regii,* [1828 ?] 8°. **7383***. b. **6**. (**5**.)

CACCIA (JOSEPH) *See* FERRARI (C.) Grand dictionnaire français-italien et italien-français . . . Par C. Ferrari et J. Caccia. 1874. 8°. **12942**. g. **7**.

—— —— 1879. 8°. **12902**. h. **10**.

—— —— [1916.] 8°. **12944.i.1.**

—— Guide universel de l'étranger dans Marseille . . . Suivi d'une excursion à Aix et à Toulon. Par J. Caccia [and Antonin Palliès] . . . Ouvrage accompagné d'un plan . . . et des vues, *etc.* pp. vi. 312. *Paris,* 1876. 16°. **10171**. a. **10**.

A later edition is entered under PALLIÈS (*A.*).

—— Nouveau guide général du voyageur en Italie . . . Ouvrage accompagné d'une carte . . . d'un grand nombre de vues et de plans. pp. xvi. 514. *Paris,* [1875.] 16°. **10136**. de. **17**.

—— Le Serment, son origine dans l'antiquité. pp. 32. *Paris,* 1870. 8°. **6025**. aaa. **12**.

CACCIA (MAXIMILIEN) *Count.* Des vertus militaires et du mérite de la carrière des armes en temps de paix. pp. xx. 291. *Paris,* 1846. 8°. **1387**. i. **1**.

CACCIA (NATALE) Note su la fortuna di Luciano nel Rinascimento. Le versioni e i dialoghi satirici di Erasmo da Rotterdam e di Ulrico Hutten. pp. 149. *Milano,* [1914.] 8°. **11313**. dd. **37**.

CACCIA (VINCENTIUS) Metritidis et hepatitidis in hydropem ferme catholicum versæ historia, quam ceu inaugurale tentamen . . . una cum thesibus adnexis, publicæ disquisitioni submittebat V. Caccia. pp. 20. *Ticini Regii,* [1831.] 8°. **7383***. b. **12**. (**18**.)

CACCIA (VIRGINIO) Trattato delle malattie della bocca e dei denti, *etc.* 2 pt. pp. xi. 1081. *Torino,* 1900. 8°. **7611**. cc. **30**.

CACCIACONTI (ASCANIO) *See* also STRAFALCIONE, *pseud.* [i.e. A. Cacciaconti.]

—— Filastoppa. Comedia. [In verse.] [*Sienna ?* 1550 ?] 8°. **11427**. b. **23**.

—— [Another edition.] [*Luca Bonetti*:] *Siena,* [c. 1575.] 8°. **162**. a. **31**.

—— Pelagrilli. Commedia. [In verse.] *Ad instantia delle herede di G. d'Alisandro: Siena,* 1552. 8°. **162**. a. **32**.

—— [Another edition.] [*Luca Bonetti*:] *Siena,* 1576. 12°. **1071**. c. **39**.

CACCIAGUERRA (BUONSIGNORE) *See* KERR (*Lady* Amabel) A Precursor of St. Philip—Buonsignore Cacciaguerra. 1903. 8°. **4864**. de. **6**.

—— Dialogo spirituale del Ven. Prete Buonsignore Cacciaguerra con Felice, vergine di Barbarano, sua penitente; di cui anche scrive dopo di esso la . . . vita. Si aggiunge . . . una lettera di Bernardino Scardeone . . . alle monache di S. Stefano in Padova . . . Il tutto . . . corretto, e illustrato con varie annotazioni, *etc.* [Edited by Gaetano Volpi.] pp. xxxviii. 267. *Padova,* 1740. 8°. **224**. g. **21**.

—— Pie e divote meditazioni . . . Opera postuma . . . Ora ripulita, e adornata con alcune annotazioni, con un indice . . . e col compendio della vita dell'autore. Si aggiunge . . . la . . . meditazione di S. Luigi Gonzaga intorno a' SS. Angeli. [Edited by Gaetano Volpi.] pp. xxiv. 363. *Padova,* 1740. 8°. **223**. g. **7**.

CACCIAGUERRA (BUONSIGNORE)

—— Trattato della Cõmunione . . . Nouamente ristampato, et con più cose agiũte dall'istesso autore. ff. 200. *G. M. di Pellippari: Vercelli,* 1561. 16°. Voyn. **26.**

—— Trattato della tribolatione . . . Nuouamente ristampato, & ricorretto. ff. 99. *F. Franceschini: Venetia,* 1567. 16°. **1018.** a. **39.**

CACCIAGUERRI (CACCIAGUERRA) *See* VILLA (A.) Risposta . . . alle scritture del Capitano C. Cacciaguerri. 1562. 4°. **10631.** c. **46. (2.)**

CACCIALANZA (JOSEPH) Quam arduum sit tutam graviditatis diagnosim efformare. Dissertatio inauguralis, *etc.* pp. 24. *Ticini Regii,* [1827.] 8°. **7383*.** d. **5. (2.)**

CACCIALUPUS (JOANNES BAPTISTA) *Begin.* [fol. 1 *recto*:] [C]Vm viderem sepissimè iudices ꝛ officiales egredi terminos iuris, *etc. End.* [fol. 30 *verso*:] Hic finiunt solemnes ꝛ aurei tractatus. s. de debitoribus fugitiuis. de pactis ꝛ de transactionibus, *etc.* G.L. *per Petruȝ maufer: Mutine,* die .xviij. mensis Iunij, 1492. fol. IC. **32316.**
30 *leaves. Sig.* a–f⁶·⁴. *Double columns,* 62 *lines to a column.*

—— Tractat⁹ de debitoribus suspec. et fugiti. Et Tractat⁹ de pactis, *etc.* G.L. MS. NOTES. [*Pavia,* 1495 ?] fol. IC. **31695.**
16 *leaves. Sig.* a⁴ b⁴ A⁴ B⁴. *Double columns,* 73 *lines to a column.*

—— Tractatus de Pactis.—Tractatus . . . de Transactionibus.—Tractatus de Aduocatis, *etc. See* TRACTATUS. Primum [*etc.*] volumen tractatuum, *etc.* vol. 3. 1549. fol. **5305.** i.

—— Tractatus . . . de Vnionibus, *etc.*—Joã. Baptiste Caccialupi . . . de Pensionibus questiones triginta. *See* TRACTATUS. Primum [*etc.*] volumen tractatuum, *etc.* vol. 15. 1549. fol. **5305.** i.

—— Ioannis Baptistæ Caccialupi . . . Tractatus de Pactis. —Io. Baptistae Caccialupi, De Transactionibus. *See* TRACTATUS. Tractatus vniuersi iuris, *etc.* tom. 6. pt. 1. 1584. fol. **499.** f. **7.**

—— Tractatus . . . de Vnionibus, *etc.*—Tractatus . . . de Pensionibus, *etc. See* TRACTATUS. Tractatus vniuersi iuris, *etc.* tom. 15. pt. 1. 1584. fol. **499.** g. **10.**

—— D. Ioannis Baptiste de Caccialupis de Aduocatis. *See* TRACTATUS. Tractatus vniuersi iuris, *etc.* tom. 3. pt. 1. 1584. fol. **499.** f. **3.**

—— De modo studendi ꝛ uita doctorũ tctatus. *See* REPETITIONES. *Begin.* [fol. 2 *recto*:] Incipit solẽnis Repetitõ, *etc.* 1472. fol. IC. **19559.**

—— [Another edition.] De modo studendi in vtroq; Iure: cũ noib⁹ omniũ scribentiũ in iure. Interpretationes oĩm tituloꝝ legũ et canonum. [fol. 2 *recto*:] Modus studend [*sic*] in iure accuratissimus . . . p . . . dñm iohannẽ baptistã de gazalupis, *etc.* [fol. 13 *recto*:] Expositiones siue declarationes omnium titulorum iuris tam Ciuilis q̃ Canonici per Sebastianũ Brãt. collecte et reuise. G.L. *per Michaelem furter: Basilee,* kal'. septẽbrib⁹ [1 Sept.], 1500. 4°. IA. **37816.**
164 *leaves, the last blank. Sig.* a⁸ b⁴ ; A–T⁸. 46 *lines to a page. Without the blank leaf.*

—— [Another copy.] IA. **37817.**
Imperfect ; containing only the Expositiones of S. Brant.

CACCIALUPUS (JOANNES BAPTISTA)

—— [Another edition.] Modus studẽdi in iure accuratissim⁹, *etc. See* BRANT (S.) [*Miscellaneous Works.*] Expositiones siue declaratiões omniũ titulorũ iuris, *etc.* 1508. 4°. **500.** d. **3.**

—— [Another edition.] *See* BRANT (S.) [*Miscellaneous Works.*] Expositiões siue declarationes omniũ tituloꝝ iuris, *etc.* 1514. 8°. **877.** g. **11.**

—— [Another edition.] *See* BRANT (S.) [*Miscellaneous Works.*] Expositiones siue declaratiões omnium titulorum iuris, *etc.* 1514. 4°. **500.** d. **4.**

—— [Another edition.] *See* BRANT (S.) [*Miscellaneous Works.*] Expositiones siue declarationes omnium titulorum iuris, *etc.* 1521. 8°. C. **64.** b. **6. (3.)**

—— [Another edition.] *See* BRANT (S.) [*Miscellaneous Works.*] Titulorum omnium iuris . . . expositiones, *etc.* 1547. 8°. **1480.** a. **37. (2.)**

—— [Another edition.] *See* BRANT (S.) [*Miscellaneous Works.*] Titulorum omnium iuris . . . expositiones, *etc.* 1552. 8°. **877.** g. **12.**

—— [Another edition.] *See* BRANT (S.) [*Miscellaneous Works.*] Titulorum omnium iuris . . . expositiones, *etc.* 1555. 8°. **5306.** a. **3.**

—— [Another edition.] In: VOCABULARIUS. Vocabularium vtriusque iuris, *etc.* pp. 691–720. 1559. 8°. **5205.** aa. **9.**

—— [Another edition.] *See* BRANT (S.) [*Miscellaneous Works.*] Titulorum omnium iuris . . . expositiones, *etc.* 1587. 8°. **5306.** a. **11.**

—— De Pẽsionibus Tractatus uere aureus . . . Addito indice per Didacum Sanctium. pp. 93. MS. NOTES. *Apud F. M. Caluum: Romae,* 1531. 4°. **697.** g. **34. (1.)**

—— Joannis Baptistæ de Gazalupis Succincta historia interpretum et glossatorum juris. *See* PANCIROLI (G.) Guidi Panziroli . . . De claris legum interpretibus libri quatuor, *etc.* 1721. 4°. **1130.** e. **1.**

—— Tractatus . . . de debitore suspecto ꝛ fugitiuo. *See* TRACTATUS. Primum [*etc.*] volumen tractatuum, *etc.* vol. 8. 1549. fol. **5305.** i.

—— [Another edition.] *See* TRACTATUS. Selecti tractatus iuris varii, *etc.* 1570. fol. **5306.** f. **7.**

—— [Another edition.] *See* TRACTATUS. Tractatus vniuersi iuris, *etc.* tom. 3. pt. 2. 1584. fol. **499.** f. **4.**

—— [Another edition.] *See* FEYERABEND (S.) Corpus selectorum tractatuum de pignoribus et hypothecis. 1586. fol. **5510.** f. **5.**

—— [Another edition.] *See* MERCATURA. De mercatura decisiones, *etc.* 1621. fol. **499.** c. **10.**

—— [Another edition.] *See* MERCATURA. Benevenuti Stracchæ aliorumque . . . jurisconsultorum De mercatura . . . decisiones & tractatus, *etc.* 1669. fol. **502.** k. **11.**

—— Tractatus . . . de ludo, *etc. See* TRACTATUS. Primum [*etc.*] volumen tractatuum, *etc.* vol. 4. 1549. fol. **5305.** i.

—— [Another edition.] *See* TRACTATUS. Tractatus vniuersi iuris, *etc.* tom. 7. 1584. fol. **499.** f. **9.**

—— Ioannis Baptistæ Caccialupi . . . Tractatus de pactis. *See* TRACTATUS. Tractatus de pactis clarissimorum iureconsultorum, *etc.* 1582. 4°. **5605.** ccc. **13.**

CACCIALUPUS (JOANNES BAPTISTA)

—— Tractatus . . . de vnionibus. *See* TRACTATUS. Tractatus vniuersi iuris, *etc.* tom. 15. pt. 2. 1584. fol. **499**. g. **11**.

—— Tractatus per modum repetitionis c. 1. de feu. cogni. in vsibus feudorum, *etc.* *See* TRACTATUS. Primum [*etc.*] volumen tractatuum, *etc.* vol. 13. 1549. fol. **5305**. i.

—— [Another edition.] *See* TRACTATUS. Tractatus vniuersi iuris, *etc.* tom. 10. pt. 1. 1584. fol. **499**. g. **2**.

—— Begin. [fol. 1 *recto*:] Repetitio solēpnis et vtilis domini Io. baptiste de Caccialupis de sancto seuerino super .l. imperiuȝ. Et .l. iubere cauere .ff. de iurisd. om. iudi. Cum. questionibus ptinentibus ad eas In Senensi gymnasio demane legētis Feliciter incipit, *etc.* G.L. *Per Henricū de Haerlem: Senis*, Die .XI. mensis maij, 1493. fol. IC. **34647**.

16 leaves, the last blank. Sig. a—d⁴. *Double columns, 60 lines to a column.*

CACCIAMALI (GIOVANNI BATTISTA) Morfogenesi delle Prealpi lombarde, ed in particolare di quelle della provincia di Brescia, *etc.* [With a map.] pp. xi. 308. *Brescia*, 1930. 8°. **7108**. g. **1**.

—— Studii . . . sulla collina di Castenedolo, *etc.* pp. 93. pl. II. 1896. *See* BRESCIA.—*Ateneo di Brescia.* Commentarj, *etc.* 1896. 1808, *etc.* 4°. Ac. **28**.

CACCIAMALI (LINA CUCCO) *See* CUCCO-CACCIAMALI.

CACCIAMANUS (SANCTUS) *See* ROME, *Church of.*—Alexander VII. [1655–1667.] *Begin.* Alexander Papa VII., *etc.* [A brief appointing S. Cacciamanus Prefect General of the Congregatio Clericorum Regularium Ministrantium Infirmis. Dated 3 Feb. 1657.] 1657. 4°. **1897**. b. **14**. (**48**.)

CACCIANEMICI (LUCIO) *See* ALBERTI (Leandro) Libro secondo (terzo) della deca seconda dell'Historie di Bologna. Di nouo aumentato, et ricorretto per opra del R^do^ Padre F. L. Caccianemici. 1589, *etc.* 4°. **658**. c. **6**. (**2**, **3**.)

—— *See* ALBERTI (Leandro) Di F. Leandro Alberti . . . Dell'Historie della sua Patria Libro primo, *etc.* [With a dedicatory epistle by L. Caccianemici.] 1599. 4°. **658**. c. **5**.

CACCIANEMICI (ROSANESE DE') *See* HUMILITY, *Saint.* [R. de' Caccianemici.]

CACCIANEMICI PALCANI (LUIGI) Le Prose italiane di Luigi Palcani. Con figure in rame. pp. 156. *Milano*, 1817. 16°. **1340**. b. **13**.

—— Opuscoli. (Del fuoco di Vesta.—Del natro orientale.—Del platino.) *See* RACCOLTA. Raccolta di operette filosofiche e filologiche scritte nel secolo XVIII. vol. 2. 1832. 8°. **12201.p.1/352.**

—— Lettere. 1830. *See* RACCOLTA. Raccolta di prose e lettere scritte nel secolo XVIII. vol. 2. 1829, *etc.* 8°. **12201.p.1/351.**

—— Aloysii Caccianimici Palcani De prodigiosis solis defectibus sermo, iterum editus curante Petro Napoli-Signorelli. pp. xi. 44. *Neapoli*, 1791. 8°. **898**. c. **19**. (**3**.)

—— De vita Eustachii Zanotti commentarius. Iterum editus. [With a dedicatory epistle by G. Garatonius.] pp. 47. *Romæ*, 1785. 8°. **10631**. c. **33**.

—— [Another copy.] **10630**. c. **7**.

—— [Another edition.] Iterum editus curante Clementino Vannettio. pp. 36. *Parmae*, 1785. 8°. **10630**. c. **6**.

CACCIANEMICI PALCANI (LUIGI)

—— [Another edition.] [With the dedicatory epistles prefixed to previous editions by G. Garatonius, C. Vannetti and A. Fabroni.] pp. 51. [*Bologna*, 1785?] 8°. **10630**. d. **12**.

—— Elogio di Eustachio Zanotti, tradotto dal Latino. *See* ZANOTTI (E.) Trattato-teorico-pratico di prospettiva. 1825. 8°. **12201.p.1/337.**

—— Del fuoco di Vesta. Ragionamento, *etc.* [With plates.] pp. 55. *Bassano*, 1794. 8°. **899**. d. **6**. (**2**.)

—— [Another copy.] **898**. c. **19**. (**2***.)

—— Elogio d'Anton-Mario Lorgna. [By L. Caccianemici Palcani.] pp. 25. [1800?] 8°. *See* LORGNA (A. M.) **10630**. d. **4**. (**2**.)

—— [Another edition.] *See* GAMBA (B.) Elogi di Italiani illustri, *etc.* 1829. 12°. **10630**. a. **14**.

—— [Another edition.] *See* RACCOLTA. Raccolta di prose e lettere scritte nel secolo XVIII. vol. 1. 1829. 8°. **12201.p.1/350.**

—— Elogio di Leonardo Ximenes. [Edited by the Marquis A. Bovio Silvestri.] pp. 32. [*Bologna*, 1791.] 8°. **10630**. d. **4**. (**1**.)

CACCIANIGA (ANTONIO) Il Bacio della contessa Savina. pp. 355. *Milano*, 1875. 8°. **12471**. bb. **18**.

—— Bozzetti morali ed economici. [Edited, with a biographical introduction, by L. Bailo.] pp. xv. 196. *Treviso*, 1868. 8°. **8404**. d. **10**.

—— Brava gente. [Essays.] pp. 349. *Milano*, 1889. 8°. **12356**. d. **35**.

—— Il Convento. Racconto . . . Seconda edizione. pp. 372. *Milano*, 1883. 8°. **12471**. e. **31**.

—— Il Dolce far niente. Scene della vita veneziana del secolo passato. pp. 287. *Milano*, 1869. 8°. **12471**. bb. **31**.

—— La Famiglia Bonifazio. Racconto. pp. 395. *Milano*, 1886. 8°. **12471**. g. **32**.

—— Il Roccolo di Sant'Alipio. Racconto. pp. 359. *Milano*, 1881. 8°. **12471**. cc. **29**.

—— Sotto i ligustri. (Racconti e novelle.—Reminiscenze dell'esilio.—Impressioni rurali.) pp. xvi. 340. *Milano*, 1881. 8°. **12471**. e. **21**.

—— La Vita campestre. Studi morali ed economici. pp. vii. 244. *Milano*, 1867. 8°. **8404**. bb. **6**.

CACCIANIMICI (FRANCESCO MARIA) Rime. pp. 94. *B. Cocchi: Bologna*, 1608. 4°. **C.107.e.4.(2.)**

The titlepage is engraved.

CACCIANIMICI (ROSANESE DE') *See* HUMILITY, *Saint.* [R. de' Caccianemici.]

CACCIANIMICUS PALCANUS (ALOYSIUS) *See* CACCIANEMICI PALCANI (Luigi)

CACCIANOTTI (SERENO) *See* VERCELLI.—*Archivio.* Summarium monumentorum . . . quae in tabulario Municipii Vercellensis continentur . . . Ab incerto auctore concinnatum et nunc primum editum curante S. Caccianottio. 1868. 8°. **10131**. g. **9**.

CACCIARI (PIETRO TOMMASO) *See* LEO I., *Saint*, surnamed *the Great, Pope.* Sancti Leonis Magni . . . Opera omnia . . . Accedunt . . . exercitationes in universa opera S. Leonis Magni auctore P. T. Cacciari. 1846. 4°. [MIGNE (*J. P.*) *Patrologiæ cursus completus, etc.* tom. 54–56.] **2000**. b.

CACCIARI (PIETRO TOMMASO)

—— Della vita, virtù e doni sopranaturali del Venerabile Servo di Dio P. Angiolo Paoli, Carmelitano . . . libri III. Con un appendice de miracoli, *etc.* pp. xx. 342. *Roma,* 1756. 4°. **1231.** e. **25.**

CACCIATORE. Lo Cacciatore modiesto e speretuso. Devertimento carnevalesco. [In verse.] [*Naples?* 1820?] 12°. **1071.** c. **14.** **(30.)**

—— [Another edition.] Lo Cacciatore. Divertemiento carnevalesco. [*Naples?* 1820?] 12°. **11436.** a. **13.**

CACCIATORE ITALIANO. *See* ITALIAN HUNTER.

CACCIATORE (ANDREA) Esame della Storia del reame di Napoli di Pietro Colletta dal 1794 al 1825. 2 vol. *Napoli,* 1850. 8°. **1057.** k. **24.**

CACCIATORE (GAETANO) *See* PALERMO.—*Real Osservatorio.* Annuario, *etc.* [Anno 1–13 edited by G. Cacciatore.] 1842, *etc.* 16° & 8°. Ac. **4122.**

CACCIATORE (GIUSEPPE)

—— Enciclopedia del sacerdozio, diretta dal Rev. Prof. G. Cacciatore. pp. xii. 1689. pl. XII. 1953. 8°. *See* ENCYCLOPAEDIAS. **4499.** k. **10.**

—— S. Alfonso de' Liguori e il giansenismo. Le ultime fortune del moto giansenistico e la restituzione del pensiero cattolico nel secolo XVIII. pp. 622. *Firenze,* 1944. 8°. **4824.** df. **27.**

CACCIATORE (INNOCENZO) Osservazioni sulla cometa apparsa in gennaio 1831, *etc.* pp. 15. *Palermo,* 1831. 8°. **8561.** cc. **31.** **(1.)**

CACCIATORE (NICCOLÒ) Biografia di Niccolò Cacciatore, astronomo dell'Osservatorio di Palermo, scritta da se medesimo . . . corredata di aggiunte e di note da Erasmo Fabri Scarpellini, *etc.* [With a portrait.] pp. 8. *Roma,* 1845. 4°. **898.** i. **3.** **(6.)**

—— De redigendis ad unicam seriem comparabilem meteorologicis ubique factis observationibus conventio proposita et tabulae supputatae. pp. 81. *Panormi,* 1832. 4°. **8756.** d. **45.** **(2.)**

—— Della cometa apparsa in settembre del 1807. Osservazioni, e risultati. pp. 47. *Palermo,* 1808. 4°. B. **530.** **(21.)**

—— Sull'origine del sistema solare. Discorso . . . Seconda edizione. pp. 30. *Palermo,* 1826. 8°. **8561.** e. **31.** **(2.)**

CACCINI (G. SIGISMONDO UIFALUSSI) *See* UIFALUSSI CACCINI.

CACCINI (GIULIO) called ROMANO.

—— *See* EHRICHS (K. A.) Giulio Caccini, *etc.* 1908. 8°. Hirsch **2841.**

—— *See* GANDOLFI (Riccardo) Alcune considerazioni intorno alla riforma melodrammatica a proposito di Giulio Caccini, *etc.* [1896.] 8°. Hirsch **1171.** (5.)

—— *See* GHISI (F.) Del " Fuggilotio musicale " di Giulio Romano-Caccini, *etc.* 1934. 8°. **07899.** ee. **30.**

CACCINI (TOMMASO) *See* RICCI-RICCARDI (A.) Galileo Galilei e Fra Tommaso Caccini, *etc.* 1902. 8°. **10629.** cc. **38.**

CACCINI (TOMMASO)

—— Storia ecclesiastica del Primo Concilio Niceno, *et*[c.] pp. 337. *P. Bidelli: Lucca,* 1637. 4°. **1230.** a. [ ]
The titlepage is engraved.

CACCIOLI (ANDREA) *See* ADIAFORO (Filalete) *pseu*[d.] Lettere . . . sopra la controversia di qual'ordine d[e] Minori sia il B. A. Caccioli. 1727. 4°. **636.** i. 2[ ]

CACCIOPPOLI (RENATO)

—— Ovaloidi di metrica assegnata. *In Civitate Vatican*[a] 1940. 8°. [*Pontificia Academia Scientiarum. Commenta*[*]tiones.* vol. 4. no. 1.] Ac. **101.** b/[ ]

CACCURI. Saggi analitici su l'acqua solfurea di Caccur[i] Di A. S. [1838.] 8°. *See* S., A. **7462.** e. **4.** (7[.)]

ČAĆE (IVE)

—— Nogometna lopta. Igrokaz iz pionirskog života. pp. [ ] *Zagreb,* 1946. 8°. **11758.** pp. **4**[ ]
Part of a series entitled " Omladinsko kazalište."

—— Sa vrela slobode. pp. 79. *Zagreb,* 1945. 8°. **11587.** b. **54**[ ]
Partizanska književnost. knj. 5.

—— Stipe Jarbolina i drugi čakavski stihovi. pp. 45. *Zagreb,* 1950. 8°. **11588.** de. **4**[ ]
The titlepage headed: Narodna kjižnica [sic].

—— Za slobodu. [With a portrait.] pp. 120. *Zagre*[*b,*] 1946. 8°. **11588.** bb. **1**[ ]

CACEGAS (LUIS DE) Primeira (–terceira) parte d[a] Historia de S. Domingos, particular do reino, e conquista[s] de Portugal . . . Reformada em estilo, e ordem, e ampli[-] ficada em successos, e particularidades por Fr. Luis d[e] Sousa. (Quarta parte . . . por Fr. Lucas de S[t] Catharina.) 4 pt. *Lisboa,* 1767. fol. **1232.** g. **3–6**[ ]

—— Vida de Dom Frei Bertolameu dos Martyres . . . Arcebisp[o] e Senhor de Braga . . . Reformada em estilo & ordem [&] ampliada . . . por Frey Luis de Sousa. [With a portrait.] ff. 280 [282]. *N. Carualho: Viana,* 1619. fol. **487.** i. **3**[ ]

—— [Another edition.] 2 tom. *Lisboa,* 1763. 8°. **4865.** a. **1**[ ]

CÁCERES. [Fuero granted to Cáceres by Alphonso IX., King of Leon and confirmed by Ferdinand III., King o[f] Castile and Leon.] *See* USAGRE. Fuero de Usagre . . . Anotado con las variantes del de Cáceres, *etc.* 1907. 8°. **5384.** e. **10**[ ]

—— *Archivo Municipal.* Documentación Histórica de[l] Archivo Municipal de Cáceres. Catálogo comentado y anotado por Antonio C. Floriano. *Cáceres,* 1934– . 8°. W.P. **12332.**

Jefatura Provincial del Movimiento.—Departamento de Seminarios.

—— Realidades y esperanzas de la Alta Extremadura[.] Cuarto ciclo de conferencias, *etc.* pp. vi. 226. *Cáceres* 1953. 8°. **10163.** f. **26**[ ]
Biblioteca extremeña. vol. 10.

CÁCERES (ANDRÉS AVELINO) *President of the Republic o*[*f*] *Peru.*

—— *See* ALAYZA Y PAZ SOLDÁN (L.) La Breña. (2. 1882. Cáceres el campeador.) 1954. 8°. **12493.** de. **11.**

CÁCERES (ANDRÉS AVELINO) *President of the Republic of Peru.*

—— Rasgos Militares del . . . General Andrés Avelino Cáceres . . . Homenaje a sus relevantes méritos en el día de su cumpleaños, noviembre 10 de 1886. [With a portrait.] pp. 15. *Lima*, 1886. 8º. **10601**. ee. **5**. (**1**.)

CÁCERES (ANTONIO DE) Verdadera, y nueua relacion, y copia de carta, escrita de la Ciudad de Mastrique por vn capitan español . . . en que se dà quenta de los tres mayores sucessos, y dos felizes victorias, que han tenido las armas de su Magestad . . . y las del señor Emperador en las ciudades de Mastrique en Flandes, y Lieja en Alemania, contra las de Francia, *etc.* *M. Ramos: Seuilla*, 1676. 4º. **1445**. f. **17**. (**61**.)

CÁCERES (AURORA) *See* CÁCERES (Zoila A. E.)

CACÉRÈS (**BÉNIGNO**)

—— Regards neufs sur Paris . . . avec la collaboration de P. Barlatier [and others], *etc.* [With illustrations.] pp. 229. *Paris*, 1952. 8º. **10175**. e. **36**.
Part of the series " Peuple et Culture."

—— La Rencontre des hommes. Roman. pp. 218. *Paris*, 1950. 8º. **12519**. e. **18**.

CÁCERES (BENITO CALERO DE) *See* CALERO DE CÁCERES.

CÁCERES (FRANCISCO DE) *See* DELFINO (D.) Libro intitulado Uision Deleytable y sumario de todas las sciencias. Traducido de Italiano . . . por F. de Caceres, *etc.* 1663. 4º. **525**. f. **24**.

—— *See* FRANCIS [Bernardoni], *of Assisi, Saint, Archconfraternity of the Girdle of.* Forma y modo de fundar las cofradias del cordon de nr̃o P. S. Frãcisco, *etc.* [With an address to the reader by F. de Cáceres.] 1589. 8º. C. **36**. b. **11**.

—— Dialogos Satyricos. pp. 304. *Francaforte*, 1616. 8º. **12352**. aa. **24**.

CÁCERES (JOAN BATISTA FELICES, DE) *See* FELICES DE CÁCERES.

CÁCERES (JOSÉ MARÍA) Geografía de Centro-América . . . escrita en compendio . . . Precedida de las nociones preliminares más necessarias. [With maps.] pp. 71. *Paris*, 1880. 8º. **10481**. bbb. **13**.

CÁCERES (JOSÉ NÚÑEZ DE) *See* NÚÑEZ DE CÁCERES.

CÁCERES (NICANOR) *See* ORTIZ (S.) Apuntes Biográficos del General de la Nacion, Nicanor Cáceres. 1867. 8º. **10882**. aa. **35**.

CÁCERES (RODRIGO) Ni los Espíritus ni el Diablo; ó sea Teoría científica del sueño magnético y las mesa giratorias, modo de magnetizar, *etc.* pp. 88. *Madrid*, 1880. 8º. **7410**. df. **4**.

CÁCERES (ROSA AMELIA) Siemprevivas. En la tumba de Rosa Amelia Cáceres. Homenaje a su memoria. [Obituary notices and contributions by various authors in prose and verse.] pp. 48. *Lima*, 1889. 8º. **10882**. f. **33**.

CÁCERES (ZOILA AURORA EVANGELINA) Mi Vida con Enrique Gómez Carrillo. pp. 302. *Madrid, Buenos Aires*, [1929.] 8º. **10632**. s. **19**.

CÁCERES E FARIA (LEANDRO DOREA) *See* DOREA CÁCERES E FARIA.

CÁCERES I LAREDO (TEODORO) *See* CÁCERES Y LAREDO.

CÁCERES O. (ANGÉLICA) *See* AILLÓN TAMAYO (Z.) and CÁCERES O. (A.) La Escuela Ecuatoriana frente al problema de la cultura indígena. 1935. 8º. **08385**. df. **13**.

CACERES PATIECUS (ANTONIUS) Antonii Caceris Patieci . . . In Hæresiarchas orationes quatuor. Ad Reginam Galliæ, & regni proceres orationes duæ. Ad principes Germaniæ, oratio una. Ad populum Germanum, oratio una. ff. 44. *Apud I. Accoltum: Romæ*, 1570. 4º. C. **48**. g. **6**.
With the arms of Pope Pius V. on the binding.

CÁCERES PLA (FRANCISCO) Lorca. Noticias históricas, literarias, estadísticas, etc., de la antigua Ciudad del Sol. [With a preface by S. Mellado Benitez.] pp. xii. 263. *Madrid*, 1902. 8º. **10162**. dd. **3**.

CÁCERES PRAT (ACACIO) *See* CÁCERES Y PRAT.

CÁCERES Y HEREDIA (MANUEL DE) *Begin.* Señor. El Capitan do M. de Caceres y Heredia, *etc.* [A petition addressed to the King of Spain, recalling the writer's former services, giving an account of his unjust condemnation, afterwards revoked, and asking for rehabilitation.] [1630 ?] 4º. **1324**. i. **2**. (**79**.)

CÁCERES Y LAREDO (TEODORO) *See* METASTASIO (P. A. D. B.) Ciro Reconocido . . . traducido por el Abate T. Cacéres, i Laredo. [1790 ?] 4º. **1342**. e. **11**. (**37**.)

CÁCERES Y PRAT (ACACIO) El Vierzo. Su descripcion é historia. Tradiciones y leyendas. [With a preface by Enrique G. Ceñal.] pp. xv. 163. *Madrid*, 1883. 8º. **10161**. bb. **14**.

—— Pozuelo de Alarcón, *etc.* pp. 99. *Madrid*, 1891. 8º. [*Biblioteca de la Provincia de Madrid.* tom. 14.] **10160**. bbb. **43**.

CÁCERES Y SOTOMAYOR (ANTONIO DE) *Bishop of Astorga.* Paraphrasis de los Psalmos de Dauid: reduzidos al phrasis, y modos de hablar de la lengua Española, en el sentido que los dixo el Propheta segun que los entienden los Sanctos . . . Va despues del estilo ordinario, el Psalmo Lætatus, y el de Profundis, en el que el Auctor solia predicar los Psalmos, *etc.* [With the Latin text.] ff. 304. 1616. fol. *See* BIBLE.—*Psalms.* [*Latin.*] **700**. k. **19**.

—— [Another edition.] Edición e introducción del P. Luis G. Alonso Getino. 2 tom. 1920. 8º. *See* BIBLE.—*Psalms.* [*Latin.*] **03089**. g. **31**.

CACHAN (P.)

—— Les Termites de Madagascar et leurs dégâts. [With illustrations.] pp. 28. *Tananarive-Tsimbazaza; Paris* printed, 1950. 8º. [*Publications de l'Institut de Recherche Scientifique.* vol. hors série.] Ac. **2683**. c. (**2**.)

CACHARD (HENRY) *See* FRANCE. [*Laws, etc.*—I. *Code Civil.*] The French Civil Code . . . By [i.e. translated by] H. Cachard. 1895. 8º. **5408.h.32.**

CACHASSIN (J. AUGUSTE) Questions tirées au sort . . . Thèse . . . pour obtenir le grade de docteur en médecine. pp. 36. *Montpellier*, 1839. 4º. **1181**. i. **6**. (**14**.)

CACHAZA ( ) *Ciudadano, pseud.* El Partido de la Union Liberal en Mangas de Camisa. Folleto político por el ciudadano Cachaza. pp. 47. *Madrid*, 1870. 8º. **8042**. cc. **19**. (**10**.)

CACHAZA ( ) *Licenciado, pseud.* Cortadillos de imprenta de coco y almendra por el licenciado Cachaza. [In verse.] *México*, 1820. 4º. **11451**. bbb. **45**. (**44**.)

CACHELEU (JULES DE) L'Église, Napoléon III, et l'Europe. pp. 32. *Paris*, 1861. 8°. **8010**. e. **30**. (**10**.)

—— Solution du problème vital des sociétés et variétés scientifiques. pp. iv. 484. *Paris*, 1869. 8°. **8404**. dd. **7**.

CACHELIÈVRE (ADRIEN ADOLPHE) Essai sur la variole, *etc.* pp. 24. *Strasbourg*, 1830. 4°. [*Collection genérale des dissertations de la Faculté de Médecine de Strasbourg.* vol. 42.] **7381**.* b.

CACHEMAILLE (ERNEST PETER) *See* BIBLE.—*Daniel.*—*Selections.* [*English.*] A Harmony of the Visions of Daniel . . . By the Rev. E. P. Cachemaille. [1926.] 8°. **03187**. h. **86**.

—— *See* GUINNESS (Henry G.) *the Elder, D.D.*, and (F. E.) Light for the Last Days . . . Edited and revised by the Rev. E. P. Cachemaille. 1917. 8°. **03187**. de. **98**.

—— Historicist, Præterist, Futurist; what are these? . . . Prophetic Symbolism . . . Second edition. pp. 72. *Prophecy Investigation Society: London*, 1928. 8°. [*Aids to Prophetic Study.* no. 7, 8.] W.P. **2834/7a**.
The head and running titles of no. 8 *read:* "*Symbolism of the Visions of Revelation.*"

—— A Church Sunday School Handbook: a manual of practical instructions . . . Second edition. pp. viii. 271. *Church of England Sunday School Institute: London*, 1873. 8°. **4192**. bb. **39**.

—— Third edition. pp. xii. 246. *Church of England Sunday School Institute: London*, 1875. 8°. **4192**. bbb. **1**.

—— Daniel's Prophecies now being Fulfilled. With a harmony in the words of the Revised Version. pp. 133. *Hodder & Stoughton: London*, 1888. 8°. **3186**. df. **27**.

—— The First Two Visions of Daniel, with continuous-historic explanation and a harmony of the two visions. pp. 79. pl. 4. *Prophecy Investigation Society: London*, [1915.] 8°. [*Aids to Prophetic Study.* no. 1.] W.P. **2834/1**.

—— Second edition. pp. 59. pl. 3. *Prophecy Investigation Society: London*, 1928. 8°. [*Aids to Prophetic Study.* no. 1.] W.P. **2834/36**.

—— The Five Great Monarchies, in Daniel's Prophecies, and in History. Being a brief historical exposition of the first two visions in the Book of Daniel . . . With a harmony of the two visions . . . and . . . illustrations. pp. xviii. 23. *F. B. Kitto: London*, 1870. 8°. **3187**. aa. **34**.

—— Historicist, Præterist, Futurist: what are these? An historicist review. pp. 47. *Prophecy Investigation Society: London*, 1916. 8°. [*Aids to Prophetic Study.* no. 7.] W.P. **2834/7**.

—— History of the Papacy in the Words of Prophetic Scripture. pp. 16. *C. J. Thynne & Jarvis: London*, [1929.] 8°. **3186**. de. **54**.

—— Instruction for Confirmation . . . with some suggestions as to instruction for Baptism. pp. ix. 141. *Church of England Sunday School Institute: London*, 1876. 8°. **4324**. c. **4**.

—— Our Present Peril: whence comes it? [On Revelation XVI, 13–16.] pp. 14. *C. J. Thynne & Jarvis: London*, 1924. 16°. **3205**. a. **33**.

—— The Prophetic Outlook To-day. Where are we now in prophecy? Essays on Second Advent subjects. [With special reference to the Book of Revelation. With plates.] pp. viii. 164. *Morgan & Scott: London*, 1918. 8°. **03187**. i. **37**.

CACHEMAILLE (ERNEST PETER)

—— Rev. XIV. Counterview of Christ and His Faithful Ones. *See* WASHINGTON (Marmaduke) The Period of Judgment and the Saved Remnant, *etc.* 1919. 8°. W.P. **2834/16**.

—— The Seventy Weeks and the Messiah. Dan. IX, *etc.* pp. 45. *Prophecy Investigation Society: London*, 1918. 8°. [*Aids to Prophetic Study.* no. 13.] W.P. **2834/13**.

—— Sir Isaac Newton on the Prophetic Symbols. Symbolism of the Visions of Revelation. pp. 31. *Prophecy Investigation Society: London*, 1916. 8°. [*Aids to Prophetic Study.* no. 8.] W.P. **2834/8**.

—— The Three Angels of Rev. XIV. 6–11, and their parallels, *etc.* pp. 21. *C. J. Thynne: London*, [1922.] 8°. **3187**. aaa. **77**.

—— Turkey; past, present, and future, in prophecy. Continuous-historic explanation. Illustrated. pp. 48. *Prophecy Investigation Society: London*, 1916. 8°. [*Aids to Prophetic Study.* no. 9.] W.P. **2834/9**.

—— XXVI Present Day Papers on Prophecy. An explanation of the visions of Daniel and of the Revelation, on the continuous-historic system. With maps and diagrams. pp. xii. 694. *Seeley, Service & Co.: London*, 1911. 8°. **03187**. de. **29**.

—— The Warfare of the End. By Rev. E. P. Cachemaille . . . and Mr. W. E. Vine . . . Russia in Prophecy; or, Gog and Magog. By Rev. E. Bendor Samuel and Dr. A. H. Burton . . . Addresses . . . with remarks by other speakers. pp. 79. *Prophecy Investigation Society: London*, 1920. 8°. [*Aids to Prophetic Study.* no. 19.] W.P. **2834/19**.

—— Palestine: and the Warfare of the End . . . New edition . . . A paper read to the Prophecy Investigation Society, revised and enlarged, *etc.* pp. 29. *C. J. Thynne: London*, [1921.] 8°. **3187**. aaa. **75**.

—— The Work of the Church amongst Aborigines of South America. pp. 4. *Society for Promoting Christian Knowledge: London*, 1908. 8°. [*Pan-Anglican Papers.* S.E. 4b.] **4108**. cc. **35**.

CACHEMAILLE (ERNEST PETER) and **CLOSE** (ALBERT W.)

—— The Divine Scale of Prophetic Times. [A wall-sheet.] *Oliphants: London & Edinburgh*, [1940.] *s. sh.* fol. Cup. **1247**. i. **38**.

CACHEMAILLE (JAMES LOUIS VICTOR) The Island of Sark. [Translated from the French by Louisa Harvey.] Edited by Laura E. Hale. pp. 305. *A. G. Reynolds & Co.: London* 1928. 8°. **010360**. aaa. **63**.

—— Narrative of a Journey to the Holy Land during the Millennium, to keep the Feast of Tabernacles. Translated from the French, *etc.* pp. vi. 72. *Smart & Allen: London; Frederick Clarke: Guernsey*, 1873. 16°. **4411**. de. **58**. (**1**.)

CACHERA (RENÉ)

—— *See* VILLARET (M.) Physiologie pathologique des acro-asphyxies. Par le prof. M. Villaret . . . R. Cachera. 1932. 8°. [*Congrès Français de Médecine.* session 22. Rapports. vol. 2.] **Ac.3712.b/22.**

CACHERANO DI BRICHERASIO (G. FRANCESCO M.) De' mezzi per introdurre ed assicurare stabilmente la coltivazione e la popolazione nell'agro Romano. pp. xiii. lxxx. 406. *Roma*, 1785. 8°. **659**. e. **12**.
Printed on blue paper.

CACHERANO D'OSASCO (CARLO) *Count di Rocca d'Arazzo.* See CACHERANO D'OSASCO (O.) *Count di Rocca d'Arazzo.* Consilia siue Responsa . . . Opus . . . nunc primum limatius . . . editum [by C. Cacherano d'Osasco], *etc.* 1599. fol. **500**. g. **1**. (**2**.)

—— See PIEDMONT.—*Senate.* Decisiones Sacri Senatus Pedemontani, ab O. Cacherano . . . collectæ, & nunc secundum . . . editæ, *etc.* 1599. fol. **500**. g. **1**. (**1**.)

—— Consilia, siue Responsa . . . Opus . . . nunc primum limatius et castigatius editum [by Carlo Cacherano d'Osasco, Count di Rocca d'Arazzo], *etc.* pp. 399. *Paltheniana, curante I. Feyrabendio: Francofurti,* 1599. fol. **500**. g. **1**. (**2**.)

—— Disputatio an principi Christiano fas sit . . . foedus inire, ac amicitia infidelibus iungi, *etc.* See PIEDMONT.—*Senate.* Decisiones Sacri Senatus Pedemontani, *etc.* 1599. fol. **500**. g. **1**. (**1**.)

CACHERANO D'OSASCO (OTTAVIO) See CLARETTA (G.) Un Nobile piemontese musico (O. Cacherano d'Osasco) al principio del secolo XVII, *etc.*

CACHERANUS OSASCUS (CAROLUS) *Comes Rochae Arazii.* See CACHERANO D'OSASCO (Carlo) *Count di Rocca d'Arazzo.*

CACHERANUS OSASCUS (OCTAVIANUS) *Comes Rochae Aratii.* See CACHERANO D'OSASCO (Ottaviano) *Count di Rocca d'Arazzo.*

CACHERAT (GUILLAUME) Le Capucin deffendu, contre les calomnies de Mr. Pierre du Moulin ministre; ou Traicté apologetic, contenant les iustes raisons pour lesquelles le Parlement de Bordeaux a faict brusler . . . le libelle diffamatoire contre les Capucins, composé & mis en lumiere à Sedan par ce ministre . . . Avec la refutation sommaire des calomnies & impietés qui y sont contenues. pp. 171. *A. Vitray: Paris,* 1642. 8°. **4071**. de. 5.

CACHERO (JOSÉ MARÍA MARTÍNEZ) See MARTÍNEZ CACHERO (J. M.)

CACHET (AUGUSTE) Considérations sur l'onyxis. pp. 34. *Paris,* 1874. [*Collection des thèses soutenues à la Faculté de Médecine de Paris.* An 1874. tom. 3.] **7374**. a. **8**.

CACHET (CHRISTOPHE) See MOUSIN (J.) [Discours de l'yvresse et yvrongnerie.] Pandora bacchica furens, medicis armis oppugnata . . . Opus . . . latiné redditum, auctum, & locupletatum. Opera C. Cacheti. 1614. 12°. **1037**. b. **1**.

—— Apologia dogmatica in hermetici cuiusdam anonymi scriptum de curatione calculi. In qua chymicarum ineptiarum vanitas exploditur, *etc.* pp. 160. *Apud S. Philippum: Tulli,* 1617. 8°. **1189**. d. **3**. (**3**.)

—— Controuersiæ theoricæ practicæ, in primam Aphorismorum Hippocratis sectionem . . . Pars prima. [With the text.] pp. 799. 1612. 8°. See HIPPOCRATES. [*Aphorismi.—Greek and Latin.*] **539**. d. **20**.

—— Vray et asseuré preservatif de petite verole & rougeole, *etc.* pp. 749. *S. Philippe: Toul,* 1617. 8°. **1174**. e. **2**. (**1**.)

The titlepage and the preliminary matter are duplicated in this copy.

CACHET (FRANS LION) Een en twintig dagen. Brieven aan een vriend, over een reisje naar Schotland, over de Vrije Schotsche Kerk en de opwekking, *etc.* pp. 44. *Leeuwarden,* 1874. 8°. **4175**. e. **1**.

—— Een Jaar op reis in dienst der zending. [With illustrations.] pp. viii. 879. *Amsterdam,* 1896. 8°. **4766.g.13.**

CACHET (JAN LION)

—— See NIENABER (P. J.) Jan Lion Cachet met sy sewe duiwels. [With a portrait and a facsimile.] 1940. 8°. **W.P.79/13.**

—— Eenige opmerkingen over het boekje: "Mijne overkomst tot de Nederd. Gereformeerde Kerk in Zuid Afrika, verklaard door M. P. A. Coetzee, Jr." pp. 92. *Paarl,* 1894. 8°. **4183**. c. **58**.

—— Feestrede, gehouden te Burgersdorp, 30 November, 1889, bij gelegenheid van het twintigjarig bestaan van de Theol. School der Geref. Kerk van Zuid-Afrika. See POSTMA (D.) Vier gelegenheids redevoeringen, *etc.* [1890.] 8°. **4426**. df. **6**. (**9**.)

CACHET DE GARNERANS (CLAUDE) Abrégé de l'histoire de la souveraineté de Dombe, *etc.* pp. 52. *J. le Blanc: Thoissei,* [1696.] fol. **10172**. i. **12**.

CACHETUS (CHRISTOPHORUS) See CACHET (Christophe)

CACHEUR.

—— Le Cacheur de pain dans la cave, ou le Boulanger à la lanterne. pp. 8. [*Paris,* c. 1790.] 8°. R. **221**. (**14**.)

CACHEUX (ÉMILE)

—— See CONGRÈS INTERNATIONAL DE SAUVETAGE. [Paris, 1889.] Congrès international de sauvetage. Compte rendu des travaux du Congrès . . . Par M. E. Cacheux [and others], *etc.* pp. 246. 1890. 8°. 8227. h. 36.

—— See MULLER (Émile) *Ingénieur Civile,* and CACHEUX (E.) Les Habitations ouvrières en tous pays, *etc.* 1879. 8°. **7820**. ff. **10**.

—— —— 1889. 8°. **7816**. aa. **10**.

—— L'Économiste pratique. Construction et organisation des crèches, salles d'asile, écoles, *etc.* pp. viii. 814. *Paris,* 1885 [1884]. 8°. **7816**. de. **7**.

—— Atlas. pl. 72. *Paris,* 1885 [1884]. fol. **7815**. f. **10**.

—— État actuel en France du patronage et de l'enseignement des apprentis. pp. 114. *Paris,* 1889. 8°. [*Mémoires et documents scolaires publiés par le Musée Pédagogique.* sér. 2. fasc. 45.] **S.E.124/52.**

—— État des habitations ouvrières á la fin du XIXe siècle, *etc.* [With plates.] pp. 184. *Paris,* 1891. 8°. **8275**. h. **16**.

CACHEUX (N.) De la philosophie de St Thomas d'Aquin. pp. xxviii. 640. *Paris,* 1858. 8°. **8465**. h. 5.

—— Discussion théologique et philosophique avec le protestantisme sur tous les points qui le séparent de la religion catholique; suivie de la réfutation de la lettre du Pasteur Puaux à l'évêque du Puy: Rome a-t-elle les caractères de l'Église de Jésus-Christ? pp. 557. *Paris,* 1855. 8°. **3901**. g. **6**.

—— Essai sur la philosophie du Christianisme, considérée dans ses rapports avec la philosophie moderne. 2 tom. *Paris; Strasbourg,* 1839, 41. 8°. **1351**. f. **15**.

CACHIN (ALEXANDER F.)

—— Die Organisation der touristischen Werbung in der Schweiz und die Rechtslage der Schweizerischen Zentrale für Verkehrsförderung. Dissertation, *etc.* pp. 137. *Brig,* 1952. 8°. **8224**. de. **20**.

CACHIN (Alfred Caraven) *See* Caraven-Cachin.

CACHIN (Joseph Marie François) *See* Batailler (A. P. E.) Description générale des travaux exécutés à Cherbourg . . . d'après les projets et sous la direction de feu J. M. F. Cachin. 1848. fol. **1261**. f. **11**.

CACHIN (Marcel)

—— *See* France.—*Parti Communiste Français.—Comité Central.—Bureau politique.* En avant! Pour le rassemblement des masses populaires contre le fascisme et la guerre! Lettre du Parti communiste au Parti socialiste. Lettre du Parti socialiste au Parti communiste. Préface de M. Cachin. 1935. 8°. **8029**. ee. **1**.

—— *See* Sokolov (Boris Th.) Le Voyage de Cachin et de Frossard dans la Russie des Soviets, *etc.* [1920.] 8°. **9455**. aa. **46**.

—— War Preparations against the Soviet Union. pp. 79. *Modern Books: London,* [1931.] 8°. [*XIth Plenum Series.*] **8277**. t. **51/1**.

—— [Another issue.] [War Preparations against the Soviet Union.] Preparation for War against the Soviet Union, *etc.* *Co-operative Publishing Society of Foreign Workers in the USSR: Moscow,* 1931. 8°. **8029**. ee. **56**.

CACHO (Celedonio Nicolas Arce y) *See* Arce y Cacho.

CACHO (Manuel de Rivas) *See* Rivas Cacho.

CACHO-HONDO (Inocencio) *pseud.* *See* London.—III. *Club Español de los Doce Apostolos.* El Club Español de los Doce Apóstolos, *etc.* [Satirical verses, with an introduction signed: Inocencio Cacho-Hondo.] 1875. 8°. **8042**. bb. **3**.

CACHON (Eugène Mermet de) *See* Mermet de Cachon.

CACHOT (Rebecca Carrión) *See* Carrión Cachot de Girard.

CACHOUD (François Charles) Exhibition of the Paintings by F. C. Cachoud . . . at the Anderson Galleries, *etc.* [With reproductions and a portrait.] pp. 25. *Privately printed: New York,* [1917.] 4°. **7860**. g. **12**.

CACHUCA. *See* Cachucha.

CACHUCHA. The Cachuca.—The Charity Boy. [Songs.] *Pitts: [London,* 1840?] *s. sh.* 4°. C. **116**. i. **1**. (**45**.)

—— The Cachuca.—Katty Looney. Parody on Jenny Jones. [Songs.] *Birt: [London,* 1840?] *s. sh.* 4°. C. **116**. i. **1**. (**44**.)

CACHUPIN (Francisco) [Vida y Virtudes del Venerable Padre Luis de la Puente.] Vita del Venerabile Padre Luigi della Ponte della Compagnia di Gesù . . . portata in Italiano da un Sacerdote della Compagnia stessa. pp. xvi. 664. *Venezia,* 1733. 8°. **4867**. a. **14**.

—— Epitome de la Vida del Venerable Padre Luis de la Puente de la Compañia de Iesus . . . Dispuesto por el Padre Bernardo Sartolo. *See* Puente (L. de la) Obras Espirituales. tom. 1. 1690. fol. **3677**. dd. **1**.

CACHUTO (Juan Agapito Canelon y) *See* Canelon y Cachuto.

CAÇI (Aleks)

—— On nous a enlevé notre toit. *In:* Courtade (P.) L'Albanie, *etc.* pp. 19–39. 1950. 8°. **10215**. r. **27**.

—— They took our Roof away. *In:* Courtade (P.) Albania, *etc.* pp. 16–31. [1951.] 8°. **W.P.13321/3.**

CACIA ( ) L'Ipocrisia, satira. *See* Gamba (B.) Collezione delle migliori opere scritte in dialetto Veneziano. (Poeti moderni. vol. 11.) 1817. 8°. **11431**. a. **23**.

CACIALLI (Giuseppe) Collezione dei disegni di nuove fabbriche e ornati fatti nella Regia Villa del Poggio Imperiale, proposti e diretti dall'architetto Giuseppe Cacialli. (Collection des dessins des bâtiments et ornements nouveaux, *etc.*—Parte seconda . . . la quale contiene i disegni dei nuovi ornamenti aggiunti e da aggiungersi all'I. e R. Palazzo Pitti.) [With descriptive letterpress in Italian and French.] 2 pt. *Firenze,* 1823. fol. **562***. g. **7**.

CACIALLI (Joseph) *See* Cacialli (Giuseppe)

CACIALUPUS (Joannes Baptista) *See* Caccialupus.

CACICS (Andreas) *See* Kačić Miošić (Andrija)

CÄCILIA. [For Saints, Sovereigns and Princesses of Sovereign Houses of this name:] *See* Cecilia.

—— Cäcilia, eine Zeitschrift für die musikalische Welt. *See* Periodical Publications.—*Mainz.*

—— Cäcilia. Organ für katholische Kirchenmusik. *See* Periodical Publications.—*Luxemburg.*

—— Cäcilia. Zeitschrift für katholische Kirchenmusik. *See* Periodical Publications.—*Breslau.*

CÄCILIE. [For Saints, Sovereigns and Princesses of Sovereign Houses of this name:] *See* Cecilia.

CÄCILIEN-VEREIN. Cäcilien-Verein für alle Länder deutscher Zunge. *See* Ratisbon.

CÄCILIUS. *See* Caecilius.

CACIQUE INDIEN. *See* Indian Cacique.

CACKETT (S. W. Gentle) The Antioch Cup reputed to be associated with the Holy Grail, *etc.* pp. 35. *Palestine & Bible Lands Exhibition: London,* [1935.] 8°. **07805**. e. **52**.

—— Does God——? A remarkable record of incidents that happened in this and other countries associated with the bringing of orphan girls to England for training. pp. 40. *Bible Lands Press: London,* 1940. 8°. **8288**. de. **46**.

—— The First Christmas. (Reprinted from "The English Churchman.") *Bible Lands Missions' Aids Society: London,* [1943.] 8°. **20041**. dd. **22**.

—— Palestine Portrayed. Camera pictures reproduced with descriptions and explanations. pp. 63. *Palestine & Bible Lands Exhibition: London; Marshall, Morgan & Scott: London, Edinburgh,* [1938.] 8°. **010075**. g. **4**.

CACLAMANOS (Demetrius) *See* Kaklamanos (Demetrios)

CACOCEPHALUS. Cacocephalus, sive De plagiis opusculum . . . Authore R.P. J. S. [i.e. J. Salier.] 1694. 16°. *See* S., J., *R.P.* **616**. a. **33**.

CACODOXUS (Acesias) *See* Philalethes (Eudoxus) *pseud.* [i.e. Girolamo Donzellini.]

CACOËTHES SCRIBENDI, *pseud.* *See* Periodical Publications.—*London.* The St. George's Magazine . . . Edited by Cacoëthes Scribendi. 1873. 8°. P.P. **5992**. k.

CACOLET. The Cacolet: journal of the Australian Camel Field Ambulance. *See* Australia.—*Military Forces.—Australian Contingent, British Expeditionary Force.—Medical Services.—Camel Field Ambulance.*

CACOPARDO (Salvatore)

—— In tema di libertà dell'aria. pp. 12. *Roma,* 1945. 4°. [*Quaderni aeronautici.* no. 132.] **8772.** d. **14/2.**

—— Principles of Public International Law Applicable to Air Transports. *See* League of Nations.—*Communications and Transit Organisation.* Enquiries into the Economic, Administrative and Legal Situation of Air Navigation. 1930. 4°. **U.N.v.47.**

CACOPHONIE. La Cacophonie, comédie en un acte et en prose, *etc.* [By J. J. C. Renout.] pp. 43. *Amsterdam,* 1782. 8°. **11738.** m. **10.** (**1.**)

CACOT (Francis) *See* Perkins (William) *Fellow of Christ's College, Cambridge.* A Christian and Plaine Treatise of the manner . . . of Predestination . . . First written in Latine . . . and carefully translated into English by F. Cacot and T. Tuke. 1606. 8°. **4256.** aa. **47.**

CACOUACS. Catéchisme et décisions de cas de conscience, à l'usage des Cacouacs; avec un discours du patriarche des Cacouacs, pour la réception d'un nouveau disciple. [A satire. By O. J. de Vaux de Giry.] pp. xlii. 107. *Cacopolis* [*Paris*], 1758. 8°. **1103.** b. **3.** (**3.**)

—— [Another copy.] **527.** f. **36.**

—— Nouveau mémoire pour servir à l'histoire des Cacouacs. (Premier mémoire sur les Cacouacs, inséré dans le Mercure de France . . . sous le titre d'Avis utile.) [A satire. By J. N. Moreau.] pp. 108. *Amsterdam,* 1757. 8°. **1103.** a. **11.** (**2.**)

—— [Another edition.] Mémoire pour servir à l'histoire des Cacouacs. (Premier mémoire sur les Cacouacs, *etc.*) [By J. N. Moreau.] Suivi d'un supplément à l'histoire des Cacouacs jusqu'à nos jours. (Par un membre de la direction de la Société Catholique des Bons Livres.—Catéchisme et décisions de cas de conscience à l'usage des Cacouacs, *etc.* [By O. J. de Vaux de Giry.]) 2 pt. *Paris,* 1828. 8°. **838.** c. **33.**

CACOUAULT DE LA MIMARDIÈRE (Élisabeth)

—— Dialogues raisonnés d'Hortence & de Julie, sur les principes fondamentaux de la sagesse, ou philosophie morale . . . à l'usage des jeunes demoiselles, *etc.* pp. xii. 143. *Londres,* 1785. 12°. **8410.** e. **68.** (**2.**)

—— Étrennes aux dames: ou Recueil de pièces choisies, en vers, tirées des meilleurs auteurs françois; avec quelques lettres en vers & en prose; précédées du joli Voyage de Bachaumont & La Chapelle, *etc.* pp. viii. 290. [*Imprimé*] *aux dépens de l'auteur: Londres,* 1787. 12°. **11475.** de. **39.**

The titlepage is mutilated.

—— Portraits historiques des reines de France & d'Angleterre, précédés de l'histoire abrégée des femmes des douze Césars, *etc.* 2 tom. *Imprimé aux dépens de l'auteur: Londres,* 1794. 12°. **10602.** c. **9.**

—— Traité sur les principes fondamentaux de la sagesse, ou philosophie morale. A l'usage de la jeunesse. pp. viii. 123. *Londres,* 1781. 12°. **8410.** e. **68.** (**1.**)

—— Le Triomphe de la raison; ou Lettres de deux jeunes dames de qualité, *etc.* pp. viii. 280. *C. Dilly: Londres,* 1785. 12°. **527.** e. **32.**

CACQUERAY (René de) Le Jugement des prises maritimes et la Convention de la Haye du 18 octobre 1907. pp. 260. *Rennes,* 1910. 8°. **6875.** ee. **31.**

CACTICULTURE SERIES.

—— Cacticulture Series. *Cleaver-Hume Press: London,* 1955– . 8°. W.P. d. **587.**

CACTUS AND SUCCULENT JOURNAL.

—— Cactus and Succulent Journal of Great Britain. *See* England.—*Cactus and Succulent Society of Great Britain.*

CACTUS AND SUCCULENT SOCIETY. Cactus and Succulent Society of Great Britain. *See* England.

CACTUS JOURNAL. *See* England.—*Cactus and Succulent Society, etc.*

—— *See* also Periodical Publications.—*London.*

CACTUS (Mirliflor) *pseud.* A Dandy . . . Második kiadás. pp. 90. *Budapest,* 1888. 16°. **012314.** e. **15.**

CACULA (Bartholomeus) *See* Cucala (Bartolomé)

CACURRI-GONNELLI (Enrichetta) Ricordo del pellegrinaggio nazionale alla tomba del primo re d'Italia Vittorio Emanuele ii. (ix gennaio mdccclxxxiv.) [In verse.] *Roma,* [1884.] 12°. **1871.** e. **1.** (**175.**)

CADA. Comedia famosa. Cada qual con su cada qual. De un Ingenio Complutense. [In verse. Variously attributed to M. Fernández de León and M. de León Marchante.] pp. 24. *Salamanca,* [1747 ?] 4°. T. **1733.** (**11.**)

—— [Another edition.] pp. 24. [*Madrid,*] 1793. 4°. **11726.** f. **18.**

—— [Another copy.] **1342.** e. **1.** (**33.**)

ČÁDA (František) *See* Bohemia. [*Codes.*] Nejvyššího sudího Království Českého Ondřeje z Dubé Práva zemská česká. Vydal . . . Dr. F. Čáda. 1930. 8°. [*Historický archiv České Akademie Věd a Umění.* čís. 48.] Ac. **799/6.**

—— *See* Moravia. Zemské zřízení moravské z roku 1535 spolu s tiskem z roku 1562 nové vydaným. Vydal . . . F. Čáda. 1937. 8°. [*Historický archiv.* čís. 50.] Ac. **799/6.**

—— Československá literatura právnická a státovědecká vydaná od počátku republiky v letech 1918–1925. Soupis knižní literatury a důležitých článků právnických a státovědeckých s doplňký za rok 1926. Sestavil . . . F. Čáda. pp. 254. *v Praze,* 1926. 8°. **11900.** aaa. **66.**

—— Hynovo dušesloví. Příspěvek k historii počátků psychologie české, *etc.* pp. vi. 135. *v Praze,* 1902. 8°. [*Rozpravy České Akademie Císaře Františka Josefa.* třída 1. roč. 10. čís. 2.] Ac. **799/2.**

—— Naše právo a stát. Sborník k šedésatému výročí založení spolku československých právníků "Všehrd." Uspořádán redakčním sborem. (Redigoval F. Čáda spolu s redakčním kruhem.) pp. 262. 1928. 8°. *See* Prague.—*Spolek Československých Právníků "Všehrd."* **5551.** i. **18.**

—— Noetická záhada u Herbarta a Stuarta Milla, *etc.* pp. 176. *v Praze,* 1894. 8°. [*Rozpravy České Akademie Císaře Františka Josefa.* třída 1. roč. 3. čís. 5.] Ac. **799/2.**

—— Soupis české literatury právnické a státovědecké. Sestavil . . . F. Čáda. pp. 160. *v Praze,* 1922. 8°. **011903.** c. **32.**

CADAFALCH (José Puig y) *See* Puig y Cadafalch.

CADAHALSO (José) *See* Cadalso (J. J. A. I. F. de B. de)

CADAHALSO (Joseph) *See* Cadalso (José J. A. I. F. de B. de)

CADALEN (J. P. François) Essai sur la dysenterie; présenté et . . . soutenu à la Faculté de Médecine de Montpellier, *etc.* pp. 22. *Montpellier*, 1818. 4°. **1180**. i. **1**. (**11**.)

CADALSO. De Nada sirven las Glorias siendo el Caudillo Traidor, o sea: Segunda parte de El cadalso se prepara para los hombres de bien. *Mexico*, 1832. 4°. **9770**. bb. **21**. (**46**.)

The first part, the title of which continues: "o sean los Ultimos sucesos de Puebla," is entered under Puebla de los Angeles.

CADALSO (Alejandro Ruiz y) *See* Ruiz y Cadalso.

CADALSO (Fernando) El Anarquismo y los Medios de Represión. pp. 134. *Madrid*, 1896. 8°. **08275**. h. **9**.

—— Diccionario de Legislación Penal, Procesal y de Prisiones. [With supplement.] 4 vol. *Madrid*, [1899–1908.] 8°. **5384**. ee. **1**.

—— Instituciones Penitenciarias y similares en España. pp. viii. 876. *Madrid*, 1922. 8°. **6056**. y. **12**.

CADALSO (José Juan Antonio Ignacio Francisco de Borja de) *See also* Vásquez (Josef) *pseud.* [i.e. J. J. A. I. F. de B. de Cadalso.]

—— Obras. 3 tom. *Madrid*, 1818. 8°. **830**. b. **27–29**.

—— Obras Inéditas . . . Publicadas por R. Foulché-Delbosc. pp. 8C. *Madrid*, 1894. 8°. **12230**. g. **8**.

—— Cartas Marruecas. pp. 224. *Madrid*, 1793. 4°. **12354**. d. **11**.

—— [Another edition.] pp. 224. *Barcelona*, 1796. 8°. **10909**. g. **3**.

—— Nueva edicion. pp. xii. 300. *Isla de Leon*, 1820. 12°. **1081**. d. **17**.

—— Nueva edicion, revista y . . . corregida. pp. 303. *Paris*, 1835. 12°. **10909**. aa. **13**.

—— [Another edition.] *See* Ochoa y Ronna (E. de) Epistolario Español, *etc.* tom. 1. 1850, *etc.* 8°. [*Biblioteca de Autores Españoles.* tom. 13.] **12232.f.1/13.**

—— [Another edition.] Edición y prólogo de Azorín. pp. 321. *Madrid*, 1917. 8°. **10905**. a. **35**.

—— [Another edition.] Prólogo, edición y notas de Juan Tamayo y Rubio. pp. 302. *Madrid*, 1935. 8°. **010910**. aa. **45**.

—— *See* Guentzel (A.) Die Cartas Marruecas des Don José de Cadalso, *etc.* 1938. 8°. **11861**. g. **5**.

—— *See* Mulertt (W.) Die Stellung der "Marokkanischen Briefe" innerhalb der Aufklärungsliteratur. Beitrag zum Verständnis der Schriften J. Cadalsos. 1937. 8°. **11859**. d. **9**.

—— Cartas marruecas . . . A selection. Edited with introduction, notes and vocabulary by L. B. Walton. pp. vii. 149. *G. Bell & Sons: London*, 1954. 8°. [*Bell's Spanish Classics.*] W.P. **14123/5**.

—— Los Eruditos a la Violeta . . . Con el suplemento del mismo autor y otros anexos. Textos de las primeras ediciones, *etc.* [The editor's preface signed: R. M. P.] pp. xl. 327. *Madrid*, 1928. 16°. **012356**. de. **40**.

—— Noches Lúgubres, por el coronel D. José Cadalso; seguido del Delincuente Honrado, drama en prosa, por D. Melchor Gaspar de Jovellanos. Segunda edicion. pp. 249. *Burdeos*, 1823. 12°. **1480**. a. **27**.

CADALSO (José Juan Antonio Ignacio Francisco de Borja de)

—— Noches Lúgubres. Historia de los amores del coronel don Jose de Cadalso, escritas por él mismo. Nueva edicion, corregida y aumentada. pp. 24. *Madrid*, 1847. 4°. **12330**. h. **23**. (**12**.)

—— [Another edition.] Historia de los Amores del coronel don José de Cadalso, *etc.* pp. 24. *Madrid*, 1858. 4°. **12330**. h. **24**. (**17**.)

—— [Another edition.] pp. 24. *Madrid*, 1879. 4°. **12330**. l. **5**. (**15**.)

—— [Another edition.] Noches Lúgubres . . . Notas y un prólogo del autor. pp. 63. *Madrid*, [1919.] 8°. **012350**. df. **70**

—— [Another edition.] Edited, with introduction and bibliography, by Emily Cotton. pp. 64. *Liverpool*, 1933. 8°. [*Publications of the Bulletin of Spanish Studies.* Plain Text Series. no. 2.] W.P. **10292/2**.

—— Noches lúgubres. Edición e introducción de Edith F. Helman. [With a portrait.] pp. 143. *Santander, Madrid*, 1951. 8°. **12360**. ff. **49**.

"El Viento Sur." vol. 7.

—— Óptica del Cortejo. Espejo claro en que con demostraciones prácticas del entendimiento se manifiesta lo insubstancial de semejante empleo. Ocios políticos. pp. 62. *Barcelona*, 1790. 4°. **11825**. dd. **38**. (**3**.)

—— Poesías. (Noticias de D. José de Cadalso.) pp. 228. *Madrid*, 1821. 12°. **11450**. aaa. **13**.

—— [Another issue.] *Paris*, 1821. 12°. **11451**. a. **9**.

—— [Another edition.] *See* Quintana (M. J.) Poesías Selectas Castellanas, *etc.* tom. 4. 1830. 8°. **1464**. b. **21**.

—— [Another edition.] *See* Quintana (M. J.) Tesoro del Parnaso Español, *etc.* 1838. 8°. **12230**. h. **1/15**.

—— [Another edition.] *See* Cueto (L. A. de) Poetas Líricos del Siglo xviii, *etc.* tom. 1. 1869, *etc.* 8°. [*Biblioteca de Autores Españoles.* tom. 61.] **12232.f.1/61.**

CADALVÈNE (Edmond de) and **BARRAULT** (Émile) Deux années de l'histoire d'Orient 1839–1840, faisant suite à l'Histoire de la guerre de Méhémed-Ali en Syrie et en Asie-mineure 1832–1833. 2 tom. *Paris*, 1840. 8°. **802**. i. **27**.

—— *See* MacCarthy (Justin W.) and Karatheodore (K.) Relation officielle de la maladie et de la mort du sultan Mahmoud ii., en réponse aux allégations publiées (dans un ouvrage intitulé: Deux années de l'histoire d'Orient) par MM. de Cadalvène et E. Barrault. 1841. 8°. **8028**. ee. **19**. (**1**.)

—— Histoire de la guerre de Méhémed-Ali contre la Porte Ottomane, en Syrie et en Asie-Mineure, 1831–1833. Ouvrage enrichi de cartes, *etc.* pp. xi. 512. *Paris*, 1837. 8°. **1053**. g. **27**.

CADALVÈNE (Edmond de) and **BREUVERY** (J. de)

—— L'Egypte et la Turquie de 1829 à 1836. tom. 1, 2. Égypte et Nubie. *Paris*, 1836. 8°. **1046**. f. **10**.

—— Atlas. livr. 1, 2. *Paris*, 1836. fol. **557***. g. **19**.

No more published.

CADALVÈNE (EDMOND DE) and **BREUVERY** (J. DE)

— El Ejipto y la Nubia, *etc.* *See* FERNÁNDEZ CUESTA (N.) Nuevo Viajero Universal, *etc.* tom. 1. 1859, *etc.* 8°. **10005**. g. **14**.

CADALVÈNE (ÉDOUARD DE) Recueil de médailles grecques, inédites . . . Europe. pp. x. 260. pl. v. *Paris*, 1828. 4°. **602**. g. **34**.
The volume dealing with Asia was not published.

CÀ DA MOSTO (ALVISE DA)

VOYAGES.

Fracan's Text.

— [For the Italian text of A. da Cà da Mosto's account of his own and Pedro de Sintra's voyages to Africa contained in M. Fracan's "Paesi novamente retrovati," and there entitled "Libro della prima navigatione per l'Oceano a le terre de Nigri" :] *See* FRACAN (M.)

— The Voyages of Cadamosto and other documents on Western Africa in the second half of the fifteenth century. Translated and edited by G. R. Crone. With the principal additions of G. B. Ramusio. With maps.] pp. xlv. 159. 1937. 8°. *See* LONDON.—III. *Hakluyt Society*. Ac. **6172/131**.

— Die Schipvaert Aloysij Cadamusti tot den vremden ende onbekenden landen. [Translated by C. Albyn from the German version.] *See* PORTUGUESE. Die niuwe weerelt, *etc.* 1563. fol. **569**. i. **3**.

— [Voyages.] *Fr.* *See* VESPUCCI (A.) Sensuyt le Nouueau monde . . . Translate de ytaliē, *etc.* [1510?] 4°. C. **20**. b. **23**.

— [Another edition.] *See* VESPUCCI (A.) Sensuyt le Nouueau monde, *etc.* [1515?] 4°. G. **6698**.

— *Begin.* Anfang des Buchleins von der ersten schyffarthe . . . in die Landtschaffte der Moren, *etc.* [Translated from the Italian.] *See* LANDE. Newe unbekanthe landte, *etc.* 1508. fol. C. **20**. e. **33**.

— Die Schiffart Aloysij Cadamusti, zu den frembden vnd vnerfarnen Landen. [Translated from the Latin of A. Madrignanus by Michael Herr.] *See* PORTUGUESE. Die New Welt, *etc.* 1534. fol. **601**. l. **5**.

— *Begin.* Cum ego Ludouicus Cadamustius, *etc.* [Translated by Archangelus Madrignanus.] *See* FRACAN (M.) Itinerariū Portugallēsiū, *etc.* 1508. fol. C. **20**. e. **17**.

— [Another edition.] Nauigatio ad terras ignotas A. Cadamusti, *etc.* *See* GRYNAEUS (S.) Nouus orbis, *etc.* 1532. fol. **985**. h. **17**.

— [Another edition.] *See* GRYNAEUS (S.) Nouus orbis, *etc.* 1532. fol. **798**. cc. **2**.

— [Another edition.] *See* GRYNAEUS (S.) Nouus orbis, *etc.* 1537. fol. **9604**. i. **5**.

— [Another edition.] *See* GRYNAEUS (S.) Nouus orbis, *etc.* 1555. fol. **216**. d. **1**.

Ramusio's Text.

— Nauigationi di Al. da Mosto. [Including the voyage of Pedro de Sintra. Edited by G. B. Ramusio.] *See* NAVIGAZIONI. Primo volume delle Nauigationi, *etc.* 1550. fol. C. **46**. i. **3**.

— [Another edition.] *See* RAMUSIO (G. B.) Primo volume & seconda editione delle nauigationi, *etc.* vol. 1. 1554, *etc.* fol. **566**. k. **1**.

— [Another edition.] *See* RAMUSIO (G. B.) Primo volume, & terza editione delle nauigationi, *etc.* vol. 1. 1563, *etc.* fol. **679**. h. **8**.

— [Another edition.] *See* RAMUSIO (G. B.) Primo volume, & quarta editione, delle nauigationi, *etc.* vol. 1. 1588, *etc.* fol. C. **79**. e. **4**.

— [Another edition.] *See* RAMUSIO (G. B.) Delle nauigationi et viaggi, *etc.* vol. 1. 1606. fol. **566**. i. **8**.

— [Another edition.] *See* RAMUSIO (G. B.) Delle nauigationi, *etc.* vol. 1. 1613, *etc.* fol. **566**. i. **5**.

— Navigazioni di Messer Alvise da Ca da Mosto, *etc.* *See* RAMUSIO (G. B.) Il Viaggio di Giovan Leone e le navigazioni di A. da Ca da Mosto . . . quali si leggono nella raccolta di G. Ramusio, *etc.* 1837. fol. **789**. bb. **4**.

— [Another edition.] Delle Navigazioni di Messer Alvise da Cà da Mosto. [With a portrait.] *See* CADDEO (R.) Le Navigazioni atlantiche di Alvise da Cà da Mosto, *etc.* 1928. 8°. **10496**. a. **35**.

— The Voyage of A. da Cada Mosto, in 1455, along the coast of Africa as far as Rio Grande. Written by himself. Translated from the Italian.—The second voyage of A. da Cada Mosto . . . in 1456, in which the Cape de Verde Islands were discovered.—The voyage of Captain Piedro de Cintra . . . to Sierra Leona. Written by A. de Cada Mosto. *See* COLLECTION. A New General Collection of Voyages, *etc.* vol. 1. 1745, *etc.* 4°. **2354**. h. **8**.

— Navigations de Alouys de Cademoste.—La Navigation du Capitaine Pierre Sintre . . . escrite par Messer Alouys de Cademoste. [Translated by J. Temporal.] *See* LEO (J.) *Africanus.* Historiale description de l'Afrique, *etc.* tom. 1. 1556. fol. **567**. k. 25.

— [Another edition.] *See* LEO (J.) *Africanus.* De l'Afrique, *etc.* tom. 2. 1830. 8°. **790**. e. **13**.

— [Another edition.] Relation des Voyages à la Côte occidentale d'Afrique d'Alvise de Ca' da Mosto, 1455–1457. Publiée par M. Charles Schefer. pp. xix. 206. *Paris*, 1895. 8°. **010097**. g. **11**.

— Reise des Aluise da Cada Mosto, im Jahre 1455, längst der africanischen Küste bis Rio Grande, *etc.*—Die zweyte Reise . . . nach der Küste von Africa, im Jahre 1456, auf welcher die Jnseln des grünen Vorgebirges entdeckt worden, *etc.*—Reise des Hauptmanns Piedro de Cintra . . . nach Sierra Leona. Beschrieben durch A. da Cada Mostro. [Translated from the English version in the "New General Collection of Voyages."] 1748. *See* SCHWABE (J. J.) Allgemeine Historie der Reisen, *etc.* Bd. 2. 1747, *etc.* 4°. **10025**. dd.

— Navegações de Luiz de Cadamosto : a que se ajuntou a Viagem de Pedro de Cintra, capitão portuguez. Traduzidas do italiano. 1812. *See* LISBON.—*Academia das Sciencias de Lisboa.* Collecção de Noticias para a Historia e Geografia das Nações Ultramarinas, *etc.* tom. 2. 1812, *etc.* 8°. **1446**. i. 3.

— The Voyage of A. da Cada Mosto, in 1455, along the Coast of Africa, as far as Rio Grande. [Abridged from the version in the "New General Collection of Voyages."] *See* MOORE (John H.) A New and Complete Collection of Voyages and Travels, *etc.* vol. 1. [1785?] fol. **10003**. f. **2**.

CÀ DA MOSTO (Alvise da)

PORTOLANO.

—— *Begin.* [fol. 2 *recto*:] Questa e vna opera necessaria a tutti li nauigāti chi vano in diuerse parte del mondo, *etc. End.* [fol. 81 *verso*:] Finito lo libro chiamado portolano composto per vno zentilomo veniciano, *etc.* [Attributed to A. da Cà da mosto.] 1490. 4°. *See* Portolano. G. **7309**.

—— [Another copy.] IA. **22645**.

—— Nuouo portolano non piu stampato. Molto particolare de'l levante e de'l ponente. [Attributed to A. da Cà da Mosto. An altered and abridged version of the edition of 1490.] ff. 48. 1544. 4°. *See* Portolano. **795**. e. **38**.

—— [Another edition.] Il Portolano del mare, nel qual si dichiara minutamente del sito di tutti i porti, quali sono da Venetia in Leuante, & in Ponente: & d'altri cose vtilissime, & necessarie à i nauiganti . . . Di nuouo . . . corretto, & ristampato. [Attributed to A. da Cà da mosto.] ff. 39. 1576. 4°. *See* Portolano. **1127**. g. **18**. (**2**.)

—— [Another copy.] **502**. c. **11**. (**1***.)

—— [Another edition.] ff. 38. 1584. 4°. *See* Portolano. **10498**. b. **2**.

—— [Another edition.] ff. 37. 1612. 4°. *See* Portolano. **1127**. g. **19**.

—— [Another edition.] pp. 68. *See* Consolato. Il Consolato del Mare, *etc.* 1737. 4°. **6835**. d. **11**.

—— [Another edition.] pp. 44. *See* Consolato. Il Consolato del Mare, *etc.* 1806. 4°. **6835**. e. **9**.

APPENDIX.

—— *See* Zurla (P.) *Cardinal.* Dei viaggi e delle scoperte africane di Alvise da Cà da Mosto . . . Dissertazione. 1815. 8°. **1298**. d. **17**.

CADAMOSTO (Lodovico) *See* Cusano (L.) *Marquis di Ponte.* Risposta al capitolo vii. del libro i. della Ricerca di Giacomo Cassano, il quale fonda le pretensioni della corona di Francia sopra il ducato di Milano . . . Tradotta dalla lingua spagnuola nell'italiana da L. Cadamosto. [1645.] 4°. **8026**. b. **1**.

CADAMOSTO (Luiz de) *See* Cà da Mosto (Alvise da)

CADAMOSTO (Marco) *See* Liburnio (N.) Elegantissime sentenze et aurei detti . . . raccolti da N. Liburnio . . . tradotti da M. Cadamosto. 1543. 8°. **721**. b. **2**. (**2**.)

—— Sonetti et altre rime . . . con alcune novelle . . . et stanze. ff. 60. *A. Blado Asolano: Roma,* 1544. 8°. G. **10948**.

—— Novelle . . . Edizione formata sulla prima . . . di Roma, per Antonio Blado Asolano, del 1544. pp. 78. 1799. 12°. **12470**. ee. **22**.

One of an edition of eighty copies.

—— [The sixth Novella.] *See* Italian Novelist. Del Novelliero italiano volume primo, *etc.* vol. 2. 1754. 8°. **634**. e. **21**.

—— [The sixth Novella.] *Eng. See* Roscoe (Thomas) The Italian Novelists, *etc.* vol. 2. 1825. 8°. **634**. f. **21**.

CADAMOSTO (Paolo Emilio) *See* Alciatus (A.) Emblemi di A. Alciati, *etc.* (Emblemata . . . latinè ac italicè edita P. Æ. Cadamusto interprete.) 1626. 8°. **637**. d. **22**.

CADAMUSTUS (Aloysius) *See* Cà da Mosto (Alvise da)

CADANA (Salvatore) Santuario commune. [Sermons. With a portrait.] pp. 192. *C. S. Como: Milano,* 1642. 8°. **4424**. aaa. **12**.

CADANO (Salomon Neugebauerus a) *See* Neugebauer (S.)

CADAQUES. Copia de una carta escrita a sa Excelencia per los Consols de Cadaques. [Giving an account of an unsuccessful attack on the town by the Spaniards.] *P. Lacaualleria: Barcelona,* 1643. 4°. **9180**. e. **2**. (**50**.)

CADARID RESTREPO (Tomás) *See* Medellin.—*Liga Patriótica por Colombia y por Antioquia.* Antioquia por Colombia. Documentos relacionados con el proyecto de ferrocarril troncal del occidente colombiano, *etc.* [Edited by T. Cadarid Restrepo.] 1925. 8°. **8179**. c. **55**.

CADARS (Ozil de) *See* Ozil, *de Cadars.*

CADART (Alfred) Catalogue complet d'eaux-fortes originales composées et gravées par les artistes eux-mêmes avec huit planches types divers, par Veyrassat, Feyen-Perrin, *etc.* [Compiled, with an introduction, by A. Cadart.] [With plates.] pp. 32. *Paris,* 1873. 12°. **7857**. aa. **3**.

CADART (Alfred Boucher) *See* Boucher-Cadart.

CADART (Charles Remy) De l'organisation défensive du territoire. pp. 25. *Paris,* 1873. 8°. [*Publication de la Réunion des Officiers.*] **8832**. i. **14**. (**1**.)

—— Souvenirs de Constantine. Journal d'un lieutenant du Génie, rédigé en 1838–39, et coordonné en 1893. pp. viii. 385. *Paris,* 1894. 12°. **10095**. aaa. **7**.

CADART (Jacques)

—— *See* Laski (Harold J.) [Parliamentary Government in England.] Le Gouvernement parlementaire en Angleterre . . . Traduction française de J. Cadart et Jacqueline Prélot, *etc.* 1950. 8°. **8140**. aaa. **49**.

—— Le Régime électoral des États Généraux de 1789 et ses origines, 1302–1614. pp. 212. *Paris,* 1952. 8°. [*Annales de l'Université de Lyon.* ser. 3. Droit. fasc. 11.] Ac. **365**. (d.

—— Régime électoral et régime parlementaire en Grande Bretagne, *etc.* pp. 224. *Paris,* 1948. 8°. [*Cahiers de la Fondation nationale des sciences politiques.* no. 5.] W.P. **14427**/

—— Les Tribunaux judiciaires et la notion de service publ La notion judiciaire de service public. Contribution l'étude du problème de la répartition des compétenc entre les deux ordres de jurisdictions. pp. 127. *Par* 1954. 8°. [*Annales de l'Université de Lyon.* sér. Droit. fasc. 12.] Ac. **365**. (

CADART (Jean)

—— Les Escargots. Helix pomatia l. et helix aspersa Biologie, élevage, parcage, histoire, gastronomie, co merce, *etc.* [With illustrations.] pp. 420. *Par* 1955. 8°. **07206**. e.

Savoir en histoire naturelle. vol. 24.

CADART (M.) *Mlle.* Le Conseiller français; or French it ought to be spoken. pp. xi. 162. *Dulau & C London,* 1865. 12°. **12953**. aaa.

—— Le Correcteur; or, Niceties of French conversati Submitted to the English student. pp. vi. 120 *Du & Co.; P. Rolandi: London,* 1861. 12°. **12953**. aa.

CADART (M.) *Mlle.*

—— Dictionnaire des genres de la langue française . . . Seconde édition. pp. 35. *Rolandi: Londres; Paris* [printed], [1860?] 12°. **12954. a. 58.**

CADAS (J. C. F. Casimir) Considérations générales sur les maladies héréditaires ou de famille. Tribut académique, *etc.* pp. 43. *Montpellier*, 1811. 4°. **1180. g. 5. (19.)**

CADASSUS (Célestin) Quelques considérations sur une maladie observée à bord d'un vaisseau de l'état. Thèse, *etc.* pp. 18. *Montpellier*, 1829. 4°. **1181. e. 11. (22.)**

CADAVAL, Jayme Alvares Pereira de Mello, *3rd Duke de. See* Alvares Pereira de Mello.

——, Nuño Alvares Pereira de Mello, *1st Duke de. See* Alvares Pereira de Mello.

——, Nuño Caetano Alvares Pereira de Mello, *6th Duke de. See* Alvares Pereira de Mello.

CADAVERAZ (Agustín de) *See* Cardaberaz.

CADBURY BROTHERS. [Miscellaneous pamphlets, chiefly on technical and administrative aspects of the Bournville Works.] *Bournville Works*, 1913–48. 8°. 27 pt. **08248.m.9.**

—— Bournville. A descriptive account of the growth of Cocoa and of its manufacture by Cadbury Brothers. Reprinted from the "British Trade Journal," *etc.* pp. 24. *H. Scott & Co.: Carlisle*, [1880.] 8°. **7054. df. 1. (4.)**
The running title reads: "Cocoa and its Manufacture."

—— The Bournville Works Magazine. vol. 7. no. 4., vol. 9. no. 1, *etc.* Feb. 1909, Jan. 1911, *etc.* *Bournville*, 1909– . 4°. P.P. **1423.** dia.

—— Cadbury's of Bournville. The building of a modern business. [With illustrations.] pp. 23. *Bournville*, 1948. 8°. **8232. e. 59.**

—— Camps and Tours for Industrial Workers. An account of travel schemes designed to assist young employees at Bournville Works in the fuller use of their leisure. By C. A. Harrison. [With illustrations.] pp. 32. *Bournville Works*, [1932.] 8°. **10107. dd. 10.**

—— A Century of Progress, 1831–1931. Cadbury, Bournville. By T. B. Rogers. [With illustrations.] pp. 88. [*Bournville*, 1931.] 4°. **8246. s. 20.**

—— Cocoa and Chocolate from Grower to Consumer. [With illustrations.] pp. 16. *Bournville*, 1948. 8°. **8219. c. 30.**

—— The Cococub News. *Cadbury Bros.: Bournville*, 1936– . 8°. P.P. **5793.** bch.

—— Employees of Cadbury Brothers Limited and associated companies . . . who lost their lives in the Second World War, 1939–1945. [A list.] [*Bournville?* 1947.] 4°. **09101. b. 7.**

—— Industrial Record, 1919–1939. A review of the inter-war years. pp. 84. *Bournville*, [1945.] 4°. **8232. d. 61.**

—— Industrial Record, 1919–1939 . . . Second impression, *etc.* pp. 84. *Bournville*, 1945. 4°. **08286. f. 52.**

—— The Prospects of Growing Cacao in the British Solomon Islands. With notes on Malaya, Ceylon, and Java. By D. H. Urquhart . . . Report. Prepared for and published by Cadbury Brothers Ltd. [With illustrations.] pp. 44. *Bournville*, 1951. 4°. **8219. d. 37.**

CADBURY BROTHERS.

—— Report on the Prospects of Extending the Growing of Cacao in the Territory of Papua and New Guinea. By D. H. Urquhart . . . and R. E. P. Dwyer . . . With notes on current experiments, soils, pests, and meteorological data, by various authorities. Prepared for and published by Cadbury Brothers Ltd. [With illustrations and a map.] pp. 39. *Bournville*, 1951. 4°. **8219. d. 38.**

—— Sweet-Shop Success. A handbook for the sweet retailer. Produced by the Bourneville Studio. [With illustrations.] pp. 197. xxxi. *Sir Isaac Pitman & Sons: London*, 1949 [1950.] 8°. **7949.** bb. **19.**

—— A Works Council in Action. An account of the scheme in operation at Bournville Works. [With illustrations.] pp. 48. *Bournville*, 1950. 8°. **08276. c. 83.**

—— A World-Wide Business. Text by Robert Finch. Designed and edited by Paul Redmayne. [On the economics of chocolate production. With illustrations.] pp. 64. *Bournville*, 1948. 4°. **8245.** h. **28.**

—— A Series of 6 Wall Charts . . . Issued in connection with "A World-Wide Business," *etc.* *Bournville*, [1949.] fol. 8245. h. 28a.

—— A World Wide Business, *etc.* [Teaching notes adapted for a series of film strips from the work by Robert J. Finch.] *University of London Press: London*, [1949– .] 4°. W.P. **845.**
Reproduced from typewriting.

—— *Bournville Works Youths' Club*, afterwards *Bournville Youths' Club.* The Camaraderie. The monthly record of the Bournville Works Youths' Club. no. 1–7. [*Bournville?*] 1901, 02. 4°. **1866. b. 10. (22.)**

—— The School Rag. By the students of the Bournville Day Continuation School (College) & the members of the Bournville Youths' Club. vol. 2. no. 10—vol. 14. no. 130. April 1922—April 1949. 1922–49. 8°. *See* Birmingham. *Bournville Day Continuation College.* P.P. **6148.** eaa.

CADBURY (Edward) Experiments in Industrial Organization . . . With a preface by W. J. Ashley. pp. xxi. 296. *Longmans & Co.: London*, 1912. 8°. **08248.** aaa. **6.**

—— Women's Work and Wages. A phase of life in an industrial city. By E. Cadbury, M. C. Matheson and George Shann. pp. 368. *T. Fisher Unwin: London*, 1906. 8°. **2238. a. 29.**

CADBURY (Edward) and SHANN (George) *M.A.*

—— Sweating. pp. 145. *Headley Bros.: London*, 1907. 8°. [*Social Service Handbooks, etc.* no. 5.] **08282. f. 67/5.**

CADBURY (Elizabeth) *See* Baynes (Joseph) Consolation suggested under the loss of Christian Friends. A sermon, occasioned by the death of Miss E. Cadbury, *etc.* 1829. 8°. **4920. e. 2.**

CADBURY (Elizabeth Mary) *D.B.E.*

—— *See* Scott (Richenda) Elizabeth Cadbury, 1858–1951. [With portraits.] 1955. 8°. **10864. i. 14.**

—— *See* Stempel (Therese D.) Physical Exercises for Girls, *etc.* (Introduction by Mrs. G. Cadbury.) [1904.] 8°. **7912.** aaa. **46.**

—— *See* Taylor (Mary J.) A Dear Memory. Pages from the letters of M. J. Taylor. Chosen and edited by E. M. Cadbury. 1914. 8°. **10922. c. 21.**

CADBURY (ELIZABETH MARY) *D.B.E.*

—— Adult Schools. *See* MUIRHEAD (John H.) Birmingham Institutions, *etc.* 1911. 8º. **010352. f. 15.**

—— Historical Rhymes. By Elsie Taylor [afterwards Cadbury]. With additions and reminiscences by Elizabeth M. Cadbury. pp. 78. *Printed for private circulation by John Bellows: [Gloucester,]* 1937. 4º. **09506. k. 21.**

—— Woodbrooke Presidential Address, 1927. pp. 8. *Woodbrooke Extension Committee: Birmingham,* [1927.] 8º. **08286. a. 51.**

—— [Another edition.] pp. 8. *Woodbrooke Extension Committee: Birmingham,* [1928.] 8º. **08286. aa. 76.**

CADBURY (GEORGE) *the Elder.* *See* GARDINER (Alfred G.) Life of George Cadbury . . . With . . . illustrations [including portraits]. 1923. 8º. **010856. bb. 25.**

—— *See* MANSBRIDGE (Albert) George Cadbury, Adult Schools, & Education, *etc.* [1927.] 8º. **8367. b. 39.**

—— Town Planning, with special reference to the Birmingham schemes . . . With illustrations and maps. pp. xvi. 201. *Longmans & Co.: London,* 1915. 8º. **07816. i. 43.**

CADBURY (GEORGE) *the Elder,* and **BRYAN** (TOM)

—— The Land and the Landless. pp. vii. 182. *Headley Bros.: London,* [1908.] 8º. [*Social Service Handbooks.* no. 3.] **08282. f. 67/3.**

CADBURY (GEORGE) *the Younger.* Industry and Transport . . . A paper read at the Congress of the Institute of Transport, Birmingham, *etc.* pp. 16. [*Bournville,* 1927.] 8º. **8287. c. 40.**

CADBURY (GEORGE) *the Younger,* and **DOBBS** (SEALEY PATRICK)

—— Canals and Inland Waterways. pp. xv. 160. *London,* 1929. 8º. [*Pitman's Transport Library.*] **8232. e. 27/11.**

CADBURY (*Mrs.* GEORGE) *D.B.E.* *See* CADBURY (Elizabeth M.)

CADBURY (GERALDINE SOUTHALL)

—— *See* WHITNEY (Janet P.) Geraldine S. Cadbury, 1865–1941. A biography, *etc.* [With portraits.] 1948. 8º. **10862. ee. 20.**

—— Young Offenders, yesterday and to-day. [With plates.] pp. 149. *G. Allen & Unwin: London,* 1938. 8º. **6057. p. 23.**

CADBURY (HENRY JOEL)

—— *See* BRAITHWAITE (William C.) The Beginnings of Quakerism . . . Revised by H. J. Cadbury. 1955. 8º. **4151. f. 46.**

—— *See* FOX (George) *Founder of the Society of Friends.* George Fox's ' Book of Miracles.' Edited with an introduction and notes by H. J. Cadbury, *etc.* 1948. 8º. **7409. h. 30.**

—— The Book of Acts in History. pp. vi. 170. *Adam & Charles Black: London,* 1955. 8º. **3228. de. 19.**

—— George Fox's Later Years. *In:* The Journal of George Fox, *etc.* pp. 713–756. 1952. 8º. **4907. aa. 51.**

—— Letters to William Dewsbury and Others. Transcribed and edited by H. J. Cadbury. pp. 68. *Bannisdale Press: London,* 1948. 8º. [*Journal of the Friends' Historical Society.* suppl. no. 22.] Ac. **2069.**

CADBURY (HENRY JOEL)

—— The Making of Luke-Acts. pp. x. 385. *Macmillan & Co.: London; printed in U.S.A.,* 1927. 8º. **03226. e. 57.**

—— The Peril of Modernizing Jesus. pp. vi. 216. *Macmillan Co.: New York,* 1937. 8º. **4225. g. 42.**

—— Quaker Relief during the Siege of Boston. *In:* Publications of the Colonial Society of Massachusetts. vol. 34. pp. 39–179. 1943. 8º. Ac. **8400.** d.

—— The Style and Literary Method of Luke. pp. xi. 205. *Cambridge, Mass.,* 1919, 20. [*Harvard Theological Studies.* no. 6.] Ac. **2692/24.**

—— The Swarthmore Documents in America. Edited by H. J. Cadbury. pp. 90. *London,* 1940. 8º. [*Journal of the Friends' Historical Society.* suppl. no. 20.] Ac. **2069.**

CADBURY (JAMES) A New History of Banbury, before and after a Maine Liquor Law. pp. 68. *W. Tweedie: London,* 1855. 8º. **8435. d. 22.**

CADBURY (LAURENCE JOHN)

—— The Newsprint Shortage. Statement made at the Annual General Meeting of the Daily News, Ltd. . . . by the chairman, Mr. L. J. Cadbury. *Caxton Press: London,* [1948.] 4º. **8218. d. 18.**

—— Post War Problems in the Cocoa & Chocolate Industry. Addresses at a conference of sales representatives of Cadbury Brothers Ltd. by Mr. L. Cadbury . . . and Mr. W. M. Hood . . . Bournville, 31st May, 1946. pp. 15. [*Bournville,* 1946.] 8º. **08229. s. 58.**

—— This Question of Populations. Europe in 1970. [With a map.] pp. 24. " *News Chronicle* " *Publications Department: London,* [1945.] 8º. **8288. b. 82.**

CADBURY (M. CHRISTABEL) Robert Barclay. His life and work. pp. 117. *Headley Bros.: London,* 1912. 8º. **4920. eee. 6.**

—— The Story of Robert Barclay. Told for children. pp. 40. *London; New York,* 1926. 8º. [*Friends Ancient and Modern.* no. 21.] **4804.aa.48.**

CADBURY (M. H.) The Life of Amanda Smith, " the African Sybil, the Christian Saint " . . . With an Introduction by J. Rendel Harris. [With a portrait.] pp. 84. *Cornish Bros.: Birmingham,* 1916. 8º. **4987. aaa. 18.**

CADBURY (PAUL STRANGMAN)

—— Birmingham—Fifty Years on. [With illustrations.] pp. 94. *Bournville Village Trust: Bournville,* 1952. 4º. **10358. l. 38.**

CADBURY (RICHARD) *the Elder.* *See* also HISTORICUS, *pseud.* [i.e. R. Cadbury.]

—— *See* ALEXANDER (Helen C.) Richard Cadbury of Birmingham, *etc.* 1906. 8º. **4908. bb. 11.**

CADBURY (RICHARD) *the Younger.* Everyday Life in Cape Colony in time of Peace. By X. C. [i.e. R. Cadbury.] With three illustrations. pp. 127. 1902. 8º. *See* C., X. **010097. g. 25.**

—— Memories of The Welcome Mission Hall, Worcester. [By R. Cadbury.] pp. 38. [1926.] 8º. *See* WORCESTER.—*Welcome Mission Hall.* **4192. eee. 43.**

CADBURY (RICHARD) *the Younger.*

—— 9000 Miles in the Track of the Jew . . . With . . . illustrations. pp. 63. *Marshall Bros.: London & Edinburgh,* [1923.] 4°. **10077. pp. 1.**

CADBURY (WILLIAM ADLINGTON) Labour in Portuguese West Africa . . . Second edition, with an added chapter. pp. xii. 187. *G. Routledge & Sons: London,* 1910. 8°. **08226. b. 47.**

—— Third—popular—edition. pp. xi. 147. *G. Routledge & Sons: London,* 1910. 8°. **08276. bb. 30.**

—— The Pumphrey Pedigree. [Charts and plates. Edited by W. A. Cadbury.] ff. 14. *Birmingham,* 1909. fol. **K.T.C. 38. b. 7.**
One of an edition of eighty copies.

CADBURY (WILLIAM EDWARD)

—— *See* UNITED STATES OF AMERICA.—*Survey of Medical Education.—Subcommittee on Preprofessional Education.* Preparation for Medical Education in the Liberal Arts College . . . [By] A. E. Severinghaus . . . and W. E. Cadbury. 1953. 8°. **8312. de. 48.**

CADBURY (WILLIAM WARDER) *See* KITT (T.) Text Book of Comparative General Pathology . . . Authorized translation by Dr. W. W. Cadbury, *etc.* 1906. 8°. **07293. m. 31.**

CADBURY (WILLIAM WARDER) and **JONES** (MARY HOXIE)

—— At the Point of a Lancet. One hundred years of the Canton Hospital, 1835–1935. [With plates.] pp. xvii. 304. *Kelly & Walsh: Shanghai,* 1935. 8°. **20029. f. 33.**

CADBY (CARINE) *See* CADBY (Will) and (C.) Switzerland in Summer, *etc.* 1922, *etc.* 8°. **10195.aaa.36.**

—— *See* CADBY (Will) and (C.) Switzerland in Winter, *etc.* 1914. 8°. **10196. dd. 9.**

—— —— 1921. 8°. **10195. de. 11.**

—— The Brownies in Switzerland. A children's winter sport holiday . . . Illustrated with twenty-four photographs by Will Cadby. pp. 118. *Mills & Boon: London,* [1923.] 8°. **012803. c. 45.**

—— The Dolls' Day . . . Illustrated with twenty-nine photographs by Will Cadby. pp. viii. 103. *Mills & Boon: London,* 1915. 8°. **012807. c. 25.**

—— Finding a Fairy . . . Illustrated with thirty-one photographs by Will Cadby. pp. viii. 58. *Mills & Boon: London,* 1917. 8°. **12801. aa. 5.**

—— Puppies and Kittens, and other stories . . . Illustrated with 39 photographs by Will Cadby. pp. 112. *Mills & Boon: London,* [1918.] 12°. **12801. a. 12.**

—— Topsy and Turvy. A book of holidays . . . Illustrated with 40 photographs by Will Cadby. pp. 124. *Mills & Boon: London,* 1919. 8°. **12801. a. 28.**

CADBY (CARINE) and **CADBY** (WILL)

—— Dogs and Doggerel . . . Fully illustrated. *Art Record Press: London,* 1902. *obl.* 8°. **12808. e. 91.**

CADBY (CHARLES) *See* GEORGE (Benjamin) A Series of Views on Stone . . . illustrative of a walk through C. Cadby's Patent Piano-forte Manufactory. [1854.] fol. **1299.n.22**

CADBY (E. E.) A Cape Colonist Abroad. Illustrated. pp. 46. *D. Edwards & Co.: Cape Town,* [1898.] 8°. **10025. eee. 6.**

CADBY (PHILIP) Should Women Preach? What Saith the Scriptures. pp. viii. 79. *Elliot Stock: London,* 1892. 8°. **8416. df. 7.**

CADBY (WILL) [For works by C. Cadby, illustrated with photographs by W. Cadby:] *See* CADBY (Carine)

—— *See* CADBY (Carine) and (W.) Dogs and Doggerel, *etc.* 1902. *obl.* 8°. **012808. e. 91.**

CADBY (WILL) and **CADBY** (CARINE)

—— Switzerland in Summer. Discursive information for visitors.

1. The Bernese Oberland . . . Illustrated with twenty-seven photographs and a map. pp. 121. 1922.
2. The Grisons . . . Illustrated with twenty-one photographs and a map. pp. 128. [1923.]

Mills & Boon: London, 1922, [23.] 8°. **10195. aaa. 36.**
No more published.

—— Switzerland in Winter. Discursive information for visitors . . . Illustrated with fifty-two photographs by the authors. pp. xii. 232. *Mills & Boon: London,* 1914. 8°. **10196. dd. 9.**

—— (Second issue.) pp. 127. *Mills & Boon: London,* 1921. 8°. **10195. de. 11.**

CADDEL'S YEAR BOOK AND DIRECTORY OF GRAVESEND. *See* DIRECTORIES.—*Gravesend.*

CADDEL (ROBERT) A Sermon preached on the xxx of January 1703. pp. 12. *Edinburgh,* 1703. 4°. **4475. b. 33.**

CADDELL (CECILIA MARY) Blind Agnese: or, the Little spouse of the Blessed Sacrament . . . Second edition. pp. 235. *James Duffy: Dublin,* 1856. 8°. **4414. b. 27.**

—— Agnese la povera cieca . . . Versione dall'inglese per Alfonso Maria Galea. pp. 176. *Malta,* 1898. 8°. **4411. k. 1.**

—— Flower and Fruit; or, the Use of tears. pp. vii. 216. *James Duffy: Dublin,* 1856. 16°. **4407. b. 81.**
With an additional titlepage, reading: "Flowers and Fruit," etc. and dated 1855.

—— Hidden Saints. Life of Marie Bonneau de Miramion, *etc.* pp. 188. *T. Richardson & Son: London; H. H. Richardson & Co.: New York,* 1870. 16°. **4867. a. 15.**

—— Marie Bonneau de Miramion . . . New edition. pp. 188. *Art & Book Co.: London,* 1893. 16°. **4864. a. 3.**

—— Hidden Saints. Life of Sœur Marie, the workwoman of Liege. By the author of "Wild Times" [i.e. C. M. Caddell], *etc.* pp. 223. 1869. 8°. *See* MARIE, *Sœur.* **4863. cc. 18.**

—— A History of the Missions in Japan and Paraguay. 2 pt. *Burns & Lambert: London,* 1856. 8°. **4765. a. 40.**

—— The Cross in Japan. A history of the missions of St. Francis Xavier and the early Jesuits . . . A new edition [of pt. 1 of "A History of the Missions in Japan and Paraguay"], with preface & supplementary chapter by the Bishop of Salford. pp. xiii. 192. *Burns & Oates: London,* 1904. 8°. **4767. de. 12.**

—— Home and the Homeless; a novel. 3 vol. *T. C. Newby: London,* 1858. 12°. **12629. b. 2.**

—— The Martyr Maidens of Ostend. A legend of the 18th century. *See* TALES. Historical Tales and Legends. 1858. 12°. **12620. a. 22.**

CADDELL (Cecilia Mary)

—— Nellie Netterville; or, One of the transplanted . . . By . . . the author of "Wild Times" [i.e. C. M. Caddell], *etc.* pp. vii. 319. [1867.] 8°. *See* Netterville (Nellie) **12707**. bbb. **21.**

—— Never Forgotten: or, the Home of the lost child. pp. iv. 292. *Burns, Oates & Co.: London,* 1871. 8°. **4413**. h. **11.**

—— Summer Talks about Lourdes. pp. 158. *Burns & Oates: London,* 1874. 32°. **4808**. a. **21.**

—— [Another edition.] pp. 158. *Burns & Oates: London,* [1897.] 12°. **4807**. a. **3.**

—— Wild Times. A tale of the days of Queen Elizabeth . . . New edition. pp. iv. 311. *Burns, Oates & Co.: London,* 1872. 8°. **12624**. k. **12.**

CADDELL (Henry) Sermons preached in St. John's Church, Fulham, *etc.* pp. xl. 416. *Printed for the subscribers: Chelsea,* 1843. 8°. **4477**. h. **10.**

CADDELL (Peter) *See* Harris (Paul) *Roman Catholic Priest.* The Excommunication published by the L. Archbishop of Dublin . . . against the Inhabitants of the Diocese of Dublin, for hearing the Masses of P. Caddell . . . proved . . . of no validity, *etc.* 1632. 4°. G. **5591.**

CADDELL (Walter Buckingham) *See* Morgan (Frederick C.) Handbook of Artillery Matériel . . . Seventh edition, revised by W. B. Caddell, *etc.* 1913. 8°. **08821**. de. **44.**

—— Handbook for Proficiency Pay, Royal Garrison Artillery. (Manning fixed armament.) pp. 32. *W. Clowes & Sons: London,* 1912. 16°. **8823**. e. **17**. (4.)

CADDELL (Walter Waithman De V.) *See* Blackburn (Douglas) and Caddell (W. W. De V.) The Detection of Forgery, *etc.* 1909. 8°. **2230**. e. **19.**

—— *See* Blackburn (Douglas) and Caddell (W. W. De V.) Secret Service in South Africa. 1911. 8°. **8157**. f. **10.**

CADDEO (Rinaldo)

—— *See* Cattaneo (Carlo) *Giureconsulto.* Epistolario di Carlo Cattaneo. Raccolto e annotato da R. Caddeo, *etc.* 1949, *etc.* 8°. **10923.k.3.**

—— *See* Colombo (C.) [Collected Writings.] Relazioni di viaggio e lettere di Cristoforo Colombo . . . A cura di R. Caddeo, *etc.* 1943. 8°. **010632**. aa. **34.**

—— *See* Colombo (F.) Le Historie della vita e dei fatti di Cristoforo Colombo . . . A cura di R. Caddeo, *etc.* 1930. 8°. **10633**. r. **1.**

—— *See* Laghi (A. M.) I Primi anni del risorgimento ticinese nella Cronaca inedita di A. M. Laghi. [Edited by R. Caddeo.] 1938. 8°. W.P. **1538/21.**

—— Le Edizioni di Capolago. Storia e critica. Bibliografia ragionata, nuovi studi sulla tipografia elvetica, il Risorgimento italiano e il canton Ticino, documenti inediti, *etc.* pp. 472. pl. x. *Milano,* 1934. 4°. **2704.fs.2.**

—— Le Navigazioni atlantiche di Alvise da Ca da Mosto, Antoniotto Usodimare e Niccoloso da Recco. A cura di R. Caddeo, con prefazione, note, *etc.* [With plates, and maps.] pp. 340. *Milano,* 1928. 8°. **10496**. a. **35.**

—— La Typografia Elvetica di Capolago, *etc.* [With plates, including portraits and facsimiles.] pp. 588. *Milano,* 1931. 4°. **2704.fs.1.**

CADDICK (Arthur)

—— Lyrics from Nancledra. pp. 32. *Fortune Press: Lond* 1950. 8°. **11657**. l.

—— Quiet Lutes and Laughter. Selected poems, grave a gay. pp. 39. *Fortune Press: London,* 1955. 8°. **11659**. b.

—— Respectable Persons. A novel. pp. 224. *Hutchinson & Co.: London & Melbourne,* [1940.] 8°. NN. **315**

—— The Speech of Phantoms. pp. 14. *Latin Pr Saint Ives,* 1951. 8°. [*Crescendo Poetry Series.* no. 1 **Cup.510.acd.3**

CADDICK (David W.) Commercial Do's and Don pp. vi. 58. *Methuen & Co.: London,* 1925. 8°. **08228**. e.

—— The Outline of British Trade. A text-book, *etc.* pp. 1 *G. G. Harrap & Co.: London,* 1924. 8°. **08229**. aa.

—— Political Principles and Motives, *etc.* [Essays.] pp. xi. 97. *Methuen & Co.: London,* 1925. 8°. **08139**. aa.

—— The Republic of Chile. A popular description of country; its people, and its customs. pp. 64. *A. H. Stockwell: London,* [1912.] 8°. **10481**. p.

CADDICK (Frederick)

—— Decontamination of Foodstuffs. Arranged in tab form. pp. 15. *Sanitary Publishing Co.: Lon* [1941.] 8°. **7385**. aa

—— Decontamination of Foodstuffs. Revised edition, pp. 15. *Sanitary Publishing Co.: London,* [1943.] 8°. **7392**. a

—— Decontamination of Foodstuffs affected with Bli Gases. (A reproduction of tables iv, v, and vi of booklet "Decontamination of Foodstuffs.") *Sani Publishing Co.: London,* [1942.] *s. sh.* fol. **1865**. c. **20.**

CADDICK (H. C.) The Bride's Book; a code of m and conduct selected from works of eminent wri for the use of young married women. pp. 126. *H. Fi R. Fisher & P. Jackson: London,* [1835.] 16°. **713**. a.

—— Tales of the Affections: being sketches from real pp. v. 199. *Longman & Co.: London,* [1828.] 8°. N. **680.**

CADDICK (Helen) A White Woman in Central Afr pp. viii. 242. *T. Fisher Unwin: London,* 1900. 8°. **010095**. de.

CADDICK (Richard) *See* Bible. [*English.*] The I Bible, *etc.* copious ms. notes [by R. Caddick]. 1698. 12°. **1411**. c

—— *See* Bible.—*New Testament.* [*Hebrew.*] The New T ment . . . in Hebrew. Corrected . . . By the Rev Caddick. 1798. 8°. **01901**. a.

—— *See* Bible.—*New Testament.* [*Polyglott.*] The Testament . . . in Hebrew and English . . . Corre . . . By the Rev. R. Caddick. 1798, *etc.* 8°. **01902**. a.

—— Hebrew made easy; or, a Short and plain introduc to the sacred Hebrew language, compiled in a new met *etc.* pp. xii. 192. *T. Plummer: London,* 1799. 12°. **12903**. aa.

CADDIE.

—— Caddie, a Sydney Barmaid. An autobiography written by herself. With an introduction by Dymphna Cusack. pp. xxi. 274. *Constable & Co.: London,* 1953. 8º. **10863.** de. **18.**

CADDIE (Albert) Index-Catalogue of the Books in the Lending and Reference Departments. (Compiled by A. Caddie.) pp. 149. 1887. 8º. *See* Stoke-on-Trent.—*Public Free Library.* **11900.** n. **13.**

CADDINGTON.

—— The Parish Register of Caddington, 1558–1812. 1942. *See* Bedford, *County of.—County Record Society.* Bedfordshire Parish Registers, *etc.* vol. 25. 1931, *etc.* fol. **10362.dd.4/25.**

CADDY (Alex. F.) The Secret of Pixy Hall. An original farcical comedy in the Cornish dialect in two acts. pp. 17. [*Teddington,* 1932.] 4º. **11778.** h. **32.** *Typewritten.*

—— Treculliacks Parish Council. A humorous sketch in the Cornish dialect, in one act. pp. 12. [*Teddington,* 1931.] 4º. **11779.** l. **73.** *Typewritten.*

CADDY (Arnold) The Transport of Wounded. Compiled for the use of the Calcutta Light Horse. pp. 21. *City Press & Bengal Printing Co.: Calcutta,* 1916. 8º. **8828.** aa. **50.**

CADDY (Florence) Adrian Bright. [A novel.] 3 vol. *Hurst & Blackett: London,* 1883. 8º. **12635.** p. **11.**

—— Artist and Amateur; or, the Surface of life. A novel. 3 vol. *Chapman & Hall: London,* 1878. 8º. **12639.** e. **1.**

—— Footsteps of Jeanne d'Arc. A pilgrimage. pp. xvi. 375. *Hurst & Blackett: London,* 1886. 8º. **10663.** g. **4.**

—— Household Organization. pp. xvi. 209. *Chapman & Hall: London,* 1877. 8º. **7944.** b. **5.**

—— Lares and Penates; or, the Background of life. pp. 325. *Chatto & Windus: London,* 1881. 8º. **12643.** a. **11.**

—— Through the Fields with Linnæus. A chapter in Swedish history. 2 vol. *Longmans & Co.: London,* 1887. 8º. **10761.** bbb. **24.**

—— To Siam and Malaya in the Duke of Sutherland's Yacht 'Sans Peur.' pp. x. 362. *Hurst & Blackett: London,* 1889. 8º. **10027.** f. **7.**

[C]ADDY (Glenna Garratt)

—— *See* Walke (Nelson S.) Good Health for you, your Family, and your Community. [By] N. S. Walke . . . G. G. Caddy. 1955. 8º. W.P. **3407/16.**

[C]ADDY (John Archibald)

—— *See* Jocelyn (Julian R. J.) Some Notes on the History of the Advanced Class [of the Royal Artillery], 1866–1939. [The notes on the period 1927–39 written by J. A. Caddy.] [1955.] 8º. **10818.** a. **22.**

[C]ADDY (William) and **WARD** (Nicholas) To the Supream Authority, the Parliament of the Commonwealth of England. The humble Petition of William Caddy of Taunton, and Nicholas Ward of Chard, *etc.* [*London,* 1654.] *s. sh.* fol. **669.** f. **19.** (**12.**)

[C]ADDY (William Henry) Twenty-six Full-size Working Drawings for Wood Carving . . . With descriptive notes. *W. H. Caddy: Brighton,* [1892.] *obl.* 4º. **7817.** e. **17.**

—— [Another copy.] **7817.** g. **26.**

CADE, *Family of. See* Simpson (Llewellyn L.) Pedigree of Beresford, Blythe, Cheney, Wright, and Cade, *etc.* [1912.] fol. Cup. **649.** d. **10.** (**10.**)

CADE (André)

—— Les Incunables médicaux lyonnais. Discours, *etc.* [With facsimiles.] pp. 44. pl. x. 1942. 8º. *See* Lyons.—*Académie des Sciences, Belles-Lettres et Arts.* **11915.** i. **10.**

CADE (André) and **RAVAULT** (Pierre P.)

—— Syndromes pancréatiques chroniques, avec prédominance des troubles de la sécrétion externe. Par A. Cade . . . et P. P. Ravault . . . avec la collaboration radiologique de Roger Cade. 1934. *See* Congrès Français de Médecine. [Quebec, 1934.] Congrès Français de Médecine . . . Procès-verbaux, *etc.* session 23. Rapports. vol. 1. 1895, *etc.* Ac. **3712.** b/**23.**

CADE (Anthony) A Iustification of the Church of England. Demonstrating it to be a true Church of God, *etc.* pp. 315. 112. *For George Lathum: London,* 1630. 8º. **3936.** bb. **40.**

—— Saint Paules Agonie. A sermon . . . specially touching the motions of sinne, remaining in the regenerate. pp. 39. *Imprinted by Bernard Alsop: London,* 1618. 4º. **4256.** b. **8.**

—— A Sermon of the Nature of Conscience which may well be tearmed, A Tragedy of Conscience in Her. First, a Wakning. Secondly, Wrastling. Thirdly, Scourging, *etc.* pp. 46. *Bernard Alsop for Thomas Iones: London,* 1621. 4º. **4477.** aaa. **122.**

—— [Another edition.] A Sermon necessarie for these Times, shewing the nature of Conscience . . . To which is adjoyned a necessarie, brief and pithy treatise of the Ceremonies of the Church of England. pp. 63. *Printed by the Printers to the Universitie of Cambridge; sold by John Sweeting:* [*London,*] 1639. 4º. **4477.** b. **122.** (**4.**) *Imperfect; wanting the "Treatise of the Ceremonies."*

—— [A reissue.] Conscience, it's Nature and Corruption, with it's repairs and means to inform it aright. In a vindication of the Publick Prayers and Ceremonies of the Church of England, *etc.* (An Appendix to the foregoing sermon, concerning the Ceremonies of the Church of England.) pp. 63. 44. *For John Williams: London,* 1661. 8º. **3475.** b. **8.** *The appendix has a separate titlepage dated* 1636.

CADE (Charles R.) The Chandos Cross Word Puzzle Book, *etc.* pp. 59. *F. Warne & Co.: London & New York,* [1930.] 16º. **7913.** aa. **94.**

CADE (Coulson T.) The Cornish Penny. A novel. pp. 311. *Grant Richards: London; printed in U.S.A.,* 1922. 8º. NN. **7751.**

—— Dandelions. [A novel.] pp. 321. *Martin Secker: London,* 1917. 8º. NN. **4557.**

CADE (David W.) Dream Cargoes. [Poems.] pp. 64. *Dean & Co.: New York,* 1928. 8º. **011686.** g. **95.**

CADE (Francis Joseph) *See* Pruen (George G.) The Jubilee of Cheltenham College 1891. [Compiled by G. G. Pruen, F. J. Cade and A. A. Hunter.] [1892.] 4º. **8365.** f. **31.**

CADE (J. François) De l'inoculation de la petite vérole, essai, *etc.* pp. 31. *Montpellier,* an vii [1798/9]. 4º. **1180.** d. **5.** (**19.**)

CADE (JACK) *See* CLAYTON (Joseph) The True Story of Jack Cade, Captain of Kent, A.D. 1450. A vindication. 1909. 8°. **10816**. df. **33**.

—— *See* COOPER (William D.) John Cade's Followers in Kent. [1865.] 8°. **9904**. r. **13**. (**1**.)

—— *See* KING (William L.) A Pedigree of the House of De Fynes, illustrating Jack Cade's rebellion, *etc.* 1907. 8°. **9904**. i. **38**.

—— —— 1908. 8°. C. **60**. i. **24**.

—— *See* LYLE (Helen M.) The Rebellion of Jack Cade, 1450. 1950. 8°. W.P. **3175/16**.

—— *See* ORRIDGE (Benjamin B.) Illustrations of Jack Cade's Rebellion, *etc.* 1869. 4°. **9505**. ff. **1**.

—— Jack Cade; or, the Rebel of London. A play, *etc.* [Signed: W. T. T.] [1867?] 8°. *See* T., W. T. **11781**. f. **45**. (**3**.)

CADE (JAMES) London's Disease and Remedie: or, a Short and plain discourse, pointing at some probable causes of this present judgement that lies upon us, *etc.* pp. 61. *Ja. Cotterel for O. Pulleyn: London*, 1665. 8°. **4374**. de. **38**.

CADE (JEAN ANTOINE AUGUSTIN) Considérations sur la fluxion de poitrine muqueuse. Tribut academique, *etc.* pp. 28. *Montpellier*, 1825. 4°. **1181**. d. **3**. (**3**.)

CADE (JOHN) *Captain.* The last Speeches and Confession of Captain John Cade and John Mils constable: who were hanged at Weymouth for endeavouring to betray that Garrison to the enemie, with all the severall examinations . . . With a coppie of Sir Lewis Dives letter to Colonell Sydenham about the same, and Colonell Sydenham his answere. pp. 14. *Imprinted by Jane Coe: London*, 1645. 4°. E. **274**. (**28**.)

CADE (JOHN) *of Kidwelly.* The State of the Town of Kidwillie in South Wales in the Reign of Queen Elizabeth, with a plan for its improvements. *See* LELAND (John) *the Antiquary.* Joannis Lelandi De rebus Britannicis collectanea, *etc.* vol. 2. 1770. 8°. **2072**. a. **16**.

CADE (JOHN) *Quaker. See* ASHBY (Richard) The True Light owned and vindicated, *etc.* [Signed: R. Ashby, J. Fiddeman, J. Cade.] 1699. 4°. **4152**. bb. **67**.

CADE (JOHN) *Rebel. See* CADE (Jack)

CADE (LAURENCE HERBERT) The Book of the Rudge, *etc.* *Sir I. Pitman & Sons: London*, 1927. 8°. [*Motor-Cyclist's Library.*] W.P. **8199/10**.
Later editions, by L. H. Cade and F. Anstey, are entered under CADE *(L. H.) and* ANSTEY *(F.) B.Sc., A.M.I.A.E.*

—— Common Sense Contract. pp. 240. *Hurst & Blackett: London*, [1933.] 8°. **7916**. c. **38**.

—— The Modern World Book of Motors. [With plates.] pp. 159. [*Sampson Low, Marston & Co.: London*, [1950.] 4°. **8764**. aa. **61**.

CADE (LAURENCE HERBERT) and **ANSTEY** (FRANK) *B.Sc., A.M.I.A.E.*

—— The Book of the Rudge . . . Second edition, *etc.* pp. vii. 96. *Sir I. Pitman & Sons: London*, 1933. 8°. [*Motor-Cyclist's Library.*] W.P. **8199/38**.
The first edition, by L. H. Cade, is entered under CADE *(L. H.).*

CADE (LAURENCE HERBERT) and **ANSTEY** (FRANK) *B.Sc., A.M.I.A.E.*

—— [Another edition.] Revised by W. C. Haycraft . . . Third edition. pp. vii. 108. *London*, 1935. 8°. [*Pitman's Motor Cyclists Library.*] W.P. **8199/47**.

—— Fourth edition. pp. vii. 108. *London*, 1938. 8°. [*Pitman's Motor Cyclists Library.*] W.P. **8199/66**.

—— The Book of the Rudge . . . Revised by W. C. Haycraft . . . Fifth edition. pp. vii. 108. *Sir Isaac Pitman & Sons: London*, 1953. 8°. [*Pitman's Motor-Cyclists' Library.*] W.P. **8199/108**.

CADE (M. A. AMABLE) Considérations nouvelles sur le diagnostic différentiel et le traitement de quelques ophthalmies spéciales . . . Thèse, *etc.* pp. 34. *Paris*, 1837. 4°. **1184**. h. **5**. (**26**.)

CADE (M. S. A. EDME) De la saignée dans le traitement de l'eclampsie puerpérale, *etc.* pp. 58. *Paris*, 1867. 4°. [*Collection des thèses soutenues à la Faculté de Médecine de Paris.* An 1867. tom. 3.] **7373**. h. **6**.

CADE (PAUL) Death Slams the Door. pp. 180. *Modern Age Books: New York*, [1937.] 8°. **012643**. o. **6**.

CADE (REGINALD COURTNEY)

—— Handbook on British Colonial Stamps in Current Use, September 1949. Comprising historical, geographical and general information . . . Compiled by R. C. Cade. pp. 103. 1950–. 8°. *See* ENGLAND. [*Miscellaneous Official Publications.*] [Various editions.] B.S. **68/37**.

CADE (ROGER)

—— *See* CADE (A.) and RAVAULT (P. P.) Syndromes pancréatiques chroniques . . . Par A. Cade . . . et P. P. Ravault . . . avec la collaboration radiologique de R. Cade. 1934. 8°. [*Congrès Français de Médecine.* session 23. Rapports. vol. 1.] **Ac.3712.b/23.**

CADE (SALISBURY) *See* BYFIELD (Timothy) A Letter to the Fatal Triumvirate [i.e. J. Freind, R. Mead and S. Cade]: in answer to that pretended to be written by Dr. Byfield, *etc.* [By John Harris.] 1719. 8°. **1172**. g. **8**. (**2**.)

—— Bibliotheca Cadeana: being a catalogue of part of the library of the late learned Salisbury Cade, *etc.* pp. 28. [1721.] 8°. S.C. **466**. (**4**.)

CADE (*Sir* STANFORD) *K.B.E.*

—— *See* BUTLIN (*Sir* Henry T.) *Bart.* Diseases of the Tongue. By W. G. Spencer . . . and S. Cade . . . Being the third edition of Butlin's "Diseases of the Tongue," *etc.* 1931. 8°. **2256**. f. **18**.

—— *See* CANTLIE (*Sir* James) *K.B.E.* British Red Cross Society First Aid Manual . . . By Sir Harold E. Whittingham . . . and Sir S. Cade, *etc.* 1949. 8°. W.P. **1831/1d**.

—— *See* CANTLIE (*Sir* James) *K.B.E.* British Red Cross Society First Aid Manual . . . By Sir H. E. Whittingham . . . and Sir S. Cade, *etc.* 1952. 8°. W.P. **1831/1e**.

—— Chemotherapy of Cancer. The inaugural Florence Blair Bell Lecture delivered at the Liverpool Medical Institution on 16th November, 1950. [An account of the work of William Blair Bell on cancer. With portraits.] pp. 31. pl. 4. *University Press: Liverpool* 1951 [1952]. 8°. **7444**. aaa. **15**

CADE (*Sir* STANFORD) *K.B.E.*

—— Malignant Disease and its Treatment by Radium, *etc.* pp. xi. 1280. *J. Wright & Sons: Bristol*, 1940. 8°. **7462.** s. **28.**

—— Malignant Disease and its Treatment by Radium . . . Second edition. *John Wright & Sons: Bristol*, 1948– . 8°. W.P. **6154.**

—— Radium Treatment of Cancer, *etc.* pp. x. 158. pl. XIII. *J. & A. Churchill: London*, 1929. 8°. **7470.** dd. **49.**

CADE (THOMAS JEFFERSON) The King's Speech on the Presidential Contest, to the people of the United States. pp. 14. *Philadelphia*, 1836. 8°. **8177.** aaa. **80.** (2)

CADE (W. T.) Metric Weights converted into Pounds and Ounces. pp. 22. *E. Punt & Co.: London*, [1911.] 8°. **08533.de.20.(3.)**

CADE (WILLIAM) *Deputy of the Ward of St. Botolph, Bishopsgate.* See LAKE (John) successively *Bishop of Sodor & Man, of Bristol* and *of Chichester.* *Στεφανος πιστου*: or, the True Christian's character & crown. Described in a sermon . . . At the funeral of Mr. W. Cade. 1671. 4°. **1416.** d. **66.**

CADE (WILLIAM) *Priest of the Church of England.* The Foundation of Popery Shaken: or, the Bishop of Rome's supremacy opposed in a sermon, upon Matth. XVI. 18, 19. pp. 31. *T. M. for Robert Clavel: London*, 1678. 4°. **226.** h. **3.** (**7.**)

CADÉAC (A.) *See* MARCHAND (Henri F.), and CADÉAC (A.) Découvertes préhistoriques dans la région de Médéa, *etc.* 1932. 8°. **07707.** i. **78.**

CADÉAC (CÉLESTIN) *See* LE BLANC (Paul) *of Lyons.* Pathologie chirurgicale générale. By P. Le Blanc, C. Cadéac. Translated, *etc.* 1907. 8°. [*MERILLAT (L. A.) Veterinary Surgery.* vol. 2.] **07294.** l. **2.**

—— —— 1916. 8°. [*MERILLAT (L. A.) The Principles of Veterinary Surgery, etc.*] **07294.** i. **16.**

—— Pathologie générale et anatomie pathologique générale des animaux domestiques, par C. Cadéac . . . avec la collaboration de J. Bournay, *etc.* pp. viii. 478. *Paris*, 1893. 12°. **7421.** aaa. **28.**

CADÉAC (CÉLESTIN) and MEUNIER (ALBIN)

Contribution à l'étude de l'alcoolisme, recherches expérimentales sur les essences, *etc.* 1892, 93. *See* LYONS.—*Société d'Agriculture, etc.* Annales, *etc.* sér. 6. tom. 4, 5. 1838, *etc.* 8°. Ac. **362/3.**

CADÉAC (J. M. L.) De la rigidité du col de l'utérus pendant le travail de l'accouchement. pp. 32. *Paris*, 1859. 4°. [*Collection des thèses soutenues à la Faculté de Médecine de Paris.* An 1859. tom. 3.] **7373.** b. **15.**

CADEAU. Le Cadeau du premier jour de l'an . . . Par Mad. de G . . . . 1809. 12°. *See* G . . . . . ., *Mad. de.* **012807.** de. **27.**

CADEAU (ÉMILE) Influence des suppurations prolongées sur la production de la tuberculisation pulmonaire, *etc.* pp. 44. *Paris*, 1874. 4°. [*Collection des thèses soutenues à la Faculté de Médecine de Paris.* An 1874. tom. 3.] **7374.** a. **8.**

CADEAU DE FESSEL (BENITA PAULINA) Curso Elemental de Partos. pp. 146. *Lima*, 1827. 8°. **1176.** h. **16.**

CADEC (JAN) Tragedien Sacr, commancet en Jardin an Olivet beté Menes Calvar. Pe meditation var pep mister a bassion hon salver Jesus Christ . . . Dresset ha corriget ha neves gant M. P. D. pp. 22. *G. Buitingh: Quemper*, 1688. 12°. **1019.** g. **21.** (**2.**)
Cropped.

CADEDDU (GAETANO) *See* BRUNDO (C.) Ricordi storici di Gaetano Cadeddu, *etc.* 1887. 8°. **10602.** d. **23.** (**2.**)

CADEI (ANTONIO) Sui componimenti d'ogni forma e sui buoni scrittori. Trattato speciale. pp. 186. *Milano*, 1875. 8°. **11824.** bb. **8.**

CADEL (ATTILIO) and **GOSETTI** (FRANCESCO) La Fognatura delle città in rapporto alle malattie endemiche ed epidemiche, *etc.* pp. 4. 284. pl. VIII. *Torino, Roma*, 1891. 8°. **8777.** bbb. **20.**

CADEL (ISIDORE FERDINAND) Essai sur la phthisie pulmonaire tuberculeuse. Tribut académique, *etc.* pp. 35. *Montpellier*, 1835. 4°. **1181.** g. **12.** (**7.**)

CADELL AND DAVIES. *See* CADELL (T.) and DAVIES (W.) *Publishing Firm.*

CADELL, *Family of.* *See* STEVENSON (John R. H.) The Cadells of Banton, Grange, Tranent, Cockenzie, *etc.* 1890. fol. **1860.** cc. **1.**

CADELL, *Family of, of Tranent.* Cadells of Tranent. [By J. P. Dunlop.] ff. 4. [*London*, 1936.] 4°. **1860.** cc. **1.** (**2.**)
Typewritten.

CADELL (CECILIA MARY) Massenburg. A tale. [By C. M. Cadell.] 3 vol. 1825. 12°. *See* MASSENBURG. N. **277.**

—— The Reformer. By the author of "Massenburg" [i.e. C. M. Cadell]. 3 vol. 1832. 12°. *See* REFORMER. N. **904.**

CADELL (CHARLES) Narrative of the Campaigns of the Twenty-eighth Regiment, since their return from Egypt in 1802. pp. xx. 281. *Whittaker & Co.: London*, 1835. 12°. **806.** c. **26.**

CADELL (ELIZABETH) *See* CADELL (Violet E.)

CADELL (FRANCIS CAMPBELL BOILEAU)

—— *See* HONEYMAN (Tom J.) Three Scottish Colourists. S. J. Peploe, F. C. B. Cadell, Leslie Hunter. [With reproductions and portraits.] 1950. 8°. **7868.** f. **30.**

—— Jack and Tommy. Twenty drawings. pl. 20. *Grant Richards: London*, 1916. 4°. **1874.** c. **28.**

CADELL (HENRY MOUBRAY) The Geology and Scenery of Sutherland . . . Second edition, revised and enlarged. [With plates and maps.] pp. 108. *David Douglas: Edinburgh*, 1896. 8°. **7105.** aa. **9.**

—— Geology as a Branch of Technical Education, *etc.* [With plates.] pp. 29. *Neill & Co.: Edinburgh*, 1887. 8°. **7106.** h. **30.** (**7.**)

—— Rhymes for the Times. Kaiser William the Hun and his place in the Sun . . . Second edition. pp. vii. 23. *T. & A. Constable: Edinburgh*, 1917. 8°. **011648.** ee. **38.**

—— The Rocks of West Lothian. An account of the geological and mining history of the West Lothian District . . . With eighty illustrations, orographical and geological maps. pp. xvi. 390. *Oliver & Boyd: Edinburgh, London*, 1925. 8°. **07109.** h. **57.**

CADELL (HENRY MOUBRAY)

—— The Story of the Forth . . . With 75 illustrations and 8 maps. pp. xvii. 299. *J. Maclehose & Sons: Glasgow,* 1913. 8°. **10370**. v. **7**.

CADELL (HENRY MOUBRAY) and **WILSON** (JAMES SIMPSON GRANT)

—— The Geology of the Oil-Shale Fields. *See* LOTHIANS. The Oil-Shales of the Lothians, *etc.* 1906. 8°. **B.S.38.Gb/1.(3.)**

—— *See* CARRUTHERS (Robert G.) The Geology of the Oil-Shale Fields . . . based on the work of H. M. Cadell and J. S. G. Wilson. 1912. 8°. [*The Oil-Shales of the Lothians.*] **B.S.38.Gb/1.(3a.)**

—— *See* CARRUTHERS (Robert G.) The Geology of the Oil-Shale Fields . . . Based on the work of H. M. Cadell and J. S. Grant Wilson. 1927. 8°. [*The Oil-Shales of the Lothians.*] **B.S.38.Gb/1.(3b.)**

CADELL (*Mrs.* HENRY MOUBRAY) *See* CADELL (Jessie E.)

CADELL (JAMES)

—— Black Niklas. pp. 254. *Victor Gollancz: London,* 1954. 8°. NNN. **5342**.

—— Roast Pigeon. [A novel.] pp. 213. *MacGibbon & Kee: London,* 1951. 8°. NNN. **2023**.

CADELL (JANET SYDSERFF) Fisher-Folk. pp. 88. *Macniven & Wallace: Edinburgh,* [1884 ?] 8°. **012600**. aa. **24**.

CADELL (JESSIE ELLEN) *See* 'UMAR KHAIYĀM. [*Other Versions.—English.*] The Ruba'yat of Omar Khayam. Translated by Mrs. H. M. Cadell, *etc.* 1899. 8°. **757**. d. **50**.

—— Ida Craven. [A novel.] 2 vol. *H. S. King & Co.: London,* 1876. 8°. **12637**. k. **5**.

—— Worthy. A study of friendship. [Edited by John F. Cadell.] pp. viii. 518. *Remington & Co.: London,* 1895. 8°. **012628**. e. **31**.

CADELL (JOHN FRANCIS) *See* CADELL (Jessie E.) Worthy, *etc.* [Edited by J. F. Cadell.] 1895. 8°. **012628**. e. **31**.

CADELL (*Sir* PATRICK ROBERT)

—— *See* INDIA. [*Laws, etc.*—I.] The Bengal Manual of the Sea Customs and Tariff Laws, *etc.* (Compiled by P. R. Cadell.) 1911. 8°. I.S. BE. **284/7**.

—— *See* REED (*Sir* Stanley) *K.B.E.*, and CADELL (*Sir* P. R.) India: the new phase. 1928. 8°. **012210.bbb.4/15.**

—— *See* TAYLOR (Philip Meadows) *Colonel.* The Letters of P. M. Taylor to Henry Reeve. Edited . . . by Sir P. Cadell. 1947. 8°. **10923**. aaa. **5**.

—— History of the Bombay Army . . . With two coloured plates and eleven maps. pp. xv. 362. *Longmans & Co.: London,* 1938. 8°. **08820**. d. **11**.

CADELL (ROBERT) Particulars and Conditions of Sale of Copyrights, the property of the trustees of the late Robert Cadell, Publisher, Edinburgh; consisting of the entire copyrights, steel plates, woodcuts, stereotype plates, &c. of the works of Sir Walter Scott, Bart. . . . to be sold by auction . . . at the London Coffee House, Ludgate Hill, London. pp. 11. *T. Constable: Edinburgh,* [1851.] 4°. **824**. i. 5. (4.)

CADELL (*Sir* ROBERT) *K.C.B.* Sir John Cope and the Rebellion of 1745. [Edited by Thomas Cadell. With maps.] pp. xii. 282. *W. Blackwood & Sons: Edinburgh & London,* 1898. 8°. **9509**. l. **5**.

CADELL (THOMAS) and **DAVIES** (WILLIAM) *Publishing Firm.* The Publishing Firm of Cadell & Davies. Select correspondence and accounts, 1793–1836. Edited with an introduction and notes by Theodore Besterman. pp. xxxv. 189. *Oxford University Press: London* 1938. fol. **010921**. m. **5**

—— A Catalogue of Approved English Books . . . printed for and sold by T. Cadell, jun. and W. Davies, *etc.* pp. 132 [*London,*] 1802. 8°. S.C. **738**. (3.

—— Catalogue of Valuable Books . . . printed . . . for T. Cadell and W. Davies. pp. 24. [*London,*] 1803. 12°. S.C. **736**. (1.

—— Catalogue of Valuable Books . . . printed . . . for T. Cadell and W. Davies. pp. 26. *G. Sidney:* [*London,* 1816. 8°. S.C. **768**. (1.

—— New Books, published during the years 1796 and 1797 by T. Cadell, jun. and W. Davies . . . Being a supplement to their catalogue of approved English books, *etc.* pp. 22. [*London,* 1798.] 8°. S.C. **732**. (3.

CADELL (THOMAS) *Brother of Sir Robert Cadell, K.C.B.* *See* CADELL (*Sir* R.) *K.C.B.* Sir John Cope, *etc.* [Edited by T. Cadell.] 1898. 8°. **9509**. l. **5**

CADELL (VIOLET ELIZABETH)

—— The Cuckoo in Spring. pp. 190. *Hodder & Stoughton: London,* 1954. 8°. NN. **2906**

—— Fishy, said the Admiral. pp. 192. *Robert Hale: London,* 1948. 8°. NN. **38110**

—— The Frenchman and the Lady. pp. 254. *Hodder & Stoughton: London,* 1952. 8°. NNN. **2808**

—— Gay Pursuit. pp. 255. *Robert Hale: London,* 1950. 8°. NNN. **482**

—— The Gentlemen go by. pp. 190. *Hodder & Stoughton: London,* 1954. 8°. NNN. **5071**

—— The Greenwood Shady. pp. 255. *Hodder & Stoughton: London,* 1951. 8°. NNN. **2147**

—— Iris in Winter. pp. 272. *Robert Hale: London,* 1951. 8°. NNN. **1350**

—— Journey's Eve. pp. 254. *Hodder & Stoughton: London,* 1953. 8°. NNN. **390**

—— The Lark shall sing. pp. 191. *Hodder & Stoughton: London,* 1955. 8°. NNN. **7183**

—— Men and Angels. pp. 192. *Hodder & Stoughton: London,* 1952. 8°. NNN. **317**

—— Money to burn. pp. 189. *Hodder & Stoughton: London,* 1954 [1955]. 8°. NNN. **616**

—— My Dear Aunt Flora. pp. 252. *Robert Hale:* [*London,*] 1946. 8°. NN. **3628**

—— River Lodge. pp. 223. *Robert Hale: London,* [1948.] 8°. NN. **3886**

—— Spring Green. pp. 190. *Hodder & Stoughton: London,* 1953. 8°. NNN. **416**

—— Sun in the Morning, *etc.* pp. 255. *Hodder & Stoughton: London,* 1951. 8°. NNN. **158**

CADELL (WILLIAM ARCHIBALD) A Journey in Carniola, Italy, and France, in the years 1817, 1818, *etc.* 2 vol. pl. XXXIII. *A. Constable & Co.: Edinburgh,* 1820. 8°. **982**. d. **11, 12**

CADELL (William Archibald)

—— On the Lines that divide each Semidiurnal Arc into six equal parts . . . From the Transactions of the Royal Society of Edinburgh, *etc.* pp. 21. *Neill & Co.: Edinburgh*, 1816. 4°. **441**. g. **22**. (**6**.)

CADEMAN (Thomas) *See* London.—ii. *Livery Companies. —Distillers.* The Distiller of London, *etc.* [Edited by T. de Mayerne and T. Cademan.] 1639. fol. **717**. i. **10**.

—— —— 1652. 12°. **1400**. a. **32**.

—— The Earle of Bedfords Passage to the Highest Court of Parliament, May the ninth, 1641, about tenne a clocke in the morning. Observed by his Lordship's Physitian Doctor Cademan. pp. 6. *For Hugh Perry: London*, 1641. 4°. **113**. a. **29**.

—— [Another copy.] E. **158**. (**17**.)

CADEMANN (Augustus) Jucundissimum ex physicis problema de basilisci existentia et essentia, *etc. Praes.* G. C. Kirchmaierus. *Literis hæred. M. Oelschlegelii: [Wittenberg,]* 1659. 4°. B. **426**. (**5**.)

—— [Another edition.] De basilisco, *etc. See* Kirchmaier (G. C.) Georgii Casp. Kirchmajeri . . . De basilisco, unicornu . . . dissertationes aliquot, *etc.* disp. 1. 1669. 8°. **987**. a. **31**. (**2**.)

—— [Another edition.] Jucundissimum ex physicis problema de basilisci existentia et essentia, *etc. Typis M. Henckelii: [Wittenberg,]* 1670. 4°. **444**. d. **21**. (**9**.)

—— [Another edition.] De basilisco, *etc. See* Kirchmaier (G. C.) Georg. Casp. Kirchmaieri . . . disputationes zoologicæ, *etc.* disp. 1. 1736. 4°. B. **333**. (**1**.)

CADEMANNUS (Augustus) De mensium provocatione. *See* Kroes (A.) De matricis præfocatione, *etc.* [1614.] 4°. T. **560**. (**9**.)

CADEMARTORI (Ernest) Il faut en finir quand même. Les droits du pape et du catholicisme. pp. 16. *Marseille*, 1867. 8°. **3902**. cc. **33**. (**6**.)

CADEMOSTE (Alouys de) *See* Cà da Mosto (Alvise da)

CADEMOSTO (Marco) *See* Cadamosto.

CADENA, Ramón La Cadena y Laguna, *Marquis de la. See* La Cadena y Laguna.

CADENA, Ramón Lacadena y Brualla, *Marquis de la. See* Lacadena y Brualla.

CADENA (Antonio Osorio de la) *See* Osorio de la Cadena.

CADENA (Carlos) Descripcion de las Reales Exequias, que á la Tierna Memoria de nuestro . . . monarca . . . Carlos iii. Rey de España . . . se hicieron . . . en la . . . ciudad de Guatemala, *etc.* (Caroli Tertii . . . elogium funebre.) [With plates.] pp. 64. lxx. [1789.] 4°. **10632**. c. **54**.

—— Lenguas indígenas de Centro América en el siglo xviii, según copia del Archivo de Indias, hecha por . . . don León Fernández y publicada por Ricardo Fernández Guardia y Juan Fernández Ferraz, *etc.* [A series of vocabularies compiled in Guatemala in 1788–89, by C. Cadena and others, on instructions from King Charles iii. of Spain, issued in response to a request from Catherine the Great.] pp. vii. 110. *San José de Costa Rica*, 1892. 8°. **12911**. v. **3**.

CADENA (Diego Velazquez de la) *See* Velazquez de la Cadena.

CADENA (Felipe) La Vida Muerta, y la Muerte Viva. Oracion fúnebre, que en tiernos recuerdos de . . . Doña Isabel de Farnecio predicó . . . el M. R. P. Fr. P. Cadena. *See* Fernandez de Cordova (M.) El Sentimiento de el Alma, y Llanto de la Monarquia de España, *etc.* [1768.] 4°. **811**. e. **31**.

CADENA (Joseph Onofre Antonio de la) Cartilla musica, y primera parte; que contiene un methodo facil de aprehenderla à cantar. pp. 30. *Lima*, 1763. 4°. M.K. **8**. f. **14**.

CADENA (Manuela Velazquez de la) *See* Velazquez de la Cadena.

CADENA (Mariano Velazquez de la) *See* Velazquez de la Cadena.

CADENA (Peregrin Garcia) *See* Garcia Cadena.

CADENAS. Les Cadenas et ceintures de chasteté. [By Alcide Bonneau.] Notice historique, suivie du Plaidoyer de Freydier, avocat à Nîmes. Avec figures. pp. xl. 65. *Paris*, 1883. 8°. Tab. **603**. a. **59**.

CADENAS (José Juan) *See* Vélez de Guevara (L.) Inés de Castro . . . Adaptación lírica . . . por J. J. Cadenas, *etc.* 1903. 8°. **11726**. e. **26**. (**10**.)

CADENAS (Manuel) La Provincia de Toledo de la Compañía de Jesús, 1880–1914. Reseña histórica ilustrada de su formación, casas y ministerios. [Translated from the Latin and completed by Enrique del Portillo.] pp. ix. 291. *Madrid*, 1916. 8°. **04782**. h. **35**.

CADENAS (Pedro) De Pedro Cadenas. Romance de las valentias de Pedro Cadenas, y otros tres soldados de las Galeras de España. [In verse.] *Madrid*, 1764. 4°. T. **1957**. (**5**.)

—— [Another edition.] *Madrid*, 1820. 4°. **1072**. g. **27**. (**4**.)

—— [Another edition.] *Valladolid*, [1830?] 4°. **11451**. ee. **39**. (**28**.)

—— [Another edition.] Pedro Cadenas. Relacion verdadera de los amores y desafíos que tuvieron en Barcelona cuatro valerosos soldados de la marina española. [In verse.] *Madrid*, 1858. 4°. **11450**. f. **25**. (**2**.)

CADENAS DELGADO (Manuel) [For official documents issued by M. Cadenas Delgado as Secretario de Hacienda of the Republic of Venezuela:] *See* Venezuela.—*Ministerio de Hacienda.*

CADENAT (J.)

—— Poissons de mer du Sénégal. pp. 345. *Dakar*, 1950. 8°. [*Institut Français d'Afrique Noire. Initiations africaines.* no. 3.] Ac. **6917**. b/5.

CADENA Y ELETA (José) Proyecto de código procesal canónico. pp. xv. 413. *Madrid*, 1895. 8°. **05107**. i. **1**.

CADENBACH (Carl August) *See* Loehle (S.) De Aristophanis fabula, quae inscribitur Aves. [With a preface by C. A. Cadenbach.] 1865. 8°. **11705**. g. **19**. (**7**.)

—— Commentationum sophoclearum specimen. pp. 23. *Heidelbergae*, 1852. 8°. **11705**. df. **24**.

—— Das Lyceum zu Heidelberg in seiner geschichtlichen Entwickelung . . . 1808–1858. pp. iv. 80. *Heidelberg*, 1859. 8°. **8365**. c. **53**. (**6**.)

CADENBERG (Josephus Slop de) *See* Slop de Cadenberg.

CADÈNE (JEAN) L'Église réformée de Bordeaux. Aperçu historique. pp. 88. *Bordeaux*, 1892. 8°. 4534. a. 33. (2.)

CADENEDUS (JACOBUS) Astrææ Venetae Plausus in Caroli II. Stuarti Magnæ Britan: Franc: & Hiber: regis gloriosissimi et priscæ cum eodem monarcha amicitiæ instauratione sapientissimis Pat. lycei moderatoribus ab J. Cadenedo . . . sacrati 1661. x Kal. Dec. pp. 15. *Typis P. Frambotti: Patavii*, [1661.] 4°. E. 1957. (4.)

—— Pallas Pronuba in Faustissimis Nuptiis Caroli Secundi & Catherinæ Magnæ Britan. Franc: & Hiber: Reg: potentissimorum, *etc.* *Typis P. Frambotti: Patavii*, 1662. 4°. E. 1957. (10.)

CADENET, *the Troubadour.* Der Trobador Cadenet. Von Carl Appel. [The French text, with a German translation and notes.] pp. 123. *Halle*, 1920. 8°. 011483. k. 65.

CADENET (AUGUSTE) De la dysenterie épidémique, considerée particulièrement chez l'homme de guerre. Thèse, *etc.* pp. 28. *Montpellier*, 1844. 4°. 1182. d. 7. (18.)

CADENET (PIERRE DE) *Sieur de Brieulle.* *See* ENRIQUEZ (A.) Resolution courageuse et louable de la comtesse de Tirconel . . . Traduicte d'Espagnol en François par P. de Cadenet, *etc.* 1628. 12°. 1204. b. 10.

CADENHEAD, *Family of.* *See* CADENHEAD (George) The Family of Cadenhead. 1887. 8°. 9905. c. 31.

CADENHEAD (GEORGE) The Family of Cadenhead. pp. xix. 57. *J. & J. P. Edmond & Spark: Aberdeen*, 1887. 8°. 9905. c. 31.

—— Sketch of the Territorial History of the Burgh of Aberdeen, *etc.* pp. 43. MS. NOTE. *Lewis Smith: Aberdeen*, 1878. 8°. 10370. e. 37.

CADENHEAD (J. F.) The Canadian Scottish. Christmas Day. An impression. pp. 7. *Rosemount Press: Aberdeen*, 1916. 8°. 9081. de. 21.

—— The Canadian Scottish. Stray papers by a private, *etc.* pp. xii. 34. *Rosemount Press: Aberdeen*, 1915. 4°. 9083. g. 9.

CADENHEAD (J. W.) *See* RAYMOND (J. W.) *pseud.* [i.e. J. W. Cadenhead.]

CADENHEAD (WILLIAM) The New Book of Bon-Accord; or, Guide to the city of Aberdeen. Second edition, thoroughly revised and enlarged. [With a map.] pp. 116. *L. & J. Smith: Aberdeen*, 1862. 8°. 10370. aa. 6. *The date on the cover is* 1864.

CADENUS. Cadenus and Vanessa. A poem. [By Jonathan Swift.] pp. 37. *J. Roberts: London*, 1726. 8°. C. 71. h. 10.

—— [Cadenus and Vanessa. A poem, *etc.*] [By Jonathan Swift.] pp. 32. [*Dublin*, [1726.] 8°. 11659. c. 74. *Imperfect; wanting the titlepage, which bears the date* 2726.

—— [Another edition.] [*Allan Ramsay: Edinburgh*,] 1726. 8°. 992. h. 7. (4.) *Pp.* 83–114 *of a collection. With a separate titlepage.*

—— Cadenus and Vanessa. A poem. By Dr. S—T. [i.e. Jonathan Swift.] The second edition. 1726. 8°. *See* S—T, *Dr.* 11659. c. 75

—— Cadenus and Vanessa. A poem. [By J. Swift.] The second edition. pp. 32. *Dublin*, 1726. 8°. 11661. aa. 40.

—— Cadenus and Vanessa . . . By Dr. S—T. [i.e. Jonathan Swift.] The sixth edition. 1726. 8°. *See* S—T, *Dr.* 11660. e. 40.

CADÉOT (JEAN BAPTISTE) Dissertation sur la vaccine, *etc.* pp. 24. *Montpellier*, 1811. 4°. 1180. g. 3. (16.)

CADERAS (GIAN FADRI) *See* MAXFIELD (Mildred E.) Studies in Modern Romansh Poetry in the Engadine, with special consideration of . . . G. F. Caderas, *etc.* 1938. 4°. 11859. dd. 15.

—— *See* VITAL (A.) *Romansch Scholar.* Gian Fadri Caderas. 1899. 8°. [*Annalas della Società Reto-Romantscha.* Ann. 13.] Ac. 9817.

—— Fluors alpinas. Rimas. pp. 185. *Coira*, 1883. 8°. 11431. eee. 1.

—— Nouvas rimas. pp. 135. *Coira*, 1879. 8°. 11452. cc. 3.

—— Rimas. pp. vii. 107. *Coira*, 1865. 8°. 11436. aa. 36.

—— Sorrirs e larmas. Rimas. pp. 92. *Samedan*, 1887. 8°. 885. g. 3.

CADERAS (MATHIS ANTON) *Begin.* Hohe Oberherrlichkeit der Ehrs. Räthe und Gemeinden! Getreue, liebe Bundsgenossen. Die drei Bünde von hohen Rhätien sind ein freier Staat, *etc.* [Signed by M. A. Caderas, G. Planta and others.] [*Coire?* 1795.] fol. 9304. g. 9. (6.)

—— Protesta wider das Verfahren des grossen Kongresses des Jahrs 1795, *etc.* [Signed by M. A. Caderas, G. Planta, and others.] [*Coire*, 1795.] fol. 9304. g. 9. (7.)

—— *See* DERMONT (T.) *Begin:* Die Ihro Weisheiten denen Herren Häuptern eingereichte Protesta der Herren Präsident Caderas, V. G. Planta [and others] . . . nöthiget uns . . . gegenwärtige . . . Verantwortung ab, *etc.* [1795.] fol. 9304. g. 7. (11.)

CADERE (VICTOR G.) Questions juridiques et diplomatiques roumaines, *etc.* pp. iii. 146. *Paris*, 1936. 8°. 5756. p. 25.

—— Tratat de procedură civilă după legile de unificare şi legile provinciale in vigoare . . . Ediţia a II-a. pp. 606. *Bucureşti*, [1936.] 8°. 5756. s. 16.

CADEREITA, LOPE DIEZ DE AUXARMENDARIZ, *Marquis de.* *See* DIEZ DE AUXARMENDARIZ (L.) *Marquis de Cadereyta.*

CADEREYTA, LOPE DIEZ DE AUXARMENDARIZ, *Marquis de.* *See* DIEZ DE AUXARMENDARIZ.

CADERNO.

—— Caderno da doutrina pella lingoa dos Manaos. *See* MANAOS.

CADERNOS.

—— Cadernos de folclore. *See* SÃO PAULO.—*Departamento Estadual de Informações.—Divisão de Turismo e Expansão Cultural.*

CADES (HAZEL RAWSON) Any Girl can be Good-Looking. pp. vi. 197. *D. Appleton & Co.: New York; London*, 1927. 8°. 7383. c. 31.

—— Handsome is as Handsome does. How to make your daughter better looking. [With plates.] pp. v. 104. *D. Appleton-Century Co.: New York; London*, 1938. 8° 7383. tt. 18

CADET. The Cadet. *See* LIVERPOOL.—*H.M.S. Conway School Ship.*

—— The Cadet; a poem, in six parts: containing Remarks on British India. To which is added, Egbert and Amelia in four parts; with other poems. By a late Resident in the East [i.e. John H. Caunter]. 2 vol. *Robert Jennings: London*, 1814. 12°. 993. d. 46

CADET.

—— The Cadet. The official monthly journal of the 6th Cadet Batt., The Royal Hampshire Regiment. *See* ENGLAND.—*Army.*—*Cadets.*—*6th Cadet Battalion, Royal Hampshire Regiment.*

—— Scraps and Scrappers. By Cadet. pp. 96. *Drane's: London,* [1922.] 8°. **012354**. df. **50**.

CADET JOURNAL. *See* ENGLAND.—*Army Cadet Force Association.*

CADET NURSE CORPS NEWS. *See* UNITED STATES OF AMERICA.—*Public Health Service.—Division of Nurse Education.*

CADET REVIEW. *See* ENGLAND.—*Army Cadet Force Association.*

CADET ( ) Les Journées mémorables de juillet 1830. [A song.] *See* GARDY (J. A.) Jérôme Buteux et le père Chopin aux barricades, *etc.* 1830. 12°. **11474**. e. **7**. **(2.)**

CADET ( ) and **LANGET** ( )

—— Adresse aux Français. La liberté ou la mort, guerre éternelle aux traîtres et aux intrigans. [Signed: Cadet, Langet.] pp. 8. *Paris,* [1793.] 8°. **R. 212**. **(19.)**

CADET (AUGUSTE) *See* CADET (Louis A.)

CADET (CHARLES LOUIS) *See* CADET DE GASSICOURT.

CADET (ERNEST) Les Caisses des écoles. pp. 27. *Paris,* 1889. 8°. [*Mémoires et documents scolaires publiés par le Musée Pédagogique.* sér. 2. fasc. 40.] **S.E.124/52.**

—— Dictionnaire de la législation usuelle. Comprenant les éléments du droit civil, commercial, *etc.* pp. 746. *Paris,* 1869. 12°. **5423**. aaa. **10**.

—— Études morales sur la société contemporaine. Le mariage en France. Statistique, réformes, *etc.* [With plates and a map.] pp. xiv. 249. *Paris,* 1870. 8°. **8416**. g. **34**.

CADET (FÉLIX) *See* AUBIGNÉ (F. d') *Marchioness de Maintenon.* [*Letters, etc.—Selections.*] Madame de Maintenon . . . Choix de lettres . . . par F. Cadet . . . et . . . E. Darin. 1884. 12°. **8310**. aaa. **16**.

—— *See* PASCAL (B.) Opuscules philosophiques . . . Édition . . . précédée d'une introduction . . . et accompagnée de notes critiques par F. Cadet. 1864. 12°. **8464**. aaa. **46**. (**4**.)

—— *See* PIGEONNEAU (H.) Manuel encyclopédique du commerce, rédigé par MM. Pigeonneau . . . F. Cadet, *etc.* 1879. 8°. **8229**. p. **16**.

—— *See* SENECA (L. A.) [*Letters.—French.*] Lettres choisis de Sénèque à Lucilius. Édition . . . précédée d'une introduction . . . et accompagnée de notes critiques par F. Cadet. 1864. 8°. **10905**. c. **27**.

—— L'Éducation à Port-Royal. Saint-Cyran, Arnauld, Lancelot, Nicole, De Saci, Guyot, Coustel, Fontaine, J. Pascal. Extraits précédés d'une introduction par F. Cadet. pp. 316. *Paris,* 1887. 8°. **8356**. aaa. **23**.

—— Port-Royal Education . . . Translated, with an index, by Adnah D. Jones. pp. iv. 260. *Swan Sonnenschein & Co.: London,* 1898. 8°. **8311**. bb. **20**.

—— Examen du Traité des devoirs de Cicéron, *etc.* pp. 140. *Reims,* 1865. 8°. **8460**. f. **5**.

CADET (FÉLIX)

—— Histoire de l'économie politique. Les précurseurs. Boisguilbert. Vauban. Quesnay. Turgot. pp. 248. 1869. 8°. *See* RHEIMS.—*Société Industrielle de Reims.* **8207**. h. **4**.

—— Pierre de Boisguilbert, précurseur des économistes, 1646–1714. Sa vie, ses travaux, son influence. pp. x. 442. *Paris,* 1870. 8°. **10659**. w. **10**.

—— Turgot, 1727–1781. [With a portrait.] pp. 190. *Paris,* [1873.] 16°. [*Bibliothèque Franklin.* no. 12.] **12209**. a. **34**.

CADET (JEAN MARCEL) *See* BOOK. [*Book of the Dead.—Papyri, etc. written for special individuals.—Khaās-Ast.*] Copie figurée d'un rouleau de papyrus trouvé à Thèbes dans un tombeau des Rois, publiée par M. Cadet. 1805. 4°. **879**. m. **6**.

—— Corse. Restauration de cette île. pp. 30. [*Paris,* 1824.] 4°. T. **74***. (**8**.)

—— Du sol, de l'air et des eaux d'Espagne, précautions qu'ils exigent. pp. xii. 65. *Paris,* 1823. 8°. T. **2052**. (**9**.)

—— Mémoire sur les bois de Corse, et observations générales sur l'époque de la coupe des arbres. pp. 29 [33]. *Paris,* 1791. 8°. F. **532**. (**1**.)

—— Mémoire sur les jaspes et autres pierres précieuses de l'isle de Corse. Suivi de notes sur l'histoire naturelle, de la traduction du Critias et de divers morceaux du Timée de Platon. pp. 239. *Bastia,* 1785. 8°. **987**. a. **25**.

CADET (JOSEPH LUCIEN THÉOPHILE) Essai sur la pneumatose gastro-intestinale des hystériques, *etc.* pp. 60. *Paris,* 1871. 4°. [*Collection des thèses soutenues à la Faculté de Médecine de Paris.* An 1871. tom. 2.] **7373**. m. **16**.

CADET (LOUIS) Oromazes, Prince de Perse. Tragédie. [In verse.] pp. 63. *A. Lesselin: Paris,* 1651. 4°. **164**. c. **53**.

CADET (LOUIS AUGUSTE) Hygiène, inhumation, crémation ou incinération des corps . . . Avec huit gravures hors texte. Deuxième édition. pp. 252. *Paris,* [1877.] 8°. **7390**. de. **5**.

CADET (MARIANNA) Le Benignità del sommo pontefice papa Pio IX. Canto, *etc.* [By M. Cadet.] pp. 15. [1846.] 8°. *See* PIUS IX., *Pope.* **899**. e. **14**. (**3**.)

CADET (MATHURIN JEAN BAPTISTE) Des différentes espèces de gravelles, et de leurs rapports avec le régime alimentaire, *etc.* pp. 23. *Paris,* 1847. 4°. [*Collection des thèses soutenues à la Faculté de Médecine de Paris.* An 1847. tom. 2.] **7372**. a. **10**.

CADET (P.) Université de France. Académie de Strasbourg. Acte public pour la licence, *etc.* (Jus romanum. De servitutibus, *etc.*—Droit civil français. Des servitudes, *etc.*) pp. 65. *Strasbourg,* 1863. 8°. **5408**. b. **8**.

CADET (THÉODORE FERDINAND) Quelques considérations générales sur l'iritis. Thèse, *etc.* pp. 25. *Paris,* 1837. 4°. **1184**. h. **14**. (**26**.)

CADET DE GASSICOURT (CHARLES JULES ERNEST) Recherches sur la rupture des kystes hydatiques du foie à travers la paroi abdominale et dans les organes voisins, *etc.* pp. 83. *Paris,* 1856. 4°. [*Collection des thèses soutenues à la Faculté de Médecine de Paris.* An 1856. tom. 1.] **7372**. i. **4**.

—— Traité clinique des maladies de l'enfance, *etc.* 3 vol. *Paris,* 1880–84. 8°. **7580**. f. **27**.

CADET DE GASSICOURT (Charles Louis) *See* Alissan de Chazet (A. R. P.) and Cadet de Gassicourt (C. L.) Finot, *etc.* 1805. 8°. **11738.** c. **1.** (**4.**)

—— *See* Periodical Publications.—*Paris.* Bulletin de pharmacie, rédigé par Parmentier, C. L. Cadet, *etc.* 1809, *etc.* 8°. P.P. **3188.** c.

—— L'Anti-Novateur, ou les Lectures de M. Jérome. Par le C. C. G. [Signed: C. G. C. D. V., i.e. C. L. F. Cadet de Gassicourt.] pp. 46. 1797. 8°. *See* V., C. G. C. D. R. **671.** (**9.**)

—— [Another copy.] F. **422.** (**2.**)

—— [Another copy.] L'Anti-novateur, *etc.* [Signed: C. G. C. D. V., i.e. C. L. Cadet de Gassicourt.] 1797. 8°. *See* V., C. G. C. D. R. **214.** (**4.**)

—— [Another copy.] L'Anti-novateur, *etc.* [Signed: C. G. C. D. V., i.e. C. L. Cadet de Gassicourt.] 1797. 8°. *See* V., C. G. C. D. R. **214.** (**11.**)

—— Discours prononcé par le citoyen Cadet-Gassicourt à l'inauguration des bustes de Marat et Le Pelletier, *etc.* *See* Marat (J. P.) [*Appendix.*] Fête en l'honneur de Marat, *etc.* [1793.] 8°. **645.** a. **41.** (**2.**)

—— Essai sur la vie privée d'Honoré Gabriel Riquetti de Mirabeau. *See* Riquetti (H. G.) *Count de Mirabeau.* [*Miscellaneous Works.*] Œuvres choisies. tom. 1. 1820. 8°. **1207.** g. **11.**

—— Les Initiés, anciens et modernes; suite du Tombeau de Jacques Molai. Œuvre posthume par le C. C. L. C. G. D. L. S. D. M. B. C. D. V. [i.e. C. L. Cadet de Gassicourt, de la section de Mont Blanc, condamné de Vendémiaire.] pp. 32. [1796.] 8°. *See* V., C. L. C. G. D. L. S. D. M. B. C. D., *le C.* F. **467.** (**5.**)

—— [Another copy.] **4783.** bbb. **40.** (**2.**)

—— [Another edition.] pp. 35. [1796.] 8°. *See* V., C. L. C. G. D. L. S. D. M. B. C. D., *le C.* **4783.** c. **35.** (**2.**)

—— Mémoire sur le café. *See* Cadet de Vaux (A. A.) Dissertation sur le café, *etc.* 1806. 12°. **1145.** c. **50.**

—— Opinion d'un électeur du Département de la Seine, adressée à ses collègues. [By C. L. Cadet de Gassicourt?] pp. 16. 1817. 8°. *See* Seine, *Department of the.* R. **135.** (**1.**)

—— Projet d'institut nomade. (Extrait de la Revue encyclopédique.) pp. 37. *Paris,* 1820. 8°. **733.** d. **26.**

—— Réflexions sur les élections, et sur les principes du système électoral. Par un électeur du département de la Seine [i.e. C. L. Cadet de Gassicourt?]. pp. 48. 1816. 8°. *See* Réflexions. **1141.** h. **9.** (**2.**)

—— St Géran, ou la Nouvelle langue française, anecdote récente . . . Petite parodie d'un grand voyage. Seconde édition. [By C. L. Cadet de Gassicourt. With a plate.] pp. 139. 1812. 12°. *See* Saint Géran. **1079.** f. **12.**

—— Le Tombeau de Jacques Molai, ou le Secret des conspirateurs, à ceux qui veulent tout savoir. Œuvre posthume de C. L. C. G. D. L. S. D. M. B. C. D. V. [i.e. C. L. Cadet de Gassicourt, de la section de Mont Blanc, condamné de Vendémiaire.] pp. 31. an 4 [1796?]. 8°. *See* V., C. L. C. G. D. L. S. D. M. B. C. D. **4783.** c. **35.** (**1.**)

—— [Another copy.] **4783.** bbb. **40.** (**1.**)

—— [Another edition.] Le Tombeau de Jacques Molai, ou Histoire secrète et abrégée des initiés, anciens et modernes, des templiers, francs-maçons, illuminés, etc. Et recherches sur leur influence dans la révolution française . . . Seconde édition. pp. 162. *Paris,* an 5 [1796/7]. 12°. **4783.** b. **28.**

—— Voyage en Autriche, en Moravie et en Bavière, fait à suite de l'armée française, pendant la campagne de 18 . . . Avec une carte du théâtre de la guerre de 1809 Autriche, et des plans de bataille d'Essling et de Wagra [With maps.] pp. viii. 406. *Paris,* 1818. 8°. **9073.** df.

CADET DE GASSICOURT (Charles Louis Féli Dissertation sur le jalap; these, *etc.* pp. 84. *Pari* 1817. 4°. **1183.** d. **14.** (8

—— Premiers secours avant l'arrivée du médecin, ou Pet dictionnaire des cas d'urgence, à l'usage des gens d monde; suivi d'une instruction sur les champignons, *et* pp. xxiv. 264. pl. 8. *Paris,* 1845. 12°. **1405.** b. **1**

CADET DE GASSICOURT (Ernest) *See* Cadet d Gassicourt (Charles J. E.)

CADET DE GASSICOURT (Félix Clément Léo Histoire de l'abbaye de Cordillon . . . Illustrée de planches hors texte . . . Tome 1er.—Histoire, *et* pp. xxxiv. 260. pl. xii. *Caen,* 1906. 4°. **4633.** dd. *No more published.*

CADET DE GASSICOURT (Félix Clément Léon) an **DU FOURNEL DU ROURE DE PAULIN** (Edmon *Baron.*

—— L'Hermétisme dans l'art héraldiq . . . Avec 55 illustrations, 3 tableaux et 7 planches ho texte. pp. 182. *Paris,* 1907. 8°. **9902.** aa.

CADET DE VAUX (Antoine Alexis) *See* Labori ( ) *Chemist.* Observations sur les fosses d'aisanc . . . par MM. Laborie, Cadet le jeune, *etc.* 1778. 8°. **1172.** i. **10.** (7

—— *See* Rozier (F.) Cours complet d'agriculture . . Rédigé par les citoyens Chaptal . . . Cadet de-Vaux, *etc* 1801, *etc.* 4°. **35.** c. **3–1**

—— *See* Spielmann (J. R.) [Institutiones chemicae.] In stituts de chymie . . . traduits du latin . . . par M. Cad le jeune. 1770. 12°. **8905.** a. **3**

—— [De la goutte et du rhumatisme.] Untrügliches Mitt gegen Gicht und Rheumatismus. Aus dem französische Originale . . . verdeutscht. pp. 68. *Köln,* [1825?] 8° **7630.** b. **43.** (1

—— Dissertation sur le café; son historique, ses propriété et le procédé pour en obtenir la boisson la plus agréab . . . Suivie de son analyse; par Charles-Louis Cade pp. 120. *Paris,* 1806. 12°. **1145.** c. **5**

—— Instruction sur l'art de faire le vin, *etc.* pp. 68. *Pari* an 8 [1799/1800]. 8°. **1172.** i. **11.** (13

—— [Another edition.] L'Art de faire le vin, d'après doctrine de Chaptal. Instruction destinée aux vigneron *etc.* pp. 80. *Paris,* an 9 [1801]. 8°. **1172.** i. **11.** (14

—— Mémoire sur la gélatine des os, et son application l'économie alimentaire, privée et publique, *etc.* pp. 99. *Paris,* [1803.] 8°. B. **526.** (3

—— [Another copy.] **1038.** k. **20.** (2.

—— [Another copy.] **1172.** i. **11.** (15. *With a* ms. *letter from the author inserted.*

—— Mémoire sur la peinture au lait, *etc.* pp. 14. *Paris,* an 9 [1801]. 8°. **1043.** h. **13.** (6.)

—— Le Ménage ou l'emploi des fruits dans l'économi domestique; procédés à l'usage de la mère de famille, *et* pp. xxiv. 288. *Paris,* 1810. 8°. **7949.** a.

CADET DE VAUX (Antoine Alexis)

—— Moyen de prévenir et de détruire le méphitisme des murs, *etc.* pp. 8. *Paris*, an 9 [1801]. 8°. **1172**. i. **11**. (**5**.)

—— Observations sur la préparation du bouillon d'os dans les grands établissemens. pp. 8. [*Paris*, 1804?] 4°. B. **476**. (**3**.)

—— Observations sur la sécheresse, *etc.* pp. 14. [1800?] 8°. **966**. h. **34**. (**6**.)

—— Réflexions sur la diminution progressive des eaux. pp. 8. [1798.] 8°. **F. 487**. (**2**.)

—— [Traité de la culture du tabac.] Trattato della cultura del tabacco, e della preparazione della sua foglia, ridotte ai suoi veri principj . . . Traduzione italiana, con note di un professore d'agricoltura. pp. 19–88. *Firenze*, 1811. 12°. **7074**. k. **1**. (**4**.)

CADET EUSTACHE ( ) *See* **Râpée**, ***Quai de la.*** Le Déjeuné de la Rapée . . . Nouvelle édition . . . augmentée d'une Lettre de M. Cadet Eustache à M. Jerôme Du Bois, *etc.* [1755?] 12°. **12238**. e. **6**. (**9**.)

CADET-GASSICOURT (Félix) *See* Cadet de Gassicourt (Charles L. F.)

CADET-LA-RÈSSO ( ) *See* Cadet-La-Scie.

CADET-LA-SCIE ( ) *See* Roumanille (J.) Lou Mège de Cucugnan. Lou Colera. (Le Choléra . . . Traduction française de Cadet-La-Scie.) [1869.] 4°. **12350**. m. **6**.

CADETS OWN. Cadets Own. A monthly magazine. *See* England.—*Sons of Temperance.—London Grand Division.—Cadet Council.*

CADETT AND NEALL. *See* Periodical Publications. —*Ashtead.* Dry Plates . . . Edited by Cadett & Neall. [1892, *etc.*] 8°. P.P. **1912**. ed.

—— Cadett and Neall's Booklet of Photographic Faults and Failures. *See* Lambert (Frederick C.)

CADETT (Herbert) *See* Lawrence (Boyle) and Cadett (H.) Fin-de-Siècle Stories. [1892.] 8°. **012634**. f. **17**.

—— The Adventures of a Journalist. pp. 206. *Sands & Co.: London*, 1900. 8°. **12625**. aaa. **13**.

—— The Boys' Book of Battles, *etc.* pp. 305. *C. A. Pearson: London*, 1903 [1902]. 8°. **09008**. ee. **8**.

CADETT (James) *See* Gale (J. R. C.) and Cadett (J.) First Aid in Photography, *etc.* 1896. 8°. **8909**. h. **9**.

CADETT (James) and **SHEPHERD** (E. Sanger)

—— Orthochromatic and Three-Colour Photography—simplified. (6th edition.) pp. 31. *Cadett & Neall: Ashtead*, 1901. 8°. **08909**. e. **17**.

CADETT (Thomas) Timothy Cotton. A poem. 2 vol. *J. C. Hotten: London*, 1871, [73?] 8°. **11652**. aa. **2**.
Printed for the author. The author's name occurs in vol. 2 only.

CADEU, *Saint.* *See* Cadoc.

CADEY (Prudence) Broken Pattern, *etc.* pp. 359. *Fenland Press: London*, 1933. 8°. NN. **21580**.

—— Claudia Decides. pp. 352. *Constable & Co.: London* 1928. 8°. NN. **14308**'

CADFAN. *See* Cadvan.

CADFRYN-ROBERTS (John Augustus) *See* Roberts (J. A. C.)

CADGE (William) *See* Morton (Thomas) *Assistant Surgeon to University College Hospital.* The Surgical Anatomy of the Principal Regions of the Human Body. By T. Morton and W. Cadge. 1850, *etc.* 8°. **781**. h. **33**.

CADGER. Cager's Ball. Bold Robin Hood. [Two songs.] *Hodges: [London*, 1860?] *s. sh.* 4°. C. **116**. i. **1**. (**163**.)

—— The Cadgers Tear. (The Old Woman and her Cats.) [Two songs.] [*E. Hodges: London*, 1850?] *s. sh.* 4°. C. **116**. i. **1**. (**43**.)

—— Rummy Old Cadger am I, Home. [Two songs.] *E. Hodges:* [*London*, 1846?] *s. sh.* 4°. **11621**. k. **4**. (**69**.)

CADI. The Cadi: or, Amours among Moors. A comic opera in two acts, *etc.* [A translation of "Le Caïd" by T. M. F. Sauvage.] pp. 40. *S. G. Fairbrother: London*, [1851.] 8°. **1344**. l. **18**.

—— Le Cadi dupé, opéra-comique en un acte; par l'auteur du Maître en droit [i.e. P. R. Lemonnier], *etc.* [With musical notes.] pp. 64. *Paris*, 1761. 8°. [*Nouveau théâtre de la Foire.* tom. 5.] **11735**. d. **2**.

—— [Another issue.] *Paris*, 1761. 8°. **11738**. h. **23**. (**2**.)

—— [Another issue.] pp. 50. *Paris*, 1761. 8°. **11737**. b. **10**.
Pp. 1–48 are another issue of pp. 1–48 of the preceding, pp. 49–50 a resetting of pp. 53–54.

—— [Another edition.] pp. 39. *Paris*, 1771. 8°. [*Recueil général des opéra bouffons.* tom. 5.] **11735**. b. **2**.

CADIAT (Ernest) *See* Ledieu (A.) and Cadiat (E.) Le Nouveau matériel naval, *etc.* 1889, *etc.* 8° & 4°. **8807**. d. **28**.

CADIAT (Ernest) and **DUBOST** (Lucien)

—— Traité pratique d'électricité industrielle, *etc.* pp. iii. 496. *Paris*, 1885. 8°. **8757**. dd. **11**.

—— Deuxième édition, *etc.* pp. v. 583. *Paris*, 1886. 8°. **8757**. g. **13**.

—— Cinquième édition, *etc.* pp. vi. 721. *Paris*, 1896. 8°. **8758**. dd. **3**.

CADIAT (L. Oscar) Étude sur l'anatomie normale et les tumeurs du sein chez la femme, *etc.* pp. 62. pl. iii. *Paris*, 1875. 4°. [*Collection des thèses soutenues à la Faculté de Médecine de Paris.* An 1875. tom. 4.] **7374**. b.

—— Traité d'anatomie générale appliquée à la médecine . . . Avec une introduction de M. le professeur Ch. Robin, *etc.* 2 tom. *Paris*, 1879, 81. 8°. **7421**. h. **30**.

CADIC (François) Contes & légendes de Bretagne . . avec commentaires explicatifs. tom. 1. pp. x. 334. *Paris, Hennebont*, 1914. 8°. **12430**. r. **2**.
No more published.

CADIC (Jean Mathurin) En Est. Guerz brehonek é pemb loden. La Moisson. Poème breton, *etc. Bret. & Fr.* pp. x. 95. *Vannes*, 1897. 8°. **11595**. g. **17**.

CADICAMO (Giuseppe) Dèlia. Romanza orientale. pp. 12. *Milano*, 1875. 12°. **11436**. d. **49**.

CADIER, *Frères.* Au Pays des isards . . . Seconde édition, *etc.* [With illustrations and maps.] 2 pt. *Osse*, 1903, 04. 8°. **10162**. cc. **20**.
Pt. 1 only is of the second edition.

CADIER (Albert) *Docteur.* Manuel de laryngoscopie et de laryngologie, *etc.* pp. 245. *Paris,* 1880. 12°. **7616. a. 12.**

—— Quelques considérations sur les blessures d'artères, *etc.* pp. 46. *Paris,* 1866. 4°. [*Collection des thèses soutenues à la Faculté de Médecine de Paris.* An 1866. tom. 2.] **7373. g. 5.**

CADIER (Albert) *Pastor at Pau.* A French Mission in Spain. The story of evangelisation in Haut Aragon . . . Translated from the French. [With plates.] pp. 36. *R.T.S.: London,* 1925. 8°. **4767. de. 63.**

CADIER (Alfred) Osse. Histoire de l'Église réformée de la vallée d'Aspe, *etc.* [With a map.] pp. xv. 391. *Paris,* 1892. 8°. **4629. k. 24.**

CADIER (Jacobus Petrus Haksteen de) Dissertatio inauguralis juridica, de emancipatione, *etc.* pp. 24. *Leodii,* [1830.] 4°. **498. f. 16. (17.)**

CADIER (Jean)

—— *See* Calvin (Jean) [*Institutio Christianae Religionis.—French.*] Institution de la religion chrétienne . . . Édition nouvelle, *etc.* [Prepared by J. Cadier and P. Marcel.] 1955, etc. 8°. **03560.m.6.**

—— *See* Vernier (J. F.) Jean-Frédéric Vernier . . . d'après son autobiographie . . . Par J. Cadier. 1934. 8°. **010665. de. 39.**

CADIER (Léon) *See* Béarn.—*États.* Le Livre des syndics des états de Béarn . . . Publié . . . par L. Cadier. 1889. 8°. [*Archives historiques de la Gascogne.* fasc. 18.] **Ac. 6772/2.**

—— *See* Faith, *Saint, Priory of, at Morlàas.* Cartulaire de Sainte Foi de Morlàas. Publié par L. Cadier. 1884. 8°. **04782. h. 50.**

—— *See* Merry, *Saint, Church of, at Paris.* Cartulaire et censier de Saint-Merry de Paris, *etc.* (Publié par L. Cadier.) 1891. 8°. [*Mémoires de la Société de l'Histoire de Paris.* tom. 18.] **Ac. 6883/2.**

—— Bulles originales du xiiie siècle conservées dans les archives de Navarre. 1887. *See* Rome.—*École Française.* Mélanges d'archéologie et d'histoire. année 7. [1881, *etc.*] 8°. **Ac. 5233.**

—— Essai sur l'administration du royaume de Sicile sous Charles Ier et Charles II d'Anjou. pp. viii. 310. *Paris,* 1891. 8°. [*Bibliothèque des Écoles Françaises d'Athènes et de Rome.* fasc. 59.] **Ac. 5206/2.**

—— Les États de Béarn depuis leurs origines jusqu'au commencement du xvie siècle. Étude sur l'histoire et l'administration d'un pays d'états. pp. xxiv. 483. *Paris,* 1888. 8°. **9226. k. 7.**

—— Manuscrits de la Bibliothèque d'Auch. [By L. Cadier.] 1886. 8°. [*Catalogue général des manuscrits des bibliothèques publiques de France.* Départements. tom. 4.] *See* Auch.—*Bibliothèque.* **Bar T. 2. a.**

—— Manuscrits de la Bibliothèque de Bayonne. [By L. Cadier.] 1888. 8°. [*Catalogue général des manuscrits des bibliothèques publiques de France.* Départements. tom. 9.] *See* Bayonne.—*Bibliothèque.* **Bar T. 2. a.**

—— Manuscrits de la Bibliothèque de Carcassonne. [By L. Cadier.] 1891. 8°. [*Catalogue général des manuscrits des bibliothèques publiques de France.* Départements. tom. 13.] *See* Carcassonne.—*Bibliothèque.* **Bar.T.3.b.**

—— Manuscrits de la Bibliothèque de Perpignan. [By L. Cadier.] 1891. 8°. [*Catalogue général des manuscrits des bibliothèques publiques de France.* Départements. tom. 13.] *See* Perpignan.—*Bibliothèque.* **Bar.T.3.b.**

CADIÈRE (Catherine) *See* Cadière (Marie C.)

CADIÈRE (Estienne Thomas) *See* Cadière (M. Recueil des mémoires ou factums qui ont paru pardev le Parlement de Provence: pour et contre la demois C. Cadière, F. E.-T. Cadière, *etc.* 1731. fol. **5405. g.**

CADIÈRE (François) *See* Cadière (M. C.) Recueil mémoires ou factums qui ont paru pardevant le Parlem de Provence: pour et contre la demoiselle C. Cadière . F. E.-T. Cadière, *etc.* 1731. fol. **5405. g.**

CADIÈRE (Léopold)

—— Croyances et pratiques religieuses des viêtnamiens, [With illustrations and a portrait.] pp. 343. vol. 2, ***Saigon; Limoges*** **[printed], 1955, 57. 8°.** **Ac. 8814. f. 4.**

One of the " Publications hors série de l'École Franç d'Extrême Orient."

Tom. 3 was published in Paris.

—— Paul Khiêm, clerc minoré, élève du gr séminaire de Phu-Xuân—Hué. (Extrait des " Ann de la Société des Missions-Étrangères.") pp. 38. *Hongkong,* 1905. 8°. **4804. g. 7.**

—— Phonétique annamite, dialecte du Haut-Ann pp. xiii. 113. *Paris,* 1902. 8°. [*Publications de l'É Française d'Extrême-Orient.* vol. 3.] **Ac. 8814.**

—— Tableau chronologique des dynasties annamites. 19 *See* Saigon.—*École Française d'Extrême Orient.* Bulle *etc.* tom. 5. no. 1, 2. 1901, *etc.* 8°. **15012.**

CADIÈRE (Léopold) and **PELLIOT** (Paul)

—— Première étude sur les sour annamites de l'histoire d'Annam. 1904. *See* Saigon *École Française d'Extrême-Orient.* Bulletin, *etc.* tom. no. 3. 1901, *etc.* 8°. **15012.**

CADIÈRE (Marie Catherine) *See* Chaudon (*Avocat.* Dénonciation des écrits de Me Chaudon, [With reference to the action brought against J. B. Gir by M. C. Cadière.] 1731. fol. **1244. l.**

—— *See* Girard (J. B.) *Jesuit.* A Compleat Translatior the Memorial of the Jesuit Father John Baptist Gir . . . against M. C. Cadiere, *etc.* 1732. 12°. **5405. aa**

—— *See* Girard (J. B.) *Jesuit.* A Defence of F. J Baptist Girard . . . against the accusation of M. Cadiere. 1732, *etc.* 8°. **1131. h. 33.**

—— —— 1731. 8°. **4866. c.**

—— *See* Girard (J. B.) *Jesuit.* Jugement du procez entr père Girard et la D^{lle} Cadière. [1731.] *s. sh.* fol. **1244. l.**

—— *See* Girard (J. B.) *Jesuit.* Mémoire instructif pou père Jean-Baptiste Girard . . . contre M.-C. Cadière, 1731. 8°. **4092. dd. 13.**

—— *See* Girard (J. B.) *Jesuit.* The Tryal of Father Jo Baptist Girard . . . at the instance of Miss M. C. Cadi *etc.* 1732. 4°. **1131. h. 33.**

—— *See* Henley (John) called " *Orator* Henley." A Lect on High Fits of Zeal; or Mrs. Cadiere's raptures, *etc.* [1732 ?] 8°. **4376. aaa.**

—— *See* Provence.—*Parlement.* Reflexions sur l'arrêt Parlement d'Aix, intervenu dans l'affaire de la Demois Cadière, contre le P. Girard Jésuite. 1731. 4°. **1482. c.**

—— *See* Smith (Michael) *Vicar of South Mimms.* Fat Girard and Miss Cadière, *etc.* 1840. 8°. **11645. df.**

CADIÈRE (MARIE CATHERINE)

—— The Case of Mary Katherine Cadiere, against the Jesuite Father John Baptist Girard, *etc.* pp. viii. 6–47. *Printed for the Proprietor: London,* 1731. 12°. **1131**. h. **33**. (**7**.)

—— Factum pour Marie Catherine Cadière contre le père Jean Baptiste Girard, Jésuite, où ce religieux est accusé de l'avoir portée . . . aux plus criminels excès de l'impudicité, *etc.* pp. 164. *Aix,* 1731. 8°. **4092**. dd. **13**. (**1**.)

—— [Another issue.] *La Haye,* 1731. 8°. **4092**. cc. **23**.

—— A Compleat Translation of the whole Case of Mary Catherine Cadiere, against the Jesuite Father John Baptist Girard . . . The sixth edition. [A translation of "Factum pour Marie Catherine Cadière."] pp. 214. *J. Millan: London,* 1732. 12°. **5405**. aa. **8**.

—— [Another edition.] pp. 184. *J. Millan: London,* 1732. 12°. **881**. c. **2**.

—— The Case of Mrs. Mary Catharine Cadiere, against the Jesuit Father John Baptiste Girard . . . With a preface by the publisher . . . The fifth edition. [An abridged translation of "Factum pour Marie Catherine Cadière."] pp. vi. 96. *J. Roberts: London,* 1732. 8°. **1131**. h. **33**. (**8**.)

—— The sixth edition corrected. pp. vi. 96. *J. Roberts: London,* 1732. 8°. **518**. c. **21**. (**2**.)

—— The tenth edition corrected. pp. vi. 80. *Allan Ramsay & Gavin Hamilton: Edinburgh,* 1730 [1732 ?]. 8°. **1131**. f. **36**.

—— The eleventh edition corrected. pp. vi. 96. *J. Roberts: London,* 1732. 8°. **1132**. f. **49**.

—— Histoire du procez entre Demoiselle Cadière, & P. Cadière jacobin, Mre. Cadière prêtre, P. Nicolas prieur des Carmes déchaussez de Toulon, d'une part ; & le P. Girard jésuite, Recteur du Séminaire royal de Toulon, de l'autre. pp. 40. [1731.] 8°. **1132**. a. **36**.

—— Memoirs of Miss Mary Catherine Cadiere, and Father Girard, Jesuit . . . In an epistle from a person of quality at Paris to his correspondent in London. pp. 32. *J. Isted: London,* 1731. 8°. **518**. c. **20**. (**5**.)

—— Recueil des mémoires ou factums qui ont paru pardevant le Parlement de Provence: pour et contre la demoiselle Catherine Cadière, F. Estienne Thomas Cadière, et Messire François Cadière, ses frères, le P. Girard, et le P. Nicolas. 30 pt. *Marseille,* 1731. fol. **5405**. g. **3**.
A collection of separately published items, with a general titlepage.

—— Recueil général des pièces concernant le procez entre la demoiselle Cadière . . . et le père Girard. 2 tom. 1731. fol. **1244**. l. **13**.
A collection of separately published items, with a general titlepage, and list of contents for each tom. In this copy portraits have been inserted, and additional MS. *and printed matter has been bound in at the end.*

—— [Another edition.] 8 tom. *La Haye,* 1731. 12°. **1132**. a. **1–8**.
Another edition, of which the titlepage reads "Recueil général des pièces contenues au procez du père Jean-Baptiste Girard . . . et de demoiselle Catherine Cadière," is entered under GIRARD (*J. B.*) *Jesuit.*

—— Suite des procédures de Catherine Cadière, contre le R. Père Girard, contenant la réponse au mémoire instructif de ce Jésuite, et plusieurs autres pièces, *etc.* 2 pt. *La Haye,* 1731. 8°. **1244**. b. **3**.

CADIÈRE (MARIE CATHERINE)

—— A Compleat Translation of the Sequel of the Proceedings of Mary Catherine Cadière, against the Jesuit Father John Baptist Girard, *etc.* pp. 255. *J. Millan: London,* 1732. 12°. **878**. f. **1**.

—— The second edition. pp. 255. *J. Millan: London,* 1732. 12°. **5405**. aa. **10**.

—— Thirty two Pieces, never before translated, of the Proceedings upon the Tryal of M. Cadiere, and F. Girard. Which, with the 3 vols. intituled, The Compleat Translations, is a full account of that . . . affair. pp. 164. *J. Millan: London,* 1732. 12°. **5405**. aa. **11**.

CADIÈRES (RAOUL) *See* BAUDIN (P.) and CADIÈRES (R.) Les grandes journées populaires, *etc.* [1899.] 8°. **09200**. i. **2**.

CADIERGUES (GEORGES) Histoire de la Seigneurie de La Capelle-Merlival—La Capelle-Merlival, Saint Maurice, Labathude & Rudelle—depuis ses origines jusqu'à 1789 . . . Avec de nombreuses illustrations, plans, cartes, *etc.* pp. iii. 270. lxxxvii. *Cahors,* 1906 [1905]. 8°. **010169**. g. **12**.

CADIERUS (NICOLAUS) *See* VINAC (H. de) *de Prato Florido.* Sermones dñicales sup. Euãgelia et epistolas de tempore hyemali, *etc.* [Edited by N. Cadierus.] 1528. 8°. **846**. k. **6**.

CADIEU (M. J. C.) Essai sur l'hydrophobie, ou la rage communiquée ; thèse, *etc.* pp. 22. *Paris,* 1812. 4°. **1182**. i. **6**. (**3**.)

CADIEUX ET DERÔME. *See* EPHEMERIDES. Le Canada ecclésiastique. Almanach-annuaire . . . publié par Cadieux & Derôme, *etc.* [1889, *etc.*] 12°. **P.P. 2539**. f.

CADIEUX (JOSEPH) Livre généalogique de la famille. pp. 226. *Montréal,* 1897. 4°. **9906**. b. **18**.

CADIEUX (LOUIS EDOUARD) Practical Talks with the Christian Child. A brief manual of manners and morals. pp. 59. *American Book Co.: New York,* [1914.] 16°. **8410**. de. **56**.

CADIGAN (JEANA JOSEPHINE)

—— Management Mechanised Accounting, *etc.* pp. xv. 145. *Gee & Co.: Potters Bar,* 1943. 8°. **8231**. bb. **61**.

CADIGAN (ROBERT J.)

—— September to June. (Stories of school and college life.) Edited by R. J. Cadigan. pp. x. 424. *D. Appleton-Century Co.: New York,* [1942.] 8°. **08385**. g. **12**.

CADIGO. The Game of Cadigo. (Brancaster Golf Course. The eighteen original sketches by Major Oswald Ames.) *Unwin Bros.: [London,* 1908.] 4°. N.L. Tab. **1**. e. **6**.

ČADÍK (JINDŘICH)

—— Augustin Němejc, *etc.* [With plates, including reproductions and a portrait.] pp. 178. *v Praze,* 1940. 8°. [*Česká akademie věd a umění. Separately published obituaries.*] Ac. **799/20**. (**47**.)

CADILHAC (ANTOINE DE LA MOTHE) *See* LA MOTHE CADILHAC.

CADILHAC (ARTHUR MARIO AGRICOLA COLLIER GALLETTI DI) *See* GALLETTI DI CADILHAC.

CADILHAC (Désiré) Hommage funèbre à la mémoire de Monseigneur Charles-Thomas Thibault [in verse] . . . Suivi de Les Trois hôtes, souvenir poétique dédié à Mgr. Ramadié . . . à l'occasion de son sacre et de son prochain départ de Béziers. [Edited by E. Séguin.] pp. 19. *Montpellier*, 1865. 8°. **4865**. dd. **41**. (7.)

—— Renouveau. [Poems.] pp. 364. *Paris*, 1865. 18°. **11482**. ccc. **19**.

CADILHAC (*Hon.* Margaret Isabella Galletti di) *See* Galletti di Cadilhac.

CADILHAC (Paul Émile) Les Projets de régionalisme administratif. pp. 138. *Paris*, 1921. 8°. **08052**. dd. **3**.

CADILHAC (R. C. Galletti di) *See* Galletti di Cadilhac.

CADILHAC DE MADIÈRES (Paulin) Essai de la chlorose. Thèse, *etc.* pp. 58. *Montpellier*, 1850. 4°. **7379**. b. **2**. (4.)

CADILHON (F. J.) De l'impaludisme chronique, *etc.* pp. 64. *Paris*, 1869. 4°. [*Collection des thèses soutenues à la Faculté de Médecine de Paris.* An 1869. tom. 3.] **7373**. k. **9**.

CADILLAC, *Ship.* The 'Cadillac' Magazine. vol. 1. no. 5. *Bristol*, [1912.] 8°. **08806**. c. **41**.

CADILLA DE MARTINEZ (Maria) La Poesía Popular en Puerto Rico . . . Tésis doctoral. [With a bibliography.] pp. 366. *Madrid*, 1933. 8°. **11855**. dd. **15**.

—— Rememorando el pasado heroico. [A history of Puerto Rico.] pp. 667. *Arecibo*, 1946. 8°. **9773**. aaa. **22**.

CA' DI MASSER (Leonardo da) *See* Leonardo, *da Ca' di Masser.*

CADINOUCHE (Moëdine A.) Corps cancérigènes, corps cancéricides. Les données actuelles du problème étiologique du cancer et leurs conséquences thérapeutiques. pp. 78. *Paris*, 1935. 8°. **7439**. ppp. **13**.

CADIOLI (Giovanni) Descrizione delle pitture, sculture ed architetture che si osservano nella città di Mantova, e ne' suoi contorni, *etc.* pp. 136. *Mantova*, 1763. 8°. **7807**. a. **7**.

—— *See* Susani (G.) Nuovo prospetto delle pitture, sculture ed architetture di Mantova, *etc.* [Based in part on "Descrizione delle pitture, sculture ed architetture di Mantova" by G. Cadioli.] 1818. 8°. **10132**. f. **8**.

CADIOT (Clara) *See* Loti (P.) *pseud.* [Pêcheur d'Islande.] An Iceland Fisherman . . . Copyright translation by C. Cadiot. [1888.] 8°. **012547**. f. **1**.

CADIOT (Émile) Les Catholiques allemands. *See* Gachow (E.) Histoire de la théophilanthropie, *etc.* 1870. 8°. **4629**. aaa. **34**.

—— Université de France. Faculté de Théologie protestante de Strasbourg. Essai sur les conditions d'une traduction populaire de la Bible en langue française. Thèse, *etc.* pp. 106. *Strasbourg*, 1868. 8°. **3678**. bb. **20**. (8.)

CADIOT (J. A.) An Authentic Narrative of the Conversion to the Protestant Faith, and of the Death of J. A. Cadiot, . . . Translated from the French. pp. 96. *James Nisbet: London*, 1827. 8°. **1126**. c. **8**.

CADIOT (Marcellin) Tablettes des révolutions de la France de 1789 à 1848 . . . ou Précis historique des conflits des pouvoirs souverains dans les affaires d'état. pp. 100. *Paris*, 1848. 16°. **8052**. b. **12**.

CADIOT (Pierre Juste) [Études de pathologie et clinique.] Studies in Clinical Veterinary Medicine and Surgery . . . Translated, edited and supplemented w 49 new articles . . . by Jno. A. W. Dollar. pp. xv. 6 *David Douglas: Edinburgh*, 1900. 8°. **07293**. m.

—— Roaring in Horses: its pathology and treatment . Translated . . . by Thomas J. Watt Dollar, *etc.* pp. *Swan Sonnenschein & Co.: London*, 1892. 8°. **7293**. bbb.

CADIOT (Pierre Juste) and **ALMY** (J.)

—— [Traité de thérapeutique chirurgi des animaux domestiques.] A Treatise on Surg Therapeutics of Domestic Animals . . . Translated A. Liautard. vol. 1. pp. xv. 580. *Baillière & C London*, 1907. 8°. **07291**. h.
No more published.

CADIOT (Prosper) De la pneumonie fibrineuse, *etc.* pp *Paris*, 1855. 4°. [*Collection des thèses soutenues Faculté de Médecine de Paris.* An 1855. tom. 3.] **7372**. **I**

CADIOU (Paul) Les Chants de la Corse. pp. 93. *Ren* 1897. 8°. **011483**.

CADIOU (René) *See* Origen. Commentaires inédits Psaumes. Étude sur les textes d'Origène contenus da manuscrit Vindobonensis 8. Par R. Cadiou. 1936. **03089**. i.

—— Introduction au système d'Origène. pp. 115. *P* 1932. 8°. **3670**. bb.

—— La Jeunesse d'Origène. Histoire de l'école d'Alexan au début du IIIe siècle. pp. 424. *Paris*, 1935. [*Études de Théologie Historique.*] **2201**. dd. **I**
The date on the wrapper is 1936.

CADISCH (Anita Elsa Steiner) *See* Steiner-Cal (A. E.)

CADISCH (Joos)

—— Geologie der Schweizer Alpen . . . Zweite Auflage, fasst unter Mitarbeit von Dr. E. Niggli. [With illu tions.] pp. xi. 480. *Basel*, 1953. 8°. **7111**. ee

CADISCH (Joos) and **STRECKELSEN** (Albert)

—— Geologisches Panorama von der Weissfluh bei Da Bearbeitet von J. Cadisch und A. Streckeisen. Bei Geologisches Panorama vom Cotschnagrat. Bearb von A. Streckeisen und R. Gees. (Gebirgszeichnung M. Adrian.) Herausgegeben von der Naturforsche Gesellschaft Davos, *etc.* [With maps.] pp. 12. [1950.] 8°. *See* Davos.—*Naturforschende Gesellscha* **7111**. e

CADIVEC (Edith)

—— Bekenntnisse und Erlebnisse. [With a portrait.] pp. 346. *Privately printed*, [1930?] 8°. Cup. **363**. **I**

CADIX. *See* Cadiz.

CADIX (Albert) L'Immoralité de la morale cléri pp. viii. 40. *Besançon*, 1901. 8°. **3902**. c. **36**.

CADIX (Maurice) Essai historique sur la réforr Besançon au XVIe siècle d'après des documents iné Avec plan et illustrations, *etc.* pp. 175. *Montai* 1905. 8°. **4632**. df

CADIZ.

OFFICIAL DOCUMENTS.

—— Por parte de la Ciudad de Cadiz, informando con le ha mandado, de las conueniencias, y vtilidades q seguiran, de despachar en su puerto y bahia las arm y flotas, y las objeciones que contra esto se han pues satisfaziendo a ellas. ff. 6. [*Cadiz?* 1630?] fol. C. **62**. i. **18**.

Begin. Señor. La Ciudad de Cadiz, *etc.* [A petition o the King protesting against the request of the city of Seville for a monopoly of the sea-trade of Spain.] ff. 17. *Cadiz,* 1695.] fol. **1323.** k. **16.** (**21.**)

Bando. D. Andres Lopez, *etc.* [Prohibiting games of chance. 16 May 1810.] [*Cadiz,* 1810.] *s. sh.* fol. **1323.** k. **18.** (**22.**)

Edicto. D. Andres Lopez, *etc.* [Regulating the coach-fares between Cadiz and the Isle of Leon. 28 May 1810.] *Cadiz,* 1810.] *s. sh.* fol. **1323.** k. **18.** (**23.**)

MUNICIPAL INSTITUTIONS.

CABILDO.

Manifiesto. Bien consta á este respetable público, *etc.* Announcing the names of local representatives chosen to elect a deputy to the Cortes. 24 July 1810.] [*Cadiz,* 1810.] *s. sh.* fol. **1323.** k. **18.** (**29.**)

Edicto. Sin embargo, *etc.* [Announcing the preliminary elections for the Cortes. 26 July 1810.] [*Cadiz,* 1810.] *s. sh.* fol. **1323.** k. **18.** (**27.**)

Manifiesto. Por virtud del edicto, *etc.* [Announcing the election of Don Andres Morales as deputy to the Cortes. 18 Aug. 1810.] [*Cadiz,* 1810.] *s. sh.* fol. **1323.** k. **18.** (**34.**)

JUNTA DE PRESIDENCIA DE ELECCIONES PARA CORTES.

Edicto. Habitantes de Cadiz, *etc.* [On the forthcoming elections for the Cortes. 17 July 1810.] [*Cadiz,* 1810.] fol. **1323.** k. **18.** (**28.**)

JUNTA SUPERIOR DE GOBIERNO.

Coleccion de Providencias Dadas en la Ciudad de Cadiz para el Establecimiento de su Junta Superior de Gobierno, *etc.* pp. 24. *Mexico,* 1810. 4°. **9180.** d. **1.** (**26.**)

Resumen . . . de la entrada y salida de caudales de la tesorería . . . desde 1.° de febrero (hasta 30 de junio), *etc.* 4 pt. [*Cadiz,* 1810.] fol. **1323.** k. **18.** (**39–42.**)

La Junta Superior de Cadiz á la América Española. (Para enteraros de la verdad de los acontecimientos, manifestaros la serie de sus operaciones, y mostraros el rumbo por donde vuestra lealtad debe seguirnos para la salvacion de la patria.) [28 Feb. 1910.] [*Cádiz,* 1810.] fol. **1323.** k. **18.** (**16.**)

Caudales invertidos en los objetos que se expresan, desde primero de febrero hasta quince de marzo, *etc.* [16 March 1810.] [*Cadiz,* 1810.] fol. **1323.** k. **18.** (**43.**)

La Junta Superior de Gobierno de Cádiz a las Señoras de su Vecinario, *etc.* [Commending the women of Cadiz for their aid in making clothing for the army. 23 June 1810.] [*Cadiz,* 1810.] *s. sh.* fol. **1323.** k. **18.** (**24.**)

— *Begin.* Gaditanos, *etc.* [A proclamation announcing the forthcoming election of the Cortes. 8 July 1810.] [*Cadiz,* 1810.] fol. **1323.** k. **18.** (**25.**)

— *Begin.* La Junta Superior de Gobierno de esta ciudad acaba de recibir del Virreynato y Consulado de México y del muy ilustre Ayuntamiento de Vera Cruz, los apreciables oficios, que á la letra se copian, *etc.* [4 July 1810.] [*Cadiz,* 1810.] *s. sh.* fol. **1323.** k. **18.** (**26.**)

— *Begin.* La Junta Superior de Gobierno en cumplimiento de la promesa que hizo . . . inserta en este á la letra los oficios que ha recibido de los capitanes generales de la Habana y Puerto Rico, *etc.* [16 July 1810.] [*Cadiz,* 1810.] *s. sh.* fol. **1323.** k. **18.** (**30.**)

—— Manifiesto, *etc.* (La Contextacion dada por el Ayuntamiento de la Imperial Ciudad de México á su circular de 28 de febrero último.) [3 Aug. 1810.] [*Cadiz,* 1810.] *s. sh.* fol. **1323.** k. **18.** (**31.**)

—— Edicto. Públicas y notorias, *etc.* [Ordering all persons in the city engaged in building to help in the completion of the fortress of San Fernando. 14 Sept. 1810.] [*Cadiz,* 1810.] *s. sh.* fol. **1323.** k. **18.** (**36.**)

—— *Begin.* Vecinos de Cadiz, *etc.* [A proclamation ordering general conscription. 22 Sept. 1810.] [*Cadiz,* 1810.] *s. sh.* fol. **1323.** k. **18.** (**35.**)

—— Bando. La Junta Superior, *etc.* [Publishing a decree of the Regency commanding immigrants from provinces not occupied by the French to leave the city. 4 Oct. 1810.] [*Cadiz,* 1810.] *s. sh.* fol. **1323.** k. **18.** (**37.**)

—— Edicta. La Junta Superior, *etc.* [Giving directions for the conduct of the civil and military population during trial raid alarms. 29 Oct. 1810.] [*Cadiz,* 1810.] *s. sh.* fol. **1323.** k. **18.** (**38.**)

—— *Begin.* Excelentísimo señor, *etc.* [Correspondence relating to the complaints of the Duke de Alburquerque as to the equipment of the army.] [*Cadiz,* 1810.] *s. sh.* fol. **1323.** k. **18.** (**44.**)

—— Reglamento y Convenio propuesto por la Junta Superior de Cádiz. (Haciendose cargo provisionalmente en su distrito, de todas las rentas de la corona.) *See* SPAIN.—Ferdinand VII., *King.* [*Documents issued by the Council of Regency, etc.*] Real Aprobacion y Decreto, *etc.* 1810. 4°. **9180.** d. **1.** (**27.**)

REAL JUNTA DE SANIDAD.

—— *Begin.* Don Andres Lopez y Sagastizabal, *etc.* [A proclamation warning captains of vessels against infringement of the quarantine regulations. 10 May 1810.] [*Cadiz,* 1810.] *s. sh.* fol. **1323.** k. **18.** (**19.**)

—— *Begin.* Don Andres Lopez y Sagastizabal, *etc.* [A proclamation imposing fines for vessels infringing the quarantine regulations. 17 Aug. 1810.] [*Cadiz,* 1810.] *s. sh.* fol. **1323.** k. **18.** (**32.**)

MISCELLANEOUS INSTITUTIONS.

ASOCIACIÓN DE CERVANTISTAS.

—— Aniversario de Cervántes. Fiesta literaria . . . para conmemorar la muerte del príncipe de nuestros ingenios, *etc.* año 1–3. *Cádiz,* 1874–76. 8°. Cerv. **572–574.**
The titlepage of año 3 *reads: Asociación de Cervantistas. Aniversario* CCLX. *de la muerte de Miguel de Cervantes Saavedra. Festividad, etc.*

—— [Another copy of año 1, 2.] **11840.** d. **63.**

ATENEO DE CÁDIZ.

—— Ateneo de Cádiz. Científico, artístico y literario. (Director y editor responsable, Don M. Ayllon y Altolaguirre.) no. 1–51. 22 ag. 1858—15 dic. 1859. *Cádiz,* 1858, 59. fol. **1880.** b. **38.**
No more published.

BANCO NACIONAL DE SAN CÁRLOS.

—— Caxa de Descuentos del Banco Nacional de San Cárlos en Cádiz. (Reglas, que la direccion del Banco . . . acordó, y deberán observarse en la formacion y gobierno de la caxa de descuentos.) pp. 27. *Madrid,* 1785. 4°. **8229.** aaaa. **4.** (**2.**)

—— Real cédula de S. M. y señores del Consejo, por la qual se crea, erige y autoriza un Banco nacional y general para facilitar las operaciones del comercio . . . con la denominacion de Banco de San Cárlos . . . Van añadidas las modificaciones hechas á esta real cédula, *etc.* pp. liv. 297. *Madrid*, 1789. 4°. **8229**. aaaa. **2**.

—— Relacion de los pueblos que han impuesto acciones en el Banco Nacional de San Cárlos en consecuencia de las reales cédulas de 2 de junio y 27 de agosto de 1782. pp. 51. *Madrid*, 1784. 4°. **8229**. aaaa. **3**. (**2**.)

—— Segunda(–Séptima) Junta General del Banco Nacional de San Cárlos, *etc.* 6 pt. *Madrid*, [1783–89.] 8°. **8229**. aaaa. **3**, **4**.

COLEGIO DE HUMANIDADES DE ISABEL II.

—— Exámen público á que se presentan los alumnos del Colegio de Humanidades de Isabel II. de esta ciudad de Cádiz, *etc.* pp. 27. *Cádiz*, 1836. 4°. **1444**. e. **8**. (**17**.)

COLEGIO SEMINARIO DE SAN BARTOLOME.

—— Constituciones y Reglas del Colegio Seminario de san Bartolome de la ciudad de Cadiz. ff. 51. *Madrid*, 1594. 8°. **715**. d. **21**. (**2**.)

COMERCIO.

—— Informe dirigido a S.M. por el Consulado y Comercio de esta plaza en 24 de julio, sobre los perjuicios que se originarian de la concesion del comercio libre de los extrangeros con nuestras Américas. pp. 37. *Cádiz*, 1811. 4°. **1477**. b. **11**. (**11**.)

—— Memoria sobre los males que sufre el comercio español, y medios de repararlos . . . Dirigida á las Córtes por una Comision del Comercio de Cádiz. pp. 237. *Cádiz*, 1820. 4°. **9180**. e. **3**. (**4**.)

COMISION DE LA EMPRESA DEL TEATRO.

—— *See* CORRAL Y PUENTE (P. del) and LIZAUR (D. de) Notas para la mejor inteligencia de la esposicion que pública la Comision de la Empresa del Teatro. [With extracts from the " esposicion."] 1834. 4°. **1444**. e. **8**. (**8**.)

COMPAGNIE DU CHEMIN DE FER DE CADIX À XÉRÈS ET SÉVILLE.

—— *See* SEVILLE.—*Compañia de los Ferro-Carilles de Sevilla, á Jérez y Puerto-Real á Cádiz.*

CONSULADO Y COMERCIO.

—— *See* supra: COMERCIO.

CORRILLO DEL PÓPULO.

—— Catálogo de la I Exposición retrospectiva de asuntos de la mar . . . organizada por el Corrillo del Pópulo . . . Octubre, 1946. pp. 30. *Cadiz*, [1946.] 8°. **11926**. aaa. **28**.

OBSERVATORIO REAL.

—— [For works referring to the Observatorio Real, originally situated in Cadiz, but removed in 1801 to San Fernando:] *See* SAN FERNANDO, *Isle of Leon.*

REAL ACADEMIA GADITANA DE CIENCIAS Y LETRAS.

—— Obras escogidas del Excmo. Sr. D. Francisco Flores Arenas . . . Tomo 1. Obras poéticas. [With a biographical sketch by Vicente Rubio y Diaz, and a critical note by Alfonso Moreno Espinosa.] pp. viii. 278. *Cadiz*, 1878. 8°. **11451**. g. **39**.
No more published.

REAL ACADEMIA HISPANO AMERICANA DE CIENCIAS Y ARTES.

—— Discursos leidos ante la Real Academia Hispa Americana en la recepción del Sr. D. Francisco de l Barras de Aragón, el día 8 de diciembre de 1912. (Primer pasos de España en América. [By F. de las Barras Aragón.] Contestación, por el académico Don Ju Reina.) pp. 53. *Cádiz*, 1912. 8°. **09009**. c. **19**. (

—— Novelas Ejemplares de D. Miguel de Cervantes Saaved . . . Prólogo de Doña Blanca de los Ríos. [With illustr tions.] pp. xxi. 448. *Cádiz*, 1916. 8°. Ac. **14**

—— El Romancero del Quijote. Aventuras del Ingenio Hidalgo, descritas en CXIII romances, por D. Federic Lafuente. pp. 394. *Cádiz*, 1926. 4°. Ac. **140/**

—— Sillerías de Coro en las Iglesias Españoles . . . Segun edición. [By Pelayo Quintero Atauri. With plates pp. 214. *Cádiz*, 1928. **7875**. cc. **2**

SOCIEDAD ECONÓMICA DE AMIGOS DEL PAÍS.

—— Memoria dirigida á la Regencia provisional del reino . sobre un tratado de comercio con la Inglaterra, *etc.* pp. 5 *Cádiz*, 1841. 8°. **8245**. b. .

—— Una Residencia de Invierno. Estudio meteorológico médico del clima de Alicante, como estación inverna *etc.* [Compiled by C. Sanchez Palacio.] (Inforn facultativo sobre el clima de Alicante, redactado p Don V. Navarro y Albero.) pp. 32. *Alicante*, 1882. 8° **7687**. f.

APPENDIX.

—— [For editions of " A briefe and true report of t honorable voyage vnto Cadiz, 1596," contained Hakluyt's Voyages:] *See* HAKLUYT (Richard) T principal navigations . . . and discoveries of the Englis nation, *etc.*

—— [For editions of " A briefe and true report of th honorable voyage vnto Cadiz, 1596" contained Samuel Purchas's " Pilgrimes ":] *See* PURCHAS (Samue *the Elder.* Purchas his Pilgrimes, *etc.*

—— Canal de navegacion desde la bahia de Cádiz á Chiclan pasando por San Fernando. Importancia y bases d esta empresa, *etc.* [Extracts from the " Revista popular d Cádiz" and from official documents.] pp. 32. *Madri* 1849. 8°. **8775**. c. **3**

—— Le Coffre, ou le Médecin de Cadix, comédie en un act et en prose, *etc.* [By J. M. Piccini.] pp. 30. *Pari* 1798. 8°. **11738**. a. **18**. (**1**

—— Copia de carta remitida de la ciudad de Cadiz a esta d Sevilla, en que dà cuenta de lo sucedido en dicha ciuda de Cadiz, con el huracàn que le sobrevino en 15. de marc deste presente año de 1671. *Sevilla*, 1671. 4°. **1323**. g. **1**. (**5**

—— [Another edition.] Contribuição Documental para Historia da Cidade de Cadiz. (Relacion verdadera, copia de carta, escrita de la Ciudad de Cadiz à esta Cort donde declara el lamentable sucesso de dicha Ciudad d Cadiz con el Huracàn, que le sobreuino en quinzc [*sic*] d Março deste presente año de mil y seiscientos y setenta vno.) [A type facsimile edited by Moses Bensaba Amzalak.] pp. 8. *Lisboa*, 1926. fol. **10160**. i. **14**

—— Documentos relativos á la toma y saco de Cádiz por lo ingleses en julio de 1596. 1860. *See* FERNÁNDEZ D NAVARRETE (M.) Coleccion de documentos, *etc.* tom. 36 1842, *etc.* 8°. **9195**. d

—— Guia de Cádiz, para el año de 1846. pp. 220. *Cádiz* 1845. 16°. **795**. c. **20**

— The History of Cales Passion: Or as some will by-name it, The Miss-taking of Cales presented in Vindication of the Sufferers, to forewarne the future. By G: T: Esq; [i.e. George Tooke.] 1652. 4°. *See* T: G: *Esq.* **114.** k. **20.**

— Nombres Antiguos de las Calles y Plazas de Cádiz. Sus orígenes, sus cambios . . . Por un individuo de la Academia Española de Arqueología. (Diccionario de voces gaditanas.) pp. xvi. 85. xviii. *Cádiz,* 1857. 8°. **12231.** e. **13.** (**1.**)

— Nueva relacion y curioso romance, de la mas prodigiosa historia, que han oido los mortales en que se declara la feliz fortuna que tuvo el hijo de un cortante de la ciudad de Cadiz, llevándosele un mercader á las Indias, *etc.* [In verse.] pp. 8. *Barcelona,* [1850 ?] 4°. **11450.** f. **27.** (**1.**)

— Paseo Histórico-Artístico por Cádiz, *etc.* [With a plan.] pp. 261. *Cádiz,* 1853. 8°. **10161.** aa. **28.**

— Prodigiosa vida, admirable doctrina, preciosa muerte de los venerables hermanos los filósofos liberales de Cadiz; su entierro y oracion fúnebre hasta el Requiescant Amen . . . Por D. F. A. y B., Filósofo de Antaño, *etc.* [1815 ?] 4°. *See* A. y B., F., *D., Filósofo de Antaño.* **8042.** bbb. **22.** (**1.**)

— Reflexiones acerca de la epidemia que reyna en Cadiz, y medios de atajar los estragos de una peste. pp. 47. *Madrid,* 1800. 4°. **11451.** c. **55.** (**5.**)

— Relatione di quanto é sucesso trà li capitani del . . . Re Cattolico et l'armata inglese nel porto de Cadice, dal primo giorno di Nouembre . . . fino alli 7 del detto mese, *etc.* 1626. 12°. *See* SPAIN.—*Army.* [*Appendix.*—I.] **9077.** aaa. **5.**

— Sucessos de Cadiz, desde sabado primero de noviembre, que el Ingles entrò en la baya, hasta sabado ocho del mismo, que salio della, *etc.* [*Seville?*] 1625. fol. **593.** h. **17.** (**59.**)

— Sucessos de Cadiz, y entrada del enemigo olandes en su baìa. *G. de Contreras: Lima,* 1626. fol. **593.** h. **22.** (**66.**)

— Traurige Zeitung aus Cadix in Spanien, von dem am 10/20 Octob. des 1683-sten Jahrs allda in der Bay durch eine unversehene Feuersbrunst verunglücktem Convoy-Schiff, das Wapen von Hamburg genand, *etc.* [1684 ?] 4°. **591.** c. **24.** (**5.**)

— Villancicos que se cantan en Cadiz por Noche-Buena. *Madrid,* 1856. 4°. **11450.** f. **24.** (**20.**)

ADIZ, *Diocese of.—Sínodo.* Crónica del Sínodo Diocesano de Cádiz, celebrado en los días 15, 16 y 17 de febrero de 1882. Publícase . . . por el cronista del Sínodo D. José Maria Leon y Dominguez. pp. 66. *Cádiz,* 1882. 8°. **5017.** c. **3.**

ADIZ, *Province of.—Junta Censoria.* Calificacion del Diccionario Critico-Burlesco. *See* G., B. J. Contestacion del Autor del Diccionario Critico-Burlesco, *etc.* 1820. 12°. **12942.** a. **24.** (**2.**)

ADIZ, BENEDICTUS, *Bishop of.* [1511–1526.] *See* ACCOLTI (Benedetto) *Cardinal.*

—, DOMINGO, *Bishop of.* [1825–1853.] *See* SILOS MORENO.

— FRANCISCO XAVIER, *Bishop of.* [1819–1824.] *See* CIENFUEGOS Y JOVELLANOS (F. X.) *Cardinal, etc.*

—, JOSÉ, *Bishop of.* [1691–1695.] *See* BARZIA Y ZAMBRANA.

—, JUAN JOSÉ, *Bishop of.* [1853–1863.] *See* ARBOLÍ.

CADIZ DRAMATIC GALLERY. Galería Dramática Gaditana. 4 tom. *Cadiz,* 1845, 46. 12°. **11726.** d. **12.**

CADIZ (CHARLES FITZWILLIAM) *See* NATAL. Natal Ordinances, Laws, and Proclamations. Compiled and edited . . . by C. F. Cadiz [and others], *etc.* 1879, *etc.* 8°. **6606.** l. **11.**

CÁDIZ (DIEGO JOSÉ DE) *See* DIEGO JOSÉ, *de Cadiz* [José Francisco Juan Maria Caamaño].

CÁDIZ (ENRIQUE GÓMEZ DE) *See* GÓMEZ DE CÁDIZ.

CADIZ (LEILA)

—— Mercy and Justice. Songs. pp. 12. *Rapid Printing Co.: Dublin,* [1945.] 8°. **11658.** aa. **69.**

CÁDIZ (MANUEL GÓMEZ DE) *See* GÓMEZ DE CÁDIZ.

CADLE (RICHARD DUNBAR)

—— Particle Size Determination. [With illustrations.] pp. xv. 303. *Interscience Publishers: New York,* 1955. 8°. [*Interscience Manuals.* no. 7.] W.P. B. **61/7.**

CADŁUBCUS (VINCENTIUS) *See* VINCENT [Kadłubek], *Saint, etc.*

CADMAN (CECIL FRANK MILES)

—— No Confidence. [A speech delivered in the Union House of Assembly.] pp. 20. *Cape Town & Wynberg,* [1946.] 8°. **12302.** a. **30.**

—— Padre Punches. pp. 211. *Rustica Press: Cape Town & Wynberg,* [1944.] 8°. **08157.** de. **109.**

—— Silver Lamps. [Sermons.] pp. viii. 76. *Warren & Son: Winchester,* 1917. 8°. **4476.** de. **70.**

—— Socialism for South Africa. pp. 186. [1942.] 8°. *See* AFRICA, *South.—Union of South Africa.—South African Labour Party.* **08286.** g. **85.**

CADMAN (CHARLES WAKEFIELD) Carlos Troyer. A biographical appreciation. *See* TROYER (C.) Indian Music Lecture, *etc.* [1913.] 8°. **7898.** bbb. **46.** (**3.**)

CADMAN (DANIEL) School Stenography. A system of lineal short hand; illustrated by a set of engraved copies and specimens, *etc.* pp. 22. pl. VI. *Simpkin & Marshall: London,* [1835.] **1043.** l. **22.** (**1.**)

CADMAN (ELIJAH) *See* WALLIS (Humphrey) The Happy Warrior. The life story of Commissioner E. Cadman. [With portraits.] 1928. 8°. **4908.** k. **19.**

CADMAN (ELSIE JANE)

—— A First Biology. pp. viii. 148. *G. Bell & Sons: London,* 1952. 8°. **07001.** f. **68.**

—— A First Biology. (Second edition.) pp. viii. 152. *G. Bell & Sons: London,* 1954. 8°. **7008.** ff. **8.**

CADMAN (HENRY) Harry Druidale, Fisherman from Manxland to England, *etc.* [With plates.] pp. xvi. 321. *Macmillan & Co.: London,* 1898. 8°. **7906.** cc. **1.**

CADMAN (HENRY ASHWELL) Gomersal Past and Present . . . With a map, *etc.* pp. 232. *Hunters: Leeds,* 1930. 8°. **010360.** b. **29.**

CADMAN (JAMES)

—— *See* NORTON-IN-THE-MOORS.—*Old Nortonian Society.* Records of ye Old Nortonian Society. From 1925 to 1947. [Collected by J. Cadman.] 1947. 8°. **010368.** t. **12.**

—— The Corporation in New Jersey. Business and politics, 1791–1875. pp. xvi. 462. *Harvard University Press: Cambridge, Mass.*, 1949. 8°. [*Studies in Economic History.*] W.P. **5425/5.**

CADMAN (JOSIAH) Particular Account of the Last Speech and Dying Declaration of Josiah Cadman, for issuing forged five pound notes of the Bank of England, and of other seven men, *etc.* (Execution. A Full, True and Particular Account of the Execution of Mrs. Margaret Tyndal, or Shuttleworth.) [*London?* 1821.] *s. sh.* fol. **1851. c. 19. (43.)**

—— Remarkable Speech of Cadman. Executions at Newgate. Nov. 21. *Catnach:* [*London*, 1821.] *s. sh.* 8°. **1880. c. 10. (12.)**

CADMAN (MARY) *See* NOCTROFF (Alethes) *pseud.* Perjury, the Proof of Forgery: or, Mr. Crofton's civilitie justified by Cadmans falsitie, *etc.* 1657. 4°. **E. 931. (1.)**

CADMAN (SAMUEL PARKES) *See* HAMLIN (Fred) S. Parkes Cadman, pioneer radio minister, *etc.* [With a portrait.] 1930. 8°. **4987. a. 15.**

—— *See* RIDGE (Francis M.) S. Parkes Cadman. 1936. 8°. **3628.aa.7/34.**

—— Adventure for Happiness. pp. 312. *Macmillan Co.: New York*, 1935. 8°. **08408. g. 52.**

—— Ambassadors of God. pp. 353. *Funk & Wagnalls Co.: London; printed in U.S.A.*, 1920. 8°. **4498. ff. 22.**

—— Answers to Everyday Questions, *etc.* [With a portrait.] pp. 365. *Abingdon Press: New York*, [1930.] 8°. **08408. f. 13.**

—— Charles Darwin and other English Thinkers, with reference to their religious and ethical value . . . A series of lectures, *etc.* pp. ix. 284. *J. Clarke & Co.: London; Norwood, Mass.* [printed], [1911.] 8°. **10803. de. 29.**

—— The Christ of God. pp. 180. *Macmillan Co.: New York*, 1929. 8°. **4223. bb. 36.**

—— Christianity and the State . . . A series of lectures, *etc.* pp. xi. 370. *Macmillan Co.: New York*, 1924. 8°. **08285. e. 34.**

—— Imagination and Religion . . . The Cole Lectures for 1924, *etc.* pp. 208. *Macmillan Co.: New York*, 1926. 8°. **04375. df. 56.**

—— The Prophets of Israel . . . Illustrated by Frank O. Salisbury. pp. 195. *Macmillan Co.: New York*, 1933. 4°. **2216. d. 11.**

—— The Three Religious Leaders of Oxford and their Movements: John Wycliffe, John Wesley, John Henry Newman. pp. xvii. 596. *Macmillan Co.: New York*, 1916. 8°. **4902. f. 16.**

—— William Owen. Born September 13, 1822, died October 28, 1896. A saint of the Methodist household of faith. [With a portrait.] pp. 121. *C. H. Kelly: London*, [1912.] 8°. [*Library of Methodist Biography.*] **4907. a. 15/3.**

CADMAN (WILLIAM) *See* J., A. J. Barley Loaves . . . With introduction by . . . W. Cadman. 1877. 16°. **11652. df. 45.**

—— *See* SHELFORD (Leonard E.) "Full of the Holy Ghost and of Faith" . . . A sermon preached . . . in loving remembrance of . . . W. Cadman, *etc.* [1891.] 8°. **4906. dd. 38. (7.)**

—— *See* SHELFORD (Leonard E.) A Memorial of the Re William Cadman, *etc.* [With a portrait.] 1899. 8°. **4907. ee. 1**

—— The Acknowledgment of the Divine Attributes in t Person of Christ at the Second Advent. *See* DATT (William) *Vicar of St. Paul's, Wolverhampton.* Go Dealings with Israel, *etc.* 1850. 12°. **1356. g. 1**

—— An Address delivered . . . at the Funeral of the Re W. Conway, *etc.* pp. 8. *Seeley, Jackson & Hallida London*, 1876. 8°. **4902. bb. 45. (1**

—— [Another copy.] An Address . . . at the Funeral of t Rev. W. Conway, *etc.* *London*, 1876. 8°. **4481. b. 29. (1**

—— The Ark of Christ's Church. A sermon, *etc.* pp. 23. *Kerby & Endean: London*, 1881. 8°. **4478. h. 10. (1**

—— Can the Ethiopian change his Skin? A sermon . . Twelfth thousand. pp. 16. *Seeley, Jackson & Hallida London*, 1857. 8°. **4478. a. 126. (**

—— Can the Ethiopian Change his Skin? *See* LONDON.— III. *Exeter Hall.* Exeter Hall Sermons for the Worki Classes, *etc.* 1857. 8°. **4463. d. 1**

—— Christian Assurance. [A sermon.] *See* THINGS. "Thin that accompany Salvation," *etc.* 1858. 8°. **4463. d. 3**

—— The Christian Minister: his true position, and t purpose of his office. *See* CHURCHMAN. The Churchm Armed. A course of lectures, *etc.* [1864.] 8°. **4464. aaa.**

—— Christian Warriors. *See* ENGLAND.—*Church of Englan —Young Men's Society for Aiding Missions, e* Lectures, *etc.* 1856. 8°. **4193. d. 6**

—— Church Pastoral-Aid Society. A sermon in behalf the above society, *etc.* pp. 32. *Wertheim & Macintos London*, [1855.] 16°. **4477. a. 1**

—— Conquering and to conquer. A sermon, *etc.* pp. 23. *Kerby & Endean: London*, 1881. 8°. **4478. h. 10. (1**

—— The Destinies of the Holy Places. *See* FREMANT (William R.) *Dean of Ripon.* Present Times and Futu Prospects, *etc.* 1854. 8°. **1356. g. 1**

—— The Duty of the Young Men of England to aid in t Missionary Work. *See* ENGLAND.—*Church of England.- Church of England Young Men's Society for Aidi Missions, etc.* The Claims of Missions, *etc.* 1846. 8°. **1369. f. 3**

—— England in the Reign of James the Second. *S* ENGLAND.—*Church of England.—Church of Engla Young Men's Society for Aiding Missions, etc.* Lecture *etc.* 1851. 8°. **4193. d. 6**

—— The Exaltation of Christ. *See* PAUL, *Saint and Apost —Cathedral Church of, in London.* Sermons, *etc.* 1859. 8°. **4477. a. 12**

—— The Gathering of the Saints at the Appearing of Chri *See* DALLAS (Alexander R. C.) Lift up your Heads, *etc.* 1848. 12°. **1356. g. 1**

—— The Hidden Manna, the White Stone, the New Nam or, the Choice gifts of the kingdom. *See* BICKERSTE (Robert) *Bishop of Ripon.* The Gifts of the Kingdo Being lectures, *etc.* 1855. 8°. **1356. g. 1**

—— The Liberty of Christ's Kingdom. *See* FREMANT (William R.) *Dean of Ripon.* The Millennial Kingdo *etc.* 1852. 8°. **1356. g. 1**

CADMAN (WILLIAM)

—— The Lord's Day: its divine authority and perpetual obligation. *See* PAPERS. Papers for the Times. [1866.] 8°. **4378**. bb. **24**.

—— The Parables Prophetically Explained; being lectures delivered during Lent, 1853, at St. George's, Bloomsbury. By twelve clergymen of the Church of England. With a preface by the Rev. W. Cadman. pp. xvi. 356. *J. F. Shaw: London*, 1853. 8°. **1356**. g. **17**.

—— Park Chapel Remembrancer. Being the substance of sermons preached in Park Chapel, Chelsea. no. 1. A daily message for 1850. [By W. Cadman.] pp. 24. 1850. 12°. *See* LONDON.—III. *Park Chapel, Chelsea*. **4461**. d. **30**.

—— Pastoral Visitation. *See* ELLICOTT (Charles J.) *Bishop of Gloucester and Bristol*. Homiletical and Pastoral Lectures, *etc.* 1879. 8°. **4499**. cc. **8**.

—— Prophecy a Motive to Prayer for the Holy Spirit. *See* HOARE (Edward) *Canon of Canterbury*. The Light of Prophecy, *etc.* 1856. 8°. **1356**. g. **20**.

—— Rabbinism and Romanism Compared. *See* SIGNS. The Signs of the Times, *etc.* pt. 1. 1854. 8°. **4461**. b. **38**.

—— A Retrospect. (Lecture.) *See* SIGNS. The Signs of the Times, *etc.* pt. 2. 1854. 8°. **4461**. b. **38**.

—— Saints in Glory. *See* HOLLAND (Charles) *Rector of Petworth, Sussex*. The Scripture Expositor, *etc.* vol. 1. 1848. 12°. **3127**. d. **16**.

—— [Another edition.] *See* DRUMMOND (David T. K.) The Preacher in the House, *etc.* 1851. 8°. **4464**. a. **19**.

—— [A sermon on Daniel IV. 27.] *In:* The Fast-Day Sermons, *etc.* no. 11. pp. 127–137. [1857.] 8°. **4463**. d. **22**.

—— A Sermon preached at Trinity Church . . . Holborn, *etc.* 1855. *See* LONDON.—III. *London Society for Promoting Christianity among the Jews*. The Forty-seventh Report, *etc.* 1810, *etc.* 8°. P.P. **1149**.

—— A Sermon preached before the Church Pastoral Aid Society, *etc.* 1853. *See* ENGLAND.—*Church of England.—Church Pastoral Aid Society*. The Eighteenth Annual Report, *etc.* 1836, *etc.* 8°. P.P. **1025**.

—— Spread of the Knowledge of the Glory of the Lord. *See* PYM (William W.) Good Things to Come, *etc.* 1847. 12°. **1356**. g. **11**.

—— The Teaching of the Church of England concerning the Presence of Christ in the Lord's Supper. *See* QUESTIONS. Questions of the Day, *etc.* 1867. 8°. **4255**. aaa. **60**.

—— The Testimony of St. Stephen. *See* PAUL, *Saint and Apostle.—Cathedral Church of, in London*. Twenty-two Sermons, *etc.* 1859. 8°. **4477**. f. **69**.

—— The Traditions of the Church of Rome contrasted with the Truths of the Bible. A lecture, *etc.* *See* ENGLAND.—*Church of England.—Church of England Young Men's Society for Aiding Missions, etc.* Six Lectures on Protestantism, *etc.* 1852. 8°. **3939**. d. **56**.

—— The Wide Proclamation of the Gospel among the Heathen. *See* BAYLEY (*Sir* John R. L. E.) *Bart.* Twelve Lent Lectures, *etc.* [1858.] 8°. **3185**. d. **11**.

—— The Word of Prophecy, a light in these perilous times. *See* AURIOL (Edward) Popish Darkness and Millennial Light, *etc.* 1851. 12°. **1356**. g. **15**.

ADMAN (WILLIAM ARTHUR)

—— Shelterbelts for Welsh Hill Farms. [With illustrations.] pp. 31. *London*, 1953. 8°. [*Forest Record*. no. 22.] B.S. **15/30**.

ADMAN (WILLIAM GEORGE) The Quarries of Syracuse, and other verses. pp. 40. *H. Rawson & Co.: Manchester*, 1915. 8°. **011649**. ee. **55**.

ADMAN (WILLIAM HEALEY) The Last Journey of Jesus to Jerusalem: its purpose in the light of the Synoptic Gospels. pp. 159. *Humphrey Milford: London*, 1923. 8°. **4227**. e. **42**.

CADMUS. *See* ANSELME DE PUISAYE (H. d') *Marquis*. Du héros phénicien Cadmus et de sa famille, *etc.* 1888. 8°. **7706**. b. **33**.

—— Cadmus et Hermione, tragédie, *etc.* [By Philippe Quinault.] pp. 64. *Suivant la copie imprimée à Paris; [Abraham Wolfgang: Amsterdam,]* 1682. 12°. [*Recueil des opéra*. tom. 1.] **242**. a. **9**.

—— [A reissue.] Cadmus et Hermione, tragedie, *etc.* [By Philippe Quinault.] [*Amsterdam,*] 1687. 12°. C. **69**. bb. **2**. (**1**.)

—— [A reissue.] Cadmus et Hermione, tragédie en musique. [By P. Quinault.] [*Amsterdam,*] 1687. 12°. [*Recueil des opera, etc.* tom. 1.] C. **65**. hh. **7**.

CADMUS, *the Milesian*. Le Palais du silence. Conte philosophique. (Ouvrage de Cadmus de Milet.) [Purporting to be a translation from the Greek of Cadmus, but actually written by P. A. de Sainte Foix.] 2 vol. *Amsterdam*, 1754. 12°. **12514**. a. **53**.

—— The Palace of Silence: a philosophic tale . . . Translated from the French by a Lady. 2 vol. *J. Bew: London*, 1775. 12°. **12548**. aa. **24**.

CADMUS, *pseud.*, and **HARMONIA,** *pseud.* The Island of Sheep. By Cadmus and Harmonia. pp. 193. *Hodder & Stoughton: London*, 1919. 8°. **012601**. b. **9**.

CADMUS (BRADFORD) and **CHILD** (ARTHUR J. E.)

—— Internal Control against Fraud and Waste . . . Developed as a project of the Institute of Internal Auditors. pp. xii. 318. 1953. 8°. *See* NEW YORK.—*Institute of Internal Auditors*. **8231**. i. **29**.

CADMUS (CHRISTOPHER) *pseud.* [i.e. NATHAN BROWN.] Ꞇe Histori ov Magnus Mahárba and ꞇe Blak Dragun. Bai Kristofur Kadmus. pp. 122. *Ꞇe Filolojikal Gemána: Nũ-York*, 1866. 8°. **12991**. aaa. **1**.

CADMUS (NANCY E.) A Manual of Obstetrical Nursing, *etc.* pp. xv. 100. *G. P. Putnam's Sons: New York & London*, 1922. 8°. **07580**. ee. **60**.

CADMUSTUS (PAULUS AEMILIUS) *See* CADAMOSTO (Paolo E.)

CADNESS (HENRY) Decorative Brush-Work & Elementary Design, *etc.* pp. xii. 174. pl. XXXVIII. *B. T. Batsford: London*, 1902. 8°. **7858**. o. **18**.

—— Second edition. Revised and enlarged, *etc.* pp. xiv. 184. pl. XLII. *B. T. Batsford: London*, 1904. 8°. **07807**. f. **19**.

—— Third edition. Revised and enlarged, *etc.* pp. xiv. 194. pl. XLVI. *B. T. Batsford: London*, 1909. 8°. **07807**. f. **36**.

—— Stencil-Craft, *etc.* (Edited by F. Morley Fletcher.) pp. x. 105. *Sir I. Pitman & Sons: London*, 1921. 8°. **07942**. d. **75**.

CADO (LÉON) Du traitement de la sciatique par les courants continus. pp. 51. *Paris*, 1872. 4°. [*Collection des thèses soutenues à la Faculté de Médecine de Paris*. An 1872. tom. 3.] **7373**. n. **9**.

CADOC, *Saint*.

—— *See* DOBLE (Gilbert H.) "Cornish Saints" Series (no. 40. St. Cadoc in Cornwall and Brittany.) [1933,] *etc.* 8°. **4832**. aaa. **2/40**.

—— Llyma Ddoethineb Catwg Ddoeth o' Lancarfan, *etc.* [Collected by Thomas ab Ievan.] *See* JONES (Owen) called OWAIN MYFYR. The Myvyrian Archaiology of Wales, *etc.* vol. 3. 1801. 8°. **872**. m. **5**.

—— [Another edition.] *See* JONES (Owen) called OWAIN MYFYR. The Myvyrian Archaiology of Wales, *etc.* 1870. 8°. **2288**. g. **6**.

CADOC, *Saint.*

—— [Selections.] *See* DYFERION. Dyferion y Beirdd, *etc.* 1842. 16°. **11595.** aa. **14.** (**10.**)

—— Cannen spirituel é inour Sant Cadeu . . . péhani e inourér é paræs Belz, é escobty Güénèd, *etc.* pp. 7. *Güénèd*, [1860 ?] 16°. **3434.** bbb. **15.**

CADOGAN BOOKLETS. Cadogan Booklets. 15 pt. *Gowans & Gray: London, Glasgow*, 1905–08. 16°. **944.** bb. **3.**

CADOGAN OFFICE SOCIAL CLUB. *See* LONDON.—III.

CADOGAN (*Lady* ADELAIDE) Drawing-Room Plays. Selected and adapted from the French by Lady Adelaide Cadogan. Illustrated by E. L. Shute, *etc.* pp. 126. *Sampson Low & Co.: London*, 1888. 4°. **11781.** h. **9.**

—— Illustrated Games of Patience . . . Second edition. 2 ser. *Sampson, Low & Co.: London*, 1875, 87. 4°. **7913.** f. **20.**

CADOGAN (*Lady* AUGUSTA SARAH) *See* BIBLE.—*Ruth.* [*English.*] The Book of Ruth. Illustrated by the Lady A. Cadogan. 1850. 4°. **3165.** e. **9.**

CADOGAN (*Lady* AUGUSTA SARAH) and **CADOGAN** (*Lady* HONORIA LOUISA)

—— Recollections of Rome in 1843. [Coloured lithographs, from designs.] By the Ladies A. and H. C. [i.e. Cadogan.] [1845 ?] fol. *See* C., *Lady* A., and *Lady* H. Dept. of Prints & Drawings.

CADOGAN (CHARLES) *Baron Cadogan.* An Act for Vesting the Manor of Okeley, and other lands in the county of Bucks, in —— and —— in trust for Charles Lord Cadogan and his heirs, and for settling other lands . . . to the same uses in lieu thereof. [The draft of a proposed act of parliament.] pp. 10. [*London?* 1740 ?] fol. **816.** m. **5.** (**30.**)

CADOGAN (*Hon. Sir* EDWARD CECIL GEORGE) *K.B.E.*

—— The India We Saw. pp. vii. 310. *John Murray: London*, 1933. 8°. **010055.** a. **54.**

—— The Life of Cavour . . . With a portrait. pp. ix. 385. *Smith, Elder & Co.: London*, 1907. 8°. **10633.** cc. **7.**

—— Makers of Modern History. Three types: Louis Napoleon, Cavour, Bismarck. pp. ix. 216. *John Murray: London*, 1905. 8°. **10603.** f. **4.**

—— The Roots of Evil. Being a treatise on the methods of dealing with crime and the criminal during the eighteenth and nineteenth centuries in relation to those of a more enlightened age. [With plates.] pp. xiii. 314. *John Murray: London*, 1937. 8°. **6055.** s. **31.**

CADOGAN (GEORGE) *Earl Cadogan.* A Letter from an Inhabitant of Chelsea to . . . the Earl Cadogan . . . relative to the ecclesiastical condition of the parish. pp. 15. *Ridgway & Son: London*, 1835. 8°. **4105.** d. **8.**

CADOGAN (GEORGE) *Lieutenant in General Oglethorpe's Regiment.* The Spanish Hireling Detected: being a refutation of the several calumnies and falshoods in a late pamphlet [by James Edward Oglethorpe], entitul'd An Impartial Account of the late Expedition against St. Augustine under General Oglethorpe. pp. 68. *J. Roberts: London*, 1743. 8°. **1061.** g. **21.**

CADOGAN (GULIELMUS) *See* CADOGAN (William) *M.D.*

CADOGAN (H.) "Why do the Nations . . ." [On the prevention of war. With plates.] pp. 90. *A. H. Stockwell: London*, [1933.] 8°. **08425.** e. **68.**

CADOGAN (*Lady* HONORIA LOUISA) *See* C., *Lady* A., and *Lady* H. Recollections of Rome in 1843. By the Ladies A. and H. C. [i.e. Cadogan.] [1845 ?] fol. Dept. of Prints & Drawings.

CADOGAN (PRIMROSE LILIAN) *Countess Cadogan.*

—— The Miracle Tree . . . Illustrations by Astrid Walford. [Tales for children.] pp. 120. *Geoffrey Bles: London*, 1950. 8°. **12833.** e. **11.**

CADOGAN (WILLIAM) *Earl Cadogan. Begin.* Hauts & puissants seigneurs, *etc.* [A protest to the States General of the Netherlands against the award of the prize court at Curaçao in respect of the English sloop "Saint James" captured by Willem de Groot off the Barbadoes.] [*The Hague*, 1715.] *s. sh.* fol. **1324.** k. **1.** (**1.**)

—— A Catalogue of the Rich Furniture of the Right Honourable the Earl of Cadogan . . . As likewise an excellent collection of pictures . . . Which will be sold by auction . . . the 14th of February, 1726–7, *etc.* pp. 20. [*London*, 1727.] 4°. **C.119.h.3.(6.)**

—— Catalogue des tableaux, de l'argenterie, vaisselle dorée, et pierries [*sic*] appartenants son excellence [*sic*] le comte de Cadogan . . . qui seront vendu [*sic*] par encan, *etc.* pp. 14. [*London*, 1727.] 8°. **S.C. 550.** (**14.**)

CADOGAN (WILLIAM) *M.D.* A Dissertation on the Gout, and all chronic diseases, jointly considered, as proceeding from the same causes, *etc.* pp. viii. 88. *J. Dodsley: London*, 1771. 8°. **T. 59.** (**1.**)

—— [Another copy.] A Dissertation on the Gout, *etc.* *London*, 1771. 8°. **6497.** bb. **5.** (**7.**)

—— The second edition. pp. 99. *J. Dodsley: London*, 1771. 8°. **1172.** h. **3.** (**7.**)

—— The third edition. pp. 99. *J. Dodsley: London*, 1771. 8°. **T. 178.** (**1.**)

—— The fifth edition. pp. 100. *J. Dodsley: London*, 1771. 8°. **7630.** f. **30.**

—— The tenth edition. pp. 100. *J. Dodsley: London*, 1772. 8°. **48.** a. **1.** (**1.**)

—— The tenth edition. pp. 76. 3. *Henry Knox: Boston*, 1772. 8°. **7620.** aaa. **21.**

—— The eleventh edition. pp. 100. *J. Dodsley: London*, 1772. 8°. **1188.** d. **37.**

—— *See* BERKENHOUT (John) Doctor Cadogan's Dissertation on the Gout . . . examined and refuted, *etc.* 1772. 8°. **T. 178.** (**3.**)

—— *See* CARTER (William) *late Fellow of Oriel College, Oxford.* A Free and Candid Examination of Dr. Cadogan's Dissertation on the Gout, *etc.* [1772 ?] 8°. **7305.** de. **19.** (**1.**)

—— *See* FALCONER (William) *M.D.* Observations on Dr. Cadogan's Dissertation on the Gout, *etc.* 1772. 8°. **T. 178.** (**2.**)

—— An Address to Doctor Cadogan, occasioned by his Dissertation on the gout and other chronic diseases: with remarks and observations. [By William Falconer.] pp. 36. *J. Almon: London*, 1771. 8°. **7630.** e. **30.**

—— An Essay upon Nursing, and the management of children . . . By a Physician [i.e. W. Cadogan], *etc.* pp. 34. 1748. 8°. *See* PHYSICIAN. **1178.** e. **2.** (**2.**)

—— The fourth edition, with additions. pp. 38. *J. Roberts: London*, 1750. 8°. **T. 185.** (**7.**)

—— The fifth edition, with further additions. pp. 43. *J. Roberts: London*, 1752. 8°. **T. 1664.** (**7.**)

—— The sixth edition. pp. 43. *J. Roberts: London*, 1753. 8°. **1178.** e. **2.** (**3.**)

—— The eighth edition. pp. 43. *Robert Horsfield: London*, 1764. 8°. **T. 178.** (**4.**)

—— The tenth edition, revised and corrected by the author. pp. 53. *Robert Horsfield: London*, 1772. 8°. **1172.** k. **3.** (**3.**)

—— Oratio anniversaria in theatro Collegii Regalis Medicorum Londinensium ex Harvæi Instituto habita, *etc.* pp. 23. *J. Whiston: Londini*, 1764. 4°. **T. 46.** (**5.**)

—— Oratio anniversaria in theatro Collegii Regalis Medicorum Londinensium ex Harvæi Instituto habita, die xviii Octobris, 1792. pp. 22. *J. Dodsley: Londini*, 1792. 4°. **7680.** c. **11.**

CADOGAN (*Hon.* WILLIAM BROMLEY) *See* BIDDULPH (Thomas T.) An Elegy, occasioned by the death of . . . W. B. Cadogan, *etc.* 1797. 4°. **11632**. g. **6**.

—— *See* CECIL (Richard) The Works of the Rev. Richard Cecil, *etc.* (Memoirs of the Honourable and Reverend W. B. Cadogan.) [With a portrait.] 1811. 8°. **493**. d. **22**.

—— —— 1822. 8°. **4920**. aaaa. **43**.

—— *See* CECIL (Richard) Life of the Honourable and Reverend W. B. Cadogan . . . Abridged. [1832.] 12°. **864**. f. **11/24**.

—— *See* COOKE (John) *Minister of the Independent Church at Maidenhead.* Five Letters to a Friend, occasioned by the death of . . . W. B. Cadogan. 1797. 8°. **4902**. e. **2**.

—— *See* DE COETLOGON (Charles E.) The True Greatness . . . of the Ministerial Character, illustrated in a sermon, preached on occasion of the death of . . . W. B. Cadogan, *etc.* 1797. 8°. **4476**. g. **16**.

—— *See* GOODE (William) *Rector of St. Andrew, Wardrobe and St. Ann, Blackfriars.* The Gospel Treasure . . . A sermon, occasioned by the death of . . . W. B. Cadogan, *etc.* 1797. 8°. **1415**. e. **1**.

—— *See* N., J. A Few Words of Advice & Consolation to the Worshippers at St. Lawrence's, who . . . lament the removal of their faithful pastor. [Letters written in 1797 on the occasion of the death of W. B. Cadogan.] 1812. 8°. **4139**. cc. **54**.

—— *See* WILLATS (Thomas C.) An Apology for the Church of Christ and the Church of England; with a vindication of the doctrines of . . . W. B. Cadogan, *etc.* 1798. 8°. **4108**. de. **42**.

—— Discourses of the Honourable and Reverend W. B. Cadogan. To which are now added short observations on the Lord's Prayer, and letters to several of his friends . . . With memoirs of his life by Richard Cecil. [With a portrait.] pp. cxxxi. 438. *F. & C. Rivington: London,* 1798. 8°. **1021**. i. **5**.

—— An Address from a Clergyman to his Parishioners. pp. iv. 38. *Mess. Rivington: London,* 1785. 8°. **702**. h. **3**. (**2**.)

—— The Continuance and Constancy of the Friendship of God, as a covenant God with his people, considered in a sermon . . . upon the death of . . . W. Romaine. pp. 39. *Printed for the Author: London,* 1795. 8°. **1419**. f. **42**.

—— [Another copy.] **1419**. f. **43**.

—— [Another edition.] Funeral Sermon, occasioned by the death of the Rev. W. Romaine, *etc.* pp. 32. *G. Thompson: London,* 1795. 8°. **1419**. f. **44**.

—— God's Mercy to the Fatherless, considered in a sermon, *etc.* pp. 35. *A. M. Smart & T. Cowslade: Reading,* [1786.] 8°. **4474**. dd. **6**.

—— Liberty, and Equality, two sermons. pp. 76. *Smart & Cowslade: Reading,* 1792. 8°. **1103**. k. **63**.

—— The Life of the Rev. William Romaine. (A Catalogue of the writings of the Rev. W. Romaine.) pp. iv. 96. *T. Bensley: London,* 1796. 8°. **613**. k. **16**. (**1**.)

—— [Another edition.] *See* ROMAINE (William) Works of the late Reverend William Romaine. vol. 7. 1796. 8°. **3752**. bb. **13**.

—— [Another edition.] *See* ROMAINE (William) The Works of the late Rev. W. Romaine, *etc.* vol. 1. 1813. 8°. **3753**. c. **9**.

—— A new edition. pp. iv. 96. *Ebenezer Palmer: London,* 1827. 8°. **4906**. cc. **3**.

—— [Another edition.] *See* ROMAINE (William) The Whole Works of the late Reverend William Romaine, *etc.* 1837. 8°. **3755**. cc. **12**.

—— [Another edition, abridged.] pp. 72. *R.T.S.: London,* [1832.] 12°. [*Christian Biography.*] **864**. f. **11/62**.

—— The Love of Christ the Portion and Principle of the Children of God. Proved in a sermon . . . upon the death of Mrs. Talbot, *etc.* pp. 45. *A. M. Smart & T. Cowslade: Reading,* [1785.] 8°. **1417**. h. **21**.

CADOGAN (*Hon.* WILLIAM BROMLEY)

—— The Power of Faith: considered in a sermon, *etc.* pp. 30. *J. F. & C. Rivington: London,* 1780. 8°. **1026**. f. **4**. (**1**.)

—— Psalms and Hymns. Collected by W. B. Cadogan. . . . Second edition. pp. x. 264. 1787. 12°. *See* BIBLE.—*Psalms.—Selections.* [*English.*] **3436**. cc. **37**.

—— Third edition. pp. xx. 264. 1794. 24°. *See* BIBLE.—*Psalms.—Selections.* [*English.*] **3436**. c. **37**.

—— Sixth edition. pp. xii. 258. 1817. 18°. *See* BIBLE.—*Psalms.—Selections.* [*English.*] **3436**. aa. **34**.

—— A new edition. pp. 329. 1824. 24°. *See* BIBLE.—*Psalms.—Selections.* [*English.*] **3437**. d. **1**. (**1**.)

—— An Elegy on the much lamented Death of the Hon. and Rev. William Bromley Cadogan. *Printed for the Author: London,* [1797.] *s. sh.* 8°. **644**. k. **25**. (**10**.)

CADOINE (JOSEPH JULES PAUL MARIE FRANÇOIS DE) *Marquis de Gabriac.* Souvenirs diplomatiques de Russie et d'Allemagne, 1870–1872. pp. vii. 337. *Paris,* 1896. 8°. **9077**. eee. **41**.

CADOL (ÉDOUARD) *See* CADOL (Victor E.)

CADOL (VICTOR ÉDOUARD) *See* also MARGALIERS (P. de) *pseud.* [i.e. V. E. Cadol.]

—— *See* DAIGNÉ (D.) Les Comédies indépendantes . . . Précédées d'une lettre de M. E. Cadol. 1880. 12°. **11740**. e. **9**.

—— *See* JALLAIS (A. de) La Corde du pendu . . . par MM. A. de Jallais, C. Cabot et E. Cadol. 1854. 8°. **11739**. g. **88**. (**9**.)

—— *See* JALLAIS (A. de) and CADOL (V. E.) La Question d'Occident, *etc.* [1854.] 8°. **11739**. g. **51**.

—— *See* VARIN (C. V.) and CADOL (V. E.) Le Jeune homme au riflard. Vaudeville . . . par MM. Varin et Cadol, *etc.* 1860. 8°. [*Bibliothèque dramatique.* tom. 89.] **2296**. d. **27**.

—— —— 1862. fol. [*Théâtre contemporain illustré.* liv. 546, 547.] **2296**. h.

—— Une Amourette. Comédie en quatre actes, *etc.* pp. 108. *Paris,* 1871. 8°. **11740**. f. **2**. (**1**.)

—— La Belle affaire. Comédie en trois actes, *etc.* pp. xv. 107. *Paris,* 1881. 12°. **11739**. e. **51**. (**2**.)

—— La Belle Virginie . . . Deuxième édition. pp. 300. *Paris,* 1883. 18°. **12518**. e. **17**.

—— Cathi. pp. 403. *Paris,* 1883. 12°. **12516**. d. **18**.

—— Le Cheveu du Diable. Voyage fantastique au Japon. pp. 299. *Paris,* 1875. 12°. **12517**. f. **4**.

—— La Colonie étrangère. (Feuilleton du Rappel.) 83 pt. [*Paris,* 1882.] fol. **1871**. a. **23**.
The portions of the newspaper containing the "Feuilleton" cut off and bound together.

—— Les Créanciers du bonheur. Comédie en trois actes, *etc.* pp. 93. *Paris,* 1871. 12°. **11739**. c. **15**. (**12**.)

—— La Diva. pp. 350. *Paris,* 1879. 12°. **12517**. ccc. **15**.

—— Un Enfant d'Israël. pp. 334. *Paris,* 1881. 12°. **12518**. g. **33**.

—— L'Enquête. Drame en trois actes, *etc.* pp. 67. *Paris,* [1873.] 12°. **11740**. b. **12**. (**2**.)

—— La Fausse monnaie. Comédie en cinq actes, *etc.* pp. 143. *Paris,* 1869. 12°. **11736**. c. **36**.

—— Gilberte. pp. 327. *Paris,* 1887. 8°. **12491**. p. **23**.

—— La Grand'maman. Comédie en quatre actes, en prose, *etc.* pp. 108. *Paris,* [1878.] 12°. **11740**. b. **13**. (**1**.)

—— Hortense Maillot. pp. 359. *Paris,* 1885. 18°. **12511**. l. **10**.

—— Les Inutiles. pp. xv. 314. *Paris,* 1877. 12°. **12517**. ff. **6**.

CADOL (VICTOR ÉDOUARD)

—— [Another edition.] pp. 155. *Paris,* 1880. 12°. **11740.** e. **8.**

—— Jacques Cernol. Comédie en trois actes, *etc.* pp. 87. *Paris,* 1870. 12°. **11737.** bb. **23.**

—— Lettre à M. le marquis de Carabas sur les partis. pp. 30. *Paris,* 1862. 8°. **8052.** d. **91.** (**8.**)

—— Lucette. pp. 361. *Paris,* 1886. 12°. **12511.** ᴜ. **24.**

—— Madame Élise. pp. 254. *Paris,* 1874. 12°. **12516.** h. **6.**

—— Madeleine Houdard . . . Deuxième édition. pp. 314. *Paris,* 1895. 18°. **012551.** i. **27.**

—— Mademoiselle. pp. 380. *Paris,* 1887. 8°. **12491.** r. **13.**

—— Marguerite Chauveley. pp. xx. 316. *Paris,* 1878. 12°. **12517.** eee. **20.**
The titlepage is mutilated.

—— Le Monde galant. pp. 272. *Paris,* 1873. 12°. **12515.** df. **11.**

—— Le Mystère. Comédie en un acte et en prose, *etc.* pp. 34. *Paris,* 1870. 12°. **11739.** cc. **19.** (**2.**)

—— Les Parents riches. pp. 384. *Paris,* 1885. 18°. **12511.** l. **25.**

—— Paris pendant le siége, *etc.* pp. 107. *Bruxelles,* 1871. 8°. **9078.** ccc. **37.** (**6.**)

—— Le Secrétaire particulier. 2ᵉ édition. pp. 349. *Paris,* 1893. 12°. **012550.** f. **37.**

—— Son Altesse. pp. 371. *Paris,* 1883. 18°. **12516.** d. **17.**

—— Son Excellence Satinette, Affaires Étrangères. pp. 365. *Paris,* 1882. 12°. **12518.** b. **28.**

—— Le Spectre de Patrick. Drame fantastique en cinq actes et neuf tableaux. pp. 103. *Paris,* 1872. 12°. **11739.** cc. **22.** (**2.**)

—— Suzanne Herbain. pp. 263. *Paris,* 1894. 12°. **012550.** i. **1.**

—— La Vie en l'air. pp. 351. *Paris,* 1884. 12°. **12510.** l. **25.**

CADOLINI (ALOYSIUS) Enumeratio carabicorum Ticinensium sistens insecta hujus familiæ in agro Ticinensi hucusque inventa. Dissertatio inauguralis, *etc.* pp. 36. *Ticini Regii,* [1830.] 8°. **7383.*** d. **15.** (**8.**)

CADOLINI (ANTONIUS MARIA) *Cardinal.* Antonius Maria Cadolini . . . Episcopus Caesenatensis . . . gratiam Domini Nostri Iesu Christi, et charitatem Dei, et communicationem Sancti Spiritus. [A pastoral letter of A. M. Cadolini on his consecration. Dated: 21 April 1822.] pp. xi. *Romæ,* 1822. 4°. **898.** i. **5.** (**6.**)

CADOLINI (GEMMA MANFRO) *See* MANFRO-CADOLINI.

CADOLINI (GIOVANNI) Discorso (intorno alle interpellanze sulla politica generale del Ministero). *See* MORDINI (A.) Discorsi, *etc.* 1862. 8°. **8033.** aa. **53.** (**4.**)

—— Memorie del Risorgimento, dal 1848 al 1862. [With plans.] pp. 508. *Milano,* 1911. 8°. **9165.** bbb. **42.**

—— Il Quarto reggimento dei volontari ed il corpo d'operazione in Valcamonica nella campagna del 1866. Ricordi. pp. 100. *Firenze,* 1867. 8°. **9165.** c. **36.**

CADOLINI (GIUSEPPE) *See* SGANZIN (J. M.) Programma . . . delle lezioni di . . . costruzione . . . Prima versione italiana . . . dall'ingegnere G. Cadolini. 1832. 4°. **8776.** ff. **1.**

CADOLINI (IGNATIUS JOANNES) *Cardinal.* Epistola pastoralis ad clerum et populum universum Ficodensis dioeceseos. pp. xvi. *Romæ,* [1827.] 4°. **4445.** g. **8.**

CADOLINI (RAFFAELE)

—— *See* BOLOGNA.—*Liceo Musicale.* Catalogo della biblioteca del Liceo Musicale, *etc.* (vol. 4. Compiuto e pubblicato dal Dr. R. Cadolini.) 1890, *etc.* 8°. **11907.** g. **19.**

CADOMUM. *See* CAEN.

CADONAU (PEDER PAUL)

—— *See* BIBLE.—*Selections.* [*Romansch.—Oberland Dialect.*] Il Niev Testament. Ils Psalms, *etc.* (Versiun procurada da P. P. Cadonau cun agid de H. Bertogg.) 1954. 8°. **3042.** de. **15.**

CADONI (ANTIOCO) Sull'economia rurale della Sardegna . . . Articoli estratti dal Corriere di Sardegna. pp. 39. *Cagliari,* 1865. 8°. **7076.** aa. **52.** (**6.**)

CADONICI (GIOVANNI) Informazione sopra il famoso ed agitato fenomeno della giovane cremonese vomitante sassi ed altri corpi strani, *etc.* pp. xlix. *Brescia,* 1749. 4°. **8630.** e. **3.**

CADOR (L.) Subsistances et populations. pp. 464. *Paris,* 1850. 8°. **8205.** d. **10.**

CADORE. Statuta communitatis Cadubrii cum additionibus nouiter impressa. [Compiled by Philippus Almericus.] ff. lxxxvi. *Per Ioannem Patauinum: Venetiis,* 1545. fol. **5326.** g. **14.**

CADORE, JEAN BAPTISTE NOMPÈRE DE CHAMPAGNY, *Duke de.* *See* NOMPÈRE DE CHAMPAGNY.

CADORÉ (ÉMILE) Les Appareils plâtrés en staff. Leur application aux blessures de guerre. pp. 82. pl. XVI. *Paris,* 1917. 8°. **7482.** l. **27.**

CADORET (   ) *See* TERODAK (   ) *Le Sieur, pseud.* [i.e. —— Cadoret.]

CADORET (EUGÈNE) Le Droit de César. Doctrine catholique sur la légitimité du pouvoir royal. pp. xliii. 235. *Paris,* 1853. 8°. **4051.** cc. **7.**

CADORET (FERDINAND) Études cliniques sur la rougeole. Thèse, *etc.* pp. 35. *Montpellier,* 1854. 4°. **7379.** c. **4.** (**7.**)

CADORET (L. S.) Le Souhait du pasteur. *See* ROUSSEL (N.) Galerie de quelques prédicateurs de l'Église Réformée de France, *etc.* sér. 1. 1835, *etc.* 8°. **4426.** cc. **6.** (**2.**)

CADORET (PIERRE) L'Industrie sardinière en Bretagne. Thèse, *etc.* pp. 174. *Paris,* 1912. 8°. **08227.** bb. **30.**

CADORIN (GIOVANNI BATTISTA) *See* ONGARO (F. dall') La Betulia liberata. Poemetto . . . pubblicato da G. B. Cadorin. 1874. 4°. **11436.** i. **7.** (**5.**)

CADORIN (GIUSEPPE) Dello amore ai Veneziani di Tiziano Vecellio, delle sue case in Cadore e in Venezia, e delle vite de' suoi figli. Notizie. pp. 123. *Venezia,* 1833. 4°. **1267.** h. **2.**

—— Pareri di XV architetti e notizie storiche intorno al palazzo ducale di Venezia. Con illustrazioni dell'ab. G. Cadorin. pp. 196. *Venezia,* 1838. 8°. **1401.** h. **18.**

CADORIN (MATTEO) *See* CADORINO.

CADORINO (MATTEO) *See* SCHOTTUS (F.) Itinerario, overo Nova descrittione de' viaggi principali d'Italia, *etc.* [With plates by M. Cadorin.] 1688. 8°. **10129.** aa. **19.**

CADORNA (CARLA) La Guerra nelle retrovie. pp. 136. *Firenze,* 1917. 8°. **08248.** b. **45.**

CADORNA (CARLO) *See* ALIBERTI (V.) Sul progetto di riordinamento delle amministrazioni centrali e provinciali . . . proposto dal Ministro dell'Interno Senatore Cadorna, *etc.* 1868. 8°. **8033**. bb. **34**. (**7**.)

—— *See* CHIODO (A.) Risposte dei cessati ministri Chiodo, Cadorna e Tecchio alla relazione . . . del general maggiore A. Chrzanowski, *etc.* 1849. 8°. **9165**. bb. **32**.

—— Del primo ed unico principio del diritto pubblico clericale. Estratto della Rassegna di scienze sociali e politiche, *etc.* pp. 96. *Roma,* 1888. 8°. **05107**. i. **26**.

—— L'Espansione coloniale dell'Italia. pp. 23. *Firenze,* 1885. 8°. **8154**. ee. **31**. (**2**.)

—— Le Interpretazioni abusive dei convegni internazionali, e in specie di quelli di Londra per l'Egitto e di Skiernewicz . . . Ritratto dalla Rassegna di scienze sociali e politiche, *etc.* pp. 14. *Firenze,* 1884. 8°. **08028**. g. **50**.

—— Lettera dei fatti di Novara del marzo 1849 . . . Terza edizione. pp. 43. *Roma,* 1889. 8°. **8032**. ccc. **2**. (**4**.)

—— Il Potere temporale dei papi. La legge delle garanzie e la garanzia delle garanzie. [Reprinted from the "Rassegna di scienze sociale e politiche."] pp. 72. *Firenze,* 1884. 8°. **4051**. e. **54**.

—— Il Principio della rinascenza e uno strascico del medio evo, *etc.* (Estratto dalla Rassegna di scienze sociali e politiche.) pp. 30. *Roma,* 1887. 8°. **8033**. h. **44**.

—— Le Relazioni internazionali dell'Italia e la questione dell'Egitto. pp. 88. *Torino,* 1882. 8°. **8028**. g. **8**.

—— Religione, diritto, libertà. Delle condizione giuridica delle associazioni e delle autorità religiose negli stati civili . . . Edizione postuma curata dal generale Cadorna, con cenni biografici del senatore M. Tabarrini. 2 vol. *Milano,* 1893. 8°. **3900**. i. **24**.

—— Le Seicento delegazioni governative. Osservazioni . . . sul disegno di legge della Commissione della Camera dei Deputati intorno al riordinamento dell'amministrazione centrale e provinciale dello stato. pp. 76. *Firenze,* 1869. 8°. **8033**. bb. **34**. (**10**.)

—— Vita e scritti di Carlo Bagnis. Commemorazione. pp. 64. *Roma,* 1880. 4°. **10629**. f. **24**.

—— Le Riforme amministrative del ministro Cadorna. pp. 47. *Firenze,* 1868. 8°. **8032**. bb. **56**. (**5**.)

CADORNA (LUIGI) *See* MONTECUCCOLI (R.) *Prince.* Le Più belle pagine di R. Montecuccoli. Scelte da L. Cadorna. 1922. 12°. **012226**. a. **1/3**.

—— Il Generale Raffaele Cadorna nel Risorgimento italiano. Con 5 carte topografiche. [With a portrait.] pp. 400. *Milano,* 1922. 8°. **9168**. c. **30**.

—— La Guerra alla fronte italiana fino all'arresto sulla linea della Piave e del Grappa, 24 maggio 1915—9 novembre 1917. Con 3 carte corografiche. 2 vol. *Milano,* 1921. 8°. **09083**. d. **42**.

—— Pagine polemiche, *etc.* [With a map.] pp. xxviii. 364. *Milano,* 1950. 8°. **9087**. bbb. **15**.
Part of the series "Memorie e documenti." The date in the colophon is 1951.

CADORNA (RAFFAELE) *the Elder.*

—— *See* CADORNA (C.) Religione, diritto, libertà . . . Edizione postuma curata dal generale Cadorna, *etc.* 1893. 8°. **3900**. i. **24**.

CADORNA (RAFFAELE) *the Elder.*

—— *See* CADORNA (L.) Il Generale R. Cadorna nel Risorgimento italiano, *etc.* 1922. 8°. **9168**. c. **30**.

—— *See* CORSELLI (R.) Cadorna. 1937. 8°. **10635**. b. **4**.

—— Lettera . . . all'arcivescovo di Palermo dopo il sollevamento del 1866. *See* ROME, *Church of.*—Pius IX., *Pope.* [1846–1878.] La Bolla di composizione o della S. Crociata in Sicilia, *etc.* 1875. 8°. **3902**. de. **25**. (**7**.)

—— La Liberazione di Roma nell'anno 1870 ed il plebiscito. Narrazione politico-militare corredata di tre carte . . . Seconda edizione. pp. ix. 601. *Torino,* 1889. 8°. **9167**. e. **7**.

—— Terza edizione—postuma—riveduta ed accresciuta dall'autore nel 1896 e pubblicata dal figlio. pp. xi. 627. *Torino,* 1898. 8°. **9166**. ee. **29**.

CADORNA (RAFFAELE) *the Younger.*

—— La Difesa di Roma. Discorso commemorativo pronunciato in campidoglio per l'8 settembre 1943. pp. 17. *Roma,* [1953.] 8°. **12302**. b. **73**.

—— La Riscossa. Dal 25 luglio alla liberazione. [With plates and plans.] pp. 397. *Milano,* 1948. 8°. **9102**. fff. **33**.
La seconda guerra mondiale. vol. 26.

CADORNA-VIANI-VISCONTI (CAROLINA) L'Amico del popolo. Racconti. pp. 265. *Milano,* 1876. 8°. **12471**. c. **8**.

—— Dall'alba al tramonto, o sia la vita della donna. pp. 210. *Milano,* 1874. 8°. **8416**. bb. **7**.

—— Favole, poesie e commedie pei fanciulli. pp. 144. *Milano,* 1870. 8°. **12226**. b. **10**.

CADORNEGA (ANTÓNIO DE OLIVEIRA DE) *See* OLIVEIRA DE CADORNEGA.

CADOT (ALFRED DEGORCE) *See* DEGORCE CADOT.

CADOT (ANTOINE) Observations sur les effets de l'arnica montana, dans le traitement d'une fièvre de nature mucoso-putride . . . qui a régné dans le département de Seine et Marne à la fin de l'an 12. et au commencement de l'an 13. pp. 29. *Paris,* 1805. 4°. **1182**. f. **16**. (**6**.)

CADOT (B. CH. H.) Note sur l'invasion des Helvètes dans les Gaules et la première campagne de Jules César. pp. 24. *Lyon,* [1862.] 4°. **9039**. h. **21**.

CADOT (CH.) *See* CADOT (B. Ch. H.)

CADOT (HARRIETTE) *See* TILLY, afterwards CADOT.

CADOT (J. L.) L'Amusette des Français, ou Recueil de chansons . . . Choisis ou composés par J. L. Cadot, *etc.* *Paris,* [1810.] 12°. **F. 1920**. (**2**.)

—— Assemblées du Champ-de-Mai. (Le Champ de Mai. L'Amour de la patrie. [Two patriotic songs.]) pp. 2. [*Paris,* 1815.] *s. sh.* fol. **168**. k. **3**. (**6**.)

—— Départ volontaire des nouvelles Amazones françaises. (Marches des Amazones françaises.—Pas de charge des héroines lorraines et alsaciennes.) pp. 3. [*Paris,* 1815.] 4°. **112**. e. **8**. (**38**.)

CADOT (LOUIS) La Vérité sur le siége de Péronne. Réponse au général Faidherbe. pp. 24. *Paris,* 1872. 8°. **9079**. bb. **6**. (**7**.)

CADOT (Louis Félix) Des fistules salivaires de la parotide et du canal de Sténon. pp. 52. *Paris*, 1872. 4°. [*Collection des thèses soutenues à la Faculté de Médecine de Paris.* An 1872. tom. 3.] **7373. n. 9.**

CADOT (Pierre) *See* Alucci (C.) Institution et préceptes pour le Iubilé de l'Année Saincte . . . Traduit . . . par P. C. A. (P. Cadot.) Augmenté & enrichy d'annotations . . . par ledit P. C. A. 1653. 12°. **3478. a. 12.**

CADOT (Roger)

—— Chants dans la tempête . . . Poèmes des deux guerres. pp. 179. *Paris*, [c. 1942.] 8°. **11484. b. 21.**

CADOT (Thibaut) Le Blason de France, ou Notes curieuses sur l'Edit concernant la police des armoiries. (Dictionnaire ou table . . . et explication des termes, figures et pièces du blason les plus ordinaires et usitez en France.—Planches.) [The author's dedicatory epistle signed: C * * *, i.e. T. Cadot.] 2 pt. 1697. 8°. *See* C * * *. **137. a. 32.**

CADOU (René Guy)

—— Les Biens de ce monde 1944–1950. Avec un dessin par Toulouse. pp. 34. *Paris*, 1951. 8°. **11484. df. 34.**
Collections P.S. no. 72.

—— Guillaume Apollinaire ou l'artilleur de Metz. Avec un portrait inédit par Roger Toulouse. pp. 150. *Nantes*, 1948. 8°. **011840. cc. 73.**

—— Testament d'Apollinaire. Témoignage. pp. 190. *Paris*, 1945. 8°. **11866. a. 52.**

—— René Guy Cadou. Une étude par Michel Manoll. Inédits, poèmes et textes choisis, bibliographie, portraits et documents. pp. 229. *Paris*, 1954. 8°. [*Poètes d'aujourd'hui.* no. 41.] **W.P. 1567/41.**

CADOUDAL (Georges) *See* Cadoudal (L. G. de) Georges Cadoudal et la Chouannerie, *etc.* 1887. 8°. **10664. g. 21.**

—— *See* Drake (Francis) *British Envoy at Munich.* Procédure contre Georges [Cadoudal], Pichegru, etc. Correspondance de M. Drake. [1804 ?] 8°. **911. c. 21. (2.)**

—— *See* Grandin (L.) Georges Cadoudal. [1890.] 8°. **10602.dd.16/3.**

—— *See* Lachouque (H.) and Arnna (J.) Cadoudal et les chouans. 1951. 8°. **010665. k. 14.**

—— *See* Lenôtre (G.) *pseud.* Georges Cadoudal. [With a portrait.] 1929. 8°. **W.P. 8349/1.**

—— *See* Muret (T. C.) Vie populaire de Georges Cadoudal. 1845. 12°. **10660. a. 47. (3.)**

—— *See* Seine, *Department of the.—Tribunal Criminel.* Tribunal criminel et spécial du département de la Seine. Liste des individus [G. Cadoudal and others] mis en état d'accusation, prévenus d'être auteurs ou complices d'une conspiration, *etc.* [1804.] 4°. **F. 52*. (9*.)**

—— *See* Seine, *Department of the.—Tribunal Criminel.* Notice abrégée sur la vie, le caractère et les crimes des principaux assassins aux gages de l'Angleterre [i.e. G. Cadoudal and others], *etc.* 1804. 8°. **F. 1258. (19.)**

—— Acte d'accusation de Georges, Pichegru, Moreau, et autres, prévenus de conspiration contre la personne du Premier Consul, et contre la sûreté intérieure et extérieure de la République. (Pièces justificatives.) pp. 448. *Paris*, 1804. 8°. **911. c. 21. (1.)**
Imperfect; wanting the half-title.

CADOUDAL (Georges)

—— [Another copy.] **934. c. 10. (**
Imperfect; wanting pp. 341–448, *containing the* "*Pièc justificatives.*"

—— [Another copy.] **F. 1270. (**
Imperfect; wanting the "*Pièces justificatives.*"

—— Arrestation du fameux chef de brigands, Georges, et de ses affidés. pp. 4. *Paris*, [1804.] 4°. **F. 52*. (9**

—— Arrêt de la cour de justice criminelle et spéciale séan à Paris, qui condamne à la peine de mort, Georg Cadoudal, Louis Ducorps, *etc.* pp. 4. [*Paris*, 1804.] 4° **R. 692. (**

—— Cour de Justice criminelle séante à Paris. Bulletin procès instruit . . . Contre Georges, Moreau et autres, 11 pt. [*Paris*, 1804.] 4°. **707. g. 1**

—— [Another copy.] **F. 52*. (1**

—— Interrogatoire subi devant M. Thuriot par Georg Cadoudal, prévenu d'être un des chefs principaux d brigands envoyés par l'Angleterre pour assassiner majesté l'Empereur des Français, *etc.* pp. 4. [*Paris*, 1804.] 4°. **R. 692. (**

—— Procès instruit par la Cour de Justice criminelle spéciale du département de la Seine, séante à Pa contre Georges, Pichegru et autres, prévenus de conspir tion contre la personne du Premier Consul; recueilli p des sténographes. 8 tom. *Paris*, 1804. 8°. **878. i. 6–**

—— [Another copy.] **1131. f. 2–1**
Imperfect; wanting the titlepages and half-titles tom. 1–4, *the Tables des matières of tom.* 2, 3, 5, *and t* "*Rapport du Grand-Juge . . . au Gouvernement,*" *whi stands at the beginning of tom.* 1.

—— Vie privée de Georges Cadoudal contenant sa correspo dance particulière, et des notes propres à le faire connaitr Terminée par une Complainte des plus intéressante [The Complainte signed: P. C.] pp. 24. [*Pari* 1804.] 12°. **F. 1302. (1**

CADOUDAL (Georges de) *See* Cadoudal (Louis G. de)

CADOUDAL (Louis Georges de) *See* Camusat Riancey (C. L.) Le Troisième commandement . . précédé d'une notice sur l'auteur par G. de Cadoudal. 1861. 12°. **4355. aa. 64. (5**

—— Auray et Quiberon, Morbihan. 1892. *See* Robuch (J.) Paysages et monuments. livr. 1–13. 1892, *etc.* f **1790. c.**

—— Le 10 Août. pp. 35. *Paris*, 1875. 12°. **9230. bb.**

—— Faits et récits contemporains. Nouveau recueil ane dotique. pp. v. 224. *Paris*, 1860. 12°. **12356. bb.**

—— Georges Cadoudal et la Chouannerie. Par son nev G. de Cadoudal . . . Ouvrage orné d'un portrait accompagné d'une carte. pp. xi. 476. *Par* 1887. 8°. **10664. g. 2**

—— Histoires et anecdotes des temps présents, recueilli et mises en ordre par M. G. de Cadoudal. pp. 259. *Paris*, 1863. 12°. **12804. ccc.**

—— Honnêtes facéties et menus propos, recueillis et mis e ordre par M. G. de Cadoudal. pp. 259. *Paris*, 1863. 12 **12354. aaa.**

—— Madame Acarie. Étude sur la société religieuse au xvie et xviie siècles. pp. 232. *Paris*, 1863. 12°. **4865. aa. 1.**

—— Les Serviteurs des hommes. pp. x. 271. *Pari* 1864. 12°. **10603. bb. 2**

CADOUDAL (Louis Georges de)

—— Les Signes du temps. Critiques littéraires et morales. pp. iii. 404. *Paris*, 1862. 12°. **11826**. bbb. **25**.

—— Souvenirs de quinze années, 1845–1861. Esquisses morales, historiques et littéraires. pp. 352. *Paris*, 1862. 12°. **12236**. aaa. **3**.

CADOUIN.

—— Le Suaire de Cadouin. (Le Saint suaire de Cadouin.) [With plates.] pp. 39. *Bergerac*, [1930?] 8°. **4633**. e. **23**.

CADOUSTEAU (Jean Baptiste) *See* Dormoy (G.) and ( ) *Madame*. Vocabulaire tahitien-français, *etc.* (Révisé par MM. Cadousteau et Butteaud.) 1890. 8°. **12910**. a. **65**.

—— —— 1894. 8°. **12910**. a. **59**.

CADOUX (Arthur Temple) Essays in Christian Thinking. pp. 188. *London*, 1922. 8°. [*Christian Revolution Series*. no. 14.] **012201**. aaa. **2/14**.

—— The Gospel that Jesus preached and the Gospel for To-day. pp. 248. *G. Allen & Unwin: London*, 1925. 8°. **4223**. bb. **32**.

—— Jesus and Civil Government. A contribution to the problem of Christianity and coercion. pp. 163. *G. Allen & Unwin: London*, 1923. 8°. **04018**. de. **44**.

—— *See* Walsh (Walter) *Leader of the "Free Religious Movement."* Jesus: War or Peace? *etc.* [A reply to "Jesus and Civil Government," by A. T. Cadoux.] [1924.] 8°. **8425**. tt. **22**.

—— Morals for Ministers. By R. E. X. [i.e. A. T. Cadoux.] pp. 127. 1928. 8°. *See* X., R. E. **4499**. eee. **17**.

—— A New Orthodoxy of Jesus and Personality. pp. 207. *I. Nicholson & Watson: London*, 1934. 8°. **4223**. d. **17**.

—— Onesimus . . . Adapted for stage presentation. pp. vi. 30. *Religious Drama Society of Great Britain: London*, 1952. 8°. **011781**. n. **53**.

—— The Parables of Jesus: their art and use. pp. 255. *J. Clarke & Co.: London*, [1931.] 8°. **03226**. ee. **61**.

—— Shakespearian Selves. An essay in ethics. [Studies of characters in the plays of Shakespeare.] pp. 175. *Epworth Press: London*, 1938. 8°. **11764**. l. **16**.

—— Songs of Self and God. [Poems. With a portrait.] pp. 130. *James Clarke & Co.: London*, [1950.] 8°. **11655**. d. **39**.

—— The Sources of the Second Gospel. pp. 296. *J. Clarke & Co.: London*, [1935.] 8°. **03226**. de. **100**.

—— The Theology of Jesus. pp. 304. *Nicholson & Watson: London*, 1940. 8°. [*International Library of Christian Knowledge*.] W.P. **11719/12**.

—— The Thought of St. James. pp. 101. *J. Clarke & Co.: London*, 1944. 8°. **3228**. aa. **6**.

CADOUX (Cecil John)

—— *See* Bartlet (James V.) Church Life and Church-Order during the First Four Centuries . . . Edited by C. J. Cadoux, *etc.* 1943. 8°. **4536.ccc.7.**

—— *See* Bible.—*Old Testament*. [*English*.] Books of the Old Testament in colloquial speech. (no. 9. The Book of Deuteronomy. Translated . . . by C. J. Cadoux.) [1920, *etc.*] 8°. W.P. **6532/9**.

CADOUX (Cecil John)

—— Ancient Smyrna. A history of the city from the earliest times to 324 A.D. [With plates and maps.] pp. xlv. 438. *Basil Blackwell: Oxford*, 1938. 8°. **9042**. g. **4**.

—— An Appeal to the People of the Christian Church. pp. 27. *Fellowship of Reconciliation: London*, 1919. 8°. **4381**. bb. **35**.

—— The Case for Evangelical Modernism. A study of the relation between Christian faith and traditional theology. pp. xvii. 182. *Hodder & Stoughton: London*, 1938. 8°. **04374**. k. **15**.

—— Catholicism and Christianity. A vindication of progressive Protestantism, *etc.* pp. xl. 708. *G. Allen & Unwin: London*, 1928. 8°. **3942**. f. **13**.

—— The Character of the Gospel-Record . . . Reprinted from the "Bulletin of the John Rylands Library", *etc.* pp. 19. *Manchester*, 1946. 8°. **3228**. d. **4**.

—— The Christian Crusade. A study in the supreme purpose of life. pp. vii. 126. *J. M. Dent & Sons: London & Toronto*, 1924. 8°. **4406**. i. **30**.

—— Christian Pacifism Re-examined. pp. xx. 245. *Basil Blackwell: Oxford*, 1940. 8°. **8425**. w. **29**.

—— The Congregational Way, *etc.* pp. 46. *Basil Blackwell: Oxford*, 1945. 8°. **4140**. aa. **6**.

—— The Early Christian Attitude to War, *etc.* pp. xxxii. 272. *Headley Bros.: London*, 1919. 8°. [*Christian Revolution Series*.] **012201**. aaa. **2/3**.

—— [A reissue.] The Early Christian Attitude to War, *etc.* *G. Allen & Unwin: London*, 1940. 8°. **8425**. tt. **44**.

—— *See* Todorov (Ya.) Отношението на първитѣ християни къмъ войната и военната служба. [Based on C. J. Cadoux's "The Early Christian Attitude to War."] 1924. 8°. **20002**. e. **86**.

—— The Early Church and the World. A history of the Christian attitude to pagan society and the state down to the time of Constantinus. pp. lii. 675. *T. & T. Clark: Edinburgh*, 1925. 8°. **4533**. eee. **23**.

—— The Guidance of Jesus for To-day, *etc.* pp. 178. *G. Allen & Unwin: London*, 1920. 8°. **4223**. aaa. **45**.

—— The Historic Mission of Jesus. A constructive re-examination of the eschatological teaching in the Synoptic Gospels. pp. xxiv. 376. *Lutterworth Press: London & Redhill*, 1941. 8°. [*Lutterworth Library*. vol. 12.] W.P. **4629/12**.

—— The Life of Jesus. [With a map.] pp. 224. *Penguin Books: West Drayton*, 1948. 8°. [*Pelican Books*. no. 189.] **012209**. d. **4/189**.

—— The Message about the Cross. A fresh study of the doctrine of the Atonement. pp. 92. *G. Allen & Unwin: London*, 1924. 8°. **4255**. de. **39**.

—— The Meaning of the Cross for Christian Ethics. (The sixth . . . section of . . . "The Message about the Cross.") pp. 24. *H. O. Hodgkin: Leeds*, 1924. 8°. **4223**. de. **49**.

—— Philip of Spain and the Netherlands. An essay on moral judgments in history. pp. xv. 251. *Lutterworth Press: London & Redhill*, 1947. 8°. **09073** b. **40**.

—— A Pilgrim's Further Progress. Dialogues on Christian teaching. pp. xvi. 211. *Basil Blackwell: Oxford*, 1943. 8°. **04018**. k. **5**.

CADOUX (Cecil John)

—— [A reissue.] A Pilgrim's Further Progress, *etc. Oxford*, 1945. 8°. **04018. f. 70.**

—— The Possibility of a United Christendom: from the standpoint of the Congregational Communion. pp. 24. *London*, [1937.] 8°. [*Union of Christendom.* section 4. no. 5c.] **04374. g. 45/4. (5c.)**

—— The Reformation. Addresses delivered to the Assembly of the Congregational Union . . . I. The Spiritual Principles of the Reformation. By C. J. Cadoux . . . II. The Reformation and the Free Churches. By Bernard L. Manning. pp. 38. *Independent Press: London*, 1938. 8°. **20033. aa. 33.**

—— The Resurrection and Second Advent of Jesus. pp. 30. *Independent Press: London*, 1927. 8°. **4808. cc. 8.**

—— Roman Catholicism and Freedom. pp. 191. *Independent Press: London*, 1936. 8°. **3942. ee. 35.**

—— Second impression. pp. 191. *Independent Press: London*, 1936. 8°. **3939. ccc. 46.**

—— Third edition, with supplementary notes. pp. 207. *Independent Press: London*, 1937. 8°. **3939. ccc. 47.**

—— Roman Catholicism and Freedom. (Fourth edition.) pp. 207. *Independent Press: London*, 1947. 8°. **3942. eee. 83.**

CADOUX (Gaston) Les Attachés commerciaux et les consulats. Rapport . . . Préface de M. de Lanessan. pp. 72. *Paris*, [1891.] 8°. **08227. g. 47. (3.)**

—— Les Finances de la ville de Paris de 1798 à 1900. Suivies d'un essai de statistique comparative des charges communales des principales villes françaises et étrangères, de 1878 à 1898. [With a bibliography.] pp. viii. 821. *Paris, Nancy*, 1900. 8°. **08228. i. 48.**

—— Relation officielle des fêtes organisées par la ville de Paris pour la visite des officiers et marins de l'escadre russe . . . 1893. pp. vii. 244. 1896. 4°. *See* Paris.—*Municipalité.* **9930. i. 21.**

—— La Vie des grandes capitales. Études comparatives sur Londres—Paris—Berlin. Préface de M. André Lefèvre. pp. xiii. 259. *Paris, Nancy*, 1908. 8°. **010107. g. 16.**

—— Deuxième édition. (Études comparatives sur Londres—Paris—Berlin—Vienne—Rome.) pp. vii. 372. *Paris, Nancy*, 1913. 8°. **10108. de. 19.**

CADOVIUS (Christianus Arnoldus) *See* Arrhenius (J.) Historia Academiæ Upsaliensis, *etc.* (Partem secundam . . . sistunt præses Petrus L. Arrhenius . . . et respondens . . . C. A. Cadovius.) [1752, *etc.*] 4°. **272. e. 27. (2.)**

CADOVIUS (Nicolaus Garleffus) Ad locum Plinii, ex libr. II. cap. XIII. Exercitatio mathematica de admiranda vi refractionis circa defectus lunæ horizontales, *etc. Praes.* J. B. Roeschelius. *M. Henckelius: Wittenbergæ*, [1681.] 4°. **531. l. 8. (14.)**

CADOVIUS-MUELLER (Johann) Memoriale linguæ frisicae . . . Mit Zugrundelegung der in Aurich befindlichen Originalhandschrift zum ersten Male herausgegeben von Dr. L. Kükelhan. [With plates.] pp. 118. *Leer*, 1875. 8°. **12972. d. 6.**

—— [Another edition.] Nach der Jeverschen Originalhandschrift herausgegeben von Erich König. Mit zehn Tafeln. pp. 136. *Norden & Leipzig*, 1911. 8°. [*Forschungen herausgegeben vom Verein für niederdeutsche Sprachforschung.* Bd. 4.] **Ac. 9822/5.**

CADOZ (François) *See* 'Abd al-Raḥmān ibn Abī Ba[kr] (Jalāl al-Dīn) *al-Suyūṭī.* [al-Jāmi 'al-ṣaghīr.] Civil[ité] musulmane, ou recueil de sentences et de maxim[es] extraites de l'ouvrage du célèbre auteur arabe l'Im[am] Essiyouthi, avec une traduction . . . par F. Cadoz. 1851. 12°. **14521. a.**

—— Droit musulman malékite. Examen critique de [la] traduction officielle qu'a faite M. Perron du livre [de] Khalil contenant la solution de questions intéressant[es,] *etc.* pp. 206. *Bar-sur-Aube*, 1870. 8°. **5319. bb.**

—— Initiation à la science du droit musulman. Variét[és] juridiques. pp. xii. 99. *Oran*, 1868. 8°. **5319. cc. 1**

—— Le Secrétaire de l'Algérie, ou le Secrétaire français-arab[e] contenant des modèles de lettres et d'actes sur toutes sort[es] de sujets, *etc.* pp. 180. *Alger*, 1850. 12°. **14586. a. 3**
Lithographed.

CADRAN. *See* England.—*Ministry of Informati[on]* [1939–].

CADRANS. Des cadrans solaires. pp. 40. [*Pari[s]*, 1680 ?] 8°. **533. b. 25. (**
Apparently extracted from a larger work.

CADRATUS (Petrus) *Bishop of Orange. Begin.* [fol. [1] *recto*:] Oratio Reuerendi in xp̄o patris ⁊ dn̄i dn̄i Pe[tri] Cadrati Ep̄i Antiacen̄ [*sic*] . . . oratoris christianissi[mi] Frācorum regis: ad Sanctissimū dn̄m nostrū dn̄ Innocentium papam Octauū. [fol. 3 *verso*:] Orat[io] R̄ndi dn̄i. A. de Shinuccijs Ep̄i Suanen̄ ad Sāctissim[um] dn̄m Innocentiū papā .viii. pro republica Senen̄. G.[L.] [*Stephan Planck: Rome*, 1485 ?] 4°. **IA. 1840**
Four leaves, without signatures. 33 lines to a page.

—— [Another copy.] **IA. 184**

—— [Another copy.] **IA. 184**

—— [Another edition.] *Begin.* [fol. 1 *recto*:] Oratio Reuere[n]dissimoꝝ ac nobilissīoꝝ dn̄oꝝ oratoruʒ xp̄ianissi[mi] francorum regis ad sanctissimum dominū nostruʒ d. Inn[o]centium papam viii. in publico consistorio habita. die [?] februarii. anno. m. cccc. lxxxv., *etc.* G.L. [*Bartholomaeus Guldinbeck: Rome*, 1485.] 4°. **IA. 1812**
2 leaves, without signatures. 35 lines to a page.

CADRAWD, *Bardic name of Thomas C. Evans. See* Eva[ns] (Thomas C.) *of Llangynwyd, etc.*

CADRÈS (Alphonse) *See* Cadrès (Antoine A.)

CADRÈS (Antoine Alphonse) *See* Guilleminot (. La Sagesse chrétienne . . . Nouvelle édition . . . p[ar] A. A. Cadrès. 1857, *etc.* 12°. **3557. a. 2**

—— *See* Marie (Pierre) *Jesuit.* Jesus Crucified, or t[he] Science of the Cross . . . Edited by A. Cadrès, *etc.* 1918. 12°. **03456. df.**

—— Notice sur la vie et les ouvrages du père Jean-Nicol[as] Grou . . . Accompagnée d'un fac-simile. pp. 94. *Par[is]*, 1862. 8°. **4866. bb. 1**

—— [Another edition.] *See* Grace (J. N.) L'Intérieur [de] Jésus et de Marie, *etc.* 1862. 12°. **4378. aaa. 2**

CADRÈS (Émile) Code de procédure commerciale mis e[n] rapport avec la doctrine et la jurisprudence, suivi d[es] lois organiques et des dispositions réglementaires co[n]cernant les tribunaux de commerce. pp. xxiv. 448. *Paris*, 1844. 8°. **882. g. 1**

—— Traité des enfants naturels mis en rapport avec [la] doctrine et la jurisprudence. pp. xxxii. 440. *Pari[s]*, 1846. 8°. **5425. e.**

CADRIEU (Jean Guillaume) Essai sur la dothinenterite. Tribut académique, *etc.* pp. 31. *Montpellier*, 1835. 4°. **1181.** g. **10.** (**11.**)

CADROY (Paul) *See* Isnard (M.) Corps législatif. Conseil des Cinq-Cents. Éclaircissemens donnés . . . sur la dénonciation faite contre . . . Cadroy, Chambon, *etc.* [1795.] 8°. F. **1025.** (**14.**)

—— Convention nationale. Arrêtés et correspondance avec le Comité de salut public, *etc.* pp. 40. [*Paris*,] an 3 [1795]. 8°. F. **1236.** (**5.**)

—— Cadroy, membre du Conseil des Cinq-Cents, à ses collègues, sur le Mémoire de Fréron. pp. 24. *Paris*, an 4 [1796]. 8°. F. **1018.** (**7.**)

—— Cadroy, représentant du peuple, à ses collègues, membres du Corps législatif. Pour servir de suite au compte rendu de ses diverses missions dans les départemens méridionaux. pp. 8. [*Paris*,] an IV [1795]. 8°. F. **1206.** (**8.**)

—— [Another copy.] F. **1236.** (**14.**)

—— [Another copy.] Cadroy . . . à ses collègues, membres du Corps législatif, *etc.* [*Paris*,] an IV [1794]. 8°. R. **101.** (**25.**)

—— Convention nationale. Motion d'ordre . . . lue à la séance au 24 brumaire. pp. 10. *Paris*, an 3 [1794]. 8°. F. **788.** (**7.**)

—— Convention nationale. Opinion sur la garantie de la représentation nationale. pp. 16. [*Paris*,] an III [1794]. 8°. F. **593.** (**13.**)

—— [Another copy.] F. **787.** (**7.**)

—— Convention nationale. Opinion . . . sur le jugement de Louis XVI. pp. 7. *Paris*, 1793. 8°. F. **914.** (**15.**)

—— Convention nationale. Rapport du représentant du peuple Cadroy sur ses diverses missions dans les départemens méridionaux. (Errata dans le Rapport, *etc.*) 2 pt. *Paris*, an 4 [1795]. 8°. F. **1236.** (**1, 15.**)

—— Rapport fait à la Convention nationale . . . sur la situation, les rapports et les besoins du département des Bouches-du-Rhône. pp. 72. 2 pt. *Lyon*, [1796.] 8°. F. **1244.** (**5.**)

—— Convention nationale. Rapport sur l'approvisionnement, *etc.* pp. 30. *Paris*, an V [1796]. 8°. F. **476.** (**18.**)

—— [Another copy.] Convention nationale. Rapport sur l'approvisionnement, fait à la Convention, *etc.* *Paris*, an IV [1795]. 8°. R. **101.** (**26.**)

CADRUVI (Pieder Donat)

—— Die Gemeindelöser nach bündnerischem Recht. Dissertation, *etc.* pp. 116. *Ilanz*, 1952. 8°. **05551.** i. **33.**

CADRY (Jean Baptiste) *See* Bible.—*Appendix.—New Testament.* [*Miscellaneous.*] Histoire du livre des reflexions morales sur le Nouveau Testament et de la constitution Unigenitus, *etc.* [tom. 1 by J. Louail; tom. 2-4 by J. B. Cadry.] 1726, *etc.* 4°. **856.** l. **1-4.**

CADSANT. *See* Cadzand.

CADUBRIUM. *See* Cadore.

CADUCEO. El Caduceo. *See* Periodical Publications.—*Puebla de los Angeles.*

CADUCEUS. Caduceus Sinicus. *See* Chinese Caduceus.

CADUF (Fidel) *See* Jaeger (P.) Comedia de Cont Heinrich de Eichenfels . . . Augmentada tras canzuns e publicada da Sur F. Caduf. 1891. 8°. [*Annales della Societad Rhaeto-Romanscha.* ann. 6.] Ac. **9817.**

CADUFF (Gion Christian) Testamen dell'Olma, ù Kunst da ventireivlameing virer, à beadameing murir, *etc.* pp. 634. *Panaduz*, 1705. 12°. **885.** g. **13.**

—— Squicciau la tiarza gada. pp. 483. *Claustra de Mustêr* [*Disentis*], 1755. 12°. **885.** g. **17.**

—— [Another edition. Edited by Manrus Nager.] pp. 396. *Cuera*, 1785. 12°. **885.** g. **19.**
Pp. 213–216 *are mutilated.*

CADUFF (Julius) Aus der Schweiz. Gedichte. pp. xii. 100. *Chur*, 1859. 16°. **11525.** aaa. **63.** (**1.**)

CADUGANUS (Maredydius) *pseud.* [i.e. Thomas Richard, *Rector of Llanfyllin.*]

—— *Χοιροχωρογραφια*: sive, Hoglandiæ descriptio. (Augusto heroi Domino H - - S - - Maredydius Caduganus Pymlymmonensis. S.P.D.) [A satire in verse, in answer to the "Muscipula" of E. Holdsworth.] pp. vi. 16. *Londini*, 1709. 8°. **1078.** m. **6.** (**2.**)

CADURCUM. *See* Cahors.

CADUTA. Caduta ed esilio dei tiranni. [In verse.] [*Genoa*, 1848.] *s. sh.* fol. **804.** k. **13.** (**329.**)

CADVALLA, *King of Wessex.* *See* Cadwalla.

CADVAN, *Bardic name of Hugh Williams.* *See* Williams (Hugh) called Cadvan.

CADVAN, *Bardic name of John Cadvan Davies.* *See* Davies (J. C.) called Cadvan.

CADVAN STONE.

—— The "Cadvan Stone," Towyn, Mer. The inscribed words arranged as 'The Lord's Prayer' with explanatory notes. [Signed: D. R. P., i.e. D. R. Pugh.] 1939. 8°. *See* P., D. R. **07709.** bb. **3.**

CADWALADER (John) *General.* A Reply to Genl. Joseph Reed's Remarks on a late publication in the Independent Gazetteer; with some observations on his address to the people of Pennsylvania, *etc.* *See* Smith (Horace W.) Nuts for Future Historians to Crack, *etc.* 1856. 8°. **9602.** d. **14.**

CADWALADER (John) *Jurist.* Memoir of Charles John Biddle, *etc.* *See* Philadelphia.—*Bar.* Proceedings of a Meeting of the Bar of Philadelphia, *etc.* 1874. 8°. **10882.** i. **10.** (**1.**)

CADWALADER (John Lambert) Digest of the Published Opinions of the Attorneys-General, and of the leading decisions of the Federal Courts, with reference to international law, treaties and kindred subjects. pp. vii. 268. 1877. 8°. *See* United States of America.—*Department of State.* **6616.** df. **2.**

—— Revised edition. pp. vii. 290. 1877. 8°. *See* United States of America.—*Department of State.* **6616.** e. **2.**

—— [Another copy, with a different titlepage.] *See* United States of America.—*Department of State.* **6616.** ccc. **7.**

—— In memoriam John L. Cadwalader. November 17, 1836—March 11, 1914. pp. 27. *Privately printed: New York*, 1914. 8°. **10882.** gg. **16.**

CADWALADER (Thomas) An Essay on the West-India Dry-Gripes, *etc.* [Revised by A. Spencer.] pp. 42. *B. Franklin: Philadelphia*, 1745. 4°. T. **61.** (**2.**)

CADWALADER (Williams Biddle) Diseases of the Spinal Cord, *etc.* pp. xvii. 204. *Baillière & Co.: London; printed in U.S.A.*, 1932. 8°. **07630.** f. **16.**

CADWALADR (DILYS)

—— 'Bara.' Y bryddest a ddyfarnwyd yn orau . . . yng Nghystadleuaeth y Goron yn Eisteddfod Genedlaethol . . . 1945. pp. 12. *Gwasg Gomer: Llandysul*, 1945. 8°. **11595. h. 70.**

—— Storïau. pp. 130. *Hughes a'i Fab: Wrecsam*, 1936. 8°. **875. h. 123.**

CADWALADR (J. J.) Songs for Music, and other verses. pp. 66. *Drane's: London*, [1914.] 8°. **011652. i. 94.**

CADWALADYR (DAFYDD) Ehediadau y meddwl, ar yr achlysur o farwolaeth y Parchedig Thomas Charles . . . o'r Bala . . . a Mrs. Sarah Charles, ei wraig, *etc.* [In verse.] pp. 16. *R. Saunderson: Bala*, 1815. 8°. **C.117.a.47.(3.)**

—— Marwnad, er coffadwriaeth am y diweddar Mr. John Evans o'r Bala, *etc.* pp. 8. *R. Saunderson: Bala*, 1817. 8°. **C.117.a.47.(5.)**

CADWALLA, *King of Wessex.* *See* EBNER AB ESCHENBACH (J. G.) Dissertatio academica de Cadvalla, rege Saxonum, *etc.* [1736.] 4°. **G. 1571.**

CADWALLADER (GEORGE) *pseud.* [i.e. JAMES RALPH.] *See* PERIODICAL PUBLICATIONS.—*London.* The Remembrancer (or, National Advocate). By G. Cadwallader. 1748–51. fol. & 12°. (Burney.)

—— —— 1748. 12°. **P.P. 3557. o.**

CADWALLADER (LAURA HANES) The Career of the Earl of Essex from the Islands voyage 1597 to his execution in 1601 . . . A thesis, *etc.* pp. 128. *University of Pennsylvania: Philadelphia*, 1923. 8°. **010856. aa. 2.**

CADWALLADER (PHYLLIS)

—— Skippy's Mishap. [A tale for children.] pp. 17. *Arthur H. Stockwell: Ilfracombe*, 1955. 8°. **12838. df. 15.**

CADWALLADER (PRISCILLA) Memoir of Priscilla Cadwallader, *etc.* [The preface signed: J. J.] 1864. 12°. *See* J., J. **4986. aa. 18.**

CADWALLADER (RAWLINS) Handbook of Obstetrics, *etc.* pp. xii. 370. *F. A. Davis Co.: Philadelphia*, 1908. 8°. **07581. ee. 43.**

CADWELL (FLORALYN) The Wicked Wang-Pah Meets a Dragon. A Chinese fantasy in three acts. pp. 47. *Samuel French: New York; London*, [1925.] 8°. **11791. de. 19.**

—— [A reissue.] *New York; London*, [1926.] 8°. [*French's Acting Edition.*] **11791. t. 1/38.**

CADWELL (GRACE) How to Tap Dance. pp. 43. *Simon: St. Louis*, 1931 [1930]. 8°. **07911. ee. 54.**

CADWELL (J. W.) Full and Comprehensive Instructions how to Mesmerize . . . Fifth edition. pp. 144. *The Author: Boston*, 1885. 8°. **7410. b. 57.**

—— Sixth edition. pp. 128. *The Author: Boston*, 1885. 8°. **7410. a. 79.**

CADWYN.

—— Y Gadwyn. *See* CARDIFF.—*Crwys Road Calvinistic Methodist Church.*

CADY (A. HOWARD)

—— Poker: the modern game, *etc.* pp. 37. *American Sports Publishing Co.: New York*, 1895. 8°. **7917. e. 6.** *Vol. 1 no. 4 of "Spalding's Home Library."*

CADY (BERTHA CHAPMAN) and **CADY** (VERNON MOSHE[R])

—— The Way Life begins. An introduction to sex edu[ca]tion, *etc.* pp. 80. pl. IX. *American Social Hyg[iene] Association: New York*, 1924. 8°. **7008. b.**

CADY (CALVIN BRAINERD) *See* PERIODICAL PUBLICATI[ONS.] —*Boston, Mass.* The Boston Musical Year-book, (The Musical Year-book of the United States. vol. By G. H. Wilson and C. B. Cady.) 1884, *etc.* 12°. **P.P. 2523.**

—— Music-Education, *etc.* vol. 1–vol. 3. bk. 3. *C. F. Summy Co.: Chicago*, 1902, 03[–18]. 8° & 4°. **7899. g. 25 & 1.**

No more published.

—— Children's Song Studies . . . Teacher's Material Par[t] [A separate issue of pp. 49–69 of vol. 2. of "M[usic-] Education."] *C. F. Summy Co.: Chicago*, [1904.] 4[°]. **7899. 1.**

—— Melo-Rhythmic Technical Studies . . . Teach[er's] Material Part VII. [A separate issue of pp. 109–12[?] vol. 2. of "Music-Education."] *C. F. Summy C[o.:] Chicago*, [1904.] 4°. **7899. 1.**

CADY (CHARLES W.) The Indiana Annual Register, Pocket Manual, for the year 1845, *etc.* pp. 208. 1844. *See* PERIODICAL PUBLICATIONS.—*Indianapolis.* **P.P. 2533**

CADY (DANIEL) Opinion of Hon. Judge Cady in Supr[eme] Court. The People of the State of New York vs. Ge[orge] Clarke . . . Judgment for defendant, George Cla[rke.] pp. 41. *Joel Munsell: Albany*, 1851. 8°. **6736. b**

CADY (DANIEL R.) Memorial of Lieut. Joseph P. Burr[age,] a funeral sermon, *etc.* pp. 48. *Gould & Lincoln: Bos[ton,]* 1864. 12°. **4985. aaa.**

CADY (EDWIN HARRISON)

—— The Gentleman in America. A literary study in Am[eri]can culture. pp. 232. *Syracuse University P[ress:]* [*Syracuse, N.Y.*, 1949.] 8°. **11860. ff.**

CADY (EDWIN LAIRD)

—— Industrial Purchasing. With hints on working [with] purchasing agents. pp. vi. 256. *J. Wiley & S[ons:] New York*, [1945.] 8°. **8234. bb.**

—— Precision Investment Castings. pp. vi. 356. *Rein[hold] Publishing Corporation: New York*, 1948. 8°. **8773. b.**

CADY (EMILIE) *See* CADY (H. E.)

CADY (ERNEST)

—— We adopted Three, *etc.* [An account of child adopt[ion.]] pp. 189. *Ernest Benn: London*, 1954. 8°. **8417. f.**

CADY (FRANCIS ELMORE) and **DATES** (HENRY BALD[WIN]) Illuminating Engineering. Prepared by a staff [of] specialists for students and engineers. Editors: F. Cady . . . H. B. Dates, *etc.* pp. xiii. 486. *J. Wiley & Sons: New York*, 1925. 8°. **08715. dd.**

—— Second edition, thoroughly revised. pp. xv. 515. *J. Wiley & Sons: New York*, 1928. 8°. **08715. cc.**

CADY (GILBERT HAVEN) *See* STARVED ROCK STATE P[ARK.] Starved Rock State Park, *etc.* (Geology by G. H. Cad[y.]) 1918. 8°. [*Geographic Society of Chicago. Bulletin.* no] **Ac. 6**

—— Classification and Selection of Illinois Coals. pp. *Urbana*, 1935. 8°. [*Illinois State Geological Su[rvey.] Bulletin.* no. 62.]

—— Supplement. Analyses of Illinois Coals. pp *Urbana*, 1948. 8°. A.S. 1

CADY (GILBERT HAVEN)

—— Coal Resources of District I (II and VI). [With illustrations and maps.] 3 pt. *Urbana*, 1915–17. 8º. [*Illinois Coal Mining Investigations. Bulletin.* no. 10, 15, 16.] **07107.r.23/1.**

—— Geology and Mineral Resources of the Hennepin and La Salle Quadrangles. pp. 136. pl. VI. *Urbana*, 1919. 8º. [*Illinois State Geological Survey. Bulletin.* no. 37.] A.S. I. **26.**

CADY (H. EMILIE) Miscellaneous Writings . . . Revised and authorized. pp. 118. *L. N. Fowler: London*, 1917. 8º. **04376. e. 59.**

—— The Best Theology. pp. 111. *Power Book Co.: Wimbledon*, [1907.] 8º. [*New Life Booklets.*] **7409.a.40/2.**

—— The Best Theology. pp. 111. *Power Book Co.: Wimbledon*, [1907.] 8º. **7409. a. 40/11.**

—— God a Present Help. pp. 113. *Power Book Co.: London*, [1912.] 8º. **04403. i. 14.**

—— Revised and enlarged. pp. 120. *L. N. Fowler & Co.: London*, 1913. 8º. **04403. i. 15.**

—— Lessons in Truth. A course of twelve lessons in practical Christianity. pp. 199. *Power Book Co.: London*, [1912.] 8º. **04403. i. 16.**

—— Revised edition. pp. 157. *L. N. Fowler & Co.: London*, 1913. 8º. **04403. i. 17.**

—— Revised and enlarged edition. pp. 157. *L. N. Fowler & Co.: London*, [1922.] 8º. **04403. i. 68.**

CADY (H. KEITH)

—— *See* GRANT (Charlotte L.) American High School Biology. By C. L. Grant . . . H. K. Cady, *etc.* [1948.] 8º. **7008. c. 15.**

—— *See* GRANT (Charlotte L.) [American High School Biology.] High School Biology. [By] C. L. Grant . . . H. K. Cady, *etc.* [1952.] 8º. **7008. c. 27.**

CADY (HAMILTON PERKINS) General Chemistry. pp. xiv. 522. *McGraw-Hill Book Co.: New York*, 1916. 8º. [*International Chemical Series.*] **8711. c. 1/7.**

CADY (HARRISON) *See* BURGESS (Thornton W.) Green Forest Series. With illustrations by H. Cady. 1921, *etc.* 8º. **012809. bbb. 13.**

—— *See* BURGESS (Thornton W.) Tommy and the Wishing Stone . . . With illustrations by H. Cady. 1915. 8º. **012807. bb. 38.**

—— *See* WELLS (Carolyn) The Happychaps . . . With illustrations by H. Cady. 1908. 8º. **12804. w. 17.**

CADY (JOHN FRANK) Foreign Intervention in the Rio de la Plata, 1838–50. A study of French, British, and American policy in relation to the dictator Juan Manuel Rosas. [With maps, and a bibliography.] pp. xiv. 296. *University of Pennsylvania Press: Philadelphia*, 1929. 8º. **9773. ccc. 6.**

—— La Intervención Extranjera en el Río de la Plata, 1838–1850. Estudio de la política seguida por Francia, Gran Bretaña y Norteamérica con respecto al dictador Juan Manuel de Rosas. Traducción de Juan M. Uteda, *etc.* pp. 307. *Buenos Aires*, 1943. 8º. [*Biblioteca de la Sociedad de Historia Argentina.* no. 14.] Ac. **8592.** d.

—— The Roots of French Imperialism in Eastern Asia. [With a bibliography.] pp. xii. 322. *Published for the American Historical Association [by] Cornell University Press: Ithaca, N.Y.*, 1954. 8º. **9231. k. 24.**

CADY (LOUISE LINCOLN)

—— Nursing in Tuberculosis, *etc.* pp. xvi. 481. *W. B. Saunders Co.: Philadelphia & London*, 1948. 8º. **7689. c. 8.**

CADY (MAGLOIRE THÉODORE) Des causes et de la prophylaxie de la phthisie pulmonaire. pp. 32. *Paris*, 1854. 4º. [*Collection des thèses soutenues à la Faculté de Médecine de Paris.* An 1854. tom. 4.] **7372. g. 4.**

CADY (RICHARD CARLYSLE)

—— *See* WENZEL (Leland K.) Geology and Ground-Water Resources of Scotts Bluff County, Nebraska. By L. K. Wenzel, R. C. Cady, *etc.* 1946. 8º. [*U.S. Geological Survey. Water-Supply Paper.* no. 943.] A.S. **212.**

—— Effect upon Ground-water Levels of Proposed Surface-Water Storage in Flathead Lake, Montana, *etc.* *Washington*, 1941. 8º. [*U.S. Geological Survey. Water-Supply Paper.* no. 849B.] A.S. **212.**

CADY (RICHARD CARLYSLE) and **SCHERER** (OLIVER J.)

—— Geology and Ground-Water Resources of Box Butte County, Nebraska . . . Prepared in cooperation with the Conservation and Survey Division, University of Nebraska. [With maps.] pp. v. 102. pl. 6. *Washington*, 1946. 8º. [*U.S. Geological Survey. Water Supply Paper.* 969.] A.S. **212.**

CADY (VERNON MOSHER)

—— *See* CADY (Bertha C.) and CADY (V. M.) The Way Life begins, *etc.* 1924. 8º. **7008. b. 39.**

—— The Estimation of Juvenile Incorrigibility. A report of experiments . . . by means of certain non-intellectual tests, *etc.* [With tables.] pp. 140. *California Bureau of Juvenile Research: Whittier*, 1923. 8º. **8311. ff. 27.**

Monograph no. 2 of the "Journal of Delinquency."

CADY (WALLACE M.)

—— Stratigraphy and Structure of West-Central Vermont. 1945. *See* UNITED STATES OF AMERICA.—*Geological Society of America.* Bulletin, *etc.* vol. 56. 1890, *etc.* 8º. Ac. **3187.**

CADY (WALTER GUYTON) *See* BENEDICT (Francis G.) and CADY (W. G.) A Bicycle Ergometer with an Electric Brake. 1912. 8º. [*Carnegie Institution of Washington. Publications.* no. 167.] Ac. **1866.**

—— Piezoelectricity. An introduction to the theory and applications of electromechanical phenomena in crystals. pp. xxiii. 806. *McGraw-Hill Book Co.: New York, London*, 1946. 8º. [*International Series in Pure and Applied Physics.*] W.P. **7225/35.**

CADY (WILHELMINA W.) *See* AMICIS (E. de) Military Life in Italy . . . Translated by W. W. Cady, *etc.* 1882. 8º. **12331. f. 28.**

—— *See* AMICIS (E. de) Studies of Paris. Translated . . . by W. W. Cady, *etc.* [1887.] 8º. **10168. bbb. 38.**

CADY (WILLOUGHBY MILLER)

—— Radar Scanners and Radomes. Edited by W. M. Cady . . . M. B. Karelitz . . . Louis A. Turner, *etc.* pp. xvi. 491. *McGraw-Hill Book Co.: New York*, 1948. 8º. [*Massachusetts Institute of Technology, Radiation Laboratory Series.* vol. 26.] **Ac.4484/6.**

CADYOW CASTLE. Cadyow Castle: or the Minstrel. [A ballad. By Sir Walter Scott.] pp. 8. *Falkirk*, [1840?] 12º. C. **116.** h. 2. (4.)

CADZAND.

—— Coutume de l'île de Cadsant. [With a French translation of the Dutch texts.] 1891. *See* GILLIODTS VAN SEVEREN (L.) Coutumes des pays et comté de Flandre. Quartier de Bruges. (Coutumes des petites villes et seigneuries enclavées. tom. 2.) 1879, *etc.* 4°. **5686.g.1/2e.**

—— —*Walloon Church.* Register of the Walloon Church of Cadzand in Holland, 1685–1724. Edited . . . by Doctor Johannes de Hullu and William Minet. pp. 86. *Frome,* 1934. 4°. [*Publications of the Huguenot Society of London.* vol. 36.] **Ac. 2073/4.**

CAE, *Aunt, pseud.* [i.e. HENRY COURTNEY SELOUS.] The Children of the Parsonage. By the author of "Gerty and May" . . . "New Baby," etc., etc. (Aunt Cae.) With illustrations by K. Greenaway. pp. viii. 136. *Griffith & Farran: London,* 1874. 8°. **4413. d. 21.**

CAECILIA. Cäcilia. Organ für katholische Kirchenmusik. *See* PERIODICAL PUBLICATIONS.—*Luxemburg.*

—— Cäcilia. Zeitschrift für katholische Kirchenmusik. *See* PERIODICAL PUBLICATIONS.—*Breslau.*

—— Cäcilia, eine Zeitschrift für die musikalische Welt. *See* PERIODICAL PUBLICATIONS.—*Mainz.*

CAECILIA. [For Saints, Sovereigns and Princesses of Sovereign Houses of this name:] *See* CECILIA.

CAECILIANER. *See* CECILIAN.

CAECILIEN KALENDER. *See* EPHEMERIDES.

CAECILIENVEREIN.

—— Caecilienverein Chur. *See* COIRE.

CAECILIEN-VEREIN.

—— Cäcilien-Verein, Frankfort on the Main. *See* FRANKFORT ON THE MAIN.

CAECILIEN-VEREINE. Cäcilien-Vereine in der Erzdiöcese Cöln und den Diöcesen Hildesheim, Mainz, Münster, Osnabrück und Paderborn. *See* GERMANY.

CAECILIUS. Cäcilius und Octavius, oder Gespräche über die vornehmsten Einwendungen gegen die christliche Wahrheit. [By Carl Friedrich Goeschel.] Nebst einem Vorworte von Dr. Tholuck. pp. 208. *Berlin,* 1828. 8°. **4016. a. 14.**

CAECILIUS, *Calactinus.* *See* MARTENS (L.) De libello *Περι ὑψους*. [With a chapter on the work by Caecilius of the same title.] 1877. 8°. **11312. h. 41. (4.)**

—— *See* SCHWAB (Theodor) Alexander Numeniu *Περι σχηματων* in seinem Verhältnis zu Kaikilios, *etc.* 1916. 8°. **W.P. 2119/5.**

—— *See* SUIDAS. [Lexicon Graecum.] *Begin.* [fol. 1 *recto*:] *διαλογος Στεφανου του μελανος, etc.* [fol. 3 *recto*:] *Το μεν παρον βιβλιον, Σουιδα· οἱ δε συνταξαμενοι τουτο ἀνδρες σοφοι· Εὐδημος ῥητωρ . . . Κεκιλιος Σικελιωτης, etc.* 1499. fol. **IC. 26913.**

—— Cæcili Rhetoris fragmenta collegit, disposuit et commentatus est Theophilus Burckhardt . . . Dissertatio philologica, *etc.* pp. 54. *Basileae,* 1863. 8°. **11396. bbb. 1.**

—— Caecilii Calactini fragmenta. Collegit Ernestus Ofenloch. pp. xl. 242. *Lipsiae,* 1907. 8°. **2048. b. 26.**
Part of the "Bibliotheca scriptorum graecorum et romanorum Teubneriana."

CAECILIUS, *Fabrianensis.* *See* HUSAIN IBN 'ABD ALLĀH (Abū 'Alī) called *Ibn Sīnā, etc.* [*Two or more Works.*] Auicēne . . . opera . . . Alpharabius de Intelligentiis, *etc.* [Edited by Caecilius Fabrianensis.] 1508. fol. **542. g. 2. (1.)**

CAECILIUS (LUCIUS) [For editions of the treatise "De mortibus persecutorum," sometimes attributed to L. Caecilius:] *See* LACTANTIUS (L. C. F.)

CAECILIUS (SEXTUS) *Africanus.* *See* VÉCSEY (T.) Sextus Caecilius Africanus jogtudós. Székfoglaló értekezés, *etc.* 1889. 8°. [*Magyar Tudományos Akadémia. Értekezések a társadalmi tudományok köréből.* köt. 10. sz. 6.] **Ac. 825/46.**

CAECILIUS CYPRIANUS, *Saint, Bishop of Carthage.* *See* CYPRIAN.

CAECILIUS METELLUS, *Family of.* *See* WENDE (M.) De Caeciliis Metellis, *etc.* 1875. 8°. **9041. c. 13**

CAECILIUS SECUNDUS (CAIUS PLINIUS) *See* PLINIUS CAECILIUS SECUNDUS.

CAECILIUS STATIUS (CAIUS) *See* SAGITTARIUS (C.) Casparis Sagittarii . . . Commentatio de vita et scripti[s] Livii Andronici . . . Cæcilii, *etc.* 1672. 8°. **1089. e. 1[...]**

—— *See* TEUFFEL (W. S.) Caecilius Statius, Pacuvius, *et*[*c.*] 1858. 4°. [*TUBINGEN.—Eberhard-Karls-Universitä*[*t.*] *Einladung zur Akademischen Feier des Geburtsfestes* . . . *des Königs Wilhelm von Württemberg.*] **11312. h. 3[...]**

—— Ex Cæcilio. [Fragments.] *See* ESTIENNE (R.) *t*[*he*] *Elder.* Fragmenta poetarum veterum Latinorum, *etc.* 1564. 8°. **680. a. 28. ([...]**

—— S. Cæcilii fragmenta quæ exstant. (S. Cæcilii Vita, [...] Petro Crinito desumpta.) *See* G., A. P. B. P. Corp[us] omnium veterum poetarum Latinorum, *etc.* pt. 1. 1611. 4°. **11352. e.**

—— Fragmenta. *See* LATIN POETS. Corpus omnium ve[te]rum poetarum Latinorum, *etc.* 1627. 4°. **833. i.**

—— S. Cæcilii fragmenta. *See* AMATI (P.) Collectio Pisa[u]rensis omnium poematum . . . Latinorum, *etc.* tom. 4. 1766. fol. **653. d.**

—— Caii Caecilii Statii . . . deperditarum fabularum fr[ag]menta. Edidit Leonhardus Spengel. pp. 62. *Monachii,* 1829. 4°. **T. 5*.**

—— [Another copy.] **833. k. 19.**

—— [Fragments.] 1855. *See* RIBBECK (O.) Scenicae Ro[ma]norum poesis fragmenta, *etc.* vol. 2. 1852, *etc.* 8°. **11707. g.**

—— [Fragments.] *Lat. & Eng.* *See* WARMINGTON (Eric [...]) Remains of Old Latin, *etc.* vol. 1. 1935, *etc.* 8°. **2282. h.**

—— Fragmenta. *Lat. & Fr.* *See* LEVÉE (J. B.) and MONNIER (G. A.) Théâtre complet des Latins, *etc.* vol. 1823. 8°. **11707.**

CAECUS (VENTURA) *See* FALCONETTI (V.) called VENT[URA] CAECUS.

CAEDICIUS, *pseud.* *See* CONSTANTINOPLE. Ancien [...] de Constantinople imprimé entre 1566 et 1574, avec [...] explicatives par Caedicius. [1890.] 8°. **10106. i. 3.**

CÆDMON.

WORKS.

—— The Cædmon Poems, translated into English prose by Charles W. Kennedy . . . With an introduction, and facsimiles of the illustrations in the Junius MS. [and a bibliography.] pp. lxx. 258. *G. Routledge & Sons: London,* 1916. 8°. **11623**. e. **27**.

HYMN.

—— Cædmon's Hymn. *See* SMITH (Albert Hugh) Three Northumbrian Poems, *etc.* 1933. 8°. W.P. **8632/1**.

—— *See* DOBBIE (Elliott van K.) The Manuscripts of Cædmon's Hymn and Bede's Death Song, *etc.* 1937. 8°. [*Columbia University Studies in English and Comparative Literature.* no. 128.] Ac. **2688/16**. **(69.)**

PARAPHRASE.

—— Cædmonis Monachi Paraphrasis poetica Genesios ac præcipuarum Sacræ paginæ historiarum, abhinc annos M.LXX. Anglo-Saxonicè conscripta, & nunc primùm edita à Francisco Junio. [Containing a paraphrase of Genesis, Exodus and Daniel, together with poems on the Lamentations of the fallen angels, the Harrowing of Hell, and the Temptation. With plates.] pp. 106. 1655. 4°. *See* BIBLE.—*Pentateuch.* [*Anglo-Saxon.*] **219**. **f**. **15**.

—— The Cædmon Manuscript of Anglo-Saxon Biblical Poetry, Junius XI in the Bodleian Library. [A facsimile.] With introduction by Sir Israel Gollancz. pp. cxxvii. 229. 1927. fol. *See* BIBLE.—*Pentateuch.* [*Anglo-Saxon.*] L.R. **262**. d. **4**.

—— The Junius Manuscript. Edited by George Philip Krapp, *etc.* pp. lviii. 247. 1931. 8°. [*Anglo-Saxon Poetic Records.* no. 1.] *See* BIBLE.—*Pentateuch.* [*Anglo-Saxon.*] **11626.m.4/1.**

—— Cædmon's Metrical Paraphrase of parts of the Holy Scriptures, in Anglo-Saxon. With an English translation, notes and a verbal index, by Benjamin Thorpe. pp. xxxv. 341. 1832. 8°. *See* BIBLE.—*Pentateuch.* [*Polyglott.*] Ac. **5665/5**.

—— Cædmon's des Angelsachsen biblische Dichtungen. (Ein angelsächsisches Glossar.) Herausgegeben von K. W. Bouterwek . . . Mit zwei Facsimiles, *etc.* *Anglo-Saxon & Ger.* 2 Tl. 1847–54. 8°. *See* BIBLE.—*Pentateuch.* [*Polyglott.*] **3149**. **h**. **13**.

Selections.

—— Cädmons Genesis (Exodus, Daniel). 1857. 8°. [GREIN (*C. W. M.*) *Bibliothek der angelsächsischen Poesie, etc.* Bd. 1.] *See* BIBLE.—*Pentateuch.* [*Anglo-Saxon.*] **11595**. dd. **3**.

—— Genesis. [Comprising lines 235–851 of the Junius Manuscript of Cædmon's paraphrase of Genesis, known as "Genesis B."] 1875. 8°. [SIEVERS (*E.*) *Der Heliand und die angelsächsische Genesis.*] *See* BIBLE.—*Genesis.* [*Anglo-Saxon.*] **4999**. ee. **12**. **(1.)**

—— Cædmon's Exodus and Daniel. Edited from Grein. By Theodore W. Hunt. pp. 124. 1883. 8°. *See* BIBLE.—*Exodus.* [*Anglo-Saxon.*] **11595**. e. **43**.

—— Die altsächsische Genesis in angelsächsischer Sprache. [Comprising lines 235–851 of the Junius Manuscript of Cædmon's paraphrase of Genesis, known as "Genesis B."] 1897. 8°. [PIPER (*P.*) *Denkmäler der aelteren deutschen Litteratur.* Bd. 1.] *See* BIBLE.—*Genesis.* [*Anglo-Saxon.*] **012252**. m. **4**.

CÆDMON. [PARAPHRASE.]

—— Die altenglischen Dichtungen [attributed to Cædmon] Daniel' und 'Azarias.' (Bearbeiteter Text, mit metrischen, sprachlichen und textkritischen Bemerkungen, sowie einem Wörterbuche.) [Edited by Wilhelm Schmidt.] 1907. 8°. [*Bonner Beiträge zur Anglistik.* Hft. 23.] *See* BIBLE.—*Daniel.* [*Anglo-Saxon.*] **011851**. i. **46**.

—— Exodus and Daniel; two Old English poems . . . Edited by F. A. Blackburn. pp. xxxvi. 231. 1907. 8°. *See* BIBLE.—*Exodus.* [*Anglo-Saxon.*] **12204**. p. **5/26**.

—— The Later Genesis (Genesis B) and other Old English and Old Saxon texts relating to the Fall of Man. Edited by Fr. Klaeber. pp. 69. 1913. 8°. [*Englische Textbibliothek.* Hft. 15.] *See* BIBLE.—*Genesis.* [*Anglo-Saxon.*] **12273**. c. **21/15**.

—— Die ältere Genesis. Mit Einleitung, Anmerkungen, Glossar und der lateinischen Quelle, herausgegeben von F. Holthausen. Mit einer Tafel. [The text of the Junius Manuscript of Cædmon's paraphrase of Genesis, omitting "Genesis B."] 1914. 8°. [*Alt- und mittelenglische Texte.* Bd. 7.] *See* BIBLE.—*Genesis.* [*Anglo-Saxon.*] **12272**. p.

—— The Later Genesis . . . Edited by Fr. Klaeber . . . New edition with supplement. pp. 12. 69. 1931. 8°. [*Englische Textbibliothek.* Hft. 15.] *See* BIBLE.—*Genesis.* [*Anglo-Saxon.*] **12273**. c. **21/15**a.

—— The Later Genesis. Edited from MS. Junius II by B. J. Timmer. [Comprising lines 235–818 of the Junius Manuscript of Cædmon's paraphrase of Genesis known as Genesis B, together with Old Saxon Genesis fragments.] pp. 135. 1948. 8°. *See* BIBLE.—*Pentateuch.* [*Anglo-Saxon.*] **3054**. bb. **20**.

—— Caedmon's Schöpfung und Abfall der bösen Engel, aus dem Angelsächsischen übersetzt, nebst Anmerkungen von J. P. E. Greverus. [Extracted from Cædmon's paraphrase of Genesis.] Programm zum Osterexamen des Gymnasium. *Anglo-Saxon & Ger.* pp. 61. 1852. 8°. *See* BIBLE.—*Genesis.*—*Selections.* [*Polyglott.*] **11595**. d. **15**.

—— The Fall of Man, or Paradise Lost of Cædmon [extracted from his paraphrase of Genesis]. Translated in verse from the Anglo-Saxon, with a new metrical arrangement of the lines of part of the original text, and an introduction on the versification of Cædmon, by W. H. F. Bosanquet. pp. xxxviii. 63. 1860. 8°. *See* BIBLE.—*Genesis.*—*Selections.* [*English.*] **11623**. c. **8**.

—— Cædmon, the Anglo-Saxon Poet. [A translation in verse of selected passages from Cædmon's paraphrase of Genesis, Exodus and Daniel, with connecting passages in prose, and with an introduction. The translator's preface signed: R. T. G., i.e. Robert T. Gaskin.] pp. 64. 1873. 8°. *See* BIBLE.—*Pentateuch.*—*Selections.* [*English.*] **03051**. ff. **58**.

—— Genesis A. Translated from the Old English by Lawrence Mason. [Sometimes attributed to Cædmon.] pp. vii. 61. 1915. 8°. [*Yale Studies in English.* no. 48.] *See* BIBLE.—*Genesis.* [*English.*] Ac. **2692**. ma/3.

DOUBTFUL OR SUPPOSITITIOUS WORKS.

—— [For editions of "The Dream of the Rood," sometimes attributed to Cædmon:] *See* CROSS.

APPENDIX.

—— *See* BOUTERWEK (C. W.) De Cedmone poëta Anglo-Saxonum vetustissimo brevis dissertatio. 1845. 8°. **641**. i. **27**.

CÆDMON. [Appendix.]

—— *See* Braasch (T.) Vollständiges Wörterbuch zur sog. Caedmonschen Genesis. 1933. 8°. **12981.** p. **1/76.**

—— *See* Bradley (Henry) *M.A.* The 'Caedmonian' Genesis. 1920. 8°. [*Essays and Studies by Members of the English Association.* vol. 6.] Ac. **2664/4.**

—— *See* Duff (John W.) Caedmon: an essay. 1901. 8°. **011853.** f. **7.**

—— *See* Ellis (*Sir* Henry) *Principal Librarian of the British Museum.* Account of Cædmon's Metrical Paraphrase of Scripture History, *etc.* 1833. 4°. **7709.** h. **28.**

—— *See* Gajšek (S. von) Milton und Caedmon. 1911. 8°. **12984.** h. **1.** (**35.**)

—— *See* Gaskin (Robert T.) Cædmon, the first English poet, *etc.* 1902. 8°. **C4429.** b. **14.**

—— *See* Goetzinger (E.) Ueber die Dichtungen des Angelsachsen Caedmon und deren Verfasser, *etc.* 1860. 8°. **11623.** c. **16.**

—— *See* Graz (F.) Beiträge zur Textkritik der sogenannten Caedmonschen Genesis. 1896. 8°. [*Festschrift zum siebzigsten Geburtstage O. Schade.*] **011851.** i. **3.**

—— *See* Graz (F.) Die Metrik der sog. Caedmonschen Dichtungen mit Berücksichtigung der Verfasserfrage. 1894. 8°. [*Studien zum germanischen Alliterationsvers.* Hft. 3.] **11825.** q. **46.**

—— *See* Gurteen (Stephen H.) The Epic of the Fall of Man. A comparative study of Cædmon, Dante and Milton. 1896. 8°. **11421.** dd. **6.**

—— *See* Muerkens (G.) Untersuchungen über das altenglische Exoduslied [attributed to Caedmon]. 1899. 8°. [*Bonner Beiträge zur Anglistik.* Hft. 2.] **011851.** i. **46.**

—— *See* Sandras (E. G.) De carminibus Anglo-Saxonicis Cædmoni adjudicatis disquisitio, *etc.* 1859. 8°. **11595.** d. **5.**

—— *See* Watson (Robert S.) Cædmon, the first English poet. 1875. 8°. **11824.** c. **13.**

—— *See* Wrenn (Charles L.) The Poetry of Cædmon, *etc.* [1947.] 8°. [*Sir Israel Gollancz Memorial Lecture, British Academy.* 1946.] Ac. **1186/18.**

—— The Cædmon Memorial. Being a description of the cross, with explanation of lettering and figures thereon, *etc.* pp. 14. *Horne & Son: Whitby,* [1899.] 8°. **10348.** aaa. **59.** (**3.**)

—— Cædmon, the Father of English Sacred Poetry. [With illustrations.] pp. 11. *St. Mary's Parish Church Domestic Council: Whitby,* [1954?] 12°. **4908.** k. **59.**

—— Figuræ quædam antiquæ ex Cædmonis Monachi paraphraseos in Genesin exemplari pervetusto in bibliotheca Bodleiana adservato delineatæ, *etc.* 1754. 4°. *See* Bible.—*Appendix.—Genesis.* [*Pictorial Illustrations.*] **786.** l. **16.**

—— A Song of Cædmon, and other poems. By G. E. D. 1871. 8°. *See* D., G. E. **11646.** cc. **16.**

CÆDWALLA, *King of Wessex.* *See* Cadwalla.

CAELEBS. *See* Coelebs.

CAELESTINUS. [For Saints, Sovereigns, and Princes of Sovereign Houses of this name:] *See* Celestine.

CAELESTINUS, *Abbot of Saint Emmeram, at Ratisb* *See* Coelestinus.

CAELESTINUS (Bartholomaeus) *See* Celestino (B tolommeo)

CAELESTINUS (Claudius)

—— De his quę mundo mi biliter eueniunt: vbi de sensuum erroribus, & potent animę, ac de influentijs cælorum, F. C. Cælestini opusc lum. De mirabili potestate artis et naturæ, vbi de philos phorum lapide, F. Rogerij Bachonis . . . libellus. H duo gratissima, & non aspernanda opuscula, Oront F. (Fineus) Delph. . . . recognoscebat, & in sua redigebat harmoniam. ff. 52. *Apud S. Colinæu Lutetiæ Parisiorum,* 1542. 4°. **784.** m.

—— Des choses merueilleuses en nature, où est traicté erreurs des sens, des puissances de l'ame, & des influen des cieux, traduit en François par Iaques Girard Tornus. *See* Bacon (Roger) [*Two or more Works. French.*] Le Miroir d'alquimie, *etc.* 1557. 8°. **1034.** e.

CAELESTIUS. *See* Bertius (P.) Twee disputatien: eene D. Petri Bertii, Van de ketterije Pelagij ende Cæles *etc.* 1609. 4°. T. **2239.** (

CAELIA. Cælia: or, the Perjur'd lover. A play, [By Charles Johnson. With a prologue by T. Cibber a an epilogue by H. Fielding.] pp. 60. *J. Watts: Lond* 1733. 8°. **643.** g. **14.** (

—— [Another copy.] **161.** d.

CAELINA. Cælina; or, a Tale of mystery: a drama two acts. Taken from a French play [by R. C. Guilb de Pixérécourt], called, Cælina [or rather, Cœlina], l'Enfant du mystère. By John Wallace. pp. 25. *Prin for the Translator: London,* 1802. 8°. **11735.** e.

CAELIO (Gaspar) *See* Coelho (Gasparo)

CAELIUS APICIUS. *See* Apicius (Coelius)

CAELIUS AURELIANUS. *See* Aurelianus (Caeliu

CAELIUS (Antoninus) Antonini Caelii . . . Introduc universalis ad medicam facultatem; ac brevis method curandi particulares . . . corporis humani affectus: n non de pulsibus tractatio: quibus additur Comm tarius in primum librum Aphorismorum Hippocra pp. 214. *Ex typographia P. Breæ, ad instantiam F. Rode & I. Kalamuneri: Messanæ,* 1618. 4°. **539.** e. **21.** (

CAELIUS (Joannes) De motu in genere, continuo infinito. *See* Romanus (A.) A. Romani . . . Lamp *etc.* 1614. 4°. **536.** e.

CAELIUS (Ludovicus) *Rhodiginus.* *See* Richerius (L.

CAELIUS (Michael) *of Breslau.* Oratio de causis pes *etc.* *G. Baumann: Vratislaviæ,* [1626.] 4°. **1179.** d. **12.** (1

CAELIUS (Michael) *Schlossprediger zu Mansfeld.*

—— *See* Bugenhagen (J.) *Pommer.* [*Single Works.*] W man Christum ynn der Schrifft sol süchen vnd erkenne Von gutten Wercken vnd dem Gesetz, widder ein Grawen Münch, Michael Coelius, *etc.* 1530. 4°. **3907.** b.

—— Jonas (J.) Vom Christlichen abschied aus dies tödlichen leben des . . . Herrn D. M. Lutheri, beric durch D. J. Jonam, M. M. Celium, *etc.* 1546. 4°. **4885.** aaa.

—— —— 1564. 12°. [Melanchthon (*P.*) *Vita Luthe etc.*] **1371.** a. **26.** (

—— —— 1845. 8°. **4885.** c. **47.** (

—— —— 1846. 8°. **4885.** c. **47.** (

CAELIUS (Michael) *Schlossprediger zu Mansfeld.*

—— *See* Jonas (J.) The true hystorie of the Christen departynge of . . . Martyne Luther, collected by J. Jonas, M. Celius, *etc.* [1546.] 8°. **3906. aa. 29.**

—— *See* Jonas (J.) Narratio de morte . . . M. Lutheri . . . a J. Jona, M. Celio, et aliis . . . conscripta. [1547?] 8°. [*Pollicarius (J.) Carmen de beneficiis, etc.*] **701. b. 54.**

—— —— 1555. 8°. [*Melanchthon (P.) Historia de vita . . . D. M. Lutheri, etc.*] **1371. a. 30. (1.)**

—— —— 1847. 8°. [*Melanchthon (P.) De vita . . . D. M. Lutheri, etc.*] **1371. g. 32. (1.)**

—— Acht Zeichen, Eines waren seligmachenden Glaubens, aus dem Euangelio Matthei am fünfften Capitel. Mit ablenung des missverstands vom verdienst guter werck, so hinein ist getragen. *Gedruckt durch V. Kaubisch: Eisleben,* 1558. 8°. **C. 65. c. 19. (5.)**

—— Auslegung vber den Spruch Salomonis, Prouerbiorum achtzehenden Capitel. Wer eine Ehefraw findet, der findet was guts, Vnd bekömet wolgefallen vom Herrn. Zu trost vnd lere, allen Christlichen fromen Eheleuten, *etc. Gedruckt durch V. Kaubisch: Eisleben,* 1557. 4°. **4427. f. 13.**

—— Newer jrthumb vnd schwermerey vom Sacrament: Sampt etzlichen lügen, so Georg Witzel gepredigt . . . Mit einer langen Vorrhede, von Cochlei und Witzels lere [by Conradus Cordatus]. *Gedruckt durch G. Rhaw: Wittemberg,* 1534. 4°. **3905. f. 47.**

—— Michael Cölius' Predigten. [Two sermons.] *See* Beste (A. F. W.) Die bedeutendsten Kanzelredner der älteren lutherschen Kirche, *etc.* Bd. 1. 1856, *etc.* 8°. **4428. e. 8.**

—— Sermon über der seligen Leiche Doctor Martini Luthers zu Eisleben am xx. tag Februarii . . . gethan, anno 1546. *See* Jonas (J.) Zwo Tröstliche Predigt, *etc.* 1546. 4°. **3906. cc. 52.**

—— M. Michaelis Coelii Leichen-Predigt, die er . . . am 19. Februar, 1546. in Eissleben D. Martin Luthern zu Ehren gehalten. *See* Hofmann (Carl G.) Memoriam saecularem funeris et sepulcri D. Martini Lutheri recolere studet D. C. G. Hofmannus. 1746. 4°. **4888. c. 8. (1.)**

—— [Another edition.] Predigt über der Leich Herrn Dr. M. Luther . . . 1546, *etc.* *See* Stichart (F. O.) Dr. M. Luther's Tod, *etc.* 1845. 8°. **1371. h. 28.**

—— [Another edition.] M. M. Cölii Leichenpredigt Lutheri, *etc.* *See* Bresler (C. H.) Dr. Luther's Tod und Begräbniss, *etc.* [1846.] 8°. **4885. d. 49. (3.)**

—— [Another edition.] *See* John (G. A.) Getreue und ausführliche Nachricht von D. M. Luthers . . . Abscheiden, *etc.* 1846. 8°. **4885. d. 22.**

—— Wie man die Sünde erkennen, beichten, vnnd vergebung derselben, durch die Absolution vnd Hochwirdiges Sacrament erlangen sol, vermanung an die Kirche zu Mansfeldt, *etc.* [*Heirs of G. Rhaw: Wittenberg,*] 1549. 8°. **3906. a. 16.**

CAELIUS ANTIPATER (Lucius) *See* Antipater.

CAELIUS RUFUS (Marcus) *See* Rufus.

CAELLIEU (Colijn) *See* Michault (P.) Le Pas de la mort, poëme inédit de P. Michault [or by Amé de Montgesoie], suivi d'une traduction flamande de Colyn Coellin, *etc.* 1869. 8°. [*Société des Bibliophiles de Belgique. Publications.* no. 2.] **Ac. 9033.**

CAELLO (Antonio) *See* Coello.

CAELS (Theodoricus Petrus) Theodorici Petri Caels . . . de Belgii plantis qualitate quadam hominibus cæterisve animalibus nociva seu venenata præditis, symptomatibus ab earum usu productis, nec non antidotis adhibendis dissertatio, *etc.* pp. 66. *Bruxellis,* 1774. 4°. **B. 3. (10.)**

CAEM, *pseud.* [i.e. Chas. A. E. MacHenry.]

—— The Canadian Stamp Directory, containing the addresses of over one hundred stamp collectors in Canada, a list of Canadian dealers: and a few names of American dealers. Edited by Caem. pp. 16. 1896. 32°. *See* Directories.—*Stamp Dealers and Collectors.* Crawford **783. (4.)**

CAEMMERER (August Friedrich) Untersuchung von der Seelen, *etc.* pp. 86. *Leipzig,* 1714. 8°. **1019. k. 1. (5.)**

CAEMMERER (Erich) Die Alteburg bei Arnstadt. Ein Beitrag zur Kenntnis der Vorgeschichte Thüringens, *etc.* pp. 38. *Leipzig,* 1924. 8°. [*Mannus-Bibliothek.* no. 37.] **7705. t. 1/37.**

CAEMMERER (Frz.) Sammlung neuer ausgewaehlter Bau-Entwürfe zu einfachen Kirchen, Bet- & Wohngebaeuden . . . 2te Auflage. [Twenty-one plates without letterpress.] *Leipzig,* 1861. fol. **1732. e. 12.**

CAEMMERER (Hans Paul)

—— A Manual on the Origin and Development of Washington. [With illustrations.] pp. xi. 365. *Washington,* 1939. 4°. [*U.S. Senate Document.* 75th Congress. 3rd Session. no. 178.] **A.S. 10/4.**

—— Washington, the National Capital. [With illustrations.] pp. xxv. 736. *Washington,* 1932. 4°. [*U.S. Senate Document.* 71st Congress, 3rd Session. no. 332.] **A.S. 10/4.**

CAEMMERER (Heinrich) R. M. Rilkes Duineser Elegien. Deutung der Dichtung. pp. vii. 151. *Stuttgart,* 1937. 8°. **11859. aa. 26.**

CAEMMERER (Hermann von) *See* Hohenzollern, *House of.* Die Testamente der Kurfürsten von Brandenburg und der beiden ersten Könige von Preussen. Herausgegeben von H. von Caemmerer. 1915. 8°. [*Veröffentlichungen des Vereins für Geschichte der Mark Brandenburg.*] **Ac. 7325/2. (17.)**

—— Das Regensburger Religionsgespräch im Jahre 1546. (Berliner Inaugural-Dissertation.) pp. 77. *Berlin,* 1901. 8°. **4662. h. 21.**

CAEMMERER (Rudolf Carl Fritz von)

—— *See* Holleben (A. H. L. von) Geschichte des Frühjahrsfeldzuges 1813 und seine Vorgeschichte. (Bd. 2. Die Ereignisse von Ende April bis zum Waffenstillstand. Bearbeitet von v. Caemmerer.) 1904, *etc.* 8°. **09078. dd. 32/4.**

—— Die Befreiungskriege 1813–1815. Ein strategischer Überblick . . . Mit 1 Karte in Steindruck, *etc.* pp. vii. 146. *Berlin,* 1907. 8°. **9079. cc. 33.**

—— [Betrachtungen zur Schlacht am Schaho.] Comments on the Battle on the Scha Ho. [From the "Militär-Wochenblatt."] Authorised translation by Karl von Donat. *See* Sha-ho. The Battle on the Scha Ho, *etc.* 1906. 8°. **9055. cc. 19.**

—— [Betrachtungen zur Schlacht bei Mukden.] Comments on the Battle of Mukden. [From the "Militär-Wochenblatt." Translated by Karl von Donat.] *See* Mukden. The Battle of Mukden, *etc.* 1906. 8°. **9055. de. 31.**

CAEMMERER (Rudolf Carl Fritz von)

—— Die Entwickelung der strategischen Wissenschaft im 19. Jahrhundert. pp. ix. 213. *Berlin*, 1904. 8°. **08821**. g. **19**.

—— The Development of Strategical Science during the 19th century . . . Authorized translation by Karl von Donat. pp. xvi. 277. *Hugh Rees: London*, 1905. 8°. **8832**. d. **8**.

—— Friedrich des Grossen Feldzugsplan für das Jahr 1757. Vortrag, *etc*. pp. 52. *Berlin*, 1883. 8°. **8831**. b. **16**. (**5**.)

—— Magenta. Der Feldzug von 1859 bis zur ersten Entscheidung . . . Mit . . . Kartenbeilagen, *etc*. pp. x. 216. *Berlin*, 1902. 8°. **9166**. ee. **31**.

CAEMMERER (Rudolf Carl Fritz von) and **ARDENNE** (Armand Leon von) *Baron*.

—— In Wehr und Waffen. Ein Buch von Deutschlands Heer und Flotte . . . Herausgegeben von den Generalleutnants z. D. von Caemmerer und Baron von Ardenne. Mit 510 Abbildungen im Text und 49 Kunstbeilagen. 2 Tl. *Stuttgart*, [1911.] fol. **1866**. d. **6**.

CAEN.

MUNICIPAL INSTITUTIONS.

Assises de Caumont.

—— Compte-rendu de la 11e session tenue à Rouen, les 15–18 juin 1896. pp. xviii. 438. *Rouen*, 1897. 8°. **12203**. h. **9**.

—— Mémoires sur la musique sacrée en Normandie. Par le R.P. Dom Joseph Pothier . . . l'abbé A. Collette . . . l'abbé Bourdon. [With musical notes.] pp. 41. viii. *Ligugé*, 1896. 8°. **7897**. t. **46**.
The date on the wrapper is 1897.

—— Rapport sur l'état moral et les progrès de l'instruction (dans la région comprenant les départements suivants: Seine-Inférieure, Eure, Calvados, Orne, Manche, Sarthe, Mayenne, Maine-et-Loire et Loir-et-Cher). Présenté par A. Héron. pp. 168. *Rouen*, 1896. 4°. **8356**. m. **8**.

—— Rapport sur le mouvement littéraire en Normandie de 1898 à 1902. Par Maurice Sourian. pp. 133. *Caen*, 1903. 8°. **11859**. i. **20**.

—— Rapport sur le mouvement scientifique, industriel et agricole (dans les cinq départements de la Normandie et dans ceux de la Sarthe, de la Mayenne, du Maine-et-Loire et du Loir-et-Cher, pendant les cinq dernières années). Présenté par M. Th. Canonville-Deslys. pp. 168. 47. *Caen*, 1896. 4°. **12203**. h. **17**.
Partly lithographed.

Bibliothèque Municipale.

—— Catalogue des manuscrits de la Bibliothèque municipale de Caen. Précédé d'une notice historique sur la formation de la Bibliothèque par Gaston Lavalley. pp. lix. 274. *Caen*, 1880. 8°. **11905**. g. **23**.

—— Catalogue des ouvrages normands de la Bibliothèque municipale de Caen . . . Par Gaston Lavalley. 3 tom. *Caen*, 1910–12. 8°. **011904**. i. **30**.

—— Manuscrits de la Bibliothèque de Caen. [By Gaston Lavalley.] 1890. *See* France.—*Ministère de l'Instruction Publique*. Catalogue général des manuscrits des bibliothèques publiques de France. Départements. tom. 14. 1885, *etc*. 8°. **Bar.T.3.b.**

CAEN. [Municipal Institutions.]

Bureau des Finances.

—— Lettres et chevauchées du Bureau des Finances de Cae sous Henry iv. Avec introduction, notes et tables, p Lucien Romier. pp. xxv. 332. 1910. 8°. *See* Rouen.—*Société de l'Histoire de Normandie*. Ac. **6890/4**

Comité Général et National de la ville de Caen.

—— Extrait du procès-verbal du Comité général & nation de la ville de Caen, relatif à la mort de M. de Belzunc pp. 58. *Caen*, 1789. 8°. **F. 981**. (**1**

Commune.

—— Conduite révolutionnaire des Commune & Société pop laire de Caen. pp. 18. *Caen*, [1794.] 4°. **R. 674**. (**1**

—— Observations soumises à Nosseigneurs de l'Assemb nationale, au nom de la Commune de Caen, par ses Déput extraordinaires. pp. 15. *Caen*, 1790. 8°. **F. 652**. (**1**

—— [Another copy.] **F. 43**. (

—— Observations sur la division territoriale de la Normand et sur le département de Caen en particulier; présenté par les députés extraordinaires de la commune de Ca à nosseigneurs de l'Assemblée nationale, *etc*. pp. 16. [1789.] 8°. **R. 233**. (

Conseil Municipal.

—— Arrêté du Conseil municipal de la ville de Caen. [Wi regard to the posting up of two anonymous addresses the National Assembly and the King respectively.] pp. *Caen*, [1792.] 8°. **F. 652**. (**1**

—— Précis sommaire de l'ordre qui sera suivi lors de fédération des Gardes Nationales & troupes de ligne département du Calvados. (Extrait du Registre délibérations du Corps Municipal.) pp. 7. *Ca* [1790?] 4°. **8828**. i.

Corps Municipal.

—— *See* supra: Conseil Municipal.

Musée d'Histoire Naturelle.

—— Annuaire du Musée d'histoire naturelle de Caen, pub par M. E. Eudes-Deslongchamps, *etc*. tom. 1. pp. xviii. 598. pl. v. *Caen, Paris*, 1880. 8°. Ac. **28**
No more published.

—— Catalogue descriptif des trochilidés ou oiseaux-mouc aujourd'hui connus. Revue d'après les exemplaires Musée de Caen par M. Eug. Eudes-Deslongchamps . Avec planches. fasc. 1. pp. 489. pl. vi. *Caen, Pa* 1880. 8°. **7285**. e.

Parlement.

—— *See* Normandy.—*Parlement*.

Tribunal Criminel Militaire.

—— Jugement rendu par le tribunal criminel militaire, éta près l'armée des côtes de Cherbourg, séant au quarti général de Caen, qui condamne Louis Belaize . . . à peine de mort . . . Extrait des registres du Tribu criminel militaire, *etc*. *Caen*, [1794.] *s. sh*. fol. **1865**. c. **4**. (**6**

MISCELLANEOUS INSTITUTIONS.

Abbaye aux Hommes.

—— *See* Stephen, *Saint and Martyr, Abbey Church of, Caen*. *See* also infra: Collège du Mont, afterwa Collège Royal.

ACADÉMIE DES SCIENCES, ARTS ET BELLES LETTRES.

—— Mémoires. 1823–1924. 60 tom. *Caen, etc.,* 1825–1924. 8°.

—— Tables . . . 1754–1883 (1884–1893, 1894–1903). *Caen,* 1884–1903. 8°.

—— Nouvelle série. *Caen,* 1925– . 8°. Ac. **305/2**.

—— Rapport général sur les travaux de l'Académie . . . jusqu'au premier janvier 1811. (Rapports . . . pour les années 1811, 1812, 1813, 1814 et 1815.) Par P. F. T. Delarivière. 2 vol. *Caen,* 1811, [16?] 8°. Ac. **305**.

—— Lettres inédites de P.-D. Huet, évêque d'Avranches, à son neveu, M. de Charsigné . . . Publiées par A. Gasté. pt. 1. pp. xiii. 404. *Caen,* 1901. 8°. Ac. **305/4**. *No more published.*

—— Mémoire, qui a remporté le prix en 1788, sur la question proposée par l'Académie royale des Belles-Lettres de Caen; " Existe-t-il des mines de charbon-de-terre dans les environs de Caen? Quels sont les moyens les plus économiques de les exploiter?" pp. 37. *Caen,* 1789. 8°. B. **233**. (**5**.)

—— Prix le Sauvage. Rapport sur le concours ouvert le 26 février 1858, lu dans une séance extraordinaire . . . le 4 déc. 1861, par M. Roulland, au nom d'une commission composée de MM. Vastel, Roulland, *etc.* pp, 119. *Caen,* 1862. 8°. Ac. **305/3**.

ASSEMBLÉE CENTRALE DE RÉSISTANCE À L'OPPRESSION.

—— Départemens réunis. Assemblée centrale de résistance à l'oppression. Déclaration que fait à la France entière, l'Assemblée centrale des départemens du Nord-Ouest, des motifs et de l'objet de sa formation. pp. 16. *Caen,* 1793. 8°. F. **652**. (**15**.)

—— Proclamation de l'Assemblée centrale de résistance à l'oppression, réunie à Caen, aux citoyens français. [Together with an address of General Félix Wimpffen to the citizens of Paris.] pp. 4. *Caen,* 1793. 8°. F. **652**. (**16**.)

ASSOCIATION NORMANDE.

—— Règlement constitutif de l'Association Normande. pp. 8. *Caen,* [c. 1830.] 8°. **08230**. bb. **40**. (**5**.) *Imperfect; wanting the titlepage.*

—— Annuaire des cinq départements de l'ancienne Normandie, publié par l'Association normande. année 1–56. *Caen,* 1834–90. 8°.

—— Table générale . . . Par M. de Roissy, 1835–1859. *Caen,* 1863. 8°. Ac. **412**.

—— Association normande. (Plan d'une statistique générale des cinq départemens de l'ancienne Normandie, proposé par M. de Pracomtal.) pp. xiv. 27. *Caen,* 1833. 8°. Ac. **412**. (**2**.)

Comité de Décentralisation.

—— Organisation cantonale. Question de la suppression ou de la conservation des Sous-Préfectures-Conseils cantonaux. pp. vi. 106. *Caen,* 1871. 8°. **5424**. df. **12**.

—— Organisation départementale, *etc.* pp. vi. 60. *Caen,* 1871. 8°. **8051**. cc. **38**.

—— Procès-verbaux des séances, *etc.* pp. vi. 138. *Caen,* 1871. 8°. **8051**. cc. **39**.

CADOMENSIS ACADEMIA.

—— *See* infra: UNIVERSITÉ DE CAEN.

CHAMBRE DE COMMERCE.

—— Enquête sur les principes et les faits généraux qui régissent la circulation monétaire et fiduciaire. Réponses adressées à la Commission d'enquête . . . sur le rapport de M. C. Paulmier . . . Abrégés des réponses. pp. 73. *Caen,* 1865. 4°. **8228**. i. **36**.

CHAMBRE DES CONFÉRENCES DES AVOCATS STAGIAIRES PRÈS LA COUR IMPÉRIALE DE CAEN.

—— Procès-verbal de la séance de rentrée . . . 25 janvier 1862. Allocution de M. Leblond, bâtonnier de l'Ordre. Étude sur Michel de Marillac. Par M. Exupère Caillemer. pp. 48. *Caen,* 1862. 8°. **5425**. eee. **11**.

COLLÉGE DU MONT, afterwards COLLÈGE ROYAL.

—— Les Élèves du Collège du Mont au Roi Louis XVI à son entrée à Caen, 1786. [Three poems. A facsimile of the edition published at Caen in 1786.] Introduction par Tony Genty. pp. xii. 11. *Rouen,* 1922. 4°. [*Recueil de poësies scolaires composées dans les Collèges de Rouen et de Caen.*] Ac. **8938/79**.

—— Sujets des pièces dramatiques, qui seront représentées au College royal de Bourbon, de la Compagnie de Jésus de la très célèbre Université de Caen, pour la distribution des prix . . . le vendredi 9e d'août 1748 . . . A Caen . . . M.DCCXLVIII. [A reprint.] pp. 14. [1900?] *See* ROUEN.—*Société des Bibliophiles Normands.* Ancien théâtre scolaire. Pièces, *etc.* fasc. 4. [1897, *etc.*] 4°. Ac. **8938/57**.

—— Visite au College royal de Caen, ancienne Abbaye de St. Étienne fondée dans le XIe siècle par Guillaume-le-Conquérant. [With plates.] pp. 39. *Caen, Paris,* 1829. 8°. **10168**. bb. **14**.

COLLÉGE ROYAL.

—— *See* supra: COLLÉGE DU MONT, ETC.

COMPAGNIE DU SAINT SACREMENT, called L'HERMITAGE.

—— Mémoire pour faire connoistre l'esprit & la conduite de la Compagnie establie en la ville de Caën, appellée l'Hermitage. [By C. Du Four and others.] [*Paris?* 1660?] 4°. **698**. h. **46**.

ÉGLISE PROTESTANTE.

—— The Registers of the Protestant Church at Caen, Normandy. Edited by C. E. Lart. vol. 1. [Baptisms and marriages. 1560–1572.] pp. xxiv. 712. *Imprimerie Lafolye Frères: Vannes,* 1907. 8°. **9902**. a. **18**. *No more published.*

FACULTÉ DES LETTRES DE CAEN.

—— *See* infra: UNIVERSITÉ DE CAEN.

SOCIÉTÉ D'AGRICULTURE ET DE COMMERCE.

—— Annuaire de la Société d'Agriculture et de Commerce de Caen, pour l'année 1812. pp. 36. *Caen,* 1812. 8°. B. **665**. (**5**.)

SOCIÉTÉ D'HISTOIRE DU DROIT NORMAND.

—— Bibliothèque d'histoire du droit normand. Publiée . . . par Ch. Astoul et R. Génestal. *Caen,* 1910– . 8°. **5408**. f.

SOCIÉTÉ DES AMIS DE LA CONSTITUTION.

—— Adresse de la Société des amis de la constitution à Caen aux sociétés patriotiques du Calvados & à toutes les sociétés civiques de France. pp. 4. *Caen*, [1791.] 8°. R. **234**. (**17**.)

—— Adresse des Amis de la constitution à Caen, à leurs frères, les habitans des campagnes. pp. 5. *Caen*, [1791.] 8°. R. **234**. (**16**.)

—— Extrait du Registre des délibérations de la Société des amis de la constitution . . . du 27 septembre 1791. (Discours de M. Bonnet de Meautry.—Discours de Claude Fauchet.) pp. 7. *Caen*, [1791.] 8°. R. **234**. (**22**.)

SOCIÉTÉ DES ANTIQUAIRES DE LA NORMANDIE.

—— Bulletin, *etc.* 34 tom. *Paris; Caen*, 1860–1921. 8°. *Tom.* 7–34 *were published at Caen.*

—— Table générale alphabétique et analytique des matières contenus dans les cinq premiers volumes . . . 1860–1869, par M. Renault. pp. vi. 203. *Caen*, 1872. 8°. Ac. **5320**.

—— Mémoires, *etc.* 1824–36. 10 tom. *Caen, Paris*, 1825–38. 8°.

—— Atlas. 1825–36. 7 pt. *Caen*, 1825–37. *obl.* 4°. Ac. **5320/2**.

—— Mémoires . . . 2e série. 10 tom. *Paris, Caen*, 1840–53. 4°.

—— 3e série. 10 tom. *Paris*, 1855–80. 4°.

—— 4e série. 4 tom. *Caen*, 1883–1911. 4°.

—— Table . . . des vingt-quatre premiers volumes. Par M. le conseiller Renault. pp. viii. 151. *Paris*, 1863. 4°. Ac. **5320/3**.

—— A Monsieur le Ministre de l'Intérieur, la Société des Antiquaires de Normandie. [An address, requesting him to take steps for the preservation of the church of St. Étienne-le-Vieux at Caen. With plates.] *Caen*, 1850. fol. **1259**. e. **6**.

Musée.

—— Catalogue et description des objets d'art de l'antiquité, du moyen âge, de la renaissance, et des temps modernes exposés au Musée. Rédigé par M. Gervais. pp. 136. *Caen*, 1864. 8°. **07708.aaa.10.**

SOCIÉTÉ DES BEAUX-ARTS DE CAEN.

—— Bulletin, *etc.* 8 vol. *Caen*, 1856–88[91]. 8°. Ac. **4538**.

SOCIÉTÉ DES CARABOTS.

—— Arrestés de la Société des Carabots. *Caen*, 1793. *s. sh.* fol. **Tab.443.a.3.(26.)**

SOCIÉTÉ LINNÉENNE DU CALVADOS, afterwards SOCIÉTÉ LINNÉENNE DE NORMANDIE.

—— Bulletin, *etc.* 10 vol. *Caen*, 1856–66. 8°.

—— 2e série. 10 vol. *Caen*, 1868–76. 8°.

—— 3e série. 10 vol. *Caen*, 1877–87. 8°.

—— 4e série. 10 vol. *Caen*, 1888–97. 8°.

—— 5e série. 10 vol. *Caen*, 1897–1907. 8°.

—— 6e série. 10 vol. *Caen*, 1909–19. 8°.

—— 7e série. 10 vol. *Caen*, 1919–28. 8°.

—— 8e série. *Caen*, 1929– . 8°. Ac. **2842**.

—— Mémoires, *etc.* vol. 1–26. *Caen; Paris*, 1824–1924. 8° & 4°.

—— Nouvelle série.

Section zoologique. vol. 1. fasc. 1, *etc.*
Section botanique. vol. 1. fasc. 1, *etc.*
Section géologique. vol. 1. fasc. 1, *etc.*

Caen, 1925– . 4°. Ac. **2842/3**.

—— Mémoires . . . Publiés par M. de Caumont . . . Seconde série. Premier volume. Première partie. pp. iv. 193. *Paris*, 1829. 4°. **7107**. e. **5**.
No more published. This was intended to be the first volume of the 4° *series, which was in fact started in* 1835 *with vol.* 5 *of the series of Mémoires placed at* Ac. 2842/3.

—— Séance publique . . . tenue . . . le 5 juin 1834 (le 4 juin 1835, le 24 mai 1836). 3 vol. *Caen*, 1834–36. 8°. Ac. **2842/2**.

SOCIÉTÉ PHILHARMONIQUE DU CALVADOS.

—— Statuts, *etc.* pp. 24. 4. *Caen*, 1827. 8°. **898**. c. **18**. (**5**.)

SOCIÉTÉ RÉPUBLICAINE.

—— La Société républicaine de Caen aux sociétés populaires de l'empire. pp. 4. *Caen*, [1793.] 8°. R. **234**. (**31**.)

SOCIÉTÉ ROYALE D'AGRICULTURE ET DE COMMERCE.

—— Précis des travaux de la Société . . . depuis son rétablissement en 1801, jusqu'en 1810. Par M. Pierre-Aimé Lair, secrétaire. *Caen*, 1827. 8°.
[Continued as :]
Mémoires de la Société, *etc.* tom. 2–7. *Caen*, 1827–58. 8°.
[Continued as :]
Bulletin mensuel, *etc.* année 1858–68. *Caen*, 1859–69. 8°.

—— Nouvelle série. année 1869–89. *Caen*, 1869–89. 8°. Ac. **3398**.

UNIVERSITÉ DE CAEN.

—— ve Centenaire de la fondation de l'Université de Caen, 1432–1932. Livre d'or. (Le volume composé par A. Bigot.) [With plates, including portraits.] pp. 236. *Caen*, 1933. 8°. **8355**. ff. **10**.

—— Dénonciation à la très-célèbre Université de Caen, de plusieurs propositions extraites des thèses & cahiers des Jésuites du Collège du Mont, renouvellant la doctrine déja condamnée par cette Université. pp. 21. [*Caen?*] 1762. 12°. **5374.a.40.**

—— [Another copy.] Dénonciation à la très-célèbre Université de Caën, *etc.* 1762. 12°. **4071**. aa. **48**. (**1**.)

—— Mémoires adressés au Parlement de Normandie par l'Université de Caen; le premier, au sujet de Lettres de Maître-ès-Arts de Bourges, vendues par ceux qui se disoient ci-devant Jésuites dans le Collège du Mont à Caen; le second, sur l'usurpation faite par les mêmes, du Collège du Mont . . . sur leurs différens égaremens & entreprises, & sur la manière de les remplacer. pp. 96. [*Caen?* 1762.] 12°. **4092**. bb. **4**.

—— Prælectiones in Hippocratis librum De internis affectionibus, in publicis Medicor. Scholis . . . Cadomensis Academiæ, pro solenni Cathedræ vacantis disputatione habitæ . . . Edente M. Francisco de St. André. pp. 148. *J. Cavelier: Cadomi*, 1687. 12°. **539**. c. **32**.

CAEN. [MISCELLANEOUS INSTITUTIONS.]

—— L'Université de Caen, 1432–1932. Son passé, son présent. (Publié sous la direction de A. Bigot.) pp. 296. *Caen,* 1933. 8°. **8355.** ff. **9.**

Faculté de Droit.

—— Travaux de la Semaine d'histoire du droit normand tenue à Jersey du 24 au 27 mai 1923 avec la concours de la Société de Droit de Jersey, de la Société Jersiaise et de la Société d'Histoire du Droit normand, *etc.* pp. xiv. 418. *Caen,* 1925. 8°. Ac. **303/3.**

—— Travaux de la Semaine d'histoire du droit normand tenue à Guernesey du 26 au 30 mai 1927, *etc.* pp. xvi. 368. *Caen,* 1928. 8°. Ac. **303/4.**

Faculté des Lettres.

—— Annales de la Faculté des Lettres de Caen. année 1–6. *Paris, Caen,* 1885–90. 8°. Ac. **303.**

—— Bulletin mensuel. (Faculté des Lettres de Caen.) année 1–7; année 8. livr. 1–9. *Caen,* 1885–92. 8°. Ac. **303/2.**

No more published.

APPENDIX.

—— Adresse à tous les corps administ-atifs de Caen. [On priests who did not subscribe to the "serment civique."] pp. 6. [1791.] 8°. R. **234.** (**20.**)

—— Adresse des citoyens de la ville de Caen . . . à l'Assemblée nationale. (Au roi. Adresse des citoyens.) pp. 7. *Caen,* [1791.] 8°. R. **234.** (**23.**)

—— Déclaration des curés de la ville de Caen, au sujet du serment prescrit par le décret de l'Assemblée nationale, du 27 novembre 1790. pp. 7. [*Caen?* 1791.] 8°. F.R. **139.** (**32.**)

—— Description d'une feste donnée à Caen . . . le dix decembre 1738 . . . par Messieurs les Pensionnaires sujets du Roy de la Grande Bretagne, à l'occasion de l'aniversaire de la Naissance de Sa Majesté Britannique. pp. 4. *Caen,* [1738.] 4°. **835.** h. **19.** (**11.**)

—— Mémoire pour les quatre-vingt-qua[tre] citoyens détenus dans la tour de Caen, dep[uis] le 5 novembre 1791. pp. 72. *Paris,* 1792. 8°. R. **234.** (**28.**)
The titlepage and the last leaf are mutilated.

—— Obseruations addressées aux spectables Catholiques de la ville de Caen. [Signed: F. D. Auditeur théologien.] [1610?] 8°. *See* D., F., *Auditeur théologien.* **3902.** aaa. **41.** (**4.**)

—— Les Origines de la ville de Caen, et des lieux circonvoisins. [By P. D. Huet, Bishop of Avranches.] pp. 652. *Rouen,* 1702. 8°. **575.** f. **5.**

—— [Another edition.] Revûes, corrigées, et augmentées. Seconde édition. pp. 442. *Rouen,* 1706. 8°. **282.** d. **35.**

—— Recueil de pièces non imprimées, extraites des registres du Parlement de Rouen, et de l'Hôtel-de-Ville de Caen, pour prouver que les Jésuites sont coupables de toutes sortes d'excès, notamment du crime de lèze-Majesté, dont ils sont accusés dans la dénonciation faite au Parlement de Normandie. pp. 131. 1762. 12°. *See* NORMANDY.—*Parlement.* **4071.** aa. **48.** (**2.**)

—— Révolutions de Caen . . . ou Récit exact de ce qui s'est passé dans cette capitale, & particulièrement de la prise de la forteresse. Juillet, 1789. pp. 7. [*Paris,*] 1789. 8°. F. **842.** (**8.**)

CAEN.

—— Révolutions de Caen . . . Introduction par R. N. Sauvage. [A facsimile reprint of the edition of 1789.] pp. xiv. 7. 1944. 4°. *See* ROUEN.—*Société des Bibliophiles Normands.* Ac. **8938/92.**

—— Strenæ ad Senatum Populumque Cadomensem. [The dedication signed: N. M.] 1598. 8°. *See* M., N. **12301.** aaa. **16.** (**2.**)

—— Société des Amis de la Constitution, séante aux Jacobins, à Paris. Adresse des citoyens de la ville de Caen . . . à l'Assemblée nationale. (Au Roi. Adresse des citoyens, *etc.*) pp. 7. [*Paris,* 1792.] 8°. **935.** b. **9.** (**40.**)

—— [Another copy.] F. **333.** (**1.**)

CAEN, *Bailliage de.* Rôle du ban et de l'arrière-ban du bailliage de Caen en 1552. Publié pour la première fois avec introduction, notes, additions et corrections par Émile Travers. pp. xvii. 399. 1901. 8°. *See* ROUEN.—*Société de l'Histoire de Normandie.* Ac. **6890/34.**

CAEN, *Département de.—Bureau Intermédiaire.* Ordonnance de MM. les Président et Deputés composant le Bureau intermédiaire du département de Caen . . . par laquelle il est enjoint aux Syndics municipaux de chaque paroisse, d'assembler leur Municipalité . . . pour faire & arrêter la déclaration des personnes ci-devant privilégiées, & qui jouissoient . . . d'exemption de tailles . . . & de déposer lesdites déclarations . . . pour être de suite procédé à la plus juste répartition desdites impositions, *etc.* pp. 7. *Caen,* [1789.] 4°. **8225.** f. **5.**

CAEN, *Généralité de.—Assemblée Provinciale.* Procès-verbal de la séance préliminaire de l'Assemblée provinciale de Basse-Normandie, tenue à Caen le lundi 20e jour d'août 1787. pp. 47. *Caen,* 1787. 4°. **1476.** d. **14.**

—— Procès-verbal des séances de l'Assemblée provinciale de Basse-Normandie, tenues à Caen en novembre & décembre 1787. pp. 343. 29. *Caen,* 1788. 4°. **180.** d. **13.**

—— *Assemblées Municipales.* Instructions pour les Assemblées municipales (de Basse Normandie). pp. 19. *Caen,* [1789?] 4°. **5402.** aa. **5.**

CAEN (ANTONIUS DE) *Praes.* *See* MAILLARD (F.) Quæstio medica . . . Sunt-ne tam variæ morborum, quàm ægrorum facies? [1682.] 4°. **1182.** e. **2.** (**16.**)

—— *Praes.* *See* POIRIER (L.) Quæstio medica . . . Est ne cibis sumendis ordo servandus? [1676.] 4°. **1182.** e. **1.** (**160.**)

CAEN (CHARLES MATHIEU ISIDORE DE) *Count.* *See* DECAEN.

CAEN (HERBERT EUGENE)

—— Baghdad: 1951. [On San Francisco.] pp. 120. *Doubleday & Co.: Garden City, N.Y.,* 1950. 8°. **010410.** k. **33.**

CAEN (JANINE LÉVY) *See* LÉVY-CAEN.

CAEN (JULIEN) *See* LOMBARD (J.) and CAEN (J.) Le Contremaître mécanicien. 1906. 8°. **08766.** b. **35.**

CAEN (MAURICE) Traité de blanchisserie mécanique, désinfection et nettoyage à sec . . . Avec 116 figures dans le texte. pp. xvi. 240. *Paris & Liége,* 1938. 8°. **7944.** v. **24.**

CAEN (RAOUL DE) *See* RAOUL, *de Caen.*

CAENAZZO (TOMASO) Del prodigioso approdo del corpo di S. Eufemia Calcedonese in Rovigno. *See* PARENZO.—*Società Istriana di Archeologia, etc.* Atti e memorie, *etc.* vol. 1. 1885, *etc.* 8°. Ac. **5230.**

CAENDLER (AGNELLUS) Arnolphus, malè Malus cognominatus, seu justa defensio, qua Arnolphi, Bavariæ ducis . . . facta, fata, fama a veterum æquè ac recentiorum scriptorum obtrectationibus, fabulis & convitiis vindicantur . . . per Fr. A. C. Augustinianum [i.e. A. Caendler]. pp. 162. 1735. 4°. *See* C., A., *Fr., Augustinianus.* **1199. h. 5.**

CAENEGEM (FRANZ VAN) La Guerre des Paysans. Quelques noms et quelques faits, 1798–1799 . . . 2e édition, revue et augmentée. pp. 291. *Bruxelles,* 1897. 8°. **9414. h. 20.**

CAENEGEM (J. VAN) Het Kanalenvraagstuk in Noord-Oost-België, in verband met eene Rijn-Scheldevaart en een kolenafvoerkanaal in Limburg, *etc.* [With maps.] pp. 158. *Hasselt,* 1922. 8°. **08235. d. 55.**

CAENEGHEM (R. VAN)

—— Hekserij bij de BaLuba van Kasai, *etc.* [With a summary in French.] pp. 280. *Bruxelles,* 1955. 8°. [*Académie Royale des Sciences Coloniales. Classe des sciences morales et politiques. Mémoires in-8°.* Nouvelle série. *Ethnographie.* tom. 3. fasc. 1.] Ac. **6261.**

—— Over het godsbegrip der Baluba van Kasai. pp. 179. *Bruxelles,* 1952. 8°. [*Institut Royal Colonial Belge. Section des Sciences Morales et Politiques. Mémoires.* Collection in-8°. tom. 22. fasc. 2.] Ac. **6261.**

—— Studie over de gewoontelijke strafbepalingen tegen het overspel bij de Baluba en Ba Lulula van Kasai. pp. 55. *Bruxelles,* 1938. 8°. [*Institut Royal Colonial Belge. Section des Sciences Morales et Politiques. Mémoires.* Collection in-8°. tom. 7. fasc. 3.] **Ac.6261.**

CAENEGEM (R. C. VAN)

—— Geschiedenis van het strafrecht in Vlaanderen van de XIe tot de XIVe eeuw. Avec résumé français. pp. xxii. 399. *Brussel,* 1954. 8°. [*Verhandelingen van de Koninklijke Vlaamse Academie voor Wetenschappen, Letteren en Schone Kunsten van België. Klasse der Letteren.* no. 19.] Ac. 988. ec/2.

CAENIGA (MARIUS DE) *See* GRANDI (G.) Clarissimi viri D. Guidonis Grandi . . . Epistola mathematica de momento gravium in planis inclinatis; deque directione fulcri . . . Ex autographo iterum edidit . . . adnotationibus illustravit . . . M. de Caeniga. 1711. 4°. **529. g. 11. (9.)**

CAEPHALUS (JOANNES) D. Ioannis Cæphali Consilium XXXI. lib. I., *etc. See* BUDELIUS (R.) De monetis et re numaria, *etc.* 1591. 4°. **714. h. 10.**

CAEPIANUS (JOANNES) *See* CEPIANUS.

CAEPOLA (BARTHOLOMAEUS) *See* CAEPOLLA.

CAEPOLA (IZAIÁŠ) *See* CAEPOLLA.

CAEPOLLA (BARTHOLOMAEUS) *See* PAULUS, *de Castro.* [Consilia.] *Begin.* [fol. 1 *recto:*] Abbas, Absolutio, *etc. End.* [fol. 439 *recto:*] Cum . . . Pauli castrensis dilapsa undiq͂ neq͂ in unum corpus redacta consilia cernerentur . . . Bartholomeus cepolla . . . singula queq͂ ab eo . . . consulta colligere elaborauit, *etc.* [1475 ?] fol. IC. **20718.**

—— —— 1485. fol. IC. **7334.**

—— *Begin.* [fol. 1 *verso:* Incipit. Tabula. Seruitutum. Vrbanoꝝ p̄dioruȝ.] [fol. 40 *recto:*] Incipit Tabula Cautelarum Domini Bartholamei [*sic*] Cepolla de Verona. [fol. 69 *verso:*] Finiunt Cautele vtriusq͂ iuris monarche Domini Bartholomei Cepole. Veronensis, *etc.* [fol. 71 *verso:* Incipit Tabula tractatus de Seruitutibus rusticorum prediorum.] G.L. *per Andream de Bonetis: Venetijs,* [die .xx. Augusti, 1485.] fol. IC. **22095.**

108 *leaves, ff.* 5, 39 *and* 70 *blank. Sig.* A4 a8 b8 c6 d8 c4 f10 g8 h6 i8 [*4] k8 l–n6 o8. *Double columns,* 75 *lines to a column. A fragment, consisting of quires* f–i, *containing the Cautelae.*

CAEPOLLA (BARTHOLOMAEUS)

—— *Begin.* [Pt. 1. fol. 2 *recto:*] Incipit tabula seruitutuȝ vrbanoruȝ predioruȝ. [fol. 5 *recto:*] Tractatus vberrimus de seruitutibus vrbanorum prediorum per eximium iurecconsultuȝ Bartholomeū cepollaȝ veronēsem sūmopere confectus. [fol. 43 *recto:*] Incipit tabula tractatus de seruitutibus rusticoruȝ prediorum. [Pt. 2. fol. 1 *recto:*] Incipit tabula cautelarum domini Bartholomei cepolle de verona. *End.* [fol. 33 *recto:*] Finiunt cautele . . . Bartholomei cepolle veronensis. G.L. 3 pt. *Ioanneantonio birreta īpressionis huius auctore: Papie,* Kalendis Aprilis [1 April], 1492. fol. IC. **31418.**

Pt. 1. 84 *leaves, the first blank, ff.* 5–41 *numbered* 1–37, *ff.* 47–84 *numbered* 1–38. *Sig.* a4; a–d8 e6; aa4; aa–dd8 ee6. *Pt.* 2. 34 *leaves, the last blank, ff.* 3–33 *numbered* 1–31. *Sig.* A2; A–D8. *Double columns,* 68 *lines to a column. Without the last blank.*

—— Cautele domini Bertholomei [*sic*] cepolle de verona cum tractatu de seruitutibus. G.L. *per Bernardinū d' Tridino: venetijs,* die .xvij. mēsis februarij, die xx. februarij, 1493. fol. IC. **22173.**

108 *leaves. Sig.* a4; AA–EE6 FF4; aa4; AAA–EEE6 FFF4; A2; A–E6. *Double columns,* 70 *lines to a column.*

—— *Begin.* [fol. 2 *recto:*] Cautelle famosissimi Iuris .V. doctoris domini Bartholomei Cepolla Veronensis. *per Xp̄oforum Vualdarfer, Impensis Petriantonii de burgo dicti de casteliono & Philippi de lauania: Mediolani,* die .xv. Septembris, 1475. fol. IC. **26211.**

50 *leaves, the first blank. Without signatures. Double columns,* 53 *lines to a column. Without the blank leaf.*

—— [Another edition.] *Begin.* [fol. 2 *recto:*] Bartholomei veroneñ vulgariter nūcupati Cepole vtriusq͂ iuris doctoris aduocati Cōsistorialis Padue legentis Cautele vtilissime feliciter Incipiunt, *etc.* G.L. *industria Egidii vāder heerstraten: Louanii,* Iunii die octaua, 1486. 4°. IA. **49346.**

104 *leaves, the first blank. Sig.* a–n8. 28 *lines to a page. Without the blank leaf.*

—— [Another edition.] *Begin.* [fol. 2 *recto:*] Bartholomei Veroneñ vulgariter nūcupati Cepole, vtriusq͂ iuris doctoris aduocati Cōsistorialis Padue legētis cautele vtilissime feliciter Incipiunt, *etc.* G.L. *industria Egidij vander heerstraten: Louanij,* Februarij die .xxv., 1487. 4°. IA. **49348.**

100 *leaves, the first blank. Sig.* a–d8 e6 f–l8 m6 n8. 28 *lines to a page.*

—— [Another edition.] Dissertissimi juris vtriusq͂ monarche dn̄i Bartholomei veronenſ. Cepolle nūcupati Cautele iuris vtilissime, quibꝰ et aduocati et ꝓcuratores suis clientulis in omni strepitu iudicioꝝ facile subuenire possunt. G.L. [*Johann Prüss: Strasburg,*] Februarij die .xxv., 1490. 4°. IB. **1667.**

86 *leaves,* 2–86 *numbered* I–LXXXV. *Sig.* [a8 b6 c6 d8] c6 f6 g8 h–m6 n8. 44 *lines to a page.*

—— *Begin.* [fol. 2 *recto:*] Incipiunt cōsilia criminalia Clarissimi ⁊ excellentissimi vtriusq͂ iuris doctoris ⁊ militis .D. Bartho. Cepole tūc legētis ī florētissimo gymnasio patauino, *etc.* G.L. *studio Bonini de Boninis: Brixie,* xij. Kalendas Aprilis [21 March], 1490. fol. IC. **31108.**

98 *leaves, the first and last blank. Sig.* a–e6 f4 g–m6 n4 o4 p–s6·4. *Double columns,* 64 *lines to a column.*

—— [Another edition.] Consi. Cepo. Consilia criminalia celeberrimi ac prestantissimi vtriusq͂ juris illuminatoris domini Bartholomei Cepole. Veronēsis: nuper dilgentissime [*sic*] ex manuscripto exēplari ipsius authoris recognita, ⁊ emēdata. Additis quoq͂ summarijs ac repertorio (dn̄i Luce Panetij) non mediocri diligētia elaborato feliciter incipiunt. G.L. ff. clxxii. *Opera A. du Ry ac impensis J. de Giuncta: Lugduni,* 1531. 8°. **5305. a. 19.**

The titlepage is engraved. The date in the colophon is 1530.

CAEPOLLA (Bartholomaeus)

—— Tractatus de cognitione libroruȝ iuris canonici . . . ad reue. D. Nicol. Donatum, *etc.* *See* Tractatus. Primum volumen tractatuum, *etc.* vol. 1. 1549. fol. **5305.** i.

—— [Another edition.] *See* Tractatus. Tractatus vniversi iuris, *etc.* tom. 1. 1584. fol. **499.** f. **1.**

—— *Begin.* [fol. 2 *recto*:] Bartholomei Cepole Veronensis . . . ad. R. In xp̄o patrem do. dn̄m Hermolaum Barbarum Venetum . . . Libellus de cōtractibus emptionum et locationum cum pacto de retrouēdendo simulatis. [*In domo Antonii et Raphaelis de Vulterris*:] *Rome*, die prima menſ. Septembris, 1474. fol. IC. **17686.**
28 *leaves, the first and last blank. Without signatures. Double columns,* 55 *lines to a column.*

—— [Another edition.] *Begin.* [fol. 2 *recto*:] Bartholomei. Cepole Veronensis . . . ad R. In xp̄o patrē. do. dn̄m Hermolaum Barbarum . . . Libellus de contractibus emptionū et locationum cum pacto de retrouendendo simulatis. [fol. 19 *verso*:] Incipit Tractatus peregrinus de Renunciationibus consuetis apponi in contractibus. G.L. ms. notes. [*Georgius Lauer*: *Rome*, 1480?] fol. IC. **17527.**
22 *leaves, the first blank. Without signatures. Double columns,* 65 *lines to a column.*

—— [Another edition.] *Begin.* [fol. 2 *recto*:] Bartholomei Cepole Veronēsis iur. vtriusq; doctoris . . . Libellus de cōtractibus emptionū et locationū cū pacto de retrouendendo simulatis. [*Johann Neumeister*: *Albi*, 1480?] fol. IB. **43010.**
60 *leaves, the first blank. Without signatures. Double columns,* 36 *lines to a column.*

—— [Another edition.] *Begin.* [fol. 1 *recto*:] Bartholomei Cepolle Veronēsis . . . Libellus de cōtractibus emptionuȝ et locationū cū pacto de retrouēdendo simulatus [*sic*]. G.L. *p henricū harlem*: *Senis*, die xviij. menſ. Madij, 1493. fol. IC. **34648.**
18 *leaves. Sig.* A⁶ B⁴ C⁶ D². *Double columns,* 60 *lines to a column.*

—— [Another edition.] Tractatus . . . de cōtractibus emptionum ꝛ locationum, *etc.* *See* Tractatus. Primum volumen tractatuum, *etc.* vol. 5. 1549. fol. **5305.** i.

—— [Another edition.] Bartholomei Caepollae . . . de contractibus simulatis. *See* Tractatus. Tractatus vniuersi iuris, *etc.* tom. 7. 1584. fol. **499.** f. **9.**

—— *Begin.* [fol. 2 *recto*:] Bartholomei Cepole veronēſ. . . . Ad insignē equiteȝ . . . zachariam Triuisanum virum patricium de Impatore Militū deligendo. Prohemiū foeliciter Incipit, *etc.* *End.* [fol. 18 *recto*:] Explicit solēnis tractatus de re militari cum cōclusionibus eiusdem in fine additus [*sic*]. editus er [*sic*] Famosissimum utriusq; iuris doctorem dn̄m Bartholomeum Cepolla Veronenſ. G.L. [*Georgius Lauer*: *Rome*, 1480?] fol. IC. **17531.**
18 *leaves, the first blank. Without signatures. Double columns,* 65 *lines to a column.*

—— [Another edition.] Bartholomei Cepolle . . . de imperatore militum deligendo, *etc.* *See* Tractatus. Primum volumen tractatuum, *etc.* vol. 12. 1549. fol. **5305.** i.

—— [Another edition.] *See* Tractatus. Tractatus vniuersi iuris, *etc.* tom. 16. 1584. fol. **499.** h. **1.**

—— *Begin.* [fol. 2 *recto*:] Incipit tabula hui⁹ libri. [fol. 6 *verso*:] Incipit tabula alterius tractatus de Seruitutibus rusticorū p̄diorū. [fol. 15 *recto*:] [Q]Vi alicuius artis uel doctrine scientiā profitent̃, *etc.* [fol. 70 *verso*:] Tractatus dn̄i Bartholomei Cepolla de Verona. de seruitutibus urbanorum & rusticorū prediorū Finit feliciter. [fol. 71 *recto*:] Tractatus seruitutuȝ rusticoꝝ p̄dioꝝ dn̄i Bartholomei Cepolla . . . Incipit feliciter. [fol. 131 *verso*:] Tractatus de seruitutib⁹ rusticoꝝ prediorū . . . finit feliciter. [*Petrus Petri & Johannes Nicolai*: *Perugia*, 1475?] fol. IC. **32702.**
132 *leaves, the first and last blank. Without signatures. Double columns,* 52 *lines to a column.*

CAEPOLLA (Bartholomaeus)

—— [Another edition.] *Begin.* [fol. 2 *recto*:] Incipit tabula de seruitutibus rusticoꝝ p̄dioꝝ. [fol. 7 *recto*:] Tractatus seruitutum rusticorum predioruȝ dn̄i Bartholomei Cepolla . . . Incipit feliciter. [fol. 62 *recto*:] Incipit Tabula Seruitutum Urbanoꝝ p̄diorum. [fol. 66 *recto*:] Tractatus seruitutuȝ urbanorum predioruȝ dn̄i Bartholomei Cepolla, *etc.* ms. notes. *Apud Sanctum Marcū*: *Rome*, die Nona Mensis Septembris, 1475. fol. IC. **17983.** & IC. **17950.**
108 *leaves, ff.* 1 *and* 61 *blank. Without signatures. Double columns,* 62 *lines to a column.*

—— [Another copy.] IC. **17951.**
Imperfect; wanting ff. 1–60, 102, 107.

—— [Another edition.] Tractatus seruitutum rusticorum prediorum, *etc.*—Bartholomei Cepolle . . . Tractatus . . . de seruitutibus vrbanorum prediorum, *etc.* *See* Tractatus. Primum volumen tractatuum, *etc.* vol. 4. 1549. fol. **5305.** i.

—— [Another edition.] Bartholomæi Cæpolæ . . . de seruitutibus vrbanorum prædiorum. — Bartholomæi Coepollæ . . . de seruitutibus rusticorum prædiorum. *See* Tractatus. Tractatus vniuersi iuris, *etc.* tom. 6. pt. 2. 1584. fol. **499.** f. **8.**

—— [Another edition.] Tractatus . . . de seruitutibus tam vrbanorum quàm rusticorum prædiorum. Cui accessit, D. Martini Laudensis I.C. Repetitio ad L. Seruitutes 14 ff. de Seruitutibus. Item D. Ioannis Superioris I.C. in singulas L. quæ sunt sub tit. ff. de Seruit. Comment. succenturiati. Editio postrema . . . recognita & . . . expurgata. pp. 532. *H. Boissat & G. Remeus*: *Lugduni*, 1660. 4°. **496.** e. **1.**

—— *Begin.* [fol. 1 *verso*:] Rubrice huius tractatus, *etc.* [fol. 2 *recto*:] Incipit Tabula tractatus de Seruitutibus rusticoꝝ p̄dioꝝ. [fol. 9 *recto*:] Tractatus seruitutū rusticorum predioꝝ dn̄i Bartholomei Cepolla . . . Incipit feliciter. [*In domo Antonii et Raphaelis de Vulterris*: *Rome*, 1474?] fol. IC. **17689.**
72 *leaves, without signatures. Double columns,* 56 *lines to a column. Imperfect; wanting ff.* 66, 69.

CAEPOLLA (Izaiáš) *See* Bible. [*Bohemian.*] Biblj České. [Translated from the Vulgate for the use of the Bohemian Brethren by I. Caepolla and others.] 1579, *etc.* 4°. **3035.** b. **6.**

CAER.

—— Y Gaer. *See* Periodical Publications.—*Cardiff.*

CAËR (Théophile de) Causerie sur l'aumônerie militaire . . . précédée d'une préface par Monseigneur de Ségur. Deuxième édition. pp. 75. *Paris*, 1874. 12°. **8829.** a. **9.**

—— Un Ex-Voto à N.-D. de Lourdes. Histoire intime et authentique d'une guérison . . . Deuxième édition. pp. 443. *Paris*, 1890. 8°. **4378.** g. **2.**

CAERDEN (Paulus van)

—— Kort Verhael ofte Journael van de reyse gedaen naer de Oost Indien met 4. schepen . . . Onder den Admirael Pieter Both . . . in den iaren 1599. 1600. ende 1601. Gehouden by Capiteyn P. van Caerden. pp. 20. *See* Nederlandse Oostindische Compagnie. Begin ende voortgangh van de . . . Oost Indische Compagnie, *etc.* dl. 1. 1646. 4°. **983.** ff. **8.**

—— Voyage de P. van Caerden aux Indes Orientales. Fait dans les annees 1599, 1600. & 1601, *etc.* *See* Constantin (de) *pseud.* Recueil des voyages, *etc.* tom. 3. 1725. 12°. **1047.** a. **15.**

CAERDEN (Paulus van)

—— [Another edition.] *See* Constantin (de) *pseud.* Recueil des voiages, *etc.* tom. 2. 1754. 12°. **303. a. 10.**

—— Loffelijcke Voyagie op Oost-Indien, met 8 schepen . . . int jaer 1606. onder het beleyt van den Admirael P. van Caerden, *etc.* pp. 48. *See* Nederlandsse Oost Indische Compagnie. Begin ende voortgangh van de . . . Oost Indische Compagnie, *etc.* dl. 2. 1646. 4°. **983. ff. 8.**

—— Relation du II. Voiage de P. van Caerden aux Indes Orientales, *etc.* *See* Constantin (de) *pseud.* Recueil des voyages, *etc.* tom. 6. 1725. 12°. **1047. a. 20.**

—— [Another edition.] *See* Constantin (de) *pseud.* Recueil des voiages, *etc.* tom. 3. pt. 2. 1754. 12°. **303. a. 13.**

CAERDYDD. *See* Cardiff.

CAERFALLWCH, *Bardic name of Thomas Edwards.* *See* Edwards (Thomas) called Caerfallwch.

CAERFYRRDIN. *See* Carmarthen.

CAERGWRLE.

—— Caergwrle . . . Official guide. Issued under the auspices of the Caergwrle Development Association. pp. 40. *E. J. Burrow & Co.: Cheltenham,* [1929.] 8°. **10354. a. 166.**

CAERGYSTENIN. *See* Constantinople.

CAERHYDON (Patience) Patience Caerhydon. A story. By the author of 'Beneath the Wheels' [i.e. Fanny Eliza Millett Notley], *etc.* 3 vol. *Tinsley Bros.: London,* 1870. 8°. **12627. l. 2.**

CAERIOLANUS (Fridericus Furius) *See* Furio Ceriol (Federico)

CAERLAVEROCK. The Siege of Carlaverock in the XXVIII Edward I. A.D.MCCC, with the arms of the earls, barons, and knights, who were present on the occasion; with a translation, a history of the castle, and memoirs of the personages commemorated by the poet [here identified as Walter of Exeter]. By Nicholas Harris Nicolas. pp. xxxii. 380. *J. B. Nichols & Son: London,* 1828. 4°. **600. i. 10.**

—— [Another copy.] **G. 5417.**

—— The Roll of Arms of the Princes, Barons, and Knights who attended King Edward I. to the Siege of Caerlaverock, in 1300; edited . . . with a translation and notes, by Thomas Wright . . . With the coat-armours emblazoned in gold and colours. pp. viii. 39. *J. C. Hotten: London,* 1864. 4°. **9917. h. 15.**

—— *See* Harrison (Arthur P.) Roll of Karlaverock, containing the banners and shields of the knights in arms at the seige of 10th July 1300. (Emblazoned by A. P. Harrison, and Son.) [1846?] 4°. **1328. i. 5. (2.)**

—— *See* Prinet (M.) Les Armoiries des Français dans le poème du siège de Carlaverock, *etc.* 1932. 8°. **11855. dd. 45.**

CAERLEON.

—— The Roman Amphitheatre, Caerleon, Monmouthshire. (A condensed version of the larger illustrated guide [by R. E. M. Wheeler and T. V. Wheeler].) *London,* 1943. 8°. [*Ministry of Works. Ancient Monuments Inspectorate. Ancient Monuments and Historic Buildings. Leaflet Guides.*] **B.S. 46/32. (17.)**

CAERLEON.—*Caerleon Antiquarian Association,* afterwards *Monmouthshire and Caerleon Antiquarian Association.* Proceedings . . . for the years 1927–28. pp. 35. [*Caerleon,* 1929.] 4°. **Ac. 5755. b.**
No more published.

—— An Account of some of the Rude Stone Monuments and Ancient Burial Mounds in Monmouthshire. By M. E. Bagnall-Oakeley, assisted by . . . W. Bagnall-Oakeley. pp. 22. *Newport,* 1889. 8°. **7705. ee. 24. (2.)**

—— The Crosses of Monmouthshire. By Elizabeth E. H. Mitchell. [With illustrations.] pp. ix. 45. *Newport,* 1893. 4°. **7709. h. 35.**

—— Goldcliff, and the ancient Roman inscribed stone found there, 1878. Together with other papers by Octavius Morgan. pp. iv. 35. *Newport,* 1882. 8°. **Ac. 5755/6.**

—— The Lordship, Castle & Town of Chepstow, otherwise Striguil. With an appendix on the Lordship of Caerleon. By James G. Wood. [With illustrations.] pp. 90. *Newport,* 1910. 4°. **10368. g. 51.**

—— Notes on Penhow Castle, by Octavius Morgan . . . and Thomas Wakeman. pp. 27. *Newport,* 1867. 8°. **7703. g. 18. (1.)**

—— Notes on the Ancient Domestic Residences of Pentre-Bach, Crick, Ty-Mawr, the Garn, Crindau, and St. Julian's, by Octavius Morgan . . . and Thomas Wakeman. pp. 29. pl. IX. *Newport,* 1860. 8°. **Ac. 5755.**

—— Notes on the Ancient Domestic Residences of Tre-Owen, Killwch, and the Waen, by Octavius Morgan . . . and Thomas Wakeman. pp. 19. pl. VIII. *Newport,* 1861. 8°. **Ac. 5755/2.**

—— Notes on the Architecture and History of Caldicot Castle, Monmouthshire. By Octavius Morgan . . . and Thomas Wakeman. pp. 45. pl. XII. *Newport,* [1854.] 8°. **Ac. 5755/5.**

—— Notes on Wentwood, Castle Troggy, and Llanvair Castle, by Octavius Morgan . . . and Thomas Wakeman. pp. 49. pl. VII. *Newport,* 1863. 8°. **Ac. 5755/8.**

—— Notice of a Tessellated Pavement, discovered in the Churchyard, Caerleon, by Octavius Morgan . . . together with an Essay on Mazes and Labyrinths by the Rev. Edward Trollope . . . with notes by Albert Way. [With plates.] pp. 25. *Newport,* 1866. 8°. **Ac. 5755/4.**

—— Notices of Pencoyd Castle and Langstone, by Octavius Morgan . . . and Thomas Wakeman. pp. 38. pl. VI. *Newport,* 1864. 8°. **Ac. 5755/3.**

—— Papers on Monmouth Castle and Priory. The Raglan Castle. Grosment. Skenfrith. Whitecastle. Pembridge *etc.* pp. 103. *Gloucester,* [1896.] 8°. **10352. k. 23**

—— Papers relating to the History of Monmouthshire Read at the meeting of the Cambrian Archæological Association . . . in 1885. pp. vi. 78. [*Newport,* 1886. 8°. **Ac. 5755/7**

—— *Monmouthshire and Caerleon Antiquarian Association* *See* supra: *Caerleon Antiquarian Association, etc.*

Urban District Council.

—— Historic Caerleon. The official guide to the urban district of Caerleon. [With illustrations.] pp. 48. *Caerleon,* 1955. 8°. **010370. h. 65**

CAERLEON, *pseud.* Waifs and Strays. By Caerleon. [Poems.] pp. iv. 95. *Provost & Co.: London,* [1876.] 8°. **11652.** g. 5.

CAERLION (Hoel) Sundial Songs. pp. 90. *John Long: London,* 1910. 8°. **011650.** de. **36.**

CAERLUDD. Social Religion exemplify'd, in an account of the first settlement of Christianity in the city of Caerludd [i.e. London]. In several dialogues. [By Matthias Maurice.] The second edition. 2 pt. *J. Buckland: London,* 1750. 8°. **4409.** ee. **22.**
The titlepage from a copy of the edition of 1740 *has been mounted on the flyleaf at the beginning of the volume.*

—— The third edition. pp. viii. 552. *J. Buckland; T. Field: London,* 1759. 8°. **4410.** dd. **13.**

CAERMAN (Antonius) Disputatio physica de aëre, *etc.* *Praes.* J. de Bruyn. *T. ab Ackersdijck, & G. à Zyll: Trajecti ad Rhenum,* 1554 [1654]. 4°. **536.** f. **17.** (**1.**)

CAERMARTHEN. *See* Carmarthen.

CAERNARVON. *See* Carnarvon.

CAERNARVONSHIRE GOLF CLUB. *See* Conway, *Carnarvonshire.*

CAERNARVONSHIRE HISTORICAL SOCIETY. *See* Carnarvon, *County of.*

CAERNARVONSHIRE MOUNTAINS. *See* Carnarvonshire Mountains.

CAERNARVONSHIRE RECORD OFFICE. *See* Carnarvon, *County of.*

CAERPHILLY CASTLE. A Guide to Caerphilly Castle. pp. 35. *D. Owen & Co.: Cardiff,* 1880. 8°. **10369.** cc. **2.**

CAERS (Jean Baptiste) Veritas et æquitas Constitutionis Unigenitus [issued by Clement xi.] theologicè demonstrata, seu 101. Quenelli propositiones confutatæ ex locis theologicis . . . Editio altera. [The dedication signed: J. B. C., i.e. J. B. Caers.] pp. 134. 1724. 12°. *See* C., J. B. **5015.** a. **13.**

CAES (Lucien) and **HENRION** (Roger)

—— Collectio bibliographica operum ad ius romanum pertinentium.

ser. 1. Opera edita in periodicis miscellaneis encyclopaediisque. 1949— .
ser. 2. Theses. 1950– .

Bruxelles, 1949– . 8°. **2017.a.**

CAESAENA. *See* Cesena.

CAESALPINUS (Andreas) *See* Fuchs (C.) Andreas Caesalpinus. De cujus viri ingenio, doctrina, et virtute pauca delibat . . . C. Fuchs. 1798. 4°. B. **339.** (**1.**)

—— *See* Sundström (C. J.) Framställning af hufvudpunkterna i Andreæ Cæsalpini filosofi, *etc.* 1860. 8°. **8466.** bb. **41.** (**5.**)

—— *See* Taurellus (N.) Alpes cæsae, hoc est, Andr. Cæsalpini . . . dogmata, discussa & excussa, *etc.* 1597. 8°. **716.** c. **35.**

—— *See* Viviani (U.) Vita ed opere di Andrea Cesalpino, *etc.* [With plates, including portraits.] 1922. 8°. **012209.cc.1/6.**

—— Andreæ Cæsalpini . . . Quæstionum peripateticarum lib. v . . . Dæmonum inuestigatio peripatetica . . . Secunda editio. Quæstionum medicarum libri ii. De medicament. facultatibus lib. ii . . . Nunc primum editi. ff. 290. *Apud Iuntas: Venetiis,* 1593. 4°. **461.** b. **2.**

CAESALPINUS (Andreas)

—— Il Trattato sui Sapori (De saporibus), inedito . . . ed il carteggio, in gran parte inedito . . . con Baccio Valori, col Granduca di Toscana, con Bianca Cappello, con Belisario Vinta e con l'Albercotti, con l'aggiunta delle sue lettere dedicatorie, delle tre sue testimonianze sulla malattia e sull'esumazione di S. Filippo Neri, *etc.* *See* Viviani (U.) Vita ed opere di Andrea Cesalpino, *etc.* 1922. 8°. **012209.cc.1/6.**

—— Appendix ad libros de plantis et quæstiones peripateticas. pp. 32. *Apud A. Zannettum: Romæ,* 1603. 4°. **447.** b. **2.** (**2.**)

—— [Another edition of pt. 1.] Appendix ad libros de plantis. *See* Boccone (P., afterwards S.) Museo di piante rare della Sicilia, Malta, Corsica, Italia, Piemonte, e Germania, *etc.* 1697. 4°. **448.** h. **6.**

—— Dæmonum. Inuestigatio Peripatetica. In quâ explicatur locus Hippocratis in Progn., Si quid diuinum in morbis habetur. ff. 24. *Apud Iuntas: Florentiæ,* 1580. 4°. **719.** f. **13.**

—— De metallicis, libri tres. pp. 222. *Ex Typographia A. Zannetti: Romæ,* 1596. 4°. **457.** c. **13.**

—— [Another copy.] **444.** c. **3.** (**1.**)

—— [Another copy.] **34.** a. **5.**

—— [Another edition.] [Edited by Philippus Scherbius.] pp. 222. *C. Agricola: Noribergæ,* 1602. 4°. **990.** f. **2.**

—— De plantis libri xvi. pp. 621. *Apud G. Marescottum: Florentiæ,* 1583. 4°. **447.** b. **2.** (**1.**)

—— [Another copy.] **36.** b. **17.**

—— Praxis vniuersæ artis medicæ . . . in duas partes diuisa, & multis adiectis in hac vltima editione correcta. 2 pt. *Typis L. Marchesini: Venetiis,* 1680. 12°. **545.** b. **17, 18.**

—— Andreæ Cæsalpini . . . Quæstionum peripateticarum libri quinque. *See* Tractationes. Tractationum philosophicarum tomus vnus, *etc.* 1588. fol. **526.** n. **6.**

CAESAR. Cæsar, the Watch Dog of the Castle. A romantic drama, in two acts. Adapted from the French. pp. 34. *London,* [1868 ?] 12°. [*Lacy's Acting Edition of Plays.* vol. 79.] **2304.** f. **24.** (**2.**)

—— Cæsars Dialogue, or, a Familiar Communication containing the first Institution of a Subiect, in allegiance to his Soueraigne. [The preface signed: E. N., i.e. E. Nisbet.] 1601. 16°. *See* N., E. **4409.** aa. **42.**

—— Ce que coûte un César, ou le " Garde-à-vous " d'un caporal de l'armée du Rhin. Par A. D. 1888. 8°. *See* D., A. **9080.** b. **44.**

—— A Friend to Cæsar. Or, an Humble proposition for the more regular, speedy, and easie payment of his Majesties treasure, granted, or to be granted by the Lords and Commons assembled in Parliament, for the carrying on of his Majesties expences . . . By a Person of Honour. pp. 28. *For Robert Harford: London,* 1681. fol. **8223.** c. **22.**

—— [Another copy.] A Friend to Cæsar . . . By a Person of Honour. *London,* 1681. fol. **1474.** dd. **21.** (**1.**)

—— The Things that are Cæsar's rendered unto Cæsar, and the Things that are God's, rendered unto God. By . . . M. W. [i.e. Morgan Watkins.] 1666. 4°. *See* W., M. **4152.** f. **20.** (**12.**)

CAESAR.

—— Tributo de Cesar pagado a Cesar, librado en las Musas y cobrado por el Tiempo. (Publícalo Santiago Alvarez Gamero.) 1917. *See* PERIODICAL PUBLICATIONS.—*Paris.* Revue hispanique, *etc.* tom. 40. 1894, *etc.* 8°. **P.P. 4331.** aea.

CAESAR [DE BOURBON], *Duke de Vendôme.* *See* DUPUY DE MONTBRUN (J.) La Défaite du Sieur de Montbrun . . . par . . . le Duc de Vendosme, *etc.* 1622. 8°. **1193.** h. **14.** (4.)

—— *See* FRANCE.—Henry IV., *King.* [1589–1610.] Lettres de légitimation de César de Vendosme, *etc.* [1682.] 8°. **878.** i. **22.** (3.)

—— *See* FRANCE.—Louis XIII., *King.* [1610–1643.] Lettres de declaration du Roy pour le restablissement du Sieur Duc de Vendosme en son gouvernement de Bretagne, *etc.* 1614. 8°. **1192.** h. **8.** (2.)

—— *See* FRANCE.—Louis XIII., *King.* [1610–1643.] Declaration du Roy contre les Ducs de Vendosme, de Mayenne, *etc.* 1617. 8°. **1192.** h. **1.** (10.)

—— *See* LANOUVELLE (E. de) Gabrielle d'Estrées et les Bourbon-Vendôme. [With special reference to Caesar, Duke de Vendôme.] 1936. 8°. **010665.** g. **34.**

—— Copie de la lettre enuoyée au Roy par Monsieur de Vendosme. [Protesting his loyalty, and against being deprived of his province. Dated: 1 Mar. 1614.] pp. 8. 1614. 12°. **285.** e. **34.** (4.)

—— [Another edition.] pp. 8. [1614.] 8°. **8051.** a. **60.** (1.)

—— Seconde lettre de Monsieur de Vendosme, au Roy. [Dated: 27 Mar. 1614.] pp. 12. *P. Chevalier: Paris,* 1614. 8°. **285.** e. **34.** (5.)

—— [Another edition.] Auec vne lettre à la Royne. pp. 7. *M. Mondiere: Paris,* 1614. 8°. **8051.** a. **60.** (1*.)

—— Lettre de Monsieur de Vendosme adressee au Roy. [A protestation of his fidelity. Dated: 15 Feb. 1616.] pp. 16. 1616. 8°. **1058.** b. **30.** (11.)

—— La Capitulation de la ville de Seurre ou Bellegarde, faite entre le Duc de Vendosme, & le Comte de Tavannes . . . Avec les soins que Sa Majesté a pris en personne au siége de cette place, *etc.* *M. Stael: la Haye,* 1650. 4°. **1058.** h. **15.** (26.)

—— [Another copy.] **8050.** h. **43.** (30.)

—— Le Herault d'armes à Monsieur le Duc de Vendosme. [Commanding him in the King's name to lay down his arms.] pp. 5. [*Paris ?*] 1616. 8°. **C. 32.** c. **14.** (31.)

—— Recit veritable de ce qui s'est passé à Blauet . . . entre Monseigneur le Duc de Vendosme, et le sieur de Soubize. Auec le sortie dudit sieur de Soubize hors de Blauet, et sa retraitte sur la mer, *etc.* [A reprint of the edition of 1625.] pp. 15. *Nantes,* 1881. 8°. **1192.** f. **5.** (4.)

CAESAR [DE BOURBON], *Duke de Vendôme,* and **FRANCIS** [DE VENDÔME], *Duke de Beaufort, Grandson of Henry* IV., *King of France.*

—— A Nosseigneurs de Parlement. [A petition with respect to the process instituted against them.] pp. 8. [*Paris ?* 1649 ?] 4°. **1199.** g. **22.** (9.)

CAESAR [D'ESTE], *Duke of Modena.* *See* ROME, *Church of* —Clement VIII., *Pope.* [1592–1605.] Sanctissimi D. Clementis Papæ VIII. Declaratio et promulgatio majoris excommunicationis contra Cæsarem Estensem, *etc.* 1597. 4°. **T. 2223.** (10.)

—— —— 1598. 4°. **697.** e. **37.**

—— *See* ROSSI (B. de') Descrizione del magnificentiss. apparato e de' maravigliosi intermedi fatti . . . nelle . . . nozze degl'Illustrissimi . . . Signori il Sig. Don Cesare d'Este e la Signora Donna Virginia Medici. 1585. 4°. **811.** e. **60.**

—— *See* TERZANIUS (F.) Ad S. D. N. Clementem VIII. . . oratio, habita cùm eidem nomine Alphonsi II. Estensis Ducis Ferrariæ . . . obedientiam præstaret . . . Cæsar Estensis, *etc.* 1592. 4°. **805.** d. **41**

—— *See* TERZANIUS (F.) Oratio ad Sixtum V. Pontificem Max. pro . . . Alphonso II. Estense Duce Ferrariæ obedientiam præstante . . . Cæsare Estense eiusdem Ducis patruele, *etc.* 1586. 4°. **805.** d. **36**

—— Narratione della partenza del . . . Sig. D. Cesare da Este . . . Con le feste et trionfi fatte nell'intrata dell'illustriss. . . . Cardinale Aldobrandino Legato. Nella città di Ferrara, il dì 29. di Genaro, M.D.XCVIII. *A. Viani. Pavia,* 1598. 4°. **811.** d. **54.** (4.)

CAESAR, *Edward VII.'s Dog.* Where's Master? By Cæsar *etc.* [With a frontispiece by Maud Earl.] pp. 54. *Hodder & Stoughton: London,* 1910. 8°. **12352.** s. **32**

CAESAR, *Grammarian.* Une Grammaire latine inédit du XIIIe siècle [being a work by Caesar, a Grammarian entitled "Compendium Grammaticæ"], extraite de manuscrits no. 465 de Laon et no. 15462, fonds latin de la Bibliothèque nationale, par C. Fierville. pp. xxvi. 201. *Paris,* 1886. 8°. **12934.** h. **10**

CAESAR [D'ESTE], *Marquis di Montecchio.* *See* CAESAR [d'Este], *Duke of Modena.*

CAESAR (ALFRED AUGUSTUS LEVI)

—— North-East England. pp. 24. *George Philip & Son London,* 1954. *obl.* fol. [*Pictorial Survey of England & Wales.* sect. 4.] **W.P. 12687/**

CAESAR (ANTONIUS) Antonii Caesaris Maria Theresi Romanorum Imperatrix . . . seu bellum Germanicum *etc.* [A poem. With a portrait.] pp. 264. *Florentiae* 1768. 4°. **837.** i. **27**

With the autograph of Robert Southey. The titlepage is engraved.

CAESAR (AQUILIN JULIUS) Annales ducatus Styriæ, cum adjecta finitimarum provinciarum . . . historia . . . e antiquis historiae monumentis collecti. tom. 1–3. *Græcii; Viennæ,* 1768–77. fol. **170.** i. **10–12**

No more published. Tom. 3 was published at Vienna.

—— Beschreibung des Herzogthums Steyermark. [Based on the "Annales ducatus Styriæ."] 2 Tl. **F.P.** *Grätz* 1773. 8°. **9314.** f. **2**

—— Beschreibung der kaiserl. königl. Hauptstadt Grätz und aller daselbst befindlichen Merkwürdigkeiten nach der berliner und potsdammer Beschreibung eingerichtet 3 Tl. *Salzburg,* 1781. 8°. **573.** d. **1**

CAESAR (ARNOLDUS) *See* KEYSERE (Arnaud de)

CAESAR (Barptholomeus) Auslegunge Dreyer Iudischeñ Benedeyũg als nemlich So sie den Regenbogeñ sehen. dõnerñ höreñ vnnd eyñ gemeyne wye dan hernach. [With the Hebrew text of the benedictions, and with a woodcut.] [1515?] *s. sh.* fol. Dept. of Prints & Drawings.

—— *See* Eisemann (H.) Bartholomaeus Kaiser. Deutsch-hebräisches Flugbatt um 1515. [With a reproduction.] [1931.] fol. **7853**. s. **34**.

CAESAR (Caius) *Adopted Son of the Emperor Augustus. See* Noris (E.) *Cardinal.* Cenotaphia Pisana Caii et Lucii Cæsarum dissertationibus illustrata . . . Cæsaris vtriusque vita, gesta, & annuæ eorundem inferiæ exponuntur, *etc.* 1681. fol. **574**. m. **10**.

—— —— 1704. fol. **664**. h. **11**.

—— —— 1764. 4°. **661**. i. **19**.

CAESAR (Caius Julius)

Arrangement.

WORKS.

Latin.

—— *Begin.* [fol. 2 *recto*:] [De bello gallico.] [G]Allia est omnis diuisa in partes tres, *etc.* [fol. 76 *recto*:] [De bello civili.] [L]Itteris a Fabio. C. cesaris consulibus redditis, *etc.* [fol. 124 *recto*:] [De bello alexandrino.] [B]Ello Alexandrino cõflato, *etc.* [fol. 139 *verso*:] [De bello africano.] [C]Aesar itineribus iustis cõfectis, *etc.* [fol. 158 *recto*:] [De bello hispaniensi.] [P]Harnace superato: Africa recepta, *etc.* [fol. 167 *recto*:] [D]Ictatoris Cesaris cõmentarios: iam pridem multa diligentia me recognouisse memineram, *etc.* [fol. 167 *verso*:] [Table of contents.]

Iohannis andree. Episcopi Aleriensis epistola, *etc.* [The Commentaries of Caesar, edited by Joannes Andreas, Bishop of Aleria.] ed. pr. ms. notes. [*Conradus Sweyheym & Arnoldus Pannartz;*] *in domo Petri de Maximis: Rome,* die .xii. mensis maii, 1469. fol. C. **19**. d. **12**.
168 *leaves, the first and last blank. Without signatures.* 38 *lines to a page. Without the blank leaves.*

—— [Another copy.] C. **2**. c. **7**.
Without the blank leaves.

—— [Another copy.] G. **9181**.
Without the blank leaves.

—— *Begin.* [fol. 2 *recto*:] Caii Iulii Caesaris commentariorum liber primus(—septimus) de bello gallico ab ipso confecto. [fol. 59 *recto*:] A. Hirtii belli gallici commentarius nouissimus. [fol. 67 *recto*:] Caii Iulii Caesaris belli ciuilis pompeiani commentarius primus(—iii). [fol. 109 *verso*:] Caii Iulii Caesaris belli alexandrini Opii aut Hirtii commentarius quartus. [fol. 123 *verso*:] Caii Iulii Caesaris belli africi Opii aut Hirtii commentarius quintus. [fol. 140 *recto*:] Caii Iulii Caesaris belli hispaniensis Opii aut Hirtii commentarius sextus. *Nicolaus Ienson: Venetiis,* 1471. fol. IB. **19632**.
148 *leaves, the first and last blank. Without signatures.* 39 *lines to a page. Without the blank leaves.*

CAESAR (Caius Julius) [Works.—*Latin.*]

—— [Another copy.] **167**. i. **11**.
Without the blank leaves.

—— [Another copy.] G. **9182**.

—— *Begin.* [fol. 2 *recto*:] C. Iulii Cesaris. belli gallici. Commentarius Primus(—septimus). [fol. 66 *verso*:] A. Hirtii belli gallici cõmentarius nouissimus. [fol. 76 *recto*:] C. Iulii Cesaris belli ciuilis Põpeiani cõmētarius p̉mus (—tertius). [fol. 124 *recto*:] C. Iulii Cesaris. belli Allexãdrini. Opii aut Hircii Commentarius Quartus. [fol. 139 *verso*:] C. Iulii Cesaris belli Africi. Opii uel Hircii Cõmētarius Quintus. [fol. 158 *recto*:] C. Iulii Cesaris belli Hispaniensis. Opii aut Hirtii cõmētarius. sextus. [fol. 167 *recto*:] [D]Ictatoris Cesaris cõmentarios: iam pridem multa diligentia me recognouisse memineram, *etc.* [fol. 167 *verso*:] [Table of contents.] Iohannis andree. Episcopi Aleriensis epistola, *etc.* [*Conradus Sweynheym & Arnoldus Pannartz;*] *in domo Petri de Maximis: Rome,* die .xxv. mensis augusti, 1472. fol. G. **9183**.
168 *leaves, the first and last blank. Without signatures.* 38 *lines to a page. Without the blank leaves.*

—— [Another copy.] **167**. i. **12**.
Without the blank leaves. Ff. 2, 9, 11–62, 63, 65, 70, 72, 86, 89, 93–102, 113, 122, 136–143 *are made up from a copy of the* 1469 *edition. Fol.* 122 *is misbound before* 144.

—— *Begin.* [fol. 1 *verso*:] Petrus Iustinus Philelphus sal. pl. dicit Iohanni Simonetae ducali secretario. [fol. 2 *recto*:] G. Iulii Caesaris commentariorum de bello gallico liber primus(—septimus). [fol. 58 *verso*:] A. Hircii præfatio in octauũ librum: quem ipse addidit libro septĩo Cõmentarioꝝ G: Iulii Cæsaris de bello gallico. [fol. 67 *recto*:] G. Iulii Caesaris commentariorum de bello ciuili liber primus(—tertius). [fol. 108 *recto*:] A. Hirtii aut Opii commentariorum de bello alexandrino liber quartus. [fol. 121 *recto*:] A. Hirtii aut Opii commentariorum de bello africo liber quintus. [fol. 137 *verso*:] A. Hirtii aut Opii commentariorum de bello hispaniensi liber sextus. [fol. 147 *recto*: Index commentariorum. G. Iulii Caesaris: & earum rerum: quas . . . Raymundus Marlianus inuenit: atq; addidit.] [Edited by Petrus Justinus Philelphus.] few ms. notes.
Antonius zarothus: [*Milan,*] Die .x. mensis Februarii, 1477. fol. **167**. i. **13**.
168 *leaves, fol.* 146 *blank. Sig.* a–g⁸ h¹⁰ i–s⁸; [A⁸ B⁸ C⁶]. 41 *lines to a page. Imperfect; wanting quires* A–C *containing the index by Marlianus.*

—— *Begin.* [fol. 1 *recto*:] G. Iulii Caesaris commentariorum de bello gallico liber primus(—septimus). [fol. 52 *verso*:] A. Hircii præfatio in octauum librum: quē ipse addidit libro septimo Commentariorum. G: Iulii Cæsaris de bello gallico. [fol. 60 *recto*:] C. Iulii Caesaris commentariorum de bello ciuili. liber primus(—tertius). [fol. 97 *verso*:] A. Hirtii aut Opii commentariorum de bello alexandrino liber quartus. [fol. 109 *verso*:] A. Hirtii aut Opii commentariorum de bello aphrico liber quintus. [fol. 124 *verso*:] A. Hirtii aut Opii commentariorum de bello hispaniensi liber sextus. [fol. 133 *recto*:] Index commentariorum. G. Iulii Cæsaris: & earum reꝝ: quas . . . Raymundus Marlianus inuenit: atq; addidit. *Philippus Lauagnia: Mediolani,* sexto idus apriles [8 April], 1478. fol. IB. **26152**.
152 *leaves, fol.* 132 *blank. Sig.* a–p⁸ q⁶ r⁶ A⁸ B⁸ C⁴. 42 *lines to a page.*

—— *Begin.* [fol. 2 *recto*:] G. Iulii Caesaris commentariorum de bello gallico liber primus(—septimus). [fol. 58 *verso*:] A. Hircii præfatio ĩ octauũ librum: quē ipse addidit libro septimo Commentariorum. G. Iulii Cæsaris de bello gallico. [fol. 67 *recto*:] G. Iulii Caesaeis [*sic*] commentariorum de bello ciuili liber primus(—tertius). [fol. 108

CAESAR (CAIUS JULIUS) [WORKS.—*Latin.*]

recto:] A. Hirtii aut Opii commentariorum de bello alexandrino liber quartus. [fol. 121 *recto:*] A. Hirtii aut Opii commentariorum de bello africo liber quintus. [fol. 137 *verso:*] A. Hirtii aut Opii commentariorum de bello hispaniensi. liber sextus. [fol. 147 *recto:*] Index commentariorum G. Iulii Cæsaris: & earum rerum: quas . . . Raymundus Marlianus inuenit: atque addidit. [Edited by Hieronymus Bononius.] *Michael Manzolinus: Taruisii,* 1480. fol. **IB. 28362.**

168 *leaves, the first blank. Sig.* a–u$^{8\cdot6}$ x^6; A^8 B^8 C^6. 44 *lines to a page. Without the blank leaf.*

—— *Begin.* [fol. 2 *recto:*] G. Iulii Caesaris commentariorum de bello gallico liber primus(—septimus). [fol. 52 *recto:*] A. Hircii præfatio ī octauum librum: quem ipse addidit libro septimo Commentariorum. G. Iulii Cæsaris de bello gallico. [fol. 59 *verso:*] G. Iulii Caesaris commentariorum de bello ciuili liber primus(—tertius). [fol. 95 *verso:*] A. Hirtii aut Opii commentariorum de bello alexandrino liber quartus. [fol. 107 *verso:*] A. Hirtii aut Opii commentariorum de bello africo liber quintus. [fol. 121 *verso:*] A. Hirtii aut Opii commentariorum de bello hispaniensi. liber sextus. [fol. 129 *verso:*] Index commentariorum. G. Iulii Cæsaris: & earum rerum: quas . . . Raymundus Marlianus īuenit: atque addidit. [Edited by Hieronymus Bononius.] *opera & expensis Octauiani Scoti: Venetiis,* xii. kal. septēbris [21 Aug.], 1482. fol. **IB. 21184.**

148 *leaves, the first blank. Sig.* a^8 b–x$^{8\cdot6}$. 41 *lines to a page.*

—— *Begin.* [fol. 2 *recto:*] C. Iulii Caesaris commentariorum de bello gallico liber primus, *etc.* [Followed by the rest of the Commentaries. Edited by Hieronymus Bononius. With an index by Raimundus Marlianus.] *per Theodorum de Regazonibus de Asula: Venetiis,* Die uero xiii. Iulii, 1490. fol. **IB. 23547.**

134 *leaves, the first blank.* Sig. a–q^8 r^6. 45 *lines to a page.*

—— [Another copy.] **IB. 23548.**

A fragment, consisting of ff. 2–5, 7, 8, *sheets* c1, d1, o1, o3, o4, q1 *and quire* r; *fol.* 6 *being supplied in* MS. *and the rest made up from a copy of the* 1494 *edition.*

—— Commentarius Caesaris. [With the supplementary commentaries ascribed to Hirtius and others. Edited by Hieronymus Bononius. With an index by Raimundus Marlianus.] *per Philippum de Pinciis: Venetiis,* die .xxv. octobris, 1494. fol. **167. c. 19.**

134 *leaves. Sig.* a–q^8 r^6. 45 *lines to a page.*

—— Commentarij Cæsaris recogniti per Philippum Beroaldum. [With the supplementary commentaries ascribed to Hirtius and others.] ff. 252. [*B. de Gabiano: Lyons,*] 1508. 8°. **803. b. 18.**

One of the counterfeit imitations of the Aldine editions.

—— Caij Iulij Caesaris: Inuictissimi īperatoris cōmentaria: seculoꝝ iniuria antea difficilia: ⁊ valde mendosa. Nunc primum a viro docto [i.e. Lucas Panaetius] expolita: ⁊ optime recognita. Additis de nouo apostillis: vna cū figuris suis locis apte dispositis, *etc.* [With the supplementary commentaries ascribed to Hirtius and others.] ff. 110. *Impressa per A. de Zannis de Portesio: Venetiis,* 1511. fol. **IB.24059/3.**

—— Commentarii Cæsaris recogniti per Philippum Beroaldum. ff. 220. [*B. de Gabiano: Lyons,* 1512.] 8°. **803. b. 23.**

Previous edition 1508.

—— Hoc uolumine continentur hæc. Commentariorum de bello Gallico libri VIII. (A. Hircii derelictorum de bello Gallico liber VIII.) De bello ciuili pompeiano libri IIII. De bello Alexandrino liber I. De bello Africano liber I. De bello Hispaniensi liber I, *etc.* (Index eorum, quæ in commentariis C. Iulij Cæsaris habentur per ordinem alphabeti per Raimundum Marlianum.) [Edited by Joannes Jucundus.] ff. 296. *In ædibus Aldi et Andreæ Soceri: Venetiis,* 1513. 8°. **678. b. 5.**

The inscriptions Massilia and Uxellodunum which appear in MS. *on the plans of those two fortresses are in the handwriting of Aldus.*

CAESAR (CAIUS JULIUS) [WORKS.—*Latin.*]

—— [Another copy.] FEW MS. NOTES. **803. d. 28.**

—— [Another copy.] **C. 16. d. 14.**

—— [Another copy.] **G. 9048.**

—— [Another edition.] Commentaria Cæsaris . . . diligentissime reuisa, *etc.* ff. 281. ON VELLUM. *P. de Giunta: Florentiæ,* 1514. 8°. **C. 19. f. 12.**

—— Caij Iulij Cæsaris: Inuictissimi īperatoris cōmentaria: seculorū iniuria antea difficilia: ⁊ valde mēdosa, *etc.* ff. 110. *Per A. de Zannis: Venetiis,* 1517. fol. **C. 56. f. 5.**

Previous edition 1511.

—— Hoc uolumine continentur hæc. Commentariorum de bello Gallico libri VIII. De bello ciuili pompeiano libri IIII, *etc.* ff. 296. *In ædibus Aldi et Andreæ soceri: Venetiis,* 1518, 19. 8°. **C. 16. d. 15.**

Previous edition 1513. *The second of the two leaves between the commentaries and index bears the Aldine imprint with the date " Mense Ianuario* 1518."

—— Commentaria Cæsaris . . . diligentissime reuisa, *etc.* ff. 285. *ꝑ hæredes P. Iuntæ: Florentiæ,* 1520. 8°. **293. e. 29.**

Previous edition 1514.

—— Commentariorum Cæsaris Elenchus. De bello Gallico libri VIII, *etc.* ff. 310. *Excudebat T. Vuolff: Basileæ,* 1521. 8°. **9039. aaa. 15.**

Previous edition 1518, 19.

—— [C. Iulii Cæsaris commentariorum libri octo.] [With the " De bello civili " and the supplementary commentaries ascribed to Hirtius and others.] ff. 243. *Imprimebat P. Vidouęus; sumptibus P. Viartij: Lutecię,* 1522. 4°. **587. g. 1.**

Imperfect; wanting the titlepage.

—— Commentariorum C. Cæsaris elenchus. De bello Gallico libri VIII, De bello ciuili Pompeiano libri III, De bello Alexandrino liber I, De bello Africano liber I, De bello Hispaniensi liber I. pp. 648. *Apud I. Badiū & I. Roigny: Parisijs,* 1533. 8°. **586. b. 27.**

—— C. Iulii Cæsaris commentarij. [With the supplementary commentaries ascribed to Hirtius and others.] pp. 602. *Per N. Brylingerum: Basileæ,* 1539. 8°. **1307. b. 19.**

—— C. Iulii Cæsaris rerum ab se gestarum commentarii . . . [With the supplementary commentaries ascribed to Hirtius and others.] Omnia . . . accuratè emendata . . . Veterum Galliæ locorum, populorum, urbium, montium, ac fluuiorum breuis descriptio. Eutropii epitome belli Gallici ex Suetonii Tranquilli monumentis quæ desiderantur. ff. 128. *Ex officina M. Vascosani: Parisiis,* 1543. fol. **C.108.i.4.**

—— [Another copy.] C. Iulii Cæsaris rerum ab se gestarum commentarii, *etc. Parisiis,* 1543. fol. **C. 132. h. 49.**

In an elaborate Parisian gilt calf binding of c. 1550 *with the ownership inscription and motto of Thomas Mahieu tooled on the covers.*

—— C. Iulii Cæsaris rerum ab se gestarum commentarii, *etc.* [With the supplementary commentaries ascribed to Hirtius and others.] (Veterum Galliæ locorum, populorum, urbium, montium ac fluuiorum breuis descriptio . . . authore Raimundo Marliano.) pp. 523. *Ex officina R. Stephani: Lutetiæ,* 1544. 8°. **294. d. 17. (1.)**

—— C. Iulii Cæsaris rerum ab se gestarum commentarii . . . summa diligentia castigati. [With the supplementary commentaries ascribed to Hirtius and others.] pp. 695. *Apud S. Gryphium: Lugduni,* 1546. 16°. **293. a. 31.**

—— C. Iulii Cæsaris commentariorum libri VIII. [With the "De bello civili" and the supplementary commentaries ascribed to Hirtius and others.] Quibus adiecimus suis in locis D. Henrici Glareani annotationes, *etc.* pp. 741. *Per N. Bryling: Basileæ,* 1548. 8°. **586.** c. **1.**
Previous edition 1539.

—— Hoc uolumine continentur, commentariorum de bello Gallico libri VIII, De bello ciuili Pompeiano libri III, De bello Alexandrino liber I, De bello Africano liber I, De bello Hispaniensi liber I . . . Cum correctionibus Pauli Manutii. ff. 318. *Aldus: Venetiis,* 1559. 8°. **803.** b. **12.**
Previous edition 1518, 19.

—— [Another edition.] ff. 318. *Aldus: Venetiis,* 1561. 8°. **803.** d. **27.**

—— C. Iulii Cæsaris commentariorum libri VIII. De bello ciuili Pompeiano lib. III., *etc.* pp. 635. *Per N. Bryling: Basileæ,* 1561. 8°. **586.** c. **2.**
Previous edition 1548.

—— C. Iulii Cæsaris commentariorum de bello Gallico libri VIII, ciuili Pompeiano, lib. III . . . Ioannis Michaelis Bruti scholia, quibus loci plurimi obscuriores explicantur. ff. 318. *Aldus: Venetiis,* 1564. 8°. **803.** d. **30.**
Previous edition 1561.

—— C. Iulii Cæsaris commentariorum de bello Gallico, libri VIII, ciuili Pompeiano libri III, Alexandrino liber I, Africano liber I, Hispaniensi liber I . . . Eutropii epitome belli Gallici ex Suetonii Tranquilli monumentis quae desiderantur. pp. 674. *H. de Marnef: Parisiis,* 1564. 16°. C. **19.** a. **15.**

—— C. Iul. Cæsaris rerum ab se gestarum commentarii. Ad vetustissimorum codicum fidem summa cura diligentiaq; castigati. (Eutropii epitome belli Gallici, ex Suetonij Tranquilli monumentis.) pp. 752. FEW MS. NOTES. *Apud A. Gryphium: Lugduni,* 1565. 16°. **586.** a. **13.**
Previous edition 1546. *The titlepage and last leaf of the index are mutilated.*

—— C. Iulii Cæsaris commentariorum de bello Gallico, libri IIX, ciuili Pompeiano, lib. III . . . Corrigente Aldo Manutio. ff. 320. FEW MS. NOTES. *In ædibus Manutianis: Venetiis,* 1566. 8°. **1306.** b. **15.**
Previous edition 1564.

—— [Another edition.] Cum scholiis Errici Glareani. ff. 398. FEW MS. NOTES. *Ex bibliotheca Aldina: Venetiis,* 1569. 8°. **1306.** b. **14.**

—— C. Iulii Cæsaris commentarii . . . emendati, & studiosissimè recogniti à Ioanni Rosseto . . . Hisce, cum locorum, vrbium & populorum nominibus, & expositionibus, ac item rerum, & verborum copiosissimo indice, accessit variarum lectionum libellus . . . eodem Rosseto collectore. [With the supplementary commentaries ascribed to Hirtius and others.] pp. 256. *Excudebat I. Probus: Lausannæ,* 1571. fol. **586.** k. **8.**

—— C. Iulii Cæsaris de bello Gallico commentarii VIII. A. Hircii de eodem liber octauus. C. Cæsaris de bello ciuili Pompeiano commentarij III. A. Hircii de bello Alexandrino lib. I. De bello Africano lib. I. De bello Hispaniensi lib. I. Cum scholiis Franc. Hotomani . . . Ful. Vrsini . . . Ald. Manutii. 2 pt. *Apud B. Vincentium: Lugduni,* 1574. fol. C. **80.** f. **7.**

—— [Another edition.] pp. 386. COPIOUS MS. NOTES [and autograph of Isaac Casaubon]. *Apud B. Vincentium: Lugduni,* 1574. 8°. **586.** c. **4.**

CAESAR (Caius Julius) [Works.—*Latin.*]

—— C. Iulii Cæsaris commentarii, nouis emendationibus illustrati. Eiusdem librorum, qui desiderantur, fragmenta. Ex bibliotheca Fului Vrsini . . . Scholia Aldi Manutij . . . Ioannis Sambuci spicilegia, *etc.* [With the supplementary commentaries ascribed to Hirtius and others.] pp. 487. *Excudebat C. Plantinus: Antuerpiæ,* 1574. 8°. **586.** c. **3.**

—— C. Iulii Cæsaris rerum gestarum commentarii XIV . . . Omnia collatis antiquis manuscriptis exemplaribus . . . emendatè restituta . . . Eutropii epitome belli Gallici ex Suetonii Tranquilli monumentis . . . Cum doctiss. annotationibus Henrici Glareani, Francisci Hotomani . . . Fuluii Vrsini . . . Aldi Manutii, P. F. Ex musæo & impensis Iacobi Stradæ. [Edited by J. Strada.] 3 pt. *Apud G. Coruinum: Francofurti,* 1575. fol. **587.** l. **13.**

—— [Another copy.] **198.** g. **7.**

—— C. Iulii Caesaris commentarii ab Aldo Manutio . . . emendati et scholiis illustrati. [With the supplementary commentaries ascribed to Hirtius and others, and the fragments.] pp. 676. *Apud Aldum: Venetiis,* 1575. 8°. G. **17222.**

—— [Another edition.] pp. 676. *Apud Aldum: Venetiis,* 1576. 8°. **160.** c. **12.**

—— [Another copy.] **586.** c. **5.**
Some of the leaves are mutilated.

—— C. Iulii Cæsaris rerum ab se gestarum commentarii: Io. Iocundi . . . opera . . . accuratissimè olim collati, nunc vero Fuluij Vrsini scholijs, & doctissimorum quorundam virorum aliquot annotationibus & castigationibus illustrati. [With the supplementary commentaries ascribed to Hirtius and others.] pp. 734. *Apud A. de Harsy: Lugduni,* 1576. 16°. **586.** a. **14.**

—— C. Iulii Cæsaris rerum ab se gestarum commentarii. [With the supplementary commentaries ascribed to Hirtius and others.] (Paulli Manutij ad Paullum Rhamnusium epistola. Excerpta quædam è Vegetio & Petro Victorio de instrumentis bellicis. De Galliæ diuisione Aldi Manutij commentarius. Fuluij Vrsini emendationes in Cæsaris comment.) pp. 903. MS. NOTES. *Apud A. Gryphium: Lugduni,* 1576. 16°. **586.** a. **15.**

—— C. Iulii Cæsaris commentarii; nouis emēdationibus, & aliquot ad marginem adiectis lectionum varietatibus illustrati. pp. 556. MS. NOTES. *Ex officina C. Plantini: Antuerpiæ,* 1578. 16°. **293.** a. **38.**
Previous edition Antwerp, 1574.

—— Caii Iulii Cæsaris commentariorum libri VIII. Multo quàm antehac vnquam emendatiores editi, *etc.* pp. 630. *Ex officina Brylingeriana: Basileæ,* 1581. 12°. **586.** c. **6.**
Previous edition Basle, 1561.

—— C. Iulii Cæsaris commentarii; nouis emendationibus, & aliquot ad marginem adiectis lectionum varietatibus illustrati. [With the supplementary commentaries ascribed to Hirtius and others.] pp. 607. *Apud Arnoldum Hatfildum & Nin. Newtonum: Londini,* 1585. 8°. C. **56.** a. **3.**

—— C. Iulii Cæsaris rerum ab se gestarum commentarii. pp. 772. *Apud A. Gryphium: Lugduni,* 1586. 8°. **586.** c. **7.**
Previous edition Lyons, 1576.

—— C. Iulii Caesari commentarii ab Aldo Manuccio . . . emendati et scholiis illustrati. pp. 596. *Apud Aldum: Venetiis,* 1588. 8°. **1306.** b. **17.**
Previous edition Venice, 1576.

—— [Another copy.] MS. NOTES. **160.** c. **1.**
Imperfect; wanting the titlepage and the last leaf.

—— C. Iulii Cæsaris commentarii, nouis emendationibus illustrati, *etc.* [With the supplementary commentaries ascribed to Hirtius and others.] pp. 80. 490. *Ex officina typographica M. Nutij: Antuerpiae*, 1595. 8°.
9041. b. 34.

—— C. Iulii Cæsaris commentarii, *etc.* pp. 107. *Excudebat Arnoldus Hatfildus: Londini*, 1601. 16°. **586.** a. 28.
Previous edition 1585.

—— C. Iulii Cæsaris quæ exstant, ex nuperâ viri docti [J. J. Scaliger] accuratissima recognitione. [With the supplementary commentaries ascribed to Hirtius and others.] Accedit nunc vetus interpres Græcus librorum VII de bello Gallico . . . Præterea notæ, adnotationes, commentarii partim veteres, partim noui, in quibus notæ . . . Io. Brantii . . . Adhæc indices . . . vtiles . . . Editio adornata opera & studio Gothofredi Iungermani. (Nomenclator geographicus . . . excerptus . . . potissimum è thesauro geographico Abrahami Ortelii.) 2 vol. *Apud C. Marnium & heredes I. Aubrii: Francofurti*, 1606. 4°. **587.** g. **2.**

—— [Another copy.] **197.** d. **12.**

—— C. Iulii Cæsaris quæ exstant: ex noua et accuratissima viri docti [J. J. Scaliger] recognitione. [With the supplementary commentaries ascribed to Hirtius and others.] pp. 480. *Ex officina Plantiniana Raphelengii: [Leyden,]* 1606. 8°. **586.** c. 8.

—— C. Iul. Cæsaris commentaria. [With the supplementary commentaries ascribed to Hirtius and others.] *See* La Rovière (P. de) Historiæ Romanæ scriptores Latini veteres, qui extant omnes, *etc.* tom. 1. 1609. fol.
9042. i. **4.** (**1.**)

—— C. Iulii Cæsaris quæ exstant. [With the supplementary commentaries ascribed to Hirtius and others.] pp. 550. *Ex officina Plantiniana Raphelengii: [Antwerp,]* 1614. 16°.
C. **20.** f. **28.**

—— C. Iulii Cæsaris Commentarii ab Aldo Manutio . . . emendati atque correcti, *etc.* [With the supplementary commentaries ascribed to Hirtius and the "Veterum. Galliae locorum . . . descriptio" of R. Marlianus. With illustrations and a map.] 2 pt. *Apud Iacobum Sarzinam: Venetiis*, 1616. 8°. **1483.** aa. **16.**
The second part, containing the commentary of Aldo Manuzio, has a separate titlepage. The map has been mutilated.

—— C. Iul. Cæsaris commentaria. [With the supplementary commentaries ascribed to Hirtius and others.] *See* Roman History. Historiæ Romanæ scriptores Latini veteres, qui extant omnes, *etc.* tom. 1. 1621. fol.
198. f. 5.

—— C. Iulii Cæsaris rerum a se gestarum commentarij. [With the supplementary commentaries ascribed to Hirtius and others.] Editio nouissima, auctior & emendatior: in qua sunt typi, seu figuræ, quatuor præcipuarum Galliæ vrbium à Cæsare expugnatarum; necnon & fabricæ pontis in Rheno, *etc.* pp. 879. *Apud I. Tornæsium: [Geneva,]* 1623. 16°. **1482.** a. **16.**

—— C. Iulii Cæsaris quæ extant, ex emendatione Ios. Scaligeri. [With the supplementary commentaries ascribed to Hirtius and others.] (Nomenclator geographicus . . . excerptus . . . e thesauro geographico Abrahami Ortelii.) pp. 561. *Ex officina Elzeviriana: Lugduni Batavorum*, 1635. 12°. **673.** a. **13.**
The titlepage is engraved.

—— [Another copy.] C. **16.** b. **13.**

—— [Another issue.] **586.** a. 1
In this issue the misprints in pagination have bee corrected.

—— [Another copy.] **586.** a. **1**

—— [Another copy.] G. **1719**
With the arms of Count Hoym on the binding.

—— [Another edition.] pp. 526. *Ex officina Elzeviriana Lugduni Batavorum*, 1635. 12°. **165.** b.

—— [Another copy.] **673.** a. **1**

—— [Another copy.] C. **67.** b. **2**
With the arms of Charterhouse School on the binding.

—— C. Iulii Cæsaris quæ extant. Ex emendatione Io Scaligeri. [With maps.] pp. 526. *Ex officin Elzeviriana: Amstelodami*, 1635. 12°. **1477.** d. **2**
The titlepage is engraved. A different edition from th preceding.

—— [Another edition.] pp. 456. *J. Janss. E. Weyerstraet: Amstelod.*, [1650?] 16°. **586.** a. **1**
Imperfect; wanting the preliminary matter and pp. 1– of the text.

—— C. Iulii Cæsaris quæ exstant, cum selectis variorum com mentariis, quorum plerique novi, opera et studio Arnol Montani. [With the supplementary commentari ascribed to Hirtius and others.] Accedunt notitia Galli et notæ auctiores ex autographo Iosephi Scaliger pp. 838. *A. Wyngaerden: Lugd. Bat.*, 1651. 8°.
587. d.
The titlepage is engraved.

—— C. Iulii Cæsaris quæ extant, ex recensione Ios. Scaliger [With the supplementary commentaries ascribed Hirtius and others.] pp. 532. *Apud J. Janssonium Amstelodami*, 1657. 12°. **586.** a. **1**
The titlepage is engraved.

—— [Another edition.] pp. 890. *Ex officina Elzeviriana Amstelodami*, 1661. 8°. **587.** d.
The titlepage is engraved.

—— [Another copy.] **586.** c. **2**

—— [Another edition.] *Ex officina Elzeviriana: Amstelodam* 1661. 12°. C. **69.** bb. **2**
The titlepage is engraved. With the arms of the Pamfi family stamped on the binding.

—— [Another edition.] pp. 456. *Typis D. Elzeviri Amstelodami*, 1664. 16°. **1306.** a. **2**
The titlepage is engraved.

—— [Another edition.] pp. 918. *Ex officina Elzeviriana Amstelodami*, 1670. 8°. **999.** ee.
The titlepage is engraved.

—— [Another edition.] pp. 456. *Typis D. Elzeviri Amstelodami*, 1675. 16°. **1306.** a. 2
The titlepage is engraved.

—— C. Julii Cæsaris quæ exstant, interpretatione et not illustravit Joannes Goduinus . . . in usum serenissir Delphini. [With the supplementary commentari ascribed to Hirtius and others.] (Index vocabuloru omnium, quæ in Cæsare leguntur.) pp. 490. *P. Le Peti Lutetiæ Parisiorum*, 1678. 4°. **586.** h. 1
The date in the colophon is 1677.

—— [Another copy.] **53.** d. 1

—— [Another copy.] G. **1755**

CAESAR (Caius Julius) [Works.—*Latin.*]

—— C. Julii Cæsaris quæ extant. [With the supplementary commentaries ascribed to Hirtius and others.] 2 vol. pp. 566. *D. a Gaasbeek: Lugduni Batavorum,* 1684. 12º. **989**. a. **20, 21.**
The titlepage of vol. 1 *is engraved.*

—— C. Julii Cæsaris quæ exstant, interpretatione et notis illustravit Joannes Goduinus . . . in usum Delphini. Juxta editionem Parisiensem. pp. 490. *Impensis Abelis Swall: Londini,* 1693. 8º. **9039**. bbb. **13.**
Previous edition 1678.

—— C. Julii Cæsaris quæ extant cum notis & animadversionibus Dionysii Vossii, ut & qui vocatur Julius Celsus de vita et rebus gestis C. Julii Cæsaris, ex musæo Joannis Georgii Graevii. [With the supplementary commentaries ascribed to Hirtius and others.] 2 pt. *P. & J. Blaeu: Amstelodami,* 1697. 8º. **584**. d. **37.**
With an additional titlepage, engraved.

—— C. Julii Cæsaris quæ exstant; interpretatione et notis illustrauit Joannes Goduinus . . . in usum Delphini. Juxta editionem Parisiensem. Editio secunda. pp. 490. *Tho. Newborough: Londini,* 1706. 8º. **587**. d. **3.**
Previous edition 1693.

—— C. Julii Cæsaris quæ exstant omnia. Ex recensione Joannis Davisii . . . cum ejusdem animadversionibus ac notis Pet. Ciacconii, Fr. Hotomanni, Joan. Brantii, Dionys. Vossii et aliorum. [With the supplementary commentaries ascribed to Hirtius and others.] Accessere metaphrasis Græca librorum VII. de bello Gallico, necnon indices necessarii. pp. 751. 96. *Typis academicis: Cantabrigiæ,* 1706. 4º. **587**. g. **3.**

—— C. Julii Cæsaris quae extant. [With the supplementary commentaries ascribed to Hirtius and others.] Accuratissimè cum libris editis & MSS. optimis collata, recognita & correcta. Accesserunt annotationes Samuelis Clarke . . . Item indices locorum, rerumque & verborum utilissimæ. Tabulis æneis ornata. pp. 560. *Sumptibus & typis Jacobi Tonson: Londini,* 1712. fol. K.T.C. **23**. b. **1.**

—— [Another copy.] G. **8047, 48.**

—— [Another copy.] Tab. **1314**. a. **1.**

—— [Another copy.] C. **2**. e. **11.**
Mutilated.

—— C. Julii Cæsaris quæ extant omnia. [With the supplementary commentaries ascribed to Hirtius and others.] Cum animadversionibus integris Dion. Vossii, J. Davisii . . . aliorumque variis notis; ut & . . . Julius Celsus de vita et rebus gestis C. Julii Cæsaris, ex Musæo Joannis Georgii Græevii. 2 tom. *Lugduni Batavorum; Delphis,* 1713. 8º. **197**. a. **6.**
With an additional titlepage, engraved.

—— C. Julii Cæsaris et A. Hirtii de rebus à C. Julio Cæsari gestis commentarii. Cum C. Jul. Cæsar. fragmentis. [Edited by Michael Maittaire.] pp. 424. **L.P.** *J. Tonson & J. Watts: Londini,* 1716. 8º. **679**. b. **8.**

—— [Another copy.] **160**. k. **1.**

—— [Another copy.] G. **9086.**
Imperfect; wanting the frontispiece.

—— C. Julii Cæsaris quæ extant . . . Accesserunt annotationes Samuelis Clarke, item indices locorum rerumque et verborum. pp. 512. *Sumptibus Jacobi Tonson: Londini,* 1720. 8º. **587**. d. **4.**
Previous edition 1712.

CAESAR (Caius Julius) [Works.—*Latin.*]

—— C. Julii Cæsaris et Auli Hirtii quæ exstant omnia. Recensuit . . . Joannes Davisius, *etc.* 2 pt. **L.P.** *Typis academicis: Cantabrigiæ,* 1727. 4º. **197**. d. **14.**
Previous edition Cambridge, 1706.

—— [Another copy.] COPIOUS MS. NOTES [by the editor]. C. **45**. e. **8.**
Imperfect; wanting pp. 737–753, *the Index rerum and Index auctorum, and the map.*

—— C. Julii Cæsaris de bellis Gallico et civili Pompejano . . . [With the supplementary commentaries ascribed to Hirtius and others.] Cum integris notis Dionysii Vossii, Joannis Davisii et Samuelis Clarkii. Cura et studio Francisci Oudendorpii, qui suas animadversiones, ac varias lectiones adjecit. (Dissertatio Henrici Dodwelli de lib. oct. B. Gall. & Alex. Afric. atque Hisp. auctore.) 2 pt. pp. 1035. FEW MS. NOTES. *Ludg. Bat.; Rotterodami,* 1737. 4º. **586**. h. **17, 18.**

—— [Another copy.] **L.P.** **673**. k. **3.**

—— [Another copy.] **L.P.** **53**. h. **12.**

—— [Another copy.] G. **9161.**

—— C. Julii Cæsaris commentariorum de bello Gallico libri VII (liber VIII. scriptore A. Hirtio Pansa). [The text of Gottfried Jungermann.]—Ex C. Julii Cæsaris commentariis de bello civili. *See* Bouquet (M.) Recueil des historiens des Gaules, *etc.* tom. 1. 1738, *etc.* fol. **Circ.8–9.b.**

—— C. Julii Cæsaris quæ extant . . . Accesserunt annotationes Samuelis Clarke, *etc.* pp. 510. *J. & R. Tonson & J. Watts: Londini,* 1739. 8º. **09039**. d. **33.**
Previous edition 1720.

—— C. Julii Cæsaris quæ extant. [With the supplementary commentaries ascribed to Hirtius and others.] 2 vol. *J. Brindley: Londini,* 1744. 12º. **989**. a. **22.**

—— [Another copy.] **165**. b. **2.**

—— C. Julii Cæsaris commentariorum qui exstant libri. [With the supplementary commentaries ascribed to Hirtius and others.] 1748. *See* Haurisius (B. C.) Scriptores historiæ Romanæ Latini veteres, *etc.* tom. 3. 1743, *etc.* fol. **198**. h. **11.**

—— Caii Julii Caesaris et A. Hirtii de rebus a Caesare gestis commentarii. Cum fragmentis. Accesserunt indices locorum rerumque et verborum. Omnia, ex recensione Samuelis Clarke fideliter expressa. pp. 378. **L.P.** *Robertus & Andreas Foulis: Glasguae,* 1750. fol. **197**. f. **12.**

—— [Another edition.] pp. 500. *Robertus & Andreas Foulis: Glasguæ,* 1750. 4º. **294**. f. **3.**

—— [Another edition.] 3 vol. *Robertus & Andreas Foulis: Glasguae,* 1750. 12º. **800**. a. **2–4.**

—— C. Julii Cæsaris quæ extant . . . Accesserunt annotationes Samueli Clarke, *etc.* pp. 510. *J. & R. Tonson & J. Watts: Londini,* 1753. 8º. **587**. d. **5.**
Previous edition 1739.

—— C. Julii Cæsaris quæ exstant opera; cum A. Hirtii sive Oppii commentariis de bellis Gall. Alexand. Afric. et Hispaniensi. Accesserunt ejusdem Cæsaris fragmenta, necnon et nomina populorum, oppidorum et fluviorum, quæ apud Cæsarem reperiuntur. (De Cæsaris vita et scriptis. Ex Ger. Joan. Vossio.—Dissertatio Henrici Dodwelli, de lib. oct. B. Gall. et Alex. Afric. atque Hisp. auctore.) 2 tom. *Parisiis,* 1755. 16º. **159**. a. **13, 14.**

CAESAR (Caius Julius) [Works.—*Latin.*]

—— C. Julii Cæsaris quæ extant. Interpretatione & notis illustravit Joannes Godvinus . . . in usum Delphini . . . Editio sexta. pp. iii. 490. *W. Innys & S. Richardson, etc.: Londini*, 1755. 8°. **588. f. 16.**
Previous edition 1745.

—— C. Julii Caesaris et A. Hirtii De rebus à C. Julio Caesare gestis commentarii . . . Editio nova accuratissima. [Edited by Michael Maittaire. With maps.] pp. 422. *J. & R. Tonson: Londini*, 1764. 12°. **9041. e. 19.**
Previous edition 1716.

—— C. Julii Cæsaris de bellis Gallicis et civili Pompeiano; nec non A. Hirtii, aliorumque de bellis Alexandrino, Africano, et Hispaniensi, commentarii; ex optimis et accuratissimis Francisci Oudendorpii et Samuelis Clarke editionibus expressi. pp. 357. *J. Dickson: Edinburgi*, 1771. 12°. **9040. b. 13.**

—— C. Julii Cæsaris quæ extant. Interpretatione & notis illustravit Joannes Godvinus . . . Editio nona, et prioribus longè accuratior. pp. 490. *J. F. & R. Rivington: Londini*, 1778. 8°. **9040. dd. 12.**
Previous edition London, 1755.

—— C. Julii Cæsaris quæ extant . . . Accesserunt annotationes Samuelis Clarke . . . Editio quarta. pp. 510. *G. Strahan: Londini*, 1778. 8°. **9042. aaa. 5.**
Previous edition 1753.

—— C. Julii Cæsaris et aliorum de bellis Gallico civili Pompeiano Alexandrino Africano et Hispaniensi commentarii juxta editionem Oudendorpii. Accedunt tabulæ et index geographicus auctiores. pp. 506. **L.P.** *E Typographeo Clarendoniano: Oxonii*, 1780. 8°. **196. b. 14.**

—— C. Julii Cæsaris et A. Hirtii de rebus à C. Julio Cæsare gestis commentarii. Cum . . . fragmentis, *etc.* pp. 422. *J. F. & C. Rivington & T. Longman: Londini*, 1784. 12°. **9039. bb. 17.**

—— Caii Julii Cæsaris opera omnia. [With the supplementary commentaries ascribed to Hirtius and others.] (Nomenclator geographicus . . . excerptus potissimum e thesauro geographico Abrahami Ortelii.—Josephi Justi Scaligeri notitia Galliæ. Item ejusdem notæ super appellationibus locorum aliquot, & gentium apud Cæsarem.—Nomina populorum, oppidorum, fluviorum, &c. quæ apud Cæsarem reperiuntur, a S. Clarkio ordine alphabetico digesta.—Dissertatio Henrici Dodwelli de lib. oct. B. Gall. & Alex. Afric. atque Hisp. auctore.) [Edited by Henry Homer.] 2 tom. **L.P.** *Sumtibus editoris: Londini*, 1790. 8°. **673. g. 12, 13.**

—— [Another copy.] **L.P.** **51. h. 13.**

—— C. Julii Cæsaris commentarii de bello Gallico et civili. Accedunt libri de bello Alexandrino Africano et Hispaniensi. E recensione Christoph. Cellarii, cumque selectis ejusdem notis, et indice Latinitatis Sam. Fr. Nathan. Mori. Edidit Esaias Budai. pp. 745. MS. NOTES. *Debrecini*, 1797. 8°. **1307. b. 9.**

—— C. Iulii Caesaris de bello Gallico et civili nec non aliorum de bello Alexandrino Africano et Hispaniensi commentarii . . . Praemittitur notitia literaria (ex Ger. Ioan. Vossio lib. I. de hist. Lat. cap. XIII). (Henrici Dodwelli dissertatio de auctore lib. VIII. de bello Gall. & Alex. Afric. atque Hispan.—Index editionum C. Iulii Caesaris auctior Fabriciano et in v. aetates digestus.—C. Iulii Caesaris fragmenta.) Accedit index rerum et verborum. Editio secunda, emendatior et auctior. 2 vol. *Argentorati*, 1803. 8°. **159. f. 5, 6.**

CAESAR (Caius Julius) [Works.—*Latin.*]

—— C. Iulii Caesaris commentarii de bello Gallico et civili. Accedunt libri de bello Alexandrino Africano et Hispaniensi. E recensione Francisci Oudendorpii. Post Cellarium et Morum denuo curavit Ier. Iac. Oberlinus. (Henrici Dodwelli dissertatio de auctore lib. oct. de B. Gall. et Alex. Afric. atque Hisp.—Comparatio epocharum belli civilis Pompeii et Caesaris.—Nomina populorum, oppidorum, fluviorum etc. quae apud Caesarem reperiuntur, a S. Clarkio ordine alphabetico digesta.) pp. 902. *Lipsiae*, 1805. 8°. **587. d. 6.**

—— [Another copy.] **F.P.** **294. f. 1.**

—— C. Julii Cæsaris de bellis Gallico et civili Pompeiano, nec non A. Hirtii, aliorumque de bellis Alexandrino, Africano, et Hispaniensi, commentarii, ex editione Francisci Oudendorpii, sedulâ recensione accurati. [Edited by John Carey.] pp. 468. *Rodwell & Martin, etc.: Londini*, 1816. 12°. **832. a. 12.**

—— C. Julii Cæsaris de bello Gallico et civili commentarii, ad usum Lycæorum. [With the continuation of the "De bello Gallico" ascribed to Hirtius.] Stereotypa Herhan. pp. 428. *Parisiis*, 1818. 12°. **1306. a. 15.**

—— C. Julii Cæsaris opera omnia. Ex editione Oberliniana cum notis et interpretatione in usum Delphini, variis lectionibus, notis variorum, J. Celsi commentariis . . . accurate recensita. 5 vol. *A. J. Valpy: Londini*, 1819. 8°. [*Delphin and Variorum Classics.*] **11388. d. 3.**

—— Caius Julius Cæsar . . . Cum varietate lectionum, Julii Celsi commentariis, tabulis geographicis et selectissimis eruditorum notis quibus suas adjecerunt N. L. Achaintre et N. E. Lemaire. [With the supplementary commentaries ascribed to Hirtius and others.] (*Πλουταρχου . . . Γαιος Ἰουλιος Καισαρ.—Γαιου Ἰουλιου Καισαρος ἀπομνημονευματα του ἐν τῃ Γαλατιᾳ πολεμου.* C. Julii Cæsaris commentariorum de bello Gallico libri septem in Græcum sermonem translati [by M. Planudes, or T. Gaza].—Notæ ad interpretem Græcum Gothofredi Jungermani.) 4 vol. *Parisiis*, 1819–22. 8°. [*Bibliotheca classica latina.* vol. 1–4.] **11305. f. 18.**

—— C. Julii Caesaris itemque Auli Hirtii quae extant omnia recensita et illustrata cura et studio Joannis Baptistae Giani, *etc.* 3 vol. *Mediolani*, 1820. 8°. [*Classicorum latinorum nova editio.* vol. 5–7.] **11304. dd. 2/3.**

—— [Another copy.] **L.P.** **1308. l. 12–14.**

—— C. Julii Caesaris de bellis Gallico et civili Pompejano nec non A. Hirtii aliorumque de bellis Alexandrino Africano et Hispaniensi commentarii ad MSStorum fidem expressi, cum integris notis Dionysii Vossii, Joannis Davisii et Samueli Clarkii, cura . . . Francisci Oudendorpii, qui suas animadversiones ac varias lectiones adjecit. Editio nova auctior, *etc.* 2 tom. *Stutgardiae*, 1822. 8°. **9041. b. 19.**

—— C. Julii Cæsaris, de bellis Gallico et civili Pompeiano . . . commentarii, sedula recensione accurati. [Edited by John Carey.] pp. 468. *Rodwell & Martin: Londini*, 1822. 12°. **11312. a. 1.**
Previous edition 1816.

—— C. Julii Cæsaris quæ extant, interpretatione et notis illustravit Joannes Goduinus . . . Juxta editionem Parisienem [*sic*]. Editio decima quarta, prioribus longe accuratior. pp. 490. 127. *R. Bensley: Londini*, 1824. 8°. **9039. ccc. 13.**

Previous edition London, 1778.

—— C. Julii Cæsaris quæ extant, interpretatione et notis illustravit Johannes Godvinus . . . in usum Delphini. [With the supplementary commentaries ascribed to Hirtius and others.] The notes and interpretations translated and improved by Thomas Clark. Fourth edition. pp. viii. 410. *H. C. Carey: Philadelphia*, 1824. 8º. **1308**. g. **10**.

—— C. Julii Cæsaris commentarii de bello Gallico et civili . . . E recensione Francisci Oudendorpii. Post Cellarium et Morum denuo curavit Jer. Jac. Oberlinus . . . Editio nova. pp. xxviii. 675. *Apud Ricardum Priestley: Londini*, 1825. 8º. **9039**. dd. **3**.
Previous edition 1805.

—— C. Julii Cæsaris commentarii de bello Gallico et civili. Accedunt libri de bello Alexandrino Africano et Hispaniensi. Mit geographischen, historischen, kritischen und grammatischen Anmerkungen . . . von Anton Möbius. Mit zwei Kupfertafeln. 2 Bd. *Hannover*, 1826, 30. 8º. **9040**. e. **16**.

—— Caii Iulii Caesaris commentarii de bello Gallico et civili . . . bearbeitet von Anton Baumstark. [With the continuation of the " De bello Gallico " ascribed to Hirtius.] pp. 587. *Freiburg*, 1832. 8º. **587**. g. **4**.

—— Caii Julii Cæsaris Opera omnia . . . notulis sermone anglicano exaratis illustrata . . . in usum scholarum. Studio Joannis Dymock. Editio decima. pp. 476. *Bell & Bradfute, etc.: Edinburgi*, 1833. 12º. **9042**. de. **14**.

—— Commentarii de bellis C. Iulii Caesaris. Recensuit et illustravit Car. Ern. Christ. Schneider. pt. 1, 2. *Halis*, 1840–55. 8º. **803**. e. **25**.
Containing the " De bello Gallico " only; no more published.

—— C. Iulii Caesaris commentarii de bello Gallico et civili etc. Cum fragmentis et indice historico et geographico. Nova editio stereotypa. [With the supplementary commentaries ascribed to Hirtius and others.] pp. 554. *Lipsiae*, 1844. 8º. **9039**. aa. **3**.

—— C. Julii Caesaris commentarii cum supplementis A. Hirtii et aliorum. Caesaris Hirtiique fragmenta. Carolus Nipperdeius recensuit optimorum codicum auctoritates annotavit quaestiones criticas praemisit. pp. 814. *Lipsiae*, 1847. 8º. **1308**. g. **7**.

—— Caii Julii Cæsaris commentarii, cum supplementis Auli Hirtii et aliorum. pp. 515. *J. H. Parker: Oxonii*, 1852. 16º. **1307**. a. **4**.

—— C. Julii Caesaris Commentarii. Cum supplementis A. Hirtii et aliorum. Recognovit Franciscus Oehler. pp. viii. 460. *Lipsiae*, 1860. 8º. **9042**. de. **11**.

—— C. Iuli Caesaris commentarii cum A. Hirti aliorumque supplementis. Recognovit Bernardus Dinter. 3 vol. *Lipsiae*, 1864–76. 8º. **11340**. cc. **2**.
Part of the " Bibliotheca scriptorum graecorum et romanorum Teubneriana."

—— C. Julii Caesaris commentarii de bellis Gallico et civili, aliorum de bellis Alexandrino, Africano et Hispaniensi. Annotatione critica instruxit F. Dübner. Imprimé par ordre de l'Empereur . . . par les soins de M. Anselme Petetin.) 2 vol. *Parisiis*, 1867. 4º. **9040**. h. **21**.

—— C. Iulii Caesaris commentarii cum supplementis A. Hirtii et aliorum. Iterum recognovit Emanuel Hoffmann. 2 vol. *Vindobonae*, 1888. 8º. **9040**. a. **10**.

—— C. Iulii Caesaris commentarii cum A. Hirtii aliorumque supplementis ex recensione Bernardi Kübleri . . . Editio maior. (Commentarius de bello Africo. Rec. Ed. Wölfflin.) 3 vol. *Lipsiae*, 1893–97. 8º. **011306.a.9.**
Part of the " Bibliotheca scriptorum graecorum et romanorum Teubneriana."

—— C. Iuli Cæsaris commentariorum pars prior qua continentur libri VII de bello Gallico cum A. Hirti supplemento (pars posterior qua continentur libri III de bello civili cum libris incertorum auctorum de bello Alexandrino Africo Hispaniensi). Recensuit brevique adnotatione critica instruxit Renatus Du Pontet. 2 pt. *Oxonii*, [1900.] 8º. [*Scriptorum classicorum bibliotheca Oxoniensis.*] **2046**. a.

—— C. Iuli Caesaris commentarii. [With the supplementary commentaries ascribed to Hirtius and others.] Edidit Alfredus Klotz . . . Editio minor. 3 vol. *Lipsiae*, 1920–27. 8º. **011306.a.10.**
Part of the " Bibliotheca scriptorum graecorum et latinorum Teubneriana."

—— C. Iuli Caesaris commentarii. Edidit Alfredus Klotz . . . Editio quarta. *Lipsiae*, 1952, 50, 27. 8º. **2049**. f. **7**.
Part of " Bibliotheca scriptorum graecorum et romanorum teubneriana." Vol. 2 is of the second edition. Vol. 3 is of the first edition.

Latin and French.

—— Les Commentaires de César . . . de la traduction de N. Perrot, Sieur d'Ablancourt. [With the supplementary commentaries ascribed to Hirtius and others.] Nouvelle édition, revuë et corrigée. (Remarques sur la carte de l'ancienne Gaule par le Sieur Samson d'Abbeville.) 2 tom. *A. & H. Molin: Lyon*, 1689. 12º. **803**. d. 6.

—— Nouvelle édition: revue & retouchée . . . par M. de Wailly. 2 tom. *Paris*, 1775. 12º. **9039**. aaa. **16**.

—— Commentaires de César; avec des notes historiques, critiques et militaires, par M. le comte Turpin de Crissé. [With the supplementary commentaries ascribed to Hirtius and others.] 3 tom. *Montargis*, 1785. 4º. **198**. e. **11–13**.

—— Les Commentaires de César; traduction nouvelle, le texte en regard, avec des notes critiques et littéraires, un index géographique et six cartes de la Gaule; précédée d'un coup-d'œil sur l'histoire, l'état politique, religieux &c. des Gaulois et d'un aperçu des institutions militaires des Romains. On y a joint l'abrégé de la vie de César et . . . un précis des affaires de Rome, année par année. [With the supplementary commentaries ascribed to Hirtius and others.] Par M. le Déist de Botidoux. 5 tom. *Paris*, 1809. 8º. **587**. d. **8–10**.

—— Mémoires . . . Traduction nouvelle par M. Artaud. [With the supplementary commentaries ascribed to Hirtius and others.] (Notice sur Jules César [by J. L. Laya].) 3 tom. *Paris*, 1832, 28. 8º. [*Bibliothèque latine-française.*] **11306**. e. **7–9**.

—— Jules César. [Works, with the supplementary commentaries ascribed to Hirtius and others, and a French translation by T. C. E. Baudement and J. J. S. A. Damas-Hinard, and a life of Caesar by the former.] 1850. *See* Nisard (J. M. N. D.) Collection des auteurs latins, *etc.* 1850, *etc.* 8º. **11306**. m. **17**.

Latin and Italian.

—— C. Julii Cæsaris quae extant omnia, italica versione [by Francesco Baldelli] e MS. codice ad hodiernum stylum accommodata; tabulis æneis . . . notis tum variorum . . . tum in usum Sereniss. Delphini, tum suis . . . auxit Hermolaus Albritius, *etc.* [With the supplementary commentaries ascribed to Hirtius and others.] pp. 686. xxxx. [*Venice*, 1737.] 4º. **1306**. m. **10**.

—— [Another copy.] ON VELLUM. C. **5**. c. **8**.

—— I Comentarj di C. Giulio Cesare in nostra volgar lingua recati. Edizione prima Napoletana nella quale si è aggiunto il testo latino ricavato dalle migliori edizioni. Con le note di Cristoforo Cellario. [With the supplementary commentaries ascribed to Hirtius and others.] (Vita di C. Giulio Cesare compendiata da Enea Vico.—Proemio di Andrea Palladio intorno a' disegni, ed alle fatiche da lui fatte, per facilitar la lezione de' comentarj di C. Giulio Cesare.—Indice geografico.) 3 tom. *Napoli,* 1782. 8°. **196**. a. **5–7**.

Latin and Spanish.

—— Los Commentarios de Cayo Julio Cesar, traducidos por D. Joseph Goya y Muniain, *etc.* (Supplemento . . . entresacado y traducido en castellano de la vida . . . escrita . . . por Cayo Suetonio Tranquilo, y . . . por Plutarco.) 2 tom. *Madrid,* 1798. 4°. **588**. f. **17, 18**.

English.

—— Obseruations upon Caesar's Comentaries. [With a translation of the text.] By Clement Edmundes, *etc.* 2 pt. *For Math. Lownes: London,* 1609. 4°. **9041**. d. **1**.

The titlepage is engraved. Without books 6 *and* 7 *of the "De bello Gallico."*

—— [Another copy.] **1305**. l. **12**.

With the arms of James I. *stamped in gold on the binding.*

—— [Another copy.] **197**. e. **14**.

Imperfect; wanting the "De bello Gallico."

—— [Another copy.] 3 pt. [*London,* 1609.] fol. C. **60**. n. **3**.

This issue contains books 6 *and* 7 *of the "De bello Gallico" and "The Maner of our Moderne Training, or Tacticke Practise" from the edition printed by Lownes in* 1604. *The engraved titlepage is of the proof-state, before the addition of the imprint. With the autographs of Edmondes and Ben Jonson.*

—— [Another edition.] The Commentaries of C. Julius Cæsar . . . with . . . observations thereupon: also the Art of our modern training, or, tactick practise; by Clement Edmonds . . . Whereunto is adjoyned the eighth commentary of the warres in Gallia (by A. Hirtius) . . . Together with the life of Cæsar . . . Revised, corrected, and enlarged. 2 pt. *Printed by R. Daniel: London,* 1655. fol. **586**. i. **19**.

With an additional titlepage, engraved.

—— [Another edition.] pp. 332. *Tho. Newcomb for Jonathan Edwin:* [*London,*] 1677. fol. **198**. f. **11**.

—— [Another edition.] pp. 309. *Edward Jones for Matthew Gillyflower & Richard Bentley:* [*London,*] 1695. fol. **586**. k. **9**.

—— C. Julius Cæsar's Commentaries . . . To which is added Aulus Hirtius, or Oppius's supplement of the Alexandrian, African and Spanish wars. With the author's life. Adorn'd with sculptures from the designs of . . . Palladio. Made English . . . by Captain Martin Bladen. The second edition, improv'd, *etc.* pp. 363. *R. Smith: London,* 1706. 8°. **1481**. aaa. **17**.

—— The third edition, *etc.* pp. 432. *J. Knapton: London,* 1719. 8°. **587**. d. **7**.

—— The fourth edition, *etc.* pp. 432. *J. Knapton & D. Midwinter: London,* 1726. 8°. **587**. e. **22**.

—— The seventh edition, *etc.* pp. 430. *J. & P. Knapton: London,* 1750. 8°. **294**. g. **16**.

—— The Commentaries of Cæsar, translated into English [With the supplementary commentaries ascribed t Hirtius and others.] To which is prefixed a discours concerning the Roman art of war. By William Dunca . . . Illustrated with cuts. pp. civ. 335. *J.* *R. Tonson: London,* 1753. fol. **L.1.f.5**

—— [Another copy.] The Commentaries of Cæsar, *etc.* *London,* 1753. fol. **198**. h. **1**

—— [Another edition.] 2 vol. *J. & R. Tonson: Londo* 1755. 8°. **9039**. d.

—— C. Julius Cæsar's Commentaries . . . Made Englis . . . by Col. Martin Bladen. The eighth edition, revise *etc.* pp. xxxii. 430. *J. Fuller: London,* 1770. 8°. **9039**. cc. **1**

Previous edition 1750.

—— Cæsar, translated by William Duncan. [With th supplementary commentaries ascribed to Hirtius an others.] 2 vol. *A. J. Valpy: London,* 1832. 16°. **11305**. aa. **1**. (**1**

—— [Another edition.] pp. viii. 368. *Jones & Co.: Londo* 1833. 8°. **9039**. g. **1**. (**1**

—— Cæsar's Commentaries on the Gallic and Civil Wars with the supplementary books attributed to Hirti . . . Literally translated [by W. A. Macdevitt], with note *etc.* pp. iv. 572. *London,* 1851. 8°. [*Bohn's Classic Library.*] **2500**. e. **1**

—— "De bello Gallico" & other commentaries. (The W in Gaul. [With the continuation ascribed to Hirtius.]- The Civil War.) (Translated by W. A. Macdevitt. Wi an introduction by Thomas de Quincey.) pp. xxiii. 360. *J. M. Dent & Sons: London; E. P. Dutton & Co New York,* [1915.] 8°. [*Everyman's Library.*] **12206.p.1/53**

—— Julius Caesar's Commentaries. A modern rendering b Somerset de Chair. Engravings by Clifford Web pp. 311. *Golden Cockerel Press: London,* 1951. 8°. **Cup.510.af.15**

—— Caesar's War Commentaries . . . Edited and translat by John Warrington. pp. xvi. 304. *J. M. Dent & Son London; E. P. Dutton & Co.: New York,* 1953. 8 [*Everyman's Library.* no. 702.] **12206**. p. **1/78**

French.

—— Les Commentaires de Iules Cesar. De la guerre ciui . . . De la guerre Alexandrine . . . De la guerre Daffriq . . . De la guerre Despaigne . . . Translatez par . . Estienne Delaigue dict Beauuoys. Des batailles conquestz faictz par Cesar au pays de Gaul. Translat par . . . Robert Gaguin . . . Auec les portraictz descriptios des lieux, fortz, pontz, machines, & aultr choses . . . Ensemble les nos des lieux, villes, & peupl du pays de Gaule. [With woodcuts.] 2 pt. *P. Vido pour P. Le Preux & G. Du Pre: Paris,* 1531. fol. **586**. k. **1**

—— [Another edition.] vol. 1. *Par I. Petit: Paris,* 1539. 8 C. **27**. h. **18**. (**1**

Imperfect; wanting vol. 2, *containing the "De bel Gallico."*

—— [Another edition.] ff. 423. *Chez O. Petit; imprimé p P. Gaultier: Paris,* 1546. 16°. **802**. a. **3**

—— Commentaires de Iules Cesar, de la guerre ciuile d Romains, & autres expeditions militaires par luy fait és Gaules, & Afrique [i.e. the supplementary comme taries ascribed to Hirtius and others]. Auec portrait [Translated by Étienne de l'Aigue and Robert Gaguin ff. 342. *Pour G. du Pre: Paris,* [1550?] 16°. **9040**. aaa. **1**

—— Les Commentaires de Iules Cesar, des guerres de la Gaule, plus ceux des guerres ciuiles, contre la part Pompeienne. [With the supplementary commentaries ascribed to Hirtius and others.] Le tout de la version de Blaise de Vigenere, & illustré d'annotations. (Sommaire d'Europe des faictes et gestes de Iulles Cesar, extraict des memoires de Suetone.—Abregez de Flore, sur l'onze, et douziesme decades de Tite-Lieu, concernans la plus-part les faicts & gestes de Iulles Cesar.) 2 vol. *Chez A. l'Angelier: Paris*, 1589. fol. C. **79**. f. **11**.
With the arms of Henry, Prince of Wales, son of James I., *stamped on the binding.*

—— [Another edition.] 2 pt. *A. Langellier: Paris*, 1603, 02. 4°. C. **77**. d. **7**.

—— Les Commentaires de Iules Cesar, et les annotations de Blaise de Vigenere. [With the supplementary commentaries ascribed to Hirtius and others.] Auec les Paralleles de Cesar, et de Henry IIII. De nouueau illustrez de maximes politiques. Par Anthoine de Bandole. Derniere edition. 3 pt. *I. Rebuffé: Paris*, 1625. 4°. **587**. g. **7**.

—— Les Commentaries, de Cesar. [With the supplementary commentaries ascribed to Hirtius and others. Translated by Nicolas Perrot d'Ablancourt.] (Remarques sur la carte de l'ancienne Gaule tirée des commentaires de César. Par le sieur Sanson d'Abbeville. Remarques sur la traduction.) 3 pt. *Veuue de J. Camusat: Paris*, 1652. 4°. **197**. c. **7**.

—— Troisiesme édition, reueue et corrigée. 3 pt. *A. Courbé: Paris*, 1658, 1657. 4°. **9039**. g. **5**.

—— Édition nouvelle, reveue & corrigée. pp. lx. 444. *A. Wolfgang: Amsterdam*, 1678. 8°. **587**. b. **32**.

—— Les Commentaires de César, d'une traduction toute nouvelle [or rather, slightly altered from the translation of N. Perrot d'Ablancourt]. [With the supplementary commentaries ascribed to Hirtius and others.] 2 tom. *La Haye*, 1743. 12°. **9041**. aa. **2**.

—— Les Commentaires de César, traduits par J. B. Varney. [With the supplementary commentaries ascribed to Hirtius and others.] 2 tom. *Paris*, 1810. 8°. **587**. d. **11**.

—— Commentaires. [With the supplementary commentaries ascribed to Hirtius and others. Translated by N. Perrot d'Ablancourt.] 1850. *See* Liskenne (F. C.) and Sauvan (J. B. B.) Bibliothèque historique et militaire. tom. 3. 1851, 40, *etc.* 8°. **1309**. i. **5**.

—— Œuvres complètes. Commentaires sur la guerre des Gaules avec les réflexions de Napoléon Ier, suivis des commentaires sur la guerre civile et de la vie de César par Suétone (traduite en français par M. de Golbéry). Traduction d'Artaud. Nouvelle édition . . . revue par M. Félix Lemaistre, et précédée d'une étude sur César par M. Charpentier. 2 tom. *Paris*, [1892.] 12°. **9040**. ccc. **7**.

German.

—— Julius der erst Römisch Keiser von seinen kriegē, erst mals vss dem Latin in Tütsch bracht [by Matthias Ringmann]. [With the supplementary commentaries ascribed to Hirtius and others.] (Das leben Julij Cesaris nach beschrybung des Kriechischen lerers Plutarchi.) [With woodcuts.] ff. cxxvi. MS. NOTES. *Gedruckt durch I. Grüninger: Strassburg*, 1507. fol. C. **38**. h. **10**.
Cropped.

—— [Another edition.] [With woodcuts.] *Gedruckt durch I. Grüninger: Strassburg*, 1508. fol.
Dept. of Prints & Drawings.

—— Caij Julij Cesaris des grossmechtigen ersten Römischen Keysers Historien vom Gallier vn der Römer Burgerische krieg: so er selbst beschriben: vñ durch sondere grosse manheyt seiner ritterlichen tugent gefüret hat. [With the supplementary commentaries ascribed to Hirtius and others. Translated by Matthias Ringmann. With woodcuts.] ff. clxiii. *Getruckt durch J. Schöffer: Meyntz*, 1530. fol. C. **38**. i. **2**.

—— [Another edition.] ff. clxvi. *Getruckt durch J. Schöffer: Meyntz*, 1532. fol. C.125.f.1.

—— C. Julij des Ersten Rö. Keysers, Warhafftige Beschreibunge aller namhafften fürtrefflichen Kriege . . . Sampt den Büchern Auli Hircij . . . Jetzt auffs newe nach M. Ringmanni Philesij verteutschung . . . gebessert, mit schönen Figuren, *etc.* (Das Leben des . . . C. Julij Cesaris . . . durch . . . Plutarchum . . . beschrieben.) pp. 482. *Getruckt durch P. Schmidt; in verlegung S. Feyrabends & S. Hüters: Franckfurt*, 1565. fol. **805**. h. **10**.

—— K. Julius Cäsars und anderer Schriftsteller historische Nachrichten vom gallischen, bürgerlichen, alexandrinischen, afrikanischen und spanischen Kriege. Ins Deutsche übersetzt von M. Johann Franz Wagner. pp. xiv. 582. *Stutgart*, 1765. 8°. **9040**. d. **8**.

—— [Another copy.] **196**. a. **4**.
Imperfect; wanting the last four leaves, containing the index.

—— C. Julius Cäsars Denkwürdigkeiten aus dem gallischen und bürgerlichen Kriege, übersetzt von Philipp Ludwig Haus . . . [With the supplementary commentaries ascribed to Hirtius and others.] Dritte Ausgabe. Durchaus umgearbeitet von D. Friedrich Strack. 2 Bd. *Frankfurt*, 1817. 8°. **803**. c. **19, 20**.

—— Memoiren über den Gallischen Krieg. Deutsch von Prof. Dr. H. Köchly und Oberst W. Rüstow. Siebente Auflage. (Memoiren über den Bürger-Krieg. Deutsch von H. Köchly.) 2 pt. *Berlin*, [1889.] 8°. [*Langenscheidtsche Bibliothek sämtlicher griechischen und römischen Klassiker in neueren deutschen Muster-Übersetzungen.* Bd. 77.] **012213**. g. **1/77**.
Pt. 2 has a separate titlepage bearing the imprint: Stuttgart, 1868.

Hungarian.

—— C. Julius Caesar' minden munkái. [With the supplementary commentaries ascribed to Hirtius and others.] Fordítá és jegyzeteivel bővíté Szenczy Imre. 2 köt. *Budán*, 1839, 40. 8°. [*Magyar Tudós Társaság. Romai classicusok magyar fordításokban.* köt. 3, 4.] Ac. **825/22**.

Italian.

—— Commentarii di C. Iulio Cesare tradotti in volgare per Agostino Ortica. ff. ccxxxi. *Per G. de Gregorii: Venegia*, 1523. 8°. **586**. c. **11**.

—— [Another edition.] ff. 262. *P. Alex. Pag. Benacenses. F. Bena. V.V.: [Toscolano*, 1525?] 8°. **293**. a. **5**.
Imperfect; wanting the titlepage.

—— [Another edition.] ff. cclxxii. *Stampato per F. di Alessandro Bindoni & M. Pasini: Vinegia*, 1528. 8°. **586**. c. **12**.

—— Commentarii di Caio Giulio Cesare, tradotti di latino in volgar lingua per Agostino Ortica de la Porta, Genouese, nuouamente reuisti & . . . corretti & Historiati. ff. 247. *Francesco Bindoni & Mapheo Pasini: Vinegia*, 1531. 8°. **1471. de. 34.**

—— [Another edition.] ff. 242. *Per A. de Torti: Venetiis*, 1539. 8°. **586. c. 13.**

—— [Another edition.] ff. 256. *Nelle case de' figliuoli di Aldo: Venetia*, 1547. 8°. **C. 16. d. 16.**

—— I Commentari di C. Giulio Cesare da M. Francesco Baldelli nuouamente di lingua Latina tradotti in Thoscana. [With the supplementary commentaries ascribed to Hirtius and others.] Con figure e tauole, *etc.* pp. 384 [784]. *Appresso G. Giolito e fratelli: Vinegia*, 1554. 8°. **293. d. 21.**

—— [Another edition.] pp. 773. *Appresso G. Giolito: Vinegia*, 1557. 8°. **293. d. 16.**

—— [Another issue.] *Appresso G. Giolito: Vinegia*, 1558. 8°. **586. a. 20.**
The date in the colophon is 1557. *Imperfect; wanting sig.* ***7, 8. *Sig.* ***7 *is supplied in* ms.

—— [Another edition.] pp. 407. *Appresso P. de' Franceschi: Venetia*, 1575. 4°. **587. d. 12.**
The date in the colophon is 1574.

—— [Another copy.] **L.P.** **672. d. 3.**

—— [Another copy.] **293. g. 15.**

—— [Another edition.] pp. 407. *Appresso G. Foglietti: Venetia*, 1618. 4°. **587. d. 13.**
The date in the colophon is 1598, *probably the correct date.*

—— [Another edition.] pp. 407. *N. Misserini: Venetia*, 1619. 4°. **293. h. 11.**
The titlepage is engraved.

Roumanian.

—— Comentariele lui Caiu Juliu Cesare de belulu Galicu. Traduse de C. Copacinianu. (Comentariele lui Caiu Juliu Cesare de belulu civile, urmate de comentariele lui A. Hirtiu db [*sic*] belele Alexandrinu si Africanu precumu si de comentariele de belulu Ispanicu ale unui autoru anonimu; traduse de D. Caianu.) 2 pt. *Bucuresci*, 1872, 77. 8°. **9041. c. 27.**
The title on the wrapper reads: " Operile lui Caiu Juliu Cesare traduse Romanescu," etc. The date on the wrapper is 1877.

Russian.

—— Записки Юлия Цезаря и его продолжателей О галльской войне, О гражданской войне, Об александрийской войне, Об африканской войне. Перевод и комментарии . . . М. М. Покровского. (C. Iuli Caesaris aliorumque scriptorum commentarii, *etc.*) [With plates.] pp. 559. *Москва, Ленинград*, 1948. 8°. [*Литературные памятники.*] **Ac. 1125/225. (2.)**

Spanish.

—— Los comentarios de Gayo Iulio Cesar. [fol. 2 *recto:*] Tabla delos comentarios, *etc.* [fol. 10 *recto:*] Trasladaçiō d'los comētarios de Gayo iulio çesar de latin en romāçe fecha por frey Diego lopez de Toledo comendador de Castilnouo, *etc.* [fol. 64 *verso:*] Prohemio de Aulo hirçio enel octauo libro dela guerra de françia que añadio en los comentarios de Gayo julio çesar. [fol. 119 *verso:*] Libro quarto delos comentarios d' Aulo hirçio o opio dela guerra de Alexandria. [fol. 133 *verso:*] Libro quinto delos comentarios d' Aulo hirçio o opio dela guerra de Africa. [fol. 151 *recto:*] Libro sexto delos comentarios . . . dela guerra de España. **G.L.** *a costa del mercader Melchior goriçio; por Pedro hagembach: Toledo*, A quatorze del mes de Iulio, 1498. fol. **IB. 53527.**
176 *leaves, ff.* 11–169 *numbered* i–clix, *ff.* 170, 176 *probably blank. Sig.* a⁶ b⁴ a–z⁶ A–C⁶ D⁴ (i–iiii). *Double columns,* 41, 42 *lines to a column. Without the blank leaves.*

—— [Another edition.] Nueuamēte impressos y corregido **G.L.** ff. clxviii. *Impressos en casa de M. de Eguia: Alcala*, 1529. fol. **C. 125. e.**

—— [Another edition.] Libro de los comentarios de Gayo Julio Cesar, *etc.* ff. 343. [*J. Du Puys:*] *Paris*; *A. Birckman: Anueres*, 1549. 8°. **C. 63. f. 2**

—— [Another edition.] Los Commentarios de Gayo Iuli Cesar . . . Añadido vn argumento de las guerras de Francia, y vna declaracion de su diuision para concorda a Cesar con otros autores. ff. 244. *Viuda de A. Martin: Madrid*, 1621. 4°. **803. g. 4**

DE BELLO CIVILI.

Latin.

—— C. Julii Caesaris commentariorum de bello civili libri III. Grammatisch, kritisch und historisch erklärt von M. Christian Gottlob Herzog. pp. xii. 547. *Leipzig*, 1834. 8°. **9040. dd. 1.**

—— C. Iulii Caesaris commentarii de bello civili erklärt von Friedrich Kraner. Achte Auflage von Dr. Friedrich Hofmann . . . Mit zwei Karten von H. Kiepert. pp. 26 *Berlin*, 1881. 8°. **11306. dd. 3. (2**

—— C. Julii Cæsaris commentarii de bello civili. (Reprinted from the complete edition of Caesar's commentaries in the " Oxford Pocket Classics.") *Apud Parker & Socios: Oxonii*, [1883.] 8°. **11304. b. 6**

—— C. Iulii Caesaris commentarii de bello civili. Für den Schulgebrauch erklärt von Dr. Rudolf Menge. pp. viii. 250. *Gotha*, 1893. 8°. **9040. ccc. 2**

—— C. Iuli Caesaris Belli Civilis libri III. In usum scholarum iterum recognovit Bernardus Dinter. Editio stereotyp pp. vi. 207. *Lipsiae*, 1896. 8°. **9042. aa. 34. (2**

—— The Commentaries of C. Julius Caesar. The Civil War. Edited by Charles E. Moberly . . . New edition. [With maps.] pp. viii. 231. *Clarendon Press: Oxford*, 1897. 8 [*Clarendon Press Series.*] **2320. f.**

—— C. Iuli Caesaris belli civilis libri III. Recensuit Alfr Holder. pp. viii. 250. *Lipsiae*, 1898. 8°. **9040. dd. 2**

—— C. Iulii Caesaris commentarii de bello civili. Recensu praefatus est, brevi appendice critica instruxit Dominic Bassi. pp. vii. 165. *Aug. Taurinorum*, 1916. 8°. [*Corp scriptorum latinorum Paravianum.* no. 3.] **011306.a.2/3**

—— The Commentaries of C. Julius Caesar on the Civil Wa Edited by Charles E. Moberly . . . New illustrated editic with an introduction by Hugh Last. pp. xlviii. 227. *Clarendon Press: Oxford*, 1925. 8°. **09039. aa.**
Previous edition 1897.

—— Civil War in Spain. C. Iuli Caesaris De Bello Civil liber primus, chapters 37–55 and 59 to the end. Wit introduction, notes and vocabulary by H. E. Gould . . and J. L. Whiteley, *etc.* [With illustrations.] pp. xxiii. 14 *Macmillan & Co.: London*, 1939. 8°. [*Modern Scho Classics.*] **W.P. 6076/**

Latin and English.

—— The Civil Wars. With an English translation by A. (Peskett. [With maps.] pp. x. 369. *William Heineman London; Macmillan Co.: New York*, 1914. 8°. [*Lo Classical Library.*] **2282. d. 2**

Latin and French.

— La Guerre civile, suivi de la Guerre d'Alexandrie. Texte traduit et annoté par Maurice Rat. pp. xvii. 547. *Paris*, 1933. 8°. **9042**. a. **26**.

— La Guerre civile . . . Texte établi et traduit par Pierre Fabre . . . Troisième édition. [With maps.] 2 tom. *Paris*, 1947. 8°. [*Collection des Universités de France.*] **2319**. c. **74**.

Latin and Greek.

— C. Julii Cæsaris commentarii de bello civili. *Γ. 'Ιουλιου Καισαρος Τα περι του ἐμφυλιου πολεμου ἀπομνημονευματα. Χαριν των μαθητων ἐκδοθεντα, ἐξελληνισθεντα και σημειωσεσι πλουτισθεντα ὑπο Σ. Κ. Σακελλαροπουλου.* τευχος α'. pp. 156. *'Εν 'Αθηναις*, 1877. 8°. **9041**. c. **4**.
No more published.

English.

— The Commentaries of C. Julius Caesar on the Civil War. Literally translated by Rev. James Rice. bk. 1, 2. *E. Ponsonby, etc.: Dublin; Simpkin, Marshall & Co.: London*, 1887, 88. 8°. **11304**. bb. **9**.
No more published.

— Caesar's Civil War with Pompeius. Translated with introduction and notes by the Rev. F. P. Long. pp. xxviii. 228. *Clarendon Press: Oxford*, 1906. 8°. **9041**. eee. **21**.

— Civil War . . . A literal translation. 3 bk. *James Brodie: London*, [c. 1950.] 8°. [*Brodie's Interleaved Classical Translations.*] W.P. **11526/55**.
Bk. 1, 3 *are reissues of the edition of* [1935], *which is entered below under* [*Selected and Single Books.—English*].

Danish.

— Borgerkrigen. Oversat af Joh. B. Koch. pp. 239. *København*, 1925. 8°. [*Skrifter udgivne af Selskabet til historiske Kildeskrifters Oversættelse.* Række 10. no. 10–14.] Ac. **7623/31**.

French.

— Commentaires de Jules César. Campagne d'Espagne. Traduction nouvelle par Victor Develay. livre 1. pp. 111. *Paris*, 1863. 8°. **9040**. dd. **22**. **(4.)**
No more published.

German.

— Der Bürgerkrieg . . . Aus dem Lateinischen mit Einleitung und Erläuterung von Dr. M. Oberbreyer. pp. 182. *Leipzig*, [1878.] 16°. **012207**. f. **10**. **(1.)**

Selected and Single Books.

Latin.

— Caii Julii Cæsaris commentariorum de bello civili liber I. With English notes. pp. xi. 45. *Walton & Maberly: London*, 1859. 12°. **9040**. b. **9**.

— The Commentaries of C. Julius Caesar. The Civil War. Book I. Edited by Charles E. Moberly. pp. 85. *Oxford*, 1872. 8°. [*Clarendon Press Series.*] **12205**. m. **17**.

— C. Iulii Caesaris commentarii de bello civili liber primus. With introduction and notes by G. U. Pope. pp. 110. *See* Madras.—*Madras University.* The Latin Text Books . . . for the Entrance Examination of 1880. 1879. 12°. **12934**. c. **38**.

— Gai Iuli Caesaris commentariorum de bello civili liber primus. With introduction, notes and maps by A. G. Peskett, *etc.* pp. xx. 172. *University Press: Cambridge*, 1890. 8°. [*Pitt Press Series.*] **12204**. d. **5/84**.

—— Gai Iuli Caesaris commentariorum de bello civili liber secundus. Edited by A. G. Peskett. pp. xii. 88. *University Press: Cambridge*, 1890. 8°. [*Pitt Press Series.*] **2322**. cc. **9**.

—— Gai Iuli Caesaris de bello civili commentariorum I. Edited with notes and vocabulary for the use of schools by Malcolm Montgomery. pp. xxvii. 141. *Macmillan & Co.: London*, 1891. 16°. [*Elementary Classics.*] **11305**. bb. **3**.

—— Gai Iuli Caesaris commentariorum de bello civili liber tertius. Edited, with introduction, notes and maps by A. G. Peskett. pp. xxiv. 184. *University Press: Cambridge*, 1900. 8°. [*Pitt Press Series.*] **12204**. d. **5/79**.

—— Caesar: Civil War, book I. Edited by A. H. Allcroft. pp. 109. *London*, [1902.] 8°. [*University Tutorial Series.*] **12205**. c. **504**.

—— C. Iuli Caesaris commentariorum de bello civili liber primus. Edited with introduction, notes and vocabulary by the Rev. W. J. Bensly, *etc.* pp. xi. 236. *London*, 1909. 8°. [*Bell's Illustrated Classics.* Intermediate series.] **11305**. c. **38/4**.

—— Caesar: Civil War, book III. Edited by H. B. Stanwell. pp. 137. *London*, 1909. 8°. [*University Tutorial Series.*] **12205**. e. **136**.

—— C. Iuli Caesaris commentariorum de bello civili liber primus. Edited by the Rev. W. J. Bensly. [With maps.] pp. vii. 213. *London*, 1932. 8°. [*Bell's Illustrated Classics.*] **11304**. d. **44**.
Previous edition 1909.

—— Gai Iuli Caesaris commentariorum de bello civili liber tertius. Edited, with introduction, notes and maps, by A. G. Peskett. pp. xxiv. 214. *University Press: Cambridge*, 1933. 8°. [*Pitt Press Series.*] **2322**. dd. **21**.
A reissue of the edition of 1900, *with a vocabulary.*

—— Gai Iuli Caesaris commentariorum de bello civili liber primus. Edited by A. G. Peskett. (Reprinted with vocabulary.) pp. xx. 196. *University Press: Cambridge*, 1934. 8°. [*Pitt Press Series.*] **2322**. d. **51**.
Previous edition 1890.

—— C. Iuli Caesaris Commentariorum de bello civili liber tertius. Julius Caesar. Civil War, Book III. Edited with introduction, notes and vocabulary by E. C. Kennedy. pp. xxxix. 280. *Macmillan & Co.: London*, 1941. 8°. [*Modern School Classics.*] W.P. **6076/6**.

—— C. Iuli Cæsaris Commentariorum de Bello Civili liber tertius. Julius Cæsar, Civil War, Book III, Chapters 73–112. Edited with introduction, notes and vocabulary by E. C. Kennedy. pp. xxix. 134. *Macmillan & Co.; London*, 1941. 8°. [*Modern School Classics.*] **W.P.6076/4.**

Latin and English.

—— Cæsar, De bello civili. Books I. and II. Literally and interlinearly translated . . . by John Gibson. pp. 152. *J. Cornish & Sons: London*, [1890.] 8°. [*Gibson's Interlinear Translations.*] **11305**. ee.

English.

—— Caesar, de bello civili, bk. I. Translated into English by H. W. Hunting. pp. 59. *J. Palmer: Cambridge*, 1890. 8°. **9041**. aaa. **35**.

—— Caesar de bello civili book I, translated into literal English, by John Perkins. pp. 60. *J. Hall & Son: Cambridge*, 1890. 8°. **9041**. aa. **8**.

—— De bello civili . . . Books i. & ii. Literally translated by J. A. Prout. pp. 72. *J. Cornish & Sons: London,* [1892.] 12°. [*Kelly's Classical Keys.*] **11305.** dd. **45.**

—— Caesar's Civil War. Book i. Literally translated . . . by A. D. C. Amos. pp. 63. *E. Johnson: Cambridge,* 1896. 8°. **9039.** b. **37.**

—— Cæsar de bello civili . . . Book iii. Literally translated by J. A. Prout. pp. 64. *J. Cornish & Sons: London,* [1903.] 12°. [*Kelly's Classical Keys.*] **11305.** dd. **88.**

—— Civil War, book iii. A translation by H. B. Stanwell. pp. 69. *London,* [1909.] 8°. [*University Tutorial Series.*] **12205.** e. **137.**

—— Caesar's Civil War. Book i. Translated by W. A. M'Devitte. *London,* [1928.] 8°. **11306.** bbbb. **19.**
One of " Bell's Classical Translations."

—— Cæsar: Civil War. Book i (iii). A literal translation. 2 pt. *London,* [1935.] 8°. [*Brodie's Interleaved Classical Translations.*] W.P. **11526/3.**

—— De Bello Civili, i. A translation by Harold Osborne. pp. 66. *University Tutorial Press: London,* [1937.] 8°. **012933.** c. **49.**

Selections and Abridgments.

Latin.

—— An Easy Abridgment of Cæsar's De bello civili. By H. Awdry . . . With maps, *etc.* pp. xxxii. 143. *Rivingtons: London,* 1888. 8°. **9040.** bb. **8.**

—— Tales of the Civil War from Caesar's Commentaries. Adapted for the use of beginners, with vocabulary, notes, and exercises by Charles Haines Keene. pp. x. 98. *Macmillan & Co.: London,* 1894. 16°. [*Elementary Classics.*] **11305.** bb. **4.**

—— Tales of the Civil War from the third book of Caesar's Civil War. Edited, with historical introduction, notes, maps, vocabularies and English exercises by W. D. Lowe. pp. 100. *Clarendon Press: Oxford,* 1906. 8°. **09039.** bbb. **11.**

—— [Selections from the " De bello civili," bk. 3.] *See* infra: De Bello Gallico.—Selections and Abridgments.—*Latin.* Cæsar in Gaul, *etc.* [1917.] 8°. **09039.** b. **4.**

—— Books i and ii of the Civil War, partly in the original and partly in F. P. Long's translation. Edited by H. N. P. Sloman. pp. 141. *Oxford,* 1923. 8°. [*Clarendon Series of Greek and Latin Authors.*] W.P. **6801/10.**

—— Book iii of the Civil War. Partly in the original and partly in F. P. Long's translation. Edited by W. C. Compton . . . and C. E. Freeman . . . With an introduction by Hugh Last. pp. 160. *Oxford,* 1923. 8°. [*Clarendon Series of Latin and Greek Authors.*] W.P. **6801/11.**

—— The Shorter Caesar—Civil War . . . Arranged and edited for the use of schools by T. G. Wells. pp. xviii. 159. *London,* 1928. 8°. [*Bell's Shorter Classics.*] W.P. **6418/6.**

Appendix.

This section contains references to works which deal primarily with the text. References to works which deal primarily with historical questions are entered below under Appendix.—Campaigns.

—— *See* Barwick (C.) Caesars Bellum civile. Tendenz Abfassungszeit und Stil. 1951. 8°. [*Berichte über di Verhandlungen der Sächsischen Akademie der Wissenschaften.* Phil.-hist. Klasse. Bd. 99. Hft. 1.] Ac. **700/2**

—— *See* Elberling (C. W.) Observationes criticæ ad Caii Iulii Cæsaris commentarios de bello civili. 1828. 8°. **803.** f. **11**

—— *See* Gloede (H.) Caesars historische Glaubwürdigkeit in den Commentarien vom Bürgerkrieg. 1871. 8°. **9040.** f. **26. (8.)**

—— *See* Goeler (A. von) *Baron.* Bürgerkrieg zwischen Cäsar und Pompeius . . . Nach Cäsars bell. civ. lib. i. bearbeitet, *etc.* 1861. 8°. **9040.** e. **3.**

—— *See* Goeler (A. von) *Baron.* Die Kämpfe bei Dyrrhachium und Pharsalus . . . Eine kriegswissenschaftliche und philologische Forschung nach Cäsars drittem Buche des Bürgerkriegs, *etc.* 1854. 8°. **9040.** f. **9.**

—— *See* Hefner-Alteneck (J. H. von) Geographie zu C. Julius Caesar's Commentarien de bello civili, *etc.* 1836. 8°. **803.** f. **12.**

—— *See* Lightfoot (George C.) Students' Aids to the Study of the Classics, *etc.* (Caesar: Civil War, book i.) 1937, *etc.* 8°. **011313.aaa.15/5.**

—— *See* Loritus (H.) *Glareanus.* In C. Iulii Cæsaris commentariorum de bello ciuili librũ i(—librum vi) . . . annotationes. 1544. 8°. [*Eutropii epitome belli gallici, etc.*] **803.** b. **17.**

—— *See* Mattirolo (O.) A quale pianta corrisponde la " Chara " ricordata da Giulio Cesare nei commentari " de bello civili," lib. iii, xlviii. 1939. 8°. [*Memorie della R. Accademia Nazionale dei Lincei.* Classe di scienze fisiche, mathematiche e naturali. ser. 6. vol. 7. fasc. 7.] Ac. **102/11.**

—— *See* Schneider (T. H.) Loci Caesaris de bello civili commentariorum nonnulli explicati et emendati. [1859.] 8°. **9040.** ccc. **15.**

—— Caesar. Civil War Book iii. A vocabulary and test papers, *etc.* pp. 26. *London,* [1909.] 8°. [*University Tutorial Series.*] **12205.** e. **170**

—— Quaestio habetur, num Caesar bellum civile scripserit. [By Heinrich Mosmer.] pp. 8. *Culmbach,* [1865.] 8°. **11312.** c. **10.**

DE BELLO GALLICO.

Latin.

—— *Begin.* [fol. 1 *recto:*] [G]ay Iuly cesaris dictatoris exordia. Vt pleraq; mortaliũ fragilia, *etc.* [The life of Caesar, from the " De viris illustribus " of Francesco Petrarca.] [fol. 83 *recto:*] [G]Allia est omnis diuisa in partes tres, *etc.* [fol. 144 *recto:*] Suprascriptos .vij. libros de bello gallico composuit ipse cesar. Sequentem autẽ. Iulius celsus cesaris familiaris. [fol. 153 *recto:*] Finiunt feliciter libri cõmentarioꝝ Iulij cesaris de bello gallico. lxxiii. [fol. 154 *verso:*] Tabula siue registrũ, *etc.* G.L. [*Conrad Fyner: Esslingen,*] 1473. fol. C. **2.** c. **8.**
156 *leaves, the last three blank. Without signatures.* 38 *lines to a page. Without the blank leaves.*

—— [Another copy.] G. **9160.**
Without the blank leaves.

—— *Begin.* [fol. 1 *recto:*] Liber primus. G. iulii Cęsaris commentariorum De bello gallico liber primus. [fol. 38 *recto:*] Liber septimus. *End.* [fol. 50 *verso:*] his rebus litteris Cęsaris cognitis romę dierum uiginti supplicatio redditur. G.L. *in officina ioannis burgiensis: burgis* mense aprili, 1491. fol. IB. **53296**
50 *leaves. Sig.* a–g⁶ h⁸. 41 *lines to a page. In quire* b *leaves* 3, 4 *are misbound between* 5 *and* 6.

—— C. Iulii Cæsaris commentariorum de bello Gallico lib. vii. Item A. Hirtii de eodem lib. viii. pp. 251. *I. Mayer: Dilingæ*, 1654. 8°. **586. b. 28.**

—— Caii Iulii Cæsaris commentarii de bello Gallico. Ad optimorum librorum fidem edidit et varietatem lectionis maxime memorabilem adiecit Carolus Guil. Elberling. (Incerti auctoris Auli Hirtii ut videtur commentariorum de bello Gallico liber octavus.) pp. x. 479. *Havniæ*, 1827. 8°. **586. c. 23.**

—— C. Julius Cæsar's Commentaries on the Gallic War; from the text of Oudendorp: with a selection of notes . . . To which are added examination questions . . . By E. H. Barker. pp. viii. 268. *Longman & Co.: [London,]* 1831. 12°. **1211. h. 17.**

—— Gaji Julii Cæsaris de bello Gallico commentariorum libri septem et octavus A. Hirtii. Recensuit et praefatus est Joannes Kofod Whitte. pp. xxxiii. 180. *Havniae*, 1844. 8°. **803. c. 18.**

—— Cæsar's Commentaries on the Gallic War; and the first book of the Greek paraphrase; with English notes, critical and explanatory, plans of battles, sieges, etc., and historical, geographical, and archæological indexes by Charles Anthon. pp. xvii. 498. *Harper & Bros.: New-York*, 1845. 12°. **803. b. 15.**

—— C. Iulii Cæsaris commentarii de bello Gallico. pp. iv. 231. *Edinburgh*, 1847. 8°. [*Chambers's Educational Course.* Classical section.] **012211.a.1/42.**

—— Cæsar's Commentaries on the Gallic War: and a specimen of the Greek paraphrase; with English notes . . . by Charles Anthon. Sixth edition, corrected and enlarged, with additional annotations by . . . G. B. Wheeler. pp. 508. *W. Tegg & Co.: London*, 1853. 12°. **1307. b. 10.**

—— A new edition. Revised, corrected and enlarged by the Rev. C. Hawkins. pp. xvi. 340. *Longman & Co.: London*, 1855. 8°. **1307. d. 16.**

—— C. Julii Cæsaris commentarii de bello Gallico . . . with notes and a geographical register . . . By Henry Young. [With the continuation ascribed to Hirtius.] pp. xv. 215. *John Weale: London*, 1854. 12°. **11306. b. 11.**

—— C. Julii Caesaris commentarii de bello Gallico. With notes by George Long. pp. xvi. 442. *Whittaker & Co.; George Bell: London*, 1853. 12°. [*Grammar School Classics.*] **11305. b. 10.**

—— C. Julii Caesaris commentarii de bello Gallico. Erklaert von Friedrich Kraner. Mit einer Karte von Gallien von H. Kiepert. Zweite Auflage. pp. vi. 377. *Berlin*, 1855. 8°. **11306. dd. 3. (1.)**

—— C. Julius Cæsar's Commentaries on the Gallic War. With English notes, critical and explanatory, a lexicon, indexes, etc. By Rev. J. A. Spencer, *etc.* pp. 408. *D. Appleton & Co.: New York*, 1857. 8°. **1308. c. 22.**

—— C. Julii Cæsaris commentarii de bello Gallico. pp. xvi. 240. *Edinburgh*, 1860. 8°. [*Chambers's Educational Course.* Classical section.] **012211.a.1/148.**
Previous edition 1847.

—— C. Julii Caesaris commentarii de bello Gallico. With notes, by George Long. Second edition. pp. xix. 482. *Whittaker & Co.; George Bell: London*, 1860. 12°. [*Grammar School Classics.*] **11305. b. 11.**
Previous edition 1853.

CAESAR (Caius Julius) [De Bello Gallico.—*Latin.*]

—— C. Julii Cæsaris commentarii de bello Gallico. Recognovit Geo. Long. pp. 187. *Deighton, Bell & soc.: Cambridge*, 1861. 8°. [*Cambridge Greek and Latin Texts.*] **11306. a. 5.**

—— C. Julii Cæsaris commentarii de bello Gallico. pp. x. 235. *J. H. & J. Parker: Oxonii*, 1862. 16°. **11304. b. 54.**

—— C. Julii Caesaris commentarii de bello Gallico. Libri i.–vii. From the text of Schneider, carefully revised, with . . . a vocabulary of all the words in the text . . . By A. K. Isbister. pp. v. 163. 90. *Longmans & Co.: London*, 1866. 12°. **9025. bb. 22.**

—— Cæsar's Commentaries on the Gallic War. With a vocabulary and notes. By Wm. Bingham. pp. 348. *E. H. Butler & Co.: Philadelphia*, 1871. 8°. **9039. c. 16.**

—— Caii Julii Cæsaris commentarii de bello Gallico. With explanatory notes, lexicon, map, indexes, etc. By George Stuart . . . Sixth edition. pp. viii. 345. *Eldredge & Brother: Philadelphia*, 1871. 8°. **9039. b. 18.**

—— The Commentaries of C. Julius Cæsar, the Gallic War, with the supplement of Hirtius. Edited by Charles E. Moberly, *etc.* 2 vol. *Oxford*, 1871, 77. 8°. [*Clarendon Press Series.*] **2320. d. 32. & f. 32.**

—— The First(—Seventh) Book of Cæsar's Gallic War. With a vocabulary. Edited by John T. White. 7 pt. *Longmans & Co.: London*, 1872–81. 16°. [*White's Grammar School Texts.*] **11306. aaa. 8.**

—— C. J. Cæsaris commentarii de bello Gallico. Édition classique, accompagnée de remarques et notes . . . par Ed. Feugère. pp. xvi. 198. *Paris*, [1873.] 8°. **9039. bb. 16.**

—— Gaji Julii Cæsaris de bello Gallico commentariorum libri septem et octavus A. Hirtii. Tertium recensuit Dr. Ioannes Kofod Whitte. pp. 180. *Hauniæ*, 1877. 8°. **1307. c. 25.**
Previous edition 1844.

—— C. Julii Cæsaris commentarii de bello Gallico libri septem. With introduction, examination questions . . . notes . . . maps . . . and a geographical index. Edited by Leonard Schmitz. pp. 336. *London & Glasgow*, 1878. 8°. [*Collins' School Series.*] **12204. c. 20/23.**

—— Gai Iuli Caesaris de bello Gallico commentariorum i. ii. (—octavus.) With English notes by A. G. Peskett. 6 pt. *Cambridge*, 1879, 78–85. 8°. [*Pitt Press Series.*] **2322. c. 2.**

—— Gai Iuli Caesaris de bello Gallico commentariorum i (–vii). Edited . . . by Arthur S. Walpole (ii, iii by W. G. Rutherford; iv by Clement Bryans; v, vi by C. Colbeck; vii by Rev. John Bond and Arthur S. Walpole) . . . With notes and vocabulary. 5 pt. *Macmillan & Co.: London*, 1879–89. 16°. [*Elementary Classics.*] **11305. bb. 5–10.**

—— The Commentaries of Caius Julius Caesar. The Gallic War. Based on Kraner's text. pp. 312. *Rivingtons: London*, 1881. 16°. **9041. a. 4.**

—— C. Iuli Caesaris Belli Gallici libri vii. Accessit A. Hirti liber octavus. Recensuit Alfred Holder. pp. vi. 396. *Freiburg i. B. & Tübingen*, 1882. 8°. **09039. cc. 27.**

—— C. Iulii Caesaris commentarii de bello Gallico. [With the continuation ascribed to Hirtius.] Scholarum in usum edidit Ignatius Prammer, *etc.* pp. xxx. 164. *Pague; Lipsiae*, 1883. 8°. [*Bibliotheca scriptorum graecorum et romanorum.*] **11305. bbb. 12. (1.)**

—— The Commentaries of C. Julius Caesar. The Gallic war, with the supplement of Hirtius. Edited by Charles E. Moberly. pp. xiv. 351. *Oxford*, 1884. 8°. [*Clarendon Press Series.*] **2320. d. 32*.**
Previous edition 1871, 77.

—— Commentaires . . . Guerre des Gaules. Nouvelle édition . . . avec une introduction, des notes, un appendice et une carte de la Gaule ancienne par M. Ch. Lebaigue. pp. xxiv. 311. *Paris*, 1887. 12°. **9039. b. 8.**

—— Gai Iuli Caesaris de bello Gallico commentarii. After the German of Kraner-Dittenberger. By Rev. John Bond . . . and A. S. Walpole. pp. lxxx. 419. *Macmillan & Co.: London*, 1887. 8°. **9040. a. 8.**

—— The Commentaries of C. Julius Caesar. The Gallic War. Edited by the Rev. Charles E. Moberly. 3 pt. *Oxford*, 1888–90. 8°. [*Clarendon Press Series.*] **2319. a. 3–5.**
Previous edition 1884.

—— C. Iulii Caesaris commentarii de bello Gallico. [With the continuation ascribed to Hirtius.] Edidit Ignatius Prammer. pp. 215. *Cassell: Londini; printed in Germany*, 1890. 8°. **9041. b. 18.**

—— C. Iulii Caesaris belli Gallici libri VII. A. Hirtii liber VIII. Recensuit, apparatu critico instruxit Henricus Meusel. pp. xii. 261. *Berolini*, 1894. 8°. **9040. gg. 4.**

—— Des C. Julius Cæsar gallischer Krieg. Herausgegeben von Dr. Franz Fügner. 3 pt. *Leipzig*, 1894. 8°. **9041. h. 10.**

—— Cæsar's Gallic War. Books I. and II. Edited by T. W. Haddon . . . and G. C. Harrison, *etc.* (Books III.–V., VI. and VII. Edited by M. T. Tatham.) 3 pt. *Edward Arnold: London*, [1894–97.] 8°. **9041. eee. 11.**

—— C. Iulii Caesaris commentarii de bello Gallico. Für den Schulgebrauch herausgegeben und erklärt von Dr. Karl Hamp . . . Mit . . . Plänen, *etc.* pp. viii. 259. *Bamberg*, 1895. 8°. **9039. dd. 17.**

—— Caesar. Gallic War. Book I (–VII). Edited, with introduction, notes, and a full Latin-English vocabulary, and map, by J. F. Davis. 7 pt. *Hachette & Co.: London*, 1897, 94–1903. 8°. **09039. bbb. 7.**

—— C. Iuli Caesaris Belli Gallici libri VII cum A. Hirti libro octavo. In usum scholarum iterum recognovit, adiecit Galliam antiquam tabula descriptam Bernardus Dinter. Editio stereotypa. pp. xvi. 253. *Lipsiae*, 1898. 8°. **9042. aa. 34. (1.)**

—— Caesar. De bello Gallico. Books I–VII. According to the text of Emanuel Hoffmann, Vienna, 1890. Edited with introduction and notes by St. George Stock. 2 vol. *Clarendon Press: Oxford*, 1898. 8°. **9041. h. 5.**

—— [Another copy.] **L.P.** **9043.aa.9.**

—— Gai Iuli Caesaris de bello Gallico commentarius secundus [*etc.*]. With English notes by A. G. Peskett. *University Press: Cambridge*, 1899– . 8°. [*Pitt Press Series.*] **2322. de. 96.**
Previous edition 1879, 78–85.

—— C. Iulii Caesaris de bello Gallico liber primus (secundus). Edited by A. C. Liddell. (Liber tertius by F. H. Colson and G. M. Gwyther.—Liber quartus by A. W. Upcott.—Liber quintus by Arthur Reynolds.—Liber sextus by J. T. Phillipson.—Liber septimus by S. E. Winbolt.) 7 pt. *London*, 1899–1910. 8°. [*Bell's Illustrated Classical Series.*] **11304.d.2–8.**

—— Caesar. The Gallic War. Book I(–VII). Edited b John Brown, *etc.* 7 pt. *London*, 1900–03. 8°. [*Blackie Latin Series.*] **11305. aaaa. 20/**

—— Cæsar—Gallic War. Books I., II., III. By J. Manis Hardwich. (Books IV., V. By St. J. Basil Wyn Willson.—Books VI., VII. By C. A. A. Dupontet.) 3 p *Edinburgh & London*, 1901, 1899, 1901. 8°. [*Blackwood Classical Texts.*] **11304. bb. 25/2, 4,**

—— Caesar's Commentaries on the Gallic War. With intr duction, notes, and vocabulary by Albert Harkness . . assisted by Charles H. Forbes. pp. 593. *America Book Co.: New York*, [1901.] 8°. **09039. d.**

—— C. Iuli Caesaris de bello Gallico libri VII. Caesar's Gal War. With introduction, notes, and vocabulary by J. Westcott. pp. lxxi. 226. 197. 93. *D. Appleton & Co New York*, 1902. 8°. [*Twentieth Century Series of Tex Books.*] **012201. h. 4/1**

—— Gai Iuli Caesaris de bello Gallico commentarii. Aft the German of Kraner-Dittenberger. By Rev. Joh Bond . . . and Rev. A. S. Walpole. pp. lxxx. 419. *Macmillan & Co.: London*, 1905. 8°. **09039. bbb. 1**
Previous edition 1887.

—— C. Iuli Caesaris de bello Gallico liber I(–VIII). Edited b W. H. D. Rouse. 8 pt. *London*, 1906, 07. 8°. [*Blackie Latin Texts.*] **11304. cc. 2/**

—— Gai Iuli Caesaris commentarii rerum in Gallia gestaru VII. Accedit Auli Hirti commentarius. Ex recensio T. Rice Holmes. pp. xi. 249. *P. H. L. Warne Londini*, 1914. 8°. [*Scriptorum classicorum bibliothe Riccardiana.* no. 15.] **C. 98. i. 3/**

—— C. Iuli Caesaris commentarii rerum in Gallia gestaru VII. A. Hirti commentarius VIII. Edited by T. Ri Holmes. pp. lxvi. 462. *Clarendon Press: Oxford*, 1914. 8 **9041. c. 2**

—— [Another edition of bk. 1–7.] (A vocabulary. Compile by George G. Loane. [Bound up with each part.]) 7 p *Oxford*, 1914. 8°. [*New Clarendon Press Series of Classic Authors.*] **011306.aa.1/1**

Latin and English.

—— Cæsar's Commentaries on the Gallic War. Boo I(–VII). With a literal interlinear translation . . . B T. J. Arnold. 5 pt. *London*, [1886–92.] 16°. [*Cornish Interlinear Keys.*] **11305. a. 2/**

—— Cæsar's Commentaries on the Gallic War. Construe . . . word for word. By . . . Dr. Giles. Second editio revised. 2 vol. *Cornish & Sons: London*, [1886.] 16 [*Key to the Classics.*] **11305. a. 6**

—— Caesar: the Gallic War. With an English translatio by H. J. Edwards. pp. xxii. 619. *William Heinemann London; Macmillan Co.: New York*, 1917. 8°. [*Loe Classical Library.*] **2282. d. 45**

Latin and French.

—— Commentaires . . . Guerre des Gaules. Traductio nouvelle, avec le texte, des notes, et un index. Par C Louandre. pp. xx. 476. *Paris*, 1860. 12°. **9040. c.**

—— Les Commentaires sur la Guerre des Gaules expliqué littéralement, traduits en français et annotés par Sommer. 2 vol. *Paris*, 1863, 65. 12°. [*Les Auteur latins expliqués.*] **11304. ccc.**

—— Commentaires . . . Guerre des Gaules, *etc.* *Paris* 1873. 12°. **9039. b. 1**
A reissue of the edition of 1860.

CAESAR (Caius Julius) [De Bello Gallico.]

—— **La Guerre des Gaules. Texte traduit et annoté par Maurice Rat. tom. 1. pp. vi. 325.** ***Paris,*** **1932. 8°. 9042. aa. 31.**

—— Guerre des Gaules . . . Texte établi et traduit par L. A. Constans. Quatrième édition revue et corrigée. 2 tom. *Paris*, 1947. 8°. [*Collection des Universités de France.*] **2319.** c. **44.**

Latin and Portuguese.

—— Commentarios de Caio Julio Cesar, traduzidos em portuguez por Francisco Sotero dos Reis, *etc.* [" De bello Gallico ", bk. 1–5, xxviii.] livr. 1–3. *San Luiz,* 1863, 64. 8°. **9039.** dd. **5.**
No more published.

English.

—— The eyght bookes of Caius Iulius Cæsar conteyning his martiall exploytes in the Realme of Gallia and the Countries bordering vppon the same translated oute of latin into English by Arthur Goldinge G. 𝕭.𝕷. ff. 272. *Imprinted by Willyam Seres: London,* 1565. 8°. **9039.** a. **19.**
With the translator's autograph on the titlepage.

—— [Another copy.] G. **9049.**

—— [Another edition.] 𝕭.𝕷. ff. 123. *Imprinted by Thomas Este: London,* 1590. 4°. C. **21.** b. **9.**

—— [Another copy.] **294.** e. **1.**

—— Obseruations, vpon the fiue first bookes of Cæsars Commentaries, setting fourth the practise of the art military, in the time of the Roman Empire. Wherein are handled all the chiefest points of their discipline, with the true reasons of euery part, together with such instructions as may be drawn from their proceedings, for the better direction of our moderne warres. By Clement Edmunds. (Obseruations vpon Cæsars Commentaries, *etc.* bk. 6, 7. —The Maner of our Moderne Training, or Tacticke Practise.) [With engravings.] 2 pt. pp. 199. 138. *Printed by Peter Short: London,* 1600, 04. fol. **C.114.g.2.**
The titlepage of pt. 2 *is engraved, and bears the imprint: Printed at London for Mathew Lownes.*

—— **[Another copy of the first part.] 197. e. 18.**

—— Cæsar's Commentaries on the Gallic War: new and literal translation . . . By Roscoe Mongan. pp. iv. 100. *M. W. Rooney: Dublin,* 1850. 8°. **1307.** c. **20.**

—— Cæsar's Commentaries on the Gallic War, complete, literally translated . . . by J. B. Owgan . . . and C. W. Bateman. pp. 213. *Dublin,* [1882.] 8°. [*Kelly's Classical Keys.* vol. 19.] **11305.** dd. **5.**

—— Cæsar's Gallic War. Books i–vii. Literally translated from the text of Hoffmann. By St. George Stock. pp. 145. *A. T. Shrimpton & Son: Oxford,* 1894. 8°. **9041.** f. **11.**

—— Caesar's Commentaries on the Gallic War. Translated into English by T. Rice Holmes. pp. xx. 297. *Macmillan & Co.: London,* 1908. 8°. **09039.** dd. **12.**

—— Caesar's Gallic War. Translated by the Rev. F. P. Long. pp. viii. 278. *Clarendon Press: Oxford,* 1911. 8°. **09039.** aaa. **4.**

—— Gallic War. Book i(–vii). A literal translation. 7 pt. *London,* [1935.] 8°. [*Brodie's Interleaved Classical Translations.*] W.P. **11526/1.**

CAESAR (Caius Julius) [De Bello Gallico.—*English.*]

—— Cæsar's Commentaries . . . on the Gallic War. Literally translated into English prose by Joseph B. Owgan [and C. W. Bateman]. pp. 213. *J. Cornish & Sons: London,* [1939.] 8°. [*Kelly's Keys to the Classics.*] **11305.** dd. **91.**
A reissue of the edition of 1882.

—— Gallic War. Book i(–vii). A literal translation. 7 pt. *James Brodie: London,* [c. 1950.] 8°. [*Brodie's Interleaved Classical Translations.*] W.P. **11526/25.**
A reissue of the edition of [1935], *without the blank pages.*

—— Caesar. The Conquest of Gaul. A new translation by S. A. Handford. pp. 283. *Penguin Books: Harmondsworth,* 1951. 8°. [*Penguin Classics.* no. L21.] W.P. **513/21.**

Czech.

—— G. Julia Caesara paměti o válce gallské. Přeložil S. K. Macháček. pp. xvi. 1–188. *v Praze,* 1872–[74]. 8°. [*Bibliotéka klassikův řeckých a římských.*] **11304.** c. **10.**

—— C. Julia Caesara zápisky o válce gallské. Přeložil P. Slavíček. [With the continuation ascribed to Hirtius.] pp. 230. *v Praze,* 1882. 8°. **9041.** b. **26.**

French.

—— [LEs commentaires de iulius cesar.] *End.* [fol. 113 *verso:*] La translation des cōmentaires iulius cesar sur le faict de la conqste du pays de gaule faicte ⁊ mise en francois . . . par frere Robert gaguin . . . Lan Mil. cccc. octante viii. [With woodcuts.] *Imprime par Anthoine verard* [*or rather, by Pierre Le Caron for Vérard*]: *Paris,* [1488.] fol. **166.** i. **22.**
114 *leaves, the last blank. Sig.* a–n⁸ o⁶ p⁴. *Double columns,* 37 *lines to a column. The year* 1488 *which is given as that of Gaguin's translation is really that of printing. Imperfect; wanting the first leaf and the blank last leaf.*

—— [Another edition.] Les oeuures Et briefues expositions de Julius cesar sur le faict des batailles de Gaule. 𝕲.𝕷. *Imprime par la veufue feu M. le Noir: Paris,* [1525?] 4°. **9039.** bbb. **17.**

—— Les Commentaires de Cesar des guerres de la Gaule. [With the continuation ascribed to Hirtius.] Mis en françois par Blaise de Vigenere: auec quelques annotations dessus. 2 pt. *Chez N. Chesneau & I. Poupy: Paris,* 1576. 4°. **587.** g. **5.**

—— La Guerre . . . dans les Gaules. [Translated with notes by — de Pecis.] 3 vol. **L.P.** *De l'Imprimerie Royale* [*Bodoni*]: *Parme,* 1786. 8°. **293.** h. **1–3.**

—— Guerre des Gaules, traduite des mémoires dits commentaires . . . Avec un grand nombre de notes . . . par Théophile Berlier. pp. xii. 400. *Paris,* 1825. 8°. **803.** f. **10.**

—— Guerre des Gaules. Traduction française par N. A. Dubois. pp. 228. *Paris,* 1863. 12°. **9039.** aa. **4.**

—— Guerre des Gaules. Traduction nouvelle [by Justin Bellanger], avec notes et un index géographique. pp. 437. *Paris,* 1892. 12°. **9041.** eee. **4.**

—— Les Commentaires de la Guerre Gallique. [Translated by Albertus Pighius in 1520 and illustrated by Godofredus Batavus.] Reproduits en fac-simile d'après le manuscrit original. 3 tom. 1894. 8°. *See* Paris.—*Société des Bibliophiles Français.* K.T.C. **28.** a. **3.**

German.

—— Der gallische Krieg. Verdeutscht und erläutert von Viktor Stegemann. Mit 9 Abbildungen und 14 Karten. pp. lxviii. 360. *Leipzig,* [1939.] 8°. **9041.** e. **7.**

CAESAR (Caius Julius) [De Bello Gallico.—*Greek.*

—— C. Julii Cæsaris commentariorum de bello Gallico interpretatio græca Maximi quæ fertur Planudis . . . Edidit et brevi annotatione critica instruxit Antonius Baumstark. pp. xxvi. 187. *Friburgi*, 1834. 8°. **9040.** dd. 9.

Italian.

—— Commentarii (della guerra Gallica) . . . tradocti in lingua Fiorentina per Dante Popoleschi. [Edited by Carlo Aldobrandi.] *Impressi p̄ I. Stephano di Carlo di Pavia: Firenze*, 1518. 4°. **293.** f. **27.**

—— La Guerra gallica. Tradotta e commentata da Francesco Arnaldi. Con note militari del generale Ottavio Zoppi. 2 vol. *Roma*, anno XVII [1938]. 8°. [*La Guerra e la milizia negli scrittori italiani d'ogni tempo.*] **8839.d.1/12.**

Polish.

—— Gaiusa Juliusza Cezara o woynie francuskiey, ksiąg siedmioro. Osme, przez . . . Aulusa Hircyusza Panze, przekładania Andrzeia Wargockiego. pp. 302. *w Warszawie*, 1803. 8°. [Mostowski (T.) *Wybór pisarzów polskich. Historya.*] **899.** b. **23.** (2.)

Selected and Single Books.

Latin.

—— Ex C. Julii Cæsaris commentariis de bello Gallico libri quinque. pp. 118. *L. Hansard: Londini; Pote & Williams: Etonæ*, 1806. 8°. **9039.** bbb. **6.**

—— C. Julii Cæsaris de bello Gallico commentariorum libri v, *etc.* pp. 175. *E. Williams: Etonæ*, 1829. 12°. **9040.** a. **27.**

—— C. Julii Cæsaris de bello Gallico commentariorum libri v, *etc.* pp. 175. *E. P. Williams: Etonæ*, 1839. 12°. **9040.** aa. **25.**

—— C. Julii Cæsaris de bello Gallico commentariorum libri VI. Editio nova. pp. xi. 184. *C. P. Williams: Etonæ*, 1845. 12°. **803.** c. **13.**

—— Cæsar's Commentaries [De bello Gallico], books I. to III. For the use of junior classes. With English notes by George Long, *etc.* pp. vi. 123. *Whittaker & Co.; George Bell: London*, 1857. 12°. [*Grammar School Classics.*] **11305.** b. **8.**

—— C. Julii Cæsaris commentariorum de bello Gallico libri IV . . . With notes . . . by the Rev. J. R. Major. pp. 100. *William Tegg: London*, [1861.] 8°. **9040.** b. **10.**

—— Cæsar's Gallic War. The first six books . . . with a synopsis of each book, and notes in English by W. G. Cookesley, *etc.* pp. 257. *E. P. Williams: Eton*, 1861. 12°. **9040.** b. **11.**

—— Cæsar de bello Gallico. Cæsar's commentaries, books I.–III. With short English notes, for the use of schools. pp. ix. 83. *J. H. & J. Parker: Oxford*, 1861. 16°. **11304.** b. **39.**

—— C. Julii Cæsaris commentarii de bello Gallico. Libri I–V. From the text of Schneider, carefully revised; with various readings . . . notes . . . and . . . a lexicon of all the words in the text . . . By A. K. Isbister. pp. xxxii. 176. *Longman & Co.: London*, 1863. 12°. **9040.** c. **26.**

—— Second edition, enlarged, *etc.* pp. xlix. 176. *Longman & Co.: London*, 1864. 12°. **9040.** bbb. **23.**

CAESAR (Caius Julius) [De Bello Gallico.—Select and Single Books.—*Latin.*]

—— First Book (Second and Third Books) of Cæsar's Co[mmentaries] on the Gallic War. With notes and vocabula[ry] . . . intended for the use of schools . . . By Dr. Ken[nedy]. 2 vol. *Longman & Co.: London*, 1864, 65. 12°. **9040.** a. [...]

—— First Book of Cæsar's Commentaries on the Gal[lic] War. With notes and vocabulary . . . By Dr. Ken[nedy]. Second edition . . . revised, *etc.* pp. 66. *Longm[an] & Co.: London*, 1864. 12°. **9040.** a. [...]

—— The First Book of Cæsar's Gallic War. With a vocab[u]lary, and a series of easy reading lessons for beginn[ers] . . . By A. K. Isbister. pp. xlix. 49. *Longman & C[o.]: London*, 1865. 12°. **9039.** bb. [...]

—— Caesar's Commentaries, books I to III . . . With E[ng]lish notes by George Long . . . A new edition. pp. vii. 133. *Whittaker & Co.; George Bell: Lond[on]*, 1868. 8°. [*Grammar School Classics.*] **11305.** b. [...]
Previous edition 1857.

—— Selections from Cæsar, comprising the first, second, a[nd] extracts from the fourth, fifth, and sixth books of t[he] Gallic War, *etc.* pp. 184. 1869. 8°. *See* Edinburgh.—*Scottish School-Book Association.* **9039.** c. [...]

—— C. Julii Caesaris de bello Gallico. Lib. V. and VI. Wi[th] copious notes. Edited by J. S. Laurie. pp. 96. *Cent[ral] School Depôt: London*, [1877.] 12°. [*Laurie's La[tin] Course.*] **12199.** ccc. **1**[...]

—— Cæsar de bello Gallico. Books I. to III. . . . Edited [by] J. H. Merryweather . . . and C. C. Tancock. pp. iv. 2[...] *Rivingtons: London*, 1879. 8°. **9041.** aaa. [...]

—— C. Julii Cæsaris commentariorum de bello Gallico lib[er] primus(—sextus). With notes . . . by E. Forbes Lankest[er] (Herbert Bendall). 6 pt. *London*, 1880. 16°. [*Allma[n's] Classics.*] **11305.** aaa. **17.** ([...]

—— The First Book of Cæsar's Gallic War. Text on[ly]. pp. 42. *Longmans & Co.: London*, 1881. 16°. [*Whit[e's] Grammar School Texts.*] **11306.** aaa. **8**[...]
A reissue of part of the complete edition of 1872.

—— C. Julii Caesaris commentarii de bello Gallico. Liber [I.] With notes . . . and a life of the author, by Pierce Ega[n] (Liber II. With notes by A. C. Maybury.) 2 pt. *Baillière & Co.: London*, 1882. 12°. [*Aids to the Classic[s.]*] **11305.** aaaa. [...]

—— Cæsar's Gallic War. First book, with vocabulary a[nd] notes. By W. M'Dowall . . . New edition. pp. 35. 7[...] *Oliver & Boyd: Edinburgh*, 1882. 8°. **9041.** aaa. **2**[...]

—— The First Book of Cæsar's Gallic War, with note[s]. pp. 68. *Longmans & Co.: London*, 1883. 16°. **9040.** aaa. **2**[...]

—— C. Julii Cæsaris commentarii de bello Gallico liber I . [...] Edited by Leonhard Schmitz. *William Collins, So[ns] & Co.: London & Glasgow*, [c. 1885.] 8°. [*Collins' Scho[ol] Series.*] **12204.** c. **20/23**[...]
A reissue of parts of the complete edition of 1878.

—— Caesar de bello Gallico. Books I–III. With prefac[e,] introductions, maps, plans . . . Edited by J. H. Merr[y]weather and C. C. Tancock. New edition. pp. iv. 234. *Rivingtons: London*, [1886.] 8°. **9040.** a. [...]
Previous edition 1879.

—— Cæsar's Commentaries. Books VI. and VII. . . . Wit[h] English notes by George Long. *Whittaker & Co.; G. Bell & Sons: London*, 1886. 8°. [*Grammar Scho[ol] Classics.*] **11305.** b. **2**[...]

—— Caesar de bello Gallico. Book I. With notes and vocabulary. pp. 60. *Edinburgh,* [1886.] 8°. [*Chambers's Educational Course.*] **012211.a.1/232.**

—— Caesar's Commentaries, Books I. to III . . . With English notes by George Long . . . A new edition. pp. vii. 133. *Whittaker & Co.; George Bell & Sons: London,* 1887. 8°. [*Grammar School Classics.*] **11305.** b. **9a.**
Previous edition 1868.

—— Caesar de bello Gallico. [Bk. 1–6. With notes and vocabularies.] 6 pt. [*Rivingtons: London,* 1887.] 8°. **9040.** aaa. **20.**

—— The First Book of Cæsar's Gallic War, with an introduction, notes, and a vocabulary. pp. 112. *George Gill & Sons: London,* [1887?] 8°. [*Oxford & Cambridge Classics.*] **12202.** df. **9/37.**

—— C. Julii Cæsaris de bello Gallico. Liber primus. Edited with introduction, notes, and maps by Alexander M. Bell. pp. viii. 124. *Williams & Norgate: London,* 1888 [1887]. 8°. **9039.** b. **7.**

—— The Seventh Book of Cæsar's Gallic War . . . By John T. White . . . New edition, sixth and seventh thousand. pp. viii. 254. *Longmans, Green & Co.: London,* 1888. 8°. [*White's Grammar School Texts.*] **11306.** aaa. **27.**
A reissue of part of the complete edition of 1872–81.

—— Caesar's Seventh Campaign in Gaul. B.C. 52. De bello Gallico lib. VII. Edited, with notes, excursus, and tables of idioms, by W. Cookworthy Compton . . . With illustrations from sketches by E. T. Compton, and maps. pp. xix. 138. *G. Bell & Sons: London,* 1889. 8°. **9041.** aaa. **34.**

—— Caesar. The Gallic War. Book I(—V). With maps, notes, vocabulary and exercises for translation. Edited by E. H. Couchman (II–V by M. J. F. Brackenbury). 5 pt. *Percival & Co.: London,* 1890, 91. 8°. **9040.** aa. **13.**

—— The Sixth Book of Cæsar's Gallic War; with introduction, notes, and vocabulary, by Roscoe Mongan. pp. 90. *G. Gill & Sons: London,* [1890.] 8°. [*Oxford & Cambridge Classics.*] **12202.** df. **9/5.**

—— Caesar. The Gallic War. Book I (II, IV, V) . . . Edited by E. H. Couchman (II, IV, V by M. J. F. Brackenbury). Second edition. 4 pt. *Percival & Co.: London,* 1892–95. 8°. **9040.** aa. **21.**
Previous edition 1890, 91.

—— Caesar de bello Gallico. Book I. Containing brief notes . . . Exercises . . . and vocabularies, by J. Brown. pp. 128. *Blackie & Son: London,* 1892. 8°. **9040.** aa. **16.**

—— Caesar, Book I., and English Sentences for Translation into Latin. With notes and vocabularies. [Edited by Thomas T. M'Lagan.] pp. 78. *London & Edinburgh,* 1892. 8°. [*Chambers's Educational Course.*] **012211.** a. **1/211*.**

—— The Gallic War . . . Book I(–VI). With introduction, notes, and appendices by John Brown, *etc.* 6 pt. *Blackie & Son: London,* 1893–97. 8°. **09039.** bbb. **22.**

—— Cæsar: Gallic War, book I. Edited by A. H. Allcroft . . . and F. G. Plaistowe. pp. xvi. 80. *W. B. Clive & Co.: London,* [1893.] 8°. [*Univ. Corr. Coll. Tutorial Series.*] **12205.** c. **99.**

—— Caesar's Bellum Gallicum, books II, III & IV, with introductory notices, notes, complete vocabulary . . . by John Henderson . . . and E. W. Hagarty. *Copp, Clark Co.: Toronto,* [1895.] 8°. **9040.** bbb. **27.**

—— Cæsar, De bello Gallico. Books II., III. and IV. With introduction, notes . . . and a complete vocabulary . . . By J. C. Robertson. pp. xxiii. 165. *W. J. Gage Co.: Toronto,* 1896. 8°. **9040.** b. **29.**

—— Caesar. The Gallic War. Book I(–VI) . . . Edited by E. H. Couchman (II–VI by M. J. F. Brackenbury) . . . New edition. 6 pt. *Rivington & Co.: London,* 1897–1900. 8°. **9041.** eee. **14.**
Previous edition 1892–95.

—— Cæsar de bello Gallico books I–III. With preface, introduction, maps, plans . . . and . . . notes . . . Edited by J. H. Merryweather . . . and C. C. Tancock . . . New and revised edition. pp. 234. *Longmans & Co.: London,* 1897. 8°. **9041.** eee. **16.**
Previous edition 1886.

—— Gai Iuli Caesaris de bello Gallico liber II. The War with the Belgae. Edited with notes and vocabulary for beginners by E. S. Shuckburgh. pp. xvii. 78. *Cambridge,* 1897. 8°. [*Pitt Press Series.*] **2322.** d. **44.**

—— The Second Book of Cæsar's Gallic War. Edited for the use of schools by W. C. Collar. pp. ix. 96. *Ginn & Co.: Boston & London,* 1897. 8°. **9041.** a. **14.**

—— Gai Iuli Caesaris de bello Gallico liber I (III–VII) . . . Edited with notes and vocabulary for beginners by E. S. Shuckburgh. 6 pt. *University Press: Cambridge,* 1899–1901. 8°. [*Cambridge Series for Schools.*] **012201.** e. **4/3.**

—— Caesar's Gallic War, book I. With notes, introduction, and vocabulary by J. W. Bartram. pp. 152. *London,* 1899. 8°. [*Longmans' Illustrated Classics.*] **11304.** bb. **23/1.**

—— C. Iuli Caesaris commentariorum de bello Gallico liber quartus (quintus [1–23]). *See* HENDERSON (John) *of Toronto,* and FLETCHER (J.) *M.A., LL.D.* Latin Reader, *etc.* 1900. 8°. **12932.** c. **57.**

—— C. Julii Caesaris commentarii de bello Gallico. Liber quartus (quintus [1–23]). *See* CARRUTHERS (Adam) and ROBERTSON (J. C.) The New Primary Latin Book, *etc.* 1900. 8°. **12935.** bbb. **5.**

—— Cæsar—Gallic War. Books IV., V. By St. J. Basil Wynne Willson. With imitative exercises for re-translation by W. L. Grant. pp. xxviii. 179. 31. *Toronto,* [1901.] 8°. [*Morang's Educational Series.*] **12200.** b. **32/1.**

—— C. Iulii Caesaris de bello Gallico commentariorum liber primus(—quintus). Edited with introduction, notes and vocabulary by A. S. Wilkins, *etc.* 3 pt. *London,* 1902, 03. 8°. [*Dent's Temple Series of Classical Texts.*] **11306.** bb. **49.** (1–3.)

—— C. Iuli Caesaris de bello Gallico libri IV. The first four books of Caesar's Gallic War. With introduction, notes, and vocabulary by J. H. Westcott. pp. lxx. 103. 139. 93. *D. Appleton & Co.: New York,* 1902. 8°. [*Twentieth Century Series of Text-Books.*] **012201.** h. **4/16.**

—— Preparatory Caesar. De bello Gallico, book II (III). By Frank Ritchie. 2 pt. *Longmans & Co.: London,* 1905, 07. 8°. **9039.** ccc. **25.**

CAESAR (Caius Julius) [De Bello Gallico.—Selected and Single Books.—*Latin.*]

—— Gallic War. Book vii. (The text . . . of the edition prepared by Dr. Shuckburgh.) pp. 67. *University Press: Cambridge*, 1906. 8°. **09039**. bbb. **13**.

—— Gallic War, book ii. (iii., iv. 20–v. 23, v., ch. 25–28 [or rather, 58], vi.) Edited by Ll. M. Penn. 5 pt. *W. B. Clive: London*, [1914, 12–14.] 8°. [*School Latin Classics.*] **12935.f.54/1.**

—— Caesar de bello Gallico, iv., v. By A. H. Allcroft . . . With an introduction by Ll. M. Penn. 3 pt. *W. B. Clive: London*, [1912.] 8°. [*University Tutorial Series.*] **12205**. c. **435**.

—— Gallic War. Book iv (v). Edited by E. S. Shuckburgh. (New edition.) 2 pt. *University Press: Cambridge*, 1912. 8°. **09039**. bbb. **17, 18**.

—— Caesar's Gallic War, books i & ii, edited with notes . . . by Ernst Riess and Arthur L. Janes. pp. 305. 56. *American Book Co.: New York*, [1914.] 8°. **09039**. d. **28**.

—— Gallic War. Book ii (iii, vi, vii). Edited by E. S. Shuckburgh. (New edition.) 4 pt. *Cambridge*, 1915. 8°. [*Cambridge Elementary Classics.*] W.P. **1788/7**.

—— Caesar's Belgian Campaign. [" De bello Gallico," bk. 2.] Edited, with introduction, notes and vocabulary, by S. E. Winbolt. pp. 107. *London*, 1915. 8°. [*Bell's Simplified Classics.*] **12204**. de. **12/10**.

—— Caesar in Britain . . . De bello Gallico commentarii quartus—xx–xxxviii—et quintus. Edited by T. Rice Holmes . . . With a vocabulary compiled by George G. Loane. pp. 160. *Oxford*, 1916. 8°. [*New Clarendon Press Series of Classical Authors.*] **011306.aa.1/3.**

—— Cæsar in Gaul [" De bello Gallico," bk. 1–4 and selections from bk. 5–7], and selections from the third book of the Civil War. With introduction, review of first-year syntax, grammar, prose composition, and vocabularies. By Benjamin L. D'Ooge . . . and Frederick C. Eastman. pp. xl. 460. 120. *Ginn & Co.: Boston*, [1917.] 8°. **09039**. b. 4.

—— Caesar's Gallic War Book v. Edited by R. C. Carrington. [With maps.] pp. viii. 157. *G. Bell & Sons: London*, 1939. 8°. [*Alpha Classics.*] **12213.de.4/10.**

—— C. Iuli Caesaris de Bello Gallico commentarius quintus. Edited with introduction, notes and vocabularies by H. E. Gould . . . and J. L. Whiteley. pp. xliii. 199. *Macmillan & Co.: London*, 1940. 8°. [*Modern School Classics.*] W.P. **6076/2**.

—— Caesar: De Bello Gallico, ii. Mairġréad ní Éiṁṫiġ . . . do ċuir i n-eagar. pp. xv. 248. Brún ⁊ Ó Nualláin: Áṫ Cliaṫ, 1940. 8°. **9042**. aa. **32**.

—— Caesar. From De Bello Gallico Book i, cc. 1–29. Edited with introductions, vocabularies, notes and composition exercises by W. J. Williams. pp. xi. 79. *Browne & Nolan: Dublin*, [1941.] 8°. [*New Secondary School Series.*] **12213.aa.6/3.**

—— C. Iuli Caesaris De bello gallico commentariorum liber ii Edited for the use of schools, with introduction and complete vocabulary, and with notes and exercises on chapters i–xxvii, by James J. Carey. [With a map.] pp xxiv. 131. *Dublin*, 1944. 8°. [*Gill's Elementary Classics.*] **11304.bbb.3/1.**

CAESAR (Caius Julius) [De Bello Gallico.—Select and Single Books.—*Latin.*]

—— Caesar: De Bello Gallico iv. Edited with notes a vocabulary by John Gallagher. pp. xliv. 163. *Dubl* 1945. 8°. [*Browne & Nolan's Latin Classics.*] W.P. **14100**

—— C. Iuli Caesaris commentariorum de bello Gallico li secundus. Edited with introduction, notes, and voca laries by H. E. Gould . . . and J. L. Whiteley. pp. xxxii. 126. *Macmillan & Co.: London*, 1947. [*Modern School Classics.*] W.P. **6076/**

—— C. Iuli Caesaris commentariorum de bello Galli Liber quartus. Edited . . . By H. E. Gould and J. Whiteley. pp. xxvii. 122. *Macmillan & Co.: Lond* 1952. 8°. [*Modern School Classics.*] W.P. **6076/**

—— Caesar: Gallic War. Books ii & iii. Edited by S. Handford, *etc.* pp. vii. 107. *Methuen & Co.: Lond* 1952. 8°. [*Methuen's Classical Texts.*] W.P. **336**

—— C. Juli Caesaris commentarium de bello Gallico. Li tertius. Edited with introduction, notes, and vocabul by H. E. Gould . . . and J. L. Whiteley. pp. xxxiii. 10 *Macmillan & Co.: London*, 1954. 8°. [*Modern Sc Classics.*] W.P. **6076/**

Latin and English.

—— Caii Julii Cæsaris commentariorum libri quinque prio The first five books of Cæsar's Commentaries, with analytical and interlineal translation . . . by Ja Hamilton. 2 pt. *Hamilton: London*, 1829. 12°. **1211**. g.

—— The Handy-Book to Cæsar, a manual for preparat for the military, civil-service . . . and other exami tions . . . With copious notes, a parsing praxis, (C. Julii Cæsaris commentariorum de bello Gallico li primus.) pp. 142. *Simpkin, Marshall & Co.: Lond* 1861. 8°. **9039**. cc.

—— The First Book of C. Julius Cæsar's Commentaries the Gallic War. With grammatical analysis, translati and explanatory notes. pp. viii. 231. *Simpk Marshall & Co.: London*, 1877. 8°. [*Analytical Se of Greek and Latin Classics.*] **11305**. d. **2**

—— Second edition. pp. viii. 231. *Simpk Marshall & Co.: London*, 1878. 8°. [*Analytical Se of Greek and Latin Classics.*] **11305**. d. **2**

—— The First Book of C. Julius Cæsar's Commentaries the Gallic War. With translation and notes, *etc.* pp. *Simpkin, Marshall & Co.: London*, 1884. 16°. [*La English Series of Classical Authors.*] **12216**. a.

—— Caii Julii Caesaris de bello Gallico commentariorum lil With a literal translation, a set of exercises . . . Alphonse Estoclet. pp. xxii. 139. *W. Stewart & C London*, 1884. 8°. [" *Practical Series.*"] **12204**. c

—— Caesar de bello Gallico, book i. With two translatio one phrase by phrase and literal, the other free, by J Hugh Hawley. pp. 151. *Relfe Bros.: London*, [1885.] **9040**. bb

—— C. Julii Caesaris commentarii de bello Gallico. Book & vi. With translation and notes . . . by A. C. M bury. pp. 113. *Baillière & Co.: London*, [1885.] [*Aids to the Classics.*] **11305**. aaaa

—— Cæsar de bello Gallico. Book iii. Interlinearly tr lated into English by J. A. Prout. pp. 24. " *Notes* ": *London*, 1887. 8°. [*Gibson's Interlinear Tr lations.* no. 7.] **11305**.

—— Cæsar: Gallic War, book i. Edited by A. H. Allc . . . and F. G. Plaistowe. 3 pt. *W. B. Clive & London*, [1893.] 8°. [*Univ. Corr. Coll. Tutorial Serie* **12205**. c.

AESAR (CAIUS JULIUS) [DE BELLO GALLICO.—SELECTED AND SINGLE BOOKS.]

— Caesar: Gallic War. Book II (III, V–VII). Edited by A. H. Allcroft . . . and W. F. Masom. [The translation of bk. 2 and 3 by A. A. Irwin Nesbitt.] 5 vol. *W. B. Clive & Co.: London,* [1896, 91–94.] 8°. [*Univ. Corr. Coll. Tutorial Series.*] **12205.** c. **295.**

— Caesar: Gallic War, book IV. Edited by A. H. Allcroft . . . and T. R. Mills. (A translation by A. A. Irwin Nesbitt.) 3 pt. *W. B. Clive & Co.: London,* [1899.] 8°. [*University Tutorial Series.*] **12205.** c. **421.**

English.

— Cæsar's Commentaries of the Gallic War, literally translated into English prose. [Bk. 1–4.] By Joseph B. Owgan. pp. 98. *Dublin,* 1858. 8°. [*Kelly's Series of Classical Keys.* vol. 18.] **1349.** a. **35.**

— A Literal Translation of Caesar: De bello Gallico. Books I.–IV. . . . By the Rev. T. A. Blyth. pp. 96. *A. T. Shrimpton & Son: Oxford,* 1883. 8°. **11306.** bbb. **17.**

— Cæsar de bello Gallico. Book III. pp. 27. *London,* [1883.] 8°. [*Moffatt's Interleaved Verbatim Translations.*] **11306.** b. **31.**

— Cæsar de bello Gallico, books IV. & V., literally translated, with notes, by J. W. Rundall. pp. 55. *J. Hall & Son: Cambridge,* 1884. 8°. **9040.** bb. **4.**

— Caesar: de bello Gallico V., VI. A translation. By A. A. Irwin Nesbitt. pp. 24. *W. B. Clive: London,* [1906.] 8°. [*University Tutorial Series.*] **12205.** e. **54.**

— Caesar's Commentaries on the War in Gaul. Books IV & V. Literally translated from the text in the Pitt Press Series by C. H. Prichard. pp. 53. *E. Johnson: Cambridge,* 1912. 8°. **09004.** aa. **3.** (4.)

Gaelic.

— De bello Gallico V. Ar n-a chur i nEagar fara gluais, nótaí, foclóir, &rl. i nGaedhilg don Athair Tomás Tóibín. pp. 127. *Oifig Díolta Foillseacháin Rialtais: Baile Atha Cliath,* 1934. 8°. **012933.** a. **102.**

German.

— [De bello Gallico, bk. 1.] *See* MUELINEN (H. F. von) Divico, *etc.* 1898, *etc.* 8°. **9039.** de. **12.**

SELECTIONS AND ABRIDGMENTS.

Latin.

— *Begin.* [fol. 1 *verso:* Ad Cesarem. Vt possem niueam tuam referre, *etc.* [fol. 2 *recto:*] Ad Xystum .iiii. Pont. max. Andree Brentii Patauini . . . epistola. [fol. 2 *verso:*] Andreę Brentii Patauini In. C. Iulii orationem prẹfatio ad quirites. [fol. 3 *recto:*] C. Iul. Cęsaris oratio Vesontione belgicę ad milites habita. [Compiled from Caesar De bello gallico i, 40, and Dion Cassius xxxviii, 36–46, by A. Brentius.] [*Bartholomaeus Guldinbeck: Rome,* 1481?] 4°. IA. **18193.**
10 *leaves. Without signatures.* 34 *lines to a page.*

— *Begin.* [fol. 1. *recto:*] Ad Cesarem. Vt possem niueam tuam referre, *etc.* [*ibid.* l. 12:] Ad Xystum quartum Pontificem maximum Andree Brentij Patauini . . . epistola . . . [fol. 1 *verso:*] Andree Brentij Patauini In. C. Iulij orõeȝ p̃fatio ad quirites. [*fol.* 2 *recto:*] G. Iul. Cesaris oratio Vesontione belgice ad milites habita. [Compiled from Caesar De Bello Gallico i, 40, and Dion Cassius xxxviii, 36–46, by A. Brentius.] G.L. [*Stephan Planck: Rome,* 1483?] 4°. IA. **18610.**
8 *leaves, without signatures.* 33 *lines to a page.*

CAESAR (CAIUS JULIUS) [DE BELLO GALLICO.—SELECTIONS AND ABRIDGMENTS.—*Latin.*]

—— Selectæ historiæ ex C. Julio Cæsare, Justino, et L. A. Floro. In usum Scholæ Wintoniensis. Editio altera et recognita. pp. 298. *J. Robbins: Wintoniæ,* 1814. 12°. **9039.** c. **7.**

—— [Selections from the "De Bello Gallico."] *See* TROGUS POMPEIUS. [*Latin.*] Select Sentences from Justin, Caesar, *etc.* 1828. 12°. **1211.** f. **30.**

—— Abridged Extracts from Cæsar's Commentaries, with notes and a copious index of words, phrases and proper names. pp. iv. 119. *Bell & Bradfute: Edinburgh,* 1839. 12°. **9039.** aaa. **14.**

—— A New Latin Reading-Book: consisting of short sentences, easy narrations and descriptions selected from Cæsar's Gallic War . . . With a dictionary. pp. viii. 135. *Taylor & Walton: London,* 1841. 12°. **12935.** b. **34.**

—— An Epitome of part of Cæsar's Commentaries, with an etymological vocabulary, a geographical outline, and a map of Cæsar's Gaul . . . By Edward Woodford . . . Second edition. pp. xxxvii. 216. *Maclachlan, Stewart & Co.: Edinburgh,* 1848. 16°. **803.** b. **24.**

—— Third edition. pp. lii. 219. *Maclachlan & Stewart: Edinburgh,* 1852. 12°. **9039.** aa. **8.**

—— Cæsar, for Beginners, with a classified vocabulary and copious notes. By Joseph Currie. pp. vi. 154. *R. Griffin & Co.: London & Glasgow,* 1854. 12°. **803.** b. **25.**

—— A New Latin Reading-Book . . . selected from Cæsar's Gallic War . . . Second edition, revised. pp. viii. 103. *Walton & Maberly: London,* 1855. 12°. **12933.** a. **15.**
Previous edition 1841.

—— Cæsar's Invasions of Britain. [Extracts from bk. 4, 5.] *See* ABBOTT (Edwin) *Head Master of the Philological School, London.* A Second Latin Book, *etc.* 1858. 12°. **12934.** a. **32.**

—— An Epitome of part of Cæsar's Commentaries . . . By Edward Woodford. Fourth edition. pp. lii. 219. *Maclachlan & Stewart: Edinburgh,* 1860. 8°. **9040.** a. **17.**
Previous edition 1852.

—— Cæsar. Select passages for the use of schools. With notes by the Rev. F. B. Butler. pp. iv. 54. *Seeley, Jackson & Halliday: London,* 1871. 16°. **12201.** cc. **4.**

—— Selections from Cæsar. The Gallic War. By G. L. Bennett. pp. xix. 154. *Rivingtons: London,* 1880. 8°. **9041.** aaa. **13.**

—— Cæsar. Scenes from the fifth and sixth books of the Gallic War. Edited . . . by C. Colbeck. pp. xxxi. 75. *Macmillan & Co.: London,* 1881. 16°. [*Elementary Classics.*] **11305.** bb. **11.**

—— An Epitome of part of Cæsar's Commentaries . . . by Edward Woodford . . . Thirteenth edition. pp. xlvii. 219. *MacLachlan & Stewart: Edinburgh,* 1882. 8°. **9043.** df. **4.**
Previous edition 1860.

—— Cæsar's Invasion of Britain. Adapted . . . by W. Welch . . . and C. G. Duffield . . . With notes, exercises and vocabularies. pp. xvii. 97. *Macmillan & Co.: London,* 1884. 16°. [*Elementary Classics.*] **11305.** bb. **13.**

—— Caesar's Invasion of Britain. Adapted . . . by W. Welch . . . and C. G. Duffield . . . New edition. pp. xvii. 97. *Macmillan & Co.: London,* 1886. 8°. [*Elementary Classics.*] **11305.** bb. **132.**

CAESAR (Caius Julius) [De Bello Gallico.—Selections and Abridgments.—*Latin.*]

—— Caesar's Helvetian War. Adapted . . . by W. Welch . . . and C. G. Duffield. With notes, exercises and vocabularies. pp. 95. *Macmillan & Co.: London,* 1887. 16°. [*Elementary Classics.*] **11305.** bb. **12.**

—— Selections from Cæsar. The Gallic War. By G. L. Bennett. pp. xix. 154. *Rivingtons: London,* 1887. 8°. **9040.** b. 2.

A reissue of the edition of 1880.

—— Selection from Caesar, *etc. See* Trogus Pompeius. [*Latin.*] Selecta ex Justino, *etc.* 1889. 8°. **11306.** c. **25.**

—— Caesar's Invasions of Britain. Gallic War, iv. 20–38.—v. 1–23. With introduction, notes, imitative exercises, &c. by J. Brown. pp. xix. 91. *Blackie & Son: London,* 1894. 8°. **9510.** aaa. **7.**

—— Caesar's Bellum Britannicum [bk. 4, ch. 20–38, 5, ch. 1–23], with introductory notices, notes . . . By John Henderson . . . and E. W. Hagarty. 2 pt. *Copp, Clark Co.: Toronto,* [1895.] 8°. **9040.** bbb. **26.**

—— Caesar, Bellum Britannicum, being book iv. chap. 20–38 and book v. chap. 1–23 of the Bellum Gallicum, with introduction, maps and illustrations . . . and a complete vocabulary to Caesar. By J. C. Robertson. *W. J. Gage Co.: Toronto,* 1895. 8°. **9039.** aaa. **36.**

—— The History of the Helvetian War. C. Iulius Caesar de bello Gallico i, 1–29. Edited with notes and vocabulary for beginners by E. S. Shuckburgh. pp. xx. 76. *Cambridge,* 1896. 8°. [*Pitt Press Series.*] **2322.** d. **39.**

—— Caesar: Gallic War, book i., chapters 1–29. Edited by A. H. Allcroft . . . and F. G. Plaistowe. pp. xvi. 60. *W. B. Clive: London,* [1896.] 8°. [*Preceptors' Series.*] **12202.** dh. **1/1.**

—— Selections from Caesar. *See* Nepos (C.) Selecta ex Cornelio Nepote . . . Caesare, *etc.* 1897. 8°. **11304.** c. **4.**

—— Introduction to Caesar. [The first thirty chapters of the "De bello Gallico" in a simplified form.] By M. L. Brittain. pp. 171. *American Book Co.: New York,* 1901. 8°. **9040.** d. 2.

—— Selections from Caesar. *See* Nepos (C.) Selecta ex Cornelio Nepote, *etc.* 1901. 8°. **11305.** d. **19.**

—— [Selections from the "De bello Gallico."] *See* Henderson (John) *of Toronto,* and Fletcher (J.) *M.A., LL.D.* Exercises in Latin Sight Translation, *etc.* [1901.] 8°. **12934.** bb. **52.**

—— First Steps in Caesar. The expeditions to Britain. De bello Gallico, iv., 20–36; and v., 8–23. By Frank Ritchie. pp. vi. 95. *Longmans & Co.: London,* 1903. 8°. **9041.** aa. **14.**

—— Caesar in Britain. [Extracts from bk. 4, 5.] Edited, with introduction and vocabulary, by J. F. Dobson. pp. 64. *London,* [1905.] 8°. [*Arnold's Latin Texts.*] **11305.** aaa. **18/1.**

—— Caesar: Gallic War, book v., ch. 8–23; book vi., ch. 11–28. Edited by A. H. Allcroft . . . and W. F. Masom. pp. xix. 45. *W. B. Clive: London,* [1906.] 8°. [*University Tutorial Series.*] **12205.** e. **63.**

—— Caesar and Vergil for Junior Matriculation. Caesar: De bello Gallico, iv, 20–38; v, 1–23. Vergil: Aeneid, ii, 1–505. Edited, with introduction, notes, exercises and vocabularies by E. W. Hagarty. 2 pt. *Toronto,* 1906. 8°. [*Morang's Modern Text-Books.*] **012203.** g. **11/9.**

CAESAR (Caius Julius) [De Bello Gallico.—Selections and Abridgments.—*Latin.*]

—— Simplified Caesar. A first Latin reader and e[...] book. Arranged with notes, exercises and vocabul[...] W. F. Witton. pp. vi. 112. *Edward Arnold: L*[...] [1908.] 8°. **9039.**[...]

—— Caesar's Expeditions to Britain. De bello [...] iv. 20–36; v. 1–23. By William A. Edward, *etc.* pp. xxxix. 103. *Longmans & Co.: London,* 1909. **9041.**[...]

—— Caesar's Invasions of Britain. De bello Gallico, [...] c. xx–v, c. xxiii. Edited, with introduction and [...] by the Rev. A. W. Upcott . . . and Arthur Re[...] pp. viii. 119. xxxi. *London,* 1909. 8°. [*Bell's Ill*[...] *Classical Series.*] **1130**[...]

—— Matriculation Caesar. Bell. Gall., B. iv., chapter[...] and, Bell. Gall. B. v., chapters 1–23. By [...] Henderson . . . and R. A. Little. pp. iv. 226. *Copp, Clark Co.: Toronto,* [1909.] 8°. **09039**[...]

—— Caesar for Junior Matriculation. Caesar: d[...] Gallico, iv, 20–38; v, 1–23. Edited, with intro[...] notes, exercises and vocabularies by E. W. H[...] pp. iv. 122. *Toronto,* 1909. 8°. [*Morang's C*[...] *Series.* no. 1.] **012199.**[...]

—— Caesar in Britain: selections from the fourth a[...] books of Caesar's Gallic War. Edited, with hi[...] introduction, notes, vocabularies and English e[...] by W. D. Lowe. pp. 95. *Clarendon Press:* [...] 1910. 8°. **09039.** [...]

—— Caesar's Fifth Campaign. From De bello [...] book v. Edited, with introduction, notes and voc[...] by S. E. Winbolt. pp. xi. 90. *London,* 1911. 8°. [...] *Simplified Classics.*] **12204.** d[...]

—— Caesar and the Germans. Adapted from Caes[...] bello Gallico,' and edited, with introduction, [...] vocabulary, &c., by A. H. Davies, *etc.* pp. xl. 156. *Macmillan & Co.: London,* 1915. 16°. [*Elementa*[...] *sics.*] **11305.** [...]

—— Caesar's Wars with the Germans. Part of [...] "Gallic War." Adapted and edited, with intro[...] notes, exercises, and vocabularies, by W. Chalmer[...] *etc.* pp. xii. 85. *B. H. Blackwell: Oxford,* 1916. **9041**[...]

—— Caesar. Books iv, 20–38 and v. (Books vi a[...] of the Gallic War, partly in the original and p[...] translation. Edited by R. W. Livingstone . . . a[...] Freeman. 2 pt. *Clarendon Press: Oxford,* 19[...] [*Clarendon Series of Latin and Greek Authors.*] W.P.

—— Caesar. Books i to iii of the Gallic War. Partl[...] original and partly in translation. Edited by C. [...] pp. 160. *Oxford,* 1927. 8°. [*Clarendon Latin* [...] *Series.*] W.P. [...]

—— Caesar. The Invasion of Britain—De bello [...] iv. 20–v. 24. Edited by A. H. Allcroft . . . an[...] Mills. pp. 82. 32. *W. B. Clive: London,* [1927.] **01293**[...]

—— Caesar and Vercingetorix. Bellum Gallicu[...] Abridged and simplified text, with historical intr[...] . . . notes and vocabulary. By the Rev. J. [...] Norris. pp. xxv. 162. *University Press: Ca*[...] 1931. 8°. **01293**[...]

—— An Introduction to Caesar. De bello Gallic[...] Selected extracts . . . arranged, with test pape[...] cises and vocabulary, by C. F. C. Letts. 2 pt. *U*[...] *Press: Cambridge,* 1931, 32. 8°. **01293**[...]

ESAR (Caius Julius) [De Bello Gallico.—Selections and Abridgments.—*Latin.*]

— Graded Caesar. [Passages from bk. 3. With exercises and vocabulary.] By E. G. A. Atkinson . . . and G. E. J. Green, *etc.* pp. 94. *Longmans & Co.: London,* 1935. 8°. **012933. aa. 87.**

— An Introduction to Caesar. De bello Gallico I. Selected extracts graded and arranged . . . by C. F. C. Letts. (Second edition.) pp. vi. 88. *University Press: Cambridge,* 1937. 8°. [*Cambridge Elementary Classics.*] W.P. **1788/26.**
Previous edition 1931.

— Caesar's Invasions of Britain—Gallic War, book IV, ch. 20—book V, ch. 24. Edited by R. C. Carrington. pp. ix. 118. pl. XII. *G. Bell & Sons: London,* 1938. 8°. [*Alpha Classics.*] **12213.de.4/1.**

— Caesar's Gallic War. Books I–VII. Selected passages. Edited with introduction, notes, vocabulary and maps. By G. W. Irvine. pp. 203. *Juta & Co.: Cape Town & Johannesburg,* [1939.] 8°. **9042. aa. 30.**

— Caesar: De Bello Gallico I, 1–29. Helvetian War. Edited with notes and vocabulary by John Gallagher. pp. xliv. 197. *Dublin,* 1945. 8°. [*Browne and Nolan's Latin Classics.*] W.P. **14100/1.**

— The Rising of the Gauls. Being chapters one to thirty of Caesar's Gallic War Book VII with exercises on the constructions by Harry Broadbent. pp. ix. 90. *John Murray: London,* 1950. 8°. **012935. bb. 6.**

— The Helvetian War. Chapters 1–29 of the Commentarii de Bello Gallico, book I. Edited with introduction, notes and vocabulary by H. E. Gould . . . and J. L. Whiteley. pp. xxv. 118. *Macmillan & Co.: London,* 1953. 8°. [*Modern School Classics.*] W.P. **6076/25.**

Latin and English.

— Julius Cesar's Commentaryes. Newly translatyd owte of laten in to englyshe [by John Tiptoft, Earl of Worcester], as much as cōcernyth thys realm of England sumtyme callyd Brytayne: whych is the eldyst hystoryes of all other that can be found, that ever wrote of thys realme of England. B.L. pp. xix. [*William Rastell: London,*] 1530. fol. C. **32. m. 6.**

— Cæsar's Invasion of Britain: from the Commentaries. [Extracts from bk. 4 and 5.] With a literal interlinear translation on the plan recommended by Mr. Locke, critical explanatory notes, *etc.* 2 pt. *John Taylor: London,* 1829. 8°. **1211. g. 1. (1.)**

— Cæsar for Beginners. The Helvetic War. [Bk. 1, ch. 1–29.] 2 pt. *Taylor & Walton: London,* 1841. 12°. **1211. h. 34.**

— Cæsar's Helvetic War. [Extracts from bk. 1.] With interlinear translation, notes and queries . . . By T. H. Key. 2 pt. *James Walton: London,* 1872. 8°. **9039. b. 19.**

— Caesar: the Invasion of Britain. De bello Gallico, IV. 20–V. 23. Edited by A. H. Allcroft . . . and T. R. Mills. 3 pt. *W. B. Clive & Co.: London,* [1899.] 8°. [*University Tutorial Series.*] **12205. c. 404.**

— Caesar's Invasions of Britain. (Extracted from De bello Gallico, lib. IV, V.) Edited, with notes, exercises, and vocabulary by S. E. Winbolt. pp. vi. 87. *London,* 1911. 8°. [*Bell's Simplified Classics.* no. 1.] **12204. de. 12/2.**

English.

— Translations from Cæsar and Cicero for retranslation into Latin, *etc.* [With a key.] 2 pt. *Longmans & Co.: London,* 1886. 8°. **12935. df. 47.**

CAESAR (Caius Julius) [De Bello Gallico.—Selections and Abridgments.]

—— Extracts from Caesar. Translated into English for retranslation. Books I–IV. By R. E. Macnaghten . . . and H. V. Macnaghten. pp. 55. *Rivingtons: London,* 1887. 12°. **9040. aa. 8.**

—— The Invasion of Britain. De Bello Gallico, chaps. IV. 20—V. 24. pp. 24. *James Brodie: London,* [1936.] 8°. [*Brodie's Interleaved Classical Translations.*] W.P. **11526/64.**

French.

—— La Guerre des Suisses, traduite du I. livre des Commentaires . . . par Louys XIV. . . . Roy de France, *etc.* pp. 18. *Imprimerie Royale: Paris,* 1651. fol. **198. g. 5.**

—— Traduction d'une partie des Commentaires . . . par Henri IV. [Bk. 1, ch. 1–4.] *See* Boutrays (R.) Nouvelle histoire de Henri IV, *etc.* 1816. 12°. **284. b. 1.**

Appendix.

This section contains references to works which deal primarily with the text. References to works which deal primarily with historical questions are entered below under Appendix.—*Campaigns.*

—— *See* Apitz (J. I.) Schedæ criticæ in C. I. Cæsaris commentarios de bello Gallico. 1835. 8°. **803. e. 21.**

—— *See* Arbois de Jubainville (M. H. d') Les Noms gaulois chez César et Hirtius de bello Gallico, *etc.* 1891, *etc.* 12°. **12978. c. 19.**

—— *See* Beckmann (Franz) *Privatdozent an der Universität Berlin.* Geographie und Ethnographie in Caesars Bellum Gallicum. 1930. 8°. **9042. aaa. 7.**

—— *See* Boehm (F. C.) C. Iuli Caesaris libri VII de bello Gallico. Index verborum, *etc.* [1934.] 8°. **012933. b. 11.**

—— *See* Brancaccio (L.) Il Brancatio della vera disciplina et arte militare sopra i Comentari di Giulio Cesare [i.e. "De bello Gallico"], da lui ridotti in compendio per commodità de' soldati. 1582. fol. **536. l. 31. (3.)**

—— *See* Brancaccio (L.) Della nuoua disciplina & vera arte militare . . . secondo i precetti di Cesare [in his "De bello Gallico"], *etc.* 1585. fol. M.L. **e. 21.**

—— *See* Brinker (C.) Wie weit ist der Wortschatz in Caesars b. gall. I–VII . . . im lateinischen Lesebuch der unteren Klassen zu verwerten? *etc.* 1891. 4°. **12902. h. 17. (2.)**

—— *See* Bryans (Clement) Latin Prose Exercises based upon Cæsar's Gallic War, *etc.* 1884. 8°. **12933. bbb. 16.**

—— —— 1886. 8°. **12933. bbb. 32.**

—— *See* Colomb (G.) L'Énigme d'Alésia. Solution proposée d'après le livre VII des commentaires de César. 1922. 8°. **010169. ee. 40.**

—— *See* Creak (Albert) A Complete Dictionary to Caesar's Gallic War. 1870. 12°. **9039. c. 15.**

—— *See* Davis (John F.) *M.A.* A Complete Latin-English Vocabulary to Caesar's Gallic War book IV, *etc.* 1895. 8°. **12935. de. 51.**

—— *See* Davis (John F.) *M.A.* A Complete Latin-English Vocabulary to Caesar's Gallic War book V, *etc.* 1895. 8°. **12935. de. 52.**

—— *See* Davis (John F.) *M.A.* A Complete Latin-English Vocabulary to Caesar's Gallic War book VII, *etc.* 1894. 8°. **12934. cc. 36.**

—— *See* Devic (   ) *Abbé.* Étude sur les IIe et VIIIe livres des commentaires de César; pour servir à l'histoire des Bellovaques, des Ambianois et des Atrébates. 1865. 8°. **9039. h. 11.**

—— *See* Deville (J. A.) Considérations sur Alésia des commentaires de César. 1859. 8°. **7705. c. 31. (4.)**

—— *See* Eisen (E.) Der pädagogische Werth von C. Julius Caesar's Commentarien über den gallischen Krieg, *etc.* 1868. 8°. **11312. n. 1. (1.)**

—— *See* Fabia (P.) De orationibus quæ sunt in commentariis Cæsaris de bello Gallico thesim proponebat . . . P. Fabia. 1889. 8°. **11312. l. 43.**

—— *See* Fallue (L.) Conquête des Gaules. Analyse raisonné des commentaires de Jules César, *etc.* 1862. 8°. **9040. e. 20.**

—— *See* Feret (P. J.) Colonies des Celtes. Londres fille d'un bourg du continent. Étude d'après le texte de Jules César. 1864. 8°. **10347. c. 6. (4.)**

—— *See* Fiedler (F. A. M.) Geographie des transalpinischen Galliens nach C. Julius Caesars Commentarien de bello Gallico, *etc.* 1828. 8°. **10173. bbb. 28.**

—— *See* Flade (C. G.) Ad Memoriam Io. Christophori Richteri . . . pie riteque recolendam . . . invitat M. C. G. Flade. Præmittitur comparatio Julii Caesaris graeci cum latino. [On the Greek version of the "De bello Gallico."] 1815. 4°. **9039. e. 8.**

—— *See* Frigell (A.) Svar på en recension af mag. F. W. Häggström. [On A. Frigell's edition of the "De bello Gallico."] 1857. 12°. **9040. c. 2.**

—— *See* Froehlich (Franz) *Dr. phil.* Die Glaubwürdigkeit Caesars in seinem Bericht über den Feldzug gegen die Helvetier, *etc.* 1903. 4°. **9040. h. 29.**

—— *See* Graham (A.) *M.A.* A General Vocabulary to Caesar's Gallic War, *etc.* 1908. 8°. **12934. dd. 13.**

—— *See* Häggström (F. W.) Granskning af A. Frigells skrift: "Caesaris commentarii de bello Gallico med förklaringar och anmärkningar." 1857. 8°. **9040. e. 23. (3.)**

—— *See* Huber (P.) Die Glaubwürdigkeit Cäsars in seinem Bericht über den gallischen Krieg, *etc.* 1931. 8°. **9042. aaa. 9.**

—— *See* Hughes (Arthur A.) Via Caesaris. [Sentences, etc., adapted from the "De bello Gallico."] 1925. 8°. **012933. a. 24.**

—— *See* Jenner (William A.) and Wilson (H. E.) Caesar's First Campaign. A beginner's Latin book, *etc.* [1910.] 8°. **09039. bb. 15.**

—— *See* Koechly (A. H. T.) and Ruestow (F. W.) Einleitung zu C. Julius Cäsar's Commentarien über den gallischen Krieg. 1857. 8°. **9040. f. 26. (4.)**

—— *See* Lachanal (A.) Notes d'un chercheur sur l'Alésia de Vercingétorix décrite par César, *etc.* 1887. 12°. **10168. b. 43.**

—— *See* Lenormant (F.) Mémoire sur l'Alesia des commentaires de César, *etc.* 1860. 4°. [*Académie des Inscriptions et Belles-Lettres. Mémoires présentés par divers savants.* sér. 1. tom. 6. pt. 1.] **Ac.420/10.(1.)**

—— *See* Leutsch (C. C. von) *Baron.* Ueber die Belgen des Julius Cäsar, *etc.* 1844. 8°. **9039. e. 7.**

—— *See* Lightfoot (George C.) Students' Aids to the Stud of the Classics, *etc.* (Caesar: Gallic War, book I.-V. Invasion of Britain, De bello Gallico, IV. 20.-V. 24.) 1937, *etc.* 8°. **011313.aaa.15/1**

—— *See* Loane (George G.) Caesar's Gallic War. A vocab lary. 1915. 8°. **12933. bbb. 3**

—— *See* Loritus (H.) *Glareanus.* In C. Cæsaris comme tariorum de bello gallico libros . . . annotationes. 1544. 8°. [*Eutropii epitome belli gallici, etc.*] **863. b. 1**

—— *See* Maxa (R.) Die Rheinbrücke in Cæsar's Commen de B. G. IV., 17, *etc.* [1880.] 8°. **20012. eee.**

—— *See* Mitchell (George W.) Latin Composition based Caesar [i.e. on the "De bello Gallico"]. 1908. 8°. **12933. bb. 1**

—— *See* Paepke (W.) Präparation zu Cäsars Bellu Gallicum. 1894, *etc.* 8°. **12924. bbb. 5**

—— *See* Perrin (J. B.) *Ingénieur des Arts et Métiers.* Ur Solution au problème d'Alésia. [With reference to th "De bello Gallico," bk. 7.] 1938. 8°. **07707. eee. 4**

—— *See* Sanson (N.) Remarques sur la carte de l'ancien Gaule tirée des commentaires de César. 1649. 4°. **568. e. 16. (6**

—— *See* Sarrette (A.) Quelques pages des commentair de César . . . Études d'archéologie militaire, *etc.* (Ra port sur l'ouvrage de M. Sarrette. Par M. A. Delacroix 1863, *etc.* 8°. **9039. f.**

—— *See* Serrure (C. A.) Études sur la numismatiqu gauloise des commentaires de César, *etc.* 1885, *etc.* 8°. **7757. b.**

—— *See* Sihler (E. G.) A Complete Lexicon of the Latinit of Caesar's Gallic War. 1891. 8°. **12935. e. 1**

—— *See* Thomas (Hubertus) *Leodius.* De Tungris et Eburon bus, aliisque inferioris Germaniæ populis . . . con mentarius, utilis omnibus qui Cæsaris de bello Gallic historiam recte intelligere cupiunt. 1541. 8°. **1193. i.**

—— —— [1574.] fol. [*Schardius* (*S.*) *Historicum opus, et* tom. 1.] **9366. i. 1**

—— —— 1585. 8°. [*Pirckheimer* (*B.*) *Descriptio Ge maniæ.*] **574. c. 1**

—— —— 1673. fol. [*Schardius Redivivus.* tom. 1.] **9366. l.**

—— *See* Touflet du Mesnil (G.) Onomastique de la Gau Sceltane . . . Caesar. [A commentary on the "D bello Gallico."] 1884, *etc.* 8°. **2276. g. 1**

—— *See* Walkowski (Sz.) Słowniczek łacińsko-polsk G. Iulii Caesaris De bello gallico. Liber primus. 1946. 8°. **12936. b. 1**

—— *See* Wuras (H.) Helps to the Study of Caesar's Galli War. 1938. 12°. **12934. aa. 6**

—— *See* Wyss (E.) Stilistische Untersuchungen zur Darste lung von Ereignissen in Caesars bellum Gallicum, *etc.* 1930. 8°. **9042. bb. 2**

—— Caesar. De bello gallico, I. A vocabulary and te papers. By Tutors of University Correspondence Colleg pp. 24. *W. B. Clive & Co.: London,* [1893.] 8°. [*Tutori Series.*] **12205. c. 20**

—— Dissertation sur l'emplacement du champ de bataille ou César défit l'armée des Nervii et de leurs alliés, par M. de C..... Membre de l'Académie d'Amiens [i.e. Louis N. J. J. de Cayrol]. 1832. 8°. *See* C....., *M. de, Membre de l'Academie d'Amiens.* **803. f. 14.**

—— Examples of the Latin Rules. Taken out of Cæsar de bello Gallico book 1 and book 7. *Relfe Bros.: London,* [1880.] *s. sh.* 4°. **1881. c. 16. (93.)**

—— Jules César. [A description of Gaul, Germany and Britain, based on the "De bello Gallico."] *See* Charton (E.) Voyageurs anciens et modernes, *etc.* tom. 1. 1854, *etc.* 8°. **10027. g. 2.**

—— Nouns and Verbs of the first ten chapters of Cæsar's Gallic War. pp. 15. *Relfe Bros.: London,* [1895.] 16°. **12901. a. 36. (5.)**

—— Präparation zu Cäsars gallischem Kriege, *etc.* pp. 480. *Leipzig,* [1861.] 8°. [*Freund's Schüler-Bibliothek.*] **11306. aa. 4.**

SELECTIONS.

Latin.

—— C. Cæsaris Orationes. *See* Livius (T.) *Patavinus.* T. Liuii Patauini . . . Orationes . . . Quibus accesserunt orationes omnes, quæ iam extant apud C. Crispum Sallustium, Q. Curtium, *etc.* [1600?] 8°. **803. d. 26.**

—— Caesar. Episodes from the Gallic and the Civil Wars. With an introduction, notes, and vocabulary by Maurice W. Mather. pp. 549. *American Book Co.: New York,* [1905.] 8°. [*Morris and Morgan's Latin Series.*] **11304. c. 11/11.**

—— Second Year Latin for Sight Reading. Selections from Caesar and Nepos. By Arthur L. James. pp. 238. *American Book Co.: New York,* [1911.] 8°. **09039. bb. 17.**

—— Gallic and Civil Wars. Selected passages. Edited with introduction, notes, vocabulary and maps by G. W. Irvine . . . Second edition. pp. 261. *Juta & Co.: Cape Town & Johannesburg,* [1950.] 8°. **9043. e. 2.**

Latin and Italian.

—— Eleganze de' Commentari di Giulio Cesare, raccolte dal reuerendo M. Pre. F. Grossa. pp. 162. *Appresso G. Angelieri: Vinetia,* 1588. 8°. **293. d. 32.**

English.

—— [Selections.] *See* Rohan (H. de) *Duke de Rohan.* The Complete Captain, *etc.* 1640. 8°. **9039. b. 17.**

—— [Another edition.] An Abridgment of the Wars in Cæsars Commentaries, *etc. See* Rohan (H. de) *Duke de Rohan.* The Duke of Rohan's Manual, *etc.* 1708. 8°. **1398. a. 7.**

—— Gallic and Civil Wars. Selected passages. An English translation by G. W. Irvine. pp. 92. *Juta & Co.: Cape Town & Johannesburg,* [1950.] 8°. **9043. e. 1.**

French.

—— Harangues militaires extraictes des œuures de Iule Cesar, *etc. See* Belleforest (F. de) Harengues militaires, *etc.* 1572. fol. **M.L.tt.4.**

—— Abregé des guerres de Gaule (Abregé des guerres ciuiles) des commentaires de Cesar. *See* R., H. D. Le Parfaict Capitaine, *etc.* 1636. 4°. **C. 66. c. 7.**

—— [Another edition.] *See* Rohan (H. de) *Duke de Rohan.* Le Parfait Capitaine, *etc.* 1638. 4°. **534. e. 16.**

—— [Another edition.] *See* R., H. D. Le Parfaict Capitaine, *etc.* 1638. 12°. **9040. aaa. 12.**

—— [Another edition.] *See* Rohan (H. de) *Duke de Rohan.* Le Parfaict Capitaine, *etc.* 1644. 4°. **294. f. 5.**

—— Abregé des guerres des commentaires de Cesar. *See* Rohan (H. de) *Duke de Rohan.* Le Parfaict Capitaine, *etc.* 1648. 12°. **9039. a. 14.**

—— [Another edition.] *See* R., H. D. Le Parfait capitaine, *etc.* 1744. 12°. **9039. aa. 2.**

—— [Another edition.] *See* R., H. D. Le Parfait capitaine, *etc.* 1745. 8°. **8828. b. 50.**

DOUBTFUL OR SUPPOSITITIOUS WORKS.

—— Caesar at Alexandria. De bello Alexandrino 1–33. Edited with introduction, notes and vocabulary by J. C. Wykes. *Lat.* pp. xxiii. 94. *Macmillan & Co.: London,* 1951. 8°. [*Modern School Classics.*] W.P. **6076/22.**

—— Caesar at Alexandria. Chapters i–xxxiii.—A literal translation. pp. 16. *James Brodie: London,* [1953.] 8°. [*Brodie's Interleaved Classical Translations.*] W.P. **11526/62.**

—— Guerre d'Alexandrie. Texte établi et traduit par Jean Andrieu. [With plates, including maps.] pp. xciii. 103. *Paris,* 1954. 8°. [*Collection des Universités de France.*] **2319. c. 86.**

APPENDIX.

Biography.

—— *See* Abbott (Jacob) History of Julius Caesar. [1849.] 12°. **10602. aa. 9.**

—— *See* Alexander, *the Great, King of Macedon.* [*Appendix.*—ii.] Judgment on Alexander and Cæsar, *etc.* 1672. 12°. **832. c. 48.**

—— *See* Allulli (R.) Giulio Cesare. [1926.] 8°. **10607. de. 45.**

—— *See* B., J. B. Obseruations vpon the liues of Alexander, Caesar, Scipio. Newly Englished [from G. Botero's "I Prencipi"]. 1602. 8°. **10605. aa. 4.**

—— *See* Bailly (A.) Jules César. 1932. 8°. **10607. ee. 47.**

—— *See* Berg (E. van den) Jules César. 1881. 16°. **12206. c. 21.**

—— *See* Brandes (G. M. C.) Cajus Julius Cæsar. 1918. 8°. **10607. f. 3.**

—— *See* Bréan (A.) J. C. César dans la Gaule . . . Abrégé de la vie de César, *etc.* 1864. 8°. **9039. h. 22.**

—— *See* Buchan (John) *Baron Tweedsmuir.* Julius Caesar, *etc.* [With a portrait.] 1932. 8°. **10607. c. 17.**

—— —— [*Buchan (J.) Baron Tweedsmuir. Men and Deeds.*] 1935. 8°. **09004. de. 4.**

—— —— 1936. 8°. **10607. aa. 54.**

—— *See* Butenschoen (J. F.) Caesar, Cato und Friedrich von Preussen, *etc.* 1789. 8°. **9004. bb. 8.**

—— *See* Castello (C. de) *Begin.* [fol. 2 *recto*:] [C]Omenciase el primo libro Imperiale. Oue rratterimo [*sic*] de le conditione e modo de Iulio Cesaro, *etc.* 1488. 4°. **IA. 19490.**

— See Castille (H.) Parallèle entre César, Charlemagne, et Napoléon, *etc.* 1858. 8°. **8006. d. 12.**

— See Clarke (Samuel) *Minister of St. Bennet Fink.* The Life and Death of Julius Cæsar. 1665. 4°. **276. i. 14. (3.)**

— See Curtius Rufus (Q.) Incomincia la historia dAlexandro magno, *etc.* (La Comparatione di Caio Julio Cesare Imperadore ed Alexandro Magno da P. Candido ordinata.) 1478. fol. **IB. 27038.**

— — 1524. 8°. **294. a. 21.**

— — 1530. 8°. **294. a. 26.**

— — 1531. 8°. **9026. a. 12.**

— See Deutsch (Monroe E.) The Plot to Murder Caesar on the Bridge. 1916. 8°. [*University of California Publications in Classical Philology.* vol. 2. no. 14.] Ac. **2689. g/5.**

— See Duggan (Alfred) Julius Cæsar. [With a portrait.] 1955. 8°. W.P. d. **597/2.**

— See Dumas (Alexandre) *the Elder.* [*Les Grands Hommes en Robe de Chambre.*] Les Grands hommes en robe de chambre. César. 1857, *etc.* 8°. **10605. d. 10.**

— — 1866. 8°. **2334. c. 11.**

— See Dunan (R.) [La Vie ardente de Jules César.] The Love Life of Julius Caesar. 1930. 8°. **10607. d. 12.**

— See Dunnett ( ) Debate on the Character of Julius Cæsar, *etc.* 1882. 12°. **11602. bbb. 30. (1.)**

— See Enriquez de Zuñiga (J.) Historia de la vida del primer Cesar. 1633. 4°. **10606. c. 22.**

— See Fabricius (J. S.) C. Julius Cæsar nomismaticus, *etc.* 1678. 8°. **602. a. 16.**

— See Ferrero (G.) The Life of Cæsar, *etc.* [An abridged translation of the first two volumes of "Grandezza e decadenza di Roma."] 1933. 8°. **9042. c. 12.**

— See Floridus (F.) Francisci Floridi Sabini in M. Actii Plauti . . . calumniatores apologia . . . Eiusdem de C. Iulij Cæsaris præstantia libri iii, *etc.* 1540. fol. **C.81.i.9.**

— See Foschini (A.) Cesare. [With portraits.] 1936. 8°. **20010. cc. 58.**

— See Froude (James A.) Cæsar. A sketch. 1879. 8°. **10606. f. 3.**

— See Gastineau (B.) Les Femmes de Jules César, sa vie privée, *etc.* 1865. 12°. **10605. aaa. 37. (3.)**

— See Giovannetti (E.) La Religione di Cesare, *etc.* [With portraits.] 1937. 8°. **10607. ee. 59.**

— See Goddard (Edgar H.) and Cook (J.) *M.A.* Caesariana. An intermediate Latin reader. [A short life of Caesar compiled from various sources.] [1934.] 8°. **012933. a. 101.**

— See Goltz (H.) C. Julius Cæsar, *etc.* 1563. fol. **138. e. 6.**

— See Grendon (Felix) No Other Caesar. [A biography of Julius Caesar.] 1941. 8°. **10608. ccc. 12.**

— See Guarnieri (L.) Giulio Cesare, *etc.* [With a portrait.] 1936. 8°. **10608. d. 3.**

— See Hardinge (Hilary) Julius Caesar, *etc.* 1912. 8°. **12215.ee.1/20.**

— See Henriquez de Villegas (D.) Aula militar i, politicas ideas, deducidas de las acciones de C. Iul Cesar, *etc.* 1649. 8°. **8823. f. 1**

— See Jean, *de Tuim.* Li hystore de Julius Cesar, *etc.* 1881. 8°. **12403. ff.**

— See Klass (J.) Cicero und Caesar. Ein Beitrag z Aufhellung ihrer gegenseitigen Beziehungen. 1939. 8°. **09010. d. 1/35**

— See Lamartine de Prat (M. L. A. de) Vie de César. 1865. 8°. **10605. ee. 3**

— See Lepeletier de Saint-Fargeau (L. M.) *Cou* César, *etc.* 1865. 12°. **10605. aaa. 2**

— See Louvet de Couvray (A.) Les Hommes pro dentiels. Alexandre—César—Napoléon. 1865. 8°. **10604. bbbb. 1**

— See Malim (Herbert) Two Conquerors, Alexander a Cæsar. 1921. 8°. **10607. aaa.**

— See Meissner (A. G.) Leben des C. Julius Cäsar, *etc.* 1799, *etc.* 8°. **10605. df.**

— See Mess (A. von) Caesar, sein Leben, seine Zeit u seine Politik bis zur Begründung seiner Monarchie, *etc.* 1913. 8°. **07702. c. 29**

— See Montgon (A. de) Jules César, *etc.* 1933. 8°. **10607. aaaa.**

— [For editions of Napoleon iii.'s "Histoire de Ju César":] See Napoleon iii., *Emperor of the Frenc* [*Works.*]

— [For the account of the assassination of Caesar co tained in the fragmentary life of Augustus by Nicola Damascenus:] See Nicolaus, *Damascenus.*

— See Pearce (John W. E.) Caesar Imperator. An e mentary Latin reader, *etc.* 1909. 8°. **12935. ccc. 1**

— See Petrarca (F.) [*De Viris Illustribus.—Lati* Francisci Petrarchæ historia Julii Cæsaris, *etc.* 1827. 8 **609. e. 1**

— See Petrarca (F.) [*De Viris Illustribus.—Lati* Pétrarque. Vie de César. Reproduction phototypiq du manuscrit autographe, manuscrit latin 5784 de Bibliothèque nationale, *etc.* 1906. fol. MS. Facs. 8

— [For editions of Plutarch's life of Caesar:] See Plutarc [*Vitae Parallelae.*]

— See Pratt (Fletcher) Hail, Caesar! *etc.* 1938. 8°. **10608. c.**

— See Rodrigues de Almada (A.) O Perfeito herois na preferencia de Julio Cesar á Alexandre Magno. 1762. 4°. **12301. e. 35. (**

— See Rogberg (C. E. J.) Caesar och hans tidehvarf, e 1854. 8°. **10605. cc. 1**

— See Rosseeuw Saint-Hilaire (E. F. A.) Jules Cés *etc.* 1866. 8°. **10605. aaa.**

— See Rovani (G.) La Giovinezza di Giulio Cesare, e 1873. 8°. **10606. g.**

— See Russell (Ada) Julius Caesar, *etc.* 1915. 8°. **010603. c. 1**

— See Sada (C.) Cesare, *etc.* 1936. 8°. **20011. e.**

CAESAR (CAIUS JULIUS) [APPENDIX.—*Biography.*]

— *See* SALLUSTIUS CRISPUS (C.) [*Appendix.*] Cesariano. Incomēcia el libro extracto de Salustio Historiographo ⁊ Lucano sūmo poeta, *etc.* 1492. fol. IB. **23903.**

— *See* SCHIAPPALARIA (S. A.) La Vita di C. Iulio Cesare, *etc.* 1578. 4°. C. **80.** a. **10.**

— *See* SILVAGNI (U.) Giulio Cesare. 1930. 8°. **10607.** h. **25.**

— *See* SIMONE (G. de) G. Giulio Cesare e la caduta della Repubblica. 1902. 8°. **09004.** aa. **10.** (**5.**)

— *See* SOELTL (J. M. von) Cajus Julius Cäsar, *etc.* 1826. 8°. **1448.** d. **4.**

— *See* STRASBURGER (H.) Caesars Eintritt in die Geschichte. 1938. 8°. **10608.** cc. **2.**

— [For editions of Suetonius's life of Caesar:] *See* SUETONIUS TRANQUILLUS (C.)

— *See* THADDEUS (Victor) Julius Caesar & the Grandeur that was Rome, *etc.* 1928. 8°. **10607.** d. **5.**

— *See* WADDELL (William) Caesar's Character, *etc.* 1907. 8°. **10606.** l. **6.**

— *See* WALTER (Gérard) *Historian.* [César.] Caesar, *etc.* [With a portrait and a bibliography.] 1953. 8°. **10608.** ee. **31.**

— *See* WILLIAMS (John) *Archdeacon of Cardigan.* The Life of Julius Caesar. 1854. 8°. **10605.** a. **35.**

— *See* ZUMPT (A. W.) Aug. Wilh. Zumptii De dictatoris Caesaris die et anno natali commentatio. 1874. 8°. **10605.** g. **1.**

— Koe biokalafi. Jiuliasi Sisa. Alifaleti. Kolomibusi. (Koe biokalafi ʻo Keio Jiuliasi Sisa, koe Tikitato ʻo Loma.—Koe biokalafi ʻo Alifaleti, koe Tuʻi Haohaoa.—Koe biokalafi ʻo Kalisitofa Kolomibusi, koe Amilali; ʻaia naʻa ne ʻilo ki he Mama Foʻou.) pp. 164. *J. Walker & Co.: Lonitoni,* 1883. 8°. **010603.** a. **4.**

— I Fatti di Cesare; testo di lingua inedito del secolo XIV, pubblicato a cura di Luciano Banchi. pp. lxxvii. 388. *Bologna,* 1863. 8°. [*Collezione di opere inedite . . . pubblicata per cura della R. Commissione pe' testi di lingua nelle Provincie dell'Emilia.* vol. 6.] **12225.** g. **2.**

— Life of Julius Cæsar. pp. 192. *R.T.S.: London,* [1846.] 16°. **4420.f.9.(1.)**

— De schoone Historie van Julius Cæsar en de Romeynen, hoe sy dese Nederlanden eerst gewonnen en daer naer verloren hebben . . . Desen druk vermeerderd met de beschryvinge van den geheelen levens-loop van J. Cæsar. Als ook de korte beschrijvinge van de Nederlanden . . . getrokken uyt verscheyde oude historie-schrijvers. Van nieuws overzien en op veele plaetsen verbetert. pp. 77. *J. H. Heyliger: Antwerpen,* [1625?] 4°. **12410.** f. **27.** (**13.**)

— [Another edition.] pp. 77. *Gend,* [1750?] 4°. **12450.** d. **19.** (**2.**)

— [Another edition.] pp. 77. *Gend,* [1750?] 4°. **12450.** e. **4.**

— [Another edition.] pp. 77. *Gend,* [1750?] 4°. **12450.** e. **5.**

— [Another edition.] pp. 77. *Gend,* [1750?] 4°. **12450.** e. **6.**

— Vie de Jules César. (La Mort de César.) 2 pt. *Paris,* 1864, 67. 8°. **10605.** f. **32.**

CAESAR (CAIUS JULIUS) [APPENDIX.—]

Campaigns.

References to works which deal primarily with the text of the "De bello civili" and the "De bello Gallico" are entered above under DE BELLO CIVILI.—*Appendix, and* DE BELLO GALLICO.—*Appendix respectively.*

—— *See* AFRICAN WAR. César. Guerre d'Afrique. Texte établi et traduit par A. Bouvet. 1949. 8°. **2319.** d. **22.**

—— *See* APPACH (F. H.) Caius Julius Caesar's British Expeditions from Boulogne to the Bay of Apuldore, *etc.* 1868. 8°. **10358.** bbb. **31.**

—— *See* BAILLY (A.) Les Gaulois courageux. César en Belgique, *etc.* [1910.] 8°. **9415.** h. **5.**

—— *See* BELL (Thomas C.) Rutuparum reliquiæ . . . with remarks on Julius Caesar's landing-place in Britain. 1831. 4°. **7703.** f. **18.** (**2.**)

—— *See* BERNARD (H.) *of Montmorency.* Mœurs des Bohémiens, *etc.* (Jules César et Vercingétorix.) 1869. 8°. **886.** k. **9.**

—— —— 1869. 8°. **10126.** a. **24.**

—— *See* BLANCHO (A. M.) Guerre maritime de César contre les Vénètes, *etc.* 1899. 8°. **09004.** cc. **7.** (**3.**)

—— *See* C . . . . ., *M. de, Membre de l'Académie d'Amiens.* Dissertation sur l'emplacement du champ de bataille ou César défit l'armée des Nervii et de leurs alliés, *etc.* 1832. 8°. **803.** f. **14.**

—— *See* CADOT (C.) Note sur l'invasion des Helvètes dans les Gaules et la première campagne de Jules César. [1862.] 4°. **9039.** h. **21.**

—— *See* CAIGNART DE SAULCY (L. F. J.) Les Expéditions de César en Grande-Bretagne. 1860. 8°. **9040.** f. **7.**

—— *See* CAIGNART DE SAULCY (L. F. J.) Les Campagnes de Jules César dans les Gaules. Études d'archéologie militaire. 1862. 8°. **9040.** g. **9.**

—— *See* CHAPEL (T. A. F. A.) Jules César à Izernore. [On the topography of the siege of Alesia.] 1892. 8°. **9004.** dd. **4.** (**13.**)

—— *See* CHAPMAN (Henry S.) The Story of Dola, Julius Cæsar's landing place, *etc.* [1921.] 8°. **010352.** de. **38.**

—— *See* CHIFFLET (J. J.) Portus Iccius Iulii Cæsaris demonstratus, *etc.* 1626. 4°. **569.** d. **31.** (**1.**)

—— —— 1627. 4°. C. **77.** b. **26.**

—— *See* COHAUSEN (A. von) Cäsar's Rheinbrücken philologisch, militärisch und technisch untersucht. 1867. 8°. **9039.** g. **27.** (**1.**)

—— *See* CONSTANS (L. A.) Guide illustré des campagnes de César en Gaule, *etc.* 1929. 8°. **W.P.253/3.**

—— *See* CUCHERAT (F.) Alexia et les Aulerci-Brannovices au tribunal de vingt siècles et de J. César. 1863. 8°. **7708.** c. **34.** (**10.**)

—— *See* DEDERICH (A.) Julius Caesar am Rhein, *etc.* 1870. 8°. **9039.b.12.**

—— *See* DESJARDINS (A. E. E.) Alesia, septième campagne de Jules César . . . suivie d'un appendice renfermant des notes inédites écrites de la main de Napoléon Ier sur les commentaires de Jules César. 1859. 8°. **9040.** f. **11.**

—— *See* DODGE (Theodore A.) Great Captains. (Cæsar.) 1890, *etc.* 8°. **10600. f. 3.**

—— *See* DODGE (Theodore A.) Great Captains. A course of six lectures showing the influence on the art of war of the campaigns of Alexander, Cæsar, *etc.* 1889. 8°. **9009. i. 14.**

—— *See* DOMASZEWSKI (A. von) Die Phalangen Alexanders und Caesars Legionen. 1926. 8°. [*Sitzungsberichte der Heidelberger Akademie der Wissenschaften.* Phil.-hist. Klasse. Jahrg. 1925/26. Abh. 1.] Ac. **892/2.**

—— *See* EICHHEIM (M.) Cäsar's Feldzüge gegen die germanischen Belgier, *etc.* 1864. 8°. **9039. bbb. 20.**

—— *See* EICHHEIM (M.) Die Kämpfe der Helvetier und Sueben gegen C. J. Cäsar. Eine kritische Studie. 1876. 8°. **9305. b. 5.**

—— *See* EICHHEIM (M.) Die Kämpfe der Helvetier, Sueben u. Belgier gegen C. Julius Cäsar, *etc.* 1866. 8°. **9039. bbb. 31. (6.)**

—— *See* ESSELLEN (M. F.) Zur Frage, wo Julius Cäsar die beiden Rheinbrücken schlagen liess, *etc.* 1864. 8°. **9039. dd. 10.**

—— *See* FLEMING (L.) *Count.* De trajectu J. Cæsaris in Britanniam dissertatio, *etc.* [1697.] 8°. **1472. aa. 3.**

—— *See* FROEHLICH (Franz) *Dr. phil.* Das Kriegswesen Cäsars. 1889, *etc.* 8°. **9041. i. 10.**

—— *See* GANTIER (V.) La Conquête de la Belgique par Jules César. 1882. 8°. **9041. c. 38.**

—— *See* GOELER (A. von) *Baron.* Cäsar's Gallischer Krieg . . . eine kriegswissenschaftliche und philologische Forschung, *etc.* 1858. 8°. **9040. g. 7.**

—— *See* GOELER (A. von) *Baron.* Treffen bei Ruspina, nebst Beleuchtung einiger andern Stellen in Rüstow's Heerwesen und Kriegführen Cäsars. 1855. 8°. **1307. h. 20. (2.)**

—— *See* GRAZIOLI (F. S.) Il Genio militare di Cesare. 1937. 8°. [*Quaderni Augustei.* Studi italiani. no. 2.] Ac. **103. b/4. (1.)**

—— *See* GUILLEMOT (P.) Excursions archéologiques, *etc.* (Dissertation sur l'expédition de J. César contre les Helvètes et sur le lieu de leur défaite dans les montagnes éduennes.) 1861. 8°. **7702. bb. 12.**

—— *See* HAIGNERÉ (D.) Étude sur le Portus Itius de Jules César. Réfutation d'un mémoire de M. F. de Saulcy. 1862. 8°. **7702. c. 2. (9.)**

—— *See* HENRARD (P. J. J.) Jules César et les Éburons, *etc.* 1882. 8°. [*Académie Royale de Belgique. Mémoires couronnés, etc.* Collection in-8°. tom. 33.] Ac. **985/4.**

—— *See* HEUZEY (L.) Les Opérations militaires de Jules César, etudiées sur le terrain par la Mission de Macédoine, *etc.* 1886. 8°. **9040. h. 2.**

—— *See* HICKS (Hastings E.) Secret of Success in the Field. Précis of Cæsar's Despatches. 1903. 4°. **9039. g. 29.**

—— *See* HOCK (A.) Études sur quelques campagnes de Jules César dans la Gaule-Belgique, *etc.* 1897. 8°. **9041. m. 9.**

—— *See* HOLMES (Thomas R. E.) Ancient Britain and the Invasions of Julius Caesar. 1907. 8°. **2394. f. 2.**

—— *See* HOLMES (Thomas R. E.) Cæsar's Conquest of Gaul. 1899. 8°. **9041. h. 7.**

—— *See* HOLMES (Thomas R. E.) Caesar's Conquest c Gaul . . . Being part I. of the larger work on the sam subject. 1903. 8°. **9041. l. 5**

—— *See* HOLMES (Thomas R. E.) Caesar's Conquest o Gaul, *etc.* 1911. 8°. **9042.gg.4.**

—— *See* JAL (A.) La Flotte de César, *etc.* 1861. 12°. **7702. a. 16**

—— *See* JUDEICH (W.) Caesar im Orient, *etc.* 1885. 8°. **9039. g. 2**

—— *See* JUDSON (Harry P.) Cæsar's Army, *etc.* 1888. 8°. **8826. bb. 4**

—— *See* KAMPEN (A. von) Fifteen Maps illustrating Cæsar' Gallic War, *etc.* 1879. *obl.* 4°. Maps **26. b. 51**

—— *See* LA RAMÉE (P. de) Petri Rami . . . Liber d Cæsaris militia. 1559. 8°. **534. d. 38**

—— *See* LEWIN (Thomas) The Invasion of Britain by Juliu Caesar. 1859. 8°. **1326. e. 4**

—— —— 1862. 8°. **1326. d. 17**

—— *See* MAISSIAT (J.) Jules César en Gaule. 1865, *etc.* 8°. **10605. ee. 46**

—— *See* MARQUE (B.) Le Dernier oppidum gaulois assiég par César, *etc.* 1917. 8°. **9232. cc. 3**

—— *See* MATHIEU (P. P.) Vercingétorix et César à Gergovi chez les Arvernes, *etc.* 1862. 8°. **7708. aaa. 17**

—— *See* MAURER (Theodor) *of Mainz.* Noch einmal Juliu Cäsars Brücke über den Rhein. Vademecum für Herr A. Rheinhard. 1883. 8°. **7708. aaa. 45. (4.**

—— *See* MELLEVILLE (M.) Le Passage de l'Aisne par J César, l'assiette de son camp et la situation de Bibrax, *etc* 1864. 8°. **9039. e. 4**

—— *See* MEYER (Clemens F.) and KOCH (A.) Atlas z Caesars bellum gallicum, *etc.* 1879. 8°. **9166. bb. 8**

—— *See* NAPOLEON I., *Emperor of the French.* [*Works.* Précis des guerres de César, *etc.* 1836. 8°. **587. d. 28**

—— *See* NAPOLEON I., *Emperor of the French.* [*Works.* Uebersicht der Kriege Cäsars, *etc.* 1836. 8°. **M.L.aa.36.**

—— *See* OERTZEN (A. von) Die Unterwerfung Galliens durch Cäsar verglichen mit der Bezwingung Frankreichs durch die deutsche Armee im Feldzuge 1870/71. 1904. 8°. **09008. f. 10. (5.)**

—— *See* PECIS (de) Observations sur la campagne de Jules César en Espagne, *etc.* 1782. 8°. **803. f. 13.**

—— *See* PEIGNÉ-DELACOURT (A.) Étude nouvelle sur la campagne de J. César contre les Bellovaques, *etc.* 1869. 8°. **9039. dd. 16. (9.)**

—— *See* POQUET (A. E.) Jules César et son entrée dans la Gaule-Belgique. 1864. 8°. **10170. ccc. 14.**

—— *See* POSTE (Beale) Cæsar's Place of Landing in Britain. 1844. 8°. **10350. cc. 22. (2.)**

—— *See* QUINCHE (E.) Les Helvètes. Divico contre César *etc.* 1948. 8°. **9043. aa. 12**

—— *See* RENNELL (James) Concerning the Place where Julius Cæsar landed in Britain, *etc.* 1827. 4°. G. **13894. (5.)**

— See Rheinhard (A.) C. Jul. Caesar's Rhein-Brücke. Eine technisch-kritische Studie, *etc.* 1883. 8°. **7706**. c. **33**. (**8**.)

— See Ruestow (F. W.) Heerwesen und Kriegführung C. Julius Cäsars. 1855. 8°. **7702**. d. **28**.

— See Saint-Hypolite ( ) Recherches sur quelques points historiques relatif au siége de Bourges . . . exécuté par César, *etc.* 1842. 8°. **1443**. g. **13**. (**3**.)

— See Sandiford (R.) Le Azioni di Cesare sul mare, *etc.* 1938. 8°. [*Quaderni Augustei*. Studi italiani. no. 12.] Ac. **103**. b/**4**. (**1**.)

— See Schlossmann (A.) Die Kämpfe Julius Cäsars an der Aisne, *etc.* 1916. 8°. **9042**. bb. **3**.

— See Schlumberger (J.) Cäsar und Ariovist, *etc.* 1877. 8°. **9041**. c. **9**.

— See Sharpe (*Sir* Montagu) Bregant-Forda and the Hanweal. A paper on the passage of the army of Julius Cæsar across the Thames at Brentford, *etc.* 1904. 8°. **010349**. i. **33**.

— See Simeoni (G.) Cesar renouuellé. Par les obseruations militaires du S. G. Symeon. 1558. 8°. **534**. d. **32**.

— See Simeoni (G.) Liure premier de Caesar renouuellé par le S. G. Simeon, *etc.* (Liure second de Caesar renouuellé. Par F. de S. Thomas.) 1570. 8°. **586**. c. **10**.

— See Simon (Matth.) Die ältesten Nachrichten von den Bewohnern des linken Rheinufers. Julius Cäsar und seine Feldzüge in Gallien, *etc.* 1833, *etc.* 8° & fol. **7705**. aaaa. **14**. & **7703**. c. **26**.

— See Somner (William) Julii Cæsaris Portus Iccius illustratus, *etc.* 1694. 8°. **577**. e. **36**.

— See S . . . . t. L'Œuvre de Jacques Maissiat. Annibal et César en Gaule, *etc.* 1892. 8°. **9004**. dd. **5**. (**13**.)

— See Stoffel (E. G. H. C.) *Baron.* Guerre de César et d'Arioviste, *etc.* 1890. 4°. **9041**. dd. **9**.

— See Stoffel (E. G. H. C.) *Baron.* Histoire de Jules César. Guerre civile. 1887. 4° & fol. **9039**. l. **1**.

— See Surtees (Scott F.) Julius Cæsar: did he cross the Channel? 1866. 8°. **10360**. bb. **4**.

— See Surtees (Scott F.) Julius Cæsar: showing . . . that he never crossed the Channel; but sailed from Zeeland, and landed in Norfolk, *etc.* 1868. 12°. **10360**. bb. **5**.

— See Trollope (Anthony) The Commentaries of Cæsar. 1870. 8°. **11306**. bbb. **29**.

— See Vaccà Berlinghieri (L.) Examen des opérations et des travaux . . . de César au siège d'Alesia, *etc.* 1812. 8°. B. **509**. (**9**.)

— See Valentin-Smith (J. E.) Fouilles dans la vallée du Formans . . . Documents pour servir à l'histoire de la campagne de Jules César contre les Helvètes, *etc.* 1888. 8°. **9225**. i. **19**.

— See Veith (Georg) *k. und k. Hauptmann.* Der Feldzug von Dyrrhachium zwischen Caesar und Pompejus, *etc.* 1920. 8°. **9042**. d. **2**.

— See Veith (Georg) *k. und k. Hauptmann.* Geschichte der Feldzüge C. Julius Caesars, *etc.* 1906. 8°. **9039**. h. **18**.

— See Vine (Francis T.) Cæsar in Kent. The landing of Julius Cæsar and his battles with the ancient Britons, *etc.* 1886. 8°. **9505**. bb. **10**.

—— See Wainwright (John) Julius Caesar; did he cross the Channel? [by Scott F. Surtees] reviewed. 1869. 8°. **10360**. c. **5**.

—— See Zama (C.) Historia dos tres grandes Capitães da antiguidade. Alexandre, Annibal e Cesar. 1894. 8°. **10606**. i. **2**.

—— Alesia. Étude sur la septième campagne de César en Gaule. [By Henry Eugene Philip Louis, d'Orléans, Duke d'Aumale.] pp. viii. 245. *Paris,* 1859. 8°. **9040**. f. **10**.

—— [Another copy.] **800**. k. **27**.

—— Mélange de remarques, sur-tout sur César; et autres militaires anciens et modernes. Pour servir de continuation au Commentaires des commentaires de Turpin sur Montecuculi, et sur la Tactique de Guibert, par le général-major de W. [i.e. C. E. de Warnéry.] 1782. 8°. *See* W., de, *Général-Major.* **717**. c. **51**.

—— Le Parfaict Capitaine. Autrement, l'abregé des guerres de Gaule (abregé des guerres ciuiles) des Commentaires de Cesar. Auec quelques remarques sur icelles, *etc.* [The dedication signed: H. D. R., i.e. Henri, Duke de Rohan.] 1636. 4°. *See* R., H. D. C. **66**. c. **7**.

—— [Another edition.] 1638. 12°. *See* R., H. D. **9040**. aaa. **12**.

—— [Another edition.] 1744. 12°. *See* R., H. D. **9039**. aa. **2**.

—— [Another edition.] 1745. 8°. *See* R., H. D. **8828**. b. **50**.

Literary Criticism.

—— See Allen (Henry E.) Observationes aliquot in C. Julii Caesaris utriusque belli commentarios, *etc.* [Notes on the text.] 1874. 8°. **9039**. bb. **15**.

—— See Barwick (Carolus) Caesars Commentarii und das Corpus Caesarianum. 1938. 8°. [*Philologus.* Supplementbd. 31. Hft. 2.] P.P. **5043**.

—— See Bossuat (R.) Traductions françaises des Commentaires de César à la fin du xve siècle, *etc.* 1942. 8°. [*Bibliothèque d'humanisme et renaissance.* tom. 3.] **P.P.4331.ebg.**

—— See Crusius (G. C.) Vollständiges Wörterbuch zu den Werken des Julius Cäsar. 1838. 8°. **011313**. a. **16**.

—— See Cserép (J.) C. Julius Cæsar commentariusainak folytatásai és Asinius Pollio. 1906. 8°. [*Értekezések a nyelv- és széptudományi osztály köréből.* köt. 19. sz. 8.] Ac. **825**/**20**.

—— See Dernoscheck (P. O.) De elegantia Caesaris, sive de commentariorum de B. G. et de B. C. differentiis animadversiones, *etc.* 1903. 8°. **11313**. c. **4**. (**2**.)

—— See Ebeling (H.) Schulwörterbuch zu den Schriften des Caius Julius Caesar, *etc.* 1871. 8°. **12935**. bbb. **3**.

—— See Fischer (F. H. T.) Die Rectionslehre bei Caesar. 1854. 4°. [*Programm der Lateinischen Hauptschule zu Halle für das Schuljahr* 1853–1854.] **11312**. h. **13**.

—— See Forchhammer (J. N. G.) Quæstiones criticæ de vera commentarios de bellis civili, Alexandrino, Africano, Hispaniensi emendandi ratione, *etc.* 1852. 8°. **9040**. d. **1**.

—— See Frese (R. B. J.) Beiträge zur Beurteilung der Sprache Caesars. Mit besonderer Berücksichtigung des Bellum Civile, *etc.* 1900. 8°. **11313**. c. **4**. (**1**.)

—— *See* FROEHLICH (Franz) *Dr. phil.* Realistisches und Stilistisches zu Cäsar und dessen Fortsetzern, *etc.* 1887. 8°. **11312.** l. **38.** (4.)

—— *See* GAMBARELLIUS (A.) Oppositorum quae Augustinus Gambarellius . . . e Plauto, Terentio . . . Cæsare, & Cicerone collegit liber, *etc.* 1606. 4°. **12934.** g. **6.**

—— *See* GLUECK (C. W.) Die bei Caius Julius Caesar vorkommenden keltischen Namen in ihrer Echtheit festgestellt und erläutert. 1857. 8°. **12978.** e. **2.**

—— *See* GRONOVIUS (Joannes F.) *the Elder.* Joh. Fred. Gronovii . . . lectiones Plautinæ, quibus . . . Cæsar . . . aliique scriptores veteres . . . illustrantur, *etc.* 1740. 8°. **1000.** l. **5.**

—— *See* HODERMANN (M.) Unsere Armeesprache im Dienste der Caesar-Übersetzung. 1899. 8°. **012901.** l. **4.** (**11.**)

—— *See* KALINKA (E.) Cäsars und seiner Fortsetzer Schriften, 1898–1928. 1929. 8°. [*Jahresbericht über die Fortschritte der klassischen Altertumswissenschaft.* Bd. 224.] P.P. **1897.** f.

—— *See* KINDSCHER (F.) Francisci Kindscheri Quæstiones Cæsarianæ. 1864. 4°. **11312.** h. **49.**

—— *See* KINDSCHER (F.) Universitati litterariae Fridericiae Guilelmiae Berolinensi semisæcularibus idibus Octobribus a. MDCCCLX. pie laeteque gratulabundus F. Kindscher, *etc.* (Emendationes Caesarianae.) 1860. 4°. **836.** i. **19.** (4.)

—— *See* LANDGRAF (G.) Untersuchungen zu Caesar und seinen Fortsetzern, *etc.* 1888. 8°. **11312.** i. **57.**

—— *See* LEHMANN (A.) De verborum compositorum quae apud Sallustium, Caesarem, Tacitum leguntur cum dativo structura commentatio. [1863.] 8°. **8363.** c. **2.** (**6.**)

—— *See* MERGUET (P. A. H.) Lexikon zu den Schriften Cäsars, *etc.* 1884, *etc.* 8°. **2049.h.**

—— *See* MEUSEL (H.) Lexicon Caesarianum. 1887. 8°. **12935.** g. **2.**

—— *See* MUELLER (Wernerus) De Caesaris quod fertur Belli Africi recensione, *etc.* 1893. 8°. **9004.** m. **13.** (**2.**)

—— *See* NISARD (J. M. N. D.) Les Quatre grands historiens latins, *etc.* (César.) 1874. 12°. **11852.** bbb. **18.**

—— *See* NUTTING (Herbert C.) Caesar's Use of Past Tenses in Cum-Clauses. 1918. 8°. [*University of California Publications in Classical Philology.* vol. 5. no. 1.] Ac. **2689.** g/5.

—— *See* POETTER (H.) Untersuchungen zum Bellum Alexandrinum und Bellum Africanum. Stil und Verfasserfrage. 1932. 8°. **9042.** aaa. **10.**

—— *See* PREUSS (S.) Vollständiges Lexikon zu den pseudocäsarianischen Schriftwerken, *etc.* 1884. 8°. **12934.** dd. **5.**

—— *See* PROCKSCH (A.) Die consecutio temporum bei Cäsar, *etc.* 1874. 8°. **11312.** cc. **46.** (**9.**)

—— *See* RAMBAUD (M.) L'Art et la déformation historique dans les Commentaires de César. 1953. 8°. [*Annales de l'Université de Lyon.* sér. 3. fasc. 23.] Ac. **365.** (c.)

—— *See* SCALIGER (J. J.) Quædam loca in C. Julii Cæsaris commentariis discussa. 1636. fol. [*Historiæ Francorum scriptores.* tom. 1.] **805.** i. **12.**

—— *See* SCHLITTE (A. C. F.) De Gaio Julio Caesare grammatico, *etc.* [1865.] 8°. **8363.** f. **3.** (**23.**)

—— *See* SNELLMAN (W. J.) Die bei Caesar gebräuchlichen Stellungsformen eines adjektivischen Attributs und attributiven Genetivs als nähere Bestimmungen desselben Substantivs. 1920. 8°. [*Suomalaisen Tiedeakatemian toimituksia.* sarja B. nid. 11. no. 8.] Ac. **1094.** c

—— *See* STEELE (R. B.) Chiasmus in Sallust, Caesar, *etc.* 1891. 8°. **11312.** q. **6.** (**9.**

—— *See* URSINUS (F.) Fului Vrsini notæ . . . ad Cæsarem 1595. 8°. [*Fragmenta historicorum collecta ab Antonio Augustino.*] C. **76.** a. **1**

—— *See* VOGEL (W. S.) Zur Stellung von esse bei Caesar und Sallust, *etc.* 1937. 8°. **12933.** e. **33**

Politics.

—— *See* ADCOCK (Frank E.) From the Conference of Luca to the Rubicon . . . Caesar's Dictatorship. 1932, *etc.* 8°. [*Cambridge Ancient History.* vol. 9.] **2070.e–f.** & **09004.** de

—— *See* ALFÖLDI (A.) Studien über Caesars Monarchie 1953. 8°. [*Kungl. Humanistiska Vetenskapssamfundet Lund. Årsberättelse.* 1952/1953.] Ac. **1068**

—— *See* ANCHEMAN DE MARTIGNAC ( ) Révolution de l'état populaire en monarchique par le différend de César et de Pompée. 1679. 12°. **584.** a. **17**

—— *See* BARILLI FILOPANTI (Q.) Cesare al Rubicone, *etc.* 1866. 8°. **9039.** a. **13**

—— *See* BETTI (E.) Le Origine giuridiche e lo svolgimento politico del conflitto tra Giulio Cesare e il senato romano *etc.* 1915. 8°. **9042.** cc. **22**

—— *See* DENNIS (John) *the Critic.* Julius Cæsar acquitted and his Murderers condemned . . . Shewing that it was not Cæsar who destroy'd the Roman liberties, but the corruptions of the Romans themselves, *etc.* 1722. 8°. E. **2016.** (**1.**

—— *See* FOWLER (William W.) *Sub-Rector of Lincoln College Oxford.* Julius Cæsar and the Foundation of the Roman Imperial System. 1892. 8°. **10601.f.12.**

—— *See* GRENIER (A. S.) L'Opera di Cesare e di Augusto nella Gallia, *etc.* 1938. 8°. [*Quaderni Augustei.* Studi stranieri. no. 9.] Ac. **103.** b/4. (**2.**

—— *See* GUARINI (A.) Il Cesare, overo l'apologia di Cesare *etc.* 1632. 4°. **196.** b. **15**

—— *See* HARDY (Ernest G.) Some Problems in Roman History. Ten essays bearing on the administrative and legislative work of Julius Caesar. 1924. 8°. **9042.** b. **6**

—— *See* HOLMES (Thomas R. E.) The Roman Republic and the Founder of the Empire. 1923. 8°. **2382.** f. **7**

—— *See* MEYER (Eduard) *Professor der Geschichte an der Universität Berlin.* Caesars Monarchie und das Principat des Pompejus, *etc.* 1918. 8°. **09039.** dd. **22**

—— *See* OMAN (*Sir* Charles W. C.) *K.B.E.* Seven Roman Statesmen of the Later Republic. The Gracchi . . . Caesar, *etc.* 1902. 8°. **2402.** b. **2**

—— *See* PALLU DE LESSERT (A. C.) Les Colonies attribuées à César—coloniae Juliae—dans l'Afrique romaine. 1912. 8°. [*Mémoires de la Société Nationale des Antiquaires de France.* sér. 8. tom. 1.] Ac. **5331**

CAESAR (Caius Julius) [Appendix.—*Politics.*]

—— *See* Prideaux (Humphrey) *Dean of Norwich.* The Judgment of Dr. Prideaux in condemning the murder of Julius Cæsar . . . maintain'd, *etc.* 1721. 8°. **1093**. d. **55**.

—— *See* Ramée (D.) Le Grand perturbateur romain. César, *etc.* 1870. 8°. **1308**. g. **12**.

—— *See* Roos (A. G.) De Verleening van tribunicische bevoegheden aan Caesar en Augustus. 1941. 8°. [*Mededeclingen der Nederlandsche Akademie van Wetenschappen.* Afd. Letterkunde. Nieuwe reeks. dl. 4. no. 16.] Ac. **944**. (**2**.)

—— *See* Rosenthal (Ferdinand) Die Erlässe Cäsars und die Senatsconsulte im Josephus Alterth. xiv, 10 . . . untersucht. [1885?] 8°. **9004**. l. **2**. (**4**.)

—— *See* Roux (Georges) *Political Writer.* La Leçon de César. 1932. 8°. **10607**. aaa. **35**.

—— *See* Saalfeld (G. A. E. A.) C. Julius Cäsar. Sein Verfahren gegen die gallischen Stämme vom Standpunkte der Ethik und Politik, *etc.* 1881. 8°. **9041**. b. **20**.

—— *See* Seitz (C.) L'Œuvre politique de César jugée par les historiens de Rome au xixme siècle. 1889. 8°. **9041**. b. **36**.

—— *See* Smith (William) *of Exeter, U.S.* Some Remarks on the Assassination of Julius Cæsar. 1827. 8°. **10882**. d. **29**.

—— *See* Taylor (Lily R.) Party Politics in the Age of Caesar. 1949. 8°. [*Sather Classical Lectures.* vol. 22.] Ac. **2689**. g/**17**.

—— *See* Wiegandt (L.) C. Julius Caesar und die tribunizische Gewalt. 1890. 8°. **10604**. e. **16**. (**7**.)

—— An Enquiry into the Merit of Assassination: with a view to the character of Cæsar, and his designs on the Roman Republick. [By Aaron Hill.] pp. 99. *T. Cooper: London,* 1738. 8°. E. **2029**. (**3**.)

Miscellaneous.

—— *See* Bensemann (W.) Beiträge zur Caesarforschung. I. C. J. Caesars Unterfeldherren und seine Beurteilung derselben. 1896. 8°. **9039**. dd. **21**.

—— *See* Bibikov (I.) Юлій Цезарь въ исторіи и на сценѣ . . . съ 15-ью фотографіями. 1904. 8°. **10600**. ff. **20**. (**2**.)

—— *See* Boehringer (E.) Der Caesar von Acireale. [With portraits.] [1933.] 8°. **7876**. f. **38**.

—— *See* Cesano (S. L.) Le Monete di Cesare. 1950. 8°. [*Atti della Pontificia Accademia Romana di Archeologia.* ser. 3. Rendiconti. vol. 23/24.] Ac. **5236**.

—— *See* Geiger (C. A.) Der römische Kalender und seine Verbesserung durch Julius Caesar. 1936. 8°. **08560**. f. **16**.

—— *See* Grenier (A. S.) L'Opera di Cesare e di Augusto nella Gallia, *etc.* 1938. 8°. [*Quaderni Augustei.* Studi stranieri. no. 9.] Ac. **103**. b/**4**. (**2**.)

—— *See* Gundelfinger (F.) Caesar in der deutschen Literatur. 1904. 8°. [*Palaestra.* Bd. 33.] **12203**. ff. **1**/**33**.

—— *See* Gundolf (F.) *pseud.* Caesar. Geschichte seines Ruhms. 1925. 8°. **10607**. g. **16**.

—— *See* Gundolf (F.) *pseud.* [Caesar. Geschichte seines Ruhms.] The Mantle of Caesar, *etc.* [1929.] 8°. **10607**. dd. **5**.

CAESAR (Caius Julius) [Appendix.—*Miscellaneous.*]

—— *See* Gundolf (F.) *pseud.* Caesar im neunzehnten Jahrhundert. 1926. 8°. **10607**. e. **18**.

—— *See* Italy.—*Confederazione Nazionale Sindacati Fascisti Professionisti ed Artisti.* Celebrazioni di Romagna. Cesare-Dante, *etc.* 1933. 8°. **11856**. ff. **44**.

—— *See* Jordanus (H.) Henrici Jordani de suasoriis ad Caesarem senem de re publica inscriptis commentatio. 1868. 8°. **11312.c.44.(7.)**

—— *See* Lamont (Roscoe) The Roman Calendar and its Reformation by Julius Caesar, *etc.* [1920.] 8°. **08548**. f. **36**.

—— *See* Nocca (D.) Illustratio usus et nominis plantarum quæ in Julii Caesaris commentariis indigitantur. 1812. 4°. **448**. h. **28**.

—— *See* Palagi (B.) Giulio Cesare nella poesia drammatica italiana e straniera. [With a bibliography.] 1918. 8°. **011850**. k. **45**.

—— *See* Parodi (E. G.) Le Storie di Cesare nella letteratura italiana dei primi secoli. 1889. 8°. [*Studj di filologia romanza pubblicati da Ernesto Monaci.* vol. 4.] **12941**. n.

—— *See* Poulsen (F.) Billeder af Pompejus og Cæsar. 1935. 8°. [*Studier fra Sprog- og Oldtidsforskning.* no. 168.] Ac. **9877**/**2**.

—— *See* Saatmann (C.) Caesars Rheinbrücke, *etc.* 1938. 8°. [*Bonner Jahrbücher.* Hft. 143/44. Tl. 1.] Ac. **5453**.

—— *See* Sandiford (R.) Le Azioni di Cesare sul mare, *etc.* 1938. 8°. [*Quaderni Augustei.* Studi italiani. no. 12.] Ac. **103**. b/**4**. (**1**.)

—— *See* Scott (Frank J.) Portraits of Julius Caesar. The Scott Collection of casts exhibited under the auspices of the Classical Department of Harvard University, *etc.* 1904. 8°. **07808**. g. **23**. (**2**.)

—— *See* Scott (Frank J.) Portraitures of Julius Cæsar. A monograph. 1903. 8°. **10606**. h. **34**.

—— *See* Weimann (J. G.) J. G. Weimann . . . tractatus botanico-criticus de chara-Caesaris, cujus lib. iii. de bello civ. c. xlviii. meminit. Praemittitur laus Caesaris. 1769. 8°. B. **204**. (**4**.)

—— *See* Zumpt (A. W.) De imperatoris Augusti die natali fastisque ab dictatore Caesare emendatis, commentatio chronologica, *etc.* 1875. 8°. [*Jahrbücher für Philologie und Pädagogik.* Neue Folge der Supplemente. Bd. 7. Hft. 4.] P.P. **4986**.

—— Aut Cæsar, aut nihil! [A political pamphlet advocating German unity.] *Ger.* pp. 97. *Berlin,* 1862. 8°. **8072**. cc. **63**. (**7**.)

—— Les Avantures de Jules Cesar, et de Murcie, dans les Gaules, ou le Modele de l'amour parfait. [By P. de Lesconvel.] pp. 131. *Veuve C. Coignard: Paris,* 1695. 12°. **12513**. aaa. **3**.

—— Caius Julius Cæsar: a poem. By K. [1846.] 8°. *See* K. **11646**. dd. **13**. (**6**.)

—— Cesare in Egitto. Drama da rappresentarsi nel pubblico Teatro di Pesaro nell'autunno dell'anno 1729, *etc.* [By Giacomo Francesco Bussani.] pp. 56. *Pesaro,* 1729. 12°. **905**. l. **4**. (**4**.)

—— Les Commentaires de Cesar. [An edition of "L'Anti-Caquet de l'accouchée," a reply to the "Recueil general des Caquets de l'accouchée."] pp. 14. 1622. 8°. **1192**. f. **10**. (**5**.)

CAESAR (Caius Julius) [Appendix.—*Miscellaneous*.]

—— De Doodt van Julius Cezar. Treurspel. [Altered from M. A. Barbier's "La Mort de César."] pp. 78. *Rotterdam*, 1728. 8°. **11735**. a. 5.

—— [Another copy.] **11755**. bb. **78**. (4.)

—— Entwurf einer Oratorisch-Dramatischen Vorstellung von dem Dictator Julius Cäsar [by Johann Martin Müller ?], welche den 13. 14. 15 und 16 Februar 1781 im Hamburgischen Johanneo wird gehalten werden. [A programme of this and other events.] [1781.] fol. *See* Hamburg.—*Johanneum*. Hirsch **1231**.

—— Giulio Cesare in Egitto. A serious opera in two acts. [By Niccolò F. Haym.] *Ital. & Eng.* pp. 51. *D. Stuart: London*, 1787. 8°. **1342**. k. **34**.
Earlier editions, with a somewhat different English version, are entered under the author's name.

—— La Liberte vangee, ou Cesar poignardé. [A tragedy. By J. Guérin.] pp. 46. *R. du Petit Val: Rouen*, 1606. 12°. **11737**. a. **11**.

—— Nova tragedia intitulada Morte de Cezar, ou Do Mundo a Maior Crueldade. [In verse.] pp. 38. *Lisboa*, 1783. 4°. **11728**. g. **43**. (9.)

—— La Morte di Cesare, dramma per musica, *etc.* [In verse. By Gaetano Sertor.] pp. 64. *Milano*, [1791.] 8°. **11715**. df. **11**.

—— Parallele entre César, Cromwel, Monck et Bonaparte. Fragment traduit de l'anglais. [A Bonapartist pamphlet, variously attributed to J. C. D. de Lacretelle, to the Marquis de Fontanes, and to Napoleon and Lucien Bonaparte.] pp. 16. *Paris*, [1800.] 8°. F. **1189**. (**10**.)

—— [Another copy.] Parallèle entre César, Cromwel, Monck et Bonaparte, *etc.* [1800.] 8°. R. **119**. (**18**.)

—— [Another edition.] pp. 15. [*Paris*, 1800.] 8°. F. **1331**. (**11**.)

—— Santa-Anna vil y traidor quiere ser emperador. [Signed: Julio Cesar—Agustin Iturbide—Sila.] *México*, 1834. *s. sh.* fol. **9770**. k. **12**. (**99**.)

—— Comedia nueva. Ser Vencido y Vencedor. Julio Cesar y Caton. [By G. Zavala y Zamora.] pp. 32. [*Madrid*,] 1801. 4°. **1342**. e. **1**. (**34**.)

—— The Tragedie of Cæsar and Pompey. Or Cæsars Reuenge. Priuately acted by the Studentes of Trinity Colledge in Oxford. [In verse.] [*G. Eld*] *For Nathaniel Fosbrooke & Iohn Wright: London*, 1607. 4°. C. **34**. b. **7**.

—— [Another edition.] The Tragedy of Caesar's Revenge. [Edited by F. S. Boas and W. W. Greg.] *Oxford University Press: London*, 1911. 4°. [*Malone Society Reprints*.] Ac. **9923**. (**22**.)

—— [Another edition.] *London*, 1913. 4°. [*Tudor Facsimile Texts*.] K.T.C. **119**. a. **31**.

CAESAR (Cajus Julius) *pseud.* [i.e. Joseph Linck.]

—— De bello civili. Partistriden vid 1883 års riksdag. pp. 206. *Stockholm*, 1883. 8°. **8092**. de. **32**.

CAESAR (Carl Adolph) Hat Sachsen im 18ten Jahrhundert an Denkfreiheit gewonnen ? *See* Schulze (Johann D.) Abriss einer Geschichte der Leipziger Universität, *etc.* 1810. 8°. **8355**. bbb. **18**.

CAESAR (Carl Julius) *See* Dilich (W.) Urbs et Academia Marpurgensis succincte descripta . . . Edidit J. Caesar. 1867. 4°. **10231**. i. 5.

CAESAR (Carl Julius)

—— *See* Hegesippus, *Historical Writer*. Hegesippus, q dicitur, sive Egesippus De bello judaico . . . Edi C. F. Weber. Opus morte Weberi interruptum absol J. Caesar, *etc.* 1864. 4°. **4515**. f.

—— *See* Hyperides. Hyperidis oratio pro Euxenippo orationis pro Lycophrone fragmenta. Cum adnotatio critica . . . edidit J. Caesar. 1857. 8°. **11391**. f. **18**. (

—— *See* Jena.—*Versammlung der Lehrer deutscher Hoc schulen*. Beschlüsse der Versammlung der Leh deutscher Hochschulen zu Jena, 21.–24. Sept. 184 zusammengestellt von J. Cäsar. 1848. 8°. **8307**. g. **4**. (

—— *See* Marburg.—*Academia Marburgensis*. Academi Marpurgensis privilegia, leges generales et statuta special anno mdcliii. promulgata, edidit J. Caesar. 1868. 4°. **8355**. g. **23**. (

—— *See* Marburg.—*Academia Marburgensis*. Catalog studiosorum Scholae Marpurgensis . . . Edidit I. Caesa 1875, *etc.* 4°. **8356**. i. 1

—— Ein Beitrag zur Charakteristik Otfried Müller's Mytholog, *etc.* pp. 16. *Marburg*, 1859. 8°. **10707**. ff. **29**. (

—— Fasti Prorectorum et Rectorum Universitatis Marbu gensis a saeculari eius anno mdcccxxvii usque ad h tempus deducti, *etc.* pp. iv. 38. *See* Marburg.—*Academia Marburgensis*. Inclutae Academiae Eberha dinae Carolinae Tubigensi . . . quarta saecularia solle niter celebraturae . . . gratulantur Universitatis Ma burgensis Rector et Senatus, *etc.* 1877. 4°. **836**. i. **21**. (1

—— Die Grundzüge der griechischen Rythmik im Anschlu an Aristides Quintilianus erläutert von J. Caesa pp. xii. 292. *Marburg*, 1861. 8°. **12932**. dd.

—— Der Prometheus des Aeschylus. Zur Revision d Frage über seine theologische Bedeutung. pp. viii. 57. *Marburg*, 1860. 8°. **11705**. g. **16**. (2

CAESAR (Carolus) Observationes ad aetatem tituloru Latinorum Christianorum definiendam spectantes. pp. 7 *Bonnae*, 1896. 8°. **11312**. r.

CAESAR (Carolus Gulielmus Eduardus) De obscur tionibus corneae. Dissertatio inauguralis medica, *et* pp. 30. *Berolini*, [1836.] 8°. **7385**. a.* (8

CAESAR (Charles) Numerus Infaustus. (A short vie of the unfortunate reigns of six Kings of England William the Second ; Henry the Second ; Edward t Second ; Richard the Second ; James the Second.) *S* Caesar (*Sir* Julius) Life of Sir Julius Cæsar, *etc.* 1810. 4°. **613**. l.

—— [Another edition.] *See* Lodge (Edmund) Life of S Julius Cæsar, *etc.* 1827. 4°. **613**. l. **1**

CAESAR (Charles Edward) Notes on North West Canad and Missionary Work among Red Indians & Eskim carried on by the Bible Churchmen's Missionary Societ pp. 63. *Bible Churchmen's Missionary Society: Londo* 1925. 8°. **4764**. i. **2**

CAESAR (Drusus Julius)

—— *See* Rogers (Robert S.) Studies in the Reign Tiberius. Some imperial virtues of Tiberius and Drus Julius Caesar. 1943. 8°. **09039**. d. **3**

CAESAR (Eunice Lee)

—— For This My Mother Wrapped Me Warm. [A novel.] pp. 247. *D. Appleton-Century Co.: New York & London,* [1947.] 8°. **12729.** cc. **13.**

CAESAR (F.) *of the Handelskammer, Frankfort. See* Frankfort on the Main.—*Handelskammer.* Geschichte der Handelskammer zu Frankfurt a. M. 1707–1908, *etc.* (Geld-, Mass- und Gewichtswesen, Privatrecht und Rechtspflege, von F. Caesar.) 1908. 8°. **8248.** k. **31.**

CAESAR (Ferdinand) Der preussische Civil-Prozess, oder praktische Anleitung für preussische Juristen zu Verhandlungen im summarischen-, Bagatell- und Mandats-Prozesse, *etc.* pp. xi. 454. *Halle,* 1845. 8°. **5655.** b. **7.**

—— Vierte mit Rücksicht auf die neuere Gesetzgebung berichtigte Auflage. pp. 243. *Halle,* 1874. 8°. **5656.** b. **3.**

CAESAR (Franciscus Maria) Francisci Mariæ Cæsaris Theresia: sive Ostenta Dei O.M. edita pro Augusta Maria Theresia Romanorum Imperatrice, *etc.* [A poem.] pp. 728. *Viennæ Austriæ,* 1752. 4°. **78.** f. **28.**

CAESAR (Gaius) *Adopted Son of the Emperor Augustus. See* Caesar (Caius)

CAESAR (Gaius) *Emperor of Rome. See* Caligula.

CAESAR (Gaius Julius) *See* Caesar (Caius J.)

CAESAR (Gene)

—— Mark of the Hunter. [A novel.] pp. 250. *William Sloane Associates: New York,* [1953.] 8°. **12732.** b. **15.**

CAESAR (Germanicus) *Adopted Son of the Emperor Tiberius. See* Germanicus.

CAESAR (Gothofredus) De avium pulcherrima, pavone, *etc. Praes.* V. Friderici. *Typis viduæ J. Wittigau: Lipsiæ,* [1676.] 4°. **B. 450.** (**15.**)

CAESAR (Gustav Adolph) Ueber Haematocele periuterina. Medicinische Inaugural-Dissertation, *etc.* pp. 34. *Halle,* [1867.] 8°. **7386.c.13.(5.)**

CAESAR (Hermannus) De Plauti memoria apud Nonium servata, *etc.* pp. 159. *Argentorati,* 1886. 8°. [*Dissertationes philologicae Argentoratenses.* vol. 11. fasc. 4.] **12901.** e. **25.**

CAESAR (Irving) *See* Harbach (Otto) Nina Rosa. A musical play . . . The lyrics by I. Caesar, *etc.* [1934.] 4°. **11791.** tt. **1/241.**

CAESAR (Joachimus)

—— *See also* Major (Aeschacius) *pseud.* [i.e. Joachimus Caesar.]

—— *See* Melz (Christian F.) An Evaluation of the Earliest German translation of "Don Quixote": "Junker Harnisch aus Fleckenland." [Identifying the translator, Pahsch Bastel von der Sohle, with J. Caesar.] 1945. 8°. [*University of California Publications in Modern Philology.* vol. 27. no. 5.] Ac. **2689.** g/4.

CAESAR (Johannes Christophorus) Dissertationem inauguralem de asthmate . . . publico examini submittit J. C. Cæsar, *etc.* pp. 23. *Literis Schönnerstædtianis: Altdorffj,* 1680. 4°. **1179.** k. **8.** (**4.**)

CAESAR (John) A Sermon preach'd at Croydon . . . at the Assizes held there, March the 10th, 1707, *etc.* pp. iv. 20. *Samuel Crouch: London,* 1708. 4°. **4474.** bbb. **21.**

CAESAR (John James) The Glorious Memory of a Faithful Prince by a thankful Posterity; in a sermon preach'd upon the most lamented death of King William III . . . to the High German Prussian Congregation in the Savoy. Dedicated in its native language to the King of Prussia; and . . . translated into English by the author. pp. 30. *Henry Mortlock: London,* 1702. 4°. **1419.** i. **39.**

—— God's Inevitable Judgments on Perjured Princes: a sermon, *etc.* pp. 24. *Awnsham & John Churchil: London,* 1704. 4°. **226.** f. **19.** (**18.**)

—— The Great Happiness of a Faithful Princess in Child-bearing. Set forth in a thanksgiving-sermon upon the entire recovery of her Royal Highness the Princess of Wales, *etc.* pp. 27. *George Mortlock: London,* 1716. 8°. **225.** g. **16.** (**17.**) *Imperfect; wanting a leaf before the beginning of the text.*

—— The Royal Pilgrim. A funeral sermon upon the most lamented death of His Majesty Frederic, late King of Prussia, *etc.* [Translated from the German by the author.] pp. 31. *Rich. Smith: London,* 1713. 4°. **1416.** g. **32.**

—— The Victorious Deborah. A thanksgiving sermon for the most glorious success of the arms of Her Majesty . . . and her allies, *etc.* pp. 26. *Thomas Bennet: London,* 1702. 4°. **696.** f. **10.** (**9.**)

CAESAR (Julius) *of Berlin.*

—— Neuester Almanach für Spieler, enthaltend die gründlichste Anweisung zu einer leichten Erlernung des Whist-l'Hambre-Quadrille . . . Kegel- und Ballspiel, herausgegeben von Julius Cäsar. pp. 385. *Berlin,* 1799. 8°. **7906.** aa. **11.**

—— Das Schach- und Tokkategli-Spiel . . . Abgedruckt aus dem neuesten vollständigen Spiel-Almanach von Julius Cäsar. Durchaus verbessert von G. W. v. Abenstein. pp. 81. *Berlin,* 1810. 8°. **7913.** ccc. **24.** (**1.**)

CAESAR (Julius) *Patavinus.* Inuention nouuelle et asseuree d'une pratique generale d'Arithmetique . . . Nouellement corrige & augmentee par l'autheur . . . Auec les plus notables foires de plusieurs pays. *A. Bertram: Strasburg,* 1619. 8°. **C. 54.** g. **6.**

—— A newe and a most excellent Inuention for the buying and selling of all sortes of Merchandizes in all places, and with all kinds of money, *etc. See* Pathway. The Pathway to Knowledge, *etc.* [1596.] 4°. **C. 54.** e. **9.**

CAESAR (Julius) *Professor at Marburg. See* Caesar (Carl J.)

CAESAR (*Sir* Julius) The Ancient State, Authoritie, and Proceedings of the Court of Requests, *etc.* [By Sir Julius Caesar.] pp. 162. ms. note [by the author]. 1597. 4°. *See* England.—*Court of Requests.* **6282.** b. **26.**

—— *See* Lodge (Edmund) Life of Sir Julius Cæsar, *etc.* 1827. 4°. **613.** l. **10.**

—— A Catalogue of the Manuscripts of . . . Sir Julius Cæsar . . . which will be sold by auction . . . on Wednesday 23d and Thursday 24th of November 1757, *etc.* [By Samuel Paterson.] pp. 12. [*London,* 1757.] 4°. **11903.** i. **29.**

—— [Another edition.] A Catalogue of Several Thousands of the most singular and interesting Heads in the Collection of Manuscripts of . . . Sir Julius Cæsar . . . which will be sold by auction . . . on Wednesday the 14th of December, 1757, and the two following evenings . . . By Samuel Paterson, *etc.* pp. ii. 94. ms. notes of prices. *Brindley, etc.: London,* [1757.] 8°. **824.** b. **17.** (**10.**)

CAESAR (*Sir* JULIUS)

—— Life of Sir Julius Cæsar, Knt. . . . With memoirs of his family and descendants. [By Edmund Lodge.] Illustrated by seventeen portraits . . . To which is added, Numerus infaustus, an historical work, by Charles Cæsar. pp. 116. *Robert Wilkinson: London,* 1810. 4°. **613**. l. **9**.

—— [Another copy.] **L.P.** **134**. f. **15**.

CAESAR (JULIUS P.) Letters on Christian Missions. By a Layman of the Church of England. [The preface signed: J. P. C., i.e. J. P. Caesar. Reprinted from the "New Era and the Press."] 1858. 8°. *See* C., J. P. **4193**. c. **24**.

CAESAR (KARL ADOLPH) *See* CAESAR (Carl A.)

CAESAR (LAWSON)

—— Insects Troublesome in the Home. pp. 52. *Toronto,* 1941. 8°. [*Ontario Department of Agriculture. Bulletin.* 416.] C.S. E. **252/35**.

CAESAR (LEONARDUS) *See* LAYMANNUS (P.) Quæstiones canonicæ de prælatorum ecclesiasticorum electione. [With a dedicatory epistle by L. Caesar.] 1627. 8°. **5061**. a. **19**.

CAESAR (LONGINUS) Trinum magicum, siue Secretorum magicorum opus: continens I. De magia naturali, artificiosa & superstitiosa disquisitiones axiomaticas. II. Theatrum naturæ, præter curam magneticam, & veterum sophorum sigilla & imagines magicas, etiam conclusiones physicas, elementales, cœlestes & infernales exhibens. III. Oracula Zoroastris, & mysteria mystica philosophiæ . . . Accessere nonnulla secreta secretorum & mirabilia mundi. Editum à Cæsare Longino. pp. 635. *Impensis A. Hummij: Francofurti,* 1614. 12°. **1035**. a. **5**. (**3**.)

—— [Another edition.] pp. 603. *Ex officina typographica A. Hummii: Francofurti,* 1616. 12°. **719**. a. **8**.

—— Trinum magicum, siue secretorum naturalium . . . cœlestium, infernalium opus . . . continens I. Marci Antonii Zimaræ conclusiones physicas . . . II. Alexandri Aphrodisei quæstiones et solutiones physico-mathematicas (Angelo Politiano interprete). III. Alberti magni tractatus tres de virtutibus herbarum, lapidum et animalium . . . Accessere eiusdem Alberti libelli De mirabilibus mundi et secretis mulierum, vt & Auerrois ac Aristotelis propositiones ac solutiones physicæ. Nunc primum in lucem editum à Longino Cæsare. pp. 328. *Sumptibus A. Hummij: Francofurti,* 1609. 8°. **1141**. a. **7**.

CAESAR (LUCIUS) *Adopted Son of the Emperor Augustus. See* NORIS (E.) *Cardinal.* Cenotaphia Pisana Caii et Lucii Cæsarum dissertationibus illustrata . . . Cæsaris vtriusque vita, gesta, & annuæ eorundem inferiæ exponuntur, *etc.* 1681. fol. **574**. m. **10**.

—— —— [1704.] fol. **664**. h. **11**.

—— —— 1764. 4°. **661**. i. **19**.

CAESAR (OCTAVIUS) *Emperor of Rome. See* AUGUSTUS (C. J. C. O.)

CAESAR (PHILIPPUS) *Professor of Theology at Bremen.* Captivitatis babylonicæ theologica pericope princeps, historiam sacram, quo ad res in Judæa gestas, inde a morte Josiæ . . . usque ad primam Hierosolymorum destructionem complexa, *etc. Praes.* R. Eglinus Iconius. *See* HELVICUS (C.) D. Christoph. Helvici Elenchi judaici, *etc.* 1702. 8°. **4034**. bb. **18**.

CAESAR (PHILIPPUS) *Professor of Theology at Breme*

—— Triapostolatus septentrionis. Vita et gesta, S. Willeha S. Ansgarii, S. Rimberti, trium principalium Eccles Bremensis episcoporum . . . Ex prævetusto & authenti Hamburgensis Ecclesiæ codice MS. in lucem public producta per P. Cæsarem. 1710. *See* FABRICIUS (J. Memoriæ hamburgenses, *etc.* vol. 2. 1710, *etc.* 8°. **614**. d.

CAESAR (PHILIPPUS) *Superintendent at Gottingen.* Vniue propemodum doctrina de vsura, testimonijs sacrosanc Scripturæ & doctorum purioris Ecclesiæ . . . funda stabilita & confirmata, *etc.* pp. 100. *Basil* [1569.] 8°. **3837**. aaa. **9**. (

—— A General Discourse against the Damnable Sect Vsurers . . . [Translated by Thomas Rogers.] Whe unto is annexed another godlie treatise concernyng t lawfull vse of ritches. [Adapted by Thomas Rogers fr N. Hemmingsen's Commentaries.] 2 pt. *Iohn Kyngst for Andrew Maunsell: London,* 1578. 4°. **4374**. d.

CAESAR (SEBASTIANUS) successively *Bishop of Oporto a of Coimbra. See* CESAR DE MENEZES (Sebastião)

CAESAR (SEBASTIANUS) *Themarensis.* De hydrope thes *etc. Praes.* T. Erastus. *Excudebat I. Maier: Heidelberg* 1572. *s. sh.* fol. **7306**. f. **6**. (**1**

—— De incubo theses. *Praes.* S. Grynaeus. *Excudebat Maior: Heidelbergæ,* [1570 ?] *s. sh.* fol. **7306**. f. **6**. (

CAESAR (THEOPHILUS) *See* MORIENUS, *Roman* Alchimy Spiegel: oder Kurtz entworffene Practick d gantzen chymischen Kunst . . . in vnser Teutsche Spra vbergesetzt durch T. Cæsarem August. 1613. 8°. **1033**. c. **3**. (

CAESAR (THOMAS) Thomas Cæsar, Sen., a thorough-br Hampshire Briton, commenced a gentleman travelli macaroni stationer. [1793.] *s. sh.* 4°. **8135**. c. **93**. (

—— Thomas Cæsar, Sen., a thorough-bred Hampshi Briton . . . His advice to young men, particularly young tradesmen, *etc.* pp. 11. 1793. 8°. **8135**. c. **93**. (

CAESAR (WILLIAM) The Gospel of St John, its authorsh and authenticity. pp. vii. 262. *W. Blackwood & Son Edinburgh,* 1877. 8°. **3227**. df.

CAESARAUGUSTA. *See* SARAGOSSA.

CAESAR-AUGUSTA (JOANNES PETRUS A) *See* JU PEDRO, *de Saragoza, etc.*

CAESARE (AMADAEUS DE) Hæreseologia, in qua omn errores, hæresesque ab mundi primordio ad hæc usq tempora . . . referuntur, & refutantur, *etc.* 2 tom. *Romæ,* 1736. fol. **L.19.a.3**

CAESARE (CAIO GIULIO) *See* CÆSAR (Caius J.)

CAESAREA, *in Cappadocia,* ANDREAS, *Archbishop* [c. 490.] *See* ANDREAS.

——, ARETHAS, *Archbishop of.* [c. 914.] *See* ARETHAS.

——, ARISTACES, *Archbishop of.* [1826–1854.] *S* AZARÈAN (Aristakes)

——, BASIL, *Archbishop of.* [370–379.] *See* BASIL, *Sain etc.*

——, BASILEIOS, *Metropolitan of.* [945–956.] *See* BASILEIO

——, FIRMUS, *Bishop of.* [431–438.] *See* FIRMUS.

CAESAREA, *in Cappadocia*,

——, JUAN MANUEL, *Archbishop of*. [1848.] *See* IRISARRI Y PERALTA.

——, THALASSIUS, *Bishop of*. [438–452.] *See* THALASSIUS.

CAESAREA, *in Palestine*, EUSEBIUS, *Bishop of*. [c. 315–c. 338.] *See* EUSEBIUS, *Pamphili, etc.*

——, GELASIUS, *Bishop of*. [c. 476.] *See* GELASIUS.

——, HAYMARUS MONACHUS, *Archbishop of*. [1187–1194.] *See* MONACHUS (H.) successively *Archbishop of Caesarea in Palestine* and *Patriarch of Jerusalem*.

——, HENRICUS, *Archbishop of*. [1458–1465.] *See* KALTEISEN (H.) successively *Archbishop of Trondhjem* and *of Caesarea in Palestine*.

——, PARTHENIOS, *Bishop of*. [c. 1737.] *See* PARTHENIOS, successively *Metropolitan of Caesarea in Palestine* and *Patriarch of Jerusalem*.

——, THEOPHILUS, *Bishop of*. [c. 190.] *See* THEOPHILUS, *Saint, Bishop of Caesarea in Palestine*.

——, THOMAS, *Archbishop of*. [1474–1491.] *See* BASIN (T.) successively *Bishop of Lisieux* and *Archbishop of Caesarea in Palestine*.

CAESAREA ACADEMIA. Caesarea Academia Litterarum Vindobonensis. *See* VIENNA.—*Oesterreichische Akademie der Wissenschaften*.

—— Caesarea Academia Medico-Chirurgica Vilnensis. *See* WILNA.

—— Caesarea Academia Scientiarum. *See* VIENNA.—*Oesterreichische Akademie der Wissenschaften*.

CAESAREA FERDINANDEA UNIVERSITAS PRAGENSIS. *See* PRAGUE.—*Universita Karlova*.

CAESAREA REGIA SOCIETAS ZOOLOGICO-BOTANICA. *See* VIENNA.—*Zoologisch-Botanischer Verein, etc.*

CAESAREIUS DE LEONIBUS (FRANCISCUS) *Cardinal*. Epistola pastoralis ad clerum populumque universum Aesinae dioeceseos. pp. xx. *Romae*, 1817. 4°. **1356**. k. **6**. **(22.)**

—— [Another copy.] T. **79***. **(16.)**

CAESAREUS (JANUS) *Consentinus*. *See* CAESARIUS.

CAESAREUS (NICOLAUS) *Leucopetraeus*. Bedeutung und Offenbarung wahrer Himlischer Influxion, nemblich der Finsternissen, so die folgenden sieben Jhar nacheinander geschehen, auch von der grossen Coniunction Saturni und Jouis im 1563. Jhar . . . zukünfftigk, darinn grosse vorenderung der Reich uñ anderer ding angezeigt werden, vom 1559. Jhar, bis ins 1565. Jar werende. 1558. 4°. **8632**. ccc. **32**. (**2**.)

CAESARI (EDGAR HERBERT)

—— The Science and Sensations of Vocal Tone. A school of natural vocal mechanics, *etc.* pp. xxiv. 199. *J. M. Dent & Sons: London*, 1936. 8°. **7406**. ppp. **26**.

—— The Voice of the Mind, *etc.* [With a portrait of the author.] pp. 366. *Robert Hale: London*, 1951. 8°. **7891**. bb. **36**.

CAESARIANUS (CAESAR) *See* CESARIANO (Cesare)

CAESARIBUS (FRANCISCUS DYSTENUS DE) Augustissimæ Dominæ Elisabethæ Romanorum Imperatrici Franciscus Dystenus de Cæsaribus d.d.d. (Pro electione in Augustos Serenissimorum principum Stephani Francisci Solymorum Regis—et Mariæ Theresiæ Austriacæ panegyris.) [1745.] 4°. **11408**. bbb. **22**.

CAESARIENSIS, *pseud*. Reminiscences of Church Life in Jersey. [Signed: Cæsariensis.] pp. 24. *For private circulation: London*, [1917.] 8°. **04705**. a. **22**.

CAESARINIS (JULIANUS DE) *Cardinal*. *See* CAESARINUS (J.)

CAESARINUS (JULIANUS) *Cardinal*. *See* BECKER (Paul) *of Iserlohn*. Giuliano Cesarini, *etc.* 1935. 8°. **20003**. d. **36**.

—— *See* BRACCIOLINI (P.) Poggii Florentini Oratio in funere reverendissimi Cardinalis D. Iuliani de Caesarinis, *etc.* 1844. 8°. [*Spicilegium romanum*. tom. 10.] **832**. k. **16**.

—— *See* CARLERIUS (A.) Narratio vetus de morte Juliani Cæsarini Cardinalis, *etc.* 1680. 8°. [*Stephani Baluzii Miscellaneorum liber tertius*.] **1087**. h. **23**.

—— —— 1751. fol. [*Stephani Baluzii Tutelensis Miscellanea*. tom. 1.] **13**. e. **9**.

—— *See* FRÁNKL, afterwards FRAKNÓI (V.) Cesarini Julián bibornok magyarországi papai követ élete. 1890. 8°. **4888**. e. **7**.

—— *See* JENKINS (Robert C.) The Last Crusader or, the Life and times of Cardinal Julian, *etc.* 1861. 8°. **4863**. d. **18**.

—— Exemplum literarum quas Iulianus Cardinalis sancti Angeli Legatus in Germania, mira libertate scripsit ad Eugenium Pont. Romanũ, conantem dissoluere Basiliense Concilium.—Exemplum alterius epistolæ eiusdem domini legati, missæ ad Eugenium Pontificem Romanum. *See* PIUS II., *Pope*. Commentariorum Æneæ Syluii Piccolominei Senensis, de Concilio Basileæ celebrati libri duo, *etc.* [1525 ?] fol. **4520**. e. **6**.

—— [Another edition.] *See* GRATIUS (O.) Fasciculus rerum expetendarum ac fugiendarum, *etc.* 1535. fol. **4520**. e. **2**.

—— [Another edition.] *See* GRATIUS (O.) Fasciculi rerum expetendarum & fugiendarum, *etc.* tom. 1. 1690. fol. **7**. c. **10**.

—— [Another edition.] *See* PIUS II., *Pope*. Æneæ Sylvii postea Pii II . . . Commentariorum historicorum libri III de Concilio Basiliensi. 1700. 4°. **5016**. b. **22**.

—— Denkschrift des Kardinals Cesarini über das Symbolum. Erstausgabe des lateinischen Textes, verbesserte Ausgabe der griechischen Übersetzung [by Nicolaus Sagundinus]. [Edited by Georg Hofmann.] (Concilium Florentinum. III.) pp. 62. *Roma*, 1931. 8°. [*Orientalia Christiana*. no. 68.] **Ac. 2002**. bb.

—— Iuliani Caesarinj . . . de inserenda in symbolum particula Filioque dissertatio ἀνεκδοτος habita in Concilio Florentino [in the Greek translation by Nicolaus Sagundinus]. E MSS. Bibliothecae Caesareae Mediceae Laurentianae eruit et nunc primum ex Graeco latine reddidit Rudesindus Andosilla. *Gr. & Lat.* pp. xxxi. lxiii. *Florentiae*, 1762. 4°. **4226**. i. **11**.

—— Die Handakten des Konzilspräsidenten Cesarini. Herausgegeben von Heinrich Dannenbauer. 1936. *See* BASLE, *Council of*. Concilium Basiliense, *etc.* Bd. 8. 1896, *etc.* 8°. **5015**. ee.

CAESARINUS (VIRGINIUS) *See* CESARINO (Virginio)

CAESARION. Cæsarion, or Historical, political, and moral discourses. *See* CÉSARION.

CAESARIS (GIOVANNI DE) Medaglioni abruzzesi. Con prefazione del Senatore prof. Filippo Masci. pp. vi. 257. *Teramo*, 1913. 8°. **10632**. v. 5.

—— Verso la vita, *etc.* [A novel.] pp. vi. 266. *Lanciano*, 1907. 8°. **12471**. tt. 22.

CAESARIS (PETRUS) *See* WAGENER (P.) called CAESARIS.

CAESARISM. Skilnaden emellan Cæsarism och Voltairism de moderna politiska idéerna, samt några ord om 1789 års principer. Ett gif akt till Swenska folket af A. 1868. 8°. *See* A. **8010**. dd. 10.

CAESARIUS. *Σπουδογελοιος* de coma dialogus primus. Cæsarius et Curtius interlocutores. [By C. de Saumaise.] pp. 115. [*Leyden*,] 1645. 8°. **810**. c. 3. (2.)

—— [Another copy.] **1080**. h. 44.

CAESARIUS, *Brother of Saint Gregory of Nazianzus.* *See* GREGORY, *of Nazianzus, Saint, etc.* D. Gregorij Nazianzeni . . . in laudem Cæsarij fratris & sororis suæ Gorgoniæ, orationes funebres, *etc.* *Gr.* 1589. 8°. **834**. b. 34.

—— *See* GREGORY, *of Nazianzus, Saint.* *Εἰς Καισαριον . . . ἐπιταφιος λογος, etc.* 1850. 12°. [GENOUILLE (*J. C.*) *Choix de discours des pères grecs.*] **3627**. b. 21.

—— —— 1855. 12°. [GENOUILLE (*J. C.*) *Choix de discours des pères grecs.*] **3627**. b. 22.

—— —— 1867. 12°. [GENOUILLE (*J. C.*) *Choix de discours des pères grecs.*] **3670**. aa. 19.

—— *See* GREGORY, *of Nazianzus, Saint, etc.* Oraison funèbre de Césaire, *etc.* 1855. 12°. **3627**. b. 23.

—— —— 1898. 8°. **4829**. cc. 29. (3.)

—— *See* PALMIERI (A.) Vita di San Cesario medico. 1850. 8°. **898**. d. 1. (1.)

—— Quæstiones theologicæ et philosophicæ . . . Græcè & latine nunc primùm editæ ab Elia Ehingero, *etc.* [Containing the 78 problems which the editor considers genuine.] pp. 229. *Typis I. Prætorii: Augustæ Vindelicorum*, 1626. 4°. **862**. i. 3.

—— [Another edition.] *Καισαριου . . . Διαλογοι τεσσαρες* . . . Cæsarii . . . Dialogi IV . . . Interpretatio latina primùm in lucem prodijt . . . Basileæ ann. 1571. opera Ioan. Leuuenclaij. *Gr. & Lat.* *See* LA BIGNE (M. de) Magna bibliotheca veterum patrum, *etc.* tom. 11. 1654. fol. **3624**. e.

—— Sancti Cæsarii . . . Dialogi IV. Interprete Joanne Leunclavio, *etc.* *Gr. & Lat.* 1770. *See* GALLANDIUS (A.) Bibliotheca veterum patrum, *etc.* tom. 6. 1765, *etc.* fol. **469**. h. 6.

—— *Καισαριου . . . Διαλογοι τεσσαρες* . . . Caesarii . . . Dialogi quatuor. 1858. *See* GREGORY, *of Nazianzus, Saint, etc.* *Του ἐν ἁγιοις πατρος ἡμων Γρηγοριου . . . τα εὑρισκομενα παντα.* *Gr. & Lat.* 1857, *etc.* 8°. [MIGNE (*J. P.*) *Patrologiae cursus completus . . . Series graeca.* tom. 38.] **2001**. d.

—— Cæsarii, viri illustris . . . Dialogi iiii . . . Hos nunc primum Io. Leuuenklaius & luce donauit & latinam in linguam transcripsit, *etc.* *See* GREGORY, *of Nazianzus, Saint, etc.* Operum Gregorii Nazianzeni tomi tres, *etc.* tom. 3. 1571. fol. **3623**. e. 19.

CAESARIUS, *Brother of Saint Gregory of Nazianz*

—— Cæsarii, viri illustris, Dialogi IIII., *etc.* *Lat.* 1618. LA BIGNE (M. de) Magna bibliotheca veterum patr *etc.* tom. 4. 1618, *etc.* fol. **469**. e

—— [Another edition.] 1677. *See* LA BIGNE (M. de) Max bibliotheca veterum patrum, *etc.* tom. 5. 1677, *etc.* fol. **464**. f

—— Sancti Cæsarii Medici, et Sancti Phoebadii Aginne Episcopi, opera, *etc.* (Didymi Cæci Alexandrini L unus de Spiritu Sancto, liber contra Manichæos.) pp. 474. *Parisiis*, 1842. 8°. [CAILLAU (*A. B.*) *Pa apostolici.* tom. 53.] **362**

—— Четыре бесѣды Кесарія, или Вопросы святаго Си вестра и отвѣты Преподобнаго Антонія. Текстъ рукописи XV вѣка, принадлежащей Московской Ду ной Академіи. Сообщилъ Архимандритъ Леон *Slav.* pp. xv. cꙃ. 20. 1890. 8°. *See* LENINGRAD. —*Общество Любителей Древней Письменности.* Ac. **9086**

—— Cæsarii . . . Dialogus II. *Gr.* *See* CURETON (Will Spicilegium syriacum, *etc.* 1855. 8°. **753.bh.1**

CAESARIUS, *Heisterbacensis.* *See* BEITZ (E.) Caesa von Heisterbach und die bildende Kunst. 1926. 8°. **07807**. l.

—— *See* BETHANY (M.) Cäsarius von Heisterbach, *etc.* 1896. 8°. **011851** i. 16.

—— *See* KAUFMANN (Alexander) *Archivrath.* C. von Heis bach . . . Mit einem Bruchstück aus des Caesarius libri miraculorum, *etc.* 1862. 8°. **4888**. aaa.

—— *See* KOENIGER (A. M.) Die Beicht nach Cäsarius Heisterbach. 1906. 8°. [*Veröffentlichungen aus kirchenhistorischen Seminar München.* Reihe 2. no. **03560**. i.

—— *See* PONCELET (A.) Note sur les Libri viii Miraculo de Césaire d'Heisterbach. 1902. 8°. **4824**. df. 7. (

—— *See* SCHMIDT (P.) *Lic. theol.* Der Teufels- Daemonenglaube in den Erzählungen des Cæsarius Heisterbach. 1926. 8°. **3832**. c.

—— *See* SCHOENBACH (A. E.) Studien zur Erzählu literatur des Mittelalters. (Tl. 4, 7, 8. Ueber Caesa von Heisterbach.) 1898, *etc.* 8°. [*Sitzungsberichte Kaiserlichen Akademie der Wissenschaften.* Phil.- Klasse. Bd. 144, 159, 161.] Ac. **8**

—— Die Wundergeschichten des Caesarius von Heisterb Herausgegeben von Dr. Alfons Hilka. *Lat.*

Bd. 1. Einleitung, Exempla und Auszüge aus Predigten des Caesarius von Heisterbach. pp. 28. 1933.
Bd. 3. Die beiden ersten Bücher der Libri VIII mi lorum. Bearbeitet von Dr. Alfons Hilka.—L Leiden und Wunder des Heiligen Engelbert, Erzbis von Köln. Bearbeitet von Dr. Fritz Zschae Die Schriften über die Heilige Elisabeth von Thüri Bearbeitet von Dr. Albert Huyskens. pp. 27. 1937.

Bonn, 1933– . 8°. [*Publikationen der Gesellschaf rheinische Geschichtskunde.* no. 43.] Ac. **7028**.

—— Caesarii Heisterbacensis Catalogus archiepiscopo Coloniensium 94–1230. 1845. *See* BOEHMER (J. Fontes rerum germanicarum, *etc.* Bd. 2. 1843, *etc.* **1315**. e.

—— *Begin.* [fol. 2 *recto*:] Prologus Cesarij cisterciēsis mon ī Heysterbacho in dyalogū miraculorum Incipit felic *End.* [fol. 310 *recto*:] Duodecime distinctiōis dy miraculorum Cesarij Cistercieẽ mōchi: et ꝑ cōse tocius dyalogi finis est felicit', *etc.* [*Ulrich Cologne*, 1475 ?] fol. IB. 2

310 *leaves, the first blank. Without signatures. D columns*, 35 *lines to a column.*

CAESARIUS, *Heisterbacensis.*

—— [Another edition.] Illustrium miraculorum et historiarum memorabilium lib. XII. Nunc ab innumeris mendis repurgati, & recèns in lucem editi. [Edited by J. Fischerus.] 2 pt. *In officina Birckmannica, sumptibus A. Mylij: Coloniæ Agrippinæ*, 1591. 8°. **4827**. bb. **12**.

—— [Another edition.] Cæsarii monachi Vallis S. Petri . . . Dialogi. pp. 364. *Bono-fonte*, 1662. fol. [*TISSIER (B.) Bibliotheca patrum Cisterciensium.* tom. 2.] **487**. k. 4.

—— [Another edition.] Caesarii Heisterbacensis . . . Dialogus miraculorum. Textum ad quatuor codicum manuscriptorum editionisque principis fidem accurate recognovit Josephus Strange. Accedunt specimina codicum, in tabula lithogr. 2 vol. *Coloniae*, 1851. 8°. **4061**. bbb. 3.

—— The Dialogue on Miracles . . . Translated by H. von E. Scott and C. C. Swinton Bland, with an introduction by G. G. Coulton. [With plates.] 2 vol. *G. Routledge & Sons: London*, 1929. 8°. [*Broadway Medieval Library.*] **012210.c.3/4.**

—— Johann Hartliebs Übersetzung des Dialogus Miraculorum von Caesarius von Heisterbach. Aus der einzigen Londoner Handschrift herausgegeben von Karl Drescher, *etc.* pp. xxiii. 474. pl. II. *Berlin*, 1929. 8°. [*Deutsche Texte des Mittelalters.* Bd. 33.] Ac. **855/15**.

—— Index in Caesarii Heisterbacensis Dialogum. pp. 47. *Confluentiae*, 1857. 8°. **4061**. bbb. 4.

—— Fasciculus moralitatis . . . homilias de infantia seruatoris Jesu Christi complectens. Pars prima(—tertia) . . . Per R. P. F. Ioannem Andream Coppenstein . . . nunc primum ex peruetusto MS. cod. ad typos elaborata: additis ad marginem lemmatis & citationibus adnotatis. 3 pt. *Sumptibus P. Henningij: Coloniæ Agrippinæ*, 1615. 4°. **4423**. c. **44**. (1.)

—— Homiliæ festiuæ . . . super festis anni totius. Per R. P. F. Ioannem Andream Coppenstein . . . nunc primum ex peruetusto MS. Cod. ad typos in lucem productæ, & marginalibus nonnihil adiutæ, citationibus adnotatis. pp. 260. *Apud P. Henningium: Coloniæ*, 1615. 4°. **4423**. c. 44. (2.)

—— Die Fragmente der Libri VIII. Miraculorum des Caesarius von Heisterbach. Herausgegeben von Dr. Aloys Meister. *Lat.* pp. xliii. 221. *Rom*, 1901. 8°. [*Römische Quartalschrift für christliche Altertumskunde.* Supplementhft. 13.] P.P. **1931**. dk.

—— Caesarii Heisterbacensis Vita Sancti Engelberti Archiepiscopi Coloniensis. 1204–1225. [Bk. 4 and 5 of "Libri octo miraculorum."] 1845. *See* BOEHMER (J. F.) Fontes rerum germanicarum, *etc.* Bd. 2. 1843, *etc.* 8°. **1315**. e. **10**.

—— [Vita Beatae Elizabethae.] Des Cäsarius von Heisterbach Schriften über die hl. Elisabeth von Thüringen. Herausgegeben und erläutert von Albert Huyskens. 1908. 8°. *See* COLOGNE.—*Historischer Verein für den Niederrhein.* Hft. 86. 1855, *etc.* 8°. Ac. **7335**.

—— Wunderbare und denkwürdige Geschichten aus den Werken des Cäsarius von Heisterbach. Ausgewählt, übersetzt, und erläutert von Alexander Kaufmann. 2 Tl. 1888, 91. 8°. [*Annalen des Historischen Vereins für den Niederrhein.* Hft. 47, 53.] Ac. **7335**.

CAESARIUS, *Medicus.* *See* CAESARIUS, *Brother of Saint Gregory of Nazianzus.*

CAESARIUS, *Saint, Bishop of Arles.* *See* ARNOLD (Carl F.) Caesarius von Arelate und die Gallische Kirche seiner Zeit. 1894. 8°. 4629. e. 35.

CAESARIUS, *Saint, Bishop of Arles.*

—— *See* CHAILLAN (M.) Saint Césaire, 470–543. 1912. 8°. **4826**. ee. **43**.

—— *See* CYPRIANUS, *Bishop of Toulon.* Vita S. Cæsarii episcopi Arelatensis. 1668. fol. [*Acta Sanctorum Ordinis S. Benedicti.* sæculum 1.] **484**. g. **1**.

—— —— 1733. fol. [*Acta Sanctorum Ordinis S. Benedicti.* sæculum 1.] **4824**. f. **1**.

—— —— 1743. fol. [*BOLLANDUS (J.) and HENSCHENIUS (G.) Acta Sanctorum, etc.* Aug. tom. 6.] **485**. g. **8**.

—— —— 1753. fol. [*BOLLANDUS (J.) and HENSCHENIUS (G.) Acta Sanctorum, etc.* Aug. tom. 6.] **1228**. g. **6**.

—— —— 1848. 4°. [*MIGNE (J. P.) Patrologiae cursus completus.* tom. 67.] **2000**. c.

—— —— 1868. fol. [*BOLLANDUS (J.) and HENSCHENIUS (G.) Acta Sanctorum, etc.* Aug. tom. 6.] **L.23.a.1.**

—— —— 1896. 4°. [*KRUSCH (B.) Passiones vitaeque sanctorum aevi Merovingici.*] **2087.e.**

—— *See* GELLERT (B. F.) Caesarius von Arelate. 1892, *etc.* 4°. **4829**. ee. **11**.

—— *See* HAUTKAPPE (F.) Über die altdeutschen Beichten, und ihre Beziehungen zu Cäsarius von Arles. 1917. 8°. [*Forschungen und Funde.* Bd. 4. Hft. 5.] **11840**. tt.

—— *See* MALNORY (A.) Saint Césaire, *etc.* 1894. 8°. [*Bibliothèque de l'École pratique des Hautes Études. Sciences philologiques et historiques.* fasc. 103.] Ac. **8929**.

—— *See* MARSDIN, afterwards COOPER-MARSDIN (Arthur C.) Cæsarius, Bishop of Arles, claimed as the author of the Athanasian Creed. 1903. 8°. **03504**. f. **19**.

—— *See* THIBAUT (J. B.) L'Ancienne liturgie gallicane, son origine et sa formation en Provence . . . sous l'influence . . . de Saint Césaire d'Arles, *etc.* 1929. 8°. **3475**. ff. **51**.

—— Sermones et homiliæ.—Opuscula et epistolæ. 1848. *See* MIGNE (J. P.) Patrologiæ cursus completus, *etc.* tom. 67. 1844, *etc.* 4°. **2000**. c.

—— Sancti Caesarii . . . Opera omnia nunc primum in unum collecta (studio et diligentia D. Germani Morin.) 2 vol. *Maretioli*, 1937, 42. fol. **3623**. d. **8**.
Vol. 1 *is in* 2 *pt.*

—— Caesarii Arelatensis opera.

1. Sermones . . . collecti . . . studio . . . Germani Morin . . . Editio altera (curante Cyrillo Lambot). 2pt. 1953.

Turnholti, 1953- . 8°. [*Corpus christianorum. Series latina.* tom. 103, 104, *etc.*] **X.0100/8.(103.)**

—— S. Caesarii . . . Homilia I(–XLVI).—Exhortatio . . . ad tenendam vel custodiendam caritatem.—Incipit Epistola Sancti Cæsarii ad quosdam Germanos.—Item Sancti Cæsarii De decem virginibus. 1618. *See* LA BIGNE (M. de) Magna bibliotheca veterum patrum, *etc.* tom. 5. pt. 3. 1618, *etc.* fol. **469**. e. 5.

—— Exhortatio . . . ad tenendam vel custodiendam charitatem.—Epistola . . . ad quosdam Germanos.—Item S. Cæsarii De decem virginibus.—Regula Cæsarii. *See* BIGNE (M. de) Magna bibliotheca veterum patrum, *etc.* tom. 5. 1654. fol. **3624**. e. **1**.

CAESARIUS, *Saint, Bishop of Arles.*

—— S. Cæsari . . . Homilia I (-XLVI).—Exhortatio ad tenendam vel custodiendam charitatem.—Epistola . . . ad quosdam Germanos.—Item Sancti Cæsarii De decem virginibus.—Regula Sanctimonalium. 1677. *See* LA BIGNE (M. de) Maxima bibliotheca veterum patrum, *etc.* tom. 8. 1677, *etc.* fol. **464.** f. **9.**

—— Homiliæ XIV. Stephanus Baluzius Tutelensis nunc primùm edidit notisque illustrauit.—Eiusdem S. Cæsarii Sermo de decem virginibus. Ex codice regularum Lucae Holstenij duæ sequentes homiliæ dantur hic integræ, quorum fragmenta iam fuerant edita sæculo quinto huius Bibl. part. 3.—Eiusdem Sancti Cæsarii . . . Admonitio, seu correctio ad eos qui vxores habentes, adulteria committere non erubescunt.—Epistola . . . ad Cæsariam Abbatissam eiusque congregationem.—Eiusdem Sancti Cæsarii Epistola hortatoria ad virginem Deo dedicatam. 1677. *See* LA BIGNE (M. de) Maxima bibliotheca veterum patrum, *etc.* tom. 27. 1677, *etc.* fol. **465.** f. **12.**

—— Sancti Cæsarii . . . Homiliæ XIV. Accessere alia nonnulla opuscula ex codice regularium Holsteniano desumpta. 1776. *See* GALLANDIUS (A.) Bibliotheca veterum patrum, *etc.* tom. 11. 1765, *etc.* fol. **469.** h. **11.**

—— S. Caesarii . . . Regula sanctarum virginum, aliaque opuscula ad sanctimoniales directa. Ad normam codicum nunc primum edidit Germanus Morin . . . Adiectis tribus tabulis phototypicis. pp. 55. *Bonnae,* 1933. 8°. [*Florilegium patristicum.* fasc. 34.] **3623.** df. **20/34.**

—— Omelie ⁊ admonitiões btĩ Cesarij arelatensis epĩ. *See* ZENO, *Saint, Bishop of Verona.* In p̃senti opusculo infrascripta continentur, *etc.* 1508. 8°. **4426.** de. **19.** (**2.**)

—— Cæsarii Episcopi Arelatensis Homiliæ XL, è tenebris in lucem reuocatæ, à Gilberto cognato Nozereno. *See* GRYNAEUS (J. J.) Monumenta S. Patrum orthodoxographa, *etc.* vol. 3. 1569. fol. **3833.** d. **17.**

—— S. Cæsarii . . . Homilia I(-XLVI). 1610. *See* LA BIGNE (M. de) Bibliothecæ veterum patrum . . . tomi octo, *etc.* tom. 2. 1609, *etc.* fol. C. **79.** i. **2.**

—— S. Cæsarii . . . Homelia I(-XLVI). *See* LA BIGNE (M. de) Magna bibliotheca veterum patrum, *etc.* tom. 2. 1654. fol. **3624.** e. **1.**

—— Sancti Cæsarii . . . Homiliæ xiv. Stephanus Baluzius . . . nunc primùm edidit, notisque illustravit. pp. 130. *F. Muguet: Parisiis,* 1669. 8°. **3627.** b. **14.**

—— [Another copy.] **1412.** c. **18.**

—— Estratto delle profezie di San Cesario . . . che trovasi . . . nel libro intitolato mirabilis, esistente nella biblioteca nazionale di Parigi, *etc.* [Supposititious.] *Lat. & Ital.* pp. 7. *Milano,* 1814. 12°. **3166.** df. **36.**

—— The Extraordinary Prophecy of Cesaire, Bishop of Arles, in the Year 512. which foretels . . . the events of the French Revolution, *etc.* [From the "Liber mirabilis."] *See* WIZARD. The Wizard, *etc.* 1816. 12°. **8631.** b. **37.** (**1.**)

CAESARIUS, *Saint, Quaestor of Bithynia.* *See* CAESARIUS, *Brother of Saint Gregory of Nazianzus.*

CAESARIUS, *von Heisterbach.* *See* CAESARIUS, *Heisterbacensis.*

CAESARIUS (DOMINICUS) Dominici Cæsarij . . . epistolarum selectarum centuriæ II., *etc.* pp. 262. *Impensis H. Tamburini: Bononiæ,* 1621. 8°. C. **79.** a. **20.**
The titlepage is engraved.

—— Dominici Cæsarii . . . epistolarum centuria v. moralis, *etc.* pp. 360. *Impensis P. Golfarini: Bononie,* 1624. 8°. **10920.** aa. **2.**

The titlepage is engraved.

CAESARIUS (HENRICUS) Danck Sermoon over het teghenwoordighe ghemaeckte bestant van twaelf jaeren . . . Mitsgaeders Totstichtinghe van allen staten der menschen, *etc.* pp. 71. *J. a Meliszoon: Utrecht,* 1609. 4°. T. **2421.** (**9.**)

—— Staet van Regeringhe, nae den wijsen raedt van Iethro Priester in Midian, tot Moses zijnen swager . . . voorgestelt alle overheeden hooge ende leege . . . Een tractaet weesende schriftuerlick, historisch, politijck, ende morael. Met . . . ghetuygenissen ende exempelen, *etc.* pp. 331. *J. Amelissz: Utrecht,* 1625. 4°. **8081.** e. **3.**

CAESARIUS (JANUS) *Consentinus.* *See* HORATIUS FLACCUS (Q.) [*Carmina.—Latin.*] Commentarius Ioannis Cæsarii Consentini in triginta duas Q. Horatii Flacci odas. 1566. 8°. **11385.** b. **20.**

—— *See* PLUTARCH. [*De Vitiosa Verecundia.—Latin.*] Plutarchi opusculum de immoderata verecundia a Io. Caesario Consentino latine redditum, *etc.* 1565. 8°. **8461.** a. **5**

—— [Selected Latin poems.] *See* GHERUS (R.) *pseud* Delitiæ CC. italorum poetarum, *etc.* vol. 1. pt. 1. 1608. 12°. **238.** i. **1**

—— [Another edition.] 1719. *See* ITALIAN POETS. Carmin illustrium poetarum italorum. tom. 3. 1719, *etc.* 8°. **657.** a. **1**

CAESARIUS (JOANNES) *Amstelodamensis.* Disputati medica inauguralis de apoplexia, *etc.* pp. 8. *M. Yvon: Cadomi,* 1628. 4°. **1179.** d. **9.** (**7**

CAESARIUS (JOANNES) *Consentinus.* *See* CAESARIU (Janus)

CAESARIUS (JOANNES) *Juliacensis.* *See* BERTRUCI (N.) Bertrucii Bononiensis . . . Compendium siue . collectorium artis medicæ . . . nunc demum recognitu & suæ integritati restitutum per D. I. Cæsarium, *e* 1537. 4°. **1481.** c. **2**

—— *See* BOETHIUS (A. M. T. S.) [*De Consolatione Phi sophiae.—Latin.*] D. Seuerini Boethii . . . De conso tione philŏsophiæ . . . libri quinque . . . Recognouit . I. Cæsarius. 1535. 8°. **8407.** bbb.

—— *See* CELSUS (A. C.) Aurelii Cornelii Celsi, De re medi libri . . . Q. Sereni Samonici præcepta medica . . . Rhemnij Fannij Palæmonis, De ponderibus & mensu . . . Hos libros D. I. Cæsarius . . . castigavit, *etc.* 1528. 8°. **1477.** a.

—— —— 1538. 8°. **774.** b.

—— *See* CELSUS (A. C.) Aur. Corn. Celsi De medicina li octo. Cum notis integris J. Caesarii, R. Constantini, 1746. 8°. **58.** n.

—— *See* CELSUS (A. C.) A. Cornelii Celsi Medicinae l octo, *etc.* [With the dedications and prefaces of Caesarius.] 1785. 4°. **541.** f.

—— —— 1806. 8°. **159.** g.

—— *See* CLICHTOVEUS (J.) Fundamentum logicæ. In ductio in terminorum cognitionem . . . unà cum Cæsarii commentariis. 1538. 8°. **12932.** b. **4.**

ESARIUS (JOANNES) *Juliacensis.*

— *See* DIOMEDES, *the Grammarian.* Diomedis Grammatici Opus, ab Iohanne Cæsario, ita emendatum . . . ut nulla porrò labes insideat. Item Donati De octo orationis partibus, & barbarismo libellus, ab eodem recognitus. 1526. 8°. **624.** a. **1.**

— *See* HORATIUS FLACCUS (Q.) [*Epistolae.—Latin.*] Institutio moralis philosophie metrica: Continentur in hoc codice Horatii Flacci morales epistole, *etc.* [Edited by J. Caesarius.] 1504. 4°. **11385.** c. **12.**

— *See* LE FÈVRE (Jacques) *d'Étaples.* Ars moralis philosophie, *etc.* [fol. 3 *verso*:] Ioannis Cesarii Iuliacēsis epitome in moralem philosophiam ex morali introductione Iacobi fabri Stapulensis in ethicen Aristotelis deprompta adiectis insup breuiusculis cōmentariis . . . feliciter incipit. [1500 ?] 4°. IA. **47924.**

— *See* LE FÈVRE (J.) *d'Étaples.* Introductio . . . in Arithmeticam Diui Seuerini Boetij, *etc.* [With a prefatory epistle by J. Caesarius.] [1507 ?] 4°. **529.** g. **8.** (**1.**)

— *See* OPPIAN. Oppiani poctae Alieuticon . . . libri quinq; . . . C. Plinij Secundi Naturalis historiæ libri duo . . . Pauli item Iouij De piscibus liber vnus . . . Hos . . . authores I. Cæsarius . . . recognouit, castigauit, simulq; & scholijs passim explanauit. 1534. 4°. **956.** c. **15.**

— *See* OROSIUS (P.) Pauli Orosii . . . Aduersus paganos, quos uocant, historiarum libri septem, *etc.* [Edited by J. Caesarius.] 1536. 8°. **856.** d. **1.**

— —— 1542. 8°. **9009.** aa. **23.**

— *See* PLINIUS SECUNDUS (C.) [*Latin.*] C. Plinii Secundi naturalis historiæ opus, ab innumeris mendis à D. I. Cæsario Iuliaceñ . . . uindicatum . . . & breuiusculis simul in margine scholiis, ab eodem illustratum. 1524. fol. **456.** c. **12.**

— —— 1524. 8°. **7002.** a. **34.**

— *See* PLINIUS SECUNDUS (C.) [*Latin.*] C. Plinij Secundi Historiæ naturalis liber secundus. Cum . . . annotationibus I. Cæsarij & P. I. Oliuarij. 1536. 8°. **975.** b. **23.**

— *See* PRISCIANUS. Prisciani Periegesis . . . cui accedunt ejusdem Carmen de ponderibus et mensuris et Epitome phænomenon . . . Recensuit et notis . . . Jo. Cæsarii, Eliæ Vineti . . . in Carmen de pond. et mensuris . . . illustravit J. C. W. 1825. 8°. [*Bibliotheca classica latina.* vol. 137.] **11305.** m. **5.**

— *See* SERENUS SAMMONICUS (Q.) Q. Sereni Samonici, De medicina, præcepta saluberrima, per D. Cæsarium ab omnibus quibus scatebant mendis . . . emaculata. Item Q. Rhemnij Fannij Palæmonis, De ponderibus & mensuris, liber vtilissimus. 1533. 8°. **539.** b. **37.**

— *Begin.* In hoc opusculo hæc continentur. Epistola Ioannis Cæsarij Iuliacensis ad . . . Hermannum Comitem Nuenarium. Apologia eiusdem in mali consulentes. Dialectica eiusdem in decem tractatus digesta, iuxta præceptoꝝ decalogi numeꝝ, *etc.* ff. 79. FEW MS. NOTES. *Excudebat Eucharius Ceruicornus:* [*Cologne,* 1525 ?] 4°. **520.** d. **6.** (**2.**)

— Compendiaria artis grammaticae institutio per Ioannem Cæsarium nuper cōgesta, autoribus cū primis Aspero iuniore, Aelio Donato & Phoca, cum epitome de constructione partium orationis, *etc.* *Expensis P. Quentell: Coloniae,* 1525. 4°. **12932.** bb. **22.**

CAESARIUS (JOANNES) *Juliacensis.*

—— Dialectica . . . Cui adiecimus Ioannis Murmellij Isagogen in decem Aristotelis Prædicamenta. Praeterea accessit Tractatus de decē prædicamentis, ex Diui Seuerini Boetij de Trinitate libro, per Ioannem Cæsarium in compendium contractus & scholijs illustratus. *Apud hæredes A. Birckmanni: Coloniæ,* 1558. 8°. **1384.** a. **5.** (**1.**)

—— *See* RAYANUS (Hermannus) *Welsdalius.* Scholia . . . in Dialecticam I. Caesarii, *etc.* 1559. 8°. **1384.** a. **5.** (**3.**)

—— Saphicum. *See* SIBUTUS (G.) *Daripinus.* Ars memoratiua, *etc.* 1506. 4°. **11408.** bb. **41.**

CAESARIUS (VALENTINUS) Fides Bohemo-Palatina pro Ferdinando II. Austriaco . . . contra Friderici Comitis Palatini &c. declarationem publicam: cur regni Bohemiæ, annexarumque prouinciarum regimen in se susceperit. Cui adiecta mantissa, aduersus breuem causarum coniectionem: quibus moti status regni Bohemiæ & incorporatarum prouinciarum, non admisso Ferdinando &c. ad noui regis electionem processeruut [*sic*] . . . Accessit adhæc Sacræ Cæsareæ, et Hungaricæ, Bohemiæque Regiæ Maiestatis, edictalis cassatio & annullatio, *etc.* pp. 178. *Viennæ Austriæ,* 1620. 8°. **1054.** a. **6.**

CAESARMONTANUS (JOSEPHUS ANTONIUS) *See* LITURGIES.—*Latin Rite.*—*Missals.*—I. [*Abridgments and Extracts.*—*Latin.*] Rubricæ Missalis Romani, cum earum expositione . . . ex variis rubricarum expositoribus collecta; à P. F. J. A. Cæsaremontano. 1820. 8°. T. **2483.** (**2.**)

CAESAROTTUS (MELCHIOR) *See* CESAROTTI.

CAESARS. *See* VICO (E.) Primorum XII. Caess. genealogiarum, stemmatum, consanguinitatum, affinitatumq; vera delineatio. [1553.] *s. sh.* fol. **131.** h. **5.** (**7.**)

—— Ad sex primorum Cæsarum genealogicam arborem commentaria Pio VI. P. M. dicata. [With a dedicatory letter by J. B. Rotundus. With a genealogical tree.] pp. 210. *Neapoli,* 1787. 4°. C. **64.** d. **6.**
With the arms of Pope Pius VI. stamped on the binding.

—— Het Leven der hedendaagse aansprekers, of de Cæsars op hun troon. Klugtspel. pp. 18. *Amsterdam,* 1735. 8°. **11755.** aaa. **58.** (**1.**)

—— [Another copy.] **11754.** a. **80.** (**8.**)
Imperfect; wanting all before sig. A2.

—— Primorum XII. Caess. genealogiarum stemmatum, consanguinitatum affinitatumq; vera delineatio. [By E. Vico.] *Jo. Jacobi de Rubeis formis: Romę,* [1660 ?] fol.
Dept. of Prints & Drawings.

CAESARUS (ANTONIUS) *See* CESARI (Antonio).

CAESEMAKER (CAROLINE DE) Het Fabriekmeisje. Oorspronkelijk tooneelspel in één bedrijf, *etc.* [With musical notes.] pp. 20. 8. *Gent,* 1884. 8°. **11754.** e. **26.** (**1.**)

CAESENA. *See* CESENA.

CAESENATES. *See* CESENESE.

CAESIEN (FILIP) *See* ZESEN (Philipp von)

CAESII, *Family of.* *See* CESI.

CAESIUS (BERNARDUS) Mineralogia, siue Naturalis philosophiæ thesauri, *etc.* pp. 626. *I. & P. Prost: Lugduni,* 1636. fol. **459.** c. **18.**

—— [Another copy.] **32.** g. **11.**

CAESIUS (Carolus) *See* Cesio (Carlo)

CAESIUS (Ferdinandus Calorius) *See* Pico della Mirandola (G. F.) *Count della Concordia, the Younger.* Joannis Francisci Pici . . . Liber de veris calamitatum causis nostrorum temporum . . . Nunc primum prodidit ex incognita Mirandulana editione anni MDXIX. brevem Pici notitiam adjectam F. C. Caesius. 1860. 8°.
4535. bbb. **17**. (**6**.)

CAESIUS (Fridericus) *Duke d'Aquasparta. See* Cesi (Federico)

CAESIUS (Georgius) Catalogus, nunquam antea visus, omnium cometarum secundum seriem annorum à diluuio conspectorum, vsq; ad hunc præsentem post Christi natiuitatem 1579 annum . . . ex multorum historicorum, philosophorum & astronomorum . . . scriptis . . . diligentissima inquisitione collectus . . . à M. Georgio Cæsio . . . Et eiusdem iudicium de Cometa nuper in fine anni 77 elapsi viso. *Excudebat V. Furmannus: Norībergæ*, 1579. 8°. **8560**. aa. **32**.

—— Chronick, oder ordenliche verzeichnuss vnnd beschreibung aller Cometen, von der algemeinen Sündflut an . . . bis auff dis . . . 1579. Jar, *etc.* *Gedrnckt* [sic] *bey V. Fuhrman: Nürnberg*, 1579. 8°. **8561**. aa. **9**.

—— Prognosticon Astrologicum auff das Jar . . . M.D.LXXXV., *etc. Gedruckt durch V. Fuhrman: Nürnberg*, [1584.] 4°.
8610. bbb. 8. (**6**.)

—— Prognosticon astrologicum, oder Teutsche Practick: auff das Jahr . . . M.DCII., *etc. V. Fuhrmann: Nürnberg*, [1601.] 4°. **8610**. bbb. **16**. (**10**.)
The date is given in a chronogram.

CAESIUS (Petrus Donatus) *Cardinal. See* Cesi (Pietro D.)

CAESIUS (Philippus) *See* Zesen (Philipp von)

CAESIUS A ZESEN (Philippus) *See* Zesen (Philipp von)

CAESIUS BASSUS. *See* Bassus.

CAETANI, *Family of. See* Caetani (G. B.) Documenti dell'archivio Caetani. 1920, *etc.* fol. **9906**. s. **8**.

—— *See* Caetani (G. B.) XXIX maggio MCMXX. Nozze di Michelangelo Caetani con Cora degli Antinori. (Documenti famigliari dell'archivio Caetani.) 1920. 8°.
9907. ff. **16**.

—— *See* Carinci (G. B.) Documenti scelti dell'archivio della eccm̃a famiglia Caetani di Roma, *etc.* 1846. 8°.
9907. de. **32**.

—— Origine dell'antichissima e nobilissima casa Caetani con li suoi stati, che possiede. [By Francesco Molinari ?] pp. viii. 38. *Roma*, 1911. 8°. **9907**. f. **27**.

CAETANI (Benedetto) *See* Boniface VIII., *Pope.*

CAETANI (Enrichetta) *Duchess di Sermoneta.* Alcuni ricordi di Michelangelo Caetani, duca di Sermoneta. Raccolti dalla sua vedova, 1804–1862, e pubblicati pel suo centenario. Seconda edizione, *etc.* pp. 179. *Milano*, 1904. 8°. **10631**. g. **53**.

CAETANI (Enrico) *Cardinal.*

—— [For official documents issued by E. Caetani as legate of Bologna :] *See* Bologna. [*Acts of Legates.*]

—— *See* Paris.—*Parlement.* Arrest de la Cour de Parlement contre toutes prouisions de bénéfices décernées par les Cardinaux Cajetan & de Plaisance eux disans Legats de Notre S. Père le Pape, *etc.* [11 Aug. 1594.] 1595. 8°. **9200**. aaa. **44**.

CAETANI (Enrico) *Cardinal.*

—— *See* Rome, *Church of.*—[*Popes.*]—Sixtus v. [1585–1590 Le Pouuoir et Commission de Monseigneur l'Illustrissim et Réuérendissime Cardinal Caietan, Legat deputé p le S. Siége Apostolique au Royaume de France, *etc.* 1590. 8°. **9200**. aaa. 4

—— *See* Vannozzi (B.) Delle lettere Miscellanee del Si Bonifatio Vannozzi . . . Insieme con le lettere di attio importantissime nella legatione di Monsignor Illustrissim Caetano Legato à latere di Nostro Signore in Polonia. 1606. 4°. **831**. b. 2

—— Instructions for Young Gentlemen; or, the instru tions of Cardinall Sermonetta [E. Caetani] to his cous Petro Caetano, at his first going into Flanders to t Duke of Parma, to serue Philip King of Spaine. pp. 12 *John Lichfield for Thomas Huggins: Oxford*, 1633. 12°.
722. a.

—— [Another edition.] *See* Instructions. Instructio for Youth. Gentlemen and Noblemen, *etc.* 1722. 12°.
1031. d.

—— [Another edition.] *See* INSTRUCTIONS. Walsingham's Manual, *etc.* 1728. 12°. **8005**. b. 3

—— Harangue au Reuerendissime et Illustrissime Leg Henry Caietan, faicte par aucuns Bourgeois de Par Au moys de Feburier, 1590. pp. 16. *Chez D. Millic Paris*, 1590. 8°. **901**. a. 4

—— Harangue prononcée à Monseigneur l'Illustrissime Réuérendiss^me^ Henry Cardinal Caietan, *etc.* pp. 47. *Chez N. Niuelle & R. Thierry: Paris*, 1590. 8°.
1192. g. 5. (3

CAETANI (Gelasio Benedetto)

—— *See* Dante Alighieri. [*Divina Commedia.—Comple Texts.—Italian.*] Comedia Dantis Aldigherii, *etc.* (Ripr duzione del Codice Caetani. Editor a cura di G. Caetan 1930. fol. **Cup.500.g.3**

—— *See* Ebner (*Captain.* La Battaglia di ottobre del 1915 sul Col Lana, *etc.* [Edited by G. B. Caetani.] 1921. 8°.
09083. b. 5

—— *See* Peele (Robert) Gelasio Caetani. A biographic memorial. [With a portrait.] 1936. 8°.
20003. aa. 9

—— Documenti dell'archivio Caetani. [Edited and in pa written by G. B. Caetani. With plates, including portrait of the editor.] 11 vol.

Caetanorum genealogia. Indice genealogico e cen biografici della familia Caetani dalle origini all'anr MDCCCLXXXII. pp. 122. 1920.
Regesta chartarum. 5 vol. 1922–30.
Epistolarium Honorati Caietani. Lettere familiari d Cardinale Scarampo e corrispondenza della Guer Angioina, 1450–1467. pp. xvii. 263. 1926.
Domus Caietana. Storia documentata della famil Caetani. 2 vol. 1927, 33.
Varia. Raccolte delle carte più antiche dell'archiv Caetani e regesto delle pergamene del fondo Pisan Con introduzione di Cesare Ramadori. pp. xxvi. 42 1936.

Perugia ; Sancasciano ; Città del Vaticano, 1920–36. fo
9906. s.

—— [Another copy of the "Varia."] **9907**. t. 2

—— XXIX maggio MCMXX. Nozze di Michelangelo Caeta con Cora degli Antinori. (Documenti famiglia dell'archivio Caetani.) pp. 29. *Perugia*, 1920. 8°.
9907. ff. 1

CAETANI (Gelasio Benedetto)

— La Prima stampa del Codice Caetani della Divina Commedia, *etc.* pp. 13. *Sancasciano Val di Pesa,* 1930. 8°. **Cup.500.d.21.**

CAETANI (Leone) *Duke di Sermoneta.*

— *See* Aḥmad ibn Muḥammad (Abu 'Alī) called Ibn Miskawaih. The Tajârib al-Umam or History of Ibn Miskawayh . . . Reproduced . . . with a preface and summary by L. Caetani Principe di Teano, *etc.* 1909, *etc.* 8°. **14005.** g. **7.**

— *See* Pantanelli (P.) Notizie storiche della terra di Sermoneta . . . Edite da L. Caetani. 1909. 8°. **10151.** f. **36.**

— Annali dell'Islām. Compilati da L. Caetani. vol. 1–10. *Milano,* 1905–26. 4°. **4504.** i. **13.**
No more published.

— Chronographia islamica, ossia riassunto cronologico della storia di tutti i popoli musulmani dall anno 1 all'anno 922 della Higrah, 622–1517 dell' era volgare, corredato della bibliografia di tutte le principali fonti stampate e manoscritte. 5 fasc. pp. xiv. 1716. *Paris,* 1912–[22.] 4°. **9057.** d. **20.**
Covering the period A.D. 622–750 *only.*

— La Funzione dell'Islam nell'evoluzione della civiltà. Estratto da "Scientia," *etc.* pp. 32. *Bologna,* [1912.] 8°. **4504.** g. **42.**

— Registro generale alfabetico, *etc.* (A–DAR.) pp. 248. *Roma,* 1904. 4°. **15001.** d.
No more published.

— Studi di storia orientale. vol. 1, 3. *Milano,* 1911, 14. 8°. **9057.** ff. **6.**
Vol. 2 *was not published.*

CAETANI (Leone) *Duke di Sermoneta,* and **GABRIELI** (Giuseppe)

— Onomasticon Arabicum, ossia repertorio alfabetico dei nomi di persona e di luogo contenuti nelle principali opere storiche, biografiche e geografiche, stampate e manoscritte, relative all'Islām. vol. 1, 2 [containing the introduction and entries A'ābil—'Abdallah]. *Roma,* 1915. 4°. **10608.** i. **1.**
No more published.

CAETANI (Marguerite)

— An Anthology of New Italian Writers. Edited by M. Caetani and selected from the pages of the review Botteghe oscure. pp. 477. *John Lehmann: London; Rome* printed, 1951. 8°. **012227.** cc. **2.**

CAETANI (Michelangelo) *Duke di Sermoneta. See* Caetani (E.) *Duchess di Sermoneta.* Alcuni ricordi di Michelangelo Caetani, *etc.* 1904. 8°. **10631.** g. **53.**

— Carteggio dantesco del duca di Sermoneta con Giambattista Giuliani . . . ed altri insigni dantofili, con ricordo biografico di A. di Gubernatis. pp. 179. *Milano,* 1883. 8°. **11421.** cc. **19.**

— Epistolario del duca Michelangelo Caetani di Sermoneta. [With plates, including portraits, and including in vol. 2 a fifth edition of "Tre chiose nella Divina Commedia." Edited by G. L. Passerini.] 2 vol. *Firenze,* 1902, 03. 8°. **010920.** m. **19.**
Printed for private circulation.

— Della dottrina che si asconde nell'ottavo e nono canto dell'Inferno della Divina Commedia di Dante Allighieri esposizione nuova. pp. 21. *Roma,* 1852. 8°. **11420.** d. **1.** (**6.**)

CAETANI (Michelangelo) *Duke di Sermoneta*

— [Another edition.] *See* Fabricatore (B.) Del veltro allegorico de' Ghibellini, *etc.* 1856. 8°. **11421.** g. **18.**

— Di una più precisa dichiarazione intorno ad un passo della Divina Comedia di Dante Alighieri nel xviii canto del Paradiso, proposta agli amici di questi studj da M. Caetani. pp. 10. [1859.] 8°. **11805.** i. **24.**

— Matelda nella divina foresta della Commedia di Dante Allighieri. Disputazione tusculana. [By M. Caetani, Duke di Sermoneta.] pp. 24. 1857. *See* Dante Alighieri. [*Divina Commedia.—Appendix.—Purgatorio.*] **11420.** dd. **37.**

— La Materia della Divina Commedia . . . dichiarata in vi tavole da M. Caetani. *Roma,* 1855. fol. **1875.** b. **14.**
Lithographed throughout.

— Seconda edizione. *Rome,* 1872. fol. **1872.** a. **28.**

— Seconda edizione fiorentina con un proemio di Raffaello Fornaciari. pp. xix. 18. *Firenze,* 1886. 32°. **11421.** a. **2.**

— Tre chiose . . . nella Divina Commedia di Dante Allighieri. Seconda edizione. [With plates.] pp. 67. *Roma,* 1876. 8°. **11422.** ff. **2.**

— Terza edizione. pp. 63. *Roma,* 1881. 8°. **11420.** g. **20.** (**7.**)

— [Another edition.] Terza edizione, *etc.* pp. 66. *Città di Castello,* 1894. 8°. [*Collezione di opuscoli danteschi inediti o rari.* vol. 11.] **011420.** a. **1/8.**

CAETANI (Onorato) *Capitan Generale delle Fanterie Pontificie.* Lettere di Onorato Caetani . . . nella battaglia di Lepanto. Pubblicate da G. B. Carinci. Seconda edizione. pp. 235. *Roma,* 1893. 8°. **010905.** e. **48.**

CAETANI (Onorato) *Protonotario Apostolico.* Lettera al sig. abate Francesco Cancellieri editore del frammento liviano scritta l'anno mdcclxxxi . . . Seconda edizione. (Saggio della vita letteraria di Monsignor Onorato Caetani.) 2 pt. *Roma,* 1799. 8°. **899.** d. **7.** (**4.**)

— Observations sur la Sicile . . . en 1774. Osservazioni sulla Sicilia, *etc. Fr. & It.* pp. 24. [*Rome,* 1775 ?] 4°. **899.** e. **5.** (**15.**)

— Des römischen Prälaten Herrn Caetani Bemerkungen über Sicilien. 1774. Aus dem Französischen. *See* Bernoulli (Johann) *the Younger.* Johan Bernoulli's Sammlung kurzer Reisebeschreibungen, *etc.* Bd. 1. 1781, *etc.* 8°. **1045.** b. **1.**

— Orazione in morte dell'Imperatrice Regina Maria Teresa Walburga di Austria, *etc.* pp. xxxviii. *Napoli,* 1780. 4°. **1356.** k. **7.** (**32.**)

CAETANI (Onorato) *Signore di Sermoneta.* Epistolarium Honorati Caietani. Lettere familiari del Cardinale Scarampo e corrispondenza della Guerra Angioina, 1450–1467. pp. xvii. 263. *Sancasciano,* 1926. fol. [*Caetani* (*G. B.*) *Documenti dell'Archivio Caetani.*] **9906.** s. **8.**

CAETANI (Vittoria) *Duchess di Sermoneta.* Things Past, *etc.* [With plates, including portraits.] pp. 287. *Hutchinson & Co.: London,* [1929.] 8°. **10634.** dd. 32.

— The Locks of Norbury. The story of a remarkable family in the xviiith and xixth centuries. [With portraits.] pp. xii. 389. *John Murray: London,* 1940. 8°. 9906. r. 8.

CAETANI (VITTORIA) *Duchess di Sermoneta.*

—— Sparkle Distant Worlds. [Reminiscences. With plates, including portraits.] pp. 288. *Hutchinson & Co.: London,* [1947.] 8°. **010632**. bb. **26**.

CAETANI LOVATELLI (ERSILIA) *Countess.* Amor und Psyche. *See* MUENZ (S.) Ferdinand Gregorovius und seine Briefe an Gräfin Ersilia Caetani Lovatelli. 1896. 8°. **10920**. ccc. **39**.

—— Antichi monumenti illustrati. pp. 247. *Roma,* 1889. 8°. **7706**. a. **32**.

—— Attraverso il mondo antico. pp. 347. *Roma,* 1901. 8°. **7701**. aa. **41**.

—— Miscellanea archeologica. pp. 291. *Roma,* 1891. 8°. **7706**. a. **40**.

—— Nuova miscellanea archeologica. pp. 134. *Roma,* 1894. 8°. **7708**. aa. **66**.

—— Ricerche archeologiche. pp. 229. *Roma,* 1903. 8°. **07703**. e. **22**.

CAETANO, *de Santo José.* Vida do B. Fr. Simão de Roxas, da ordem da SS. Trindade, *etc.* pp. 304. *Lisboa,* 1772. 8°. **4865**. aaa. **12**.

CAETANO (CAMILLO) *See* GAETANI.

CAETANO (ENRICO) *Cardinal. See* CAETANI.

CAETANO (FERNANDO DE MONCADA ARAGON LA CERDA Y) *Duke de San Juan. See* MONCADA ARAGON LA CERDA Y CAETANO.

CAETANO (FILIPPO) *Duke di Sermoneta.* Le Tre comedie famose del Signor D. Filippo Caetano . . . cioe La Schiaua, L'Ortentio, Li Due vecchi. [Edited by G. A. Gregoriis.] pp. 324. *E. Cicconio: Naples,* 1644. 4°. **162**. g. **15**.

CAETANO (IGNACIO DE SANTO) *See* IGNACIO, *de São Caietano.*

CAETANO (JOSÉ) Additamento ao papel, intitulado Alvarista defendido . . . no qual em duas cartas dos cegos Lucas, e Pascoal se aclara, e expende a differença dos modos potencial, e conjunctivo, tocada no primeiro papel, e agora totalmente dicidida por seu author J. Caetano. pp. 14. *Lisboa,* 1757. 4°. **10632**. bbb. **19**. **(14.)**

—— Juizo grammatical, ou primeira audiencia, feita na casinha da almotaçaria . . . Pelo almotacel da semana [i.e. J. Caetano], *etc.* pp. 15. 1754. 4°. *See* JUIZO. **12943**. bb. **12**. **(1.)**

—— Segunda audiencia grammatical, feita na cazinha da almotaçaria, *etc.* pp. 31. *Lisboa,* 1755. 4°. **12943**. bb. **12**. **(2.)**

CAETANO (RUGGIERO) Le Memorie de l'anno santo 1675, celebrato da Papa Clemente X. . . . descritta in forma di giornale. pp. 526. *M. A. & O. Campana: Roma,* 1691. 4°. **4570**. cc. **6**.

—— Orationem de Christi Domini nece . . . D. Francisco Caietano Sermonetæ Duci, &c. R. Caietanus D.D.D. pp. 32. *Typis J. Phæi: Romæ,* 1653. 8°. G. **5484**. **(2.)**

—— Il Trifauce infernale abbattuto dal Gerione celeste per li trè memorabili portenti successi nel mondo alli 2 di settembre 1686, *etc.* [A sonnet.] *Eredi del Sarti: Bologna,* 1686. *s. sh.* fol. **838**. m. **22**. **(114.)**

CAETANO (TOMMASO) *Cardinal. See* VIO (Thomas de) *Cardinal.*

CAETANO DE ABREU FREIRE EGAS MONI[Z] (ANTÓNIO) *See* EGAS MONIZ (A.)

CAETANO DE LIMA (LUIZ) *See* BEZERRA E LIMA (J. A[...]) Elogio do Padre D. Luiz Caetano de Lima, *etc.* 1759. 4°. **4864**. ccc. **3**

—— Ludovici Caietani de Lima . . . carminum libri I[...] Antiquioris benevolique amici curâ in lucem editi. pp. 13[...] *Olisipone,* 1743. 4°. **11405**. bb.

—— Ludovici Caietani de Lima . . . epigrammata, quib[...] aliquot gesta Augustissimmi [*sic*] Lusitanorum Reg[...] Joannis V. memoriæ produntur. 2 pt. *Olissipon[...]* 1730, 32. 4°. **11405**. bb.

—— [Another copy of pt. 2.] **11405**. bb. **8**

—— Geografia historica de todos os estados soberanos [...] Europa, com as mudanças, que houve nos seus Domini[...] . . . Tomo primeiro (segundo), em que se trata [...] Portugal. [With plates and maps.] 2 tom. *Lisbo[...]* 1734, 36. 4°. **179**. e. **15**, **[...]**
No more published.

—— Grammatica Franceza, ou Arte para aprender o Franc[...] por meyo da lingua portugueza, *etc.* pp. 311. *Lisbo[...]* 1710. 8°. **236**. e. **3**

—— Grammatica Franceza, ou Arte para apprender o Franc[...] por meyo da lingua portugueza, *etc.* 2 pt. *Lisboa Occidental,* 1733, 32. 4°. **825**. d. **3**
A different work from the preceding.

CAETANO DE SOUSA (ANTONIO) *See* SOUSA.

CAETANO DE SOUSA (MANOEL) Reportorio Milit[...] das Ordens do Exercito do Estada da India . . . des[...] 1851 a 1860 . . . Coordenado . . . por M. Caetano [...] Sousa. pp. 546. 1862. 4°. *See* PORTUGAL.—*Colonies.*—*East Indies.*—*Army.* **8830**. c. **4**

CAETANO DIAS (ANTONIO)

—— Catálogo das obras raras ou valiosas da Biblioteca [...] Escola Nacional de Belas Artes. pp. vii. 67. pl. xv. 1945. 8°. *See* RIO DE JANEIRO.—*Escola Nacional [...] Belas Artes.—Biblioteca.* **2774.d.1/5**

CAETANO DIAS (ANTÓNIO) and **COSME** (LUÍS)

—— Compêndio de classifacação decimal e índice alfabéti[...] . . . Segunda edição, revista, aumentada e melhorad[...] pp. viii. 322. *Rio de Janeiro,* 1950. 8°. [*Instituto Nacion[...] do Livro.* Coleção B.2. Biblioteconomia. no. 5.] W.P. **8740**[...]

CAETANO DO ROSARIO E NORONHA (ISIDOR[...]) *See* JORDÃO (L. M.) *Viscount de Pavia Manso.* Reflexõ[...] sobre a materia da Petição de Aggravo, que em defens[...] do Prelado de Moçambique (I. Caetano do Rosario [...] Noronha) fez . . . L. M. Jordão, *etc.* 1860. 4°. **4767**. d. **11**. **(1[...]**

—— Um Brado pelas colonias, ou as Colonias salvas pe[...] missão e Portugal salvo pelas colonias. Collecção [...] artigos, publicados no Jornal do Commercio, *etc.* pp. 7[...] *Lisboa,* 1870. 8°. **8180**. f. **4**

CAETANO GONSALVES (JOSÉ) Oração funebre, q[...] nas solemnes exequias do ex.[mo] e rd.[mo] Sr. D. [...] Manuel de S. Galdino, Arcebispo Metropolitano de G[...] . . . recitou J. Caetano Gonsalves. pp. 13. *Nova-G[...]* 1868. 8°. **4867**. g.

CAETANUS (ANTONIUS) *Cardinal, Archbishop of Capua.*

—— Epistulae et acta Antonii Caetani, 1607–1611. Pars [...] Pars 3 sectio 1, 2.) Edidit Milena Linhartová. 4 [...] *Pragae,* 1932–46. 8°. [*Epistulae et acta nuntiorum ap[...] tolicorum apud Imperatorem,* 1592–1628. tom. 4.] **4572**. bbb. **2**
[Part 2.]

ÆTANUS (Constantinus) *See* Caietanus.

ÆTANUS (Nicolaus) *Cardinal.* [For official documents issued by N. Caetanus as Archbishop of Capua:] *See* Capua, *Province of.*

ÆTANUS (Thomas Devius) *Cardinal.* *See* Vio (T. de)

ÆTI. Cæti de donne ai treuggi coa protesta de Portolianne. [A dialogue, in verse.] [*Genoa,* 1848.] *s. sh.* fol. **804.** k. **13.** (**270.**)

ÆTSPEL. *See* Kaatspel.

ÆVALLOS (Hieronymus de) Hieronymi de Cævallos . . . opus exquisitissimum, in quo præcipue de cognitione per viam violentiæ in causis ecclesiasticis et inter personas ecclesiasticas agitur, *etc.* pp. 458. *Sumptibus hæredum J. Weidenfeldt & G. de Berges: Coloniæ Agrippinæ* 1687. fol. **5107.** h. **4.**

ÆYRO (Franciscus) Opusculum morale de bulla Cruciatæ Lusitana, & de monitorijs. pp. 313. *Eboræ,* 1717. 8°. **5017.** a. **5.**

— [Another edition.] pp. 313. *Ulyssipone Occidentali,* 1723. 8°. **5017.** a. **6.**

— [Another edition.] *See* Nogueira (L.) R. P. Ludovici Nogueira . . . Expositio bullæ Cruciatæ, *etc.* 1744. fol. **5005.** g. **5.**

AF (Oroslav) *See* Štrekelj (K.) Pisma in zapiski iz Cafove ostaline. 1900. 8°. [*Zbornik znanstvenih in poučnih spisov.* zvez. 2.] Ac. **3434/2.**

AFANDARIS (Georges) *See* Kaphantares (Georgios)

AFARDO (Giuseppe) Avventure maravigliose ed interessanti del famoso Giuseppe Cafardo nobile romano date alla luce da un suo amico fedelissimo, colle annotazioni tedesche, *etc.* (Seltsame und merkwürdige Begebenheiten, *etc.*) [A translation of parts of " Les Aventures de Joseph Pignata, echappé de l'Inquisition de Rome," with the name Cafardo substituted for that of Pignata, and the dates altered, and with additional material from " L'Infortuné Napolitain ou les Aventures du Seigneur Rozelli " by the Abbé —— Olivier.] *Ital.* pp. 400. *Augsburg,* 1768. 8°. **10630.** a. **6.**

AFARELLI (Francesco)

— Lunario perpetuo secondo la nuoua reforma. Segno pretioso del christiano, nouamente posto in luce. [A diagram, with explanatory text.] *G. Orliens: Milano,* [1585 ?] *s. sh.* fol. Tab. **597.** d. **1.** (**8.**)

AFARGÀMALA. Identificazione Cafargàmala=Beitgemâl. Documenti, *etc.* (Studi Stefaniani.) [Articles by various writers.] 3 ser. *Beitgemal,* 1934. 4°. **07702.** aaa. **36.**

AFARO (Paolo) *See* Alphonso Maria [de' Liguori], *Saint, Bishop of Sant' Agata dei Goti.* [*Two or more Works.*] Life of Father D. Paul Cafaro, *etc.* 1849. 8°. [*Lives of the Companions of St. Alphonso Liguori.*] **4826.** bbb. **15.**

— *See* Rome, *Church of.—Congregatio Rituum.* Nucerina Paganorum seu Compsana. Beatificationis et canonizationis . . . P. Cafaro . . . Positio super introductione causae. 1908. fol. **5052.** e. **48.**

— *See* Rome, *Church of.—Congregatio Rituum.* Nucerina Paganorum seu Compsana. Beatificationis et canonizationis . . . P. Cafaro . . . Positio super non-cultu. 1908. fol. **5207.** g. **14.**

CAFARUS, *Genuensis.* *See* Caffarus, *de Taschifellone.*

CAFASSO (Giuseppe) *See* Rome, *Church of.—Congregatio Rituum.* Taurinen. Beatificationis et canonizationis . . . J. Cafasso . . . Novissima positio super virtutibus. 1920. fol. **5052.** ee. **5.**

—— *See* Rome, *Church of.—Congregatio Rituum.* Taurinen. Beatificationis et canonizationis . . . J. Cafasso . . . Positio super introductione causae. 1906. fol. **5052.** e. **25.**

—— Il Venerabile Giuseppe Cafasso. Nuova vita compilata sui processi di beatificazione. pp. 340. *Torino,* 1920. 8°. **4864.** df. **21.**

CAFAZZO (Girolamo Orlando) *See* Orlando-Cafazzo.

CAFÉ. Le Café des artistes, vaudeville en un acte . . . par trois auteurs [C. G. Étienne, P. C. Gaugiron-Nanteuil and —— Morel], *etc.* pp. 36. *Paris,* an 8 [1799/1800]. 8°. **11738.** f. **32.** (**5.**)

—— Le Café des halles, comédie en un acte, *etc.* [By C. J. Guillemain.] pp. 44. *Londres, et se trouve à Paris ;* [*Paris* printed,] 1781. 8°. **11738.** g. **4.** (**5.**)

—— La Comedia Nueva, ó el Café, *etc.* [By L. Fernandez de Moratin.] [1790 ?] 4°. *See* Comedia. **1342.** e. **1.** (**35.**)

—— [Another edition.] [1800 ?] 4°. *See* Comedia. **11726.** c. **5.** (**2.**)

—— Saynete nuevo. Intitulado. El Café, *etc.* [In verse.] pp. 8. *Valencia,* 1816. 4°. **1342.** f. **5.** (**26.**)

—— Café Parisien. *See* Paris.

CAFÉ AND MILK BAR CATERING.

—— Café & Milk Bar Catering. Contributors: Joan N. Marks, George Reeson [and others] . . . With 78 illustrations. pp. vii. 246. *Heywood & Co.: London,* 1952. 8°. **08229.** h. **73.**

CAFERRI (Niccolò Angelo) Vita Bartholomæi Platinæ, et doctorum virorum de eius scriptis iudicia ex bibliotheca Pamphilia historica, siue de historicis, quorum opera extant. *See* Sacchi (B.) *de Platina.* Bartolomeo Platina Delle vite de' pontefici, *etc.* 1666. 4°. **4855.** cc. **6.**

—— [Another edition.] *See* Sacchi (B.) *de Platina.* Le Vite de' pontifici, *etc.* 1715. 4°. **484.** b. **6.**

—— [Another edition.] *See* Sacchi (B.) *de Platina.* Le Vite de' pontefici, *etc.* 1730, *etc.* 8°. **4855.** dd. **15.**

CAFÉS-CONCERTS.

—— Les Cafés-concerts en 1866. *See* Ephemerides.

CAFEZOGLE (Spiridion) *See* Kaphezoglou (Spuridon)

CAFFA. *See* Theodosia.

CAFFA (Carolus) *See* Paolo, *Servita.* F. Pauli Sarpi Tractatus de materiis beneficiariis . . . Ex italico in latinum versus . . . a Carolo Caffa. 1681. 12°. **5107.** aa. **19.**

—— Caroli Caffæ . . . Diæta studiosi nobilis, ital. lat. gallica. Juxta quam vitam ordine suo dignam componat . . . Secundâ jàm vice luci edita, adjectis juxta 22. opellæ num. totidem italico-latino-gallicis dissertationibus. pp. 368. *J. Bielcke: Jenæ,* 1690. 4°. **525.** f. **27.**

CAFFAREL (Marie François Ernst) Der Skandal Caffarel-Boulanger und die Corruption in Frankreich von ***. pp. 54. *Berlin,* 1887. 8°. **8051.** de. **9.** (**2.**)

CAFFARELLA, afterwards **ORSINI** (ANNA MARIA) *Princess.* *See* ORSINI.

CAFFARELLI (AUGUSTE DE) *Count.* *See* CAFFARELLI DU FALGA (Marie F. A. de)

CAFFARELLI (COSTANZA MARIA MATTEI) *Duchess d'Asergio.* *See* MATTEI CAFFARELLI.

CAFFARELLI (FRANCESCO) [For official documents issued by F. Caffarelli as Governor of Rome:] *See* ROME.—*The City.*—*[Official Documents issued by the Governors of the City.]*—Caffarelli (F.) *Governor.*

CAFFARELLI (FRANCESCO DI) Gli Strumenti ad arco e la musica da camera. pp. x. 235. *Milano,* 1894. 8°. **012200.** i. **13.**
One of the "Manuali Hoepli."

CAFFARELLI (LOUIS MARIE JOSEPH DE) *Count.* [For reports made by Count L. M. J. de Caffarelli to the Conseil d'État, 1810, 11:] *See* FRANCE.—*Conseil d'État.*

CAFFARELLI DU FALGA (JOSEPH MAXIMILIEN DE) *See* ALDÉGUIER (F. d') Étude historique sur la vie privée et militaire de Joseph-Maximilien de Caffarelli du Falga, *etc.* [With a portrait.] 1849. 8°. **10660.** i. **1.**

CAFFARELLI DU FALGA (LOUIS MARIE JOSEPH MAXIMILIEN) *See* GERANDO (J. M. de) *Baron.* Vie du général Louis-Marie-Joseph-Maximilien Caffarelli du Falga, *etc.* 1801. 8°. **F. 1318. (1.)**

CAFFARELLI DU FALGA (MARIE FRANÇOIS AUGUSTE DE) *Count.* *See* ALDÉGUIER (F. d') Étude historique sur la vie privée et militaire de Joseph-Maximilien de Caffarelli du Falga, *etc.* (Notice historique sur le lieutenant-général comte Auguste de Caffarelli.) 1849. 8°. **10660.** i. **1.**

CAFFARINI (TOMMASO NACCI) *See* THOMAS [Nacci Caffarini], *de Senis.*

CAFFARO. *See* CAFFARUS, *de Taschifellone.*

CAFFARO (ALBINO) L'Arte del lanificio in Pinerolo e gli statuti di essa. 1893. *See* TURIN.—*Deputazione di Storia Patria.* Miscellanea di storia italiana, *etc.* tom. 30. 1862, *etc.* 8°. *Subalpina* Ac. **6550.**

CAFFARO (FRANCESCO) Lettre d'un théologien [i.e. F. Caffaro] consulté pour savoir si la comédie peut être permise, ou doit être absolument défenduë. [BOURSAULT (E.) *Œuvres, etc.* tom. 1.] 1721. 12°. *See* THÉOLOGIEN. **636.** a. **8.**

—— [Another edition.] Lettre d'un homme d'érudition & de mérite [i.e. F. Caffaro], consulté par l'auteur pour sçavoir, si la comédie peut être permise, ou doit être absolument défenduë. pp. 84. 1725. 12°. [BOURSAULT (E.) *Théâtre, etc.* tom. 1.] *See* LETTRE. **242.** g. **27.**

—— Discourse of the Lawfulness and Unlawfulness of Plays. *See* MOTTEUX (Peter A.) Beauty in Distress, *etc.* 1698. 8°. **841.** c. **8. (12.)**

—— [Another edition.] *See* MANSEL (Robert) *Manager of the Sheffield Theatre.* Free Thoughts upon Methodists, Actors, *etc.* 1814. 12°. **1343.** l. **32.**

—— [Another edition.] *In:* F., D. A Defence of the Drama, *etc.* pp. 97–163. 1826. 8°. **840.** c. **27.**

CAFFARO (PIETRO) Famiglie pinerolesi descritte negli archivi parrocchiali di Pinerolo dal 1565 al 1604. vol. 1. pp. 348. *Pinerolo,* 1910. 8°. **9914.** r. **14.**
No more published.

—— Notizie e documenti della chiesa pinerolese, raccolta . . . da P. Caffaro. 6 tom. *Pinerolo,* 1893–1903. 8°. **4606.** ee. **2.**

CAFFARUS, *de Taschifellone.* Caffari ejusque continuatorum Annales Genuenses ab anno MC ad annum usque MCCXCIII e manuscriptis codicibus nunc primum in lucem prodeunt. 1725. *See* MURATORI (L. A.) Rerum italicarum scriptores, *etc.* tom. 6. 1723, *etc.* fol. **L.1.h.1/6.**

—— MXCIX–MCCLXXXVII. Cafari et continuatorum Annale Januenses. [A facsimile of a MS. in the archives of th city of Genoa.] [*Genoa,* 1899.] fol. Tab. **439.** a. **4**

—— [Another edition.] Annali genovesi di Caffaro e de suoi continuatori dal MXCIX al MCCXCIII. Nuova edizione a cura di Luigi Tommaso Belgrano. (vol. 2 a cura d L. T. Belgrano e di Cesare Imperiale; vol. 3–5 a cura di C. Imperiale.) 5 vol. *Genova,* 1890–1929. 8°. [*Fonti per la storia d'Italia.*] Ac. **6543. (9.**

—— Ex Annalibus genuensibus, auctoribus Caffaro, Oberto cancellario et aliis, *etc.* 1781. *See* BOUQUET (M.) Recueil des historiens des Gaules, *etc.* tom. 12. 1738, *etc.* fol. **Circ.8–9.b.**

—— Cafari Genuensis de liberatione civitatum Orientis 1886. *See* PARIS.—*Académie des Inscriptions et Belles Lettres.* Recueil des historiens des Croisades. Historiens occidentaux. tom. 5. 1841, *etc.* fol. **1899.m.31.**

CAFFÉ. Il Caffé, o la Scozzeze. Commedia. 1762. 8° [DIODATI (O.) *Biblioteca teatrale, etc.* tom. 1.] *See* SCOTCHWOMAN. **240.** i. **26**

—— Il Caffé, ossia brevi e varj discorsi distributi in fogl periodici, *etc.* *See* PERIODICAL PUBLICATIONS.—*Brescia*

CAFFE-SCHALE. *See* KAFFEE-SCHALE.

CAFFE (CHARLES JOSEPH) *See* CORNIL (A. V.) Un Patriote savoisien pendant la Révolution française. Biographie de C.-J. Caffe, *etc.* [With a portrait.] 1892. 8°. **10661.** e. **17**

—— Le Capitaine Caffe aux républicains françois. Tableau des vexations exercées contre le capitaine Caffe pour son amour passionné de la liberté et son attachement à la révolution. pp. 10. [1794.] 8°. R. **172. (32.**

CAFFE (JEAN MARIE JÉRÔME) *Physician.* Les Hôpitaux *See* PARIS. [*Appendix.—History.*] Paris révolutionnaire tom. 4. 1838. 8°. **10170.** ccc. **2**

CAFFE (JEAN MARIE JÉRÔME) *Religieux Dominicain* Portraits savoisiens. Le Père Caffe, religieux dominicai de Chambéry. pp. 45. *Chambéry,* 1859. 8°. **4866.** c. **1**

CAFFÉ (P. P. A.) Considérations sur les avantages de l méthode des bains mercuriels dans le traitement de l siphilis et de la plupart des affections cutanées; thèse *etc.* pp. 49. *Paris,* 1815. 4°. **1183.** c. **6. (28.**

CAFFE (PAUL LOUIS BALTHAZAR) *See* JEANDET (J. P. A. Méthode unique pour rendre complète l'histoire de hommes et des choses. Lettre à M. le docteur Caffe (Réponse de M. le docteur Caffe.) 1858. 12°. **07305.** f. **16. (6**

—— *See* PERIODICAL PUBLICATIONS.—*Paris.* Journal hebdomadaire de médecine. (Journal universel et hebdomadaire de médecine et de chirurgie pratiques et des institutions médicales. Par MM. Begin, Caffe [and others], *etc.* 1828, *etc.* 8°. P.P. **2905**

—— Propositions de médecine et de chirurgie, et d'institut médical ; thèse, *etc.* pp. 31. *Paris,* 1833. 4°. **1184.** e. **14. (13.)**

CAFFEE. *See* KAFFEE.

CAFFEE-HAUS. *See* KAFFEEHAUS.

CAFFEE- UND THE-LOGIA. *See* KAFFEE- UND TEE-LOGIA.

CAFFEE (NATHANIEL MONTIER)

—— *See* READ (William A.) Studies for William A. Read . . . Edited by N. M. Caffee and T. A. Kirby. 1940. 8°. **012902**. i. **61**.

CAFFERATA (HENRY TAYLOR) The Catechism Simply Explained . . . Seventh edition, thirtieth thousand. pp. xvi. 172. *Art & Book Co.: Westminster*, 1910. 8°. **03504**. f. **42**.
The cover bears the words "Sixth edition, twenty-fifth thousand."

—— Tenth edition, *etc.* pp. viii. 180. *Burns, Oates & Co.: London*, 1922. 8°. **03504**. g. **34**.

—— The Catechism Simply Explained for Little Children. pp. vi. 83. *St. Anselm's Society: London*, [1911.] 8°. **03504**. f. **52**.

—— The Little Child's First Communion Book, *etc.* pp. ix. 22. *St. Anselm's Society: London*, 1911. 16°. **3455**. df. **76**.

CAFFETIST. *See* KAFFETIST.

CAFFEY (FRANCIS GORDON) A Brief Statutory History of the United States Department of Agriculture. pp. 26. 1916. 8°. *See* UNITED STATES OF AMERICA.—*Department of Agriculture.—Office of the Solicitor.* A.S. **803/5**.

CAFFI (ANDREA) *See* MURATOV (P. P.) L'Ancienne peinture russe. Traduction du manuscrit russe par A. Caffi. 1925. 8°. **7852**. s. **16**.

—— *See* ZANOTTI-BIANCO (U.) and CAFFI (A.) La Pace di Versailles, *etc.* 1919. 8°. **08028**. i. **16**.

—— Santi e guerrieri di Bisanzio nell'Italia meridionale. *See* ORSI (P.) Le Chiese basiliane della Calabria, *etc.* 1929. 4°. **7820**. r. **23**.

CAFFI (ENRICO) I Ragni di Calabria. Studio. pp. 62. *Bergamo*, 1895. 8°. **7298**. a. **10**.

CAFFI (ERNESTO) Nietzsches Stellung zu Machiavellis Lehre. Ein literarisch-philosophischer Essai. pp. 46. *Wien*, 1912. 8°. **08462**. f. **2**. (**1**.)

CAFFI (EUSTORGIO) Nozze Ticozzi-Guidini. (Un' Episodio della guerra 1848.) pp. 23. *Mestre*, 1875. 4°. **9166**. h. **6**.

CAFFI (FRANCESCO)

—— Della vita e del comporre del poeta lirico Giacopo Vittorelli, *etc.* [With a portrait.] pp. 24. ON VELLUM. *Venezia*, 1835. 8°. C. **42**. b. **24**.

—— Della vita e del comporre di Benedetto Marcello . . . sovrannominato principe della musica, *etc.* pp. 31. *Venezia*, 1830. 8°. **10601**. bb. **3**. (**2**.)

—— Della vita e del comporre di Bonaventura Furlanetto . . . maestro della Capella ducale di S. Marco, *etc.* [With a portrait.] pp. 40. *Venezia*, 1820. 8°. T. **2356**. (**12**.)

—— Della vita e delle opere del prete Gioseffo Zarlino, *etc.* pp. 32. *Venezia*, 1836. 8°. **4865**. dd. **13**.

—— [Another copy.] Della vita e delle opere del prete Gioseffo Zarlino, *etc.* *Venezia*, 1836. 8°. Hirsch **5080**.
Imperfect; wanting the frontispiece.

—— Della vita e delle opere di Bartolomeo Gamba, *etc.* pp. 33. *Venezia*, 1841. 8°. **10630**. b. **20**.

—— [Another copy.] **1450**. e. **11**. (**3**.)

CAFFI (FRANCESCO)

—— Novella inedita. [Edited by Andrea Tessier.] pp. 20. *Venezia*, 1855. 8°. **12470**. f. **27**. (**3**.)

—— Novelle tre . . . recitate nell'Ateneo di Castel Franco. pp. 16. *Venezia*, 1816. 8°. T. **2271**. (**9**.)
No. 22 of an edition of fifty copies.

—— [Another copy.] G. **18063**.
No. 40 of an edition of fifty copies.

—— Storia della musica sacra nella già Cappella ducale di San Marco in Venezia dal 1318 al 1797. [With portraits.] 2 vol. *Venezia*, 1854, 55. 8°. Hirsch **1444**.
With an additional titlepage, engraved.

—— [A reissue.]

Storia della musica sacra nella già Cappella ducale di San Marco in Venezia dal 1318 al 1797. [A reissue of the Venice edition of 1854, 55.] 2 vol. *Milano*, 1931. 8°. **7896**. e. **21**.

CAFFI (IPPOLITO) *See* CODEMO GERSTENBRAND (L.) Ippolito Caffi, cenni artistici e biografici. 1866. 8°. **10631**. f. **39**. (**12**.)

—— La Mia prigionia. Al marchese Antinari . . . lettera. *Venezia*, 1848. 8°. **8033**. d. **27**. (**12**.)

—— Nozze Giuseppe Rizzani, Luisa Galeazzi. (I Prigionieri del 1848 e il Sentimento dei veri Goriziani.) [Comprising "La Mia prigionia, lettera di Ippolito Caffi al marchese Antinori" and "Proclama dei veri Goriziani agli Udinesi." The preface signed: D. B.] pp. 30. *Udine*, 1896. 4°. **10631**. h. **39**.

CAFFI (JOSEPH THEOBALDUS) De influxu corporis in animum, dissertatio, *etc.* pp. 36. *Ticini Regii*, [1826.] 8°. **7383***. d. **2**. (**10**.)

CAFFI (MICHELE) Dei lavori d'intaglio in legname e di tarsia pittorica nel coro della cattedrale di Ferrara: lettera di M. Caffi a G. Campori. Estratto dall'Indicatore modenese, *etc.* pp. 14. [*Modena*, 1851?] 8°. **7875**. b. **40**.

—— Dell'abbazia di Chiaravalle in Lombardia. Illustrazione storico-monumentale-epigrafica. [With plates.] pp. 158. *Milano*, 1842. 8°. **4605**. e. **8**.
The title on the wrapper reads: "Dell'abbazia di Chiaravalle in Lombardia. Iscrizioni e monumenti. Aggiuntavi la storia dell'eretica Guglielmina Boema."

—— [Another copy.] **1367**. f. **11**.

—— Della chiesa di Sant' Eustorgio in Milano. Illustrazione storico-monumentale epigrafica. pp. xxii. 206. *Milano*, 1841. 8°. **702**. i. **27**.

—— [Another copy.] **4605**. d. **2**.

—— Di alcuni architetti e scultori della Svizzera italiana. (Estratto dall'Archivio storico lombardo.) pp. 21. *Milano*, 1885. 8°. **7706**. ee. **18**. (**5**.)

CAFFIAUX (HENRI) *See* CHORICIUS. Choricius de Gaza. Éloge funèbre de Procope traduit . . . par H. Caffiaux. 1862. 8°. **11391**. cc. **15**.

—— *See* HENNIN (H. de) La Ville de Valenciennes assiégée par Louis XIV. en 1677, a-t-elle été prise par force ou par trahison? Par H. Caffiaux. [Consisting of "Relation du siége & de la prise de Valenciennes . . . recueillie par H. de Hennin" with introduction and notes by H. Caffiaux.] 1875. 8°. **9226**. f. **2**. (**8**.)

CAFFIAUX (Henri)

—— Abattis de maisons à Gommegnies, Crespin et Saint-Saulve, 1348–1382. Extraits tirés des comptes du Massart et annotés par H. Caffiaux. pp. 30. *Valenciennes*, 1863. 8°. **7711.bb.24.**

—— De l'oraison funèbre dans la Grèce païenne. pp. vi. 288. *Valenciennes*, 1861. 8°. **11391.** g. **8.**

—— Essai sur le régime économique, financier et industriel de Hainaut après son incorporation à la France, *etc.* pp. xxiv. 487. *Valenciennes*, 1873. 8°. **8229.** dd. **29.**

—— Hannonia Ludovico xiv. regnante, thesim proponebat Facultati Litterarum Parisiensi H. Caffiaux. pp. 78. *Valencenis*, 1860. 8°. **9414.** b. **34.**

CAFFIAUX (Philippe Joseph) Défenses du beau sexe, ou Mémoires historiques, philosophiques et critiques, pour servir d'apologie aux femmes. [By P. J. Caffiaux.] 4 tom. 1753. 12°. *See* Défenses. **8416.** i. **19.**

CAFFIERI, *Family of.* *See* Guiffrey (J. J.) Les Caffiéri, sculpteurs et fondeurs-ciseleurs, *etc.* 1877. 8°. **2264.** cc. **9.**

—— *See* Tyssandier (L.) Un Gouverneur de Paris. Le général Lecointe. Les Buzot et les Caffieri. 1897. 18°. **010664.** f. **11.**

CAFFIERI (Jean Jacques) *See* Jouin (H.) Jean-Jacques Caffieri . . . son portrait par L.-J.-F. Lagrénee, l'aîné. 1891. 8°. **7854.** h. **32.**

—— *See* M***. Lettre d'un amateur des beaux arts à M***. [With reference to a statue by J. J. Caffieri in the Église royale des Invalides.] [1789 ?] 8°. F.R. **236.** (**3.**)

—— *See* Marquet de Vasselot (A. J. J.) Trois œuvres inconnues de S. Mazière, J. J. Caffieri, et C.-A. Bridan au Musée de Versailles. 1901. 8°. **7875.** c. **29.**

CAFFIERI (Joseph Corentin) *See* Buzot (C. A.) and Caffieri (J. C.) Au Conseil des Cinq-cents, les héritiers Buzot. [1797 ?] *s. sh.* 8°. F. **949.** (**12.**)

CAFFIERI (Philippe)

—— Catalogue d'une belle collection de tableaux, sculptures, desseins, estampes encadrées & en feuilles, livres d'estampes, livres & autres objets de curiosité. Provenant du cabinet de M.*** [i.e. P. Caffieri]. Dont la vente se fera . . . le mardi 10 octobre 1775, & jours suivans, *etc.* pp. 55. 1775. 8°. *See* Catalogues. **562.** e. **19.** (**4.**)

—— Panneaux et frisses propres aux sculpteurs et peintres inventez et dessignes par Caffieri. [Six engravings.] *H. Bonnart: Paris*, [1680 ?] fol. Dept. of Prints & Drawings.

CAFFIN (Benjamin Charles) *See* Gloag (Paton J.) i Thessalonians (ii Thessalonians). Exposition and homiletics by Rev. P. J. Gloag . . . Homilies by various authors. Rev. Prof. T. Croskery . . . Rev. B. C. Caffin, *etc.* 1887. 8°. [*Pulpit Commentary.*] **3131.d.1/50.**

—— *See* Redford (Robert A.) Song of Solomon. Exposition by Rev. R. A. Redford . . . Homiletics by Rev. B. C. Caffin, *etc.* 1893. 8°. [*Pulpit Commentary.*] **3131.d.1/20.**

—— *See* Williams (Arthur L.) St. Matthew. Exposition by Rev. A. L. Williams. Homiletics by Rev. B. C. Caffin, *etc.* 1894. 8°. [*Pulpit Commentary.*] **3131.d.1/38.**

—— i Peter (ii Peter). Exposition and homiletics by Rev. B. C. Caffin. 2 vol. *Kegan Paul & Co.: London*, 1889. 8°. [*Pulpit Commentary.*] **3131.d.1/56.**

CAFFIN (Benjamin Charles)

—— Philippians. Exposition and homiletics by Rev. B. C. Caffin . . . Homilies by various authors, *etc.* pp. xiii. 199. iii. *Kegan Paul & Co.: London*, 1886. 8°. [*Pulpit Commentary.*] **3131.d.1/48.**

—— The Second Book of Kings and corresponding part of ii. Chronicles. pp. 128. *J. Nisbet & Co.: London*, 1894. 8°. [*Comprehensive Scripture Lesson-Scheme.* Dept. 3. Teacher's Classified Lesson-Material. pt. 9.] **3107.** df. **16.**

CAFFIN (Benoit) *See* Periodical Publications.—*Arras.* Annuaire statistique et administratif du département du Pas-de-Calais . . . publié . . . par M. B. Caffin. 1845, *etc.* 8°. P.P. **2410.** a.

CAFFIN (Charles Henry) *See* Cole (Timothy) Old Spanish Masters. Engraved by T. Cole. With historical notes by C. H. Caffin, *etc.* 1907. 8°. **7857.** k. **14.**

—— *See* Small (Herbert) Handbook of the New Library of Congress . . . With essays on the architecture, sculpture and painting, by C. Caffin, *etc.* 1897. 8°. **11899.** c. **24.**

—— The ABC Guide to Pictures. [With plates.] pp. 253. *Stanley Paul & Co.: London*, [1916.] 8°. **7859.** de. **7.**

—— American Masters of Painting. Being brief appreciations of some American painters. Illustrated with examples of their work. pp. x. 195. *Grant Richards: London; Norwood, Mass.* [printed], 1903. 8°. **7855.** cc. **32.**

—— American Masters of Sculpture. Being brief appreciations of some American sculptors and of some phases of sculpture in America. [With plates.] pp. xiii. 234. *Doubleday, Page & Company: Garden City, New York*, 1913. 8°. **7877.** b. **13.**

—— Art for Life's Sake. An application of the principles of art to the ideals and conduct of individual and collective life. pp. 287. *Prang Co.: New York*, [1913.] 8°. **07808.** de. **21.**

—— How to Study Pictures, by means of a series of comparisons of paintings and painters from Cimabue to Monet, with historical and biographical summaries and appreciations of the painters' motives and methods. [With illustrations.] pp. xv. 513. *Century Co.: New York*, 1905. 8°. **7856.** i. **9.**

—— [Another copy, with a different titlepage.] *Hodder & Stoughton: London; [printed in U.S.A.,]* 1906. 8°. **7857.** s. **8.**

—— How to Study Pictures . . . With additions by Roberta M. Fansler . . . Edited by Alfred Busselle. pp. xiv. 544. *D. Appleton-Century Co.: New York, London*, 1941. 8°. **7866.** pp. **23.**

—— How to Study the Modern Painters, by means of a series of comparisons of paintings and painters from Watteau to Matisse, with historical and biographical summaries and appreciations of the painters' motives and methods. [With plates.] pp. xxi. 255. *Hodder & Stoughton: London*, [1914.] 8°. **7859.** b. **6.**

—— How to Study the Old Masters, by means of a series of comparisons of paintings and painters from Cimabue to Lorrain, with historical and biographical summaries and appreciations of the painters' motives and methods. [With plates.] pp. xvi. 281. *Hodder & Stoughton: London*, 1914. 8°. **7859.** b. **5.**

—— Photography as a Fine Art. The achievements and possibilities of photographic art . . . Illustrated. pp. xv. 191. *Grant Richards: London; New York* printed, 1902. 4°. **8903.** dd. **7.**

[C]AFFIN (CHARLES HENRY)

—— The Story of American Painting. The evolution of painting in America from colonial times to the present. [With illustrations.] pp. xiii. 396. *Hodder & Stoughton: London ; New York* printed, [1908.] 8°. **7856. i. 32.**

—— The Story of Dutch Painting. [With plates.] pp. xi. 210. *Century Co.: New York*, 1909. 8°. **7875. t. 11.**

—— [Another copy, with a different titlepage.] *T. Fisher Unwin: London ; [printed in U.S.A.,]* 1910. 8°. **7855. bbb. 40.**

—— The Story of French Painting. [With illustrations.] pp. xiv. 232. *Century Co.: New York*, 1911. 8°. **7860. pp. 2.**

—— The Story of Spanish Painting. [With illustrations.] pp. xi. 203. *Century Co.: New York*, 1910. 8°. **7855. bb. 54.**

—— [Another copy, with a different titlepage.] *T. Fisher Unwin: London ; printed in U.S.A.*, 1910. 8°. **7856. c. 36.**

[C]AFFIN (ERNEST) Code électoral pratique, *etc.* pp. 148. *Bordeaux*, 1869. 16°. **5423. a. 17.**

—— Des droits de propriété, des communes et des sections des communes sur les biens communaux, de la mise en valeur de ces biens, de l'emploi de leurs prix, de locations et de ventes. pp. 192. *Limoges*, 1860. 8°. **5425. bb. 3.**

[C]AFFIN (GEORGE CRAWFORD) Some Thoughts for Holy Advent, Christmas, the Feast of the Holy Innocents, and Epiphany-tide, *etc.* pp. 35. *J. Masters & Co.: London*, 1880. 8°. **4372. de. 20.** (7.)

—— Words about our Lord ; being four sermons for Good Friday, Easter Day and Low Sunday, *etc.* pp. 24. *J. Masters & Co.: London*, 1879. 8°. **4473. g. 3.** (3.)

[C]AFFIN (JACQUES FRANÇOIS) Aux chambres et à Mgr le Ministre de l'Instruction publique ; à tous les médecins, observations sur la réorganisation de l'enseignement de la médecine. pp. 55. *Paris*, 1844. 8°. **1406. g. 29.** (2.)

—— Considérations sur la nature, le siège, et les causes des maladies scrophuleuses des glandes lymphatiques, *etc.* [A thesis.] pp. 37. *Paris*, 1805. 4°. **1182. g. 2.** (9.)

[C]AFFIN (MATTHEW) *See* CAFFYN.

[C]AFFIN (PETER) *See* GREENFIELD (Edmund) Christ the Judge of All. A funeral sermon, preached after the fearful backsliding life, distressing death, and burial of a Senior Deacon of a Christian Protestant Church (P. Caffin). 1842. 8°. **4476. f. 52.**

[C]AFFIN D'ORSIGNY (JEAN LOUIS PIERRE HENRI) Grignon, Institution royale et agronomique. Quinze ans d'exploitation et de direction, *etc.* pp. vii. 218. *Paris*, 1845. 8°. **1254. e. 36.**

[C]AFFINIÈRE (MAURICE GAUDIN DE LA) *See* GAUDIN DE LA CAFFINIÈRE.

[C]AFFOCI (ANDRÉS JIRON) *See* JIRON CAFFOCI.

[C]AFFOL (JEAN DEVALZ DE) *See* DEVALZ DE CAFFOL.

[C]AFFORT ( ) *Abbé.* Œuvres complètes. 1856. *See* MIGNE (J. P.) Collection intégrale et universelle des orateurs sacrés, *etc.* tom. 79. 1844, *etc.* 4°. **3676. b. 11.**

CAFFORT (J. P.) Concours pour la Chaire de Pathologie Externe . . . De la certitude en chirurgie et de ses sources. Thèse, *etc.* pp. 62. *Montpellier*, 1840. 4°. **1181. i. 19*.** (3.)

—— Essai sur les affections vermineuses. Dissertation inaugurale, *etc.* pp. 24. *Montpellier*, 1823. 4°. **1181. c. 8.** (16.)

—— Faculté de Médecine de Montpellier. Concours pour la Chaire de Pathologie Externe. (Exposer le plan d'une pathologie générale chirurgicale.) pp. 23. [*Montpellier*, 1839.] 4°. **1182. d. 3.** (1.)
A lithographed MS. *facsimile.*

—— Prouberbis et redits narbouneses recullits et rengats per letro alfabetico per Moussu Caffort. pp. 86. *Narbonne*, 1913. 8°. **012305. m. 26.** (2.)

CAFFO SANTORO (FRANCESCO) Il Naturalismo del popolo nella letteratura italiana del dugento e del trecento. pp. 251. *Siracusa*, 1916. 8°. **011853. w. 12.**

CAFFRARIA. *See* KAFFRARIA.

CAFFRE WARS. *See* KAFFIR WARS.

CAFFRES. *See* KAFIRS.

CAFFREY (A. A.)

—— American Bombsight. [A novel.] pp. 82. *The World's Work: Kingswood, Surrey*, [1943.] 8°. **012633. ppp. 16.**

CAFFREY (DONALD JOHN)

—— *See* WORTHLEY (Leon H.) and CAFFREY (D. J.) Scouting, Quarantine and Control for the European Corn Borer, 1917–1926. 1927. 8°. [*U.S. Department of Agriculture. Technical Bulletin.* no. 53.] **A.S. 800/2.**

CAFFREY (DONALD JOHN) and **BARBER** (GEORGE W.) The Grain Bug. pp. 35. *Washington*, 1919. 8°. [*U.S. Department of Agriculture. Bulletin.* no. 779.] **A.S. 800.**

CAFFREY (DONALD JOHN) and **WORTHLEY** (LEON HOWARD)

—— A Progress Report on the Investigations of the European Corn Borer. pp. 155. *Washington*, 1927. 8°. [*U.S. Department of Agriculture. Bulletin.* no. 1476.] **A.S. 800.**

CAFFREY (GEORGE) *See* PAPPENHEIM (M.) [Die Lumbalpunktion.] Lumbar Puncture . . . Translated by G. Caffrey. 1925. 8°. **07641. ee. 3.**

CAFFREY (LUKE) Luke Caffrey's Gost. To which is added, Luke Caffreys Kilmainham Minit. [Songs.] pp. 8. *W. Goggin: Limerick*, [1790 ?] 8°. **11622. df. 34.** (35.)

CAFFRIS (ANDREA VACA Y) *See* VACA Y CAFFRIS.

CAFFYN (J. E.)

—— *See* BLAIR (George W. S.) and VEINOGLOU (B. C.) Rheological Properties of Dielectric and other Materials. By G. W. S. Blair . . . and B. C. Veinoglou . . . in co-operation with J. E. Caffyn. 1946. 8°. **W.P. 9138/232.**

CAFFYN (KATHLEEN MANNINGTON) *See* also IOTA, *pseud.* [i.e. K. M. Caffyn.]

—— Anne Mauleverer. pp. 349. *Methuen & Co.: London*, 1899. 8°. **012642. cc. 1.**

—— At a Rest House of the Foot-Hills. [By K. Caffyn.] ff. 7. [1904.] 8°. *See* REST HOUSE. **012632. aa. 53.** (5.)

CAFFYN (KATHLEEN MANNINGTON)

—— Dorinda and her Daughter. pp. 351. *Hurst & Blackett: London*, 1910. 8°. **012623. b. 19.**

—— The Fire-Seeker. pp. 415. *Eveleigh Nash: London*, 1911. 8°. **012618. bb. 24.**

—— He for God only. pp. 358. *Hurst & Blackett: London*, 1903. 8°. **012638. c. 6.**

—— Mary Mirrilies. pp. 352. *Hurst & Blackett: London*, 1916. 8°. NN. **3757.**

—— The Minx. pp. 384. *Hutchinson & Co.: London*, 1900. 8°. **012641. b. 13.**

—— Two Ways of Love. pp. 364. *Hurst & Blackett: London*, 1913. 8°. NN. **1321.**

—— Victims of Circe. *See* MARTIN (*Mrs.* H. P.) Coo-ëe, *etc.* [1891.] 8°. **012631. k. 29.**

—— " Whoso Breaketh an Hedge." pp. 344. *Hurst & Blackett: London*, 1909. 8°. **012623. b. 18.**

CAFFYN (MANNINGTON) *See* CAFFYN (Stephen M.)

CAFFYN (*Mrs.* MANNINGTON) *See* CAFFYN (Kathleen M.)

CAFFYN (MATTHEW) *See* GREGG (Florence) Matthew Caffin, *etc.* 1890. 8°. **4907. aaa. 45.**

—— *See* LAWSON (Thomas) *Quaker, of Lancashire*, and SLEE (J.) An Untaught Teacher witnessed against . . . That is to say, the unsound . . . doctrines of M. Caffyn, Baptist-teacher, laid open, *etc.* 1655. 4°. E. **854. (12.)**

—— *See* WHITEHEAD (George) *Quaker*. The Pernicious Way of the Rigid Presbyter and antichristian Ministers, detected . . . To which is annexed something . . . in answer to M. Caffin his great error . . . in his book entituled, Faith in God's Promises, the Saints best Weapon. 1662. 4°. **4152. f. 18. (19.)**

—— The Deceived, and deceiving Quakers Discovered. Their damnable heresies . . . and dishonesty laid open . . . By M. Caffyn . . . Antichrist made known; or the Romish whore of Babylon proved not to bee the Antichrist, or man of sin, in seven particulars . . . By William Jeffery. pp. 80. *R. I. for Francis Smith: London*, 1656. 4°. E. **873. (2.)**

—— *See* NAYLER (James) The Light of Christ . . . occasioned by laying open some deceipts in a booke titled, The Deceived and Deceiving Quakers discovered; subscribed M. Caffin and W. Jeffery, *etc.* 1656. 4°. E. **877. (1.)**

CAFFYN (STEPHEN MANNINGTON) Miss Milne and I. A story . . . Third edition. pp. viii. 324. *Remington & Co.: London*, 1889. 8°. **012632. k. 11.**

—— A Poppy's Tears. pp. viii. 152. *Chapman & Hall: London*, 1890. 8°. **012631. e. 66.**

CAFFYN (W. H.) *See* BOSWELL (James) *the Elder*. [*Journal of a Tour to the Hebrides.*] A Journal of a Tour to the Hebrides . . . With twelve drawings in pen and ink by W. H. Caffyn, *etc.* 1928. 8°. **010369. f. 40.**

CAFFYN (WILLIAM) Seventy-one Not Out. The reminiscences of William Caffyn . . . Edited by " Mid-on." [With plates, including portraits.] pp. xiv. 265. *W. Blackwood & Sons: Edinburgh & London*, 1899. 8°. **07905. g. 30.**

CAFIERO (CARLO) *See* BAKUNIN (M. A.) Dieu et l'état. [With a preface by C. Cafiero and E. Reclus.] 1882. 12°. **8009. aaa. 13.**

CAFIERO (CARLO)

—— —— 1892. 8°. **08275. ee. 23. (1.**

—— *See* BAKUNIN (M. A.) God and the State . . . With a preface by C. Cafiero and E. Reclus, *etc.* 1883. 8°. **8275. dd. 6. (3.**

—— —— 1894. 8°. **08276. i. 21**

—— *See* MARX (C.) Il Capitale . . . Brevemente compendiato da C. Cafiero. 1879. 8°. **8275. bbb. 9**

—— Anarchia e comunismo. Discorso. pp. 11. *Ancona* 1891. 8°. **8277. de. 29. (10.**

—— Anarchie et communisme. Discours prononcé en 188 . . . Extrait du Révolté. pp. 20. *Foix*, 1890. 8°. **8277. ee. 2. (10.**

CAFIERO (G.) New Method for preventing Collisions a Sea. Signals for use in fog, mist or falling snow. pp. 5. *L. A. Smart: Glo'ster*, [1886.] 8°. **8807. c. 20. (5.**

CAFIERO (PASQUALE) Italiano e cattolico. Soluzione pratica di un problema di coscienza. pp. 16. *Roma* 1883. 8°. **3900. e. 19. (1.**

CAFISI (GIUSEPPE) Relazione degli effetti di un fier turbine accaduto nella terra della Favara in Sicilia il d 10 marzo 1772. 1774. *See* SICILIAN AUTHORS. Opuscol di autori siciliani. tom. 15. 1758, *etc.* 4°. **663. g. 8**

CAFLISCH (FRIEDRICH) *See* CAFLISCH (Johann F.)

CAFLISCH (HANS) *See* BAXTER (Richard) [A Call to th Unconverted to turn and live.] La Vusch da Deus, c chomma ils pucconts tiers la Penitentia. Mess giu e Rumonsch. [The translator's dedicatory letter signed H. C., i.e. H. Caflisch.] 1669. 12°. **4411. aa. 2**

CAFLISCH (JOHANN FRIEDRICH) Excursions-Flora fü das südöstliche Deutschland. Ein Taschenbuch zum Bestimmen der in den nördlichen Kalkalpen, der Donau-Hochebene . . . und dem bayerischen Walde vorkommenden Phanerogamen oder Samenpflanzen. pp. xlviii. 374. *Augsburg*, 1878. 8°. **7033. b. 10.**

—— Uebersicht der Flora von Augsburg, enthaltend, die in der Umgebung Augsburgs wildwachsenden und allgemeinen cultivirten Phanerogamen. Bearbeitet von J. F. Caflisch unter Mitwirkung von Dr. Gustav Körbe und Gottfried Deisch. pp. viii. 103. *Augsburg*, 1850. 8°. **7055. c. 12.**

CAFLISCH (LEONHARD)

—— Der junge Mozart in Zürich. Ein Beitrag zur Mozart-Biographie auf Grund bisher unbekannter Dokumente vo L. Caflisch und M. Fehr. pp. 19. pl. 4. *Zürich* 1952. 4°. [*Neujahrsblatt der Allgemeinen Musikgesellschaft Zürich.* no. 140.] Ac. **5132**

CAFLISCH (NINA) Carlo Maderno. Ein Beitrag zur Geschichte der römischen Barockarchitektur, *etc.* [With portraits.] pp. x. 158. pl. XXXI. *München*, 1934. 4°. **07815. b. 23.**

CAFMEYER (PETRUS DE) Hooghweirdighe historie van het Alder-Heylighste Sacrament van Mirakel, in desen nieuwe druck merckelyck verbetert ende vermeerdert . . . verciert met schoone copere figuren. (Eerste[—tweede] vervolgh . . . Op-gestelt ende by een vergaedert door G. D. B. [i.e. G. D. Backer.]) pp. x. 48. 70. *Brussel*, 1720. fol. **9917. k. 1. (2.)**

—— Vénérable histoire du Très-Saint Sacrement de Miracle, notablement améliorée & augmentée en cette nouvelle édition . . . Enrichie de très-belles figures en taille douce . . . traduite en françois par G. D. B. (G. de Backer.) (Première[—seconde] suite de la vénérable histoire du Très-Saint Sacrement . . . Composé & recueïlli par G. D. B. [i.e. G. de Backer.]) pp. viii. 46. 70. *Bruxelles*, 1720. fol. **3834. g. 4.**

AFMEYER (Petrus de)

— Hooghweerdighe historie van het Alder-Heylighste Sacrament van Mirakel, in desen druck door den autheur merckelyck vermeerdert . . . Alles getrocken uyt . . . geapprobeerde autheurs. Verciert met schoone kopere figuren. pp. iii. 64. *Brussel*, 1735. fol. **9917. k. 1. (3.)**

A different work from the preceding.

AFRA (Estéban de) *See* Zafra (E. de)

AGA (Lars) *See* Kagg.

AGABRAGAS, *el Bachiller, pseud.* Sermon burlesco de gran divertimento para una funcion, predicado en Pamplona . . . por el bachiller Cagabragas. [In verse.] pp. 8. *Valladolid*, [1830?] 4°. **11451. ee. 39. (4.)**

AGE. The Gilded Cage, and other stories. pp. 42. *American Baptist Publication Society: Philadelphia*, [1864.] 24°. **12805. aa. 8.**

AGE BIRDS.

— [For the magazine "Cage Birds," see the Catalogue of Newspapers.]

— [For works published by "Cage Birds":] *See* Periodical Publications.—London.—*Cage Birds.*

— Our National Cage Birds. A treatise on their breeding and management. pp. 34. *W. Welham: Brixton*, [1888.] 8°. **7291. c. 3. (5.)**

AGE BIRDS ANNUAL. *See* Periodical Publications.—London.—*Cage Birds.*

AGÉ ( ) Quelques observations de Cagé. [Defending himself against the charge of having lowered the level of the river Hallu.] pp. 16. [*Paris*, 1809?] 4°. **5403. b. 6. (95.)**

AGE (John M.)

— Theory and Application of Industrial Electronics. [By] J. M. Cage . . . With the assistance of C. J. Bashe. pp. xi. 290. *McGraw-Hill Book Co.: New York*, 1951. 8°. [*McGraw-Hill Electrical and Electronic Engineering Series.*] **W.P. 13470/8.**

AGE (Margaret) *See* Cage (Thornton) The Case betwixt Thornton Cage, Esq. and his Wife (M. Cage). [1684?] fol. **816. m. 5. (31.)**

AGE (Thornton) The Case betwixt Thornton Cage, Esq. and his Wife (Margaret Cage). pp. 4. [1684?] fol. **816. m. 5. (31.)**

AGE (William) *Begin.* London, November 19. 1701. To all the Enemies of the King, the Government, and themselves, within the City of Rochester, that appear on the behalf of Collonel Cage. [A manifesto against his parliamentary candidature.] [1701.] *s. sh.* fol. **816. m. 3. (135.)**

AGED BIRD FUND. *See* London.—iii. *Royal Society for the Prevention of Cruelty to Animals.—Bird Fund.*

AGED BIRD POSTER FUND. *See* London.—iii. *Royal Society for the Prevention of Cruelty to Animals.—Bird Fund.*

AGELOT. De Cagelot. Monstrum horrendum, *etc.* [A satire in verse against Ernest Louis, Duke of Brunswick.] pp. 15. *Brunsvici* [*The Hague*], 1785. 8°. **934. g. 17. (27.)**

AGÈRE (François) Essai sur les plaies de tête, et sur les heureux succès obtenus de la méthode évacuante dans les accidens de la commotion, avec quelques vues sur les méprises que l'on peut commettre dans l'opération du trépan, *etc.* [A thesis.] pp. 34. *Montpellier*, [1806.] 4°. **1180. f. 4. (3.)**

ČAGEVIĆ (Stevan) О трговинском Уговору са Аустро-Угарском, *etc.* pp. 29. *Београд*, 1908. 8°. **8074. aaaa. 44.**

CAGGESE (Romolo) *See* Florence. Statuti della Repubblica Fiorentina: editi . . . da R. Caggese. 1910, *etc.* 8°. **5357.e.23.**

—— L'Alto medioevo. Con duecentodieci illustrazioni nel testo. pp. xii. 613. *Torino*, 1937. 4°. [*Grande storia d'Italia.*] **9171.c.2/1.**

—— Classi e comuni rurali nel medio evo italiano. Saggio di storia economica e giuridica. 2 vol. *Firenze*, 1907, 08. 8°. **9168. bb. 15.**

Vol. 1 forms part of the "Pubblicazioni del R. Istituto di Scienze Sociali 'Cesare Alfieri' in Firenze." The date on the wrapper of vol. 2 is 1909.

—— Un Comune libero alle porte di Firenze nel secolo xiii, Prato in Toscana. Studi e ricerche. pp. 250. *Firenze*, 1905. 8°. **10132. k. 8.**

—— Dal Concordato di Worms alla fine della prigionia di Avignone, 1122–1377. Con trecento illustrazioni nel testo. pp. viii. 536. *Torino*, 1939. 8°. [*Grande storia d'Italia.*] **9171.c.2/4.**

—— Firenze dalla decadenza di Roma al risorgimento d'Italia . . . Con prefazione di Guido Mazzoni. [With a bibliography.] 3 vol. *Firenze*, 1912–[21]. 8°. **9150. bb. 30.**

—— Foggia e la Capitanata. Con 150 illustrazioni. pp. 144. *Bergamo*, 1910. 8°. [*Collezione di monografie illustrate.* ser. 1. Italia artistica. no. 56.] **7814. ccc. 1/54.**

—— Italy, 1313–1414. 1932, *etc.* *See* Bury (John B.) The Cambridge Medieval History, *etc.* vol. 7. 1911, *etc.* 8°. [Latest edition.] **2070.f.** [Earlier editions.] **09004. g.**

—— Mirabeau. pp. xi. 361. *Bologna*, [1924.] 8°. **10657. aaa. 36.**

—— Prato nell'età di Dante. *See* Dante Alighieri. [*General Appendix.—Biography and Criticism.*] Dante e Prato, *etc.* 1922. 8°. **011420. c. 41.**

—— La Repubblica di Siena e il suo contado nel secolo decimoterzo. 1906. *See* Sienna.—*Reale Accademia dei Rozzi.—Commissione Senese di Storia Patria.* Bullettina senese di storia patria. anno 13. fasc. 1, 2. 1894, *etc.* 8°. **Ac. 6521/4.**

—— Roberto d'Angiò e i suoi tempi. 2 vol. *Firenze*, 1922, 30. 8°. **10633. v. 6.**

CAGGEVINNE. Coutume de Caggevinne. *Dutch & Fr.* *See* Casier (C.) Coutumes de la ville d'Aerschot, de Neder-Assent et de Caggevinne, *etc.* 1894. 4°. **5686. g. 1/1a.**

CAGGIANO (Gianfrancesco da) Undici discorsi o conferenze intorno all'Immacolato Concepimento di Maria Santissima. pp. 284. *Parigi*, 1858. 8°. **4806. g. 14.**

CAGGIANO (Giulio) Libertà e progresso. Anarchia e socialismo discorso agli operai. pp. 16. *Napoli*, 1890. 16°. **8277. a. 60. (3.)**

CAGGIO (Paolo)

—— Flamminia prudente. Novelletta, *etc.* ff. 19. [*A. Arrivabene:*] *Al segno del Pozzo: Vinegia*, 1551. 8°. **11715. bb. 16.**

—— Iconomica del Signor Paolo Caggio . . . nella quale s'insegna breuemente per modo di dialogo il gouerno Famigliare, *etc.* ff. 64. *Al segno del Pozzo* [*A. Arrivabene*]: *Vinegia*, 1552. 8°. **721. c. 9. (2.)**

—— [Another copy.] **8407. b. 19.**

CAGGIO (PAOLO)

—— Ragionamenti di P. Chaggio, ne quali egli introduce tre suoi amici, che naturalmente discorrono intorno à una uaga fontana, in ueder se la uita cittadinesca sia più felice, del uiuer solitario fuor le città, e nelle uille. ff. 79. [*A. Arrivabene:*] *Al segno del Pozzo: Venetia*, 1551. 8°. **8009**. a. **27**.

CAGGIOLI (AGOSTINO) Un Anno di prigione in Milano. Reminiscenze politiche secrete. pp. 191. *Bergamo*, 1866. 16°. **10630**. aa. 25.

CAGIANO DE AZEVEDO (ANTONIUS MARIA) *Cardinal.* Epistola pastoralis ad clerum et populum universum Dioeceseos Tusculanæ. pp. 15. *Romæ*, 1854. 4°. **898**. i. **1**. (**11**.)

CAGIANO DE AZEVEDO (MICHELANGELO)

—— Aquinum, *etc. Ital.* pp. 82. pl. x. *Roma*, 1949. 8°. [*Italia romana: municipi e colonie.* ser. 1. vol. 9.] Ac. **103**. b/2.

—— I " Capitolia " dell'Impero romano. pp. 76. pl. XVI. [*Vatican City*,] 1940. 4°. [*Atti della Pontificia Accademia Romana di Archeologia.* ser. 3. Memorie. vol. 5. no. 1.] Ac. **5236**.

—— Interamna Lirenas vel Sucasina, presso Pignataro Interamna, *etc.* pp. 58. pl. IV. *Roma*, 1947. 8°. [*Italia romana: municipi e colonie.* ser. 2. vol. 2.] Ac. **103**. b/**2**. (**3**.)

CAGIANUT (B.)

—— Beitrag zur Wirkung von Sexualhormonen auf die Primitiventwicklung von Triton alpestris. Die Beeinflussung der hormonalen Störung durch SH-Glutathion . . . Mit 2 Textabbildungen. pp. 249. *Genève*, 1949. 8°. [*Revue suisse de zoologie.* tom. 56. fasc. 1.] Ac. **2870**. b.

CAGIATI (MEMMO) *See* BORRELLI (N.) *Historical Writer.* Memmo Cagiati, *etc.* 1928. 8°. **10634**. ee. **37**.

—— *See* PERIODICAL PUBLICATIONS.—*Naples.* Annuario italiano per i numismatici e raccoglitori di monete e medaglie. Diretto da M. Cagiati. 1926. 8°. Dept. of Coins & Medals.

—— *See* PERIODICAL PUBLICATIONS.—*Naples.* Miscellanea numismatica. Periodico mensile diretto da M. Cagiati, *etc.* 1920, *etc.* 8°. Dept. of Coins & Medals.

—— Le Monete del re Manfredi nel reame delle Due Sicilie. (Istituto italiano di Numismatica. Estratto dal vol. II degli " Atti e memorie.") pp. 32. *Roma*, 1915. 8°. Dept. of Coins & Medals.

—— Le Monete del reame delle Due Sicilie da Carlo I. d'Angiò a Vittorio Emmanuele II. 2 pt.

pt. 1. La Zeccha di Napoli. fasc. 1–5. 1911, 12.
pt. 2. Le Zecche minore del reame di Napoli. fasc. 6–8. 1913–16.

Napoli, 1911–16. 8°.
Imperfect; wanting pt. 3, *fasc.* 9, *entitled* " *Zecche di Messina da Carlo* I. *d'Angiò a Ferdinando il Cattolico*," *after which no more was published.*

—— Il Supplemento all'opera " Le Monete del reame delle Due Sicilie da Carlo I. d'Angiò a Vittorio Emmanuele II," a cura dell'autore M. Cagiati. anno 1–4. *Napoli*, 1911–13. 8°. Dept. of Coins & Medals.

—— [Another copy.] **7756**. r. 9.
Imperfect; wanting fasc. 8, 9 *of the original work, and anno* 1. *no.* 1, *anno* 2, *no.* 2, 5–12, *anno* 3 *and* 4 *of the supplement.*

CAGIĆ (MIHAILO)

—— Лирске исповести. Песме. pp. 73. *Београд*, 1951. 8°. **11588**. eee. **82**.
Part of a series entitled " *Савремена поезија.*"

CAGIGAL (FRANCISCO MARIANO NIFO Y) *See* NIFO Y CAGIGAL.

CAGIGAL (LUIS CANDELAS Y) *See* CANDELAS Y CAGIGAL.

CAGIGAS (C. DE LAS) Almanaque de la Civilizacion, por C. de las Cagigas. [1850, *etc.*] 16°. *See* EPHEMERIDES. P.P. **2589**. i.

—— Almanaque Popular . . . para el año 1853. Por C. de las Cagigas, *etc.* pp. 79. [1852.] 16°. *See* EPHEMERIDES. P.P. **2589**. g. (**8**.)

—— Almanaque Universal. Para el año 1854. Por C. de las Cagigas, *etc.* pp. 80. [1853.] 16°. *See* EPHEMERIDES. P.P. **2589**. g. (**10**.)

—— Primer Calendario de C. de las Cagigas, arreglado al meridiano de México, para el año de 1850. pp. 72. [1850.] 16°. *See* EPHEMERIDES. P.P. **2589**. g. (4.)

CAGIGAS (DIONISIO DE LAS) El Ataque de Nelson a Tenerife relatado por un marino montañés (D. de las Cagigas). [Edited by Fernando Barreda. With illustrations.] pp. 37. *Santander*, 1936. 8°. **09077**. aaa. **52**.

CAGIGAS (ISIDRO DE LAS)

—— *See* MOROCCO. Tratados y convenios referentes a Marruecos. [Edited by I. de las Cagigas.] 1952. 8°. **S.0.65/2.**

—— Minorías étnico-religiosas de la edad media española.

1. Los Mozárabes. 2 tom. pp. 588. 1947, 48.
2. Los Mudéjares. 2 tom. pp. 572. 1948, 49.

Madrid, 1947– . 8°. **4626**. d. **4**.

CAGIN (PAUL) *See* LITURGIES.—*Latin Rite.—Missals.*—I. [*Sources of the Missal, etc.*] Le Sacramentaire gélasien d'Angoulême, *etc.* [Edited by P. Cagin.] [1919.] 8°. **03366**. k. 3.

—— L'Euchologie latine, étudiée dans la tradition de ses formules et de ses formulaires. 2 vol.

1. Te Deum ou illatio? *etc.* pp. xxxi. 594. 1906.
2. L'Eucharista, canon primitif de la messe, *etc.* [With plates.] pp. 334. 1912.

Appuldurcombe; Liège [printed], 1906, 12. 8°. [*Scriptorium Solesmense.*] **2202**. d. **11**.
Vol. 1 *only published at Appuldurcombe; the imprint of vol.* 2 *reads: Rome, Paris, Tournai.*

—— Le Manuscrit latin M VI., 2 du Musée Borgia. (Extrait de la Revue des bibliothèques.) pp. 37. *Paris*, 1902. 8°. **3478**. h. **25**. (**4**.)

—— Plainchant and Solesmes. By Dom Paul Cagin . . . and Dom André Mocquereau. [With letters from Popes Pius X and Leo XIII.] pp. vi. 70. *Burns & Oates: London*, [1905.] 8°. **7898**. gg. **6**.

—— Le Sacramentarium Triplex de Gerbert. (Extrait de la Revue des bibliothèques.) pp. 29. *Paris*, 1900. 8°. **3478**. h. **25**. (**3**.)

CAGLI, ALFONSO, *Bishop of.* [1806–1817.] *See* CINGARI.

——, GEORGIUS, *Bishop of.* [1507–1513.] *See* BENIGNUS (G.) successively *Bishop of Cagli* and *Archbishop of Nazareth.*

——, LODOVICO AGOSTINO, *Bishop of.* [1754–1802.] *See* BERTOZZI.

AGLI (Cesare) G. D. Romagnosi . . . La vita—i tempi —le opere. [With plates, including portraits, and a bibliography.] pp. 379. *Roma*, 1935. 8°. **20010**. f. **29**.

AGLI (Emma C.) *See* Carroll (Lewis) *pseud.* [Alice in Wonderland.] Nel paese delle meraviglie . . . Fatto italiano da E. C. Cagli. [1924.] 4°. **12802**. d. **52**.

AGLI (Paolo Antonio Agostino Zamperoli di) *Bishop of San Angelo in Vado and Urbania. See* Zamperoli di Cagli.

AGLIÀ-FERRO (Antonino) Indirizzo di Antonio Caglià Ferro. A miei fratelli, *etc.* [On political events in Sicily.] (Le Capitolazioni militari svizzere. [By Carlo du Coster.]) *Genova*, [1848.] *s. sh.* fol. **804**. k. **13**. (**34**.)

—— Nomenclatura familiare siculo-italica. Seguita da una breve fraseologia. pp. xvi. 119. *Messina*, 1840. 8°. **1331**. f. **2**.

AGLIARI.

Camera di Commercio ed Arti.

—— Relazione sovra la statistica e l'andamento del commercio e delle industrie della provincia di Cagliari nel 1867, *etc.* pp. xviii. 115. *Cagliari*, 1869. fol. **8244**. h. **11**.

Club Alpino Sardo.

—— Bolletino del Club Alpino Sardo. annata 1893, 94. *Cagliari*, 1893–95. 8°.
[Continued as:]
Annuario del Club Alpino Sardo. anno 3–5. *Cagliari*, 1896–98. 8°. Ac. **6008**.

Deputazione di Storia Patria per la Sardegna.

—— Archivio storico sardo. [From vol. 23. fasc. 1/4 onwards published by the Regia Deputazione di Storia Patria per la Sardegna.] *See* infra: *Società Storica Sarda*. Archivio storico sardo. 1905, *etc.* 8°. Ac. **6501**.

Reale Università.

—— *See* infra: Università degli Studi.

Regio Archivio di Stato.

—— Inventario del R. Archivio di Stato di Cagliari e notizie delle carte conservate nei più notevoli archivi comunali vescovili e capitolari della Sardegna. [Compiled by Silvio Lippi.] pp. xxii. 175. *Cagliari*, 1902. fol. **11907**. g. **46**.

Società Dante Alighieri, Comitato di Cagliari.

—— *See* Italy.

Società Storica Sarda.

—— Archivio storico sardo. *Cagliari*, 1905– . 8°. Ac. **6501**.
Imperfect; wanting fasc. 1. *From vol.* 23. *fasc.* 1/4 *onwards published by the Regia Deputazione di Storia Patria per la Sardegna.*

—— Indici dei volumi i–xxv. A cura di Francesco Artizzu. pp. 21. *Padova*, 1959. 8°. Ac. **6501**. (**a**.)

—— Biblioteca storica sarda. (Biblioteca della Società storica sarda.) 3 vol. *Cagliari, Sassari*, 1907–17. 4° & 8°. Ac. **6501**. b.

Università degli Studi.

—— Cenni sulla attuali condizioni della R. Università di Cagliari. pp. 27. *Cagliari*, 1872. 8°. **8309**. df. **36**. (**8**.)

—— Studi di storia e filologia. [By B. R. Motzo.] vol. 1. pp. viii. 182. *Cagliari*, 1927. 8°. Ac. **40**.
No more published.

CAGLIARI.

—— L'Università di Cagliari e il progetto Gianturco. Relazione della Commissione . . . letta all'Assemblea generale del Corpo Accademico della R. Università di Cagliari il 23 maggio 1897. pp. 31. *Cagliari*, 1897. 8°. **8304**. f. **7**. (**5**.)

Istituto per gli Studi Sardi.

—— Studi sardi. *Sassari*, 1934– . 8°. Ac. **6501**. c.
Wanting vol. 3. *fasc.* 2, *vol.* 6.

APPENDIX.

—— I Cittadini di Cagliari agli amatissimi fratelli Piemontesi, Genovesi, Savojardi e Nizzardi. (Inno del popolo Sardo a S. M. il Re Carlo Alberto.—Inno popolare alla patria.— I Piemontesi ai Sardi. [Poems.]) *Genova*, 1847. 8°. **804**. k. **13**. (**63**.)

CAGLIARI, *Province of.—Consiglio.* All'onorevole Commissione d'Inchiesta. Il Consiglio della Provincia di Cagliari. pp. 55. [*Cagliari*, 1869.] 4°. **8223**. c. **15**. (**3**.)

CAGLIARI, Lucifer, *Bishop of.* [353–371.] *See* Lucifer.

CAGLIARI, *Ship.* Difesa del Cagliari presso la Commissione delle Prede, e de' Naufragi. [By F. Castriota and G. and R. Damora.] [1858.] 4°. *See* Castriota Scanderbeg (F.) **6825**. f. 14.

CAGLIARI (Paolo) called Paolo Veronese. *See* Caliari.

CAGLIERI (Liborio) Compendio delle vite de santi orefici ed argentieri, raccolto da diversi autori da L. Caglieri, *etc.* [With illustrations.] pp. 102. *Roma*, 1727. 4°. **4805**. g. **8**.

CAGLIERO (Giovanni) *Cardinal. See* Imperatori (U. E.) Giovanni Cagliero, 1838–1926. [With a portrait.] [1931.] 8°. **4606.p.1/10.**

CAGLIOLA (Adelia Bonincontro) *See* Bonincontro Cagliola.

CAGLIOLA (Filippo)

—— Almæ Siciliensis Prouinciæ Ordinis Minorum Conuentualium S. Francisci manifestationes nouissimæ, sex explorationibus complexæ. Quibus Seraphici Conuentualis Ordinis in hoc Siculo regno exordia . . . præstantur, *etc.* pp. 195. *Ex typographia P. Turini: Venetiis*, 1644. 4°. **4785**. bbb. 4.

CAGLIOSTRO. L'Almanach illustré, le Cagliostro. *See* Ephemerides.

CAGLIOSTRO, *Madame.* Auch noch Etwas für Ordens- und Nichtordens-Leute, durch Madame Cagliostro und durch das Rosen-System nunmehro beyderley Geschlechts. Zum Aufschluss aller und jeder Bundesladen nach zeitüblichem Geschmack. [By E. A. A. von Göchhausen?] 2 Tl. *Philadelphia* [*Eisenach*], 178–[1787]. 8°. **8630**. ccc. **1**.

CAGLIOSTRO (Alessandro di) *Count. See* Balsamo (G.) calling himself *Count* Alessandro di Cagliostro.

CAGLIOSTRO (Alexandre de) *Count. See* Balsamo (G.) calling himself *Count* Alessandro di Cagliostro.

CAGLIOSTRO (Serafina di) *Countess. See* Feliciani (Lorenza) afterwards Balsamo (L.) calling herself *Countess* Serafina di Cagliostro.

CAGNA (Achille Giovanni) Falene dell'amore, *etc.* pp. 219. *Milano*, 1878. 8° **12471**. cc. 3.

—— Maria, ovvero Così cammina il mondo. Dramma in quattro atti. pp. 87. *Milano*, 1869. 16°. **11715**. de. 41. (2.)

CAGNA (Achille Giovanni)

—— Quando amore spira.... pp. xii. 495. *Milano*, 1894. 8°. **12471**. i. **15**.

—— Racconti umoristici, *etc.* 2 vol. *Milano*, 1873. 16°. **12471**. aa. **6**.

—— La Rivincita dell'amore. pp. 235. *Milano*, 1891. 8°. **12471**. h. **41**.

CAGNA (Giacopo) Sommario dell'origine et nobiltà d'alcune famiglie della Città di Padoua. [Edited by Antonio Rossetti.] pp. 64. *Appresso L. Pasquati: Padoua*, 1589. 4°. **142**. a. **8**.

—— [Another edition.] pp. 58 [59]. *G. Criuellari: Padoua*, 1623. 4°. **661**. a. **19**.

CAGNAC (Moïse) *See* Salignac de la Mothe Fénelon (F. de) *Archbishop of Cambrai.* Lettres de direction. Introduction et notes par M. Cagnac, *etc.* 1906. 8°. **10905**. cc. **10**.

—— Fénelon. Études critiques. pp. xii. 404. *Paris*, 1910. 8°. **4864**. de. **28**.

—— Fénelon, apologiste de la foi . . . Leçons données à l'Université Catholique de Paris, *etc.* pp. 375. *Paris*, 1917. 8°. **4864**. dg. **18**.

—— Les Lettres spirituelles en France, *etc.* 2 tom. *Paris*, 1928, 29. 8°. **4863**. aa. **31**.

CAGNACCI (Carlo) Giuseppe Mazzini e i fratelli Ruffini. Lettere raccolte e annotate dal prof. C. Cagnacci. pp. 570. *Porto Maurizio*, 1893. 8°. **10921**. cc. **38**.

—— Luigi Banchero. Racconto storico. pp. 150. *Torino*, 1875. 8°. **12471**. c. **16**.

CAGNACCI (E.)

—— *See* Caspani (E.) and Cagnacci (E.) Afghanistan crocevia dell'Asia. 1951. 8°. **010058**. pp. **4**.

CAGNACCI (Guido) *See* Costa (G.) Lettere varie, e documenti autentici intorno le opere, e vero nome, cognome, e patria di Guido Cagnacci. 1752. [*Calogierà* (*A.*) *Raccolta d'opuscoli scientifici e filologici.* tom. 47.] **247**. c. **16**.

CAGNACCI (Ottavio) Octavii Cagnacci e soc. Iesu odae. Editio altera auctior. pp. 131. *Mediolani*, 1902. 8°. **11408**. g. **48**.

CAGNACINUS (Alphonsus) Alphonsi Cagnacini fragmentum historicum antiquitatis nobilissimæ urbis Ferrariæ . . . latine ex italico vertit, præfationem, atque indicem addidit Bernardinus Morettus. [Ascribed in error to A. Cagnacinus; in fact by P. Ligorio.] pp. 15. 1722. *See* Graevius (J. G.) Thesaurus antiquitatum et historiarum Italiæ. tom. 7. pt. 1. 1725, *etc.* fol. **L.R.302.a.2/7.**

CAGNANI (A.) Documents sur les troubles de Bastia, 1er, 2 et 3 juin 1791. Publiés par M. A. Cagnani. pp. 117. *Bastia*, 1894. 8°. [*Bulletin de la Société des Sciences historiques & naturelles de la Corse.* fasc. 158.] Ac. **2861**.

CAGNANI (Cammillo) Relazione della pellegrinazione, che hà fatto la Ven. Compagnia di Sta Maria di Loreto della Città di Fiorenza alla Santa Casa nel mese di Maggio dell'anno MDCXXXX. e di molte grazie concedute dal suo santissimo crocifisso, *etc.* pp. 56. *Nella stamperia de' Landi: Fiorenza*, 1640. 4°. **1193**. m. **1**. (**39**.)

CAGNANI (Eugenio) Raccolta d'alcune rime di scrittori mantouani. Fatta per Eugenio Cagnani. Con vna lettera cronologica & altre prose, & rime dello stesso. pp. 125. *A. & L. Osanni: Mantoua*, 1612. 4°. **84**. b. **28**. (**1**.)

CAGNANI (Francesco Maria) *See* Oeio (Eustasio) *pseud* [i.e. F. M. Cagnani.]

CAGNARD (Louis) Les Martyrs ignorés. Précédés d'un lettre de M. Barthélemy Saint-Hilaire. pp. viii. 402. *Paris*, 1875. 12°. **12516**. f. **5**

CAGNARONUS (Caesar) *See* Trieste. Statut. inclytæ civitatis Tergesti, per fel. record. Ferdinandum I Imperatorem . . . et Carolum VI. . . . confirmata . . Et marginalibus textualibus annotationibus . . . locuple tata per excellentiss. D. C. Cagnaronum, *etc.* 1727. 4°. **5549**. e. **40**

CAGNASSI ( ) Gli Assassinii in Africa. Rive lazioni sul processo Cagnassi-Livraghi che si svolge a Massaua. pp. 31. *Napoli*, 1891. 8°. **8154**. a. **17**. (**4**.

CAGNASSI (Michele) Le Stelle cadenti di agosto 1879 osservate dal prof. M. Cagnassi in Salerno. pp. 12. *Salerno*, 1879. 12°. **8563**. aa. **7**. (**1**.

CAGNAT (René Louis Victor) *See* Ballu (A.) and Cagnat (R. L. V.) Musée de Timgad. 1903. 4°. **7703.b.32/12.**

—— *See* Berlin.—*Koenigliche Akademie der Wissenschaften etc.* [*Miscellaneous Publications.*] Corpus inscriptionum Latinarum, *etc.* (vol. 8. Supplementum. pt. 1. Inscriptionum Africae Proconsularis Latinarum supplementum. Ediderunt R. Cagnat et Iohannes Schmidt —pt. 2. Inscriptionum Provinciae Numidiae Latinarum supplementum. Ediderunt R. Cagnat et Iohannes Schmidt.—pt. 3. Inscriptionum Mauretaniae Latinarum miliariorum et instrumenti domestici in Provinciis Africanis repertorum supplementum. Ediderunt Iohannes Schmidt R. Cagnat Hermannus Dessau.) 1863, *etc.* 4° **L.R.300.a.1/8.**

—— *See* Bœswillwald (E.) Timgad . . . Par E. Bœswillwald . . . R. Cagnat . . . A. Ballu, *etc.* 1905. 4°. **7701**. ccc. **3**

—— *See* Boulanger (A.) Antiquités puniques. [Edited by R. Cagnat.] 1913. 4°. **7703**. b. **32/8**

—— *See* Douël (M.) Au pays de Salammbô. Préface de R. Cagnat. 1911. 8°. **010097**. k. **11**

—— *See* France.—*Ministère de l'Instruction Publique, etc.* Atlas archéologique de la Tunisie. Édition spéciale des cartes topographiques publiées par le Ministère de la Guerre, avec un texte explicatif par MM. E. Babelon, R. Cagnat, *etc.* 1893, *etc.* fol. Maps **12**. e. **39**.

—— *See* Goyau (P. L. T. G.) Chronologie de l'empire romain. Publiée sous la direction de R. Cagnat. 1891. 8°. **09039**. aa. **1**.

—— *See* Goyau (P. L. T. G.) Lexique des antiquités romaines. Rédigé sous la direction de R. Cagnat, *etc.* 1895. 8°. **7706**. b. **37**

—— *See* Periodical Publications.—*Paris.* L'Année épigraphique . . . Par R. Cagnat. 1889, *etc.* 8°. P.P. **1927**. be

—— *See* Tunis.—*Musée Alaoui.* Catalogue du Musée Alaoui, *etc.* [With a preface by R. Cagnat.] 1897. 8°. **7703.b.32/15.**

—— *See* Tunisia.—*Direction des Antiquités et Arts.* Les Monuments historiques de la Tunisie. (pt. 1. Les Monuments antiques. Publiés par R. Cagnat, P. Gauckler, *etc.*) 1898, *etc.* fol. **7701**. k. **19**

—— A travers le monde romain. pp. 300. *Paris*, 1912. 8°. **09039**. bb. **20**.

CAGNAT (René Louis Victor)

— L'Armée romaine d'Afrique et l'occupation militaire de l'Afrique sous les Empereurs. [With plates and maps.] pp. xxiv. 812. 1892. 4°. *See* France.—*Ministère de l'Instruction Publique, etc.* **9039. i. 10.**

— [Another edition.] pp. xxviii. 802. 1913 [1912, 13]. 4°. *See* France.—*Ministère de l'Instruction Publique, etc.* **9040. i. 15.**

— Bibliographie critique de l'épigraphie latine. pp. 24. *Paris,* 1901. 8°. [*Bibliothèque de bibliographies critiques.* no. 13.] **11926. p. 36.**

— Cours d'épigraphie latine. Deuxième édition entièrement refondue et accompagnée de planches, *etc.* pp. xxvi. 436. *Paris,* 1889. 8°. **07708. f. 11.**

— Cours élémentaire d'épigraphie latine. pp. x. 226. *Paris,* 1886 [1885]. 8°. **7705. e. 28.**

— Étude historique sur les impôts indirects chez les Romains jusqu'aux invasions des barbares, d'après les documents littéraires et épigraphiques. pp. xiv. 256. *Paris,* 1882. 8°. **7705. f. 15.**

— Inscriptiones Graecae ad res Romanas pertinentes. Auctoritate et impensis Academiae Inscriptionum et Litterarum Humaniorum collectae et editae. [Edited by R. L. V. Cagnat.] 1911 [1901]- . 8°. *See* Paris.—*Académie des Inscriptions et Belles-Lettres.* **Ac. 420/8.**

— Inventaire des mosaïques de la Gaule et de l'Afrique, *etc.* [Edited by R. L. V. Cagnat. With plates.] 8 pt. 1909–25. 8°. *See* Paris.—*Académie des Inscriptions et Belles Lettres.* **Ac. 420. d/3.**

— Lambèse. [With illustrations.] pp. 72. *Paris,* 1893. 12°. **10096. bb. 15.**
One of the "Guides en Algérie à l'usage des touristes et des archéologues."

— Musée de Lambèse. pp. 89. pp. vii. *Paris,* 1895. 4°. [*Musées et collections archéologiques de l'Algérie et de la Tunisie.*] **7703.b.32/5.**

— Rapport sur une mission en Tunisie. 1882–88. *See* France.—*Ministère de l'Instruction Publique, etc.* Archives des missions scientifiques et littéraires, *etc.* sér. 3. tom. 9, 11, 12, 14. 1873, *etc.* 8°. **P.P. 1424. ks.**

— Mélanges Cagnat. Recueil de mémoires concernant l'épigraphie et les antiquités romaines dédié par ses anciens élèves . . . à M. René Cagnat . . . à l'occasion du 25ᵉ anniversaire de sa nomination comme professeur au Collège de France. [With a portrait and a bibliography.] pp. 452. *Paris,* 1912. 8°. **7704. cc. 39.**

CAGNAT (René Louis Victor) and **CHAPOT** (Victor)

— Manuel d'archéologie romaine. [With illustrations.] tom. 1, 2. *Paris,* 1916, 20. 8°. **07704. ee. 34.**
No more published.

CAGNAT (René Louis Victor) and **MERLIN** (Alfred)

— Inscriptions latines d'Afrique, Tripolitaine, Tunisie, Maroc. Par MM. R. Cagnat . . . et A. Merlin . . . avec la collaboration de M. Louis Chatelain. pp. iii. 223. *Paris,* 1923. 8°. **7701. g. 20.**

CAGNAT (René Louis Victor) and **SALADIN** (Henri)

— Voyage en Tunisie, *etc.* pp. vi. 419. *Paris,* 1894. 8°. **010097. g. 3.**

CAGNATI (Marsilio) De continentia, vel de sanitate tuenda liber primus, *etc.* pp. 151. *Apud A. & H. Donangelos: Romæ,* 1591. 4°. **1039. h. 14. (1.)**

CAGNATI (Marsilio)

— [Another edition.] Marsilij Cagnati . . . De sanitate tuenda libri duo, *etc.* ff. 196. *Apud F. Bolzettam: Patauij,* 1605. 4°. **1039. i. 6. (2.)**

— De morte caussa partus medica quidem disputatio sed forensibus negotijs tractandis necessaria. (De ligno sancto prima [—altera] disputatio.) *Apud A. Zannettum: Romæ,* 1602. 4°. **1176. i. 1. (1.)**
With "Appendix Disputationis de morte caussa partus. Ad Iulium Benignum . . . Marsilius Cagnatus," forming pp. xxix–xxxii of another work.

— De Romani aeris salubritate commentarius. [With a map.] pp. 53. *Apud A. Zannettum: Romæ,* 1599. 4°. **659. c. 12. (6.)**

— [Another copy.] **1170. h. 2. (1.)**

— De Tiberis inundatione medica dissertatio . . . Epidemia Romana, disputatio scilicet de illa populari ægritudine, quæ anno 1591, & de altera quæ anno 1593, in vrbem Romam inuasit. pp. 73. *Apud A. Zannettum: Romæ,* 1599. 4°. **551. b. 4.**

— De vrbana febres curandi ratione commentarius apologeticus. pp. 45. *Apud A. Zannettum: Romæ,* 1601. 4°. **551. b. 59.**

— Marsilij Cagnati . . . in Aphor. Hyppoc. xxii. sectionis primæ germana quamuis noua expositio . . . nuper edita per Philandrum Colutium . . . cui additus est Comm: in Hypp. Aphor. ij. sect. xxiv . . . ab ipso Philandro illustrata, & aucta. pp. 110. *Apud B. Zannettum: Romæ,* 1619. 8°. **539. d. 22. (1.)**

— *See* Cletus (A.) Aetij Cleti . . . Dilucidatio in Aphor. 22. primæ sect. pro defensione interpretationis M. Cagnati, *etc.* 1621. 8°. **539. d. 22. (3.)**

— *See* Manelphus (J.) Ioannis Manelphi . . . Responsio breuis . . . in commentationem M. Cagnati . . . super Aphorismo Concocta 22. lib. i. Hippocratis. 1621. 8°. **539. d. 22. (2.)**

— *See* Martianus (P.) Breuis Annotatio super expositionem Aphorismi. Concocta medicari M. Cagnati . . . nuper impressam, *etc.* 1619. 4°. **549. e. 10. (1.)**

— In Hippocratis Aphorismum secundæ sectionis vicesimum quartum commentarius Marsilij Cagnati. pp. 31. *Apud A. & H. Donangelos: Romæ,* 1591. 4°. **542. f. 2.**

— Relatione dell'infermita del Cardinale Saluiati. pp. 15. *L. Zannetti: Roma,* 1603. 4°. **1176. i. 1. (2.)**

— Marsilij Cagnati . . . variarum obseruationum libri duo. Eiusdem disputatio de ordine in cibis seruando. 2 pt. *Ex typographia G. Ferrarij; apud V. Accoltum: Romæ,* 1581. 8°. **957. e. 3.**

— Marsilij Cagnati . . . variarum obseruationum libri quatuor, quorum duo posteriores nunc primum accessere. Eiusdem disputatio de ordine in cibis seruando. 2 pt. *Apud B. Donangelum; excudebat A. Gardanus, & F. Coattinus: Romæ,* 1587. 8°. **1169. d. 5. (1, 2.)**

— [Another edition.] [1604.] *See* Gruterus (J.) Lampas, siue fax artium liberalium, *etc.* tom. 3. 1602, *etc.* 8°. **1087. i. 3.**

— Ex quinto libro variarum obseruationum Marsilij Cagnati nomina hæc parum nota enarrantur, Pharmacopola, Aromatarius, Seplasiarius, Ropopla, Catholicus, Unguentarius. pp. 11. [*Rome,* 1602 ?] 4°. **1176. i. 1. (1*.)**

CAGNATI (MARSILIO)

—— *See* ROME.—*Collegium Aromatariorum.* Collegij Aromatariorum almæ vrbis nominis pharmacopolæ, & seplasarij, pro defensione, animaduersio. [Together with a reply beginning, " Marsilius Cagnatus Vniuersitatis Aromatariorum vrbis Consulibus fælicitatem."] 1603. 4°. **1172. i. 2. (4.)**

CAGNATIUS (JOANNES) *de Tabia.* *See* CAGNAZZO (J.)

CAGNATUS (MARSILIUS) *See* CAGNATI (Marsilio)

CAGNAZZI (LUCA DE SAMUELE)

—— La Mia vita. Memorie inedite a cura di Alessandro Cutolo, *etc.* [With plates, including a portrait.] pp. 356. *Milano,* 1944. 8°. **10656. n. 26.**

—— Saggio sulla popolazione del regno di Puglia ne' passati tempi e nel presente. [With a map.] 2 pt. *Napoli,* 1820, 39. 8°. **1138. g. 6.**

—— [Another copy of pt. 1.] **10131. d. 18.**

—— Su i valori delle misure e dei pesi degli antichi Romani, desunti dagli originali esistenti nel Real Museo Borbonico di Napoli, *etc.* [With plates.] pp. 153. *Napoli,* 1825. 8°. **811. i. 8.**

—— Su la varia indole delle forze agenti nell'universo. pp. xi. 303. *Napoli,* 1845. 8°. **1393. h. 28.**

—— Sul dissodamento de' pascoli del tavoliere di Puglia e sull'affrancazione de' suoi canoni. pp. 53. *Napoli,* 1832. 8°. **8227. c. 70. (2.)**

—— [Another copy.] **8246. bbb. 49. (10.)**

—— Tonographiae excogitatio. [With a plate.] pp. 47. *Neapoli,* 1841. 8°. **785. g. 32.**

CAGNAZZO (JOANNES) Summa Summarum (de Casibus cõscientia) quæ Tabiena dicitur. ff. 503. *Impressa in edibus B. Hectoris : Bononie,* 1517. 4°. **854. h. 8.**

CAGNE (ANDRÉ) Le Secretariat général de la Société des Nations. Thèse, *etc.* pp. 155. *Paris,* 1936. 8°. **8028. dd. 39.**

CAGNETTO (GIOVANNI) and **ZANCAN** (ADELCHI) Anatomische und experimentelle Untersuchungen über die typhöse Nephritis. 1907. *See* ZIEGLER (Ernst) *Professor der Pathologie in Freiburg i. B.,* and NAUWERCK (C.) Beiträge zur pathologischen Anatomie, *etc.* Bd. 41. Hft. 3. 1886, *etc.* 8°. **P.P.3206.aa.**

CAGNEY (CHARLES FRANCIS) *See* BROOM (Herbert) A Selection of Legal Maxims . . . The sixth edition. By H. F. Manisty . . . and C. Cagney. 1884. 8°. **6146. k. 16.**

—— *See* LONDON.—III. *Council of Law Reporting.* The Law Reports . . . Compilers, P. B. Hutchins . . . C. F. Cagney. 1892. 8°. **5807.a.16.**

—— *See* POWELL (Edmund) Powell's Principles and Practice of the Law of Evidence. Sixth edition. By J. Cutler . . . and C. F. Cagney. 1892. 8°. **6281. de. 24.**

—— —— 1898. 8°. **6282. ee. 7.**

—— —— 1904. 8°. **6191. d. 12.**

—— Compensation. The publican's case. pp. 91. *W. H. Allen & Co.: London,* 1888. 8°. **8436. bb. 24.**

CAGNEY (JAMES) *See* BROWNE (Lennox) The Throat and Nose . . . With special assistance as follows . . . Nervous Diseases, J. Cagney, *etc.* 1899. 8°. **7615. g. 10.**

CAGNEY (JAMES)

—— *See* ERB (W. H.) [Handbuch der Elektrotherapie. Electrotherapeutics . . . Translated by A. de Watteville . . . with the assistance of J. Cagney, *etc.* 1887. 8°. [*Von Ziemssen's Handbook of General Therapeutics* vol. 6.] **7439. e. 10**

—— *See* JAKSCH (F. von) Clinical Diagnosis . . . Translated . . . and enlarged by J. Cagney, *etc.* 1890. 8°. **7442. h. 20**

—— —— 1893. 8°. **7442. ee. 6**

—— —— 1897. 8°. **7442. ee. 14**

—— —— 1899. 8°. **7439. e. 2**

CAGNEY (KARIN H.) *See* MOLANDER (H.) The Fortune Hunter. Translated . . . by K. H. Cagney. 1905. 8°. **012631. bbb. 38**

CAGNI (GIOVANNI) Miniere di zolfo in Italia, *etc.* pp. xi. 275. *Milano,* 1903. 8°. **012200. i. 98**

CAGNI (MANFREDO) Egitto . . . Con 25 fototipie, *etc.* pp. 224. *Torino,* 1897. 8°. **010095. h. 5**

CAGNI (PIETRO) Amedeo di Savoia. Discorso, *etc.* pp. 38 *Piazza Armerina,* 1890. 8°. **10601. ee. 5. (6.**

CAGNI (UMBERTO) Relazione del capitano di fregata Umberto Cagni. *See* LOUIS AMADEUS JOSEPH MARIA FERDINAND FRANCIS [of Savoy], *Duke degli Abruzzi.* Osservazioni scientifiche eseguite durante la spedizione polare di S. A. R. Luigi Amedeo, *etc.* 1903. 4°. **8706. h. 10**

—— Relazione sulla spedizione colle slitte verso il polo *See* LOUIS AMADEUS JOSEPH MARIA FERDINAND FRANCIS [of Savoy], *Duke degli Abruzzi.* La " Stella Polare " ne mare artico, *etc.* 1903. 8°. **10460. df. 2**

—— Report of Commander Umberto Cagni on the Sledge Expedition towards the Pole. *See* LOUIS AMADEUS JOSEPH MARIA FERDINAND FRANCIS [of Savoy], *Duke degli Abruzzi.* On the " Polar Star " in the Arctic Sea *etc.* vol. 2. 1903. 8°. **2370. g. 6**

CAGNIARD (ESPÉRANCE) *See* BORDEAUX (G.) Le Président Carnot en Normandie, *etc.* [Edited by E. Cagniard. 1889. 4°. **1763. d. 27**

CAGNIARD (LOUIS PAUL ÉMILE)

—— La Prospection géophysique. pp. 203. pl. VIII. *Paris,* 1950. 8°. **07107. f. 44**
Part of a series entitled " La Science vivante."

—— Réflexion et réfraction des ondes séismiques progressives. pp. xi. 255. *Paris,* 1939. 8°. **07108. d. 12**

CAGNIARD-LATOUR (CHARLES) *Baron.* Notice sur les travaux scientifiques de M. Cagniard-Latour. pp. 25. *Paris,* 1851. 4°. **8705. f. 31. (4**

CAGNIAT (CH.) De l'inflammation rhumatismale des synoviales tendineuses et des bourses séreuses, *etc.* pp. 52 [58]. *Paris,* 1875. 4°. [*Collection des thèses soutenues à la Faculté de Médecine de Paris.* An 1875. tom. 4.] **7374. [illegible]**

CAGNIN (FRANÇOYS) *See* BULLIOUD (P.) Vie de Françoys Cagnin, *etc.* 1897. 8°. **4866. i. [illegible]**

CAGNION (A. N.) Dissertation sur la leucorrhée. pp. 1[illegible] *Paris,* 1819. 4°. **1183. e. 9. (15**

CAGNION (J. P.) Vues sur la puberté de la femme, et sur la chlorose ; dissertation, *etc.* pp. 19. *Paris,* 1809. 4 **T. 543. (21**

—— [Another copy.] **1182. h. 6. (8**

AGNOLA (ANGELO) Esposizione topografica del viaggio israelitico nel deserto, *etc.* pp. 231. *Lodi*, 1829. 8°. **571.** f. **26.**

AGNOLA (FRANCESCO) La Questione sociale e le autonomie. Ampliazione della conferenza tenuta dal deputato F. Cagnola ai suoi elettori, in Codogno, *etc.* pp. 365. *Lodi*, 1884. 4°. **8275.** ee. **15.**

— Relazione sulle acque e diritti inerenti letta dall' on. deputato avv. F. Cagnola al Congresso agrario di Lodi. pp. 28. *Milano*, 1883. 8°. **7073.** de. **7.** (**3.**)

AGNOLA (GIOVANNI PIETRO) Storia di Milano, dall'anno 1023, omesso il libro primo, sino al 1497. 1842. *See* ITALIAN HISTORICAL ARCHIVES. Archivio storico italiano, *etc.* tom. 3. 1842, *etc.* 8°. **P.P. 3557.**

AGNOLA (JOSEPHUS) *Marquis.* De augustissimo Trinitatis mysterio oratio, *etc.* pp. xii. *Romæ*, 1786. 4°. **1356.** k. **8.** (**7.**)

AGNOLA (LUIGI) *Marquis.* Le Solenni esequie di Monsignor Filippo Visconti, arcivescovo di Milano, celebrate nella Metropolitana il giorno xv di Febrajo, l'anno CIƆIƆCCCII. [With a portrait.] pp. 12. pl. IV. *Milano*, 1802. fol. **1864.** c. **2.**
The titlepage is engraved.

— Necrologia del marchese Luigi Cagnola. [Signed: G. With a portrait.] 1833. 8°. *See* G. **10630.** dd. **2.** (**4.**)

AGNOLI (AGOSTINO) *See* CRESCIMANNO TOMASI (G.) Alcuni poeti alla corte di Francesco IV di Modena . . . A. Cagnoli, *etc.* 1900. 8°. **10632.** cc. **40.**

— Poesie. 2 vol. *Reggio*, 1844. 8°. **11431.** de. **57.**

AGNOLI (ANTOINE) *See* CAGNOLI (Antonio)

AGNOLI (ANTONIO) *See* AGOSTINELLI (B.) Istruzione popolare per ben regolare gli orologi a tempo medio, coll' uso delle tavole di equazione, desunte dalle notizie astronomiche del professore cav. sig. A. Cagnoli. 1873. 8°. **8506.** g. **1.** (**3.**)

— *See* PINDEMONTE (I.) Tributo alla memoria dell'insigne astronomo cavaliere A. Cagnoli. 1821. 8°. **T. 68*.** (**1.**)

— Catalogue de 501 étoiles suivi des tables relatives d'aberration et de nutation. pp. viii. 280. *Modène*, 1807. 4°. **1395.** f. **24.**

— De' due orologj, italiano e francese, ossia degl'inconvenienti che nascono dal regolare gli orologj al tramontar del sole, o come anche dicesi all'italiana. Dissertazione, *etc.* pp. 44. *Venezia*, 1787. 8°. **T. 2363.** (**6.**)

— [Another edition.] pp. 16. *Venezia*, 1797. 4°. **8766.** ee. **22.** (**1.**)

— Notizie astronomiche . . . Seconda edizione accresciuta di annotazioni per opera de' professori G. Bianchi, F. Carlini, A. Colla. [With plates.] 2 vol. *Parma*, 1851. 8°. **8560.** b. **21.**
Each vol. has an additional titlepage, engraved.

— [Nuovo e sicuro mezzo per riconoscere la figura della terra.] Memoir on a New and Certain Method of ascertaining the Figure of the Earth by means of occultations of the fixed stars . . . With notes and an appendix by Francis Baily. pp. 44. *Privately printed: London*, 1819. 8°. **B. 731.** (**3.**)

— [Another copy.] **8560.** e. **20.**

— Trigonometria piana e sferica. pp. xv. 461. pl. IX. *Parigi*, 1786. 4°. **60.** d. **16.**

CAGNOLI (ANTONIO)

— Trigonométrie rectiligne et sphérique, traduite . . . par N. M. Chompré. Seconde édition considérablement augmentée. [With plates.] pp. xvi. 508. *Paris, 1808. 4°.* **530.k.25.**

CAGNOLI (BELMONTE) *See* also PAPAGNO, *da Bisceglia, pseud.* [i.e. B. Cagnoli.]

— Di Aquilea distrutta . . . libri venti . . . Con gli argomenti à ciascun libro di Dionisio Dionigi. pp. 657. *F. Baba: Venetia*, 1625. 12°. **1063.** b. **10.**
The titlepage is engraved.

— [Another edition.] In questa seconda impressione corretta, e migliorata . . . Con aggiunta de gli argomenti in ottaua rima. pp. 272. *F. Baba: Venetia*, 1628. 4°. **11427.** g. **1.**

— La Vita di S. Giuliano, martire in Anazarbe . . . La Morte del peccatore, e del giusto del medesimo. [In verse.] 2 pt. *A. Pinelli: Venetia*, 1622. 8°. **11427.** df. **15.**

CAGNOLI (LUIGI) *See* EPIRINO, *pseud.* Opuscoli concernenti la poesia. Quinterno primo. (Epirino al celeberrimo autore [L. Cagnoli] del famoso sonetto pubblicato il dì 6 giugno 1822.) [1822.] 8°. **T. 2281.** (**9.**)

— A Fortunato Viaschi Reggiano cui si conferisce in Modena la laurea di medicina. Ode. pp. vii. [*G. B. Bodoni: Parma*,] 1795. 8°. **L.R. 233.** a. **10.** (**1.**)

CAGNOLI (OTTAVIO) Cenni statistici di Verona, e della sua provincia, colla pianta di Verona nel 1849. pp. viii. 130. *Verona*, 1849. 8°. **10131.** e. **6.**

CAGNOLO (NICOLÒ) Lucrezia Borgia in Ferrara, sposa a Don Alfonso d'Este. Memorie storiche estratte dalla Cronaca ferrarese di Bernardino Zambotto, dov' è inserita la Relazione di N. Cagnolo, *etc.* pp. 77. *Ferrara*, 1867. 8°. **10630.** aaa. **17.**

CAGNOLUS (BAPTISTA) *See* CAGNOLUS (H.) Hieronymi Cagnoli . . . Commentaria . . . in primam & secundam Digesti Veteris, & Codicis partem, *etc.* [Edited by B. Cagnolus.] 1576. fol. **5309.** h. **4.**

CAGNOLUS (HIERONYMUS) Hieronymi Cagnoli . . . Commentaria doctissima in primam & secundam Digesti Veteris, & Codicis partem, maximeꝗ in quatuor ordinarias, vt appellant, lecturas matutinas . . . Nunc tertia vice diligentius excusa, *etc.* (Petri Violæ . . . oratio in funere . . . Hieronymi Cagnoli habita.) [Edited by Baptista Cagnolus.] pp. 547. *Apud Iuntas: Venetiis*, 1576. fol. **5309.** h. **4.**

— Splendidissimi Iurisconsulti Domini Hieronymi Cagnoli . . . in Constitutiones & Leges primi, secundi, quinti, & duodecimi Pandectarum . . . aurearum enarrationum liber primus . . . Post primam impressionem denuo ex typographo, authoris . . . aucta, *etc.* G.L. 2 tom. *Apud H. Scotum: Venetiis*, 1554, 53. fol. **5322.** ee. **5.**
Tom. 2 is of the second edition.

— Excellētissimi Jureconsulti ac insignis equitis. Hieronymi cagnoli . . . septē perutiles atꝗ elegātissime repetitiones . . . His addita est repetitio legis curabit .C. de actio empti., *etc.* G.L. ff. 80. *Typis A. Ransti: in vrbe Taurini*, 1528. fol. **5254.** h. **1.** (**2.**)

CAGNONE (GIUSEPPE) Pietro Gravina, umanista del sec. XVI. pp. viii. 107. *Catania*, 1901. 8°. **10630.** e. **22.**

CAGNONI (ACHILLE) Descrizione di Caprera. Preceduta da un sunto storico sulla vita del generale Garibaldi, e sue principali gesta, *etc.* pp. 98. *Milano*, 1865. 4°. **10129.** ee. **24.**

CAGNO-POLITI (N. DI) Giulio Cesare Vanini . . . Saggio bio-bibliografico. 2ª edizione . . . ampliata. pp. xv. 159. *Roma,* 1894. 8°. **10629.** cc. **34.**

CAGNUCCI (ANGELA ELETTA) *See* VINCENZO, *da Porto S. Giorgio, Franciscan.* Vita della beata Battista Varani, *etc.* [With a dedication by A. E. Cagnucci.] 1874. 8°. **4867.** bb. **9.**

CAGNY (PAUL) *See* PARIS.—*Société Impériale et Centrale de Médecine Vétérinaire.* Bulletin et mémoires de la Société centrale de Médecine vétérinaire, rédigés et publiés . . . par M. P. Cagny. 1885, *etc.* 8°. [*Recueil de médecine vétérinaire.*] **P.P.3284.(2.)**

—— Formulaire des vétérinaires praticiens, comprenant environ 1500 formules et rédigé d'après les nouvelles méthodes thérapeutiques . . . Avec la collaboration de Paul Cantiget . . . Troisième édition revue et augmentée. pp. xii. 348. *Paris,* 1900. 12°. **7293.** aa. **25.**

CAGNY (PAUL DE) Notice historique sur la commune et la seigneurie de Caulincourt. (Extrait de la "Picardie.") pp. 32. *Amiens,* 1872. 8°. **9904.** dd. **41.** (**6.**)

CAGNY (PERCEVAL DE) Chroniques de P. de Cagny, publiées pour la première fois . . . par H. Moranvillé. pp. xviii. 288. 1902. 8°. *See* PARIS.—*Société de l'Histoire de France.* Ac. **6884/95.**

CAGOT. The Cagot; or, Heart for heart. A play in five acts. [In verse. By Edmund O'Rourke.] pp. 99. *John Mitchell: London,* 1856. 8°. **11781.** e. **38.** (**11.**)

CAHAGNE (FRANÇOIS ARSÈNE CHAIZE DE) *See* CHAIZE DE CAHAGNE.

CAHAGNES (JACQUES) *See* CAHAIGNES (Jacques de)

CAHAGNESIUS (JACOBUS) *See* CAHAIGNES (Jacques de)

CAHAGNET (GUILLAUME PIERRE FRANÇOIS) Aperçu sur quelques symptômes de fièvres pernicieuses ou ataxiques, en Zélande, et sur leur traitement, *etc.* [A thesis.] pp. 15. *Paris,* 1807. 4°. **1182.** g. **11.** (**30.**)

CAHAGNET (HENRI ERNEST) Thèse pour le doctorat en médecine, *etc.* (Questions sur diverses branches des sciences médicales.) pp. 23. *Paris,* 1838. 4°. **1184.** i. **5.** (**4.**)

CAHAGNET (LOUIS ALPHONSE) Études sur l'homme. pp. 80. *Argenteuil; Paris,* 1858. 12°. **8406.** c. **38.** (**2.**)

—— Force et matière [i.e. "Kraft und Stoff" by F. C. C. L. Büchner], ou Réfutation des doctrines de cet ouvrage. pp. 35. [*Paris;*] *Argenteuil,* 1866. 18°. **8466.** b. **39.** (**4.**)

—— Lumière des morts, ou Études magnétiques philosophiques, et spiritualistes, dédiées aux libres penseurs du XIX siècle. pp. viii. 322. *Paris,* 1851. 12°. **8465.** c. **23.**

—— [Lumière des morts.] Blicke in das Leben der Todten. Die Lehre von Gott und den geheimen Kräften der Natur. pp. viii. 235. *Leipzig,* 1853. 16°. **8631.** a. **8.**

—— Magie magnétique, ou Traité historique et pratique de fascinations . . . possessions . . . nécromancie . . . Troisième édition, corrigée et augmentée. pp. 519. *Paris,* 1895. 8°. **08631.** g. **13.**

—— Magnétisme. Arcanes de la vie future dévoilés, *etc.* 3 tom. *Paris,* 1848–54. 12°. **8465.** aaa. **29.**

—— [Magnétisme.] The Celestial Telegraph; or, the Secrets of the life to come revealed through magnetism, *etc.* pp. viii. 243. *Geo. Peirce: London,* [1850.] 12°. **8465.** c. **22.**

CAHAGNET (LOUIS ALPHONSE)

—— Méditations d'un penseur, ou Mélanges de philosophi et de spiritualisme, *etc.* 2 tom. *Paris,* 1860. 12°. **4409.** g. **1**

—— Révélations d'outre-tombe par les esprits Galilé Hypocrate, Franklin, etc., sur Dieu, la préexistence de âmes, *etc.* pp. 383. *Paris,* 1856. 12°. **8631.** c. **4**

—— Sanctuaire du spiritualisme; étude de l'âme humain et de ses rapports avec l'univers, d'après le somnambulism et l'extase. pp. 382. *Paris,* 1850. 12°. **8630.** f. **1**

—— Das Heiligthum der Geisterwelt, d. ·.· Offenbarunge über die menschliche Seele . . . nach den Ergebnisse des Somnambulismus, *etc.* pp. vi. 370. *Grimma c Leipzig,* 1859. 8°. **8631.** b. **24**

—— La Vie et les œuvres philosophiques de Alphons Cahagnet. Par ses disciples et ses amis les Étudiant Swedenborgiens libres. pp. 59. *Paris,* 1898. 8°. **3716.** df. **43.** (**3**

CAHAIGNE (JOSEPH) La Couronne impériale, satir [In verse.] A Louis-Napoléon-Werhuel, dit Bonapart Avec notes historiques. pp. 81. *Imprimerie Universelle Jersey,* 1853. 8°. **11483.** e. **2**

CAHAIGNES (JACQUES DE) *See* LE PAULMIER DE GREN TEMESNIL (J.) Traité du vin et du sidre . . . Tradui . . . par J. de Cahaignes, *etc.* 1896, *etc.* 8°. Ac. **8938/5**

—— *See* PLAUTUS (T. M.) [*Aulularia.—French.*] L'Ava ricieux. Comédie traduite librement . . . par J. d Cahaignes, *etc.* 1899. 4°. Ac. **8939/4**

—— Brevis facilisque methodus curandarum febrium. pp. 153. *P. Poisson: Cadomi,* 1616. 8°. **1166.** d. **20.** (**2**

—— Brevis facilisque methodus curandorum capit affectuum. pp. 338. *P. Poisson: Cadomi,* 1618. 8°. **1188.** a. **11.** (**1.**

—— Censori prælectionis meæ de aqua medicata font Hebecreuonij, nomen Fr. Chicotij ementito, Iacobu Cahagnesius. pp. 26. *E typographia I. Bassi:* [*Caen,* 1614. 12°. **1171.** f. **27.** (**3.**

—— Iac. Cahagnesii . . . De morte Ioannis Ruxelij orati funebris, habita Cadomi, die 7. Octobr. 1586. (Oraiso funebre, *etc.* [A translation by J. Vauquelin de l Fresnaye.]—Le Tombeau de Monsieur Rouxel, recueil de plusieurs doctes personnages [including Cahaigne "Lachrymæ ad tumulum I. Ruxellii".]) 2 pt. pp. 11 *I. le Bas: Cadomi,* 1586. 4°. **1090.** m. **5.** (**5, 6.**

—— Le Tombeau de Jean Rouxel, suivi de son oraiso funèbre, et précédé d'une introduction par R. N. Sauvage [A facsimile of the work published by J. de Cahaignes i 1586, without the Latin version of the oration. With portrait of Rouxel.] pp. xxiv. 56. 1931. 4°. *See* ROUEN —*Société de Bibliophiles Normands.* Ac. **8938/85**

—— Discours de l'entrée du duc d'Épernon à Caen, le 14 mai 1588. Publié, avec introduction, par R. de Formigny d la Londe. pp. xl. 23. a–n. 1903. 8°. *See* ROUEN.—*Société des Bibliophiles Normands.* Ac. **8938/64**

—— Elogiorum civium Cadomensium centuria prima. pp. 152. *Ex typographia I. Bassi: Cadomi,* 1609. 4°. **276.** h. **23**

—— Éloges des citoyens de la ville de Caen. Première cen turie. Traduction d'un Curieux. pp. vi. 421. *Caen* 1880. 4°. **10664.** f. **1**

HAIGNES (JACQUES DE)

— Les Premiers vers de F. de Malherbe. Traduction de l'épitaphe de Geneviève Rouxel [with the original Latin of Cahaignes]. Publiés . . . par F. G. S. Trebutien. pp. 31. *Caen*, 1872. 8°. **11403**. aaa. **2**.

HAISSE (A. H.) *See* CAHAISSE (H. A.)

HAISSE (HENRI ALEXIS) Mémoires de Préville et de Dazincourt, revus . . . corrigés, et augmentés d'une notice sur ces deux comédiens, par M. Ourry. pp. 384. *Paris*, 1823. 8°. [*Collection des mémoires sur l'art dramatique.*] **840**. e. **16**. (**2**.)

— Mémoires de Dazincourt, comédien . . . par H. A. K * * * s [i.e. H. A. Cahaisse] . . . Seconde édition. [With a portrait.] pp. viii. 199. 1810. 8°. *See* K * * * s, H. A. **10660**. d. **11**.

— Mémoires de Préville . . . comédien français ; par K. S. H. [i.e. H. A. Cahaisse.] [With a portrait.] pp. 288. 1812. 8°. *See* H., K. S. G. **14498**. (**2**.)

— L'Observateur des maisons de jeu. Par A. H. [or rather, H. A.] Cahaisse. pp. 86. *Paris*, 1819. 8°. **8050**. d. **60**. (**1**.)

HALANE (CORNELIUS FRANCIS) Police Practice and Procedure . . . With 12 illustrations. pp. iv. 241. xii. *E. P. Dutton & Co.: New York*, 1914. 8°. **6056**. aaaa. **8**.

— The Policeman's Guide. A manual of study and instruction. pp. viii. 276. *Harper & Bros.: New York*, [1952.] 8° **6059**. ee. **21**.

HALL (RAYMOND DU BOIS) The Sovereign Council of New France. A study in Canadian constitutional history. [With a bibliography.] pp. 274. *New York*, 1915. 8°. [*Studies in History, Economics and Public Law.* vol. 65. no. 1.] Ac. **2688/2**.

HAN (ABRAHAM)

— *See* JESHURIN (E. H.) אב· קאהאן ביבליאגראפיע· מיט ביאגראפישע דאטעם . . . Abraham Cahan Bibliography, *etc.* [With portraits.] 1941. 8°. **11914**. b. **33**.

— *See* NEW YORK.—*United Vilner Relief Committee.* דער ווילנער [Der Vilner.] (Dedicated to Abraham Cahan's 80th birthday.) [Appreciations by various authors. With a bibliography and portraits.] 1941. 4°. P.P. **15**. abg.

— בלעטער פון מיין לעבען [Bletter fun mein Leben.] [An autobiography. With a portrait.] *Judaeo-Ger.* 5 Bd. [" *Vorwärts* " *Association: New York*,] 1926–31. 8°. **10888**. b. **14**.

— היסטאריע פון די פעראייניגטע שטאאטען [Historye fun die fereinigte Staaten.] *Judaeo-Ger.* 2 vol. [" *Vorwärts* ": *New York*,] 1910, 12. 8°. **9616**. c. 3.

— The Rise of David Levinsky. A novel. pp. 529. *Harper & Bros.: New York & London*, 1917. 8°. NN. **4495**.

— The White Terror and the Red. A novel of revolutionary Russia. pp. viii. 430. *Hodder & Stoughton: London*, 1905. 8°. **012631**. aaa. **36**.

— Yekl. A tale of the New York ghetto. pp. v. 190. *D. Appleton & Co.: New York*, 1896. 8°. **012704**. e. 3.

HAN (JACOB) Zur Kritik des Geniebegriffs. pp. 64. *Bern*, 1911. 8°. [*Berner Studien zur Philosophie und ihrer Geschichte.* Bd. 73.] **8461**. eee. **1/73**.

CAHAN (JUDAH LOEB)

—— שטודיעס וועגן יידישער פאלקסשאפונג· [Shtudies vegn yidisher folksshafung.] (Studies in Yiddish Folklore. Edited by Max Weinreich.) [With an introduction in English and portraits.] pp. 274. *Yiddish Scientific Institute—Yivo: New York*, 1952. 8°. **10010**. cc. **12**.

CAHAN (YEHUDE LEYB) *See* CAHAN (J. L.)

CAHANIN (LOUIS) Des passions expansives, et de l'heureuse influence qu'elles exercent dans les maladies. Thèse, *etc.* pp. 35. *Paris*, 1818. 4°. **1183**. e. **6**. (**7**.)

CAHANNES (GION) *See* CARNOT (M.) Venantius . . . Per romontsch da Dr. G. Cahannes. 1909. 8°. [*Annalas della Societa Reto-Romantscha.* Annada 24.] Ac. **9817**.

—— Die Jerusalemreise des Abtes Jakob Bundi im Jahre 1591. 1923. *See* COIRE.—*Geschichtforschende Gesellschaft von Graubünden, etc.* Achter [*etc.*] Jahresbericht, *etc.* Jahrg. 1922. [1879, *etc.*] 8°. Ac. **6930/3**.

CAHARD (FERDINAND ALEXANDRE) Faculté de Droit de Paris. Thèse pour la licence, *etc.* (Jus romanum. Qui potiores in pignore vel hypotheca habeantur et de his qui in priorum creditorum locum succedunt.—Droit français. De l'hypothèque.) pp. 44. *Paris*, 1857. 4°. **5405**. f. **26**. (**8**.)

CAHEN (A.) *Dramatist*, and **SUJOL** (G.) A l'essai. Comédie en un acte. pp. 34. *Paris*, 1880. 12°. **11740**. f. **19**. (**3**.)

—— [Another edition.] 1881. *See* THÉÂTRE. Théâtre de campagne, *etc.* sér. 7. 1876, *etc.* 12°. **2296**. a. 8.

CAHEN (ABRAHAM) Inscriptions puniques et néo-puniques de Constantine, El-Hofra. Extrait du Recueil des notices et mémoires de la Société archéologique de Constantine, *etc.* pp. 32. *Constantine*, 1879. 8°. **7706**. cc. **5**. (**6**.)

—— Les Juifs dans l'Afrique septentrionale. 1867. *See* CONSTANTINE, *Algeria.—Société archéologique du Departement de Constantine.* Recueil des notices et memoires de la Société, *etc.* vol. 11. 1863, *etc.* 8°. Ac. **5349**.

—— Notice historique sur les Israélites des l'Algérie. *See* FRANCE. [*Laws, etc.*—II.] Recueil des lois . . . concernant les Israélites depuis 1850, *etc.* 1878. 8°. **1376**. g. **9**. (**2**.)

CAHEN (ALBERT) *See* BOILEAU-DESPRÉAUX (N.) [*Single Works.*] Épistres. Édition critique avec commentaire par A. Cahen. 1937. 8°. Ac. **9812/49**.

—— *See* BOILEAU-DESPRÉAUX (N.) [*Single Works.*] Satires. Édition critique, avec introduction et commentaire. Par A. Cahen. 1932. 8°. Ac. **9812/41**.

—— *See* MANUEL (E.) Mélanges en prose, publiés avec une introduction par A. Cahen, *etc.* 1905. 8°. **12355**. de. **33**.

—— *See* SALIGNAC DE LA MOTHE FÉNELON (F. de) *Archbishop of Cambrai.* Les Aventures de Télémaque. Nouvelle édition, publiée avec une recension complète des manuscripts authentiques, une introduction et des notes, par A. Cahen. 1920. 8°. **12240.k.1/20.**

—— *See* SALIGNAC DE LA MOTHE FÉNELON (F. de) *Archbishop of Cambrai.* Lettre à l'Académie . . . Avec une introduction . . . par A. Cahen. 1899. 16°. **011824**. ee. **33**.

—— *See* SALIGNAC DE LA MOTHE FÉNELON (F. de) *Archbishop of Cambrai.* Lettre à l'Académie . . . Avec une introduction par A. Cahen, *etc.* 1914. 8°. **11863**. a. **17**.

CAHEN (Albert)

—— Lettres du XVIIIe siècle. Lettres choisies de Voltaire, Mme du Deffand, Diderot, Mme Roland et de divers auteurs publiées avec une introduction, des notices et des notes par A. Cahen. pp. xxii. 536. *Paris*, 1894. 12°. **10909**. ccc. **31**.

—— Albert Cahen, 1857–1937. [Funeral discourses. By various speakers. With a portrait.] pp. 16. *Paris*, [1938.] 8°. **010665**. m. **7**.

CAHEN (Alfred)

—— *See* Stone (Nahum I.) Productivity of Labor in the Cotton-Garment Industry. Prepared by N. I. Stone assisted by A. Cahen, *etc.* 1939. 8°. [*U.S. Bureau of Labor Statistics. Bulletin.* no. 662.] A.S. **111**.

—— Statistical Analysis of American Divorce, *etc.* [A thesis.] pp. 151. [*Columbia University Press*:] *New York*, 1932. 8°. **5176**. ee. **37**.

—— [Another issue.] *New York*, 1932. 8°. [*Studies in History, Economics and Public Law.* no. 360.] Ac. **2688/2**.
Without the last leaf containing the author's Vita.

CAHEN (Claude)

—— La Première pénétration turque en Asie-Mineure—seconde moitié du XIe s. 1948. *See* Periodical Publications.—*Brussels.* *Βυζαντιον.* Revue internationale, *etc.* tom. 18. 1924, *etc.* 8°. P.P. **4748**. pc.

—— Quelques aspects de l'administration égyptienne médiévale vus par un de ses fonctionnaires. *In*: Bulletin de la Faculté des lettres de Strasbourg. année 26. pp. 97–118. 1948. 8°. Ac. **2633**. e/3.

—— Un Traité d'armurerie composé pour Saladin. [On the treatise of Murḍā ibn 'Alī al-Ṭarsūsī contained in Bodleian MS. Hunt. 264. With extracts.] *In*: Bulletin d'études orientales. tom. 12. pp. 103–163. pl. III. 1948. 4°. Ac. **5200**. b.

CAHEN (Coralie) Souvenirs de la guerre de 1870–71. Conférence, *etc.* pp. 27. [*Paris*, 1888.] 8°. **9004**. gg. **17**. (4.)

CAHEN (Edmond) Le Juif et l'Auvergnat. Roman. pp. 237. *Paris*, 1932. 8°. **12514**. pp. **18**.

CAHEN (Édouard) *See* Cerbelaud (G.) and Dumont (G.) Le Génie civil et les travaux publics à l'Exposition universelle de 1878 . . . Sous la direction de M. E. Cahen. 1879. 8°. **7959**. h. **7**.

—— Canal des Deux-Mers. Réunion . . . organisée par le Cercle républicain radical de Toulouse . . . Conférence. pp. 23. *Toulouse*, [1888.] 4°. **08235**. m. **16**. (2.)

CAHEN (Edward) and **WOOTTON** (William Ord) The Mineralogy of the Rarer Metals. A handbook for prospectors . . . With a foreword by F. W. Harbord. pp. xxvii. 211. *C. Griffin & Co.*: *London*, 1912. 8°. **07108**. f. **13**.

—— Second edition, revised by E. Cahen. pp. xxxii. 246. *C. Griffin & Co.*: *London*, 1920. 8°. **07108**. f. **22**.

CAHEN (Émile) *See* Bouches-du-Rhône, *Department of the.—Conseil Général.* Les Bouches-du-Rhône. Encyclopédie départementale, *etc.* (tom. 4. vol. 1. Archéologie. Par E. Cahen, R. Doré, B. Durand.) 1932, *etc.* fol. **10167**. r. **1/4**.

—— *See* Callimachus. [*Collections.*] Callimaque . . . Texte établi et traduit par E. Cahen. 1922. 8°. **2319**. c. 9.

CAHEN (Émile)

—— *See* Callimachus. [*Collections.*] Callimaque . . . Texte établi et traduit par E. Cahen, *etc.* 1940. 8°. **2319**. c. **82**

—— *See* Couat (A.) Alexandrian Poetry under the first three Ptolemies . . . With a supplementary chapter by E. Cahen, *etc.* 1931. 8°. **11313**. cc. **32**

—— Callimaque et son œuvre poétique. pp. 654. *Paris* 1929. 8°. [*Bibliothèque des Écoles Françaises d'Athènes et de Rome.* fasc. 134.] Ac. **5206/2**

CAHEN (Eugène) Éléments de la théorie des nombres. Congruences, formes quadratiques, nombres incommensurables, *etc.* pp. viii. 403. *Paris*, 1900. 8°. **08533**. k. **19**

—— Théorie des nombres. 2 tom. *Paris*, 1914, 24. 8°. **8529**. i. **3**

CAHEN (François)

—— Problems of Power Transmission at Voltages above 225 kV. pp. 64. *British Electrical & Allied Manufacturers' Association*: *London*, 1952. 4°. [*BEAMA Publication.* no. 146.] W.P. **1861/18**

CAHEN (Fritz Max) Men against Hitler . . . [Reminiscences.] Adapted with an introduction by Wythe Williams. pp. 258. *Bobbs-Merrill Co.*: *Indianapolis*, *New York*, [1939.] 8°. **08073**. d. **31**

—— [Another edition.] pp. 223. *Jarrolds*: *London* [1939.] 8°. **08073**. d. **30**

CAHEN (Gaston) *See* Russia. [*Appendix.—Agriculture and Commerce.*] Le Livre de comptes de la caravane russe à Pékin en 1727–1728 (Щетные книги и прочи дѣла касающияся до каравана.) Texte—traduction—commentaire par G. Cahen. 1911. 8°. **8248**. c. **13**

—— Histoire des relations de la Russie avec la Chine sous Pierre le Grand, 1689–1730. pp. 274. ccxvii. *Paris* 1912. 8°. **09057**. cc. **27**

CAHEN (Georges) Le Logement dans les villes. La crise parisienne. pp. 292. *Paris*, 1913. 8°. **08248**. ff. **27**

CAHEN (Gustave) Eugène Boudin. Sa vie et son œuvre . . . Avec une préface d'Arsène Alexandre . . . huit eaux-fortes par L. Delteil, *etc.* (Carnets d'Eugène Boudin.) pp. 199. *Paris*, 1900. 4°. **10658**. l. **14**

CAHEN (Isidore) *See* Brecher (G.) L'Immortalité de l'âme chez les Juifs . . . traduit . . . et précédé d'une introduction par I. Cahen. 1857. 12°. **4034**. c. **7**

—— *See* Periodical Publications.—*Paris.* Archives israélites de France, *etc.* [tom. 22–62 edited by I. Cahen.] 1840, *etc.* 8°. P.P. **13**

—— Deux libertés en une. pp. 71. *Paris*, 1848. 12°. **8052**. d. **9**

CAHEN (Israel) Esquisse sur la philosophie du poëme de Job. 1851. *See* Bible.—*Old Testament.* [*Polyglott.*] La Bible, traduction nouvelle, *etc.* tom. 15. 1831, *etc.* 8°. **01903**. a. **1**

CAHEN (Jacques Gabriel)

—— Le Vocabulaire de Racine. pp. 249. *Paris*, 1946. 8°. [*Revue de linguistique romane.* tom. 16. no. 59–64.] Ac. **9809**. b

CAHEN (L.) *Geologist.*

—— Bibliographie géologique du Congo Belge et du Ruanda-Urundi, *etc.* (Bibliographie géologique du Congo, du Rwanda et du Burundi.) [By L. Cahen.] 1955, 52- . 8°. *See* BRUSSELS.—*Musée Royal de l'Afrique Centrale.* **Ac. 2959. c/4.**

—— Le Calcaire de Sekelolo, le complexe tillitique et la dolomie rose C dans l'anticlinal de Congo dia Kati, Bas-Congo. pp. 55. pl. x. *Tervuren,* 1950. 8°. [*Annales du Musée du Congo belge.* Série in 8°. *Sciences géologiques.* vol. 7.] Ac. **2959.** c/2. (b.)

CAHEN (L.) *Geologist,* and **LEPERSONNE** (J.)

—— Notes sur la géomorphologie du Congo occidental. pp. 95. pl. II. *Tervuren,* 1948. 8°. [*Annalen van het Museum van Belgisch Congo. Reeks in* 8°. Geologische Wetenschappen. dl. 1.] **Ac.2959.c/2.(b.)**

CAHEN (LÉON) *See* LETACONNOUX (J.) and CAHEN (L.) La Vie parisienne au XVIIIe siècle, *etc.* 1914. 8°. **010170.** i. **25.**

—— L'Angleterre au XIXe siècle. Son évolution politique. pp. 204. *Paris,* 1924. 8°. **09525.** de. **5.**

—— Condorcet et la Révolution française. pp. xxxi. 592. *Paris,* 1904. 8°. **010661.** b. **44.**

—— L'Évolution constitutionnelle de la France. *See* INTERNATIONAL COMMITTEE OF HISTORICAL SCIENCES.—*Commission d'Histoire Constitutionnelle.* La Costituzione degli stati nell'età moderna, *etc.* vol. 1. 1933, *etc.* 8°. W.P. **7858/1.**

—— Le Grand Bureau des Pauvres de Paris au milieu du XVIIIe siècle. Contribution à l'histoire de l'assistance publique. pp. 78. *Paris,* 1904. 8°. [*Bibliothèque d'histoire moderne.* tom. 1. fasc. 3.] **09009.** d. **1/3.**

—— Histoire du monde de 1919 à 1937. [By L. Cahen, Raymond Ronze and Émile Folinais.] pp. 414. *Paris,* 1937. 8°. **9011.** aa. **14.**

—— Les Querelles religieuses & parlementaires sous Louis XV . . . Ouvrage illustré de six gravures. pp. vi. 111. *Paris,* 1913. 8°. [*L'Histoire par les contemporains.*] **09200.g.12/5.**

—— La Révolution et le clergé catholique, 1789–1795. *See* W., M. L'Œuvre sociale de la Révolution française, *etc.* [1901.] 8°. **9231.** b. **3.**

CAHEN (LÉON) and **GUYOT** (RAYMOND)

—— L'Œuvre législative de la Révolution. pp. iii. 486. *Paris,* 1913. 8°. **05402. aa. 12.**

CAHEN (LOUIS) Džepni Srpsko-Engleski i Englesko-Srpski Rečnik . . . Serbian-English and English-Serbian Pocket Dictionary. pp. iv. 268. *Kegan Paul & Co.: London,* 1916. 8°. **12975.** bbb. **13.**

—— Second impression, revised. pp. iv. 268. *Kegan Paul & Co.: London,* 1916. 8°. **12975.** b. **17.**

—— (Third impression.) pp. iv. 268. *Kegan Paul & Co.: London,* 1918. 8°. **12975.** b. **21.**

—— Džepni Srpsko-Engleski i Englesko-Srpski Rečnik . . . Serbian-English and English-Serbian Pocket Dictionary. (Fifth impression.) pp. iv. 268. *Kegan Paul & Co.: London,* 1941. 8°. **12976.** cc. **23.**

CAHEN (LOUIS) and **FORBES** (NEVILL)

—— English-Serbian Phrase-Book, with easy grammar. pp. 48. *B. H. Blackwell: Oxford,* 1915. 8°. **12975.** c. **11.**

CAHEN (MAURICE) Études sur le vocabulaire religieux du vieux-scandinave. La libation. pp. 325. *Paris,* 1921. 8°. [*Collection linguistique.* no. 9.] Ac. **9810/3.**

—— Morphologie du verbe allemand. pp. 95. *Paris,* 1929. 8°. [*Publications de la Faculté des Lettres de l'Université de Strasbourg.* Série initiation et méthodes. fasc. 3.] **Ac.2633.e/6.**

—— Le Mot " dieu " en vieux-scandinave. pp. 81. *Paris,* 1921. 8°. [*Collection linguistique.* no. 10.] Ac. **9810/3.**

CAHEN (MAURICE) and **OLSEN** (MAGNUS)

—— L'Inscription runique du coffret de Mortain . . . Avec un appendice sur le décor du coffret par C. Osieczkowska. [With plates.] pp. 66. *Paris,* 1930. 8°. [*Collection linguistique.* no. 32.] Ac. **9810/3.**

CAHEN (MAYER) De la néphrite albumineuse chez les femmes enceintes. pp. 58. *Paris,* 1846. 4°. [*Collection des thèses soutenues à la Faculté de Médecine de Paris.* An 1846. tom. 2.] **7371.** f. **16.**

CAHEN (MOYSE) Dissertation sur la circoncision, envisagée sous les rapports religieux, hygiéniques, et pathologiques, *etc.* pp. 19. *Paris,* 1816. 4°. **1183.** c. **15.** (2.)

CAHEN (PAUL) L'Abolition du cours forcé en Russie et en Autriche. *See* QUESTIONS. Questions monétaires contemporaines, *etc.* 1905. 8°. **08226.** dd. **8.**

CAHEN (RAYMOND) Mensura membrorum rhythmica cum metrica comparatur. Exempla petuntur ex Ouidi Metamorphoseon libris. pp. 120. *Paris,* 1910. 8°. **11313.** g. **31.** (4.)

—— Le Rythme poétique dans les Métamorphoses d'Ovide. pp. xii. 626. *Paris,* 1910. 8°. [*Bibliothèque de la Fondation Thiers.* fasc. 24.] Ac. **443.**

—— Le Satiricon [of Petronius] et ses origines. pp. 108. *Lyon, Paris,* 1925. 8°. [*Annales de l'Université de Lyon.* Nouvelle série. II. Droit, lettres. fasc. 38.] Ac. **365.**(b)

CAHEN (SAMUEL) *See* BEN LEVI (G.) *pseud.* Les Matinées du samedi . . . Avec une préface, par S. Cahen. 1842. 12°. **4515.** c. **4.**

—— *See* BIBLE.—*Old Testament.* [*Polyglott.*] La Bible, traduction nouvelle . . . avec des notes . . . Par S. Cahen. 1831, *etc.* 8°. **01903.** a. **1.**

—— *See* LUZZATTO (F.) Mémoire sur les Juifs d'Abyssinie, *etc.* [Edited by S. Cahen.] [1853?] 8°. **10095.** bbb. **11.**

—— *See* PERIODICAL PUBLICATIONS.—*Paris.* Archives israélites de France. Revue mensuelle religieuse . . . sous la direction de S. Cahen. 1840, *etc.* 8°. P.P. **13.**

—— Manuel d'histoire universelle . . . depuis le commencement du monde jusqu'en 1836. pp. 418. *Paris,* 1836. 18°. [*Encyclopédie-Roret.*] **12207.** a. **1/120.**

—— [Précis élémentaire d'instruction religieuse.] Principios elementales de instruccion religiosa y moral, para la enseñanza de la juventud hebrea. Traducidos segun la última edicion francesa . . . y precedidos de un " Ligero Bosquejo de la Historia Hebrea " por Angel J. Jesurun. pp. 66. *Carácas,* 1845. 16°. **4034.** aa. **7.**

CAHEN (ZACHARIA) De adventu Sancti Spiritus oratio, *etc.* pp. 11. *Romae,* [1851.] 4°. **898.** i. **1.** (18.)

CAHEN-SALABELLE (R.)

—— *See* JUNG (C. G.) Aspects du drame contemporain. Préface et traduction de R. Cahen-Salabelle. 1948. 8°. **11868**. ff. **1**.

CAHEN-SALVADOR (GEORGES)

—— Un Grand humaniste, Peiresc, 1580–1637. pp. 312. pl. VIII. *Paris*, 1951. 8°. **010665**. l. **36**.

—— Les Prisonniers de guerre, 1914–1919. pp. 316. *Paris*, 1929. 8°. **09081**. d. **29**.

—— Le Procès du Général Boulanger, 1886–1891. pp. 27. *Paris*, 1953. 8°. [*France Illustration. Supplément théâtral et littéraire.* no. 124.] P.P. **4283**. m. (**1**.)

CAHENSLY (PETER PAUL) Die deutschen Auswanderer und der St. Raphael-Verein. pp. 26. *Frankfurt, Luzern*, 1887. 8°. [*Frankfurter zeitgemässe Broschüren.* Neue Folge. Bd. 8.] **12209**. g.

CAHIER. Cahier Angellier. *See* PERIODICAL PUBLICATIONS.—*Lille.*

—— Cayer commun des trois ordres du bailliage de * * *. [With two inserted leaves printed at Chaumont, in which this work is stated to be an inexact and incomplete copy of the "Cahier des trois ordres du bailliage de Langres."] pp. 141. MS. NOTES. *Paris*, 1789. 8°. F.R. **43**. (**5**.)

—— Le Cahier d'amour. Confidences inédites. Par une adoratrice de Maupassant (Mlle X . . .). [With an introduction by Pierre Borel.] 1939. 8°. [*Les Œuvres libres.* no. 216.] *See* X . . ., *Mlle.* Edited. **12208**. ee. **216**.

—— Cahier d'un philosophe, commissaire de la Noblesse dans deux bailliages; ou doléances d'un Américain persécuté. [Signed: De P * * * * * * * * *.] [1789.] 8°. *See* P * * * * * * * * *, de. R. **41**. (**13**.)

—— Cahier d'une assemblée primaire au mois de juin 1791. pp. 62. *Châtillon sur Seine*, 1791. 8°. F. **70****. (**15**.)

—— Cahier de courriers. (Impressions sur la vie Japonaise. [By] Félicien Challage.—La Russie vue de la Vistule. [By] Edmond Bernus.—Courrier de Finlande. [By] Jean Deck.) pp. 70. *Paris*, 1902. 8°. [*Cahiers de la quinzaine.* sér. 3. no. 17.] **12208**. pp. **1/16**.

—— Cahier de la quinzaine. (Cahier pour le vingt-cinquième anniversaire de la fondation des Cahiers de la quinzaine.) pp. 15. *Paris*, [1925.] 8°. [*Cahiers de la quinzaine.* sér. 16. no. 1.] **12208.pp.1/147.**

—— Cahier de poésie. Saint Jean de la Croix, Paul Claudel [and others], *etc.* pp. 102. *Neuchâtel*, 1942. 8°. [*Les Cahiers du Rhône.* no. 2.] W.P. **2953/2**.

—— Cahier des doléances et réclamations des femmes. Par Madame B * * * B * * *. 1789. 8°. *See* B * * *, B * * *, *Madame.* F. **26**. (**3**.)

—— Cahier des pauvres. [By J. F. Lambert.] pp. 16. [1789.] 8°. R. **190**. (**1**.)

—— Cahier des représentations & doléances du beau sexe, au moment de la tenue des États-généraux. [A satire.] pp. 18. [*Paris*,] 1789. 8°. F. **393**. (**6**.)

—— Cahier national. [Suggestions for the reform of abuses.] pp. 42. [1789?] 8°. F.R. **43**. (**6**.)

CAHIER (AUGUSTE) Famille Bra. Notice historique sur une famille d'artistes douaisiens, etc. [With a portrait.] pp. 104. *Douai*, 1863. 8°. **10661**. bb. **36**.

CAHIER (AUGUSTE)

—— Notice sur l'origine et les progrès des Musées de Peinture & de Sculpture de Douai. pp. xxi. *See* DOUAI.—*Musée de Douai.* Catalogue des ouvrages de peinture, *etc.* 1869. 12°. **7857**. aa. **34**.

CAHIER (BON CLAUDE) *See* CAHIER DE GERVILLE.

CAHIER (CHARLES) *See* LITURGIES.—*Latin Rite.*—*Hours.*—I. [*French.*] Œuvre de Jehan Foucquet, *etc.* [Facsimiles of miniatures by J. Foucquet, with descriptive notices by C. Cahier.] 1866, *etc.* 4°. C. **44**. g. **8, 9**.

—— *See* MARTIN (Arthur M.) and CAHIER (C.) Monographie de la cathédrale de Bourges, *etc.* 1841, *etc.* fol. **1899.c.3.**

—— Caractéristiques des saints dans l'art populaire, énumérées et expliquées. 2 tom. *Paris*, 1867. 4°. **2009**. g.

—— Ébauche d'études à faire sur les calendriers chrétiens du temps passé . . . Extrait de la Revue de l'art chrétien, *etc.* pp. 58. *Arras*, 1878. 8°. **7709**. g. **6**.

—— Quelque six mille proverbes et aphorismes usuels empruntés à notre âge et aux siècles derniers. pp. xiii. 579. *Paris*, 1856. 12°. **12305**. d. 5.

CAHIER (CHARLES) and **MARTIN** (ARTHUR MARIE)

—— Mélanges d'archéologie, d'histoire et de littérature, rédigés ou recueillis par . . . C. Cahier et A. Martin. Collection de mémoires, *etc.* 4 vol. *Paris*, 1847–56. fol. **7708**. eee. **1**.

—— Suite aux Mélanges d'archéologie, rédigés ou recueillis par . . . les PP. C. Cahier et A. Martin. Publiée par le survivant (C. Cahier). Première série. Correlages et tissus. 2 vol. *Paris*, 1868. fol. **7708**. eee. **1**.

—— Nouveaux mélanges d'archéologie, d'histoire et de littérature sur le moyen âge. Par . . . C. Cahier et feu A. Martin . . . Collection publiée par le P. Ch. Cahier. Curiosités mystérieuses. (Ivoires, *etc.*—Décorations d'églises.—Bibliothèques.) 4 vol. *Paris*, 1874–77. fol. **7708**. eee. **1**.

CAHIER (LOUIS GILBERT) Discours . . . sur les événemens du 20 juin 1792, *etc.* pp. 4. *See* PARIS.—*Municipalité.* Conseil général de la Commune. Conduite tenue par M. le Maire de Paris, *etc.* 1792. 4°. F. **6***. (**11**.)

—— Mémoire pour Pierre Carette, menuisier, citoyen de la section du Mont-Blanc. [Exculpating him from the charge of having made a faulty gun-carriage for the service of the Republic.] pp. 8. [*Paris*, 1793.] 4°. F. **38***. (**7**.)

CAHIER DE GERVILLE (BON CLAUDE) *See* DUVEYRIER (H. N. M.) *Baron*, and CAHIER DE GERVILLE (B. C.) Rapport de MM. Duveyrier et B. C. Cahier, commissaires nommés . . . pour l'exécution des décrets de l'Assemblée nationale, relatifs aux troubles de Nanci. 1790. 8°. F. **328**. (**15**.)

—— *See* MARSEILLES. Démenti formel des assertions du Ministère de l'Intérieur [B. C. Cahier de Gréville] à l'Assemblée nationale [to the effect that J. E. B. Duprat had been expelled from Marseilles]. [1792.] 8°. F. **594**. (**12**.)

—— Compte rendu en exécution du décret du 20 février 1792, par B. C. Cahier, sur les mesures qu'il a prises pour prévenir la suite des troubles élevés dans le département des Bouches-du-Rhône, notamment dans la ville d'Arles. pp. 12. [*Paris*, 1792.] 8°. F. **654**. (**9**.)

CAHIER DE GERVILLE (Bon Claude)

—— Compte rendu par B.-C. Cahier, Ministre de l'Intérieur, à l'Assemblée nationale, *etc.* pp. 74. *Paris*, 1792. 8°. **F. 1206.** (4.)

—— Municipalité de Paris. Procureur de la Commune . . . Monsieur le Président, *etc.* [A letter giving an account of the changes made in the number of parishes in Paris, and their condition.] pp. 10. [*Paris*, 1791.] 4°. **F. 10*.** (26.)

—— Objets soumis à l'Assemblée nationale, par le Ministre de l'Intérieur [B. C. Cahier de Gerville], et sur lesquels il n'a point été statué. pp. 46. *Paris*, 1792. 8°. **F. 475.** (9.)

—— Rapport du Ministre de l'Intérieur à l'Assemblée nationale, sur l'exécution de la loi du 14 mars 1792, *etc.* [On the purchase of foreign corn, and the relief of distressed areas.] pp. 18. *Paris*, 1792. 4°. **F. 1217.** (12.)

CAHIERRE (Édouard Henri). De la fièvre typhoïde chez les enfants. pp. 54. *Paris*, 1865. 4°. [*Collection des thèses soutenues à la Faculté de Médecine de Paris.* An 1865. tom. 2.] **7373. f. 8.**

CAHIERRE (Jacques Isidore Louis François Calixte Prosper) Faculté de Droit de Paris. Thèse pour la licence, *etc.* (Jus romanum. De inofficioso testamento. —Droit français. Dispositions générales.) pp. 25. *Paris*, 1857. 4°. **5405. f. 26.** (9.)

CAHIERRE (Loïc)

—— Notions générales sur la lithographie et l'offset. Applications à l'impression des cartes géographiques. pp. 374. 1945. 4°. *See* Paris.—*Institut Géographique National.* **7947. dd. 4.**

CAHIERRE (Michel) Le Déclin des Chambres Hautes. Thèse, *etc.* pp. vi. 159. *Rennes*, 1925. 8°. **08027. i. 112.**

CAHIERS. Cahiers Alfred de Musset. *See* Paris.—*Société Alfred de Musset.*

—— Cahiers alsaciens d'archéologie, d'art et d'histoire. *See* Strasburg.—*Société pour la Conservation des Monuments Historiques d'Alsace.* Anzeiger für elsässische Altertumskunde, *etc.*

—— Cahiers antiracistes. *See* Periodical Publications.—*Algiers.*

—— Cahiers archéologiques. *See* Periodical Publications.—*Paris.*

—— Les Cahiers balzaciens. *See* Periodical Publications. —*Paris.*

—— Les Cahiers belges. *See* Belgian Pamphlets.

—— Les Cahiers CIBA. *See* Gesellschaft für Chemische Industrie in Basel.

—— Cahiers d'archéologie et d'histoire d'Alsace. *See* Strasburg.—*Société pour la Conservation des Monuments Historiques d'Alsace.* Anzeiger für elsässische Altertumskunde.

—— Cahiers d'art. *See* Periodical Publications.—*Paris.*

—— Cahiers d'art Arca. 4 pt. *Montréal*, [1942–48.] 8°. **7813. l. 1.**

No more published.

—— Les Cahiers d'aujourd'hui. *See* Periodical Publications.—*Paris.*

CAHIERS.

—— Cahiers d'enseignement illustrés . . . Dessins par Armand Dumaresq (M. Roy), *etc.* no. 1–87. [*Paris*, 1886–90.] 8°. **12204. h. 2.**

—— Cahiers d'Études Cathares. *See* Arques.—*Société du Souvenir et des Études Cathares.*

—— Cahiers d'études européennes. *See* Berlin.—*Office d'Échanges Culturels Inter-universitaires.*

—— Cahiers d'histoire mondiale. *See* Commission Internationale pour une Histoire du Développement Scientifique et Culturel de l'Humanité.

—— Cahiers d'informations françaises. *See* Periodical Publications.—*Paris.*

—— Les Cahiers d'un bibliophile. no. 1–6; no. 7. pp. 1–48. *Paris*, [1900–04.] 8°. **11737. ee. 49.**
Imperfect; wanting the rest of no. 7, and no. 8.

—— Cahiers d'Uriage, *etc.* *See* Uriage.—*École Nationale des Cadres d'Uriage.* Jeunesse France, *etc.*

—— Cahiers de Beyrouth. *See* Beyrout.—*Institut Polski.* Teka bejrucka.

—— Cahiers de Bruges. Recherches européennes, *etc.* *See* Bruges.—*College of Europe.*

—— Cahiers de Byrsa. *See* Carthage.—*Musée Lavigerie de Saint-Louis de Carthage.*

—— Cahiers de Caux. *See* Moral Rearmament.

—— Cahiers de droit fiscal international. *See* International Fiscal Association.

—— Cahiers de France. *See* Periodical Publications.—*Paris.*

—— Cahiers de l'Afrique et l'Asie. *See* Periodical Publications.—Paris.—*L'Afrique et l'Asie.*

—— Les Cahiers de l'Alpe. ser. 1. no. 1–4. *Grenoble*, 1938, 39. 8°. **012208. aa. 7.**

—— Cahiers de l'art sacré. *See* Periodical Publications.—Paris.—*L'Art sacré.*

—— Cahiers de l'Association Marc Bloch de Toulouse. Études d'histoire méridionale. *See* Toulouse.—*Association Marc Bloch de Toulouse.*

—— Cahiers de l'École Française d'Extrême Orient. *See* Paris.—*Société des Amis de l'École Française d'Extrême Orient.*

—— Les Cahiers de l'Institut de Sociologie Solvay. *See* Brussels.—*Instituts Solvay.*—*Institut de Sociologie.*

—— Cahiers de la Compagnie Madeleine Renaud—Jean-Louis Barrault. *See* Compagnie Madeleine Renaud—Jean-Louis Barrault

—— Les Cahiers de la documentation. *See* Brussels.—*Association Belge de Documentation.*

—— Cahiers de la Fondation nationale des sciences politiques. *See* France.—*Fondation Nationale des Sciences Politiques.*

—— Cahiers de la nouvelle époque. *See* Periodical Publications.—*Paris.*

—— Les Cahiers de la pléiade. *See* Periodical Publications. —*Paris.*

—— Cahiers de la presse. *See* PARIS.—*Université de Paris.—Institut de Science de la Presse.*

—— Cahiers de la quinzaine. [Edited by C. Péguy.] sér. 2, *etc.* *Paris*, 1901- . 8°. **12208.** pp. 1.
The indexes, etc. for the first seven series will be found in sér. 6. *no.* 1, *sér.* 7. *no.* 1, *and sér.* 8. *no.* 1, *bound together at* 12208. pp. 1/56.

—— Cahiers de la réconciliation. *See* INTERNATIONAL FELLOWSHIP OF RECONCILIATION.—*Groupe Français.*

—— Cahiers de la Révolution Française. *See* PARIS.—*Université de Paris.—Faculté des Lettres.—Institut d'Histoire de la Révolution Française.*

—— Cahiers de la revue d'histoire et de philosophie religieuse. *See* STRASBURG.—*Université de Strasbourg.—Faculté de Théologie protestante.*

—— Les Cahiers de libération. *See* PERIODICAL PUBLICATIONS.—*Algiers.*

—— Cahiers de notre jeunesse. *See* PERIODICAL PUBLICATIONS.—*Paris.*

—— Les Cahiers de Patrie. *See* PERIODICAL PUBLICATIONS.—*Algiers.* Patrie, *etc.*

—— Cahiers de pensée et action. *See* PERIODICAL PUBLICATIONS.—*Brussels.* Pensée et action. (Les Cahiers pensée et action.)

—— Les Cahiers de Tunisie. Revue des sciences humaines. *See* TUNIS.—*Université de Tunis.*

—— Les Cahiers des Amis des Livres. *See* PARIS.—*Société Amis des Livres.*

—— Les Cahiers des Dix. *See* MONTREAL.—*Les Dix.*

—— Les Cahiers des Hommes de bonne volonté. Cahier 1(-4.) [With special reference to the work of Jules Romains.] 4 pt. *Paris*, 1948, 49. 8°. **11869.** bb. **33.**
No more published.

—— Cahiers des relations artistiques. *See* LEAGUE OF NATIONS.—*International Institute of Intellectual Co-operation.*

—— Cahiers documentaires. (La guerre de 1914–16.) *See* BELGIUM.—*Bureau Documentaire Belge.*

—— Cahiers du bolchevisme. *See* FRANCE.—*Parti Communiste Français.—Comité Central.*

—— Les Cahiers du Centre. *See* PERIODICAL PUBLICATIONS.—*Nevers.* Les Cahiers nivernais et du Centre.

—— Cahiers du communisme. *See* FRANCE.—*Parti Communiste Français.—Comité Central.*

—— Cahiers du monde nouveau. Revue mensuelle. *See* PERIODICAL PUBLICATIONS.—*Paris.*

—— Cahiers du Musée Ingres. *See* MONTAUBAN.—*Musée Ingres.*

—— Les Cahiers du pacifisme. *See* WAR RESISTERS' INTERNATIONAL.—*Ligue d'Action Pacifiste et Sociale.*

—— Les Cahiers du silence. *See* DIVONNE DE BOISGELIN (C.)

—— Cahiers du Sud. *See* PERIODICAL PUBLICATIONS.—*Marseilles.*

—— Les Cahiers du travail. sér. 1. no. 2–11. *Paris*, 1921. 8°. **08282.** ff. **87.**

—— Les Cahiers du Vieux-Colombier. *See* COPEAU (J.)

—— Cahiers Ferdinand de Saussure. *See* GENEVA.—*Société Genevoise de Linguistique.*

—— Les Cahiers français. (Revue bimensuelle d'information.) *See* FRANCE.—*La France Combattante.—Service de Presse et de l'Information.* Documents d'information.

—— Les Cahiers français. Directeur : J. Le Marchand. *See* LE MARCHAND (J.)

—— Cahiers français d'information. *See* FRANCE.—*Ministère de l'Information.* [1944–46.]

—— Cahiers franco-allemands. *See* PERIODICAL PUBLICATIONS.—*Berlin.—Deutsch-Französische Monatshefte.*

—— Les Cahiers indépendants. 9 pt. *Bruxelles*, 1919. 8°. **012209.** bb. **1**

—— Cahiers internationaux de sociologie. *See* PERIODICAL PUBLICATIONS.—*Paris.*

—— Cahiers juifs. Revue paraissant tous les deux mois. *See* PERIODICAL PUBLICATIONS.—*Alexandria.*

—— Cahiers Laënnec. *See* MOUVEMENT INTERNATIONAL DES INTELLECTUELS CATHOLIQUES.—*Centre de Recherches et de Déontologie Médicales.*

—— Les Cahiers Marcel Proust. *See* FERNANDEZ (Ramón) *Literary Critic.*

—— Cahiers mauriciens. *See* PORT LOUIS.—*Société de Écrivains Mauriciens.*

—— Les Cahiers nivernais et du Centre. *See* PERIODICAL PUBLICATIONS.—*Nevers.*

—— Cahiers nord-africains. *See* PARIS.—*Études Sociales Nord-Africaines.* E.S.N.A. Cahiers nord-africains.

—— Les Cahiers pensée et action. *See* PERIODICAL PUBLICATIONS.—*Brussels.* Pensée et action, *etc.*

—— Les Cahiers politiques. *See* PERIODICAL PUBLICATIONS.—*Paris.*

—— Cahiers préparés d'écriture sans modèles gravés, *etc.* 4 no. *Paris*, [1887.] 4°.

—— Cahiers préparés, *etc.* [Large copies for the above books.] 5 no. [1887.] *obl.* fol. **1880. a. 1**

—— Cahiers rhodaniens. *See* BORDIGHERA.—*Istituto di Studi Liguri.—Section Valentinoise.* Cahiers valentinois.

—— Cahiers Sextil Pușcariu, *etc.* *See* PERIODICAL PUBLICATIONS.—*Rome.*

—— Les Cahiers techniques de l'art. *See* RUMPLER (M.)

—— Cahiers valentinois. *See* BORDIGHERA.—*Istituto di Studi Liguri.—Section Valentinoise.*

—— Les Cahiers verts. *See* HALÉVY (D.)

—— Le Plus original des cahiers. Extrait de celui d'un fou qui a de bons momens. [A satirical pamphlet on current abuses. By A. F. Le Maître.] pp. 70. *Au Greluchon* [*Paris ?*], 1789. 8°. **F. 395.** (4

—— [Another copy.] **R. 41.** (8

CAHILL (BERNARD J. S.) An Account of a Land Map of the World on a new and original projection, invented by B. J. S. Cahill. (Reprinted from the Journal of the Association of Engineering Societies.) [With "A Brief Account of the Cahill World Map."] 2 pt. [1913.] 8°. **10001.** ff. **19**

CAHILL (CHARLES) Anecdotes and Reminiscences of the Road in the Coach Days. By an Old Commercial Traveller, *etc.* pp. 100. *Stead & Lashmar: London,* [1892.] 8°. **012330. e. 5.**

CAHILL (DANIEL RAYMOND)

—— The Custody of the Holy Eucharist. A historical synopsis and commentary. A dissertation, *etc.* pp. xvi. 178. *Catholic University of America Press: Washington,* 1950. 8°. [*Catholic University of America Canon Law Studies.* no. 292.] Ac. **2692. y/21.**

CAHILL (DANIEL WILLIAM) *See* ANDERSON (William) *LL.D.* Exposure of the Rev. Dr. Cahill's Reply [to W. Anderson's challenge to a public debate]. 1853. 8°. **4175. df. 26. (5.)**

—— *See* CAMPBELL (Theophilus) Transubstantiation. Reply to the sermon of the Rev. Dr. Cahill. 1852. 8°. **3940. d. 3.**

—— *See* CARSON (James C. L.) Twelve Letters on Transubstantiation: containing two challenges to the Rev. Dr. Cahill, as well as a critique on the sermon delivered by him . . . the 26th of May, 1853. 1853. 12°. **3940. d. 36.**

—— *See* KINSELLA (William) *R.C. Bishop of Ossory,* and CAHILL (D. W.) Letter on the subject of the New Reformation, *etc.* 1827. 12°. **3942. a. 14.**

—— *See* MAXWELL (David) *of Belfast.* Protestant Truth against Romish Error: a reply to . . . Dr. Cahill, *etc.* [1856.] 12°. **3940. c. 18.**

—— *See* MINTON, afterwards MINTON-SENHOUSE (Samuel) Complete Exposure of Dr. Cahill, *etc.* 1853. 12°. **3940. d. 39.**

—— Letters, addressed to several members of the British Cabinet: and speeches on various subjects, delivered in . . . England, Ireland and Scotland. pp. viii. 470. *James Duffy: Dublin,* 1856. 12°. **1205. f. 13.**

—— The Case of the Madiais. Letter . . . to the Earl of Carlisle [on a letter written by him to the "Leeds Mercury"]. pp. 8. *T. Smith: Manchester,* [1853.] 8°. **3939. aa. 41. (5.)**

—— The Rev. Dr. Cahill's First(—Fifth) Letter to Lord John Russell, relative to his Lordship's epistle to the Bishop of Durham [on papal aggression]. 5 pt. *T. Smith: Manchester,* [1850.] 8°. **3939. aa. 41. (4.)**

—— The Holy Eucharist: a lecture, *etc.* pp. 19. *Munsell & Rowland: Albany,* 1860. 8°. **4327. dd. 2.**

—— Letter . . . to the Rev. J. Burns . . . on the Adorable Sacrament of the Eucharist. pp. 23. *J. Shanley: Melbourne,* 1854. 12°. **3942. aa. 26.**

—— Letter to the Right Honourable Lord Viscount Palmerston [relating to the alleged enlistment of Irishmen in the United States for the British Service]. pp. 12. *M. T. Gason: Melbourne,* 1856. 8°. **3940. dd. 17.**

—— Dr. Cahill answered: a reply to the letter of the 21st of October, 1852, addressed by the Rev. D. W. Cahill . . . to the Earl of Derby. By an English Protestant. pp. 18. *H. C. Barton: Preston,* 1852. 8°. **3942. b. 11.**

—— The Life, Letters, and Lectures of Dr. Cahill. (pt. 1. Biographical sketch.) pp. 1–16. *P. C. D. Warren: Dublin,* [1886.] 8°. **12273. c. 11.**
Imperfect; wanting all after p. 16.

CAHILL (EDWARD) The Catholic Social Movement. pp. 24. "*Irish Messenger*": *Dublin,* 1931. 8°. **08282. a. 145.**

CAHILL (EDWARD)

—— The Framework of a Christian State. An introduction to social science. pp. xxvii. 701. *M. H. Gill & Son: Dublin,* 1932. 8°. **20016. eee. 3.**

—— Freemasonry and the Anti-Christian Movement. pp. xxiii. 186. *M. H. Gill & Son: Dublin,* 1929. 8°. **04784. de. 64.**

—— Second edition, revised and enlarged. pp. xxix. 271. *M. H. Gill & Son: Dublin,* 1930. 8°. **04784. de. 72.**

—— Freemasonry. (Mainly a summary of the writer's book, "Freemasonry and the Anti-Christian Movement.") 2 pt. *Catholic Truth Society of Ireland: Dublin,* 1944. 8°. **20048. a. 27.**

—— Wolnomularstwo-masonerja. Przekład, *etc.* pp. 43. *F. Mildner & Sons: London,* 1947. 8°. **4786. df. 21.**

—— Ireland's Peril. pp. 29. *M. H. Gill & Son: Dublin,* 1930. 8°. **10390. c. 35.**

—— The Monastery of Mungret. pp. 40. *Catholic Truth Society of Ireland: Dublin,* 1908. 8°. **4534. a. 34. (2.)**

CAHILL (EDWARD F.) Revision and Purchase of Tithe Rent Charge. pp. 32. *E. Ponsonby: Dublin,* 1871. 8°. **5157. a. 16.**

CAHILL (EMILY)

—— The Arsenic Content of some Tissues of the Albino Rat as a Function of Ingested Sodium Arsenite. A dissertation, *etc.* pp. vii. 26. *Washington,* 1936. 8°. [*Catholic University of America. Biological Series.* no. 21.] Ac. **2692. y/22.**

CAHILL (FRED VIRGIL)

—— Judicial Legislature. A study in American legal theory. pp. ix. 164. *Ronald Press Co.: New York,* [1952.] 8°. **6618. bb. 35.**

CAHILL (HOLGER) *See* NEW YORK.—*Museum of Modern Art.* American Folk Art, *etc.* [With an introduction by H. Cahill.] [1932.] 4°. **07805. k. 46.**

—— *See* NEW YORK.—*Museum of Modern Art.* American Sources of Modern Art. [With an introduction by H. Cahill.] 1933. 8°. **07805. k. 50.**

—— *See* NEW YORK.—*Museum of Modern Art.* New Horizons in American Art. With an introduction by H. Cahill. 1936. 8°. **7810. t. 23.**

—— *See* UNITED STATES OF AMERICA.—*Work Projects Administration.—Federal Art Project.* Emblems of Unity and Freedom, *etc.* [With an introduction by H. Cahill.] [1942.] 8°. **07806. ee. 75.**

—— Profane Earth. pp. 383. *Macaulay Co.: New York,* [1927.] 8°. **12713. b. 4.**

—— A Yankee Adventurer. The story of Ward and the Taiping rebellion. [With plates, including a portrait.] pp. 296. *Macaulay Co.: New York,* 1930. 8°. **10880. v. 14.**

CAHILL (HOLGER) and **BARR** (ALFRED HAMILTON)

—— Art in America in Modern Times. Edited by H. Cahill and A. H. Barr. [With illustrations.] pp. 110. *Methuen & Co.: London; printed in U.S.A.,* [1934.] 4°. **7817. r. 14.**

—— Art in America. A complete survey. Edited by H. Cahill and A. H. Barr. [With illustrations.] pp. viii. 162. *Halcyon House: New York,* 1939. 4°. **7811. v. 2.**

Part 2 is a reprint of "Art in America in Modern Times."

CAHILL (JAMES)

—— The Black Pirate. pp. 128. *Lutterworth Press: London & Redhill*, 1946. 8°. **12828**. bb. **45**.

—— Flying with the Mounties. [A tale.] pp. viii. 248. *A. & C. Black: London*, 1937. 8°. **20059**. d. **38**.

—— M'Bonga's Trek. pp. 127. *Lutterworth Press: London & Redhill*, 1947. 8°. **12830**. eee. **25**.

—— The Pilot of Indian Leap, *etc.* pp. 288. *Oxford University Press: London*, 1939. 8°. **12824**. bb. **23**.

CAHILL (JOHN) *Novelist.*

—— Wheal Certainty: a Cornish story. pp. vi. 277. *Ward & Downey: London*, 1890 [1889]. 8°. **012632**. l. **9**.

CAHILL (JOHN) *O.P.*

—— The Development of the Theological Censures after the Council of Trent, 1563–1709. A dissertation, *etc.* pp. xxii. 194. *University Press: Fribourg*, 1955. 8°. [*Studia Friburgensia.* New series. no. 10.] Ac. **607/9**.

CAHILL (LAWRENCE WILLIAM) and **PANTING** (PETER JAMES)

—— Cacti and Succulents. [With illustrations.] pp. 102. *W. & G. Foyle: London*, 1953. 8°. [*Foyles Handbooks.*] W.P. **2940/96**.

—— [A reissue.] Cacti and Succulents. *Frederick Muller: London*, 1953. 8°. **7032**. r. **54**.

CAHILL (M.) *See* FORBES (Frances A. M.) and CAHILL (M.) A Scottish Knight-Errant. A sketch of the life and times of John Ogilvie, Jesuit. [1920.] 8°. **4956**. ee. **25**.

CAHILL (MARION COTTER) Shorter Hours. A study of the movement since the Civil War. [A thesis.] pp. 301. [*Columbia University Press*:] *New York*, 1932. 8°. **8282**. tt. **30**.

—— [Another issue.] pp. 300. *New York*, 1932. 8°. [*Studies in History, Economics and Public Law.* no. 380.] Ac. **2688/2**.
Without the last leaf containing the author's Vita.

CAHILL (MARY CAMILLA)

—— The Absolute and the Relative in St. Thomas and in Modern Philosophy. A dissertation, *etc.* pp. viii. 130. *Catholic University of America Press: Washington*, 1939. 8°. [*Catholic University of America. Philosophical Studies.* vol. 45.] Ac. **2692**. y/**14**.

CAHILL (MICHAEL FREDERICK) The Householders' Duty respecting Repairs. pp. 280. *Effingham Wilson: London*, 1909. 8°. **6325**. i. **16**.

—— Second edition, revised by R. Borregaard. pp. xxxix. 231. *Effingham Wilson: London*, 1930. 8°. **6326**. df. **20**.

CAHILL (MICHAEL J.) The Customs Manual of Water-guard and Waterside Duties. 1897–98. pp. 184. *E. T. Olver: Falmouth*, 1897. 8°. **08228**. e. **9**.

CAHILL (PATRICK)

—— *See* BELLOC (Joseph H. P.) [*Selections.*] One Thing and another . . . Selected by P. Cahill. 1955. 8°. **12356**. ss. **47**.

—— The English First Editions of Hilaire Belloc. A chronological catalogue of 153 works attributed to that author . . . With an open letter to H. Belloc by G. K. Chesterton. pp. 51. *The Compiler: London*, 1953. 8°. **11926**. n. **4**.

CAHILL (PAUL) *pseud.*

—— Very High Finance. [Reprinted from "The Word." *Candour Publishing Co.: South Croydon*, [1955.] 8°. **8205**. v. **2**

CAHILL (THOMAS W.) De la coqueluche, ou toux con vulsive; dissertation, *etc.* pp. 25. *Paris*, 1814. 4°. **1183**. c. 3. (9

CAHIR, THOMAS, *Baron.* *See* BUTLER.

CAHIRA. *See* CAIRO.

CAHITA LANGUAGE.

—— Arte de la Lengua Cahita . . . Compuesto por un Pad de la Compañia de Jesus, Missionero de mas de treint años en la Provincia de Cynaloa [i.e. Tomás Basilio], *et* pp. 118. *Mexico*, 1737. 8°. C. **33**. a. **32**. (1

CAHLENUS (FRIEDRICH) *See* VIRGILIUS MARO (P.) [*Buc lica.—German.*] Zehen auserlesene Hirten-Lieder . . . i deutsche Reime übersetzet und . . . erkläret [by Cahlenus]. 1648. 8°. **11355**. a. **6**. (2

CAHN HILL IMPROVEMENT SCHEME. *S* ABERYSTWYTH.—*University College of Wales.*

CAHN (ALVIN ROBERT) An Ecological Study of Souther Wisconsin Fishes, *etc.* pp. 151. pl. XVI. *Urban* 1927. 8°. [*Illinois Biological Monographs.* vol. 11. no. 1 Ac. **2692**. u/2

—— The Spiny Dogfish. A laboratory guide. pp. xii. 94. *Macmillan Co.: New York*, 1926. 8°. **07290**. e. **1**

—— The Turtles of Illinois. With 31 plates, *etc.* pp. 21 *Urbana*, 1937. 8°. [*Illinois Biological Monograph* vol. 16. no. 1, 2.] Ac. **2692**. u/2

CAHN (CHARLES MONTAGUE) *See* BURROWS (Roland) an CAHN (C. M.) The Evidence Act, 1938, *etc.* 1938. 8°. **6282**. dg. **1**

—— *See* COCKLE (Ernest) Cases and Statutes on the Law Evidence . . . Fifth edition, by C. M. Cahn. 1932. 8 **6282**. r. **1**

—— —— 1938. 8°. **6282**. r. **2**

—— *See* ODGERS (William B.) and ODGERS (Walter B Odgers on the Common Law of England . . . Third editio By R. Burrows . . . assisted by . . . C. M. Cahn, *et* 1927. 8°. **2016.f**

—— *See* PHIPSON (Sidney L.) The Law of Evidence . . Seventh edition, by R. Burrows . . . assisted by C. M Cahn. 1930. 8°. **6282**. s. **1**

—— *See* PHIPSON (Sidney L.) Manual of the Law of Ev dence . . . Fifth edition. By R. Burrows . . . assiste by C. M. Cahn. 1938. 8°. **6190**. dd. **2**

CAHN (EDMOND NATHANIEL)

—— Supreme Court and Supreme Law. Edited by Edmon Cahn. pp. ix. 250. *Indiana University Press Bloomington*, 1954. 8°. **6618**. d. **1**

CAHN (ELIAS BENEDICT) Leitfaden für den Unterricht i der israelitischen Religion. pp. viii. 96. *Main* 1850. 8°. **4033**. a. **1**

—— Zweite . . . vermehrte Auflage. pp. viii. 96. *Main* 1860. 8°. **4034**. cc. **36**. (2.

CAHN (ERNST) Das Schlafstellenwesen in den deutsche Grossstädten und seine Reform, mit besonderer Berück sichtigung der Stadt München. pp. xiv. 121. *Stuttgart* 1898. 8°. [*Münchener volkswirtschaftliche Studien* Stück 28.] **08248**. f. **7**. (5.

CAHN (Ernst)

—— Das Verhältniswahlsystem in den modernen Kulturstaaten. Eine staatsrechtlich-politische Abhandlung. pp. xii. 369. *Berlin*, 1909. 8°. **8007. eee. 13.**

CAHN (Frances) *See* Adler (Herman M.) The Incidence of Delinquency in Berkeley, 1928–1932. By H. Adler, F. Cahn, *etc.* 1934. 8°. Ac. **2689**. gf. (**1**.)

CAHN (Frances) and **BARY** (Valeska)

—— Welfare Activities of Federal, State, and Local Governments in California, 1850–1934. pp. xxiv. 422. *Berkeley*, 1936. 8°. [*Publications of the Bureau of Public Administration, University of California.*] Ac. **2689**. gf. (**5**.)

CAHN (Frances T.)

—— Federal Employees in War and Peace. Selection, placement, and removal. pp. xiii. 253. *Brookings Institution: Washington*, 1949. 8°. **8290. e. 4.**

CAHN (Fritz)

—— *See* Germany. [*Laws, etc.*—ii. *Civil Law.*] Privatrechtliche Gesetze ausserhalb des BGB . . . Text-Ausgabe . . . unter Mitwirkung von Dr F. Cahn . . . systematisch zusammengestellt von Prof. Dr H. Hoeniger. 1921. 8°. **5607. a. 13.**

—— *See* Hoeniger (H.) Handelsrechtliche Aktenstücke und Formulare zur Einführung in das Handels-, Schiffahrts-, Wechsel- und Scheckrecht. Von Dr H. Hoeniger . . . unter Mitwirkung von Dr F. Cahn. 1922. 8°. **5607. c. 13.**

CAHN (Hans Joseph)

—— Das Kriegsschadenrecht der Nationen. *Zürich, New York*, [1947- .] 8°. **W.P. 200.**

CAHN (Herbert Adolf)

—— Die Münzen der sizilischen Stadt Naxos. Ein Beitrag zur Kunstgeschichte des griechischen Westens. *Dissertation, etc.* pp. 168. pl. xii. *Basel*, 1944. 8°.

7758.b.14.

CAHN (Herman) Capital To-Day. A study of recent economic development. pp. x. 313. *G. P. Putnam's Sons: New York & London*, 1915. 8°. **08227. cc. 49.**

—— Second edition, revised and enlarged. pp. xii. 376. *G. P. Putnam's Sons: New York & London*, 1918. 8°. **08229. aa. 1.**

CAHN (Joseph) Découverte intéressante à l'usage des administrations, avoués, notaires, commerçants et autres personnes, pour faire soi-même toutes sortes de couleurs à l'usage des timbres-griffes . . . pour papier et linge, *etc.* [Signed by the inventor, J. Cahn.] pp. 8. *Strasbourg*, 1852. 16°. **7954. a. 49. (3.)**

CAHN (Julius) Frankfurter Medailleure im 16. Jahrhundert . . . Sonder-Abdruck aus Festschrift zur Feier des 25jährigen Bestehens des Städtischen Historischen Museums in Frankfurt a. M., *etc. Frankfurt*, 1903. 4°. **Dept. of Coins & Medals.**

—— German Renaissance Medals in the British Museum . . . Reprinted from the "Numismatic Chronicle," *etc.* [With plates.] pp. 25. *London*, 1904. 8°. **7754. b. 7. (14.)**

—— Die Medaillen und Plaketten der Kunstsammlung W. P. Metzler in Frankfurt am Main, *etc.* pp. 63. pl. xxvi. *Frankfurt*, 1898. 4°.

—— Zusätze und Nachträge. pp. 9. pl. xxvii–xxx. *Frankfurt*, 1903. 4°. **7755. g. 32.**

CAHN (Julius)

—— Münz- und Geldgeschichte der im Grossherzogtum Baden vereinigten Gebiete . . . Bearbeitet von Dr. J. Cahn. i. Teil: Konstanz und das Bodenseegebiet im Mittelalter. pp. x. 460. pl. x. 1911. 8°. *See* Carlsruhe.—*Badische Historische Commission.* Ac. **7066/15.**

—— Münz- und Geldgeschichte der Stadt Strassburg im Mittelalter. pp. viii. 176. *Strassburg*, 1895. 8°. **7756. d. 33.**

—— Der Rappenmünzbund. Eine Studie zur Münz- und Geld-Geschichte des oberen Rheinthales. [With four plates.] pp. v. 218. *Heidelberg*, 1901. 8°. **7757. b. 18.**

CAHN (Lester Richard) The Modern Practice of Tooth-Extraction. pp. viii. 132. *Macmillan Co.: New York*, 1924. 8°. **07611. de. 11.**

CAHN (Michael) *Commentator. See* Mishnāh.—*Nĕzīkīn.*—*Ābhōth.* Pirke Aboth . . . erläutert . . . von Dr. M. Cahn. 1875. 8°. **4033. b. 60.**

CAHN (Michael) *Provinzial-Rabbiner in Fulda.* Die religiösen Strömungen in der zeitgenössischen Judenheit. pp. xx. 448. *Frankfurt*, 1912. 8°. **04034. h. 18.**

CAHN (Philipp) *See* Eliasberg (H.) and Cahn (P.) Die Behandlung der kindlichen Lungentuberkulose mit dem künstlichen Pneumothorax. 1924. 8°. [*Abhandlungen aus der Kinderheilkunde und ihren Grenzgebieten.* Hft. 1.] **P.P. 3033. (2.)**

CAHN (R. W.)

—— The Preparation of Uranium Crystals. [With plates.] pp. 15. *Harwell*, 1951. fol. [*Atomic Energy Research Establishment. Report.* no. M/R 744.] B.S. **62/40. (7.)**

CAHN (Rudolf Edwin)

—— *See* Way (Eugene I.) Motion Pictures in Argentina and Brazil. (Based on reports by R. E. Cahn [and others].) 1929. 8°. [*U.S. Bureau of Foreign and Domestic Commerce. Trade Information Bulletin.* no. 630.] A.S. **128/3.**

CAHN (Simon) Die Wechsel-Arbitrage. Theoretisch und practisch durch viele Beispiele erläutert zum Gebrauche für den Selbstunterricht, *etc.* pp. 107. *Frankfurt*, 1879 [1878]. 8°. **8507. e. 4. (10.)**

CAHN (Théophile) and **HOUGET** (Jacques) Glucides, décembre 1936—décembre 1937. [With a bibliography.] pp. 66. *Paris*, 1938. 8°. [*Physiologie.* année 1. no. 1.] **P.P. 3136. ac.**

—— Lipides et stérides, *etc.* pp. 69. *Paris*, 1939. 8°. [*Physiologie.* 1939. no. 2.] **P.P. 3136. ac.**

CAHN (Wilhelm) *See* Lasker (E.) *Politician.* Aus Eduard Lasker's Nachlass. Herausgegeben von Dr. W. Cahn. 1902. 8°. **8072. eee. 35.**

—— Pariser Gedenkblätter. Tagebuchaufzeichnungen aus der Zeit des grossen Kriegs, der Belagerung und der Commune. 2 Bd. *Berlin*, 1898. 8°. **09078. bb. 13.**

CAHN-SPEYER (Rudolf Simon)

—— Franz Seydelmann als dramatischer Komponist. Inaugural-Dissertation, *etc.* [With musical examples.] pp. 301. *Leipzig*, 1909. 8°. Hirsch **4667.**

—— Handbuch des Dirigierens. pp. viii. 284. *Leipzig*, 1919. 8°. **7894. e. 28.**

—— [Another copy.] Handbuch des Dirigierens. *Leipzig*, 1919. 8°. Hirsch **5239.**

CAHOKIA.—*Court of the District of Cahokia.* Cahokia Records, 1778–1790. Edited . . . by Clarence Walworth Alvord. pp. clvi. 663. *Springfield, Ill.*, 1907. 8°. [*Collections of the Illinois State Historical Library.* vol. 2. Virginia series. vol. 1.] **Ac. 8526/2.**

CAHON (ALBERT) Essai sur la contusion du cerveau. pp. 31. *Paris*, 1872. 4°. [*Collection des thèses soutenues à la Faculté de Médecine de Paris.* An 1872. tom. 3.] **7373. n. 9.**

—— Les Picards. Scènes de la vie picarde à l'époque des communes. [Poems.] Avec une préface d'Ernest Vaughan. pp. xii. 312. *Paris*, 1910. 8°. **011483. a. 1.**

—— Les Vaincus. [A poem.] pp. 279. *Paris*, 1877. 8°. **11482. i. 9.**

CAHOON (GUYBERT PHILLIPS)

—— *See* RICHARDSON (John S.) and CAHOON (G. P.) Methods and Materials for Teaching General and Physical Science. 1951. 8°. **8713. e. 22.**

CAHOON (HARYOT HOLT) What One Woman Thinks. Essays . . . edited by C. M. Westover. pp. vii. 269. *T. Fisher Unwin: London*, [1894.] 8°. **012357. e. 87.**

CAHOON (HERBERT)

—— *See* SLOCUM (Jonn J.) and CAHOON (H.) A Bibliography of James Joyce, *etc.* 1953. 8°. **2785.aa.1/5.**

—— Thanatopsis. [Poems.] pp. 25. *Tiger's Eye: New York*, 1949. 8°. **11689. cc. 29.**

CAHOON (JOHN BRADLEY)

—— Formulating X-Ray Technics. Third edition. [With plates.] pp. xiii. 229. *Duke University Press: Durham, N.C.*, 1953. 8°. **7471. b. 35.**

CAHOONE (SARAH S.) Visit to Grand-papa; or, a Week at Newport. pp. 213. *Taylor & Dodd: New York*, 1840. 12°. **12805. h. 18.**

CAHORS. Pétition des citoyens réunis des quatre sections de la commune de Cahors, à la Convention nationale. [Relating chiefly to the recent arrest of thirty-two deputies.] pp. 6. *Cahors*, [1793.] 4°. **F. 64*. (20.)**

—— Cahors. Inventaire raisonné & analytique des archives municipales. [By Edmond Albe.] Première partie. XIIIe siècle. pp. 217. *Cahors*, [1915.] 8°. **10167. f. 26.**
No more published.

—— Discours des choses memorables aduenues à Caors & païs de Quercy, en l'an M.CCCC.XXVIII. Extraict des Annalles Consulaires dudict Caors. (Premiere [—douziesme] Annotation.—Annotation dixiesme en laquelle est declaré quelles estoient les machines & artilleries du temps passé auec leurs pourtraicts.) 2 pt. *Par I. Rousseau: Caors*, 1586. 8°. **G. 15230.**

Bibliothèque.

—— Catalogue de la Bibliothèque de la ville de Cahors. (Rédigé par F. Cangardel.) (Catalogue des manuscrits . . . rédigé par M. C. Couderc.) pp. xxxiv. 720. *Cahors*, 1887. 8°. **011903. m. 4.**

CAHORS, *Diocese of.* Pouillé du diocèse de Cahors, publié par A. Longnon. 1877. 4°. *See* FRANCE. [*Appendix.—History and Politics.—Miscellaneous.*] Collection de documents inédits, *etc.* (Mélanges historiques, *etc.* tom. 2.) 1835, *etc.* 4°, *etc.* **1885. e. 8/2.**

—— [Another issue.] pp. 186. *Paris*, 1877. 4°. **4629. g. 12.**

—— Mandement des vicaires généraux du diocèse de Cahors, le siége vacant, qui ordonne que le Te Deum sera chanté . . . en actions de grâces de l'heureuse élection de . . . Pie VII. pp. 4. [1800.] 4°. **1356. d. 5. (7.)**

CAHORS, *Diocese of.*

—— *Synod.* Statuta synodalia Cadurcensis, Ruthenensis, et Tutelensis ecclesiarum. *See* MARTÈNE (E.) and DURAND (U.) Thesaurus novus anecdotorum, *etc.* tom. 4. 1717. fol. **10. f. 5.**

CAHORS, ALAIN, *Bishop of.* [1637–1659.] *See* SOLMINIAC (A. de) *Count, etc.*

——, AMBROSE, *Bishop of.* [c. 752–770.] *See* AMBROSE, *Saint.*

——, DESIDERIUS, *Bishop of.* [629–654.] *See* DESIDERIUS, *Saint, etc.*

——, HUGUES, *Bishop of.* [1312–1316.] *See* GÉRALDI.

——, JEAN JACQUES DAVID, *Bishop of.* [1842–1863.] *See* BARDOU.

——, JOSEPH DOMINIQUE, *Bishop of.* [1766–1777.] *See* CHEYLUS (J. D. de) successively *Bishop of Tréguier, of Cahors* and *of Bayeux.*

——, LOUIS ANTOINE, *Bishop of.* [1679–1680.] *See* NOAILLES (L. A. de) *Cardinal.*

CAHOS. *See* CHAOS.

CAHOUR (ABEL) Essai de statistique du clergé nantais tant séculier que régulier, à l'époque de la Révolution française. pp. 75. *Nantes*, 1862. 8°. **4632. dd. 4.**

—— Notice historique & critique sur Saint-Émilien, évêque de Nantes, mort à Autun, au VIIIe siècle. [With a map.] pp. 235. *Nantes*, 1859. 12°. **4828. a. 10.**

—— Vie de M. Orain, prêtre, confesseur de la foi pendant la Révolution . . . Deuxième édition. pp. 395. *Nantes*, 1861. 12°. **4866. aa. 16.**

CAHOUR (ARSÈNE M.) Baudouin de Constantinople. Chronique de Belgique et de France en 1225. [The story of the pretender Bertrand de Rayns.] pp. 356. *Paris*, 1850. 12°. **9135. aaa. 26.**

—— Balduinus van Constantinopelen, kronyk van Belgie en van Frankryk in 1225. pp. 348. *Doornik*, 1852. 8°. **10759. d. 11.**

—— Bibliothèque critique des poëtes français. 3 tom. *Paris*, 1863. 8°. **11475. e. 7.**

—— Chefs-d'œuvre d'éloquence française accompagnés de notes historiques, morales et littéraires, *etc.* pp. 630. *Paris*, 1854. 8°. **4426. e. 8.**

—— Des études classiques et des études professionnelles. pp. 280. *Paris*, 1852. 8°. **8308. f. 27.**

—— Des Jésuites. Par un Jésuite. [A reply to the lectures of J. Michelet and E. Quinet, published under the title: "Des Jésuites."] Seconde édition, augmentée. 2 pt. *Paris*, 1844. 18°. **1356. c. 7.**
Pt. 1 only is of the second edition.

CAHOUR (JOSEPH) Manuel pour l'étude de la langue latine adaptée aux usages de la vie moderne. pp. 244. *Paris*, 1928. 8°. **012933. a. 71.**
The date on the wrapper is 1929.

—— Notice sur la Bibliothèque de Laval. Son histoire, ses conservateurs, ses collections. pp. 24. *Laval*, 1916. 8°. **11901. b. 61.**

—— Petit lexique pour l'étude de la " Vita Karoli " d'Eginhard. pp. 59. *Paris*, 1928. 8°. **012933. c. 32.**

CAHOURS (ALBERT) Du cathétérisme dans les engorgements chroniques de la prostate. pp. 26. *Paris* 1857. 4°. [*Collection des thèses soutenues à la Faculté de Médecine de Paris.* An 1857. tom. 3.] **7373. a. 3**

CAHOURS (Auguste)

—— Histoire des radieaux organiques. *See* Paris.—*Société Chimique de France.* Leçons de chimie professées en 1860 [*etc.*]. 1861, *etc.* 8°. Ac. **3895/4.**

—— Leçons de chimie générale élémentaire, professées à l'École centrale des Arts et Manufactures. 2 tom. *Paris,* 1856. 12°. **8905.** b. **28.**

CAHOURS (Auguste) and **RICHE** (Alfred)

—— Chimie des demoiselles. Leçons professées à la Sorbonne. pp. iii. 344. *Paris,* [1868.] 8°. **8907.** f. **24.**

CAHOURS (B. A.) Quelques considérations sur l'anurie comme cause d'accidents cérébraux, *etc.* pp. 24. *Strasbourg,* 1860. 4°. [*Collection générale des dissertations de la Faculté de Médecine de Strasbourg.* sér. 2. tom. 24.] **7381.*** e.

CAHU (Raymond) Comment l'Angleterre gouverne ses colonies? Étude sur le Colonial Office. pp. 77. *Paris,* 1910. 8°. **8156.** f. **55.**

CAHU (Théodore) *See* Bué (H. J.) called Alphonse Bué. La Main du général Boulanger . . . Préface de T. Cahu. 1889. 12°. **8632.** bb. **55.**

—— Amante et mère. pp. 295. *Paris,* 1894. 12°. **012550.** f. **74.**

—— Un Amour dans le monde. pp. 366. *Paris,* [1895.] 12°. **12511.** o. **22.**

—— Au pays des Mauresques. pp. 338. *Paris,* [1888.] 8°. **10097.** bb. **36.**

—— Celles qui se donnent. Roman dialogué. pp. 312. *Paris,* [1899.] 18°. **012551.** b. **27.**

—— Chez les Allemands . . . Illustrations de Caran d'Ache et de Job. Sixième édition. pp. 340. *Paris,* 1887. 12°. **10240.** bb. **14.**

—— Des Batignolles au Bosphore. pp. 376. *Paris,* 1890. 8°. **10126.** cc. **11.**

—— Les Enfants de cigarette, *etc.* [With illustrations.] pp. 425. *Paris,* [1893.] 8°. **12830.** a. **125.** *Part of "Bibliothèque enfantine."*

—— L'Europe en armes en 1889. Étude de politique militaire. pp. liii. 402. *Paris,* 1889. 18°. **8026.** bb. **27.**

—— Georges et Marguerite . . . Troisième édition. pp. 363. *Paris,* 1893. 8°. **012550.** c. **61.**

—— L'Homme aux papillons. pp. 361. *Paris,* 1911. 8°. **12550.** pp. **18.**

—— Une Jeune marquise. Roman, *etc.* pp. 352. *Paris,* 1889. 12°. **012548.** e. **58.**

—— Les Mémoires de Cigarette. Par Théo-Critt (T. Cahu). pp. 100. *Paris,* [1888.] 8°. **12806.** p. **34.**

—— La Mobilisation et le général Boulanger. pp. 8. *Asnières,* 1889. 8°. **8824.** a. **16.** (**4.**)

—— La Montée des races. Roman. pp. ix. 337. *Paris,* [1903.] 8°. **012550.** c. **26.** *The running title reads: Yvonne Godel & Cie.*

—— Pardonnée? Cinquième édition. pp. 307. *Paris,* 1890. 12°. **012547.** g. **74.**

—— Perdus dans l'espace. Grand roman d'aventures. Illustrations, *etc.* pp. 316. *Paris,* 1894. 8°. **012547.** m. **52.**

—— [A reissue.] *Paris,* 1895. 8°. **12491.** u. **1.**

CAHU (Théodore)

—— Rires francs. pp. 118. *Paris,* [1895.] 8°. **012550.** de. **35.**

—— Russes et Autrichiens en robe de chambre. pp. 247. *Paris,* [1888.] 8°. **12354.** cc. **20.**

—— Second mariage. Roman. Quatrième édition. pp. 342. *Paris,* 1891. 12°. **012548.** e. **33.**

—— Tendresse qui tue. Roman. pp. 238. *Paris,* [1906.] 8°. **012548.** d. **51.**

—— Théo-Critt à Saumur. Illustré, *etc.* pp. 378. *Paris,* 1889. 8°. **012330.** k. **12.**

CAHU (Théodore) and **AZCO** (Jean d')

—— Le Printemps d'une femme. Roman moderne. pp. 298. *Paris,* [1910.] 8°. **12551.** v. **24.**

CAHU (Théodore) and **FOREST** (Louis)

—— L'Oubli? 1877–1899 . . . Illustrations de L. Sabattier. pp. 120. [*Paris,*] 1899. fol. [*L'Illustration.* no. 2944–58. suppl. 29 juillet—4 nov. 1899.] P.P. **4283.** m. (**1.**)

CAHU (Théodore) and **LE LOIR** (Maurice)

—— Richelieu. Avant propos de Gabriel Hanotaux. pp. iv. 84. *Paris,* 1901. fol. **1764.** b. **29.**

CAHU (Théodore) and **SÉMANT** (Paul de)

—— Rose Bonheur. Sous la haine. (Vers l'amour.) 2 pt. *Paris,* [1905.] 8°. **012548.** aaa. **62.**

CAHUAC (J. Cyprien) La Vérité contre l'erreur, ou contre Renan. [In verse.] pp. 3. *Agen,* [1865.] 8°. **11482.** d. **13.**

CAHUAC (Jean Homobon) Dissertation sur les anévrysmes du cœur; thèse, *etc.* pp. 27. *Paris,* 1828. 4°. **1184.** c. **5.** (**24.**)

CAHUAC (John)

—— *See* Palmer (Elihu) Principles of Nature . . . A new edition, revised and corrected by J. Cahuac, *etc.* 1819. 12°. **4016.** c. **36.**

—— J. Cahuac's Letter to Lord Sidmouth, on his oppressive arrest for the sale of an alledged libel. pp. 15. *John Cahuac: London,* 1819. 8°. C.T. **69.** (**5.**)

CAHUET (Albéric) Les Abeilles d'or. Île d'Elbe 1815. Roman. pp. 283. *Paris,* 1939. 8°. **12549.** ee. **9.**

—— Les Amants du lac . . . Illustrations . . . de Carlos S. de Tejada. 4 pt. pp. 100. *Paris,* 1927. fol. [*La Petite Illustration.* Roman. no. 144–47.] P.P. **4283.** m. (**1.**)

—— Après la mort de l'Empereur [i.e. Napoleon I.] . . . Documents inédits. Deuxième édition. pp. 315. *Paris,* 1913. 8°. **010662.** a. **10.**

—— Claude-Adolphe Nativelle, 1812–1889. Histoire d'une vie dans l'histoire d'une époque. [With illustrations, including a portrait.] pp. 126. [*Paris,*] 1937. 8°. **10657.** g. **47.**

—— Les Dernières joies de Séverin Chantal. Roman. pp. 308. *Paris,* 1910. 8°. **012548.** dd. **54.**

—— La Femme aux images . . . Illustrations de Léon Fauret. 3 pt. pp. 79. *Paris,* 1937. fol. [*La Petite Illustration.* Roman. no. 401–03.] P.P. **4283.** m. (**1.**)

—— [Another edition.] pp. 190. *Paris,* 1938. 8°. **012548.** eeee. **70.**

CAHUET (Albéric)

—— Irène, femme inconnue . . . Illustrations de Léon Fauret. 3 pt. pp. 87. *Paris*, 1930. fol. [*La Petite Illustration*. Roman. no. 211–13.] P.P. **4283**. m. (**1**.)

—— [Another edition.] pp. 285. *Paris ; Édimbourg* printed, 1939. 8°. [*Collection Nelson*.] **012199**. g. **1/360**.

—— Irène, femme inconnue. pp. 285. *Paris ; Édimbourg* printed, 1939. 8°. [*Collection Nelson*.] **012199**. g. **1/360**.

—— Lucile de Chateaubriand. (Un Werther féminin.) Illustré avec des gravures du temps et des reconstitutions documentaires. 4 pt. pp. 119. *Paris*, 1935. fol. [*La Petite Illustration*. Roman. no. 340–43.] P.P. **4283**. m. (**1**.)

—— [Another edition.] pp. 286. *Paris*, 1935. 8°. **010665**. e. **14**.

—— Mademoiselle de Milly . . . Illustrations de Jean Droit. 2 pt. pp. 36. *Paris*, 1928. fol. [*La Petite Illustration*. Roman. no. 169, 70.] P.P. **4283**. m. (**1**.)

—— Le Missel d'Amour . . . Illustrations de René Lelong. 3 pt. pp. 62. *Paris*, 1923. fol. [*La Petite Illustration*. Roman. Nouvelle série. no. 53–55.] P.P. **4283**. m. (**1**.)

—— [Another edition.] pp. viii. 215. *Paris*, 1923. 8°. **012547**. ccc. **24**.

—— [Another edition.] pp. 190. *Paris ; Édimbourg* printed, 1931. 8°. [*Collection Nelson*.] **012199**. g. **1/277**.

—— Moussia, ou la Vie et la mort de Marie Bashkirtseff. pp. 251. *Paris*, 1926. 8°. **010795**. aa. **29**.

—— Moussia et ses amis. [With portraits.] pp. 232. *Paris*, [1930.] 8°. **010795**. a. **66**.

—— Napoléon délivré . . . Documents et témoignages inédits. pp. 374. *Paris*, 1914. 8°. **010662**. aa. **33**.

—— La Nuit espagnole . . . Compositions de J. Simont. 3 pt. pp. 84. *Paris*, 1934. fol. [*La Petite Illustration*. Roman. no. 304–06.] P.P. **4283**. m. (**1**.)

—— [Another edition.] pp. 243. *Paris*, 1934. 8°. **12513**. ppp. **37**.

—— Pontcarral. Roman. pp. 283. *Paris*, 1937. 8°. **012551**. n. **2**.

—— Colonel Pontcarral . . . Translated . . . by Claud W. Sykes. pp. 320. *John Hamilton: London*, [1938.] 8°. **12549**. aa. **12**.

—— La Question d'Orient dans l'histoire contemporaine, 1821–1905. Préface de M. Frédéric Passy. pp. iii. 537. *Paris*, 1905. 8°. **2240**. aa. **7**.

—— Régine Romani . . . Illustrations de René Lelong. 3 pt. pp. 72. *Paris*, 1925. fol. [*La Petite Illustration*. Roman. no. 93–95.] P.P. **4283**. m. (**1**.)

—— Retours de Sainte-Hélène, 1821–40. pp. 237. *Paris*, 1932. 8°. **10655**. e. **17**.

—— Sainte-Hélène, petite île . . . Illustrations de Carlos S. de Tejada. [With plates.] 4 pt. pp. 107. *Paris*, 1932. fol. [*La Petite Illustration*. Roman. no. 263–66.] P.P. **4283**. m. (**1**.)

—— [Another edition.] pp. 283. *Paris*, 1932. 8°. **12514**. pp. **19**.

CAHUET (Albéric) and **SORBETS** (Gaston)

—— Le Roi s'ennuie. Comé[die] en un acte. pp. 6. 1909. *See* Periodical Publicatio[ns] —*Paris*. L'Illustration, *etc*. (L'Illustration théâtra[le] no. 128.) 1843, *etc*. fol. P.P. **4283**. m. (

CAHUET (Albert) La Liberté du théâtre. Thèse, [etc.] pp. iii. 253. *Paris*, 1902. 8°. **5402**. d.

CAHUN (B.) Jessod Haamuna, the Thirteen Articles [of] Faith [i.e. the "Sh^e^lōsh 'eśrēh 'iḳḳārīm" of Moses [b.] Maimon], demonstrated from the Holy Bible. By Cahun. (Jessod Haamuna, les Treize Articles de Foi, e[tc.]) [pt. 1. Containing the Hebrew text of the first Fun[da]mental Principle and its four attributes.] *Eng. &* pp. 61. 1855. 8°. *See* Moses, *ben Maimon*. [*Sh^e^l 'eśrēh 'iḳḳārīm*.] **4033**. e. **42**.

CAHUN (David Léon) Les Aventures de capitaine Mag[o] ou une Exploration phénicienne mille ans avant l'[ère] chrétienne. Ouvrage illustré de 72 gravures dessinées [sur] bois par P. Philippoteaux et accompagné d'une ca[rte]. pp. 424. *Paris*, 1875. 8°. **12514**. k

—— The Adventures of Captain Mago ; or, a Phœnic[ian] expedition, b.c. 1000 . . . Illustrated by P. Philip[po]teaux, and translated . . . by Ellen E. Frewer. pp. viii. 344. *Sampson Low & Co.: London*, 1876. 8° **12516**. k

—— La Bannière bleue. Aventures d'un musulman, d[']un chrétien et d'un païen à l'époque des Croisades et d[e la] conquête mongole . . . Ouvrage illustré de 73 grav[ures] dessinées sur bois par J. Lix. pp. 430. *Paris*, 1877. **12514**. k

—— The Blue Banner ; or, the Adventures of a Mussulm[an,] a Christian, and a Pagan in the time of the Crusades [and] Mongol Conquest . . . Translated . . . by W. C. Sand[...] With 76 wood engravings by J. Lix. pp. xvi. 351. *Sampson Low & Co.: London*, 1877. 8°. **12517**. h

—— Excursions sur les bords de l'Euphrate. pp. 294. *Pa[ris,]* [1885.] 18°. **10075**. aaa.

—— Hassan le janissaire. 1516. pp. xiv. 370. *Pa[ris,]* 1891. 12°. **012548**. df.

—— Introduction à l'histoire de l'Asie. Turcs et Mongols [des] origines à 1405. pp. xiii. 519. *Paris*, 1896. 8°. **09055**. bb.

—— Les Mercenaires. Ouvrage illustré, *etc*. pp. vii. 327 *Paris*, 1882. 8°. **12510**. i.

—— Les Pilotes d'Ango. Ouvrage illustré de 45 grav[ures] . . . par Sahib. pp. 315. *Paris*, 1878. 8°. **12510**. h.

—— Les Rois de mer . . . Ouvrage illustré de soix[ante] dessins par C. Gilbert. pp. 302. *Paris*, [1890.] 8°. **12512**. k.

—— La Tueuse. 1241. pp. 348. *Paris*, 1893. 12°. **012550**. e.

CAHUN (Léon) *See* Cahun (David L.)

CAHUSAC (Francis H. E.) What think you of Chr[ist?] Is the Christ of the Catholic Church the Christ of [the] Gospels ? pp. v. 104. *R. & T. Washbourne: Lon[don,]* 1914. 8°. **3942**. de.

CAHUSAC (Louis de) L'Algérien, ou les M[uses] comédiennes, comédie-ballet, en trois actes & en vers, pp. 128. *Paris*, 1744. 8°. **164**. c.

CAHUSAC (LOUIS DE)

—— Fragments, composés de l'acte de Bacchus et Hégémone, entrée des Amours de Tempé [by L. de Cahusac], de l'acte de la Femme, troisième entrée des Fêtes de Thalie [by Joseph de la Font], et du Devin du village, intermède en un acte [by J. J. Rousseau]. Représentés par l'Académie-Royale de Musique, *etc.* 2 pt. 1765. 4°. *See* TEMPE. **11736.** h. **11.** (6.)

—— La Danse ancienne et moderne, ou Traité historique de la danse. 3 tom. *La Haye,* 1754. 12°. **1042.** a. **14.**

—— [Another copy.] **56.** a. **35–37.**

—— [Another copy.] C. **67.** a. **16.**
Imperfect; wanting the titlepage of tom. 1, in place of which a duplicate of that of tom. 2 has been inserted. With the arms of Montmorency, Duke of Luxembourg, on the binding.

—— Des Herrn von Cahüsac historische Abhandlung von der alten und neuen Tanzkunst . . . Aus dem Französischen übersetzt. 2 pt. 1759. *See* SAMMLUNG. Sammlung vermischter Schriften zur Beförderung der schönen Wissenschaften, *etc.* Bd. 1, 2. 1759, *etc.* 8°. **821.** g. **42.**

—— Les Fêtes de l'Himen et de l'Amour; ou les Dieux d'Éigipte; ballet-héroïque, *etc.* pp. 46. *Paris,* 1765. 4°. **11736.** k. **8.**

—— Les Festes de Polimnie; ballet héroïque, *etc.* pp. 54. *Paris,* 1753. 4°. **11736.** h. **11.** (3.)

—— Grigri, histoire véritable. Traduite du japonnois en portugais par Didaque Hadeczuca . . . & du portugais en françois par l'abbé de ***. [By L. de Cahusac.] 2 pt. [1739.] 8°. *See* GRIGRI. **12511.** d. **9.**

—— [Another edition.] 2 pt. 1745. 12°. *See* GRIGRI. **1080.** c. **24.**

—— Naïs; opéra pour la paix, *etc.* pp. 59. FEW MS. NOTES. [*Paris,*] 1749. 4°. **11736.** k. **5.** (7.)

—— La Naissance d'Osiris, ou la Feste Pamilie, ballet allégorique.—Anacréon, ballet héroique. [1754.] *See* FONTAINEBLEAU. Spectacles donnés à Fontainebleau. vol. 2. [1753, *etc.*] 4°. **84.** i. **8.**

—— Pharamond, tragédie. Par Monsieur de C * * * [i.e. L. de Cahusac]. pp. 76. 1736. 8°. *See* C * * *, *Monsieur de.* **164.** c. **52.**

—— Zénéïde, comédie en un acte, en vers, avec un divertissement, *etc.* pp. 42. *Paris,* 1744. 8°. **164.** c. **55.**

—— [Another edition.] pp. 40. *La Haye,* 1750. 8°. [*Théâtre de la Haye.* tom. 5.] **242.** g. **22.**

—— Zeneide, ein Lustspiel von einem Aufzuge. Nach dem Französischen des Herrn von Cahüsac. [Translated by J. J. Salamon.] pp. 48. *Leipzig,* 1760. 8°. **11747.** g. **7.** (3.)

—— Zoroastre; opéra, *etc.* pp. 76. MS. NOTES. *Paris,* 1756. 4°. **11736.** h. **11.** (12.)

CAHUZAC (ALBERT) Essai sur les institutions et le droit malgaches. tom. 1. pp. 506. *Paris,* 1900. 8°. **05319.** f. **54.**

No more published?

CAHUZAC (EMMANUEL DE) *Viscount.* La Loi Dufaure et l'Internationale. Les Communeux jugés par l'Internationale . . . Deuxième édition. pp. 16. *Bruxelles,* 1871. 8°. **8050.** i. **4.**

CAHUZAC (J. A. LOUIS) Des constitutions médicales. Thèse, *etc.* pp. 39. *Montpellier,* 1847. 4°. **7379.** a. **4.** (3.)

CAHUZAC (JEAN LOUIS) Esquisse sur les eaux thermales d'Amélie-les-Bains. Thèse, *etc.* pp. 35. *Montpellier,* 1857. 4°. **7379.** d. **10.** (7.)

CAHUZAC DE CAUX (SÉBASTIEN CHARLES PHILIBERT) successively *Bishop of Assure* and *of Aire.* Lettre pastorale de l'évêque d'Aire au clergé séculier et régulier de son diocèse. pp. 53. [1791.] 8°. F. **107.** (2.)

CAHZET (ANDRÉ RENÉ BALTHAZAR D'ALISSAN DE) *See* ALISSAN DE CHAZET.

CAIADUS (HENRICUS)

—— Hermici Oratio (habita publice Pataui nono calendas nouembris .M.D.III.) cum epistola ad Bartholomeum Blanchinum Bononiensem. *Bernardinus Vitalis: Venetiis,* 1504. 4°. **1482.** bb. **1.**

—— Hermicus Cayado, iure consultus Ulyssiponensis. (Ecloga I–IX.—Silva I–III.—Epigrammatum liber I, II.) [With a life of the author.] *See* REYS (A. dos) Corpus illustrium poetarum lusitanorum, *etc.* tom. 1. 1745, *etc.* 4°. **78.** h. **1.**

—— *Begin.* [fol. 1 *recto:*] Sacratissimo Hemanueli prĩo Portugaliae Algarabiorumq̧ . . . regi dominoq̧ Guinee seruulus Henricus Caiadus. [fol. 3 *recto:*] Henrici Caiadi Lusitani Aegloga prĩa(—sexta), *etc.* G.L.
Iustinianus de Ruberia: Bononiae, x. kalendas augustas [23 July], [1496.] 4°. IA. **29199.**
30 *leaves. Sig.* a–c[6] d[8]. 25 *lines to a page.*

—— The Eclogues of Henrique Cayado. Edited, with introduction and notes, by Wilfred P. Mustard. pp. 98. *Johns Hopkins Press: Baltimore; Oxford University Press: London,* 1931. 8°. [*Studies in the Renaissance Pastoral.* no. 6.] **11858.a.64/6.**

—— [Another copy.] **20020.** a. **48.**

—— Aus den lateinischen Gedichten des Hermicus Cayado. [Selections from the Epigrammata.] *Lat. & Ger. See* BUDIK (P. A.) Leben und Wirken der vorzüglichsten lateinischen Dichter des XV.–XVIII. Jahrhunderts, *etc.* Bd. 3. 1828. 8°. **817.** c. **13.**

CAIAN. The Caian. *See* CAMBRIDGE.—*University of Cambridge.—Gonville and Caius College.*

—— Caian, ou l'Idolatre converty. Tagi-comedie [*sic*], de F. G. B. [i.e. Frère Girard, Barnabite.] 1656. 8°. *See* B., F. G. **11737.** aa. **12.**

CAIANU (D.) *See* CAESAR (C. J.) [*Works.—Roumanian.*] Comentariele lui C. Juliu Cesare de belulu Galicu, *etc.* (Comentariele lui C. Juliu Cesare de belulu civile, urmate de comentariele lui A. Hirtiu de belele Alexandrinu si Africanu . . . traduse D. Caianu.) 1872, *etc.* 8°. **9041.** c. **27.**

CAIAPHAS, *High Priest of the Jews. See* COPPENS (U.) The Palace of Caiphas, *etc.* [1904.] 8°. **10077.** bbb. **37.**

—— *See* LEE (Edward H. H.) The Plan of Caiaphas. [1924.] 8°. **03226.** e. **33.**

—— Een Toast van Cajaphas. [A satire on contemporary theology.] pp. 16. *Hoorn,* 1864. 8°. **3925.** bbb. **40.** (3.)

CAIBANI (AUGUSTO) Gingillini d'amore. Un Marito che affitta la moglie. Di A. Caibani. Il settimo comandamento: Non far adulterio. Dell'Eruditucolo. pp. 190. *Milano,* [1888.] 32°. **12470.** aaa. **40.**

CAICEDO (DE) *Marquis.* El Oro; su explotacion y consideraciones acerca de los yacimientos auríferos de las Islas Filipinas. pp. 42. *Madrid,* 1880. 8°. **8229.** i. **11.** (**1.**)

CAICEDO (DOMINGO) [For official documents issued by D. Caicedo as Vice-President of the Republic of New Granada:] *See* NEW GRANADA, *Republic of.*—[1831–58.]—Caicedo (D.) *Vice-President.*

CAICEDO (FERNANDO CUERO I) *Bishop of Popayan. See* CUERO I CAICEDO.

CAICEDO (JOSÉ MARIA TORRES) *See* TORRES CAICEDO.

CAICEDO CASTILLA (JOSÉ JOAQUÍN)

—— [Two speeches in the Colombian Senate on the "Protocol of Friendship and Cooperation between the Republic of Colombia and the Republic of Peru."] *In:* COLOMBIA. [Republic of Colombia, 1886– .]—*Senado.*—*Comisión de Relaciones Exteriores.* Debate del Protocolo, *etc.* 1936. 8°. L.A.S. **382/5.**

CAICEDO I CUERO (JOAQUIN) *See* ORTIZ (José J.) Noticia biografica de J. Caicedo i Cuero. 1854. 8°. **10881.** f. **20.** (**3.**)

CAICEDO I TAMACHO (FERNANDO) *See* ORTIZ (José J.) Noticia biografica de J. Caicedo i Cuero. [With an address to the author by F. Caicedo i Tamacho.] 1854. 8°. **10881.** f. **20.** (**3.**)

CAICEDO R. (JOSÉ) *See* CAICEDO ROJAS.

CAICEDO ROJAS (JOSÉ) *See* CUADROS. Cuadros de Costumbres de R. E. Santander . . . J. Caicedo Rojas, *etc.* 1936. 8°. **12213.** b. **1/22.**

—— *See* ESPINOSA (J. M.) Memorias de un Abanderado. [With an introduction signed: J. Caicedo R.] 1876. 8°. **10882.** bbb. **10.**

—— Las Memorias de un Abanderado. [On the publication of the work of this title by J. M. Espinosa. Signed: J. Caicedo R.] *Bogotá,* 1878. *s. sh.* 8°. **1881.** c. **16.** (**36.**)

CAICEDO Y FLÓREZ (FERNANDO) *See* CAYCEDO Y FLÓREZ.

CAICO (LINA) *See* TRINE (Ralph W.) In armonia coll'infinito. Versione di Luisa e Lina Caico, *etc.* 1910. 8°. **8411.** k. **26.**

CAICO (LOUISA) *See* CERVESATO (A.) [Latina tellus.] The Roman Campagna . . . Translated by L. Caico, *etc.* 1913. 8°. **10151.** f. **27.**

—— *See* LEOPARDI (G.) *Count, the Poet.* [*Canti.*—*Single Poems and Selections.*—*French.*] Choix de poésies. Version française de L. Caico. 1923. 8°. **11431.** ccc. **47.**

—— *See* TRINE (Ralph W.) In armonia coll'infinito. Versione di Luisa e Lina Caico, *etc.* 1910. 8°. **8411.** k. **26.**

—— Sicilian Ways and Days . . . With one hundred and twenty-eight illustrations. pp. 279. *John Long: London,* 1910. 8°. **10136.** dd. **13.**

CAICOS ISLANDS. [For laws and other official documents of the Caicos Islands:] *See* TURKS AND CAICOS ISLANDS.

CAÏD BEN SHERIF. *See* ḲĀʻID IBN SHARĪF.

CAIDIN (MARTIN)

—— Rockets beyond the Earth . . . Drawings by Fred. L. Wolff and Jerry J. Schlamp. [With illustrations.] pp. 319. *Arco Publishers: London; printed in U.S.A.,* 1955. 8°. **8764.** s. **2.**

CAIDIN (MARTIN)

—— Worlds in Space . . . Illustrated by Fred L. Wol pp. x. 212. pl. 64. *Sidgwick & Jackson: Lond* 1954. 8°. **08560.** b.

CAIE (GEORGE JOHNSTONE) Family Prayers for five weel With a few prayers for special occasions, and priva prayers for one week. pp. 194. *J. G. Hitt: Edinbur* 1896. 8°. **3456.** ee.

CAIE (JOHN MORRISON) The Kindly North. Verse Scots and English, *etc.* pp. xvi. 110. *D. Wyllie & So Aberdeen,* 1934. 8°. **011641.** ee.

—— 'Twixt Hills and Sea. Verse in Scots and English, *e* pp. xvi. 111. *D. Wyllie & Son: Aberdeen,* 1939. 8°. **11656.** i.

CAIE (NORMAN MACLEOD) The Mount of Expiation. study of the seven deadly sins. pp. 95. *Hodder Stoughton: London,* 1923. 8°. **04403.** i.

—— Night-Scenes of Scripture. pp. 195. *Alexander Gardn Paisley,* 1921. 8°. **03128.** f.

—— The Secret of a Warm Heart, and other papers. pp. 1 *H. R. Allenson: London,* [1927.] 8°. **04403.** k.

—— Seven Words of Love. The sayings of Jesus on Cross. pp. 63. *A. H. Stockwell: London,* [1925.] 8°. **4224.** cc.

—— The Vintage. Studies in the fruit of the Spirit. pp. 1 *R.T.S.: London,* [1925.] 8°. **04403.** k.

CAIETAN (CONSTANTIN) *See* CAIETANUS (Constantinus)

CAIETAN (HENRI) *Cardinal. See* CAETANI (Enrico)

CAIETAN (THOMAS) *Cardinal. See* VIO (T. de)

CAIETANO DE ARAGONIA (BERNARDUS) *See* CA *Monastery of.* Codex diplomaticus Cavensis . Accedit appendix qua praecipua Bibliothecae MS. memb nacea describuntur per D. B. Caietano de Aragonia. 1873, *etc.* 4°. **9150.** i.

CAIETANUS, *ab Assumptione.* Vita R. P. F. Epiphani SS. Trinitate Tridentini, Carmelitae Discalceati. [Wit portrait.] pp. lv. *Venetiis,* 1765. 4°. **4867.** f.

CAIETANUS, *Saint. See* CAJETAN [Tiene], *Saint.*

CAIETANUS (CONSTANTINUS) *See* HESER (G.) Geo Heseri . . . Dioptra Kempensis, *etc.* (Summula Appa tui Constantini Caietani abbatis ad Joannem Ger restitutum [contained in the 1644 edition of the " imitatione Christi"] opposita. Argumenta collegit dissolvit Georgius Heser.) 1650. 12°. I.X. App. **106.**

—— *See* JESUS CHRIST. [*De Imitatione Christi.*—*Lat* Venerabilis viri Joannis Gessen Abbatis Ord. S. Bened De Imitatione Christi libri quatuor, a Domno C. Caiet . . . recensiti . . . Accessit eiusdem Domni C. Abb Caietani Defensio pro hoc ipso librorum auctore, nec r eorumdem librorum Methodus practica et breuis epito *etc.* 1616. 12°. I.X. Lat.

—— —— 1616. 12°. I.X. Lat.

—— *See* JESUS CHRIST. [*De Imitatione Christi.*—*Englis* The Followinc [*sic*] of Christ, *etc.* [Translated from edition of C. Caietanus, with his dedicatory epistle.] 1673. 12°. I.X. Eng. **1**

—— *See* NAUDÉ (G.) Raisons peremptoires de Mai G. Naudé . . . Contre P. Roussel, R. Quatremaire, F. Valgrave, Religieux Benedictins . . . pour monst que les IV. MSS. de Rome dont les dits Benedictins servent pour oster le livre de l'Imitation de Jesus-Ch a T. de Kempis sont falsifiez . . . par . . . C. Cajet Religieux Benedictin, ou par quelque autre du me ordre. [1652 ?] 4°. **1127.** i. **13.**

CAIETANUS (Constantinus)

—— *See* Pandulphus, *Pisanus.* Sanctiss. D. N. Gelasii Papæ. II. . . . vita . . . nunc primùm edita, & commentarijs illustrata a Domno C. Caietano. (Vita et passio S. Erasmi Antiochiæ episc. . . . scripta a Ioanne Caietano, qui & Gelasius Papa II. Edita . . . ac scholijs illustrata a Domno C. Abbate Caietano.) 1638. 4°. **1371. e. 10.**

—— *See* Peter [Damiano], *Saint, Cardinal, etc.* B. Petri Damiani operum tomus primus(—tertius), *etc.* (Tomus tertius, continens opuscula . . . argumentis notisq. illustrata atque nunc primum excusa opera ac studio C. Caietani.) 1606, *etc.* fol. **3675. f. 3.**

—— —— 1663. fol. **3625. b. 10.**

—— —— 1743. fol. **689.ee.8,9.**

—— —— 1783. 4°. **1219. k. 18.**

—— —— 1853. 4°. [*Patrologiæ cursus completus.* tom. 144, 145.] **2000. f.**

—— *See* Peter [Damiano], *Saint, Cardinal, etc.* B. Petri Damiani . . . Epistolarum libri octo . . . collecti et argumentis notisque illustrati opera C. Caetani. 1610. 4°. **1009. c. 8.**

—— *See* Werlinus (S.) Rosweydus redivivus, id est, Vindiciæ vindiciarum Kempensium . . . pro libello Thomæ a Kempis de imitatione Christi adversus . . . Constantini Caietani duplicem defensionem hanc Romæ anno 1644, illam Parisiis anno 1638 editas. 1649. 12°. I.X. App. **103.**

—— Constantini Caietani . . . De singulari primatu S. Petri solius. Commentarius, *etc.* 1698. *See* Rocaberti (J. T. de) *Archbishop of Valencia.* Bibliotheca maxima pontificia, *etc.* tom. 7. 1698, *etc.* fol. **484. e. 6.**

—— Leiteræ . . . de auctore libri de imitatione J. C. *See* Thuillier (V.) Historia concertationis de auctore libelli de imitatione Christi, *etc.* 1726. 12°. I.X. App. **113.**

—— Domni Constantini Caietani . . . Pro Ioanne Gersen, Abbate Vercellensi, librorum de imitatione Christi auctore. Concertatio priori editione auctior. Accessit Apologetica eiusdem responsio pro hoc ipso librorum auctore: aduersus Heribertum Rosvueydum. 1618. 8°. I.X. App. **101.**

—— D. Constantini Caetani . . . Responsio apologetica, pro . . . Io. Gersen . . . germano auctore librorum quatuor de imitatione Christi . . . aduersum vindicias Kempenses Heriberti Rosweydi, *etc.* pp. 239. *See* Jesus Christ. [*De Imitatione Christi.—Latin.*] Magni, & Venerabilis Serui Dei, Ioannis Gersen, Abbatis Italo-Benedictini, De imitatione Christi libri quatuor, *etc.* 1644. 8°. **I.X.Lat.306.**

—— Sanctoꝝ trium episcopoꝝ relig^is bened^næ luminum Isidori Hispalens. Ildefonsi Tolet. Gregorii Card. Ost. vitæ, et actiones . . . Addita sunt . . . aliquot eiusdem S. Isidori scripta nondum edita ad Philippum III. Hispꝝ . . . Regem Catholicum. pp. 156. *Apud I. Mascardum: Romæ,* 1606. 4°. **487. h. 14.**

CAIETANUS (Daniel) *See* Priscianus, *of Caesarea.* Habes candide lector in hoc opere Prisciani uolumē maius . . . Habes insuper eiusdem uolumē minus: & de duodecim carminibus: ac etiam de accētibus cū expositione . . . Danielis Caietani nūc primū edita, *etc.* 1496. fol. **IB. 22938.**

—— —— 1500. fol. **IB. 23693.**

—— *See* Seneca (L. A.) [*Tragedies.—Latin.*] *Begin.* [fol. 2 *recto*:] Ad magnificum ac generosum Leonardum Mocenigum . . . Danielis Gaietani Cremonensis apologia. [fol. 5 *recto*:] L. Annei Senecæ Tragœdiæ cū duobus cōmentis [of D. Caietanus and G. B. Marmita]. 1493. fol. **IB. 22748.**

CAIETANUS (Daniel)

—— —— 1498. fol. **IB. 24083.**

—— 1514. fol. **833. l. 29.**

—— —— 1522. fol. **C. 39. i. 21.**

CAIETANUS (Henricus) *Cardinal.* *See* Caetani.

CAIETANUS (Honoratus) *See* Caetani (Onorato) *Signore di Sermoneta.*

CAIETANUS (Jacobus) *Cardinal.* *See* Gaietanus.

CAIETANUS (Joannes) afterwards *Pope Gelasius II.* *See* Gelasius II., *Pope* [Giovanni Caetani].

CAIETANUS (Joannes) *Theatine.* *See* Aresi (P.) *Bishop of Tortona.* Illustrissimi . . . Dn. Pauli Aresii . . . Sacrorum phrenoschematum liber . . . Opus a F. I. Cajetano . . . Latinitate donatum. 1702. fol. **4855. h. 7.**

CAIETANUS (Josephus) De sapientia, et insipientia Salomonis paræenesis scholastico-expositiva, *etc.* 2 pt. *Conimbricæ,* 1741. 4°. **3166. ee. 9.**

—— Theo-Rhetoris simulacrum, seu Vera effigies concionatoris evangelici, opusculum prævium ad Divini Verbi hierologiam, sive artem . . . ponderandi Sacram Scripturam per conceptus, ut vocant, prædicabiles, *etc.* 6 vol. *Conimbricæ,* 1730–35. 4°. **3125. ee. 24.**

CAIETANUS (Nicolaus) *Duke of Laurenzana.* *See* Gaetano d'Aragona (Niccolò)

CAIETANUS (Octavius) *See* Theodosius, *a Monk of Syracuse.* Theodosii Monachi epistola de Syracusanæ urbis expugnatione cum animadversionibus O. Cajetani. 1725. fol. [*Muratori (L. A.) Rerum italicarum scriptores.* tom. 1. pt. 2.] **L.1.h.1/1.**

—— Icones aliquot, et origines illusrium [*sic*] ædium Sanctissimæ Deiparæ Mariæ, quæ in Siciliæ insula coluntur. Accesserunt Meditationes de vita eiusdem Deiparæ (auctore I. A. Confalonerio). [Edited by T. Tamburini.] 2 pt. *P. de Isola: Panormi,* 1663, 64. 4°. **664. a. 16.**
Imperfect; wanting the plates.

—— Octauii Caietani . . . Idea operis de vitis Siculorum sanctorum famaue sanctitatis illustrium Deo volente bonis iuuantibus in lucem prodituri. pp. 150. *Apud E. Simeonem & socios: Panhormi,* 1617. 4°. **662. c. 38.**

—— Isagoge ad historiam sacram siculam . . . Opus posthumum, *etc.* [With plates.] pp. 403. *Panormi,* 1707. 4°. **664. a. 12.**

—— [A reissue.] *Panormi,* 1708. 4°. **864. m. 9.**

—— Editio novissima, auctior, & emendatior. coll. 234. *Lugduni Batavorum,* 1723. fol. [*Thesaurus antiquitatum et historiarum Siciliae.* vol. 2.] **L.R.302.a.2/10.**

—— Vitæ sanctorum Siculorum, ex antiquis Græcis Latinisque monumentis, & vt plurimum ex M.S.S. codicibus nondum editis collectæ, aut scriptæ, digestę iuxta seriem annorum Christianæ Epochæ, & animaduersionibus illustratæ a R. P. O. Caietano . . . Opus posthumum . . . cui perficiendo operam contulit R. P. Petrus Salernus . . . Accessit auctoris opusculum, vbi origines illustrium ædium SS. Deiparæ Mariæ in Sicilia . . . explicantur. 2 tom. *Apus Civillos: Panormi,* 1657. fol. **487. l. 7, 8.**

—— [Another copy.] **663. k. 13, 14.**

CAIETANUS (Octavius)

—— *See* Joannes, *Diaconus Ecclesiae S. Januarii Neapoli.* Martyrium S. Procopii Episcopi Tauromenitani . . . cum animadversionibus . . . O. Cajetani . . . secundo tomo Sanctorum Siculorum. 1725. [*Muratori* (*L. A.*) *Rerum italicorum scriptores.* tom. 1. pt. 2.] **L.1.h.1/1.**

CAIETANUS (Rogerius) *See* Caetano (Ruggiero)

CAIETANUS (Thomas de Vio) *Cardinal.* *See* Vio (T. de)

CAIETANUS (Thomas Devius) *Ordinis Praedicatorum Generalis.* *See* Vio (T. de) *Cardinal.*

CAIETANUS DE LIMA (Ludovicus) *See* Caetano de Lima (Luiz)

CAIETANUS PALMA (Petrus Victor) *See* Palma Cayet (Pierre V.)

CAIETE. *See* Gaeta.

CAIFASSI (Ildebrando) Sulle acque minerali e termali di Rapolano nella provincia senese e particolarmente sulle antiche termo sulfuree di proprietà del sig. Achille Marii, *etc.* pp. 31. *Siena,* 1863. 8°. **7462.** ee. **6. (9.)**

CAIGER (Frederick Foord) The Diagnosis and Management of Doubtful Cases of Diphtheria. Being an address, *etc.* pp. 16. 1904. 8°. *See* London.—iii. *Medical Officers of Schools Association.* **07305.** m. **6. (11.)**

CAIGER (George)

—— The Australian Way of Life. Edited by G. Caiger, *etc.* pp. xvi. 158. pl. xi. *William Heinemann: London,* 1953. 8°. [*Way of Life Series.*] W.P. b. **634/1.**

—— Britain behind the Guns . . . Second edition. pp. 14. *British Embassy: Tokyo,* 1940. 8°. [*British Information Series.* no. 4.] **B.S.14/158.(4.)**

—— Tojo Say No. Japanese ideas and ideals. [With plates.] pp. viii. 165. *Angus & Robertson: Sydney,* 1943. 8°. **010055.** aa. **88.**

CAIGER (Herbert) A Nation's Best Asset: its childhood's health. Suggestions on school and home hygiene to teachers and parents. pp. 25. *J. C. Juta & Co.: Cape Town,* [1906.] 8°. **07305.** i. **38. (1.)**

CAIGER (Hugh) Sunday Afternoon: twenty-seven children's services, containing an address, prayers, lessons, hymns, etc. Advent to Whitsuntide. pp. x. 163. *S.P.C.K.: London,* 1938. 8°. **03456.** f. **95.**

—— Sunday Afternoon. [Fifty-two children's services.] 2 pt. *S.P.C.K.: London,* 1940. 8°. **03456.** ff. **85.**
Pt. 1 *is a reissue of "Sunday Afternoon . . . Advent to Whitsuntide."*

—— What We Believe and What We Do. Fifty-two lessons on the Church Catechism for use in Sunday schools and at the children's service. pp. vii. 213. *S.P.C.K.: London,* 1936. 8°. **03504.** f. **87.**

—— [A reissue.] What we believe and what we do, *etc.* pp. vii. 213. *National Society; S.P.C.K.: London,* 1941. 8°. [*Church Education Publications.*] W.P. **6246/13.**

—— Worship and Prayer. Fifty-two talks to young people. pp. viii. 226. *S.P.C.K.: London,* 1937. 8°. **03456.** f. **80.**

CAIGER (M. T.)

—— *See* Harrop (R.) *Writer on Aeronautics.* The Design and Testing of Supersonic Nozzles. By R. Harrop . . . M. T. Caiger. 1953. 4°. [*Aeronautical Research Council. Reports and Memoranda.* no. 2712.] B.S. **2/2.**

CAIGER (Stephen Langrish) Archæology and the New Testament . . . With . . . plates, *etc.* pp. x. 194. *Cassell & Co.: London,* 1939. 8°. **07703.** e. **7[illegible]**

—— Bible and Spade. An introduction to biblical archaeology. pp. xii. 218. pl. 24. *Oxford University Press London,* 1936. 8°. **07704.** de. **7[illegible]**

—— British Honduras Past and Present. pp. 240. *George Allen & Unwin: London,* 1951. 8°. **010481.** f. **3[illegible]**

—— Edlaston. Church and parish. pp. 20. [*The Author Osmaston,*] 1953. 8°. **010368.** aa. **8[illegible]**

—— Honduras ahoy! The Church at work in Central America. [With plates.] pp. 46. *Society for the Propagation of the Gospel in Foreign Parts: London* 1949. 8°. **4768.** a. **4[illegible]**

—— Lives of the Prophets. 10 pt. *S.P.C.K.: London* [1936.] 8°. [*Little Books on Religion.* no. 106–115.] W.P. **1307/106–115**

—— [Another edition.] pp. vii. 307. *S.P.C.K.: London* [1936.] 8°. **20029.** a. **37**

—— Lives of the Prophets, *etc.* (Revised and enlarged edition.) pp. 333. *S.P.C.K.: London,* 1949. 8°. **03187.** i. **93**

—— The Old Testament and Modern Discovery. [With plates.] pp. xii. 102. *S.P.C.K.: London,* 1938. 8°. [*Biblical Handbooks.*] **3130.f.48/4.**

—— Shepherd's Pie. A comedy in one act. pp. 28. *S.P.C.K.: London,* 1951. 8°. **11783.** ff. **3[illegible]**

—— Westward Ho! A glimpse at the diocese of British Honduras, Central America. [With plates and a map.] pp. 24. *S.P.G. & S.P.C.K.: London,* 1935. 8°. **20020.** f. **20**

CAIGHTON (Arthur) Recitations Grave and Gay. pp. 51 *Reynolds & Co.: London,* [1914.] 8°. **012331.** e. **102**

—— Six Recitations. pp. 16. *Reynolds & Co.: London* [1919.] 8°. **011648.** e. **114**

CAIGNARD DE MAILLY (Thomas Joseph Charles) *See* Caignart de Mailly.

CAIGNART, *Family of.* Notes généalogiques et biographiques sur la famille Caignart de Saint-Quentin et ses alliances. pp. 45. *Amiens,* 1890. 8°. **9906.** b. **8. (3.**

CAIGNART DE MAILLY (Thomas Joseph Charles) *See* also Duchesne, *Père, pseud.* [i.e. L. J. P. Ballois and T. J. C. Caignart de Mailly.]

—— *See* France. [*Appendix.—History and Politics.—Revolution of* 1789.] Histoire de la Révolution de 1789, [tom. 16, 17 by T. J. C. Caignart de Mailly.] 1790, *etc.* 8°. **2085.**

—— —— 1792, *etc.* 8°. **9220.** [illegible]

—— *See* Periodical Publications.—*Paris.* Annales maç. *etc.* [Edited by T. J. C. Caignart de Mailly.] [1807, *etc.*] 18°. **4783.** b. **1[illegible]**

—— Le Premier qui s'attroupera . . . Extrait de l'Ami de la patrie. [An attack on the proposal of V. Duplantier to restrict the activity of the clubs.] pp. 4. [*Paris,* 1797.] 8°. **F. 1120. (5**

—— Voilà le détail du grand départ du directeur Carnot avec le cousin Jacques et sa famille. [A satirical song.] pp. 4. [*Paris,* 1797.] 8°. **F. 410. (25**

CAIGNART DE SAULCY (LOUIS FÉLICIEN JOSEPH)

See BOURGUIGNAT (J. R.) Testacea novissima quæ Cl. de Saulcy in itinere per Orientem annis 1850 et 1851 collegit. 1852. 8°. **7298. d. 37. (2.)**

—— *See* DELESSERT (E.) Voyage aux Villes Maudites . . . Suivi de notes scientifiques et d'une carte par F. de Saulcy. 1853. 12°. **10075. a. 10.**

—— *See* LIÈVRE (E.) Les Collections célèbres d'œuvres d'art . . . Textes historiques et descriptifs par MM. F. de Saulcy, A. de Longpérier [and others], *etc.* 1866. fol. **1812. b. 29.**

—— *See* MADDEN (Frederick W.) Remarks in reply to the new observations on "Jewish Numismatics" by M. F. de Saulcy [published in the "Revue numismatique" for 1864 and 1865], *etc.* 1865. 8°. **7758.g.15.**

—— *See* MARCHANT (Nicolas D.) *Baron.* Lettres du baron Marchant sur la numismatique et l'histoire, annotées par . . . F. de Saulcy [and others], *etc.* 1851. 8°. **7756. dd. 9.**

—— *See* PERIODICAL PUBLICATIONS.—*Mans.* Mélanges de numismatique, publiés par F. de Saulcy, *etc.* 1874, *etc.* 8°. **P.P. 1877. c.**

—— *See* PERIODICAL PUBLICATIONS.—*Paris.* L'Athenæum français . . . Fondé et dirigé par MM. L. Vivien de Saint Martin, F. de Saulcy [and others]. 1852, *etc.* 4°. **P.P. 4291.**

—— *See* PIOBERT (G.) École d'Application de l'Art[e] et du Génie. Cours d'artillerie. Partie théorique . . . Rédigée par MM. Didion et de Saulcy. 1841. 4°. **1397. g. 1.**

—— *See* SCHLUMBERGER (G. L.) Des bractéates d'Allemagne . . . avec une lettre de M. de Saulcy. 1873. 8°. **7755. dd. 1.**

—— *See* SCHLUMBERGER (G. L.) Éloge de M. de Saulcy, *etc.* [With a portrait and a bibliography.] 1881. 4°. **010655. h. 40.**

—— *See* WALLON (H. A.) Éloges académiques. (tom. 2. Notice sur la vie et les travaux de M. L. F. J. Caignart de Saulcy.) 1882. 8°. **10664. c. 19.**

—— Analyse grammaticale du texte démotique du décret de Rosette. [With plates.] tom. 1. pt. 1. pp. 264. *Paris,* 1845. 4°. **813. f. 53.**
No more published.

—— Armurerie. ff. xxvi. pl. 25. 1851. *See* LACROIX (Paul) Le Moyen âge et la Renaissance, *etc.* tom. 4. 1848, *etc.* 4°. **1310. k. 9.**

—— Les Campagnes de Jules César dans les Gaules. Études d'archéologie militaire. [With plans.] pt. 1. pp. iii. 452. *Paris,* 1862. 8°. **9040. g. 9.**
No more published.

—— Catalogue des collections dont se compose le Musée de l'Artillerie. pp. xi. 312. 1855. 8°. *See* PARIS.—*Musée d'Artillerie.* **8827. b. 63.**

—— Les Derniers jours de Jérusalem. [With plans.] pp. 448. *Paris,* 1866. 8°. **4516. eee. 29.**

—— Dictionnaire des antiquités bibliques. (Appendice. Réponses aux critiques soulevées par mes publications sur la Terre Sainte.) coll. 1032. *Paris,* 1859. 4°. [*Troisième et dernière encyclopédie théologique.* tom. 45.] **L.R. 272. c. 1.**

—— Dictionnaire topographique abrégé de la Terre Sainte. pp. 324. *Paris,* 1887. 8°. **2356. b. 9.**

—— Éléments de l'histoire des ateliers monétaires du royaume de France depuis Philippe-Auguste jusqu'à François Ier inclusivement. pp. vi. 166. *Paris,* 1877. 4°. **7755. e. 2. (12.)**

—— Essai de classification des monnaies autonomes de l'Espagne. [With plates and a map.] pp. x. 219. *Metz,* 1840. 8°. **811. k. 34.**

—— Essai de classification des suites monétaires byzantines. pp. xiv. 488. *Metz,* 1836. 8°. **602. h. 15.**

—— Planches. pl. XXXIII. *Metz,* 1836. 4°. **602. i. 25.**

—— Étude chronologique des livres d'Esdras et de Néhémie. pp. 107. *Paris,* 1868. 8°. **3166. e. 39.**

—— Les Expéditions de César en Grande-Bretagne. pp. 42. *Paris,* 1860. 8°. **9040. f. 7.**

—— *See* HAIGNERÉ (D.) Étude sur le Portus Itius . . . Réfutation d'un mémoire de F. de Saulcy [entitled: "Les Expéditions de César en Grande-Bretagne"]. 1862. 8°. **7702. c. 2. (9.)**

—— Histoire d'Hérode, roi des Juifs. pp. 387. *Paris,* 1867. 8°. **10606. h. 16.**

—— Histoire d'un livre [the "Recueil de documents relatifs à l'histoire des monnaies frappées par les rois de France depuis Philippe II jusqu'à François Ier"]. pp. 58. *Paris,* 1880. 8°. **11840. f. 19. (6.)**

—— Histoire de l'art judaïque, tirée des textes sacrés et profanes. pp. 425. *Paris,* 1858. 8°. **2217. d. 4.**

—— Histoire des Machabées ou princes de la dynastie asmonéenne. pp. 319. *Paris,* 1880. 8°. **4516. eee. 30.**

—— Histoire monétaire de Jean le Bon, roi de France. [With plates.] pp. 139. *Paris,* 1880. 4°. **7757. f. 11.**

—— Histoire numismatique de Henri V et Henri VI rois d'Angleterre pendant qu'ils ont régné en France. pp. 122. pl. IV. *Paris,* 1878. 4°. **7755. h. 4.**

—— Histoire numismatique du règne de François Ier, roi de France. pp. v. 259. *Paris,* 1876. 4°. **7756. e. 1.**

—— Jérusalem. pp. 336. *Paris,* 1882. 8°. **10077. i. 5.**

—— Mémoire sur les monnaies datées des Séleucides. pp. 89. *Paris,* 1871. 8°. **7704. k. 8. (4.)**

—— Numismatique de la Terre Sainte. Description des monnaies autonomes et impériales de la Palestine et de l'Arabie Pétrée, ornée de 25 planches, *etc.* pp. xv. 406. *Paris,* 1874. 4°. **7755. dd. 23.**

—— Numismatique des Croisades. pp. viii. 174. *Paris,* 1847. 4°. **7755. h. 22.**

—— *See* FRIEDLAENDER (J.) [Die Münzen des Johanniter-Ordens.] Recherches sur les monnaies frappées dans l'Île de Rhodes par les Grands Maîtres de l'ordre . . . de Saint-Jean de Jérusalem. Ouvrage . . . servant de complément à la "Numismatique des Croisades," de M. F. de Saulcy. 1855. 4°. **7756. e. 12.**

—— Observations numismatiques. 5 no. *Metz; Nancy,* 1834–36. 8°. **7756. c. 29. (3.)**

—— Observations sur l'alphabet Tifinag. (Extrait du Journal asiatique.) pp. 20. [*Paris,*] 1849. 8°. **12910. aaa. 28. (1.)**

CAIGNART DE SAULCY (Louis Félicien Joseph)

—— La Palestine, le Jourdain et la Mer-Morte. Examen du rapport de M. Isambert, inséré dans le Bulletin de la Société de Geographie. (Extrait de la Revue de l'Orient.) pp. vii. 87. *Paris*, 1854. 8°. **10076. f. 13.**

—— Recherches sur l'écriture cunéiforme assyrienne. Inscriptions de Van. pp. 44. *Paris*, 1848. 4°. Dept. of Egyptian & Assyrian Antiquities.

—— Recherches sur l'emplacement véritable du tombeau d'Hélène, reine d'Adiabène. pp. 45. *Paris*, 1869. 4°. **7704. l. 19. (6.)**

—— Recherches sur la numismatique judaïque. pp. i. 192. pl. xx. *Paris*, 1854. 4°. **7756. e. 5.**

—— Recherches sur les monnaies de la cité de Metz. pp. 120. pl. 3. *Metz*, 1836. 8°. **603. f. 30.**

—— Recherches sur les monnaies des comtes et ducs de Bar, pour faire suite aux recherches sur les monnaies des ducs héréditaires de Lorraine. pp. 44. pl. vii. *Paris*, 1843. 4°. **810. m. 13.**

—— Recherches sur les monnaies des ducs héréditaires de Lorraine. pp. x. 247. pl. xxxvi. *Metz*, 1841. 4°. **810. m. 12.**

—— Recherches sur les monnaies des évêques de Metz. pp. 95. pl. iii. [*Metz*, 1845 ?] 8°. **7755. b. 13.**

—— Recueil de documents relatifs à l'histoire des monnaies frappées par les rois de France depuis Philippe ii jusqu'à François Ier. [tom. 4 edited by W. Froehner.] 4 tom. *Paris*, 1879–92. 4°. [*Collection de documents inédits sur l'histoire de France.* sér. 3.] **1885. f. 11.**

—— Souvenirs numismatiques de la Révolution de 1848. Recueil complet des médailles, monnaies et jetons qui ont paru en France depuis le 22 février jusqu'au 20 décembre 1848. [By L. F. J. Caignart de Saulcy.] pp. 111. pl. 60. [1850.] 4°. *See* France. [*Appendix.—History and Politics.—Revolution of* 1848.] **7755. e. 12.**

—— Système monétaire de la République romaine à l'époque de Jules César. pp. 32. pl. ix. *Paris*, 1873. 4°. [*Mémoires de la Société française de Numismatique et d'Archéologie. Section d'attributions numismatiques.*] **Ac. 5812/4.**

—— Voyage autour de la mer Morte et dans les terres bibliques, exécuté de décembre 1850 à avril 1851.

Relation du voyage. 2 tom. 8°. **10076. f. 2.**
Atlas. pl. lviii. 4°. **10076. i. 5 (1.)**
Catalogue raisonné des mollusques terrestres et fluviatiles recueillis par M. F. de Saulcy . . . Par J. R. Bourguignat. pp. xxvi. 96. pl. 4. **10076. i. 5. (2.)**
Catalogue des plantes observées en Syrie et en Palestine . . . par MM. de Saulcy et Michon. Rédigé par MM. E. Cosson et Kralik. pp. vii. 19. **10076. i. 5. (3.)**

Paris, 1853. 8° & 4°. **10076. f. 2. & i. 5.**

—— Narrative of a Journey round the Dead Sea and in Bible Lands, in 1850 and 1851 . . . Edited, with notes, by Count Edward de Warren. [With a map.] 2 vol. *Richard Bentley: London*, 1853. 8°. **10075. cc. 23.**

—— Voyage autour de la mer Morte. [An abridgment.] 2 tom. *Paris*, 1858. 8°. **10077. a. 17.**

—— *See* Isaacs (Albert A.) The Dead Sea; or notes . . . made during a journey to Palestine . . . on M. De Saulcy's supposed discovery of the Cities of the Plain [as related in his " Voyage autour de la mer Morte "]. 1857. 8°. **10075. d. 8.**

—— Voyage en Terre Sainte. 2 tom. *Paris*, 1865. 8°. **10076. h. 8.**

—— [Another edition.] Souvenirs d'un voyage en Terre Sainte. [Without the appendices. Edited by G. Richard.] pp. 382. *Paris*, 1867. 12°. **10076. aa. 11.**

CAIGNART DE SAULCY (Louis Félicien Joseph) and **HUGUENIN** (Jean François)

—— Relation du siége de Metz en 1444, par Charles vii. et René d'Anjou publié sur les documens originaux. [With plates and maps.] pp. 343. *Metz*, 1835. 8°. **805. d. 15**

CAIGNÉ (François) Dissertation sur la dentition des enfants du 1er âge, et les accidents qui l'accompagnent, etc. pp. 20. *Paris*, 1805. 4°. **1182. f. 14. (39**

CAIGNIEZ (Louis Charles) Les Amans en poste, ou la Magicienne supposée, comédie en trois actes, *etc.* pp. 48. *Paris*, 1804. 8°. **11738. bbb. 25. (2**

—— André, ou la Maison des bois, comédie en un acte, *etc.* pp. 30. *Paris*, 1821. 8°. **11738. bbb. 24. (5**

—— Azendai, ou, le Nécessaire et le superflu, mélodrame comique en trois actes . . . Sujet tiré d'un conte de M. Adrien de Sarrazin, *etc.* pp. 56. *Paris*, 1818. 8°. **11738. bbb. 23. (3**

—— Les Corbeaux accusateurs, ou, la Forêt de Cercotte, mélodrame historique en trois actes et en prose, *etc.* pp. 62. *Paris*, 1816. 8°. **11738. bbb. 23. (2**

—— Edgar, ou la Chasse aux loups, mélodrame en trois actes, en prose, *etc.* pp. 62. *Paris*, 1812. 8°. **11738. bbb. 24. (1**

—— L'Enfant de l'amour, mélodrame en trois actes et en prose, imité de l'allemand, de Kotzebue, *etc.* pp. 62. *Paris*, 1813. 8°. **11738. bbb. 24. (4**

—— L'Enfant venu par la fenêtre, comédie en trois actes en prose . . . Seconde édition. pp. 56. *Paris*, 1814. 8 **11738. bbb. 25. (**

—— Le Faux Alexis, ou le Mariage par vengeance, mélodrame . . . Seconde édition. pp. 56. *Paris*, 1811. 8°. **11738. bbb. 22. (**

—— La Fille adoptive, ou les Deux mères, mélodrame en quatre actes, et en prose, tiré du roman de Madame de Genlis, *etc.* pp. 56. *Paris*, 1810. 8°. **11738. bbb. 25. (1**

—— La Fille de la nature, ou, Louise et Valborn, comédie en trois actes et en prose, imitée de l'allemand, d'Augus Lafontaine . . . Quatrième édition. pp. 63. *Pari* 1825. 8°. **11738. bbb. 22. (2**

—— La Folle de Wolfenstein, mélodrame en trois actes, *et* pp. 46. *Paris*, 1813. 8°. **11738. bbb. 25. (8**

—— La Forêt d'Hermanstad, ou la Fausse épouse, mélodrame en trois actes, *etc.* pp. 56. *Paris*, 1810. 8°. **11738. bbb. 22. (7**

—— La Forêt enchantée, ou la Belle au bois dormant mélodrame féerie en trois actes, *etc.* pp. 32. *Pari* 1822. 8°. **11738. bbb. 24. (**

—— L'Hermite du Mont-Pausilippe, mélodrame en trois actes, tiré du roman des " Quatre espagnols," *etc.* pp. 6 *Paris*, 1805. 8°. **11738. bbb. 25. (**

—— L'Illustre aveugle, mélodrame en trois actes et en prose *etc.* pp. 63. *Paris*, 1808. 8°. **11738. bbb. 24. (**

—— Jean-de-Calais, mélodrame . . . en trois actes et en prose, *etc.* pp. 64. *Paris*, 1810. 8°. **11738. bbb. 22. (**

—— Le Jugement de Salomon, mélodrame en trois actes mêlé de chants, *etc.* pp. 39. *Paris*, 1802. 8°. **11738. bbb. 22. (**

[C]AIGNIEZ (Louis Charles)

— The Voice of Nature: a play, in three acts . . . By James Boaden. [A translation by J. Boaden of " Le Jugement de Salomon " by L. C. Caigniez.] pp. vii. 43. *James Ridgway: London*, 1803. 8°. **161**. g. **52**.

— Le Juif errant, mélodrame en trois actes, *etc.* pp. 59. *Paris*, 1812. 8°. **11738**. bbb. **23**. (**4**.)

— La Méprise de diligence, comédie en trois actes et en prose, *etc.* pp. 86. *Paris*, 1819. 8°. **11738**. bbb. **22**. (**1**.)

— La Morte vivante, mélodrame en trois actes, *etc.* pp. 55. *Paris*, 1813. 8°. **11738**. bbb. **25**. (**5**.)

— Nourjahad et Chérédin, ou, l'Immortalité à l'épreuve, mélodrame en trois actes et en prose, mêlé de chants, *etc.* pp. 40. *Paris*, 1803. 8°. **11738**. bbb. **24**. (**3**.)

— La Petite Bohémienne, mélodrame comique en trois actes et en prose, imité de Kotzbüe, *etc.* pp. 56. *Paris*, 1816. 8°. **11738**. bbb. **22**. (**8**.)

— Richardet et Bradamante, mélodrame en trois actes, sujet tiré du poëme de l'Arioste, chant 25e, *etc.* pp. 55. *Paris*, 1805. 8°. **11738**. bbb. **25**. (**9**.)

— Les Souvenirs des premières amours, comédie en un acte et en prose, *etc.* pp. 35. *Paris*, 1808. 8°. **11738**. bbb. **22**. (**9**.)

— Le Triomphe de David, mélodrame en trois actes, *etc.* pp. 39. *Paris*, 1806. 8°. **11738**. bbb. **25**. (**7**.)

— Le Volage, ou, le Mariage difficile, comédie en trois actes et en prose, *etc.* pp. 92. *Paris*, 1807. 8°. **11738**. bbb. **23**. (**5**.)

[C]AIGNIEZ (Louis Charles) and **BAUDOUIN D'AUBIGNY** (Jean Marie Théodore)

— La Pie voleuse, ou la servante de Palaiseau, mélodrame historique en trois actes et en prose, *etc.* pp. 64. *Paris*, 1815. 8°. **11738**. bbb. **22**. (**6**.)

— [Another copy.] **11738**. cc. **10**. (**4**.) *Slightly mutilated.*

— [Another edition.] *Paris*, 1842. 8°. [*La France dramatique au dix-neuvième siècle.* tom. 12.] **2296**. f. **12**.

— The Magpie or the Maid ? A melo drame, in three acts. Translated and altered from the French, by I. Pocock, *etc.* [An adaptation of " La Pie voleuse " by L. C. Caigniez and J. M. T. Baudouin d'Aubigny.] pp. 52. 1815. 8°. *See* Magpie. **11779**. c. **76**.

— The Magpie; or, the Maid of Palaiseau. A melo-dramatic romance. In three acts . . . Second edition. [An adaptation of " La Pie voleuse " by L. C. Caigniez and J. M. T. Baudouin d'Aubigny.] pp. 48. 1815. 8°. *See* Magpie. **643**. f. **18**. (**2**.)

— The Maid and the Magpye ; or, which is the Thief ? A musical entertainment, in two acts. Freely translated, with alterations, from the French, by S. J. Arnold, *etc.* pp. 52. *John Miller: London*, 1815. 8°. **643**. f. **18**. (**1**.)

— The Magpie or the Maid ? . . . Second edition [of Pocock's version]. pp. 56. 1816. 8°. *See* Magpie. **11779**. c. **77**.

— The Magpie ; or, the Maid of Palaiseau. A melo-drame, *etc.* (Oxberry's Edition.) [An adaptation of " La Pie voleuse " by L. C. Caigniez and J. M. T. Baudouin d'Aubigny.] pp. ii. 36. 1820. 8°. [*New English Drama.* vol. 11.] *See* Magpie. **11770**. f. **11**.

CAIGNIEZ (Louis Charles) and **BAUDOUIN D'AUBIGNY** (Jean Marie Théodore)

—— Ninetta, or, the Maid of Palaiseau : an opera . . . translated and altered from the French (of MM. D'Aubigny and Caigniez) and Italian [i.e. the libretto of " La Gazza ladra " by G. M. S. C. Gherardini] . . . by Henry R. Bishop, *etc.* pp. 47. [1830.] 8°. *See* Baudouin d'Aubigny (J. M. T.) and Caigniez (L. C.) T. **1317**. (**8**.)

—— [Another edition of Pocock's version.] The Magpie or the Maid ? *etc.* pp. 48. 1831. 12°. [*Cumberland's British Theatre.* vol. 27.] *See* Pocock (Isaac) **642**. a. **14**.

—— [Another edition.] The Maid and the Magpie, *etc.* pp. 48. [1870.] 12°. [*Lacy's Acting Edition.* vol. 87.] *See* Maid. **2304**. g. **5**.

—— [Another edition.] pp. 16. [1888.] 8°. [*Dicks' Standard Plays.* no. 948.] *See* Pocock (Isaac) **11770**. bbb.

—— [For editions of " La Gazza ladra," the opera-libretto adapted by G. M. S. C. Gherardini from " La Pie voleuse " by L. C. Caigniez and J. M. T. Baudouin d'Aubigny :] *See* Gherardini (G. M. S. C.)

—— *See* E., M. La Pie voleuse. The narrative of the Magpie ; or the Maid of Palaiseau [taken from the melodrama, by L. C. Caigniez and J. M. T. Baudouin d'Aubigny], *etc.* 1815. 8°. **11736**. h. **40**.

CAIGNIEZ (Louis Charles) and **BERNARD** (François) calling himself Bernard-Valville.

—— Henriette et Adhémar, ou la Bataille de Fontenoy, mélodrame en trois actes et en prose, imité du théâtre allemand, *etc.* pp. 71. *Paris*, 1810. 8°. **11738**. bbb. **23**. (**1**.)

CAIGNIEZ (Louis Charles) and **BRISSET** (Mathurin Joseph)

—— Honneur et séduction, mélodrame en trois actes. pp. 69. *Paris*, 1822. 8°. **11738**. bbb. **21**. (**4**.)

CAIGNIEZ (Louis Charles) and **DEB** . . . [i.e. — Debotières.]

—— Androcles, ou le Lion reconnaissant, mélodrame en trois actes, *etc.* pp. 38. *Paris*, 1804. 8°. **11738**. bbb. **24**. (**9**.)

CAIGNIEZ (Louis Charles) and **FONTENAY** ( )

—— La Belle-mère et les deux orphelins, mélodrame en trois actes et en prose, *etc.* pp. 56. *Paris*, 1808. 8°. **11738**. bbb. **25**. (**4**.)

CAIGNIEZ (Louis Charles) and **LEMAIRE** (Henri) *Novelist.*

—— Les Enfans du bucheron, comédie en trois actes, en prose, *etc.* pp. 63. *Paris*, 1809. 8°. **11738**. bbb. **24**. (**7**.)

CAIGNIEZ (Louis Charles) and **LOUIS** ( ) *pseud.* [i.e. *Baron* Ludwig Benedict Franz von Bilderbeck.]

—— Imposture et vérité, mélodrame en trois actes et en prose, *etc.* pp. 52. *Paris*, 1816. 8°. **11738**. bbb. **24**. (**2**.)

—— Le Mandarin Hoang-Pouf, ou l'Horoscope, folie en un acte. pp. 32. *Paris*, 1821. 8°. **11738**. bb. **25**. (**8**.)

CAIGNIEZ (Louis Charles) and **VILLIERS** (Pierre) *Dramatist.*

—— Rosalba d'Arandès, pièce en trois actes, *etc.* pp. 39. *Paris,* 1821. 8°. **11738.** o. **37.** (**13.**)

CAIGNOU (Érasme de) Dissertation sur l'empyème. pp. 15. *Paris,* 1819. 4°. **1183.** e. **9.** (**22.**)

CAIL (Jane) Love Me and Die. pp. 128. *London,* [1937.] 8°. [*Pearson's Big Threepennies.* no. 72.] **012632.n.1/72.**

CAIL (Jean François) *See* Du Saussois (A.) Galerie des hommes utiles. (Cail, Jean François.) 1875, *etc.* 16°. **10606.** aa. **39.** (3.)

CAIL (William)

—— *See* Chicken (Edward) The Collier's Wedding, *etc.* [The editor's preface signed: W. C., i.e. W. Cail.] 1829. 8°. **1077.** f. **35.**

CAILA (Pierre Martin de) *Baron.* *See* Berchon (J. A. E.) Le Baron de Caila, *etc.* [With a portrait.] 1891. 8°. Ac. **297.**

CAILAR (Paulus du) Dissertatio theologica de regina stante ad dextram regis in auro Ophir; ad Psalm. xlv. 10, *etc.* *Praes.* J. Wessel. pp. 29. *Lugduni Batavorum,* 1733. 4°. T. **2198.** (**10.**)

—— Dissertatio theologica de vinculo foederis, ad locum Ezechiel. xx: 37, *etc.* *Praes.* J. Wessel. pp. 13. *Lugduni Batavorum,* 1734. 4°. T. **2177.** (**12.**)

CAILHASSON (François Marie) *See* Cailhassou.

CAILHASSOU (François Marie) *See* Le Brun (C. F.) *Duke de Plaisance.* Parallèle du plan donné par M. Le Brun, pour remédier aux effets du papier-monnoie, avec ceux de M.M. Clavier . . . Caillasson, *etc.* [1796.] 8°. **F. 183.** (**11.**)

—— Rapport fait à l'Assemblée nationale au nom des Comités de l'ordinaire & de l'extraordinaire des finances. [Recommending a new issue of assignats.] pp. 19. [*Paris,* 1792?] 8°. **F. 183.** (**7.**)

—— Rapport sur les pétitions des communes de Metz, Bordeaux & Nancy [for a grant of public money]; fait à l'Assemblée nationale, au nom du Comité de l'extraordinaire des finances. pp. 22. [*Paris,* 1792.] 8°. **F. 215.** (**7.**)

CAILHAU (Durand) D. Cailhau . . . aux citoyens régisseurs, composant la Régie générale de l'enrégîtrement, et du domaine national. pp. 8. [*Paris,* 1799.] 8°. **F. 531.** (**5.**)

CAILHAVA (Léon) *See* France. [*Appendix.—History and Politics.—Miscellaneous.*] De tristibus Franciae libri quatuor . . . nunc primum in lucem editi cura et sumptibus L. Cailhava. 1840. 4°. **837.** l. **8.**

—— *See* Vingtrinier (M. E. A.) L. Cailhava, bibliophile lyonnais, *etc.* 1877. 8°. **10664.** dd. **4.**

CAILHAVA D'ESTENDOUX (Jean François) *See* Bracia. Trzey bracia bliznięta. Komedyia . . . z francuzkiéy . . . przełożona [by W. Bogusławski from "Les Trois jumeaux vénitiens," by A. Collalto, with dialogue by T. d'Hèle and J. F. Cailhava d'Estendoux]. 1791. 8°. [Bogusławski (*W.*) *Dzieła dramatyczne.* tom 12.] **1343.** i. **32.**

—— *See* Figliuola. La Buona figliuola, opéra comique en trois actes, parodiée en François [by J. F. Cailhava d'Estendoux, from the opera of that name by Carlo Goldoni]. 1777. 8°. [*Recueil général des opéra bouffons, etc.* tom. 7.] **11735.** b. **2.**

CAILHAVA D'ESTENDOUX (Jean François)

—— *See* Matteucci (A.) called Collalto. Les Trois jumeaux vénitiens. Comédie italienne . . . Par A. Collalto. [The dialogue by Th. d'Hèle and J. F. Cailhava d'Estendoux.] 1792. 8°. **11738.** a. **25.** (3.

—— *See* Picard (L. B.) Institut Impérial de France. Funérailles de M. Cailhava . . . Discours. [1813.] 4°. **733.** g. **17.** (**33.**

—— Théatre de M. Cailhava. 3 tom. *Paris,* 1781, 82. 8°. **86.** a. **7,** 8

Tom. 3 *contains only* "*Les Journalistes anglais.*"

—— Athènes pacifiée, comédie en trois actes et en prose tirée des onze pièces d'Aristophane. pp. 62. *Paris* an v [1797]. 8°. **997.** l. **9**

—— Cailhava aux citoyens composant le Comité du Théâtre Français de la République. [Two letters on the non performance of his plays.] pp. 3. [*Paris,* 1797.] 4°. **936.** f. **10.** (**14.**

—— Les Contes de l'abbé de Colibri. *See* infra: Le Soupé des petits-maîtres, *etc.*

—— De l'art de la comédie, ou Détail raisonné des diverses parties de la comédie, et de ses différents genres; suivi d'un Traité de l'imitation . . . Terminé par l'exposition des causes de la décadence du théâtre et des moyens de le faire réfleurir. 4 tom. *Paris,* 1772. 8°. **1343.** g. **8–11**

—— Troisieme edition. 2 tom. *Paris,* 1792. 8°. **840.** d. **19**

—— Études sur Molière, ou Observations sur la vie, les moeurs les ouvrages de cet auteur, et sur la manière de jouer ses pièces, *etc.* pp. 355. *Paris,* 1802. 8°. **640.** f. **25**

—— Le Mariage interrompu, comédie, en trois actes, *etc.* pp. 78. *Paris,* 1769. 8°. **11737.** bb. **2.** (**2.**

—— Mémoire pour J. F. Cailhava, en réponse à des défenses faites par les Comédiens françois, aux Directeurs du Théatre du Palais-Royal, de jouer ses pièces. pp. 22 [*Paris,* 1790?] 4°. **936.** f. **10.** (**4.**

—— Les Menechmes grecs, comédie en prose & en quatre actes, précédés d'un prologue. [Adapted from the "Menaechmi" of Plautus.] pp. xvi. 87. 1791. 8° *See* Plautus (T. M.) [*Menaechmi.—Imitations, etc.*] **1000.** l. **20**

—— Le Nouveau marié, ou les Importuns, opéra comique en un acte . . . Les paroles sont de M. de Cailhava, *etc.* pp. 31. *Paris,* 1771. 8°. [*Recueil général des opéra bouffons, etc.* tom. 4.] **11735.** b. **2**

—— Réflexions presentées au Comité d'instruction publique en réponse aux Mémoires de quelques directeurs de spectacles de Province, contre les droits des auteurs dramatiques. pp. 4. [*Paris,* 1792?] 4°. **936.** f. **10.** (**9.**

—— Le Soupé des petits-maîtres . . . Ouvrage moral [By J. F. Cailhava d'Estendoux.] 2 pt. [1772?] 12°. *See* Souper. **012551.** a. **35.**

—— Les Contes de l'abbé de Colibri. Nouvelle édition [of "Le Soupé des petits maîtres"], avec préface par un homme de lettres fort connu. [The preface signed: Ch. M. i.e. Pierre Charles Monselet.] pp. xvii. 190. *Paris,* 1881. 8°. **12518.** n. **5.**

With an additional titlepage, engraved.

—— [Another edition.] Le Soupé des petits-maîtres, *etc.* pp. 154. *Bruxelles,* [1890.] 12°. **012547.** g. **59**

CAILHAVA D'ESTENDOUX (JEAN FRANÇOIS)

—— Le Tuteur dupé, comédie en cinq actes et en prose. Sujet tiré de Plaute, acte deuxième du Soldat Fanfaron, *etc.* pp. 106. *Paris,* 1765. 12°. **11740**. de. **8**. (**4**.)

CAILHAVA D'ESTENDOUX (JEAN FRANÇOIS) and **LÉGER** (FRANÇOIS PIERRE AUGUSTE)

—— Ziste et Zeste, ou les Importuns, folie en un acte et en vaudevilles, *etc.* pp. 35. *Paris,* an v [1797]. 8°. **11738**. h. **11**. (**6**.)

CAILHOL (JACQUES)

—— Le Marché de Marseille, vo lei Doues coumaires, comédie en deux actes et en vers. [By J. Cailhol? or — Carvin?] pp. 45. 1785. 8°. *See* MARSEILLES. **1343**. g. **27**.

—— [Another edition.] pp. 32. 1821. 8°. *See* MARSEILLES. **11740**. f. **23**. (**4**.)

—— Moussu Jus, comédie en un acte et en vers, représentée . . . en décembre 1784. Revue et corrigée par l'auteur. [By J. Cailhol?] *Prov.* pp. 20. 1804. 8°. *See* JUS ( ) *Maître d'hôtel.* **11498**. f. **53**. (**3**.)

—— Moussu Jus, comédie, *etc.* [By J. Cailhol?] *Prov.* pp. 20. *See* JUS ( ) *Maître d'hôtel.* **1343**. g. **16**. (**3**.)

CAILL (ANTONY) La Question des vacances scolaires. pp. 41. *Paris,* 1891. 8°. **8304**. b. **21**. (**4**.)

CAILLARD ( )

—— Notice d'une collection de tableaux anciens et modernes, des trois écoles . . . dont la vente après le décès de M. Caillard, aura lieu . . . les . . . 3 et . . . 4 mai 1830, *etc.* pp. 16. [*Paris,*] 1830. 8°. **562**. e. **74**. (**14**.)

CAILLARD ( ) called *L'Abbé Raillard.* La Friquassée crotestillonnée . . . Reproduit littéralement d'après l'imprimé de 1604 et accompagné d'une notice par A. Pottier. pp. xv. 28. 1863. 4°. *See* ROUEN.—*Société des Bibliophiles Normands.* Ac. **8938/4**.

—— Réimpression textuelle, faite sur l'édition de Rouen 1604; précédée d'un avant-propos de Philomneste, junior [i.e. P. G. Brunet], et enrichie d'annotations de M. E. Sidredoulx, *etc.* pp. x. 74. *Rouen; Genève* [printed], 1867. 12°. **12234**. ccc. **17**.
One of a series called "Raretés bibliographiques." No. 91 *of an edition of* 100 *copies.*

—— [Another edition.] Commentée par Me E. Sidredoulx. Avec une préface de Prosper Blanchemain. pp. vi. 160. *Paris,* 1878. 12°. **11474**. bb. **14**.

CAILLARD (ANTOINE BERNARD) *See* LAVATER (J. C.) [Physiognomische Fragmente, *etc.*] Essai sur la physiognomonie, *etc.* [Translated by A. B. Caillard and others.] [1781, *etc.*] 4°. **29**. g. **5**.

—— *See* LAVATER (J. C.) [Physiognomische Fragmente, *etc.*] L'Art de connaître les hommes par la physionomie. [Translated by A. B. Caillard and others.] 1806, *etc.* 4°. **721**. l. **4–8**.

—— Catalogue des livres composant la bibliothèque de feu M. Caillard . . . dont la vente se fera le mardi 21 décembre 1830, *etc.* pp. 175. MS. NOTES. *Paris,* 1830. 8°. S.C. **1213**.

—— Catalogue des livres du Cabinet de Mr. A. B. Caillard. pp. xii. 462. **F.P.** *Paris,* 1805. 8°. **11904**. i. **14**.
The half-title and head-title read " Catalogue de mes livres." One of an edition of twenty-five copies.

CAILLARD (ANTOINE BERNARD)

—— [Another edition.] Catalogue des livres . . . de la bibliothèque de feu M. A. B. Caillard. (Notice sur M. A. B. Caillard.) pp. xxiii. 423. **L.P.** MS. NOTES OF PRICES. *Paris,* 1808. 8°. **11904**. i. **15**.
One of an edition of twenty-five copies.

—— [A reissue.] *Paris,* 1810. 8°. **821**. f. **22**.

—— Mémoire sur la révolution de Hollande. *See* SÉGUR (L. P. de) *Count.* Histoire des principaux événements du règne de F. Guillaume II, roi de Prusse, *etc.* tom. 1. 1800. 8°. **981**. b. **13**.

CAILLARD (AUGUSTE JOSEPH) Quelques considérations sur l'étiologie et le traitement prophylactique de la phthisie pulmonaire. pp. 36. *Paris,* 1869. 4°. [*Collection des thèses soutenues à la Faculté de Médecine de Paris.* An 1869. tom. 3.] **7373**. k. **9**.

CAILLARD (CHARLES CAMILLE) The French Correspondent; consisting chiefly of selections from letters of the most eminent French and English authors and others on familiar, commercial, and historical subjects. To which are added fac-similes of the autographs of celebrated French writers, *etc.* pp. 218. *Whittaker & Co.: London; T. C. Browne: Leicester,* [1860.] 12°. **10909**. b. **17**.

—— [Another issue.] The French Correspondent, *etc.* *Whittaker & Co.: London; T. Chapman Browne; the Author: Leicester,* [c. 1860.] 8°. **012955**. b. **26**.

CAILLARD (CHARLES FRANCIS) Les Vivantes. [Poems.] Préface de Léo Claretie. pp. xii. 245. *Paris,* 1907. 8°. **11483**. dd. **37**.

CAILLARD (CHARLES FRANCIS) and **BÉRYS** (JOSÉ DE) *pseud.* [i.e. JOSÉ BLOCH.]

—— Le Cas Debussy. Une opinion de M. Claude Debussy; un article de M. Raphaël Cor; une enquête de la " Revue du Temps Présent "; le secret de M. Debussy. pp. 144. *Paris,* [1910.] 8°.
Hirsch 2941.

—— [Another copy.] **7896**. r. **17**.
Imperfect; wanting the last leaf bearing the colophon.

CAILLARD (E. G. P.) Propositions de médecine et de chirurgie; thèse, *etc.* pp. 23. *Paris,* 1833. 4°. **1184**. f. **3**. (**13**.)

CAILLARD (EMMA MARIE) Charlotte Corday, and other poems. pp. ix. 98. *Kegan Paul & Co.: London,* 1884. 8°. **11653**. ccc. **24**.

—— The Church and the New Knowledge. pp. 221. *Longmans & Co.: London,* 1915. 8°. [*Layman's Library.*] **3624**. a. **5/6**.

—— Electricity, the science of the nineteenth century. A sketch for general readers, *etc.* pp. xiii. 310. *John Murray: London,* 1891. 8°. **8757**. aa. **28**.

—— The Garden, the Wilderness, and the City. pp. 62. *S.P.C.K.: London,* 1907. 16°. **4430**. aa. **54**.

—— Individual Immortality. pp. xii. 136. *John Murray: London,* 1903. 8°. **4255**. dd. **11**.

—— The Invisible Powers of Nature. pp. xix. 252. *John Murray: London,* 1888. 8°. **8704**. ee. **29**.

—— Law and Freedom. pp. ix. 154. *J. Nisbet & Co.: London,* 1899. 8°. **8410**. g. **11**.

—— A Living Christianity. pp. viii. 120. *John Murray: London,* 1918. 8°. **03558**. ee. **47**.

CAILLARD (EMMA MARIE)

—— The Lost Life, and other poems. pp. viii. 189. *Eyre & Spottiswoode: London,* 1889. 8°. **011653. f. 81.**

—— The Many-Sided Universe: a study specially addressed to young people. By C. M. E. [i.e. E. M. Caillard.] pp. xvi. 159. 1906. 8°. *See* E., C. M. **4378. ff. 16.**

—— A Poem of Life. pp. vii. 120. *London Literary Society: London,* [1884]. 8°. **11653. ccc. 25.**

—— Progressive Revelation; or, Through nature to God. pp. xvi. 267. *John Murray: London,* 1895. 8°. **4371. aaaa. 39.**

—— Reason in Revelation; or, the Intellectual aspect of Christianity. pp. 122. *J. Nisbet & Co.: London,* [1898.] 8°. **4371. de. 31.**

CAILLARD (FRANCIS CHARLES) *See* CAILLARD (Charles F.)

CAILLARD (GASPAR) Sermons sur divers textes de l'Ecriture Sainte. pp. 372. *J. Smith & W. Bruce: Dublin,* 1728. 8°. **4425. b. 5.**

—— [Another edition.] 2 tom. *Amsterdam,* 1738. 8°. **4428. b. 12.**

CAILLARD (GASTON) L'Indochine . . . Kouang-Tchéou-Wan . . . 4 cartes, *etc.* pp. 124. *Paris,* [1922.] 8°. [*Notre domaine colonial.* vol. 8.] **10002.i.20/2.**

CAILLARD (JACQUES LOUIS) Exposé des expériences faites sur les fébrifuges indigènes, à la clinique de M. le professeur Bourdier. [A thesis.] pp. 54. *Paris,* 1809. 4°. **1182. h. 4. (4.)**

CAILLARD (MABEL) A Lifetime in Egypt. 1876–1935. [With a portrait.] pp. 279. *Grant Richards: London,* 1935. 8°. **010822. e. 39.**

CAILLARD (PAUL) Les Chasses en France et en Angleterre. Histoires de sport. pp. 338. *Paris,* 1864. 12°. **7907. aaa. 24.**

—— Les Chiens d'arrêt. Races anglaises—dressage—hygiène du chenil. Avec douze aquarelles . . . par Olivier de Penne, et cinquante vignettes, *etc.* pp. viii. 148. *Paris,* 1890. *obl.* 4°. **1821. c. 9.**

—— Des chiens anglais de chasse et de tir, et de leur dressage . . . Préface du Marquis de Cherville. pp. xxiv. 272. *Paris,* 1882. 18°. **7908. aaa. 28.**

CAILLARD (V.) La Vénérable Anne-Marie Javouhey, fondatrice de la Congrégation de Saint-Joseph de Cluny, 1779–1851 . . . Deuxième édition. pp. ii. 221. *Paris,* 1909. 8°. **4826. ee. 33.**

CAILLARD (*Sir* VINCENT HENRY PENALVER) *See* CAILLARD (Zöe) *Lady.* Sir Vincent Caillard speaks from the Spirit World, *etc.* [With a portrait.] 1932. 8°. **8633. bbb. 39.**

—— Imperial Fiscal Reform. pp. xx. 288. *Edward Arnold: London,* 1903. 8°. **08225. f. 20.**

—— Report on the Revenues ceded by Turkey to the Bondholders of the Ottoman Public Debt . . . and some remarks on cognate subjects. [With tables.] pp. 82. viii. *Effingham Wilson: London,* [1888.] 8°. **8227. f. 43.**

—— A New Conception of Love. By Sir V. Caillard. Written on his communigraph. [Transcribed and with an appendix by Lady Caillard. With plates, including portraits.] pp. 254. *Rider & Co.: London,* [1934.] 8°. **08632. h. 44.**

CAILLARD (ZÖE) *Lady.* *See* CAILLARD (*Sir* Vincent H. P.) A New Conception of Love, *etc.* [Transcribed and with an appendix by Lady Caillard. With a portrait.] [1934.] 8°. **08632. h. 44.**

CAILLARD (ZÖE) *Lady.*

—— An Extraordinary Flight . . . A story written from the "Great Beyond" by the actual spirit hand of the author on the communigraph, *etc.* (The medium—Mrs. Louisa Bolt.) pp. 100. *A. H. Stockwell: London,* [1940.] 8°. **8634. f. 54.**

—— Sir Vincent Caillard Speaks from the Spirit World, *etc.* [With plates, including a portrait.] pp. 15. *Rider & Co.: London,* 1932. 8°. **8633. bbb. 39.**

CAILLARD-BILONNIÈRE (ABRAHAM JACQUES) Dissertation sur les luxations originelles ou congénitales des fémurs; thèse, *etc.* [With plates.] pp. 24. *Paris,* 1828. 4°. **1184. c. 8. (26.)**

CAILLAS (ALIN) Les Pêches d'amateur au bord de la mer. Ouvrage illustré, *etc.* pp. iii. 280. *Paris,* 1934. 8°. **7915. p. 7.**

CAILLASSON (FRANÇOIS MARIE) *See* CAILHASSOU.

CAILLAT (J.) *Writer on Free Trade.* Le Sentier de la vie, ou Grèves et ouvriers. pp. 35. *Paris,* 1872. 8°. **8276. cc. 32. (8.)**

CAILLAT (JOS. M.) Essai sur la menstruation; thèse, *etc.* pp. 57. *Paris,* 1836. 4°. **1184. h. 1. (5.)**

—— Le Source des Yeux au Bains d'Hercule en Hongroie, procédé particulier d'application des eaux minérales au traitement de l'appareil oculaire, *etc.* pp. 85. *Paris,* [1862.] 8°. **7470. aa. 70. (1.)**

CAILLAT (JULES) Essai sur l'hygiène des jeunes gens dans les établissements d'instruction publique. Thèse, *etc.* pp. 35. *Montpellier,* 1846. 4°. **1182. d. 17. (18.)**

CAILLAT (ROGER)

—— Contribution à l'étude du fluorure de silicium et des fluosilicates. 1945. *See* PERIODICAL PUBLICATIONS.—*Paris.* Annales de chimie, *etc.* sér. 11. tom. 20. 1914, *etc.* 8°. **P.P. 1495. aa.**

CAILLAU (ARMAND BENJAMIN) *See* AUGUSTINE, *Saint, Bishop of Hippo.* [*Works.—Latin.*] Sancti Aurelii Augustini operum supplementum . . . cura et studio D. A. B. Caillau. 1836, *etc.* fol. **691. k. 20.**

—— *See* GREGORY, *of Nazianzus, Saint, Patriarch of Constantinople.* Του . . . πατρος . . . Γρηγοριου του θεολογου . . . τα εὑρισχομενα [*sic*] παντα. Sancti patris . . . Gregorii theologi . . . opera omnia, quæ extant, *etc.* [tom. 2 edited by A. B. Caillau.] 1778, *etc.* fol. **475. i. 10–11.**

—— *See* JUSTE (L.) and CAILLAU (A. B.) Histoire complète et illustrée de la vie des Saints, *etc.* 1845. 8°. **1372. k. 1.**

—— *See* SCHEFFMACHER (J. J.) Lettres . . . Revues . . . par A. B. Caillau. 1839, *etc.* 8°. **1351. h. 19.**

—— Patres apostolici (Patres tertii–quinti Ecclesiæ sæculi). Editio nova [of "Collectio selecta SS. Ecclesiæ Patrum"], accurantibus A. B. Caillau (M. N. S. Guillon, B. Saint-Yves), nonnullisque Cleri Gallicani Presbyteris. tom. 1–62, 70–94, 97, 98, 108–148. [With two volumes containing indexes to the works of St. Augustine and of St. Chrysostom, by F. P. Du Tripon.] *Parisiis,* 1842, 36, 43. 8°. **3622. h–k.**
Tom. 63–69, 96, 99–107 *were not published in this edition. Tom.* 97, 98 *are of the earlier edition. Tom.* 131 *is in* 2 *pt.*

—— Histoire critique et religieuse de Notre-Dame de Lorette. pp. xxvii. 638 [438]. *Paris,* 1843. 8°.

—— Atlas. *obl.* 4°. **871.h.94.**

CAILLAU (ARMAND BENJAMIN)

—— Histoire critique et religieuse de Notre-Dame de Roc-Amadour, suivie d'une neuvaine d'instructions et de prières, *etc.* [With plates.] pp. 432. *Paris,* 1834. 8°. **491. e. 11.**

—— Introductio ad Sanctorum Patrum lectionem, *etc.* 2 vol. pp. 1180. *Mediolani,* 1830, 31. 8°. **3675.b.3.** *First issued as vol.* 8, 9 *of "Thesaurus Patrum."*

—— Patres apostolici, *etc.* *See* supra : Collectio selecta SS. Ecclesiæ Patrum, *etc.*

—— Thesaurus Patrum floresque doctorum qui cum in theologia tum in philosophia olim claruerunt. Hoc est: dicta, sententiæ et exempla ex SS. Patribus probatissimisque scriptoribus collecta et per locos communes distributa cura et opere plurimorum rebus sacris addictorum. [Edited by A. B. Caillau.] (vol. 8, 9. Introductio ad Sanctorum Patrum lectionem . . . auctore A. B. Caillau.) 9 vol. *Mediolani,* 1827–30. 8°. **1125. d. 1–9.**

—— [Another issue in nine volumes of vol. 1–7.] **3675. b. 2.**

CAILLAU (ARMAND BENJAMIN) and **SAINTYVES** (P. M. B.)

—— Lectiones variantes Sermonum genuinorum Sancti Augustini a Benedictinis editorum, collectæ . . . ab A. B. Caillau et B. Saint-Yves. 1849. *See* MIGNE (J. P.) Patrologiæ cursus completus, *etc.* tom. 47. 1844, *etc.* 4°. **2000. b.**

CAILLAU (FABIEN) Considérations sur les difficultés du diagnostic des maladies de l'estomac. pp. 42. *Paris,* 1873. 4°. [*Collection des thèses soutenues à la Faculté de Médecine de Paris.* An 1873. tom. 4.] **7373. o.**

CAILLAU (JEAN MARIE) *See* DUBREUILH (C.) Éloge de Jean-Marie Caillau, *etc.* 1868. 8°. **10662. dd. 29. (10.)**

—— *See* QUILLET (C.) La Callipédie . . . Traduction nouvelle . . . par J. M. Caillau. [1799.] 12°. **1080. l. 3.**

—— Avis aux mères de famille sur l'éducation physique, morale et les maladies des enfans . . . jusqu'à l'âge de six ans. 3 pt. pp. xvi. 272. *Bordeaux,* [1796.] 12°. **1031. d. 18.**

—— Medicinæ infantilis brevis delineatio ; cui subjunguntur considerationes quædam de infantiâ et morbis infantilibus, *etc.* [A thesis.] pp. 8. *Parisiis,* 1803. 4°. **1182. f. 4. (12.)**

—— Mémoire sur le croup. pp. xvi. 182. *Bordeaux,* 1812. 8°. **7615. b. 12.**

CAILLAU (SIMONNET) Le Débat de deux demoyselles l'une nommée la noyre, et l'autre la tannée, suivi de la vie de Saint Harence, et d'autres poésies du xve siècle, *etc.* [The "Débat" attributed to S. Caillau.] pp. viii. 175. 1825. 8°. *See* DÉBAT. **11475. e. 19.**

—— [Another copy.] **11475. g. 44. (1.)**

—— [Another edition.] 1856. 16°. [MONTAIGLON (*A. de*) *Recueil de poésies françoises, etc.* tom. 5.] *See* DÉBAT. **12234.aa.20.** ^COURDE DE

CAILLAUD (AIMÉ L.) Des accidents syphilitiques consécutifs à la vaccination considérés au point de vue médico-légal. pp. 36. *Paris,* 1863. 4°. [*Collection des thèses soutenues à la Faculté de Médecine de Paris.* An 1863. tom. 2.] **7373. e. 6.**

CAILLAUD (FRÉDÉRIC) Catalogue des radiaires, des annélides, des cirrhipèdes et des mollusques marins, terrestres et fluviatiles recueillis dans le département de la Loire-Inférieure. pp. 323. pl. IV. *Nantes,* 1865. 8°. **7298. d. 11.**

CAILLAUD (FRÉDÉRIC ROMANET DU) *See* ROMANET DU CAILLAUD.

CAILLAUD (JEAN) Considerations générales sur la saignée, *etc.* [A thesis.] pp. 40. *Paris,* 1806. 4°. **1182. g. 7. (20.)**

CAILLAUD (JEAN FRANÇOIS XAVIER) Histoire de Notre-Dame-de-Vaudouant. pp. xxviii. 119. *Bourges,* 1858. 18°. **4629. a. 10.**

—— Martyrs du diocèse de Bourges pendant la révolution de 1793. pp. xvi. 396. *Bourges,* 1857. 18°. **4826. a. 8.**

—— Notice sur le précieux sang de Neuvy-Saint-Sépulcre. pp. iv. 277. *Bourges,* 1865. 12°. **4629. aa. 37.**

CAILLAUD (JOHN)

—— *See* BENGAL.—*Governor and Council.* Proceedings of the Governor and Council at Bengal, during Colonel Caillaud's absence, in consequence of the orders received from the Court of Directors, *etc.* [Being the investigation of a charge made against him, of "offering a reward to assassinate the Shahżadah," i.e. 'Alī Gaubar, afterwards Shāh 'Ālam, Emperor of Hindustan.] [1763.] 4°. **102. i. 48.**

CAILLAUD (LOUIS) De l'obésité. pp. 32. *Paris,* 1865. 4°. [*Collection des thèses soutenues à la Faculté de Médecine de Paris.* An 1865. tom. 2.] **7373. f. 8.**

CAILLAUD (MAURICE) Notions d'acoustique physiologique et musicale, *etc.* pp. ii. 165. *Paris,* 1923. 8°. **7896. tt. 41.**

CAILLAULT (CHARLES) Traité pratique des maladies de la peau chez les enfants. pp. viii. 392. *Paris,* 1859. 12°. **7640. b. 9.**

—— A Practical Treatise on Diseases of the Skin in Children: from the French of Caillault. With notes by Robert Howarth Blake. pp. xii. 277. *John Churchill: London,* 1861. 12°. **7640. e. 4.**

—— Second edition. With notes, appendix, and formulæ, by Robert Howarth Blake. pp. xii. 331. *J. Churchill & Sons: London,* 1863. 12°. **7640. c. 10.**

CAILLAULT (CHARLES FERDINAND MARIE) Du signe stéthoscopique du décollement du placenta. pp. 28. *Paris,* 1852. 4°. [*Collection des thèses soutenues à la Faculté de Médecine de Paris.* An 1852. tom. 3.] **7372. e. 7.**

CAILLAULT (LÉON) Faculté de Droit de Paris. Thèse pour la licence, *etc.* (Jus romanum. De collatione bonorum.—Droit français. Des rapports, *etc.*) pp. 36. *Paris,* 1858. 8°. **5406. aaa. 4. (17.)**

CAILLAUX (D.) Thèse pour le doctorat en médecine, *etc.* (De l'apoplexie, *etc.*—Questions sur diverses branches des sciences médicales.) pp. 31. *Paris,* 1838. 4°. **1184. h. 18. (17.)**

CAILLAUX (HENRIETTE) *Diplômée de l'École du Louvre.* Aimé-Jules Dalou, 1838–1902, *etc.* [With a portrait.] pp. 158. pl. XVI. *Paris,* 1935. 8°. **10655.m.17.**

CAILLAUX (HENRIETTE) *Wife of Joseph Marie Auguste Caillaux.* *See* RAPHAEL (John N.) The Caillaux Drama. [With portraits.] 1914. 8°. **8050. dd. 46.**

CAILLAUX (Joseph) Dissertation sur l'inflammation du péritoine, *etc.* pp. 21. *Paris*, 1812. 4º. **1182**. i. 3. (**21**.)

CAILLAUX (Joseph Marie Auguste) *See* Ajam (M.) Problèmes algériens . . . Avec une préface de M. J. Caillaux. 1913. 8º. **8157**. bb. **27**.

—— *See* Bernard (R.) and Aymard (C.) L'Œuvre française au Maroc . . . Préface de M. Caillaux. [1914.] 8º. **08026**. aa. **9**.

—— *See* Fabre-Luce (A. E. A.) Caillaux, *etc.* 1933. 8º. **10655**. e. **40**.

—— *See* Fleurieu (R. de) Joseph Caillaux, *etc.* 1951. 8º. **10666**. a. **46**.

—— *See* Letellier (Albert) Joseph Caillaux, l'empereur des crédules. 1922. 8º. **08052**. c. **25**.

—— *See* Martin (Gaston) Joseph Caillaux. 1931. 8º. **10655**. bbb. **14**.

—— *See* Paix-Séailles (C.) Jaurès et Caillaux, *etc.* [1920.] 8º. **10658**. ee. **8**.

—— *See* Raphael (John N.) The Caillaux Drama. [With portraits.] 1914. 8º. **8050**. dd. **46**.

—— *See* Vergnet (P.) Joseph Caillaux. 1918. 8º. **10657**. de. **15**.

—— *See* Wellhoff (E.) L'Emprunt forcé. Préface de J. Caillaux. 1923. 8º. **08229**. dd. **11**.

—— Agadir. Ma politique extérieure. pp. 243. *Paris*, [1919.] 8º. **08052**. aaa. **19**.

—— D'Agadir à la grande pénitence. pp. 284. *Paris*, 1933. 8º. **8004**. df. **7**.

—— L'Impôt sur le revenu. [A collection of speeches.] pp. viii. 538. *Paris, Nancy*, 1910. 8º. **08228**. ff. **72**.

—— Les Impôts en France. Traité technique. Par J. Caillaux . . . A. Touchard . . . G. Privat-Deschanel. 2 tom. *Paris*, 1896, 1904. 8º. **08228**. i. **76**.

—— Deuxième édition revue et mise à jour. 2 tom. *Paris*, 1911. 8º. **8227**. p. **1**.

—— Mes mémoires, *etc.* [With plates, including portraits.] *Paris*, 1947– . 8º. W.P. **9619**.

—— Mes prisons. (Devant l'histoire.) pp. v. 349. *Paris*, 1921. 8º. **10657**. aa. **31**.

—— Notre système d'impôts. pp. iv. 128. *Paris*, 1904. 8º. **08226**. cc. **20**.

—— Où va la France ? Où va l'Europe ? pp. 293. *Paris*, 1922. 8º. **08052**. aaa. **31**.

—— Whither France ? Whither Europe ? . . . Translated . . . by K. M. Armstrong. [With a portrait.] pp. xiii. 207. *T. Fisher Unwin: London*, 1923. 8º. **08027**. c. **105**.

—— A dónde va Francia ? A dónde va Europa ? Versión española por Javier Bueno. pp. 187. *Berlin, Buenos Aires*, [1923.] 8º. [*Biblioteca de Política y Economía.* tom. 4.] **08028.ddd.19/4.**

—— The World Crisis: the lessons which it teaches and the adjustments of economic science which it necessitates . . . Translated . . . by Hamilton Marr. pp. 27. *Cobden-Sanderson: London*, 1932. 8º. [*Richard Cobden Lecture.* no. 4.] W.P. 9785/4.

CAILLAUX (L. Ch.) Qu'est-ce que l'Antechrist ? pp. 20 *Nice*, 1887. 8º. **3186**. i. **1**

CAILLAVET (Gaston Arman de) [For works writte by G. A. de Caillavet in collaboration with Robert d Flers in which the latter's name stands first:] *See* Fler (Robert de) and Caillavet (G. A. de)

—— La Belle aventure. Comédie en trois actes par G. A de Caillavet, R. de Flers & E. Rey. pp. 38. *Pari* 1914. fol. [*La Petite Illustration.* Théâtre. no. 37.] P.P. **4283**. m. (2

—— [Another edition.] pp. 253. *Paris*, 1920. 8º. **11735**. k. **2**

—— [La Choix d'une carrière.] Choosing a Career: farce in one act . . . Adapted by Barrett H. Clark pp. 19. *Samuel French: New York*, [1915.] 8º. [*World Best Plays.*] **12205.v.19/33**

—— La Montansier. Pièce en quatre actes dont un prologu [By G. A. de Caillavet, R. de Flers & Jeoffrin pp. 277. *Paris*, 1904. 8º. **11736**. f. **1**

—— Le Roi. Comédie en quatre actes par G. A. de Caillave Robert de Flers et Emmanuel Arène. pp. 36. *Pari* 1908. fol. [*L'Illustration théâtrale.* no. 99.] P.P. **4283**. m. (2

—— [Another edition.] pp. 247. *Paris*, 1909. 8º. **11735**. e. **5**

CAILLAVET (Gaston Arman de) and **FLERS** (Rober de)

—— L'Amour veille. pp. 3 *Paris*, 1907. fol. [*L'Illustration théâtrale.* no. 71.] P.P. **4283**. m. (2

—— [Another edition.] pp. 300. *Paris*, 1908. 8º. **11736**. e. **2**

—— Le Bois sacré. Comédie en trois actes. pp. 36. *Pari* 1910. fol. [*L'Illustration théâtrale.* no. 147.] P.P. **4283**. m. (2

—— Deuxième édition. pp. 215. *Paris*, 1911. 8º. **11735**. f. **3**

—— La Chance du mari. Comédie en un acte. *Pari* 1906. fol. [*L'Illustration théâtrale.* no. 40.] P.P. **4283**. m. (2

—— Cydalise et le chèvre-pied. Ballet en deux actes et troi tableaux, *etc.* [Scenario.] pp. 16. *Paris*, [1923.] 8º. **11735**. b. **28**

—— Papa. (Comédie.) Le sire de Vergy. (Opéra-bouffe. [With illustrations.] pp. 126. *Paris*, [1918.] 8º. **11737**. dd. **7**

—— Primerose. Comédie en trois actes. pp. 32. *Paris* 1912. fol. [*L'Illustration théâtrale.* no. 200.] P.P. **4283**. m. (2.

—— [Another edition.] Edited with introduction, notes exercises, and vocabulary by Alexander Green . . . an S. A. Rhodes. [With a portrait.] pp. xiv. 192. *Boston*, [1936.] 8º. [*Heath's Modern Language Series.*] **12213**. a. **1/374**

CAILLAVET (Léontine Arman de) *See* Brousson (J. J.) Les Vêpres de l'Avenue Hoche, *etc.* [Reminiscences o Anatole France and of Madame Arman de Caillavet.] 1932. 8º. **10655**. g. **24**

—— *See* Pouquet (J. M.) Le Salon de Madame Arman d Caillavet, *etc.* [With portraits.] 1926. 8º. **010662**. cc. **63**

CAILLAVET (Léontine Arman de)

—— *See* Pouquet (J. M.) The Lost Salon. [A translation of " Le Salon de Madame Arman de Caillavet."] 1927. 8°. **10656**. bbb. **24**.

CAILLAVET (Simone de) Les Heures latines. [Poems.] Préface de M. Anatole France. pp. 201. *Paris*, [1918.] 8°. **011483**. aa. **32**.

CAILLÉ (Adolphe Alexandre) *See* Favre (Léopold) A. Caillé. Notice biographique. 1888. 8°. **10604**. e. **12**. **(7.)**

—— L'Empereur et ses détracteurs. [In reply to a speech by Frédéric Mestreau.] pp. 88. *Niort*, 1872. 12°. **8051**. b. **42**.

—— Deuxième édition. pp. 88. *Niort*, 1872. 12°. **8051**. aaa. **9**.

—— Les Français et les Espagnols à Nice et dans les Alpes-Maritimes au xviiime siècle. Opérations militaires dans les Alpes et les Apennins, pendant la guerre de la succession d'Autriche, 1742–1748. pt. 1, 2. 1886. *See* Nice.—*Société Niçoise des Sciences Naturelles et Historiques.* Bulletin, *etc.* Nouvelle série. tom. 2. 1885, *etc.* 8°. Ac. **2846**.

CAILLE (Alexis) Au pays du printemps éternel. La Guatémala et son avenir économique. pp. 72. *Paris*, 1914. 8°. **8180**. aa. **54**. **(2.)**

—— Le Brésil et la commandite française. pp. 159. *Paris*, 1914. 8°. **08228**. f. **63**.

CAILLE (Alphonse) Un Jaloux. Comédie en deux actes, en vers, précédée d'un prologue. pp. 47. *Rouen*, 1873. 8°. **11736**. h. **3**.

CAILLE (André) *See* Coster (F.) R. P. Francisci Costeri . . . Ad analyticam assertionem A. Calliæ . . . breuis responsio. 1596. 12°. **3908**. a. **11**.

—— Apologie pour le tressainct & tresparfaict sacrifice faict & parfaict vne seule fois en la Croix par nostre Seigneur & seul sauueur Iesus Christ: contre le feinct & supposé sacrifice de la Messe, maintenu par Pierre Cotton. pp. 355. [*Geneva*,] 1601. 8°. **3901**. b. **6**.

CAILLÉ (Augustus) Differential Diagnosis and Treatment of Disease, *etc.* pp. xxix. 867. *D. Appleton & Co.: New York & London*, 1906. 8°. **7439**. ee. **2**.

—— Postgraduate Medicine. Prevention and treatment of disease, *etc.* pp. xxxviii. 1023. *D. Appleton & Co.: New York & London*, 1918. 8°. **07305**. e. **50**.

—— [A reissue.] *New York & London*, 1922. 8°. **7305**. eee. **6**.

CAILLÉ (Dominique F.) Édith au cou de cygne. [In verse.] pp. 32. *Paris*, 1886. 8°. **11483**. eee. **1**. **(8.)**

CAILLE (E. d'Audibert) *See* Audibert Caille.

CAILLE (Isaac de) *See* Brun de Castellane (I. de) *Seigneur de Caille.*

CAILLE (J. M. d'Audibert) *See* Audibert Caille.

CAILLÉ (Jacques)

—— *See* Burel (A.) La Mission du capitaine Burel au Maroc en 1808. Documents . . . avec introduction et commentaire par J. Caillé, *etc.* 1953. 4°. [*Institut des Hautes Études Marocaines. Notes et documents.* no. 13.] Ac. **17**. b/4.

CAILLÉ (Jacques)

—— Charles Jagerschmidt, Chargé d'affaires de France au Maroc, 1820–1894, *etc.* [With portraits.] pp. 311. pl. ix. *Paris; Tanger printed*, 1951. 8°. [*Publications de l'Institut des Hautes-Études Marocaines.* tom. 51.] **Ac.17.b.**

—— De l'action en dommages-intérêts pour adultère. pp. 160. *Rennes*, 1925. 8°. **5175**. dd. **17**.

—— Une Mission de Léon Roches à Rabat en 1845. [With a portrait and with maps.] pp. 132. *Casablanca*, 1947. 8°. [*Publications de l'Institut des Hautes Études Marocaines.* tom. 43.] Ac. **17**. b.

—— La Mosquée de Hassan à Rabat, *etc.* (Plans et dessins de Jean Hainaut.) 2 pt. pp. 171. pl. xlviii. fig. 44–63. *Paris*, 1954. 4°. [*Publications de l'Institut des Hautes-Études Marocaines.* tom. 57.] Ac. **17**. b.
Fig. 1–44 are in the text.

—— Organisation judiciaire et procédure marocaines, *etc.* pp. 459. *Paris*, 1948. 8°. [*Institut des Hautes Études Marocaines. Collection des centres d'études juridiques.* tom. 25.] Ac. **17**. b/2.

—— La Représentation diplomatique de la France au Maroc. pp. 86. *Paris*, 1951. 8°. **Ac.17.b/4.** [*Institut des hautes études marocaines. Notes et documents.* no. 8.]

—— La Ville de Rabat jusqu'au protectorat français. Histoire et archéologie. [With plans.] 3 vol. pp. 596. pl. lxxx. *Vanoest*, 1949. 8°. [*Publications de l'Institut des Hautes-Études Marocaines.* tom. 44.] Ac. **17**. b.

CAILLE (Louis) Ode à l'occasion de la paix signée à Lunéville, le 20 pluviôse an 9 . . . au Premier Consul. pp. 10. *Paris*, 1801. 8°. F. **1169**. (10.)

—— [Another copy.] **1065**. l. **43**. (22.)

—— [Another copy.] **8051**. de. **13**. (4.)

CAILLE (Nicolas) Thèse pour le doctorat en médecine, *etc.* (Questions sur diverses branches des sciences médicales.) pp. 46. *Paris*, 1843. 4°. [*Collection des thèses soutenues à la Faculté de Médecine de Paris.* An 1843. tom. 3.] **7371**. d. **13**.

CAILLÉ (P. F.) *See* Anchel (R.) and Caillé (P. F.) Histoire des décorations françaises contemporaines, *etc.* 1933. 4°. **09917**. i. **13**.

CAILLÉ (Pierre) *See* Mathieu (Albert) and Roux (J. C.) Pathologie gastro-intestinale . . . Quatrième édition revue, corrigée et augmentée par MM. J. C. Roux . . . P. Caillé, *etc.* 1923, *etc.* 8°. **07620**. h. **39**.

CAILLE (Pierre) *Poet.*

—— Archives. [Verses.] pp. 202. *Paris*, 1936. 8°. **20011**. e. **34**.

CAILLE (Pierre) *Potter.*

—— *See* Fierens (P.) Trois sculpteurs belges . . . P. Caille, *etc.* [Reproductions and portraits, with an introduction and notes.] 1949. 8°. **7877**. i. **2**.

—— *See* Rotterdam.—*Museum Boijmans.* Charles Leplae: beeldhouwwerken—teekeningen. Pierre Caille: ceramiek. [A catalogue of an exhibition.] 1947. 8°. **7877**. d. **28**.

—— Pierre Caille, *etc.* [Reproductions. With a portrait and with an introductory essay by Paul Fierens.] pp. 15. pl. 24. *Anvers*, [1950.] 8°. [*Monographies de l'art belge.* sér. 4. no. 4.] W.P. a. **48**. d/4.

CAILLE (RUTH KENNEDY) Resistant Behavior of Preschool Children, *etc.* [A thesis.] pp. xv. 142. *Teachers College, Columbia University: New York*, 1933. 8°. **08311.** cc. **88.**

CAILLEAU (ANDRÉ) Catalogue des livres nouveaux, qui se vendent à Paris, chez André Cailleau . . . et Charles Huguier . . . 1727. pp. 4. [*Paris*, 1727.] 4°. **S.C.1034./10.**

—— Catalogue des livres qui se vendent à Paris chez André Cailleau, provenans du fond de M. Roulland & autres imprimez en 1731. [*Paris*, 1731.] *s. sh.* 4°. **S.C.1034/14.**

CAILLEAU (ANDRÉ CHARLES)

—— [For editions of the "Dictionnaire bibliographique" attributed by J. C. Brunet to R. Duclos and A. C. Cailleau, but in fact by R. Duclos:] *See* DICTIONNAIRE.

—— Almanach des Grâces, étrennes chantantes; dédié au beau sexe, par M. C * * [i.e. A. C. Cailleau] pour l'année . . . M.DCC.LXXXIV. pp. 276. 1784. 12°. *See* C * *, M. **011483.** de. **48.**

—— L'Automatie des animaux ; suivie de quelques réflexions sur le Mahométisme et l'agriculture. Par un partisan de Descartes [i.e. A. C. Cailleau]. pp. 188. 1783. 12°. *See* AUTOMATIE. **1146.** b. **27.**

—— Nouveaux bouquets poissards. Nouvelle édition, augmentée de bouquets grivois, chantans et galans, dediés à l'ombre de Vadé. [By A. C. Cailleau.] pp. 48. [1770?] 12°. *See* BOUQUETS. **1065.** e. **35.**

—— Les Philosophes manqués, comédie nouvelle en un acte . . . [A satire on "Les Philosophes" by C. Palissot de Montenoy. By A. C. Cailleau.] Nouvelle édition, corrigée et augmentée. pp. 27. 1760. 12°. *See* PHILOSOPHES. **241.** i. **26.** (**5.**)

—— Le Veuvage de Figaro, ou la Fille retrouvée, comédie en trois actes, *etc.* [By A. C. Cailleau.] pp. 80. 1785. 8°. *See* FIGARO. **11738.** a. **15.** (**5.**)

—— Vie privée et criminelle d'Antoine-François Desrues, *etc.* [By A. C. Cailleau.] pp. 96. 1777. 12°. *See* DERUES (A. F.) **5405.** a. **20.**

—— [Another edition.] pp. 120. [1778?] 12°. *See* DERUES (A. F.) **10662.** aa. **3.** (**1.**)

—— [Another edition.] pp. 118. 1779. 12°. *See* DERUES (A. F.) G. **14688.**

—— Le Waux-Hall populaire, ou les Fêtes de la guinguette, poème grivois et poissardi-lyri-comique, *etc.* [By A. C. Cailleau.] pp. 127. [1769.] 12°. *See* VAUXHALL. **11483.** c. **29.**

CAILLEAU (ARMAND BENJAMIN) *See* CAILLAU.

CAILLEAU (CATHÉRINE) Trois nouveaux contes des fées. [1786.] *See* CABINET. Le Cabinet des fées, *etc.* tom. 32. 1785, *etc.* 8°. **89.** d. **19.**

—— Feen-Märchen. [A translation of "Trois nouveaux contes des fées."] *See* BIBLIOTHEK. Die blaue Bibliothek, *etc.* Bd. 1. 1790, *etc.* 8°. **12410.** b. **2.**

CAILLEBOTTE (JEAN FRANÇOIS RENÉ) Essai sur l'histoire et les antiquités de la ville et arrondissement de Domfront. Troisième édition. pp. xiv. 124. *Domfront*, 1827. 12°. **1050.** b. **7.**

CAILLE DU FOURNY (HONORÉ) *See* ANSELME, *de la Vierge Marie.* Histoire généalogique et chronologique de la maison royale de France . . . continuée par M. Du Fourny, *etc.* 1726, *etc.* fol. **2098.f.**

—— —— 1868, *etc.* 4°. **1860.** a. **10.**

CAILLEMER (CHARLES FRANÇOIS LOUIS)

—— *See* DERIES (L.) Un Haut fonctionnaire normand d'avant et d'après la Révolution. Charles-Louis-François Caillemer. [1923.] 8°. [*Comité des Travaux historiques et scientifiques. Notices, inventaires & documents.* vol. 8.] Ac. **437/7.**

—— Corps législatif. Commission du Conseil des Anciens. Rapport . . . sur une résolution de la commission des Cinq-Cents, relative à la reconnoissance de l'identité d'un individu condamné, évadé et repris. Séance du 9 frimaire an 8. pp. 6. *Paris*, an 8 [1799]. 8°. F.R. **219.** (**6.**)

—— Corps législatif. Discours par Caillemer . . . pour exprimer son vœu sur le projet de loi relatif à l'établissement des tribunaux spéciaux. Séance du 18 pluviose an 9. pp. 14. *Paris*, an 9 [1801]. 8°. F.R. **222.** (**40.**)

—— Tribunat. Opinion . . . sur le projet de loi concernant la poursuite des délits jugés par les tribunaux correctionnels et criminels. Dans la séance du 2 nivose an 9. pp. 12. *Paris*, an 9 [1801]. 8°. F.R. **222.** (**1.**)

—— Tribunat. Opinion . . . sur le projet de loi organique du tribunal de cassation. Séance du 9 pluviose an 8. pp. 6. *Paris*, an 8 [1800]. 8°. F.R. **183.** (**14.**)

—— Tribunat. Opinion . . . sur le projet de loi relatif à la division du territoire de la République. Séance du 24 pluviose, an 8. pp. 7. [*Paris*,] an 8 [1800]. 8°. F.R. **115.** (**43.**)

—— Tribunat. Opinion . . . sur le projet de loi relatif à la poursuite des délits dont la connoissance appartient aux tribunaux criminels et correctionnels. Séance du 8 pluviose an 9. pp. 11. *Paris*, an 9 [1801]. 8°. F.R. **222.** (**28.**)

—— Tribunat. Opinion . . . sur le projet de loi relatif à la suppression des assesseurs des justices de paix. Séance du 26 ventose an 9. pp. 6. *Paris*, an 9 [1801]. 8°. F.R. **185.** (**47.**)

—— Tribunat. Opinion . . . sur le projet de loi relatif aux actes de l'état civil. Séance du 6 nivose an 10. pp. 6. [*Paris*,] nivôse, an 10 [1801/02]. 8°. F.R. **194.** (**11.**)

—— Tribunat. Opinion . . . sur le projet de loi relatif aux justices de paix. Séance du 15 frimaire an 9. pp. 11. *Paris*, an 9 [1800]. 8°. F.R. **185.** (**36.**)

—— Tribunat. Rapport . . . sur la pétition du citoyen Regnaud . . . Séance du 2 brumaire an 10. pp. 4. [*Paris*,] an 10 [1801]. 8°. F.R. **99.** (**47.**)

—— Tribunat. Rapport . . . sur le projet de loi concernant l'acquisition des bâtimens de l'ancien évêché d'Avanches, pour y placer le tribunal civil de l'arrondissement et autres établissemens publics. Séance du 19 frimaire an 9. pp. 4. *Paris*, an 9 [1800]. 8°. F.R. **249.** (**10.**)

—— Tribunat. Rapport . . . sur le projet de loi organique des tribunaux. Séance du 21 ventose an 8. pp. 15. *Paris*, an 8 [1800]. 8°. F.R. **181.** (**3.**)

—— Tribunat. Rapport . . . sur le projet de loi organique des tribunaux. Séance du 25 ventose an 8. pp. 4. *Paris*, an 8 [1800]. 8°. F.R. **181.** (**8.**)

CAILLEMER (EXUPÈRE) *See* POLIS. Compilation anonyme sur la défense des places fortes [entitled "Ὅπως χρὴ τὸν τῆς πολιορκουμένης πόλεως στρατηγὸν πρὸς τὴν πολιορκίαν ἀντιτάττεσθαι"]. Traduite . . . par M. E. Caillemer. 1872. 8°. [*Mémoires de la Société d'Émulation du Doubs.* sér. 4. vol. 6.] Ac. **283**

—— Des intérêts. Thèse, *etc.* pp. 275. *Caen*, 1861. 8°. **5423.** bb. **13**

CAILLEMER (Exupère)

—— Le Droit civil dans les provinces anglo-normandes au XIIe siècle. (Extrait des Mémoires de l'Académie nationale des Sciences, Arts et Belles-Lettres de Caen.) pp. 72. *Caen*, 1883. 8°. **6005**. de. **14**.

—— Étude sur Michel de Marillac. *See* Caen.—*Chambre des Conférences des Avocats stagiaires près la Cour impériale de Caen*. Procès-verbal de la séance de rentrée, *etc.* 1862. 8°. **5425**. eee. **11**.

—— [Another edition.] Chambre des Conférences des Avocats stagiaires près la Cour impériale de Caen. Étude sur Michel de Marillac. Discours, *etc.* pp. 40. *Caen*, 1862. 8°. **10663**. g. **20**. (4.)

—— Études sur les antiquités juridiques d'Athènes.

La Propriété littéraire, *etc.* [1868.]
La Droit de succession legitime, *etc.* pp. 209. 1879.
La Naturalisation, *etc.* pp. 40. 1880.

Paris; Caen, [1868]–80. 8°. **5205**. bb. **2**.

—— Jean de Blanot. *See* Appleton (C.) Mélanges Ch. Appleton, *etc.* [With a preface by E. Caillemer.] 1903. 8°. [*Annales de l'Université de Lyons.* Nouvelle série. II. Droit, Lettres. fasc. 13.] **Ac.365.(b.)**

—— M. Frédéric Taulier, sa vie et ses œuvres, 1806–1861. Discours, *etc.* pp. 40. *Paris; Grenoble*, 1864. 8°. **10661**. dd. **23**. (5.)

—— Les Manuscrits Bouhier, Nicaise et Peiresc de la Bibliothèque du Palais des Arts de Lyon. (Description des manuscrits.) pp. viii. 48. 1880. 8°. [*Collection des opuscules lyonnais.* no. 1.] *See* Lyons.—*Palais des Arts.—Bibliothèque.* **10168**. d. **3**.

—— Notes pour la biographie du jurisconsulte Gaius. pp. 15. [*Paris*,] 1865. 8°. **10601**. d. **11**. (2.)

—— Notices et extraits de manuscrits de la Bibliothèque de Lyon. (Extrait des Mémoires de l'Académie des sciences, belles-lettres et arts de Lyon.) pp. 50. *Lyon*, 1881. 8°. **11900**. ee. **2**.

CAILLEMER (Louis Charles Urbain) Thèse pour le doctorat en médecine. (Questions sur diverses branches des sciences médicales.) pp. 29. *Paris*, 1838. 4°. **1184**. i. **4**. (5.)

CAILLEMER (Robert) *See* Schatz (A.) and Caillemer (R.) Le Mercantilisme libéral à la fin du XVIIe siècle, *etc.* 1906. 8°. **08226**. dd. **32**. (4.)

—— Études sur les successions au moyen âge. 2 vol. pp. 740. *Lyon*, 1901. 8°. **06005**. k. **23**.

CAILLER (Charles)

—— Introduction géométrique à la mécanique rationnelle . . . Ouvrage publié par H. Fehr et R. Wavre. pp. xii. 627. *Genève; Paris*, 1924. 8°. [*Veröffentlichungen der Schweizerischen Mathematischen Gesellschaft.* tom. 1.] Ac. **4216**. (**1**.)

—— Sur la notion de courbure et sur quelques points de géometrie infinitésimale non-euclidienne. 1911. *Genève; Paris*, 1911. 4°. [*Mémoires de la Société de Physique et d'Histoire naturelle de Genève.* vol. 37. fasc. 2.] Ac. **2870**.

CAILLER (Claude Alexandre)

—— La Politique balkanique de l'Italie entre 1875 et 1914. Thèse, *etc.* pp. 238. *La Tour de Peilz*, 1951. 8°. **8029**. dd. **13**.

CAILLER (Gaetano La Corte) *See* La Corte-Cailler.

CAILLER (Pierre)

—— Monographies photographiques de Grèce . . . Collection publiée sous la direction de P. Cailler. 1938– . 8°. *See* Switzerland.—*Société des Études Grecques et Byzantines en Suisse.* W.P. **12666**.

CAILLER (Raoul) Elegie. [On the death of Ronsard.] *See* Binet (C.) Discours de la vie de Pierre de Ronsard, *etc.* 1586. 4°. **1073**. i. **22**.

CAILLERS (François de) *See* Callières.

CAILLET ( ) *Sous-Lieutenant.* Le Nouvel officier d'infanterie en guerre. Ce qu'il doit savoir. pp. 49. *Paris*, 1916. 8°. **8829**. aaa. **49**.

CAILLET (Albert Louis)

—— Aperçu général sur le traitement mental, *etc.* [With plates.] pp. 23. *Paris*, [1912.] 8°. **4184**. cc. **5**.

—— Manuel bibliographique des sciences psychiques ou occultes. 3 tom. *Paris*, 1912 [1913]. 8°. **B.B.A.e.3.**

—— Traitement mental et culture spirituelle. La santé et l'harmonie dans la vie humaine. pp. xiii. 399. *Paris*, 1912. 8°. **7410**. aaaa. **39**.

CAILLET (Ambroise Marie) Thèse pour le doctorat en médecine. (Questions sur diverses branches des sciences médicales.) pp. 18. *Paris*, 1839. 4°. [*Collection des thèses soutenues à la Faculté de Médecine de Paris.* An 1839. tom. 3.] **7371**. a. **3**.

CAILLET (Blaise) Vies des saints; avec le martyrologe romain et des réflexions morales en forme de lecture de piété pour chaque jour de l'année. 4 tom. *Lyon*, 1864. 8°. **4823**. dd. **1**.

CAILLET (C.) Classifications, diagnostic et pronostic des présentations et positions. pp. 30. *Paris*, 1867. 4°. [*Collection des thèses soutenues à la Faculté de Médecine de Paris.* An 1867. tom. 3.] **7373**. h. **6**.

CAILLET (Félix) L'Amnistie. [In verse.] pp. 7. *Paris*, 1859. 8°. **11481**. d. **51**. (**4**.)

—— La Maison d'Autriche. pp. 101. *Paris*, 1867. 8°. **9315**. g. **19**.

CAILLET (Gérard)

—— *See* Figueiredo (G.) Un Dieu a dormi dans la maison, *etc.* (Adaptation de G. Caillet.) 1952. 8°. [*France Illustration. Supplément théâtral et littéraire.* no. 117.] P.P. **4283**. m. (**1**.)

CAILLET (Henri) *Lieutenant.* Réponse de Caillet. *See* Lebrasse (M. F.) Réponse aux tardives dénonciations dirigées contre les citoyens Lebrasse, Caillet, *etc.* [1793?] 4°. F. **45***. (**9**.)

CAILLET (Henri) *of Tours.* De la chlorose pendant la grossesse, et de sa véritable proportion. pp. 26. *Paris*, 1856. 4°. [*Collection des thèses soutenues à la Faculté de Médecine de Paris.* An 1856. tom. 4.] **7372**. i. **4**.

CAILLET (Jules) *See* Bouillet (M. N.) Atlas universel d'histoire et de géographie, contenant 1° la chronologie (avec la collaboration de M. Caillet), *etc.* 1865. 8°. **10002**. h. **8**.

—— —— 1877. 8°. **12224**. de. **2**.

—— *See* Mangin (E.) Nouveau traité complet du jeu de billard . . . Préface par M. J. C. [i.e. J. Caillet.] 1876. 12°. **7915**. bbb. **4**.

CAILLET (JULES)

—— *See* MANGIN (E.) Complément du Nouveau traité du jeu de billard . . . Préface par M. J. Caillet. 1880. 12°. **7915**. bbb. **4**. (**2**.)

—— De l'administration en France sous le ministère du cardinal de Richelieu. pp. xi. 548. *Paris*, 1857. 8°. **8050**. f. **24**.

—— Deuxième édition, refondue. 2 tom. *Paris*, 1861. 12°. **8050**. d. **10**.

—— De ratione in imperio Romano ordinando ab Hadriano imperatore adhibita dissertationem scripsit ad gradum . . . doctoris obtinendum J. Caillet. pp. 152. *Parisiis*, 1857. 8°. **1307**. f. **19**.

CAILLET (L.) Trucs et procédés, par un groupe de practiciens . . . A l'usage de . . . menuisiers, ébénistes, *etc.* [Compiled by L. Caillet.] pp. viii. 174. *Paris*, [1920.] 8°. **07942**. a. **17**.

CAILLET (L. N.) Dissertation sur les hémorrhagies uterines en général, *etc.* pp. 25. *Paris*, 1817. 4°. **1183**. d. **10**. (**26**.)

CAILLET (LOUIS) *See* GADAGNE (T. de) Acte du 12 décembre 1539 concernant la famille de Gadagne. Par L. Caillet, *etc.* 1913. 8°. **9916**. bb. **25**.

—— *See* VAREY (T. de) Lettre de Thomas de Varey, otage en Angleterre, 1364, aux bourgeois de Lyon. [Edited by L. Caillet.] [1908.] 8°. **10921**. h. **37**. (**3**.)

—— *See* VAULX (J. de) Compte de Jean de Vaulx, *etc.* [Edited by L. Caillet.] 1909. 8°. **10600**. g. **28**. (**2**.)

—— Étude sur les relations de la Commune de Lyon avec Charles VII. et Louis XI, 1417–1483. pp. xlv. 720. *Lyon ; Paris*, 1909. 8°. [*Annales de l'Université de Lyon.* Nouvelle série. II. Droit, Lettres. fasc. 21.] Ac. **365**. (**6**.)

—— Études sur les relations de Lyon avec le Mâconnais et la Bresse au XVe siècle. 1909. *See* MACON.—*Société des Sciences, etc.* Annales, *etc.* sér. 3. tom. 14. 1851, *etc.* 8°. Ac. **366/3**.

—— [Another edition.] pp. vi. 90. *Paris*, 1909. 8°. [*Bibliothèque du XVe siècle.* tom. 10.] **12203**. h. **1/9**.

—— Lettres inédites des ducs et duchesses de Bourbon antérieures à 1503 conservées aux Archives municipales de Lyon. pp. 38. *Moulins*, 1909. 8°. [*Curiosités bourbonnaises.* no. 20.] **010171**. l. **26**.

—— Rapport sur le fonctionnement de la Bibliothèque Communale de Limoges durant l'année 1912 (1913). 2 pt. 1913, 15. fol. *See* LIMOGES.—*Bibliothèque Communale.* **11903**. a. **25**.

CAILLET (MAURICE) *See* CAILLET (R.) and (M.) La Bibliothèque Inguimbertine de Carpentras, *etc.* 1929. 8°. **667.m.10.**

—— Fers de reliures et ex-libris de la Bibliothèque Municipale de Valence. pp. 52. 1941. 8°. *See* VALENCE.—*Bibliothèque Municipale.* **11898**. d. **19**.

CAILLET (PIERRE) Épis et bluets. Poésies, *etc.* pp. vii. 156. *Paris*, 1864. 8°. **11481**. i. **20**.

—— Les Garibaldiennes. Poésies. [With a preface by A. Bonneau.] pp. iv. 103. *Paris*, 1861. 12°. **11481**. bbb. **10**.

CAILLET (ROBERT) Le Canal de Carpentras. Contribution à l'histoire du Comtat Venaissin, 1561–1925. Ouvrage illustré de huit planches et d'une carte . . . Suivi d'une étude technique avec croquis par M. Victorin Espert, *etc.* pp. xv. 254. *Carpentras*, 1925. 8°. **8235**. r. **12**.

CAILLET (ROBERT) and **CAILLET** (MAURICE)

—— La Bibliothèque Inguimbertine de Carpentras. Son histoire, ses reliures. [With plates, including a portrait of J. D. d'Inguimbert.] pp. 107. 1929. 8°. *See* CARPENTRAS.—*Bibliothèque.* **667.m.10.**

CAILLET (VINCENT MARIE) Tables de réfractions astronomiques . . . précédées d'un rapport fait au Bureau des Longitudes, par M. Largeteau. pp. 40. *Paris*, 1854. 8°. **8561**. e. **31**. (**6**.)

—— Traité élémentaire de navigation . . . 2e édition, revue et corrigée. pp. xi. 433. pl. IX. *Paris*, 1857. 8°. **8806**. d. **3**.

CAILLET-BOIS (HORACIO)

—— Las Ciudades de Santa Fe y Corrientes. *Span., Eng. & Fr.* pp. 55. pl. CXXXIV. *Buenos Aires*, 1945. 4°. [*Documentos de arte argentino.* cuaderno 17.] W.P. **3787**.

CAILLET-BOIS (RICARDO RODOLFO)

—— La América española y la Revolución francesa. *In:* Boletín de la Academia Nacional de la Historia. año 16. vol. 13. pp. 159–216. 1940. 8°. Ac. **8592/12**.

—— Bio-bibliografía de Carlos Ramón Correa Luna. 1939. *See* BUENOS AIRES.—*Universidad de Buenos Aires.—Facultad de Filosofía y Letras.—Sección de Historia,* afterwards *Instituto de Investigaciones Históricas.* Boletín, *etc.* tom. 23. no. 77/80. 1922, *etc.* 8°. Ac. **2694**. ca.

—— Ensayo sobre el Río de la Plata y la Revolución francesa. 2 pt. *Buenos Aires*, 1929. 8°. [*Universidad de Buenos Aires.—Facultad de Filosofía y Letras. Publicaciones del Instituto de Investigaciones Históricas.* no. 49.] Ac. **2694**. ca/3.

—— Las Islas Malvinas. (Una tierra argentina.) Ensayo basado en una nueva y desconocida documentación. Segunda edición, *etc.* [With maps.] pp. 453. *Buenos Aires*, 1952. 8°. **10482**. m. **39**

—— El Patriota y su Editor Pedro Feliciano Sáenz de Cavia. [On the periodical " El Patriota." With extracts.] 1942. *See* BUENOS AYRES.—*Sociedad de Historia Argentina.* Anuario de Historia Argentina. año 1941. 1942, *etc.* 4° Ac. **8592**. d/2

—— La Revolución en el Virreinato. 1939. *See* LEVENE (R. Historia de la Nación Argentina, *etc.* vol. 5. 1936, *etc.* 8° **Ac.8592/5.**

CAILLET-BOIS (TEODORO)

—— *See* OLAZÁBAL (M. de) Memorias del coronel Manuel d Olazábal, *etc.* [With an introduction by T. Caillet-Bois 1942. 8°. [*Biblioteca del Instituto Sanmartiniano.* vol. 5 Ac. **973**

—— *See* SAN MARTÍN (J. de) *Protector of Peru.* Epistolar entre los libertadores San Martín y Bolívar. Recopilado anotado por T. Caillet Bois y I. Bucich Escobar. 1941. 8 [*Biblioteca del Instituto Sanmartiniano.* vol. 4.] Ac. **973**

—— Costa Sur y Plata. *Buenos Aires*, 1939– . 8°. W.P. **1039**

—— Patagonia. (Selección y prólogo de T. Caillet-Boi [With plates.] pp. 111. *Buenos Aires*, [1944.] 8°. **010481**. e.

—— El Proceso de Bouchar pp. 47. xi. *Buenos Aires*, 1936. fol. [*Universidad Buenos Aires.—Facultad de Filosofía y Letras. Publi ciones del Instituto de Investigaciones Históricas.* no. 6 Ac. **2694**. ca

CAILLETEAU (Émile) Étude sur l'origine des pustules vaccinales secondaires. pp. 34. *Paris,* 1869. 4°. [*Collection des thèses soutenues à la Faculté de Médecine de Paris.* An 1869. tom. 3.] **7373. k. 9.**

CAILLETEAU (Théodore R. J. B.) Dissertation sur les fièvres intermittentes; thèse, *etc.* pp. 24. *Paris,* 1830. 4°. **1184. d. 6. (9.)**

CAILLETET (Cyrille) Essai et dosage des huiles . . . des savons et de la farine de blé, *etc.* pp. iii. 104. *Paris,* 1859. 12°. **7953. d. 4.**

CAILLETET (Ernest) De la rétroversion de l'utérus pendant la grossesse. pp. 52. *Paris,* 1868. 4°. [*Collection des thèses soutenues à la Faculté de Médecine de Paris.* An 1868. tom. 3.] **7373. i. 7.**

CAILLETET (Louis Paul) Le Jubilé académique de Monsieur L. P. Cailletet, 18 janvier 1910. [With a preface by Alphonse Berget. With portraits and a bibliography.] pp. 47. *Paris,* [1910.] 8°. **010655. b. 33.**

CAILLETTE. La vie et trespassement de caillette. [In verse. A type facsimile. The editorial note signed: G. V., i.e. Giraud and A. A. Veinant.] *Paris,* 1831. 4°. **T. 1472. (13.)**

One of an edition of forty-two copies.

CAILLETTE (Rodolphe) De la propagation des affections de la plèvre au péritoine par le système lymphatique. pp. 52. *Paris,* 1874. 4°. [*Collection des thèses soutenues à la Faculté de Médecine de Paris.* An 1874. tom. 3.] **7374. a. 8.**

CAILLETTE DE L'HERVILLIERS (Edmond) Le B. Josaphat Kuncewicz, archevêque de Polotsk, martyr, *etc.* pp. 108. *Paris,* 1865. 12°. **4886. b. 15.**

—— De l'entomologie dans ses rapports avec l'agriculture. pp. 16. *Bar-sur-Aube,* 1864. 8°. **7296. c. 43. (4.)**

—— Le Mont Gannelon à Clairoix près de Compiègne, étude d'archéologie, de philologie & d'histoire. pp. 126. *Compiègne ; Paris,* 1860. 8°. **10172. dd. 29.**

—— Notre-Dame-de-Bon-Secours de Compiègne, recherches historiques sur l'origine de cette Chapelle et sur le pélerinage dont elle est le but chaque année. pp. viii. 100. *Compiègne ; Paris,* 1861. 8°. **4632. ee. 3.**

—— Pierrefonds, Saint Jean aux Bois, La Folie, Saint Pierre en Chastres. Souvenirs historiques et archéologiques de la forêt de Compiègne. pp. 88. *Paris,* [1858.] 8°. **10171. ff. 10.**

—— Saint Pierre à Rome. pp. 58. *Paris ; Lyon,* 1867. 8°. **3902. g. 41. (2.)**

CAILLEUX (Alphonse de) *See* Nodier (J. E. C.) Voyages pittoresques et romantiques de l'ancienne France. Par MM. C. Nodier, J. Taylor et A. de Cailleux. 1820, *etc.* fol. **445. i. 7–15. & 446. l. 1–10.**

CAILLEUX (Amédée) De la métrite granuleuse du col utérin et d'un nouveau mode de traitement par l'acide chlorhydrique et le sous-nitrate de bismuth. pp. 32. *Paris,* 1866. 4°. [*Collection des thèses soutenues à la Faculté de Médecine de Paris.* tom. 2.] **7373. g. 5.**

CAILLEUX (André)

—— *See* Duplaix (S.) and Cailleux (A.) Étude minéralogique et morphoscopique de quelques sables des grands fonds de l'océan atlantique occidental, *etc.* 1952. 8°. [*Göteborgs Kungl. Vetenskaps- och Vitterhets-Samhälles handlingar.* följd 6. ser. B. bd. 6. no. 5.] Ac. **1063.**

CAILLEUX (André)

—— *See* Romanovsky (V.) and Cailleux (A.) La Glace et les glaciers. 1953. 8°. **8716. aaa. 60.**

—— Les Actions éoliennes périglaciaires en Europe. pp. 176. pl. v. *Paris,* 1942. 4°. [*Mémoires de la Société Géologique de France.* Nouvelle sér. no. 46.] Ac. **3115/2.**

CAILLEUX (André) and **TAYLOR** (Gérald)

—— Cryopédologie. Étude des sols gelés. pp. 218. pl. xii. *Paris,* 1954. 8°. [*Expéditions polaires françaises. Missions Paul-Émile Victor.* no. 4.] W.P. a. **204/4.**
Actualités scientifiques et industrielles. no. 1203.

CAILLEUX (Édouard) L'Impôt sur la richesse mobiliaire en Italie, *etc.* 1901. *See* Paris.—*École Libre des Sciences Politiques.—Société des Anciens Élèves, etc.* Congrès des sciences politiques de 1900, *etc.* 1901. 8°. Ac. **2311.**

—— La Question chinoise aux États-Unis et dans les possessions des puissances européennes. pp. viii. 277. *Paris,* 1898. 8°. **8022. d. 1.**

CAILLEUX (Henri Girard de) *See* Girard de Cailleux.

CAILLEUX (Joseph Adrien) Résumé analytique, théorique et pratique de l'hémorrhagie utérine . . . thèse, *etc.* pp. 25. *Paris,* 1836. 4°. **1184. g. 11. (25.)**

CAILLEUX (Ludovic de) Le Monde antédiluvien. Poëme biblique en prose. pp. xix. 446. *Paris,* 1845. 8°. **1161. g. 34.**

CAILLEUX (Marie Françoise) *See* Thilorier (J. C.) Tribunal criminel de la Seine. Accusation d'attentat contre la liberté individuelle. Mémoire pour la demoiselle Bretin, accusée ; contre la dame Cailleux, sa sœur, *etc.* 1801. 4°. **F. 49*. (7.)**

—— Mémoire pour une veuve (Marie-Françoise Bretin, veuve de Remi Jean Cailleux) spoliée de son héritage, et détenue arbitrairement par sa famille. (Contre Jeanne Sophie Bretin et consorts.) pp. 18. [*Paris,* 1798/99.] 8°. **F. 989. (1.)**

CAILLEUX (Pierre Théophile) La Judée en Europe. La vérité sur les Juifs, leur origine et leur religion. Précédé d'un préface par Ch. M. Limousin, *etc.* pp. xl. 221. *Paris,* 1894. 8°. **4516. aa. 17.**

—— Origine celtique de la civilisation de tous les peuples. Théorie nouvelle. pp. viii. 535. *Paris ; Bruxelles* [printed], 1878. 8°. **10007. c. 4.**

CAILLEUX (Roland) Essai critique sur la doctrine homœopathique. pp. 101. *Paris,* 1933. 8°. **7462. r. 28.**

—— Une Lecture. Roman. pp. 358. [*Paris,*] 1948. 8°. **012550. pp. 26.**

—— Saint-Genès, ou la Vie brève. Roman. pp. 332. [*Paris,*] 1943. 8°. **12519. c. 27.**

CAILLEUX (Théophile) *See* Cailleux (Pierre T.)

CAILLEZ (Maurice) L'Organisation du crédit au commerce extérieur en France et à l'étranger. [With graphs.] pp. 376. *Paris,* 1923. 8°. **08229. cc. 10.**

CAILLI. *See* Cailly.

CAILLIAUD (Frédéric) *See* Raffeneau Delile (A.) Centurie de plantes d'Afrique du voyage à Méroé, recueillies par M. Cailliaud, *etc.* 1826. 8°. **1145. i. 3.**

CAILLIAUD (FRÉDÉRIC)

—— *See* Y. Les Abyssiniennes et les femmes du Soudan oriental d'après les relations de Bruce . . . Cailliaud, *etc.* 1876. 8º. **8416**. d. **31**.

—— Recherches sur les arts et métiers, les usages de la vie civile et domestique des anciens peuples de l'Égypte, de la Nubie et de l'Éthiopie . . . Accompagné d'une carte géographique, et des planches représentant des objets d'art, *etc.* *Paris*, 1831. fol. **789**. g. **11**.
Imperfect; containing only the plates.

—— Voyage à l'Oasis de Thébes, et dans les déserts situées à l'orient et à l'occident de la Thébaïde, fait pendant les années 1815, 1816, 1817 et 1818, par M. Frédéric Cailliaud . . . Rédigé et publié par M. Jomard . . . Contenant 1.º Le voyage à l'Oasis de Dakel, par M. le chevalier Drovetti . . . 2.º Le journal du premier voyage de M. Cailliaud en Nubie; 3.º Des recherches sur les oasis, *etc.* pp. xvii. 120. pl. xxiv. *Paris*, 1821. fol. **560***. g. **17**.
The second volume, containing "Des recherches sur les oasis, etc." does not appear to have been published.

—— Travels in the Oasis of Thebes, and in the deserts situated east and west of the Thebaid; in the years 1815, 16, 17, and 18 . . . Edited by M. Jomard . . . Translated from the French. pp. xii. 72. pl. 18. *Sir R. Phillips & Co.: London*, 1822. 8º. [*New Voyages and Travels.* vol. 7.] **P.P. 3904**. i.

—— [Another copy.] **7704**. aaa. **51**.

—— Voyage à Méroé, au Fleuve Blanc, au-delà de Fâzoql dans le midi du royaume de Sennâr, à Syouah et dans cinq autres oasis; fait dans les années 1819, 1820, 1821 et 1822, *etc.* [Edited by the author and E. F. Jomard.] 4 tom. [*Paris*,] 1826, 27. 8º. **744**. e. **2**.

—— [Plates, with descriptive letterpress.] 2 vol. *Paris*, 1823. fol. **747**. c. **19**.

CAILLIÉ (RENÉ) *Traveller.*

—— *See* WELCH (G.) The Unveiling of Timbuctoo. The astounding adventures of Caillié. [With portraits.] 1938. 8º. **010093**. f. **49**.

—— Journal d'un voyage à Temboctou et à Jenné, dans l'Afrique centrale . . . pendant les années 1824, 1825, 1826, 1827, 1828 . . . Avec une carte itinéraire, et des remarques géographiques, par M. Jomard. [With a portrait.] 3 tom. *Paris*, 1830. 8º. **10095**. dd. **4**.

—— Atlas. **10095**. i. **3**.

—— [Another copy.] **10096**. bbb. **16**.
Imperfect; wanting the 'Atlas.'

—— [Another edition.] [1842.] *See* DUPONCHEL (A.) Nouvelle bibliothèque des voyages, *etc.* tom. 9. [1841, *etc.*] 8º. **1424**. e. **5**.

—— Travels through Central Africa to Timbuctoo; and across the Great Desert, to Morocco, performed in the years 1824–1828. [With a portrait.] 2 vol. *H. Colburn & R. Bentley: London*, 1830. 8º. **1047**. h. **12**, **13**.

—— Promenades autour du monde, ou Extraits des voyages de MM. Caillé, Mollien [and others] . . . Publiés par M. J. O. D. [i.e. Joseph J. Odolant-Desnos.] [1834.] 12º. *See* D., J. O., *M.* **10024**. aa. **3**.

CAILLIÉ (RENÉ) *Writer on Spiritualism.* *See* RENUCCI (J. E.) Conciliation scientifique du matérialisme et du spiritualisme . . . Avec préface de R. Caillié. 1894. 8º. **8632**. g. **24**. (**10**.)

CAILLIÈRE (JACQUES DE) *Marshal of France.* CALLIÈRES.

CAILLIÈRES (FRANÇOIS DE) *See* CALLIÈRES.

CAILLIÈRES DE LÉTANG (P. J. G. DE) *See* CALLIÈ DE L'ÉTANG.

CAILLIET (ÉMILE) *Directeur du Cours complementaire Morhange.* Les Origines du mouvement sinn-fein Irlande. pp. 61. [*Metz*, 1921.] 8º. **8146**. de.

CAILLIET (ÉMILE) *Professor in Scripps College.*

—— The Beginning of Wisdom. The 1946–47 Otts lecture Davidson College, North Carolina. pp. 192. *Fleming H. Revell Co.: New York*, [1947.] 8º. **4018**. eee.

—— The Clue to Pascal, *etc.* pp. 128. *S.C.M. Pr* *London*, 1944. 8º. **4379**. ee.

—— Mysticis et "mentalité mystique." Étude d'un problème p par les travaux de M. Lévy-Bruhl sur la menta primitive. pp. 195. *Paris*, 1938. 8º. [*Études d'hist et de philosophie religieuses.* no. 36.] **Ac. 2633**.

—— Pascal. pp. 40. *Inter-Varsity Fellowship: Lon* [1950.] 16º. [*University Booklets.* no. 13.] **W.P. 15044**

—— [La Prohibition de l'occulte.] Why We Oppose Occult . . . Translated by George Franklin Cole. pp. *University of Pennsylvania Press: Philadelphia*, 1931. **08632**. ee.

—— [Another copy.] **08632**. gg.

—— Symbolisme et âmes primitives. pp. 306. *P* 1936. 8º. **010006**. g.

—— La Tradition littéraire des idéologues, *etc.* pp. xxi. 3 *Philadelphia*, 1943. 8º. [*Memoirs of the American P sophical Society.* vol. 19.] **Ac. 18**

—— The Themes of Magic in Nineteenth Century Fr Fiction . . . English translation by Lorraine Ha pp. xii. 228. *Les Presses Universitaires de France: P* 1932. 8º. **11855**. d.

CAILLIEU (COLIJN) *See* MONTGESOIE (A. de) [Le de la mort.] Colijn Caillieu's Dal sonder Wederkeere Pas der doot, *etc.* [With the text of the origi 1936. 8º. [*Universiteit te Gent. Werken uitge door de Faculteit der Wijsbegeerte en Letteren.* afl. 73.] **Ac. 26**

CAILLIEU (NORBERT) *See* LAUNOY (J. de) Ioa Launoii . . . Censura Responsionis, qua Fr. Norb Caillocius sese mendaciis . . . irretiuit. 1663. 8º. **848**. f. **12**.

CAILLIN, *Saint, Bishop.* [For editions of the Boo Fenagh, sometimes attributed to Saint Caillin:] FENAGH, *Book of.*

CAILLIOT (AMÉDÉE) Concours pour la chaire de chim de toxicologie . . . Histoire et appréciation des pr de la chimie au dix-neuvième siècle. Thèse, *etc.* pp. *Strasbourg*, 1838. 4º. [*Collection générale des disserta de la Faculté de Médecine de Strasbourg.* sér. 2. tom. **738**

—— Essai chimique sur la térébenthine des sapins à redressée, *etc.* pp. 86. *Strasbourg*, 1830. 4º. [*Colle générale des dissertations de la Faculté de Médecin Strasbourg.* vol. 42.] **738**

AILLIOT (ÉMILE AMÉDÉE)

— Observations de méningo-périencéphalite chronique et primitive. Considérations sur cette affection, *etc.* pp. 52. *Strasbourg*, 1864. 4°. [*Collection générale des dissertations de la Faculté de Médecine de Strasbourg.* sér. 2. tom. 35.] **7381.*** e.

AILLIOT (EUGÈNE) Essai sur l'encéphaloïdes ou fongus médullaire, *etc.* pp. 56. pl. III. *Strasbourg*, 1823. 4°. [*Collection générale des dissertations de la Faculté de Médecine de Strasbourg.* vol. 31.] **7381.*** b.

AILLIOT (LOUIS) De la convalescence qui succède aux maladies fébriles, *etc.* pp. 32. *Strasbourg*, 1802. 4°. [*Collection générale des dissertations de l'École Spéciale de Médecine de Strasbourg.* vol. 2.] **7381.*** b.

AILLIOT (RENÉ) Essai sur l'anévrysme, présenté et soutenu à l'École de Médecine de Paris, *etc.* pp. 100. *Paris*, an VII [1799]. 8°. **1182.** b. **1.** (4.)

AILLOCIUS (NORBERTUS) *See* CAILLIEU (Norbert)

AILLOIS (ROGER)

— *See* SECONDAT (C. de) *Baron de Montesquieu.* Histoire véritable. Édition critique par R. Caillois. 1948. 8°. W.P. **2063/22.**

— Babel. Orgueil, confusion et ruine de la littérature. pp. 307. [*Paris*,] 1948. 8°. **11865.** cc. **29.**

— Circonstancielles, 1940–1945 . . . 2e édition. pp. 151. [*Paris*,] 1946. 8°. **12360.** df. **13.**

— La Communion des forts. Études sociologiques. pp. 181. *Marseille*, 1944. 8°. **8289.** de. **71.**

— L'Homme et le sacré. pp. xi. 146. *Paris*, 1939. 8°. [*Mythes et religions.*] W.P. **13335/3.**

— Les Impostures de la poésie. pp. 87. [*Paris*,] 1945. 8°. **11867.** e. **12.**

— Le Mythe et l'homme. pp. 222. *Paris*, 1938. 8°. **12359.** b. **22.**

— Poétique de St.-John Perse. pp. 212. *Paris*, 1954. 8°. **11871.** aa. **15.**

— Le Rocher de Sisyphe. pp. 179. [*Paris*,] 1946. 8°. **12359.** a. **51.**

— Vocabulaire esthétique. pp. 137. *Paris*, 1946. 8°. **11866.** a. **53.**

AILLOIS (ROLAND)

— *See* SPINOZA (B. de) [*Works.*] Œuvres complètes . . . Texte nouvellement traduit ou revu, présenté et annoté par R. Caillois [and others], *etc.* 1954. 8°. **12257.** e. **4.**

AILLOL (HENRI) *See* BOUCHES-DU-RHÔNE, *Department of the.—Conseil Général.* Les Bouches-du-Rhône. Encyclopédie départementale, *etc.* (tom. 12. Le Sol . . . Biogéographie. Par H. Caillol [and others].) 1932, *etc.* fol. **10167.** r. **1/12.**

— Catalogue des coléoptères de Provence . . . Extrait des Annales de la Société des Sciences naturelles de Provence, *etc.* 2 pt. *Marseille*, 1908, 13. 8°. **7296.** ccc. **19.**
Pt. 2 forms Mémoire no. 3 of the Société Linnéenne de Provence. The date on the wrapper of pt. 2 is 1913–1914.

AILLON (E. M. E.)

— Deux mots sur la nouvelle constitution. Par un employé. [The foreword signed: E. M. E. Caillon.] pp. 16. [*Paris*,] an VIII [1799]. 8°. R. **154.** (2.)

CAILLON (GUILLAUME SÉBASTIEN) *See* ARNAULD ( ) *Instituteur.* Liberté, Égalité, Justice. Arnauld . . . aux autorités constituées . . . Mémoire . . . Suivi d'une réponse à la dénonciation de Caillon. [1794.] 8°. R. **649.** (1.)

CAILLOT (A. C. EUGÈNE) Histoire de l'île Oparo ou Rapa. pp. 85. *Paris*, 1932. 8°. **10493.** ff. **30.**

—— Histoire de la Polynésie orientale. pp. 606. *Paris*, 1910. 8°. **10492.** gg. **4.**

—— Histoire des religions de l'archipel Paumotu, *etc.* pp. 144. *Paris*, 1932. 8°. **20003.** dd. **4.**

—— Mythes, légendes et traditions des Polynésiens. Textes polynésiens recueillis, publiés, traduits en français et commentés par A. C. E. Caillot. pp. 340. *Paris*, 1914. 8°. **12431.** t. **7.**

—— Les Polynésiens orientaux au contact de la civilisation, *etc.* pp. 291. pl. XCII. *Paris*, 1909. 8°. **10491.** g. **39.**

CAILLOT (ANTOINE)

—— *See* CREVIER (J. B. L.) Abrégé de l'Histoire des empereurs, de Crévier, suivant le plan de cet auteur; par Ant. C** [i.e. A. Caillot]. 1819. 12°. **9040.** bbb. **1.**

—— *See* DARES, *the Phrygian.* Histoire de la guerre de Troie, attribuée à Darès de Phrygie. (Traduite par A. Caillot.) 1813. 12°. [DICTYS, *of Crete. Histoire de la guerre de Troie, etc.*] **802.** d. **12.**

—— *See* PERIODICAL PUBLICATIONS.—*Paris.* Annales maç.·. dédiées à Son Altesse . . . le Prince Cambacérès . . . par Caillot. [1807, *etc.*] 18°. **4783.** b. **17.**

—— Beautés naturelles et historiques des îles, des montagnes, et des volcans . . . Avec six figures. pp. x. 420. *Paris*, 1822. 12°. **10027.** aa. **20.**

—— Ça ne va pas, ça n'ira pas: non, c'est le chat. [A political pamphlet.] Par l'auteur de la Lanterne magique de la rue Impériale, et de N'en parlons plus et parlons-en toujours [i.e. A. Caillot]. pp. 7. [1814.] 8°. *See* CHAT. **934.** c. **14.** (**14.**)

—— Dictionnaire portatif de littérature françoise, composé d'après les principes des littérateurs françois les plus célèbres, *etc.* pp. 411. *Paris*, 1810. 8°. **1091.** b. **18.**

—— Mémoires pour servir à l'histoire des mœurs et usages des Français . . . pendant le règne de Louis XVI . . . et jusqu'à nos jours. 2 tom. *Paris*, 1827. 8°. **1322.** f. **18.**

—— [Another copy of tom. 2.] **1322.** e. **26.**

—— Mes vingt ans de folies, d'amour et de bonheur; ou Mémoires d'un abbé petit-maître; où l'on trouve une esquisse des mœurs qui régnoient à Paris il y a vingt ans. Publiés par un de ses amis. [By Antoine Caillot.] 3 tom. 1807. 8°. *See* ANS. **1154.** c. **24.**

—— [Another edition.] tom. 1, 2. 1808. 12°. *See* ANS. **012548.** aa. **32.**

—— Morceaux choisis des lettres édifiantes et curieuses, écrites des missions étrangères . . . précédés de réflexions sur les missions et les missionnaires; et suivis . . . d'un coup-d'œil général sur les missions . . . Quatrième édition, corrigée, augmentée, et ornée de huit gravures. 2 tom. *Paris*, 1823. 12°. **4766.** b. **10.**

—— N'en parlons plus et parlons-en toujours. [A political pamphlet.] Par l'auteur de la Lanterne magique de la rue Impériale [i.e. A. Caillot]. pp. 8. [1814.] 8°. *See* NE. **934.** c. **14.** (**15.**)

CAILLOT (Antoine)

—— Nouveau dictionnaire proverbial, satirique et burlesque, *etc.* pp. x. 538. *Paris*, 1826. 12°. **12304. d. 22.**

—— Plus de printemps, plus de violettes: vivent les lis et les œillets blancs. [Signed: Ant. C**, i.e. A. Caillot.] pp. 4. [1815.] 8°. *See* C** (Ant.) R. **130. (16.)**

—— Le Rollin de la jeunesse; ou morceaux choisis des Histoires ancienne et romaine, précédés d'un abrégé de la vie de Rollin . . . Deuxième édition, revue et augmentée, *etc.* [By A. Caillot. With plates.] 2 tom. 1816. 12°. *See* Rollin (Charles) **9005. aaa. 23.**

—— Tableau des exercices et de l'enseignement en usage dans un pensionnat de jeunes demoiselles dirigé par une sage institutrice . . . Avec figures. 2 tom. *Paris*, 1816. 12°. **8305. aa. 14.**

—— Le Thermomètre, ou Chaud et froid; par l'auteur de la Lanterne magique de la rue Impériale [i.e. A. Caillot], *etc.* [A political pamphlet.] pp. 8. [1814.] 8°. *See* Thermomètre. **8052. l. 2. (15.)**

—— Vie de Bossuet, évêque de Meaux, *etc.* pp. x. 380. *Paris*, 1825. 12°. **4864. bb. 8.**

—— Voyage autour de ma bibliothèque, roman bibliographique, où les gens du monde et les dames peuvent apprendre à former une bibliothèque de bons ouvrages, dans quelque genre que ce soit. 3 tom. *Paris*, 1809. 12°. **271. b. 24–26.**

CAILLOT (Cathérine) *See* Cailleau.

CAILLOT (Ernest) *See* Desroziers (C.) and Caillot (E.) Commentaire des racines grecques. 1865. 12°. **12924. aaa. 48. (5.)**

—— Les Prussiens à Chartres, 21 octobre 1870—16 mars 1871. pp. 119. *Chartres*, 1871. 8°. **9078. cc. 22.**

CAILLOT (Jules Séverin) Contes après les contes. pp. v. 184. *Paris*, [1919.] 8°. **012547. aa. 36.**

CAILLOT (Napoléon) Dissertation sur l'hystérie; thèse, *etc.* pp. 27. *Paris*, 1833. 4°. **1184. f. 2. (22.)**

CAILLOT DE MONTUREUX (H. E.) Du rhumatisme articulaire aigu. pp. 30. *Paris*, 1852. 4°. [*Collection des thèses soutenues à la Faculté de Médecine de Paris.* An 1852. tom. 3.] **7372. e. 7.**

CAILLOT-DUVAL ( ) *pseud.* [i.e. *Count* Alphonse Toussaint Joseph André Marie Marseille de Fortia de Piles and Pierre Marie Louis de Boisgelin de Kerdu.] *See* Fortia de Piles (A. T. J. A. M. M. de) *Count*, and Boisgelin de Kerdu (P. M. L. de)

CAILLOU (Alan) *pseud.* [i.e. Alan Lyle-Smythe.]

—— Rogue's Gambit. pp. vii. 242. *Peter Davies: London*, 1955. 8°. NNN. **7175.**

—— The World is Six Feet Square. [An account of the author's experiences after his capture in North Africa in 1943.] pp. 214. *Peter Davies: London*, 1954. 8°. **10864. aa. 33.**

CAILLOUÉ (Denis) *See* Charles i., *King of Great Britain and Ireland.* [*Eikon Basilike.*] Εἰκων βασιλικη. Ou portrait roial, *etc.* [Translated by D. Cailloué. The translator's dedication prefixed to the first part signed: Φιλαναξ; that prefixed to the second part signed: D. C.] 1649. 12°. E. **1255.**

CAILLOUÉ (Denis)

—— *See* Charles i., *King of Great Britain and Irelan* [*Eikon Basilike.*] Εἰκων βασιλικη. Le Portrait du Ro de la Grand' Bretagne, *etc.* [Translated by D. Caillou Revised and altered by J. Porrée.] 1649. 12°. **8122. a. 2**

—— —— 1649. 12°. **8135. a.**

—— —— 1649. 4°. **293. k. 2**

—— *See* Charles ii., *King of Great Britain and Irelan* [*Biography.—ii.*] Boscobel, ou Abrégé de ce qui s'est pass dans la retraite memorable de Sa Majesté Britanniq après la bataille d'Worcester, *etc.* [Translated by I Cailloué.] 1676. 12°. **599. c. 2**

—— *See* Grebner (P.) Prediction, où se voit comme le Ro Charles ii. . . . doit estre remis aux royaumes d'Angl terre, Escosse & Irlande, *etc.* [The editor's dedicatio signed: D. C., i.e. D. Cailloué.] 1650. 16°. **600. a. 2**

—— Métamorphose des Isles Fortunées. A la reyne douairiè de la Grande Bretagne. Ode. [The dedicatory lett signed: D. C., i.e. D. Cailloué.] pp. 56. 1649. 12 [*Charles i., King of Great Britain and Ireland.* Εἰκω βασιλικη. *Ou portrait roial, etc.*] *See* C., D. E. **125**

CAILLOUX (Pousse) *pseud.* *See* Pousse Cailloux.

CAILLOUX-POUGET (François René) *Baro* Souvenirs de guerre du général baron Pouget. Publiés pa Mme de Boisdeffre, née Pouget. pp. vii. 323. *Pari* 1895. 12°. **9080. e. 1**

—— *See* Grabinski (G.) *Count.* Souvenirs de guerre d général baron Pouget, *etc.* [A review.] [1895 ?] 8 **011852. i. 17. (2**

CAILLY. Cailly en Normandie; son histoire dès les siècl les plus reculés, la liste de ses anciens seigneurs, les chart et donations à diverses abbayes. [By A. Lemarchan Edited by William Sealy.] pp. 71. *Rouen London & Aylesbury* printed, 1895. 8°. **10174. h. 2**

—— [Another issue.] [With extracts relating to the famil of Cailly from Burke's "Dormant and Extinct Peerages and other works.] pp. 88. 1896. 8°. **10174. h. 22. (1**

CAILLY, *Family of.* *See* Cailly. Cailly en Normandie, *et* [With extracts relating to the family of Cailly fro Burke's "Dormant and Extinct Peerages" and oth works.] 1896. 8°. **10174. h. 22. (1**

—— *See* Sealy (William) Notes sur Cailli . . . sur s seigneurs et leurs descendants en Angleterre, *etc.* 1891. 8 **9915. de. 2**

CAILLY ( ) *See* also Ulliac, *pseud.* [i.e. — Cailly

—— Griefs et plaintes des femmes mal mariées. [By — Cailly.] pp. 42. [1789.] 8°. *See* Griefs. F. **389. (9**

CAILLY (Adrien Guillaume) Contes en vers, chansons e pièces fugitives. pp. 288. *Paris*, an ix [1800]. 12°. **011483. de. 4**

CAILLY (Charles) Corps législatif. Conseil des Ancien Opinion . . . sur la résolution du 24 prairial, relative au transactions passées pendant la dépréciation du papie monnoie. Séance du 4 thermidor an 6. pp. 4. *Pari* an 6 [1798]. 8°. F.R. **200. (31**

—— Corps législatif. Conseil des Anciens. Opinion . . . sur la résolution relative au droit de successibilité de l République sur les biens des émigrés, depuis la loi d 9 floréal an 3, *etc.* pp. 11. *Paris*, an 7 [1799]. 8°. F. **738. (17.**

CAILLY (Charles)

—— Corps législatif. Conseil des Anciens. Rapport fait . . . au nom d'une commission spéciale, sur la résolution du premier floréal dernier, relative à l'organisation du notariat . . . Séance du 12 prairial an 7. pp. 46. [*Paris*,] an 7 [1799]. 8°. **F.R. 190. (16.)**

—— Un Mot sur le milliard décrété pour les défendeurs de la patrie. pp. 16. [*Paris*, 1797.] 8°. **F. 207. (8.)**

CAILLY (Jacques de) Poësies du chevalier d'Aceilly (de Cailly). *See* Le Coigneaux de Bachaumont (F.) and Lhuillier-Chapelle (C. E.) Voyage de Messieurs Bachaumont et La Chapelle, *etc.* 1708. 8°. **1065. b. 7.**

—— [Another edition.] *See* Recueil. Recueil de pièces choisies, *etc.* pt. 1. 1714. 8°. **12237. aaa. 16.**

—— [Another edition.] *See* Lhuillier-Chapelle (C. E.) and Le Coigneux de Bachaumont (F.) Voyage de Messieurs Chapelle et Bachaumont. 1742. 12°. **12314. aa. 30.**

—— [Another edition.] *See* La Suze (H. de) *Countess.* Recueil de pièces galantes, *etc.* tom. 5. 1748. 8°. **12234. cccc. 18.**

—— Epigrammes. *See* Bibliothèque. Bibliothèque poëtique, *etc.* tom. 2. 1745. 4°. **84. h. 2.**

—— Diverses petites poésies du chevalier d'Aceilly (J. de Cailly). pp. xv. cxlvi. *Paris*, 1825. 16°. [*Collection de petits classiques françois.*] **831. a. 7.**

CAIMARY (Jaime Escalas) *See* Escalas Caimary (J.)

CAIMBEAL (Aonghas) *See* Campbell (Angus) *of Ness, Lewis.*

CAIMBEAL (Imhear) *See* Orme (William) *Congregational Minister.* Leabhar Cheist mu Shuidheachadh agus Orduighean Rioghachd Chriosd . . . Air eadar-theangachadh . . . gu Gaelic, le I. Caimbeal. 1825. 12°. **3505. a. 43.**

CAIMBEUL (Do'nall) Smuaintean Cudthromacha, mu Bhas agus fhulangas ar Slanui'-fhir . . . Air an tiundadh gu Gailig Albannuich, le D. Macphairlain . . . 'An dara uair. pp. vi. 144. *D. Frier: Peairt*, 1800. 12°. **4226. aaa. 19.**

CAIMBEUL (Iain Latharna) *See* Campbell (John Lorne)

CAIMBEUL (Mairearad) Laoidhean Spioradail, air an Cnuasachadh. pp. 83. *Mundell, Doig & Stevenson: Dun-Eidin*, 1810. 12°. **4411. aa. 7.**

CAIMBEUL (Seonaidh) Orain Ghaidhlig le Seonaidh Caimbeul . . . Ar an toirt sìos le Iain Mac Aonghuis. Air an deasachadh le Iain Latharna Caimbeul. pp. xvii. 130. *I. B. Mac Aoidh & a Ch.: Dun Pharlain*, 1936. 8°. **875. k. 74.**

CAIMI (Antonio) L'Accademia di belle arti in Milano. Sua origine, suo incremento e suo stato attuale. pp. 40. 1873. 8°. *See* Milan.—*Reale Accademia delle Belle Arti.* **7807. k. 21.**

—— Cenno storico sul Museo patrio di archeologia in Milano. pp. 27. *Milano*, 1873. 8°. **7704. g. 5. (3.)**

—— Delle arti del disegno, e degli artisti nelle provincie di Lombardia, dal 1777 al 1862. Memoria, *etc.* pp. vi. 231. *Milano*, 1862. 8°. **7805. bb. 3.**

—— La Pinacoteca della R. Accademia di belle arti di Milano. pp. 21. *Milano*, 1873. 8°. **7704. g. 5. (4.)**

CAIMI (Aristide) Giornale delle operazioni di guerra eseguite dalla legione di guardia nazionale mobile a difesa dello Stelvio e Tonale nella campagna del 1866. [With a map.] pp. 54. *Torino*, 1868. 8°. **9165. c. 37.**

CAIMI (Aristide)

—— Pier Luigi Farnese. Dramma in cinque atti. pp. 86. *Milano*, 1848. 8°. **1342. l. 22.**

CAIMI (Bernardino) Il Beato Bernardino Caimi, fondatore del Santuario di Varallo. Documenti e lettere inedite. [Edited by Emilio Motta.] (Bibliografia del Santuario di Varallo.) pp. 30. *Milano*, 1891. 8°. **010910. d. 1. (3.)**

CAIMI (Carlo) Nuovo Galateo. Consigli di un nonno a' suoi nipoti. (Seconda edizione.) pp. 137. *Milano*, 1869. 8°. **8409. aaa. 2.**

CAIMI (Gaetano) Notizie storiche del grand' ospitale di Milano. Prospetto cronologico dei ritratti de' suoi benefattori, coll'eterico degli autori, *etc.* 2 pt. *Milano*, 1857. 8°. **10132. h. 3.**
The half-title reads : "Guida storico-artistica dell'Ospitale Maggiore di Milano."

CAIMI (Pietro) Cenni sulla importanza e coltura dei boschi, con norme di legislazione e amministrazione forestale. pp. xxi. 140. *Milano*, 1857. 8°. **7030. e. 8.**

CAIMI (Pio)

—— Le Aziende municipalizzate di Lugano. Genesi, sviluppo, finalità. Tesi di laurea, *etc.* pp. 134. *Lugano*, 1954. 8°. **08230. eee. 52.**

CAIMO (Giacomo) *See* Caimo (P.) Pompeij Caimi . . . De nobilitate . . . liber. [Edited by G. Caimo.] 1634. 8°. **1088. c. 17. (2.)**

—— *See* Caimo (P.) Dialogo delle tre vite riputate migliori, *etc.* [Edited by G. Caimo.] 1640. 4°. **716. b. 14.**

CAIMO (Joannes Robertus Gislenus) *Bishop of Bruges. See* Flanders.—*Capuchins.* Applausus panegyrocongratulatorius et anagrammatice panegyricus . . . a Provinciæ Flandro-Belgicæ Capucinis exhibitus . . . Domino Joanni Roberto Gisleno Caïmo xvi. Brugensium episcopo . . . cathedram Brugensem adeunti die 30. Junii 1754. [1754.] fol. **1482. f. 1. (2.)**

CAIMO (Norberto) Della vita del venerabile Lupo d'Olmedo . . . libri quattro, *etc.* pp. xxxiv. 274. *Bologna*, 1754. 8°. **12410. aaa. 28. (2.)**

—— Della vita di Santa Paola . . . fondatrice dell'ordine Girolamino, libri quattro scritti da un monaco del medesimo ordine della congregazione d'Italia [i.e. N. Caimo], *etc.* pp. xxiv. 149. 1752. 8°. *See* Paula, *Saint.* **4829. bb. 3.**

—— Lettere [signed: N. N.] d'un vago italiano, ad un suo amico. [By N. Caimo.] tom. 1, 2. [1761 ?] 8°. *See* N., N. **10160. bb. 22.**

—— Voyage d'Espagne, fait en l'année 1755 : avec des notes historiques, géographiques & critiques ; et une table raisonnée des tableaux . . . de Madrid, de l'Escurial . . . Traduit de l'italien ; par le P. De Livoy. (Lettere d'un vago italiano.) [By N. Caimo. Abridged from tom. 1 and 2.] 2 pt. 1772. 12°. *See* Italian. **281. c. 9.**

—— Briefe eines Italiäners über eine im Jahre 1755 angestellte Reise nach Spanien . . . Aus der französischen Uebersetzung des P. Livoy [i.e. his abridged translation of tom. 1 and 2 of N. Caimo's "Lettere d'un vago italiano"]. pp. 276. 1774. 8°. *See* Italian. **10160. c. 12.**

—— Vita del venerabile Onofrio Orobuoni, *etc.* [With a portrait.] pp. xxiv. 159. *Milano*, 1760. 8°. **4864. c. 19.**

CAIMO (Pompeo) De callido innato libri tres, *etc.* pp. 455. *Apud H. Piutum: Venetiis*, 1626. 4°. **549. e. 12.**

CAIMO (POMPEO)

—— De febrium putridarum indicationibus iuxta Galeni methodum colligendis, & adimplendis, libri duo. pp. 265. *Apud P. P. Tozium: Patauij*, 1628. 4°. **543. d. 19.**

—— [Another copy.] **1166. e. 19. (1.)**

—— Pompeij Caimi . . . De nobilitate . . . liber. [Edited by Giacomo Caimo.] pp. 95. *Typis N. Schiratti: Vtini*, 1634. 8°. **1088. c. 17. (2.)**

—— Dialogo delle tre vite riputate migliori, delitiosa, ambitiosa, studiosa, *etc.* [Edited by Giacomo Caimo.] pp. 170. *Creuellari: Padoua*, 1640. 4°. **716. b. 14.**

—— Parallelo politico delle republiche antiche, e moderne, in cui coll'essame de' veri fondamenti de' gouerni ciuili, si antepongono li moderni a gli antichi, e la forma della Repub. Veneta, a qualunque altra forma delle republiche antiche. pp. 156. *P. P. Tozzi: Padoua*, 1627. 4°. **232. h. 31.**

—— [Another edition.] In questa seconda impressione di varie considerationi accresciuto dall'autore. pp. 246. *Tozzi: Padoua*, 1627. 8°. **522. c. 14.**

CAIMPENTA (UGO) L'Impero abissino. [With plates.] pp. 319. *Milano*, 1935. 8°. **010094. de. 73.**

—— L'Impero italiano d'Etiopia. [With plates.] pp. 331. *Milano*, 1936. 8°. **010093. de. 49.**

—— L'Italia in Africa. Dall'Impero Romano ad oggi, *etc.* pp. 381. pl. XXXII. *Milano*, 1937. 8°. **9060. i. 2.**

—— Lo Spionaggio inglese—Intelligence Service—dalle origini ai tempi nostri. pp. 246. *Milano*, 1936. 8°. **09505. g. 8.**

CAIMUS (JACOBUS) *See* CAIMO (Giacomo)

CAIMUS (POMPEIUS) *See* CAIMO (Pompeo)

CAIN. *See* APTOWITZER (V.) Kain und Abel in der Agada, den Apokryphen, hellenistischen, christlichen und muhammedanischen Literatur. 1922. 8°. **04504. g. 28.**

—— *See* BOEKLEN (E. A.) Adam und Qain. Im Lichte der vergleichenden Mythenforschung. 1907. 8°. [*Mythologische Bibliothek.* Bd. 1. Hft. 2, 3.] **Ac. 5387. d.**

—— *See* CAMILLE (J. E. de) Caïn père de la franc-maçonnerie. [1875 ?] 8°. **4783. aaa. 5.**

—— Another Cain. A poem. [A reply to Lord Byron's "Cain."] pp. 15. *Hatchard & Son: London*, 1822. 8°. **T. 1063. (6.)**

—— Cain; a mystery. By the author of Don Juan [i.e. Lord Byron]. pp. 93. *Printed for the Booksellers: London*, 1822. 12°. **11779. a. 22.**

—— Cain and Patsy, the Gospel preached to the poor. A story of slave life. pp. 47. *Book Society: London*, [1863.] 16°. **4415. a. 23.**

—— Cain the Wanderer: a Vision of Heaven: Darkness: and other poems. By —— [i.e. John Edmund Reade]. pp. 330. *Whittaker, Treacher & Co.: London*, 1829. 8°. **841. h. 27.**

—— Caines Bloudy Race known by their fruits, *etc.* [The address to the reader signed: F. H., i.e. Francis Howgill ?] 1657. 4°. *See* H., F. **4152. f. 22. (9.)**

—— Cain's Lamentations over Abel. In six books. pp. 241. *G. A. Stephens: Portsea*, [1810 ?] 12°. **11522. cc. 1. (4.)**

—— Concerning this present Cain in his generation, the unbelieving and wicked Heathen, *etc.* [A rhapsodical prophesy. By Ludwig Friedrich Gifftheyl.] pp. 8. *Printed by I. L.: London*, 1648. 4°. **E. 435. (2.)**
A MS. note by G. Thomason on the titlepage reads, "Writen by Henry Guifthaile ye German profitt of ye tribe of Juda."

CAIN.

—— The Death of Cain. [By William Henry Hall.] *Se* MISCELLANY. The Sacred Miscellany, *etc.* 1800. 8°. **4400. b.**

—— The Death of Cain [by W. H. Hall], intended as companion to the Death of Abel [of S. Gessner]. Carefull corrected and abridged by G. Stephens. pp. 76. *G. A. Stephens: Portsea*, [1810 ?] 12°. **11522. cc. 1. (2**

—— The Death of Cain; in five books. To which is prefixe an introductory view of the principal events in the histo of man from the Creation until the death of Abel. [B W. H. Hall.] *In:* GESSNER (S.) The Death of Abe *etc.* pt. 1. pp. 133–234. 1821. 8°. **12557. bb. 2**

CÁIN DOMNAIG. *See* PRIEBSCH (R.) Quelle und Abfa sungszeit der Sonntagsepistel in der irischen "Cái Domnaig," *etc.* 1907. 8°. **11852. s. 18. (8**

CAIN (ARTHUR JAMES)

—— Animal Species and their Evolution. pp. 190. *Hutchinson's University Library: London*, 1954. 8 [*Hutchinson's University Library.*] **W.P. 1413/10**

—— A Revision of Trichoglossus Haematodus and of t Australian Platycercine Parrots. *In:* The Ibis. vol. 9 no. 3. pp. 432–479. 1955. 8°. **P.P. 203**

—— Subdivisions of the Genus Ptilinopos—Aves, Columba *etc.* [With plates.] *London*, 1954. 8°. [*Bulletin of t British Museum (Natural History). Zoology.* vol. no. 8.] **Ac. 1325. a. (**

CAIN (CHARLES WILLIAM) and **VOADEN** (DENYS JOAN)

—— Military Aircraft of the U.S.S.R. . . . With drawin and silhouettes by Björn Karlström. pp. 72. *Herbert Jenkins: London*, 1952. 8°. **08773. de. 3**

CAIN (DANIEL J.) *See* PERIODICAL PUBLICATIONS.—*Charleston, South Carolina.* The Southern Journal Medicine, *etc.* (The Charleston Medical Journal, *et* vol. 5–9 edited by D. J. Cain and F. Peyre Porcher vol. 10 edited by C. Happoldt . . . assisted by D. Cain, *etc.*) 1846, *etc.* 8°. **P.P. 289**

CAIN (EDME) Considérations physiologiques et path logiques sur la digestion, *etc.* [A thesis.] pp. 55. *Pari* 1809. 4°. **1182. h. 4. (24**

CAIN (ERNEST EDMUND)

—— Cyclone! Being an illustrated offici record of the hurricane and tidal wave which destroyed th city of Belize, British Honduras on the . . . 10th Se tember 1931 . . . With some personal experience [With plates.] pp. xv. 135. *A. H. Stockwell: Londo* [1933.] 8°. **10482. aa. 3**

CAIN (FRANCIS) Execution. An account of the execution . . . Frances Cain and George Laidlaw at Glasgow on . . the 29th Oct. 1823. for housebreaking & theft . . . Fro the Edinburgh Star. *B. Brown: [Edinburg* 1823.] *s. sh.* fol. **1888. c. 10. (39**

CAIN (GEORGES JULES AUGUSTE) *See* BALZAC (H. d [*Single Works.*] La Cousine Bette. Dix compositions p G. Caïn, *etc.* 1888. 8°. **012547. g.**

—— *See* BOURNAND (F.) L'Amour sous la Révolution . . Notices et documents historiques de J. Claretie . . . G. Cain. 1909. 8°. **09225. f. 2**

—— *See* CALLET (A.) L'Agonie du vieux Paris. Préface G. Cain, *etc.* 1911. 8°. **010171. h. 4**

CAIN (Georges Jules Auguste)

—— *See* Leblanc (Henri) *Collector.* Collection Henri Leblanc . . . La Grande Guerre . . . Préface de G. Cain. 1916, *etc.* 8°. **11916. e. 1.**

—— *See* Paris.—*Musée Carnavalet.* Guide explicatif du Musée Carnavalet, par MM. C. Sellier et P. Dorbec, sous la direction de M. G. Cain. 1903. 8°. **7958. aaa. 33.**

—— *See* Silvestre (P. A.) Floréal. Illustrations de G. Cain, *etc.* [1891.] 4°. **1873. a. 4.**

—— A travers Paris. Ouvrage orné de 148 illustrations et de 16 plans, *etc.* pp. 424. *Paris,* [1909.] 8°. **10169. ee. 12.**

—— Anciens théâtres de Paris. Le Boulevard du Temple. Les théâtres du boulevard, *etc.* pp. xii. 390. *Paris,* 1906. 12°. **011795. aaa. 6.**

—— Quatrième mille. pp. xii. 390. *Paris,* 1920. 12°. **011795. c. 30.**

—— Coins de Paris. Préface de Victorien Sardou . . . Avec 100 illustrations documentaires. pp. 335. *Paris,* [1905.] 8°. **10169. d. 41.**

—— Nooks & Corners of Old Paris . . . With a preface by Victorien Sardou. (Translation by Frederick Lawton.) With over a hundred illustrations. pp. 326. *E. Grant Richards: London,* 1907. 4°. **10172. f. 29.**

—— Environs de Paris. [With illustrations and plans.] 2 sér. *Paris,* [1911, 13.] 8°. **010169. f. 20.**

—— Le Long des rues. Ouvrage orné de 124 illustrations et de plans, *etc.* pp. 382. *Paris,* [1912.] 8°. **010169. ee. 12.**

—— Nouvelles promenades dans Paris. Ouvrage orné de 135 illustrations et de 20 plans, *etc.* (Dixième mille.) pp. 414. *Paris,* [1910.] 8°. **010169. ee. 10.**

—— Paris. Les anciens quartiers . . . Publié sous la direction artistique de M. G. Cain. [Plates with prefaces by various writers.] 11 vol. *Paris,* [1902–08.] *obl.* 8°. **10174. dg. 7.**

—— Les Pierres de Paris. Ouvrage orné de 133 illustrations et de 6 plans, *etc.* pp. 402. *Paris,* [1910.] 8°. **010168. f. 21.**

—— [Les Pierres de Paris.] The Byways of Paris . . . With one hundred and thirty-three illustrations and six . . . maps and plans. Translated by Louise Seymour Houghton. pp. xiv. 315. *Duffield & Co.: New York,* 1912. 8°. **10174. c. 21.**

—— La Place Vendôme. Précédé d'une notice de Frédéric Masson. [With illustrations.] pp. xxviii. 129. 10. *Paris,* 1908. 4°. **10171. i. 12.**

—— Promenades dans Paris. Ouvrage orné de 107 illustrations et de 18 plans, *etc.* (Quatorzième mille.) pp. 404. *Paris,* [1910.] 8°. **010169. ee. 9.**

—— Walks in Paris . . . Translated by Alfred Allinson . . . With . . . illustrations and plans. pp. xi. 334. *Methuen & Co.: London,* 1909. 8°. **010168. h. 52.**

—— Tableaux de Paris. Ouvrage orné de 96 illustrations et de 17 plans, *etc.* pp. 345. *Paris,* [1920.] 8°. **010169. ee. 37.**

CAIN (H. Thomas)

—— Petroglyphs of Central Washington. [With illustrations.] pp. ix. 57. *University of Washington Press: Seattle,* 1950. 8°. **10413. k. 43.**

CAIN (Henri) *See* Claretie (J.) and Cain (H.) La Navarraise, *etc.* 1894. 8°. **11740. eee. 2. (11.)**

—— —— 1895. 12°. **11740. d. 16. (4.)**

—— —— 1899. 12°. **11740. eee. 22. (7.)**

—— —— 1904. 8°. **11735. f. 34. (1.)**

—— *See* Croisset (F. de) *pseud.*, and Cain (H.) Chérubin, *etc.* 1905. 8°. **11741. b. 33.**

—— *See* Daudet (E.) and Cain (H.) La Citoyenne Cotillon, *etc.* 1904. 8°. **11737. c. 10.**

—— *See* Ferrare (H.) and Cain (H.) La Danseuse de Pompéi, *etc.* 1912. 8°. **906. i. 11. (5.)**

—— *See* Kufferath (M.) and Cain (H.) Obéron, *etc.* 1911. 8°. **11735. bb. 29. (2.)**

—— *See* Le Lorrain (J.) Don Quichotte. Comédie lyrique . . . Poème de H. Cain d'après la comédie héroïque de Le Lorrain [i.e. " Le Chevalier de la longue figure "]. [1910.] 8°. **11736. d. 25. (4.)**

—— *See* Le Lorrain (J.) Don Quixote . . . Written by H. Cain after Le Lorrain [i.e. after his play " Le Chevalier de la longue figure "], *etc.* [1911.] 8°. **11735. dd. 3.**

—— *See* Lemonnier (C.) and Cain (H.) Cachaprès, *etc.* [1914.] 8°. **11735. ccc. 33. (6.)**

—— *See* Lenôtre (G.) *pseud.*, and Cain (H.) Les Grognards, *etc.* 1921. fol. [*La Petite Illustration théâtrale.* Nouvelle série. no. 37.] **P.P. 4283. m. (2.)**

—— *See* Parodi (D. A.) Roma. Opéra tragique . . . de H. Cain, d'après Rome vaincue, d'Alexandre Parodi. [1912.] 12°. **11736. bbb. 39. (4.)**

—— *See* Richepin (J.) and Cain (H.) La Belle au bois dormant, *etc.* 1908. fol. [*L'Illustration théâtrale.* no. 79.] **P.P. 4283. m. (2.)**

—— —— 1908. 8°. **11737. ee. 45.**

—— *See* Richepin (J.) and Cain (H.) La Glu. Drame musical, *etc.* 1910. 8°. **11735. bb. 28. (4.)**

—— *See* Rostand (E.) Cyrano de Bergerac. Comédie lyrique . . . Adaptation de H. Cain, *etc.* 1936. 8°. **11740. k. 24.**

—— *See* Sardou (V.) Gismonda, *etc.* [Adapted by H. Cain and L. Payen.] [1919.] 12°. **11735. k. 73.**

—— *See* Silvestre (P. A.) and Cain (H.) Le Chevalier d'Éon, *etc.* 1908. 8°. **11736. bbb. 38. (2.)**

—— Cendrillon. Conte de fées en quatre actes et six tableaux d'après Perrault, *etc.* [In verse.] pp. 57. *Paris,* 1899. 18°. **11740. eee. 28. (1.)**

—— Cendrillon—Cinderella . . . English version by Henry Grafton Chapman. *Fr. & Eng.* pp. 46. *New York,* [1911.] 8°. [*G. Schirmer's Collection of Opera-Librettos.*] **7896. p. 1/4.**

—— La Flamenca. Drame musical en quatre actes, *etc.* [By H. Cain and Eugène and Édouard Adenis.] pp. 95. *Paris,* 1903. 8°. **11739. e. 65.**

—— Marcella. Idillio moderno in tre episodi. Di Henry Cain, Édouard Adenis e Lorenzo Stecchetti, *etc.* pp. 47. *Milano,* [1903.] 8°. **11714. ccc. 10.**

—— Quatre-vingt-treize! Épopée lyrique en 4 actes et 5 tableaux d'après l'œuvre de Victor Hugo, *etc.* pp. 54. *Paris,* [1936.] 8°. **20012. ee. 64.**

CAIN (Henri)

—— Quo Vadis? From the book of Henryk Sienkiewicz. Translated by B. Kozakiewicz and L. de Janasz. [An opera, adapted by H. Cain.] English libretto by A. St. John Brenon, *etc.* pp. 55. [1911.] 8°. *See* Sienkiewicz (H.) **906.** i. **16.** **(6.)**

—— La Vivandière. Opéra-comique en trois actes, *etc.* pp. 65. *Paris*, 1895. 18°. **11740.** de. **21.** **(1.)**

CAIN (Henri) and **BERNÈDE** (Arthur)

—— Sapho, pièce lyrique en cinq actes d'après le roman de Alphonse Daudet, *etc.* pp. 48. *Paris*, 1897. 8°. **11740.** e. **44.** **(3.)**

—— [Another edition.] pp. 56. *Paris*, [1908.] 18°. **11736.** bbb. **38.** **(1.)**

CAIN (Henri) and **GASTAMBIDE** (Raoul)

—— Graziella. Poème romantique en quatre actes et cinq tableaux, d'après le roman de Lamartine, *etc.* pp. 68. *Paris*, [1913.] 8°. **11735.** ccc. **15.** **(6.)**

CAIN (Henri) and **PAYEN** (Louis)

—— L'Aigle. Épopée lyrique en 3 parties et 10 tableaux, *etc.* pp. 82. *Paris*, 1912. 8°. **11737.** d. **35.** **(4.)**

—— Carmosine. Conte romanesque en quatre actes, d'après Boccace & Musset [i.e. his comedy "Carmosine"], *etc.* pp. 85. *Paris*, [1913.] 12°. **11735.** bbb. **28.** **(2.)**

CAIN (Henri) and **SOLVAY** (Lucien)

—— Thyl Uylenspiegel. Drame lyrique en trois actes et quatre tableaux, *etc.* pp. 77. *Paris*, 1899. 18°. **11739.** de. **45.** **(2.)**

—— Nouvelle version, *etc.* pp. 55. *Paris*, [1920.] 8°. **11735.** de. **20.**

CAIN (Henry) *Captain.* *See* Hall (Thomas) *of Timaru, N.Z.* Report of the Trial of Thomas Hall, charged with the wilful murder of Captain Cain, *etc.* 1887. 8°. **6495.** e. **23.**

CAIN (Henry) *Dramatist.* *See* Cain (Henri)

CAIN (Henry Edney Conrad) *See* Metzgen (M. S.) and Cain (H. E. C.) The Handbook of British Honduras, *etc.* 1925. 8°. **P.P. 2587.** de.

—— When the Angel says: "Write!" [Verses.] pp. 69. *Arthur H. Stockwell: Ilfracombe*, 1948. 8°. **11658.** aaa. **215.**

CAIN (Henry Edward)

—— James Clarence Mangan and the Poe-Mangan Question. A dissertation, *etc.* pp. xiii. 93. *J. H. Furst Co.: Washington*, 1929. 8°. **11871.** ee. **12.**

CAIN (James Mallahan)

—— Three of a Kind. (Career in C Major.—The Embezzler.—Double Indemnity.) pp. 288. *Robert Hale: London*, [1945.] 8°. **NN. 35717.**

—— Three of Hearts. (Love's Lovely Counterfeit.—Past all Dishonour.—The Butterfly.) pp. 405. *Robert Hale: London*, 1949. 8°. **12728.** e. **26.**

—— Double Indemnity and The Embezzler. pp. 218. *Pocket Books: London*, 1950. 8°. **12707.** b. **45.**

—— Galatea. pp. 189. *Robert Hale: London*, 1954. 8°. **12733.** a. **1.**

CAIN (James Mallahan)

—— Jealous Woman. pp. 224. *Robert Hale: London*, 1955. 8°. NNN. **6156.**

—— Mildred Pierce. [A novel.] pp. 264. *Robert Hale: London*, 1943. 8°. **12728.** a. **13.**

—— Mildred Pierce. pp. 323. *Pocket Books (G. B.): London*, 1950. 8°. **12703.** bbb. **41.**

—— The Moth. pp. 356. *Robert Hale: London; Sydney* printed, [1950.] 8°. NNN. **709.**

—— Our Government. pp. x. 241. *A. A. Knopf: New York*, 1930. 8°. **08176.** aa. **26.**

—— The Postman always Rings Twice. pp. 192. *Jonathan Cape: London*, 1934. 8°. **12601.** r. **19.**

—— The Postman Always Rings Twice. pp. 96. *Jonathan Cape: London*, 1947. 8°. [*Guild Books.* no. 233.] W.P. **10101/17.**

—— The Postman always rings twice. pp. 122. *Penguin Books: Harmondsworth*, 1952. 8°. [*Penguin Books.* no. 874.] **12208.** a. **1/874.**

—— The Root of his Evil. pp. 190. *Robert Hale: London*, 1954. 8°. NNN. **5498.**

—— Serenade. pp. 314. *A. A. Knopf: New York*, 1937. 8°. **12716.** bbb. **22.**

—— [Another edition.] pp. 286. *Jonathan Cape: London*, 1938. 8°. **12717.** b. **15.**

—— Serenade. pp. 206. *Penguin Books: London*, 1953. 8°. [*Penguin Books.* no. 902.] **12208.** a. **1/902.**

CAIN (John) *See* Bible.—*Luke.* [*Gondi.—Koi dialect.*] The Gospel of Luke, *etc.* [Translated by F. Haig, revised by J. Cain.] 1889. 32°. **14178.** h. **37.**

—— The Koi. A southern tribe of the Gonds. pp. 16. [1880?] 8°. **10058.** a. **35.** **(3.)**

CAIN (John Cannell) *See* Roscoe (*Right Hon. Sir* Henry E.) and Schorlemmer (C.) A Treatise on Chemistry . . . New edition completely revised by Sir H. E. Roscoe, assisted by Dr. J. C. Cain, *etc.* 1911, *etc.* 8°. **8901.** bbb. **18.**

—— *See* Roscoe (*Right Hon. Sir* H. E.) and Schorlemmer (C.) A Treatise on Chemistry . . . Revised by Dr. J. C. Cain, *etc.* 1920, *etc.* 8°. **8904.e.30.**

—— The Chemistry of the Diazo-Compounds. pp. x. 172. *Edward Arnold: London*, 1908. 8°. **8904.** bb. **16.**

—— The Chemistry and Technology of the Diazo-Compounds . . . Second edition. pp. xi. 199. *Edward Arnold: London*, 1920. 8°. **8903.** aaa. **24.**

—— The Manufacture of Dyes. [Edited by Jocelyn F. Thorpe.] pp. ix. 274. *Macmillan & Co.: London*, 1922. 8°. **07943.** b. **3.**

—— The Manufacture of Intermediate Products for Dyes, *etc.* pp. xi. 263. *Macmillan & Co.: London*, 1918. 8°. **08909.** b. **49.**

CAIN (John Cannell) and **THORPE** (Jocelyn Field)

—— The Synthetic Dyestuffs and the Intermediate Products from which they are derived. pp. xv. 405. *C. Griffin & Co.: London*, 1905. 8°. **07945.** k. **37.**

—— Second edition, revised. pp. xvii. 423. *C. Griffin & Co.: London*, 1913. 8°. **7945.** dd. **15.**

CAIN (JOHN CANNELL) and **THORPE** (JOCELYN FIELD)

—— Third edition, revised. pp. xvii. 423. *C. Griffin & Co.: London*, 1917. 8°. **07495**. m. **53**.

—— Fourth edition, revised. pp. xvii. 423. *C. Griffin & Co.: London*, 1918. 8°. **8904**. e. **14**.

—— Sixth edition, revised. pp. xvii. 423. *C. Griffin & Co.: London*, 1923. 8°. **8901**. cc. **27**.

—— Seventh edition . . . rewritten and enlarged by J. F. Thorpe . . . and Reginald Patrick Linstead. pp. xv. 472. *C. Griffin & Co.: London*, 1933. 8°. **07945.m.53.**

CAIN (JOHN RICE) and **HOSTETTER** (J. C.) A Rapid Method for the Determination of Vanadium in Steels, Ores, etc., based on its quantitative inclusion by the phosphomolybdate precipitate. pp. 20. *Washington*, 1912. 8°. [*Technologic Papers of the Bureau of Standards.* no. 8.] A.S. **145/2**.

CAIN (JUDE) Memoir of Jude Cain, who died in Liverpool, Feb. 3, 1829, aged twelve years. pp. 16. *American Sunday School Union: Philadelphia*, 1831. 12°. **864**. h. **45**. **(1.)**

CAIN (JULIEN) *See* LEDOS (E. G.) Histoire des catalogues des livres imprimés de la Bibliothèque nationale . . . Préface par J. Cain. 1936. 8°. **11913**. b. **56**.

—— *See* PARIS.—*Exposition Internationale des Arts et Techniques*, 1937. Bibliothèques . . . Introduction par J. Cain. 1938. 4°. **11911**. dd. **50**.

—— Le Catalogue des imprimés de la Bibliothèque nationale. Une expérience d'un siècle. [Reprinted from the preface to "Histoire des catalogues du Département des Imprimés," by E. G. Ledos.] pp. 22. 1936. 8°. *See* PARIS.—*Bibliothèque Nationale.* [*Imprimés.*] **11900**. ee. **45**.

—— Ébauche et premiers éléments d'un musée de la littérature, présenté sous la direction de J. Cain, *etc.* [With plates.] pp. xvi. 92. 1938. 4°. *See* PARIS.—*Exposition Internationale des Arts et Techniques*, 1937. **11859**. dd. **14**.

—— Les Transformations de la Bibliothèque nationale et le dépôt annexe de Versailles. [With illustrations.] pp. 51. *Paris*, [1936.] 8°. [*Bulletin des bibliothèques.* Special number.] P.P. **6475**. bh. **(2.)**

—— [Another issue.] 1936. 4°. *See* PARIS.—*Bibliothèque Nationale.* **11908**. dd. **21**.

CAIN (LEO F.)

—— *See* BELL (Reginald) *of Stanford University.* Motion Pictures in a Modern Curriculum . . . By R. Bell, L. F. Cain, *etc.* 1941. 8°. **08385**. g. **26/3**.

CAÏN (LÉON) Souvenirs du siège de Strasbourg, 1870. Le combat du pont d'Illkirch, sortie du 16 août. Récit d'un témoin. [With a map.] pp. 40. *Paris*, 1902. 8°. **9079**. l. **16**.

CAIN (MARY CLOUGH)

—— The Historical Development of State Normal Schools for White Teachers in Maryland, *etc.* [A thesis.] pp. viii. 184. *Bureau of Publications, Teachers College, Columbia University: New York*, 1941. 8°. **08385**. ee. **68**.

CAIN (NEVILLE) The Fairies' Circus, *etc.* [With illustrations.] *Harper & Bros.: London*, 1903. 4°. **12812**. d. **7**.

CAIN (PATRICK) *See* KANE.

CAIN (PAUL) Fast One. [A novel.] pp. 304. *Doubleday, Doran & Co.: Garden City, N.Y.*, 1933. 8°. **12709**. e. **8**.

—— [Another edition.] pp. 308. *Constable: London*, 1936. 8°. NN. **25420**.

CAIN (ROY F.) Studies of Coprophilous Sphaeriales in Ontario. pp. 126. *Toronto*, 1934. 8°. [*University of Toronto. Biological Series.* no. 38.] Ac. **2702/5**.

CAIN (STANLEY ADAIR)

—— Foundations of Plant Geography. pp. xiv. 556. *Harper & Bros.: New York & London*, [1944.] 8°. **7034**. c. **21**.

CAIN (THOMAS)

—— Curtain Up! New ten-minute plays. pp. 93. *University of London Press: London*, [1952.] 8°. **11784**. aaa. **29**.

—— Dramatised Civics. [Plays for use in the teaching of civics.] *University of London Press: London*, 1948– . 8°. W.P. **14156**.

—— **Notes for Teachers. pp. 48.** ***University of London Press: London,*** **[1949.] 8°.** W.P. **14156**. a.

—— Ten More Ten-Minute Plays. pp. 112. *University of London Press: London*, 1949. 8°. **11783**. de. **64**.

—— Ten Ten-Minute Plays for Seniors. pp. 126. ***University of London Press: London,*** 1938. 8°. **011781**. f. **86**.

CAIN (WILLIAM) A Brief Course in the Calculus . . . Second edition. pp. x. 280. *Blackie & Son: London*, 1909. 8°. **8505**. bbb. **42**.

—— Earth Pressure, Retaining Walls and Bins. pp. x. 287. *J. Wiley & Sons: New York*, 1916. 8°. **08768**. c. **50**.

CAÏNA. Caïna and other poems. By the author of 'The King's Sacrifice,' &c. pp. viii. 67. *Smith, Elder & Co.: London*, 1876. 8°. **11652**. ee. **42**.

CAINA (SOPHIA DEL) *See* MILL (Sophia)

CAINE (CAESAR) *See* GARRIGILL. Garrigill. St. John's Church . . . The Register—Baptisms, Marriages, and Deaths—from 1699 to 1730, edited by C. Caine. 1901. 8°. **9903**. b. **15**.

—— *See* MALCOLM (Thomas) Barracks and Battlefields in India; or, the Experiences of a soldier of the 10th Foot—North Lincoln—in the Sikh wars and Sepoy Mutiny. Edited by the Rev. C. Caine, *etc.* 1891. 8°. **9057**. bb. **14**.

—— *See* STROTHER ( ) *of Hull.* Strother's Journal . . . Edited by C. Caine. [1913.] 8°. **10854**. aaa. **23**.

—— *See* WIDDRINGTON (*Sir* Thomas) Analecta Eboracensia . . . Edited and annotated by the Rev. C. Caine. 1897. 8°. **10358**. l. **12**.

—— All Saints' Parish, Ipswich. A record of thirty years' work . . . Twelve illustrations. pp. 92. *W. E. Harrison: Ipswich*, 1902 et seq. [1910.] 8°. **4707**. a. **58**.

—— The Archiepiscopal Coins of York, *etc.* [Reprinted from the "Yorkshire Gazette." With illustrations.] pp. 74. "*Yorkshire Gazette*": *York*, 1908. 8°. **7757**. bb. **28**.

—— A Brief Chronicle of Wesleyan Methodism in Leyton, Essex, 1750–1895 . . . Nine illustrations. pp. 96. **L.P.** *T. Hubbard: Leyton*, [1896.] 4°. **4715**. g. **13**.
One of an edition of twenty-five copies.

—— Brief Notes on North Fambridge and its Church, taken chiefly from the registers. pp. 7. *Privately printed: Maldon*, 1905. 8°. **9904**. d. **6**.

CAINE (Caesar)

—— Capella de Gerardegile, or the Story of a Cumberland chapelry, Garrigill. [With plates, including a map.] pp. xxv. 248. *R. M. Saint: Haltwhistle*, 1908. 8°. **010360**. g. 4.

—— A Catechism of the Sects . . . Reprinted from the National Church. pp. 34. *Church Defence & Instruction Committee: London*, 1907. 8°. **4380**. df. **12**. (5.)

—— [Another copy.] **4535**. a. **8**. (6.)

—— [Another copy.] **4531**. aa. **11**. (1.)

—— A Catechism on the Blessed Eucharist for Confirmation Candidates and others. pp. 23. *A. R. Mowbray & Co.: London, Oxford*, 1905. 16°. **4324**. a. **68**.

—— [Another copy.] **4324**. a. **64**.

—— Cleator and Cleator Moor: past and present. Seventy illustrations [including maps]. pp. xviii. 475. *Titus Wilson: Kendal*, 1916. 8°. **010368**. h. 2.

—— The Difficulty of Godparents in the Confirmation of Adults educated in Dissent . . . Paper read before . . . the Ipswich Clerical Union. pp. 8. *Goose & Son: Norwich*, [1908.] 8°. **4380**. df. **12**. (6.)

—— First Lessons in Question and Answer Form on Confirmation or the Laying on of Hands. pp. 39. *A. R. Mowbray & Co.: London, Oxford*, 1907. 16°. **04420**. de. **65**. (7.)

—— History of Wesleyan Methodism in the Crewe Circuit. pp. 79. *J. Hinchsliff: Crewe*, 1883. 8°. **4715**. aa. **18**.

—— The Iron Mines of Cleator. pp. 3 [33]. *W. Halton & Sons: Whitehaven*, 1911. 8°. **07108**. f. **14**. (2.)

—— Kessingland . . . Suffolk . . . Brief facts for the use of visitors. pp. 7. [1910.] 8°. **010352**. de. **18**. (2.)

—— The Martial Annals of the City of York . . . Sixty illustrations. pp. xi. 287. *C. J. Clark: London*, 1893. 8°. **10360**. h. 27.

—— "The Methodist Recorder" and the Church in Garrigill. [A reply to three paragraphs of an article in the "Methodist Recorder" signed H. K., i.e. the Rev. Nehemiah Curnock. With the text of the paragraphs in question.] [1901.] *s. sh.* fol. **1865**. c. **18**. (20.)

—— Notes on the Castle & Church of Egremont. pp. 14. *W. Halton & Sons: Whitehaven*, [1913.] 12°. **10368**. aa. **69**. (6.)

—— The Pauline View of Natural Truth. An exposition and an appeal, *etc.* [An address.] pp. 16. *Church Newspaper Co.: London*, [1903.] 8°. **03128**. g. **47**. (3.)

—— The Story of Mashonaland and the Missionary Pioneers. With map . . . and illustrations . . . Edited by the Rev. F. W. Macdonald. [With extracts from the journal of the Rev. Owen Watkins and the letters of the Rev. Isaac Shimmin.] pp. 63. *Wesleyan Mission House: London*, [1893.] 16°. **4767**. a. **13**.

—— William Pearce, of Poplar. A chapter in the history of Methodism in East London . . . Twelve illustrations [including a portrait]. pp. 104. *C. H. Kelly: London*, [1894.] 8°. **4907**. b. **37**.

CAINE (*Sir* Derwent Hall) *See* Caine (*Sir* Thomas H. H.) *K.B.E.* Life of Christ. [Edited by G. R. H. Caine and Sir D. H. Caine.] 1938. 8°. **20032**. f. **38**.

—— —— 1938. 8°. **20018**. b. **35**.

CAINE (Frederick)

—— Job Evaluation for Launderers and Dry Cleaners. pp. 53. *Trader Publishing Co.: London*, 1947. 8°. [*"Power Laundry" Handbook.* New ser. no. 2.] W.P. **2024/2**.

CAINE (Frederick)

—— Production Control in the Laundry. [With a portrait.] pp. 56. *London*, 1947. 8°. [*"Power Laundry" Handbook. New ser.* no. 1.] W.P. **2024/1**.

—— Proficiency Incentives for Launderers & Dry Cleaners. pp. 63. *Trader Publishing Co.: London*, 1947. 8°. [*"Power Laundry" Handbook.* New ser. no. 3.] W.P. **2024/3**.

CAINE (Gordon Ralph Hall) *See* Bussy (Frederick M.) and Caine (G. R. H.) Gems of Oratory, *etc.* [1909.] 8°. **012301**. e. **78**.

—— *See* Caine (*Sir* Thomas H. H.) *K.B.E.* Life of Christ. [Edited by G. R. H. Caine and Sir D. H. Caine.] 1938. 8°. **20032**. f. **38**.

—— —— 1938. 8°. **20018**. b. **35**.

CAINE (Hall) *See* Caine (*Sir* Thomas H. H.) *K.B.E.*

CAINE (M. R.) *See* Schultz (William J.) and Caine (M. R.) Financial Development of the United States. 1937. 8°. **08230**. ee. **16**.

CAINE (Nathaniel) *See* Caine (William S.) and Caine (N.) Tables for Use in the Tin Plate Trade. 1877. 8°. **8245**. gg. **5**.

—— *See* Caine (William S.) and Caine (N.) W. S. & N. Caine, Iron & Tinplate Merchants. [Telegraphic codes for use in the tin-plate trade.] [1875.] fol. **1802**. c. **10**.

CAINE (Oliver Vernon)

—— The Coming of Navarre. An English boy's adventures in the days of Guise and Henry of Navarre. pp. v. 372. *J. Nisbet & Co.: London*, 1909. 8°. **012804**. aa. **16**

—— Face to Face with Napoleon. An English boy's adventures in the great French war, *etc.* pp. vii. 367. *J. Nisbet & Co.: London*, 1898. 8°. **012804**. ff. **11**.

—— In the Year of Waterloo. (Illustrations by Chris. Hammond.) pp. 365. *J. Nisbet & Co.: London*, 1899. 8°. **012643**. k. **28**

—— Sons of Victory. A boy's story of the coming of Napoleon pp. vii. 394. *J. Nisbet & Co.: London*, 1904. 8°. **012803**. cc. **30**

—— Wanderer and King . . . With illustrations by Henry Austin. pp. 367. *J. Nisbet & Co.: London*, 1903. 8°. **012628**. aa. **1**

CAINE (Philip W.)

—— Now I'm Awake! and other poems. pp. 39. *Fortune Press: London*, 1954. 8°. **11657**. l. **73**.

—— When I was Young, and other poems pp. 95. *Brown & Sons: Douglas*, [1931.] 8°. **11640**. e. **62**

CAINE (*Sir* Thomas Henry Hall) *K.B.E.* *See* Albert *King of the Belgians.* King Albert's Book, *etc.* [Edited by Sir T. H. Hall Caine.] 1914. 4°. K.T.C. **104**. b. **3**

—— *See* Bell (Henry T. M.) Charles Whitehead . . With an appreciation of Whitehead by Mr. Hall Caine. 1894. 8°. **10854**. bbb. **30**

—— *See* Bojer (J.) [Troens magt.] The Power of a Li[e] . . . with an introduction by Hall Caine. 1908. 8°. **012581**. c. **14**

—— *See* Dickens (Charles) [*Works.*] The Waverley Edition of the Works of Charles Dickens. (The Personal History of David Copperfield . . . With an introduction by Hal[l] Caine.) [1913, *etc.*] 8°. **12272**. s. **1/8**

— *See* DICKENS (Charles) [*Single Tales and Plays.*] A Christmas Carol . . . With an introduction by H. Caine. 1906. 8°. **012203. e. 6/11.**

— *See* DICKENS (Charles) [*Single Tales and Plays.*] The Cricket on the Hearth . . . With an introduction by H. Caine, *etc.* 1906. 8°. **012203. e. 6/11*.**

— *See* KENYON (C. F.) Hall Caine. The man and the novelist. [With a portrait.] 1901. 8°. [*English Writers of To-day.* no. 4.] **10856. ff.**

— *See* MAETERLINCK (M. P. M. B.) The Princess Maleine . . . and the Intruder . . . With an introduction by Hall Caine. 1892. 8°. **11735. f. 50.**

— *See* NORRIS (Samuel) Two Men of Manxland. Hall Caine, novelist, T. E. Brown, poet. [With portraits.] 1947. 8°. **10861. de. 28.**

— *See* TIREBUCK (William E.) 'Twixt God and Mammon . . . With a memoir of the author by Hall Caine. 1903. 8°. **012638. c. 38.**

— Address on Policemanship, written by Hall Caine and read by Irene Vanbrugh at George Robey's concert in aid of The Metropolitan & City Police Orphanage, *etc.* [With portraits, and a facsimile.] *C. Knight & Co.: London,* 1917. 8°. **6056. v. 19.**

— Arthur Osborne Montgomery Jay . . . The boxing parson. The story of a life's sacrifice. *See* N., D. Father and Son, *etc.* [1914 ?] 8°. **4905. bb. 66.**

— Barbed Wire. *See* infra: The Woman of Knockaloe.

— The Bondman. A new saga. 3 vol. *William Heinemann: London,* 1890. 8°. **012639. l. 6.**

— (Fourth edition.) [With a portrait.] pp. x. 340. *William Heinemann: London,* 1895. 8°. **12646. ff. 7.**

— [Another edition.] pp. 158. *William Heinemann: London,* 1908. 8°. **012640. b. 57.**

— [Another edition.] pp. 319. *William Heinemann: London,* 1912. 8°. **012621. k. 5.**

— [Another edition.] pp. 479. *T. Nelson & Sons: London,* [1919.] 8°. **12619. pp. 24.**

— [Another edition.] pp. 376. *Readers Library Publishing Co.: London,* [1928.] 8°. **012601. bbb. 42.**

— O Escravo. Tradução . . . por Januário Leite. 4.ª edição. pp. 391. *Lisboa,* 1943. 8°. **12650. de. 33.**

— The Bondman Play. pp. xvi. 240. *Daily Mail: London,* 1906. 8°. **11778. dd. 11.**

— Capt'n Davy's Honeymoon. The Last Confession. The Blind Mother. pp. 273. *William Heinemann: London,* 1893 [1892]. 8°. **012641. k. 34.**

— The Christian. A story. pp. 452. *William Heinemann: London,* 1897. 8°. **012625. f. 39.**

— Second edition. pp. 453. *William Heinemann: London,* 1897. 8°. **012632. a. 54.**

— Third edition. pp. 453. *William Heinemann: London,* 1897. 8°. **012632. a. 57.**

— [Another edition.] pp. 539. *G. N. Morang: Toronto,* 1897. 8°. **012621. l. 20.**

— [Another edition.] pp. 215. *William Heinemann: London,* 1910. 8°. **012640. b. 58.**

— [Another edition.] pp. 478. *T. Nelson & Sons: London,* [1919.] 8°. **012603. df. 3.**

— Chrześcijanin. Powieść na tle stosunków amerykańskich. Przekład C. N. [i.e. by C. Niewiadomska.] pp. 626. *Warszawa,* 1898. 8°. **012618. fff. 13.**

— [The Christian.] O Apóstolo. Tradução . . . de L. de C. e Almeida. 5.ª edição. pp. 292. *Lisboa,* 1943. 8°. **12650. de. 18.**

— Cobwebs of Criticism. A review of the first reviewers of the 'Lake,' 'Satanic,' and 'Cockney' Schools. pp. xxiv. 266. *Elliot Stock: London,* 1883. 8°. **11825. o. 9.**

— (Second edition.) pp. xxxviii. 294. *G. Routledge & Sons: London,* 1908 [1907]. 8°. [*New Universal Library.*] **12204. p. 2/118.**

— Y Ddiod . . . (Ffugchwedl yn ymdrin ag un o brif gwestiynau yr oes.) Gyda rhagarweiniad gan Mr. William George. pp. 76. *Cwmni y Cyhoeddwyr Cymreig: Caernarfon,* [1907.] 8°. **012613. ee. 20.**

— The Deemster. A romance. 3 vol. *Chatto & Windus: London,* 1887. 8°. **012638. g. 2.**

— Library edition. pp. viii. 365. *Chatto & Windus: London,* 1895. 8°. **012621. g. 38.**

— New edition. pp. 154. *Chatto & Windus: London,* 1898. 8°. **012624. k. 5.**

— Fine-paper edition. pp. viii. 391. *Chatto & Windus: London,* 1902. 8°. **012613. de. 2.**

— [Another edition.] pp. viii. 365. *William Heinemann: London,* 1921. 8°. **012614. b. 18.**

— [Another edition.] pp. 288. *J. Leng & Co.: London,* 1927. 8°. ["*People's Friend*" *Library.* no. 195.] **12645. dd. 1/195.**

— The Drama of Three Hundred & Sixty-Five Days. Scenes in the Great War, *etc.* (Reprinted, with certain additions, from "The Daily Telegraph.") pp. 126. *William Heinemann: London,* 1915. 8°. **9082. f. 36.**

— The Eternal City. pp. 606. *William Heinemann: London,* 1901. 8°. **012639. a. 41.**

— [Another edition.] pp. 638. *G. N. Morang & Co.: Toronto,* 1901. 8°. **012622. k. 7.**

— His Majesty's Theatre edition. pp. viii. 383. *William Heinemann: London,* 1902. 8°. **012641. cc. 38.**

— [Another edition.] pp. 212. *Hodder & Stoughton: London,* [1913.] 8°. **12601. t. 4.**

— [Another edition.] pp. 478. *T. Nelson & Sons: London,* [1919.] 8°. **012603. df. 9.**

— Cidade Eterna. Tradução de L. de C. e Almeida. 6.ª edição. pp. 398. *Lisboa,* 1943. 8°. **12650. de. 36.**

— [The Eternal City.] Doña Roma. Novela. pp. ix. 376. *Chicago,* 1905. 8°. **012613. ee. 16.**

— The Eternal Question. A new dramatisation of "The Eternal City." pp. viii. 102. *Printed for private circulation: London,* 1910. 8°. **11779. dd. 37.**

— King Edward, a Prince and a Great Man. A pen portrait. (Reprinted from the Daily Telegraph.) pp. 43. *Collier & Co.: London,* 1910. 8°. **10806. aa. 41.**

— Life of Christ. [Edited by G. R. Hall Caine and Sir Derwent Hall Caine.] pp. xx. 1270. *Collins: London,* 1938. 8°. **20032. f. 38.**

CAINE (*Sir* THOMAS HENRY HALL) *K.B.E.*

—— [Another edition.] pp. xxi. 1310. *Doubleday, Doran & Co.: New York*, 1938. 8°. **20018. b. 35.**

—— Life of Samuel Taylor Coleridge. [With a bibliography by J. P. Anderson.] pp. 154. xxi. *Walter Scott: London*, 1887. 8°. [“*Great Writers.*”] **10601. dd. 11.**

—— The Little Man Island. Scenes and specimen days in the Isle of Man. pp. 50. *Isle of Man Steam Packet Co.: Douglas*, 1894. 8°. **10368. cc. 51.**

—— [Another copy.] **10369. ccc. 29.**

—— The Little Manx Nation. pp. 159. *William Heinemann: London*, 1891. 8°. **10368. ccc. 37.**

—— The Manxman. pp. 439. *William Heinemann: London*, 1894. 8°. **012629. f. 15.**

—— [Another edition.] pp. 445. *T. Nelson & Sons: London*, [1919.] 8°. **12619. pp. 12.**

—— [Another edition.] pp. 288. *J. Leng & Co.: London*, 1927. 8°. [“*People's Friend*” *Library.* no. 192.] **12645. dd. 1/192.**

—— [Another edition.] pp. 378. *Readers Library Publishing Co.: London*, [1929.] 8°. **012601. bbb. 72.**

—— [The Manxman.] A Vélha Tragédia . . . Tradução . . . por Januário Leite . . . 2.ª edição. 2 vol. *Lisboa*, 1941. 8°. **12650. de. 1.**

—— Mary Magdalene. The new Apocrypha. pp. 1–8. *Hall Caine: London*, 1891. 8°. **012631. e. 72.**

—— The Master of Man. The story of a sin. pp. 432. *William Heinemann: London*, 1921. 8°. **NN. 7194.**

—— [The Master of Man.] O Juiz . . . Traduzido . . . por Frederico de Carvalho. 3.ª edição. 2 vol. *Lisboa*, 1942. 8°. **12650. de. 4.**

—— My Story. pp. xii. 398. *William Heinemann for Collier & Co.: London*, 1908. 8°. **010854. de. 4.**

—— [Another issue.] pp. xii. 406. *William Heinemann: London*, 1908. 8°. **10856. m. 5.**

—— [Another edition.] pp. 254. *Readers Library Publishing Co.: London*, [1931.] 8°. **012601. b. 46.**

—— Our Girls. Their work for the war . . . With 15 illustrations, *etc.* pp. 127. *Hutchinson & Co.: London*, 1916. 8°. **08415. e. 30.**

—— The Prodigal Son. pp. 426. *William Heinemann: London*, 1904. 8°. **012629. dd. 47.**

—— [Another edition.] pp. 192. *London*, [1908.] 8°. [*Newnes' Sixpenny Copyright Novels.* no. 143.] **012604.f.1/102.**

—— [Another edition.] pp. 478. *T. Nelson & Sons: London*, [1919.] 8°. **012603. df. 11.**

—— [The Prodigal Son.] Syn Marnotrawny . . . Przekład C. N. [i.e. C. Niewiadomska.] Bezpłatny dodatek do Tygodnika illustrowanego. pp. 560. *Warszawa*, 1905. 8°. **012612. ff. 20.**

—— O Filho Pródigo. Tradução . . . por Januário Leite . . . 7.ª edição, *etc.* pp. xv. 443. *Lisboa*, 1941. 8°. **12650. de. 12.**

—— The Prophet. A parable. pp. 10. *William Heinemann: London*, 1890. 8°. **12631. b. 2.**

CAINE (*Sir* THOMAS HENRY HALL) *K.B.E.*

—— Quamdiu, Domine! [An essay.] *See* REID (A.) *Political Writer.* Vox Clamantium, *etc.* 1894. 8°. **8409. h. 19.**

—— Recollections of Dante Gabriel Rossetti. [With a portrait.] pp. xiii. 297. *Elliot Stock: London*, 1882. 8°. **2408. cc. 1.**

—— [Another edition.] pp. x. 259. *Cassell & Co.: London*, 1928. 8°. **010856. aaa. 47.**

—— Richard III. and Macbeth: the spirit of romantic play in relationship to the principles of Greek and of Gothic art, and to the picturesque interpretations of Mr. Henry Irving: a dramatic study. pp. 46. *Simpkin, Marshall & Co.: London; Edward Howell: Liverpool*, 1877. 8°. **11840. f. 1. (14.)**

—— The Scapegoat. A romance . . . Second edition. 2 vol. *William Heinemann: London*, 1891. 8°. **012631. m. 30.**

—— (Fourth edition.) pp. 318. *William Heinemann: London*, 1892. 8°. **012618. f. 17.**

—— [Another edition.] pp. 174. *London*, [1907.] 8°. [*Newnes' Sixpenny Copyright Novels.* no. 131.] **012604.f.1/101.**

—— [The Scapegoat.] A Expiação. Tradução de J. C. de Barros. 2.ª edição. pp. 382. *Lisboa*, 1942. 8°. **12650. de. 20.**

—— The Shadow of a Crime. 3 vol. *Chatto & Windus: London*, 1885. 8°. **12619. s. 1.**

—— A new edition. pp. 138. *Chatto & Windus: London*, 1899. 8°. **012624. k. 11.**

—— A Sombra dum Crime. Tradução . . . por Januário Leite. 2 vol. *Lisboa*, 1937. 8°. **12650. de. 3.**

—— A Son of Hagar. A romance of our time. 3 vol. *Chatto & Windus: London*, 1887. 8°. **12636. k. 16.**

—— [Another edition.] pp. 480. [*London*, 1910.] 8°. [*Nelson's Library.*] **12202.y.1/62.**

—— [Another edition.] pp. ix. 377. *Liverpool*, [1919.] 8°. [“*World's Best*” *Library.*] **12621. p. 1/3.**

—— Um Filho de Agar. Tradução . . . por Januário Leite. 2 vol. *Lisboa*, 1938. 8°. **12650. de. 2.**

—— Sonnets of Three Centuries: a selection . . . Edited by T. H. Caine. pp. xxxvi. 331. *Elliot Stock: London*, 1882. 4°. **2288. f. 5.**

—— The Spiritual Brotherhood of Mankind, *etc.* *See* CAMPBELL (Reginald J.) The New Theology, *etc.* [1909.] 8°. **4136. df. 7.**

—— The White Prophet . . . Illustrated by R. Caton Woodville. 2 vol. *London*, 1909. 8°. [*Heinemann's Library of Modern Fiction.*] **12601. bb. 1/6.**

—— New and revised edition. pp. vii. 372. *William Heinemann: London*, 1911. 8°. **NN. 418.**

—— [Another edition.] pp. 218. *London*, [1913.] 8°. [*Newnes' Sixpenny Copyright Novels.*] **012604. f.1/202.**

—— O Profeta Branco. Tradução . . . por Januário Leite. 3.ª edição. pp. 483. *Lisboa*, 1941. 8°. **12650. de. 17.**

—— “Why I wrote ‘The White Prophet.’” pp. 58. *Privately printed for the Author: London*, [1909.] 8°. **11850. bb. 46. (4.)**

AINE (*Sir* THOMAS HENRY HALL) *K.B.E.*

— The Woman of Knockaloe. A parable. pp. xvi. 207. *Cassell & Co.: London,* 1923. 8°. **NN. 9092.**

— [Another edition.] Barbed Wire. pp. 247. *Readers Library Publishing Co.: London,* [1927.] 8°. **012603. ee. 65.**

— The Woman Thou Gavest Me. Being the story of Mary O'Neill, *etc.* pp. vii. 585. *William Heinemann: London,* 1913. 8°. **NN. 1051.**

— Popular edition, *etc.* pp. vii. 585. *William Heinemann: London,* 1917. 8°. **NN. 4343.**

— [Another edition.] pp. xi. 584. *William Heinemann London,* 1921. 8°. **012614. b. 17**

— Yan, the Icelander; Home, Sweet Home. A lecture-story, *etc.* pp. 49. *Hall Caine: Greeba Castle, Isle of Man,* [1896.] 16°. **012629. de. 23.**
One of an edition of 100 *copies.*

— Arame Farpado. Tradução . . . por Januário Leite. 2.ª edição. pp. 234. *Lisboa,* 1943. 8°. **12650. de. 11.**

AINE (WILLIAM) *Chaplain of the County Gaol, Manchester.* Central Association for Stopping the Sale of Intoxicating Liquors on Sunday . . . Legislative enactments relative to the Sunday liquor traffic. A paper, *etc.* pp. 16. *J. Broad & Co.: Manchester,* [1869.] 8°. **8435. cc. 15.**

AINE (WILLIAM) *Novelist.* An Angler at Large, *etc.* pp. xii. 306. *Kegan Paul & Co.: London,* 1911. 8°. **7904. bbb. 19.**

— The Author of "Trixie." pp. 247. *Herbert Jenkins: London,* 1924 [1923]. 8°. **NN. 9182.**

— Bildad the Quill-driver, *etc.* pp. 315. *John Lane: London, New York,* 1916. 8°. **NN. 3233.**

— Boom! A novel of the century. pp. 314. *Greening & Co.: London,* 1909. 8°. **012623. b. 20.**

— [A reissue.] *London,* 1911. 8°. **012623. a. 38.**

— Sixth edition. pp. 255. *Stanley Paul & Co.: London,* 1926. 8°. **012604. aa. 28.**

— The Brave Little Tailor; or, Seven at a blow. An entertainment, embroidered by W. Caine upon a pantomime of the same name . . . by George Calderon & W. Caine, after the narrative . . . by the brothers Grimm, *etc.* pp. 323. *Grant Richards: London,* 1923. 8°. **012802. bbb. 50.**

— But She Meant Well. pp. 300. *John Lane: London,* 1914. 8°. **NN. 2316.**

— The Devil in Solution . . . Illustrated by George Morrow. pp. 320. *Greening & Co.: London,* 1911. 8°. **012618. bb. 27.**

— Third edition. pp. 320. *Stanley Paul & Co.: London,* [1926.] 8°. **012604. aa. 29.**

— Drones. pp. 316. *Methuen & Co.: London,* 1917. 8°. **NN. 4394.**

— The Fan, and other stories. pp. 301. *Methuen & Co.: London,* 1917. 8°. **NN. 4087.**

— Fish, Fishing & Fishermen. [Articles reprinted from periodicals.] pp. xii. 253. *P. Allan & Co.: London,* 1927. 8°. **7920.cc.32.**

— The Glutton's Mirror. By W. Caine. Illustrated by himself. pp. 87. *T. Fisher Unwin: London,* 1925. 4°. **12316. w. 16.**

CAINE (WILLIAM) *Novelist.*

—— Great Snakes! A variation on a classical theme. pp. 248. *John Lane: London, New York,* 1916. 8°. **012600. e. 6.**

—— Hoffman's Chance. pp. 376. *John Lane: London, New York; Bell & Cockburn: Toronto,* 1912. 8°. **NN. 419.**

—— The Irresistible Intruder. pp. 324. *John Lane: London, New York; Bell & Cockburn: Toronto,* 1914. 8°. **NN. 1512.**

—— Lady Sheba's Last Stunt. pp. 251. *Herbert Jenkins: London,* 1924. 8°. **NN. 10250.**

—— Mendoza and a Little Lady. pp. 287. *G. P. Putnam's Sons: London & New York,* [1921.] 8°. **NN. 7408.**

—— Monsieur Segotin's Story. pp. 45. *Chatto & Windus: London,* 1917. 8°. **12602. i. 5.**

—— The New Foresters . . . With . . . map. pp. viii. 247. *J. Nisbet & Co.: London,* 1913. 8°. **012354. f. 34.**

—— Old Enough to Know Better. pp. 320. *Greening & Co.: London,* 1911. 8°. **012618. bb. 26.**

—— Pilkington. pp. 254. *Ward, Lock & Co.: London,* 1906. 8°. **012632. c. 5.**

—— A Prisoner in Spain. A romance. pp. 320. *Greening & Co.: London,* 1910. 8°. **012623. b. 21.**

—— Third edition. pp. 320. *Stanley Paul & Co.: London,* [1926.] 8°. **012604. aa. 30.**

—— The Pursuit of the President. A distraction in five flights, *etc.* pp. 259. *G. Routledge & Sons: London,* 1907. 8°. **012634. ccc. 36.**

—— The Revolt at Roskelly's. pp. 316. *Greening & Co.: London,* 1910. 8°. **012623. b. 22.**

—— Third edition. pp. 316. *Stanley Paul & Co.: London,* [1926.] 8°. **012604. aa. 31.**

—— Save us from our Friends! pp. 320. *Greening & Co.: London,* 1912. 8°. **012618. bb. 22.**

—— Smoke Rings. pp. 131. *Stanley Paul & Co.: London,* 1926. 4°. **012316. f. 14.**

—— The Strangeness of Noel Carlton. pp. 304. *Herbert Jenkins: London,* 1920. 8°. **NN. 6161.**

—— Three's a Crowd. An Anglo-American comedy. pp. 436. *Houghton Mifflin Co.: Boston & New York,* 1917. 8°. **NN. 4575.**

—— The Victim and the Votery. A guignolerie. pp. 158. *Greening & Co.: London,* 1908. 8°. **012629. k. 58.**

—— What a Scream! and other stories . . . Illustrated by H. M. Bateman. pp. viii. 279. *P. Allan & Co.: London,* 1927. 8°. **NN. 12695.**

—— The Wife Who Came Alive. pp. 319. *Herbert Jenkins: London,* 1919. 8°. **NN. 5341.**

CAINE (WILLIAM) *Novelist,* and **FAIRBAIRN** (JOHN) *Novelist.*

—— The Confectioners. pp. 314. *J. W. Arrowsmith: Bristol,* 1906. 8°. **012633. dd. 10.**

CAINE (WILLIAM RALPH HALL) *See* LANCASTER, *County of.* Lancashire. Biographies, Rolls of Honour. Introduction by W. R. H. Caine. 1917. 8°. **10803.** f. **24.**

—— [Pamphlets relating to the Isle of Man.] 8 pt. [1914–25.] 8°. **10353.** aa. **42.**

—— Annals of the Magic Isle. pp. xxix. 356. *Cecil Palmer: London,* 1926. 8°. **012643.** gg. **18.**

—— Can We Comprehend God? A study of the Divine Name. [With a portrait.] pp. 103. *C. W. Daniel Co.: London,* 1940. 8°. **04374.** de. **20.**

—— The Challenge of Lancashire . . . Souvenir volume of the Lancashire Authors' Association. pp. lxxiv. *Privately printed: London,* 1927. 8°. **010368.** i. **51.**
A reissue, with an additional sheet containing a new title-page and "a personal note," of W. R. H. Caine's introduction to "Lancashire. Biographies, etc." Interleaved.

—— The Children's Hour. An anthology of poems, stories, sketches, etc., by leading authors: illustrated by the chief artists of the day . . . Edited by R. H. Caine. [With an introduction by the Countess of Jersey.] pp. xv. 127. *George Newnes: London,* [1907.] 8°. **012803.** h. **62.**

—— The Cruise of the Port Kingston. [With plates.] pp. xxxi. 351. *Collier & Co.: London,* 1908. 8°. **010480.** g. **20.**

—— Humorous Poems of the Century. Edited, with biographical notes, by R. H. Caine. pp. xiii. 328. *Walter Scott: London,* [1889.] 8°. [*Canterbury Poets.*] **11604.** aa. **17.**

—— Isle of Man . . . With 20 illustrations in colour by A. Heaton Cooper. pp. xvi. 240. *A. & C. Black: London,* 1909. 8°. **10368.** p. **7.**

—— Love Songs of English Poets, 1500–1800, *etc.* [Edited by W. R. H. Caine.] pp. xxv. 278. *William Heinemann: London,* 1892. 8°. **11601.** dd. **6.**

—— [Another copy.] **L.P.** **11601.** d. **18.**

—— T. E. Brown: the last phase of the poet's life. *Printed for private circulation: Douglas,* [1924.] 8°. **10827.** h. **30.**

—— The Three Legs of Man, the Swastika . . . an Examination of the Medieval History of Sir Ray Lankester, *etc.* [Articles reprinted from various periodicals.] pp. 23. [1920.] 8°. **12274.** dd. **3.**

CAINE (WILLIAM SPROSTON) *See* BROWN (Hugh S.) Hugh Stowell Brown . . . A memorial volume, edited by . . . W. S. Caine. 1887. 8°. **4905.** bb. **60.**

—— *See* NEWTON (John) *of Plymouth.* W. S. Caine, M.P. A biography, *etc.* [With portraits.] 1907. 8°. **010817.** k. **6.**

—— *See* ŚIŚIRAKUMĀRA GHOSHA. Indian Sketches . . . With an introduction by W. S. Caine. 1898. 8°. **12354.** de. **39.**

—— —— 1923. 8°. **12356.** ppp. **31.**

—— India as seen by Mr. W. S. Caine. pp. 7. 76. *G. P. Varma & Bros. Press: Lucknow,* 1889. 8°. **8023.** g. **32.** (3.)

—— The Indian National Congress.—The Congress: what it aims at, *etc.*—The Congress: mode of election of delegates. *See* INDIA.—*Indian National Congress.* The Indian National Congress . . . Impressions, *etc.* 1889. 8°. **8023.** ee. **26.** (8.)

CAINE (WILLIAM SPROSTON)

—— Local Option. By W. S. Caine . . . William Hoyle . . . and Rev. Dawson Burns. pp. 132. *Swan Sonnenschein & Co.: London,* 1885. 8°. [*The Imperial Parliament.* vol. 6.] **8139.** bbb. **44/6.**

—— Third edition. pp. 136. *Swan Sonnenschein & Co.: London,* 1896. 8°. [*The Imperial Parliament.* vol. 6.] **8139.** bbb. **44/6**a.

—— A new standard edition. pp. 133. 1909. 8°. [*The Imperial Parliament.* vol. 6.] *See* BURNS (James D.) **8139.** bbb. **44/6**b.

—— Picturesque India. A handbook for European travellers, *etc.* [With maps.] pp. xliv. 624. *G. Routledge & Sons: London,* 1890. 8°. **010057.** ee. **7.**

—— [Another edition.] pp. xlv. 662. *G. Routledge & Sons: London & New York,* [1898.] 8°. **010057.** g. **13.**

—— A Trip round the World in 1887–8 . . . Illustrated by John Pedder . . . and the author. Second edition. pp. xxiv. 398. *G. Routledge & Sons: London,* 1888. 8°. **10024.** f. **17.**

CAINE (WILLIAM SPROSTON) and **CAINE** (NATHANIEL)

—— Tables for Use in the Tin Plate Trade. *Liverpool Printing & Stationery Co.: Liverpool,* 1877. 8°. **8245.** gg. **5.**

—— W. S. & N. Caine, Iron & Tinplate Merchants. [Telegraphic codes for use in the tin-plate trade.] 2 pt. [*Liverpool?* 1875.] fol. **1802.** c. **10.**

CAINER (SCIPIONE) *See* TURIN.—*Club Alpino Italiano.* Revista alpina italiana, *etc.* (vol. 4–11. Redattore Dott. S. Cainer.) 1882, *etc.* 8°. Ac. **6012/3.**

CAINES (CLEMENT) Letters on the Cultivation of the Otaheite Cane; the manufacture of sugar and rum, the saving of melasses, the care and preservation of stock, *etc.* pp. xv. 301. *Messrs. Robinson: London,* 1801. 8°. **7076.** aaa. **13.**

CAINES (GEORGE) *See* CLINTON (George W.) A Digest of the Decisions at Law and in Equity . . . contained in the . . . reports of Johnson, Caines, *etc.* 1852, *etc.* 8°. **6625.** h. **7.**

—— *See* COLEMAN (William) *Lawyer.* Reports of Cases of Practice, *etc.* [By W. Coleman and G. Caines.] 1808. 8°. **6622.** ff. **3.**

—— *See* SELFRIDGE (Thomas O.) Trial of Thomas O. Selfridge . . . Taken in shorthand by T. Lloyd . . . and G. Caines, *etc.* [1806.] 8°. **1247.** c. **4.**

—— Cases argued and determined in the Court for the Trial of Impeachments and Correction of Errors in the State of New-York. 2 vol. 1810. 8°. *See* NEW YORK, *State of.*—*Court for the Trial of Impeachments and Correction of Errors.* **6622.ff.4.**

—— New-York Term Reports of Cases argued and determined in the Supreme Court of that State. Second edition, with corrections and additions. By [or rather edited with notes by] G. Caines. [May Term, 1803—Nov Term, 1805.] 3 vol. 1813, 14. 8°. *See* NEW YORK *State of.*—*Supreme Court.* **6622.** ff. **6**

—— A Summary of the Practice of the Supreme Court of the State of New-York. pp. xviii. 536. *Isaac Riley: New-York,* 1808. 8°. **6736.** i. **1.**

AINES (W. S.) *Printing Firm.*

—— Type Specimen Book, 1950. Second post-war edition., pp. 90. *W. S. Caines: [London,* 1950.] 8°. **11908.** d. **26.**

AINES (W. S.) *Writer of Verse.*

—— My Changeless Friend, *etc.* [Verses.] pp. 40. *Elliot Stock: London,* 1909. 8°. **3437.** ee. **55.**

AINNEACH, *O.S.F.C.* *See* CANICE.

AINSCROSS.—*Cainscross and Ebley Co-operative Society.* Cainscross & Ebley Co-operative Economist. Edited by Bramwell Hudson. no. 241, *etc.* *Stroud,* 1913– . 8°. P.P. **1423.** lxa.

—— *St. Matthew's Church.* *See* MATTHEW, *Saint and Apostle, Church of, at Cainscross.*

AINSCROSS AND EBLEY CO-OPERATIVE ECONOMIST. *See* CAINSCROSS.—*Cainscross and Ebley Co-operative Society.*

AIPHAS. *See* CAIAPHAS.

CAIR (MARY) After All—. [A novel.] pp. 288. *Thornton Butterworth: London,* 1927. 8°. NN. **12588.**

CAIR (STANLEY HERBERT) The Responsible Citizen. pp. 192. *T. Nelson & Sons: London,* 1938. 8°. [*Discussion Books.* no. 6.] **012209.d.3/6.**

CAIRA, *le Chevalier de, pseud.* Le Bonnet rebuté. Anecdote. [Signed: le ci-devant Chevalier de Çaira.] (Petit catéchisme national.) pp. 8. [*Paris,* 1790?] 8°. F. **367.** (**11.**)

CAIRANO (ONORATO ROSA DA) *See* ROSA DA CAIRANO.

CAIRASCO DE FIGUEROA (BARTOLOMÉ) Canto de la Curiosidad, en elogio del famoso templo del Escorial [and other poems], *etc.* 1774. *See* LOPEZ DE SEDANO (J. J.) Parnaso Español, *etc.* tom. 8. 1768, *etc.* 8°. **242.** k. **35.**

—— Canto de la Sabiduria en la Festividad de la Venida del Espíritu Santo. 1771. *See* LOPEZ DE SEDANO (J. J.) Parnaso Español, *etc.* tom. 5. 1768, *etc.* 8°. **242.** k. **32.**

—— Definiciones Poéticas, Morales y Cristianas. 1857. *See* ARIBAU (B. C.) Biblioteca de Autores Españoles, *etc.* tom. 42. 1849, *etc.* 8°. **12232.f.1/42.**

—— Poesías. 1855. *See* ARIBAU (B. C.) Biblioteca de Autores Españoles, *etc.* tom. 35. 1849, *etc.* 8°. **12232.f.1/35.**

—— Templo Militante, Flos Santorum, y Triumphos de sus Virtudes, *etc.* 3 pt. *P. Crasbeeck: Lisboa,* 1613–18. fol. **11451.** k. **7.**

CAIRD, *Family of.* *See* CAIRD (Rennie A.) A History of, or Notes upon, Family of Caird, Scotland, *etc.* 1913, *etc.* 8°. **9907.** bb. **2.**

CAIRD (ALEXANDER MACNEEL) The Cry of the Children. An address . . . Second edition. pp. 16. *W. Blackwood & Son: Edinburgh & London,* 1849. 8°. **8305.** d. **46.** (**3.**)

—— The Land Tenancy Laws: an address . . . Revised and enlarged, *etc.* (Seventh thousand.) pp. 20. *Seton & Mackenzie; J. Menzies & Co.: Edinburgh,* [1871.] 8°. **6573.** d. **3.**

—— [A reissue.] *Seton & Mackenzie: Edinburgh,* [1876.] 8°. **6145.** cc. **20.** (**4.**)

CAIRD (ALEXANDER MACNEEL)

—— Local Government and Taxation in Scotland. *See* LONDON.—III. *Cobden Club.* Cobden Club Essays. Local Government, *etc.* 1875. 8°. **2240.** d. **16.**

—— Mary Stuart, her guilt or innocence. An inquiry into the secret history of her times. pp. xxi. 271. *A. & C. Black: Edinburgh,* 1866. 8°. **10805.** ee. **24.**

—— The Poor-Law Manual for Scotland: carefully revised, greatly enlarged, and brought down to the present time . . . Sixth edition. pp. xviii. 481. *A. & C. Black: Edinburgh,* 1851. 12°. **1384.** e. **5.**

—— Special Evils of the Scottish Poor-Law, *etc.* pp. 40. *Edmonston & Douglas: Edinburgh,* 1877. 8°. **8275.** ee. **2.** (**13.**)

CAIRD (ALICE MONA) *See* also HATTON (G. Noel) *pseud.* [i.e. A. M. Caird.]

—— *See* FOERSTER (Ernst) Die Frauenfrage in den Romanen englischer Schriftstellerinnen der Gegenwart (George Egerton, Mona Caird, Sarah Grand). 1907. 8°. **11851.** s. **16.**

—— *See* QUILTER (Harry) Is Marriage a Failure? *etc.* [A newspaper correspondence suggested by an article on marriage by A. M. Caird.] [1888.] 8°. **012207.** h. **2.**

—— Beyond the Pale. An appeal on behalf of the victims of vivisection. pp. 71. *William Reeves: London,* [1897.] 8°. [*Bijou Library.* no. 8.] **12200.** ee. **7.**

—— The Daughters of Danaus. pp. 491. *Bliss, Sands & Co.: London,* 1894. 8°. **012629.** ee. **56.**

—— The Great Wave. pp. 515. *Wishart & Co.: London,* 1931. 8°. NN. **18101.**

—— The Inquisition of Science. pp. 24. *National Anti-Vivisection Society: London,* 1903. 8°. **8425.** ee. **26.** (**5.**)

—— The Logicians. An episode in dialogue. pp. 36. [1905.] 8°. **11778.** l. **43.** (**2.**)

—— The Morality of Marriage, and other essays on the status and destiny of woman. pp. xvi. 239. *George Redway: London,* 1897. 8°. **08416.** k. **1.**

—— The Pathway of the Gods. A novel. pp. 339. *Skeffington & Son: London,* 1898. 8°. **012643.** cc. **45.**

—— Personal Rights. A presidential address delivered to the forty-first annual meeting of the Personal Rights Association, *etc.* pp. 11. *Personal Rights Association: London,* [1913.] 8°. **08248.** ff. **28.** (**5.**)

—— A Romance of the Moors. pp. 182. *Bristol,* [1891.] 8°. [*Arrowsmith's Bristol Library.* vol. 47.] **12207.** g.

—— Romantic Cities of Provence . . . Illustrated from sketches by Joseph Pennell and Edward M. Synge. pp. 416. *T. Fisher Unwin: London,* 1906. 8°. **10168.** h. **35.**

—— A Sentimental View of Vivisection. pp. 48. *William Reeves: London,* [1895.] 8°. [*Bijou Library.* no. 3.] **12200.** ee. **7.**

—— The Stones of Sacrifice. pp. 460. *Simpkin, Marshall & Co.: London,* 1915. 8°. NN. **3016.**

—— The Wing of Azrael. 3 vol. *Trübner & Co.: London,* 1889. 8°. **012638.** m. **12.**

CAIRD (C. M.)

—— Lady Hetty. A story of Scottish and Australian life. [By C. M. Caird.] 3 vol. 1875. 8°. *See* HETTY, *Lady*. **12633**. n. **6**.

—— "Lady Hetty." Roman aus dem schottischen und australischen Leben . . . Aus dem Englischen von Helene Lobedan. 2 vol. *Leipzig*, 1876. 8°. **012638**. pp. **39**.

CAIRD (DAVID) Church and State in Wales. A plain statement of the case for disestablishment. pp. 104. *Liberation Society: London*, [1912.] 8°. **4136**. f. **11**.

—— Second edition, revised and enlarged. pp. 136. *Liberation Society: London*, [1912.] 8°. **4136**. f. **13**.

CAIRD (EDWARD) *Master of Balliol College, Oxford*. *See* CAIRD (John) *Principal of the University of Glasgow*. The Fundamental Ideas of Christianity . . . With a memoir by E. Caird. 1899. 8°. **4371**. dd. **25**.

—— *See* CAIRD (John) *Principal of the University of Glasgow*. University Addresses, *etc*. [Edited by E. Caird.] 1898. 8°. **08365**. g. **5**.

—— *See* CAIRD (John) *Principal of the University of Glasgow*. University Sermons, *etc*. [Edited by E. Caird.] 1898. 8°. **4477**. g. **20**.

—— *See* JONES (*Sir* Henry) and MUIRHEAD (J. H.) The Life and Philosophy of Edward Caird, *etc*. [With portraits.] 1921. 8°. **010855**. bb. **22**.

—— *See* PLATO. [*Two or more Works.—English*.] The Four Socratic Dialogues of Plato . . . With a preface by E. Caird. 1903. 8°. **8461**. aaa. **35**.

—— *See* SETH (Andrew) afterwards PATTISON (A. S. P.) and HALDANE (R. B.) *Viscount Haldane*. Essays in Philosophical Criticism . . . With a preface by E. Caird. 1883. 8°. **8463**. f. **2**.

—— *See* WALLACE (William) *Whyte's Professor of Moral Philosophy, etc*. Lectures and Essays on Natural Theology and Ethics . . . Edited, with a biographical introduction, by E. Caird. 1898. 8°. **8411**. d. **1**.

—— *See* WARREN (William P.) Pantheism in Neo-Hegelian Thought. [With special reference to the philosophy of E. Caird and of A. S. Pringle-Pattison.] 1933. 8°. [*Yale Studies in Religion*. no. 3.] Ac. **2692**. ma/**15**.

—— *See* WORDSWORTH (William) *Poet Laureate*. Selections from the Poetry of William Wordsworth . . . With an introduction by Dr. E. Caird. 1899. 8°. **12274**. bb.

—— A Critical Account of the Philosophy of Kant, with an historical introduction. pp. xx. 673. *James Maclehose: Glasgow*, 1877. 8°. **08461**. h. **68**.

—— The Critical Philosophy of Immanuel Kant. 2 vol. *J. Maclehose & Sons: Glasgow*, 1889. 8°. **8467**. df. **5**.

—— Second edition. 2 vol. *J. Maclehose & Sons: Glasgow*, 1909. 8°. **2236**. cc. **12**.

—— Essays on Literature and Philosophy. 2 vol. *J. Maclehose & Sons: Glasgow*, 1892. 8°. **012357**. f. **53**.

—— [Another edition of vol. 1.] Essays on Literature. pp. 259. *J. Maclehose & Sons: Glasgow*, 1909. 8°. **012355**. g. **46**.

—— *See* BLAKENEY (Edward H.) Caird's Essays; a critical review, *etc*. [1893.] 8°. **11825**. q. **22**. (**11**.)

—— The Evolution of Religion. The Gifford lectures delivered before the University of St. Andrews in sessions 1890–91 and 1891–92. 2 vol. *J. Maclehose & Sons: Glasgow*, 1893. 8°. **2206**. d. **4**.

CAIRD (EDWARD) *Master of Balliol College, Oxford*.

—— Second edition. 2 vol. *J. Maclehose & Sons: Glasgow*, 1894. 8°. **4376**. i. **21**.

—— The Evolution of Religion . . . Third edition. 2 vol. *J. Maclehose & Sons: Glasgow*, 1899. 8°. **4398**. bb. **28**.

—— The Evolution of Theology in the Greek Philosophers. The Gifford Lectures delivered in the University of Glasgow in sessions 1900–1 and 1901–2. 2 vol. *J. Maclehose & Sons: Glasgow*, 1904. 8°. **08465**. df. **4**.

—— [Another edition.] 2 vol. *MacLehose, Jackson & Co.: Glasgow*, 1923. 8°. **2236**. b. **4**.

—— Hegel. [With a portrait.] pp. viii. 224. *W. Blackwood & Sons: Edinburgh & London*, 1883. 8°. [*Philosophical Classics for English Readers*.] **2326**. a. **12**.

—— Lay Sermons and Addresses delivered in the Hall of Balliol College, Oxford. pp. 312. *J. Maclehose & Sons: Glasgow*, 1907. 8°. **012355**. ee. **31**.

—— The Problem of Philosophy at the Present Time: an introductory address, *etc*. pp. 43. *J. Maclehose & Sons: Glasgow*, 1881. 8°. **8463**. bb. **21**. (**4**.)

—— The Social Philosophy and Religion of Comte. pp. xx. 249. *J. Maclehose & Sons: Glasgow*, 1885. 8°. **8468**. bb. **17**.

CAIRD (ELIZA) Christian Songs and Elegies . . . Edited by John Caird. pp. 49. *Published for private circulation: Perth*, [1846.] 8°. **11645**. aa. **24**.

CAIRD (FRANCIS MITCHELL) *See* CATHCART (Charles W.) and CAIRD (F. M.) Johnston's Students' Atlas of Bones and Ligaments. 1885. 4°. **1832**. c. **16**.

CAIRD (FRANCIS MITCHELL) and **CATHCART** (CHARLES WALKER)

—— A Surgical Handbook: for the use of students, practitioners, *etc*. pp. xv. 262. *C. Griffin & Co.: London*, 1889. 8°. **7481**. aa. **24**.

—— Fifth edition, revised. pp. xv. 278. *C. Griffin & Co.: London*, 1893. 8°. **07481**. de. **1**.

—— Eighth edition, revised throughout. pp. xv. 321. *C. Griffin & Co.: London*, 1897. 8°. **07481**. de. **5**.

—— Eleventh edition. pp. xv. 323. *C. Griffin & Co.: London*, 1902. 8°. **07481**. g. **6**.

—— Thirteenth edition. pp. xv. 325. *C. Griffin & Co.: London*, 1905. 8°. **07481**. g. **11**.

—— Fourteenth edition. pp. xv. 325. *C. Griffin & Co.: London*, 1907. 8°. **07481**. g. **13**.

—— Fifteenth edition, revised. pp. xv. 331. *C. Griffin & Co.: London*, 1910. 8°. **07481**. g. **18**.

—— Sixteenth edition, revised and enlarged. pp. xv. 364. *C. Griffin & Co.: London*, 1914. 8°. **07481**. g. **22**.

—— Seventeenth edition, with appendix. pp. xv. 364. *C. Griffin & Co.: London*, 1916. 8°. **07481**. g. **23**.

CAIRD (GEORGE BRADFORD)

—— *See* BIBLE.—*Selections*. [*English*.] The Shorter Oxford Bible. Abridged and edited by G. W. Briggs, G. B. Caird, N. Micklem. 1951. 8°. **03051**. k. **44**.

—— The Apostolic Age. pp. 222. *Gerald Duckworth & Co.: London*, 1955. 8°. [*Studies in Theology*.] **12207**. d. **1**/**50**.

CAIRD (George Bradford)

—— The Truth of the Gospel. pp. vii. 168. *Oxford University Press: London*, 1950. 8°. [*Primer of Christianity*. no. 3.] W.P. **5953/1**. b.

CAIRD (*Right Hon. Sir* James) *K.C.B.* Agriculture. *See* Ward (Thomas H.) The Reign of Queen Victoria, *etc.* vol. 2. 1887. 8°. **09504.h.34.**

—— The British Land Question. pp. 47. *Cassell, Petter, Galpin & Co.: London*, 1881. 8°. **8207**. aaa. **13**. **(6.)**

—— English Agriculture in 1850–51. pp. xxvii. 550. *Longman & Co.: London*, 1851. 8°. **7076**. d. **7**.

—— High Farming under Liberal Covenants the best substitute for Protection . . . Third edition. pp. 32. *W. Blackwood & Sons: Edinburgh & London*, 1849. 8°. **7077**. d. **14**.

—— Fifth edition. pp. 33. *W. Blackwood & Sons: Edinburgh & London*, 1849. 8°. **7077**. d. **15**.

—— High Farming vindicated and further illustrated . . . Second edition. pp. 37. *A. & C. Black: Edinburgh*, 1850. 8°. **7076**. c. **10**.

—— *See* Cato, *the Censor, pseud.* Caird's High Farming harrowed, *etc.* 1850. 8°. **8246**. d. **13**.

—— India: the land and the people, *etc.* pp. xii. 216. *Cassell & Co.: London*, 1883. 8°. **10075**. ff. **10**.

—— Third edition. pp. xv. 255. *Cassell & Co.: London*, 1884. 8°. **10058**. d. **18**.

—— The Irish Land Question. pp. 32. *Longmans & Co.: London*, 1869. 8°. **8145**. bbb. **3**. **(8.)**

—— The Landed Interest and the Supply of Food. pp. xv. 160. *Cassell & Co.: London*, 1878. 8°. **07077**. g. **63**.

—— Our Daily Food, its price, and sources of supply . . . Second edition. pp. 40. *Longmans & Co.: London*, 1868. 8°. **8245**. bbb. **63**. **(3.)**

—— The Plantation Scheme; or, the West of Ireland as a field for investment. [With a map.] pp. vii. 191. *W. Blackwood & Sons: Edinburgh & London*, 1850. 8°. **8275**. e. **50**.

—— Prairie Farming in America. With notes by the way on Canada and the United States. [With a map.] pp. viii. 128. *Longman & Co.: London*, 1859. 8°. **10412**. b. **4**.

—— Caird's Slanders on Canada [in "Prairie Farming in America"] answered & refuted. pp. 40. *Lovell & Gibson: Toronto*, 1859. 8°. **8154**. b. **31**.

CAIRD (James Renny) Sermons . . . With memoir by the Rev. Robert Munro. pp. xxx. 204. *Alexander Gardner: Paisley*, 1908. 8°. **4478**. k. **8**.

CAIRD (John) *Confectioner*. The Complete Confectioner and Family Cook . . . Illustrated with copperplates and woodcuts. pp. vi. 454. *Archibald Allardice: Leith; The Author: Edinburgh*, 1809. 12°. **1037**. f. **19**.

CAIRD (John) *Principal of the University of Glasgow*. *See* Caird (Eliza) Christian Songs and Elegies . . . Edited by J. Caird. [1846.] 8°. **11645**. aa. **24**.

—— *See* Jones (*Sir* Henry) Principal Caird. An address, *etc.* 1898. 8°. **4804**. h. **8**. **(7.)**

—— *See* MacEwan (Charles) *Author of "Dangerous Divinity."* Dangerous Divinity in High Places: being a review of the late lecture [on "Bishop Butler and his Theology"] by the Rev. Principal Caird, *etc.* [1882.] 8°. **4380**. l. **28**. **(9.)**

CAIRD (John) *Principal of the University of Glasgow*.

—— *See* Warr (*Sir* Charles L.) *K.C.V.O.* Principal Caird. 1926. 8°. **3606**. b. **3/3**.

—— *See* Watson (Archibald) *D.D.* Christ's Authority, and other sermons . . . With a preface by J. Caird. 1883. 8°. **4466**. i. **7**.

—— Christian Manliness. A sermon, *etc.* pp. 31. *James Maclehose: Glasgow*, 1871. 8°. **4478**. dd. **2**. **(13.)**

—— Corporate Immortality.—Union with God. *See* Scotch Sermons. Scotch Sermons. 1880. 8°. **4464**. i. **2**.

—— Essays for Sunday Reading . . . With an introduction by the Very Rev. Donald Macleod. pp. xxi. 245. *Sir I. Pitman & Sons: London*, 1906. 8°. **04403**. eee. **28**.

—— The Fundamental Ideas of Christianity . . . (The Gifford Lectures . . . 1892–3 and 1895–6.) With a memoir by Edward Caird. 2 vol. *J. Maclehose & Sons: Glasgow*, 1899. 8°. **4371**. dd. **25**.

—— In memoriam. A sermon preached . . . on occasion of the death of the Very Rev. Thomas Barclay, *etc.* pp. 30. *James Maclehose: Glasgow*, 1873. 8°. **4955**. d. **26**. **(18.)**

—— An Introduction to the Philosophy of Religion. pp. xi. 358. *James Maclehose: Glasgow*, 1880. 8°. **4373**. f. **5**.

—— Introductory Address in the Faculty of Divinity. *See* Glasgow.—*University of Glasgow*. Introductory Addresses, *etc.* 1870. 4°. **8365**. bb. **8**.

—— Mind and Matter. A sermon, *etc.* pp. 27. *J. Maclehose & Sons: Glasgow*, 1888. 8°. **4473**. g. **28**. **(13.)**

—— Religion in Common Life. A sermon, *etc.* pp. 32. *W. Blackwood & Sons: Edinburgh & London*, 1855. 8°. **4485**. d. **3**.

—— New edition. pp. 30. *W. Blackwood & Sons: Edinburgh & London*, 1856. 8°. **4478**. aaa. **10**.

—— [Another edition.] pp. 24. *W. Blackwood & Sons: Edinburgh & London; Hobart Town* [printed], 1856. 12°. **4478**. aa. **120**. **(2.)**

—— Authorised Australian edition, *etc.* pp. 32. *George Robertson: Melbourne*, 1856. 8°. **4478**. h. **2**.

—— [Another edition.] With introduction by Jonathan Nield, *etc.* pp. 62. *H. R. Allenson: London*, [1905.] 8°. [*Heart and Life Booklets*. no. 8.] **04402**. fff. **1/8**.

—— [Another edition.] pp. 35. *Gowans & Gray: London, Glasgow*, 1906. 16°. **4400**. g. **30**.

—— Diadhaidheachd am measg Ghnothuichean an t-Saoghail: searmoin, *etc.* pp. 30. *Paton & Ritchie: Dun-Eidean*, 1856. 8°. **4478**. aa. **17**.

—— Die Religion im gemeinen Leben. Eine Predigt . . . Mit einem Vorwort von Christian Carl Julius Bunsen. Zweite verbesserte und vermehrte Auflage. pp. xx. 38. *Leipzig*, 1857. 8°. **4427**. i. **3**. **(6.)**

—— Náboženství ve všedním životě. Reč . . . Z anglického jazyka přeložil Jan Váňa. pp. 20. *v Praze*, 1882. 8°. [*Anglicko-slovanská knihovna*. 4.] **12205**. i. **1**.

—— *See* Henri (G. W.) Our National Errors, viewed in connection with the Rev. Mr. Caird's sermon . . . on Religion in Common Life. 1856. 8°. **4175**. c. **40**.

CAIRD (John) *Principal of the University of Glasgow.*

—— Religions of India: Vedic period—Brahmanism. (Buddhism.) 2 pt. *W. Blackwood & Sons: Edinburgh & London,* [1881.] 8°. [*Faiths of the World.* Lectures 1, 2.] **4466.** dd. **10/2.**

—— [Another edition.] *See* Oriental Religions. Oriental Religions. 1882. 8°. **4503.** cc. **25.**

—— Sermons. pp. vi. 327. *W. Blackwood & Sons: Edinburgh & London,* 1858. 8°. **4463.** d. **5.**

—— Aspects of Life . . . A new edition of "Sermons," *etc.* pp. vii. 304. *H. R. Allenson: London,* [1906.] 8°. **4462.** ee. **25.**

—— Spinoza. (An examination of his philosophical system.) [With a portrait.] pp. 315. *W. Blackwood & Sons: Edinburgh & London,* 1888. 8°. [*Philosophical Classics for English Readers.*] **2326.** a. **17.**

—— Spiritual Influence. [A sermon.] *See* Wilson (Daniel) *Bishop of Calcutta.* Regeneration, *etc.* [1860.] 8°. **4256.** aa. **55.**

—— The Unity of the Sciences. A lecture, *etc.* pp. 39. *James Maclehose: Glasgow,* 1874. 8°. **8710.** aa. **11.** (**2.**)

—— The Universal Religion. A lecture delivered in Westminster Abbey on the day of intercession for missions. November 30, 1874. pp. 32. *James Maclehose: Glasgow,* 1874. 8°. **04018.** p. **2.**

—— University Addresses: being addresses on subjects of academic study delivered to the University of Glasgow. [Edited by Edward Caird. With a portrait.] pp. x. 383. *J. Maclehose & Sons: Glasgow,* 1898. 8°. **08365.** g. **5.**

—— University Sermons preached before the University of Glasgow, 1873–1898. [Edited by Edward Caird. With a portrait.] pp. viii. 402. *J. Maclehose & Sons: Glasgow,* 1898. 8°. **4477.** g. **20.**

—— What is Religion? A sermon, *etc.* pp. 30. *James Maclehose: Glasgow,* 1871. 8°. **4476.** dd. **41.** (**1.**)

—— A Vallás a munkás életben. Egyházi beszéd, melyet Crathie-Churchben 1855. oktober 14-kén Ő Felsége az Aug. Királyne s Albert Kir. Hg. előtt Caird J. . . . tartott. Magyar forditotta I. S. reform. tanár. [i.e. Sándor Imre.] pp. 48. *Pest,* 1858. 8°. **4398.** b. **79.**

CAIRD (Lindsay Henryson) The History of Corsica. pp. xi. 179. *T. Fisher Unwin: London,* 1899. 8°. **9167.** f. **7.**

—— Talks about the Border Regiment. pp. 32. *T. Fisher Unwin: London,* 1903. 8°. **8821.** a. **5.** (**2.**)

CAIRD (Mona) *See* Caird (Alice M.)

CAIRD (Rennie Alexander) A History, or Notes upon, Family of Caird, Scotland. 2 pt. *Raithby, Lawrence & Co.: Leicester,* 1913, 15. 8°. **9907.** bb. **2.**

CAIRD (William John) *See* Don (John) and Caird (W. J.) Chambers's Navigation, *etc.* 1911. 8°. **08806.** aaa. **6.**

—— —— 1930. 8°. **8804.** bb. **9.**

CAIRD (William R.) An Address on the Instant Coming of the Lord, and the Preparation of the Church for His Coming, *etc.* pp. 23. *Thomas Bosworth: London,* 1867. 8°. **764.** i. **17.** (**2.**)

—— A Letter to the Rev. R. H. Story . . . respecting certain misstatements contained in his memoir of the late Rev. R. Story. pp. 44. *Thomas Laurie: Edinburgh,* 1863. 8°. **764.** i. **17.** (**3.**)

CAIRD (William R.)

—— Notes on the "Feast of the Lord," prescribed to the Jews, and their bearing upon the faith and hope of the Christian Church. By the author of "Worship in Spirit and in Truth" [i.e. W. R. Caird]. pp. 233. 1884. 8°. *See* Jews. **764.** i. **17.** (**5.**)

—— On Worship in Spirit and in Truth. An exposition of the right order of the public worship of the Church. [By W. R. Caird.] pp. xiii. 203. 1877. 8°. *See* Worship. **3478.** bbb. **16.**

—— [Another copy.] **764.** i. **17.** (**4.**)

—— Scripture References on the Gifts and Fruits of the Holy Spirit, *etc.* [Signed: W. R. C., i.e. W. R. Caird.] pp. 12. 1832. 8°. *See* C., W. R. **764.** i. **17.** (**1.**)

—— To the Reverend the Ministers of the Established Church; the Right Reverend the Bishops and their Clergy; and the Rev. the Clergy of all other Christian Congregations in Scotland. [On the schisms within the Church of Scotland. Signed: W. R. Caird, Micaiah Smith, Martin Lindsay.] pp. 3. [1842.] 8°. **764.** m. **6.** (**6.**)

CAIRD (William R.) and **LUTZ** (Johann Evangelist Georg)

—— God's Purpose with Mankind and the Earth. An introduction to a right understanding of the Scriptures . . . Translated . . . from the German . . . A second, improved, and enlarged edition. 2 vol. *Mason, Firth & M'Cutcheon: Melbourne; Thomas Bosworth: London,* 1876, 78. 8°. **3109.** ccc. **1.**

—— [Another copy.] **764.** i. **18.**

CAIRE (de) *Count.* Observations sur un ouvrage de M. de Jarry, ayant pour titre: Projet de formation de l'armée françoise, &c. pp. 69. [*Paris,* 1790.] 8°. **F.R. 275.** (**12.**)

CAIRE (Antonin) Thèse pour le doctorat en médecine, *etc.* (Questions sur diverses branches des sciences médicales.) pp. 30. *Paris,* 1842. 4°. [*Collection des thèses soutenues à la Faculté de Médecine de Paris.* An 1842. tom. 3.] **7371.** c. **17.**

CAIRE (César) La Législation sur le travail industriel des femmes et des enfants. pp. 339. *Paris,* 1896. 8°. **05402.** ff. **6.**

CAIRE (Claudius) Eaux thermo-minérales de Plombières. Étude sur les maladies constitutionnelles des voies digestives, *etc.* pp. 32. *Cannes,* 1868. 8°. **7470.** g. **32.** (**3.**)

—— Essai sur la nostalgie. pp. 27. *Paris,* 1852. 4°. [*Collection des thèses soutenues à la Faculté de Médecine de Paris.* An 1852. tom. 3.] **7372.** e. **7.**

CAIRE (Ferdinando) *See* Ricci (Francesco) *Avvocato.* Corso teorico-pratico di diritto civile . . . Nuova edizione, riveduta . . . dall'avvocato G. Piola (vol. 6–10 dall' avvocato F. Caire). 1907. 8°. **5357.** e. **13.**

—— L'Economia politica applicata in relazione alla legislazione speciale vigente. pp. xv. 361. *Casale,* 1891. 8°. **08207.** g. **21.**

CAIRE (Gaudenzio) Dell'utilità ed importanza degli studi giuridici, economici e statistici nell'insegnamento professionale e industriale. Discorso, *etc.* pp. 30. *Novara,* 1873. 8°. **6006.** bb. **30.**

CAIRE (N. R.) Dissertation sur les hémorrhoïdes, *etc.* pp. 19. *Paris,* 1817. 4°. **1183.** d. **14.** (**9.**)

CAIRE (Paulin Constantin) Étude sur le chlorure de sodium, *etc.* pp. 64. *Paris*, 1873. 4°. [*Collection des thèses soutenues à la Faculté de Médecine de Paris.* An 1873. tom. 4.] **7373.** o.

CAIRE (Pietro) Di una moneta di Pisa ed altra di Bologna trovata presso Novara . . . Digressione. pp. 12. *Novara*, 1875. 8°. **7755.** cc. **9.**

—— Numismatica e sfragistica novarese . . . Memoria i. ii. e iii. pp. vi. 359. *Novara*, 1882. 8°. **7757.** c. **5.**

CAIRE (Pietro Luigi) La Questione del confine occidentale d'Italia sotto il rapporto geografico-strategico, etnografico e linguistico . . . in risposta al libro del barone Severino Cassio "Il Limite naturale d'Italia ad Occidente." pp. 74. *Torino*, 1867. 8°. **8032.** h. **40.** (**5.**)

—— Saggio sul dialetto nizzardo in confronto colle lingue romanze e coi dialetti italiani. pp. 44. *Sanremo*, 1884. 8°. **12902.** d. **24.** (**9.**)

CAIRE (René) *See* Dekobra (M.) *pseud.*, and Caire (R.) Le Voyage sentimental de Lord Littlebird, *etc.* 1919. 8°. **11735.** k. **9.**

CAIREL (Barthélemy) De la douleur. Thèse, *etc.* pp. 40. *Montpellier*, 1870. 4°. **7379.** h. **16.** (**16.**)

CAIREL (Elias) Der Trobador Elias Cairel. Kritische Textausgabe mit Uebersetzungen und Anmerkungen, sowie einer historischen Einleitung . . . Von Dr. Hilde Jaeschke. pp. 223. *Berlin*, 1921. 8°. [*Romanische Studien.* Hft. 20.] **12952.** ppp. **1/20.**

CAIRE-MORANT (A.) La Science des pierres précieuses, appliquée aux arts, *etc.* pp. viii. 423. pl. xvi. *Paris*, 1826. 8°. **973.** c. **26.**

CAIRES (H. S. de) *See* De Caires.

CAIRES (Theophilus) *See* Kaïres.

CAIRLON QUARTERLY. *See* London.—iii. *Anglo-Egyptian Society.*

CAIRN. The Cairn. A gathering of precious stones from many hands. [Poems, anecdotes, etc. The preface "to the reader" signed: "A soldier's daughter," i.e. Sarah, Lady Nicolas.] pp. xvi. 254. *George Bell: London*, 1846. 8°. **1388.** b. **11.**

—— The Cairn. Edinburgh College of Art Magazine. *See* Edinburgh.—*Edinburgh College of Art.*

CAIRN TERRIER ASSOCIATION. *See* England.

CAIRN (James)

—— The Heart of Hollywood. Biographies in miniature of film artists, *etc.* [With portraits.] pp. 202. *Richard Madley: London*, [1942.] 8°. **010604.** bb. **7.**

—— The Heart of Hollywood . . . Second series. [With portraits.] pp. 224. *D. S. Smith: London*, 1945. 8°. **010604.** a. **38.**

—— The Heart of Hollywood. Third series. [With portraits.] pp. 79. *Richard Madley: London*, 1946. 8°. **11797.** a. **60.**

—— Today's Stars. A Hollywood portrait album with biographies. *Hollywood Publications: London*, [1947.] 8°. **11797.** eee. **22.**

CAIRNCROSS (Alec Kirkland) *See* Cairncross (Alexander K.)

CAIRNCROSS (Alexander Kirkland)

—— *See* Glasgow.—*University of Glasgow.—Department of Social and Economic Research.* Social and Economic Studies. (General editor: A. K. Cairncross.) 1953, *etc.* 8°. Ac. **1487.** e/**3.**

CAIRNCROSS (Alexander Kirkland)

—— Home and Foreign Investment, 1870–1913. Studies in capital accumulation. pp. xvi. 251. *University Press: Cambridge*, 1953. 8°. **8219.** pp. **33.**

—— Introduction to Economics. pp. vi. 430. *Butterworth & Co.: London*, 1944. 8°. **08206.** eee. **85.**

—— Introduction to Economics . . . Second edition. pp. viii. 592. *Butterworth & Co.: London*, 1951. 8°. **08207.** l. **14.**

—— The Scottish Economy. A statistical account of Scottish life by members of the staff of Glasgow University. Edited by A. K. Cairncross. pp. xv. 319. *University Press: Cambridge*, 1954. 8°. [*Publications of the Department of Social and Economic Research, University of Glasgow. Social and Economic Studies.* no. 2.] Ac. **1487.** e/**3.**

CAIRNCROSS (Andrew Scott) *See* Parkman (Francis) *the Younger.* On the Warpath . . . Arranged by A. S. Cairncross. [1934.] 8°. W.P. **4834/15.**

—— *See* Peacock (Thomas L.) Maid Marian . . . Edited by A. S. Cairncross. [1935.] 8°. W.P. **7492/3.**

—— *See* Shakespeare (William) [*Works.*] The Arden Shakespeare. (The First Part of King Henry vi. Completely revised and reset. Edited by A. S. Cairncross.) 1899, *etc.* 8°. **11763.** p. **26.** (**1.**)

—— *See* Shakespeare (William) [*Works.*] The Arden Shakespeare, *etc.* (The Second Part of King Henry vi. Third edition, revised. Edited by A. S. Cairncross. 1899. *etc.* 8°. **11763.p.26.b.**

—— Eight Essayists . . . Edited by A. S. Cairncross. pp. xii. 268. *Macmillan & Co.: London*, 1937. 8°. [*Scholar's Library.*] **012209.d.1/56.**

—— Fact and Fiction. Selected and edited by A. S. Cairncross. pp. xiii. 276. *Macmillan & Co.: London*, 1936. 8°. [*Scholar's Library.*] **012209.d.1/48.**

—— Longer Poems, old and new. Selected and edited by A. S. Cairncross. pp. ix. 303. *Macmillan & Co.: London*, 1934. 8°. [*Scholar's Library.*] 012209.d.1/22.

—— Modern Essays in Criticism. Edited by A. S. Cairncross. pp. xi. 301. *Macmillan & Co.: London*, 1938. 8°. [*Scholar's Library.*] **012209.d.1/63.**

—— Poems for Youth. Selected and edited by A. S. Cairncross. pp. xii. 205. *Macmillan & Co.: London*, 1935. 8°. [*Scholar's Library.*] **012209.d.1/35.**

—— Poems Old and New . . . Selected and edited by A. S. Cairncross. pp. xiii. 232. *Macmillan & Co.: London*, 1933. 8°. [*Scholar's Library.*] **012209.d.1/8.**

—— Practical Intermediate English. A three years' course, *etc.* 3 vol. *Oliver & Boyd: Edinburgh, London*, [1932–34.] 8°. **12980.** i. **34.**

—— The Problem of Hamlet. A solution. pp. xix. 205. *Macmillan & Co.: London*, 1936. 8°. **11767.** bb. **10.**

CAIRNCROSS (Andrew Scott) and **SCOBBIE** (James K.)

—— More Poems Old and New. Selected and edited by A. S. Cairncross . . . and J. K. Scobbie. pp. xiii. 215. *Macmillan & Co.: London*, 1939. 8°. [*Scholar's Library.*] **012209.d.1/69.**

CAIRNCROSS (David) The Origin of the Silver Eel, with remarks on bait & fly fishing. pp. viii. 96. *G. Shield: London*, 1862. 8°. **7290.** a. **43.**

CAIRNCROSS (Henry) *See* Burrows (John N.) and Plimpton (W.) Ritual Notes . . . By the editors of "The Order of Divine Service" (H. C., E. C. R. L. [i.e. H. Cairncross, E. C. R. Lamburn]), *etc.* 1926. 8°. **3474.** aa. **2.**

—— —— 1935. 8°. **3474.** aa. **34.**

CAIRNCROSS (Joseph Edward Morrow) and **EMMERSON** (Walter Leslie) Home Health, Happiness and Beauty. Edited by J. E. Cairncross . . . W. L. Emmerson, *etc.* pp. 96. *Good Health Association: Watford,* [1938.] 8°. **7383.** tt. **10.**

CAIRNCROSS (Stanley Everett)

—— The Preparation of Certain Quinazolines by the Reaction of Formaldehyde on Parasubstituted Anilines . . . Dissertation . . . Reprinted from the Collection of Czechoslavak [*sic*] Chemical Communications, *etc.* 2 pt. *New York,* 1938. 8°. **8897.** f. **24.**

CAIRNCROSS (Thomas Scott) The Appeal of Jesus. pp. 198. *J. Clarke & Co.: London,* [1915.] 8°. **4226.** ff. **24.**

—— Blawearie. [A novel.] pp. xvi. 231. *Hodder & Stoughton: London,* [1911.] 8°. **012618.** bb. **25.**

—— From the Kilpatrick Hills. Poems. pp. 152. *Alexander Gardner: Paisley,* [1921.] 8°. **011648.** g. **49.**

—— The Making of a Minister. pp. 189. *J. Clarke & Co.: London,* 1914. 8°. **4499.** bbb. **22.**

—— The Return of the Master, and other poems. pp. viii. 106. *Robert Scott: Langholm; J. Menzies & Co.: Edinburgh & Glasgow,* [1905.] 8°. **11650.** ff. **47.**

—— The Scot at Hame. [Poems.] pp. vi. 74. *Constable & Co.: London,* 1922. 8°. **011650.** k. **79.**

—— The Steps of the Pulpit. pp. xv. 260. *Hodder & Stoughton: London,* 1910. 8°. **4499.** i. **11.**

CAIRNCROSS (W. M.) The Book for Officers. Showing the way to victory, efficiency, honour & health. pp. xviii. 202. *Bennett, Coleman & Co.: Bombay,* 1916. 16°. **8825.** aaa. **61.**

CAIRNES, *Family of. See* Lawlor (Henry C.) A History of the Family of Cairnes, *etc.* 1906. 4°. **9904.** p. **4.**

CAIRNES (Clive Elmore) Coquihalla Area, British Columbia. [With plates and maps.] pp. 187. *Ottawa,* 1924. 8°. [*Canada. Geological Survey. Memoir.* no. 139.] C.S. E. **16/9.**

—— Descriptions of Properties, Slocan Mining Camp, British Columbia. [With maps.] pp. v. 274. pl. II. *Ottawa,* 1935. 8°. [*Canada. Geological Survey. Memoir.* no. 184.] C.S. E. **16/9.**

—— Geology and Mineral Deposits of Bridge River Mining Camp, British Columbia. [With maps.] pp. 140. vi. *Ottawa,* 1937. 8°. [*Canada. Geological Survey. Memoir.* no. 213.] C.S. E. **16/9.**

—— Slocan Mining Camp, British Columbia. [With maps.] pp. iv. 137. pl. XIII. *Ottawa,* 1934. 8°. [*Canada. Geological Survey. Memoir.* no. 173.] C.S. E. **16/9.**

CAIRNES (De Lorme Donaldson) Moose Mountain District of Southern Alberta. [With maps.] pp. 55. *Ottawa,* 1907. 8°. [*Reports submitted to the Geological Survey of Canada.*] **7106.de.1.(11.)**

—— Second edition. pp. 62. *Ottawa,* 1914. 8°. [*Canada. Geological Survey. Memoir.* no. 61.] C.S. E. **16/9.**

—— Portions of Atlin District, British Columbia: with special reference to lode mining. [With a map.] pp. ix. 129. pl. XXXII. *Ottawa,* 1913. 8°. [*Canada. Geological Survey. Memoir.* no. 37.] C.S. E. **16/9.**

CAIRNES (De Lorme Donaldson)

—— Preliminary Memoir on the Lewes and Nordenskiöld Rivers Coal District, Yukon Territory. [With maps.] pp. 70. *Ottawa,* 1910. 8°. [*Canada. Geological Survey. Memoir.* no. 5.] C.S. E. **16/9.**

—— Report on a Portion of Conrad and Whitehorse Mining Districts, Yukon. [With a map.] pp. 38. *Ottawa,* 1908. 8°. [*Reports submitted to the Geological Survey of Canada.*] **7106.de.1.(17.)**

—— Scroggie, Barker, Thistle, and Kirkman Creeks, Yukon Territory. [With plates.] pp. 47. *Ottawa,* 1917. 8°. [*Canada. Geological Survey. Memoir.* no. 97.] C.S. E. **16/9.**

—— Upper White River District, Yukon. pp. iv. 191. pl. XVII. *Ottawa,* 1915. 8°. [*Canada. Geological Survey. Memoir.* no. 50.] C.S. E. **16/9.**

—— Wheaton District, Yukon Territory. [With a supplement.] 2 pt. *Ottawa,* 1912, 15. 8°. [*Canada. Geological Survey. Memoir.* no. 31.] C.S. E. **16/9.**

—— The Yukon-Alaska International Boundary, between Porcupine and Yukon Rivers. pp. iii. 161. pl. XVI. *Ottawa,* 1914. 8°. [*Canada. Geological Survey. Memoir.* no. 67.] C.S. E. **16/9.**

CAIRNES (John Elliott) The Character & Logical Method of Political Economy; being a course of lectures, *etc.* pp. xii. 184. *Longman & Co.: London,* 1857. 8°. **8205.** b. **13.**

Imperfect; wanting pp. 1, 2.

—— Second and enlarged edition. pp. xvii. 229. *Macmillan & Co.: London,* 1875. 8°. **8206.** cc. **25.**

—— [Another edition.] pp. 235. *Macmillan & Co.: London,* 1888. 8°. **8207.** g. **38.**

—— Colonization and Colonial Government: a lecture. *See* Dublin.—*Young Men's Christian Association.* Lectures delivered . . . during the year 1864. 1865. 8°. **4463.** dd. **16.**

—— England's Neutrality in the American Contest . . . Reprinted with additions from "Macmillan's Magazine." pp. 23. *Emancipation Society: London,* 1864. 8°. **8177.** aaa. **13.**

—— Essays in Political Economy, theoretical and applied. pp. vii. 371. *Macmillan & Co.: London,* 1873. 8°. **8206.** c. **34.**

—— An Examination into the Principles of Currency involved in the Bank Charter Act of 1844. pp. 78. *Hodges & Smith: Dublin,* 1854. 8°. **8229.** aaaa. **21.** (**13.**)

—— Political Essays. pp. viii. 350. *Macmillan & Co.: London,* 1873. 8°. **8009.** bbb. **29.**

—— The Revolution in America: a lecture, *etc. See* Dublin.—*Young Men's Christian Association.* Lectures delivered . . . during the year 1862. 1863. 8°. **4463.** d. **12.**

—— (Seventh edition, revised and enlarged.) pp. 48. *Hodges, Smith & Co.: Dublin,* [1863.] 8°. **8175.** de. **44.**

—— The Slave Power; its character, career, & probable designs: being an attempt to explain the real issues involved in the American contest. pp. xviii. 304. *Parker, Son & Bourn: London,* 1862. 8°. **8156.** d. **6.**

—— Second edition. Much enlarged and with a new preface. pp. xliv. 410. *Macmillan & Co.: London & Cambridge,* 1863. 8°. **8156.** d. **7.**

[CA]IRNES (JOHN ELLIOTT)

— Some Leading Principles of Political Economy newly expounded. pp. xix. 506. *Macmillan & Co.: London,* 1874. 8°. **8207**. g. **16**.

— [Another edition.] pp. 421. *Macmillan & Co.: London,* 1884. 8°. **8205**. ee. **27**.

— A Few Remarks on Professor Cairnes' Recent Contribution to Political Economy [i.e. "Some Leading Principles of Political Economy newly expounded."] By a former Member of the Political Economy Club. pp. 18. *Simpkin, Marshall & Co.: London,* 1875. 8°. **8207**. bb. **21**.

— The Southern Confederacy and the African Slave Trade. The correspondence between Professor Cairnes . . . and George M'Henry . . . Reprinted from the "Daily News." With an introduction and notes by the Rev. George B. Wheeler. pp. xxviii. 61. *McGlashan & Gill: Dublin,* 1863. 8°. **8156**. aaa. **17**.

— University Education in Ireland . . . Reprinted from the Theological Review. pp. 43. *Macmillan & Co.: London,* 1866. 8°. **8364**. bb. **17**.

— *See* MACDEVITT (John) University Education in Ireland and "Ultramontanism." Being an examination of arguments lately published by . . . G. [or rather J.] E. Cairnes, *etc.* 1866. 8°. **8364**. bb. **27**.

— University Education in Ireland: a letter to J. S. Mill, Esq. M.P. pp. 63. *Macmillan & Co.: London,* 1866. 8°. **8365**. c. **13**.

— University Education in Ireland . . . Extract from a letter to J. S. Mill, Esq. pp. 15. *Printed for private circulation: Dublin,* 1873. 8°. **8366**. bb. **55**. (**5**.)

— Who are the Canters? pp. 8. *Emily Faithfull: London,* [1863.] 12°. **8177**. a. **82**. (**8**.)

— Woman Suffrage: a reply [to Goldwin Smith] . . . Reprinted from Macmillan's Magazine, *etc.* pp. 24. *A. Ireland & Co.: Manchester,* 1874. 8°. **8416**. cc. **1**. (**16**.)

[CA]IRNES (MAUD) *pseud.* [i.e. *Lady* MAUD KATHLEEN CAIRNES CURZON-HERRICK.] *See* also HERRICK (*Lady* M. K. C. C.)

— Strange Journey. pp. 248. *Cobden-Sanderson: London,* 1935. 8°. **NN**. **23485**.

[CA]IRNES (THOMAS PLUNKET) Thomas Plunket Cairnes, J.P. A memento of the address and presentation . . . made to T. P. Cairnes . . . Together with various biographical sketches and pulpit references. pp. viii. 56. *Printed for private circulation: London,* [1894.] 4°. **4956**. f. **12**.

[CA]IRNES (WILLIAM ELLIOT) An Absent-Minded War. Being some reflections on our reverses [in South Africa] and the causes which have led to them. By a British Officer [i.e. W. E. Cairnes]. pp. vii. 183. 1900. 8°. *See* WAR. **8832**. aa. **38**.

— The Army from Within. By the author of "An Absent-Minded War" [i.e. W. E. Cairnes]. pp. viii. 180. 1901. 8°. *See* ENGLAND.—*Army.* [*Appendix.*] **8822**. aaa. **8**.

— The Coming Waterloo . . . Second impression. pp. 364. *A. Constable & Co.: Westminster,* 1901. 8°. **012640**. c. **42**.

— Lord Roberts as a Soldier in Peace and War. A biography. pp. 331. *Hodder & Stoughton: London,* 1901. 8°. **010817**. e. **21**.

CAIRNES (WILLIAM ELLIOT)

— Social Life in the British Army. By a British officer [i.e. W. E. Cairnes]. With . . . illustrations by R. C. Woodville. pp. xx. 224. 1900. 8°. *See* ENGLAND.—*Army.* [*Appendix.*] **8822**. aaa. **6**.

CAIRNEY (JOHN)

— *See* GOWLAND (William P.) and CAIRNEY (J.) Anatomy and Physiology for Nurses, *etc.* 1955. 8°. **7423**. d. **11**.

— Gynaecology for Senior Students of Nursing, *etc.* pp. 211. pl. II. *N. M. Peryer: Christchurch,* 1954. 8°. **7583**. b. **54**.

— Surgery for Students of Nursing, *etc.* pp. 326. *N. M. Peryer: Christchurch, N.Z.,* 1952. 8°. **7484**. m. **27**.

CAIRNGORM CLUB. *See* ABERDEEN, *City of.*

CAIRNS, *Family of.* *See* LAWLOR (Henry C.) A History of the Family of Cairnes or Cairns, *etc.* 1906. 4°. **9904**. p. **4**.

CAIRNS (ADAM) *See* BALLANTYNE (James) *Rev., of Melbourne.* Report of the Proceedings in connection with the consummation of Presbyterian Union . . . With prefatory note by the Rev. Dr. Cairns. 1859. 8°. **4175**. bb. **31**.

— *See* CUMMING (John) *D.D., etc.* A Lecture on Labor, Rest, and Recreation . . . With an introduction by Dr. Cairns. 1856. 8°. **8282**. d. **48**. (**3**.)

— *See* NEW (Isaac) The Boaster rebuked: remarks on Dr. Cairns' insulting attack on the Baptists, *etc.* 1863. 8°. **4135**. e. **3**. (**7**.)

— Church and State. A lecture, *etc.* pp. 28. *Wilson, Mackinnon & Fairfax: Melbourne,* 1856. 8°. **4183**. bb. **84**. (**10**.)

— State Aid Question. Strictures on the pamphlets of Dr. Cairns [i.e. "Church and State"] & T. T. A'Beckett [entitled: "A Defence of State Aid to Religion"]. By a Scotch Catholic. pp. 16. *James Caple: Melbourne,* 1856. 8°. **8307**. f. **16**.

— The Dangers and Duties of the Young Men of Victoria . . . Lecture delivered before the Victoria Early Closing Association, *etc.* pp. 29. *Wilson, Mackinnon & Fairfax: Melbourne,* 1856. 8°. **8406**. dd. **17**. (**2**.)

— England's Policy and Prospects in connection with the Eastern War: a discourse, *etc.* pp. 16. *Hugh M'Coll: Melbourne,* 1854. 8°. **4477**. f. **1**. (**5**.)

— Historic Sketches of Gibraltar & its neighbourhood. A lecture, *etc.* pp. 25. *Hugh M'Coll: Melbourne,* 1854. 8°. **10107**. ff. **5**. (**2**.)

— Inaugural Address delivered at the opening of the Theological Hall of the Presbyterian Church of Victoria, *etc.* pp. 16. *A. J. Smith: Melbourne,* 1866. 8°. **4183**. bb. **63**.

— The Inauguration of the Political Independence of Victoria . . . A lecture, *etc.* pp. 19. *Wilson, Mackinnon & Fairfax: Melbourne,* 1856. 8°. **8154**. c. **21**.

— The Jews; their fall and restoration. Two discourses, *etc.* pp. 32. *J. J. Blundell & Co.: Melbourne,* 1854. 8°. **4034**. e. **55**. (**2**.)

— New Year's Sermon; with remarks suggested by the decease of . . . Sir Charles Hotham. pp. 22. *Wilson, Mackinnon & Fairfax: Melbourne,* 1856. 8°. **4920**. cc. **46**. (**11**.)

CAIRNS (Adam)

—— The Second Woe; a popular exposition of the tenth and eleventh chapters of Revelation, showing that the theory of the Rev. Mr. Elliott, and the author of the "Seventh Vial," as to the death and resurrection of the witnesses, is inconsistent both with prophetic Scripture and profane history. pp. v. 163. *Johnstone & Hunter: Edinburgh,* 1852. 8°. **3186. c. 7.**

—— Some Objections to Universal Atonement stated, and the objections to a particular and efficacious Atonement considered: in two discourses . . . Second edition. pp. 32. *Fife Sentinel Office: Cupar,* 1844. 8°. **4257. d. 17.**

With newspaper-cuttings inserted.

CAIRNS (Alexander) *See* Eversley (William P.) Eversley's Law of the Domestic Relations . . . Fourth edition by A. Cairns. 1926. 8°. **6326. i. 25.**

—— —— 1937. 8°. **6327.g.1.**

—— *See* Montefiore (Arthur J. H.) afterwards Brice (A. J. H. M.) Look upon the Prisoner . . . Edited by A. Cairns, *etc.* [1928.] 8°. **06055. ee. 19.**

—— The County Court Pleader. A guide to pleadings and evidence in actions in the County Courts, with precedents of claims and defences. pp. xxvii. 608. *Sweet & Maxwell; Stevens & Sons: London,* 1937. 8°. **6191. g. 8.**

—— The County Court Pleader . . . Second edition. By E. Dennis Smith. pp. xxix. 779. *Sweet & Maxwell; Stevens & Sons: London,* 1949. 8°. **6192. bbb. 9.**

—— Leading Cases on Rent Restriction. With an introductory outline. pp. xi. 162. *Stevens & Sons: London,* 1923. 8°. **6325. c. 49.**

—— The Practising Lawyer's Repertory. An alphabetical commonplace book of statute and case law and rules of procedure, *etc.* pp. xvi. 433. *Sweet & Maxwell; Stevens & Sons: London,* 1933. 8°. **6120. f. 17.**

CAIRNS (Alison H.)

—— *See* Cairns (David S.) David Cairns. An autobiography . . . Edited by his son and daughter, *etc.* 1950. 8°. **4957. bb. 4.**

CAIRNS (C. C.) A Book of Noble Women . . . With seven photogravure portraits. pp. xi. 368. *T. C. & E. C. Jack: London,* [1911.] 8°. **010603. d. 5.**

—— [A reissue.] Noble Women, *etc.* *London & Edinburgh,* [1912.] 8°. **10601. w. 7.**

CAIRNS (Charlotte)

—— Tea Time Tips. pp. 124. *Ettrick Press: Edinburgh, London,* [1948.] 8°. **7948. aa. 23.**

—— With Ring and Grill. [Recipes.] pp. 95. *Ettrick Press: London, Edinburgh,* 1951. 8°. **7949. de. 31.**

CAIRNS (Christiana Victoria) Fugitive Poems. pp. 248. *Jones & Causton: London,* 1860. 8°. **11647. c. 30.**

CAIRNS (Cicely)

—— Murder goes to Press. pp. 211. *Constable: London,* 1950. 8°. **NNN. 840.**

CAIRNS (D.) *of the New Zealand Department of Scientific and Industrial Research.*

—— *See* Poole (A. L.) *of the New Zealand Department of Scientific and Industrial Research,* and Cairns (D.) Botanical Aspects of Ragwort . . . Control. 1940. 8°. [*New Zealand. Department of Scientific and Industrial Research. Bulletin.* no. 82.] **C.S. G. 681.**

CAIRNS (D.) *Son of David Smith Cairns.*

—— *See* Cairns (David S.) David Cairns. An autobiography . . . Edited by his son and daughter, *etc.* 1950. 8°. **4957. bb. 4.**

CAIRNS (David) *See* Cairns (John) *Principal of the United Presbyterian College, Edinburgh.* Christ, the Morning Star; and other sermons. By . . . J. Cairns. Edited by his brothers (William Cairns, David Cairns). 1892. 8°. **4478. dd. 26.**

—— *See* Smith (David) *D.D., of Biggar.* Sermons and Letters . . . With a memoir of the author by D. Cairns. 1869. 8°. **4462. cc. 30.**

CAIRNS (David Smith) *See* Brunner (E.) The Church and the Oxford Group. Translated by D. Cairns. 1937. 8°. **4106. i. 57.**

—— *See* Brunner (E.) God and Man . . . Translated with an introduction by D. Cairns. 1936. 8°. **04374. de. 79.**

—— *See* Small (Annie H.) An Act of Prayer . . . Introduction by Professor D. S. Cairns. 1912. 8°. **03558.de.50/4.**

—— *See* Stirling (John) The Study Bible, *etc.* (St. John . . . By D. S. Cairns.) 1926, *etc.* 8°. **03126. h. 2/10.**

—— *See* Young (W. P.) *Rev.* A Soldier to the Church . . . With an introduction by Prof. D. S. Cairns. 1919. 8°. **4106. e. 63.**

—— The Army and Religion. An enquiry and its bearing upon the religious life of the nation, *etc.* pp. xxxi. 455. 1919. 8°. *See* England.—*Committee of Enquiry upon the Army and Religion.* **04018. e. 4.**

—— Christianity and Macht-Politik. pp. 20. *Evangelical Information Committee: London,* 1918. 8°. **4014. d. 60.**

—— Christianity in the Modern World. pp. xv. 314. *Hodder & Stoughton: London,* 1906. 8°. **4375. ee. 29.**

—— The Crisis and the Non-Christian Races. *See* Kempthorne (J. A.) *successively Bishop of Hull and of Lichfield.* Christianity and the World-Crisis. Addresses, *etc.* [1915.] 8°. **4017. dd. 17.**

—— Faith. pp. 16. *C.M.S.: London,* 1911. 8°. **4767. aa. 28. (3.)**

—— The Faith that Rebels. A re-examination of the miracles of Jesus. pp. 260. *Student Christian Movement: London,* 1928. 8°. **4224. h. 28.**

—— (Third, revised, edition.) pp. 260. *Student Christian Movement: London,* 1929. 8°. **4225. ff. 38.**

—— [Another edition.] pp. 256. *Student Christian Movement Press: London,* 1933. 8°. [*Torch Library.*] **3606.aa.7/3.**

—— The Faith that rebels, *etc.* (Sixth edition.) pp. xi. 260. *SCM Press: London,* 1954. 8°. **04227. a. 16.**

—— The German Reaction to Defeat. An address given to the seventh meeting of the British Council of Churches . . . October 3rd, 1945. pp. 10. [1945.] 8°. *See* England.—*British Council of Churches.—Department of International Friendship.* **12301. b. 41.**

—— The Image of God in Man. pp. 255. *SCM Press London,* 1953 8°. **4381. h. 36**

—— Jesus on Faith. pp. 8. *Layman Publishing Co. Goring,* [1954.] 8°. [*Linking Christianity with Citizenship.* no. 11.] **W.P. c. 536/11**

CAIRNS (David Smith)

—— Life and Times of Alexander Robertson MacEwen, *etc.* [With portraits.] pp. xii. 308. *Hodder & Stoughton: London*, 1925. 8°. **4956. k. 17.**

—— God the Hope of the World. Address, *etc.* pp. 23. *Macniven & Wallace: Edinburgh*, [1923.] 8°. **4473. h. 44.**

—— Hope . . . Reprinted from the International Review of Missions, *etc.* pp. 12. *Student Christian Movement: London*, [1916.] 8°. **4016. h. 27.**

—— The Reasonableness of the Christian Faith. pp. vi. 221. *Hodder & Stoughton: London*, 1918. 8°. **4014. ee. 37.**

—— The Riddle of the World. [Based on the Baird Lectures for 1932.] pp. vii. 378. *Student Christian Movement Press: London*, 1937. 8°. **04374. e. 37.**

—— David Cairns. An autobiography. Some recollections . . . and selected letters, edited by his son and daughter [i.e. D. Cairns and Alison H. Cairns], with a memoir by . . . D. M. Baillie. [With plates, including a portrait.] pp. 220. *SCM Press: London*, 1950. 8°. **4957. bb. 4.**

CAIRNS (Dorothy) Your Healthy Diet. pp. 37. *Lutterworths: London*, [1926.] 8°. **7391. aa. 48.**

CAIRNS (*Hon.* Douglas Halyburton) On Shooting. *See* Letters. Letters to Young Sportsmen, *etc.* 1920. 8°. **7911. e. 27.**

CAIRNS (Ebenezer Adam) *See* Dykes (James O.) " Weep not." A funeral sermon. [On the death of E. A. Cairns.] 1866. 8°. **4906. cc. 1.**

CAIRNS (Elizabeth) Memoirs of the Life of Elizabeth Cairns . . . written by herself, *etc.* [Edited by John Greig.] pp. 173. *John Brown: Glasgow*, 1762. 8°. **1416. a. 23.**

—— [Another edition.] [With a preface by Peter Drummond.] pp. 94. *Nisbet & Co.: London*, 1857. 8°. **4804. f. 25. (2.)**

CAIRNS (Ethel) *See* Cairns (John A. R.) Drab Street Glory, *etc.* [Edited by T. Allen and E. Cairns.] [1934.] 8°. **8286. aa. 35.**

CAIRNS (Frank) *See* MacIver (Kenneth I.) In Memoriam. Some sermons by the Rev. K. I. MacIver . . . With biographical sketch by the Rev. F. Cairns, *etc.* [1931.] 8°. **04478. g. 55.**

—— The Prophet of the Heart. Being the Warrack Lectures on Preaching for 1934. pp. 205. *Hodder & Stoughton: London*, 1934. 8°. **20018. ee. 12.**

CAIRNS (Gwendoline Olga) and **CAIRNS** (James Ford)

—— Australia, *etc.* [With plates.] pp. vi. 90. *Adam & Charles Black: London*, 1953. 8°. [*Lands and Peoples Series.*] **W.P. 123/9.**

CAIRNS (Hugh MacCalmont) *Earl Cairns. See* Barrister-at-Law. The Law of Mutual Life Assurance with special reference to the decision of Lord Cairns in the Kent Mutual Society's case. To which is appended . . . a verbatim report of Lord Cairns's judgment, *etc.* 1872. 8°. **8227. bb. 47.**

—— *See* Blake (John A.) The Salmon Fisheries of Ireland. Replies to arguments advanced against Mr. M'Mahon's Fishery Bill by Lord Stuart de Decies and Sir H. Cairns. 1863. 4°. **7290. e. 48.**

CAIRNS (Hugh MacCalmont) *Earl Cairns.*

—— *See* Cecil (Robert A. T. G.) *Marquis of Salisbury*, and Cairns (H. M.) *Earl Cairns.* London Chatham and Dover Railway Arbitration. Award, *etc.* 1870. 8°. **8235. i. 45. (7.)**

—— —— [1871.] 8°. **6376. f. 17. (3.)**

—— *See* England.—*Church of England.—Clergy.* [*Appendix.*] The Ornaments of the Minister. Case submitted to counsel . . . together with the joint opinion thereon of the Attorney-General, Sir H. M. Cairns, *etc.* 1866. 8°. **5155. aaa. 32.**

—— *See* Hawkins (Francis V.) The Title to Landed Estates Bills, and the Solicitor-General's [Sir H. M. C. Cairns's] speech, considered. 1859. 8°. **6305. b. 3. (12.)**

—— *See* Kelly (*Right Hon. Sir* Fitzroy) On the Repeal of the xxixth Canon of 1603. The opinions of Sir F. Kelly, Sir H. McC. Cairns . . . on behalf of the Lord Archbishop of Armagh. 1861. 8°. **5175. c. 20.**

—— *See* Senex. Chancery Lunatics. A reply to the address made to the House of Commons . . . by Sir H. Cairns . . . in defence of the two acts of Parliament, passed in 1853, relating to Chancery Lunatics, *etc.* 1861. 8°. **8304. ff. 13. (5.)**

—— Addresses delivered by Sir H. Cairns . . . Rev. T. R. Birks; and the Rev. Canon Hugh McNeile . . . on the identity in the interests of the two branches of the United Church of England and Ireland; that church's present danger; her duty and safeguard in the impending crisis; at the Irish Church Missions' Anniversary Breakfast, 1864. pp. 23. *Hatchard & Co.: London*, 1864. 12°. **4165. b. 17.**

—— Albert Arbitration. Lord Cairns's decisions. [With Appendix A–P.] Reported by F. S. Reilly. 3 pt. pp. 268. lxxvi. *Stevens & Haynes: London*, 1872–75. 8°. **6121. b. 2.**

—— Belfast Nurses' Home and Training School. Speech. pp. 7. *Adair's Steam Printing Works: Belfast*, 1873. 8°. **07306. g. 19. (2.)**

—— For the English Working Classes. The Irish Church. An address delivered in 1864 . . . Re-issued by B. A. Heywood. pp. 16. *Hatchard & Co.: London*, 1868. 8°. **4165. aaa. 23.**

—— Third edition. pp. 23. *Hatchard & Co.: London*, 1868. 8°. **4165. aaa. 24.**

—— Four Speeches . . . on behalf of the Church Missionary Society. pp. 10. *Church Missionary House: London*, 1885. 8°. **4766. d. 13. (10.)**

—— India Debate. Speech of the Solicitor General delivered in the House of Commons . . . in opposition to Mr. Cardwell's motion. Reprinted from the " Times." Second edition. pp. 24. *I. R. Taylor: London*, [1858.] 8°. **8023. d. 13.**

—— Third edition. pp. 24. *I. R. Taylor: London*, [1858.] 8°. **08023. bb. 4. (2.)**

—— Judgment delivered . . . on behalf of Her Majesty's Most Honorable Privy Council in the case of Martin v. Mackonochie. Edited by W. E. Browning. pp. 32. *Butterworths: London*, 1869. 8°. **5157. bb. 4.**

—— Opinions of Lord Chancellor Cairns and Lord Selborne on the Public Worship Regulation Bill. pp. 8. [*London*, 1874.] 8°. **4109. b. 7. (14.)**

—— Some Last Words of Earl Cairns. Earl Cairns' speech at . . . Exeter Hall . . . March 24th, 1885, on the claims of the heathen and Mohammedan world. Together with a few of his dying words. pp. 15. *C.M.S.: London*, [1885.] 8°. **4766. aa. 8. (1.)**

CAIRNS (Hugh MacCalmont) *Earl Cairns.*

—— The Speech of the Lord Chancellor delivered in the House of Lords, June 29th 1868, on the motion for the second reading of a Bill, intituled ' An Act to prevent, for a limited time, new appointments in the Church of Ireland.' pp. 48. *Seeley, Jackson & Halliday: London,* 1868. 8°. **4165.** aaa. **25.**

—— [Another edition.] pp. 47. *Seeley, Jackson & Halliday: London,* 1868. 8°. **4165.** aa. **25.**

—— Titles to Landed Estates. Speech of the Solicitor General, on the introduction of bills to simplify the titles to landed estates, and to establish a registry of titles to landed estates. pp. 30. *William Amer: London,* 1859. 8°. **6305.** b. **3. (11.)**

—— Answer to the Land-Titles' Speech of the Solicitor General, shewing the objections to his bills. pp. 28. *Law Times Office: London,* [1859.] 8°. **6305.** c. **3.**

—— Words to Young Men. (An address.) pp. 7. *Hodder & Stoughton: London,* [1881.] 16°. **4422.** b. **16.** (**2.**)

—— Brief Memories of Hugh McCalmont, first Earl Cairns. By the author of " Memoir of the Rev. W. Marsh, D.D." [i.e. Miss C. M. Marsh] . . . Sixth thousand, with additions. pp. 114. *J. Nisbet & Co.: London,* 1885. 8°. **4956.** aaa. **17.**

CAIRNS (*Sir* Hugh William Bell) *K.B.E.*

—— *See* Florey (Sir Howard W.) and Cairns (Sir H. W. B.) K.B.E. Investigation of War Wounds. Penicillin, *etc.* 1943. 8°. B.S. **45/86.**

—— A Study of Intracranial Surgery. pp. 83. *London,* 1929. 8°. [*Medical Research Council. Special Report Series.* no. 125.] B.S. **25/8.**

CAIRNS (Huntington) Law and the Social Sciences, *etc.* pp. xiv. 279. *Kegan Paul & Co.: London,* 1935. 8°. [*International Library of Psychology, Philosophy and Scientific Method.*] **08458.** c. **1/31.**

—— Legal Philosophy from Plato to Hegel. pp. xv. 583. *Johns Hopkins Press: Baltimore.* 1949. 8°. **6003.cc.31.**

—— The Limits of Art. Poetry and prose chosen by ancient and modern critics. Collected and edited by H. Cairns. pp. xliv. 1473. *Routledge & Kegan Paul: London,* 1951. 8°. **12299.** ee. **20.**

CAIRNS (Huntington) and **WALKER** (John) *of the National Gallery of Art, Washington.*

—— Masterpieces of Painting from the National Gallery of Art. [Reproductions.] Edited by H. Cairns and J. Walker. (Third edition.) pp. 182. 1946. fol. *See* Washington, *D.C.—Smithsonian Institution.—National Gallery of Art.* [1937- .] L.R. **296.** dd. **14.**

—— Masterpieces of Painting from the National Gallery of Art. [Reproductions.] Edited by H. Cairns and J. Walker. pp. 183. 1952. fol. *See* Washington, *D.C.—Smithsonian Institution.—National Gallery of Art.* [1937- .] L.R. **401.** d. **13.**

CAIRNS (J. M.) *See* Donnegan (James) A New Greek and English Lexicon . . . Arranged . . . by J. M. Cairns, *etc.* 1843. 12°. **12923.** a. **46.**

CAIRNS (J. S.)

—— The Life Force and the Body Image. *J. S. Cairns: Sunderland.* [1954.] 4°. 1865. c. 20. (72.)

CAIRNS (Jacques) Considérations physiologiques sur le système nerveux; thèse, *etc.* pp. 30. *Paris,* 1824. 4°. **1183.** h. **7.** (**12.**)

CAIRNS (James) *B.D.* The Grading of the Sunday School. pp. 93. *S.P.C.K.: London,* 1909. 8°. **4192.** de. **19.**

CAIRNS (James) *of Hawick.* Report of the Trial of Cairns, Turnbull, Smith, and Lamb . . . for the crimes of mobbing and rioting, and assault . . . By Archibald Swinton. pp. 40. *Thomas Clark: Edinburgh,* 1838. 8°. **6583.** cc. **24.**

CAIRNS (James) *Poetical Writer.* Sunshine and Shadow. [Poems.] pp. xi. 92. *Moray Press: Edinburgh & London,* 1934. 8°. **11654.** aa. **29.**

CAIRNS (James Ford)

—— *See* Cairns (Gwendoline O.) and Cairns (J. F.) Australia, *etc.* 1953. 8°. W.P. **123/9.**

CAIRNS (John) *Esq.* A Practical Treatise on the Growing and Curing of Tobacco in Ireland. pp. 30. *M. H. Gill & Son: Dublin,* 1886. 8°. **7031.** bb. **31.** (**3.**)

CAIRNS (John) *of Dumfries.* Principal Cairns. pp. 157. *Oliphant, Anderson & Ferrier: Edinburgh,* 1903. 8°. [*Famous Scots Series.*] **10803.** ccc. **7.**

CAIRNS (John) *Presbyterian Minister, of Woolwich.* John Hawkes, and his successors. A biographical and historical account, from 1662 to 1912, of the Presbyterian ministry of the congregation now known as New Road, Woolwich. pp. 32. *W. J. Squires: Woolwich,* 1913. 8°. **4715.** aa. **48.**

CAIRNS (John) *Principal of the United Presbyterian College, Edinburgh. See* Anderson (William) *LL.D.* An Exposure of Popery . . . With an introduction by . . . J. Cairns, *etc.* 1878. 8°. **3940.** bb. **4.**

—— *See* Andrew (Alexander) John Cairns . . . his life story, *etc.* [1898.] 8°. **4804.** cc. **4.** (**5.**)

—— *See* Bacon (F.) *Viscount St. Albans.* [*Selections.*] Thoughts on Holy Scripture . . . With preface by J. Cairns. 1862. 8°. **03128.** h. **7.**

—— *See* Bible.—*Thessalonians.* [*Polyglott.*] A Commentary on the Greek Text of the Epistles . . . to the Thessalonians . . . With a preface by . . . Professor Cairns. 1877. 8°. **03265.** eee. **16.**

—— *See* Cairns (John) *of Dumfries.* Principal Cairns. 1903. 8°. **10803.** ccc. **7.**

—— *See* Culverwell (Nathaniel) Of the Light of Nature. A discourse . . . With a critical essay . . . by J. Cairns. 1857. 8°. **4375.** d. **18.**

—— *See* Henderson (James) *D.D., of Galashiels.* Sermons . . . With memoir by J. Cairns. 1859. 8°. **4464.** c. **24.**

—— *See* Krummacher (F. W.) Elijah the Tishbite . . . New translation, by the Rev. J. Cairns. 1846. 12°. **4785.** aa. **3.**

—— *See* Krummacher (F. W.) Friedrich Wilhelm Krummacher: an autobiography . . . With a preface by Professor Cairns. 1869. 8°. **4886.** h. **45.**

—— —— 1871. 8°. **4887.** b. **34.**

—— *See* MacEwen (Alexander R.) Life and Letters of John Cairns, *etc.* [With a portrait.] 1895. 8°. **4956.** h. **5.**

—— —— 1898. 8°. **4907.** k. **2.**

CAIRNS (John) *Principal of the United Presbyterian College, Edinburgh.*

—— *See* Murray (Nicholas) *Rev., etc.* Kirwan's Letters to . . . John Hughes, Roman Catholic Bishop of New York . . . With recommendatory preface by J. Cairns. [1875.] 8°. **3942.** a. **1.**

—— *See* Probation. Future Probation . . . By S. Leathes . . . W. Cairns, *etc.* 1886. 8°. **3605.** i. **2/1.**

—— *See* Smith (Alexander Skene) Holiday Recreations . . . With a preface by . . . Principal Cairns. 1888. 8°. **011653.** e. **28.**

—— *See* Wilson (George) *M.D., F.R.S.E.* Counsels of an Invalid, *etc.* [Edited by J. Cairns.] 1862. 8°. **4407.** aaa. **32.**

—— Christ the Central Evidence of Christianity, and other present day tracts. 6 pt. *R.T.S.: [London,]* 1893. 8°. **4429.** df. **32.**

—— Argument for Christianity from the Experience of Christians. pp. 40. *R.T.S.: London,* [1889.] 8°. [*Present Day Tracts.* ser. 2. no. 61.] **4018.** ee. **1/11.**

—— Christ and the Christian Faith. Present day papers. pp. 113. *R.T.S.: London,* 1904. 8°. **4430.** f. **13.**

—— Christ the Central Evidence of Christianity. pp. 36. *R.T.S.: London,* 1882. 8°. [*Present Day Tracts.* no. 3.] **4018.** ee. **1/1.**

—— Christ, the Morning Star; and other sermons. By . . . J. Cairns. Edited by his brothers (William Cairns, David Cairns). pp. xi. 365. *Hodder & Stoughton: London,* 1892. 8°. **4478.** dd. **26.**

—— Christianity and Miracles at the Present Day. pp. 44. *R.T.S.: London,* 1882. 8°. [*Present Day Tracts.* no. 1.] **4018.** ee. **1/1.**

—— Dr. Guthrie as an Evangelist. A sermon, *etc.* pp. 14. *W. Oliphant & Co.: Edinburgh,* 1873. 8°. **4906.** f. **26.** (**8.**)

—— An Examination of Professor Ferrier's "Theory of Knowing and Being." pp. 31. *T. Constable & Co.: Edinburgh,* 1856. 8°. **8466.** d. **9.**

—— The Faithful Minister's Farewell. A discourse on the death of the Rev. David M. Inglis . . . With an address at the interment, by the Rev. William Ritchie. pp. 15. *W. Oliphant & Co.: Edinburgh,* 1867. 8°. **4955.** d. **26.** (**12.**)

—— False Christs and the True, or the Gospel history maintained in answer to Strauss and Renan. A sermon, *etc.* pp. 32. *Edmonston & Douglas: Edinburgh,* 1864. 8°. **4805.** cc. **5.**

—— Fragments of College and Pastoral Life: a memoir of the late Rev. John Clark, of Glasgow. With selections from his essays, lectures, and sermons. pp. 227. *W. Oliphant & Sons: Edinburgh,* 1851. 12°. 4955. b. 5.

—— The Gospel the Power of God unto Salvation. A sermon, *etc.* pp. 23. *W. Oliphant & Co.: Edinburgh,* 1876. 8°. **4473.** c. **17.** (**12.**)

—— The Greatest Historical Marvel: how to account for it? [A lecture.] See JEWS. The Jews in relation to the Church and the World, *etc.* 1877. 8°. **4034.** de. **4.**

—— The Indian Crisis, viewed as a call to prayer. A discourse. pp. 16. *Melrose & Plenderleith: Berwick,* 1857. 8°. **4477.** d. **24.**

—— Is the Evolution of Christianity from mere natural sources credible? pp. 56. *R.T.S.: London,* [1887.] 8°. [*Present Day Tracts.* no. 49.] **4018.** ee. **1/9.**

—— Memoir of John Brown, D.D. (Supplementary chapter . . . A letter to Rev. John Cairns, D.D., by J. Brown, M.D.) [With a portrait.] pp. xii. 516. *Edmonston & Douglas: Edinburgh,* 1860. 8°. **4955.** c. **20.**

—— The Moral Greatness of the Temperance Enterprise. A sermon. pp. 16. *Scottish Temperance League: Glasgow,* [1879.] 8°. **4478.** e. **88.** (**8.**)

—— The Offering of the Gentiles. A sermon, *etc.* pp. 36. *John Snow: London,* 1859. 12°. **4478.** aa. **120.** (**3.**)

—— On the Disestablishment of the Church of Scotland. pp. 22. *W. Oliphant & Co.: Edinburgh,* 1872. 8°. **4175.** bb. **1.** (**5.**)

—— *See* Juror. Reply to Dr. Cairns on Disestablishment, *etc.* 1872. 8°. **4175.** bb. **1.** (**3.**)

—— On the Membership of the Christian Church, and the purity of her communion. pp. 47. *J. Nisbet & Co.: London,* 1866. 8°. **4103.** c. **15.**

—— On the Sufficiency of the Voluntary Principle. *See* Whyte (R.) *of Edinburgh.* Lectures on Disestablishment, *etc.* 1882. 8°. **4175.** de. **31.**

—— Outlines of Apologetical Theology. An introductory lecture. pp. 31. *W. Oliphant & Co.: Edinburgh,* 1867. 8°. **3554.** aa. **6.**

—— Oxford Rationalism and English Christianity. [A reply to "Essays and Reviews."] pp. 23. *William Freeman: London,* [1861.] 12°. **4374.** c. **8.**

—— Present Duty with regard to Union. A speech delivered in the United Presbyterian Synod, Edinburgh, *etc.* pp. 16. *W. Oliphant & Co.: Edinburgh,* 1870. 8°. **4175.** bb. **36.**

—— Present State of the Christian Argument from Prophecy. pp. 64. *R.T.S.: London,* [1884.] 8°. [*Present Day Tracts.* no. 27.] **4018.** ee. **1/5.**

—— Rochdale Discourses: a memorial contribution by fourteen clergymen connected with the United Presbyterian Synod in England. With a preface by . . . J. Cairns. Second edition. pp. viii. 327. *Johnstone, Hunter & Co.: Edinburgh,* 1870. 8°. **4462.** dd. **13.**

—— Romanism and Rationalism as opposed to pure Christianity. pp. 60. *A. Strahan & Co.: London & Edinburgh,* 1863. 8°. **3942.** a. **42.**

—— Sanctification. pp. 24. *Drummond's Tract Depôt: Stirling,* [1899.] 8°. **4422.** bbb. **70.** (**2.**)

—— The Scottish Philosophy; a vindication, and reply [to J. Smith's "Examination of Cairns' 'Examination of Professor Ferrier's Theory of Knowing and Being'"]. pp. 26. *T. Constable & Co.: Edinburgh,* 1856. 8°. **8466.** d. **10.**

—— Sermon. *See* Brown (John) *D.D., of Edinburgh.* The Jubilee Services of the Rev. John Brown, *etc.* 1856. 8°. **4955.** a. **54.** (**5.**)

—— Sermon. *See* Young (David) *D.D., of Perth.* Sermons preached . . . on occasion of the death of the Rev. Alexander Macewen, *etc.* 1875. 8°. **4465.** aaa. **37.**

—— Sketch of Mr. Kirkwood's Character. *See* Kirkwood (Alexander) Memoir of the Rev. Alexander Kirkwood, *etc.* 1858. 8°. **4955.** a. **40.**

CAIRNS (John) *Principal of the United Presbyterian College, Edinburgh.*

—— Speech on the Subordinate Standards . . . With the report of the Committee and declaratory statement adopted by the United Presbyterian Synod, May 1878. pp. 22. *W. Oliphant & Co.: Edinburgh*, 1878. 8°.
4175. df. **2**. (**7**.)

—— The Success of Christianity an argument for its divine origin. A discourse, *etc.* pp. 20. *Hamilton, Adams & Co.: London*, 1862. 8°. **4478**. b. **14**.

—— The Success of Christianity, and modern explanations of it. pp. 54. *R.T.S.: London*, [1882.] 8°. [*Present Day Tracts.* no. 6.] **4018**. ee. **1/1**.

—— The Trial of Patience: a sermon, preached at the opening of the United Presbyterian Synod, *etc.* pp. 15. *W. Oliphant & Co.: Edinburgh*, 1873. 8°.
4479. cc. **48**. (**6**.)

—— Unbelief in the Eighteenth Century as contrasted with its earlier and later history. Being the Cunningham Lectures for 1880. pp. ix. 309. *A. & C. Black: Edinburgh*, 1881. 8°. **4463**. i. 4.

—— A Full Account of the Call of the Rev. John Cairns . . . of Berwick-on-Tweed, from Greyfriars Church, Glasgow: with . . . the address of the Rev. J. Cairns. pp. 14. *Thomas Melrose: Berwick*, 1855. 8°. **4175**. dd. 4.

CAIRNS (John Arthur Robert) Careers for Girls. Compiled by J. A. R. Cairns. pp. 288. *Hutchinson & Co.: London*, [1928.] 8°. **08246**. e. **42**.

—— Drab Street Glory, *etc.* [Impressions of life in the slums. Edited by Trevor Allen and Ethel Cairns. With a portrait.] pp. 219. *Hutchinson & Co.: London*, [1934.] 8°. **8286**. aa. **35**.

—— The Loom of the Law . . . The experiences and reflections of a Metropolitan Magistrate, *etc.* [With a portrait.] pp. 320. *Hutchinson & Co.: London*, [1922.] 8°.
6056. v. **30**.

—— The Problem of a Career solved by 36 men of distinction. Compiled by J. A. R. Cairns. pp. 311. *Arrowsmith: London*, 1926. 8°. **8311**. ff. **6**.

—— The Sidelights of London. pp. 307. *Hutchinson & Co.: London*, 1923. 8°. **010349**. d. **6**.

CAIRNS (*Mrs.* John Arthur Robert) *See* Cairns (Ethel)

CAIRNS (John B.)

—— Bright and Early. A bookseller's memories of Edinburgh and Lasswade, *etc.* [With plates, including a portrait.] pp. xii. 292. *Cairns Bros.: Edinburgh*, 1953. 8°.
10863. de. **30**.

CAIRNS (John C.)

—— Great Britain and the Fall of France. A study in allied disunity. *In:* The Journal of Modern History. vol. 27. no. 4. pp. 365–409. 1955. 8°. Ac. **2691**. d/**43**.

CAIRNS (Julia) *See* London.—iii. *Press Art School.* Fashion Drawing & Designing. [By J. Cairns and others.] [1936.] fol. **7742**. w. **16**.

—— Heaven's Gate. In search of everyday happiness. pp. 62. *Frederick Muller: London*, 1937. 8°.
08408. h. **68**.

—— Home Making, *etc.* [With illustrations, including a portrait.] pp. 334. *Waverley Book Co.: London*, [1950.] 8°. **7949**. bb. **23**.

CAIRNS (Julia)

—— [A reissue.] Home Making. *London*, [1953.] 8°.
7940. g. **34**

—— More Stardust. In search of everyday happiness. pp. 62. *Weldons: London*, [1936.] 8°. **08408**. h. **43**

—— More Stardust, *etc.* (Second edition.) pp. 62. *Frederick Muller: London*, 1944. 8°. **8412**. aa. **22**

—— Stardust. In search of everyday happiness. pp. 62. *Weldons: London*, 1935. 8°. **12357**. r. **39**.

—— White Heather. In search of quiet comfort. pp. 61. *Frederick Muller: London*, 1941. 8°. **04401**. e. **11**.

—— Wings Have We, *etc.* pp. 62. *Frederick Muller: London*, 1943. 8°. **12356**. p. **45**

CAIRNS (Laura) A Scientific Basis for Health Instruction in Public Schools. [With tables.] *Berkeley, Cal.*, 1929. 8°. [*University of California Publications in Education.* vol. 2. no. 5.] Ac. **2689**. g/**7**.

CAIRNS (Mary Bell)

—— The Law of Tort in Local Government. pp. xxiii. 142. *Shaw & Sons: London*, 1954. 8°. **6429**. bb. **73**

CAIRNS (Thomas) Disputatio medica inauguralis de pleuritide, et peripneumonia. *Praes.* L. van de Poll. pp. 8. *Trajecti ad Rhenum*, 1705. 4°. **1185**. k. **17**. (**7**.)

CAIRNS (William) *J.P.*

—— Mr. Cairn's Children's Choir, Edinburgh 1901–1931. A singing pilgrimage. [With illustration, including portraits.] pp. 41. *Colin A. Maclean: Edinburgh*, [1931.] 8°.
7891. bbb. **62**.

CAIRNS (William) *of Edinburgh. See* Cairns (John) *Principal of the United Presbyterian College, Edinburgh.* Christ, the Morning Star; and other sermons. By . . . J. Cairns. Edited by his brothers (William Cairns, David Cairns). 1892. 8°. **4478**. dd. **26**.

—— *See* Chisholm (Walter) Poems . . . Edited . . . by W. Cairns. 1879. 8°. **11653**. de. **17**.

CAIRNS (William) *Professor of Logic and Belles Lettres at Belfast College. See* Young (John) *Professor of Moral Philosophy, etc.* Lectures on Intellectual Philosophy . . . . . . Edited by W. Cairns. 1835. 8°. **528**. h. **27**.

—— On the Mutual Dependence of Mankind for intellectual, moral and religious improvement. A sermon, *etc.* pp. 32. *Longman & Co.: London*, 1822. 8°. **4473**. f. **21**. (**3**.)

—— Outlines of Lectures on Logic and Belles Lettres. 2 pt. *Thomas Mairs: Belfast*, 1829. 12°. **1091**. f. **20**.

—— A Treatise on Moral Freedom; containing inquiries into the operations of the intellectual principles, in connexion generally with moral agency and responsibility, but especially with volition and moral freedom. pp. xxiv. 496. *Longmans & Co.: London*, 1844. 8°.
1386. g. **10**.

CAIRNS (William) *Writer of Fiction.* A Day after the Fair. pp. 150. *Swan Sonnenschein & Co.: London*, 1887. 8°. **12614**. l. **39**.

CAIRNS (William B.) *See* Franklin (Benjamin) *LL.D.* Benjamin Franklin's Autobiography. Edited . . . by W. B. Cairns. 1905. 8°. [*Longman's English Classics.*]
12274.bbb.15/5.

CAIRNS (William B.)

—— American Literature for Secondary Schools. pp. xiii. 341. *Macmillan Co.: New York*, 1914. 8°. **11825**. ccc. **21**.

—— British Criticisms of American Writings, 1783–1815. A contribution to the study of Anglo-American literary relationships. pp. 97. *Madison*, 1918. 8°. [*University of Wisconsin Studies in Language and Literature*. no. 1.] Ac. **1792/7**.

—— British Criticisms of American Writings, 1815–1833, *etc.* pp. 319. *Madison*, 1922. 8°. [*University of Wisconsin Studies in Language and Literature*. no. 14.] Ac. **1792/7**.

—— The Forms of Discourse. With an introductory chapter on style . . . Revised edition. pp. xiv. 358. *Ginn & Co.: Boston*, [1909.] 8°. **11852**. t. **2**.

—— A History of American Literature. pp. vii. 502. *Oxford University Press: New York; Henry Frowde: London*, 1912. 8°. **011852**. bb. **33**.

—— Revised edition. pp. ix. 569. *Oxford University Press: New York*, 1930. 8°. **20017**. a. **9**.

—— On the Development of American Literature from 1815 to 1833, with especial reference to periodicals. pp. iv. 87. *Madison*, 1898. 8°. [*Bulletin of the University of Wisconsin*. Philology and Literature Series. vol. 1. no. 1.] Ac. **1792**.

—— Selections from Early American Writers, 1607–1800. Edited by W. B. Cairns. pp. xii. 493. *Macmillan Co.: New York*, 1909. 8°. **012296**. aa. **8**.

CAIRNS (William Thomas) The Bible in Scottish Life and History. pp. 32. *Edinburgh*, 1937. 8°. [*Church of Scotland Booklets*. no. 12.] **4431.bb.26/12.**

—— The Religion of Dr. Johnson and other essays. pp. xiii. 137. *Oxford University Press: London*, 1946. 8°. **12359**. f. **49**.

CAIRNS (Zoé Percy) "He that Will not." [A tale.] pp. 146. *Claude Stacey: London*, [1925.] 8°. **012643**. aa. **65**.

—— Santa Caterina. The story of an island. pp. 181. *Claude Stacey: London*, [1926.] 8°. **012640**. c. **49**.

CAIRO.

MISCELLANEOUS INSTITUTIONS AND SOCIETIES.

Abbassia Observatory.

—— *See* Egypt.—*Ministry of Public Works.—Survey Department.*

American University.

—— Oriental Studies. *London*, 1925– . 8°. Ac. **12**. b.

Department of Education.

—— The Effects of Centralization on Education in Modern Egypt. By Russell Galt, *etc.* pp. 134. *Cairo*, 1936. 8°. **08355**. f. **40**.

Association des Amis de l'Art Copte.

—— *See* infra: Société d'Archéologie Copte.

Association des Amis des Églises et de l'Art Coptes.

—— *See* infra: Société d'Archéologie Copte.

Association Littéraire d'Égypte.

—— Miscellanea Ægyptiaca. Anno 1842. vol. 1. pt. 1. pp. 124. *Alexandria*, [1842.] 4°. Ac. **13**. b.

Bibliothèque Khédiviale, afterwards Bibliothèque Égyptienne.

—— Rapport . . . pour l'année 1887. *Fr. & Arab.* 2 pt. 1888. 8°. *See* Egypt.—*Ministère de l'Instruction Publique.—Administration des Wakfs.* **14598**. c. **9**.

—— Arabic Palaeography. A collection of Arabic texts from the first century of the Hidjra till the year 1000. Edited by B. Moritz. pp. ix. pl. 188. *Cairo; Leipzig; Vienna* [printed], 1905. fol. Or. **70**. e. **2**.
Publications of the Khedivial Library, Cairo. no. 16.

—— Arabic Papyri in the Egyptian Library. [Texts, with translations and notes.] By Adolf Grohmann . . . volume II. Legal texts. With twenty four plates. pp. viii. 259. pl. XXIV. *Cairo*, 1936. 4°. **14546**. f. **11**.

—— Bulletin of Additions. European Section. English edition. *Cairo*, 1928– . 8°. W.P. **9784**.

—— Bulletin des additions. Section européenne. Édition française. *Le Caire*, 1928– . 8°. W.P. **9783**.

—— Catalogue de la section européenne. I. L'Égypte. [By Carl Vollers.] pp. vi. 205. *Le Caire*, 1892. 8°. **011900**. ee. **71**.

—— Deuxième édition. [By B. Moritz.] pp. xiii. 589. *Le Caire*, 1901. 8°. **011900**. ee. **78**.

—— Catalogue of the Collection of Arabic Coins preserved in the Khedivial Library at Cairo. By S. Lane-Poole. pp. xv. 384. *B. Quaritch: London*, 1897. 8°. **7756**. d. **37**.

—— Guide de la Salle d'Exposition. *Eng. & Arab.* 2 pt. *Le Caire*, 1887. 8°. **14598**. c. **7**.

Cairo Museum.

—— *See* infra: Musée Égyptien.

Cairo Scientific Society.

—— Cairo Scientific Journal. *See* Periodical Publications.—*Cairo.* Survey Notes.

ΧΙΑΚΗ ΠΑΡΟΙΚΙΑ 'Ο 'ΟΜΗΡΟΣ.

—— *Κανονισμος, etc.* pp. 16. *ἐν Καιρῳ*, 1905. 8°. **8288**. a. **10**.

Comité de Conservation des Monuments de l'Art Arabe.

—— I. Procès-verbaux des séances; II. Rapports de la deuxième Commission. 3 pt. *Le Caire*, 1884–90. 4° & 8°. **7702**. g. **38**.

—— La Mosquée du sultan Hassan au Caire. Par Max Herz Bey. [With plates.] pp. 34. *Le Caire*, 1899. fol. **1736**. b. **13**.

Commission Internationale réunie au Caire pour l'Examen des Réformes proposées par le Gouvernement Égyptien dans l'Administration de la Justice en Égypte.

—— Impressions sur le Rapport de la Commission . . . Les capitulations et la réforme judiciaire. pp. 60. *Paris*, 1870. 8°. **5319**. b. **36**.

Dar-el-Salam.

—— Les Mardis de Dar el-Salam, 1952. [Lectures by various authors.] pp. 242. *Le Caire*, [1952.] 8°. **12360**. m. **23**.

Deutsches Institut für Ägyptische Altertumskunde.

—— *See* Berlin.—*Deutsches Archaeologisches Institut.—Abteilung Kairo.*

DIVAN DU KAIRE.

—— *See* EGYPT.—*Al-Dīwān al-Khuṣūṣī.*

EGYPTIAN SOCIETY.

—— Laws and Regulations. pp. 8. *Alexandrie,* [1840?] 4°. Ac. **12**.

—— Fifth (Sixth) Report, 1841 (42). [*Cairo?* 1841, 42.] fol. **1881**. a. **1**. (**125**, **126**.)

—— A Hieroglyphical Vocabulary. [With a prospectus of work proposed to be carried out by the Society in publishing facsimiles of inscriptions.] [*London?* 1845?] 4°. G. **16666**.

—— Mémoire sur le lac Moeris . . . Par Linant de Bellefonds. [With a map.] pp. 28. *Alexandrie,* 1843. 4°. **7703**. g. **7**. (**1**.)

EGYPTIAN SOCIETY OF HISTORICAL STUDIES.

Founded as the Royal Society of Historical Studies. Name changed to Egyptian Society of Historical Studies in 1952.

—— Proceedings. 1951, *etc.* *Cairo,* 1952– . 8°. Ac. **8629**.

ʽΕΛΛΗΝΙΚΟΣ ΦΙΛΕΚΠΑΙΔΕΥΤΙΚΟΣ ΣΥΛΛΟΓΟΣ "ʽΗ ʽΕΝΟΤΗΣ."

—— *Κεκροψ, συγγραμμα περιοδικον του ἐν Καΐρῳ ʽΕλληνικου Φιλεκπαιδευτικου συλλογου ʽΗ ʽΕνοτης. ʼΕκδιδομενον δις του μηνος* [by D. I. Oikonomopoulos]. no. 15, 19, 20, 21. *ἐν Καΐρῳ, ἐν ʼΑλεξανδρειᾳ,* 1876, 77. 8°. Ac. **13**.

ENGLISH SCHOOL.

—— Report and Balance Sheet for the year ending September 30th 1937 [*etc.*]. *Cairo,* [1937– .] 8°. **8356**. p. 2.

—— The English School, Cairo. A short record of its foundation and development since 1916, *etc.* pp. 27. *Cairo,* 1937. 8°. **8356**. p. 3.

—— The English School Magazine. *Cairo,* 1938– . 8°. P.P. **6231**. eg.

FOUAD I. UNIVERSITY.

—— *See* infra: UNIVERSITÉ ÉGYPTIENNE.

GEOLOGICAL MUSEUM.

—— Catalogue des invertébrés fossiles de l'Égypte représentés dans les collections du Geological Museum au Caire. Par R. Fourtau. [With plates.] 6 no. *Le Caire,* 1913–24. 4°. [*Geological Survey of Egypt. Palaeontological Series.* no. 1–6.] **7203**. e. **45**.

INSTITUT D'ÉGYPTE. [1798–1801.]

—— Procès verbaux des séances de l'Institut des sciences et des arts d'Égypte, imprimés en exécution d'un arrêté de l'Institut national des sciences et des arts. pp. 26. an VII [1798/99]. 4°. *See* PARIS.—*Institut de France.* **733**. g. **11**. (**2**.)

—— [Another copy.] F. **56***. (**2**.)

—— [Another copy.] F. **53***. (**9**.)

—— Annuaire de la République française calculé pour le méridien du Kaire l'an VIII de l'ère française. (Composé par une commission de l'Institut de Kaire.) [With a "Tableau militaire de l'armée d'Orient."] pp. 108 [122]. *Au Kaire,* [1799.] 4°. P.P. **2581**. d.

—— Annuaire de la République française, calculé pour le méridien du Kaire, l'an IX de l'ère française. [With "Tableau militaire."] 2 pt. *Au Kaire,* [1800.] 4°. **280**. d. 4. (3.)

—— Mémoires sur l'Égypte, publiés pendant les campagnes du général Bonaparte, dans les années VI et VII (VIII et IX). 4 tom. *Paris,* an VIII–XI [1800–03]. 8°. **978**. g. **16**–**19**.

—— [Another copy.] **280**. d. **7**.

INSTITUT D'ÉGYPTE. [1918– .]

—— [For publications of the Institute up to 1918:] *See* ALEXANDRIA.—*Institut Égyptien.*

—— Bulletin. 1918–1919 [*etc.*]. *Le Caire,* 1919– . 8°. Ac. **10**/**4**.

—— Index des communications et mémoires publiés par l'Institut d'Égypte, 1859–1952 [i.e. the "Institut d'Égypte" and by the "Institut Égyptien" at Alexandria]. pp. xvi. 194. [6.] pl. VII. 1952. 8°. *See* ELLUL (J.) **11927**. r. **19**.

—— Mémoires présentés à l'Institut d'Égypte, *etc.* *Le Caire,* 1919– . 4°. **Ac.10/8.**

INSTITUT DU KAIRE.

—— *See* supra: INSTITUT D'ÉGYPTE.

INSTITUT FRANÇAIS D'ARCHÉOLOGIE ORIENTALE.

—— Bulletin . . . Publié sous la direction de M. E. Chassinat. *Le Caire,* 1901– . 4°. Ac. **5200**.

—— Art islamique. *Le Caire,* 1953– . 4°. Ac. **5200**/**7**.

—— Bibliothèque des arabisants français, contenant les mémoires des orientalistes français relatifs aux études arabes parus dans des périodiques . . . Publiée sous la direction de M. Émile Chassinat (George Foucart).

Silvestre de Sacy, 1758–1838. Par M. Georges Salmon. 2 tom.

Le Caire, 1905, 23. 8°. Ac. **5200**/**2**.
No more published.

—— Catalogue des signes hiéroglyphiques de l'imprimerie de l'Institut français du Caire. Par M. E. Chassinat. [With supplement.] 2 pt. *Le Caire.* 1907, 30. 8°. **11913**. b. **3**.

—— Conférences de l'Institut Français d'Archéologie Orientale. *Le Caire,* 1948– . 8°. W.P. D. **268**.

—— Contribution à une étude de la méthodologie canonique de Taḳī-d-dīn Aḥmad b. Taimīya. Traduction annotée: 1) du Maʻāriğ al-wuṣūl ilā maʻrifat anna uṣūl ad-dīn wa furūʻahu ḳad bayyanahā ar-Rasūl, et 2) d'al-Ḳiyās fī-š-šarʻ ʻal-islāmī. [By Henri Laoust.] pp. 247. *Le Caire,* 1939. 8°. **4507**. d. **14**.
Textes et traductions d'auteurs orientaux. tom. 4.

—— Documents de fouilles de l'Institut Français d'Archéologie Orientale du Caire, publiés sous la direction de M. Pierre Jouguet. *Le Caire,* 1934– . fol. Ac. **5200**/**6**.

—— Études historiques. *Au Caire,* 1944– . 4°. W.P. **3991**.

—— Fouilles de l'Institut français d'Archéologie orientale du Caire. Années 1921–1923 [*etc.*] . . . Rapports préliminaires. *Le Caire,* 1924– . fol. Dept. of Egyptian & Assyrian Antiquities.

—— Fouilles franco-polonaises. Rapports. I. Tell Edfou 1937. Par B. Bruyère, J. Manteuffel, K. Michałowski, J. Sainte Fare Garnot. Contribution de Ch. Kuentz. Plans et dessins de Mlle. G. Jourdain. (II. Tell Edfou 1938. Par K. Michałowski, J. de Linage, J. Manteuffel, J. Sainte Fare Garnot. Plans et dessins de A. Czeczot.) (Wykopaliska Polsko-Francuskie. Sprawozdanie.) 3 fasc. 1937–39. 4°. *See* WARSAW.—*Królewski Uniwersytet Warszawski, etc.* Ac. **1147/16.**

—— Fouilles franco-suisses. Rapports. *Le Caire*, 1950– . fol. W.P. D. **890.**

—— Le Martyre de Saint Hélias et l'encomium de l'évêque Stéphanos de Hnès sur Saint Hélias. Transcrits . . . par . . . Geo. P. G. Sobhy. *Coptic & Fr.* pp. viii. 122. *Le Caire*, 1919. 4°. **07705.** d. **11.**
Tom. 1. *of the "Bibliothèque d'études coptes" of the Institute.*

—— Mémoires publiés par les membres de l'Institut . . . sous la direction de M. E. Chassinat (Pierre Jouguet, Ch. Kuentz, Jean Sainte Fare Garnot). 1902– . fol. **1710.** d.
Tom. 79 *and* 80 *were also published as tom.* 12 *and* 13 *of "Mémoires de la Délégation Archéologique Française en Afghanistan."*

—— Recherches d'archéologie, de philologie et d'histoire. Publiées sous la direction de M. Pierre Jouguet. *Le Caire*, 1930– . 8°. Ac. **5200/3.**

—— Répertoire chronologique d'épigraphie arabe . . . Publié . . . sous la direction de Ét. Combe, J. Sauvaget et G. Wiet. *Le Caire*, 1931– . . 4°. **15005.a.2.**

—— Le Temple de Dendara. [By Émile Chassinat. With plates.] 5 tom. *Le Caire*, 1934–52. fol. Ac. **5200/5.**
Tom. 5 *comprises* 2 *fascicules.*

KHEDIVIAL AGRICULTURAL SOCIETY.

—— Journal of the Khedivial Agricultural Society and the School of Agriculture . . . Editors: G. P. Foaden . . . W. C. Mackenzie. vol. 1. Jan. & Feb.—Nov. & Dec. 1899. *Cairo*, 1899. 8°.
[Continued as:]
Year-book of the Khedivial Agricultural Society, Cairo. 1905 (1906). *Cairo*, 1906, 07. 8°. Ac. **3547.**

LYCÉE FRANÇAIS.

—— Latina ephemeris aegyptiaca et universa. codex 6–8. Dec. 1936—May 1937. *Kahirae*, [1936, 37.] fol. P.P. **8.** ga.
Reproduced from typewriting.

MIDDLE EAST SUPPLY CENTRE.

—— The Agricultural Development of the Middle East. By B. A. Keen . . . A report . . . May, 1945. pp. xii. 126. pl. 15. *H.M. Stationery Office: London*, 1946. 8°. **07078.** g. **80.**

—— Middle East Science. A survey of subjects other than agriculture. By E. B. Worthington . . . A report . . . August, 1945. [With a map.] pp. xiii. 239. pl. xvi. *H.M. Stationery Office: London*, 1946. 8°. **7007.** d. **6.**

—— The Proceedings of the Conference on Middle East Agricultural Development, Cairo, February 7th–10th, 1944. [With plates.] pp. x. 220. *Cairo*, 1944. 8°. **07076.** l. **55.**
Agricultural Report no. 6 *of the Centre.*

—— Rural Education and Welfare in the Middle East. By H. B. Allen . . . A report . . . September 1944. pp. v. 24. *H.M. Stationery Office: London*, 1946. 8°. **8356.** n. **31.**

MISSION ARCHÉOLOGIQUE FRANÇAISE.

—— Mémoires publiés par les membres de Mission archéologique française au Caire sous la direction de M. Maspero (E. Grébaut, V. Bouriant, P. Jouget). tom. 1–13, 15, 17–24, 26–31. 1889 [1884]–1934. fol. *See* FRANCE.—*Ministère de l'Instruction publique, etc.* **7703.** k.
tom. 18: **1708.** d. **4.**

MUSÉE ARABE.

—— *See* infra: MUSÉE NATIONAL DE L'ART ARABE.

MUSÉE COPTE.

—— A Brief Guide to the Coptic Museum and to the Principal Ancient Coptic Churches of Cairo. By Marcus H. Simaika Pasha . . . Translated . . . by G. H. Costigan. pp. xvi. 91. pl. XCVII. *Cairo*, 1938. 8°. **7802.** b. **42.**

—— Une Collection de pierres sculptées au Musée copte du Vieux-Caire. Collection Abbâs el-Arabî. Par Hilde Zaloscer. [A catalogue.] pp. xxiii. 63. pl. XXI. *Le Caire*, 1948. 4°. **7877.** dd. **39.**
One of the "Publications de la Société d'Archéologie Copte. Bibliothèque d'art et d'archéologie."

—— The Coptic Museum. [With illustrations.] *Éditions Universitaires d'Égypte: Cairo*, 1955. 8°. **07813.** ee. **53.**

—— Guide sommaire du Musée Copte et des principales églises du Caire. Par Marcus H. Simaika Pacha. pp. xiii. 94. pl. CLXI. *Le Caire*, 1937. 8°. **7809.** ppp. **57.**

MUSÉE ÉGYPTIEN.

—— A Brief Description of the Principal Monuments. (Objects from the Tomb of Tutankhamûn). [With plans.] pp. 134. xxiii. *Cairo*, 1934. 8°. **07708.** aaa. **33.**

—— A Brief Description of the Principal Monuments exhibited in the Egyptian Museum, Cairo. By G. Daressy . . . Third edition. [With plans.] pp. xvi. 56. *Cairo*, 1925. 8°. **07703.** k. **33.**

—— 1927 edition. (By the curators of the Museum.) pp. xvi. 134. *Cairo*, 1927. 8°. **07703.** k. **33**a.

—— [Another edition.] pp. xxiii. 182. *Cairo*, 1930. 8°. **07703.** k. **33**b.

—— [Another edition.] pp. xxiii. 186. *Cairo*, 1931. 8°. **07703.** k. **33**c.

—— Catalogue général des antiquités égyptiennes du Musée du Caire. 1901– . 4°. *See* EGYPT.—*Service des Antiquités de l'Égypte.* **07701.** a. **1**, etc.

—— The Egyptian Museum. [With illustrations.] pp. 86. *Éditions Universitaires d'Égypte: Cairo*, 1955. 8°. **07708.** pp. **2.**

—— Encyclopédie photographique de l'art. The Photographic Encyclopædia of Art. Le Musée du Caire. Photographies inédites d'André Vigneau. Préface et notices par Étienne Drioton. *Fr. & Eng.* pp. 47. [*Paris*, 1949.] fol. **7812.** tt. **54.**

—— [Führer durch das Museum von Gizeh.] A Guide for the Museum of Ghizeh. Compiled by Leo Thude. pp. xvi. 165. *The Author: Cairo*, [1891.] 8°. **07703.** k. **40.**

—— Griechische Urkunden des Ägyptischen Museums zu Kairo. Herausgegeben von F. Preisigke. pp. viii. 58. *Strassburg*, 1911. 8°. [*Schriften der Strassburger Wissenschaftlichen Gesellschaft.* Hft. 8.] Ac. **548.**

—— Guide du visiteur au Musée du Caire. Par G. Maspero. pp. viii. 441. *Le Caire*, 1902. 8°. **7704.** a. **57.**

—— Deuxième édition. pp. xxii. 538. *Le Caire*, 1912. 8°. **07805.** aaa. **24.**

—— Guide to the Cairo Museum. [By G. Maspero.] Translated by J. E. and A. A. Quibell. [With plans.] pp. vi. 544. *Cairo*, 1903. 8°. **07703**. k. **41**.

—— Guide to the Cairo Museum. ([By] G. Maspero.) Translated by J. E. and A. A. Quibell. Fifth edition. pp. viii. 526. *Cairo*, 1910. 8°. Dept. of Egyptian & Assyrian Antiquities.

—— [Kunstwerke aus dem ägyptischen Museum zu Kairo.] Works of Art from the Egyptian Museum at Cairo. With explanations by Ludwig Borchardt. Translated by George A. Reisner. pp. 19. pl. 50. *Cairo; Dresden*, [1908?] fol. L.R. **294**. d. **13**.

—— Le Musée égyptien. [A guide. With illustrations.] pp. 86. *Le Caire*, 1955. 8°. **07705**. n. **24**.

—— Le Musée égyptien. Recueil de monuments et de notices sur les fouilles d'Égypte. Publié par M. E. Grébaut. (tom. 2, 3. Par M. G. Maspero.) tom. 1–3. 1890–1915. 4°. *See* Egypt.—*Ministry of Public Works*. Ac. **5200**. c.

—— Notice des principaux monuments exposés au Musée de Gizeh. pp. xxvii. 341. 1892. 8°. *See* Egypt.—*Service des Antiquités de l'Égypte*. **7704**. a. **44**.

—— The New Egyptian Museum and Research Institute at Cairo. [Plans of a projected rebuilding of the Museum.] pp. 37. pl. xv. [1931.] *obl.* fol. Dept. of Egyptian & Assyrian Antiquities.

—— Papyrus de Philadelphie édités par Jean Scherer. [Musée Égyptien, Cairo, papyri 49280–49365. The texts, with commentary and reproductions.] pp. xiv. 140. pl. viii. *Le Caire*, 1947. 4°. [*Publications de la Société Fouad I de Papyrologie*. Textes et documents. 7.] Ac. **13**. d.

—— Répertoire généalogique et onomastique du Musée du Caire. Par Georges Legrain. Monuments de la xviie et de la xviiie dynastie. pp. 304. 1908. 8°. *See* Egypt. —*Service des Antiquités de l'Égypte*. **7704**. k. **29**.

—— A Short Description of the Objects from the Tomb of Tutankhamûn . . . Second edition. pp. 45. *Le Caire*, 1927. 8°. **07704**. df. **54**.

Bibliothèque.

—— Catalogue de la Bibliothèque . . . Par M. Henri Munier. 2 fasc. pp. vii. 1010. 1928. 8°. *See* Egypt.—*Service des Antiquités de l'Égypte*. **011900**. c. **10**.

Musée National de l'Art Arabe.

—— Bois sculptés d'églises coptes, époque Fatimide. Par Edmond Pauty, *etc.* pp. vii. 38. pl. xlv. *Le Caire*, 1930. fol. L.R. **400**. a. **18**.
One of the "Publications du Musée Arabe du Caire."

—— Catalogue général du Musée arabe du Caire.

Lampes et bouteilles en verre émaillé. Par M. Gaston Wiet. pp. 193. pl. xcii. 1929. **7813**. h. **1/1**.
Les Bois à épigraphes jusqu'à l'époque mamlouke. Par M. Jean David Weill. pp. viii. 89. pl. xxi. 1931. **7813**. h. **1/2**.
Les Bois sculptés jusqu'à l'époque ayyoubide. Par M. Edmond Pauty. pp. vii. 81. pl. xcvii. 1931. **7813**. h. **1/3**.
Les Filtres de gargoulettes. Par M. Pierre Olmer. pp. viii. 124. pl. lxxix. 1932. **7813**. h. **1/4**.
Objets en cuivre. Par M. Gaston Wiet. [With a catalogue of Egyptian copper-work in the museums and private collections of the world.] pp. viii. 315. pl. lxxvi. 1932. **7813**. h. **1/5**.
Stèles funéraires. [By various authors. With plates.] 1932– . **7813**. h. **1/6**.

Le Caire, 1929– . fol. **7813**. h.

—— Catalogue of the National Museum of Arab Art. B Max Herz . . . Edited by S. Lane-Poole, *etc.* [Wit plates.] pp. xxxii. 91. *Gilbert & Rivington: London* [1896.] 8°. **7807**. a. **5**

—— Catalogue sommaire des monuments exposés dans l Musée national de l'Art arabe. [By Max Herz.] pp. lxv. 187. *Le Caire*, 1895. 8°. **7807**. aa. **4**

—— La Céramique égyptienne de l'époque musulman pl. 142. *Bale*, 1922. fol. L.R. **39**. c.

—— La Céramique musulmane de l'Égypte. Par Aly Be Bahgat et Félix Massoul. [Plates, with an introduction pp. 96. *Le Caire*, 1930. fol.
Dept. of Oriental Antiquities

—— Fouilles d'Al Fousṭaṭ . . . Par Aly Bahgat Bey e Albert Gabriel. pp. viii. 128. pl. xxxii. *Paris* 1921. fol. **7700**. k. 4

—— Gaibī et les grands faïenciers égyptiens d'époqu mamlouke. Avec un catalogue de leurs œuvres con servées au Musée d'Art arabe du Caire. Par M. Arman Abel. pp. vii. 114. pl. xxxi. *Le Caire*, 1930. 4°. **7803**. r. **1**

—— La Necropoli musulmana di Aswān, di Ugo Monneret d Villard. pp. viii. 54. pl. xxix. *Le Caire*, 1930. fol. L.R. **400**. a. **1**
One of the "Publications du Musée Arabe du Caire."

Near East Christian Council.

—— News Bulletin. June 1948. *Cairo*, 1948. 4°. P.P. **657**.
For private circulation.

Ophthalmological Society of Egypt.

—— *See* infra: Société d'Ophtalmologie d'Égypte.

Royal Society of Historical Studies.

—— *See* supra: Egyptian Society of Historical Studies

School of Agriculture.

—— Journal of the Khedivial Agricultural Society and th School of Agriculture . . . Editors: G. P. Foaden . . W. C. Mackenzie. vol 1. 1899. 8°. *See* supra Khedivial Agricultural Society. Ac. **3547**

Société d'Archéologie Copte.

Association des Amis des Églises et de l'Art Coptes, 1935.
Association des Amis de l'Art Copte, 1936, 37.
Société d'Archéologie Copte, 1938– .

—— Bulletin de l'Association des Amis des Églises et d l'Art coptes. (Bulletin de la Société d'Archéologie copte. *Le Caire*, 1936– . 8°. Ac. **13**.

—— Exposition d'art copte, décembre 1944. Guide. [By Ala J. B. Wace and E. Drioton.] pp. xiv. 92. v. 25. pl. xii *Le Caire*, 1944. 8°. **7960**. i. **71**

Société d'Études Historiques Juives d'Égypte.

—— Revue de l'histoire juive en Égypte. *Le Caire* 1947– . 8°. P.P. **3809**. fc

Société d'Ophtalmologie d'Égypte.

—— Bulletin. *Oxford*, [1914– .] 8°. Ac. **3695**. b.

Société de Géographie d'Égypte.

Société Khédiviale de Géographie du Caire, 1875–1917.
Société Sultanieh de Géographie, 1917–1921.
Société Royale de Géographie d'Égypte, 1922–1953.
Société de Géographie d'Égypte, 1953– .

From 1936 *onwards, works published by the Societ and not forming parts of series are entered only unde their authors.*

—— Statuts. pp. 15. *Alexandrie*, 1875. 8°. Ac. **6042**. c/2. (**1**.)

—— Bulletin. *Le Caire*, 1894- . 8°. Ac. **6042**. c.

—— Mémoires. *Caire*, 1919- . 4°. Ac. **6042**. d.

—— Publications spéciales . . . Sous la direction de M. Adolphe Cattaui Bey. *Au Caire*, 1923- . 8°. Ac. **6042**. d/2.

—— [For reports of the Eleventh International Geographical Congress held at Cairo, 1925 :] *See* Congresses.—*Congrès International de Géographie*. Compte-rendu, *etc*. 11th Congress.

—— Bibliographie géographique de l'Égypte. Publiée sous la direction de M. Henri Lorin. (tom. 1. Géographie physique et géographie humaine. Par Mlle. Henriette Agrel, MM. Georges Hug, Jean Lozach et René Morin.—tom. 2. Géographie historique. Par M. Henri Munier.) 2 tom. [*Cairo*,] 1928, 29. 8°. **BB.J.e.3.**

—— Con Sua Maestà il Re Fuad all'oasi di Ammone. [By Evaristo Breccia. With a portrait.] pp. 54. pl. xxxviii. *Le Caire*, 1929. 8°. **10094**. r. **14**.

—— Dictionnaire des noms géographiques contenus dans les textes hiéroglyphiques. [By Henri Gauthier.] 7 tom. *Le Caire*, 1925–31. 4°. **7701**. f. **28**.

—— Discours prononcé . . . à la séance d'inauguration . . . par le Dr. G. Schweinfurth. pp. 18. *Alexandrie*, 1875. 8°. Ac. **6042**. c/2. (**2**.)

—— Dizionario dei nomi geografici e topografici dell'Egitto greco-romano. [By Aristide Calderini.] *Cairo*, 1935- . 4°. Ac. **6042**. d/**5**.

—— L'Égypte d'aujourd'hui. Le pays et les hommes. [By Henri Lorin. With portraits and maps.] pp. xxxi. 220. pl. xxvi. *Le Caire*, 1926. 8°. **10094**. r. **15**.

—— L'Égypte et la géographie. Sommaire historique des travaux géographiques exécutés . . . sous la dynastie de Mohammed Aly. Par le Dr. Frédéric Bonola Bey. pp. 118. *Le Caire*, 1889. 8°. Ac. **6042**. c/**3**. (**2**.)

—— L'Habitat rural en Égypte. Par . . . J. Lozach et G. Hug, *etc*. [With plates and maps.] pp. xxiii. 218. *Le Caire*, 1930. 8°. Ac. **6042**. c/**6**.

—— Motifs décoratifs d'art arabe, Salle du Congrès international de Géographie, le Caire, 1925. (Adolfo Brandani, architecte.) pl. xxxiii. [*Cairo*, 1925.] fol. Ac. **6042**. d/**4**.

—— Programme of Work. pp. 16. *Cairo*, 1918. 8°. Ac. **6042**. c/**3**. (**1**.)

—— Questionnaire préliminaire d'ethnologie africaine. Par M. George Foucart. pp. xxxi. 162. *Le Caire*, 1919. 8°. Ac. **6042**. d/2. (**10**.)

—— Introductory Questions on African Ethnology. By George Foucart. pp. xxxii. 159. *Cairo*, 1919. 8°. Ac. **6042**. c/4.

Ethnographical Museum.

—— Catalogue of the Ethnographical Museum of the Roya Geographical Society of Egypt. By E. S. Thomas. (Extrait du "Bulletin de la Société Royale de Géographie d'Égypte.") [With plates.] pp. 130. *Le Caire*, 1924. 8°. **010006**. i. **31**.

Société Fouad Ier d'Entomologie.

Société Entomologique d'Égypte, 1907–22.
Société Royale Entomologique d'Égypte, 1923–37.
Société Fouad Ier d'Entomologie, 1937–

—— Bulletin de la Société entomologique d'Egypte. année 1912. fasc. 1 ; année 13. jan./mars 1912 ; 1920 *Le Caire*, 1913, 21. 8°. Ac. **3662**.

[Continued as :]

—— Bulletin de la Société royal entomologique d'Égypte. année 17. fasc. 2/4. *Le Caire*, 1925. 8°. Ac. **3662/2**a.

—— Nouvelle série. vol. 13, fasc. 1/3.—vol. 14, fasc. 1 ; vol. 14. fasc. 4—vol. 16. fasc. 1/2 ; vol. 19. *Le Caire*, 1929–35. 8°.

[Continued as ;]

—— Bulletin de la Société Fouad Ier d'entomologie. vol. 24–26, 28–30, 32, 33. *Le Caire*, 1940–49. 8°. Ac. **3662/2**b.

Société Fouad I. de Papyrologie.

Société Royale Égyptienne de Papyrologie, 1930–39.
Société Fouad I de Papyrologie, 1939- .

—— Études de papyrologie. *Le Caire*, 1932- . 8°. Ac. **13**. d/**2**.

—— Les Papyrus Fouad I. Nos. 1–89 [*etc*.]. Édités par A. Bataille, O. Guéraud [and others], *etc*. [The Greek texts, with translations and notes. With facsimiles.] *Le Caire*, 1939- . fol. [*Publications de la Société Fouad I. de Papyrologie. Textes et documents.* no. 3, *etc*.] Ac. **13**. d.

—— Publications... Textes et documents. *Le Caire*, 1931- . fol. Ac. **13**. d.

—— Zenon papyri. Nos. 59801–59853. P. Cairo Zenon. vol. v. By C. C. Edgar. Ouvrage posthume édité par . . . O. Guéraud et P. Jouguet. 2 pt. pp. xiv. 62. pl. viii. *Le Caire*, 1940, 51. fol. [*Publications de la Société Fouad I. de Papyrologie. Textes et documents.* no. 5.] Ac. **13**. d.

Société Littéraire Hellénique "L'Union."

—— *See* supra : ʽΕΛΛΗΝΙΚΟΣ ΦΙΛΕΚΠΑΙΔΕΥΤΙΚΟΣ ΣΥΛΛΟΓΟΣ "ʽΗ ʽΕΝΟΤΗΣ."

Société Royale de Géographie d'Égypte.

—— *See* supra : Société de Géographie d'Égypte.

Université Egyptienne.

Bibliothèque.

—— Règlement provisoire de la Bibliothèque. *Fr. & Arab.* pp. 6. *Rome*, 1910. 8°. **11907**. aa. **2**. (**4**.)

—— Bulletin de la Bibliothèque. Première (deuxième) année. *Le Caire*, 1910, 11. 8°. Ac. **14**.

—— Fuad I. University Papyri. Edited by David S. Crawford. pp. vii. 138. *Alexandrie*, 1949. 4°. [*Publications de la Société Fouad I. de papyrologie. Textes et documents.* no. 8.] Ac. **13**. d.

Faculté de Droit.

—— Annuaire de la Faculté de droit. Année 1935–1936. pp. xv. 155. *Le Caire*, [1935.] 8°. **8356**. m. **23**.

—— Publications of the Faculty of Law. no. 1, 5, 6. *Cairo*, [1933,] 38. 8°. Ac. **14**. d.

Faculté des Lettres.

—— Réglement de la Faculté des Lettres. pp. 21. *Le Caire*, 1911. 8°. Ac. **14/2**. (**1**.)

CAIRO. [Miscellaneous Institutions and Societies.]

—— Bulletin of the Faculty of Arts. [With contributions in English, French and Arabic.] vol. 1. pt. 1—vol. 5. pt. 1; vol. 9. pt. 2, *etc.* May 1933—May 1937; Dec. 1947, *etc.* *Giza*, 1933- . 8°. Ac. **14**. c.
This set contains two editions of vol. 4. pt. 1.

—— Recueil de travaux publiés par la Faculté des Lettres. (Collection of works published by the Faculty of Arts.) *Le Caire*, 1927- . 8° & 4°. Ac. **14**. c/**2**.
Two parts have the series number 2. Guido Ignazio's "Summarium," erroneously numbered fasc. 2, forms fasc. 3. Other parts do not bear series title or number.

Faculté des Sciences.

—— Report for the Session 1928–29 [*etc.*]. *Eng. & Arab.* *Cairo*, 1930- . 8°. Ac. **14**. b.

—— Bulletin of the Faculty of Science. no. 28, *etc.* *Cairo*, 1950- . 8°. Ac. **14**. b/**3**.

—— Publications of the Faculty of Science. *Cairo*, 1932- . 8° & 4°. Ac. **14**. b/**2**.
Part of the series does not bear series title or number.

—— *Faculty of Arts.* *See* supra: *Faculté des Lettres.*

Faculty of Commerce.

—— [Publications.] *Fouad I. University Press: Cairo*, 1946- . 8°. Ac. **14**. e.

—— *Faculty of Law.* *See* supra: *Faculté de Droit.*

Faculty of Medicine.

—— First (—Fourth) Annual Report of Ophthalmic Section, Kasr el-Aini Hospital, *etc.* *Cairo*, [1929–32.] 8°. [*Egyptian University. Publications of the Faculty of Medicine.* no. 10.] Ac. **14**. f.

—— Publication no. 1, *etc.* *Cairo*, 1931- . 8°. Ac. **14**. f.

—— The Third Pandemic of Plague in Egypt . . . By A. W. Wakil. [With diagrams.] pp. 169. *Cairo*, 1932. 8°. **7688**. h. **26**.

Museum of Moslem Art.

—— Moslem Art in the Fouad I University Museum. By Zeky M. Hassan. [An illustrated catalogue.] *Eng. & Arab.* *Fouad I University Press: Cairo*, 1950- . 8°. Ac. **14**. ba.

Victoria Hospital.

—— The Victoria Hospital Cairo. (Report of the Egyptian Relief Fund . . . Foundation Rules of the Victoria Hospital . . . List of Subscribers.) pp. 39. *London*, 1883. 8°. [*Report of the Chapter of the Order of St. John of Jerusalem in England.*] A.R.534.

APPENDIX.

—— Dagverhaal van eene reize van Groot Cairo na den Berg Sinai en te rug; opgesteld en gedaan in 't jaar 1722, by en door den Præfect [of the Franciscans] van Egypten, in gezelschap van eenige zendelingen der Societeit de Propaganda Fide te Groot Cairo . . . Waarby gevoegd zyn aanmerkingen over den oorsprong der beeldsprak en fabel-kunde der aloude heidenen. Opgedragen aan de Hollandsche Maatschappy der Wetenschap . . . en door den autheur aan 't Genootschap der Oudheidsonderzoekers te Londen. Door . . . Robert, Bisschop van Clogher . . . vertaald door J. J. Dusterhoop. pp. 193. *Amsterdam*, 1754. 8°. **10098**. a. **19**.

CAIRO. [Appendix.]

—— Descriptio Alcahiræ vrbis quæ Mizir, et Mazar dicitu[r] [By Guillaume Postel.] *Apud M. Paganum: Veneti[is]*, 1549. 12°. C. **107**. bb. **17**. (
Imperfect; wanting the map.

—— A Journal from Grand Cairo to Mount Sinai and bac[k] again. Translated from a manuscript, written by th[e] Prefetto [of the Franciscans] of Egypt in company wi[th] the Missionaries de propaganda fide at Grand Cairo. T[o] which are added Some Remarks on the Origin of Hier[o]glyphics . . . By Robert Lord Bishop of Clogher. [Wi[th] plates.] pp. 139. *William Bowyer: London*, 1753. 4°. **789**. bb. **1**

—— [Another copy.] few ms. notes. B. **284**. (1
Inserted in this copy are a reply from the Society [of] Antiquities to the Bishop of Clogher's dedicatory epist[le] in ms.*, a map, an engraving, and an extract from Geor[ge] Sandys "Travels."*

—— The second edition, corrected. pp. 168. *William Bowyer: London*, 1753. 8°. **280**. e. **1**

—— [Another edition.] *See* Maundrell (H.) A Journ[ey] from Aleppo to Jerusalem, *etc.* 1810. 12°. **10076**. f. **3**

—— [Another edition.] *See* Pinkerton (John) A Gener[al] Collection of Voyages, *etc.* vol. 10. 1811. 4°. L.R. **80**. c.

—— [Another edition.] *See* Maundrell (H.) A Journ[ey] from Aleppo to Jerusalem, *etc.* 1812. 12°. **10076**. aa. **1**

—— Scandals at Cairo in connection with Slavery. Publish[ed] with the sanction . . . of the British and Foreign An[ti-] Slavery Society . . . By an English Resident at Cai[ro.] pp. 18. *Cairo*, 1885. 8°. **8156**. cc. 5. (

—— [Another copy.] **8155**. b. **3**. (

—— Tage-Reisen von Gross-Cairo nach dem Berge Sinai u[nd] wieder zurük. Aus einer Handschrift des Präfektus d[er] Franciskaner in Egipten übersezet. Mit Anmerkung[en] über den Ursprung der Hieroglifen u. Mythologie der alt[en] Heiden. Der Gesellschaft der Allerthümer in Lond[on] zugeeignet, von dem hochwürdigen Robert—Clayton Bischof zu Clogher. Aus der verbesserten englisch[en] Ausgabe übersezet von J. P. Cassell, *etc.* pp. 162. pl. *Hannover*, 1754. 8°. **10095**. a.

CAIRO, *Illinois*, Charles Reuben, *Bishop of.* [189- 1900.] *See* Hale.

CAIRO BUSINESS MIRROR. Cairo Business Mirr[or] and City Directory. *See* Directories.—*Cairo, Illinois.*

CAIRO MUSEUM. *See* Cairo.—*Musée Égyptien.*

CAIRO SCIENTIFIC JOURNAL. *See* Periodic[al] Publications.—*Cairo.* Survey Notes.

CAIRO SCIENTIFIC SOCIETY. *See* Cairo.

CAIRO (Alessionna Scarampi del) *See* Scarampi d[el] Cairo.

CAIRO (Gio) and **GIARELLI** (Francesco) Codogno il suo territorio nella cronaca e nella storia. 2 vol. *Codogno*, 1897, 98. 8°. **10132**. g. **4**

CAIRO (Jack)

—— Cocksure Dame. [A novel.] pp. 112. *Sci[...]* *London*, [1952.] 8°. Cup. **367**. bb.

CAIRO (Petrus) De abusu methodi antiphlogisticæ, dissertatio inauguralis, *etc.* pp. 52. *Picini Regii*, 1819. 8°. **7383**. c. **2**. (**13**.)

CAIROL ( ) *Avocat au Parlement de Paris*. Conférences de jurisprudence, sur l'édit concernant ceux qui ne font pas profession de la religion catholique. pp. xii. 104. *Paris*, 1788. 8°. F. **27**. (**11**.)

CAIROL (François) Recherches sur le terrain crétacé inférieur de la Clape et des Corbières. [With plates.] pp. 177. 1872. *See* Periodical Publications.—*Paris*. Annales des sciences géologiques, *etc.* tom. 3. 1869, *etc.* 8°. P.P. **2084**. b.

—— [Another issue.] *Paris*, 1872. 8°. [*Bibliothèque de l'École Pratique des Hautes Études*. Section des sciences naturelles. tom. 6.] Ac. **8929**. (5.)

CAIROLI, *Family of*.

—— *See* Marchi (L. de) *Librarian, University of Pavia*. La Famiglia Cairoli, *etc.* [1900.] 4°. **1762**. d. **27**.

—— *See* Rosi (M.) I Cairoli. 1908. 8°. **9168**. a. **1/1**.

—— —— 1929. 8°. **9905**. a. **25**.

—— *See* Venosta (F.) I Fratelli Cairoli, 1848–1867. 1868. 8°. **10629**. a. **52**.

—— La Famiglia Cairoli. Dall'Inglese. [Translated by Francesco Torraca from the Westminster Review.] pp. 127. *Napoli*, 1879. 12°. **10629**. aa. **19**.

CAIROLI (A. G.) *See* Stanhope (Philip D.) *4th Earl of Chesterfield*. [*Appendix*.] Guida della vita umana . . . Tradotta nell'idioma italiano [by A. G. Cairoli]. 1816. 8°. T. **2489**. (2.)

CAIROLI (Adelaide) *See* Beccari (G. A.) Ad Adelaide Cairoli le donne italiane. [A collection of short pieces in prose and verse.] 1873. 8°. **12226**. g. **4**.

—— *See* Ghighlione Giulietti (E.) Adelaide Cairoli e i suoi figli. Lettere inedite dal 1847 al 1871. 1952. 8°. **10922**. g. **14**.

—— *See* Maineri (B. E.) Il Monumento ad Adelaide Cairoli in Gropello-Lomellino (24 ottobre 1875). Memorie, *etc.* [1876.] 8°. **10602**. i. 3. (**13**.)

—— Lettere di Adelaide Cairoli. [Edited by E. Casanova.] *In:* Archivi. ser. 2. anno 18. fasc. 4. pp. 191–218. 1951. 8°. P.P. **3557**. dba.

—— In morte di Adelaide Cairoli Bono. Raccolta di versi e prose di illustri signore italiane. pp. 67. *Ragusa*, 1871. 8°. **10631**. bbb. **42**. (**7**.)

CAIROLI (Benedetto) *See* Cardillo Brigandì (S.) Benedetto Cairoli nella storia d'Italia, *etc.* 1881. 8°. **10629**. aa. **28**.

—— Il Re. Benedetto Cairoli. Il paese. Note di un Ex-Ministro. 1879. 8°. *See* N., N., *Ex-Ministro*. **8032**. aaa. **4**.

CAIROLI (Giovanni) *See* Ferrari (P. V.) Villa Glori . . . Seguono in appendice il " Giornaletto di Campo " ed altre note e ricordi scritti . . . da G. Cairoli. 1899. 8°. **9169**. de. **1/16**.

—— Poesie patrie. *See* Maineri (B. E.) Il Monumento ai fratelli Cairoli, *etc.* pt. 2. 1883. 8°. **10629**. aa. **34**. (**3**.)

—— Spedizione dei Monti Parioli, 23 ottobre 1867 . . . Con proemio e note di B. E. Maineri. pp. 187. *Milano*, 1878. 8°. **9166**. bbb. **10**.

CAIROLI (Joannes) De summa inter urolithiasim et podagram affinitate, dissertatio inauguralis, *etc.* pp. 22. *Ticini Regii*, [1830.] 8°. **7383***. b. **1**. (**17**.)

CAIROLI (Josephus) De dysenteria ejusque natura, dissertatio inauguralis, *etc.* pp. 19. *Ticini Regii*, [1821.] 8°. **7383***. b. **5**. (**8**.)

CAIRON (Claude Antoine Jules) *See* Noriac (Jules) *pseud.* [i.e. C. A. J. Cairon.]

CAIRRIGE (Seán Ó Muirthile) *See* Ó Muirthile Cairrige.

CAIS DE PIERLAS (Eugenio) *Count*. *See* Nice.—*Cathedral*. Cartulaire de l'ancienne cathédrale de Nice, publié par le comte E. Cais de Pierlas. 1888. 4°. **4629**. k. **4**.

—— *See* Pons, *Saint, Benedictine Abbey of, at Nice*. Chartrier de l'abbaye de Saint-Pons hors les murs de Nice, publié . . . par le comte E. Cais de Pierlas, *etc.* 1903. 4°. [*Collection de documents historiques publiés par ordre de S.A.S. le prince Albert I, prince souverain de Monaco*.] **9170.f.1/5.**

—— Le Fief de Chateauneuf dans les Alpes maritimes du XIe au XVe siècle, *etc.* 1892. *See* Turin.-Deputazione Subalpina *di Storia Patria*. Miscellanea, *etc.* tom. 29. 1862, *etc.* 8°. Ac. **6550**.

—— Le XIe siècle dans les Alpes maritimes. Études généalogiques. 1889. *See* Turin.—*Accademia delle Scienze*. Memorie. ser. 2. tom. 39. pt. 2. 1839, *etc.* 4°. Ac. **2816**.

—— Gli Statuti della gabella di Nizza sotto i Conti di Provenza. 1894. *See* Turin.-Deputazione Subalpina di Storia *Patria*. Miscellanea, *etc.* tom. 31. 1862, *etc.* 8°. Ac. **6550**.

—— La Ville de Nice pendant le premier siècle de la domination des Princes de Savoie, *etc.* pp. 558. *Turin*, 1898. 8°. **010168**. h. **1**.

CAISE (Albert) Cartulaire de Saint-Vallier, ou Relevé des chartes et documents concernant Saint-Vallier . . . Ouvrage orné de planches, *etc.* pp. 166. *Paris*, 1870. 12°. **10169**. bbb. **18**.

—— Diane de Poitiers, dame de Saint-Vallier. Ses actes, ses prédécesseurs et ses successeurs dans la communauté de Saint-Vallier. (Extrait du Bulletin de la Société d'Archéologie et de Statistique de la Drôme.) pp. 20. *Valence*, 1891. 8°. **10601**. ff. **3**. (**6**.)

—— [Another copy.] **10601**. ff. **11**. (**2**.)

—— Exploration archéologique au tombeau de Juba II, dit, Tombeau de la Chrétienne. Guide du touriste accompagné de vues et d'un plan du mausolée, *etc.* (Le Tombeau de Juba II., et les légendes arabes du K'bar-er-Roumia.) pp. 18. *Blida*, 1893. 8°. **07703**. i. **2**. (**12**.)

—— Histoire de Saint-Vallier ; de son abbaye, de ses seigneurs et de ses habitants . . . Avec un plan de la ville, *etc* pp. xii. 300. *Paris*, 1867. 12°. **10169**. aaa. **14**.

—— Le Jugement de Jésus-Christ. [On an ancient document so styled.] *Blidah*, [1893.] *s. sh.* fol. **1897**. c. **8**. (**114**.)

—— Monuments historiques d'Algérie. Le tombeau de Juba II dit Tombeau de la Chrétienne. pp. 7. *Blida*, 1892. 8°. **07703**. f. **2**. (**4**.)

—— Origine d'Alger, Icosium. (Notes archéologiques inédites.) *Blidah*, [1893.] *s. sh.* 8°. **1882**. c. **2**. (**23**.)

CAISE (ALBERT)

—— Le Prieuré de l'Île de Saint-Vallier. (Extrait du Bulletin de la Société d'Archéologie et de Statistique de la Drôme.) pp. 7. *Valence*, 1890. 8°. **4530. ee. 28. (2.)**

—— Le Registre baptistaire de Saint-Vallier, 2 mai 1568—17 décembre 1575. Étude sur l'état des personnes de cette paroisse et l'origine de leurs noms patronymiques. pp. 19. *Valence*, 1892. 8°. **9906. b. 12. (6.)**

—— Teurkia . . . Mœurs algériennes. [A novel.] pp. 323. *Paris*, [1889.] 12°. **012547. h. 17.**

CAISE (ALBERT) and **DREUX** (ALFRED)

—— Le Volontaire d'un an, comédie en un acte, *etc.* pp. 32. *Paris*, 1873. 12°. **11739. e. 2.**

CAISE (ALBERT) and **PAILLARD** (ÉDOUARD)

—— La Famille du conscrit. Drame populaire en cinq actes . . . Suivi des documents relatifs à l'incident désigné dans le Figaro sous le titre Scandale du Théatre-Montmartre. pp. 13. *Paris*, 1875. 4°. **11739. k. 68. (13.)**

CAISLEY (LANCE)

—— *See* COOK (Kenneth) and CAISLEY (L.) Music through the Brass Band, *etc.* [1953.] 8°. **W.P. c. 503/1.**

CAISLEY (WALTER BRADFORD)

—— London's River and Guide to the Middle Thames. [With illustrations and maps.] *Thames Launches: [Twickenham*, 1954.] 8°. **010349. w. 21.**

CAISSAN (JACQUES) Recette très-veritable pour la guerison des personnes & animaux mordus de chiens, loups & autres animaux enragez. pp. 29. *A. Saugrain: Paris*, 1615. 8°. **783. c. 4. (3.)**

CAISSE. Caisse Auxiliaire. *See* PARIS.

—— Caisse Centrale de Secours Mutuels Agricoles. *See* FRANCE.

—— Caisse Coloniale des Pensions et Allocations Familiales pour Employés. *See* BELGIUM.

—— Caisse d'Épargne. *See* PARIS.

—— Caisse d'Escompte. *See* PARIS.

—— Caisse de Chômage attachée au Ministère du Travail et de l'Assistance Publique. *See* POLAND.—*Ministerstwo Pracy i Opieki Społecznej.—Fundusz Bezrobocia.*

—— Caisse de Placemens en Viager. *See* PARIS.

—— Caisse de Prévoyance des Ouvriers Mineurs. *See* HAINAULT.

—— Caisse de Prévoyance en faveur des Ouvriers Mineurs [of the province of Liége]. *See* LIÉGE, *Province of.*

—— Caisse de Prévoyance établie à Charleroy en faveur des Ouvriers Mineurs. *See* CHARLEROY.

—— Caisse de prévoyance établie à Mons en faveur des ouvriers mineurs. *See* HAINAULT.—*Caisse de Prévoyance des Ouvriers Mineurs.*

—— Caisse des Arrérages. *See* FRANCE.

—— Caisse des Propriétaires. *See* PARIS.

—— Caisse Générale d'Épargne et de Retraite. *See* BELGIUM.

CAISSE.

—— Caisse-hypothécaire d'Agriculture. *See* PARIS.

—— Caisse J. Mianowski. *See* WARSAW.—*Komitet zarządają kasą pomocy dla osób pracujących na polu naukow imienia Józefa Mianowskiego.*

—— Caisse Mutuelle Nationale d'Allocations Familia *See* BELGIUM.

—— Caisse nationale d'assurance. Par M. C. F. Ingénie géographe, *etc.* [i.e. C. F. Ribart?] 1790. 8°. *See* M. C. F., *Ingénieur-Géographe des Camps & Armées Roi.* **F. 206. (1**

—— Caisse Nationale d'Assurance en Cas d'Accidents. FRANCE.

—— Caisse Nationale d'Assurances sur la Vie. *See* FRANC

—— Caisse Nationale d'Épargne. *See* FRANCE.—*Minist des Postes, Télégraphes et Téléphones.*

—— Caisse Nationale de Crédit Professionnel. *See* BELGIU

—— Caisse Nationale des Assurances Sociales. *See* ITALY *Istituto Nazionale della Previdenza Sociale.*

—— Caisse Nationale des Recherches Scientifiques. FRANCE.—*Ministère de l'Instruction Publique.*

—— Caisse ouverte pour l'Extinction de la Mendicité. FRANCE.

—— Caisse Régionale d'Assurance-Vieillesse des Travaille Salariés des Départements du Haut-Rhin, du Bas-R et de la Moselle. *See* STRASBURG.

—— Caisse Régionale de Sécurité Sociale des Départements Haut-Rhin, du Bas-Rhin et de la Moselle. *See* STRASBU

CAISSEL (DE) Relation de ce qui s'est passé Catalogne. (Suite de la Relation.) [The dedicat epistle signed: D. C., i.e. — de Caissel.] 2 pt. 1678, 79. 12°. *See* C., D. **9078. aaa.**

CAISSELET (L.) Essai sur le traitement de la chlor Thèse, *etc.* pp. 61. *Montpellier*, 1854. 4°. **7379. c. 6.**

CAISSES. Caisses d'Épargne. *See* FRANCE.

—— Caisses des Veuves et Orphelins. *See* BELGIUM.

CAISSO (ÉMILE) De l'exclusivisme en médecine. Th *etc.* pp. 94. *Montpellier*, 1853. 4°. **7379. b. 13.** (

CAISSO (FIRMIN) Considérations sur les avantages et conditions des topographies médicales. Tribut aca mique, *etc.* pp. 30. *Montpellier*, 1819. 4°. **1180. i. 8.**

CAISSO (JEAN BENJAMIN) Recherches anatomo-pat logiques sur la fièvre typhoïde . . . Thèse, *etc.* pp. 33 *Montpellier*, 1864. 4°. **7379. f. 6.**

CAISSON (A. ÉLIE) Qu'est-ce que le prêtre? Expl tion de divers passages de la Bible, *etc.* (Sec discours.) 2 pt. *Paris*, [1830.] 8°. **523. e. 19.**

CAISSOTTI DI CHIUSANO (PIETRO GIOACHI Orazione. [Concerning the ransoming of Christian sl in Algiers, Tripoli, etc.] *See* ROMUALDO, *di San Gi battista.* La Redenzione degli schiavi, *etc.* [1761.] 4 **8156. df.**

CAISTOR.—*Society of Industry.* Reports of the sev institutions of the Society of Industry, establishe Caistor, A.D. 1800, *etc.* [Edited by William Di Visitor.] 3 vol. *J. Whitham: Caistor*, 1821. 8°. **1390. g.**

AISTOR, *Rural District of.*

— The Official Guide to Caistor Rural District, Lincs., *etc.* (Caistor Rural District, Lincs. The official guide.) [By L. Elgar Pike. Various editions.] [1949– .] 8°. *See* PIKE (Leslie E.) **010368**. k. **65**.

ÁIT. Cáit agus Cól. (Scéilín Nodlag.) [With illustrations by Marion King.] pp. 15. Oifig an tSoláthair: Baile Átha Cliath, [1937.] fol. **12812**. dd. **50**.

AITANYA. *See* CHAITANYA.

AITHBAT. The Battle of the Genii; a fragment. In three cantos. Taken from an ancient Erse manuscript, supposed to be written by Caithbat, the father of Cuchullin . . . Done into English by the Author of Homer Travestie. [A burlesque of bk. 6 of " Paradise Lost." By Thomas Bridges.] pp. 63. *S. Hooper: London,* 1765. 4°. **11630**. e. **9**. (**6**.)

ITHNESS. Diplomatarium Katanense et Sutherlandense. Fornbréfasafn Katnesinga og Suðrlendinga. Caithness & Sutherland Records. Collected and edited by Alfred W. Johnston and Amy Johnston. vol. 1. pp. lviii. 332. *London,* 1909–28. 8°. [*Viking Society for Northern Research. Old Lore Series.* vol. 10.] Ac. **9939/4**. (**3**.)

No more published.

— A Note of Various Measures, calculated for the Improvement of the County of Caitness, carrying on, anno 1801. pp. 8. *D. Willison: Edinburgh,* [1801 ?] 8°. B. **495**. (**5**.)

— *Commissariot.* The Commissariot Record of Caithness. Register of Testaments, 1661–1664. Edited by F. J. Grant. pp. 7. *Edinburgh,* 1902. 8°. [*Scottish Record Society. Publications.* pt. 18.] **2100.f.(2.)**

ITHNESS, *Diocese of.* [For the united Diocese of Moray, Ross and Caithness:] *See* MORAY, ROSS AND CAITHNESS, *Diocese of.*

— Two Ancient Records of the Bishopric of Caithness from the Charter-Room at Dunrobin. With a prefatory notice, by Cosmo Innes. 1855. *See* EDINBURGH.—*Bannatyne Club.* The Bannatyne Miscellany. vol. 3. 1827, *etc.* 4°. Ac. **8248/19**.

ITHNESS, GEORGE, *Bishop of.* [1600–1606.] *See* GLADSTANES.

—, JAMES, 14*th Earl of.* [1821–1881.] *See* SINCLAIR.

—, JOHN, *Bishop of.* [1624–1638.] *See* ABERNETHY.

—, MARIE, *Countess of.* [1830–1895.] *See* SINCLAIR.

—, WILLIAM, 1*st Earl of.* [d. 1480.] *See* SINCLAIR.

—, WILLIAM, 10*th Earl of.* [1727–1779.] *See* SINCLAIR.

ITHNESS ALMANAC. *See* EPHEMERIDES.

ITHNESS AND SUTHERLAND ALMANAC. *See* EPHEMERIDES.

ITHNESS (JAMES BALHARRIE) Pastime Poems. pp. 168. *Erskine Macdonald: London,* 1924. 8°. **011645**. ee. **96**.

ITHNESS (JAMES WALKER) Practical Mathematics. pp. viii. 318. *W. & R. Chambers: London, Edinburgh,* [1923.] 8°. **08531**. e. **24**.

ITICIOSMA GAOIDHEILGE. *See* IRISH CATECHISM.

IUBY (AMANDO)

— O Mysterio do cabaré. Novella policial. pp. 249. *São Paulo,* 1931. 8°. **12492**. e. **3**.

CAIUS, *Presbyter Romanus.* Caii qui circiter initia sæculi tertii floruit fragmenta. *Gr. & Lat.* 1846. *See* ROUTH (M. J.) Reliquiae sacræ. vol. 2. 1846, *etc.* 8°. **2204**. c. **6**.

—— Fragmenta. *Gr. & Lat.* 1857. *See* MIGNE (J. P.) Patrologiæ cursus completus, *etc.* Series Græca. tom 10. 1857, *etc.* 4°. **2001**. b.

CAIUS, *Saint, Pope.* S. Caii papæ epistola ad Felicem episcopum de accusatoribus. De diuinitate, ac vera humanitate Christi, *etc.* *See* MARNAVIĆ (I. T.) *Bishop of Bosnia.* Unica gentis Aureliæ Valeriæ Salonitanæ Dalmaticæ nobilitas. 1628. 4°. **9903**. dd. **8**.

CAIUS (BERNARDINUS) Bernardini Caii De alimentis, quæ cuiq; naturæ conueniant liber. In quo etiam de voluptatis natura, de saporibus . . . disputatur, *etc.* pp. 174. *Apud E. Deuchinum, & I. B. Pulcianum socios: Venetiis,* 1608. 4°. **1038**. h. **11**.

—— Bernardini Caii De sanguinis effusione disputatio, *etc.* pp. 128. *Apud E. Deuchinum: Venetiis,* 1607. 4°. **783**. l. **3**.

—— Disputatio . . . de vesicantium usu. pp. 87. *Apud E. Deuchinum: Venetiis,* 1606. 4°. **783**. l. **2**.

CAIUS (JEAN FERNAND)

—— *See* GENSE (James H.) J. F. Caius of the Society of Jesus, 1877–1944. [With portraits.] [1945.] 8°. **4887**. e. **54**.

CAIUS (JOANNES) *See* CAIUS (John)

CAIUS (JOHN) *See* also LONDINENSIS, *pseud.* [i.e. J. Caius.]

—— *See* BAKER (*Sir* George) *Bart., M.D.* Oratio ex Harveii instituto habita . . . Accedit commentarius quidam de Joanne Caio, *etc.* 1761. 4°. T. **52**. (**13**.)

—— *See* CAIUS (Thomas) Thomæ Caii . . . Vindiciæ antiquitatis Academiæ Oxoniensis contra J. Caium, *etc.* 1730. 8°. **08364.ee.100.**

—— *See* GALEN. [*Works.—Latin.*] Cl. Galeni . . . opera in latinam linguam conuersa, *etc.* (Cl. Galeni de decretis Hippocratis & Platonis liber primus, sine principio, Ioanne Caio Britanno interprete.) 1550. fol. **L.20.a.1.**

—— *See* GALEN. [*Two or more Works.—Greek.*] Cl. Galeni . . . libri aliquot græci partim hactenus non uisi, partim . . . repurgati . . . annotationibusq; illustrati per I. Caium, *etc.* 1544. 4°. **540**. e. **8**.

—— *See* GALEN. [*Two or more Works.—Greek.*] *Γαληνου . . . Βιβλια περι ἑπταμηνων βρεφων* . . . Galeni . . . libri de septimestri partu . . . emendati per I. Caium. [1557 ?] 8°. **540**. b. **15**. (**3**.)

—— *See* GALEN. [*De Sanitate Tuenda.—Greek.*] *Κλαυδιου Γαληνου . . . περι ὑγιεινων λογοι ἑξ* . . . Claudii Galeni . . . de tuenda valetudine libri sex . . . castigati per I. Caium. 1549. 8°. **540**. d. **9**.

—— *See* HALLIWELL, afterwards HALLIWELL-PHILLIPPS (James O.) The Life of St. Katharine . . . and an account of the magical manuscript of Dr. Caius. 1848. 4°. **11631**. h. **25**.

—— Ioannis Caii . . . opera aliquot et versiones, partim iam nata, partim recognita atque aucta. (C. Galeni . . . opera aliquot, partim non ante edita: partim emendata, & per Ioannem Caium . . . versa.) [With a portrait.] pp. 355. *A. M. Bergagne: Louanii,* 1556. 8°. G. **12260**.

CAIUS (JOHN)

—— [Another copy.] **246. k. 6.**
Imperfect; wanting the second leaf, containing the table of contents and the portrait of the author.

—— [Another copy.] **1172. f. 5. (1.)**
Imperfect; containing only "De medendi methodo" and "De ephemera Britannica."

—— The Works of John Caius, M.D., Second Founder of Gonville and Caius College and Master of the College, 1559–1573. With a memoir of his life by John Venn . . . Edited . . . by E. S. Roberts . . . in commemoration of the four-hundredth anniversary of the birth of John Caius in 1910. [Including Abraham Fleming's translation of "De canibus britannicis." With plates, including a portrait.] 9 pt. 1912. 8°. *See* CAMBRIDGE.—*University of Cambridge.—Gonville and Caius College.* **012273. g. 1.**

—— Joannis Caii . . . De canibus britannicis, liber unus; De rariorum animalium & stirpium historia, liber unus; De libris propriis, liber unus; De pronunciatione græcæ et latinæ linguæ, cum scriptione nova, libellus; ad optimorum exemplarium fidem recogniti à S. Jebb. pp. xv. 249. *Car. Davis: Londini,* 1729. 8°. **957. c. 11.**

—— [Another copy.] **L.P.** **446. c. 22.**

—— [Another copy.] **L.P.** G. **19292.**

—— The Annals of Gonville and Caius College . . . Edited by John Venn. *Lat.* pp. xiii. 431. *Cambridge,* 1904. 8°. [*Cambridge Antiquarian Society. Publications.* Octavo series. no. 40.] Ac. **5624.**

—— A Boke, or counseill against the disease commonly called the sweate, or sweatyng sicknesse, *etc.* **B.L.** ff. 39. *Richard Grafton: London,* 1552. 8°. **1167. a. 52.**
Imperfect; wanting ff. 35, 38.

—— A Boke, or Counsell against the Disease commonly called the Sweate . . . 1552. *See* GRUNER (C. G.) Scriptores de sudore anglico superstites, *etc.* 1847. 8°. **7561. h. 48.**

—— [Another edition.] *See* HECKER (J. F. C.) [Die grossen Volkskrankheiten des Mittelalters.] The Epidemics of the Middle Ages, *etc.* 1844. 8°. **1146. h. 23.**

—— [A facsimile of the edition of 1552.] Edited by Alexander Malloch. pp. xix. ff. 39. *New York,* 1937. 8°. [*Scholars' Facsimiles & Reprints.*] W.P. **9530/7.**

—— De antiquitate Cantebrigiensis Academiæ libri duo. Aucti ab ipso authore plurimum. In quorum secundo de Oxoniensis quoq; Gymnasii antiquitate disseritur, & Cantebrigiense longè eo antiquius esse definitur . . . Adiunximus assertionem antiquitatis Oxoniensis Academiæ, ab Oxoniensi quodam [i.e. Thomas Caius] annis iam elapsis aliquot ad Reginam Elizabeth. conscriptam, *etc.* 2 pt. *In ædibus Johannis Daij: Londini,* 1574. 4°. **731. i. 2. (1, 2.)**

—— [Another copy.] **731. b. 4. (1, 2.)**

—— [Another copy.] C. **32. h. 15. (1, 2.)**

—— [Another copy.] FEW MS. NOTES [by Matthew Parker, Archbishop of Canterbury]. **672. d. 12. (1, 2.)**

—— [Another copy.] G. **3612. (1, 4.)**

—— [Another copy.] C. **24. a. 27. (1, 2.)**
The volume of which this work forms part is a presentation copy to King James I. *from John Parker, son of Archbishop Parker. The original titlepage has been replaced by a special titlepage.*

CAIUS (JOHN)

—— [Another edition.] *See* CAIUS (Thomas) Thomæ Cai . . . Vindiciæ antiquitatis Academiæ Oxoniensis contra J. Caium, *etc.* 1730. 8°. **08364.ee.100.**

—— Ioannis Caii . . . De canibus britannicis, liber unus. De rariorum animalium et stirpium historia, liber unus. De libris propriis, liber unus. Iam primum excusi. 3 pt. *Per G. Seresium: Londini,* 1570. 8°. C. **31. a. 44**

—— [Another copy.] G. **12261. (2.**

—— [Another copy.] G. **2319**

—— [Another copy.] **234. a. 39**
Imperfect; wanting the general titlepage, and the first named work.

—— Joh. Caji . . . De canibus britannicis libellus. *See* PAULLINI (C. F.) Cynographia curiosa, *etc.* 1685. 4°. **461. c. 6**

—— [Another edition.] *See* GRATIUS, *Faliscus.* Grati Falisci Cynegeticon, *etc.* 1699. 8°. **1213. k. 8**

—— [Another edition.] *See* VLIET (Jan van) Poetæ latin rei venaticæ scriptores, *etc.* 1728. 4°. **454. b. 4**

—— [Another edition.] *See* BURMANNUS (P.) *the Elder.* Poetæ latini minores, *etc.* tom. 2. 1731. 4°. **655. b. 19**

—— [Another edition.] 1824. *See* LEMAIRE (N. E.) Bibliotheca classica latina, *etc.* vol. 134. 1819, *etc.* 8°. **11305. m. 5**

—— Of Englishe Dogges, the diuersities, the names, th natures and the properties. A short treatise written i latine by Johannes Caius . . . and newly drawne int Englishe by Abraham Fleming. **B.L.** pp. 44. *Rychard Johnes: London,* 1576. 4°. C. **31. g. 4**

—— [Another edition.] pp. 44. *A. Bradley: London* 1880. 8°. **7291. de. 5**

—— [Another edition.] 1880. *See* ARBER (Edward) An English Garner, *etc.* vol. 3. 1877, *etc.* 8°. **12269. cc. 12**

—— [Another edition.] 1903. *See* ARBER (Edward) A English Garner. (Social England Illustrated.) 1903, *etc.* 8°. **2324. e. 9/7**

—— Annalium Collegii medicorum Londini liber, *etc.* (The first book of the Annals of the Royal College of Physicians London, compiled by J. Caius, comprising the year 1518–1572. Printed for the first time, 1911.) pp. 71. *See* supra: The Works of John Caius, *etc.* 1912. 8°. **012273. g. 1**

—— Ioannis Caii . . . De ephemera britannica, liber unus non ante æditus. [With a portrait.] *See* supra: Ioann Caii . . . opera aliquot, *etc.* 1556. 8°. G. **1226**

—— [Another edition.] Summâ curâ recognitus. pp. 133. *Gul. & J. Innys: Londini,* 1721. 8°. **1167. c. 4**

—— [Another copy.] **43. e.**

—— [Another copy.] G. **1918**

—— Iohannis Caii . . . De ephemera Britannica liber . . Londini, 1721. *See* GRUNER (C. G.) Scriptores de sudo anglico superstites, *etc.* 1847. 8°. **7561. h. 48**

—— Ioannis Caii . . . De medendi methodo libri duo, e Cl. Galeni Pergameni, & Io. Baptistæ Montani Veronensi . . . sententia. Opus . . . iam primum natum. 2 lib pp. 107. *Apud H. Frobenium & N. Episcopium Basileae,* 1544. 8°. **540. d. 7. (4.**

CAIUS (JOHN)

—— [Another edition.] *See* MONTANUS (J. B.) Ioan. Baptistæ Montani . . . opuscula uaria, *etc.* tom. 1. 1558. 8°. **545.** c. 2.

—— I. Caii . . . De pronunciatione grecæ & latinæ linguæ cum scriptione noua libellus. pp. 23. *In ædibus Johannis Daij: Londini,* 1574. 4°. **672.** d. **12.** (4.)

—— [Another copy.] **731.** b. **4.** (4.)

—— [Another copy.] **731.** i. **2.** (4.)

—— [Another copy.] C. **32.** h. **15.** (4.)

—— [Another copy.] G. **3612.** (3.)

—— Historiæ Cantebrigiensis Academiæ ab vrbe condita, liber primus (secundus). pp. 135. *In ædibus Johannis Daij: Londini,* 1574. 4°. **731.** b. **4.** (3.)

—— [Another copy.] FEW MS. NOTES. **731.** i. **2.** (3.)

—— [Another copy.] FEW MS. NOTES [by Matthew Parker, Archbishop of Canterbury]. **672.** d. **12.** (3.)

—— [Another copy.] C. **32.** h. **15.** (3.)

—— [Another copy.] G. **3612.** (2.)

—— [Another copy.] C. **24.** a. **27.** (3.)
The volume of which this work forms part is a presentation copy to King James I. *from John Parker, son of Archbishop Parker. The original titlepage has been replaced by a special titlepage. The volume also contains three plates: a map of Cambridge by Richard Lyne, the arms of the colleges, and elevations of the Common Schools.*

—— Caii Spectrum: or, Dr Keyes's Charge against Dr M— [i.e. Dr. Richard Mead]. [With special reference to Mead's "Short Discourse concerning Pestilential Contagion."] pp. 22. *For A. Moore: London,* 1721. 8°. **1172.** g. **8.** (3.)

CAIUS (JOHN FERNAND) *See* KĀNHOBĀ RAṆCHHODDĀS KĪRTIKAR. Indian Medicinal Plants . . . Edited, revised, enlarged, and mostly rewritten by E. Blatter . . . J. F. Caius, *etc.* [1936.] 8°. **7032.** ppp. **9.**

CAIUS (THOMAS)

—— *See* BIBLE.—*New Testament.* [*English.*] The first tome or volume of the Paraphrase of Erasmus vpon the newe testamente. [Translated by T. Caius and others.] 1548 [O.S.]. fol. C. **110.** g. **12.**

—— *See* LONGLAND (John) *Bishop of Lincoln.* J. Longlondi . . . tres conciones, *etc.* [Translated from the English by T. Caius?] [1527?] fol. C. **40.** l. **5.**

—— Assertio antiquitatis Oxoniensis Academiæ incerto authore eiusdem Gymnasii [i.e. T. Caius], *etc.* *See* LONDINENSIS, *pseud.* [i.e. J. Caius.] De antiquitate Cantabrigiensis Academiæ libri duo, *etc.* 1568. 8°. **731.** a. **6.** (1, 2.)

—— [Another edition.] *See* CAIUS (John) De antiquitate Cantebrigiensis Academiæ libri duo, *etc.* 1574. 4°. **731.** i. **2.** (2.)

—— [Another edition.] *See* infra: Thomæ Caii . . . Vindiciæ antiquitatis Academiæ Oxoniensis, *etc.* vol. 1. 1730. 8°. **08364.ee.100.**

—— Thomæ Caii . . . Vindiciæ antiquitatis Academiæ Oxoniensis contra Joannem Caium, Cantabrigiensem. In lucem ex autographo emisit Tho. Hearnius. Qui porro non tantum Antonii à Wood vitam . . . & Humphredi Humphreys . . . de viris claris Cambro Britannicis observationes, sed & reliquias quasdam, ad familiam . . . Ferrariorum, de Gidding Parva . . . pertinentes, subnexuit. [Including also "De antiquitate Cantabrigiensis Academiæ libri duo" by John Caius.] 2 vol. pp. cviii. 834. *E Theatro Sheldoniano: Oxonii,* 1730. 8°. **08364.ee.100.**

—— [Another copy.] L.P. **166.** h. **8, 9.**

—— [Another copy.] L.P. G. **12522, 23.**

CAIVANO (TOMMASO) *See* ARONA (Juan de) *pseud.* Inno a Lesseps . . . Tradotto . . . da T. Caivano. 1886. 8°. **10601.** dg. **6.** (4.)

—— Il Guatemala. pp. viii. 310. *Firenze,* 1895. 8°. **10480.** df. **3.**

—— Por qué sube el oro? Conferencia, *etc.* pp. 34. *Buenos Ayres,* 1891. 8°. [*Revista del Paraguay.* Supplemento. año 1. no. 3.] P.P. **4126**/b.

—— Religione e filosofia. I destini umani, ricerche e studi. pp. 426. *Milano,* 1881. 8°. **4374.** h. **18.**

—— Storia della guerra d'America fra il Chilì, il Perù e la Bolivia . . . Con una carta, *etc.* pp. 562. *Torino,* 1882. 8°. **9772.** aaa. **11.**

—— Il Venezuela. pp. 360. *Milano,* 1897. 8°. **9772.** bb. **27.**

CAIVANO-SCHIPANI (FELICE) Dizionario biografico de' soci dell'Accademia Pittagorica. pp. 203. *Napoli,* 1881. 8°. **10629.** aaa. **37.**

CAIX (ALFRED DE) Histoire du Bourg d'Écouché, département de l'Orne. pp. 265. *Caen,* 1862. 8°. **10170.** ccc. **17.**

—— Notice sur le prieuré de Briouze. pp. 48. *Caen,* 1856. 4°. **7703.** f. **22.** (4.)

CAIX (C. NAPOLEONE) Le origini della lingua poetica italiana, principii di grammatica storica italiana ricavati dallo studio dei manoscritti, con una introduzione sulla formazione degli antichi canzonieri italiani. pp. 284. [1880.] *See* FLORENCE.—Università di Firenze. Pubblicazioni, *etc.* Sezione di filosofia e filologia. vol. 2. 1875, *etc.* 8°. Ac. **8848.**

—— Saggio sulla storia della lingua e dei dialetti d'Italia, con un'introduzione sopra l'origine delle lingue neolatine. pp. lxxii. 1–256. *Parma,* 1872. 8°. **12941.** g. **31.**
No more published.

—— Studi di etimologia italiana e romanza. Osservazioni ed aggiunte al "Vocabolario etimologico delle lingue romanze" di F. Diez. pp. xxxv. 213. *Firenze,* 1878. 8°. **12942.** bb. **28.**

—— In memoria di Napoleone Caix e Ugo Angelo Canello. Miscellanea di filologia e linguistica per G. I. Ascoli [and others], *etc.* [With biographical notices of C. N. Caix and U. A. Canello.] pp. xxxviii. 478. *Firenze,* 1886. 4°. **12902.** i. **1.**

CAIX (ROBERT DE) *See* LABOULAYE (E. de) Les Chemins de fer de Chine . . . Préface de M. R. de Caix, *etc.* 1911. 8°. **08235.** f. **96.**

—— Fachoda. La France et l'Angleterre. [With maps.] pp. viii. 321. *Paris,* 1899. 12°. **8028.** aaaa. **19.**

—— Terre-neuve, Saint Pierre et le French Shore. La question des pêcheries et le traité du 8 avril 1904, *etc.* pp. 100. *Paris,* 1904. 8°. **8155.** de. **46.**

CAIXA.

—— Caixa de Amortização. *See* RIO DE JANEIRO.

—— Caixa de Crédito do Huambo. *See* NOVA LISBOA.

CAIXA.

—— Caixa Economica e Monte de Soccorro da Capital Federal. *See* Rio de Janeiro.

CAIXAL Y ESTRADÉ (Joseph) *Bishop of Urgel.* Veni-mecum pii sacerdotis, quod ex variis devotis libris excerptum, ex sui exilii loco, tanquam amoris pignus, suo clero . . . offert . . . I Caixal et Estrade . . . Accedit manuale ordinandorum, ipsis imo et sacerdotibus omnibus pernecessarium. pp. 456. *Barcinone,* 1856. 16°. **3477. a. 66.**

CAIX DE SAINT-AMOUR (Amédée de) *See* Caix de Saint-Aymour.

CAIX DE SAINT-AYMOUR (Amédée de) *Count. See* France.—*Commission des Archives Diplomatiques.* Recueil des instructions données aux ambassadeurs et ministres de France, *etc.* (tom. 3. Portugal. Avec une introduction et des notes par le Vte de Caix de Saint-Aymour.) 1884, *etc.* 8°. **09076. d.**

—— *See* Periodical Publications.—*Paris.* Annuaire des sciences historiques . . . Publié par A. de Caix de Saint-Aymour. 1877. 8°. **P.P. 3472. g.**

—— *See* Periodical Publications.—*Paris.* Le Musée archéologique . . . Publié sous la direction de A. de Caix de Saint-Aymour. 1876, *etc.* 4°. **P.P. 1931. dab.**

—— Anne de Russie reine de France, puis comtesse de Valois. Notice extraite . . . des Causeries du besacier, *etc.* pp. 48. *Senlis,* 1894. 8°. **10601. aa. 35. (6.)**

—— Autour de Noyon. Sur les traces des barbares, *etc.* pp. xii. 340. pl. xl. *Paris,* 1917. 4°. **9081. g. 5.**

—— Études sur quelques monuments mégalithiques de la vallée de l'Oise. pp. 39. *Paris,* 1874. 8°. **7704. cc. 5.**

—— Une Famille d'artistes et de financiers aux xviie et xviiie siècles. Les Boullongne . . . Ouvrage illustré de cinq portraits . . . et renfermant le catalogue raisonné de 588 œuvres des artistes de cette famille, *etc.* pp. xi. 337. *Paris,* 1919. 8°. **10657. dd. 6.**

—— La France en Éthiopie. Histoire des relations de la France avec l'Abyssinie chrétienne sous les règnes de Louis xiii. et de Louis xiv., 1634–1706, d'après les documents inédits des Archives du Ministère des Affaires Étrangères. pp. xv. 373. *Paris,* 1886. 8°. **9061. de. 27.**

—— La Grande voie romaine de Senlis à Beauvais et l'emplacement de Litanobriga ou Latinobriga. Solutions du problème proposées jusqu'à ce jour. Études de M. l'abbé Caudel. Recherches de MM. G. Millescamps et Hahn . . . Rapport, accompagné de deux cartes par A. de Caix de Saint-Aymour. pp. 84. *Paris,* 1873. 8°. **7705. b. 1.**

—— Guerre de 1914. La Marche sur Paris de l'aile droite allemande. Ses derniers combats, 26 août—4 septembre 1914. Avec trois cartes. 4e édition. pp. 137. *Paris,* 1916. 8°. **09082. a. 26.**

—— 8e édition, revue et considérablement augmentée. pp. 181. *Paris,* 1917. 8°. **09082. bbb. 47.**

—— Les Intérêts français dans le Soudan éthiopien, *etc.* pp. 142. *Paris,* 1884. 12°. **8027. bb. 4.**

—— La Langue latine étudiée dans l'unité indo-européenne, *etc.* pp. 452. *Paris,* 1868. 8°. **12934. i. 13.**

—— Mémoire sur l'origine de la ville et du nom de Senlis, *etc.* pp. 23. *Senlis,* 1863. 8°. **10172. ee. 28. (6.)**

CAIX DE SAINT-AYMOUR (Amédée de) *Count.*

—— Mémoires et documents pour servir à l'histoire des pays qui forment aujourd'hui le département de l'Oise, *etc.* 2 sér. *Paris,* 1898, 1916. 8°. **09231. k. 19.**

—— Un Million pour nos musées nationaux s'il vous plaît! pp. 48. *Paris,* 1878. 8°. **7959. bb. 12. (6.)**

—— Note sur quelques lécythes blancs d'Érétrie. 1893. *See* Paris.—*Société Nationale des Antiquaires de France.* Mémoires, *etc.* sér. 6. tom. 3. 1891, *etc.* 8°. **Ac. 5331.**

—— Note sur un temple romain découvert dans la forêt d'Halatte . . . lue à la réunion des sociétés savantes à la Sorbonne le 9 avril 1874. pp. 35. *Paris,* 1874. 16°. **7704. a. 3.**

—— Notes et documents pour servir à l'histoire d'une famille picarde au moyen-âge, xi–xvie siècles. La Maison de Caix. Rameau mâle des Boves-Coucy. pp. viii. 252. ccxxxviii. 83. *Paris,* 1895. 8°. **9906. bb. 12**

—— Les Pays sud-slaves de l'Austro-Hongrie . . . Ouvrage illustré de . . . gravures et d'une carte. pp. iv. 301. *Paris,* 1883. 18°. **10205. ccc. 10.**

—— Le Plébiscite et l'hérédité. pp. 36. *Paris,* 1870. 8°. **8051. f. 5. (1.)**

—— La Question de l'enseignement des langues classiques et des langues vivantes, *etc.* pp. 31. *Paris,* 1866. 8°. **8309. h. 13. (11.)**

—— Questions algériennes. Arabes et Kabyles. pp. 287. *Paris,* 1891. 12°. **8027. bb. 14**

—— Vieux manoirs et gentilshommes bas-normands: promenades historiques dans le Val d'Orne. Soixante-dix illustrations. pp. 311. *Caen,* [1914.] 8°. **10170. i. 19**

CAIZERGUES (César) *See* Caizergues (Fulcrand C.)

CAIZERGUES (Fulcrand César) *See* Rogery (S.) and Caizergues (F. C.) Rapport fait à l'École de Médecine de Montpellier, *etc.* [1800.] 4°. [*Opinion de l'École de Médecine de Montpellier sur la nature . . . de la fièvre, etc.*] **1180. e. 4. (2.)**

—— Fragment de physiologie médicale, *etc.* pp. 42. *Montpellier,* an 8 [1800]. 4°. **1180. d. 7. (18.)**

—— Séance solennelle de rentrée des Facultés de l'Académie de Montpellier du 2 novembre 1840. Rapport sur les travaux de la Faculté de Médecine de Montpellier, pendant l'année scolaire 1839–1840. pp. 41. 1840. 4°. *See* Montpellier.—*École de Médecine.* **1181. i. 15. (1.)**

CAIZERGUES (L.) Du névrome. Observations et réflexions. Thèse, *etc.* pp. 107. *Montpellier,* 1867. 4°. **7379. g. 12. (13.)**

CAIZERGUES (Raymond) Des myélites syphilitiques. Thèse, *etc.* pp. 186. *Montpellier,* 1878. 4°. **7379. l. 11. (4.)**

CAIZZI (Bruno)

—— Antologia della questione meridionale. A cura di Bruno Caizzi, *etc.* pp. 462. *Milano,* 1950. 8°. **8032. ccc. 19**

—— Benelux. Organisation et perspectives. [By B. Caizzi with the collaboration of M. C. L. Ameye.] pp. 34. *Genève,* [1950.] 8°. **8204. e. 42**
Les Cahiers d'actualité économique. no. 23.

CAIZZI (Luigi) Analisi scacchistica. Compendio prospettico. pp. vii. 434. *Napoli*, 1928. *obl.* 8°. **7915**. de. **42**.

CAJA.

— Caja de Ahorros de Caracas. *See* Caracas.

— Caja de Ahorros de Empleados Públicos. *See* Chile.

— Caja de Ahorros de Madrid. *See* Madrid.

— Caja de Ahorros de Mexico. *See* Mexico, *City of.*

— Caja de Crédito Agrario. *See* Chile.—*Ministerio de Fomento.*

— Caja de Crédito Minero. *See* Chile.

— Caja Dominicana de Seguros Sociales. *See* Dominican Republic.

— Caja General de Depósitos. *See* Spain.

— Caja Nacional de Jubilaciónes y Pensiónes de Empleados Ferroviarios. *See* Buenos Ayres.

CAJACIA. *See* Cajazzo.

CAJADO (Hermicus) *See* Caiadus (Henricus)

CAJAK (Jan) *the Elder.*

— Преглед савремене словачке литературе. 3 pt. 1905, 06. *See* Novi Sad.—*Матица Српска* Сербскій Лѣтописъ, *etc.* (Летопис Матице Српске.) књ. 234, 236, 237. [1842, *etc.*] 8°. Ac. **8984**.

CAJAK (Ján) *the Younger.*

— Po stopách Generála Viesta. [With plates.] pp. 54. 1947. 8°. *See* Slovakia.—*Povereníctvo Informácií.* **12593**. g. **23**.

CAJAL (Rosa María)

— Juan Risco. [A novel.] pp. 233. *Barcelona*, 1948. 8°. **12492**. de. **13**.
Colección "Áncora y delfín." vol. 41.

CAJAL (Santiago Ramón y) *See* Ramón y Cajal.

CAJALÉN (Anders) Afhandling om sättet at utöda mask på stickelbärs busken, *etc.* *Praes.* P. Kalm. pp. 8. *Åbo*, [1778.] 4°. B. **600**. (**13**.)

CAJAMAI, *Island of.* The Present State of Physick in the Island of Cajamai [i.e. Jamaica]. To the Members of the R. S. [i.e. Royal Society.] [A satire on Sir Hans Sloane. By William King, LL.D. ?] no. 1. pp. 7. [*London*, 1710 ?] 4°. **551**. a. **9**. (**6**.)
No more published ?

— [Another copy.] **117**. l. **60**.

CAJAN (Johan Fredrik) *See* Kajaani.

CAJANDER (Aimo Kaarle) Beiträge zur Kenntniss der Vegetation der Alluvionen des Nördlichen Eurasiens. 3 pt. 1906. *Helsingfors*, 1906–09. 4°. [*Societas Scientiarum Fennica. Acta.* tom. 32. no. 1; tom. 33. no. 6; tom. 37. no. 5.] Ac. **1094**/**2**.

— Studien über die Moore Finnlands. pp. 208. *Helsingfors*, 1913. 8°. [*Fennia.* vol. 35. no. 5.] Ac. **6113**.

— Ueber Waldtypen. pp. iv. 175. *Helsingfors*, 1909. 8°. [*Fennia.* vol. 28. no. 2.] Ac. **6113**.

CAJANDER (Gabriel Johannes) Dissertationis de origine literarum latinarum pars prior (posterior). *Praes.* H. G. Porthan. 2 pt. pp. 32. *Aboæ*, [1786.] 4°. **817**. c. **23**. (**9**.)

CAJANDER (Karl Alexander) Uudenkaupungin muinaisia. Koonnut K. A. Cajander, *etc.* I. 1616–1647. pp. 334. *Turku*, [1889,] 95. 8°. **10292**. h. **34**.
No more published.

CAJANDER (Paavo Eemil) *See* Runeberg (Johan L.) Vänrikki Stoolin Tarinat. Suomentanut P. Cajander, *etc.* 1924. 12°. **011557**. ee. **6**.

— *See* Shakespeare (W.) [*Works.—Finnish.*] Shakespeare'n Dramoja. (Suomentanut P. Cajander.) 1879, *etc.* [*Suomalaisen Kirjallisuuden Seuran Toimituksia.* osa 60.] Ac. **9080**.

— *See* Zschokke (J. H. D.) [Das Goldmacher-Dorf.] Kultala. [The translation by C. N. Keckman.] (Tämän painoksen kielellistä asua on walwonut maisteri P. Cajander.) 1888. 12°. **884**. e. **5**.

CAJANDER (Zakarias) Sammandrag af tre föredrag i landthushållning, på Läne-styrelsens anmodan . . . hållna i Luleå stad . . . mars 1857. pp. 24. *Luleå*, 1857. 8°. **7074**. c. **45**. (**3**.)

CAJANELLO, Anne Charlotte del Pezzo, *Duchess di.* *See* Leffler, afterwards Edgren (A. C.) afterwards Pezzo (A. C. del) *Duchess di Cajanello.*

CAJANI (Angelo) *See* Euclid. [*Elementa.*] Ευκλειδου στοιχειων βιβλια ιε'. Euclidis Elementorum libri xv. [Edited by A. Cajani.] 1545. 8°. **717**. d. **42**.

— *See* Euclid. [*Elementa.*] I quindici libri degli elementi di Euclide, di Greco tradotti in lingua thoscana. [By A. Cajani.] 1545. 8°. **530**. b. **13**.

CAJANI (F.) *See* X * * *. Histoire de la Révolution de 1830, *etc.* [Edited by F. Cajani.] 1870. 8°. **9220**. h. **5**.

CAJANUS (Abrahamus) *See* Holstius (J.) and Cajanus (A.) Dissertatio chemica, de silica ex solutione alkalina per barytam præcipitata, *etc.* [1801.] 4°. B. **387**. (**13**.)

CAJANUS (Angelus) *See* Cajani (Angelo)

CAJANUS (Aug.) Våra nomader, framställning med en blick på nybyggesväsendet i Lappmarken. pp. 129. *Stockholm*, 1870. 12°. **10281**. aa. **24**.

CAJANUS (Eric) Historisk och oeconomisk beskrifning öfwer Cronoby sokn uti Österbotn. *Praes.* P. Kalm. pp. 34. *Åbo*, [1755.] 4°. B. **669**. (**16**.)

CAJANUS (G.)

— *See* Helsinki.—*Juridiska Föreningen i Finland.* Tidskrift, *etc.* (Sakregister. Årgångarne I–XX. 1865–1884. Utarbetadt af G. Cajanus.) 1910, *etc.* 8°. Ac. **2145**. (**3**.)

CAJAROTTI (Ilario) La Lettura de' poeti: canto pubblicato nelle faustissime nozze Lavagnoli e da Mula. [By I. Cajarotti. The dedication signed: N. P.] pp. 29. 1809. 8°. *See* Lavagnoli (E.) T. **2272**. (**11**.)

CAJAS (Virgilio A.) Campañas de la República del Ecuador. pp. 34. *Quito*, 1898. 8°. **09004**. aaa. **10**. (**4**.)

CAJAZZO, Jacobus, *Bishop of.* *See* Lutiis (J. de)

CAJETAN [Tiene], *Saint.* *See* Barzisa (G. B.) Le Azioni di S. Gaetano, *etc.* [With a portrait.] 1733. 4°. **4867**. f. **16**.

— *See* Caracciolus (A.) De vita Pauli quarti Pont. Max. collectanea . . . Item Cajetani Thienæi, Bonifacii a Colle . . . vitæ, *etc.* 1612. 4°. C. **81**. c. **13**. (**1**.)

CAJETAN [Tiene], *Saint.*

—— *See* Castaldo (G. B.) Vita del B. G. Tiene, *etc.* 1616. 4°. **205.** b. **15.** (**2.**)

—— *See* Cirino (N.) Inno a San Gaetano Thiene. (Documenti che riguardano la vita di S. Gaetano.) 1877. 8°. **11431.** de. **53.**

—— *See* Magenis (G. M.) Nuova e più copiosa storia dell'ammirabile . . . vita di S. Gaetano Tiene, *etc.* 1726. 4°. **4828.** d. **20.**

—— *See* Magenis (G. M.) Vita di S. Gaetano Tiene, *etc.* 1776. 4°. **4828.** d. **21.**

—— *See* Magenis (G. M.) Neu vermehrte . . . Lebens Geschicht des Heiligen Cajetans von Thiene, *etc.* 1754. 4°. **4807.** d. **9.**

—— *See* Maulde La Clavière (M. A. R. de) Saint Gaëtan, *etc.* 1902. 8°. **4826.** ee. **13.**

—— *See* Maulde La Clavière (M. A. R. de) Saint Cajetan, *etc.* 1902. 8°. **4830.** b. **15.**

—— *See* Negrone (G.) R.P. J. Nigroni . . . Historica disputatio de S. Ignatio . . . & de B. Caietano Thienæo, *etc.* 1630. 4°. **1371.** d. **8.**

—— *See* Norbert, *Saint, Archbishop of Magdeburg.* Saint Norbert, archevêque de Magdebourg (Saint Gaétan). 1860. 8°. **4824.** c. **31.**

—— *See* Nuñez da Sylva (A.) Hecatombe sacra . . . em que se conthem as principaes acções da vida do glorioso patriarca S. Caetano Thiene. 1686. 8°. **1464.** a. **10.**

—— *See* Paschini (P.) S. Gaetano Thiene, Gian Pietro Carafa e le origini dei chierici regolari teatini. 1926. 8°. **04785.** m. **52.**

—— *See* Paternò (N.) *Baron di Recalcacci.* Idillio in lode di S. Gaetano Tiene. 1758. 4°. [*Opuscoli di autori siciliani.* tom. 1.] **663.** g. **1.**

—— *See* Pepe (S.) Vita del B. Gaetano Tiene, *etc.* 1657. 4°. **1373.** f. **17.**

—— *See* Rome, *Church of.*—Innocent xii., *Pope.* Bulla . . . canonizationis S. Caietani Thienæi. [15 July 1691.] 1692. fol. **1897.** b. **15.** (**73.**)

—— *See* Silvestro, da Volsanzibio, O.F.M.Cap. Vita e dottrina di Gaetano di Thiene . . . Con un'appendice di documenti inediti e rari. [With a portrait.] 1949. 8°. **4828.** dd. **33.**

—— *See* Zinelli (G. M.) Memorie istoriche della vita di S. Gaetano, *etc.* 1753. 4°. **4825.** f. **35.**

—— Le Lettere di San Gaetano da Thiene. A cura di D. Francesco Andreu. [With facsimiles.] pp. xxxiv. 144. *Città del Vaticano,* 1954. 8°. [*Studi e testi.* vol. 177.] **012211.** b. **1/177.**

—— Relatione delle cerimonie, & apparato, fatto . . . nella canonizatione de' cinque Santi, cioè di S. Gaetano Tieneo, di S. Francesco Borgia, di S. Filippo Benitii, di S. Ludovico Beltrando, e di S. Rosa di S. Maria, fatta dalla Santità di N. S. PP. Clemente x. *G. Dragondelli: Roma,* 1671. 4°. **1193.** m. **1.** (**68.**)

CAJETAN [Tiene], *Saint, Congregation of Regular Clerks of. See* Theatines.

CAJETAN (Thomas de Vio) *Cardinal. See* Vio (T. de)

CAJEX.

—— Cajex. Magazine of the Association of Jewish Ex-Servicemen and Women, Cardiff. *See* Cardiff.—*Association of Jewish Ex-Servicemen and Women.*

ČAJKANOVIĆ (Veselin)

—— Вергилије и његови савременици. pp. iv. 197. *Београд,* 1930. 8°. [*Српска Књижевна Задруга.* бр. 222.] **012216.** de. **1/222.**

—— О српском врховном богу. (О врховном богу у старој српској религији.) pp. 208. *Београд,* 1941. 8°. [*Српска Краљевска Академија. Посебна издања.* књ. 132.] Ac. **1131.**

—— Расправе и грађа . . . Уредио В. Чајкановић, *etc.* *Београд,* 1934– . 8°. [*Српски Етнографски Зборник.* књ. 50, *etc.*] Ac. **1131/4.**

—— Српске народне приповетке . . . Уредио В. Чајкановић. *Београд-Земун,* 1927– . 8°. [*Српски Етнографски Зборник.* књ. 41, *etc.*] Ac. **1131/4.**

—— Студије из религије и фолклора. pp. 182. *Београд,* 1924. 8°. [*Српски Етнографски Зборник.* књ. 31.] Ac. **1131/4.**

ČAJKOVAC (Sigismund)

—— Druga čitanka za niže pučke škole u Hrvatskoj i Slavoniji. Drugo izdanje. Priredio Dr. Sigismund Čajkovac, *etc.* pp. 160. *u Zagrebu,* 1921. 8°. **12976.** t. **16.**

CAJO (Andrea) Sermone. (Omaggio poetico al sacro oratore Giuseppe Barbieri.) *See* Barbieri (G.) Saggi di sacra eloquenza, *etc.* 1833. 12°. **1367.** h. **17.** (**9.**)

CAJOLI (Renato)

—— *See* Italy.—Enrico De Nicola, *Provisional Chief of State.* [1946–48.] L'Autonomia del Trentino-Alto Adige. Commento [by R. Cajoli] allo Statuto speciale e alle norme d'attuazione, *etc.* 1952. 8°. **5357.** c. **13.**

CAJORI (Florian) *See* Archibald (Raymond C.) Cajori's Edition of Sir Isaac Newton's Mathematical Principles of Natural Philosophy, *etc.* [1936.] 8°. **08535.** h. **35.**

—— *See* Archibald (Raymond C.) Florian Cajori, *etc.* [With a portrait.] [1932.] 8°. **010885.** g. **14.**

—— *See* Newton (*Sir* I.) [*Principia.*] Sir Isaac Newton's Mathematical Principles . . . The translations revised, and supplied with an historical and explanatory appendix, by F. Cajori. 1934. 8°. **08534.** h. **5.**

—— Arithmetik. Gleichungslehre. Zahlentheorie. 1907. *See* Cantor (M.) Vorlesungen über Geschichte der Mathematik, *etc.* Bd. 4. 1894, *etc.* 8°. 8530.i.46.

—— The Chequered Career of Ferdinand Rudolph Hassler, first Superintendent of the United States Coast Survey. A chapter in the history of science in America. [With plates, including a portrait.] pp. 245. *Christopher Publishing House: Boston,* [1929.] 8°. **010880.** e. **28.**

—— The Early Mathematical Sciences in North and South America . . . Illustrated. pp. 156. *R. G. Badger: Boston,* [1928.] 8°. **08560.** df. **24.**

—— A History of Elementary Mathematics. With hints on methods of teaching. pp. viii. 304. *Macmillan Co.: New York,* 1896. 8°. **2242.** d. **15.**

—— A History of Mathematical Notations. 2 vol. *Open Court Publishing Co.: Chicago,* 1928, 29. 8°. **8503.** h. **15.**

—— *See* Schulte (Mary L.) Additions in Arithmetic, 1483–1700, to the Sources of Cajori's "History of Mathematical Notations," *etc.* 1935. 8°. **08535.** ee. **6.**

—— A History of Mathematics. pp. xiv. 422. *Macmillan & Co.: New York & London,* 1894. 8°. **08532.** f. **39.**

—— Second edition, revised and enlarged. pp. viii. 514. *Macmillan Co.: New York,* 1919. 8°. 2023.c.

CAJORI (FLORIAN)

—— A History of Physics in its Elementary Branches, including the evolution of physical laboratories. pp. viii. 322 *Macmillan Co.: New York*, 1899. 8°. **8707**. dd. **18**

—— Revised and enlarged edition. pp. xiii. 424. *Macmillan Co.: New York*, 1929. 8°. **08710**. bb. **3**.

—— A History of the Arithmetical Methods of Approximation to the Roots of Numerical Equations of one Unknown Quantity. 2 pt. *Colorado Springs*, 1910. 8°. [*Colorado College Publication*. Science series. vol. 12. no. 7.] Ac. **2691**. f/**7**.

—— A History of the Conceptions of Limits and Fluxions in Great Britain from Newton to Woodhouse . . . With portraits of Berkeley and Maclaurin. pp. viii. 299. *Chicago & London*, 1919. 8°. [*Open Court Series of Classics of Science and Philosophy*. no. 5.] **8708**. a. **37/5**.

—— A History of the Logarithmic Slide Rule and Allied Instruments. [With a bibliography.] pp. vii. 126. x. *A. Constable & Co.: London; New York* [printed], 1909. 8°. **8548**. ccc. **11**.

—— The History of Zeno's Arguments on Motion: phases in the development of the theory of limits . . . Reprinted from the American Mathematical Monthly, *etc.* [1915.] 8°. **08532**. eee. **3**.

—— An Introduction to the Modern Theory of Equations. pp. ix. 239. *Macmillan Co.: New York*, 1904. 8°. **8530**. ff. **2**.

—— A List of Oughtred's Mathematical Symbols, with historical notes. *Berkeley*, 1920. 8°. [*University of California Publications in Mathematics*. vol. 1. no. 8.] Ac. **2689**. g/**21**.

—— On the History of Gunter's Scale and the Slide Rule during the seventeenth century. *Berkeley*, 1920. 8°. [*University of California Publications in Mathematics*. vol. 1. no. 9.] Ac. **2689**. g/**21**.

—— The Teaching and History of Mathematics in the United States. pp. 400. *Washington*, 1890. 8°. [*U.S. Bureau of Education. Circular of Information*. 1890. no. 3.] A.S. **203**.

—— William Oughtred, a great seventeenth-century teacher of mathematics. pp. vi. 100. *Open Court Publishing Co.: Chicago*, 1916. 8°. **010826**. de. **48**.

CAJORI (FLORIAN) and **ODELL** (LETITIA REBEKAH)

—— Elementary Algebra. First year course. [With answers.] 2 pt. *Macmillan Co.: New York*, 1915, 16. 8°. **08532**. ee. **18**.

CAJOT (JOSEPH) Les Antiquités de Metz, ou Recherches sur l'origine des Médiomatriciens; leur premier établissement dans les Gaules, leurs mœurs, leur religion. pp. xii. 318. *Metz*, 1760. 8°. **284**. b. **2**.

—— Histoire critique des coqueluchons. [By J. Cajot.] pp. 173. 1762. 12°. *See* HISTOIRE. **4091**. a. **4**.

—— Les Plagiats de M. J. J. R. de Genève (Jean-Jacques Rousseau), sur l'éducation. [By] D. J. C. B. [i.e. J. Cajot Bénédictin.] pp. xxii. 378. 1766. 12°. *See* B., D. J. C. **716**. a. **24**.

CAJTHAML (FRANTIŠEK)

—— Obrázky z "Deutschböhmen." Kresby starého menšináře. pp. 209. *v Praze*, 1923. 8°. **10215**. c. **39**.

CAJU (JAN DU) Blauwe schenen, blyspel met zang in een bedryf. pp. 37. *Antwerpen*, 1854. 8°. **11755**. b. **8**.

—— Hedendaegsche jongheid. Dry verhalen. pp. 107. *Antwerpen*, 1855. 8°. **12580**. g. **14**.

ČAKAVSKA LIRIKA.

—— Antologija nove čakavske lirike. Drugo prošireno izdanje. [With contributions by V. Nazor and others.] pp. 154. *Zagreb*, 1947. 8°. **11588**. bb. **21**. *Part of a series entitled "Suvremeni pisci Hrvatske."*

CAKCHIQUEL LANGUAGE. A Grammar of the Cakchiquel Language of Guatemala. Translated from a MS. (Arte de la lengua cakchiquel) in the library of the American Philosophical Society, with an introduction and additions, by Daniel G. Brinton. [With a map.] pp. 72. *McCalla & Stavely: Philadelphia*, 1884. 8°. **12902**. dd. **12**.

CAKCHIQUELS.

—— The Annals of the Cakchiquels. (By a member of the Xakila family [or rather, by F. H. Arana and F. Díaz].) The original text, with a translation, notes and introduction by D. G. Brinton. pp. 234. *Philadelphia*, 1885. 8°. [*Library of Aboriginal American Literature*. no. 6.] **2398**. e. **3**.

—— The Annals of the Cakchiquels. [Compiled by Francisco Hernández Arana and Francisco Díaz.] Translated from the Cakchiquel Maya by Adrián Recinos and Delia Goetz. Title of the Lords of Totonicapán. Translated from the Quiché text into Spanish by Dionisio José Chonay. English version by Delia Goetz. pp. ix. 217. [1953.] 8°. *See* HERNÁNDEZ ARANA (F.) **W.P.14865/37.**

CAKE BOOK. The Everyday Cake Book . . . By G. P. [1920.] 8°. *See* P., G. **07942**. aa. **57**.

CAKE (DAVID) and **EYRE** (THOMAS) Remarks on Various Parts of the Holy Scriptures . . . And various miscellaneous selections. [Edited by T. Eyre.] pp. lxxii. 288. *Printed for the Author: Ringwood*, 1827. 12°. **1109**. c. **12**.

CAKE (EDWIN W.)

—— *See* RASMUSSEN (Marius P.) Retail Outlets for Fruit in New York City. By M. P. Rasmussen . . . E. W. Cake. 1941. 8°. [*U.S. Farm Credit Administration. Cooperative Research and Service Division. Bulletin*. no. 52.] A.S. **929**/**6**.

—— Operation of Small-Lot Country Fruit and Vegetable Auctions. pp. iv. 40. *Washington*, 1940. 8°. [*U.S. Farm Credit Administration. Cooperative Research and Service Division. Circular*. no. C118.] A.S. **929**/**5**.

CAKELESS.

—— Cakeless. [A satirical play in verse on Dean H. J. Liddell, C. L. Dodgson and other Christ Church characters. By John Howe Jenkins.] pp. 15. MS. NOTES. [*Mowbray: Oxford*, 1874.] 8°. **11779**. b. **5**. (**3**.)

CAKES. Cakes and Other Good Things. By the author of "Supper Dishes for people with small means," &c. [i.e. E. de V. Mathew.] pp. xiv. 52. *Simpkin & Marshall: London; Pawsey & Hayes: Ipswich*, [1886.] 8°. **7944**. aaa. **57**. (**1**.)

—— Hye, for Cakes and Ale; a new poem on a certain young Miss Lady in F—— st - - - t and a brewers son call'd W——, of the City of Dublin, *etc.* 1726. fol. *See* W—, *a Brewer's Son, of the City of Dublin*. **1890**. e. **5**. (**116**.)

ČAKOVAR. *See* DIAKOVAR.

ČAKRA (EMIL) Словенска азбука. Кирилица и латиница една прама другой. pp. 60. *у Новом Саду*, 1859. 8°. **12976. c. 32. (4.)**

ČAKS (ALEKSANDRS)

—— Cīnai un darbam. Dzejas. [With a portrait.] pp. 132. *Rīgā*, 1951. 8°. **11588. f. 37.**

—— Mūžības skartie. pp. 115. *Stockholm*, 1950. 8°. **11588. c. 7.**

CAL. *Begin.* Sendo a Cal o material mais consideravel, que intervém na construcçaõ dos edificios, *etc.* [On the uses of lime in building.] [1770?] fol. **9181. e. 4. (24.)**

CAL (ERNESTO GUERRA DA) *See* GUERRA DA CAL (E.)

CAL. (PO. QUARTANO DI) *See* QUARTANO (PO.)

CALÀ (CARLO) *Duke di Diano* and *Marquis di Ramonte.* *See* NAPLES, *Kingdom of.* [*Laws, etc.*—I.] Pragmaticæ, edicta, decreta, interdicta regiæque sanctiones regni Neapolitani quæ . . . collegerunt P. Caravita . . . C. Cala, *etc.* 1772. fol. **706. m. 11.**

—— Historia de' Suevi nel conquisto de' regni di Napoli, e di Sicilia per l'imperadore Enrico Sesto. Con la vita del beato Giovanni Calà . . . Coll'aggiunta dell'opere d'antichissimi autori sopra la vita . . . del medesimo Beato. pp. 358. *N. de Bonis: Napoli*, 1660. fol. **662. h. 22.**

—— [Another copy.] **592. h. 10.**

—— [Another copy.] **178. e. 4.**

—— Memorie historiche dell'apparitione delle croci prodigiose. pp. 189. *N. de Bonis: Napoli*, 1661. 4°. **485. b. 3. (2.)**

CALÀ (GIOVANNI) *See* CALÀ (C.) *Duke di Diano and Marquis di Ramonte.* Historia de' Suevi . . . con la vita del beato G. Calà, *etc.* [With a portrait.] 1660. fol. **662. h. 22.**

CALA (RAMON DE) *See* GARRIDO (Fernando) Legalidad de la Internacional. Discursos . . . precedidos de una introduccion de R. de Cala. 1871. 4°. **8042. cc. 16. (3.)**

CALABAZA. La Calabaza y el Vino. Relacion jocosa . . . Compuesta por un Ingenio que se meneaba. [In verse.] *Barcelona*, [1850?] 4°. **11450. f. 27. (2.)**

CALÁBEK (LEOPOLD)

—— Administrativní příručka pro lidovýchovné pracovníky a knihovníky. [Compiled by] L. Calábek. Druhé doplněné a přepracované vydání. [With the text of the relevant laws and regulations.] pp. 227. 1928. 8°. *See* CZECHOSLOVAKIA. [*Collections of Laws, etc.*] **05551. e. 19.**

CALABER (CHRYSOSTOMUS) *See* CHRYSOSTOMUS, *of Calabria.*

CALABER (JEAN B. AUGUSTIN) Essai sur la question sociale. Gouvernants et gouvernés. pp. 217. *Paris; Angers*, 1893. 8°. **08275. f. 3.**

CALABER (NICOLAUS) *See* NICOLAUS, *Rheginus.*

CALABER (QUINTUS) *See* QUINTUS, *Smyrnaeus.*

CALABI (AUGUSTO) L'Arte tipografica in Italia nella III Fiera internazionale del Libro, *etc.* pp. xxvi. 1928. 8°. *See* FLORENCE.—*Fiera Internazionale del Libro*, 1928. **011904. bb. 49.**

CALABI (AUGUSTO)

—— Il Filo di Arianna, o sia come iniziare alle arti figurative e insegnarne la storia. pp. 41. *Milano*, 1926. 8°. **7803. p. 2.**

—— La Gravure italienne au XVIIIe siècle. pp. vi. 74. pl. LXXXIV. *Paris*, 1931. 4°. **7852. v. 8.**

—— L'Incisione italiana. pp. 30. pl. CXCIII. *Milano*, 1931. 4°. **7852. v. 4.**

—— Odor di stampa. pp. 152. *Milano*, 1934. 8°. **011903. c. 59.**

—— Questioni attuali delle arti figurative. I. La produzione contemporanea. pp. 101. *Firenze*, [1921.] 8°. **07805. ee. 103.**

CALABI (AUGUSTO) and **CORNAGGIA** (G.)

—— Matteo dei Pasti. La sua opera medaglistica distinta da quella degli anonimi Riminesi del XV secolo in relazione ai medaglioni Malatestiani, aggiunte le falsificazioni. Studio critico e catalogo ragionato . . . Con ottantatre riproduzioni, *etc.* pp. 145. *Milano*, [1926.] fol. Dept. of Coins & Medals.

—— Pisanello. L'opera medaglistica paragonata a quella pittorica, distinte dalla produzione di seguaci e falsificatori dei secoli XV e XVI in relazione ai medaglioni decorativi coevi. Studio critico italiano e inglese e catalogo ragionato . . . Con CXX riproduzioni, *etc.* pp. 253. *Guido Modiano: Milano*, 1928. 4°. **7755. i. 29.**

CALABI (EMMA)

—— La Pittura a Brescia nel Seicento e Settecento. Catalogo della mostra . . . a cura della dott. Emma Calabi. pp. xxxix. 129. pl. XXXIII. 1935. 8°. *See* BRESCIA.—*Comune.* **7868. a. 65.**

CALABI (IDA)

—— I Commentarii di Silla come fonte storica. *Roma*, 1950. 8°. [*Atti dell'Accademia Nazionale dei Lincei. Memorie.* Classe di scienze morali, storiche e filologiche. ser. 8. vol. 3. fasc. 5.] Ac. **102/10.**

CALABIANA (ALOYSIUS NAZARI DE) *Count, Bishop of Casale.* *See* NAZARI DE CALABIANA.

CALABRE. *See* CALABRIA.

CALABRE (E.) Dissertation sur l'influence de l'éducation, des habitudes et des passions, dans les maladies nerveuses. pp. 84. *Paris*, 1804. 4°. **1182. f. 10. (9.)**

CALABRELLA (E. C. DE) *Baroness.* The Double Oath; or, the Rendezvous. 3 vol. *Richard Bentley: London*, 1850. 12°. **12623. e. 17.**

—— Evenings at Haddon Hall. Edited by the Baroness de Calabrella. With illustrations, from designs by George Cattermole. pp. 453. *Henry Colburn: London*, 1846. 8°. **1457. k. 5.**

—— [A reissue.] Evenings at Haddon Hall, *etc.* *Henry G. Bohn: London*, 1848. 8°. **12643. s. 16.**

—— [Another edition.] pp. vi. 432. *London*, [1849.] 8°. [*Bohn's Illustrated Library.*] **2502. b. 9.**

—— The Prism of Imagination. (The illustrations to the tales by Henry Warren: the borders and ornamental titles by Owen Jones.) *Longman & Co.: London*, 1844. 8°. **1457. h. 9.**

—— The Prism of Thought. *Longman & Co.: London*, 1843. 16°. **1387. a. 31.**

—— The Tempter and the Tempted. 3 vol. *Thomas Miller: London*, 1842. 12°. **N. 2270.**

CALABRE-PÉRAU (GABRIEL LOUIS) *See* AUGIER DE MARIGNI (F.) Histoire des Arabes sous le gouvernement des califes. [Edited by G. L. Calabre-Pérau.] 1750. 12°. **280. f. 17-20.**

—— *See* BOSSUET (J. B.) successively *Bishop of Condom* and *of Meaux*. [*Works*.] Œuvres. [Edited by G. L. Calabre-Pérau.] 1748, *etc.* 4°. **477. d. 1-12.**

—— *See* DU CASTRE D'AUVIGNY (J.) Les Vies des hommes illustres de la France, *etc.* (tom. 13–22. Par Monsieur l'abbé Pérau.) 1739, *etc.* 12°. **612. c. 1-23.**

—— *See* FRANCE. [*Appendix.—Miscellaneous.*] Les Vies des hommes illustres de la France, *etc.* [tom. 13–23 by G. L. Calabre-Pérau.] 1739, *etc.* 12°. **275. f. 2-27.**

—— *See* MADAILLAN DE LESPARRE (A. L. de) *Marquis de Lassay.* Recueil de différentes choses. [Edited by G. L. Calabre-Pérau.] 1756. 8°. **830. b. 4.**

—— *See* MORITZ, *of Saxony, Count, etc.* Mes rêveries. Ouvrage posthume de Maurice comte de Saxe . . . augmenté d'une histoire abrégeé de sa vie . . . par Monsieur l'abbé Pérau. 1757. 4°. **62. f. 14, 15.**

—— *See* PAS (M. de) *Marquis de Feuquières.* Lettres et négociations du marquis de Feuquières, *etc.* [Edited by G. L. Calabre-Pérau.] 1753. 12°. **8050. bb. 18.**

—— Description historique de l'Hôtel Royal des Invalides . . . Avec les plans, coupes, élévations géométrales de cet édifice, & les peintures & sculptures de l'église, dessinées & gravées par le sieur Cochin. pp. xii. 104. pl. 108. *Paris*, 1756. fol. **1782. d. 7.**

—— L'Ordre des Francs-Maçons trahi, et le secret des Mopses révélé. [By G. L. Calabre-Pérau.] pp. xxx. 240. 34. 1745. 12°. *See* FREEMASONS. [*Appendix.*] **C. 67. c.10.**

—— [Another edition.] pp. xxxii. 195. 1763. 8°. *See* FREEMASONS. [*Appendix.*] **4785. d. 35.**

—— [Another edition.] pp. xxxii. 195. 31. 1771. 8°. *See* FREEMASONS. [*Appendix.*] **1369. a. 15.**

—— [Another edition.] pp. 131. 1781. 12°. *See* FREEMASONS. [*Appendix.*] **4782. a. 26. (2.)**

—— Die offenbarte Freymäurerey und das gedeckte Geheimniss der Mopse. Aus dem Französischen übersetzt von dem Bruder Phidias, mit einem Schreiben des Uebersetzers für die Glaubwürdigkeit dieses Buchs und einem Anhange einiger Freymäurer Lieder und Reden vermehret. Mit Kupfern. pp. 243. *Leipzig*, 1745. 8°. **4785. aaa. 39.**

—— Recueil A(—Z, &). [A collection of historical essays. Edited successively by G. L. Calabre-Pérau, A. G. Meusnier de Querlon, B. Mercier-Saint-Léger, J. de la Porte, E. de Barbazan, B. C. Graillard de Graville.] 24 pt. 1745–62. 12°. *See* RECUEIL. **012208. ee. 1.**

—— Le Secret des francs-maçons [by G. L. Calabre-Pérau], avec un recueil de leurs chansons, précédé de quelques péeces [*sic*] de poësies [compiled by J. J. Naudot]. pp. x. 136. 1714 [1744 ?] 18°. *See* FREEMASONS. [*Appendix.*] **1486. aa. 28.**

—— Le Secret des francs-maçons [by G. L. Calabre-Pérau], avec un recueil de leurs chansons, précédé de quelques pièces de poësies [compiled by J. J. Naudot]. pp. x. 160. 1744. 12°. *See* FREEMASONS. [*Appendix.*] **4785. aa. 27. (1.)**

—— Vie de Jerôme Bignon, avocat général et conseiller d'état. 2 pt. *Paris*, 1757. 12°. **612. d. 1.**

—— [Another copy.] **276. f. 16.**

CALABRESE (FRANCO)

—— Incontri con Leopardi. pp. 121. *Milano*, 1951. 8°. **11869. dd. 33.**
Part of the series "Cultura."

CALABRESE (GIUSEPPE) Origini del melodramma sacro in Roma, *etc.* pp. xix. 273. *Gravina*, [1907.] 8°. **11851. w. 16.**

CALABRESI (RENATA) La Determinazione del presente psichico. [With plates.] pp. xi. 188. *Firenze*, 1930. 8°. [*Pubblicazioni della R. Università degli Studi di Firenze. Facoltà di lettere e di filosofia.* N.S. vol. 10.] **Ac. 8848.**

CALABRIA. The Brigands of Calabria. A romantic drama, in one act. pp. 18. *London*, [1866 ?] 12°. [*Lacy's Acting Edition of Plays.* vol. 65.] **2304. f. 10. (8.)**

—— [Another edition.] Adapted by W. E. Lane. 1871. *See* BRITISH DRAMA. The British Drama. Illustrated. vol. 5. 1864, *etc.* 8°. **11770. bbb. 12. (14.)**

—— [A reissue.] *London*, [1879 ?] 8°. [*Dicks' Standard Plays.* no. 150.] **11770. bbb. 4.**

—— La Calabria. Rivista di letteratura popolare, *etc.* *See* PERIODICAL PUBLICATIONS.—*Monteleone.*

—— Calabria during a Military Residence of Three Years, *etc.* *See* infra: Séjour d'un officier françois en Calabre, *etc.*

—— Compassioneuole relazione delli spauentosi terremoti occorsi nella Calabria, & altri luoghi. Col nome delle città, e terre sommerse, e rouinate da detti terremoti. Seguiti questo presente anno 1638. alli 27. di Marzo. *Pietro Nesti: Fiorenza*, 1638. 4°. **7108. aaa. 14.**

—— Dreadfull Newes: or a true relation of the great, violent and late earthquake. Hapned the 27. day of March . . . last, at Callabria, *etc.* [A translation of an Italian original.] pp. 17. *I. Okes, for R. Mab: London*, 1638. 4°. **444. a. 34.**

—— Ricerche di storia medioevale e moderna in Calabria. *See* PUTORTÌ (N.)

—— Saggio di fenomeni antropologici relativi al tremuoto, ovvero riflessioni . . . fatte per occasion de' tremuoti avvenuti nelle Calabrie l'anno 1783. e seguenti. Dall'Ab . . . . S . . . . . *See* S . . . ., Ab . . . . . **662. c. 23.**

—— Séjour d'un officier français [i.e. — Duret de Tavel] en Calabre, ou Lettres propres à faire connaître l'état ancien et moderne de la Calabre . . . et les événemens politiques et militaires qui s'y sont passés pendant l'occupation des Français. pp. xii. 312. *Paris, Rouen*, 1820. 8°. **1057. h. 17. (2.)**

—— Calabria, during a Military Residence of Three Years: in a series of letters by a General Officer of the French Army. From the original MS. [A translation of "Séjour d'un officier français en Calabre" by — Duret de Tavel.] pp. xvi. 360. *Effingham Wilson: London*, 1832. 8°. **1049. k. 12.**

—— *Begin.* [Sig. A ii *verso*:] The Preface to the Reader. [Sig. A iii *verso*:] Straunge Newes out of Calabria: Prognosticated in the yere 1586, vpon the yere 87. and what shall happen in the said yere, *etc.* [With a woodcut on the recto of Sig. A ii.] [*For John Perrin: London*, 1587 ?] 4°. **C. 40. g. 9.**
Imperfect; wanting Sig. A 1. *The plate is cropped.*

—— Vera relatione del spauentevole terremoto successo alli 27. di marzo . . . nelle Prouincie di Calabria Citra, & Vltra, *etc.* *Appresso L. Grignani: Roma*, 1638. 4°. **444. b. 20. (3.)**

—— Verdadera relacion del espantable terremoto, sucedido a los veynte y siete de Março de 1638 . . . en la prouincia de Calabria . . . Traduzida de Italiano en Castellano, por Francisco de Firmamante. *G. Nogues: Barcelona*, 1638. 4°. **12331. dd. 16. (19.)**

CALABRIA.

—— Warhaffter Bericht von dem vorgangenen grewlichen Erdbidem, in Nider Calabrien, den 17—27—Martii, Anno 1638. auff den Abend geschehen . . . Erstlich gedruckt zu Venedig, vnd auss den Italianischen verteutscht. *Bey J. Dümlern: Nürnberg*, [1639?] 4°. **7108. aa. 14.**

CALABRIA CITERIORE.—*Commessione delle Ferrovie Napolitane.* Sulla Ferrovia Calabra relazione della commessione nominata dal Consiglio Provinciale della Calabria Citeriore. [With a map.] pp. 30. *Cosenza*, 1862. 8°. **8235. i. 8.**

CALABRIA CITRA. *See* CALABRIA CITERIORE.

CALABRIA SECONDA. *See* CALABRIA ULTERIORE.

CALABRIA ULTERIORE. Gli Abitanti della Seconda Calabria. Ai cittadini Liberatori della nazione. [*Catanzaro*, 1820.] *s. sh.* fol. **8032. m. 9. (7.)**

—— [Another copy.] **8032. m. 9. (12.)**

CALABRIA ULTRA. *See* CALABRIA ULTERIORE.

CALABRIAN INSURRECTION. Documenti storici riguardanti l'insurrezione calabra. Preceduti dalla storia degli avvenimenti di Napoli del 15 maggio [by Count Gennaro Marulli]. pp. 641. *Napoli*, 1849. 8°. **9165. f. 13.**

CALABRIEN. *See* CALABRIA.

CALABRITTI (ANTONIO) *See* JEROCADES (A.) La Lira Focense . . . ristampata per cura di A. Calabritti. 1809. 12°. **1161. d. 20.**

CALABRITTO (ALFREDO) Nuovi elettori e vecchi partiti. pp. 171. *Napoli*, 1882. 8°. **8032. bb. 22.**

CALABRITTO (GIOVANNI) *See* FOSCOLO (N. U.) Sulla fortuna dei " Sepolcri " in Inghilterra, *etc.* [An essay by G. Calabritto on English translations of the poem, with the text of the versions.] 1932. 8°. **11857. a. 4.**

CALABRÒ (FERDINANDO) *See* CONTI (S. de') Sigismondo dei Conti da Foligno. Le storie de' suoi tempi, *etc.* [tom. 2 translated by F. Calabrò.] 1883. 8°. **9167. k. 12.**

CALABRÒ (GIUSEPPE MARIA) *See* MAZZINI (G.) La Dottrina religioso-sociale nelle opere di Giuseppe Mazzini. Le religioni del passato. Studio di critica storica. [Selections. Edited by G. M. Calabrò.] 1910. 8°. **11825. ppp. 11.**

—— *See* MAZZINI (G.) Mazzini. La dottrina storica. Studio di critica storica. [Selections. Edited by G. M. Calabrò.] 1916. 8°. **9004. c. 10.**

CALABUIG REVERT (J. JOSÉ) Derecho Penal Eclesiástico vigente en Ibero-América y su proceso histórico. pp. xv. 253. *Totana*, [1930.] 8°. **5107. eee. 20.**

CALACE DE FERLUC (ANTOINE) and **DESCHARD** (HERVÉ)

—— Comment interpréter la particule? pp. 28. *Paris*, 1947. 16°. **12955. a. 45.**

CALADE (MCE. DE DURANTI LA) *See* DURANTI LA CALADE.

CALADO (JOSEPH IGNACIO RUIZ) *See* RUIZ CALADO.

CALADO (MANOEL) O Valeroso Lucideno, e triumpho da liberdade. Primeira parte. pp. 356. *P. Craesbeeck: Lisboa*, 1648. fol. **601. l. 13.**
No more published.

CALADO (RAFAEL SALINAS) *See* SALINAS CALADO.

CALADO (RAPHAEL RUIZ) *See* RUIZ CALADO.

CALADONIA. *See* CALEDONIA.

CALADOU (A.) La Police correctionnelle et municipale à Montpellier en 1791–1792. pp. 173. *Montpellier*, 1930. 8°. **10167. pp. 16.**

CALAFATO (VINCENZO)

—— *See* BALLATORE (V.) Elogio del poeta Vincenzo Calafato, *etc.* 1953. 8°. **11436. m. 32.**

CALAGIUS (ANDREAS)

—— *See* BERNAVUS (P.) Ex nomine M. Andr. Cal. Vrat. ad iter et fortunam eiusdem allusio. [With other complimentary verses addressed to A. Calagius.] 1595. 4°. **1474. b. 56. (4.)**

—— Aulæum a Viadri Nymphis textum, atq̃ . . . Iohanni . . . Episcopo Vratisl. &c. ipsa electionis die, quæ fuit 18. Iulij, anni elapsi 1600. datum dono, *etc.* [In verse.] *Typis I. Rhambæ: Gorlicii*, 1601. 4°. **11409. f. 35. (7.)**

—— Biblidos sive miraculorum divinorum serie biblica descriptorum liber I.(–X.) . . . Editum a M. Andrea Calagio. [In verse.] 10 pt. *Typis Sartorianis: Lygnicii*, 1595–1600. 4°. **C. 66. c. 19.**

—— [Another edition.] pp. 294. *M. Lantzenberger: Lipsiæ*, 1600. 16°. **11409. aa. 25.**

—— D. D. Theologorum in corruptam Evangelii doctrinam Vratislaviæ sonantium symbola, singulis singula octostichis explicata, *etc.* [With a portrait.] *Typis Sartorianis: Lignicii*, [1603.] 4°. **11409. ee. 34. (7.)**

—— De Varadino Hungariæ propugnaculo, strenue, nec citra divinum auxilium asserto. [In verse.] *Typis Sartorianis: Lignicii*, 1599. 4°. **11409. f. 32.**

—— D. Rudolpho II. Rom. Imperatori . . . missæ dono Gallinæ Zedlicianæ Metamorphosis: carmine . . . adumbrata. *A. Fritsch imprimebat: Gorlicii*, 1591. 4°. **11409. f. 35. (5.)**

—— Diuo Rodulpho II. Romanorum Imperatori . . . primùm Vratislauiam ingresso. Anno Saluatoris: M.D.LXXVII, *etc.* [In verse.] *Ex officina typographica C. Scharffenbergii: Vratislauiæ*, [1577.] 4°. **11409. f. 35. (1.)**

—— Duo epithetorum tomi, ille propriis nominibus, hic appellatiuis adiiciendorum, omnium: ex antiquioribus . . . poetis septendecim . . . selectorum ab A. Calagio . . . Tomus prior. *Ex officina typographica G. Baumanni: Vratislauiæ*, 1590. fol. **C.68.k.11.**

—— Epigrammatum . . . centuriæ sex. pp. 199. *Typis Sciurinis: Francofurti ad Oderam*, 1602. 8°. **11403. aa. 51.**

—— Hortus Doct. Laurentii Scholzii . . . celebratus carmine. *In officina typographica G. Baumanni: Vratislauiæ*, 1592. 4°. **11409. c. 36. (2.)**

—— M. Andreæ Calagii . . . Laurea: et huic gratulantia, amicorum . . . epigrammata. *In officina typographica G. Bauman: Vratislauiæ*, 1597. 4°. **11409. f. 35. (6.)**

—— Prognosticon anni Christiani M.D.LXXXVIII., *etc.* [In verse.] *Typis A. Fritschii: Gorlicii*, 1588. 4°. **11409. c. 36. (1.)**

—— Suggestum Magdalæum Vratislauiense nouum. Succincto adumbratum carmine. *Ex officina typographica I. Scharffenbergii: Vratislauiæ*, 1581. 4°. **11409. f. 35. (2.)**

CALAGIUS (ANDREAS)

—— [Another edition.] 1728. *See* CRUSIUS (T. T.) Miscellanea silesiaca, *etc.* (Miscellanea silesiaca continuata.) 1722, *etc.* 8°. **168.** a. **4.**

—— Terræ motus, passim in Silesia xv. Sept. anno M.D.LXXXX. . . . animaduersus, *etc.* [In verse.] *A. Fritsch excudebat : Gorlicii,* 1590. 4°. **11409.** f. **35.** (**4.**)

CALAHAN (HAROLD AUGUSTIN) Back to Treasure Island . . . With illustrations, *etc.* pp. 246. *A. & C. Black: London,* [1936.] 8°. **20055.** i. **4.**

—— Gadgets and Wrinkles. A compendium of man's ingenuity at sea . . . Illustrated. pp. xiv. 311. *Macmillan Co.: New York,* 1938. 8°. **08805.** b. **8.**

—— Geography for Grown-Ups . . . Illustrated by Stephen J. Voorhies, *etc.* pp. viii. 351. *Harper & Bros.: New York & London,* [1946.] 8°. **010006.** g. **63.**

—— Hurrah's Nest . . . Illustrated by Rico Tomaso. [A novel.] pp. x. 244. *Vanguard Press: New York,* 1937. 8°. **12715.** d. **37.**

—— Learning to Cruise . . . Illustrated. pp. xii. 286. *Macmillan Co.: New York,* 1935. 8°. **8805.** df. **17.**

—— Learning to Race . . . Illustrated. pp. xv. 319. *Macmillan Co.: New York,* 1934. 8°. **08806.** bb. **54.**

—— Learning to Sail. [With illustrations.] pp. xxii. 316. *Macmillan Co.: New York,* 1932. 8°. **8804.** e. **9.**

—— Rigging. [With plates.] pp. x. 276. *Macmillan Co.: New York,* 1940. 8°. **8809.** aa. **5.**

—— Sailing Technique. [With plates.] pp. xv. 459. *Macmillan Co.: New York,* 1950. 8°. **7920.** e. **22.**

—— The Ship's Husband. A guide to yachtsmen in the care of their craft, *etc.* pp. xiv. 323. *Macmillan Co.: New York,* 1937. 8°. **8805.** df. **31.**

—— The Sky and the Sailor. A history of celestial navigation. [With plates.] pp. xiii. 262. *Harper & Bros.: New York,* [1952.] 8°. **8803.** bb. **38.**

—— So You're Going to Buy a Boat . . . Illustrated. pp. viii. 269. *Macmillan Co.: New York,* 1939. 8°. **08805.** b. **11.**

CALAHAN (HAROLD AUGUSTIN) and **TREVOR** (JOHN B.) *A.B.*

—— Wind and Tide in Yacht Racing . . . Illustrated . . . and containing new instruments for the navigation of a yacht in a race. pp. xiv. 145. *G. G. Harrap & Co.: London,* 1936. 4°. **8807.** l. **7.**

CALAHORRA, JUAN BERNARDO, *Bishop of.* [1470–77.] *See* DIAZ DE LUCO.

——, RODERICUS, *Bishop of.* [1468–70.] *See* SANCIUS DE AREVALO.

CALAHORRA AND LA CALZADA, ANTOLIN, *Bishop of.* [1861–65.] *See* MONESCILLO.

CALAHORRA (DIEGO ORTUÑEZ DE) *See* ORTUÑEZ DE CALAHORRA.

CALAHORRA (JUAN DE) *See* JUAN, *de Calahorra, etc.*

CALAHORRA DE LA ÓRDEN (ENRIQUE) Curso elemental de materia farmacéutica mineral y animal. 2 pt. pp. 448. *Madrid,* 1875. 8°. **7482.** g. **1.**

CALAHUMANA (ANDRÉS SANTA CRUZ Y) *See* SANTA CRUZ Y CALAHUMANA, *President of Bolivia.*

CALAINN. *See* CALLAN.

CALAIS.

MUNICIPAL INSTITUTIONS.

Bibliothèque.

—— Manuscrits de la Bibliothèque de Calais. [By H. Loriquet.] 1886. *See* FRANCE.—*Ministère de l'Instruction Publique.* Catalogue général des manuscrits des bibliothèques publiques de France. Départements. tom. 4. 1886, *etc.* 8°. Bar T. **2.** a.

Conseil Général.

—— Nécessité d'un port militaire dans la Manche : emplacement désigné et reconnu le plus propre à la construction de ce port. pp. 6. *Paris,* [1794.] 4°. **936.** f. **11.** (**39.**)

MISCELLANEOUS INSTITUTIONS

Chambre de Commerce.

—— Calais, son port, son industrie. Conférence par M. F. Lennel. pp. 78. *Paris,* 1908. 8°. **10174.** e. **6.**

APPENDIX.

98

—— An Admonition to the towne of Callays. [Signed: R. P.] 1557. 16°. *See* P., R. C. **38.** c. **32.**

—— Annuaire commercial & général de Calais & Saint Pierre. *See* PERIODICAL PUBLICATIONS.—*London.*

—— Copia di vna lettera della presa di Cales per il Re Christianissimo. [Signed: V. D.] Con le capitulationi fatte con essa terra. [1558.] 4°. *See* D., V. C. **55.** c. **1.**

—— Discorso sopra la presa della inespugnabile città d Calès, tradotto di lingua Francese . . . per Bartolomeo Maraffi Fiorentino. [With a plan of the fortress.] pp. 8. *Appresso F. Portonaris: Vinegia,* 1558. 4°. **9220.** c. **33.**

—— [Another edition.] Narratione de la presa di Cales. [1558?] 4°. **1319.** e. **23.**

—— Encore un mot pour les naufragés de Calais. pp. 4. [*Paris,* 1799.] 8°. F. **745.** (**2*.**)

—— [Another copy.] F. **70*.** (**1*.**)

—— Gewisse vnd Warhafftige Zeitung, was sich mit der weitberhümpten Stadt vnd fästen Schloss Cales . . . zugetragen hat mit . . . Herrn Alberten, des H. Römischen Stuls Cardinal vnd Ertzhertzogen zu Oesterreich . . . wie seine . . . Durchlaucht dieselbige Statt vnd Schloss . . . mit gewalt eingenom̃en hat . . . Auss Niderländischer spraach vertiert in Hochteutsch, durch Conrad Löw. *Bey W. von Lützenkirchen: Cölln,* 1596. 4°. **1319.** e. **22.**

—— Histoire veritable de la cruauté exercée . . . vers les peres capucins par les heretiques de . . . Calais en Picardie. [Reprinted from the edition of 1625.] pp. 18. *See* ÉDOUARD, *d'Alençon, Capuchin.* Trois histoires, *etc.* 1892. 8°. **4804.** h. **2.** (**5.**)

—— The Maner of the tryumphe at Caleys and Bulleyn. [With a woodcut.] B.L. *Wynkyn de Worde for Johan Gowgh: [London,* 1532.] 4°. C. **21.** b. **20.**

—— The second pryntyng, with mo addiciõs as it was done in dede. B.L. *Wynkyn de Worde, for Johan Gowgh: [London,* 1532.] 4°. C. **21.** b. **21.**

—— [Another edition.] 1879. *See* ARBER (Edward) An English Garner, *etc.* vol. 2. 1877, *etc.* 8°. **12269.** cc. **12.**

CALAIS. [APPENDIX.]

—— [Another edition.] pp. vii. 37. 1884. *See* GOLDSMID (Edmund M.) Bibliotheca curiosa, *etc.* 1883, *etc.* 8°. **012202.** de. **21.**

—— [Another edition.] 1903. *See* ARBER (Edward) An English Garner. (Tudor Tracts.) 1903, *etc.* 8°. **2324.** e. **9/1.**

—— Moralite nouuelle de la prinse de Calais, *etc.* pp. 12. *See* LE ROUX DE LINCY (A. J. V.) and MICHEL (F.) Recueil de farces, *etc.* tom. 1. 1837, *etc.* 8°. **1343.** e. **18.**

—— Newe Zeittung. Welcher massen die alte vnd veste Stat, Schloss vñ Port, Cales, von . . . Alberto, Hertzogen zu Oesterreich . . . in namen Philippi Königs in Hispanien, den 17. vnd 24. tag . . . Aprilis, in disem 1596. Jar, erobert, vnd dem König Henrico . . . dem vierdten, in Franckreich vnd Navarra, mit stürmender hand abgedrungen worden. *Bey B. Käppeler: Augspurg,* [1596.] *s. sh.* fol. **1870.** d. **2.** (**17.**)

—— Nouvelles réflexions sommaires pour les naufragés de Calais. pp. 4. [*Paris,* 1799.] 8°. **F. 745.** (**2****.)

—— [Another copy.] **F. 70*.** (**1****.)

—— Oblęzenie miasta Kale. *See* infra: Le Siège de Calais.

—— Observations pour les naufragés de Calais. pp. 8. [*Paris,* 1799.] 8°. **F. 745.** (**2.**)

—— [Another copy.] **F. 70*.** (**1.**)

—— La Reduction de Calais au Royaume de France, detenue par l'Anglois depuis l'an 1347. pp. 43. *C. Micard: Paris,* [15]58. 8°. **1193.** g. **22.** (**2.**)

—— Le Siége de Calais, nouvelle historique. [By C. A. Guérin de Tencin.] 2 tom. *La Haye,* 1739. 12°. **12512.** aaa. **21.**

—— Deuxième édition. 2 tom. *La Haye,* 1739. 12°. **12511.** bb. **27.**

—— [Another edition.] 2 tom. *La Haye,* 1740. 12°. **012550.** de. **14.**

—— [Another edition.] *See* BIBLIOTHÈQUE. Bibliothèque de campagne, *etc.* tom. 11. 1749. 12°. **244.** f. **11.**

—— [Another edition.] Augmenté de l'Histoire d'Eustache de Saint-Pierre, sous le regne de Philippe de Vallois, roi de France & de Navarre, en 1346 & 1347, avec le portrait. [By M. A. Poisson de Gomez.] Nouvelle édition. pp. 227. *Amsterdam,* 1765. 8°. **1479.** aaa. **14.**

—— Oblężenie miasta Kale. Wiadomość historyczna. Z francuzkiego przełożona. [A translation by J. Niemcewicz of "Le Siége de Calais" by C. A. Guérin de Tencin.] pp. 268. *w Wilnie,* 1782. 8°. **1459.** a. **51.**

—— Songs, Duets, Choruses, &c. in the Surrender of Calais, a play [by George Colman the Younger] . . . Third edition. pp. 19. *W. Woodfall, for T. Cadell: London,* 1791. 8°. **11778.** f. **10.**

—— The Surrender of Calais. An historical drama. [In verse.] pp. 80. *G. Peacock: York,* 1801. 8°. **1346.** f. **16.**

A different play from that of the same name by George Colman the Younger.

—— [Another copy.] **163.** k. **40.**

—— Varia doctissimorum virorum Galliæ poemata de capto Caleto. *See* SCHARDIUS (S.) Historicum opus, *etc.* tom. 3. [1574.] fol. **9366.** i. **11.**

CALAIS ET ARDRES, *Bailliages de.—Tiers-État.* Cahier général du Tiers-État des bailliages de Calais et Ardres. pp. 36. *Calais,* 1789. 8°. **F.R. 25.** (**25.**)

CALAIS PACKET. The Calais Packet. [A song.] [*London,* 1820?] *s. sh.* 4°. **C. 116.** i. **1.** (**39.**)

CALAIS (A. I.) Exercises on the Longer Syntax. Adapted to Eve and De Baudiss' French Grammar. pp. 101. *David Nutt: London,* 1888. 8°. **12954.** c. **23.**

—— French Phrase Book; containing a selection of expressions and idioms with their English equivalents. pp. viii. 172. *David Nutt: London,* 1890. 8°. **12952.** df. **32.**

—— The Wellington College French Exercise Book. Adapted to the "Wellington College French Grammar," and containing copious exercises, *etc.* pp. 262. *David Nutt: London,* 1886. 8°. **12950.** bbb. **35.**

—— Second edition, revised. pp. 213. *David Nutt: London,* 1889. 8°. **12950.** df. **44.**

—— *See* CAUMONT (L. A.) A Key to A. I. Calais' Wellington College French Exercise Book, *etc.* 1894. 8°. **12953.** de. **33.**

CALAIS (JEAN) *See* SAVOYARD. Néron Lambesc vit-il toujours?—toujours vit. Ou, réponse d'un Savoyard au Sieur Calais. [1791?] 8°. **F. 405.** (**5.**)

—— Grand détail exact et circonstancié de l'expédition de M. de Bouillé à Nancy. pp. 8. [*Paris,* 1790.] 8°. **F. 328.** (**8.**)

CALAIS (JEAN DE) *See* JEAN, *de Calais, etc.*

CALAISIS. Précis des motifs présentés par les citoyens du ci-devant Calaisis, à l'effet de prouver l'abolition de la Dixme à laquelle étoient assujetties leurs terres. pp. 24. [*Paris,* 1791?] 8°. **F.R. 241.** (**2.**)

CALA ******** JO.** Bulletin du pape. [A satire. Signed: Cala ********** Jo.] pp. 30. [*Paris,* 1791.] 8°. **F. 463.** (**5.**)

CALAMA, POSSIDIUS, *Bishop of. See* POSSIDIUS, *Saint, Bishop of Calama.*

CALAMA (JOSEPH PEREZ) *Bishop of Quito. See* PEREZ CALAMA.

CALAMAI (LUIGI) Analisi chimica dell'acqua salino-purgativa di Casale . . . Estratta dalla Gazz. tosc. delle scienze medico-fisiche, *etc.* pp. 12. *Firenze,* 1847. 8°. **7462.** e. **9.** (**2.**)

—— Analisi chimica delle acque minerali di S. Quirico . . . Estratta dalla Gazz. tosc. delle scienze medico-fisiche, *etc.* pp. 16. *Firenze,* 1847. 8°. **7462.** e. **9.** (**3.**)

—— Dei mezzi impiegati al riscaldamento delle acque dei bagni di Chiecinella, *etc. See* FILIPPESCHI (G.) Dell'efficacia terapeutica della acque dei bagni di Chiecinella, *etc.* 1845. 8°. **7462.** e. **4.** (**9.**)

—— Dell'acqua minerale acidola dei bagni di Chiecinella, illustrazione e analisi chimica. pp. 62. *Firenze,* 1844. 8°. **7462.** ee. **6.** (**2.**)

—— Di una nuova acqua minerale salino-purgativa denominata Acqua del Pino di S. Luce, relazione. (Articolo estratto dalla Gazzetta toscana delle scienze medico-fisiche.) pp. 23. *Firenze,* 1844. 8°. **7462.** e. **4.** (**8.**)

—— Notizia sull'acqua minerale di Quarrata presso Pescia e su la di lei analisi chimica. pp. 6. *Firenze,* 1843. 8°. **7462.** ee. **6.** (**1.**)

CALAMAI (Luigi)

—— Sopra le acque minerali di Rio nell'Isola dell'Elba, *etc.* pp. 50. *Firenze*, 1847. 8°. **7462.** ee. **5.** (**10.**)

—— Sulle acque minerali saline dette della Croce dei possessi del sig. marchese G. Mansi, *etc.* pp. 98. *Firenze*, 1850. 8°. **7462.** ee. **5.** (**12.**)

CALAMANDRANA (Giulio Cordara di) *See* Cordara (Giulio Cesare)

CALAMANDREI (E. Polidori) *See* Polidori Calamandrei.

CALAMANDREI (Piero)

—— Elogio dei giudici scritto da un avvocato. Seconda edizione aumentata. pp. xxiv. 169. *Firenze*, 1938. 8°. **6003.** b. **9.**

—— [Elogio dei giudici.] Eulogy of Judges. Written by a lawyer . . . Translated by John Clarke Adams and C. Abbott Phillips, Jr. pp. 121. *Princeton University Press: Princeton*, 1942. 8°. **6003.** c. **9.**

—— Il Manganello, la cultura e la giustizia. *In:* Periodical Publications.—*Florence.* Non mollare. 1925. Riproduzione fotografica . . . con tre saggi storici di G. Salvemini, E. Rossi, P. Calamandrei. pp. 69–112. 1955. 8°. P.P. **3556.** iag.

CALAMANDREI (Piero) and **LEVI** (Alessandro)

—— Commentario sistematico alla Costituzione italiana. [By various authors.] Diretto da Piero Calamandrei e Alessandro Levi, *etc.* 2 vol. *Firenze*, 1950. 8°. **5373.** l. **12.**

CALAMANDREI (Rodolfo) Belino. Profili e ricordi. pp. 189. *Firenze*, 1886. 8°. **10256.** aa. **18.**

—— Definizione del commercio. pp. xi. 137. *Firenze*, 1896. 8°. **08228.** h. **14.**

—— Del fallimento. Commento al libro iii. e al capo iii. titolo i. libro iv. del Nuovo Codice di Commercio Italiano, *etc.* 2 vol. *Torino*, 1883. 8°. **6825.** ee. **12.**

—— Delle società e delle associazioni commerciali. Commento al libro i, titolo ix del Nuovo Codice di Commercio Italiano. 2 vol. *Torino*, 1884. 8°. **5359.** ee. **1.**

—— Monarchia e repubblica rappresentative. 1886. *See* Brunialti (A.) Biblioteca di scienze politiche, *etc.* vol. 2. 1883, *etc.* 8°. **8005.** i.

CALAMARI (Giuseppe) Il Confidente di Pio ii, Card. Iacopo Ammannati-Piccolomini, 1422–1479, *etc.* 2 vol. pp. xiv. 610. *Roma, Milano*, 1932. 8°. **4517.df.34.**

—— Leopoldo Galeotti e il moderatismo toscano. pp. 184. *Modena*, 1935. 8°. [*Collezione storica del Risorgimento italiano.* ser. 1. vol. 14.] W.P. **1538/14.**

CALAMARO, LAREDO ET CIE. Code télégraphique de la maison Calamaro, Laredo & Cie. pp. 123. *Thomas Brakell: Liverpool*, 1906. 8°. **08755.** i. **13.**

CALAMARTE (Antonio Pérez) *See* Pérez Calamarte.

CALAMATI (Federico) Sul Tebro. Armonie poetiche. pp. 157. *Roma*, 1879. 8°. **11431.** aaa. **25.**

CALAMATO (Alexander) *See* Nissenus (D.) R.P. Didaci Nisseni . . . opera omnia, *etc.* (Appendix de festivitatibus B. V. Mariæ, aliorumque . . . sanctorum, *etc.* [By C. de Avendanno, A. Calamato and others.]) 1738. fol. **3678.** g. **5.**

CALAMATO (Alexander)

—— Reverendi Domini Alexandri Calamato Conciones sacræ ac morales: in duos tomos distributæ. Tomus primus continet Sylvam variorum discursuum . . . Cui accesserunt R^di D. Francisci Maidalchini sermones . . . Tomus secundus continet eiusdem A. Calamato Quadragesimale . . . Quibus adiunctæ sunt Laudes & encomia Deiparæ Virginis pro diebus Sabbathinis, *etc.* 2 tom. *H. Aertssens & C. Woons: Antverpiæ*, 1652. 4°. **4424.** dd. **10.**
With an additional titlepage, engraved.

CALAMATTA (Luigi) *See* Alvin (L. J.) Notice sur Louis Calamatta, *etc.* [With a portrait.] 1882. 8°. Dept. of Prints & Drawings.

—— *See* Gautier (Théophile) *the Elder.* Les Dieux et les demidieux de la peinture . . . Illustrations par M. Calamatta. 1864. 8°. **7854.** h. **24.**

CALAMBRONE, *pseud.* [i.e. Francesco Frediani.] *See* Frediani (F.)

CALAME (Alexandre) *Artist.*

—— *See* Rambert (E.) Alexandre Calame, sa vie et son œuvre, *etc.* [With a portrait.] 1884. 8°. **010661.** i. **37.**

—— *See* Toepffer (R.) Voyages en zigzac . . . Ornés de 15 grands dessins par M. Calame. 1844. 8°. **1429.** k. **5.**

CALAME (Henri Florian) Droit privé d'après la coutume neuchâteloise. Cours professé à Neuchâtel de 1829 à 1830. pp. xxiv. 491. *Neuchâtel*, 1858. 8°. **5551.** aaa. **6.**

CALAMIANES ISLANDS. Naufrage d'une patache portugaise sur un banc de sable, vis-a-vis des îles Calamianes, mer des Indes, en 1688. 1789. *See* Voyages. Voyages imaginaires, songes, *etc.* (Supplément. tom. 3.) 1787, *etc.* 8°. **303.** g. **28.**

CALAMIE (Edmund) *See* Calamy (E.) *B.D., etc.*

CALAMINUS (Anton Leopold) Hülfe in der Noth. Erinnerungen aus Hanaus Vorzeit in Sage und Geschichte, gesammelt von A. L. Calaminus. pp. vi. 138. *Hanau*, 1847. 8°. **12430.** f. **9.**

—— Nachricht über die Gründung der evangelischen Marienkirche und Johanneskirche zu Hanau. Ein Beitrag zur . . . Reformationsgeschichte, *etc.* [With a plate.] pp. vii. 80. *Hanau*, 1858. 8°. **4660.** b. **5.**

CALAMINUS (Georgius) *See* Euripides. [*Phoenissae.—Greek and Latin.*] Phœnissæ Euripidis, tragœdia Latino metro versa a M. G. Calamino, *etc.* 1577. 8°. **11705.** aa. **20.**

—— G. Calamini Silesij liber, vel epistola Mnemosynes ad Eugeniam, de litterarum origine & propagatione. Elegiarum liber i. Lyricorum lib. i. Epithalamicω̄n lib. i. Epigrammatum lib. i. ms. notes. *N. Wyriot: Argentorati*, 1583. 8°. **11408.** aaa. **50.**

—— Rudolphottocarus: Austriaca tragœdia noua [in verse]: Rudolphi i. Habsburgi seculum et res gestas continens: adiunctis notis historicis. Rudolphidos liber: res Austriadum a Rudolpho i. ad ii. usque nostrum . . . subijciens [*sic*], *etc.* 2 pt. *Per I. Rihelium: Argentorati*, 1594. 8°. **11712.** aa. **22.**

CALAMINUS (Petrus) *Praes.* *See* Gomarus (F.) Theses de Coena Domini, *etc.* 1594. 4°. **4376.** de. **16.** (**47.**)

CALAMITA (Carlos)

—— Figuras y semblanzas del Imperio. Francisco López de Villalobos, médico de reyes y príncipe de literatos. pp. 309. *Madrid*, 1952. 8°. **10636.** d. **5.**
Part of the " Colección ' La Nave.' "

CALAMITIES. Calamities of Authors; including some inquiries respecting their moral and literary characters. By the author of "Curiosities of Literature" [i.e. Isaac D'Israeli]. 2 vol. *John Murray: London*, 1812. 8°. **616.** b. **32, 33.**

—— [Another copy.] **91.** a. **16, 17.**

—— [Another copy.] **L.P.** G. **785.**

CALAMNIUS (EDVIN) *See* VIRTALA (E.) *pseud.* [i.e. E. Calamnius.]

CALAMNIUS (GABRIEL) *the Elder.* Gabriel Calamniuksen vähäinen cocous suomalaisista runoista, Turusa 1755. Käsinkirjoitetum kopion mukaan uudestaan painattanut Kustavi Grotenfelt. [1889.] *See* PERIODICAL PUBLICATIONS.—*Helsinki.* Suomi, *etc.* Kolmas Jakso. osa 3. 1841, *etc.* 8°. P.P. **4852.** d.

CALAMNIUS (GABRIEL) *the Younger.* Korta anmärckningar, wid inbyggarenas näringar och hushållning, uti Cala-Joki Sochn i Österbotn, med wederbörandes samtycke, *etc. Praes.* P. Kalm. pp. 10. *Åbo*, [1753.] 4°. B. **588.** (8.)

CALAMNIUS, afterwards **KIANTO** (ILMARI)

—— *See* KIANTO (U.) Ilmari Kiannon kirjalliset julkaisut, 1896–1954, *etc.* 1954. 8°. **11927.** aa. **39.**

—— Hiljaisina hetkinä. Toinen kokoelma. Laulurunoja. Kirjoittanut I. Calamnius. pp. 95. *Porvoossa*, 1898. 8°. **011586.** h. **64.**

—— Lauluja ja runoelmia. pp. 132. *Porwoossa*, 1900. 8°. **11586.** f. **20.**

—— Nuori runoilijamaisteri. Papin Poika muistelee menneitä. [With plates, including portraits.] pp. 469. *Helsingissä*, 1931. 8°. **10797.** b. **9.**

—— Omat koirat purivat. Pidätetyn päiväkirja vuodelta 1940. pp. 188. *Helsinki*, 1948. 8°. **10794.** b. **19.**

—— Papin Poika. Kirja elämästä. [Reminiscences of childhood. With plates, including portraits.] pp. 398. *Helsingissä*, 1928. 8°. **10796.** b. **27.**

—— Patruunan tytär. Romaani Ämmän ja Kurimon rautaruukien ajoilta. pp. 247. *Helsingissä*, 1933. 8°. **12593.** a. **13.**

—— Punainen wiiwa. Seitsemäs painos. [A novel. With decorations by G. Paaer.] pp. 181. *Helsingissä*, 1934. 8°. **12592.** f. **8.**

—— Ryysyrannan Jooseppi. Köyhälistötarina suomesta . . . Toinen painos. pp. 389. *Helsingissä*, 1925. 8°. **012591.** aaa. **97.**

—— Soutajan lauluja. Kokoelma pieniä runoja. Kirjoitti I. Calamnius. pp. 158. *Porvoossa*, 1897. 8°. **011586.** h. **104.**

—— Väärällä uralla. [A novel.] Kertoillut I. Calamnius. pp. 183. *Porvoossa*, 1896. 8°. **012590.** ee. **46.**

—— Vanha postineiti. Korpiromaani. pp. 368. [*Hämeenlinna*,] 1935. 8°. **12593.** a. **19.**

CALAMNIUS (JOHAN WIKTOR) Saarna, jonka Martti Lutheruksen 400 syntymäpäiwän juhlana . . . 1883. Kuopion Tuomiokirkossa piti T:ri J. W. Calamnius. pp. 18. *Kuopiossa*, 1883. 8°. **4427.** cc. **19.** (14.)

CALAMÓN DE LA MATA Y BRIZUELA (JOSEP[illegible]) Glorias sagradas, aplausos festivos, y elogios poeticos en [illegible] perfeccion del . . . templo de la santa iglesia cathedr[illegible] de Salamanca, y colocacion de el . . . sacramento en s[illegible] nuevo . . . tabernaculo, *etc.* pp. 391. *Salamanc[illegible]* 1736. fol. **4625.** f. **1**[illegible]

CALAMOTTA. Der Kanal von Calamotta. [By Arch[illegible] duke Louis Salvator. With plates.] pp. 44. *Pra[illegible]* 1910. 4°. **10125.** ff. **2**[illegible]

CALAMUS. Calamus. The quarterly journal of the Orde[illegible] of the Great Companions. *See* ENGLAND.—*Order of th[illegible] Great Companions.*

—— Calamus. The quarterly journal of the Threefol[illegible] Movement. *See* LONDON.—III. *Threefold Movement.*

CALAMUS, *pseud.* [i.e. FRANK WILD REED.] *See* RE[illegible] (F. W.)

CALAMUS LEAVES. *See* DUBLIN.—*Order of the Gre[illegible] Companions.*

CALAMY (BENJAMIN) *See* NEEDHAM (Robert) *Fellow [illegible] Queen's College, Cambridge.* Six Sermons, *etc.* [Edit[illegible] by B. Calamy.] 1679. 8°. **1024.** c. **1**[illegible]

—— *See* SHERLOCK (William) *Dean of St. Paul's.* A Serm[illegible] preached at the Funeral of the Reverend Benj. Calam[illegible] . . . Jan. 7th 168$\frac{5}{6}$. 1686. 8°. **1415.** e. [illegible]

—— The Authentic Narrative of Poor Joseph. pp. 16. *R.T.S.: London*, [1830?] 16°. **864.** a. 5. ([illegible]

—— The Certainty of our Resurrection Proved. [A sermon[illegible] 1795. *See* FAMILY LECTURES. Family Lectures, *e[illegible]* vol. 2. 1791, *etc.* 8°. **224.** k. [illegible]

—— A Discourse about a Scrupulous Conscience, preached [illegible] the Parish-Church of St. Mary Aldermanbury, Londo[illegible] pp. 41. *For Rowland Reynolds: London*, 1683. 4°. **4473.** c. **1.** ([illegible]

—— The second edition. pp. 41. *For Rowland Reynold[illegible] London*, 1683. 4°. **226.** f. **9.** (1[illegible]

—— [Another edition, slightly abridged.] *See* DISSENTE[illegible] A Collection of Cases . . . written to recover Dissente[illegible] *etc.* 1694. fol. **700.** m. [illegible]

—— [Another edition.] *See* DISSENTERS. A Collection [illegible] Cases . . . written to recover Dissenters, *etc.* vol. 2[illegible] 1718. 8°. **226.** b. [illegible]

—— *See* DELAUNE (Thomas) A Plea for the Non-Co[illegible] formists . . . in a letter to Dr. B. Calamy, upon h[illegible] sermon, called, Scrupulous Conscience, *etc.* 1684. 4°. **873.** e. **12**[illegible]

—— —— 1704. 4°. **110.** f. **4**[illegible]

—— —— 1706. 4°. **1355.** d. **4**[illegible]

—— —— 1712. 8°. **1355.** c. [illegible]

—— —— 1720. 8°. **4135.** b. [illegible]

—— —— 1733. 8°. **3914.** b. [illegible]

—— —— 1800. 12°. **4106.** a. [illegible]

—— —— 1817, *etc.* 8°. **4135.** aaa. [illegible]

—— —— 1845. 8°. **4139.** bb. **2**[illegible]

—— Animadversions upon Dr Calamy's Discourse in t[illegible] Conformists Cases against Dissenters, concerning [illegible] scrupulous conscience. Wherein the nature of [illegible] doubting, tender conscience is considered: togeth[illegible] with the duty of such as are possessed of it. pp. 30[illegible] *A. Baldwin: London*, 1700. 4°. **T. 675.** ([illegible]

—— [Another copy.] **4135.** c. [illegible]

—— The Hazard of a Death-bed Repentance. [A sermon.] 1795. *See* Family Lectures. Family Lectures, *etc.* vol. 2. 1791, *etc.* 8º. **224.** k. **3.**

—— The Important Concern of a Future State. [A sermon.] 1795. *See* Family Lectures. Family Lectures, *etc.* vol. 2. 1791, *etc.* 8º. **224.** k. **3.**

—— Life and Immortality brought to Light by the Gospel. [A sermon.] *See* Protestant Writers. The Practical Preacher, *etc.* vol. 1. 1762. 8º. **4454.** f. **16.**

—— Passive Obedience the Doctrine of the Church of England; and doing evil that good may come, a damnable sin. A Sermon preach'd before the . . . Lord-Mayor, &c. Sept. 30. 1683. By B. Calamy. Not printed in his volume of sermons. pp. 24. *John Morphew: London,* 1710. 8º. **693.** d. **8.** (**1.**)

—— A Sermon preached at St. Lawrence-Jury, London, upon the 9th of September, being the day of thanksgiving for the deliverance of the King & Kingdom from the late treasonable conspiracy. pp. 35. *R. E. for W. Kettilby: London,* 1683. 4º. **226.** h. **15.** (**11.**)

—— A Sermon preached before the Artillery-Company of London . . . December 2, 1684, *etc.* pp. 28. *For John Baker: London,* 1685. 4º. **226.** h. **18.** (**28.**)

—— [Another copy.] **226.** i. **2.** (**11.**)

—— A Sermon preached before the Lord Mayor, Aldermen and Citizens of London . . . the 29th of May 1682. pp. 35. *J. M. for Walter Kettilby: London,* 1682. 4º. **694.** f. 5. (2.)

—— The second edition. pp. 35. *J. M. for Walter Kettilby: London,* 1682. 4º. **694.** f. 5. (3.)

—— [Another copy.] **226.** h. **15.** (**10.**)

—— A Sermon preached before the Right Honorable the Lord Mayor . . . the 13th. of July, 1673. pp. 28. *For Nathaniel Brooke: London,* 1673. 4º. **226.** h. **18.** (**26.**)

—— A Sermon preached before the Right Honourable the Lord Mayor . . . September the Second, 1684. Being the anniversary fast for the dreadful fire in . . . 1666. pp. 32. *For Walter Kettilby: London,* 1685. 4º. **226.** i. 2. (5.)

—— [Another copy.] **226.** h. **15.** (**13.**)

—— A Sermon preached before the Right Honourable the Lord Mayor . . . the 30th of September, 1683. pp. 32. *For W. Kettilby: London,* 1683. 4º. **226.** h. **15.** (**12.**)

—— [Another copy.] **693.** f. **6.** (**2.**)
Without the preliminary page stating that the sermon is printed by desire of the Court.

—— [Another copy.] **226.** h. **18.** (**27.**)
Without the preliminary page.

—— Sermons preached upon Several Occasions. Never before printed. [Edited by James Calamy.] pp. 495. *M. Flesher for Henry Dickenson & Richard Green: London,* 1687. 8º. **1022.** a. **18.**

—— The second edition, corrected. pp. 495. *M. Clark for Henry Dickenson & Richard Green: London,* 1690. 8º. **4460.** aa. **5.**

—— The fourth edition corrected. To which is added a sermon preached at his funeral by William Sherlock. [With a portrait.] pp. 403. *D. Brown; J. Nicholson & J. Sprint: London,* 1704. 8º. **4461.** cc. **9.**

—— The fifth edition corrected, *etc.* [With a portrait.] pp. xi. 403. *Daniel Browne: London,* 1715. 8º. **4453.** bb. **12.**

—— The seventh edition, *etc.* pp. xi. 404. *William Mears: London,* 1738. 8º. **4455.** bb. **4.**

—— Three Sermons. [No. 1, 5, 11 of the "Sermons preached on Several Occasions," slightly abridged.] 1825. *See* Wesley (John) A Christian Library, *etc.* vol. 23. 1819, *etc.* 8º. **495.** e. **12.**

—— Some Considerations about the Case of Scandal, or giving offence to weak brethren. [By B. Calamy.] pp. 60. 1683. 4º. *See* Considerations. **698.** i. **1.** (**9.**)

—— [Another edition.] pp. 50. 1685. 4º. *See* Considerations. **4106.** c. **15.**

—— [Another edition.] pp. 60. *See* Dissenters. A Collection of Cases . . . written to recover Dissenters, *etc.* vol. 1. 1685. 4º. **4106.** h. **1.**

—— [Another edition.] *See* Dissenters. A Collection of Cases . . . written to recover Dissenters, *etc.* 1694. fol. **700.** m. **13.**

—— [Another edition.] *See* Dissenters. A Collection of Cases . . . written to recover Dissenters, *etc.* vol. 2. 1718. 8º. **226.** b. **19.**

CALAMY (E.) *of Liverpool.* Help! Help! The Church in Danger! as shewn in a series of letters. [An attack on the Church of England.] pp. 16. *E. Smith & Co.: Liverpool,* 1836. 8º. **4108.** bb. **6.**

CALAMY (Edmund) *B.D., Minister of St. Mary's, Aldermanbury. See* also Smectymnuus, *pseud.* [i.e. S. Marshall, E. Calamy and others.]

—— *See* Anonymus, *Londinensis.* A Letter to Dr. Calamy [Edmund Calamy, D.D.], shewing that Mr. Archdeacon Echard has done the part of a faithful historian in branding Mr. Edmund Calamy, the Doctor's grandfather, as a promoter of rebellion, *etc.* [1718?] 8º. E. **2012.** (5.)

—— *See* Barber (Edward) *Baptist.* A Declaration and Vindication of the carriage of Edward Barber at the parish meeting-house of Benetfinck . . . after the morning exercise of Mr. Callamy was ended, *etc.* [1648.] 4º. E. **458.** (**8.**)

—— *See* Bible.—*Selections.* [*English.*] Cromwell's Soldier's Bible: being a reprint in facsimile of "The Souldier's Pocket Bible," compiled [or rather, here stated to have been compiled] by E. Calamy, *etc.* 1895. 8º. **3149.** e. **13.**

—— *See* Bible.—*Minor Prophets.* [*English.*] A Brief Exposition on the xii. Smal Prophets . . . By G. Hutcheson. [With an epistle to the reader by E. Calamy.] 1657. fol. **3166.** f. **5.**

—— *See* Blake (Thomas) *Puritan Divine.* Mr Blake's Answer to Mr Tombes . . . in vindication of the birth-priviledge . . . of beleevers, *etc.* [With a recommendatory preface by E. Calamy and R. Vines.] 1646. 4º. E. **349.** (**16.**)

—— *See* Bolton (Samuel) *D.D.* The Dead Saint speaking, to Saints and Sinners living, *etc.* [With an address to the reader by E. Calamy.] 1657, *etc.* fol. **4452.** g. 3.

—— *See* Clarke (Samuel) *Minister of St. Bennet Fink.* The Marrow of Ecclesiastical Historie, *etc.* [With a recommendatory preface by E. Calamy.] 1650. 4º. E. **591.**

CALAMY (Edmund) *B.D., Minister of St. Mary's, Aldermanbury.*

—— *See* Fenner (William) *B.D.* The Works of . . . W. Fenner . . . published by his over-seers [i.e. T. Hill and E. Calamy], *etc.* 1651, *etc.* 8°. **3752.** aaa. **1.**

—— *See* Fenner (William) *B.D.* A Divine Message to the Elect Soule, *etc.* [Edited by E. Calamy and J. Goodwin.] 1647. 8°. **4453.** b. **13.** (**1.**)

—— —— 1651. 8°. **4452.** b. **6.**

—— *See* Fenner (William) *B.D.* A Divine Message to the Elect Soul, *etc.* [Edited by J. Goodwin and E. Calamy.] 1676. 8°. **4481.** de. **11.**

—— *See* Fenner (William) *B.D.* The Soul's Looking-glasse, *etc.* [The epistle to the reader signed: Edm. C., i.e. Edmund Calamy.] 1640. 8°. **4408.** c. **23.**

—— *See* Hudibras. Hudibras on Calamy's Imprisonment, *etc.* [1663.] fol. Lutt. ii. **28.**

—— *See* Hudson (Samuel) A Vindication of the Essence and Unity of the Church Catholike Visible, *etc.* [With an epistle to the reader by E. Calamy.] 1650. 4°. **4106.** a. **42.**

—— —— 1658. 4°. E. **960.** (**2.**)

—— *See* Love (Christopher) The Christians Duty and Safety in evill times, *etc.* [Edited by E. Calamy and others.] 1653. 8°. E. **1434.** (**3.**)

—— *See* Love (Christopher) The Dejected Soules Cure, *etc.* [Edited by E. Calamy and others.] 1657. 4°. **4452.** bb. **2.** (**1.**)

—— *See* Love (Christopher) The Penitent Pardoned, *etc.* [Edited by E. Calamy and others.] 1657. 4°. **4452.** bb. **2.** (**2.**)

—— *See* Love (Christopher) The Zealous Christian taking Heaven by Holy Violence, *etc.* [Edited by E. Calamy and others.] 1657. 4°. **4452.** bb. **2.** (**3.**)

—— *See* Marshall (Stephen) Smectymnuus Redivivus . . . Composed by five . . . divines (S. Marshall, E. Calamy [and others]). 1669. 4°. **4105.** bb. **21.**

—— *See* R., J. An Answer for Mr. Calamie to a poem congratulating his imprisonment in Newgate, *etc.* 1663. fol. Lutt. ii. **27.**

—— *See* Roberts (Francis) *D.D.* Clavis Bibliorum. The Key of the Bible, *etc.* [With a recommendatory epistle by E. Calamy.] 1648. 8°. E. **1123.**

—— *See* Robinson (Ralph) *Puritan Divine.* Christ All and in All, *etc.* [Edited by E. Calamy and others.] 1656. 8°. **4452.** bb. **14.**

—— *See* Shepard (Thomas) *the Elder.* The Parable of the Ten Virgins, opened and applied, *etc.* [With a prefatory note by E. Calamy and others.] 1797. 8°. **3224.** l. **21.**

—— *See* Stephens (Nathaniel) A Plain and Easie Calculation of the Name, Mark, and Number . . . of the Beast. Whereunto is prefixed, a commendatory epistle . . . by Mr. E. Calamy. 1656. 4°. E. **879.** (**6.**)

—— *See* Taylor (Thomas) *D.D., Fellow of Christ's College, Cambridge.* The Works of . . . Dr. Thom. Taylor, *etc.* [With a dedicatory epistle by E. Calamy.] 1653. fol. **3752.** f. **12.**

—— *See* Tombes (John) *B.D.* An Apology for the . . . Treatises . . . concerning Infant Baptisme . . . together with a postscript by way of reply to Mr. Blakes answer to Mr. Tombes his letter, and Mr. E. Calamy and Mr. R. Vines' preface to it, *etc.* 1646. 4°. E. **352.** (**1.**)

CALAMY (Edmund) *B.D., Minister of St. Mary's, Alder*
manbury.

—— *See* Udall (O.) Perez Uzza. Or, a Serious letter se
to . . . E. Calamy January the 17th 1663, touching h
sermon at Aldermanbury, December the 28th intimati
his close design and dangerous insinuation against t
publick peace, *etc.* 1663. 4°. **4105.** bb. **4**

—— *See* Wild (Robert) *D.D.* A Poem upon the Impriso
ment of Mr Calamy in Newgate. [1662.] fol.
Lutt. ii. **2**

—— —— [1764?] fol. C. **20.** f. **2.** (8

—— *See* Wild (Robert) *D.D.* Dr. Wild's Echo: or, a F
answer to his poem on the inprisonment of Master Calam
[1663?] *s. sh.* 4°. C. **121.** g. **6.** (

—— *See* Yearwood (Randolph) The Penitent Murder
. . . Whereunto is annexed a serious advice to the i
habitants of London from many reverend ministers there
[signed by E. Calamy and others]. 1657. 8°.
1244. a.

—— Farewel Sermons preached by Mr. Calamy, Dr. Mant
[and others] . . . Together with Mr. Calamies sermon at t
funeral of Mr. Ash. His serm. Decemb. 28. at Alderma
bury . . . Revised and corrected, *etc.* [The preface signe
L. R., N.S.] 1663. 4°. *See* R., L., and N., S.
1470. b.

—— Sermon . . . August 17. 1662.—The Righteous Ma
Death Lamented. A sermon, preached at St. Austi
London, August 23. 1662. at the funeral of . . . M
Simeon Ash, *etc.* *See* London.—iii. *Ministers.* T
London-Ministers Legacy, *etc.* 1662. 8°. **695.** b.

—— Mr. Calamy's Sermon, preached, August 17. 1662.
Mr. Calamy's Sermon at the funeral of Mr. Ash.—M
Calamy's Sermon, preached December 28. 1662. S
Collection. A Compleat Collection of Farewell Sermo
. . . With Dr. Wilde's poem on Mr. Calamy's impris
ment, *etc.* 1663. 8°. **695.** a.

—— Mr Calamy's Sermon preached August 17, 1662.—M
Calamy's Sermon [on Eli, preached 28. Dec. 1662]. S
Nonconformist Ministers. Farewell Sermons of so
of the most Eminent of the Nonconformist Ministers,
1816. 8°. **1026.** e.

—— An Answer [by E. Calamy] to the Articles agai
Master Calamy, Master Martiale, Master Burton, Mas
Peters, Master Moleigne, Master Case, M. Sedgwic
M. Evans, &c. and many other painfull divines who w
impeached of high treason by his Majesty. Fi
answering particularly the articles themselves, th
shewing the mis-information of his Majestie by t
bishops, concerning the same, *etc.* pp. 5.
William Bond: London, 1642. 4°. E. **132.** (

—— The Art of Divine Meditation. Or, a Discourse of
nature, necessity, and excellency thereof. With moti
to . . . the better-performance of that most importa
Christian duty. In several sermons on Gen. 24.
[Taken down from the author's preaching.] pp. 208.
For Tho. Parkhurst: London, 1680. 8°. **4454.** aaa.
Imperfect; wanting the portrait.

—— The City Remembrancer. Or, a Sermon preached
the native citizens, of London, at their solemn assem
in Pauls . . . the 23 of June, A.D. mdclvii. pp. 74.
S. G. for John Baker: London, 1657. 12°. E. **1676.** (

—— The Doctrine of the Bodies Fragility. *See* infra: T
Saints Transfiguration.

CALAMY (EDMUND) *B.D., Minister of St. Mary's, Aldermanbury.*

—— The Door of Truth opened: or, a Brief narrative of . . . how Mr Henry Burton came to shut himself out of the church-doors of Aldermanbury . . . In answer to a paper [by H. Burton] called, Truth shut out of Doors, *etc.* [By E. Calamy.] pp. 18. 1645. 4°. *See* BURTON (Henry) *Rector of St. Matthew's, Friday Street.* **E. 311. (13.)**

—— Eli trembling for fear of the Ark. A sermon, preached at St. Mary Aldermanbury, Dec. 28. 1662: by E. Calamy, B.D. late Minister there: upon the preaching of which he was committed prisoner to . . . Newgate . . . Together with the Mittimus and manner of his imprisonment, annexed hereunto. pp. 19. *Oxford,* 1663. 4°. **114. f. 34.**

—— *See* WILD (Robert) *D.D.* Anti-Boreale, *etc.* (A discourse occasioned by Mr Calamies late sermon, intituled Eli trembling for fear of the Ark.) [1663.] 4°. **873. k. 8.**

—— *See* WOMOCK (Laurence) *Bishop of Saint David's.* An Antidote to Cure the Calamites of their Trembling for fear of the Arke, *etc.* (A discourse occasioned by Mr Calamies late sermon, intituled Eli trembling for fear of the Ark.) 1663. 4°. **4135. a. 84.**

—— Englands Antidote, against the Plague of Civil Warre. Presented in a sermon before the Honorable House of Commons, on their late extraordinary solemne fast, October 22. 1644. pp. 45. *I. L. for Christopher Meredith: London,* 1645. 4°. **E. 17. (17.)**

—— England's Looking-Glasse, presented in a sermon preached before the . . . House of Commons, at their late solemne fast, December 22. 1641. pp. 62. *I. Raworth for Chr. Meredith: London,* 1642. 4°. **E. 131. (29.)**

—— The fourth . . . edition. pp. 32. *For Cadwallader Greene: London,* 1642. 4°. **4474. d. 51.**

—— Gods Free Mercy to England, presented as a pretious, and powerful motive to humiliation in a sermon preached before the . . . House of Commons, at their late solemne fast, Feb. 23. 1641. pp. 50. *For Christopher Meredith: London,* 1642. 4°. **E. 133. (18.)**

—— [Another edition.] pp. 51. *For Christopher Meredith: London,* 1642. 4°. **4474. d. 29.**

—— The Godly Mans Ark, or, City of Refuge, in the day of his distresse. Discovered in divers sermons, the first of which was preached at the funerall of Mistresse Elizabeth Moore . . . Hereunto are annexed Mris. Moores evidences for heaven, *etc.* pp. 254. *For Jo. Hancock & Tho. Parkhurst: London,* 1657. 8°. **E. 1616. (1.)**

—— The second edition, corrected and amended. pp. 254. *For John Hancock & Tho. Parkhurst: London,* 1658. 8°. **4454. aaa. 5.**

—— The eighth edition, corrected and amended. pp. 34 [221]. *For John Hancock & Thomas Parkhurst: London,* 1678. 12°. **874. b. 1.**
Cropped.

—— The 17th edition, corrected and amended. pp. 142. *For Thomas Parkhurst & John Hancock: London,* 1693. 12°. **4452. a. 14.**

—— New edition. [The editor's preface signed: M. F. Without the "Brief Repetition," *etc.*] pp. v. 208. *J. Nisbet & Co.: London,* 1865. 16°. **4454. aa. 14.**

CALAMY (EDMUND) *B.D., Minister of St. Mary's, Aldermanbury.*

—— A Brief Repetition of what was said of Mris. Elizabeth Moore at her Burial. [By E. Calamy. Being pp. 195–221 of an edition of "The Godly Mans Ark."] [1656?] 16°. *See* MOORE (Elizabeth) *Mrs., of London.* **1418. i. 29.**

—— The Great Danger of Covenant-refusing, and Covenant-breaking. Presented in a sermon preached before the . . . Lord Mayor, and . . . the Sheriffes . . . Jan. 14. 1645. Upon which day the solemne League and Covenant was renued by them, *etc.* pp. 40. *M. F. for Christopher Meredith: London,* 1646. 4°. **E. 327. (6.)**

—— [Another edition.] *See* ENGLAND. [*Solemn League and Covenant,* 1643.] A Phenix or the solemn League and Covenant, *etc.* [1661.] 12°. **4175. a. 29.**

—— [Another edition.] *See* ENGLAND. [*Solemn League and Covenant,* 1643.] The Memorial of the Presbyterians, exemplified in the Solemn League and Covenant, *etc.* 1706. 4°. **4175. bb. 14.**

—— The Happinesse of those who Sleep in Jesus . . . Delivered in a sermon preached at the funeral of . . . the Lady Anne Waller . . . Oct. 31, 1661. pp. 32. *J. H. for Nathanael Webb: London,* 1662. 4°. **1419. h. 37.**

—— [Another copy.] **114. f. 33.**

—— An Indictment against England because of her selfe-murdering Divisions: together with an exhortation to an England-preserving unity and concord. Presented in a sermon, preached before the . . . House of Lords . . . at the late solemn fast, Dec. 25. 1644. [With "A catalogue of the sermons preached and printed by order of both or either Houses of Parliament from January 1643 to January 1644."] pp. 41. *I. L. for C. Meredith: London,* 1645. 4°. **E. 23. (5.)**

—— A Just and Necessary Apology against an unjust Invective, published by Mr. Henry Burton in a late book of his, entituled, Truth still Truth, though shut out of doors. pp. 12. *For Christopher Meredith: London,* 1646. 4°. **E. 320. (9.)**

—— [Another copy.] **E. 319. (25.)**

—— Master E. Calamies Leading Case. [On his being committed to Newgate by the Lord Mayor for an unlawful sermon.] pp. 16. *London,* 1663. 4°. **4135. a. 20.**

—— Mr. Edmond Calamy his speech in Guild-Hall . . . the sixt of October, 1643. *See* LONDON.—II. *Livery of the City.* Four Speeches, *etc.* 1646. 4°. **102. a. 76.**

—— The Noble-Mans Patterne of true and reall Thankfulnesse. Presented in a sermon before the . . . House of Lords; at their late solemne day of thanksgiving, June 15 1643 for the discovery of a . . . designe, tending to the utter subversion of the Parliament and of the famous City of London. pp. 59. *G. M. for Christopher Meredith: London,* 1643. 4°. **E. 56. (3.)**

—— Of the Resurrection. [A sermon.] *See* CASE (Thomas) *M.A.* The Morning Exercise Methodized, *etc.* 1660. 4°. **E. 1008.**

—— [Another edition.] 1845. *See* ANNESLEY (Samuel) *LL.D., etc.* The Morning Exercises, *etc.* vol. 5. 1844, *etc.* 8°. **1356. h. 5.**

—— A Patterne for all, especially for Noble and Honourable Persons, to teach them how to die nobly and honourably. Delivered in a sermon preached at the solemne interment of the corps of the Right Honourable Robert Earle of Warwick . . . May 1. 1658, *etc.* pp. 39. *For Edward Brewster: London,* 1658. 4°. **1417. i. 7.**

CALAMY (EDMUND) *B.D., Minister of St. Mary's, Aldermanbury.*

—— [Another copy.] **1417**. i. 8.

—— [Another copy.] **113**. f. 24.

—— [Another copy.] E. **947**. (**1**.)

—— The Saints Rest: or their happy Sleep in Death. As it was delivered in a sermon, Aug. 24, 1651. pp. 19. *Printed by A.M.: London*, 1651. 4°. E. **641**. (**19**.)
A MS. note on the titlepage reads: "said to be for Mr. Loue."

—— [Another edition.] A Sermon preached . . . at Aldermanbury London, Aug. 24. 1651. Being a funeral sermon for Mr. Love on the Sabbath Day following after he was executed, *etc. For G. Horton: London*, [1651.] 4°. **106**. e. **18**. (4.)
Cropped.

—— [Another edition.] *See* LOVE (Christopher) A Christians Duty and Safety in evill times, *etc.* 1653. 8°. E. **1434**. (3.)

—— The Doctrine of the Bodies Fragility: with a divine project, discovering how to make these vile bodies of ours glorious by getting gracious souls. Represented in a sermon at the funerall of . . . D[r] Samuel Bolton. [A surreptitious edition of "The Saints' Transfiguration."] pp. 19. *For Joseph Moore: London*, 1655. 4°. E. **814**. (8.)

—— The Saints Transfiguration: or, the Body of Vilenesse changed into a Body of Glory. A sermon preached . . . at the funerall of . . . D[r] Samuel Bolton . . . With a short account of his death . . . To which are annexed verses upon his death, composed by divers of his friends, *etc.* pp. 35. *For Joseph Cranford: London*, 1655. 4°. **1415**. b. **46**.

—— [Another copy.] **1415**. b. **47**.

—— [Another copy.] **113**. f. **3**.

—— Two Solemne Covenants made between God and Man . . . Clearly laid open, distinguished, and vindicated, *etc.* pp. 14. *For Thomas Banks: London*, 1647. 4°. **4378**. c. **11**.
The author's name occurs only on the portrait prefixed.

—— [Another copy.] E. **373**. (6.)
Imperfect; wanting the portrait.

—— [Extracts from E. Calamy's "Indictment against England," "Speech at Guildhall, October the sixth, 1643," "The Noble-Mans Patterne," and "A Just and Necessary Apology."] *See* EVANGELIUM. Evangelium Armatum. A specimen . . . of . . . doctrines . . . preached . . . by . . . Mr. Calamy, Mr. Jenkins, *etc.* 1663. 4°. **4135**. c. **31**.

—— Mr. Edmund Calamy his Exhortations to the Service of the Lord.—Divine Sentences, collected from the works of Mr. E. Calamy, lately deceased. [With a portrait.] *See* SAINTS. Saints Memorials, *etc.* 1674. 8°. **873**. e. **37**.

—— Old Mr. E. Calamy's Former and Latter Sayings upon several Occasions. *For W. B.: London*, 1674. *s. sh.* fol. **816**. m. **21**. (6.)

—— A Conspiracie of the Twelve Bishops in the Tower, against Mr. Calamie, Mr. Burton, Mr. Martiall, and many other worthy divines, &c. As also how they obscurely made those articles, wherein Mr. Pym and the other Parliament-men were impeached, *etc. For W. Bond: London*, 1641. 4°. E. **181**. (**32**.)

CALAMY (EDMUND) *B.D., Minister of St. Mary's, Aldermanbury.*

—— On the Death of Mr. Calamy, *etc.* [Verses by R. Wild.] *London*, 1667. *s. sh.* fol. C. **20**. f. **2**. (**75**.)

—— [Another copy.] Lutt. II. **29**.

—— The Pulpit Incendiary: or, the Divinity and devotion of Mr. Calamy, Mr. Case . . . and other Sion-Colledge preachers in their Morning-Exercises, with the keen and angry application thereof unto the parliament and army. Together with a true vindication of the Covenant from the false glosses put upon it, *etc.* [By John Price.] pp. 62. *Printed by C. S.: [London,]* 1648. 4°. E. **438**. (**10**.)

—— The Pulpit Incendiary anatomized: or a vindication of Sion Colledge, and the Morning Exercises, *etc.* pp. 16. *For Ralph Smith: London*, 1648. 4°. E. **442**. (**5**.)

CALAMY (EDMUND) *D.D., Son of Edmund Calamy, M.A.* *See* CHANDLER (Benjamin) An Apology which I Benjamin Chandler do make for my standing by Mr. Joseph Stedman, in opposition to Dr. Calamy, Mr. Tong, *etc.* 1720. 8°. **698**. i. **8**. (**7**.)

—— *See* EARLE (Jabez) A Sermon preach'd . . . upon occasion of the Ordination of W. Hunt . . . With a charge given to the said W. Hunt . . . by E. Calamy, *etc.* 1725. 8°. **225**. h. **24**. (**1**.)

—— *See* GORDON (Alexander) *Principal of the Unitarian Home Missionary College, Manchester.* Calamy as a Biographer. [1914.] 8°. **11850**. d. **29**.

—— *See* MATHER (Increase) Memoirs . . . With a preface by the Reverend E. Calamy. 1725. 8°. **491**. c. **15**. (**3**.)

—— *See* MAYO (Daniel) A Funeral Sermon, occasioned by the . . . death of . . . E. Calamy, *etc.* 1732. 8°. **1415**. e. **6**.

—— *See* STEDMAN (Joseph) Presbyterian Priest-craft: being a full and true account of the proceedings of Dr. Calamy [and others] . . . in Salters-Hall, *etc.* 1720. 8°. **698**. i. **8**. (**9**.)

—— *See* THEOLOGICO-LAICUS, *pseud.* The Uncharitableness of Modern Charity, and the infidelity of modern faith, expos'd in a new way . . . In a letter to . . . Dr. Calamy, *etc.* 1722. 8°. **4135**. c. **82**.

—— *See* TROSSE (George) The Life of the Reverend M[r] George Trosse . . . With a . . . preface by the Rev[d] Dr. Calamy, Mr. Tong, and Mr. Evans. 1715. 8°. **1418**. h. **34**.

—— *See* VRIES (G. de) *Professor of Philosophy at Utrecht.* Exercitationis . . . de fictis innatarum idearum mysteriis pars prima (pars secunda, quam . . . proponit E. Calamy). 1688, *etc.* 4°. **525**. d. **12**. (**19**.)

—— An Abridgment of Mr. Baxter's History of his Life and Times. With an account of many others of those worthy ministers who were ejected, after the Restauration of King Charles the Second . . . And a continuation of their history, till the year 1691. By E. Calamy. pp. 701. 1702. 8°. *See* BAXTER (Richard) [*Single Works.*] **488**. b. **2**.

—— [Another edition.] An Abridgement of Mr. Baxter's History of his Life and Times . . . and the continuation . . . to . . . 1711. The second edition. 2 vol. 1713. 8°. *See* BAXTER (Richard) [*Single Works.*] **487**. b. **34**.

—— The Nonconformist's Memorial; being an account of the ministers who were ejected or silenced after the Restoration, particularly by the Act of Uniformity . . . 1662 . . . Originally written by . . . E. Calamy, D.D. Now abridged and corrected . . . by Samuel Palmer. To which is prefixed an introduction, containing a brief

CALAMY (Edmund) *D.D., Son of Edmund Calamy, M.A.*

history of the times in which they lived, *etc.* (An English version of the Latin epitaphs in the Nonconformist's Memorial: to which is added a poem . . . By Thomas Gibbons.) [A recast of Calamy's Abridgment. With portraits.] 2 vol. *W. Harris: London,* 1775. 8°. **204.** b. **5, 6.**

— [Another copy.] G. **20189, 90.**

— [Another copy.] The Nonconformists' Memorial, *etc.* *London,* 1775. 8°. **4716.** b. **14.**

— The second edition. 2 vol. *J. Harris: London,* 1777. 8°. **4905.** bbb. **21.**

— [Another issue.] *Alex. Hogg: London,* 1778. 8°. **1126.** h. **15, 16.**

— The second edition. [With a portrait.] 3 vol. *Button & Son; T. Hurst: London,* 1802, 03. 8°. **2012.d.**

— [Another copy.] **4715.** d. **3.**

— *See* Baxter (Richard) [*Single Works.*] A Vindication of the Royal Martyr King Charles i. from the Irish Massacre cast upon him in the Life of Richard Baxter [i.e. Reliquiae Baxterianae] . . . And since in the Abridgment by E. Calamy, *etc.* 1704. 4°. **010807.** i. **22.**

— *See* Baxter (Richard) [*Single Works.*] A Vindication of the Royal Martyr King Charles i, from the Irish Massacre in the year 1641, cast upon him in the Life of Richard Baxter, wrote by himself. And since in the Abridgment by E. Calamy, *etc.* 1750. 4°. [*Somers* (*John*) *Baron Somers. A Second Collection of Scarce and Valuable Tracts, etc.* vol. 2.] **184.** a. **6.**

— — 1811. 4°. [*Somers* (*John*) *Baron Somers. A Collection of Scarce and Valuable Tracts, etc.* vol. 5.] **750.** g. **5.**

— *See* Carte (Thomas) The Irish Massacre set in a Clear Light. Wherein Mr. Baxter's account of it in the history of his own life, and the abridgment thereof by Dr. Calamy, are fully consider'd, *etc.* [1714.] 4°. **8145.** ee. **5.**

— — 1715. 4°. **601.** f. **22.** (**10.**)

— *See* Case. A Case of Present Concern, in a letter to a member of the House of Commons [on certain statements affecting the character of King Charles i. contained in E. Calamy's "Abridgment of Mr. Baxter's History of his Life and Times"]. [1702.] 4°. **10806.** b. **24.**

— *See* Hoadly (Benjamin) successively *Bishop of Bangor, of Hereford, etc.* The Reasonableness of Conformity to the Church of England . . . In answer to the tenth chapter of Mr. Calamy's Abridgment of Mr. Baxter's History of his Life and Times, *etc.* 1703. 8°. **1019.** d. **18.** (**1.**)

— *See* Matthews (Arnold G.) Calamy Revised. Being a revision of Edmund Calamy's "Account" of the ministers and others ejected and silenced, 1660–2. 1934. 8°. **2012.d.**

— *See* Maurice (Matthias) Monuments of Mercy; or, Some of the distinguishing favours of Christ to his Congregational Church at Rowel . . . as held forth in the evangelical labours . . . of Mr. Richard Davis; being . . . a just vindication of his memory from the false aspersions cast thereupon by Dr. Calamy, in the continuation of his account of the ejected ministers. 1729. 8°. **1022.** a. **35.**

— *See* Ollyffe (John) A Defence of Ministerial Conformity . . . in answer to the misrepresentations of . . . Mr. Calamy in . . . his Abridgment of the History of Mr. Baxter's Life and Times. 1702. 8°. **698.** a. **52.**

— *See* Philalethes, *pseud.* [i.e. Isaac Sharpe.] Animadversions on Some Passages of Mr. Edmund Calamy's Abridgment of Mr. Richard Baxter's History of his Life and Times, *etc.* (With an answer to Mr. Calamy's—unprinted—defence.) 1704. 4°. **488.** c. **28.**

— *See* Presbyterian Preachers. A Century of Eminent Presbyterian Preachers . . . To which is added, an appendix, with the short characters of several of these preachers . . . taken from Dr. Calamy's Abridgment of Baxter's Life. 1723. 8°. **700.** h. **22.**

— *See* Walker (John) *D.D., etc.* An Attempt towards recovering an Account of the Numbers and Sufferings of the Clergy of the Church of England . . . occasion'd by the ninth chapter . . . of Dr. Calamy's Abridgment of the Life of Mr. Baxter, *etc.* 1714. fol. **490.** k. **10.**

— *See* Wallis (John) *D.D., Savilian Professor.* The Rule for Finding Easter . . . vindicated against . . . the misrepresentations of . . . Mr. Calamy [in his "Abridgment of Mr. Baxter's History of his Life and Times"], *etc.* 1712. 12°. **8562.** aa. **23.**

— — 1714. 12°. **3478.** bbb. **33.**

— Seditious Preachers, Ungodly Teachers. Exemplified in the case of the ministers, ejected by the Act of Uniformity 1662 . . . Opposed chiefly to Mr. Calamy's Abridgment, where he has canonized them for so many saints and confessors, *etc.* pp. 58. copious ms. notes. *J. Morphew: London,* 1709. 4°. **111.** g. **60.**

— [Another edition.] pp. 48. 1887. *See* Edinburgh—*Clarendon Historical Society.* Reprints. ser. 3. no. 1. 1882, *etc.* 4°. **Ac. 8251.**

— A Caveat against New Prophets, in two sermons at the Merchants Lecture in Salters Hall. pp. 55. *T. Parkhurst, etc.: London,* 1708. 8°. **695.** c. **6.** (**4.**)

— *See* Bulkeley (*Sir* Richard) *Bart.* An Answer to several Treatises lately publish'd on the subject of the Prophets [i.e. to "A Caveat against New Prophets," by E. Calamy, and other works], *etc.* 1708. 8°. **695.** c. **6.** (**6.**)

— The Church and the Dissenters compar'd, as to Persecution. In some remarks on Dr. Walker's attempt to recover the names and sufferings of the clergy that were sequestred, &c. between 1640, and 1660. pp. 98. *John Clark: London,* 1719. 8°. **698.** i. **9.** (**3.**)

— Comfort and Counsel to Protestant Dissenters. With some serious queries to such as hate and cast them out . . . In two sermons, *etc.* pp. 43. *John Lawrence, etc.: London,* 1712. 8°. **111.** f. **11.**

— The second edition. pp. 43. *John Lawrence: London,* 1712. 8°. **4106.** b. **33.**

— A Continuation of the Account of the Ministers, Lecturers . . . who were ejected and silenced after the Restoration in 1660, by or before the Act for Uniformity. To which is added, the Church and Dissenters compar'd as to persecution, in some remarks on Dr. Walker's attempt to recover the names and sufferings of the clergy that were sequestred, &c. between 1640 and 1660. And also some free remarks on the twenty-eighth chapter of Dr. Bennet's Essay on the 39 Articles of Religion. 2 vol. pp. xlviii. viii. 1005. 146. 63. *R. Ford: London,* 1727. 8°. **487.** b. **35.**

—— [Another copy.] **859**. i. **19, 20.**

—— [Another copy.] G. **2145, 46.**

—— A Defence of Moderate Non-conformity. In answer to the reflections of Mr. Ollyffe and Mr. Hoadly, on the tenth chapter of the Abridgment of the Life of the Reverend Mr. Rich. Baxter. Part I. With a postscript containing some remarks on a tract of Mr. Dorringtons, entituled, The Dissenting Ministry in Religion, censur'd . . . from the Holy Scriptures. (Part II. With a postscript, containing an answer to Mr. Hoadly's Serious Admonition, *etc.*—Part III. . . . To which are added three letters: one to Mr. Ollyffe, in answer to his Second Defence of Ministerial Conformity. Another to Mr. Hoadly, in answer to his Defence of the Reasonableness of Conformity. And, a third to the author, from Mr. Rastrick . . . giving an historical account of his Nonconformity.) 3 vol. *Tho. Parkhurst: London*, 1703–05. 8°. **4106**. b. **32.**

—— *See* HOADLY (Benjamin) successively *Bishop of Bangor, of Hereford, etc.* A Brief Defense of Episcopal Ordination . . . To which are added, a reply to the introduction to the second part: and a postscript relating to the third part of Mr. Calamy's Defense of Moderate Non-conformity. 1707. 8°. **858**. f. **1.**

—— *See* HOADLY (Benjamin) successively *Bishop of Bangor, of Hereford, etc.* A Defence of the Reasonableness of Conformity to the Church of England, &c. In answer to the objections of Mr. Calamy, in his Defence of Moderate Non-Conformity, *etc.* 1705. 8°. **1019**. d. **18**. (**3**.)

—— *See* HOADLY (Benjamin) successively *Bishop of Bangor, of Hereford, etc.* The Reasonableness of Conformity to the Church of England . . . With the defense of it [against E. Calamy] . . . Together with the reply to the introduction to the second part; and a postscript relating to the third part, of Mr. Calamy's Defense of Moderate Nonconformity. 1712. 8°. **4106**. cc. **4.**

—— *See* HOADLY (Benjamin) successively *Bishop of Bangor, of Hereford, etc.* A Serious Admonition to Mr. Calamy, occasion'd by the first part of his Defence of Moderate Nonconformity. 1703. 8°. **701**. f. **9**. (**1**.)

—— —— 1705. 8°. **1019**. d. **18**. (**2**.)

—— *See* OLLYFFE (John) A Second Defence of Ministerial Conformity to the Church of England: in answer to Mr. Calamy's objections against the first; in his pretended vindication of . . . his Abridgment of Mr. Baxter's Life and Times. 1705. 8°. **4139**. b. **100**. (**3**.)

—— *See* OLLYFFE (John) A Third Defence of Ministerial Conformity to the Church of England. In answer to Mr. Calamy's objections against the former, *etc.* 1706. 8°. **4139**. b. **100**. (**4**.)

—— A Letter [signed: A. L.] from a Congregational Minister in the Country, to Mr. Calamy: occasion'd by his late book, entitul'd, A Defence of Moderate Nonconformity. 1704. 8°. *See* L., A. **4106**. b. **69.**

—— A Discourse concerning the Rise and Antiquity of Cathedral Worship. In a letter to a friend. [Signed: N. N., i.e. E. Calamy.] pp. 36. 1699. 4°. *See* N., N. **698**. i. **2**. (**18**.)

—— Divine Mercy Exalted: or, Free grace in its glory. Being a sermon on Rom. IX. xvi. Preached at the Merchants Lecture at Salters-Hall, *etc.* pp. viii. 48. *Tho. Parkhurst: London*, 1703. 16°. **4256**. aa. **11.**

—— [Another copy.] **1416**. a. **24.**

—— A Funeral Sermon for the late Reverend Mr. John Mottershed, *etc.* pp. 43. *S. Billingsley: London*, 1729. 8°. **1417**. e. **44.**

—— A Funeral Sermon for the late Reverend Mr. John Sheffield, *etc.* pp. 45. *J. Clark & R. Hett; Samuel Chandler: London*, 1726. 8°. **1418**. g. **13.**

—— [Another copy.] **1418**. g. **14.**

—— [Another copy.] **225**. h. **18**. (**14**.)

—— [Another copy.] **225**. h. **20**. (**10**.)

—— A Funeral Sermon for the late Reverend Mr. Joseph Bennet, *etc.* pp. 47. *J. Clark & R. Hett; Samuel Chandrer* [sic] *: London*, 1726. 8°. **1416**. c. **60.**

—— [Another copy.] **4474**. cc. **117**. (**6**.)

—— A Funeral Sermon occasion'd by the decease of Mr. Michael Watts, *etc.* pp. 47. *T. Parkhurst, etc.: London*, 1708. 8°. **1417**. i. **24.**

—— [Another copy.] **1417**. i. **25.**

—— A Funeral Sermon, occasioned by the much lamented death of Mrs. Frances Lewis, *etc.* pp. 46. *T. Parkhurst, etc.: London*, 1708. 8°. **1417**. c. **9.**

—— [Another copy.] **1417**. c. **10.**

—— [Another copy.] **1417**. c. **8.**

—— A Funeral Sermon, occasion'd by the sudden death of the Reverend Mr. Matthew Sylvester, *etc.* pp. 46. *T. Parkhurst, etc.: London*, 1708. 8°. **1417**. h. **15.**

—— A Funeral Sermon, preach'd at the interment of Mr. Samuel Stephens, *etc.* pp. 31. *For Abraham Chandler: London*, 1694. 4°. **1419**. g. **35.**

—— A Funeral Sermon, preached on the occasion of the decease of . . . Mrs. Elizabeth Williams, *etc.* pp. 92. *For J. Lawrence: London*, 1698. 16°. **1419**. a. **38.**

—— [Another copy.] **1419**. a. **39.**

—— God's Concern for his Glory in the British Isles; and the Security of Christ's Church from the Gates of Hell: in three sermons at the Merchants Lecture in Salters-Hall. pp. 91. *John Clark: London*, 1715. 8°. **225**. e. **27.**

—— An Historical Account of My Own Life, with some reflections on the times I have lived in, 1671–1731 . . . Now first printed. Edited and illustrated with notes, historical and biographical, by John Towill Rutt. [With a portrait.] 2 vol. *H. Colburn & R. Bentley: London*, 1829. 8°. **490**. b. **3, 4.**

—— The History of Jonathan Brown, the Bargeman. (From Dr. Calamy's "Historical Account of his own Life and Times.") pp. 16. *Religious Tract Society: London* [c. 1820.] 12°. **4421**. c. **23**. (**52**.)

—— The History of Jonathan Brown, the Bargeman. [Extracted from E. Calamy's "An Historical Account of My Own Life," vol. 2.] pp. 16. *R.T.S.: London* [1830?] 12°. [*First Series Tracts.* no. 131.] **863**. k. **9**

—— [Another edition.] *See* CHRISTIAN HOUSEHOLD Favourite Narratives, *etc.* 1860. 8°. **4416**. f. **25**

—— The Inspiration of the Holy Writings of the Old and New Testament consider'd and improv'd. In fourteen sermons . . . [An answer to "Five Letters concerning the Inspiration of the Holy Scriptures" by J. Leclerc. To which is added, a single sermon in vindication of the Divine Institution of the Office of the Ministry, *etc* pp. 422. *T. Parkhurst: London*, 1710. 8°. **4016**. b. **13**

— A Letter to a Divine in Germany, giving a brief but true account of the Protestant Dissenters in England. *See* infra: The Principles and Practice of Moderate Nonconformists, *etc.*

— A Letter to Archdeacon Echard upon occasion of his History of England: wherein the true principles of the Revolution are defended, the Whigs and Dissenters vindicated . . . and a number of historical mistakes rectify'd. pp. 121. *John Clark: London,* 1718. 8°. **T. 1763. (13.)**

— [Another copy.] **B. 151. (5.)**

— [Another copy.] **117. b. 39.**

— [Another copy.] **195. c. 2.**

— [Another copy.] **G. 16897. (4.)**

— The third edition. pp. 100. *John Clark: London,* 1718. 8°. **598. d. 28.**

— [Another copy.] **E. 2012. (4.)**

— *See* ANONYMUS, *Londinensis.* A Letter to Dr. Calamy [in reply to his "Letter to Archdeacon Echard"], shewing that Mr. Archdeacon Echard has done the part of a faithful historian, in branding Mr. Edmund Calamy, the Doctor's grandfather, as a promoter of rebellion, *etc.* [1718?] 8°. **E. 2012. (5.)**

— *See* PHILALETHES, *pseud.* [i.e. Isaac Sharpe.] An Answer to Dr. Edmund Calamy's Letter to Mr. Archdeacon Echard, upon occasion of his History of England, *etc.* 1718. 8°. **8139. b. 26. (2.)**

— Memoirs of the Life of the late Rev[d] Mr. John Howe. pp. 268. *Sam. Chandler: London,* 1724. 8°. **1124. d. 6.**

— [Another copy.] **1416. i. 54.**

— [Another copy.] **202. b. 20.**

— [Another edition.] pp. 88. *See* HOWE (John) *of Magdalen College, Oxford.* The Works of . . . J. Howe, *etc.* vol. 1. 1724. fol. **L.5.h.5.**

— Life of the Rev. John Howe . . . Abridged. pp. 72. *R.T.S.: London,* [1832.] 12°. [*Christian Biography.*] **864. f. 11/26.**

— The Life of the Rev. J. Howe . . . Slightly abridged. 1839. *See* JACKSON (Thomas) *Wesleyan Minister.* A Library of Christian Biography, *etc.* vol. 11. 1837, *etc.* 12°. **1124. a. 4.**

— The Ministry of the Dissenters vindicated: in an ordination sermon preached at Ailsbury . . . June 11. 1724. pp. 38. *J. Clark & R. Hett: London,* 1724. 8°. **693. d. 8. (3.)**

— [Another edition.] To which is added, a Letter to the Author [i.e. Zachary Grey] of a Pamphlet, intitled, The Ministry of Dissenters proved to be null and void, from Scripture and Antiquity . . . The second edition. pp. 42. *J. Clark & R. Hett: London,* 1724. 8°. **4474. e. 13.**

— [Another edition of the "Letter."] *J. Clark & R. Hett: London,* 1724. 8°. **701. g. 19. (7.)**
Pp. 37–42 of the second edition of Calamy's "Ministry of the Dissenters vindicated," with a special titlepage prefixed.

— The Ministry of the Dissenters proved to be null and void, from Scripture and Antiquity. In answer to Dr. Calamy's sermon: entitled, The Ministry of the Dissenters vindicated, &c. . . . By a Presbyter of the Church of England [i.e. Zachary Grey]. (Appendix. [An answer to the "Letter" annexed to the second edition of Calamy's "Ministry of the Dissenters vindicated."]) 2 pt. MS. NOTES. *Tho. Warner: London,* 1725. 8°. **112. d. 46. (6.)**

— The Nonconformist's Memorial, *etc.* *See* supra: An Abridgment of Mr. Baxter's History, *etc.*

— Obadiah's Character. A sermon to young people, preach'd . . . December the 28th 1713. pp. 31. *Andrew Bell: London,* 1714. 8°. **4474. e. 11.**

— A Practical Discourse concerning Vows; with special reference to Baptism and the Lord's Supper. pp. 310. *Printed by Geo. Larkin Jun.; sold by John Lawrence: London,* 1697. 8°. **4323. c. 15.**

— [Another edition.] pp. 214. *Tho. Parkhurst: London,* 1704. 12°. **4327. b. 14.**

— The Principles and Practice of Moderate Nonconformists with respect to Ordination, exemplify'd: in a sermon preach'd at the ordination of Mr. John Munckley, January the 19th 1717, and a charge given to Mr. James Read . . . and Mr. S. Chandler . . . Dec. 19th 1716. To which is added, a Letter to a Divine in Germany giving a brief but true account of the Protestant Dissenters in England. pp. 48. *John Clark: London,* 1717. 8°. **T. 1805. (4.)**

— [Another copy.] **693. d. 8. (2.)**

— The second edition. pp. 48. *John Clark: London,* 1717. 8°. **4474. e. 12.**

— A Letter to a Divine in Germany, giving a brief, but true, account of the Protestant Dissenters in England. By E. Calamy, D.D. Reprinted from his sermon at the ordination of the Reverend Mr. Samuel Chandler. pp. 15. *Richard Hett: London,* 1736. 8°. **4106. c. 57.**

— [Another edition.] pp. 13. *See* ENGLAND.—*Church of England.* [*Appendix.*] Plain Reasons. I. For dissenting from the Communion of the Church of England, *etc.* 1736. 8°. **4136. b. 70. (1.)**

— The Prudence of the Serpent, and Innocence of the Dove. A sermon preach'd . . . May the 6th 1713. before a numerous assembly of the Dissenting Ministers of Devon and Cornwall, *etc.* pp. 32. *John Clark: London,* 1713. 8°. **4475. aaa. 19.**

— The Seasonableness of Religious Societies. A sermon preach'd . . . April the 23d, 1714. pp. 27. *J. & J. Marshall: London,* 1714. 8°. **4474. cc. 16.**

— A Sermon at the Merchants Lecture . . . Decemb. the 7th. 1708. Upon occasion of the many late bankrupts, *etc.* pp. 16. *T. Parkhurst, etc.: London,* 1709. 8°. **4476. aaa. 28.**

— A Sermon, preach'd before the Societies for Reformation of Manners in London and Middlesex. pp. 53. *For John Lawrence: London,* 1699. 12°. **4474. b. 15.**

— Sir Richard Bulkeley's Remarks on the Caveat against New Prophets [by E. Calamy] consider'd, in a letter to a friend. [Signed: E. C., i.e. E. Calamy. In reply to "An Answer to several Treatises lately publish'd on the subject of the Prophets" by Sir R. Bulkeley.] pp. 16. 1708. 8°. *See* C., E. **4105. bb. 32.**

CALAMY (Edmund) *D.D., Son of Edmund Calamy, M.A.*

—— Sobermindedness recommended: in a sermon preach'd . . . April the 22d. 1717, *etc.* pp. 30. *John Clark; John Marshall: London,* 1717. 8°. **4474.** cc. **17.**

—— Thirteen Sermons concerning the Doctrine of the Trinity. Preach'd at the Merchant's-Lecture . . . Together with a vindication of that celebrated text, 1 John v. 7. from being spurious; and an explication of it, upon the supposition of its being genuine: in four sermons, preach'd . . . An. 1719, 1720. [With a portrait.] pp. 559. *John Clark: London,* 1722. 8°. **226.** b. **24.**

—— Truth and Love. A discourse from Ephesians iv. 15 at the Merchants-Lecture . . . November 29. 1720. pp. 36. *John Clark: London,* 1720. 8°. **4474.** aaa. **10.**

CALAMY (Edmund) *Son of Edmund Calamy, D.D.* Disputatio theologica de veritate historiarum Novi Testamenti, *etc. Praes.* J. A. Marck. pp. 26. *Lugduni Batavorum,* 1720. 4°. T. **45*.** (**7.**)

CALAMY (Étienne) Quelques considérations générales sur le choléra dit asiatique; thèse, *etc.* pp. 16. *Paris,* 1833. 4°. **1184.** f. **2.** (**28.**)

CALAMY (James) *See* Calamy (Benjamin) Sermons, *etc.* [Edited by J. Calamy.] 1687. 8°. **1022.** a. **18.**

—— —— 1690. 8°. **4460.** aa. **5.**

—— —— 1738. 8°. **4455.** bb. **4.**

CALAN (Charles de la Lande de) *Viscount. See* La Lande de Calan.

CALAN (Charles Joseph de la Lande de) *Count. See* La Lande de Calan.

CALANCA. Beleuchtung der von zweien der Herren Deputirten einer obern Bundssession für die Ehrs. Räthe und Gemeinden eingereichten Einlage, welche sie zu datiren beliebten, "Ruschein den 22sten Juli 1796." [On the judicature in the valley of Mesocco. Dated: 23 Aug. 1796. Signed: Die Völker der 11 Gemeinden von Calanka und in deren Nahmen. Peter Demenga, Bevollmächtigter.] [*Coire,* 1796.] fol. **9304.** g. **8.** (**19.**)

—— [Another copy.] **S.P.31.(30.)**

—— *See* Toggenburg (C.) Sehr kurze Gegenbeleuchtung von Seiten derer in der Einlage vom 22sten Juli 1796. benannten Deputirten des obern grauen Bundes, gegen jene des Thals Calanca, *etc.* [1796.] fol. **9304.** g. **8.** (**20.**)

—— Memorial [dated: 3 Nov. 1795] presentau à sias sabienschas ils Signurs Caus dil Stand per part dils Deputai (Peter De Menga, Carl Vidua) dallas indisch vischneuncas della Vall Calanca. (Aulta Superioritat dils Ludeivels Cusseilgs, a Cummins, de Cumminas treis Ligias! [A petition, dated: 11 Mar. 1796, signed by P. Demenga on behalf of the inhabitants of the valley of Calanca.]—Aggionta tier il Memorial, *etc.*) [*Coire,* 1796.] fol. **9304.** g. **3.** (**4.**)

—— Einlage [dated: 3 Nov. 1795] an Ihre Weisheiten die Herren Standeshäupter von den Deputirten der Eilf Gemeinden, des Thals Calanca. (Hohe Oberherrlichkeit der Ehrs. Räthe, und Gemeinden gemeiner dreier Bünden! [Dated: 11 Mar. 1796.]—Nachtrag, *etc.*) [*Coire,* 1796.] fol. **9304.** g. **6.** (**9.**)

—— [Another copy.] **S.P.31.(18.19.)**

CALANCHA (Antonio de la) Coronica Moralizada del Orden de San Augustin en el Perù, con sucesos egenplares en esta monarquia, *etc.* [tom. 2 edited by Bernardo de Torres.] 2 tom. *P. Lacavalleria: Barcelona;* [*J. Lopez de Herrera: Lima,*] 1638, [53.] fol. **203.** f. **6.** & **493.** k. **11*.**

Imperfect; wanting the titlepage to tom. 2. *Tom.* 1 *has an additional titlepage, engraved. Tom.* 2, *published at Lima, contains six leaves of preliminary matter, sig.* b–d; *lib. I., ff.* 1–4, *pp.* 15–268; *editor's preface to lib. II., in one leaf; lib. II., pp.* 1–42 [48], *ending abruptly in the middle of cap. X.; lib. V., pp.* 1–92, *and a table in two leaves. No more published.*

—— [Another copy of tom. 1, with a different titlepage.] *Barcelona,* 1639. fol. **493.** k. **11.**

—— *See* Brulius (J.) Historiæ Peruanæ Ordinis Eremitarum S. P. Augustini libri octodecim, *etc.* [Based on the "Coronica Moralizada" of A. de la Calancha.] 1651. fol. **493.** i. **23.**

CALANCO. La Calanco. Recuei de literaturo prouvençalo. *See* Marseilles.—*Felibre de la Mar.*

CALAND (A.) *Leeraar aan de R.H.B.S. te Leeuwarden.*

—— *See* Cowan (Frederick M.) and Maatjes (A. B.) Leercursus ter beoefning der Engelsche taal. 1891, *etc.* 8°. **12981.** c. **45.**

CALAND (Abraham) Beschouwingen over den gezondheidstoestand van Nederland en bijzonder van Middelburg. pp. 42. vi. *Middelburg,* 1857. 8°. **7686.** d. **41.** (**4.**)

—— Eenige beschouwingen over eene Noordzeehaven voor Amsterdam en de afdamming van het IJ bij het Pampus. pp. xi. 70. *Middelburg,* 1863. 8°. **8775.** cc. **8.**

—— Iets over het algemeen reglement voor de polders der provincie Zeeland, hetwelk eerstdaags bij de provinciale staten op nieuw in behandeling komt. [A criticism of a pamphlet entitled "Beschouwingen over het ontwerp van een algemeen reglement voor de polders der provincie Zeeland."] pp. 20. *Middelburg,* 1859. 8°. **8776.** c. **41.** (**5.**)

—— Nader betoog hoe en door wien eene zeehaven te Scheveningen moet worden aangelegd, en belangrijkheid daarvan voor de ingezetenen van 's Gravenhage. pp. vi. 38. *Middelburg,* 1862. 8°. **8806.** ee. **29.** (**3.**)

—— Nadere beschouwingen over het herstel en de verbetering der Middelburgsche haven. pp. 35. *Middelburg,* 1858. 8°. **8776.** c. **41.** (**4.**)

—— Nog een woord over eene Noordzeehaven van Amsterdam, in verband beschouwd met de toekomst van die stad. pp. 20. *Middelburg,* 1868. 8°. **8245.** dd. **26.** (**4.**)

—— Ontwerp voor een open vaarwater van Amsterdam naar de Noordzee, met de vereischten waaraan het moet voldoen en de voordeelen aan hetzelve verbonden. [With a map.] pp. 32. *Middelburg,* 1868. 8°. **8775.** bb. **50.** (**7.**)

—— Open brief aan den Heer Mr. K. Wagtho, betrekkelijk zijne verdediging van het onlangs ontworpen polderreglement van Zeeland [entitled "Overzigt der handelingen van de provinciale staten van Zeeland, betreffende der calamiteuse polders"]. pp. 40. *Middelburg,* 1857. 8°. **8775.** c. **71.** (**3.**)

—— Verhandeling over het nut der afgezaagde palen-hoofden, en de beste wijze van verdediging der Zeeuwsche Stranden. pp. 107. 1821. *See* Flushing.—*Zeeuwsch Genootschap der Wetenschappen, etc.* Nieuwe verhandelingen, *etc.* dl. 3. 1807, *etc.* 8°. **964.** h. **12.**

—— Vrije beoordeeling van het ontwerp-reglement van administratie der polders in Zeeland. pp. 157. *Middelburg,* 1856. 8°. **8776.** d. **6.**

CALAND (Frederik) *See* Geluk (A.) Beschrijving der stad Reimerswaal . . . bewerkt door F. Caland. 1877. 8°. **10271**. ff. **5**.

—— *See* Periodical Publications.—*Rotterdam*. Annuaire de la noblesse et des familles patriciennes des Pays-Bas. Publié avec la coöpération de MM. F. Caland, A. Fahre, *etc*. 1871. 8°. P.P. **3884**.

CALAND (Gulielmus) *See* Caland (Willem)

CALAND (Pieter) *See* Bruinings (C.) and Caland (P.) Memorie over den toestand van den . . . waterstaat der provincie Friesland. 1871. 8°. **8775**. eee. **27**. (**5**.)

—— Amélioration de la Barre de Rio Grande do Sul. Rapport présenté au Gouvernement brésilien . . . 1885. 1897. *See* Costa Couto (A. J. da) Quarto Relatorio. Melhoramentos da Barra do Rio Grande do Sul, *etc*. pt. 3. 1898, *etc*. 8°. L.A.S. **165/10**.

CALAND (Willem) *See* Āpastamba. Das Śrautasūtra . . . Übersetzt von Dr. W. Caland . . . 1.–7. Buch. 1921. 8°. [*Quellen der Religionsgeschichte*. Gruppe 7. Bd. 8.] Ac. **670**. c.

—— *See* Āpastamba. Das Śrautasūtra des Āpastamba, achtes bis fünfzehntes [*etc*.] Buch aus dem Sanskrit übersetzt von W. Caland. 1924, *etc*. 8°. [*Verhandelingen der Koninklijke Akademie van Wetenschappen te Amsterdam*. Afd. Letterkunde. Nieuwe reeks. dl. 24. no. 2 ; dl. 26. no. 4.] Ac. **944/3**.

—— *See* Brāhmaṇas.—*Pañchaviṃṣabrāhmaṇa*. Pañcaviṃśabrāhmaṇa . . . Translated by Dr. W. Caland. [With a portrait.] 1931. 8°. [*Bibliotheca Indica*. vol. 252.] **14002**. a.

—— *See* Brāhmaṇas.—*Talavakārabrāhmaṇa*. Das Jaiminiya-Brāhmana in Auswahl. Text, Übersetzung, Indices von W. Caland. 1919. 8°. [*Verhandelingen der Koninklijke Akademie van Wetenschappen te Amsterdam*. Afd. Letterkunde. Nieuwe reeks. dl. 19. no. 4.] Ac. **944/3**.

—— *See* Buddhaghosa. [Manoratha-pūraṇī.] Boeddhistische verhalen. Uit het Pāli vertaald door Dr. W. Caland. 1923. 8°. **14098**. a. **56**.

—— *See* Coromandel, *Coast of*. Twee oude Fransche verhandelingen over het Hindoeïsme. Uitgegeven en toegelicht door W. Caland. 1923. 8°. [*Verhandelingen der Koninklijke Akademie van Wetenschappen te Amsterdam*. Afd. Letterkunde. Nieuwe reeks. dl. 23. no. 3.] Ac. **944/3**.

—— *See* Jaimini. De Literatuur van den Samaveda en het Jaiminigṛhyasūtra, door W. Caland. 1905. 8°. [*Verhandelingen der Koninklijke Akademie van Wetenschappen de Amsterdam*. Afd. Letterkunde. Nieuwe reeks. dl. 6. no. 2.] Ac. **944/3**.

—— *See* Jongh (W. G. de) De Remonstrantie van W. Geleynssen de Jongh. Uitgegeven door Prof. Dr. W. Caland, *etc*. 1929. 8°. [*Werken uitgegeven door de Linschoten-Vereeniging*. vol. 31.] Ac. **6095**.

—— *See* Kauṣika. Altindisches Zauberritual. Probe einer Uebersetzung der wichtigsten Theile des Kauśika Sūtra. Von Dr. W. Caland. 1900. 4°. [*Verhandelingen der Koninklijke Akademie van Wetenschappen te Amsterdam*. Afd. Letterkunde. Nieuwe reeks. dl. 3. no. 2.] Ac. **944/3**.

—— *See* Maṣaka. Der Ārṣeyakalpa des Sāmaveda. Herausgegeben und bearbeitet von W. Caland. 1908. 8°. [*Abhandlungen für die Kunde des Morgenlandes*. Bd. 12. no. 3.] **753**. f. **20**.

CALAND (Willem)

—— *See* Rāmakṛishṇa, *son of Devajī*. Een Onbekend Indisch tooneelstuk (Gopālakelicandrikā). Tekst met inleiding door W. Caland. 1917. 8°. [*Verhandelingen der Koninklijke Akademie van Wetenschappen te Amsterdam*. Afd. Letterkunde. Nieuwe reeks. dl. 17. no. 3.] Ac. **944/3**.

—— *See* Roger (Abraham) De Open-deure tot het verborgen heydendom . . . Uitgegeven door W. Caland. 1915. 8°. [*Werken uitgegeven door de Linschoten-Vereeniging*. no. 10.] Ac. **6095**.

—— *See* Vaitāna-sūtra. Das Vaitānasūtra des Atharvaveda, übersetzt von W. Caland. 1910. 8°. [*Verhandelingen der Koninklijke Akademie van Wetenschappen te Amsterdam*. Afd. Letterkunde. Nieuwe reeks. dl. 11. no. 2.] Ac. **944/3**.

—— *See* Vikhanas. Vaikhánasasmārtasūtram . . . Translated by Dr. W. Caland. 1929. 8°. [*Bibliotheca Indica*. vol. 249.] **14002**. a.

—— *See* Ziegenbalg (B.) B. Ziegenbalg's kleinere Schriften. Herausgegeben von W. Caland. 1930. 8°. [*Verhandelingen der Koninklijke Akademie van Wetenschappen*. Afd. Letterkunde. Nieuwe reeks. dl. 29. no. 2.] Ac. **944/3**.

—— *See* Ziegenbalg (B.) Ziegenbalg's Malabarisches Heidenthum. Herausgegeben . . . von W. Caland. 1926. 8°. [*Verhandelingen der Koninklijke Akademie van Wetenschappen*. Afd. Letterkunde. Nieuwe reeks. dl. 25. no. 3.] Ac. **944/3**.

—— Altindische Zauberei. Darstellung der altindischen " Wunschopfer." pp. xiv. 143. *Amsterdam*, 1908. 8°. [*Verhandelingen der Koninklijke Akademie van Wetenschappen*. Afd. Letterkunde. Nieuwe reeks. dl. 10. no. 1.] Ac. **944/3**.

—— Die altindischen Todten- und Bestattungsgebräuche. Mit Benützung handschriftlicher Quellen dargestellt von Dr. W. Caland. pp. xiv. 191. *Amsterdam*, 1896. 8°. [*Verhandelingen der Koninklijke Akademie van Wetenschappen*. Afd. Letterkunde. Nieuwe reeks. dl. 1. no. 6.] Ac. **944/3**.

—— Altindischer Ahnencult. Das Çrāddha nach den verschiedenen Schulen mit Benutzung handschriftlicher Quellen dargestellt. pp. xii. 266. *Leiden*, 1893. 8°. **4503**. ee. **29**.

—— De nummis M. Antonii IIIviri vitam et res gestas illustrantibus commentatio. Specimen litterarium inaugurale, *etc*. pp. 83. *Lugduni-Batavorum*, 1883. 8°. Dept. of Coins & Medals.

—— Drie oude Portugeesche verhandelingen over het Hindoeïsme. Toegelicht en vertaald door W. Caland en A. A. Fokker. [Comprising " Breve Relação das Escrituras dos Gentios da India Oriental " and " Noticia Summaria do Gentilismo da Asia " translated by A. A. Fokker, and " Over der Oost Indianen goden en godheden " translated by A. Moubach from a French version of a Portuguese original. Edited by W. Caland.] pp. viii. 216. *Amsterdam*, 1915. 8°. [*Verhandelingen der Koninklijke Akademie van Wetenschappen*. Afd. Letterkunde. Nieuwe reeks. dl. 16. no. 2.] Ac. **944/3**.

—— On the Sacred Books of the Vaikhānasas. *Amsterdam*, 1928. 8°. [*Mededeelingen der Koninklijke Akademie van Wetenschappen*. Afd. Letterkunde. dl. 65. ser. A. no. 7.] Ac. **944**.

—— Over het Vaikhānasasūtra. *Amsterdam*, 1926. 8°. [*Mededeelingen der Koninklijke Akademie van Wetenschappen*. Afd. Letterkunde. dl. 61. ser. A. no. 8.] Ac. **944**.

CALAND (WILLEM)

—— Over Ziegenbalg's Malabarisches Heidenthum. pp. 17. *Amsterdam*, 1924. 8°. [*Mededeelingen der Koninklijke Akademie van Wetenschappen*. Afd. Letterkunde. dl. 57. ser. A. no. 4.] Ac. **944**.

—— Über das rituelle Sūtra des Baudhāyana. pp. viii. 65. *Leipzig*, 1903. 8°. [*Abhandlungen für die Kunde des Morgenlandes*, etc. Bd. 12. no. 1.] **753**. f. **20**.

—— Ueber Totenverehrung bei einigen der indo-germanischen Völker. pp. 80. *Amsterdam*, 1888. 4°. [*Verhandelingen der Koninklijke Akademie van Wetenschappen*. Afd. Letterkunde. dl. 17.] Ac. **944/3**.

—— Zur Syntax der Pronomina im Avesta. pp. 66. iv. *Amsterdam*, 1891. 4°. [*Verhandelingen der Koninklijke Akademie van Wetenschappen*. Afd. Letterkunde. dl. 20.] Ac. **944/3**.

CALAND (WILLEM) and **HENRY** (VICTOR)

—— L'Agniṣṭoma. Description complète de la forme normale du sacrifice de soma dans le culte védique, etc. 2 tom. pp. lvii. xv. 520. pl. IV. *Paris*, 1906, 07. 8°. **4506**. f. **27**.

CALANDER (PHILIPPUS) *See* CALANDRI (Filippo)

CALANDRA (CLAUDIO) Di una questione di acque in relazione alla condotta di Torino. Memoria. pp. 51. *Torino*, 1880. 8°. **8768**. l. **2**. (5.)

—— Olaszország vizjogi törvényei. C. Calandra . . . összeállitása után forditotta és előszóval ellátta György Endre. pp. 246. *Budapest*, 1877. 8°. [*Közmunkaés Közlekedési Magyar Királyi Ministerium kiadmányai*. füz. 12.] S.455.

CALANDRA (EDOARDO) *See* MASCHERPA (M.) Edoardo Calandra, *etc.* [With a portrait and a bibliography.] 1933. 8°. **10633**. s. 20.

—— A guerra aperta. La signora di Riondino, 1690. La marchesa Falconis, 1705–1706. pp. 335. *Roma, Torino*, 1906. 8°. **12471**. t. 35.

—— La Bell'Alda. Leggenda. pp. 119. *Tornio*, 1884. 8°. **12470**. ff. **16**.

—— La Falce. Punizione, l'enigma. [Tales.] pp. 271. *Torino, Roma*, 1902. 8°. **12471**. s. 20.

—— Juliette. Romanzo. pp. 278. *Torino*, 1909. 8°. **12471**. r. **10**.

—— La Straniera. Novelle e teatro. [With a life of the author by Dino Mantovani.] pp. 264. *Torino*, 1914. 8°. **12470**. p. **9**.

—— Vecchio Piemonte, *etc.* [Tales.] pp. 204. *Torino*, 1895. 8°. **10136**. bbb. **32**.

CALANDRA (SILVIO) Rime. *See* BORGOGNI (G.) Rime di diuersi illust: poeti, *etc.* 1599. 12°. **1070**. a. **18**. (3.)

CALANDRELLI (GIUSEPPE) Opuscoli astronomici, e fisici di Giuseppe Calandrelli, e Andrea Conti (e Giacomo Ricchebach). 8 tom. *Roma*, 1803–24. 4°. **533**. h. **17–21**.

Tom. 5 *is entitled* "*Tavole delle parallassi di altezza di longitudine e di latitudine.*"

—— Ragionamento sopra il conduttore elettrico Quirinale, *etc.* pp. xxxvi. *Roma*, 1789. 8°. **8755**. bbb. **42**.

CALANDRELLI (IGNAZIO) Elementi di algebra e geometria (di trigonometria), *etc.* 3 tom. *Roma*, 1836, 37. 8°. **716**. e. **17**.

CALANDRELLI (IGNAZIO)

—— Osservazioni e calcolo delle orbite delle due prime comete telescopiche dell'anno 1857 ed esame delle diverse opinioni sulla fisica costituzione di questi astri . . . Estratta dagli Annali di scienze matematiche e fisiche, *etc.* pp. 42. *Roma*, 1857. 8°. **899**. e. **12**. (**1**).

—— Prelezioni all'algebra, ovvero Lezioni sul sistema ordinario di numerazione, *etc.* pp. 45. *Roma*, 1837. 8°. **716**. c. **4**. (2.)

—— Sulla gran cometa apparsa nel marzo dell'anno 1843. Memoria, *etc.* pp. 79. *Roma*, 1844. 4°. **898**. i. **3**. (1.)

CALANDRELLI (MATÍAS) *See* LOPEZ (V. F.) Introduccion al diccionario filológico-comparado de la lengua castellana de M. Calandrelli, *etc.* 1880. 8°. **12943**. b. **37**.

—— *See* NAVARRO VIOLA (A.) Juicio crítico del diccionario filológico-comparado de la lengua castellana. [A comparison of the dictionary of M. Calandrelli with that of R. Barcia.] 1884. 8°. **12901**. b. **47**. (2.)

—— Gramática Comparada de las Lenguas Latina y Griega, con arreglo al método filológico . . . Fonología. pp. 28. *Buenos Aires*, 1875. 8°. **12933**. dd. **4**. (**10**.)
No more published.

—— Gramática Filológica de la Lengua Latina segun el método de Bopp . . . Primera y segunda parte. Fonologia—Morfologia—Derivacion y composicion de las palabras. pp. xxiii. 149. *Buenos Aires*, 1873. 8°. **12934**. bbb. **17**.

No more published.

—— Lecciones de Historia correspondientes al programa de primer año. pp. 104. *Buenos Aires*, 1872. 8°. **9004**. i. **2**.

CALANDRI (ANTONIO) L'Italia ed i sommi letterati del nostro secolo. In morte di Gino Capponi, pensieri. pp. 22. *Pontremoli*, 1876. 8°. **11825**. i. **19**. (**12**.)

CALANDRI (FILIPPO) *Begin.* [fol. 2 *recto*:] Philipp Calandri ad nobilem et studiosuꝫ Iulianum Laurentii Medicẽ de arimethrica [*sic*] opusculũ. [With woodcuts.] *Ital.* G. L. *per Lorenzo de Morgiani et Giouanni Thedesco da Maganza: Firenze*, a di primo di Gẽnaio, 1491. 8°. G. **2317**.
104 *leaves. Sig.* a⁴ b–i⁸ l–o⁸ p⁴. 26 *lines to a page. The verso of fol.* 1 *bears a woodcut headed* "*Pictagoras arithmetrice introductor.*"

—— [Another edition.] Pictagoras Arithmetrice introductor. [fol. 2 *recto*:] Philippi Calandri . . . de Arimethrica [*sic*] opusculum. [With woodcuts.] *per B. Zucchecta: Firẽze*, 1518. 8°. C. **54**. aa. **5**.

CALANDRI (FRANCESCO) *See* RININO (M.) Francesco Calandri C. R. S. Note biografiche. 1883. 8°. **10629**. bb. **40**.

CALANDRI (PIETRO MARIA) Petri Mariae Calandri Compendium de agrorum corporumque dimensione. *See* SODERINI (G. V.) Le Opere di G. V. Soderini, *etc.* vol. 1. 1902, *etc.* 8°. **12225**. k. **5**.

CALANDRINI ( ) *of the Geneva Ordnance. See* WATSON (*Sir* William) *M.D.* Observations upon the Effects of Lightning . . . being answers to certain questions proposed by M. Calandrini, *etc.* 1764. 4°. **440**. g. **17**.

CALANDRINI (FILIPPO) Relazione sopra la pubblica mostra di frutti e di fiori avvenuta nel settembre 1858, *etc.* (Parole del Presidente.) pp. 16. [1858.] 8°. *See* FLORENCE.—*Imperiale e Reale Società Toscana d'Orticoltura.* **7075**. cc. **53**. (5.)

CALANDRINO (IGNAZIO)

—— G. A. Cesareo. Saggio critico. [With a portrait.] pp. 290. *Mazara*, 1948. 8°. **11861**. a. **15**.

CALANDRINUS (BENEDICTUS) *See* TURRETINUS (F.) Francisci Turrettini . . . De satisfactione Christi disputationes, *etc.* (Disputatio octava. Quæ sexta est de satisfactionis Christi veritate. *Resp.* B. Calandrinus.) 1666. 4°. **860**. l. **19**.

CALANDRINUS (CAESAR) *See* RUYTINCK (S.) Gheschiedenissen ende handelingen die voornemelick aengaen de Nederduytsche natie ende gemeynten, wonende in Engelant . . . vergadert door S. Ruytinck, C. Calandrinus, *etc.* 1873. 8°. [*Werken der Marnix-Vereeniging.* ser. 3. dl. 1.] Ac. **2043**.

CALANDRINUS (PHILIPPUS) Epithalamium in nuptias præstantissimi viri domini Philippi Calandrini sponsi & lectissimæ virginis Margaritæ Van der Meulen sponsæ. [Signed: Non ut voluit, sed ut valuit. P. C. F. Sursum.] (Epithalamium, *etc.*) [Signed: Ho. C. F. Sursum.] [1610?] 4°. **11408**. f. **59**. (**1**.)

CALANDRIUS (STEPHANUS) Breuissima chirurgicæ facultatis compendiaria, *etc.* pp. 130. *Apud C. Strabellam: Sauiliani*, 1623. 12°. **782**. b. **23**. (**4**.)

CALANDRO (FILENIO) Vna Lettera da l'ultimo di Giugno, la qual narra, l'apparecchio d'vna noua armata, & altre prouisioni, qual fa il Serenissimo Rè Catholico, per andare alla ruina del Turco . . . Et narra di alcune scaramuzze fatte tra Christiani e Turchi, *etc.* *Per P. Bonardo: [Bologna*, 1560.] 4°. **1312**. b. **33**.

—— Lettera Notabile, doue narra tutte le battaglie seguite tra Christiani, & Turchi sotto il forte delle Gerbe; et narra . . . il conflitto dell'armata Christiana, *etc.* *Per P. Bonardo: [Bologna*, 1560.] 4°. **1312**. b. **32**.

CALANDRUCCI (GIACINTO) Breve relazione del famosissimo quadrone della gloriosa S. Rosalia . . . da esporsi à 7 di Novembre del 1703. alla publica divozione . . . dipinto in Roma . . . del Signor G. Calandrucci. [By G. V. Auria?] pp. 7. [*Palermo?* 1703?] 4°. **12225**. b. **5**. (**9**.)

CALANI (AMELIA CARLETTI) *See* CARLETTI CALANI.

CALANI (ARISTIDE) Scène dell'insurrezione indiana descritte dal cavaliere A. Calani. pp. 951. *Milano, Verona*, 1858. 8°. **09057**. b. **11**.

CALANIUS (PROSPER) Prosperi Calani . . . Paraphrasis in librum Galeni de inæquali intemperie. Huic alia quædam, eodem autore . . . subiecimus. pp. 287. *Apud S. Gryphium: Lugduni*, 1538. 8°. **540**. d. **16**.

CALANO (PHILARETUS) *pseud.* Epistola quæ vere exponit obitum Adriani Turnebi . . . Adiecta sunt nonnulla epitaphia . . . ab amicis . . . conscripta. *Parisiis*, 1565. 4°. **837**. h. **13**. (**1**.)

CALANQUE. La Calanque. Recueil de littérature provençale. *See* MARSEILLES.—*Felibre de la Mar.* La Calanco, *etc.*

CALANSO (GUIRAUT DE) *See* GUIRAUT, *de Calanso.*

CALANUS (JUVENCUS CAELIUS) *Bishop of Fünfkirchen.* Attilae vita per Iuuencum Celium Calanum Dalmatam edita. *See* PLUTARCH. [*Vitae Parallelae.—Latin.*] Plutarchi Vitæ, *etc.* 1502. fol. **10607**. k. **2**.

—— Tertium recusus, recognitus, et notis vberrimis illustratus. 1735. *See* BEL (M.) Adparatus ad historiam Hungariæ, *etc.* Decas 1. Monumentum 3. 1735, *etc.* fol. **149**. f. **14**.

CALANUS (MAURITIUS) Mauritii Calani . . . Exercitationum libri primi pars prima de proprietatibus individualibus, *etc.* pp. 132. *Apud I. Gironum: Ferrariæ*, 1645. 4°. **1172**. f. **6**. (**1**.)

CALAORRA (GIOVANNI DI) *See* JUAN, *de Calahorra, Franciscan.*

CALAR (GABRIEL DE AIROLO) *See* AIROLO CALAR.

CALARD (TH. F.) De l'application pratique et de la fabrication des feuilles métalliques perforées. Historique de la première fabrication créée en France par M. T. F. Calard . . . Rapports de sociétés savantes, *etc.* pp. 64. *Paris*, 1862. 8°. **8766**. ee. **39**. (**1**.)

CALARIS. *See* CAGLIARI.

CALART (JEAN BAPTISTE) *See* POSTEL (N.) Factum pour Maistre Nicolas Postel . . . contre, Maistres Mathieu Maheult, Iean-Baptiste Calart, *etc.* 1685. 12°. **1172**. a. **6**. (**2**.)

CALART (MELCHIOR) *See* CALARTUS.

CALARTUS (MELCHIOR) *See* EBERTUS (T.) M. Theodori Eberti . . . Manuductionis aphoristicæ . . . sectiones sedecim. (Sectio undecima in qua continetur Oeconomica, *etc.* *Resp.* M. Calartus.) [1620.] 4°. **819**. f. **6**.

CALARY (B. J. ADRIEN) Thèse pour le doctorat en médecine, *etc.* (Questions sur diverses branches des sciences médicales.) pp. 30. *Paris*, 1843. 4°. [*Collection des thèses soutenues à la Faculté de Médecine de Paris.* An 1843. tom. 3.] **7371**. d. **13**.

CALARY (ÉMILE) Des fièvres larvées intermittentes. pp. 39. *Paris*, 1873. 4°. [*Collection des thèses soutenues à la Faculté de Médecine de Paris.* An 1873. tom. 4.] **7373**. o.

CALARY (JEAN BAPTISTE) Essai sur les pertes utérines hors l'état de grossesse, *etc.* pp. 19. *Paris*, 1817. 4°. **1183**. d. **10**. (**2**.)

CALARY DE LAMAZIÈRE (R.) Les Capitulations en Bulgarie. pp. 234. *Paris*, 1905. 8°. **8027**. i. **22**.

CALAS, *Family of.* *See* PHILOSOPHE. Le Philosophe ignorant. Avec un avis au public sur les parricides imputés aux Calas & aux Sirven. 1766. 8°. **1390**. h. **60**.

—— *See* VOL . . . . ., *M. de.* Lettre de M. de Vol . . . . . à M. d'Am . . . Sur deux événemens tragiques . . . dans la persécution des deux familles de Calas et de Sirven, *etc.* 1765. 8°. **611**. b. **15**. (**3**.)

CALAS (ADOLPHE) Considérations sur le traitement des ophthalmies. Thèse, *etc.* pp. 48. *Montpellier*, 1854. 4°. **7379**. c. **7**. (**7**.)

CALAS (ALEXANDRE) Auguste Comte médecin. Thèse, *etc.* pp. 91. *Paris*, 1889. 4°. **7680**. e. **3**.

CALAS (ALEXANDRE DU VOISIN) *See* DU VOISIN-CALAS.

CALAS (ANNE ROSE) *See* ÉLIE DE BEAUMONT (J. B. J.) Mémoire à consulter et consultation pour la dame A. R. Cabibel, veuve Calas, *etc.* 1762. 4°. **503**. e. **21**. (**13**.)

—— *See* ÉLIE DE BEAUMONT (J. B. J.) Mémoire pour Dame Anne-Rose Cabebel, veuve Calas, et pour ses enfans, *etc.* 1765. 4°. **503**. e. **21**. (**15**.)

—— *See* VIGUIÈRE (J.) Déclaration juridique de la servante de Madame Calas au sujet de la . . . calomnie qui persécute encore cette . . . famille. 1767. 8°. **831**. d. **25**. (**7**.)

CALAS (Donat) Mémoire de Donat Calas pour son père, *etc.* (Lettre de Donat Calas, fils, à la veuve dame Calas, sa mère.) *See* Voltaire (F. M. A. de) [*Miscellaneous Pieces.*] Histoire d'Elizabeth Canning et de Jean Calas, *etc.* 1762. 8°. **E. 2221.** (3.)

—— Lettre de Donat Calas, fils, à la veuve dame Calas, *etc.* (Mémoire de Donat Calas pour son père, *etc.*) *Fr. & Eng.* *See* Voltaire (F. M. A. de) [*Miscellaneous Pieces.*] Original Pieces relative to the Trial and Execution of Mr John Calas, *etc.* 1762. 8°. **5423.** bbb. **6.**

—— The Memorial of Mr. Donatus Calas . . . concerning the execution of his father, Mr. John Calas . . . with remarks by M. de Voltaire. [Translated by John Lockman.] pp. 14. *See* Lockman (John) A History of the Cruel Sufferings of the Protestants, *etc.* 1763. 12°. **490.** a. **35.**

CALAS (H. M.) Les Petits poèmes de l'enfance. pp. 216. *Paris,* 1866. 12°. **11482.** ccc. **20.**

—— Les Petits poèmes de l'enfance et de l'adolescence . . . 2e édition considérablement augmentée. pp. 364. *Paris,* 1869. 12°. **11482.** bb. **9.**

—— Simple histoire de Jésus d'après les Évangiles. pp. 207. *Paris,* 1864. 12°. **4824.** bb. **19.**

CALAS (Jean) *See* Allier (R. S. P.) Voltaire et Calas, *etc.* 1898. 8°. **05402.** eee. **16.**

—— *See* Bezard (F. S.) Convention nationale. Rapport et projet de décret sur la proposition d'indemniser les enfans de Jean Calas, de la ruine que son procès leur a occasionnée, *etc.* [1794?] 8°. **F. 1242.** (12.)

—— *See* Calas (D.) The Memorial of Mr. Donatus Calas . . . concerning the execution of his father, Mr. John Calas, *etc.* 1763. 12°. **490.** a. **35.**

—— *See* Chassaigne (M.) [L'Affaire Calas.] The Calas Case, *etc.* [With a portrait.] [1930.] 8°. **5408.** aaa. **15.**

—— *See* Coquerel (A. J.) Jean Calas et sa famille, *etc.* 1858. 12°. **4866.** b. **14.**

—— —— 1869. 8°. **4867.** e. **25.**

—— *See* Labat (L.) Le Drame de la rue des Filatiers, 1761. Jean Calas. Son procès, *etc.* 1910. 8°. **06005.** e. **55.** (2.)

—— *See* Laya (J. L.) Jean Calas, tragédie en cinq actes . . . précédée d'une préface historique sur J. Calas, *etc.* 1791. 8°. **640.** g. **20.** (4.)

—— *See* Mangold (W. J.) Jean Calas und Voltaire, *etc.* 1861. 8°. **4865.** bb. **50.** (2.)

—— *See* Maugham (Frederic H.) Viscount *Maugham.* The Case of Jean Calas. 1928. 8°. **5423.** de. **21.**

—— *See* Salvan (A.) Histoire du procès de Jean Calas, *etc.* 1863. 8°. **5425.** aa. **44.**

—— *See* Traité. Traité sur la tolérance (à l'occasion de la mort de Jean Calas). 1763. 8°. **1248.** d. **1.**

—— *See* Voltaire (F. M. A. de) [*Traité sur la Tolérance.*] Traité sur la tolérance à l'occasion de la mort de Jean Calas. 1901. 16°. **4372.** aa. **25.**

—— *See* Voltaire (F. M. A. de) [*Traité sur la Tolérance.*] A Treatise on Religious Toleration. Occasioned by the execution of . . . John Calas, *etc.* 1764. 8°. **4378.** cc. **5.**

—— —— 1765. 12°. **4372.** aaa. **45.**

—— —— 1820. 12°. **4377.** aaa. **8.**

CALAS (Jean)

—— *See* Voltaire (F. M. A. de) [*Traité sur la Tolérance.*] Histoire abrégée de la mort de Jean Calas, *etc.* 1791. 8°. [*Lemaire d'Argy* (*A. J.*) *Calas, ou le Fanatisme.*] **640.** g. **20.** (5.)

—— *See* Voltaire (F. M. A. de) [*Miscellaneous Pieces.*] Histoire d'Elizabeth Canning et de Jean Calas. 1762. 8°. **E. 2221.** (3.)

—— *See* Voltaire (F. M. A. de) [*Miscellaneous Pieces.*] Original Pieces relative to the Trial and Execution of Mr John Calas, *etc.* 1762. 8°. **5423.** bbb. **6.**

—— *See* Wege (B.) Der Prozess Calas im Briefwechsel Voltaires. 1896, *etc.* 4°. **5402.** i. **2.**

—— Calas, sur l'échafaud, à ses juges. [In verse.] pp. 7. 1765. 8°. **11475.** df. **34.** (4.)

—— The History of the Misfortunes of John Calas, a victim to fanaticism. To which is added a letter [in verse] from M. Calas to his wife and children; written by M. de Voltaire [or rather by A. M. H. Blin de Sainmore]. pp. 33. 8. *T. Sherlock: London,* 1772. 8°. **1415.** e. **8.**

—— [Another copy of the second part: Lettre de Jean Calas.] **11474.** b. **22.**

—— [Another edition.] pp. 48. *P. Williamson: Edinburgh,* 1776. 8°. **1414.** f. **43.** (1.)

CALAS (Jean Joseph Marie) De l'abus dans les alimens et dans les boissons, considéré comme cause des maladies, *etc.* [A thesis.] pp. 23. *Montpellier,* 1808. 4°. **1180.** f. **12.** (24.)

CALAS (Jules) Le Massacre de Vassy. pp. 32. *Rouillac,* 1888. 8°. **9004.** c. **13.** (2.)

—— La Révocation de l'édit de Nantes. Conférence, *etc.* pp. 61. *Paris,* 1886. 8°. Ac. **2015/8.** (3.)

CALAS (M. D.) *See* Teule (A. E. de) Annales du prieuré de Notre-Dame de Prouille, *etc.* [With a biographical sketch of the author by M. D. Calas.] 1902. 8°. Ac. **262/3.**

CALAS (Nicolas)

—— *See* Mead (Margaret) and Calas (N.) Primitive Heritage, *etc.* 1954. 8°. **10010.** bb. **18.**

—— Foyers d'incendie. [A philosophical essay.] pp. 261. *Paris,* 1938. 8°. **8471.** f. **2.**

CALAS (Nicolas Claude Fabry de) *See* Fabri de Peiresc.

CALAS (Pierre) Déclaration de Pierre Calas. *See* Voltaire (F. M. A. de) [*Miscellaneous Pieces.*] Histoire d'Elizabeth Canning et de Jean Calas, *etc.* 1762. 8°. **E. 2221.** (3.)

—— Déclaration de Pierre Calas. (The Declaration of Peter Calas.) *Fr. & Eng.* *See* Voltaire (F. M. A. de) [*Miscellaneous Pieces.*] Original Pieces relative to the Trial and Execution of Mr John Calas, *etc.* 1762. 8°. **5423.** bbb. **6.**

CALASANCTIUS, *Capuchin* [Jos. Joosen].

—— De Beeldspraak bij den heiligen Basilius den Grote. Met een inleiding over de opvattingen van de Griekse en Romeinse rhetoren aangaande beeldspraak. pp. 331. *Nijmegen, Utrecht,* 1941. 8°. [*Studia graeca Noviomagensia.* fasc. 2.] W.P. **14415/2.**

CALASANCTIUS (Josephus) *Saint.* *See* Joseph [Calasanzio], *Saint.*

CALASANS (José)

—— Cachaça, moça branca. Um estudo de folclore. pp. 112. *Bahia*, 1951. 8°. [*Publicações do Museu do Estado da Bahia.* no. 13.] W.P. **2885/13.**

CALASANS (Pedro de) Uma Scena de Nossos Dias. pp. vi. 95. *Leipzig*, 1864. 8°. **11726.** aaa. **55.** (**5.**)

—— Wiesbade. Aquarella. [Verses.] pp. vi. 64. *Leipzig*, 1864. 8°. **11452.** bb. **13.**

CALASANZ DE LLEVANERAS (José) Biografía Hispano-Capuchina . . . Memorias históricas recopiladas . . . por F. C. de Ll. Cap. [i.e. J. Calasanz de Llevaneras.] cuad. 1–3. 1891–93. 8°. *See* Ll., F. C. de, *Cap.* **4865.** i. **5.**

CALASANZIO (Giuseppe) *Saint. See* Joseph [Calasanzio], *Saint.*

CALASANZ-LICHTNEGEL (Josef) Sistematische Darstellung der Grundsätze im neuen österreichischen Civil-Cassa-, Rechnungs- und Controlswesen. Nebst einem Anhange, enthaltend: eine kurze theoretisch-practische Anleitung über die Conto-corrente-Buchführung, *etc.* pp. xii. 244. *Wien*, 1868. 8°. **8228.** f. **27.**

CALASCIONE, *Don.* Don Calascione. Drama giocoso per musica. Per il Gran Teatro di Brussella, *etc.* [By Giovanni Barlocci.] pp. 47. *Bruxelles*, [1755 ?] 12°. **906.** d. **3.** (**1.**)

This work also appeared as " La Finta cameriera."

—— Don Calascione. Drama giocoso per musica, per il Teatro di S. M. B. *Ital. & Eng.* pp. 103. *G. Woodfall: London*, 1749. 8°. **907.** i. **6.** (**9.**)

CALASIO (Marius de) *See* Marius, *de Calasio.*

CALASSANTI-MOTYLIŃSKI (Gustave Adolphe de) *See* Ibn al-Ṣaghīr. Chronique d'Ibn Ṣaghir sur les Imams Rostemides du Tahert. 1908. 8°. [*Actes du XIVe Congrès International des Orientalistes.* pt. 3. Suite.] **Ac.8806/14.**

—— *See* Ibrāhīm ibn Sulaimān, *Shemmākhī.* Le Djebel Nefousa. Transcription, traduction française et notes, avec une étude grammaticale par A. de Calassanti-Motylinski. 1898, *etc.* 8°. [*Publications de l'École des Lettres d'Alger. Bulletin de correspondance africaine.* no. 22.] Ac. **5350/2.**

—— *See* Muḥammad ibn Shaṭawī ibn Sulaimān. Notes historiques sur le Mzab Guerara depuis sa fondation. Par A. de Calassanti-Motylinski. (Traduction d'une relation redigée par Si Mohammed ben Chetioui ben Slimane.) 1885. 8°. **14555.** e. **7.** (**1.**)

—— Le Dialecte berbère de R'Edamès. pp. xxxii. 334. *Paris*, 1904. 8°. [*Publications de l'École des Lettres d'Alger. Bulletin de correspondance africaine.* no. 28.] Ac. **5350/2.**

—— Grammaire, dialogues et dictionnaire touaregs. Publiés . . . par René Basset . . : Tome premier. Grammaire et dictionnaire français-touareg. [Revised and completed by C. E. de Foucauld.] pp. 328. *Alger*, 1908. 8°. **12910.** p. **46.**

No more published. A " Dictionnaire abrégé touareg-français," written in continuation of this, is entered under Foucauld *(Charles Eugène de) Viscount.*

CALASSARE (   )

—— Appendix ad opusculum: Missionarius instructus, etc., in qua de quotidianis pietatis exercitiis particulariter agitur. [By — Calassare. With " Additamenta et correctiones " to the " Missionarius instructus."] pp. 51. 4. 1896. 8°. *See* Missionarius. **3455.** ff. **8.**

CALASSO (Francesco)

—— Gli Ordinamenti giuridici del rinascimento medievale. Seconda edizione. pp. 322. *Milano*, 1949. 8°. **5373.** m. **7**

CALATABIANO (Salvatore Majorana) *See* Majorana Calatabiano.

CALATAFIMI. Il Figlio prodigo. Processione sacro-allegorico-ideale da rappresentarsi in Calatafimi nei giorni 2 e 3 maggio 1903 in ricorrenza della solenne festività di Gesù Crocifisso. pp. 14. *Palermo*, 1903. 8°. **03366.** ee. **6.** (**1.**)

—— Gesù Cristo Re dei Secoli. Processione sacro-allegorico-ideale per la solenne festività del SS. Crocifisso da celebrarsi nel Comune di Calatafimi nei giorni 2 e 3 maggio 1905. pp. 14. *Alcamo*, 1905. 8°. **03366.** ee. **6.** (**3.**)

—— Giuseppe il Giusto proclamato Salvatore del Mondo. Figura dell'Uomo Dio redentore dell'umano genere. Processione sacro-allegorico-ideale da rappresentarsi in Calatafimi nei giorni 2 e 3 maggio 1904 in ricorrenza della solenne festività di Gesù Crocifisso. pp. 15. *Palermo*, 1904. 8°. **03366.** ee. **6.** (**2.**)

CALATAYUD. Fuero de Calatayud, 1131. *Lat. & Ger. See* Wohlhaupter (E.) Altspanisch-gotische Rechte, *etc.* 1936. 8°. **Ac.2121.**

—— *Iglesia Bilbilitana.* Villancicos, que se cantaron la noche de Navidad en la Santa Iglesia Bilbilitana este año 1669, *etc.* *Por A. Verges: Zaragoça*, 1669. 4°. **1073.** k. **22.** (**36.**)

—— *Orden del Santo Sepulcro de Jerusalén. See* Holy Sepulchre.—*Order of the Holy Sepulchre, at Calatayud.*

CALATAYUD (Antonio Lopez de) *See* Lopez de Calatayud.

CALATAYUD (Juan Joseph de Escalona y) *Bishop of Michoacan. See* Escalona y Calatayud.

CALATAYUD (Mariano Madramany y) *See* Madramany y Calatayud.

CALATAYUD (Pedro de) Doctrinas Practicas, que suele explicar en sus missiones . . . el padre Pedro de Calatayud . . . dispuestas para desenredar, y dirigir las conciencias, *etc.* 3 tom. *Valençia; Logroño*, 1737–54. fol. **4071.** h. **3.**

Tom. 3 is entitled " Opusculos y Doctrinas Practicas," etc., and was printed at Logroño.

—— [Another copy of tom. 3.] C. **64.** f. **2.**

In a satin binding embroidered with the arms of Diego de Roxas y Contreras, Bishop of Cartagena, to whom the work is dedicated.

CALATAYUD (Pedro Lopez Henriquez de) *See* Lopez Henriquez de Calatayud.

CALATAYUD (Vicente) *See* Mayáns y Siscár (G.) Carta . . . escrita al Dotor Don Vicente Calatayud. 1760. 4°. **819.** g. **31.** (**2.**)

—— Divus Thomas cum Patribus ex Prophetis locutus, priscorum ac recentium errorum . . . tenebras . . . angelice dissipans. Sive dissertationes theologicæ scholastico-dogmaticæ, et mystico-doctrinales ad sensum et litteram Divi Thomæ, *etc.* 5 tom. *Valentiæ in Hispania Tarraconensi*, 1744–52. fol. **L.19.c.3.**

CALATAYUD Y BONMATÍ (Vicente) El Culto Externo cual lo practica la Iglesia Católica, tiene un sentido profundamente racional y filosófico . . . Memoria, *etc.* pp. 71. *Alicante*, 1889. 8°. **3475.** de. **24.** (**4.**)

—— Necesidad del Principado Civil del Romano Pontífice para mejor realizar la misión divina que á éste se ha confiado, *etc.* pp. 42. *Alicante*, 1890. 8°. **8033.** f. **21.** (**4.**)

CALATAYUD Y BORDA (Cypriano Gerónimo de) Oracion Funebre que en las solemnes exequias de la R. M. Maria Antonia de San Joseph . . . dixo . . . el R.P. Pr. Fr. C. G. de Calatayud y Borda. *Lima,* 1783. 8°. **486.** c. **27.**

Imperfect; wanting all after p. 142.

CALATE. Cala-te! Emmudece! [Signed: J. C. R., i.e. J. C. Ryle.] [1855.] 12°. *See* R., J. C. [Thirteen tracts, etc.] **4419.** cc. **47.** (**3.**)

CALATIN, *Family of.* *See* Doederlein (J. A.) M. à Bappenhaim . . . continuatus. Das ist: Historische Nachrichten von dem . . . Hauss der . . . Marschallen von Calatin und der davon abstammenden, *etc.* 1739. 4°. **1328.** h. **15.**

CALATINUS, *pseud.* [i.e. Luigi Caruso.]

—— Luigi Sturzo, sacerdote, studioso e artista, uomo di azione, *etc.* (2ª edizione.) [With a portrait.] pp. 65. *Rovigo,* 1947. 8°. **10630.** k. **27.**

CALATRAVA, *Order of.* Bullarium Ordinis Militiæ de Calatrava . . . Opus D. Ignatij Josephi de Ortega et Cotes . . . directione, D. Joannis Francisci Alvarez de Baquedano . . . diligentia, et D. Petri de Ortega Zuñiga et Aranda . . . labore completum. Cui accessit catalogus Summorum Pontificum ac bullarum, seu indultorum, quæ ab eisdem emanarunt, *etc.* pp. 872. *Matriti,* 1761. fol. **5005.** cc. **6.**

—— Diffiniciones de la Orden y Caualleria de Calatraua conforme al Capitulo General celebrado en Madrid, año de 1600. pp. 456. *L. Sāchez: Valladolid,* 1603. fol. **608.** k. **21.**

The date in the colophon is 1604.

—— [Another edition.] pp. 675. *D. Diaz de la Carrera: Madrid,* 1661. fol. **608.** k. **19.**
The titlepage is engraved.

—— [Another copy.] **4783.** d. **8.**
Imperfect; wanting the plate of the Virgin Mary at p. 200.

—— Índice de los Documentos de la Orden Militar de Calatrava existentes en el Archivo Histórico Nacional. Del Boletín de la Real Academia de Historia, *etc.* [By F. R. de Uhagón y Guardamino, Marqués de Laurencín.] pp. 167. 1899. 8°. *See* Madrid.—*Archivo Histórico Nacional.* **04785.** k. **35.**

CALATRAVA (Francisco) *See* Calatrava y Ogayar.

CALATRAVA (José María) *See* Pando (J. M. de) Carta al Excmo Sr. D. José María Calatrava, *etc.* 1837. 4°. **9180.** d. **2.** (**10.**)

—— Carta . . . a los Editores del Español-Constitucional y la contextacion que por encargo de estos ha dado Don Alvaro Florez Estrada. pp. 68. [*London,* 1825.] 8°. **1141.** i. **13.** (**6.**)

—— Continuacion y Conclusion de la Respuesta de Don José María Calatrava á un libelo publicado contra él. pp. 128. *Boosey & Hijo; D. V. Salvá: Londres,* 1825. 4°. **9180.** ccc. **8.** (**5.**)

CALATRAVA (Luis de) Orán. Orígenes del desastre de Sáida . . . Segunda edicion. pp. 31. *Madrid,* 1881. 16°. **8042.** a. **9.**

CALATRAVA Y OGAYAR (Francisco) La Abolicion de los Fueros Vasco-Navarros. Estudio político, histórico, crítico y filosófico de la sociedad española . . . Precedido de un discurso preliminar por el ilmo. Señor Don Manuel Ortiz de Pinedo . . . Segunda edicion. pp. xlviii. 336. *Madrid,* 1876. 8°. **8042.** g. **2.**

—— Estudios Político-Históricos. pp. 72. *Madrid,* 1874. 8°. **8042.** e. **7.**

CALATRAVEÑO (Fernando) Calculo Pulmonar. La lucha antituberculosa en Portugal, *etc.* pp. 44. *Madrid,* 1907. 8°. **7616.** ee. **22.**

CALATRONI ( ) *Medico.* *See* Rigamonti ( ) All'amico medico Tetoni sul segno diagnostico della diatesi stenica e quello dell'astenica del sig. medico Calatroni. 1807. 8°. **7383*.** c. **5.** (**3.**)

CALÀ ULLOA (Pietro) *Duke di Lauria.*

—— Agrippina. Tragedia. pp. 88. *Napoli,* 1826. 12°. [*L'Ape teatrale.* fasc. 20.] **11716.** a. **6/20.**

—— Dell'amministrazione della giustizia criminale nel regno di Napoli, *etc.* pp. xxiii. 304. *Napoli,* 1835. 8°. **5326.** aaa. **1.**

—— Delle presenti condizioni del reame delle Due Sicilie. pp. 64. 1862. 8°. **8032.** a. **11.** (**1.**)

—— The Present Condition of the Kingdom of the Two Sicilies. pp. 79. *Robert Hardwicke: London,* 1862. 8°. **8033.** b. **71.** (**7.**)

—— État actuel du royaume des Deux-Siciles. pp. 48. *Paris,* 1862. 8°. **8032.** h. **44.** (**4.**)

—— Delle vicissitudini e de' progressi del dritto penale in Italia, dal risorgimento delle lettere sin oggi . . . Terza edizione. pp. 136. *Palermo,* 1842. 8°. **1376.** d. **14.**

—— Intorno alla storia del reame di Napoli di Pietro Colletta. Annotamenti. pp. 463. *Napoli,* 1877. 8°. **9166.** cc. **2.**

—— Lettres d'un ministre émigré. Suite aux Lettres napolitaines. pp. 298. *Marseille,* 1870. 8°. **8051.** e. **23.**

—— Lettres napolitaines. pp. 216. *Paris,* 1864. 8°. **8032.** i. **6.**

—— *See* Micciarelli (T. V.) Appel au journalisme sur les Lettres napolitaines de M. le marquis P.-C. Ulloa. 1864. 8°. **8052.** h. **46.** (**9.**)

—— Un Re in esilio. La corte di Francesco ii a Roma dal 1861 al 1870. Memorie e diario inediti, pubblicati con introduzione e note da Gino Doria. pp. xl. 248. *Bari,* 1928. 8°. **10634.** e. **15.**

CALAURIA.

—— The Exile of Calauria; or, the Last days of Demosthenes. [A drama, in verse, by Stratford Canning, Viscount Stratford de Redcliffe.] [1872.] 8°. *See* Demosthenes. [*Appendix.*] **011779.** ff. **60.**

CALAVAR. Calavar; or the Knight of the Conquest: a romance of Mexico. [By Robert M. Bird.] 2 vol. *Carey, Lea & Blanchard: Philadelphia,* 1834, 37. 12°. **12703.** e. **11.**

Vol. 2 *is of the third edition.*

CALAVERONUS (Joannes Gulielmus) *See* Chalcus (T.) Tristani Calchi . . . Historiæ patriæ libri viginti . . . cum notis [by J. G. Calaveronus]. 1627. fol. **178.** g. **9.** (**1.**)

—— —— 1704. fol. [*Graevius* (*J. G.*) *Thesaurus antiquitatum et historiarum Italiæ, etc.* tom. 2. pt. 1.] **L.R.302.a.2/2.**

CALAVIA (Mariano) España y la Democracia. Consideraciones crítico-históricas sobre la Revolucion de Setiembre [1868]. pp. 303. *Madrid,* 1879. 8°. **8042.** b. **20.**

—— Estudios Críticos sobre el Fausto de Goëthe. pp. 87. *Madrid,* 1871. 4°. **011824.** f. **66.** (**1.**)

—— Reflexiones acerca de la Gloriosa Revolucion de Setiembre de 1868. pp. 66. *Madrid,* 1868. 8°. **8042.** cc. **18.** (**4.**)

CALAVIA (Mariano) and **CALDERÓN LLANES** (José)

—— La Interinidad, escritos políticos . . . precedidos del discurso pronunciado por D. Nicolás Salmeron y Alonso en la reunion democrática de 18 de Octubre de 1868. pp. 192. *Madrid,* 1870. 16°. **8042. a. 1.**

CALAVROS (Néoclès M.) *See* Kalabros (Neokles M.)

CALAVRYTA. *See* Kalabruta.

CALA Y HARANA DEL OJO (Antonio Martínez de) *See* Antonio, *de Lebrixa, the Elder.*

CALA Y HINOJOSA (Antonio Martínez de) *See* Antonio, *de Lebrixa, the Elder.*

CALAYNOS. Romãce del moro calaynos de como req̃ria de amores ala infanta Sebilla y ella le demando en arras tres cabeças delos doze pares. (Coplas heches por juã dꝰ lēzina.) [With a woodcut.] **G. L.** [1550?] 4°. **G. 11022. (2.)**

CALA Y SÁNCHEZ (Miguel) Geología del Término de Morón y descripción de su yacimiento diatomífero. 1897. *See* Madrid.—*Sociedad Española de Historia Natural.* Anales, *etc.* serie 2. tom. 6. 1872, *etc.* 8°. **Ac. 2826.**

CALA Y VALCARCEL (Lorenzo) Réfutacion á la Carta publicada en contestacion á la del Rey de España el S. D. Carlos v. de Borbon [entitled " Breve Contestacion á la Carta de D. Carlos "] . . . Obra traducida del idioma Español ae [*sic*] Frances. Por el Sr. Conde A. de Brunet de la Renoudière. [With the Spanish text.] Yllustrada con la representacion hecha á . . . Padre Gregorio xvi. por la yglesia de España: traducida del idioma Latino en Español y Frances. [With the Latin text.] (Réfutation de la lettre publiée en réponse à celle du Roi d'Espagne, *etc.*) 2 pt. *Paris,* 1841. 8°. **8042. e. 18.**

CALBAIN. Farce Nouuelle dung sauetier nomme Calbain: fort ioyeuse : lequel se maria a vne sauetiere: a troys personnages : cestassauoir. Calbain. La femme. Et le galland. [In verse.] **G. L.** *En la maison de feu B. Chaussard : Lyon,* 1548. 4°. **C. 20. e. 13. (33.)**

—— [Another edition.] 1854. *See* Viollet le Duc (E. L. N.) Ancien théâtre françois, *etc.* tom. 2. 1854, *etc.* 8°. **12234. bb. 6/2.**

CALBASY (Seraphino) *pseud.* [i.e. François Rabelais.] *See* Rabelais (F.)

CALBE (Loewe) *See* Loewe-Calbe (   )

CALBEN (M. L.) Au peuple souverain. Dénonciation contre les intrigans des Jacobins. pp. 7. [*Paris,* 1794.] 8°. **935. b. 12. (13.)**

—— [Another copy.] **F. 351. (6.)**

—— Réponse à un écrit [by — Baraly] intitulé, Les Jacobins démasqués. pp. 7. *Paris,* [1794.] 8°. **F. 349. (5.)**

—— [Another copy.] **F. 357. (12.)**

CALBERLA (Georg Moritz) Karl Marx, " Das Kapital " und der heutige Sozialismus. Kritik einiger ihrer Fundamentalsätze. pp. 73. *Dresden,* 1877. 8°. [*Sozialwissenschaftliches.* Hft. 1.] **8276. de. 21.**

—— Die Löhnung nach der Arbeitsleistung in einer sächsischen Landwirthschaft. Vortrag, *etc.* pp. 19. *Dresden,* [1875.] 8°. **8275. ee. 2. (6.)**

CALBET (Antonin) *See* Castanier (P.) La Courtisane de Memphis . . . Illustrations de A. Calbet. 1900. 8°. **012551. aa. 68.**

—— *See* Louÿs (P.) Aphrodite . . . Illustrations de A. Calbet. 1896. 12°. **012551. k. 40.**

—— *See* Louÿs (P.) La Femme et le pantin . . . Illustrations de A. Calbet, *etc.* 1899. 12°. **12550. v. 14.**

—— *See* Ronsard (P. de) Les Amours . . . Cinq illustrations . . . de A. Calbet. [1937.] 8°. **11484. aa. 5.**

CALBETUS (L. Porcius) *pseud.* [i.e. Albertus Piccolus.] Apologetica expostulatio pro S. P. Q. Mamertino. [With a prefatory epistle by G. Aliprandus.] pp. 68. *Apud N. Misserinum: Venetiis,* 1623. 4°. **489. g. 29. (2.)**

—— [A reissue.] *Ex typographia A. Castellani : Cosentiæ,* 1628. 4°. **C. 74. c. 8. (1.)**

—— *Φυλακτηριον* adversus Mamertinae immunitatis calumniatores. pp. 148. *Ex typographia N. Misserini: Venetiis,* 1623. 4°. **489. g. 29. (1.)**

—— [A reissue.] *Ex typographia A. Castellani: Cosentiæ,* 1628. 4°. **C. 73. b. 17. (2.)**

CALBI (Ruggero) La Filosofia esposta in sonetti. pp. xxiii. 202. *Faenza,* 1715. 12°. **11427. df. 31.**

CALBIUS (Caspar Adamus) De jure cratium, *etc.* 1750. *See* Strykius (S.) Viri quondam illustris . . . Samuelis Strykii . . . opera omnia, *etc.* vol. 12. disp. 9. 1743, *etc.* fol. **498. g. 14.**

CALBIUS (Joannes Adamus) De privilegiis advocatorum, *etc.* *See* Strykius (S.) Viri quondam illustris . . . Samuelis Strykii . . . opera omnia. vol. 1. disp. 15. 1743, *etc.* fol. **498. g. 3.**

CALBO (Andrea) *See* Kalbos (Andreas I.)

CALBO (Baltasar) Manifiesto de la Causa formada por el Señor D. Joseph Maria Manescau . . . por comision de la Junta Suprema de Gobierno, contra Don Baltasar Calbo. pp. 34. *Valencia,* 1808. 4°. **T. 1545. (12.)**

—— [Another copy.] **636. g. 16. (3.)**

—— [Another edition.] pp. 34. [*Valencia?* 1808.] 4°. **1444. e. 6. (22.)**

—— [Another edition.] Dado á luz por . . . D. Juan Lopez Cancelada. pp. 31. [*Mexico,* 1808?] 4°. **9180. e. 5. (40.)**

CALBÓ (Enrique Gay) *See* Gay-Calbó.

CALBO (José Julian de Acosta y) *See* Acosta y Calbo.

CALBO (Juan) *See* Calvo.

CALBÓ (Raphael) Dissertation sur les angines. pp. 48. *Paris,* 1858. 4°. [*Collection des thèses soutenues à la Faculté de Médecine de Paris.* An 1858. tom. 3.] **7373. b. 1.**

CALBO CROTTA (Francesco) *Count.* Memoria che può servire alla storia politica degli ultimi otto anni della Repubblica di Venezia. [Contributions by various authors. Signed: A. B., i.e. Abbate Boni? Also attributed to F. Calbo Crotta as compiler.] pp. 400. 1798. 8°. *See* B., A. **9166.bb.17.**

CALBO DE ROZAS (Lorenzo) *See* Calvo de Rozas.

CALBOLI (Giacomo Paulucci di) *Baron.* *See* Paulucci di Calboli.

CALBOLI (Raniero da) *See* Atti Astolfi (L.) Una Pergamena del 1280 contenente un codicillo al testamento di Raniero da Calboli. 1901. 4°. **7701**. c. **8**. (**3**.)

CALBOLI (Raniero Paulucci di) *Marquis*. *See* Paulucci di Calboli.

CALBOLI PAULUCCI (Francesco di) La Giuditta. Canti. pp. xiii. 207. *Parma*, 1813. 4°. L.R. **233**. b. **2**.

CALBO Y ROCHINA DE CASTRO (Damaso) Historia de Cabrera y de la guerra civil en Aragon, Valencia y Murcia. Redactada con presencia de documentos y datos de una y otra parte . . . 2a edicion. (Apéndice.) [With a "Note to the several lives of Marshal Cabrera," signed: T. C. G. H., i.e. T. C. G. Hornyold, and dated 1889, inserted.] pp. vi. 682. 38. *Madrid*, 1846, 45. 8°. **9181**. e. **9**.

CALBRECHT (Jozef) De Oorsprong der Sinte Peetersmannen, hunne voorrechten, hunne inrichting, en de evolutie dezer instelling tot bij den aanvang der xvie eeuw. pp. xiv. 186. *Leuven*, 1922. 8°. [*Université de Louvain. Recueil de travaux publiés par les membres des conférences d'histoire et de philologie.* sér. 2. fasc. 2.] Ac. **2646**/**4**.

—— De Vlamingen en de Spaansche ontdekkingsreizen tijdens de xvie eeuw in het Oosten. pp. 278. *Antwerpen, Eindhoven*, 1927. 8°. **010028**. k. **10**.

CALBRIS (B.) *A.M.* The Rational Guide to the French Tongue. Containing . . . rules for learning the language without disgust, and for speaking it with facility. Part ii. A French Plaidoyer between five young ladies . . . in the course of which the French syntax is elucidated, the idiom discussed, *etc.* 2 pt. *Debrett: London*, 1797. 8°. **1212**. e. **15**.

CALBRIS (B.) *Vasseius*. De lymphaticorum œconomia, dissertatio, *etc.* pp. 27. *Parisiis*, anno xii [1804]. 4°. **1182**. f. **10**. (**10**.)

CALBRIS (Ferdinand) De l'hémorrhagie puerpérale. pp. 36. *Paris*, 1861. 4°. [*Collection des thèses soutenues à la Faculté de Médecine de Paris.* An 1861. tom. 2.] **7373**. d. **3**.

CALBRIS (Jacques) De l'étendue des sciences médicales. pp. 31. *Paris*, 1848. 8°. [*Collection des thèses soutenues à la Faculté de Médecine de Paris.* An 1848. tom. 2.] **7372**. b. **5**.

CALBURN (Clemencia) *See* Rogers (Caroline) *pseud.* [i.e. C. Calburn.]

CALBUS (Joannes Marcus) *See* Laste (N. dalle) De Joanne Marco Calbo . . . oratio, *etc.* 1765. 4°. **113**. e. **6**.

CALÇA (Franciscus) *See* Calza.

CALCAGNI (Diego) Memorie istoriche della città di Recanati nella marca d'Ancona, *etc.* pp. 374. ms. notes. *Messina*, 1711. fol. **658**. h. **17**.

—— [Another copy.] **178**. f. **7**.

CALCAGNI (Gennaro) Trattato di chimica generale e inorganica, *etc.* pp. 591. pl. iv. *Torino, Genova*, [1920.] 8°. **8903**. cc. **10**.

CALCAGNI (Menotti) Viltà nefandezze e delitti delle grandi assemblee politiche. Il senato romano, *etc.* 2 vol. *Arce*, 1929. 8°. **9042**. a. **16**.

CALCAGNI (Michele) *See* Drayton (Michael) Sonetto liv del cav. Michael Drayton . . . tradotto dal signor M. Calcagni. 1775. 4°. [*Opuscoli di autori siciliani.* tom. 16.] **663**. g. **8**.

CALCAGNI (Michele)

—— De' re di Siracusa, Finzia e Liparo non ricordati dalle storie riconosciuti ora con le monete. 2 tom. *Palermo*, 1808, 09. 4°. **811**. k. **13**.

CALCAGNINI (Celio) *See* Aristotle. [*Works.—Greek and Latin.*] Aristotelis opera omnia, *etc.* (tom. 2. Aristotelis . . . De coloribus liber. C. Calcagnino interprete.) 1654. fol. **517**. m. **9–12**.

—— *See* Aristotle. [*Works.—Latin.*] Aristotelis opera, *etc.* (tom. 3. Aristotelis . . . De coloribus liber, C. Calcagnino interprete.) 1542. fol. C. **76**. f. **5**.

—— *See* Aristotle. [*Doubtful or Supposititious Works.—De Coloribus.—Latin.*] Aristotelis . . . De coloribus liber, C. Calcagnino interprete. 1548. 8°. [*Actuarii . . . Libri* vii. *De urinis, etc.*] **541**. a. **23**.

—— —— 1670. 8°. [*Actuarii . . . De urinis libri* vii., *etc.*] **540**. d. **22**.

—— *See* Calcagnini (T. G.) Della vita e degli scritti di Monsignor Celio Calcagnini . . . Commentario. 1818. 4°. **815**. l. **23**.

—— *See* Cavedoni (C.) Delle monete antiche . . . descritte da C. Calcagnini, *etc.* 1825. 4°. **7755**. e. **2**. (**3**.)

—— *See* Hipler (F.) Die Vorläufer des Nikolaus Coppernicus, insbesondere Celio Calcagnini, *etc.* 1882. 8°. [*Mitteilungen des Coppernicus-Vereins für Wissenschaft und Kunst zu Thorn.* Hft. 4. no. 3.] Ac. **727**.

—— *See* Lucian, *of Samosata*. [*Judicium Vocalium.*] Luciani . . . *Δικη φωνηεντων*. i. iudiciū uocaliū, eiusq; translatio C. Calcagnino interprete. 1510. 4°. [*Constantini Lascaris Institutiones uniuersæ, etc.*] **624**. c. **11**.

—— —— 1539. 8°. [*Giraldus* (*L. G.*) *Huic libello insunt Lilii Gregorii Gyraldi . . . Herculis Vita, etc.*] C. **46**. b. **17**. (**1**.)

—— —— 1542. 4°. [*Constantini Lascaris . . . Græcæ Institutiones, etc.*] **624**. c. **15**.

—— Coelii Calcagnini . . . Opera Aliquot. [Edited by A. M. Brasavola.] pp. 657. *Per H. Frobenium & N. Episcopium: Basileæ*, 1544. fol. C. **80**. f. **12**.

—— Cœlii Calcagnini Carminum. Liber primus(—tertius). *See* Pigna (G. B.) Io. Baptistæ Pignæ Carminum, lib. quatuor, *etc.* 1553. 8°. **238**. m. **24**.

—— [Select poems.] *See* Gherus (Ranutius) *pseud.* Delitiæ italorum poetarum, *etc.* pt. 1. 1608. 12°. **238**. i. **1**.

—— Cælii Calcagnini in funere Beatricis Pannoniarum reginæ, oratio.—In funere Hippolyti Cardinalis Estensis, oratio.—In funere Alphonsi primi, ducis Ferrariæ iii. oratio.—In funere Antonij Constabilis, oratio.—In funere Herculis Strozzæ, oratio. *See* Rome, *Church of.—Popes.* Orationes funebres in morte Pontificum, *etc.* 1613. 8°. **1090**. k. **5**. (**3**.)

—— Cælii Calcagnini Pro oratoribus Fauentinis oratio ad Iulium ii. Pont. Max.—Pro Alphonso primo, duce Ferrariæ tertio apologia, ad Iulium ii. Pont. Max.—Pro Alfonso primo . . . oratio ad Leonem x. Pont. Max.—Pro oratoribus Fauentinis, oratio, ad Hadrianum vi. Pont. Max.—Pro Hercule secundo, duce Ferrariæ quarto, ad Paullum tertium Pontificem Maximum oratio. *See* I., A. F. G. G. Orationes gratulatoriæ, *etc.* 1613. 8°. **1090**. k. **5**. (**1**.)

—— [Select poems.] 1719. *See* Italian Poets. Carmina illustrium poetarum italorum. tom. 3. 1719, *etc.* 8°. **657**. a. **18**.

CALCAGNINI (CELIO)

— Ad Io. Baptistam Cynthium Gyraldum physicum Coelii Calcagnini super imitatione commentatio. *See* GIRALDI (G. B.) Cynthii Ioannis Baptistae Gyraldi . . . De obitu diui Alfonsi Estensis . . . epicedion, *etc.* 1537. 4°. **11408.** bbb. **54.**

— [Another edition.] *See* GIRALDI (G. B.) Cynthii Ioannis Baptistæ Gyraldi . . . Poematia, *etc.* 1540. 8°. **11409.** b. **3.**

— Annotatiunculæ seu glossemata e libro Cœlii excerpta quæ in margine legebantur. (Cœlii Calcagnini Obseruatio super Sardanapalo Tarso, et Anchiale Rhemniāiꝗ carminis pēsitatio, e libro ānotationū eius excerpta.) *See* DIONYSIUS, *Periegetes.* Dionysii Afri de situ orbis opus, *etc.* 1512. 4°. **672.** f. **4.** (**1.**)

— Coelii Calcagnini Apologia festiuissima pro *Ταυ* contra *Σιγμα*, Lucianicæ accusationi respondens. *See* GIRALDUS (L. G.) *Begin.* Huic libello insunt Lilii Gregorii Gyraldi . . . Herculis Vita, *etc.* 1539. 8°. C. **46.** b. **17.** (**1.**)

— De re nautica commentatio. 1701. *See* GRONOVIUS (J.) Thesaurus graecarum antiquitatum, *etc.* vol. 11. 1697, *etc.* fol. **1709.** b. **4.**

— De talorum ac tesserarum et calculorum ludis, *etc.* 1699. *See* GRONOVIUS (J.) Thesaurus graecarum antiquitatum, *etc.* vol. 7. 1697, *etc.* fol. **1709.** b. **4.**

— Disquisitiones aliquot in libros Officiorum M. T. Ciceronis, *etc.* *See* CICERO (M. T.) [*De Republica.—Somnium Scipionis.—Latin.*] In M. T. Ciceronis De somnio Scipionis fragmentum, Petri Ioannis Oliuarii Valentini Scholia, *etc.* 1538. 4°. **30.** a. **21.** (**1.**)

— M. Tullii Ciceronis defensiones contra Celii Calcagnini Disquisitiones in eius officia per Iacobum Grifolum. [With the text of the "Disquisitiones."] ff. 75. *Apud Aldi filios: Venetiis,* 1546. 8°. **1385.** b. **5.**

— [Another copy.] **232.** k. **9.**

— [Another edition.] *See* FERRARIUS (H.) *of Correggio.* Hieronymi Ferrarii ad Paulum Manutium emendationes in Philippicas Ciceronis, *etc.* 1552. 8°. **835.** d. **13.**

— [Another edition.] Disquisitiones aliquot in libros officiorum M. T. Ciceronis, *etc.* *See* CICERO (M. T.) [*Two or more Works.—Latin.*] M. Tul. Ciceronis De officiis libri III., *etc.* 1556. 4°. **8404.** g. **3.**

— [Another edition.] *See* CICERO (M. T.) [*De Officiis.—Latin.*] M. T. Ciceronis De officiis libri tres, *etc.* 1560. 4°. **525.** i. **5.**

— [Another edition.] *See* CICERO (M. T.) [*Two or more Works.—Latin.*] M. T. Ciceronis De officiis libri tres, *etc.* 1688. 8°. **57.** h. **2.**

— [Another edition.] *See* CICERO (M. T.) [*Two or more Works.—Latin.*] M. T. Ciceronis De officiis libri tres, *etc.* 1710. 8°. **999.** e. **6, 7.**

— *See* NIZOLIUS (M.) Marii Nizolii . . . Defensiones aliquot locorum Ciceronis in libro de Officijs, contra Disquisitiones Cœlij Calcagnini. 1572. fol. [*Ciceronis De officiis libri III, etc.*] **722.** m. **14.** (**1.**)

— Cœlii Calcagnini Encomium pulicis. *See* ARGUMENTA. Argumentorum ludicrorum . . . scriptores varij, *etc.* 1623. 8°. **1080.** h. **6.**

— [Another edition.] *See* DISSERTATIONES. Dissertationum ludicrarum . . . scriptores varii. 1638. 12°. **1080.** d. **13.**

CALCAGNINI (CELIO)

— [Another edition.] *See* DISSERTATIONES. Dissertationum ludicrarum . . . scriptores varii. 1644. 12°. **671.** a. **10.**

— [Another edition.] *See* PALLAS. Admiranda rerum admirabilium encomia, *etc.* 1666. 12°. **1080.** d. **19.**

— [Another edition.] *See* PALLAS. Admiranda rerum admirabilium encomia, *etc.* 1676. 12°. **1080.** d. **20.**

— Oratio tumultuario habita . . . in funere Herculis Strozæ. *See* STROZZI (T. V.) Strozii Poetae pater et filius. 1513. 8°. **1070.** c. **1.**

CALCAGNINI (SCIPIONE) *See* STIGLIANI (T.) Delle rime del Signor Tomaso Stigliani, parte prima, con breui dichiarationi . . . fatte dal Signor S. Calcagnini. 1608. 12°. **1062.** a. **4.**

CALCAGNINI (TEOFILO) *Count.* *See* LAZZARI (Alfonso) Le Prime nozze di Maria Stuarda, *etc.* [With a letter from Count T. Calcagnini to Hercules II., Duke of Ferrara, describing the ceremony.] 1921. 8°. **10805.** dd. **13.**

CALCAGNINI (TOMMASO GUIDO) Della vita e degli scritti di Monsignor Celio Calcagnini . . . commentario pp. viii. 71. **L.P.** *Roma,* 1818. 4°. **815.** l. **23**

— *See* CANCELLIERI (F.) Lettera . . . a . . . Monsignor T. G. Calcagnini . . . in lode del suo Commentario della vita e degli scritti di Monsignor C. Calcagnini. 1818. 4°. **1450.** k. **7.**

— Relazione del solenne funebre anniversario alla ch. memoria di S. E. il Marchese Ercole Calcagnini, celebrato da Monsignor Tommaso Guido suo figlio. *Roma,* 1818. 4°. T. **40*.** (**21.**)

CALCAGNINI ZAVAGLIA (MARIA) *Marchioness.* Per nozze De Bassetti di Trento e Revedin di Venezia. [Poems edited by Marchioness M. Calcagnini Zavaglia.] pp. 16. *Ferrara,* 1826. 8°. **11436.** bb. **51.** (**2.**)

CALCAGNINO (AGOSTINO) Dell'imagine edessena libri due. Con osseruationi historiche. pp. 485. *G. M. Farroni, N. Pesagno, & P. F. Barberi: Genoua,* 1639. 4°. **486.** b. **8.**

— Le Sacre palme genouesi, cioè vite de' santi martiri genouesi Desiderio vescouo di Langres et Vrsicino medico . . . Con vna breue relatione di XVIII. fanciulli Giustiniani de' Signori di Scio, del P. Carlo Spinola . . . e del P. Ferdinando Isola, *etc.* pp. 138. *B. Guasco: Genoua,* 1655. 4°. **662.** e. **22.**

CALCAGNINUS (AUGUSTINUS) *See* CALCAGNINO.

CALCAGNINUS (CAELIUS) *See* CALCAGNINI (Celio)

CALCAGNINUS (CAROLUS LEOPOLDUS) Caroli Leopoldi Calcagnini . . . De variatione ultimæ voluntatis. Trebellianica. Variisque, etiam ad Feudalem materiam, observationibus, *etc.* 3 tom. *Romæ,* 1745–47. fol. **5305.** bb. **17.**

— Supplex libellus Sac. Congregationi in Præsynodali Congregatione designatæ porrectus . . . De exemptione Ferrariensis ecclesiæ, & respectiuè immediata subiectione Romano Pontifici. *Romæ,* 1725. 4°. T. **38*.** (**25.**)

CALCAGNO ( ) *Begin.* O Maluasio rio vilā, *etc.* *End.* Finita e la frottola del Villan per el Venerabile homo ditto Calcagno. Viua Viua Calcagno. [In verse.] G.L. [*Bologna?* 1505?] 4°. **11429.** c. **32.**

CALCAGNO (DIEGO CUMBO) *See* CUMBO CALCAGNO.

CALCAGNO (FRANCISCO) *See* MERLIN (M.) *Countess.* Mis Doce Primeros Años, *etc.* [With a biography by F. Calcagno.] 1922. 8°. **10634.** aa. **25.**

—— Diccionario Biográfico Cubano. pp. 724. *New-York,* 1878. 8°. **10883.** dd. **10.**

CALCAGNO (GUIDO) Biblioteche scolastiche. pp. 145. pl. 13. *Milano,* 1938. 8°. [*Enciclopedia del libro.*] **2715.b.4/8.**

—— Una Mostra di topografia romana. Cenni illustrativi (pubblicati nei fascicoli di luglio ed agosto 1903 della rivista " Emporium "). pp. 43. *Bergamo,* 1903. 4°. **10107.** h. **4.** (**1.**)

CALCAGNO (LORENZO) *See* CALCANEUS.

CALCANEUS (LAURENTIUS) Consilia Do. Laurentii Calcanei . . . consultoribus utilissima, summarijs uberrimóque repertorio illustrata, necnon recognita, *etc.* G.L. ff. 176. *Apud hæredes I. Giuntæ; excu. F. ꝛ C. Marchãtz fratres: Lugduni,* 1549. fol. **1887.** d. **1.**

CALCAÑO (EDUARDO) *See* CALCAÑO Y PANIZA.

CALCAÑO (JOSÉ ANTONIO) *See* CALCAÑO Y PANIZA.

CALCAÑO (JUAN BAUTISTA) *See* CALCAÑO Y PANIZA.

CALCAÑO (JULIO) *See* HERNÁNDEZ (D. R.) Flores y Lágrimas . . . Con un prólogo por J. Calçaño, *etc.* 1889. 12°. **11450.** d. **7.**

—— *See* PARDO (F. G.) D. Francisco G. Pardo. [Select poems. With an introduction by J. Calcaño.] 1890. 8°. [*Parnaso Venezolano.* ser. 1. tom. 11.] **11450.** ccc. **38.**

—— *See* PEREZ (Arbonio) Herculano. Drama historico, *etc.* [With a preface by J. Calcaño.] 1869. 12°. **11726.** aaa. **55.** (**7.**)

—— *See* PERIODICAL PUBLICATIONS.—*Carácas.* El Semanario . . . Redactor: J. Calcaño, *etc.* 1878. 4°. **P.P. 4105.** hb.

—— *See* SALUZZO (M. A.) Leyenda de la Tumba. [With a preface by J. Calcaño.] 1878. 8°. **11450.** ee. **29.**

—— *See* YEPES (J. R.) Don José Ramón Yepes. [Select poems. With an introduction by J. Calcaño.] 1889. 8°. [*Parnaso Venezolano.* ser. 1. tom. 7.] **11450.** ccc. **38.**

—— Blanca. Novella original . . . Editor, Rafael Hernandez Gutierrez. [With a preface by J. Gonzalez Rodil.] pp. 162. *Carácas,* 1865. 16°. **12490.** b. **4.**

—— El Castellano en Venezuela. Estudio crítico. pp. xviii. 707. *Carácas,* 1897. 8°. **12941.** d. **15.**

—— El Castellano en Venezuela. Estudio crítico. pp. xxix. 571. [*Caracas;*] *Madrid* [printed], 1950. 8°. [*Biblioteca venezolana de cultura. Colección " Andrés Bello."*] **W.P.** B. **547/3.**

—— Parnaso Venezolano. Colección de poesías de autores venezolanos desde mediados del siglo XVIII hasta nuestros dias. Precedida de una introducción acerca del orígen y progreso de la poesía en Venezuela, *etc.* tom. 1. pp. xxi. 574. *Carácas,* 1892. 8°. **11450.** h. **37.**

—— Tres Poetas Pesimistas del siglo XIX. (Lord Byron. Shelley. Leopardi.) Estudio crítico. pp. 322. *Carácas,* 1907. 8°. **11840.** t. **21.**

CALCAÑO Y PANIZA (EDUARDO) *See* GARCÍA DE QUEVEDO (J. H.) D. José Heriberto García de Quevedo. [Select poems. With an introduction by E. Calcaño y Paniza.] 1889. 8°. [*Parnaso Venezolano.* ser. 1. tom. 6.] **11450.** ccc. **38.**

—— *See* RIOS (J. M. de los) Médicos Venezolanos . . . precedidos de un prólogo del Dr. E. Calcaño. 1893. 8°. **10881.** f. **26.**

—— *See* TAVIEL DE ANDRADE (E.) Centenario de Simon Bolívar . . . y carta de los Señores D. E. Calcaño y D. Hector Varela. 1883. 8°. **10601.** c. **11.** (**4.**)

—— De la Justicia Criminal. pp. iii. 25. *Carácas,* 1890. 8°. **6785.** d. **9.** (**5.**)

—— Historia patria. La familia Jugo. pp. 59. *Carácas,* [1878?] 8°. **10880.** cc. **5.** (**2.**)

—— Protócolo. Artículos editoriales de la " Gaceta Oficial " sobre la cuestion agrícola-industrial, *etc.* pp. 105. *Carácas,* 1879. 8°. **8228.** i. **40.**

—— Tratado de Derecho Internacional. pp. xv. 101. *Carácas,* 1897. 8°. **06955.** g. **17.**

CALCAÑO Y PANIZA (JOSÉ ANTONIO) *See* ROJAS (A.) Un Libro en Prosa . . . Con una introduccion por J. A. Calcaño. 1876. 8°. **12230.** f. **1.**

—— Obras Poéticas. pp. 439. *París,* 1895. 18°. **11450.** d. **11.**

—— [Select poems.] *See* SPANISH POETICAL ALBUM. Album Poético Español, *etc.* 1874. 8°. **11450.** i. **1.**

—— [Select poems.] *See* RÓJAS (J. M.) Biblioteca de Escritores Venezolanos Contemporáneos, *etc.* 1875. 8°. **12230.** f. **6.**

—— El Canto de Primavera. pp. 68. *Carácas,* 1865. 8°. **11450.** e. **35.**

—— Contribución al estudio de la música en Venezuela. [With plates.] pp. 127. *Caracas,* 1939. 8°. **7899.** aaaa. **42.**

—— El Leñador. Leyenda Americana. pp. 40. *Carácas,* 1857. 8°. **11450.** f. **44.**

CALCAÑO Y PANIZA (JUAN BAUTISTA) *See* VENEZUELA.—*Comision Revisora de Leyes Fiscales.* Código de Aduanas para la República de Venezuela. Redactado . . . por una Comision (Projecto del Presidente de la Comision revisora, J. B. Calcaño), *etc.* 1859. 8°. **8226.** ff. **2.**

—— Los Verbos Castellanos que rigen preposicion ilustrados con ejemplos, *etc.* pp. xii. 113. *Curazao,* 1887. 8°. **12943.** d. **24.**

CALCAR (ALBERTUS VAN) Responsio ad quaestionem . . . Comparetur veterum doctrina cum recentiorum theoria de ista affectione pathologica in homine, quae vocatur metastasis, *etc.* 1822. *See* UTRECHT.—*Academia Rheno-Trajectina.* Annales, *etc.* 1821–22. 1817, *etc.* 8°. **Ac. 936.**

CALCAR (ELISA VAN) *See* CALCAR (Eliza C. F. van)

CALCAR (ELIZA CAROLINA FERDINANDA VAN) *See* SIKEMEIER (J. H.) Elise van Calcar-Schiotling, haar leven en omgeving, haar arbeid, haar geestesrichting . . . Versierd met . . . portretten, *etc.* 1921. 8°. **010760.** i. **1.**

—— De Eedgenooten. Historische roman uit de 16de eeuw. 2 dl. *'s Gravenhage,* 1888. 8°. **12580.** l. **2.**

CALCAR (Eliza Carolina Ferdinanda van)

—— Emanuel Swedenborg, de ziener. pp. xvi. 335. *'s Gravenhage*, 1882. 8°. **3716**. e. 5.

—— Het Feest te Wolfhezen, 14 Julij 1864. pp. 46. *'s Gravenhage*, 1864. 8°. **3925**. bbb. **40**. (4.)

—— Johan Stephen van Calcar. Historische novelle uit de zestiende eeuw. pp. vi. 302. *Amsterdam*, 1862. 8°. **12580**. i. **16**.

—— Kinderen der eeuw. 3 dl. *Arnhem*, 1872, 73. 8°. **12581**. k. 1.

—— Die Kleine papierwerkers. Wat men van een stukje papier al maken kan. 4 pt. *Amsterdam*, 1863–65. 8°. **7953**. dd. 5.

—— Sophia Frederika Mathilda, Koningin der Nederlanden, als vorstin en moeder geschetst . . . Met portret. pp. 101. *Haarlem*, 1877. 8°. **10760**. bbb. **5**.

—— De Tweede Pinksterdag. Roman, *etc.* 2 dl. *'s Gravenhage*, 1891. 8°. **12580**. i. **28**.

—— Wat is noodig? eene vraag over vrouwelijke opvoeding, aan het Nederlandsche volk. pp. 45. *Amsterdam*, 1864. 8°. **3925**. bbb. **43**. (1.)

—— De Zoon van den klepperman. Eene vertelling. 3de uitgave. pp. 263. *Antwerpen*, 1867. 12°. **12580**. aaa. **14**.

CALCAR (Reinder Pieters van) Klinisch-biologische studiën over het mechanisme der infectieziekten. Eerste gedeelte: Pneumonie. pp. 71. pl. iii. *Amsterdam*, 1904. 8°. [*Verhandelingen der Koninklijke Akademie van Wetenschappen te Amsterdam.* sect. 2. dl. 10. no. 6.] *No more published.* **Ac.944/2.(b.)**

CALCARA (Pietro) Descrizione dell'isola di Lampedusa. [With a map.] pp. 45. *Palermo*, 1847. 4°. **10151**. bb. **17**.

—— Descrizione dell'isola di Linosa. [With a map.] pp. 29. *Palermo*, 1851. 8°. **10132**. bb. **40**.

—— Memoria sopra alcune conchiglie fossili rinvenute nella contrada d'Altavilla. [With a plate.] pp. 16. *Palermo*, 1841. 8°. **7203**. bb. **19**.

CALCARE, *pseud.* Cement Users' and Buyers' Guide. A book for daily use of all those . . . who are interested in any way in buying, using or storing of Portland Cement. By Calcare. pp. 115. *E. & F. N. Spon: London*, 1901. 16°. **7817**. aa. **13**.

CALCATERRA (Carlo) *See* Arborio Gattinara di Breme (L. A.) Polemiche . . . Introduzione e note di C. Calcaterra, *etc.* 1923. 8°. **011850**. b. **74**.

—— *See* Salvadori (G.) Liriche e saggi. A cura di C. Calcaterra. 1933. 8°. **20000**. k. **12**.

—— *See* Settembrini (L.) Dalle ricordanze della mia vita. Pagine scelte e coordinate da C. Calcaterra. 1933. 8°. **20001**. ee. **5**.

—— Il Barocco in Arcadia, e altri scritti sul Settecento. pp. viii. 528. *Bologna*, 1950. 8°. **11867**. ccc. **47**.

—— Con Guido Gozzano e altri poeti. [On Italian poetry in the early twentieth century.] pp. xii. 391. *Bologna*, 1944. 8°. **11868**. aaa. **14**.

—— Ideologismo e italianità nella trasformazione linguistica della seconda metà del Settecento. Ricerche nuove. Lezioni di storia della lingua italiana tenute nell'Università di Bologna, l'anno accademico 1945–1946. pp. 171. *Bologna*, [1946.] 4°. **12944**. d. **12**.

CALCATERRA (Carlo)

—— Il Nostro imminente Risorgimento. Gli studi e la letteratura in Piemonte nel periodo della Sampaolina e della Filopatria. pp. xv. 651. *Torino*, 1935. 8°. **11857**. cc. **12**.

—— Novelle d'ogni secolo della nostra letteratura. Scelte e annotate da C. Calcaterra . . . iii edizione riveduta. pp. xiv. 395. *Torino*, 1933. 8°. **12470**. i. **24**.

—— Poesia e canto. Studi sulla poesia melica italiana e sulla favola per musica. pp. xix. 369. *Bologna*, 1951. 8°. **11867**. m. **17**.

—— Storia della poesia frugoniana. pp. xv. 528. *Genova*, 1920. 8°. **011853**. r. **74**.

CALCATERRA (Nicola) Proclamazione agli amici della patria. [An exhortation to order and support of the constitution.] [*Naples*, 1820.] *s. sh.* fol. **8032**. m. **7**. (**16**.)

—— Saggio di cosmogonia e cosmologia, ovvero dell'origine ed organizzazione de sistemi mondani. 2 tom. *Messina*, 1838. 8°. **1254**. i. **24**.

CALCATOGGIO (Paul Matthieu) Considérations générales sur l'auscultation, la percussion, et sur leur importance pratique. Thèse, *etc.* pp. 44. *Montpellier*, 1843. 4°. **1182**. c. **16**. (5.)

CALCE (D. G. L.) Italia o Crispalia? Pensieri e rivelazioni. pp. 176. *Sondrio*, 1895. 8°. **8033**. h. **23**.

—— Lettere d'amore di un generale d'Africa, edite dal dottor Calce [or rather, written by him?]. pp. viii. 214. *Sondrio*, 1896. 8°. **10920**. b. **39**.

—— Satan délivré et la Bête, 666, déchainée. Lettres en italien, en français, et en anglais, *etc.* vol. 1. pp. 127. *San Remo*, 1919. 8°. *No more published.* **3186**. b. **48**.

CALCEBIGI (Ranieri de') *See* Calsabigi.

CALCÉDOINE. *See* Chalcedon.

CALCEDON. *See* Chalcedon.

CALCEOLARI (Francesco) *See* Calzolari.

CALCEOLARIUS (Franciscus) *See* Calzolari (Francesco)

CALCETERAS. Saynete nuevo. Intitulado Las Calceteras, *etc.* [By R. F. de la Cruz Cano y Olmedilla.] pp. 8. *Valencia*, 1813. 4°. **1342**. f. **5**. (143.)

CALCHAS. Le Calchas moderne, ou Oracle divertissant, *etc.* *See* Ephemerides. Petit chansonnier, Calcas moderne, *etc.*

CALCHEIM (Wilhelm von) called Lohausen. *See* Calchum.

CALCHI (Carlina) *See* Cravenna (C.) *Countess.*

CALCHI (Tristano) *See* Chalcus (Tristanus)

CALCHI-NOVATI (Giulio) Il Divorzio. pp. 46. *Milano*, 1892. 8°. **08416**. ff. **30**. (4.)

CALCHOFF (Joannes Christianus) *See* Kalckhoff.

CALCHOU. *See* Kelso.

CALCHUM (Wilhelm von) called Lohausen. Zusammfassung etlicher geometrischen Aufgaben: so durch die Rechenkunst allein aufzulösen. [With diagrams.] pp. 136. *Bremen*, 1629. fol. **8505**. f. **3**. (**1**.)

CALCHUS (Tristanus) *See* Chalcus.

CALCIATI (Alessandro) *of Piacenza.*

—— *See* Bible.—*Ruth.* [*Italian.*] Il Libro di Rut. Versione libera in ottava rima di A. Calciati. 1876. 8°. **3149**. h. **11**.

CALCIATI (Alessandro) *of the University of Turin.*

—— *See* Lichtendorff-Clairville (A.) Dictionnaire polyglotte des termes médicaux, *etc.* (Versione italiana del dott. A. Calciati.) 1950, *etc.* 8°. **2024**. e.

CALCIATI (Cesare) *Count*, and **BRACCIANI** (Luigi) Nel Paese dei Cunama. Missione Corni-Calciati-Bracciani in Eritrea, 1922–1923 . . . Con oltre 400 fotografie . . . 1 cartina, *etc.* pp. xiii. 315. pl. 25. *Milano*, 1927. 8°. **010094**. l. **40**.

CALCIATI (Cesare) *Count*, and **KONCZA** (Mathias)

—— The Basin of the Hispar Glacier. *See* Workman (William H.) and (F. B.) The Call of the Snowy Hispar, *etc.* 1910. 8°. **10056**. pp. **8**.

CALCIUS (Ignatius) Linguæ sanctæ rudimenta, in usum tironum versibus concinnata, *etc.* pp. 214. *Neapoli*, 1753. 8°. **12904**. aaa. **9**.

CALCIUS CAPPAVALLIS (N.) *See* Caux de Cappeval (N. de)

CALCKHOFF (Joannes Christianus) *See* Kalckhoff.

CALCO (Ludovico Maria) Vita del servo di Dio P. Ludovico Maria Calco dell'Ordine dei Predicatori della Congregazione di Santa Sabina. Descritta da un religioso dell'ordine stesso, e della medesima congregazione. [With a portrait.] pp. xii. 184. *Venezia*, 1754. 4°. **4867**. e. **22**.

CALCOCONDYLAS (Laonicus) *See* Chalcocondylas.

CALCODONTÈO (Argino) *Pastor Arcade, Vicecustode della Colonia Mitirtea, pseud.* Saggio delle rime di Argino Calcodontèo, *etc.* pp. 44. *Napoli*, 1778. 4°. **11429**. f. **6**. (**2**.)

CALCOEN. *See* Calicut.

CALCOEN (Gerard Gillis) *See* Calkoen.

CALCOGRAFIA.

—— Calcografia Camerale. *See* Rome.—*The City.*—*Calcografia Nazionale.*

—— Calcografia di belle statue antiche degli dei degli antichi Romani, e di altre nazioni, che veggonsi ancora in Roma, *etc.* pl. 48. *Roma*, 1779. 4°. **1899.cc.40.**

—— Calcografia Nazionale. *See* Rome.—*The City.*

CALCOLO. Calcolo sopra il valore dell'opinioni, e sopra i piaceri, e i dolori della vita umana. [By G. M. Orles.] pp. 70. **L.P.** *Venezia*, 1757. 4°. **1342**. k. **2**. (**3**.)

—— [Another copy.] **232**. h. **32**. *Imperfect; wanting the titlepage.*

—— Calcolo delle frazioni decimali exposto per iniziare la gioventù al conteggio de' pesi, e delle misure giusta il nuovo sistema della Legge 15. Piovoso Anno ix. E. F. pp. 29. *Cesena*, 1803. 8°. **899**. e. **5**. (**1**.)

CALCONDILA (Demetrio) *See* Chalcocondylas (D.)

CALCOT GOLF CLUB. *See* Reading.

CALCOTE (James L.) *See* Glenn (David C.) Opinion . . . in the case of J. L. Calcote vs. F. Stanton and H. S. Buckner, *etc.* [1854.] 8°. **6617**. bb. **27**. (**5**.)

CALCOTT (J. Berkeley) Stanzas, by Miss Berkeley Calcott, eleven years of age. pp. 16. *George Folds: Dublin*, 1834. 8°. **11641**. c. **10**.

CALCOTT (John Wall) *See* Callcott.

CALCOTT (M. E. Berkeley) Faith's Triumphs, and other Scripture subjects. pp. viii. 295. *S. W. Partridge & Co.: London*, [1884.] 8°. **3128**. ee. **31**.

CALCOTT (Wellins) A Candid Disquisition of the Principles and Practices of the . . . Society of Free and Accepted Masons; together with some strictures on the origin, nature, and design of that institution. pp. xxxii. 244. *Printed for the Author: London*, 1769. 8°. **4784**. cc. **4**.

—— [Another edition.] pp. xiii. 256. *William McAlpine: Boston*, 1772. 8°. **4784**. bb. **7**.

—— [Another edition.] With copious notes by the Rev. George Oliver. [With additional chapters by George Smith and William Dodd respectively.] pp. 303. *Richard Spencer: London*, 1847. 12°. [*Golden Remains of the Early Masonic Writers.* vol. 2.] **4784**. c. **21**.

—— [Another edition.] Calcott's Masonry, with considerable additions and improvements, *etc.* pp. 5. 208. *Robert Desilver: Philadelphia*, 1817. 24°. **4783**. b. **15**.

—— Thoughts Moral and Divine . . . The second edition with improvements, *etc.* pp. xlviii. 320. *Printed for the Author: Birmingham*, 1758. 8°. **722**. g. **4**.

—— The third edition, with improvements. pp. x. 432. *Printed for the Author: Coventry*, 1759. 8°. **4405**. dd. **21**.

—— The fourth edition, with improvements. pp. viii. 429. *Printed for the Author: Manchester*, 1761. 8°. **4407**. g. **28**.

—— A Collection of Thoughts, Moral and Divine . . . Fifth edition, with improvements. pp. xlvi. 439. *Printed for the Author: Exeter*, 1764. 8°. **12270**. f. **4**.

—— [Another copy.] **L.P.** **12270**. e. **36**.

CALCOTT (Wilfrid Hardy) Santa Anna. The story of an enigma who once was Mexico. [With plates, including portraits.] pp. xiv. 391. *University of Oklahoma Press: Norman*, 1936. 8°. **010886**. f. **22**.

CALCOTT (William Stansfield) *See* Perry (John H.) Chemical Engineers' Handbook . . . W. S. Calcott . . . assistant editor. 1934. 8°. W.P. **4318/7**.

CALCRAFT (E.) *Writer on Foreign Missions.*

—— A Dream come True. The story of an African girl. [With illustrations.] pp. 30. *Church Missionary Society: London*, 1948. 8°. **4767**. c. **2**.

CALCRAFT (Emily)

—— A Sketch of the Character of the late Lord Erskine. [By E. Calcraft.] pp. 16. 1823. 8°. *See* Erskine (Thomas) *Baron Erskine.* **10817**. bbb. **13**.

—— A Sketch of the Character of the late Lord Erskine. Extracted from the Morning Chronicle, with some slight alterations and additions. [Signed: E. C., i.e. E. Calcraft.] 1824. 8°. [*The Pamphleteer.* vol. 23.] *See* C., E. P.P. **3557**. w.

CALCRAFT (Emily)

— A Sketch of the Character of the late Rev. Samuel Parr, LL.D., *etc.* [By E. Calcraft.] pp. 19. 1825. 8°. *See* Parr (Samuel) *LL.D.* **4906**. h. **21**. (**9**.)

CALCRAFT (Helen)

— Uncle Dan's Bird Book . . . Pictures by F. C. Holleyman and W. Sawyer. pp. 46. *Harper: London*, [1944.] 8°. **7288**. a. **6**.

CALCRAFT (*Right Hon.* John) To the Worthy and Independent Freemen of the City of Rochester. [An address, dated 17 April 1818.] *Caddel: Rochester*, 1818. *s. sh.* fol. **10368**. e. **2**. (**10**.)

— To the Worthy and Independent Freemen of the City of Rochester. [An address, dated 10 May 1818.] *Caddel: Rochester*, 1818. *s. sh.* fol. **10368**. e. **2**. (**8**.)

— A Dispassionate Appeal to the Legislature Magistrates and Clergy against Mr Calcraft's proposed Bill, for throwing open the retail trade in malt liquor. By a County Magistrate. pp. 35. *Effingham Wilson: London*, 1830. 8°. **T. 1294**. (**4**.)

CALCRAFT (John William) *pseud.* [i.e. John William Cole.] *See* Masers de Latude (J. H.) Memoirs . . . Translated . . . by J. W. Calcraft. 1834. 8°. **613**. b. **14**.

— — 1892. 8°. [*The Escapes of Casanova and Latude from Prison.*] 012207.k.1/13.

— An Address to the Public, containing observations on some late criticisms connected with the Edinburgh Theatre. *Edinburgh*, 1822. 8°. **P.P. 5197**. ba. (**2**.)

— The Bride of Lammermoor. A drama in five acts. [Based on the novel by Sir Walter Scott.] pp. viii. 62. *John Anderson, jun.: Edinburgh; Simpkin & Marshall: London*, 1823. 8°. 643.f.25.(1.)

— The Bride of Lammermoor, *etc.* pp. 44. *G. H. Davidson: London*, [1850?] 12°. [*Cumberland's British Theatre.* vol. 45. no. 369.] **642**. a. **24**.

— [A reissue.] The Bride of Lammermoor, *etc.* *London*, [c. 1865.] 12°. [*Cumberland's British Theatre.*] **642**. a. **24a**.

The wrapper bears the imprint: "Thomas Hailes Lacy: London."

— [Another edition.] pp. 48. *London*, [1852.] 12°. [*Duncombe's Edition of the British Theatre.* vol. 60.] **2304**. a. **30**. (**9**.)

— [Another edition.] pp. 48. *London*, [1857.] 12°. [*Lacy's Acting Edition.* vol. 28.] **2304**. e. **2**. (**8**.)

— [Another edition.] pp. 20. *London*, [1882?] 8°. [*Dicks' Standard Plays.* no. 344.] **11770**. bbb. **4**.

— A Defence of the Stage, or an Inquiry into the real qualities of theatrical entertainments, their scope and tendency, being a reply to a sermon entitled: "The Evil of the Theatrical Amusements stated and illustrated" . . . by the Rev. Dr. John B. Bennett, *etc.* pp. vii. 175. *Milliken & Son: Dublin*, 1839. 8°. **11795**. f. **27**.

CALCRAFT (William) Calcraft's Lament! or, the Hangman in a Hobble. [In verse.] *Printed for the Author: London*, [1850?] *s. sh.* 8°. **6495**. bb. **3**. (**24**.)

— The Groans of the Gallows, in the past and present life of William Calcraft, the living hangman of Newgate. pp. 12. *E. Hancock:* [*London*, 1846?] 12°. **10825**. aaa. **30**. (**4**.)

— Second edition. pp. 12. *E. Hancock: London*, [1847?] 12°. **6495**. bb. **3**. (**19**.)

CALCRAFT (William)

— Groans of the Gallows: or a Sketch of the life of Wm. Calcraft, English hangman, commonly called Jack Ketch. With a general review of the causes of crime, *etc.* pp. 7. [1850?] 12°. **10855**. dh. **23**.

— The Groans of the Gallows! or, a Sketch of the past & present life of Wm. Calcraft the English hangman! commonly called Jack Ketch. pp. 7. *Rial: London*, [c. 1850.] 12°. **1878**. d. **12** (**52**.)

— [Another edition.] A Voice from the Goal [*sic*]; or, the Horrors of the condemned cell! Being the life of W. Calcraft, the present hangman. pp. 8. *The Bookseller: London*, [1857?] 8°. **6495**. bb. **3**. (**23**.)

— The Groans of the Gallows; or, the Lives and exploits of William Calcraft and Nathaniel Howard, the living rival hangmen of London and York. pp. 16. *C. Elliot: London*, [1855?] 8°. **10825**. b. **17**.

— The Hangman's Letter to the Queen; in reply to the "Groans of the Gallows," vindicating his life, character and profession; with his proposed new machine to be substituted for the gallows, *etc.* pp. 16. *C. Elliot: London*, [1855?] 8°. **6495**. bb. **3**. (**21**.)

— Life and Recollections of Calcraft. no. 1. pp. 16. [1870?] 8°. **10601**. g. **9**. (**3**.)

CALCUL. Calcul des cyclones [in the Island of Mauritius]. pp. 12. [*Mauritius*,] 1902. 8°. **08755**. e. **13**.

— Calcul du jeu appellé par les François le trente-et-quarante, et que l'on nomme à Florence le trente-et-un . . . Par Mr D. M. 1739. 4°. *See* M., D., *Mr.* **7913**. ff. **21**.

CALCULATEUR. Le Calculateur universel . . . The Universal Calculator, *etc.* pp. 24. *Fr. & Eng.* *Librairie Granger: Montreal*, [1903.] 8°. **8548**. de. **52**.

CALCULATION. A Probable Calculation of the annual income to be raised by a tax on marriages, burials, and legacies. [*London*, 1695?] *s. sh.* fol. **816**. m. **6**. (**82**.)

CALCULATIONS. Calculations and Facts relative to Lottery Insurances, *etc.* pp. vii. 31. *Printed for the Author: London*, 1795. 16°. **8503**. dg. **3**. (**1**.)

— Calculations and Tables relating to the attractive virtue of Loadstones, *etc.* [By James Hamilton, Earl of Abercorn.] pp. 14. 1729. 8°. **537**. b. **27**.

— Calculations deduced from First Principles . . . for the use of the societies instituted for the benefit of old age: intended as an introduction to the study of the doctrine of annuities. By a Member of one of the Societies [i.e. W. Dale]. pp. cxvi. 247. *J. Ridley: London*, 1772. 8°. **50**. b. **26**.

— Calculations of Taxes for a Family of each rank, degree or class: for one year. [By Joseph Massie.] pp. 16. *Thomas Payne: London*, 1756. 8°. **8226**. b. **15**.

— Chemical Calculations. Worked examples with revision notes on chemical theory and the principles of volumetric analysis. pp. 88. *R. Gibson & Sons: Glasgow*, [1936.] 8°. **8902**. ff. **21**.

— Historical Calculations . . . Compiled and arranged from a work entitled "The Mystery of God finished," *etc.* 1851. 8°. *See* Mystery. **3185**. bb. **48**.

— Simple Calculations for Sanitary Officials & Students. pp. 34. *Sanitary Publishing Co.: London*, [1911.] 8°. **08768**. b. **12**. (**2**.)

CALCULATIONS.

—— Some Calculations on certain Prophetic Periods. Translated from the French. Geneva, January, 1834. With a few additional remarks. pp. 16. *George Herbert: Dublin*, 1855. 8°. **3185.** a. **58.**

CALCULATOR. The Calculator. [A card and tape in a box, with "Directions for using the Calculator" pasted on the lid of the box.] [1878.] **8507.** a. **9.**

—— Calculator for Weights of Steel Sections per Linear Inch. *High Speed Steel Alloys: Widnes*, [1937.] 8°. **1860.** cc. **5.** (**3.**)

—— The 'Compact' Calculator [of dates]. [*London*, 1914.] *s. sh.* fol. **1865.** c. **1.** (**82.**)

—— Counting-House Manual, and Introduction to Business, being an outline of practical book-keeping . . . By Calculator. pp. 64. *Simpkin, Marshall & Co.: London*, 1843. 8°. **8223.** c. **4.**

—— General Calculator: to facilitate the invoicing and checking of accounts, &c. from ⅛d. to 25s., or ⅛ to 300. pp. vi. *McCorquodale & Co.: London*, [1887.] 8°. **8533.** bbb. **35.** (**5.**)

Imperfect; wanting the pages of the calculator from ¼*d. to* 24*s.* 10*d. inclusive.*

—— An Ingenious and Educative Calculator on Industrial and Commercial Percentages from 1/16th to 100 per cent. on amounts from 1d. to a £1000. pp. 40. *Evan Evans: Merthyr Tydfil*, [1914.] 8°. **8548.** bb. **70.**

—— Key to the Intellectual Calculator, or Manual of practical arithmetic [of John T. Crossley and William Martin], *etc.* pp. 180. *Hamilton, Adams, & Co., etc.: London*, [1862?] 12°. **8533.** a. **43.**

—— Observations on the Report of the Committee of Weights and Measures. By Calculator. 1814. *See* PERIODICAL PUBLICATIONS.—*London*. The Pamphleteer, *etc.* vol. 4. 1813, *etc.* 8°. **P.P. 3557.** w.

—— A Ready Calculator: showing computations of sums from 1 to 1,000 . . . from 1d. to 4d. . . . from 4d. to 9d. . . . and 9d. to 2s., *etc.* pp. 149. *Rylands & Sons: Manchester*, 1863. 8°. **8529.** ee. **18.**

—— The Short Calculator: or, Short rules for shortening ordinary calculations. pp. 12. *J. & J. Barwick: Lancaster*, 1861. 24°. **8504.** a. **56.** (**1.**)

—— The Speedy Calculator. [A card.] [1911.] 32°. **944.** c. **6.**

—— [Another edition.] [1911.] 32°. **944.** c. **7.**

—— The Universal Metric Calculator on the decimal system for obtaining the value of precious stones, pearls, etc. . . . also special Ready Reckoner for Pearls, *etc.* pp. 254. *Calipe, Dettmer & Co.: London*, [1914.] 16°. **8548.** aa. **89.**

—— [Another edition.] pp. 110. *Calipe, Dettmer & Co.: London*, [1914.] 32°. **8548.** a. **30.**

Without the "Ready Reckoner."

—— The Vivid Mental Calculator and Table Tester. [With description.] *Blackie & Son: London*, [1894.] *s. sh.* fol. **1860.** cc. **5.** (**7.**)

CÁLCULO. Calculo de la Poblacion del Mundo y los Gentiles que mueren y se condenan por falta de ministros de evangelio, que los entiendan y conviertan en la Asia y en las Americas. [*Mexico*, 1810?] *s. sh.* 4°. **4767.** df. **9.** (**5.**)

CALCULUS. Calculus Made Easy . . . By F. R. S. [i.e. Silvanus P. Thompson.] 1910. 8°. *See* S., F. R. **8530.** df. **33.**

—— [Another edition.] 1914. 8°. *See* S., F. R. **08532.** df. **1.**

—— The Calculus of Form. [By Oliver Byrne.] [1870?] 4°. **C. 40.** i. **5.**

The whole edition was cancelled except two copies.

CALCULUS, *pseud.* Remarks on some of the proposed Railway Projects, for connecting Rochester, Chatham, and Strood, with Gravesend or Rosherville; with a map of the country shewing the two competing lines. By Calculus. pp. 21. *James Burrill: Chatham*, 1844. 8°. **10368.** e. **4.** (**20.**)

CALCULUS, *pseud.* [i.e. MYER LAUTENBERG.] Constant Factor. The intelligent person's guide to racing. By Calculus. pp. 27. [*Constant Factor Publishing: Manchester*, 1937.] 8°. **07908.** f. **50.**

—— Speed from the Sports Car. Tuning for efficiency. A textbook for the sports car enthusiast. By "Calculus." pp. 190. *Motor World Publishing Co.: Glasgow*, 1950. 8°. **8767.** e. **44.**

—— The Sports Car Engine. Factors in performance. A popular handbook . . . By "Calculus." pp. 111. *Motor World Publishing Co.: Glasgow*, [1949.] 8°. **8773.** a. **40.**

—— [A reissue.] The Sports Car Engine, *etc.* *Glasgow*, 1950. 8°. **8767.** e. **34.**

CALCULUS (GULIELMUS) *Monachus Gemmeticensis. See* GULIELMUS, *Gemeticensis.*

CALCULUS (WILHELMUS) *Monachus Gemmeticensis. See* GULIELMUS, *Gemeticensis.*

CALCUS (LUDOVICUS MARIA) *See* CALCO (Ludovico M.)

CALCUS (TRISTANUS) *See* CHALCUS.

CALCUTT (JOSEPHINE ELEANOR) *See* HINTON (John P.) and CALCUTT (J. E.) Sterilization, *etc.* 1935. 8°. **08416.** aa. **81.**

CALCUTTA.

OFFICIAL DOCUMENTS.

—— [For "Rules, Ordinances, and Regulations, for the good order and civil government of the Settlement of Fort William in Bengal":] *See* BENGAL. [*Collections of Laws.*—II. *Calcutta.*]

—— Hand-book of Bye-laws, Rules, Regulations, &c. Second edition. [With addenda and corrigenda.] 5 pt. *Calcutta*, 1913. 8°. **08285.** k. **18.**

REPORTS OF PUBLIC MEETINGS AND MEMORIALS FROM MIXED BODIES OF INHABITANTS.

—— Remarks on the Petition of the British Inhabitants of Bengal, Bahar, and Orissa, to Parliament, by the Gentlemen of the Committee at Calcutta, appointed to transmit the Petition to England, *etc.* [Signed: H. Cottrell and others.] (Appendix to the Comment on the Petition of the British Inhabitants, *etc.*) 2 pt. [*London*, 1780?] 4°. **800.** k. **8.** (**1*.**)

—— [Another copy.] **708.** i. **26.** (**6.**)

CALCUTTA. [REPORTS OF PUBLIC MEETINGS AND MEMORIALS FROM MIXED BODIES OF INHABITANTS.]

—— The Whole Proceedings of the Meeting held at the Theatre in Calcutta, on the 25th of July, 1785, to take into consideration "an act for the better regulation of the affairs of the East-India Company" . . . Together with the resolutions of the said meeting, and the speeches of Messrs. Dallas and Purling. To which are annexed, the resolutions agreed on by the officers of the Third Brigade, stationed at Cawnpore. pp. 46. *W. Richardson: London,* [1786?] 8°. **8022.** b. **19.**

—— Report of the Proceedings at a General Meeting of the Inhabitants of Calcutta, on the 15th of December, 1829. Extracted from the Bengal Hurkaru, *etc.* pp. 20. *T. Breteli: London,* [1830.] 8°. **08223.** h. **29.** (**1.**)

—— Meeting at the Town Hall. [A report, reprinted from the "Bengal Hurkaru," of the proceedings of a meeting held on 5 Jan. 1835.] pp. 26. [1835.] 4°. **8023.** g. **48.**

—— Report of the Meeting of the Inhabitants of Calcutta, held at the Town Hall, on the 5th January, 1835, to take into consideration the propriety of petitioning the Governor-General in Council or the Legislative Council of India, to repeal the press regulation passed in 1823 . . . Taken in short hand by M. A. Bignell. pp. 26. *S. Smith & Co.: Calcutta,* 1835. 8°. **8022.** e. **36.** (**1.**)

—— To the Honorable the Court of Directors of the East India Company. The memorial of the undersigned inhabitants of Calcutta, *etc.* [An appeal against the Act no. 11 of 1836.] [*Calcutta,* 1837?] fol. **9055.** f. **10.**
Lithographed.

—— Report of a Public Meeting held at the Town Hall, Calcutta, on the 24th November, 1838. pp. 52. *Stewart & Murray: London,* 1839. 8°. **1434.** e. **7.** (**1.**)

—— Report of the Proceedings of a Public Meeting of the Native Community held in the Town Hall . . . the 29th July, 1853. [With a petition to Parliament, requesting Indian representation and protesting against Sir Charles Wood's Indian Bill.] pp. 57. *J. F. Bellamy: Calcutta,* 1853. 8°. **8023.** c. **83.** (**1.**)

—— Corrected Report of Proceedings of a Public Meeting at the Town Hall, Calcutta, in favour of the extension of the jurisdiction of the Mofussil Criminal Courts. pp. 89. *J. E. Gomes:* [*Calcutta,*] 1857. 8°. **5319.** a. **36.**

—— Report of a Public Meeting of the Inhabitants of Calcutta, held on the 12th September, 1859. To petition both Houses of Parliament, against a Bill entitled a Bill for the Licensing of Trades and Professions, *etc.* pp. iii. 22. *J. M. Gaumisse: Calcutta,* [1859.] 8°. **8226.** f. **40.** (**1.**)

—— A Full and Corrected Report of the Proceedings of the Meeting of the Inhabitants of Calcutta and its vicinity, held at the Town Hall, on the 25th February, 1862, for the purpose of testifying public respect and gratitude to his Excellency Earl Canning . . . for his general administration of the country. pp. 24. *Thakoordoss Doss: Calcutta,* [1862.] 8°. **8022.** cc. **2.** (**3.**)

—— Proceedings of the Public Meeting on the Civil Service Question held at the Town Hall of Calcutta. [24 Mar. 1877.] pp. 69. *K. K. Chakravarti: Calcutta,* 1879. 8°. **8022.** de. **10.** (**5.**)

—— A Full Report of a Public Meeting held at the Town Hall of Calcutta on the 2nd March, 1878, regarding Indian expenditure and taxation. pp. 26. *"Englishman" Press: Calcutta,* 1878. 8°. **8226.** f. **40.** (**2.**)

CALCUTTA. [REPORTS OF PUBLIC MEETINGS AND MEMORIALS FROM MIXED BODIES OF INHABITANTS.]

—— Report of the Proceedings of the Second Public Meeting held at the Town Hall, on Friday, the 6th September 1878, in connection with the Vernacular Press Act. pp. 52. *Jogesh Chunder Banerjea: Calcutta,* 1878. 8°. **8023.** bbb. **11.**

—— The Full Proceedings of a Public Meeting held on the 22nd January, 1891 . . . to protest against the Age of Consent Bill. pp. 58. *Sabhabazar Standing Committee: Calcutta,* 1891. 8°. **8415.** g. **62.** (**4.**)

—— Programme. [The agenda of a public meeting held to devise ways and means to perpetuate the memory of Sir Abd al-Karīm abu Aḥmad Khān Ghaznawī.] pp. 4. [*Calcutta,* 1938.] 4°. **20030.** d. **41.**

MUNICIPAL INSTITUTIONS.

CORPORATION.

Under this subheading are included reports, etc. issued by the Commissioners for the Improvement of the Town of Calcutta, 1848–63, *the Justices of the Peace,* 1863–76, *and the Municipal Commissioners,* 1876–1900.

—— Administration Report of the Calcutta Municipality for 1866 (–1878). *Calcutta,* 1867–79. fol.
[Continued as:]
Administration Report of the Commissioners of the Town of Calcutta (of the Commissioners of Calcutta) for 1879 (–1898-99). *Calcutta,* 1880–99. fol.
[Continued as:]
Report of (on) the Municipal Administration of Calcutta for . . . 1899–1900 [*etc.*]. *Calcutta,* 1900– . fol. P.P. **3800.** gc.
Imperfect; wanting the report for 1919–20.

—— **Chairman's (Chief Executive Officer's) Report on the Municipal Administration of Calcutta for the year 1922-23 (1923-24, 1924-25, 1935-36 [*etc.*]. *Calcutta,* [1923– .] fol. 8287. h. 1.**

—— Cholera in Calcutta in 1894, and anti-choleraic inoculation. [Two reports by W. T. Simpson, Health Officer.] pp. 17. 10. [*Calcutta,* 1895.] fol. **7560.** k. **7.**

—— The Drainage of Calcutta. [A letter from the Commissioners for the Improvement of Calcutta on the subject of a proposed new system of drainage of that city, with the report of Messrs. M. and G. Rendel, and observations thereon by W. Clark and A. M. Dowleans.] pp. 5. 49. 12. [*Calcutta,*] 1859. 8°. **8776.** b. **53.**

—— First (Third—Seventh) Half Yearly Report of the Commissioners for the Improvement of Calcutta, *etc.* 6pt. *Calcutta,* 1848[–51]. 8° & 4°.
[Continued as:]
[Tenth—Thirteenth Annual Report of the Commissioners. 1853–1856.] [*Calcutta,* 1854]–57. 8°.
Imperfect; wanting the titlepages for the 10*th and* 11*th Reports.*
[Continued as:]
General Report of the Commissioners for the Improvement of the Town of Calcutta for the year 1857(–59). 3 pt. *Calcutta,* 1858–60. 8°. P.P. **3800.** gca.

—— Letter from the Municipal Commissioners to the Government of Bengal, forwarding a report on the drainage of Calcutta, by W. Clark . . . dated the 29th December, 1855. [With the report.] pp. 104. pl. 3. *Calcutta,* [1855.] 8°. **08777.** aaaa. **4.**

—— Proceedings of an Ordinary Meeting of the Municipal Corporation of Calcutta held at the Town Hall . . . 7th March 1864, containing a full report of Baboo Ramgopaul Ghose's speech regarding the suppression of burning Ghats on the banks of the Hooghly. Reprinted from the Hindoo Patriot. pp. 14. *Calcutta,* 1864. 8°. **8023.** bbb. **70.** (**12.**)

—— Report of the Health Officer of Calcutta for the year 1909 [*etc.*]. *Calcutta*, 1910– . fol. P.P. **2888**. g.
Imperfect; wanting the reports for 1931 *and* 1933.

—— Report on the Census of Calcutta in 1866. pp. ii. 228. *Calcutta*, 1866. fol. **8287**. h. **2**.

—— Report on the Census of the Town of Calcutta. Taken on the 6th April 1876. By H. Beverley. [With a map.] pp. 63. cxxiv. *Calcutta*, 1876. fol. **8287**. h. **3**.

CALCUTTA IMPROVEMENT TRUST.

—— Annual Report . . . 1914–1915. [With maps.] pp. 106. [*Calcutta*,] 1915. fol. **8277**. i. **30**.

COMMISSIONERS FOR MAKING IMPROVEMENTS IN THE PORT OF CALCUTTA.

—— *See* infra: PORT TRUST.

COMMISSIONERS FOR THE IMPROVEMENT OF THE TOWN OF CALCUTTA, 1848–1863.

—— [For reports, etc., issued by the Commissioners for the Improvement of the Town of Calcutta:] *See* supra: CORPORATION.

COMMISSIONERS FOR THE PORT OF CALCUTTA.

—— *See* infra: PORT TRUST.

COMMISSIONERS OF THE TOWN OF CALCUTTA, 1876–1900.

—— *See* infra: MUNICIPAL COMMISSIONERS.

HEALTH DEPARTMENT.

—— Annual Report of the Health Officers of the Port of Calcutta for 1900(–1918). 1901–19. fol. & 8°.
[Continued as:]
Reports of the Health Departments of the Ports of Calcutta and Chittagong for the year 1919(–1935). 1921–36. 8°. *See* BENGAL.—*Public Health Department.* I.S. BE. **11/2** & **213/4**.

—— Biological Investigation of the Water Purification Plants of Calcutta Corporation. *Calcutta*, [1929– .] 8°. W.P. **9495**.

HISTORICAL RECORD ROOM.

See BENGAL.—RECORD ROOM.

JUSTICES OF THE PEACE.

—— [For reports and other documents relating to the municipal administration, issued by the Justices of the Peace between 1863 and 1876:] *See* supra: CORPORATION.

MUNICIPAL COMMISSIONERS, 1876–1900.

—— [For reports, etc., issued by the Municipal Commissioners:] *See* supra: CORPORATION.

MUNICIPALITY.

—— *See* supra: CORPORATION.

POLICE.

—— The Calcutta Police Pocket Directory. pp. iii. 61. [*Calcutta*, 1904.] 12°. I.S. BE. **286/3**.

—— Manual containing Rules and Regulations for the Guidance of the European Reserve Force, Calcutta Police. pp. 59. [*Calcutta*, 1898.] 16°. I.S. BE. **286**.

—— Manual containing Rules and Regulations for the Guidance of the European Reserve Force, Calcutta Police. pp. 78. [*Calcutta*, 1906.] *obl.* 12°. I.S. BE. **286/2**.

—— Parade Manual. pp. 13. [*Calcutta*, 1903.] 16°. I.S. BE. **286/4**.

—— Police Rules for the Regulation of Traffic in Calcutta . . . May 1st 1912 (—1st March 1922). 4 pt. *Calcutta*, 1912–22. 12°. I.S. BE. **286/5**.

—— Strength and Disposition of the Police Force under the Commissioner of Police, Calcutta. Corrected up to 24th February 1900. pp. 9. [*Calcutta*,] 1900. fol. I.S. BE. **9/3**.

PORT TRUST.

—— Commissioners for making Improvements in the Port of Calcutta. Administration Report for the year 1875-76 (1876-77, 1881-82, 1882-83). 4 pt. *Calcutta*, 1877–83. fol. I.S. BE. **8/4**.

—— Administration Report for 1896–97 [*etc.*] of the Commissioners for the Port of Calcutta. *Calcutta*, 1897– . fol. 1896–97, *etc.* P.P. **3800**. gk.
Imperfect; wanting the reports for 1897-98–1908-09, 1933-34 *and* 1934-35.

—— The Calcutta Port Trust. A brief history . . . 1870–1920. [With plates and maps.] pp. 44. *Thacker, Spink & Co.: Calcutta & Simla*, 1920. 4°. **10055**. cc. **33**.

—— The Commissioners for the Port of Calcutta. Ferry Service. Time table and general information. [With a frontispiece and a plan.] pp. 17. *Calcutta*, 1909. *obl.* fol. **1890**. a. **39**.

PUBLIC LIBRARY.

—— Catalogue of the Calcutta Public Library. pp. xx. 487. *Calcutta*, 1846. 8°. **11902**. d. **22**.

—— Catalogue of the Calcutta Public Library. pp. vi. 645. lvi. *Calcutta*, 1855. 8°. **11904**. c. **35**.

RECORD ROOM.

—— *See* BENGAL.

MISCELLANEOUS INSTITUTIONS.

AGRICULTURAL AND HORTICULTURAL SOCIETY OF INDIA.

—— List of Members of the Agricultural & Horticultural Society of India. January 1st 1841. pp. 23. [*Calcutta*, 1841.] 8°. Ac. **3541/5**.

—— List of Members of the Agricultural & Horticultural Society of India. January 1st 1842. pp. 25. [*Calcutta*, 1842.] 8°. **07078**. df. **78**.

—— Report of the Agricultural and Horticultural Society of India for the year 1841 [*sic*] (1841, 1842). 3 pt. *Calcutta*, 1841–43. 8°. **7054**. e. **12**.
Other reports are included in the " Transactions " and the " Journal " of the Society.

—— Proceedings. Jan.–June 1838; Oct., Nov. 1839; Dec. 1840; Jan., March–May, Sept., Nov., Dec. 1841; Jan.–June 1842. *Calcutta*, [1838–42.] 8°. Ac. **3541/4**.
The " Journal " of the Society, which from Jan. 1887 *to Nov.* 1891 *bears the title on the wrapper " Proceedings of the Agricultural and Horticultural Society of India," and from Jan. to Mar.* 1892 *" Proceedings & Journal, etc.," is entered above.*

—— Journal, *etc.* vol. 1–14. *Calcutta*, 1842–67. 8°.
The caption title of the separate numbers of vol. 1 *reads: " The Monthly Journal."*

CALCUTTA. [Miscellaneous Institutions.]

—— New series. vol. 1–12. *Calcutta*, 1867–1901. 8°.
From Jan. 1887 *to Nov.* 1891 *the title on the wrapper of each part reads "Proceedings of the Agricultural and Horticultural Society of India," from Jan.—Mar.* 1892 *"Proceedings & Journal," etc.*

—— Index to vol. 1–9 [of the original series]. pp. 63. *Calcutta*, 1857. 8°. Ac. **3541/2**

—— Transactions, *etc.* vol. 1–8. *Calcutta*, 1838, 37–41. 8°. Ac. **3541.**
No more published. Vol. 1–3 *are of a later edition.*

—— Index to the Transactions of the Agricultural and Horticultural Society of India. Volumes I to VIII. pp. 33. *Calcutta*, 1857. 8°. Ac. **3541.** (a.)

—— Suggestions received by the Agricultural & Horticultural Society of India for extending the cultivation and introduction of useful and ornamental plants, with a view to the improvement of the agricultural and commercial resources of India. Compiled by Henry Harpur Spry . . . Published by authority of Government. pp. viii. iii. 208. *Bishop's College Press: Calcutta*, 1841. 8°. **7077.** dd. **23.**

All India Cow Conference Association.

—— The Condition of Cattle in India. Being an enquiry into the causes of the present deterioration of cattle, with suggestions for their remedy. By Nilananda Chatterjee . . . Illustrated. pp. vii. 647. iv. 16. xv. *Calcutta*, 1926. 8°. **07295.** dd. **4.**

"Antarjatik Banga" Parishat.

—— *See* infra: International Bengal Institute.

Anti-Fascist Writer's and Artist's Association.

—— Us. A people's symposium. Edited by Hiren Mukerjee. pp. vii. 116. *Calcutta*, [1943.] 8°. **012359.** cc. **31.**

Armenian Philanthropic Academy.

—— New Rules and Regulations of the Armenian Philanthropic Academy. *Armenian & Eng.* pp. 85. *Calcutta*, 1843. 8°. **17030.** cc. **2.**

Ārya Sāhitya Samiti.

—— *See* infra: Aryan Literary Club.

Aryan Literary Club.

—— *See* Bible.—*Matthew.* [*Bengali.*] সুসমাচার । সাধু ম্যাথু । [Translated from the English, with copious notes, by the Aryan Literary Club.] [1895.] 8°. **14123.** b. **19.**

—— The Scientific and Commercial Secret Revealer. Compiled . . . by the Arya Sahitya Samiti or the Aryan Literary Club . . . New edition. pp. 2. 192. xi. *R. C. Ghosh: Calcutta*, 1896. 12°. **07944.** ee. **44.**

Asiatic Society of Bengal, afterwards Royal Asiatic Society of Bengal.

—— Rules of the Asiatic Society of Bengal, *etc.* pp. 24. *Calcutta*, 1869. 8°. **10055.** ee. **1.** (7.)

—— [Another edition.] Revised to November 15th, 1876. pp. 24. *Calcutta*, 1876. 8°. Ac. **8826/7.**

—— Annual Report . . . for 1848. pp. 34. *Calcutta*, 1849. 8°. Ac. **8826/3.**

—— Financial Report [for the year 1848–49]. pp. 16. [*Calcutta*, 1849.] 8°. Ac. **8826/3.** (2.)

CALCUTTA. [Miscellaneous Institutions.—Asiatic Society of Bengal, afterwards Royal Asiatic Society of Bengal.]

—— Asiatick Researches; or, Transactions of the Society, instituted in Bengal, for inquiring into the history and antiquities, the arts, sciences and literature of Asia. vol. 1–20. *Calcutta*, 1788–1839. 4°. Ac. **8826.** b.
Imperfect; wanting vol. 5.

—— [Another copy of vol. 1–14.] T.C. **14.** b. **6–19.**

—— [Another copy of vol. 1–12.] **434.** e. **1–12.**

—— Index to the first eighteen volumes of the Asiatic Researches, *etc.* pp. 228. *Calcutta*, 1835. 4°. Ac. **8826.** b.

—— [Another edition.] Printed verbatim from the Calcutta edition. vol. 1–11. *J. Sewell: London*, 1801–12. 8°. Ac. **8826/4.**

—— [Another edition.] Republished . . . by Bihārilāla Mitra and Mahendranath Ghosh . . . A new edition. vol. 1. pp. xi. 47. *B. Mitra & M. Ghosh: Calcutta*, 1875. 8°. Ac. **8826/8.**

—— Recherches asiatiques, ou Mémoires de la Société établie au Bengale pour faire des recherches sur l'histoire et les antiquités, les arts, les sciences et la littérature de l'Asie; traduits de l'anglois par A. Labaume . . . Publiés par A. Duquesnoy. [A prospectus, containing "Avertissement de l'éditeur" and two essays from vol. 2. With two plates.] pp. i–viii. 1–17. 1–16. *Paris*, 1802. 4°. B. **473.** (8.)

—— Recherches asiatiques; ou, Mémoires de la Société établie au Bengale pour faire des recherches sur l'histoire et les antiquités, les arts, les sciences et la littérature de l'Asie; traduits de l'anglois par A. Labaume; revus et augmentés de notes, pour la partie orientale, philologique et historique, par M. Langlès . . . et pour la partie des sciences exactes et naturelles, par les Cens Cuvier, Delambre, Lamarck et Olivier, *etc.* [A translation of vol. 1–7.] 2 tom. *Paris*, 1805. 4°. Ac. **8826/5.**

—— Abhandlungen über die Geschichte und Alterthümer, die Künste, Wissenschaften und Literatur Asiens von Sir William Jones und andern Mitgliedern der im Jahr 1784 zu Calcutta in Indien errichteten gelehrten Gesellschaft . . . Aus dem Englischen übersetzt von Johann Christian Fick . . . durchgesehen, und mit Anmerkungen, ausführlichen Erläuterungen und Zusätzen bereichtet von D. Johann Friederich Kleuker. (Bd. 4. Das Brahmanische Religionssystem im Zusammenhange dargestellt . . . wie auch von den verschiedenen Ständen Indiens mit besonderer Rücksicht auf Fr. Paullini a S. Bartholomæo Systema Brahmanicum, etc. . . . von Dr. J. F. Kleuker. [Translations of selected articles from "Asiatick Researches."] 4 Bd. *Riga*, 1795–97. 8°. **817.** a. **17–18.**

—— *See* Sédillot (J. J. E.) Notice des Recherches asiatiques, ou Mémoires de la Société etablie au Bengale . . . Traduits de l'anglais par A. la Beaume, *etc.* [1807.] 8°. **817.** b. **4.** (8.)

—— Analyse des Mémoires contenus dans le xive volume des Asiatick Researches . . . avec des notes et un appendice; par L. Langlès. pp. vii. 114. *Paris*, 1825. 4°. Ac. **8826/6.**

—— Notice du huitième volume des Asiatick Researches, *etc.* (Extrait de la Revue philosophique, littéraire et politique.) [By Count C. F. Chasseboeuf de Volney.] pp. 38. ms. notes. [*Paris*, 1808.] 8°. **817.** b. **4.** (9.)

CALCUTTA. [MISCELLANEOUS INSTITUTIONS.—ASIATIC SOCIETY OF BENGAL, afterwards ROYAL ASIATIC SOCIETY OF BENGAL.]

—— Asiatick Researches. Transactions of the Physical Class, *etc.* [With plates.] pt. 1. pp. vi. 265. vii. *Calcutta,* 1829. 4°. Ac. **8826**. ba.
No more published.

—— The Journal of the Asiatic Society of Bengal. Edited by James Prinsep. vol. 1–7. *Calcutta,* 1832–38. 8°.

—— New series. vol. 8–75. *Calcutta,* 1840–1936. 8°. Ac. **8826**.
Vol. 74 *and* 75, *issued in parts between* 1904 *and* 1936, *were special volumes added to complete King and Gamble's "Materials for a Flora of the Malayan Peninsula," which began in vol.* 58. *The series proper, which was closed in* 1904 *with vol.* 73, *and the "Proceedings," which were also closed with the volume for* 1904 *were continued together.*

[Continued as :]

—— Journal and Proceedings of the Asiastic Society of Bengal. New series. vol. 1–30. *Calcutta,* 1905–1934. 8°. Ac. **8826**. **(2.)**

[Continued in three parts :]

—— Year-Book of the Asiatic Society of Bengal. *Calcutta,* 1935– . 8°. Ac. **8826**. **(7.)**

—— Journal of the Asiatic Society of Bengal. Letters. vol. 1. no. 1—vol. 23. no. 2. 1935–1957. *Calcutta,* 1935–58. 8°. Ac. **8826**. **(4.)**
Wanting vol. 24.

—— Journal of the Asiatic Society of Bengal. Science. vol. 1. no. 1—vol. 23. no. 2. 1935–1957. *Calcutta,* 1935–59. 8°. Ac. **8826**. **(5.)**
Wanting vol. 24.

[The two series of the Journal recombined as :]

—— Journal of the Asiatic Society. vol. 1. no. 1, *etc.* 1959, *etc. Calcutta,* 1961– . 8°. Ac. **8826**. **(8.)**

—— Index to the Numismatic Supplements I to XVI (XVII–XXXII) in the Journal, Asiatic Society of Bengal, 1904–1911 (1912–1913). 2 pt. *Calcutta,* 1912, 20. 8°. Ac. **8826**. **(3.)**

—— [Another copy.] Journal of the Asiatic Society of Bengal. vol. 71. pt. 1. extra no. 1. *Calcutta,* 1902. 8°. **12910**. t. **18**.

—— Useful Tables, forming an Appendix to the Journal of the Asiatic Society, *etc.* [By James Prinsep.] 2 pt. *Calcutta,* 1834. 8°. Ac. **8826/9**.
Another edition containing the author's name is entered under PRINSEP (*James*).

—— Memoirs of the Asiatic Society of Bengal. *Calcutta,* 1905– . 4°. Ac. **8826**. b/2.

—— Presidential Address (Annual Address), 1929 [*etc.*]. *Calcutta,* [1929– .] 8°. Ac. **8826/11**.

—— Proceedings, *etc.* 1865–1904. 40 vol. *Calcutta,* 1866–1905. 8°. Ac. **8826**. **(6.)**
Imperfect; wanting no. 8 *of* 1873 *and pp.* 138–152 *of no.* 9 *of* 1891. *From* 1905 *the "Proceedings" were issued with the "Journal" under the title "Journal and Proceedings."*

—— Bibliotheca Indica; a collection of Oriental works, *etc. Calcutta,* 1848– . 8° & 4°. **14002**. a, b.

—— Bibliography of Meteorological Papers in the publications of the Asiatic Society of Bengal, 1788–1928. By V. V. Sohoni. (From the Journal and Proceedings, Asiatic Society of Bengal.) [*Calcutta,*] 1929. 8°. **11907**. d. 3.

CALCUTTA. [MISCELLANEOUS INSTITUTIONS.—ASIATIC SOCIETY OF BENGAL, afterwards ROYAL ASIATIC SOCIETY OF BENGAL.]

—— A Brief Sketch of the Activities of the Asiatic Society of Bengal. pp. 7. *Calcutta,* 1927. 8°. Ac. **8826/12**.

—— Catalogue of the Scientific Serial Publications in the Principal Libraries of Calcutta. Compiled . . . by Stanley Kemp, *etc.* pp. xii. 292. *Calcutta,* 1918. 8°. Ac. **8826/13**.

—— Centenary Review of the Asiatic Society of Bengal from 1784 to 1883, *etc.* (pt. 1. History of the Society. By Dr. Rajendralala Mitra.—pt. 2. Archæology, History, Literature, &c. By Dr. A. F. R. Hoernle.—pt. 3. Natural Science, &c. By Baboo P. N. Bose.—Proceedings of the Special Centenary Meeting.) 4 pt. *Calcutta,* 1885. 8°. Ac. **8826/10**.

—— Descriptions of new Indian Lepidopterous Insects from the Collection of the late Mr. W. S. Atkinson . . . Rhopalocera, by William C. Hewitson . . . Heterocera . . . by Frederic Moore . . . With an introductory notice by Arthur Grote, *etc.* 3 pt. pp. xi. 299. pl. VIII. *Calcutta; London* [printed], 1879–88. 4°. **7296**. h. **11**.

—— Descriptive Ethnology of Bengal. By Edward Tuite Dalton. Illustrated by lithograph portraits copied from photographs. Printed for the government of Bengal, under the direction of the Council of the Asiatic Society of Bengal. pp. 327. pl. XXXVII. 1872. 4°. *See* BENGAL. [*Miscellaneous Public Documents and Official Publications.*] **10007**. y. **1**.

—— 150th Jubilee of the Royal Asiatic Society of Bengal, 1784–1934, and the Bicentenary of Sir William Jones, 1746–1946. [Extracts from proceedings relating to the bicentenary and anniversary addresses.] pp. 28. *Calcutta,* [1946.] 8°. Ac. **8826/16**.

—— Indian Science Congress. Eleventh Annual Meeting . . . 1924, to be held at the Central College, Bangalore. (Programme.) pp. xxi. *Calcutta,* [1924.] 8°. Ac. **8826/14**. **(1.)**

—— A Key to Professor H. H. Wilson's System of Transliteration. Published by order of the Philological Committee of the Asiatic Society of Bengal. pp. 7. [*Calcutta,* 1865.] 8°. **12902**. **d**. **1**. **(4.)**

—— List of Arabic and Persian MSS. acquired on behalf of the Government of India; by the Asiatic Society of Bengal during 1903–1907 (1908–1910). 2 pt. *Calcutta,* [1908, 13.] 4°. Ac. **8826**. **b/3**.

—— The Oriental Biographical Dictionary. By the late Thomas William Beale . . . Edited by the Asiatic Society of Bengal, under the superintendence of Henry George Keene. pp. v. 291. *Calcutta,* 1881. 4°. **14003**. g. **9**.

—— Proceedings of the Twelfth Indian Science Congress. Benares, 1925. pp. xxiii. 356. *Calcutta,* 1925. 8°. Ac. **8826/14**. **(2.)**

—— Proposals made by the Royal Asiatic Society of Bengal in connection with cultural reconstruction in India. 2p. *Calcutta,* [1945.] 8°. **Ac.8826./17.**

—— Report on the Search of Sanskrit Manuscripts, 1895 to 1900 (1901-1902 to 1905-1906). By Mahāmahopādhyāya Haraprasad Shāstrī. 2 pt. *Calcutta,* 1901, 05. fol. **14096**. dd. **6**.

—— Sir William Jones. Bicentenary of his birth. Commemoration volume, 1746–1946. [By various authors. Edited by Kālidāsa Nāga. With plates, including portraits.] pp. xi. 173. *Calcutta,* 1948. 8°. **012359**. d. **30**.

CALCUTTA. [MISCELLANEOUS INSTITUTIONS.—ASIATIC SOCIETY OF BENGAL, afterwards ROYAL ASIATIC SOCIETY OF BENGAL.]

Library.

—— Catalogue of the Library of the Asiatic Society of Bengal. Compiled by Walter Arnold Bion. pp. 418. *Calcutta*, 1884. 8°. **011899. l. 26.**

—— A Catalogue of Printed Books in European Languages in the Library of the Asiatic Society of Bengal. 4 pt. pp. 664. *Calcutta*, 1908–10. 8°. **011904.** bb. **50.**

—— List of Additions to the Library . . . January to June, 1907 (1908). 2 pt. [*Calcutta*, 1907, 08.] 8°. Ac. **8826/15.**
Printed on one side of the leaf only.

—— List of Periodicals and Publications received in the Library of the Asiatic Society of Bengal. pp. 6. *Calcutta*, 1878. 8°. **11905. k. 21. (9.)**

—— The Sanskrit Buddhist Literature of Nepal. By Rájendralála Mitra. [A systematic catalogue of the collection of MSS. presented to the Society by Brian H. Hodgson, preceded by a memoir of the donor.] pp. xlvii. 340. *Calcutta*, 1882. 8°. **14096. b. 12.**

Museum.

—— Catalogue of Curiosities of the Museum of the Asiatic Society, Calcutta. Prepared by the Librarian. pp. 67. *Calcutta*, 1849. 8°. Ac. **8826/2.**

—— Catalogue of the Mammalia in the Museum, Asiatic Society. By Edward Blyth. pp. 187. xiii. *Calcutta*, 1863. 8°. **7207.** dd. **13.**

—— Catalogue of the Recent Shells in the Museum, Asiatic Society of Bengal. By W. Theobald, Junior, *etc.* pp. 4. 160. 5. *Calcutta*, 1860. 8°. **7207.** dd. **31.**

ASSOCIATION FOR THE PROVISION OF HEALTH AND MATERNITY SUPERVISORS.

—— Maternity and Infant Welfare. A handbook . . . By Ruth Young. pp. iii. ii. 183. *Calcutta*, 1920. 8°. **07580.** e. **81.**

ASSOCIATION OF BAPTIST CHURCHES IN BENGAL.

—— The Oriental Baptist. Published under the auspices of the Association of Baptist Churches in Bengal. *See* PERIODICAL PUBLICATIONS.—*Calcutta.*

ASSOCIATION OF ENGINEERS.

—— Journal of the Association of Engineers. vol. 19. no. 1, *etc.* March 1943, *etc. Calcutta*, 1943– . 8°. P.P. **1660.** ra.

ASTRONOMICAL SOCIETY OF INDIA.

—— The Journal of the Astronomical Society of India. Edited by J. J. Meikle. vol. 1. no. 1—vol. 4. no. 4. Nov. 1910—Feb. 1914. *Calcutta*, 1910–14. 8°. Ac. **4194.**

BAṄGĪYA-JANA-SABHĀ.

—— *See* infra: BENGAL PEOPLES' ASSOCIATION.

BANGIYA SAHITYA PARISHAD.

—— Handbook to the Sculptures in the Museum of the Bangiya Sahitya Parishad. By Manomohan Ganguly, *etc.* pp. viii. 146. 5. pl. XXVII. *Calcutta*, 1922. 8°. **7876.** e. **1.**

BENGAL BRITISH INDIA SOCIETY.

—— Evidences relative to the Efficiency of Native Agency in the administration of the affairs of this country. pp. xvi. 56. *Calcutta*, 1844. 8°. **08023.** aa. **13.** (**2.**)

CALCUTTA. [MISCELLANEOUS INSTITUTIONS.]

—— Evidences relating to the Efficiency of Native Agency in India . . . Reprinted with a supplement, by the British Indian Association. pp. xvi. 95. 1853. 8°. *See* INDIA.—*British Indian Association.* **8022.** bbb. **39.**

BENGAL CHAMBER OF COMMERCE AND INDUSTRY.

—— Half-yearly Report (Reports) of the Committee of the Bengal Chamber of Commerce, *etc.* 1854–69. 22 pt. *Calcutta*, 1854–69. **8231.** b. **8.**
Imperfect; wanting various numbers.

—— [A letter from the Secretary of the Bengal Chamber of Commerce to the Officiating Secretary to the Government of Bengal, acknowledging the receipt of a copy of "The Cyclone in the Bay of Bengal in June, 1872," with a commentary.] [*Calcutta*, 1872.] *s. sh.* fol. **1890.** e. **4.** (**114.**)

BENGAL CLUB.

—— A Short History of the Bengal Club, 1827–1927. By H. R. Panckridge. [With plates.] pp. 64. *Calcutta*, 1927. 8°. **010055.** b. **22.**

—— [Another copy.] **010055.** bb. **49.**

BENGAL COUNCIL OF MEDICAL REGISTRATION.

—— Rules and Regulations of the Bengal Council of Medical Registration, based on Bengal Act no. VI. of 1914,—the Bengal Medical Act, 1914. pp. iii. 65. *Calcutta*, 1916. 8°. **05318.** eee. **2.**

—— The Annual Medical List . . . 1916–17 [*etc.*]. *Calcutta*, [1917– .] 8°. P.P. **2548.** oba.

BENGAL ECONOMIC ASSOCIATION.

—— Bengal Economic Journal. The journal of the Bengal Economic Association, *etc.* vol. 1. no. 1–3, vol. 2. no. 1, 2. April 1916—April 1918. *Calcutta*, 1916–18. 8°. P.P. **1423.** yf.

BENGAL ECONOMIC MUSEUM.

—— Report on the Dyes and Tans of Bengal. Compiled by Hugh W. M'Cann. pp. x. 214. *Calcutta*, 1883. 8°. **7944.** d. **3.**

BENGAL MEDICAL LIBRARY.

—— The Bengal Medical Library Catalogue. Third edition. Revised and rewritten, *etc.* pp. 2. xv. 315. *Calcutta*, 1917. 8°. **011903.** dd. **11.**

BENGAL MILITARY ORPHAN SOCIETY.

—— Abstract of the more important Rules and Regulations of the Bengal Military Orphan Society. pp. 25. *Calcutta*, 1847. 8°. **7305.** ee. **13.** (**18.**)

—— Rules and Regulations of the Lower Branch of the Military Orphan Society. pp. 43. v. iii. *Calcutta*, 1850. 8°. **7305.** ee. **13.** (**19.**)

BENGAL MUSIC SCHOOL.

—— Public Opinion and Official Communications, about the Bengal Music School and its President (Dr. Sourindro Mohun Tagore). [With a supplement.] 2 pt. *Calcutta*, 1877. 8°. **07896.** i. **23.**

BENGAL PEOPLES' ASSOCIATION.

—— Report of the Non-Official Commission on the Calcutta Disturbances, 1918. pp. 91. *Calcutta*, 1919. 8°. **9058.** aaa. **5.**

CALCUTTA. [Miscellaneous Institutions.]

—— Some Papers relating to the Proposed Constitutional Reforms in India. [Edited by Viṣveṣvara Chakravartī.] *Calcutta*, [1919.] fol. **8022**. g. **44**.

Bengal Photographic Society.

—— Journal, *etc*. vol. 1. no. 1—vol. 5. no. 13. May 1862—Sept. 1865. *Calcutta*, 1862–65. 8°.

—— New series. vol. 1. no. 1—vol. 2. no. 6. March 1867—April 1871. *Calcutta*, 1867–71. 4°. P.P. **1912**. ma.

Bengal Provincial Conference.

—— The Report of the Proceedings of the Bengal Provincial Conference held in Calcutta on 25th, 26th and 27th October, 1888. pp. 117. *Calcutta*, 1888. 8°. **8022**. bb. **23**.

—— Report on Reform Proposals. pp. 58. *Calcutta*, 1918. 8°. **08023**. aaa. **44**.

Bengal Radical Club.

—— Study Circle Series. *Calcutta*, [1940– .] 8°. W.P. **1298**.

Bengal Secretariat Library.

—— Catalogue of the Bengal Secretariat Library. [Compiled by Kālī-prasanna Vandyopādhyāya.] Revised by C. S. McLean. pp. iii. 516. cii. xlvii. *Calcutta*, 1895. 8°. **11899**. d. **29**.

—— Catalogue of the Bengal Secretariat Library. Compiled by Kally Prosunno Banerjea; revised by C. S. McLean, with index. pp. iii. 718. cci. *Calcutta*, 1901. 8°. **011907**. ee. **8**.

—— Catalogue. [Compiled by Kālī-prasanna Vandyopādhyāya.] Revised and rewritten by Prasanna Kumar Das. Sixth edition, *etc*. pp. ix. 662. *Calcutta*, 1906. 8°. **11908**. e. **16**.

—— Catalogue. [Compiled by Kālī-prasanna Vandyopādhyāya.] Revised and re-written by Prasanna Kumar Das. Vol. I. General books and official publications. Seventh edition, *etc*. pp. xii. 710. *Calcutta*, 1914. 8°. **011899**. d. **10**.

Bengal Social Science Association.

—— Transactions, *etc*. vol. 1–7. *Calcutta*, 1867–78. 8°. Ac. **2294**.

—— The Bengal Social Science Association. Annual Meeting of 1877. pp. 37. *Calcutta*, 1877. 8°. Ac. **2294/2**.

Bengal United Service Club.

—— Rules for the Government of the Bengal United Service Club. (Alphabetical list of members.) pp. 54. *Calcutta*, 1864. 8°. **8830**. aa. **21**.

Bengal Veterinary College.

Bengal Veterinary Institution, 1893–99.
Bengal Veterinary College, 1899– .

—— [Curricula and rules.] 5 pt. [*Calcutta*, 1894–1901.] 8°. **07299**. b. **26**.
Various editions.

—— Annual Report of the Bengal Veterinary College (Institution), *etc*. 1895/96–1934/35. *In:* Annual Report of the Civil Veterinary Department, Bengal, for the year 1895-96(–1934-35). [1896, *etc*.] fol. & 8°. I.S. BE. **110**. & **299/13**.

CALCUTTA. [Miscellaneous Institutions.]

Bengalee Ex-Service Association.

—— Bengalees and Military Training. Being a resumé of the work done by the Bengalee Ex-Service Association since March, 1939. [With plates.] pp. 36. *Calcutta*, [1941.] 8°. **8821**. g. **26**.

Benoy Sarkar Academy.

—— Bulletin. no. 1, 3. June 1953, June 1954. *Calcutta*, 1953, 54. fol. Ac. **1930**. g.
Reproduced from typewriting.

Bethune Society.

—— The Proceedings of the Bethune Society for the sessions of 1859–60, 1860–61. (The Proceedings and Transactions of the Bethune Society from November 10th 1859 [1861], to April 20th 1869.) [The editor's preface signed: J. L., i.e. James Long.] 2 vol. *Calcutta*, 1862, 70. 8°. Ac. **1930/2**.

—— Bethune Society. At a monthly meeting of the Bethune Society held . . . on the 10th November, 1859(—12th April 1860). [Proceedings.] 6 pt. [*Calcutta*, 1859, 60.] 8°. **8355**. bb. **26**. (**1**.)

—— Popular Lecture on the Laws of England. By Joseph Goodeve. pp. 25. *Calcutta*, 1861. 8°. **7305**. ee. **13**. (**16**.)

—— Selections from the Bethune Society's Papers. no. 1, 2. *Calcutta*, 1854, 55. 8°. Ac. **1930**.

Bihar Planters' Association.

—— Report of the Indigo Research Station, Sirsiah . . . for the year 1909–1910. By C. Bergtheil. pp. 7. *Calcutta*, 1910. 8°. **07076**. f. **71**.

Biochemical Society.

—— Proceedings of the Biochemical Society, Calcutta. vol. 1–3. 1934/1935–1936/1937. *Calcutta*, [1935–37.] 8°. Ac. **3955**.

Bishop's College.

—— Statutes of the Missionary Institution of the Incorporated Society for the Propagation of the Gospel in Foreign Parts; to be called and known as Bishop's College, near Calcutta. pp. 12. *London*, 1825. 4°. **4193**. l. **4**.

Bishop's College Press.

—— Specimen of Printing Types for book and other works, used at Bishop's College Press. *Calcutta*, 1854. 8°. **11899**. bbb. **24**. (**5**.)

Library.

—— Catalogue of Manuscripts in the Bishop's College Library . . . Prepared by . . . Hara Prasad Shastri. pp. 57. *Calcutta*, 1915. 8°. **14096**. cc. **8**. (**3**.)

Appendix.

—— Notice of Bishop's College, etc. From a review of the Churchman's Almanack copied from the Calcutta Christian Advocate. [An attack on the objects and administration of the College.] pp. 12. *Baptist Mission Press: [Calcutta*, 1845?] 12°. **8305**. aa. **26**. (**1**.)

Bose Research Institute.

—— Transactions of the Bose Research Institute. (Bose Institute Transactions.) 2 vol. *Calcutta*, 1918, 27. 8°. Ac. **1931**. d.

Brahmananda Keshub Chunder Sen Centenary Committee.

—— Prayers. [By] Keshub Chunder Sen. Centenary publication. pp. 8. xxv. 394. *Calcutta*, 1943. 8°. **3458**. b. **46**.

BUDDHIST TEXT SOCIETY OF INDIA.

—— Journal . . . Edited by Sárat Cándra Dás. vol. 1. pt. 1—vol. 7. pt. 4. Jan. 1893—Mar. 1906. *Calcutta*, 1893–1904. 8°. **14003**. b. **19**.

CALCUTTA APPRENTICING SOCIETY.

—— The Third Report of the Calcutta Apprenticing Society, *etc.* pp. viii. 17. *Calcutta*, 1828. 8°. **8285**. bb. **3**.

CALCUTTA ART SOCIETY.

—— Tagore and China. Editor: Dr. Kalidas Nag, *etc.* (Published by Federation of Indian Music and Dancing and Calcutta Art Society.) [With plates, including a portrait.] pp. viii. 63. [1945.] 8°. *See* infra: *Federation of Indian Music and Dancing.* **11865**. dd. **21**.

CALCUTTA AUXILIARY BIBLE SOCIETY.

—— The Bible in India. Extracted from the fortieth report of the Calcutta Auxiliary Bible Society. pp. 55. *W. H. Dalton: London*, 1853. 8°. **3127**. f. **32**.

—— The Fifty-Seventh Report of the Calcutta Auxiliary Bible Society, for MDCCCLIX. pp. 56. *Calcutta*, 1870. 8°. **3129**. ee. **1**.

CALCUTTA BIBLE ASSOCIATION.

—— The Second (fifth) Report of the Calcutta Bible Association, MDCCCXXIV (MDCCCXXVII). With an appendix, a list of subscribers and donors, &c. &c. 2 pt. *Calcutta*, 1824, 27. 8°. **4193**. cc. **2**. (**3, 4**.)

—— [Another copy of the fifth Report.] **4193**. cc. **2**. (**5**.)

CALCUTTA CHRISTIAN TRACT AND BOOK SOCIETY.

—— The Fortieth Report of the Calcutta Christian Tract & Book Society, *etc.* pp. 71. *Calcutta*, 1870. 8°. **4192**. cc. **3**.

CALCUTTA CITY MISSION.

—— The Eighth Report of the Calcutta City Mission for 1860, *etc.* pp. 23. *Calcutta*, 1861. 8°. **4766**. d. **23**.

—— City Missions. By a member of the Committee of the Calcutta City Mission. (Circulated by the Committee.) pp. 32. *Calcutta*, 1853. 8°. **4193**. dd. **30**.

CALCUTTA COMMITTEE OF THE CHURCH MISSIONARY SOCIETY.

—— The Second (fifth, thirty-eighth, forty-second) Report of the Calcutta Committee (Calcutta Corresponding Committee) of the Church Missionary Society, *etc.* 4 pt. *Calcutta*, 1819–62. 8°. **4193**. cc. **69**.

CALCUTTA DOMICILED COMMUNITY ENQUIRY COMMITTEE.

—— Report . . . 1918–19. pp. vi. 233. *Calcutta*, 1920. fol. **8285**. g. **43**.

CALCUTTA EXHIBITION, 1923.

—— Calcutta Exhibition. Official Handbook & Guide. [With plates.] pp. 353. *Calcutta*, 1923. 8°. **010056**. g. **43**.

CALCUTTA GEOGRAPHICAL SOCIETY.

—— *See* infra: GEOGRAPHICAL SOCIETY OF INDIA.

CALCUTTA HIGH SCHOOL.

—— First(—tenth) Annual Report, *etc.* 10 pt. *Calcutta*, 1831–40. 8°. **1030**. g. **19**.

CALCUTTA HISTORICAL SOCIETY.

—— Bengal, Past & Present. Journal of the Calcutta Historical Society. *Calcutta*, 1907– . 4°.

—— Index to vol. I–VIII (IX–XVIII). 2 pt. [*Calcutta*, 1916, 28.] 4°. Ac. **8603**.

—— [Another copy.] vol. 1—vol. 16. pt. 1. July 1907—Mar. 1918. *Calcutta*, 1907–18. 4°.

—— Index to vol. I–VIII. [*Calcutta*, 1916.] 4°. Ac. **8603/2**.

—— Calcutta Faces and Places in pre-camera days. By Wilmot Corfield. pp. 60. *Calcutta*, 1910. 4°. **10056**. t. **13**.

—— [Another copy.] **10056**. s. **10**.

—— The Diaries of Three Surgeons of Patna [William Anderson, Peter Campbell and William Fullarton], 1763. Edited by Walter K. Firminger. pp. 74. *Calcutta*, 1909. 4°. **9057**. g. **2**.

—— The Narrative of the Life of a Gentleman long resident in India. By G. F. Grand. A new edition edited . . . with introduction, notes and additional letters by Walter K. Firminger. pp. xix. 335. *Calcutta*, 1910. 8°. **010854**. de. **33**.

CALCUTTA MADRASAH.

—— [Annual reports for 1846/47, 1847/48, 1849/50–1851/52 and 1853/54.] 6 pt. 1848–54. *See* infra: HINDU COLLEGE. Annual Reports of the Hindu College . . . Calcutta Mudrussa, *etc.* 1848, *etc.* 8°. **8365**. cc. **35**.

Library.

—— Catalogue of the Arabic and Persian Manuscripts in the Library of the Calcutta Madrasah. By Kamálu 'd-Dín Aḥmad . . . and 'Abdu 'l-Muqtadir. With an introduction by E. Denison Ross. pp. iv. 38. 115. 1905. 8°. *See* BENGAL. [*Miscellaneous Public Documents, etc.*] **14598**. d. **34**.

CALCUTTA MATHEMATICAL SOCIETY.

—— Bulletin, *etc.* *Calcutta*, 1909– . 8°. Ac. **4283**.

CALCUTTA MISSIONARY CONFERENCE.

—— The Educational Destitution in Bengal and Behar; and the London Christian Vernacular Education Society for India. pp. 35. *Calcutta*, 1858. 8°. **8308**. cc. **26**.

—— [Another copy.] **8305**. bbb. **37**. (**2**.)

—— Petition adopted by the Calcutta Missionary Conference in August, 1852, in reference to the East India Company's charter, *etc.* pp. 13. [*Calcutta*, 1852.] 8°. **8022**. ee. **25**.

—— Petitions to Parliament by the Calcutta Missionary Conference (against the Grant to Juggernath, and the connection of the East India Company with the Hindu and Mussalman religions). pp. 19. *Calcutta*, 1853. 8°. **4766**. f. **21**. (**6**.)

—— Petition of the Calcutta Missionaries, for a Royal Commission to enquire into the condition of the people of Bengal. pp. 16. *Sanders, Cones & Co.: [Calcutta*, 1856.] 8°. **8023**. cc. **2**. (**3**.)

—— The Missionary Petition to Parliament. (Petition of the Calcutta Missionaries for a Royal Commission to enquire into the condition of the people of Bengal.) [Reprinted from the Christian Intelligencer.] pp. 12. [1857.] 8°. **8023**. d. **14**.

—— Report of the Sub-Committee of the Calcutta Missionary Conference for the establishment of a Native Christian Family Fund, with proposed rules for its management. pp. 14. [*Calcutta*, 1860?] 8°. **4768.aa.99.(6.)**

—— Statement concerning Sir Mordaunt Wells's Judgment in the case of Hema Nath Bose . . . With notes and appendices. pp. 51. *Baptist Mission Press: Calcutta*, 1863. 8°. **4765**. eee. **21**. (**8**.)

—— Statistical Tables of Protestant Missions in India, Ceylon, and Burma, for 1871. Prepared at the request of the Calcutta Missionary Conference. pp. iv. 48. *Calcutta*, 1873. 8°. **4766**. f. **18**.

—— Statistical Tables of Protestant Missions in India, Burma and Ceylon, prepared on information collected at the close of 1890, at the request of the Calcutta Missionary Conference. pp. xv. 66. *Calcutta*, 1892. fol. **4766**. g. **10**.

CALCUTTA MUSIC ASSOCIATION.

—— Music of India. Quarterly magazine. Organ of the Calcutta Music Association. vol. 2. no. 1. April 1938. *Calcutta*, 1938. 8°. P.P. **1948**. bo.

CALCUTTA PSYCHICAL SOCIETY.

—— Bulletin, *etc.* *Calcutta*, 1932– . 8°. Ac. **3834**. h.

CALCUTTA SANSKRIT COLLEGE.

—— *See* infra: GOVERNMENT SANSCRIT COLLEGE.

CALCUTTA SCHOOL-BOOK SOCIETY.

—— The Nineteenth Report of the Proceedings of the Calcutta School-Book Society . . . 1856. (The Twenty-eighth Report of the Proceedings of the Calcutta School-Book Society, with which is now amalgamated the Vernacular Literary Society. 1872 & 1873.) 2 pt. *Calcutta*, 1857, 74. 8°. **4193**. dd. **90**.

—— An Epitome of Ancient History, containing a concise account of the Egyptians, Assyrians, Persians, Grecians and Romans. [Compiled by James Prinsep. With a Bengali version mainly by J. D. Pearson.] pp. 623. *Calcutta*, 1830. 8°. **14127**. b. **50**.

—— The Leading Principles of English Grammar. [With a Persian version by A'ẓam al-Dīn Ḥasan, Balgrāmī.] pp. 177. *Calcutta*, 1833. 8°. **757**. c. **20**.

—— The Persian Reader; or, select extracts from various Persian writers. *Eng. & Pers.* 3 vol. *Calcutta*, 1824, 25. 8°. **757**. d. **36**.

CALCUTTA STOCK EXCHANGE ASSOCIATION.

—— The Calcutta Stock Exchange Official Year Book 1940 (1942 [*etc.*]). *Calcutta*, [1940– .] 8°. P.P. **2550**. f. *Imperfect; wanting the issue for* 1941.

CALCUTTA TRADE ASSOCIATION.

—— Report of the Proceedings of the Calcutta Trade Association, from its foundation in 1830, to Dec. 1850. pp. 56. 317. iv. [*Calcutta*,] 1852. 8°. **08229**. df. **10**.

CALCUTTA TURF CLUB.

—— The Racing Calendar, *etc.* vol. 8, 9, 12. 1895-96, 1896-97, 1899-1900. *Calcutta*, 1896–1900. 8°. P.P. **2546**. c.

CANNING INSTITUTE.

—— Report . . . for the sessions 1866–68. pp. 105. *Calcutta*, 1868. 8°. **8364**. cc. **59**.

CARMICHAEL MEDICAL COLLEGE.

—— The Carmichael Medical College. Report & Proceedings of the Silver Jubilee Celebration, 1941. [With illustrations.] pp. 174. *Calcutta*, [1942.] *obl.* 8°. **7689**. a. **60**.

CATHEDRAL CHURCH.

—— Report of the New Cathedral of St. Paul, Calcutta, from June 1839 to October 1841. [Drawn up by Daniel Wilson, Bishop of Calcutta. With a plan.] pp. 74. *Bishop's College Press: Calcutta*, 1841. 8°. **4765**. bbb. **3**.

—— Final Report of St. Paul's Cathedral, Calcutta. To which is prefixed the sermon delivered on the occasion of the consecration by the Bishop. With an appendix containing documents. [With plates.] 2 pt. *Bishop's College Press: Calcutta*, 1847. 8°. **4765**. cc. **15**.

—— [Another copy.] **4765**. df. **2**. (**7***.)

—— Report on St. Paul's Cathedral Funds, and the commencement of the Cathedral Mission. To which is prefixed a sermon delivered by the Bishop on occasion of the commemoration of the third anniversary of the consecration. pp. 33. *Sanders, Cones & Co.: Calcutta*, 1850. 8°. **4765**. df. **2**. (**8**.)

—— [Another copy.] **4473**. cc. **10**. (**25**.)

Library.

—— Catalogue of the Cathedral Library. pp. ii. 122. *Calcutta*, 1861. 8°. **11900**. bb. **44**. (**3**.)

CHRIST CHURCH SCHOOLS.

—— A Brief Report of Christ Church Schools, in connection with the Calcutta Diocesan Committee of the Christian Knowledge Society for M.DCCCXLIV. pp. 13. *Bishop's College Press: Calcutta*, 1845. 8°. **4765**. df. **10**. (**5**.)

CHRISTIAN INSTRUCTION SOCIETY.

—— Third Report of the Calcutta Christian Instruction Society, 1835 to 1838. pp. 20. *Calcutta*, 1838. 8°. **4193**. aaa. **69**.

CHRISTIAN VERNACULAR EDUCATION SOCIETY FOR INDIA, BENGAL BRANCH.

—— *See* LONDON.—III. *Christian Literature Society for India and Africa.*

COLLEGE OF FORT WILLIAM.

—— Rules and Regulations of the College of Fort William, enacted . . . on the 23d June, 1841, and ordered to be in force from that date instead of the preceding statutes, *etc.* pp. 10. MS. NOTES. *Calcutta*, 1841. fol. Ac. **2696/6**.

—— The College of Fort William in Bengal. [Containing the official papers and the literary proceedings of the college during its first four years. Edited by Claudius Buchanan.] pp. vii. 240. *London*, 1805. 4°. **731**. l. **13**.

—— [Another copy.] **128**. e. **13**.

—— Essays by the Students of the College of Fort William in Bengal. To which are added the theses pronounced at the public disputations in the oriental languages, *etc.* (vol. 2, 3. Primitiæ orientales. Containing the theses in the oriental languages, *etc.*) 3 vol. *Calcutta*, 1802–04. 8°. **14005**. ee. **2**.

—— Public Disputation of the Students of the College of Fort William . . . before . . . Lord Minto . . . together with his Lordship's discourse. 27th February, 1808. pp. 52. *Black, Parry & Kingsbury: London*, 1808. 8°. **8365**. b. **57**.

CALCUTTA. [MISCELLANEOUS INSTITUTIONS.]

—— Public Disputation of the Students of the College of Fort William . . . before . . . Lord Minto . . . together with his Lordship's discourse. 15. September, 1810. pp. 60. *Black, Parry & Kingsbury: London,* 1811. 8°.
T. **1081**. (**7**.)

—— Public Disputation of the Students of the College of Fort William . . . before . . . Lord Minto . . . together with his Lordship's discourse. 30th September, 1812. pp. 65. *Black, Parry & Co.: London,* 1813. 8°.
8366. cc. **39**. (**2**.)

—— Public Disputation of the Students of the College of Fort William . . . before . . . Lord Minto . . . together with his Lordship's discourse. 20th September, 1813. pp. 48. *Black, Parry & Co.: London,* 1814. 8°.
8366. cc. **39**. (**3**.)

—— Public Disputation of the Students of the College of Fort William . . . before . . . Earl Moira . . . together with his Lordship's discourse. 20th June 1814. pp. 67. *Black, Parry & Co.: London,* 1815. 8°. **731**. h. **5**. (**2**.)

—— [Another copy.] **117**. e. **55**.

Library.

—— Catalogue of Books in European Languages in the Library of the Board of Examiners, late College of Fort William. Prepared under the superintendence of Lieutenant-Colonel Ranking. [With indexes.] 3 pt. 1903, 04. 4°. *See* BENGAL.—*Board of Examiners.*
11908. i. **14**.

—— Catalogue of Books in Oriental Languages in the Library of the Board of Examiners, late College of Fort William. Prepared under the superintendence of Lieutenant-Colonel Ranking. [With indexes.] 3 pt. 1903-05. 4°. *See* BENGAL.—*Board of Examiners.* **11908**. i. **13**.

CONFERENCE OF THE BAPTIST MISSIONARIES OF BENGAL.

—— The Minutes and Reports of a Conference of the Baptist Missionaries of Bengal, held at Calcutta from Augt. 22nd to Sept. 12th, 1855: with a letter from the secretary of the [Baptist Missionary] Society, and an appendix of documents. pp. 127. *Calcutta,* 1855. 8°.
20030. ff. **3**. (**3**.)

DISTRICT CHARITABLE SOCIETY.

—— Second(—forty-fifth) Report of the District Charitable Society, *etc. Calcutta,* 1833–76. 8°. **8282**. ff. **20**.
Imperfect; wanting the 1*st,* 3*rd*–6*th,* 8*th,* 9*th,* 15*th,* 25*th,* 26*th, and* 41*st*–43*rd Reports.*

EAST INDIANS' PETITION COMMITTEE.

—— Report of Proceedings connected with the East Indians' Petition to Parliament read at a public meeting held at the Town Hall, Calcutta, March 28, 1831; with an appendix. pp. xxxii. 113. *Baptist Mission Press: Calcutta,* 1831. 8°. **8023**. bbb. **29**.

—— [Another copy.] T. **2014**. (**2**.)

ENGINEERING ASSOCIATION OF INDIA.

—— Seven Problems of Planning. Being the presidential address of . . . Darab Cursetjee Driver at the annual general meeting of the Engineering Association of India, held on 9th August, 1944. pp. 17. *Calcutta,* [1944.] 8°.
12301. l. **40**.

FAMILY LITERARY CLUB.

—— The Second (third) Anniversary Report (the eighth and ninth annual reports—the thirteenth, fourteenth annual report—the fifteenth, sixteenth anniversary report) of the Family Literary Club, *etc.* 7 pt. *Calcutta,* 1859–73. 8°. **8305**. dd. **23**.

CALCUTTA. [MISCELLANEOUS INSTITUTIONS.]

FEDERATION OF INDIAN MUSIC AND DANCING.

—— Tagore and China. Editor: Dr. Kalidas Nag, *etc.* (Published by Federation of Indian Music and Dancing and Calcutta Art Society.) [With plates, including portraits.] pp. viii. 63. *Calcutta,* [1945.] 8°.
11865. dd. **21**.

FREE SCHOOL.

—— Rules and Regulations of the Calcutta Free School. pp. 40. xlvi. *Calcutta,* 1850. 8°. **8365**. bb. **12**.

—— A Short Account of the Present State of the Free School in Calcutta. (An Account of the Free School, *etc.* —Report of the Free School, *etc.*) 6 pt. *Calcutta,* 1817–23. 8°. **8365**. b. **32**. (**2**.)

FREE SCHOOL SOCIETY.

—— Proposals for the Institution of a Free School Society, in Bengal. pp. 13. *Thomas Watley: Calcutta,* 1791. 4°.
C.T.72.(4.)

—— Proposals for the Institution of a Free-School Society in Bengal, *etc.* pp. 17. *Honorable Company's Press: Calcutta,* 1796. 8°. **8365**. b. **32**. (**1**.)

GENERAL ASSOCIATION OF MISSIONARIES.

—— A Statement respecting a Central Institution or College, in order to the improvement and increased efficiency of school operations, conducted by missionaries of various denominations in Calcutta. pp. 56. *Baptist Mission Press: Calcutta,* 1831. 8°. **4765**. eee. **21**. (**9**.)

GENERAL CONFERENCE OF BENGAL PROTESTANT MISSIONARIES, 1855.

—— Proceedings of a General Conference of Bengal Protestant Missionaries held at Calcutta, September 4–7, 1855. pp. 183. *Calcutta,* 1855. 8°. **4766**. f. **9**.

—— [Another copy.] **4765**. df. **21**. (**6**.)

—— [Another copy.] **4765**. eee. **21**. (**13**.)

—— On Vernacular Christian Literature. [By James Long.] pp. 9. [*Calcutta,* 1855.] 8°. **11826**. h. **9**.

GENERAL TRADERS ASSOCIATION.

—— Shopping Guide, *etc.* pp. 73. *Calcutta,* [1944.] 8°.
8218. c. **35**.

GEOGRAPHICAL SOCIETY OF INDIA.

Calcutta Geographical Society, 1933–1950.
Geographical Society of India, 1951– .

—— Calcutta Geographical Review. vol. 1. no. 1—vol. 12. no. 4. Sept. 1936—Dec. 1950. *Calcutta,* 1936–50. 8°.
[Continued as:]
Geographical Review of India. vol. 13. no. 1, *etc.* March 1951, *etc. Calcutta,* 1951– . 8°. Ac.6208.

—— Publication no. 3 [*etc.*]. *Calcutta,* 1940– . 8°.
Ac. **6208**/**2**.

GOOD PARENTS ASSOCIATION.

—— Keys to Success. pp. 80. *Baroda,* 1954. 8°.
Cup. **363**. e. **16**.

GOVERNMENT ART GALLERY.

—— Annual Report on the Working of the Government Art Gallery, Calcutta, for the year 1917-18(–1919-20; 1921-22). *Calcutta,* 1918–22. fol. I.S. BE. **79**.

GOVERNMENT HOUSE.

—— Descriptive List of Pictures at Government House, Calcutta, *etc.* [By A. G. A. Durand.] pp. xx. 49. iv. *Calcutta*, 1897. 4°. I.S. **337.**

GOVERNMENT SANSCRIT COLLEGE.

—— [Annual reports for 1846/47, 1847/48, 1849/60–1851/52, and 1853/54.] 6 pt. 1848–54. *See* infra: HINDU COLLEGE. Annual Reports of the Hindu College . . . Sanskrit College, *etc.* 1848, *etc.* 8°. **8365.** cc. **35.**

—— Annual Report of the Government Sanscrit College of Bengal. Sessions 1851-52 and 1852-53. pp. 15. lxxv. *Calcutta*, 1853. 8°. I.S. BE. **231/4.**

Library.

—— Catalogue of Printed Books in the Sanskrit College Library. pp. iv. 314. *Calcutta*, 1919. 8°. **011903.** d. **55.**

—— A Descriptive Catalogue of Sanskrit Manuscripts in the Library of the Calcutta Sanskrit College. Prepared . . . by Hṛishíkeśa Śástrí . . . and Siva Chandra Gui. (vol. x [12]. By Hṛīshikeśa Śāstrī and Nīlamaṇi Cakravartti.) 12 vol. *Calcutta*, 1895–1909. 8°. **14096.** cc. **10.**
Published in parts; the wrappers are dated 1892–1915.

HAYGIAN MARTASIRAGAN JEMARAN.

—— *See* supra: ARMENIAN PHILANTHROPIC ACADEMY.

HEALTH AND CHILD WELFARE EXHIBITION.

—— Health and Child Welfare Exhibition, Calcutta, 1920. [With an appendix containing lectures delivered at the Exhibition.] pp. 31. cxlii. *Calcutta*, 1921. 8°. **07580.** c. **28.**

HIGH COURT.

—— *See* BENGAL.—*Courts of Law.*

HINDU COLLEGE.

—— Annual Reports of the Hindu College, Patshalla, Branch School, Sanscrit College, Calcutta Mudrussa, Russapuglah School, for 1846-47 (1847-48, 1849-50–1851-52, 1853-54). 6 vol. *Calcutta*, 1848–54. 8°. **8365.** cc. **35.**

—— Scholarship Examinations of 1845-46 (1846-47), *etc.* [Edited by F. J. Mouat.] 2 pt. *Calcutta*, 1847, 48. 8°. **8365.** bbb. **49.**

—— Scholarship Examinations of the Hindu, Hooghly, Dacca and Kishnaghur Colleges for 1848-49. [Edited by F. J. Mouat.] pp. ii. 131. *Calcutta*, 1849. 8°. **8365.** cc. **34.**

HINDU THEOPHILANTHROPIC SOCIETY.

—— Discourses read at the meetings of the Hindu Theophilanthropic Society. vol. 1. pp. iv. 143. *Calcutta*, 1844. 8°. **4766.** c. **11.**

INCORPORATED LAW SOCIETY OF CALCUTTA.

—— The Rules and Orders of the High Court of Judicature at Fort William in Bengal, Original Side. With appendices of forms. pp. iv. 360. *Calcutta*, 1939. 8°. **5319.df.3.**

INDIAN ASSOCIATION FOR THE CULTIVATION OF SCIENCE.

—— Proceedings, *etc.* vol. 5–8. *Calcutta*, 1919–23. 8°.
Imperfect; wanting vol. 9.
[Continued as:]
Indian Journal of Physics, vol. I [*etc.*] . . . and Proceedings . . . vol. x [*etc.*]. *Calcutta*, 1926– . 8°. Ac. **1930.** b/**2.**

—— Bulletin no. 12(–15). 4 pt. *Calcutta*, 1914–18. 8°. Ac. **1930.** b.

—— Active Nitrogen—a New Theory. By S. K. Mitra. (Joykissen Mookerjee Medal Lecture for 1945.) pp. 73. *Calcutta*, 1945. 8°. **08909.** f. **62.**

—— Copper in Ancient India. By Panchanan Neogi. pp. ii. 64. *Calcutta*, 1918. 8°. Ac. **1930.** b/**3.**
Special Publication no. 1 *of the Association.*

INDIAN CHAMBER OF COMMERCE.

—— Annual Report of the Committee for the year 1931. pp. 71. *Calcutta*, 1932. 8°. **8230.** ff. **35.**

—— Representation made by the Indian Commercial Associations of Calcutta to His Excellency the Viceroy. pp. 7. *London*, [1930.] 8°. **08023.** dd. **48.**

INDIAN CHEMICAL SOCIETY.

—— Industrial & News Edition of the Journal of the Indian Chemical Society. vol. 1. no. 1/2–vol. 3. no. 3/4; vol. 6 no. 1; vol. 7. no. 3/4; vol. 19. no. 3/4–vol. 20. no. 3/4. 1938–1940; 1943; 1944; 1956, 1957. *Calcutta*, 1938–57. 8°.
[Continued as:]
Indian Journal of Applied Chemistry. vol. 21. no. 1, *etc.* 1958, *etc.* *Calcutta*, 1958– . 8°. Ac. **3954/2.**

—— Quarterly Journal, *etc.* *Calcutta*, 1924– . 8°. Ac. **3954.**

Lahore Branch.

—— Sir Shanti Swarup Bhatnagar Commemoration Volume [Essays by various authors.] (Editors: V. S. Puri, P. L Kapur.) pp. vi. 112. *Lahore*, [1941.] 4°. **8898.** g. **37**

INDIAN JUTE MILLS ASSOCIATION.

Research Department.

—— Jute Abstracts . . . Summaries of current literature. *Calcutta*, 1937– . 8°. P.P. **1423.** yel.

—— The Moisture Relationships of Jute. pp. x. 153. *Calcutta*, 1939. 4°. **07941.** t. **1.**

—— Private and Confidential Reports.
no. 1. The chemical composition of the jute fibre. pp. 30. *Calcutta*, 1937. 8°. **7081.** g. **14.**

INDIAN MINING FEDERATION.

—— Indian Mining Federation. Report of the Committee for the year 1936 [*etc.*]. *Calcutta*, 1937– . 8°. W.P. **9793.**

INDIAN MUSEUM.

—— Minutes of the Trustees. Sept. 1866–Mar. 1868, Apr. 1868–Mar. 1869—Apr. 1873–Mar. 1874. *Calcutta*, 1868–74. 8°.
[Continued as:]
Extracts from the Minutes of the Trustees of the Indian Museum. 1 Apr. 1874–31 Mar. 1875—1 Apr. 1877–31 Mar. 1878. *Calcutta*, 1875–78. 8°.
[Continued as:]
Annual Report, List of Accessions and Selected Extracts of Minutes. Apr. 1878–Mar. 1879—Apr. 1879–Mar. 1880. *Calcutta*, 1879, 80. 8°.
[Continued as:]
Annual Report and List of Accessions. Apr. 1880–Mar. 1881—Apr. 1888–Mar. 1889. *Calcutta*, 1881–89. 8°.
[Continued as:]
Annual Report. Apr. 1889–Mar. 1890—Apr. 1914–Mar. 1915. *Calcutta*, 1890–1915. 8°. **7959.** de. **2.**
Imperfect; wanting the Report for 1909–10. *This issue of the Annual Report does not always contain the reports of both sections of the Museum.*

—— Indian Museum Notes. 5 vol. *Calcutta*, 1889–1903. 8°. **Ac. 3693.**

—— Memoirs. *Calcutta*, 1907– . 4°. **Ac. 3693.** b.

—— Notes on Economic Entomology. no. 1, 2. *Calcutta*, 1888. 8°. **7297.** h. **13.**
Replaced by Indian Museum Notes.

—— Records of the Indian Museum. A journal of Indian zoology. *Calcutta*, 1907– . 8°.

—— General Index to vols. I–XX, 1907–1920. *Calcutta*, 1923. 8°. **Ac. 3693/4.**

—— Abanindranath Tagore. His early work. Edited by Ramendranath Chakravorty. [Reproductions with introductory text. With portraits.] pp. 19. pl. XIII. *Calcutta*, 1951. 4°. **7871.** d. **9.**

—— An Account of the Alcyonarians collected by the Royal Indian Marine Survey Ship Investigator in the Indian Ocean. By J. Arthur Thomson . . . and W. D. Henderson. (I. The Alcyonarians of the deep sea. II. The Alcyonarians of the littoral area. By J. A. Thomson and J. J. Simpson.) 2 vol. *Calcutta*, 1906, 09. 4°. **1829.** h. **6.**

—— An Account of the Deep-Sea Brachyura collected by the Royal Indian Marine Survey Ship Investigator. By A. Alcock. pp. ii. 85. 2. pl. IV. *Calcutta*, 1899. 4°. **7297.** l. **9.**

—— [Another copy.] **7297.** l. **12.**

—— An Account of the Deep-Sea Madreporaria collected by the Royal Indian Marine Survey Ship Investigator. By A. Alcock. pp. 2. 29. pl. III. *Calcutta*, 1898. 4°. **7297.** l. **10.**

—— An Account of the Indian Triaxonia collected by the Royal Indian Marine Survey Ship Investigator, by Franz Eilhard Schulze . . . The German original translated into English by Robert von Lendenfeld. pp. 113. pl. XXIII. *Calcutta*, 1902. 4°. **7297.** l. **18.**

—— Aids to the Identification of Rats connected with Plague in India, with suggestions as to the collection of specimens. By W. C. Hossack. pp. 10. *Allahabad*, 1907. 8°. **7002.** h. **21.** (4.)

—— Annotated List of the Asiatic Beetles in the collection of the Indian Museum . . . Part I. Family Carabidæ, Subfamily Cicindelinæ. By N. Annandale . . . and Dr. Walther Horn. pp. 31. pl. 1. *Calcutta*, [1909.] 8°. **7297.** h. **32.**

—— Catalogue and Hand-book of the Archæological Collections in the Indian Museum. By John Anderson. 2 vol. *Calcutta*, 1883. 8°. **07708.** e. **20.**

—— Supplementary Catalogue of the Archaeologica Collection of the Indian Museum. By . . . Theodor Bloch. pp. ii. 96. *Calcutta*, 1911. 8°. **07708.** e. **20.**

—— Catalogue of Mammalia in the Indian Museum, Calcutta: by John Anderson. (pt. 2 by W. L. Sclater.) 2 pt. *Calcutta*, 1881, 91. 8°. **7206.** f. **9.**

—— Catalogue of Mollusca in the Indian Museum, Calcutta. By Geoffrey Nevill. fasc. E. pp. 42. *Calcutta*, 1877. 8°. **7298.** b. **21.**
No more published?

—— Catalogue of the Coins of the Indian Museum. By Chas. J. Rodgers. 4 pt. *Calcutta*, 1893–96. 8°. **7757.** bb. **6.**

—— Catalogue of the Coins in the Indian Museum, Calcutta, including the Cabinet of the Asiatic Society of Bengal, *etc.* (vol. 1 by Vincent A. Smith; vol. 2, 3 by H. Nelson Wright; vol. 4 edited by John J. Allan.) 4 vol. *Oxford*, 1906–28. 8°. **2261.** a. **11.**

—— Supplementary Catalogue of the Coins in the Indian Museum. Non-Muhammadan series. Volume 1. By Pandit B. B. Bidyabinod. pp. iii [viii]. 103. pl. I. *Calcutta*, 1923. 8°. **2261.** a. **12.**

—— A Supplement to Volume II of the Catalogue of Coins in the Indian Museum, Calcutta—The Sultans of Delhi and their contemporaries. By Shamsuddin Ahmad. pp. ix. 152. pl. V. 1939. 8°. *See* INDIA.—*Archaeological Survey.* **7754.** b. **22.**

—— A Supplement to Volume III of the Catalogue of Coins in the Indian Museum, Calcutta—the Mughal Emperors of India. By Shamsuddin Ahmed. pp. ix. 240. pl. III. 1939. 8°. *See* INDIA.—*Archaeological Survey.* **7754.** b. **23.**

—— Catalogue of the Indian Decapod Crustacea in the collection of the Indian Museum . . . By A. Alcock. 4 vol. *Calcutta*, 1901–10. 4°. **7297.** l. **29.**

—— A Catalogue of the Mantodea, with descriptions of new genera and species, and an enumeration of the specimens, in the collection of the Indian Museum, Calcutta. By J. Wood-Mason. 2 pt. pp. 66. pl. II. *Calcutta*, 1889, 91. 8°. **7297.** bb. **39.**

—— A Catalogue of the Moths of India, compiled by E. C. Cotes . . . and Colonel C. Swinhoe. 7 pt. pp. 812. *Calcutta*, 1887–89. 8°. **7297.** e. **16.**

—— Catalogue of the Remains of Pleistocene and Prehistoric Vertebrata, contained in the Geological Department of the Indian Museum, Calcutta. By Richard Lydekker. pp. 16. *Calcutta*, 1886. 8°. **7203.** b. **1.**

—— Catalogue of the Remains of Siwalik Vertebrata contained in the Geological Department of the Indian Museum, Calcutta. By Richard Lydekker. 2 pt. *Calcutta*, 1885, 86. 8°. **7203.** b. **2.**

—— Catalogue raisonné of the Prehistoric Antiquities in the Indian Museum at Calcutta. By J. Coggin Brown . . . Edited by Sir John Marshall. pp. 155. pl. X. 1917. 8°. *See* INDIA.—*Archaeological Survey of India.* **7700.** e. **6.**

—— Craniological Data from the Indian Museum, Calcutta. [By B. A. Gupte.] pp. 70. 1909. 4°. *See* INDIA.—*Ethnographical Survey of India.* **10007.** y. **3.**

—— A Descriptive Catalogue of the Indian Deep-Sea Crustacea Decapoda Macrura and Anomala in the Indian Museum. Being a revised account of the deep-sea species collected by the Royal Indian Marine Survey Ship Investigator. By A. Alcock. pp. 286. iv. pl. III. *Calcutta*, 1901. 4°. **7297.** l. **14.**

—— A Descriptive Catalogue of the Indian Deep-Sea Fishes in the Indian Museum. Being a revised account of the deep-sea fishes collected by the Royal Indian Marine Survey Ship Investigator. By A. Alcock. pp. iii. 211. viii. *Calcutta*, 1899. 4°. **7297.** l. **8.**

—— [Another copy.] **7297.** l. **11.**

—— Echinoderma of the Indian Museum.

pt. 1. Ophiuroidea. An Account of the Deep-Sea Ophiuroidea collected by the Royal Indian Marine Survey Ship Investigator. By R. Koehler. *Fr.* pp. 76. 11. pl. xiv. 1899.
pt. 2. Ophiuroidea. Illustrations of the Shallow-Water Ophiuroidea collected by the . . . Investigator. By R. Koehler. *Fr.* pp. 4. pl. xxi. 1900.
pt. 3. Holothurioidea. An Account of the Deep-Sea Holothurioidea collected by the . . . Investigator. By R. Kœhler and C. Vaney. *Fr.* pp. 123. ii. pl. xv. 1905.
pt. 4. Holothurioidea. An Account of the Litoral Holothurioidea collected by the . . . Investigator. By R. Koehler and C. Vaney. *Fr.* pp. 54. pl. iii. 1908.
pt. 5. Asteroidea i. An Account of the Deep-Sea Asteroidea collected by the . . . Investigator. By René Koehler. *Fr.* pp. 143. pl. xiii. 1909.
pt. 6. Asteroidea ii. An Account of the Shallow-Water Asteroidea. By René Koehler. *Fr.* pp. 191. pl. xx. 1910.
pt. 7. Crinoidea. The Crinoids of the Indian Ocean. By Austin Hobart Clark. pp. iii. 325. 1912.
pt. 8. Echinoidea i. An Account of the Echinoidea. (Spatangidés.) By René Kœhler. *Fr.* pp. 258. pl. xx. 1914.
pt. 9. Echinoidea. ii. An Account of the Echinoidea. (Clypeastridés et Cassidulidés.) By René Kœhler. *Fr.* pp. 161. pl. xv. 1922.
pt. 10. Echinoidea iii. An Account of the Echinoidea. (Échinides reguliers.) By René Kœhler. *Fr.* pp. 158. 1927.

10 vol. *Calcutta,* 1899–1927. 4°. **7297.** l. **28.**

—— Figures and Descriptions of Nine Species of Squillidæ from the Collection in the Indian Museum. By the late James Wood-Mason. pp. 11. pl. iv. *Calcutta,* 1895. 4°. **7296.** g. **14.**

—— A Guide to the Zoological Collections exhibited in the Bird Gallery of the Indian Museum. By F. Finn. pp. 2. 131. *Calcutta,* 1900. 8°. **7285.** aa. **16.**

—— [Another copy.] Ac. **3693/3.**

—— A Guide to the Zoological Collections exhibited in the Fish Gallery of the Indian Museum. [By A. Alcock.] pp. 92. *Calcutta,* 1899. 8°. **7290.** b. **13.**

—— A Guide to the Zoological Collections exhibited in the Invertebrate Gallery of the Indian Museum. pp. 155. *Calcutta,* 1894. 8°. **7298.** c. **18.**

—— A Guide to the Zoological Collections exhibited in the Reptile and Amphibia Gallery of the Indian Museum. pp. 47. *Calcutta,* 1894. 8°. **7204.** df. **6.** **(8.)**

—— Hand List of Mollusca in the Indian Museum, Calcutta. By Geoffroy Nevill. 2 vol. *Calcutta,* 1878, 84. 8°. **7299.** f. **34.**

—— —— Index of the Genera and Species of Mollusca in the Hand List of the Indian Museum . . . Gastropoda. By W. Theobald. 2 pt. *Calcutta,* 1889. 8°. Ac. **3693/2.**

—— An Illustrated Catalogue of the Asiatic Horns and Antlers in the Collection of the Indian Museum. By T. Bentham. [With plates.] pp. 96. *Calcutta,* 1908. 8°. **7204.** i. **3.**

—— Indian Fish of Proved Utility as Mosquito-Destroyers. By R. B. Seymour Sewell . . . and B. L. Chaudhurī. pp. 24. *Calcutta,* 1912. 4°. **7002.** bb. **12.** **(4.)**

—— The Indian Museum, 1814–1914. pp. xi. 136. lxxxvii. *Calcutta,* 1914. 8°. Ac. **3693/5.**

—— [Another copy.] **10008.** r. **7.**

—— List of the Batrachia in the Indian Museum. By W. L. Sclater. pp. viii. 43. *London,* 1892. 8°. **7290.** b. **11.**

—— List of the Birds in the Indian Museum . . . By F. Finn. pt. 1. pp. xxv. 115. *Calcutta,* 1901. 8°. **7001.** bb. **33.** **(1.)**

—— List of Snakes in the Indian Museum. By W. L. Sclater. pp. x. 79. *Calcutta,* 1891. 8°. **7290.** b. **8.**

—— A Short Guide to the Indian Museum. By A. F. M. Abdul Ali. pp. 28. *Calcutta,* 1928. 8°. Ac. **3693/7.** **(1.)**

Archaeological Section.

—— Indian Museum. Archaeological Section. [An account of the exhibits.] pp. 9. *Calcutta,* 1922. 8°. **7702.** p. **6.**

Art Section.

—— Introductory Guide to the Art Section of the Indian Museum, Calcutta. By Percy Brown, *etc.* pp. 18. pl. ix. *Calcutta,* 1916. 8°. **7805.** bb. **41.**

—— Quinquennial Report of the Art Section of the Indian Museum, Calcutta, for the years 1912-13 to 1916-17. pp. 4. *Calcutta,* 1917. fol. I.S. **BE. 69.**

Library.

—— Catalogue of the Books in the Library of the Indian Museum. Corrected to August, 1887. Compiled by R. Leonard Chapman. (Supplement i, September, 1887, to August, 1891. Compiled by Henry W. Fleming.—Supplement ii, September 1891 to August, 1895. Compiled by H. B. Perie. Supplement iii, September, 1895 to August, 1899, Supplement iv, September, 1899 to August 1903. Compiled by C. O. Bateman.) 5 vol. *Calcutta,* 1889–1905. 8°. **011903.** e. **20.**

Indian Psychological Association.

—— Indian Journal of Psychology. *Calcutta,* 1926– . 8°. P.P. **1247.** o.

Indian Research Fund Association.

—— The Indian Journal of Medical Research. *Calcutta,* 1913– . 8°. P.P. **2888.** ca.

—— Indian Medical Research Memoirs. Supplementary series to " The Indian Journal of Medical Research." *Calcutta,* 1924– . 8°. P.P. **2888.** caa.

—— Records of the Malaria Survey of India. vol. 1. no. 2, 3; vol. 2. no. 1. March, Oct. 1930; March 1931. *Calcutta,* 1930, 31. 8°. P.P. **2888.** cad.

Scientific Advisory Board.

—— Report of the Scientific Advisory Board for the year 1st January to 31st December, 1936(–1949). *New Delhi,* [1937–50.] 8°. A.R. **1224.**
Wanting the Reports for the years 1945, 1946.

Indian Research Institute.

—— D. R. Bhandarkar Volume. Edited by Bimala Churn Law. [With plates, including a portrait.] pp. xxx. 382. *Calcutta,* 1940. 8°. **15010.f.2.**

—— Indian Culture. Journal of the Indian Research Institute. *Calcutta,* 1934– . 8°. P.P. **656.** bg.

—— Indian Research Institute Publications. Fine Art Series. *Calcutta,* 1934– . 4°. **Ac.1930.e.**

—— Indian Research Institute Publications. Indian History Series. no. 2, *etc.* *Calcutta*, 1939– . 8°. Ac. **1930**. e/**3**.

—— Indian Research Institute Publications. Indian Positive Sciences Series. *Calcutta*, 1935– . 8°. **14053**. ddd. **1**, *etc.*

—— Indian Research Institute Publications. Linguistic Series. *Calcutta*, 1937– . 8°. Ac.1930.e/2.

—— Indian Research Institute Publications. Tutorial series. *Calcutta*, [1940– .] 8°. **8011**. de. **52**.

—— Indian Research Institute Publications. Vedic Series. *Calcutta*, 1933– . 4°. **14010**. eee. **1**, *etc.*

INDIAN RESEARCH SOCIETY.

—— Research and Review. Journal of the Indian Research Society. vol. 1. pt. 1–3. *Calcutta*, 1908, 09. 8°. Ac. **8825**. d.

—— The Eagle and the Captive Sun, a study in comparative mythology. By Jnanendralal Majumdar. pp. xii. 231. *Calcutta*, 1909. 8°. **4505**. eee. **35**.

INDIAN SOCIETY OF ORIENTAL ART.

—— Journal, *etc.* *Calcutta*, 1933– . 4°. Ac. **4728**.

—— Indian Society of Oriental Art. Catalogue of Ancient and Modern Pictures and Sculpture, exhibited at the United Provinces Exhibition, 1910–11. [Compiled by N. Blount and A. K. Coomaraswamy.] pp. 42. [*Calcutta*, 1910.] 8°. **7807**. i. **27**. (**4**.)

—— Sadanga, or, the Six limbs of painting. By Abanindranath Tagore. [Reprinted from the "Modern Review."] pp. iii. 25. *Calcutta*, [1921.] 4°. **7859**. t. **34**.

—— Some Notes on Indian Artistic Anatomy. By Abanindranath Tagore. (Translated by Sukumar Ray. Illustrated by Nanda Lal Bose and Venkatappa.) pp. ii. 17. [*Calcutta*, 1914.] 4°. **7806**. de. **26**.

—— [Another edition.] pp. ii. 15. *Calcutta*, [1921.] 4°. **7859**. t. **35**.

—— South Indian Bronzes. A historical survey of South Indian sculpture with iconographical notes based on original sources. By O. C. Gangoly . . . 95 full-page illustrations and 45 smaller plates in the text. pp. xiii. 80. pl. XCIV. *Calcutta*, 1915. 4°. **7700**. f. **4**.

INDIAN SOCIETY OF SOIL SCIENCE.

—— Proceedings of the Indian Society of Soil Science, 1943–44. pp. 9. *Calcutta*, 1944. 8°. Ac. **3541**. c/**2**.

—— Bulletin no. 1, [*etc.*]. *Calcutta*, [1938– .] 8°. Ac. **3541**. b.

—— The Soils of the Central Provinces and Berar. By . . . D. V. Bal. pp. 9. *Calcutta*, 1943. 8°. **07078**. ff. **69**.

—— Symposium on the Black and Red Soils of Southern India. Held at the Poona Agricultural College on the 11th October, 1938. pp. 59. *Calcutta*, 1939. 8°. **7080**. b. **3**.

Forms Bulletin no. 2 *of the Society.*

INDIAN SUGAR MILLS ASSOCIATION.

—— List of Sugar Mills in India working and projected, 1945. pp. 46. *Calcutta*, 1945. 8°. **8219**. pp. **8**.

INSTITUTION OF CHEMISTS (INDIA).

—— The Fuel Problem in India. By H. K. Sen, *etc.* pp. 48. *Calcutta*, 1928. 8°. **8715**. ee. **53**.

INTERNATIONAL BENGAL INSTITUTE.

Sociological Division.

—— Sociological Papers. (1. The Aboriginals of West Bengal.—2. Animal sacrifice.) pp. 4. *Calcutta*, [1936.] 8°. **10008**. pp. **15**.

INTERNATIONAL EXHIBITION, 1883–84.

—— Official Report of the Calcutta International Exhibition. 2 vol. *Bengal Secretariat Press: Calcutta*, 1885. 8°. **7958**. h. **7**.

—— Catalogue of Articles of the Madras Presidency and of Travancore, collected and forwarded to the Calcutta International Exhibition of 1883, by the Madras and Travancore Committees. Compiled by G. Bidie. pp. x. 96. *Government Press: Madras*, 1883. 8°. **7958**. h. **5**.

LADIES' SOCIETY FOR NATIVE FEMALE EDUCATION.

—— Report . . . 1852. pp. 30. *Calcutta*, 1853. 12°. **4033**. aa. **49**.

LIBRARY OF THE HOME DEPARTMENT, GOVERNMENT OF INDIA.

—— Catalogue of Books belonging to the Library of the Government of India. pt. 2. pp. 220. *Calcutta*, 1861. 8°. **11901**. g. **17**.

—— Catalogue of Books belonging to the Library of the Home Department, Government of India. 2 pt. *Calcutta*, 1867, 70. 8°. **11904**. dd. **20**.

LORD'S DAY UNION FOR INDIA.

—— A Brief History of the Repeal of the Lord's Day Act and of efforts to restore the legal "dies non." pp. 28. *Calcutta*, 1894. 8°. **05319**. e. **21**. (**6**.)

MAHA-BODHI SOCIETY.

—— Report . . . From 1891 to 1915, *etc.* pp. 24. *Calcutta*, [1915.] 8°. Ac. **2094/2**.

—— Journal of the Maha-Bodhi Society. Edited by H. Dharmapala. vol. 1. no. 1—vol. 9. no. 12. May 1892—Apr. 1901. *Calcutta*, 1892–1901. 4°.
[Continued as:]
The Maha-Bodhi and the United Buddhist World, *etc.* vol. 10. no. 1—vol. 31. no. 12. May 1901—Dec. 1923. *Calcutta*, 1901–23. 4° & 8°.
[Continued as:]
The Maha-Bodhi. The journal of the Maha-Bodhi Society, *etc.* vol. 32. no. 1, *etc.* Jan. 1924, *etc.* *Calcutta*, 1924– . 8°. Ac. **2094**.

—— [Leaflets relating to certain Buddhist relics presented to the Society.] 4 pt. 1916. fol. Ac. **2094**. b.

—— Buddha Gaya, *etc.* [A petition to the Viceroy, and other documents relating to the Buddhist Rest-house at Buddha Gaya.] pp. 27. *Calcutta*, [1907.] fol. **8022**. g. **40**.

—— Buddhagaya Temple. Contents: proposed Buddha Gaya Temple Act, 1935; Congress and Hindu Maha Sabha Report; views of prominent Indians and Europeans. pp. 69. *Calcutta*, 1935. 8°. **20020**. k. **10**.

—— Oppression and Tyranny at Buddha Gaya. Buddhist pilgrims forcibly ejected from the Great Temple by the menials of the Saivite Mahant. The visit of the Lieutenant Governor of Bengal to the Temple on December 3rd, 1909. [With illustrations.] pp. 11. *Colombo*, [1910.] 8°. **8156**. f. **56**. (**3**.)

MAHOMEDAN LITERARY SOCIETY.

—— Abstract of Proceedings of the Mahomedan Literary Society of Calcutta at a meeting held . . . on . . . the 23rd November, 1870. Lecture by Moulvie Karamat Ali, of Jounpore, on a question of Mahomedan Law, involving the duty of Mahomedans in British India towards the ruling power. pp. 23. *Calcutta*, 1871. 8°. **8023**. dd. **30**.

—— A Practical View of the Age of Consent Act, for the benefit of the Mahomedan community in general, by the Committee of the Mahomedan Literary Society of Calcutta. pp. 6. *Calcutta*, 1891. 8°. **8415**. g. **62**. (**5**.)

—— Professor Vambery to Islam in Hind Greeting. [Containing a letter from Professor A. Vambery to Nawāb 'Abd al-Laṭīf Khān Bahādur and a leading article on it reprinted from " Reis & Rayyet."] pp. 8. [1889.] 8°. **08023**. aa. **10**. (**3**.)

—— A Quarter Century of the Mahomedan Literary Society of Calcutta. A resumé of its work from 1863 to 1889, *etc.* pp. 26. *Calcutta*, 1889. 8°. **011853**. h. **12**. (**1**.)

LA MARTINIERE.

—— Rules and Regulations of La Martiniere, founded in Calcutta under the will of Major General Claude Martin. With an extract of the will of the testator . . . and other documents, *etc.* pp. 103. *Calcutta*, 1835. 8°. **8365**. c. **2**.

—— [Another edition.] pp. 103. *Calcutta*, 1847. 8°. **8355**. c. **46**.

—— Report of La Martiniere Institution . . . 1846–47 (1847–48—Annual Report of La Martiniere, Calcutta, for MDCCCL). 3 pt. *Calcutta*, 1847–51. 8°. **8355**. cc. **40**.

MARWARI ASSOCIATION.

—— Marwari Association Topical Publication, no. 1 [*etc.*]. Editor-in-chief . . . Madangopal Poddar . . . Associate editors . . . J. N. Varma . . . & S. K. Chatterjee. *J. N. Varma: Calcutta*, 1944– . 8°. W.P. **4827**.

MEDICAL AND PHYSICAL SOCIETY OF CALCUTTA.

—— Laws and Regulations of the Medical and Physical Society of Calcutta. 1833. pp. 15. *Calcutta*, 1833. 8°. **7686**. aa. **6**.

—— Transactions. vol. 1—vol. 9. pt. 1. *Calcutta*, 1825–45. 8°. Ac. **3870/4**.
No more published.

MEDICAL COLLEGE OF BENGAL.

—— Rules and Regulations of the Medical College of Bengal. pp. 49. *Calcutta*, 1849. 8°. I.S.BE.231/6.

—— Rules and Regulations of the Medical College in the Presidency of Bengal. pp. iv. 54. *Calcutta*, 1860. 8°. **7680**. aa. **72**. (**1**.)

—— Annual Report . . . Session 1845-46(–1852-53). *Calcutta*, [1846]–53. 8°. I.S. BE. **231/3**.

—— [Report on the First General Examination in Chemistry, September 1836.] pp. 86. [*Calcutta*, 1836.] 8°. **8708**. c. **18**. (**1**.)
Imperfect; wanting the titlepage.

—— Catalogue of Books. pp. 114. *Calcutta*, 1903. 8°. **011908**. ff. 8.

—— The Centenary of the Medical College, Bengal. pp. xi. 163. *Calcutta*, 1935. 8°. **7680**. e. 58.

—— Transactions of the Medical College Re-Union. *Calcutta*, [1938– .] 8°. P.P. **2888**. bg.

Pathological Museum.

—— Catalogue of the Pathological Museum, Medical College, Calcutta. By J. F. P. McConnell . . . Revised by Leonard Rogers. 2 vol. pp. iii. 951. *Calcutta*, 1910, 12. 8°. **7439**. de. **32**.

MESMERIC HOSPITAL.

—— Record of Cases treated in the Mesmeric Hospital from November 1846 to May 1847 (June to Dec. 1847): with reports of the official visitors. 2 pt. *W. Ridsdale: Calcutta*, 1847, [48.] 8°. **7410**. ee. **36**.

—— [Another copy of vol. 1.] **7409**. h. **6**.

MINING AND GEOLOGICAL INSTITUTE OF INDIA.

—— Memorandum of Association. (Articles of Association.) pp. 25. *Calcutta*, [1909.] fol. Ac. **3199/4**. (**1**.)

—— Transactions . . . Edited by E. H. Roberton. *Calcutta*, 1906– . 4°. Ac. **3199**.

—— Indian Mining. A concise handbook for laymen and specialists. By J. A. Dunn. pp. xi. 262. *Calcutta*, 1943. 8°. **07107**. e. **88**.

—— Mining and Geological Institute of India . . . 1908 (–1921). Member List. *Calcutta*, [1908–21.] fol. Ac. **3199/3**.
Imperfect; wanting the lists for 1910 *and* 1920.

Library.

—— Catalogue of Books in the Library of the Mining & Geological Institute of India. pp. 22. *Calcutta*, 1916. fol. Ac. **3199/4**. (**2**.)

MISSION CHURCH.

—— *See* infra: OLD CHURCH.

MOHAMMADAN SPORTING CLUB.

—— The Calcutta Monthly. A monthly review devoted to literary sporting, scientific, social and moral subjects. Issued under the auspices of the members of the Mohammadan Sporting Club. *See* PERIODICAL PUBLICATIONS.—*Calcutta*.

MOSLEM INSTITUTE.

—— Journal . . . Honorary editor: A. F. M. Abdul Ali. vol. 1. no. 1.—vol. 6. no. 1. July–Sept. 1905—July–Sept. 1910. *Calcutta*, 1905–10. 8°.
Imperfect; wanting vol. 5. *no.* 3, 4.

—— New series. vol. 1. no. 1. July–Sept. 1915. *Calcutta*, 1915. 8°.
[Continued as:]
The Muslim Review. vol. 1. no. 1—vol. 4. no. 4. July–Sept. 1926—April–June 1930. *Calcutta*, 1926–1930. **14005**. ee. **1**.
No more published.

MUDRUSSA.

—— *See* supra: CALCUTTA MADRASAH.

MUTLAH ASSOCIATION.

—— The Mutlah as an Auxiliary Port to Calcutta: its progress and prospects, *etc.* pp. 43. *Calcutta*, 1858. 8°. **10058**. d. **11**. (**6**.)

—— The Port of Calcutta and 'the Port of Mutlah,' considered in connection by a railway or a ship canal. By a Member of the Mutlah Association, *etc.* pp. 47. *Calcutta*, 1858. 8°. **8235**. bb. **74**. (**4**.)

—— Report of the Committee of the Mutlah Association, established in February, 1858, with the object of promoting the progress of the Mutlah as an auxiliary port, and containing a summary of their proceedings up to March 1861. pp. 16. *Calcutta*, 1861. 8°. **10056.** e. **7.** (**1.**)

NATIONAL CHRISTIAN COUNCIL OF INDIA, BURMA AND CEYLON.

—— *See* infra: NATIONAL MISSIONARY COUNCIL, ETC.

NATIONAL INSTITUTE OF SCIENCES OF INDIA.

—— Proceedings, *etc.* *Calcutta*, 1935– . 8°. Ac. **1930.** d.

—— Transactions, *etc.* *Calcutta*, 1935– . 4°. Ac. **1930.** d/2.

—— Annual Address to the National Institute of Sciences of India. 1936 [*etc.*]. *Calcutta*, 1936– . 8°. W.P. **1725.**

—— Indian Science Abstracts. Being an annotated bibliography of science in India. 1935 [*etc.*]. *Calcutta*, 1936– . 8°. Ac. **1930.** d/3.

—— Opening Address of Sir Jnan Chandra Ghosh . . . on the occasion of the Symposium on Post-War Organisation of Scientific Research in India held at Calcutta on September 27 and 28, 1943. pp. 11. *Calcutta*, [1943.] 8°. **12302.** b. **17.**

—— Symposium on the Factors influencing the Spawning of Indian Carps. pp. 28. *Calcutta*, [1945.] 8°. **7290.** f. **51.**

NATIONAL LIBRARY.

Imperial Library, 1903–48.
National Library, 1948– .

—— Annual Report for the year 1903–(1910). *Calcutta*, 1903–1911. 4°.
Imperfect; wanting the report for 1909.
[Continued as:]
Report on the Working of the Imperial Library, *etc.* *Calcutta*, 1912– . 4° & 8°. **11908.** e.

—— Author Catalogue of Printed Books in European Languages. *Calcutta*, 1941–. 8°. W.P. **4153.**

—— Catalogue. Part I. Author-catalogue of printed books in European Languages. With a supplementary list of newspapers. 2 vol. pp. xii. coll. 1643. *Calcutta*, 1904. 4°.

—— [Another copy.] Catalogue, *etc.* *Calcutta*, 1904, *etc.* 4°. **11916.** m. **16.**
Imperfect; wanting vol. 2 *of the supplement.*

—— —— First supplement. 2 vol. coll. 1336. 94. *Calcutta*, 1917, 18. 4°. **11908.** i. **19.**

—— Catalogue. Part II. Subject-Index to the Author Catalogue. 2. vol. *Calcutta*, 1908, 10. 8°.

—— —— First [*etc.*] Supplement. *Calcutta*, 1929– . 8°. **11900.** s. **33.**

—— Catalogue. Part IV. Catalogue of Indian Official Publications. Vol. I., A–L. pp. 543. *Calcutta*, 1909. 4°. **11900.** v. **10.**
No more published.

—— Catalogue of Books and Serial Articles relating to Language. [Compiled by A. T. Pringle.] pp. iii. coll. 760. 30. *Calcutta*, 1899. fol. **11907.** i. **12.**

—— Catalogue of Books in the Reading Room. With supplement and index. pp. 95. 27. *Calcutta*, 1903. 4°. **11907.** g. **47.**

—— Second edition. coll. 146. 4. 38. *Calcutta*, 1906. 4°. **11907.** t. **3.**

—— Catalogue of Sanskrit, Pali and Prakit Books. *Calcutta*, 1951– . 8°. **14096.** dd. **11.**

—— Catalogue raisonné of the Bûhâr Library. 2 vol.

vol. 1. Catalogue of the Persian Manuscripts . . . Begun by Maulavî Qâsim Ḥasîr Raḍavî. Revised and completed by Maulavî 'Abd-ul-Muqtadir. pp. ix. 382.
vol. 2. Catalogue of the Arabic Manuscripts . . . By Shams-ul-'Ulamā' M. Hidāyat Ḥusain. pp. viii. 619.

Calcutta, 1921, 23. 8°. **15008.c.20.**

—— Eighteenth Century Pamphlets, Maps and Prints, with a few MSS. [A special number of the Accessions Catalogue.] pp. 18. [*Calcutta*, 1904.] 4°. **11907.** t. **2.**

—— Guide to the Imperial Library. Fourteenth edition. By K. M. Asadullah. pp. 20. *Calcutta*, 1931. 16°. **11902.** aaa. **61.**

—— Hints to Readers. Sixth and revised edition. pp. 13. *Calcutta*, 1908. 8°. **011903.** g. **15.** (**1.**)

—— List of Additions. Third series. no. 14–172. Oct. 1905—Dec. 1919. *Calcutta*, 1905–20. 4°. **11908.** i. **18.**
Imperfect; wanting all before no. 14 *and all after no.* 172.

—— List of Periodicals received in the Imperial Library. pp. 11. *Calcutta*, 1913. 8°. **11901.** b. **60.** (**2.**)

—— Second edition. pp. 17. *Calcutta*, 1933. 8°. **11911.** bb. **37.**

—— The National Library of India. Golden Jubilee souvenir. Sunday, 1st February, 1953. pp. 54. pl. 20. *Calcutta*, 1953. 4°. I.S. **427/3.**

—— Rules for compiling the Catalogues of Printed Books, Maps, etc. in the Imperial Library. *Calcutta*, 1913. 8°. **11901.** b. **60.** (**3.**)

—— The Ta'ríkh Náma-i-Harát—the History of Harát—of Sayf ibn Muḥammad ibn Ya'qúb al-Harawí. Edited with introduction by Muḥammad Zubayr aṣ-Ṣiddíqí. pp. xxvi. 821. *Calcutta*, 1944. 8°. **14773.** cc. **23.**

NATIONAL MAHOMMEDAN ASSOCIATION.

—— The Rules and Objects of the National Mahommedan Association, with a list of the members. pp. 24. *Calcutta*, 1882. 8°. **4503.** f. **24.** (**4.**)

NATIONAL MISSIONARY COUNCIL, afterwards NATIONAL CHRISTIAN COUNCIL OF INDIA, BURMA AND CEYLON.

—— The National Christian Council Review, formerly The Harvest Field. *See* PERIODICAL PUBLICATIONS.—*Mysore*. The Harvest Field.

—— Proceedings of the First [*etc.*] Meeting of the . . . Council . . . 1924 [*etc.*]. *Calcutta*, [1924– .] 8°. W.P. **8549.**

—— The Christian Minister in India: his vocation and training. A study based on a survey of theological education by the National Christian Council. By C. W. Ranson. pp. 317. *United Society for Christian Literature: London & Redhill*, 1946. 8°. **4768.** bb. **4.**

—— Directory of Churches and Missions in India, Pakistan, Burma and Ceylon, 1947–1949. pp. 411. *Nagpur*, 1948. 8°. **4767**. eee. **32**.

—— Opium in India. [Results of an enquiry undertaken by the National Christian Council of India, Burma and Ceylon, edited by William Paton.] pp. 81. *Calcutta*, 1924. 8°. **8435**. g. **45**.

NATIVE CHRISTIAN TEMPORAL AID SOCIETY.

—— The Fifth Report of the Native Christian Temporal Aid Society, with a list of subscribers and donors for 1849, *etc*. pp. 42. *Calcutta*, 1850. 8°. **4225**. aa. **14**.

NATIVE HOSPITAL.

—— Report of the Transactions of the Native Hospital and its dependent dispensaries, during the year 1851. pp. 75. *Calcutta*, 1852. 8°. **7686**. aaa. **15**.

NORMAL SCHOOL.

—— India. Special appeal on behalf of the Calcutta Normal School. pp. 18. [*London*,] 1858. 8°. **8306**. df. **25**. (**7**.)

NUMISMATIC SOCIETY OF INDIA.

—— Journal of the Numismatic Society of India. vol. 4. pt. 1, *etc*. June 1942, *etc*. *Bombay*, 1942– . 8°. Ac. **5899**/**1**.

OFFICE LIBRARY OF THE INSPECTOR-GENERAL OF CIVIL HOSPITALS, BENGAL.

—— Catalogue of Books in the Office Library of the Inspector-General of Civil Hospitals, Bengal. 2 pt. *Calcutta*, 1909. 8°. **011907**. h. 3.

—— [Another edition of pt. 1.] pp. 167. *Calcutta*, 1909. 8°. **11907**. pp. **18**.
Interleaved.

OLD CHURCH.

—— The Old Church, Calcutta, Parish Magazine. vol. 3. no. 8—vol. 8. no. 10. Aug. 1895—Oct. 1899. *Calcutta*, 1895–99. 4°. P.P. **910**. cha.
Imperfect; wanting vol. 4. *no.* 5; *vol.* 6. *no.* 11, 12; *vol.* 7. *no.* 8; *vol.* 8. *no.* 5, 9.

—— The Centenary of the Old or Mission Church. [Signed: J. L., i.e. James Long.] pp. 7. [1870.] 8°. *See* L., J. **10055**. ee. **1**. (**6**.)

ORIENTAL SEMINARY.

—— Report of the Oriental Seminary and its Branch Schools for the year 1853-54(–1858-59, 1860-61). 6 pt. *Calcutta*, 1854–61. 8°. **8355**. b. **54**.

—— Report of the Distribution of Prizes at the Town-hall. Feb. 22, 1851 (Feb. 12, 1853) to the successful students of the Oriental Seminary, *etc*. 2 pt. *Calcutta*, 1851, 53. 8°. **8365**. bb. 52.

PHILATELIC SOCIETY OF BENGAL.

—— The Philatelic World. A monthly journal for stamp collectors. Official organ of the Philatelic Society of Bengal . . . Edited by B. Gordon Jones. vol. 1. no. 1—vol. 3. no. 7 & 8. July 1894—Feb. 1897. *Calcutta*, 1894–97. 8°. P.P. **1424**. apg.
Imperfect; wanting vol. 2. *no.* 7–10.

PHILATELIC SOCIETY OF INDIA.

—— The Philatelic Journal of India. vol. 23. no. 1, *etc*. Jan. 1919, *etc*. *Lahore, Birmingham*, 1919– . 4°. P.P. **1424**. apk.

—— Publications, *etc*. vol. 1–9. *Calcutta*, 1897–1908. 8°. **08247**. h. **38**.
Imperfect; wanting all after vol. 9.

—— The Four Annas Lithographed Stamps of India, 1854–55. By D. R. Martin . . . and E. A. Smythies. pp. xix. 50. pl. 12. *Stanley Gibbons: London*, 1930. 4°. **8247**. f. **32**.

PHOTOGRAPHIC SOCIETY OF BENGAL.

—— The Journal of the Photographic Society of Bengal. no. 2, 3. Jan., May 1857. *Calcutta*, 1857. 4°. P.P. **1912**. m.

—— Catalogue of Pictures in the Exhibition of the Photographic Society of Bengal. 4th March 1857. pp. 14. *Calcutta*, 1857. 8°. **8907**. f. **22**.

—— [Another edition.] pp. 14. *Calcutta*, 1857. 8°. **8907**. f. **23**.

—— To the Members of the Photographic Society of Bengal. [An address, signed: " A Member," opposing an intended resolution to expel the Rājendralāla Mitra for speaking against the Indigo Planters at a public meeting.] pp. 12. *Calcutta*, 1857. 8°. **1414**. f. **75**. (**12**.)

PHOTOGRAPHIC SOCIETY OF INDIA.

—— The Journal of the Photographic Society of India, *etc*. vol. 12. no. 1–6, 8, 10; vol. 36. no. 400—vol. 64. no. 463. Jan.–June, Aug., Oct. 1899; Apr. 1921—May-June 1927. *Calcutta*, 1899–1927. fol. & 4°. Ac. **5064**.
The numeration is irregular.

PRESIDENCY COLLEGE.

—— Calendar for 1911-12(–1913-14, 1919-20). 4 pt. *Calcutta*, 1911–19. 8°. P.P. **2549**. c.

—— The Presidency College Magazine. vol. 23. no. 2, *etc*. Jan. 1937, *etc*. *Calcutta*, 1937– . 8°. P.P. **3779**. hl.

Chemical Society.

—— Proceedings . . . from November, 1908 to April, 1909. pp. 43. [*Calcutta*, 1909.] 8°. **8905**. c. **25**.

Library.

—— Catalogue of Books in the Presidency College Library. pp. ii. 386. *Calcutta*, 1897. 8°. **011904**. f. **10**.

—— [Another edition.] pp. iii. 510. *Calcutta*, 1907. 8°. **011901**. g. **39**.

—— [Another edition.] Presidency College Library Catalogue. Author-catalogue of printed books. pp. 742. *Calcutta*, 1909. 8°. **011904**. bb. **3**.

—— [Another edition.] Catalogue of Books in the Presidency College Library. 2 pt. *Calcutta*, 1914, 15. 8°. **011904**. h. **39**.

PRESIDENCY GENERAL HOSPITAL.

—— Rules for the Management of the Presidency General Hospital, Calcutta. pp. 16. v. [*Calcutta*,] 1899. 8°. I.S. BE. **215**/**9**.

—— [A reissue.] Rules for the Management of the Presidency General Hospital, Calcutta. [*Calcutta*,] 1900. 8°. I.S. BE. **215**/**10**.

PUBLISHERS' ASSOCIATION OF BENGAL.

—— The Publisher. The official organ of the Publishers' Association of Bengal. vol. 1. no. 1–3. Sept.—Dec. 1934. *Calcutta*, 1934. 4°. P.P. **6491**. nb.

QUEEN VICTORIA MEMORIAL.

—— Illustrated Catalogue of the Exhibits. pp. 140. [*Calcutta*,] 1925. 4°. **07959**. e. **7**.

RAMAKRISHNA MISSION INSTITUTE OF CULTURE.

—— Bulletin, *etc.* vol. 4. no. 4, *etc.* April 1953, *etc.* *Calcutta*, 1953– . 8°. P.P. **3800**. gaf.

RAMAKRISHNA VEDANTA MATH.

—— The Memoirs of Ramakrishna, *etc.* (A reprint, with emendation, from the American edition of the "Gospel of Ramakrishna," 1907.) [Edited by Swami Abhedananda. With portraits.] pp. xiii. 437. *Calcutta*, [1939.] 8°. **04504**. c. **15**.

RAMMOHUN ROY CENTENARY COMMITTEE.

—— The Father of Modern India. Commemoration volume of the Rammohun Roy Centenary Celebrations, 1933. Compiled & edited by Satis Chandra Chakravarti, *etc.* [With a portrait.] pp. xxxviii. 572. *Calcutta*, 1935. 8°. **20031**. c. **5**.

ROYAL ASIATIC SOCIETY OF BENGAL.

—— *See* supra: ASIATIC SOCIETY OF BENGAL, *etc.*

ROYAL BOTANIC GARDEN.

See SIBPUR.

RUSSAPUGLAH SCHOOL.

—— [Annual reports for 1846/47, 1847/48, 1849/50—1851/52, and 1853/54.] 6 pt. 1848–54. *See* supra: HINDU COLLEGE. Annual Reports of the Hindu College . . . Russapuglah School, *etc.* 1848, *etc.* 8°. **8365**. cc. **35**.

SANSCRIT COLLEGE.

—— *See* supra: GOVERNMENT SANSCRIT COLLEGE.

SAT-SĀHITYA-SAṄGHA.

—— Makers of Indian History. [Reprints of speeches and writings of historical importance.] *Calcutta*, [1934– .] 8°. W.P. **11952**.

SCHOOL OF TROPICAL MEDICINE AND HYGIENE.

Pasteur Institute.

—— First [*etc.*] Annual Report . . . for the year 1924 [*etc.*]. *Calcutta*, 1926– . 8°. I.S. **115/7**.

SOCIETY FOR THE ACQUISITION OF GENERAL KNOWLEDGE.

—— Selection of Discourses read at the meetings of the Society for the Acquisition of General Knowledge. vol. 3. pp. iv. 91. *Calcutta*, 1843. 8°. **012215**. h. **1**.

SOCIETY FOR THE PROMOTION OF INDIAN INDUSTRIES.

—— Journal, *etc.* vol. 1. no. 1. pp. 37. *Calcutta*, [1892.] 8°. **08276**. i. **19**.

SOCIETY FOR THE PROMOTION OF INDUSTRIAL ARTS.

—— Annual Report . . . for the year 1858. [With plates.] pp. 23. *Calcutta*, 1858. 8°. **7943**. bb. **54**.

SOCIETY FOR THE RESUSCITATION OF INDIAN LITERATURE.

—— The Oriental. A monthly journal devoted to the resuscitation of Indian literature, *etc.* vol. 1. no. 1.—vol. 12. no. 2. Oct. 1898—Feb. 1910. *Calcutta*, 1898–1910. 8°. Ac. **8825**. b.

—— Ayurveda; or, the Hindu system of medical science. [By Manmathnātha Datta.] pp. 131. *Calcutta*, 1899. 12°. Ac. **8825**. c.

—— Hindu Dramatic Works. Translated from the original Sanskrit into English by H. H. Wilson . . . 1. Malati-Madhava [by Bhavabhūti]. 2. Ratnavali [by Harsha-deva]. 3. The Mrichchhakati [by Sūdraka]. 3 pt. *Calcutta*, 1901. 8°. **14080**. b. **13**.

—— Works of Kalidasa . . . 1. Shakuntala [in the translation of Sir W. Jones]. 2. Vikrama-Urvashi [translated by H. H. Wilson]. 3. Kumara-Sambhavam. 4. Megha-Duta [translated by H. H. Wilson]. 5. Ritu-Samhara. 6. Raghu-Vamsha. 6 pt. *Calcutta*, 1901. 12°. **14080**. b. **10**.

SOCIETY OF SAINT VINCENT DE PAUL.

—— *See* VINCENT [de Paul], *Saint, Society of, in Calcutta.*

SOCIETY OF THE SISTERS OF THE POOR.

—— First (second) Report of the Society of the Sisters of the Poor, Calcutta. 2 pt. *Calcutta*, 1866, 67. 8°. **4783**. cc. **6**.

SRI AUROBINDO PATHAMANDIR.

—— Sri Aurobindo Mandir Second [*etc.*] Annual . . . 1943 [*etc.*]. On the occasion of the 71st [*etc.*] birthday of Sri Aurobindo. *Calcutta*, 1943– . 8°. P.P. **1253**. ma. *Wanting the annuals for* 1944–46.

SRI RAMAKRISHNA CENTENARY COMMITTEE.

—— The Cultural Heritage of India. Sri Ramakrishna Centenary Memorial. [With plates, including portraits.] 3 vol. *Calcutta*, 1937. 4°. **010056**. dd. **55**.

Parliament of Religions.

—— The Religions of the World. [Addresses, messages and papers delivered in the Parliament of Religions. With plates.] 2 vol. pp. xx. xiii. 1044. xx. xiii. *Calcutta*, 1938. 8°. **04504**. c. **1**.

STANDING COMMITTEE ON THE HINDU SEA-VOYAGE QUESTION.

—— The Hindu Sea-Voyage Movement in Bengal. pp. v. 67. xxii. *Calcutta*, 1894. 8°. **4503**. cc. **7**.

TEA DISTRICTS LABOUR ASSOCIATION.

—— Hand-book of Castes and Tribes employed on tea estates in North-East India, *etc.* pp. ii. ii. 360. *Printed for private circulation: Calcutta*, 1924. 8°. **010007**. h. **24**.

—— Language Hand-book. Gondi. pp. 99. *Calcutta*, 1926. 8°. **14178**. f. **46**.

—— Language Hand-book. Kharia. pp. 92. *Calcutta*, 1929. 8°. **14178**. h. **35**.

—— Language Hand-book. Kui. pp. 100. *Calcutta*, 1926. 8°. **14178**. f. **44**.

—— Language Hand-Book. Nepali. pp. 86. *Calcutta*, 1927. 8°. **14160**. de. **2**.

—— Language Hand-book. Oraon. [Including "A Short Grammar of the Oraon Language," by A. Grignard.] pp. 131. *Calcutta*, 1926. 8°. **14178**. f. **45**.

—— Language Hand-book. Oriya. pp. 104. *Calcutta*, 1926. 8°. **14121**. g. **33**.

—— Language Hand-Book. Savara. pp. 137. *Calcutta*, 1927. 8°. **14178**. i. **7**.

CALCUTTA. [Miscellaneous Institutions.]

Union Debating Society.

—— Rules, *etc.* pp. 4. *Calcutta*, 1871. 8°. **8364. a. 49.**

United Provinces Historical Society.

—— *See* infra: **Uttar Pradesh Historical Society.**

University of Calcutta.

—— University of Calcutta. Regulations. pp. xxi. 409. *Calcutta*, 1914. 8°. Ac. **1931/72.**

—— The Calcutta University Calendar. *Calcutta*, 1858– . 8°. P.P. **2549. a.**

—— University of Calcutta. Minutes for the year 1857 (–1863/64, 1866/7–1880/81, 1906. pt. 2., 1908. pt. 2—1911). 39 vol. *Calcutta*, 1860–1912. 8°. P.P. **2549. b.**

—— Calcutta University. Entrance Examination, 1860. Alphabetical list of passed candidates. *Calcutta*, 1861. *s. sh.* fol. L.R. **270. a. 8.**

—— A Complete Alphabetical List of the Graduates of the Calcutta University from 1858 to 1881, with their degrees and occupations. pp. 40. vi. *See* Krishnachandra Rāya. High Education and the Present Position of the Graduates in Arts and Law of the Calcutta University, *etc.* 1882. 8°. **8309. dd. 31.** (3.)

—— Descriptive Catalogue of University Publications. January 1930 (August 1931, September 1932). 3 pt. *Calcutta*, 1930–32. 4°. Ac. **1931/56.**

—— Post-graduate Teaching in the University of Calcutta. 1918–1919 (1919–1920). [A report.] 2 pt. *Calcutta*, [1919, 20.] 8°. Ac. **1931/7.**

Examination Papers.

—— Subjects of Examination in the English Language, appointed by the Senate . . . for the Entrance Examination of December, 1860. [An edition of the prescribed texts.] pp. 221. pl. xii. *Baptist Mission Press: Calcutta*, 1859. 8°. **12201. f. 4.**

—— Subjects of Examination in the English Language appointed by the Senate . . . for the First Examination in Arts of December, 1879. [An edition of the prescribed texts.] pp. 385. *Calcutta*, 1877. 8°. **12269. dd. 1.**

—— Entrance Examination Papers of the Calcutta University from the year 1858, in four parts. Part i.—English. (Part iv.—Mathematics.) 2 pt. *Bose & Co.: Calcutta*, 1879. 8°. **8367. b. 6.**

—— English Translation of the Revised Persian F.A. Course, Calcutta University: with explanatory notes . . . Translated by Moulavi Syed Husain Ali . . . with . . . help from . . . the compiler of the text-book Shams-ul-Ulama Moulavi Ahmad. pp. 148. *The Compiler: Calcutta*, 1898. 8°. **757. g. 59.**

—— Question Papers for the B.A. and B.Sc. Examinations, 1907. pp. 131. *Calcutta*, 1908. 8°. P.P. **2549. ba.**

—— Question Papers for the M.A. and P.R.S. Examinations. 1907. pp. 233. *Calcutta*, 1908. 8°. P.P. **2549. bb.**

—— An English Translation of the Persian Course for the Matriculation Examination of the Calcutta University 1910–1911. With various notes. Translated by Syed Husain Ali. pp. 168. iii. *The Translator: Calcutta*, [1909.] 8°. **14822. d. 13.**

—— [Another edition.] pp. 168. iii. *The Translator: Calcutta*, [1909.] 8°. **14822. d. 18.**

—— An English Translation of the Persian Course for the Matriculation Examination of the Calcutta University for 1913 . . . By Maulavi Abul Makarem Fazlul Wahhab . . . & Maulavi Syed Hasan Askari, *etc.* pp. iv. 140. *The Translators: Calcutta*, 1911. 8°. **14822. d. 15.**

—— The University Question Papers for the year 1920 [*etc.*]. *Calcutta*, 1923– . 8°. P.P. **2549. aa.**
Previously published as Part iii of the Calendar.

—— Calcutta University Questions, 1926–1940. Matriculation. With University regulations, syllabus & other useful information for examinees. pp. xvi. 274. 74. *Sen, Ray & Co.: Calcutta*, 1940. 8°. **8355. de. 76.**

—— Calcutta University Questions, 1909–1940 [or rather, 1941]. I.A. & I.Sc. With university regulations, syllabus, *etc.* 4 pt. *Sen, Ray & Co.: Calcutta*, 1941. 8°. **8367. aa. 51.**

Miscellaneous Publications.

From 1947 onward works by individual authors published by the University of Calcutta are entered under their authors.

—— The Aborigines of the Highlands of Central India. By B. C. Mazumdar. pp. vi. 84. *Calcutta*, 1927. 8°. **010006. f. 14.**

—— Administrative System of the Marathas. From original sources. By Surendranath Sen. pp. xvi. 633. *Calcutta*, 1923. 8°. **9058. de. 2.**

—— Second edition, revised and enlarged. pp. xx. 699. *Calcutta*, 1925. 8°. Ac. **1931/27.**

—— Agricultural Indebtedness in India and its Remedies: being selections from official documents. Compiled by S. C. Ray. pp. xi. 466. 14. *Calcutta*, 1915. 8°. Ac. **1931/5.**

—— Algebra. Lectures delivered to post-graduate students of Calcutta University. By Friedrich Wilhelm Levi. *Calcutta*, 1936– . 8°. Ac. **1931/63.**

—— Analytical Key to the Commonly Occurring Natural Orders of Bengal. By Surendra Chandra Banerji. pp. viii. 127. *Calcutta*, 1934. 8°. **7207. aaa. 31.**

—— Anthropological Papers . . . New series. *Calcutta*, 1927– . 8°. Ac. **1931/29.**

—— The Arab Kingdom and its Fall. By J. Wellhausen. Translated by Margaret Graham Weir. pp. xvii. 592. *Calcutta*, 1927. 8°. Ac. **1931/32.**

—— Art and Archæology Abroad. A report intended primarily for Indian students desiring to specialize in those subjects in the research centres of Europe and America. Submitted by Kalidas Nag . . . Ghose Travelling Fellow. pp. ix. 125. pl. xix. *Calcutta*, 1937. 8°. **7811. ppp. 2.**

—— The Aryan Trail in Iran and India. A naturalistic study of the Vedic hymns and the Avesta. By Nagendranath Ghose. pp. xiii. 333. *Calcutta*, 1937. 8°. **11859. g. 20**

—— Asoka. By D. R. Bhandarkar. (The Carmichael Lectures, 1923.) pp. xviii. 346. *Calcutta*, 1925. 8°. **10607. e. 14.**

—— Second edition, revised, *etc.* pp. xxvi. 404. *Calcutta*, 1932. 8°. Ac. **1931/59.**

CALCUTTA. [MISCELLANEOUS INSTITUTIONS.—UNIVERSITY OF CALCUTTA.—*Miscellaneous Publications.*]

—— Aspects of Bengali Society from old Bengali Society. By Tamonash Chandra Das Gupta. [With plates.] pp. xl. 371. *Calcutta*, 1935. 8°. **010056.** c. **27.**

—— Barhut Inscriptions. Edited and translated with critical notes by Benimadhab Barua . . . and Kumar Ganganada Sinha. pp. 139. *Calcutta*, 1926. 8°. **14058.** c. **24.**

—— The Basic Conception of Buddhism. By Vidhushekhara Bhattacharya. (Adharchandra Mookerjee Lectures, 1932.) pp. x. 103. *Calcutta*, 1934. 8°. **20017.** l. **19.**

—— Bengali Prose Style . . . By Rai Sahib Dinesh Chandra Sen. pp. xv. 153. *Calcutta*, 1921. 8°. Ac. **1931/14.**

—— The Bengali Ramayanas . . . By Rai Saheb Dineshchandra Sen. pp. xviii. 305. *Calculta*, 1920. 8°. Ac. **1931/13.**

—— The Blind in India and abroad. By Subodh Chandra Roy. [With plates.] pp. xviii. 255. [*Calcutta*,] 1944. 8°. **8288.** b. **117.**

—— Brahmanical Gods in Burma. A chapter of Indian art and iconography. By Nihar-ranjan Ray. pp. ix. 99. pl. XXIII. *Calcutta*, 1932. 8°. **04504.** k. **65.**

—— Calcutta University Readership Lectures. (Calcutta University Special Readership Lectures.) *See* infra: University of Calcutta Readership Lectures.

—— Chaitanya and his Age. Ramtanu Lahiri Fellowship Lectures . . . 1919 and 1921. By Rai Bahadur Dinesh Chandra Sen. pp. xxviii. 417. *Calcutta*, 1922. 8°. Ac. **1931/20.**

—— Chaitanya and his Companions . . . Lectures . . . By Rai Sahib Dinesh Chandra Sen. pp. xxii. 309. *Calcutta*, 1917. 8°. Ac. **1931/6.**

—— Cheap Balanced Diets—for Bengalis. By Nishikanta Ray. (Calcutta University Jubilee Research Prize.) pp. xii. 125. *Calcutta*, 1939. 8°. **7391.** v. **28.**

—— Chronology of Ancient India, from the times of the Rigvedic King Divōdāsa to Chandragupta Maurya, with glimpses into the political history of the period. [By] Sita Nath Pradhan. pp. xxix. 291. *Calcutta*, 1927. 8°. Ac. **1931/33.**

—— Civil Service in India under the East India Company. A study in administrative development. Thesis . . . by Akshoy Kumar Ghosal, *etc.* pp. xii. 508. *Calcutta*, 1944. 8°. **9057.** ff. **16.**

—— Conflict and Co-operation in Modern History. Lectures delivered at the Calcutta University March, 1943, by H. G. Alexander. pp. 54. *Calcutta*, 1944. 8°. **9011.** ee. **22.**

—— The Constitutional System of India. A critical and comparative analysis. By Naresh Chandra Roy. pp. xii. 380. *Calcutta*, 1937. 8°. **20031.** d. **19.**

—— The Contribution of Christianity to Ethics. Stephanos Nirmalendu Ghosh Lectures, 1930-31. By Clement C. J. Webb. pp. 121. *Calcutta*, 1932. 8°. **8404.** ee. **29.**

—— [Another copy.] **8408.** i. **26.**
With an erratum slip added.

—— Contributions to the History of Islamic Civilization. By S. Khuda Bukhsh. Second edition. 2 vol. *Calcutta*, 1929, 30. 8°. Ac. **1931/42.**
Vol. 2 is of the first edition.

CALCUTTA. [MISCELLANEOUS INSTITUTIONS.—UNIVERSITY OF CALCUTTA.—*Miscellaneous Publications.*]

—— Contributions to the History of the Hindu Revenue System. By U. N. Ghoshal. pp. xv. 313. *Calcutta*, 1929. 8°. Ac. **1931/46.**

—— " Courtesy " in Shakespeare. [With special reference to the influence of Castiglione's " Libro del cortegiano."] By M. M. Bhattacherje, *etc.* pp. xix. 225. *Calcutta*, 1940. 8°. **11767.** b. **32.**

—— Cynewulf and the Cynewulf Canon. [By] Satyendra Kumar Das. pp. xx. 259. *Calcutta*, 1942. 8°. Ac. **1931/84.**

—— The Deśīnāmamālā of Hemacandra. Edited . . . with an introduction, index to the text and commentary and English translation . . . by Muralydhar Banerjee. *Calcutta*, 1931- . 8°. **14092.** ab. **1.**

—— Development of Indian Railways. By Nalinaksha Sanyal. [With plates and maps.] pp. xvi. 397. *Calcutta*, 1930. 8°. Ac. **1931/51.**

—— Dhātukosha. Forming a supplement to the Elementary Sanskrit Grammar [of G. F. W. Thibaut] published by the Calcutta University. By Bahuballabh Shastri. pp. 276. *Calcutta*, 1912. 8°. **14092.** aa. **19.**

—— Early Career of Kanhoji Angria, and other papers. By Surendra Nath Sen. pp. ix. 225. *Calcutta*, 1941. 8°. **09059.** b. **33.**

—— The Early Heroes of Islam. By S. A. Salik. pp. xiv. 514. *Calcutta*, 1926. 8°. **9059.** aa. **9.**

—— Eastern Bengal Ballads. Mymensing. (Eastern Bengali Ballads.) Ramtanu Lahiri Research Fellowship Lectures for 1922–24 (1924–26, 1926–28, 1929–31). Compiled and edited by Dineschandra Sen, *etc.* *Bengali & Eng.* 4 vol. *Calcutta*, 1923–32. 8°. **14129.** h. **15.**

—— The Economic and Commercial Publications of the Post-Graduate Teachers of Calcutta University. [By] Satis Chandra Ghosh. pp. vi. 80. *Calcutta*, 1948. 8°. **11926.** ee. **31.**

—— Economic Reconstruction of India. A study in economic planning . . . [By] Khagendra N. Sen. pp. ix. 500. *Calcutta*, 1939. 8°. **08246.** i. **32.**

—— The Economics of Leather Industry, with special reference to Bengal. By B. Ramachandra Rau. pp. x. 184. *Calcutta*, 1925. 8°. **08244.** ff. **16.**

—— Elementary Banking for Indian Beginners. By B. Ramachandra Rau. pp. ix. 197. *Calcutta*, 1925. 8°. **08225.** b. **21.**

—— Second edition, revised and enlarged. pp. xv. 353. *Calcutta*, 1934. 8°. **8231.** b. **47.**

—— An Elementary Sanskrit Grammar for use in the upper classes of higher English schools. By G. Thibaut C.I.E., assisted by Pandit Bahuballabha Shastri. pp. xii. 244. *Calcutta*, 1911. 8°. **14092.** aa. **12.**

—— Elements of Social Anthropology. By B. C. Mazumdar. pp. x. 139. *Calcutta*, 1936. 8°. **010007.** e. **43.**

—— Elements of the Science of Language. By Irach Jehangir Sorabji Taraporewala. [With charts.] pp. xxix. 484. *Calcutta*, 1932. 8°. Ac. **1931/61.**

—— The Ethics of the Hindus. By Sushil Kumar Maitra. pp. xvii. 344. 8. *Calcutta*, 1925. 8°. Ac. **1931/28.**

—— The European Alliance, 1815–1825. By C. K. Webster. pp. 89. *Calcutta*, 1929. 8°. **9075.** bb. **9.**

—— The Evolution of Indian Industries. By Rohinimohan Chaudhuri. pp. ix. 456. *Calcutta*, 1939. 8°. **08277. i. 60.**

—— Evolution of Indian Polity. By R. Shama Sastri. pp. xvi. 176. *Calcutta*, 1920. 8°. **09057. b. 23.**

—— Evolution of the Khalsa . . . By Indubhusan Banerjee. *Calcutta*, 1936– . 8°. **W.P. 10254.**

—— Exploration in Tibet. [By] Swami Pranavānanda, *etc.* [With plates, including a portrait, and maps.] pp. xx. 160. *Calcutta*, 1939. 8°. **10055. t. 18.**

—— Extracts and Documents relating to Mārāṭhā History.

vol. 1. Śiva Chhatrapati. Being a translation of Sabhāsad Bakhar with extracts from Chiṭṇis and Sivadigvijaya, with notes. By Surendranath Sen. pp. ix. ii. 272. 1920.
vol. 2. Foreign Biographies of Shivaji. By Surendra Nath Sen. [With a portrait.] pp. lvii. 492. [1927.]

2 vol. *Calcutta*, 1920, 27. 8°. **9058. de. 7.**

—— The Federal System of the United States of America. A study in federal-state relations. By Naresh Chandra Roy. pp. xii. 308. *Calcutta*, 1940. 8°. **08175. c. 45.**

—— Finite Geometrical Systems. Six public lectures delivered in February, 1940 . . . by . . . F. W. Levi. pp. 51. *Calcutta*, 1942. 8°. **Ac. 1931/82.**

—— Folk Art of Bengal. By Ajitcoomar Mookerjee, *etc.* pp. xv. 50. pl. XLII. *Calcutta*, 1939. 4°. **Ac. 1931/75.**

—— Food. By Chunilal Bose. (Adharchandra Mookerjee Lectures for 1929.) [With a portrait.] pp. 117. *Calcutta*, 1930. 8°. **Ac. 1931/54.**

—— The Foundations of Living Faiths. An introduction to comparative religion. By Haridas Bhattacharyya. (Stephanos Nirmalendu Ghosh Lectures.) *Calcutta*, 1938– . 8°. **Ac. 1931/67.**

—— The Ganges Delta. [By] Kanangopal Bagchi. [With maps and plans.] pp. x. 157. *Calcutta*, 1944. 8°. **010058. n. 18.**

—— A Genetic History of the Problems of Philosophy. By . . . Muraly Dhar Banerjee . . . Developed and completed by . . . Hiranmay Banerjee. pp. xii. 297. *Calcutta*, 1935. 8°. **08459. ee. 73.**

—— The German Primer for Science Students. By Haragopal Biswas. pp. xiii. 258. *Calcutta*, 1938. 8°. **Ac. 1931/70.**

—— Girls' Education in India, in the secondary and collegiate stages. By Jyotiprora Dasgupta. [With plates.] pp. xiii. 269. *Calcutta*, 1938. 8°. **8312. bbb. 29.**

—— Gleanings from my Researches . . . By Sir Upendranath Brahmachari. *Calcutta*, 1940– . 8°. **Ac. 1931/80.**

—— Handbook for the Guidance of Geography Students—Teachers' Training Certificate Course in Geography. Edited by Dr. S. P. Chatterjee. pp. 89. *Calcutta*, 1939. 8°. **10004. pp. 30.**

—— Hindu Law of Evidence, or, a Comparative study of the law of evidence according to the Smṛtis. By Amareswar Thakur. pp. xvi. 277. *Calcutta*, 1933. 8°. **20017. k. 19.**

—— A Historical Study of the terms Hinayāna and Mahāyāna and the Origin of Mahāyāna Buddhism. By Ryukan Kimura. pp. xx. 203. *Calcutta*, 1927. 8°. **Ac. 1931/35.**

—— A History of American Anthropology. [By] Panchanan Mitra. [With a bibliography.] pp. x. 239. *Calcutta*, 1933. 8°. **010006. i. 39.**

—— A History of Brajabuli Literature. Being a study of the Vaisnava lyric poetry and poets of Bengal. By Sukumar Sen. [With plates, including portraits.] pp. xv. 600. *Calcutta*, 1935. 8°. **11857. cc. 33.**

—— A History of Factory Legislation in India. Compiled by J. C. Kydd. pp. viii. 190. *Calcutta*, 1920. 8°. **5318. aaa. 16.**

—— A History of Indian Literature. By M. Winternitz . . . Translated . . . by Mrs. S. Ketkar (and Miss H. Kohn), and revised by the author. 2 vol. *Calcutta*, 1927, 33. 8°. **Ac. 1931/34.**

—— History of Indian Medicine. Containing notices, biographical and bibliographical, of the Āyurvedic physicians and their works on medicine . . . By Girindranāth Mukhopādhyāya . . . Griffith Prize Essay for 1911. 3 vol. *Calcutta*, 1923–29. 8°. **Ac. 1931/18.**

—— History of Police Organisation in India and Indian Village Police. Being select chapters of the Report of the Indian Police Commission, 1902–03. pp. 53. *Calcutta*, 1913. 8°. **Ac. 1931/3. (1.)**

—— History of Political Thought from Rammohun to Dayananda, 1821–84 . . . [By] Bimanbehari Majumdar. *Calcutta*, 1934– . 8°. **W.P. 11268.**

—— A History of Pre-Buddhistic Indian Philosophy. By Benimadhab Barua. pp. xxiv. 444. *Calcutta*, 1921. 8°. **4503. h. 16.**

—— A History of Sanskrit Literature. Classical period . . . General editor: S. N. Dasgupta. *Calcutta*, 1947– . 8°. **15010.b.20.**

—— The History of the Bengali Language. By Bijaychandra Mazumdar. pp. xvii. 298. *Calcutta*, 1920. 8°. **12906. o. 18.**

—— Second edition. pp. xix. 323. *Calcutta*, 1927. 8°. **Ac. 1931/37.**

—— A History of the Islamic Peoples. Translated from the German of Dr. Weil's Geschichte der islamitischen Völker by S. Khuda Bukhsh. pp. vii. 170. *Calcutta*, [1915.] 8°. **09055. c. 53.**

—— Indian Cultural Influence in Cambodia. By Bijan Raj Chatterji. pp. xv. 303. *Calcutta*, 1928. 8°. **07704. e. 37.**

—— Indian Steel and Protection. By K. Khosla. pp. x. 133. *Calcutta*, 1939. 8°. **8218. e. 34.**

—— Indian Writers of English Verse. By Lotika Basu. pp. xiii. 156. *Calcutta*, 1933. 8°. **11856. b. 19.**

—— Industrial Finance in India. A study in investment banking and state-aid to industry with special reference to India. By Saroj Kumar Basu. (Thesis.) pp. xvii. 436. *Calcutta*, 1939. 8°. **08244. h. 69.**

—— Inland Transport and Communication in Mediæval India. By Bejoy Kumar Sarkar. pp. ii. 87. *Calcutta*, 1925. 8°. **08235. d. 66.**

—— An Introduction to Adwaita Philosophy, Sankara School of Vedanta. By Kokileswar Sastri, Vidyaratna. pp. xv. 194. *Calcutta*, 1924. 8°. **Ac. 1931/19.**

—— Second edition. pp. xvii. 247. *Calcutta*, 1926. 8°. **04504. i. 36.**

—— An Introduction to Indian Philosophy. By S. C. Chatterjee . . . and D. M. Datta. pp. xviii. 464. *Calcutta*, 1939. 8°. Ac. **1931/76.**

—— An Introduction to Indian Philosophy. By Satischandra Chatterjee . . . and Dhirendramohan Datta . . . Second edition, revised and enlarged. pp. xviii. 496. *Calcutta*, 1944. 8°. **8459.** tt. **24.**

—— An Introduction to the Geometry of the Fourfold . . . By Surendra Mohan Ganguli. pp. xxi. 427. *Calcutta*, 1934. 8°. **08534.** h. **12.**

—— An Introduction to the Theory of Elliptic Functions and Higher Transcendentals. By Ganesh Prasad. pp. x. 99. *Calcutta*, 1928. 8°. **8504.** dd. **38.**

—— The Jubilee French Course . . . By J. Buffard. *Calcutta*, 1936– . 4°. W.P. **9110.**

—— Juristic Personality of Hindu Deities. Asutosh Mookerjee Lectures, 1931. By S. C. Bagchi. pp. vi. 78. *Calcutta*, 1933. 8°. **20017.** l. **26.**

—— Kamala Lectures. *Calcutta*, 1925– . 8°. Ac. **1931/26.**

—— The Khaṇḍakhādyaka. An astronomical treatise of Brahmagupta. Translated into English with an introduction, notes, illustrations and appendices by Prabodh Chandra Sengupta. pp. xxx. 204. *Calcutta*, 1934. 8°. **14055.** ddd. **3.**

—— Kindred Sayings on Buddhism. By Mrs. Rhys Davids. pp. viii. 108. *Calcutta*, 1930. 8°. **04504.** de. **79.**

—— Lahiri's Select Poems. Revised edition, *etc.* [An anthology of English verse.] pp. x. 189. *Calcutta*, 1928. 8°. Ac. **1931/62.**

—— [Another edition.] pp. x. 199. *Calcutta*, 1930. 8°. Ac. **1931/50.**

—— The Law of Fixtures in British India. [By] Manmathanath Ray. pp. ii. 165. *Calcutta*, 1928. 8°. Ac. **1931/36.**

—— Lectures on Ancient Indian Numismatics. Delivered by D. R. Bhandarkar. (The Carmichael Lectures, 1921.) pp. xii. 229. *Calcutta*, 1921. 8°. **7757.** aaa. **43.**

—— Lectures on Arabic Historians. Delivered before the University of Calcutta, February, 1929. By D. S. Margoliouth. pp. 160. *Calcutta*, 1930. 8°. Ac. **1931/45.**

—— Lectures on Comparative Religion. By Arthur Anthony Macdonell. pp. 190. *Calcutta*, 1925. 8°. Ac. **1931/23.**

—— Lectures on Ethnography. By Rao Bahadur L. K. Anantha Krishna Iyer, *etc.* [With plates.] pp. xiv. ii. 277. *Calcutta*, 1925. 8°. **010007.** h. **25.**

—— Lectures on the Ancient History of India, on the period from 650 to 325 B.C. . . . By D. R. Bhandarkar. (The Carmichael Lectures, 1918.) pp. xii. 218. *Calcutta*, 1919. 8°. **9056.** ee. **22.**

—— [Another copy.] **9058.** aa. **11.**

—— Lectures on the Economic Condition of Ancient India. [By] J. N. Samaddar. pp. xiv. 165. *Calcutta*, 1922. 8°. **08245.** h. **41.**

—— Lectures on Wave Mechanics delivered before the Calcutta University by Arnold Sommerfeld. pp. vii. 120. *Calcutta*, 1929. 8°. **8710.** a. **25.**

—— The Legal Aspects of Strikes, and the course, efficacy and justification of legislation to prevent them. By Probodhchandra Ghosh. pp. 60. *Calcutta*, 1920. 8°. **5310.** aaa. **6.**

—— The Linguistic Speculations of the Hindus. By Prabhatchandra Chakravarti. pp. xviii. 496. *Calcutta*, 1933. 8°. **12904.** dd. **27.**

—— The Little Clay Cart. A play in ten acts by King Shudraka. Translated from the original Sanskrit by Satyendra Kumar Basu, *etc.* pp. xxvi. 153. *Calcutta*, 1939. 8°. **14079.** c. **74.**

—— Mādhva Logic. Being an English translation of the Pramāṇacandrikā [of Chalāri Seshāchārya] with an introductory outline of Mādhva philosophy and the text in Sanskrit. By Susil Kumar Maitra. pp. xxvi. 166. *Calcutta*, 1936. 8°. **14049.** da. **6.**

—— Magadha Architecture and Culture. [By] Sris Chandra Chatterjee. pp. xxviii. 112. pl. xxx. *Calcutta*, 1942. 4°. **7711.** aaa. **16.**

—— Manu-Smṛti. The Laws of Manu. With the Bhāṣya of Medhātithi. Translated by Gangānātha Jhā. 5 vol. *Calcutta*, 1920–26. 8°. **14038.** e. **24.**

—— Manu Smrti. Notes. By Ganganatha Jha. 3 vol. *Calcutta*, 1924–29. 8°. Ac. **1931/24.**

—— [Another copy.] **14038.** e. **24.**

—— A Manual of Buddhist Historical Traditions—Saddhamma-Sañgaha [by Dhammakitti]. Translated into English . . . by Bimala Churn Law. pp. vi. 140. *Calcutta*, 1941. 8°. **14097.** e. **10.**

—— Materials for the Study of the Early History of the Vaishnava Sect. By Hemchandra Raychaudhuri. pp. viii. 146. *Calcutta*, 1920. 8°. **04503.** f. **56.**

—— Second edition, revised and enlarged. pp. xiv. 226. *Calcutta*, 1936. 8°. **20031.** d. **21.**

—— Molecular Diffraction of Light. By C. V. Raman. pp. x. 103. *Calcutta*, 1922. 8°. **8716.** f. **2.**

—— Museum Method and the Process of Cleaning and Preservation. By Minendra Nath Basu. pp. viii. 34. *Calcutta*, 1943. 8°. Ac. **1931 79.**
No. 2 of the "Asutosh Museum Series."

—— Mussulman Culture. [By Vasily Vladimirovich Bartol'd.] Translated from the Russian by Shahid Suhrawardy, *etc.* pp. xxviii. 146. *Calcutta*, 1934. 8°. **9058.** df. **5.**

—— Negative Fact, Negation and Truth. By Adhar Chandra Das. pp. xxiii. 294. *Calcutta*, 1942. 8°. **8472.** d. **35.**

—— Newness of Life. Stephanos Nirmalendu Lectures. By Maurice A. Canney. pp. 178. *Calcutta*, 1928. 8°. **4375.** dd. **18.**

—— The Nyāya Theory of Knowledge. A critical study of some problems of logic and metaphysics. By S. C. Chatterjee. pp. xix. 421. *Calcutta*, 1939. 8°. **8459.** v. **26.**

—— Old Brāhmī Inscriptions in the Udayagiri and Khaṇḍagiri Caves. Edited with new readings and critical notes by Benimadhab Barua. pp. xxii. 324. *Calcutta*, 1929. 8°. Ac. **1931/41.**

—— On the Chemistry and Toxicology of Nerium Odorum. With a description of a newly-separated active principle. By Chunilal Bose . . . Coates Memorial Prize thesis. pp. 28. pl. iv. *Calcutta*, 1912. 8°. **07509.** h. **42.**

—— On the Fundamentals of Analysis. Six public lectures delivered . . . 1938 at the University of Calcutta by the Hardinge Professor F. W. Levi. pp. 56. *Calcutta* 1939. 8°. **08535**. h. **129**.

—— On the Poetry of Matthew Arnold, Robert Browning and Rabindranath Tagore. By Amulyachandra Aikat. pp. 346. *Calcutta*, 1921. 8°. **011850**. aaa. **65**.

—— Organic Thio-compounds. With special reference to tautomeric changes and the formation of polysulphonium derivatives. By Sir Prafulla Chandra Ray. pt. 1. pp. iii. 70. *Calcutta*, 1919. 8°. Ac. **1931/10**.

—— Organization of Railways. By S. C. Ghose. pp. 33. *Calcutta*, 1927. 8°. **08235**. bb. **71**.

—— The Orient under the Caliphs. Translated from Von Kremer's Culturgeschichte des Orients by S. Khuda Bukhsh. pp. xii. 463. *Calcutta*, 1920. 8°. **09057**. b. **22**.

—— The Original and Developed Doctrines of Indian Buddhism, in charts. By Ryukan Kimura. pp. vi. 73. *Calcutta*, 1920. 4°. **4503**. h. **17**.

—— Orissa in the Making . . . By B. C. Mazumdar. pp. iii. xi. 247. [*Calcutta*,] 1925. 8°. Ac. **1931/25**.

—— Othello, the Moor of Venice. With introduction and notes by John C. Scrimgeour. pp. lxxxii. 299. *Calcutta*, 1921. 8°. **11765**. t. **28**.

—— Pāli Literature and Language. By Wilhelm Geiger . . . Authorized English translation by Batakrishna Ghosh. pp. xviii. 250. *Calcutta*, 1943. 8°. **012904**. k. **69**.

—— Paper Currency in India. By B. B. Das Gupta, *etc.* pp. xviii. 331. *Calcutta*, 1927. 8°. **08229**. cc. **74**.

—— The Payment of Wages and Profit-Sharing. With a chapter on Indian conditions. By R. N. Gilchrist. pp. 422. *Calcutta*, 1924. 8°. Ac. **1931/21**.

—— Philosophical Currents of the Present Day. By Dr. Ludwig Stein. Translated by Shishirkumar Maitra. 3 vol. pp. xvi. iii. viii. 623. *Calcutta*, 1918–24. 8°. Ac. **1931/8**.

—— Philosophical Essays. By Surendranath Dasgupta. pp. 388. *Calcutta*, 1941. 8°. **8467**. i. **25**.

—— The Philosophy of Sanskrit Grammar. By Prabhat Chandra Chakravarti. pp. xiv. 344. *Calcutta*, 1930. 8°. Ac. **1931/48**.

—— The Philosophy of the Upanishads. By Sures Chandra Chakravarti. pp. xv. 274. *Calcutta*, 1935. 8°. **20020**. d. **28**.

—— The Pilgrimage of Faith in the World of Modern Thought. Stephanos Nirmalendu Ghosh Lectures, 1927–28. By Douglas Clyde Macintosh. pp. 299. *Calcutta*, 1931. 8°. Ac. **1931/55**.

—— Poetical Selections. Second and enlarged edition. pp. xviii. 615. *Calcutta*, 1920. 8°. Ac. **1931/11**.

—— Poetry Monads and Society. Sir George Stanley Lectures, 1941. [By] Humayun Kabir. pp. 203. *Calcutta*, 1941. 8°. Ac. **1931/81**.

—— Political History of Ancient India from the accession of Parikshit to the extinction of the Gupta dynasty. By Hemchandra Raychaudhuri. pp. xvi. v. 350. *Calcutta*, 1923. 8°. Ac. **1931/31**.

—— Second edition, revised and enlarged. pp. xix. 416. *Calcutta*, 1927. 8°. **20018**. dd. **37**.

—— Third edition, revised and enlarged. pp. xix. 469. *Calcutta*, 1932. 8°. **9059**. c. **8**.

—— Political History of Ancient India . . . By Hemchandra Raychaudhuri . . . Fourth edition, revised and enlarged. [With maps.] pp. xxiii. 582. *Calcutta*, 1938. 8°. **09059**. cc. **2**.

—— The Post-Caitanya Sahajiā Cult of Bengal. By Manindra Mohan Bose. pp. xviii. 320. *Calcutta*, 1930. 8°. Ac. **1931/47**.

—— Post-War Europe, 1918–1937. By Sudhindranath Ghosh. (University Extension Lectures.) pp. 33. *Calcutta*, 1939. 8°. **9100**. f. **24**.

—— Prakrit Dhammapada. Based upon M. Senart's Kharoṣṭhī manuscript. With text, translation & notes by Benimadhab Barua . . . and Sailendranath Mitra. pp. lv. 238. 10. *Calcutta*, 1921. 8°. **14013**. c. **4**.

—— Pre-Aryan and Pre-Dravidian in India. [Articles.] By Sylvain Lévi, Jean Przyluski and Jules Bloch. Translated from French [and edited] by Prabodh Chandra Bagchi. pp. xxix. 184. *Calcutta*, 1929. 8°. Ac. **1931/40**.

—— Prehistoric India, its place in the world's cultures. By Panchanan Mitra. [With plates.] pp. xiii. 285. *Calcutta*, 1923. 8°. **07704**. e. **18**.

—— Second edition, revised and enlarged. pp. xxviii. 512. pl. LIII. *Calcutta*, 1927. 8°. Ac. **1931/30**.

—— Present-Day Banking in India. By B. Ramachandra Rau. pp. viii. 301. *Calcutta*, 1922. 8°. **08228**. cc. **77**.

—— Second edition, revised and enlarged. pp. 311. ii. *Calcutta*, 1925. 8°. **08225**. b. **48**.

—— Third edition, rewritten and enlarged. pp. xviii. 686. *Calcutta*, 1930. 8°. **8224**. g. **25**.

—— Present-Day Banking in India. By Basavarsu Ramachandra Rau . . . Fourth edition, rewritten and enlarged. pp. xx. 784. *Calcutta*, 1938. 8°. **08230**. h. **48**.

—— The Principles of Philosophy. By Hari Mohan Bhattacharyya. pp. xv. 437. [*Calcutta*,] 1944. 8°. **8471**. c. **57**.

—— The Principles of Training for Historical Investigation. By Arthur Percival Newton. pp. 93. *Calcutta*, 1929. 8°. Ac. **1931/43**.

—— The Problem of Minorities. [By] Dhirendranath Sen. pp. xxxi. 793. *Calcutta*, 1940. 8°. **8024**. c. **3**.

—— Problems of Rural India. Being a collection of addresses . . . by Nagendra Nath Gangulee. pp. xi. 155. *Calcutta*, 1928. 8°. Ac. **1931/38**.

—— Prolegomena to a History of Buddhist Philosophy. By B. M. Barua. pp. 47. *Calcutta*, 1918. 8°. Ac. **1931/9**.

—— Protection for Indian Steel. By E. H. Solomon. pp. xiv. 106. *Calcutta*, 1924. 8°. **8245**. ee. **32**.

—— Public Administration in India—historical, structural and functional. By Akshaya K. Ghose. (University Extension Lectures for 1925.) pp. xxi. 743. *Calcutta*, 1930. 8°. **08023**. dd. **54**.

—— Public Health as a Social Service. By John B. Grant. pp. 65. *Calcutta*, 1941. 8°. **7393**. aaa. **30**.

—— Ranjit Singh. [By] Narendra Krishna Sinha. [With a portrait.] pp. x. 216. *Calcutta*, 1933. 8°. **10607**. cc. **17**.

—— Readership Lectures. *See* infra: University of Calcutta Readership Lectures.

—— Reports on the State of Education in Bengal, 1835 & 1838 . . . By William Adam. Edited by Anathnath Basu. pp. lxvii. 578. *Calcutta*, 1941. 8°. **8356**. p. **18**.

—— Researches on Bengal Polyporaceae. By S. R. Bose. pp. 85. pl. IV. *Calcutta*, 1942. 4°. **7033**. i. **26**.

—— Rig-Vedic India. By Abinas Chandra Das. vol. 1. pp. xxii. 592. *Calcutta*, 1921. 8°. Ac. **1931/74**.
No more published.

—— Rise of the Sikh Power. By Narendra Krishna Sinha. [With a map.] pp. xii. 240. *Calcutta*, 1936. 8°. **9059**. d. **11**.

—— A Roman Alphabet for India. By Suniti Kumar Chatterji . . . Reprinted from the Journal of the Department of Letters, *etc.* pp. 58. [*Calcutta*,] 1935. 8°. **7941**. s. **6**.
No. 4 *of the Calcutta University Phonetic Studies.*

—— Rural Self-Government in Bengal. By Naresh Chandra Roy. pp. xii. 202. *Calcutta*, 1936. 8°. **08285**. k. **50**.

—— Śakti or Divine Power. A historical study based on original Sanskrit texts. By Sudhendu Kumar Das. pp. xiv. 298. *Calcutta*, 1934. 8°. **20017**. l. **20**.

—— The Sāṅkhya Conception of Personality . . . By Abhay Kumar Majumdar . . . Edited by Jatindra Kumar Majumdar, *etc.* pp. xvi. 158. *Calcutta*, 1930. 8°. Ac. **1931/49**.

—— Select Readings from English Prose. pp. vi. 276. *Calcutta*, 1920. 8°. Ac. **1931/12**.

—— Selections from Avesta and Old Persian. Edited with translations and notes by Irach Jehangir Sorabji Taraporewala. ser. 1. pt. 1. pp. xiii. 242. *Calcutta*, 1922. 8°. **14990**. b. **2**.

—— Selections from the Historical Records of the Hereditary Minister of Baroda . . . Collected [and translated] by Rai Bahadur B. A. Gupte. [With portraits.] pp. viii. 127. *Calcutta*, 1922. 8°. **14139**. eee. **9**.

—— Self-Government and the Bread Problem . . . By J. W. Petavel. Second edition. pp. xx. 108. *Calcutta*, 1921. 8°. Ac. **1931/15**.

—— The Separation of Executive and Judicial Functions. A study in the evolution of the Indian magistracy. By R. N. Gilchrist. pp. iv. 240. *Calcutta*, 1923. 8°. **08023**. cc. **34**.

—— Shree Gopal Basu Mallik Lectures on Vedānta Philosophy. Delivered, December, 1925, by S. K. Belvalkar. Part 1: lectures 1–6. pp. xv. 240. *Poona*, 1929. 8°. Ac. **1931/73**.

—— Sino-Indica. Publications de l'Université de Calcutta. *Paris*, 1927– . 8°. **11093**. b. **9**. & **11095**. c. **46**.

—— Sir Asutosh Mookerjee Silver Jubilee Volumes. [A symposium.]

vol. 1. Arts and Letters. [With plates.] pp. vii. 614. 1921.
vol. 2. Science. [With plates.] pp. vii. 476. 1922.
vol. 3. Orientalia. [With plates.] pt. 1, 3. 2 vol. 1922, 27.

4 vol. *Calcutta*, 1921–27. 8°. Ac. **1931/16**.
Imperfect; wanting vol. 3. *pt.* 2.

—— Six Lectures on Recent Researches in the Theory of Fourier Series. By Ganesh Prasad. pp. xiv. 139. *Calcutta*, 1928. 8°. **8505**. dd. **24**.

—— Six Lectures on the Mean-Value Theorem of the differential Calculus . . . By Ganesh Prasad. pp. x. 107. *Calcutta*, 1931. 8°. **08531**. i. **17**.

—— Social and Rural Economy of Northern India. Cir. 600 B.C.—200 A.D. . . . By Atindranath Bose. vol. 1. pp. xxx. 148. *Calcutta*, 1942. 8°. **8289**. d. **29**.

—— The Social Organization in North-East India in Buddha's Time. By Richard Fick. Translated by Shishirkumara Maitra. pp. xvii. 365. *Calcutta*, 1920. 8°. **09057**. b. **24**.

—— Some Bengal Villages. An economic survey. Edited by N. C. Bhattacharyya . . . and L. A. Natesan, *etc.* pp. xii. 225. *Calcutta*, 1932. 8°. **20017**. d. **9**.

—— Some Historical Aspects of the Inscriptions of Bengal. Pre-Muhammadan epochs. By Benoychandra Sen. pp. lxxviii. 613. *Calcutta University Press: Calcutta*, 1942. 8°. **15010.e.18.**

—— The Spirit of Indian Civilization. By Dhirendra Nath Roy. pp. xix. 296. *Calcutta*, 1938. 8°. Ac. **1931/78**.

—— Sri Aurobindo and the Future of Mankind . . . By Adhar Chandra Das. pp. xii. 130. *Calcutta*, 1934. 8°. **08632**. gg. **46**.

—— Studies in Indian Antiquities. By Hemchandra Raychaudhuri. pp. xvi. 225. *Calcutta*, 1932. 8°. Ac. **1931/60**.

—— Studies in Indian History. By Surendranath Sen. pp. viii. 266. *Calcutta*, 1930. 8°. Ac. **1931/52**.

—— Studies in Post-Śaṁkara Dialectics. By Ashutosh Bhattacharyya Shastri. pp. xxii. 322. *Calcutta*, 1936. 8°. Ac. **1931/64**.

—— Studies in Shelley. By Amiyakumar Sen. pp. xvi. 343. *Calcutta*, 1936. 8°. **11857**. d. **18**.

—— Studies in Spenser. By Mohinimohan Bhattacherje, *etc.* pp. xii. 93. *Calcutta*, 1929. 8°. Ac. **1931/39**.

—— Studies in the Dimensions of Erythrocytes of Man. By Hemendra Nath Chatterjee. (Griffith Memorial Prize.) pp. 35. pl. 4. *Calcutta*, 1939. 8°. Ac. **1931/77**.

—— Studies in the History of the Bengal Subah, 1740–70 . . . By Kalikinkar Datta. *Calcutta*, 1936– . 8°. Ac. **1931/65**.

—— Studies in the History of the British in India. By A. P. Dasgupta. pp. xiii. 165. *Calcutta*, 1942. 8°. **9058**. e. **8**.

—— Studies in the Tantras . . . By Prabodh Chandra Bagchi. *Calcutta*, 1939– . 8°. W.P. **2561**.

—— A Study of the Vedānta. Sreegopal Basumallik Fellowship Lectures for 1929. By Saroj Kumar Das . . . Second edition [of " Towards a Systematic Study of the Vedanta "]. pp. xxi. 404. *Calcutta*, 1937. 8°. **20032**. b. **50**.

—— The Supernatural in English Romantic Poetry, 1780–1830. By Sukumar Dutt. pp. xviii. 415. *Calcutta*, 1938. 8°. Ac. **1931/66**.

—— The Surgical Instruments of the Hindus. With a comparative study of the surgical instruments of the Greek, Roman, Arab and the modern European surgeons. By Girindranāth Mukhopādhyāya . . . Griffith Prize Essay for 1909. 2 vol. pp. xxxi. 444. pl. LXXXII. *Calcutta*, 1913, 14. 8°. **7679**. aa. **31**.

—— The System of Vedantic Thought and Culture. By Mahendranath Sircar. pp. xi. 328. *Calcutta*, 1925. 8°. **04504**. g. **60**.

—— Tagore Law Lectures, 1870 [*etc.*]. *Calcutta*, 1870– . 8°. **05318**. e. **1**, *etc.*

—— The Theory of Plane Curves. By Surendramohan Ganguli . . . Second edition, *etc.* 2 vol. *Calcutta*, 1925, 26. 8°. **08531**. ee. **37**.

—— Third edition . . . revised and enlarged. *Calcutta*, 1931– . 8°. Ac. **1931/58**.

—— The Theory of Profits. By Prafulla Chandra Ghosh. pp. xx. 442. *Calcutta*, 1933. 8°. **08206**. e. **79**.

—— Tort by Animals . . . By Nirmal Kumar Sen. (Onauthnauth Deb Law Research Prize Thesis.) pp. vi. 137. *Calcutta*, 1936. 8°. **06004**. eee. **24**.

—— Training in Leadership and Citizenship for Young India. By S. C. Roy. pp. 298. *Calcutta*, 1942. 8°. Ac. **1931/83**.

—— Translation of the Sûrya-Siddhânta, a text-book of Hindu astronomy, with notes and an appendix, by Rev. Ebenezer Burgess . . . Reprinted from the edition of 1860. Edited by Phanindralal Gangooly . . . With an introduction by Prabodhchandra Sengupta. pp. lvi. 409. *Calcutta*, 1935. 8°. **14055**. c. **14**.

—— University of Calcutta Readership Lectures. *Calcutta*, 1913– . 8°. Ac. **1931/2**.
The first of the series was published at the Cambridge University Press.

—— University Studies. 8 vol. *Calcutta*, 1909–11. 8°. Ac. **1931**.
Imperfect; wanting no. 4, *no.* 8, *and all after no.* 10.

—— Vanaspati. Plants and plant-life as in Indian treatises and traditions. Griffith Memorial Prize Essay for 1925. By Girija Prasanna Majumdar. pp. xx. 254. ii. *Calcutta*, 1927. 8°. **07028**. b. **26**.

—— The Vedānta: its place as a system of metaphysics. Sreegopal Basumallik Fellowship Lectures for 1926. By N. K. Dutt. pp. viii. 249. *Calcutta*, 1931. 8°. Ac. **1931/57**.

—— Volpone, or the Fox. By Ben Jonson. pp. 132. *Calcutta*, 1917. 8°. **011779**. f. **12**.

—— Water Supplies in Bengal. Calcutta University Jubilee Research Prize, 1927. By Nishi Kanta Ray. pp. vii. 169. *Calcutta*, 1936. 8°. **08777**. aa. **3**.

—— Western Influence in Bengali Literature. [By] Priyaranjan Sen. pp. xiii. 417. *Calcutta*, 1932. 8°. **20017**. bb. **10**.

—— Yoga Philosophy in relation to other Systems of Indian Thought. By S. N. Dasgupta. pp. x. 380. *Calcutta*, 1930. 8°. Ac. **1931/44**.

Appointments and Information Board.

—— Career-Lectures. pp. 447. *Calcutta*, 1939. 8°. Ac. **1931**. f.

Asutosh Museum.

—— Excavations at Bangarh, 1938–41. By Kunja Gobinda Goswami. [With a map.] pp. ix. 42. pl. XXXIII. *Calcutta*, 1948. 4°. **07705**. c. **83**.
Asutosh Museum Memoir. no. 1.

Calcutta University Institute.

Society for the Higher Training of Young Men, 1893–1897.
Calcutta University Institute, 1898– .

—— The Calcutta University Magazine. A monthly newspaper and review. vol. 1; vol. 5. no. 12—vol. 8. no. 4. Jan.—Dec. 1894, Dec. 1898—Apr. 1901. *Calcutta*, 1894–1901. 4°. P.P. **1219**. lf.
Imperfect; wanting vol. 2–4, *vol.* 6. *no.* 5, *vol.* 7. *no.* 2–4, 10, *and all after vol.* 8. *no.* 4.

Department of Letters.

—— Journal, *etc.* *Calcutta*, 1920– . 8°. Ac. **1931**. ca.

Department of Science.

—— Journal, *etc.* vol. 1–10. 1919–33. *Calcutta*, 1919–33. 8°.

—— New series. vol. 1. no. 1, *etc.* *Calcutta*, 1937– . 8°. Ac. **1931**. c.

Library.

—— **Catalogue of Books. 2 pt. [*Calcutta*,] 1925, 31. 8°. 11911. d. 50.**

—— A General Catalogue of Bengali Manuscripts in the Library of the University of Calcutta . . . Edited by Manindramohan Bose. *Calcutta*, 1940– 4°.
15009.a.9.

Senate.

—— University of Calcutta. Convocation Addresses. (vol. 1. 1858–1879.—vol. 2. 1880–1898.) 2 vol. *Calcutta*, 1914. 8°. Ac. **1931/4**.

—— University of Calcutta. Convocation of the Senate for conferring degrees. The 13th February, 1904. pp. 17. *Calcutta*, [1904.] 8°. **8304**. ee. **9**. (**3**.)

—— Address by the Hon'ble Sir Asutosh Mookerjee . . . at the Annual Convocation held on the 15th March 1913. pp. 34. [*Calcutta*, 1913.] 8°. Ac. **1931/3**. (**2**.)

Society for the Higher Training of Young Men.

—— **See supra: *Calcutta University Institute.***

University Law College.

—— The University Law College Magazine. vol. 1. no. 1. Apr. 1931. *Calcutta*, 1931. 8°. Ac. **1931**. e.

Appendix.

—— Proposed Plan of the University of Calcutta. pp. 14. *Sanders & Cones*: [*Calcutta*, 1845.] 8°. **8304**. e. **14**. (**2**.)

CALCUTTA. [MISCELLANEOUS INSTITUTIONS.—UNIVERSITY OF CALCUTTA.]

—— Studies of the Calcutta University. [A criticism of the University's policy. By Charles H. Tawney. Reprinted from the Calcutta Review.] pp. 21. [*Calcutta*, 1865.] 8°. **8023**. ee. **9**. (**5**.)

UTTAR PRADESH HISTORICAL SOCIETY.

United Provinces Historical Society, 1917–49.
Uttar Pradesh Historical Society, 1950– .

—— The Journal of the United Provinces Historical Society, *etc. Calcutta*, 1917– . 8°. Ac. **8604**.

VERNACULAR LITERATURE SOCIETY.

—— First Report of the Vernacular Literature Committee (1854–55). Report of the Transactions of the Vernacular Literature Society. Feb. 1856—30 June 1861). 6 pt. *Calcutta*, 1852. 8°. Ac. **8825**.

—— [Another copy of the report for 1858–59.] Report of the Transactions of the Vernacular Literature Society, *etc. Calcutta*, 1860. 8°. **4768**. c. **88**. (**8**.)

—— [An appeal on behalf of the Vernacular Literature Society, May 1856.] [*Calcutta*, 1856.] 4°. **1881**. a. **2**. (**98**.)

VIṢVA-VAISHṆAVA-RĀJA-SABHĀ.

—— Vaishnavism : real & apparent. pp. ii. 30. *Ananta Vasudeva Brahmachari, Vidyabhusan : Calcutta*, [1926.] 8°. **4507**. a. **30**.

ZOOLOGICAL GARDENS.

—— Report of the Honorary Committee for the Management of the Zoological Gardens for the year 1893-94 (1904-05–1925-26). [*Calcutta*, 1894]–1926. fol. & 8°. I.S. BE. **112**. & **217**.
Wanting the report for 1906–07.

APPENDIX.

—— [A collection of papers relating to the drainage system of Calcutta carried out by W. Clark.] 8 pt. [*Calcutta, etc.*, 1869–71.] fol. & 8°. **1803**. d. **2**.

—— Advantages of the Use of Gas in Private Houses in Calcutta, with a description of the manufacture of coal-gas. pp. 49. pl. VI. *Calcutta Gazette : Calcutta*, [1854.] 8°. **7106**. g. **21**.

—— Alphabetical List of Winter Residents in Calcutta. pp. 8. *India Publishers : Calcutta*, 1895. fol. **10057**. h. **23**. (**3**.)

—— The Black Pamphlet of Calcutta. The Famine of 1874. By a Bengal Civilian [i.e. Charles J. O'Donnell]. English edition. pp. viii. 82. *William Ridgway : London*, 1876. 8°. **8023**. bbb. **5**.

—— A Brief History of the Cyclone at Calcutta and Vicinity, 5th October 1864. pp. xi. 332. 1865. 8°. *See* BENGAL. [*Miscellaneous Public Documents, etc.*] I.S. BE. **214/4**.

—— Calcutta : a poem. With notes. pp. 128. *J. J. Stockdale : London*, 1811. 12°. **11641**. c. **11**.

—— Calcutta in the Olden Time—its localities. From the Calcutta Review . . . Map of Calcutta, 1792–3. By A. Upjohn. [With a plate.] pp. 46. [*Calcutta*, 1852.] 8°. **010058**. ee. **13**. (**1**.)
Imperfect ; wanting the map.

—— Calcutta Sanitation : being a series of editorial articles reprinted from the Indian Medical Record. pp. ii. 35. *Record Press : Calcutta*, 1896. 8°. **8707**. e. **26**. (**2**.)

CALCUTTA. [APPENDIX.]

—— Calcutta to Liverpool, by China, Japan, and America in 1877. By H. W. N. [i.e. Sir Henry W. Norman.] 1878. 8°. *See* N., H. W. **10026**. a. **1**.

—— From Calcutta to the Snowy Range . . . By an Old Indian. [The preface signed : F. F. W., i.e. Frederick F. Wyman.] 1866. 8°. *See* W., F. F. **10057**. bb. **36**.

—— Observations on the Advantages of a Wet-Dock for the Port of Calcutta. pp. 27. *P. Crichton : Calcutta*, 1824. 8°. **8776**. bb. **48**.

—— The Port of Calcutta and 'the Port of Mutlah' ; considered in connection by a railway and a ship canal. By a Member of the Mutlah Association, *etc.* pp. 47. 1850. 8°. *See* supra : MUTLAH ASSOCIATION. **8235**. bb. **74**. (**4**.)

—— The Social Evil in Calcutta . . . [By R. Kerr.] 3rd edition. pp. xii. 112. *T. S. Smith : Calcutta*, [1886.] 12°. **8277**. aa. **62**.

—— The Tourists' Guide to the Principal Stations between Calcutta and Mooltan and Allahabad and Bombay. On the East Indian Railway, *etc.* (Fourth edition.) pp. vi. 172. *W. Newman & Co. : Calcutta*, [1875 ?] 8°. **10058**. b. **27**.

CALCUTTA, *Diocese of.—Church Association.* Rules of the Church Association for the Diocese of Calcutta, and special form of prayer. pp. 14. *Calcutta*, 1867. 8°. **4371**. de. **24**. (**5**.)

—— *Calcutta Diocesan Committee of the Society for Promoting Christian Knowledge.* Report of the Calcutta Diocesan Committee of the Society for Promoting Christian Knowledge for the year M.DCCC.LIX (1867, 1868, 1870). 4 pt. *Calcutta*, 1859–71. 8°. **4421**. b. **3**.

CALCUTTA, *R.C. Province of.* Acta et decreta Concilii Calcuttensis primi. 1894. pp. 11. 180. *Calcuttae*, 1905. 8°. **5016**. f. **9**.

CALCUTTA, DANIEL, *Bishop of.* [1832–1858.] *See* WILSON.

——, EDWARD RALPH, *Bishop of.* [1876–1898.] *See* JOHNSON.

——, GEORGE ALFRED, *Bishop of.* [1913–1919.] *See* LEFROY (G. A.) successively *Bishop of Lahore* and *of Calcutta.*

——, GEORGE EDWARD LYNCH, *Bishop of.* [1858–1867.] *See* COTTON.

——, JAMES EDWARD COWELL, *Bishop of.* [1898–1902.] *See* WELLDON.

——, JOHN MATTHIAS, *Bishop of.* [1829–1832.] *See* TURNER.

——, JOHN THOMAS, *Bishop of.* [1827–1829.] *See* JAMES.

——, REGINALD, *Bishop of.* [1823–1827.] *See* HEBER.

——, REGINALD STEPHEN, *Bishop of.* [1902–1913.] *See* COPLESTON (R. S.) successively *Bishop of Colombo* and *of Calcutta.*

——, ROBERT, *Bishop of.* [1867–1876.] *See* MILMAN.

——, THOMAS FANSHAW, *Bishop of.* [1814–1823.] *See* MIDDLETON.

CALCUTTA ANNUAL DIRECTORY. The Calcutta Annual Directory and Kalendar. *See* DIRECTORIES.—*Calcutta.* [The Original Calcutta Annual Directory, *etc.*]

—— The Calcutta Annual Directory and First Quarterly Register. *See* DIRECTORIES.—*Calcutta.* The Calcutta Annual Register and Directory.

CALCUTTA ANNUAL DIRECTORY.

—— The Calcutta Annual Directory and Register. *See* DIRECTORIES.—*Calcutta.* The Calcutta Annual Register and Directory.

CALCUTTA ANNUAL REGISTER. The Calcutta Annual Register. *See* PERIODICAL PUBLICATIONS.—*Calcutta.*

—— The Calcutta Annual Register and Directory. *See* DIRECTORIES.—*Calcutta.*

CALCUTTA APPRENTICING SOCIETY. *See* CALCUTTA.

CALCUTTA AUXILIARY BIBLE SOCIETY. *See* CALCUTTA.

CALCUTTA BABOOS. The Intolerant and Persecuting Section of the Calcutta Baboos Exposed!!! [Extracts from newspapers referring to a meeting of Hindus opposed to missionary proselytism, letters to the Bengal Hurkaru on the same subject by Alexander Duff and editorial comment thereon.] pp. 22. *Baptist Mission Press: Calcutta*, 1847. 12°. **4193. bb. 8.**

CALCUTTA BIBLE ASSOCIATION. *See* CALCUTTA.

CALCUTTA CHRISTIAN OBSERVER. *See* PERIODICAL PUBLICATIONS.—*Calcutta.*

CALCUTTA CHRISTIAN TRACT AND BOOK SOCIETY. *See* CALCUTTA.

CALCUTTA CHRONICLE. *See* PERIODICAL PUBLICATIONS.—*Calcutta.*

CALCUTTA CITY MISSION. *See* CALCUTTA.

CALCUTTA COMMERCIAL GUIDE. *See* PERIODICAL PUBLICATIONS.—*Calcutta.*

CALCUTTA COMMITTEE. Calcutta Committee of the Church Missionary Society. *See* CALCUTTA.

CALCUTTA COURT.

—— Calcutta Court of Small Causes. *See* BENGAL.—*Courts of Justice.*

CALCUTTA DIOCESAN COMMITTEE. Calcutta Diocesan Committee of the Society for Promoting Christian Knowledge. *See* CALCUTTA, *Diocese of.*

CALCUTTA DOMICILED COMMUNITY ENQUIRY COMMITTEE. *See* CALCUTTA.

CALCUTTA EXCHANGE PRICE CURRENT. *See* PERIODICAL PUBLICATIONS.—*Calcutta.*

CALCUTTA EXHIBITION. *See* CALCUTTA.

CALCUTTA GAZETTE.

—— The Calcutta Gazette. *See* BENGAL, *West.* [*Miscellaneous Official Publications.*]

CALCUTTA GEOGRAPHICAL REVIEW.

—— ***See* CALCUTTA.—*Geographical Society of India.***

CALCUTTA GEOGRAPHICAL SOCIETY.

—— ***See* CALCUTTA.—*Geographical Society of India.***

CALCUTTA HIGH SCHOOL. *See* CALCUTTA.

CALCUTTA HISTORICAL SOCIETY. *See* CALCUTTA.

CALCUTTA HOUSING AND COMMUNICATIONS COMMITTEE. *See* BENGAL.

CALCUTTA IMPROVEMENT TRUST. *See* CALCUTTA.

CALCUTTA JOURNAL. The Calcutta Journal of Medicine, *etc.* *See* PERIODICAL PUBLICATIONS.—*Calcutta.*

—— The Calcutta Journal of Natural History. *See* PERIODICAL PUBLICATIONS.—*Calcutta.*

CALCUTTA LAW JOURNAL. *See* PERIODICAL PUBLICATIONS.—*Calcutta.*

CALCUTTA LIBERAL. Prospectus of the Calcutta Liberal; comprising the preliminary consultations of the seven editors; and the frank declaration of their principles. In prose and verse. [By James Atkinson.] (Second edition.) 2 pt. *Calcutta*, 1824. 8°. **12350. cc. 11.**

CALCUTTA LITERARY GAZETTE. *See* PERIODICAL PUBLICATIONS.—*Calcutta.*

CALCUTTA MADRASAH. *See* CALCUTTA.

CALCUTTA MAGAZINE. The Calcutta Magazine and Monthly Register. *See* PERIODICAL PUBLICATIONS.—*Calcutta.*

CALCUTTA MATHEMATICAL SOCIETY. *See* CALCUTTA.

CALCUTTA MISSIONARY CONFERENCE. *See* CALCUTTA.

CALCUTTA MONTHLY. *See* PERIODICAL PUBLICATIONS.—*Calcutta.*

CALCUTTA MONTHLY JOURNAL. *See* PERIODICAL PUBLICATIONS.—*Calcutta.*

CALCUTTA MONTHLY REGISTER. *See* PERIODICAL PUBLICATIONS.—*Calcutta.*

CALCUTTA MUDRISSA. *See* CALCUTTA.—*Calcutta Madrasah.*

CALCUTTA MUSIC ASSOCIATION. *See* CALCUTTA.

CALCUTTA NERICKH. *See* PERIODICAL PUBLICATIONS.—*Calcutta.*

CALCUTTA NEW PRICE CURRENT. *See* PERIODICAL PUBLICATIONS.—*Calcutta.*

CALCUTTA ORIENTAL JOURNAL. *See* PERIODICAL PUBLICATIONS.—*Calcutta.*

CALCUTTA PSYCHICAL SOCIETY. *See* CALCUTTA.

CALCUTTA RENT ENQUIRY COMMITTEE. *See* BENGAL.

CALCUTTA REVIEW. *See* PERIODICAL PUBLICATIONS. *Calcutta.*

CALCUTTA SANSKRIT COLLEGE. *See* CALCUTTA. —*Government Sanscrit College.*

CALCUTTA SCHOOL BOOK SOCIETY. *See* CALCUTTA.

CALCUTTA STOCK EXCHANGE ASSOCIATION *See* CALCUTTA.

CALCUTTA TECHNICAL INSTITUTE COMMITTEE. *See* BENGAL.

CALCUTTA TRADE ASSOCIATION. *See* CALCUTTA.

CALCUTTA TRAMWAYS COMMITTEE. *See* BENGAL.

CALCUTTA TURF CLUB. *See* CALCUTTA.

CALCUTTA UNIVERSITY. *See* CALCUTTA.—*University of Calcutta.*

CALCUTTA UNIVERSITY COMMISSION. *See* INDIA.

CALCUTTA UNIVERSITY INSTITUTE. *See* CALCUTTA.—*University of Calcutta.*

CALCUTTA UNIVERSITY MAGAZINE. *See* CALCUTTA.—*University of Calcutta.—Calcutta University Institute.*

CALCUTTA UNIVERSITY READERSHIP LECTURES. Calcutta University Readership Lectures. (Calcutta University Special Readership Lectures.) *See* CALCUTTA.—*University of Calcutta.* University of Calcutta Readership Lectures.

CALCUTTA WEEKLY NOTES. *See* PERIODICAL PUBLICATIONS.—*Calcutta.*

CALCUTTA WEEKLY PRICE CURRENT. *See* PERIODICAL PUBLICATIONS.—*Calcutta.*

CALD (FREDERICK) *See* CALDER.

CALDA (GIUSEPPE) I Ministri del Culto e gli articoli 173, 174, 175 e 176, del codice penale per il regno d'Italia, *etc.* pp. 93. *Piacenza*, 1888. 8°. **3900.** f. **6.** (**4.**)

CALDAAD ( ) Confession générale d'un député du côté gauche. pp. 48. *Paris*, 1791. 8°. F. **386.** (**4.**)

CALDANA (PETRONIO PETRONIO) *See* PETRONIO CALDANA.

CALDANI (FLORIANO) *See* CALDANI (L. M. A.) and CALDANI (F.) Icones anatomicæ, *etc.* [With a portrait.] 1801, *etc.* fol. Tab. **819.** c.

—— *See* CALDANI (L. M. A.) and CALDANI (F.) Engravings of the Ligaments copied from the original works of the Caldanis, *etc.* 1836. 4°. **7420.** g. **48.**

—— *See* PERIODICAL PUBLICATIONS.—*Padua.* Giornale di medicina pratica, *etc.* (Nuovi commentarij di medicina . . . pubblicati dai signori V. L. Brera . . . F. Caldani.) 1812, *etc.* 8°. P.P. **2910.**

—— Delle fasee per uso de' bambini. Lettera all'illustrissimo signor Fortunato Naccari. pp. 24. *Padova*, 1794. 8°. **1178.** c. **11.**

—— Discorso inaugurale letto nella grand'aula dell' I.R. Università di Padova per l'apertura di tutti gli studii nel giorno XXV di novembre MDCCCXXVII. pp. 36. *Padova*, 1828. fol. **8365.** ff. **6.**

—— Discorso pronunciato nella Basilica di S. Antonio in Padova il giorno XXVII di aprile MDCCCXI . . . solennizzandosi dalla Regia Università di Padova la nascita di Sua Maestà il Re di Roma. pp. 28. **F.P.** *Padova*, 1811. 4°. **814.** k. **26.**

—— Lettera nella quale si esaminano alcune riflessioni circa le nuove ricerche sulla elettricità animale [i.e. "Memoria intorno all'elettricità animale" by G. Aldini] pubblicate nel tom. XVII. part IV. degli Opuscoli scelti sulle scienze e sulle arti. pp. 16. *Padova*, 1795. 8°. **8755.** bbb. **43.**

—— Veridica relazione dell'ultima malattia e della morte del signor marchese Tommaso degli Obizzi, *etc.* pp. 12. [*Padua*, 1803.] 8°. **899.** cc. **6.** (**7.**)

CALDANI (LEOPOLDO MARCO ANTONIO) L. M. A. Caldanii . . . Institutiones physiologicae et pathologicae. Edidit, praefatus est, indicemque addidit Eduardus Sandifort. 2 tom. pp. 739. *Lugduni Batavorum*, 1784. 8°. **1403.** i. **2.**

CALDANI (LEOPOLDO MARCO ANTONIO)

—— Institutiones physiologicæ. (Institutiones pathologicæ.) Editio tertia italica, aucta & emendata. 2 vol. *Venetiis*, 1786. 8°. **784.** h. **6.**

—— Leopoldi M. Antonij Caldani ad Albertum Allerum epistola. [An account of experiments carried out at Haller's request.] Alberti Halleri ad nuperum scriptum Roberti Whyttij apologia. [With reference to the 1761 edition of Whytt's "Physiological Essays" with an appendix containing an answer to Haller on the subjects of sensibility and irritability.] [1764?] 8°. T. **437.** (**3.**)

—— Brevi riflessioni sul calore animale . . . Inserite nel tomo XIII della Società italiana delle Scienze. pp. 16. *Modena*, 1806. 4°. **899.** i. **2.** (**6.**)

—— Innesto felice del vajuolo instituito e descritto da L. M. A. Caldani. pp. liv. *Padova*, 1768. 8°. **117.** k. **24.**

—— L. M. A. Caldanii . . . Institutiones physiologicae . . . Editio novissima. pp. 385. *Lipsiæ*, 1785. 8°. **784.** h. **5.**

—— Lettera terza . . . sopra l'irritabilità e insensitività Halleriana. pp. 23. *Bologna*, 1759. 8°. **117.** n. **6.** (**2.**)

—— Riflessioni fisiologiche . . . sopra due dissertazioni del signor Claudio Nicola Le Cat, *etc.* pp. xvi. 283. *Venezia*, 1767. 8°. **236.** k. **43.**

—— Sull'insensitività, ed irritabilità di alcune parti degli animali. Lettera, *etc.* *See* FABRI (G. B.) Sulla insensitività ed irritabilità Halleriana, *etc.* pt. 1. 1757. 4°. **43.** g. **14.** (**2.**)

CALDANI (LEOPOLDO MARCO ANTONIO) and **CALDANI** (FLORIANO)

—— Icones anatomicae, quotquot sunt celebriores ex optimis neotericorum operibus summa diligentia depromtae et collectae. Tabulas selegerunt et nonnullas ex cadaveribus ad vivum delineatas addere curarunt Leopoldus Marcus Antonius et Florianus Caldani. [With portraits.] 3 vol. pl. CCLXIV. *Venetiis*, 1801–13. fol. Tab. **819.** c.

—— Iconum anatomicarum explicatio. 5 vol. *Venetiis*, 1802–14. fol. **775.** n. **28.**

—— Engravings of the Ligaments copied from the original works of the Caldanis with descriptive letter-press by Edward Mitchell . . . Revised and carefully compared with nature by Robert Knox. *Peter Brown: Edinburgh*, 1836. 4°. **7420.** g. **48.**

CALDANI (PETRONIO MARIA) In morte della eccellente donzella Ruffina Battoni Romana, fra gli Arcadi Corintea, rime . . . Edizione seconda e in questa accresciute. pp. 39. *Bologna*, 1794. 8°. **11431.** e. **18.**

CALDANI (ULISSE) Osservazioni sul discorso inaugurale [i.e. "La Scienza e la vita"] letto dal prof. F. De Sanctis nell' Università di Napoli. pp. 80. *Matera*, 1873. 8°. **8463.** b. **1.** (**5.**)

CALDARA (ALESSANDRA) I Connotati personali nei documenti d'Egitto dell'età greca e romana. pp. vii. 131. *Milano*, 1924. 8°. [*Studi della Scuola Papirologica.* vol. 4. pt. 2.] Ac. **2810.** c.

CALDARA (POLIDORO) called *da Caravaggio.* *See* GALESTRUZZI (G. B.) [A collection of engravings by G. B. Galestruzzi, chiefly from designs by P. da Caravaggio.] [1660?] 4°. **673.** i. **13.** (**2.**)

—— Polydori Carauagiensis insignia Monocromata, *etc.* [Eight plates, engraved by P. Santi Bartoli.] [*Rome*, 1660?] *obl.* 4°. **1322.m.5.(1.)**

CALDARELLA (ANTONINO)

—— Il Governo di Pietro d'Aragona in Sicilia. *In:* Atti dell'Accademia di Scienze Lettere e Arti di Palermo. ser. 4. vol. 13. pt. 2. fasc. 3. pp. 5–78. 1953. 8°. Ac. **99**.

—— L'Impresa di Martino I, re di Sicilia, in Sardegna, a. 1408–1409. *In:* Atti della Accademia di Scienze Lettere e Arti di Palermo. ser. 4. vol. 14. pt. 2. pp. 5–90. 1954. 8°. Ac. **99**.

CALDARELLI (NAZARENO) *See* CARDARELLI (Vincenzo) *pseud.* [i.e. N. Caldarelli.]

CALDARERA (FRANCESCO) Introduzione allo studio della geometria superiore. vol. 1. pp. v. 620. pl. VIII. *Palermo*, 1882. 8°. **8529**. h. **9**.
No more published.

CALDARI (FERDINANDO) *See* BIBLE.—*Genesis.* [*Italian.*] La Genesi ridotta in ottava rima . . . dal dottore F. Caldari, *etc.* 1747, *etc.* 4°. **3**. b. **10, 11**.

CALDARINI (GIULIO FRANCESCO) *See* PERI (G.) San Giulio il santo delle vaste idee . . . Orazione, *etc.* [Edited by G. F. Caldarini.] 1760. 4°. **4828**. cc. **5**.

CALDAROLA. Volumen statutorum iurisq. municipalis ecclesiasticæ terræ Calderolæ. [Edited by G. Piccha, assisted by O. Paulonius and C. Novellus.] pp. 135. *Apud S. Martellinum: Maceratiæ*, 1586. fol. **1239**. h. **2**.

CALDART (CASIMIRO) La Metrica tedesca. Sviluppo storico, la poesia classicizzante tedesca e la poesia barbara italiana, la metrica moderna. pp. 69. *Livorno*, 1909. 8°. **011852**. i. **81**. (**2**.)

CALDAS, *Department of.*

MESSAGES, ETC., OF GOVERNORS.

—— Mensaje del Gobernador de Caldas [Jorge Gartner] a la Asamblea de 1934. pp. 51. *Manizales*, [1934.] 4°. L.A.S. **396/2**.

MISCELLANEOUS OFFICIAL PUBLICATIONS.

—— Los Municipios de Caldas en 1931. Estadísticas comparadas con las de 1930. [By Rafael Arango Villegas.] pp. 288. *Manizales*, 1932. 8°. **10482**. cc. **19**.

DEPARTMENTS OF STATE AND PUBLIC INSTITUTIONS.

—— *Oficina Departamental de Estadística.* Labores de la Oficina Departamental de Estadística en el año de 1931 [*etc.*]. *Manizales*, [1932– .] 1 **L.A.S.396/10.**

—— *Policía.* Compilación de las Disposiciones sobre Régimen de esta Institución. pp. 70. *Manizales*, 1935. 8°. L.A.S. **397/2**.

Secretaría de Hacienda.

—— Informe rendido por el Secretarío de Hacienda al Gobernador del Departamento. pp. 170. *Manizales*, 1935. 8°. L.A.S. **396/3**.

CALDAS (ALCIDES)

—— *See* HOZBEN (Lancelot T. [Science for the Citizen.] O Homem e a ciência . . . Tradução de Alcides Caldas [and others], *etc.* 1952. 8°. **8714**. f. **1**.

CALDAS (ANTONIO PEREIRA DE SOUZA) *See* PEREIRA DE SOUZA CALDAS.

CALDAS (ANTONIO PINHEIRO) *See* PINHEIRO CALDAS.

CALDAS (FRANCISCO ANTONIO DE) Poesías filosofico-morales. pp. 168. *Oviedo*, 1860. 8°. **11451**. aaa. **13**.

CALDAS (FRANCISCO JOSÉ DE) *See* CALDAS Y TENORIO.

CALDAS (JOSÉ) *See* OPORTO. Corpus codicum Latinorum et Portugalensium, *etc.* [Edited, with an introduction in Latin and Portuguese, by J. Caldas.] 1891, *etc.* 4°. L.R. **261**. d. **2**.

—— Cartas de um Vencido. pp. xiii. 230. *Lisboa*, [1911.] 8°. **8042**. aaa. **64**.

CALDAS (JOSÉ JOAQUIM DE SILVA PEREIRA) *See* SILVA PEREIRA CALDAS.

CALDAS (ROBERTO GOMES) *See* GOMES CALDAS.

CALDAS AULETE (FRANCISCO JULIO) Diccionario Contemporaneo da Lingua Portugueza, *etc.* [The compilation begun by F. J. Caldas Aulete, and completed under the direction of A. Lopes dos Santos Valente.] 2 vol. pp. xxiii. 1913. *Lisboa*, 1881. 8°. **12942**. h. **10**.

—— Grammatica Nacional . . . Adoptada pelo Conselho Geral de Instrucção Publica. Oitava edição, *etc.* pp. 144. *Lisboa*, 1874. 8°. **12942**. aaa. **22**. (**5**.)

CALDAS BARBOZA (DOMINGOS) *See* also LERENO, *pseud.* [i.e. D. Caldas Barboza.]

—— Descripçaõ da Grandiosa Quinta dos Senhores de Bellas, e noticia do seu melhoramento, *etc.* pp. 87. *Lisboa*, 1799. 4°. **10160**. c. **13**.

—— Viola de Lereno: collecção das suas cantigas, *etc.* [With a portrait.] 2 vol. 1798, 1826. 8°. *See* LERENO, *pseud.* **11452**. b. **21**.

—— Viola de Lereno . . . Prefácio de Francisco de Assis Barbosa. 2 vol. *Rio de Janeiro*, 1944. 8°. [*Biblioteca popular brasileira.* no. 14, 15.] W.P. **11936/14, 15**.

CALDAS DE MONTBUY, CARLOS SANLLEHY Y GIRONA, *Marquis of.* *See* SANLLEHY Y GIRONA.

CALDAS PEREYRA ET CASTRO (FRANCISCUS DE) Dn. Francisci de Caldas Pereyra et Castro . . . Receptarum sententiarum, seu, Quæstionum forensium et controuersiarum ciuilium, libri duo. (Solemnis et analyticæ [*sic*] relectio . . . tituli De inofficioso testamento, ad Institutiones Imperiales D. Iustiniani . . . enucleata.—Relectio noua ad Diocletiani et Maximiani . . . decisionem in legem vnicam cod. ex delicto defuncti in quantum heredes conueniantur.—Domini Francisci Caldas Pereyra et Castro . . . Consilium primum[—LIII].) 3 pt. *In D. Z. Palthenii, Librarii Francofurtensis Officina: [Frankfort,]* 1612. fol. **499**. c. **9**.

CALDAS XAVIER (ALFREDO)

—— O Major Caldas Xavier. [With plates, including portraits.] pp. 198. 1953. 8°. *See* PORTUGAL.—*Ministério do Ultramar.—Agência Geral do Ultramar.* **10632**. v. **38**.

CALDAS XAVIER (ALFREDO AUGUSTO)

—— *See* CALDAS XAVIER (A.) O Major Caldas Xavier. [With portraits.] 1953. 8°. **10632**. v. **38**.

—— Reconhecimento do Limpopo. Os territorios ao sul do Save e os vatuas. [With a map.] 1894. *See* LISBON.—*Sociedade de Geographia de Lisboa.* Boletim, *etc.* ser. 13. no. 3. 1877, *etc.* 8°. Ac. **6020**.

CALDAS Y TENORIO (FRANCISCO JOSÉ DE) *See* PERIODICAL PUBLICATIONS.—*Bogotá.* Año de 1810. Continuacion del Semanario del Nuevo Reyno de Granada. [Edited by F. J. de Caldas y Tenorio.] 1810. 8°. P.P. **3707**.

CALDAS Y TENORIO (Francisco José de)

—— Obras . . . Recopiladas y publicadas por Eduardo Posada. pp. xxvii. 596. *Bogotá*, 1912. 8°. [*Biblioteca de Historia Nacional.* vol. 9.] **9773.i.2/9.**

—— Semanario de la Nueva Granada. Miscelanea de ciencias, literatura, artes é industria. Publicada por una sociedad . . . bajo la direccion de F. J. de Caldas. Nueva edicion [of the greater part of the papers for 1808 and 1809 and no. 1 of 1810] . . . con varios opusculos inéditos de F. J. de Caldas . . . y adornada con su retrato, *etc.* [Edited by A. Lasserre. Corrected and annotated by J. Acosta.] pp. x. 572. 1849. 8°. *See* Periodical Publications.—*Bogotá.* **P.P. 4101.**

—— Memorias científicas. (Cartas . . . dirigidas á Mutis.) [Edited by D. Mendoza. With a portrait.] *See* Mendoza (Diego) Expedición Botánica de José Celestino Mutis al Nuevo Reino de Granada, *etc.* 1909. 8°. **7031. r. 11.**

—— Viajes. Viaje al corazón de Barnuevo. (Viajes al Sur de Quito.—Viaje de Paute.—Cuenca.) [With extracts from "Memoria histórica sobre la vida . . . de Francisco José de Caldas" by L. de Pombo.] pp. 161. *Bogotá*, 1936. 8°. [*Biblioteca Aldeana de Colombia.* no. 41.] **12213. b. 1/41.**

—— Cartas . . . Recopiladas y publicadas por Eduardo Posada. pp. xvi. 512. *Bogotá*, 1917. 8°. [*Biblioteca de Historia Nacional.* vol. 15.] **9773.i.2/15.**

—— Estudios varios. Precedidos de la biografía del sabio por Lino de Pombo. pp. 113. *Bogotá*, 1941. 16°. [*Biblioteca del maestro.* sección 2. no. 1.] **W.P. 14109/2.**

—— Relación de un Viaje hecho a Cotacache, la Villa, Imbadura, Cayambe, etc., comenzado el 23 de julio de 1802, *etc.* [Edited by Agustín J. Barreiro.] pp. 214. *Madrid*, 1933. 8°. **10482. dd. 11.**

CALDAY GRANGE GRAMMAR SCHOOL. *See* West Kirby.

CALDBECK.—*St. Mungo's Church.* *See* Kentigern, *Saint, etc.*—Caldbeck.—*St. Mungo's Church.*

CALDBECK (Mary Costello) Sefton Hall. A tale. 2 vol. *T. C. Newby: London*, 1870. 8°. **12627. f. 6.**

CALDBECK (William Roper) The Nation and the Army. A plea for a practical & thorough military policy. pp. 264. *Grant Richards: London*, 1910. 8°. **8822. a. 39.**

CALDCLEUGH (Alexander)

—— Meteorological Observations in Brazil, and on the Equator. *In:* Daniell (John F.) Meteorological Essays, *etc.* pp. 335–348. 1823. 8°. **538. e. 19.**

—— [Another edition.] *In:* Daniell (John F.) Meteorological Essays, *etc.* pp. 335–348. 1827. 8°. **1136. l. 30.**

—— Travels in South America, during the years 1819–20–21; containing an account of the present state of Brazil, Buenos Ayres, and Chile. [With plates and maps.] 2 vol. *John Murray: London*, 1825. 8°. **1050. h. 17, 18.**

CALDECOTE, Thomas Walter Hobart, *Viscount.* *See* Inskip.

CALDECOTT COMMUNITY. *See* Caldecott Nursery School.

CALDECOTT NURSERY SCHOOL, afterwards **CALDECOTT COMMUNITY.** First (third, fifth–seventeenth) Annual Report, *etc.* (Annual Report, 1935–1936 [*etc.*].) *London*, [1912– .] 8°. **A.R. 328.**
Imperfect; wanting the second and fourth Annual Reports.

—— The Caldecott Community. A forecast, 1932. pp. 6. [*Cheshunt*, 1932.] 8°. **08364. f. 84.**

—— The Caldecott Community, Hyde Heath, Wareham, Dorset. A social experiment. [With illustrations.] pp. 31. [1941.] 8°. **8365. ee. 1.**

—— The Caldecott Community, The Mote, Maidstone. A social experiment. [With illustrations.] pp. 22. *Maidstone*, [1937.] 8°. **08364. f. 89.**

—— New Foundations. Some aspects of the work of the Caldecott Community. By Enid Coggin. [With plates.] pp. 26. *Cole & Co.: London*, [1925.] 8°. **8365. dd. 22.**

CALDECOTT, *Family of.*

—— *See* Wood (Hilda M. C.) Record of the Caldecott Family in South Africa. [1939.] 4°. **09915. t. 24.**

CALDECOTT (Alfred) *See* Aesop. [*English.—Selections.*] Some of Æsop's Fables . . . shewn in designs by R. Caldecott, from new translations by A. Caldecott, *etc.* 1883. 4°. **12304. l. 13.**

—— *See* Watson (Frederick) *Rector of Starston.* Inspiration. [Edited by A. Caldecott.] 1906. 8°. **04429. aaa. 26.**

—— *See* Whately (Arnold R.) The Inner Light . . . With introductory note by A. Caldecott. 1908. 8°. **4373. df. 13.**

—— The Argument from the Emotions. *See* Matthews (Walter R.) *K.C.V.O.*, successively *Dean of Exeter* and *of St. Paul's.* King's College Lectures on Immortality. 1920. 8°. **4255. dd. 37.**

—— The Being of God, in the Light of Philosophy. *See* Swete (Henry B.) Essays on some Theological Questions of the Day. 1905. 8°. **4379. h. 33.**

—— The Church in the West Indies . . . With a map. pp. 275. *S.P.C.K.: London*, 1898. 8°. [*Colonial Church Histories.*] **2208.a.5/5.**

—— The Emotional Element in Religion: a vindication. *See* London.—iii. *University of London.* London Theological Studies, *etc.* 1911. 8°. **4379. i. 12.**

—— English Colonization and Empire. [With maps.] pp. viii. 277. *John Murray: London*, 1891. 8°. [*University Extension Manuals.*] **12204. f. 7/3.**

—— The Indo-Chinese Opium Trade. pp. 8. *Society for Promoting Christian Knowledge: London*, 1908. 8°. [*Pan-Anglican Papers.* S.D. 3h.] **4108. cc. 35.**

—— Pantheism and Christian Thought. pp. 8. *Society for Promoting Christian Knowledge: London*, 1908. 8°. [*Pan-Anglican Papers.* S.B. 7.] **4108. cc. 35.**

—— The Philosophy of Religion in England and America. pp. xvi. 434. *Methuen & Co.: London*, 1901. 8°. **4372. cc. 29.**

—— The Religious Sentiment illustrated from the lives of Wesley's helpers. An essay read before the Aristotelian Society. pp. 32. *Robert Culley: London*, [1909.] 8°. **4376. ee. 34.**

CALDECOTT (Alfred) and **MACKINTOSH** (Hugh Ross)

—— Selections from the Literature of Theism. Edited, with introduction and explanatory notes, by A. Caldecott . . . and H. R. Mackintosh. pp. xiii. 472. *T. & T. Clark: Edinburgh,* 1904. 8°. **08464.** f. **40.**

—— Third edition. pp. xv. 490. *T. & T. Clark: Edinburgh,* 1931. 8°. **08486.** eee. **38.**

CALDECOTT (*Sir* Andrew) *G.C.M.G.*

—— Fires burn Blue. [Short stories.] pp. 222. *Edward Arnold & Co.: London,* 1948. 8°. NN. **38878.**

—— The Governor-Designate. *In:* De Lanerolle (H. C. N.) and Joseph (E. M. W.) "Well, Mudaliyar!" and other plays, *etc.* pp. 227–236. [1954.] 8°. **11783.** d. **19.**

—— Not Exactly Ghosts. [Tales.] pp. 213. *Edward Arnold & Co.: London,* 1947. 8°. **12646.** f. **49.**

CALDECOTT (C.) *See* Bible.—*Proverbs.* [*English.*] Sacra Ethica; or, the Proverbs of Solomon, in verse . . . By C. Caldecott. 1819. 12°. **1164.** b. **50.**

—— *See* Bible.—*Proverbs.* [*English.*] Horæ Sacræ. Divine Ethics, *etc.* [1830?] 12°. **3165.** a. **1.**

CALDECOTT (C. H.) *See* Zulu Kafirs. Descriptive History of the Zulu Kafirs . . . Revised by C. H. Caldecott. 1853. 8°. **7959.** b. **41.** (**1.**)

CALDECOTT (Harry Stratford)

—— The Bacons and Shakspere. Their lives in parallel lines. With incidental discussions of the plays and poems of 'Shakespeare.' pp. 148. *Gay & Hancock: London,* 1908. 8°. Lamb. **72.**

—— Spoils. Studies in Shakespeare . . . Revised and enlarged. pp. xi. 44. *Printed for private circulation: London,* [1891?] 8°. **11763.** cc. **18.** (**10.**)

CALDECOTT (John) An Essay on the Qualifications and Duties of Accountants and Auditors, *etc.* pp. 52. *Letts, Son & Co.: London,* [1875.] 8°. **8244.** bbb. **34.**

—— A Practical Guide for Retail Tradesmen and others to Book-Keeping by Double Entry, or according to the Italian method of debtor and creditor, *etc.* pp. xiv. 307. *W. & T. Piper: London,* [1851.] 8°. **8505.** c. **17.**

—— [Another edition.] A Practical Guide . . . to Account Keeping . . . Second edition. pp. xiv. 315. *Piper, Stephenson & Co.: London,* [1855?] 8°. **08532.** e. **5.**

CALDECOTT (Marian) Agnes Beaumont. A true story of the year 1670. pp. 109. *Houghton & Co.: London,* [1874.] 16°. **4418.** cc. **3.**

—— [Another copy.] **4418.** ccc. **30.**

CALDECOTT (R. M.) *See* Bābar, *Emperor of Hindustan.* The Life of Baber . . . By R. M. Caldecott. [An abridgment of the translation by J. Leyden and W. Erskine.] 1844. 8°. **14456.** d. **23.**

CALDECOTT (Randolph) *See* Aesop. [*English.—Selections.*] Some of Æsop's Fables, with modern instances, shewn in designs by R. Caldecott, *etc.* 1883. 4°. **12304.** l. **13.**

—— *See* Blackburn (Henry G.) Breton Folk . . . With . . . illustrations by R. Caldecott. 1880. 4°. **10174.** h. **10.**

CALDECOTT (Randolph)

—— *See* Blackburn (Henry G.) Randolph Caldecott. A personal memoir of his early art career . . . With . . . illustrations [by Caldecott]. [With a portrait.] 1886. 4°. **10854.** h. **2.**

—— *See* Carr (Alice) North Italian Folk . . . Illustrated by R. Caldecott. 1878. 8°. **10151.** bb. **24.**

—— *See* D., A. Y. The Owls of Olynn Belfry . . . Illustrated by R. Caldecott. [1886.] 16°. **12811.** a. **43.**

—— *See* Davis (Mary G.) Randolph Caldecott . . . An appreciation. [With a portrait.] [1946.] 8°. **10890.** dd. **13.**

—— *See* Ewing (Juliana H.) Daddy Darwin's Dovecote . . . Illustrated by R. Caldecott. [1884.] 8°. **12810.** cc. **52.**

—— *See* Ewing (Juliana H.) Jackanapes . . . With illustrations by R. Caldecott. 1884. 8°. **4429.** d. **2.**

—— *See* Ewing (Juliana H.) Lob Lie-by-the-Fire . . . Illustrated by R. Caldecott, *etc.* [1885.] 8°. **12805.** t. **44.**

—— *See* Irving (Washington) Bracebridge Hall . . . Illustrated by R. Caldecott. 1877. 8°. **12355.** b. **1.**

—— *See* Irving (Washington) Old Christmas . . . Illustrated by R. Caldecott. 1876. 8°. **12703.** bbb. **2.**

—— *See* La Fontaine (J. de) [*Fables.—French.*] Fables de la Fontaine. A selection . . . With illustrations by R. Caldecott. 1885. 8°. **12200.** eee. **1.**

—— *See* Loffelt (A. C.) Beschrijvende catalogus van Engelsche prentkunst voor groote en kleine kinderen. W. Crane . . . R. Caldecott, *etc.* 1893. 4°. **7808.** cc. **8.** (**3.**)

—— *See* Manchester.—*Brasenose Club.* Catalogue of a Loan Collection of the Works of Randolph Caldecott exhibited at the Brasenose Club, *etc.* [With a memoir by George Evans.] 1888. 8°. **7858.** bb. **48.**

—— *See* Morgan (Louisa) Baron Bruno . . . and other fairy stories . . . With illustrations by R. Caldecott. 1875. 8°. **12410.** bbb. **3.**

—— *See* Society Novelettes. Society Novelettes . . . Illustrated . . . from designs by R. Caldecott, *etc.* 1883. 8°. **12643.** m. **1.**

—— *See* Tennyson (Hallam) *Baron Tennyson.* Jack and the Beanstalk . . . Illustrated by R. Caldecott. 1886. 4°. **12807.** ff. **8.**

—— Fac similes of Original Sketches by Caldecott. Reproduced from "Will o' the Wisp" 1868, by J. Galloway. ff. 16. *J. Galloway: Manchester,* [1887.] *obl.* 4°. **7857.** e. **40.**

—— Gleanings from the "Graphic." [With a portrait.] pp. 83. *G. Routledge & Sons: London,* 1889 [1888]. *obl.* 4°. **1869.** b. **31.**

—— Randolph Caldecott's "Graphic" Pictures. pp. 96. *G. Routledge & Sons: London,* 1883 [1882]. *obl.* fol. **1762.** b. **11.**

—— Randolph Caldecott's Last "Graphic Pictures." pp. 71. *G. Routledge & Sons: London,* 1888 [1887]. *obl.* fol. **1762.** a. **9.**

—— More "Graphic" Pictures. pp. 71. *G. Routledge & Sons: London,* 1887 [1886]. *obl.* 4°. **1762.** b. **14.**

CALDECOTT (Randolph)

—— Randolph Caldecott's Painting Book. *S.P.C.K.: London*, [1895.] 8°. **4429.** dd. **10.**

—— Randolph Caldecott's Painting Book. (First series.) *F. Warne & Co.: London & New York*, [1902.] 4°. **7858.** q. **22.**
A different work from the preceding.

—— R. Caldecott's Picture Books. 16 pt.
The House that Jack Built.
The Diverting History of John Gilpin.
The Mad Dog.
The Babes in the Wood.
The Milkmaid.
Sing a Song for Sixpence.
The Queen of Hearts.
The Farmer's Boy.
Hey Diddle Diddle and Baby Bunting.
The Three Jovial Huntsmen.
A Frog he would a-wooing go.
The Fox Jumps over the Parson's Gate.
Come Lasses and Lads.
Ride a-Cock Horse to Banbury ✠ & A Farmer went trotting upon his Grey Mare.
An Elegy on the Glory of her Sex, Mrs. Mary Blaize. By Dr. Oliver Goldsmith.
The Great Panjandrum himself.
G. Routledge & Sons: London, [1878–84.] 4°. & *obl.* 4°. **12805.** k. **61.**

—— R. Caldecott's Picture Book, *etc.* (R. Caldecott's Picture Book. no. 2.) 2 vol. *G. Routledge & Sons: London*, [1879, 81.] 4°. **12805.** s. **17.**
Another issue of the first eight parts of "R. Caldecott's Picture Books."

—— R. Caldecott's Collection of Pictures & Songs, *etc.* 8 pt. *G. Routledge & Sons: London*, [1881.] 4°. **12809.** n. **36.**
Another issue in one volume of the first eight parts of "R. Caldecott's Picture Books."

—— The Hey Diddle Diddle Picture Book. 4 pt. *G. Routledge & Sons: London*, [1883.] *obl.* 4°. **12805.** r. **53.**
Another issue in one volume of four parts of "R. Caldecott's Picture Books."

—— The Panjandrum Picture Book, *etc.* 4 pt. *G. Routledge & Sons: London*, [1885.] *obl.* 4°. **12810.** cc. **54.**
Another issue in one volume of four parts of "R. Caldecott's Picture Books."

—— R. Caldecott's Picture Books. 4 pt. *G. Routledge & Sons: London*, [1889, 92.] 16°. **12806.** n. **49.**
Another edition of the first four parts of "R. Caldecott's Picture Books," 1878, *etc.*

—— R. Caldecott's Second Collection of Pictures and Songs, *etc.* 8 pt. *F. Warne & Co.: London*, [1895.] *obl.* 4°. **12806.** s. **51.**
A reissue in one volume of "The Hey Diddle Diddle Picture Book" and "The Panjandrum Picture Book."

—— R. Caldecott's Collection of Pictures & Songs, *etc.* 8 pt. *F. Warne & Co.: London*, [1896.] 4°. **12809.** t. **3.**
A reissue of the edition of 1881.

—— R. Caldecott's Picture Book. no. 1(–4). 4 vol. *F. Warne & Co.: London & New York*, [1906, 07.] 16°. **012807.** de. **97.**
Another edition of fourteen parts of "R. Caldecott's Picture Books."

—— A Sketch-Book of R. Caldecott's, *etc.* pp. 48. *G. Routledge & Sons: London*, [1883.] *obl.* 8°. **1780.** a. **16.**

CALDECOTT (Randolph)

—— Randolph Caldecott's Sketches. With an introduction by Henry Blackburn. pp. 94. *Sampson Low & Co.: London*, 1890 [1889]. 4°. **12330.** k. **53.**

—— Catalogue of the Whole of the Remaining Works of . . . Randolph Caldecott, *etc.* [A sale catalogue.] pp. 12. *W. Clowes & Sons: London*, [1886.] 8°. **S.C.Christie.**

CALDECOTT (Thomas) *See* England.—*Courts of Law and Equity.* [*Reports.*] Reports of Cases relative to the Duty and Office of a Justice of the Peace, from Michaelmas Term 1776, inclusive, to Trinity [and thence to Michaelmas] Term 1785, inclusive. By T. Caldecott. 1786, *etc.* 4°. **1243.** h. **24, 25.**

—— *See* Milton (J.) [*Minor Poems.*] Poems upon Several Occasions, *etc.* copious ms. notes [by T. Caldecott]. 1785. 8°. C. **45.** e. **14.** (**1.**)

—— *See* Milton (J.) [*Minor Poems.*] Poems upon Several Occasions, *etc.* copious ms. notes [by T. Caldecott]. 1791. 8°. **11630.** c. **21.**

—— *See* Shakespeare (W.) [*Works.*] The Plays of William Shakespeare, *etc.* copious ms. notes [by T. Caldecott]. 1813. 8°. **11762.** dd.

—— *See* Shakespeare (W.) [*Smaller Collections of Plays.*] Hamlet and As You Like It, *etc.* [Edited by T. Caldecott.] 1819. 8°. **642.** k. **10.**

—— [Another copy.] copious ms. corrections and additions [by T. Caldecott]. **11766.** k. **20.**

—— *See* Shakespeare (W.) [*Smaller Collections of Plays.*] Hamlet and As You Like It. A specimen of a new edition of Shakespeare. By T. Caldecott. copious ms. corrections and additions [by T. Caldecott]. 1820. 8°. **11766.** k. **21.**

—— *See* Shakespeare (W.) [*Smaller Collections of Plays.*] Hamlet, and As You Like It. A specimen of an edition of Shakespeare. By T. Caldecott. 1832. 8°. **642.** k. **11.**

—— Catalogue of the Exceedingly Curious Collection of Books, illustrative of Early English Literature, formed by the late Thomas Caldecott, *etc.* [A sale catalogue.] ms. notes of prices. pp. 87. [*London*, 1833.] 8°. **821.** i. **26.**

CALDECOTT (Watson) *See* Eutropius (F.) Eutropius, books i. and ii. . . . Edited by W. Caldecott. 1893. 8°. **9041.** a. **12.**

—— Exercises on Edwards's "The Story of the Kings of Rome." pp. 24. *University Press: Cambridge*, 1910. 8°. **012902.** ee. **29.** (**2.**)

CALDECOTT (William Shaw) *See* Cape Town.—*Cape of Good Hope Society for the Prevention of Cruelty to Animals.* The Animal Friend . . . Editor, W. S. Caldecott. 1899, *etc.* 4°. **1866.** b. **7.** (**24.**)

—— Good Works; or, "Things that accompany salvation": being a series of chapters on the Methodist Rules. pp. vi. 184. *Elliot Stock: London*, 1875. 8°. **4139.** aa. **1.**

—— Herod's Temple. Its New Testament associations and its actual structure. [In part written by Henry T. Hooper. With plates and plans.] pp. xv. 395. *C. H. Kelly: London*, [1913.] 8°. **07709.** b. **5.**

—— Leaves of a Life . . . [Autobiographical reminiscences.] With an introduction by the Rev. Henry T. Hooper. [With plates.] pp. xxviii. 180. *C. H. Kelly: London*, 1912. 8°. **4920.** h. **3.**

CALDECOTT (William Shaw)

—— The Second Temple in Jerusalem. Its history and its structure. [With plates and plans.] pp. xvi. 396. *John Murray: London*, 1908. 8°. **4516**. cc. **31**.

—— Solomon's Temple. Its history and structure . . . With a preface by the Rev. A. H. Sayce. [With plates and a plan.] pp. xiii. 358. *R.T.S.: London*, 1907. 8°. **04430**. g. **13**.

—— Synthetic Studies in Scripture . . . Foreword by Harold M. Wiener. pp. xx. 181. *Robert Scott: London*, 1913. 8°. **03127**. ee. **24**.

—— The Tabernacle. Its history and structure . . . With a preface by the Rev. A. H. Sayce. [With plates.] pp. xix. 236. *R.T.S.: London*, 1904. 8°. **04429**. l. **34**.

CALDEIAN. *See* West Kirby.—*Calday Grange Grammar School*.

CALDEIRA (Antonio Corrêa) *See* Corrêa Caldeira.

CALDEIRA (Carlos José) *See* Periodical Publications.—*Lisbon*. Revista Peninsular. [Edited by C. J. Caldeira.] 1855, *etc.* 8°. P.P. **4123**. b.

—— Apontamentos d'uma Viagem de Lisboa á China, e da China a Lisboa. 2 tom. *Lisboa*, 1852, 53. 8°. **10025**. b. **2**.

—— Considerações sobre o Estado das Missões e da Religião Christã na China, seguidas de dois artigos publicados no Boletim do Governo de Macao, relativos ao mesmo assumpto. pp. 27. *Lisboa*, 1851. 8°. **4766**. e. **19**. (**17**.)

CALDEIRA (Gaspar)

—— *See* Bourdon (L.) [Articles on historical subjects, *etc.*] (Deux aventuriers portugais: G. Caldeira et A. Luis, 1564–1568. 1955.) 1951, *etc.* 8°. W.P. **378/2**.

CALDEIRA (Gonçalo Gomes) *See* Gomes Caldeira.

CALDEIRA (Jozé) Tratado dos Afetos, e Costumes Oratorios. pp. 135. *Lisboa*, 1825. 8°. **11805**. aa. **22**. (**1**.)

CALDEIRA BRANT PONTES (Felisberto) *Marquis de Barbacena*. *See* Aguiar (A. A. de) Vida do Marquez de Barbacena. 1896. 8°. **010882**. k. **18**.

CALDEIRA PIRES (António) História do Palácio Nacional de Queluz. Prefácio-estudo de Affonso de Dornellas, *etc.* [With plates.] 2 vol. *Coimbra*, 1924, 26. 8°. [*Subsídios para a História da Arte Portuguesa*. no. 14.] W.P. **8747/14**.

CALDELAR (Adèle) Fables morales et religieuses . . . [In verse.] Dessins par Eustache Lorsay. pp. vii. 327. *Paris*, 1844. 8°. **1347**. k. **1**.

—— Un Pot de terre contre vingt pots de fer. Curieuses révélations sur l'Athénée et plusieurs autres sociétés de Paris, *etc.* pp. 106. *Paris*, 1865. 8°. **011840**. h. **51**.

CALDENBACH (Christoff) *See* Kaldenbach (Christoph)

CALDENBACHIUS (Christophorus) *See* Kaldenbach (Christoph)

CALDENBACHIUS (Samuel) *See* Kaldenbach.

CALDENBORN, *Augustinian Monastery at*. *See* Kaltenborn.

CALDER, *Mid*. *See* Mid Calder.

CALDER, *River*. Reasons for Extending the Navigation of the River Calder from Wakefield to Halifax. pp. 4. [*London*, 1758?] fol. **(S.P.R.) 358.b.3.(41.)**

CALDER AND HEBBLE NAVIGATION. Tables for the Calculation of Lock Dues, payable upon the Calder and Hebble Navigation, *etc.* 1825. 8°. *See* Company of Proprietors of the Calder and Hebble Navigation. **10347**. e. **13**.

CALDER BRAES.

—— A New and much Admir'd Song, called, The Lass of Calder Braes. To which is added, The lass of Torrance Glen. The praise of Scottish whisky. And the French fleet dismantled, *etc.* pp. 8. *T. Johnston: Falkirk*, [1810?] 12°. **11606**. aa. **22**. (**21**.)

—— [Another copy.] A New and much admir'd Song, called The Lass of Calder Braes, *etc.* *Falkirk*, [1810?] 8°. **1078**. k. **27**. (**12**.) *Mutilated*.

CALDER FARM REFORMATORY SCHOOL. *See* Mirfield.

CALDER HIGH SCHOOL. *See* Liverpool.

CALDER MARSHALL, SON & IBOTSON. Book-keeping. pp. xi. 380. *Cassell & Co.: London*, 1907. 8°. **8507**. h. **23**.

CALDER (Albert R.) The Forward Movement and the Monstrous Selfishness of the People. By a Lover of the Church (A. R. Calder). pp. 16. *W. Blackwood & Sons: Edinburgh & London*, [1931.] 8°. **4175**. de. **59**.

CALDER (Alex.) The Bacon Pig. A guide to producers under the Pigs Marketing Scheme. pp. 11. *J. Truscott & Son: London*, [1936.] 8°. **8234**. a. **39**.

—— Some Problems facing the Pig Industry. (Unrevised proof.) [1951.] fol. **1865**. c. **14**. (**29**.)

CALDER (Alexander) *Officer of the Order of the Legion of Honour*. The Coming Era. pp. 422. *Trübner & Co.: London*, 1879. 8°. **4015**. h. **2**.

—— For Happiness. pp. 340. *Trübner & Co.: London*, 1886. 8°. **4373**. g. **19**.

—— The Man of the Future. An investigation of the laws which determine happiness. pp. xiv. 341. *Chapman & Hall: London*, 1872. 8°. **4379**. h. **15**.

—— The Presidential Address to the National Conference of Spiritualists, February 7th, 1877. pp. 12. 1877. **8630**. f. **4**.

CALDER (Alexander) *Writer on Drawing*. *See* Aesop. [*English.—Collections.*] Fables of Æsop according to Sir R. L'Estrange. With fifty drawings by A. Calder. 1931. 4°. **Cup.510.bb.26.**

—— Alexander Calder. Mobiles, stabiles, constellations. (Exposition du 25 octobre au 16 novembre 1946.) [With a portrait.] pp. 35. 1946. 16°. *See* Paris.—*Galerie Louis Carré*. **7960**. a. **52**.

—— Animal Sketching. pp. 62. *John Lane: London; printed in U.S.A.*, 1926. 8°. **7859**. aa. **11**.

CALDER (Augustus Barclay) Lectures on Midwifery for Midwives. pp. xi. 274. *Baillière & Co.: London*, 1906. 8°. **07581**. ee. **25**.

—— Second edition. pp. vii. 258. *Baillière & Co.: London*, 1912. 8°. **07580**. i. **7**.

—— Questions and Answers on Midwifery for Midwives. With syllabus of lectures for the "L.O.S." delivered at the Fulham Midwifery Training School. pp. xiv. 143. *Baillière & Co.: London*, 1904. 16°. **7581**. ccc. **32**.

CALDER (AUGUSTUS BARCLAY)

—— (Second edition.) pp. xiv. 141. *Baillière & Co.: London*, 1906. 16°. **7581**. ccc. **41**.

—— Third edition. pp. vii. 155. *Baillière & Co.: London*, 1909. 16°. **7580**. a. **24**.

—— Fourth edition. pp. viii. 175. *Baillière & Co.: London*, 1915. 16°. **07580**. de. **4**.

CALDER (CHARLES) Three Sermons . . . With a preface by the editor, the Rev. Malcolm Macgregor. pp. 84. *Maclaren & Macniven: Edinburgh*, 1877. 8°. **4474**. b. **1**.

CALDER (CHARLES CUMMING) List of Species and Genera of Indian Phanerogams not included in Sir J. D. Hooker's Flora of British India. By C. C. Calder, V. Narayanaswami and M. S. Ramaswami. 1926. *See* INDIA.—*Botanical Survey*. Records of the Botanical Survey, *etc.* vol. 11. no. 1. 1893, *etc.* 8°. **7028**. r.

CALDER (CHARLES MACLEAR) *See* GRIFFITH (*Sir* William B.) An Index to the Acts and Laws of Jamaica . . . With three appendices . . . by C. M. Calder. 1900. 4°. **C.S.F.153/2.(2.)**

—— John Vassall and his Descendants. By one of them. [The foreword signed: C. M. C., i.e. C. M. Calder.] pp. 40. [1920.] 8°. *See* C., C. M. **9906**. e. **33**.

CALDER (E. H. S.) *See* MEYER (Hans, H.T.) [Ostafrikanische Gletscherfahrten.] Across East African Glaciers . . . Translated . . . by E. H. S. Calder, *etc.* 1891. 8°. **10097**. m. **21**.

CALDER (FANNY L.) and **MANN** (E. E.) *Teacher*. A Teachers' Manual of Elementary Laundry Work. pp. viii. 76. *Longmans & Co.: London*, 1891. 8°. **7944**. de. **42**.

—— Second edition. pp. viii. 83. *Longmans & Co.: London*, 1892. 8°. **7943**. aa. **60**.

—— Third edition. pp. x. 83. *Longmans & Co.: London*, 1894. 8°. **7942**. aaa. **54**.

—— New impression. With illustrations. (Fourth edition.) pp. viii. 82. *Longmans, Green & Co.: London*, 1901. 12°. **07944**. df. **7**.

CALDER (FRANCIS WILLIAM GRANT) Practical Hints on the Cure of Squinting by Operation. pp. viii. 96. *Henry Renshaw: London*, 1841. 8°. **1186**. h. **19**.

CALDER (FREDERICK) *Rev., M.A.* A Collection of Arithmetical Questions with Answers; forming a complete set of examples upon Calder's Arithmetic. pp. 46. *Whittaker & Co.: London*, 1849. 12°. **8505**. b. **32**.

—— Second edition. pp. 55. *Whittaker & Co.: London*, 1851. 12°. **8505**. a. **78**. (3.)

—— Exercises in Mensuration, with their Solutions, forming a key to all the exercises in Part III. of Lund's Geometry and Mensuration. pp. 72. *Longman & Co.: London*, 1859. 12°. **8531**. b. **26**.

—— A Familiar Explanation of the Higher Parts of Arithmetic . . . Designed as an introduction to algebra. pp. x. 167. *Whittaker & Co.: London*, 1848. 12°. **8505**. b. **31**.

—— A Familiar Explanation of the Elementary Rules of Arithmetic; being an introduction to the Higher Parts of Arithmetic already published. (A Familiar Explanation of the Higher Parts of Arithmetic . . . Second edition. [Including the questions from "A Collection of Arithmetical Questions."]) 2 pt. *Whittaker & Co.: London*, 1852. 12°. **8505**. b. **63**.
The title on the cover reads: "Calder's Arithmetic. Part I. & II."

CALDER (FREDERICK) *Rev., M.A.*

—— A Familiar Explanation of Arithmetic . . . New edition. [With answers.] 2 pt. *Longman & Co.: London*, 1861. 12°. **8504**. b. **3**.

—— [A reissue of pt. 1.] *London*, 1862. 12°. **8504**. aaa. **68**.

—— Arithmetic for Schools . . . Abridged from the author's 'Familiar Explanation of Arithmetic.' pp. viii. 237. *Longmans & Co.: London*, 1869. 8°. **8506**. aaa. **22**.

—— Answers to Part 1 of Calder's Arithmetic. pp. 15. *Whittaker & Co.: London*, 1852. 8°. **8505**. b. **33**.

—— Answers to Calder's Arithmetic [i.e. "A Familiar Explanation of the Higher Parts of Arithmetic"]. pp. 41. *Whittaker & Co.: London*, 1851. 8°. **8505**. b. **30**.

—— The Proposed Decimal Coinage, and its application to the various rules of arithmetic, with an explanation of the Chinese abacus, or swanpan. pp. 23. *Whittaker & Co.: London*, 1854. 12°. **8505**. a. **78**. (5.)

—— Scripture Stories for the Young . . . With illustrations by D. H. Friston. pp. viii. 287. *J. Hogg & Sons: London*, [1862.] 8°. **3128**. d. **25**.

—— [A reissue.] Scripture Stories and Bible Narratives for Children, *etc.* *Ward, Lock & Co.: London*, [1872.] 8°. **3128**. ccc. **14**.

—— [A reissue.] Bible Narratives; or, Scripture stories, *etc.* *London*, [1875.] 8°. **3128**. ccc. **13**.

—— Thoughts on the Work of the New Education Commission. pp. 30. *Longman & Co.: London*, 1865. 8°. **8355**. bbb. **23**.

CALDER (FREDERICK) *Wesleyan Methodist Minister.* Memoirs of Simon Episcopius . . . To which is added a brief account of the Synod of Dort, *etc.* pp. 549. *Simpkin & Marshall; John Mason: London*, 1835. 8°. **1124**. f. **26**.

CALDER (FREDERICK C.) Nutshell Theology. pp. 94. *The Author: Brighton*, 1936. 8°. **04018**. g. **69**.

CALDER (GEORGE) *See* AURAICEPT. Auraicept na n'Éces . . . Edited . . . with introduction, translation of the Ballymote text, notes and indices by G. Calder. 1917. 8°. **12978**. g. **27**.

—— *See* ROSS (William) *Schoolmaster at Gairloch.* Gaelic Songs . . . New edition revised, with metrical translation, memoir, glossary, and notes, by G. Calder. 1937. 8°. **11595**. h. **36**.

—— *See* STATIUS (P. P.) [*Thebais.—Irish and English.*] Togail na Tebe. The Thebaid . . . The Irish text. Edited . . . with introduction, translation, vocabulary and notes by G. Calder. 1922. 8°. **11386**. h. **34**.

—— *See* VIRGILIUS MARO (P.) [*Æneis.—Polyglott.*] Imtheachta Æniasa, the Irish Æneid . . . The Irish text, with translation into English, introduction, vocabulary, and notes. By Rev. G. Calder. 1907. 8°. Ac. **9955**.

—— A Gaelic Grammar, *etc.* pp. xiv. 352. *A. MacLaren & Sons: Glasgow*, [1923.] 8°. **12978**. bb. **30**.

CALDER (GRACE J.)

—— The Writing of "Past and Present." A study of Carlyle's manuscripts. pp. viii. 216. *Yale University Press: New Haven*, 1949. 8°. [*Yale Studies in English.* vol. 112.] Ac. 2692. ma/3.

CALDER (H. K.) Rubber " Form " at a Glance. A guide to investors in rubber shares, *etc.* 2 no. *Effingham Wilson: London*, 1918, 19. 8°. **08230**. ee. **44**.

CALDER (ISABEL MACBEATH) *See* DAVENPORT (John) *B.D.* Letters of John Davenport . . . Edited by I. M. Calder. 1937. 8°. **010921**. p. 5.

—— *See* STILES (E.) Letters & Papers of Ezra Stiles . . . Edited by I. M. Calder. 1933. 8°. Ac. **9726/3**.

—— Colonial Captivities, Marches and Journeys. Edited . . . by I. M. Calder. pp. vii. 255. 1935. 8°. *See* UNITED STATES OF AMERICA.—*National Society of the Colonial Dames of America.* **9555**. r. **18**.

—— [Another copy.] **9555**. r. **22**.

—— The New Haven Colony. [With a map.] pp. vi. 301. *Yale University Press: New Haven*, 1934. 8°. [*Yale Historical Publications. Miscellany.* vol. 28.] Ac. **2692**. md/3.

—— [Another copy.] **9555**. r. **19**.

CALDER (J. A.)

—— *See* SAVILE (Douglas B. O.) and CALDER (J. A.) Notes on the Flora of Chesterfield Inlet, *etc.* [1952.] 8°. **7036**. d. **7**.

CALDER (JAMES) *Minister of Croy.* Diary of J. Calder . . . Edited from the original MSS., with illustrative notes, by the Rev. William Taylor. pp. vi. 121. *Peter Drummond: Stirling*, 1875. 8°. **4955**. aa. **8**.

CALDER (JAMES) *of Forgandenny.* Leaves from a Diary. [Journal of a tour in South Africa, Australia, New Zealand and Canada.] pp. 219. *Cowan & Son: Perth*, 1906. 4°. **010025**. df. **57**.

CALDER (JAMES ERSKINE) *Begin.* Macquarie-street, 26th August, 1864. Dear Sir, In compliance with the request . . . that I would . . . prepare a Return exhibiting the condition of Tasmania for several years past, *etc.* [A return to the Colonial Treasurer.] pp. 4. ff. 5–12. [1864.] fol. *See* TASMANIA. [*Miscellaneous* Public *Documents.*] **8223**. f. **1**.

—— Oyster Culture. A compilation of facts. [With plates.] pp. 30. 1868. 8°. *See* TASMANIA. [*Miscellaneous Official* Publications.] **7905**. cc. **23**.

—— Some Account of the Wars, Extirpation, Habits, &c., of the Native Tribes of Tasmania. pp. 115. iii. *Henn & Co.: Hobart Town*, 1875. 8°. **10492**. aaa. **4**.

—— [Another copy, with two additional leaves, bearing a dedication, dated June 1876, and a note by the author.] **10492**. aaa. **36**.

—— Tasmanian Industries: with some notices of those of the Australian colonies and New Zealand, *etc.* pp. 101. 1869. 8°. *See* TASMANIA. [*Miscellaneous Official* Publications.] **7956**. bb. **53**. (**2**.)

CALDER (JAMES MORISON)

—— Scotland's March Past. The share of Scottish Churches in the London Missionary Society. [With plates.] pp. 35. *Livingstone Press: London*, 1945. 8°. **4767**. de. **42**.

CALDER (JAMES TRAILL) Sketch of the Civil and Traditional History of Caithness, from the Tenth Century. pp. xvi. 294. *T. Murray & Son: Glasgow*, 1861. 8°. **10369**. c. **26**.

—— Second edition. With historical notes by Thomas Sinclair . . . Maps and illustrations. pp. xxiv. 368. *William Rae: Wick*, 1887. 8°. **010369**. g. **30**.

CALDER (JEAN MCKINLAY)

—— The Story of Nursing . . . Illustrated by Roy Spencer. pp. 76. *Methuen & Co.: London*, 1954. 8°. [*Methuen's Outlines.*] W.P. A. **543/11**.

CALDER (JOHN) *D.D.* The Nature, the Object, the Distinctions, and the Season of Charity Considered. A sermon preached at St. Thomas's, Jan. 1, 1772, for the benefit of the Children educated at the Charity-School in Gravel-Lane, Southwark. pp. 27. *Printed at the Request of the Managers: London*, 1772. 8°. **4475**. bb. **31**.

—— A Catalogue of the Entire and Select Library of the late Rev. John Calder . . . which will be sold by auction, *etc.* pp. 63. *Wright & Murphy: London*, 1816. 8°. **130**. k. **7**. (**6**.)

CALDER (JOHN) *Inspector of Factories.* Capital's Duty to the Wage-Earner, *etc.* pp. xii. 326. *Longmans & Co.: New York, London*, 1923. 8°. **08285**. b. **112**.

—— Course in Modern Production Methods. John Calder, director, *etc.* 6 vol. *Business Training Corporation: New York, Chicago*, [1920, 21.] 8°. **08228**. a. **61**.

—— The Prevention of Factory Accidents, *etc.* pp. xvi. 325. *Longmans & Co.: London*, 1899. 8°. **08282**. e. **35**.

CALDER (JOHN) *Inspector of Factories*, and **BLOOMFIELD** (MEYER)

—— American Industry. A cooperative course of reading and lectures . . . John Calder, Meyer Bloomfield, directors. 5 pt. *Business Training Corporation: New York, Chicago*, 1920. 8°. **08282**. a. **12**.

CALDER (JOHN B.)

—— Price List of American and Foreign Postage Stamps (Descriptive Price Catalogue of Government Postage Stamps), for sale by J. B. Calder. ([First,] third—sixth edition.) 5 pt. *John B. Calder: Providence, R.I.*, [1871–73.] 8°. Crawford **118**. (**1–5**.)

CALDER (JOHN WILLIAM)

—— *See* HILGENDORF (Frederick W.) Pasture Plants and Pastures of New Zealand . . . Revised by J. W. Calder, *etc.* [1949.] 8°. W.P. **6064/21**.

—— *See* HILGENDORF (Frederick W.) Weeds of New Zealand and how to eradicate them . . . Revised by J. W. Calder, *etc.* [1949.] 8°. **7035**. a. **61**.

—— *See* HILGENDORF (Frederick W.) Weeds of New Zealand and how to eradicate them . . . Revised by J. W. Calder. 1952. 8°. **7032**. r. **44**.

CALDER (MILDRED BUSSING) *See* PHILLIPS (Dorothy W.) Dear Mrs. Bender . . . Illustrated by . . . M. B. Calder. [1937.] 8°. **20059**. d. **16**.

CALDER (PETER) *See* MELVIN (James) *LL.D.* Latin Exercises. To which are prefixed, Dissertations on a variety of . . . Latin idioms and constructions. By P. Calder. [Edited by P. Calder.] 1858. 8°. **12934**. b. **24**, **25**.

—— —— 1873. 8°. **12935**. bbb. **13**.

—— *See* MELVIN (James) *LL.D.* Latin Exercises . . . to which are prefixed dissertations . . . by . . . P. Calder. 1884. 8°. **012935**. b. **4**.

CALDER (PETER RITCHIE)

—— *See* WOODLANDS (Archibald F.) ' Jungle in Retreat ! ' R. Calder's mission of inquiry in South-East Asia for the United Nations Organisations. [1952.] 8°. **10058**. ppp. **50**.

CALDER (PETER RITCHIE)

—— Atomer, radar, penicillin, vitaminer. *See* infra: Profile of Science.

—— The Birth of the Future, *etc.* [With plates.] pp. xiv. 298. *Arthur Barker: London,* 1934. 8°. **08709.** l. **49.**

—— Carry On, London. [With plates.] pp. 163. *English Universities Press: London,* 1941. 8°. **9101.** a. **26.**

—— The Conquest of Suffering, *etc.* pp. xvi. 166. *Methuen & Co.: London,* 1934. 8°. **7391.** p. **7.**

—— Dawn over Asia. pp. 48. *News Chronicle: London,* 1952. 8°. [*Background to the News.* no. 5.] W.P. **4246/5.**

—— Health of a Nation. pp. 20. *Bureau of Current Affairs: London,* 1946. 8°. [*Current Affairs.* no. 3.] P.P. **3610.** gkl.

—— The Lamp is lit. [An account of the work of the World Health Organization.] 1951. 8°. *See* WORLD HEALTH ORGANIZATION.—*Division of Public Information.* U.N. o. **106/2.**

—— The Lesson of London. pp. 127. *Secker & Warburg: London,* 1941. 8°. [*Searchlight Books.* no. 3.] W.P. **10146/3.**

—— Man and the Soil. Edited by R. Calder. [With illustrations.] pp. 26. *British Council: London,* 1952. 8°. [*Study Box.*] W.P. B. **872/5.**

—— Men against the Desert, *etc.* [On a tour of desert research stations in North Africa and the Middle East. With plates.] pp. 186. *George Allen & Unwin: London,* 1951. 8°. **10028.** r. **28.**

—— Men against the Jungle . . . Illustrations by Eric Schwab, *etc.* [An account of a journey made to report on the United Nations Technical Assistance Programme in Indonesia, Thailand, Burma, India, Pakistan and Afghanistan. With a portrait.] pp. 231. pl. 15. *George Allen & Unwin: London,* 1954. 8°. **010055.** b. **85.**

—— [Men against the Jungle.] Gevecht met het oerwoud. (Vertaling Emy Sandberg-Frankamp.) [With plates.] pp. 257. *Arnhem,* 1954. 8°. **10058.** t. **28.**

—— Profile of Science. pp. 326. *George Allen & Unwin: London,* 1951. 8°. **08710.** b. **12.**

—— [Profile of Science.] Wegbereiter der Zukunft. Atom —Radar—Penizillin—Vitamine und ihre Entdecker. (Übersetzung von Max Müller und Hans Scheurich.) pp. 304. *Wiesbaden,* 1953. 8°. **8713.** f. **21.**

—— Perfil de la ciencia. Traducción de César de Madariaga. pp. 361. *Buenos Aires,* 1953. 8°. **8714.** e. **23.**
Part of the "Colección Ciencia y cultura."

—— [Profile of Science.] Atomer, radar, penicillin, vitaminer. Naturvetenskap av i dag. (Till svenska av Sten Söderberg.) pp. 230. *Stockholm,* [1952.] 8°. **8711.** b. **14.**

—— Roving Commission . . . With eight plates. pp. xi. 227. *Methuen & Co.: London,* 1935. 8°. **010360.** cc. **59.**

—— Science makes Sense. pp. 192. *George Allen & Unwin: London,* 1955. 8°. **8714.** b. **44.**

—— Start Planning Britain Now, *etc.* pp. 63. *Kegan Paul & Co.: London,* 1941. 8°. [*The Democratic Order.* no. 5.] **8289.a.60/5.**

—— Unesco's Task. pp. 23. *United Nations Association: London,* [1947.] 8°. [*Peacefinder Series.* no. 3.] **W.P.3472/3.**

CALDER (PETER RITCHIE)

—— War of the Hemispheres. (Reprinted . . . from The New Statesman.) pp. 7. *Peace News: London,* 1947. 8°. [*P.N. Pamphlet.*] W.P. **2429/7.**

—— West meets East. [An account of the work in South-East Asia of the Specialised Agencies of the United Nations. With illustrations.] pp. 40. *News Chronicle: London,* 1952. 8°. [*Background to the News.* no. 6.] W.P. **4246/6.**

CALDER (RALPH FORMAN GODLEY)

—— *See* INTERNATIONAL CONGREGATIONAL COUNCIL. Proceedings of the Seventh International Congregational Council . . . Edited by R. F. G. Calder. 1953. 8°. **04715.** h. **15.**

—— *See* INTERNATIONAL CONGREGATIONAL COUNCIL. To introduce the Family. Edited by R. F. G. Calder. 1953. 8°. **4716.** aa. **45.**

CALDER (RITCHIE) *See* CALDER (Peter R.)

CALDER (ROBERT) *See* IGNATIUS, *Saint, Bishop of Antioch.* [*English.*] The Genuine Epistles of St. Ignatius . . . [Edited by R. Calder.] To which is added, A Short Answer to Mr. William Jameson's Nazianzeni Querela, where he impugns the authority of the foresaid epistles. By R. C. (R. Calder.) 1708. 8°. **3805.** a. **41.**

—— An Answer [by Robert Calder] to a Pamphlet [by John Anderson]: called, A Dialogue betwixt a Curat and a Country-Man, concerning the English-Service, or Common-Prayer-Book of England. pp. 47. 1711. 4°. *See* LITURGIES.—*Church of England.—Common Prayer.* [*Appendix.—Miscellaneous.*] **478.** b. **28.**

—— [Another copy.] **478.** b. **29.**

—— *See* LITURGIES.—*Church of England.—Common Prayer.* [*Appendix.—Miscellaneous.*] An Answer to the Dialogue between the Curat and the Countrey-Man concerning the English-Service, or Common-Prayer-Book of England examined. In a familiar letter to the author of the answer. 1712. 4°. **4175.** e. **3.**

—— The Lawfulness and Expediency of Set Forms of Prayer, Maintained . . . By the Rev. Mr. Robert Calder . . . and by the Rev. Bishops Taylor, Comber and King. pp. vi. 184. *Alex. Robertson: Leith,* 1766. 12°. **3477.** b. **75.**

—— Miscellany Numbers; relating to the controversies about the Book of Common-Prayer, episcopal government, the power of the Church in ordaining rites and ceremonies, &c. defended by Scripture, reason, antiquity, and the sentiments of the learn'dest reformers, *etc.* 30 no. pp. 116. 4. *Edinburgh,* 1713. fol. **695.** k. **13.**

—— The Priesthood of the Old and New Testament by Succession, *etc.* 2 pt. pp. 279. *J. Wilson: Edinburgh,* [1720?] 12°. **4105.** a. **10.**
The titlepage of pt. 2 reads "The Second part of the Succession of the Priesthood in the Old and New Testament."

—— Reasons for a Toleration to the Episcopal Clergie; and objections against it answer'd. [By R. Calder.] pp. 27. 1703. 8°. *See* SCOTLAND.—*Episcopal Church.—Clergy.* **4175.** a. **2.**

—— The Spirit of Slander Exemplified in a Scandalous Pamphlet called, the Jacobite Curse . . . To which the principal person Mr. R - - - - - C - - ld - - r [i.e. R. Calder] that is traduced in page 8th, gives this reply, *etc.* pp. 16. 1714. 8°. *See* C - - LD - - R (R - - - - -) **115.** a. **3.**

CALDER (Robert)

—— Schola Sepulchri: the School of the Grave, or, the many practicall lessons of wisdom, which the Scriptures teach us, from the consideration of mortalitie. pp. 23. 88. *Iohn Forbes: Aberdeen*, 1701. 8°. **852**. f. **16**.

—— A True Copy of Letters past betwixt Mr. Robert Calder, Minister of the Gospel, and Mr. James Cuninghame of Barns, concerning the trial of the mission of these people, that pass under the name of prophets, in Scotland and England. With a relation of the failing of their prophecies, and the true character of an enthusiast. pp. viii. 72. *James Watson: Edinburgh*, 1710. 8°. **1369**. a. **3**.

—— The True Difference betwixt the Principles and Practices of the Kirk and the Church of Scotland, exemplified in several instances . . . London . . . MDCCXII. [The editor's preface signed: T. S., i.e. Thomas Stephen.] pp. 24. *Andrew Moffat: London*, 1841. 12°. **4175**. aa. **17**.

—— Mr Robert Calder's Vindication of his Sermon preach'd January 30, 1703. from the malice and ignorance of an anonymous . . . enemy, who published some few notes thereof. pp. 56. *Edinburgh*, 1703. 12°. **4474**. a. **5**.

CALDER (*Sir* Robert) *Bart.* Minutes of the Proceedings at a Court Martial, assembled on board His Majesty's Ship Prince of Wales, in Portsmouth Harbour, on . . . the 23d day of December, 1805, and the three following days, for the trial of Sir Robert Calder, Bart., *etc.* pp. 108. *London; J. C. Mottley: Portsmouth*, 1806. 8°. **1103**. i. **77**.

CALDER (Robert Hogg) *See* also Camlach, *pseud.* [i.e. R. H. Calder.]

—— Deeside Ditties. By a Native [i.e. R. H. Calder]. pp. 48. 1912. 8°. *See* Native. **011649**. de. **12**.

—— Gleanings from a Deeside Parish. (Song-fragments, rhymes, proverbs and sayings.) By a Native [i.e. R. H. Calder]. pp. 15. 1920. 8°. *See* Native. **12450**. p. **4**.

—— The Scottish National Dances: their origin, nature, and history. By R. H. C. [i.e. R. H. Calder.] pp. 21. 1928. 8°. *See* C., R. H. **7908**. g. **36**.

—— Songs of the Plough. pp. 19. *W. Smith & Sons: Aberdeen*, 1919. 8°. **011648**. e. **183**.

CALDER (Robert McLean) *See* Hartig (P.) Die Edinburger Dialektgruppe. Sprachgeschichtliche Studie über Satzproben . . . und über den Berwickshire-Lokaldichter Calder. 1923. 8°. **12203**. ff. **1/161**.

—— A Berwickshire Bard. The songs and poems of Robert McLean Calder. Edited, with introductory memoir, by W. S. Crockett. [With illustrations and a portrait.] pp. 306. *J. & R. Parlane: Paisley*, 1897. 8°. **011652**. ee. **99**.

CALDER (Ronald Bain) *See* Savage (*Sir* William G.) The Bacteriology of Canned Meat and Fish. By W. G. Savage . . . R. B. Calder. 1922. 8°. [*Food Investigation Board. Special Report.* no. 11.] B.S. **38**. d/3.

CALDER (Royall Mann) Bacteriology for Nurses. With a laboratory manual, *etc.* pp. 285. pl. vi. *W. B. Saunders Co.: Philadelphia & London*, 1932. 8°. **07560**. df. **18**.

—— Second edition, *etc.* pp. 320. pl. vi. *W. B. Saunders Co.: Philadelphia & London*, 1937. 8°. **07560**. df. **31**.

CALDER (Royall Mann)

—— Microbiology . . . Third edition, entirely reset. pp. ix. 317. pl. vii. *W. B. Saunders Co.: Philadelphia & London*, 1943. 8°. **7564**. aaa. **3**.

CALDER (William) *See* Chaucer (Geoffrey) [*Canterbury Tales.—Modernized Versions.*] Chaucer's Canterbury Pilgrimage, epitomised by W. Calder. 1892. 8°. **11623**. e. **17**.

—— County of Sutherland. [With illustrations.] pp. 80. [*The Author: Dornoch*, 1955.] 8°. **010370**. pp. **20**.

—— The Estate and Castle of Skibo. [With plates.] pp. 80. *Albyn Press: Edinburgh*, 1949. 8°. **10370**. d. **18**.

CALDER (William) *Mechanic.* Poems Moral & Miscellaneous, with a few songs, by a Journeyman Mechanic [i.e. W. Calder]. (Appendix, consisting of pieces written since 1838.) pp. 94. 1838, [42 ?] 8°. *See* Poems. **1414**. g. **29**. (**7**.)

CALDER (*Sir* William Moir)

—— *See* Asia Minor. Monumenta Asiae Minoris antiqua. (vol. 1. Edited by W. M. Calder.—vol. 4. Monuments and documents from Eastern Asia and Western Galatia. Edited by W. H. Buckler, W. M. Calder, W. K. C. Guthrie. —vol. 6. Monuments and documents from Phrygia and Caria. Edited by W. H. Buckler, W. M. Calder.—vol. 7. Monuments from Eastern Phrygia. Edited by Sir W. M. Calder.—vol. 8. Monuments from Lycaonia, the Pisido-Phrygian Borderland, Aphrodisias. Edited by Sir W. M. Calder and J. M. R. Cormack.) 1928, *etc.* 4°. [*Publications of the American Society for Archæological Research in Asia Minor.* vol. 1, 4, 6, 7, 8.] Ac. **5211**.

—— *See* Buckler (William H.) Anatolian Studies Presented to W. H. Buckler. Edited by W. M. Calder and J. Keil. 1939. 8°. **Ac.2671/16.(26.)**

—— *See* Maximilian Alexander Frederick William, *Prince of Baden.* The Memoirs of Prince Max of Baden . . . Translation by W. M. Calder and C. W. H. Sutton. 1928. 8°. **010703**. f. **44**.

—— *See* Ramsay (*Sir* William M.) Anatolian Studies presented to Sir William Mitchell Ramsay. Edited by W. H. Buckler & W. M. Calder. 1923. 8°. **Ac.2671/16.(12.)**

—— *See* Sachs (H.) Selections from Hans Sachs. Chosen by W. M. Calder. 1948. 8°. W.P. **8866/23**.

—— Leaves from an Anatolian Notebook . . . Reprinted from "The Bulletin of the John Rylands Library," *etc.* pp. 20. *Manchester University Press: Manchester*, 1929. 8°. **07703**. l. 39.

—— Philadelphia and Montanism . . . With three plates. Reprinted from "The Bulletin of the John Rylands Library," *etc.* pp. 46. *University Press: Manchester; Longmans & Co.: London*, 1923. 8°. **4530**. f. **13**.

—— Some Monuments of the Great Persecution . . . Reprinted from "The Bulletin of the John Rylands Library," *etc.* pp. 20. *University Press: Manchester; Longmans & Co.: London*, 1924. 8°. **4530**. dd. **18**.

CALDERA-BROSSA MELOPIANO. Melopiano Caldera-Brossa. Giudizi della stampa nazionale ed estera su questa invenzione italiana. [With a preface by L. Caldera.] pp. 56. *Torino*, 1873. 8°. **7806**. aaa. **1**. (**13**.)

CALDERA CLIPPINGS. The Caldera Clippings. [A journal produced on board the ship "Caldera."] pp. 30. *P. Davis & Sons: Pietermartizburg*, 1877. 8°. **10496**. a. **27**.

CALDERA (Benito) *See* Camoens (L. de) Los Lusiadas . . . traduzidos en octaua rima Castellana por B. Caldera. 1580. 4°. **87.** b. **19.**

CALDERA (Eduardus) De erroribus pragmaticorum libri quatuor, totidem variarum lectionum. 1752. *See* Meerman (G.) Novus thesaurus juris civilis et canonici, *etc.* tom. 3. 1751, *etc.* fol. **18.** h. **8.**

CALDERA (Luigi) *See* Caldera-Brossa Melopiano. Melopiano Caldera-Brossa, *etc.* [With a preface by L. Caldera.] 1873. 8°. **7806.** aaa. **1.** (**13.**)

CALDERA (Rafael) *See* Caldera Rodríguez (R.)

CALDERA DE HEREDIA (Caspar) *See* Caldera de Heredia (Gaspar)

CALDERA DE HEREDIA (Gaspar) Casparis Calderæ de Heredia . . . Tribunal medicum, magicum, et politicum. 2 pt. *Apud J. Elsevirium: Lugduni Batavorum,* 1658. fol. **543.** h. **11.**

—— Casparis Calderæ de Heredia . . . Tribunalis medici illustrationes et obseruationes practicæ. Accessit liber aureus de facile parabilibus, *etc.* (Index sectionum, stationum et capitum, qui in Medico nostro tribunali desideratur.) pp. 354. *Apud I. Meursium: Antuerpiæ,* 1663. fol. **L.20.a.6.**

—— Vista, visita, y reconocimiento del cuerpo del venerable siervo de Dios el Rey Don Fernando el Santo. [*Seville?* 1668?] fol. T. **16*.** (**36.**)

CALDERAI (Talete) Della vita e delle opere del commendatore Domenico Chiodo, maggiore generale del Genio. [With a portrait and maps.] pp. 119. *Firenze,* 1871. 8°. **10631.** ee. **34.**

CALDERANI (Giuseppe) Lettera . . . scritta al signor Giovanni Lapi in risposta di alcune domande intorno alla fattoria di Camugliano . . . di cui occorse parlare nel . . . discorso sull'esterminio del loglio, *etc.* *See* Lapi (G.) Discorso sull'esterminio del loglio, *etc.* 1767. 8°. **7074.** k. **1.** (**8.**)

CALDERARA (Mario) and **BANET-RIVET** (P.) Manuel de l'aviateur-constructeur . . . Deuxième édition, revue et notablement augmentée. pp. viii. 320. *Paris,* 1910. 8°. **08767.** aa. **14.**

CALDERARI (Giovanni Battista) La Schiaua, comedia. pp. 175. *A. dalla Noce: Vicenza,* 1589. 8°. **1071.** k. **2.** (**3.**)

CALDERARI (Giulio Cesare) Poesie d'argomento religioso e melanconico. pt. 1. pp. 176. *Milano,* 1875. 8°. **11431.** cc. **40.**

CALDERARI (Ottone) *Count.* *See* Le Breton (J.) Notice historique sur la vie et les ouvrages de M. le comte Ottone-Calderari, *etc.* [1808.] 4°. [*Séance publique de la Classe des Beaux Arts de l'Institut de France du premier octobre* 1808.] **733.** h. **14.** (**20.**)

—— Disegni e scritti d'architettura. [Edited by A. Diedo, G. Marangoni, A. Rigato and A. Vivorio.] vol. 1, 2. *Vicenza,* 1808–17. fol. **557*.** i. **4.**
Wanting vol. 3 *containing the "Scritti."*

CALDERARO (Agostino) *See* Gentildonna. Il Terremoto delle Calabrie . . . Poema . . . con prefazione e commenti dell'Ex-tenente Calderaro Agostino. 1889. 8°. **11429.** ee. **35.** (**4.**)

CALDERARO (Giulia) Alessandro Manzoni e il mondo latino e greco. pp. 239. *Firenze,* 1937. 8°. **20013.** c. **25.**

CALDERA RODRÍGUEZ (Rafael)

—— *See* Caracas.—*Academia de Ciencias Políticas y Sociales.* Discurso de incorporación del individuo de número Doctor Arturo Uslar Pietri . . . Contestación del académico Doctor R. Caldera. 1955. 8°. **8181.** b. **18.**

—— Academia de Ciencias Políticas y Sociales. Discurso de incorporación del individuo de número Doctor R. Caldera. Tema: idea de una sociología venezolana, *etc.* pp. 101. 1953. 8°. *See* Caracas.—*Academia de Ciencias Políticas y Sociales.* **8295.** d. **10.**

—— Andrés Bello. Ensayo, *etc.* pp. 167. [*Caracas,*] 1935. 8°. **20003.** h. **9.**

—— Derecho del Trabajo. Ensayo de una exposición doctrinal de la materia analizando la situación venezolana y la legislación y jurisprudencia venezolanas. pp. xxix. 867. *Caracas,* 1939. 8°. **8288.** h. **22.**

CALDERERO. Sainete Nuevo. Intitulado: El Calderero y Vecindad. [By R. F. de la Cruz Cano y Olmedilla.] pp. 8. *Valencia,* 1822. 4°. **1342.** f. 5. (**27.**)

CALDEREROS. Entremes nuevo de los Caldereros. pp. 16. [*Madrid?* 1770?] 16°. **11725.** aa. **1.** (**35.**)

—— [Another edition.] Entremes de los Caldereros. pp. 16. [*Valencia?* 1810?] 16°. **11452.** aaaa. **1.** (**19.**)

CALDERFORD (M.) Willie. A story of a children's hospital. pp. 49. *Swan Sonnenschein & Co.: London,* 1899. 8°. **04410.** e. **49.**

CALDERIA (Joannes) Concordantiæ poetarum philosophorum & theologorum, *etc.* [Edited by M. A. Biondo.] ff. 179. *Apud Cominum de Tridino Montisferati: Venetijs,* 1547. 8°. **11824.** aaa. **15.**
Printed on tinted paper.

CALDERINI (Aristide) *See* Calderini De-Marchi (R.) Jacopo Corbinelli et les érudits français, *etc.* [Edited by A. Calderini.] 1914. 8°. **10633.** a. **25.**

—— *See* Calderini De-Marchi (R.) and Calderini (A.) Autori greci nelle epistole di Jacopo Corbinelli, *etc.* 1915. 8°. **11313.** ee. **1.**

—— *See* De Marchi (A.) I Romani . . . Libro . . . di A. de Marchi . . . e di A. Calderini, *etc.* 1931. 8°. **07702.** bb. **27.**

—— *See* Homer. [*Iliad.—Greek.*] Ilias Ambrosiana, *etc.* [Edited by A. Calderini.] 1953. fol. W.P. **12809/28.**

—— *See* Milan.—*Basilica di S. Lorenzo Maggiore.* La Basilica di S. Lorenzo Maggiore in Milano. [By A. Calderini, G. Chierici and C. Cecchelli.] [1951.] 4°. **07822.** v. 3.

—— Aquileia romana. Ricerche di storia e di epigrafia. pp. cxxxvi. 594. *Milano,* 1930. 8°. [*Pubblicazioni dell'Università Cattolica del Sacro Cuore.* ser. 5. vol. 10.] **7704.** g. **51.**

—— Bibliografia metodica degli studi di egittologia e di papirologia. *In:* Aegyptus, *etc.* anno. 1. no. 1—anno 18. fasc. 3/4, anno 23. fasc. 2, anno. 29. fasc. 1/2, *etc.* 1920–38, 1943, 1949, *etc.* 1920– . 8°. P.P. **3807.** bd.
The 'Bibliografia' was continued in the issues between anno 19 *and anno* 23. *fasc.* 1, *but these numbers are missing from this set. It was discontinued between anno* 24 *and anno* 28.

—— Di un'ara greca dedicatoria agli dei inferi esistente nel Museo Archeologico di Milano. [With plates.] pp. 34. *Milano,* 1907. 8°. **7707.** df. **25.**

CALDERINI (Aristide)

—— Dizionario dei nomi geografici e topografici dell'Egitto greco-romano. 1935- . 4°. *See* Cairo.—*Société de Géographie d'Égypte.* Ac. **6042**. d/5.

—— Echi elettorali. Votate per M. Tullio Cicerone. [On the consular elections of 64 B.C.] pp. 15. *Milano,* 1948. 8°. [*Quaderni di studi romani.* no. 1.] Ac. **103**. ca.

—— Giacomo Lumbroso. Estratto dalla "Raccolta di scritti in onore di Giacomo Lumbroso," *etc.* pp. xviii. *Milano,* 1925. 8°. **10634**. d. **56**.

—— La Manomissione e la condizione dei liberti in Grecia, *etc.* pp. xix. 464. *Milano,* 1908. 8°. **8157**. ee. **25**.

—— Papiri latini. Appunti delle lezioni di papirologia. [Texts. Edited, with an introduction and notes, by A. Calderini. With facsimiles.] pp. ix. 138. pl. iv *Milano,* 1945. 8°. **07705. aaa. 9.**

—— La Religione degli Egiziani. *See* Tacchi Venturi (P.) Storia delle religioni, *etc.* vol. 1. 1934, *etc.* 8°. **4508.1.2/1.**

—— Scolî greci all'Antologia Planudea. Memoria, *etc.* 1912. *See* Milan.—*Reale Istituto Lombardo di Scienze, Lettere ed Arti.* Memorie, *etc.* Classe di lettere e scienze morali e storiche. vol. 22. 1843, *etc.* 4°. Ac. **110**/5.

—— I Severi. La crisi dell'Impero nel III secolo. [With a bibliography.] pp. 645. *Bologna,* 1949. 8°. [*Storia di Roma.* vol. 7.] W.P. **12791/7**.

—— Gli Studi greci di Francesco Novati. *See* Novati (F.) Francesco Novati, *etc.* 1917. 8°. Ac. **6525/5**.

—— *Θησαυροι.* Ricerche di topografia e di storia della pubblica amministrazione nell'Egitto greco-romano. pp. 132. *Milano,* 1924. 8°. [*Studi della Scuola Papirologica.* vol. 4. pt. 3.] Ac. **2810**. c.

—— La Zona di Piazza S. Sepolcro. A cura di A. Calderini. [With a plan.] pp. 70. pl. xv. *Milano,* 1940. 8°. [*Instituto di Studi Romani, Sezione Lombarda. Ricerche della Commissione per la Forma Urbis Mediolani.* vol. 4.] Ac. **103**. c.

—— La Zona monumentale di S. Lorenzo in Milano, *etc.* pp. 232. pl. xxxiv. 1934. 8°. *See* Milan.—*Comitato per l'Archeologia e l'Arte in Lombardia.* **07815**. ee. **75**.

CALDERINI (Carlo Ampelio) *See* Periodical Publications.—*Milan.* Annali universali di medicina. (vol. 93–155. Continuati dal dottore C. A. Calderini.) [1827, *etc.*] 8°. P.P. **2923**.

—— Specimen pathologicum circa studii inflammationis praestantiam. Dissertatio inauguralis, *etc.* pp. 39. *Ticini Regii,* 1831. 8°. **7383***. b. **1**. (**2**.)

CALDERINI (Carolus) *Almi Collegii Borromaeorum alumnus. See* Calderini (Carlo A.)

CALDERINI (Carolus) *I.R. Collegii Ghisleriorum alumnus.* De cutis adsociatione cum reliquo organismo, dissertatio inauguralis, *etc.* pp. 27. *Ticini Regii,* [1821.] 8°. **7383***. d. **3**. (**12**.)

CALDERINI (Emma) Il Costume popolare in Italia . . . Introduzione di Amy A. Bernardy. pp. 166. pl. 200. *Milano,* 1934. fol. **7742**. w. **2**.

CALDERINI (Giovanni) *Dottore. See* Parma.—*Università di Parma.—Reale Istituto Ostetrico.* R. Istituto Ostetrico annesso all'Ospizio di Maternità nell'Università di Parma. 1°. Rendiconto del dottor G. Calderini, *etc.* 1877. 8°. Ac. **106**.

CALDERINI (Giovanni) *Dottore.*

—— Calendario della gravidanza, dedotto dal Calendario circolare del prof. cav. D. Tibone, *etc.* (Supplemento al N. 39. della Gazzetta delle cliniche.) [*Turin,* 1869.] *s. sh. obl.* fol. **1830**. c. **1**. (**15**.)

—— Del contatto dell'iride colla lente cristallina nell'occhio umano, *etc.* pp. 23. *Torino,* 1868. 8°. **7610**. e. **31**. (**6**.)

—— L'Osteomalacia . . . Memoria presentata pel Concorso di Aggregazione, al Collegio medico-chirurgico di Torino. pp. 83. *Torino & Firenze,* 1870. 8°. **7298**. dd. **15**.

CALDERINI (Giovanni) *Jurist. See* Calderinus (Joannes)

CALDERINI (Guglielmo) *See* Petersen (E. A. H.) Die Marcus-Säule auf Piazza Colonna in Rom. Herausgegeben von E. Petersen, A. von Domaszewski, G. Calderini. 1896. fol. Tab. **1294**. b.

—— Le Opere architettoniche di Guglielmo Calderini. [With an introduction by G. B. Milani.] pl. 88. *Milano,* [1918.] fol. L.R. **32**. b. **6**.

—— Schiarimenti del secondo progetto per la facciata del duomo di Firenze, *etc.* pp. 15. *Perugia,* 1867. 8°. **7815**. aaa. **39**. (**7**.)

CALDERINI (Marco) Carlo Marochetti. Monografia con ritratti, fac-simile e riproduzioni di opere dell'artista. pp. 64. *Torino,* [1928.] fol. **7876**. h. **25**.

CALDERINI (Nazareno) *See* Isola (M. dall') La Trasimenide, *etc.* [With a dedication by N. Calderini.] 1846. 8°. **11405**. e. **19**.

CALDERINI (Sandra)

—— Ricerche sull'industria e il commercio dei tessuti in Egitto. 1947. *See* Periodical Publications.—*Milan.* Aegyptus, *etc.* anno 26. fasc. 1/2. 1920, *etc.* 8°. P.P. **3807**. bd.

CALDERINI (Vincenzo) L'Omicidio per gelosia. Il furto immaginario. Una sognata ricettazione dolosa. Difesa . . . [of L. Martignani and others of his family] innanzi al Tribunale Criminale di Ravenna. (Sentenza.) pp. 101. 4. *Forlì,* 1853. 8°. **898**. d. **1**. (**11**.)

CALDERINI DE-MARCHI (Rita) Jacopo Corbinelli et les érudits français d'après la correspondance inédite Corbinelli-Pinelli, 1566–1587. [Edited by A. Calderini.] pp. xi. 288. *Milano,* 1914. 8°. **10633**. a. **25**.

CALDERINI DE-MARCHI (Rita) and **CALDERINI** (Aristide)

—— Autori greci nelle epistole di Jacopo Corbinelli, MSS. Ambros. B 9 inf.; T. 167 sup. pp. 86. *Milano,* 1915. 8°. **11313**. ee. **1**.

CALDERINIS (Joannes de) *See* Calderinus (Joannes)

CALDERINO (Cesare Mirani)

—— *See* Galesino (P.) Dittionario, ouero Tesoro della lingua volgare . . . Con il dittionario latino . . . accommodato alle voci volgari d'esso tesoro . . . di M. C. M. Calderino, *etc.* 1618. 8°. **1480**. aa. **43**.

—— Dictionariolum, siue Thesauri linguæ latinæ, et omnibus [*sic*] à vocibus latinis incipientium dictionariorum compendium. Italicis etiam, & praecipuè D. Petri Galesini . . . Thesauro accommodatum . . . Hac postrema editione aliquibus vocibus, quæ deerant, locupletatum. *See* Galesino (P.) Il Perfetto dittionario, *etc.* 1659. 8°. **627**. c. **3**.

CALDERINO (CESARE MIRANI)

—— [Another edition.] Dictionariolum, siue Thesauri linguæ latinæ, et omnium à vocibus latinis incipientium dictionariorum compendium, *etc.* *See* GALESINO (P.) Il Perfetto dittionario, *etc.* 1684. 8°. **627.** c. **4.**

CALDERINO (DOMIZIO) *See* CALDERINUS (Domitius)

CALDERINUS (DOMINICUS) *See* CALDERINUS (Domitius)

CALDERINUS (DOMITIUS) [For editions of the Satires of Juvenal with the commentary of D. Calderinus:] *See* JUVENALIS (D. J.) [*Satirae.—Latin.*]

—— [For editions of Martial with the commentary of D. Calderinus:] *See* MARTIALIS (M. V.) [*Latin.*]

—— *See* MERULA (G.) *Begin.* [fol. 2 *recto*:] Ad inuictissimum principem Federicum de Monteferetro Vrbini ducem: Georgii Merulae Alexandrini praefatio in satyrarum Iuuenalis enarrationes. [fol. 100 *recto*:] Georgii Merulae Alexandrini aduersus Domitii commentarios (in Martialem) praefatio, *etc.* 1478. fol. IB. **19942.**

—— —— 1478. fol. IB. **28402.**

—— [For editions of the "Epistolae Heroidum" of Ovid with the commentary of D. Calderinus on the epistle of Sappho published with one or more of the other works of Ovid:] *See* OVIDIUS NASO (P.) [*Two or more Works.—Latin.*]

—— [For editions of the "Ibis" of Ovid with the commentary of D. Calderinus, published with one or more of the other works of Ovid:] *See* OVIDIUS NASO (P.) [*Two or more Works.—Latin.*]

—— *See* PAUSANIAS, *the Traveller.* Pausanias Historicus. Domitius Calderinus E Græco traduxit. Atticæ descriptio. [1500?] 4°. IA. **24610.**

—— *See* PROPERTIUS (S. A.) *Begin.* [fol. 1 *verso*:] Vita Propertii. [fol. 2 *recto*:] Propertii . . . Elegiarum liber primus ad Tullum. [With the commentary of D. Calderinus.] 1486. fol. IB. **31093.**

—— —— 1500. fol. [*Tibullus cum commentariis, etc.*] IB. **24101.**

—— *See* PTOLEMAEUS (C.) [*Geographia.—Latin.*] *Begin.* [fol. 1 *verso*:] Claudii Ptholemei Alexandrini Philosophi Cosmographia. [Edited by D. Calderinus.] 1478. fol. C. **3.** d. **6.**

—— *See* STATIUS (P. P.) [*Works.—Latin.*] *Begin.* [fol. 2 *recto*:] Placidi Lactantii interpretetio in primum librum Thebaidos. [fol. 153 *recto*:] Ex emendatione & interpretatione Domitii calderini Veronensis Statii papini Neapolitani Syluarū Liber primus (—v.), *etc.* [fol. 217 *recto*:] Domitius in Sapho Ouidii. [fol. 223 *verso*:] Domitii elucubratio in quædā ꝑpertii loca. quæ difficiliora uidebāt͂, *etc.* [fol. 228 *recto*:] Ex tertio libro obseruationum domitii. 1483. fol. IB. **21203.**

—— —— 1490. fol. IB. **23305.**

—— —— 1494. fol. IB. **23711.**

—— —— 1498. fol. IB. **24172.**

—— —— 1600. 4°. **681.** g. **19.**

—— —— 1618. 4°. **654.** b. **15.**

—— —— 1671. 8°. **11375.** c. **31.**

CALDERINUS (DOMITIUS)

—— *See* STATIUS (P. P.) [*Silvae.—Latin.*] *Begin.* [fol. 1 *verso*:] ἐπωπιδων. Hoc volumine Domitius inseruit. Syluarum Statii papinii libros quinque a se emendatos. Commentariolos in Sappho Ouidii quos edidit. propertii loca obscura a se elucubrata. Particulam ex tertio libro suarum obseruationum, *etc.* [1482?] fol. IB. **22018.**

—— *See* SUETONIUS TRANQUILLUS (C.) [*Vitae XII. Caesarum.*] *Begin.* [fol. 2 *recto*:] Bonus Accursius Pisanus Salutem dicit plurimā . . . primo ducali secretario Ciccho Simonetæ. [fol. 3 *verso*:] Domitii Calderini . . . de uita Caii Suetonii tranquilli, *etc.* 1475. fol. C. **2.** c. **10.**

—— —— 1490. fol. IB. **23139.**

—— [For editions of the works of Virgil with the commentaries of D. Calderinus on some of the minor poems:] *See* VIRGILIUS MARO (P.) [*Works.*]

—— *See* VIRGILIUS MARO (P.) [*Minor Poems.*] Vergiliana opuscula, *etc.* [With the commentary of D. Calderinus.] [1501.] fol. Hirsch III. **1133.** (**3.**)

—— *See* VITELLIUS (C.) *Begin.* [fol. 2 *recto*:] Cornelii Vitellii Corythii in defensionem Plinii & Domitii Calderini contra Georgium Merulam Alexandrinum . . . Epistola. [1482?] 4°. IA. **21342.**

—— *Begin.* [fol. 2 *recto*:] Domitius Calderinus Ioanni Francisco Lodouici Principis Mantuani filio salutem. [fol. 2 *verso*:] Domitii Calderini Vfronensis [*sic*] Commentarii in .M. Valerium Martialem, *etc.* [fol. 173 *recto*:] Domitii Calderini Veronensis Cōmētarioli ī Ibin Ouidii, *etc.* [Edited by Joannes Calphurnius.] *arte & ingenio Iacobi de Rubeis: Venetiis,* Idibus Septembris [13 Sept.], 1474. fol. **167.** c. **23.**
186 *leaves, ff.* 1 *and* 172 *blank. Without signatures.* 50 *lines to a page. Imperfect; wanting ff.* 79–84 *and the blank leaves.*

—— *Begin.* [fol. 1 *recto*:] Ad Franciscum Aragoneum Ferdinandi Regis Neap. F., *etc.* [fol. 1 *verso*:] Domitius in Sapph. Ouidii. [fol. 17 *verso*:] Domitii Elucubratio in quædam Propertii loca: Quæ difficiliora uideantur, *etc.* [fol. 30 *recto*:] Domitii ad Franciscum Aragonum Epilogus et De obseruationibus. G. L. *Henricus de colonia: Brixiæ,* die Iunii .viii, 1476. 8°. IA. **31043.**
38 *leaves. Sig.* a–d⁸ e⁶. 30–32 *lines to a page.*

—— *Begin.* [fol. 2 *recto*:] Domitii Calderini Veronensis secretarii apostolici in commentarios Iuuenalis ad . . . Iulianum Medicen Petri Cosmi filium Florentinum. [fol. 3 *recto*:] Domitii Calderini Veronensis . . . Commentarii In Satyras Iuuenalis, *etc.* [fol. 64 *verso*:] Domitii Calderini Verōsis . . . Defēsio aduersus Brotheū [i.e. Nicolaus Perottus] Grāmaticū Cōmtarioꝝ Mart. Calūniatorē: Cū Recriatōe Retaxatōis Pliiāæ In Qua Brotheus Ducētis Et. lxxv. Locis Præstātissīū Scriptorē Deprauauit. [Edited by Joannes Calphurnius.] [*Venice?* 1477?] fol. **G.9810.(2.)**
70 *leaves, the first blank. Sig.* a–k$^{8 \cdot 6}$. 42 *lines to a page. Without the blank leaf.*

—— *Begin.* [fol. 2 *recto*:] [dOmitius calderinus Iohanni francisco Lodouici principis mantuani filio Salutem, *etc.*] [fol. 4 *recto*:] [Domitii Calderini Veronensis Commentarii in .M. Valerium Martialem, *etc.*] [fol. 10 *recto*:] bArbara Pyramidum. Hoc primo epigrāmate assentatur Domitiano, *etc.* *End.* [fol. 315 *verso*:] Domitii calderini ueronensis commentarii in .M. Valeriuȝ martialem. cum defensione finiunt, *etc.* [fol. 316 *recto*:] M. Lucidi phosphori Epigramma. *per Iohannem genſberg, auspicio et fauore iohannis Aloisii tuscani: rome,* die martis .xxii. mensis martii, 1474. fol. IB. **17665.**
316 *leaves, ff.* 1 *and* 9 *blank. Without signatures.* 33 *lines to a page. Imperfect; wanting ff.* 1–9, 19–26.

CALDERINUS (Domitius)

—— [Another edition.] *Begin.* [fol. 2 *recto:*] dOmitius Calderinus Iohāni Frācisco Lodouici principis mantuani filio Salutē, *etc.* [fol. 3 *recto:*] Domitii Calderini ueronēsis cōmentarii in .M. Valerium Martialem, *etc.* *End.* [fol. 276 *recto:*] Domitii caldermi [*sic*] ueronēsis cōmētarii ī .M. Valeriū Martialē cū defēsiōe finiūt, *etc.* *opa & īpēdio Iohannis de Colonia Agripinēsi at Iohānis māthen: Venetiis,* 1474. fol. IB. **20220.**
276 *leaves, the first blank. Sig.* a^6; a^8 b^{10} c^{10} d^8 e–m^{10} n–s^8 t^6 u^6 x–z^{10} aa^8 bb^6 cc^{10} dd^8 ee^{10} ff^{10} gg^{12}. 34 *lines to a page.*

—— [Commentarii in quaedam Virgilii opuscula.] *Begin.* [fol. 1 *recto:*] Domitii Calderini Veronēsis cōmētarii ī. p. uir. Marōis Culicō. pAstor oues de more ad umbrā cōpellens, etc. *End.* [fol. 25 *verso:*] Finis Ciricis. FEW MS. NOTES. [*Simon Magniagus: Milan,* 1480?] 4° & 8°. IA. **26603.**
26 *leaves, the last blank. Sig.* a^8 b^8 c^6 d^4. 30 *lines to a page. Without the blank leaf.*

—— [For editions of "Defensio adversus Brotheum grammaticum Commentariorum Martialis calumniatorem" by D. Calderinus published with the Satires of Juvenal:] *See* JUVENALIS (D. J.) [*Satirae.—Latin.*]

—— Ex tertio libro obseruationum domitii. *See* BEROALDUS (P.) *the Elder.* [*Two or more Works.*] Ecce tibi lector humanissime: Philippi Beroaldi Annotationes Centum, *etc.* 1496. fol. IB. **31254.**

—— [Another edition.] *See* COCCIUS (M. A.) *Sabellicus.* In hoc volumine hæc continentur, Marci Antonii Sabellici Annotationes, *etc.* 1502. fol. **837.** m. **32.**

—— [Another edition.] *See* COCCIUS (M. A.) *Sabellicus.* In hoc volumine hec continentur. Marci Antonii Sabellici annotationes, *etc.* 1508. fol. **630.** l. **3.** (**2.**)

—— [Another edition.] *See* BADIUS (J.) *Ascensius.* Annotationes doctorum virorū in grammaticos, *etc.* [1511.] fol. C. **76.** d. **11.**

CALDERINUS (Gaspar) [Consilia.] *Begin.* [fol. 2 *recto:*] De constitutionibus. Rubrica. [fol. 24 *recto:*] Consilia domini Io. Cal. Et do. Gas. eius filii redacta sub congruis rubricis et decurtata. assumptis rationibus substantificis per dominum Dominicum de sancto Geminiano. Incipiunt feliciter. 1472. fol. *See* CALDERINUS (Joannes) IC. **17578.**

—— [Another copy.] IC. **17577.**

—— [Another edition.] *Begin.* [fol. 2 *recto:*] Tabula Cōsiliorū Iohānis calderini ꝛ Gasparis ei⁹ filj ꝛ Dominici de sancto geminiāo. [fol. 15 *recto:*] D. Iohannis calderini ꝛ Gasparis eius filii ꝛ Dominici de sancto Geminiano incipiunt Consilia sub Rubricis decretaliū instituta ꝛ sub earuȝ numero ordīata. [The Consilia of J. and G. Calderinus, edited by Dominicus de Sancto Geminiano.] 𝕲.𝕷. 1491. fol. *See* CALDERINUS (Joannes) IC. **26732.**

CALDERINUS (Joannes) *Begin.* [fol. 2 *recto:*] Auctoritates decretorum oēm effectum tam textus ꝙ glosarū nuclialiter et compendiose in se continentes Incipiunt, *etc.* [By J. Calderinus.] 𝕲.𝕷. 147[7]. fol. *See* AUCTORITATES. C. **13.** b. **2.**

—— [Consilia.] *Begin.* [fol. 2 *recto:*] De constitutionibus. Rubrica. [fol. 24 *recto:*] Consilia domini Io. Cal. Et do. Gas. eius filii. redacta sub congruis rubricis et decurtata. assumptis rationibus substantificis per dominum Dominicum de sancto Geminiano. Incipiunt feliciter. *Per Adaȝ rot: Rome,* xxiiii. Mensis Decēbris, 1472. fol. IC. **17578.**
186 *leaves, ff.* 1, 23, 185 *and* 186 *blank. Without signatures. Double columns,* 50 *lines to a column.*

—— [Another copy.] IC. **17577.**
Without the blank first leaf.

CALDERINUS (Joannes)

—— [Another edition.] *Begin.* [fol. 2 *recto:*] Tabula Cōsiliorū Iohānis calderini ꝛ Gasparis ei⁹ filj ꝛ Dominici de sancto geminiāo. [fol. 15 *recto:*] D. Iohannis calderini ꝛ Gasparis eius filii ꝛ Domini de sancto Geminiano incipiunt Consilia sub Rubricis decretaliū instituta ꝛ sub earuȝ numero ordīata. [The Consilia of J. and G. Calderinus, edited by Dominicus de Sancto Geminiano.] 𝕲.𝕷. *per Vldericuȝ scinzenzeler Opera ꝛ īpensa Petriantonij de Castelliono: Ml'i* [*Milan*], die .xxv. mensis augusti, 1491. fol. IC. **26732.**
94 *leaves, the first blank. Sig.* A^8 B^6 a–k^8. *Double columns,* 70 *lines to a column.*

—— [Repertorium utriusque iuris.] *Begin.* [fol. 2 *recto:*] Hec dictio A interdum includit, *etc.* *End.* [fol. 489 *verso:*] Diuini ac humani iuris. res tam supnas ꝙ subt'nas bñ disponētis repertoriū disertissimi doctoris Caldrini . . . felicit' Explicit. 𝕲.𝕷. [*Michael Wenssler: Basle,*] pmo yd⁹ decemb' [12 Dec.], 1474. fol. IC. **37063.**
490 *leaves, the first and last blank. Without signatures. Double columns,* 47 *lines to a column.*

—— [Tabula Bibliae auctoritatum et sententiarum, *etc.*] *Begin.* [fol. 2 *recto:*] [C]Vm ego thomas Dorniberg de mēingen . . . nup quosdam libros reuoluerē in manus venerat tractatus . . . dñi īohannis Caldrini . . . ꝯcordantias auctoritatum ꝛ sentēciaꝝ Biblie decretoꝝ ac decretaliū ordīe alphabetico cōprehendēs, *etc.* [fol. 2 *verso:*] Incipit igitur Caldrini Tabula. *End.* [fol. 77 *verso:*] Biblie auctoritatū ꝛ sentēciaꝝ q̄ in deċtoꝝ et decretaliū ꝯpilatōnibꝫ solēt induci tabula p Iohānē Caldrini . . . ꝯpilata et p Thomā Dorniberg . . . correcta . . . explicit felicit'. 𝕲.𝕷. *p Petrū Drach impssa:* [*Spires,*] 1481. fol. IB. **8499.**
78 *leaves, the first and last blank. Sig.* a^8 b^8 c^{10} d–g^8 h^6 i^8 k^8. 42 *lines to a page. Without the first blank leaf.*

—— *Begin.* [fol. 2 *recto:*] Tractatus de ecclesiastico interdicto. Iohannis Calderini doctoris eximii. [fol. 23 *recto:*] Repetitio capituli ꝑposuisti de foro cōpetenti dñi Friderici de Senis incipit. [*Theobaldus Schencbecher: Rome,* 1472?] fol. IC. **17615.**
24 *leaves, ff.* 1, 22 *and* 24 *blank. Without signatures. Double columns,* 52 *lines to a column.*

—— [Another edition.] *See* TRACTATUS. Primum [*etc.*] volumen tractatuum, *etc.* vol. 16. 1549. fol. **5305.** i.

—— [Another edition.] *See* TRACTATUS. Tractatus vniuersi iuris, *etc.* tom. 14. 1584. fol. **499.** g. **9.**

—— Tractatus nouus aureus et solemnis de hæreticis . . . Ioannis Calderini. In quo omnia quæ ad officium inquisitorum contra hæreticam prauitatem spectant . . . tractantur . . . cui adiecta est Noua forma procedendi contra de hæresi inquisitos, *etc.* [Edited by D. Zenarus.] ff. 98. *Ad Candentis Salamandræ Insigne: Venetijs,* 1571. 4°. **5051.** b. **17.**

—— [For editions of "Tractatus seu Forma procedendi contra de hæresi inquisitos" sometimes attributed to J. Calderinus:] *See* TRACTATUS.

CALDERISI (Raffaele) Nel sesto centenario della morte di Dante Alighieri. Note e chiose su alcuni punti oscuri della Divina Commedia. pp. 75. *Aversa,* 1921. 8°. **011420.** b. **45.**

—— Saggio critico. Antonio Sebastiano Minturno, poeta e trattatista del cinquecento dimenticato. Vita e opere. pp. 102. *Aversa,* 1921. 8°. **011851.** dd. **42.**

CALDERIUS (Franciscus) *See* CHALDERIA.

CALDER-MARSHALL (Arthur) *See* Marshall.

CALDEROLA. *See* Caldarola.

CALDERÓN, Felix María Calleja del Rey Bruder Losada Flores Campeño Montero de Espinosa, *Count de.* *See* Calleja del Rey Bruder Losada Flores Campeño Montero de Espinosa.

CALDERÓN (Adolfo) Necesidad y justicia de la prescripción en general, y cuestiones particulares en orden á la prescripción de que tratan el derecho común y la ordenanza de minas del Perú. 1889. *See* Latorre (E. C.) Memorias y Discursos Universitaríos sobre el Código Civil Chileno, *etc.* tom. 2. 1888, *etc.* 8°. **6784.** h. **12.**

CALDERÓN (Alfredo) *See* Giner de los Rios (F.) Obras completas. (1. Principios de derecho natural, sumariamente expuestos por F. Giner y A. Calderón.) 1916, *etc.* 8°. **12233.i.1.**

—— *See* Giner de los Ríos (F.) *Profesor.* Obras completas, *etc.* (13, 14. Resumen de filosofía del derecho. Por F. Giner y A. Calderón.) 1916, *etc.* 8°. **12233.** i. **1.**

—— *See* Giner de los Rios (F.) and Calderón (A.) Resumen de Filosofía del Derecho. 1898. 8°. **06005.** e. **36.**

—— A Punta de Pluma. pp. 186. *Barcelona,* [1902.] 8°. **012357.** g. **6.**

—— Nonadas. [With a portrait.] pp. 318. *Bilbao,* 1896. 8°. **012357.** k. **34.**

—— Treinta Artículos. pp. 202. *Valencia,* 1902. 8°. **012356.** i. **70.**

CALDERÓN (Andrés García) *See* García Calderón.

CALDERÓN (Andrés Gonzalez) *See* Gonzalez Calderón.

CALDERÓN (Andrés Josef Roxo y) *See* Roxo y Calderón.

CALDERÓN (Antonio) *Archbishop of Granada.* Parte Primera de las Excelencias del Glorioso Apostol Santiago, *etc.* [Edited by G. Pardo.] (Parte Segunda de las Excelencias y primacias del . . . Apostol Santiago . . . Por el Reuerendissimo Padre Geronymo Pardo.) 2 pt. *G. Rodriguez: Madrid,* 1658. fol. **487.** i. **35.**
The titlepage of pt. 2 bears the date 1657.

CALDERÓN (Antonio Moreno) *See* Moreno Calderón.

CALDERÓN (Baltasar Isaza y) *See* Isaza y Calderón.

CALDERÓN (Baltezar) Alabanças de la insigne ciudad de Barcelona, y de las cosas mas insignes della, y de los seys cuerpos Santos que tiene, *etc.* [In verse.] *G. Graells & G. Dotil: Barcelona,* 1604. 4°. **11450.** e. **25.** (**22.**)

CALDERÓN (Diego) Tiernos Afectos de Amor, Temor, Humildad, y Confianza; con que clama en dulces soliloquios una alma que . . . suspira por su verdadero bien. Dispuestos en decimas, *etc.* [53 of the 150 stanzas by D. Calderón, the rest by F. de las Llagas.] pp. 52. *México,* 1784. 4°. **11450.** d. **19.**

CALDERÓN (Eduardo Caballero) *See* Caballero Calderón.

CALDERÓN (Emmanuel) Clarissimo viro . . . Josepho Antonio Areche . . . D. E. Calderon D. O. C. Q. Elegia. *See* Cabello (E.) Pro publico totius philosophiæ examine . . . sequentia . . . exponunt candidati, qui subscribuntur, *etc.* [1787?] 8°. **731.** f. 29. (4.)

CALDERÓN (Evaristo Correa) *See* Correa Calderón.

CALDERÓN (Felipe de la Corte y Ruano) *See* Corte y Ruano Calderón.

CALDERÓN (Fernando) Obras Poéticas. [With a preface by M. Payno y Bustamante, and a portrait.] pp. xxi. 390. *México,* 1844. 8°. **11450.** dd. **25.**

—— Nueva edicion. [With a biographical introduction by R. B. de la Colina.] pp. xx. 404. *Vera Cruz; Corbeil* [printed], 1883. 18°. **11450.** bb. **17.**

—— Obras . . . Poesias y teatro. [With a biographical introduction by R. B. de la Colina.] pp. xxxiii. 482. *México,* 1902. 8°. **12231.** cc. 9.

—— Poems. *Span. & Eng.* *See* Mexican Poems. Mexican and South American Poems, *etc.* 1892. 8°. **11450.** c. **34.**

—— Hermán o la Vuelta del Cruzado, *etc.* pp. 92. *México,* 1945. 8°. [*Biblioteca enciclopédica popular.* tom. 70.] **12214.** ee. **1/70.**

CALDERÓN (Fernando Iglesias) *See* Iglesias Calderón.

CALDERÓN (Francisco García) *See* García Calderón.

CALDERÓN (Francisco R.)

—— *See* Cosío Villegas (D.) Historia moderna de México, *etc.* (1. La República restaurada. 2. La Vida económica. Por F. R. Calderón.) 1955. 8°. W.P. d. **328/1b.**

CALDERÓN (Franciscus de Castillo) *See* Castillo Calderón.

CALDERÓN (Gabriel) Sermon Predicado en la Santa Iglesia de Seuilla, dia de la Conuersion de San Pablo. ff. 11. *F. Perez: Seuilla,* 1608. 4°. **4423.** g. **1.** (**15.**)

CALDERÓN (Gabriel Díaz Vara) *See* Díaz Vara Calderón.

CALDERÓN (Gaspar de Alvarado) *See* Alvarado Calderón.

CALDERÓN (Gaspar de Zeballos y) *Marquis de Casa-Calderón.* *See* Zeballos y Calderón.

CALDERON (George Leslie) *See* Caine (William) *Novelist.* The Brave Little Tailor . . . Embroidered by W. Caine upon a pantomime of the same name . . . by G. Calderon & W. Caine, *etc.* 1923. 8°. **012802.** bbb. **50.**

—— *See* Chekhov (A. P.) [*Smaller Collections.*—1. *Plays.*] Two Plays . . . Translated, with an introduction and notes, by G. Calderon. 1912. 8°. **11758.** cc. **1.**

—— —— 1924. 8°. **11758.** h. **45.**

—— *See* Hankin (St. John E. C.) and Calderon (G. L.) Thompson. A comedy in three acts. [1913.] 8°. **11778.** k. **37.**

—— *See* Lubbock (Percy) George Calderon, *etc.* [With portraits.] 1921. 8°. **010855.** dd. **6.**

—— *See* Shperk (Th.) Ontology . . . Translated . . . by G. L. Calderon. 1897. 8°. **08464.** g. **12.**

—— *See* Tolstoi (I. L.) *Count.* Reminiscences of Tolstoy . . . Translated by G. Calderon. 1914. 8°. **010790.** g. **50.**

—— The Adventures of Downy V. Green, Rhodes Scholar at Oxford . . . With illustrations by the author. pp. 184. *Smith, Elder & Co.: London,* 1902. 8°. **012314.** g. **59.**

CALDERON (George Leslie)

—— Dwala. A romance. pp. 244. *Smith, Elder & Co.: London*, 1904. 8°. **012629.** bbb. **35.**

—— Eight One-Act Plays. [Edited by Katharine Calderon.] pp. 189. *Grant Richards: London*, 1922. 8°. **011779.** i. **19.**

—— The Fountain. A comedy in three acts, *etc.* pp. 161. *Gowans & Gray: London, Glasgow*, 1911. 8°. [*Repertory Plays.* no. 2.] **11778.** pp. **1/2.**

—— The Little Stone House. A play in one act. pp. 32. *London*, 1913. 8°. [*Sidgwick & Jackson's Series of One-Act Plays.*] **11773.c.10/1.**

—— The Organisation of Buying. A policy for women. pp. 14. *Priory Press: Hampstead*, [1911.] 8°. **8228.** aa. **51.** (**1.**)

—— [Another copy.] **8228.** aa. **51.** (**2.**)

—— The Russian Stage. A sketch of recent Russian drama . . . From the "Quarterly Review," July, 1912. [1912.] 8°. **011853.** bb. **18.** (**2.**)

—— Tahiti. [Edited by Katharine Calderon. With plates, including a portrait.] pp. 260. *Grant Richards: London*, 1921. 8°. **10493.** e. **16.**

—— Three Plays and a Pantomime. pp. 352. *Grant Richards: London*, 1922. 8°. **011779.** i. **22.**

—— The Two Talismans. A comedy in one act. (From Eight One-Act Plays.) pp. 31. *Sidgwick & Jackson: London*, 1928. 8°. **011781.** ee. **71.**

—— Woman in relation to the State. A consideration of the arguments advanced for the extension of the parliamentary suffrage to women. pp. 60. *Priory Press: Hampstead*, 1908. 8°. **8415.** bb. **58.**

—— Правда о Графѣ Львѣ Толстомъ. (The Wrong Tolstoi.) [Translated by K. P. Pobyedonostsev from an article in the "Monthly Review."] pp. 24. *Москва*, 1901. 8°. **3925.** cc. **50.**

CALDERÓN (Germán Torres) *See* Torres Calderón.

CALDERON (Hermogenes) *See* Calderon (Philip H.)

CALDERÓN (Joannes) *See* Calderón (Juan)

CALDERON (Joannes Sendin) *See* Sendin y Calderon (Juan)

CALDERÓN (José Antonio Villacorta) *See* Villacorta Calderón.

CALDERÓN (José Eulalio) Relacion de los Méritos del Bachiller José Eulalio Calderon, *etc.* pp. 7. *México*, 1849. 8°. **10882.** c. **30.** (**9.**)

CALDERÓN (José María) [For official documents issued by J. M. Calderón as Governor of the State of Puebla:] *See* Puebla de los Angeles, *State of.*—Calderon (J. M.) *Governor.*

—— *See* López de Santa-Anna (A.) *President of the Republic of Mexico.* Armisticio convenido entre los Señores Generales D. Antonio Lopez de Santa-Anna y D. J. M. Calderon. 1832. *s. sh.* fol. **9770.** k. **10.** (**61.**)

—— No Sea que Salga Mentira, la Noticia del Gobierno. Suplemento al Registro Oficial num. 66. anotado. Parte del general Calderon avisando la total destruccion de las fuerzas rebeldes de Veracruz. *México*, 1832. *s. sh.* fol. **9770.** k. **10.** (**106.**)

CALDERÓN (José María)

—— Derrota de los Americanos en el Estado de Puebla por el general Calderon. [Signed: Muchos militares.] *México*, 1827. *s. sh.* fol. **9770.** k. **9.** (**28.**)

CALDERÓN (Juan) *Franciscan Friar, of Saragossa. See* Dexter (F. L.) *pseud.* Fragmentum Chronici . . . Flavij Lucij Dextri . . . In lucem editum, & viuificatum zelo, & labore P. Fr. I. Calderon, *etc.* 1619. 4°. **C. 69.** e. **17.**

—— *See* Murillo (D.) Divina, dulce, y provechosa poesia . . . Sacada a luz por Fray I. Calderon, *etc.* 1616. 8°. **011451.** e. **30.**

CALDERÓN (Juan) *Professor de Humanidades. See* Bible.—*New Testament.* [*Spanish.*] El Nuevo Testamento de Nuestro Señor Jesu-Cristo, *etc.* [Edited by J. Calderon.] 1852. 8°. **3022.** e. **6.**

—— *See* Liturgies.—*Church of England.*—*Common Prayer.* [*Spanish.*] Liturgia Anglicana, ó Libro de Oracion Comun, *etc.* [Edited by J. Calderon.] 1852. 24°. **3407.** a. **41.**

—— *See* Periodical Publications.—*London.* El Examen Libre, *etc.* (Editor y redactor, J. Calderon.) [1851, *etc.*] 8°. **P.P. 23.** f.

—— Análisis Lógica y Gramatical de la Lengua Española. pp. 105. *Madrid*, 1843. 8°. **12943.** dd. **2.** (**1.**)

—— Segunda edicion, anotada por Don Francisco Merino Ballesteros. pp. 96. *Madrid*, 1852. 8°. **12943.** cc. **5.** (**2.**)

—— Cervantes vindicado en ciento y quince pasajes del texto del Ingenioso Hidalgo D. Quijote de la Mancha, que no han entendido, ó que han entendido mal, algunos de sus comentadores ó críticos. [Edited by L. de Usoz i Rio.] pp. xxiii. 256. *Madrid*, 1854. 8°. **12491.** c. **36.**

—— Friendly Discussions with my Priest. From the manuscript of the late Rev. Juan Calderon, a Protestant Spaniard. [Translated from the Spanish.] pp. vi. 190. *Jackson & Walford: London*, 1854. 8°. **3940.** d. **62.**

CALDERÓN (Juan Alonso) Memorial historico, iuridico, politico, de la S. Iglesia Catedral de la Puebla de los Angeles, en la Nueua-España. Sobre restituirla las Armas Reales . . . de que ha sido despojada injustamente, *etc.* ff. 89. [*Madrid?* 1652?] **573.** l. **3.** (**3.**)

—— Memorial, y Discurso historico-iuridico-politico que dio a la Magestad Catolica del Rey . . . Don Philipe Quarto, el Doctor Iuan Alonso Calderon . . . representando sus seruicios personales, y lo que contienen los treinta libros que ha escrito del Imperio de la Monarquia de España, *etc.* ff. 25. *D. Diaz de la Carrera: Madrid*, 1651. fol. **573.** l. **3.** (**4.**)

—— [Another copy.] **9181.** e. **10.** (**1.**)

CALDERÓN (Juan Antonio González) *See* González Calderón.

CALDERÓN (Juan de La Peña) *See* La Peña Calderón.

CALDERÓN (Juan de Salas) *See* Salas Calderón.

CALDERÓN (Juan Manuel) Orden particular al Primer Batallon Activo del Estado. *Mérida de Yucatan*, 1828. *s. sh.* fol. **9770.** k. **9.** (**78.**)

CALDERON (Katharine) *See* Calderon (George L.) Eight One-Act Plays. [Edited by K. Calderon.] 1922. 8°. **011779.** i. **19.**

—— *See* Calderon (George L.) Tahiti. [Edited by K. Calderon.] 1921. 8°. **10493.** e. **16.**

CALDERÓN (Luis Felipe) *See* Sargent (*Sir* Percy W. G.) and Russell (A. E.) Emergencias en la Práctica de la Medicina y de la Cirugía . . . Primera traducción española . . . editada bajo la dirección del Doctor L. F. Calderón. 1917. 8°. **20036.a.1/106.**

—— *See* Woodwark (*Sir* Arthur S.) Manual de Medicina . . . Obra traducida y editada bajo la dirección del Doctor L. F. Calderón. 1917. 8°. **20036.a.1/167.**

CALDERÓN (Luisa) *See* Picton (*Sir* Thomas) Evidence taken at Port of Spain . . . in the case of Luisa Calderon, *etc.* 1806. 8°. **C.T. 232. (6.)**

—— *See* Picton (*Sir* Thomas) The Trial of Governor Picton, for having maliciously and with a view to oppress Louisa Calderon . . . by inflicting the torture on her, *etc.* [1806?] 8°. **1131.** h. **30.**

CALDERÓN (Manuel) *See* Espinosa de los Monteros Medrano (J. de) El Aprendiz de Rico, *etc.* [With M. Calderón's notes.] 1902. 4°. [*Mendiburu (M. de) Apuntes Históricos del Perú.*] **9770.** f. **19.**

CALDERÓN (Manuel Pérez) *See* Pérez Calderón.

CALDERÓN (Mathias de Peralta) *See* Peralta Calderón.

CALDERÓN (Nicolás) Mystica Basa del Sacro Illipulitano Monte de Granada, sermon panegyrico historial, *etc.* pp. 30. *See* Heredia Barnuevo (D. N. de) Mystico Ramillete, *etc.* 1741. fol. **4855.** f. **6.**

CALDERÓN (Pedro) *Dramatist. See* Calderón de la Barca.

CALDERÓN (Pedro) *Jesuit.* Memorial del Reverendissimo Padre Maestro Pedro Calderon, de la Compañia de Jesus . . . presentado en el Real, y Supremo Consejo de las Indias en 30. de Março de 1693. En respuesta de otro impresso del . . . Padre Maestro Fr. Ignacio de Quesada, del Orden de Santo Domingo . . . Dalo à la estampa Don Geronimo Lezcano, y Sepulbeda. [Written by A. M. Jaramillo from notes by P. Calderón?] ff. 54. *H. Dehmen: Colonia,* 1695. fol. **1228.** d. **14.**

CALDERÓN (Pedro) *Profesor de Medicina Chirúrgica.* Memoria á cerca de la Utilidad que resulta de la union de Medicina y Cirujia; leida á la Academia Médico Chirurgica de Puebla . . . Julio 15 de 1826. pp. 55. [*Puebla,* 1826.] 16°. **7321.** a. **29.**

CALDERÓN (Pedro P.) *See* Larrain (N.) El País de Cuyo . . . Revisada y anotada por Pedro P. Calderón. 1906. 8°. **9770.v.9.**

CALDERON (Philip Hermogenes) *See* Gatty (Margaret) Parables from Nature . . . With illustrations by C. W. Cope . . . H. Calderon, *etc.* 1861, *etc.* 8°. **12807.** e. **17.**

—— *See* Henley (William E.) The Graphic Gallery of Shakspeare's Heroines. A series of studies in Goupilgravure from paintings by L. Alma Tadema . . . P. H. Calderon, *etc.* 1888. fol. **1899.p.16.**

—— *See* Lund (Thomas W. M.) The Religion of Art in three pictures; "An Idyll," "S. Elizabeth of Hungary's Great Act of Renunciation" (by P. H. Calderon), *etc.* 1891. 8°. **7808.** a. **38.**

CALDERÓN (R. Venancio) [Select poems.] *See* Fernández (M.) Lira Costarricense, *etc.* tom. 1. 1890. 8°. **11450.** ccc. **31.**

CALDERÓN (Rafael Castejón) *See* Castejón Calderón (R.)

CALDERÓN (Rodrigo) *Marquis de Siete Iglesias. See* Gascón de Torquemada (G.) Nacimiento, Vida, Prision y Muerte de Don Rodrigo Calderon, *etc.* 1789. 8°. **10632.** aa. **49.**

—— *See* Histoire. Histoire admirable, et declin pitoyable, aduenu en la personne d'vn fauory de la Cour d'Espagne [i.e. R. Calderón]. 1633. 8°. **1055.** a. **36.**

—— —— 1885. 15°. [*Fournier (E.) Variétés historiques et littéraires, etc.* tom. 1.] **12234.** aa. **8.**

—— *See* Manojo (F.) Relacion de la Muerte de D. Rodrigo Calderon, *etc.* [1621.] fol. **707.** h. **28.** (3.)

—— *See* Manojo (F.) Newes from Spaine. A relation of the death of Don Rodrigo Calderon, *etc.* 1622. 4°. **10632.** b. **28.**

—— *See* Ocampo (M. de) Oracion Lamentable a la muerte de Don Rodrigo Calderon, *etc.* 1621. fol. **707.** h. **28.** (4.)

—— —— 1622. 4°. **12231.** de. **16.** (6.)

—— *See* Ossorio y Gallardo (A.) Los Hombres de Toga en el proceso de D. Rodrigo Calderón. [1918.] 8°. **5384.** de. **10.**

—— *See* Pérez Gómez (A.) Romancero de don Rodrigo Calderón . . . Introducción Bibliográfica de A. Pérez Gómez. 1955. 8°. **11454.** c. **15.**

—— *See* Ponce (M.) Oracion Funebre, en la muerte de don Rodrigo Calderon, *etc.* [1621.] fol. **707.** h. **28.** (5.)

—— Memorial que Don Rodrigo Calderon dio a su Magestad del Rey Felipe iiii. . . . en su abono. ms. additions. [*Madrid,* 1621.] fol. **707.** h. **28.** (2.)

—— Calderon, the Courtier: a tale. By the author of "Leila" [i.e. E. G. E. Bulwer Lytton, Baron Lytton], *etc.* pp. 144. *Carey, Lea & Blanchard: Philadelphia,* 1838. 12°. **12620.** aaa. **18.**

—— Para que se haya de executar la sentencia de muerte, a que esta condenado don Rodrigo Calderon, y repelerse la peticion de suplicacion por su parte interpuesta, se representa lo siguiente. ff. 28. ms. notes. [*Madrid,* 1621.] fol. **707.** h. **28.** (1.)

—— Siete Romances de Don Rodrigo Calderon, con algunas cosas de su muerte, y un romance muy famoso de la muerte del Rey Felipe Tercero. [In verse.] *Valencia,* [1760?] 4°. **T. 1955. (17.)**

—— Waerachtich Verhael hoe dat de Justitie gheschiet is binnen Madril . . . ouer Don Rodrigo Calderon. Ouergheseedt wt het Spaens, *etc.* pp. 7. *A. Verhoeuen: Hantwerpen,* 1621. 4°. [*Gazette of Antwerp.* Nov. 1621. no. 168.] **P.P. 3444.** af. (313.)

CALDERÓN (S. G.) *See* Fernández (D. E.) and Calderón (S. G.) Vocabulario Tagalog-Castellano-Inglés, *etc.* 1913. *obl.* 8°. **12910.** m. **15.**

CALDERÓN (Salvador) *See* Calderón y Arana.

CALDERÓN (Sebastián López de Llergo y) *See* López de Llergo y Calderón.

CALDERÓN (Senén Suárez) *See* Suárez Calderón.

CALDERÓN (Serafín Estébanez) *See* Estébanez Calderón.

CALDERÓN (Sofronio) *See* Bible.—*New Testament.* [*Tagalog.*] Ang Bagong Tipan, *etc.* [Translated by S. Calderón and others.] 1907. 8°. **03068.** e. **109.**

CALDERÓN (TELÉSFORO R.)

—— La Traición de Sebastián Rodríguez Lora y Oscar de Moya Hernández. [Documents relating to the alleged treason of Rodríguez Lora and Moya Hernández. Edited by T. R. Calderón. With facsimiles of correspondence.] pp. 56. *Ciudad Trujillo*, [1951.] 8°. **10899**. l. **5**.

CALDERÓN (VENTURA GARCÍA) *See* GARCÍA CALDERÓN.

CALDERÓN (VICENTE) Memoria sobre el Alumbrado de Gas. pp. vi. 53. *Madrid*, 1848. 8°. **1142**. i. **13**. (**2**.)

CALDERON (WILLIAM FRANK) *See* REYNARD THE FOX. [*English*.] The Most Delectable History of Reynard the Fox . . . Done into pictures by W. F. Calderon. 1895. 8°. **12411**. b. **7**.

—— Animal Painting & Anatomy. [Illustrated by the author.] pp. 336. *Seeley, Service: London*, 1936. 4°. [*New Art Library*.] **7876**. bb. **1/4**.

CALDERÓN ALTAMIRANO DE CHAVES HINOJOSA Y PAREDES (LUIS FRANCISCO) Opusculos de Oro, Virtudes Morales Christianas. pp. 720. *Madrid*, 1707. 4°. **4407**. h. **19**.

CALDERÓN COUSIÑO (ADOLFO)

—— *See* CHILE. [*Appendix*.] Chile y la independencia del Perú, 1821–1921, *etc.* [The introduction signed: A. Calderón Cousiño.] 1921. 8°. **9773**. e. **9**.

—— Breve Historia Diplomática de las Relaciones Chileno-Peruanas . . . 2ª edición. pp. 235. *Santiago de Chile*, 1919. 8°. **9773**. de. **11**.

—— Short Diplomatic History of the Chilean-Peruvian Relations 1819–1879. pp. 255. *Imprenta Universitaria: Santiago de Chile*, 1920. 8°. **9773**. de. **21**.

CALDERÓN DE CABALLERO (MARÍA DEL CARMEN) *See* NIETO CABALLERO (L. E.) Maria del Carmen Calderón de Caballero. [Obituary notices, with a portrait.] 1924. 24°. **10883**. a. **12**.

CALDERÓN DE LA BARCA (FERNANDO DE SETTIÉN) *See* SETTIÉN CALDERÓN DE LA BARCA.

CALDERÓN DE LA BARCA (FRANCES ERSKINE) *Marchioness*. *See* BARTOLI (D.) History of the Life and Institute of St. Ignatius de Loyola . . . Translated by the author of " Life in Mexico " [i.e. the Marchioness F. E. Calderón de la Barca]. 1856. 8°. **4827**. b. **8**.

—— The Affianced One. By the author of " Gertrude " [i.e. F. E. Calderón de la Barca], *etc.* 3 vol. 1832. 8°. *See* ONE. N. **884**.

—— The Attaché in Madrid; or, Sketches of the court of Isabella II. Translated from the German [or rather, written in English by the Marchioness F. E. Calderón de la Barca]. pp. xi. 368. 1856. 8°. *See* MADRID. **10160**. b. **15**.

—— Madrid hace cincuenta años á los ojos de un diplomático extranjero. Obra alemana anónima escrita y publicada hacia el año 1854. Traducida al inglés en 1856, con el título de The Attaché in Madrid, por otro anónimo, y de este último idioma al castellano por Don Ramiro. Con un prólogo, notas y comentarios del mismo. [A translation of " The Attaché in Madrid," by the Marchioness F. E. Calderón de la Barca.] pp. 504. 1904. 8°. *See* MADRID. **10162**. b. **7**.

—— Gertrude: a tale of the sixteenth century, *etc.* [By F. E. Calderón de la Barca.] 2 vol. 1830. 8°. *See* GERTRUDE. N. **718**.

CALDERÓN DE LA BARCA (FRANCES ERSKINE) *Marchioness*.

—— Life in Mexico, during a residence of two years in that country. By Madame C— de la B— [i.e. the Marchioness F. E. Calderón de la Barca]. With a preface, by W. H. Prescott. pp. xiv. 437. 1843. 8°. *See* LA B—, C— de, *Madame*. **12205**. dd. **19**.

—— [Another edition.] (With an introduction by Henry Baerlein.) pp. xxxviii. 542. *J. M. Dent & Sons: London; E. P. Dutton & Co.: New York*, [1913.] 8°. [*Everyman's Library*.] **12206.p.1/475.**

—— [A reissue.] Life in Mexico. Introduction by Manuel Romero de Terreros, Marqués de San Francisco. pp. xxviii. 542. *London; New York*, 1954. 8°. [*Everyman's Library*. no. 664.] **12206**. p. **1/876**.

—— Life in Mexico . . . Abridged from the original. pp. 240. *Simms & M'Intyre: London*, 1852. 8°. [*The Bookcase*. no. 5.] **1155**. l. **9**. (**1**.)

—— La Vida en México. Prólogo y selección de Antonio Acevedo Escobedo. [An abridgment.] pp. ix. 94. *México*, 1944. 8°. [*Biblioteca enciclopédica popular*. tom. 14.] **12214**. ee. **1/14**.

CALDERÓN DE LA BARCA (JOSEPH) *See* CALDERÓN DE LA BARCA (P.) [*Comedias.—Collections.—Spanish*.] Segunda parte de comedias . . . recogidas por Don I. Calderon de la Barca. 1637. 4°. C. **57**. c. **40**.

CALDERÓN DE LA BARCA (JOSEPH MARIA) Gloriosa Defensa de Malta contra el Formidable Exército de Soliman 11. por los Caballeros de San Juan de Jerusalem. pp. 215. *Madrid*, 1796. 8°. **9135**. ff. **9**.

CALDERÓN DE LA BARCA (MANUEL) *See* CALDERÓN DE LA BARCA Y ABREGO.

CALDERÓN DE LA BARCA (MIGUEL) *See* ISEQUILLA PALACIO (J. de la) Manifiesto juridico por el Señor Don Miguel Calderon de la Barca . . . en defensa de los capitulos puestos . . . por Don J. de Urive, *etc.* [1715 ?] fol. **9771**. h. **1**. (**5**.)

—— *See* MEXICO, *Province of*.—*Real Audiencia de Nueva España*. Reales Aranzeles de los Ministros de la Real Audiencia . . . formados . . . por los Señores Oydores de esta Real Audiencia Lic. Don M. Calderón de la Varca y Don Balthazar de Tovar, *etc.* 1727. fol. **145**. e. **17**.

CALDERÓN DE LA BARCA (PEDRO)

ARRANGEMENT.

COMEDIAS.

COLLECTIONS.

Spanish.

—— Segunda Parte de Comedias de Don Pedro Calderon . . . Recogidas por Don Ioseph Calderon de la Barca, *etc.* (Tercera Parte de Comedias. [Edited by Sebastian Ventura de Vergara Salcedo.]) 2 vol. *Madrid*, 1637, [64.] 4°. C. **57**. c. **40**.
The titlepage of pt. 3 *is mutilated.*

CALDERÓN DE LA BARCA (PEDRO) [COMEDIAS.—COLLECTIONS.—*Spanish.*]

—— La Dama Duende.—La Vida es Sueño. *See* COMEDIAS. Comedias parte treinta, *etc.* 1638. 4°. **11726. g. 30.**

—— La Vanda y la Flor.—El Principe Constante. 1649. *See* SPAIN. [*Appendix.—Miscellaneous.*] Primera [*etc.*] parte de Comedias escogidas, *etc.* pt. 6. 1652, *etc.* 4°. **11725. b. 6.**

—— No ay Burlas con el Amor.—El Secreto a Vozes.—El Pintor de su Deshonra.—El Rey abaxo Ninguno. *See* COMEDIAS. Parte quarenta y dos de Comedias, *etc.* 1650. 4°. **11725. d. 10.**

—— El Garrote mas bien dado.—Mañana serà otro dia.—Los Empeños que se ofrecen.—El guardarse a si mismo. *See* ALFAY (T. de) El Mejor de los Mejores Libro, *etc.* 1651. 4°. **11725. d. 11.**

—— No siempre lo Peor es Cierto.—La Exaltacion de la Cruz.—Mejor està que estaua.—Luis Perez el Gallego.—Con quien vengo vengo. *See* SPAIN. [*Appendix.—Miscellaneous.*] Primera [*etc.*] parte de Comedias, *etc.* 1652, *etc.* 4°. **11725. b. 1.**

—— Amigo, Amante, y Leal.—Enfermar con el remedio . . . De tres ingenios. De Don P. Calderon, L. Velez de Guevara, y Don G. Cancer. 1653. *See* SPAIN. [*Appendix.—Miscellaneous.*] Primera [*etc.*] parte de Comedias escogidas, *etc.* pt. 4. 1652, *etc.* 4°. **11725. b. 4.**

—— El Garrote mas bien dado.—Mañana serà otro dia.—La Guarda de si mismo.—Los Empeños que se ofrecen. *See* ALFAY (T. de) El Mejor de los Mejores Libros, *etc.* 1653. 4°. **1072. h. 1.**

—— Darlo todo, y no dar nada.—Los Empeños de Seis Horas. De Don P. Calderon [or rather, by Antonio Coello].—Gustos y Disgustos son no mas que Imaginacion.—El Pastor Fido. [The third jornada by Calderon.]—La Tercera de si misma. De Don P. Calderon [or rather, by A. Mira de Mescua].—Amado y Aborrecido.—Agua Mansa. 1657. *See* SPAIN. [*Appendix.—Miscellaneous.*] Primera [*etc.*] parte de Comedias escogidas, *etc.* pt. 8. 1652, *etc.* 4°. **11725. b. 8.**

—— Las Manos Blancas no ofenden.—El Escondido y la Tapada.—El Mejor Amigo el Muerto. [The third jornada by Calderon.] 1657. *See* SPAIN. [*Appendix.—Miscellaneous.*] Primera [*etc.*] parte de Comedias escogidas, *etc.* pt. 9. 1652, *etc.* 4°. **11725. b. 9.**

—— Fuego de Dios en el querer bien.—Los tres Afectos de Amor, Piedad, Desmayo, y Valor.—El Joseph de los Mugeres. 1660. *See* SPAIN. [*Appendix.—Miscellaneous.*] Primera [*etc.*] parte de Comedias escogidas, *etc.* pt. 13. 1652, *etc.* 4°. **11725. b. 13.**

—— El Conde Lucanor.—El Mejor Padre de Pobres, de Don P. Calderón [or rather, by J. Pérez de Montalbán].—Los Empeños de un Plumaje.—Las tres Justicias en una.—Cada uno para si. 1661. *See* SPAIN. [*Appendix.—Miscellaneous.*] Primera [*etc.*] parte de Comedias escogidas, *etc.* pt. 15. 1652, *etc.* 4°. **11725. b. 15.**

—— Dicha y Desdicha del Nombre.—Seneca y Neron.—Amigo, Amante y Leal. 1662. *See* SPAIN. [*Appendix.—Miscellaneous.*] Primera [*etc.*] parte de Comedias escogidas, *etc.* pt. 18. 1652, *etc.* 4°. **11725. b. 18.**

—— La gran comedia de Dar Tiempo al Tiempo.—Antes que Todo es mi Dama.—No ay Cosa como callar.—Muger, llora y venceras. 1662. *See* SPAIN. [*Appendix.—Miscellaneous.*] Primera [*etc.*] parte de Comedias escogidas, *etc.* pt. 17. 1652, *etc.* 4°. **11725. b. 17.**

CALDERÓN DE LA BARCA (PEDRO) [COMEDIAS.—COLLECTIONS.—*Spanish.*]

—— El Maxico prodigioso.—Auristela y Lisidante.—El Rigor de las Desdichas.—Saber desmentir sospechas. 1663. *See* SPAIN. [*Appendix.—Miscellaneous.*] Primera [*etc.*] parte de Comedias escogidas, *etc.* pt. 20. 1652, *etc.* 4°. **11725. b. 20.**

—— Qual es Mayor Perfeccion.—Fortunas de Andromeda y Perseo.—La Margarita Preciosa. [The third jornada by Calderon.] 1663. *See* SPAIN. [*Appendix.—Miscellaneous.*] Primera [*etc.*] parte de Comedias escogidas, *etc.* pt. 21. 1652, *etc.* 4°. **11725. b. 21.**

—— Las Armas de la Hermosura.—La Señora y la Criada. 1679. *See* SPAIN. [*Appendix.—Miscellaneous.*] Primera [*etc.*] parte de Comedias escogidas, *etc.* pt. 46. 1652, *etc.* 4°. **11725. d. 5.**

—— Verdadera Quinta Parte de Comedias . . . que publica Don Iuan de Vera Tassis y Villaroel, *etc.* pp. 542. *F. Sanz: Madrid,* 1682. 4°. **C. 57. c. 40*.**

—— *See* GUERRA Y RIBERA (M. de) El Buen Zelo, o Examen de un papel, que con nombre de . . . Manuel Guerra, y Ribera . . . corre en vulgar, impresso por aprobacion de la Quinta parte verdadera de comedias de Don Pedro Calderon, *etc.* 1683. fol. **9181. e. 10. (3.)**

—— Primera(—Octava) Parte de Comedias del Celebre Poeta Español, Don Pedro Calderon De La Barca . . . que nueuamente corregidas publica Don Iuan de Vera Tassis y Villaroel, *etc.* [With a portrait.] *F. Sanz: Madrid,* 1685, 83–94. 4°. **11725. f. 5.**

—— Primera(—Novena) Parte de Comedias Verdaderas . . . que nuevamente corregidas publicò Don Juan de Vera Tassis y Villarroel. 9 pt. *Madrid,* 1726, 1698–1730. 4°. **87. a. 13.**

—— [Another edition.] 9 pt. *Madrid,* 1726, 1691–1760. 4°. **11725. cc. 3.**

Some of the vols. are duplicates of those of the preceding collection.

—— Judas Macabeo.—Los Cabellos de Absalon. *See* SPAIN. [*Appendix.—Miscellaneous.*] Comedias Nuevas, *etc.* 1726. 4°. **11725. cc. 8.**

—— Comedias . . . que saca à luz Don Juan Fernandez de Apontes, *etc.* 11 tom. *Madrid,* 1760–63. 4°. **11725. e. 1.**

—— [Another copy.] **11726. h. 6.**

—— Bien vengas mal, si vienes solo.—Los Empeños de un acaso. *See* GARCÍA DE LA HUERTA (V. A.) Theatro Hespañol, *etc.* pt. 2. tom. 4. 1785. 8°. **243. b. 12.**

—— Casa con dos puertas mala es de guardar.—No hay burlas con el amor. *See* GARCÍA DE LA HUERTA (V. A.) Theatro Hespañol, *etc.* pt. 2. tom. 6. 1785. 8°. **243. b. 14.**

—— Dar tiempo al tiempo.—Tambien hay duelo en las damas. *See* GARCÍA DE LA HUERTA (V. A.) Theatro Hespañol, *etc.* pt. 2. tom. 3. 1785. 8°. **243. b. 11.**

—— Mejor esta, que estaba.—Primero soy yo. *See* GARCÍA DE LA HUERTA (V. A.) Theatro Hespañol, *etc.* pt. 2. tom. 8. 1785. 8°. **243. b. 16.**

—— No siempre lo peor es cierto.—Con quien vengo, vengo. *See* GARCÍA DE LA HUERTA (V. A.) Theatro Hespañol, *etc.* pt. 2. tom. 5. 1785. 8°. **243. b. 13.**

—— Qual es mayor perfeccion.—El Escondido, y la tapada. *See* GARCÍA DE LA HUERTA (V. A.) Theatro Hespañol, *etc.* pt. 2. tom. 7. 1785. 8°. **243. b. 15.**

—— La Devocion de la Cruz.—La Vida es Sueño.—El Principe Constante.—Los Empeños de un Acaso.—La Gran Cenobia.—Eco y Narciso.—Dicha y Desdicha del Nombre.—La Desdicha de la Voz. 1809, 10. *See* Norwich (A.) Teatro Español, *etc.* tom. 1, 2. 1809, *etc.* 8°. **11728.** cc. **1.**

—— La Dame Duende.—El Secreto á Voces.—Gustos y Disgustos son no mas que Imaginacion.—La Vida es Sueño.—Peor esta que estaba. 1820. *See* Spanish Theatre. El Teatro Español, *etc.* tom. 2. 1817, *etc.* 8°. **243.** l. **2.**

—— Las Comedias de D. Pedro Calderon de la Barca, cotejadas con las mejores ediciones . . . corregidas y dadas á luz por J. J. Keil. [With a portrait.] 3 tom. *Leipsique,* 1820–22. 12°. **11725.** bb. **15.**

—— Casa con Dos Puertas Mala es de Guardar.—Lances de Amor, y Fortuna.—La Devocion de la Cruz.—Para vencer á amor, qüerer vencerle.—La Puente de Mantible. 1821. *See* Spanish Theatre. El Teatro Español, *etc.* tom. 3. 1817, *etc.* 8°. **243.** l. **3.**

—— Comedias Escogidas. 4 tom. *Madrid,* 1826–33. 8°. **1342.** a. **27–30.**

—— [Another copy.] **11725.** aaa. **6.**

—— Las Comedias de D. Pedro Calderon de la Barca, corregidas y dadas á luz por Juan Jorge Keil Senior. [With a portrait.] 4 tom. *Leipsique,* 1827–30. 8°. **2298.** i. **4.**

—— Comedias Escogidas . . . El Mágico Prodigioso. La Vida es Sueño. Y El Príncipe Constante. [With a portrait.] pp. xi. 299. *C. y H. Senior: Londres,* 1837. 8°. **640.** b. **35.**

—— Teatro Escogido de Calderon de la Barca. Con una introduccion y la biografía por Don E. de Ochoa. [With a portrait.] pp. ii. 823. *Paris,* 1838. 8°. [*Coleccion de los Mejores Autores Españoles.* tom. 12.] **12230.** h. **1/12.**

—— La Vida es Sueño.—Casa con dos puertas mala es de guardar.—La Devocion de la Cruz.—El Mayor Monstruo los Zelos.—La Cena de Baltasar. 1840. *See* Spanish Authors. Coleccion de los Mejores Autores Españoles. tom. 17. 1835, *etc.* 8°. **12230.** h. **1/17.**

—— El Príncipe Constante.—El Mágico Prodigioso. *See* Vega Carpio (L. F. de) Seleccion de obras maestras dramáticas de Lope de Vega y Calderon de La Barca, *etc.* 1844. 8°. **11726.** b. **77.**

—— La Vida es Sueño.—El Mágico Prodigioso.—El Alcalde de Zalamea.—Casa con dos puertas mala es de guardar.—Mañanas de Abril y Mayo. *See* Schuetz (D. C.) Teatro Español, *etc.* 1846. 8°. **1342.** g. **26.**

—— Comedias . . . Coleccion mas completa que todas las anteriores hecha e ilustrada por Don J. E. Hartzenbusch. 4 tom. *Madrid,* 1848–50. 8°. [*Biblioteca de Autores Españoles.* tom. 7, 9, 12, 14.] **12232.f.1/7,9.13.14.**

—— Teatro Escojido de Calderon de la Barca. *See* Spanish Theatre. Coleccion Selecta del Antiguo Teatro Español, *etc.* 1854. 8°. **2298.** i. **3.**

—— Casa con dos puertas mala es de guardar, *etc.*—Á secreto agravio secreta venganza, *etc.* 1864. *See* Museo. Museo Dramático Ilustrado, *etc.* tom. 2. 1863, *etc.* 4°. **2298.** i. **2.**

—— El Alcalde de Zalamea, comedia en tres jornadas. Entremeses (La Plazuela de Santa Cruz.—El Desafío de Juan Rana.—Las Jácaras.—La Casa holgona). pp. 189. *Madrid,* 1876. 16°. [*Biblioteca Universal.* tom. 24.] **739.** a. **24.**

—— Teatro Escogido. 3 tom. *Leipzig,* 1876, 77. 8°. [*Coleccion de Autores Españoles.* tom. 35–37.] **12230.bb.6/35–37.**

—— Calderon según sus Obras, sus Críticos y sus Admiradores, y crónica del segundo centenario de su muerte, festejado en Madrid . . . 1881. Por J. Alonso del Real. Obra adornada con grabados . . . Contiene El Alcalde de Zalamea . . . Lances de Amor y Fortuna . . . El Gran Teatro del Mundo . . . El Dragoncillo . . . El Mellado, *etc.* pp. 366. *Barcelona,* 1881. 8°. **11725.** aa. **23.**

—— Obras Dramáticas Escogidas. pp. 487. *Salamanca,* 1881. 8°. **2298.** h. **1.**

—— Teatro Selecto . . . precedido de un estudio crítico de D. Marcelino Menéndez Pelayo. 4 tom. *Madrid,* 1881. 8°. **2298.** g. **5.**

—— La Vida es Sueño, comedia . . . El Médico de su Honra, comedia . . . La Vida es Sueño, auto sacramental . . . precedidas de una reseña biográfica por D. Emilio Sanchez Pastor. [With a portrait.] pp. xii. 326. *Madrid,* 1881. 16°. **11726.** a. **3.**

—— Das Leben ist Traum.—Der standhafte Prinz. (Der wundertätige Zauberer.—Der Richter von Zalamea, nebst dem gleichnamigen Stücke des Lope de Vega.) *Span.* 3 vol. *Leipzig,* 1881–87. 8°. [*Klassische Bühnendichtungen der Spanier.* vol. 1–3.] **12230.** c. **20.**

—— Teatro . . . Con un estudio crítico-biográfico y apuntes históricos y bibliográficos sobre cada comedia por Garcia-Ramon. 4 tom. *Paris,* 1882, 83. 18°. **11725.** df. **2.**

—— Select Plays . . . Edited, with introductions and notes by Norman Maccoll. [With a portrait.] pp. lix. 507. *Macmillan & Co.: London,* 1888. 8°. **11726.** g. **16.**

—— La Vida es Sueño . . . Entremeses (El Dragoncillo.—La Casa de los linajes.—La Franchota). pp. 183. *Madrid,* 1896. 16°. [*Biblioteca Universal.* tom. 138.] **739.** b. **59.**

—— Teatro . . . Edición anotada por Miguel de Toro Gisbert. [Containing "La Vida es Sueño" and "El Purgatorio de San Patricio."] pp. viii. 360. *Paris,* 1913. 8°. **011853.** pp. **42.**

—— Teatro. 1. El Alcalde de Zalamea—La Vida es Sueño—El Mágico Prodigioso—El Principe Constante . . . Prólogo de Justo Gómez Ocerín. pp. 284. *Madrid,* 1920. 8°. **11728.** de. **12.**
No more published.

—— Three Plays . . . Casa con dos puertas mala es de guardar, La vida es sueño, La cena del Rey Baltasar. Edited with introduction and notes by George Tyler Northup. pp. lv. 358. *Boston,* [1926.] 8°. [*Heath's Modern Language Series.*] **12213.** a. **1/211.**

—— Comedias Religiosas . . . Prólogo y edición de Angel Valbuena. *Madrid,* 1930– . 8°. W.P. **10467.**
Part of the "Clásicos Castellanos."

—— Obras Completas. Textos íntegros según las primeras ediciones y los manuscritos autógrafos, que saca a luz Luis Astrana Marín. Dramas. [Containing selected Comedias only. With a portrait.] pp. lxiii. 2310. *Madrid,* 1932. 8°. **2043.e.**

CALDERÓN DE LA BARCA (Pedro) [Comedias.—Collections.—*Spanish.*]

—— Obras Escogidas de Don Pedro Calderón de la Barca. Edición y prólogo de Luis Astrana Marín. pp. 458. *Madrid*, 1940. 8°. **11729.** b. **1.**

—— Comedias de capa y espada. II. La Dama duende y No hay cosa como callar. Edición, prólogo y notas de Ángel Valbuena Briones. pp. xcii. 223. *Madrid*, 1954. 8°. **11726.** d. **75.**
Clásicos castellanos. no. 137.

—— La Vida es sueño. El Alcalde de Zalamea. Estudio, edición y glosario por Augusto Cortina. pp. lxi. 238. *Madrid*, 1955. 8°. **11729.** c. **16.**
Clásicos castellanos. no. 138.

Spanish and English.

—— Love the Greatest Enchantment: The Sorceries of Sin: The Devotion of the Cross . . . Attempted strictly in English asonante and other imitative verse, by Denis Florence Mac-Carthy. With an introduction to each drama, and notes by the translator, and the Spanish text from the editions of Hartzenbusch, Keil, and Apontes. pp. xiii. 316. *Longman & Co.: London*, 1861. 4°. **2298.** g. **3.**

English.

—— I be Fairy Lady, from la Dama duende. Keep your own secret, from Nadie fie su secreto. *See* Spanish Language. Three Comedies, translated from the Spanish. 1807. 8°. **839.** e. **19.**

—— Dramas of Calderon, tragic, comic, and legendary. Translated from the Spanish, principally in the metre of the original, by Denis Florence M'Carthy. 2 vol. *Charles Dolman: London*, 1853. 8°. **2298.** f. 4.

—— Six Dramas of Calderon. Freely translated by Edward Fitzgerald. pp. viii. 273. *William Pickering: London*, 1853. 8°. **11726.** c. **11.**

—— Life's a Dream: The Great Theatre of the World. From the Spanish of Calderon. With an essay on his life and genius by Richard Chenevix Trench. pp. vi. 229. *J. W. Parker & Son: London*, 1856. 8°. **11726.** c. **1.**

—— The Mighty Magician. ("Such Stuff as dreams are made of." A drama, taken from Calderon's "Vida es sueño.") [Translated by Edward Fitzgerald.] *J. Childs & Son: [Bungay*, 1865.] 8°. C. **58.** b. **20.**

—— [Another copy.] The Mighty Magician. [*Bungay*, 1865.] 8°. Ashley **737.**

—— Calderon's Dramas. The Wonder-Working Magician: Life is a Dream: The Purgatory of Saint Patrick. Now first translated fully from the Spanish in the metre of the original by Denis Florence Mac-Carthy. pp. xvi. 377. *H. S. King & Co.: London*, 1873. 8°. **2298.** g. **4.**

—— An Essay on the Life and Genius of Calderon. With translations from his 'Life's a Dream' and 'Great Theatre of the World' . . . Second edition, revised and improved. pp. vi. 229. *Macmillan & Co.: London*, 1880. 8°. **2306.** a. **10.**
Previous edition 1856.

—— Six Dramas of Calderon, freely translated by Edward Fitzgerald. Edited by H. Oelsner. [With a portrait.] pp. xxxiv. 497. *Alexander Moring: London*, 1903. 8°. [*The King's Classics.*] **012209.** h. **1/2.**

—— Six Dramas of Calderon. Translated from the Spanish by Edward Fitzgerald. pp. ix. 243. *G. Routledge & Sons: London*, 1904. 8°. [*Morley's Universal Library.*] **12204.gg.2/2.**

CALDERÓN DE LA BARCA (Pedro) [Comedias.—Collections.]

—— Eight Dramas of Calderon. Freely translated by Edward Fitzgerald. pp. 517. *Macmillan & Co.: London*, 1906. 8°. **11725.** df. **4.**

—— Six Plays of Calderon. (Translated by Edward Fitz-Gerald.) *See* 'Umar Khaiyām. [*FitzGerald's Version.*] The Rubaiyat, *etc.* [1928.] 8°. **12206.p.1/613.**

French.

—— Le Viol puni, en espagnol, L'Alcalde de Zalamea.—La Cloison, en espagnol, El Escondido y la tapada.—Se défier des apparences, en espagnol, Nunca lo peor es cierto.—La Journée difficile, en espagnol, los Empeños de seis horas. *See* L * * *. Théâtre espagnol. tom. 2. 1770. 12°. **11725.** aa. **16.**

—— Chefs-d'œuvre du théâtre espagnol. Caldéron. [Eight plays, translated by V. L. S. M. Angliviel de la Beaumelle and J. B. d'Esménard. With a biographical notice of Calderon by Angliviel de La Beaumelle, and a portrait.] 2 tom. *Paris*, 1822. 8°. [*Chefs-d'œuvre des théâtres étrangers.* tom. 14, 15.] **1342.** h. **14, 15.**

—— Calderon. [Seventeen plays, translated by J. J. S. A. Damas-Hinard.] 3 sér. *Paris*, 1841, 43. 8°. [*Chefs-d'œuvre du théâtre espagnol.*] **11725.** e. **2.**

—— Œuvres dramatiques de Calderon. Traduction de M. A. de Latour, avec une étude sur Calderon, *etc.* 2 pt. *Paris*, 1871, 73. 8°. **11726.** g. **7.**

—— L'Amour lui-même n'échappe pas à l'amour. Ni amor se libra de amor. (Autos sacramentels de Calderon sur Psyché. [An analysis of the two autos entitled "Psiquis y Cupido."]) *See* Latour (A. de) Psyche en Espagne. 1879. 12°. **11824.** de. **15.**

German.

—— Schauspiele . . . Übersetzt von August Wilhelm Schlegel. 2 Bd. *Berlin*, 1809. 8°. **11725.** aaa. **15.**
With an additional titlepage, reading "Spanisches Theater."

—— Schauspiele . . . Uebersetzt von J. D. Gries. Zweite, durchgesehene Ausgabe . . . Mit dem Bildnisse Calderon's. (Supplementband von der Verfasserin der Roland's Abenteuer [i.e. Wilhelmine Schmidt].) [With a preface signed: N. D., i.e. Nicolaus Delius.] 9 Bd. *Berlin*, 1840–50. 16°. **11725.** a. **14.**

—— Schauspiele . . . Übersetzt von Adolf Martin. 3 Tl. *Leipzig*, 1844. 12°. [*Ausgewählte Bibliothek der Classiker des Auslandes.* Bd. 36–38.] **1154.** e. **10.**

—— Schauspiele . . . Übersetzt von August Wilhelm von Schlegel. Zweite Ausgabe, besorgt von Eduard Böcking. 2 Bd. *Leipzig*, 1845. 16°. **11725.** a. **40.**
Previous edition 1809. *With an additional titlepage reading: "Spanisches Theater."*

—— Calderon's grösste Dramen religiösen Inhalts. Aus dem Spanischen übersetzt und mit den nöthigsten Erläuterungen versehen von Dr. F. Lorinser. 7 Bd. *Freiburg i. B.*, 1875, 76. 12°. **11725.** bb. **1.**

—— Obras de Calderon de la Barca. Dramatische Dichtungen von Calderon de la Barca in wortgetreuer Uebersetzung, *etc.* pp. 204. *Erlangen*, 1884. 8°. **11725.** bb. **4.**

Russian.

—— Сочиненія . . . Переводъ . . . К. Д. Бальмонта. вып. 1, 2. *Москва*, 1900, 02. 8°. **11725.** bb. **35.**

CALDERÓN DE LA BARCA (PEDRO) [COMEDIAS.—COLLECTIONS.]

Swedish.

—— Trenne dramer af don Pedro Calderon . . . i svensk öfversättning af Theodor Hagberg. pp. 427. *Upsala*, 1870. 8°. **11726**. aaa. **9**.

SINGLE COMEDIAS.

—— Comedia famosa. A Secreto Agravio, Secreta Venganza. Por otro titulo, Vengarse con Fuego, y Agua. pp. 30. *Sevilla*, [1720?] 4°. **11728**. b. **59**.

—— [Another edition.] Vengarse con Fuego, y Agua, *etc.* [1740?] 4°. **11725**. ee. **2**. (**2**.)

—— [Another edition.] Comedia famosa. A Secreto Agravio, Secreta Venganza, *etc.* pp. 31. *Barcelona*, 1757. 4°. **11725**. ee. **2**. (**10**.)

—— [Another edition.] *Barcelona*, [1770?] 4°. **11728**. h. **16**. (**13**.)

—— Comedia famosa. Afectos de Odio y Amor, *etc.* MS. NOTE [by J. R. Chorley]. *Barcelona*, [1770?] 4°. **11728**. h. **15**. (**1**.)

—— Letra de la Musica, que se canta en la famosa comedia intitulada: Afectos de odio, y amor [by Calderon]. [1810?] 4°. *See* AFECTOS. **11726**. aaa. **14**. (**9**.)

—— La gran comedia, Agradecer y no Amar. 1653. *See* SPAIN. [*Appendix.—Miscellaneous.*] Primera [*etc.*] parte de Comedias escogidas, *etc.* pt. 5. 1652, *etc.* 4°. **11725**. b. **5**.

—— [Another edition.] [1730?] 4°. **11728**. h. **15**. (**2**.)

—— El Alcaide de sí mismo. *See* infra: El Alcayde de sí mismo.

—— [El Alcalde de Zalamea.] El Garrote mas bien dado. Comedia famosa. [1735?] 4°. T. **1737**. (**9**.)

—— [Another edition.] *Valladolid*, [1760?] 4°. **11728**. h. **15**. (**3**.)

—— [Another edition.] Comedia famosa. El Alcalde de Zalamea. *Barcelona*, [1770?] 4°. **11728**. a. **56**.

—— [Another edition.] Edited by Ida Farnell. pp. xlviii. 126. *Manchester, London*, 1921. 8°. [*Spanish Texts and Studies.*] W.P. **6502/4**.

—— [Another edition.] pp. 151. *Madrid*, [1924.] 8°. **11728**. aaa. **11**.

—— [Another edition.] Ilustrado con litografías por José de Togores. [With a portrait.] pp. 221. *Barcelona*, 1933. 4°. **11729**. dd. **1**.

—— Dommeren i Zalamea. Drama i tre Akten. Oversat af A. Richter. pp. x. 166. *Kjøbenhavn*, 1882. 8°. **11726**. b. **6**.

—— De Rechter van Zalamea. Drama in zeven tafereelen . . . In het Nederlandsch bewerkt door W. G. Nieuwenkamp. pp. 109. *Amsterdam*, 1889. 8°. **11726**. e. **5**.

—— L'Alcade de Zalamea . . . Adaptation française d'Alexandre Arnoux. pp. 23. *Paris*, 1953. 8°. [*France Illustration. Supplément théâtral et littéraire.* no. 125.] P.P. **4283**. m. (**1**.)

—— Der Schulze von Zalamea. Schauspiel in drei Aufzügen . . . Bearbeitet von Otto Freiherrn von Taube. pp. 95. *Leipzig*, [1923.] 8°. [*Insel-Bücherei.* no. 354.] **012213**. de. **1/354**.

CALDERÓN DE LA BARCA (PEDRO) [COMEDIAS.—SINGLE COMEDIAS.]

—— Der Richter von Zalamea. Schauspiel in drei Aufzügen —acht Bildern . . . Freie Nachdichtung von Wilhelm von Scholz. pp. 77. *Breslau*, [1937.] 8°. **11725**. e. **37**.

—— A Zalameai Biró. Szinmű három felvonásban . . . Fordította Győry Vilmos. *Hung.* pp. 156. *Budapest*, 1883. 8°. [*Kisfaludy-Társaság. Spanyol szinműtár.* füz. 5.] Ac. **8983/4**.

—— L'Alcalde di Zalamea. Commedia . . . Tradotta dal signor Pietro Andolfati. pp. 80. *Venezia*, 1799. 8°. [*Teatro moderno applaudito.* tom. 33.] **639**. b. **11**.

—— *See* COLLOT D'HERBOIS (J. M.) Il y a bonne justice, ou le Paysan magistrat, drame en cinq actes et en prose, imité de l'espagnol de Calderon. 1778. 8°. **11738**. c. **16**. (**1**.)

—— *See* CORNEILLE (T.) [*Single Plays.*] Le Geolier de soy-mesme, comedie. [Based on "El Alcayde de si mismo" by P. Calderón de la Barca.] 1661. 12°. **11736**. aa. **11**.

—— —— 1662. 12°. **11737**. de. **8**.

— 1689. 12°. **637**. a. **5**. (**1**.)

—— *See* FAUR (L. F.) Isabelle et Fernand, ou l'Alcade de Zalamea, comédie. [Based on Calderon's "El Alcalde de Zalamea."] 1784. 8°. **11738**. e. **35**. (**4**.)

—— El Alcayde de si mismo. Comedia famosa. [*Madrid?* 1650?] 4°. **C.108.bbb.20.(7.)**

—— [Another edition.] pp. 32. *Valencia*, 1764. 4°. **11728**. a. **57**.

—— [Another edition.] pp. 28. *Sevilla*, [1770?] 4°. **11725**. ee. **5**. (**16**.)

—— Comedia famosa. Amado y Aborrecido, *etc.* *Barcelona*, [1770?] 4°. **11728**. a. **59**.

—— La gran comedia, Amar despues de la Muerte. ff. 20. [1720?] 4°. **11728**. h. **15**. (**4**.)

—— [Another edition.] [*Barcelona?* 1750?] 4°. T. **1737**. (**2**.)

—— [Another edition.] *Barcelona*, [1770?] 4°. **11725**. ee. **4**. (**11**.)

—— Comedia famosa, Amigo, Amante, y Leal. [*Madrid?* 1720?] 4°. **11728**. h. **15**. (**5**.)

—— [Another edition.] Refundida por Cesáreo Saenz de Heredia. pp. 103. *Madrid*, 1924. 8°. **11725**. e. **35**.

—— Comedia famosa. El Amor haze discretos. De vn ingenio de esta corte [P. Calderón de la Barca]. 1671. 4°. [*Primera parte (parte treinta y siete) de Comedias escogidas de los mejores de España.*] *See* AMOR. **11725**. c. **16**.

—— [Another edition.] De una causa dos efetos [*sic*]. Comedia famosa. [*Madrid?* 1700?] 4°. **C.108.bbb.20.(1.)**

—— [Another edition.] La gran comedia, El Amor haze Discretos. *Salamanca*, [1740?] 4°. **11728**. a. **60**. *Imperfect; wanting two leaves of the first Act.*

—— [Another edition.] Comedia famosa. De una causa dos efectos. pp. 28. *Sevilla*, [1765?] 4°. T. **1486**. (**3**.)

—— [Another copy.] T. **1488**. (**3**.)

—— [Another copy.] **11728**. h. **15**. (**15**.)

— [Amor, Honor y Poder.] La Industria contra el Poder, y el honor contra la fuerza. Comedia famosa. De L. de Vega Carpio. [Or rather, "Amor, Honor y Poder," by Calderon.] 1634. 4°. [*Parte veynte y ocho de Comedias de varios autores.*] *See* VEGA CARPIO (L. de) [*Separate Plays.*] **11726.** g. **29.**

— [Another edition.] [*Madrid?* 1700?] 4°. **C.108.bbb.20.(3.)**

— [Another edition.] Comedia famosa. Amor, Honor y Poder. pp. 32. *Madrid,* 1754. 4°. **11725.** ee. **3.** (**12.**)

— [Another edition.] [*Madrid,* 1790?] 4°. **11728.** a. **61.**

— *See* CHARRIN (P. J.) Amour, honneur et devoir, ou le Rapt, drame . . . imité du théâtre espagnol de Caldéron, *etc.* 1815. 8°. **11738.** bbb. **38.** (**12.**)

— Comedia famosa. Antes que Todo es mi Dama. *Barcelona,* [1770?] 4°. **11728.** a. **64.**

— Comedia famosa, Apolo y Climene. ff. 28. [*Madrid?* 1730?] 4°. **11728.** a. **65.**

— Comedia famosa. Argenis y Poliarco. ff. 24. [1700?] 4°. **11728.** a. **66.**

— Comedia famosa. Las Armas de la Hermosura, *etc.* *Barcelona,* 1766. 4°. T. **1737.** (**1.**)

— [Another edition.] pp. 42. *Valencia,* 1769. 4°. **11728.** a. **67.**

— Comedia nova intitulada As Lagrimas da Belleza, sam as armas que mais vencem. [Translated and adapted from Las Armas de la Hermosura of Calderon.] pp. 31. 1784. 4°. *See* LAGRIMAS. **11728.** g. **44.** (**12.**)

— Comedia famosa. El Astrologo Fingido. *Barcelona,* [1760?] 4°. **1342.** e. **6.** (**7.**)

— [Another edition.] El Astrologo Finjido . . . Comedia escrita en tres actos . . . refundida en cinco por Don Pablo Mendibil. pp. 148. *M. Calero: Londres,* 1826. 16°. **11725.** aa. **22.** (**3.**)
Tom. 1 *of "Revista del Antiguo Teatro Español, etc." edited by P. Mendibil.*

— *See* CORNEILLE (T.) [*Single Plays.*] Le Feint astrologue, comedie. [Based on "El Astrólogo fingido" by P. Calderón de la Barca.] 1688. 12°. **637.** a. **2.** (**2.**)

— Comedia famosa. Auristela y Lisidante, *etc.* *Barcelona,* 1766. 4°. **11725.** ee. **4.** (**8.**)

— [Another edition.] *Barcelona,* [1770?] 4°. **11728.** a. **68.**

— Comedia famosa. La Aurora en Copacabana. pp. 52. [*Barcelona?* 1785?] 4°. **11728.** a. **69.**

— La Banda y la Flor. *See* infra: La Vanda y la Flor.

— Comedia famosa. Basta callar. pp. 32. *Sevilla,* [1750?] 4°. **11728.** h. **15.** (**6.**)

— [Another edition.] [1760?] 4°. **11725.** ee. **3.** (**14.**)

— [Another edition.] *Barcelona,* [1770?] 4°. **11728.** a. **71.**

— Bien vengas mal, si vienes solo, *etc.* pp. 28. *Sevilla,* [1730?] 4°. **11725.** ee. **5.** (**12.**)

— [Another edition.] FEW MS. NOTES. [*Madrid,* 1760.] 4°. **11728.** a. **73.**
Pp. 89–128 *of tom.* 2 *of the collection "Comedias del celebre poeta . . . Calderon, etc." edited by J. F. de Apontes. Imperfect; wanting the end of Act* 3.

CALDERÓN DE LA BARCA (PEDRO) [COMEDIAS.— SINGLE COMEDIAS.]

— [Another edition.] Refundida y acomodada á la escena moderna, en cuatro actos por D. Angel María Dacarrete. pp. 76. *Madrid,* 1861. 8°. **11726.** bb. **47.** (**8.**)

— Los Cabellos de Absalon. Comedia famoso. [*Madrid?* 1650?] 4°. **C.108.bbb.20.(9.)**

— [Another edition.] pp. 28. *Sevilla,* [1750?] 4°. **11725.** ee. **5.** (**1.**)

— [Another edition.] [*Madrid,* 1750?] 4°. **11728.** a. **74.**

— Cada uno para sì. Comedia famosa. pp. 40. *Sevilla,* [1730?] 4°. **11728.** h. **15.** (**7.**)

— [Another edition.] [*Madrid?* 1750?] 4°. **11726.** e. **2.** (**4.**)

— [Another edition.] [*Madrid,* 1760.] 4°. **11728.** a. **76.**
Pp. 57–110 *of tom.* 1 *of the collection "Comedias del celebre poeta . . . Calderon, etc." edited by J. F. de Apontes.*

— Las Cadenas del Demonio, comedia famosa. [*Madrid?* 1700?] 4°. **C.108.bbb.20.(11.)**

— [Another edition.] [1760?] 4°. **11728.** a. **77.**

— [Another copy.] **11728.** h. **16.** (**18.**)

— [Another edition.] *Barcelona,* 1766. 4°. **11725.** ee. **4.** (**9.**)

— La gran comedia: Casa con dos Puertas mala es de guardar. pp. 34. *Madrid,* [1770?] 4°. **11725.** ee. **2.** (**15.**)

— [Another edition.] *Barcelona,* [1770?] 4°. **11728.** a. **79.**

— [Another edition.] pp. 34. *Valencia,* 1796. 4°. **11728.** h. **15.** (**9.**)

— Huset med to Indgange. Komedie i tre Akter . . . Oversat af A. Richter. pp. 185. *Kjøbenhavn,* 1887. 8°. **11728.** bb. **6.**

— Das Haus mit zwei Thüren. (Übersetzt im Versmasse der Urschrift.) Von Georg Nicolaus Bärmann. pp. 119. *Wien,* 1827. 16°. **11725.** a. **12.**

— La gran comedia, El Castillo de Lindabridis, *etc.* [*Madrid,* 1760.] 4°. **11728.** a. **81.**
Pp. 35–40 *of tom.* 2 *of the collection "Comedias del celebre poeta . . . Calderon, etc." edited by J. P. de Apontes. Imperfect; comprising a portion of Act* 1 *only.*

— [Another edition.] *Barcelona,* 1766. 4°. **11725.** ee. **4.** (**10.**)

— [Another edition.] *Barcelona,* [1771.] 4°. **11728.** a. **80.**

— Comedia burlesca, Cefalo, y Pocris, *etc.* [*Madrid,* 1760.] 4°. **11728.** a. **82.**
Pp. 1–34 *of tom.* 2 *of the collection "Comedias del celebre poeta . . . Calderon, etc." edited by J. F. de Apontes.*

— [Another edition.] *Barcelona,* [1770?] 4°. **11728.** a. **83.**

— Cefalo und Pocris, Burleske . . . übersetzt von C. A. Dohrn. pp. iv. 165. *Stettin,* 1879. 8°. **11725.** c. **22.**

— Celos aun del Aire matan. *See* infra: Zelos, *etc.*

— La Cisma de Inglaterra. Comedia famosa. pp. 32. *Sevilla,* [1700?] 4°. **11728.** h. **15.** (**11.**)

— [Another edition.] pp. 32. *Madrid,* 1785. 4°. **11728.** a. **84.**

—— See SCHMIDT (Friedrich W. V.) Ueber die Kirchentrennung von England, Schauspiel des Don G. Calderon de la Barca, *etc.* 1819. 8°. **11725. e. 6.**

—— La gran comedia de Con quien vengo vengo [by Calderon]. *See* COMEDIAS. Parte treynta una, de las mejores comedias, *etc.* 1638. 4°. **11725. d. 12.**

—— [Another edition.] pp. 36. *Madrid*, 1746. 4°. **11725. ee. 4. (1.)**

—— [Another edition.] *Barcelona*, [1770?] 4°. **11728. a. 88.**

—— La gran comedia del Conde Lucanor. [*Madrid?* 1661?] 4°. **11728. a. 87.**

—— [Another edition.] ff. 20. [*Madrid?* 1750?] 4°. **11725. ee. 3. (3.)**

—— [Another edition.] *Barcelona*, [1770?] 4°. **11728. a. 86.**

—— La Cruz en la Sepultura. *See* infra: La Devocion de la Cruz.

—— La Dama Duende. Comedia famosa. [*P. Crasbeeck: Lisbon*, 1647.] 4°. **11728. h. 15. (14.)**
Forming fol 167–191 *of the collection* " *Doze comedias las mas grandiosas, etc.*"

—— [Another edition.] [*Madrid?* 1760?] 4°. **11725. ee. 2. (13.)**

—— [Another edition.] *Barcelona*, 1771. 4°. **11728. a. 91.**

—— [Another edition.] *See* GARCÍA DE LA HUERTA (V. A.) Theatro Hespañol, *etc.* pt. 2. tom. 2. 1785. 8°. **243. b. 10.**

—— La Dama Duende. Comedia en zinco actos, refundida de la que con el mismo título escribió don P. Calderon de la Barca. Por don José Fernandez Guerra. pp. 111. *Malaga*, 1826. 8°. **1342. b. 15. (1.)**

—— *See* BULLOCK (Christopher) Woman is a Riddle; a comedy, *etc.* [Based on "La Dama Duende" by Calderon.] 1717. 4°. **161. g. 64.**

—— —— 1729. 12°. **11775. b. 13.**

—— —— 1731. 12°. **11775. b. 14.**

—— —— 1759. 12°. **1342. n. 8. (5.)**

—— —— 1770. 8°. **11775. e. 6.**

—— Comedia famosa. Dar Tiempo al Tiempo. *Barcelona*, [1770?] 4°. **11728. a. 93.**

—— Comedia famosa. Darlo todo, y no dar nada, *etc.* *Barcelona*, 1763. 4°. **11725. ee. 4. (7.)**

—— [Another edition.] *Barcelona*, [1770?] 4°. **11728. a. 92.**

—— De un Castigo tres Venganzas. *See* infra: Un Castigo en tres Venganzas.

—— De una Causa dos Efectos. *See* supra: El Amor haze discretos.

—— La Desdicha de la Voz, comedia famosa. [*Madrid?* 1700?] 4°. **C.108.bbb.20.(4.)**

—— [Another edition.] pp. 44. [1720?] 4°. T. **1737. (6.)**

—— [La Devocion de la Cruz.] La Cruz en la Sepultura. Comedia famosa. De L. de Vega Carpio. [Or rather, "La Devocion de la Cruz, by Calderon.] 1634. 4°. [*Parte veynte y ocho, de Comedias de varios autores.*] *See* VEGA CARPIO (L. de) [*Separate Plays.*] **11726. g. 29.**

—— [Another edition.] [*Madrid?* 1700?] 4°. **C.108.bbb.20.(5.)**

—— [Another edition.] Comedia famosa, La Devocion de la Cruz. ff. 20. [1760?] 4°. **11728. a. 94.**

—— [Another edition.] La Cruz en la Sepultura. *Barcelona*, [1810.] 4°. **11728. a. 90.**

—— La Dévotion à la Croix. *See* DIEULAFOY (M.) Le Théâtre édifiant, *etc.* 1907. 8°. **11725. bb. 16.**

—— Comedia famosa. Dicha, y Desdicha del Nombre. pp. 52. [1760?] 4°. T. **1486. (2.)**

—— [Another copy.] **11728. h. 15. (16.)**

—— Comedia famosa. Los Dos Amantes del Cielo, Crisanto y Daria. *Barcelona*, [1770?] 4°. **11728. a. 96.**

—— The Two Lovers of Heaven: Chrysanthus and Daria . . . With dedicatory sonnets to Longfellow, etc. By D. F. Mac-Carthy. pp. 60. *J. F. Fowler: Dublin; J. C. Hotten: London*, 1870. 8°. **11726. h. 7.**

—— Chrysanthus und Daria. *See* SCHACK (A. F. von) Spanisches Theater, *etc.* Tl. 2. 1845. 8°. **11726. aaa. 48.**

—— Kochankowie nieba. Przez K. Balińskiego. pp. 192. *Poznań*, 1858. 12°. **11726. b. 23.**
Tom 1 *of* " *Wybór dzieł Kalderona.*"

—— Duelos de Amor, y Lealtad. Comedia famosa. pp. 36. *Sevilla*, [1730?] 4°. **11728. b. 2.**

—— [Another edition.] [*Madrid?* 1760?] 4°. **11725. ee. 2. (14.)**

—— [Another edition.] *Barcelona*, [1810?] 4°. **11728. b. 1.**

—— Eco y Narciso. *See* GARCÍA DE LA HUERTA (V. A.) Theatro Hespañol, *etc.* pt. 3. tom. 2. 1785. 8°. **243. b. 18.**

—— [Another edition.] *Barcelona*, [1810?] 4°. **11728. b. 3.**

—— Los Empeños de un Acaso. Comedia famosa. [1700?] 4°. **C.108.bbb.20.(8.)**

—— [Another edition.] pp. 32. *Sevilla*, [1720?] 4°. **11728. h. 15. (17.)**

—— [Another edition.] [1760?] 4°. **11728. b. 6.**

—— [Another edition.] *Barcelona*, [1770?] 4°. **11728. b. 5.**

—— Die Verwicklungen des Zufalls. Lustspiel in drei Aufzügen . . . Uebersetzt von Ernst Friedrich Freyh. von der Malsburg. pp. 190. *Berlin*, 1819. 8°. **11725. a. 11.**

—— Comedia famosa. El Encanto sin Encanto. pp. 40. *Salamanca*, [1750?] 4°. **11728. b. 9.**

—— Comedia famosa. El Escondido, y la Tapada. pp. 36. *Salamanca*, [1750?] 4°. **11728. h. 15. (18.)**

—— [Another edition.] *Barcelona*, [1770?] 4°. **11728. b. 13.**

—— 'Tis Well it's no Worse: a comedy, *etc.* [Adapted from "El Escondído y la Tapada," by Isaac Bickerstaffe.] pp. xii. 104. *W. Griffin: London,* 1770. 8°. **11777.** d. **7.**

—— The second edition. pp. xii. 104. *W. Griffin: London,* 1770. 8°. **161.** c. **45.**

—— The third edition. pp. xii. 104. *W. Griffin: London,* 1770. 8°. **643.** h. **10. (11.)**

—— The Pannel. An entertainment of three acts. Altered [by J. P. Kemble] from the comedy of 'Tis well it's no worse. pp. 47. *C. Stalkerd, etc.: London,* 1789. 8°. **161.** f. 4.

—— The second edition. pp. iv. 47. *C. Stalkerd, etc.: London,* 1789. 8°. **643.** g. **15.** (**5.**)

—— [Another edition.] 1871. 8°. *See* KEMBLE (John P.) **11770.** bbb. **12.** (**28.**)

—— [A reissue.] [1875?] 8°. [*Dicks' Standard Plays.* no. 112.] *See* KEMBLE (John P.) **11770.** bbb. 4.

—— Der Verschlag, oder Hier wird Versteckens gespielt. Ein Lustspiel . . . nach Calderan [*sic*], von Bock. [In prose.] pp. 124. *Leipzig,* 1781. 8°. **11747.** e. **8.** (**4.**)

—— *See* COLLÉ (C.) L'Esprit follet, ou la Dame invisible. Comédie, *etc.* [Founded on "El Escondído y la Tapada."] 1770. 8°. **11738.** c. **14.** (**1.**)

—— [Las Espigas de Ruth.] *See* KRALIK VON MEYRSWALDEN (R.) Die Ähren der Ruth. Ein geistliches Festspiel mit Chören nach Calderon, *etc.* [1905.] 8°. **11748.** de. 14.

—— Comedia famosa, de la Estatua de Prometeo. [*Madrid?* 1750?] 4°. **11725.** ee. **3.** (**4.**)

—— Des Prometheus Götterbildnis . . . Mit Einleitung, theilweiser Übersetzung, Anmerkungen und einem metrischen Anhange von K. Pasch. pp. 80. *Wien,* 1887. 8°. **11726.** i. **8.** (**2.**)

—— Comedia famosa. La Exaltacion de la Cruz. pp. 36. *Salamanca,* [1780?] 4°. **11726.** e. **1.** (**9.**)

—— Loa para la comedia de Fieras Afemina Amor. (Comedia famosa. Fieras Afemina Amor.) [*Madrid?* 1760?] 4°. **11726.** e. **3.** (**4.**)

—— [Another edition.] *Barcelona,* [1770?] 4°. **11728.** b. 15.

—— Pantomima y canto de una parte de la zarzuela . . . titulada Fieras Afemina Amor. [1845.] *See* GALERÍA. Galería Dramática, *etc.* vol. 57. 1836, *etc.* 8°. **1342.** g. **6.** (**8.**)

—— Comedia famosa. Fineza contra Fineza. pp. 39. *Barcelona,* 1758. 4°. **11725.** ee. **2.** (**9.**)

—— [Another edition.] *Barcelona,* 1765. 4°. **11728.** b. 16.

—— La gran comedia. Fortunas de Andromeda, y Perseo, *etc.* [1750?] 4°. **11728.** a. 62.

—— Comedia famosa. Fuego de Dios en el querer bien. [1750?] 4°. **11725.** ee. **2.** (**5.**)

—— [Another edition.] *Barcelona,* [1770?] 4°. **11728.** b. **17.**

—— [Another copy.] **11728.** h. **15.** (**20.**)

—— Comedia famosa. El Galan Fantasma. [1725?] 4°. **11728.** b. 18.

—— [Another edition.] [*Madrid?* 1730?] 4°. **11728.** h. **16.** (**1.**)

—— Der Liebhaber als Gespenst . . . Frei bearbeitet von der Verfasserin der Roland's Abentheuer [i.e. Wilhelmine Schmidt]. pp. 124. *Gotha,* 1825. 12°. **11725.** a. **37.** (**2.**)

—— El Garrote más bien dado. *See* supra: El Alcalde de Zalamea.

—— Comedia famosa. El Golfo de las Sirenas. [*Madrid?* 1730?] 4°. **T. 1737.** (**10.**)
Pp. 493–516 *of a collection of plays. Imperfect; wanting the last leaf, which is supplied in MS.*

—— [Another edition.] pp. 24. *Sevilla,* [1740?] 4°. **11725.** ee. **5.** (**4.**)

—— Comedia famosa. La Gran Cenobia. pp. 28. *Sevilla,* [1750?] 4°. **11725.** ee. **5.** (**5.**)

—— [Another edition.] *Barcelona,* 1763. 4°. **T. 1737.** (**4.**)

—— [Another edition.] *Barcelona,* [1770?] 4°. **11728.** b. **20.**

—— Comedia famosa. El Gran Principe de Fez, Don Balthasar de Loyola. *Barcelona,* [1770?] 4°. **11728.** b. **21.**

—— Comedia famosa. Guardate de la Agua Mansa. *Barcelona,* [1772?] 4°. **11728.** b. **22.**

—— [Another copy.] **11728.** h. **16.** (**2.**)

—— Comedia famosa. Gustos, y Disgustos son no mas que Imaginacion. pp. 36. *Madrid,* 1748. 4°. **11725.** ee. **3.** (**2.**)

—— *See* GOZZI (C.) *Count.* Zwey unruhige Nächte, oder Neigung und Abneigung, *etc.* [Adapted from Carlo Gozzi's play "Le due notti affannose," which is based on Calderon's "Gustos y disgustos no son más que imaginación."] 1794. 8°. **752.** a. **1/63.**

—— La gran comedia. Hado, y Divisa de Leonido, y de Marfisa, *etc.* pp. 57. [*Barcelona,* 1760?] 4°. **11728.** b. 23.

—— Hazer del Amor Agravio. *See* infra: La Vanda y la Flor.

—— Comedia famosa. La Hija del Ayre. Primera parte. *Barcelona,* 1763. 4°. **T. 1737.** (**11.**)

—— Comedia famosa. La Hija del Ayre. Parte segunda, *etc.* *Barcelona,* 1763. 8°. **T. 1737.** (**11*.**)

—— [Another edition.] Precedido de un prólogo escrito por S. Olmedo y Estrada. pp. vi. 97. *Madrid,* 1881. 8°. **11726.** a. **25.** (**4.**)

—— Semíramis ó la Hija del Aire. Segunda parte. Drama en tres jornadas . . . arreglado y refundido por José Echegaray. pp. 70. *Madrid,* 1896. 8°. **11728.** cc. **2.** (**4.**)

—— *See* RAUPACH (E. B. S.) The Daughter of the Air: a mythic tragedy . . . after the idea of P. Calderon, *etc.* 1831. 12°. **839.** f. **20.**

—— Comedia famosa. El Hijo del Sol, Faeton, *etc.* *Barcelona,* [1770?] 4°. **11728.** b. 25.

—— Comedia famosa. Los Hijos de la Fortuna, Teagenes, y Clariclea. pp. 44. *Barcelona,* 1757. 4°. **11725.** ee. **4.** (**4.**)

—— Comedia famosa, El Hombre Pobre Todo es Trazas. [*Madrid?* 1730?] 4°. **11728.** b. 26.

CALDERÓN DE LA BARCA (PEDRO) [COMEDIAS.—SINGLE COMEDIAS.]

—— *See* GALANT. Le Galand doublé, comedie. [By T. Corneille. Based on P. Calderón de la Barca's " El Hombre pobre todo es trazas."] 1690. 12°. **637. a. 3. (1.)**

—— La Industria contra el Poder, y el Honor contra la Fuerza. *See* supra: Amor, Honor, y Poder.

—— Comedia famosa. El Jardin de Falerina, *etc.* pp. 24. *Sevilla*, [1750?] 4°. **11725. ee. 5. (6.)**

—— [Another edition.] pp. 31. [*Barcelona?* 1755?] 4°. **T. 1486. (4.)**

—— [Another copy.] **11728. h. 16. (3.)**

—— Comedia famosa. El Joseph de las Mugeres. pp. 36. *Salamanca*, [1760?] 4°. **11725. ee. 5. (13.)**

—— [Another edition.] *Barcelona*, 1766. 4°. **11728. b. 29.**

—— Comedia famosa. Judas Macabeo. ff. 20. [1750?] 4°. **11728. b. 4.**

—— [Another edition.] pp. 28. *Sevilla*, [1750?] 4°. **11725. ee. 5. (7.)**

—— Comedia famosa de los Lances de Amor y Fortuna. [*Valencia?* 1735?] 4°. **T. 1737. (13.)**
Ff. 171–194 *of a collection of plays.*

—— [Another edition.] pp. 32. *Madrid*, 1754. 4°. **11725. ee. 4. (5.)**

—— [Another edition.] [*Barcelona?* 1776?] 4°. **11728. b. 30.**

—— Comedia famosa. El Laurel de Apolo, *etc.* [*Madrid?* 1750?] 4°. **11725. ee. 2. (6.)**

—— [Another edition.] pp. 24. *Sevilla*, [1780?] 4°. **11725. ee. 5. (19.)**

—— Comedia famosa. Luis Perez el Gallego. Primera parte. *Madrid*, 1751. 4°. **11725. ee. 3. (10.)**

—— Comedia famosa. El Maestro de Danzar. pp. 32. *Sevilla*, [1750?] 4°. **11725. ee. 5. (8.)**

—— El Magico Prodigioso. Comedia famosa. pp. 32. *Sevilla*, [1730?] 4°. **11728. h. 16. (16.)**

—— [Another edition.] pp. 36. *Salamanca*, [1760?] 4°. **11725. ee. 5. (14.)**

—— [Another edition.] *Barcelona*, [1770?] 4°. **11728. b. 31.**

—— [Another edition.] Publiée d'après le manuscrit original de la bibliothèque du duc d'Osuna, avec deux fac-simile, une introduction, des variantes et des notes par Alfred Morel-Fatio. pp. lxxvi. 255. *Heilbronn*, 1877. 8°. **11728. bb. 1.**

—— [Another edition.] With introduction, notes and vocabulary by James N. Birch. pp. vii. 184. *Methuen & Co.: London*, 1929. 8°. **11728. aaa. 20.**

—— [El Mágico Prodigioso.] Justina; a play. Translated . . . by J. H. [i.e. D. F. MacCarthy.] pp. iv. 138. *James Burns: London*, 1848. 16°. **1342. g. 24.**

—— Le Prodigieux magicien, drame . . . Traduit pour la première fois en français par Th. de Puymaigre. pp. 64. *Metz*, 1852. 8°. **11726. dd. 7.**

CALDERÓN DE LA BARCA (PEDRO) [COMEDIAS.—SINGLE COMEDIAS.]

—— *See* BEYSCHLAG (J. H. C. W.) De Cypriano mago et martyre tragœdiæ Calderonis [i.e. " El Mágico Prodigioso "] persona primaria. 1866. 4°. [*Academiæ Fridericianæ Halensis . . . rector . . . nomina civium suorum qui in certamine literario . . . praemia reportaverunt renunciat, etc.*] **8357. l. 39. (7.)**

—— *See* CARRIERE (M.) Calderon's wunderthätiger Magus und Goethe's Faust, *etc.* 1876. 8°. **011840. m. 12. (1.)**

—— *See* KAENDERS (P.) Her Only Love, *etc.* (Based on Calderon's " El magico prodigioso.") 1914. 8°. **11791. d. 38.**

—— *See* OWEN (John) *Rector of East Anstey, etc.* The Five Great Skeptical Dramas of History. (El Magico Prodigioso.) 1896. 8°. **11824. i. 10.**

—— *See* ROSENKRANZ (J. C. F.) Ueber Calderon's Tragödie vom wunderthätigen Magus, *etc.* 1829. 8°. **1464. c. 17.**

—— La gran comedia. Mañana será otro dia. pp. 36. *Córdoba*, [1750?] 4°. **11725. ee. 5. (9.)**

—— [Another edition.] *Barcelona*, [1770?] 4°. **11728. b. 32.**

—— Comedia famosa, Mañanas de Abril y Mayo. [1720?] 4°. **11728. h. 16. (4.)**

—— Comedia famosa. Las Manos Blancas no ofenden, *etc.* [*Barcelona*, 1770?] 4°. **11728. b. 33.**

—— El Mayor Encanto Amor. Comedia famosa. *Sevilla*, [1740?] 4°. **11728. h. 16. (5.)**

—— [Another edition.] *Barcelona*, 1785. 4°. **11728. b. 34.**

—— Comedia famosa. El Mayor Monstruo los Zelos, y Tetrarca de Jerusalem. pp. 38. *Barcelona*, 1790. 4°. **11725. ee. 4. (16.)**

—— [Another edition.] pp. 39. *Cadiz*, 1799. 4°. **11728. h. 16. (6.)**

—— [Another edition.] pp. 40. [*Madrid*,] 1801. 4°. **11728. b. 35.**

—— Relacion, El Mayor Monstruo los Zelos, *etc.* [An extract.] 2 pt. *Valencia*, 1758. 4°. **T. 1953. (45.)**

—— Relacion de Hombre. El mayor monstruo los zelos. [An extract.] *Córdoba*, [1810?] 4°. **11450. h. 6. (8.)**

—— Comedia famosa, El Medico de su Honra. *Barcelona*, [1770?] 4°. **11728. b. 36.**

—— [Another copy.] **11728. b. 37.**

—— Lékarz swoiego honoru, traiedya w pięciu aktach . . . przez J. N. Kamińskiego dla teatru polskiego przerobiona. pp. 123. *we Lwowie*, 1827. 8°. **11726. g. 15.**

—— *See* PARIS (Léon) Le Médecin de son honneur. Drame . . . inspiré de Calderon, *etc.* 1912. 8°. **11735. h. 14. (2.)**

—— Comedia famosa, Mejor esta que estava. pp. 44. [*Madrid?* 1700?] 4°. **T. 1741. (15.)**

—— [Another edition.] pp. 32. *Sevilla*, [1765?] 4°. **T. 1486. (5.)**

—— [Another copy.] **11728. h. 16. (7.**

—— [Another edition.] *Barcelona*, [1770?] 4°. **11728**. b. **38**.

—— [Mejor está que estaba.] Fortune Mends: a comedy, in three acts, translated . . . by Fanny Holcroft. 1805. *See* PERIODICAL PUBLICATIONS.—*London*. The Theatrical Recorder, *etc.* vol. 2. 1805, *etc.* 8°. P.P. **5203**.

—— Il y a du mieux, en espagnol, Mejor esta que estava, comédie. [In verse.] *See* L * * *. Théâtre espagnol. tom. 1. 1770. 12°. **11725**. aa. **16**.

—— Comedia famosa. El Monstruo de los Jardines. pp. 32. *Sevilla*, [1750?] 4°. **11725**. ee. **5**. (**10**.)

—— [Another edition.] *Barcelona*, 1764. 4°. **11728**. b. **41**.

—— Comedia famosa. Muger, llora, y vencerás, *etc.* pp. 36. *Madrid*, 1756. 4°. **11728**. b. **42**.

—— La gran comedia. Nadie fie su Secreto. [*Madrid?* 1750?] 4°. **11725**. ee. **4**. (**2**.)

—— [Another edition.] *Salamanca*, [1750?] 4°. **11728**. b. **43**.

Cropped.

—— Comedia famosa. Ni Amor se libra de Amor. *Barcelona*, 1763. 4°. **11726**. e. **3**. (**6**.)

—— Comedia famosa. La Niña de Gomez Arias. pp. 36. *Madrid*, [1760?] 4°. **11725**. ee. **3**. (**13**.)

—— [Another edition.] pp. 36. *Valencia*, 1782. 4°. **11728**. b. **44**.

—— [Another edition.] Refundida en cinco actos por Don Gabino Tejado. pp. 84. *Madrid*, 1848. 8°. **11726**. d. **1**. (**6**.)

—— Das Mädchen des Gomez Arias . . . Frei bearbeitet von der Verfasserin der Rolands Abentheuer [i.e. Wilhelmine Schmidt]. pp. 172. *Gotha*, 1825. 12°. **11725**. a. **37**. (**1**.)

—— Comedia famosa. No guardas tu tu secreto. 1652. *See* SPAIN. [*Appendix.—Miscellaneous.*] Primera [*etc.*] parte de Comedias escogidas, *etc.* pt. 2. 1652, *etc.* 4°. **11725**. b. **2**.

—— Comedia famosa. No ay Burlas con el Amor. pp. 40. [*Valencia?* 1755?] 4°. T. **1486**. (**1**.)

—— [Another copy.] **11728**. h. **16**. (**8**.)

—— Relacion: No hay Burlas con el Amor. [An extract.] *Valencia*, 1758. 4°. T. **1953**. (**35**.)

—— [Another edition.] *Córdoba*, [1813?] 4°. **12330**. l. **1**. (**91**.)

—— On ne badine point avec l'amour, en espagnol, No ai burlas con el amor, comédie. [In prose.] *See* L * * *. Théâtre espagnol. tom. 3. 1770. 12°. **11725**. aa. **16**.

—— Comedia famosa. No hay Cosa como Callar. *Barcelona*, [1770?] 4°. **11728**. b. **45**.

—— Comedia famosa de Nunca lo Peor es Cierto. *D. Garcia y Morras: Madrid*, 1652.] 4°. T. **1737**. (**14**.)
Ff. 16–38 *of the* "*Primera parte de comedias escogidas de los mejores de España.*" *Imperfect; wanting ff.* 36 *and* 37, *which are supplied in* MS.

—— [Another edition.] Comedia famosa. No Siempre lo Peor es Cierto. [*Madrid?* 1750?] 4°. **11725**. ee. **3**. (**5**.)

—— [Another edition.] *Barcelona*, [1770?] 4°. **11728**. b. **46**.

—— *See* MARGUERITTE (V.) La Double méprise, ou "Le Pire n'est pas toujours certain," d'après Calderon [i.e. based on Calderon's "No siempre lo peor es cierto"], *etc.* 1898. 12°. **11740**. de. **18**.

—— Comedia famosa. Origen, Perdida, y Restauracion de la Virgen del Sagrario. ff. 20. [*Madrid?* 1750?] 4°. **11725**. ee. **3**. (**6**.)

—— [Another edition.] Comedia famosa. La Virgen del Sagrario, su origen, perdida y restauracion. *Barcelona*, 1771. 4°. **11728**. b. **68**.

—— La gran comedia, Para vencer a amor, querer vencerle. 1654. *See* SPAIN. [*Appendix.—Miscellaneous.*] Primera [*etc.*] parte de Comedias escogidas, *etc.* pt. 7. 1652, *etc.* 4°. **11725**. b. **7**.

—— [Another edition.] pp. 36. *Madrid*, 1754. 4°. **11728**. b. **48**.

—— [Another edition.] pp. 36. *Valencia*, 1769. 4°. **11728**. h. **16**. (**9**.)

—— [Another edition.] *Barcelona*, 1771. 4°. **11725**. ee. **4**. (**12**.)

—— Relacion: Para vencer, amor, querer vencerle. [An extract.] *Valencia*, [1758?] 4°. T. **1953**. (**9**.)

—— Comedia famosa. Peor està, que estaba. ff. 20. [*Barcelona?* 1750?] 4°. **11725**. ee. **4**. (**3**.)

—— [Another edition.] *Barcelona*, [1770?] 4°. **11728**. b. **49**.

—— From Bad to Worse . . . Translated from the Spanish by Fanny Holcroft. *See* PERIODICAL PUBLICATIONS.—*London*. The Theatrical Recorder. vol. 1. no. 4. 1805, *etc.* 8°. P.P. **5203**.

—— Comedia famosa. El Pintor de su Deshonra. ff. 18. [*Madrid?* 1650?] 4°. **C.108.bbb.20.(10.)**

—— [Another edition.] [*Madrid?* 1750?] 4°. **11725**. ee. **2**. (**7**.)

—— [Another edition.] pp. 32. *Sevilla*, [1760?] 4°. **11728**. b. **50**.

—— El Polyfemo. *See* infra: WORKS WRITTEN IN COLLABORATION.

—— Comedia famosa. El Postrer Duelo de España. *Barcelona*, [1770?] 4°. **11728**. b. **51**.

—— Comedia famosa. Primero soy yo. *Barcelona*, [1771?] 4°. **11728**. b. **52**.

—— [Another edition.] pp. 34. *Valencia*, 1782. 4°. **11725**. ee. **4**. (**13**.)

—— Comedia famosa, El Principe Constante, y Martyr de Portugal. *F. Sanz:* [*Madrid*, 1680?] 4°. **11728**. b. **53**.

—— [Another edition.] pp. 32. *Sevilla*, [1740?] 4°. **11728**. h. **16**. (**11**.)

—— [Another edition.] pp. 32. *Madrid*, 1749. 4°. **11728**. b. **54**.

—— [Another edition.] [Edited by A. A. Parker.] pp. vii. 94. *University Press: Cambridge*, 1938. 8°. [*Cambridge Plain Texts.*] W.P. **6501/52**.

—— Der standhafte Prinz. *See* PETZ (L.) Tetralogie tragischer Meisterwerke, *etc.* 1824. 8°. **1343**. k. **21**.

—— Der standhafte Prinz . . . Tragödie . . . Frei bearbeitet. pp. 106. *Gotha*, 1826. 12°. **11725**. a. **37**. (**4**.)

—— Der standhafte Prinz. Schauspiel . . . In deutsche Iamben übertragen von R. Baumstark. pp. xix. 93. *Frankfurt*, 1891. 8°. **11726. aaa. 6.**

—— Der standhafte Prinz . . . Übertragen und für die Vereinsbühne eingerichtet von B. M. Steinmetz. pp. 48. *Paderborn*, [1910.] 8°. **11747.** d. **35.** (3.)
No. 415 *of the "Kleines Theater."*

—— [El Principe Constante.] Az állhatatos Fejedelem. Szinmű három felvonásban . . . Fordították Greguss Gyula és Győry Vilmos. pp. 146. *Pesten*, 1870. 8°. [*Kisfaludy-Társaság. Spanyol szinműtár.* füz. 1.] Ac. **8983/4.**

—— [El Principe Constante.] J. Słowackiego Xiążę Niezłomny. Z Calderona de la Barca. Tragedja we trzech częściach. pp. 172. *Paryż*, 1844. 12°. **11758. aaa. 8.**

—— *See* SCHULZE (Johann) *Prussian Minister of Education.* Ueber den standhaften Prinzen des Don Pedro Calderon. 1811. 8°. **011840.** e. **65.**

—— *See* SLOMAN (Albert E.) The Sources of Calderón's El Príncipe constante, *etc.* 1950. 8°. W.P. **5736/9.**

—— La Puente de Mantible . . . De Lope de Vega Carpio [or rather, by Calderon]. [1700?] 4°. *See* VEGA CARPIO (L. F. de) **11728.** h. **21.** (2.)

—— [Another edition.] [*Madrid?* 1750?] 4°. **11728.** b. **55.**

—— Comedia famosa. El Purgatorio de San Patricio. pp. 36. *Madrid*, 1743. 4°. **11728.** h. **16.** (19.)

—— [Another edition.] *Barcelona*, [1770?] 4°. **11728.** b. **56.**

—— Comedia famosa. La Purpura de la Rosa, *etc.* (Loa para la comedia de la Purpura de la Rosa.) [*Madrid?* 1750?] 4°. **11725.** ee. **3.** (7.)

—— Comedia famosa. Qual es Mayor Perfeccion, Hermosura, o Discrecion? pp. 40. *Barcelona*, 1758. 4°. **11728.** h. **15.** (13.)

—— Comedia famosa. Saber del mal, y del bien. pp. 35. *Salamanca*, [1750?] 4°. **11728.** h. **16.** (12.)

—— [Another edition.] *Barcelona*, 1763. 4°. **11728.** b. **58.**

—— El Secreto a Vozes. Comedia famosa. [1720?] 4°. **11728.** h. **16.** (14.)

—— [Another edition.] pp. 36. [1740?] 4°. T. **1737.** (16.)

—— [Another edition.] pp. 40. *Madrid*, 1753. 4°. **11725.** ee. **3.** (11.)

—— [Another edition.] *See* GARCÍA DE LA HUERTA (V. A.) Theatro Hespañol, *etc.* pt. 3. tom. 1. 1785. 8°. **243.** b. **17.**

—— [Another edition.] Publícala José M. de Osma. pp. xxi. 138. *Lawrence, Kan.*, 1938. 8°. [*Bulletin of the University of Kansas. Humanistic Studies.* vol. 6. no. 2.] Ac. **2692.** i/4.

—— Comedia famosa. El Segundo Scipion, *etc.* ff. 30. [*Madrid?* 1740?] 4°. **11725.** ee. **3.** (1.)

—— [Another edition.] *Barcelona*, [1770?] 4°. **11728.** b. **60.**

—— La Selva Confusa. (Edited, with an introduction, by George Tyler Northup.) 1909. *See* PERIODICAL PUBLICATIONS.—*Paris.* Revue hispanique, *etc.* tom. 21. no. 59. 1894, *etc.* 8°. P.P. **4331.** aea.

CALDERÓN DE LA BARCA (PEDRO) [COMEDIAS.—SINGLE COMEDIAS.]

—— Semiramis ó La Hija del Aire. *See* supra: La Hija del Ayre.

—— Comedia famosa. La Señora, y la Criada, *etc.* pp. 32. *Salamanca*, [1760?] 4°. **11725.** ee. **5.** (15.)

—— [Another edition.] *Barcelona*, [1770?] 4°. **11728.** b. **61.**

—— Comedia famosa. La Sibila del Oriente, y Gran Reyna de Saba. pp. 32. [*Madrid?* 1750?] 4°. **11725.** ee. **3.** (8.)

—— Die Seherin des Morgens. Schauspiel nach Don Pedro Calderon de la Barca frei bearbeitet. pp. 91. *Gotha*, 1830. 12°. **11725.** a. **37.** (3.)

—— *See* MEYER (Wilhelm) *of Spires.* Ueber Calderon's Sibylle des Orients, *etc.* 1879. 4°. **732.** i. **25.** (9.)

—— Comedia famosa, El Sitio de Breda. *Barcelona*, [1770?] 4°. **11728.** b. **62.**

—— Sueños ay que Verdad son. Comedia famosa. [*Seville?* 1740?] 4°. **11728.** b. **63.**
Cropped.

—— Tambien ay Duelo en las Damas. Comedia famosa. [*Barcelona?* 1740?] 4°. T. **1737.** (17.)

—— [Another edition.] *Barcelona*, 1764. 4°. T. **1737.** (18.)

—— Comedia famosa. Los Tres Afectos de Amor. Piedad, desmayo, y valor. [*Madrid?* 1730?] 4°. **11728.** b. **64.**

—— [Another edition.] *Barcelona*, [1760?] 4°. **11725.** ee. **4.** (6.)

—— Comedia Famosa. Las Tres Justicias en una. *Barcelona*, 1771. 4°. **11728.** b. **65.**

—— [Another edition.] pp. 32. *Valencia*, 1782. 4°. **11725.** ee. **4.** (14.)

—— Comedia famosa. Los Tres Mayores Prodigios. *Barcelona*, [1810?] 4°. **11728.** b. **66.**

—— Troya Abrasada. *See* infra: WORKS WRITTEN IN COLLABORATION.

—— Un Castigo en Tres Venganças. *See* COMEDIAS. Parte veynte y ocho, de Comedias de varios autores. 1634. 4°. **11726.** g. **29.**

—— [Another edition.] Comedia famosa. De un Castigo tres Venganzas. *Valladolid*, [1750?] 4°. **11725.** ee. **5.** (2.)

—— [Another edition.] Comedia famosa. Un Castigo en tres Venganzas. [*Barcelona?* 1770?] 4°. T. **1737.** (3.)

—— La Vanda y la Flor. Comedia famosa. [*Madrid?* 1650?] 4°. C 108.bbb.20.(2.)

—— [Another edition.] Comedia famosa, Hazer del Amor Agrauio. De vn Ingenio de esta Corte [i.e. Calderon]. [In verse.] 1668. 4°. *See* AMOR. **11725.** c. **9.**

—— [Another edition.] *Madrid*, 1728. 4°. **11728.** b. **67.**

—— [Another edition.] pp. 32. *Valencia*, 1782. 4°. **11725.** ee. **4.** (15.)

—— Relacion, La Vanda, y la Flor. [An extract.] [*Valencia?* 1758?] 4°. T. **1953.** (58.)

—— [Another edition.] [*Madrid?* 1820?] 4°. **1072. g. 27. (59.)**

—— Vengarse con Fuego, y Agua. *See* supra: A Secreto Agravio, Secreta Venganza.

—— La Vida es Sueño. Comedia famosa. [*P. Crasbeeck: Lisbon,* 1647.] 4°. **11728. h. 16. (17.)**
Forming fol. 192–215 *of the collection* " *Doze comedias las mas grandiosas, etc.*"

—— [Another edition.] ff. 18. [*Madrid?* 1650?] 4°. **C.108.bbb.20.(12.)**

—— Comedia famosa. La Vida es Sueño. [*Madrid,* 1720?] 8°. **11728. f. 100. (12.)**

—— [Another edition.] [*Barcelona?* 1740?] 4°. **T. 1737. (19.)**

—— [Another edition.] *See* MUSEO. Museo Dramático Ilustrado. tom. 1. 1863, *etc.* 4°. **2298. i. 2.**

—— Edicion ilustrada con grabados. Primera edicion. pp. 44. *Madrid,* 1881. 8°. **11725. dd. 2.**

—— [Another edition.] pp. 123. *Madrid,* 1881. 16°. **11726. a. 5.**

—— [Another edition.] *See* infra: APPENDIX. Homenaje á Calderon, *etc.* 1881. 4°. **1869. b. 20.**

—— [Another edition.] Texto cotejado con el de las mejores ediciones por D. J. E. Hartzenbusch, y biografía del autor por D. C. A. de la Barrera. pp. 128. *Madrid,* 1881. 8°. **11726. b. 5.**

—— [Another edition.] With notes and vocabulary by William Wistar Comfort. pp. 180. *American Book Co.: New York,* [1904.] 8°. **11725. df. 3.**

—— [Another edition.] pp. 94. *Chatto & Windus: London; Strassburg* [printed, 1907.] 16°. [*Bibliotheca Romanica.* no. 8.] **012207.f.22/6.**

—— [Another edition.] Edited by Milton A. Buchanan . . . Vol. I. [The text.] pp. 135. *Toronto; Edinburgh* printed, 1909. 8°. [*University of Toronto Studies. Philological series.* Extra vol.] **Ac.2702/11.**
No more published.

—— [Another edition.] Edited . . . by H. J. Chaytor. pp. xiii. 116. *London,* 1923. 8°. [*Blackie's Spanish Series.*] **W.P. 7248/4.**

—— [Another edition.] pp. 154. *Madrid,* [1924.] 8°. **11728. aaa. 9.**

—— Das Leben als ein Traum . . . Aus dem Italiänischen übersetzt . . . D. F. H. W. M. (La Vie est un songe, *etc.*) [A translation by M. J. F. Scharfenstein of G. A. Cicognini's Italian version of Calderon's "La Vida es Sueño." With the French translation of T. S. Gueullette printed opposite.] pp. 167. 1750. 8°. *See* LEBEN. **11725. f. 11.**

—— Life's a Dream . . . Translated . . . by Frank Birch and J. B. Trend, *etc.* pp. xiii. 72. *W. Heffer & Sons: Cambridge,* 1925. 8°. **11726. bbb. 47.**

—— Life is a Dream. Translated . . . by H. Carter. pp. 125. *The Author: Sanderstead,* 1928. 16°. **11728. de. 11.**

—— Sigismundus, Prinse van Polen: of, het Leven is een droom. Den laatsten druk. [By Calderon, translated by — Schouwenbergh.] pp. 80. 1705. 8°. *See* SIGISMUND, *Prince of Poland.* **11725. a. 28.**

—— Sigismundus Prins van Polen, of het Leeven is een droom, *etc.* (Aldus verändert en herrymt door N: W: op den Hooff.) pp. 72. 1767. 8°. *See* SIGISMUND, *Prince of Poland.* **11755. aa. 35. (3.)**

—— Het Leven een droom . . . Uit het Spaansch vertaald door A. S. Kok. Voorafgegaan door eene verhandeling over Calderon en het Spaansche drama. [With a portrait.] pp. 215. *Amsterdam,* 1871. 8°. **11726. aaa. 30.**

—— La Vie est un songe . . . Traduction en vers par Louis Vasco. [With a portrait.] 1892. *See* DUNKIRK.—*Société Dunkerquoise pour l'Encouragement des Sciences, des Lettres et des Arts.* Mémoires, *etc.* vol. 26. 1853, *etc.* 8°. **Ac. 322.**

—— La Vie est un songe. Comédie . . . Traduite de l'espagnol par Alexandre Arnoux. pp. 31. *Paris,* 1922. 8°. [*Collection nouvelle de la France dramatique.* no. 10.] **P.P. 4296. h. (2.)**

—— Das Leben ein Traum. Schauspiel in fünf Acten . . . neu übersetzt und für die deutsche Bühne bearbeitet von Paul Herlth. pp. xxxv. 97. *Berlin,* 1868. 8°. **11726. aaa. 29.**

—— Das Leben ein Traum. Schauspiel in fünf Akten. [Translated by Joseph Schreyvogel.] pp. x. 59. *Stuttgart,* 1868. 8°. **11747. bb. 7.**

—— [Another edition.] Nach dem Spanischen, von C. A. West [pseudonym of J. Schreyvogel]. pp. 67. *Leipzig,* [1871.] 16°. **012207. f. 1. (1.)**

—— Az Élet Álom. Szinmű három felvonásban . . . Fordította Győry Vilmos. pp. 160. *Pesten,* 1870. 8°. [*Kisfaludy-Társaság. Spanyol szinműtár.* füz. 3.] **Ac. 8983/4.**

—— La Vita è un sogno. Comedia del Signor . . . Giacinto Andrea Cicognini. [An adaptation of "La Vida es Sueño."] pp. 128. 1663. 12°. *See* CICOGNINI (G. A.) **638. b. 7. (3.)**

—— [Another edition.] 1664. 12°. *See* COCIGNINI (G. A.) **638. b. 9. (3.)**

—— Życie snem . . . Dramat . . . dziejący się w Polsce w przekładzie J. Szujskiego. pp. 138. *we Lwowie,* 1882. 8°. **11728. bb. 8.**

—— Lifvet en dröm. Skådespel i fem akter. Fri bearbetning af F. A. Dahlgren. pp. 81. *Stockholm,* 1858. 12°. **11726. b. 22.**

—— Relacion de la Comedia: La Vida es Sueño. [An extract.] *Valencia,* 1758. 4°. **T. 1953. (29.)**

—— La Vida es Sueño . . . adaptado á manera de cuento para los niños por Ramón María Tenreiro, e ilustrado por Marco. pp. 119. *Madrid,* [1915.] 8°. **11725. aa. 30.**

—— *See* BOEDO (F.) Iberismo de Lope de Vega. Dos Españas. Segismundo ¿es el Contraquijote? 1935. 8°. **11858. aa. 4.**

—— *See* CUBAS (M.) La Vida es Sueño. Novela tomada del célebre drama de D. Pedro Calderon de la Barca, *etc.* 1881. 8°. **11726. aaa. 3.**

—— *See* FARINELLI (A.) La Vita è un sogno. [With a portrait.] 1916. 8°. **11876.m.1/2.**

—— *See* FUNES (E.) Segismundo. Estudio crítico. [Essays on "La Vida es Sueño."] 1899. 8°. **011852. e. 19.**

CALDERÓN DE LA BARCA (PEDRO) [COMEDIAS.—SINGLE COMEDIAS.]

—— *See* GONZÁLEZ OLMEDO (F.) Las Fuentes de "La Vida es Sueño," *etc.* 1928. 8°. **011824. b. 70.**

—— *See* RÍOS DE LAMPÉREZ (B. dle os) "La Vida es Sueño" y los diez Segismundos de Calderón. 1926. 8°. **011840.** d. **33.**

—— *See* RISCO (A. L.) El Segismundo histórico de "La Vida es sueño." 1949. 8°. [*Revista de la Universidad de Buenos Aires.* no. 336.] Ac. **2694.** a/**10.**

—— *See* WILSON (Edward M.) La Vida es sueño, *etc.* 1947. 8°. **11861.** h. **12.**

—— La Virgen del Sagrario. *See* supra: Origen, Pérdida, y Restauracion de la Virgen, *etc.*

—— La gran comedia, Zelos aun del ayre matan, *etc.* 1663. *See* SPAIN. [*Appendix.—Miscellaneous.*] Primera [*etc.*] parte de Comedias escogidas, *etc.* pt. 19. 1652, *etc.* 4°. **11725.** b. **19.**

—— [Another edition.] [1675?] *See* SPAIN. [*Appendix.—Miscellaneous.*] Primera [*etc.*] parte de Comedias escogidas, *etc.* pt. 41. 1652, *etc.* 4°. **11725.** c. **20.**

—— [Another edition.] [*Madrid?* 1750?] 4°. **11725.** ee. **3.** (**9.**)

—— [Another edition.] *Barcelona,* [1770?] 4°. **11728.** b. **69.**

—— Beaucoup de bruit pour rien, comédie . . . imitée de l'espagnol de Caldéron, *etc.* [1794.] 8°. **11738.** dd. **25.** (3.)

AUTOS.

—— [For Autos included in collections of the Comedias:] *See* supra: COMEDIAS.—*Collections.*

COLLECTIONS.

Spanish.

—— Auto de las plantas.—Del pleito matrimonial del cuerpo, y el alma.—El cubo de la Almudena.—El teatro del mundo. *See* AUTOS. Autos Sacramentales, *etc.* 1655. 4°. **1072.** l. **2.**

—— El Diuino Iason.—La Cena del Rey Baltasar. *See* ROBLES (J. de) Navidad y Corpus Christi, *etc.* 1664. 4°. **11726.** d. **27.**

—— Autos Sacramentales, Alegoricos, y Historiales . . . Primera parte. [With an engraved portrait.] pp. 459. *I. Fernandez de Buendia: Madrid,* 1677. 4°. C. **63.** b. **39.**

No more published.

—— Autos Sacramentales, Alegoricos, y Historiales . . . Obras posthumas que . . . saca originales à luz Don Pedro de Pando y Mier, *etc.* [With a portrait.] 6 pt. *Madrid,* 1717. 4°. **11725.** g. **5.**

—— Autos sacramentales . . . Parte quinta. pp. 423. *Madrid,* 1717. 4°. **11729.** b. **25.**

A different edition from the preceding. Imperfect; wanting pt. 1–4, 6.

—— Autos Sacramentales, Alegoricos, y Historiales . . . Obras posthumas, que saca à luz Don Juan Fernandez de Apontes. 6 tom. *Madrid,* 1759, 60. 4°. **11725.** d. **14.**

—— [Another copy.] **11725.** cc. **4.**

—— Autos Sacramentales. Edición y notas de Angel Valbuena Prat. 2 vol. *Madrid,* 1926, 27. 8°. **11728.** e. **102.**

Part of the "Clásicos Castellanos."

CALDERÓN DE LA BARCA (PEDRO) [AUTOS.—COLLECTIONS.]

English.

—— Mysteries of Corpus Christi. From the Spanish. By Denis Florence Mac-Carthy. [Containing "Belshazzar's Feast" and "The Divine Philothea."] (With a commentary and an introductory discourse . . . from the German of Dr. Franz Lorinser; and an essay . . . from the Spanish of Don Eduardo Gonzalez Pedroso.) *James Duffy: Dublin,* 1867. 8°. **11725.** a. **16.**

German.

—— Geistliche Schauspiele . . . Uebersetzt von Joseph Freiherrn von Eichendorff. pp. 346. *Stuttgart & Tübingen,* 1846. 8°. **1342.** g. **27.**

—— Don Pedro Calderon's de la Barca Geistliche Festspiele. In deutscher Übersetzung mit erklärendem Commentar und einer Einleitung über die Bedeutung und den Werth dieser Dichtungen herausgegeben von Franz Lorinser. Bd. 1, 2. *Regensburg,* 1856, 57. 8°. **11726.** e. **36.**

Imperfect; wanting Bd. 3–18.

SINGLE AUTOS.

—— La Cena de Baltasar. pp. vii. 56. *University Press: Cambridge,* 1925. 8°. [*Cambridge Plain Texts.*] W.P. **6501.**

—— Relacion del auto sacramental intitulado: La Devocion de la Missa. [*Cordoba?* 1813?] **12330.** l. **1.** (**86.**)

—— [Another copy.] **12330.** l. **1.** (**87.**)

—— [Another copy.] **12330.** l. **1.** (**90.**)

—— Relacion del auto sacramental intitulado: La Divina Philotea. *Cordoba,* [1813?] 4°. **12330.** l. **1.** (**84.**)

—— Auto inédito "El Divino Orfeo." *In:* CABAÑAS (P.) El Mito de Orfeo en la literatura española, *etc.* pp. 239–287. 1948. 8°. [*Anejos de Cuadernos de Literatura.* no. 1.] Ac. **132/16.** (**3.**)

—— [Las Espigas de Ruth.] *See* KRALIK VON MEYRSWALDEN (R.) Die Ähren der Ruth. Ein geistliches Festspiel mit Chören nach Calderon, *etc.* [1913.] 8°. **11748.** ff. **15.**

—— [El Gran Teatro del Mundo.] Das grosse Welttheater. Sakramentsspiel . . . Nach Josef von Eichendorffs Übersetzung für die Einsiedler Aufführung bearbeitet. pp. 56. 1935. 8°. *See* EINSIEDELN.—*Gesellschaft der Geistlichen Spiele.* **20010.** ee. **11.**

—— Lo Que va del Hombre á Dios. Auto sacramental, alegórico. [1750?] 4°. **12330.** l. **14.** (**13.**)

Imperfect; wanting all after p. 16.

—— [Los Misterios de la Misa.] *See* KRALIK VON MEYRSWALDEN (R.) Die Geheimnisse der Messe. Ein geistliches Festspiel nach Calderon, *etc.* [1914.] 16°. **11747.** aaaa. **18.**

—— No hay más fortuna que Dios. Edited with introduction and notes by Alexander A. Parker. pp. xl. 91. *Manchester University Press:* [*Manchester,*] 1949 [1950]. 8°. [*Spanish Texts.*] Ac. **2671/50.** (**2.**)

—— [Las Ordenes Militares.] Die geistlichen Ritterorden. Auto sacramental . . . übersetzt von Franz Lorinser. pp. 175. *Regensburg,* 1855. 16°. **11725.** a. **15.**

—— Relacion del auto sagramental intitulado: Las Ordenes Militares. [An extract.] *Cordoba,* [1813?] 4°. **12330.** l. **1.** (**89.**)

—— Auto sacramental alegorico, Protestacion de la Fè. [*Madrid*, 1760 ?] 4°. **11728**. a. **70**.

—— Relacion del auto sacramental intitulado: El Veneno y la Triaca. *Cordoba*, [1815 ?] 4°. **11450**. h. **6**. (**7**.)

—— El Verdadero Dios Pan. Auto sacramental alegórico de don P. Calderón de la Barca. Texto y estudio por José M. de Osma. pp. 149. *Lawrence*, 1949. 8°. [*University of Kansas Publications. Humanistic Studies.* no. 28.] Ac. **2692**. i/4.

—— La Vida es Sueño. Auto sacramental. *See* infra: APPENDIX. Homenaje á Calderon, *etc.* 1881. 4°. **1869**. b. **20**.

APPENDIX.

—— *See* MACGARRY (Mary F. de S.) The Allegorical and Metaphorical Language in the Autos Sacramentales of Calderón, *etc.* 1937. 8°. [*Catholic University of America. Department of Romance Languages and Literatures. Publications.* no. 16.] Ac. **2692**. yab.

—— *See* PARKER (Alexander A.) The Allegorical Drama of Calderon. An introduction to the Autos Sacramentales. 1943. 8°. **11865**. ff. **20**.

—— *See* VALBUENA PRAT (A.) Los Autos Sacramentales de Calderón, *etc.* 1924. 8°. [*Revue hispanique.* tom. 61. no. 139.] P.P. **4331**. aea.

POEMS.

—— Poesías . . . Con anotaciones y un discurso . . . sobre los plagios, que . . . cometió Le Sage, al escribir su Gil Blas de Santillana. Por Adolfo de Castro. pp. 128. *Cádiz*, 1845. 8°. **11451**. d. **9**.

—— [Selected poems.] 1855. *See* ARIBAU (B. C.) Biblioteca de Autores Españoles, *etc.* tom. 35. 1849, *etc.* 8°. **12232.f.1/35.**

—— Poesías. pp. 96. *Madrid*, 1874. 32°. **528**. m. **23/85**.

—— Poesías Inéditas. [The editor's preface signed: F. P.] pp. 189. *Madrid*, 1881. 16°. [*Biblioteca Universal.* tom. 71.] **739**. a. **71**.

—— Afectos de un corazon arrepentido, hablando con Dios en forma de confession. pp. 36. *Madrid*, 1755. 4°. **1077**. l. **41**. (**1**.)

—— [Another edition.] *See* BIBLE.—*Psalms.—Selections.* [*Polyglott.—Single Psalms.*] Traduccion en verso del Salmo L. de David, *etc.* 1879. 8°. **03089**. e. **2**.

—— Discurso metrico-ascetico, sobre la inscripción Psalle, et Sile, que esta gravada en la verja del choro de la santa iglesia de Toledo . . . Sácale á luz Don Antonio Fernandez de Azevedo, *etc.* pp. 16. *Madrid*, 1741. 4°. **1077**. l. **41**. (**3**.)

—— Lagrimas, que vierte una alma arrepentida á la hora de la muerte á los pies de Christo crucificado. pp. 18. *Madrid*, 1757. 4°. **11451**. e. **39**. (**5**.)

MINOR WORKS.

—— [For Entremeses, Loas, etc. included in collections of the Comedias:] *See* supra: COMEDIAS.—*Collections.*

—— Entremes de las Carnestolendas.—Entremes de la Plazuela de Santa Cruz. *See* RASGOS. Rasgos del Ocio, *etc.* 1661. 8°. **11725**. aa. **18**.

—— Loa Sacramental de Los Siete Sabios de Grecia.—Entremes de Pelicano, y Raton.—Entremes de las Lenguas. *See* SPAIN. [*Appendix.—Miscellaneous.*] Entremeses Varios, *etc.* [c. 1660.] **11725**. a. **29**.

—— El Labrador Gentilhombre.—Loa (para la comedia Hado y divisa de Leonido y de Marfisa). *See* CUBAS (M.) La Vida es Sueño. Novela tomada del célebre drama de D. Pedro Calderon de la Barca, *etc.* 1881. 8°. **11726**. aaa. **3**.

—— Deposicion . . . en favor de los profesores de la pintura, *etc.* *See* NIPHO (F. M.) Cajon de Sastre Literato, *etc.* 1781. 12°. **12352**. bb. **38**.

—— Calderón und die Malerei. Von Ernst Robert Curtius. [The text and a German translation of the "Deposicion." With a commentary.] 1936. 8°. [*Romanische Forschungen.* Bd. 50. Hft. 2.] P.P. **5044**. ad.

—— Entremes de la Franchota. [By Calderon.] [1780 ?] 16°. *See* FRANCHOTA. **11725**. aa. **2**. (**19**.)

—— Entremes de las Carnestolendas. [By Calderon.] pp. 16. [1750 ?] 16°. *See* CARNESTOLENDAS. **11726**. aa. **1**. (**3**.)

—— Entremes. Del Desafio de Juan Rana. [By Calderon.] [1760 ?] 16°. *See* RANA (J.) **11725**. aa. **3**. (**14**.)

—— [Another edition.] [1780 ?] 16°. *See* RANA (J.) **11726**. aa. **1**. (**34**.)

—— Entremes del Dragoncillo. *Barcelona*, [1750 ?] 16°. **11725**. aa. **1**. (**19**.)

—— [Another copy.] **11726**. aa. **4**. (**26**.)

—— Loa Sacramental del Relox. *See* ARCADIA. Arcadia de Entremeses, *etc.* 1723. 8°. **11725**. a. **9**.

—— Tratado defendiendo la nobleza de la pintura. *See* supra: Deposicion . . . en favor de los profesores de la pintura.

WORKS WRITTEN IN COLLABORATION.

—— [For editions of plays written in part by Calderón included in collections of the Comedias:] *See* supra: COMEDIAS.—*Collections.*

—— *See* AMIGO. Comedia famosa. El Mejor Amigo el Muerto . . . la primera jornada de L. de Velmonte . . . la tercera de don P. Calderon. [1700 ?] 4°. **1072**. h. **14**. (**12**.)

—— —— [1700 ?] 4°. **11728**. a. **44**.

—— —— [1740 ?] 4°. **11728**. a. **45**.

—— —— [1760 ?] 4°. **11728**. h. **8**. (**10**.)

—— *See* CABANI (F. de') *Countess di Montorio*, called FILIPPA CATANESE. Comedia famosa, El Monstruo de la Fortuna. De tres ingenios. [The first jornada by Calderon.] 1666. 4°. [*Primera, etc., parte de Comedias escogidas de los mejores de España.* pt. 24.] **11725**. c. **3**.

—— —— [1760 ?] 4°. **1342**. e. **1**. (**44**.)

—— *See* PASTOR. Comedia famosa. El Pastor Fido . . . La jornada primera es de Don A. Solès . . . la tercera de Don P. Calderòn. 1751. 4°. **1342**. f. **2**. (**11**.)

—— *See* REMEDIO. Comedia famosa, Enfermar con el Remedio, *etc.* [The first jornada by Calderon.] [1730 ?] 4°. T. **1733**. (**22**.)

—— —— [1730 ?] 4°. **11726**. f. **35**.

CALDERÓN DE LA BARCA (PEDRO) [WORKS WRITTEN IN COLLABORATION.]

—— El Polyfemo. Comedia famosa. De Don Pedro Calderon [or rather, the first jornada by A. Mira de Mescua, the second by J. Pérez de Montalbán, and the third by Calderon]. [*P. Crasbeeck: Lisbon*, 1647.] 4°. **11728**. h. **16**. (**10**.)
Forming ff. 23–42 of the collection entitled " Doze comedias las mas grandiosas, etc."

—— Troya Abrasada. Tragi-comedia en tres actos, *etc.* [By Calderon and J. de Zabaleta?] pp. 32. 1791. 4°. *See* TROY. **1342**. e. **4**. (**41**.)

—— [Another edition.] [Edited by George Tyler Northup.] 1913. *See* PERIODICAL PUBLICATIONS.—*Paris*. Revue hispanique, *etc.* tom. 29. 1894, *etc.* 8°. P.P. **4331**. aea.

—— Yerros de Naturaleza y Aciertos de la Fortuna. Comedia de Don Pedro Calderón de la Barca y Don Antonio Coello y Ochoa. Edición y observaciones preliminares de Eduardo Juliá Martínez. [With facsimiles.] pp. 174. *Madrid*, 1930. 8°. **20011**. e. **44**.

SELECTIONS.

—— Obra Lírica, *etc.* [Consisting chiefly of extracts from the plays.] pp. xviii. 194. *Barcelona*, 1943. 16°. **11453**. a. **14**.

DOUBTFUL OR SUPPOSITITIOUS WORKS.

—— [For editions of plays erroneously attributed to Calderón included in collections containing also authentic works of Calderón :] *See* supra : COMEDIAS.—*Collections*.

—— Comedia famosa. Vencerse es Mayor Valor. De Don Pedro Calderon [or rather, by D. and J. de Figueroa y Córdoba ?].
1658. *See* SPAIN. [*Appendix.—Miscellaneous.*] Primera [*etc.*] parte de Comedias escogidas, *etc.* pt. 11. 1652, *etc.* 4°. **11725**. b. **11**.

—— Dos Comedias atribuídas a Calderón de la Barca. (La Más Dichosa Venganza. Amor con Valor se Obliga.) [Edited, with an introduction, by E. Juliá Martínez.] pp. 223. *Madrid*, 1931. 8°. **20001**. dd. **49**.

—— [La Adúltera Penitente.] *See* CASTRO Y ROSSI (A. de) Una Joya Desconocida de Calderon [i.e. La Adúltera Penitente, here attributed to Calderon]. Estudio acerca de ella, *etc.* [With extracts.] 1881. 8°. **11840**. f. **17**. (**2**.)

—— El Alva con siete Soles. Comedia famosa. [Not by Calderon.] [*Madrid ?* 1700 ?] 4°. **11728**. a. **58**.

—— El Angel dela Guarda. Comedia famosa. [Sometimes attributed to J. de Valdivieso.] [*Madrid ?* 1700 ?] 4°. **11728**. a. **63**.

—— [Another edition.] MS. NOTE [by J. R. Chorley]. ff. 16. [*Madrid ?* 1700 ?] 4°. **11728**. h. **14**. (**19**.)

—— La Batalla de Sopetran. Comedia famosa. [Not by Calderon.] ff. 16. [*Madrid ?* 1750 ?] 4°. **11728**. a. **72**.

—— Cada uno con su igual. Comedia famosa. De Don Pedro Calderon [or rather by Blas de Mesa]. [*Madrid ?* 1720 ?] 4°. **11728**. a. **75**.

—— Comedia famosa, Las Canas en el Papel, y Dudoso en la Venganza. De Don Pedro Calderon [or rather, by Guillen de Castro]. 1661. *See* SPAIN. [*Appendix.—Miscellaneous.*] Primera [*etc.*] parte de Comedias escogidas, *etc.* pt. 14. 1652, *etc.* 4°. **11725**. b. **14**.

CALDERÓN DE LA BARCA (PEDRO) [DOUBTFUL OR SUPPOSITITIOUS WORKS.]

—— [Another edition.] ff. 16. [*Madrid*, 1700 ?] 4°. **87**. b. **1**. (**5**.)

—— [Another edition.] [*Seville ?* 1720 ?] 4°. **11728**. h. **15**. (**8**.)

—— [Another edition.] pp. 36. *Zaragoza*, [1750 ?] 4°. **11728**. a. **78**.

—— Casarse por Vengarse. Comedia famosa de Don Pedro Calderon [or rather, by F. de Rojas Zorrilla]. pp. 54. [*Madrid ?* 1700 ?] 4°. **11728**. h. **15**. (**10**.)

—— La Codicia rompe el Saco. Comedia famosa. [Not by Calderon.] pp. 32. *Sevilla*, [1720 ?] 4°. **11728**. h. **15**. (**12**.)

—— [Another copy.] **11725**. ee. **2**. (**3**.)

—— [Another edition.] pp. 32. *Barcelona*, 1756. 4°. **11728**. a. **85**.

—— La Conquista del Alma. [Not by Calderon.] pp. 32. *Salamanca*, [1790 ?] 4°. **11728**. a. **89**.

—— La Critica del Amor. Comedia famosa. [Not by Calderon.] [*Barcelona ?* 1720 ?] 4°. T. **1737**. (**5**.)

—— De Alcala a Madrid. Comedia famosa. De Don Pedro Calderon [or rather, by A. de Claramonte]. ff. 16. MS. NOTE [by J. R. Chorley]. [*Madrid ?* 1730 ?] 4°. **11728**. h. **8**. (**12**.)
Cropped.

—— Los Desdichados Dichosos. 1658. *See* SPAIN. [*Appendix.—Miscellaneous.*] Primera [*etc.*] parte de Comedias escogidas, *etc.* pt. 12. 1652, *etc.* 4°. **11725**. b. **12**.

—— El Dia de San Blas en Madrid. Comedia famosa. [Not by Calderon.] ff. 16. [*Madrid ?* 1700 ?] 4°. **11728**. a. **95**.

—— La Dicha del Retraydo. Comedia famosa. [Not by Calderon.] [*Barcelona ?* 1700 ?] 4°. T. **1737**. (**7**.)

—— Duelo de Honor, y Amistad. Comedia famosa. [*Madrid ?* 1740 ?] 4°. **11725**. ee. **2**. (**1**.)

—— Los Empeños de Seis Horas. Comedia famosa, de Don Pedro Calderon [or rather, by Antonio Coello]. pp. 32. *Sevilla*, [1720 ?] 4°. **11728**. b. **8**.

—— [For editions of " The Adventures of Five Hours " adapted by Sir Samuel Tuke from " Los Empeños de Seis Horas," sometimes attributed to Calderón :] *See* TUKE (*Sir* S.) *Bart.*

—— Los Empeños de un Plumage, y Origen de los Guevaras. Comedia famosa. [Not by Calderon.] pp. 32. *Sevilla*, [1730 ?] 4°. **11728**. b. **7**.

—— [Another edition.] [*Madrid ?* 1750 ?] 4°. **11725**. ee. **2**. (**4**.)

—— [Another edition.] pp. 32. 1782. 4°. *See* INGENIO. **1342**. e. **2**. (**41**.)

—— Engañar para Reynar, comedia famosa. De Don Pedro Calderon [or rather, by Antonio Enriquez Gomez]. pp. 24. [*Seville ?* 1750 ?] 4°. **11725**. ee. **5**. (**3**.)

—— [Another edition.] pp. 32. *Valencia*, 1762. 4°. **11728**. b. **10**.

—— Enseñarse a ser Buen Rey. Comedia famosa. [*Madrid ?* 1650 ?] 4°. **C.108.bbb.20.(6.)**

—— Comedia famosa. El Escandalo de Grecia contra las Santas Imagenes. 1658. *See* SPAIN. [*Appendix.—Miscellaneous.*] Primera [*etc.*] parte de Comedias escogidas, *etc.* pt. 11. 1652, *etc.* 4°. **11725**. b. **11**.

—— Comedia famosa. El Escandalo de Grecia contra las Santas Imágenes. [Not by Calderon.] pp. 28. *Salamanca*, [1790?] 4°. **11728**. b. **11**.

—— [Another copy.] **11728**. i. **21**. (**10**.)

—— El Esclavo de Maria. Comedia famosa. [Not by Calderon.] [*Madrid?* 1740?] 4°. **11728**. b. **12**.

—— Comedia famosa. La Española de Florencia. De Don Pedro Calderon [or rather by Lope de Vega?] 1658. *See* SPAIN. [*Appendix.—Miscellaneous.*] Primera [*etc.*] parte de Comedias escogidas, *etc.* pt. 12. 1652, *etc.* 4°. **11725**. b. **12**.

—— La Española de Florencia. Comedia famosa. De Don Pedro Calderon de la Barca [or rather, by Lope de Vega?]. pp. 32. *Sevilla*, [1720?] 4°. **11728**. b. **14**.

—— [Another copy.] **11728**. h. **15**. (**19**.)

—— [Another edition.] Edited, with an introduction and notes, by S. L. Millard Rosenberg. A dissertation, *etc.* pp. xlii. 132. *Philadelphia*, 1911. 8°. [*Publications of the University of Pennsylvania. Series in Romanic Languages and Literatures.* no. 5.] Ac. **2692**. p/**10a**.

—— Comedia famosa. El Galàn sin Dama. De Don Pedro Calderon de la Barca [or rather, by Antonio Hurtado de Mendoza]. pp. 36. *Valladolid*, [1750?] 4°. **11728**. b. **19**.

—— Entremes de Guardadme las Espaldas. [Sometimes attributed to Calderon.] [1780?] 16°. *See* ESPALDAS. **11726**. aa. **4**. (**37**.)

—— Haz bien, y Guardate. Comedia famosa. [Not by Calderon.] ff. 16. [*Madrid?* 1700?] 4°. **11728**. b. **24**.

—— El Impossible mas Facil. Comedia famosa. De Don Pedro Calderon [or rather, by J. de Matos Fragoso?]. [*Valencia?* 1720?] 4°. T. **1737**. (**12**.)

—— [Another edition.] [*Madrid?* 1730?] 4°. **11728**. b. **27**.

—— [Another edition.] [*Madrid?* 1730?] 4°. **87**. b. **1**. (**4**.)
Other editions, in which the work is attributed to Matos Fragoso, are entered under his name.

—— El Ingrats. Corona de comedias. Comedia famosa. [Not by Calderon.] pp. 32. *Sevilla*, [1720?] 4°. **11728**. b. **28**.

—— [Another copy.] MS. NOTE [by J. R. Chorley]. **11728**. h. **4**. (**8**.)

—— Lo que haze un Manto en Madrid. Comedia famosa. ff. 18. [*Madrid?* 1750?] 4°. **11725**. ee. **2**. (**8**.)

—— El Lucero de Castilla y Privado Perseguido. Comedia en tres actos, inedita. De D. Pedro Calderon de la Barca [or rather, by L. Velez de Guevara]. pp. 113. *Madrid*, 1837. 16°. **11725**. a. **13**.

—— Comedia famosa, El Mejor Padre de Pobres. De Don Pedro Calderon [or rather, by J. Perez de Montalbán]. [*Seville?* 1700?] 4°. **11728**. h. **14**. (**14**.)

—— [Another edition.] [*Seville?* 1720?] 4°. **11728**. b. **39**.

—— El Mercader de Toledo, Vara de Medir, y Accion del Mejor Testigo. Comedia famosa. [Not by Calderon.] pp. 31. *Sevilla*, [1720?] 4°. **11728**. b. **40**.

—— Comedia famosa. No avrá mal donde ay Mugèr. pp. 28. *Sevilla*, [1750?] 4°. **11725**. ee. **5**. (**11**.)

—— [Another copy.] **11725**. ee. **2**. (**11**.)

—— No son Todos Ruyseñores. Comedia famosa, de Don Pedro Calderon [or rather, by Lope de Vega]. pp. 32. *Sevilla*, [1700?] 4°. **11728**. b. **47**.

—— Entremes de Pelicano y Raton. De Calderon [or rather, by G. de Cancer y Velasco]. *Valladolid*, [1750?] 16°. **11726**. aa. **4**. (**63**.)

—— La gran comedia, Quien calla, otorga. [*Barcelona?* 1710?] 4°. T. **1737**. (**15**.)

—— La Respuesta está en la Mano. Comedia famosa. [Not by Calderon.] [*Madrid?* 1700?] 4°. **11728**. b. **57**.

—— Comedia famosa. El Rigor de las Desdichas, y Mudanzas de Fortuna. De un ingenio de la corte [i.e. P. Calderon de la Barca?]. pp. 40. [1750?] 4°. *See* RIGOR. **11726**. f. **81**.

—— Relacion de la comedia intitulada: El Rigor de las Desdichas, y Mudanzas de Fortuna. *Valencia*, 1758. 4°. T. **1953**. (**76**.)

—— [Another edition.] *Malaga*, 1782. 4°. T. **1986**. (**12**.)

—— Relacion segunda: El Rigor de las Desdichas, *etc.* *Valencia*, 1758. 4°. T. **1953**. (**75**.)

—— La Roca de el Honor. Comedia famosa. pp. 28. *Sevilla*, [1730?] 4°. **11725**. ee. **2**. (**16**.)

—— [Another copy.] **11725**. ee. **5**. (**17**.)

—— Seneca, y Neron. Comedia famosa. [*Madrid?* 1700?] 4°. **11726**. e. **1**. (**2**.)

—— El Texedor de Segovia, comedia famosa. De Don Pedro Calderon [or rather, by J. Ruiz de Alarcon y Mendoza]. Primera parte. pp. 31. [*Madrid?* 1670?] 4°. T. **1741**. (**18**.)

—— El Texedor de Segovia, Comedia famosa. De Don Pedro Calderon [or rather, by J. Ruiz de Alarcon y Mendoza]. Segunda parte. pp. 31. [*Madrid?* 1670?] 4°. T. **1741**. (**19**.)

—— Vencer Amor, y Ambicion. Comedia famosa. ff. 16. [*Madrid?* 1760?] 4°. **11725**. ee. **2**. (**12**.)

—— Comedia famosa. El Vencimiento de Turno. De Don P. Calderon [or rather, by A. M. del Campo]. 1658. *See* SPAIN. [*Appendix.—Miscellaneous.*] Primera [*etc.*] parte de Comedias escogidas, *etc.* vol. 12. 1652, *etc.* 4°. **11725**. b. **12**.

—— Zelos no ofenden al Sol. Comedia famosa. [*Barcelona?* 1730?] 4°. T. **1737**. (**20**.)

—— [Another edition.] pp. 32. *Salamanca*, [1750?] 4°. **11728**. h. **16**. (**15**.)

—— [Another edition.] pp. 28. *Sevilla*, [1770?] 4°. **11725**. ee. **5**. (**18**.)

—— [Another edition.] pp. 34. 1782. 4°. *See* INGENIO. **1342**. e. **4**. (**61**.)

—— Láska v nárožním domě. Veselohra ve 2 jednáních dle Calderona a Cosmara vzdělána od Jos. K. Tyla. *See* MOSENTHAL (S. H.) Svatojanský dvůr, *etc.* 1871. 8°. [*Divadelní ochotník.* Nové sbírky. sv. 35.] **11758**. p. **6**. (**5**.)

APPENDIX.

—— *See* ABERT (J.) Schlaf und Traum bei Calderon. 1880. 8°. [URLICHS (*C. L.*) *Strena philologa Ludovico Urlichsio . . . oblata.*] **11312**. k. **32**.

—— *See* ARNESEN KALL (B. M.) Den Spanske Trilogi, *etc.* (Calderon de la Barca.) 1884. 8°. **11825. df. 29.**

—— *See* BAUMGARTNER (Alexander) Calderon: Festspiel zum 25. Mai 1881. Mit einer Einleitung über Calderons Leben und Werke. 1881. 8°. **11747. d. 24. (4.)**

—— *See* BAUMGARTNER (Alexander) Calderón; poemita dramático precedido de una introducción sobre la vida y las obras del poeta español, *etc.* 1882. 8°. **11746. f. 15. (1.)**

—— *See* BREYMANN (H.) Calderon-Studien. (Die Calderon-Literatur.) 1905. 8°. **11853. c. 21.**

—— *See* CASTRO Y ROSSI (A. de) Discurso acerca de las costumbres públicas y privadas de los Españoles en el siglo XVII. fundado en el estudio de las comedias de Calderón, *etc.* 1881. 8°. **11840. l. 26.**

—— *See* COMMELERÁN Y GÓMEZ (F. A.) D. Pedro Calderon de la Barca . . . Estudio biográfico-crítico. 1881. 8°. **10632. aaa. 13.**

—— *See* COTARELO Y MORI (E.) Ensayo sobre la vida y obras de Don Pedro Calderón de la Barca. (Primera parte.) [With portraits.] 1921, *etc.* 8°. [*Boletín de la Real Academia Española.* tom. 8, 9, 10.] Ac. **144/16.**

—— *See* DORER (E.) Beiträge zur Calderon-Literatur. 1884, *etc.* 8°. **11840. e. 53.**

—— *See* DORER (E.) Die Calderon-Literatur in Deutschland, *etc.* 1881. 8°. **819. h. 44. (7.)**

—— *See* DORER (E.) Goethe und Calderon, *etc.* 1881. 8°. **638. e. 43. (5.)**

—— *See* D'ORSEY (Alexander J. D.) Calderon: a poem in honour of the second centenary of the immortal poet. 1881. 8°. **11647. f. 20. (5.)**

—— *See* EGUÍA RUIZ (C.) Cervantes, Calderón, *etc.* (Don Pedro Calderón de la Barca. Indagaciones gentilicias y etnográficas.) 1951. 8°. [*Anejos de Cuadernos de Literatura.* no. 8.] Ac. **132/16. (3.)**

—— *See* ELLITS ( ) Othello and Desdemona . . . With a notice of Calderon's debt to Shakespeare. 1887. 12°. **11764. bb. 9.**

—— *See* FASTENRATH (J.) Calderon de la Barca, *etc.* 1881. 8°. **11525. f. 10. (8.)**

—— *See* FREDÉN (N. G. T. M.) La Cena del amor. Estudios sobre Calderón de la Barca. 1954. 8°. **11871. e. 14.**

—— *See* GARCÍA (P. de A.) Calderon de la Barca. Su vida y su teatro, *etc.* 1881. 8°. **10632. aaa. 12.**

—— *See* GONZÁLEZ RUIZ (N.) and PEERS (E. A.) Six Tales from Calderon, *etc.* [1934.] 8°. **012941. a. 35.**

—— *See* GRINDA Y FORNER (J.) Las Ciencias Positivas en Calderón de la Barca, *etc.* 1881. 8°. **11826. bbb. 2.**

—— *See* GUENTHNER (Engelbert) Calderon und seine Werke. 1888. 8°. **011840. h. 34.**

—— *See* GUERRA Y RIBERA (M. de) Apelacion al tribunal de los doctos, justa defensa de la aprobacion a las comedias de Don Pedro Calderon de la Barca, *etc.* 1752. 4°. **1421. g. 2.**

—— *See* HASELL (Elizabeth J.) Calderon. 1879. 8°. [*Foreign Classics for English Readers.*] **2322. a.**

—— *See* HEIBERG (J. L.) De poëseos dramaticæ genere hispanico, præsertim de Petro Calderone de la Barca, *etc.* 1817. 8°. **1342. d. 2.**

—— *See* HILBORN (Harry W.) A Chronology of the Plays of D. P. Calderón de la Barca. 1938. 8°. **11865. bb. 11.**

—— *See* JIMÉNEZ Y HURTADO (M.) Cuentos españoles contenidos en las producciones dramáticas de Calderon de la Barca, *etc.* [1881.] 8°. **11725. bb. 3.**

—— *See* LAGARRIGUE (J.) L'Espagne et Calderon de la Barca. 1881. 8°. **011853. b. 13.**

—— *See* LARA (G. A. de) Obelisco funebre, pyramide funesto . . . á la inmortal memoria de D. Pedro Calderon de la Barca, *etc.* 1684. 8°. **11450. dd. 41.**

—— *See* LASSO DE LA VEGA Y ARGÜELLES (A.) Calderon de la Barca. Estudio, *etc.* 1881. 8°. **11825. ee. 18.**

—— *See* LECHANTEUR DE PONTAUMONT (E.) De la littérature espagnole et de Calderon. 1847. 8°. **11852. r. 31.**

—— *See* LEWES (George H.) The Spanish Drama. Lope de Vega and Calderon. 1846. 12°. **1156. d. 2. (2.)**

—— *See* LINDNER (E.) *Dr.* Die poetische Personifikation in den Jugendschauspielen Calderon's, *etc.* 1904. 8°. **11822. r. 4/32.**

—— *See* LOPEZ DE AYALA (A.) La Mejor Corona. Loa para celebrar el aniversario del nacimiento de Don Pedro Calderon, *etc.* 1868. 8°. **11726. bbb. 30. (9.)**

—— *See* MADARIAGA (S. de) Shelley & Calderon, *etc.* 1920. 8°. **011851. c. 5.**

—— *See* MENÉNDEZ Y PELAYO (M.) Calderón y su Teatro . . . Conferencias, *etc.* 1881. 12°. **11726. aaa. 4.**

—— *See* MENÉNDEZ Y PELAYO (M.) Edición nacional de las obras completas de Menéndez Pelayo, *etc.* (vol. 8. Calderón y su teatro.) 1940, *etc.* 8°. **12232. e. 1.**

—— *See* MANTEROLA (J.) Euskal-Oroitza. Calderon aundiari berebigarren eunteko mugaldian. (Recuerdo basco. Al gran Calderon en el segundo centenario de su muerte.) [1881.] 4°. **11586. i. 2.**

—— *See* NEUBAUER (H.) Calderon. Eine Würdigung, *etc.* 1892. 8°. **011850. g. 8. (10.)**

—— *See* ORTIZ (G.) Die Weltanschauung Calderons. 1897. 8°. **8461. eee. 1/5.**

—— *See* PEREIRA (A. J.) Shakspeare y Calderón. Notas para un paralelo entre ambos autores, *etc.* [1881?] 8°. **011768. bb. 6.**

—— *See* PÉREZ PASTOR (C.) Documentos para la Biografía de D. Pedro Calderón de la Barca, *etc.* 1905, *etc.* 8°. **10633. h. 12.**

—— *See* PFANDL (L.) Ausdrucksformen des archaischen Denkens und des Unbewussten bei Calderón. 1937. 8°. [FINKE (*H.*) *Gesammelte Aufsätze zur Kulturgeschichte Spaniens, etc.* Bd. 6.] Ac. **2026/10. (1.)**

—— *See* PICATOSTE (F.) Centenario de Calderon. Memoria, *etc.* (Tema. Conceptos de la naturaleza y de sus leyes que de las obras de Calderon resulta, *etc.*) 1881. 8°. **11825. o. 15. (1.)**

—— *See* PUTMAN (J. J.) Mijne "Studiën" over Calderon en zijne geschriften verdedigd, *etc.* 1881. 8°. **11850. k. 10. (1.)**

—— *See* RIBEIRO (J. P.) Don Pedro Calderon de la Barca. Rapido esboço da sua vida e escriptos. 1881. 8°. **10631. f. 9.**

CALDERÓN DE LA BARCA (Pedro) [Appendix.]

—— *See* Rubió y Lluch (A.) El Sentimiento del Honor en el Teatro de Calderón, *etc.* 1882. 8°. **011795. e. 26.**

—— *See* Sanchez-Moguel (A.) Calderon et Goethe . . . Mémoire, *etc.* 1883. 8°. **11840. b. 37.**

—— *See* Savine (A.) Pedro Calderon de la Barca d'après de récentes publications, *etc.* 1890. 8°. **011824. h. 31. (6.)**

—— *See* Schmidt (F. W. V.) Die Schauspiele Calderon's dargestellt und erläutert, *etc.* 1857. 8°. **2306. g. 6.**

—— *See* Schmidt (Leopold Valentin) Ueber die vier bedeutendsten Dramatiker der Spanier . . . Calderon, *etc.* 1858. 8°. **11795. cc. 42. (1.)**

—— *See* Silva (R.) The Religious Dramas of Calderón. 1946. 8°. [Peers (*Edgar A.*) *Liverpool Studies in Spanish Literature.* ser. 2.] W.P. **11367/4.**

—— *See* Sofer (J.) Die Welttheater Hugo von Hofmannsthals und ihre Voraussetzungen bei Heraklit und Calderon. 1934. 8°. **11797. eee. 27.**

—— *See* Soler y Arqués (C.) Los Españoles segun Calderón. Discurso, *etc.* 1881. 8°. **11840. l. 31. (5.)**

—— *See* Toro y Duran (R. del) Apuntes biográficos de Pedro Calderon de la Barca, *etc.* 1881. 8°. **11450. ee. 24. (9.)**

—— *See* Ullrich (C. A. H.) Quaestiones Calderonianae. Dissertatio philologica, *etc.* [1865.] 8°. **8363. b. 5. (14.)**

—— *See* Ulrici (H.) Ueber Shakspeare's dramatische Kunst, und sein Verhältniss zu Calderon und Göthe. 1939. 8°. **840. f. 16.**

—— *See* Valbuena Prat (A.) Calderón. Su personalidad, su arte dramático, *etc.* 1941. 8°. **10630. k. 17.**

—— *See* Vilar y Pascual (L.) Historia genealógica, heráldica y biográfica del gran Calderon de la Barca, *etc.* 1881. 8°. **10603. c. 26. (1.)**

—— *See* Weir (Lucy E.) The Ideas embodied in the Religious Drama of Calderon. 1940. 8°. [*University of Nebraska. Studies in Language, Literature and Criticism.* no. 18.] Ac. **2692. 1/10.**

—— *See* Wille (J.) Calderóns Spiel der Erlösung, *etc.* 1932. 8°. **11878.aa.4.**

—— Album Calderoniano. Homenaje que rinden los escritores portugueses y españoles al esclarecido poeta Don Pedro Calderon de la Barca en la solemne conmemoracion de su centenario celebrada en el mes de mayo de 1881. pp. viii. 124. *Madrid,* 1881. 4°. **10632. h. 4.**

—— El Ateneo de Madrid en el Centenario de Calde ron Disertaciones, poesías y discursos de los señores Sanchez Moguel, Revilla, Ruiz Aguilera, Fernandez y Gonzalez, Palacio, Campillo, Moreno Nieto, Moret y Echegaray. pp. xv. 213. *Madrid,* 1881. 8°. **10631. bbb. 27.**

—— Discursos y poesías leidos el dia 25 de mayo de 1881 en el paraninfo de la Universidad Literaria de Salamanca en honor del insigne poeta dramático Don Pedro Calderon de la Barca, con ocasion del segundo centenario de su muerte. pp. 119. *Salamanca,* 1881. 4°. **10631. h. 7.**
Pp. 71–74 are mutilated.

—— Funebres elogios a la memoria de D. Pedro Calderon de la Barca. Escritos por algunos apassionados suyos del Alcaçar, *etc.* pp. 19. *F. Mestre: Valencia,* 1681. 4°. **T. 40*. (1.)**

—— Homenage á Calderon. Monografías, *etc.* (Biografía . . . Por D. Felipe Picatoste y Rodriguez.—Iconografía Calderoniana. Por D. Pascual Millán.—La Vida es Sueño. Consideraciones críticas por D. Rafael Ginard de la Roso.) [With the text of the comedia La Vida es Sueño, and the auto La Vida es Sueño.] pp. 339. *Madrid,* 1881. 4°. **1869. b. 20.**

CALDERÓN DE LA BARCA GONZÁLEZ DE HENAO (Pedro) *See* Calderón de la Barca (P.)

CALDERÓN DE LA BARCA Y ABREGO (Manuel) Preceptos Útiles para las Primeras Clases, ó Breve explicacion de las partes de la oracion, y de sus principales accidentes, *etc.* pp. 51. *México,* 1782. 12°. **12943. aa. 7.**

CALDERÓN DE PINILLOS (Carmen Torres) *See* Torres Calderon de Pinillos.

CALDERÓN DE ROBLES (Joannes) *See* Alcántara, *Orden y Cavalleria de.* Privilegia selectiora Militiæ Sancti Iuliani de Pereiro . . . à Summis Pontificibus hactenus concessa. Opera Doctoris Fr. I. Calderon de Robles. 1662. fol. **4625. f. 6. (2.)**

CALDERONE (Casimiro) L'Amore e la natura nell'Ariosto. pp. 52. *Palermo,* 1902. 8°. **11853. aa. 29.**

—— Il Borghi in Sicilia. pp. 77. *Palermo,* 1886. 8°. **10106. ccc. 8. (2.)**

CALDERONE COLAJANNI (Innocenzo) Il Socialismo repubblicano. Studio. pp. 118. *Palermo,* 1875. 8°. **8277. b. 17.**

CALDERÓN HERZE Y COLLANTES (Pedro) Filantropía, Caridad y Beneficencia; legislacion de España sobre establicimientos públicos y particulares de beneficencia. Discurso, *etc.* pp. 14. *Madrid,* 1861. 8°. **5385.aaa.38.(5.)**

CALDERONI (Alessandro) L'Esilio amoroso, tauola boschereccia, *etc.* [In verse.] pp. 127. *V. Baldinj: Ferrara,* 1607. 12°. **638. b. 33. (1.)**

CALDERONI (Gianfranco)

—— *See* Bazin (A.) Vittorio De Sica . . . Nota biografica, filmografia e bibliografia a cura di G. Calderoni. 1953. 8°. **11714. aa. 54.**

—— *See* Mida (M.) Roberto Rossellini . . . Nota biografica, filmografia e bibliografia a cura di G. Calderoni. 1953. 8°. **11799. a. 6.**

CALDERONI (Giuseppe Maria) Allocuzione estemporanea fatta nella sala del Palazzo Senatorio dell'inclita città di Velletri . . . in occasione del solenne possesso della giurisdizione temporale della medesima eseguito dall'Illustrissimo . . . Silvestro Scarani . . . suffraganeo a nome, e per . . . il signor Cardinal Errico, duca d'York . . . a xxvii. settembre mdccciii. pp. x. *Velletri,* [1803.] 4°. **1897. b. 6. (8.)**

CALDERONI (T.) *See* Bione, *d'Amatunta, pseud.* Doride ed Erimnete. Favola nuziale, *etc.* [The dedication signed: T. Calderoni.] 1874. 8°. **12304. cc. 38.**

CALDERÓN LLANES (José) *See* Calvía (M.) and Calderón Llanes (J.) La Interinidad, escritos políticos, *etc.* 1870. 16°. **8042. a. 1.**

CALDERÓN LYNCH (ALFONSO)

—— Enfermedades parasitarias e infecto-contagiosas que más atacan a la ganadería del Departamento de Puno. pp. 40. 1944. 8°. *See* PERU.—*Ministerio de Agricultura.* —*Dirección de Ganadería.*—*Granja Modelo de Puno-Chuquibambilla.* L.A.S. **603/5.**

CALDERÓN QUIJANO (JOSÉ ANTONIO)

—— *See* ABASCAL Y SOUSA (J. F. de) Memoria de gobierno . . . Edición preparada par V. Rodríguez Casado y J. A. Calderón Quijano, *etc.* 1944. 8°. **9774.** de. **1.**

—— Belice, 1663?–1821. Historia de los establecimientos británicos del río Valis hasta la independencia de Hispanoamérica, *etc.* [With plates, including maps.] pp. xix. 503. pl. xxxii. *Sevilla,* 1944. 8°. [*Escuela de Estudios Hispano-Americanos.* no. 5.] **09555.** ee. **6.**

—— El Fuerte de San Fernando de Omoa: su historia e importancia que tuvo en la defensa del Golfo de Honduras. 1942, 43. *See* SPAIN.—*Consejo Superior de Investigaciones Científicas.*—*Instituto Gonzalo Fernández de Oviedo.* Revista de Indias. año 3. no. 9; año 4. no. 11. 1940, *etc.* 8°. Ac. **132.**

—— Historia de las fortificaciones en Nueva España, *etc.* [With plates.] pp. xxxvi. 334. *Sevilla,* 1953. fol. L.R. **400.** b. **3.**
Publicaciones de la Escuela de Estudios Hispano-Americanos de Sevilla. no. 60.

—— Ingenieros militares en Nueva España. *In:* Anuario de estudios americanos. tom. 6. pp. 1–72. 1949. 8°. Ac. **161.** a/**2.**

CALDERÓN Y ARANA (SALVADOR) *See* TENNE (C. F. A.) and CALDERÓN Y ARANA (S.) Die Mineralfundstätten der Iberischen Halbinsel. 1902. 8°. **07107.** i. **18.**

—— Los Fosfatos de Cal Naturales, *etc.* 1890. *See* MADRID.—*Sociedad Española de Historia Natural.* Anales, *etc.* tom. 19. 1872, *etc.* 8°. Ac. **2826.**

—— Los Minerales de España. 2 tom. 1910. 8°. *See* MADRID.—*Junta para Ampliación de Estudios é Investigaciones Científicas.* Ac. **145/2.**

—— Organizacion y Arreglo de los Museos de Historia Natural. pp. 244. *Madrid,* 1884. 8°. **7006.** bb. **24.**

—— Reseña de las Rocas de la Isla Volcánica Gran Canaria. [Reprinted from the "Anales de la Sociedad Española de Historia Natural."] pp. 33. *Madrid,* 1876. 8°. **7106.** g. **9.** (**5.**)

—— Reseña Geológica de la Provincia de Guadalajara. [With a map.] pp. 97. *Madrid,* 1874. 8°. **7106.** c. **1.** (**8.**)

—— La Sal Común y su Papel en el Organismo del Globo. 1888. *See* MADRID.—*Real Sociedad Española de Historia Natural.* Anales, *etc.* tom. 17. 1872, *etc.* 8°. Ac. **2826.**

CALDERÓN Y COLLANTES (SATURNINO) Oda, leida por el licenciado Don S. Calderon y Collantes, *etc.* pp. 16. *Santiago,* [1830?] 4°. **899.** c. **23.** (**13.**)

CALDERÓN Y RÁVAGO (FRANCISCO) Semanero Santo, o Manual devoto para considerar la passion de Nro. Señor Jesu-Christo, en la Semana Santa: adornado con estampas: con un diario utilissimo para la vida Christiana, *etc.* pp. 208. *Barcelona,* 1765. 12°. **4403.** aaa. **21.**

CALDERÓN Y SANABRIA (DIEGO) Examen Analítico-Legal de los Bienes Vinculados, y de su Supresion. 2 tom. *Cádiz,* 1847. 8°. **5385.** a. **10.**

CALDERWOOD (CARMELITA)

—— *See* FUNSTEN (Robert V.) and CALDERWOOD (C.) Orthopedic Nursing, *etc.* 1943. 8°. **7689.** b. **22.**

—— *See* FUNSTEN (Robert V.) and CALDERWOOD (C.) Orthopedic Nursing . . . Second edition. 1949. 8°. **7689.** aa. **29.**

CALDERWOOD (DANIEL SCOTT) *See* SHAKESPEARE (W.) [*Smaller Collections of Plays.*] The Swan Shakespeare. (Coriolanus. With notes by D. S. Calderwood.) 1899, *etc.* 8°. **011765.** g. **16.**

CALDERWOOD (DAVID) *See* also DIDOCLAVIUS (Edwardus) *pseud.* [i.e. D. Calderwood.]

—— *See* also PHILADELPHUS (Hieronymus) *pseud.* [i.e. D. Calderwood.]

—— *See* SCOTLAND.—*Church of Scotland.* [*Books of Discipline.*] The First and Second Booke of Discipline, *etc.* [Edited by D. Calderwood.] 1621. 4°. **1230.** a. **2.**

—— Altare Damascenum, seu Ecclesiæ Anglicanæ politia, Ecclesiæ Scoticanæ obtrusa, à formalista quodam delineata, illustrata et examinata sub nomine olim E. Didoclavii studio & opera D. Calderwood, cui locis suis interserta confutatio Paræneseos Tileni ad Scotos . . . et adjecta epistola Hieronymi Philadelphi de regimine Ecclesiæ Scoticanæ, ejusque vindiciæ contra calumnias Johannis Spotsvodi . . . per Anonymum. Editio . . . emendatior. pp. 782. *Lugduni Batavorum,* 1708. 4°. **491.** g. **12.**

—— De regimine Ecclesiæ Scoticanæ brevis relatio. [By D. Calderwood.] pp. 29. 1618. 8°. *See* SCOTLAND.—*Church of Scotland.* [*Appendix.*] C. **53.** aa. **14.**

—— A Defence of our Arguments against kneeling in the act of receiving the Sacramentall elements of bread and wine impugned by Mr. Michelsone. [By D. Calderwood.] pp. 79. 1620. 8°. *See* MICHAELSON (J.) **1219.** a. **39.**

—— A Dialogue betwixt Cosmophilus and Theophilus anent the urging of new ceremonies upon the Kirke of Scotland. [By D. Calderwood?] pp. 43. 1620. 8°. *See* COSMOPHILUS. **698.** c. **34.**

—— A Dispute upon communicating at our confused Communions. [By D. Calderwood.] pp. 74. 1624. 12°. *See* DISPUTE. **4327.** aa. **10.** (**3.**)

—— An Epistle of a Christian Brother exhorting an other to keepe himself vndefiled from the present corruptions brought in to the ministration of the Lords Supper. [By D. Calderwood.] pp. 27. 1624. 12°. *See* EPISTLE. **4327.** aa. **10.** (**1.**)

—— An Exhortation of the Particular Kirks of Christ in Scotland to their Sister Kirk in Edinburgh. [By D. Calderwood.] pp. 23. 1624. 12°. *See* SCOTLAND.—*Church of Scotland.* [*Appendix.*] **4327.** aa. **10.** (**2.**)

—— The History of the Kirk of Scotland . . . Edited . . . by the Rev. Thomas Thomson. 8 vol. 1842–49. 8°. *See* EDINBURGH.—*Wodrow Society.* Ac. **2081/7.**

—— Parasynagma Perthense et juramentum Ecclesiæ Scoticanæ, *etc.* [By D. Calderwood.] pp. 47. 1620. 4°. *See* *See* SCOTLAND.—*Church of Scotland.*—*General Assembly.* [*Separate Transactions.*] **4175.** c. **72.**

CALDERWOOD (DAVID)

—— The Pastor and the Prelate; or, Reformation and conformity shortly compared by the Word of God, *etc.* [By D. Calderwood.] pp. 47. 1692. 4°. *See* PASTOR. **4175**. a. **69**.

—— [Another edition.] *See* PRESBYTERIAN. The Presbyterian's Armoury. vol. 3. 1843. 8°. **1354**. k. **3**.

—— Perth Assembly. Containing 1. The proceedings thereof . . . 2. The proofe of the nullitie thereof, *etc.* [By D. Calderwood.] pp. 101. 1619. 4°. *See* SCOTLAND.—*Church of Scotland.—General Assembly.* [*Separate Transactions.*] **110**. a. **2**.

—— A Re-examination of the five Articles enacted at Perth anno 1618, *etc.* [By D. Calderwood.] pp. 237. 1636. 4°. *See* SCOTLAND.—*Church of Scotland.—General Assembly.* [*Separate Transactions.*] **851**. e. **3**.

—— Scoti *του τυχοντος* Paraclesis, contra Danielis Tileni . . . Parænesin . . . Cuius pars prima est, De episcopali ecclesiæ regimine. [By D. Calderwood.] pp. 232. 1622. 4°. *See* TILENUS (D.) **4175**. c. **74**.

—— A Solution of Doctor Resolutus [i.e. David Lindsay, Bishop of Brechin]; his resolutions for kneeling. [By D. Calderwood.] pp. 55. 1619. 4°. *See* RESOLUTUS, *Doctor.* **4323**. bb. **17**.

—— The Speach of the Kirk of Scotland to her beloved Children. [By D. Calderwood.] pp. 125. 1620. 8°. *See* SCOTLAND, *Church of.* [*Appendix.*] **873**. b. **31**.

—— The True History of the Church of Scotland, from the beginning of the Reformation, unto the end of the reigne of King James VI. pp. 839. 8. 1678. fol. **491**. l. **19**.

—— [Another copy.] G. **11947**.
Imperfect; wanting the index.

—— [A reissue.] [*Sold by R. Boulter: London,* 1680.] fol. **210**. d. **10**.

—— Calderwoods Recantation: or, a Tripartite Discourse directed to such of the ministrie, and others in Scotland, that refuse Conformitie to the ordinances of the Church. [A fabrication by Patrick Scot.] pp. 50. *Bernard Alsop: London,* 1622. 4°. **4175**. a. **13**.

CALDERWOOD (HENRY) *See* COOPER (John) *Rev.* Jesus Christ's Mode of Presenting Himself to the World, *etc.* [With a prefatory note by H. Calderwood.] 1880. 8°. **4227**. e. **10**.

—— *See* CALDERWOOD (William L.) and WOODSIDE (D.) The Life of Henry Calderwood, *etc.* [With portraits.] 1900. 8°. **4956**. bbb. **17**.

—— *See* FLEMING (William) *D.D.* The Vocabulary of Philosophy . . . Edited by H. Calderwood. 1876. 8°. **8464**. bb. **49**.

—— —— 1878. 8°. **8463**. d. **9**.

—— —— 1887. 8°. **2234**. b. **9**.

—— *See* KANT (I.) The Metaphysic of Ethics . . . With an introduction by H. Calderwood, *etc.* 1869. 8°. **8404**. bbb. **27**.

—— —— 1871. 8°. **2236**. a. **13**.

—— Caffres and Caffre Missions; with preliminary chapters on the Cape Colony as a field for emigration and basis of missionary operation. pp. xii. 234. *J. Nisbet & Co.: London,* 1858. 8°. **4765**. a. **42**.

CALDERWOOD (HENRY)

—— David Hume. pp. 158. *Oliphant & Co.: Edinburgh,* [1898.] 8°. [*Famous Scots Series.*] **10803**. ccc. **21**.

—— Evolution and Man's Place in Nature. pp. xv. 349. *Macmillan & Co.: London,* 1893. 8°. **7006**. b. **48**.

—— Second edition. pp. xx. 316. *Macmillan & Co.: London,* 1896. 8°. **7006**. f. **19**.

—— Handbook of Moral Philosophy. pp. vii. 277. *Macmillan & Co.: London,* 1872. 8°. **8409**. c. **42**.

—— Fourteenth edition, largely rewritten. pp. x. 376. *Macmillan & Co.: London,* 1888. 8°. **8409**. i. **14**.

—— The Moral Law in its relation to Christian Life. *See* REVELATION. Divine Revelation Explained, *etc.* 1866. 8°. **4014**. aaa. **33**.

—— Moral Philosophy; as a science and as a discipline. An inaugural lecture. pp. 18. *Edmonston & Douglas: Edinburgh,* 1868. 8°. **08464**. f. **8**. (**3**.)

—— On Teaching: its ends and means. pp. ix. 114. *Edmonston & Douglas: Edinburgh,* 1874. 8°. **8306**. aaa. **13**.

—— Third edition. pp. x. 126. *Macmillan & Co.: London,* 1881. 8°. **8307**. bb. **21**.

—— The Parables of Our Lord interpreted in view of their relations to each other. pp. xv. 443. *Macmillan & Co.: London,* 1880. 8°. **3224**. k. **10**.

—— The Philosophy of the Infinite. With special reference to the theories of Sir William Hamilton and M. Cousin. pp. viii. 241. *T. Constable & Co.: Edinburgh,* 1854. 8°. **1248**. k. **11**.

—— Second edition, greatly enlarged. pp. xix. 520. *Macmillan & Co.: Cambridge, London,* 1861. 8°. **8466**. e. **10**.

—— *See* VERA (A.) An Inquiry into Speculative and Experimental Science, with special reference to Mr. Calderwood [i.e. to his "Philosophy of the Infinite"] and Professor Ferrier's recent publications, *etc.* 1856. 8°. **8466**. c. **16**.

—— The Relations of Mind and Brain. pp. xvi. 435. *Macmillan & Co.: London,* 1879. 8°. **8468**. h. **17**.

—— Second edition. pp. xx. 527. *Macmillan & Co.: London,* 1884. 8°. **8462**. f. **5**.

—— Third edition. pp. xxii. 551. *Macmillan & Co.: London,* 1892. 8°. **2236**. c. **6**.

—— The Relations of Science and Religion. The Morse lecture, 1880, *etc.* pp. 323. *Macmillan & Co.: London,* 1881. 8°. **4014**. ff. **2**.

—— Speeches delivered at a meeting held in Queen Street Hall, Edinburgh on Wednesday, February 17, 1886 to uphold the legislative union between Great Britain and Ireland, by Professor Calderwood, L.L.D., and Professor Butcher, L.L.D. pp. 12. *Irish Loyal and Patriotic Union: Dublin, London,* 1886. 8°. **8146**. d. **9**. (**18**.)

—— Vocabulary of Philosophy and student's book of reference. On the basis of Fleming's Vocabulary. pp. vi. 359. *Griffin & Co.: London,* 1894. 8°. **8462**. bb. **29**.

CALDERWOOD (HOWARD NEWTON)

—— *See* GALTSOFF (Paul S.) Ecological and Physiological Studies of the effect of Sulfate Pulp Mill Wastes on Oysters in the York River, Virginia. By P. S. Galtsoff . . . and H. N. Calderwood. 1947. 4°. [*U.S. Fish and Wildlife Service. Fishery Bulletin.* no. 43.] A.S. **96**.

CALDERWOOD (James Park) *See* Moyer (James A.) Elements of Engineering Thermodynamics. By J. A. Moyer . . . J. P. Calderwood, *etc.* 1920. 8°. **8764**. c. **11**.

—— —— 1923. 8°. **8763**. ee. **7**.

—— —— 1925. 8°. **8763**. f. **23**.

—— —— 1929. 8°. **8769**. d. **18**.

—— —— 1933. 8°. **08769**. dd. **28**.

—— —— 1935. 8°. **08770**. c. **27**.

—— *See* Moyer (James A.) and Calderwood (J. P.) Engineering Thermodynamics. 1915. 8°. **08715**. d. **45**.

—— *See* Potter (Andrey A.) and Calderwood (J. P.) Elements of Steam and Gas Power Engineering. 1920. 8°. **08767**. eee. **46**.

—— —— 1930. 8°. **08769**. b. **19**.

—— —— 1938. 8°. **8771**. aa. **5**.

CALDERWOOD (Lizzie Greenleaf) *See* Calderwood (William) Brief Memorial of Mrs. Lizzie G. Calderwood. [1860.] 16°. **4986**. a. **12**.

CALDERWOOD (Margaret) Letters and Journals . . . from England, Holland and the Low Countries, in 1756. Edited by Alexander Fergusson. pp. lviii. 386. *D. Douglas: Edinburgh,* 1884. 8°. **10921**. cc. **22**.

CALDERWOOD (Robert George Matheson)

—— Prophets of the Old Testament, *etc.* [Reprinted from "Listen."] pp. 15. *Sheldon Press: London,* [1943.] 8°. [*African Home Library.* no. 30.] W.P. **1606/30**.

CALDERWOOD (William) Brief Memorial of Mrs. Lizzie G. Calderwood, of the Saharunpur Mission, Northern India. pp. 74. *American Tract Society: New York,* [1860.] 16°. **4986**. a. **12**.

—— Things New and Old. (Second edition.) pp. 28. *John Heywood: Manchester, London,* 1888. 8°. **4372**. f. **36**. **(7.)**

—— The True Church. pp. 12. *John Heywood: Manchester,* 1889. 8°. **4109**. e. **15**. **(5.)**

CALDERWOOD (William Leadbetter)

—— The Common Eel, and its Capture; with suggestions applicable to Scotland. pp. 16. 1918. 8°. *See* England.—*Scottish Office.—Scottish Fresh-Water Fisheries Committee.* B.S. **39/4**. (5.)

—— The Life of the Salmon, with reference more especially to the fish in Scotland. pp. xxiv. 160. *Edward Arnold: London,* 1907. 8°. **7290**. d. **18**.

—— Mussel Culture and the Bait Supply; with reference more especially to Scotland. pp. vii. 121. *Macmillan & Co.: London,* 1895. 8°. **7290**. a. **24**.

—— Salmon! Experiences and reflections. [With plates.] pp. 175. *E. Arnold & Co.: London,* 1938. 8°. **7908**. eee. **53**.

—— Salmon and Sea Trout. With chapters on hydro-electric schemes, fish passes, *etc.* [With plates.] pp. xi. 242. *E. Arnold & Co.: London,* 1930. 8°. **07290**. ee. **15**.

—— Salmon Hatching and Salmon Migrations. Being the Buckland Lectures for 1930. [With plates.] pp. 95. *E. Arnold & Co.: London,* 1931. 8°. **07295**. a. **21**.

CALDERWOOD (William Leadbetter)

—— The Salmon Rivers and Lochs of Scotland . . . Illustrated. pp. x. 442. *Edward Arnold: London,* 1909. 4°. **7908**. i. **10**.

—— Second edition, revised, *etc.* pp. ix. 438. *E. Arnold & Co.: London,* 1921. 8°. **07290**. ee. 3.

CALDERWOOD (William Leadbetter) and **WOODSIDE** (David)

—— The Life of Henry Calderwood, LL.D., F.R.S.E. . . . With a special chapter on his philosophical works by A. S. Pringle-Pattison. [With portraits.] pp. viii. 447. *Hodder & Stoughton: London,* 1900. 8°. **4956**. bbb. **17**.

CALDÉS ARÚS (Vicens)

—— *See* Shakespeare (William) [*Works.—Catalan.*] Obres completes, *etc.* (vol. 11. Conte d'hivern. Traducció de V. Caldés Arús.) 1907, *etc.* 8°. **11768**. ee. **1/11**.

CALDESI (Giovanni Battista) Osservazioni anatomiche . . . intorno alle tartarughe marittime d'acqua dolce e terrestri. pp. 91. pl. 9. *P. Matini: Firenze,* 1687. 4°. **462**. e. **18**.

—— [Another copy.] **446**. f. **2**. **(4.)**

—— [Another copy.] MS. ADDITIONS. **39**. a. **18**.

CALDESI (Leonida) The National Gallery. A selection of pictures by the old masters photographed by Signor L. Caldesi. With descriptive and historical notices by Ralph N. Wornum. 8 pt. *Virtue & Co.: London,* [1868–73.] fol. **1755**. g. **2**.

—— Photographs by Cav^e^ Leonida Caldesi, of Ancient Marbles, Bronzes, Terracottas, &c. . . . in the British Museum . . . Published . . . under the direction of C. T. Newton. 2 vol. *C. B. Caldesi & Co.: London,* [1873, 74.] fol. **1704**. d. **10**.

CALDESI (Leonida) **AND CO.** The Photographic Historical Portrait Gallery. Consisting of a series of portraits . . . in the most celebrated collections in England. Photographed by L. Caldesi and Co. With descriptive letter-press by Amelia B. Edwards. vol. 1. pp. 102. pl. L. *P. & D. Colnaghi, Scott, & Co.: London,* 1864. 4°. **1752**. b. **31**.

CALDEY BOOKS. Caldey Books. 2 no. 1909, 11. 8°. *See* Prinknash.—*Benedictine Monastery.* **4379**. eee. **6**.

CALDEY ISLAND.—*Benedictine Monastery.* [For the Benedictine Community housed successively at Painsthorpe, Caldey Island, and Prinknash:] *See* Prinknash.—*Benedictine Monastery.*

CALDEY NOTES.

—— *See* Prinknash Park.—*Benedictine Monastery.* Notes for the Month, *etc.*

CALDI (Giuseppe) La Coscienza e l'io nel loro valore psicologico elementare, *etc.* vol. 1. pp. 93. *Udine,* 1896. 8°. **8468**. l. **21**.
No more published.

—— Metodologia generale della interpretazione scientifica. 2 vol. *Torino, Palermo,* 1893, 94. 8°. **8468**. k. **22**.

CALDICOTT (Arthur E.) *See* Caldicott (Charles) A Guide to the City of Hereford . . . Illustrated by Mr. C. Caldicott and Mr. A. E. Caldicott. [1897.] 8°. **10352**. e. **50**.

—— *See* Caldicott (Charles) The Way about Herefordshire . . . Illustrated by C. Caldicott and A. E. Caldicott, *etc.* [1896.] 8°. **010358**. e. **70**.

—— *See* Caldicott (Charles) The Way about Worcestershire . . . With . . . illustrations by Messrs. C. Caldicott and A. E. Caldicott. [1898.] 8°. **010358**. e. **80**.

CALDICOTT (Charles) The Guide to Llandudno, its scenery, walks, *etc.* pp. 103. *Iliffe & Son: London,* [1896.] 8°. **10369.** aaa. **53.**

—— A Guide to the City of Hereford: its beauties and antiquities . . . Illustrated by Mr. C. Caldicott and Mr. Arthur E. Caldicott. pp. 118. *Iliffe & Son: London,* [1897.] 8°. **10352.** e. **50.**

—— Walks Through Coventry; being a guide to visitors, *etc.* pp. 40. *F. Caldicott: Coventry,* 1884. 8°. **10347.** cc. **13.** (**1.**)

—— The Way about Herefordshire . . . Written by C. Caldicott and illustrated by C. Caldicott and A. E. Caldicott. With a comprehensive county gazetteer, edited by A. Baines. (2nd edition.) pp. 210. *Iliffe & Son: London,* [1896.] 8°. [*Way-About Series.* no. 9.] **010358.** e. **70.**

—— The Way about Worcestershire and Gazetteer of the County . . . With map and illustrations by Messrs. C. Caldicott and A. E. Caldicott. pp. 206. *Iliffe & Son: London,* [1898.] 8°. [*Way-About Series.* no. 19.] **010358.** e. **80.**

CALDICOTT (John William) *Antique Dealer.* The Values of Old English Silver and Sheffield Plate, from the xvth to the xixth centuries . . . Edited by J. Starkie Gardner. pp. 293. pl. lxxxvii. *Bemrose & Sons: London,* 1906. 4°. **7709.** r. **4.**

—— [Another edition.] Values of Antiques. The values of old English silver, Sheffield plate, pewter, china, furniture, clocks, etc. From the fifteenth century. pp. xi. 735. *J. W. Caldicott: Bath,* [1929.] 8°. **07805.** e. **33.**

CALDICOTT (John William) *M.A.* Analysis of the Poll-Book in the recent election of two burgesses to serve in Parliament for the University of Oxford, *etc.* *Rivingtons: London,* 1866. 8°. **8364.** cc. **56.** (**7.**)

—— In usum tironum apud Scholam Bristoliensem erudiendorum. [Notes to be used with sections 102–200 of Kennedy's Progressive Latin Grammar. By the Rev. J. W. Caldicott.] pp. 16. 1878. 8°. *See* Bristol.—*Bristol Grammar School.* **12902.** bb. **21.** (**8.**)

—— Religious Education and Religious Freedom, from a Churchman's point of view. A letter addressed to the Right Hon. W. E. Gladstone, *etc.* pp. 20. *National Education League: Birmingham,* 1872. 8°. **4105.** cc. **18.** (**7.**)

—— Unsectarian Education, a reply to the Bishop of Peterborough. pp. 4. *National Education League: Bristol,* [1870.] 8°. **1897.** c. **19.** (**10.**)

CALDICOTT (Oswald Holt) Executorship Accounts. An address, *etc.* pp. 80. *Gee & Co.: London,* 1889. 8°. **6355.** aaa. **36.**

—— Third edition. pp. 82. *Gee & Co.: London,* 1898. 8°. **6355.** aaa. **40.**

CALDICOTT (Thomas Ford) Hannah Corcoran: an authentic narrative of her conversion from Romanism, her abduction from Charlestown, *etc.* pp. 130. *Gould & Lincoln: Boston,* 1853. 12°. **4986.** aa. **2.**

CALDIN (Edward Francis Hussey)

—— The Power and Limits of Science. A philosophical study. pp. ix. 196. *Chapman & Hall: London,* 1949. 8°. **08467.** df. **31.**

—— Science and Christian Apologetic. An essay in the comparison of methods, *etc.* pp. 44. *Blackfriars: London,* 1951. 8°. [*Aquinas Paper.* no. 17.] W.P. **6218/17.**

CALDINE (D.) Corridas de Toros. Illustrations de C. Roussel, *etc.* (Troisième édition.) pp. xxxv. 304. *Paris,* 1900. 8°. **7912.** e. **8.**

CALDIS (Calliope G.)

—— The Council of Four as a Joint Emergency Authority in the European Crisis at the Paris Peace Conference, 1919. A political study. Submitted as a thesis, *etc.* pp. xx. 228. *Ambilly,* 1953. 8°. **9088.** c. **3.**

CALDO (Lorenzo) Osservazioni meridiane di stelle di Eros. pp. 17. *Palermo,* 1937. fol. [*Giornale di scienze naturali ed economiche.* vol. 39.] Ac. **2814.**

CALDOGNO (Francesco) *Count.* Una Relazione ai Rettori di Vicenza del conte Francesco Caldogno, Deputato dal Senato della Repubblica Veneta alle montagne ed ai confini. (Nozze faustissime Bucchia-Bertagnoni.) pp. 15. *Vicenza,* 1878. 8°. **012301.** i. **13.**

CALDORA (Nicolaus) *Bishop of Venosa.* Epistola pastoralis ad clerum et populum ecclesiæ Venusinæ. pp. vi. *Romæ,* 1818. 4°. **1356.** k. **6.** (**45.**)

CALDRINUS (Joannes) *See* Calderinus.

CALDWALL (E.) *See* Morus (Horatius) Tables of Surgerie, *etc.* [Edited by E. Caldwall.] 1585. fol. **549.** l. **7.** (**1.**)

CALDWALL (Richard) *See* Morus (Horatius) Tables of Surgerie . . . translated out of Latine . . . by R. Caldwall. 1585. fol. **549.** l. **7.** (**1.**)

CALDWALL (Thomas)

—— A Select Collection of Ancient and Modern Epitaphs, and Inscriptions: to which are added some on the decease of eminent persons. Collected by T. Caldwall. [With a portrait.] pp. iv. 416. *The Compiler: London,* 1796. 12°. **12299.** eee. **25.**

—— [A reissue.] A Collection of Epitaphs and Inscriptions, ancient and modern; distinguished either for their wit, humour, and singularity; elegance of composition; morality of sentiment, or celebrity of character. Carefully selected from preceding publications, including many never before printed. [Compiled by T. Caldwall.] 1802. 12°. *See* Collection. **277.** d. **35.**

CALDWELL. Caldwell, the Magic City in the Boise Valley, Idaho. Facts pertaining to the magic city and its great tributary resources, *etc.* pp. 23. *Rule & Cole: Caldwell,* 1891. 8°. **10411.** g. **39.** (**6.**)

CALDWELL BROTHERS. Caldwell's Systematic Guide to Edinburgh. *See* Couston (John)

CALDWELL (Alfred Betts) Coffee for None. pp. 319. *E. Mathews & Marrot: London,* 1934. 8°. NN. **22525.**

—— No Tears Shed. pp. x. 279. *Doubleday, Doran & Co.: Garden City, N.Y.,* 1937. 8°. **12716.** b. **24.**

—— Turquoise Hazard. pp. 276. *Doubleday, Doran & Co.: Garden City, N.Y.,* 1936. 8°. A.N. **3207.**

CALDWELL (Allan)

—— Screw Tug Design. pp. ix. 154. *Hutchinson's Scientific & Technical Publications: London,* [1947.] 8°. **8809.** cc. **2.**

CALDWELL (Anne) *See* Marsh, afterwards Marsh Caldwell (A.)

CALDWELL (Arthur Bunyan) History of the American Negro and his Institutions. Georgia edition. Edited by A. B. Caldwell, *etc.* [Biographies and portraits of prominent negroes.] vol. 1. pp. 688. *A. B. Caldwell Publishing Co.: Atlanta*, 1917. 8°. **10888.** d. **15.**
No more published.

CALDWELL (Augustin) The Rich Legacy. Memories of Hannah Tobey Farmer, *etc.* [With a portrait.] pp. xii. 631. *Privately printed: Boston*, 1892. 8°. **4986.** eee. **1.**

CALDWELL (Benjamin Palmer) On the State of Equilibrium of certain Double Iodides, cyanides, nitrates and sulphates in aqueous solution. Dissertation, *etc.* pp. 55. *Chemical Publishing Co.: Easton, Pa.*, 1901. 8°. **08909.** f. **33.**

CALDWELL (Cal)

—— Catch Fire. Poems. pp. 38. *Arthur H. Stockwell: Ilfracombe*, 1956. 8°. **11661.** de. **16.**

CALDWELL (Charles) *See* Alibert (J. L.) *Baron.* A Treatise on Malignant Intermittents . . . Translated . . . with an introductory discourse . . . by C. Caldwell. 1807. 8°. **7561.** f. **13.**

—— An Address on the Vice of Gambling, *etc.* pp. 37. *J. Clarke & Co.: Lexington, Ky.*, 1834. 8°. **8425.** g. **20.** (**2.**)

—— An Anniversary Oration on the Subject of Quarantines, delivered to the Philadelphia Medical Society, *etc.* pp. 30. *Fry & Kammerer: Philadelphia*, 1807. 8°. T. **117.** (**4*.**)

—— An Attempt to establish the Original Sameness of three Phenomena of Fever . . . described by medical writers under the several names of Hydrocephalus internus, Cynanche trachealis, and Diarrhœa infantum. pp. 69. *Thomas Dobson: Philadelphia*, 1796. 8°. T. **173.** (**1.**)

—— Autobiography of Charles Caldwell, M.D. With a preface, notes, and appendix by Harriot W. Warner. [With a portrait.] pp. 454. *Lippincott, Grambo & Co.: Philadelphia*, 1855. 8°. **7679.** e. **42.**

—— [Another copy.] **10880.** e. **44.**

—— Character of General Washington. pp. 15. *"The True American": Philadelphia*, 1801. 8°. T. **203.** (**2.**)

—— Discourse . . . on the Advantages of a National University, *etc.* *See* Bishop (Robert H.) Oxford Addresses, *etc.* 1835. 8°. **8355.** cc. **21.**

—— A Discourse on the Genius and Character of the Rev. Horace Holley, LL.D. late President of Transylvania University . . . With an appendix, containing copious notes biographical and illustrative. pp. viii. 294. *Hilliard, Gray & Co.: Boston*, 1828. 8°. **1372.** i. **4.**

—— An Elegiac Poem on the Death of General Washington. pp. 12. *"The True American": Philadelphia*, 1806. 8°. T. **184.** (**9.**)
Printed on blue paper.

—— Medical & Physical Memoirs, containing, among other subjects, a particular enquiry into the origin and nature of the late pestilential epidemics of the United States. pp. 348. *T. & W. Bradford: Philadelphia*, 1801. 8°. **7561.** f. **17.**

—— Memoirs of the Life and Campaigns of the Hon. Nathaniel Greene. [With a portrait.] pp. xxiii. 452. *Robert Desilver: Philadelphia*, 1819. 8°. **1453.** d. **18.**

—— New Views of Penitentiary Discipline and moral education and reform. pp. viii. 52. *William Brown: Philadelphia*, 1829. 8°. **6056.** b. **9.**

—— An Oration commemorative of the Character and Administration of Washington, *etc.* pp. 37. *Bradford & Inskeep: Philadelphia*, 1810. 8°. T. **86.** (**3.**)

CALDWELL (Charles)

—— Phrenology vindicated, and Antiphrenology unmasked. pp. 156. *Samuel Colman: New York*, 1838. 12°. **7410.** b. **17.**

—— A Reply to Dr. Haygarth's Letter to Dr. Percival, on infectious fevers, *etc.* pp. 50. *T. & W. Bradford: Philadelphia*, 1802. 8°. T. **378.** (**1.**)

—— A Semi-annual Oration, on the Origin of Pestilential Diseases, *etc.* pp. 59. *T. & S. F. Bradford: Philadelphia*, 1799. 8°. T. **96.** (**3.**)
Printed on blue paper.

—— Thoughts on Physical Education: being a discourse delivered to a convention of teachers in Lexington, Ky., *etc.* pp. 133. *Marsh, Capon & Lyon: Boston*, 1834. 8°. **8308.** b. **16.**

—— Thoughts on Physical Education . . . and on the study of the Greek and Latin languages. With notes by Robert Cox; and a . . . preface by George Combe. pp. xv. 190. *A. & C. Black: Edinburgh*, 1836. 8°. **1030.** f. **21.**

—— Thoughts on the Original Unity of the Human Race. pp. x. 178. *E. Bliss: New York*, 1830. 8°. **10006.** c. **13.**

—— A Valedictory Address on some of the duties and qualifications of a physician delivered to the graduates of the medical Department of Transylvania University, *etc.* [An extract.] [1830.] 8°. **7680.** bb. **65.** (**1.**)

CALDWELL (Cy)

—— Henry Ford . . . Illustrated by Edd Ashe. [With plates, including a portrait.] pp. 206. *Bodley Head: London*, 1955. 8°. [*Men of the Modern Age.* no. 6.] W.P. b. **633/6.**

—— Speak the Sin Softly. [A novel.] pp. 320. *Macdonald & Co.: London*, 1947. 8°. NN. **37540.**

CALDWELL (Daniel Richard)

—— *See* Hongkong.—*Commission to enquire into the charges against Mr. D. R. Caldwell, Registrar General.* [Report of the Commission, with minutes of evidence, etc.] [1858.] fol. C.S. b. **91.**

CALDWELL (David Hume)

—— *See* Babbitt (Harold E.) and Caldwell (D. H.) The Free Surface around, and Interference between, Gravity Wells. 1948. 8°. [*University of Illinois Engineering Experiment Station. Bulletin series.* no. 374.] Ac. **2692.** u/**4.**

—— *See* Babbitt (Harold E.) and Caldwell (D. H.) Turbulent Flow of Sludges in Pipes. 1940. 8°. [*University of Illinois Engineering Experiment Station. Bulletin series.* vol. 38. no. 13.] Ac. **2692.** u/**4.**

CALDWELL (Edmund G.) *See* Bryden (Henry A.) Animals of Africa . . . Illustrated by E. Caldwell. 1900. 8°. **7003.** aaaa. **30/1.**

—— *See* Haviland, afterwards Brindley (Maud D.) Lives of the Fur Folk . . . Illustrated by E. Caldwell. 1910. 8°. **7204.** de. **14.**

—— *See* Prichard, afterwards Hesketh-Prichard (Hesketh V.) Hunting Camps in Wood and Wilderness . . . Illustrated by . . . E. G. Caldwell, *etc.* 1910. 8°. **7904.** d. **14.**

CALDWELL (Elizabeth) *See* Dugdale (Gilbert) A True Discourse of the practises of Elizabeth Caldwell . . . on the parson of T. Caldwell, *etc.* 1604. 4°. C. **27.** c. **27.**

CALDWELL (Ella Stewart) *See* also Stewart (Caldwell) *pseud.* [i.e. E. S. Caldwell.]

—— Ah Me! When one loves. And other poems, *etc.* pp. 48. *A. H. Stockwell: London,* [1926.] 8°. **011645.** g. **119.**

—— Opened Eyes. A novel. pp. 203. *A. H. Stockwell: London,* [1926.] 8°. **4412.** dd. **45.**

—— Till Thou hast Paid, *etc.* pp. 224. *A. H. Stockwell: London,* [1927.] 8°. NN. **13284.**

CALDWELL (Elsie Noble)

—— In a Changing Brazil. [With plates.] pp. 198. *Richard R. Smith: New York,* 1946. 8°. **010481.** ee. **24.**

CALDWELL (Erskine)

—— *See* Kirkland (Jack) La Route au tabac. Pièce en trois actes . . . d'après le roman d'E. Caldwell. Adaptation française de M. Duhamel. 1947. fol. [*France illustration, littéraire et théâtrale.* no. 4.] P.P. **4283.** m. (**2.**)

—— *See* White (Margaret B.) Russia at War. Photographs by M. Bourke-White. Described by E. Caldwell, *etc.* [1942.] 4°. **9101.** dd. **12.**

—— All Night Long. pp. 191. *Cassell & Co.: London,* 1943. 8°. NN. **34009.**

—— All-Out on the Road to Smolensk. pp. 230. *Duell, Sloan & Pearce: New York,* [1942.] 8°. **9100.** aa. **33.**

—— American Earth. pp. 255. *Martin Secker: London,* 1935. 8°. A.N. **2396.**

—— Call it Experience. [An autobiography.] pp. 160. *Hutchinson: London,* 1952. 8°. **10890.** fff. **14.**

—— The Courting of Susie Brown, and other stories. pp. 170. *Falcon Press: London,* 1952. 8°. **12701.** ee. **9.**

—— Episode in Palmetto. pp. 208. *Falcon Press: London,* 1951. 8°. **12731.** bb. **48.**

—— Georgia Boy. pp. 139. *Falcon Press: London,* 1947. 8°. **12829.** aa. **7.**

—— [Georgia Boy.] Мальчик из Джорджии. Перевод . . . Н. Волжиной и Ив. Кашкина, *etc.* pp. 125. *Москва,* 1945. 8°. **12707.** b. **42.**

—— God's Little Acre. pp. 318. *Martin Secker: London,* 1933. 8°. **12721.** aaa. **5.**

—— God's Little Acre. pp. 218. *Falcon Press: London,* 1948 [1949]. 8°. NN. **39341.**

—— God's Little Acre. pp. 212. *William Heinemann: London,* 1955. 8°. NNN. **6679.**

—— *See* Viking Press. The Viking Press, New York. "God's Little Acre" by Erskine Caldwell. Appendix to the fifth printing. [The judgment of the New York City Magistrate dismissing the charge of obscenity brought against the Viking Press as publishers of the book.] [1933.] fol. **11853.** v. **58.**

—— A House in the Uplands. pp. 176. *Falcon Press: London,* 1947. 8°. **12728.** aaa. **8.**

—— Jackpot. The short stories of Erskine Caldwell. pp. ix. 756. *Duell, Sloan & Pearce: New York,* [1940.] 8°. **12723.** dd. **18.**

—— Jackpot. Collected short stories. pp. 756. *Falcon Press: London,* 1950. 8°. **12730.** ff. **22.**

CALDWELL (Erskine)

—— Journeyman. pp. 253. *Secker & Warburg: London,* 1938. 8°. **12718.** aa. **10.**

—— Journeyman. pp. 146. *Falcon Press: London,* 1948. 8°. **12729.** i. **20.**

—— A Lamp for Nightfall. pp. 199. *Falcon Press: London,* 1952. 8°. **12701.** ee. **8.**

—— Love and Money. pp. 206. *William Heinemann: London,* 1955. 8°. **12733.** i. **39.**

—— Moscow Under Fire. A wartime diary: 1941. pp. 111. *Hutchinson & Co.: London,* [1942.] 8°. **9101.** e. **13.**

—— Place called Estherville. pp. 215. *Falcon Press: London,* 1950. 8°. **12730.** ppp. **30.**

—— Southways. pp. 175. *Falcon Press: London,* 1953. 8°. **12731.** p. **13.**

—— [A reissue.] Southways. *William Heinemann: London,* 1955. 8°. NNN. **7031.**

—— The Sure Hand of God. pp. 175. *Falcon Press: London,* 1948 [1949]. 8°. NN. **39460.**

—— This very Earth. pp. 196. *Falcon Press: London,* 1949. 8°. NN. **39771.**

—— Tobacco Road. pp. 241. *C. Scribner's Sons: New York,* 1932. 8°. A.N. **1421.**

—— [Another edition.] pp. 243. *Cresset Press: London,* 1933. 8°. **12709.** eee. **11.**

—— Tobacco Road. pp. 180. *Falcon Press: London,* 1948. 8°. **12729.** de. **10.**

—— *See* Kirkland (Jack) Tobacco Road. A play . . . from the novel by E. Caldwell. 1937. 8°. **20031.** e. **40.**

—— *See* Kirkland (Jack) Tobacco Road. A three act play . . . From the novel by E. Caldwell. 1949. 8°. **11791.** pp. **58.**

—— Tragic Ground. pp. 195. *Falcon Press: London,* 1947. 8°. **12725.** aaa. **23.**

—— Tragic Ground. (Sixth printing.) pp. 237. *Duell, Sloan & Pearce: New York,* [1947.] 8°. **12728.** aaa. **37.**

—— Trouble in July. pp. 250. *Jonathan Cape: London,* 1940. 8°. **12721.** cc. **19.**

—— Trouble in July. pp. 159. *Falcon Press: London,* 1948. 8°. **12729.** g. **7.**

—— We Are the Living. pp. 301. *Martin Secker: London,* 1934. 8°. **12709.** g. **9.**

CALDWELL (Eugene Wilson) *See* Pusey (William A.) and Caldwell (E. W.) The Practical Application of the Röntgen Rays in Therapeutics and Diagnosis, *etc.* 1903. 8°. **7462.** g. **13.**

—— —— 1904. 8°. **7462.** g. **16.**

CALDWELL (Francis Cary) Electrical Engineering Problems. pp. v. 105. *McGraw-Hill Book Co.: New York, London,* 1914. 8°. **8756.** c. **50.**

—— Electrical Engineering Test Sheets for the dynamo laboratory. *McGraw-Hill Book Co.: New York, London,* 1911. 8°. **08767.** aa. **19.**

—— Modern Lighting. pp. xi. 386. *Macmillan Co.: New York,* 1930. 8°. [*Engineering Science Series.*] W.P. **3467/10.**

CALDWELL (Fred) Aunt Susie Shoots the Works! A mystery farce in three acts. pp. 124. *Samuel French: New York,* [1938.] 8°. **11792**. aaa. **21**.

—— Bashful Bertie. A bright, new comedy in three acts. pp. 107. *Samuel French: New York,* [1947.] 8°. **011791**. bb. **30**.

—— Miss Chatterbox. A . . . comedy in three acts. pp. 105. *Samuel French: New York, Los Angeles,* [1946.] 8°. **11791**. pp. **54**.

—— This Freedom of Ours. A . . . comedy drama in three acts. pp. 129. *Samuel French: New York,* [1943.] 8°. **011791**. b. **17**.

—— Uncle Cy Hits a New High! A sea-going farce with a gallon of laughs in three acts. pp. 117. *Samuel French: New York,* [1939.] 8°. **011791**. a. **24**.

CALDWELL (G. P.) Causa Causæ; primary laws of liberty and freedom. pp. 54. *Holmes & Son: London,* 1892. 8°. **8007**. de. **2**. (**6**.)

—— Humorous and Religious Verse. pp. 27. *Bennet & Davis: Durban, South Africa,* [1900.] 8°. **11602**. dd. **16**. (**2**.)

CALDWELL (George Alfred) Speech . . . on the Tariff. Delivered in the House of Representatives, *etc.* pp. 11. *"Globe": Washington,* 1844. 8°. **8177**. cc. **51**. (**27**.)

CALDWELL (George Chapman) The Fatty Acids contained in the Oil of the Arachis Hypogæa and the Oleic Acid Series. Inaugural dissertation, *etc.* pp. 47. *University Press: Göttingen,* 1856. 8°. **8905**. bbb. **40**. (**1**.)

CALDWELL (George Walter) Legends of Southern California, *etc.* [In verse and prose.] pp. 101. *Phillips & Van Orden Co.: San Francisco,* [1919.] 8°. **012403**. df. 3.

—— The Master Key. [A poem.] pp. 58. *G. W. Caldwell: Oakland, California,* [1923.] 8°. **011686**. g. **47**.

CALDWELL (Grace F.) English Contributions to Scientific Thought.—The English Gift to World Literature. *See* Larned (Joseph N.) English Leadership, *etc.* 1918. 8°. **09506**. de. **5**.

CALDWELL (H.) *of Edinburgh.* Princess Beauty's Pimples. A fairy story, *etc.* pp. 14. *A. H. Stockwell: London,* [1926.] 8°. **12805**. ccc. **46**.

CALDWELL (H. G.)

—— *See* Cudmore (Sedley A.) and Caldwell (H. G.) Rural and Urban Composition of the Canadian Population. 1938. 8°. [*Dominion Bureau of Statistics. Census Monograph.* no. 6.] C.S. e. **9/31**.

CALDWELL (H. H.)

—— *See* Hilliker (Katharine) and Caldwell (H. H.) Poor Little Me. A three act play. [1940.] 8°. **011781**. g. **1/472**.

CALDWELL (Halwin) The Art of doing our Best; as seen in the lives and stories of some thorough workers . . . The illustrations by John Absolon, H. K. Browne, and the brothers Dalziel. pp. xi. 351. *J. Hogg & Sons: London,* [1860.] 8°. **10604**. a. **33**.

—— [Another edition.] pp. 284. *Gall & Inglis: London, Edinburgh,* [1873.] 8°. **10602**. bb. **11**.

CALDWELL (Harry R.)

—— *See* Caldwell (John C.) Our Friends the Tigers. [An account of the life of H. R. Caldwell and his family as missionaries in China. With a portrait.] 1954. 8°. **4768**. e. **19**.

CALDWELL (Harry R.)

—— Blue Tiger, *etc.* [Accounts of missionary work and sport in China.] pp. xiv. 242. *Duckworth: London,* 1925. 8°. **010055**. f. **32**.

CALDWELL (Harry R.) and **CALDWELL** (John C.)

—— South China Birds . . . Stories and legends by Muriel E. Caldwell. [With plates.] pp. 447. *Hester May Vanderburgh: Shanghai,* 1931. 8°. **7288**. c. **8**.

CALDWELL (Helen)

—— *See* Machado de Assis (J. M.) Dom Casmurro . . . Translated by H. Caldwell, *etc.* 1953. 8°. **12492**. aa. **48**.

—— *See* Machado de Assis (J. M.) Dom Casmurro . . . Translated by H. Caldwell. 1953. 8°. **12493**. cc. **7**.

CALDWELL (Henry) The Invasion of Canada in 1775. Letter attributed to . . . H. Caldwell, *etc.* pp. 20. *Quebec,* 1887. 8°. [*Literary and Historical Society of Quebec. Historical Documents.* ser. 2. no. 5.] **Ac. 8560/4**.

CALDWELL (Henry Swan) Essai sur la circulation, considérée dans ses rapports avec l'anévrisme du cœur; thèse, *etc.* pp. 20. *Paris,* 1827. 4°. **1183**. i. **10**. (**10**.)

CALDWELL (Howard H.) Oliatta, and other poems. pp. 200. *Redfield: New York,* 1855. 12°. **11687**. bb. **33**.

—— Poems. pp. 134. *Whittemore, Niles & Hall: Boston,* 1858. 12°. **11686**. bb. **21**.

CALDWELL (Howard Walter) *See* Fling (F. M.) and Caldwell (H. W.) Studies in European and American History, *etc.* [1897.] 8°. **9009**. c. **29**.

—— Education in Nebraska. pp. 268. *Washington,* 1902. 8°. [*U.S. Bureau of Education. Circular of Information.* no. 3, 1902.] A.S. **203**.

CALDWELL (James) *A.M.I.Mech.E.*

—— *See* Hislop (George S.) and Caldwell (J.) Tests of Model Propellers in the High Speed Tunnel Thrust and Torque Measurements on a 2-Blade, 6 per cent. Thick, Clark Y Section Propeller, *etc.* 1951. 4°. [*Aeronautical Research Council. Reports and Memoranda.* no. 2595.] B.S. **2/2**.

CALDWELL (James) *Manufacturer.*

—— A Letter, to the Manufacturers, and Inhabitants of the Parishes of Stoke, Burslem and Wolstanton, in the County of Stafford, on Courts of Request, occasioned by the bill intended to be brought into Parliament this sessions, for the establishment of that jurisdiction in the Potteries; by a Manufacturer [i.e. J. Caldwell?] pp. 14. [1794.] 8°. *See* Manufacturer. **6283**. bb. **12**.

CALDWELL (James) *of Paisley. See* Kilbarchan. Register of Marriages and Baptisms in the Parish of Kilbarchan, *etc.* [Transcribed by J. Caldwell.] 1912. 8°. [*Scottish Record Society.* pt. 58.] **2100.f.(10.)**

CALDWELL (James) *of Pennycuick.* An Explanation of the Song of Solomon: the Shorter Catechism and part of the Second Epistle to the Thessalonians. [With the texts.] pp. 256. 1836. 8°. *See* Bible.—*Song of Solomon.* [*English.*] **3165**. de. **4**.

CALDWELL (James) *Preacher at Fawkirke.* The Countesse of Marres Arcadia, or Sanctuarie. Containing morning, and evening meditations for the whole weeke . . . Enriched with a godlie treatise, called, An Ascension of the soule of Heaven, by meditation on the Passion of our Lord Iesus Christ. [Edited by P. Anderson.] pp. 444. *Iohn Wreittoun: Edinburgh,* 1625. 12°. C. **65**. aa. **1**.

CALDWELL (*Sir* James) *Bart.* *See* Ireland.—*Parliament.* —iii. *House of Commons.* [*Debates.*] Debates relative to the affairs of Ireland in . . . 1763 and 1764. Taken by a Military Officer. To which are added, his remarks on the trade of Ireland, *etc.* [The dedication signed: J. C., i.e. Sir J. Caldwell.] 1766. 8°. **G. 4805.**

—— *See* Taylor (Frank) *M.A., of Manchester University.* Johnsoniana from the Bagshawe Muniments in the John Rylands Library: Sir James Caldwell, Dr. Hawkesworth, Dr. Johnson, and Boswell's use of the 'Caldwell minute,' *etc.* 1952. 8°. **11867. p. 9.**

—— Sir James Caldwell's Account of the Speeches in both Houses of Parliament, at the Opening of the Session in 1762. *See* England.—*Parliament.*—*House of Commons.* —*Proceedings.*—i. Sir Henry Cavendish's Debates of the House of Commons, *etc.* vol. 1. 1841. 8°. **807. f. 20.**

—— An Address to the Commons of Ireland: by a Freeholder [i.e. Sir J. Caldwell]. pp. 43. 1771. 8°. *See* Freeholder. **8145. aaa. 41.**

—— An Address to the House of Commons of Ireland: by a Freeholder [i.e. Sir J. Caldwell] . . . The third edition. pp. 43. 1771. 8°. *See* Freeholder. **8145. b. 118.**

—— A Brief Examination of the Question whether it is expedient, either in a religious or political view to pass an Act to enable Papists to take real securities for money which they may lend . . . The second edition. pp. 35. *S. Powell: Dublin,* 1764. 8°. **702. h. 2. (2.)**

—— An Enquiry, how far the Restrictions laid upon the Trade of Ireland by British Acts of Parliament are a benefit or disadvantage to the British Dominions in general, and to England in particular . . . With an address to the gentlemen concerned in the woollen commerce of Great Britain . . . To which is added a letter to Sir John Duntze, Bart. in which a union between the two kingdoms is discussed. pp. xii. 113. *Henry Mugg: Exeter,* 1779. 8°. **117. h. 59.**

—— [Another edition.] pp. 100. *R. Marchbank: Dublin,* 1779. 8°. **8145. dd. 9.**

—— An Essay on the Character and Conduct of His Excellency Lord Visc. Townshend, *etc.* [By Sir J. Caldwell.] pp. 26. 1771. 8°. *See* Townshend (George) *1st Marquis Townshend.* **8145. bb. 121.**

CALDWELL (James Ernest) The Yellow Bag: a drama. pp. 74. *C. H. Thorburn: Ottawa,* 1907. 8°. **11778. k. 2.**

CALDWELL (James Ralston) *See* Eger, *Sir.* Eger and Grime . . . With an introductory study by J. R. Caldwell. 1933. 8°. [*Harvard Studies in Comparative Literature.* vol. 9.] **Ac. 2692/14.**

—— John Keats' Fancy. The effect on Keats of the psychology of his day. pp. ix. 206. *Cornell University Press: Ithaca, N.Y.,* 1945. 8°. **11865. i. 15.**

—— The Origin of the Story of Bǫthvar-Bjarki. 1939. *See* Periodical Publications.—*Oslo.* Arkiv för nordisk filologi, *etc.* bd. 55. hft. 3. 1883, *etc.* 8°. **P.P. 5044. e.**

CALDWELL (James Stamford) A Digest of the Laws relating to the Poor. pp. xv. 456. *J. Butterworth & Son: London,* 1821. 12°. **516. b. 27.**

—— Results of Reading. pp. vii. 351. *John Murray: London,* 1843. 8°. **1457. g. 18.**

—— A Treatise of the Law of Arbitration. With an appendix of precedents. pp. xv. 501. *J. Butterworth & Son: London,* 1817. 8°. **518. l. 18.**

CALDWELL (James Stamford)

—— The second edition. pp. xxiv. 310. *J. Butterworth & Son: London,* 1825. 8°. **517. f. 6.**

—— Second American . . . edition, with notes and references . . . by Chauncey Smith. pp. xii. 539. *Chauncey Goodrich: Burlington,* 1853. 8°. **6625. bb. 6.**

CALDWELL (Janet Taylor)

—— The Arm and the Darkness. pp. 512. *Collins: London,* 1943. 8°. **NN. 34267.**

—— The Beautiful is Vanished. pp. 511. *Collins: London,* 1951. 8°. **12730. d. 6.**

—— Dynasty of Death. [A novel.] pp. 780. *Collins: London,* 1939. 8°. **12719. dd. 8.**

—— The Eagles Gather. pp. 383. *Collins: London,* 1940. 8°. **12721. d. 11.**

—— The Earth is the Lord's. A tale of the rise of Genghis Khan. pp. 400. *Collins: London,* 1941. 8°. **NN. 32575.**

—— The Final Hour. pp. 511. *Collins: London,* 1945. 8°. **12727. bb. 18**

—— Let Love come Last. pp. 512. *Collins: London,* 1950. 8°. **12730. h. 19.**

—— Maggie—her Marriage, *etc.* pp. 172. *Frederick Muller: [London,* 1954.] 8°. *Gold Medal Books.* no. 25. **12732. a. 32.**

—— Melissa, pp. 448. *Collins: London,* 1949. 8°. **12730. b. 7.**

—— Never Victorious, never Defeated. pp. 639. *Collins: London,* 1954. 8°. **12731. cc. 31.**

—— The Strong City. pp. 512. *Collins: London,* 1942. 8°. **12725. bbb. 9.**

—— There was a Time. pp. 512. *Collins: London,* 1948. 8°. **12726. b. 59.**

—— This Side of Innocence. pp. 512. *Collins: London,* 1947. 8° **12729. bb. 1.**

—— The Turnbulls. pp. 480. *Collins: London,* 1944. 8°. **12724. aa. 30.**

—— The Wide House. pp. 512. *Collins: London,* 1946. 8°. **12727. bbb. 22.**

CALDWELL (Joannes) Dissertatio medica inauguralis de hysteria, *etc.* pp. 72. *Balfour & Smellie: Edinburgi,* 1780. 8°. **T. 291. (5.)**

CALDWELL (John) *A.M.* An Impartial Trial of the Spirit operating in this part of the world . . . A sermon preached at New London-derry, *etc.* pp. viii. 47. *Robert Foulis: Glasgow,* 1742. 8°. **4486. a. 57. (1.)**

CALDWELL (John) *of Texas.*

—— Desperate Voyage, *etc.* [An autobiographical account of a voyage in a cutter from Panama to Sydney. With plates, including portraits.] pp. 324. *Little, Brown & Co.: Boston,* 1949. 8°. **010498. b. 2.**

—— [A reissue.]

Desperate Voyage. [On the voyage of the author, alone, from Panama to Australia. With a portrait.] pp. xviii. 324. *Victor Gollancz: London,* 1950. 8°. **010498. bb. 3.**

CALDWELL (John) *Parson of Winwick.* A Sermon preached before the right honorable Earle of Darbie and diuers others assembled in his honors Chappell at Newparke in Lankashire, *etc.* **B.L.** MS. NOTES. *Imprinted by Thomas East: London,* 1577. 8°. **C. 21. a. 10. (3.)**

CALDWELL (JOHN COPE)

—— *See* CALDWELL (Harry R.) and CALDWELL (J. C.) South China Birds, *etc.* 1931. 8°. **7288**. c. **8**.

—— *See* GAYN (Mark) and CALDWELL (J.C.) American Agent. [1947.] 8°. **09059**. aaa. **30**.

—— Our Friends the Tigers. [An account of the life of Harry R. Caldwell and his family as missionaries in China. With a portrait.] pp. 176. *Hutchinson: London,* 1954. 8°. **4768**. e. **19**.

CALDWELL (JOHN H.) The Thurstons of the Old Palmetto State: or, Varieties of southern life, *etc.* pp. 406. *Joseph Russell: New York,* 1861. 8°. **12704**. dd. **18**.

CALDWELL (JOHN R.) *See* PERIODICAL PUBLICATIONS.—*Glasgow.* The Northern Witness. Edited by J. R. Caldwell. 1878, *etc.* 8°. P.P. **291**. aa.

—— Because Ye Belong to Christ, *etc.* pp. 32. *Pickering & Inglis: London, Glasgow,* [1929.] 8°. **4401**. g. **48**.

—— The Charter of the Church. Revised notes of an exposition of the First Epistle to the Corinthians. 2 vol. *Pickering & Inglis: Glasgow,* [1912, 32.] [*Every Christian's Library.*] **03560**. h. **1/10**.

—— The Christian Life: its experience and development. [With a portrait.] pp. 162. *Pickering & Inglis: London, Glasgow,* [1927.] 8°. **04403**. i. **94**.

—— Epitome of Christian Experience in Psalm XXXII., with the Development of Christian Life . . . With photo and brief record of life. pp. xxxiv. 162. *Pickering & Inglis: Glasgow,* [1917.] 8°. [*Every Christian's Library.*] **03560**. h. **1/15**.

—— The Gathering and Receiving of Children of God. pp. 31. *Pickering & Inglis: London, Glasgow,* [1929.] 8°. **4401**. g. **47**.

—— Leaven. pp. 48. *The Publishing Office: Glasgow,* [1883.] 16°. **4422**. aa. **44**. (**3**.)

—— Separation from the World, Jehoshaphat, and other papers. pp. 64. *Turner & Co.: Glasgow,* [1883.] 16°. **4401**. k. **21**.

—— Things to Come; being a short outline of some of the great events of prophecy. pp. 112. "*Northern Witness*": *Glasgow,* [1883.] 8°. **3185**. df. **5**.

—— Tenth edition, *etc.* pp. 112. *Pickering & Inglis: Glasgow,* [1919.] 8°. **03187**. de. **102**.

—— Thoughts concerning Fellowship. pp. 19. *The Publishing Office: Glasgow,* [1884.] 16°. **4372**. df. **21**. (**5**.)

CALDWELL (JOHN WILLIAM) Oration, pronounced at Worcester, Mass., July 4, 1803. pp. 16. *Sewall Goodridge: Worcester,* 1803. 4°. **8175**. c. **22**.

CALDWELL (JOHN WILLIAM GRANT)

—— Understand your Diabetes. A guide-book for the diabetic patient. pp. xv. 146. *Oxford University Press: Toronto,* 1949. 8°. **7642**. a. **40**.

CALDWELL (JOSEPH BLAKE) An Oration pronounced on the thirty second anniversary of American Independence . . . To which is added an appendix, containing fourteen spirited resolutions adopted on the occasion. pp. 31. *Isaiah Thomas: Worcester,* 1808. 8°. **8177**. cc. **9**.

CALDWELL (JOSEPH STUART) *See* RITCHIE (John W.) and CALDWELL (J. S.) Primer of Hygiene, *etc.* 1923. 8°. **7405**. pp. **10**.

—— *See* RITCHIE (John W.) and CALDWELL (J. S.) Cartilla de Higiene personal, *etc.* 1913. 8°. **7404**. pp. **19**.

CALDWELL (JOSEPH STUART)

—— Hydrion Concentration Changes in relation to Growth and Ripening in Fruits. pp. 54. *Washington,* 1934. 8°. [*U.S. Department of Agriculture. Technical Bulletin.* no. 403.] A.S. **800/2**.

CALDWELL (KEITH)

—— Report of a Faunal Survey in Eastern and Central Africa, January to April, 1947. pp. 38. [*London,*] 1948. 8°. [*Society for the Preservation of the Fauna of the Empire. Occasional Paper.* no. 8.] Ac. **3585**. e/**2**.

CALDWELL (LYNTON KEITH)

—— The Administrative Theories of Hamilton & Jefferson: their contribution to thought on public administration. pp. ix. 244. *Chicago* 1944. 8°. [*University of Chicago Studies in Public Administration.*] **Ac.2691.d/53.(10.)**

—— Contributions to Thought on Public Administration. Hamilton and Jefferson. A part of a dissertation submitted . . . March, 1943. [Typescript.] pp. 188–201, 431–451. *Chicago,* 1945. Mic. A. **36**.
MICROFILM. *Issued by the University of Chicago Libraries Dept. of Photographic Reproduction.*

CALDWELL (MERRITT) The Philosophy of Christian Perfection, *etc.* [By M. Caldwell.] pp. 159. 1848. 12°. *See* CHRISTIAN PERFECTION. **4408**. bbb. **32**.

CALDWELL (MURIEL E.)

—— *See* CALDWELL (Harry R.) and CALDWELL (J. C.) South China Birds . . . Stories and legends by M. E. Caldwell. 1931. 8°. **7288**. c. **8**.

CALDWELL (N. E. H.)

—— The Control of Banana Rust Thrips. pp. 73. *Brisbane,* 1938. 8°. [*Queensland. Department of Agriculture and Stock. Division of Plant Industry—Research—Bulletin.* New series. no. 16.] C.S. G. **195/2**.

CALDWELL (NORMAN JAMES)

—— About Cancer. A reassurance to every man and woman. pp. 48. *Buck Bros. & Harding: London,* [1949.] 16°. **7443**. a. **18**.
Part of "Buck Bros. Pocket Series."

—— General Elementary Science for Students of Chiropody, *etc.* pp. 231. *Charlesworth & Wiles: London,* 1948. 8°. **8713**. a. **53**.

CALDWELL (NORMAN WARD)

—— Fangs of the Sea. By N. Caldwell, in collaboration with Norman Ellison. [On shark-catching. With plates, including portraits.] pp. x. 282. *Angus & Robertson: Sydney,* 1936. 8°. **10496**. cc. **29**.

—— [A reissue.] *Quality Press: London; Sydney* printed, 1937. 8°. **010460**. e. **27**.

—— The French in the Mississippi Valley, 1740–1750. pp. 113. *University of Illinois Press: Urbana,* 1941. 8°. [*Illinois Studies in the Social Sciences.* vol. 26. no. 3.] Ac. **2692**. u/**14**.

—— Titans of the Barrier Reef. Further adventures of a shark fisherman . . . Photographs by the author. [With portraits.] pp. 248. *Angus & Robertson: Sydney & London,* 1938. 8°. **07206**. ff. **5**.

CALDWELL (ORESTES HAMPTON) and **DENNIS** (STANLEY A.) How to Retail Radio . . . By the Editors of Electrical Merchandising (O. H. Caldwell and S. A. Dennis). pp. xiv. 226. *McGraw Hill Book Co.: New York,* 1922. 8°. **8759**. b. **4**.

CALDWELL (Oscar T.) Trial of Oscar T. Caldwell, late a conductor on the Chicago and Burlington Railroad Line, for embezzlement . . . reported by J. V. Smith, *etc.* pp. 35. *Daily Democratic Press: Chicago*, 1855. 8°. **6673**. d. **2**.

CALDWELL (Otis William) *See* Bergen (J. Y.) and Caldwell (O. W.) Introduction to Botany. [1914.] 8°. **07028**. k. **51**.

—— *See* Curtis (Francis D.) Biology for Today. By F. D. Curtis . . . O. W. Caldwell, *etc.* [1934.] 8°. **7002**. pp. **11**.

—— *See* Curtis (Francis D.) Everyday Biology. By F. D. Curtis . . . O. W. Caldwell, *etc.* [1940.] 8°. **7006**. r. **22**.

—— Biological Foundations of Education. By O. W. Caldwell . . . Charles Edward Skinner . . . and J. Winfield Tietz. [With illustrations.] pp. vii. 534. *Ginn & Co.: Boston*, [1931.] 8°. **7384**. r. **18**.

—— Elements of General Science. Laboratory Problems. By O. W. Caldwell . . . W. L. Eikenberry . . . and Earl R. Glenn. pp. viii. 188. *Ginn & Co.: Boston*, [1920.] 8°. **08709**. a. **50**.

Interleaved.

—— New edition, *etc.* pp. ix. 196. *Ginn & Co.: Boston*, [1924.] 8°. **8703**. df. **24**.

—— A Laboratory Manual for Work in General Science. By O. W. Caldwell, W. L. Eikenberry, and Charles J. Pieper. pp. xi. 134. *Ginn & Co.: Boston*, [1915.] 4°. **8709**. d. **10**.

—— Science remaking the World. [Lectures by various authors.] By O. W. Caldwell . . . and E. E. Slosson. [With plates.] pp. x. 292. *William Heinemann: London; printed in U.S.A.*, 1923. 8°. **08709**. b. **39**.

CALDWELL (Otis William) and **COURTIS** (Stuart Appleton)

—— Then & Now in Education, 1845: 1923, *etc.* pp. ix. 400. *World Book Co.: Yonkers-on-Hudson, New York*, 1924. 8°. **8385**. aa. **13**.

CALDWELL (Otis William) and **CURTIS** (Francis Day)

—— Science for Today. pp. xvi. 733. xxii. *Ginn & Co.: Boston*, [1936.] 8°. **8712**. a. **27**.

CALDWELL (Otis William) and **EIKENBERRY** (William Lewis)

—— Elements of General Science. pp. xiv. 308. *Ginn & Co.: Boston*, [1914.] 8°. **08709**. aa. **12**.

—— Revised edition. pp. xii. 404. *Ginn & Co.: Boston*, [1918.] 8°. **08709**. aa. **25**.

—— New edition. pp. xiii. 455. *Ginn & Co.: Boston*, [1924.] 8°. **8709**. l. **13**.

—— New edition. pp. xv. 600. *Ginn & Co.: Boston*, [1926.] 8°. **08709**. b. **49**.

—— A Laboratory Manual for Work in General Science . . . Revised edition. pp. xi. 139. *Ginn & Co.: Boston*, [1919.] 4°. **8706**. ee. **33**.

CALDWELL (Otis William) and **LUNDEEN** (Gerhard Emmanuel)

—— Do you Believe it? [On superstitions.] pp. x. 307. *Doubleday, Doran & Co.: Garden City, N.Y.*, 1934. 8°. **08632**. gg. **39**.

CALDWELL (Otis William) and **MEIER** (William Herman Dietrich)

—— Open Doors to Science. pp. x. 333. *Ginn & Co.: Boston*, [1925.] 8°. **8709**. l. **16**.

CALDWELL (Peter Scott) Gas and Oil Engines, *etc.* pp. 125. *Constable & Co.: London*, 1925. 8°. **08767**. a. **78**.

CALDWELL (R. B.) *See* Perez (Venancio) and Ferrer (R.) Correspondencia comercial en español e ingles . . . Version inglesa por R. B. Caldwell. 1929. 8°. **012942**. bbb. **11**.

CALDWELL (Robert) *Coadjutor Bishop of Madras.* *See* Day (Ernest H.) Mission Heroes. Bishop Caldwell. [1896.] 8°. **4429**. d. **39**. (**1**.)

—— Christianity and Hinduism. A lecture addressed to educated Hindus, *etc.* pp. 63. *S.P.C.K.: London*, [1879.] 8°. **4372**. d. **4**. (**8**.)

—— A Comparative Grammar of the Dravidian or South Indian Family of Languages. pp. viii. 528. *Harrison: London*, 1856. 8°. **12907**. cc. **15**.

—— Second edition, revised and enlarged. pp. xlii. 608. *Trübner & Co.: London*, 1875. 8°. **12907**. s. **4**.

—— Third edition, revised and edited by the Rev. J. L. Wyatt . . . and T. Ramakrishna Pillai. pp. xl. 640. *Kegan Paul & Co.: London*, 1913. 8°. **12908.cc.1.**

—— A Description of Roman Imperial Aurei found near Calicut on the Malabar Coast, and now in the possession of His Highness the Rajah of Travancore. *Government Press: Trevandrum*, 1851. 8°. **7754.a.1.**

—— Evangelistic Work amongst the Higher Classes and Castes in Tinnevelly. Rev. Dr. Caldwell's Third Journal. pp. 13. [1876.] 8°. **4765**. bbb. **44**.

—— The First Centenary of the Tinnevelly Mission . . . A paper, *etc.* pp. 6. *Church Mission Press: Palamcottah*, 1880. 8°. **4766**. d. **13**. (**2**.)

—— The Inner Citadel of Religion. pp. 32. *S.P.C.K.: London*, [1879.] 8°. **4372**. d. **4**. (**9**.)

—— Lectures on the Tinnevelly Missions, descriptive of the field, the work, and the results, *etc.* pp. 134. *Bell & Daldy: London*, 1857. 8°. **4193**. d. **47**.

—— Observations on the Kudumi. pp. 8. *J. J. Craen: [Madras?]* 1867. 8°. **4506**. d. **18**. (**1**.)

—— A Political and General History of the District of Tinnevelly, in the Presidency of Madras, from the earliest period to its cession to the English Government in A.D. 1801. pp. x. 300. *E. Keys: Madras*, 1881. 8°. **9057**. cc. **11**.

—— The Prince of Wales in Tinnevelly, and "From Delahay Street to Edeyengoody." pp. 36. *S.P.C.K.: London*, 1876. 8°. **10056**. a. **45**.

—— Records of the Early History of the Tinnevelly Mission, *etc.* pp. xi. 356. *Higginbotham & Co.: Madras*, 1881. 8°. **4765**. ee. **11**.

—— The Relation of Christianity to Hinduism. pp. 19. *R. Clay, Sons, & Taylor: London*, [1885.] 8°. **4503**. f. **24**. (**6**.)

—— [Another copy.] **4766**. f. **10**. (**9**.)

CALDWELL (Robert) *Coadjutor Bishop of Madras.*

—— Reminiscences . . . Edited by . . . Rev. J. L. Wyatt. pp. 195. *Addison & Co.: Madras,* 1894. 8°. **4906**. ee. **33**.

—— The Three Way-marks. pp. iv. 60. *Christian Vernacular Education Society: Madras,* 1860. 8°. **4411**. bb. **5**.

—— The Tinnevelly Shanars: a sketch of their religion and their moral condition . . . with special reference to the facilities and hindrances to the progress of Christianity amongst them. pp. 77. *R. Twigg: Madras,* 1849. 8°. **4765**. eee. **21**. (**6**.)

—— The Unsearchable Riches of Christ. A sermon, *etc.* pp. 23. *S.P.C.K.: Madras,* 1851. 8°. **4473**. cc. **10**. (**28**.)

CALDWELL (Robert) *F.R.C.S.* Military Hygiene. pp. xi. 416. *Baillière & Co.: London,* 1905. 8°. **7391**. c. 52.

—— Second edition. pp. xiv. 580. *Baillière & Co.: London,* 1910. 8°. **7391**. d. 34.

—— The Prevention of Disease in Armies in the Field. pp. viii. 182. *Baillière & Co.: London,* 1904. 8°. **7406**. de. **33**.

CALDWELL (Robert) *F.R.G.S.* Chi-Nyanja Simplified. pp. 88. *Zambesi Industrial Mission: London,* [1897.] 8°. **12910**. m. **1**.
Interleaved.

—— Second edition, with key. pp. 46. *Zambesi Industrial Mission: London,* [1897.] 8°. **12910**. m. **2**.

—— The Greatest Need of the Age. [A religious tract.] pp. 55. *Thomas Williams: London,* 1897. 8°. **4380**. e. **18**.

—— Third edition. pp. 55. *Thomas Williams: London,* 1908. 8°. **4380**. ee. **16**. (**5**.)

—— Fourth edition. pp. 40. *Thos. Williams: London,* 1908. 16°. **4372**. a. **48**. (**2**.)

—— Fifth edition. pp. 47. *Morgan & Scott: London,* [1920.] 8°. **04403**. i. **50**.

—— The March of the Unsaved. [A religious tract.] pp. 14. *G. Stoneman: London,* [1896.] 24°. **4418**. aaa. **31**. (**4**.)

—— Papers on Prayer. pp. 32. *Zambesi Industrial Mission: London,* [1907.] 16°. **04420**. e. **8**. (**4**.)

—— [Another edition.] pp. 39. *Zambesi Industrial Mission: London,* [1908.] 16°. **04420**. f. **20**. (**2**.)

—— In Everything by Prayer . . . Fifth edition [of "Papers on Prayer"]. pp. 39. *Morgan & Scott: London,* [1920.] 8°. **03456**. de. **18**.

—— The Revelation of Jesus Christ. pp. vii. 240. *Morgan & Scott: London,* [1920.] 8°. **4226**. ff. **37**.

CALDWELL (Robert) *M.A.* Masimulizi ya Afrika . . . Geographical History of Africa: Swahili. pp. v. 154. *Sheldon Press: London,* 1930. 8°. **010094**. ee. **21**.

CALDWELL (Robert) *Merchant.* The Gold Era of Victoria; being the present and the future of the colony in its commercial, statistical and social aspects. [With a map.] pp. 142. *W. S. Orr & Co.: London,* 1855. 8°. **10491**. d. **4**.

CALDWELL (Robert C.) The Chit-Chat Papers, reprinted from the Athenæum and Daily News . . . By the Silent Member of the Club [i.e. R. C. Caldwell], *etc.* [Reprinted from the edition of 1873.] pp. 216. *Higginbotham & Co.: Madras,* 1893. 8°. **012357**. k. **18**.

CALDWELL (Robert C.)

—— The Chutney Lyrics. A collection of comic pieces in verse, *etc.* [By R. C. Caldwell.] pp. 63. 1871. 4°. *See* Chutney Lyrics. **11651**. g. **6**.

—— Second edition, *etc.* pp. vi. 63. *Higginbotham & Co.: Madras,* 1889. 8°. **12316**. l. **12**.

—— Constance Lorn, and other poems. pp. 123. *A. W. Bennett: London,* 1867. 8°. **11647**. bb. **37**.

CALDWELL (Robert Graham)

—— The New Castle County Workhouse, Greenbank, Delaware. pp. x. 257. *University of Delaware: Newark,* [1940.] 8°. [*Delaware Notes.* ser. 13.] W.P. **11924**.

CALDWELL (Robert Granville) James A. Garfield, party chieftain. [With plates, including portraits.] pp. xi. 383. *Dodd, Mead & Co.: New York,* 1931. 8°. **010885**. ee. **13**.

—— The Lopez Expeditions to Cuba, 1848–1851. A dissertation, *etc.* pp. 138. *Princeton University Press: Princeton,* 1915. 8°. **9771**. eee. **28**.

—— A Short History of the American People . . . With maps. 2 vol. *G. P. Putnam's Sons: New York & London,* 1925, 27. 8°. **9616**. eee. **3**.

CALDWELL (Robert J.) The Economic Situation in Czechoslovakia in 1920. pp. 48. 1921. 8°. *See* United States of America.—*Department of Labor.* A.S. **108/7**.

CALDWELL (Sallie K.)

—— *See* Gaddis (Maxwell P.) The Sacred Hour. [On S. K. Caldwell. With her correspondence and portrait.] 1856. 8°. **4986**. aa. **63**.

CALDWELL (Samuel Andrew Gailey)

—— The Preparation and Spinning of Flax Fibre. [With illustrations.] pp. xii. 364. *Emmott & Co.: London,* 1931. 8°. **7941**. g. **22**.

—— Rayon Staple Fibre Spinning. pp. 170. *Emmott & Co.: London & Manchester,* 1953. 8°. **7745**. aa. **1**.

CALDWELL (Samuel Lunt) *See* Williams (Roger) The Bloudy Tenent of Persecution. Edited by S. L. Caldwell. 1867. 4°. [*Publications of the Narragansett Club.* ser. 1. vol. 3.] Ac. **9510**.

—— *See* Williams (Roger) The Bloody Tenent yet More Bloody. (Edited by S. L. Caldwell.) 1870. 4°. [*Publications of the Narragansett Club.* ser. 1. vol. 4.] Ac. **9510**.

—— Church Worship. *See* New York.—*Madison Avenue Baptist Church.* The Madison Avenue Lectures. [1867.] 12°. **4486**. aaa. **89**.

—— A Discourse preached in Warren at the completion of the first century of the Warren Association, *etc.* pp. 19. *Hammond, Angell & Co.: Providence,* 1867. 8°. **4486**. cc. **18**. (**23**.)

CALDWELL (Samuel Lunt) and **GORDON** (Adoniram Judson)

—— The Service of Song for Baptist Churches. [Compiled by S. L. Caldwell and A. J. Gordon.] pp. 793. *Gould & Lincoln: Boston,* 1872. 12°. **3440**. ee. **11**.

CALDWELL (Sibyl) "The Deceitful Miss Smiths." pp. 12. *London, New York,* [1906.] 12°. [*French's Acting Edition of Plays.* vol. 153.] **2304**. h. **44**.

—— A Domestic Entanglement. pp. 12. *London, New York,* [1905.] 12°. [*French's Acting Edition of Plays.* vol. 153.] **2304**. h. **44**.

CALDWELL (Sibyl)

—— The Ejection of Aunt Lucinda. pp. 10. *London, New York,* [1907.] 12°. [*French's Acting Edition of Plays.* vol. 154.] **2304. h. 45.**

—— The Final Rehearsal. pp. 10. *London, New York,* [1908.] 12°. [*French's Acting Edition of Plays.* vol. 155.] **2304. h. 46.**

—— Five Sketches for Women's Institutes, Girl Guides, etc., etc. pp. 82. *London, New York,* [1924.] 8°. [*French's Acting Edition.*] **11791. t. 1/3.**

—— The Misses Primrose's Deception. pp. 12. *London, New York,* [1907.] 12°. [*French's Acting Edition of Plays.* vol. 154.] **2304. h. 45.**

—— That Horrid Major. pp. 11. *London, New York,* [1907.] 12°. [*French's Acting Edition of Plays.* vol. 155.] **2304. h. 46.**

—— Their New Paying Guest. A farce. pp. 11. *London, New York,* [1905.] 12°. [*French's Acting Edition of Plays.* vol. 153.] **2304. h. 44.**

—— Two Aunts at a Time. pp. 14. *London, New York,* [1908.] 12°. [*French's Acting Edition of Plays.* vol. 155.] **2304. h. 46.**

—— Up-to-Date. pp. 16. *London, New York,* [1905.] 12°. [*French's Acting Edition of Plays.* vol. 153.] **2304. h. 44.**

CALDWELL (Stephen Adolphus) A Banking History of Louisiana. pp. 138. *Baton Rouge,* 1935. 8°. [*Louisiana State University Studies.* no. 19.] **Ac. 2685. e.**

CALDWELL (Taylor) *See* Caldwell (Janet T.)

CALDWELL (Thomas) *See* Dugdale (Gilbert) A True Discourse of the practises of Elizabeth Caldwell, J. Bownd . . . on the parson of T. Caldwell, *etc.* 1604. 4°. **C. 27. c. 27.**

CALDWELL (Thomas) *Editor of "The Golden Book of Modern English Poetry."* The Golden Book of Modern English Poetry, 1870–1920. Selected & arranged by T. Caldwell, *etc.* pp. xxviii. 395. *J. M. Dent & Sons: London & Toronto,* 1922. 8°. **11607. c. 32.**

—— Revised edition. *J. M. Dent & Sons: London & Toronto,* 1923. 8°. **011604. ff. 25.**

—— Revised and enlarged edition. pp. xxxii. 413. *J. M. Dent & Sons: London & Toronto,* 1930. 8°. **11601. l. 7.**

—— [Another edition.] (With additional selections by Philip Henderson.) pp. xxv. 404. *J. M. Dent & Sons: London,* 1935. 8°. [*Everyman's Library.*] **12206.p.1/709.**

—— School edition (slightly abridged). pp. xxxl. 344. *J. M. Dent & Sons: London & Toronto,* 1926. 8°. **011604. g. 38.**

—— [Another edition.] pp. xxxi. 344. *J. M. Dent & Sons: London & Toronto,* 1926. 8°. **011604. g. 42.**

CALDWELL (W.) *Mining Engineer.*

—— Methods of Working the Oil-Shales. *See* Lothians. The Oil-Shales of the Lothians, *etc.* 1906. 8°. **B.S.38.Gb/1.(3.)**

—— Methods of Working the Oil-Shales. *See* Lothians. The Oil-Shales of the Lothians, *etc* 1912. 8°. **B.S.38.Gb/1.(3a.)**

—— Methods of Working the Oil-Shales. *See* Lothians. The Oil-Shales of the Lothians, *etc.* 1927. 8°. **B.S.38.Gb/1.(3b.)**

CALDWELL (Wallace Everett) *See* Capart (J.) Thebes, *etc.* [Translated by W. E. Caldwell.] 1926. 4°. **7704. h. 13.**

—— The Ancient World. [With plates and maps.] pp. xvii. 590. *Farrar & Rinehart: New York,* [1937.] 8°. [*Civilization of the Western World.* vol. 1.] **09008. bb. 35/1.**

—— Hellenic Conceptions of Peace, *etc.* pp. 141. *New York,* 1919. 8°. [*Columbia University Studies in Political Science.* vol. 84. no. 2.] **Ac. 2688/2.**

—— [Another copy, with a different titlepage.] **08425. f. 2.**

CALDWELL (William) *Professor of Moral Philosophy, McGill University.* Pragmatism and Idealism. pp. ix. 268. *A. & C. Black: London,* 1913. 8°. **08461. e. 42.**

—— Schopenhauer's System in its Philosophical Significance. pp. xviii. 538. *W. Blackwood & Sons: Edinburgh & London,* 1896. 8°. **08461. i. 1.**

CALDWELL (William) *Senior Moderator, Trinity College, Dublin.* Elementary Qualitative and Volumetric Analysis, inorganic and organic, *etc.* pp. xxiv. 418. *J. & A. Churchill: London,* 1924. 8°. **8903. ee. 20.**

CALDWELL (William Elmer)

—— *See* King (George B.) and Caldwell (W. E.) The Fundamentals of College Chemistry. [1949.] 8°. **08909. d. 56.**

—— *See* King (George B.) and Caldwell (W. E.) The Fundamentals of College Chemistry, *etc.* [1954.] 8°. **8896. aa. 8.**

CALDWELL (William Elmer) and **KING** (George Brooks)

—— A Brief Course in Semimicro Qualitative Analysis. pp. vi. 163. *American Book Co.: New York,* [1953.] 8°. **8902. h. 4.**

CALDWELL (William Thomas)

—— Organic Chemistry. (Under the editorship of Herman T. Briscoe.) pp. x. 763. *Houghton Mifflin Co.: Boston,* [1943.] 8°. **8902. dd. 26.**

CALDWELL-JOHNSTON (John) *See* Johnston.